MACEDONIA

THRACE

Constantinople
(Byzantium) ★

PROPONTIS

Thessalonike •

ASIA MINOR

THESSALY

AEGEAN

MYTILENE
(LESBOS)

ITHACA

EUBOEA

Thebes ★

Athens ★

• Smyrna

Corinth ★

PELOPONNESUS

Mycene ★

Argus ★

Olympia

SEA

★ Sparta

DELOS

ANCIENT GREECE
and the
AEGEAN SEA

ARAL
SEA

OXUS RIVER

CHINA

PERSIA

TIBET

IAN GULF

INDIA

INDIAN

OCEAN

AVAILABLE IN TWO FORMS

Our Heritage of World Literature

THE COMPLETE WORK, COMPRISING BOOK ONE AND
BOOK TWO: "LITERATURE IN TRANSLATION" AND
"LITERATURE IN OUR OWN TONGUE"

Literature in Translation

BOOK ONE, "LITERATURE IN TRANSLATION," ONLY,
OMITTING BRITISH AND AMERICAN WRITERS

OUR HERITAGE OF WORLD LITERATURE

REVISED EDITION

STITH THOMPSON
INDIANA UNIVERSITY

AND

JOHN GASSNER
STERLING PROFESSOR OF PLAYWRITING
YALE UNIVERSITY

HOLT, RINEHART AND WINSTON   NEW YORK

6   7   8   9

PREFACE TO THE REVISED EDITION

Our Heritage of World Literature has been prepared in the belief that a certain, rather definite part of the literature of the world has come to belong to our cultural inheritance. This is by no means confined to works written in English. Homer and the Bible, Æschylus and Dante, Cervantes and Molière, are as truly within our great literary tradition as are Chaucer, Milton, and Shakespeare. Indeed, a considerable number of writers in foreign tongues have had so much vitality that even under the handicap of translation they have entered into the very bloodstream of our culture. It is from such men that selections for this anthology have been chosen. On the other hand, many authors have been important in their own time or their own land but have failed to extend their influence to us. They are felt to be exotic: though they may at some time have been important to us or may be so in the future, they are not now part of our intellectual or artistic life. These men have been excluded to make more room for those really significant to us of the English-speaking world.

In preparing the revised edition of this work care has been taken to retain all the features that recommended *Our Heritage of World Literature* to teachers and students.

While retaining the basic organization of the material into national strains in roughly chronological order, the editors have rearranged some of the chapters in order to highlight certain periods. Accordingly the anthology is divided into five parts. *Part I,* following Matthew Arnold's suggestion, groups the Hellenic and Hebraic Worlds. The literature of the Orient is treated in *Part II.* The Medieval World of Saga and Romance constitutes *Part III,* and it is followed by The Renaissance and Modern Worlds, *Part IV.* The last section of the anthology, *Part V,* treats the writings of Britain and America. It is hoped that this slight reorganization will serve to clarify the structure of the whole and to trace our literary heritage in a meaningful pattern.

Some two hundred pages of new text have been added for the purpose of ensuring more satisfactory representation for various periods and for verious forms of writing. While there have been some additions to Parts I, II, and III, it is Part IV that has been most extensively amplified. The additions to this modern section bring the reader nearer to our own day, without violating the principle that all selections must be in some respect part of our literary heritage.

Wherever possible substantial selections have been provided. Though this practice has caused the omission of novels and long treatises, except where a real unit could be separated from the whole, it has permitted very generous representation of Homer, Herodotus, Plato, Aristotle, Virgil, the Bible, Horace, Dante, Cervantes, Villon, Montaigne, Rabelais, Voltaire, Heine, Zola, and others. Among the foreign authors represented by *complete* works are Æschylus, Sophocles, Euripides, Aristophanes, Plautus, Molière, Racine, Balzac, Flaubert, Anatole France, Goethe, Ibsen, Hauptmann, Gogol, Tolstoy, Dostoyevsky, and Chekhov. By this plan, rather than by the inclusion of fragments from a multitude of lesser writers, the reader is made keenly aware of certain important men and movements and is not confused by a mass of overwhelming details.

In order to promote the reader's understanding of the selections and relieve him of the necessity of resorting to many supplementary texts, the introductions to Book One: Literature in Translation (pages 1-984) have been revised and extended. Taken together, they constitute a brief history of comparative literature. As a further help toward the understanding of the old literatures, some appropriate essays, such as Arnold's "Hebraism and Hellenism" and his "On Celtic Literature" and Gilbert Murray's discussion of the special contribution of the Greeks, have been included.

The notes have been prepared on the assumption that the reader has a good dictionary available and knows how to use the special aids that it supplies. Aids in the understanding of literature have been given by (1) the maps in the end-papers, (2) the mythological sketches, in which, at appropriate places, the essential part of Bulfinch's work appears, (3) the account of Greek philosophy, (4) the material on the Greek theater—Sheldon Cheney's "Attending a Greek Play" and the editorial interpolation of some facts about Greek staging, and (5) the introduction to poetic form.

Standard translations have been used throughout. Special attention should be given to Nicholson's version of *The Canterbury Tales*, Banks's *Sir Gawain and the Green Knight* (in the original alliterative meter), and Leppar's translation of Villon's *Little Testament*. Dean Selatie E. Stout of Indiana University contributed from his exhaustive knowledge of Pliny's letters and has permitted some of his new renderings to be published here for the first time. Professors Manchester and Lancaster of Vanderbilt University have contributed selections from their translation of *La Araucana,* the first real epic to have been written in our hemisphere. In many cases the editors have chosen translations made by such notable poets as Crashaw, Byron, Shelley, Arnold, Dryden, Pope, Emreson, Longfellow, Rossetti, Morris, and others.

The entire volume has been set in the same large type-face which was used in the original edition. An effort has been made by the publisher to present our literary heritage in a fitting and congenial typographical format.

Our Heritage of World Literature is comprised of Book One: Literature in Translation (pages 1-984) and Book Two: British and American Literature (pages 985-1418). For the convenience of those whose study of world literature omits writings in our own tongue, Book One: Literature in Translation has been made available in a single volume. Teachers, therefore, can select either the complete anthology or Literature in Translation only.

In preparing the revised edition the editors have not altered the section devoted to British and American writing. The introductions for Book One have been almost entirely the work of Mr. Gassner.

The editors have taken upon themselves many obligations in preparing this anthology and many people have helped with suggestions. To publishers and authors who have been good enough to grant permission for the use of copyrighted material acknowledgment is given at appropriate places.

S. T.
J. G.

May, 1942

TABLE OF CONTENTS

Book One: *Literature in Translation*

OUR INHERITANCE FROM OTHER LITERATURES

PART ONE

Hellenic and Hebraic Worlds

PART TWO
The Oriental World

PART THREE
The Medieval World

PART FOUR

The Renaissance and Modern World

Book Two: Literature in Our Own Tongue

PART FIVE: THE WELL OF ENGLISH

Appendices

OUR LITERARY HERITAGE

The struggle to find and to fill one's place in the amazing welter of forces in the modern world is so insistent that little time is left to consider the forces themselves. We are thrust into such a world without our will or knowledge. We enjoy good roads and schools, parks and transportation. With the slightest expenditure, we have conveniences and pleasures that wealth could not purchase in the days of our fathers. And we have burdens which have come from their misdeeds, or their bungling, or possibly from no fault of theirs—poverty, disease, and the continual threat of world catastrophes.

Such is the world we come to at birth. It is our inheritance as truly as is the fortune handed down from father to son. We cannot escape this inheritance but must make the best of it. We may improve it. We may make greatest use of its goods and strive to remedy its evils. We may leave the great estate enlarged for those who come after if only we will enter wholeheartedly into possession of what the untold ages have given us.

This heritage from the past is of many kinds. That which first impresses us is perhaps the material conquest of nature which our ancestors have accomplished and which they have handed on to us. Not to speak of the great recent developments whereby time and space and drudgery and disease are conquered—railways, steam power, electricity, immunity—we are likewise heirs of the man who first learned to plow, to thresh, to sail a ship, to mine and work in iron. To only the slightest degree can we call our present physical comforts our own work. They come to us from the past.

The greatest inheritance we enter into from those who have gone before us, however, is not these physical comforts. For thousands of years our ancestors have been thinking and feeling and have gradually built up a great tradition of the finest of these thoughts and emotions. They have evolved great religious systems. They have worked out political and philosophical principles. They have sung and played on instruments and have left us a great heritage of music. They have striven to catch beauty of form and color and have slowly learned the secret of sculpture and painting. They have told tales and chanted poems and through long centuries have recorded for us their thoughts and feelings. They have, also, through all these means and many others, established agelong mental and emotional habits. All these activities and tendencies together we call a people's culture.

We are all born into some type of cultural surroundings. As children we think and feel as our parents do and usually as our community does. We are little Americans or Englishmen or Russians. Thousands of years of tradition have gone to make us what we are. Such general patterns of thought and feeling come to us unconsciously. They are the very air we breathe as children.

But there are other parts of our culture—in many ways the most precious parts—which we may never come to possess. We have inherited them, but they are like a fortune which is held in trust till the heir is able to spend it profitably. Such is true of music, of art, of literature. Bach and Beethoven and Wagner may be had for the asking, but the full possession of their marvelous gift to us comes only as we ourselves grow in appreciation and understanding. Watch any true music lover and see how the greatest music becomes a lasting passion that grows always stronger and adds a beauty to all his days. It is the same with great art. At first the taste may be for the garish, the sensational, or the tawdry, but with time and loving study, one comes to know his values and to be satisfied only with the best. And when this happens, one has truly entered into his inheritance and his life has been made rich.

It is literature that needs most of all to be made one's own if one is ever to possess it. Symphonies may come to us over the radio and great statues and pictures may surround us or look down at us daily. They may gradually and imperceptibly influence us until we come to cherish them. But books are on shelves and between covers, and unless they are taken from the shelves and the covers are opened and the words read and understood, they are lifeless. When one approaches them, however, with good intelligence and sympathetic feeling, they may well be the most valuable inheritance that has come from the past.

"A good book is the precious life blood of a master spirit," wrote one of the greatest of these masters. As I see this inscription facing me each day over the portal of my own university library, I think of the hundreds of thousands of books ranged in the long rows of stacks inside. After all, it is only the great book that Milton meant, and most books are not great. They give information, or facts, or pile up records. But on those same shelves are, nevertheless, many books of many kinds that are truly great. They give to us the very best in thought or imagination or observation or emotion that the greatest spirits of the past have left us. They have enriched the lives of readers for many generations.

Happy is the man who truly comes under the spell of great books. His enjoyment continually increases. Each time he makes real contact with a masterpiece, his capacity for appreciation grows. His thought, usually sluggish, may be stirred by one of the world's thinkers and he thrills to see light appearing in many a region that was dark before. Such an experience leads him to long for its repetition, and soon a passion for clear thinking brings him to seek the guidance of others and still others. Or he may have been seeing the earth with half-closed eyes, little aware of its wealth of shapes and colors, and of its interesting beasts and men. And then for a little, with the aid of a book, he sees all with new eyes. What was dull and commonplace is now filled with wonder and fascination. Other writers will carry him with them because of their exuberant imagination or their power to understand or express emotions, or their habit of seeing the humor of life. When once a man has learned the joy of such companionship, he seeks it more and more. Life becomes too short for its full enjoyment.

Even in the hurry of the modern world, the great books have never lost their power. With Homer we may still give overselves up to the glory of adventure and noble achievement in a heroic world. We may go with Herodotus and see Egypt of twenty-five centuries ago. We may explore the depths of human tragedy with Sophocles or Shakespeare. We may join Plato and Socrates and discuss the great problems of life and death, of right and wrong, of the soul and the after life. With Theocritus we may make an afternoon call and attend a great festival in Alexandria and marvel how little change twenty-two centuries have wrought in our manners and actions. We may stand with Ruth amid the alien corn or wonder at the dignity and profound beauty of scripture, hallowed as it has been by a thousand sacred associations. We may give ourselves up to the witchery of Deirdre and luxuriate in its imaginative richness. Chaucer and Don Quixote and Milton and Emerson, and a hundred others, need only to be taken from the shelves and read. There they stand, those silent books, waiting. They are our literary heritage. Shall we not go and take possession, like heirs who have come of age?

S. T.

BOOK ONE

LITERATURE IN TRANSLATION

Those of us who use the English language have a vast inheritance. It comes to us not only from the literature of two great nations, the British Empire and the United States, but from many races and nations of the globe. The internationalism of culture has nowhere been exemplified so fully as in our assimilation of nearly three thousand years of civilization from the banks of the Nile to the shores of China, from sunny Sicily and Athens to the arctic regions of Iceland. This became our own gradually, through translation and through absorption by British and American writers.

Time, the mighty winnower, has eliminated a great deal that was written in our own and other languages. Much that was accounted superb before the age of printing, was lost by flood, fire, and the ravages of conquest and fanaticism. Thus only a small portion of the work of Homer's predecessors, and of Æschylus, Sophocles, Euripides, and Menander has come down to our generation. Time has also leveled many reputations that had once been exaggerated by the special tastes or needs of different periods. Remote sectors of the world like India and the Far East have fostered some literature that has not been found directly assimilable because of its dependence upon esoteric mythologies and philosophies. The productions of small and distant countries separated from us by long-enduring linguistic barriers also have failed to become a part of our heritage, while other nations attained

maturity or distinctness too late to exert a literary influence on us.

However, no important literary culture has been wholly withheld from us. Even exotic writings, unassimilable for the average reader, have permeated the body of English letters through the interest of writers and thinkers whose own work has been widely read by us. Many of us who would find it hard to respond to Hindu mystical literature have made informal contact with it through Sir Edwin Arnold, Emerson, Schopenhauer, and Yeats. The strongest link between different national literatures is our basic humanity. Adventure, physical struggle between man and man, or man and nature, spiritual gropings, and the elemental virtues of courage, generosity, kindliness, and love speak a common language. The words of the Roman playwright Terence, *"Homo sum; humani nil a me alienum puto"*—I am a man and nothing human can be alien to me—sum up the relation of literature to life; and it is life that is the international language of the world's literature. British writers, moreover, have been mighty translators, with the result that many foreign classics have become English classics.

How this heritage became our property is told by nearly sixteen centuries of history. The process started with the dawn of Anglo-Saxon civilization, when the material of *Beowulf* was brought to England by its Teutonic conquerors. By the end of the sixth century, with the conversion of the

1

country to Christianity, we were also beginning to receive portions of Hebrew literature. The English people acquired a rapidly increasing number of Anglo-Saxon redactions of biblical episodes, as well as a good deal of the theological and legendary matter from the early Christian Church. By the end of the ninth century, during the civilizing reign of Alfred the Great in Wessex, we were already also adding to our stock some Latin literature through translations of the late Roman philosopher Bœthius' *Consolations of Philosophy* and *The Universal History* of Orosius. French verse forms established themselves in England along with the Norman barons who came in the wake of William the Conqueror's triumph in 1066; and French romance, itself based on Celtic legend, found a new homeland in England. By the middle of the fourteenth century, the early renaissance of Dante's and Boccaccio's Italy began to filter through in the work of Chaucer and his contemporaries, and the full-blown renaissance of the succeeding centuries became English property in the sixteenth century.

It was at this time, too, that such ancient classics as Homer and Plutarch, the English Bible, Rabelais and Montaigne, were added to our literary store. Then in the seventeenth century, largely through contact between the French and the exiled English courts, French neo-classicism was brought to our shores, and Molière became a valuable acquisition. In the eighteenth century, as the British empire began to spread over the Orient, our ancestors fell under the spell of the *Arabian Nights* and the glamorous Moslem world, and became interested in the Sanskrit literature of India. At this time they also discovered the long-neglected writings of the Anglo-Saxon period, along with the lays and sagas of Scandinavia and Iceland. Finally, the eighteenth century gave us the masters of the French Enlightenment, Voltaire, Montesquieu, Rousseau, and others.

At the beginning of the nineteenth century, the English-speaking world made the acquaintance of Goethe and other German romanticists. Then, as our knowledge of the East was enlarged, a variety of exotic literatures entered our consciousness. Chinese, Persian, and Japanese, as well as more Hindu, masterpieces became known to us. Egyptology recovered specimens of one of the world's oldest cultures; and our growing knowledge of Celtic literature culminated in the popularization of Gaelic poetry and legend by the Irish nationalist movement. Toward the end of the century, con-

tinued familiarity with French culture and contact with hitherto remote Russia brought us such masters of realistic fiction as Balzac, Flaubert, Maupassant, Zola, Turgenev, Tolstoy, and Dostoyevsky. About this time, too, Scandinavia contributed Ibsen's realistic plays to the English theater. Since that time, many other foreign works have enjoyed vogues, although it is too early to say whether they will endure as a vital part of our literary culture. Personal taste alone will dictate any predictions one may venture on this score. All that can be said is that some writers, most notably Marcel Proust and Thomas Mann, have already made strong bids for inclusion in our heritage with one or more of their works.

The present collection of *Literature in Translation* brings together some of the greatest of the writings that have come into our heritage. They were produced in many different times and places, but they were so filled with life that they have transcended geographical and linguistic boundaries. They have kept their power in a new and different world than that in which they were created, and they have been sufficiently rich and rewarding to survive even the inevitable reduction they have had to suffer, in many instances, by translation.

Each of the foreign literatures that have contributed masterpieces to us has added something significant, whose loss would leave us poorer. We cannot fail to see how distinctly the Hebrew and Greek classics left their mark on all that we think and feel, as well as on all that we create in our own tongue. Indeed, as Matthew Arnold noted, they have dominated all that is fundamental in our culture. Much that is most pleasantly fanciful in our reading has come to us, as Arnold also observed, directly and indirectly from the Celtic world. We have shared in the courtesy and the wit and clear thinking of the French, and in the brilliant narrative skill of the Italians, as well as in the florid imagination of the Arabian story-tellers and the mysticism of the Hindu sages. We have enjoyed the romanticism of the German, the penetrating social analysis of the Norwegian, the sympathetic realism of the Russian. And other lands have bestowed their characteristic gifts. From them all we have received much sustenance and strength. It remains only to be added that to those nations that could avail themselves of the privilege we made generous payment in kind, for the literature that contains the writings of Chaucer, Shakespeare, Milton, Swift, Byron, Dickens, Whitman, and many other masters has had currency enough to pay all debts.

INTRODUCTION TO PART ONE

HELLENIC AND HEBRAIC WORLDS

Our heritages from the Hellenic world of Greece and Rome and from the Hebraic world of Palestine have usually appeared to be in conflict with each other, but have just as often appeared in some form of synthesis. Because of their importance, their seeming conflict, and the balance which they can provide (and have provided) when taken together, the masterpieces of classic and Hebraic literature are collected in this book into a single division. Together they form the foundation of our culture and of its literary expression.

The moral fervor of the Hebrews, along with their sense of social justice and of divine retribution for evil, may be traced through the greater part of our literature. One cannot read Spenser, Shakespeare, Milton, Wordsworth, Dickens, and Carlyle, not to mention numerous minor writers, without realizing this. With it, however, most important writers have combined the love of beauty, awareness of form, and enjoyment of natural gratifications which we associate with Greece.

It was the noble and penetrating English critic Matthew Arnold who succeeded in defining most sharply the respective merits and shortcomings of our dual heritage, in pointing out their clash of principles, and emphasizing the importance of finding the proper balance between them. In the light of modern research, it is possible to qualify Arnold's distinctions somewhat. Neither Hellenism nor Hebraism was a full-grown and static concept; actually, they both grew up slowly and naturally in relation to historical circumstances, and they did not for long follow any single path undiverted by influences from without and impulses from within. The Greeks were by no means consistently beauty-loving and joy-seeking pagans; the ancient Hebrews were not always conscience-burdened puritans—as *The Song of Songs* alone would attest. Examples of puritanism, suppression of individualism and of free thought, moral fervor, consciousness of sin, and of the necessity of purification through mystic rites can be adduced from the his-

3

tory of Greece. At a late stage Hebrew literature was veering toward a Hellenistic skepticism, and Greek philosophical literature toward Hebraic moralism and oriental mysticism.

Nevertheless, we find that only the features singled out by Arnold impressed themselves upon the consciousness of the English-speaking peoples, and to this extent his essay, herewith reprinted, correctly analyzes the two pivots around which they and their literature have revolved.

MATTHEW ARNOLD

Hebraism and Hellenism

Both Hellenism and Hebraism arise out of the wants of human nature, and address themselves to satisfying those wants. But their methods are so different, they lay stress on such different points, and call into being by their respective disciplines such different activities, that the face which human nature presents when it passes from the hands of one of them to those of the other, is no longer the same. To get rid of one's ignorance, to see things as they are, and by seeing them as they are to see them in their beauty, is the simple and attractive ideal which Hellenism holds out before human nature; and from the simplicity and charm of this ideal, Hellenism, and human life in the hands of Hellenism, is invested with a kind of aërial ease, clearness, and radiancy; they are full of what we call sweetness and light. Difficulties are kept out of view, and the beauty and rationalness of the ideal have all our thoughts. "The best man is he who most tries to perfect himself, and the happiest man is he who most feels that he *is* perfecting himself,"—this account of the matter by Socrates, the true Socrates of the *Memorabilia*,[1] has something so simple, spontaneous, and unsophisticated about it, that it seems to fill us with clearness and hope when we hear it. But there is a saying which I have heard attributed to Mr. Carlyle about Socrates—a very happy saying, whether it is really Mr. Carlyle's or not—which excellently marks the essential point in which Hebraism differs from Hellenism. "Socrates," this saying goes, "is terribly *at ease* in Zion." Hebraism—and here is the source of its wonderful strength—has always been severely preoccupied with an awful sense of the impossibility of being at ease in Zion; of the difficulties which oppose themselves to man's pursuit or attainment of that perfection of which Socrates talks so hopefully and, as from this point of view one might almost say, so glibly. It is all very well to talk of getting rid of one's ignorance, of seeing things in their reality, seeing them in their beauty; but how is this to be done when there is something which thwarts and spoils all our efforts?

This something is sin; and the space which sin fills in Hebraism, as compared with Hellenism, is indeed prodigious. This obstacle to perfection fills the whole scene, and perfection appears remote and rising away from earth, in the background. Under the name of sin, the difficulties of knowing oneself and conquering oneself which impede man's passage to perfection, become, for Hebraism, a positive, active entity hostile to man, a mysterious power which I heard Dr. Pusey the other day, in one of his impressive sermons, compare to a hideous hunchback seated on our shoulders, and which it is the main business of our lives to hate and oppose. The discipline of the Old Testament may be summed up as a discipline teaching us to abhor and flee from sin; the discipline of the New Testament, as a discipline teaching us to die to it. As Hellenism speaks of thinking clearly, seeing things in their essence and beauty, as a grand and precious feat for man to achieve, so Hebraism speaks of becoming conscious of sin, of awakening to a sense of sin, as a feat of this kind. It is obvious to what wide divergence these differing tendencies, actively followed, must lead. As one passes and repasses from Hellenism to Hebraism, from

Hebraism and Hellenism. In this long essay Matthew Arnold has been discussing the contribution of the Greek world (Hellenism) and the Jewish. This English essayist and poet (1822-1888) is also represented in this anthology. See page 1156 for some facts concerning his life and works.
[1] Socrates as presented in Xenophon's *Memorabilia of Socrates.*

Plato to St. Paul, one feels inclined to rub one's eyes and ask oneself whether man is indeed a gentle and simple being, showing the traces of a noble and divine nature; or an unhappy chained captive, laboring with groanings that cannot be uttered to free himself from the body of this death.

Apparently it was the Hellenic conception of human nature which was unsound, for the world could not live by it. Absolutely to call it unsound, however, is to fall into the common error of its Hebraizing enemies; but it was unsound at that particular moment of man's development, it was premature. The indispensable basis of conduct and self-control, the platform upon which alone the perfection aimed at by Greece can come into bloom, was not to be reached by our race so easily; centuries of probation and discipline were needed to bring us to it. Therefore the bright promise of Hellenism faded, and Hebraism ruled the world. Then was seen that astonishing spectacle, so well marked by the often-quoted words of the prophet Zechariah, when men of all languages and nations took hold of the skirt of him that was a Jew, saying:—"*We will go with you, for we have heard that God is with you.*" And the Hebraism which thus received and ruled a world all gone out of the way and altogether become unprofitable, was, and could not but be, the later, the more spiritual, the more attractive development of Hebraism. It was Christianity; that is to say, Hebraism aiming at self-conquest and rescue from the thrall of vile affections, not by obedience to the letter of a law, but by conformity to the image of a self-sacrificing example. To a world stricken with moral enervation Christianity offered its spectacle of an inspired self-sacrifice; to men who refused themselves nothing, it showed one who refused himself everything;—"*my Saviour banished joy!*" says George Herbert. When the *alma Venus,* the life-giving and joy-giving power of nature, so fondly cherished by the Pagan world, could not save her followers from self-dissatisfaction and ennui, the severe words of the apostle came bracingly and refreshingly: "Let no man deceive you with vain words, for because of these things cometh the wrath of God upon the children of disobedience." Through age after age and generation after generation, our race, or all that part of our race which was most living and progressive, was *baptized into a death;* and endeavored, by suffering in the flesh, to cease from sin. Of this endeavor, the animating labors and afflictions of early Christianity, the touching asceticism of mediæval Christianity, are

the great historical manifestations. Literary monuments of it, each in its own way incomparable, remain in the *Epistles* of St. Paul, in St. Augustine's *Confessions,* and in the two original and simplest books of the *Imitation.*

Of two disciplines laying their main stress, the one, on clear intelligence, the other, on firm obedience; the one, on comprehensively knowing the ground of one's duty, the other, on diligently practicing it; the one, on taking all possible care (to use Bishop Wilson's words again) that the light we have be not darkness, the other, that according to the best light we have we diligently walk,—the priority naturally belongs to that discipline which braces all man's moral powers, and founds for him an indispensable basis of character. And, therefore, it is justly said of the Jewish people, who were charged with setting powerfully forth that side of the divine order to which the words *conscience* and *self-conquest* point, that they were "entrusted with the oracles of God"; as it is justly said of Christianity, which followed Judaism and which set forth this side with a much deeper effectiveness and a much wider influence, that the wisdom of the old Pagan world was foolishness compared to it. No words of devotion and admiration can be too strong to render thanks to these beneficent forces which have so borne forward humanity in its appointed work of coming to the knowledge and possession of itself; above all, in those great moments when their action was the wholesomest and the most necessary.

But the evolution of these forces, separately and in themselves, is not the whole evolution of humanity,—their single history is not the whole history of man; whereas their admirers are always apt to make it stand for the whole history. Hebraism and Hellenism are, neither of them, the *law* of human development, as their admirers are prone to make them; they are, each of them, contributions to human development,—august contributions, invaluable contributions; and each showing itself to us more august, more invaluable, more preponderant over the other, according to the moment in which we take them, and the relation in which we stand to them. The nations of our modern world, children of that immense and salutary movement which broke up the Pagan world, inevitably stand to Hellenism in a relation which dwarfs it, and to Hebraism in a relation which magnifies it. They are inevitably prone to take Hebraism as the law of human development, and not as simply a contribution to it, however precious,

And yet the lesson must perforce be learned, that the human spirit is wider than the most priceless of the forces which bear it onward, and that to the whole development of man Hebraism itself is, like Hellenism, but a contribution.

Perhaps we may help ourselves to see this clearer by an illustration drawn from the treatment of a single great idea which has profoundly engaged the human spirit, and has given it eminent opportunities for showing its nobleness and energy. It surely must be perceived that the idea of immortality, as this idea rises in its generality before the human spirit, is something grander, truer, and more satisfying than it is in the particular forms by which St. Paul, in the famous fifteenth chapter of the Epistle to the Corinthians, and Plato, in the *Phædo,* endeavor to develop and establish it. Surely we cannot but feel that the argumentation with which the Hebrew apostle goes about to expound this great idea is, after all, confused and inconclusive; and that the reasoning, drawn from analogies of likeness and equality, which is employed upon it by the Greek philosopher, is over-subtle and sterile. Above and beyond the inadequate solutions which Hebraism and Hellenism here attempt, extends the immense and august problem itself, and the human spirit which gave birth to it. And this single illustration may suggest to us how the same thing happens in other cases also.

But meanwhile, by alternations of Hebraism and Hellenism, of a man's intellectual and moral impulses, of the effort to see things as they really are, and the effort to win peace by self-conquest, the human spirit proceeds; and each of these two forces has its appointed hours of culmination and seasons of rule. As the great movement of Christianity was a triumph of Hebraism and man's moral impulses, so the great movement which goes by the name of the Renascence was an uprising and reinstatement of man's intellectual impulses and of Hellenism. We in England, the devoted children of Protestantism, chiefly know the Renascence by its subordinate and secondary side of the Reformation. The Reformation has been often called a Hebraizing revival, a return to the ardor and sincereness of primitive Christianity. No one, however, can study the development of Protestantism and of Protestant churches without feeling that into the Reformation, too,—Hebraizing child of the Renascence and offspring of its fervor, rather than its intelligence, as it undoubtedly was,—the subtle Hellenic leaven of the Renascence found its way, and that the exact respective parts, in the Reformation, of Hebraism and of Hellenism, are not easy to separate. But what we may with truth say is, that all which Protestantism was to itself clearly conscious of, all which it succeeded in clearly setting forth in words, had the characters of Hebraism rather than of Hellenism. The Reformation was strong, in that it was an earnest return to the Bible and to doing from the heart the will of God as there written. It was weak, in that it never consciously grasped or applied the central idea of the Renascence,—the Hellenic idea of pursuing, in all lines of activity, the law and science, to use Plato's words, of things as they really are. Whatever direct superiority, therefore, Protestantism had over Catholicism was a moral superiority, a superiority arising out of its greater sincerity and earnestness,—at the moment of its apparition at any rate,—in dealing with the heart and conscience. Its pretensions to an intellectual superiority are in general quite illusory. For Hellenism, for the thinking side in man as distinguished from the acting side, the attitude of mind of Protestantism towards the Bible in no respect differs from the attitude of mind of Catholicism towards the Church. The mental habit of him who imagines that Balaam's ass spoke, in no respect differs from the mental habit of him who imagines that a Madonna of wood or stone winked; and the one, who says that God's Church makes him believe what he believes, and the other, who says that God's Word makes him believe what he believes, are for the philosopher perfectly alike in not really and truly knowing, when they say *God's Church* and *God's Word,* what it is they say, or whereof they affirm.

In the sixteenth century, therefore, Hellenism re-entered the world, and again stood in presence of Hebraism,—a Hebraism renewed and purged. Now, it has not been enough observed, how, in the seventeenth century, a fate befell Hellenism in some respects analogous to that which befell it at the commencement of our era. The Renascence, that great re-awakening of Hellenism, that irresistible return of humanity to nature and to seeing things as they are, which in art, in literature, and in physics, produced such splendid fruits, had, like the anterior Hellenism of the Pagan world, a side of moral weakness and of relaxation or insensibility of the moral fiber, which in Italy showed itself with the most startling plainness, but which in France, England, and other countries was very apparent, too. Again this loss of spiritual balance, this exclusive preponderance given to man's perceiving and knowing side, this unnatural defect of his feeling and acting side, provoked a reaction. Let us trace that reaction where it most nearly concerns us.

Science has now made visible to everybody the great and pregnant elements of difference which lie in race, and in how signal a manner they make the genius and history of an Indo-European people vary from those of a Semitic people. Hellenism is of Indo-European growth, Hebraism is of Semitic growth; and we English, a nation of Indo-European stock, seem to belong naturally to the movement of Hellenism. But nothing more strongly marks the essential unity of man than the affinities we can perceive, in this point or that, between members of one family of peoples and members of another. And no affinity of this kind is more strongly marked than that likeness in the strength and prominence of the moral fiber, which, notwithstanding immense elements of difference, knits in some special sort the genius and history of us English, and our American descendants across the Atlantic, to the genius and history of the Hebrew people. Puritanism, which has been so great a power in the English nation, and in the strongest part of the English nation, was originally the reaction in the seventeenth century of the conscience and moral sense of our race, against the moral indifference and lax rule of conduct which in the sixteenth century came in with the Renascence. It was a reaction of Hebraism against Hellenism; and it powerfully manifested itself, as was natural, in a people with much of what we call a Hebraizing turn, with a signal affinity for the bent which was the master-bent of Hebrew life. Eminently Indo-European by its *humor*, by the power it shows, through this gift, of imaginatively acknowledging the multiform aspects of the problem of life, and of thus getting itself unfixed from its own over-certainty, of smiling at its own over-tenacity, our race has yet (and a great part of its strength lies here), in matters of practical life and moral conduct, a strong share of the assuredness, the tenacity, the intensity of the Hebrews. This turn manifested itself in Puritanism, and has had a great part in shaping our history for the last two hundred years. Undoubtedly it checked and changed amongst us that movement of the Renascence which we see producing in the reign of Elizabeth such wonderful fruits. Undoubtedly it stopped the prominent rule and direct development of that order of ideas which we call by the name of Hellenism, and gave the first rank to a different order of ideas. Apparently, too, as we said of the former defeat of Hellenism, if Hellenism was defeated, this shows that Hellenism was imperfect, and that its ascendancy at that moment would not have been for the world's good.

Yet there is a very important difference between the defeat inflicted on Hellenism by Christianity eighteen hundred years ago, and the check given to the Renascence by Puritanism. The greatness of the difference is well measured by the difference in force, beauty, significance, and usefulness, between primitive Christianity and Protestantism. Eighteen hundred years ago it was altogether the hour of Hebraism. Primitive Christianity was legitimately and truly the ascendant force in the world at that time, and the way of mankind's progress lay through its full development. Another hour in man's development began in the fifteenth century, and the main road of his progress then lay for a time through Hellenism. Puritanism was no longer the central current of the world's progress, it was a side stream crossing the central current and checking it. The cross and the check may have been necessary and salutary, but that does not do away with the essential difference between the main stream of man's advance and a cross or side stream. For more than two hundred years the main stream of man's advance has moved towards knowing himself and the world, seeing things as they are, spontaneity of consciousness; the main impulse of a great part, and that the strongest part, of our nation has been towards strictness of conscience. They have made the secondary the principal at the wrong moment, and the principal they have at the wrong moment treated as secondary. This contravention of the natural order has produced, as such contravention always must produce, a certain confusion and false movement, of which we are now beginning to feel, in almost every direction, the inconvenience. In all directions our habitual causes of action seem to be losing efficaciousness, credit, and control, both with others and even with ourselves. Everywhere we see the beginnings of confusion, and we want a clue to some sound order and authority. This we can only get by going back upon the actual instincts and forces which rule our life, seeing them as they really are, connecting them with other instincts and forces, and enlarging our whole view and rule of life.

ANCIENT CLASSICAL LITERATURES

The term "classic" has been freely applied to any work that has become a standard of excellence for a particular period, nation, or group of nations. We may thus speak of a "classic of romanticism," a "classic of English literature," or a "European classic." The word was first used by the Romans, when only members of the chief class of the state were called *classici*, as compared with the poorer people who were described as *infra classem*—that is, below the true class. Used in a figurative sense, a "classic" was a writer of prime distinction. Sainte-Beuve's definition in his essay *What Is a Classic?* refers to the classic writer as "an old author canonized by admiration, and an authority in his particular style." He sets forth the essential qualities that in the long run assure such canonization:

"A true classic, as I should like to see it defined, is an author who has enriched the mind of man, increased its treasure, and enabled it to advance a step; who has discovered a moral and unequivocal truth or revealed some eternal passion in that heart in which all seemed known and revealed; who has expressed his thought, observation, or invention, in no matter what form, provided only it be broad and great, refined, sane, and beautiful in itself; who has spoken to all in his own peculiar style, but a style which is found to be also the property of the whole world and is new without neologism, new and yet old, contemporary with all time."

Many writers who wrote after the fall of Rome would qualify under Sainte-Beuve's catholic definition, but the terms "classic," "classics," and "classical literature" have long been employed in a strict sense as a synonym for Greek and Roman writing. To the Romans, the Greeks were the classics. Later ages made the Romans classics too. During the medieval centuries, in Western Europe, while the Greek language and its masterpieces were largely unknown, men looked back on Latin writings with admiration and sometimes even with the kind of reverence that Dante displayed toward Virgil. During the Renaissance this veneration was extended to Greek authors whose general superiority became ultimately recognized.

THE MAIN PERIODS OF GREEK AND ROMAN LITERATURE

The Greek and Latin masterpieces develop out of two related and long-evolving cultures. They arise in different, more or less well-defined, ages, and represent their highest achievements. A preliminary review of the main periods of classical literature may help to relate a richly diversified heritage. For convenience they may be listed in the following order:

1. *The Homeric Age*

In this period (*circa* 850 B.C.) the Greek epics, the *Iliad* and the *Odyssey*, were created. This age was no doubt preceded by a good deal of "floating" or unwritten literature about which very little is known. In the succeeding and less exalted centuries, from the eighth to the end of the sixth, more floating literature was composed by rhapsodists who elaborated the epic material that provided subjects for many a later Greek tragedy. From these narratives, that took the form of "cycles," only fragments have come down to us. In addition we have the didactic and largely uninspired poetry of the Bœotian poet Hesiod, who was considered by some ancient writers as Homer's contemporary and by others as his junior by several generations. His lowly *Works and Days* or *Erga* recounts the workaday life of an agricultural community, retails such common superstitions as the lucky and unlucky days of the year, and contains popular saws that reflect the complaints and the wry wisdom of a hard-pressed peasantry. In contrast to Homer's admiration for the primitive kings, Hesiod's social animus is democratic; his philosophy has been aptly described by Gilbert Murray as bitter insurgency against the oligarchy of noblemen who oppress the common people. His poem also includes the classic myths of Pandora and the Four Ages—of gold, silver, bronze, and iron. Hesiod's other poem, the *Theogony*, is an attempt to systematize Greek religion and to correlate its myths and local cults. This codification of religious material gave to later centuries a kind of lay Bible and a source for literary references. Comic war poems, an extant example of which is *The Battle of the Frogs and Mice*, also abounded in the seventh and sixth centuries, and a series of hymns, believed to have been associated with the recital of epic poetry, have survived from that time. Long philosophical works, of which only fragments survive, were written in verse, and the authors—Thales, Solon, Xenophanes, Parmenides, Heraclitus, and others—are significant in the early history of philosophy. The seventh and sixth centuries also gave rise to various forms of lyric poetry and were graced by the well-known names of Sappho, Anacreon, and Simonides, who were succeeded in the next century by the great Theban poet Pindar.

2. *The Attic Age*

During the Attic Age of the fifth and fourth centuries B.C. the city-state of Athens was culturally predominant. This is the period of the superb playwrights Æschylus, Sophocles, Euripides, and Aristophanes; of the great historians Herodotus and Thucydides; and of the philosophers Anaxagoras and Socrates. Their work belongs for the most part to the fifth century, the time of the political supremacy of Athens after the battles of Marathon and Salamis. In the main, this period, the most glorious in ancient history, revolves around its political leader, Pericles, and is conse-

quently known as the "Periclean Age." But, although Athens was defeated by Sparta in 404 B.C. and became so politically weakened that it lost its independence under Philip of Macedonia and Alexander the Great, Athens retained cultural primacy for nearly another remarkable century. The fourth century B.C. is noted for the comedies of Menander and many other playwrights whose work has been lost; for the philosophical masterpieces of Plato and Aristotle; the historical writings of Xenophon, and the oratory of Demosthenes.

3. *The Hellenistic or Alexandrian Age*

This age may be said to begin in 322 B.C., the year of the death of both Demosthenes and Aristotle, the year politically punctuated by the division of Alexander's empire by his generals, after his death in 323. The literary predominance of Athens passed to Alexandria, the city in Egypt founded by Alexander, which became the capital of his successors, the Ptolemies. Only in one respect did Athens retain its intellectual leadership; it remained the home of philosophers, and it was there that Epicurus and Zeno established their influential schools of thought. Alexandria, enjoying royal patronage and a magnificent library, became the metropolis of the Hellenistic world—that is, of Greek-dominated Mediterranean civilization. Although largely derivative and academic, Alexandrian culture produced, in addition to such scholars and scientists as Euclid, Eratosthenes, and Hipparchus, some notable poets: the third-century writers of idylls Theocritus, Bion, and Moschus. It was here, too, that followers of Plato became permeated with oriental mysticism and produced neo-platonic systems of thought that were later used by Christian apologists to establish a connection between Christian theology and Greek philosophy.

Alexandria, however, was only one center of Hellenism, and the late products of Greek genius appeared throughout the Mediterranean world, especially in Rome. Notable work graced the declining years of Hellenism—the histories of Polybius (205-123 B.C.) and the Hellenized Jew, Josephus (A.D. 37?-95?), the geography of Strabo (63 B.C.-A.D. 21), the biographies and essays of Plutarch (A.D. 46?-120?), the philosophical lectures of Epictetus (A.D. 97-175), and the satires of Lucian (A.D. 125?-200?). It was during this period, too, that the Greek Anthology was enriched with many short lyrics and epigrams by minor poets. Hellenic literary activity continued until the fourth century

A.D. with diminishing results, until classic Greek literature became virtually extinct owing to the opposition of Christianity, the infiltration of the Orient, the corruption of the Greek language, and a succession of political catastrophes.

4. Early Roman Literature

Literature written in the Latin language started after the First Punic War. It began about the middle of the third century B.C. with imitations of Greek epic poetry by Livius Andronicus. He was followed by a more original writer of epic verse and comedy, Nævius, and by the dramatic and epic poet Ennius (239-169 B.C.) who was highly regarded by Cicero and Horace. None of their work became part of our literary heritage, but the third and the second centuries were noteworthy for the development of Roman comedy by its two masters, Plautus (254-184 B.C.) and Terence (194-159 B.C.), whose work influenced all European comedy. This period also witnessed the dawn of Roman satire, oratory, and history.

5. The Age of Cicero and the Augustan Period

This period covers roughly the first century B.C. and the first two decades of the first century A.D. (100 B.C.-A.D. 14), when the Roman Empire was master of western and southern Europe and of the Mediterranean areas of Asia and Africa. It includes the reign of Augustus Cæsar (27 B.C.-A.D. 14), the greatest of Roman emperors.

The republican period of the first century before Christ, which preceded the reign of Augustus, produced the orations, essays, and letters of Cicero (106-43 B.C.); the *Commentaries* of Julius Cæsar (100-44 B.C.); the histories of Sallust (86-34 B.C.) and Livy (59-17 B.C.), who also belongs to the age of Augustus, who befriended him; the great philosophical poem *De Rerum Natura* (The Nature of Things) by Lucretius (96-55 B.C.), and the lyric poetry of Catullus (87-54 B.C.).

To the Augustan Age belongs the best poetry of Virgil (70-19 B.C.), Horace (65-8 B.C.), Propertius (50?-15? B.C.), and Ovid (43 B.C.-A.D. 17).

6. The Post-Augustan Period

The period from the death of Augustus to the close of the reign of Theodoric in A.D. 526 and the end of the Roman Empire marked the gradual decline of Roman culture, with intermittent interludes of revival. Roman satire developed in the work of Persius, Juvenal, Martial, and Petronius during the first century A.D.; Seneca wrote his in-fluential closet dramas during Nero's reign; and epic poetry continued to be written by Lucan, Statius, and others. History and biography achieved notable extension at the hands of Tacitus (A.D. 55?-120), and about the same time Suetonius wrote his terrifying portraits of some of the decadent Emperors in his *Lives of the Twelve Cæsars*. Pliny the Younger established letter writing on a high plane, and picaresque or adventure fiction made its appearance in Petronius' satirical novel *The Satyricon* and Apuleius' romance *The Golden Ass*. In the third, fourth, and fifth centuries A.D., considerable literary activity continued, but only some of the poetry of Ausonius (310-394), Claudius Claudianus (365?-408?), Sidonius Apollinaris (5th century), and the anonymous *Vigil of Venus* have any claim to attention.

For the convenience and instruction of the reader, we have presented the vast field of Greek and Roman writing telescopically in this anthology. We have singled out a few periods, such as the Periclean Age, because of its well-defined unity; but wherever such unity is of secondary importance, the selections are grouped under some unifying heading (such as Greek and Latin Poetry).

The reader should remember that the selections in the classic section have been culled from a literature that stretched over thirteen centuries, if not more. The people who expressed themselves in this literature faced so vast a variety of circumstances and conflicts that their experience may be said to sum up the entire history of man's glory and travail on this earth. In the selections that follow we may, above all, see the peculiar blend of the intellectual and the emotional, of the physical and the mental, that made these people the originators of so much that we prize in civilization. We may also learn much about their way of life—their social systems, politics, religious practices, and even their intimate human interests. Despite their many differences, the ancient classical literatures reveal considerable literary continuity. A distinct style sets the genuinely classical author apart from, let us say, medieval and romantic writers. We discover in his work scrupulous attention to literary form, clarity of observation and statement, and fundamental directness and balance.

MYTHOLOGY

One other thing that the Greeks and Romans held in common and passed on to later generations is a mythology. Ignorance of this wealth of traditional matter to which classic writers refer constantly is the principal barrier to an understanding of their work. For this reason, and because classic mythology has an inherent charm and interest, the first selection in this section is an account of the best-known myths as given by Thomas Bulfinch. (Stories referring to the Trojan War, the *Odyssey*, and some great tragic cycles are, however, postponed until the Homeric poems and the Greek tragedies are reached.)

Although variously modified and elaborated by later writers, mythology was originally a "floating" or oral literature stemming from primitive times; consequently it is shrouded in obscurity. Parallels to the myths of Greece will be found in other cultures; in Egypt, Syria, and Persia, and among the ancient Hindus, who were related to the classic Greeks as members of the Indo-European family, which has a common linguistic basis. All myths are obviously rooted in primitive society, in ritual and magic-making, and ultimately, of course, in primitive psychology.

Some important scholars have stressed Nature mythology, but the extremists among them have been criticized for maintaining that primitive man is "highly interested in natural phenomena, and that his interest is predominantly of a theoretical, contemplative, and poetical character."[1] In expressing or interpreting nature, man creates personified concepts and stories, and each myth therefore contains some kernel of natural fact elaborated beyond easy recognition. The objection to accepting this theory strictly is that primitive man "has to a very limited extent the purely artistic or scientific interest in nature," and that "there is but little room for symbolism in his ideas and tales." Yet nature appears in many myths.

Another view of mythology has stressed the historical record of the past. Unquestionably, primitive history and the deeds of remote heroes, or the founders of powerful ruling families, left an imprint on the myths. But this is not the whole explanation by any means. It is also possible to find imbedded in mythology primitive sexual conflicts from which neurotic modern man has by no means found release, such as incest (and the taboo against it), and the tensions that must have existed between the all-powerful fathers of patriarchal societies and their sons. No doubt some myths reflect the struggle against such antisocial impulses.

The most authoritative contemporary opinion, however, puts the main stress on the myth's service to primitive society or culture, largely in connection with established magical practices and religious rites, with moral regulations that restrain antisocial impulses, and such social facts as the existence of distinct tribes and of useful customs. The myth becomes "a warrant of antiquity, reality, and sanctity" for a magic-making rite, a ceremony, or a social or moral rule. It embodies a cultural fact, and is often regarded by primitive peoples "to be the real cause which has brought about the moral rule, the social grouping, the rite, or the custom"; it states a precedent, so to speak. When it expresses some idea of immortality, it voices a belief inherent in human nature and in social practices; when it deals with the origins of families, tribes, or dynasties, it expresses the gregarious instincts of man and gives sanction to the social organization of a given period. When it revolves, as it often does, around the recurrent cycle of life and death—as in the death and resurrection stories of mythological figures like Osiris, Attis, Adonis, Orpheus, Dionysus, and the Mexican god Quetzalcoatl—the myth releases its believer from fears of death and of loss of potency on the one hand, and on the other hand, it gives explanatory sanction to magic intended to further such a practical end as assuring the return of the fruitful season. Rites undertaken for the promotion of fertility, tribal unity, and tribal order are similarly justified by the tale; that is, the myth of magic justifies the claims of the practitioner to potency, warrants the correctness of his procedure, and vouches for the truth of its underlying belief.

Whatever may be the actual uses of myths in any society, it is clear that the various stories in any mythology have often had a long and complicated history before they were worked into the larger pattern of a mythological system or adapted to the uses of the people where they are found. But a really adequate study of the origins and wanderings of the various myths has hardly begun.

What interests us here, however, is not this extensive anthropological background (although it serves to counteract a naïve or flippant attitude toward mythology) but the literary aspect of this abundant material. Myth contains the seeds of later epics, romances, and dramas. Its beliefs are close to the desires, obsessions, fears, and aspirations of

[1] The quotations in this paragraph are from Bronislaw Malinowski's *Myth in Primitive Psychology*, Norton, 1926.

humanity. "Myths of love and death, stories of the loss of immortality, of the passing of the Golden Age, and of the banishment from Paradise, myths of incest and of sorcery play with the very elements which enter into the artistic forms of tragedy, of lyric, and of romantic narrative."[2] Moreover, in strengthening tradition, they promote culture, which is the source of later literature; and as the first works of fiction of any society, they set examples for future and more consciously created literary art.

The magnificence of Greek mythology foreshadows the genius that later expressed itself in the work of the Greek masters. "A nation less gifted loads the name of its god with epithets and his idol with attributes; the Greek, because dowered with imagination, *feels* his god as a *personality*, with a live human history."[3] In their myths, the people of Hellas began the art of humanization, of beauty, of blitheness, and of release from fear that glows in the greatest Greek literature.

[2] *Ibid.,* p. 88.
[3] Jane Ellen Harrison, *Mythology,* Marshall Jones, 1924.

THOMAS BULFINCH

Myths of Greece and Rome

The Greek Gods

The religions of ancient Greece and Rome are extinct. The so-called divinities of Olympus have not a single worshiper among living men. They belong now not to the department of theology, but to those of literature and taste. There they still hold their place, and will continue to hold it, for they are too closely connected with the finest productions of poetry and art, both ancient and modern, to pass into oblivion.

We propose to tell the stories relating to them which have come down to us from the ancients, and which are alluded to by modern poets, essayists, and orators. Our readers may thus at the same time be entertained by the most charming fictions which fancy has ever created, and put in possession of information indispensable to everyone who would read with intelligence the elegant literature of his own day.

In order to understand these stories, it will be necessary to acquaint ourselves with the ideas of the structure of the universe which prevailed among the Greeks—the people from whom the Romans, and other nations through them, received their science and religion.

The Greeks believed the earth to be flat and circular, their own country occupying the middle of it, the central point being either Mount Olympus,

the abode of the gods, or Delphi, so famous for its oracle.

The circular disk of the earth was crossed from west to east and divided into two equal parts by the *Sea,* as they called the Mediterranean, and its continuation the Euxine, the only seas with which they were acquainted.

Around the earth flowed the *River Ocean,* its course being from south to north on the western side of the earth, and in a contrary direction on the eastern side. It flowed in a steady, equable current, unvexed by storm or tempest. The sea, and all the rivers on earth, received their waters from it.

The northern portion of the earth was supposed to be inhabited by a happy race named the Hyperboreans, dwelling in everlasting bliss and spring beyond the lofty mountains whose caverns were supposed to send forth the piercing blasts of the north wind, which chilled the people of Hellas (Greece). Their country was inaccessible by land or sea. They lived exempt from disease or old age, from toils and warfare.

On the south side of the earth, close to the stream of Ocean, dwelt a people happy and virtuous as the Hyperboreans. They were named the Ethiopians. The gods favored them so highly that they were wont to leave at times their Olympian abodes and go to share their sacrifices and banquets.

Myths of Greece and Rome. From Bulfinch, *The Age of Fable.*

On the western margin of the earth, by the stream of Ocean, lay a happy place named the Elysian Plain, whither mortals favored by the gods were transported without tasting of death, to enjoy an immortality of bliss. This happy region was also called the "Fortunate Fields," and the "Isles of the Blessed."

We thus see that the Greeks of the early ages knew little of any real people except those to the east and south of their own country, or near the coast of the Mediterranean. Their imagination meantime peopled the western portion of this sea with giants, monsters, and enchantresses; while they placed around the disk of the earth, which they probably regarded as of no great width, nations enjoying the peculiar favor of the gods, and blessed with happiness and longevity.

The Dawn, the Sun, and the Moon were supposed to rise out of the Ocean, on the eastern side, and to drive through the air, giving light to gods and men. The stars, also, except those forming the Wain or Bear, and others near them, rose out of and sank into the stream of Ocean. There the sun-god embarked in a winged boat, which conveyed him round by the northern part of the earth, back to his place of rising in the east.

The abode of the gods was on the summit of Mount Olympus, in Thessaly. A gate of clouds, kept by the goddesses named the Seasons, opened to permit the passage of the Celestials to earth, and to receive them on their return. The gods had their separate dwellings; but all, when summoned, repaired to the palace of Jupiter, as did also those deities whose usual abode was the earth, the waters, or the underworld. It was also in the great hall of the palace of the Olympian king that the gods feasted each day on ambrosia and nectar, their food and drink, the latter being handed round by the lovely goddess Hebe. Here they conversed of the affairs of heaven and earth; and as they quaffed their nectar, Apollo, the god of music, delighted them with the tones of his lyre, to which the Muses sang in responsive strains. When the sun was set, the gods retired to sleep in their respective dwellings.

The following lines from the *Odyssey* will show how Homer conceived of Olympus:

So saying, Minerva, goddess azure-eyed,
Rose to Olympus, the reputed seat
Eternal of the gods, which never storms
Disturb, rains drench, or snow invades, but calm
The expanse and cloudless shines with purest day.
There the inhabitants divine rejoice
Forever.

The robes and other parts of the dress of the goddesses were woven by Minerva and the Graces, and everything of a more solid nature was formed of the various metals. Vulcan was architect, smith, armorer, chariot builder, and artist of all work in Olympus. He built of brass the houses of the gods; he made for them the golden shoes with which they trod the air or the water, and moved from place to place with the speed of the wind, or even of thought. He also shod with brass the celestial steeds, which whirled the chariots of the gods through the air, or along the surface of the sea. He was able to bestow on his workmanship self-motion, so that the tripods (chairs and tables) could move of themselves in and out of the celestial hall. He even endowed with intelligence the golden handmaidens whom he made to wait on himself.

Jupiter, or Jove (Zeus), though called the father of gods and men, had himself a beginning. Saturn (Cronos) was his father, and Rhea (Ops) his mother. Saturn and Rhea were of the race of Titans, who were the children of Earth and Heaven, which sprang from Chaos, of which we shall give a further account in our next chapter.

There is another cosmogony, or account of the creation, according to which Earth, Erebus, and Love were the first of beings. Love (Eros) issued from the egg of Night, which floated on Chaos. By his arrows and torch he pierced and vivified all things, producing life and joy.

Saturn and Rhea were not the only Titans. There were others, whose names were Oceanus, Hyperion, Iapetus, and Ophion, males; and Themis, Minemosyn, Eurynome, females. They are spoken of as the elder gods, whose dominion was afterwards transferred to others. Saturn yielded to Jupiter, Oceanus to Neptune, Hyperion to Apollo. Hyperion was the father of the Sun, Moon, and Dawn. He is therefore the original sun-god, and is painted with the splendor and beauty which were afterwards bestowed on Apollo.

Ophion and Eurynome ruled over Olympus till they were dethroned by Saturn and Rhea.

The representations given of Saturn are not very consistent; for on the one hand his reign is said to have been the golden age of innocence and purity, and on the other he is described as a monster who devoured his children. Jupiter, however, escaped this fate, and when grown up espoused Metis (Prudence), who administered a draught to Saturn which caused him to disgorge his children. Jupiter, with his brothers and sisters, now rebelled against their father Saturn and his brothers the Titans, vanquished them, and imprisoned some of them in Tartarus, inflicting other penalties on others. Atlas was condemned to bear up the heavens on his shoulders.

On the dethronement of Saturn, Jupiter with his brothers Neptune (Poseidon) and Pluto (Dis) divided his dominions. Jupiter's portion was the heavens, Neptune's the ocean, and Pluto's the realms of the dead. Earth and Olympus were common property. Jupiter was king of gods and men. The thunder was his weapon, and he bore a shield called Ægis, made for him by Vulcan. The eagle was his favorite bird, and bore his thunderbolts.

Juno (Hera) was the wife of Jupiter, and queen of the gods. Iris, the goddess of the rainbow, was her attendant and messenger. The peacock was her favorite bird.

Vulcan (Hephæstos), the celestial artist, was the son of Jupiter and Juno. He was born lame, and his mother was so displeased at the sight of him that she flung him out of heaven. Other accounts say that Jupiter kicked him out for taking part with his mother in a quarrel which occurred between them. Vulcan's lameness, according to this account, was the consequence of his fall. He was a whole day falling, and at last alighted on the Island of Lemnos, which was thenceforth sacred to him. Milton alludes to this story in *Paradise Lost,* Book I:

> . . . From morn
> To noon he fell, from noon to dewy eve,
> A summer's day; and with the setting sun
> Dropped from the zenith, like a falling star,
> On Lemnos, the Ægean isle.

Mars (Ares), the god of war, was the son of Jupiter and Juno.

Phœbus Apollo, the god of archery, prophecy, and music, was the son of Jupiter and Latona, and brother of Diana (Artemis). He was god of the sun, as Diana, his sister, was the goddess of the moon.

Venus (Aphrodite), the goddess of love and beauty, was the daughter of Jupiter and Dione. Others say that Venus sprang from the foam of the sea. The zephyr wafted her along the waves to the Isle of Cyprus, where she was received and attired by the Seasons, and then led to the assembly of the gods. All were charmed with her beauty, and each one demanded her for his wife. Jupiter gave her to Vulcan, in gratitude for the service he had rendered in forging thunderbolts. So the most beautiful of the goddesses became the wife of the most

ill-favored of gods. Venus possessed an embroidered girdle called Cestus, which had the power of inspiring love. Her favorite birds were swans and doves, and the plants sacred to her were the rose and the myrtle.

Cupid (Eros), the god of love, was the son of Venus. He was her constant companion; and, armed with bow and arrows, he shot the darts of desire into the bosoms of both gods and men. There was a deity named Anteros, who was sometimes represented as the avenger of slighted love, and sometimes as the symbol of reciprocal affection. The following legend is told of him:

Venus, complaining to Themis that her son Eros continued always a child, was told by her that it was because he was solitary, and that if he had a brother he would grow apace. Anteros was soon afterwards born, and Eros immediately was seen to increase rapidly in size and strength.

Minerva (Pallas, Athene), the goddess of wisdom, was the offspring of Jupiter, without a mother. She sprang forth from his head completely armed. Her favorite bird was the owl, and the plant sacred to her the olive.

Mercury (Hermes) was the son of Jupiter and Maia. He presided over commerce, wrestling, and other gymnastic exercises, even over thieving, and everything, in short, which required skill and dexterity. He was the messenger of Jupiter, and wore a winged cap and winged shoes. He bore in his hand a rod entwined with two serpents, called the caduceus.

Mercury is said to have invented the lyre. He found, one day, a tortoise, of which he took the shell, made holes in the opposite edges of it, and drew cords of linen through them, and the instrument was complete. The cords were nine, in honor of the nine Muses. Mercury gave the lyre to Apollo, and received from him in exchange the caduceus.

Ceres (Demeter) was the daughter of Saturn and Rhea. She had a daughter named Proserpine (Persephone), who became the wife of Pluto, and queen of the realms of the dead. Ceres presided over agriculture.

Bacchus (Dionysus), the god of wine, was the son of Jupiter and Semele. He represents not only the intoxicating power of wine, but its social and beneficent influences likewise, so that he is viewed as the promoter of civilization, and a lawgiver and lover of peace.

The Muses were the daughters of Jupiter and Mnemosyne (Memory). They presided over song, and prompted the memory. They were nine in number, to each of whom was assigned the presidence over some particular department of literature, art, or science. Calliope was the muse of epic poetry, Clio of history, Euterpe of lyric poetry, Melpomene of tragedy, Terpsichore of choral dance and song, Erato of love poetry, Polyhymnia of sacred poetry, Urania of astronomy, Thalia of comedy.

The Graces were goddesses presiding over the banquet, the dance, and all social enjoyments and elegant arts. They were three in number. Their names were Euphrosyne, Aglaia, and Thalia.

The Fates were also three—Clotho, Lachesis, and Atropos. Their office was to spin the thread of human destiny, and they were armed with shears, with which they cut it off when they pleased. They were the daughters of Themis (Law), who sits by Jove on his throne to give him counsel.

The Erinnyes, or Furies, were three goddesses who punished by their secret stings the crimes of those who escaped or defied public justice. The heads of the Furies were wreathed with serpents, and their whole appearance was terrific and appalling. Their names were Alecto, Tisiphone, and Megæra. They were also called Eumenides.

Nemesis was also an avenging goddess. She represents the righteous anger of the gods, particularly towards the proud and insolent.

Pan was the god of flocks and shepherds. His favorite residence was in Arcadia.

The Satyrs were deities of the woods and fields. They were conceived to be covered with bristly hair, their heads decorated with short, sprouting horns, and their feet like goats' feet.

Momus was the god of laughter, and Plutus the god of wealth.

Roman Divinities

The preceding are Grecian divinities, though received also by the Romans. Those which follow are peculiar to Roman mythology:

Saturn was an ancient Italian deity. It was attempted to identify him with the Grecian god Cronos, and fabled that after his dethronement by Jupiter he fled to Italy, where he reigned during what was called the Golden Age. In memory of his beneficent dominion, the feast of Saturnalia was held every year in the winter season. Then all public business was suspended, declarations of war and criminal executions were postponed, friends made presents to one another, and the slaves were indulged with great liberties. A feast was given them at which they sat at table, while their masters served them, to show the natural equality of men, and that all things belonged equally to all, in the reign of Saturn.

Faunus, the grandson of Saturn, was worshiped as the god of fields and shepherds, and also as a prophetic god. His name in the plural, Fauns, expressed a class of gamesome deities, like the Satyrs of the Greeks.

Quirinus was a war god, said to be no other than Romulus, the founder of Rome, exalted after his death to a place among the gods.

Bellona, a war goddess.

Terminus, the god of landmarks. His statue was a rude stone or post, set in the ground to mark the boundaries of fields.

Pales, the goddess presiding over cattle and pastures.

Pomona presided over fruit trees.

Flora, the goddess of flowers.

Lucina, the goddess of childbirth.

Vesta (the Hestia of the Greeks) was a deity presiding over the public and private hearth. A sacred fire, tended by six virgin priestesses called Vestals, flamed in her temple. As the safety of the city was held to be connected with its conservation, the neglect of the virgins, if they let it go out, was severely punished, and the fire was rekindled from the rays of the sun.

Liber is the Latin name of Bacchus; and Mulciber of Vulcan.

Janus was the porter of heaven. He opens the year, the first month being named after him. He is the guardian deity of gates, on which account he is commonly represented with two heads, because every door looks two ways. His temples at Rome were numerous. In war time the gates of the principal one were always open. In peace they were closed; but they were shut only once between the reign of Numa and that of Augustus.

The Penates were the gods who were supposed to attend to the welfare and prosperity of the family. Their name is derived from Penus, the pantry, which was sacred to them. Every master of a family was the priest to the Penates of his own house.

The Lares, or Lars, were also household gods, but differed from the Penates in being regarded as the deified spirits of mortals. The family Lars were held to be the souls of the ancestors, who watched over and protected their descendants. The words Lemur and Larva more nearly correspond to our word Ghost.

The Romans believed that every man had his

Genius, and every woman her Juno: that is, a spirit who had given them being, and was regarded as their protector through life. On their birthdays men made offerings to their Genius, women to their Juno.

The Creation and First Ages

Before earth and sea and heaven were created, all things wore one aspect, to which we give the name of Chaos—a confused and shapeless mass, nothing but dead weight, in which, however, slumbered the seeds of things. Earth, sea, and air were all mixed up together; so the earth was not solid, the sea was not fluid, and the air was not transparent. God and Nature at last interposed, and put an end to this discord, separating earth from sea, and heaven from both. The fiery part, being the lightest, sprang up, and formed the skies; the air was next in weight and place. The earth, being heavier, sank below; and the water took the lowest place, and buoyed up the earth.

Here some god—it is not known which—gave his good offices in arranging and disposing the earth. He appointed rivers and bays their places, raised mountains, scooped out valleys, distributed woods, fountains, fertile fields, and stony plains. The air being cleared, the stars began to appear, fishes took possession of the sea, birds of the air, and four-footed beasts of the land.

But a nobler animal was wanted, and Man was made. It is not known whether the creator made him of divine materials, or whether in the earth, so lately separated from heaven, there lurked still some heavenly seeds. Prometheus took some of this earth, and kneading it up with water, made man in the image of the gods. He gave him an upright stature, so that while all other animals turn their faces downward, and look to the earth, he raises his to heaven, and gazes on the stars.

Prometheus was one of the Titans, a gigantic race who inhabited the earth before the creation of man. To him and his brother Epimetheus was committed the office of making man, and providing him and all other animals with the faculties necessary for their preservation. Epimetheus undertook to do this, and Prometheus was to overlook his work when it was done. Epimetheus accordingly proceeded to bestow upon the different animals the various gifts of courage, strength, swiftness, sagacity; wings to one, claws to another, a shelly covering to a third, etc. But when man came to be provided for, who was to be superior to all other animals, Epimetheus had been so prodigal of his resources that he had nothing left to bestow upon him. In his perplexity he resorted to his brother Prometheus, who, with the aid of Minerva, went up to heaven, and lighted his torch at the chariot of the sun, and brought down fire to man. With this gift man was more than a match for all other animals. It enabled him to make weapons wherewith to subdue them; tools with which to cultivate the earth; to warm his dwelling, so as to be comparatively independent of climate; and finally to introduce the arts and to coin money, the means of trade and commerce.

Woman was not yet made. The story (absurd enough!) is that Jupiter made her, and sent her to Prometheus and his brother, to punish them for their presumption in stealing fire from heaven; and man, for accepting the gift. The first woman was named Pandora. She was made in heaven, every god contributing something to perfect her. Venus gave her beauty, Mercury persuasion, Apollo music, etc. Thus equipped, she was conveyed to earth, and presented to Epimetheus, who gladly accepted her, though cautioned by his brother to beware of Jupiter and his gifts. Epimetheus had in his house a jar, in which were kept certain noxious articles, for which, in fitting man for his new abode, he had had no occasion. Pandora was seized with an eager curiosity to know what this jar contained; and one day she slipped off the cover and looked in. Forthwith there escaped a multitude of plagues for hapless man,—such as gout, rheumatism, and colic for his body, and envy, spite, and revenge for his mind,—and scattered themselves far and wide. Pandora hastened to replace the lid! but, alas! the whole contents of the jar had escaped, one thing only excepted, which lay at the bottom, and that was *hope*. So we see at this day, whatever evils are abroad, hope never entirely leaves us; and while we have *that,* no amount of other ills can make us completely wretched.

Another story is that Pandora was sent in good faith, by Jupiter, to bless man; that she was furnished with a box, containing her marriage presents, into which every god had put some blessing. She opened the box incautiously, and the blessings all escaped, *hope* only excepted. This story seems more probable than the former; for how could hope, so precious a jewel as it is, have been kept in a jar full of all manner of evils, as in the former statement?

The world being thus furnished with inhabitants, the first age was an age of innocence and happiness, called the *Golden Age.* Truth and right prevailed, though not enforced by law, nor was there any magistrate to threaten or punish. The forest had not yet been robbed of its trees to furnish timbers for vessels, nor had men built fortifications round their towns. There were no such things as swords, spears, or helmets. The earth brought forth all things necessary for man, without his labor in plowing or sowing. Perpetual spring reigned, flowers sprang up without seed, the rivers flowed with milk and wine, and yellow honey distilled from the oaks.

Then succeeded the *Silver Age,* inferior to the *Golden,* but better than that of brass. Jupiter shortened the spring, and divided the year into seasons. Then, first, men had to endure the extremes of heat and cold, and houses became necessary. Caves were the first dwellings, and leafy coverts of the woods, and huts woven of twigs. Crops would no longer grow without planting. The farmer was obliged to sow the seed, and the toiling ox to draw the plow.

Next came the *Brazen Age,* more savage of temper, and readier to the strife of arms, yet not altogether wicked. The hardest and worst was the *Iron Age.* Crime burst in like a flood; modesty, truth, and honor fled. In their places came fraud and cunning, violence, and the wicked love of gain. Then seamen spread sails to the wind, and the trees were torn from the mountains to serve for keels to ships, and vex the face of ocean. The earth, which till now had been cultivated in common, began to be divided off into possessions. Men were not satisfied with what the surface produced, but must dig into its bowels, and draw forth from thence the ores of metals. Mischievous *iron,* and more mischievous *gold,* were produced. War sprang up, using both as weapons; the guest was not safe in his friend's house; and sons-in-law and fathers-in-law, brothers and sisters, husbands and wives, could not trust one another. Sons wished their fathers dead, that they might come to the inheritance; family love lay prostrate. The earth was wet with slaughter, and the gods abandoned it, one by one, till Astræa alone was left, and finally she also took her departure.

Jupiter, seeing this state of things, burned with anger. He summoned the gods to council. They obeyed the call, and took the road to the palace of heaven. The road, which anyone may see in a clear night, stretches across the face of the sky, and is called the Milky Way. Along the road stand the palaces of the illustrious gods; the common people of the skies live apart, on either side. Jupiter addressed the assembly. He set forth the frightful condition of things on the earth, and closed by announcing his intention to destroy the whole of its inhabitants, and provide a new race, unlike the first, who would be more worthy of life, and much better worshipers of the gods. So saying he took a thunderbolt, and was about to launch it at the world, and destroy it by burning; but recollecting the danger that such a conflagration might set heaven itself on fire, he changed his plan, and resolved to drown it. The north wind, which scatters the clouds, was chained up; the south was sent out, and soon covered all the face of heaven with a cloak of pitchy darkness. The clouds, driven together, resound with a crash; torrents of rain fall; the crops are laid low; the year's labor of the husbandman perishes in an hour. Jupiter, not satisfied with his own waters, calls on his brother Neptune to aid him with his. He lets loose the rivers, and pours them over the land. At the same time, he heaves the land with an earthquake, and brings in the reflux of the ocean over the shores. Flocks, herds, men, and houses are swept away, and temples, with their sacred enclosures, profaned. If any edifice remained standing, it was overwhelmed, and its turrets lay hid beneath the waves. Now all was sea, sea without shore. Here and there an individual remained on a projecting hilltop, and a few, in boats, pulled the oar where they had lately driven the plow. The fishes swim among the treetops; the anchor is let down into a garden. Where the graceful lambs played but now, unwieldy sea calves gambol. The wolf swims among the sheep, the yellow lions and tigers struggle in the water. The strength of the wild boar serves him not, nor his swiftness the stag. The birds fall with weary wing into the water, having found no land for a resting-place. Those living beings whom the water spared fell a prey to hunger.

Parnassus alone, of all the mountains, overtopped the waves; and there Deucalion, and his wife Pyrrha, of the race of Prometheus, found refuge—he a just man, and she a faithful worshiper of the gods. Jupiter, when he saw none left alive but this pair, and remembered their harmless lives and pious demeanor, ordered the north winds to drive away the clouds, and disclose the skies to earth, and earth to the skies. Neptune also directed Triton to blow on his shell, and sound a retreat to the waters. The waters obeyed, and the sea returned to its shores, and the rivers to their channels. Then Deucalion thus addressed Pyrrha: "O wife, only surviving woman, joined to me first by the ties of kindred and marriage, and now by a common danger, would that we possessed the power of our ancestor Prometheus, and could renew the race as he at first made it! But as we cannot, let us seek yonder temple, and inquire of the gods what remains for us to do." They entered the temple, deformed as it was with slime, and approached the altar, where no fire burned. There they fell prostrate on the earth, and prayed the goddess to inform them how they might retrieve their miserable affairs. The oracle answered, "Depart from the temple with head veiled and garments unbound, and cast behind you the bones of your mother." They heard the words with astonishment. Pyrrha first broke silence: "We cannot obey; we dare not profane the remains of our parents." They sought the thickest shades of the wood, and revolved the oracle in their minds. At length Deucalion spoke: "Either my sagacity deceives me, or the command is one we may obey without impiety. The earth is the great parent of all; the stones are her bones; these we may cast behind us; and I think this is what the oracle means. At least, it will do no harm to try." They veiled their faces, unbound their garments, and picked up stones, and cast them behind them. The stones (wonderful to relate) began to grow soft, and assume shape. By degrees, they put on a rude resemblance to the human form, like a block half finished in the hands of the sculptor. The moisture and slime that were about them became flesh; the stony part became bones; the veins remained veins, retaining their name, only changing their use. Those thrown by the hand of the man became men, and those by the woman became women. It was a hard race, and well adapted to labor, as we find ourselves to be at this day, giving plain indications of our origin.

Prometheus has been a favorite subject with the poets. He is represented as the friend of mankind, who interposed in their behalf when Jove was incensed against them, and who taught them civilization and the arts. But as, in so doing, he transgressed the will of Jupiter, he drew down on himself the anger of the ruler of gods and men. Jupiter had him chained to a rock on Mount Caucasus, where a vulture preyed on his liver, which was renewed as fast as devoured. This state of torment might have been brought to an end at any time by Prometheus, if he had been willing to submit to his oppressor; for he possessed a secret which involved the stability of Jove's throne, and if he would have revealed it, he might have been at once taken into favor. But that he disdained to do. He has therefore become the symbol of magnanimous endurance of unmerited suffering, and strength of will resisting oppression.

The Python

The slime with which the earth was covered by the waters of the flood produced an excessive fertility, which called forth every variety of production, both bad and good. Among the rest, Python, an enormous serpent, crept forth, the terror of the people, and lurked in the caves of Mount Parnassus. Apollo slew him with his arrows—weapons which he had not before used against any but feeble animals, hares, wild goats, and such game. In commemoration of this illustrious conquest he instituted the Pythian games, in which the victor in feats of strength, swiftness of foot, or in the chariot race was crowned with a wreath of beech leaves; for the laurel was not yet adopted by Apollo as his own tree.

The famous statue of Apollo called the Belvedere represents the god after this victory over the serpent Python.

Apollo and Daphne

Daphne was Apollo's first love. It was not brought about by accident, but by the malice of Cupid. Apollo saw the boy playing with his bow and arrows; and being himself elated with his recent victory over Python, he said to him, "What have you to do with warlike weapons, saucy boy? Leave them for hands worthy of them. Behold the conquest I have won by means of them over the vast serpent who stretched his poisonous body over acres of the plain! Be content with your torch, child, and kindle up your flames, as you call them, where you will, but presume not to meddle with my weapons." Venus's boy heard these words, and rejoined, "Your arrows may strike all things else, Apollo, but mine shall strike you." So saying, he took his stand on a rock of Parnassus, and drew from his quiver two arrows of different workmanship, one to excite love, the other to repel it. The former was of gold and sharp-pointed, the latter blunt and tipped with lead. With the leaden shaft he struck the nymph Daphne, the daughter of the river god Peneus, and with the golden one Apollo, through the heart. Forthwith the god was seized with love for the maiden, and she abhorred the thought of loving. Her delight was in woodland sports and in the spoils of the chase. Many lovers sought her, but she spurned them all, ranging the woods, and taking no thought of Cupid nor of Hymen. Her father often said to her, "Daughter, you owe me a son-in-law; you owe me grandchildren." She, hating the thought of marriage as a crime, with her beautiful face tinged all over with blushes, threw her arms around her father's neck, and said, "Dearest father, grant me this favor, that I may always remain unmarried, like Diana." He consented, but at the same time said, "Your own face will forbid it."

Apollo loved her, and longed to obtain her; and he who gives oracles to all the world was not wise enough to look into his own fortunes. He saw her hair flung loose over her shoulders, and said, "If so charming in disorder, what would it be if arranged?" He saw her eyes bright as stars; he saw her lips, and was not satisfied with only seeing them. He admired her hands and arms, naked to the shoulder, and whatever was hidden from view he imagined more beautiful still. He followed her; she fled, swifter than the wind, and delayed not a moment at his entreaties. "Stay," said he, "daughter of Peneus; I am not a foe. Do not fly me as a lamb flies the wolf, or a dove the hawk. It is for love I pursue you. You make me miserable, for fear you should fall and hurt yourself on these stones, and I should be the cause. Pray run slower, and I will follow slower. I am no clown, no rude peasant. Jupiter is my father, and I am lord of Delphos and Tenedos, and know all things, present and future. I am the god of song and the lyre. My arrows fly true to the mark; but, alas! an arrow more fatal than mine has pierced my heart! I am the god of medicine, and know the virtues of all healing plants. Alas! I suffer a malady that no balm can cure!"

The nymph continued her flight, and left his plea half uttered. And even as she fled she charmed him. The wind blew her garments, and her unbound hair streamed loose behind her. The god grew impatient to find his wooings thrown away, and, sped by Cupid, gained upon her in the race. It was like a hound pursuing a hare, with open jaws ready to seize, while the feebler animal darts forward, slipping from the very grasp. So flew the god and the virgin—he on the wings of love, and she on those of fear. The pursuer is the more rapid, however, and gains upon her, and his panting breath blows upon her hair. Her strength begins to fail, and, ready to sink, she calls upon her father, the river god: "Help me, Peneus! open the earth to enclose me, or change my form, which has brought me into this danger!" Scarcely had she spoken, when a stiffness seized all her limbs; her bosom began to be enclosed in a tender bark; her hair became leaves; her arms became branches; her foot stuck fast in the ground, as a root; her face became a tree-top, retaining nothing of its former self but its beauty. Apollo stood amazed. He touched the stem, and felt the flesh tremble under the new bark. He embraced the branches, and lavished kisses on the wood. The branches shrank from his lips. "Since you cannot be my wife," said he, "you shall assuredly be my tree. I will wear you for my crown; I will decorate with you my harp and my quiver; and when the great Roman conquerors lead up the triumphal pomp to the Capitol, you shall be woven into wreaths for their brows. And, as eternal youth is mine, you also shall be always green, and your leaf know no decay." The nymph, now changed into a laurel tree, bowed its head in grateful acknowledgment.

Io

Juno one day perceived it suddenly grow dark, and immediately suspected that her husband had raised a cloud to hide some of his doings that would not bear the light. She brushed away the cloud, and saw her husband on the banks of a glassy river, with a beautiful heifer standing near him. Juno suspected the heifer's form concealed some fair nymph of mortal mold—as was, indeed, the case; for it was Io, the daughter of the river god Inachus, whom Jupiter had been flirting with, and, when he became aware of the approach of his wife, had changed into that form.

Juno joined her husband, and noticing the heifer, praised its beauty, and asked whose it was, and of what herd. Jupiter, to stop questions, replied that it was a fresh creation from the earth. Juno asked to have it as a gift. What could Jupiter do? He was loath to give his mistress to his wife; yet how refuse so trifling a present as a simple heifer? He could not, without exciting suspicion; so he consented. The goddess was not yet relieved of her suspicions; so she delivered the heifer to Argus, to be strictly watched.

Now Argus had a hundred eyes in his head, and never went to sleep with more than two at a time, so that he kept watch of Io constantly. He suffered her to feed through the day, and at night tied her up with a vile rope round her neck. She would have stretched out her arms to implore freedom of Argus, but she had no arms to stretch out, and her voice was a bellow that frightened even herself. She saw her father and her sisters, went near them, and suffered them to pat her back, and heard them admire her beauty. Her father reached her a tuft of grass, and she licked the outstretched hand. She longed to make herself known to him, and would have uttered her wish; but, alas! words were wanting. At length she bethought herself of writing, and inscribed her name—it was a short one—with her hoof on the sand. Inachus recognized it, and discovering that his daughter, whom he had long sought in vain, was hidden under this disguise, mourned over her, and, embracing her white neck, exclaimed, "Alas! my daughter, it would have been a less grief to have lost you altogether!" While he thus lamented, Argus, observing, came and drove her away, and took his seat on a high bank, from whence he could see all round in every direction.

Jupiter was troubled at beholding the sufferings of his mistress, and calling Mercury told him to go and despatch Argus. Mercury made haste, put his winged slippers on his feet, and cap on his head, took his sleep-producing wand, and leaped down from the heavenly towers to the earth. There he laid aside his wings, and kept only his wand, with which he presented himself as a shepherd driving his flock. As he strolled on he blew upon his pipes. These were what are called the Syrinx or Pandean pipes. Argus listened with delight, for he had never seen the instrument before. "Young man," said he, "come and take a seat by me on this stone. There is no better place for your flocks to graze in than hereabouts, and here is a pleasant shade such as shepherds love." Mercury sat down, talked, and told stories till it grew late, and played upon his pipes his most soothing strains, hoping to lull the watchful eyes to sleep, but all in vain; for Argus still contrived to keep some of his eyes open though he shut the rest.

Among other stories, Mercury told him how the instrument on which he played was invented. "There was a certain nymph, whose name was Syrinx, who was much beloved by the satyrs and spirits of the wood; but she would have none of them, but was a faithful worshiper of Diana, and followed the chase. You would have thought it was Diana herself, had you seen her in her hunting dress, only that her bow was of horn and Diana's of silver. One day, as she was returning from the chase, Pan met her, told her just this, and added more of the same sort. She ran away, without stopping to hear his compliments, and he pursued till she came to the bank of the river, where he overtook her, and she had only time to call for help on her friends the water nymphs. They heard and consented. Pan threw his arms around what he supposed to be the form of the nymph, and found he embraced only a tuft of reeds! As he breathed a sigh, the air sounded through the reeds, and produced a plaintive melody. The god, charmed with the novelty and with the sweetness of the music, said, 'Thus, then, at least, you shall be mine.' And he took some of the reeds, and placing them together, of unequal lengths, side by side, made an instrument which he called Syrinx, in honor of the nymph." Before Mercury had finished his story he saw Argus's eyes all asleep. As his head nodded forward on his breast, Mercury with one stroke cut his neck through, and tumbled his head down the rocks. O hapless Argus! the light of your hundred eyes is quenched at once! Juno took them and put them as ornaments on the tail of her peacock, where they remain to this day.

But the vengeance of Juno was not yet satiated. She sent a gadfly to torment Io, who fled over the whole world from its pursuit. She swam through the Ionian Sea, which derived its name from her, then roamed over the plains of Illyria, ascended Mount Hæmus, and crossed the Thracian strait, thence named the Bosphorus (cow-ford), rambled on through Scythia, and the country of the Cimmerians, and arrived at last on the banks of the Nile. At length Jupiter interceded for her, and upon his promising not to pay any more attentions to her Juno consented to restore her to her form. It was curious to see her gradually recover her former self. The coarse hairs fell from her body, her horns shrank up, her eyes grew narrower, her mouth shorter; hands and fingers came instead of hoofs to her forefeet; in fine there was nothing left of the heifer, except her beauty. At first she was afraid to speak, for fear she should low, but gradually she recovered her confidence and was restored to her father and sisters.

Callisto

Callisto was another maiden who excited the jealousy of Juno, and the goddess changed her into a bear. "I will take away," said she, "that beauty with which you have captivated my husband." Down fell Callisto on her hands and knees; she tried to stretch out her arms in supplication—they were already beginning to be covered with black hair. Her hands grew rounded, became armed with crooked claws, and served for feet; her mouth, which Jove used to praise for its beauty, became a horrid pair of jaws; her voice, which if unchanged would have moved the heart to pity, became a growl, more fit to inspire terror. Yet her former disposition remained, and with continual groaning, she bemoaned her fate, and stood upright as well as she could, lifting up her paws to beg for mercy, and felt that Jove was unkind, though she could not tell him so. Ah, how often, afraid to stay in the woods all night alone, she wandered about the neighborhood of her former haunts; how often, frightened by the dogs, did she, so lately a huntress, fly in terror from the hunters! Often she fled from the wild beasts, forgetting that she was now a wild beast herself; and, bear as she was, was afraid of the bears.

One day a youth espied her as he was hunting. She saw him and recognized him as her own son, now grown a young man. She stopped and felt inclined to embrace him. As she was about to approach, he, alarmed, raised his hunting spear, and was on the point of transfixing her, when Jupiter, beholding, arrested the crime, and snatching away both of them, placed them in the heavens as the Great and Little Bear.

Juno was in a rage to see her rival so set in honor, and hastened to ancient Tethys and Oceanus, the powers of ocean, and in answer to their inquiries thus told the cause of her coming: "Do you ask why I, the queen of the gods, have left the heavenly plains and sought your depths? Learn that I am supplanted in heaven—my place is given to another. You will hardly believe me; but look when night darkens the world, and you shall see the two of whom I have so much reason to complain exalted to the heavens, in that part where the circle is the smallest, in the neighborhood of the pole. Why should anyone hereafter tremble at the thought of offending Juno, when such rewards are the consequence of my displeasure? See what I have been able to effect! I forbade her to wear the human form—she is placed among the stars! So do my punishments result—such is the extent of my power! Better that she should have resumed her former shape, as I permitted Io to do. Perhaps he means to marry her, and put me away! But you, my foster-parents, if you feel for me, and see with displeasure this unworthy treatment of me, show it, I beseech you, by forbidding this guilty couple from coming into your waters." The powers of the ocean assented, and consequently the two constel-lations of the Great and Little Bear move round and round in heaven, but never sink, as the other stars do, beneath the ocean.

Diana and Actæon

Thus in two instances we have seen Juno's severity to her rivals; now let us learn how a virgin goddess punished an invader of her privacy.

It was midday, and the sun stood equally distant from either goal, when young Actæon, son of King Cadmus, thus addressed the youths who with him were hunting the stag in the mountains:

"Friends, our nets and our weapons are wet with the blood of our victims; we have had sport enough for one day, and tomorrow we can renew our labors. Now, while Phœbus parches the earth, let us put by our implements and indulge ourselves with rest."

There was a valley thick enclosed with cypresses and pines, sacred to the huntress queen, Diana. In the extremity of the valley was a cave, not adorned with art, but nature had counterfeited art in its construction, for she had turned the arch of its roof with stones as delicately fitted as if by the hand of man. A fountain burst out from one side, whose open basin was bounded by a grassy rim. Here the goddess of the woods used to come when weary with hunting and lave her virgin limbs in the sparkling water.

One day, having repaired thither with her nymphs, she handed her javelin, her quiver, and her bow to one, her robe to another, while a third unbound the sandals from her feet. Then Crocale, the most skillful of them, arranged her hair, and Nephele, Hyale, and the rest drew water in capacious urns. While the goddess was thus employed in the labors of the toilet, behold Actæon, having quitted his companions, and rambling without any especial object, came to the place, led thither by his destiny. As he presented himself at the entrance of the cave, the nymphs, seeing a man, screamed and rushed towards the goddess to hide her with their bodies. But she was taller than the rest and overtopped them all by a head. Such a color as tinges the clouds at sunset or at dawn came over the countenance of Diana thus taken by surprise. Surrounded as she was by her nymphs, she yet turned half away, and sought with a sudden impulse for her arrows. As they were not at hand, she dashed the water into the face of the intruder, adding these words: "Now go and tell, if you can, that you have seen Diana unappareled." Immediately a pair of branching stag's horns grew out of his head, his neck gained in length, his ears grew sharp-pointed, his hands became feet, his arms long legs, his body was covered with a hairy spotted hide. Fear took the place of his former boldness, and the hero fled. He could not but admire his own speed; but when he saw his horns in the water, "Ah, wretched me!" he would have said, but no sound followed the effort. He groaned, and tears flowed down the face which had taken the place of his own. Yet his consciousness remained. What shall he do?—go home to seek the palace, or lie hid in the woods? The latter he was afraid, the former he was ashamed, to do. While he hesitated the dogs saw him. First Melampus, a Spartan dog, gave the signal with his bark, then Pamphagus, Dorceus, Lelaps, Theron, Nape, Tigris, and all the rest, rushed after him swifter than the wind. Over rocks and cliffs, through mountain gorges that seemed impracticable, he fled and they followed. Where he had often chased the stag and cheered on his pack, his pack now chased him, cheered on by his huntsmen. He longed to cry out, "I am Actæon; recognize your master!" but the words came not at his will. The air resounded with the bark of the dogs. Presently one fastened on his back, another seized his shoulder. While they held their master, the rest of the pack came up and buried their teeth in his flesh. He groaned,—not in a human voice, yet certainly not in a stag's,—and falling on his knees, raised his eyes, and would have raised his arms in supplication, if he had had them. His friends and fellow-huntsmen cheered on the dogs, and looked everywhere for Actæon, calling on him to join the sport. At the sound of his name, he turned his head, and heard them regret that he should be away. He earnestly wished he was. He would have been well pleased to see the exploits of his dogs, but to feel them was too much. They were all around him, rending and tearing; and it was not till they had torn his life out that the anger of Diana was satisfied.

Midas

Bacchus, on a certain occasion, found his old schoolmaster and foster-father, Silenus, missing. The old man had been drinking, and in that state wandered away, and was found by some peasants, who carried him to their king, Midas. Midas recognized him, and treated him hospitably, entertaining him for ten days and nights with an unceasing round of jollity. On the eleventh day he brought Silenus back, and restored him in safety to his pupil. Whereupon Bacchus offered Midas his choice of a reward, whatever he might wish. He asked that whatever he might touch should be changed into *gold*. Bacchus consented, though sorry that he had not made a better choice. Midas went his way, rejoicing in his new-acquired power, which he hastened to put to the test. He could scarce believe his eyes when he found a twig of an oak, which he plucked from the branch, become gold in his hand. He took up a stone; it changed to gold. He touched a sod; it did the same. He took an apple from the tree; you would have thought he had robbed the garden of the Hesperides. His joy knew no bounds, and as soon as he got home, he ordered the servants to set a splendid repast on the table. Then he found to his dismay that whether he touched bread, it hardened in his hand; or put a morsel to his lips, it defied his teeth. He took a glass of wine, but it flowed down his throat like melted gold.

In consternation at the unprecedented affliction, he strove to divest himself of his power; he hated the gift he had lately coveted. But all in vain; starvation seemed to await him. He raised his arms, all shining with gold, in prayer to Bacchus, begging to be delivered from his glittering destruction. Bacchus, merciful deity, heard and consented. "Go," said he, "to the River Pactolus, trace the stream to its fountainhead, there plunge your head and body in, and wash away your fault and its punishment." He did so, and scarce had he touched the waters before the gold-creating power passed into them, and the river sands became changed into *gold,* as they remain to this day.

Thenceforth Midas, hating wealth and splendor, dwelt in the country, and became a worshiper of Pan, the god of the fields. On a certain occasion Pan had the temerity to compare his music with that of Apollo, and to challenge the god of the lyre to a trial of skill. The challenge was accepted, and Tmolus, the mountain god, was chosen umpire. The senior took his seat, and cleared away the trees from his ears to listen. At a given signal Pan blew on his pipes, and with his rustic melody gave great satisfaction to himself and his faithful follower Midas, who happened to be present. Then Tmolus turned his head toward the Sun-god, and all his trees turned with him. Apollo rose, his brow wreathed with Parnassian laurel, while his robe of Tyrian purple swept the ground. In his left hand he held the lyre, and with his right hand struck the strings. Ravished with the harmony, Tmolus at once awarded the victory to the god of the lyre, and all but Midas acquiesced in the judgment. He dissented, and questioned the justice of the award. Apollo would not suffer such a depraved pair of ears any longer to wear the human form, but caused them to increase in length, grow hairy, within and without, and movable on their roots; in short, to be on the perfect pattern of those of an ass.

Mortified enough was King Midas at this mishap; but he consoled himself with the thought that it was possible to hide his misfortune, which he attempted to do by means of an ample turban or head-dress. But his hair-dresser of course knew the secret. He was charged not to mention it, and threatened with dire punishment if he presumed to disobey. But he found it too much for his discretion to keep such a secret; so he went out into the meadow, dug a hole in the ground, and stooping down, whispered the story, and covered it up. Before long a thick bed of reeds sprang up in the meadow, and as soon as it had gained its growth, began whispering the story, and has continued to do so, from that day to this, every time a breeze passes over the place.

Venus and Adonis

Venus, playing one day with her boy Cupid, wounded her bosom with one of his arrows. She pushed him away, but the wound was deeper than she thought. Before it healed she beheld Adonis, and was captivated with him. She no longer took any interest in her favorite resorts—Paphos, and Cnidos, and Amathos, rich in metals. She absented herself even from heaven, for Adonis was dearer to her than heaven. Him she followed and bore him company. She who used to love to recline in the shade, with no care but to cultivate her charms, now rambles through the woods and over the hills, dressed like the huntress Diana; and calls her dogs, and chases hares and stags, or other game that it is safe to hunt, but keeps clear of the wolves and bears, reeking with the slaughter of the herd. She charged Adonis, too, to beware of such dangerous animals. "Be brave towards the timid," said she; "courage against the courageous is not safe. Beware how you expose yourself to danger and put my happiness to risk. Attack not the beasts that Nature has armed with weapons. I do not value your glory so high as to consent to purchase it by such exposure. Your youth, and the beauty that charms Venus, will not touch the hearts of lions and bristly boars. Think of their terrible claws and prodigious strength! I hate the whole race of them. Do you ask me why?" Then she told him the story of Atalanta and Hippomenes, who were changed into lions for their ingratitude to her.

Having given him this warning, she mounted her chariot drawn by swans, and drove away through the air. But Adonis was too noble to heed such counsels. The dogs had roused a wild boar from his lair, and the youth threw his spear and wounded the animal with a sidelong stroke. The beast drew out the weapon with his jaws, and rushed after Adonis, who turned and ran; but the boar overtook him, and buried his tusks in his side, and stretched him dying upon the plain.

Venus, in her swan-drawn chariot, had not yet reached Cyprus, when she heard coming up through mid-air the groans of her beloved, and turned her white-winged coursers back to earth. As she drew near and saw from on high his lifeless body bathed in blood, she alighted and, bending over it, beat her breast and tore her hair. Reproaching the Fates, she said, "Yet theirs shall be but a partial triumph; memorials of my grief shall endure, and the spectacle of your death, my Adonis, and of my lamentation shall be annually renewed. Your blood shall be changed into a flower; that consolation none can envy me." Thus speaking, she sprinkled nectar on the blood; and as they mingled, bubbles rose as in a pool on which raindrops fall, and in an hour's time there sprang up a flower of bloody hue like that of the pomegranate. But it is short-lived. It is said the wind blows the blossoms open, and afterwards blows the petals away; so it is called Anemone, or Wind Flower, from the cause which assists equally in its production and its decay.

Echo and Narcissus

Echo was a beautiful nymph, fond of the woods and hills, where she devoted herself to woodland sports. She was a favorite of Diana, and attended her in the chase. But Echo had one failing; she was fond of talking, and whether in chat or argument, would have the last word. One day Juno was seeking her husband, who, she had reason to fear, was amusing himself among the nymphs. Echo by her talk contrived to detain the goddess till the nymphs made their escape. When Juno discovered it, she passed sentence upon Echo in these words: "You shall forfeit the use of that tongue with which you have cheated me, except for that one purpose you are so fond of—*reply*. You shall still have the last word, but no power to speak first."

This nymph saw Narcissus, a beautiful youth, as he pursued the chase upon the mountains. She loved him and followed his footsteps. Oh, how she longed to address him in the softest accents, and win him to converse! but it was not in her power. She waited with impatience for him to speak first, and had her answer ready. One day the youth, being separated from his companions, shouted aloud, "Who's here?" Echo replied, "Here." Narcissus looked around, but seeing no one, called out, "Come." Echo answered, "Come." As no one came, Narcissus called again, "Why do you shun me?" Echo asked the same question. "Let us join one another," said the youth. The maid answered with all her heart in the same words, and hastened to the spot, ready to throw her arms about his neck. He started back, exclaiming, "Hands off! I would rather die than you should have me!" "Have me," said she; but it was all in vain. He left her, and she went to hide her blushes in the recesses of the woods. From that time forth she lived in caves and among mountain cliffs. Her form faded with grief, till at last all her flesh shrank away. Her bones were changed into rocks and there was nothing left of her but her voice. With that she is still ready to reply to anyone who calls her, and keeps up her old habit of having the last word.

Narcissus's cruelty in this case was not the only instance. He shunned all the rest of the nymphs, as he had done poor Echo. One day a maiden who had in vain endeavored to attract him uttered a prayer that he might some time or other feel what it was to love and meet no return of affection. The avenging goddess heard and granted the prayer.

There was a clear fountain, with water like silver, to which the shepherds never drove their flocks, nor the mountain goats resorted, nor any of the beasts of the forest; neither was it defaced with fallen leaves or branches; but the grass grew fresh around it, and the rocks sheltered it from the sun. Hither came one day the youth, fatigued with hunting, heated and thirsty. He stooped down to drink, and saw his own image in the water; he thought it was some beautiful water-spirit living in the fountain. He stood gazing with admiration at those bright eyes, those locks curled like the locks of Bacchus or Apollo, the rounded cheeks, the ivory neck, the parted lips, and the glow of health and exercise over all. He fell in love with himself. He brought his lips near to take a kiss; he plunged his arms in to embrace the beloved object.

It fled at the touch, but returned again after a moment and renewed the fascination. He could not tear himself away; he lost all thought of food or rest, while he hovered over the brink of the fountain gazing upon his own image. He talked with the supposed spirit: "Why, beautiful being, do you shun me? Surely my face is not one to repel you. The nymphs love me, and you yourself look not indifferent upon me. When I stretch forth my arms you do the same; and you smile upon me and answer my beckonings with the like." His tears fell into the water and disturbed the image. As he saw it depart, he exclaimed, "Stay, I entreat you! Let me at least gaze upon you, if I may not touch you." With this, and much more of the same kind, he cherished the flame that consumed him, so that by degrees he lost his color, his vigor, and the beauty which formerly had so charmed the nymph Echo. She kept near him, however, and when he exclaimed, "Alas! alas!" she answered him with the same words. He pined away and died; and when his shade passed the Stygian river, it leaned over the boat to catch a look at itself in the waters. The nymphs mourned for him, especially the water-nymphs; and when they smote their breasts Echo smote hers also. They prepared a funeral pile and would have burned the body, but it was nowhere to be found; but in its place a flower, purple within, and surrounded with white leaves, which bears the name and preserves the memory of Narcissus.

Perseus and Medusa

Perseus was the son of Jupiter and Danaë. His grandfather Acrisius, alarmed by an oracle which had told him that his daughter's child would be the instrument of his death, caused the mother and child to be shut up in a chest and set adrift on the sea. The chest floated towards Seriphus, where it was found by a fisherman who conveyed the mother and infant to Polydectes, the king of the country, by whom they were treated with kindness. When Perseus was grown up Polydectes sent him to attempt the conquest of Medusa, a terrible monster who had laid waste the country. She was once a beautiful maiden whose hair was her chief glory, but as she dared to vie in beauty with Minerva, the goddess deprived her of her charms and changed her beautiful ringlets into hissing serpents. She became a cruel monster of so frightful an aspect that no living thing could behold her without being turned into stone. All around the cavern where she dwelt might be seen the stony figures of men and animals which had chanced to catch a glimpse of her and had been petrified with the sight. Perseus, favored by Minerva and Mercury, the former of whom lent him her shield and the latter his winged shoes, approached Medusa while she slept and taking care not to look directly at her, but guided by her image reflected in the bright shield which he bore, he cut off her head and gave it to Minerva, who fixed it in the middle of her Ægis.

The Sea-Monster

Perseus, continuing his flight, arrived at the country of the Æthiopians, of which Cepheus was king. Cassiopeia his queen, proud of her beauty, had dared to compare herself to the Sea-Nymphs, which roused their indignation to such a degree that they sent a prodigious sea-monster to ravage the coast. To appease the deities, Cepheus was directed by the oracle to expose his daughter Andromeda to be devoured by the monster. As Perseus looked down from his aërial height he beheld the virgin chained to a rock, and waiting the approach of the serpent. She was so pale and motionless that if it had not been for her flowing tears and her hair that moved in the breeze, he would have taken her for a marble statue. He was so startled at the sight that he almost forgot to wave his wings. As he hovered over her he said, "O virgin, undeserving of those chains, but rather of such as bind fond lovers together, tell me, I beseech you, your name, and the name of your country, and why you are thus bound." At first she was silent from modesty, and, if she could, would have hid her face with her hands; but when he repeated his questions, for fear she might be thought guilty of some fault which she dared not tell, she disclosed her name and that of her country, and her mother's pride of beauty. Before she had done speaking, a sound was heard off upon the water, and the sea-monster appeared, with his head raised above the surface, cleaving the waves with his broad breast. The virgin shrieked, the father and mother who had now arrived at the scene, wretched both, but the mother more justly so, stood by, not able to afford protection, but only to pour forth lamentations and to embrace the victim. Then spoke Perseus: "There will be time enough for tears; this hour is all we have for rescue. My rank as the son of Jove and my renown as the slayer of the Gorgon might make me acceptable as a suitor; but I will try to win her by services rendered, if the gods will

only be propitious. If she be rescued by my valor, I demand that she be my reward." The parents consent (how could they hesitate?) and promise a royal dowry with her.

And now the monster was within the range of a stone thrown by a skillful slinger, when with a sudden bound the youth soared into the air. As an eagle, when from his lofty flight he sees a serpent basking in the sun, pounces upon him and seizes him by the neck to prevent him from turning his head round and using his fangs, so the youth darted down upon the back of the monster and plunged his sword into its shoulder. Irritated by the wound, the monster raised himself into the air, then plunged into the depth; then, like a wild boar surrounded by a pack of barking dogs, turned swiftly from side to side, while the youth eluded its attacks by means of his wings. Wherever he can find passage for his sword between the scales he makes a wound, piercing now the side, now the flank, as it slopes towards the tail. The brute spouts from his nostrils water mixed with blood. The wings of the hero are wet with it, and he dares no longer trust to them. Alighting on a rock which rose above the waves, and holding on by a projecting fragment, as the monster floated near he gave him a death stroke. The people who had gathered on the shore shouted so that the hills re-echoed with the sound. The parents, transported with joy, embraced their future son-in-law, calling him their deliverer and the savior of their house, and the virgin, both cause and reward of the contest, descended from the rock.

The Golden Fleece

In very ancient times there lived in Thessaly a king and queen named Athamas and Nephele. They had two children, a boy and a girl. After a time Athamas grew indifferent to his wife, put her away, and took another. Nephele suspected danger to her children from the influence of the stepmother, and took measures to send them out of her reach. Mercury assisted her, and gave her a ram with a *golden fleece,* on which she set the two children, trusting that the ram would convey them to a place of safety. The ram vaulted into the air with the children on his back, taking his course to the east, till when crossing the strait that divides Europe and Asia, the girl, whose name was Helle, fell from his back into the sea, which from her was called the Hellespont,—now the Dardanelles. The ram continued his career till he reached the kingdom of Colchis, on the eastern shore of the Black Sea, where he safely landed the boy Phryxus, who was hospitably received by Æetes, king of the country. Phryxus sacrificed the ram to Jupiter, and gave the *Golden Fleece* to Æetes, who placed it in a consecrated grove, under the care of a sleepless dragon.

There was another kingdom in Thessaly near to that of Athamas, and ruled over by a relative of his. The king Æson, being tired of the cares of government, surrendered his crown to his brother Pelias on condition that he should hold it only during the minority of Jason, the son of Æson. When Jason was grown up and came to demand the crown from his uncle, Pelias pretended to be willing to yield it, but at the same time suggested to the young man the glorious adventure of going in quest of the *Golden Fleece,* which it was well known was in the kingdom of Colchis, and was, as Pelias pretended, the rightful property of their family. Jason was pleased with the thought and forthwith made preparations for the expedition. At that time the only species of navigation known to the Greeks consisted of small boats or canoes hollowed out from trunks of trees, so that when Jason employed Argus to build him a vessel capable of containing fifty men, it was considered a gigantic undertaking. It was accomplished, however, and the vessel named "Argo," from the name of the builder. Jason sent his invitation to all the adventurous young men of Greece, and soon found himself at the head of a band of bold youths, many of whom afterwards were renowned among the heroes and demigods of Greece. Hercules, Theseus, Orpheus, and Nestor were among them. They are called the Argonauts, from the name of their vessel.

The "Argo" with her crew of heroes left the shores of Thessaly and having touched at the Island of Lemnos, thence crossed to Mysia and thence to Thrace. Here they found the sage Phineus, and from him received instruction as to their future course. It seems the entrance of the Euxine Sea was impeded by two small rocky islands, which floated on the surface, and in their tossings and heavings occasionally came together, crushing and grinding to atoms any object that might be caught between them. They were called the Symplegades, or Clashing Islands. Phineus instructed the Argonauts how to pass this dangerous strait. When they reached the islands they let go a dove, which took her way between the rocks, and passed in safety, only losing some feathers of her tail.

Jason and his men seized the favorable moment of the rebound, plied their oars with vigor, and passed safe through, though the islands closed behind them, and actually grazed their stern. They now rowed along the shore till they arrived at the eastern end of the sea, and landed at the kingdom of Colchis.

Jason made known his message to the Colchian king, Æetes, who consented to give up the golden fleece if Jason would yoke to the plow two fire-breathing bulls with brazen feet, and sow the teeth of the dragon which Cadmus had slain, and from which it was well known that a crop of armed men would spring up, who would turn their weapons against their producer. Jason accepted the conditions, and a time was set for making the experiment. Previously, however, he found means to plead his cause to Medea, daughter of the king. He promised her marriage, and as they stood before the altar of Hecate, called the goddess to witness his oath. Medea yielded, and by her aid, for she was a potent sorceress, he was furnished with a charm, by which he could encounter safely the breath of the fire-breathing bulls and the weapons of the armed men.

At the time appointed, the people assembled at the grove of Mars, and the king assumed his royal seat, while the multitude covered the hillsides. The brazen-footed bulls rushed in, breathing fire from their nostrils that burned up the herbage as they passed. The sound was like the roar of a furnace, and the smoke like that of water upon quicklime. Jason advanced boldly to meet them. His friends, the chosen heroes of Greece, trembled to behold him. Regardless of the burning breath, he soothed their rage with his voice, patted their necks with fearless hand, and adroitly slipped over them the yoke, and compelled them to drag the plow. The Colchians were amazed; the Greeks shouted for joy. Jason next proceeded to sow the dragon's teeth and plow them in. And soon the crop of armed men sprang up, and, wonderful to relate! no sooner had they reached the surface than they began to brandish their weapons and rush upon Jason. The Greeks trembled for their hero, and even she who had provided him a way of safety and taught him how to use it, Medea herself, grew pale with fear. Jason for a time kept his assailants at bay with his sword and shield, till, finding their numbers overwhelming, he resorted to the charm which Medea had taught him, seized a stone and threw it in the midst of his foes. They immediately turned their arms against one an-

other, and soon there was not one of the dragon's
brood left alive. The Greeks embraced their hero,
and Medea, if she dared, would have embraced
him too.

It remained to lull to sleep the dragon that
guarded the fleece, and this was done by scattering
over him a few drops of a preparation which
Medea had supplied. At the smell he relaxed his
rage, stood for a moment motionless, then shut
those great round eyes, that had never been known
to shut before, and turned over on his side, fast
asleep. Jason seized the fleece and with his friends
and Medea accompanying, hastened to their vessel
before Æetes the king could arrest their departure,
and made the best of their way back to Thessaly,
where they arrived safe, and Jason delivered the
fleece to Pelias, and dedicated the "Argo" to Neptune. What became of the fleece afterwards we do
not know, but perhaps it was found after all, like
many other golden prizes, not worth the trouble it
had cost to procure it.

Medea and Æson

Amid the rejoicings for the recovery of the
Golden Fleece, Jason felt that one thing was wanting, the presence of Æson, his father, who was
prevented by his age and infirmities from taking
part in them. Jason said to Medea, "My spouse,
would that your arts, whose power I have seen so
mighty for my aid, could do me one further service, take some years from my life and add them to
my father's." Medea replied, "Not at such a cost
shall it be done, but if my art avails me, his life
shall be lengthened without abridging yours." The
next full moon she issued forth alone, while all
creatures slept; not a breath stirred the foliage, and
all was still. To the stars she addressed her incantations, and to the moon; to Hecate, the goddess of the under-world, and to Tellus the goddess
of the earth, by whose power plants potent for enchantment are produced. She invoked the gods of
the woods and caverns, of mountains and valleys,
of lakes and rivers, of winds and vapors. While
she spoke the stars shone brighter, and presently
a chariot descended through the air, drawn by flying serpents. She ascended it, and borne aloft made
her way to distant regions, where potent plants
grew which she knew how to select for her purpose. Nine nights she employed in her search, and
during that time came not within the doors of her
palace nor under any roof, and shunned all intercourse with mortals.

She next erected two altars, the one to Hecate,
the other to Hebe, the goddess of youth, and sacrificed a black sheep, pouring libations of milk and
wine. She implored Pluto and his stolen bride that
they would not hasten to take the old man's life.
Then she directed that Æson should be led forth,
and having thrown him into a deep sleep by a
charm, had him laid on a bed of herbs, like one
dead. Jason and all others were kept away from
the place, that no profane eyes might look upon
her mysteries. Then, with streaming hair, she
thrice moved round the altars, dipped flaming
twigs in the blood, and laid them thereon to burn.
Meanwhile the cauldron with its contents was got
ready. In it she put magic herbs, with seeds and
flowers of acrid juice, stones from the distant east,
and sand from the shore of the all-surrounding
ocean; hoarfrost, gathered by moonlight, a screech
owl's head and wings, and the entrails of a wolf.
She added fragments of the shells of tortoises, and
the liver of stags—animals tenacious of life—and
the head and beak of a crow, that outlives nine
generations of men. These with many other things
"without a name" she boiled together for her purposed work, stirring them up with a dry olive
branch; and behold! the branch when taken out
instantly became green, and before long was covered with leaves and a plentiful growth of young
olives; and as the liquor boiled and bubbled, and
sometimes ran over, the grass wherever the sprin-
klings fell shot forth with a verdure like that of
spring.

Seeing that all was ready, Medea cut the throat
of the old man and let out all his blood, and
poured into his mouth and into his wound the
juices of her cauldron. As soon as he had completely imbibed them, his hair and beard laid by
their whiteness and assumed the blackness of
youth; his paleness and emaciation were gone; his
veins were full of blood, his limbs of vigor and
robustness. Æson is amazed at himself, and remembers that such as he now is, he was in his
youthful days, forty years before.

Medea used her arts here for a good purpose, but
not so in another instance, where she made them
the instruments of revenge. Pelias, our readers will
recollect, was the usurping uncle of Jason, and
had kept him out of his kingdom. Yet he must
have had some good qualities, for his daughters
loved him, and when they saw what Medea had
done for Æson, they wished her to do the same
for their father. Medea pretended to consent, and
prepared her cauldron as before. At her request an

old sheep was brought and plunged into the cauldron. Very soon a bleating was heard in the kettle, and when the cover was removed, a lamb jumped forth and ran frisking away into the meadow. The daughters of Pelias saw the experiment with delight, and appointed a time for their father to undergo the same operation. But Medea prepared her cauldron for him in a very different way. She put in only water and a few simple herbs. In the night she with the sisters entered the bed chamber of the old king, while he and his guards slept soundly under the influence of a spell cast upon them by Medea. The daughters stood by the bedside with their weapons drawn, but hesitated to strike, till Medea chid their irresolution. Then turning away their faces, and giving random blows, they smote him with their weapons. He, starting from his sleep, cried out, "My daughters, what are you doing? Will you kill your father?" Their hearts failed them and their weapons fell from their hands, but Medea struck him a fatal blow, and prevented his saying more.

Then they placed him in the cauldron, and Medea hastened to depart in her serpent-drawn chariot before they discovered her treachery, or their vengeance would have been terrible. She escaped, however, but had little enjoyment of the fruits of her crime. Jason, for whom she had done so much, wishing to marry Creusa, princess of Corinth, put away Medea. She, enraged at his ingratitude, called on the gods for vengeance, sent a poisoned robe as a gift to the bride, and then killing her own children, and setting fire to the palace, mounted her serpent-drawn chariot and fled to Athens, where she married King Ægeus, the father of Theseus, and we shall meet her again when we come to the adventures of that hero.

Meleager

One of the heroes of the Argonautic expedition was Meleager, son of Œneus and Althea, king and queen of Calydon. Althea, when her son was born, beheld the three destinies, who as they spun their fatal thread, foretold that the life of the child should last no longer than a brand then burning upon the hearth. Althea seized and quenched the brand, and carefully preserved it for years, while Meleager grew to boyhood, youth, and manhood. It chanced, then, that Œneus, as he offered sacrifices to the gods, omitted to pay due honors to Diana; and she, indignant at the neglect, sent a wild boar of enormous size to lay waste the fields of Calydon. Its eyes shone with blood and fire, its bristles stood like threatening spears, its tusks were like those of Indian elephants. The growing corn was trampled, the vines and olive trees laid waste, the flocks and herds were driven in wild confusion by the slaughtering foe. All common aid seemed vain; but Meleager called on the heroes of Greece to join in a bold hunt for the ravenous monster. Theseus and his friend Pirithous, Jason, Peleus, afterwards the father of Achilles, Telamon the father of Ajax, Nestor, then a youth, but who in his age bore arms with Achilles and Ajax in the Trojan War—these and many more joined in the enterprise. With them came Atalanta, the daughter of Iasius, king of Arcadia. A buckle of polished gold confined her vest, an ivory quiver hung on her left shoulder, and her left hand bore the bow. Her face blent feminine beauty with the best graces of martial youth. Meleager saw and loved.

But now already they were near the monster's lair. They stretched strong nets from tree to tree; they uncoupled their dogs; they tried to find the footprints of their quarry in the grass. From the wood was a descent to marshy ground. Here the boar, as he lay among the reeds, heard the shouts of his pursuers, and rushed forth against them. One and another is thrown down and slain. Jason throws his spear, with a prayer to Diana for success; and the favoring goddess allows the weapon to touch, but not to wound, removing the steel point of the spear in its flight. Nestor, assailed, seeks and finds safety in the branches of a tree. Telamon rushes on, but stumbling at a projecting root, falls prone. But an arrow from Atalanta at length for the first time tastes the monster's blood. It is a slight wound, but Meleager sees and joyfully proclaims it. Anceus, excited to envy by the praise given to a female, loudly proclaims his own valor, and defies alike the boar and the goddess who had sent it; but as he rushes on, the infuriated beast lays him low with a mortal wound. Theseus throws his lance, but it is turned aside by a projecting bough. The dart of Jason misses its object, and kills instead one of their own dogs. But Meleager, after one unsuccessful stroke, drives his spear into the monster's side, then rushes on and despatches him with repeated blows.

Then rose a shout from those around; they congratulated the conqueror, crowding to touch his hand. He, placing his foot upon the head of the slain boar, turned to Atalanta and bestowed on her the head and the rough hide which were the trophies of his success. But at this, envy excited the rest to strife. Plexippus and Toxeus, the brothers of Meleager's mother, beyond the rest opposed the gift, and snatched from the maiden the trophy she had received. Meleager, kindling with rage at the wrong done to himself, and still more at the insult offered to her whom he loved, forgot the claims of kindred, and plunged his sword into the offenders' hearts.

As Althea bore gifts of thankfulness to the temples for the victory of her son, the bodies of her murdered brothers met her sight. She shrieks, and beats her breast, and hastens to change the garments of rejoicing for those of mourning. But when the author of the deed is known, grief gives way to the stern desire of vengeance on her son. The fatal brand, which once she rescued from the flames, the brand which the destinies had linked with Meleager's life, she brings forth, and commands a fire to be prepared. Then four times she essays to place the brand upon the pile; four times she draws back, shuddering at the thought of bringing destruction on her son. The feelings of the mother and the sister contend within her. Now she is pale at the thought of the proposed deed, now flushed again with anger at the act of her son. As a vessel, driven in one direction by the wind, and in the opposite by the tide, the mind of Althea hangs suspended in uncertainty. But now the sister prevails above the mother, and she begins as she holds the fatal wood: "Turn, ye Furies, goddesses of punishment! turn to behold the sacrifice I bring! Crime must atone for crime. Shall Œneus rejoice in his victor's son, while the house of Thestius is desolate? But, alas! to what deed am I borne along? Brothers, forgive a mother's weakness! my hand fails me. He deserves death, but not that I should destroy him. But shall he then live, and triumph, and reign over Calydon, while you, my brothers, wander unavenged among the shades? No! thou hast lived by my gift; die, now, for thine own crime. Return the life which twice I gave thee, first at thy birth, again when I snatched this brand from the flames. O that thou hadst then died! Alas! evil is the conquest; but, brothers, ye have conquered." And, turning away her face, she threw the fatal wood upon the burning pile.

It gave, or seemed to give, a deadly groan. Meleager, absent and unknowing of the cause, felt a sudden pang. He burns, and only by courageous pride conquers the pain which destroys him. He mourns only that he perishes by a bloodless and unhonored death. With his last breath he calls upon his aged father, his brother, and his fond sisters, upon his beloved Atalanta, and upon his mother, the unknown cause of his fate. The flames increase, and with them the pain of the hero. Now both subside; now both are quenched. The brand is ashes, and the life of Meleager is breathed forth to the wandering winds.

Althea, when the deed was done, laid violent hands upon herself. The sisters of Meleager mourned their brother with uncontrollable grief; till Diana, pitying the sorrows of the house that once had aroused her anger, turned them into birds.

Atalanta

The innocent cause of so much sorrow was a maiden whose face you might truly say was boyish for a girl, yet too girlish for a boy. Her fortune had been told, and it was to this effect: "Atalanta, do not marry; marriage will be your ruin." Terrified by this oracle, she fled the society of men, and devoted herself to the sports of the chase. To all suitors (for she had many) she imposed a condition which was generally effectual in relieving her of their persecutions,—"I will be the prize of him who shall conquer me in the race; but death must be the penalty of all who try and fail." In spite of this hard condition some would try. Hippomenes was to be judge of the race. "Can it be possible that any will be so rash as to risk so much for a wife?" said he. But when he saw her lay aside her robe for the race, he changed his mind, and said, "Pardon me, youths, I knew not the prize you were competing for." As he surveyed them he wished them all to be beaten, and swelled with envy of anyone that seemed at all likely to win. While such were his thoughts, the virgin darted forward. As she ran she looked more beautiful than ever. The breezes seemed to give wings to her feet; her hair flew over her shoulders, and the gay fringe of her garment fluttered behind her. A ruddy hue tinged the whiteness of her skin, such as a crimson curtain casts on a marble wall. All her competitors were distanced, and were put to death without mercy. Hippomenes, not daunted by this result, fixing his eyes on the virgin, said, "Why boast of beating those laggards? I offer myself for the contest." Atalanta looked at him with a pitying countenance, and hardly knew whether she would rather conquer him or not. "What god can tempt one so young and handsome to throw himself away? I pity him, not for his beauty (yet he is beautiful), but for his youth. I wish he would give up the race, or if he will be so mad, I hope he may outrun me." While she hesitates, revolving these thoughts, the spectators grow impatient for the race, and her father prompts her to prepare. Then Hippomenes addressed a prayer to Venus: "Help me, Venus, for you have led me on." Venus heard and was propitious.

In the garden of her temple, in her own island of Cyprus, is a tree with yellow leaves and yellow branches and golden fruit. Hence she gathered three golden apples, and unseen by anyone else, gave them to Hippomenes, and told him how to use them. The signal is given; each starts from the goal and skims over the sand. So light their tread, you would almost have thought they might run over the river surface or over the waving grain without sinking. The cries of the spectators cheered Hippomenes,—"Now, now, do your best! haste, haste! you gain on her! relax not! one more effort!" It was doubtful whether the youth or the maiden heard these cries with the greater pleasure. But his breath began to fail him, his throat was dry, the goal yet far off. At that moment he threw down one of the golden apples. The virgin was all amazement. She stopped to pick it up. Hippomenes shot ahead. Shouts burst forth from all sides. She redoubled her efforts, and soon overtook him. Again he threw an apple. She stopped again, but again came up with him. The goal was near; one chance only remained. "Now, goddess," said he, "prosper your gift!" and threw the last apple off at one side. She looked at it, and hesitated; Venus impelled her to turn aside for it. She did so, and was vanquished. The youth carried off his prize.

But the lovers were so full of their own happiness that they forgot to pay due honor to Venus; and the goddess was provoked at their ingratitude. She caused them to give offense to Cybele. That powerful goddess was not to be insulted with impunity. She took from them their human form and turned them into animals of characters resembling their own: of the huntress-heroine, triumphing in the blood of her lovers, she made a lioness, and of her lord and master a lion, and yoked them to her car, where they are still to be seen in all representations, in statuary or painting, of the goddess Cybele.

Hercules

Hercules was the son of Jupiter and Alcmena. As Juno was always hostile to the offspring of her husband by mortal mothers, she declared war against Hercules from his birth. She sent two serpents to destroy him as he lay in his cradle, but the precocious infant strangled them with his own hands. He was, however, by the arts of Juno rendered subject to Eurystheus and compelled to perform all his commands. Eurystheus enjoined upon him a succession of desperate adventures, which are called the "Twelve Labors of Hercules." The first was the fight with the Nemean lion. The valley of Nemea was infested by a terrible lion. Eurystheus ordered Hercules to bring him the skin of this monster. After using in vain his club and arrows against the lion, Hercules strangled the animal with his hands. He returned carrying the dead lion on his shoulders; but Eurystheus was so frightened at the sight of it and at this proof of the prodigious strength of the hero, that he ordered him to deliver the account of his exploits in future outside the town.

His next labor was the slaughter of the Hydra. This monster ravaged the country of Argos, and dwelt in a swamp near the well of Amymone. This well had been discovered by Amymone when the country was suffering from drought, and the story was that Neptune, who loved her, had permitted her to touch the rock with his trident, and a spring of three outlets burst forth. Here the Hydra took up his position, and Hercules was sent to destroy him. The Hydra had nine heads, of which the middle one was immortal. Hercules struck off its heads with his club, but in the place of the head knocked off, two new ones grew forth each time. At length with the assistance of his faithful servant Iolaus, he burned away the heads of the Hydra, and buried the ninth or immortal one under a huge rock.

Another labor was the cleaning of the Augean stables. Augeas, king of Elis, had a herd of three thousand oxen, whose stalls had not been cleansed for thirty years. Hercules brought the rivers Alpheus and Peneus through them, and cleansed them thoroughly in one day.

His next labor was of a more delicate kind. Admeta, the daughter of Eurystheus, longed to obtain the girdle of the queen of the Amazons, and Eurystheus ordered Hercules to go and get it. The Amazons were a nation of women. They were very warlike and held several flourishing cities. It was their custom to bring up only the female children; the boys were either sent away to the neighboring nations or put to death. Hercules was accompanied by a number of volunteers, and after various adventures at last reached the country of the Amazons. Hippolyta, the queen, received him kindly, and consented to yield him her girdle, but Juno, taking the form of an Amazon, went and persuaded the rest that the strangers were carrying off their queen. They instantly armed and came in great numbers down to the ship. Hercules, thinking that Hippolyta had acted treacherously, slew her, and taking her girdle made sail homewards.

Another task enjoined him was to bring to Eurystheus the oxen of Geryon, a monster with three bodies, who dwelt in the island of Erytheia (the red), so called because it lay at the west, under the rays of the setting sun. This description is thought to apply to Spain, of which Geryon was king. After traversing various countries, Hercules reached at length the frontiers of Libya and Europe, where he raised the two mountains of Calpe and Abyla, as monuments of his progress, or, according to another account, rent one mountain into two and left half on each side, forming the straits of Gibraltar, the two mountains being called the Pillars of Hercules. The oxen were guarded by the giant Eurytion and his two-headed dog, but Hercules killed the giant and his dog and brought away the oxen in safety to Eurystheus.

The most difficult labor of all was getting the golden apples of the Hesperides, for Hercules did not know where to find them. These were the apples which Juno had received at her wedding from the goddess of the Earth, and which she had intrusted to the keeping of the daughters of Hesperus, assisted by a watchful dragon. After various adventures Hercules arrived at Mount Atlas in Africa. Atlas was one of the Titans who had warred against the gods, and after they were subdued, Atlas was condemned to bear on his shoulders the weight of the heavens. He was the father of the Hesperides, and Hercules thought that he, if anyone, could find the apples and bring them to him. But how to send Atlas away from his post, or bear up the heavens while he was gone? Hercules took the burden on his own shoulders, and sent Atlas to seek the apples. He returned with them, and though somewhat reluctantly, took his burden upon his shoulders again, and let Hercules return with the apples to Eurystheus.

Milton, in his *Comus,* makes the Hesperides the daughters of Hesperus and nieces of Atlas:

> . . . amidst the gardens fair
> Of Hesperus and his daughters three,
> That sing about the golden tree.

The poets, led by the analogy of the lovely appearance of the western sky at sunset, viewed the west as a region of brightness and glory. Hence they placed in it the Isles of the Blest, the ruddy Isle Erytheia, on which the bright oxen of Geryon were pastured, and the Isle of the Hesperides. The apples are supposed by some to be the oranges of Spain, of which the Greeks had heard some obscure accounts.

A celebrated exploit of Hercules was his victory over Antæus. Antæus, the son of Terra, the Earth, was a mighty giant and wrestler, whose strength was invincible so long as he remained in contact with his mother Earth. He compelled all strangers who came to his country to wrestle with him, on condition that if conquered (as they all were) they should be put to death. Hercules encountered him, and finding that it was of no avail to throw him, for he always rose with renewed strength from every fall, he lifted him up from the earth and strangled him in the air.

Cacus was a huge giant, who inhabited a cave on Mount Aventine, and plundered the surrounding country. When Hercules was driving home the oxen of Geryon, Cacus stole part of the cattle, while the hero slept. That their footprints might not serve to show where they had been driven, he dragged them backward by their tails to his cave; so their tracks all seemed to show that they had gone in the opposite direction. Hercules was deceived by this stratagem, and would have failed to find his oxen, if it had not happened that in driving the remainder of the herd past the cave where the stolen ones were concealed, those within began to low, and were thus discovered. Cacus was slain by Hercules.

The last exploit we shall record was bringing Cerberus from the lower world. Hercules descended into Hades, accompanied by Mercury and Minerva. He obtained permission from Pluto to carry Cerberus to the upper air, provided he could do it without the use of weapons; and in spite of the monster's struggling, he seized him, held him fast, and carried him to Eurystheus, and afterwards brought him back again. When he was in Hades he obtained the liberty of Theseus, his admirer and imitator, who had been detained a prisoner there for an unsuccessful attempt to carry off Proserpine.

Hercules in a fit of madness killed his friend Iphitus, and was condemned for this offense to become the slave of Queen Omphale for three years. While in this service the hero's nature seemed changed. He lived effeminately, wearing at times the dress of a woman, and spinning wool with the handmaidens of Omphale, while the queen wore his lion's skin. When this service was ended he married Dejanira and lived in peace with her three years. On one occasion as he was traveling with his wife, they came to a river, across which the Centaur Nessus carried travelers for a stated fee. Hercules himself forded the river, but gave Dejanira to Nessus to be carried across. Nessus attempted to run away with her, but Hercules heard her cries and shot an arrow into the heart of Nessus. The dying Centaur told Dejanira to take a portion of his blood and keep it, as it might be used as a charm to preserve the love of her husband.

Dejanira did so, and before long fancied she had occasion to use it. Hercules in one of his conquests had taken prisoner a fair maiden, named Iole, of whom he seemed more fond than Dejanira approved. When Hercules was about to offer sacrifices to the gods in honor of his victory, he sent to his wife for a white robe to use on the occasion. Dejanira, thinking it a good opportunity to try her love-spell, steeped the garment in the blood of Nessus. We are to suppose she took care to wash out all traces of it, but the magic power remained, and as soon as the garment became warm on the body of Hercules the poison penetrated into all his limbs and caused him the most intense agony. In his frenzy he seized Lichas, who had brought him the fatal robe, and hurled him into the sea. He wrenched off the garment, but it stuck to his flesh, and with it he tore away whole pieces of his body. In this state he embarked on board a ship and was conveyed home. Dejanira, on seeing what she had unwittingly done, hung herself. Hercules, prepared to die, ascended Mount Œta, where he built a funeral pile of trees, gave his bow and arrows to Philoctetes, and laid himself down on the pile, his head resting on his club, and his lion's skin spread over him. With a countenance as serene as if he were taking his place at a festal board he commanded Philoctetes to apply the torch. The flames spread apace and soon invested the whole mass.

Theseus

Theseus was the son of Ægeus, king of Athens, and of Æthra, daughter of the king of Trœzen. He was brought up at Trœzen, and when arrived at manhood was to proceed to Athens and present himself to his father. Ægeus on parting from Æthra, before the birth of his son, placed his sword and shoes under a large stone and directed her to send his son to him when he became strong enough to roll away the stone and take them from under it. When she thought the time had come, his mother led Theseus to the stone, and he removed it with ease and took the sword and shoes. As the roads were infested with robbers, his grandfather pressed him earnestly to take the shorter and safer way to his father's country—by sea; but the youth, feeling in himself the spirit and the soul of a hero, and eager to signalize himself like Hercules, with whose fame all Greece then rang, by destroying the evil-doers and monsters that oppressed the country, determined on the more perilous and adventurous journey by land.

His first day's journey brought him to Epidaurus, where dwelt a man named Periphetes, a son of Vulcan. This ferocious savage always went armed with a club of iron, and all travelers stood in terror of his violence. When he saw Theseus approach he assailed him, but speedily fell beneath the blows of the young hero, who took possession of his club and bore it ever afterwards as a memorial of his first victory.

Several similar contests with the petty tyrants and marauders of the country followed, in all of which Theseus was victorious. One of these evildoers was called Procrustes, or the Stretcher. He had an iron bedstead, on which he used to tie all travelers who fell into his hands. If they were shorter than the bed, he stretched their limbs to make them fit it; if they were longer than the bed, he lopped off a portion. Theseus served him as he had served others.

Having overcome all the perils of the road, Theseus at length reached Athens, where new dangers awaited him. Medea, the sorceress, who had fled from Corinth after her separation from Jason, had become the wife of Ægeus, the father of Theseus. Knowing by her arts who he was, and fearing the loss of her influence with her husband if Theseus should be acknowledged as his son, she filled the mind of Ægeus with suspicions of the young stranger, and induced him to present him a cup of poison; but at the moment when Theseus stepped forward to take it, the sight of the sword which he wore discovered to his father who he was, and prevented the fatal draught. Medea, detected in her arts, fled once more from deserved punishment, and arrived in Asia, where the country afterwards called Media received its name from her. Theseus was acknowledged by his father, and declared his successor.

The Athenians were at that time in deep affliction, on account of the tribute which they were forced to pay to Minos, king of Crete. This tribute consisted of seven youths and seven maidens, who were sent every year to be devoured by the Minotaur, a monster with a bull's body and a human head. It was exceedingly strong and fierce, and was kept in a labyrinth constructed by Dædalus, so artfully contrived that whoever was enclosed in it could by no means find his way out unassisted. Here the Minotaur roamed, and was fed with human victims.

Theseus resolved to deliver his countrymen from this calamity, or to die in the attempt. Accordingly, when the time of sending off the tribute came, and the youths and maidens were, according to custom, drawn by lot to be sent, he offered himself as one of the victims, in spite of the entreaties of his father. The ship departed under black sails, as usual, which Theseus promised his father to change for white, in case of his returning victorious. When they arrived in Crete, the youths and maidens were exhibited before Minos; and Ariadne, the daughter of the king, being present, became deeply enamored of Theseus, by whom her love was readily returned. She furnished him with a sword, with which to encounter the Minotaur, and with a clue of thread by which he might find his way out of the labyrinth. He was successful, slew the Minotaur, escaped from the labyrinth, and taking Ariadne as the companion of his way, with his rescued companions sailed for Athens. On their way they stopped at the island of Naxos, where Theseus abandoned Ariadne, leaving her asleep. His excuse for this ungrateful treatment of his benefactress was that Minerva appeared to him in a dream and commanded him to do so.

On approaching the coast of Attica, Theseus forgot the signal appointed by his father, and neglected to raise the white sails, and the old king, thinking his son had perished, put an end to his own life. Theseus thus became king of Athens.

One of the most celebrated of the adventures of Theseus is his expedition against the Amazons. He assailed them before they had recovered from the attack of Hercules, and carried off their queen Antiope. The Amazons in their turn invaded the country of Athens and penetrated into the city itself; and the final battle in which Theseus overcame them was fought in the very midst of the city. This battle was one of the favorite subjects of the ancient sculptors, and is commemorated in several works of art that are still extant.

The friendship between Theseus and Pirithous was of a most intimate nature, yet it originated in the midst of arms. Pirithous had made an irruption into the plain of Marathon, and carried off the herds of the king of Athens. Theseus went to repel the plunderers. The moment Pirithous beheld him, he was seized with admiration; he stretched out his hand as a token of peace, and cried, "Be judge thyself—what satisfaction dost thou require?" "Thy friendship," replied the Athenian, and they swore inviolable fidelity. Their deeds corresponded to their professions, and they ever continued true brothers in arms. Each of them aspired to espouse a daughter of Jupiter. Theseus fixed his choice on Helen, then but a child, afterwards so celebrated as the cause of the Trojan War, and with the aid of his friend he carried her off. Pirithous aspired to the wife of the monarch of Erebus; and Theseus, though aware of the danger, accompanied the ambitious lover in his descent to the under-world. But Pluto seized and set them on an enchanted rock at his palace gate, where they remained till Hercules arrived and liberated Theseus, leaving Pirithous to his fate.

After the death of Antiope, Theseus married Phædra, daughter of Minos, king of Crete. Phædra saw in Hippolytus, the son of Theseus, a youth endowed with all the graces and virtues of his father, and of an age corresponding to her own. She loved him, but he repulsed her advances, and her love was changed to hate. She used her influence over her infatuated husband to cause him to be jealous of his son, and he imprecated the vengeance of Neptune upon him. As Hippolytus was one day driving his chariot along the shore, a sea-monster raised himself above the waters, and frightened the horses so that they ran away and dashed the chariot to pieces. Hippolytus was killed, but by Diana's assistance Æsculapius restored him to life. Diana removed Hippolytus from the power of his deluded father and false stepmother, and placed him in Italy under the protection of the nymph Egeria.

Theseus at length lost the favor of his people, and retired to the court of Lycomedes, king of Scyros, who at first received him kindly, but afterwards treacherously slew him. In a later age the Athenian general Cimon discovered the place where his remains were laid, and caused them to be removed to Athens, where they were deposited in a temple called the Theseum, erected in honor of the hero.

Dædalus

The labyrinth from which Theseus escaped by means of the clue of Ariadne was built by Dædalus, a most skillful artificer. It was an edifice with numberless winding passages and turnings opening into one another, and seeming to have neither beginning nor end, like the river Mæander, which returns on itself, and flows now onward, now backward, in its course to the sea. Dædalus built the labyrinth for King Minos, but afterwards lost the favor of the king, and was shut up in a tower. He contrived to make his escape from his prison, but could not leave the island by sea, as the king kept strict watch on all the vessels, and permitted none to sail without being carefully searched. "Minos may control the land and sea," said Dædalus, "but not the regions of the air. I will try that way." So he set to work to fabricate wings for himself and his young son Icarus. He wrought feathers together, beginning with the smallest and adding larger, so as to form an increasing surface. The larger ones he secured with thread and the smaller with wax, and gave the whole a gentle curvature like the wings of a bird. Icarus, the boy, stood and looked on, sometimes running to gather up the feathers which the wind had blown away, and then handling the wax and working it over with his fingers, by his play impeding his father in his labors. When at last the work was done, the artist, waving his wings, found himself buoyed upward, and hung suspended, poising himself on the beaten air. He next equipped his son in the same manner and taught him how to fly, as a bird tempts her young ones from the lofty nest into the air. When all was prepared for flight he said, "Icarus, my son I charge you to keep at a moderate height, for if you fly too low the damp will clog your wings, and if too high the heat will melt them. Keep near me and you will be safe." While he gave him these instructions and fitted the wings to his shoulders, the face of the father was wet with tears, and his hands trembled. He kissed the boy, not knowing that it was for the last time. Then rising on his wings, he flew off, encouraging him to follow, and looked back from his own flight to see how his son managed his wings. As they flew the plowman stopped his work to gaze, and the shepherd leaned on his staff and watched them, astonished at the sight, and thinking they were gods who could thus cleave the air.

They passed Samos and Delos on the left and Lebynthos on the right, when the boy, exulting in his career, began to leave the guidance of his companion and soar upward as if to reach heaven. The nearness of the blazing sun softened the wax which held the feathers together, and they came off. He fluttered with his arms, but no feathers remained to hold the air. While his mouth uttered cries to his father it was submerged in the blue waters of the sea, which thenceforth was called by his name. His father cried, "Icarus, Icarus, where are you?" At last he saw the feathers floating on the water, and bitterly lamenting his own arts, he buried the body and called the land Icaria in memory of his child. Dædalus arrived safe in Sicily, where he built a temple to Apollo, and hung up his wings, an offering to the god.

Orpheus and Eurydice

Orpheus was the son of Apollo and the Muse Calliope. He was presented by his father with a lyre and taught to play upon it, which he did to such perfection that nothing could withstand the charm of his music. Not only his fellow-mortals, but wild beasts were softened by his strains, and gathering round him laid by their fierceness, and stood entranced with his lay. Nay, the very trees and rocks were sensible to the charm. The former crowded round him and the latter relaxed somewhat of their hardness, softened by his notes.

Hymen had been called to bless with his presence the nuptials of Orpheus with Eurydice; but though he attended, he brought no happy omens with him. His very torch smoked and brought tears into their eyes. In coincidence with such prognostics, Eurydice, shortly after her marriage, while wandering with the nymphs, her companions, was seen by the shepherd Aristæus, who was struck with her beauty and made advances to her. She fled, and in flying trod upon a snake in the grass, was bitten in the foot, and died. Orpheus sang his grief to all who breathed the upper air, both gods and men, and finding it all unavailing resolved to seek his wife in the regions of the dead. He descended by a cave situated on the side of the promontory of Tænarus and arrived at the Stygian realm. He passed through crowds of ghosts and presented himself before the throne of Pluto and Proserpine. Accompanying the words with the lyre, he sung, "O deities of the under-world, to whom all we who live must come, hear my words, for they are true. I come not to spy out the secrets of Tartarus, nor to try my strength against the three-headed dog with snaky hair who guards the entrance. I come to seek my wife, whose opening years the poisonous viper's fang has brought to an untimely end. Love has led me here, Love, a god all powerful with us who dwell on the earth, and, if old traditions say true, not less so here. I implore you by these abodes full of terror, these realms of silence and uncreated things, unite again the thread of Eurydice's life. We all are destined to you, and sooner or later must pass to your domain. She too, when she shall have filled her term of life, will rightly be yours. But till then grant her to me, I beseech you. If you deny me I cannot return alone; you shall triumph in the death of us both."

As he sang these tender strains, the very ghosts shed tears. Tantalus, in spite of his thirst, stopped for a moment his efforts for water, Ixion's wheel stood still, the vulture ceased to tear the giant's liver, the daughters of Danaüs rested from their task of drawing water in a sieve, and Sisyphus sat on his rock to listen. Then for the first time, it is said, the cheeks of the Furies were wet with tears. Proserpine could not resist, and Pluto himself gave way. Eurydice was called. She came from among the new-arrived ghosts, limping with her wounded foot. Orpheus was permitted to take her away with him on one condition, that he should not turn round to look at her till they should have reached the upper air. Under this condition they proceeded on their way, he leading, she following, through passages dark and steep, in total silence, till they had nearly reached the outlet into the cheerful upper world, when Orpheus, in a moment of forgetfulness, to assure himself that she was still following, cast a glance behind him, when instantly she was borne away. Stretching out their arms to embrace each other, they grasped only the air! Dying now a second time, she yet cannot reproach her husband, for how can she blame his impatience

to behold her? "Farewell," she said, "a last farewell,"—and was hurried away, so fast that the sound hardly reached his ears.

Orpheus endeavored to follow her, and besought permission to return and try once more for her release; but the stern ferryman repulsed him and refused passage. Seven days he lingered about the brink, without food or sleep; then bitterly accusing of cruelty the powers of Erebus, he sang his complaints to the rocks and mountains, melting the hearts of tigers and moving the oaks from their stations. He held himself aloof from womankind, dwelling constantly on the recollection of his sad mischance. The Thracian maidens tried their best to captivate him, but he repulsed their advances. They bore with him as long as they could; but finding him insensible one day, excited by the rites of Bacchus, one of them exclaimed, "See yonder our despiser!" and threw at him her javelin. The weapon, as soon as it came within the sound of his lyre, fell harmless at his feet. So did also the stones that they threw at him. But the women raised a scream and drowned the voice of the music, and then the missiles reached him and soon were stained with his blood. The maniacs tore him limb from limb, and threw his head and his lyre into the river Hebrus, down which they floated, murmuring sad music, to which the shores responded a plaintive symphony. The Muses gathered up the fragments of his body and buried them at Libethra, where the nightingale is said to sing over his grave more sweetly than in any other part of Greece. His lyre was placed by Jupiter among the stars. His shade passed a second time to Tartarus, where he sought out his Eurydice and embraced her with eager arms. They roam the happy fields together now, sometimes he leading, sometimes she; and Orpheus gazes as much as he will upon her, no longer incurring a penalty for a thoughtless glance.

THE HOMERIC POEMS

A few minutes' study of a map of the Ancient World will show the Greek Peninsula jutting southwards into the Mediterranean Sea. It is a mountainous land, with some plains, divided by small streams. And the entire peninsula is almost cut in two at the Isthmus of Corinth. The whole contour of this land promoted from the beginning the growth of small, independent states. Outside the peninsula proper the Greek World consisted of a large number of islands which formed stepping stones completely across the Ægean Sea and encouraged the colonization of the further shores in Asia Minor. There was a time when the Greeks were settled about the Black Sea and on many a coast of the Mediterranean in North Africa, southern Italy and France, as well as on the island of Sicily.

We first learn of this world of the Greeks before the Greeks themselves entered it. For many centuries before 1200 B.C., a very vigorous and progressive civilization had existed on the island of Crete. Looking as it does toward Egypt in one direction, the eastern shores of the Mediterranean in another, and continental Greece in a third, it served for a thousand years or more as a prosperous center of trade. Enormous palaces were built, equipped with many conveniences—baths, "modern" plumbing, and the like.

In this pre-Greek world were also other centers of activity and of advancing civilization. At Mycene and Argos and Tiryns on the Greek mainland and at Troy on the Asiatic coast, trade centers had been built up, kingdoms established, and certain achievements reached in arts and crafts.

By a series of waves of migration, tribes from the country north of Greece, belonging to the Indo-European family of peoples, pushed southward and gradually overthrew these early kingdoms. These newcomers are the Greeks.

Whatever may have been the exact relation of the various groups of Greeks, there can be no doubt of an age of conflict and eventual conquest after which Greek-speaking peoples were in control of Greece and all the Ægean Islands as well as the Asiatic coast. To us this period of wars is more important than its mere historical significance would justify. For the memory of this age persisted and came to be the subject of songs—among them the world's greatest epic poems, the *Iliad* and the *Odyssey*.

We shall begin our reading of Greek literature with its oldest, and in many ways its best, poems, the *Iliad* and *Odyssey* of Homer. We shall see depicted in these poems a heroic time in which gods and heroes and supernatural events abound. The author is looking back to an age known only in tradition and he is free to invent as he will. There is no doubt that his stories have a solid basis of history and that Troy once did yield to hosts from across the Ægean. But the whole of this war is placed on a noble plane. Everything is glorified. The warriors were godlike, and even at times the sons of gods.

The audience who listened to these poems of Homer were already steeped in the stories of the gods and heroes. A large part of the Greek mythology had already been elaborated and it had come to be an indispensable background for all the heroic poetry.

The Greek audience for Homer's poems also knew much about the Greek world. They could, at least in imagination, follow Odysseus in his wanderings. They knew where Egypt and Troy and Sparta and Athens are. It is not hard with the aid of a map for us to see the relation of these places or to follow the historian when he tells us of how a very remarkable civilization even before Homer had arisen in Crete and was destroyed by the ancestors of the Greeks when they came from the north. On a good map we can also see why the Greeks on the mainland tended to live in small communities and how they came to settle the islands of the Ægean and the coasts of Asia Minor, not to speak of more remote regions such as the northern shores of the Black Sea and the coast of Southern France. All this we can see on a map.

And in the works that we shall read we shall see that peculiar blend of the intellectual and the emotional, of the physical and the mental, that made these people the originators of so much that we hold precious in civilization. We can find in these same works much of their way of life—of their social systems, their politics, their religious practices, and even their kitchen utensils.

About these two poems there are many matters of uncertainty, but scholars are generally agreed that they must be based on some kind of historic foundation. Not that they represent real history, for it is clear that the wars and adventures treated in the poems have already become distant memories. There has been time for legends to grow up. Kings and warriors have taken on supernatural qualities and become heroes and demigods, while the gods themselves consort familiarly with men. The hosts arrayed in war have been multiplied in the telling until their number seems fabulous. Strange creatures of folk legend or superstition aid or hinder Odysseus on his prodigious wanderings. Even the world of the dead shows us its secrets. Centuries of retelling have obscured the facts. At last the poet looks back at them through a haze of poetic imaginings. Perhaps scores of bards have made their contributions, each adding his bit to the splendor of the tradition until over all these battles and adventures there has been cast a sheen of glory and nobility not of this earth.

The facts about the two poems are relatively simple. They are written in a six-foot dactylic meter that for long afterward was considered the proper form for an epic poem. It is impossible to show with any exactness the effect of this meter; for the basic principle of the Greek verse was not *accent*, as with us in English, but quantity, or the length or shortness of a syllable. The six-foot dactylic in English, as seen in Longfellow's *Evangeline*, is too light and tripping a measure for comparison with the Greek. The English poem is like a tune played on a piano with its accented beat;

the Greek like the same tune on an organ with its long and stately tones.

Fortunately there is much in these great epic poems besides the music, so that even if we read them in English, whether in prose or some poetic form, we have a memorable experience. The Siege of Troy and the Wanderings of Odysseus have become part of the dream world of all poets and artists since Homer's day. Listen to what John Keats, a young English poet who knew no Greek, but loved the Greeks, says of his first discovery "On First Looking into Chapman's Homer:"

Much have I traveled in the realms of gold,
And many goodly states and kingdoms seen;
Round many western islands have I been
Which bards in fealty to Apollo hold.
Oft of one wide expanse had I been told
That deep-browed Homer ruled as his demesne—
Yet did I never breathe its pure serene
Till I heard Chapman speak out loud and bold
Then felt I like some watcher of the skies
When a new planet swims into his ken;
Or like stout Cortez, when with eagle eyes
He stared at the Pacific—and all his men
Looked at each other with a wild surmise—
Silent, upon a peak in Darien.

The poems are now divided into twenty-four books each, the books corresponding to the twenty-four letters of the Greek alphabet. These divisions were made long after Homer's own time, though most of them represent logical stopping places in the poems, pauses that would be convenient to the old bards.

There is no doubt that for many generations these poems were handed down by memory and that there was a professional class of bards who recited or sang these at the courts of nobles and kings. The holding of such long poems in memory was an everyday occurrence, and will excite no wonder in those who have heard old men in the west of Ireland tell tales hour after hour, word for word as they have told them for years and as they will tell them for years hence. The ancient bard, however, differed from our Irish tale-teller in that his was an aristocratic tradition. He was singing or reciting for kings and great nobles and his attitude was that of his masters. Homer was probably himself such a minstrel, if indeed there ever was a Homer. His glorifying of kings and warriors appears on nearly every page. And in the few places where common men are mentioned they are despised. Or if they are admirable it will appear that they are really nobles by birth.

That the poems come from this world of bards and noble or royal patrons none can doubt. Seven cities claimed Homer as theirs and no one now knows whether he ever lived. For more than a century, scholars were inclined to speak of the poems as resulting from the gradual growth of songs about the same subject, and the final bringing of these together by a combiner or editor. Such work was actually done in 1835 for the epic songs of Finland and made into the epic *Kalevala*, so that the idea is not utterly fantastic. The tendency recently, however, has been to think of a Homeric poem as the result of an author's conscious artistic creation. There may, these later critics agree, have been a different author for the *Iliad* than for the *Odyssey*, and most agree that the *Odyssey* seems the later of the two poems. Both may be roughly placed in the ninth or tenth century before Christ. All critics agree that many changes have crept into the poems since their first composition—changes due to faulty memory, errors in copying, and even deliberate falsification. Such would be the inevitable fate of any poem produced and preserved for centuries by professional bards. For the poems were probably not reduced to writing until the sixth century before Christ—not less than three or four hundred years after they were composed and almost twice that long after the events which furnished their subject.

The presentation of the stories may well be left to the poet himself, for he did not write for a learned audience. They were simple kings and nobles who had never been to a school in their lives. They knew life at first hand just as each of us may know it if we will. They were touched by sorrow; they laughed at humor; they gloried in great deeds; they rejoiced in their hero's good fortune and grieved at his misfortunes; they marveled at the world of wonder.

Of course, these kings and nobles had some special knowledge of their own, knowledge that we can attain only from books. They knew their neighbors, the history of their own generation and perhaps something of that gone before. They had in mind something of the geography of the Mediterranean and Ægean world. The latter knowledge would help them much in their listening to the *Odyssey*.

This kind of information the modern student must obtain if he is to enjoy the poems as they were first enjoyed. The geography he can learn from his map. What he must learn from books in order to enjoy Homer is really very little if he already knows something of the Greek gods and heroes. But it would be well if, before beginning the *Iliad*, he reads the mythological background as Mr. Bulfinch has retold it.

THE LITERARY QUALITIES OF THE HOMERIC EPICS

The literary qualities of the *Iliad* and the *Odyssey* are too transparent to require extensive explanation. These poems are the best examples we have of that form of literature which we call the *folk epic*, by which we mean an epic or long narrative poem that developed gradually out of the national consciousness of a people. Such an epic reflects a people's traditions and beliefs, its customs and its manner of living. Although the *Iliad* and the *Odyssey* were composed several generations after the events recorded by the poems, we have evidence that life could not have changed so radically in the interim as to alienate their poet from the heroic age. The state in which we now find both poems reveals the shaping hand of a later age, but this does not invalidate them as folk literature, for the shaping was made in the spirit of a people close to its roots. This is conclusively revealed not only by the lighthearted, amoral treatment of the gods, which reflected the common view (despite some suggestions of a later morality and the incorporation of a later mystical view of the underworld in the *Odyssey*), but also by the fact that all Greece accepted the *Iliad* and *Odyssey* as a national bible.

For the shaping hand we must be exceedingly grateful. Although the presence of a few episodes suggests that the various tales of the Trojan War sung by early minstrels were not completely fused, the *Iliad* and the *Odyssey* are basically unified. The *Iliad* deals with one major crisis in the long war and is further unified by its theme— the wrath of Achilles and its consequences. Its high points are Achilles' quarrel with the leader of the Greeks, Agamemnon, and his retirement from the battle; the subsequent defeat of the Greeks; Achilles' reconciliation with his comrades and his return to the battlefield, which stems the success of the Trojans and culminates in the death of their hero and mainstay, Hector. The funeral rites for Achilles' friend Patroclus, the return of Hector's body to his father Priam, and the burial of Hector then round out the story. If some events seem arbitrarily inserted into the epic, they do not seriously violate the sequence of the narrative; in a war, separate occurrences are neither incredible nor inappropriate. The *Odyssey*, for all its multiplicity of incident and geographical spread, is as unified as any romance can be, for it is the account of a hero's attempt to return to his country and regain his wife and kingdom. Its progression is not constant, it is true; but far from marring this masterpiece, the flashback method that returns us to the Trojan War and the divergences from a steady voyage to Ithaca, including Odysseus' visit to Hades, only sustain suspense while enriching the narrative.

Characteristic of the epic style, which will also be found in the folk epics of other nations, is the use of such poetic devices as the epithet and the descriptive simile. The *heroic epithet* not only identifies characters or things, but it facilitates one's identification of them by constant reminders of their chief characteristic or the main impression they leave on the poet and his public. The *simile* not only intensifies our perception of some detail or event in an economical manner—that is, without interrupting the flow of narrative—but it enables the poet to dwell pleasurably on familiar natural phenomena and social activities. The descriptiveness of both epics is, indeed, one of their major achievements; by means of apt similes and longer passages, such as the account of Achilles' shield and of the various places visited by Odysseus, the Homeric poems attain remarkable vividness.

Particularly notable is the humanizing power of the poems. Heroes who would normally have been shrouded in obscurity come down to us as living and highly individualized characters. They are drawn with broad but incisive strokes, and without formal stiffness despite their antiquity. Men like Agamemnon, Achilles, Hector, Odysseus, or the lowly swineherd Eumæus, and women like Helen, Andromache, Nausicaä, or Penelope appear before us as though we had known them personally. Contradictions in human nature are observed objectively. Achilles may be a redoubtable hero in battle, but he is also a devoted friend; he may be reckless, but he also dreads death; he can be savage in grief and triumph, when he avenges his friend cruelly and mistreats Hector's body, but he is also capable of respect and pity when visited by Hector's aged father. The humorous side of character is also present to the poet when he portrays Odysseus' guile and his love of prevarication.

This humanization extends to the supernatural. The gods are only larger human beings, and they are endowed with the same passions and failings. Even mighty Zeus has his domestic troubles and skirmishes; the goddesses quarrel like their mundane counterparts; and they can even be wounded by mortals. The presence of some ancient superstitions, including a melancholy picture of the shadowy dead in the *Odyssey*, cannot cloud the vision that conceives the gods in the image of man. Even in the presence of monsters and terrors, Odysseus retains his confidence in human resourcefulness and intellect. Despite an acute realization of pain and struggle, moreover, the world of the Greek epics is beautiful, and man is constantly aware of its wonder and magnificence. The superb language and music, the imagery and the rapture of the poems, arise naturally and effortlessly from this consciousness of beauty that Matthew Arnold held to be the soul of Hellenism. "You Greeks are always children," said an Egyptian priest to the Greek law-giver Solon. But this youthfulness is a precious spirit so long as it remains uncorrupted.

Equally remarkable, however, is the fact that such a national epic of war as the *Iliad* should in its ultimate form exhibit such fairness to the enemy and such sympathy for human beings regardless of their nationality. In the *Iliad* the common man is still disregarded, his deeds and sufferings in battle are overlooked, and his voice of protest is ridiculed in the characterization of the rebellious Thersites. But ordinary people begin to receive their due in the *Odyssey*, a work of probably later composition. The Trojans, Priam, Hector, and the latter's wife, Andromache, are the most sympathetic characters of the *Iliad*. The pathos of Hector's parting from Andromache and of Priam's visit to his son's murderer, from whom he reclaims the body of Hector, has rarely been equalled in the world's literature. Thus justice and fellow-feeling are added to the loveliness and excitement of the poetry. Here, in the words of Gilbert Murray, is "the true pathos of war: the thing seen on both sides," and in this respect the poem foreshadows the later achievements of Greek literature. "This power of entering vividly into the feelings of both parties in a conflict is perhaps the most characteristic gift of the Greek genius; it is the spirit in which Homer, Æschylus, Herodotus, Euripides, Thucydides, find their kinship, and which enabled Athens to create the drama."[1]

[1] Gilbert Murray, *A History of Ancient Greek Literature*, p. 43.

THOMAS BULFINCH

Myths of the Trojan War

Minerva was the goddess of wisdom, but on one occasion she did a very foolish thing; she entered into competition with Juno and Venus for the prize of beauty. It happened thus: At the nuptials of Peleus and Thetis all the gods were invited with the exception of Eris, or Discord. Enraged at her exclusion, the goddess threw a golden apple among the guests, with the inscription, "For the fairest." Thereupon Juno, Venus, and Minerva each claimed the apple. Jupiter, not willing to decide in so delicate a matter, sent the goddesses to Mount Ida, where the beautiful shepherd Paris was tending his flocks, and to him was committed the decision. The goddesses accordingly appeared before him. Juno promised him power and riches, Minerva glory and renown in war, and Venus the fairest of women for his wife, each attempting to bias his decision in her own favor. Paris decided in favor of Venus and gave her the golden apple, thus making the two other goddesses his enemies. Under the protection of Venus, Paris sailed to Greece, and was hospitably received by Menelaus, king of Sparta. Now Helen, the wife of Menelaus, was the very woman whom Venus had destined for Paris, the fairest of her sex. She had been sought as a bride by numerous suitors, and before her decision was made known, they all, at the suggestion of Ulysses, one of their number, took an oath that they would defend her from all injury and avenge her cause if necessary. She chose Menelaus, and was living with him happily when Paris became their guest. Paris, aided by Venus, persuaded her to elope with him, and carried her to Troy, whence arose the famous Trojan War, the theme of the greatest poems of antiquity, those of Homer and Virgil.

Menelaus called upon his brother chieftains of Greece to fulfill their pledge, and join him in his efforts to recover his wife. They generally came forward, but Ulysses, who had married Penelope, and was very happy in his wife and child, had no disposition to embark in such a troublesome affair. He therefore hung back and Palamedes was sent to urge him. When Palamedes arrived at Ithaca Ulysses pretended to be mad. He yoked an ass and an ox together to the plow and began to sow salt. Palamedes, to try him, placed the infant Telemachus before the plow, whereupon the father turned the plow aside, showing plainly that he was no madman, and after that could no longer refuse to fulfill his promise. Being now himself gained for the undertaking, he lent his aid to bring in other reluctant chiefs, especially Achilles. This hero was the son of that Thetis at whose marriage the apple of Discord had been thrown among the goddesses. Thetis was herself one of the immortals, a sea-nymph, and knowing that her son was fated to perish before Troy if he went on the expedition, she endeavored to prevent his going. She sent him away to the court of King Lycomedes, and induced him to conceal himself in the disguise of a maiden among the daughters of the king. Ulysses, hearing he was there, went disguised as a merchant to the palace and offered for sale female ornaments, among which he had placed some arms. While the king's daughters were engrossed with the other contents of the merchant's pack, Achilles handled the weapons and thereby betrayed himself to the keen eye of Ulysses, who found no great difficulty in persuading him to disregard his mother's prudent counsels and join his countrymen in the war.

Priam was king of Troy, and Paris, the shepherd and seducer of Helen, was his son. Paris had been brought up in obscurity, because there were certain ominous forebodings connected with him from his infancy that he would be the ruin of the state. These forebodings seemed at length likely to be realized, for the Grecian armament now in preparation was the greatest that had ever been fitted out. Agamemnon, king of Mycenæ, and brother of the injured Menelaus, was chosen commander-in-chief. Achilles was their most illustrious warrior. After him ranked Ajax, gigantic in size and of great courage, but dull of intellect; Diomede, second only to Achilles in all the qualities of a hero; Ulysses, famous for his sagacity; and Nestor, the oldest of the Grecian chiefs, and one to whom they all looked up for counsel. But Troy was no feeble enemy. Priam, the king, was now

Myths of the Trojan War. From Bulfinch, *The Age of Fable.*

old, but he had been a wise prince and had strengthened his state by good government at home and numerous alliances with his neighbors. But the principal stay and support of his throne was his son Hector, one of the noblest characters painted by heathen antiquity. He felt, from the first, a presentiment of the fall of his country, but still persevered in his heroic resistance, yet by no means justified the wrong which brought this danger upon her. He was united in marriage with Andromache, and as a husband and father his character was not less admirable than as a warrior. The principal leaders on the side of the Trojans, besides Hector, were Æneas and Deiphobus, Glaucus and Sarpedon.

After two years of preparation the Greek fleet and army assembled in the port of Aulis in Bœotia. Here Agamemnon in hunting killed a stag which was sacred to Diana, and the goddess in return visited the army with pestilence, and produced a calm which prevented the ships from leaving the port. Calchas, the soothsayer, thereupon announced that the wrath of the virgin goddess could only be appeased by the sacrifice of a virgin on her altar, and that none other but the daughter of the offender would be acceptable. Agamemnon, however reluctant, yielded his consent, and the maiden Iphigenia was sent for under the pretense that she was to be married to Achilles. When she was about to be sacrificed the goddess relented and snatched her away, leaving a hind in her place, and Iphigenia, enveloped in a cloud, was carried to Tauri, where Diana made her priestess of her temple.

HOMER

The Iliad

BOOK I

How Agamemnon and Achilles fell out at the siege of Troy; and Achilles withdrew himself from battle, and won from Zeus a pledge that his wrong should be avenged on Agamemnon and the Achaians.

Sing, goddess, the wrath of Achilles Peleus' son, the ruinous wrath that brought on the Achaians woes innumerable, and hurled down into Hades many strong souls of heroes, and gave their bodies to be a prey to dogs and all winged fowls; and so the counsel of Zeus wrought out its accomplishment from the day when first strife parted Atreides king of men and noble Achilles.

Who then among the gods set the twain at strife and variance? Even the son of Leto and of Zeus; for he in anger at the king sent a sore plague upon the host, that the folk began to perish, because Atreides[1] had done dishonor to Chryses the priest. For he had come to the Achaians' fleet ships to win his daughter's freedom, and brought a ransom beyond telling; and bare in his hands the fillet of Apollo the Far-darter upon a golden staff; and made his prayer unto all the Achaians, and most of all to the two sons of Atreus, orderers of the host: "Ye sons of Atreus and all ye well-greaved Achaians, now may the gods that dwell in the mansions of Olympus grant you to lay waste the city of Priam, and to fare happily homeward; only set ye my dear child free, and accept the ransom in reverence to the son of Zeus, far-darting Apollo."

Then all the other Achaians cried assent, to reverence the priest and accept his goodly ransom; yet the thing pleased not the heart of Agamemnon son of Atreus, but he roughly sent him away, and laid stern charge upon him, saying: "Let me not find thee, old man, amid the hollow ships, whether tarrying now or returning again hereafter, lest the staff and fillet of the god avail thee naught. And her will I not set free; nay, ere that shall old age come on her in our house, in Argos, far from her native land, where she shall ply the loom and serve my couch. But depart, provoke me

The Iliad. Translated by Lang, Leaf, and Myers. By permission of The Macmillan Co. Although seven cities claimed to be Homer's birthplace, nothing is certainly known about him, not even whether he actually lived. The value of the poems is not affected by anything we may know or not know of Homer's life.

[1] Son of Atreus, that is, Agamemnon and Menelaus. Here only the former is meant.

not, that thou mayest the rather go in peace."

So said he, and the old man was afraid and obeyed his word, and fared silently along the shore of the loud-sounding sea. Then went that aged man apart and prayed aloud to king Apollo, whom Leto of the fair locks bare: "Hear me, god of the silver bow, that standest over Chryse and holy Killa, and rulest Tenedos with might, O Smintheus! If ever I built a temple gracious in thine eyes, or if ever I burnt to thee fat flesh of thighs of bulls or goats, fulfill thou this my desire; let the Danaans pay by thine arrows for my tears."

So spake he in prayer, and Phœbus Apollo heard him, and came down from the peaks of Olympus wroth at heart, bearing on his shoulders his bow and covered quiver. And the arrows clanged upon his shoulders in his wrath, as the god moved; and he descended like to night. Then he sate him aloof from the ships, and let an arrow fly; and there was heard a dread clanging of the silver bow. First did he assail the mules and fleet dogs, but afterward, aiming at the men his piercing dart, he smote; and the pyres of the dead burnt continually in multitude.

Now for nine days ranged the god's shafts through the host; but on the tenth Achilles summoned the folk to assembly, for in his mind did goddess Hera of the white arms put the thought, because she had pity on the Danaans when she beheld them perishing. Now when they had gathered and were met in assembly, then Achilles fleet of foot stood up and spake among them: "Son of Atreus, now deem I that we shall return wandering home again—if verily we might escape death—if war at once and pestilence must indeed ravage the Achaians. But come, let us now inquire of some soothsayer or priest, yea, or an interpreter of dreams—seeing that a dream too is of Zeus—who shall say wherefore Phœbus Apollo is so wroth, whether he blame us by reason of vow or hecatomb; if perchance he would accept the savor of lambs or unblemished goats, and so would take away the pestilence from us."

So spake he and sate him down; and there stood up before them Kalchas son of Thestor, most excellent far of augurs, who knew both things that were and that should be and that had been before, and guided the ships of the Achaians to Ilios by his soothsaying that Phœbus Apollo bestowed on him. He of good intent made harangue and spake amid them: "Achilles, dear to Zeus, thou biddest me tell the wrath of Apollo, the king that smiteth afar. Therefore will I speak; but do thou make

covenant with me, and swear that verily with all thy heart thou wilt aid me both by word and deed. For of a truth I deem that I shall provoke one that ruleth all the Argives with might, and whom the Achaians obey. For a king is more of might when he is wroth with a meaner man; even though for the one day he swallow his anger, yet doth he still keep his displeasure thereafter in his breast till he accomplish it. Consider thou, then, if thou wilt hold me safe."

And Achilles fleet of foot made answer and spake to him: "Yea, be of good courage, speak whatever soothsaying thou knowest; for by Apollo dear to Zeus, him by whose worship thou, O Kalchas, declarest thy soothsaying to the Danaans, no man while I live and behold light on earth shall lay violent hands upon thee amid the hollow ships; no man of all the Danaans, not even if thou mean Agamemnon, that now avoweth him to be greatest far of the Achaians."

Then was the noble seer of good courage, and spake: "Neither by reason of a vow is he displeased, nor for any hecatomb, but for his priest's sake to whom Agamemnon did despite, and set not his daughter free and accepted not the ransom; therefore hath the Far-darter brought woes upon us, yea, and will bring. Nor will he ever remove the loathly pestilence from the Danaans till we have given the bright-eyed damsel to her father, unbought, unransomed, and carried a holy hecatomb to Chryse; then might we propitiate him to our prayer."

So said he and sate him down, and there stood up before them the hero son of Atreus, wide-ruling Agamemnon, sore displeased; and his dark heart within him was greatly filled with anger, and his eyes were like flashing fire. To Kalchas first spake he with look of ill: "Thou seer of evil, never yet hast thou told me the thing that is pleasant. Evil is ever the joy of thy heart to prophesy, but never yet didst thou tell any good matter nor bring it to pass. And now with soothsaying thou makest harangue among the Danaans, how that the Far-darter bringeth woes upon them because, forsooth, I would not take the goodly ransom of the damsel Chryseis, seeing I am the rather fain to keep her own self within mine house. Yea, I prefer her before Klytaimnestra my wedded wife; in no wise is she lacking beside her, neither in favor nor stature, nor wit nor skill. Yet for all this will I give her back, if that is better; rather would I see my folk whole than perishing. Only make ye me ready a prize of honor forthwith, lest I alone of all the Argives be disprized, which thing beseemeth not; for ye all behold how my prize is departing from me."

To him then made answer fleet-footed goodly Achilles: "Most noble son of Atreus, of all men most covetous, how shall the great-hearted Achaians give thee a meed of honor? We know naught of any wealth of common store, but what spoil soe'er we took from captured cities hath been apportioned, and it beseemeth not to beg all this back from the folk. Nay, yield thou the damsel to the god, and we Achaians will pay thee back threefold and fourfold, if ever Zeus grant us to sack some well-walled town of Troy-land."

To him lord Agamemnon made answer and said: "Not in this wise, strong as thou art, O godlike Achilles, beguile thou me by craft; thou shalt not outwit me nor persuade me. Dost thou wish, that thou mayest keep thy meed of honor, for me to sit idle in bereavement, and biddest me give her back? Nay, if the great-hearted Achaians will give me a meed suited to my mind, that the recompense be equal—but if they give it not, then I myself will go and take a meed of honor, thine be it or Aias', or Odysseus' that I will take unto me; wroth shall be he to whomsoever I come. But for this we will take counsel hereafter; now let us launch a black ship on the great sea, and gather picked oarsmen, and set therein a hecatomb, and embark Chryseis of the fair cheeks herself, and let one of our counselors be captain, Aias or Idomeneus or goodly Odysseus, or thou, Peleides, most redoubtable of men, to do sacrifice for us and propitiate the Fardarter."

Then Achilles fleet of foot looked at him scowling and said: "Ah me, thou clothed in shamelessness, thou of crafty mind, how shall any Achaian hearken to thy bidding with all his heart, be it to go a journey or to fight the foe amain? Not by reason of the Trojan spearmen came I hither to fight, for they have not wronged me; never did they harry mine oxen nor my horses, nor ever waste my harvest in deep-soiled Phthia, the nurse of men; seeing there lieth between us long space of shadowy mountains and sounding sea; but thee, thou shameless one, followed we hither to make thee glad, by earning recompense at the Trojans' hands for Menelaos and for thee, thou dog-face! All this thou reckonest not nor takest thought thereof; and now thou threatenest thyself to take my meed of honor, wherefor I travailed much, and the sons of the Achaians gave it me. Never win I meed like unto thine, when the Achaians sack any populous citadel of Trojan men; my hands bear the brunt of furious war, but when the apportioning cometh then is thy meed far ampler, and I betake me to the ships with some small thing, yet mine own, when I have fought to weariness. Now will I depart to Phthia, seeing it is far better to return home on my beaked ships; nor am I minded here in dishonor to draw thee thy fill of riches and wealth."

Then Agamemnon king of men made answer to him: "Yea, flee, if thy soul be set thereon. It is not I that beseech thee to tarry for my sake; I have others by my side that shall do me honor, and above all Zeus, lord of counsel. Most hateful art thou to me of all kings, fosterlings of Zeus; thou ever lovest strife and wars and fightings. Though thou be very strong, yet that I ween is a gift to thee of God. Go home with thy ships and company and lord it among thy Myrmidons; I reck not aught of thee nor care I for thine indignation; and this shall be my threat to thee: seeing Phœbus Apollo bereaveth me of Chryseis, her with my ship and my company will I send back; and mine own self will I go to thy hut and take Briseis of the fair cheeks, even that thy meed of honor, that thou mayest well know how far greater I am than thou, and so shall another hereafter abhor to match his words with mine and rival me to my face."

So said he, and grief came upon Peleus' son, and his heart within his shaggy breast was divided in counsel, whether to draw his keen blade from his thigh and set the company aside and so slay Atreides, or to assuage his anger and curb his soul. While yet he doubted thereof in heart and soul, and was drawing his great sword from his sheath, Athene came to him from heaven, sent forth of the white-armed goddess Hera, whose heart loved both alike and had care for them. She stood behind Peleus' son and caught him by his golden hair, to him only visible, and of the rest no man beheld her. Then Achilles marveled, and turned him about, and straightway knew Pallas Athene; and terribly shone her eyes. He spake to her winged words, and said: "Why now art thou come hither, thou daughter of ægis-bearing Zeus? Is it to behold the insolence of Agamemnon, son of Atreus? Yea, I will tell thee that I deem shall even be brought to pass: by his own haughtinesses shall he soon lose his life."

Then the bright-eyed goddess Athene spake to him again: "I came from heaven to stay thine anger, if perchance thou wilt hearken to me, being sent forth of the white-armed goddess Hera, that loveth you twain alike and careth for you. Go to now, cease from strife, and let not thine hand draw the sword; yet with words indeed revile him, even as it shall come to pass. For thus will I say to thee, and so it shall be fulfilled; hereafter shall goodly gifts come to thee, yea, in threefold measure, by reason of this despite; hold thou thine hand, and hearken to us."

And Achilles fleet of foot made answer and said to her: "Goddess, needs must a man observe the saying of you twain, even though he be very wroth at heart; for so is the better way. Whosoever obeyeth the gods, to him they gladly hearken."

He said, and stayed his heavy hand on the silver hilt, and thrust the great sword back into the sheath, and was not disobedient to the saying of Athene; and she forthwith was departed to Olympus, to the other gods in the palace of ægisbearing Zeus.

Then Peleus' son spake again with bitter words to Atreus' son, and in no wise ceased from anger: "Thou heavy with wine, thou with face of dog and heart of deer, never didst thou take courage to arm for battle among thy folk or to lay ambush with the princes of the Achaians; that to thee were even as death. Far better booteth it, forsooth, to seize for thyself the meed of honor of every man through the wide host of the Achaians that speaketh contrary to thee. Folk-devouring king! seeing thou rulest men of naught; else were this despite, thou son of Atreus, thy last. But I will speak my word to thee, and swear a mighty oath therewith: verily by this staff that shall no more put forth leaf or twig, seeing it hath for ever left its trunk among the hills, neither shall it grow green again, because the ax hath stripped it of leaves and bark; and now the sons of the Achaians that exercise judgment bear it in their hands, even they that by Zeus' command watch over the traditions—so shall this be a mighty oath in thine eyes—verily shall longing for Achilles come hereafter upon the sons of the Achaians one and all; and then wilt thou in no wise avail to save them, for all thy grief, when multitudes fall dying before manslaying Hector. Then shalt thou tear thy heart within thee for anger that thou didst in no wise honor the best of the Achaians."

So said Peleides [2] and dashed to earth the staff studded with golden nails, and himself sat down; and over against him Atreides waxed furious. Then in their midst rose up Nestor, pleasant of speech, the clear-voiced orator of the Pylians, he from whose tongue flowed discourse sweeter than honey. Two generations of mortal men already had he seen perish, that had been of old time born and nurtured with him in goodly Pylos, and he was king among the third. He of good intent made harangue to them and said: "Alas, of a truth sore lamentation cometh upon the land of Achaia. Verily Priam would be glad and Priam's sons, and all the Trojans would have great joy of heart, were they to hear all this tale of strife between you twain that are chiefest of the Danaans in counsel and chiefest in battle. Nay, hearken to me; ye are younger both than I. Of old days held I converse with better men even than you, and never did they make light of me. Yea, I never beheld such warriors, nor shall behold, as were Peirithoos and Dryas shepherd of the host and Kaineus and Exadios and godlike Polyphemos [and Theseus son of Aigeus, like to the immortals]. Mightiest of growth were they of all men upon the earth; mightiest they were and with the mightiest fought they, even the wild tribes of the mountain caves, and destroyed them utterly. And with these held I converse, being come from Pylos, from a distant land afar; for of themselves they summoned me. So I played my part in fight; and with them could none of men that are now on earth do battle. And they laid to heart my counsels and hearkened to my voice. Even so hearken ye also, for better is it to hearken. Neither do thou, though thou art very great, seize from him his damsel, but leave her as she was given at the first by the sons of the Achaians to be a meed of honor; nor do thou, son of Peleus, think to strive with a king, might against might; seeing that no common honor pertaineth to a sceptered king to whom Zeus apportioneth glory. Though thou be strong, and a goddess mother bare thee, yet his is the greater place, for he is king over more. And thou, Atreides, abate thy fury; nay, it is even I that beseech thee to let go thine anger with Achilles, who is made unto all the Achaians a mighty bulwark of evil war."

Then lord Agamemnon answered and said: "Yea verily, old man, all this thou sayest is according unto right. But this fellow would be above all others, he would be lord of all and king among all and captain to all; wherein I deem none will hearken to him. Though the immortal gods made him a spearman, do they therefore put revilings in his mouth for him to utter?"

Then goodly Achilles brake in on him and answered: "Yea, for I should be called coward and

[2] Son of Peleus.

man of naught, if I yield to thee in every matter, howsoe'er thou bid. To others give now thine orders, not to me [play master; for thee I deem that I shall no more obey]. This, moreover, will I say to thee, and do thou lay it to thy heart. Know that not by violence will I strive for the damsel's sake, neither with thee nor any other; ye gave and ye have taken away. But of all else that is mine beside my fleet black ship, thereof shalt thou not take anything or bear it away against my will. Yea, go to now, make trial, that all these may see; forthwith thy dark blood shall gush about my spear."

Now when the twain had thus finished the battle of violent words, they stood up and dissolved the assembly beside the Achaian ships. Peleides went his way to his huts and trim ships with Menoitios' son and his company; and Atreides launched a fleet ship on the sea, and picked twenty oarsmen therefor, and embarked the hecatomb for the god, and brought Chryseis of the fair cheeks and set her therein; and Odysseus of many devices went to be their captain.

So these embarked and sailed over the wet ways; and Atreides bade the folk purify themselves. So they purified themselves, and cast the defilements into the sea and did sacrifice to Apollo, even unblemished hecatombs of bulls and goats, along the shore of the unvintaged sea; and the sweet savor arose to heaven eddying amid the smoke.

Thus were they busied throughout the host; but Agamemnon ceased not from the strife wherewith he threatened Achilles at the first; he spake to Talthybios and Eurybates that were his heralds and nimble squires: "Go ye to the tent of Achilles Peleus' son, and take Briseis of the fair cheeks by the hand and her lead hither; and if he give her not, then will I myself go, and more with me, and seize her; and that will be yet more grievous for him."

So saying he sent them forth, and laid stern charge upon them. Unwillingly went they along the beach of the unvintaged sea, and came to the huts and ships of the Myrmidons. Him found they sitting beside his hut and black ship; nor when he saw them was Achilles glad. So they in dread and reverence of the king stood, and spake to him no word, nor questioned him. But he knew in his heart, and spake to them: "All hail, ye heralds, messengers of Zeus and men, come near; ye are not guilty in my sight, but Agamemnon that sent you for the sake of the damsel Briseis. Go now, heaven-sprung Patroklos, bring forth the damsel, and give them her to lead away. Moreover, let the twain

themselves be my witnesses before the face of the blessed gods and mortal men, yea and of him, that king untoward, against the day when there cometh need of me hereafter to save them all from shameful wreck. Of a truth he raveth with baleful mind, and hath not knowledge to look before and after, that so his Achaians might battle in safety beside their ships."

So said he, and Patroklos hearkened to his dear comrade, and led forth from the hut Briseis of the fair cheeks, and gave them her to lead away. So these twain took their way back along the Achaians' ships, and with them went the woman all unwilling. Then Achilles wept anon, and sat him down apart, aloof from his comrades on the beach of the gray sea, gazing across the boundless main: he stretched forth his hands and prayed instantly to his dear mother: "Mother, seeing thou didst of a truth bear me to so brief span of life, honor at the least ought the Olympian to have granted me, even Zeus that thundereth on high; but now doth he not honor me, no, not one whit. Verily Atreus' son, wide-ruling Agamemnon, hath done me dishonor; for he hath taken away my meed of honor and keepeth her of his own violent deed."

So spake he weeping, and his lady mother heard him as she sate in the sea-depths beside her aged sire. With speed arose she from the gray sea, like a mist, and sate her before the face of her weeping son, and stroked him with her hand, and spake and called on his name: "My child, why weepest thou? What sorrow hath entered into thy heart? Speak it forth, hide it not in my mind, that both may know it."

Then with heavy moan Achilles fleet of foot spake to her: "Thou knowest it; why should I tell this to thee that knowest all! We had fared to Thebe, the holy city of Eëtion, and laid it waste and carried hither all the spoils. So the sons of the Achaians divided among them all aright; and for Atreides they set apart Chryseis of the fair cheeks. But Chryses, priest of Apollo the Far-darter, came unto the fleet ships of the mail-clad Achaians to win his daughter's freedom, and brought a ransom beyond telling, and bare in his hands the fillet of Apollo the Far-darter upon a golden staff, and made his prayer unto all the Achaians, and most of all to the two sons of Atreus, orderers of the host. Then all the other Achaians cried assent, to reverence the priest and accept his goodly ransom; yet the thing pleased not the heart of Agamemnon son of Atreus, but he roughly sent him away and laid stern charge upon him. So the old man went back in anger, and Apollo heard his prayers, seeing he loved him greatly, and he aimed against the Argives his deadly darts. So the people began to perish in multitudes, and the god's shafts ranged everywhither throughout the wide host of the Achaians. Then of full knowledge the seer declared to us the oracle of the Far-darter. Forthwith I first bade propitiate the god; but wrath gat hold upon Atreus' son thereat, and anon he stood up and spake a threatening word, that hath now been accomplished. Her the glancing-eyed Achaians are bringing on their fleet ship to Chryse, and bear with them offerings to the king; and the other but now the heralds went and took from my hut, even the daughter of Briseus, whom the sons of the Achaians gave me. Thou therefore, if indeed thou canst, guard thine own son; betake thee to Olympus and beseech Zeus by any deed or word whereby thou ever didst make glad his heart. For oft have I heard thee proclaiming in my father's halls and telling that thou alone amid the immortals didst save the son of Kronos, lord of the storm-cloud, from shameful wreck, when all the other Olympians would have bound him, even Hera and Poseidon and Pallas Athene. Then didst thou, O goddess, enter in and loose him from his bonds, having with speed summoned to high Olympus him of the hundred arms whom gods call Briareus, but all men call Aigaion; for he is mightier even than his father—so he sate him by Kronion's side rejoicing in his triumph, and the blessed gods feared him withal and bound not Zeus. This bring thou to his remembrance and sit by him and clasp his knees, if perchance he will give succor to the Trojans; and for the Achaians, hem them among their ships' sterns about the bay, given over to slaughter; that they may make trial of their king, and that even Atreides, wide-ruling Agamemnon, may perceive his blindness, in that he honored not at all the best of the Achaians."

Then Thetis weeping made answer to him: "Ah me, my child, why reared I thee, cursed in my motherhood? Would thou hadst been left tearless and griefless amid the ships, seeing thy lot is very brief and endureth no long while; but now art thou made short-lived alike and lamentable beyond all men; in an evil hour I bare thee in our halls. But I will go myself to snow-clad Olympus to tell this thy saying to Zeus, whose joy is in the thunder, if perchance he may hearken to me. But tarry thou now amid thy fleet-faring ships, and continue wroth with the Achaians, and refrain utterly from battle: for Zeus went yesterday to Okeanos, unto the noble Ethiopians for a feast, and all the gods followed with him; but on the twelfth day will he return to Olympus, and then will I fare to Zeus' palace of the bronze threshold, and will kneel to him and think to win him."

So saying she went her way and left him there, vexed in spirit for the fair-girdled woman's sake, whom they had taken perforce despite his will: and meanwhile Odysseus came to Chryse with the holy hecatomb. When they were now entered within the deep haven, they furled their sails and laid them in the black ship, and lowered the mast by the forestays and brought it to the crutch with speed, and rowed her with oars to the anchorage. Then they cast out the mooring stones and made fast the hawsers, and so themselves went forth on to the sea-beach, and forth they brought the hecatomb for the Far-darter Apollo, and forth came Chryseis withal from the seafaring ship. Then Odysseus of many counsels brought her to the altar and gave her into her father's arms, and spake unto him: "Chryses, Agamemnon king of men sent me hither to bring thee thy daughter, and to offer to Phœbus a holy hecatomb on the Danaans' behalf, wherewith to propitiate the king that hath now brought sorrow and lamentation on the Argives."

So saying he gave her to his arms, and he gladly took his dear child; and anon they set in order for the god the holy hecatomb about his well-builed altar; next washed they their hands and took up the barley meal. Then Chryses lifted up his hands and prayed aloud for them: "Hearken to me, god of the silver bow that standest over Chryse and holy Killa, and rulest Tenedos with might; even as erst thou heardest my prayer, and didst me honor, and mightily afflictedst the people of the Achaians, even so now fulfill me this my desire: remove thou from the Danaans forthwith the loathly pestilence."

So spake he in prayer, and Phœbus Apollo heard him. Now when they had prayed and sprinkled the barley meal, first they drew back the victims' heads and slaughtered them and flayed them, and cut slices from the thighs and wrapped them in fat, making a double fold, and laid raw collops thereon, and the old man burnt them on cleft wood and made libation over them of gleaming wine; and at his side the young men in their hands held five-pronged forks. Now when the thighs were burnt and they had tasted the vitals, then sliced they all the rest and pierced it through with spits, and roasted it carefully, and drew all off again. So when they had rest from the task and had made ready the banquet, they feasted, nor was their heart aught stinted of the fair banquet. But when they had put away from them the desire of meat and drink, the young men crowned the bowls with wine, and gave each man his portion after the drink-offering had been poured into the cups. So all day long worshiped they the god with music, singing the beautiful pæan, the sons of the Achaians making music to the Far-darter; and his heart [10] was glad to hear. And when the sun went down and darkness came on them, they laid them to sleep beside the ship's hawsers; and when rosy-fingered Dawn appeared, the child of morning, then set they sail for the wide camp of the Achaians; and Apollo the Far-darter sent them a favoring gale. They set up their mast and spread the white sails forth, and the wind filled the sail's belly and the dark wave sang loud about the stem as the ship made way, and she sped across the [20] wave, accomplishing her journey. So when they were now come to the wide camp of the Achaians, they drew up their black ship to land high upon the sands, and set in line the long props beneath her; and themselves were scattered amid their huts and ships.

But he sat by his swift-faring ships, still wroth, even the heaven-sprung son of Peleus, Achilles fleet of foot; he betook him neither to the assembly that is the hero's glory, neither to war, but con- [30] sumed his heart in tarrying in his place, and yearned for the war-cry and for battle.

Now when the twelfth morn thereafter was come, then the gods that are for ever fared to Olympus all in company, led of Zeus. And Thetis forgat not her son's charge, but rose up from the sea-wave, and at early morn mounted up to great heaven and Olympus. There found she Kronos' son of the far-sounding voice sitting apart from all on the topmost peak of many-ridged Olympus. So [40] she sat before his face and with her left hand clasped his knees, and with her right touched him beneath his chin, and spake in prayer to king Zeus son of Kronos: "Father Zeus, if ever I gave thee aid amid the immortal gods, whether by word or deed, fulfill thou this my desire: do honor to my son, that is doomed to earliest death of all men: now hath Agamemnon king of men done him dishonor, for he hath taken away his meed of honor and keepeth her of his own violent deed. [50] But honor thou him, Zeus of Olympus, lord of counsel; grant thou victory to the Trojans the

while, until the Achaians do my son honor and exalt him with recompense."

So spake she; but Zeus the cloud-gatherer said no word to her, and sat long time in silence. But even as Thetis had clasped his knees, so held she by him clinging, and questioned him yet a second time: "Promise me now this thing verily, and bow thy head thereto; or else deny me, seeing there is naught for thee to fear; that I may know full well how I among all gods am least in honor."

Then Zeus the cloud-gatherer, sore troubled, spake to her: "Verily it is a sorry matter, if thou wilt set me at variance with Hera, whene'er she provoketh me with taunting words. Even now she upbraideth me ever amid the immortal gods, and saith that I aid the Trojans in battle. But do thou now depart again, lest Hera mark aught; and I will take thought for these things to fulfill them. Come now, I will bow my head to thee, that thou [20] mayest be of good courage; for that, of my part, is the surest token amid the immortals; no word of mine is revocable nor false nor unfulfilled when the bowing of my head hath pledged it."

Kronion[3] spake, and bowed his dark brow, and the ambrosial locks waved from the king's immortal head; and he made great Olympus quake.

Thus the twain took counsel and parted; she leapt therewith into the deep sea from glittering Olympus, and Zeus fared to his own palace. All the [30] gods in company arose from their seats before their father's face; neither ventured any to await his coming, but they stood up all before him. So he sate him there upon his throne; but Hera saw, and was not ignorant how that the daughter of the Ancient of the sea, Thetis the silver-footed, had devised counsel with him. Anon with taunting words spake she to Zeus the son of Kronos: "Now who among the gods, thou crafty of mind, hath devised counsel with thee? It is ever thy good [40] pleasure to hold aloof from me and in secret meditation to give thy judgments, nor of thine own good will hast thou ever brought thyself to declare unto me the thing thou purposest."

Then the father of gods and men made answer to her: "Hera, think not thou to know all my sayings; hard they are for thee, even though thou art my wife. But whichsoever it is seemly for thee to hear, none sooner than thou shall know, be he god or man. Only when I will to take thought aloof [50] from the gods, then do not thou ask of every matter nor make question."

Then Hera the ox-eyed queen made answer to

---

[3] Son of Kronos or Cronus; that is, Zeus.

him: "Most dread son of Kronos, what word is this thou hast spoken? Yea, surely of old I have not asked thee nor made question, but in very quietness thou devisest all thou wilt. But now is my heart sore afraid lest thou have been won over by silver-footed Thetis, daughter of the Ancient of the sea, for she at early morn sat by thee and clasped thy knees. To her I deem thou gavest a sure pledge that thou wilt do honor to Achilles, and lay many low beside the Achaians' ships." 10

To her made answer Zeus the cloud-gatherer: "Lady, good lack! ever art thou imagining, nor can I escape thee; yet shalt thou in no wise have power to fulfill, but wilt be the further from my heart; that shall be even the worse for thee. And if it be so, then such must my good pleasure be. Abide thou in silence and hearken to my bidding, lest all the gods that are in Olympus keep not off from thee my visitation, when I put forth my hands unapproachable against thee." 20

He said, and Hera the ox-eyed queen was afraid, and sat in silence, curbing her heart; but throughout Zeus' palace the gods of heaven were troubled. Then Hephaistos the famed craftsman began to make harangue among them, to do kindness to his dear mother, white-armed Hera: "Verily this will be a sorry matter, neither any more endurable, if ye twain thus fight for mortals' sakes, and bring wrangling among the gods; neither will there any more be joy of the goodly feast, seeing that evil 30 triumpheth. So I give counsel to my mother, though herself is wise, to do kindness to our dear father Zeus, that our father upbraid us not again and cast the banquet in confusion. What if the Olympian, the lord of the lightning, will to dash us from our seats! for he is strongest far. Nay, approach thou him with gentle words, then will the Olympian forthwith be gracious unto us."

So speaking he rose up and set in his dear mother's hand the twy-handled cup, and spake to 40 her: "Be of good courage, mother mine, and endure, though thou art vexed, lest I behold thee, that art so dear, chastised before mine eyes, and then shall I not be able for all my sorrow to save thee; for the Olympian is a hard foe to face. Yea, once ere this, when I was fain to save thee, he caught me by my foot and hurled me from the heavenly threshold; all day I flew, and at the set of sun I fell in Lemnos, and little life was in me. There did the Sintian folk forthwith tend me for 50 my fall."

He spake, and the white-armed goddess Hera smiled, and smiling took the cup at her son's hand.

Then he poured wine to all the other gods from right to left, ladling the sweet nectar from the bowl. And laughter unquenchable arose amid the blessed gods to see Hephaistos bustling through the palace.

So feasted they all day till the setting of the sun; nor was their soul aught stinted of the fair banquet, nor of the beauteous lyre that Apollo held, and the Muses singing alternately with sweet voice.

Now when the bright light of the sun was set, these went each to his own house to sleep, where each one had his palace made with cunning device by famed Hephaistos the lame god; and Zeus the Olympian, the lord of lightning, departed to his couch where he was wont of old to take his rest, whenever sweet sleep visited him. There went he up and slept, and beside him was Hera of the golden throne.

[*Agamemnon now tries to carry on the war without Achilles' help. After various incidents which retard the action he is ready to open the combat which he hopes will capture Troy. But it is now agreed that the issue shall be decided by a single combat between Menelaos and Paris, who are the real causes of the war. In the duel Paris is overcome and is about to be killed when Aphrodite, who is his protectress, takes him unseen to the city where he visits Helen. Meantime, in spite of the truce, Menelaos has been wounded by Pandaros, an ally of the Trojans. This act causes a renewal of the battle, which is in progress as Book VI opens.*]

BOOK VI

How Diomedes and Glaukos being about to fight, were known to each other, and parted in friendliness. And how Hector returning to the city bade farewell to Andromache his wife.

So was the dread fray of Trojans and Achaians left to itself, and the battle swayed oft this way and that across the plain, as they aimed against each other their bronze-shod javelins, between Simoeis and the streams of Xanthos.

First Aias son of Telamon, bulwark of the Achaians, brake a battalion of the Trojans and brought his comrades salvation, smiting a warrior that was chiefest among the Thracians, Eussoros' son Akamas the goodly and great. Him first he smote upon his thick-crested helmet-ridge and drave into his forehead, so that the point of bronze pierced into the bone; and darkness shrouded his eyes.

Then Diomedes of the loud war-cry slew Axylos Teuthranos' son that dwelt in stablished Arisbe, a man of substance dear to his fellows; for his dwelling was by the roadside and he entertained all men. Howbeit of all these was there then not one to meet the foe before his face and save him from fell destruction; but Diomedes took the life of both of them, even of him and Kalesios his squire that now was the driver of his chariot; so passed both below the earth.

And Euryalos slew Dresos and Opheltios, and followed after Aisepos and Pedasos whom erst the fountain-nymph Abarbarea bare to noble Boukolion. Now Boukolion was son of proud Laomedon, his eldest born, begotten of a mother unwedded; and as he tended his flocks he had converse with the nymph in love, and she conceived and bare twin sons. And lo, the strength of these and their glorious limbs Mekisteus' son unstrung, and stripped the armor from their shoulders. And stubborn Polypoites slew Astyalos, and Odysseus with spear of bronze laid low Pidytes of Perkote, and so did Teukros to goodly Aretaon. Then was Ableros killed by the glistening spear of Antilochos, Nestor's son, and Elatos by Agamemnon king of men; beside the banks of fair-flowing Satnioeis dwelt he in steep Pedasos. And Leïtos the warrior caught Phylakos, as he fled; and Eurypylos slew Melanthios.

Now did Menelaos of the loud war-cry take Adrestos alive; for his horses took flight across the plain, and stumbling in a tamarisk bough brake the curved car at the pole's foot; so they themselves fared towards the city where the rest were fleeing in rout, and their lord rolled from out the car beside the wheel, prone in the dust upon his face. Then came Atreus' son Menelaos to his side bearing his far-shadowing spear. Thereat Adrestos caught him by his knees and besought him: "Take me captive, thou son of Atreus, and accept a worthy ransom; many a treasure is stored up in my father's rich palace, bronze and gold and smithied iron; thereof would my father yield thee ransom beyond the telling, if he but heard that I am alive at the ships of the Achaians."

So spake he, and moved the spirit in his breast. And now had he forthwith given him to his squire to lead him to the Achaians' fleet ships, but that Agamemnon came running to meet him, and spake a word of chiding to him: "Good Menelaos, why art thou so careful of the foemen? Have then such good deeds been wrought thee in thy house by Trojans? Of them let not one escape sheer destruction at our hands, not even the man-child that the mother beareth in her womb; let not even him escape, but all perish together out of Ilios, uncared for and unknown."

So spake the hero and turned his brother's mind with righteous persuasion; so with his hand he thrust the hero Adrestos from him, and lord Agamemnon smote him in the flank, and he was overthrown, and Atreus' son set his heel upon his chest and plucked forth his ashen spear.

Then Nestor called to the Argives with far-reaching shout: "My friends, Danaan warriors, men of Ares' company, let no man now take thought of spoils to tarry behind, that he may bring the greatest burden to the ships; but let us slay the foemen. Thereafter shall ye at your ease also strip of their spoil the dead corpses about the plain."

So spake he and stirred the spirit and soul of every man. Now had the Trojans been chased again by the Achaians, dear to Ares, up into Ilios, in their weakness overcome, but that Priam's son Helenos, far best of augurs, stood by Aineias' side and Hector's, and spake to them: "Aineias and Hector, seeing that on you lieth the task of war in chief of Trojans and Lykians, because for every issue ye are foremost both for fight and counsel, stand ye your ground, and range the host everywhither to rally them before the gates, ere yet they fall fleeing in their women's arms, and be made a rejoicing to the foe. Then when ye have aroused all our battalions we will abide here and fight the Danaans, though in sore weariness; for necessity presseth us hard: but thou, Hector, go into the city, and speak there to thy mother and mine; let her gather the aged wives to bright-eyed Athene's temple in the upper city, and with her key open the doors of the holy house; and let her lay the robe, that seemeth to her the most gracious and greatest in her hall and far dearest unto herself, upon the knees of beauteous-haired Athene; and vow to her to sacrifice in her temple twelve sleek kine, that have not felt the goad, if she will have mercy on the city and the Trojans' wives and little children. So may she perchance hold back Tydeus' son from holy Ilios, the furious spearman, the mighty deviser of rout, whom in good sooth I deem to have proved himself mightiest of the Achaians. Never in this wise feared we Achilles prince of men, who they say is born of a goddess; nay, but he that we see is beyond measure furious; none can match him for might."

So spake he, and Hector disregarded not his

brother's word, but leapt forthwith from his chariot in his armor to earth, and brandishing two sharp spears passed everywhere through the host, rousing them to battle, and stirred the dread war-cry. So they were rallied and stood to face the Achaians, and the Argives gave ground and ceased from slaughter, and deemed that some immortal had descended from starry heaven to bring the Trojans succor, in such wise rallied they. Then Hector called to the Trojans with far-reaching shout: "O high-souled Trojans and ye far-famed allies, quit you like men, my friends, and take thought of impetuous courage, while I depart to Ilios and bid the elders of the council and our wives pray to the gods and vow them hecatombs."

So saying Hector of the glancing helm departed, and the black hide beat on either side against his ankles and his neck, even the rim that ran uttermost about his bossed shield.

Now Glaukos son of Hippolochos and Tydeus' son met in the mid-space of the foes, eager to do battle. Thus when the twain were come nigh in onset on each other, to him first spake Diomedes of the loud war-cry: "Who art thou, noble sir, of mortal men? For never have I beheld thee in glorious battle ere this, yet now hast thou far outstripped all men in thy hardihood, seeing thou abidest my far-shadowing spear. Luckless are the fathers whose children face my might. But if thou art some immortal come down from heaven, then will not I fight with heavenly gods. Nay more-over even Dryas' son mighty Lykurgos was not for long when he strove with heavenly gods, he that erst chased through the goodly land of Nysa the nursing-mothers of frenzied Dionysos; and they all cast their wands upon the ground, smitten with murderous Lykurgos' ox-goad. Then Dionysos fled and plunged beneath the salt seawave, and Thetis took him to her bosom, affrighted, for a mighty trembling had seized him at his foe's rebuke. But with Lykurgos the gods that live at ease were wroth, and Kronos' son made him blind, and he was not for long, because he was hated of all the immortal gods. So would neither I be fain to fight the blessed gods. But if thou art of men that eat the fruit of the field, come nigh, that anon thou mayest enter the toils of destruction."

Then Hippolochos' glorious son made answer to him: "Great-hearted Tydeides,[4] why enquirest thou of my generation? Even as are the generations of leaves such are those likewise of men; the leaves that be the wind scattereth on the earth, and the forest buddeth and putteth forth more again, when the season of spring is at hand; so of the generations of men one putteth forth and another ceaseth. Yet if thou wilt, have thine answer, that thou mayest well know our lineage, whereof many men have knowledge. There is a city Ephyre in the heart of Argos, pasture-land of horses, and there dwelt Sisyphos that was craftiest of men, Sisyphos son of Aiolos; and he begat a son, even Glaukos, and Glaukos begat noble Bellerophon. To him the gods granted beauty and lovely manhood; but Proitos in his heart devised ill for him, and being mightier far drave him from the land of the Argives, whom Zeus had made subject to his scepter. Now Proitos' wife, goodly Anteia, lusted after him, to have converse in secret love, but no whit prevailed she, for the uprightness of his heart, on wise Bellerophon. Then spake she lyingly to king Proitos: 'Die, Proitos, or else slay Bellerophon, that would have converse in love with me against my will.' So spake she, and anger gat hold upon the king at that he heard. To slay him he forbare, for his soul had shame of that; but he sent him to Lykia, and gave him tokens of woe, graving in a folded tablet many deadly things, and bade him shew these to Anteia's father, that he might be slain. So fared he to Lykia by the blameless convoy of the gods. Now when he came to Lykia and the stream of Xanthos, then did the king of wide Lykia honor him with all his heart; nine days he entertained him and killed nine oxen. And when on the tenth day rosy-fingered Dawn appeared, then he questioned him and asked to see what token he bare from his son-in-law, even Proitos. Now when he had received of him Proitos' evil token, first he bade him slay Chimaira the unconquerable. Of divine birth was she and not of men, in front a lion, and behind a serpent, and in the midst a goat; and she breathed dread fierceness of blazing fire. And her he slew, obedient to the signs of heaven. Next fought he with the famed Solymi; this, said he, was the mightiest battle of warriors wherein he entered. And thirdly he slew the Amazons, women peers of men. And as he turned back therefrom, the king devised another cunning wile; he picked from wide Lykia the bravest men, and set an ambush. But these returned nowise home again; for noble Bellerophon slew them all. So when the king now knew that he was the brave offspring of a god, he kept him there, and plighted him his daughter, and gave him the half of all the honor of his kingdom; moreover the Lykians

---

[4] Son of Tydeus.

meted him a domain pre-eminent above all, fair with vineyards and tilth to possess it. And his wife bare wise Bellerophon three children, Isandros and Hippolochos and Laodameia. With Laodameia lay Zeus the lord of counsel, and she bare godlike Sarpedon, the warrior with arms of bronze. But when even Bellerophon came to be hated of all the gods, then wandered he alone in the Aleian plain, devouring his own soul, and avoiding the paths of men; and Isandros his son was slain by Ares insatiate of battle, as he fought against the famed Solymi, and his daughter was slain in wrath of gold-gleaming Artemis. But Hippolochos begat me, and of him do I declare me to be sprung; he sent me to Troy and bade me very instantly to be ever the best and to excel all other men, nor put to shame the lineage of my fathers that were of noblest blood in Ephyre and in wide Lykia. This is the lineage and blood whereof I avow myself to be."

So said he, and Diomedes of the loud war-cry was glad. He planted his spear in the bounteous earth and with soft words spake to the shepherd of the host: "Surely then thou art to me a guest-friend of old times through my father: for goodly Oineus of yore entertained noble Bellerophon in his halls and kept him twenty days. Moreover they gave each the other goodly gifts of friendship; Oineus gave a belt bright with purple, and Bellerophon a gold twy-handled cup, the which when I came I left in my palace. But of Tydeus I remember naught, seeing I was yet little when he left me, what time the Achaian host perished at Thebes. Therefore now am I to thee a dear guest-friend in midmost Argos, and thou in Lykia, whene'er I fare to your land. So let us shun each other's spears, even amid the throng; Trojans are there in multitudes and famous allies for me to slay, whoe'er it be that God vouchsafeth me and my feet overtake; and for thee are there Achaians in multitude, to slay whome'er thou canst. But let us make exchange of arms between us, that these also may know how we avow ourselves to be guest-friends by lineage."

So spake the twain, and leaping from their cars clasped each the other by his hand, and pledged their faith. But now Zeus son of Kronos took from Glaukos his wits, in that he made exchange with Diomedes Tydeus' son of golden armor for bronze, the price of five score oxen for the price of nine.

Now when Hector came to the Skaian gates and to the oak-tree, there came running round about him the Trojans' wives and daughters, enquiring of sons and brethren and friends and husbands. But he bade them thereat all in turn pray to the gods; but sorrow hung over many.

But when he came to Priam's beautiful palace, adorned with polished colonnades—and in it were fifty chambers of polished stone, builded hard by one another, wherein Priam's sons slept beside their wedded wives; and for his daughters over against them on the other side within the courtyard were twelve roofed chambers of polished stone builded hard by one another, wherein slept Priam's sons-in-law beside their chaste wives—then came there to meet him his bountiful mother, leading with her Laodike, fairest of her daughters to look on; and she clasped her hand in his, and spake, and called upon his name: "My son, why hast thou left violent battle to come hither? Surely the sons of the Achaians—name of evil!—press thee hard in fight about thy city, and so thy spirit hath brought thee hither, to come and stretch forth thy hands to Zeus from the citadel. But tarry till I bring thee honey-sweet wine, that thou mayest pour libation to Zeus and all the immortals first, and then shalt thou thyself also be refreshed if thou wilt drink. When a man is awearied wine greatly maketh his strength to wax, even as thou art awearied in fighting for thy fellows."

Then great Hector of the glancing helm answered her: "Bring me no honey-hearted wine, my lady mother, lest thou cripple me of my courage and I be forgetful of my might. Moreover I have awe to make libation of gleaming wine to Zeus with hands unwashen; nor can it be in any wise that one should pray to the son of Kronos, god of the storm-cloud, all defiled with blood and filth. But go thou to the temple of Athene, driver of the spoil, with offerings, and gather the aged wives together; and the robe that seemeth to thee the most gracious and greatest in thy palace, and dearest unto thyself, that lay thou upon the knees of beauteous-haired Athene, and vow to her to sacrifice in her temple twelve sleek kine, that have not felt the goad, if she will have mercy on the city and the Trojans' wives and little children. So may she perchance hold back Tydeus' son from holy Ilios, the furious spearman, the mighty deviser of rout. So go thou to the temple of Athene, driver of the spoil; and I will go after Paris, to summon him, if perchance he will hearken to my voice. Would that the earth forthwith might swallow him up! The Olympian fostered him to be a sore bane to the Trojans and to great-hearted Priam, and to Priam's sons. If I but saw him going down to the gates of death, then might I deem that my heart had forgotten its sorrow."

So said he, and she went into the hall, and called to her handmaidens, and they gathered the aged wives throughout the city. Then she herself went down to her fragrant chamber where were her embroidered robes, the work of Sidonian women, whom godlike Alexandros himself brought from Sidon, when he sailed over the wide sea, that journey wherein he brought home high-born Helen. Of these Hekabe took one to bear for an offering to Athene, the one that was fairest for adornment and greatest, and shone like a star, and lay nethermost of all. Then went she her way and the multitude of aged wives hasted after her.

Now when they came to the temple of Athene in the citadel, fair-cheeked Theano opened them the doors, even Kisseus' daughter, wife of horse-taming Antenor; for her the Trojans had made priestess of Athene. Then lifted they all their hands to Athene with lamentation: and fair-cheeked Theano took the robe and laid it on the knees of beauteous-haired Athene, and lifted up her voice and prayed to the daughter of great Zeus: "Lady Athene, savior of the city, fair among goddesses, break now Diomedes' spear, and grant moreover that himself may fall prone before the Skaian gates; that we may sacrifice thee now forthwith in thy temple twelve sleek kine, that have not felt the goad, if thou wilt have mercy on the city and the Trojans' wives and little children." So spake she praying, but Pallas Athene denied the prayer.

So were these praying to the daughter of great Zeus; and Hector was come to Alexandros' fair palace, that himself had builded with them that were most excellent carpenters then in deep-soiled Troy-land; these made him his chamber and hall and courtyard hard by to Priam and Hector, in the upper city. There entered in Hector dear to Zeus, and his hand bare his spear, eleven cubits long: before his face glittered the bronze spear-point, and a ring of gold ran round about it. And he found Paris in his chamber busied with his beauteous arms, his shield and breastplate, and handling his curved bow; and Helen of Argos sate among her serving-women and appointed brave handiwork for her handmaidens. Then when Hector saw him he rebuked him with scornful words: "Good sir, thou dost not well to cherish this rancor in thy heart. The folk are perishing about the city and high wall in battle, and for thy sake the battle-cry is kindled and war around this city; yea

thyself wouldest thou rail out with another, didst thou see him shrinking from hateful war. Up then, lest the city soon be scorched with burning fire."

And godlike Alexandros[5] answered him: "Hector, since in measure thou chidest me and not beyond measure, therefore will I tell thee; lay thou it to thine heart and hearken to me. Not by reason so much of the Trojans, for wrath and indignation, sate I me in my chamber, but fain would I yield me to my sorrow. Even now my wife hath persuaded me with soft words, and urged me into battle; and I moreover, even I, deem that it will be better so; for victory shifteth from man to man. Go to then, tarry awhile, let me put on my armor of war; or else fare thou forth, and I will follow; and I think to overtake thee."

So said he, but Hector of the glancing helm answered him not a word. But Helen spake to him with gentle words: "My brother, even mine that am a dog, mischievous and abominable, would that on the day when my mother bare me at the first, an evil storm-wind had caught me away to a mountain or a billow of the loud-sounding sea, where the billow might have swept me away before all these things came to pass. Howbeit, seeing the gods devised all these ills in this wise, would that then I had been mated with a better man, that felt dishonor and the multitude of men's reproachings. But as for him, neither hath he now sound heart, nor ever will have; thereof deem I moreover that he will reap the fruit. But now come, enter in and sit thee here upon this bench, my brother, since thy heart chiefly trouble hath encompassed, for the sake of me, that am a dog, and for Alexandros' sin; on whom Zeus bringeth evil doom, that even in days to come we may be a song in the ears of men that shall be hereafter."

Then great Hector of the glancing helm answered her: "Bid me not sit, Helen, of thy love; thou wilt not persuade me. Already my heart is set to succor the men of Troy, that have great desire for me that am not with them. But rouse thou this fellow, yea let himself make speed, to overtake me yet within the city. For I shall go into mine house to behold my housefolk and my dear wife, and infant boy; for I know not if I shall return home to them again, or if the gods will now overthrow me at the hands of the Achaians."

So spake Hector of the glancing helm and departed; and anon he came to his well-stablished house. But he found not white-armed Andromache in the halls; she with her boy and fair-robed hand-

---

[5] Another name of Paris.

maiden had taken her stand upon the tower, weeping and wailing. And when Hector found not his noble wife within, he came and stood upon the threshold, and spake amid the serving-women: "Come tell me now true, my serving-women. Whither went white-armed Andromache forth from the hall? Hath she gone out to my sisters or unto my brothers' fair-robed wives, or to Athene's temple, where all the fair-tressed Trojan women propitiate the awful goddess?"

Then a busy housedame spake in answer to him: "Hector, seeing thou straitly chargest us tell thee true, neither hath she gone out to any of thy sisters or thy brothers' fair-robed wives, neither to Athene's temple, where all the fair-tressed Trojan women are propitiating the awful goddess; but she went to the great tower of Ilios, because she heard the Trojans were hard pressed, and great victory was for the Achaians. So hath she come in haste to the wall, like unto one frenzied; and the nurse with her beareth the child."

So spake the housedame, and Hector hastened from his house back by the same way down the well-builded streets. When he had passed through the great city and was come to the Skaian gates, whereby he was minded to issue upon the plain, then came his dear-won wife, running to meet him, even Andromache daughter of great-hearted Eëtion, Eëtion that dwelt beneath wooded Plakos, in Thebe under Plakos, and was king of the men of Kilikia; for his daughter was wife to bronze-harnessed Hector. So she met him now, and with her went the handmaid bearing in her bosom the tender boy, the little child, Hector's loved son, like unto a beautiful star. Him Hector called Skamandrios, but all the folk Astyanax; for only Hector guarded Ilios. So now he smiled and gazed at his boy silently, and Andromache stood by his side weeping, and clasped her hand in his, and spake and called upon his name. "Dear my lord, this thy hardihood will undo thee, neither hast thou any pity for thine infant boy, nor for me forlorn that soon shall be thy widow; for soon will the Achaians all set upon thee and slay thee. But it were better for me to go down to the grave if I lose thee; for never more will any comfort be mine, when once thou, even thou, hast met thy fate, but only sorrow. Moreover I have no father nor lady mother: my father was slain of goodly Achilles, for he wasted the populous city of the Kilikians, even high-gated Thebe, and slew Eëtion; yet he despoiled him not, for his soul had shame of that, but he burnt him in his inlaid armor and raised a barrow over him; and all about were elm-trees planted by the mountain nymphs, daughters of ægis-bearing Zeus. And the seven brothers that were mine within our halls, all these on the self-same day went within the house of Hades; for fleet-footed goodly Achilles slew them all amid their kine of trailing gait and white-fleeced sheep. And my mother, that was queen beneath wooded Plakos, her brought he hither with the other spoils, but afterward took a ransom untold to set her free; but in her father's halls was she smitten by the Archer Artemis. Nay, Hector, thou art to me father and lady mother, yea and brother, even as thou art my goodly husband. Come now, have pity and abide here upon the tower, lest thou make thy child an orphan and thy wife a widow. And stay thy folk beside the fig-tree, where best the city may be scaled and the wall is assailable. Thrice came thither the most valiant that are with the two Aiantes and famed Idomeneus and the sons of Atreus and Tydeus' valiant son, and essayed to enter; whether one skilled in soothsaying revealed it to them, or whether their own spirit urgeth and biddeth them on."

Then great Hector of the glancing helm answered her: "Surely I take thought for all these things, my wife; but I have very sore shame of the Trojans and Trojan dames with trailing robes, if like a coward I shrink away from battle. Moreover mine own soul forbiddeth me, seeing I have learnt ever to be valiant and fight in the forefront of the Trojans, winning my father's great glory and mine own. Yea of a surety I know this in heart and soul; the day shall come for holy Ilios to be laid low, and Priam and the folk of Priam of the good ashen spear. Yet doth the anguish of the Trojans hereafter not so much trouble me, neither Hekabe's own, neither king Priam's, neither my brethren's, the many and brave that shall fall in the dust before their foemen, as doth thine anguish in the day when some mail-clad Achaian shall lead thee weeping and rob thee of the light of freedom. So shalt thou abide in Argos and ply the loom at another woman's bidding, and bear water from fount Messeis or Hypereia, being grievously entreated, and sore constraint shall be laid upon thee. And then shall one say that beholdeth thee weep: 'This is the wife of Hector, that was foremost in battle of the horse-taming Trojans when men fought about Ilios.' Thus shall one say hereafter, and fresh grief will be thine for lack of such an husband as thou hadst to ward off the day of thraldom. But me in death may the heaped-up earth be covering, ere I hear thy crying and thy carrying into captivity."

So spake glorious Hector, and stretched out his arm to his boy. But the child shrunk crying to the bosom of his fair-girdled nurse, dismayed at his dear father's aspect, and in dread at the bronze and horse-hair crest that he beheld nodding fiercely from the helmet's top. Then his dear father laughed aloud, and his lady mother; forthwith glorious Hector took the helmet from his head, and laid it, all gleaming, upon the earth; then kissed he his dear son and dandled him in his arms, and spake in prayer to Zeus and all the gods, "O Zeus and all ye gods, vouchsafe ye that this my son may likewise prove even as I, pre-eminent amid the Trojans, and as valiant in might, and be a great king of Ilios. Then may men say of him, 'Far greater is he than his father,' as he returneth home from battle; and may he bring with him blood-stained spoils from the foeman he hath slain, and may his mother's heart be glad."

So spake he, and laid his son in his dear wife's arms; and she took him to her fragrant bosom, smiling tearfully. And her husband had pity to see her, and caressed her with his hand, and spake and called upon her name: "Dear one, I pray thee be not of oversorrowful heart; no man against my fate shall hurl me to Hades; only destiny, I ween, no man hath escaped, be he coward or be he valiant, when once he hath been born. But go thou to thine house and see to thine own tasks, the loom and distaff, and bid thine handmaidens ply their work; but for war shall men provide and I in chief of all men that dwell in Ilios."

So spake glorious Hector, and took up his horse-hair-crested helmet; and his dear wife departed to her home oft looking back, and letting fall big tears. Anon she came to the well-stablished house of man-slaying Hector, and found therein her many handmaidens, and stirred lamentation in them all. So bewailed they Hector, while yet he lived, within his house: for they deemed that he would no more come back to them from battle, nor escape the fury of the hands of the Achaians.

Neither lingered Paris long in his lofty house, but clothed on him his brave armor, bedight with bronze, and hasted through the city, trusting to his nimble feet. Even as when a stalled horse, full-fed at the manger, breaketh his tether and speedeth at the gallop across the plain, being wont to bathe him in the fair-flowing stream, exultingly; and holdeth his head on high, and his mane floateth about his shoulders, and he trusteth in his glory, and nimbly his limbs bear him to the haunts and pasturage of mares; even so Priam's son Paris, glittering in his armor like the shining sun, strode down from high Pergamos laughingly, and his swift feet bare him. Forthwith he overtook his brother noble Hector, even as he was on the point to turn him away from the spot where he had dallied with his wife. To him first spake godlike Alexandros: "Sir, in good sooth I have delayed thee in thine haste by my tarrying, and came not rightly as thou badest me."

And Hector of the glancing helm answered him and said: "Good brother, no man that is right-minded could make light of thy doings in fight, seeing thou art strong: but thou art willfully remiss and hast no care; and for this my heart is grieved within me, that I hear shameful words concerning thee in the Trojans' mouths, who for thy sake endure much toil. But let us be going; all this will we make good hereafter, if Zeus ever vouchsafe us to set before the heavenly gods that are for everlasting the cup of deliverance in our halls, when we have chased out of Troy-land the well-greaved Achaians."

[The next books describe in detail the battles. At length the Trojans have driven the Achaians back and it looks as if the promise of Zeus to avenge the injury done to Achilles is to be fulfilled. Agamemnon sends an embassy to ask Achilles' help, but he refuses and continues sulking in his tent. The battle is renewed. The gods take sides and give success to the Trojans, then to the Greeks, and finally to the Trojans. In these difficult straits, Achilles permits his friend Patroklos to enter the battle, disguised in Achilles' own armor. Now the Trojans are driven back but Patroklos is killed and Achilles' armor taken.]

BOOK XVIII

How Achilles grieved for Patroklos, and how Thetis asked for him new armor of Hephaistos; and of the making of the armor.

Thus fought the rest in the likeness of blazing fire, while to Achilles came Antilochos, a messenger fleet of foot. Him found he in front of his ships of upright horns, boding in his soul the things which even now were accomplished. And sore troubled he spake to his great heart: "Aye me, wherefore again are the flowing-haired Achaians flocking to the ships and flying in rout over the plain? May the gods not have wrought against me the grievous fears at my heart, even as my mother revealed and told me that while I am yet alive the best man of the Myrmidons must by deed of the men of Troy forsake the light of the sun. Surely now must Menoitios' valiant son be dead—foolhardy! surely I bade him when he should have beaten off the fire of the foe to come back to the ships nor with Hector fight amain."

While thus he held debate in his heart and soul, there drew nigh unto him noble Nestor's son, shedding hot tears, and spake his grievous tidings: "Aye me, wise Peleus' son, very bitter tidings must thou hear, such as I would had never been. Fallen is Patroklos, and they are fighting around his body, naked, for his armor is held by Hector of the glancing helm."

Thus spake he, and a black cloud of grief enwrapped Achilles, and with both hands he took dark dust and poured it over his head and defiled his comely face, and on his fragrant doublet black ashes fell. And himself in the dust lay mighty and mightily fallen, and with his own hands tore and marred his hair. And the handmaidens, whom Achilles and Patroklos took captive, cried aloud in the grief of their hearts, and ran forth around valiant Achilles, and all beat on their breasts with their hands, and the knees of each of them were unstrung. And Antilochos on the other side wailed and shed tears, holding Achilles' hands while he groaned in his noble heart, for he feared lest he should cleave his throat with the sword. Then terribly moaned Achilles; and his lady mother heard him as she sate in the depths of the sea beside her ancient sire. And thereon she uttered a cry, and the goddesses flocked around her, all the daughters of Nereus that were in the deep of the sea. There were Glauke, and Thaleia, and Kymodoke, Nesaia and Speio and Thoë and ox-eyed Halië and Kymothoë and Aktaie and Limnoreia and Melite and Iaira and Amphithoë and Agauë and Doto and Proto and Pherusa and Dynamene and Dexamene and Amphinome and Kallianeira, Doris and Panope and noble Galateia, and Nemertes, and Apseudes and Kallianassa, and there were Klymene and Ianeira and Ianassa and Maira, and Oreithuia, and fair-tressed Amathyia, and other Nereïds that were in the deep of the sea. With these the bright cave was filled, and they all beat together on their breasts, and Thetis led the lament: "Listen, sister Nereids, that ye all hear and know well what sorrows are in my heart. Aye me unhappy, aye me that bare to my sorrow the first of men! For after I had borne a son noble and strong, the chief of

heroes, and he shot up like a young branch, then when I had reared him as a plant in a very fruitful field I sent him in beaked ships to Ilios to fight against the men of Troy; but never again shall I welcome him back to his home, to the house of Peleus. And while he yet liveth in my sight and beholdeth the light of the sun, he sorroweth, neither can I help him any whit though I go unto him. But I will go, that I may look upon my dear child, and learn what sorrow hath come to him though he abide aloof from the war."

Thus spake she and left the cave; and the nymphs went with her weeping, and around them the surge of the sea was sundered. And when they came to deep-soiled Troy-land they went up upon the shore in order, where the ships of the Myrmidons were drawn up thickly around fleet Achilles. And as he groaned heavily his lady mother stood beside him, and with a shrill cry clasped the head of her child, and spake unto him winged words of lamentation: "My child, why weepest thou? what sorrow hath come to thy heart? Tell it forth, hide it not. One thing at least hath been accomplished of Zeus according to the prayer thou madest, holding up to him thy hands, that the sons of the Achaians should all be pent in at the ships, through lack of thee, and should suffer hateful things."

Then groaning heavily spake unto her Achilles fleet of foot: "My mother, that prayer truly hath the Olympian accomplished for me. But what delight have I therein, since my dear comrade is dead, Patroklos, whom I honored above all my comrades as it were my very self? Him have I lost, and Hector that slew him hath stripped from him the armor great and fair, a wonder to behold, that the gods gave to Peleus a splendid gift, on the day when they laid thee in the bed of a mortal man. Would thou hadst abode among the deathless daughters of the sea, and Peleus had wedded a mortal bride! But now, that thou mayest have sorrow a thousandfold in thy heart for a dead son, never shalt thou welcome him back home, since my soul biddeth me also live no longer nor abide among men, if Hector be not first smitten by my spear and yield his life, and pay for his slaughter of Patroklos, Menoitios' son."

Then answered unto him Thetis shedding tears: "Short-lived, I ween, must thou be then, my child, by what thou sayest, for straightway after Hector is death appointed unto thee."

Then mightily moved spake unto her Achilles fleet of foot: "Straightway may I die, since I might not succor my comrade at his slaying. He hath fallen afar from his country and lacked my help in his sore need. Now therefore, since I go not back to my dear native land, neither have at all been succor to Patroklos nor to all my other comrades that have been slain by noble Hector, but I sit beside my ships a profitless burden of the earth, I that in war am such an one as is none else of the mail-clad Achaians, though in council are others better—may strife perish utterly among gods and men, and wrath that stirreth even a wise man to be vexed, wrath that far sweeter than trickling honey waxeth like smoke in the breasts of men, even as I was wroth even now against Agamemnon king of men. But bygones will we let be, for all our pain, curbing the heart in our breasts under necessity. Now go I forth, that I may light on the destroyer of him I loved, on Hector: then will I accept my death whensoever Zeus willeth to accomplish it and the other immortal gods. For not even the mighty Herakles escaped death, albeit most dear to Kronian Zeus the king, but Fate overcame him and Hera's cruel wrath. So also shall I, if my fate hath been fashioned likewise, lie low when I am dead. But now let me win high renown, let me set some Trojan woman, some deep-bosomed daughter of Dardanos, staunching with both hands the tears upon her tender cheeks and wailing bitterly; yea, let them know that I am come back, though I tarried long from the war. Hold not me then from the battle in thy love, for thou shalt not prevail with me."

Then Thetis the silver-footed goddess answered him saying: "Yea, verily, my child, no blame is in this, that thou ward sheer destruction from thy comrades in their distress. But thy fair glittering armor of bronze is held among the Trojans. Hector of the glancing helm beareth it on his shoulders in triumph, yet not for long, I ween, shall he glory therein, for death is hard anigh him. But thou go not yet down into the mellay of war until thou see me with thine eyes come hither. In the morning will I return, at the coming up of the sun, bearing fair armor from the king Hephaistos."

Thus spake she and turned to go from her son, and as she turned she spake among her sisters of the sea: "Ye now go down within the wide bosom of the deep, to visit the Ancient One of the Sea and our father's house, and tell him all. I am going to high Olympus to Hephaistos of noble skill, if haply he will give unto my son noble armor shining gloriously."

Thus spake she, and they forthwith went down beneath the surge of the sea. And the silver-footed goddess Thetis went on to Olympus that she might bring noble armor to her son.

So her unto Olympus her feet bore. But the Achaians with terrible cries were fleeing before man-slaying Hector till they came to the ships and to the Hellespont. Nor might the well-greaved Achaians drag the corpse of Patroklos Achilles' squire out of the darts, for now again overtook him the host and the horses of Troy, and Hector son of Priam, in might as it were a flame of fire. Thrice did glorious Hector seize him from behind by the feet, resolved to drag him away, and mightily called upon the men of Troy. Thrice did the two Aiantes, clothed on with impetuous might, beat him off from the dead man, but he nathless, trusting in his might, anon would charge into the press, anon would stand and cry aloud, but he gave ground never a whit. As when shepherds in the field avail no wise to chase a fiery lion in fierce hunger away from a carcase, so availed not the two warrior Aiantes to scare Hector son of Priam from the dead. And now would he have won the body and gained renown unspeakable, had not fleet wind-footed Iris come speeding from Olympus with a message to the son of Peleus to array him, unknown of Zeus and the other gods, for Hera sent her. And she stood anigh and spake to him winged words: "Rouse thee, son of Peleus, of all men most redoubtable! Succor Patroklos, for whose body is terrible battle afoot before the ships. There slay they one another, these guarding the dead corpse, while the men of Troy are fierce to hale him unto windy Ilios, and chiefliest noble Hector is fain to drag him, and his heart biddeth him fix the head on the stakes of the wall when he hath sundered it from the tender neck. But arise, lie thus no longer! let awe enter thy heart to forbid that Patroklos become the sport of dogs of Troy. Thine were the shame if he go down mangled amid the dead."

Then answered her fleet-footed noble Achilles: "Goddess Iris, what god sent thee a messenger unto me?"

And to him again spake wind-footed fleet Iris: "It was Hera that sent me, the wise wife of Zeus, nor knoweth the high-throned son of Kronos nor any other of the Immortals that on snowy Olympus have their dwelling-place."

And Achilles fleet of foot made answer to her and said: "And how may I go into the fray? The Trojans hold my arms; and my dear mother bade me forbear to array me until I behold her with my eyes returned, for she promised to bring fair armor from Hephaistos. Other man know I none whose noble armor I might put on, save it were the shield of Aias Telamon's son. But himself, I ween, is in the fore-front of the press, dealing death with his spear around Patroklos dead."

Then again spake unto him wind-footed fleet Iris: "Well are we also aware that thy noble armor is held from thee. But go forth unto the trench as thou art and show thyself to the men of Troy, if [10] haply they will shrink back and refrain them from battle, and the warlike sons of the Achaians take breath [amid their toil, for small breathing-time is in the thick of fight]."

Thus spake fleet-footed Iris and went her way. But Achilles dear to Zeus arose, and around his strong shoulders Athene cast her tasseled ægis, and around his head the bright goddess set a crown of a golden cloud, and kindled therefrom a blazing flame. And as when a smoke issueth from a city [20] and riseth up into the upper air, from an island afar off that foes beleaguer, while the others from their city fight all day in hateful war,—but with the going down of the sun blaze out the beacon-fires in line, and high aloft rusheth up the glare for dwellers round about to behold, if haply they may come with ships to help in need—thus from the head of Achilles soared that blaze toward the heavens. And he went and stood beyond the wall beside the trench, yet mingled not among the [30] Achaians, for he minded the wise bidding of his mother. There stood he and shouted aloud, and afar off Pallas Athene uttered her voice, and spread terror unspeakable among the men of Troy. Clear as the voice of a clarion when it soundeth by reason of slaughterous foemen that beleaguer a city, so clear rang forth the voice of Aiakides. And when they heard the brazen voice of Aiakides, the souls of all of them were dismayed, and the horses of goodly manes were fain to turn the chariots [40] backward, for they boded anguish in their hearts. And the charioteers were amazed when they saw the unwearying fire blaze fierce on the head of the great-hearted son of Peleus, for the bright-eyed goddess Athene made it blaze. Thrice from over the trench shouted mightily noble Achilles, and thrice were the men of Troy confounded and their proud allies. Yea there and then perished twelve men of their best by their own chariot wheels and spears. But the Achaians with joy drew Patroklos [50] forth of the darts and laid him on a litter, and his dear comrades stood around lamenting him; and among them followed fleet-footed Achilles, shed-

ding hot tears, for his true comrade he saw lying on the bier, mangled by the keen bronze. Him sent he forth with chariot and horses unto the battle, but home again welcomed never more.

Then Hera the ox-eyed queen sent down the unwearying Sun to be gone unwillingly, unto the streams of Ocean. So the Sun set, and the noble Achaians made pause from the stress of battle and the hazardous war.

Now the men of Troy on their side when they were come back out of the violent fray loosed their swift horses from the chariots and gathered themselves in assembly or ever they would sup. Upon their feet they stood in the assembly, neither had any man heart to sit, for fear was fallen upon all because Achilles was come forth, after long ceasing from fell battle. Then began to speak among them wise Polydamas, son of Panthoos, for he alone saw before and after. Comrade of Hector [20] was he, and in the same night were both born, but the one in speech was far the best, the other with the spear. So with good intent toward them he made harangue and spake: "Take good heed on both sides, O my friends; for my part I would have ye go up now to the city, not wait for bright morning on the plain beside the ships, for we are far off from the wall. So long as this man was wroth with noble Agamemnon, so long were the Achaians easier to fight against, aye and I too re-[30] joiced when I couched nigh their swift ships, trusting that we should seize the curved ships for a prey. But now am I sore afraid of the fleet son of Peleus; so exceeding fierce is his heart, he will not choose to abide on the plain where Trojans and Achaians both in the midst share the spirit of war, but the prize he doeth battle for will be our city and our wives. Now go we up to our fastness; hearken unto me, for thus will it be. Now hath divine night stayed the fleet son of Peleus, but if [40] tomorrow full-armed for the onset he shall light upon us abiding here, well shall each know that it is he, for gladly will whosoever fleeth win to sacred Ilios, and many of the men of Troy shall dogs and vultures devour—far be that from my ear. But if, though loth, we hearken unto my words, this night in counsel we shall possess our strength, and the city shall be guarded of her towers and high gates and tall well-polished doors that fit thereon close-shut. But at dawn of day in armor harnessed [50] will we take our stand along the towers. Ill will he fare if he come forth from the ships to fight with us for our wall. Back to his ships shall he betake him when in vain chase he hath given his strong-necked horses their fill of hasting everywhither beneath the town. But within it never will he have heart to force his way, nor ever lay it waste; ere then shall he be devoured of swift dogs."

Then with stern gaze spake unto him Hector of the glancing helm: "Polydamas, no longer to my liking dost thou speak now, in that thou biddest us go back and be pent within the town. Have ye not had your fill already of being pent behind the towers? Of old time all mortal men would tell of this city of Priam for the much gold and bronze thereof, but now are its goodly treasures perished out of its dwellings, and much goods are sold away to Phrygia and pleasant Maionia, since mighty Zeus dealt evilly with us. But now when the son of crooked-counseling Kronos hath given me to win glory at the ships and to pen the Achaians beside the sea, no longer, fond man, put forth such counsels among the folk. No man of Troy will hearken unto thee, I will not suffer it. But come let us all be persuaded as I shall say. Sup now in your ranks throughout the host, and keep good ward, and each watch in his place. And whoso of the Trojans is grieved beyond measure for his goods, let him gather them together and give them to the people to consume in common, for it is better they have joy thereof than the Achaians. Then at dawn of day in armor harnessed at the hollow ships we will arouse keen war. What though in very truth noble Achilles be arisen beside the ships, ill shall he fare, if he will have it so. I at least will not flee from him out of the dread-sounding war, but full facing him will I stand, to try whether he win great victory, or haply I. The war-god is alike to all and a slayer of him that would slay."

Thus Hector spake, and the men of Troy applauded with fond hearts, for Pallas Athene bereft them of their wit. And they gave assent to the ill advising of Hector, but none hearkened to Polydamas who devised good counsel. Then they supped throughout the host; but the Achaians all night made moan in lamentation for Patroklos. And first of them in the loud lamentation was the son of Peleus, laying upon the breast of his comrade his man-slaying hands and moaning very sore, even as a deep-bearded lion whose whelps some stag-hunter hath snatched away out of a deep wood; and the lion coming afterward grieveth, and through many glens he rangeth on the track of the footsteps of the man, if anywhere he might find him, for most bitter anger seizeth him;—thus Achilles moaning heavily spake among the Myrmidons: "Aye me, vain verily was the word I uttered on that day when I cheered the hero Menoitios in his halls and said that I would bring back to Opœis his son in glory from the sack of Ilios with the share of spoil that should fall unto him. Not all the purposes of men doth Zeus accomplish for them. It is appointed that both of us redden the same earth with our blood here in Troy-land, for neither shall the old knight Peleus welcome me back home within his halls, nor my mother Thetis, but even here shall earth keep hold on me. Yet now, O Patroklos, since I follow thee under earth, I will not hold thy funeral till I have brought hither the armor and the head of Hector, thy high-hearted slayer, and before thy pyre I will cut the throats of twelve noble sons of the men of Troy, for mine anger thou art slain. Till then beside the beaked ships shalt thou lie as thou art, and around the deep-bosomed women, Trojan and Dardanian, shall mourn thee weeping night and day, even they whom we toiled to win by our strength and our long spears when we sacked rich cities of mortal men."

Thus spake noble Achilles, and bade his comrades set a great tripod on the fire, that with all speed they might wash from Patroklos the bloody gore. So they set a tripod of ablution on the burning fire, and poured therein water and took wood and kindled it beneath; and the fire wrapped the belly of the tripod, and the water grew hot. And when the water boiled in the bright bronze, then washed they him and anointed with olive oil, and filled his wounds with fresh ointment, and laid him on a bier and covered him with soft cloth from head to foot, and thereover a white robe. Then all night around Achilles fleet of foot the Myrmidons made lament and moan for Patroklos.

Meanwhile Zeus spake unto Hera his sister and wife: "Thou hast accomplished this, O Hera, ox-eyed queen, thou hast aroused Achilles fleet of foot. Verily of thine own children must the flowing-haired Achaians be."

Then answered unto him Hera the ox-eyed queen: "Most dread son of Kronos, what is this word thou hast said? Truly even a man, I ween, is to accomplish what he may for another man, albeit he is mortal and hath not wisdom as we. How then was I who avow me the first of goddesses both by birth and for that I am called thy wife, and thou art king among all Immortals—how was I not in mine anger to devise evil against the men of Troy?"

So debated they on this wise with one another.

But Thetis of the silver feet came unto the house of Hephaistos, imperishable, starlike, far seen among the dwellings of Immortals, a house of bronze, wrought by the crook-footed god himself. Him found she sweating in toil and busy about his bellows, for he was forging tripods twenty in all to stand around the wall of his stablished hall, and beneath the base of each he had set golden wheels, that of their own motion they might enter the assembly of the gods and again return unto his house, a marvel to look upon. Thus much were they finished that not yet were the ears of cunning work set thereon; these was he making ready, and welding chains. While hereat he was laboring with wise intent, then drew nigh unto him Thetis, goddess of the silver feet. And Charis went forward and beheld her, fair Charis of the shining chaplet whom the renowned lame god had wedded. And she clasped her hand in hers and spake and called her by her name: "Wherefore, long-robed Thetis, comest thou to our house, honored that thou art and dear? No frequent comer art thou hitherto. But come onward with me that I may set guest-cheer before thee."

Thus spake the bright goddess and led her on. Then set she her on a silver-studded throne, goodly, of cunning work, and a footstool was beneath her feet; and she called to Hephaistos, the famed artificer, and said unto him: "Hephaistos, come forth hither, Thetis hath need of thee."

And the renowned lame god made answer to her: "Verily a dread and honored goddess in my sight is she that is within, seeing that she delivered me when pain came upon me from my great fall though the ill-will of my shameless mother who would fain have hid me away, for that I was lame. Then had I suffered anguish of heart had not Eurynome and Thetis taken me into their bosom—Eurynome daughter of Ocean that floweth back ever upon himself. Nine years with them I wrought much cunning work of bronze, brooches and spiral arm-bands and cups and necklaces, in the hollow cave, while around me the stream of Ocean with murmuring foam flowed infinite. Neither knew thereof any other of gods or of mortal men, save only Thetis and Eurynome who delivered me. And now cometh Thetis to our house; wherefore behoveth it me verily in all wise to repay fair-tressed Thetis for the saving of my life. But do thou now set beside her fair entertainment, while I put away my bellows and all my gear."

He said, and from the anvil rose limping, a huge bulk, but under him his slender legs moved nim-bly. The bellows he set away from the fire, and gathered all his gear wherewith he worked into a silver chest; and with a sponge he wiped his face and hands and sturdy neck and shaggy breast, and did on his doublet, and took a stout staff and went forth limping; but there were handmaidens of gold that moved to help their lord, the semblances of living maids. In them is understanding at their hearts, in them are voice and strength, and they have skill of the immortal gods. These moved beneath their lord, and he gat him haltingly near to where Thetis was, and set him on a bright seat, and clasped her hand in his and spake and called her by her name: "Wherefore, long-robed Thetis, comest thou to our house, honored that thou art and dear? No frequent comer art thou hitherto. Speak what thou hast at heart; my soul is fain to accomplish it, if accomplish it I can, and if it be appointed for accomplishment."

Then answered unto him Thetis shedding tears: "Hephaistos, hath there verily been any of all goddesses in Olympus that hath endured so many grievous sorrows at heart as are the woes that Kronian Zeus hath laid upon me above all others? He chose me from among the sisters of the sea to enthrall me to a man, even Peleus Aiakos' son, and with a man I endured wedlock sore against my will. Now lieth he in his halls forspent with grievous age, but other griefs are mine. A son he gave me to bear and nourish, the chief of heroes, and he shot up like a young branch. Like a plant in a very fruitful field I reared him and sent him forth on beaked ships to Ilios to fight against the men of Troy, but never again shall I welcome him back to his home within the house of Peleus. And while he yet liveth in my sight and beholdeth the light of the sun, he sorroweth, neither can I help him any whit though I go unto him. The maiden whom the sons of the Achaians chose out to be his prize, her hath the lord Agamemnon taken back out of his hands. In grief for her wasted he his heart; while the men of Troy were driving the Achaians on their ships, nor suffered them to come forth. And the elders of the Argives entreated him, and told over many noble gifts. Then albeit himself he refused to ward destruction from them, he put his armor on Patroklos and sent him to the war, and much people with him. All day they fought around the Skaian gates and that same day had sacked the town, but that when now Menoitios' valiant son had wrought much harm, Apollo slew him in the forefront of the battle, and gave glory unto Hector. Therefore now come I a suppliant unto thy knees, if haply thou be willing to give my short-lived son shield and helmet, and goodly greaves fitted with ankle-pieces, and cuirass. For the armor that he had erst, his trusty comrade lost when he fell beneath the men of Troy; and my son lieth on the earth with anguish in his soul."

Then made answer unto her the lame god of great renown: "Be of good courage, let not these things trouble thy heart. Would that so might I avail to hide him far from dolorous death, when dread fate cometh upon him, as surely shall goodly armor be at his need, such as all men afterward shall marvel at, whosoever may behold."

Thus saying he left her there and went unto his bellows and turned them upon the fire and bade them work. And the bellows, twenty in all, blew on the crucibles, sending deft blasts on every side, now to aid his labor and now anon howsoever Hephaistos willed and the work went on. And he threw bronze that weareth not into the fire, and tin and precious gold and silver, and next he set on an anvil-stand a great anvil, and took in his hand a sturdy hammer, and in the other he took the tongs.

First fashioned he a shield great and strong, adorning it all over, and set thereto a shining rim, triple, bright-glancing, and therefrom a silver baldrick. Five were the folds of the shield itself; and therein fashioned he much cunning work from his wise heart.

There wrought he the earth, and the heavens, and the sea, and the unwearying sun, and the moon waxing to the full, and the signs every one wherewith the heavens are crowned, Pleiads and Hyads and Orion's might, and the Bear that men call also the Wain, her that turneth in her place and watcheth Orion, and alone hath no part in the baths of Ocean.

Also he fashioned therein two fair cities of mortal men. In the one were espousals and marriage feasts, and beneath the blaze of torches they were leading the brides from their chambers through the city, and loud arose the bridal song. And young men were whirling in the dance, and among them flutes and viols sounded high; and the women standing each at her door were marveling. But the folk were gathered in the assembly place; for there a strife was arisen, two men striving about the blood-price of a man slain; the one claimed to pay full atonement, expounding to the people, but the other denied him and would take naught; and both were fain to receive arbitrament at the hand of a daysman. And the folk were cheering both, as they took part on either side. And heralds kept order among the folk, while the elders on polished stones were sitting in the sacred circle, and holding in their hands staves from the loud-voiced heralds. Then before the people they rose up and gave judgment each in turn. And in the midst lay two talents of gold, to be given unto him who should plead among them most righteously.

But around the other city were two armies in siege with glittering arms. And two counsels found favor among them, either to sack the town or to share all with the townsfolk even whatsoever substance the fair city held within. But the besieged were not yet yielding, but arming for an ambushment. On the wall there stood to guard it their dear wives and infant children, and with these the old men; but the rest went forth, and their leaders were Ares and Pallas Athene, both wrought in gold, and golden was the vesture they had on. Goodly and great were they in their armor, even as gods, far seen around, and the folk at their feet were smaller. And when they came where it seemed good to them to lay ambush, in a river bed where there was a common watering-place of herds, there they set them, clad in glittering bronze. And two scouts were posted by them afar off to spy the coming of flocks and of oxen with crooked horns. And presently came the cattle, and with them two herdsmen playing on pipes, that took no thought of the guile. Then the others when they beheld these ran upon them and quickly cut off the herds of oxen and fair flocks of white sheep, and slew the shepherds withal. But the besiegers, as they sat before the speech-places and heard much din among the oxen, mounted forthwith behind their high-stepping horses, and came up with speed. Then they arrayed their battle and fought beside the river banks, and smote one another with bronze-shod spears. And among them mingled Strife and Tumult, and fell Death, grasping one man alive fresh-wounded, another without wound, and dragging another dead through the mellay by the feet; and the raiment on her shoulders was red with the blood of men. Like living mortals they hurled together and fought, and haled the corpses each of the other's slain.

Furthermore he set in the shield a soft fresh-plowed field, rich tilth and wide, the third time plowed; and many plowers therein drave their yokes to and fro as they wheeled about. Whensoever they came to the boundary of the field and turned, then would a man come to each and give into his hands a goblet of sweet wine, while others would be turning back along the furrows, fain to reach the boundary of the deep tilth. And the field grew black behind and seemed as it were a-plowing, albeit of gold, for this was the great marvel of the work.

Furthermore he set therein the demesne-land of a king, where hinds were reaping with sharp sickles in their hands. Some armfuls along the swathe were falling in rows to the earth, whilst others the sheaf-binders were binding in twisted bands of straw. Three sheaf-binders stood over them, while behind boys gathering corn and bearing it in their arms gave it constantly to the binders; and among them the king in silence was standing at the swathe with his staff, rejoicing in his heart. And henchmen apart beneath an oak were making ready a feast, and preparing a great ox they had sacrificed; while the women were strewing much white barley to be a supper for the hinds.

Also he set therein a vineyard teeming plenteously with clusters, wrought fair in gold; black were the grapes, but the vines hung throughout on silver poles. And around it he ran a ditch of cyanus, and round that a fence of tin; and one single pathway led to it, whereby the vintagers might go when they should gather the vintage. And maidens and striplings in childish glee bare the sweet fruit in plaited baskets. And in the midst of them a boy made pleasant music on a clear-toned viol, and sang thereto a sweet Linos-song with delicate voice; while the rest with feet falling together kept time with the music and song.

Also he wrought therein a herd of kine with upright horns, and the kine were fashioned of gold and tin, and with lowing they hurried from the byre to pasture beside a murmuring river, beside the waving reed. And herdsmen of gold were following with the kine, four of them, and nine dogs fleet of foot came after them. But two terrible lions among the foremost kine had seized a loud-roaring bull that bellowed mightily as they haled him, and the dogs and the young men sped after him. The lions rending the great bull's hide were devouring his vitals and his black blood; while the herdsmen in vain tarred on their fleet dogs to set on, for they shrank from biting the lions but stood hard by and barked and swerved away.

Also the glorious lame god wrought therein a pasture in a fair glen, a great pasture of white sheep, and a steading, and roofed huts, and folds.

Also did the glorious lame god devise a dancing-place like unto that which once in wide Knosos Daidalos wrought for Ariadne of the lovely tresses. There were youths dancing and maidens of costly wooing, their hands upon one another's wrists. Fine linen the maidens had on, and the youths well-woven doublets faintly glistening with oil. Fair wreaths had the maidens, and the youths daggers of gold hanging from silver baldrics. And now would they run round with deft feet exceeding lightly, as when a potter sitting by his wheel that fitteth between his hands maketh trial of it whether it run: and now anon they would run in lines to meet each other. And a great company stood round the lovely dance in joy; [and among them a divine minstrel was making music on his lyre,] and through the midst of them, leading the measure, two tumblers whirled.

Also he set therein the great might of the River of Ocean around the uttermost rim of the cunningly-fashioned shield.

Now when he had wrought the shield great and strong, then wrought he him a corslet brighter than a flame of fire, and he wrought him a massive helmet to fit his brows, goodly and graven, and set thereon a crest of gold, and he wrought him greaves of pliant tin.

So when the renowned lame god had finished all the armor, he took and laid it before the mother of Achilles. Then she like a falcon sprang down from snowy Olympus, bearing from Hephaistos the glittering arms.

[*The rest of the poem tells of the defeat of the Trojans; the slaying of Hector by Achilles, who pursues him three times around the walls; the dragging of the dead body of Hector; the embassy of King Priam to secure Hector's body; and finally the funeral rites of Hector. The* Iliad *implies, but does not relate, the fall of Troy. For this see Book II of Virgil's Æneid (pp. 279-289).*]

The Odyssey

[*The poem begins at Ithaca, the home of Odysseus, one of the heroes of the Trojan War. The home is in possession of suitors who are insisting that Penelope, Odysseus' wife, choose one of them as husband since Odysseus has been unheard of for ten years. The youthful Telemachus is helpless to resist his mother's suitors. Athene, patroness of Odysseus, now advises Telemachus to search for his father. In spite of the suitors' opposition, Te-* ¹⁰ *lemachus goes first to Pylos the home of Nestor and then to Sparta where he is entertained by Menelaos and Helen but learns little about Odysseus.*

The action now moves to an island where Odysseus is being detained by the goddess Calypso. Being at length ordered by the gods, Calypso permits Odysseus to leave on a raft. He is, however, wrecked by Poseidon, who has never forgiven Odysseus for blinding Polyphemus, the Cyclops. Odysseus swims and finally reaches land where he ²⁰ *falls into a deep sleep. At this point Book VI begins.*]

BOOK VI

Nausicaa, going to a river near that place to wash the clothes of her father, mother, and brethren, while the clothes were drying played with her maids at ball; and Odysseus coming forth is fed and clothed, and led on his way to the house of her father, King Alcinous.

So there he lay asleep, the steadfast goodly Odys- ³⁰ seus, fordone with toil and drowsiness. Meanwhile Athene went to the land and the city of the Phæacians, who of old, upon a time, dwelt in spacious Hypereia; near the Cyclôpes they dwelt, men exceeding proud, who harried them continually, being mightier than they. Thence the godlike Nausithous made them depart, and he carried them away, and planted them in Scheria, far off from men that live by bread. And he drew a wall around the town, and builded houses and made ⁴⁰ temples for the gods and meted out the fields. Howbeit ere this had he been stricken by fate, and had gone down to the house of Hades, and now Alcinous was reigning, with wisdom granted by the gods. To his house went the goddess, gray-eyed Athene, devising a return for the great-hearted Odysseus. She betook her to the rich-wrought bower, wherein was sleeping a maiden like to the gods in form and comeliness, Nausicaa, the daughter of Alcinous, high of heart. Beside her on either hand of the pillars of the door were two handmaids, dowered with beauty from the Graces, and the shining doors were shut.

But the goddess, fleet as the breath of the wind, swept towards the couch of the maiden, and stood above her head, and spake to her in the semblance of the daughter of a famous seafarer, Dymas, a girl of like age with Nausicaa, who had found grace in her sight. In her shape the gray-eyed Athene spake to the princess, saying:

"Nausicaa, how hath thy mother so heedless a maiden to her daughter? Lo, thou hast shining raiment that lies by thee uncared for, and thy marriage-day is near at hand, when thou thyself must needs go beautifully clad, and have garments to give to them who shall lead thee to the house of the bridegroom! And, behold, these are the things whence a good report goes abroad among men, wherein a father and lady mother take delight. But come, let us arise and go a-washing with the breaking of the day, and I will follow with thee to be thy mate in the toil, that without delay thou mayst get thee ready, since truly thou art not long to be a maiden. Lo, already they are wooing thee, the noblest youths of all the Phæacians, among that people whence thou thyself dost draw thy lineage. So come, beseech thy noble father betimes in the morning to furnish thee with mules and a wain to carry the men's raiment, and the robes, and the shining coverlets. Yea and for thyself it is seemlier far to go thus than on foot, for the places where we must wash are a great way off the town."

So spake the gray-eyed Athene, and departed to Olympus, where, as they say, is the seat of the gods that standeth fast for ever. Not by winds is it shaken, nor ever wet with rain, nor doth the snow come nigh thereto, but most clear air is spread about it cloudless, and the white light floats over it. Therein the blessed gods are glad for all their days, and thither Athene went when she had shown forth all to the maiden.

Anon came the throned Dawn, and awakened Nausicaa of the fair robes, who straightway marveled on the dream, and went through the halls to

Homer, *The Odyssey.* Translated by Butcher and Lang. By permission of The Macmillan Co.

tell her parents, her father dear and her mother. And she found them within, her mother sitting by the hearth with the women her handmaids, spinning yarn of sea-purple stain, but her father she met as he was going forth to the renowned kings in their council, whither the noble Phæacians called him. Standing close by her dear father she spake, saying: "Father, dear, couldst thou not lend me a high wagon with strong wheels, that I may take the goodly raiment to the river to wash, so much as I have lying soiled? Yea and it is seemly that thou thyself, when thou art with the princes in council, shouldst have fresh raiment to wear. Also, there are five dear sons of thine in the halls, two married, but three are lusty bachelors, and these are always eager for new-washen garments wherein to go to the dances; for all these things have I taken thought."

This she said, because she was ashamed to speak of glad marriage to her father; but he saw all and answered, saying:

"Neither the mules nor aught else do I grudge thee, my child. Go thy ways, and the thralls shall get thee ready a high wagon with good wheels, and fitted with an upper frame."

Therewith he called to his men, and they gave ear, and without the palace they made ready the smooth-running mule-wain, and led the mules beneath the yoke, and harnessed them under the car, while the maiden brought forth from her bower the shining raiment. This she stored in the polished car, and her mother filled a basket with all manner of food to the heart's desire, dainties too she set therein, and she poured wine into a goatskin bottle, while Nausicaa climbed into the wain. And her mother gave her soft olive oil also in a golden cruse, that she and her maidens might anoint themselves after the bath. Then Nausicaa took the whip and the shining reins, and touched the mules to start them; then there was a clatter of hoofs, and on they strained without flagging, with their load of the raiment and the maiden. Not alone did she go, for her attendants followed with her.

Now when they were come to the beautiful stream of the river, where truly were the unfailing cisterns, and bright water welled up free from beneath, and flowed past, enough to wash the foulest garments clean, there the girls unharnessed the mules from under the chariot, and turning them loose they drove them along the banks of the eddying river to graze on the honey-sweet clover. Then they took the garments from the wain, in their hands, and bore them to the black water, and briskly trod them down in the trenches, in busy rivalry. Now when they had washed and cleansed all the stains, they spread all out in order along the shore of the deep, even where the sea, in beating on the coast, washed the pebbles clean. Then having bathed and anointed them well with olive oil, they took their mid-day meal on the river's banks, waiting till the clothes should dry in the brightness of the sun. Anon, when they were satisfied with food, the maidens and the princess, they fell to playing at ball, casting away their tires, and among them Nausicaa of the white arms began the song. And even as Artemis, the archer, moveth down the mountain, either along the ridges of lofty Taygetus or Erymanthus, taking her pastime in the chase of boars and swift deer, and with her the wild wood-nymphs disport them, the daughters of Zeus, lord of the ægis, and Leto is glad at heart, while high over all she rears her head and brows, and easily may she be known,—but all are fair; even so the girl unwed outshone her maiden company.

But when now she was about going homewards, after yoking the mules and folding up the goodly raiment, then gray-eyed Athene turned to other thoughts, that so Odysseus might awake, and see the lovely maiden, who should be his guide to the city of the Phæacian men. So then the princess threw the ball at one of her company; she missed the girl, and cast the ball into the deep eddying current, whereat they all raised a piercing cry. Then the goodly Odysseus awoke and sat up, pondering in his heart and spirit:

"Woe is me! to what men's land am I come now? say, are they froward, and wild, and unjust, or are they hospitable, and of God-fearing mind? How shrill a cry of maidens rings round me, of the nymphs that hold the steep hill-tops, and the river-springs, and the grassy water meadows! It must be, methinks, that I am near men of human speech. Go to, I myself will make trial and see."

Therewith the goodly Odysseus crept out from under the coppice, having broken with his strong hand a leafy bough from the thick wood, to hold athwart his body, that it might hide his nakedness withal. And forth he sallied like a lion mountain-bred, trusting in his strength, who fares out blown and rained upon, with flaming eyes; amid the kine he goes or amid the sheep or in the track of the wild deer; yea, his belly bids him go even to the good homestead to make assay upon the flocks.

Even so Odysseus was fain to draw nigh to the fair-tressed maidens, all naked as he was, such need had come upon him. But he was terrible in their eyes, being marred with the salt sea foam, and they fled cowering here and there about the jutting spits of shore. And the daughter of Alcinous alone stood firm, for Athene gave her courage of heart, and took all trembling from her limbs. So she halted and stood over against him, and Odysseus considered whether he should clasp the knees of the lovely maiden, and so make his prayer, or should stand as he was, apart, and beseech her with smooth words, if haply she might show him the town, and give him raiment. And as he thought within himself, it seemed better to stand apart, and beseech her with smooth words, lest the maiden should be angered with him if he touched her knees: so straightway he spake a sweet and cunning word:

"I supplicate thee, O queen, whether thou art a goddess or a mortal! If indeed thou art a goddess of them that keep the wide heaven; to Artemis, then, the daughter of great Zeus, I mainly liken thee, for beauty and stature and shapeliness. But if thou art one of the daughters of men who dwell on earth, thrice blessed are thy father and thy lady mother, and thrice blessed thy brethren. Surely their souls ever glow with gladness for thy sake, each time they see thee entering the dance, so fair a flower of maidens. But he is of heart the most blessed beyond all other who shall prevail with gifts of wooing, and lead thee to his home. Never have mine eyes beheld such an one among mortals, neither man nor woman; great awe comes upon me as I look on thee. Yet in Delos once I saw as goodly a thing: a young sapling of a palm tree springing by the altar of Apollo. For thither too I went, and much people with me, on that path where my sore troubles were to be. Yea, and when I looked thereupon, long time I marveled in spirit, —for never grew there yet so goodly a shoot from ground,—even in such wise as I wonder at thee, lady, and am astonied and do greatly fear to touch thy knees, though grievous sorrow is upon me. Yesterday, on the twentieth day, I escaped from the wine-dark deep, but all that time continually the wave bare me, and the vehement winds drave, from the isle Ogygia. And now some god has cast me on this shore, that here too, methinks, some evil may betide me; for I trow not that trouble will cease; the gods ere that time will yet bring many a thing to pass. But, queen, have pity on me, for after many trials and sore to thee first of all

am I come, and of the other folk, who hold this city and land, I know no man. Nay show me the town, give me an old garment to cast about me, if thou hadst, when thou camest here, any wrap for the linen. And may the gods grant thee all thy heart's desire: a husband and a home, and a mind at one with his may they give—a good gift, for there is nothing mightier and nobler than when man and wife are of one heart and mind in a house, a grief to their foes, and to their friends great joy, but their own hearts know it best."

Then Nausicaa of the white arms answered him, and said: "Stranger, forasmuch as thou seemest no evil man nor foolish—and it is Olympian Zeus himself that giveth weal to men, to the good and to the evil, to each one as he will, and this thy lot doubtless is of him, and so thou must in anywise endure it:—and now, since thou hast come to our city and our land, thou shalt not lack raiment, nor aught else that is the due of a hapless suppliant, when he has met them who can befriend him. And I will show thee the town, and name the name of the people. The Phæacians hold this city and land, and I am the daughter of Alcinous, great of heart, on whom all the might and force of the Phæacians depend."

Thus she spake, and called to her maidens of the fair tresses: "Halt, my maidens, whither flee ye at the sight of a man? Ye surely do not take him for an enemy? That mortal breathes not, and never will be born, who shall come with war to the land of the Phæacians, for they are very dear to the gods. Far apart we live in the wash of the waves, the outermost of men, and no other mortals are conversant with us. Nay, but this man is some helpless one come hither in his wanderings, whom now we must kindly entreat, for all strangers and beggars are from Zeus, and a little gift is dear. So, my maidens, give the stranger meat and drink, and bathe him in the river, where withal is a shelter from the winds."

So she spake, but they had halted and called each to the other, and they brought Odysseus to the sheltered place, and made him sit down, as Nausicaa bade them, the daughter of Alcinous, high of heart. Beside him they laid a mantle, and a doublet for raiment, and gave him soft olive oil in the golden cruse, and bade him wash in the streams of the river. Then goodly Odysseus spake among the maidens, saying: "I pray you stand thus apart, while I myself wash the brine from my shoulders, and anoint me with olive oil, for truly oil is long a stranger to my skin. But in your sight I will not bathe, for I am ashamed to make me naked in the company of fair-tressed maidens."

Then they went apart and told all to their lady. But with the river water the goodly Odysseus washed from his skin the salt scurf that covered his back and broad shoulders, and from his head he wiped the crusted brine of the barren sea. But when he had washed his whole body, and anointed him with olive oil, and had clad himself in the raiment that the unwedded maiden gave him, then Athene, the daughter of Zeus, made him greater and more mighty to behold, and from his head caused deep curling locks to flow, like the hyacinth flower. And as when some skillful man overlays gold upon silver—one that Hephæstus and Pallas Athene have taught all manner of craft, and full of grace is his handiwork—even so did Athene shed grace about his head and shoulders.

Then to the shore of the sea went Odysseus apart, and sat down, glowing in beauty and grace, and the princess marveled at him, and spake among her fair-tressed maidens saying:

"Listen, my white-armed maidens, and I will say somewhat. Not without the will of all the gods who hold Olympus hath this man come among the godlike Phæacians. Erewhile he seemed to me uncomely, but now he is like the gods that keep the wide heaven. Would that such an one might be called my husband, dwelling here, and that it might please him here to abide! But come, my maidens, give the stranger meat and drink."

Thus she spake, and they gave ready ear and hearkened, and set beside Odysseus meat and drink, and the steadfast goodly Odysseus did eat and drink eagerly, for it was long since he had tasted food.

Now Nausicaa of the white arms had another thought. She folded the raiment and stored it in the goodly wain, and yoked the mules strong of hoof, and herself climbed into the car. Then she called on Odysseus, and spake and hailed him: "Up now, stranger, and rouse thee to go to the city, that I may convey thee to the house of my wise father, where, I promise thee, thou shalt get knowledge of all the noblest of the Phæacians. But do thou even as I tell thee, and thou seemest a discreet man enough. So long as we are passing along the fields and farms of men, do thou fare quickly with the maidens behind the mules and the chariot, and I will lead the way. But when we set foot within the city,—whereby goes a high wall with towers, and there is a fair haven on either side of the town, and narrow is the entrance, and

curved ships are drawn up on either hand of the mole, for all the folk have stations for their vessels, each man one for himself. And there is the place of assembly about the goodly temple of Poseidon, furnished with heavy stones, deep bedded in the earth. There men look to the gear of the black ships, hawsers and sails, and there they fine down the oars. For the Phæacians care not for bow nor quiver, but for masts, and oars of ships, and gallant barques, wherein rejoicing they cross the gray sea. Their ungracious speech it is that I would avoid, lest some man afterward rebuke me, and there are but too many insolent folk among the people. And someone of the baser sort might meet me and say: 'Who is this that goes with Nausicaa, this tall and goodly stranger? Where found she him? Her husband he will be, her very own. Either she has taken in some shipwrecked wanderer of strange men,—for no men dwell near us; or some god has come in answer to her instant prayer; from heaven has he descended, and will have her to wife for evermore. Better so, if herself she has ranged abroad and found a lord from a strange land, for verily she holds in no regard the Phæacians here in this country, the many men and noble who are her wooers.' So will they speak, and this would turn to my reproach. Yea, and I myself would think it blame of another maiden who did such things in despite of her friends, her father and mother being still alive, and was conversant with men before the day of open wedlock. But, stranger, heed well what I say, that as soon as may be thou mayest gain at my father's hands an escort and a safe return. Thou shalt find a fair grove of Athene, a poplar grove near the road, and a spring wells forth therein, and a meadow lies all around. There is my father's demesne, and his fruitful close, within the sound of a man's shout from the city. Sit thee down there and wait until such time as we may have come into the city, and reached the house of my father. But when thou deemest that we are got to the palace, then go up to the city of the Phæacians, and ask for the house of my father Alcinous, high of heart. It is easily known, and a young child could be thy guide, for nowise like it are builded the houses of the Phæacians, so goodly is the palace of the hero Alcinous. But when thou art within the shadow of the halls and the court, pass quickly through the great chamber, till thou comest to my mother, who sits at the hearth in the light of the fire, weaving yarn of sea-purple stain, a wonder to behold. Her chair is leaned against a pillar, and her maidens sit behind her. And there my father's throne leans close to hers, wherein he sits and drinks his wine, like an immortal. Pass thou by him, and cast thy hands about my mother's knees, that thou mayest see quickly and with joy the day of thy returning, even if thou art from a very far country. If but her heart be kindly disposed toward thee, then is there hope that thou shalt see thy friends, and come to thy well-builded house, and to thine own country."

She spake, and smote the mules with the shining whip, and quickly they left behind them the streams of the river. And well they trotted and well they paced, and she took heed to drive in such wise that the maidens and Odysseus might follow on foot, and cunningly she plied the lash. Then the sun set, and they came to the famous grove, the sacred place of Athene; so there the goodly Odysseus sat him down. Then straightway he prayed to the daughter of mighty Zeus: "Listen to me, child of Zeus, lord of the ægis, unwearied maiden; hear me even now, since before thou heardest not when I was smitten on the sea, when the renowned Earth-shaker smote me. Grant me to come to the Phæacians as one dear, and worthy of pity."

So he spake in prayer, and Pallas Athene heard him; but she did not yet appear to him face to face, for she had regard unto her father's brother, who furiously raged against the godlike Odysseus, till he should come to his own country.

BOOK VII

Odysseus being received at the house of the king Alcinous, the queen after supper, taking notice of his garments, gives him occasion to relate his passage thither on the raft. Alcinous promises him a convoy for the morrow.

So he prayed there, the steadfast goodly Odysseus, while the two strong mules bare the princess to the town. And when she had now come to the famous palace of her father, she halted at the gateway, and round her gathered her brothers, men like to the immortals, and they loosed the mules from under the car, and carried the raiment within. But the maiden betook her to her chamber; and an aged dame from Aperæa kindled the fire for her, Eurymedusa, the handmaid of the chamber, whom the curved ships upon a time had brought from Aperæa; and men chose her as a prize for Alcinous, seeing that he bare rule over all the Phæacians, and the people hearkened to

him as to a god. She waited on the white-armed Nausicaa in the palace halls; she was wont to kindle the fire and prepare the supper in the inner chamber.

At that same hour Odysseus roused him to go to the city, and Athene shed a deep mist about Odysseus for the favor that she bare him, lest any of the Phæacians, high of heart, should meet him and mock him in sharp speech, and ask him who he was. But when he was now about to enter the pleasant city, then the goddess, gray-eyed Athene, met him, in the fashion of a young maiden carrying a pitcher, and she stood over against him, and goodly Odysseus inquired of her:

"My child, couldst thou not lead me to the palace of the lord Alcinous, who bears sway among this people? Lo, I am come here, a stranger travelworn from afar, from a distant land; wherefore of the folk who possess this city and country I know not any man."

Then the goddess, gray-eyed Athene, answered him saying: "Yea now, father and stranger, I will show thee the house that thou bidst me declare, for it lies near the palace of my noble father; behold, be silent as thou goest, and I will lead the way. And look on no man, nor question any. For these men do not gladly suffer strangers, nor lovingly entreat whoso cometh from a strange land. They trust to the speed of their swift ships, wherewith they cross the great gulf, for the Earth-shaker hath vouchsafed them this power. Their ships are swift as the flight of a bird, or as a thought."

Therewith Pallas Athene led the way swiftly, and he followed hard in the footsteps of the goddess. And it came to pass that the Phæacians, mariners renowned, marked him not as he went down the city through their midst, for the fair-tressed Athene suffered it not, that awful goddess, who shed a wondrous mist about him, for the favor that she bare him in her heart. And Odysseus marveled at the havens and the gallant ships, yea and the places of assembly of the heroes, and the long high walls crowned with palisades, a marvel to behold. But when they had now come to the famous palace of the king, the goddess, gray-eyed Athene, spake first and said:

"Lo, here, father and stranger, is the house that thou wouldst have me show thee: and thou shalt find kings at the feast, the fosterlings of Zeus; enter then, and fear not in thine heart, for the dauntless man is the best in every adventure, even though he come from a strange land. Thou shalt find the queen first in the halls: Arete is the name whereby men call her, and she came even of those that begat the king Alcinous. First Nausithous was son of Poseidon, the Earth-shaker, and of Periboea, the comeliest of women, youngest daughter of great-hearted Eurymedon, who once was king among the haughty Giants. Howbeit, he destroyed his infatuate people, and was himself destroyed; but Poseidon lay with Periboea and begat a son, proud Nausithous, who sometime was prince among the Phaeacians; and Nausithous ¹⁰ begat Rhexenor and Alcinous. While Rhexenor had as yet no son, Apollo of the silver bow smote him, a groom new wed, leaving in his halls one only child Arete; and Alcinous took her to wife, and honored her as no other woman in the world is honored, of all that now-a-days keep house under the hand of their lords. Thus she hath, and hath ever had, all worship heartily from her dear children and from her lord Alcinous and from all the folk, who look on her as on a goddess, and ²⁰ greet her with reverend speech, when she goes about the town. Yea, for she too hath no lack of understanding. To whomso she shows favor, even if they be men, she ends their feuds. If but her heart be kindly disposed to thee, then is there good hope that thou mayest see thy friends, and come to thy high-roofed home and thine own country."

Therewith gray-eyed Athene departed over the unharvested seas, and left pleasant Scheria, and came to Marathon and wide-wayed Athens, and ³⁰ entered the good house of Erechtheus. Meanwhile Odysseus went to the famous palace of Alcinous, and his heart was full of many thoughts as he stood there or ever he had reached the threshold of bronze. For there was a gleam as it were of sun or moon through the high-roofed hall of great-hearted Alcinous. Brazen were the walls which ran this way and that from the threshold to the inmost chamber, and round them was a frieze of blue, and golden were the doors that closed in the ⁴⁰ good house. Silver were the door-posts that were set on the brazen threshold, and silver the lintel thereupon, and the hook of the door was of gold. And on either side stood golden hounds and silver, which Hephaestus wrought by his cunning, to guard the palace of great-hearted Alcinous, being free from death and age all their days. And within were seats arrayed against the wall this way and that, from the threshold even to the inmost chamber, and thereon were spread light coverings finely ⁵⁰ woven, the handiwork of women. There the Phaeacian chieftains were wont to sit eating and drinking, for they had continual store. Yea, and there were youths fashioned in gold, standing on firm-set bases, with flaming torches in their hands, giving light through the night to the feasters in the palace. And he had fifty handmaids in the house, and some grind the yellow grain on the millstone, and others weave webs and turn the yarn as they sit, restless as the leaves of the tall poplar tree: and the soft olive oil drops off that linen, so closely is it woven. For as the Phaeacian men are skilled beyond all others in driving a swift ship upon the deep, even so are the women the most cunning at the loom, for Athene hath given them notable wisdom in all fair handiwork and cunning wit. And without the courtyard hard by the door is a great garden, of four plow-gates, and a hedge runs round on either side. And there grow tall trees blossoming, pear-trees and pomegranates, and apple-trees with bright fruit, and sweet figs, and olives in their bloom. The fruit of these trees never ²⁰ perisheth neither faileth, winter nor summer, enduring through all the year. Evermore the West Wind blowing brings some fruits to birth and ripens others. Pear upon pear waxes old, and apple on apple, yea and cluster ripens upon cluster of the grape, and fig upon fig. There too hath he a fruitful vineyard planted, whereof the one part is being dried by the heat, a sunny plot on level ground while other grapes men are gathering and yet others they are treading in the wine-press. In ³⁰ the foremost row are unripe grapes that cast the blossom, and others there be that are growing black to vintaging. There too, skirting the furthest line, are all manner of garden beds, planted trimly, that are perpetually fresh, and therein are two fountains of water, whereof one scatters his streams all about the garden, and the other runs over against it beneath the threshold of the courtyard and issues by the lofty house, and thence did the townsfolk draw water. These were the splendid gifts of the gods in the palace of Alcinous.

There the steadfast goodly Odysseus stood and gazed. But when he had gazed at all and wondered, he passed quickly over the threshold within the house. And he found the captains and the counselors of the Phaeacians pouring forth wine to the keen-sighted god, the slayer of Argos; for to him they poured the last cup when they were minded to take rest. Now the steadfast goodly Odysseus went through the hall, clad in a thick ⁵⁰ mist, which Athene shed around him, till he came to Arete and the king Alcinous. And Odysseus cast his hands about the knees of Arete, and then it was that the wondrous mist melted from off him, and a silence fell on them that were within the house at the sight of him, and they marveled as they beheld him. Then Odysseus began his prayer:

"Arete, daughter of godlike Rhexenor, after many toils am I come to thy husband and to thy knees and to these guests, and may the gods vouchsafe them a happy life, and may each one leave to his children after him his substance in his halls and whatever dues of honor the people have rendered unto him. But speed, I pray you, my parting, that I may come the more quickly to mine own country, for already too long do I suffer affliction far from my friends."

Therewith he sat him down by the hearth in the ashes at the fire, and behold, a dead silence fell on all. And at the last the ancient lord Echeneus spake among them, an elder of the Phæacians, excellent in speech and skilled in much wisdom of old time. With good will he made harangue and spake among them:

"Alcinous, this truly is not the more seemly way, nor is it fitting that the stranger should sit upon the ground in the ashes by the hearth, while these men refrain them, waiting thy word. Nay come, bid the stranger arise, and set him on a chair inlaid with silver, and command the henchmen to mix the wine, that we may pour forth likewise before Zeus, whose joy is in the thunder, who attendeth upon reverend suppliants. And let the housewife give supper to the stranger out of such stores as be within."

Now when the mighty king Alcinous heard this saying, he took Odysseus, the wise and crafty, by the hand, and raised him from the hearth, and set him on a shining chair, whence he bade his son give place, valiant Laodamas, who sat next him and was his dearest. And a handmaid bare water for the hands in a goodly golden ewer, and poured it forth over a silver basin to wash withal, and drew to his side a polished table. And a grave dame bare wheaten bread and set it by him and laid upon the board many dainties, giving freely of such things as she had by her. So the steadfast goodly Odysseus did eat and drink; and then the mighty Alcinous spake unto the henchman:

"Pontonous, mix the bowl and serve out the wine to all in the hall, that we may pour forth likewise before Zeus, whose joy is in the thunder, who attendeth upon reverend suppliants."

So spake he, and Pontonous mixed the honey-hearted wine, and served it out to all, when he had poured for libation into each cup in turn. But when they had poured forth and had drunken to their hearts' content, Alcinous made harangue and spake among them:

"Hear me, ye captains and counselors of the Phæacians, that I may speak as my spirit bids me. Now that the feast is over, go ye home and lie down to rest; and in the morning we will call yet more elders together, and entertain the stranger in the halls and do fair sacrifice to the gods, and thereafter we will likewise bethink us of the convoy, that so without pain or grief yonder stranger may by our convoy reach his own country speedily and with joy, even though he be from very far away. So shall he suffer no hurt or harm in mid passage, ere he set foot on his own land; but thereafter he shall endure such things as Fate and the stern spinning women drew off the spindles for him at his birth when his mother bare him. But if he is some deathless god come down from heaven, then do the gods herein imagine some new device against us. For always heretofore the gods appear manifest amongst us, whensoever we offer glorious hecatombs, and they feast by our side, sitting at the same board; yea, and even if a wayfarer going all alone has met with them, they use no disguise, since we are near of kin to them, even as are the Cyclôpes and the wild tribes of the Giants."

And Odysseus of many counsels answered him, saying, "Alcinous, that thought be far from thee! for I bear no likeness either in form or fashion to the deathless gods, who keep wide heaven, but to men that die. Whomsoever ye know of human kind the heaviest laden with sorrow, to them might I liken myself in my griefs. Yea, and I might tell of yet other woes, even the long tale of toil that by the gods' will I endured. But as for me, suffer me to sup, afflicted as I am; for nought is there more shameless than a ravening belly, which biddeth a man perforce be mindful of him, though one be worn and sorrowful in spirit, even as I have sorrow of heart; yet evermore he biddeth me eat and drink and maketh me utterly to forget all my sufferings, and commandeth me to take my fill. But do ye bestir you at the breaking of the day, that so ye may set me, hapless as I am, upon my country's soil, albeit after much suffering. Ah, and may life leave me when I have had sight of mine own possessions, my thralls, and my dwelling that is great and high!"

So spake he, and they all assented thereto, and bade send the stranger on his way, for that he had spoken aright. Now when they had poured forth and had drunken to their hearts' content, they went each one to his house to lay them to rest. But goodly Odysseus was left behind in the hall, and by him sat Arete and godlike Alcinous; and the maids cleared away the furniture of the feast; and white-armed Arete first spake among them. For she knew the mantle and the doublet, when she saw the goodly raiment that she herself had wrought with the women her handmaids. So she uttered her voice and spake to him winged words: [10]

"Sir, I am bold to ask thee first of this. Who art thou of the sons of men, and whence? Who gave thee this raiment? Didst thou not say indeed that thou camest hither wandering over the deep?"

Then Odysseus of many counsels answered her, and said: "'Tis hard, O queen, to tell my griefs from end to end, for that the gods of heaven have given me griefs in plenty. But this will I declare to thee, whereof thou dost question and inquire. There is an isle, Ogygia, that lies far off in the [20] sea; there dwells the daughter of Atlas, crafty Calypso, of the braided tresses, an awful goddess, nor is any either of gods or mortals conversant with her. Howbeit, some god brought me to her hearth, wretched man that I am, all alone, for that Zeus with white bolt crushed my swift ship and cleft it in the midst of the wine-dark deep. There all the rest of my good company was lost, but I clung with fast embrace about the keel of the curved ship, and so was I borne for nine whole [30] days. And on the tenth dark night the gods brought me nigh the isle Ogygia, where Calypso of the braided tresses dwells, an awful goddess. She took me in, and with all care she cherished me and gave me sustenance, and said that she would make me to know not death nor age for all my days; but never did she win my heart within me. There I abode for seven years continually, and watered with my tears the imperishable raiment that Calypso gave me. But when the eighth year came [40] round in his course, then at last she urged and bade me to be gone, by reason of a message from Zeus, or it may be that her own mind was turned. So she sent me forth on a well-bound raft, and gave me plenteous store, bread and sweet wine, and she clad me in imperishable raiment, and sent forth a warm and gentle wind to blow. For ten days and seven I sailed, traversing the deep, and on the eighteenth day the shadowy hills of your land showed in sight, and my heart was glad,— [50] wretched that I was—for surely I was still to be the mate of much sorrow. For Poseidon, shaker of the earth, stirred up the same, who roused against me the winds and stopped my way, and made a wondrous sea to swell, nor did the wave suffer me to be borne upon my raft, as I made ceaseless moan. Thus the storm winds shattered the raft, but as for me I cleft my way through the gulf yonder, till the wind bare and the water brought me nigh your coast. Then as I strove to land upon the shore, the wave had overwhelmed me, dashing me against the great rocks and a desolate place, but at length I gave way and swam back, till I came to the river, where the place seemed best in mine eyes, smooth of rocks, and withal there was a shelter from the wind. And as I came out I sank down, gathering to me my spirit, and immortal night came on. Then I gat me forth and away from the heaven-fed river, and laid me to sleep in the bushes and strewed leaves about me, and the god shed over me infinite sleep. There among the leaves I slept, stricken at heart, all the night long, even till the morning and mid-day. And the sun sank when sweet sleep let me free. And I was aware of the company of thy daughter disporting them upon the sand, and there was she in the midst of them like unto the goddesses. To her I made my supplication, and she showed no lack of a good understanding, behaving so as thou couldst not hope for in chancing upon one so young; for the younger folk lack wisdom always. She gave me bread enough and red wine, and let wash me in the river and bestowed on me these garments. Herein, albeit in sore distress, have I told thee all the truth."

And Alcinous answered again, and spake saying: "Sir, surely this was no right thought of my daughter, in that she brought thee not to our house with the women her handmaids, though thou didst first entreat her grace."

And Odysseus of many counsels answered, and said unto him: "My lord, chide not, I pray thee, for this the blameless maiden. For indeed she bade me follow with her company, but I would not for fear and very shame, lest perchance thine heart might be clouded at the sight; for a jealous race upon the earth are we, the tribes of men."

And Alcinous answered yet again, and spake saying: "Sir, my heart within me is not of such temper as to have been wroth without a cause: due measure in all things is best. Would to father Zeus, and Athene, and Apollo, would that so goodly a man as thou art, and like-minded with me, thou wouldst wed my daughter, and be called my son, here abiding: so would I give thee house and wealth, if thou wouldst stay of thine own will:

but against thy will shall none of the Phæacians keep thee: never be this well-pleasing in the eyes of father Zeus! And now I ordain an escort for thee on a certain day, that thou mayst surely know, and that day the morrow. Then shalt thou lay thee down overcome by sleep, and they the while shall smite the calm waters, till thou come to thy country and thy house, and whatsoever place is dear to thee, even though it be much farther than Eubœa, which certain of our men say is the farthest of lands, they who saw it, when they carried Rhadamanthus, of the fair hair, to visit Tityos, son of Gaia. Even thither they went, and accomplished the journey on the self-same day and won home again, and were not weary. And now shalt thou know for thyself how far my ships are the best, and how my young men excel at tossing the salt water with the oar-blade."

So spake he, and the steadfast goodly Odysseus rejoiced; and then he uttered a word in prayer, and called aloud to Zeus: "Father Zeus, oh that Alcinous may fulfill all that he hath said, so may his fame never be quenched upon the earth, the grain-giver, and I should come to mine own land!"

Thus they spake one to the other. And white-armed Arete bade her handmaids set out bedsteads beneath the gallery, and cast fair purple blankets over them, and spread coverlets above, and thereon lay thick mantles to be a clothing over all. So they went from the hall with torch in hand. But when they had busied them and spread the good bed-stead, they stood by Odysseus and called unto him, saying:

"Up now, stranger, and get thee to sleep, thy bed is made."

So spake they, and it seemed to him that rest was wondrous good. So he slept there, the stead-fast goodly Odysseus, on the jointed bedstead, be-neath the echoing gallery. But Alcinous laid him down in the innermost chamber of the high house, and by him the lady his wife arrayed bedstead and bedding.

[In the games, held next day in his honor, Odys-seus surpasses everyone. The king eventually en-quires about his name, his country, and his adven-tures.]

BOOK IX

Odysseus relates, first, what befell him amongst the Cicones at Ismarus; secondly, amongst the Lotophagi; thirdly, how he was used by the Cyclops Polyphemus.

And Odysseus of many counsels answered him saying: "King Alcinous, most notable of all the people, verily it is a good thing to list to a min-strel such as this one, like to the gods in voice. Nay, as for me, I say that there is no more gracious or perfect delight than when a whole people makes merry, and the men sit orderly at feast in the halls and listen to the singer, and the tables by them are laden with bread and flesh, and a wine-bearer drawing the wine serves it round and pours it into the cups. This seems to me wellnigh the fairest thing in the world. But now thy heart was inclined to ask of my grievous troubles, that I may mourn for more exceeding sorrow. What then shall I tell of first, what last, for the gods of heaven have given me woes in plenty? Now, first, will I tell my name, that ye too may know it, and that I, when I have escaped the pitiless day, may yet be your host, though my home is in a far country. I am Odysseus, son of Laertes, who am in men's minds for all manner of wiles, and my fame reaches unto heaven. And I dwell in clear-seen Ithaca wherein is a mountain Neriton, with trembling forest leaves, standing manifest to view, and many islands lie around, very near one to the other, Dulichium and Same, and wooded Zacynthus. Now Ithaca lies low, furthest up the sea-line to-ward the darkness, but those others face the dawn-ing and the sun: a rugged isle, but a good nurse of noble youths; and for myself I can see nought beside sweeter than a man's own country. Verily Calypso, the fair goddess, would fain have kept me with her in her hollow caves, longing to have me for her lord; and likewise too, guileful Circe of Aia, would have stayed me in her halls, longing to have me for her lord. But never did they prevail upon my heart within my breast. So surely is there nought sweeter than a man's own country and his parents, even though he dwell far off in a rich home, in a strange land, away from them that begat him. But come, let me tell thee too of the troubles of my journeying, which Zeus laid on me as I came from Troy.

"The wind that bare me from Ilios brought me nigh to the Cicones, even to Ismarus, whereupon I sacked their city and slew the people. And from out the city we took their wives and much sub-stance, and divided them amongst us, that none through me might go lacking his proper share. Howbeit, thereafter I commanded that we should flee with a swift foot, but my men in their great folly hearkened not. There was much wine still a drinking, and still they slew many flocks of sheep by the seashore and kine with trailing feet and shambling gait. Meanwhile the Cicones went and raised a cry to other Cicones their neighbors, dwelling inland, who were more in number than they and braver withal: skilled they were to fight with men from chariots, and when need was on foot. So they gathered in the early morning as thick as leaves and flowers that spring in their season—yea and in that hour an evil doom of Zeus stood by us, ill-fated men, that so we might be sore afflicted. They set their battle in array by the swift ships, and the hosts cast at one another with 10 their bronze-shod spears. So long as it was morn and the sacred day waxed stronger, so long we abode their assault and beat them off, albeit they outnumbered us. But when the sun was wending to the time of the loosing of cattle, then at last the Cicones drave in the Achæans and overcame them, and six of my goodly-greaved company perished from each ship: but the remnant of us escaped death and destiny.

"Thence we sailed onward stricken at heart, yet 20 glad as men saved from death, albeit we had lost our dear companions. Nor did my curved ships move onward ere we had called thrice on each of those our hapless fellows, who died at the hands of the Cicones on the plain. Now Zeus, gatherer of the clouds, aroused the North Wind against our ships with a terrible tempest, and covered land and sea alike with clouds, and down sped night from heaven. Thus the ships were driven headlong, and their sails were torn to shreds by the 30 might of the wind. So we lowered the sails into the hold, in fear of death, but rowed the ships landward apace. There for two nights and two days we lay continually, consuming our hearts with weariness and sorrow. But when the fair-tressed Dawn had at last brought the full light of the third day, we set up the masts and hoisted the white sails and sat us down, while the wind and the helmsman guided the ships. And now I should have come to mine own country all unhurt, but 40 the wave and the stream of the sea and the North Wind swept me from my course as I was doubling Malea, and drave me wandering past Cythera.

"Thence for nine whole days was I borne by ruinous winds over the teeming deep; but on the tenth day we set foot on the land of the lotus-eaters, who eat a flowery food. So we stepped ashore and drew water, and straightway my company took their midday meal by the swift ships. Now when we had tasted meat and drink I sent 50 forth certain of my company to go and make search what manner of men they were who here live upon the earth by bread, and I chose out two

of my fellows, and sent a third with them as herald. Then straightway they went and mixed with the men of the lotus-eaters, and so it was that the lotus-eaters devised not death for our fellows, but gave them of the lotus to taste. Now whosoever of them did eat the honey-sweet fruit of the lotus, had no more wish to bring tidings nor to come back, but there he chose to abide with the lotus-eating men, ever feeding on the lotus, and forgetful of his homeward way. Therefore I led them back to the ships weeping, and sore against their will, and dragged them beneath the benches, and bound them in the hollow barques. But I commanded the rest of my well-loved company to make speed and go on board the swift ships, lest haply any should eat of the lotus and be forgetful of returning. Right soon they embarked and sat upon the benches, and sitting orderly they smote the gray sea water with their oars.

"Thence we sailed onward stricken at heart. And we came to the land of the Cyclôpes, a froward and a lawless folk, who trusting to the deathless gods plant not aught with their hands, neither plow: but, behold, all these things spring for them in plenty, unsown and untilled, wheat, and barley, and vines, which bear great clusters of the juice of the grape, and the rain of Zeus gives them increase. These have neither gatherings for council nor oracles of law, but they dwell in hollow caves on the crests of the high hills, and each one utters the law to his children and his wives, and they reck not one of another.

"Now there is a waste isle stretching without the harbor of the land of the Cyclôpes, neither nigh at hand nor yet afar off, a woodland isle, wherein are wild goats unnumbered, for no path of men scares them, nor do hunters resort thither who suffer hardships in the wood, as they range the mountain crests. Moreover it is possessed neither by flocks nor by plowed lands, but the soil lies unsown evermore and untilled, desolate of men, and feeds the bleating goats. For the Cyclôpes have by them no ships with vermillion cheek, not yet are there shipwrights in the island, who might fashion decked barques, which should accomplish all their desire, voyaging to the towns of men (as ofttimes men cross the sea to one another in ships), who might likewise have made of their isle a goodly settlement. Yea, it is in no wise a sorry land, but would bear all things in their season; for therein are soft water-meadows by the shores of the gray salt sea, and there the vines know no decay, and the land is level to plow;

thence might they reap a crop exceeding deep in due season, for verily there is fatness beneath the soil. Also there is a fair haven, where is no need of moorings, either to cast anchor or to fasten hawsers, but men may run the ship on the beach, and tarry until such time as the sailors are minded to be gone, and favorable breezes blow. Now at the head of the harbor is a well of bright water issuing from a cave, and round it are poplars growing. Thither we sailed, and some god guided us through the night, for it was dark and there was no light to see, a mist lying deep about the ships, nor did the moon show her light from heaven, but was shut in with clouds. No man then beheld that island, neither saw we the long waves rolling to the beach, till we had run our decked ships ashore. And when our ships were beached, we took down all their sails, and ourselves too stept forth upon the strand of the sea, and there we fell into sound sleep and waited for the bright Dawn.

"So soon as early Dawn shone forth, the rosy-fingered, in wonder at the island we roamed over the length thereof: and the Nymphs, the daughters of Zeus, lord of the ægis, started the wild goats of the hills, that my company might have wherewith to sup. Anon we took to us our curved bows from out the ships and long spears, and arrayed in three bands we began shooting at the goats; and the god soon gave us game in plenty. Now twelve ships bare me company, and to each ship fell nine goats for a portion, but for me alone they set ten apart.

"Thus we sat there the livelong day until the going down of the sun, feasting on abundant flesh and on sweet wine. For the red wine was not yet spent from out the ships, but somewhat was yet therein, for we had each one drawn off large store thereof in jars, when we took the sacred citadel of the Cicones. And we looked across to the land of the Cyclôpes who dwell nigh, and to the smoke, and to the voice of the men, and of the sheep and of the goats. And when the sun had sunk and darkness had come on, then we laid us to rest upon the sea-beach. So soon as early Dawn shone forth, the rosy-fingered, then I called a gathering of my men, and spake among them all:

"'Abide here all the rest of you, my dear companions; but I will go with mine own ship and my ship's company, and make proof of these men, what manner of folk they are, whether froward, and wild, and unjust, or hospitable and of god-fearing mind.'

"So I spake, and I climbed the ship's side, and bade my company themselves to mount, and to loose the hawsers. So they soon embarked and sat upon the benches, and sitting orderly smote the gray sea water with their oars. Now when we had come to the land that lies hard by, we saw a cave on the border near to the sea, lofty and roofed over with laurels, and there many flocks of sheep and goats were used to rest. And about it a high outer court was built with stones, deep bedded, and with tall pines and oaks with their high crown of leaves. And a man was wont to sleep therein, of monstrous size, who shepherded his flocks alone and afar, and was not conversant with others, but dwelt apart in lawlessness of mind. Yea, for he was a monstrous thing and fashioned marvelously, nor was he like to any man that lives by bread, but like a wooded peak of the towering hills, which stands out apart and alone from others.

"Then I commanded the rest of my well-loved company to tarry there by the ship, and to guard the ship, but I chose out twelve men, the best of my company, and sallied forth. Now I had with me a goat-skin of the dark wine and sweet, which Maron, son of Euanthes, had given me, the priest of Apollo, the god that watched over Ismarus. And he gave it, for that we had protected him with his wife and child reverently; for he dwelt in a thick grove of Phœbus Apollo. And he made me splendid gifts; he gave me seven talents of gold well wrought, and he gave me a mixing bowl of pure silver, and furthermore wine which he drew off in twelve jars in all, sweet wine unmingled, a draught divine; nor did any of his servants or of his handmaids in the house know thereof, but himself and his dear wife and one house-dame only. And as often as they drank that red wine honey sweet, he would fill one cup and pour it into twenty measures of water, and a marvelous sweet smell went up from the mixing bowl: then truly it was no pleasure to refrain.

"With this wine I filled a great skin, and bare it with me, and corn too I put in a wallet, for my lordly spirit straightway had a boding that a man would come to me, a strange man, clothed in mighty strength, one that knew not judgment and justice.

"Soon we came to the cave, but we found him not within; he was shepherding his fat flocks in the pastures. So we went into the cave, and gazed on all that was therein. The baskets were well laden with cheeses, and the folds were thronged with lambs and kids; each kind was penned by itself, the firstlings apart, and the summer lambs apart, apart too the younglings of the flock. Now all the vessels swam with whey, the milk-pails and the bowls, the well-wrought vessels whereinto he milked. My company then spake and besought me first of all to take of the cheeses and to return, and afterwards to make haste and drive off the kids and lambs to the swift ships from out the pens, and to sail over the salt sea water. Howbeit I hearkened not (and far better would it have been), but waited to see the giant himself, and whether he would give me gifts as a stranger's due. Yet was not his coming to be with joy to my company.

"Then we kindled a fire, and made burnt-offering, and ourselves likewise took of the cheeses, and did eat, and sat waiting for him within till he came back, shepherding his flocks. And he bore a grievous weight of dry wood, against supper time. This log he cast down with a din inside the cave, and in fear we fled to the secret place of the rock. As for him, he drave his fat flocks into the wide cavern, even all that he was wont to milk; but the males both of the sheep and of the goats he left without in the deep yard. Thereafter he lifted a huge door-stone and weighty, and set it in the mouth of the cave, such an one as two and twenty good four-wheeled wains could not raise from the ground, so mighty a sheer rock did he set against the doorway. Then he sat down and milked the ewes and bleating goats all orderly, and beneath each ewe he placed her young. And anon he curdled one half of the white milk, and massed it together, and stored it in wicker-baskets, and the other half he let stand in pails, that he might have it to take and drink against supper time. Now when he had done all his work busily, then he kindled the fire anew, and espied us, and made question:

"'Strangers, who are ye? Whence sail ye over the wet ways? On some trading enterprise or at adventure do ye rove, even as sea-robbers over the brine, for at hazard of their own lives they wander, bringing bale to alien men.'

"So spake he, but as for us our heart within us was broken for terror of the deep voice and his own monstrous shape; yet despite all I answered and spake unto him, saying:

"'Lo, we are Achæans, driven wandering from Troy, by all manner of winds over the great gulf of the sea; seeking our homes we fare, but another path have we come, by other ways: even such, methinks, was the will and the counsel of Zeus. And we avow us to be the men of Agamemnon, son of Atreus, whose fame is even now the mightiest under heaven, so great a city did he sack, and destroyed many people; but as for us we have lighted here, and come to these thy knees, if perchance thou wilt give us a stranger's gift, or make any present, as is the due of strangers. Nay, lord, have regard to the gods, for we are thy suppliants; and Zeus is the avenger of suppliants and sojourners, Zeus, the god of the stranger, who fareth in the company of reverend strangers.'

"So I spake, and anon he answered out of his pitiless heart: 'Thou art witless, my stranger, or thou hast come from afar, who biddest me either to fear or shun the gods. For the Cyclôpes pay no heed to Zeus, lord of the ægis, nor to the blessed gods, for verily we are better men than they. Nor would I, to shun the enmity of Zeus, spare either thee or thy company, unless my spirit bade me. But tell me where thou didst stay thy well-wrought ship on thy coming? Was it perchance at the far end of the island, or hard by, that I may know?'

"So he spake tempting me, but he cheated me not, who knew full much, and I answered him again with words of guile:

"'As for my ship, Poseidon, the shaker of the earth, brake it to pieces, for he cast it upon the rocks at the border of your country, and brought it nigh the headland, and a wind bare it thither from the sea. But I with these my men escaped from utter doom.'

"So I spake, and out of his pitiless heart he answered me not a word, but sprang up, and laid his hands upon my fellows, and clutching two together dashed them, as they had been whelps, to the earth, and the brain flowed forth upon the ground, and the earth was wet. Then cut he them up piecemeal, and made ready his supper. So he ate even as a mountain-bred lion, and ceased not, devouring entrails and flesh and bones with their marrow. And we wept and raised our hands to Zeus, beholding the cruel deeds; and we were at our wits' end. And after the Cyclops had filled his huge maw with human flesh and the milk he drank thereafter, he lay within the cave, stretched out among his sheep.

"So I took counsel in my great heart, whether I should draw near, and pluck my sharp sword from my thigh, and stab him in the breast, where the midriff holds the liver, feeling for the place with my hand. But my second thought withheld me, for so should we too have perished even there with utter doom. For we should not have prevailed to roll away with our hands from the lofty door the heavy stone which he set there. So for that time we made moan, awaiting the bright Dawn.

"Now when early Dawn shone forth, the rosy-fingered, again he kindled the fire and milked his goodly flocks all orderly, and beneath each ewe set her lamb. Anon when he had done all his work busily, again he seized yet other two men and made ready his mid-day meal. And after the meal, lightly he moved away the great door-stone, and drave his fat flocks forth from the cave, and afterwards he set it in his place again, as one might set the lid on a quiver. Then with a loud whoop, the Cyclops turned his fat flocks towards the hills; but I was left devising evil in the deep of my heart, if in any wise I might avenge me, and Athene grant me renown.

"And this was the counsel that showed best in my sight. There lay by a sheep-fold a great club of the Cyclops, a club of olive wood, yet green, which he had cut to carry with him when it should be seasoned. Now when we saw it we likened it in size to the mast of a black ship of twenty oars, a wide merchant vessel that traverses the great sea gulf, so huge it was to view in bulk and length. I stood thereby and cut off from it a portion as it were a fathom's length, and set it by my fellows, and bade them fine it down, and they made it even, while I stood by and sharpened it to a point, and straightway I took it and hardened it in the bright fire. Then I laid it well away, and hid it beneath the dung, which was scattered in great heaps in the depths of the cave. And I bade my company cast lots among them, which of them should risk the adventure with me, and lift the bar and turn it about in his eye, when sweet sleep came upon him. And the lot fell upon those four whom I myself would have been fain to choose, and I appointed myself to be the fifth among them. In the evening he came shepherding his flocks of goodly fleece, and presently he drave his fat flocks into the cave each and all, nor left he any without in the deep court-yard, whether through some foreboding, or perchance that the god so bade him do. Thereafter he lifted the huge door-stone and set it in the mouth of the cave, and sitting down he milked the ewes and bleating goats, all orderly, and beneath each ewe he placed her young. Now when he had done all his work busily, again he seized yet other two and made ready his supper. Then I stood by the Cyclops and spake to him, holding in my hands an ivy bowl of the dark wine:

"'Cyclops, take and drink wine after thy feast of man's meat, that thou mayest know what manner of drink this was that our ship held. And lo, I was bringing it thee as a drink offering, if haply thou mayest take pity and send me on my way home, but thy mad rage is past all sufferance. O hard of heart, how may another of the many men there be come ever to thee again, seeing that thy deeds have been lawless?'

"So I spake, and he took the cup and drank it off, and found great delight in drinking the sweet draught, and asked me for it yet a second time:

"'Give it me again of thy grace, and tell me thy name straightway, that I may give thee a stranger's gift, wherein thou mayest be glad. Yea for the earth, the grain-giver, bears for the Cyclôpes the mighty clusters of the juice of the grape, and the rain of Zeus gives them increase, but this is a rill of very nectar and ambrosia.'

"So he spake, and again I handed him the dark wine. Thrice I bare and gave it him, and thrice in his folly he drank it to the lees. Now when the wine had got about the wits of the Cyclops, then did I speak to him with soft words:

"'Cyclops, thou askest me my renowned name, and I will declare it unto thee, and do thou grant me a stranger's gift, as thou didst promise. Noman is my name, and Noman they call me, my father and my mother and all my fellows.'

"So I spake, and straightway he answered me out of his pitiless heart:

"'Noman will I eat last in the number of his fellows, and the others before him: that shall be thy gift.'

"Therewith he sank backwards and fell with face upturned, and there he lay with his great neck bent round, and sleep, that conquers all men, overcame him. And the wine and the fragments of men's flesh issued forth from his mouth, and he vomited, being heavy with wine. Then I thrust in that stake under the deep ashes, until it should grow hot, and I spake to my companions comfortable words, lest any should hang back from me in fear. But when that bar of olive wood was just about to catch fire in the flame, green though it was, and began to glow terribly, even then I came nigh, and drew it from the coals, and my fellows gathered about me, and some god breathed great courage into us. For their part they seized the bar of olive wood, that was sharpened at the point, and thrust it into his eye, while I from my place aloft turned it about, as when a man bores a ship's beam with a drill while his fellows below spin it with a strap, which they hold at either end, and the auger runs round continually. Even so did we seize the fiery-pointed brand and whirled it round in his eye, and the blood flowed about the heated bar. And the breath of the flame singed his eyelids and brows all about, as the ball of the eye burnt away, and the roots thereof crackled in the flame. And as when a smith dips an ax or adze in chill water with a great hissing, when he would temper it—for hereby anon comes the strength of iron—even so did his eye hiss round the stake of olive. And he raised a great and terrible cry, that the rock rang around, and we fled away in fear, while he plucked forth from his eye the brand bedabbled in much blood. Then maddened with pain he cast it from him with his hands, and called with a loud voice on the Cyclôpes, who dwelt about him in the caves along the windy heights. And they heard the cry and flocked together from every side, and gathering round the cave asked him what ailed him:

"'What hath so distressed thee, Polyphemus, that thou criest thus aloud through the immortal night, and makest us sleepless? Surely no mortal driveth off thy flocks against thy will: surely none slayeth thyself by force or craft?'

"And the strong Polyphemus spake to them again from out the cave: 'My friends, Noman is slaying me by guile, nor at all by force.'

"And they answered and spake winged words: 'If then no man is violently handling thee in thy solitude, it can in no wise be that thou shouldest escape the sickness sent by mighty Zeus. Nay, pray thou to thy father, the lord Poseidon.'

"On this wise they spake and departed; and my heart within me laughed to see how my name and cunning counsel had beguiled them. But the Cyclops, groaning and travailing in pain, groped with his hands, and lifted away the stone from the door of the cave, and himself sat in the entry, with arms outstretched to catch, if he might, anyone that was going forth with his sheep, so witless, methinks, did he hope to find me. But I advised me how all might be for the very best, if perchance I might find a way of escape from death for my companions and myself, and I wove all manner of craft and counsel, as a man will for his life, seeing that great mischief was nigh. And this was the counsel that showed best in my sight. The rams of the flock were well nurtured and thick of fleece, great and goodly, with wool dark as the violet. Quietly I lashed them together with twisted withies, whereon the Cyclops slept, that lawless monster. Three together I took: now the middle one of the three would bear each a man, but the other twain went on either side, saving my fellows. Thus every three sheep bare their man. But as for me I laid hold of the back of a young ram who was far the best and the goodliest of all the flock, and curled beneath his shaggy belly there I lay, and so clung face upward, grasping the wondrous fleece with a steadfast heart. So for that time making moan we awaited the bright Dawn.

"So soon as early Dawn shone forth, the rosy-fingered, then did the rams of the flock hasten forth to pasture, but the ewes bleated unmilked about the pens, for their udders were swollen to bursting. Then their lord, sore stricken with pain, felt along the backs of all the sheep as they stood up before him, and guessed not in his folly how that my men were bound beneath the breasts of his thick-fleeced flocks. Last of all the sheep came forth the ram, cumbered with his wool, and the weight of me and my cunning. And the strong Polyphemus laid his hands on him and spake to him, saying:

"'Dear ram, wherefore, I pray thee, art thou the last of all the flocks to go forth from the cave, who of old wast not wont to lag behind the sheep, but wert ever the foremost to pluck the tender blossom of the pasture, faring with long strides, and wert still the first to come to the streams of the rivers, and first didst long to return to the homestead in the evening. But now art thou the very last. Surely thou art sorrowing for the eye of thy lord, which an evil man blinded, with his accursed fellows, when he had subdued my wits with wine, even Noman, whom I say hath not yet escaped destruction. Ah, if thou couldst feel as I, and be endued with speech, to tell me where he shifts about to shun my wrath; then should he be smitten, and his brains be dashed against the floor here and there about the cave, and my heart be lightened of the sorrows which Noman, nothing worth, hath brought me!'

"Therewith he sent the ram forth from him, and when we had gone but a little way from the cave and from the yard, first I loosed myself from under the ram and then I set my fellows free. And swiftly we drave on those stiff-shanked sheep, so rich in fat, and often turned to look about, till we came to the ship. And a glad sight to our fellows were we that had fled from death, but the others they would have bemoaned with tears; howbeit I suffered it not, but with frowning brows forbade each man to weep. Rather I bade them to cast on board the many sheep with goodly fleece, and to sail over the salt sea water. So they embarked forthwith, and sate upon the benches, and sitting orderly smote the gray sea water with their oars. But when I had not gone so far, but that a man's shout might be heard, then I spoke unto the Cyclops taunting him:

"'Cyclops, so thou wert not to eat the company of a weakling by main might in thy hollow cave! Thine evil deeds were very sure to find thee out, thou cruel man, who hadst no shame to eat thy guests within thy gates, wherefore Zeus hath requited thee, and the other gods.'

"So I spake, and he was mightily angered at heart, and he brake off the peak of a great hill and threw it at us, and it fell in front of the dark-prowed ship. And the sea heaved beneath the fall of the rock, and the backward flow of the wave bare the ship quickly to the dry land, with the wash from the deep sea, and drave it to the shore. Then I caught up a long pole in my hands, and thrust the ship from off the land, and roused my company, and with a motion of the head bade them dash in with their oars, that so we might escape our evil plight. So they bent to their oars and rowed on. But when we had now made twice the distance over the brine, I would fain have spoken to the Cyclops, but my company stayed me on every side with soft words, saying:

"'Foolhardy that thou art, why wouldst thou rouse a wild man to wrath, who even now hath cast so mighty a throw towards the deep and brought our ship back to land, yea, and we thought that we had perished even there? If he had heard any of us utter sound or speech he would have crushed our heads and our ship timbers with a cast of a rugged stone, so mightily he hurls.'

"So spake they, but they prevailed not on my lordly spirit, and I answered him again from out an angry heart:

"'Cyclops, if any one of mortal men shall ask thee of the unsightly blinding of thine eye, say that it was Odysseus that blinded it, the waster of cities, son of Laertes, whose dwelling is in Ithaca.'

"So I spake, and with a moan he answered me, saying:

"'Lo now, in very truth the ancient oracles have come upon me. There lived here a soothsayer, a noble man and a mighty, Telemus, son of Eurymus, who surpassed all men in soothsaying, and waxed old as a seer among the Cyclôpes. He told me that all these things should come to pass in the aftertime, even that I should lose my eyesight at the hand of Odysseus. But I ever looked for some tall and goodly man to come hither, clad in great might, but behold now one that is a dwarf, a man of no worth and a weakling, hath blinded me of my eye after subduing me with wine. Nay come

hither, Odysseus, that I may set by thee a stranger's cheer, and speed thy parting hence, that so the Earth-shaker may vouchsafe it thee, for his son am I, and he avows him for my father. And he himself will heal me, if it be his will; and none other of the blessed gods or of mortal men.'

"Even so he spake, but I answered him, and said: 'Would god that I were as sure to rob thee of soul and life, and send thee within the house of Hades, as I am that not even the Earth-shaker will heal thine eye!'

"So I spake, and then he prayed to the lord Poseidon stretching forth his hands to the starry heaven: 'Hear me, Poseidon, girdler of the earth, god of the dark hair, if indeed I be thine, and thou avowest thee my sire,—grant that he may never come to his home, even Odysseus, waster of cities, the son of Laertes, whose dwelling is in Ithaca; yet if he is ordained to see his friends and come unto his well-builded house, and his own country, late may he come in evil case, with the loss of all his company, in the ship of strangers, and find sorrows in his house.'

"So he spake in prayer, and the god of the dark locks heard him. And once again he lifted a stone, far greater than the first, and with one swing he hurled it, and he put forth a measureless strength, and cast it but a little space behind the dark-prowed ship, and all but struck the end of the rudder. And the sea heaved beneath the fall of the rock, but the wave bare on the ship and drave it to the further shore.

"But when we had now reached that island, where all our other decked ships abode together, and our company were gathered sorrowing, expecting us evermore, on our coming thither we ran our ship ashore upon the sand, and ourselves too stept forth upon the sea-beach. Next we took forth the sheep of the Cyclops from out the hollow ship, and divided them, that none through me might go lacking his proper share. But the ram for me alone my goodly-greaved company chose out, in the dividing of the sheep, and on the shore I offered him up to Zeus, even to the son of Cronos, who dwells in the dark clouds, and is lord of all, and I burnt the slices of the thighs. But he heeded not the sacrifice, but was devising how my decked ships and my dear company might perish utterly. Thus for that time we sat the livelong day, until the going down of the sun, feasting on abundant flesh and sweet wine. And when the sun had sunk and darkness had come on, then we laid us to rest upon the sea-beach. So soon as early Dawn shone forth, the rosy-fingered, I called to my company, and commanded them that they should themselves climb the ship and loose the hawsers. So they soon embarked and sat upon the benches, and sitting orderly smote the gray sea water with their oars.

"Thence we sailed onward stricken at heart, yet glad as men saved from death, albeit we had lost our dear companions.

[Odysseus now tells of his adventures with Æolus who kept the winds in a bag. His men open the bag out of curiosity, and the ship is driven back from the very sight of their homes in Ithaca. Next he loses eleven out of his twelve ships, and then arrives at the home of the enchantress Circe, where his men are turned to swine. He visits the land of the dead and discourses with the ghosts of heroes. Odysseus resists the wiles of the Sirens and safely passes by Scylla and Charybdis. His men then commit a sacrilege by killing the sacred oxen of the Sun, and they are all destroyed. Odysseus saves himself on a plank and after nine days in the sea arrives at Ogygia where he remains seven years with Calypso.

This is the end of Odysseus' story. The Phæacians are charmed with the story and prepare for his return. In a magic ship they carry him to Ithaca and leave him asleep. Athene disguises him as a beggar. He is received by his old swineherd Eumæus, who tells him all that has happened at home.

Telemachus then returns from Sparta in spite of the intrigues of the suitors. He comes to Eumæus and welcomes the stranger. Odysseus lets Telemachus know who he is and together they plot vengeance on the suitors.

They go to the palace, first Telemachus and then Odysseus, in disguise. Here he submits to insults without revealing himself. Penelope asks him if he has learned anything of Odysseus, and he assures her that her husband will soon return. An aged nurse recognizes him by an old scar, but he bids her remain silent. The time of vengeance on the suitors approaches.]

BOOK XXI

Penelope bringeth forth her husband's bow, which the suitors could not bend, but was bent by Odysseus.

Now the goddess, gray-eyed Athene, put it into the heart of the daughter of Icarius, wise Penelope, to set the bow and the axes of gray iron, for the wooers in the halls of Odysseus, to be the weapons of the contest, and the beginning of death. So she descended the tall staircase of her chamber, and took the well-bent key in her strong hand, a goodly key of bronze, whereon was a handle of ivory. And she betook her, with her handmaidens, to the treasure-chamber in the uttermost part of the house, where lay the treasures of her lord, bronze and gold and well-wrought iron. And there lay the back-bent bow and the quiver for the arrows, and many shafts were therein, winged for death, gifts of a friend of Odysseus, that met with him in Lacedæmon, Iphitus son of Eurytus, a man like to the gods. These twain fell in with one another in Messene, in the house of wise Ortilochus. Now Odysseus had gone thither to recover somewhat that was owing to him from all the people, for the men of Messene had lifted three hundred sheep in benched ships from out of Ithaca, with the shepherds of the flock. In quest of these it was that Odysseus went on a far embassy, being yet a lad; for his father and the other elders sent him forth. Moreover, Iphitus came thither in his search for twelve brood mares, which he had lost, with sturdy mules at the teat. These same it was that brought him death and destiny in the latter end, when he came to the child of Zeus, hardy of heart, the man Heracles, that had knowledge of great adventures, who smote Iphitus though his guest in his house, in his frowardness, and had no regard for the vengeance of the gods, nor for the table which he spread before him; for after the meal he slew him, his guest though he was, and kept for himself in the halls the horses strong of hoof. After these was Iphitus asking, when he met with Odysseus, and he gave him the bow, which of old great Eurytus bare and had left at his death to his son in his lofty house. And Odysseus gave Iphitus a sharp sword and a mighty spear, for the beginning of a loving friendship; but never had they acquaintance one of another at the board; ere that might be, the son of Zeus slew Iphitus son of Eurytus, a man like to the immortals, the same that gave Odysseus the bow. But goodly Odysseus would never take it with him on the black ships, as he went to the wars, but the bow was laid by at home in the halls as a memorial of a dear guest, and he carried it on his own land.

Now when the fair lady had come even to the treasure-chamber, and had stept upon the threshold of oak, which the carpenter had on a time planed cunningly, and over it had made straight the line, —door-posts also had he fitted thereby, whereon he set shining doors,—anon she quickly loosed the strap from the handle of the door, and thrust in the key, and with a straight aim shot back the bolts. And even as a bull roars that is grazing in a meadow, so mightily roared the fair doors smitten by the key; and speedily they flew open before her. Then she stept on to the high floor, where the coffers stood, wherein the fragrant raiment was stored. Thence she stretched forth her hand, and took the bow from off the pin, all in the bright 10 case which sheathed it around. And there she sat down, and set the case upon her knees, and cried aloud and wept, and took out the bow of her lord. Now when she had her fill of tearful lament, she set forth to go to the hall to the company of the proud wooers, with the back-bent bow in her hands, and the quiver for the arrows, and many shafts were therein winged for death. And her maidens along with her bare a chest, wherein lay much store of iron and bronze, the gear of combat 20 of their lord. Now when the fair lady had come unto the wooers, she stood by the pillar of the well-builded roof, holding up her glistening tire before her face; and a faithful maiden stood on either side of her, and straightway she spake out among the wooers and declared her word, saying:

"Hear me, ye lordly wooers, who have vexed this house, that ye might eat and drink here evermore, forasmuch as the master is long gone, nor could ye find any other mark for your speech, but all 30 your desire was to wed me and take me to wife. Nay come now, ye wooers, seeing that this is the prize that is put before you. I will set forth for you the great bow of divine Odysseus, and whoso shall most easily string the bow in his hands, and shoot through all twelve axes, with him will I go and forsake this house, this house of my wedlock, so fair and filled with all livelihood, which methinks I shall yet remember, aye, in a dream."

So spake she, and commanded Eumæus, the 40 goodly swineherd, to set the bow for the wooers and the axes of gray iron. And Eumæus took them with tears, and laid them down; and otherwhere the neatherd wept, when he beheld the bow of his lord. Then Antinous rebuked them, and spake and hailed them:

"Foolish boors, whose thoughts look not beyond the day, ah, wretched pair, wherefore now do ye shed tears, and stir the soul of the lady within her, when her heart already lies low in pain, for that 50 she has lost her dear lord? Nay sit, and feast in silence, or else get ye forth and weep, and leave the bow here behind, to be a terrible contest for the wooers, for methinks that this polished bow does not lightly yield itself to be strung. For there is no man among all these present such as Odysseus was, and I myself saw him, yea I remember it well, though I was still but a child."

So spake he, but his heart within him hoped that he would string the bow, and shoot through the iron. Yet verily, he was to be the first that should taste the arrow at the hands of the noble Odysseus, whom but late he was dishonoring as he sat in the halls, and was inciting all his fellows to do likewise.

Then the mighty prince Telemachus spake among them, saying: "Lo now, in very truth, Cronion has robbed me of my wits! My dear mother, wise as she is, declares that she will go with a stranger and forsake this house; yet I laugh and in my silly heart I am glad. Nay come now, ye wooers, seeing that this is the prize which is set before you, a lady, the like of whom there is not now in the Achæan land, neither in sacred Pylos, nor in Argos, nor in Mycenæ, nor yet in Ithaca, nor in the dark mainland. Nay but ye know all this yourselves,—why need I praise my mother? Come therefore, delay not the issue with excuses, nor hold much longer aloof from the drawing of the bow, that we may see the thing that is to be. Yea and I myself would make trial of this bow. If I shall string it, and shoot through the iron, then should I not sorrow if my lady mother were to quit these halls and go with a stranger, seeing that I should be left behind, well able now to lift my father's goodly gear of combat."

Therewith he cast from off his neck his cloak of scarlet, and sprang to his full height, and put away the sword from his shoulders. First he dug a good trench and set up the axes, one long trench for them all, and over it he made straight the line and round about stamped in the earth. And amazement fell on all that beheld how orderly he set the axes, though never before had he seen it so. Then he went and stood by the threshold and began to prove the bow. Thrice he made it to tremble in his great desire to draw it, and thrice he rested from his effort, though still he hoped in his heart to string the bow, and shoot through the iron. And now at last he might have strung it, mightily straining thereat for the fourth time, but Odysseus nodded frowning and stayed him, for all his eagerness. Then the strong prince Telemachus spake among them again:

"Lo you now, even to the end of my days I shall be a coward and a weakling, or it may be I am too young, and have as yet no trust in my hands to defend me from such an one as does violence without a cause. But come now, ye who are mightier men than I, essay the bow and let us make an end of the contest."

Therewith he put the bow from him on the ground, leaning it against the smooth and well-compacted doors, and the swift shaft he propped hard by against the fair bow-tip, and then he sat down once more on the high seat, whence he had risen.

Then Antinous, son of Eupeithes, spake among them, saying: "Rise up in order, all my friends, beginning from the left, even from the place whence the wine is poured."

So spake Antinous, and the saying pleased them well. Then first stood up Leiodes, son of Œnops, who was their soothsayer and ever sat by the fair mixing-bowl at the extremity of the hall; he alone hated their infatuate deeds and was indignant with all the wooers. He now first took the bow and the swift shaft, and he went and stood by the threshold, and began to prove the bow; but he could not bend it; or ever that might be, his hands grew weary with the straining, his unworn, delicate hands; so he spake among the wooers, saying:

"Friends, of a truth I cannot bend it, let some other take it. Ah, many of our bravest shall this bow rob of spirit and of life, since truly it is far better for us to die, than to live on and to fail of that for which we assemble evermore in this place, day by day expecting the prize. Many there be even now that hope in their hearts and desire to wed Penelope, the bedfellow of Odysseus: but when such an one shall make trial of the bow and see the issue, thereafter let him woo some other fair-robed Achæan woman with his bridal gifts and seek to win her. So may our lady wed the man that gives most gifts, and comes as the chosen of fate."

So he spake, and put from him the bow, leaning it against the smooth and well-compacted doors, and the swift shaft he propped hard by against the fair bow-tip, and then he sat down once more on the high seat, whence he had risen.

But Antinous rebuked him, and spake and hailed him: "Leiodes, what word hath escaped the door of thy lips; a hard word, and a grievous? Nay, it angers me to hear it, and to think that a bow such as this shall rob our bravest of spirit and of life, and all because thou canst not draw it. For I tell thee that thy lady mother bare thee not of such might as to draw a bow and shoot arrows:

but there be others of the proud wooers that shall draw it soon."

So he spake, and commanded Melanthius, the goatherd, saying: "Up now, light a fire in the halls, Melanthius; and place a great settle by the fire and a fleece thereon, and bring forth a great ball of lard that is within, that we young men may warm and anoint the bow therewith and prove it, and make an end of the contest."

So he spake, and Melanthius soon kindled the never-resting fire, and drew up a settle and placed it near, and put a fleece thereon, and he brought forth a great ball of lard that was within. Therewith the young men warmed the bow, and made essay, but could not string it, for they were greatly lacking of such might. And Antinous still held to the task and godlike Eurymachus, chief men among the wooers, who were far the most excellent of all.

But those other twain went forth both together from the house, the neatherd and the swineherd of godlike Odysseus; and Odysseus passed out after them. But when they were now gotten without the gates and the court-yard, he uttered his voice and spake to them in gentle words:

"Neatherd and thou swineherd, shall I say somewhat or keep it to myself? Nay, my spirit bids me declare it. What manner of men would ye be to help Odysseus, if he should come thus suddenly, I know not whence, and some god were to bring him? Would ye stand on the side of the wooers or of Odysseus? Tell me even as your heart and spirit bid you."

Then the neatherd answered him, saying: "Father Zeus, if but thou wouldst fulfill this wish: —oh, that that man might come, and some god lead him hither! So shouldest thou know what my might is, and how my hands follow to obey."

In like manner Eumæus prayed to all the gods that wise Odysseus might return to his own home.

Now when he knew for a surety what spirit they were of, once more he answered and spake to them, saying:

"Behold, home am I come, even I; after much travail and sore am I come in the twentieth year to mine own country. And I know how that my coming is desired by you alone of all my thralls, for from none besides have I heard a prayer that I might return once more to my home. And now I will tell you all the truth, even as it shall come to pass. If the god shall subdue the proud wooers to my hands, I will bring you each one a wife, and will give you a heritage of your own and a house

builded near to me, and ye twain shall be thereafter in mine eyes as the brethren and companions
of Telemachus. But behold, I will likewise show
you a most manifest token, that ye may know me
well and be certified in heart, even the wound
that the boar dealt me with his white tusk long
ago, when I went to Parnassus with the sons of
Autolycus."

Therewith he drew aside the rags from the great
scar. And when the twain had beheld it and 10
marked it well, they cast their arms about the wise
Odysseus, and fell a weeping; and kissed him
lovingly on head and shoulders. And in like manner Odysseus too kissed their heads and hands.
And now would the sunlight have gone down
upon their sorrowing, had not Odysseus himself
stayed them saying:

"Cease ye from weeping and lamentation, lest
someone come forth from the hall and see us, and
tell it likewise in the house. Nay, go ye within one 20
by one and not both together, I first and you following, and let this be the token between us. All
the rest, as many as are proud wooers, will not suffer that I should be given the bow and quiver; do
thou then, goodly Eumæus, as thou bearest the
bow through the hall, set it in my hands and speak
to the women that they bar the well-fitting doors
of their chamber. And if any of them hear the
sound of groaning or the din of men within our
walls, let them not run forth but abide where they 30
are in silence at their work. But on thee, goodly
Philœtius, I lay this charge, to bolt and bar the
outer gate of the court and swiftly to tie the knot."

Therewith he passed within the fair-lying halls,
and went and sat upon the settle whence he had
risen. And likewise the two thralls of divine Odysseus went within. And now Eurymachus was handling the bow, warming it on this side and on that
at the light of the fire; yet even so he could not
string it, and in his great heart he groaned might- 40
ily; and in heaviness of spirit he spake and called
aloud, saying:

"Lo you now, truly am I grieved for myself and
for you all! Not for the marriage do I mourn so
greatly, afflicted though I be; there are many
Achæan women besides, some in sea-begirt Ithaca
itself and some in other cities. Nay, but I grieve,
if indeed we are so far worse than godlike Odysseus in might, seeing that we cannot bend the
bow. It will be a shame even for men unborn to 50
hear thereof."

Then Antinous, son of Eupeithes, answered him:
"Eurymachus, this shall not be so, and thou thy-

self too knowest it. For today the feast of the
archer god is held in the land, a holy feast. Who
at such a time would be bending bows? Nay, set it
quietly by; what and if we should let the axes all
stand as they are? None methinks will come to the
hall of Odysseus, son of Laertes, and carry them
away. Go to now, let the wine-bearer pour for libation into each cup in turn, that after the drink-
offering we may set down the curved bow. And in
the morning bid Melanthius, the goatherd, to lead
hither the very best goats in all his herds, that we
may lay pieces of the thighs on the altar of Apollo
the archer, and assay the bow and make an end of
the contest."

So spake Antinous, and the saying pleased them
well. Then the henchmen poured water on their
hands, and pages crowned the mixing-bowls with
drink, and served out the wine to all, when they
had poured for libation into each cup in turn. But
when they had poured forth and had drunken to
their hearts' desire, Odysseus of many counsels
spake among them out of a crafty heart, saying:

"Hear me, ye wooers of the renowned queen,
that I may say that which my heart within me
bids. And mainly to Eurymachus I make my
prayer and to the godlike Antinous, forasmuch as
he has spoken even this word aright, namely, that
for this present ye cease from your archery and
leave the issue to the gods; and in the morning
the god will give the victory to whomsoever he
will. Come therefore, give me the polished bow,
that in your presence I may prove my hands and
strength, whether I have yet any force such as once
was in my supple limbs, or whether my wanderings and needy fare have even now destroyed it."

So spake he and they all were exceeding wroth,
for fear lest he should string the polished bow.
And Antinous rebuked him, and spake and hailed
him:

"Wretched stranger, thou hast no wit, nay never
so little. Art thou not content to feast at ease in
our high company, and to lack not thy share of the
banquet, but to listen to our speech and our discourse, while no guest and beggar beside thee hears
our speech? Wine it is that wounds thee, honey-
sweet wine, that is the bane of others too, even of
all who take great draughts and drink out of
measure. Wine it was that darkened the mind even
of the Centaur, renowned Eurytion, in the hall
of high-hearted Peirithous, when he went to the
Lapithæ; and after that his heart was darkened
with wine, he wrought foul deeds in his frenzy,
in the house of Peirithous. Then wrath fell on all

the heroes, and they leaped up and dragged him forth through the porch, when they had shorn off his ears and nostrils with the pitiless sword, and then with darkened mind he bare about with him the burden of his sin in foolishness of heart. Thence was the feud begun between the Centaurs and mankind; but first for himself gat he hurt, being heavy with wine. And even so I declare great mischief unto thee if thou shalt string the bow, for thou shalt find no courtesy at the hand of any-one in our land, and anon we will send thee in a black ship to Echetus, the maimer of all men, and thence thou shalt not be saved alive. Nay then, drink at thine ease, and strive not still with men that are younger than thou."

Then wise Penelope answered him: "Antinous, truly it is not fair nor just to rob the guests of Telemachus of their due, whosoever he may be that comes to this house. Dost thou think if yonder stranger strings the great bow of Odysseus, in the pride of his might and of his strength of arm, that he will lead me to his home and make me his wife? Nay he himself, methinks, has no such hope in his breast; so, as for that, let not any of you fret himself while feasting in this place; that were indeed unmeet."

Then Eurymachus, son of Polybus, answered her, saying: "Daughter of Icarius, wise Penelope, it is not that we deem that he will lead thee to his home,—far be such a thought from us,—but we dread the speech of men and women, lest some day one of the baser sort among the Achæans say: 'Truly men far too mean are wooing the wife of one that is noble, nor can they string the polished bow. But a stranger and a beggar came in his wanderings, and lightly strung the bow, and shot through the iron.' Thus will they speak, and this will turn to our reproach."

Then wise Penelope answered him: "Eurymachus, never can there be fair fame in the land for those that devour and dishonor the house of a prince, but why make ye this thing into a reproach? But, behold, our guest is great of growth and well-knit, and avows him to be born the son of a good father. Come then, give ye him the polished bow, that we may see that which is to be. For thus will I declare my saying, and it shall surely come to pass. If he shall string the bow and Apollo grant him renown, I will clothe him in a mantle and a doublet, goodly raiment, and I will give him a sharp javelin to defend him against dogs and men, and a two-edged sword and sandals to bind beneath his feet, and I will send him whithersoever his heart and spirit bid him go."

Then wise Telemachus answered her, saying: "My mother, as for the bow, no Achæan is mightier than I to give or to deny it to whomso I will, neither as many as are lords in rocky Ithaca nor in the isles on the side of Elis, the pastureland of horses. Not one of these shall force me in mine own despite, if I choose to give this bow, yea once and for all, to the stranger to bear away with him. But do thou go to thine own chamber and mind thine own housewiferies, the loom and distaff, and bid thine handmaids ply their tasks. But the bow shall be for men, for all, but for me in chief, for mine is the lordship in the house."

Then in amaze she went back to her chamber, for she laid up the wise saying of her son in her heart. She ascended to her upper chamber with the women her handmaids, and then was bewailing Odysseus, her dear lord, till gray-eyed Athene cast sweet sleep upon her eyelids.

Now the goodly swineherd had taken the curved bow, and was bearing it, when the wooers all cried out upon him in the halls. And thus some one of the haughty youths would speak: "Whither now art thou bearing the curved bow, thou wretched swineherd, crazed in thy wits? Lo, soon shall the swift hounds of thine own breeding eat thee hard by thy swine, alone and away from men, if Apollo will be gracious to us and the other deathless gods."

Even so they spake, and he took and set down the bow in that very place, being affrighted because many cried out on him in the halls. Then Telemachus from the other side spake threateningly, and called aloud:

"Father, bring hither the bow, soon shalt thou rue it that thou servest many masters. Take heed, lest I that am younger than thou pursue thee to the field, and pelt thee with stones, for in might I am the better. If only I were so much mightier in strength of arm than all the wooers that are in the halls, soon would I send many an one forth on a woeful way from out our house, for they imagine mischief against us."

So he spake, and all the wooers laughed sweetly at him, and ceased now from their cruel anger toward Telemachus. Then the swineherd bare the bow through the hall, and went up to wise Odysseus, and set it in his hands. And he called forth the nurse Eurycleia from the chamber and spake to her:

"Wise Eurycleia, Telemachus bids thee bar the well-fitting doors of thy chamber, and if any of the women hear the sound of groaning or the din of men within our walls, let them not go forth, but abide where they are in silence at their work."

So he spake, and wingless her speech remained, and she barred the doors of the fair-lying chambers.

Then Philœtius hasted forth silently from the house, and barred the outer gates of the fenced court. Now there lay beneath the gallery the cable of a curved ship, fashioned of the byblus plant, wherewith he made fast the gates, and then himself passed within. Then he went and sat on the settle whence he had risen, and gazed upon Odysseus. He already was handling the bow, turning it every way about, and proving it on this side and on that, lest the worms might have eaten the horns when the lord of the bow was away. And thus men spake looking each one to his neighbor:

"Verily he had a good eye, and a shrewd turn for a bow! Either, methinks, he himself has such a bow lying by at home or else he is set on making one, in such wise does he turn it hither and thither in his hands, this evil-witted beggar."

And another again of the haughty youths would say: "Would that the fellow may have profit thereof, just so surely as he shall ever prevail to bend this bow!"

So spake the wooers, but Odysseus of many counsels had lifted the great bow and viewed it on every side, and even as when a man that is skilled in the lyre and in minstrelsy, easily stretches a cord about a new peg, after tying at either end the twisted sheep-gut, even so Odysseus straightway bent the great bow, all without effort, and took it in his right hand and proved the bow-string, which rang sweetly at the touch, in tone like a swallow. Then great grief came upon the wooers, and the color of their countenance was changed, and Zeus thundered loud showing forth his tokens. And the steadfast goodly Odysseus was glad thereat, in that the son of deep-counseling Cronos had sent him a sign. Then he caught up a swift arrow which lay by his table, bare, but the other shafts were stored within the hollow quiver, those whereof the Achæans were soon to taste. He took and laid it on the bridge of the bow, and held the notch and drew the string, even from the settle whereon he sat, and with straight aim shot the shaft and missed not one of the axes, beginning from the first ax-handle, and the bronze-weighted shaft passed clean through and out at the last. Then he spake to Telemachus, saying:

"Telemachus, thy guest that sits in the halls does

thee no shame. In nowise did I miss my mark, nor was I wearied with long bending of the bow. Still is my might steadfast—not as the wooers say scornfully to slight me. But now it is time that supper too be got ready for the Achæans, while it is yet light, and thereafter must we make other sport with the dance and the lyre, for these are the crown of the feast."

Therewith he nodded with bent brows, and Telemachus, the dear son of divine Odysseus, girt his sharp sword about him and took the spear in his grasp, and stood by his high seat at his father's side, armed with the gleaming bronze.

BOOK XXII

The killing of the wooers.

Then Odysseus of many counsels stripped him of his rags and leaped on to the great threshold with his bow and quiver full of arrows, and poured forth all the swift shafts there before his feet, and spake among the wooers:

"Lo, now is this terrible trial ended at last; and now will I know of another mark, which never yet man has smitten, if perchance I may hit it and Apollo grant me renown."

With that he pointed the bitter arrow at Antinous. Now he was about raising to his lips a fair twy-eared chalice of gold, and behold, he was handling it to drink of the wine, and death was far from his thoughts. For who among men at feast would deem that one man amongst so many, how hardy soever he were, would bring on him foul death and black fate? But Odysseus aimed and smote him with the arrow in the throat, and the point passed clean out through his delicate neck, and he fell sidelong and the cup dropped from his hand as he was smitten, and at once through his nostrils there came up a thick jet of slain man's blood, and quickly he spurned the table from him with his foot, and spilt the food on the ground, and the bread and the roast flesh were defiled. Then the wooers raised a clamor through the halls when they saw the man fallen, and they leaped from their high seats, as men stirred by fear, all through the hall, peering everywhere along the well-builded walls, and nowhere was there a shield or mighty spear to lay hold on. Then they reviled Odysseus with angry words:

"Stranger, thou shootest at men to thy hurt. Never again shalt thou enter other lists, now is utter doom assured thee. Yea, for now hast thou slain the man that was far the best of all the noble youths in Ithaca; wherefore vultures shall devour thee here."

So each one spake, for indeed they thought that Odysseus had not slain him willfully; but they knew not in their folly that on their own heads, each and all of them, the bands of death had been made fast. Then Odysseus of many counsels looked fiercely on them, and spake:

"Ye dogs, ye said in your hearts that I should never more come home from the land of the Trojans, in that ye wasted my house, and lay with the maidservants by force, and traitorously wooed my wife while I was yet alive, and ye had no fear of the gods, that hold the wide heaven, nor of the indignation of men hereafter. But now the bands of death have been made fast upon you one and all."

Even so he spake, and pale fear gat hold on the limbs of all, and each man looked about, where he might shun utter doom. And Eurymachus alone answered him, and spake: "If thou art indeed Odysseus of Ithaca, come home again, with right thou speakest thus, of all that the Achæans have wrought, many infatuate deeds in thy halls and many in the field. Howbeit, he now lies dead that is to blame for all, Antinous; for he brought all these things upon us, not as longing very greatly for the marriage nor needing it sore, but with another purpose, that Cronion has not fulfilled for him, namely, that he might himself be king over all the land of stablished Ithaca, and he was to have lain in wait for thy son and killed him. But now he is slain after his deserving, and do thou spare thy people, even thine own; and we will hereafter go about the township and yield thee amends for all that has been eaten and drunken in thy halls, each for himself bringing atonement of twenty oxen worth, and requiting thee in gold and bronze till thy heart is softened, but till then none may blame thee that thou art angry."

Then Odysseus of many counsels looked fiercely on him, and said: "Eurymachus, not even if ye gave me all your heritage, all that ye now have, and whatsoever else ye might in any wise add thereto, not even so would I henceforth hold my hands from slaying, ere the wooers had paid for all their transgressions. And now the choice lies before you, whether to fight in fair battle or to fly, if any may avoid death and the fates. But there be some, methinks, that shall not escape from utter doom."

He spake, and their knees were straightway loosened and their hearts melted within them. And Eurymachus spake among them yet again:

"Friends, it is plain that this man will not hold his unconquerable hands, but now that he has caught up the polished bow and quiver, he will shoot from the smooth threshold, till he has slain us all; wherefore let us take thought for the delight of battle. Draw your blades, and hold up the tables to ward off the arrows of swift death, and let us all have at him with one accord, and drive him, if it may be, from the threshold and the doorway and then go through the city, and quickly would the cry be raised. Thereby should this man soon have shot his latest bolt."

Therewith he drew his sharp two-edged sword of bronze, and leapt on Odysseus with a terrible cry, but in the same moment goodly Odysseus shot the arrow forth and struck him on the breast by the pap, and drave the swift shaft into his liver. So he let the sword fall from his hand, and groveling over the table he bowed and fell, and spilt the food and the two-handled cup on the floor. And in his agony he smote the ground with his brow, and spurning with both his feet he overthrew the high seat, and the mist of death was shed upon his eyes.

Then Amphinomus made at renowned Odysseus, setting straight at him, and drew his sharp sword, if perchance he might make him give ground from the door. But Telemachus was beforehand with him, and cast and smote him from behind with a bronze-shod spear between the shoulders, and drave it out through the breast, and he fell with a crash and struck the ground full with his forehead. Then Telemachus sprang away, leaving the long spear fixed in Amphinomus, for he greatly dreaded lest one of the Achæans might run upon him with his blade, and stab him as he drew forth the spear, or smite him with a down stroke of the sword. So he started and ran and came quickly to his father, and stood by him, and spake winged words:

"Father, lo, now I will bring thee a shield and two spears and a helmet all of bronze, close fitting on the temples, and when I return I will arm myself, and likewise give arms to the swineherd and to the neatherd yonder: for it is better to be clad in full armor."

And Odysseus of many counsels answered him saying: "Run and bring them while I have arrows to defend me, lest they thrust me from the doorway, one man against them all."

So he spake, and Telemachus obeyed his dear father, and went forth to the chamber, where his famous weapons were lying. Thence he took out four shields and eight spears, and four helmets of bronze, with thick plumes of horse hair, and he started to bring them and came quickly to his father. Now he girded the gear of bronze about his own body first, and in like manner the two thralls did on the goodly armor, and stood beside the wise and crafty Odysseus. Now he, so long as he had arrows to defend him, kept aiming and smote the wooers one by one in his house, and they fell thick one upon another. But when the arrows failed the prince in his archery, he leaned his bow against the door-post of the stablished hall, against the shining faces of the entrance. As for him he girt his fourfold shield about his shoulders and bound on his mighty head a well-wrought helmet, with horse hair crest, and terribly the plume waved aloft. And he grasped two mighty spears tipped with bronze.

Now there was in the well-builded wall a certain postern raised above the floor, and there by the topmost level of the threshold of the stablished hall, was a way into an open passage, closed by well-fitted folding doors. So Odysseus bade the goodly swineherd stand near thereto and watch the way, for thither was there but one approach. Then Agelaus spake among them, and declared his word to all:

"Friends, will not some man climb up to the postern, and give word to the people, and a cry would be raised straightway; so should this man soon have shot his latest bolt?"

Then Melanthius, the goatherd, answered him, saying: "It may in no wise be, prince Agelaus; for the fair gate of the court-yard is terribly nigh, and perilous is the entrance to the passage, and one man, if he were valiant, might keep back a host. But come, let me bring you armor from the inner chamber, that ye may be clad in hauberks, for, methinks, within that room and not elsewhere did Odysseus and his renowned son lay by the arms."

Therewith Melanthius, the goatherd, climbed up by the clerestory of the hall to the inner chambers of Odysseus, whence he took twelve shields and as many spears, and as many helmets of bronze with thick plumes of horse hair, and he came forth and brought them speedily, and gave them to the wooers. Then the knees of Odysseus were loosened and his heart melted within him, when he saw them girding on the armor and brandishing the long spears in their hands, and great, he saw, was the adventure. Quickly he spake to Telemachus winged words:

"Telemachus, sure I am that one of the women in the halls is stirring up an evil battle against us, or perchance it is Melanthius."

Then wise Telemachus answered him: "My father, it is I that have erred herein and none other is to blame, for I left the well-fitted door of the chamber open, and there has been one of them but too quick to spy it. Go now, goodly Eumæus, and close the door of the chamber, and mark if it be indeed one of the women that does this mischief, or Melanthius, son of Dolius, as methinks it is."

Even so they spake one to the other. And Melanthius, the goatherd, went yet again to the chamber to bring the fair armor. But the goodly swineherd was ware thereof, and quickly he spake to Odysseus who stood nigh him:

"Son of Laertes, of the seed of Zeus, Odysseus, of many devices, lo, there again is that baleful man, whom we ourselves suspect, going to the chamber; do thou tell me truly, shall I slay him if I prove the better man, or bring him hither to thee, that he may pay for the many transgressions that he has devised in thy house?"

Then Odysseus of many counsels answered saying: "Verily, I and Telemachus will keep the proud wooers within the halls, for all their fury, but do ye twain tie his feet and arms behind his back and cast him into the chamber, and close the doors after you, and make fast to his body a twisted rope, and drag him up the lofty pillar till he be near the roof beams, that he may hang there and live for long, and suffer grievous torment."

So he spake, and they gave good heed and hearkened. So they went forth to the chamber, but the goatherd who was within knew not of their coming. Now he was seeking for the armor in the secret place of the chamber, but they twain stood in waiting on either side the door-posts. And when Melanthius, the goatherd, was crossing the threshold with a goodly helm in one hand, and in the other a wide shield and an old, stained with rust, the shield of the hero Laertes that he bare when he was young—but at that time it was laid by, and the seams of the straps were loosened,—then the twain rushed on him and caught him, and dragged him in by the hair, and cast him on the floor in sorrowful plight, and bound him hand and foot in a bitter bond, tightly winding each limb behind his back, even as the son of Laertes bade them, the steadfast goodly Odysseus. And they made fast to his body a twisted rope, and dragged him up the lofty pillar till he came near the roof beams. Then didst thou speak to him and gird at him, swineherd Eumæus:

"Now in good truth, Melanthius, shalt thou watch all night, lying in a soft bed as beseems thee, nor shall the early-born Dawn escape thy ken, when she comes forth from the streams of Oceanus, on her golden throne, in the hour when thou art wont to drive the goats to make a meal for the wooers in the halls."

So he was left there, stretched tight in the deadly bond. But they twain got into their harness, and closed the shining door, and went to Odysseus, wise and crafty chief. There they stood breathing fury, four men by the threshold, while those others within the halls were many and good warriors. Then Athene, daughter of Zeus, drew nigh them, like Mentor in fashion and in voice, and Odysseus was glad when he saw her and spake, saying:

"Mentor, ward from us hurt, and remember me thy dear companion, that befriended thee often, and thou art of like age with me."

So he spake, deeming the while that it was Athene, summoner of the host. But the wooers on the other side shouted in the halls, and first Agelaus son of Damastor rebuked Athene, saying:

"Mentor, let not the speech of Odysseus beguile thee to fight against the wooers, and to succor him. For methinks that on this wise we shall work our will. When we shall have slain these men, father and son, thereafter shalt thou perish with them, such deeds thou art set on doing in these halls; nay, with thine own head shalt thou pay the price. But when with the sword we shall have overcome your violence, we will mingle all thy possessions, all that thou hast at home or in the field, with the wealth of Odysseus, and we will not suffer thy sons nor thy daughters to dwell in the halls, nor thy good wife to gad about in the town of Ithaca."

So spake he, and Athene was mightily angered at heart, and chid Odysseus in wrathful words: "Odysseus, thou hast no more steadfast might nor any prowess, as when for nine whole years continually thou didst battle with the Trojans for high born Helen, of the white arms, and many men thou slewest in terrible warfare, and by thy device the wide-wayed city of Priam was taken. How then, now that thou art come to thy house and thine own possessions, dost thou bewail thee and art of feeble courage to stand before the wooers? Nay, come hither, friend, and stand by me, and I will show thee a thing, that thou mayest know what manner of man is Mentor, son of Alcimus, to repay good deeds in the ranks of foemen."

She spake, and gave him not yet clear victory in full, but still for a while made trial of the might and prowess of Odysseus and his renowned son. As for her she flew up to the roof timber of the murky hall, in such fashion as a swallow flies, and there sat down.

Now Agelaus, son of Damastor, urged on the wooers, and likewise Eurynomus and Amphimedon and Demoptolemus and Peisandrus son of Polyctor, and wise Polybus, for these were in valiancy far the best men of the wooers, that still lived and fought for their lives; for the rest had fallen already beneath the bow and the thick rain of arrows. Then Agelaus spake among them, and made known his word to all:

"Friends, now at last will this man hold his unconquerable hands. Lo, now has Mentor left him and spoken but vain boasts, and these remain alone at the entrance of the doors. Wherefore now, throw not your long spears all together, but come, do ye six cast first, if perchance Zeus may grant us to smite Odysseus and win renown. Of the rest will we take no heed, so soon as that man shall have fallen."

So he spake and they all cast their javelins, as he bade them, eagerly; but behold, Athene so wrought that they were all in vain. One man smote the door-post of the stablished hall, and another the well-fastened door, and the ashen spear of yet another wooer, heavy with bronze, stuck fast in the wall. So when they had avoided all the spears of the wooers, the steadfast goodly Odysseus began first to speak among them:

"Friends, now my word is that we too cast and hurl into the press of the wooers, that are mad to slay and strip us beyond the measure of their former iniquities."

So he spake, and they all took good aim and threw their sharp spears, and Odysseus smote Demoptolemus, and Telemachus Euryades, and the swineherd slew Elatus, and the neatherd Peisandrus. Thus they all bit the wide floor with their teeth, and the wooers fell back into the inmost part of the hall. But the others dashed upon them, and drew forth the shafts from the bodies of the dead.

Then once more the wooers threw their sharp spears eagerly; but behold, Athene so wrought that many of them were in vain. One man smote the door-post of the stablished hall, and another the well-fastened door, and the ashen spear of another wooer, heavy with bronze, struck in the wall. Yet Amphimedon hit Telemachus on the hand by the wrist lightly, and the shaft of bronze wounded the surface of the skin. And Ctesippus grazed the shoulder of Eumæus with a long spear high above the shield, and the spear flew over and fell to the ground. Then again Odysseus, the wise and crafty, he and his men cast their swift spears into the press of the wooers, and now once more Odysseus, waster of cities, smote Eurydamas, and Telemachus Amphimedon, and the swineherd slew Polybus, and last, the neatherd struck Ctesippus in the breast and boasted over him, saying:

"O son of Polytherses, thou lover of jeering, never give place at all to folly to speak so big, but leave thy case to the gods, since in truth they are far mightier than thou. This gift is thy recompense for the ox-foot that thou gavest of late to the divine Odysseus, when he went begging through the house."

So spake the keeper of the shambling kine. Next Odysseus wounded the son of Damastor in close fight with his long spear, and Telemachus wounded Leocritus son of Euenor, right in the flank with his lance, and drave the bronze point clean through, that he fell prone and struck the ground full with his forehead. Then Athene held up her destroying ægis on high from the roof, and their minds were scared, and they fled through the hall, like a drove of kine that the flitting gadfly falls upon and scatters hither and thither in spring time, when the long days begin. But the others set on like vultures of crooked claws and curved beak, that come forth from the mountains and dash upon smaller birds, and these scour low in the plain, stooping in terror from the clouds, while the vultures pounce on them and slay them, and there is no help nor way of flight, and men are glad at the sport; even so did the company of Odysseus set upon the wooers and smite them right and left through the hall; and there rose a hideous moaning as their heads were smitten, and the floor all ran with blood.

Now Leiodes took hold of the knees of Odysseus eagerly, and besought him and spake winged words: "I entreat thee by thy knees, Odysseus, and do thou show mercy on me and have pity. For never yet, I say, have I wronged a maiden in thy halls by froward word or deed, nay I bade the other wooers refrain, whoso of them wrought thus. But they hearkened not unto me to keep their hands from evil. Wherefore they have met a shameful death through their own infatuate deeds. Yet I, the soothsayer among them, that have wrought no evil, shall fall even as they, for no grace abides for good deeds done."

Then Odysseus of many counsels looked askance at him, and said: "If indeed thou dost avow thee to be the soothsayer of these men, thou art like to have often prayed in the halls that the issue of a glad return might be far from me, and that my dear wife should follow thee and bear thee children; wherefore thou shalt not escape the bitterness of death."

Therewith he caught up a sword in his strong hand, that lay where Agelaus had let it fall to the ground when he was slain, and drave it clean through his neck, and as he yet spake his head fell even to the dust.

But the son of Terpes, the minstrel, still sought how he might shun black fate, Phemius, who sang among the wooers of necessity. He stood with the loud lyre in his hand hard by the postern gate, and his heart was divided within him, whether he should slip forth from the hall and sit down by the well-wrought altar of great Zeus of the household court, whereon Laertes and Odysseus had burnt many pieces of the thighs of oxen, or should spring forward and beseech Odysseus by his knees. And as he thought thereupon this seemed to him the better way, to embrace the knees of Odysseus, son of Laertes. So he laid the hollow lyre on the ground between the mixing-bowl and the high seat inlaid with silver, and himself sprang forward and seized Odysseus by the knees, and besought him and spake winged words:

"I entreat thee by thy knees, Odysseus, and do thou show mercy on me and have pity. It will be a sorrow to thyself in the aftertime if thou slayest me who am a minstrel, and sing before gods and men. Yea none has taught me but myself, and the god has put into my heart all manner of lays, and methinks I sing to thee as to a god, wherefore be not eager to cut off my head. And Telemachus will testify of this, thine own dear son, that not by mine own will or desire did I resort to thy house to sing to the wooers at their feasts; but being so many and stronger than I they led me by constraint."

So he spake, and the mighty prince Telemachus heard him and quickly spake to his father at his side: "Hold thy hand, and wound not this blameless man with the sword; and let us save also the henchman Medon, that ever had charge of me in our house when I was a child, unless perchance Philœtius or the swineherd have already slain him, or he hath met thee in thy raging through the house."

So he spake, and Medon, wise of heart, heard him. For he lay crouching beneath a high seat, clad about in the new-flayed hide of an ox and shunned black fate. So he rose up quickly from under the seat, and cast off the ox-hide, and sprang forth and caught Telemachus by the knees, and besought him and spake winged words:

"Friend, here am I; prithee stay thy hand and speak to thy father, lest he harm me with the sharp sword in the greatness of his strength, out of his anger for the wooers that wasted his possessions in the halls, and in their folly held thee in no honor."

And Odysseus of many counsels smiled on him and said: "Take courage, for lo, he has saved thee and delivered thee, that thou mayst know in thy heart, and tell it even to another, how far more excellent are good deeds than evil. But go forth from the halls and sit down in the court apart from the slaughter, thou and the full-voiced minstrel, till I have accomplished all that I must needs do in the house."

Therewith the two went forth and gat them from the hall. So they sat down by the altar of great Zeus, peering about on every side, still expecting death. And Odysseus peered all through the house, to see if any man was yet alive and hiding away to shun black fate. But he found all the sort of them fallen in their blood in the dust, like fishes that the fishermen have drawn forth in the meshes of the net into a hollow of the beach from out the gray sea, and all the fish, sore longing for the salt sea waves, are heaped upon the sand, and the sun shines forth and takes their life away; so now the wooers lay heaped upon each other. Then Odysseus of many counsels spake to Telemachus:

"Telemachus, go, call me the nurse Eurycleia, that I may tell her a word that is on my mind."

So he spake, and Telemachus obeyed his dear father, and smote at the door, and spake to the nurse Eurycleia: "Up now, aged wife, that overlookest all the women servants in our halls, come hither, my father calls thee and has somewhat to say to thee."

Even so he spake, and wingless her speech remained, and she opened the doors of the fair-lying halls, and came forth, and Telemachus led the way before her. So she found Odysseus among the bodies of the dead, stained with blood and soil of battle, like a lion that has eaten of an ox of the homestead and goes on his way, and all his breast and his cheeks on either side are flecked with blood, and he is terrible to behold; even so was Odysseus stained, both hands and feet. Now the nurse, when she saw the bodies of the dead and the great gore of blood, made ready to cry aloud for joy, beholding so great an adventure. But Odysseus checked and held her in her eagerness, and uttering his voice spake to her winged words:

"Within thine own heart rejoice, old nurse, and be still, and cry not aloud; for it is an unholy thing to boast over slain men. Now these hath the destiny of the gods overcome, and their own cruel deeds, for they honored none of earthly men, neither the bad nor yet the good, that came among them. Wherefore they have met a shameful death through their own infatuate deeds. But come, tell me the tale of the women in my halls, which of them dishonor me, and which be guiltless."

Then the good nurse Eurycleia answered him: "Yea now, my child, I will tell thee all the truth. Thou hast fifty women-servants in thy halls, that we have taught the ways of housewifery, how to card wool and to bear bondage. Of these twelve in all have gone the way of shame, and honor not me, nor their lady Penelope. And Telemachus hath but newly come to his strength, and his mother suffered him not to take command over the women in this house. But now, let me go aloft to the shining upper chamber, and tell all to thy wife, on whom some god hath sent a sleep."

And Odysseus of many counsels answered her, saying: "Wake her not yet, but bid the women come hither, who in time past behaved themselves unseemly."

So he spake, and the old wife passed through the hall, to tell the women and to hasten their coming. Then Odysseus called to him Telemachus, and the neatherd, and the swineherd, and spake to them winged words:

"Begin ye now to carry out the dead, and bid the women help you, and thereafter cleanse the fair high seats and the tables with water and porous sponges. And when ye have set all the house in order, lead the maidens without the stablished hall, between the vaulted room and the goodly fence of the court, and there slay them with your long blades, till they shall have all given up the ghost and forgotten the love that of old they had at the bidding of the wooers, in secret dalliance."

Even so he spake, and the women came all in a crowd together, making a terrible lament and shedding big tears. So first they carried forth the bodies of the slain, and set them beneath the gallery of the fenced court, and propped them one on another; and Odysseus himself hasted the women and directed them, and they carried forth the dead perforce. Thereafter they cleansed the fair high seats and the tables with water and porous sponges.

And Telemachus, and the neatherd, and the swineherd, scraped with spades the floor of the well-builded house, and, behold, the maidens carried all forth and laid it without the doors.

Now when they had made an end of setting the hall in order, they led the maidens forth from the stablished hall, and drove them up in a narrow space between the vaulted room and the goodly fence of the court, whence none might avoid; and wise Telemachus began to speak to his fellows, saying:

"God forbid that I should take these women's lives by a clean death, these that have poured dishonor on my head and on my mother, and have lain with the wooers."

With that word he tied the cable of a dark-prowed ship to a great pillar and flung it round the vaulted room, and fastened it aloft, that none might touch the ground with her feet. And even as when thrushes, long of wing, or doves fall into a net that is set in a thicket, as they seek to their roosting-place, and a loathy bed harbors them, even so the women held their heads all in a row, and about all their necks nooses were cast, that they might die by the most pitiful death. And they writhed with their feet for a little space, but for no long while.

Then they led out Melanthius through the doorway and the court, and cut off his nostrils and his ears with the pitiless sword, and drew forth his vitals for the dogs to devour raw, and cut off his hands and feet in their cruel anger.

Thereafter they washed their hands and feet, and went into the house to Odysseus, and all the adventure was over. So Odysseus called to the good nurse Eurycleia: "Bring sulphur, old nurse, that cleanses all pollution and bring me fire, that I may purify the house with sulphur, and do thou bid Penelope come here with her handmaidens, and tell all the women to hasten into the hall."

Then the good nurse Eurycleia made answer: "Yea, my child, herein thou hast spoken aright. But go to, let me bring thee a mantle and a doublet for raiment, and stand not thus in the halls with thy broad shoulders wrapped in rags; it were blame in thee so to do."

And Odysseus of many counsels answered her, saying: "First let a fire now be made me in the hall."

So he spake, and the good nurse Eurycleia was not slow to obey, but brought fire and brimstone; and Odysseus throughly purged the women's chamber and the great hall and the court.

Then the old wife went through the fair halls of Odysseus to tell the women, and to hasten their coming. So they came forth from their chamber with torches in their hands, and fell about Odysseus, and embraced him and kissed and clasped his head and shoulders and his hands lovingly, and a sweet longing came on him to weep and moan, for he remembered them every one.

[*In the last two books of the* Odyssey, *the hero makes himself known to Penelope and later to his aged father, Laertes. The Ithacans plan revenge on Odysseus but are defeated and submit to his rule.*]

GREEK CULTURE
ITS DEVELOPMENT
AND NATURE

After the brilliant period of Achæan culture described in the Homeric poems, these Greeks were entirely overrun by a new group of their own kinsmen, the Dorians. For some centuries there resulted a decline in civilization throughout the whole Hellenic world, a time the historians call the Greek Middle Ages. Then gradually there emerged, about the seventh or sixth century before Christ, the Greek peoples who were to become the cultural leaders of antiquity, and in many ways of all time. The change wrought by the Dorian invasion and the way in which the old and new civilizations differ are vividly described by Walter Leaf in his *Companion to the Iliad*.[1]

"Before the beginnings of European history there dwelt in Greece a people who called themselves Achaians. They had come probably from the North, through Thrace, and had settled in Thessaly and Bœotia, in the Peloponnesos, in the islands of the western coast, in Crete, and in a few of the neighboring islands which lie between Crete and the coast of Asia Minor. They were a pure Greek race, and spoke a pure Greek tongue, the parent of those dialects which the Greeks themselves in after years distinguished as Æolic.

"But they had not found Greece vacant when they came. It had been inhabited by a race or races whom the Greeks themselves called Pelasgians, and of whom we know little more than

the name. These Pelasgians still lived in the land as a plebeian class, to whom the invading Achaians held something of the same position as the feudal lords in early Norman times to their defeated Saxons.

"The main seat of the Achaians was at the inland fortress of Mykenai, in the hills between Corinth and the Gulf of Argos. But they were divided among many petty princes, who dwelt in various strong towns, chiefly along the eastern coasts and the islands, and with few important settlements—perhaps only Pylos and Kalydon—in the west. Sparta was probably their main settlement next after Mykenai.

"When they came into Greece we cannot even approximately tell. But we know that in the twelfth and thirteenth centuries B.C. they had attained to great wealth, and had produced a vigorous and beautiful school of art. They were great builders, and much of their work is still, after more than 3000 years, a marvel for boldness of conception and solidity of construction. Their rule must have lasted for several centuries, but at length it fell, about 1000 B.C., before the invading Dorians, a rude tribe of Greek mountaineers who pressed southwards from the hills round Thessaly.

"The period at which we become acquainted with the Achaians is that of the height of their civilization. Such knowledge as we have of them

[1] London, 1892, pp. 1 ff. By permission of the Macmillan Co.

at this time, the twelfth and thirteenth centuries B.C., we owe to the discoveries of Dr. Schliemann at Mykenai, since supplemented by excavations at other sites in Greece. But these great finds, though telling us much, leave much still to be guessed at. It is at a later period, probably less than a century before their destruction by the Dorians, that we gain a more intimate acquaintance with them through the two great poems which they have left us as their intellectual inheritance, the *Iliad* and the *Odyssey*.

"These poems have often been spoken of as popular poetry, *Volkspoesie,* and have even been compared to the ballad poetry of our own and other nations. It is now generally recognized that this conception is radically false. The *Iliad* and *Odyssey* are essentially and above all court poems. They were composed to be sung in the splendid palaces of a ruling aristocracy, and the commonalty have no part or lot as actors in them. Even the slave and swineherd Eumaios, the only figure of the lower class of heroic society who takes a leading part in either poem, is described as of princely birth, kidnaped when a child and sold as a slave by Phœnician traders. When the common sort are mentioned in the *Iliad* in contrast to the 'kings' it is in terms of supreme disdain; only one of them, Thersites, is given an individuality, and then only that he may be held up to ridicule and humiliation. This is the first point which must be clearly grasped by those who would enter into the spirit of Homer: that the poems are aristocratic and courtly, not popular.

"The next is, that they are not to be regarded as the outcome of a young and primitive people. They are the offspring of an advanced civilization, the growth of centuries; and of a civilization which was approaching its decline and fall. It was in some respects a civilization even more advanced than that which grew out of the ruins brought about by the invasion of the Dorians. This is clear from various traits, of which one or two may be mentioned,

"First, the position of women, the keystone of the family, was as high as any that the world has yet seen; in many ways it strikingly reminds us of the family of our own day, and was far above the status of women in classical Athens. Women were on a virtual equality with men, mixing with them freely in domestic intercourse, and subject to none of the disabilities which weighed so heavily upon them in later times. In archæological discussions on the Homeric house we hear a great deal of the 'women's chambers'; but the phrase is an incorrect one, as incorrect as it would be if used of a modern London house. The women sit habitually among the men in the great common hall. There are of course besides the bedrooms, working chambers, and offices, which are used by the domestic slaves who are, for household duties, naturally women. But there is no trace of anything resembling the *gynaikonitis*[2] of later Greece, a separate part of the house where the woman was almost a prisoner, and where no man but the master of the house might penetrate. The conception of the home was, in fact, more like that of an English than of an Attic house.

"In religion, again, the Achaians held a distinctly more advanced position than did the Greeks of the classical period. The most salient point here is the absence of superstition. Charms and witchcraft are almost entirely absent; we hardly hear of more than of the stopping of blood by a charm in one passage of the *Odyssey*. Augury is indeed practiced, but it holds a quite subordinate position, and in one very famous passage of *Iliad* XII it is spoken of in terms of anything but respect. Though an omen at times may encourage or alarm the observer, it never on any occasion suggests or prevents an action of any importance; there is nothing in the least resembling the childish observance of sacrifices or birds by which not only the classical Greeks but even the sober Romans allowed the gravest decisions to be postponed or abandoned. We miss too the crowds of local deities who received in later times a higher and more earnest share of worship than the nominally supreme gods. Especially we notice the absence of all forms of the 'Chthonian' worship of the dread powers of the under-world in which superstition in later days was allowed to run riot. All these baser forms of belief which characterize the primitive stage of thought had been purged away; and even what is left is treated with a lightness which seems hardly to conceal failing belief. The passage of arms between Zeus and Hera at the end of *Iliad* I may stand as a type of all; the gods throughout are treated with scant respect, and are not even made ideals of moral virtue; far from

[2] Women's quarters in a house.

it. Here, again, the Achaians had gone far beyond the Greeks who succeeded them in the historic age.[3]

"So too in many of the customs which mark more particularly the primitive state later Greece is far richer than the heroic age. It is indeed remarkable, considering the early age of the poems, that they should have afforded so little material for the students of survivals from the first ages of culture. Relationship is virtually the same as in modern Europe; there is hardly a trace to be found of such early institutions as maternal descent instead of paternal, and none whatever of exogamy or other artificial restraints upon the choice of a wife. And what is still more remarkable, perhaps, is the entire absence of any tribal feeling as distinct from national. The only division in the Greek army of which we hear is the purely personal quarrel between Achilles and Agamemnon; there is no sign of this having ever passed into a division between the Myrmidons and Argives; and yet the preponderance of tribal feeling over national is one of the most universal signs of early civilization. That national feeling should be supreme, is the mark of the last step in the slow process of nation-making; and it had been won by the Achaians. We have only to think of Marathon[4] and Platæa to see how far they were in this respect beyond the Greeks of the fifth century.[5]

"It is clear, then, that between the time of the Achaians and the classical age the clock of civiliza-tion had been set far back. The invasion of the rude Dorians had destroyed the earlier culture, and the delicate plant took long to grow up again; and when it recovered, it was under other circumstances which materially altered its aspect. Though the Achaians were thorough Greeks, yet there is a gulf between them and the Greeks whom we best know which cannot be too clearly conceived.

"How then did it come to pass that the Homeric poems are thus in many ways more modern than later Greece? The answer is, I believe, to be found in the descent of the Ionians. The appearance of the Ionian name is the great mark of the difference between pre-historic and historic Greece. In Homer the Greeks are a unity—the Achaians. In the historic age they are found as three sharply sundered stems—Æolians, Dorians, and Ionians. We know who the Æolians were—they were descendants of the Achaians; we know who the Dorians were and whence they came; but who were these Ionians who are to us the type of all that is most Greek in the world of intellect at least?

"The answer is given us by the traditions of the Ionians themselves, and there is no reason for doubting it. The Ionians were the old pre-Hellenic or Pelasgian population Hellenized by the Achaians. Far from being ashamed of this mixture of blood, they gloried in it; the first aim of the Ionic Athenians was to magnify their old Autochtho-

[3] Later scholarship may quarrel with Walter Leaf at this point. It is probable that the Ionian poet (Homer) who shaped the *Iliad* and the *Odyssey* out of older Achæan lays and legends is responsible for the poems' sophistication in religious matters and comparative freedom from barbaric superstitions. This is the view held by the author of the most authoritative history of Greece, J. B. Bury (*A History of Greece*, 1900): "The *Iliad* was arrayed in Ionian dress . . . It is probable also that the Ionian poet also did much to adapt the epic material which he used to the taste and moral ideas of a more refined age. The *Iliad* is notably free from the features of crude savagery which generally mark the early literature of primitive peoples; only a few slight traces remain to show that there were in the background ugly and barbarous things over which a veil has been drawn."

As Professor Walter Woodburn Hyde has noted in his *Greek Religion and Its Survivals* (p. 18-19), "The Ionian bards did not always take the gods seriously or reverently, but often in their lays used them for ornament or even burlesque." The Achæans were probably anything but free from barbaric superstitions; only the final Ionian version of Achæan epic matter is free from them. Leaf's contrast between the religious outlook of the Homeric epics and that of the later Greeks is substantially correct. But the disappearance of the playful paganism of the Homeric age is the result, not of the character of the Ionian race, but of popular religious movements of the seventh and sixth centuries, especially of the so-called Orphic mysteries which took shape in Athens and its environs. Orphism revived many ancient popular beliefs, including fear of the ghost world, at the same time that it injected ethical content into Greek religion. The *Necyia* or *Descent into Hell* in the eleventh book of the *Odyssey*, which describes Hades, is held to be a later edition, reflecting the new movement.   J. G.

[4] See Herodotus' account of Marathon, p. 111 f. below.

[5] Here, too, some qualification is necessary. The Achæans had many petty kings and were divided into many small kingdoms. Professor Bury notes, "It is uncertain how far the Greek states of that time can be described as a federation or an empire." All that can be safely maintained is that the Trojan War was a joint expedition by the princes of Greece who had a common cause against the powerful city entrenched at the entrance of the Dardanelles which probably interfered with Greek enterprise; that most of the little states recognized the supremacy of Mycenæ, and that its king, Agamemnon, "succeeded in enlisting their cooperation."

nous descent, and to minimize the share of the Achaians in their blood. . . .

"We thus have an obvious explanation of the comparative modernness of the Homeric civilization as compared with that of Athens. The Autochthonous[6] population had preserved intact all their primitive beliefs and superstitions, while adopting the forms of the Achaian civilization; that is what always happens. But when the once dominant classes were removed to perish by an artistic but otherwise inglorious death in the Æolian colonies of Asia Minor and elsewhere, the older people, impregnated with their genius, sprang rapidly into independent life. But they did not drop the more primitive phases of belief which had clung to them; these rose to the surface with the rest of that marvelous Ionic genius, and many an ancient survival was enshrined in the literature or mythology of Athens which had long passed out of all remembrance of Mykenai. . . . Wherever the Pelasgians were strongest, in Attica, in Arcadia, and in Thessaly,—for these were the three sites of traditional Pelasgianism,—there we find the most abundant evidence of primitive thought; stone-worship in Athens and Arcadia—in Arcadia the were-wolf, in Thessaly witchcraft. It was, in fact, the cropping up of an older stratum which brought to light these remains of a hoary antiquity in a land whose former masters, so far as they are in evidence, had outlived them. This, then, is the fundamental mark of the gap between Homeric and classical Greece; a fresh start is taken from an earlier level, and all classical Greece bears witness to the fact.

"It must not of course be imagined that what I have called the modernness of the heroic age extended through the whole range of life. Many departments still retained a rudimentary complexion; in polity, in law, and in mechanical invention the Achaians were far behind the Greeks as we find them when they enter into history proper. But none the less the Achaians had reached a point in art, in religion, and in domestic relations which shows that they were an old nation, not a young one. They had accumulated wealth which enabled them to enjoy the cultured luxury which is the privilege of age; and with luxury the seeds of decay had begun to sprout. The Achaians had lost the love of war and fighting for its own sake; the sense of honor and the desire of plunder were the

motives which kept up the army of the Atreidai; their ideal was the happy nation of the Phaiakians, who lived far from tumult and could give themselves to the delights of song, feast, and dance. It is impossible not to be reminded of the happy land of the Counts of Toulouse in the twelfth century, where a whole people lived in an atmosphere of luxury and song. The realm of Agamemnon, like the realm of Raymond, went down before the attack of the rude barbarians from the North. But, unlike Toulouse, Mykenai has left us two immortal treasures: first, the Ionian genius which thence drew life; and secondly, the great Epic, a monument happily more perfect and more enduring than even the Lion-gate of Mykenai itself."

As the new Greeks emerged they displayed qualities of leadership in every department of life. Though Athens became gradually the center for great cultural activity there were many other places where the Greeks lived and showed their characteristic ability. The island of Lesbos near the Asiatic shore and, in due time, Sicily produced literature of high quality. And many Greek cities made their contributions to philosophy. In the period beginning in the sixth century, culminating in the fifth in the Age of Pericles in Athens, and extending down almost to the beginning of the Christian Era, the entire world was dominated by the genius of Greece. Before actually reading the literature of these later Greeks it may be well to consider something of the nature of their contribution to the world. Gilbert Murray, whose essay follows, is one of the closest students and most understanding interpreters of the life and works of this highly gifted people.

The literary genius of the post-Homeric Greeks, as an expression of their new culture and outlook, is evident in the types of literature they developed.

Lyric poetry attains perfection as early as the seventh century, and it continues to be elaborated for centuries; its masters—Sappho, Pindar, Theocritus, and others—rank with the world's greatest lyricists. One of the most notable achievements appears in the composition of history, which reached its peak in the fifth-century work of Herodotus and Thucydides; another in their creation of drama, associated with the great fifth-century names of Æschylus, Sophocles, Euripides, and Aristophanes. The art of literary criticism also becomes established when Aristotle begins to investigate the nature of tragedy and epic poetry in the

[6] Original inhabitants.

fourth century; and satire and oratory owe their inception as a written art to the same age. Finally, these Greeks not only create Western philosophy but bring it to an eminence unsurpassed.

In most of these literary pastures the Romans merely follow them; and it is for this reason that later Latin masterpieces are grouped with their Greek antecedents in the case of certain literary forms such as comedy, lyric poetry, satire, and philosophy.

GILBERT MURRAY

The Value of Greece to the Future of the World

If the value of man's life on earth is to be measured in dollars and miles and horse-power, ancient Greece must count as a poverty-stricken and a minute territory; its engines and implements were nearer to the spear and bow of the savage than to our own telegraph and aeroplane. Even if we neglect merely material things and take as our standard the actual achievements of the race in conduct and in knowledge, the average clerk who goes to town daily, idly glancing at his morning news-paper, is probably a better behaved and infinitely better informed person than the average Athenian who sat spellbound at the tragedies of Æschylus. It is only by the standard of the spirit, to which the thing achieved is little and the quality of mind that achieved it much, which cares less for the sum of knowledge attained than for the love of knowledge, less for much good policing than for one free act of heroism, that the great age of Greece can be judged as something extraordinary and unique in value.

By this standard, if it is a legitimate and reasonable one to apply, we shall be able to understand why classical Greek literature was the basis of education throughout all later antiquity; why its re-discovery, however fragmentary and however imperfectly understood, was able to intoxicate the keenest minds of Europe and constitute a kind of spiritual "Re-birth," and how its further and further exploration may be still a task worth men's spending their lives upon and capable of giving mankind guidance as well as inspiration.

But is such a standard legitimate and reasonable? We shall gain nothing by unanalyzed phrases. But I think surely it is merely the natural standard of any philosophical historian. Suppose it is argued that an average optician at the present day knows more optics than Roger Bacon, the inventor of spectacles; suppose it is argued that therefore he is, as far as optics go, a greater man, and that Roger Bacon has nothing to teach us; what is the answer? It is, I suppose, that Roger Bacon, receiving a certain amount of knowledge from his teachers, had that in him which turned it to unsuspected directions and made it immensely greater and more fruitful. The average optician has probably added a little to what he was taught, but not much, and has doubtless forgotten or confused a good deal. So that, if by studying Roger Bacon's life or his books we could get into touch with his mind and acquire some of that special moving and inspiring quality of his, it would help us far more than would the mere knowledge of the optician.

This truth is no doubt hard to see in the case of purely technical science; in books of wider range, such as Darwin's for instance, it is easy for any reader to feel the presence of a really great mind, producing inspiration of a different sort from that of the most excellent up-to-date examination text

The Value of Greece to the Future of the World. From *The Legacy of Greece.* By permission of The Oxford University Press. Gilbert Murray, Regius Professor of Greek at Oxford, was born in Australia in 1866 and has had a distinguished career as a Greek scholar, teacher, and translator of Euripides.

book. In philosophy, religion, poetry, and the highest kinds of art, the greatness of the author's mind seems as a rule to be all that matters; one almost ignores the date at which he worked. This is because in technical sciences the element of mere fact, or mere knowledge, is so enormous, the elements of imagination, character, and the like so very small. Hence, books on science, in a progressive age, very quickly become "out of date," and each new edition usually supersedes the last. It is the rarest thing for a work of science to survive as a text-book more than ten years or so. Newton's *Principia* is almost an isolated instance among modern writings.

Yet there are some few such books. Up till about the year 1900 the elements of geometry were regularly taught, throughout Europe, in a text-book written by a Greek called Eucleides in the fourth or third century B.C. That text-book lasted over two thousand years. Now, of course, people have discovered a number of faults in Euclid, but it has taken them all that time to do it.

Again, I knew an old gentleman who told me that, at a good English school in the early nineteenth century, he had been taught the principles of grammar out of a writer called Dionysius Thrax, or Denis of Thrace. Denis was a Greek of the first century B.C., who made or carried out the remarkable discovery that there was such a thing as a science of grammar, i.e., that men in their daily speech were unconsciously obeying an extraordinarily subtle and intricate body of laws, which were capable of being studied and reduced to order. Denis did not make the whole discovery himself; he was led to it by his master Aristarchus and others. And his book had been re-edited several times in the nineteen-hundred odd years before this old gentleman was taught it.

To take a third case: all through later antiquity and the Middle Ages the science of medicine was based on the writings of two ancient doctors, Hippocrates and Galen. Galen was a Greek who lived at Rome in the early Empire, Hippocrates a Greek who lived at the island of Cos in the fifth century B.C. A great part of the history of modern medicine is a story of emancipation from the dead hand of these great ancients. But one little treatise attributed to Hippocrates was in active use in the training of medical students in my own day in Scotland and is still in use in some American Universities. It was the Oath taken by medical students in the classic age of Greece when they solemnly faced the duties of their profession. The disciple swore to honor and obey his teacher and care for his children if ever they were in need; always to help his patients to the best of his power; never to use or profess to use magic or charms or any supernatural means; never to supply poison or perform illegal operations; never to abuse the special position of intimacy which a doctor naturally obtains in a sick house, but always on entering to remember that he goes as a friend and helper to every individual in it.

We have given up that oath now: I suppose we do not believe so much in the value of oaths. But the man who first drew up that oath did a great deed. He realized and defined the meaning of his high calling in words which doctors of unknown tongues and undiscovered countries accepted from him and felt to express their aims for well over two thousand years.

Now what do I want to illustrate by these three instances? The rapidity with which we are now at last throwing off the last vestiges of the yoke of Greece? No, not that. I want to point out that even in the realm of science, where progress is so swift and books so short-lived, the Greeks of the great age had such genius and vitality that their books lived in a way that no others have lived. Let us get away from the thought of Euclid as an inky and imperfect English school-book, to that ancient Eucleides who, with exceedingly few books but a large table of sand let into the floor, planned and discovered and put together and re-shaped the first laws of geometry, till at last he had written one of the great simple books of the world, a book which should stand a pillar and beacon to mankind long after all the political world that Eucleides knew had been swept away and the kings he served were conquered by the Romans, and the Romans in course of time conquered by the barbarians, and the barbarians themselves, with much labor and reluctance, partly by means of Eucleides' book, eventually educated; so that at last, in our own day, they can manage to learn their geometry without it. The time has come for Euclid to be superseded; let him go. He has surely held the torch for mankind long enough; and books of science are born to be superseded. What I want to suggest is that the same extraordinary vitality of mind which made Hippocrates and Euclid and even Denis of Thrace last their two thousand years, was also put by the Greeks of the great age into those activities which are, for the most part at any rate, not perishable or progressive but eternal.

This is a simple point, but it is so important that

we must dwell on it for a moment. If we read an old treatise on medicine or mechanics, we may admire it and feel it a work of genius, but we also feel that it is obsolete: its work is over; we have got beyond it. But when we read Homer or Æschylus, if once we have the power to admire and understand their writing, we do not for the most part have any feeling of having got beyond them. We have done so no doubt in all kinds of minor things, in general knowledge, in details of technique, in civilization and the like; but hardly any sensible person ever imagines that he has got beyond their essential quality, the quality that has made them great.

Doubtless there is in every art an element of mere knowledge or science, and that element is progressive. But there is another element, too, which does not depend on knowledge and which does not progress but has a kind of stationary and eternal value, like the beauty of the dawn, or the love of a mother for her child, or the joy of a young animal in being alive, or the courage of a martyr facing torment. We cannot for all our progress get beyond these things; there they stand, like light upon the mountains. The only question is whether we can rise to them. And it is the same with all the greatest births of human imagination. As far as we can speculate, there is not the faintest probability of any poet ever setting to work on, let us say, the essential effect aimed at by Æschylus in the Cassandra-scene of the *Agamemnon,* and doing it better than Æschylus. The only thing which the human race has to do with that scene is to understand it and get out of it all the joy and emotion and wonder that it contains.

This eternal quality is perhaps clearest in poetry: in poetry the mixture of knowledge matters less. In art there is a constant development of tools and media and technical processes. The modern artist can feel that, though he cannot, perhaps, make as good a statue as Pheidias, he could here and there have taught Pheidias something: and at any rate he can try his art on subjects far more varied and more stimulating to his imagination. In philosophy the mixture is more subtle and more profound. Philosophy always depends in some sense upon science, yet the best philosophy seems generally to have in it some eternal quality of creative imagination. Plato wrote a dialogue about the constitution of the world, the *Timæus,* which was highly influential in later Greece, but seems to us, with our vastly superior scientific knowledge, almost nonsensical. Yet when Plato writes about the theory of knowledge or the ultimate meaning of Justice or of Love, no good philosopher can afford to leave him aside: the chief question is whether we can rise to the height and subtlety of his thought.

And here another point emerges, equally simple and equally important if we are to understand our relation to the past. Suppose a man says: "I quite understand that Plato or Æschylus may have had fine ideas, but surely anything of value which they said must long before this have become common property. There is no need to go back to the Greeks for it. We do not go back and read Copernicus to learn that the earth goes round the sun." What is the answer? It is that such a view ignores exactly this difference between the progressive and the eternal, between knowledge and imagination. If Harvey discovers that the blood is not stationary but circulates, if Copernicus discovers that the earth goes round the sun and not the sun round the earth, those discoveries can easily be communicated in the most abbreviated form. If a mechanic invents an improvement on the telephone, or a social reformer puts some good usage in the place of a bad one, in a few years we shall probably all be using the improvement without even knowing what it is or saying Thank you. We may be as stupid as we like, we have in a sense got the good of it.

But can one apply the same process to *Macbeth* or *Romeo and Juliet?* Can anyone tell us in a few words what they come to? Or can a person get the good of them in any way except one—the way of vivid and loving study, following and feeling the author's meaning all through? To suppose, as I believe some people do, that you can get the value of a great poem by studying an abstract of it in an encyclopædia or by reading cursorily an average translation of it, argues really a kind of mental deficiency, like deafness or color-blindness. The things that we have called eternal, the things of the spirit and the imagination, always seem to lie more in a process than in a result, and can only be reached and enjoyed by somehow going through the process again. If the value of a particular walk lies in the scenery, you do not get that value by taking a short cut or using a fast motor-car.

In looking back, then, upon any vital and significant age of the past we shall find objects of two kinds. First, there will be things like the Venus of Milo or the Book of Job or Plato's *Republic,* which are interesting or precious in themselves, because of their own inherent qualities; secondly, there will be things like the Roman code of the Twelve Tables or the invention of the printing press or the record of certain great battles, which are interesting chiefly because they are causes of other and greater things or form knots in the great web of history—the first having artistic interest, the second only historical interest, though, of course, it is obvious that in any concrete case there is generally a mixture of both.

Now Ancient Greece is important in both ways. For the artist or poet it has in a quite extraordinary degree the quality of beauty. For instance, to take a contrast with Rome: if you dig about the Roman Wall in Cumberland you will find quantities of objects, altars, inscriptions, figurines, weapons, boots and shoes, which are full of historic interest but are not much more beautiful than the contents of a modern rubbish heap. And the same is true of most excavations all over the world. But if you dig at any classical or sub-classical site in the Greek world, however unimportant historically, practically every object you find will be beautiful. The wall itself will be beautiful; the inscriptions will be beautifully cut; the figurines, however cheap and simple, may have some intentional grotesques among them, but the rest will have a special truthfulness and grace; the vases will be of good shapes and the patterns will be beautiful patterns. If you happen to dig in a burying-place and come across some epitaphs on the dead, they will practically all—even when the verses do not quite scan and the words are wrongly spelt—have about them this inexplicable touch of beauty.

I am anxious not to write nonsense about this. One could prove the point in detail by taking any collection of Greek epitaphs, and that is the only way in which it can be proved. The beauty is a fact, and if we try to analyze the sources of it we shall perhaps in part understand how it has come to pass.

In the first place, it is not a beauty of ornament; it is a beauty of structure, a beauty of rightness and simplicity. Compare an athlete in flannels playing tennis and a stout dignitary smothered in gold robes. Or compare a good modern yacht, swift, lithe, and plain, with a lumbering, heavily gilded, sixteenth-century galleon, or even with a Chinese state junk: the yacht is far the more beautiful though she has not a hundredth part of the ornament. It is she herself that is beautiful, because her lines and structure are right. The others are essentially clumsy and, therefore, ugly things, dabbed over with gold and paint. Now ancient Greek things for the most part have the beauty of the yacht. The Greeks used paint a good deal, but apart from that a Greek temple is almost as plain as a shed: people accustomed to arabesques and stained glass and gargoyles can very often see nothing in it. A Greek statue has as a rule no ornament at all: a young man racing or praying, an old man thinking, there it stands expressed in a stately and simple convention, true or false, the anatomy and the surfaces right or wrong, aiming at no beauty except the truest. It would probably seem quite dull to the maker of a medieval wooden figure of a king which I remember seeing in a town in the east of Europe: a crown blazing with many-colored glass, a long crimson robe covered with ornaments and beneath them an idiot face, no bones, no muscles, no attitude. That is not what a Greek meant by beauty. The same quality holds to a great extent of Greek poetry. Not, of course, that the artistic convention was the same, or at all similar, for treating stone and for treating language. Greek poetry is statuesque in the sense that it depends greatly on its organic structure; it is not in the least so in the sense of being cold or colorless or stiff. But Greek poetry on the whole has a bareness and severity which disappoints a modern reader, accustomed as he is to lavish ornament and exaggeration at every turn. It has the same simplicity and straightforwardness as Greek sculpture. The poet has something to say and he says it as well and truly as he can in the suitable style, and if you are not interested you are not. With some exceptions which explain themselves he does not play a thousand pretty tricks and antics on the way, so that you may forget the dullness of what he says in amusement at the draperies in which he wraps it.

But here comes an apparent difficulty. Greek poetry, we say, is very direct, very simple, very free from irrelevant ornament. And yet when we translate it into English and look at our translation, our main feeling, I think, is that somehow the glory has gone: a thing that was high and lordly has become poor and mean. Any decent Greek scholar when he opens one of his ancient poets feels at once the presence of something lofty and rare—something like the atmosphere of *Paradise Lost*. But the language of *Paradise Lost* is elaborately twisted and embellished into loftiness and rarity; the language of the Greek poem is simple and direct. What does this mean?

I can only suppose that the normal language of Greek poetry is in itself in some sense sublime

Most critics accept this as an obvious fact, yet, if true, it is a very strange fact and worth thinking about. It depends partly on mere euphony: *Khaireis horôn fôs* is probably more beautiful in sound than "You rejoice to see the light," but euphony cannot be everything. The sound of a great deal of Greek poetry, either as we pronounce it or as the ancients pronounced it, is to modern ears almost ugly. It depends partly, perhaps, on the actual structure of the Greek language: philologists tell us that, viewed as a specimen, it is in structure and growth and in power of expressing things, the most perfect language they know. And certainly one often finds that a thought can be expressed with ease and grace in Greek which becomes clumsy and involved in Latin, English, French or German. But neither of these causes goes, I think, to the root of the matter.

What is it that gives words their character and makes a style high or low? Obviously, their associations; the company they habitually keep in the minds of those who use them. A word which belongs to the language of bars and billiard saloons will become permeated by the normal standard of mind prevalent in such places; a word which suggests Milton or Carlyle will have the flavor of those men's minds about it. I therefore cannot resist the conclusion that, if the language of Greek poetry has, to those who know it intimately, this special quality of keen austere beauty, it is because the minds of the poets who used that language were habitually toned to a higher level both of intensity and of nobility than ours. It is a finer language because it expresses the minds of finer men. By "finer men" I do not necessarily mean men who behaved better, either by our standards or by their own; I mean men to whom the fine things of the world, sunrise and sea and stars and the love of man for man, and strife and the facing of evil for the sake of good, and even common things like meat and drink, and evil things like hate and terror, had, as it were, a keener edge than they have for us and roused a swifter and a nobler reaction.

Let us resume this argument before going further. We start from the indisputable fact that the Greeks of about the fifth century B.C. did for some reason or other produce various works of art, buildings and statues and books, especially books, which instead of decently dying or falling out of fashion in the lifetime of the men who made them, lasted on and can still cause high thoughts and intense emotions. In trying to explain this strange fact we notice that the Greeks had a great and pervading instinct for beauty, and for beauty of a particular kind. It is a beauty which never lies in irrelevant ornament, but always in the very essence and structure of the object made. In literature we found that the special beauty which we call Greek depends partly on the directness, truthfulness, and simplicity with which the Greeks say what they want to say, and partly on a special keenness and nobility in the language, which seems the natural expression of keen and noble minds. Can we in any way put all these things together so as to explain them—or at any rate to hold them together more clearly?

An extremely old and often misleading metaphor will help us. People have said: "The world was young then." Of course, strictly speaking, it was not. In the total age of the world or of man the two thousand odd years between us and Pericles do not count for much. Nor can we imagine that a man of sixty felt any more juvenile in the fifth century than he does now. It was just the other way, because at that time there were no spectacles or false teeth. Yet in a sense the world *was* young then, at any rate our western world, the world of progress and humanity. For the beginnings of nearly all the great things that progressive minds now care for were then being laid in Greece.

Youth, perhaps, is not exactly the right word. There are certain plants—some kinds of aloes, for instance—which continue for an indefinite number of years in a slow routine of ordinary life close to the ground, and then suddenly, when they have stored enough vital force, grow ten feet high and burst into flower, after which, no doubt, they die or show signs of exhaustion. Apart from the dying, it seems as if something like that happened from time to time to the human race, or to such parts of it as really bear flowers at all. For most races and nations during the most of their life are not progressive but simply stagnant, sometimes just managing to preserve their standard customs, sometimes slipping back to the slough. That is why history has nothing to say about them. The history of the world consists mostly in the memory of those ages, quite few in number, in which some part of the world has risen above itself and burst into flower or fruit.

We ourselves happen to live in the midst or possibly in the close of one such period. More change has probably taken place in daily life, in ideas, and in the general aspect of the earth during the last century than during any four other centuries since the Christian era: and this fact has tended to make us look on rapid progress as a normal condition of the human race, which it never has been. And another such period of bloom, a bloom comparatively short in time and narrow in area, but amazingly swift and intense, occurred in the lower parts of the Balkan Peninsula from about the sixth to the fourth centuries before Christ.

Now it is this kind of bloom which fills the world with hope and therefore makes it young. Take a man who has just made a discovery or an invention, a man happily in love, a man who is starting some great and successful social movement, a man who is writing a book or painting a picture which he knows to be good; take men who have been fighting in some great cause which before they fought seemed to be hopeless and now is triumphant; think of England when the Armada was just defeated, France at the first dawn of the Revolution, America after Yorktown: such men and nations will be above themselves. Their powers will be stronger and keener; there will be exhilaration in the air, a sense of walking in new paths, of dawning hopes and untried possibilities, a confidence that all things can be won if only we try hard enough. In that sense the world will be young. In that sense I think it was young in the time of Themistocles and Æschylus. And it is that youth which is half the secret of the Greek spirit.

And here I may meet an objection that has perhaps been lurking in the minds of many readers. "All this," they may say, "professes to be a simple analysis of known facts, but in reality is sheer idealization. These Greeks whom you call so 'noble' have been long since exposed. Anthropology has turned its searchlights upon them. It is not only their plows, their weapons, their musical instruments, and their painted idols that resemble those of the savages; it is everything else about them. Many of them were sunk in the most degrading superstitions: many practiced unnatural vices: in times of great fear some were apt to think that the best 'medicine' was a human sacrifice. After that, it is hardly worth mentioning that their social structure was largely based on slavery; that they lived in petty little towns, like so many wasps' nests, each at war with its next-door neighbor, and half of them at war with themselves!"

If our anti-Greek went further he would probably cease to speak the truth. We will stop him while we can still agree with him. These charges are on the whole true, and, if we are to understand what Greece means, we must realize and digest them. We must keep hold of two facts: first, that the Greeks of the fifth century produced some of the noblest poetry and art, the finest political thinking, the most vital philosophy, known to the world; second, that the people who heard and saw, nay, perhaps, even the people who produced these wonders, were separated by a thin and precarious interval from the savage. Scratch a civilized Russian, they say, and you find a wild Tartar. Scratch an ancient Greek, and you hit, no doubt, on a very primitive and formidable being, somewhere between a Viking and a Polynesian.

That is just the magic and the wonder of it. The spiritual effort implied is so tremendous. We have read stories of savage chiefs converted by Christian or Buddhist missionaries, who within a year or so have turned from drunken corroborees and bloody witch-smellings to a life that is not only godly but even philanthropic and statesmanlike. We have seen the Japanese lately go through some centuries of normal growth in the space of a generation. But in all such examples men have only been following the teaching of a superior civilization, and after all, they have not ended by producing works of extraordinary and original genius. It seems quite clear that the Greeks owed exceedingly little to foreign influence. Even in their decay they were a race, as Professor Bury observes, accustomed "to take little and to give much." They built up their civilization for themselves. We must listen with due attention to the critics who have pointed out all the remnants of savagery and superstition that they find in Greece: the slave-driver, the fetish-worshiper and the medicine-man, the trampler on women, the bloodthirsty hater of all outside his own town and party. But it is not those people that constitute Greece; those people can be found all over the historical world, commoner than blackberries. It is not anything fixed and stationary that constitutes Greece: what constitutes Greece is the movement which leads from all these to the Stoic or fifth-century "sophist" who condemns and denies slavery, who has abolished all cruel superstitions and preaches some religion based on philosophy and humanity, who claims for women the same spiritual rights as for man, who looks on all human creatures as his brethren, and the world as "one great City of gods and men." It is that movement which you will not find elsewhere, any more than the statues of Pheidias or the dialogues of Plato or the poems of Æschylus and Euripides.

From all this two or three results follow. For one thing, being built up so swiftly, by such keen effort, and from so low a starting-point, Greek civilization was, amid all its glory, curiously unstable and full of flaws. Such flaws made it, of course, much worse for those who lived in it, but they hardly make it less interesting or instructive to those who study it. Rather the contrary. Again, the near neighborhood of the savage gives to the Greek mind certain qualities which we of the safer [10] and solider civilizations would give a great deal to possess. It springs swift and straight. It is never jaded. Its wonder and interest about the world are fresh. And lastly there is one curious and very important quality which, unless I am mistaken, belongs to Greek civilization more than to any other. To an extraordinary degree it starts clean from nature, with almost no entanglements of elaborate creeds and customs and traditions.

I am not, of course, forgetting the prehistoric [20] Minoan civilization, nor yet the peculiar forms—mostly simple enough—into which the traditional Greek religion fell. It is possible that I may be a little misled by my own habit of living much among Greek things and so forgetting through long familiarity how odd some of them once seemed. But when all allowances are made, I think that this clean start from nature is, on the whole, a true claim. If a thoughtful European or American wants to study Chinese or Indian things, [30] he has not only to learn certain data of history and mythology, he has to work his mind into a particular attitude; to put on, as it were, spectacles of a particular sort. If he wants to study medieval things, if he takes even so universal a poet as Dante, it is something the same. Curious views about the Pope and the emperor, a crabbed scholastic philosophy, a strange and to the modern mind rather horrible theology, floating upon the flames of Hell: all these have somehow to be taken [40] into his imagination before he can understand his Dante. With Greek things this is very much less so. The historical and imaginative background of the various great poets and philosophers is, no doubt, highly important. A great part of the work of modern scholarship is now devoted to getting it clearer. But on the whole, putting aside for the moment the possible inadequacies of translation, Greek philosophy speaks straight to any human being who is willing to think simply, Greek art [50] and poetry to anyone who can use his imagination and enjoy beauty. He has not to put on the fetters or the blinkers of any new system in order to understand them; he has only to get rid of his own—a much more profitable and less troublesome task.

This particular conclusion will scarcely, I think, be disputed, but the point presents difficulties and must be dwelt upon.

In the first place, it does not mean that Greek art is what we call "naturalist" or "realist." It is markedly the reverse. Art to the Greek is always a form of *Sophia,* or Wisdom, a *Techné* with rules that have to be learnt. Its air of utter simplicity is deceptive. The pillar that looks merely straight is really a thing of subtle curves. The funeral bas-relief that seems to represent in the simplest possible manner a woman saying good-by to her child is arranged, plane behind plane, with the most delicate skill and sometimes with deliberate falsification of perspective. There is always some convention, some idealization, some touch of the light that never was on sea or land. Yet all the time, I think, Greek art remains in a remarkable degree close to nature. The artist's eye is always on the object, and, though he represents it in his own style, that style is always normal and temperate, free from affectation, free from exaggeration or morbidity and, in the earlier periods, free from conventionality. It is art without doubt; but it is natural and normal art, such as grew spontaneously when mankind first tried in freedom to express beauty. For example, the language of Greek poetry is markedly different from that of prose, and there are even clear differences of language between different styles of poetry. And further, the poetry is very seldom about the present. It is about the past, and that an ideal past. What we have to notice there is that this kind of rule, which has been usual in all great ages of poetry, is apparently not an artificial or arbitrary thing but a tendency that grew up naturally with the first great expressions of poetical feeling.

Furthermore, this closeness to nature, this absence of a unifying or hide-bound system of thought, acting together with other causes, has led to the extraordinary variety and many-sidedness which is one of the most puzzling charms of Ancient Greece as contrasted, say, with Israel or Assyria or early Rome. Geographically it is a small country with a highly indented coast-line and an interior cut into a great number of almost isolated valleys. Politically it was a confused unity made up of numerous independent states, one walled city of a few thousand inhabitants being quite enough to form a state. And the citizens of these states were, each of them, rather excessively capable of forming opinions of their own and fighting for them. Hence came in practice much isolation and faction and general weakness, to the detriment of the Greeks themselves; but the same cause led in thought and literature to immense variety and vitality, to the great gain of us who study the Greeks afterwards. There is hardly any type of thought or style of writing which cannot be paralleled in ancient Greece, only they will there be seen, as it were, in their earlier and simpler forms. Traces of all the things that seem most un-Greek can be found somewhere in Greek literature: voluptuousness, asceticism, the worship of knowledge, the contempt for knowledge, atheism, pietism, the religion of serving the world and the religion of turning away from the world: all these and almost all other points of view one can think of are represented somewhere in the records of that one small people. And there is hardly any single generalization in this chapter which the author himself could not controvert by examples to the contrary. You feel in general a great absence of all fetters: the human mind free, rather inexperienced, intensely interested in life and full of hope, trying in every direction for that excellence which the Greeks called *areté,* and guided by peculiar instinct toward Temperance and Beauty.

The variety is there and must not be forgotten; yet amid the variety there are certain general or central characteristics, mostly due to this same quality of freshness and closeness to nature.

If you look at a Greek statue or bas-relief, or if you read an average piece of Aristotle, you will very likely at first feel bored. Why? Because it is all so normal and truthful; so singularly free from exaggeration, paradox, violent emphasis; so destitute of those fascinating by-forms of insanity which appeal to some similar faint element of insanity in ourselves. "We are sick," we may exclaim, "of the sight of these handsome, perfectly healthy men with grave faces and normal bones and muscles! We are sick of being told that Virtue is a mean between two extremes and tends to make men happy! We shall not be interested unless someone tells us that Virtue is the utter abnegation of self, or, it may be, the extreme and ruthless assertion of self; or again, that Virtue is all an infamous mistake!

What is at the back of this sort of feeling? which I admit often takes more reasonable forms than these I have suggested. It is the same psycho-

logical cause that brings about the changes of fashion in art or dress: which loves "stunts" and makes the fortunes of yellow newspapers. It is boredom or *ennui.* We have had too much of A; we are sick of it; we know how it is done and despise it; give us some B, or better still some Z. And after a strong dose of Z we shall crave for the beginning of the alphabet again. But now think of a person who is not bored at all; who is, on the contrary, immensely interested in the world, keen to choose good things and reject bad ones; full of the desire for knowledge and the excitement of discovery. The joy to him is to see things as they are and to judge them normally. He is not bored by the sight of normal, healthy muscles in a healthy, well-shaped body; he is delighted. If you distort the muscles for emotional effect, he would say with disappointment: "But that is ugly!" or "But a man's muscles do *not* go like that!" He will have noted that tears are salt and rather warm; but if you say like a modern poet that your heroine's tears are "more hot than fire, more salt than the salt sea," he will probably think your statement ἀπίθανον "unpersuasive," and therefore ψυχρόν "chilling."

It is perhaps especially in the religious and moral sphere that we are accustomed to the habitual use of ecstatic language: expressions that are only true of exalted moments are used by us as the commonplaces of ordinary life. "It is a thousand times worse to see another suffer than to suffer oneself." "True love only desires the happiness of the beloved object." This kind of "high falutin'" has become part of our regular mental habit, just as dead metaphors by the bushel are part of our daily language. Consequently we are a little chilled and disappointed by a language in which people hardly ever use a metaphor except when they vividly realize it, and never utter heroic sentiments except when they are wrought up to the pitch of feeling them true. Does this mean that the Greek always remains, so to speak, at a normal temperature, that he never has intense or blinding emotions? Not in the least. It shows a lack of faith in the value of life to imagine such a conclusion It implies that you can only reach great emotion by pretense, or by habitually exaggerating small emotions, whereas probably the exact reverse is the case. When the great thing comes, then the Greek will have the great word and the great thought ready. It is the habitual exaggerator who will perhaps be bankrupt. And after all—the great things are sure to come!

The power of seeing things straight and knowing what is beautiful or noble, quite undisturbed by momentary boredoms or changes of taste, is a very rare gift and never perhaps possessed in full by anyone. But there is a profound rule of art, bidding a man in the midst of all his study of various styles or his pursuit of his own peculiar imaginations, from time to time *se retremper dans la nature*—"to steep himself again in nature." And in something the same way it seems as if the world ought from time to time to steep itself again in Hellenism: that is, it ought, amid all the varying affectations and extravagances and changes of convention in art and letters, to have some careful regard for those which arose when man first awoke to the meaning of truth and beauty and saw the world freely as a new thing.

Is this exaggeration? I think not. But no full defense of it can be attempted here. In this essay we have been concerned almost entirely with the artistic interest of Greece. It would be equally possible to dwell on the historical interest. Then we should find that, for that branch of mankind which is responsible for western civilization, the seeds of almost all that we count best in human progress were sown in Greece. The conception of beauty as a joy in itself and as a guide in life was first and most vividly expressed in Greece, and the very laws by which things are beautiful or ugly were to a great extent discovered there and laid down. The conception of Freedom and Justice, freedom in body, in speech and in mind, justice between the strong and the weak, the rich and the poor, penetrates the whole of Greek political thought, and was, amid obvious flaws, actually realized to a remarkable degree in the best Greek communities. The conception of Truth as an end to pursue for its own sake, a thing to discover and puzzle out by experiment and imagination and especially by Reason, a conception essentially allied with that of Freedom and opposed both to anarchy and to blind obedience, has perhaps never in the world been more clearly grasped than by the early Greek writers on science and philosophy. One stands amazed sometimes at the perfect freedom of their thought. Another conception came rather later, when the small City States with exclusive rights of citizenship had been merged in a larger whole: the conception of the universal fellowship between man and man. Greece realized soon after the Persian war that she had a mission to the world, that Hellenism stood for the higher life of man as against barbarism, for Aretê, or Excel-

lence, as against the mere effortless average. First came the crude patriotism which regarded every Greek as superior to every barbarian; then came reflection, showing that not all Greeks were true bearers of the light, nor all barbarians its enemies; that Hellenism was a thing of the spirit and not dependent on the race to which a man belonged or the place where he was born: then came the new word and conception ἀνθρωπότης, *humanitas*, which to the Stoics made the world as one brotherhood. No people known to history clearly formulated these ideals before the Greeks, and those who have spoken the words afterwards seem for the most part to be merely echoing the thoughts of old Greek men.

These ideas, the pursuit of Truth, Freedom, Beauty, Excellence, are not everything. They have been a leaven of unrest in the world; they have held up a light which was not always comforting to the eyes to see. There is another ideal which is generally stronger and may, for all we know, in the end stamp them out as evil things. There is Submission instead of Freedom, the deadening or brutalizing of the senses instead of Beauty, the acceptance of tradition instead of the pursuit of Truth, the belief in hallucination or passion instead of Reason and Temperate Thought, the obscuring of distinction between good and bad and the acceptance of all human being and all states of mind as equal in value. If something of this kind should prove in the end to be right for man, then Greece will have played the part of the great wrecker in human history. She will have held up false lights which have lured our ship to dangerous places. But at any rate, through calm and storm, she does hold her lights; she lit them first of the nations and held them during her short reign the clearest; and whether we believe in an individual life founded on Freedom, Reason, Beauty, Excellence and the pursuit of Truth, and an international life aiming at the fellowship between man and man, or whether we think these ideals the great snares of human politics, there is good cause for some of us in each generation at the cost of some time and trouble to study such important forces where they first appear consciously in the minds of our spiritual ancestors. In the thought and art of ancient Greece, more than any other, we shall find these forces, and also to some extent their great opposites, fresh, clean and comparatively uncomplicated, with every vast issue wrought out on a small material scale and every problem stated in its lowest terms.

THE AGE OF PERICLES

Although Greek lyricism begins to flourish before the fifth century and in centers other than Athens, the whole stream of post-Homeric classic literature has its fountainhead in the city dear to Pallas Athene during the years of its supremacy. We may, therefore, conclude our preface to this literature with a brief survey of this remarkable age.

It began when Athens assumed the political leadership of Greece and established an empire. The process was slow but steady. After a long and obscure early history, during which Athens mastered the sea-girt territory of Attica, the city forged ahead socially, culturally, and politically. Following class-conflicts between the old landed families and the middle classes and peasantry, Athens received a democratic constitution under Solon at the beginning of the sixth century. Simultaneously the city extended its political power by conquering Salamis and Nisæa, and became increasingly prosperous by devoting itself to trade.

More progress and stabilization was achieved under the democratic tyrant Pisistratus, who began to lead Athens to empire by gradual stages of conquest, colonial settlements, and cultural preeminence among the Ionian states. It was during his reign and that of his son Hippias that the city took the Ionian festival at Delos under its special care; made organized Homeric recitations a feature of its Panathenaic festival; encouraged the development of the theater by inaugurating dramatic contests at the popular festival known as the Great Dionysia of the city; and began to promote architecture and sculpture. Prominent poets, like Simonides of Ceos, noted for his choral odes, and Anacreon, "the singer of wine and love," were also welcomed to the court of Hippias.

In 510 B.C. Athens rid itself of its benevolent tyrants and came under the leadership of a great democratic reformer, Cleisthenes. He corrected various abuses, opened Athenian citizenship to a large number of people hitherto excluded, and won important military victories. However, at about this time Athens was suddenly exposed to the greatest threat in its history, when the Persian king Darius decided to chastise Athens and other Greek cities for aiding the revolt of the Ionian colonies in Asia Minor. It was against the massed power of the great king that the Athenians scored their great triumph, at Marathon in 490 B.C. Since the Spartan army, which came to support them, arrived too late, the prestige of victory went entirely to Athens. "The enormous prestige which she won by the single-handed victory . . . gave her new self-confidence and ambition; history seemed to have set a splendid seal on her democracy; she felt she could trust her constitution and that she might lift her head as high as any state in Hellas. The Athenians always looked back to Marathon as marking an epoch. It was as if on that day the gods said to them, Go on and prosper."[1] On the practical side, Athenian democracy underwent further extensions, and the Athenian fleet was increased by Themistocles, who realized the importance of making the city a sea-power.

This was followed by a second peril, in 480 B.C., in the form of the more ambitious and powerful invasion of Greece by Xerxes, the son of Darius. The Spartans at Thermopylæ were unable to stem it; Attica was invaded, and the Acropolis in Athens captured by the Persians. The future looked dark to the Greeks. Once more, however, Athens asserted itself, this time in the momentous sea-battle off the island of Salamis, which crushed the naval power of the enemy. Although his land forces were only temporarily checked, and were defeated only after a long struggle in which the Spartan army played the major role, it was the victory at Salamis that captured the imagination of the Greeks.

From the conclusion of this second invasion it was Athens that drew the greatest benefits. Sparta was unable to capitalize on her own glorious victories, but Athens, because of her resourcefulness and her sea-power, was able to establish herself as an empire. She became the head of a federation of states, the Confederacy of Delos, and before long had mastered most of her former allies and confederates, ultimately transferring the treasury of the Confederacy to the Acropolis, and subjugating recalcitrant states. It was at this important period that Athens had the good fortune to be guided by her greatest statesman, Pericles.

Under these auspicious circumstances was born the glorious civilization that is associated with the name of Pericles. Athens was rebuilt and made the queen of cities. Great architects, sculptors, and such painters as Ictinus, Phidias, and Polygnotus beautified her with the temples and sculpture that

---

[1] J. B. Bury, *A History of Greece*, Modern Library, p. 244.

made her the wonder of the world. And within her confines arose a short-lived age of enlightenment unparalleled in ancient history.

The Athenians became remarkably cosmopolitan in their outlook and developed an intense curiosity about the world. A scientific attitude toward nature had appeared earlier among the Ionians. Now Athens became the haven of Pericles' friend and teacher, the radical philosopher Anaxagoras, who propounded a materialistic or mechanical theory of the universe. Education became liberalized by the class of teachers known as Sophists, who subjected everything to the scrutiny of reason and taught the methods of argumentation. The Sophists, who have been greatly maligned, did not confine themselves to the teaching of rhetoric. They devoted themselves to the study of language, philosophy, religion, ethics, and politics. The greatest of these enlighteners, Protagoras, exemplified most of these interests. He founded the science of grammar, taught rhetoric, formulated a theory of democracy, and maintained a skeptical relativist position with respect to absolute knowledge. "Man," he declared, "is the measure of things"—that is, there is no truth beyond the impression something makes on the human mind. In religion he was an agnostic, writing: "About the Gods, I have no means of knowing that they are or are not." Socrates stood somewhat apart from the Sophists because he did not teach professionally—that is, for a fee. But he was closer to them, through his skepticism and rationalism, than his disciple Plato cared to admit. As Gilbert Murray noted, the greatness of these rationalists lay not in the correctness of their scientific results, but in their pioneering intellect, their courage in

struggling with ideas, and their spirit. It was in this milieu that Æschylus, Sophocles, Euripides, and Aristophanes created many of their plays, and Herodotus and Thucydides, their histories.

The Periclean age came to a disastrous end. Athenian imperialism made many enemies, and in 431 B.C. plunged the city-state into a protracted conflict with Sparta and her allies. At the conclusion of this struggle, known as the Peloponnesian War, Athens was defeated and prostrated. And even before the fall of the city in 404 B.C., her spirit had become demoralized: demagoguery and intolerance had blighted the fine flower of Periclean civilization. Pericles lost much of his influence and could not protect his friends, the artists and philosophers. The great sculptor Phidias was accused of embezzling funds intended for the public works program; Anaxagoras was accused of "impiety" and forced to flee the wrath of the citizens. The plague that decimated the city killed Pericles in 429 B.C. and the leadership of Athens passed into the hands of militaristic and narrow-minded rabble-rousers. Athenians began to look askance at the spirit of intelligent inquiry and developed the habit of persecuting its proponents. In 411 B.C., Protagoras was condemned and his skeptical book on religion was publicly burned; he boarded a ship to Sicily and was apparently drowned on the way. In 399 B.C. Athens passed the sentence of death on Socrates. However, the spirit of inquiry, the habit of close reasoning, and the love of art could not be stamped out entirely. It persisted throughout the war period, it survived the fall of Athens by a century, and then it spread over the entire Mediterranean area colonized by the Greeks and later controlled by the Romans.

GREEK HISTORIANS
THE AGE OF PERICLES

Although the recording of historical events had long been customary in other Mediterranean civilizations—in Babylonia and Egypt,—it was one of the singular achievements of the Greek mind that it developed the art and approached the science of history. Characteristically, this began in the Periclean age, with the work of Herodotus, "the father of history," and reached its zenith under the shadow of that age, in Thucydides' account of the Peloponnesian War. Then all subsequent historical writing among the Greeks—whether presented plainly as history or, in the case of Plutarch, in biographical form—followed the example. The selections given below all pertain to the great Periclean period: Herodotus conveys Athens' restless spirit of inquiry and immortalizes the epic struggle against Persia; Plutarch, writing many centuries later, gives us an account of its leader, Pericles, of his share in its triumphs and his foretaste of its decline and defeat; Thucydides sums up its ideals for us in the funeral oration Pericles delivered at the end of the first year of the Peloponnesian War.

The Greek mind favored the historical approach precisely because it was worldly, inquiring, and given to making evaluations. Even Homer's poetry is now known to be not wholly unhistorical. Historical writing was also promoted early in Greece by the love of story-telling and the development of prose. Chronicles began to be written by the Ionians, and while their accuracy may be questioned, there is a familiar ring of historical independence and conscientiousness in the words of their first historian, who traveled far in search of information: Hecatæus of Miletus speaks thus: "I write as I consider true, for the traditions of Greeks

seem to me manifold and absurd." But it was given to Herodotus (484-425 B.C.), a native of Halicarnassus in Asia Minor, to select a subject sufficiently broad and significant to make his book important, to apply rationalism and, wherever possible, some research to an epoch; to fuse diverse events into a single, logically related and meaningful narrative, and to develop a style at once critical and fluent, clear and noble.

His incidental accounts comprise many of the most interesting passages of his *History*. A Greek subject of Persia in Halicarnassus, Herodotus developed a valuable catholicity of interest and a freedom from race prejudices. Becoming involved in political struggles against Persia and the Greek tyrant of his city, he found it imperative to flee to Samos, and soon became a wanderer through the Mediterranean world.

Herodotus found a new home in Athens, where he enjoyed the friendship of the tragic poet Sophocles, and he was later made a citizen of the Athenian colony of Thurii in southern Italy. His travels before and after this event took him to Babylon, Egypt, and Libya, and even north up the Black Sea to the Crimea. He became a professional story-teller, collecting his material wherever he could and reciting it in the Greek cities. No doubt he was encouraged in this by Pericles, for the information he brought back must have been valuable to expanding Athens.

When he came to write his book, however, he was not content with fascinating his curious readers with miscellaneous accounts of Egypt and the Near East, anecdotes, and stories of absurd marvels. He set himself the task of writing a prose epic whose theme is the gathering struggle between the East and the West, between Persia and Greece, and its culmination in the triumph of Greek arms. The battles of Marathon and Thermopylæ are thus the keystone of a magnificent arch. The last three books of his *History* give us the history of the Persian invasion; the first six, the events that led up to it, starting with the mythical rivalry between Asia and Europe.

Many episodes are only loosely connected, but they gradually come together in Herodotus' plan. We first encounter Crœsus, king of Lydia, who enslaved the Greek cities in Asia Minor; then the conquest of Lydia by Cyrus and the rise of Persia to overlordship of Asia Minor; then, after a description of Egypt, the extension of Persian rule over Egypt and the organization of the Empire under Darius. This is followed by the invasion of Libya on one side, and of Europe, on the other, in the Scythian campaign. After this we see the Ionian colonies, subjects of Persia, exploding into revolt and being aided by Athens, "the mother-city of the Ionians." As a result, Persia invades Greece, and the great struggle is precipitated.

Judged by the standards of modern historical writing, Herodotus is far from perfect; he is not always accurate, repeats many dubious tales, avoids questioning acts attributed to deity, and twists historical fact in favor of Athens, gratifying not only the Athenians' hunger for fiction but their vanity and political ambitions. But he is never narrow-minded and he is truly liberal in his treatment of different religions; "about the gods," he wrote, "one man knows as much as another." He maintains a skeptical attitude toward oracles and signs, makes it clear that he is merely passing on a tradition in many instances ("the Libyans say," "the Cyrenæans say," etc.). He presents different versions of the same story with complete open-mindedness and even criticizes some traditional accounts. Many of his inaccuracies stem from his sources of information, some of which are recognizable today as folk-lore. Above all, he tries to be fair to tyrants, whom he disliked, and to the Persians. "To see really how fair he is," writes Gilbert Murray, "one needs but look for a moment at the sort of language such writers as Froude and Motley use of the average active Catholic, especially if he be French or Spanish."

Herodotus is the Homer of historical writing. This is evident in the grandeur of his theme and the simple nobility of his style, as well as in his vivid evocation of characters and events. His great-est successor, Thucydides (471-400 B.C.), is less the epic poet than the scrupulous modern historian. He weighs all available evidence, records what he knows objectively, avoids repeating anything for its purely narrative interest or oddity, and organizes his material according to a well-conceived plan. He is truly a son of Periclean "Enlightenment"— cool, tasteful, and intellectual. Herodotus was romantically patriotic, Thucydides was judicious both by inclination and experience. His experience in the declining years of Athens was not conducive to glorification of his subject, and the fact that he observed a large part of the struggle while exiled from the city gave him a vantage point of objectivity.

Thucydides was a man of position and military distinction, related to the hero of Marathon, Miltiades. In the eighth year of the war he was made a general and placed second in command of a northern expedition. The loss of the city of Amphipolis, which he was expected to defend, resulted in his being disgraced at Athens. Thucydides' only comment was "It befell to me to be an exile from my country for twenty years after my command at Amphipolis." Worse was to follow, however, for it was his lot to observe the fall of the Athenian empire, and it remained for him to record not only its military mistakes and defeats but its spiritual deterioration.

In his *History of the Peloponnesian War* he is in all respects a realist. He sets down his aims and methods himself: "I have not thought fit to write from casual information nor according to any notion of my own. Parts I saw myself; for the rest, which I learned from others, I inquired to the fulness of my power about every detail. The truth was hard to find, because eye-witnesses of the same events spoke differently as their memories or their sympathies varied. The book will perhaps seem dull to listen to, because there is no myth in it. But if those who wish to look at the truth about what happened in the war . . . judge my work to be useful, I shall be content."

Although he never completed his project, he achieved his ideal of historical writing and thereby, in the very process of recording the end of a great period, resurrected it. For it is the Periclean spirit that lives on in his work. The supernatural has no place in it; he concerns himself with facts, political reasons, psychological factors, and modes of thought. He carries on a methodical investigation in a terse and restrained style full of antitheses and compressions natural to an intellectual. He lives for us as an artist, and his *History* remains remarkably fresh not merely as the record of an ancient struggle, but also as a universal picture of man's behavior as a political animal. Anyone who wishes to pursue the parallels between his narrative and contemporary history will not be disappointed; he will find them plentiful, and he will be enlightened in unsuspected ways.

The speeches in Thucydides' *History* are the high-water mark of his achievement. Some of them are essentially historical, others are frankly contrived in order more vividly to convey the opinions of characters or parties. At no point does he deceive us, for he says plainly that he is merely approximating the actual words, and in some instances he is simply using a dramatic device. If this differentiates his procedure from that of a twentieth-century historian, it heightens his artistry; it enriches and varies his narrative, and it lights up the features of a character or nation brilliantly.

After Thucydides' death, Greek historical writing declined for some time; however, Xenophon (430?-352 B.C.) gave further evidences of its power in his *Anabasis*, a pleasing if not wholly skillful record of high adventures in the Near East, that foreshadowed the conquests of Alexander the Great. Xenophon's *Memorabilia*, his memories of Socrates, moreover, opened up the related field of biography; his account of the philosopher's life is more reliable than Plato's. His *Cyropædia*, a picture of an ideal ruler in the person of Cyrus the Great, is not strictly history, but rather an interesting semi-philosophical variant. His *Hellenica* is, in part, an inferior continuation of Thucydides' book, bringing the story of the Peloponnesian War to its end.

When next we meet a historian who can wear Thucydides' mantle with some grace, it is in the second century B.C. He is Polybius (about 205-123 B.C.), a Greek who spent sixteen years in Rome as a hostage and became a friend of those famous Roman aristocrats and generals, the Scipios. His uncompleted *Universal History*, exemplifying the shaping hand of providence in national history and tracing the rise of Rome and its subjugation of Carthage and Greece, is notably penetrative. In his historical breadth and in his sense of justice, Polybius, who is a less inspired writer than Herodotus and Thucydides, continues to exemplify the genius of Greece. This also survives in the Hellenized Jewish writer Flavius Josephus, author of the *History of the Jewish Wars*, during the first century A.D., and in Plutarch (46-120 A.D.).

Plutarch, who wrote many short philosophical and political treatises, grouped together as *Moral Works*, is best remembered for his *Lives*, vivid sketches of forty-six famous characters of the past, based on records now lost. The lives were paired, a Greek and a Roman character being treated together because of their resemblances. His writing of "parallel lives" enabled him to compare and contrast his heroes. Born in Bœotia, educated in philosophy at Athens, and located for a time in Rome as a visitor, lecturer, and ambassador, Plutarch was qualified to bridge the gap between the Greek and the Roman worlds. Moreover, as a cosmopolitan man he developed an intense interest in public characters, and his dramatic representation of them made him the world's greatest writer of biography.

His subjects, however, bring his work within the scope of history, and in presenting social and political backgrounds for his characters he is a historian despite his inaccuracies. He had access to the works of scores of authors whose writings have disappeared. He saw ancient buildings still unruined, ancient statues unbroken, and ancient paintings fresh in their colors. For many periods and places he remains our principal source of information. But as Arthur Hugh Clough, the Victorian poet who revised John Dryden's translation of the *Lives*, reminds us, Plutarch is a moralist or moralistic biographer rather than a historian: "His interest is less for politics and the changes of empires, and much more for personal character and individual actions and motives for action; duty performed and rewarded; arrogance chastised, hasty anger corrected; humanity, fair dealing, and generosity triumphing in the visible, or relying on the invisible, world. His mind is continually running on the Aristotelian ethics and the high Platonic theories, which formed the religion of the educated population of his time." And in this respect, as well as in his serene attitude and simple cheerfulness, Plutarch is closer to Periclean Athens than his dates and his exposure to the decadent Roman world of Nero and Domitian would suggest. The virtues he loved were Periclean ones, the equableness he approved was Periclean. It is no wonder, then, that his biography of Pericles is one of his best, and his account of that age restores it to the world. Athens, in his essay, is not a city of beautiful ruins, but a busy, flourishing community overflowing with life. Plutarch shows us to what a point the great age had come, and gives us a foreshadowing of its tragic end. His life of Pericles testifies to the reality of that age by recovering it in a manner worthy of it.

HERODOTUS

History

Description of Egypt

Now the Nile, when it overflows, floods not only the Delta, but also the tracts of country on both sides of the stream, which are thought to belong to Libya and Arabia, in some places reaching to the extent of two days' journey from its banks, in some even exceeding that distance, but in others falling short of it.

Concerning the nature of the river, I was not [10] able to gain any information either from the priests or from others. I was particularly anxious to learn from them why the Nile, at the commencement of the summer solstice, begins to rise, and continues to increase for a hundred days—and why, as soon as that number is past, it forthwith retires and contracts its stream, continuing low during the whole of the winter until the summer solstice comes round again. On none of these points could I obtain any explanation from the inhabitants, though I made [20] every inquiry, wishing to know what was commonly reported—they could neither tell me what special virtue the Nile has which makes it so opposite in its nature to all other streams, nor why, unlike every other river, it gives forth no breezes from its surface.

Some of the Greeks, however, wishing to get a reputation for cleverness, have offered explanations of the phenomena of the river, for which they have accounted in three different ways. Two of these I [30] do not think it worth while to speak of, further than simply to mention what they are. One pretends that the Etesian winds cause the rise of the river by preventing the Nile-water from running off into the sea. But in the first place it has often happened, when the Etesian winds did not blow,

that the Nile has risen according to its usual wont; and further, if the Etesian winds produced the effect, the other rivers which flow in a direction opposite to those winds ought to present the same phenomena as the Nile, and the more so as they are all smaller streams, and have a weaker current. But these rivers, of which there are many both in Syria and Libya, are entirely unlike the Nile in this respect.

The second opinion is even more unscientific than the one just mentioned, and also, if I may so say, more marvelous. It is that the Nile acts so strangely, because it flows from the ocean, and that the ocean flows all round the earth.

The third explanation, which is very much more plausible than either of the others, is positively the furthest from the truth; for there is really nothing in what it says, any more than in the other theories. It is, that the inundation of the Nile is caused by the melting of snows. Now, as the Nile flows out of Libya, through Ethiopia, into Egypt, how is it possible that it can be formed of melted snow, running, as it does, from the hottest regions of the world into cooler countries? Many are the proofs whereby anyone capable of reasoning on the subject may be convinced that it is most unlikely this should be the case. The first and strongest argument is furnished by the winds, which always blow hot from these regions. The second is, that rain and frost are unknown there. Now, whenever snow falls, it must of necessity rain within five days; so that, if there were snow, there must be rain also in those parts. Thirdly, it is certain that the natives of the country are black with the heat, that the kites and the swallows remain there the whole year, and that the cranes, when they fly

[1] In other chapters we shall look into the tragedies written in this period and also into one of the comedies which showed that these people could laugh at themselves.

Herodotus, *History*. Translated by George Rawlinson. Herodotus, born about 484 B.C. in Halicarnassus in Asia Minor as a Persian subject, spent much of his life as student and untiring traveler and as historian of the great Persian defeat. He died about 425 B.C.

from the rigors of a Scythian winter, flock thither to pass the cold season. If, then, in the country whence the Nile has its source, or in that through which it flows, there fell ever so little snow, it is absolutely impossible that any of these circumstances could take place.

As for the writer who attributes the phenomenon to the ocean, his account is involved in such obscurity that it is impossible to disprove it by argument. For my part I know of no river called Ocean, and I think that Homer, or one of the earlier poets, invented the name, and introduced it into his poetry.

Perhaps, after censuring all the opinions that have been put forward on this obscure subject, one ought to propose some theory of one's own. I will therefore proceed to explain what I think to be the reason of the Nile's swelling in the summer time. During the winter, the sun is driven out of his usual course by the storms, and removes to the upper parts of Libya. This is the whole secret in the fewest possible words; for it stands to reason that the country to which the Sun-god approaches the nearest, and which he passes most directly over, will be scantest of water, and that there the streams which feed the rivers will shrink the most.

To explain, however, more at length, the case is this. The sun, in his passage across the upper parts of Libya, affects them in the following way. As the air in those regions is constantly clear, and the country warm through the absence of cold winds, the sun in his passage across them acts upon them exactly as he is wont to act elsewhere in summer, when his path is in the middle of heaven—that is, he attracts the water. After attracting it, he again repels it into the upper regions, where the winds lay hold of it, scatter it, and reduce it to a vapor, whence it naturally enough comes to pass that the winds which blow from this quarter—the south and south-west—are of all winds the most rainy. And my own opinion is that the sun does not get rid of all the water which he draws year by year from the Nile, but retains some about him. When the winter begins to soften, the sun goes back again to his old place in the middle of the heaven, and proceeds to attract water equally from all countries. Till then the other rivers run big, from the quantity of rain-water which they bring down from countries where so much moisture falls that all the land is cut into gullies; but in summer, when the showers fail, and the sun attracts their water, they become low. The Nile, on the contrary, not deriving any of its bulk from rains, and being in winter subject to the attraction of the sun, naturally runs at that season, unlike all other streams, with a less burthen of water than in the summer time. For in summer it is exposed to attraction equally with all other rivers, but in winter it suffers alone. The sun, therefore, I regard as the sole cause of the phenomenon.

It is the sun also, in my opinion, which, by heating the space through which it passes, makes the air in Egypt so dry. There is thus perpetual summer in the upper parts of Libya. Were the position of the heavenly regions reversed, so that the place where now the north wind and the winter have their dwelling became the station of the south wind and of the noon-day, while, on the other hand, the station of the south wind became that of the north, the consequence would be that the sun, driven from the mid-heaven by the winter and the northern gales, would betake himself to the upper parts of Europe, as he now does to those of Libya, and then I believe his passage across Europe would affect the Ister[1] exactly as the Nile is affected at the present day.

Concerning Egypt itself I shall extend my remarks to a great length, because there is no country that possesses so many wonders, nor any that has such a number of works which defy description. Not only is the climate different from that of the rest of the world, and the rivers unlike any other rivers, but the people also, in most of their manners and customs, exactly reverse the common practice of mankind. The women attend the markets and trade, while the men sit at home at the loom; and here, while the rest of the world works the woof up the warp, the Egyptians work it down; the women likewise carry burdens upon their shoulders, while the men carry them upon their heads. They eat their food out of doors in the streets, but retire for private purposes to their houses, giving as a reason that what is unseemly, but necessary, ought to be done in secret, but what has nothing unseemly about it, should be done openly. A woman cannot serve the priestly office, either for god or goddess, but men are priests to both; sons need not support their parents unless they choose, but daughters must, whether they choose or no.

In other countries the priests have long hair, in Egypt their heads are shaven; elsewhere it is customary, in mourning, for near relations to cut their hair close; the Egyptians, who wear no hair at any

---

[1] The present-day Danube.

other time, when they lose a relative, let their beards and the hair of their heads grow long. All other men pass their lives separate from animals, the Egyptians have animals always living with them; others make barley and wheat their food; it is a disgrace to do so in Egypt, where the grain they live on is spelt, which some call *zea.* Dough they knead with their feet; but they mix mud, and even take up dirt, with their hands. They are the only people in the world—they at least, and such as have learnt the practice from them—who use circumcision. Their men wear two garments apiece, their women but one. They put on the rings and fasten the ropes to sails inside; others put them outside. When they write or calculate, instead of going, like the Greeks, from left to right, they move their hand from right to left; and they insist, notwithstanding, that it is they who go to the right, and the Greeks who go to the left. They have two quite different kinds of writing, one of which is called sacred, the other common.

They are religious to excess, far beyond any other race of men, and use the following ceremonies:—They drink out of brazen cups, which they scour every day; there is no exception to this practice. They wear linen garments, which they are specially careful to have always fresh washed. They practice circumcision for the sake of cleanliness, considering it better to be cleanly than comely. The priests shave their whole body every other day, that no lice or other impure thing may adhere to them when they are engaged in the service of the gods. Their dress is entirely of linen, and their shoes of the papyrus plant; it is not lawful for them to wear either dress or shoes of any other material. They bathe twice every day in cold water, and twice each night; besides which they observe, so to speak, thousands of ceremonies. They enjoy, however, not a few advantages. They consume none of their own property, and are at no expense for anything; but every day bread is baked for them of the sacred corn, and a plentiful supply of beef and of goose's flesh is assigned to each, and also a portion of wine made from the grape. Fish they are not allowed to eat; and beans—which none of the Egyptians ever sow or eat, if they come up of their own accord, either raw or boiled—the priests will not even endure to look on, since they consider it an unclean kind of pulse. Instead of a single priest, each god has the attendance of a college, at the head of which is a chief priest; when one of these dies, his son is appointed in his room.

They have also another sacred bird called the phœnix, which I myself have never seen, except in pictures. Indeed, it is a great rarity, even in Egypt, only coming there (according to the accounts of the people of Heliopolis) once in 500 years, when the old phœnix dies. Its size and appearance, if it is like the pictures, are as follows: The plumage is partly red, partly golden, while the general make and size are almost exactly that of the eagle. They tell a story of what this bird does, which does not seem to me to be credible: that he comes all the way from Arabia, and brings the parent bird, all plastered over with myrrh, to the temple of the sun, and there buries the body. In order to bring him, they say, he first forms a ball of myrrh as big as he finds that he can carry; then he hollows out the ball, and puts his parent inside, after which he covers over the opening with fresh myrrh, and the ball is then of exactly the same weight as at first; so he brings it to Egypt, plastered over as I have said, and deposits it in the temple of the sun. Such is the story they tell of the doings of this bird.

In the neighborhood of Thebes there are some sacred serpents which are perfectly harmless. They are of small size, and have two horns growing out of the top of the head. These snakes, when they die, are buried in the temple of Zeus, the god to whom they are sacred.

I went once to a certain place in Arabia, almost exactly opposite the city of Buto, to make inquiries concerning the winged serpents. On my arrival I saw the backbones and ribs of serpents in such numbers as it is impossible to describe: of the ribs there were a multitude of heaps, some great, some small, some middle-sized. The place where the bones lie is at the entrance of a narrow gorge between steep mountains, which there open upon a spacious plain communicating with the great plain of Egypt. The story goes that with the spring the winged snakes come flying from Arabia towards Egypt, but are met in this gorge by the birds called ibises, which forbid their entrance and destroy them all. The Arabians assert, and the Egyptians also admit, that it is on account of the service thus rendered that the Egyptians hold the ibis in so much reverence.

The ibis is a bird of a deep-black color, with legs like a crane; its beak is strongly hooked, and its size is about that of the landrail. This is a description of the black ibis which contends with the serpents. The commoner sort, for there are two quite distinct species, has the head and the whole throat bare of feathers; its general plumage is white, but the head and neck are jet black, as also are the tips of the wings and the extremity of the tail; in its beak and legs it resembles the other species. The winged serpent is shaped like the water-snake. Its wings are not feathered, but resemble very closely those of the bat. And thus I conclude the subject of the sacred animals.

With respect to the Egyptians themselves, it is to be remarked that those who live in the corn country, devoting themselves, as they do, far more than any other people in the world, to the preservation of the memory of past actions, are the best skilled in history of any men that I have ever met. The following is the mode of life habitual to them:— For three successive days in each month they purge the body by means of emetics and clysters, which is done out of a regard for their health, since they have a persuasion that every disease to which men are liable is occasioned by the substances whereon they feed. Apart from any such precautions, they are, I believe, next to the Libyans, the healthiest people in the world—an effect of their climate, in my opinion, which has no sudden changes. Diseases almost always attack men when they are exposed to a change, and never more than during changes of the weather. They live on bread made of spelt, which they form into loaves called in their own tongue *cyllêstis*. Their drink is a wine which they obtain from barley, as they have no vines in their country. Many kinds of fish they eat raw, either salted or dried in the sun. Quails also, and ducks and small birds, they eat uncooked, merely first salting them. All other birds and fishes, excepting those which are set apart as sacred, are eaten either roasted or boiled.

In social meetings among the rich, when the banquet is ended, a servant carries round to the several guests a coffin, in which there is a wooden image of a corpse, carved and painted to resemble nature as nearly as possible, about a cubit or two cubits in length. As he shows it to each guest in turn, the servant says, "Gaze here, and drink and be merry; for when you die, such will you be."

There are a set of men in Egypt who practice the art of embalming, and make it their proper business. These persons, when a body is brought to them, show the bearers various models of corpses, made in wood, and painted so as to resemble nature. The most perfect is said to be after the manner of him whom I do not think it religious to name in connection with such a matter; the second sort is inferior to the first, and less costly; the third is the cheapest of all. All this the embalmers explain, and then ask in which way it is wished that the corpse should be prepared. The bearers tell them, and having concluded their bargain, take their departure, while the embalmers, left to themselves, proceed to their task. The mode of embalming, according to the most perfect process, is the following:—They take first a crooked piece of iron, and with it draw out the brain through the nostrils, thus getting rid of a portion, while the skull is cleared of the rest by rinsing with drugs; next they make a cut along the flank with a sharp Ethiopian stone, and take out the whole contents of the abdomen, which they then cleanse, washing it thoroughly with palm wine, and again frequently with an infusion of pounded aromatics. After this they fill the cavity with the purest bruised myrrh, with cassia, and every sort of spicery except frankincense, and sew up the opening. Then the body is placed in natrum for seventy days, and covered entirely over. After the expiration of that space of time, which must not be exceeded, the body is washed, and wrapped round, from head to foot, with bandages of fine linen cloth, smeared over with gum, which is used generally by the Egyptians in the place of glue, and in this state it is given back to the relations, who enclose it in a wooden case which they have had made for the purpose, shaped into the figure of a man. Then fastening the case, they place it in a sepulchral chamber upright against the wall. Such is the most costly way of embalming the dead.

If the persons wish to avoid expense, and choose the second process, the following is the method pursued:—Syringes are filled with oil made from the cedar-tree, which is then, without any incision or disemboweling, injected into the abdomen. The passage by which it might be likely to return is stopped, and the body laid in natrum the prescribed number of days. At the end of the time the cedar-oil is allowed to make its escape; and such is its power that it brings with it the whole stomach and intestines in a liquid state. The natrum meanwhile has dissolved the flesh, and so nothing is left of the dead body but the skin and the bones. It is returned in this condition to the relatives, without any further trouble being bestowed upon it.

The third method of embalming, which is practiced in the case of the poorer classes, is to clear out the intestines with a clyster, and let the body lie in natrum the seventy days, after which it is at once given to those who come to fetch it away.

The wives of men of rank are not given to be embalmed immediately after death, nor indeed are any of the more beautiful and valued women. It is not till they have been dead three or four days that they are carried to the embalmers. This is done to prevent indignities from being offered them. It is said that once a case of this kind occurred: the man was detected by the information of his fellow-workman.

Whensoever anyone, Egyptian or foreigner, has lost his life by falling a prey to a crocodile, or by drowning in the river, the law compels the inhab- itants of the city near which the body is cast up to have it embalmed, and to bury it in one of the sacred repositories with all possible magnificence. No one may touch the corpse, not even any of the friends or relatives, but only the priests of the Nile, who prepare it for burial with their own hands— regarding it as something more than the mere body of a man—and themselves lay it in the tomb.

Till the death of Rhampsinitus, the priests said, Egypt was excellently governed, and flourished greatly; but after him Cheops succeeded to the throne, and plunged into all manner of wicked- ness. He closed the temples, and forbade the Egyp- tians to offer sacrifice, compelling them instead to labor, one and all, in his service. Some were re- quired to drag blocks of stone down to the Nile from the quarries in the Arabian range of hills; others received the blocks after they had been con- veyed in boats across the river, and drew them to the range of hills called the Libyan. A hundred thousand men labored constantly, and were re- lieved every three months by a fresh lot. It took ten years' oppression of the people to make the cause- way for the conveyance of the stones, a work not much inferior, in my judgment, to the pyramid itself. This causeway is five furlongs in length, ten fathoms wide, and in height, at the highest part, eight fathoms. It is built of polished stone, and is covered with carvings of animals. To make it took ten years, as I said—or rather to make the cause- way, the works on the mound where the pyramid stands, and the underground chambers, which Cheops intended as vaults for his own use: these last were built on a sort of island, surrounded by water introduced from the Nile by a canal. The pyramid itself was twenty years in building. It is a square, 800 feet each way, and the height the same, built entirely of polished stone, fitted to- gether with the utmost care. The stones of which it is composed are none of them less than thirty feet in length.

The pyramid was built in steps, battlementwise, as it is called, or, according to others, altarwise.

After laying the stones for the base, they raised the remaining stones to their places by means of ma- chines formed of short wooden planks. The first machine raised them from the ground to the top of the first step. On this there was another machine, which received the stone upon its arrival, and con- veyed it to the second step, whence a third machine advanced it still higher. Either they had as many machines as there were steps in the pyramid, or possibly they had but a single machine, which, be- ing easily moved, was transferred from tier to tier as the stone rose—both accounts are given, and therefore I mention both. The upper portion of the pyramid was finished first, then the middle, and finally the part which was lowest and nearest the ground. There is an inscription in Egyptian char- acters on the pyramid which records the quantity of radishes, onions, and garlic consumed by the laborers who constructed it; and I perfectly well remember that the interpreter who read the writ- ing to me said that the money expended in this way was 1600 talents of silver. If this then is a true record, what a vast sum must have been spent on the iron tools used in the work, and on the feeding and clothing of the laborers, considering the length of time the work lasted, which has already been stated, and the additional time—no small space, I imagine—which must have been occupied by the quarrying of the stones, their conveyance, and the formation of the underground apartments.

The Battle of Marathon

The Persians, having thus brought Eretria into subjection after waiting a few days, made sail for Attica, greatly straitening the Athenians as they approached, and thinking to deal with them as they had dealt with the people of Eretria. And, be- cause there was no place in all Attica so convenient for their horse as Marathon, and it lay moreover quite close to Eretria, therefore Hippias, the son of Pisistratus, conducted them thither.

When intelligence of this reached the Athenians, they likewise marched their troops to Marathon, and there stood on the defensive, having at their head ten generals, of whom one was Miltiades.

Now this man's father, Cimon, the son of Stesag- oras, was banished from Athens by Pisistratus, the son of Hippocrates. In his banishment it was his fortune to win the four-horse chariot-race at Olympia, whereby he gained the very same honor which had before been carried off by Miltiades, his half-brother on the mother's side. At the next

Olympiad he won the prize again with the same mares; upon which he caused Pisistratus to be proclaimed the winner, having made an agreement with him that on yielding him this honor he should be allowed to come back to his country. Afterwards, still with the same mares, he won the prize a third time; whereupon he was put to death by the sons of Pisistratus, whose father was no longer living. They set men to lie in wait for him secretly; and these men slew him near the government-house in the night-time. He was buried outside the city, beyond what is called the Valley Road; and right opposite his tomb were buried the mares which had won the three prizes. The same success had likewise been achieved once previously, to wit, by the mares of Evagoras the Lacedæmonian, but never except by them. At the time of Cimon's death Stesagoras, the elder of his two sons, was in the Chersonese, where he lived with Miltiades his uncle; the younger, who was called Miltiades after the founder of the Chersonesite colony, was with his father in Athens.

It was this Miltiades who now commanded the Athenians, after escaping from the Chersonese, and twice nearly losing his life. First he was chased as far as Imbrus by the Phœnicians, who had a great desire to take him and carry him up to the king; and when he had avoided this danger, and, having reached his own country, thought himself to be altogether in safety, he found his enemies waiting for him, and was cited by them before a court and impeached for his tyranny in the Chersonese. But he came off victorious here likewise, and was thereupon made general of the Athenians by the free choice of the people.

And first, before they left the city, the generals sent off to Sparta a herald, one Pheidippides, who was by birth an Athenian, and by profession and practice a trained runner. This man, according to the account which he gave to the Athenians on his return, when he was near Mount Parthenium, above Tegea, fell in with the god Pan, who called him by his name, and bade him ask the Athenians "wherefore they neglected him so entirely, when he was kindly disposed towards them, and had often helped them in times past, and would do so again in time to come." The Athenians, entirely believing in the truth of this report, as soon as their affairs were once more in good order, set up a temple to Pan under the Acropolis, and, in return for the message which I have recorded, established in his honor yearly sacrifices and a torch-race.

On the occasion of which we speak, when Pheidippides was sent by the Athenian generals, and, according to his own account, saw Pan on his journey, he reached Sparta on the very next day after quitting the city of Athens. Upon his arrival he went before the rulers, and said to them:—

"Men of Lacedæmon, the Athenians beseech you to hasten to their aid, and not allow that state, which is the most ancient in all Greece, to be enslaved by the barbarians. Eretria, look you, is already carried away captive; and Greece weakened by the loss of no mean city."

Thus did Pheidippides deliver the message committed to him. And the Spartans wished to help the Athenians, but were unable to give them any present succor, as they did not like to break their established law. It was then the ninth day of the first decade; and they could not march out of Sparta on the ninth, when the moon had not reached the full. So they waited for the full of the moon.

The barbarians were conducted to Marathon by Hippias, the son of Pisistratus, who the night before had seen a strange vision in his sleep. He dreamt of lying in his mother's arms, and conjectured the dream to mean that he would be restored to Athens, recover the power which he had lost, and afterwards live to a good old age in his native country. Such was the sense in which he interpreted the vision. He now proceeded to act as guide to the Persians; and, in the first place, he landed the prisoners taken from Eretria upon the island that is called Ægileia, a tract belonging to the Styreans, after which he brought the fleet to anchor off Marathon, and marshaled the bands of the barbarians as they disembarked. As he was thus employed it chanced that he sneezed and at the same time coughed with more violence than was his wont. Now, as he was a man advanced in years, and the greater number of his teeth were loose, it so happened that one of them was driven out with the force of the cough, and fell down into the sand. Hippias took all the pains he could to find it; but the tooth was nowhere to be seen: whereupon he fetched a deep sigh, and said to the bystanders:—

"After all, the land is not ours; and we shall never be able to bring it under. All my share in it is the portion of which my tooth has possession."

So Hippias believed that in this way his dream was out.

The Athenians were drawn up in order of battle in a sacred close belonging to Hercules, when they were joined by the Platæans, who came in full force to their aid.

The Athenian generals were divided in their opinions; and some advised not to risk a battle, because they were too few to engage such a host as that of the Medes,[1] while others were for fighting at once; and among these last was Miltiades. He therefore, seeing that opinions were thus divided, and that the less worthy counsel appeared likely to prevail, resolved to go to the polemarch, and have a conference with him. For the man on whom the lot fell to be polemarch at Athens was entitled to give his vote with the ten generals, since anciently the Athenians allowed him an equal right of voting with them. The polemarch at this juncture was Callimachus of Aphidnæ; to him therefore Miltiades went, and said:—

"With thee it rests, Callimachus, either to bring Athens to slavery, or, by securing her freedom, to leave behind thee to all future generations a memory beyond even Harmodius and Aristogeiton. For never since the time that the Athenians became a people were they in so great a danger as now. If they bow their necks beneath the yoke of the Medes, the woes which they will have to suffer when given into the power of Hippias are already determined on; if, on the other hand, they fight and overcome, Athens may rise to be the very first city in Greece. How it comes to pass that these things are likely to happen, and how the determining of them in some sort rests with thee, I will now proceed to make clear. We generals are ten in number, and our votes are divided; half of us wish to engage, half to avoid a combat. Now, if we do not fight, I look to see a great disturbance at Athens which will shake men's resolutions, and then I fear they will submit themselves; but if we fight the battle before any unsoundness show itself among our citizens, let the gods but give us fair play, and we are well able to overcome the enemy. On thee therefore we depend in this matter, which lies wholly in thine own power. Thou hast only to add thy vote to my side and thy country will be free, and not free only, but the first state in Greece. Or, if thou preferrest to give thy vote to them who would decline the combat, then the reverse will follow."

Miltiades by these words gained Callimachus; and the addition of the polemarch's vote caused the decision to be in favor of fighting. Hereupon all those generals who had been desirous of hazarding a battle, when their turn came to command the army, gave up their right to Miltiades. He, however, though he accepted their offers, nevertheless waited, and would not fight, until his own day of command arrived in due course.

Then at length, when his own turn was come, the Athenian battle was set in array, and this was the order of it. Callimachus the polemarch led the right wing; for it was at that time a rule with the Athenians to give the right wing to the polemarch. After this followed the tribes, according as they were numbered, in an unbroken line; while last of all came the Platæans, forming the left wing. And ever since that day it has been a custom with the Athenians, in the sacrifices and assemblies held each fifth year at Athens, for the Athenian herald to implore the blessing of the gods on the Platæans conjointly with the Athenians. Now, as they marshaled the host upon the field of Marathon, in order that the Athenian front might be of equal length with the Median, the ranks of the center were diminished, and it became the weakest part of the line, while the wings were both made strong with a depth of many ranks.

So when the battle was set in array, and the victims showed themselves favorable, instantly the Athenians, so soon as they were let go, charged the barbarians at a run. Now the distance between the two armies was little short of eight furlongs. The Persians, therefore, when they saw the Greeks coming on at speed, made ready to receive them, although it seemed to them that the Athenians were bereft of their senses, and bent upon their own destruction; for they saw a mere handful of men coming on at a run without either horsemen or archers. Such was the opinion of the barbarians; but the Athenians in close array fell upon them, and fought in a manner worthy of being recorded. They were the first of the Greeks, so far as I know, who introduced the custom of charging the enemy at a run, and they were likewise the first who dared to look upon the Median garb, and to face men clad in that fashion. Until this time the very name of the Medes had been a terror to the Greeks to hear.

The two armies fought together on the plain of Marathon for a length of time; and in the mid battle, where the Persians themselves and the Sacæ had their place, the barbarians were victorious, and broke and pursued the Greeks into the inner country; but on the two wings the Athenians and the Platæans defeated the enemy. Having so done, they suffered the routed barbarians to fly at their

---

[1] He means here the Persians, of whom the Medes formed a part.

ease, and joining the two wings in one, fell upon those who had broken their own center, and fought and conquered them. These likewise fled, and now the Athenians hung upon the runaways and cut them down, chasing them all the way to the shore, on reaching which they laid hold of the ships and called aloud for fire.

It was in the struggle here that Callimachus the polemarch, after greatly distinguishing himself, lost his life; Stesilaüs too, the son of Thrasilaüs, one of the generals, was slain; and Cynægirus, the son of Euphorion, having seized on a vessel of the enemy's by the ornament at the stern, had his hand cut off by the blow of an ax, and so perished; as likewise did many other Athenians of note and name.

Nevertheless, the Athenians secured in this way seven of the vessels; while with the remainder the barbarians pushed off, and taking aboard their Eretrian prisoners from the island where they had left them, doubled Cape Sunium, hoping to reach Athens before the return of the Athenians. The Alcmæonidæ were accused by their countrymen of suggesting this course to them; they had, it was said, an understanding with the Persians, and made a signal to them, by raising a shield, after they were embarked in their ships.

The Persians accordingly sailed round Sunium. But the Athenians with all possible speed marched away to the defense of their city, and succeeded in reaching Athens before the appearance of the barbarians: and as their camp at Marathon had been pitched in a precinct of Hercules, so now they encamped in another precinct of the same god at Cynosarges. The barbarian fleet arrived, and lay to off Phalerum, which was at that time the haven of Athens; but after resting awhile upon their oars, they departed and sailed away to Asia.

There fell in this battle of Marathon, on the side of the barbarians, about 6400 men; on that of the Athenians, 192.

Bridging the Hellespont

Xerxes, after this, made preparations to advance to Abydos, where the bridge across the Hellespont from Asia to Europe was lately finished. Midway between Sestos and Madytus in the Hellespontine Chersonese, and right over against Abydos, there is a rocky tongue of land which runs out for some distance into the sea. This is the place where no long time afterwards the Greeks under Xanthippus, the son of Ariphron, took Artaÿctes the Persian, who was at that time governor of Sestos, and nailed him living to a plank. He was the Artayctes who brought women into the temple of Protesilaüs at Elæus, and there was guilty of most unholy deeds.

Towards this tongue of land then, the men to whom the business was assigned, carried out a double bridge from Abydos; and while the Phœnicians constructed one line with cables of white flax, the Egyptians in the other used ropes made of papyrus. Now it is seven furlongs across from Abydos to the opposite coast. When, therefore, the channel had been bridged successfully, it happened that a great storm arising broke the whole work to pieces, and destroyed all that had been done.

So when Xerxes heard of it, he was full of wrath, and straightway gave orders that the Hellespont should receive three hundred lashes, and that a pair of fetters should be cast into it. Nay, I have even heard it said that he bade the branders take their irons and therewith brand the Hellespont. It is certain that he commanded those who scourged the waters to utter, as they lashed them, these barbarian and wicked words: "Thou bitter water, thy lord lays on thee this punishment because thou hast wronged him without a cause, having suffered no evil at his hands. Verily King Xerxes will cross thee, whether thou wilt or no. Well dost thou deserve that no man should honor thee with sacrifice; for thou art of a truth a treacherous and unsavory river." While the sea was thus punished by his orders, he likewise commanded that the overseers of the work should lose their heads.

Then they, whose business it was, executed the unpleasing task laid upon them; and other master-builders were set over the work, who accomplished it in the way which I will now describe.

They joined together triremes and penteconters, 360 to support the bridge on the side of the Euxine Sea, and 314 to sustain the other; and these they placed at right angles to the sea, and in the direction of the current of the Hellespont, relieving by these means the tension of the shore cables. Having joined the vessels, they moored them with anchors of unusual size, that the vessels of the bridge towards the Euxine might resist the winds which blow from within the straits, and that those of the more western bridge facing the Ægean, might withstand the winds which set in from the south and from the south-east. A gap was left in the penteconters in no fewer than three places, to afford a passage for such light craft as chose to enter or leave the Euxine. When all this was done, they made the cables taut from the shore by the help of wooden capstans. This time, moreover, instead of using the two materials separately, they assigned to each bridge six cables, two of which were of white flax, while four were of papyrus. Both cables were of the same size and quality; but the flaxen were the heavier, weighing not less than a talent the cubit. When the bridge across the channel was thus complete, trunks of trees were sawn into planks, which were cut to the width of the bridge, and these were laid side by side upon the tightened cables, and then fastened on the top. This done, brushwood was brought, and arranged upon the planks, after which earth was heaped upon the brushwood, and the whole trodden down into a solid mass. Lastly, a bulwark was set up on either side of this causeway, of such a height as to prevent the sumpter-beasts and the horses from seeing over it and taking fright at the water.

And now when all was prepared—the bridges, and the works at Athos, the breakwaters about the mouths of the cutting, which were made to hinder the surf from blocking up the entrances, and the cutting itself; and when the news came to Xerxes that this last was completely finished—then at length the host, having first wintered at Sardis, began its march towards Abydos, fully equipped, on the first approach of spring.

Thus rode forth Xerxes from Sardis but he was accustomed every now and then, when the fancy took him, to alight from his chariot and travel in a litter. Immediately behind the king there followed a body of a thousand spearmen, the noblest and bravest of the Persians, holding their lances in the usual manner—then came a thousand Persian horse, picked men—then ten thousand, picked also after the rest, and serving on foot. Of these last one thousand carried spears with golden pomegranates at their lower end, instead of spikes; and these encircled the other nine thousand, who bore on their spears pomegranates of silver. The spearmen too who pointed their lances towards the ground, had golden pomegranates; and the thousand Persians who followed close after Xerxes, had golden apples. Behind the ten thousand footmen came a body of Persian cavalry, likewise ten thousand; after which there was again a void space for as much as two furlongs; and then the rest of the army followed in a confused crowd.

The march of the army, after leaving Lydia, was directed upon the river Caïcus and the land of Mysia. Beyond the Caïcus the road, leaving Mount Cana upon the left, passed through the Atarnean plain, to the city of Carina. Quitting this, the troops advanced across the plain of Thebe, passing Adramyttium, and Antandrus, the Pelasgic city; then, holding Mount Ida upon the left hand, it entered the Trojan territory. On this march the Persians suffered some loss; for as they bivouacked during the night at the foot of Ida, a storm of thunder and lightning burst upon them, and killed no small number.

On reaching the Scamander, which was the first stream, of all that they had crossed since they left Sardis, whose water failed them and did not suffice to satisfy the thirst of men and cattle, Xerxes ascended into the Pergamus of Priam, since he had a longing to behold the place. When he had seen everything, and inquired into all particulars, he made an offering of a thousand oxen to the Trojan Athena, while the Magians poured libations to the heroes who were slain at Troy. The night after, a panic fell upon the camp: but in the morning they set off with daylight, and skirting on the left hand the towns Rhœteum, Ophryneum, and Dardanus (which borders on Abydos), on the right the Teucrians of Gergis, so reached Abydos.

Arrived here, Xerxes wished to look upon all his host; so, as there was a throne of white marble upon a hill near the city, which they of Abydos had prepared beforehand, by the King's bidding, for his especial use, Xerxes took his seat on it, and, gazing thence upon the shore below, beheld at one view all his land forces and all his ships. While thus employed, he felt a desire to behold a sailing-match among his ships, which accordingly took place, and was won by the Phœnicians of Sidon, much to the joy of Xerxes, who was delighted alike with the race and with his army.

And now, as he looked and saw the whole Hellespont covered with the vessels of his fleet, and all the shore and every plain about Abydos as full as possible of men, Xerxes congratulated himself on his good fortune; but after a little while, he wept.

All that day the preparations for the passage continued; and on the morrow they burnt all kinds of spices upon the bridges, and strewed the way with myrtle-boughs, while they waited anxiously for the sun, which they hoped to see as he rose. And now the sun appeared; and Xerxes took a golden goblet and poured from it a libation into the sea, praying the while, with his face turned to the sun, "that no misfortune might befall him such as to hinder his conquest of Europe, until he had penetrated to its uttermost boundaries." After he had prayed, he cast the golden cup into the Hellespont, and with it a golden bowl, and a Persian sword of the kind which they call *acinaces*. I cannot say for certain whether it was an offering to the sun-god that he threw these things into the deep, or whether he had repented of having scourged the Hellespont, and thought by his gifts to make amends to the sea for what he had done.

When, however, his offerings were made, the army began to cross; and the foot-soldiers, with the horsemen, passed over by one of the bridges— that (namely) which lay towards the Euxine— while the sumpter-beasts and the camp-followers passed by the other, which looked on the Ægean. Foremost went the Ten Thousand Persians, all wearing garlands upon their heads; and after them a mixed multitude of many nations. These crossed upon the first day.

On the next day the horsemen began the passage; and with them went the soldiers who carried their spears with the point downwards, garlanded, like the Ten Thousand;—then came the sacred horses and the sacred chariot; next Xerxes with his lancers and the thousand horse; then the rest of the army. At the same time the ships sailed over to the opposite shore. According, however, to another account which I have heard, the king crossed the last.

As soon as Xerxes had reached the European side, he stood to contemplate his army as they crossed under the lash. And the crossing continued during seven days and seven nights, without rest or pause.

The Spartans at Thermopylæ

King Xerxes pitched his camp in the region of Malis called Trachinia, while on their side the Greeks occupied the straits. These straits the Greeks in general call Thermopylæ (the Hot Gates); but the natives, and those who dwell in the neighborhood, call them Pylæ (the Gates). Here then the two armies took their stand: the one master of all the region lying north of Trachis, the other of the country extending southward of that place to the verge of the continent.

The various nations had each captains of their own under whom they served; but the one to whom all especially looked up, and who had the command of the entire force, was the Lacedæmonian, Leonidas.

He had now come to Thermopylæ, accompanied by the 300 men which the law assigned him, whom he had himself chosen from among the citizens, and who were all of them fathers with sons living. On his way he had taken the troops from Thebes, whose number I have already mentioned, and who were under the command of Leontiades the son of Eurymachus. The reason why he made a point of taking troops from Thebes, and Thebes only, was that the Thebans were strongly suspected of being well inclined to the Medes. Leonidas therefore called on them to come with him to the war, wishing to see whether they would comply with his demand, or openly refuse, and disclaim the Greek alliance. They, however, though their wishes leant the other way, nevertheless sent the men.

The force with Leonidas was sent forward by the Spartans in advance of their main body, that the sight of them might encourage the allies to fight, and hinder them from going over to the Medes, as it was likely they might have done had they seen that Sparta was backward. They intended presently, when they had celebrated the Carneian festival, which was what now kept them at home, to leave a garrison in Sparta, and hasten in full force to join the army. The rest of the allies also intended to act similarly; for it happened that the Olympic festival fell exactly at this same period. None of them looked to see the contest at Thermopylæ decided so speedily; wherefore they were content to send forward a mere advanced guard. Such accordingly were the intentions of the allies.

The Greek forces at Thermopylæ, when the Persian army drew near to the entrance of the pass, were seized with fear; and a council was held to consider about a retreat. It was the wish of the Peloponnesians generally that the army should fall back upon the Peloponnese, and there guard the Isthmus. But Leonidas, who saw with what indignation the Phocians and Locrians heard of this plan, gave his voice for remaining where they were, while they sent envoys to the several cities to ask for help, since they were too few to make a stand against an army like that of the Medes.

While this debate was going on, Xerxes sent a mounted spy to observe the Greeks, and note how many they were, and see what they were doing. He had heard, before he came out of Thessaly, that a few men were assembled at this place, and that at their head were certain Lacedæmonians, under Leonidas, a descendant of Hercules. The horseman rode up to the camp, and looked about him, but did not see the whole army; for such as were on the further side of the wall (which had been rebuilt and was now carefully guarded) it was not possible for him to behold; but he observed those on the outside, who were encamped in front of the rampart. It chanced that at this time the Lacedæmonians held the outer guard, and were seen by the spy, some of them engaged in gymnastic exercises, others combing their long hair. At this the spy greatly marveled, but he counted their number, and when he had taken accurate note of everything, he rode back quietly; for no one pursued after him, nor paid any heed to his visit. So he returned, and told Xerxes all that he had seen.

Upon this, Xerxes, who had no means of surmising the truth—namely, that the Spartans were preparing to do or die manfully—but thought it laughable that they should be engaged in such employments, sent and called to his presence Demaratus the son of Ariston, who still remained with the army. When he appeared, Xerxes told him all that he had heard, and questioned him concerning the news, since he was anxious to understand the meaning of such behavior on the part of the Spartans. Then Demaratus said:—

"I spake to thee, O king! concerning these men long since, when we had but just begun our march upon Greece; thou, however, didst only laugh at my words, when I told thee of all this, which I saw would come to pass. Earnestly do I struggle at all times to speak truth to thee, sire; and now listen to it once more. These men have come to dispute the pass with us; and it is for this that they are now making ready. 'Tis their custom, when they are about to hazard their lives, to adorn their heads with care. Be assured, however, that if thou canst subdue the men who are here and the Lacedæmonians who remain in Sparta, there is no other nation in all the world which will venture to lift a hand in their defense. Thou hast now to deal with the first kingdom and town in Greece, and with the bravest men."

Then Xerxes, to whom what Demaratus said seemed altogether to surpass belief, asked further "how it was possible for so small an army to contend with his."

"O king!" Demaratus answered, "let me be treated as a liar, if matters fall not out as I say."

But Xerxes was not persuaded any the more. Four whole days he suffered to go by, expecting that the Greeks would run away. When, however, he found on the fifth that they were not gone, thinking that their firm stand was mere impudence and recklessness, he grew wroth, and sent against them the Medes and Cissians, with orders to take them alive and bring them into his presence. Then the Medes rushed forward and charged the Greeks, but fell in vast numbers: others, however, took the places of the slain, and would not be beaten off, though they suffered terrible losses. In this way it became clear to all, and especially to the king, that though he had plenty of combatants, he had but very few warriors. The struggle, however, continued during the whole day.

Then the Medes, having met so rough a reception, withdrew from the fight; and their place was taken by the band of Persians under Hydarnes, whom the king called his "Immortals": they, it was thought, would soon finish the business. But when they joined battle with the Greeks, 'twas with no better success than the Median detachment—things went much as before—the two armies fighting in a narrow space, and the barbarians using shorter spears than the Greeks, and having no advantage from their numbers. The Lacedæmonians fought in a way worthy of note, and showed themselves far more skillful in fight than their adversaries, often turning their backs, and making as though they were all flying away, on which the barbarians would rush after them with much noise and shouting, when the Spartans at their approach would wheel round and face their pursuers, in this way destroying vast numbers of the enemy. Some Spartans likewise fell in these encounters, but only a very few. At last the Persians, finding that all their efforts to gain the pass availed nothing, and that, whether they attacked by divisions or in any other way, it was to no purpose, withdrew to their own quarters.

During these assaults, it is said that Xerxes, who was watching the battle, thrice leaped from the throne on which he sate, in terror for his army.

Next day the combat was renewed, but with no better success on the part of the barbarians. The Greeks were so few that the barbarians hoped to find them disabled, by reason of their wounds, from offering any further resistance; and so they once more attacked them. But the Greeks were drawn up in detachments according to their cities, and bore the brunt of the battle in turns,—all except the Phocians, who had been stationed on the mountain to guard the pathway. So, when the Persians found no difference between that day and the preceding, they again retired to their quarters.

Now, as the king was in a great strait, and

knew not how he should deal with the emergency, Ephialtes, the son of Eurydêmus, a man of Malis, came to him and was admitted to a conference. Stirred by the hope of receiving a rich reward at the king's hands, he had come to tell him of the pathway which led across the mountain to Thermopylæ; by which disclosure he brought destruction on the band of Greeks who had there withstood the barbarians.

Great was the joy of Xerxes on this occasion; and as he approved highly of the enterprise which Ephialtes undertook to accomplish, he forthwith sent upon the errand Hydarnes, and the Persians under him. The troops left the camp about the time of the lighting of the lamps. The pathway along which they went was first discovered by the Malians of these parts, who soon afterwards led the Thessalians by it to attack the Phocians, at the time when the Phocians fortified the pass with a wall, and so put themselves under covert from danger. And ever since, the path has always been put to an ill use by the Malians.

The Persians took this path, and, crossing the Asopus, continued their march through the whole of the night, having the mountains of Œta on their right hand, and on their left those of Trachis. At dawn of day they found themselves close to the summit. Now the hill was guarded, as I have already said, by a thousand Phocian men-at-arms, who were placed there to defend the pathway, and at the same time to secure their own country. They had been given the guard of the mountain path, while the other Greeks defended the pass below, because they had volunteered for the service, and had pledged themselves to Leonidas to maintain the post.

The ascent of the Persians became known to the Phocians in the following manner:—During all the time that they were making their way up, the Greeks remained unconscious of it, inasmuch as the whole mountain was covered with groves of oak; but it happened that the air was very still, and the leaves which the Persians stirred with their feet made, as it was likely they would, a loud rustling, whereupon the Phocians jumped up and flew to seize their arms. In a moment the barbarians came in sight, and, perceiving men arming themselves, were greatly amazed; for they had fallen in with an enemy when they expected no opposition. Hydarnes, alarmed at the sight, and fearing lest the Phocians might be Lacedæmonians, inquired of Ephialtes to what nation those troops belonged. Ephialtes told him the exact truth, whereupon he arrayed his Persians for battle. The Phocians, galled by the showers of arrows to which they were exposed, and imagining themselves the special object of the Persian attack, fled hastily to the crest of the mountain, and there made ready to meet death; but while their mistake continued, the Persians, with Ephialtes and Hydarnes, not thinking it worth their while to delay on account of Phocians, passed on and descended the mountain with all possible speed.

The Greeks at Thermopylæ received the first warning of the destruction which the dawn would bring on them from the seer Megistias, who read their fate in the victims as he was sacrificing. After this deserters came in, and brought the news that the Persians were marching round by the hills: it was still night when these men arrived. Last of all, the scouts came running down from the heights, and brought in the same accounts, when the day was just beginning to break. Then the Greeks held a council to consider what they should do, and here opinions were divided: some were strong against quitting their post, while others contended to the contrary. So when the council had broken up, part of the troops departed and went their ways homeward to their several states; part, however, resolved to remain, and to stand by Leonidas to the last.

So the allies, when Leonidas ordered them to retire, obeyed him and forthwith departed. Only the Thespians and the Thebans remained with the Spartans; and of these the Thebans were kept back by Leonidas as hostages, very much against their will. The Thespians, on the contrary, stayed entirely of their own accord, refusing to retreat, and declaring that they would not forsake Leonidas and his followers. So they abode with the Spartans, and died with them. Their leader was Demophilus, the son of Diadromes.

At sunrise Xerxes made libations, after which he waited until the time when the forum is wont to fill, and then began his advance. Ephialtes had instructed him thus, as the descent of the mountain is much quicker, and the distance much shorter, than the way round the hills and the ascent. So the barbarians under Xerxes began to draw nigh; and the Greeks under Leonidas, as they now went forth determined to die, advanced much further than on previous days, until they reached the more open portion of the pass. Hitherto they had held their station within the wall, and from this had gone forth to fight at the point where the pass was the narrowest. Now they joined battle beyond the defile, and carried slaughter among the barbarians, who fell in heaps. Behind them the captains of the squadrons, armed with whips, urged their men forward with continual blows. Many were thrust into the sea, and there perished; a still greater number were trampled to death by their own soldiers; no one heeded the dying. For the Greeks, reckless of their own safety and desperate, since they knew that, as the mountain had been crossed, their destruction was nigh at hand, exerted themselves with the most furious valor against the barbarians.

By this time the spears of the greater number were all shivered, and with their swords they hewed down the ranks of the Persians; and here, as they strove, Leonidas fell fighting bravely, together with many other famous Spartans, whose names I have taken care to learn on account of their great worthiness, as indeed I have those of all the three hundred. There fell too at the same time very many famous Persians: among them, two sons of Darius, Abrocomes and Hyperanthes, his children by Phrataguné, the daughter of Artanes. Artanes was brother of King Darius, being a son of Hystaspes, the son of Arsames; and when he gave his daughter to the king, he made him heir likewise of all his substance; for she was his only child.

Thus two brothers of Xerxes here fought and fell. And now there arose a fierce struggle between the Persians and the Lacedæmonians over the body of Leonidas, in which the Greeks four times drove back the enemy, and at last by their great bravery succeeded in bearing off the body. This combat was scarcely ended when the Persians with Ephialtes approached; and the Greeks, informed that they drew nigh, made a change in the manner of their fighting. Drawing back into the narrowest part of the pass, and retreating even behind the cross wall, they posted themselves upon a hillock, where they stood all drawn up together in one close body, except only the Thebans. The hillock whereof I speak is at the entrance of the straits, where the stone lion stands which was set up in honor of Leonidas. Here they defended themselves to the last, such as still had swords using them, and the others resisting with their hands and teeth; till the barbarians, who in part had pulled down the wall and attacked them in front, in part had gone round and now encircled them upon every side, overwhelmed and buried the remnant which was left beneath showers of missile weapons.

PLUTARCH

Pericles

Pericles[1] was of the tribe Acamantis, and the township Cholargus, of the noblest birth both on his father's and mother's side. Xanthippus, his father, who defeated the King of Persia's generals in the battle of Mycale, took to wife Agariste, the grandchild of Clisthenes, who drove out the sons of Pisistratus, and nobly put an end to their tyrannical usurpation, and, moreover, made a body of laws, and settled a model of government admirably tempered and suited for the harmony and safety of the people.

His mother, being near her time, fancied in a dream that she was brought to bed of a lion, and a few days after was delivered of Pericles, in other respects perfectly formed, only his head was somewhat longish and out of proportion. For which reason almost all the images and statues that were made of him have the head covered with a helmet, the workmen apparently being willing not to expose him.

The master that taught him music, most authors are agreed, was Damon, who, it is not unlikely, being a sophist, out of policy sheltered himself under the profession of music to conceal from people in general his skill in other things, and under this pretense attended Pericles, the young

Pericles. Translated by John Dryden; revised by Arthur Hugh Clough. Somewhat abridged. Plutarch (c. 46-120 A.D.), Greek biographer, was born at Chæronea in Bœotia, enjoyed political preferment in Rome, and died in honor in his native town. His forty-six Parallel Lives overshadow his voluminous miscellaneous works.
[1] Pericles was born about 495 B.C. and died in 429.

athlete of politics. Pericles, also, was a hearer of Zeno, the Eleatic, who treated of natural philosophy in the same manner as Parmenides did, but had also perfected himself in an art of his own for refuting and silencing opponents in argument. But he that saw most of Pericles, and furnished him most especially with a weight and grandeur of sense, superior to all arts of popularity, and in general gave him his elevation and sublimity of purpose and of character, was Anaxagoras of Clazomenæ, whom the men of those times called by the name of Nous, that is, mind, or intelligence, whether in admiration of the great and extraordinary gift he had displayed for the science of nature, or because that he was the first of the philosophers who did not refer the first ordering of the world to fortune or chance, nor to necessity or compulsion, but to a pure, unadulterated intelligence, which in all other existing mixed and compound things acts as a principle of discrimination, and of combination of like with like.

For this man, Pericles entertained an extraordinary esteem and admiration, and filling himself with this lofty and, as they call it, up-in-the-air sort of thought, derived hence not merely, as was natural, elevation of purpose and dignity of language, raised far above the base and dishonest buffooneries of mob eloquence, but, besides this, a composure of countenance, and a serenity and calmness in all his movements, which no occurrence whilst he was speaking could disturb, a sustained and even tone of voice, and various other advantages of a similar kind, which produced the greatest effect on his hearers. Nor were these the only advantages which Pericles derived from Anaxagoras's acquaintance; he seems also to have become, by his instructions, superior to that superstition with which an ignorant wonder at appearances, for example, in the heavens, possesses the minds of people unacquainted with their causes, eager for the supernatural, and excitable through an inexperience which the knowledge of natural causes removes, replacing wild and timid superstition by the good hope and assurance of an intelligent piety.

Pericles, while yet but a young man, stood in considerable apprehension of the people, as he was thought in face and figure to be very like the tyrant Pisistratus, and those of great age remarked upon the sweetness of his voice, and his volubility and rapidity in speaking, and were struck with amazement at the resemblance. Reflecting, too, that he had a considerable estate, and was descended of a noble family, and had friends of great influence, he was fearful all this might bring him to be banished as a dangerous person, and for this reason meddled not at all with state affairs, but in military service showed himself of a brave and intrepid nature. But when Aristides was now dead, and Themistocles driven out, and Cimon was for the most part kept abroad by the expeditions he made in parts out of Greece, Pericles, seeing things in this posture, now advanced and took his side, not with the rich and few, but with the many and poor, contrary to his natural bent, which was far from democratical; but, most likely fearing he might fall under suspicion of aiming at arbitrary power, and seeing Cimon on the side of the aristocracy, and much beloved by the better and more distinguished people, he joined the party of the people, with a view at once both to secure himself and procure means against Cimon.

He immediately entered, also, on quite a new course of life and management of his time. For he was never seen to walk in any street but that which led to the market-place and council-hall, and he avoided invitations of friends to supper, and all friendly visiting and intercourse whatever; in all the time he had to do with the public, which was not a little, he was never known to have gone to any of his friends to a supper, except that once when his near kinsman Euryptolemus married, he remained present till the ceremony of the drink-offering, and then immediately rose from table and went his way. For these friendly meetings are very quick to defeat any assumed superiority, and in intimate familiarity an exterior of gravity is hard to maintain. Real excellence, indeed, is most recognized when most openly looked into; and in really good men, nothing which meets the eyes of external observers so truly deserves their admiration, as their daily common life does that of their nearer friends. Pericles, however, to avoid any feeling of commonness, or any satiety on the part of the people, presented himself at intervals only, not speaking to every business, nor at all times coming into the assembly, but, as Critolaus says, reserving himself, like the Salaminian galley, for great occasions, while matters of lesser importance were despatched by friends or other speakers under his direction.

Since Thucydides describes the rule of Pericles as an aristocratical government, that went by the name of a democracy, but was, indeed, the supremacy of a single great man, while many others say, on the contrary, that by him the common people were first encouraged and led on to such evils as appropriations of subject territory, allowances for attending theaters, payments for performing public duties, and by these bad habits were, under the influence of his public measures, changed from a sober, thrifty people, that maintained themselves by their own labors, to lovers of expense, intemperance, and license, let us examine the cause of this change by the actual matters of fact.

At the first, as has been said, when he set himself against Cimon's great authority, he did caress the people. Finding himself come short of his competitor in wealth and money, by which advantages the other was enabled to take care of the poor, inviting every day someone or other of the citizens that was in want to supper, and bestowing clothes on the aged people, and breaking down the hedges and enclosures of his grounds, that all that would might freely gather what fruit they pleased, Pericles, thus outdone in popular arts, by the advice of one Damonides of Œa, as Aristotle states, turned to the distribution of the public moneys; and in a short time having bought the people over, what with moneys allowed for shows and for service on juries, and what with other forms of pay and largess, he made use of them against the council of Areopagus of which he himself was no member, as having never been appointed by lot either chief archon, or lawgiver, or king, or captain. For from of old these offices were conferred on persons by lot, and they who had acquitted themselves duly in the discharge of them were advanced to the court of Areopagus. And so Pericles, having secured his power in interest with the populace, directed the exertions of his party against this council with such success that most of these causes and matters which had been used to be tried there were, by the agency of Ephialtes, removed from its cognizance; Cimon, also, was banished by ostracism as a favorer of the Lacedæmonians and a hater of the people, though in wealth and noble birth he was among the first, and had won several most glorious victories over the barbarians, and had filled the city with money and spoils of war; as is recorded in the history of his life. So vast an authority had Pericles obtained among the people.

There was from the beginning a sort of concealed split, or seam, as it might be in a piece of iron, marking the different popular and aristocratical tendencies; but the open rivalry and contention of Pericles and Cimon made the gash deep, and severed the city into the two parties of the people and the few. And so Pericles, at that time, more than at any other, let loose the reins to the people, and made his policy subservient to their pleasure, contriving continually to have some great public show or solemnity, some banquet, or some procession or other in the town to please them, coaxing his countrymen like children with such delights and pleasures as were not, however, unedifying. Besides that every year he sent out threescore galleys, on board of which there were numbers of the citizens, who were in pay eight months, learning at the same time and practicing the art of seamanship.

He sent, moreover, a thousand of them into the Chersonese as planters, to share the land among them by lot, and five hundred more into the isle of Naxos, and half that number to Andros, a thousand into Thrace to dwell among the Bisaltæ, and others into Italy, when the city Sybaris, which now was called Thurii, was to be repeopled. And this he did to ease and discharge the city of an idle, and, by reason of their idleness, a busy meddling crowd of people; and at the same time to meet the necessities and restore the fortunes of the poor townsmen, and to intimidate, also, and check their allies from attempting any change, by posting such garrisons, as it were, in the midst of them.

That which gave most pleasure and ornament to the city of Athens, and the greatest admiration and even astonishment to all strangers, and that which now is Greece's only evidence that the power she boasts of and her ancient wealth are no romance or idle story, was his construction of the public and sacred buildings. Yet this was that of all his actions in the government which his enemies most looked askance upon and caviled at in the popular assemblies, crying out how that the commonwealth of Athens had lost its reputation and was ill spoken of abroad for removing the common treasure of the Greeks from the isle of Delos into their own custody; and how that their fairest excuse for so doing, namely, that they took it away for fear the barbarians should seize it, and on purpose to secure it in a safe place, this Pericles had made unavailable, and how that "Greece cannot but resent it as an insufferable affront, and consider herself to be tyrannized over openly, when she sees the treasure, which was contributed by her upon a necessity for the war, wantonly lavished out by us upon our city, to gild her all over, and to adorn and set her forth, as it were some vain woman, hung round with precious stones and figures and temples, which cost a world of money."

Pericles, on the other hand, informed the people that they were in no way obliged to give any account of these moneys to their allies, so long as they maintained their defense, and kept off the barbarians from attacking them; while in the meantime they did not so much as supply one horse or man or ship, but only found money for the service; "which money," said he, "is not theirs that give it, but theirs that receive it, if so be they perform the conditions upon which they receive it." And that it was good reason, that, now the city was sufficiently provided and stored with all things necessary for the war, they should convert the overplus of its wealth to such undertakings as would hereafter, when completed, give them eternal honor, and, for the present, while in process, freely supply all the inhabitants with plenty. With their variety of workmanship and of occasions for service, which summon all arts and trades and require all hands to be employed about them, they do actually put the whole city, in a manner, into state-pay; while at the same time she is both beautiful and maintained by herself. For as those who are of age and strength for war are provided for and maintained in the armaments abroad by their pay out of the public stock, so, it being his desire and design that the undisciplined mechanic multitude that stayed at home should not go without their share of public salaries, and yet should not have them given them for sitting still and doing nothing, to that end he thought fit to bring in among them, with the approbation of the people, these vast projects of buildings and designs of work, that would be of some continuance before they were finished, and would give employment to numerous arts, so that the part of the people that stayed at home might, no less than those that were at sea or in garrisons or on expeditions, have a fair and just occasion of receiving the benefit and having their share of the public moneys.

The materials were stone, brass, ivory, gold, ebony, cypresswood; and the arts or trades that wrought and fashioned them were smiths and carpenters, molders, founders and braziers, stone-cutters, dyers, goldsmiths, ivory-workers, painters, embroiderers, turners; those again that conveyed them to the town for use, merchants and mariners and ship-masters by sea, and by land, cartwrights, cattle-breeders, wagoners, rope-makers, flax-workers, shoemakers and leather-dressers, road-makers, miners. And every trade in the same nature, as a captain in an army has his particular company of soldiers under him, had its own hired company of journeymen and laborers belonging to it banded together as in array, to be as it were the instrument and body for the performance of the service. Thus, to say all in a word, the occasions and services of these public works distributed plenty through every age and condition.

As then grew the works up, no less stately in size than exquisite in form, the workmen striving to outvie the material and the design with the beauty of their workmanship, yet the most wonderful thing of all was the rapidity of their execution.

Undertakings, any one of which singly might have required, they thought, for their completion, several successions and ages of men, were every one of them accomplished in the height and prime of one man's political service. Although they say, too, that Zeuxis once, having heard Agatharchus the painter boast of despatching his work with speed and ease, replied, "I take a long time." For ease and speed in doing a thing do not give the work lasting solidity or exactness of beauty; the expenditure of time allowed to a man's pains beforehand for the production of a thing is repaid by way of interest with a vital force for the preservation when once produced. For which reason Pericles's works are especially admired, as having been made quickly, to last long. For every particular piece of his work was immediately, even at that time, for its beauty and elegance, antique; and yet in its vigor and freshness looks to this day as if it were just executed. There is a sort of bloom of newness upon those works of his, preserving them from the touch of time, as if they had some perennial spirit and undying vitality mingled in the composition of them.

Phidias had the oversight of all the works, and was surveyor-general, though upon the various portions other great masters and workmen were employed. For Callicrates and Ictinus built the Parthenon;[2] the chapel at Eleusis, where the mysteries were celebrated, was begun by Corœbus, who erected the pillars that stand upon the floor or pavement, and joined them to the architraves; and after his death Metagenes of Xypete added the frieze and the upper line of columns; Xenocles of Cholargus roofed or arched the lantern on top of the temple of Castor and Pollux; and the long wall,[3] which Socrates says he himself heard

---

[2] The large temple crowning the Acropolis. It is a master work of architecture and sculpture.
[3] A series of three walls extending from Athens to the harbor at Piræus, some five miles distant.

Pericles propose to the people, was undertaken by Callicrates.

The Odeum, or music-room, which in its interior was full of seats and ranges of pillars, and outside had its roof made to slope and descend from one single point at the top, was constructed, we are told, in imitation of the King of Persia's Pavilion; this likewise by Pericles's order.

Pericles, also eager for distinction, then first obtained the decree for a contest in musical skill to be held yearly at the Panathenæa, and he himself, being chosen judge, arranged the order and method in which the competitors should sing and play on the flute and on the harp. And both at that time, and at other times also, they sat in this music-room to see and hear all such trials of skill.

The propylæa, or entrances to the Acropolis, were finished in five years' time, Mnesicles being the principal architect. A strange accident happened in the course of building, which showed that the goddess was not averse to the work, but was aiding and co-operating to bring it to perfection. One of the artificers, the quickest and the handiest workman among them all, with a slip of his foot fell down from a great height, and lay in a miserable condition, the physicians having no hope of his recovery. When Pericles was in distress about this, Minerva appeared to him at night in a dream, and ordered a course of treatment, which he applied, and in a short time and with great ease cured the man. And upon this occasion it was that he set up a brass statue of Minerva, surnamed Health, in the citadel near the altar, which they say was there before. But it was Phidias who wrought the goddess's image in gold, and he has his name inscribed on the pedestal as the workman of it; and indeed the whole work in a manner was under his charge, and he had, as we have said already, the oversight over all the artists and workmen, through Pericles's friendship for him; and this, indeed, made him much envied, and his patron shamefully slandered with stories.

When the orators, who sided with Thucydides and his party, were at one time crying out, as their custom was, against Pericles, as one who squandered away the public money, and made havoc of the state revenues, he rose in the open assembly and put the question to the people, whether they thought that he had laid out much; and they saying, "Too much, a great deal." "Then," said he, "since it is so, let the cost not go to your account, but to mine; and let the inscription upon the buildings stand in my name." When they heard him say thus, whether it were out of a surprise to see the greatness of his spirit or out of emulation of the glory of the works, they cried aloud, bidding him to spend on, and lay out what he thought fit from the public purse, and to spare no cost, till all were finished.

At length, coming to a final contest with Thucydides which of the two should ostracize the other out of the country, and having gone through this peril, he threw his antagonist out, and broke up the confederacy that had been organized against him. So that now all schism and division being at an end, and the city brought to evenness and unity, he got all Athens and all affairs that pertained to the Athenians into his own hands, their tributes, their armies, and their galleys, the islands, the sea, and their wide-extended power, partly over other Greeks, and partly over barbarians, and all that empire, which they possessed, founded and fortified upon subject nations and royal friendships and alliances.

After this he was no longer the same man he had been before, nor as tame and gentle and familiar as formerly with the populace, so as readily to yield to their pleasures and to comply with the desires of the multitude, as a steersman shifts with the winds. Quitting that loose, remiss, and, in some cases, licentious court of the popular will, he turned those soft and flowery modulations to the austerity of aristocratical and regal rule; and employing this uprightly and undeviatingly for the country's best interests, he was able generally to lead the people along, with their own wills and consents, by persuading and showing them what was to be done; and sometimes, too, urging and pressing them forward extremely against their will, he made them, whether they would or no, yield submission to what was for their advantage. In which, to say the truth, he did but like a skillful physician, who, in a complicated and chronic disease, as he sees occasion, at one while allows his patient the moderate use of such things as please him, at another while gives him keen pains and drug to work the cure. For there arising and growing up, as was natural, all manner of distempered feelings among a people which had so vast a command and dominion, he alone, as a great master, knowing how to handle and deal fitly with each one of them, and, in an especial manner, making that use of hopes and fears, as his two chief rudders, with the one to check the career of their confidence at any time, with the other to raise them up and cheer them when under any discouragement, plainly showed by this, that rhetoric, or the art of speaking, is, in Plato's language, the government of the souls of men, and that her chief business is to address the affections and passions, which are as it were the strings and keys to the soul, and require a skillful and careful touch to be played on as they should be. The source of this predominance was not barely his power of language, but, as Thucydides assures us, the reputation of his life, and the confidence felt in his character; his mani-[10]fest freedom from every kind of corruption, and superiority to all considerations of money. Notwithstanding he had made the city of Athens, which was great of itself, as great and rich as can be imagined, and though he were himself in power and interest more than equal to many kings and absolute rulers, who some of them also bequeathed by will their power to their children, he, for his part, did not make the patrimony his father left him greater than it was by one drachma. [20]

His paternal estate, which of right belonged to him, he so ordered that it might neither through negligence be wasted or lessened, nor yet, being so full of business as he was, cost him any great trouble or time with taking care of it; and put it into such a way of management as he thought to be the most easy for himself, and the most exact. All his yearly products and profits he sold together in a lump, and supplied his household needs afterwards by buying everything that he or his family [30]wanted out of the market. Upon which account, his children, when they grew to age, were not well pleased with his management, and the women that lived with him were treated with little cost, and complained of his way of housekeeping, where everything was ordered and set down from day to day, and reduced to the greatest exactness; since there was not there, as is usual in a great family and a plentiful estate, anything to spare, or over and above; but all that went out or came in, all [40]disbursements and all receipts, proceeded as it were by number and measure.

The Lacedæmonians beginning to show themselves troubled at the growth of the Athenian power, Pericles, on the other hand, to elevate the people's spirit yet more, and to raise them to the thought of great actions, proposed a decree, to summon all the Greeks in what part soever, whether of Europe or Asia, every city, little as well as great, to send their deputies to Athens to [50]a general assembly, or convention, there to consult and advise concerning the Greek temples which the barbarians had burnt down, and the sacrifices which were due from them upon vows they had made to their gods for the safety of Greece when they fought against the barbarians; and also concerning the navigation of the sea, that they might henceforward pass to and fro and trade securely and be at peace among themselves.

Upon this errand there were twenty men, of such as were above fifty years of age, sent by commission: five to summon the Ionians and Dorians [10]in Asia, and the islanders as far as Lesbos and Rhodes; five to visit all the places in the Hellespont and Thrace, up to Byzantium; and other five besides these to go to Bœotia and Phocis and Peloponnesus, and from hence to pass through the Locrians over to the neighboring continent as far as Acarnania and Ambracia; and the rest to take their course through Eubœa to the Œtæans and the Malian Gulf, and to the Achæans of Phthiotis and the Thessalians; all of them to treat with [20]the people as they passed, and persuade them to come and take their part in the debates for settling the peace and jointly regulating the affairs of Greece.

Nothing was effected, nor did the cities meet by their deputies, as was desired; the Lacedæmonians, as it is said, crossing the design underhand, and the attempt being disappointed and baffled first in Peloponnesus. I thought fit, however, to introduce the mention of it, to show the spirit of the man [30]and the greatness of his thoughts.

In his military conduct, he gained a great reputation for wariness; he would not by his good-will engage in any fight which had much uncertainty or hazard; he did not envy the glory of generals whose rash adventures fortune favored with brilliant success, however they were admired by others; nor did he think them worthy his imitation, but always used to say to his citizens that, so far as lay in his power, they should continue immor-[40]tal, and live for ever.

Of all his expeditions, that to the Chersonese gave most satisfaction and pleasure, having proved the safety of the Greeks who inhabited there. For not only by carrying along with him a thousand fresh citizens of Athens he gave new strength and vigor to the cities, but also by belting the neck of land, which joins the peninsula to the continent, with bulwarks and forts from sea to sea, he put a stop to the inroads of the Thracians, who lay all [50]about the Chersonese, and closed the door against a continual and grievous war, with which that country had been long harassed, lying exposed to the encroachments and influx of barbarous neighbors, and groaning under the evils of a predatory population both upon and within its borders.

Pericles curbed the passion of the Athenians for foreign conquest, and unsparingly pruned and cut down their ever busy fancies for a multitude of undertakings; and directed their power for the most part to securing and consolidating what they had already got, supposing it would be quite enough for them to do, if they could keep the Lacedæmonians in check.

That he did well and wisely in thus restraining the exertions of the Athenians within the compass of Greece, the events themselves that happened afterward bore sufficient witness. For, in the first place, the Eubœans revolted, against whom he passed over with forces; and then, immediately after, news came that the Megarians were turned their enemies; and a hostile army was upon the borders of Attica, under the conduct of Plistoanax, King of the Lacedæmonians. Wherefore Pericles came with his army back again in all haste out of Eubœa, to meet the war which threatened at home; and did not venture to engage a numerous and brave army eager for battle; but perceiving that Plistoanax was a very young man, and governed himself mostly by the counsel and advice of Cleandrides, whom the ephors had sent with him, by reason of his youth, to be a kind of guardian and assistant to him, he privately made trial of this man's integrity, and, in a short time, having corrupted him with money, prevailed with him to withdraw the Peloponnesians out of Attica.

When Pericles, in giving up his accounts of this expedition, stated a disbursement of ten talents, as laid out upon fit occasion, the people, without any question, nor troubling themselves to investigate the mystery, freely allowed of it. And some historians, in which number is Theophrastus the philosopher, have given it as a truth that Pericles every year used to send privately the sum of ten talents to Sparta, with which he complimented those in office, to keep off the war; not to purchase peace neither, but time, that he might prepare at leisure, and be the better able to carry on war hereafter.

Immediately after this, turning his forces against the revolters, and passing over into the island of Eubœa with fifty sail of ships and five thousand men in arms, he reduced their cities, and drove out the citizens of the Chalcidians, called Hippobotæ, horse-feeders, the chief persons for wealth and reputation among them; and removing all the Histiæans out of the country, brought in a planta-

tion of Athenians in their room; making them his one example of severity, because they had captured an Attic ship and killed all on board.

After this, having made a truce between the Athenians and Lacedæmonians for thirty years, he ordered, by public decree, the expedition against the isle of Samos, on the ground, that, when they were bid to leave off their war with the Milesians they had not complied. And as these measures against the Samians are thought to have been taken to please Aspasia, this may be a fit point for inquiry about the woman, what art or charming faculty she had that enabled her to captivate, as she did, the greatest statesmen, and to give the philosophers occasion to speak so much about her, and that, too, not to her disparagement. That she was a Milesian by birth, the daughter of Axiochus, is a thing acknowledged. And they say it was in emulation of Thargelia, a courtesan of the old Ionian times, that she made her addresses to men of great power. Thargelia was a great beauty, extremely charming, and at the same time sagacious; she had numerous suitors among the Greeks, and brought all who had to do with her over to the Persian interest, and by their means, being men of the greatest power and station, sowed the seeds of the Median faction up and down in several cities. Aspasia, some say, was courted and caressed by Pericles upon account of her knowledge and skill in politics. Socrates himself would sometimes go to visit her, and some of his acquaintance with him; and those who frequented her company would carry their wives with them to listen to her. Her occupation was anything but creditable, her house being a home for young courtesans. Æschines tells us, also, that Lysicles, a sheep-dealer, a man of low birth and character, by keeping Aspasia company after Pericles's death, came to be a chief man in Athens. And in Plato's Menexenus, though we do not take the introduction as quite serious, still thus much seems to be historical, that she had the repute of being resorted to by many of the Athenians for instruction in the art of speaking. Pericles's inclination for her seems, however, to have rather proceeded from the passion of love. He had a wife that was near of kin to him, who had been married first to Hipponicus, by whom she had Callias, surnamed the Rich; and also she brought Pericles, while she lived with him, two sons, Xanthippus and Paralus. Afterwards, when they did not well agree, nor like to live together, he parted with her, with her own consent, to another man, and himself took Aspasia, and loved her with wonderful affection; every day, both as he went out and as he came in from the market-place, he saluted and kissed her.

When the Peloponnesian War began to break out in full tide, he advised the people to send help to the Corcyræans, who were attacked by the Corinthians, and to secure to themselves an island possessed of great naval resources, since the Peloponnesians were already all but in actual hostilities against them. And when now the Corinthians, angry and indignant with the Athenians, accused them publicly at Lacedæmon, the Megarians joined with them, complaining that they were, contrary to common right and the articles of peace sworn to among the Greeks, kept out and driven away from every market and from all ports under the control of the Athenians. The Æginetans, also, professing to be ill-used and treated with violence, made supplications in private to the Lacedæmonians for redress, though not daring openly to call the Athenians in question. In the meantime, also, the city Potidæa, under the dominion of the Athenians, but a colony formerly of the Corinthians, had revolted, and was beset with a formal siege, and was a further occasion of precipitating the war.

Yet notwithstanding all this, there being embassies sent to Athens, and Archidamus, the King of the Lacedæmonians, endeavoring to bring the greater part of the complaints and matters in dispute to a fair determination, and to pacify and allay the heats of the allies, it is very likely that the war would not upon any other grounds of quarrel have fallen upon the Athenians, could they have been prevailed with to repeal the ordinance against the Megarians, and to be reconciled to them. Upon which account, since Pericles was the man who mainly opposed it, and stirred up the people's passions to persist in their contention with the Megarians, he was regarded as the sole cause of the war.

They say, moreover, that ambassadors went, by order, from Lacedæmon to Athens about this very business, and that when Pericles was urging a certain law which made it illegal to take down or withdraw the tablet of the decree, one of the ambassadors, Polyalces by name, said, "Well, do not take it down then, but *turn* it; there is no law, I suppose, which forbids that;" which, though prettily said, did not move Pericles from his resolution. There may have been, in all likelihood, something of a secret grudge and private animosity which he had against the Megarians. Yet, upon a public and open charge against them, that they had appropriated part of the sacred land on the frontier, he proposed a decree that a herald should be sent to them, and the same also to the Lacedæmonians, with an accusation of the Megarians; an order which certainly shows equitable and friendly proceedings enough. And after that the herald who was sent, by name Anthemocritus, died, and it was believed that the Megarians had contrived his death, then Charinus proposed a decree against them, that there should be an irreconcilable and implacable enmity thenceforward betwixt the two commonwealths; and that if any one of the Megarians should but set foot in Attica, he should be put to death; and that the commanders, when they take the usual oath, should, over and above that, swear that they will twice every year make an inroad into the Megarian country; and that Anthemocritus should be buried near the Thracian Gates, which are now called the Dipylon, or Double Gate.

On the other hand, the Megarians, utterly denying and disowning the murder of Anthemocritus, throw the whole matter upon Aspasia and Pericles. The true occasion of the quarrel is not so easy to find out. But of inducing the refusal to annul the decree, all alike charge Pericles. Some say he met the request with a positive refusal, out of high spirit and a view of the state's best interest, accounting that the demand made in those embassies was designed for a trial of their compliance, and that a concession would be taken for a confession of weakness as if they durst not do otherwise; while other some there are who say that it was rather out of arrogance and a willful spirit of contention, to show his own strength, that he took occasion to slight the Lacedæmonians.

The worst motive of all, which is confirmed by most witnesses, is to the following effect: Phidias the Molder had, as has before been said, undertaken to make the statue of Minerva. Now he, being admitted to friendship with Pericles, and a great favorite of his, had many enemies upon this account, who envied and maligned him; who also, to make trial in a case of his, what kind of judges the commons would prove, should there be occasion to bring Pericles himself before them, having tampered with Menon, one who had been a workman with Phidias, stationed him in the market-place, with a petition desiring public security upon his discovery and impeachment of Phidias. The people admitting the man to tell his story, and the prosecution proceeding in the assembly, there was nothing of theft or cheat proved against him; for Phidias, from the very first beginning, by the advice of Pericles, had so wrought and wrapt the gold that was used in the work about the statue, that they might take it all off, and make out the just weight of it, which Pericles at that time bade the accuser do. But the reputation of his works was what brought envy upon Phidias, especially that where he represents the fight of the Amazons upon the goddess's shield, he had introduced a likeness of himself as a bald old man holding up a great stone with both hands, and had put in a very fine representation of Pericles fighting with an Amazon. And the position of the hand which holds out the spear in front of the face, was ingeniously contrived to conceal in some degree the likeness, which meantime showed itself on either side.

Phidias then was carried away to prison, and there died of a disease; but, as some say, of poison, administered by the enemies of Pericles, to raise a slander, or a suspicion at least, as though he had procured it. The informer Menon, upon Glycon's proposal, the people made free from payment of taxes and customs, and ordered the generals to take care that nobody should do him any hurt. About the same time, Aspasia was indicted of impiety, upon the complaint of Hermippus the comedian, who also laid further to her charge that she received into her house freeborn women for the uses of Pericles. And Diopithes proposed a decree, that public accusations should be laid against persons who neglected religion, or taught new doctrines about things above, directing suspicion, by means of Anaxagoras, against Pericles himself. The people receiving and admitting these accusations and complaints, at length, by this means, they came to enact a decree, at the motion of Dracontides, that Pericles should bring in the accounts of the moneys he had expended, and lodge them with the Prytanes; and that the judges, carrying their suffrage from the altar in the Acropolis, should examine and determine the business in the city. This last clause Hagnon took out of the decree, and moved that the causes should be tried before fifteen hundred jurors, whether they should be styled prosecutions for robbery, or bribery, or any kind of malversation. Aspasia, Pericles begged off, shedding, as Æschines says, many tears at the trial, and personally entreating the jurors. But fearing how it might go with Anaxagoras, he sent him out of the city. And finding that in Phidias's case he had miscarried with the people, being afraid of impeachment, he kindled the war, which hitherto had lingered and smothered, and blew it up into a flame; hoping, by that means, to disperse and scatter these complaints and charges, and to allay their jealousy; the city usually throwing herself upon him alone, and trusting to his sole conduct, upon the urgency of great affairs and public dangers, by reason of his authority and the sway he bore.

These are given out to have been the reasons which induced Pericles not to suffer the people of Athens to yield to the proposals of the Lacedæmonians; but their truth is uncertain.

The Lacedæmonians, for their part, feeling sure that if they could once remove him, they might be at what terms they pleased with the Athenians, sent them word that they should expel the "Pollution" with which Pericles on the mother's side was tainted, as Thucydides tells us. But the issue proved quite contrary to what those who sent the message expected; instead of bringing Pericles under suspicion and reproach, they raised him into yet greater credit and esteem with the citizens, as a man whom their enemies most hated and feared. In the same way, also, before Archidamus, who was at the head of the Peloponnesians, made his invasion into Attica, he told the Athenians beforehand, that if Archidamus, while he laid waste the rest of the country, should forbear and spare his estate, either on the ground of friendship or right of hospitality that was betwixt them, or on purpose to give his enemies an occasion of traducing him; that then he did freely bestow upon the state all his land and the buildings upon it for the public use. The Lacedæmonians, therefore, and their allies, with a great army, invaded the Athenian territories, under the conduct of King Archidamus, and laying waste the country, marched on as far as Acharnæ, and there pitched their camp, presuming that the Athenians would never endure that, but would come out and fight them for their country's and their honor's sake.

But Pericles looked upon it as dangerous to engage in battle, to the risk of the city itself, against sixty thousand men-at-arms of Peloponnesians and Bœotians; for so many they were in number that made the inroad at first; and he endeavored to appease those who were desirous to fight, and were grieved and discontented to see how things went, and gave them good words, saying, that "trees, when they are lopped and cut, grow up again in a short time, but men, being once lost, cannot easily be recovered." He did not convene the people into an assembly, for fear lest they should force him to act against his judgment; but, like a skillful steersman or pilot of a ship, who, when a sudden squall comes on, out at sea, makes all his arrangements, sees that all is tight and fast, and then follows the dictates of his skill, and minds the business of the ship, taking no notice of the tears and entreaties of the sea-sick and fearful passengers, so he, having shut up the city gates, and placed guards at all posts for security, followed his own reason and judgment, little regarding those that cried out against him and were angry at his management, although there were a great many of his friends that urged him with requests, and many of his enemies threatened and accused him for doing as he did, and many made songs and lampoons upon him, which were sung about the town to his disgrace, reproaching him with the cowardly exercise of his office of general, and the tame abandonment of everything to the enemy's hands.

Pericles, however, was not at all moved by any attacks, but took all patiently, and submitted in silence to the disgrace they threw upon him and the ill-will they bore him; and, sending out a fleet of a hundred galleys to Peloponnesus, he did not go along with it in person, but stayed behind that he might watch at home and keep the city under his own control, till the Peloponnesians broke up their camp and were gone. Yet to soothe the common people, jaded and distressed with the war, he relieved them with distributions of public moneys, and ordained new divisions of subject land. For having turned out all the people of Ægina, he parted the island among the Athenians according to lot. Some comfort, also, and ease in their miseries, they might receive from what their enemies endured. For the fleet, sailing round the Peloponnese, ravaged a great deal of the country, and pillaged and plundered the towns and smaller cities; and by land he himself entered with an army the Megarian country, and made havoc of it all. Whence it is clear that the Peloponnesians, though they did the Athenians much mischief by land, yet suffering as much themselves from them by sea, would not have protracted the war to such a length, but would quickly have given it over, as Pericles at first foretold they would, had not some divine power crossed human purposes.

In the first place, the pestilential disease, or plague, seized upon the city, and ate up all the flower and prime of their youth and strength. Upon occasion of which, the people, distempered and afflicted in their souls, as well as in their bodies, were utterly enraged like madmen against Pericles, and, like patients grown delirious, sought to lay violent hands on their physician, or, as it were, their father. They had been possessed, by his enemies, with the belief that the occasion of the plague was the crowding of the country people together into the town, forced as they were now, in the heat of the summer weather, to dwell many of them together even as they could, in small tenements and stifling hovels, and to be tied to a lazy course of life within doors, whereas before they lived in a pure, open, and free air. The cause and author of all this, said they, is he who on account of the war has poured a multitude of people in upon us within the walls, and uses all these men that he has here upon no employ or service, but keeps them pent up like cattle, to be overrun with infection from one another, affording them neither shift of quarters nor any refreshment.

With the design to remedy these evils, and do the enemy some inconvenience, Pericles got a hundred and fifty galleys ready, and having embarked many tried soldiers, both foot and horse, was about to sail out, giving great hope to his citizens, and no less alarm to his enemies, upon the sight of so great a force And now the vessels having their complement of men, and Pericles being gone aboard his own galley, it happened that the sun was eclipsed, and it grew dark on a sudden, to the affright of all, for this was looked upon as extremely ominous. Pericles, therefore, perceiving the steersman seized with fear and at a loss what to do, took his cloak and held it up before the man's face, and screening him with it so that he could not see, asked him whether he imagined there was any great hurt, or the sign of any great hurt in this, and he answering No, "Why," said he, "and what does that differ from this, only that what has caused that darkness there, is something greater than a cloak?" This is a story which philosophers tell their scholars. Pericles, however, after putting out to sea, seems not to have done any other exploit befitting such preparations, and when he had laid siege to the holy city Epidaurus, which gave him some hope of surrender, miscarried in his design by reason of the sickness. For it not only seized upon the Athenians, but upon all others, too, that held any sort of communication with the army. Finding after this the Athenians ill-affected and highly displeased with him, he tried and endeavored what he could to appease and re-encourage them. But he could not pacify or allay their anger, nor persuade or prevail with them any way, till they freely passed their votes upon him, resumed their power, took away his command from him, and fined him in a sum of money; which by their account that say least, was fifteen talents, while they who reckon most, name fifty.

After this, public troubles were soon to leave him unmolested; the people, so to say, discharged their passion in their stroke, and lost their stings in the wound. But his domestic concerns were in an unhappy condition, many of his friends and acquaintances having died in the plague time, and those of his family having long since been in disorder and in a kind of mutiny against him. For the eldest of his lawfully begotten sons, Xanthippus by name, being naturally prodigal, and marrying a young and expensive wife, the daughter of Tisander, son of Epilycus, was highly offended at his father's economy in making him but a scanty allowance, by little and little at a time. He sent, therefore, to a friend one day and borrowed some money of him in his father Pericles's name, pretending it was by his order. The man coming afterward to demand the debt, Pericles was so far from yielding to pay it, that he entered an action against him. Upon which the young man, Xanthippus, thought himself so ill-used and disobliged that he openly reviled his father; telling first, by way of ridicule, stories about his conversations at nome, and the discourses he had with the sophists and scholars that came to his house. This difference of the young man's with his father, and the breach betwixt them, continued never to be healed or made up till his death. For Xanthippus died in the plague time of the sickness. At which time Pericles also lost his sister, and the greatest part of his relations and friends, and those who had been most useful and serviceable to him in managing the affairs of state. However, he did not shrink or give in upon these occasions, nor betray or lower his high spirit and the greatness of his mind under all his misfortunes; he was not even so much as seen to weep or to mourn, or even attend the burial of any of his friends or relations, till at last he lost his only remaining legitimate son. Subdued by this blow, and yet striving still, as far as he could, to maintain his principle, and to preserve and keep up the greatness of his soul, when he came, however, to perform the ceremony of putting a garland of flowers upon the head of the corpse, he was vanquished by his passion at the sight, so that he burst into exclamations, and shed copious tears, having never done any such thing in his life before.

The city having made trial of other generals for the conduct of war, and orators for business of state, when they found there was no one who was of weight enough for such a charge, or of authority sufficient to be trusted with so great a command, regretted the loss of him, and invited him again to address and advise them, and to reassume the office of general. He, however, lay at home in dejection and mourning; but was persuaded by Alcibiades and others of his friends to come abroad and show himself to the people; who having, upon his appearance, made their acknowledgments, and apologized for their untowardly treatment of him, he undertook the public affairs again.

About the time when his son was enrolled [in the army], it should seem the plague seized Pericles, not with sharp and violent fits, as it did others that had it, but with a dull and lingering distemper, attended with various changes and alterations, leisurely, by little and little, wasting the strength of his body, and undermining the noble faculties of his soul. So that Theophrastus, in his Morals, when discussing whether men's characters change with their circumstances, and their moral habits, disturbed by the ailings of their bodies, start aside from the rules of virtue, has left it upon record, that Pericles, when he was sick, showed one of his friends that came to visit him an amulet or charm that the women had hung about his neck; as much as to say, that he was very sick indeed when he would admit of such a foolery as that was.

When he was now near his end, the best of the citizens and those of his friends who were left alive, sitting about him, were speaking of the greatness of his merit, and his power, and reckoning up his famous actions and the number of his victories; for there were no less than nine trophies, which, as their chief commander and conqueror of their enemies, he had set up for the honor of the city. They talked thus together among themselves, as though he were unable to understand or mind what they said but had now lost his consciousness. He had listened, however, all the while, and attended to all, and, speaking out among them, said that he wondered they should commend and take notice of things which were as much owing to fortune as to anything else, and had happened to many other commanders, and, at the same time, should not speak or make mention of that which was the most excellent and greatest thing of all. "For," said he, "no Athenian, through my means, ever wore mourning."

He was indeed a character deserving our high admiration not only for his equitable and mild temper, which all along in the many affairs of his life, and the great animosities which he incurred, he constantly maintained; but also for the high spirit and feeling which made him regard it the noblest of all his honors that, in the exercise of such immense power, he never had gratified his envy or his passion, nor ever had treated any enemy as irreconcilably opposed to him. And to me it appears that this one thing gives that otherwise childish and arrogant title a fitting and becoming significance; so dispassionate a temper, a life so pure and unblemished, in the height of power and place, might well be called Olympian, in accordance with our conceptions of the divine beings, to whom, as the natural authors of all good and of nothing evil, we ascribe the rule and government of the world. Not as the poets represent, who, while confounding us with their ignorant fancies, are themselves confuted by their own poems and fictions, and call the place, indeed, where they say the gods make their abode, a secure and quiet seat, free from all hazards and commotions, untroubled with winds or with clouds, and equally through all time illumined with a soft serenity and a pure light as though such were a

home most agreeable for a blessed and immortal nature; and yet, in the meanwhile, affirm that the gods themselves are full of trouble and enmity and anger and other passions, which no way become or belong to even men that have any understanding. But this will, perhaps, seem a subject fitter for some other consideration, and that ought to be treated of in some other place.

The course of public affairs after his death produced a quick and speedy sense of the loss of Pericles. Those who, while he lived, resented his great authority, as that which eclipsed themselves, presently after his quitting the stage, making trial of other orators and demagogues, readily acknowledged that there never had been in nature such a disposition as his was, more moderate and reasonable in the height of that state he took upon him, or more grave and impressive in the mildness which he used. And that invidious arbitrary power, to which formerly they gave the name of monarchy and tyranny, did then appear to have been the chief bulwark of public safety; so great a corruption and such a flood of mischief and vice followed which he, by keeping weak and low, had withheld from notice, and had prevented from attaining incurable height through a licentious impunity.

THUCYDIDES

The Funeral Oration of Pericles

In the same winter the Athenians gave a funeral at the public cost to those who had first fallen in this war.[1] It was a custom of their ancestors, and the manner of it is as follows. Three days before the ceremony, the bones of the dead are laid out in a tent which has been erected; and their friends bring to their relatives such offerings as they please. In the funeral procession cypress coffins are borne in cars, one for each tribe; the bones of the deceased being placed in the coffin of their tribe. Among these is carried one empty bier decked for

the missing, that is, for those whose bodies could not be recovered. Any citizen or stranger who pleases, joins in the procession: and the female relatives are there to wail at the burial. The dead are laid in the public sepulcher in the beautiful suburb of the city, in which those who fall in war are always buried; with the exception of those slain at Marathon, who for their singular and extraordinary valor were interred on the spot where they fell. After the bodies have been laid in the earth, a man chosen by the state, of approved

Pericles' Funeral Oration. Translated by Richard Crawley. Thucydides, author of the history of the Peloponnesian War, was born of a substantial Athenian family about 460 B.C. and lived through the great age of the flowering and decline of Athens. He died about 399 B.C.
[1] This was the great war between Athens and Sparta, the Peloponnesian War, which, though interrupted by a few years of peace, lasted from 431 B.C. to 404. This oration was given at the end of the first year of the war.

wisdom and eminent reputation, pronounces over them an appropriate panegyric; after which all retire. Such is the manner of the burying; and throughout the whole of the war, whenever the occasion arose, the established custom was observed. Meanwhile these were the first that had fallen, and Pericles, son of Xanthippus, was chosen to pronounce their eulogium. When the proper time arrived, he advanced from the sepulcher to an elevated platform in order to be heard by as many of the crowd as possible, and spoke as follows:

"Most of my predecessors in this place have commended him who made this speech part of the law, telling us that it is well that it should be delivered at the burial of those who fall in battle. For myself, I should have thought that the worth which had displayed itself in deeds, would be sufficiently rewarded by honors also shown by deeds; such as you now see in this funeral prepared at the people's cost. And I could have wished that the reputations of many brave men were not to be imperiled in the mouth of a single individual, to stand or fall according as he spoke well or ill. For it is hard to speak properly upon a subject where it is even difficult to convince your hearers that you are speaking the truth. On the one hand, the friend who is familiar with every fact of the story, may think that some point has not been set forth with that fullness which he wishes and knows it to deserve; on the other, he who is a stranger to the matter may be led by envy to suspect exaggeration if he hears anything above his own nature. For men can endure to hear others praised only so long as they can severally persuade themselves of their own ability to equal the actions recounted: when this point is passed, envy comes in and with it incredulity. However, since our ancestors have stamped this custom with their approval, it becomes my duty to obey the law and to try to satisfy your several wishes and opinions as best I may.

"I shall begin with our ancestors: it is both just and proper that they should have the honor of the first mention on an occasion like the present. They dwelt in the country without break in the succession from generation to generation, and handed it down free to the present time by their valor. And if our more remote ancestors deserve praise, much more do our own fathers, who added to their inheritance the empire which we now possess, and spared no pains to be able to leave their acquisitions to us of the present generation. Lastly, there are few parts of our dominions that have not been augmented by those of us here, who are still more or less in the vigor of life; while the mother country has been furnished by us with everything that can enable her to depend on her own resources whether for war or for peace. That part of our history which tells of the military achievements which gave us our several possessions, or of the ready valor with which either we or our fathers stemmed the tide of Hellenic or foreign aggression, is a theme too familiar to my hearers for me to dilate on, and I shall therefore pass it by. But what was the road by which we reached our position, what the form of government under which our greatness grew, what the national habits out of which it sprang; these are questions which I may try to solve before I proceed to my panegyric upon these men; since I think this to be a subject upon which on the present occasion a speaker may properly dwell, and to which the whole assemblage, whether citizens or foreigners, may listen with advantage.

"Our constitution does not copy the laws of neighboring states; we are rather a pattern to others than imitators ourselves. Its administration favors the many instead of the few; this is why it is called a democracy. If we look to the laws, they afford equal justice to all in their private differences; if to social standing, advancement in public life falls to reputation for capacity, class considerations not being allowed to interfere with merit; nor again does poverty bar the way; if a man is able to serve the state, he is not hindered by the obscurity of his condition. The freedom which we enjoy in our government extends also to our ordinary life. There, far from exercising a jealous surveillance over each other, we do not feel called upon to be angry with our neighbor for doing what he likes, or even to indulge in those injurious looks which cannot fail to be offensive, although they inflict no positive penalty. But all this ease in our private relations does not make us lawless as citizens. Against this fear is our chief safeguard, teaching us to obey the magistrates and the laws, particularly such as regard the protection of the injured, whether they are actually on the statute book, or belong to that code which, although unwritten, yet cannot be broken without acknowledged disgrace.

"Further, we provide plenty of means for the mind to refresh itself from business. We celebrate games and sacrifices all the year round, and the elegance of our private establishments forms a daily source of pleasure and helps to banish the spleen; while the magnitude of our city draws the produce of the world into our harbor, so that to the Athenian the fruits of other countries are as familiar a luxury as those of his own.

"If we turn to our military policy, there also we differ from our antagonists. We throw open our city to the world, and never by alien acts exclude foreigners from any opportunity of learning or observing, although the eyes of an enemy may occasionally profit by our liberality; trusting less in system and policy than to the native spirit of our citizens; while in education, where our rivals from their very cradles by a painful discipline seek after manliness, at Athens we live exactly as we please, and yet are just as ready to encounter every legitimate danger. In proof of this it may be noticed that the Lacedæmonians do not invade our country alone, but bring with them all their confederates; while we Athenians advance unsupported into the territory of a neighbor, and fighting upon a foreign soil usually vanquish with ease men who are defending their homes. Our united force was never yet encountered by any enemy, because we have at once to attend to our marine and to despatch our citizens by land upon a hundred different services; so that, wherever they engage with some such fraction of our strength, a success against a detachment is magnified into a victory over the nation, and a defeat into a reverse suffered at the hands of our entire people. And yet if with habits not of labor but of ease, and courage not of art but of nature, we are still willing to encounter danger, we have the double advantage of escaping the experience of hardships in anticipation and of facing them in the hour of need as fearlessly as those who are never free from them.

"Nor are these the only points in which our city is worthy of admiration. We cultivate refinement without extravagance and knowledge without effeminacy; wealth we employ more for use than for show, and place the real disgrace of poverty not in owning to the fact but in declining the struggle against it. Our public men have, besides politics, their private affairs to attend to, and our ordinary citizens, though occupied with the pursuits of industry, are still fair judges of public matters; for, unlike any other nation, regarding him who takes no part in these duties not as unambitious but as useless, we Athenians are able to judge at all events if we cannot originate, and instead of looking on discussion as a stumbling-block in the way of action, we think it an indispensable preliminary to any wise action at all.

Again, in our enterprises we present the singular spectacle of daring and deliberation, each carried to its highest point, and both united in the same persons; although usually decision is the fruit of ignorance, hesitation of reflection. But the palm of courage will surely be adjudged most justly to those who best know the difference between hardship and pleasure and yet are never tempted to shrink from danger. In generosity we are equally singular, acquiring our friends by conferring, not by receiving, favors. Yet, of course, the doer of the favor is the firmer friend of the two, in order by continued kindness to keep the recipient in his debt; while the debtor feels less keenly from the very consciousness that the return he makes will be a payment, not a free gift. And it is only the Athenians who, fearless of consequences, confer their benefits not from calculations of expediency, but in the confidence of liberality.

"In short, I say that as a city we are the school of Hellas; while I doubt if the world can produce a man, who where he has only himself to depend upon, is equal to so many emergencies, and graced by so happy a versatility as the Athenian. And that this is no mere boast thrown out for the occasion, but plain matter of fact, the power of the state acquired by these habits proves. For Athens alone of her contemporaries is found when tested to be greater than her reputation, and alone gives no occasion to her assailants to blush at the antagonist by whom they have been worsted, or to her subjects to question her title by merit to rule. Rather, the admiration of the present and succeeding ages will be ours, since we have not left our power without witness, but have shown it by mighty proofs; and far from needing a Homer for our panegyrist, or other of his craft whose verses might charm for the moment only for the impression which they gave to melt at the touch of fact, we have forced every sea and land to be the highway of our daring, and everywhere, whether for evil or for good, have left imperishable monuments behind us. Such is the Athens for which these men, in the assertion of their resolve not to lose her, nobly fought and died; and well may every one of their survivors be ready to suffer in her cause.

"Indeed if I have dwelt at some length upon the character of our country, it has been to show that our stake in the struggle is not the same as theirs who have no such blessings to lose, and also that the panegyric of the men over whom I am now speaking might be by definite proofs established.

That panegyric is now in a great measure complete; for the Athens that I have celebrated is only what the heroism of these and their like have made her, men whose fame, unlike that of most Hellenes, will be found to be only commensurate with their deserts. And if a test of worth be wanted, it is to be found in their closing scene, and this not only in the cases in which it set the final seal upon their merit, but also in those in which it gave the first intimation of their having any. For there is justice in the claim that steadfastness in his country's battles should be as a cloak to cover a man's other imperfections; since the good action has blotted out the bad, and his merit as a citizen more than outweighed his demerits as an individual. But none of these allowed either wealth with its prospect of future enjoyment to unnerve his spirit, or poverty with its hope of a day of freedom and riches to tempt him to shrink from danger. No, holding that vengeance upon their enemies was more to be desired than any personal blessings, and reckoning this to be the most glorious of hazards, they joyfully determined to accept the risk, to make sure of their vengeance and to let their wishes wait; and while committing to hope the uncertainty of final success, in the business before them they thought fit to act boldly and trust in themselves. Thus choosing to die resisting, rather than to live submitting, they fled only from dishonor, but met danger face to face, and after one brief moment, while at the summit of their fortune, escaped, not from their fear, but from their glory.

"So died these men as became Athenians. You, their survivors, must determine to have as unfaltering a resolution in the field, though you may pray that it may have a happier issue. And not contented with ideas derived only from words of the advantages which are bound up with the defense of your country, though these would furnish a valuable text to a speaker even before an audience so alive to them as the present, you must yourselves realize the power of Athens, and feed your eyes upon her from day to day, till love of her fills your hearts; and then when all her greatness shall break upon you, you must reflect that it was by courage, sense of duty, and a keen feeling of honor in action that men were enabled to win all this, and that no personal failure in an enterprise could make them consent to deprive their country of their valor, but they laid it at her feet as the most glorious contribution that they could offer. For this offering of their lives made in common by them all they each of them individually received that renown which never grows old, and for a sepulcher, not so much that in which their bones have been deposited, but that noblest of shrines wherein their glory is laid up to be eternally remembered upon every occasion on which deed or story shall call for its commemoration. For heroes have the whole earth for their tomb; and in lands far from their own, where the column with its epitaph declares it, there is enshrined in every breast a record unwritten with no tablet to preserve it, except that of the heart. These take as your model, and judging happiness to be the fruit of freedom and freedom of valor, never decline the dangers of war. For it is not the miserable that would most justly be unsparing of their lives; these have nothing to hope for: it is rather they to whom continued life may bring reverses as yet unknown, and to whom a fall, if it came, would be most tremendous in its consequences. And surely, to a man of spirit, the degradation of cowardice must be immeasurably more grievous than the unfelt death which strikes him in the midst of his strength and patriotism!

"Comfort, therefore, not condolence, is what I have to offer to the parents of the dead who may be here. Numberless are the chances to which, as they know, the life of man is subject; but fortunate indeed are they who draw for their lot a death so glorious as that which has caused your mourning, and to whom life has been so exactly measured as to terminate in the happiness in which it has been passed. Still I know that this is a hard saying, especially when those are in question of whom you will constantly be reminded by seeing in the homes of others blessings of which once you also boasted: for grief is felt not so much for the want of what we have never known, as for the loss of that to which we have been long accustomed. Yet you who are still of an age to beget children must bear up in the hope of having others in their stead; not only will they help you to forget those whom you have lost, but will be to the state at once a reinforcement and a security; for never can a fair or just policy be expected of the citizen who does not, like his fellows, bring to the decision the interests and apprehensions of a father. While those of you who have passed your prime must congratulate yourselves with the thought that the best part of your life was fortunate, and that the brief span that remains will be cheered by the fame of the departed. For it is only the love of honor that never grows old; and honor it is, not gain, as some would have it, that rejoices the heart of age and helplessness.

"Turning to the sons or brothers of the dead, I see an arduous struggle before you. When a man is gone, all are wont to praise him, and should your merit be ever so transcendent, you will still find it difficult not merely to overtake, but even to approach their renown. The living have envy to contend with, while those who are no longer in our path are honored with a good-will into which rivalry does not enter. On the other hand, if I must say anything on the subject of female excellence to those of you who will now be in widowhood, it will be all comprised in this brief exhortation. Great will be your glory in not falling short of your natural character; and greatest will be hers who is least talked of among the men whether for good or for bad.

"My task is now finished. I have performed it to the best of my ability, and in words, at least, the requirements of the law are now satisfied. If deeds be in question, those who are here interred have received part of their honors already, and for the rest, their children will be brought up till manhood at the public expense: the state thus offers a valuable prize, as the garland of victory in this race of valor, for the reward both of those who have fallen and their survivors. And where the rewards for merit are greatest, there are found the best citizens.

"And now that you have brought to a close your lamentations for your relatives, you may depart."

GREEK TRAGEDY

One of the most remarkable accomplishments of the Greek genius and of the Attic Age was the development of tragedy. In its greatest period this form of dramatic representation engaged the efforts of the best writers of the supreme century of Greek culture, and it furnished æsthetic pleasure of an unparalleled kind to tens of thousands of spectators. Since those days the three great tragic poets of Greece have taken their place at the head of all the dramatists of the world—only Shakespeare, of all the hundreds who have tried, being admitted as an equal in their company.

How such an artistic achievement was brought about has been the subject of much discussion. We are sure that tragedy developed rather rapidly toward the end of the sixth century B.C. and that it had a religious origin, but concerning the details there are many unsolved problems.

It seems clear enough that tragedy began in some way with the worship of Dionysus (or Bacchus), the wine-god, originally a vegetation god, whose life and struggle was the subject of myths and primitive rites. A chorus of people dressed as satyrs for the celebration of the Feast of Dionysus, though at first improvising their dance and song, eventually came (by the end of the sixth century) to have set songs and formal steps. A goat was given as a prize and perhaps for this reason the performance was called a *tragoidia*, a goat song. There seems to have been no attempt at impersonation in the dance or singing until in the late sixth century a real actor was introduced by a certain Thespis (from whom today we have the name "Thespian," for actors). Such a change was necessary if ever this religious celebration was to become drama. For the very essence of drama is that the actor shall represent someone else.

In 534 B.C. the City Dionysia was organized in Athens for the more effective celebration of the Feast of Dionysus. Contests were begun in which writers vied with one another in the best kind of celebration. These became more and more dramatic and realistic. The satyr masks were abandoned and the choruses appeared in any guise the playwright demanded. At length the action came to be separated from Dionysus altogether, though it remained religious in character. In 501 B.C. there was a reorganization of the Dionysia in Athens. The goat prize was abandoned and each poet who was chosen entered four plays—three tragedies and a "satyr-play"—in competition for the yearly prize.

If we think of the early Greek tragedy as having a leader and chorus who by their singing, dancing, and dialogue told one of the Greek sacred stories, we shall see that when a second actor comes on the stage with the leader the possibilities of making the story dramatic have been vastly increased. It was this service that was performed by the first of the three great tragedians, Æschylus, who also materially shifted the emphasis from the chorus to the dialogue. Indeed it may be said that the history of Greek tragedy is largely a study of the various ways in which the chorus, which at first is the only thing of importance, gradually gives way before the more interesting action of the actor. It is in Æschylus that we first find Greek tragedy in such form that we recognize it as tragedy.

Tragedy became, so to speak, the repository of Greek culture. As theater it absorbed the arts of music and the dance, which had been growing in refinement and expertness. As dramatic literature, it incorporated the grandeur and the subject matter of epic poetry, as well as that of many myths and legends, and the beauties of lyric and choral poetry, which poets like Sappho, Alcæus, and Simonides had perfected. Tragedy, moreover, absorbed and then reflected many advances in religious and philosophical thought, in rhetoric and disputation, and in psychology. For all this, tragedy found a matrix in its special form,—a form that differs in most respects from the realistic drama to which we have become accustomed in our own day. The elements that were thus brought together into dramatic synthesis consisted of choruses and dramatic episodes, acting, dancing, and music. By these means, human experience was projected from the stage in expressive, stylized form.

The typical Greek tragedy opened with a *prologue*, an introductory scene which acquainted the audience with the situation of the play. This was followed by a *parodos*, a dramatically rendered song by the chorus on its first appearance in the *orchestra* or dancing circle that faced the stage. Then came a scene, called the *episode*, in which the characters appeared on the stage and enacted a portion of the dramatic action. At its conclusion, the chorus sang an ode, known as the *stasimon*. (Sometimes a lyric passage, known as a *commus*, was substituted for the *stasimon*.) After a series of *episodes* and *stasima*, the play was rounded out by a final chorus or *exodus*. Here, in short, was an exalted and formal art, resembling opera but with sustained passages of spoken dialogue.

Life was viewed in terms of the crises and conflicts that give it significance, that reveal humanity's dreads, aspirations, and defeats, and that challenge man to some investigation of reality. With few exceptions, of which Æschylus' *The Persians* is the sole extant example, the starting point was some myth or legend rather than a contemporary event and background. But this did not hamper Athenian dramatists. The ancient tale enabled the poet to express experience with sufficient perspective to ensure universality for his work. And it is to be remembered, too, that the myth or legend was by no means academically remote to the playwright's audience; the story could be viewed as actual history, as symbolism, or as a parallel to contemporary events. Thus the story of Œdipus and his family could be regarded by Sophocles' public as a review of Thebes's past, a past that had special significance to the Athenians who at that time counted the Thebans among their enemies. Surely, too, there was a patriotic reason for Sophocles' alteration of the legend which originally had Œdipus die in Thebes. In Sophocles' *Œdipus at Colonus*, the dying Œdipus, mystically endowed with the power of blessing the soil in which he reposed, is succored and buried in Athens. Euripides' retelling of the fall of Troy in *Trojan Women* could express the Athenian peace party's revulsion at the ruthless behavior of the Athenian imperialists; and the Athenian intellectual, who did not believe in the gods, could interpret Aphrodite in the same playwright's *Hippolytus* and Dionysus in his *Bacchæ* symbolically, as the representatives of life forces.

Greek tragedy was, in the main, the creation of three great poets, Æschylus, Sophocles, and Euripides, three men who were deeply involved in Athenian life, and in its political, cultural, and intellectual aspects. We shall review their work and read their plays shortly, but before doing so it may be helpful to acquire a more vivid sense of how their tragedies appeared to the audiences for which they were written. It is well to recapture the magic of theater in which the tragedies were steeped. For this purpose, Sheldon Cheney's imaginative picture should prove helpful. Following this, Aristotle's critical analysis of Greek dramaturgy will throw light on the nature of tragic composition as practiced by the Greeks. If it also illuminates for us the art of tragedy in other ages, this is our gain.

SOME FACTS OF GREEK STAGING

The following prosaic facts of Greek staging will serve to introduce Cheney's account:

The masks, so frequently employed in primitive ritual, were not only a hallowed convention scrupulously retained by the Greek theater, but a powerful means of attracting attention, creating excitement, and expressing essential drama. All the actors wore elongated grotesque masks of linen, cork, and wood, which grew larger and more curious with time. Although fairly stereotyped, portraying general attributes like cruelty, craft, and suffering, these disguises possessed considerable variety. Special masks would be required by mythological and allegorical characters like the horned Io, the multiple-eyed Argo, the snaky-haired Furies, and allegorical figures like Death, Force, and Frenzy. That even realism was attempted is shown by the fact that at the conclusion of Sophocles' *Œdipus the King* the mask of the hero depicted a blood-stained countenance with mutilated eyes.

Boots with thickened, painted soles and a high

headdress above the mask made the actors appear taller than life. A six-foot actor would be raised to seven and a half feet or over, so that he was likely to tumble ignominiously if he took an incautious step. Mantles of saffron, purple, and gold and extravagant costumes, particularly in comedy, lent them color; and padded clothing balanced the increased height. Characters were differentiated by means of the mask, the thickness of the boot, the quality of the garments, and such details as the crowns worn by kings, the turbans of Orientals, and the crutches that assisted old men across the stage.

Heavily encumbered, the tragedians' movements were necessarily slow and their gestures broad. It is not surprising, therefore, that violent physical action was generally avoided, deaths occurring off-stage and being related by a character known as the Messenger. Nevertheless, it was unlikely that the playgoer was bored by such static devices, for there was always more than enough movement in the chorus, in the orgiastic satyr-plays which came at the close of the morning's tragedies, and in the comedies that followed in the afternoon.

Facial play was of course concealed by the mask, but this, too, was no great loss in so vast a theater as the Athenian. Nuances of emotion were expressed for the most part verbally, although mimetic gestures and expressive masks would be of help. Fortunately, the acoustics of a Greek theater were excellent, and the voice of the actor could be projected to the utmost tiers with the aid of the open-mouthed mask that served as a sounding board. Actors were in fact chosen for their voices. Good actors were so greatly in demand that they soon commanded enormous salaries, and in later times, when playwriting talent had become scarce, acting assumed greater importance than the drama itself. It even became customary to have contests between actors as well as plays. The abused "star system" began among the allegedly austere Athenians.

The stage effect was vastly enhanced by the presence of the chorus that marched in with aplomb in ranks and files from the wings, came and went as needed, and mixed with the actors from time to time. In place of a curtain, every new scene was ushered in and followed by a choral song, and any amount of time could be assumed to elapse during the singing of a choral ode. Like the actors, the chorus was variantly costumed and wore masks appropriate to the age, sex, and character of the persons represented . . .

The chorus sang or chanted odes with appropriate, highly stylized movements. A dignified dance form accompanied the more stately odes, while odes of ecstatic emotion or gladness were accompanied by a lively dance. Much of the dancing was decidedly mimetic. One favorite dancer employed by Æschylus was famous for his ability to describe dramatic events by means of gestures.

Even when the chorus remained passive this body did not stand frozen in a tableau, as has been supposed. It continued to follow the story with descriptive movements conveying emotions of anxiety, terror, pity, hope, and exaltation. Nor did the chorus always sing; for it sometimes used recitative, and even conversational speech in addressing the actors. And it did not always sing or speak in unison. During the murder of the king in the Agamemnon, for example, the old men debate helplessly what to do and each member of the chorus voices his opinion. The songs were rendered with distinctiveness of utterance, each note corresponding to a syllable, and were accompanied by a wood-wind instrument resembling our clarinet. Later on, solos were added for greater effect and virtuosos made quite a practice of it much to the distress of the purists, who were not wanting in Athens. The use of a chorus in Greek drama certainly had its disadvantages because it slowed up and interrupted the dramatic portions of the play. But it greatly enriched the spectacular qualities of the Greek stage and introduced a musical component into the theater, which has led writers to compare classic drama with modern opera.

It is no secret that in the physical theater of the fifth century much had to be imagined or reconstructed by the audience from the suggestive background, the permanent scenic façade developed from the original dressing hut, and the descriptive passages of the play. Nevertheless, there was no dearth of color in the productions, and mechanical contraptions afforded some partially realistic scenery. Thunder and lightning were reproduced. A platform known as the *eccyclema*, a form of wagon-stage, was rolled out through the doors of the scene building or pushed out (in which case it was called an *exostra*) to reveal interior scenes. Trapdoors, aptly called "Charon's Steps," enabled ghosts to rise from the nether world. A crane-like contraption, the *mechane* or machine, transported the actor who impersonated a god to the roof of the scene building, swept him across the acting area, suspended him in mid-air, and lowered him sensationally into the orchestra. Since he came by way of the machine, he was "the god from the machine" or *"deus ex machina."* Sometimes, too, the gods were exhibited "in heaven" on a special platform. Even the settings were not so inadequate as has been imagined, since they could represent anything from a hill or countryside to a building or a series of structures. Occasionally sets were even changed within a single play with the aid of revolving painted prisms.

As for the area for the actors and the chorus, what the audience saw was a level circular place called the *orchestra* (literally, "dancing place"), backed by the *skene* or scene building.[1] At first (probably throughout the fifth century) the *skene* was a wooden structure, used for changing masks and costumes; later it was supplanted by a stone building. The *skene* represented the façade of a temple, house, or palace; normally it had three doors, used as entrances and exits for the actors. Immediately in front of the building stood a level platform hardly more than a step or so above the level of the orchestra, on which much of the dramatic action occurred, though characters sometimes appeared on the roof of the *skene* and often moved into the orchesra and confronted the chorus.

The auditorium in this open-air theater was semi-circular in shape, consisted of rising rows of seats, and in the Theater of Dionysus on the south slope of the Acropolis, accommodated about 17,000 spectators.

[1] Probably not used for the earliest plays.

SHELDON CHENEY

Attending a Greek Play

The Greek theater is an extraordinarily simple, but an extraordinarily pleasing place. From the tamped circle for dancing, with surrounding benches, it has now grown into an architectural bowl, graceful in outline, symmetrical, but not yet in any way ornate. About the full round orchestra, tiers of seats rise up, two-thirds of the way round, nestled into the Acropolis slope, divided by aisles into wedge-like sections. At the far side of the dancing circle an unpretentious stage-building, the *skene,* has been erected. It probably has a portico along the front, between two wings that come forward protectingly toward the auditorium. There still is no raised stage (one must repeat it, because from our knowledge of later theaters we always look first for a platform); there is no "scenery," and there are very few properties. Close by, ever a reminder that this is a sacred precinct, is the lovely little Temple of Dionysus. Not that any of the fifteen thousand spectators is likely to forget the religious significance of the occasion, of the plays to come, even of the theater itself.

For did we not three days ago assemble with them, in the nearby Odeon, to witness the "parade" of the dramatists, actors, and chorus, all dressed up gorgeously for this ceremonial? There we heard the announcements, the names of the poet-playwrights, of the *choregi* (the patrons or "backers" of the poets, in modern parlance), and of the plays. No doubt about the seriousness, the dignity, and the significance of all this: these performers, producers, and dramatists are specially honored members of Athenian society. What they are to present during the coming holidays is to be no mere amusement to while away idle hours, but rather a sacrament—though imbedded in a festival of revelry and games. Even in this preliminary ceremony they are wearing crowns; and we are told that at the end of the contest one of the tragic poets and his *choregus* will be crowned with that more prized emblem, the ivy.

At the opening of the festival, too, we have been witnesses at a stirring ritual and procession. The citizens of Athens have gone forth in all their holiday finery to escort the statue of Dionysus back to its home.

At break of day they have begun to assemble at the shrine, till all the city seems gathered here in

Attending a Greek Play. From *The Theatre: Three Thousand Years of Drama, Acting, and Stagecraft* (New York, 1929), pp. 38-47. By permission of the author and Longmans, Green and Co. The translations from *Œdipus the King* by Gilbert Murray are used by permission of the Oxford University Press.

the precinct of Dionysus, by the theater: the *Archon,* the priests, and the city fathers, the chosen ones who are to carry the statue and those who bear the sacrifices, the guards of honor, the choruses, the actors, the groups of contesting singers, the poets, those who later will be the audiences but who now are taking personal part in the ceremony, men, women, children, aristocrat, noble, and freeman.

Swift hands disengage the statue from its pedestal when the chief priest gives the word; the appointed carriers bear it aloft, through the city, out to a park-like place in the country near the Academy, while the procession reverently follows. Now the god's image is placed on a pedestal under the olive trees, and the sacrificial rites are held. The rest of the day is a "let-down" time, given over to games, feasting, and lighter forms of amusement. Then at night the crowd gathers again at the statue, the procession back to the city starts: the crux of the celebration, annual symbol of the first bringing of the image to Athens from Eleutheræ. Here is something out of the pre-drama days, the joyous worshipers marching by torchlight back along the road to the Acropolis, bearing the statue aloft, carrying the jars of wine and the garlands and symbolic crowns, dancing, improvising, singing. Here indeed, in the revelry and the spirited bandying, are survivals of the elements and the impulses from which the seeds of theater sprang. Then the statue is placed in the theater, which the celebrants now rededicate with suitable rites for the musical and dramatic events of the morrow. Sobered from their revelry, but no less "intoxicated," their demeanor promises a finer solemnity and beauty in the plays to follow.

The next day, and perhaps another, are given up to the dithyrambic contests; five hundred men and boys, come to Athens from all parts of Greece, sing in competition for the choral prizes. Ten groups in all offer their songs before the holiday audiences, not without dancing: a parallel to that other source of tragic drama, the old-time sung poetry. But it is the morning of the following day that we await.

There is still the darkness before dawn as we make our way toward the theater. Just the first faint streaks of light have made beautiful the eastern sky, but already all Athens seems awake, excited, hurrying toward the enclosure of Dionysus.

We are soon glad that we came thus early, for we are jostled by the crowds, and it is clear that not all these ticket-holders can squeeze into the auditorium. There is room for the overflow up there on the heights above the shaped bowl, but in the dim chill light, that seems far, far away from the dancing-orchestra where the action will pass. We gaze down curiously at this consecrated circle, with the altar of Dionysus at the very center; and beyond to the low *skene,* the background building with its pillared lower story that might be a palace front or a temple, with its three doorways facing us from the main wall, and its two "wings" or *paraskenia* thrust forward at each end—as if to enclose the acting-dancing space, so that no part of the "drama," the doings, may escape.

Light, and still more light, till the theater seems bathed in the dim freshness, the pale clarity, the loveliest moment of the day. Ah, what a moment for a drama to begin! And indeed, everything is in readiness now. The priests of Dionysus are in their chairs of honor—their thrones—down on the very edge of the orchestra; and the bowl above them is like a teeming beehive, so alive is it with human beings.

A herald! Yes, now he is calling forth Sophocles, first of this year's contestants for the tragedy prize. And the play is on. For there, around the altar of the dancing-circle, a crowd of "supers" has gathered, Theban citizens, miserable, suppliant And one stands a little apart, a priest. Forth to them comes an actor, majestically, masked and in kingly robes. His voice breaks into the morning silence with startling resonance, with the measured stately beauty of words severely chosen, richly intoned.

My children, fruit of Cadmus' ancient tree
New springing, wherefore thus with bended knee
Press ye upon us, laden all with wreaths
And suppliant branches? And the city breathes
Heavy with incense, heavy with dim prayer
And shrieks to affright the Slayer.
     . . . Seeing 'tis I ye call,
'Tis I am come, world-honored Œdipus.

This then will be the story of Œdipus the King, most tragic, most terrible. This actor and the priest now are telling us what we already know (our minds flash back to the old legend), how Œdipus, having slain the Sphinx and delivered Thebes, married the widowed Queen Jocasta, ruled happily twelve years, then found a pestilence destroying his city. We know more, too horrible almost for words: that this pestilence has come from the gods, because all unwittingly Œdipus has killed his own father, the former king, and now is married to his own mother. But these characters in the play, this proud Œdipus, and the Queen whom Sophocles will make so noble, so touching, they do not know. Like the gods themselves, this day we shall watch the fearful truth unfold to these two.

Œdipus and the Priest have told us now the misery of the Theban people; and the King—oh, irony!—pledges to seek out the cause of the sorrow, to cast it out at whatever cost. But now the Suppliants crowd toward the gateway beyond the orchestra, where Creon is entering. He, the brother of Jocasta, comes from Delphi with messages from the Oracle: there is an unclean one in the land, he who slew Laïus, the former king, and he is to be punished before the blight can be lifted. We watch as Œdipus and Creon build a dialogue toward the first climax: to that moment when the King goes back through the palace door—yes, that simple proscenium has become to us a palace now—vowing to search out the slayer of Laïus.

The Suppliants give way to the Chorus of Theban Elders. Half-chanting they come, half-dancing, with slow stateliness, threading their way over the dance-circle, taking up position as prayers to Apollo:
"A voice, a voice, that is borne on the Holy Way" . . . Here is the old religious dancing-procession, here the old devotional pattern showing through the design of the new human drama. They chant, they repeat the story of the pestilence, they implore the mercy of the gods, they call on Apollo, Athena, Artemis, Zeus, Dionysus.

Œdipus is coming again forward from the palace. He speaks, he ponders, he calls on the guilty slayer of Laïus to come forth and be banished. He sends for the blind prophet Tiresias. We listen to these two, the King ruthlessly tracking down clue after clue, the old prophet holding back the knowledge—till spurred beyond control:

Thou art thyself the unclean thing!

We see the deluge of Œdipus' wrath at this incredible accusation, until the patient Tiresias pours forth his whole prophecy, foreshadows the tragedy to its end:

Thou dost seek
With threats and loud proclaim the man whose hand
Slew Laïus. Lo, I tell thee, he doth stand
Here . . .
His staff groping before him, he shall crawl
O'er unknown earth, and voices round him call:
"Behold the brother-father of his own
Children, the seed, the sower and the sown,

Shame to his mother's blood, and to his sire
Son, murderer, incest-worker."

Like a relief from storm the Chorus comes, bringing a lyrical interlude, chanting, commenting upon the ways of gods and men, affirming faith in Œdipus—and relieving the tension with the sheer visual beauty of the dance-design.

But Creon returns, eager to defend himself against Œdipus' charge that he has instigated the accusation against the King; and as these two come near to an encounter with swords, Jocasta enters before us:

Vain men, what would ye with this angry swell
Of words heart-blinded? Is there in your eyes
No pity, thus, when all our city lies
Bleeding, to ply your privy hates? . . .

And it is she who brings to her King the first gleam of self-doubt. We see him now, losing his assurance, a dread beginning to creep in. He tells how once he killed a noble in a chariot, where three roads crossed. He was fleeing from Corinth; a prophecy had said he would kill his father and marry his mother—and so he had fled the court. And meeting this old man on the way, he had killed him and his guards. But Jocasta, stirred now by a deeper dread, sends for a herdsman, since banished to the hills, who saw Laïus murdered.

We of the audience settle back, and let the strain fall a little from us as Œdipus and Jocasta go in; we note the strophes and antistrophes of the Chorus rather idly—we have come to a human suspense that lyrics and dance cannot beguile us from. Now here is Jocasta again before us saying,

So dire a storm
Doth shake the king, sin, dread and every form
Of grief . . .

But, as she prays to Apollo, a Stranger arrives by the gateway, hailing the Chorus, asking for the King. For a moment we are inclined to find relief, with Jocasta, in the news he brings. The King of Corinth, Œdipus' reputed father, is dead, and the old prophecy of patricide seems disproved. But suddenly a new dread is aroused. The Stranger discloses that Œdipus was not Corinthian at all, but was a Theban babe rescued from a wild mountainside where he had been left to die.

Ah, mark you, while this unfolds between Œdipus and the Stranger, how Jocasta turns aside, a sickness growing in her mind! Will no one there notice her as she totters?—now her head goes down into her hands. She knows! This King, her husband, is her own babe. No need to wait the coming of the herdsman. A quick effort to restrain Œdipus from seeking confirmation; then she goes, in horror, hardly daring a farewell. For us in the audience *her* tragedy is already complete. The Chorus this time interrupts only for a moment. All eyes watch for the herdsman's coming.

How crisply Œdipus questions him! On the brink of disastrous knowledge, he searches out the reluctant truth with uncanny directness, without mercy. This is an inevitable structure. We see circumstance after circumstance nailed in; till suddenly Œdipus shines out—we know it is like this in his own mind—with all the guilty knowledge on him: himself son of Laïus, murderer of his own father, incestuous husband to his own mother, brother to his own children! As he rushes into the palace, this time, we have need of the let-down of the choral interlude. Still we have little heart for the lyrical comment—for we know that at this very moment, offstage, the physical climax of the play is taking place. We know that a Messenger, as is the wont, will come and recount to us the more horrible happenings, which perchance we could never have faced in the actual acting-out, under this pitiless morning sunshine. Now the Messenger is before us speaking:

Like one entranced with passion, through the gate
She passed, the white hands flashing o'er her head,
Like blades that tear, and fled, unswerving fled,
Toward her old bridal room, and disappeared
And the doors crashed behind her. But we heard
Her voice within, crying to him of old,
Her Laïus, long dead . . .
And, after that, I know not how her death
Found her. For sudden, with a roar of wrath,
Burst Œdipus upon us. Then, I ween,
We marked no more what passion held the
    Queen . . .
He dashed him on the chamber door. The straight
Door-bar of oak, it bent beneath his weight,
Shook from its sockets free, and in he burst
To the dark chamber.
        There we saw her first
Hanged, swinging from a noose, like a dead bird.
He fell back when he saw her. Then we heard
A miserable groan, and straight he found
And loosed the strangling knot, and on the ground
Laid her.—Ah, then the sight of horror came!
The pin of gold, broad-beaten like a flame,
He tore from off her breast, and, left and right,
Down on the shuddering orbits of his sight
Dashed it: "Out! Out! Ye never more shall see

Me nor the anguish nor the sins of me. . . ."
        . . . Like a song
His voice rose, and again, again, the strong
And stabbing hand fell, and the massacred
And bleeding eyeballs streamed upon his beard,
Wild rain, and gouts of hail amid the rain.
        . . . All that eye or ear
Hath ever dreamed of misery is here.

And then Œdipus is led in before us, blinded and bleeding. The old men of the Chorus turn away to escape the sight. But in a sort of sick horror we face this broken King, this abased human being. He gropes his way forward, calling on the gods, glorying that he has made himself a dungeon, "dark, without sound . . . self-prisoned from a world of pain," cursing the shepherd who saved him as a babe.

O flesh, horror of flesh! . . .
        In God's name,
Take me somewhere far off and cover me
From sight, or slay, or cast me to the sea
Where never eye may see me any more.

But now he has one thought more: his children, his two little daughters. There they are, Creon is bringing them before us and him.

Children! Where are ye? Hither; come to these
Arms of your—brother, whose wild offices
Have brought much darkness on the once bright eyes
Of him who grew your garden; who, nowise
Seeing nor understanding, digged a ground
The world shall shudder at . . .
        Creon, thou alone art left
Their father now, since both of us are gone
Who cared for them. Oh, leave them not alone.
        . . . So young they are, so desolate—
Of all save thee. True man, give me thine hand,
And promise . . .

For a moment only he weakens, and clings to the children. But we see them dragged from him. Creon says, "Seek not to be master more." And as Œdipus is led away, the Chorus chants again. As it too disappears, we are warned:

Therefore, O Man, beware, and look toward the end
    of things that be,
The last of sights, the last of days; and no man's life
    account as gain
Ere the full tale be finished and the darkness find
    him without pain.

At the end of this utterly moving, purging, terrible drama, we spectators wake gradually to the world about us. There is something absurdly trivial about the things we do when the Chorus has finally disappeared: we stand and stretch, and perhaps turn a little away from the sun—and titter because a man is sobbing near us. Our feelings are very close to the surface, and we have a tendency to lose sight of the audience around us in recurring fits of "star-gazing." We are shaken—and yet there is a glow of beauty in our souls, a brooding, a healing ecstasy. We have been through high grief, have descended into terror and sorrow, so terrible that all the pettinesses of life have been stripped away. Now we seem to have come out on the other side, cleansed. Somehow the soul seems to stand up and take the light, naked and glorious.

What is it that puts this mood of high suffering into tragedy? What is the secret of the majesty of these Greek dramas, that brings their audiences close to the gods, that purges human life of its weaknesses, bitterness, and shallowness, that inundates the spectator in exaltation and a god-like pity? The theme and story have not been pretty.

We have been conducted through a tale of incest, suicide, murder—a very welter of revolting crime (we shudder to think what any playwright of our more "natural" time would make of the material). But we have not shuddered at Sophocles' telling, nor have we been revolted; somehow our suffering and grief have been kept on some loftier plane.

In the first place the combination that is *theater* has come right, the majestic poetry matched by nobly dramatic story, the whole set forth in stately acting and in the chanting and rhythmic movement of the Chorus. The vast and nobly proportioned playhouse has some fitting appropriateness too. This is sustained theater, without let-down to mere anecdote-telling or picturing or individual impersonation. The tragedy has passed with sweep, with unbroken passion, majestically, with a splendid inevitability. It is the art that in its completeness goes beyond dramatic literature or acting or setting or dancing.

ARISTOTLE

The Nature of Tragedy

Of the poetry which imitates in hexameter verse, and of Comedy, we will speak hereafter. Let us now discuss Tragedy, resuming its formal definition, as resulting from what has been already said.

Tragedy, then, is an imitation of an action that is serious, complete, and of a certain magnitude; in language embellished with each kind of artistic ornament, the several kinds being found in separate parts of the play; in the form of action, not of narrative; through pity and fear effecting the proper purgation of these emotions. By "language embellished," I mean language into which rhythm, "harmony," and song enter. By "the several kinds in separate parts," I mean that some parts are rendered through the medium of verse alone, others again with the aid of song.

Now as tragic imitation implies persons acting, it necessarily follows, in the first place, that Scenic equipment will be a part of Tragedy. Next, Song and Diction, for these are the means of imitation. By "Diction" I mean the mere metrical arrangement of the words: as for "Song," it is a term whose full sense is well understood.

Again, Tragedy is the imitation of an action; and an action implies personal agents, who necessarily possess certain qualities both of character and thought. It is these that determine the qualities of actions themselves; these—thought and character—are the two natural causes from which actions spring: on these causes, again, all success or failure depends. Hence, the Plot is the imitation of the action:—for by plot I here mean the arrangement of the incidents. By Character I mean that in virtue of which we ascribe certain qualities to the agents. By Thought, that whereby a statement is proved, or a general truth expressed. Every Tragedy, therefore, must have six parts, which parts determine its quality—namely, Plot, Charac-

Aristotle, *The Nature of Tragedy*. From *The Poetics* translated by S. H. Butcher. By permission of The Macmillan Co. Though Aristotle (384-322 B.C.) was born at Stagira, a Greek colonial town on the northwest coast of the Ægean, he spent most of his life in Athens, where he was associated with Plato, established his own school of philosophy, the Lyceum, and was tutor to Alexander the Great.

ter, Diction, Thought, Scenery, Song. Two of the parts constitute the means of imitation, one the manner, and three the objects of imitation. And these complete the list. These elements have been employed, we may say, by almost all poets; in fact, every play contains Scenic accessories as well as Character, Plot, Diction, Song, and Thought.

But most important of all is the structure of the incidents. For Tragedy is an imitation, not of men, but of an action and of life,—of happiness and misery; and happiness and misery consist in action, the end of human life being a mode of action, not a quality. Now the characters of men determine their qualities, but it is by their actions that they are happy or the reverse. Dramatic action, therefore, is not with a view to the representation of character: character comes in as subsidiary to the action. Hence the incidents and the plot are the end of a tragedy; and the end is the chief thing of all. Again, without action there cannot be a tragedy; there may be without character. The tragedies of most of our modern poets fail in the rendering of character; and of poets in general this is often true. It is the same in painting; and here lies the difference between Zeuxis and Polygnotus. Polygnotus delineates character well: the style of Zeuxis is devoid of ethical quality. Again, if you string together a set of speeches expressive of character, and well finished in point of diction and thought, you will not produce the essential tragic effect nearly so well as with a play, which, however deficient in these respects, yet has a plot and artistically constructed incidents. Besides which, the most powerful elements of emotional interest in Tragedy—Reversals of Fortune, and Recognition scenes—are parts of the plot. A further proof is, that novices in the art are able to elaborate their diction and ethical portraiture, before they can frame the incidents. It is the same with almost all early poets.

The Plot, then, is the first principle, and, as it were, the soul of the tragedy: Character holds the second place. A similar fact is seen in painting. The most beautiful colors, laid on confusedly, will not give as much pleasure as the chalk outline of a portrait. Thus Tragedy is the imitation of an action, and of the agents, mainly with a view to the action.

Third in order is the Thought,—that is, the faculty of saying what is possible and pertinent in given circumstances. In the case of the dramatic dialogue, this is the function of the political or the rhetorical art: for the older poets make their char-acters speak the language of civic life; the poets of our time, the language of the rhetoricians. Character is that which reveals moral purpose: it shows what kind of things, in cases of doubt, a man chooses or avoids. A dialogue, therefore, which in no way indicates what the speaker chooses or avoids, is not expressive of character. Thought, on the other hand, is that whereby we prove that something is or is not, or state a general maxim.

Fourth comes the Diction; by which I mean, as has been already said, the expression of our meaning in words; and its essence is the same both in verse and prose.

Of the remaining elements Song holds the chief place among the embellishments.

The Scenery has, indeed, an emotional attraction of its own, but, of all the parts, it is the least artistic, and connected least with poetic theory. For the power of Tragedy, we may be sure, is felt even apart from representation and actors. Besides, the production of scenic effects depends more on the art of the stage manager than on that of the poet.

These principles being established, let us now discuss the proper structure of the Plot, since this is the first and also the most important part of Tragedy.

Now, according to our definition, Tragedy is an imitation of an action that is complete, and whole, and of a certain magnitude; for there may be a whole that is wanting in magnitude. A whole is that which has beginning, middle, and end. A beginning is that which does not itself follow anything by causal necessity, but after which something naturally is or comes to be. An end, on the contrary, is that which itself naturally follows some other thing, either by necessity, or in the regular course of events, but has nothing following it. A middle is that which follows something as some other thing follows it. A well-constructed plot, therefore, must neither begin nor end at haphazard, but conform to the type here described.

Again, if an object be beautiful—either a living organism or a whole composed of parts—it must not only have its parts in orderly arrangement, it must also be of a certain magnitude. Hence no exceedingly small animal can be beautiful; for the view of it is confused, the object being seen in an almost imperceptible moment of time. Nor, again, can an animal of vast size be beautiful; for as the eye cannot take it all in at once, the unity and sense of the whole is lost for the spectator. So it would be with a creature a thousand miles long.

As, therefore, in animate bodies and living organisms, a certain magnitude is necessary, and that such as may be easily embraced in one view; so in the plot, a certain length is necessary, and that length one that may be easily embraced by the memory. The limit of length in relation to dramatic competition and sensuous presentment is no part of artistic theory. For suppose a hundred tragedies had to be played against one another, the performance would be regulated by the hour-glass, —a method, indeed, that is familiar enough otherwise. But the limit as fixed by the nature of the drama itself is this:—the greater the length, the more beautiful will the piece be in respect of such magnitude, provided that the whole be perspicuous. And as a general rule, the proper magnitude is comprised within such limits, that the sequence of events, according to the law of probability or necessity, will admit of a change from bad fortune to good, or from good fortune to bad.

Unity of plot does not, as some persons think, consist in the unity of the hero. For infinitely various are the incidents in one man's life, which cannot be reduced to unity; and so, too, there are many actions of one man out of which we cannot make one action. Hence the error, as it appears, of all poets who have composed a Heracleid, a Theseid, or other poems of the kind. They imagine that as Heracles was one man, the story of Heracles ought also to be a unity. But Homer, as in all else he is of surpassing merit, here too—whether from art or natural genius—seems to have happily discerned the truth. In composing the *Odyssey* he did not bring in all the adventures of Odysseus—such as his wound on Parnassus, or his feigned madness at the mustering of the host—incidents between which there was no necessary or probable connection: but he made the *Odyssey,* and likewise the *Iliad,* to center round an action, that in our sense of the word is one. As therefore, in the other imitative arts, the imitation is one, when the object imitated is one, so the plot, being an imitation of an action, must imitate one action and that a whole, the structural union of the parts being such that, if any one of them is displaced or removed, the whole will be disjointed and disturbed. For that which may be present or absent without being perceived, is not an organic part of the whole.

It is, moreover, evident from what has been said, that it is not the function of the poet to relate what has happened, but what may happen,—what is possible according to the law of probability or necessity. The poet and the historian differ not by writing in verse or in prose. The work of Herodotus might be put into verse, and it would still be a species of history, with meter no less than without it. The true difference is that one relates what has happened, the other what may happen. Poetry, therefore, is a more philosophical and a higher thing than history: for poetry tends to express the universal, history the particular. The universal tells us how a person of given character will on occasion speak or act, according to the law of probability or necessity; and it is this universality at which poetry aims in giving expressive names to the characters. The particular is—for example—what Alcibiades did or suffered. In Comedy this is now apparent: for here the poet first constructs the plot on the lines of probability, and then assumes any names he pleases;—unlike the lampooners who write about a particular individual. But tragedians still keep to real names, the reason being that what is possible is credible: what has not happened we do not at once feel sure to be possible: but what has happened is manifestly possible; otherwise it would not have happened. Still there are some tragedies in which one or two names only are well known, the rest being fictitious. In others, none are well known,—as in Agathon's Flower, where incidents and names alike are fictitious, and yet it pleases. We must not, therefore, at all costs keep to the received legends, which are the usual subjects of Tragedy. Indeed, it would be absurd to attempt it; for even familiar subjects are familiar only to a few, and yet give pleasure to all. It clearly follows that the poet or "maker" should be the maker of plots rather than of verses; since he is a poet because he imitates, and what he imitates are actions. And if he chances to take an historical subject, he is none the less a poet; for there is no reason why some real events should not have that internal probability or possibility which entitles the author to the name of poet.

Of all plots and actions the epeisodic are the worst. I call a plot "epeisodic" in which the episodes or acts succeed one another without probable or necessary sequence. Bad poets compose such pieces by their own fault, good poets, to please the players; for, as they write for competing rivals, they draw out the plot beyond its capacity, and are often forced to break the natural continuity.

But again, Tragedy is an imitation not only of a complete action, but of events terrible and pitiful. Such an effect is best produced when the events come on us by surprise; and the effect is heightened when, at the same time, they follow from one another. The tragic wonder will then be greater than if they happened of themselves or by accident; for even accidents are most striking when they have an air of design. We may instance the statue of Mitys at Argos, which fell upon his murderer while he was looking at it, and killed him. Such events seem not to be due to mere chance. Plots, therefore, constructed on these principles are necessarily the best.

Plots are either Simple or Complicated; for such too, in their very nature, are the actions of which the plots are an imitation. An action which is one and continuous in the sense above defined, I call Simple, when the turning point is reached without Reversal of Fortune or Recognition: Complicated, when it is reached with Reversal of Fortune, or Recognition, or both. These last should arise from the internal structure of the plot, so that what follows should be the necessary or probable result of the preceding action. It makes all the difference whether one event is the consequence of another, or merely subsequent to it.

A Reversal of Fortune is, as we have said, a change by which a train of action produces the opposite of the effect intended; and that, according to our rule of probability or necessity. Thus in the Œdipus, the messenger, hoping to cheer Œdipus, and to free him from his alarms about his mother, reveals his origin, and so produces the opposite effect. Again in the Lynceus, Lynceus is being led out to die, and Danaüs goes with him, meaning to slay him; but the outcome of the action is that Danaüs is killed and Lynceus saved.

A Recognition, as the name indicates, is a change from ignorance to knowledge, producing love or hate between the persons destined by the poet for good or bad fortune. The best form of recognition is coincident with a reversal of fortune, as in the Œdipus. There are indeed other forms. Even inanimate things of the most trivial kind may sometimes be objects of recognition. Again, the discovery may be made whether a person has or has not done something. But the form which is most intimately connected with the plot and action is, as we have said, the recognition of persons. This, combined with a reversal of fortune, will produce either pity or fear; and actions producing these effects are those which, as we have assumed, Tragedy represents. Moreover, fortune or misfortune will depend upon such incidents. Recognition, then, being between persons, it may happen that one person only is recognized by the other—when the latter is already known—or the recognition

may need to be on both sides. Thus Iphigenia is revealed to Orestes by the sending of the letter; but another means is required to make Orestes known to Iphigenia.

Two parts, then, of the Plot—Reversal of Fortune and Recognition—turn upon surprises. A third part is the Tragic Incident. The two former have been discussed. The Tragic Incident is a destructive or painful action, such as death on the stage, bodily torments, wounds and the like.

As the sequel to what has already been said, we must proceed to consider what the poet should aim at, and what he should avoid, in constructing his plots; and by what means Tragedy may best fulfill its function.

A perfect tragedy should, as we have seen, be arranged on the simple, not the complicated, plan. It should, moreover, imitate actions which excite pity and fear, this being the distinctive mark of tragic imitation. It follows plainly, in the first place, that the change of fortune presented must not be the spectacle of a perfectly good man brought from prosperity to adversity: for this moves neither pity nor fear; it simply shocks us. Nor, again, that of a bad man passing from adversity to prosperity: for nothing can be more alien to the spirit of Tragedy; it possesses no single tragic quality; it neither satisfies the moral sense, nor calls forth pity or fear. Nor, again, should the downfall of the utter villain be exhibited. A plot of this kind would, doubtless, satisfy the moral sense, but it would inspire neither pity nor fear; for pity is aroused by unmerited misfortune, fear by the misfortune of a man like ourselves. Such an event, therefore, will be neither pitiful nor terrible. There remains, then, the character between these two extremes,—that of a man who is not eminently good and just, yet whose misfortune is brought about not by vice or depravity, but by some error or frailty. He must be one who is highly renowned and prosperous,—a personage like Œdipus, Thyestes, or other illustrious men of such families.

A well-constructed plot should, therefore, be single, rather than double, as some maintain. The change of fortune should be not from bad to good, but, reversely, from good to bad. It should come about as the result not of vice, but of some great error or frailty, in a character either such as we have described, or better rather than worse. The practice of the stage bears out our view. At first the poets recounted any legends that came in their way. Now, tragedies are founded on the story of a few houses,—on the fortunes of Alcmæon, Œdipus, Orestes, Meleager, Thyestes, Telephus, and those others who have done or suffered something terrible. A tragedy, then, to be perfect according to the rules of art should be of this construction. Hence they are in error who censure Euripides just because he follows this principle in his plays, many of which end unhappily. It is, as we have said, the right ending. The best proof is that on the stage and in dramatic competition, such plays, if they are well represented, are most tragic in their effect; and Euripides, faulty as he is in the general management of his subject, yet is felt to be the most tragic of poets.

In the second rank comes the kind of tragedy which some place first. Like the *Odyssey,* it has a double thread of plot, and also an opposite catastrophe for the good and for the bad. It is generally thought to be the best, owing to the weakness of the spectators; for the poet is guided in what he writes by the wishes of his audience. The pleasure, however, thence derived is not the true tragic pleasure. It is proper rather to Comedy, where those who, in the piece, are the deadliest enemies— like Orestes and Ægisthus—go forth reconciled at last, and no one slays or is slain.

Fear and pity may be aroused by the spectacle or scenic presentment; but they may also result from the inner structure of the piece, which is the better way, and indicates a superior poet. For the plot ought to be so constructed that, even without the aid of the eye, anyone who is told the incidents will thrill with horror and pity at the turn of events. This is precisely the impression we should receive from listening to the story of the Œdipus. But to produce this effect by the mere spectacle is a less artistic method, and dependent on extraneous aids. Those who employ spectacular means to create a sense not of the terrible but of the monstrous, are strangers to the purpose of Tragedy; for we must not demand of Tragedy every kind of pleasure, but only that which is proper to it. And since the pleasure which the poet should afford is that which comes from pity and fear through imitation, it is evident that this quality must be stamped upon the incidents.

Let us then determine what are the circumstances which impress us as terrible or pitiful.

Actions capable of this effect must happen between persons who are either friends or enemies or indifferent to one another. If an enemy kills an enemy, there is nothing to excite pity either in the act or the intention,—except so far as the suffering in itself is pitiful. So again with indifferent persons. But when the tragic incident occurs between those who are near or dear to one another—if, for example, a brother kills, or intends to kill, a brother, a son his father, a mother her son, a son his mother, or any other deed of this kind is done —here we have the situations which should be sought for by the poet. He may not indeed destroy the framework of the received legends—the fact, for instance, that Clytemnestra was slain by Orestes and Eriphyle by Alcmæon—but he ought to show invention of his own, and skillfully adapt the traditional material. What is meant by skillfully, let us explain more clearly.

The action may be done willingly and with full knowledge on the part of the agents, in the manner of the older poets. It is thus, in fact, that Euripides makes Medea slay her children. Or, again, the deed of horror may be done, but done in ignorance, and the tie of kinship or friendship be discovered afterwards. The Œdipus of Sophocles is an example. Here, indeed, the incident is outside the drama proper; but cases occur where it falls within the action of the play: we may cite the Alcmæon of Astydamas, or Telegonus in the Wounded Odysseus. Again, there is a third case, where someone is just about to do some irreparable deed through ignorance, and makes the discovery before it is done. These are the only possible ways. For the deed must either be done or not done,— and that wittingly or unwittingly. But of all these ways, to be about to act knowing the consequences, and then not to act, is the worst. It is shocking without being tragic, for no disaster follows. It is, therefore, never, or very rarely, found in poetry. One instance, however, is in the Antigone, where Hæmon intends to kill Creon. The next and better way is that the deed should be perpetrated. Still better, that it should be perpetrated in ignorance, and the discovery made afterwards. There is then nothing to shock us, while the discovery produces a startling effect. But the absolutely best way is the last mentioned. Thus in the Cresphontes, Merope is in the act of putting her son to death, but, recognizing who he is, spares his life. So in the Iphigenia, the sister recognizes the brother just in time. Again in the Helle, the son recognizes the mother when on the point of giving her up. This, then, is why a few families only, as has been already observed, furnish the subjects of tragedy. It was not art, but happy chance, that led poets by tentative discovery to impress the tragic quality upon their plots. They are compelled, therefore, to have recourse to those houses in which tragic disasters have occurred.

Enough has now been said concerning the structure of the incidents and the proper constitution of the plot.

In respect of Character there are four things to be aimed at. First, and most important, it must be good. Now any speech or action that manifests a certain moral purpose will be expressive of character: the character will be good if the purpose is good. This rule applies to persons of every class. Even a woman may be good, and also a slave; though the woman may be said to be an inferior being, and the slave is absolutely bad. The second thing to aim at is propriety. There is a type of manly valor; but for a woman to be valiant in this sense, or terrible, would be inappropriate. Thirdly, character must be true to life: for this is a distinct thing from goodness and propriety, as here described. The fourth point is consistency: for even though the original character, who suggested the type, be inconsistent, still he must be consistently inconsistent. As an example of character needlessly bad, we have Menelaus in the Orestes: of character incongruous and inappropriate, the lament of Odysseus in the Scylla, and the speech of Melanippe: of inconsistency, the Iphigenia at Aulis,—for the suppliant Iphigenia in no way resembles her later self.

As in the structure of the plot, so too in the portraiture of character, the poet should always aim either at the necessary or the probable. Thus a person of a given character should speak or act in a given way, by the rule either of necessity or of probability; just as this event should follow that by necessary or probable sequence. It is therefore evident that the unraveling of the plot, no less than the complication, must be brought about by the plot itself, and not by Machinery,—as in the Medea, or in the Return of the Greeks in the *Iliad*. Machinery should be employed only for events external to the drama,—either such as are previous to it and outside the sphere of human knowledge, or subsequent to it and which need to be foretold and announced; for to the gods we ascribe the power of seeing all things. Within the action there must be nothing irrational. If the irrational cannot be excluded, it should be outside the scope of the tragedy. Such is the irrational element in the Œdipus of Sophocles.

Again, since Tragedy is an imitation of persons who are above the common level, the example of good portrait-painters should be followed. They,

while reproducing the distinctive form of the original, make a likeness which is true to life and yet more beautiful. So too the poet, in representing men quick or slow to anger, or with other defects of character, should preserve the type and yet ennoble it. In this way Achilles is portrayed by Agathon and Homer.

These are rules the poet should observe. Nor should he neglect those appeals to the senses, which, though not among the essentials, are the concomitants of poetry; for here too there is much room for error. But of this we have said enough in our published treatises.

What Recognition is has been already explained. We will now enumerate its kinds.

First, the least artistic form, which, from poverty of wit, is commonly employed—recognition by signs. Of these some are congenital,—such as "the spear which the earth-born race bear on their bodies," or the stars introduced by Carcinus in his Thyestes. Others are acquired after birth; and of these some are bodily marks, as scars; some external tokens, as necklaces, or the little ark in the Tyro by which the discovery is effected. Even these admit of more or less skillful treatment. Thus in the recognition of Odysseus by his scar, the discovery is made in one way by the nurse, in another by the herdsman. This use of tokens for purposes of proof—and, indeed, any formal proof with or without tokens—is an inartistic mode of recognition. A better kind is that which results from the turn of fortune; as in the Bath scene in the *Odyssey*.

Next come the recognitions invented at will by the poet, and on that account wanting in art. For example, Orestes in the Iphigenia reveals the fact that he is Orestes. She, indeed, makes herself known by the letter; but he, by speaking himself, and saying what the poet, not what the plot, requires. This, therefore, is nearly allied to the fault above mentioned:—for Orestes might as well have brought tokens with him. Another similar instance is the "voice of the shuttle" in the Tereus of Sophocles.

The third form of recognition is when the sight of some object calls up a train of memory: as in the Cyprians of Dicæogenes, where the hero breaks into tears on seeing a picture; or again in the Lay of Alcinoüs, where Odysseus, hearing the minstrel play the lyre, recalls the past and weeps; and hence the recognition.

The fourth kind is by process of reasoning. Thus in the Choephori:—"Someone resembling me has come: no one resembles me but Orestes: therefore Orestes has come." Again, there is the discovery made by Iphigenia in the play of Polyeidus the Sophist. It was natural for Orestes to reason thus with himself:—"As my sister was sacrificed, so too it is my lot to be sacrificed." So, again, in the Tydeus of Theodectes:—"I came to find my son, and I must perish myself." So too in the Phineidæ: the women, on seeing the place, inferred their fate:—"Here we are fated to die, for here we were exposed." Again, there is a recognition combined with a false inference on the part of one of the characters, as in the Odysseus Disguised as a Messenger. A man said he would know the bow,—which, however, he had not seen. This remark led Odysseus to imagine that the other would recognize him through the bow, and so suggested a false inference.

But, of all recognitions, the best is that which arises from the incidents themselves, where the startling effect is produced by probable means. Such is that in the Œdipus of Sophocles, and in the Iphigenia; for it was natural that Iphigenia should wish to send a letter by Orestes. These recognitions stand on their own merits, and do not need the aid of tokens invented for the purpose, or necklaces. Next come the recognitions by process of reasoning.

THE GREEK TRAGIC POETS

I. ÆSCHYLUS (524-456 B.C.)

Beneath this stone lies Æschylus, son of Euphorion, the Athenian, who perished in the wheat-bearing land of Gela; of his prowess the groves of Marathon can speak, and the long-haired Persian who knew it well." Æschylus' epitaph, allegedly written by himself, is a fitting summary of his heroic character. Austere in temper and proud of his participation in Athens' victory over Persia, the oldest of the Athenian tragic poets was closest to the heroic age of Greece. At the same time, Æschylus was also close to the pre-Periclean religious revival, which stressed piety and purification of man's soul. He was an inheritor of sixth-century philosophy's monotheistic trends and its protest against the theology of Homer and Hesiod. Often, therefore, he spoke like a Hebrew prophet and a philosophical moralist. Born in the sacred city of Eleusis, he was reared in its mystic cult. He was, in all respects, a god-intoxicated man, if also a typical Athenian intellectual in his sense of art.

He first entered the annual dramatic contests with a series of plays in 499 B.C. and won his first prize in 484 B.C. No one contributed more to the development of his art than Æschylus, who is properly known as "the father of tragedy." Notable were his addition of a second actor to the drama, his contributions to tragic costuming, his activities as a trainer of choruses, and his keen sense of theatrical effect. Athens, which awarded him thirteen first prizes, recognized his genius and respected him, even though his conservatism was in opposition to the later democrats; and Athens was justified, for it was Æschylus who brought tragedy to its high estate by virtue of his powerful language, his high-vaulting themes, and his profundity.

He wrote approximately ninety plays. Of these only seven have survived, but they are sufficient to exemplify the advances he made in the technique and human reality of the drama. His earliest works, The Suppliants and The Persians, were preponderantly choral, the latter presenting little more than a pæan for the victorious Greeks, a warning against overweening pride, and a lament for the Persian dead. His Prometheus Bound is a magnificent representation of a titanic personality though deficient in action. But in The Seven Against Thebes and in the Oresteian trilogy, which begins with the Agamemnon, Æschylus developed action and characterization. His content reveals a similar deepening and extension. His comprehensive approach to his material kept him writing his works in the form of trilogies—that is, in a series of three closely related plays.

In his Promethean trilogy, he conceived an evolutionary history of a world ruled by Zeus who, though originally willful and hostile to man, has become responsible and moral. In the extant drama, Prometheus Bound, he crystallized his thought in a glowing character, Prometheus, the friend of man and the prototype of all rebels against tyranny. In the Oresteian trilogy, Æschylus traced the course of evil in the bloodstained annals of primitive society, and concluded with the substitution of reason and social law for the barbaric blood feud. Finding democratic Athens uncongenial, this high-minded poet spent his last years at the royal court in Syracuse, the great Italian city in Sicily; but in his legacy to the world he included that which was most admirable in the new Athens—its faith in reason and order.

2. SOPHOCLES (496-406 B.C.)

Sophocles was wholly the child of the best years of Athenian civilization. Although in his long life he also witnessed the decline of that civilization, in his art he remained unspoiled and unconfused by the mistakes and misfortunes of his city. He had acquired too much poise and stability to be defeated by external circumstances, to lose his sense of artistry and his love of moderation in all things. Victorious, self-beautifying, and cultivated Athens and Sophocles were indissolubly united.

Sophocles, the son of a prosperous merchant, was born in 496 B.C. at "White Colonus," a beautiful village a mile northwest of Athens. Endowed with unusual personal beauty, a versatile actor, and a highly esteemed gentleman, Sophocles enjoyed the favor of his city as few men did. With characteristic good fortune he won first prize the very first time he entered a dramatic contest at the age of twenty-eight, and during the next sixty years he received more prizes than any of his peers. He was never placed lower than second among the contestants, and was even honored with the rank of general in the Athenian army in deference to his popularity. Sophocles became the legendary happy man of Greece, and he was eulogized as such by his compatriots.

It is of course impossible to accept this idyllic Sophocles without qualifications. There is an account of a law-suit between the aged Sophocles and his children that cannot be discounted, and his plays reveal a comprehensive knowledge of the abysses of evil and suffering. His *Ajax* is a painful study in humiliation, madness, and suicide; the *Electra* presents an unrelenting picture of primitive vengeance; *Œdipus Tyrannus* is a painful tragedy of incest, suicide, and self-mutilation; and the *Antigone*, which culminates in a triple suicide, presents a welter of passion and conflict. Sophocles, moreover, is perhaps the most perfect example of a man who does not favor easy consolations. Unlike his visionary predecessor, Æschylus, he reads no comforting moral meaning into the order of the universe, and chance or blind fate is supreme in his world. "Human life," declares one of his choruses, "even in its utmost splendor hangs on the edge of a precipice."

It is the mark of Sophocles' unique genius that he was capable of disillusionment without cynicism or despair, that the horrors of life could not obscure for him its beauty and splendor. In all his plays the dignity of man is set up against his mistakes and defeats. He holds that man can create beauty and justice in the universe by practicing the good life, retaining his sense of proportion, and exercising a healing moderation.

Humanity cannot triumph over error or evil without the aid of reason. Each of Sophocles' tragedies is precipitated by human unreason or excess. There is excessive ambition in the hero of *Ajax*, and it drives him mad; Œdipus in *Œdipus Tyrannus* may be the sport of inscrutable Fate, but he is also the victim of too much impetuousness and passion in his nature; Creon, in the *Antigone*, destroys Antigone's life and his own happiness by excessive tyranny. If man led a life of reason, these tragedies indicate, there might still be fateful accident and death in the world, but there would be no man-made tragedy.

There is always the gratification of art, moreover, in Sophocles' philosophy; a product of reason which superimposes order on the chaos of the world, art can heal the wounds of passion with the sweetness and light of beauty. And Sophocles gave himself up to art more completely than his fellow-playwrights. He cultivated dramaturgy more skillfully and earnestly than any of his contemporaries, maintaining balance in the structure of his work and insisting upon harmony between feeling and expression. To him belongs the credit of advancing Greek tragedy furthest as a dramatic form independent of primitive ritual. He reduced the choral and lyric passages of classic tragedy, strove for concise and natural dialogue, added a third actor to enlarge the scope of his plays, and ordered his situations on the principle of progressive action. Without scaling the lyric heights of Æschylus or attempting the psychological complexities of Euripides, Sophocles created the most completely dramatic works of the ancient world.

Of Sophocles' seven extant plays, the *Antigone*, written in 443 B.C., does perhaps the greatest justice to his varied genius. Though the play was the first to be written, it is thematically the middle portion of the great saga of the Theban dynasty that begins in *Œdipus Tyrannus* and ends in *Œdipus at*

Colonus. It has both tenderness and terror, and it contains one of the most appealing characters in literature. Antigone is not a romantic heroine—she is too strident and single-willed for romantic taste —and yet the sterling courage of this girl who sets the claims of love above those of a vindictive government endows her with the morning beauty of Shakespeare's Juliet.

3. EURIPIDES (480-406 B.C.)

Euripides, the last and most modern of the great Greek tragic dramatists, was the least popular of them all in Athens during his life. He had a surplus of enemies in the city and became the unfortunate butt of the comic poets. According to Aristophanes, the most devastating of them, Euripides was a lowborn panderer to popular taste and a cantankerous misogynist who insulted womanhood in his plays.

Actually Euripides was born of aristocratic parents, and in his youth he held offices reserved for the sons of prominent families. He was uncompromisingly set against popular opinion and, far from being a woman-hater, he treated women with more sympathy and understanding than did any of his fellow dramatists. But Euripides was melancholy and reserved and anything but congenial company, and he shocked his audiences with his unconventional approach to sexual and moral problems. He was, moreover, a member of the unpopular peace party during the Peloponnesian War and an opponent of Athenian imperialism.

In fifty years of writing he won only five prizes in the annual dramatic contests, and he found it necessary to spend the last year and a half of his life in virtual exile at the court of Macedonia, where he died. But his fame grew after his death. In Athens, Sophocles, who survived him by some months, clothed his chorus in black as a mark of respect, and the State raised a cenotaph in his honor. The entire Hellenic world paid tribute to the playwright.

Euripides, who approached ethical and political problems as a rationalist and a humanitarian, was aptly called by Nietzsche "the poet of esthetic Socratism." There were, in fact, stories current in Athens that Socrates admired him above all other dramatists, and even that the philosopher assisted him in the composition of his plays. Certainly Euripides, like Socrates, used much argumentation in his dialogue and maintained a skeptical attitude toward accepted beliefs. He paid scant respect to the polytheistic religion of his day: In the *Ion,* Apollo or Phoebus is guilty of gross immorality and deception, and in the *Electra,* the god is openly criticized for having ordered Orestes to kill his mother. In *The Trojan Women,* a most searing picture of the sufferings of conquered nations, and in the *Hecuba,* which condemns the malevolence of both victors and victims, Euripides made passionate attacks on the savagery of war.

It is also part of Euripides' modernity (which brings him close to Ibsen, Strindberg, and O'Neill) that he entertained a keen interest in psychological problems. His findings, as a matter of fact, often harmonize with the subtlest observations of modern psychology. Without employing any of our current labels, he treated the dangers of sexual repression in his *Hippolytus* and acknowledged the creative and demoniac power of instinct, represented by Dionysus, in his last tragedy, *The Bacchæ.* The goddess of Love, Aphrodite, punishes the too frigid Hippolytus because he has neglected her divine rights; Dionysus wreaks fearful vengeance on the too rationalistic King Pentheus for suppressing his ecstatic rites. Nature, according to this poet, hits back when it is denied! Women like Phædra, who loves her stepson Hippolytus, and Medea, who kills her children when she is betrayed by her husband Jason, filled his tragedies with their passions and problems. Approaching these characters sympathetically and with uncanny psychological penetration, Euripides succeeded in drawing many of the most poignantly real female characters in dramatic literature.

His interest in the complexities of character and his social conscience also made Euripides introduce realism into the drama. *Electra,* one of his last masterpieces, composed in 413 B.C., exemplifies many of his strongest qualities as a dramatist and social thinker. It is in the main a profoundly realistic drama. It explains the traditional heroine, who drove her brother to murder his mother Clytemnestra, as a pathetically frustrated woman, unwholesomely devoted to her father's memory and to a passion for vengeance. National figures like Admetus, Jason, Agamemnon, and Achilles, held in popular esteem as paragons of many virtues, appeared on the stage of Euripides as shoddy specimens of humanity, because he saw heroes with the eyes of a realist and social critic (as Ibsen did nearly twenty-four centuries later). Euripides is perhaps our best example of a writer who was a once a realist and a poet. If his work is often marred because his realism and argumentativeness are imperfectly fused with his poetry, and because he ended many plays too hastily with some intervention by a god,[1] he nevertheless enriched the content of Greek drama and brought it to the threshold of modern times.

Euripides' *Alcestis* is one of his earliest plays. It was written before he became hampered by his efforts to expose social evil and to make the old myths serve this purpose. This play, one of the most charming products of his genius, is a fable about womanly love and devotion. Already the later realist is apparent in this youthful work: King Admetus, who is shaken by fear of death and allows his wife to die in his place, cuts a sorry figure beside the loving and courageous Alcestis. His parents could not have been treated more incisively and less sentimentally by a twentieth-century realist. And although his friend Hercules is a demigod and endowed with mythical strength, his boisterous behavior is set down with crassly realistic humor. Nevertheless, Euripides' incipient realism does not deprive the play of the magic of poetry and wonder. The tenderly treated character of Alcestis brightens the story, and her return to life heals the eyes that have been opened to the misery of death.

[1] By means of the device known as the *deus ex machina*, the god from the machine.

ÆSCHYLUS

Agamemnon

DRAMATIS PERSONÆ

Watchman
CLYTÆMNESTRA
Chorus of Argive Elders

AGAMEMNON
Herald (TALTHYBIOS)
CASSANDRA
ÆGISTHOS

ARGUMENT

Ten years had passed since Agamemnon, son of Atreus, king of Mykenæ, had led the Hellenes to Troïa to take vengeance on Alexandros (also known as Paris), son of Priam. For Paris had basely wronged Menelaos, king of Sparta, Agamemnon's brother, in that, being received by him as a guest, he enticed his wife Helena to leave her lord and go with him to Troïa. And now the tenth year had come, and Paris was slain, and the city of the Trojans was taken and destroyed, and Agamemnon and the Hellenes were on their way homeward with the spoil and prisoners they had taken. But meanwhile Clytæmnestra too, Agamemnon's queen, had been unfaithful, and had taken as her paramour Ægisthos, son of that Thyestes whom Atreus, his brother, had made to eat, unknowing, of the flesh of his own children. And now, partly led by her adulterer, and partly seeking to avenge the death of her daughter Iphigeneia, whom Agamemnon had sacrificed to appease the wrath of Artemis, and partly also jealous because he was bringing back Cassandra, the daughter of Priam, as his concubine, she plotted with Ægisthos against her husband's life. But this was done secretly, and she stationed a guard on the roof of the royal palace to give note when he saw the beacon-fires, by which Agamemnon had promised that he would send tidings that Troïa was taken.

SCENE:—*Argos. The Palace of Agamemnon; statues of the Gods in front. Watchman on the roof. Time, night.*

WATCHMAN. I ask the Gods a respite from these toils,
This keeping at my post the whole year round,
Wherein, upon the Atreidæ's roof reclined,
Like dog, upon my elbow, I have learnt
To know night's goodly company of stars,   5
And those bright lords that deck the firmament,
And winter bring to men, and harvest-tide;

Æschylus, *Agamemnon.* Translated by Plumptre. For previous stages in the history of Agamemnon, see p. 40. Æschylus (525-456 B.C.), the father of Greek drama, took part in the Persian Wars, which he celebrated in his play, *The Persians.* He came of the old nobility of Athens and lived most of his life in that city.

[The rising and the setting of the stars.]
And now I watch for sign of beacon-torch,
The flash of fire that bringeth news from Troïa, 10
And tidings of its capture. So prevails
A woman's manly-purposed, hoping heart;
And when I keep my bed of little ease,
Drenched with the dew, unvisited by dreams,
(For fear, instead of sleep, my comrade is, 15
So that in sound sleep ne'er I close mine eyes,)
And when I think to sing a tune, or hum,
(My medicine of song to ward off sleep.)
Then weep I, wailing for this house's chance,
No more, as erst, right well administered. 20
Well! may I now find blest release from toils,
When fire from out the dark brings tidings good.

*Pauses, then springs up suddenly, seeing a light in
the distance.*

Hail! thou torch-bearer of the night, that shedd'st
Light as of morn, and bringest full array
Of many choral bands in Argos met, 25
Because of this success. Hurrah! hurrah!
So clearly tell I Agamemnon's queen,
With all speed rising from her couch to raise
Shrill cry of triumph o'er this beacon-fire
Throughout the house, since Ilion's citadel 30
Is taken, as full well that bright blaze shows.
I, for my part, will dance my prelude now;

Leaps and dances.

For I shall score my lord's new turn of luck,
This beacon-blaze may throw of triple six. 34
Well, would that I with this mine hand may touch
The dear hand of our king when he comes home!
As to all else, the word is "Hush!" An ox
Rests on my tongue; had the house a voice
'Twould tell too clear a tale. I'm fain to speak
To those who know, forget with those who know
    not. 40

*Enter Chorus of twelve Argive elders, chanting as
they march to take up their position in the center
of the stage. A procession of women bearing
torches is seen in the distance.*

Lo! the tenth year now is passing
Since, of Priam great avengers,
Menelaos, Agamemnon,
Double-throned and double-sceptered,
Power from sovran Zeus deriving— 45
Mighty pair of the Atreidæ—
Raised a fleet of thousand vessels
Of the Argives from our country,
Potent helpers in their warfare,

Shouting cry of Ares fiercely; 50
E'en as vultures shriek who hover,
Wheeling, whirling o'er their eyrie,
In wild sorrow for their nestlings,
With their oars of stout wings rowing,
Having lost the toil that bound them 55
To their callow fledglings' couches.
But on high One,—or Apollo,
Zeus, or Pan,—the shrill cry hearing,
Cry of birds that are his clients,
Sendeth forth on men transgressing, 60
Erinnys, slow but sure avenger;
So against young Alexandros
Atreus' sons the great King sendeth,
Zeus, of host and guest protector:
He, for bride with many a lover, 65
Will to Danai give and Troïans
Many conflicts, men's limbs straining,
When the knee in dust is crouching,
And the spear-shaft in the onset
Of the battle snaps asunder. 70
But as things are now, so are they,
So, as destined, shall the end be.
Nor by tears, nor yet libations
Shall he soothe the wrath unbending
Caused by sacred rites left fireless. 75
We, with old frame little honored,
Left behind that host are staying,
Resting strength that equals childhood's
On our staff: for in the bosom
Of the boy, life's young sap rushing, 80
Is of old age but the equal;
Ares not as yet is found there:
And the man in age exceeding,
When the leaf is sere and withered,
Goes with three feet on his journey; 85
Not more Ares-like than boyhood,
Like a day-seen dream he wanders.

*Enter CLYTÆMNESTRA, followed by the procession
of torch-bearers.*

Thou, of Tyndareus the daughter,
Queen of Argos, Clytæmnestra,
What has happened? what news cometh? 90
What perceiving, on what tidings
Leaning, dost thou put in motion
All this solemn, great procession?
Of the Gods who guard the city,
Those above and those beneath us, 95
Of the heaven, and of the market,
Lo! with thy gifts blaze the altars;
And through all the expanse of Heaven,
Here and there, the torch-fire rises.

With the flowing, pure persuasion 100
Of the holy unguent nourished,
And the chrism rich and kingly
From the treasure-store's recesses,
Telling what of this thou canst tell, 105
What is right for thee to utter,
Be a healer of my trouble,
Trouble now my soul disturbing,
While anon fond hope displaying
Sacrificial signs propitious, 110
Wards off care that no rest knoweth,
Sorrow mind and heart corroding.

*The Chorus, taking their places round the central
thymele, begin their song.*

STROPHE I

Able am I to utter, setting forth
  The might from omens sprung
What met the heroes as they journeyed on,
  (For still, by God's great gift, 115
  My age, yet linked with strength,
  Breathes suasive power of song,)
How the Achæans' twin-throned majesty,
Accordant rulers of the youth of Hellas,
  With spear and vengeful hand, 120
Were sent by fierce, strong bird 'gainst Teucrian
    shore,
Kings of the birds to kings of ships appearing,
  One black, with white tail one,
Near to the palace, on the spear-hand side,
  On station seen of all, 125
A pregnant hare devouring with her young,
  Robbed of all runs to come:
Wail as for Linos, wail, wail bitterly,
  And yet may good prevail!

ANTISTROPHE I

And the wise prophet of the army seeing 130
  The brave Atreidæ twain
Of diverse mood, knew those that tore the hare,
  And those that led the host;
  And thus divining spake:
  "One day this armament 135
Shall Priam's city sack, and all the herds
Owned by the people, countless, by the towers,
  Fate shall with force lay low.
Only take heed lest any wrath of Gods
Blunt the great curb of Troïa yet encamped,
  Struck down before its time; 141
For Artemis the chaste that house doth hate,
  Her father's wingèd hounds,

Who slay the mother with her unborn young,
  And loathes the eagles' feast. 145
Wail as for Linos, wail, wail bitterly;
  And yet may good prevail!

EPODE

"For she, the fair One, though so kind of heart
To fresh-dropt dew from mighty lion's womb,
  And young that suck the teats 150
  Of all that roam the fields,
  Yet prays Him bring to pass
  The portents of those birds,
The omens good yet also full of dread.
  And Pæan I invoke 155
As Healer, lest she on the Danai send
  Delays that keep the ships
  Long time with hostile blasts,
So urging on a new, strange sacrifice,
  Unblest, unfestivaled, 160
By natural growth artificer of strife,
Bearing far other fruit than wife's true fear,
  For there abideth yet,
  Fearful, recurring still,
Ruling the house, full subtle, unforgetting, 165
  Vengeance for children slain."
Such things, with great good mingled, Calchas
    spake,
  In voice that pierced the air,
As destined by the birds that crossed our path
  To this our kingly house: 170
  And in accord with them,
Wail as for Linos, wail, wail bitterly;
  And yet may good prevail.

STROPHE II

O Zeus—whate'er He be,
  If that Name please Him well, 175
  By that on Him I call:
Weighing all other names I fail to guess
Aught else but Zeus, if I would cast aside,
  Clearly, in every deed,
From off my soul this idle weight of care. 180

ANTISTROPHE II

Nor He who erst was great,
  Full of the might to war,
  Avails now; He is gone;
And He who next came hath departed too,
His victor meeting; but if one to Zeus, 185
  High triumph-praise should sing,
His shall be all the wisdom of the wise;

STROPHE III

Yea, Zeus, who leadeth men in wisdom's way,
　　And fixeth fast the law,
　　　That pain is gain;　　　　　　　　190
And slowly dropping on the heart in sleep
　　Comes woe-recording care,
And makes the unwilling yield to wiser thoughts:
And doubtless this too comes from grace of Gods,
Seated in might upon their awful thrones.　　195

ANTISTROPHE III

And then of those Achæan ships the chief,
　　The elder, blaming not
　　Or seer or priest;
But tempered to the fate that on him smote. . . .
　　When that Achæan host　　　　　　200
Were vexed with adverse winds and failing stores,
Still kept where Chalkis in the distance lies
And the vexed waves in Aulis ebb and flow;

STROPHE IV

And breezes from the Strymon sweeping down,
Breeding delays and hunger, driving forth　　205
　　Our men in wandering course,
　　On seas without a port.
Sparing nor ships, nor rope, nor sailing gear,
With doubled months wore down the Argive host;
　　And when, for that wild storm,　　　210
Of one more charm far harder for our chiefs
The prophet told, and spake of Artemis,
　　In tone so piercing shrill,
The Atreidæ smote their staves upon the ground,
　　And could not stay their tears.　　　215

ANTISTROPHE IV

And then the old king lifted up his voice,
And spake, "Great woe it is to disobey;
　　Great too to slay my child,
　　The pride and joy of home,
Polluting with the streams of maiden's blood　　220
Her father's hands upon the altar steps.
　　What course is free from ill?
How lose my ships and fail of mine allies?
'Tis meet that they with strong desire should seek
　　A rite the winds to soothe,　　　225
E'en though it be with blood of maiden pure;
　　May all end well at last!"

STROPHE V

So when he himself had harnessed
To the yoke of Fate unbending,

With a blast of strange, new feeling,　　　230
Sweeping o'er his heart and spirit,
Aweless, godless, and unholy,
He his thoughts and purpose altered
To full measure of all daring,
(Still base counsel's fatal frenzy,　　　235
Wretched primal source of evils,
Gives to mortal hearts strange boldness.)
And at last his heart he hardened
His own child to slay as victim,
Help in war that they were waging,　　　240
To avenge a woman's frailty.
Victim for the good ship's safety.

ANTISTROPHE V

All her prayers and eager callings,
On the tender name of Father,
All her young and maiden freshness,　　　245
They but set at nought, those rulers,
In their passion for the battle.
And her father gave commandment
To the servants of the Goddess,
When the prayer was o'er, to lift her,　　　250
Like a kid, above the altar,
In her garments wrapt, face downwards,—
Yea, to seize with all their courage,
And that o'er her lips of beauty
Should be set a watch to hinder　　　255
Words of curse against the houses,
With the gag's strength silence-working.

STROPHE VI

　　And she upon the ground
　　Pouring rich folds of veil in saffron dyed,
　　Cast at each one of those who sacrificed　　260
　　　A piteous glance that pierced,
　　　Fair as a pictured form;
　　　And wishing,—all in vain,—
　　　To speak; for oftentimes
　　In those her father's hospitable halls　　　265
She sang, a maiden pure with chastest song,
　　And her dear father's life
That poured its threefold cup of praise to God,
　　Crowned with all choicest good.
　　She with a daughter's love　　　270
　　Was wont to celebrate.

ANTISTROPHE VI

What then ensued mine eyes
Saw not, nor may I tell, but Calchas' arts
Were found not fruitless. Justice turns the scale

For those to whom through pain 275
At last comes wisdom's gain.
But for our future fate,
Since help for it is none,
Good-by to it before it comes, and this
Has the same end as wailing premature; 280
For with tomorrow's dawn
It will come clear; may good luck crown our fate!
So prays the one true guard,
Nearest and dearest found,
Of this our Apian land. 285

The Chief of the Chorus turns to CLYTÆMNESTRA,
and her train of handmaids, who are seen ap-
proaching.

CHOR. I come, O Clytæmnestra, honoring
Thy majesty: 'tis meet to pay respect
To a chief's wife, the man's throne empty left:
But whether thou hast heard good news, or else
In hopes of tidings glad dost sacrifice, 290
I fain would hear, yet will not silence blame.
CLYTÆM. May Morning, as the proverb runs, ap-
pear
Bearing glad tidings from his mother Night!
Joy thou shalt learn beyond thy hope to hear;
For Argives now have taken Priam's city. 295
CHOR. What? Thy words sound so strange they
flit by me.
CLYTÆM. The Achæans hold Troïa. Speak I clear
enough?
CHOR. Joy creeps upon me, drawing forth my
tears.
CLYTÆM. Of loyal heart thine eyes give token
true.
CHOR. What witness sure hast thou of these
events? 300
CLYTÆM. Full clear (how else?) unless the God
deceive.
CHOR. Reliest thou on dreams or visions seen?
CLYTÆM. I place no trust in mind weighed down
with sleep.
CHOR. Hath then some wingless omen charmed
thy soul?
CLYTÆM. My mind thou scorn'st, as though
'twere but a girl's. 305
CHOR. What time has passed since they the city
sacked?
CLYTÆM. This very night, the mother of this
morn.
CHOR. What herald could arrive with speed like
this?
CLYTÆM. Hephæstos flashing forth bright flames
from Ida:

Beacon to beacon from that courier-fire 310
Sent on its tidings; Ida to the rock
Hermæan named, in Lemnos: from the isle
The height of Athos, dear to Zeus, received
A third great torch of flame, and lifted up,
So as on high to skim the broad sea's back, 315
The stalwart fire rejoicing went its way;
The pine-wood, like a sun, sent forth its light
Of golden radiance to Makistos' watch;
And he, with no delay, nor unawares
Conquered by sleep, performed his courier's
part: 320
Far off the torch-light, to Eurîpos' straits
Advancing, tells it to Messapion's guards:
They, in their turn, lit up and passed it on,
Kindling a pile of dry and aged heath.
Still strong and fresh the torch, not yet grown
dim, 325
Leaping across Asôpos' plain in guise
Like a bright moon, towards Kithæron's rock,
Roused the next station of the courier flame.
And that far-traveled light the sentries there
Refused not, burning more than all yet named: 330
And then the light swooped o'er Gorgôpis' lake,
And passing on to Ægiplanctos' mount,
Bade the bright fire's due order tarry not;
And they, enkindling boundless store, send on
A mighty beard of flame, and then it passed 335
The headland e'en that looks on Saron's gulf,
Still blazing. On it swept, until it came
To Arachnæan heights, the watch-tower near;
Then here on the Atreidæ's roof it swoops,
This light, of Ida's fire no doubtful heir. 340
Such is the order of my torch-race games;
One from another taking up the course,
But here the winner is both first and last;
And this sure proof and token now I tell thee,
Seeing that my lord hath sent it me from
Troïa. 345
CHOR. I to the Gods, O Queen, will pray here-
after,
But fain would I hear all thy tale again,
E'en as thou tell'st, and satiate my wonder.
CLYTÆM. This very day the Achæans Troïa hold.
I trow full diverse cry pervades the town: 350
Pour in the same vase vinegar and oil,
And you would call them enemies, not friends;
And so from conquerors and from captives now
The cries of varied fortune one may hear.
For these, low-fallen on the carcases 355
Of husbands and of brothers, children too
By aged fathers, mourn their dear ones' death
And that with throats that are no longer free.

And those the hungry toil of sleepless guard,
After the battle, at their breakfast sets;   360
Not billeted in order fixed and clear,
But just as each his own chance fortune grasps,
They in the captive houses of the Troïans
Dwell, freed at last from all the night's chill frosts,
And dews of heaven, for now, poor wretches,
        they   365
Will sleep all night without the sentry's watch;
And if they reverence well the guardian Gods
Of that new-conquered country, and their shrines,
Then they, the captors, will not captured be.
Ah! let no evil lust attack the host   370
Conquered by greed, to plunder what they ought
        not:
For yet they need return in safety home,
Doubling the goal to run their backward race.
But should the host come sinning 'gainst the
        Gods,
Then would the curse of those that perishèd   375
Be watchful, e'en though no quick ill might fall.
Such thoughts are mine, mere woman though I be.
May good prevail beyond all doubtful chance!
For I have got the blessing of great joy.
    CHOR. Thou, lady, kindly, like a sage, dost
        speak,   380
And I, on hearing thy sure evidence,
Prepare myself to give the Gods due thanks;
For they have wrought full meed for all our toil.
        [*Exit* CLYTÆMNESTRA *with her train.*

O Zeus our King! O Night beloved,
Mighty winner of great glories,   385
Who upon the towers of Troïa
Casted'st snare of closest meshes,
So that none full-grown or youthful
Could o'erleap the net of bondage,
Woe or universal capture;—   390
Zeus, of host and guest protector,
Who hath brought these things, I worship;
He long since on Alexandros
Stretched his bow that so his arrow
Might not sweep at random, missing,   395
Or beyond the stars shoot idly.

STROPHE I

Yes, one may say, 'tis Zeus, whose blow they feel;
    This one may clearly trace:
    They fared as He decreed:
        Yea, one there was who said,   400
"The Gods deign not to care for mortal men
By whom the grace of things inviolable

Is trampled under foot."
    No fear of God had he:
Now is it to the children manifest   405
    Of those who, overbold,
Breathed rebel War beyond the bounds of Right,
Their houses overfilled with precious store
    Above the golden mean.
Ah! let our life be free from all that hurts,   410
    So that for one who gains
    Wisdom in heart and soul,
    That lot may be enough.
Since still there is no bulwark strong in wealth
    Against destruction's doom,   415
For one who in the pride of wantonness
Spurns the great altar of the Right and Just.

ANTISTROPHE I

Him woeful, subtle Impulse urges on,
    Resistless in her might,
    Atè's far-scheming child: 420
    All remedy is vain.
It is not hidden, but is manifest,
That mischief with its horrid gleaming light;
    And, like to worthless bronze,
    By friction tried and tests,   425
It turns to tarnished blackness in its hue:
    Since, boy-like, he pursues
A bird upon its flight, and so doth bring
Upon his city shame intolerable:
    And no God hears his prayer,   430
    But bringeth low the unjust,
    Who deals with deeds like this.
'Thus Paris came to the Atreidæ's home,
    And stole its queen away,
And so left brand of shame indelible   435
Upon the board where host and guest had sat.

STROPHE II

She, leaving to her countrymen at home
Wild din of spear and shield and ships of war,
    And bringing, as her dower,
    To Ilion doom of death,   440
Passed very swiftly through the palace gates,
    Daring what none should dare;
    And many a wailing cry
They raised, the minstrel prophets of the house,
    "Woe for that kingly home!   445
Woe for that kingly home and for its chiefs!
Woe for the marriage-bed and traces left
    Of wife who loved her lord!"
There stands he silent; foully wronged and yet
    Uttering no word of scorn,   450

In deepest woe perceiving she is gone;
And in his yearning love
  For one beyond the sea,
A ghost shall seem to queen it o'er the house;
  The grace of sculptured forms   455
  Is loathèd by her lord,
And in the penury of life's bright eyes
  All Aphroditè's charm
  To utter wreck has gone.

ANTISTROPHE II

And phantom shades that hover round in
    dreams   460
Come full of sorrow, bringing vain delight;
  For vain it is, when one
  Sees seeming shows of good,
And gliding through his hands the dream is gone,
  After a moment's space,   465
  On wings that follow still
Upon the path where sleep goes to and fro.
  Such are the woes at home
Upon the altar hearth, and worse than these.
But on a wider scale for those who went   470
  From Hellas' ancient shore,
A sore distress that causeth pain of heart
  Is seen in every house.
Yea, many things there are that touch the quick:
  For those whom each did send   475
  He knoweth; but, instead
Of living men, there come to each man's home
  Funeral urns alone,
  And ashes of the dead.

STROPHE III

For Ares, trafficking for golden coin   480
  The lifeless shapes of men,
And in the rush of battle holding scales,
  Sends now from Ilion
  Dust from the funeral pyre,
A burden sore to loving friends at home,   485
  And bitterly bewailed,
  Filling the brazen urn
With well-smoothed ashes in the place of men;
  And with high praise they mourn
This hero skilled and valiant in the fight,   490
And that who in the battle nobly fell,
  All for another's wife:
And other words some murmur secretly;
  And jealous discontent
Against the Atreidæ, champions in the suit,   495
  Creeps on all stealthily;
  And some around the wall,

In full and goodly form have sepulture
  There upon Ilion's soil,
And their foes' land inters its conquerors.   500

ANTISTROPHE III

And so the murmurs of their subjects rise
  With sullen discontent,
And do the dread work of a people's curse;
  And now my boding fear
  Awaits some news of ill,   505
As yet enwrapt in blackness of the night.
  Not heedless of the Gods
  Of shedders of much blood,
And the dark-robed Erinnyes in due time,
  By adverse chance of life,   510
Place him who prospers in unrighteousness
In gloom obscure; and once among the unseen,
  There is no help for him:
Fame in excess is but a perilous thing;
  For on men's quivering eyes   515
Is hurled by Zeus the blinding thunder-bolt.
  I praise the good success
  That rouses not God's wrath;
Ne'er be it mine a city to lay waste.
  Nor, as a prisoner, see   520
My life wear on beneath another's power!

EPODE

And now at bidding of the courier flame,
  The herald of good news,
A rumor swift spreads through the city streets,
But who knows clearly whether it be true,   525
Or whether God has mingled lies with it?
Who is so childish or so reft of sense,
  As with his heart a-glow
At that fresh uttered message of the flame,
Then to wax sad at changing rumor's sound?   530
It suits the mood that sways a woman's mind
To pour thanksgiving ere the truth is seen:
Quickly, with rapid steps, too credulous,
The limit which a woman sets to trust
  Advances evermore;   535
  And with swift doom of death
A rumor spread by woman perishes.

As the Chorus ends, a Herald is seen approaching
his head wreathed with olive.

Soon we shall know the sequence of the torches
Light-giving, and of all the beacon-fires,
If they be true; or if, as 'twere a dream,   540
This sweet light coming hath beguiled our minds
I see a herald coming from the shore,

With olive boughs o'ershadowed, and the dust,
Dry sister-twin of mire, announces this,
That neither without voice, nor kindling blaze   545
Of wood upon the mountains, he will signal
With smoke from fire, but either he will come,
With clear speech bidding us rejoice, or else . . .
    [pauses]
The word opposed to this I much mislike.
Nay, may good issue good beginnings crown!   550
Who for our city utters other prayers,
May he himself his soul's great error reap!
   HERALD. Hail, soil of this my Argive fatherland.
Now in the light of the tenth year I reach thee,
Though many hopes are shattered, gaining one.   555
For never did I think in Argive land
To die, and share the tomb that most I craved.
Now hail! thou land; and hail! thou light of day:
Zeus our great ruler, and thou Pythian king,
No longer darting arrows from thy bow.   560
Full hostile wast thou by Scamandros' banks,
Now be thou Savior, yea, and Healer found,
O king Apollo! and the Gods of war,
These I invoke; my patron Hermes too,
Dear herald whom all heralds reverence,—   565
Those heroes, too, that sent us,—graciously
To welcome back the host that war has spared.
Hail, O ye royal dwellings, home beloved!
Ye solemn thrones, and Gods who face the sun!
If e'er of old, with cheerful glances now   570
After long time receive our king's array.
For he is come, in darkness bringing light
To you and all, our monarch, Agamemnon.
Salute him with all grace; for so 'tis meet,
Since he hath dug up Troïa with the spade   575
Of Zeus the Avenger, and the plain laid waste;
Fallen their altars and the shrines of Gods;
The seed of all the land is rooted out,
This yoke of bondage casting over Troïa,
Our chief, the elder of the Atreidæ, comes,   580
A man full blest, and worthiest of high honor
Of all that are. For neither Paris self,
Nor his accomplice city now can boast
Their deed exceeds its punishment. For he,
Found guilty on the charge of rape and theft,   585
Hath lost his prize and brought his father's house,
With lands and all, to waste and utter wreck;
And Priam's sons have double forfeit paid.
   CHOR. Joy, joy, thou herald of the Achæan host!
   HER. All joy is mine: I shrink from death no
    more.   590
   CHOR. Did love for this thy fatherland so try
    thee?
   HER. So that mine eyes weep tears for very joy.

   CHOR. Disease full sweet then this ye suffered
    from . . .
   HER. How so? When taught, I shall thy mean-
    ing master.
   CHOR. Ye longed for us who yearned for you in
    turn.   595
   HER. Say'st thou this land its yearning host
    yearned o'er?
   CHOR. Yea, so that oft I groaned in gloom of
    heart.
   HER. Whence came these bodings that an army
    hates?
   CHOR. Silence I've held long since a charm for ill.
   HER. How, when your lords were absent, feared
    ye any?   600
   CHOR. To use thy words, death now would wel-
    come be.
   HER. Good is the issue; but in so long time
Some things, one well might say, have prospered
   well,
And some give cause for murmurs. Save the Gods,
Who free from sorrow lives out all his life?   605
For should I tell of toils, and how we lodged
Full hardly, seldom putting in to shore,
And then with couch full hard. . . . What gave
   us not
Good cause for mourning? What ill had we not
As daily portion? And what passed on land,   610
That brought yet greater hardship: for our beds
Were under our foes' walls, and meadow mists
From heaven and earth still left us wringing wet,
A constant mischief to our garments, making
Our hair as shaggy as the beasts'. And if   615
One spoke of winter frosts that killed the birds,
By Ida's snow-storms made intolerable,
Or heat, when Ocean in its noontide couch
Windless reclined and slept without a wave. . . .
But why lament o'er this? Our toil is past;   620
Past too is theirs who in the warfare fell,
So that no care have they to rise again.
Why should I count the number of the dead,
Or he that lives mourn o'er a past mischance?
To change and chance I bid a long Farewell: 625
With us, the remnant of the Argive host,
Good fortune wins, no ills as counterpoise.
So it is meet to this bright sun we boast,
Who travel homeward over land and sea: 629
"The Argive host who now have captured Troïa,
These spoils of battle to the Gods of Hellas
Hang on their pegs, enduring prize and joy."
Hearing these things we ought to bless our country
And our commanders; and the grace of Zeus

That wrought this shall be honored. My tale's
told. 635
  Chor. Thy words o'ercome me, and I say not
  nay;
To learn good keeps youth's freshness with the
  old.
'Tis meet these things should be a special care
To Clytæmnestra and the house, and yet
That they should make me sharer in their joy. 640

Enter CLYTÆMNESTRA.

  CLYTÆM. I long ago for gladness raised my cry,
When the first fiery courier came by night,
Telling of Troïa taken and laid waste:
And then one girding at me spake, "Dost think,
Trusting in beacons, Troïa is laid waste? 645
This heart elate is just a woman's way."
In words like these they made me out distraught;
Yet still I sacrificed, and with a strain
Shrill as a woman's, they, now here, now there,
Throughout the city hymns of blessing raised 650
In shrines of Gods, and lulled to gentle sleep
The fragrant flame that on the incense fed.
And now why need'st thou lengthen out thy
  words?
I from the king himself the tale shall learn;
And that I show all zeal to welcome back 655
My honored lord on his return (for what
Is brighter joy for wife to see than this,
When God has brought her husband back from
  war,
To open wide her gates?) tell my lord this,
"To come with all his speed, the city's idol"· 660
And "may he find a faithful wife at home,
Such as he left her, noble watch-dog still
For him, and hostile to his enemies;
And like in all things else, who has not broken
One seal of his in all this length of time." 665
No pleasure have I known, nor scandal ill
With any other more than . . . stains on bronze.
Such is my vaunt, and being full of truth,
Not shameful for a noble wife to speak.
                                        [*Exit.*
  Chor. [*to Herald*]. She hath thus spoken in thy
  hearing now 670
A goodly word for good interpreters.
But tell me, herald, tell of Menelaos,
If, coming home again in safety he
Is with you, the dear strength of this our land.
  Her. I cannot make report of false good news,
So that my friends should long rejoice in it. 676
  Chor. Ah! could'st thou good news speak, and
  also true!

These things asunder are not well concealed.
  Her. The chief has vanished from the Achæan
  host,
He and his ship. I speak no falsehood here. 680
  Chor In sight of all when he from Ilion sailed?
Or did a storm's wide evil part him from you?
  Her. Like skillful archer thou hast hit the mark,
And in few words has told of evil long.
  Chor. And was it of him as alive or dead 685
The whisper of the other sailors ran?
  Her. None to that question answer clear can
  give,
Save the Sun-God who feeds the life of earth.
  Chor. How say'st thou? Did a storm come on
  our fleet,
And do its work through anger of the Gods? 690
  Her. It is not meet a day of tidings good
To mar with evil news. Apart for each
Is special worship. But when courier brings
With louring face the ills men pray against,
And tells a city that its host has fallen, 695
That for the State there is a general wound,
That many a man from many a home is driven,
As banned by double scourge that Ares loves,
Woe doubly-barbed, Death's two-horsed chariot
  this . . . 699
When with such griefs as freight a herald comes,
'Tis meet to chant the Erinnyes' dolorous song;
But for glad messenger of good deeds wrought
That bring deliverance, coming to a town
Rejoicing in its triumph, . . . how shall I
Blend good with evil, telling of a storm 705
That smote the Achæans, not without God's wrath?
For they a compact swore who erst were foes,
Ocean and Fire, and their pledges gave,
Wrecking the ill-starred army of the Argives;
And in the night rose ill of raging storm: 710
For Thrakian tempests shattered all the ships,
Each on the other. Some thus crashed and bruised,
By the storm stricken and the surging foam
Of wind-tost waves, soon vanished out of sight,
Whirled by an evil pilot. And when rose 715
The sun's bright orb, behold, the Ægean sea
Blossomed with wrecks of ships and dead Achæans.
And as for us and our uninjured ship,
Surely 'twas someone stole or begged us off,
Some God, not man, presiding at the helm; 720
And on our ship with good will Fortune sat,
Giver of safety, so that nor in haven
Felt we the breakers, nor on rough rock-beach
Ran we aground. But when we had escaped
The hell of waters, then in clear, bright day, 725
Not trusting in our fortune, we in thought

O'er new ills brooded of our host destroyed,
And eke most roughly handled. And if still
Breathe any of them they report of us   729
As having perished. How else should they speak?
And we in our turn deem that they are so.
God send good ending! Look you, first and chief,
For Menelaos' coming; and indeed,
If any sunbeam know of him alive
And well, by help of Zeus who has not willed   735
As yet to blot out all the regal race,
Some hope there is that he'll come back again.
Know, hearing this, that thou the truth hast heard.
                                   [*Exit Herald.*

STROPHE I

Chor. Who was it named her with such won-
      drous truth?
   (Could it be One unseen,   740
In strange prevision of her destined work,
   Guiding the tongue through chance?)
Who gave that war-wed, strife-upstirring one
The name of Helen, ominous of ill?
   For all too plainly she   745
   Hath been to men, and ships,
   And towers, as doom of Hell.
From bower of gorgeous curtains forth she sailed
With breeze of Zephyr Titan-born and strong;
   And hosts of many men,   750
   Hunters that bore the shield,
Went on the track of those who steered their boat
Unseen to leafy banks of Simois,
   On her account who came,
Dire cause of strife with bloodshed in her train. 755

ANTISTROPHE I

And so the wrath which works its vengeance out
   Dear bride to Ilion brought,
(Ah, all too truly named!) exacting still
   After long lapse of time
The penalty of foul dishonor done   760
To friendship's board and Zeus, of host and guest
   The God, from those who paid
   Their loud-voiced honor then
   Unto that bridal strain,
That hymeneal chorus which to chant   765
Fell to the lot of all the bridegroom's kin.
   But learning other song,
   Priam's ancient city now
Bewaileth sore, and calls on Paris' name,
Wedded in fatal wedlock; all the time   770
   Enduring tear-fraught life
For all the blood its citizens had lost.

STROPHE II

So once a lion's cub,
A mischief in his house,
As foster child one reared,   775
While still it loved the teats;
In life's preluding dawn
Tame, by the children loved,
And fondled by the old,
Oft in his arms 'twas held,   780
Like infant newly born,
With eyes that brightened to the hand that stroked,
And fawning at the hest of hunger keen.

ANTISTROPHE II

But when full-grown, it showed
The nature of its sires;   785
For it unbidden made
A feast in recompense
Of all their fostering care,
By banquet of slain sheep;
With blood the house was stained,   790
A curse no slaves could check,
Great mischief murderous:
By God's decree a priest of Atè thus
Was reared, and grew within the man's own house.

STROPHE III

So I would tell that thus to Ilion came   795
Mood as of calm when all the air is still,
The gentle pride and joy of kingly state,
   A tender glance of eye,
The full-blown blossom of a passionate love,
   Thrilling the very soul;   800
   And yet she turned aside,
And wrought a bitter end of marriage feast,
   Coming to Priam's race,
   Ill sojourner, ill friend,
Sent by great Zeus, the God of host and guest 805
Erinnys, for whom wives weep many tears.

ANTISTROPHE III

There lives an old saw, framed in ancient days,
In memories of men, that high estate
Full-grown brings forth its young, nor childless
      dies,
   But that from good success   810
Springs to the race a woe insatiable.
   But I, apart from all,
   Hold this my creed alone;
For impious act it is that offspring breeds,
   Like to their parent stock: 815

For still in every house
That loves the right their fate for evermore
Rejoiceth in an issue fair and good.

STROPHE IV

But Recklessness of old
Is wont to breed another Recklessness,   820
　Sporting its youth in human miseries,
Or now, or then, whene'er the fixed hour comes:
　That in its youth, in turn,
　Doth full-flushed Lust beget,
And that dread demon-power unconquerable,   825
　Daring that fears not God,—
Two curses black within the homes of men,
　Like those that gendered them.

ANTISTROPHE IV

But Justice shineth bright   829
In dwellings that are dark and dim with smoke,
　And honors life law-ruled,
While gold-decked homes conjoined with hands
　　defiled
　She with averted eyes
　Hath left, and draweth near   834
To holier things, nor worships might of wealth,
　If counterfeit its praise;
But still directeth all the course of things
　Towards its destined goal.

AGAMEMNON *is seen approaching in his chariot,
followed by another chariot, in which* CASSANDRA
*is standing, carrying her prophet's wand in her
hand, and wearing fillets round her temples, and
by a great train of soldiers bearing trophies. As
they come on the stage the Chorus sings its welcome.*

Come then, king, thou son of Atreus,
Waster of the towers of Troïa,   840
What of greeting and of homage
Shall I give, nor overshooting,
Nor due need of honor missing?
Men there are who, right transgressing,
Honor semblance more than being.   845
　O'er the sufferer all are ready
Wail of bitter grief to utter,
Though the biting pang of sorrow
Never to their heart approaches;
So with counterfeit rejoicing   850
Men strain faces that are smileless;
But when one his own sheep knoweth,
The men's eyes cannot deceive him,
When they deem with kindly purpose,

And with fondness weak to flatter.   855
Thou, when thou did'st lead thine army
For Helen's sake—(I will not hide it)—
Wast to me as one whose features
Have been limned by unskilled artist,
Guiding ill the helm of reason,   860
Giving men to death's doom sentenced
Courage which their will rejected.
Now nor from the spirit's surface,
Nor with touch of thought unfriendly,
All the toil, I say, is welcome,   865
If men bring it to good issue.
And thou soon shalt know, enquiring,
Him who rightly, him who wrongly
　Of thy citizens fulfilleth
Task of office for the city.   870

AGAM. First Argos, and the Gods who guard the
　　land,
'Tis right to greet; to them in part I owe
This my return, and vengeance that I took
On Priam's city. Not on hearsay proof
Judging the cause, with one consent the Gods   875
Cast in their votes into the urn of blood
For Ilion's ruin and her people's death;
I' the other urn Hope touched the rim alone,
Still far from being filled full. And even yet
The captured city by its smoke is seen,   880
The incense clouds of Atè live on still;
And, in the act of dying with its prey,
From richest store the dust sends savors sweet.
For these things it is meet to give the Gods
Thank-offerings long-enduring; for our nets   885
Of vengeance we set close, and for a woman
Our Argive monster laid the city low,
Foaled by the mare, a people bearing shield,
Taking its leap when set the Pleiades;   889
And, bounding o'er the tower, that ravenous lion
Lapped up its fill of blood of kingly race.
This prelude to the Gods I lengthen out;
And as concerns thy feeling (this I well
Remember hearing) I with thee agree,
And thou in me may'st find an advocate.   895
With but few men is it their natural bent
To honor without grudging prosperous friend:
For ill-souled envy that the heart besets,
Doubles his woe who suffers that disease:
He by his own griefs first is overwhelmed,   900
And groans at sight of others' happier lot.
And I with good cause say, (for well I know,)
They are but friendship's mirror, phantom shade,
Who seemed to be my most devoted friends.
Odysseus only, who against his will   905
Sailed with us, still was found true trace-fellow:

And this I say of him or dead or living.
But as for all that touches on the State,
Or on the Gods, in full assembly we,
Calling our council, will deliberate: 910
For what goes well we should with care provide
How longest it may last; and where there needs
A healing charm, there we with all good-will,
By surgery or cautery will try
To turn away the mischief of disease.   915
And now will I to home and household hearth
Move on, and first give thanks unto the Gods
Who led me forth, and brought me back again.
Since Victory follows, long may she remain!

Enter CLYTÆMNESTRA, *followed by female attend-*
ants carrying purple tapestry.

CLYTÆM. Ye citizens, ye Argive senators,   920
I will not shrink from telling you the tale
Of wife's true love. As time wears on one drops
All over-shyness. Not learning it from others,
I will narrate my own unhappy life,
The whole long time my lord at Ilion stayed.   925
For first, that wife should sit at home alone
Without her husband is a monstrous grief,
Hearing full many an ill report of him,
Now one and now another coming still,
Bringing news home, worse trouble upon bad.   930
Yea, if my lord had met as many wounds
As rumor told of, floating to our house,
He had been riddled more than any net;
And had he died, as tidings still poured in,
Then he, a second Geryon with three lives,   935
Had boasted of a threefold coverlet
Of earth above, (I will not say below him,)
Dying one death for each of those his forms;
And so, because of all these ill reports,   939
Full many a noose around my neck have others
Loosed by main force, when I had hung myself.
And for this cause no son is with me now,
Holding in trust the pledges of our love,
As he should be, Orestes. Wonder not;
For now a kind ally doth nurture him,   945
Strophios the Phokian, telling me of woes
Of twofold aspect, danger on thy side
At Ilion, and lest loud-voiced anarchy
Should overthrow thy council, since 'tis still
The wont of men to kick at those who fall.   950
No trace of guile bears this excuse of mine;
As for myself, the fountains of my tears
Have flowed till they are dry, no drop remains,
And mine eyes suffer from o'er-late repose,
Watching with tears the beacons set for thee,   955

Left still unheeded. And in dreams full oft
I from my sleep was startled by the gnat
With thin wings buzzing, seeing in the night
Ills that stretched far beyond the time of sleep.
Now, having borne all this, with mind at ease,   960
I hail my lord as watch-dog of the fold,
The stay that saves the ship, of lofty roof
Main column-prop, a father's only child,
Land that beyond all hope the sailor sees,
Morn of great brightness following after storm,   965
Clear-flowing fount to thirsty traveler.
Yes, it is pleasant to escape all straits:
With words of welcome such as these I greet thee·
May jealous Heaven forgive them! for we bore
Full many an evil in the past; and now,   970
Dear husband, leave thy car, nor on the ground,
O King, set thou the foot that Ilion trampled.
Why linger ye, [*turning to her attendants*] ye
      maids, whose task it was
To strew the pathway with your tapestries?   974
Let the whole road be straightway purple-strown,
That Justice lead to home he looked not for.
All else my care, by slumber not subdued,
Will with God's help work out what fate decrees.

The handmaids advance, and are about to lay the
purple carpets on the ground.

AGAM. O child of Leda, guardian of my home,
Thy speech hath with my absence well agreed—
For long indeed thou mad'st it—but fit praise   981
Is boon that I must seek at other hands.
I pray thee, do not in thy woman's fashion
Pamper my pride, nor in barbaric guise
Prostrate on earth raise full-mouthed cries to me;
Make not my path offensive to the Gods   986
By spreading it with carpets. They alone
May claim that honor; but for mortal men
To walk on fair embroidery, to me
Seems nowise without peril. So I bid you   990
To honor me as man, and not as God.
Apart from all foot-mats and tapestry
My fame speaks loudly; and God's greatest gift
Is not to err from wisdom. We must bless
Him only who ends life in fair estate.   995
Should I thus act throughout, good hope were
      mine.
   CLYTÆM. Nay, say not this my purposes to
      thwart.
   AGAM. Know I change not for the worse my
      purpose.
   CLYTÆM. In fear, perchance, thou vowèd'st thus
      to act.

AGAM. If any, I, with good ground spoke my will.   1000

CLYTÆM. What think'st thou Priam, had he wrought such deeds . . . ?

AGAM. Full gladly he, I trow, had trod on carpets.

CLYTÆM. Then shrink not thou through fear of men's dispraise.

AGAM. And yet a people's whisper hath great might.

CLYTÆM. Who is not envied is not enviable.   1005

AGAM. 'Tis not a woman's part to crave for strife.

CLYTÆM. True, yet the prosperous e'en should sometimes yield.

AGAM. Dost thou then prize that victory in the strife?

CLYTÆM. Nay, list; with all good-will yield me this boon.

AGAM. Well, then, if thou wilt have it so, with speed   1010
Let someone loose my buskins (servants they
Doing the foot's true work), and as I tread
Upon these robes sea-purpled, may no wrath
From glance of Gods smite on me from afar!
Great shame I feel to trample with my foot   1015
This wealth of carpets, costliest work of looms;
So far for this. This stranger [pointing to CASSANDRA] lead thou in
With kindliness. On him who gently wields
His power God's eye looks kindly from afar.
None of their own will choose a bondslave's life;
And she, the chosen flower of many spoils,   1021
Has followed with me as the army's gift.
But since I turn, obeying thee in this,
I'll to my palace go, on purple treading.

CLYTÆM. There is a sea,—and who shall drain it dry?   1025
Producing still new store of purple juice,
Precious as silver, staining many a robe.
And in our house, with God's help, O my king,
'Tis ours to boast our palace knows no stint.
Trampling of many robes would I have vowed,
Had that been ordered me in oracles,   1031
When for my lord's return I then did plan
My votive gifts. For while the root lives on,
The foliage stretches even to the house,
And spreads its shade against the dog-star's rage;
So when thou comest to thy hearth and home,   1036
Thou show'st that warmth hath come in winter time;
And when from unripe clusters Zeus matures
The wine, then is there coolness in the house,
If the true master dwelleth in his home.   1040

Ah, Zeus! the All-worker, Zeus, work out for me
All that I pray for; let it be thy care
To look to what Thou purposest to work.

[Exeunt AGAMEMNON, *walking on the tapestry,* CLYTÆMNESTRA, *and her attendants.*

STROPHE I

CHOR. Why thus continually
Do haunting phantoms hover at the gate   1045
Of my foreboding heart?
Why floats prophetic song, unbought, unbidden?
Why doth no steadfast trust
Sit on my mind's dear throne,
To fling it from me as a vision dim?   1050
Long time hath passed since stern-ropes of our ships
Were fastened on the sand, when our great host
Of those that sailed in ships
Had come to Ilion's towers:

ANTISTROPHE I

And now from these mine eyes   1055
I learn, myself reporting to myself,
Their safe return; and yet
My mind within itself, taught by itself,
Chanteth Erinnys' dirge,
The lyreless melody,   1060
And hath no strength of wonted confidence.
Not vain these inner pulses, as my heart
Whirls eddying in breast oracular.
I, against hope, will pray
It prove false oracle.   1065

STROPHE II

Of high, o'erflowing health
There is no bound that stays the wish for more,
For evermore disease, as neighbor close
Whom but a wall divides,
Upon it presses; and man's prosperous state   1070
Moves on its course, and strikes
Upon an unseen rock;
But if his fear for safety of his freight,
A part, from well-poised sling, shall sacrifice,
Then the whole house sinks not,   1075
O'erfilled with wretchedness,
Nor does he swamp his boat:
So, too, abundant gift
From Zeus in bounteous fullness, and the fruit
Of glebe at harvest tide   1080
Have caused to cease sore hunger's pestilence:

ANTISTROPHE II

But blood that once hath flowed
In purple stains of death upon the ground
At a man's feet, who then can bid it back
By any charm of song? 1085
Else him who knew to call the dead to life
Zeus had not sternly checked,
As warning unto all;
But unless Fate, firm-fixed, had barred our fate
From any chance of succor from the Gods, 1090
Then had my heart poured forth
Its thoughts, outstripping speech.
But now in gloom it wails
Sore vexed, with little hope
At any time hereafter fitting end 1095
To find, unraveling,
My soul within me burning with hot thoughts.

Re-enter CLYTÆMNESTRA.

CLYTÆM. [to CASSANDRA, who has remained in
the chariot during the choral ode]. Thou too—
I mean Cassandra—go within;
Since Zeus hath made it thine, and not in wrath,
To share the lustral waters in our house, 1100
Standing with many a slave the altar nigh
Of Zeus, who guards our goods. Now get thee
down
From out this car, nor look so over proud.
They say that e'en Alcmena's son endured 1104
Being sold a slave, constrained to bear the yoke:
And if the doom of this ill chance should come,
Great boon it is to meet with lords who own
Ancestral wealth. But whoso reap full crops
They never dared to hope for, these in all,
And beyond measure, to their slaves are harsh:
From us thou hast what usage doth prescribe. 1111
CHOR. So ends she, speaking words full clear to
thee:
And seeing thou art in the toils of fate,
If thou obey, thou wilt obey; and yet,
Perchance, obey thou wilt not. 1115
CLYTÆM. Nay, but unless she, like a swallow,
speaks
A barbarous tongue unknown, I speaking now
Within her apprehension, bid obey.
CHOR. [to CASSANDRA, still standing motionless].
Go with her. What she bids is now the best;
Obey her: leave thy seat upon this car. 1120
CLYTÆM. I have no leisure here to stay without:
For as regards our central altar, there
The sheep stand by as victims for the fire;
For never had we hoped such thanks to give:
If thou wilt do this, make no more delay; 1125

But if thou understandest not my words,
Then wave thy foreign hand in lieu of speech.
CASSANDRA shudders as in horror, but makes no
sign.
CHOR. The stranger seems a clear interpreter
To need. Her look is like a captured deer's.
CLYTÆM. Nay, she is mad, and follows evil
thoughts, 1130
Since, leaving now her city, newly-captured,
She comes, and knows not how to take the curb,
Ere she foam out her passion in her blood.
I will not bear the shame of uttering more.
[Exit.
CHOR. And I—I pity her, and will not rage: 1135
Come, thou poor sufferer, empty leave thy car;
Yield to thy doom, and handsel now the yoke.

CASSANDRA leaves the chariot, and bursts into a cry
of wailing.

STROPHE I

CASS. Woe! woe, and well-a-day!
Apollo! O Apollo!
CHOR. Why criest thou so loud on Loxias? 1140
The wailing cry of mourner suits not him.

ANTISTROPHE I

CASS. Woe! woe, and well-a-day!
Apollo! O Apollo!
CHOR. Again with boding words she calls the
God,
Though all unmeet as helper to men's groans. 1145

STROPHE II

CASS. Apollo! O Apollo!
God of all paths, Apollo true to me;
For still thou dost appall me and destroy.
CHOR. She seems her own ills like to prophesy:
The God's great gift is in the slave's mind yet. 1150

ANTISTROPHE II

CASS. Apollo! O Apollo!
God of all paths, Apollo true to me;
What path hast led me? To what roof hast
brought?
CHOR. To that of the Atreidæ. This I tell, 1154
If thou know'st not. Thou wilt not find it false.

STROPHE III

CASS. Ah! Ah! Ah me!
Say rather to a house God hates—that knows

Murder, self-slaughter, rapes,
A human shamble, staining earth with blood.
   CHOR. Keen scented seems this stranger, like a
     hound, 1160
And sniffs to see whose murder she may find.

ANTISTROPHE III

CASS. Ah! Ah! Ah me!
Lo! [*looking wildly, and pointing to the house*]
    there the witnesses whose word I trust,—
Those babes who wail their death
The roasted flesh that made a father's meal. 1165
   CHOR. We of a truth had heard thy seeress fame,
But prophets now are not the race we seek.

STROPHE IV

CASS. Ah me! O horror! What ill schemes she
    now?
What is this new great woe?
Great evil plots she in this very house, 1170
Hard for its friends to bear, immedicable;
   And help stands far aloof.
   CHOR. These oracles of thine surpass my ken;
Those I know well. The whole town rings with
    them.

ANTISTROPHE IV

CASS. Ah me! O daring one! what work'st thou
    here, 1175
Who having in his bath
Tended thy spouse, thy lord, then . . .
   How tell the rest?
For quick it comes, and hand is following hand,
Stretched out to strike the blow.
   CHOR. Still I discern not; after words so dark 1180
I am perplexed with thy dim oracles.

STROPHE V

CASS. Ah, horror, horror! What is this I see?
Is it a snare of Hell?
Nay, the true net is she who shares his bed,
Who shares in working death. 1185
Ha! let the Band insatiable in hate
Howl for the race its wild exulting cry
   O'er sacrifice that calls
   For death by storm of stones.
   CHOR. What dire Erinnys bidd'st thou o'er our
    house 1190
To raise shrill cry? Thy speech but little cheers;
   And to my heart there rush
   Blood-drops of saffron hue.

Which, when from deadly wound
They fall, together with life's setting rays 1195
End, as it fails, their own appointed course:
   And mischief comes apace.

ANTISTROPHE V

CASS. See, see, I say, from that fell heifer there
Keep thou the bull: in robes
Entangling him, she with her weapon gores 1200
   Him with the swarthy horns;
Lo! in that bath with water filled he falls,
Smitten to death, and I to thee set forth
   Crime of a bath of blood,
   By murderous guile devised. 1205
   CHOR. I may not boast that I keen insight have
In words oracular; yet bode I ill.
   What tidings good are brought
   By any oracles
   To mortal men? These arts, 1210
In days of evil sore, with many words,
Do still but bring a vague, portentous fear
   For men to learn and know.

STROPHE VI

CASS. Woe, woe! for all sore ills that fall on me!
It is my grief thou speak'st of, blending it 1215
   With his.   [*Pausing, and then crying out*]
   Ah! wherefore then
   Hast thou thus brought me here,
   Only to die with thee?
   What other doom is mine? 1220
   CHOR. Frenzied art thou, and by some God's
    might swayed,
   And utterest for thyself
A melody which is no melody,
   Like to that tawny one,
   Insatiate in her wail, 1225
The nightingale, who still with sorrowing soul,
   And "Itys, Itys," cry,
Bemoans a life o'erflourishing in ills.

ANTISTROPHE VI

CASS. Ah, for the doom of clear-voiced nightin-
    gale! 1230
The Gods gave her a body bearing wings,
And life of pleasant days
With no fresh cause to weep:
But for me waiteth still
Stroke from the two-edged sword.
   CHOR. From what source hast thou these dread
    agonies 1235

Sent on thee by thy God,
Yet vague and little meaning; and thy cries
  Dire with ill-omened shrieks
  Dost utter as a chant,
And blendest with them strains of shrillest grief?
  Whence treadest thou this track   1241
Of evil-boding path of prophecy?

STROPHE VII

Cass. Woe for the marriage-ties, the marriage-ties
Of Paris that brought ruin on his friends!
  Woe for my native stream,   1245
  Scamandros, that I loved!
Once on thy banks my maiden youth was reared,
  (Ah, miserable me!)
Now by Cokytos and by Acheron's shores
I seem too likely soon to utter song   1250
  Of wild, prophetic speech.
  Chor. What hast thou spoken now
  With utterance all too clear?
Even a boy its gist might understand;
  I to the quick am pierced   1255
  With throe of deadly pain,
Whilst thou thy moaning cries art uttering
  Over thy sore mischance,
  Wondrous for me to hear.

ANTISTROPHE VII

Cass. Woe for the toil and trouble, toil and
    trouble   1260
Of city that is utterly destroyed!
  Woe for the victims slain
  Of herds that roamed the fields,
My father's sacrifice to save his towers!
  No healing charm they brought   1265
To save the city from its present doom:
And I with hot thoughts wild myself shall cast
  Full soon upon the ground.
  Chor. This that thou utterest now
  With all before agrees.   1270
Some Power above dooms thee with purpose ill,
  Down-swooping heavily,
  To utter with thy voice
Sorrows of deepest woe, and bringing death.
  And what the end shall be   1275
  Perplexes in the extreme.

Cass. Nay, now no more from out of maiden
    veils
My oracle shall glance, like bride fresh wed;
But seems as though 'twould rush with speedy
    gales

In full, clear brightness to the morning dawn;
So that a greater war than this shall surge   1281
Like wave against the sunlight. Now I'll teach
No more in parables. Bear witness ye,
As running with me, that I scent the track
Of evil deeds that long ago were wrought: 1285
For never are they absent from this house,
That choral band which chants in full accord,
Yet no good music; good is not their theme.
And now, as having drunk men's blood, and so
Grown wilder, bolder, see, the reveling band,   1290
Erinnyes of the race, still haunt the halls,
Not easy to dismiss. And so they sing,
Close cleaving to the house, its primal woe,
And vent their loathing in alternate strains
On marriage-bed of brother ruthless found   1295
To that defiler. Miss I now, or hit,
Like archer skilled? or am I seeress false,
A babbler vain that knocks at every door?
Yea, swear beforehand, ere I die, I know
(And not by rumor only) all the sins   1300
Of ancient days that haunt and vex this house.
  Chor. How could an oath, how firm soe'er con-
    firmed,
Bring aught of healing? Lo, I marvel at thee,
That thou, though born far off beyond the sea,
Should'st tell an alien city's tale as clear   1305
As though thyself had stood by all the while.
  Cass. The seer Apollo set me to this task.
  Chor. Was he a God, so smitten with desire?
  Cass. There was a time when shame restrained
    my speech.
  Chor. True; they who prosper still are shy and
    coy.   1310
  Cass. He wrestled hard, breathing hot love on
    me.
  Chor. And were ye one in act whence children
    spring?
  Cass. I promised Loxias, then I broke my vow.
  Chor. Wast thou e'en then possessed with arts
    divine?
  Cass. E'en then my country's woes I prophesied.
  Chor. How wast thou then unscathed by Loxias'
    wrath?   1316
  Cass. I for that fault with no man gained belief.
  Chor. To us, at least, thou seem'st to speak the
    truth.
  Cass. [*again speaking wildly, as in an ecstasy*].
    Ah, woe is me! Woe's me! Oh, ills on ills!
Again the dread pang of true prophet's gift   1320
With preludes of great evil dizzies me.
See ye those children sitting on the house
In fashion like to phantom forms of dreams?

Infants who perished at their own kin's hands,
Their palms filled full with meat of their own
   flesh, 1325
Loom on my sight, the heart and entrails bearing,
(A sorry burden that!) on which of old
Their father fed. And in revenge for this,
I say a lion, dwelling in his lair,
With not a spark of courage, stay-at-home, 1330
Plots 'gainst my master, now he's home returned,
(Yes mine—for still I must the slave's yoke bear;)
And the ship's ruler, Ilion's conqueror,
Knows not what things the tongue of that lewd
   bitch
Has spoken and spun out in welcome smooth,
And, like a secret Atè, will work out 1336
With dire success: thus 'tis she plans: the man
Is murdered by the woman. By what name
Shall I that loathèd monster rightly call?
An Amphisbæna? or a Skylla dwelling 1340
Among the rocks, the sailors' enemy?
Hades' fierce raging mother, breathing out
Against her friends a curse implacable?
Ah, how she raised her cry, (oh, daring one!)
As for the rout of battle, and she feigns 1345
To hail with joy her husband's safe return!
And if thou dost not credit this, what then?
What will be will. Soon, present, pitying me
Thou'lt own I am too true a prophetess. 1349

CHOR. Thyestes' banquet on his children's flesh
I know and shudder at, and fear o'ercomes me,
Hearing not counterfeits of fact, but truths;
Yet in the rest I hear and miss my path.

  CASS. I say thou'lt witness Agamemnon's death.
  CHOR. Hush, wretched woman, close those lips
    of thine! 1355
  CASS. For this my speech no healing God's at
    hand.
  CHOR. True, if it must be; but may God avert
    it!
  CASS. Thou utterest prayers, but others murder
    plot.
  CHOR. And by what man is this dire evil
    wrought. 1359
  CASS. Sure, thou hast seen my bodings all amiss.
  CHOR. I see not his device who works the deed.
  CASS. And yet I speak the Hellenic tongue right
    well.
  CHOR. So does the Pythian, yet her words are
    hard.
  CASS. [in another access of frenzy]. Ah me, this
    fire!
      It comes upon me now! 1365
Ah me, Apollo, wolf-slayer! woe is me!

This biped lioness who takes to bed
A wolf in absence of the noble lion,
Will slay me, wretched me. And, as one
Mixing a poisoned draught, she boasts that she
Will put my price into her cup of wrath, 1371
Sharpening her sword to smite her spouse with
   death,
So paying him for bringing me. Oh, why
Do I still wear what all men flout and scorn,
My wand and seeress wreaths around my neck?
Thee, ere myself I die I will destroy: [breaks her
   wand] 1376
Perish ye thus: [casting off her wreaths] I soon
   shall follow you:
Make rich another Atè in my place;
Behold Apollo's self is stripping me
Of my divining garments, and that too, 1380
When he has seen me even in this garb
Scorned without cause among my friends and kin,
By foes, with no diversity of mood.
Reviled as vagrant, wandering prophetess,
Poor, wretched, famished, I endured to live: 1385
And now the Seer who me a seeress made
Hath brought me to this lot of deadly doom.
Now for my father's altar there awaits me
A butcher's block, where I am smitten down
By slaughtering stroke, and with hot gush of
   blood. 1390
But the Gods will not slight us when we're dead;
Another yet shall come as champion for us,
A son who slays his mother, to avenge
His father; and the exiled wanderer
Far from his home, shall one day come again,
Upon these woes to set the coping-stone: 1396
For the high Gods have sworn a mighty oath,
His father's fall, laid low, shall bring him back.
Why then do I thus groan in this new home,
When, to begin with, Ilion's town I saw 1400
Faring as it did fare, and they who held
That town are gone by judgment of the Gods?
I too will fare as they, and venture death:
So I these gates of Hades now address,
And pray for blow that bringeth death at once,
That so with no fierce spasm, while the blood 1406
Flows in calm death, I then may close mine eyes.

    Goes toward the door of the palace.

  CHOR. O thou most wretched, yet again most
    wise:
Long hast thou spoken, lady, but if well
Thou know'st thy doom, why to the altar go'st
    thou, 1410
Like heifer driven of God, so confidently?

Cass. For me, my friends, there is no time to 'scape.

Chor. Yea; but he gains in time who comes the last.

Cass. The day is come: small gain for me in flight.

Chor. Know then thou sufferest with a heart full brave.   1415

Cass. Such words as these the happy never hear.

Chor. Yet mortal man may welcome noble death.

Cass. [shrinking back from opening the door]. Woe's me for thee and thy brave sons, my father!

Chor. What cometh now? What fear oppresseth thee?

Cass. [again going to the door and then shuddering in another burst of frenzy]. Fie on't, fie!   1420

Chor. Whence comes this "Fie!" unless from mind that loathes?

Cass. The house is tainted with the scent of death.

Chor. How so? This smells of victims on the hearth.

Cass. Nay, it is like the blast from out a grave.

Chor. No Syrian ritual tell'st thou for our house.   1425

Cass. Well then I go, and e'en within will wail
My fate and Agamemnon's. And for me,
Enough of life. Ah, friends! Ah! not for nought
I shrink in fear, as bird shrinks from the brake.
When I am dead do ye this witness bear,   1430
When in revenge for me, a woman, Death
A woman smites, and man shall fall for man
In evil wedlock wed. This friendly office,
As one about to die, I pray you do me.

Chor. Thy doom foretold, poor sufferer, moves my pity.   1435

Cass. I fain would speak once more, yet not to wail
Mine own death-song; but to the Sun I pray,
To his last rays, that my avengers wreak
Upon my hated murderers judgment due
For me, who die a slave's death, easy prey.   1440
Ah, life of man! when most it prospereth,
It is but limned in outline; and when brought
To low estate, then doth the sponge, full soaked,
Wipe out the picture with its frequent touch:
And this I count more piteous e'en than that.   1445

Passes through the door into the palace.

Chor. 'Tis true of all men that they never set
A limit to good fortune; none doth say,
As bidding it depart,
And warding it from palaces of pride,
"Enter thou here no more."   1450
To this our lord the Blest Ones gave to take
Priam's city; and he comes
Safe to his home and honored by the Gods;
But if he now shall pay
The forfeit of blood-guiltiness of old,   1455
And, dying, so work out for those who died,
By his own death another penalty,
Who then of mortal men,
Hearing such things as this,
Can boast that he was born   1460
With fate from evil free?

Agam. [from within]. Ah, me! I am struck down with deadly stroke.

Chor. Hush! who cries out with deadly stroke sore smitten?

Agam. Ah me, again! struck down a second time!

[*Dies.*

Chor. By the king's groans I judge the deed is done;   1465
But let us now confer for counsels safe.

Chor. a. I give you my advice to summon here,
Here to the palace, all the citizens.

Chor. b. I think it best to rush at once on them,
And take them in the act with sword yet wet.   1470

Chor. c. And I too give like counsel, and I vote
For deed of some kind. 'Tis no time to pause.

Chor. d. Who will see, may.—They but the prelude work
Of tyranny usurped o'er all the State.

Chor. e. Yes, we are slow, but they who trample down   1475
The thought of hesitation slumber not.

Chor. f. I know not what advice to find or speak:
He who can act knows how to counsel too.

Chor. g. I too think with thee; for I have no hope
With words to raise the dead again to life.   1480

Chor. h. What! Shall we drag our life on and submit
To these usurpers that defile the house?

Chor. i. Nay, that we cannot bear: To die were better;
For death is gentler far than tyranny.

Chor. k. Shall we upon this evidence of groans
Guess, as divining that our lord is dead?   1486

Chor. l. When we know clearly, then should we discuss:

To guess is one thing, and to know another.
  CHOR. So vote I too, and on the winning side,
Taking the votes all round that we should learn
How he, the son of Atreus, fareth now.   1491

Enter CLYTÆMNESTRA *from the palace, in robes
with stains of blood, followed by soldiers and
attendants. The open doors show the corpses of*
AGAMEMNON *and* CASSANDRA, *the former lying in
a silvered bath.*

  CLYTÆM. Though many words before to suit the
    time
Were spoken, now I shall not be ashamed
The contrary to utter: How could one
By open show of enmity to foes   1495
Who seemed as friends, fence in the snares of
    death
Too high to be o'erleapt? But as for me,
Not without forethought for this long time past,
This conflict comes to me from triumph old
Of his, though slowly wrought. I stand where I   1500
Did smite him down, with all my task well done.
So did I it, (the deed deny I not,)
That he could nor avert his doom nor flee:
I cast around him drag-net as for fish,
With not one outlet, evil wealth of robe: 1505
And twice I smote him, and with two deep groans
He dropped his limbs: And when he thus fell
    down
I gave him yet a third, thank-offering true
To Hades of the dark, who guards the dead.
So fallen, he gasps out his struggling soul,   1510
And breathing forth a sharp, quick gush of blood,
He showers dark drops of gory rain on me,
Who no less joy felt in them than the corn,
When the blade bears, in glad shower given of
    God.
Since this is so, ye Argive elders here,   1515
Ye, as ye will, may hail the deed, but I
Boast of it. And were't fitting now to pour
Libation o'er the dead, 'twere justly done,
Yea more than justly; such a goblet full
Of ills hath he filled up with curses dire   1520
At home, and now has come to drain it off.
  CHOR. We marvel at the boldness of thy tongue
Who o'er thy husband's corpse speak'st vaunt like
    this.
  CLYTÆM. Ye test me as a woman weak of mind;
But I with dauntless heart to you that know   1525
Say this, and whether thou dost praise or blame,
Is all alike:—here Agamemnon lies,
My husband, now a corpse, of this right hand,
As artist just, the handiwork: so stands it.

STROPHE

  CHOR. What evil thing, O Queen, or reared on
    earth,   1530
Or draught from salt sea-wave
Hast thou fed on, to bring
Such incense on thyself,
A people's loud-voiced curse?
'Twas thou did'st sentence him,   1535
'Twas thou did'st strike him down;
  But thou shalt exiled be,
Hated with strong hate of the citizens.

  CLYTÆM. Ha! now on me thou lay'st the exile's
    doom,   1539
My subjects' hate, and people's loud-voiced curse,
Though ne'er did'st thou oppose my husband
    there,
Who, with no more regard than had been due
To a brute's death, although he called his own
Full many a fleecy sheep in pastures bred,
Yet sacrificed his child, the dear-loved fruit   1545
Of all my travail-pangs, to be a charm
Against the winds of Thrakia. Shouldst thou not
Have banished him from out this land of ours,
As meed for all his crimes? Yet hearing now
My deeds, thou art a judge full stern. But I   1550
Tell thee to speak thy threats, as knowing well
I am prepared that thou on equal terms
Should'st rule, if thou dost conquer. But if God
Should otherwise decree, then thou shalt learn,
Late though it be, the lesson to be wise.   1555

ANTISTROPHE

  CHOR. Yea, thou art stout of heart, and speak'st
    big words;
And maddened is thy soul
As by a murderous hate;
And still upon thy brow
Is seen, not yet avenged,   1560
The stain of blood-spot foul;
And yet it needs must be,
  One day thou, reft of friends,
Shalt pay the penalty of blow for blow.

  CLYTÆM. Now hear thou too my oaths of solemn
    dread: 1565
By my accomplished vengeance for my child,
By Atè and Erinnys, unto whom
I slew him as a victim, I look not
That fear should come beneath this roof of mine,
So long as on my hearth Ægisthos kindles   1570
The flaming fire, as well disposed to me

As he hath been aforetime. He to us
Is no slight shield of stoutest confidence.
There lies he, [*pointing to the corpse of* AGAMEM-
NON] one who foully wronged his wife,
The darling of the Chryseïds [1] at Troïa;   1575
And there [*pointing to* CASSANDRA] this captive
slave, this auguress,
His concubine, this seeress trustworthy,
Who shared his bed, and yet was as well known
To the sailors as their benches! . . . They have
fared
Not otherwise than they deserved: for he   1580
Lies as you see. And she who, like a swan,
Has chanted out her last and dying song,
Lies close to him she loved, and so has brought
The zest of a new pleasure to my bed.

STROPHE I

CHOR. Ah me, would death might come   1585
Quickly, with no sharp throe of agony,
    Nor long bed-ridden pain,
    Bringing the endless sleep;
Since he, the watchman most benign of all,
    Hath now been smitten low,   1590
And by a woman's means hath much endured,
And at a woman's hand hath lost his life!
Alas! alas! O Helen, evil-souled,
    Who, though but one, hast slain
Many, yea, very many lives at Troïa.   1595

    .   .   .   .   .   .

But now for blood that may not be washed out
    Thou hast to full bloom brought
A deed of guilt for ever memorable,
    For strife was in the house,
    Wrought out in fullest strength,   1600
    Woe for a husband's life.
    CLYTÆM. Nay, pray not thou for destiny of
death,
    Oppressed with what thou see'st;
Nor turn thou against Helena thy wrath,
    As though she murderess were,   1605
And, though but one, had many Danaï's souls
Brought low in death, and wrought o'erwhelming
woe.

ANTISTROPHE I

CHOR. O Power that dost attack
Our palace and the two Tantalidæ,
    And dost through women wield   1610
    A might that grieves my heart!
And o'er the body, like a raven foul,

Against all laws of right,
Standing, she boasteth in her pride of heart
That she can chant her pæan hymn of praise.   1615
    CLYTÆM. Now thou dost guide aright thy speech
and thought,
    Invoking that dread Power,
The thrice-gorged evil genius of this house;
    For he it is who feeds
In the heart's depth the raging lust of blood: 1620
Ere the old wound is healed, new bloodshed
comes.

STROPHE II

CHOR. Yes, of a Power thou tell'st
Mighty and very wrathful to this house;
Ah me! ah me! an evil tale enough
    Of baleful chance of doom,   1625
    Insatiable of ill:
    Yet, ah! it is through Zeus,
The all-appointing and all-working One;
    For what with mortal men
    Is wrought apart from Zeus?   1630
What of all this is not by God decreed?
    Ah me! ah me!
My king, my king, how shall I weep for thee?
What shall I speak from heart that truly loves?
And now thou liest there, breathing out thy life,
    In impious deed of death,   1636
    In this fell spider's web,—
    (Yes, woe is me! woe, woe!
Woe for this couch of thine dishonorable!)—
    Slain by a subtle death,   1640
With sword two-edged which her right hand did
wield.
    CLYTÆM. Thou speak'st big words, as if the deed
were mine;
    Yet think thou not of me,
    As Agamemnon's spouse;
But in the semblance of this dead man's wife,   1645
The old and keen Avenger of the house
Of Atreus, that cruel banqueter of old,
    Hath wrought out vengeance full
    On him who lieth here,
    And full-grown victim slain   1650
Over the younger victims of the past.

ANTISTROPHE II

CHOR. That thou art guiltless found
Of this foul murder who will witness bear?
How can it be so, how? And yet, perchance,
    As helper to the deed,   1655

***

[1] Referring to Chryseis. over whom Achilles and Agamemnon quarreled in Book I of the *Iliad*.

Might come the avenging Fiend
Of that ancestral time;
And in this rush of murders of near kin
Dark Ares presses on,
Where he will vengeance work   1660
For clotted gore of children slain as food.
    Ah me! ah me!
My king, my king, how shall I weep for thee?
What shall I speak from heart that truly loves?
And now thou liest there, breathing out thy life,
    In impious deed of death,   1666
    In this fell spider's web,—
    (Yes, woe is me! woe, woe!
Woe for this couch of thine dishonorable!)—
    Slain by a subtle death,   1670
With sword two-edged which her right hand did
    wield.
    CLYTÆM. Nay, not dishonorable
His death doth seem to me:
    Did he not work a doom,
    In this our house with guile?   1675
Mine own dear child, begotten of this man,
Iphigeneia, wept with many a tear,
He slew; now slain himself in recompense,
    Let him not boast in Hell,
    Since he the forfeit pays,   1680
    Pierced by the sword in death,
For all the evil that his hand began.

STROPHE III

    CHOR. I stand perplexed in soul, deprived of
    power
    Of quick and ready thought,
    Where now to turn, since thus   1685
    Our home is falling low.
I shrink in fear from the fierce pelting storm
Of blood that shakes the basement of the house:
    No more it rains in drops:
And for another deed of mischief dire,   1690
    Fate whets the righteous doom
    On other whetstones still.

ANTISTROPHE III

O Earth! O Earth! Oh, would thou had'st received
    me,
    Ere I saw him on couch
Of bath with silvered walls thus stretched in
    death!   1695
Who now will bury him, who wail? Wilt thou,
When thou hast slain thy husband, have the heart
To mourn his death, and for thy monstrous deeds

Do graceless grace? And who will chant the dirge
    With tears in truth of heart,   1700
    Over our godlike chief?

STROPHE IV

    CLYTÆM. It is not thine to speak;
    'Twas at our hands he fell,
    Yea, he fell low in death,
    And we will bury him,   1705
Not with the bitter tears of those who weep
    As inmates of the house;
But she, his child, Iphigeneia, there
Shall meet her father, and with greeting kind,
E'en as is fit, by that swift-flowing ford,   1710
    Dark stream of bitter woes,
    Shall clasp him in her arms,
    And give a daughter's kiss.

ANTISTROPHE V

    CHOR. Lo! still reproach upon reproach doth
    come;
    Hard are these things to judge: 1715
    The spoiler still is spoiled,
    The slayer pays his debt;
Yea, while Zeus liveth through the ages, this
Lives also, that the doer dree his weird;
    For this is law fast fixed.   1720
Who now can drive from out the kingly house
    The brood of curses dark?
    The race to Atè cleaves.

ANTISTROPHE VI

    CLYTÆM. Yes, thou hast touched with truth
    That word oracular;   1725
    But I for my part wish,
    (Binding with strongest oath
The evil dæmon of the Pleisthenids,)
    Though hard it be to bear,
To rest content with this our present lot;   1730
And, for the future, that he go to vex
Another race with homicidal deaths.
    Lo! 'tis enough for me,
    Though small my share of wealth,
    At last to have freed my house   1735
From madness that sets each man's hand 'gainst
    each.
    Enter ÆGISTHOS.

    ÆGIS. Hail, kindly light of day that vengeance
    brings!
Now I can say the Gods on high look down,

Avenging men, upon the woes of earth,
Since lying in the robes the Erinnyes wove   1740
I see this man, right welcome sight to me,
Paying for deeds his father's hand had wrought.
Atreus, our country's ruler, this man's father
Drove out my sire Thyestes, his own brother,
(To tell the whole truth,) quarreling for rule,   1745
An exile from his country and his home.
And coming back a suppliant on the hearth,
The poor Thyestes found a lot secure,
Nor did he, dying, stain the soil with blood,
There in his home. But this man's godless sire,   1750
Atreus, more prompt than kindly in his deeds,
On plea of keeping festal day with cheer,
To my sire banquet gave of children's flesh,
His own. The feet and finger-tips of hands
He, sitting at the top, apart concealed;   1755
And straight the other, in his blindness taking
The parts that could not be discerned, did eat
A meal which, as thou see'st, perdition works
For all his kin. And learning afterwards
The deed of dread, he groaned and backward fell,   1760
Vomits the feast of blood, and imprecates
On Pelop's sons a doom intolerable,
And makes the o'erturning of the festive board,
With fullest justice, as a general curse,
That so might fall the race of Pleisthenes.   1765
And now thou see'st how here accordingly
This man lies fallen; I, of fullest right,
The weaver of the plot of murderous doom.
For me, a babe in swaddling-clothes, he banished   1769
With my poor father me, his thirteenth child;
And Vengeance brought me back, of full age grown:
And e'en far off I wrought against this man,
And planned the whole scheme of this dark device.
And so e'en death were now right good for me,
Seeing him into the nets of Vengeance fallen.   1775
  CHOR. I honor not this arrogance in guilt,
Ægisthos. Thou confessest thou hast slain
Of thy free will our chieftain here,—that thou
Alone did'st plot this murder lamentable;
Be sure, I say, thy head shall not escape   1780
The righteous curse a people hurls with stones.
  ÆGISTH. Dost thou say this, though seated on the bench
Of lowest oarsmen, while the upper row
Commands the ship? But thou shalt find, though old,
How hard it is at such an age to learn,   1785
When the word is, "keep temper." But a prison

And fasting pains are admirably apt,
As prophet-healers even for old age.
Dost see, and not see this? Against the pricks
Kick not, lest thou perchance should'st smart for it.   1790
  CHOR. Thou, thou, O Queen, when thy lord came from war,
While keeping house, thy husband's bed defiling,
Did'st scheme this death for this our hero-chief.
  ÆGISTH. These words of thine shall parents prove of tears:
But this thy tongue is Orpheus' opposite;   1795
He with his voice led all things on for joy,
But thou, provoking with thy childish cries,
Shalt now be led; and then, being kept in check,
Thou shalt appear in somewhat gentler mood.
  CHOR. As though thou should'st o'er Argives ruler be,   1800
Who even when thou plotted'st this man's death
Did'st lack good heart to do the deed thyself?
  ÆGISTH. E'en so; to work this fraud was clearly part
Fit for a woman. I was foe, of old
Suspected. But now will I with his wealth   1805
See whether I his subjects may command,
And him who will not hearken I will yoke
In heavy harness as a full-fed colt,
Nowise as trace-horse; but sharp hunger joined
With darksome dungeon shall behold him tamed.
  CHOR. Why did'st not thou then, coward as thou art,   1811
Thyself destroy him? but a woman with thee,
Pollution to our land and our land's Gods,
She slew him. Does Orestes see the light,
Perchance, that he, brought back by Fortune's grace,   1815
May for both these prove slayer strong to smite?
  ÆGISTH. Well, since thou think'st to act, not merely talk,
Thou shalt know clearly. . . .

Calling his Guards from the palace.

On then, my troops, the time for deeds is come.
  CHOR. On then, let each man grasp his sword in hand.   1820
  ÆGISTH. With sword in hand, I too shrink not from death.
  CHOR. Thou talkest of thy death; we hail the word;
And make our own the fortune it implies.
  CLYTÆM. Nay, let us not do other evil deeds,
Thou dearest of all friends. An ill-starred harvest
It is to have reaped so many. Enough of woe: 1826

Let no more blood be shed: Go thou [*to the
    Chorus*]—go ye,
Ye aged sires, to your allotted homes,
Ere ye do aught amiss and dree your weird:
This that we have done ought to have sufficed;
But should it prove we've had enough of ills,   1831
We will accept it gladly, stricken low
In evil doom by heavy hand of God.
This is a woman's counsel, if there be
That deigns to hear it.   1835
    ÆGISTH. But that these should fling
The blossoms of their idle speech at me,
And utter words like these, so tempting Fate,
And fail of counsel wise, and flout their mas-
    ter. . . .   1839
    CHOR. It suits not Argives on the vile to fawn.
    ÆGISTH. Be sure, hereafter I will hunt thee down.
    CHOR. Not so, if God should guide Orestes back.
    ÆGISTH. Right well I know how exiles feed on
        hopes.
    CHOR. Prosper, wax fat, do foul wrong—'tis thy
        day.
    ÆGISTH. Know thou shalt pay full price for this
        thy folly.   1845
    CHOR. Be bold, and boast, like cock beside his
        mate.
    CLYTÆM. Nay, care not thou for these vain howl-
        ings; I
And thou together, ruling o'er the house,
Will settle all things rightly.

                                        [*Exeunt.*

Fate of Agamemnon's Family

It was intended by the conspirators to slay his
son Orestes also, a lad not yet old enough to be an
object of apprehension, but from whom, if he
should be suffered to grow up, there might be danger. Electra, the sister of Orestes, saved her brother's
life by sending him secretly away to his uncle
Strophius, King of Phocis. In the palace of Strophius Orestes grew up with the king's son Pylades,
and formed with him that ardent friendship which
has become proverbial. Electra frequently reminded
her brother by messengers of the duty of avenging
his father's death, and when grown up he consulted the oracle at Delphi, which confirmed him
in his design. He therefore repaired in disguise to
Argos, pretending to be a messenger from Strophius, who had come to announce the death of
Orestes, and brought the ashes of the deceased in
a funeral urn. After visiting his father's tomb and
sacrificing upon it, according to the rites of the
ancients, he made himself known to his sister Electra, and soon after slew both Ægisthus and Clytemnestra.

This revolting act, the slaughter of a mother by
her son, though alleviated by the guilt of the victim
and the express command of the gods, did not fail
to awaken in the breasts of the ancients the same
abhorrence that it does in ours. The Eumenides,
avenging deities, seized upon Orestes, and drove
him frantic from land to land. Pylades accompanied him in his wanderings and watched over him.
At length, in answer to a second appeal to the
oracle, he was directed to go to Tauris in Scythia,
and to bring thence a statue of Diana which was
believed to have fallen from heaven. Accordingly
Orestes and Pylades went to Tauris, where the barbarous people were accustomed to sacrifice to the
goddess all strangers who fell into their hands. The
two friends were seized and carried bound to the
temple to be made victims. But the priestess of
Diana was no other than Iphigenia, the sister of
Orestes, who, our readers will remember, was
snatched away by Diana at the moment when she
was about to be sacrificed. Ascertaining from the
prisoners who they were, Iphigenia disclosed herself to them, and the three made their escape with
the statue of the goddess, and returned to Mycenæ.

But Orestes was not yet relieved from the vengeance of the Erinyes. At length he took refuge with
Minerva at Athens. The goddess afforded him protection, and appointed the court of Areopagus to
decide his fate. The Erinyes brought forward their
accusation, and Orestes made the command of the
Delphic oracle his excuse. When the court voted
and the voices were equally divided, Orestes was
acquitted by the command of Minerva.

"Fate of Agamemnon's Family." From Bulfinch, *The Age of Fable.*

SOPHOCLES

Sophocles wrote three plays about the life of Œdipus. The first two, *Œdipus the King* and *Œdipus at Colonus,* relate the following story and must be understood before reading the *Antigone:* [1]

Laius, king of Thebes, was warned by an oracle that there was danger to his throne and life if his new-born son should be suffered to grow up. He therefore committed the child to the care of a herdsman with orders to destroy him; but the herdsman, moved with pity, yet not daring entirely to disobey, tied up the child by the feet and left him hanging to the branch of a tree. In this condition the infant was found by a peasant, who carried him to his master and mistress, by whom he was adopted and called Œdipus, or Swollen-foot.

Many years afterwards Laius being on his way to Delphi, accompanied only by one attendant, met in a narrow road a young man also driving in a chariot. On his refusal to leave the way at their command the attendant killed one of his horses, and the stranger, filled with rage, slew both Laius and his attendant. The young man was Œdipus, who thus unknowingly became the slayer of his own father.

Shortly after this event the city of Thebes was afflicted with a monster which infested the high-road. It was called the Sphinx. It had the body of a lion and the upper part of a woman. It lay crouched on the top of a rock, and arrested all travelers who came that way, proposing to them a riddle, with the condition that those who could solve it should pass safe, but those who failed should be killed. Not one had yet succeeded in solving it, and all had been slain. Œdipus was not daunted by these alarming accounts, but boldly advanced to the trial. The Sphinx asked him, "What animal is that which in the morning goes on four feet, at noon on two, and in the evening upon three?" Œdipus replied, "Man, who in childhood creeps on hands and knees, in manhood walks erect, and in old age with the aid of a staff." The Sphinx was so mortified at the solving of her riddle that she cast herself down from the rock and perished.

The gratitude of the people for their deliverance was so great that they made Œdipus their king, giving him in marriage their queen Jocasta. Œdipus, ignorant of his parentage, had already become the slayer of his father; in marrying the queen he became the husband of his mother. These horrors remained undiscovered, till at length Thebes was afflicted with famine and pestilence, and the oracle being consulted, the double crime of Œdipus came to light. Jocasta put an end to her own life, and Œdipus, seized with madness, tore out his eyes and wandered away from Thebes, dreaded and abandoned by all except his daughters, who faithfully adhered to him, till after a tedious period of miserable wandering he found the termination of his wretched life.

Antigone

DRAMATIS PERSONÆ

CREON, *King of Thebes*	*Second Messenger*
HÆMON, *son of Creon*	EURYDIKE, *wife of Creon*
TEIRESIAS, *a seer*	ANTIGONE, ⎱ *daughters of*
Guard	ISMENE, ⎰ *Œdipus*
First Messenger	*Chorus of Theban Elders*

ARGUMENT

After the death of Œdipus, Antigone and Ismene returned to Thebes, and lived in the king's house with Eteocles, their brother. But the seven great captains from Argos, whom Polyneikes had called to help him, came against Thebes to destroy it, and were hardly driven back. And the two brothers having died by each other's hands, the people of the city made Creon their king, as being wise and prudent, and next of kin to the dead; and he issued his decree that Eteocles should be buried with due honor, but that no man should dare to bury Polyneikes, who had come purposing to lay waste the city and all the temples of the Gods.

[1] From Bulfinch, *The Age of Fable.*

Sophocles, *Antigone.* Translated by E. H. Plumptre. Sophocles (496-406 B.C.) came from Colonus, near Athens. From the time when he led a chorus celebrating the victory of Salamis in his sixteenth year until his death at ninety he was active in the production of tragedies. He was honored in his own day as he has been by posterity.

SCENE:—*Thebes, in front of the Palace. Early morning. Hills in the distance on the left; on the right the city.*

Enter ANTIGONE *and* ISMENE.

ANTIG. Ismene, mine own sister, darling one!
Is there, of ills that sprang from Œdipus,
One left that Zeus will fail to bring on us,
The two who yet remain? Nought is there sad,
Nought full of sorrow, steeped in sin or shame,   5
But I have seen it in thy woes and mine.
And now, what new decree is this they tell,
Our captain has enjoined on all the State?
Know'st thou? Hast heard? Or are they hid from
    thee,
The ills that come from foes upon our friends?   10
    ISM. No tidings of our friends, Antigone,
Pleasant or painful, since that hour have come,
When we, two sisters, lost our brothers twain,
In one day dying by a twofold blow.
And since in this last night the Argive host   15
Has left the field, I nothing further know,
Nor brightening fortune, nor increasing gloom.
    ANTIG. That knew I well, and therefore sent for
    thee
Beyond the gates, that thou may'st hear alone.   19
    ISM. What meanest thou? It is but all too clear
Thou broodest darkly o'er some tale of woe.
    ANTIG. And does not Creon treat our brothers
    twain
One with the rites of burial, one with shame?
Eteocles, so say they, he interred
Fitly, with wonted rites, as one held meet   25
To pass with honor to the dead below.
But for the corpse of Polyneikes, slain
So piteously, they say, he has proclaimed
To all the citizens, that none should give
His body burial, or bewail his fate,   30
But leave it still unwept, unsepulchered,
A prize full rich for birds that scent afar
Their sweet repast. So Creon bids, they say,
Creon the good, commanding thee and me,—
Yes, me, I say,—and now is coming here,   35
To make it clear to those who know it not,
And counts the matter not a trivial thing;
But whoso does the things that he forbids,
For him there waits within the city's walls
The death of stoning. Thus, then, stands thy case;
And quickly thou wilt show, if thou art born   41
Of noble nature, or degenerate liv'st,
Base child of honored parents.
    ISM.   How could I,
O daring in thy mood, in this our plight,

Or breaking law or keeping, aught avail?   45
    ANTIG. Wilt thou with me share risk and toil?
    Look to it.
    ISM. What risk is this? What purpose fills thy
    mind?
    ANTIG. Wilt thou help this my hand to lift the
    dead?
    ISM. Mean'st thou to bury him, when law for-
    bids?
    ANTIG. He is my brother; yes, and thine, though
    thou   50
Would'st fain he were not. I desert him not.
    ISM. O daring one, when Creon bids thee not?
    ANTIG. He has no right to keep me from mine
    own.
    ISM. Ah me! remember, sister, how our sire
Perished, with hate o'erwhelmed and infamy,   55
From evils that himself did bring to light,
With his own hand himself of eyes bereaving,
And how his wife and mother, both in one,
With twisted cordage, cast away her life;
And thirdly, how our brothers in one day   60
In suicidal conflict wrought the doom,
Each of the other. And we twain are left;
And think, how much more wretchedly than all
We twain shall perish, if, against the law,
We brave our sovereign's edict and his power.   65
This first we need remember, we were born
Women; as such, not made to strive with men.
And next, that they who reign surpass in strength,
And we must bow to this, and worse than this.
I then, entreating those that dwell below,   70
To judge me leniently, as forced to yield,
Will hearken to our rulers. Over-zeal
That still will meddle, little wisdom shows.
    ANTIG. I will not ask thee, nor though thou
    should'st wish
To do it, should'st thou join with my consent.   75
Do what thou wilt, I go to bury him;
And good it were, in doing this, to die.
Loved I shall be with him whom I have loved,
Guilty of holiest crime. More time is mine
In which to share the favor of the dead,   80
Than that of those who live; for I shall rest
For ever there. But thou, if thus thou please,
Count as dishonored what the Gods approve.
    ISM. I do them no dishonor, but I find
Myself too weak to war against the State.   85
    ANTIG. Make what excuse thou wilt, I go to rear
A grave above the brother whom I love.
    ISM. Ah, wretched me! how much I fear for
    thee!

Antig. Fear not for me. Thine own fate raise to
    safety.

Ism. At any rate, disclose this deed to none;   90
Keep it close hidden: I will hide it too.

Antig. Speak out! I bid thee. Silent, thou wilt be
More hateful to me, if thou fail to tell
My deed to all men.

Ism.   Fiery is thy mood,
Although thy deeds the very blood might chill.   95

Antig. I know I please the souls I ought to
    please.

Ism. Yes, if thou canst; thou seek'st the impos-
    sible.

Antig. When strength shall fail me, then I'll
    cease to strive.

Ism. We should not hunt the impossible at all.

Antig. If thou speak thus, my hatred wilt thou
    gain,   100
And rightly wilt be hated of the dead.
Leave me and my ill counsel to endure
This dreadful doom. I shall not suffer aught
So evil as a death dishonorable.

Ism. Go then, if so thou wilt. Of this be sure, 105
Wild as thou art, thy friends must love thee still.
                            [*Exeunt.*

Enter Chorus of Theban Elders.

STROPHE I

Chor. O light of yon bright sun,
Fairest of all that ever shone on Thebes,
    Thebes with her seven high gates,
    Thou didst appear that day,   110
    Eye of the golden dawn,
    O'er Dirké's streams advancing,
    Driving with quickened curb,
    In haste of headlong flight,
The warrior who, in panoply of proof,   115
From Argos came, with shield of glittering white;
    Whom Polyneikes brought,
    Roused by the strife of tongues
    Against our fatherland,
    As eagle shrieking shrill,   120
    He hovered o'er our land,
    With snow-white wing bedecked,
    Begirt with myriad arms,
    And flowing horsehair crests.

ANTISTROPHE I

He stood above our towers,   125
Encircling, with his spears all blood-bestained,
    The portals of our gates;

He went, before he filled
His jaw with blood of men,
Ere the pine-fed Hephæstos   130
Had seized our crown of towers.
    So loud the battle din
That Ares loves was raised around his rear,
A conflict hard e'en for his dragon foe.
    For breath of haughty speech   135
    Zeus hateth evermore;
    And seeing them advance,
    With mighty rushing stream,
    And clang of golden arms,
    With brandished fire he hurls   140
    One who rushed eagerly
    From topmost battlement
    To shout out, "Victory!"

STROPHE II

    Crashing to earth he fell,
    Down-smitten, with his torch,   145
    Who came, with madman's haste,
    Drunken, with frenzied soul,
    And swept o'er us with blasts,
    The whirlwind blasts of hate.
    Thus on one side they fare,   150
And Ares great, like war-horse in his strength
    Smiting now here, now there,
    Brought each his several fate.
For seven chief warriors at the seven gates met,
    Equals with equals matched,   155
    To Zeus, the Lord of War,
    Left tribute, arms of bronze;
    All but the hateful ones,
Who, from one father and one mother sprung,
    Stood wielding, hand to hand,   160
    Their two victorious spears,
And had their doom of death as common lot.

ANTISTROPHE II

    But now, since Victory,
    Of mightiest name, hath come
    To Thebes, of chariots proud,   165
    Joying and giving joy,
    After these wars just past,
    Learn ye forgetfulness,
And all night long, with dance and voice of hymns,
    Let us go round in state   170
    To all the shrines of Gods,
While Bacchos, making Thebes resound with dance,
    Begins the strain of joy;
    But, lo! our country's king,
    Creon, Menœkeus' son,   175

New ruler, by new change,
　And providence of God,
Comes to us, steering on some new device;
　For, lo! he hath convened,
　By herald's loud command,   180
This council of the elders of our land.

Enter CREON.

CREON. My friends, for what concerns our com-
　monwealth,
The Gods who vexed it with the billowing storms
Have righted it again; and I have sent,
By special summons, calling you to come   185
Apart from all the others. This, in part,
As knowing ye did all along uphold
The might of Laïos' throne, in part again,
Because when Œdipus our country ruled,
And, when he perished, then towards his sons   190
Ye still were faithful in your steadfast mind.
And since they fell, as by a double death,
Both on the selfsame day with murderous blow,
Smiting and being smitten, now I hold
Their thrones and all their power of sov'reignty
By nearness of my kindred to the dead.   196
And hard it is to learn what each man is,
In heart and mind and judgment, till he gain
Experience in princedom and in laws.
For me, whoe'er is called to guide a State,   200
And does not catch at counsels wise and good,
But holds his peace through any fear of man,
I deem him basest of all men that are,
And so have deemed long since; and whoso'er
As worthier than his country counts his friend,
I utterly despise him. I myself,   206
Zeus be my witness, who beholdeth all,
Would not keep silence, seeing danger come,
Instead of safety, to my subjects true.
Nor could I take as friend my country's foe;   210
For this I know, that there our safety lies,
And sailing while the good ship holds her course,
We gather friends around us. By these rules
And such as these do I maintain the State.
And now I come, with edicts, close allied   215
To these in spirit, for my citizens,
Concerning those two sons of Œdipus.
Eteocles, who died in deeds of might
Illustrious, fighting for our fatherland,
To honor him with sepulture, all rites   220
Duly performed that to the noblest dead
Of right belong. Not so his brother; him
I speak of, Polyneikes, who, returned
From exile, sought with fire to desolate
His father's city and the shrines of Gods,   225

Yes, sought to glut his rage with blood of men,
And lead them captives to the bondslave's doom;
Him I decree that none shall dare entomb,
That none shall utter wail or loud lament,
But leave his corpse unburied, by the dogs   230
And vultures mangled, foul to look upon.
Such is my purpose. Ne'er, if I can help,
Shall the vile have more honor than the just;
But whoso shows himself my country's friend,
Living or dead, from me shall honor gain.   235
　CHOR. This is thy pleasure, O Menœkeus' son,
For him who hated, him who loved our State;
And thou hast power to make what laws thou
　wilt,
Both for the dead and all of us who live.
　CREON. Be ye then guardians of the things I
　　speak.   240
　CHOR. Commit this task to one of younger years.
　CREON. Nay, watchmen are appointed for the
　　corpse.
　CHOR. What other task then dost thou lay on us?
　CREON. Not to consent with those that disobey.
　CHOR. None are so foolish as to seek for death.
　CREON. Yet that shall be the doom; but love of
　　gain   246
Hath oft with false hopes lured men to their death.

Enter Guard.

GUARD. I will not say, O king, that I have come
Panting with speed, and plying nimble feet,
For I had many halting-points of thought,   250
Backwards and forwards turning, round and
　round:
For now my mind would give me sage advice;
"Poor wretch, why go where thou must bear the
　blame?
Or wilt thou tarry, fool? Shall Creon know
These things from others? How wilt thou 'scape
　grief?"   255
Revolving thus, I came in haste, yet slow,
And thus a short way finds itself prolonged;
But, last of all, to come to thee prevailed.
And though I tell of nought, yet I will speak;
For this one hope I cling to, might and main,   260
That I shall suffer nought but destiny.
　CREON. What is it then that causes such dismay?
　GUARD. First, for mine own share in it, this I say,
The deed I did not, do not know who did,
Nor should I rightly come to ill for it.   265
　CREON. Thou feel'st thy way and fencest up thy
　　deed
All round and round. 'Twould seem thou hast
　some news.

GUARD. Yea, news of fear engenders long delay.
CREON. Wilt thou not speak, and then depart in
   peace?
GUARD. Well, speak I will. The corpse . . . Some-
   one has been   270
But now and buried it, a little dust
O'er the skin scattering, with the wonted rites.
  CREON. What say'st thou? What man dared this
    deed of guilt?
    GUARD. I know not. Neither was there stroke
    of ax,
Nor earth cast up by mattock. All the soil   275
Was dry and hard, no track of chariot wheel;
But he who did it went and left no sign.
And when the first day-watchman showed it us,
The sight caused wonder and sore grief to all;
For he had disappeared: no tomb indeed   280
Was over him, but dust all lightly strown,
As by some hand that shunned defiling guilt;
And no sign was there of wild beast or dog
Having come and torn him. Evil words arose
Among us, guard to guard imputing blame, 285
Which might have come to blows, and none was
   there
To check its course, for each to each appeared
The man whose hand had done it. Yet not one
Had it brought home, but each disclaimed all
   knowledge;
And we were ready in our hands to take   290
Bars of hot iron, and to walk through fire,
And call the Gods to witness none of us
Were privy to his schemes who planned the deed,
Nor his who wrought it. Then at last, when
   nought   294
Was gained by all our searching, someone speaks,
Who made us bend our gaze upon the ground
In fear and trembling: for we neither saw
How to oppose it, nor, accepting it,
How we might prosper in it. And his speech
Was this, that all our tale should go to thee,   300
Not hushed up anywise. This gained the day;
And me, ill-starred, the lot condemns to win
This precious prize. So here I come to thee
Against my will; and surely do I trow
Thou dost not wish to see me. Still 'tis true   305
That no man loves the messenger of ill.
  CHOR. For me, my prince, my mind some time
    has thought
If this perchance has some divine intent.
  CREON. Cease then, before thou fillest me with
    wrath,
Lest thou be found, though full of years, a fool.   310
For what thou say'st is most intolerable,

That for this corpse the providence of Gods
Has any care. What! have they buried him,
As to their patron paying honors high,
Who came to waste their columned shrines with
   fire,   315
To desecrate their offerings and their lands,
And all their wonted customs? Dost thou see
The Gods approving men of evil deeds?
It is not so; but men of rebel mood,
Lifting their head in secret long ago,   320
Still murmured thus against me. Never yet
Had they their neck beneath the yoke, content
To bear it with submission. They, I know,
Have bribed these men to let the deed be done.
No thing in use by man, for power of ill,   325
Can equal money. This lays cities low,
This drives men forth from quiet dwelling-place,
This warps and changes minds of worthiest stamp,
To turn to deeds of baseness, teaching men
All shifts of cunning, and to know the guilt   330
Of every impious deed. But they who, hired,
Have wrought this crime, have labored to their
   cost,
Or soon or late to pay the penalty.
But if Zeus still claims any awe from me,
Know this, and with an oath I tell it thee,   335
Unless ye find the very man whose hand
Has wrought this burial, and before mine eyes
Present him captive, death shall not suffice,
Till first, hung up still living, ye shall show
The story of this outrage, that henceforth,   340
Knowing what gain is lawful, ye may grasp
At that, and learn it is not meet to love
Gain from all quarters. By base profit won
You will see more destroyed than prospering.
  GUARD. May I then speak? Or shall I turn and
    go?   345
  CREON. See'st not e'en yet how vexing are thy
    words?
  GUARD. Is it thine ears they trouble, or thy soul?
  CREON. Why dost thou gauge my trouble where
    it is?
  GUARD. The doer grieves thy heart, but I thine
    ears.
  CREON. Pshaw! what a babbler, born to prate art
    thou!   350
  GUARD. May be; yet I this deed, at least, did not
  CREON. Yes, and for money; selling e'en thy soul.
  GUARD. Ah me!
How dire it is, in thinking, false to think!
  CREON. Prate about thinking: but unless ye
    show   355

To me the doers, ye shall say ere long
That scoundrel gains still work their punishment.
[*Exit.*

GUARD. God send we find him! Should we find
  him not,
As well may be, (for this must chance decide,)
You will not see me coming here again;   360
For now, being safe beyond all hope of mine,
Beyond all thought, I owe the Gods much thanks.
[*Exit.*

STROPHE I

CHOR. Many the forms of life,
Wondrous and strange to see,
But nought than man appears   365
More wondrous and more strange.
He, with the wintry gales,
O'er the white foaming sea,
'Mid wild waves surging round,
Wendeth his way across: 370
Earth, of all Gods, from ancient days the first,
  Unworn and undecayed
He, with his plows that travel o'er and o'er,
  Furrowing with horse and mule,
Wears ever year by year.   375

ANTISTROPHE I

The thoughtless tribe of birds,
The beasts that roam the fields,
The brood in sea-depths born,
He takes them all in nets
Knotted in snaring mesh,   380
Man, wonderful in skill.
And by his subtle arts
He holds in sway the beasts
That roam the fields, or tread the mountain's
  height;
And brings the binding yoke   385
Upon the neck of horse with shaggy mane,
  Or bull on mountain crest,
  Untameable in strength.

STROPHE II

And speech, and thought as swift as wind,
And tempered mood for higher life of states,   390
  These he has learnt, and how to flee
  Or the clear cold of frost unkind,
  Or darts of storm and shower,
Man all-providing. Unprovided, he   394
Meeteth no chance the coming days may bring;
  Only from Hades, still

He fails to find escape,
Though skill of art may teach him how to flee
From depths of fell disease incurable.

ANTISTROPHE II

So, gifted with a wondrous might,   400
Above all fancy's dreams, with skill to plan,
  Now unto evil, now to good,
  He turns. While holding fast the laws,
  His country's sacred rights,
That rest upon the oath of Gods on high,   405
High in the State: an outlaw from the State,
  When loving, in his pride,
  The thing that is not good;
Ne'er may he share my hearth, nor yet my
  thoughts,
Who worketh deeds of evil like to this.   410

Enter Guards, bringing in ANTIGONE.

As to this portent which the Gods have sent,
I stand in doubt. Can I, who know her, say
That this is not the maid Antigone?
O wretched one of wretched father born,
Thou child of Œdipus,   415
What means this? Surely 'tis not that they bring
Thee as a rebel 'gainst the king's decree,
And taken in the folly of thine act?
  GUARD. Yes! She it was by whom the deed was
    done.
We found her burying. Where is Creon, pray?   420
  CHOR. Back from his palace comes he just in
    time.

Enter CREON.

CREON. What chance is this, with which my com-
    ing fits?
  GUARD. Men, O my king, should pledge them-
    selves to nought;
For cool reflection makes their purpose void.
I surely thought I should be slow to come here,   425
Cowed by thy threats, which then fell thick on me;
But now persuaded by the sweet delight
Which comes unlooked for, and beyond our hopes,
I come, although I swore the contrary,
Bringing this maiden, whom in act we found   430
Decking the grave. No need for lots was now;
The prize was mine, and not another man's.
And now, O king, take her, and as thou wilt,
Judge and convict her. I can claim a right
To wash my hands of all this troublous coil.   435
  CREON. How and where was it that ye seized and
    brought her?

GUARD. She was in act of burying. Thou knowest all.

CREON. Dost know and rightly speak the tale
thou tell'st?

GUARD. I saw her burying that self-same corpse
Thou bad'st us not to bury. Speak I clear?   440

CREON. How was she seen, and taken in the act?

GUARD. The matter passed as follows:—When
we came,
With all those dreadful threats of thine upon us,
Sweeping away the dust which, lightly spread,
Covered the corpse, and laying stript and bare   445
The tainted carcase, on the hill we sat
To windward, shunning the infected air,
Each stirring up his fellow with strong words,
If any shirked his duty. This went on
Some time, until the glowing orb of day   450
Stood in mid heaven, and the scorching heat
Fell on us. Then a sudden whirlwind rose,
A scourge from heaven, raising squalls on earth,
And filled the plain, the leafage stripping bare
Of all the forest, and the air's vast space   455
Was thick and troubled, and we closed our eyes,
Until the plague the Gods had sent was past;
And when it ceased, a weary time being gone,
The girl is seen, and with a bitter cry,
Shrill as a bird's, when it beholds its nest   460
All emptied of its infant brood, she wails;
Thus she, when she beholds the corpse all stript,
Groaned loud with many moanings, and she called
Fierce curses down on those who did the deed.
And in her hand she brings some fine, dry dust,   465
And from a vase of bronze, well wrought, up-
raised,
She pours the three libations o'er the dead.
And we, beholding, give her chase forthwith,
And run her down, nought terrified at us.
And then we charged her with the former deed,
As well as this. And nothing she denied.   471
But this to me both bitter is and sweet,
For to escape one's-self from ill is sweet,
But to bring friends to trouble, this is hard
And painful. Yet my nature bids me count   475
Above all these things safety for myself.

CREON [to ANTIGONE]. Thou, then—yes, thou,
who bend'st thy face to earth—
Confesseth thou, or dost deny the deed?

ANTIG. I own I did it, and will not deny.

CREON [to Guard]. Go thou thy way, where'er
thy will may choose,   480
Freed from a weighty charge.

[Exit Guard.

[To ANTIGONE.]   And now for thee.

Say in few words, not lengthening out thy speech,
Knew'st thou the edicts which forbade these things?

ANTIG. I knew them. Could I fail? Full clear
were they.

CREON. And thou did'st dare to disobey these
laws?   485

ANTIG. Yes, for it was not Zeus who gave them
forth,
Nor Justice, dwelling with the Gods below,
Who traced these laws for all the sons of men;
Nor did I deem thy edicts strong enough,
That thou, a mortal man, should'st overpass   490
The unwritten laws of God that know not change.
They are not of today nor yesterday,
But live for ever, nor can man assign
When first they sprang to being. Not through fear
Of any man's resolve was I prepared   495
Before the Gods to bear the penalty
Of sinning against these. That I should die
I knew, (how should I not?) though thy decree
Had never spoken. And, before my time
If I shall die, I reckon this a gain;   500
For whoso lives, as I, in many woes,
How can it be but he shall gain by death?
And so for me to bear this doom of thine
Has nothing painful. But, if I had left
My mother's son unburied on his death,   505
In that I should have suffered; but in this
I suffer not. And should I seem to thee
To do a foolish deed, 'tis simply this,—
I bear the charge of folly from a fool.

CHOR. The maiden's stubborn will, of stubborn
sire   510
The offspring shows itself. She knows not yet
To yield to evils.

CREON.   Know then, minds too stiff
Most often stumble, and the rigid steel
Baked in the furnace, made exceeding hard,
Thou see'st most often split and shivered lie;   515
And I have known the steeds of fiery mood
With a small curb subdued. It is not meet
That one who lives in bondage to his neighbors
Should think too proudly. Wanton outrage then
This girl first learnt, transgressing these my laws;
But this, when she has done it, is again   521
A second outrage, over it to boast,
And laugh as having done it. Surely, then,
She is the man, not I, if, all unscathed,
Such deeds of might are hers. But be she child   525
Of mine own sister, or of one more near
Than all the kith and kin of Household Zeus,
She and her sister shall not 'scape a doom

Most foul and shameful; for I charge her, too,
With having planned this deed of sepulture. 530
Go ye and call her. 'Twas but now within
I saw her raving, losing self-command.
And still the mind of those who in the dark
Plan deeds of evil is the first to fail,
And so convicts itself of secret guilt. 535
But most I hate when one found out in guilt
Will seek to gloze and brave it to the end.

ANTIG. And dost thou seek aught else beyond my
death?

CREON. Nought else for me. That gaining, I gain
all.

ANTIG. Why then delay? Of all thy words not
one 540
Pleases me now, (and may it never please!)
And so all mine must grate upon thine ears.
And yet how could I higher glory gain
Than placing my true brother in his tomb?
There is not one of these but would confess 545
It pleases them, did fear not seal their lips.
The tyrant's might in much besides excels,
And it may do and say whate'er it will.

CREON. Of all the race of Cadmos thou alone
Look'st thus upon the deed.

ANTIG. They see it too 550
As I do, but their tongue is tied for thee.

CREON. Art not ashamed against their thoughts
to think?

ANTIG. There is nought base in honoring our
own blood.

CREON. And was he not thy kin who fought
against him?

ANTIG. Yea, brother, of one father and one
mother. 555

CREON. Why then give honor which dishonors
him?

ANTIG. The dead below will not repeat thy
words.

CREON. Yes, if thou give like honor to the godless.

ANTIG. It was his brother, not his slave, that died.

CREON. Wasting this land, while *he* died fighting
for it. 560

ANTIG. Yet Hades still craves equal rights for all.

CREON. The good craves not the portion of the
bad.

ANTIG. Who knows if this be holy deemed below?

CREON. Not even when he dies can foe be friend.

ANTIG. My nature leads to sharing love, not
hate. 565

CREON. Go then below; and if thou must have
love,
Love them. While I live, women shall not rule.

Enter ISMENE, *led in by Attendants.*

CHOR. And, lo! Ismene at the gate
Comes shedding tears of sisterly regard,
And o'er her brow a gathering cloud 570
Mars the deep roseate blush,
Bedewing her fair cheek.

CREON [*to* ISMENE]. And thou who, creeping as
a viper creeps,
Did'st drain my life in secret, and I knew not
That I was rearing two accursèd ones, 575
Subverters of my throne,—come, tell me, then,
Wilt thou confess thou took'st thy part in this,
Or wilt thou swear thou did'st not know of it?

ISM. I did the deed, if she did, go with her,
Yes, share the guilt, and bear an equal blame. 580

ANTIG. Nay, justice will not suffer this, for thou
Did'st not consent, nor did I let thee join.

ISM. Nay, in thy troubles, I am not ashamed
In the same boat with thee to share thy fate.

ANTIG. Who did it, Hades knows, and those below: 585
I do not love a friend who loves in words.

ISM. Do not, my sister, put me to such shame,
As not to let me join in death with thee,
And so to pay due reverence to the dead.

ANTIG. Share not my death, nor make thine own
this deed 590
Thou had'st no hand in. My death shall suffice.

ISM. What life to me is sweet, bereaved of thee?

ANTIG. Ask Creon there, since thou o'er him dost
watch.

ISM. Why vex me so, in nothing bettered by it?

ANTIG. 'Tis pain indeed, to laugh my laugh at
thee. 595

ISM. But now, at least, how may I profit thee?

ANTIG. Save thou thyself. I grudge not thy escape.

ISM. Ah, woe is me! and must I miss thy fate?

ANTIG. Thou mad'st thy choice to live, and I to
die.

ISM. 'Twas not because I failed to speak my
thoughts. 600

ANTIG. To these did'st thou, to those did I seem
wise.

ISM. And yet the offense is equal in us both.

ANTIG. Take courage. Thou dost live. My soul
long since
Hath died to render service to the dead.

CREON. Of these two girls, the one goes mad but
now, 605

The other ever since her life began.

Ism. E'en so, O king; no mind that ever lived
Stands firm in evil days, but goes astray.

Creon. Thine did, when, with the vile, vile deeds
thou choosest.

Ism. How could I live without her presence
here? 610

Creon. Speak not of presence. She is here no
more.

Ism. And wilt thou slay thy son's betrothèd
bride?

Creon. Full many a field there is which he may
plow.

Ism. None like that plighted troth 'twixt him
and her.

Creon. Wives that are vile I love not for my
sons. 615

Ism. Ah, dearest Hæmon, how thy father shames
thee!

Creon. Thou with that marriage dost but vex
my soul.

Chor. And wilt thou rob thy son of her he
loved?

Creon. 'Tis Death, not I, shall break the marriage off.

Chor. Her doom is fixed, it seems, then. She
must die. 620

Creon. Fixed, yes, by me and thee. No more
delay,
Lead them within, ye slaves. These must be kept
Henceforth as women, suffered not to roam;
For even boldest natures shrink in fear
When they see Hades overshadowing life. 625

[*Exeunt Guards with* Antigone *and* Ismene.

STROPHE I

Chor. Blessed are those whose life no woe doth
taste!
For unto those whose house
The Gods have shaken, nothing fails of curse
Or woe, that creeps to generations far.
E'en thus a wave, (when spreads, 630
With blasts from Thrakian coasts,
The darkness of the deep,)
Up from the sea's abyss
Hither and thither rolls the black sand on,
And every jutting peak, 635
Swept by the storm-wind's strength,
Lashed by the fierce wild waves,
Re-echoes with the far-resounding roar.

ANTISTROPHE I

I see the woes that smote, in ancient days,
The seed of Labdacos,[2] 640
Who perished long ago, with grief on grief
Still falling, nor does this age rescue that;
Some God still smites it down,
Nor have they any end:
For now there rose a gleam, 645
Over the last weak shoots,
That sprang from out the race of Œdipus;
Yet this the blood-stained scythe
Of those that reign below
Cuts off relentlessly, 650
And maddened speech, and frenzied rage of heart.

STROPHE II

Thy power, O Zeus, what haughtiness of man,
Yea, what can hold in check?
Which neither sleep, that maketh all things old,
Nor the long months of Gods that never fail, 655
Can for a moment seize.
But still as Lord supreme,
Waxing not old with time,
Thou dwellest in Thy sheen of radiancy
On far Olympos' height. 660
Through future near or far as through the past,
One law holds ever good,
Nought comes to life of man unscathed through-
out by woe.

ANTISTROPHE II

For hope to many comes in wanderings wild,
A solace and support; 665
To many as a cheat of fond desires,
And creepeth still on him who knows it not,
Until he burn his foot
Within the scorching flame.
Full well spake one of old, 670
That evil ever seems to be as good
To those whose thoughts of heart
God leadeth unto woe,
And without woe, he spends but shortest space of
time.

And here comes Hæmon, last of all thy sons: 675
Comes he bewailing sore
The fate of her who should have been his bride,
The maid Antigone,
Grieving o'er vanished joys?

Enter Hæmon.

[2] The seed of Labdacos refers to the whole family of Laius and Œdipus.

CREON. Soon we shall know much more than
    seers can tell.   680
Surely thou dost not come, my son, to rage
Against thy father, hearing his decree,
Fixing her doom who should have been thy bride;
Or dost thou love us still, whate'er we do?
   HÆMON. My father, I am thine; and thou dost
    guide   685
With thy wise counsels, which I gladly follow.
No marriage weighs one moment in the scales
With me, while thou dost guide my steps aright.
   CREON. This thought, my son, should dwell
    within thy breast,
That all things stand below a father's will;   690
For so men pray that they may rear and keep
Obedient offspring by their hearths and homes,
That they may both requite their father's foes,
And pay with him like honors to his friend.
But he who reareth sons that profit not,   695
What could one say of him but this, that he
Breeds his own sorrow, laughter to his foes?
Lose not thy reason, then, my son, o'ercome
By pleasure, for a woman's sake, but know,
A cold embrace is that to have at home   700
A worthless wife, the partner of thy bed.
What ulcerous sore is worse than one we love
Who proves all worthless? No! with loathing
   scorn,
As hateful to thee, let that girl go wed
A spouse in Hades. Taken in the act   705
I found her, her alone of all the State,
Rebellious. And I will not make myself
False to the State. She dies. So let her call
On Zeus, the lord of kindred. If I rear
Of mine own stock things foul and orderless,   710
I shall have work enough with those without,
For he who in the life of home is good
Will still be seen as just in things of state;
I should be sure that man would govern well,
And know well to be governed, and would stand
In war's wild storm, on his appointed post,   716
A just and good defender. But the man
Who by transgressions violates the laws,
Or thinks to bid the powers that be obey,
He must not hope to gather praise from me.   720
No! we must follow whom the State appoints
In things or just and trivial, or, may be,
   The opposite of these. For anarchy
Is our worst evil, brings our commonwealth
To utter ruin, lays whole houses low,   725
In battle strife hurls firm allies in flight;
But they who yield to guidance—these shall find
Obedience saves most men. Thus help should come

To what our rulers order; least of all
Ought men to bow before a woman's sway.   730
Far better, if it must be so, to fall
By a man's hand, than thus to bear reproach,
By woman conquered.
   CHOR.   Unto us, O king,
Unless our years have robbed us of our wit,
Thou seemest to say wisely what thou say'st.   735
   HÆM. The Gods, my father, have bestowed on
    man
His reason, noblest of all earthly gifts;
And that thou speakest wrongly these thy words
I cannot say, (God grant I ne'er know how
Such things to utter!) yet another's thoughts   740
May have some reason. 'Tis my lot to watch
What each man says or does, or blames in thee,
For dread thy face to one of low estate,
Who speaks what thou wilt not rejoice to hear.
But I can hear the things in darkness said,   745
How the whole city wails this maiden's fate,
As one "who of all women most unjustly,
For noblest deed must die the foulest death,
Who her own brother, fallen in the fray,
Would neither leave unburied, nor expose   750
To carrion dogs, or any bird of prey,
May she not claim the meed of golden praise?"
Such is the whisper that in secret runs
All darkling. And for me, my father, nought
Is dearer than thy welfare. What can be   755
A nobler prize of honor for the son
Than a sire's glory, or for sire than son's?
I pray thee, then, wear not one mood alone,
That what thou say'st is right, and nought but
   that;
For he who thinks that he alone is wise,   760
His mind and speech above what others have,
Such men when searched are mostly empty found.
But for a man to learn, though he be wise,
Yea to learn much, and know the time to yield,
Brings no disgrace. When winter floods the
   streams,   765
Thou see'st the trees that bend before the storm,
Save their last twigs, while those that will not yield
Perish with root and branch. And when one hauls
Too tight the mainsail rope, and will not slack,
He has to end his voyage with deck o'erturned.
Do thou then yield; permit thyself to change.   771
Young though I be, if any prudent thought
Be with me, I at least will dare assert
The higher worth of one, who, come what will,
Is full of knowledge. If that may not be   775
(For nature is not wont to take that bent,)

'Tis good to learn from those who counsel well.

Chor. My king! 'tis fit that thou should'st learn
from him,
If he speaks words in season; and, in turn,
That thou [to Hæmon] should'st learn of him, for
both speak well.   780

Creon. Shall we at our age stoop to learn from
him,
Young as he is, the lesson to be wise?

Hæm. Learn nought thou should'st not learn.
And if I'm young,
Thou should'st my deeds and not my years con-
sider.   784

Creon. Is that thy deed to reverence rebel souls?

Hæm. I would bid none waste reverence on the
base.

Creon. Has not that girl been seized with that
disease?

Hæm. The men of Thebes with one accord say,
No.

Creon. And will my subjects tell us how to rule?

Hæm. Dost thou not see thou speakest like a
boy?   790

Creon. Must I then rule for others than myself?

Hæm. That is no State which hangs on one
man's will.

Creon. Is not the State deemed his who governs it?

Hæm. Brave rule! Alone, and o'er an empty
land!

Creon. This boy, it seems, will be his bride's
ally.   795

Hæm. If thou art she, for thou art all my care.

Creon. Basest of base, against thy father pleading!

Hæm. Yea, for I see thee sin a grievous sin.

Creon. And do I sin revering mine own sway?

Hæm. Thou show'st no reverence, trampling on
God's laws.   800

Creon. O guilty soul, by woman's craft beguiled!

Hæm. Thou wilt not find me slave unto the base.

Creon. Thy every word is still on her behalf.

Hæm. Yea, and on thine and mine, and theirs
below.

Creon. Be sure thou shalt not wed her while she
lives.   805

Hæm. Then she must die, and, dying, others
slay.

Creon. And dost thou dare to come to me with
threats?

Hæm. Is it a threat against vain thoughts to
speak?

Creon. Thou to thy cost shalt teach me wisdom's
ways,
Thyself in wisdom wanting.

Hæm.   I would say   810
Thou wast unwise, if thou wert not my father.

Creon. Thou woman's slave, I say, prate on no
more.

Hæm. Wilt thou then speak, and, speaking, listen
not?

Creon. Nay, by Olympos! Thou shalt not go
free
To flout me with reproaches. Lead her out   815
Whom my soul hates, that she may die forthwith
Before mine eyes, and near her bridegroom here.

Hæm. No! Think it not! Near me she shall not
die,
And thou shalt never see my face alive,   819
That thou may'st storm at those who like to yield.
[Exit.

Chor. The man has gone, O king, in hasty
mood.
A mind distressed in youth is hard to bear.

Creon. Let him do what he will, and bear himself
As more than man, he shall not save those girls.

Chor. What! Dost thou mean to slay them both
alike?   825

Creon. Not her who touched it not; there thou
say'st well.

Chor. What form of death mean'st thou to slay
her with?

Creon. Leading her on to where the desert path
Is loneliest, there alive, in rocky cave
Will I immure her, just so much of food   830
Before her set as may avert pollution,
And save the city from the guilt of blood;
And there, invoking Hades, whom alone
Of all the Gods she worships, she, perchance,
Shall gain escape from death, or then shall know
That Hades-worship is but labor lost.   836
[Exit.

STROPHE

Chor. O Love, in every battle victor owned;
Love, rushing on thy prey,
Now on a maiden's soft and blooming cheek,
In secret ambush hid;   840
Now o'er the broad sea wandering at will,
And now in shepherd's folds;
Of all the Undying Ones none 'scape from thee,
Nor yet of mortal men
Whose lives are measured as a fleeting day;   845
And who has thee is frenzied in his soul.

Thou makest vile the purpose of the just,
　To his own fatal harm;
Thou hast stirred up this fierce and deadly strife,
　Of men of nearest kin;   850
The charm of eyes of bride beloved and fair
　Is crowned with victory,
And dwells on high among the powers that rule,
　Equal with holiest laws;
For Aphrodite, she whom none subdues,   855
Sports in her might and majesty divine,

I, even I, am borne
　Beyond the appointed laws;
I look on this, and cannot stay
　The fountain of my tears.   860
For, lo! I see her, see Antigone
　Wend her sad, lonely way
To that bride-chamber where we all must lie.
　ANTIG. Behold, O men of this my fatherland,
　I wend my last lone way,   865
Seeing the last sunbeam, now and nevermore;
　He leads me yet alive,
　Hades that welcomes all,
　To Acheron's dark shore,
　With neither part nor lot   870
　In marriage festival,
　Nor hath the marriage hymn
　Been sung for me as bride,
But I shall be the bride of Acheron.
　CHOR. And hast thou not all honor, worthiest
　　praise,   875
Who goest to the home that hides the dead,
Not smitten by the sickness that decays,
　Nor by the sharp sword's need,
But of thine own free will, in fullest life,
　Alone of mortals, thus   880
　To Hades tak'st thy way?
　ANTIG. I heard of old her [3] pitiable end,
　On Sipylos' high crag,
The Phrygian stranger from a far land come,
　Whom Tantalos begat;   885
　Whom growth of rugged rock,
　Clinging as ivy clings,
　Subdued, and made its own:
　And now, so runs the tale,
　There, as she melts in shower,   890
　The snow abideth aye,
And still bedews yon cliffs that lie below
　Those brows that ever weep.
With fate like hers God brings me to my rest.

　CHOR. A Goddess she, and of the high Gods
　　born;   895
And we are mortals, born of mortal seed.
And lo! for one who liveth but to die,
To gain like doom with those of heavenly race,
　Is great and strange to hear.
　ANTIG. Ye mock me then. Alas! Why wait ye
　　not,   900
By all our fathers' Gods, I ask of you,
　Till I have passed away,
　But flout me while I live?
　O city that I love,
　O men that claim as yours   905
　That city stored with wealth,
　O Dirkè, fairest fount,
O grove of Thebes, that boasts her chariot host,
　I bid you witness all,
　How, with no friends to weep,   91
　By what stern laws condemned,
I go to that strong dungeon of the tomb,
　For burial strange, ah me!
Nor dwelling with the living, nor the dead.
　CHOR. Forward and forward still to farthest
　　verge   915
　Of daring hast thou gone,
And now, O child, thou hast rushed violently
　Where Right erects her throne;
Surely thou payest to the uttermost
　Thy father's debt of guilt.   920
　ANTIG. Ah! thou hast touched the quick of all
　　my grief,
The thrice-told tale of all my father's woe,
　The fate which dogs us all,
The old Labdakid race of ancient fame.
　Woe for the curses dire   925
　Of that defilèd bed,
　With foulest incest stained,
　My mother's with my sire,
Whence I myself have sprung, most miserable.
　And now, I go to them,   930
　To sojourn in the grave,
　Accursèd, and unwed;
　Ah, brother, thou did'st find
　Thy marriage fraught with ill,
And thou, though dead, hast smitten down my
　　life.   935
　CHOR. Acts reverent and devout
　May claim devotion's name,
But power, in one to whom power comes as trust,
　May never be defied;
　And thee, thy stubborn mood,   94:

[3] Niobe.

Self-chosen, layeth low.
ANTIG. Unwept, without a friend,
Unwed, and whelmed in woe,
I journey on this road that open lies.
No more shall it be mine (O misery!)   945
To look upon yon daylight's holy eye;
  And yet, of all my friends,
  Not one bewails my fate,
  No kindly tear is shed.

Enter CREON.

CREON. And know ye not, if men have leave to
  speak   950
Their songs and wailings thus to stave off death,
That they will never stop? Lead, lead her on,
Without delay, and, as I said, immure
In yon cavernous tomb, and then depart.
Leave her to choose, or drear and lonely death, 955
Or, living, in the tomb to find her home.
Our hands are clean in all that touches her;
But she no more shall dwell on earth with us.
  ANTIG. [*turning towards the cavern*]. O tomb,
  my bridal chamber, vaulted home.
Guarded right well for ever, where I go   960
To join mine own, of whom the greater part
Among the dead doth Persephassa hold;
And I, of all the last and saddest, wend
My way below, life's little span unfilled.
And yet I go, and feed myself with hopes   965
That I shall meet them, by my father loved,
Dear to my mother, well-beloved of thee,
Thou darling brother: I, with these my hands,
Washed each dear corpse, arrayed you, poured
  libations,
In rites of burial; and in care for thee,   970
Thy body, Polyneikes, honoring,
I gain this recompense. [And yet in sight
Of all that rightly judge the deed was good;
I had not done it had I come to be
A mother with her children,—had not dared,   975
Though 'twere a husband dead that moldered
  there,
Against my country's will to bear this toil.
And am I asked what law constrained me thus?
I answer, had I lost a husband dear,
I might have had another; other sons   980
By other spouse, if one were lost to me;
But when my father and my mother sleep
In Hades, then no brother more can come.
And therefore, giving thee the foremost place,
I seemed in Creon's eyes, O brother dear,   985

To sin in boldest daring. Therefore now
He leads me, having taken me by force,
Cut off from marriage bed and marriage song,
Untasting wife's true joy, or mother's bliss,
With infant at her breast, but all forlorn,   990
Bereaved of friends, in utter misery,
Alive, I tread the chambers of the dead.]
What law of Heaven have I transgressed against?
What use for me, ill-starred one, still to look
To any God for succor, or to call   995
On any friend for aid? For holiest deed
I bear this charge of rank unholiness.
If acts like these the Gods on high approve,
We, taught by pain, shall own that we have sinned;
But if these sin, [*looking at* CREON] I pray they
  suffer not   1000
Worse evils than the wrongs they do to me.
  CHOR. Still do the same wild blasts
    Vex her who standeth there.
  CREON. Therefore shall these her guards
    Weep sore for this delay.   1005
  CHOR. Ah me! this word of thine
    Tells of death drawing nigh.
  CREON. I cannot bid thee hope
    For other end than this.
  ANTIG. O citadel of Thebes, my native land, 1010
    Ye Gods of ancient days,
    I go, and linger not.
Behold me, O ye senators of Thebes,
The last, lone scion of the kingly race,
What things I suffer, and from whom they come,
Revering still the laws of reverence.   1016
    [*Guards lead* ANTIGONE *away.*

STROPHE I

CHOR. So did the form of Danæ [4] bear of old,
  In brazen palace hid,
  To lose the light of heaven,
And in her tomb-like chamber was enclosed: 1020
Yet she, O child, was noble in her race,
And well she stored the golden shower of Zeus.
But great and dread the might of Destiny;
  Nor kingly wealth, nor war,
  Nor tower, nor dark-hulled ships   1025
  Beaten by waves, escape.

ANTISTROPHE I

So too was shut, enclosed in dungeon cave,
  Bitter and fierce in mood,
  The son of Dryas,[5] king

---

[4] Danæ to whom Zeus as lover appeared in her tomb-like prison, in a golden shower.
[5] Lycurgus, who opposed the entrance of Dionysus and his rites into Thrace. He was driven mad and imprisoned in a cave.

Of yon Edonian tribes, for vile reproach,   1030
By Dionysos' hands, and so his strength
And soul o'ermad wastes drop by drop away,
And so he learnt that he, against the God,
 Spake his mad words of scorn;
 For he the Mænad throng   1035
 And bright fire fain had stopped,
 And roused the Muses' wrath.

STROPHE II

And by the double sea of those Dark Rocks
 Are shores of Bosporos,
And Thrakian isle, as Salmydessos known,   1040
 Where Ares, whom they serve,
 God of the region round,
 Saw the dire, blinding wound,
 That smote the twin-born sons
Of Phineus [6] by relentless step-dame's hand,—   1045
 Dark wound, on dark-doomed eyes,
 Not with the stroke of sword,
But blood-stained hands, and point of spindle sharp.

ANTISTROPHE II

And they in misery, miserable fate,
 Wasting away, wept sore,   1050
Born of a mother wedded with a curse,
 And she who claimed descent
 From men of ancient fame,
 The old Erechtheid race,
 Amid her father's winds,   1055
Daughter of Boreas, in far distant caves
 Was reared, a child of Gods,
 Swift moving as the steed
 O'er lofty crag, and yet
The ever-living Fates bore hard on her.   1060

Enter TEIRESIAS, guided by a Boy.

TEIR. Princes of Thebes, we come as travelers
 joined,
One seeing for both, for still the blind must use
A guide's assistance to direct his steps.
 CREON. And what new thing, Teiresias, brings
 thee here?   1064
TEIR. I'll tell thee, and do thou the seer obey.
 CREON. Of old I was not wont to slight thy
 thoughts.
TEIR. So did'st thou steer our city's course full
 well.
 CREON. I bear my witness from good profit
 gained.

TEIR. Know, then, thou walk'st on fortune's
 razor-edge.
 CREON. What means this? How I shudder at
 thy speech!   1070
TEIR. Soon shalt thou know, as thou dost hear
 the signs
Of my dread art. For sitting, as of old,
Upon my ancient seat of augury,
Where every bird finds haven, lo! I hear
Strange cry of winged creatures, shouting shrill,
With inarticulate passion, and I knew   1076
That they were tearing each the other's flesh
With bloody talons, for their whirring wings
Made that quite clear: and straightway I, in fear,
Made trial of the sacrifice that lay   1080
On fiery altar. And Hephæstos' flame
Shone not from out the offering; but there oozed
Upon the ashes, trickling from the bones,
A moisture, and it smoldered, and it spat,
And, lo! the gall was scattered to the air,   1085
And forth from out the fat that wrapped them
 round
The thigh-bones fell. Such omens of decay
From holy sacrifice I learnt from him,
This boy, who now stands here, for he is still
A guide to me, as I to others am.   1090
And all this evil falls upon the State,
From out thy counsels; for our altars all,
Our sacred hearths are full of food for dogs
And birds unclean, the flesh of that poor wretch
Who fell, the son of Œdipus. And so   1095
The Gods no more hear prayers of sacrifice,
Nor own the flame that burns the victim's limbs;
Nor do the birds give cry of omen good,
But feed on carrion of a slaughtered corpse.
Think thou on this, my son: to err, indeed,   1100
Is common unto all, but having erred,
He is no longer reckless or unblest,
Who, having fallen into evil, seeks
For healing, nor continues still unmoved.   1104
Self-will must bear the charge of stubbornness:
Yield to the dead, and outrage not a corpse.
What prowess is it fallen foes to slay?
Good counsel give I, planning good for thee,
And of all joys the sweetest is to learn
From one who speaketh well, should that bring
 gain.   1110
 CREON. Old man, as archers aiming at their mark,
So ye shoot forth your venomed darts at me;
I know your augur's tricks, and by your tribe

---

[6] This is the story of Cleopatra, daughter of Boreas. the wind-god. She married Phineus and bore
him two sons. He afterward imprisoned her. Phineus' next wife blinds the sons of Cleopatra.

Long since am tricked and sold. Yes, gain your
     gains,
Get Sardis' amber metal, Indian gold;   1115
That corpse ye shall not hide in any tomb.
Not though the eagles, birds of Zeus, should bear
Their carrion morsels to the throne of God,
Not even fearing this pollution dire,
Will I consent to burial. Well I know   1120
That man is powerless to pollute the Gods.
But many fall, Teiresias, dotard old,
A shameful fall, who gloze their shameful words
For lucre's sake, with surface show of good.

TEIR. Ah me! Does no man know, does none
     consider . . . ?   1125
CREON. Consider what? What trite poor saw
     comes now?
TEIR. How far good counsel is of all things best?
CREON. So far, I trow, as folly is worst ill.
TEIR. Of that disease thy soul, alas! is full.
CREON. I will not meet a seer with evil
     words.   1130
TEIR. Thou dost so, saying I divine with lies.
CREON. The race of seers is ever fond of gold.
TEIR. And that of tyrants still loves lucre foul.
CREON. Dost know thou speak'st thy words of
     those that rule?
TEIR. I know. Through me thou rul'st a city
     saved.   1135
CREON. Wise seer art thou, yet given o'ermuch
     to wrong.
TEIR. Thou'lt stir me to speak out my soul's
     dread secrets.
CREON. Out with them; only speak them not for
     gain.
TEIR. So is 't, I trow, in all that touches thee.
CREON. Know that thou shalt not bargain with
     my will.   1140
TEIR. Know, then, and know it well, that thou
     shalt see
Not many winding circuits of the sun,
Before thou giv'st as quittance for the dead,
A corpse by thee begotten; for that thou
Hast to the ground cast one that walked on
     earth,   1145
And foully placed within a sepulcher
A living soul; and now thou keep'st from them,
The Gods below, the corpse of one unblest,
Unwept, unhallowed, and in these things thou
Can'st claim no part, nor yet the Gods above;   1150
But they by thee are outraged; and they wait,
The sure though slow avengers of the grave,
The dread Erinnyes of the mighty Gods,
For thee in these same evils to be snared.

Search well if I say this as one who sells   1155
His soul for money. Yet a little while,
And in thy house the wail of men and women
Shall make it plain. And every city stirs
Itself in arms against thee, owning those
Whose limbs the dogs have buried, or fierce
     wolves,   1160
Or wingèd birds have brought the accursèd taint
To region consecrate. Doom like to this,
Sure darting as an arrow to its mark,
I launch at thee, (for thou dost vex me sore,)
An archer aiming at the very heart,   1165
And thou shalt not escape its fiery sting.
And now, O boy, lead thou me home again,
That he may vent his spleen on younger men,
And learn to keep his tongue more orderly,
With better thoughts than this his present
     mood.   1170
                                          [Exit.

CHOR. The man has gone, O king, predicting
     woe,
And well we know, since first our raven hair
Was mixed with gray, that never yet his words
Were uttered to our State and failed of truth.
CREON. I know it too, 'tis that that troubles
     me.   1175
To yield is hard, but, holding out, to smite
One's soul with sorrow, this is harder still.
CHOR. We need wise counsel, O Menœkeus' son.
CREON. What shall I do? Speak thou, and I'll
     obey.
CHOR. Go then, and free the maiden from her
     tomb,   1180
And give a grave to him who lies exposed.
CREON. Is this thy counsel? Dost thou bid me
     yield?
CHOR. Without delay, O king, for lo! they come,
The Gods' swift-footed ministers of ill,
And in an instant lay the self-willed low.   1185
CREON. Ah me! 'tis hard; and yet I bend my
     will
To do thy bidding. With necessity
We must not fight at such o'erwhelming odds.
CHOR. Go then and act! Commit it not to others
CREON. E'en as I am I'll go. Come, come, my
     men,   1190
Present or absent, come, and in your hands
Bring axes: come to yonder eminence.
And I, since now my judgment leans that way,
Who myself bound her, now myself will loose,
Too much I fear lest it should wisest prove   1195
Maintaining ancient laws to end my life.
                                          [Exit.

STROPHE I

CHOR. O Thou of many names,
   Of that Cadmeian maid
   The glory and the joy,
   Whom Zeus as offspring owns,   1200
   Zeus, thundering deep and loud,
Who watchest over famed Italia,
And reign'st o'er all the bays that Deo claims
   On fair Eleusis' coast.
Bacchos, who dwell'st in Thebes, the mother-
    town   1205
   Of all thy Bacchant train,
   Along Ismenos' stream,
   And with the dragon's brood;

ANTISTROPHE 1

   Thee, o'er the double peak
   Of yonder height the blaze   1210
   Of flashing fire beholds,
   Where nymphs of Corycos
   Go forth in Bacchic dance,
And by the flowery stream of Castaly,
And Thee, the ivied slopes of Nysa's hills,   1215
   And vine-clad promontory,
(While words of more than mortal melody
   Shout out the well-known name,)
   Send forth, the guardian lord
   Of the wide streets of Thebes.   1220

STROPHE II

   Above all cities Thou,
With her, thy mother whom the thunder slew,
   Dost look on it with love;
And now, since all the city bendeth low
   Beneath the sullen plague,   1225
   Come Thou with cleansing tread
   O'er the Parnassian slopes,
   Or o'er the moaning straits.

ANTISTROPHE II

   O Thou, who lead'st the band,
The choral band of stars still breathing fire,   1230
   Lord of the hymns of night,
The child of highest Zeus; appear, O king,
   With Thyian maidens wild,
   Who all night long in dance,
   With frenzied chorus sing   1235
   Thy praise, their lord, Iacchos.

Enter Messenger.

MESS. Ye men of Cadmos and Amphion's house,
I know no life of mortal man which I
Would either praise or blame. 'Tis Fortune's
   chance
That raiseth up, and Fortune bringeth low,   1240
The man who lives in good or evil plight;
And prophet of men's future there is none.
For Creon, so I deemed, deserved to be
At once admired and envied, having saved
This land of Cadmos from the hands of foes; 1245
And, having ruled with fullest sovereignty,
He lived and prospered, joyous in a race
Of goodly offspring. Now, all this is gone;
For when men lose the joys that sweeten life,
I cannot deem they live, but rather count   1250
As if a breathing corpse. His heaped-up stores
Of wealth are large, so be it, and he lives
With all a sovereign's state; and yet, if joy
Be absent, all the rest I count as nought,
And would not weigh them against pleasure's
   charm,   1255
More than a vapor's shadow.
   CHOR.   What is this?
What new disaster tell'st thou of our chiefs?
   MESS. Dead are they, and the living cause their
    death.
   CHOR. Who slays, and who is slaughtered? Tell
    thy tale.
   MESS. Hæmon is dead, slain, weltering in his
    blood.   1260
   CHOR. By his own act, or by his father's hand?
   MESS. His own, in wrath against his father's
    crime.
   CHOR. O prophet! true, most true, those words
    of thine.
   MESS. Since things stand thus, we well may
    counsel take.
   CHOR. Lo! Creon's wife comes, sad Eury-
    dike.   1265
She from the house approaches, hearing speech
About her son, or else by accident.

Enter EURYDIKE.

EURYD. I on my way, my friends, as suppliant
   bound,
To pay my vows at Pallas' shrine, have heard
Your words, and so I chanced to draw the bolt 1270
Of the half-opened door, when lo! a sound
Falls on my ears, of evil striking home,
And terror-struck I fall in deadly swoon
Back in my handmaids' arms; yet tell it me,
Tell the tale once again, for I shall hear,   1275
By long experience disciplined to grief.

Mess. Dear lady, I will tell thee: I was by,
And will not leave one word of truth untold.
Why should we smooth and gloze, where all too
    soon
We should be found as liars? Truth is still   1280
The only safety. Lo! I went with him,
Thy husband, in attendance, to the edge
Of yonder plain, where still all ruthlessly
The corpse of Polyneikes lay exposed,
Mangled by dogs. And, having prayed to her,   1285
The Goddess of all pathways, and to Pluto,
To temper wrath with pity, him they washed
With holy washing; and what yet was left
We burnt in branches freshly cut, and heaped
A high-raised grave from out his native soil,   1290
And then we entered on the stone-paved home,
Death's marriage-chamber for the ill-starred maid.
And someone hears, while standing yet afar,
Shrill voice of wailing near the bridal bower,
By funeral rites unhallowed, and he comes   1295
And tells my master, Creon. On his ears,
Advancing nearer, falls a shriek confused
Of bitter sorrow, and with groaning loud,
He utters one sad cry, "Me miserable!
And am I then a prophet? Do I wend   1300
This day the dreariest way of all my life?
My son's voice greets me. Go, my servants, go,
Quickly draw near, and standing by the tomb,
Search ye and see; and where the stone torn out
Shall make an opening, look ye in, and say   1305
If I hear Hæmon's voice, or if my soul
Is cheated by the Gods." And then we searched,
As he, our master, in his frenzy bade us;
And, in the furthest corner of the vault,
We saw her hanging by her neck, with cord   1310
Of linen threads entwined, and him we found
Clasping her form in passionate embrace,
And mourning o'er the doom that robbed him of
    her,
His father's deed, and that his marriage bed,
So full of woe. When Creon saw him there,   1315
Groaning aloud in bitterness of heart,
He goes to him, and calls in wailing voice,
"Poor boy! what hast thou done? Hast thou then
    lost
Thy reason? In what evil sinkest thou?
Come forth, my child, on bended knee I ask
    thee."   1320
And then the boy, with fierce, wild-gleaming eyes,
Glared at him, spat upon his face, and draws,
Still answering nought, the sharp two-handled
    sword.
Missing his aim, (his father from the blow

Turning aside,) in anger with himself,   1325
The poor ill-doomed one, even as he was,
Fell on his sword, and drove it through his breast,
Full half its length, and clasping, yet alive,
The maiden's arm, still soft, he there breathes
    out
In broken gasps, upon her fair white cheek,   1330
Swift stream of bloody shower. So they lie,
Dead bridegroom with dead bride, and he has
    gained,
Poor boy, his marriage rites in Hades home,
And left to all men witness terrible,
That man's worst ill is want of counsel wise.   1335
                    [Exit Eurydike.
Chor. What dost thou make of this? She turn-
    eth back,
Before one word, or good or ill, she speaks.
Mess. I too am full of wonder. Yet with hopes
I feed myself, she will not think it meet,
Hearing her son's woes, openly to wail   1340
Out in the town, but to her handmaids there
Will give command to wail her woe at home.
Too trained a judgment has she so to err.
Chor. I know not. To my mind, or silence hard,
Or vain wild cries, are signs of bitter woe.   1345
Mess. Soon we shall know, within the house
    advancing,
If, in the passion of her heart, she hides
A secret purpose. Truly dost thou speak;
There is a terror in that silence hard.
Chor. [seeing Creon approaching with the
    corpse of Hæmon in his arms]. And lo! the
    king himself is drawing nigh,   1350
And in his hands he bears a record clear,
No woe (if I may speak) by others caused,
    Himself the great offender.

Enter Creon, *bearing* Hæmon's *body.*

Creon. Woe! for the sins of souls of evil mood,
    Stern, mighty to destroy!   1355
O ye who look on those of kindred race,
    The slayers and the slain,
Woe for mine own rash plans that prosper not!
Woe for thee, son; but new in life's career,
    And by a new fate dying!   1360
        Woe! woe!
    Thou diest, thou art gone,
Not by thine evil counsel, but by mine.
Chor. Ah me! Too late thou seem'st to see
    the right.
Creon.   Ah me!   1365
I learn the grievous lesson. On my head,
God, pressing sore hath smitten me and vexed,

In ways most rough and terrible, (Ah me!)
Shattering my joy, as trampled under foot.
Woe! woe! Man's labors are but labor lost.   1370

Enter Second Messenger.

SEC. MESS. My master! thou, as one who hast
    full store,
One source of sorrow bearest in thine arms,
And others in thy house, too soon, it seems,
Thou need'st must come and see.
    CREON.   And what remains
Worse evil than the evils that we bear?   1375
    SEC. MESS. Thy wife is dead, that corpse's
    mother true,
Ill starred one, smitten with a blow just dealt.
    CREON. O agony!
Haven of Death, that none may pacify,
    Why dost thou thus destroy me?   1380
[*Turning to Messenger.*] O thou who comest,
    bringing in thy train
    Woes horrible to tell,
Thou tramplest on a man already slain.
What say'st thou? What new tidings bring'st to
    me?
            Ah me! ah me!   1385
Is it that now there waits in store for me
My own wife's death to crown my misery?
    CHOR. Full clearly thou may'st see. No longer
    now
Does yon recess conceal her.

The gates open and show the dead body of
EURYDIKE.

CREON.   Woe is me!
This second ill I gaze on, miserable,   1390
What fate, yea, what still lies in wait for me?
Here in my arms I bear what was my son;
And there, O misery! look upon the dead.
Ah, wretched mother! ah, my son! my son!
    SEC. MESS. In frenzy wild she round the altar
    clung,   1395
And closed her darkening eyelids, and bewailed
The noble fate of Megareus, who died
Long since, and then again that corpse thou hast;
And last of all she cried a bitter cry
Against thy deeds, the murderer of thy sons.   1400
    CREON. Woe! woe! alas!
    shudder in my fear. Will no one strike

A deadly blow with sharp two-edgèd sword?
    Fearful my fate, alas!
And with a fearful woe full sore beset.   1405
    SEC. MESS. She in her death charged thee with
    being the cause
Of all their sorrows, these and those of old.
    CREON. And in what way struck she the murder-
    ous blow?
    SEC. MESS. With her own hand below her heart
    she stabbed,
Hearing her son's most pitiable fate.   1410
    CREON. Ah me! The fault is mine. On no one
    else,
Of all that live, the fearful guilt can come;
I, even I, did slay thee, woe is me!
I, yes, I speak the truth. Lead me, ye guards,
Lead me forth quickly; lead me out of sight,   1415
More crushed to nothing than is nothing's self.
    CHOR. Thou counselest gain, if gain there be in
    ills,
For present ills when shortest then are best.
    CREON. Oh, come thou then, come thou,
The last of all my dooms, that brings to me   1420
Best boon, my life's last day. Come then, oh come,
That never more I look upon the light.
    CHOR. These things are in the future. What is
    near,
That we must do. O'er what is yet to come   1424
They watch, to Whom that work of right belongs.
    CREON. I did but pray for what I most desire.
    CHOR. Pray thou for nothing then: for mortal
    man
There is no issue from a doom decreed.
    CREON [*looking at the two corpses*]. Lead me
    then forth, vain shadow that I am,
Who slew thee, O my son, unwillingly,   1430
And thee too—(O my sorrow!)—and I know not
Which way to look or turn. All near at hand
Is turned to evil; and upon my head
There falls a doom far worse than I can bear.
    CHOR. Man's highest blessedness,   1435
    In wisdom chiefly stands;
And in the things that touch upon the Gods,
    'Tis best in word or deed
    To shun unholy pride;
Great words of boasting bring great punishments,
    And so to gray-haired age   1441
    Teach wisdom at the last.

EURIPIDES

Alcestis

DRAMATIS PERSONÆ

APOLLO
DEATH
CHORUS, *composed of Elders of Pheræ*
HANDMAID
ALCESTIS, *daughter of Pelias, and wife of Admetus*
ADMETUS, *King of Pheræ*
EUMELUS, *son of Admetus and Alcestis*
HERCULES
PHERES, *father of Admetus*
SERVANT, *steward of the palace*
Guards, attendants, handmaids, and mourners

*The scene throughout is in front of the palace of
Admetus at Pheræ.*

Enter APOLLO.

APOLLO. Halls of Admetus, hail! I stooped my
    pride
Here to brook fare of serfs, yea I, a God!
The fault was fault of Zeus: he slew my son
Asclepius—hurled the levin through his heart.
Wroth for the dead, his smiths of heavenly fire, 5
The Cyclopes, I slew; for blood-atonement
Allfather made me serf to a mortal man.

To this land came I, tended mine host's kine,
And warded still his house unto this day.
Righteous myself, I found a righteous man, 10
The son of Pheres: him I snatched from death,
Cozening the Fates: the Sisters promised me—
"Admetus shall escape the imminent death
If he for ransom gives another life."
To all he went—all near and dear,—and asked 15
Father and gray-haired mother who gave him life;
But, save his wife, found none that would consent
For him to die and never more see light.
Now in his arms upborne within yon home
She gaspeth forth her life: for on this day 20
Her weird it is to die and fleet from life.
I, lest pollution taint me in their house,
Go forth of yonder hall's belovèd roof.

Enter DEATH.

Lo, yonder Death;—I see him nigh at hand,
Priest of the dead, who comes to hale her down 25
To Hades' halls—well hath he kept his time,
Watching this day, whereon she needs must die.
DEATH. Ha, thou at the palace! Wilt not make
    room,
Phœbus?—thou wrestest the right yet again:
Thou removest the landmarks of Gods of Gloom,
And thou makest their honors vain. 31
Did this not suffice thee, to thwart that doom
Of Admetus, when, all by thy cunning beguiled
Were the Fates, that thou now must be warding
    the wife
With thine hand made ready the bowstring to
    strain, 35
Though she pledged her from death to redeem
    with her life
Her lord,—she, Pelias' child?
APOLLO. Fear not: fair words and justice are
    with me.
DEATH. Justice with thee!—what needeth then
    the bow?
APOLLO. This?—'tis my wont to bear it ever-
    more. 40
DEATH. Yea, and to aid yon house in lawless
    wise.
APOLLO. Mine heart is heavy for my friend's mis-
    chance.
DEATH. What, wilt thou wrest from me this
    second corpse?
APOLLO. Nay, not that other did I take by force.
DEATH. Not?—why on earth then?—why not
    underground? 45
APOLLO. She was his ransom, she for whom thou
    comest.
DEATH. Yea, and will hale her deep beneath the
    earth.
APOLLO. Take her and go: I trow I shall not
    bend thee—
DEATH. To slay the victim due?—mine office
    this.
APOLLO. Nay, but to smite with death the ripe
    for death. 50

Euripides, *Alcestis.* Translated by A. S. Way. By permission of The Macmillan Co. Euripides (c. 480-
406 B.C.) was born near Athens, had military experience in his youth, and spent a busy life writing and
producing plays, but little is known of the details of his life.

DEATH. I grasp thine argument—and thine earnestness!

APOLLO. And may Alcestis never see old age?

DEATH. Never:—should I not love mine honors too?

APOLLO. 'Tis soon or late,—thou canst but take one life.

DEATH. Yet mine the goodlier prize when die the young. 55

APOLLO. Though she die old, rich obsequies still are thine.

DEATH. Lo, Phœbus making laws to shield the rich!

APOLLO. How say'st thou?—thou a sophist unawares!

DEATH. Would wealth not buy the boon of dying old?

APOLLO. So then thou wilt not grant this grace to me? 60

DEATH. Nay surely—dost not know my wonted way?

APOLLO. Hateful to mortals this, and loathed of Gods.

DEATH. All things beyond thy rights thou canst not have.

APOLLO. Surely thou shalt forbear, though ruthless thou,

So mighty a man to Pheres' halls shall come, 65
Sent of Eurystheus forth, the courser-car
From winter-dreary lands of Thrace to bring.
Guest-welcomed in Admetus' palace here,
By force yon woman shall he wrest from thee.
Yea, thou of me shalt have no thank for this, 70
And yet shalt do it, and shalt have mine hate.

[Exit APOLLO.

DEATH. Talk on, talk on: no profit shalt thou win.
This woman down to Hades' halls shall pass.
For her I go: my sword shall seal her ours:
For consecrated to the Nether Gods 75
Is every head whose hair this sword hath shorn.

[Exit DEATH.

Enter Chorus, dividing to right and left, so that the sections answer one another till they unite at str. 2.

HALF-CHOR. 1. What meaneth this hush afront of the hall?
The home of Admetus, why voiceless all?

HALF-CHOR. 2. No friend of the house who should speak of its plight 79
Is nigh, who should bid that we raise the keen

For the dead, or should tell us that yet on the light
Alcestis looketh, and liveth the Queen,
The daughter of Pelias, noblest, I ween—
Yea, in all men's sight
Most leal to her lord of all wives hath she been. 85

STROPHE I

HALF-CHOR. 1. Or hearest thou mourning or sighing
Or beating of hands,
Or the wail of bereaved ones outcrying?
No handmaid stands
At the palace-gate. 90
O Healer, appear for the dying, appear as a bright bird flying
'Twixt the surges of fate!

HALF-CHOR. 2. She lives!—were she dead, they had raised the keen.

HALF-CHOR. 1. Nay, a corpse is all that was once a queen.

HALF-CHOR. 2. But not forth of the doors is the death-train gone. 95

HALF-CHOR. 1. Whence cometh thine hope, which I boast not mine own?

HALF-CHOR. 2. Would the King without pomp of procession have yielded the grave the possession
Of so dear, of so faithful an one?

ANTISTROPHE I

HALF-CHOR. 1. Nor the cup in the gateway appeareth,
From the spring that they bear 100
To the gate that pollution feareth,
Nor the severed hair
In the porch for the dead,
Which the mourner in bitterness sheareth, neither beating of hands one heareth
On maiden's head. 105

HALF-CHOR. 2. Yet surely is this the appointed day—

HALF-CHOR. 1. Ah! what wilt thou say?

HALF-CHOR. 2. Whereon of her doom she must pass to the tomb.

HALF-CHOR. 1. With a keen pang's smart hast thou stabbed mine heart.

HALF-CHOR. 2. It is meet, when the good are as flowers plucked away, 110
That in sorrow's gloom
Should the breast of the old tried friend have part.

STROPHE 2

Chor. Though ye voyage all seas,
　　Ye shall light on no lands,
　　Nor on Lycia's leas,　　　　　　　115
　　Nor Ammonian sands,
Whence redemption shall come for the wretched,
　　or loosing of Death's dread bands.

　　Doom's chasm hard by
　　Yawns fathomless-deep.
　　What availeth to cry　　　　　　　120
　　To the Gods, or to heap
Their altars with costly oblations, to plead with
　　the slaughter of sheep?

ANTISTROPHE 2

　　Ah, once there was one!—
　　Were life's light in the eyes
　　Of Phœbus's son,　　　　　　　　125
　　Then our darling might rise
From the mansions of darkness, through portals of
　　Hades return to our skies;

　　For he raised up the dead,
　　Ere flashed from the heaven,
　　From Zeus' hand sped,　　　　　　130
　　That bolt of the levin.
But now what remaineth to wait for?—what hope
　　of her life is given?

　　No sacrifice more
　　Unrendered remaineth;
　　No God, but the gore　　　　　　　135
　　From his altars down-raineth;
Yet healing is none for our ills, neither balm that
　　the spirit sustaineth.

Enter HANDMAID.

But hither cometh of the handmaids one,
Weeping the while. What tidings shall I hear?
For all afflictions that befall thy lords　　　140
Well mayst thou grieve; but if thy lady lives
Or even now hath passed, fain would we know.
　　Handmaid. She liveth, and is dead: both mayst
　　　thou say.
　　Chor. Aye so!—how should the same be dead
　　　and live?
　　Handmaid. Even now she droopeth, gasping out
　　　her life.　　　　　　　　　　　　145
　　Chor. O stricken king—how noble a queen thou
　　　losest!

　　Handmaid. His depth of loss he knows not ere
　　　it come.
　　Chor. And hope—is no hope left her life to
　　　save?
　　Handmaid. None—for the day foredoomed con-
　　　straineth her.
　　Chor. Are all things meet, then, being done for
　　　her?　　　　　　　　　　　　　150
　　Handmaid. Yea, ready is burial-attire.
　　Chor. Let her be sure that glorious she dies
And noblest far of woman 'neath the sun.
　　Handmaid. Noblest?—how not?—what tongue
　　　will dare gainsay?
What must the woman be who passeth her?　155
How could a wife give honor to her lord
More than by yielding her to die for him?
And this—yea, all the city knoweth this;
But what within she did, hear thou, and marvel.
For when she knew that the appointed day　160
Was come, in river-water her white skin
She bathed, and from the cedar-chests took forth
Vesture and jewels, and decked her gloriously,
And before Vesta's altar stood, and prayed:
"Queen, for I pass beneath the earth, I fall　165
Before thee now, and nevermore, and pray:—
Be mother to my orphans: mate with him
A loving wife, with her a noble husband.
Nor, as their mother dieth, so may they,
My children, die untimely, but with weal　170
In the home-land fill up a life of bliss."
To all the altars through Admetus' halls
She went, with wreaths she hung them, and she
　　prayed,
Plucking the while the tresses of the myrtle,
Tearless, unsighing, and the imminent fate　175
Changed not the lovely rose-tint of her cheek.
Then to her bower she rushed, fell on the bed;
And there, O there she went, and thus she speaks:
"O couch, whereon I loosed the maiden zone
For this man, for whose sake I die today,　180
Farewell: I hate thee not. Me hast thou slain
Me only: loth to fail thee and my lord
I die; but thee another bride shall own,
Not more true-hearted; happier perchance."
Then falls thereon, and kisses: all the bed　185
Is watered with the flood of melting eyes.
But having wept her fill of many tears,
Drooping she goeth, reeling from the couch;
Yet oft, as forth the bower she passed, returned,
And flung herself again upon the bed,　　190
And the babes, clinging to their mother's robes,
Were weeping; and she clasped them in her arms,
Fondling now this, now that, as one death-doomed.

And all the servants 'neath the roof were weeping,
Pitying their lady. But to each she stretched   195
Her right hand forth; and none there was so mean
To whom she spake not and received reply.
Such are the ills Admetus' home within.
Now, had he died, he had ended; but, in 'scaping,
He bears a pain that he shall ne'er forget.   200
   CHOR. Doth not Admetus groan for this afflic-
tion
Of such a noble wife to be bereft?
   HANDMAID. Aye, weeps, and clasps his dear one
in his arms,
And prays, "Forsake me not!"—asking the while
The impossible, for still she wanes and wastes,   205
Drooping her hand, a misery-burdened weight;
But yet, albeit hardly breathing still,
To the sun's rays fain would she lift her eyes,
As nevermore, but for the last time now
Destined to see the sun's beam and his orb.   210
But I will go and make thy presence known:
For 'tis not all that love so well their kings
As to stand by them, in afflictions loyal.
But from of old my lords were loved of thee.
                           [*Exit.*

Nine members of the Chorus chant successively:

   CHOR. 1. O Zeus, for our lords is there naught
but despair?   215
No path through the tangle of evils, no loosing of
chains that have bound them?
   CHOR. 2. No tidings?—remaineth but rending of
hair,
And the stricken ones turned to the tomb with the
garments of sorrow around them?
   CHOR. 3. Even so—even so! yet uplift we in
prayer
Our hands to the Gods, for that power from the
days everlasting hath crowned them.   220
   CHOR. 4. O Healer-king,
Find thou for Admetus the balm of relief, for the
captive deliverance!
   CHOR. 5. Vouchsafe it, vouchsafe it, for heretofore
    Hast thou found out a way; even now once
more
    Pluck back our belovèd from Hades' door,   225
    Strike down Death's hand red-reeking with
gore!
   CHOR. 6. Woe's me! woe's me!—let the woe-
dirge ring!
Ah, scion of Pheres, alas for thy lot, for love's long
severance!

   CHOR. 7. For such things on his sword might a
man not fall,
Or knit up his throat in the noose 'twixt the
heaven and the earth that quivereth?   230
   CHOR. 8. For his dear one—nay, but his dearest
of all
Shall he see on this day lying dead, while her spirit
by Lethe shivereth.
   CHOR. 9. O look!—look yonder, where forth of
the hall
She cometh, and he at her side whose life by her
life she delivereth.
   CHOR., UNITED. Cry, Land Pheræan, shrill the
keen!   235
    Lift up thy voice to wail thy best
    There dying, and thy queenliest
   Slow wasting to the Gates Unseen!

   Tell me not this, that wedlock brings
    To them that wed more bliss than woe.   240
   I look back to the long-ago;
   I muse on these unhappiest things.

   Lo, here a king—he forfeiteth
    The truest heart, the noblest wife;
    And what shall be henceforth his life?   245
   A darkened day, a living death.

Enter female attendants supporting ALCESTIS, *accompanied by* ADMETUS *and Children.*

STROPHE 1

ALCES. O Sun, and the day's dear light,
And ye clouds through the wheeling heaven in the
race everlasting flying!
   ADMET. He seeth thee and me, two stricken ones,
Which wrought the Gods no wrong, that thou
shouldst die.

ANTISTROPHE 1

ALCES.   O Land, O stately height   250
Of mine halls, and my bridal couch in Iolcos my
fatherland lying!
   ADMET. Uplift thee, hapless love, forsake me not,
And pray the mighty Gods in ruth to turn.

STROPHE 2

ALCES. I see the boat with the oars twin-sweep-
ing,
And, his hand on the pole as in haste aye keeping,   255

Charon the Ferryman calleth, "What ho, wilt thou
   linger and linger?
Hasten,—'tis thou dost delay me?" he crieth with
   beckoning finger.
   ADMET. Ah me! a bitter ferrying this thou
   namest!
O evil-starred, what woes endure we now!

ANTISTROPHE 2

ALCES. One haleth me—haleth me hence to the
   mansion   260
Of the dead!—dost thou mark not the darkling
   expansion
Of the pinions of Hades, the blaze of his eyes
   'neath their caverns out-glaring?
What wouldst thou?—Unhand me!—In anguish
   and pain by what path am I faring!
   ADMET. Woeful to them that love thee: most to
   me
And to thy babes, sad sharers in this grief.   265

EPODE

ALCES. Let be—let me sink back to rest me:
There is no strength left in my feet.
   Hades is near, and the night
   Is darkening down on my sight.
   Darlings, farewell: on the light   270
Long may ye look:—I have blessed ye
Ere your mother to nothingness fleet.
   ADMET. Ah me! for thy word rusheth bitterness
   o'er me,
Bitterness passing the anguish of death!
Forsake me not now, by the Gods I implore thee.
   By the babes thou wilt orphan, O yield not thy
   breath!   276
Look up, be of cheer: if thou diest, before me
   Is nothingness. Living, we aye live thine,
   And we die in thy death; for our hearts are a
   shrine   279
Wherein for thy love passing word we adore thee!
   ALCES. Admetus,—for thou seëst all my plight,—
Fain would I speak mine heart's wish ere I die.
I, honoring thee, and setting thee in place
Before mine own soul still to see this light,
Am dying, unconstrained to die for thee.   285
I might have wed what man Thessalian
I would, have dwelt wealth-crowned in princely
   halls;
Yet would not live on, torn away from thee,
With orphaned children: wherefore spared I not
The gifts of youth still mine, wherein I joyed.   290
Yet she that bare, he that begat, forsook thee,

Though fair for death their time of life was come,
Yea, fair, to save their son and die renowned.
Their own one wert thou: no hope there was
To get them sons thereafter, hadst thou died.   295
So had I lived, and thou, to after-days:
Thou wert not groaning, of thy wife bereaved,
Thy children motherless. Howbeit this
Some God hath brought to pass: it was to be.
So be it. Remember thou what thank is due   300
For this,—I never can ask full requital;
For naught there is more precious than the life,—
And justly due; for these thy babes thou lovest
No less than I, if that thine heart be right.
Suffer that they have lordship in mine home: 305
Wed not a stepdame to supplant our babes,
Whose heart shall tell her she is no Alcestis,
Whose jealous hand shall smite them, thine and
   mine.
Do not, ah, do not this—I pray thee, I!
For the new stepdame hateth still the babes   310
Of her that's gone with more than viper-venom.
The boy—his father is his tower of strength
To whom to speak, of whom to win reply;
But, O my child, what girlhood will be thine?
To thee what would she be, thy father's yoke-
   mate?   315
What if with ill report she smirched thy name,
And in thy youth's flower marred thy marriage-
   hopes?
For thee thy mother ne'er shall deck for bridal,
Nor hearten thee in travail, O my child,
There, where naught gentler than the mother is.
For I must die; nor shall it be to-morn,   321
Nor on the third day comes on me this doom:
Straightway of them that are not shall I be.
Farewell, be happy. Now for thee, my lord,
Abides the boast to have won the noblest wife,   325
For you, my babes, to have sprung from noblest
   mother.
   CHOR. Fear not; for I am bold to speak for him:
This will he do, an if he be not mad.
   ADMET. It shall, it shall be, fear not: thou alone
Living wast mine; and dead, mine only wife   330
Shalt thou be called: nor ever in thy stead
Shall bride Thessalian hail me as her lord.
None is there of a father so high-born,
None so for beauty peerless among women.
Children enough have I: I pray the Gods   335
For joy in these—lost is our joy in thee!
Not for a year's space will I mourn for thee,
But long as this my life shall last, dear wife,
Loathing my mother, hating mine own sire,
For in word only, not in deed, they loved me.   340

Thou gav'st in ransom for my life thine all
Of precious, and didst save. Do I not well
To groan, who lose such yokefellow in thee?
Revels shall cease, and gatherings at the wine,
Garlands, and song, which wont to fill mine
    house.   345
No, never more mine hand shall touch the lyre:
Nor will I lift up heart to sing to flute
Of Libya: stolen is life's joy with thee.
Fashioned by craftsmen's cunning hands, thy form
Imaged, shall lie as sleeping on a bed,   350
Falling whereon, and clasping with mine hands,
Calling thy name, in fancy shall mine arms
Hold my belovèd, though I hold her not:—
A drear delight, I wot: yet shall I lift   354
The burden from my soul. In dreams shalt thou
Haunt me and gladden: sweet to see the loved,
Though but as fleeting phantoms of the night.
But, were the tongue and strain of Orpheus mine,
To witch Demeter's Daughter and her lord,
And out of Hades by my song to win thee,   360
I had fared down; nor Pluto's Hound had stayed
    me,
Nor Spirit-wafter Charon at the oar,
Or ever I restored thy life to light.
Yet there look thou for me, whenso I die:
Prepare a home, as who shall dwell with me.   365
For in the selfsame cedar chest, wherein
Thou liest, will I bid them lay my bones
At thy side: never, not in death, from thee,
My one true loyal love, may I be sundered!
  Chor. Yea, I withal will mourn, as friend with
    friend,   370
With thee for this thy wife, for she is worthy.
  Alces. My children, ye yourselves have heard all
    this,
Have heard your father pledge him ne'er to wed
For your oppression and for my dishonor.   374
  Admet. Yea, now I say it, and I will perform.
  Alces. On these terms take the children from
    mine hand.
  Admet. I take them—precious gift from precious
    hand.
  Alces. Thou in my stead be a mother now to
    these.
  Admet. I must, I must—they are bereft of thee!
  Alces. Darlings, when most I need to live, I
    die.   380
  Admet. Ah me!—what shall I do, forlorn of
    thee?
  Alces. Thy wound shall time heal:—nothingness
    are the dead.

  Admet. Take me, ah take me with thee to the
    grave!
  Alces. Suffice it that one dies—she dies for thee.
  Admet. O Fate, of what a wife dost thou bereave
    me!   385
  Alces. Dark—dark—mine eyes are drooping,
    heavy-laden.
  Admet. Oh, I am lost if thou wilt leave me,
    wife!
  Alces. No more—I am no more: as naught ac-
    count me.
  Admet. Uplift thy face: forsake not thine own
    children!
  Alces. Sore loth do I—yet O farewell, my babes!
  Admet. Look on them—look!   391
  Alces.   Nothing am I henceforth.
  Admet. Ah, leav'st thou us?
  Alces.   Farewell.   [Dies.
  Admet.   O wretch undone!
  Chor. Gone,—gone! No more she lives, Ad-
    metus' wife!

STROPHE

  Eum. Woe for my lot!—to the tomb hath my
    mother descended, descended!
Never again, O my father, she seëth the light of
    the sun   395
In anguish she leaves us forsaken: the story is
    ended, is ended,
  Of her sheltering love, and the tale of the moth-
    erless life is begun.
Look—look on her eyelids, her hands drooping
    nerveless! O hear me, O hear me!
  It is I—I beseech thee, my mother!—thine own
    little, own little bird!
It is I—O, I cast me upon thee—thy lips are so
    near me, so near me;   400
Unto mine am I pressing them, mother!—I
    plead for a word—but a word!
  Admet. With her who heareth not, nor seëth: ye
And I are stricken with a heavy doom.

ANTISTROPHE

  Eum. And I am but a little one, father—so
    young, and forsaken, forsaken,
  Forlorn of my mother—O hapless! a weariful
    lot shall be mine!   405
And thou, little maiden, my sister, the burden hast
    taken, hast taken,
  Which thy brother may bear not alone, and a
    weariful lot shall be thine.

O father, of long-living love was thy marriage un-
    cherished, uncherished:
  Thou hast won not the goal of old age with the
    love of thy youth at thy side;
For, or ever she came to the fullness of days, she
    hath perished, hath perished;   410
  And the home is a wreck and a ruin, for thou,
    O my mother, hast died!
  CHOR. Admetus, this affliction must thou bear.
Not first of mortals thou, nor thou the last
Hast lost a noble wife; and, be thou sure,
From us, from all, this debt is due—to die.   415
  ADMET. I know it: nowise unforeseen this ill
Hath swooped on me: long anguished I foreknew
    it.
But—for to burial must I bear my dead—
Stay ye, and, tarrying, echo back my wail
To that dark God whom no drink-offerings move.
And all Thessalians over whom I rule   421
I bid take part in mourning for this woman
With shaven head and sable-shrouding robe.
And ye which yoke the cars four-horsed, or
    steeds
Of single frontlet, shear with steel their manes.
Music of flutes the city through, or lyres,   426
Be none, while twelve moons round their circles
    out:
For dearer dead, or kinder unto me
I shall not bury: worthy of mine honor
Is she, for she alone hath died for me.   430
    [*Exit with attendants bearing in the corpse.*

STROPHE I

  CHOR. O Pelias' daughter, I hail thee:
  I wave thee eternal farewell
To thine home where the darkness must veil thee,
  Where in Hades unsunned thou shalt dwell.
Know, Dark-haired, thy gray Spirit-wafter   435
  Hath sped not with twy-plashing oar
Woman nobler, nor shall speed hereafter
        To Acheron's shore.

ANTISTROPHE I

For the seven-stringed shell, or for pæan
  Unharped, shall thy fame be a song,   440
When o'er Sparta the moon Carnean
  High rideth the whole night long.
And in Athens the wealthy and splendid
  Shall thy name on her bards' lips ring;
Such a theme hast thou left to be blended   445
        With the lays that they sing.

STROPHE 2

O that the power were but in me,
  From the chambers of Hades, to light,
And from streams of Cocytus, to win thee
  With the oar of the River of Night!   450
O dear among women, strong-hearted
  From Hades to ransom thy lord!
Never spirit in such wise departed.
  Light lie on thee, Lady, the sward!
And, if ever thine husband shall mate him   455
  Again with a bride in thy stead,
I will loathe him, his children shall hate him,
        The babes of the dead.

ANTISTROPHE 2

When his mother would not be contented
  To hide her for him in the tomb,   460
Nor his gray-haired father consented,
  Unholpen he looked on his doom.
Whom they bare—the hard-hearted!—they cared
    not,
  Though hoary their locks were, to save!
Thou art gone, for thy great love spared not   465
  Thy blossom of youth from the grave.
Ah, may it be mine, such communion
  Of hearts!—'tis vouchsafed unto few:—
Then ours should be sorrowless union
        Our life-days through.   470

Enter HERCULES.

  HERC. Strangers, who dwell in this Pheræan land,
Say, do I find Admetus in his home?
  CHOR. Hercules, in his home is Pheres' son.
Yet say, what brings thee to Thessalian land, 474
That thou shouldst come to this Pheræan town?
  HERC. A toil for King Eurystheus, lord of Tiryns.
  CHOR. And whither journeyest? To what wan-
    derings yoked?
  HERC. For Thracian Diomedes' four-horsed car.
  CHOR. How canst thou? Sure he is unknown to
    thee!   479
  HERC. Unknown: Bistonian land I never saw.
  CHOR. Not save by battle may those steeds be
    won.
  HERC. Yet flinch I may not from the appointed
    toils.
  CHOR. Thy life or his—a triumph or a grave.
  HERC. Not this the first time I have run such
    course.   484
  CHOR. What profit is it if thou slay their lord?
  HERC. Those steeds shall I drive back to Tiryns'
    king.

CHOR. Hard task, to set the bit betwixt their jaws.

HERC. That shall I, if their nostrils breathe not fire.

CHOR. Yea, but with ravening jaws do they rend men.

HERC. Go to—thus mountain-wolves, not horses, feast.   490

CHOR. Nay, thou canst see their cribs besprent with gore.

HERC. Whom boasteth he for father, he that reared them?

CHOR. Ares, the lord of Thracia's golden shields.

HERC. Thou say'st: such toil my fate imposeth still,

Harsh evermore, uphillward straining aye,   495
If I must still in battle close with sons
Gotten of Ares; with Lycaon first,
And Cycnus then; and lo, I come to grapple—
The third strife this—with yon steeds and their lord.

But the man lives not who shall ever see   500
Alcmena's son flinch from a foeman's hand.

CHOR. Lo, there himself, the ruler of the realm,
Admetus, cometh forth his palace-hall.

Enter ADMETUS.

ADMET. Joy to thee, sprung from Zeus' and Perseus' blood!   504

HERC. Admetus, joy to thee, Thessalia's king!

ADMET. [*aside*]. Joy?—would 'twere mine! [*aloud*] Thanks!—thy good heart I know.

HERC. Wherefore for mourning shaven show'st thou thus?

ADMET. This day must I commit to earth a corpse.

HERC. Now heaven forfend thou mourn'st for children dead!

ADMET. In mine home live the babes whom I begat.   510

HERC. Sooth, death-ripe were thy sire, if he be gone.

ADMET. He liveth, and my mother, Hercules.

HERC. Surely, O surely, not thy wife, Admetus?

ADMET. Twofold must be mine answer touching her.

HERC. Or hath she died, say'st thou, or liveth yet?   515

ADMET. She is, and she is not: here lies my grief.

HERC. Nothing the more I know: dark sayings thine.

ADMET. Know'st not the fate to which she is foredoomed?

HERC. I know she pledged herself to die for thee.

ADMET. How lives she then, if she to this consented?   520

HERC. Mourn not thy wife ere dead: abide the hour.

ADMET. One doomed is dead; the dead hath ceased to be.

HERC. Diverse are these—to be and not to be.

ADMET. This, Hercules, thy sentence: that is mine.

HERC. But now, why weep'st thou? What dear friend is dead?   525

ADMET. A woman—hers the memory we mourn.

HERC. Some stranger born, or nigh of kin to thee?

ADMET. A stranger born: yet near and dear to us.

HERC. How died a stranger then in house of thine?

ADMET. An orphan here she dwelt, her father dead.   530

HERC. Would I had found thee mourning not, Admetus.

ADMET. Aye so?—what purpose lurketh 'neath thy word?

HERC. On will I to another host's hearth-welcome.

ADMET. It cannot be: may no such grief befall!

HERC. A burden unto mourners comes the guest.

ADMET. Dead are the dead:—but enter thou mine house.   536

HERC. 'Twere shame to banquet in the house of weeping.

ADMET. Aloof the guest-halls are where we will lodge thee.

HERC. Let me pass on: so earn my thanks untold.   539

ADMET. Unto another's hearth thou canst not go.
[*To an attendant*] Ho thou, lead on: open the guest-halls looking
Away from these our chambers. Tell my stewards
To set on meat in plenty. Shut withal
The mid-court doors: it fits not that the guests, 544
The while they feast, hear wailings, and be vexed.
[*Exit* HERCULES.

CHOR. What dost thou?—such affliction at the door,
And guests for thee, Admetus? Art thou mad?

ADMET. But had I driven him from my home and city
Who came my guest, then hadst thou praised me more?
Nay, verily: mine affliction so had grown   550
No less, and more inhospitable were I!

And to mine ills were added this beside,
That this my home were called "Guest-hating
    Hall."
Yea, and myself have proved him kindliest host
Whene'er to Argos' thirsty plain I fared.   555
  Chor. Why hide then the dread Presence in the
    house,
When came a friend? Thyself hast named him
    friend.
    Admet. Never had he been won to pass my
    doors,
Had he one whit of mine afflictions known.
To some, I wot, not wise herein I seem,   560
Nor will such praise: but mine halls have not
    learnt
To thrust away nor to dishonor guests.

STROPHE 1

  Chor. Halls thronged of the guests ever wel-
    come, O dwelling
Of a hero, for ever the home of the free,   564
The Lord of the lyre-strings sweet beyond telling,
    Apollo, hath deignèd to sojourn in thee,
Amid thine habitations, a shepherd of sheep,
The flocks of Admetus he scorned not to keep,
  While the shepherds' bridal-strains, soft-swell-
    ing   569
  From his pipe, pealed over the slant-sloped lea.

ANTISTROPHE 1

And the spotted lynxes for joy of thy singing
  Mixed with thy flocks; and from Othrys' dell
Trooped tawny lions: the witchery-winging
  Notes brought dancing around thy shell,
Phœbus, the dappled fawn from the shadow   575
Of the tall-tressed pines tripping forth to the
    meadow,
Beating time to the chime of the rapture-ringing
  Music, with light feet tranced by its spell.

STROPHE 2

Wherefore the flocks of my lord unnumbered
  By the Bœbian mere fair-rippling stray: 580
Where the steeds of the sun halt, darkness-cum-
    bered,
  By Molossian mountains, far away
The borders lie of his golden grain,
And his rolling stretches of pasture-plain;   584
And the havenless beach Ægean hath slumbered
  Under Pelion long 'neath the peace of his sway.

ANTISTROPHE 2

And now, with the tears from his eyes fast-raining.
  Wide hath he opened his doors to the guest,
While newly his heart 'neath its burden is strain-
    ing,
  For the wife that hath died in his halls dis-
    tressed.   590
For to honor's heights are the high-born lifted,
And the good are with truest wisdom gifted;
And there broods on mine heart bright trust un-
    waning
  That the god-reverer shall yet be blest.

  Admet. O kindly presence of Pheræan men,   595
This corpse even now, with all things meet, my
    servants
Bear on their shoulders to the tomb and pyre.
Wherefore, as custom is, hail ye the dead,
On the last journey as she goeth forth.
  Chor. Lo, I behold thy sire with aged foot   600
Advancing: his attendants in their hands
Bear ornaments to deck the dead withal.

Enter Pheres *with attendants bearing gifts.*

  Pher. I come in thine afflictions sorrowing, son
A noble wife and virtuous hast thou lost,
None will gainsay: yet these calamities   605
We needs must bear, how hard to bear soever.
Receive these ornaments, and let her pass
Beneath the earth: well may the corpse be honored
Of her who for thy life's sake died, my son;
Who made me not unchilded, left me not   610
Forlorn of thee to pine in woeful eld.
In all her sisters' eyes she hath crowned her life
With glory, daring such a deed as this.
O savior of my son, who hast raised us up
In act to fall, all hail! May bliss be thine   615
Even in Hades. Thus to wed, I say,
Profiteth men—or nothing-worth is marriage.
  Admet. Not bidden of me to her burial comest
    thou,
Nor count I thine the presence of a friend.
Thine ornaments she never shall put on;   620
She shall be buried needing naught of thine.
Thou grieve!—thou shouldst have grieved in my
    death-hour!
Thou stood'st aloof—the old, didst leave the young
To die:—and wilt thou wail upon this corpse?
Wast thou not, then, true father of my body?   625
Did she that said she bare me, and was called
Mother, not give me birth? Of bondman blood
To thy wife's breast was I brought privily?

Put to the test, thou showedst who thou art,
And I account me not thy true-born son. 630
Peerless of men in soulless cowardice!
So old, and standing on the verge of life,
Thou hadst no will, no heart hadst thou to die
For thine own son? Ye let her die, a woman
Not of our house, whom I with righteous cause
Might count alone my mother and my father. 636
Yet here was honor, hadst thou dared the strife,
In dying for thy son. A paltry space
To cling to life in any wise was left.
Then had I lived, and she, through days to come,
Nor I, left lorn, should thus mine ills bemoan. 641
Yet all that may the fortunate betide
Fell to thy lot; in manhood's prime a king,
Me hadst thou son and heir unto thine house,
So that thou wast not, dying, like to leave 645
A childless home for stranger folk to spoil.
Nor canst thou say that flouting thy gray hairs
I had giv'n thee up to death, whose reverence
For thee was passing word:—and this the thank
That thou and she that bare me render me! 650
Wherefore, make haste: beget thee other sons
To foster thy gray hairs, to compass thee.
With death's observance, and lay out thy corpse.
Not I with this mine hand will bury thee.
For thee dead am I. If I see the light,— 655
Another savior found,—I call me son
To him, and loving fosterer of his age.
With false lips pray the old for death's release,
Plaining of age and weary-wearing time.
Let death draw near—who hails his coming?
    None: 660
No more is eld a burden unto them.
    CHOR. O hush! Suffice the affliction at the doors.
O son, infuriate not thy father's soul.
    PHER. Son, whom, think'st thou—some Lydian
        slave or Phrygian
Bought with thy money?—thus beratest thou? 665
What, know'st thou not that I Thessalian am,
Sprung from Thessalian sire, free man true-born?
This insolence passeth!—hurling malapert words
On me, not lightly thus shalt thou come off!
Thee I begat and nurtured, of mine house 670
The heir: no debt is mine to die for thee.
Not from my sires such custom I received
That sires for sons should die: no Greek law this.
Born for thyself wast thou, to fortune good
Or evil: all thy dues from me thou hast. 675
O'er many folk thou rulest; wide demesnes
Shall I leave thee: to me my father left them.
What is my wrong, my robbery of thee?
For me die thou not, I die not for thee.

Thou joy'st to see light—shall thy father joy not?
Sooth, I account our time beneath the earth 681
Long, and our life-space short, yet is it sweet.
Shamelessly hast thou fought against thy death:
Thy life is but transgression of thy doom
And murder of thy wife! *My* cowardice!— 685
This from thee, dastard, by a woman outdone
Who died for thee, the glorious-gallant youth!
Cunning device hast thou devised to die
Never, cajoling still wife after wife
To die for thee!—and dost revile thy friends 690
Who will not so—and thou the coward, thou?
Peace! e'en bethink thee, if thou lov'st thy life,
So all love theirs. Thou, if thou speakest evil
Of us, shalt hear much evil, and that true.
    CHOR. Ye have said too much, thou now, and he
        before. 695
Refrain, old sire, from railing on thy son.
    ADMET. Say on, say on; I have said: if hearing
        truth
Gall thee, thou shouldest not have done me wrong.
    PHER. I had done more wrong, had I died for
        thee.
    ADMET. What, for the young and old is death the
        same? 700
    PHER. One life to live, not twain—this is our due.
    ADMET. Have thy desire—one life outlasting
        Zeus.
    PHER. Dost curse thy parents, who hast had no
        wrong?
    ADMET. Aye, whom I marked love-sick for date-
        less life.
    PHER. What?—art not burying her in thine own
        stead? 705
    ADMET. A token, dastard, of thy cowardice.
    PHER. *I* did her not to death: thou canst not
        say it.
    ADMET. Mayest thou feel thy need of me some
        day!
    PHER. Woo many women, that the more may
        die.
    ADMET. This taunt strikes thee—'tis thou wast
        loth to die. 710
    PHER. Sweet is yon sun-god's light, yea, it is
        sweet.
    ADMET. Base is thy spirit, and unmeet for men.
    PHER. Not mine old corpse to the grave thou
        bear'st with glee!
    ADMET. Yet, when thou diest, in ill fame shalt
        thou die.
    PHER. Ill fame is naught to me when I have
        died. 715

ADMET. Hear him! how full of shamelessness
    is eld!
PHER. Not shameless she,—but senseless hast
    thou found her.
ADMET. Begone: leave me to bury this my dead.
PHER. I go: her murderer will bury her!   720
Thou shalt yet answer for it to her kin.
Surely Acastus is no more a man,
If he of thee claim not his sister's blood.

                      [*Exit.*
ADMET. Avaunt, with her that kenneleth with
    thee!
Childless grow old, as ye deserve, while lives
Your child: ye shall not come beneath one roof   725
With me. If need were to renounce by heralds
Thine hearth paternal, I had renounced it now.
Let us—for we must bear the present ill—
Pass on, to lay our dead upon the pyre.
    CHOR. Alas for the loving and daring!   730
        Farewell to the noblest and best!
      May Hermes conduct thee down-faring
        Kindly, and Hades to rest
      Receive thee! If any atonement
        For ills even there may betide   735
      To the good, O thine be enthronement
        By Hades' bride!
        [*Exeunt* OMNES *in funeral procession.*

Enter SERVANT.

SERV. Full many a guest, from many a land
    which came
Unto Admetus' dwelling, have I known,
Have set before them meat: but never guest   740
More pestilent received I to this hearth:
Who first, albeit he saw my master mourning,
Entered, and passed the threshold unashamed;
Then, nowise courteously received the fare   744
Found with us, though our woeful plight he knew,
But, what we brought not, hectoring bade us bring.
The ivy cup uplifts he in his hands,
And swills the darkling mother's fiery blood,
Till the wine's flame enwrapped him, heating him.
Then did he wreathe his head with myrtle sprays,
Dissonant-howling. Diverse strains were heard: 751
For he sang on, regardless all of ills
Darkening Admetus' house; we servants wept
Our mistress: yet we showed not to the guest
Eyes tear-bedewed, for so Admetus bade.   755
And now within the house must I be feasting
This guest,—a lawless thief, a bandit rogue,
While forth the house she is borne! I followed not,
Nor stretched the hand, nor wailed unto my mis-
    tress

Farewell, who was to me and all the household   760
A mother; for from ills untold she saved us,
Assuaging her lord's wrath. Do I not well
To loathe this guest, intruder on our griefs?

Enter HERCULES.

HERC. Ho, fellow, why this solemn brooding
    look?
The servant should not lower upon the guest,   765
But welcome him with kindly-beaming cheer.
Thou, seeing here in presence thy lord's friend,
With visage sour and cloud of knitted brows
Receiv'st him, fretting o'er an alien grief.
Hither to me, that wiser thou mayst grow.   770
The lot of man—its nature knowest thou?
I trow not: how shouldst thou? Give ear to me.
From all mankind the debt of death is due,
Nor of all mortals is there one that knows
If through the coming morrow he shall live: 775
For trackless is the way of fortune's feet,
Not to be taught, nor won by art of man.
This hearing then, and learning it from me,
Make merry, drink: the life from day to day
Account thine own, all else in fortune's power.
Honor withal the sweetest of the Gods   781
To men, the Cyprian Queen—a gracious Goddess!
Away with other thoughts, and heed my words,
If thou dost think I speak wise words and true:
So think I. Hence with sorrow overwrought;   785
Rise above this affliction: drink with me,
Thy brows with garlands bound. Full well I wot,
From all this lowering spirit prison-pent
Thine anchor shall Sir Beaker's plash upheave.
What, man!—the mortal must be mortal-minded.
So, for your solemn wights of knitted brows,   791
For each and all,—if thou for judge wilt take me,—
Life is not truly life, but mere affliction.
    SERV. All this we know: but now are we in
    plight
Not meet for laughter and for revelry.   795
    HERC. The woman dead is alien-born: grieve not
Exceeding much. Yet live the household's lords.
    SERV. Live, quotha!—know'st thou not the house's
    ills?
    HERC. Yea, if thy master lied not unto me.
    SERV. Guest-fain he is—ah, guest-fain overmuch!
    HERC. A stranger dead—and no guest-cheer for
    me?   801
    SERV. O yea, an alien—overmuch an alien!
    HERC. Ha! was he keeping some affliction back?
    SERV. Go thou in peace: our lord's ills are for us.

Turns away; but HERCULES *seizes him, and makes
        him face him.*

HERC. Grief for a stranger—such words mean
    not that!   805
SERV. Else had I not sore vexed beheld thy revel.
HERC. How! have I sorry handling of mine
    hosts?
SERV. Thou cam'st in hour unmeet for welcom-
    ing,
For grief is on us; and thou see'st shorn hair
And vesture of black robes.
HERC.   But who hath died?
Not of the children one, or gray-haired sire?   811
SERV. Nay, but Admetus' wife is dead, O guest.
HERC. How say'st thou?—Ha, even then ye gave
    me welcome?
SERV. For shame he could not thrust thee from
    these doors.
HERC. O hapless! what a helpmeet hast thou
    lost!   815
SERV. We have all perished, and not she alone.
HERC. I felt it, when I saw his tear-drowned eyes,
His shaven hair, his face: yet he prevailed,
Saying he bare a stranger-friend to burial.
I passed this threshold in mine heart's despite,   820
And drank in halls of him that loves the guest,
When thus his plight! And am I reveling
With wreathed head? O my friend, that thou
    shouldst say
Naught, when on thine home such affliction
    lay! . . .   824
Where doth he bury her? Where shall I find her?
  SERV. By the straight path that leads Larissa-
    wards
Shalt see the hewn-stone tomb without the walls.
  HERC. O much-enduring heart and hand of mine,
Now show what son the Lady of Tiryns bare,
Electryon's child Alcmena, unto Zeus.   830
For I must save the woman newly dead,
And set Alcestis in this house again
And render to Admetus good for good.
I go. The sabled-vestured King of Corpses,
Death, will I watch for, and shall find, I trow,   835
Drinking the death-draught hard beside the tomb.
And if I lie in wait, and dart from ambush,
And seize, and with mine arms' coil compass him,
None is there shall deliver from mine hands
His straining sides, ere he yield up his prey.   840
Yea, though I miss the quarry, and he come not
Unto the blood-clot, to the sunless homes
Down will I fare of Cora and her King,
And make demand. I doubt not I shall lead
Alcestis up, and give to mine host's hands,   845
Who to his halls received, nor drave me thence,
Albeit smitten with affliction sore,

But hid it, like a prince, respecting me.
Who is more guest-fain of Thessalians?
Who in all Hellas? O, he shall not say   850
That one so princely showed a base man kindness.
                          [*Exit*

Enter ADMETUS, *with Chorus and attendants, re-*
turning from the funeral.

  ADMET. O hateful returning!
        O hateful to see
      Drear halls full of yearning
        For the lost—ah me!   855
What aim or what rest have I?—silence or speech,
    of what help shall they be?
        Would God I were dead!
         O, I came from the womb
        To a destiny dread!
         Ah, those in the tomb—   860
How I envy them! How I desire them, and long
    to abide in their home!
        To mine eyes nothing sweet
        Is the light of the heaven,
        Nor the earth to my feet;
        Such a helpmeet is riven   865
By Death from my side, and my darling to Hades
    the spoiler hath given.

STROPHE

CHOR.   Pass on thou, and hide thee
        In thy chambers.
ADMET.   Ah woe!
CHOR.   Wail the griefs that betide thee:
        How canst thou but so?   870
ADMET. O God!
CHOR.   Thou hast passed through deep
    waters of anguish—I know it, I know.
ADMET. Woe! darkest of days!
CHOR.   No help bringeth this
        To thy love in that place.
ADMET. Woe!
CHOR.   Bitter it is   875
The face of a wife well-belovèd for ever and ever
    to miss.
ADMET. Thou hast stricken mine heart
        Where the wound will not heal.
      What is worse than to part
        From the loving and leal?   880
Would God I had wedded her not, home-bliss with
    Alcestis to feel!
        O, I envy the lot
        Of the man without wife,

        Without child: single-wrought
          Is the strand of his life: 885
No soul-crushing burden of sorrow, no strength-
    overmastering strife.
        But that children should sicken,
          That gloom of despair
        Over bride-beds should thicken,
          What spirit can bear,   890
When childless, unwedded, a man through life's
    calm journey might fare?

ANTISTROPHE

CHOR.   Thee Fortune hath met,
        Strong wrestler, and thrown;
        Yet no bounds hast thou set—
ADMET.   Woe's me!—
CHOR.   To thy moan.   895
O, thy burden is heavy!
ADMET.   Alas!
CHOR.   Yet endure it: thou art not alone.
        Not thou art the first
        Of bereaved ones.
ADMET.   Ah me!
CHOR.   Such tempest hath burst   900
        Upon many ere thee.
Unto each his mischance, when the surges roll up
    from Calamity's sea.
ADMET.   O long grief and pain
        For belovèd ones passed!
        Why didst thou restrain,   905
        When myself I had cast
Down into her grave, with the noblest to lie peace-
    lulled at the last?
        Not one soul, but two
        Had been Hades' prey,
        Souls utterly true   910
        United for aye,
Which together o'er waves of the underworld-
    mere had passed this day.

STROPHE

CHOR.   Of my kin was there one,
        And the life's light failed
        In his halls of a son,   915
        One meet to be wailed,
His only belovèd: howbeit the manhood within
    him prevailed;
        And the ills heaven-sent
        As a man did he bear,
        Though by this was he bent   920
        Unto silvered hair,

Far on in life's path, without son for his remnant
    of weakness to care.
ADMET.   O, how can I tread
        Thy threshold, fair home?
        How shelter mine head   925
        'Neath thy roof, now the doom
Of my fate's dice changeth?—ah me, what change
    upon all things is come!
        For with torches aflame
        Of the Pelian pine,
        And with bride-song I came   930
        In that hour divine,
Upbearing the hand of a wife—thine hand, O dar-
    ling mine!
        Followed revelers, raising
        Acclaim: ever broke
        From the lips of them praising,   935
        Of the dead as they spoke,
And of me, how the noble, the children of kings,
    Love joined 'neath his yoke.
        But for bridal song
        Is the wail for the dead,
        And, for white-robed throng,   940
        Black vesture hath led
Me to halls where the ghost of delight lieth
    couched on a desolate bed.

ANTISTROPHE

CHOR.   To the trance of thy bliss
        Sudden anguish was brought.
        Never lesson like this   945
        To thine heart had been taught:
Yet thy life hast thou won, and thy soul hast de-
    livered from death:—is it naught?
        Thy wife hath departed:
        Love tender and true
        Hath she left:—stricken-hearted,   950
        Wherein is this new?
Hath Death not unyoked from the chariot of Love
    full many ere you?
ADMET. Friends, I account the fortune of my
    wife
Happier than mine, albeit it seem not so.
For naught of grief shall touch her any more,   955
And glorious rest she finds from many toils.
But I, unmeet to live, my doom outrun,
Shall drag out bitter days: I know it now.
How shall I bear to enter this mine home?   959
Speaking to whom, and having speech of whom,
Shall I find joy of entering?—whither turn me?
The solitude within shall drive me forth,
Whenso I see my wife's couch tenantless,   963

And seats whereon she sat, and, 'neath the roof,
All foul the floor; when on my knees my babes
Falling shall weep their mother, servants moan
The peerless mistress from the mansion lost.
All this within: but from the world without
Me shall Thessalian bridals chase, and throngs
Where women gossip—oh, I shall not bear   970
On these, young matrons like my wife, to look!
And whatsoever foe I have shall scoff:
"Lo there who basely liveth—dared not die,
"But whom he wedded gave, a coward's ransom,
"And 'scaped from Hades. Count ye him a man?
"He hates his parents, though himself was loth   976
"To die!" Such ill report, besides my griefs,
Shall mine be. Ah, what honor is mine to live,
O friends, in evil fame, in evil plight?

STROPHE I

CHOR. I have mused on the words of the wise,
  Of the mighty in song;   981
I have lifted mine heart to the skies,
I have searched all truth with mine eyes;
  But naught more strong
Than Fate have I found: there is naught   985
  In the tablets of Thrace,
Neither drugs whereof Orpheus taught,
Nor in all that Apollo brought
  To Asclepius' race,
When the herbs of healing he severed, and out of
  their anguish delivered   990
The pain-distraught.

ANTISTROPHE I

There is none other Goddess beside
  To the altars of whom
No man draweth near, nor hath cried
To her image, nor victim hath died,   995
  Averting her doom.
O Goddess, more mighty for ill
  Come not upon me
Than in days overpast: for his will
Even Zeus may in no wise fulfill   1000
  Unholpen of thee.
Steel is molten as water before thee, but never re-
  lenting came o'er thee,
  Who art ruthless still.

STROPHE II

Thee, friend, hath the Goddess gripped: from her
  hands never wrestler hath slipped.

Yet be strong to endure: never mourning shall
  bring our belovèd returning   1005
  From the nethergloom up to the light.
Yea, the heroes of Gods begotten,
They fade into darkness, forgotten
  In death's chill night.
Dear was she in days ere we lost her,   1010
  Dear yet, though she lie with the dead.
None nobler shall Earth-mother foster
  Than the wife of thy bed.

ANTISTROPHE II

Not as mounds of the dead which have died, so
  account we the tomb of thy bride:
But O, let the worship and honor that we render to
  Gods rest upon her: 1015
  Unto her let the wayfarer pray.
As he treadeth the pathway that trendeth
Aside from the highway, and bendeth
  At her shrine, he shall say:
"Her life for her lord's was given;   1020
  With the Blest now abides she on high.
Hail, Queen, show us grace from thine heaven!"
  Even so shall they cry.
But lo, Alcmena's son, as seemeth, yonder,
Admetus, to thine hearth is journeying.   1025

Enter HERCULES, *leading a woman wholly veiled.*

HERC. Unto a friend behoveth speech outspoken,
Admetus, not to hide within the breast
Murmurs unvoiced. I came mid thine affliction:
Fair claim was mine to rank amidst thy friends:
Thou told'st me not how lay thy wife a corpse;
Thou gavest me guest-welcome in thine home,   1031
Making pretense of mourning for a stranger.
I wreathed mine head, I spilled unto the Gods
Drink-offerings in a stricken house, even thine.
I blame thee, thus mishandled, yea, I blame;   1035
Yet nowise is my will to gall thy grief.
But wherefore hither turning back I come,
This will I tell. Take, guard for me this maid,
Till, leading hitherward the Thracian mares,
I come from slaughter of Bistonia's lord.   1040
But if I fall—no, no! I *must* return!—
I give her then, for service of thine halls.
Prize of hard toil unto mine hands she came:
For certain men I found but now arraying
An athlete-strife, toil-worthy, for all comers, 1045
Whence I have won and bring this victor's meed.
Horses there were for them to take which won
The light foot's triumph; but for hero-strife,
Boxing and wrestling, oxen were the guerdon;

A woman made it richer. Shame it seemed   1050
To hap thereon, and slip this glorious gain.
But, as I said, this woman be thy care;
For no thief's prize, but toil-achieved, I bring her.
Yea, one day thou perchance shalt say 'twas well.
   ADMET. Not flouting thee, nor counting among
     foes,   1055
My wife's unhappy fate I hid from thee.
But this had been but grief uppiled on grief,
Hadst thou sped hence to be another's guest;
And mine own ills sufficed me to bewail.
Yon maid—I pray thee, if it may be, prince,   1060
Bid some Thessalian ward her, who hath not
Suffered as I: thou hast many friends in Pheræ.
Oh, waken not remembrance of my grief!
I could not, seeing her mine halls within,
Be tearless: add not hurt unto mine hurt;   1065
Burdened enough am I by mine affliction.
Nay, in mine house where should a young maid
     lodge?—
For vesture and adorning speak her young:—
What, 'neath the men's roof shall her lodging be?
And how unsullied, dwelling with young men?
Not easy is it, Hercules, to curb   1071
The young: herein do I take thought for thee.
Or shall I ope to her my dead wife's bower?
How!—cause her to usurp my lost love's bed?
Twofold reproach I dread—first, from my folk,
Lest any say that, traitor to my savior,   1076
I fall upon another woman's bed;
Then, from my dead wife—oh, she is reverence-
     worthy!—
Of her must I be heedful. Woman, thou
Whoso thou art, know that thy body's stature
Is as Alcestis, and thy form as hers.   1081
Ah me!—lead, for the Gods' sake, from my sight
This woman! Take not my captivity captive.
For, as I look on her, methinks I see
My wife: she stirs mine heart with turmoil: foun-
     tains   1085
Of tears burst from mine eyes. O wretched I!
Now first I taste this grief's full bitterness.
   CHOR. In sooth thy fortune can I not commend:
Yet all Heaven's visitations must we bear.
   HERC. O that such might I had as back to bring
To light thy wife from nethergloom abodes,   1091
And to bestow this kindness upon thee!
   ADMET. Fain would'st thou, well I know. But
     wherefore this?
It cannot be the dead to light should come.
   HERC. O'ershoot not thou the mark; bear bravely
     all.   1095

   ADMET. Easier to exhort than suffer and be
     strong.
   HERC. But what thy profit, though for aye thou
     moan?
   ADMET. I too know this; yet love drives me dis-
     traught.
   HERC. Love for the lost—aye, that draws forth
     the tear.
   ADMET. She hath undone me more than words
     can tell.   1100
   HERC. A good wife hast thou lost, who shall
     gainsay?
   ADMET. So that thy friend hath no more joy in
     life.
   HERC. Time shall bring healing; now is thy grief
     young.
   ADMET. Time—time?—O yea, if this thy Time
     be Death!
   HERC. A young wife, new love-yearning, shall
     console thee.   1105
   ADMET. Hush!—what say'st thou?—I could not
     think thereon!
   HERC. How?—wilt not wed, but widowed keep
     thy couch?
   ADMET. Lives not the woman that shall couch
     with me.
   HERC. Look'st thou that this shall profit aught
     the dead?
   ADMET. I needs must honor her where'er she
     be.   1110
   HERC. Good—good—yet this the world calls
     foolishness.
   ADMET. So be it, so thou call me bridegroom
     never.
   HERC. I praise thee, in that leal thou art to her.
   ADMET. I?—false to her, though dead?—may I
     die first!
   HERC. Receive this woman then these halls
     within.   1115
   ADMET. Nay!—I implore thee by thy father
     Zeus!
   HERC. Yet shalt thou err if thou do not this
     thing.
   ADMET. Yet shall mine heart be tortured, if I do
     it.
   HERC. Yield thou: this grace may prove per-
     chance a duty.
   ADMET. O that in strife thou ne'er hadst won
     this maid!   1120
   HERC. Yet thy friend's victory is surely thine.
   ADMET. Well said: yet let the woman hence
     depart.

HERC. Yea—if need be. First look well—need it
be?

ADMET. Needs must—save thou wilt else be
wroth with me.

HERC. I too know what I do, insisting thus. 1125

ADMET. Have then thy will: thy pleasure is my
pain.

HERC. Yet one day shalt thou praise me: only
yield.

ADMET. [to attendants]. Lead ye her, if mine
halls must needs receive.

HERC. Nay, to no servants' hands will I commit
her.

ADMET. Thou lead her in then, if it seems thee
good. 1130

HERC. Nay, but in thine hands will I place her—
thine.

ADMET. I will not touch her! Open stand my
doors.

HERC. Unto thy right hand only trust I her.

ADMET. King, thou dost force me, sore against
my will!

HERC. Be strong: stretch forth thine hand and
touch thy guest. 1135

ADMET. [turning his face away]. I do, as one
who doth behead a Gorgon.

HERC. Hast her?

ADMET.   I have.

HERC.   Yea, guard her. Thou shalt call
The child of Zeus one day a noble guest.

[Raises the veil, and discloses ALCESTIS.

Look on her, if in aught she seems to thee
Like to thy wife. Step forth from grief to bliss.

ADMET. What shall I say?—Gods! Marvel this
unhoped for! 1141
My wife do I behold in very sooth,
Or doth some god-sent mockery-joy distract me?

HERC. Not so; but this thou seëst is thy wife.

ADMET. What if this be some phantom from the
shades? 1145

HERC. No ghost-upraiser hast thou ta'en for
guest.

ADMET. How?—whom I buried do I see—my
wife?

HERC. Doubt not: yet might'st thou well mistrust thy fortune.

ADMET. As wife, as living, may I touch, address
her?

HERC. Speak to her: all thou didst desire thou
hast. 1150

ADMET. Oh, dearest!—wife!—sweet face!—belovèd form!
Past hope I have thee! Never I thought to see
thee!

HERC. Thou hast: may no God of thy bliss be
jealous.

ADMET. O scion nobly-born of Zeus most high,
Blessings on thee! The Father who begat thee 1155
Keep thee! Thou only hast restored my fortunes.
How didst thou bring her from the shades to
light?

HERC. I closed in conflict with the Lord of
Spirits.

ADMET. Where, say'st thou, didst thou fight this
fight with Death?

HERC. From ambush by the tomb mine hands
ensnared him. 1160

ADMET. Now wherefore speechless standeth thus
my wife?

HERC. 'Tis not vouchsafed thee yet to hear her
voice.
Ere to the Powers beneath the earth she be
Unconsecrated, and the third day come.
But lead her in, and, just man as thou art, 1165
Henceforth, Admetus, reverence still the guest.
Farewell. But I must go, and work the work
Set by the king, the son of Sthenelus.

ADMET. Abide with us, a sharer of our hearth.

HERC. Hereafter this: now must I hasten on. 1170

ADMET. O prosper thou, and come again in
peace!

[Exit HERCULES.

Through all my realm I publish to my folk
That, for these blessings, dances they array,
And that atonement-fumes from altars rise.
For now to happier days than those o'erpast 1175
Have we attained. I own me blest indeed.

CHOR. O the works of the Gods—in manifold
forms they reveal them:
Manifold things unhoped-for the Gods to accomplishment bring.
And the things that we looked for, the Gods deign
not to fulfill them;
And the paths undiscerned of our eyes, the Gods
unseal them. 1180
So fell this marvelous thing.

[Exeunt OMNES.

GREEK AND LATIN COMEDY

Out of remote fertility rites, full of orgiastic ribaldry, and out of folk festivals in which rudimentary satire was present, the fifth-century Greek developed a second form of drama—light-hearted, gay, and barbed—which we call comedy. In the fifth century, comedy acquired a fanciful and extravagant form, named "Aristophanic" after its leading and only surviving playwright Aristophanes. In the fourth century, arose a second form that is most aptly described as domestic comedy or comedy of manners. The marked difference between the two types was quickly recognized by the Greeks themselves when they called the early type Old Comedy and the later one New Comedy.

Aristophanic comedy was the product of the mercurial, sophisticated, and intellectual Periclean age, of its democratic tolerance of political discussion and satire, even to the point of permitting the lampooning of public characters. And for its subject-matter this comedy drew upon the follies and abuses of democracy when the rule of the people led to demagoguery, a slackening of morale, and imperialism. In form, this dramatic composition resembled modern extravaganza, contemporary musical comedy. In *The Frogs*, for example, Aristophanes selected a fanciful situation, sending Bacchus (Dionysus) down to the underworld, giving him odd and irreverent adventures on the way, and making him the judge of a literary contest between ghosts of Æschylus and Euripides who parody each other's style with exuberant aptitude. In *The Birds*, Aristophanes created a world in the clouds, peopled it with a citizenry composed of birds, and gave them the attributes of contemporary Athens. In *The Clouds*, he invented a ludicrously pretentious Socrates, whom he showed floating in a basket in order to be closer to the ether and expounding extravagant sophistries. In *Lysistrata*, one of several anti-war satires, he conceived a somewhat bawdy revolt of the Athenian women against their bellicose men.

In Aristophanes' work, the broad humor and burlesque situations, direct harangues (*parabases*) by the chorus, impersonations of public characters, and unexpectedly lovely lyrics created a unique mixture of comic improvisation on political and social themes. These comedies are frankly topical and outspoken, often having as serious a purpose as some of Dean Swift's satires; and in the interest of this purpose, as well as for the sake of greater liveliness and comprehensiveness, the plot is treated lightly—the dramatic construction is free, and the story is replete with loosely related episodes. The form resembled something that Sheridan, Shaw, Gilbert and Sullivan, Shelley (contributing his lyric gift), Ogden Nash, and Cole Porter might have put together, if they could have collaborated.

The production of an Aristophanic comedy reflected the same riotous extravagance. The cast was extravagantly costumed, the choruses sometimes being dressed as animals (hence such titles as *The Birds* and *The Frogs*); the music was lively, the dancing vigorous and playful, the acting farcical. The proceedings presented a decided contrast to the stateliness of tragic composition and staging. But the fifth-century Greeks, who were never a one-sided people, admired this effervescent type of comedy and gave it a place in their Dionysian festivals; after all, Dionysus himself had sanctioned orgiastic exhibitions. After the performance of three tragedies in the morning, came a simple animal burlesque, known as a *satyr play* because the characters were supposed to be goatish figures or satyrs. Then in the afternoon the audience was entertained with a full-blown comedy. The program continued for three days. In a minor festival (the so-called *Lenæan*) in the neighborhood of Athens, moreover, comedy held undisputed sway.

The master of this kind of uninhibited but thoughtful entertainment was Aristophanes (448?-380? B.C.). *The Frogs* abundantly exemplifies his genius—his talent for fantastication, his playful irreverence, his clever choral poetry, and his gift of inspired mimicry, for his parodies on the styles of Æschylus and Sophocles are amazingly apt. This comedy also reveals his animus, his reverence for the austere virtues of the Marathon generation when a united and heroic Athens could defeat the Persian hordes, and his deprecation of what he considered decadence in Athenian life and art. For this reason he glorifies Æschylus and underestimates Euripides. Aristophanes, himself a child of the Periclean period in his lively wit, longed for the good old days that never returned in Greece.

After the fifth century, political or topical comedy became increasingly impossible. A second Aristophanes could not have arisen during the decline of democracy and the subjugation of the city by Macedonia under Alexander the Great. Comedy consequently became comparatively timorous and directed its attention to private characters and domestic embroilments. After a transitional form, known as Middle Comedy, of which no good examples remain, it was this new type of comic drama that came to the fore.

The great virtue of the so-called New Comedy, developed by Menander (342-292 B.C.) and his contemporaries, whose work survives mostly in fragments, and adapted by the Roman playwrights Plautus (254?-184 B.C.) and Terence (190?-159? B.C.), is its closely knit plot. There is generally some intrigue, involving love affairs, tricks played on stupid fathers, mistaken identities, and the discovery of long-lost relatives. Attention is given to the manners, rather than the politics, of the times, and to characterization, which was rarely present in the caricatures of Aristophanic comedy. Although the characters are types and are therefore not strongly individualized, they are delightfully recognizable, and they highlight familiar human characteristics. In these comedies will be found the young lovers, disapproving parents, comically betrayed husbands, vainglorious boasters, parasites,

panders, and rascally servants who have peopled comedy of manners for two thousand years. Unquestionably comedy lost inventiveness and poetry, but it approached observation of common reality and so acquired a whole new world.

Plautus (254?-184 B.C.), the most lively of the writers of this type of comedy, was born in Umbria and later went to Rome. He lived in the period that laid the foundations of the great Roman empire. It was a boisterous and adventurous age, which may explain his partiality for boisterous subjects, for such unsavory professions as white slavery, and for broad jests. No one could call his comedies refined, but no one could consider them remote from the world he knew. And he had ample opportunity to know this world.

Plautus was a greatly battered man. He served Rome as a soldier, he acted in crude native farces, and he even became a merchant. Losing his fortune at sea, he was reduced to the inglorious vocation of a traveling miller; he would wander through the streets and grind corn for householders. Fortunately for him, his plays soon became successful, and his output began to mount rapidly; according to the Romans, he wrote one hundred and thirty comedies, of which twenty-one have survived.

The Roman theater before his day was a rough-and-tumble affair, and its plays were crude products, not greatly above the level of vaudeville pieces and burlesques. But Rome, after coming into contact with the Greek colonies in Italy and conquering Greece, began to feel the influence of Greek culture.

Vivacity and broad jests distinguish his comedies, which are often much nearer to what we call farce. His dialogue is breezily colloquial, and his plot is filled with activity and complication. A favorite contrivance of his was the confusion produced by the identical appearance of some characters. In his *Amphitruo*, the earliest extant Amphitryon play, Jupiter, in visiting Alcmene who became the mother of Hercules, assumes the shape of her husband. (Mercury, at the same time, assumes the likeness of a servant girl's husband.) In the *Menæchmi*, which was the model for Shakespeare's *Comedy of Errors*, the complications arise from the existence of a pair of identical twins bearing the same name.

His commoners—cooks, flute-girls, panderers, valets, and parasites—are depicted with considerable realism. A notable example is the miser Euclio, in *The Pot of Gold* or *Aulularia*, who "when he goes to sleep will tie the bellows around his throat . . . lest he should waste his breath." Other examples are the Falstaffian vainglorious soldier who enlivens the *Miles Gloriosus* (*The Braggart Soldier*) with his pretentions, and the irrepressible parasite who foists himself on persons of wealth in *The Captives*. Characters like these became the stock in trade of later writers of comedy; Euclio is the model for the miser of Molière's *L'Avare* (*The Miser*), the braggart soldier appears in Shakespeare's and Ben Jonson's comedies, the parasite plays a roguish part in the early Elizabethan play *Ralph Roister Doister*.

The Captives with its comic types, complications, and unexpected discoveries, is typical of Plautus' work. It is also closer to the more refined type of comedy written by Plautus' successor Terence, who in the second century B.C. wrote with greater restraint and polish. His best known work, *Phormio,* contains the superb parasite who lends his name to the play, as well as the resourceful and intriguing slave Geta, a prototype of Molière's intriguing servants and of Beaumarchais' resourceful Figaro.[1] Terence, a Phœnician by birth but a devotee of Greek artistry after becoming the slave of a cultivated Roman master, tried to equal the polish of fourth-century Greek comedy. As a result he was found more acceptable to the Middle Ages, but he displayed less vigor and resourcefulness. Terence wrote charming literature, but Plautus remained first and last a man of the theater.

The theater came to an inglorious end in Rome. Latin tragedy never attained any distinction, and its last products were the rhetorical melodramas of Seneca, written during Nero's reign, which were probably never intended to be staged. Their antiquity gave them considerable credit during the Renaissance, when even the dross of classic culture passed for gold, and they exercised an unfortunate influence on sixteenth-century playwrights. Comedy deteriorated rapidly after, and in fact during, the lifetime of Terence (190?-159? B.C.). At its best, the stage, which was supplanted by the circus, had some lively actors who shone in a species of farce called *mimes*. These pantomimes and dialogues, that originally had displayed some wit, became increasingly gross and licentious. They ultimately earned the condemnation of the early Christian fathers, who consequently banned the theater as an abomination. Many centuries were to elapse before the Church could become even partially reconciled to an institution that had been so badly abused.

[1] In *The Barber of Seville* and *The Marriage of Figaro*.

ARISTOPHANES

The Frogs

CHARACTERS

BACCHUS
XANTHIAS, *servant of Bacchus*
HERCULES
CHARON
ÆACUS
EURIPIDES
ÆSCHYLUS
PLUTO
Deadman
Prosperine's Servant Maid
Two Women Sutlers

Mutes
Chorus of Votaries, and Frogs

Enter BACCHUS *and* XANTHIAS.

XANTH. Master, shall I begin with the usual jokes
That the audience always laugh at?
  BACCH. If you please;
Any joke you please except "being overburthen'd."
—Don't use it yet— We've time enough before us.   5
  XANTH. Well, something else that's comical and clever?

Aristophanes, *Frogs*. Translated by John Hookham Frere. Aristophanes (448?-380? B.C.), comic dramatist of Athens, entered on his career just as the disastrous wars were beginning to break down the Athenian leadership. He lived to see its complete eclipse.

Bacch. I forbid being "overpress'd and overburthen'd."

Xanth. Well, but the drollest joke of all—?

Bacch. Remember

There's one thing I protest against—   10

Xanth. What's that?

Bacch. Why, shifting off your load to the other
shoulder,

And fidgeting and complaining of the gripes.

Xanth. What then do you mean to say, that I
must not say

That I'm ready to befoul myself?   15

Bacch. By no means—

Except when I take an emetic.

Xanth. What's the use, then,

Of my being burthen'd here with all these bundles,

If I'm to be deprived of the common jokes   20

That Phrynichus, and Lycis, and Ameipsias

Allow the servants always in their comedies,

Without exception, when they carry bundles?

Bacch. Pray, leave them off—for those ingenious
sallies

Have such an effect upon my health and spirits   25

That I feel grown old and dull when I get home.

Xanth. It's hard for me to suffer in my limbs,

To be overburthen'd and debarr'd from joking.

Bacch. Well, this is monstrous, quite, and insupportable!

Such insolence in a servant! When your master   30

Is going afoot and has provided you

With a beast to carry ye.

Xanth. What! do I carry nothing?

Bacch. You're carried yourself.

Xanth. But I carry bundles, don't I?   35

Bacch. But the beast bears all the burdens that
you carry.

Xanth. Not those that I carry myself—'tis I that
carry 'em.

Bacch. You're carried yourself, I tell ye.

Xanth. I can't explain it,

But I feel it in my shoulders plainly enough.   40

Bacch. Well, if the beast don't help you, take
and try;

Change places with the ass and carry him.

Xanth. [in a tone of mere disgust]. Oh, dear! I
wish I had gone for a volunteer,

And left you to yourself. I wish I had.

Bacch. Dismount, you rascal! Here, we're at the
house   45

Where Hercules lives.—Hello! there! who's within
there?

Enter Hercules.

Herc. Who's there? (He has bang'd at the door,
whoever he is,

With the kick of a centaur.) What's the matter,
there?

Bacch. [aside]. Ha! Xanthias!

Xanth. What?   50

Bacch. [aside]. Did ye mind how he was fright-
en'd?

Xanth. I suppose he was afraid you were going
mad.

Herc. [aside] By Jove! I shall laugh outright;
I'm ready to burst.

I shall laugh, in spite of myself, upon my life.

Bacch. Come hither, friend.—What ails ye? Step
this way;   55

I want to speak to ye.

Herc. But I can't help laughing

To see the lion's skin with a saffron robe,

And the club with the women's sandals—altogether—

What's the meaning of it all? Have you been
abroad?   60

Bacch. I've been abroad—in the Fleet—with
Cleisthenes.

Herc. You fought—?

Bacch. Yes, that we did—we gain'd a victory;

And we sunk the enemies' ships—thirteen of 'em.

Herc. "So you woke at last and found it was a
dream?"   65

Bacch. But aboard the fleet, as I pursued my
studies,

I read the tragedy of Andromeda;

And then such a vehement passion struck my
heart,

You can't imagine.

Herc. A small one, I suppose,   70

My little fellow—a moderate little passion?

Bacch. It's just as small as Molon is—that's all—

Molon the wrestler, I mean—as small as he is—

Herc. Well, what was it like? what kind of a
thing? what was it?

Bacch. No, friend, you must not laugh; it's past
a joke;   75

It's quite a serious feeling—quite distressing;

I suffer from it—

Herc. Well, explain. What was it?

Bacch. I can't declare it at once; but I'll explain
it

Theatrically and enigmatically: 80

Were you ever seized with a sudden passionate
longing

For a mess of porridge?

Herc. Often enough, if that's all.

Bacch. Shall I state the matter to you plainly at
    once;
Or put it circumlocutorily?   85
    Herc. Not about the porridge. I understand your
    instance.
    Bacch. Such is the passion that possesses me
For poor Euripides, that's dead and gone;
And it's all in vain people trying to persuade me
From going after him.   90
    Herc. What, to the shades below?
    Bacch. Yes, to the shades below, or the shades
    beneath 'em.
To the undermost shades of all. I'm quite deter-
    mined.
    Herc. But what's your object?
    Bacch. Why my object is   95
That I want a clever poet—"for the good,
The gracious and the good, are dead and gone;
The worthless and the weak are left alive."
    Herc. Is not Iophon a good one?
—He's alive sure?   100
    Bacch. If he's a good one, he's our only good
    one;
But it's a question; I'm in doubt about him.
    Herc. There's Sophocles; he's older than Eurip-
    ides—
If you go so far for 'em, you'd best bring him.
    Bacch. No; first I'll try what Iophon can do,
Without his father, Sophocles, to assist him.   106
—Besides, Euripides is a clever rascal;
A sharp, contriving rogue that will make a shift
To desert and steal away with me; the other
Is an easy-minded soul, and always was.   110
    Herc. Where's Agathon?
    Bacch. He's gone and left me too,
Regretted by his friends; a worthy poet—
    Herc. Gone! Where, poor soul?
    Bacch. To the banquets of the blest!   115
    Herc. But then you've Xenocles—
    Bacch. Yes! a plague upon him!
    Herc. Pythangelus too—
    Xanth. But nobody thinks of me;
Standing all this while with the bundles on my
    shoulder.   120
    Herc. But have not you other young ingenious
    youths
That are fit to out-talk Euripides ten times over;
To the amount of a thousand, at least, all writing
    tragedy—?
    Bacch. They're good for nothing—
"Warblers of the Grove"—   125
—"Little, foolish, fluttering things"—poor puny
    wretches.

That dawdle and dangle about the tragic muse;
Incapable of any serious meaning—
—There's not one hearty poet amongst them all
That's fit to risk an adventurous valiant phrase.
    Herc. How—"hearty"? What do you mean by
    "valiant phrases"?   131
    Bacch. I mean a . . . kind . . . of a doubtful,
    bold expression
To talk about . . . "The viewless foot of Time"--
And . . . "Jupiter's Secret Chamber in the Skies"--
And about . . . a person's soul . . . not being per-
    jured   135
When . . . the   tongue . . . forswears   itself . . .
    in spite of the soul.
    Herc. Do you like that kind of stuff?
    Bacch. I'm crazy after it.
    Herc. Why, sure, it's trash and rubbish— Don't
    you think so?
    Bacch. "Men's fancies are their own— Let mine
    alone"—   140
    Herc. But, in fact, it seems to me quite bad—
    rank nonsense.
    Bacch. You'll tell me next what I ought to like
    for supper.
    Xanth. But nobody thinks of me here, with the
    bundles.
    Bacch. —But now to the business that I came
    upon—   144
(With the apparel that you see—the same as yours)
To obtain a direction from you to your friends,
(To apply to them—in case of anything—
If anything should occur) the acquaintances
That received you there—(the time you went be-
    fore
—For the business about Cerberus)—if you'd give
    me   150
Their names and their directions, and communi-
    cate
Any information relative to the country,
The roads,—the streets,—the bridges, and the
    brothels,
The wharfs,—the public walks,—the public houses,
The fountains,—aqueducts,—and inns, and taverns,
And lodgings,—free from bugs and fleas, if pos-
    sible,   156
If you know any such—
    Xanth. But nobody thinks of me.
    Herc. What a notion! You! Will you risk it?
    Are you mad?
    Bacch. I beseech you say no more—no more of
    that,   160
But inform me briefly and plainly about my jour-
    ney:

The shortest road and the most convenient one.

Herc. Well,—which shall I tell ye first, now?—
Let me see now—
There's a good convenient road by the Rope and
Noose;
The Hanging Road.   165
Bacch. No; that's too close and stifling.
Herc. Then, there's an easy, fair, well-beaten
track,
As you go by the Pestle and Mortar—
Bacch. What, the Hemlock?
Herc. To be sure—   170
Bacch. That's much too cold—it will never do.
They tell me it strikes a chill to the legs and feet.
Herc. Should you like a speedy, rapid, downhill
road?
Bacch. Indeed I should, for I'm a sorry traveler.
Herc. Go to the Keramicus then.   175
Bacch. What then?
Herc. Stand there and watch when the Race of
the Torch begins;
And mind when you hear the people cry *"Start!*
start!"
Then start at once with 'em.
Bacch. Me? Start? Where from?   180
Herc. From the top of the tower to the bottom.
Bacch. No, not I.
It's enough to dash my brains out! I'll not go
Such a road upon any account.
Herc. Well, which way then?   185
Bacch. The way you went yourself.
Herc. But it's a long one,
For first you come to a monstrous bottomless lake.
Bacch. And what must I do to pass?
Herc. You'll find a boat there;   190
A little tiny boat, as big as that,
And an old man that ferries you over in it,
Receiving twopence as the usual fee.
Bacch. Ah! that same twopence governs every-
thing
Wherever it goes.—I wonder how it managed   195
To find its way there?
Herc. Theseus introduced it.
—Next you'll meet serpents, and wild beasts, and
monsters,
Horrific to behold!
Bacch. Don't try to fright me;   200
You'll not succeed, I promise you.—I'm deter-
mined.
Herc. Then there's an abyss of mire and floating
filth,
In which the damn'd lie wallowing and over-
whelm'd;

The unjust, the cruel, and the inhospitable;   204
And the barbarous bilking Cullies that withhold
The price of intercourse with fraud and wrong;
The incestuous, and the parricides, and the rob-
bers;
The perjurers, and assassins, and the wretches
That willfully and presumptuously transcribe
Extracts and trash from Morsimus's plays.   210
Bacch. And, by Jove! Cinesias with his Pyrrhic
dancers
Ought to be there—they're worse, or quite as bad.
Herc. But after this your sense will be saluted
With a gentle breathing sound of flutes and voices,
And a beautiful spreading light like ours on earth,
And myrtle glades and happy quires among,   216
Of women and men with rapid applause and
mirth.
Bacch. And who are all those folks?
Herc. The initiated.
Xanth. I won't stand here like a mule in a pro-
cession   220
Any longer, with these packages and bundles.
Herc. They'll tell you everything you want to
know,
For they're established close upon the road,
By the corner of Pluto's house—so fare you well;
Farewell, my little fellow.   [*Exit.*
Bacch. I wish you better.   226
[*To Xanthias.*] You, sirrah, take your bundles up
again.
Xanth. What, before I put them down?
Bacch. Yes! now, this moment.
Xanth. Nah! don't insist; there's plenty of peo-
ple going   230
As corpses with the convenience of a carriage;
They'd take it for a trifle gladly enough.
Bacch. But if we meet with nobody?
Xanth. Then I'll take 'em.
Bacch. Come, come, that's fairly spoken, and in
good time;   235
For there they're carrying a corpse out to be
buried.

A funeral, with a corpse on an open bier, crosses
the stage.

—Hello! you there—you Deadman—can't you
hear?
Would you take any bundles to hell with ye, my
good fellow?
Deadman. What are they?
Bacch. These.   240
Deadman. Then I must have two drachmas.
Bacch. I can't—you must take less.

DEADMAN. Bearers, move on.

BACCH. No, stop! we shall settle between us—
you're so hasty.

DEADMAN. It's no use arguing; I must have two
drachmas.   245

BACCH. Ninepence!

DEADMAN. I'd best be alive again at that rate.
                                               [*Exit.*

BACCH. Fine airs the fellow gives himself—a
rascal!

I'll have him punish'd, I vow, for overcharging.

   XANTH. Best give him a good beating; give me
the bundles,   250
I'll carry 'em.

   BACCH. You're a good, true-hearted fellow;
And a willing servant.—Let's move on to the ferry.

Enter CHARON.

CHARON. Hoy! Bear a hand, there— Heave
ashore.

BACCH. What's this?   255

XANTH. The lake it is—the place he told us of.

By Jove! and there's the boat—and here's old
Charon.

   BACCH. Well, Charon!—Welcome, Charon!—
Welcome kindly!

   CHARON. Who wants the ferryman? Anybody
waiting

To remove from the sorrows of life? A passage
anybody?   260

To Lethe's wharf?—to Cerberus's Reach?

To Tartarus?—to Tænarus?—to Perdition?

   BACCH. Yes, I.

   CHARON. Get in then.

   BACCH. Tell me, where are you going?   265

To Perdition really—?

   CHARON. Yes, to oblige you, I will

With all my heart— Step in there.

   BACCH. Have a care!

Take care, good Charon!—Charon, have a care!

Come, Xanthias, come!   271

   CHARON. I take no slaves aboard

Except they've volunteer'd for the naval victory.

   XANTH. I could not—I was suffering with sore
eyes.

   CHARON. You must trudge away then, round by
the end of the lake there.   275

   XANTH. And whereabouts shall I wait?

   CHARON. At the Stone of Repentance,

By the Slough of Despond beyond the Tribulations;

You understand me?

   XANTH. Yes, I understand you;   280

A lucky, promising direction, truly.

   CHARON [*to* BACCHUS]. Sit down at the oar—
Come quick, if there's more coming!

[*To* BACCHUS *again.*] Hello! what's that you're
doing?

   BACCH. What you told me.

I'm sitting at the oar.   285

   CHARON. Sit *there,* I tell you,

You Fatguts; that's your place.

   BACCH. Well, so I do.

   CHARON. Now ply your hands and arms.

   BACCH. Well, so I do.   290

   CHARON. You'd best leave off your fooling. Take
to the oar,

And pull away.

   BACCH. But how shall I contrive?

I've never served on board—I'm only a landsman;

I'm quite unused to it—   295

   CHARON. We can manage it.

As soon as you begin you shall have some music

That will teach you to keep time.

   BACCH. What music's that?

   CHARON. A chorus of Frogs—uncommon musi-
cal Frogs.   300

   BACCH. Well, give me the word and the time.

   CHARON. Whooh up, up; whooh up, up.

Enter Chorus of Frogs.

CHOR. Brekeke-kesh, koash, koash,

Shall the Choral Quiristers of the Marsh

Be censured and rejected as hoarse and harsh;   305
   And their Chromatic essays
   Deprived of praise?

No, let us raise afresh

Our obstreperous Brekeke-kesh;

The customary croak and cry   310
   Of the creatures
   At the Theaters,

In their yearly revelry,

Brekeke-kesh, koash, koash.

   BACCH. How I'm maul'd,   315

How I'm gall'd;

Worn and mangled to a mash—

There they go! *"Koash, koash!"*—

   FROGS. Brekeke-kesh, koash, koash.

   BACCH. Oh, beshrew,   320
      All your crew;

You don't consider how I smart.

   FROGS. Now for a sample of the Art!

Brekeke-kesh, koash, koash.

   BACCH. I wish you hang'd, with all my heart.

—Have you nothing else to say?   326

"Brekeke-kesh, koash" all day!

FROGS. We've a right,
We've a right;
And we croak at ye for spite. 330
We've a right,
We've a right;
Day and night,
Day and night;
Night and day, 335
Still to creak and croak away.
Phœbus and every Grace
Admire and approve of the croaking race;
And the egregious guttural notes
That are gargled and warbled in their lyrical
throats. 340
In reproof
Of your scorn
Mighty Pan
Nods his horn;
Beating time 345
To the rhyme
With his hoof,
With his hoof.
Persisting in our plan,
We proceed as we began, 350
Breke-kesh, Breke-kesh,
Kooash, kooash.
BACCH. Oh, the Frogs, consume and rot 'em,
I've a blister on my bottom.
Hold your tongues, you tuneful creatures. 355
FROGS. Cease with your profane entreaties
All in vain forever striving:
Silence is against our natures.
With the vernal heat reviving
Our aquatic crew repair 360
From their periodic sleep,
In the dark and chilly deep,
To the cheerful upper air;
Then we frolic here and there
All amidst the meadows fair; 365
Shady plants of asphodel,
Are the lodges where we dwell;
Chaunting in the leafy bowers
All the livelong summer hours,
Till the sudden gusty showers 370
Send us headlong, helter, skelter,
To the pool to seek for shelter;
Meager, eager, leaping, lunging,
From the sedgy wharfage plunging
To the tranquil depth below, 375
There we muster all a-row;
Where, secure from toil and trouble,
With a tuneful hubble-bubble,
Our symphonious accents flow.

Brekeke-kesh, koash, koash. 380
BACCH. I forbid you to proceed.
FROGS. That would be severe indeed;
Arbitrary, bold, and rash—
Brekeke-kesh, koash, koash.
BACCH. I command you to desist— 385
—Oh, my back, there! oh, my wrist!
What a twist!
What a sprain!
FROGS. Once again—
We renew the tuneful strain. 390
Brekeke-kesh, koash, koash.
BACCH. I disdain—(Hang the pain!)
All your nonsense, noise, and trash.
Oh, my blister! Oh, my sprain!
FROGS. Brekeke-kesh, koash, koash. 395
Friends and Frogs, we must display
All our powers of voice today;
Suffer not this stranger here,
With fastidious foreign ear,
To confound us and abash. 400
Brekeke-kesh, koash, koash.
BACCH. Well, my spirit is not broke,
If it's only for the joke,
I'll outdo you with a croak.
Here it goes—"Koash, koash." 405
FROGS. Now for a glorious croaking crash,
Brekeke-kesh, koash, koash.
BACCH. I'll disperse you with a splash.
FROGS. Brekeke-kesh, koash, koash.
BACCH. I'll subdue 410
Your rebellious, noisy crew—
—Have amongst you there, slap-dash.
FROGS. Brekeke-kesh, koash, koash.
We defy your oar and you.
CHARON. Hold! We're ashore just—shift your
oar. Get out. 415
—Now pay for your fare.
BACCH. There—there it is—the twopence.

CHARON *returns.* BACCHUS, *finding himself alone
and in a strange place, begins to call out.*

BACCH. Ho, Xanthias! Xanthias, I say! Where's
Xanthias?
XANTH. A-hoy!
BACCH. Come here. 420
XANTH. I'm glad to see you, master.
BACCH. What's that before us there?
XANTH. The mire and the darkness.
BACCH. Do you see the villains and the perjurers
That he told us of? 425
XANTH. Yes, plain enough, don't you?

BACCH. Ah! now I see them, indeed, quite plain
　—and now too.
Well, what shall we do next?
XANTH. We'd best move forward;
For here's the place that Hercules there inform'd
　us　　　　　　　　　　　　　　　　　　430
Was haunted by those monsters.
　BACCH. Oh, confound him!
He vapor'd and talk'd at random to deter me
From venturing. He's amazingly conceited
And jealous of other people, is Hercules;　　435
He reckon'd I should rival him, and, in fact
(Since I've come here so far), I should rather like
To meet with an adventure in some shape.
　XANTH. By Jove! and I think I hear a kind of a
　　noise.
　BACCH. Where? Where?　　　　　　440
　XANTH. There, just behind us.
　BACCH. Go behind, then.
　XANTH. There!—it's before us now.—There!
　BACCH. Go before, then.
　XANTH. Ah! now I see it—a monstrous beast in-
　　deed!　　　　　　　　　　　　445
　BACCH. What kind?
　XANTH. A dreadful kind—all kinds at once.
It changes and transforms itself about
To a mule and an ox,—and now to a beautiful
　creature;
A woman!　　　　　　　　　　　450
　BACCH. Where? Where is she? Let me seize her.
　XANTH. But now she's turned to a mastiff all of
　　a sudden.
　BACCH. It's the Weird hag! the Vampire!
　XANTH. Like enough.
She's all of a blaze of fire about the mouth.　455
　BACCH. Has she got the brazen foot?
　XANTH. Yes, there it is—
By Jove!—and the cloven hoof to the other leg,
Distinct enough—that's she!
　BACCH. But what shall I do?　　　460
　XANTH. And I, too?
　BACCH. Save me, Priest, protect and save me,
That we may drink and be jolly together hereafter.
　XANTH. We're ruin'd, Master Hercules.
　BACCH. Don't call me so, I beg;　　465
Don't mention my name, good friend, upon any
　account.
　XANTH. Well, Bacchus, then!
　BACCH. That's worse, ten thousand times.
　XANTH. Come, master, move along— Come,
　　come this way.
　BACCH. What's happened?　　　　470
　XANTH. Why, we're prosperous and victorious;

The storm of fear and danger has subsided,
And (as the actor said the other day)
"Has only left a gentle, *qualm* behind."
The Vampire's vanish'd.　　　　　475
　BACCH. Has she? Upon your oath?
　XANTH. By Jove! she has.
　BACCH. No, swear again.
　XANTH. By Jove!
　BACCH. Is she, by Jupiter?　　　480
　XANTH. By Jupiter!
　BACCH. Oh, dear; what a fright I was in with the
　　very sight of her:
It turn'd me sick and pale—but see, the priest here!
He has color'd up quite with the same alarm.
—What has brought me to this pass?—It must be
　Jupiter　　　　　　　　　　485
With his *"Chamber in the Skies,"* and the *"Foot of
　Time."*
　XANTH. Hello, you!
　BACCH. What?
　XANTH. Why, did you not hear?
　BACCH. Why, what?　　　　　490
　XANTH. The sound of a flute.
　BACCH. Indeed! And there's a smell too;
A pretty mystical ceremonious smell
Of torches. We'll watch here, and keep quite quiet.

Enter Chorus of Votaries.

　CHOR. Iacchus! Iacchus! Ho! Iacchus! Iacchus!
　　Ho!　　　　　　　　　　495
　XANTH. There, Master, there they are, the initi-
　　ated;
All sporting about as he told us we should find 'em.
They're singing in praise of Bacchus like Diagoras.
　BACCH. Indeed, and so they are; but we'll keep
　　quiet,
Till we make them out a little more distinctly.　500
　CHOR. Mighty Bacchus! Holy Power!
Hither at the wonted hour
　Come away,
　Come away,
With the wanton holiday　　　　505
Where the revel uproar leads
To the mystic holy meads,
　Where the frolic votaries fly,
　With a tipsy shout and cry;
Flourishing the Thyrsus high,　　　510
Flinging forth, alert and airy,
To the sacred old vagary,
The tumultuous dance and song,
Sacred from the vulgar throng;
Mystic orgies that are known　　　515
To the votaries alone—

To the mystic chorus solely—
Secret—unrevealed—and holy.
XANTH. Oh glorious virgin, daughter of the god-
    dess!   519
What a scent of roasted griskin reach'd my senses.
    BACCH. Keep quiet—and watch for a chance of a
    piece of the haslets.
    CHOR. Raise the fiery torches high!
Bacchus is approaching nigh,
Like the planet of the morn,
Breaking with the hoary dawn   525
    On the dark solemnity—
There they flash upon the sight;
All the plain is blazing bright,
Flushed and overflown with light:
Age has cast his years away,   530
And the cares of many a day,
Sporting to the lively lay—
Mighty Bacchus! march and lead
(Torch in hand toward the mead)
Thy devoted humble Chorus,   535
Mighty Bacchus—move before us!
Keep silence—keep peace—and let all the profane
From our holy solemnity duly refrain;
Whose souls unenlightened by taste, are obscure;
Whose poetical notions are dark and impure;   540
Whose theatrical conscience
Is sullied by nonsense;
Who never were train'd by the mighty Cratinus
In mystical orgies poetic and vinous;   544
Who delight in buffooning and jests out of season;
Who promote the designs of oppression and trea-
    son;
Who foster sedition, and strife, and debate;
All traitors, in short, to the stage and the state;
Who surrender a fort, or in private, export
To places and harbors of hostile resort,   550
Clandestine consignments of cables and pitch;
In the way that Thorycion grew to be rich
From a scoundrelly dirty collector of tribute:
All such we reject and severely prohibit: 554
All statesmen retrenching the fees and the salaries
Of theatrical bards, in revenge for the railleries,
And jests, and lampoons, of this holy solemnity,
Profanely pursuing their personal enmity,
For having been flouted, and scoff'd, and scorn'd,
All such are admonish'd and heartily warn'd;   560
    We warn them once,
    We warn them twice,
    We warn and admonish—we warn them thrice,
To conform to the law,
To retire and withdraw;   565
While the Chorus again with the formal saw

(Fixt and assign'd to the festive day)
Move to the measure and march away.
    March! march! lead forth,
    Lead forth manfully,   570
    March in order all;
    Bustling, hustling, justling,
      As it may befall;
    Flocking, shouting, laughing,
    Mocking, flouting, quaffing,   575
      One and all;
    All have had a belly-full
    Of breakfast brave and plentiful;
      Therefore
      Evermore   580
With your voices and your bodies
Serve the goddess,
    And raise
    Songs of praise;
She shall save the country still,   585
And save it against the traitor's will;
    So she says.
Now let us raise, in a different strain,
The praise of the goddess the giver of grain;
Imploring her favor   590
With other behavior,
In measures more sober, submissive, and graver.
    Ceres, holy patroness,
    Condescend to mark and bless,
    With benevolent regard,   595
    Both the Chorus and the Bard;
    Grant them for the present day
    Many things to sing and say,
    Follies intermix'd with sense;
    Folly, but without offense.   600
    Grant them with the present play
    To bear the prize of verse away.
Now call again, and with a different measure,
The power of mirth and pleasure;
The florid, active Bacchus, bright and gay,   605
    To journey forth and join us on the way.
O Bacchus, attend! the customary patron
    Of every lively lay;
    Go forth without delay
    Thy wonted annual way,   610
To meet the ceremonious holy matron:
    Her grave procession gracing,
    Thine airy footsteps tracing
With unlaborious, light, celestial motion;
And here at thy devotion   615
    Behold thy faithful quire
    In pitiful attire;
All overworn and ragged,
This jerkin old and jagged,

These buskins torn and burst,   620
  Though sufferers in the fray,
May serve us at the worst
  To sport throughout the day;
And there within the shades,
I spy some lovely maids;   625
With whom we romp'd and revel'd,
Dismantled and dishevel'd;
With their bosoms open,
With whom we might be coping.
    XANTH. Well, I was always hearty,   630
Disposed to mirth and ease,
I'm ready to join the party.
    BACCH. And I will, if you please.
[*To the Chorus.*] Prithee, my good fellows,
Would you please to tell us   635
  Which is Pluto's door,
I'm an utter stranger,
  Never here before.
    CHOR. Friend, you're out of danger,
  You need not seek it far;   640
There it stands before ye,
  Before ye, where you are.
    BACCH. Take up your bundles, Xanthias.
    XANTH. Hang all bundles;
A bundle has no end, and these have none.   645
    CHOR. Now we go to dance and sing
  In the consecrated shades;
Round the secret holy ring,
  With the matrons and the maids.
Thither I must haste to bring   650
  The mysterious early light;
Which must witness every rite
  Of the joyous happy night.
Let us hasten—let us fly—
Where the lovely meadows lie;   655
  Where the living waters flow;
Where the roses bloom and blow.
—Heirs of Immortality,
Segregated, safe and pure,
Easy, sorrowless, secure;   660
Since our earthly course is run,
We behold a brighter sun.
Holy lives—a holy vow—
Such awards await them now.
    BACCH. Well, how must I knock at the door
      now? Can't ye tell me?   665
How do the native inhabitants knock at doors?
    XANTH. Pah; don't stand fooling there; but smite
      it smartly,
With the very spirit and air of Hercules.
    BACCH. Hello!
    ÆACUS. Who's there?   670

    BACCH. 'Tis I, the valiant Hercules!
    ÆACUS. Thou brutal, abominable, detestable,
Vile, villainous, infamous, nefarious scoundrel!
—How durst thou, villain as thou wert, to seize   674
Our watchdog, Cerberus, whom I kept and tended
Hurrying him off, half-strangled in your grasp?
—But now, be sure we have you safe and fast,
Miscreant and villain!—Thee, the Stygian cliffs,
With stern adamantine durance, and the rocks
Of inaccessible Acheron, red with gore,   680
Environ and beleaguer; and the watch,
And swift pursuit of the hideous hounds of hell;
And the horrible Hydra, with her hundred heads,
Whose furious ravening fangs shall rend and tear
      thee;
Wrenching thy vitals forth, with the heart and
      midriff;   685
While inexpressible Tartesian monsters,
And grim Tithrasian Gorgons toss and scatter
With clattering claws, thine intertwined intestines.
To them, with instant summons, I repair,
Moving in hasty march with steps of speed.   690
    XANTH. Hello, you! What's the matter there—?
    BACCH. Oh dear.
I've had an accident.
    XANTH. Poh! poh! jump up!
Come! you ridiculous simpleton! don't lie there.
The people will see you.   696
    BACCH. Indeed I'm sick at heart; la!
    XANTH. Was there ever in heaven or earth such a
      coward?
    BACCH. Me?   699
A coward! Did not I show my presence of mind—
And call for a sponge and water in a moment?
Would a coward have done that?
    XANTH. What else would he do?
    BACCH. He'd have lain there stinking like a nasty
      coward;
But I jump'd up at once, like a lusty wrestler,   705
And look'd about, and wiped myself, withal.
    XANTH. Most manfully done!
    BACCH. By Jove, and I think it was;
But tell me, weren't you frighten'd with that speech?
—Such horrible expressions!   710
    XANTH. No, not I;
I took no notice—
    BACCH. Well, I'll tell you what,
Since you're such a valiant-spirited kind of fellow,
Do you be *Me*—with the club and the lion's skin,
Now you're in this courageous temper of mind;   716
And I'll go take my turn and carry the bundles.
    XANTH. Well—give us hold—I must humor you,
      forsooth;

Make haste, and now behold the Xanthian Her-
  cules,   719
And mind if I don't display more heart and spirit.
  BACCH. Indeed, and you look the character, com-
  pletely,
Like that heroic Melitensian hangdog—
Come, now for my bundles. I must mind my
  bundles.

*Enter Proserpine's Servant Maid who immediately
  addresses* XANTHIAS.

  SERV. MAID. Dear Hercules. Well, you're come at
  last. Come in,
For the goddess, as soon as she heard of it, set to
  work   725
Baking peck loaves and frying stacks of pancakes,
And making messes of furmety; there's an ox
Besides, she has roasted whole, with a relishing
  stuffing,
If you'll only just step in this way.
  XANTH. I thank you, I'm equally obliged.   730
  SERV. MAID. No, no, by Jupiter!
We must not let you off, indeed. There's wild fowl
And sweetmeats for the dessert, and the best of
  wine;
Only walk in.
  XANTH. I thank you. You'll excuse me.   735
  SERV. MAID. No, no, we can't excuse you, indeed
  we can't;
There are dancing and singing girls besides.
  XANTH. What! dancers?
  SERV. MAID. Yes, that there are; the sweetest,
  charmingest things
That you ever saw—and there's the cook this
  moment   740
Is dishing up the dinner.
  XANTH. Go before then,
And tell the girls—those singing girls you men-
  tioned—
To prepare for my approach in person presently.
[*To* BACCHUS.] You, sirrah! follow behind me
  with the bundles.   745
  BACCH. Hello, you! what, do you take the thing
  in earnest,
Because, for a joke, I drest you up like Hercules?
Come, don't stand fooling, Xanthias. You'll pro-
  voke me.
There, carry the bundles, sirrah, when I bid you.
  XANTH. Why sure? Do you mean to take the
  things away   750
That you gave me yourself of your own accord this
  instant?
  BACCH. I never mean a thing; I do it at once.

Let go of the lion's skin directly, I tell you.
  XANTH. To you, just Gods, I make my last ap-
  peal,
Bear witness!   755
  BACCH. What! the gods?—do you think they
  mind you?
How could you take it in your head, I wonder;
Such a foolish fancy for a fellow like you,
A mortal and a slave, to pass for Hercules?
  XANTH. There. Take them.—There—you may
  have them—but, please God,   760
You may come to want my help sometime or other.
  CHOR. Dexterous and wily wits,
Find their own advantage ever;
For the wind where'er it sits,
  Leaves a berth secure and clever   765
To the ready navigator;
That foresees and knows the nature;
Of the wind and weather's drift;
And betimes can turn and shift
To the sheltered easy side;   770
'Tis a practice proved and tried,
Not to wear a formal face;
Fixt in attitude and place,
Like an image on its base;
'Tis the custom of the seas,   775
Which, as all the world agrees,
Justifies Theramenes.
  BACCH. How ridiculous and strange;
What a monstrous proposition,
That I should condescend to change   780
  My dress, my name, and my condition,
To follow Xanthias, and behave
Like a mortal and a slave;
To be set to watch the door
While he wallow'd with his whore   785
Tumbling on a purple bed;
  While I waited with submission,
To receive a broken head;
  Or be kick'd upon suspicion
Of impertinence and peeping   790
At the joys that he was reaping.

*Enter two women, Sutlers or Keepers of an eating
  house.*

  FIRST WOM. What, Platana! Goody Platana!
  there! that's he,
The fellow that robs and cheats poor victualers;
That came to our house and eat those nineteen
  loaves.
  SECOND WOM. Aye, sure enough that's he, the very
  man.   795

XANTH. There's mischief in the wind for some-
  body!
FIRST WOM.—And a dozen and a half of cutlets
  and fried chops,
At a penny halfpenny apiece—
XANTH. There are pains and penalties
Impending—   800
FIRST WOM.—And all the garlic: such a quantity
As he swallowed—
BACCH. Woman, you're beside yourself;
You talk you know not what—
SECOND WOM. No, no! you reckoned   805
I should not know you again with them there
  buskins.
FIRST WOM.—Good lack! and there was all that
  fish besides.
Indeed—with the pickle, and all—and the good
  green cheese
That he gorged at once, with the rind, and the
  rush-baskets;
And then, when I called for payment, he looked
  fierce,   810
And stared at me in the face, and grinned, and
  roared—
XANTH. Just like him! That's the way wherever
  he goes.
FIRST WOM.—And snatched his sword out, and
  behaved like mad.
XANTH. Poor souls! you suffered sadly!
FIRST WOM. Yes, indeed;   815
And then we both ran off with the fright and
  terror,
And scrambled into the loft beneath the roof;
And he took up two rugs and stole them off.
XANTH. Just like him again—but something must
  be done.
Go call me Cleon, he's my advocate.   820
  SECOND WOM. And Hyperbolus, if you meet him
  send him here.
He's mine; and we'll demolish him, I warrant.
  FIRST WOM. How I should like to strike those
  ugly teeth out
With a good big stone, you ravenous greedy villain!
You gormandizing villain! that I should—   825
Yes, that I should; your wicked ugly fangs
That have eaten up my substance, and devoured
  me.
  BACCH. And I could toss you into the public pit
With the malefactors' carcasses; that I could,
With pleasure and satisfaction; that I could.   830
  FIRST WOM. And I should like to rip that gullet
  out
With a reaping hook that swallowed all my tripe,

And liver and lights—but I'll fetch Cleon here,
And he shall summon him. He shall settle him,
And have it out of him this very day.   835
                [Exeunt First and Second Woman.
  BACCH. I love poor Xanthias dearly, that I do;
I wish I might be hanged else.
  XANTH. Yes, I know—
I know your meaning— No; no more of that,
I won't act Hercules—   840
  BACCH. Now pray don't say so, my little Xanthias.
  XANTH. How should I be Hercules?
A mortal and a slave, a fellow like me?—
  BACCH. I know you're angry, and you've a right
  to be angry;
And if you beat me for it I'd not complain;   845
But if ever I strip you again, from this time for-
  ward,
I wish I may be utterly confounded,
With my wife, my children, and my family,
And the blear-eyed Archedemus into the bargain.
  XANTH. I agree then, on that oath and those con-
  ditions.   850
  CHOR. Now that you revive and flourish
In your old attire again,
You must rouse afresh and nourish
Thoughts of an heroic strain;
That exalt and raise the figure;   855
And assume a fire and vigor;
And an attitude and air
Suited to the garb you wear;
With a brow severely bent,
Like the god you represent.   860
    But beware,
    Have a care!
If you blunder, or betray
Any weakness any way;
Weakness of the heart or brain,   865
We shall see you once again
Trudging in the former track,
With the bundles at your back.
  XANTH. Friends, I thank you for your care;
Your advice was good and fair;   870
Corresponding in its tone
With reflections of my own.
—Though I clearly comprehend
All the upshot and the end
(That if any good comes of it,   875
Any pleasure, any profit—
He, my master, will recede
From the terms that were agreed),
You shall see me, notwithstanding,
Stern, intrepid, and commanding.   880

Now's the time; for there's a noise!
Now for figure, look, and voice!

Enter ÆACUS.

ÆACUS. Arrest me there that fellow that stole the
dog.
There!—Pinion him!—Quick!
BACCH. There's somebody in a scrape. 885
XANTH. Keep off, and be hanged.
ÆACUS. Oh, ho! do you mean to fight for it?
Here! Pardokas, and Skeblias, and the rest of ye
Make up to the rogue, and settle him. Come, be
quick.
BACCH. Well, is not this quite monstrous and
outrageous, 890
To steal the dog, and then to make an assault
In justification of it.
XANTH. Quite outrageous!
ÆACUS. An aggravated case!
XANTH. Well, now—by Jupiter, 895
May I die; but I never saw this place before—
Nor ever stole the amount of a farthing from you;
Nor a hair of your dog's tail— But you shall see
now,
I'll settle all this business nobly and fairly.
—This slave of mine—you may take and torture
him; 900
And if you make out anything against me,
You may take and put me to death for aught I
care.
ÆACUS. But which way would you please to have
him tortured?
XANTH. In your own way—with . . . the lash—
with . . . knots and screws,
With—the common usual customary tortures. 905
With the rack—with . . . the water-torture—any-
way—
With fire and vinegar—all sorts of ways.
There's only one thing I should warn you of:
I must not have him treated like a child, 909
To be whipp'd with fennel, or with lettuce leaves.
ÆACUS. That's fair—and if so be . . . he's maim'd
or crippled
In any respect—the valy shall be paid you.
XANTH. Oh no!—by no means! not to me!—by
no means!
You must not mention it!—Take him to the tor-
ture.
ÆACUS. It had better be here, and under your
own eye. 915
Come, you—put down your bundles and make
ready.
And mind—let me hear no lies!

BACCH. I'll tell you what:
I'd advise people not to torture me;
I give you notice—I'm a deity. 920
So mind now—you'll have nobody to blame
But your own self—
ÆACUS. What's that you're saying there?
BACCH. Why, that I'm Bacchus; Jupiter's own
son;
That fellow there's a slave. 925
ÆACUS. Do ye hear?
XANTH. I hear him—
A reason the more to give him a good beating;
If he's immortal he need never mind it.
BACCH. Why should not you be beat as well as I
then, 930
If you're immortal, as you say you are?
XANTH. Agreed—and him, and the first that you
see flinching,
Or seeming to mind it all, you may set him down
For an impostor and no real deity.
ÆACUS. Ah, you're a worthy gentleman, I'll be
bound for't; 935
You're all for the truth and the proof.
Come— Strip there both o' ye.
XANTH. But how can ye put us to the question
fairly,
Upon equal terms?
ÆACUS. Oh, easily enough, 940
Conveniently enough—a lash apiece,
Each in your turn; you can have 'em one by one.
XANTH. That's right. Now mind if ye see me
flinch or swerve.
ÆACUS. I've struck.
XANTH. Not you! 945
ÆACUS. Why, it seems as if I had not.
I'll smite this other fellow.
BACCH. When will you do it?
Oh dear! Companions of my youthful years.
XANTH. [*to* ÆACUS]. Did ye hear? he made an
outcry. 950
ÆACUS. What was that?
BACCH. A favorite passage from Archilochus.
XANTH. O Jupiter! that on the Idean height;
ÆACUS. Well, after all my pains, I'm quite at a
loss
To discover which is the true, real deity. 955
By the Holy Goddess—I'm completely puzzled;
I must take you before Proserpine and Pluto,
Being gods themselves they're likeliest to know.
BACCH. Why, that's a lucky thought. I only wish
It had happen'd to occur before you beat us. 960
CHOR. Muse, attend our solemn summons
And survey the assembled commons,

Congregated as they sit,
An enormous mass of wit,
—Full of genius, taste, and fire,   965
Jealous pride, and critic ire—
Cleophon among the rest
(Like the swallow from her nest,
A familiar foreign bird),
Chatters loud and will be heard,   970
(With the accent and the grace
Which he brought with him from Thrace);
But we fear the tuneful strain
Will be turn'd to grief and pain;
He must sing a dirge perforce   975
When his trial takes its course;
We shall hear him moan and wail,
Like the plaintive nightingale.
It behoves the sacred Chorus, and of right to them
    belongs,
To suggest the best advice in their addresses and
    their songs,   980
In performance of our office, we present with all
    humility
A proposal for removing groundless fears and dis-
    ability.
First that all that were inveigled into Phrynichus's
    treason,
Should be suffer'd and received by rules of evidence
    and reason
To clear their conduct— Secondly, that none of our
    Athenian race   985
Should live suspected and subjected to loss of fran-
    chise and disgrace,
Feeling it a grievous scandal when a single naval
    fight
Renders foreigners and slaves partakers of the city's
    right:
—Not that we condemn the measure; we con-
    ceived it wisely done,
As a just and timely measure, and the first and
    only one: 990
—But your kinsmen and your comrades, those with
    whom you fought and bore
Danger, hardship, and fatigue, or with their fathers
    long before,
Struggling on the land and ocean, laboring with
    the spear and oar
—These we think, as they profess repentance for
    their past behavior,
Might, by your exalted wisdoms, be received to
    grace and favor.   995
Better it would be, believe us, casting off revenge
    and pride,

To receive as friends and kinsmen all that combat
    on our side
Into full and equal franchise: on the other hand
    we fear,
If your hearts are fill'd with fancies, haughty, cap-
    tious, and severe;
While the shock of instant danger threatens ship-
    wreck to the state,   1000
Such resolves will be lamented and repented of too
    late.
    If the Muse foresees at all
    What in future will befall
    Dirty Cleigenes the small—
    He, the sovereign of the bath,   1005
    Will not long escape from scath;
    But must perish by and by,
    With his potash and his lye;
    With his realm and dynasty,
    His terraqueous scouring ball,   1010
    And his washes, one and all;
    Therefore he can never cease
    To declaim against a peace.
Often times have we reflected on a similar abuse,
In the choice of men for office, and of coins for
    common use;   1015
For your old and standard pieces, valued, and
    approved, and tried,
Here among the Grecian nations, and in all the
    world beside;
Recognized in every realm for trusty stamp and
    pure assay,
Are rejected and abandon'd for the trash of yester-
    day;
For a vile, adulterate issue, drossy, counterfeit, and
    base,   1020
Which the traffic of the city passes current in their
    place!
And the men that stood for office, noted for ac-
    knowledged worth,
And for manly deeds of honor, and for honorable
    birth;
Train'd in exercise and art, in sacred dances and in
    song,
All are ousted and supplanted by a base ignoble
    throng;   1025
Paltry stamp and vulgar mettle raise them to com
    mand and place,
Brazen counterfeit pretenders, scoundrels of a
    scoundrel race;
Whom the state in former ages scarce would have
    allow'd to stand,
At the sacrifice of outcasts, as the scapegoats of the
    land.

—Time it is—and long has been, renouncing all
    your follies past,   1030
To recur to sterling merit and intrinsic worth at
    last.
—If we rise, we rise with honor, if we fall, it must
    be so!
—But there was an ancient saying, which we all
    have heard and know,
That the wise, in dangerous cases, have esteem'd it
    safe and good
To receive a slight chastisement from *a wand of*
    noble wood.   1035
    ÆACUS. By Jupiter; but he's a gentleman, that
    master of yours.
    XANTH. A gentleman! To be sure he is;
Why, he does nothing else but wench and drink.
    ÆACUS. His never striking you when you took
    his name—
Outfacing him and contradicting him!   1040
    XANTH. It might have been worse for him if he
    had.
    ÆACUS. Well, that's well spoken, like a true-bred
    slave.
It's just the sort of language I delight in.
    XANTH. You love excuses?
    ÆACUS. Yes; but I prefer   1045
Cursing my master quietly in private.
    XANTH. Mischief you're fond of?
    ÆACUS. Very fond indeed.
    XANTH. What think ye of muttering as you leave
    the room
After a beating?   1050
    ÆACUS. Why, that's pleasant too.
    XANTH. By Jove, is it! But listening at the door
To hear their secrets?
    ÆACUS. Oh, there's nothing like it.
    XANTH. And then the reporting them in the
    neighborhood.   1055
    ÆACUS. That's beyond everything.—That's quite
    ecstatic.
    XANTH. Well, give me your hand. And there
    take mine—and buss me.
And there again—and now for Jupiter's sake!—
(For he's the patron of our cuffs and beatings)
Do tell me what's that noise of people quarreling
And abusing one another there within?   1061
    ÆACUS. Æschylus and Euripides, only!
    XANTH. Heh?—?—?
    ÆACUS. Why, there's a desperate business has
    broke out
Among these here dead people;—quite a tumult.
    XANTH. As how?   1066
    ÆACUS. First there's a custom we have establish'd

In favor of professors of the arts.
When any one, the first in his own line,
Comes down amongst us here, he stands entitled
To privilege and precedence, with a seat   1071
At Pluto's royal board.
    XANTH. I understand you.
    ÆACUS. So he maintains it till there comes a
    better
Of the same sort, and then resigns it up.   1075
    XANTH. But why should Æschylus be disturb'd
    at this?
    ÆACUS. He held the seat for tragedy, as the mas-
    ter
In that profession.
    XANTH. Well, and who's there now?
    ÆACUS. He kept it till Euripides appeared;   1080
But he collected audiences about him
And flourish'd and exhibited, and harangued
Before the thieves, and housebreakers, and rogues,
Cut-purses, cheats, and vagabonds, and villains,
That make the mass of population here;   1085
And they—being quite transported, and delighted
With his equivocations and evasions,
His subtleties and niceties and quibbles—
In short—they raised an uproar, and declared him
Archpoet, by a general acclamation.   1090
And he with this grew proud and confident,
And laid a claim to the seat where Æschylus sat.
    XANTH. And did not he get pelted for his pains?
    ÆACUS. Why, no— The mob call'd out, and it
    was carried,
To have a public trial of skill between them.   1095
    XANTH. You mean the mob of scoundrels that
    you mention'd?
    ÆACUS. Scoundrels indeed! Aye, scoundrels with-
    out number.
    XANTH. But Æschylus must have had good
    friends and hearty?
    ÆACUS. Yes; but good men are scarce both here
    and elsewhere.
    XANTH. Well, what has Pluto settled to be done?
    ÆACUS. To have an examination and a trial   1101
In public.
    XANTH. But how comes it?—Sophocles?—
Why does he not put forth his claim amongst
    them?
    ÆACUS. No, no!—He's not the kind of man—not
    he!   1105
I tell ye; the first moment that he came,
He went up to Æschylus and saluted him
And kiss'd his cheek and took his hand quite
    kindly;
And Æschylus edged a little from his seat

To give him room; so now the story goes,   1110
(At least I had it from Cleidemides)
He means to attend there as a stander-by,
Proposing to take up the conqueror;
If Æschylus gets the better, well and good,
He gives up his pretensions—but, if not,   1115
He'll stand a trial, he says, against Euripides.
  XANTH. There'll be strange doings.
  ÆACUS. That there will—and shortly
—Here—in this place—strange things, I promise
    you;
A kind of thing that no man could have thought
    of;   1120
Why, you'll see poetry weigh'd out and measured.
  XANTH. What, will they bring their tragedies to
    the steel-yards?
  ÆACUS. Yes, will they—with their rules and com-
    passes
They'll measure, and examine, and compare,
And bring their plummets, and their lines and
    levels,   1125
To take the bearings—for Euripides
Says that he'll make a survey, word by word.
  XANTH. Æschylus takes the thing to heart, I
    doubt.
  ÆACUS. He bent his brows and pored upon the
    ground; I saw him.
  XANTH. Well, but who decides the business?   1130
  ÆACUS. Why, there the difficulty lies—for judges,
True learned judges, are grown scarce, and Æs-
    chylus
Objected to the Athenians absolutely.
  XANTH. Considering them as rogues and villains
    mostly.   1134
  ÆACUS. As being ignorant and empty generally;
And in their judgment of the stage particularly.
In fine, they've fix'd upon that master of yours,
As having had some practice in the business.
But we must wait within—for when our masters
Are warm and eager, stripes and blows ensue. 1140
                              [Exit ÆACUS.
  CHOR. The full-mouth'd master of the tragic
    quire,
We shall behold him foam with rage and ire;
—Confronting in the list
His eager, shrewd, sharp-tooth'd antagonist.
Then will his visual orbs be wildly whirl'd   1145
And huge invectives will be hurl'd
    Superb and supercilious,
    Atrocious, atrabilious,
With furious gesture and with lips of foam,
And lion crest unconscious of the comb;   1150
Erect with rage—his brow's impending gloom

O'ershadowing his dark eyes' terrific blaze.
    The opponent, dexterous and wary,
    Will fend and parry;
While masses of conglomerated phrase,   1155
    Enormous, ponderous, and pedantic,
    With indignation frantic,
    And strength and force gigantic,
        Are desperately sped
        At his devoted head—   1160
Then in different style
The touchstone and the file,
And subtleties of art
In turn will play their part;
Analysis and rule,   1165
And every modern tool;
With critic scratch and scribble,
And nice invidious nibble;
Contending for the important choice,
A vast expenditure of human voice!   1170

Enter EURIPIDES and ÆSCHYLUS.

  EURIP. Don't give me your advice, I claim the
    seat
As being a better and superior artist.
  BACCH. What, Æschylus, don't you speak? you
    hear his language.
  EURIP. He's mustering up a grand commanding
    visage
—A silent attitude—the common trick   1175
That he begins with in his tragedies.
  BACCH. Come, have a care, my friend
—You'll say too much.
  EURIP. I know the man of old—I've scrutinized
And shown him long ago for what he is,   1180
A rude unbridled tongue, a haughty spirit;
Proud, arrogant, and insolently pompous;
Rough, clownish, boisterous, and overbearing.
  ÆSCH. Say'st thou me so? Thou bastard of the
    earth,
With thy patch'd robes and rags of sentiment   1185
Raked from the streets and stitch'd and tack'd to-
    gether!
Thou mumping, whining, beggarly hypocrite!
But you shall pay for it.
  BACCH. There now, Æschylus,   1189
You grow too warm. Restrain your ireful mood.
  ÆSCH. Yes; but I'll seize that sturdy beggar first,
And scratch and strip him bare of his pretensions.
  BACCH. Quick! Quick! A sacrifice to the winds—
    Make ready;
The storm of rage is gathering. Bring a victim.
  ÆSCH. —A wretch that has corrupted everything;
Our music with his melodies from Crete;   1196

Our morals with incestuous tragedies.

BACCH. Dear, worthy Æschylus, contain yourself,
And as for you, Euripides, move off   1199
This instant, if you're wise; I give you warning.
Or else, with one of his big thumping phrases,
You'll get your brains dash'd out, and all your
    notions
And sentiments and matter mash'd to pieces.
—And thee, most noble Æschylus, I beseech
With mild demeanor calm and affable   1205
To hear and answer.—For it ill beseems
Illustrious bards to scold like market-women.
But you roar out and bellow like a furnace.

EURIP. I'm up to it.—I'm resolved, and here I
    stand
Ready and steady—take what course you will;   1210
Let him be first to speak, or else let me.
I'll match my plots and characters against him;
My sentiments and language, and what not:
Aye! and my music too, my Meleager,
My Æolus and my Telephus and all.   1215

BACCH. Well, Æschylus,—determine. What say
    you?

ÆSCH. I wish the place of trial had been else-
    where,
I stand at disadvantage here.

BACCH. As how?

ÆSCH. Because my poems live on earth above,
And his died with him, and descended here,   1221
And are at hand as ready witnesses;
But you decide the matter: I submit.

BACCH. Come—let them bring me fire and frank-
    incense,
That I may offer vows and make oblations   1225
For an ingenious critical conclusion
To this same elegant and clever trial—
And you too,—sing me a hymn there.—To the
    Muses.

CHOR. To the Heavenly Nine we petition,
Ye, that on earth or in air are forever kindly pro-
    tecting the vagaries of learned ambition,   1230
And at your ease from above our sense and folly
    directing (or poetical contests inspecting,
Deign to behold for a while as a scene of amusing
    attention, all the struggles of style and in-
    vention),
Aid, and assist, and attend, and afford to the
    furious authors your refined and enlighten'd
    suggestions;
Grant them ability—force and agility, quick recol-
    lections, and address in their answers and
    questions,
Pithy replies, with a word to the wise, and pulling

and hauling, with inordinate uproar and
    bawling,   1235
Driving and drawing, like carpenters sawing, their
    dramas asunder:
With suspended sense and wonder,
All are waiting and attending
On the conflict now depending!

BACCH. Come, say your prayers, you two before
    the trial.   1240

ÆSCH. O Ceres, nourisher of my soul, maintain
    me
A worthy follower of thy mysteries.

BACCH. There, you there, make your offering.

EURIP. Well, I will;
But I direct myself to other deities.   1245

BACCH. Hey, what? Your own? Some new ones?

EURIP. Most assuredly!

BACCH. Well! Pray away, then—to your own
    new deities.

EURIP. Thou foodful Air, the nurse of all my
    notions;
And ye, the organic powers of sense and speech,
And keen refined olfactory discernment,   1251
Assist my present search for faults and errors.

CHOR. Here beside you, here are we,
Eager all to hear and see
This abstruse and mighty battle   1255
Of profound and learned prattle.
    But, as it appears to me,
Thus the course of it will be;
He, the junior and appellant,
Will advance as the assailant.   1260
Aiming shrewd satyric darts
At his rival's noble parts;
And with sallies sharp and keen
Try to wound him in the spleen,
While the veteran rends and raises   1265
Rifted, rough, uprooted phrases,
Wielded like a threshing staff
Scattering the dust and chaff.

BACCH. Come, now begin, dispute away, but
    first I give you notice
That every phrase in your discourse must be re-
    fined, avoiding
Vulgar absurd comparisons, and awkward silly
    joking.

EURIP. At the first outset, I forbear to state my
    own pretensions;
Hereafter I shall mention them, when his have
    been refuted;
After I shall have fairly shown, how he befool'd
    and cheated

The rustic audience that he found which Phrynichus bequeathed him.   1275

He planted first upon the stage a figure veil'd and
muffled

An Achilles or a Niobe, that never show'd their
faces;

But kept a tragic attitude, without a word to utter.
    BACCH. No more they did: 'tis very true.
    EURIP. —In the meanwhile the Chorus   1280

Strung on ten strophes right-an-end, but they
remain'd in silence.
    BACCH. I liked that silence well enough, as well,
perhaps, or better

Than those new talking characters—
    EURIP. That's from your want of judgment,

Believe me.   1285
    BACCH. Why, perhaps it is; but what was his
intention?
    EURIP. Why, mere conceit and insolence; to
keep the people waiting

Till Niobe should deign to speak, to drive his
drama forward.
    BACCH. O what a rascal. Now I see the tricks he
used to play me.

—What makes you writhe and winch about?—
    EURIP. Because he feels my censures.   1291

--Then having dragg'd and drawl'd along, half-
way to the conclusion,

He foisted in a dozen words of noisy boisterous
accent,

With lofty plumes and shaggy brows, mere bug-
bears of the language.

That no man ever heard before.—   1295
    ÆSCH. Alas! Alas!
    BACCH. Have done there!
    EURIP. He never used a simple word.
    BACCH. Don't grind your teeth so strangely.
    EURIP. But "Bulwarks and Scamanders" and
"Hippogrifs and Gorgons."   1300

'On burnish'd shields emboss'd in brass;" bloody
remorseless phrases

Which nobody could understand.
    BACCH. Well, I confess, for my part,

I used to keep awake at night, with guesses and
conjectures

To think what kind of foreign bird he meant by
griffin-horses.   1305
    ÆSCH. A figure on the heads of ships; you goose,
you must have seen them.
    BACCH. Well, from the likeness, I declare, I took
it for Eruxis.
    EURIP. So! Figures from the heads of ships are
fit for tragic diction.

    ÆSCH. Well, then—thou paltry wretch, explain.
What were your own devices?
    EURIP. Not stories about flying-stags, like yours.
and griffin-horses;   1310

Nor terms nor images derived from tapestry Persian hangings.

When I received the Muse from you I found her
puff'd and pamper'd

With pompous sentences and terms, a cumbrous
huge virago.

My first attention was applied to make her look
genteelly;

And bring her to a slighter shape by dint of
lighter diet;   1315

I fed her with plain household phrase, and cool
familiar salad.

With water-gruel episode, with sentimental jelly,

With moral mincemeat; till at length I brought
her into compass;

Cephisophon, who was my cook, contrived to
make them relish.

I kept my plots distinct and clear, and, to prevent
confusion,   1320

My leading characters rehearsed their pedigrees for
prologues.
    ÆSCH. 'Twas well, at least that you forbore to
quote your own extraction.
    EURIP. From the first opening of the scene, all
persons were in action;

The master spoke, the slave replied, the women,
young and old ones,

All had their equal share of talk—   1325
    ÆSCH. Come, then, stand forth and tell us,

What forfeit less than death is due for such an
innovation?
    EURIP. I did it upon principle, from democratic
motives.
    BACCH. Take care, my friend—upon that ground
your footing is but ticklish.
    EURIP. I taught these youths to speechify.   1330
    ÆSCH. I say so too.—Moreover

I say that—for the public good—you ought to have
been hang'd first.
    EURIP. The rules and forms of rhetoric,—the
laws of composition,

To prate—to state—and in debate to meet a question fairly:

At a dead lift to turn and shift—to make a nice
distinction.   1335
    ÆSCH. I grant it all—I make it all—my ground
of accusation.
    EURIP. The whole in cases and concerns occur
ring and recurring

At every turn and every day domestic and familiar,
So that the audience, one and all, from personal
    experience,
Were competent to judge the piece, and form a
    fair opinion   1340
Whether my scenes and sentiments agreed with
    truth and nature.
I never took them by surprise to storm their under-
    standings,
With Memnons and Tydides's and idle rattle-trap-
    pings
Of battle-steeds and clattering shields to scare them
    from their senses;
But for a test (perhaps the best) our pupils and
    adherents   1345
May be distinguish'd instantly by person and be-
    havior;
His are Phormisius the rough, Meganetes the
    gloomy,
Hobgoblin-headed, trumpet-mouth'd, grim-visaged,
    ugly-bearded;
But mine are Cleitophon the smooth,—Theramenes
    the gentle.
    BACCH. Theramenes—a clever hand, a universal
    genius.   1350
I never found him at a loss in all the turns of party
To change his watchword at a word or at a mo-
    ment's warning.
    EURIP. Thus it was that I began,
With a nicer, neater plan;
Teaching men to look about,   1355
Both within doors and without;
To direct their own affairs,
And their house and household wares;
Marking everything amiss—
"Where is that? and—What is this?"   1360
"This is broken—that is gone,"
'Tis the modern style and tone.
    BACCH. Yes, by Jove—and at their homes
Nowadays each master comes,
Of a sudden bolting in   1365
With an uproar and a din;
Rating all the servants round,
"If it's lost, it must be found.
Why was all the garlic wasted?
There, that honey has been tasted: 1370
And these olives pilfer'd here.
Where's the pot we bought last year?
What's become of all the fish?
Which of you has broke the dish?"
Thus it is, but heretofore,   1375
The moment that they cross'd the door,
They sat them down to doze and snore.

    CHOR. "Noble Achilles! you see the disaster
The shame and affront, and an enemy nigh!"
Oh! bethink thee, mighty master,   1380
    Think betimes of your reply;
Yet beware, lest anger force
Your hasty chariot from the course;
Grievous charges have been heard,
With many a sharp and bitter word,   1385
Notwithstanding, mighty chief,
Let Prudence fold her cautious reef
In your anger's swelling sail;
By degrees you may prevail,
But beware of your behavior   1390
Till the wind is in your favor:
Now for your answer, illustrious architect,
    Founder of lofty theatrical lays!
Patron in chief of our tragical trumperies!
    Open the floodgate of figure and phrase!   1395
    ÆSCH. My spirit is kindled with anger and
    shame,
To so base a competitor forced to reply,
But I needs must retort, or the wretch will report
That he left me refuted and foil'd in debate;
Tell me then, What are the principal merits   1400
Entitling a poet to praise and renown?
    EURIP. The improvement of morals, the progress
    of mind,
When a poet, by skill and invention,
Can render his audience virtuous and wise.
    ÆSCH. But if you, by neglect or intention,   1405
Have done the reverse, and from brave honest
    spirits
Depraved, and have left them degraded and base,
Tell me, what punishment ought you to suffer?
    BACCH. Death, to be sure!—Take that answer
    from me.
    ÆSCH. Observe then, and mark, what our citi-
    zens were,   1410
When first from my care they were trusted to you;
Not scoundrel informers, or paltry buffoons,
Evading the services due to the state;
But with hearts all on fire, for adventure and war,
Distinguished for hardiness, stature, and strength,
Breathing forth nothing but lances and darts,   1416
Arms, and equipment, and battle array,
Bucklers, and shields, and habergeons, and hau-
    berks,
Helmets, and plumes, and heroic attire.
    BACCH. There he goes, hammering on with his
    helmets,   1420
He'll be the death of me one of these days.
    EURIP. But how did you manage to make 'em
    so manly,

What was the method, the means that you took?
  BACCH. Speak, Æschylus, speak, and behave your-
    self better,   1424
And don't in your rage stand so silent and stern.
  ÆSCH. A drama, brimful with heroical spirit.
  EURIP. What did you call it?
  ÆSCH. "The Chiefs against Thebes,"
That inspired each spectator with martial ambition,
Courage, and ardor, and prowess, and pride.   1430
  BACCH. But you did very wrong to encourage
    the Thebans.
Indeed, you deserve to be punish'd, you do,
For the Thebans are grown to be capital soldiers,
You've done us a mischief by that very thing.
  ÆSCH. The fault was your own, if you took other
    courses;   1435
The lesson I taught was directed to you:
Then I gave you the glorious theme of "the Per-
    sians,"
Replete with sublime patriotical strains,
The record and example of noble achievement,
The delight of the city, the pride of the stage.   1440
  BACCH. I rejoiced, I confess, when the tidings
    were carried
To old King Darius, so long dead and buried,
And the chorus in concert kept wringing their
    hands,
Weeping and wailing, and crying, Alas!
  ÆSCH. Such is the duty, the task of a poet,   1445
Fulfilling in honor his office and trust.
Look to traditional history—look
To antiquity, primitive, early, remote:
See there, what a blessing illustrious poets
Conferred on mankind, in the centuries past,   1450
Orpheus instructed mankind in religion,
Reclaim'd them from bloodshed and barbarous
    rites:
Musæus deliver'd the doctrine of medicine,
And warnings prophetic for ages to come:
Next came old Hesiod, teaching us husbandry,
Plowing, and sowing, and rural affairs,   1456
Rural economy, rural astronomy,
Homely morality, labor, and thrift:
Homer himself, our adorable Homer,
What was his title to praise and renown?   1460
What, but the worth of the lessons he taught us,
Discipline, arms, and equipment of war?
  BACCH. Yes, but Pantacles was never the wiser;
For in the procession he ought to have led,
When his helmet was tied, he kept puzzling, and
    tried   1465
To fasten the crest on the crown of his head.

  ÆSCH. But other brave warriors and noble com-
    manders
Were train'd in his lessons to valor and skill;
Such was the noble heroical Lamachus;
Others besides were instructed by him;   1470
And I, from his fragments ordaining a banquet,
Furnish'd and deck'd with majestical phrase,
Brought forward the models of ancient achieve-
    ment,
Teucer, Patroclus, and chiefs of antiquity;
Raising and rousing Athenian hearts,   1474
When the signal of onset was blown in their ear,
With a similar ardor to dare and to do;
But I never allow'd of your lewd Sthenobœas,
Or filthy, detestable Phædras—not I—
Indeed, I should doubt if my drama throughout
Exhibit an instance of woman in love.   1481
  EURIP. No, you were too stern for an amorous
    turn,
For Venus and Cupid too stern and too stupid.
  ÆSCH. May they leave me at rest, and with peace
    in my breast,
And infest and pursue your kindred and you,   1485
With the very same blow that despatch'd you
    below.
  BACCH. That was well enough said; with the
    life that he led,
He himself in the end got a wound from a friend.
  EURIP. But what, after all, is the horrible mis-
    chief?   1489
My poor Sthenobœas, what harm have they done?
  ÆSCH. The example is followed, the practice has
    gain'd,
And women of family, fortune, and worth,
Bewilder'd with shame in a passionate fury,
Have poison'd themselves for Bellerophon's sake.
  EURIP. But at least you'll allow that I never
    invented it,   1495
Phædra's affair was a matter of fact.
  ÆSCH. A fact, with a vengeance! but horrible
    facts
Should be buried in silence, not bruited abroad,
Nor brought forth on the stage, nor emblazon'd
    in poetry,   1499
Children and boys have a teacher assign'd them—
The bard is a master for manhood and youth,
Bound to instruct them in virtue and truth,
Beholden and bound.
  EURIP. But is virtue a sound?
Can any mysterious virtue be found   1503
In bombastical, huge, hyperbolical phrase?
  ÆSCH. Thou dirty, calamitous wretch, recollect
That exalted ideas of fancy require

To be clothed in a suitable vesture of phrase;
And that heroes and gods may be fairly supposed
Discoursing in words of a mightier import, 1511
More lofty by far than the children of man;
As the pomp of apparel assign'd to their persons,
Produced on the stage and presented to view,
Surpasses in dignity, splendor, and luster 1515
Our popular garb and domestic attire,
A practice which nature and reason allow,
But which you disannull'd and rejected.

EURIP. As how?

ÆSCH. When you brought forth your kings, in
a villainous fashion, 1520
In patches and rags, as a claim for compassion.

EURIP. And this is a grave misdemeanor, forsooth!

ÆSCH. It has taught an example of sordid un-
truth;
For the rich of the city, that ought to equip,
And to serve with, a ship, are appealing to pity,
Pretending distress—with an overworn dress. 1526

BACCH. By Jove, so they do; with a waistcoat
brand new,
Worn closely within, warm and new for the skin;
And if they escape in this beggarly shape,
You'll meet 'em at market, I warrant 'em all, 1530
Buying the best at the fishmonger's stall.

ÆSCH. He has taught every soul to sophisticate
truth;
And debauch'd all the bodies and minds of the
youth;
Leaving them morbid, and pallid, and spare;
And the places of exercise vacant and bare:— 1535
The disorder has spread to the fleet and the crew;
The service is ruin'd, and ruin'd by you—
With prate and debate in a mutinous state;
Whereas, in my day, 'twas a different way;
Nothing they said, nor knew nothing to say, 1540
But to call for their porridge, and cry, "Pull away."

BACCH. Yes—yes, they knew this,
How to f . . . in the teeth
Of the rower beneath:
And befoul their own comrades, 1545
And pillage ashore;
But now they forget the command of the oar:—
Prating and splashing,
Discussing and dashing,
They steer here and there, 1550
With their eyes in the air,
Hither and thither,
Nobody knows whither.

ÆSCH. Can the reprobate mark in the course he
has run,

One crime unattempted, a mischief undone? 1555
With his horrible passions, of sisters and brothers,
And sons-in-law, tempted by villainous mothers,
And temples defiled with a bastardly birth,
And women, divested of honor or worth,
That talk about life "as a death upon earth"; 1560
And sophistical frauds and rhetorical bawds;
Till now the whole state is infested with tribes
Of scriveners and scribblers, and rascally scribes—
All practice of masculine vigor and pride,
Our wrestling and running, are all laid aside, 1565
And we see that the city can hardly provide
For the Feast of the Founder, a racer of force
To carry the torch and accomplish a course.

BACCH. Well, I laugh'd till I cried
The last festival tide, 1570
At the fellow that ran,—
'Twas a heavy fat man,
And he panted and hobbled,
And stumbled and wabbled,
And the pottery people about the gate, 1575
Seeing him hurried, and tired, and late,
Stood to receive him in open rank,
Helping him on with a hearty spank
Over the shoulder and over the flank,
The flank, the loin, the back, the shoulders, 1580
With shouts of applause from all beholders;
While he ran on with a filthy fright,
Puffing his link to keep it alight.

CHOR. Ere the prize is lost and won
Mighty doings will be done. 1585
Now then—(though to judge aright
Is difficult, when force and might
Are opposed with ready slight,
When the Champion that is cast
Tumbles uppermost at last) 1590
—Since you meet in equal match,
Argue, contradict and scratch,
Scuffle, and abuse and bite,
Tear and fight,
With all your wits and all your might. 1595
—Fear not for a want of sense
Or judgment in your audience,
That defect has been removed;
They're prodigiously improved,
Disciplined, alert and smart, 1600
Drill'd and exercised in art:
Each has got a little book,
In the which they read and look,
Doing all their best endeavor
To be critical and clever; 1605
Thus their own ingenious natures,
Aided and improved by learning,

Will provide you with spectators
　Shrewd, attentive, and discerning.

　　　·　　　·　　　·　　　·　　　·

　Eurip. Proceed— Continue!　　　　　1610
　Bacch. Yes, you must continue,
Æschylus, I command you to continue.
And you, keep a look-out and mark his blunders.
　Æsch. "From his sepulchral mound I call my
　　father
"To listen and hear"—　　　　　　　　1615
　Eurip. There's a tautology!
"To listen and hear"—
　Bacch. Why, don't you see, you ruffian!
It's a dead man he's calling to— Three times　1619
We call to 'em, but they can't be made to hear.
　Æsch. And you: your prologues, of what kind
　　were they?
　Eurip. I'll show ye; and if you'll point out a
　　tautology,
Or a single word clapped in to botch a verse—
That's all!—I'll give you leave to spit upon me.
　Bacch. Well, I can't help myself; I'm bound to
　　attend.　　　　　　　　　　　　　　1625
Begin then with these same fine-spoken prologues.
　Eurip. "Œdipus was at first a happy man." . . .
　Æsch. Not he, by Jove!—but born to misery;
Predicted and predestined by an oracle
Before his birth to murder his own father!　1630
—Could he have been "at first a happy man?"
　Eurip. . . . "But afterwards became a wretched
　　mortal."
　Æsch. By no means! he continued to be
　　wretched,
—Born wretched, and exposed as soon as born
Upon a potsherd in a winter's night;　　　1635
Brought up a foundling with disabled feet;
Then married—a young man to an aged woman,
That proved to be his mother—whereupon
He tore his eyes out.
　Bacch. To complete his happiness,　　　1640
He ought to have served at sea with Erasinides.

　　　·　　　·　　　·　　　·　　　·

There!—that's enough—now come to music, can't
　ye?
　Eurip. I mean it; I shall now proceed to expose
　　him
As a bad composer, awkward, uninventive,
Repeating the same strain perpetually.—　1645
　Chor. I stand in wonder and perplext
To think of what will follow next.
Will he dare to criticize
The noble bard, that did devise

Our oldest, boldest harmonies,　　　　　1650
Whose mighty music we revere?
Much I marvel, much I fear.—
　Eurip. Mighty fine music, truly! I'll give ye a
　　sample;
It's every inch cut out to the same pattern.
　Bacch. I'll mark—I've pick'd these pebbles up
　　for counters.　　　　　　　　　　　1655
　Eurip. Noble Achilles! Forth to the rescue!
Forth to the rescue with ready support!
Hasten and go,
There is havoc and woe,
Hasty defeat,　　　　　　　　　　　　1660
And a bloody retreat,
Confusion and rout,
And the terrible shout
Of a conquering foe,
Tribulation and woe!　　　　　　　　　1665
　Bacch. Whoh hoh there! we've had woes
　　enough, I reckon;
Therefore I'll go to wash away my woe
In a warm bath.
　Eurip. No, do pray wait an instant,
And let me give you first another strain,　　1670
Transferr'd to the stage from music to the lyre.
　Bacch. Proceed then—only give us no more woes.
　Eurip. The supremacy scepter and haughty com-
　　mand
Of the Grecian land—with a flatto-flatto-flatto-
　　thrat—　　　　　　　　　　　　　1674
And the ravenous sphinx, with her horrible brood,
Thirsting for blood—with a flatto-flatto-flatto-thrat,
And armies equipt for a vengeful assault,
For Paris's fault—with a flatto-flatto-flatto-thrat.
　Bacch. What herb is that same flatto-thrat?
　　Some simple,　　　　　　　　　　　1679
I guess, you met with in the field of Marathon:
—But such a tune as this! You must have learned it
From fellows hauling buckets at the well.
　Æsch. Such were the strains I purified and
　　brought
To just perfection—taught by Phrynichus,
Not copying him, but culling other flowers　1685
From those fair meadows which the Muses love—
—But he filches and begs, adapts and borrows
Snatches of tunes from minstrels in the street,
Strumpets and vagabonds—the lullabies　1689
Of nurses and old women—jigs and ballads—
I'll give ye a proof— Bring me a lyre here, some-
　body.
What signifies a lyre? the castanets
Will suit him better— Bring the castanets,
With Euripides's Muse to snap her fingers

In cadence to her master's compositions. 1695
  BACCH. This Muse, I take it, is a Lesbian Muse.
  ÆSCH. Gentle halcyons, ye that lave
  Your snowy plume,
Sporting on the summer wave;
  Ye too that around the room, 1700
On the rafters of the roof
Strain aloft your airy woof;
Ye spiders, spiders ever spinning,
Never ending, still beginning—
Where the dolphin loves to follow, 1705
Weltering in the surge's hollow,
Dear to Neptune and Apollo;
By the seamen understood
Ominous of harm or good;
In capricious, eager sallies, 1710
Chasing, racing round the galleys.
  ÆSCH. Well, now. Do you see this?
  BACCH. I see it—
  ÆSCH. Such is your music. I shall now proceed
To give a specimen of your monodies— 1715
  O dreary shades of night!
  What phantoms of affright
  Have scared my troubled sense
  With saucer eyes immense;
  And huge horrific paws 1720
  With bloody claws!
Ye maidens haste, and bring
From the fair spring
A bucket of fresh water; whose clear stream
May purify me from this dreadful dream: 1725
  But oh! my dream is out!
  Ye maidens search about!
O mighty powers of mercy, can it be;
  That Glyke, Glyke, she
(My friend and civil neighbor heretofore), 1730
Has robb'd my henroost of its feather'd store?
  With the dawn I was beginning,
  Spinning, spinning, spinning, spinning,
  Unconscious of the meditated crime;
  Meaning to sell my yarn at market-time. 1735
  Now tears alone are left me,
  My neighbor hath bereft me,
Of all—of all—of all—all but a tear!
Since he, my faithful trusty chanticleer
Is flown—is flown!—Is gone—is gone! 1740
—But, O ye nymphs of sacred Ida, bring
Torches and bows, with arrows on the string;
  And search around
  All the suspected ground:
And thou, fair huntress of the sky; 1745
Deign to attend, descending from on high—
—While Hecate, with her tremendous torch,

Even from the topmost garret to the porch
Explores the premises with search exact,
To find the thief and ascertain the fact— 1750
  BACCH. Come, no more songs!
  ÆSCH. I've had enough of 'em;
For my part, I shall bring him to the balance,
As a true test of our poetic merit,
To prove the weight of our respective verses. 1755
  BACCH. Well then, so be it—if it must be so,
That I'm to stand here like a cheesemonger
Retailing poetry with a pair of scales.
  CHOR. Curious eager wits pursue
Strange devices quaint and new, 1760
Like the scene you witness here,
Unaccountable and queer;
I myself, if merely told it,
If I did not here behold it,
Should have deem'd it utter folly, 1765
Craziness and nonsense wholly.

Enter PLUTO.

  BACCH. Move up; stand close to the balance!
  EURIP. Here are we—
  BACCH. Take hold now, and each of you repeat
  a verse,
And don't leave go before I call to you! 1770
  EURIP. We're ready.
  BACCH. Now, then, each repeat a verse.
  EURIP. "I wish that Argo with her woven wings."
  ÆSCH. "O streams of Sperchius, and ye pastured
  plains."
  BACCH. Let go!—See now—this scale outweighs
  that other 1775
Very considerably—
  EURIP. How did it happen?
  BACCH. He slipp'd a river in, like the wool-job-
  bers,
To moisten his meter—but your line was light,
A thing with wings—ready to fly away. 1780
  EURIP. Let him try once again then, and take
  hold.
  BACCH. Take hold once more.
  EURIP. We're ready.
  BACCH. Now repeat.
  EURIP. "Speech is the temple and altar of per-
  suasion." 1785
  ÆSCH. "Death is a God that loves no sacrifice."
  BACCH. Let go!—See there again! This scale sinks
  down;
No wonder that it should, with Death put into it,
The heaviest of all calamities.
  EURIP. But I put in persuasion finely express'd
In the best terms. 1791

BACCH. Perhaps so; but persuasion
Is soft and light and silly— Think of something
That's heavy and huge, to outweigh him, some-
    thing solid.
    EURIP. Let's see— Where have I got it? Some-
      thing solid?   1795
    BACCH. "Achilles has thrown twice— Twice a
      deuce ace!"
Come now, one trial more; this is the last.
    EURIP. "He grasp'd a mighty mace of massy
      weight."
    ÆSCH. "Cars upon cars, and corpses heap'd pell
      mell."
    BACCH. He has nick'd you again—   1800
    EURIP. Why so? What has he done?
    BACCH. He has heap'd ye up cars and corpses,
      such a load
As twenty Egyptian laborers could not carry—
    ÆSCH. Come, no more single lines—let him
      bring all,
His wife, his children, his Cephisophon,   1805
His books and everything, himself to boot—
I'll counterpoise them with a couple of lines.
    BACCH. Well, they're both friends of mine—I
      shan't decide
To get myself ill-will from either party;
One of them seems extraordinary clever,   1810
And the other suits my taste particularly.
    PLUTO. Won't you decide then, and conclude
      the business?
    BACCH. Suppose then I decide; what then?
    PLUTO. Then take him
Away with you, whichever you prefer,   1815
As a present for your pains in coming down here.
    BACCH. Heaven bless ye— Well—let's see now—
      Can't ye advise me?
This is the case—I'm come in search of a poet—
    PLUTO. With what design?   1820
    BACCH. With this design; to see
The City again restored to peace and wealth,
Exhibiting tragedies in a proper style.
—Therefore whichever gives the best advice
On public matters I shall take him with me.
—First then of Alcibiades, what think ye?   1826
The City is in hard labor with the question.
    EURIP. What are her sentiments towards him?
    BACCH. What?
"She loves and she detests and longs to have him."
But tell me, both of you, your own opinions.   1831
    EURIP. I hate the man, that in his country's ser-
      vice
Is slow, but ready and quick to work her harm;
Unserviceable except to serve himself.

    BACCH. Well said, by Jove!—Now you— Give us
    a sentence.   1835
    ÆSCH. 'Tis rash and idle policy to foster
A lion's whelp within the city walls,
But when he's rear'd and grown you must indulge
    him.
    BACCH. By Jove, then I'm quite puzzled; one of
    them
Has answer'd clearly, and the other sensibly: 1840
But give us both of ye one more opinion;
—What means are left of safety for the state?
    EURIP. To tack Cinesias like a pair of wings
To Cleocritus' shoulders, and dispatch them
From a precipice to sail across the seas.   1845
    BACCH. It seems a joke; but there's some sense
    in it.
    EURIP. . . . . Then being both equipp'd with little
    cruets
They might co-operate in a naval action,
By sprinkling vinegar in the enemies' eyes.
—But I can tell you and will.   1850
    BACCH. Speak, and explain then—
    EURIP. If we mistrust where present trust is
    placed,
Trusting in what was heretofore mistrusted—
    BACCH. How! What? I'm at a loss— Speak it
    again   1854
Not quite so learnedly—more plainly and simply.
    EURIP. If we withdraw the confidence we placed
In these our present statesmen, and transfer it
To those whom we mistrusted heretofore,
This seems I think our fairest chance for safety:
    If with our present counselors we fail,   1860
Then with their opposites we might succeed.
    BACCH. That's capitally said, my Palamedes!
My politician! Was it all your own?
Your own invention?
    EURIP. All except the cruets;   1865
That was a notion of Cephisophon's.
    BACCH. Now you—what say you?
    ÆSCH. Inform me about the city—
What kind of persons has she placed in office?
Does she promote the worthiest?   1870
    BACCH. No, not she,
She can't abide 'em.
    ÆSCH. Rogues then she prefers?
    BACCH. Not altogether, she makes use of 'em
Perforce as it were.   1875
    ÆSCH. Then who can hope to save
A state so wayward and perverse, that finds
No sort of habit fitted for her wear?
Drugget or superfine, nothing will suit her!   1879
    BACCH. Do think a little how she can be saved.

ÆSCH. Not here; when I return there, I shall
  speak.

BACCH. No, do pray send some good advice before you.

ÆSCH. When they regard their lands as enemy's
  ground,
Their enemy's possessions as their own,
Their seamen and the fleet their only safeguard,
Their sole resource hardship and poverty,   1886
And resolute endurance in distress—

BACCH. That's well,—but juries eat up everything,
And we shall lose our supper if we stay.

PLUTO. Decide then—   1890

BACCH. You'll decide for your own selves,
I'll make a choice according to my fancy.

EURIP. Remember, then, your oath to your poor
  friend;
And, as you swore and promised, rescue me.

BACCH. "It was my tongue that swore"—I fix
  on Æschylus.   1895

EURIP. O wretch! what have you done?

BACCH. Me? Done? What should I?
Voted for Æschylus to be sure— Why not?

EURIP. And after such a villainous act, you dare
To view me face to face— Art not ashamed?   1900

BACCH. Why, shame, in point of fact, is nothing
  real:
Shame is the apprehension of a vision
Reflected from the surface of opinion—
—The opinion of the public—they must judge.

EURIP. O cruel!—Will you abandon me to
  death?   1905

BACCH. Why, perhaps death is life, and life is
  death,
And victuals and drink an illusion of the senses;
For what is Death but an eternal sleep?
And does not Life consist in sleeping and eating?

PLUTO. Now, Bacchus, you'll come here with us
  within.   1910

BACCH. What for?

PLUTO. To be received and entertain'd
With a feast before you go.

BACCH. That's well imagined,
With all my heart—I've not the least objection.

CHOR. Happy is the man possessing   1916
The superior holy blessing
Of a judgment and a taste
Accurate, refined and chaste;
As it plainly doth appear   1920
In the scene presented here;
Where the noble worthy Bard
Meets with a deserved reward,

Suffer'd to depart in peace
Freely with a full release,   1925
To revisit once again
His kindred and his countrymen—
    Hence moreover
    You discover,
That to sit with Socrates,   1930
In a dream of learned ease;
Quibbling, counter-quibbling, prating,
Argufying and debating
With the metaphysic sect,
Daily sinking in neglect,   1935
Growing careless, incorrect,
While the practice and the rules
Of the true poetic Schools
Are renounced or slighted wholly,
Is a madness and a folly.   1940

PLUTO. Go forth with good wishes and hearty
  good-will,
And salute the good people on Pallas's hill;
Let them hear and admire father Æschylus still
In his office of old which again he must fill:
—You must guide and direct them,   1945
Instruct and correct them,
With a lesson in verse,
For you'll find them much worse;
Greater fools than before, and their folly much
  more,
And more numerous far than the blockheads of
  yore—   1950
—And give Cleophon this,
And bid him not miss,
But be sure to attend
To the summons I send:
To Nicomachus too,   1955
And the rest of the crew
That devise and invent
    New taxes and tribute,
Are summonses sent,
    Which you'll mind to distribute.   1960
Bid them come to their graves,
Or, like runaway slaves,
If they linger and fail,
We shall drag them to jail;
Down here in the dark   1965
With a brand and a mark.

ÆSCH. I shall do as you say;
But the while I'm away,
Let the seat that I held
Be by Sophocles fill'd,   1970
As deservedly reckon'd
My pupil and second

In learning and merit
And tragical spirit—
And take special care;   1975
Keep that reprobate there
Far aloof from the Chair;
Let him never sit in it
An hour or a minute,
By chance or design   1980
To profane what was mine.
   PLUTO. Bring forward the torches!—The Chorus
   shall wait'
And attend on the Poet in triumph and state
With a thundering chant of majestical tone 1984
To wish him farewell, with a tune of his own.

CHOR. Now may the powers of the earth give
   a safe and speedy departure
To the Bard at his second birth, with a prosperous
   happy revival;
And may the city, fatigued with wars and long
   revolution,
At length be brought to return to just and wise
   resolutions;
Long in peace to remain— Let restless Cleophon
   hasten   1990
Far from amongst us here—since wars are his only
   diversion,
Thrace his native land will afford him wars in
   abundance.

PLAUTUS

The Captives

DRAMATIS PERSONÆ

ERGASILUS, *a parasite*
HEGIO, *an old gentleman*
PHILOCRATES, *an Elian Knight*⎫ *the prisoners*
TYNDARUS, *son of Hegio*   ⎭
ARISTOPHONTES, *a prisoner*
PHILOPOLEMUS, *a young man, son of Hegio*
STALAGMUS, *a slave*
Overseers of slaves
A boy

*The Scene represents the house of Hegio in Ætolia.
Before the house are seen standing in chains the
two prisoners,* PHILOCRATES *and* TYNDARUS.

   PROLOGUE. You all can see two prisoners standing
   here,
Standing in bonds; they stand, they do not sit;
In this you'll witness that I speak the truth.
Old Hegio, who lives here, is this one's father;
But how he's come to be his father's slave   5
My prologue shall inform you, if you'll listen.
This old man had two sons; the one of whom
Was stolen by a slave when four years old.
He ran away to Elis and there sold him
To this one's father.
        —Do you see?—That's right!   10

Yon fellow in the gallery says he doesn't?
Let him come nearer, then! What, there's no
   room?
If there's no room to sit, there's room to walk!
You'd like to send me begging, would you, sir!
Pray, don't suppose I'll crack my lungs for *you!*
You gentlemen of means and noble rank   16
Receive the rest; I hate to be in debt.
That run-a-way, as I've already said,
When in his flight he'd stolen from his home
His master's son, sold him to this man's father, 20
Who, having bought him, gave him to his son
To be his valet; for the two lads were
Much of an age. Now he's his father's slave
In his own home, nor does his father know it;
See how the gods play ball with us poor men!   25
Now then, I've told you how he lost *one* son.
The Ætolians and the Elians being at war,
His *other* son, a not uncommon thing
In war, was taken prisoner; and a doctor
At Elis, called Menarchus, bought him there.   30
His father then began to buy up Elians,
To see if he could find one to exchange
Against his son,—the one that is a prisoner;
The other, who's at home, he doesn't know.
Now, only yesterday he heard a rumor   35

Plautus, *The Captives.* Translated by Edward H. Sugden. Titus Maccius Plautus was born in Umbria
about 254 B.C., came to Rome, suffered varying fortunes, wrote comedies, and died in Rome in 184 B.C.

How that an Elian knight of highest rank
And noblest family was taken prisoner;
He spared no cash if he might save his son;
And so, to get him home more readily,
He bought these two from the commissioners. 40
But they between themselves have laid a plot,
So that the slave may get his lord sent home.
Thus they've exchanged their clothing and their
  names;
He's called Philocrates, *he* Tyndarus,
And either plays the other's part today. 45
The slave today will work this clever dodge,
And get his master set at liberty.
By the same act he'll save his brother too,
And get him brought back free to home and father,
Though all unwitting: oft we do more good 50
In ignorance than by our best-laid plans.
Well, ignorantly, in their own deceit,
They've so arranged and worked their little trick,
That he shall still remain his father's slave.
For now, not knowing it, he serves his father. 55
What things of naught are men, when one reflects
  on 't!
This story's ours to act, and yours to see.
But let me give you one brief word of warning:
It's well worth while to listen to this play.
It's not been treated in a hackneyed fashion, 60
Nor like the rest of plays; here you'll not find
Verses that are too nasty to be quoted.
Here is no perjured pimp, or crafty girl,
Or braggart captain.—Pray, don't be afraid
Because I said a war was going on 65
Between the Ætolians and the Elians;
The battles won't take place upon the stage.
We're dressed for comedy; you can't expect
That we should act a tragedy all at once.
If anybody's itching for a fight, 70
Just let him start a quarrel; if he gets
An opposite that's stronger, I dare bet
He'll quickly see more fighting than he likes,
And never long to see a fight again.
I'm off. Farewell, ye most judicious judges 75
At home, most valiant fighters in the field!
                                        [*Exit.*

Enter ERGASILUS *from the town.*

ERG. Grace is the name the boys have given me,
Because I'm always found *before the meat!*
The wits, I know, say it's ridiculous;
But so don't I! For at the banquet-table 80
Your gamester throws the dice and asks for *grace.*
Then is *grace* there or not? Of course she is!
But, more of course, we parasites are there,

Though no one ever asks or summons us!
Like mice we live on other people's food; 85
In holidays, when folks go out of town,
Our teeth enjoy a holiday as well.
As, when it's warm, the snails lie in their shells,
And, failing dew, live on their native juices;
So parasites lie hid in misery 90
All through the holidays, living on their juices,
Whilst those they feed on jaunt it in the country.
During the holidays, we parasites
Are greyhounds; when they're over, we are mastiffs,
Bred out of "Odious" by "Prince of Bores." 95
Now here, unless your parasite can stand
Hard fisticuffs, and has no strong objection
To have the crockery broken on his pate,
He'd better go and take a porter's billet
At the Trigeminal gate; which lot, I fear, 100
Is not at all unlikely to be mine.
My patron has been captured by the foe—
The Ætolians and the Elians are at war,
(This is Ætolia); Philopolemus,
The son of Hegio here, whose house this is, 105
In Elis lies a prisoner; so this house
A house of lamentation is to me;
As oft as I behold it, I must weep.
Now for his son's sake, he's begun a trade,
Dishonorable, hateful to himself, 110
He's buying prisoners, if perchance he may
Find any to exchange against his son.
O how I pray that he may gain his wish!
Till he's recovered, I am past recovery.
The other youths are selfish, hopelessly, 115
And only he keeps up the ancient style.
I've never flattered him without reward;
And the good father takes after his son!
Now I'll go see him. Ha! the door is opening,
Whence I have often come, just drunk with gorg-
  ing. 120

Enter from the house HEGIO *and an Overseer.*

HEG. Attend to me; those prisoners that I bought
A day ago from the Commissioners
Out of the spoil, put lighter fetters on them;
Take off these heavier ones with which they're
  bound,
And let them walk indoors or out at will; 125
But watch them with the utmost carefulness.
For when a free man's taken prisoner,
He's just like a wild bird; if once he gets
A chance of running off, it's quite enough;
You needn't hope to catch your man again. 130
OVER. Why, all of us would rather far be free
Than slaves.

Heg. Why not take steps, then, to be free?

Over. Shall I give *leg-bail?* I've naught else to give!

Heg. I fancy that in that case you would *catch it!*

Over. I'll be like that wild bird you spoke about.

Heg. All right; then I will clap you in a cage.   136
Enough of this; do what I said, and go.

[*Exit Overseer into the house.*

I'll to my brother's, to my other captives,
To see how they've behaved themselves last night,
And then I'll come back home again straightway.

Erg. [*aside*]. It grieves me that the poor old man
should ply   141
This gaoler's trade to save his hapless son.
But if perchance the son can be brought back,
The father may turn hangman: what care I?   144

Heg. Who speaks there?

Erg.   One who suffers in your grief.
I'm growing daily thinner, older, weaker!
See, I'm all skin and bones, as lean as lean!
All that I eat at home does me no good;
Only a bite at a friend's agrees with me.

Heg. Ergasilus! hail!

Erg.   Heav'n bless you, Hegio!   150

Heg. Don't weep!

Erg.   Not weep for him? What, not bewail
That excellent young man?

Heg.   I always knew
You and my son to be the best of friends.

Erg. Alas! we don't appreciate our blessings
Till we have lost the gifts we once enjoyed.   155
Now that your son is in the foeman's hands,
I realize how much he was to me!

Heg. Ah, if a stranger feels his loss so much,
What must *I* feel? He was my only joy.

Erg. A stranger? I a stranger? Hegio,   160
Never say that nor cherish such a thought!
Your only joy he was, but oh! to me
Far dearer than a thousand only joys.

Heg. You're right to make your friend's distress
your own;
But come, cheer up!

Erg.   Alas! it pains me here,   165
That now the feaster's army is discharged.

Heg. And can't you meantime find another general
To call to arms this army that's discharged?

Erg. No fear! since Philopolemus was taken,
Who filled that post, they all refuse to act.   170

Heg. And it's no wonder they refuse to act.
You need so many men of divers races
To work for you; first, those of Bakerton;
And several tribes inhabit Bakerton;

Then men of Breadport and of Biscuitville,   175
Of Thrushborough and Ortolania,
And all the various soldiers of the sea.

Erg. How oft the noblest talents lie concealed!
O what a splendid general you would make,   179
Though now you're serving as a private merely.

Heg. Be of good cheer; in a few days, I trust,
I shall receive my dear son home again.
I've got a youthful Elian prisoner,
Whom I am hoping to exchange for him,
One of the highest rank and greatest wealth.   185

Erg. May Heaven grant it!

Heg.   Where've you been invited
To dine today?

Erg.   Why, nowhere that I know of.
Why do you ask?

Heg.   Because it is my birthday;
And so, I pray you, come and dine with me.

Erg. Well said indeed!

Heg.   That is if you're content
With frugal fare.

Erg.   Well, if it's not *too* frugal;   191
I get enough of that, you know, at home.

Heg. Well, name your figure!

Erg.   Done! unless I get
A better offer, and on such conditions
As better suit my partners and myself.   195
As I am selling you my whole estate,
It's only fair that I should make my terms.

Heg. I fear that this estate you're selling me
Has got a bottomless abyss within't!
But if you come, come early.

Erg.   Now, if you like!   200

Heg. Go hunt a hare; you've only caught a
weasel.
The path my guest must tread is full of stones.

Erg. You won't dissuade me, Hegio; don't think
it!
I'll get my teeth well shod before I come.

Heg. My table's really coarse.

Erg.   Do you eat brambles?   205

Heg. My dinner's from the soil.

Erg.   So is good pork

Heg. Plenty of cabbage!

Erg.   Food for invalids!
What more?

Heg.   Be there in time.

Erg.   I'll not forget.

[*Exit* Ergasilus *to the marketplace.*

Heg. Now I'll go in and look up my accounts,
To see what I have lying at my banker's;   210
Then to my brother's, as I said just now.

[*Exit* Hegio *into the house.*

Enter Overseers, Philocrates *and* Tyndarus, *each in the other's clothes, and other slaves.*

Over. Since Heaven has willed it should be so,
That you must drink this cup of woe,
Why, bear it with a patient mind,
And so your pain you'll lighter find. 215
At home, I dare say, you were free;
Now that your lot is slavery,
Just take it as a thing of course,
Instead of making matters worse;
Behave yourselves and don't be queasy 220
About your lord's commands; 'tis easy.
Prisoners. Oh, oh!
Over. No need for howls and cries!
I see your sorrow in your eyes.
Be brave in your adversities. 224
Tyn. But we're ashamed to wear these chains.
Over. My lord would suffer far worse pains,
Should he leave you to range at large out of his
custody,
Or set you at liberty whom he bought yesterday.
Tyn. Oh, he needn't fear that he'll lose his gains;
Should he release us, we know what's our duty,
sir. 230
Over. Yes, you'll run off; I know *that.* You're a
beauty, sir!
Tyn. Run off? run off where?
Over. To the land of your birth.
Tyn. Nay, truly, it never would answer
To imitate runaway slaves.
Over. Well, by Jove!
I'd advise you, if you get a chance, sir. 235
Tyn. One thing I beg of you.
Over. What's your petition, sir?
Tyn. Give us a chance of exchanging a word,
Where there's no fear that we'll be overheard.
Over. Granted! Go, leave them. We'll take our
position there.
See that your talk doesn't last too long! 240
Tyn. Oh, that's my intention. So now, come
along!
Over. Go, leave them alone.
Tyn. We ever shall own
We're in your debt for the kindness you've shown
to us;
You have the power, and you've proved yourself
bounteous. 245
Philoc. Come away farther, as far as we can
from them;
We must contrive to conceal our fine plan from
them,
Never disclose any trace of our trickery,
Else we shall find all our dodges a mockery.
Once they get wind of it, 250
There'll be an end of it;
For if you are my master brave,
And I pretend to be your slave,
Then we must watch with greatest care;
Of eavesdroppers we must beware. 255
With caution and skill keep your senses all waking;
There's no time to sleep; it's a big undertaking.
Tyn. So I'm to be master?
Philoc. Yes, that is the notion.
Tyn. And so for your head (I would pray you
remark it), 259
You want me to carry my own head to market!
Philoc. I know.
Tyn. Well, when you've gained your wish, re-
member my devotion.
This is the way that you'll find most men treating
you;
Until they have
The boon they crave, 265
They're kind as can be; but success makes the
knave!
When they have got it, they set to work cheating
you.
Now I have told you the treatment you owe to me.
You I regard as a father, you know, to me.
Philoc. Nay, let us say,—no conventions shall
hinder us,— 270
Next to my own, you're my father, dear Tyndarus.
Tyn. That will do!
Philoc. Now then, I warn you always to remem-
ber this;
I no longer am your master but your slave; don't
be remiss.
Since kind Heav'n has shown us plainly that the
way ourselves to save 275
Is for me, who was your master, now to turn into
your slave,
Where before I gave you orders, now I beg of you
in prayer,
By the changes in our fortune, by my father's
kindly care,
By the common fetters fastened on us by the
enemy,
Think of who you were and are, and pay no more
respect to me 280
Than I used to pay to you, when you were slave
and I was free.
Tyn. Well, I know that I am you and you are me!
Philoc. Yes, stick to that!
Then I hope that by your shrewdness we shall gain
what we are at.

Enter HEGIO *from his house.*

HEG. [*addressing someone inside*]. I'll be back
    again directly when I've looked into the case:
Where are those whom I directed at the door to
    take their place?   285
  PHILOC. O by Pollux! you've been careful that we
    shouldn't be to seek;
Thus by bonds and guards surrounded we have
    had no chance to sneak!
  HEG. Howsoever careful, none can be as careful
    as he ought;
When he thinks he's been most careful, oft your
    careful man is caught.
Don't you think that I've just cause to keep a care-
    ful watch on you,   290
When I've had to pay so large a sum of money for
    the two?
  PHILOC. Truly we've no right to blame you, that
    you watch and guard us thus;
And if we should get a chance and run away, you
    can't blame *us*.
  HEG. Just like you, my son is held in slavery by
    your countrymen.
  PHILOC. Was he taken prisoner?
  HEG.   Yes.
  PHILOC.   We weren't the only cowards then.
  HEG. Come aside here; there is something I
    would ask of you alone;   296
And I hope you'll not deceive me.
  PHILOC.   Everything I know I'll own;
If in aught I'm ignorant, I'll tell you so, upon my
    life.

HEGIO *and* PHILOCRATES *go aside;* TYNDARUS *stand-
    ing where he can hear their conversation.*

  TYN. [*aside*]. Now the old man's at the barber's;
    see my master whets his knife!
Why, he hasn't even put an apron on to shield his
    clothes!   300
Will he shave him close or only cut his hair? Well,
    goodness knows!
But if he has any sense, he'll crop the old man
    properly!
  HEG. Come now, tell me, would you rather be a
    slave or get set free?
  PHILOC. What I want is that which brings me
    most of good and least of ill.
Though I must confess my slavery wasn't very
    terrible;   305
Little difference was made between me and my
    master's son.

TYN. [*aside*]. Bravo! I'd not give a cent for
    Thales, the Milesian!
For, compared with this man's cunning, he is but
    a trifling knave.
Mark how cleverly he talks, as if he'd always been
    a slave!
  HEG. Tell me to what family Philocrates belongs?
  PHILOC.   The Goldings;   310
That's a family most wealthy both in honors and
    in holdings.
  HEG.   Is your master there respected?
  PHILOC. Highly, by our foremost men.
  HEG. If his influence amongst them is as great as
    you maintain,
Are his riches fat?
  PHILOC.   I guess so! Fat as suet, one
    might say.
  HEG. Is his father living?   314
  PHILOC. Well, he *was,* sir, when we came away;
Whether he still lives or not, you'll have to go to
    hell to see.
  TYN. [*aside*]. Saved again! for now he's adding
    to his lies philosophy!
  HEG. What's his name, I pray?
  PHILOC.   Thensaurocrœsonicochrysides.
  HEG. I suppose a sort of nickname given to show
    how rich he is.
  PHILOC. Nay, by Pollux! it was given him for his
    avarice and greed.   320
Truth to tell you, Theodoromedes is his name in-
    deed.
  HEG. What is this? His father's grasping?
  PHILOC. Grasping? Aye, most covetous!
Just to show you, when he sacrifices to his Genius,
All the vessels that he uses are of Samian crockery,
Lest the Genius should steal them! There's his
    character, you see.   325
  HEG. Come with me then. [*Aside.*] Now I'll ask
    the other what I want to know.
[*To* TYNDARUS.] Now, Philocrates, your slave has
    acted as a man should do,
For from him I've learnt your birth; the whole he
    has confessed to me.
If you will admit the same, it shall to your advan-
    tage be;
For your slave has told me all.
  TYN.   It was his duty so to do.   330
All is true that he's confessed; although I must ad-
    mit to you,
'Twas my wish to hide from you my birth, and
    wealth, and family;
But now, Hegio, that I've lost my fatherland and
    liberty,

Naturally he should stand in awe of you much
  more than me,
Since by force of arms our fortunes stand on an
  equality. 335
I remember when he durst not speak a word to do
  me ill;
He may strike me now; so fortune plays with mor-
  tals as she will.
I, once free, am made a slave and brought from
  high to low degree,
And instead of giving orders must obey submis-
  sively.
But if I should have a master, such as *I* was when
  at home, 340
I've no fear that his commands will prove unjust
  or burdensome.
Hegio, will you bear from me a word of warning?
  HEG. Yes, say on.
  TYN. Once I was as free and happy as your own
  beloved son.
But the force of hostile arms has robbed him of his
  freedom, too;
He's a slave amongst our people, just as I am here
  with you. 345
Certainly there is a God who watches us where'er
  we be;
He will treat your son exactly as He finds that you
  treat me.
Virtue sure will be rewarded, vice will e'er bring
  sorrow on—
I've a father misses me, as much as you your
  absent son.
  HEG. Yes, I know. Do you admit, then, what
  your slave confessed to me? 350
  TYN. I admit, sir, that my father is a man of
  property,
And that I'm of noble birth. But I beseech you,
  Hegio
Do not let my ample riches cause your avarice to
  grow,
Lest my father think it better, though I am his
  only son,
That I should continue serving you and keep your
  livery on, 355
Rather than come home a beggar to my infinite
  disgrace.
  HEG. Thanks to Heav'n and my forefathers, I've
  been wealthy all my days;
Nor is wealth, in my opinion, always useful to
  obtain—
Many a man I've known degraded to a beast by
  too much gain;

There are times when loss is better far than gain,
  in every way. 360
Gold! I hate it! Oh, how many people has it led
  astray!
Now, attend to me, and I my purpose plainly will
  declare:
There in Elis, with your people, is my son a pris-
  oner.
If you'll bring him back to me, you shall not pay
  a single cent:
I'll release you and your slave too; otherwise I'll
  not relent. 365
  TYN. That's the noblest, kindest offer! All the
  world can't find your mate!
But is he in slavery to a private man or to the
  State?
  HEG. To Menarchus, a physician.
  TYN. Ah! my client! all is plain;
Everything will be as easy as the falling of the rain.
  HEG. Bring him home as soon as may be.
  TYN. Certainly; but, Hegio— 370
  HEG. What's your wish? For I'll do aught in
  reason.
  TYN. Listen; you shall know.
I don't ask that I should be sent back until your
  son has come.
Name the price you'll take for yonder slave, to let
  me send him home,
That he may redeem your son.
  HEG. Nay, someone else I should prefer,
Whom I'll send when truce is made to go and
  meet your father there. 375
He can take your father any message that you like
  to send.
  TYN. It's no use to send a stranger; all your toil
  in smoke would end.
Send my slave, he'll do the business just as soon as
  he gets there;
You won't hit on anybody you can send who's
  trustier,
Or more faithful; he's a man who does his work
  with all his heart. 380
Boldly trust your son to him; and he will truly
  play his part.
Don't you fear! at my own peril I'll make trial of
  his truth;
For he knows my kindness to him; I can safely
  trust the youth.
  HEG. Well, I'll send him at your risk, if you
  consent.
  TYN. Oh, I agree. 384
  HEG. Let him start as soon as may be.

TYN.   That will suit me perfectly.
HEG. Well, then, if he doesn't come back here
   you'll pay me fifty pounds;
Are you willing?
   TYN.   Certainly.
   HEG.   Then go and loose
   him from his bonds;
And the other too.
   TYN.   May Heaven ever treat you graciously!
Since you've shown me so much kindness, and
   from fetters set me free.
Ah, my neck's more comfortable, now I've cast
   that iron ruff!   390
   HEG. Gifts when given to good people win their
   gratitude! Enough!
Now, if you are going to send him, teach and tell
   him what to say,
When he gets home to your father. Shall I call
   him?
   TYN.   Do so, pray!

HEGIO *crosses the stage to* PHILOCRATES *and ad-*
dresses him.

   HEG. Heav'n bless this project to my son and me,
And you as well! I, your new lord, desire   395
That you should give your true and faithful service
To your old master. I have lent you to him,
And set a price of fifty pounds upon you.
He says he wants to send you to his father
That he may ransom my dear son and make   400
An interchange between us of our sons.
   PHILOC. Well, I'm prepared to serve either one
   or t' other;
I'm like a wheel, just twist me as you please!
I'll turn this way or that, as you command.
   HEG. I'll see that you don't lose by your com-
   pliance;   405
Since you are acting as a good slave should.
Come on.
         Now, here's your man.
   TYN.   I thank you, sir,
For giving me this opportunity
Of sending him to bring my father word
About my welfare and my purposes;   410
All which he'll tell my father as I bid him.
Now, Tyndarus, we've come to an agreement,
That you should go to Elis to my father;
And should you not come back, I've undertaken
To pay the sum of fifty pounds for you.   415
   PHILOC. A fair agreement! for your father looks
For me or for some other messenger
To come from hence to him.

TYN.   Then, pray attend,
And I will tell you what to tell my father.
   PHILOC. I have always tried to serve you hitherto,
   Philocrates,   420
As you wished me, to the utmost of my poor abili-
   ties.
That I'll ever seek and aim at, heart and soul and
   strength alway.
   TYN. That is right: you know your duty. Listen
   now to what I say.
First of all, convey a greeting to my parents dear
   from me,
And to other relatives and friends, if any you
   should see.   425
Say I'm well, and held in bondage by this worthy
   gentleman,
Who has shown and ever shows me all the honor
   that he can.
   PHILOC. Oh, you needn't tell me that, it's rooted
   in my memory.
   TYN. If I didn't see my keeper, I should think
   that I was free.
Tell my father of the bargain I have made with
   Hegio,   430
For the ransom of his son.
   PHILOC.   Don't stay to tell me that. I know.
   TYN. He must purchase and restore him, then
   we both shall be set free.
   PHILOC. Good!
   HEG.   Bid him be quick, for your sake
   and for mine in like degree.
   PHILOC. You don't long to see your son more
   ardently than he does his!
   HEG. Why, each loves his own.
   PHILOC.   Well, have you any other messages?
   TYN. Yes; don't hesitate to say I'm well and
   happy, Tyndarus;   436
That no shade of disagreement ever separated us;
That you've never once deceived me nor opposed
   your master's will,
And have stuck to me like wax in spite of all this
   flood of ill.
By my side you've stood and helped me in my sore
   adversities,   440
True and faithful to me ever. When my father
   hears of this,
Tyndarus, and knows your noble conduct towards
   himself and me,
He will never be so mean as to refuse to set you
   free;
When I'm back I'll spare no effort that it may be
   brought about.

To your toil, and skill, and courage, and your wisdom, there's no doubt   445
That I owe my chance of getting to my father's
home again:
For 'twas you confessed my birth and riches to
this best of men;
So you set your master free from fetters by your
ready wit.

PHILOC. Yes, I did, sir, as you say; I'm glad that
you remember it.

But indeed, you've well deserved it at my hands,
Philocrates;   450
For if I should try to utter all your many kind-
nesses,
Night would fall before I'd finished; you have
done as much for me
As if you had been my slave.

HEG.   Good heavens, what nobility
Shines in both their dispositions! I can scarce re-
frain from tears
When I see their true affection, and the way the
slave reveres   455
And commends his master.

TYN.   Truly he has not commended me
Even a hundredth part as much as he himself deserves to be.

HEG. Well, as you've behaved so nobly, now you
have a splendid chance
Here to crown your services by doubly faithful
vigilance.

PHILOC. As I wish the thing accomplished, so I
shall do all I know;   460
To assure you of it, I call Jove to witness, Hegio!
That I never will betray Philocrates, I'll take my
oath!

HEG. Honest fellow!

PHILOC.   I will treat him as myself,
upon my troth!

TYN. From these loving protestations, mind you
never never swerve.
And if I've said less about you than your faithful
deeds deserve,   465
Pray you, don't be angry with me on account of
what I've said;
But remember you are going with a price upon
your head;
And that both my life and honor I have staked on
your return;
When you've left my sight, I pray you, don't forget
what you have sworn,
Or when you have left me here in slavery instead
of you,   470

Think that you are free, and so neglect what you
are pledged to do,
And forget your solemn promise to redeem this
good man's son.
Fifty pounds, remember, is the price that we've
agreed upon.
Faithful to your faithful master, do not let your
faith be bought;
And I'm well assured my father will do everything
he ought.   475
Keep me as your friend forever, and this good old
man as well.
Take my hand in yours, I pray you, swear an oath
unbreakable,
That you'll always be as faithful as I've ever been
to you.
Mind, you're now my master, aye, protector, and
my father too!
I commit to you my hopes and happiness.

PHILOC.   O that'll do!   480
Are you satisfied if I can carry this commission
through?

TYN. Yes.

PHILOC.   Then I'll return in such a manner as
shall please you both.
Is that all, sir?

HEG.   Come back quickly.

PHILOC.   So I will, upon my troth.

HEG. Come along then to my banker's; I'll provide you for the way.
Also I will get a passport from the prætor.

TYN.   Passport, eh?   485

HEG. Yes, to get him through the army so that
they may let him go.
Step inside.

TYN.   A pleasant journey!

PHILOC.   Fare-you-well!

HEG.   By Pollux, though,
What a blessing that I bought these men from the
Commissioners!
So, please Heav'n, I've saved my son from bondage
to those foreigners.
Dear! How long I hesitated whether I should buy
or not!   490
Please to take him in, good slaves, and do not let
him leave the spot,
When there is no keeper with him; I shall soon
be home again.
              [*Exeunt* TYNDARUS *and slaves into the house.*
Now I'll run down to my brother's and inspect
my other men.
I'll inquire if any of them is acquainted with this
youth

[*To* Philocrates.] Come along and I'll despatch
   you. That must be done first, in sooth.   495
   [*Exeunt* Hegio *and* Philocrates *to the market-place.*

Enter Ergasilus *returning from the market-place.*

  Erg. Wretched he who seeks his dinner, and
   with trouble gets a haul;
Wretcheder who seeks with trouble, and can't find
   a meal at all;
Wretchedest who dies for food, and can't get any
   anyway.
If I could, I'd like to scratch the eyes out of this
   cursed day!
For it's filled all men with meanness towards me.
   Oh, I never saw   500
Day so hungry; why, it's stuffed with famine in its
   greedy maw.
Never day pursued its purpose in so vacuous a
   way;
For my gullet and my stomach have to keep a
   holiday.
Out upon the parasite's profession: it's all gone to
   pot!
For us impecunious wits the gilded youth don't
   care a jot.   505
They no longer want us Spartans, owners of a
   single chair,
Sons of Smacked-Face, whose whole stock-in-trade
   is words, whose board is bare.
Those that they invite are fellows who can ask
   them back in turn.
Then they cater for themselves and us poor parasites they spurn;
You will see them shopping in the market with
   as little shame   510
As when, sitting on the bench, the culprit's sentence they proclaim.
For us wits they don't care twopence; keep entirely
   to their set.
When I went just now to market, there a group
   of them I met;
"Hail!" says I; "where shall we go," says I, "to
   lunch?" They all were mum.
"Who speaks first? Who volunteers?" says I. And
   still the chaps were dumb.   515
Not a smile! "Where shall we dine together? Answer." Not a word!
Then I flashed a jest upon them from my very
   choicest hoard,
One that meant a month of dinners in the old
   days, I declare.

No one smiled; and then I saw the whole was a
   got-up affair.
Why, they wouldn't even do as much as any angry
   cur;   520
If they couldn't smile, they might at least have
   shown their teeth, I swear!
Well, I left the rascals when I saw that they were
   making game;
Went to others; and to others; and to others—still
   the same!
They had formed a ring together, just like those
   who deal in oil
I' the Velabrum. So I left them when I saw they
   mocked my toil.   525
In the Forum vainly prowling other parasites I
   saw.
I've resolved that I must try to get my rights by
   Roman law.
As they've formed a plot to rob us of our life and
   victuals too,
I shall summon them and fine them, as a magis-
   trate would do.
They shall give me ten good dinners, at a time
   when food is dear!   530
So I'll do; now to the harbor; there I may to din-
   ner steer;
If that fails me, I'll return and try this old man's
   wretched cheer.
   [*Exit* Ergasilus *to the harbor.*

Enter Hegio *from his brother's with* Aristophontes.

  Heg. How pleasant it is when you've managed
   affairs
For the good of the public, as yesterday I did,
When I bought those two fellows. Why, everyone
   stares   535
And congratulates me on the way I decided.
To tell the plain truth, I am worried with standing.
   And weary with waiting;
From the flood of their words I could scarce get a
   landing,
And even at the prætor's it showed no abating.   540
   I asked for a passport; and when it had come,
   I gave it to Tyndarus; *he* set off home.
When he had departed, for home off I started;
Then went to my brother's, to question the others,
Whether any among them Philocrates knew.   545
Then one of them cries, "He's my friend, good and
   true."
   I told him I'd bought him;
He begged he might see him; and so I have
   brought him.

ı bade them loose him from his chains,
And came away. [*To* Aristophontes.] Pray fol-
    low me; 550
Your earnest suit success obtains,
Your dear old friend you soon shall see.

    [*Exeunt* Hegio *and* Aristophontes *into the*
      house; Tyndarus *immediately rushes out.*

Tyn. Alas! the day has come on which I wish I
    never had been born.
My hopes, resources, stratagems, have fled and left
    me all forlorn.
On this sad day no hope remains of saving my
    poor life, 'tis clear; 555
No help or hope remains to me to drive away my
    anxious fear.
No cloak I anywhere can find to cover up my
    crafty lies,
No cloak, I say, comes in my way to hide my tricks
    and rogueries.
There is no pardon for my fibs, and no escape for
    my misdeeds;
My cheek can't find the shelter, nor my craft the
    hiding-place it needs. 560
All that I hid has come to light; my plans lie open
    to the day;
The whole thing's out, and in this scrape I fail to
    see a single ray
Of hope to shun the doom which I must suffer for
    my master's sake.
This Aristophontes, who's just come, will surely
    bring me to the stake;
He knows me, and he is the friend and kinsman
    of Philocrates. 565
Salvation couldn't save me, if she would; there is
    no way but this,
    To plan some new and smarter trickeries.
Hang it, *what?* What shall I do? I *am* just up a
    lofty tree,
If I can't contrive some new and quite preposterous
    foolery.

Enter from the house Hegio *and* Aristophontes.

Heg. Where's the fellow gone whom we saw
    rushing headlong from the house? 570
Tyn. [*aside*]. Now the day of doom has come;
    the foe's upon thee, Tyndarus!
O, what story shall I tell them? What deny and
    what confess?
My purposes are all at sea; O, ain't I in a pretty
    mess?
O would that Heaven had blasted you before you
    left your native land,

You wretch, Aristophontes, who have ruined all
    that I had planned. 575
The game is up if I can't light on some atrocious
    villainy!
    Heg. Ah, there's your man; go speak to him.
Tyn. [*aside*]. What man is
    wretcheder than I?
    Aris. How is this that you avoid my eyes and
    shun me, Tyndarus?
Why, you might have never known me, fellow,
    that you treat me thus!
I'm a slave as much as you, although in Elis I was
    free, 580
Whilst you from your earliest boyhood were en-
    thralled in slavery.
    Heg. Well, by Jove! I'm not surprised that he
    should shun you, when he sees
That you call him Tyndarus, not, as you should,
    Philocrates.
    Tyn. Hegio, this man in Elis was considered
    raving mad.
Take no note of anything he tells you either good
    or bad. 585
Why, he once attacked his father and his mother
    with a spear;
And the epilepsy takes him in a form that's most
    severe.
Don't go near him!
    Heg. Keep your distance!
    Aris. Rascal! Did I rightly hear,
That you say I'm mad, and once attacked my
    father with a spear?
And that I have got the sickness for which men
    are wont to spit? 590
    Heg. Never mind! for many men besides your-
    self have suffered it,
And the spitting was a means of healing them,
    and they were glad.
    Aris. What, do you believe the wretch?
    Heg. In what respect?
    Aris. That I am mad!
    Tyn. Do you see him glaring at you? Better
    leave him! O beware!
Hegio, the fit is on him; he'll be raving soon!
    Take care! 595
    Heg. Well, I thought he was a madman when
    he called you Tyndarus.
    Tyn. Why, he sometimes doesn't know his *own*
    name. Oh, he's often thus.
    Heg. But he said you were his comrade.
    Tyn. Ah, no doubt! precisely so!
And Alcmæon, and Orestes, and Lycurgus, don't
    you know,

Are my comrades quite as much as he is!

ARIS.   Oh, you gallows bird, 600
Dare you slander me? What, don't I know you?

HEG.   Come, don't be absurd.
You don't know him, for you called him Tyn-
    darus: that's very clear.
You don't know the man you see; you name the
    man who isn't here.

ARIS. Nay, he says he is the man he isn't, not
    the man he is.   605

TYN. O yes! Doubtless you know better whether
    I'm Philocrates
Than Philocrates himself does!

ARIS.   You'd prove truth itself a liar,
As it strikes me. But, I pray you, look at me!

TYN.   As you desire!

ARIS. Aren't you Tyndarus?

TYN.   I'm not.

ARIS.   You say you are Philocrates?

TYN. Certainly.

ARIS.   Do you believe him?

HEG.   Yes, and shall do, if I please.
For the other, who you say he is, went home from
    here today   611
To the father of this captive.

ARIS.   Father? He's a slave.

TYN.   And, pray!
Are you not a slave, though you were free once,
    as I hope to be,
When I have restored good Hegio's son to home
    and liberty?

ARIS. What's that, gaol-bird? Do you tell me
    that you were a free-man born?   615

TYN. No! Philocrates, not Freeman, is my name.

ARIS.   Pray, mark his scorn!
Hegio, I tell you, you're being mocked and swin-
    dled by this knave;
Why, he never had a slave except himself for *he's*
    a slave.

TYN. Ah, because you're poor yourself, and have
    no means of livelihood,
You'd wish everybody else to be like you. I know
    your mood;   620
All poor men like you are spiteful, envy those
    who're better off.

ARIS. Hegio, don't believe this fellow; for he's
    doing naught but scoff;
Sure I am, he'll play some scurvy trick on you
    before he's done;
I don't like this tale of his about the ransom of
    your son.

TYN. You don't like it, I dare say; but I'll ac-
    complish it, you see!   625

I'll restore him to his father; he in turn releases
    me.

That's why I've sent Tyndarus to see my father.

ARIS.   Come, that's lame!
You are Tyndarus yourself, the only slave who
    bears that name!

TYN. Why reproach me with my bondage? I
    was captured in the fray.

ARIS. Oh, I can't restrain my fury!

TYN.   Don't you hear him? Run away!
He'll be hurling stones at us just now, if you don't
    have him bound.   631

ARIS. Oh, damnation!

TYN.   How he glares at us! I
    hope your ropes are sound.
See, his body's covered over with bright spots of
    monstrous size!
It's the black bile that afflicts him.

ARIS.   Pollux! if this old man's wise,
You will find black pitch afflict you, when it blazes
    round your breast.   635

TYN. Ah, he's wandering now, poor fellow! by
    foul spirits he's possessed!

HEG. [*to* TYNDARUS]. What do you think? Would
    it be best to have him bound?

TYN.   Yes, so I said.

ARIS. Oh, perdition take it! Would I had a stone
    to smash his head,
This whipped cur, who says I'm mad! By Jove,
    sir, I will make you smart!

TYN. Hear him calling out for stones!

ARIS.   Pray, might we have
    a word apart, Hegio?

HEG. Yes, but keep your distance; there's no
    need to come so close!   641

TYN. If, by Pollux, you go any nearer, he'll bite
    off your nose.

ARIS. Hegio, I beg and pray you, don't believe
    that I am mad,
Or that I have epilepsy as this shameless fellow
    said.
But if you're afraid of me, then have me bound;
    I won't say no,   645
If you'll bind that rascal too.

TYN.   O no, indeed, good Hegio!
Bind the man who wishes it!

ARIS.   Be quiet, you! The case stands thus;
I shall prove Philocrates the false to be true Tyn-
    darus.
What are you winking for?

TYN.   I wasn't.

ARIS.   He winks before our very face!

HEG. What, if I approached this madman?

TYN.   It would be a wild-goose chase.
He'll keep chattering till you can't make either
    head or tail of it.   651
Had they dressed him for the part, you'd say 'twas
    Ajax in his fit.
    HEG. Never mind, I *will* approach him.
    TYN. [*aside*].   Things are looking very blue.
I'm between the knife and altar, and I don't know
    what to do.
    HEG. I attend, Aristophontes, if you've anything
    to say.   655
    ARIS. You shall hear that that is true which
    you've been thinking false today.
First I wish to clear myself of all suspicion that I
    rave,
Or that I am subject to disease—except that I'm a
    slave.
So may He who's king of gods and men restore
    me home again:
He's no more Philocrates than you or I.
    HEG.   But tell me then, 660
Who he is.
    ARIS.   The same that I have told you from
    the very first.
If you find it otherwise, I pray that I may be
    accursed,
And may suffer forfeit of fatherland and freedom
    sweet.
    HEG. What say *you*?
    TYN.   That I'm your slave, and you're my
    master.
    HEG.   That's not it.
Were you free?
    TYN.   I was.
    ARIS. He wasn't. He's just lying worse and
    worse.   665
    TYN. How do *you* know? Perhaps it happened
    that you were my mother's nurse,
That you dare to speak so boldly!
    ARIS.   Why, I saw you when a lad.
    TYN. Well, I see you when a man today! So we
    are quits, by gad!
Did I meddle with your business? Just let mine
    alone then, please.
    HEG. Was his father called Thensaurocrœsoni-
    cochrysides?   670
    ARIS. No, he wasn't, and I never heard the name
    before today.
Theodoromedes was his master's father.
    TYN. [*aside*].   Deuce to pay!
O be quiet, or go straight and hang yourself, my
    beating heart!

You are dancing there, whilst I can hardly stand
    to play my part.
    HEG. He in Elis was a slave then, if you are not
    telling lies,   675
And is not Philocrates?
    ARIS.   You'll never find it otherwise.
    HEG. So I've been chopped into fragments and
    dissected, goodness knows,
By the dodges of this scoundrel, who has led me
    by the nose.
Are you sure there's no mistake though?
    ARIS.   Yes, I speak of what I know.
    HEG. Is it certain?
    ARIS.   Certain? Nothing could be
    more entirely so.   680
Why, Philocrates has been my friend from when
    he was a boy;
But where is he now?
    HEG.   Ah, that's what vexes me,
    but gives *him* joy.
Tell me though, what sort of looking man is this
    Philocrates?
    ARIS. Thin i' the face, a sharpish nose, a fair
    complexion, coal-black eyes,
Reddish, crisp, and curly hair.
    HEG.   Yes, that's the fellow to a T. 685
    TYN. [*aside*]. Curse upon it, everything has gone
    all wrong today with me.
Woe unto those wretched rods that on my back
    today must die!
    HEG. So I see that I've been cheated.
    TYN. [*aside*].   Come on, fetters, don't be shy!
Run to me and clasp my legs and I'll take care of
    you, no fear!
    HEG. Well, I've been sufficiently bamboozled by
    these villains here.   690
T' other said he was a slave, while this pretended
    to be free;
So I've gone and lost the kernel, and the husk is
    left to me.
Yes, they've corked my nose most finely! Don't I
    make a foolish show?
But this fellow here shan't mock me! Colaphus,
    Corax, Cordalio,
Come out here and bring your thongs.

Enter Overseers.

    OVER.   To bind up faggots? Here's a go!
    HEG. Come, bind your heaviest shackles on this
    wretch.   696
    TYN. Why, what's the matter? what's my
    crime?
    HEG.   Your crime!

You've sowed and scattered ill, now you shall reap
  it.
TYN. Hadn't you better say I harrowed too?
For farmers always harrow first, then sow.   700
  HEG. How boldly does he flout me to my face!
  TYN. A harmless, guiltless man, although a slave,
Should boldly face his master, of all men.
  HEG. Tie up his hands as tightly as you can.
  TYN. You'd better cut them off; for I am yours.
But what's the matter? Why are you so angry? 706
  HEG. Because my plans, as far as in you lay,
By your thrice-villainous and lying tricks
You've torn asunder, mangled limb from limb,
And ruined all my hopes and purposes.   710
Philocrates escaped me through your guile;
I thought he was the slave, and you the free;
For so you said, and interchanged your names
Between yourselves.
  TYN.   Yes, I admit all that.
'Tis just as you have said, and cunningly 715
He's got away by means of my smart work;
But I beseech you, are you wroth at that?
  HEG. You've brought the worst torments on
    yourself.
  TYN. If not for sin I perish, I don't care!
But though I perish, and he breaks his word, 720
And doesn't come back here, my joy is this:
My deed will be remembered when I'm dead,
How I redeemed my lord from slavery,
And rescued him and saved him from his foes,
To see once more his father and his home; 725
And how I rather chose to risk my life,
Than let my master perish in his bonds.
  HEG. The only fame you'll get will be in hell.
  TYN. Nay, he who dies for virtue doesn't perish.
  HEG. When I've expended all my torments on
    you,   730
And given you up to death for your deceits,
People may call it death or perishing
Just as they like; so long as you are dead,
I don't mind if they say that you're alive.
  TYN. By Pollux! if you do so, you'll repent, 735
When he comes back as I am sure he will.
  ARIS. O Heavens! I see it now! and understand
What it all means. My friend Philocrates
Is free at home, and in his native land.
I'm glad of that; nothing could please me more.
But I am grieved I've got *him* into trouble, 741
Who stands here bound because of what I said.
  HEG. Did I forbid you to speak falsely to me?
  TYN. You did, sir.
  HEG.   Then how durst you tell me lies?

  TYN. Because to tell the truth would have done
    hurt   745
To him I served; he profits by my lie.
  HEG. But *you* shall smart for it!
  TYN.   O that's all right!
I've saved my master and am glad of that,
For I've been his companion from a boy;
His father, my old master, gave me to him. 750
D' you now think this a crime?
  HEG.   A very vile one.
  TYN. *I* say it's right; I don't agree with you.
Consider, if a slave had done as much
For your own son, how grateful you would be!
Wouldn't you give that slave his liberty? 755
Wouldn't that slave stand highest in your favor?
Answer!
  HEG. Well, yes.
  TYN.   Then why be wroth with *me?*
  HEG. Because you were more faithful to your
    master
Than e'er to me.
  TYN.   What else could you expect?
Do you suppose that in one night and day 760
You could so train a man just taken captive,
A fresh newcomer, as to serve you better
Than him with whom he'd lived from earliest
    childhood?
  HEG. Then let him pay for it. Take him off,
And fit him with the heaviest, thickest chains; 765
Thence to the quarries you shall go right on.
And whilst the rest are hewing eight stones each,
You shall each day do half as much again,
Or else be nicknamed the Six-hundred-striper.
  ARIS. By gods and men, I pray you, Hegio, 770
Do not destroy him.
  HEG.   I'll take care of him!
For in the stocks all night he shall be kept,
And quarry stones all day from out the ground.
O, I'll prolong his torments day by day.
  ARIS. Is this your purpose?
  HEG.   Death is not so sure.
Go take him to Hippolytus the smith; 776
Tell him to rivet heavy fetters on him.
Then cause him to be led out of the city
To Cordalus, my freedman at the quarries,
And tell him that I wish him to be treated 780
With greater harshness than the worst slave there.
  TYN. Why should I plead with you when you're
    resolved?
The peril of my life is yours as well.
When I am dead I have no ill to fear;
And if I live to an extreme old age, 785
My time of suffering will be but short.

Farewell! though you deserve a different wish.
Aristophontes, as you've done to me,
So may you prosper; for it is through you
That this has come upon me.

HEG.   Take him off.   790

TYN. But if Philocrates returns to you,
Give me a chance of seeing him, I pray.

HEG. Come, take him from my sight or I'll destroy you!

TYN. Nay, this is sheer assault and battery!

[*Exeunt Overseers and* TYNDARUS *to the quarries.*

HEG. There, he has gone to prison as he merits.
I'll give my other prisoners an example,   796
That none of them may dare repeat his crime.
Had it not been for him, who laid it bare,
The rascals would have led me in a string.
Never again will I put trust in man.   800
Once cheated is enough. Alas! I hoped
That I had saved my son from slavery.
My hope has perished. One of my sons I lost,
Stolen by a slave when he was four years old;
Nor have I ever found the slave or him.   805
The elder's now a captive. What's my crime,
That I beget my children but to lose them?
Follow me, you! I'll take you where you were.
Since no one pities me, I'll pity none.

ARIS. Under good auspices I left my chain;   810
But I must take the auspices again.

[*Exeunt* ARISTOPHONTES *and* HEGIO *to Hegio's brother's.*

Enter ERGASILUS *from the harbor.*

ERG. Jove supreme, thou dost protect me and increase my scanty store,
Blessings lordly and magnific thou bestowest more and more;
Both thanks and gain, and sport and jest, festivity and holidays,
Processions plenty, lots of drink and heaps of meat and endless praise.   815
Ne'er again I'll play the beggar, everything I want I've got;
I'm able now to bless my friends, and send my enemies to pot.
With such joyful joyfulness this joyful day has loaded me!
Though it hasn't been bequeathed me, I've come into property!
So now I'll run and find the old man Hegio. O what a store   820
Of good I bring to him, as much as ever he could ask, and more.

I am resolved I'll do just what the slaves do in a comedy;
I'll throw my cloak around my neck, that he may hear it first from me.
For this good news I hope to get my board in perpetuity.

Enter HEGIO *from his brother's.*

HEG. How sad the regrets in my heart that are kindled,   825
As I think over all that has happened to me.
O isn't it shameful the way I've been swindled,
And yet couldn't see!
As soon as it's known, how they'll laugh in the city!
When I come to the market they'll show me no pity,   830
But chaffing say, "Wily old man up a tree!"
But is this Ergasilus coming? Bless me!
His cloak's o'er his shoulder. Why, what can it be?

ERG. Come, Ergasilus, act and act vigorously!
Hereby I denounce and threaten all who shall obstruct my way;   835
Any man who dares to do so will have seen his life's last day.
I will stand him on his head.

HEG.   'Fore me the man begins to spar!

ERG. I shall do it. Wherefore let all passers-by stand off afar;
Let none dare to stand conversing in this street, till I've passed by;
For my fist's my catapult, my arm is my artillery,
And my shoulder is my ram; who meets my knee, to earth he goes.   841
Folk will have to pick their teeth up, if with me they come to blows.

HEG. What's he mean by all this threatening? I confess I'm puzzled quite.

ERG. I'll take care they don't forget this day, this place, my mickle might.
He who stops me in my course, will find he's stopped his life as well.   845

HEG. What he's after with these threats and menaces, I cannot tell.

ERG. I proclaim it first, that none may suffer inadvertently;
Stay at home, good people all, and then you won't get hurt by me.

HEG. Oh, depend on 't, it's a dinner that has stirred his valorous bile.
Woe to that poor wretch whose food has given him this lordly style!   850

ERG. First, for those pig-breeding millers, with
    their fat and bran-fed sows,
Stinking so that one is hardly able to get past the
    house;
If in any public place I catch their pigs outside
    their pen,
With my fists I'll hammer out the bran from those
    same filthy—men!
    HEG. Here's pot-valor with a vengeance! He's as
    full as man could wish!   855
ERG. Then those fishmongers, who offer to the
    public stinking fish,
Riding to the market on a jumping, jolting, jog-
    gling cob,
Whose foul smell drives to the Forum every loafer
    in the mob;
With their fish baskets I'll deal them on their face
    a few smart blows,
Just to let them feel the nuisance that they cause
    the public nose.   860
    HEG. Listen to his proclamations! What a royal
    style they keep!
ERG. Then the butchers, who arrange to steal the
    youngsters from the sheep,
Undertake to kill a lamb, but send you home right
    tough old mutton;
Nickname ancient ram as yearling, sweet enough
    for any glutton;
If in any public street or square that ram comes in
    my view,   865
I will make them sorry persons—ancient ram and
    butcher, too!
    HEG. Bravo! he makes rules as if he were a
    mayor and corporation.
Surely he's been made the master of the market to
    our nation.
    ERG. I'm no more a parasite, but kinglier than a
    king of kings.
Such a stock of belly-timber from the port my
    message brings.   870
Let me haste to heap on Hegio this good news of
    jollity.
Certainly there's no man living who's more for-
    tunate than he.
    HEG. What's this news of gladness which he
    gladly hastes on me to pour?
    ERG. Ho! where are you?
    Who is there? Will someone open me this door?
    HEG. Ah! the fellow's come to dinner.
    ERG.   Open me the door, I say;   875
Or I'll smash it into matchwood, if there's any
    more delay.
    HEG. I'll speak to him. Ergasilus!

ERG.   Who calls my name so lustily?
HEG. Pray, look my way!
ERG. You bid me do what Fortune never did to
    me!
Who is it?
    HEG.   Why, just look at me. It's Hegio!
    ERG.   Ye Gods! It's he.
Thou best of men, in nick of time we have each
    other greeted.   880
HEG. You've got a dinner at the port; that makes
    you so conceited.
ERG. Give me your hand.
    HEG.   My hand?
    ERG.   Your hand, I say, at once!
    HEG.   I give it. There!
ERG. Now rejoice!
    HEG.   Rejoice! but why?
    ERG.   'Tis my command. Begone dull care!
HEG. Nay, the sorrows of my household hinder
    me from feeling joy.
ERG. Ah, but I will wash you clean from every
    speck that can annoy.   885
Venture to rejoice!
    HEG.   All right, though I've no rea-
    son to be glad.
ERG. That's the way. Now order—
    HEG.   What?
    ERG.   To have a mighty fire made.
HEG. What, a mighty fire?
    ERG.   I said so; have it big enough.
    HEG.   What next?
Do you think I'll burn my house down at your
    asking?
    ERG.   Don't be vexed!
Have the pots and pans got ready. Is it to be done
    or not?   890
Put the ham and bacon in the oven, have it piping
    hot.
Send a man to buy the fish—
    HEG.   His eyes are open, but he dreams!
ERG. And another to buy pork, and lamb, and
    chickens—
    HEG.   Well, it seems
You could dine well, if you'd money.
    ERG. —Perch and lamprey, if you please,
Pickled mackerel and sting-ray, then an eel and
    nice soft cheese.   895
    HEG. Naming's easy, but for eating you won't
    find facilities
At my house, Ergasilus.
    ERG.   Why, do you think I'm ordering this
For myself?

Heg. Don't be deceived; for you'll eat neither
   much, nor little,
If you've brought no appetite for just your ordi-
   nary victual.
Erg. Nay, I'll make you eager for a feast though
   I should urge you not.   900
Heg. Me?
Erg.   Yes, you.
Heg.   Then you shall be my lord.
Erg.   A kind one too, I wot!
Come, am I to make you happy?
Heg.   Well, I'm not in love with woe.
Erg. Where's your hand?
Heg.   There, take it.
Erg.   Heaven's your friend!
Heg.   But I don't mark it, though.
Erg. You're not in the *market*, that's why you
   don't *mark it*: come now, bid
That pure vessels be got ready for the offering,
   and a kid,   905
Fat and flourishing, be brought.
Heg.   What for?
Erg.   To make a sacrifice.
Heg. Why, to whom?
Erg.   To me, of course!—I'm Jupiter
   in human guise!
Yes, to you I am Salvation, Fortune, Light, De-
   light, and Joy.
It's your business to placate my deity with food,
   dear boy!
Heg. Hunger seems to be your trouble.
Erg.   Well, my hunger isn't yours.   910
Heg. As you say; so I can bear it.
Erg.   Lifelong habit that ensures!
Heg. Jupiter and all the gods confound you!
Erg.   Nothing of the sort!
Thanks I merit for re*port*ing such good tidings
   from the *port*.
Now I'll get a meal to suit me!
Heg.   Idiot, go! you've come too late.
Erg. If I'd come before I did, your words would
   come with greater weight.   915
Now receive the joyful news I bring you. I have
   seen your son
Philopolemus in harbor safe; and he'll be here
   anon.
He was on a public vessel; with him was that
   Elian youth
And your slave Stalagmus, he who ran away—it's
   naught but truth—
He who stole your little boy when four years old
   so cruelly.   920
Heg. Curse you, cease your mocking!

Erg.   So may holy Fullness smile on me,
Hegio, and make me ever worthy of her sacred
   name,
As I saw him.
Heg.   Saw my son?
Erg.   Your son, my patron: they're the same.
Heg. And the prisoner from Elis?
Erg.   *Oui, parbleu!*
Heg.   And that vile thief,
Him who stole my younger son, Stalagmus?
Erg.   *Oui, monsieur, par Crieff!*   925
Heg. What, just now?
Erg.   *Par Killiecrankie!*
Heg.   Has he come?
Erg.   *Oui, par Dundee!*
Heg. Are you sure?
Erg.   *Par Auchtermuchtie!*
Heg.   Certain?
Erg.   *Oui, par Kirkcudbright!*
Heg. Why by these barbarian cities do you
   swear?
Erg.   Because they're rude,
As you said your dinner was.
Heg.   That's just like your ingratitude!
Erg. Ah, I see you won't believe me though it's
   simple truth I say.   930
But what countryman was this Stalagmus, when
   he went away?
Heg. A Sicilian.
Erg.   Well, but he belongs to *Colo*rado now;
For he's married to a *collar*, and she squeezes him,
   I vow!
Heg. Tell me, is your story true?
Erg.   It's really true—the very truth.
Heg. O good Heav'ns! if you're not mocking,
   I've indeed renewed my youth.   935
Erg. What? Will you continue doubting when
   I've pledged my sacred troth?
As a last resource then, Hegio, if you can't believe
   my oath,
Go and see.
Heg. Of course I will; go in, prepare the feast
   at once;
Everything's at your disposal; you're my steward
   for the nonce.
Erg. If my oracle's a false one, with a cudgel
   comb my hide!   940
Heg. You shall have your board forever, if
   you've truly prophesied.
Erg. Who will pay?
Heg.   My son and I.
Erg.   You promise that?
Heg.   I do indeed

ERG. Then I promise you your son has really
    come in very deed.
HEG. Take the best of everything!
ERG.   May no delay your path impede!
                  [*Exit* HEGIO *to the harbor.*
ERG. He has gone; and put his kitchen abso-
    lutely in my hands!   945
Heav'ns! how necks and trunks will be dissevered
    at my stern commands!
What a ban will fall on bacon, and what harm on
    humble ham!
O what labor on the lard, and what calamity on
    lamb!
Butchers and pork dealers, you shall find a deal to
    do today!
But to tell of all who deal in food would cause too
    long delay.   950
Now, in virtue of my office, I'll give sentence on
    the lard,
Help those gammons, hung though uncondemned
    —a fate for them too hard.
                [*Exit* ERGASILUS *into the house.*

Enter a boy from the house of Hegio.

BOY. May Jupiter and all the gods, Ergasilus,
    confound you quite,
And all who ask you out to dine, and every other
    parasite.
Destruction, ruin, dire distress, have come upon
    our family.   955
I feared that, like a hungry wolf, he'd make a
    fierce attack on me.
I cast an anxious look at him, he licked his lips
    and glared around;
I shook with dread, by Hercules! he gnashed his
    teeth with fearsome sound.
When he'd got in, he made a raid upon the meat-
    safe and the meats;
He seized a knife—from three fat sows he cut
    away the dainty teats.   960
Save those which held at least a peck, he shattered
    every pan and pot:
Then issued orders to the cook to get the copper
    boiling hot.
He broke the cupboard doors and searched the se-
    crets of the storeroom's hoard.
So kindly watch him if you can, good slaves,
    whilst I go seek my lord.
I'll tell him to lay in fresh stores, if he wants any
    for himself,   965
For as this fellow's carrying on, there'll soon be
    nothing on the shelf.
                [*Exit boy to the harbor.*

Enter from the harbor HEGIO, PHILOPOLEMUS,
      PHILOCRATES, *and* STALAGMUS.

HEG. All praise and thanksgiving to Jove I
    would render
For bringing you back to your father again;
For proving my staunch and successful defender,
When, robbed of my son, I was tortured with
    pain;   970
For restoring my runaway slave to my hands;
For Philocrates' honor; unsullied it stands.
    PHILOP. Grieved I have enough already, I don't
    want to grow still thinner,
And you've told me all your sorrows at the harbor,
    pending dinner.
Now to business!
    PHILOC.   Tell me, Hegio, have I kept my
    promises,   975
And restored your son to freedom?
    HEG.   Yes, you have, Philocrates.
I can never, never thank you for the services
    you've done,
As you merit for the way you've dealt with me
    and with my son.
    PHILOP. Yes, you can, dear father, and the gods
    will give us both a chance,
Worthily to recompense the source of my deliver-
    ance.   980
And I'm sure, my dearest father, it will be a pleas-
    ing task.
    HEG. Say no more. I have no tongue that can
    deny you aught you ask.
    PHILOC. Then restore to me the slave whom, as
    a pledge, I left behind.
He has always served me better than himself, with
    heart and mind.
To reward him for his kindness now shall be my
    earnest care.   985
    HEG. For your goodness he shall be restored to
    you; 'tis only fair.
That and aught beside you ask for, you shall have.
    But don't, I pray,
Be enraged with me because in wrath I've pun-
    ished him today.
    PHILOC. Ah, what have you done?
    HEG.   I sent him to the quarries bound with
    chains,
When I found how I'd been cheated.
    PHILOC.   Woe is me! he bears these pains,
Dear good fellow, for my sake, because he gained
    me my release.   991
    HEG. And on that account you shall not pay for
    him a penny piece.

I will set him free for nothing.

PHILOC. Well, by Pollux! Hegio,
That is kind. But send and fetch him quickly, will
you?

HEG. Be it so.
[*To a slave.*] Ho, where are you? Run and quickly
bid young Tyndarus return. 995
Now, go in; for from this slave, this whipping-
block, I fain would learn
What has happened to my younger son, and if he's
living still.
Meanwhile you can take a bath.

PHILOP. Come in, Philocrates.

PHILOC. I will.
[*Exeunt* PHILOPOLEMUS *and* PHILOCRATES *into
the house.*

HEG. Now stand forth, my worthy sir, my slave
so handsome, good, and wise!

STAL. What can you expect from *me*, when such
a man as *you* tells lies? 1000
For I never was nor shall be fine or handsome,
good or true;
If you're building on my goodness, it will be the
worse for you.

HEG. Well, it isn't hard for you to see which way
your interest lies;
If you tell the truth, 'twill save you from the
harshest penalties.
Speak out, straight and true; although you've not
done right and true, I guess. 1005

STAL. Oh, you needn't think I blush to hear you
say what I confess.

HEG. I will make you blush, you villain; for a
bath of blood prepare!

STAL. That will be no novelty! you threaten one
who's oft been there!
But no more of that; just tell me what you want
to ask of me.
Perhaps you'll get it.

HEG. You're too fluent; kindly speak
with brevity. 1010

STAL. As you please.

HEG. Ah, from a boy he was a supple,
flattering knave.
But to business! Pray attend to me, and tell me
what I crave.
If you speak the truth, you'll find your interest
'twill best subserve.

STAL. Don't tell me! D'you think that I don't
know full well what I deserve?

HEG. But you may escape a part if not the whole
of your desert. 1015

STAL. Oh, it's little I'll escape! and much will
happen to my hurt:
For I ran away and stole your son from you, and
him I sold.

HEG. Oh, to whom?

STAL. To Theodoromedes of the
house of Gold
For ten pounds.

HEG. Good Heav'ns! Why, that's the
father of Philocrates.

STAL. Yes, I know that quite as well as you do—
better, if you please. 1020

HEG. Jupiter in Heaven, save me, and preserve
my darling son!
On your soul, Philocrates, come out! I want you.
Make haste, run!

Enter PHILOCRATES *from the house.*

PHILOC. Hegio, I am at your service.

HEG. This man says he sold my son
To your father there in Elis for ten pounds.

PHILOC. When was this done?

STAL. Twenty years ago.

PHILOC. O, nonsense! Hegio, he's telling lies.

STAL. Either you or I am lying; for when you
were little boys, 1026
He was given you by your father to be trained
along with you.

PHILOC. Well, then, tell me what his name was,
if this tale of yours is true.

STAL. Pægnium at first; in after time you called
him Tyndarus.

PHILOC. How is it that I don't know you?

STAL. Men are oft oblivious, 1030
And forget the names of those from whom they've
nothing to expect.

PHILOC. Then this child you sold my father, if
your story is correct,
Was bestowed on me as valet. Who was he?

STAL. My master's son.

HEG. Is he living, fellow?

STAL. Nay, I got the money; then I'd done.

HEG. What say *you*?

PHILOC. That Tyndarus is your lost
son! I give you joy! 1035
So at least this fellow's statements make me think;
for he's the boy
Who received his education with myself all through
our youth.

HEGIO. Well, I'm fortunate and wretched all at
once, if you speak truth;
Wretched that I treated him so cruelly, if he's my
son;

Oh, alas! I did both more and less than what I
   should have done!   1040
How I'm vexed that I chastised him! Would that I
   could alter it!
See, he comes! and in a fashion that is anything
   but fit.

Enter TYNDARUS *from the quarries.*

TYN. Well, I've often seen in pictures all the
   torments of the damned;
But I'm certain that you couldn't find a hell that's
   stuffed and crammed
With such tortures as those quarries. There they've
   got a perfect cure   1045
For all weariness; you simply drive it off by work-
   ing more.
When I got there, just as wealthy fathers oft will
   give their boys
Starlings, goslings, quills to play with in the place
   of other toys,
So when I got there, a *crow* was given me as play-
   thing pretty!
Ah, my lord is at the door; and my old lord from
   Elis city   1050
Has returned!
HEG.   O hail, my long lost son!
TYN.   What means this talk of "sons"?
Oh, I see why you pretend to be my father; yes,
   for once
You have acted like a parent, for you've brought
   me to the light.
PHILOC. Hail, good Tyndarus!
TYN.   All hail! for you I'm
   in this pretty plight.
PHILOC. Ah! but now you shall be free and
   wealthy; for you must be told,   1055
Hegio's your father. That slave stole you hence
   when four years old;
And then sold you to my father for ten pounds,
   who gave you me,
When we both were little fellows, that my valet
   you might be.
This man whom we brought from Elis has most
   certain proofs supplied.
TYN. What, am I his son?

PHILOC.   You are; your brother
   too you'll find inside.   1060
TYN. Then you have brought back with you his
   son who was a prisoner?
PHILOC. Yes, and he is in the house.
TYN.   You've done right well and nobly, sir.
PHILOC. Now you have a father; here's the thief
   who stole you when a boy.
TYN. Now that I'm grown up, he'll find that
   theft will bring him little joy.
PHILOC. He deserves your vengeance.
TYN.   Oh, I'll have him paid
   for what he's done.   1065
Tell me though, are you my father really?
HEG.   Yes, I am, my son.
TYN. Now at length it dawns upon me, and I
   seem, when I reflect,
Yes, I seem to call to mind and somewhat vaguely
   recollect,
As if looking through a mist, my father's name
   was Hegio.
HEG. I am he!
PHILOC.   Then strike the fetters off your
   son and let him go!   1070
And attach them to this villain.
HEG.   Certainly, it shall be so.
Let's go in, and let the smith be summoned to
   strike off your chains,
And to put them on this fellow.
STAL.   Right! For they're my only gains.
EPILOGUE. Gentlemen, this play's been written on
   the lines of modesty;
Here are found no wiles of women, no gay lovers'
   gallantry;   1075
Here are no affiliations, and no tricks for getting
   gold;
No young lover buys his mistress whilst his father
   is cajoled.
It's not often nowadays, that plays are written of
   this kind,
In which good folk are made better. Now then, if
   it be your mind,
And we've pleased you and not bored you, kindly
   undertake our cause,   1080
And to modesty award the prize with heartiest
   applause.

GREEK AND LATIN LYRICS

<hr>

GREEK LYRIC POETRY

One of the major achievements of the Greek genius was lyric poetry. Beginning with the seventh century B.C. and for about a thousand years, the Greeks wrote lyrics remarkable for their purity, precision, and expressiveness. Though the term lyric as used today refers to any verse that is neither dramatic nor epic, the word was originally associated with the lyre because lyrics were intended for singing. The influence of music is apparent in the development of the Greek lyric and its verse patterns can be best understood by imagining the poems as sung to musical accompaniment.

We have only a minute fraction of Greek lyric poetry, which is like having only an arm from the statue of Venus. The great loss was sustained when the library at Alexandria was partly burned down during Julius Cæsar's siege of the city; it was completely destroyed in A.D. 389 by the fanatical Christian emperor Theodosius. Today when we look at the fragments of Sappho, though they carry across twenty-five centuries some faint impression of the remarkable woman who wrote them, we realize that we shall never know her as the Greeks did. Lyrics like hers are so intensely personal that without their author's background much is lost.

The reader of translations is at a greater disadvantage in lyric verse than in any other form. The lyricist is particularly concerned with the pattern of his verse, which depends on skillful use of words and syllables. Since one cannot carry over into a new language the poet's use of word or syllable pattern, the translator can convey at best only an approximation of the original content, thought, and emotion.

LYRIC POETRY

Of the early Greek lyricists Sappho (about 600 B.C.) is easily the most important. Her characteristic metrical form can be imitated though not exactly reproduced in English. The first three lines in the stanza are of the form $-\cup|--|-\cup\cup|-\cup|-\cup$.
The last line is $-\cup\cup|-\cup$.
Swinburne has imitated it in his

All the night sleep came not upon my eyelids,
Shed not dew, nor shook nor unclosed a feather,
Yet with lips shut close and with eyes of iron
      Stood and beheld me.

The translations of Sappho that follow are loose imitations of the original form.

It is evident that she was an artist of singular accomplishment; the ancient world called her the Tenth Muse. We know little about her life except that she lived in the Ægean island of Lesbos, the leader of a group of unusually brilliant and "emancipated" women. She was made a subject of romance and was supposed to have drowned herself from unrequited love by leaping into the sea. Although her themes were erotic, her expression of them was pure and exalted, and like all true artists she sublimated her intense emotionalism. Keenly sensitive to verse forms, she was by no means inclined to artificial decorativeness. In the words of Gilbert Murray, "her love poetry, if narrow in scope, has unrivalled splendor of expression for the longing that is too intense to have any joy in it, too serious to allow room for metaphor and imaginative ornament." By reason of her remarkable fusion of personal emotion and scrupulous craftsmanship, Sappho acquired a commanding position in the world of poetry and her influence extended even to English poets.

In an entirely different mood, Anacreon (563?-478 B.C.) combined the sensuousness of Sapphic verse with the jollity of popular drinking songs (*skolia*). Forced to flee from his home in Teos when it was conquered by the Persians in 545, he attached himself to various royal personages in Samos, Athens, and Thessaly, and became a court poet. His work shows the sophistication and pleasure-seeking of the circles in which he moved. Noted for his charm, wit, and rhythmic felicity, he was not only prolific himself but he started a fashion in verse. He is, indeed, the father of light verse or *vers de société* (society verse) and his influence appears in England, especially in the Cavalier poets of the seventeenth century. The poems of his successors among the Greeks, known as *Anacreontics*, were often attributed to him. His own work has greater variety of form and theme and is also somewhat more stately. (Since his imitators continued to flourish for many centuries, his own poems and the *Anacreontics* are placed together in our selection.)

CHORAL POETRY

Another kind of verse, choral poetry, arose from the practice of celebrating occasions like birthdays, holidays, athletic games, and victories. The celebrations took the form of poems sung and danced by a choir, and the custom soon gave rise to a profession. Poets wrote choral odes or choir songs to order, and professional choruses performed them with specially composed music. This verse could not be subjective, nor could it long remain simple, since it had to satisfy the poet's moneyed patrons, who favored ostentation. The non-choral poets were "their own," said Aristotle; the choral poets were "another's."

There were many choral poets in Greece, beginning with the seventh century, among them Stesichorus (meaning *choir-setter*) and Simonides; but it is with Pindar (522-448 B.C.) that choral poetry is usually associated. Born in Thebes, he studied music and choir-training at Athens, and being of noble descent, he quickly found wealthy patrons and became a guest of the chief families of Rhodes, Corinth, and Athens and of the kings of Macedonia, Cyrene, and Syracuse. The tyrant of Syracuse, Hiero, appears to have been his favorite patron and it is for him that he composed his first Olympic odes. Although it is too much to

call him a sycophant, Pindar did make it his business to glorify men of wealth and power and to flatter them with mythical accounts of their ancestry. A convinced conservative, a votary of Apollo and a devotee of traditional religion, he enjoyed special privileges at Delphi, the official center of Greek worship. For one who witnessed the age of free thought, he was singularly untouched by the spirit of enlightenment, as he had been earlier untouched by the Greek struggle for freedom during the Persian invasion. Gilbert Murray wonders why this remarkably gifted man "is not accounted the greatest poet that ever lived, why he has not done more, matters more," but he answers his own question by surmising that Pindar was "a poet and nothing else."

Writing about athletic victories, leisure-class generosity and genealogy, the pursuit of honor in races and other competitions of the nobility, Pindar lapsed into banalities when he attempted moralizations. But these limitations cannot detract from his remarkable gift for poetic form and for expressiveness—"the organ-playing, the grave strong magic of language, the lightning flashes of half-revealed mystery" of his style. The music he provided for his verses is, of course, lost, but it was accounted exceptionally beautiful. His verse form is a complex, musically related pattern, resembling that of the choral odes in Greek tragedy. The unit consists of three stanzas, known respectively as the *strophe*, the *antistrophe*, and the *epode*, with the strophe and the antistrophe corresponding syllable for syllable, as if sung to the same tune. In other words, they are identical in structure, whereas the epode, which closes a section of the ode, is independent in its metrical structure. The singers would move to one side as they danced with the *strophe*, which means a *turn*; then they moved back to their former position with the *antistrophe* or *counter-turn*; and finally they remained stationary while rendering the *epode* or *conclusion* of any section of the ode. Underlying his traditionalism, moreover, is his admiration for heroism and splendor. Despite the ridiculous pettiness of some of his subjects—two of his best odes celebrate mule-races!—he communicates a certain sublimity of feeling.

Although he has no following in our own day, Pindar was one of the inspirers of English poetry. In looser form than Pindar's, the ode became popular in England. We owe to it Wordsworth's great *Ode on Intimations of Immortality*; and, in still freer and in simpler structure, several of the loveliest poems of Keats. The strict Pindaric ode form was introduced into English by Ben Jonson, and popularized by Thomas Gray.

During the second half of the fifth century, much of the best lyric poetry went into the writing of Athenian tragedy and comedy, instead of rising to new heights as an independent form. Choral poetry became one of the glories of Greek drama. But the beginning of the third century witnessed a revival of Hellenic lyricism, notably in Sicily. In this ancient Hellenic outpost there arose a fresh form known as the *idyll* or the pastoral form.

PASTORAL POETRY

Simple country-songs had of course existed among the people for a long time. But it was the Sicilian Greek Theocritus who shaped pastoral literature into a distinctive literary style. For this he is known as the father of pastoral or bucolic poetry, and more broadly, as the founder of the pastoral tradition which found expression not only in lyricism, but later in drama (an example is *As You Like It*) and in prose fiction. This kind of writing became artificial when the urban gentlemen of imperial Rome and Elizabethan London cast longing eyes on the countryside. In Theocritus' day, the rustic way of life may have already lost its attractiveness, and his Sicilian peasants were soon to become semi-enslaved agricultural workers of the Roman empire. It is also true that though Sicilian-born, the poet had passed much of his life in Alexandria, the center of the sophisticated world of the third century. He reflects that world in the refinement of his artistry, as well as, to cite Murray once more, in "that habit of retrospect, that yearning over the past which pervades all the poetry . . . of Alexandria." Nevertheless, the freshness of his work and the impression it gives of spontaneity of song and of simple happiness is ever present in the ten of his thirty-two idylls which have come down to us. Perhaps in the days before he became famous in Alexandria, he had caught glimpses of just that kind of simple life in his native Sicily. His *Cyclops*, an idyll of the love of the mythical shepherd Polyphemus for the sea-nymph Galatea, is composed of simple, recognizable details of farm life.

His first idyll, the *Dirge on Daphnis*, gave rise to the fashion of couching some lament in pastoral terms, with the departed one presented as a shepherd and the imagery drawn from rustic surroundings and occupations. This poem has had many imitations; not only classic dirges but English masterpieces like Milton's *Lycidas* and Shelley's famous lament for Keats, *Adonais*. But in Theocritus' poem the pastoral setting is not yet a convention; the dirge is a lovely lyric sung by one shepherd at the request of a friend, and the subject, the death of the love-lorn Daphnis, is a folk tale or legend. No effort is made to weight it with added significance or to symbolize anything.

The fifteenth idyll, *The Syracusan Ladies* (*Adoniazusæ* or Feast of Adonis), recounts a folk festival in honor of Adonis, Aphrodite's lover according to legend, but originally a vegetation spirit whose death was lamented every year with appropriate rites. This festival is vividly described in the poem through the behavior of the celebrants, and is concluded with a dirge for Adonis that is pure lyricism. A touch of reality is present throughout in the account of the two matrons who attend the celebration; here indeed we find a humorous realism one does not expect in lyric poetry. In form, too, *The Syracusan Women* is remarkable; it is a little play or *mime*, for it consists of dialogue and involves a certain amount of action.

Theocritus is, indeed, a most attractive poet, who was capable of creating not only lyric utterance, but humor, realism, and charming dramatic narrative. He knew how to arouse and sustain interest, largely by means of expressive details and dialogue. Even *The Cyclops*, which is a monologue, has dramatic vigor. Theocritus is the last Greek poet to whom the adjective great can be applied. His two third-century successors Bion and Moschus are, by comparison, florid and ornate. Although the former's *Dirge of Adonis* is rich in passion and imagery, he is distinctly a poet by secondary inspiration. Moschus, whose *Lament for Bion* is a famous tribute to a dead poet, is even further removed from the fountainhead of natural art. The pastoral form rapidly became subject to the law of diminishing returns in the Greek world.

After this, the resources of Greek poetry came to an end, but not before leaving one final legacy in the compilation known as *The Greek Anthology*. Its approximately four thousand tiny poems, many of them anonymous, came from different centuries; some were written as early as the fifth century B.C., others as late as the sixth century A.D. Their character was well expressed by the famous librarian of Alexandria, the poet and critic Callimachus: "Great is the sweep of the river of Assyria; but it bears many scourings of earth on the flood of it, and much driftwood to the sea.

Apollo's bees draw not their water everywhere; a little dew from a holy fount, the highest bloom of the flower." Maintaining that the age of epics was gone, Callimachus called for perfection in little things. The best poems of the *Greek Anthology*[1] fulfill this requirement; most of them, including Callimachus' own lovely epitaph *Heraclitus*, are brief evocations of feeling or epigrammatic distillations of wit. They may be likened to the engravings on rare Greek coins; they have a lasting quality, for they are exquisite, apt, and universal.

Among the known contributors to this collection, the most famous are Meleager of Gadara (*circa* 100 B.C.) who possessed a vein of tenderness; the polished Antipater of Sidon; the fifth-century (A.D.) Pallades; and the sixth-century A.D. poets Agathias and Paulus Silentiarius. It was Meleager who made the first collection, which was later increased by Philippus of Thessalonica about 100 A.D. and by others throughout the Dark Ages in Eastern Europe. The *Anthology* is a fitting conclusion to Greek poetry, for, in the words of John Addington Symonds, it is "coextensive with the whole current of Greek history, from the splendid period of the Persian wars to the decadence of Christianized Byzantium." In it we hear "the private utterances, the harmoniously modulated whispers of a multitude of Greek poets."

ROMAN LYRIC POETRY

The little verses with which Greek lyricism ends are the last glistening trickles of what had once been a mighty river. It remained for the slowly awakening Romans to find new fountainheads and create a new broad stream. Roman poetry is less spontaneous and inspired than Greek. As the Latin language developed it became sonorous and complex, and imperialist Roman society favored a façade of formalism and artifice. A contemporary critic, Burton Rascoe, goes so far as to maintain that for the most part, it is "simply not to be trusted to express the author's genuine feelings, emotions or convictions."[2] But although it is true that much Roman writing is rhetorical, its best examples have a grandeur that exalts the reader, and their organ music and felicitous phrasing remain memorable. Elemental emotions are rarely evoked, but the attitudes of cultivated men,

whose humanity is not any the less valid because it is polished, live vividly in Latin verse.

Personal emotion is most apparent in Rome's first great lyricist, Catullus (*c.* 87-54 B.C.). Genuine grief and tenderness are present in the touching lament for his brother which ends with the immortal phrase of *ave atque vale*, "hail and farewell." Catullus evinces tenderness even about such little things as the death of Lesbia's sparrow. Above all, there can be no doubt about the validity of his passion, born of four years of turbulent love for a married woman, who was probably Clodia, the sister of a Roman politician. She was the product of a sophisticated social set—we would label her "café society" today—and her inconstancy was notorious. As a worldly, sophisticated gentleman, he should perhaps have taken an easy view of her infidelity, but Catullus happened to be an impassioned poet for whom love and jealousy were painfully real emotions. He raged and railed, and sometimes even became vengeful. Catullus is, in short, a realist among love poets. Moreover, there is an appealing candor in his self-examination, in his oscillation between ecstasy and misery, sunshine and shadow, confidence and doubt.

There is a genuine self-revelation in all of his work, which records, in addition to his stormy infatuation, his fondness for genial friendships and for nature. His evocation of passion has power, his exuberance and petulance a captivating charm; his description of Roman life is vivid, and his picture of country life pleasurable. It is no wonder that his poems have remained fresh over the centuries.

Catullus was a child of the turbulent years of the Roman republic, and he even became involved in republican politics, joining the faction that opposed Julius Cæsar. His greatest successors belong to the reign of Augustus Cæsar, a period of greater refinement and stability. The members of the Augustan literary circle reflect this more orderly and luxurious age in poetry that is stately, even-tempered, and comparatively artificial.

Virgil (70 B.C.-19 B.C.) is the principal figure of this period. Most important for his epic, the *Æneid*, he also made substantial contributions to lyric poetry with his pastoral writings, the *Georgics* and the *Eclogues*. In the former, written in 37 B.C., he described and glorified agriculture, which had fallen on evil days and had to be revived for the

---

[1] The word *anthology* means "garland."
[2] *Titans of Literature*, p. 92.

good of the country. In these poems Virgil relied largely on the routine life he must have observed during his boyhood on his Mantuan estate. Their content is generally tedious, but one admires them for their formal perfection, picturesqueness, and incidental passages that have little or nothing to do with the business of farming. The *Eclogues*, ten in number and written between 42 and 37 B.C., are patterned after the idylls of Theocritus. Some are genuine pastorals, others are allegories expressed in the pastoral idiom. It is largely to Virgil, in fact, that we owe this convention of allegorical pastoral poetry, in which the language of the countryside is employed to set forth ideas in no way related to agriculture. The famous fourth *Eclogue*, addressed to the poet and politician Pollio who befriended Virgil, celebrates Pollio's consulship and the expected birth of a child to this patron. Here the references to rustic life merely express Virgil's courteous compliments, his tribute to the orderly and prosperous Augustan era, and his dream of a tranquil and happy Golden Age. The Christian Middle Ages regarded this eclogue erroneously as a prophecy of the coming of Christ, but it is any case the most inspired of Virgil's poems.

Most characteristic of the Augustan age was the poetry of Virgil's contemporary and friend Quintus Horatius Flaccus (65-8 B.C.), known to future generations as Horace. The son of a well-to-do farmer who provided him with an excellent education, he led a quiet and refined life, and he steered clear of political involvements after his ill-fated support of Brutus at Philippi while a student at Athens. This cost him his estate and forced him to seek clerical employment in a government office. But his poetry won him powerful friends at court, among them the famous minister of Augustus Cæsar, Mæcenas, who patronized the arts. Given his beloved Sabine farm by Mæcenas, Horace spent most of his time there, leading a simple and independent life. His aptitude was by no means rustic, for he was a worldly and sophisticated poet, but he liked to observe the busy world at a comfortable distance, and often with amusement. He was amused at himself too, and he remained discreetly detached even in love. Perhaps he exaggerated his lack of attractiveness to women, since they probably liked him for his wit and good spirits, but he never gave himself up to a consuming interest, so that he is never impassioned,

irascible, or recriminative in his amatory verses. His *Ode to Pyrrha* (I, 5), in which he assures us he will never court shipwreck in the seas of passion, typifies his detached spirit. Indeed, he pursued the golden mean in all things.

The poetry speaks for the man. It is the product of leisure and of "the labor of the file" (*labor limæ*), as he himself said. It has precision, neatness, and is a model of the apt phrase and the right word. It is not the poetry of inspiration but that of sound observation, humor, and good taste. It is worldly and charming, not vaulting and fiery, although some of his *Odes*, like his *Ship of State*, are noble in sentiment and express a high seriousness. His *Satires* are amiable and tolerant, though penetrative; only in some of the earlier satirical poems of his *Epodes* does he indulge in any invective. His later *Epistles* are easy and informal, essayistic, and invariably charming; they contain his *Art of Poetry*, an essay in literary criticism that became the bible for many critics during and after the Renaissance. No poet received the compliment of so many imitations, and his themes and style have served many eminent writers of light verse. He brought good cheer and civilized attitudes into the soul of poetry.

The rest of Latin lyric poetry is spread over several centuries. It is richest in the period of Virgil and Horace, who found companions in such poets as Tibullus (54?-18? B.C.), the author of graceful elegies inspired by various love affairs, Propertius (50?-15? B.C.), and Ovid (43 B.C.-A.D. 18). The latter became better known as a story-teller for his poetic recounting of myths in his *Metamorphoses*, but he was also a clever writer of erotic elegies in his *Amores* and a genuine lyricist in the *Tristitia* that he composed while in exile on the shores of the Black Sea. After this age some of the most interesting verse belongs to satire rather than lyricism. The anonymous *Pervigilium Veneris* (The Vigil of Venus) is the lovely swan-song of paganism. It is a pæan to nature, to the joy of spring and the ecstasies of the worshippers of nature and love. Probably associated with a pagan rite in honor of fertility, whose goddess is Venus, the poem speaks the universal language of classic paganism. When the Latin tongue again becomes ecstatic, in the hymns of the medieval Church, it speaks with the accent of Christianity, which has a radically different spiritual view of man and the world.

HOMERIC HYMN

Hymn to Earth the Mother of All

O universal Mother, who dost keep
From everlasting thy foundations deep,
Eldest of things, Great Earth, I sing of thee!
All shapes that have their dwelling in the sea,
All things that fly, or on the ground divine   5
Live, move, and there are nourished—these are
    thine;
These from thy wealth thou dost sustain; from thee
Fair babes are born, and fruits on every tree
Hang ripe and large, revered Divinity!

The life of mortal men beneath thy sway   10
Is held; thy power both gives and takes away!
Happy are they whom thy mild favors nourish;
All things unstinted round them grow and flourish;

For them, endures the life-sustaining field
Its load of harvest, and their cattle yield   15
Large increase, and their house with wealth is filled.
Such honored dwell in cities fair and free,
The homes of lovely women, prosperously;
Their sons exult in youth's new budding gladness,
And their fresh daughters free from care and
    sadness,   20
With bloom-inwoven dance and happy song,
On the soft flowers the meadow-grass among,
Leap round them sporting—such delights by thee
Are given, rich Power, revered Divinity.

Mother of gods, thou wife of starry Heaven,   25
Farewell! be thou propitious, and be given
A happy life for this brief melody,
Nor thou nor other songs shall unremembered be

SAPPHO

One Girl

Like the sweet apple which reddens upon the top-
    most bough,
A-top on the topmost twig,—which the pluckers
    forgot, somehow,—
Forgot it not, nay, but got it not, for none could
    get it till now.
Like the wild hyacinth flower which on the hills is
    found,
Which the passing feet of the shepherds for ever
    tear and wound,
Until the purple blossom is trodden in the ground.

Hesperus the Bringer

O Hesperus, thou bringest all good things—
    Home to the weary, to the hungry cheer,
To the young bird the parent's brooding wings,
    The welcome stall to the o'erlabored steer;
Whate'er of peace about our hearthstone clings,
    Whate'er our household gods protect of dear,
Are gathered round us by thy look of rest;
Thou bring'st the child too to its mother's breast.

Ode to Aphrodite

Splendor-throned Queen, immortal Aphrodite,
Daughter of Jove, Enchantress, I implore thee
Vex not my soul with agonies and anguish;

    Slay me not, Goddess!
Come in thy pity—come, if I have prayed thee;   5
Come at the cry of my sorrow; in the old times
Oft thou hast heard, and left thy father's heaven,
    Left the gold houses,
Yoking thy chariot. Swiftly did the doves fly,
Swiftly they brought thee, waving plumes of won-
    der—   10
Waving their dark plumes all across the æther,
    All down the azure
Very soon they lighted. Then didst thou, Divine
    one,
Laugh a bright laugh from lips and eyes immortal,
Ask me, What ailed me—wherefore out of heaven
    Thus I had called thee?   16
What it was made me madden in my heart so?
Question me, smiling—say to me, "My Sappho,
"Who is it wrongs thee? Tell me who refuses
    "Thee, vainly sighing.   20
"Be it who it may be, he that flies shall follow;
"He that rejects gifts, he shall bring thee many;
"He that hates now shall love thee dearly, madly—
    "Aye, though thou wouldst not."
So once again come, Mistress; and, releasing   25
Me from my sadness, give me what I sue for,
Grant me my prayer, and be as heretofore now
    Friend and protectress.

Homeric Hymn, translated by P. B. Shelley. Translations of Sappho (born *c.* 600 B.C.): *One Girl,*
D. G. Rossetti; *Hesperus the Bringer,* Lord Byron; *Ode to Aphrodite,* J. Addington Symonds.

PINDAR

Olympian Ode I

To Hiero the Syracusan

Victor in the Horse-race

STROPHE I

Water the first of elements we hold;
  And, as the flaming fire at night
  Glows with its own conspicuous light,
Above proud treasure shines transcendent gold:
  But if, my soul, 'tis thy desire   5
  For the Great Games to strike thy lyre,
Look not within the range of day
  A star more genial to descry
Than yon warm sun, whose glittering ray
  Dims all the spheres that gild the sky; 10
  Nor loftier theme to raise thy strain
  Than famed Olympia's crowded plain:
From whence, by gifted minstrels richly wove,
Th' illustrious hymn, at glory's call,
Goes forth to Hiero's affluent hall,   15
To hail his prosperous throne and sing Saturnian
  Jove.

ANTISTROPHE I

Hiero the just, that rules the fertile field,
  Where fair Sicilia's pastures feed
  Unnumber'd flocks, and for his meed
Culls the sweet flowers that all the virtues yield;
  Nor less renown'd his hand essays   21
  To wake the Muse's choicest lays,
Such as the social feast around
  Full oft our tuneful band inspire—
But wherefore sleeps the thrilling sound? 25
  Pluck from the peg thy Dorian lyre,
  If Pisa's palms have charms for thee,
  If Pherenicus' victory
Hath roused thee to the rapturous cares of song;
Tell us how swift the ungoaded steed   30
By Alpheus urged his furious speed,
And bore the distant prize from all the panting
  throng.

EPODE I

Proud of his stud, the Syracusan king
  Partook the courser's triumph. Through the
  plain

By Lydian Pelops won his praises ring— 35
  Pelops of Neptune loved (whose watery reign
Bounds the wide earth, that trembles at his
  might),
  Pelops, whose form the plastic Fate replaced,
And from the caldron bright
  Drew forth with ivory shoulder graced. 40
Life teems with wonders: yet, in Reason's spite,
  O'er the fond fascinating fiction, warm
  From Fancy's pencil, hangs a charm
That more than Nature's self her painted dreams
  delight.

STROPHE II

For Taste, whose softening hand hath power to
  give   45
  Sweetness and grace to rudest things,
  And trifles to distinction brings,
Makes us full oft the enchanting tale receive
  In Truth's disguise as Truth. The day
  Yet comes, Time's test, that tears away 50
  The veil each flattering falsehood wears.
  Beseems us then (for less the blame)
Of those that heed us from the spheres
  Becoming marvels to proclaim.
  Great son of Tantalus, thy fate   55
  Not as the fablers I relate.
Thee with the Gods thy Sire's Sipylian guest,
  When they in turn beneath his bower
  Purest repast partook, the Power
That wields the Trident, seized, and ravished from
  the feast.   60

ANTISTROPHE II

Desire his breast had conquered. Up he drove
  His trembling prize of mortal mold
  In radiant car with steeds of gold
To th' highest mansion of all-honored Jove;
  With whom the Boy, from wondering Ide 65
  Rapt long before, like place supplied.
Her Pelops lost, her vanished son
  Soon roused the frantic mother's care;
  No tidings came; the search begun
  In mystery ended in despair.   70

Olympian Ode I. Translated by Abraham Moore. Pindar (522-448? B.C.) was born near Thebes and died at Argos. He passed four years at the court of Hieron in Syracuse. Except for his brilliant series of odes, little is known of him.

Forthwith some envious foe was found
Whispering th' unseemly slander round,
How all into the bubbling caldron cast
Thy mangled limbs were seethed, and shred
In fragments on the table spread,   75
While circling Gods looked on and shared th'
    abhorred repast.

EPODE II

Far be from me and mine the thought profane,
    That in foul feast celestials could delight!
Blasphemous tale! Detraction finds its bane 79
    E'en in the wrong it works—If mortal wight
    Heaven e'er hath honored, 'twas this Tantalus;
      But soon from ill-digested greatness sprung
Presumption and abuse:
      Thence from his towering fortunes flung
(Frightful reverse!) he fell. A ponderous rock 85
    High o'er his head hung threatening (angry
      Jove
So judged him for his crimes above):
Where day and night he waits, dreading th'
    expected shock.

STROPHE III

Thus doomed is he life's hopeless load to bear,
    Torment unceasing! Three beside,   90
    Delinquents there, like pains abide.
He from th' Immortals their ambrosial fare,
    The nectarous flood that crowned their bowl,
    To feast his earth-born comrades, stole;
Food, that, by their celestial grace,   95
    Eternal youth to him had given.
Vain hope, that guilt by time or place
    Can 'scape the searching glance of heaven!
For this the blameless Son once more
    Back to man's short-lived race they bore;   100
There, when fresh youth its blooming flower had
    blown,
    And round his chin th' umbrageous beard
    Mature its manlier growth had reared,
From Pisa's Prince he sought, his nuptial couch to
    crown

ANTISTROPHE III

The famed Hippodamè; whose charms to gain,
    The fond and furious father's pride,   106
    At night's dark hour alone he hied
To the rough shore of the loud-bellowing main,
    And called the Trident-sceptered God,
    Whose form forthwith beside him stood: 110

"Oh! if th' endearing gifts," said he,
    "The Cyprian sea-born Queen bestows,
    Have still, great Neptune, grace with thee,
    Propitiate now thy suppliant's vows.
Arrest Œnomaus' brazen spear,   115
    To Elis guide my prompt career,
And bear me on thy swiftest chariot's wheel
    Victorious to the goal; for he,
    Slayer of suitors ten and three,
Still from his daughter's hope withholds the bridal
    seal.   120

EPODE III

"Majestic Danger calls but for the brave,
    Trusts not the dastard's arm: then why should
      man,
    By life's hard lot predestined to the grave,
      Waste in the dark th' unprofitable span,
      And crouch in Age's corner unrenowned,   125
    Heav'n's noblest gifts untasted? Power divine!
    Grant thou th' event be crowned,
      This peril shall at least be mine."
Thus he, with zeal not unregarded, speeds
    His ardent prayer. The God his prayer em-
      braced,   130
    Gave him his car with gold enchased,
And roused th' unwearied plumes that winged the
    immortal steeds.

STROPHE IV

Œnomaus' power th' exulting youth o'erthrows:
    The virgin spouse his arms entwine;
    From whose soft intercourse, a line   135
By all the virtues nursed, six warriors rose.
    Now in rich pomp and solemn state
    His dust heroic honors wait.
    Where Alpheus laves the hallowed glade,
      His tomb its ample range displays,   140
    And gifts by many a stranger laid
      High on his crowded altar blaze;
    But most from proud Olympia's drome,
    On distant realms, on times to come,
Shines Pelops' fame. There Speed demands his
    crown,   145
    Toil-mastering Strength the muscle strains,
    And conquerors pass life's proud remains
On Virtue's tranquil couch, the slumber of renown.

ANTISTROPHE IV

Such is the Champion's meed: the constant good,
    That lives beyond the transient hour,   150

Of all that Heaven on man can shower,
Most fires his hope, most wakes his gratitude:
  But now 'tis mine, the strain to raise,
  And swell th' Equestrian Hero's praise,
  To crown with loud Æolian song   155
    A Prince, whose peer the spacious earth
  Holds not its noblest chiefs among,
    Boasts not in wisdom, power and worth,
    A host more gifted, to display,
    Through all the mazes of the lay.   160
Hiero, some guardian god thy fame sustains
  And makes thee his peculiar care;
  If long thy deeds his smiles shall share,
A loftier flight I'll soar, and warble sweeter
  strains.

EPODE IV

Then high on Cronium's peak my post shall be;
  There, as a poet's glance informs my soul,   166
First in the burning race thy steeds to see,
  Thy bounding chariot whirl thee to the goal.
Then shall the Muse her strongest javelin fling;
  'Bove all the ranks of greatness at the top   170
Shines the consummate king—
  Beyond that height lift not thy hope.
Be thine in that bright station long to bear
  Thy upright course; mine, with the conquering
    band,
  To take my honorable stand,   175
And 'mong the bards of Greece the palm of genius
  wear.

THEOCRITUS

The Cyclops

And so an easier life our Cyclops drew,
  The ancient Polyphemus, who in youth
Loved Galatea while the manhood grew
  Adown his cheeks, and darkened round his
    mouth.
No jot he cared for apples, olives, roses;   5
  Love made him mad; the whole world was
    neglected,
The very sheep went backward to their closes
  From out the fair green pastures, self-directed.
And singing Galatea, thus, he wore
The sunrise down along the weedy shore,   10
  And pined alone, and felt the cruel wound
Beneath his heart, which Cypris' arrow bore,
  With a deep pang: but, so, the cure was found;
And, sitting on a lofty rock, he cast
His eyes upon the sea, and sang at last: 15
  "O whitest Galatea, can it be
  That thou shouldst spurn me off who love thee
    so?
More white than curds, my girl, thou art to see,
More meek than lambs, more full of leaping glee
  Than kids, and brighter than the early glow   20
On grapes that swell to ripen,—sour like thee!
Thou comest to me with the fragrant sleep,

And with the fragrant sleep thou goest from me;
Thou fliest . . . fliest as a frightened sheep
  Flies the gray wolf!—yet love did overcome me,
So long!—I loved thee, maiden, first of all   26
  When down the hills (my mother fast beside
    thee)
I saw thee stray to pluck the summer-fall
  Of hyacinth-bells, and went myself to guide thee;
And since my eyes have seen thee, they can leave
  thee   30
No more, from that day's light! But thou . . .
  by Zeus,
Thou wilt not care for *that,* to let it grieve thee!
  I know thee, fair one, why thou springest loose
From my arm round thee. Why? I tell thee, dear!
  One shaggy eyebrow draws its smudging road   35
Straight through my ample front, from ear to ear;
  One eye rolls underneath; and yawning, broad,
Flat nostrils feel the bulging lips too near.
Yet . . . ho, ho!—I,—whatever I appear,—   39
  Do feed a thousand oxen! When I have done,
I milk the cows, and drink the milk that's best!
  I lack no cheese, while summer keeps the sun;
And after, in the cold, it's ready prest!
  And then, I know to sing, as there is none
Of all the Cyclops can, . . . a song of thee,   45
Sweet apple of my soul, on love's fair tree,

Theocritus, *The Cyclops.* Translated by E. B. Browning. Theocritus lived in the early part of the third century B.C. Though he passed much of his time in Alexandria, his idylls reflect the shepherd life of Sicily, where he was born.

And of myself who love thee . . . till the west
Forgets the light, and all but I have rest.
I feed for thee, besides, eleven fair does,   49
   And all in fawn; and four tame whelps of bears.
Come to me, sweet! thou shalt have all of those
   In change for love! I will not halve the shares.
Leave the blue sea, with pure white arms extended
   To the dry shore; and, in my cave's recess,
Thou shalt be gladder for the noon-light ended;   55
   For here be laurels, spiral cypresses,
Dark ivy, and a vine whose leaves infold
Most luscious grapes; and here is water cold,
   The wooded Ætna pours down through the trees
From the white snows, which gods were scarce too
     bold   60
   To drink in turn with nectar. Who with these
   Would choose the salt wave of the lukewarm
     seas?
Nay, look on me! If I am hairy and rough,
   I have an oak's heart in me; there's a fire
In these gray ashes which burns hot enough;   65
   And, when I burn for *thee,* I grudge the pyre
No fuel . . . not my soul, nor this one eye,—
Most precious thing I have, because thereby
I see thee, fairest! Out, alas! I wish
My mother had borne me finnèd like a fish,   70
That I might plunge down in the ocean near thee,
   And kiss thy glittering hand between the weeds,
If still thy face were turned; and I would bear thee
   Each lily white, and poppy fair that bleeds   74
Its red heart down its leaves!—one gift, for hours
   Of summer,—one for winter; since to cheer thee,
I could not bring at once all kinds of flowers.
Even now, girl, now, I fain would learn to swim,

If stranger in a ship sailed nigh, I wis,
   That I may know how sweet a thing it is   80
To live down with you in the deep and dim!
Come up, O Galatea, from the ocean,
   And, having come, forget again to go!
As I, who sing out here my heart's emotion,
   Could sit forever. Come up from below!   85
Come, keep my flocks beside me, milk my kine;
   Come, press my cheese, distrain my whey and
     curd!
Ah, mother! she alone . . . that mother of mine . . .
   Did wrong me sore! I blame her! Not a word
Of kindly intercession did she address   90
Thine ear with for my sake; and ne'ertheless
   She saw me wasting, wasting, day by day:
   Both head and feet were aching, I will say,
All sick for grief, as I myself was sick.
   O Cyclops, Cyclops! whither hast thou sent   95
   Thy soul on fluttering wings? If thou wert bent
On turning bowls, or pulling green and thick
   The sprouts to give thy lambkins, thou wouldst
    make thee
   A wiser Cyclops than for what we take thee.
Milk dry the present! Why pursue too quick   100
That future which is fugitive aright?
   Thy Galatea thou shalt haply find,
   Or else a maiden fairer and more kind;
For many girls do call me through the night,
   And, as the call, do laugh out silverly.   105
I, too, am something in the world, I see!"

While thus the Cyclops love and lambs did fold,
Ease came with song, he could not buy with gold.

The Syracusan Ladies

GORGO. Is Praxinoë at home?

PRAXINOË. Dear Gorgo, how long it is since you have been here! She *is* at home. The wonder is that you have got here at last! Eunoë, see that she has a chair. Throw a cushion on it too.

GORGO. It does most charmingly as it is.

PRAXINOË. Do sit down.

GORGO. Oh, what a thing spirit is! I have scarcely 10 got to you alive, Praxinoë! What a huge crowd, what hosts of four-in-hands! Everywhere cavalry boots, everywhere men in uniform! And the road is endless: yes, you really live *too* far away!

PRAXINOË. It is all the fault of that madman of

mine. Here he came to the ends of the earth and took—a hole, not a house, and all that we might not be neighbors. The jealous wretch, always the same, ever for spite!

GORGO. Don't talk of your husband, Dinon, like that, my dear girl, before the little boy,—look how he is staring at you! Never mind, Zopyrion, sweet child, she is not speaking about papa.

PRAXINOË. Our Lady! the child takes notice.

GORGO. Nice papa!

PRAXINOË. That papa of his the other day—we call every day "the other day"—went to get soap and rouge at the shop, and back he came to me with salt—the great big endless fellow!

GORGO. Mine has the same trick, too, a perfect

Theocritus, *The Syracusan Ladies.* Translated by Andrew Lang. By permission of The Macmillan Co.

spendthrift—Diocleides! Yesterday he got what he meant for five fleeces, and paid seven shillings a piece for—what do you suppose?—dog-skins, shreds of old leather wallets, mere trash—trouble on trouble. But come, take your cloak and shawl. Let us be off to the rich Ptolemy, the King, to see the Adonis; I hear the Queen has provided something splendid!

PRAXINOË. Fine folks do everything finely.

GORGO. What a tale you will have to tell about 10 the things you have seen, to anyone who has not seen them! It seems nearly time to go.

PRAXINOË. Idlers have always holiday. Eunoë, bring the water and put it down in the middle of the room, lazy creature that you are. Cats like always to sleep soft! Come, bustle, bring the water; quicker. I want water first, and how she carries it! give it me all the same; don't pour out so much, you extravagant thing. Stupid girl! Why are you wetting my dress? There, stop, I have washed my 20 hands, as heaven would have it. Where is the key of the big chest? Bring it here.

GORGO. Praxinoë, that full body becomes you wonderfully. Tell me how much did the stuff cost you just off the loom?

PRAXINOË. Don't speak of it, Gorgo! More than eight pounds in good silver money,—and the work on it! I nearly slaved my soul out over it!

GORGO. Well, it is *most* successful; all you could wish.

PRAXINOË. Thanks for the pretty speech! Bring my shawl, and set my hat on my head, the fashionable way. No, child, I don't mean to bite. Boo! Bogies! There's a horse that bites! Cry as much as you please, but I cannot have you lamed. Let us be moving. Phrygia, take the child, and keep him amused, call in the dog, and shut the street door.

[*They go into the street.*

Ye gods, what a crowd! How on earth are we ever to get through this coil? They are like ants 40 that no one can measure or number. Many a good deed have you done, Ptolemy; since your father joined the immortals, there's never a malefactor to spoil the passer-by, creeping on him in Egyptian fashion—oh! the tricks those perfect rascals used to play. Birds of a feather, ill jesters, scoundrels all! Dear Gorgo, what will become of us? Here come the King's war-horses! My dear man, don't trample on me. Look, the bay's rearing, see, what temper! Eunoë, you foolhardy girl, will you never 50 keep out of the way? The beast will kill the man that's leading him. What a good thing it is for me that my brat stays safe at home.

GORGO. Courage, Praxinoë. We are safe behind them, now, and they have gone to their station.

PRAXINOË. There! I begin to be myself again. Ever since I was a child I have feared nothing so much as horses and the chilly snake. Come along, the huge mob is overflowing us.

GORGO [*to an old Woman*]. Are you from the Court, mother?

OLD WOMAN. I am, my child.

PRAXINOË. Is it easy to get there?

OLD WOMAN. The Achæans got into Troy by trying, my prettiest of ladies. Trying will do everything in the long run.

GORGO. The old wife has spoken her oracles, and off she goes.

PRAXINOË. Women know everything, yes, and how Zeus married Hera!

GORGO. See, Praxinoë, what a crowd there is about the doors.

PRAXINOË. Monstrous, Gorgo! Give me your hand, and you, Eunoë, catch hold of Eutychis; never lose hold of her, for fear lest you get lost. Let us all go in together; Eunoë, clutch tight to me. Oh, how tiresome, Gorgo, my muslin skirt is torn in two already! For heaven's sake, sir, if you ever wish to be fortunate take care of my shawl!

STRANGER. I can hardly help myself, but for all that I will be as careful as I can.

PRAXINOË. How close-packed the mob is, they 30 hustle like a herd of swine!

STRANGER. Courage, lady, all is well with us now.

PRAXINOË. Both this year and for ever may all be well with you, my dear sir, for your care of us. A good kind man! We're letting Eunoë get squeezed —come, wretched girl, push your way through. That is the way. We are all on the right side of the door, quoth the bridegroom, when he shut himself in with his bride.

GORGO. Do come here, Praxinoë. Look first at 40 these embroideries. How light and how lovely! You will call them the garments of the gods.

PRAXINOË. Lady Athene, what spinning women wrought them, what painters designed these drawings, so true they are? How naturally they stand and move, like living creatures, not patterns woven. What a clever thing is man! Ah, and himself—Adonis—how beautiful to behold he lies on his silver couch, with the first down on his cheeks, the thrice-beloved Adonis,—Adonis beloved even 50 among the dead.

A STRANGER. You weariful women, do cease your endless cooing talk! They bore one to death with their eternal broad vowels!

GORGO. Indeed! And where may this person come from? What is it to you if we *are* chatterboxes! Give orders to your own servants, sir. Do you pretend to command ladies of Syracuse? If you must know, we are Corinthians by descent, like Bellerophon himself, and we speak Peloponnesian. Dorian women may lawfully speak Doric, I presume?

PRAXINOË. Lady Persephone, never may we have more than one master. I am not afraid of *your* putting me on short commons.

GORGO. Hush, hush, Praxinoë—the Argive woman's daughter, the great singer, is beginning the *Adonis;* she that won the prize last year for dirge-singing. I am sure she will give us something lovely; see, she is (preluding) commencing with her airs and graces.

THE PSALM OF ADONIS

O Queen that lovest Golgi, and Idalium, and the steep of Eryx, O Aphrodite, that playest with gold, lo, from the stream eternal of Acheron they have brought back to thee Adonis—even in the twelfth month they have brought him, the dainty-footed Hours. Tardiest of the Immortals are the beloved Hours, but dear and desired they come, for always, to all mortals, they bring some gift with them. O Cypris, daughter of Diônê, from mortal to immortal, so men tell, thou hast changed Berenice, dropping softly in the woman's breast the stuff of immortality.

Therefore, for thy delight, oh thou of many names and many temples, doth the daughter of Berenice, even Arsinoë, lovely as Helen, cherish Adonis with all things beautiful.

Before him lie all ripe fruits that the tall trees' branches bear, and the delicate gardens, arrayed in baskets of silver, and the golden vessels are full of incense of Syria. And all the dainty cakes that women fashion in the kneading-tray, mingling blossoms manifold with the white wheaten flour, all that is wrought of honey sweet, and in soft olive oil, all cakes fashioned in the semblance of things that fly, and of things that creep, lo, here they are set before him.

Here are built for him shadowy bowers of green, all laden with tender anise, and children flit overhead—the little Loves—as the young nightingales perched upon the trees fly forth and try their wings from bough to bough.

O the ebony, O the gold, O the twin eagles of white ivory that carry to Zeus the son of Cronos his darling, his cup-bearer! O the purple coverlet strewn above, more soft than sleep! So Miletus will say, and whose sheep feeds in Samos.

Another bed is strewn for beautiful Adonis, one bed Cypris keeps, and one the rosy-armed Adonis. A bridegroom of eighteen or nineteen years is he, his kisses are not rough, the golden down being yet upon his lips! And now, good-night to Cypris, in the arms of her lover! But lo, in the morning we will all of us gather with the dew, and carry him forth among the waves that break upon the beach, and with locks unloosed, and ungirt raiment falling to the ankles, and bosoms bare will we begin our shrill sweet song.

Thou only, dear Adonis, so men tell, thou only of the demigods dost visit both this world and the stream of Acheron. For Agamemnon had no such lot, nor Aias, that mighty lord of the terrible anger, nor Hector, the eldest born of the twenty sons of Hecabe, nor Parocius, nor Pyrrhus, that returned out of Troyland, nor the heroes of yet more ancient days, the Lapithæ and Deucalion's sons, nor the sons of Pelops, and the chiefs of Pelasgian Argos. Be gracious now, dear Adonis, and propitious even in the coming year. Dear to us has thine advent been, Adonis, and dear shall it be when thou comest again.

GORGO. Praxinoë, the woman is cleverer than we fancied! Happy woman to know so much, thrice happy to have so sweet a voice. Well, all the same, it is time to be making for home. Diocleides has not had his dinner, and the man is all vinegar,—don't venture near him when he is kept waiting for dinner. Farewell, beloved Adonis, may you find us glad at your next coming!

THE GREEK ANTHOLOGY

Undying Thirst

This rudely sculptured porter-pot
Denotes where sleeps a female sot;
Who passed her life, good easy soul,
In sweetly chirping o'er her bowl.
Not for her friends or children dear   5
She mourns, but only for her beer.
E'en in the very grave, they say,
She thirsts for drink to wet her clay;
And, faith, she thinks it very wrong
This jug should stand unfilled so long.   10

Antipater, *tr. by Robert Bland*

Heraclitus

They told me, Heraclitus, they told me you were
   dead,
They brought me bitter news to hear and bitter
   tears to shed.
I wept as I remembered how often you and I
Had tired the sun with talking and sent him down
   the sky.

And now that thou art lying, my dear old Carian
   guest,
A handful of gray ashes, long, long ago at rest,
Still are thy pleasant voices, thy nightingales,
   awake;
For Death, he taketh all away, but them he cannot
   take.

Callimachus, *tr. by William Cory*

A Garland for Heliodora

I'll frame, my Heliodora! a garland for thy hair,
Which thou, in all thy beauty's pride, mayst not
   disdain to wear;
For I with tender myrtles white violets will twine,
White violets, but not so pure as that pure breast
   of thine;
With laughing lilies I will twine narcissus, and the
   sweet
Crocus shall, in its yellow hue, with purple hya-
   cinth meet.

And I will twine with all the rest, and all the rest
   above,
Queen of them all, the red red rose, the flower
   which lovers love.

Meleager, *tr. by Christopher North*

My Star

Star-gazing, O my Star; would I could be
Heaven, with a host of eyes to gaze on thee.

—Plato, *tr. by Alexander Lothian*

An Irony

A man found a treasure; and, what's very strange,
Running off with the cash, left a rope in exchange:
The poor owner, at missing his gold, full of grief,
Hung himself with the rope which was left by the
   thief.

—Plato, *tr. by Sir Alexander Croke*

Writ in Water

In holy night we made the vow;
   And the same night, that long before
Had seen our early passion grow,
   Was witness to the faith we swore.
Did I not swear to love her ever?   5
   And have I ever dared to rove?
Did she not vow a rival never
   Should shake her faith, or steal her love?
Yet now she says those words are air;
   Those vows were written in the water;   10
And, by the lamp that heard her swear,
   Hath yielded to the first who sought her.

—Meleager, *tr. by C. Merivale*

No Matter

My name, my country, what are they to thee?
What, whether proud or base my pedigree?
Perhaps I far surpassed all other men;
Perhaps I fell below them all. What then?
Suffice it, stranger, that thou seest a tomb.
Thou knowst its use. It hides—no matter whom.

—Paulus Silentiarius, *tr. by William Cowper*

ODES OF ANACREON

I

I saw the smiling bard of pleasure,
The minstrel of the Teian measure;
'Twas in a vision of the night,
He beamed upon my wondering sight.
I heard his voice, and warmly prest   5
The dear enthusiast to my breast.
His tresses wore a silvery dye,
But beauty sparkled in his eye;
Sparkled in his eyes of fire,
Through the mist of soft desire.   10
His lip exhaled, whene'er he sighed,
The fragrance of the racy tide;
And, as with weak and reeling feet
He came my cordial kiss to meet,
An infant, of the Cyprian band,   15
Guided him on with tender hand.
Quick from his glowing brows he drew
His braid, of many a wanton hue;
I took the wreath, whose inmost twine
Breathed of him and blushed with wine.   20
I hung it o'er my thoughtless brow,
And ah! I feel its magic now:
I feel that even his garland's touch
Can make the bosom love too much.

II

Give me the harp of epic song,   25
Which Homer's finger thrilled along;
But tear away the sanguine string,
For war is not the theme I sing.
Proclaim the laws of festal right,
I'm monarch of the board tonight;   30
And all around shall brim as high,
And quaff the tide as deep as I.
And when the cluster's mellowing dews
Their warm enchanting balm infuse,
Our feet shall catch the elastic bound,   35
And reel us through the dance's round.
Great Bacchus! we shall sing to thee,
In wild but sweet ebricty;
Flashing around such sparks of thought,
As Bacchus could alone have taught.   40

Then, give the harp of epic song,
Which Homer's finger thrilled along;
But tear away the sanguine string,
For war is not the theme I sing.

III

Listen to the Muse's lyre,   45
Master of the pencil's fire!
Sketched in painting's bold display,
Many a city first portray;
Many a city, reveling free,
Full of loose festivity.   50
Picture then a rosy train,
Bacchants straying o'er the plain;
Piping, as they roam along,
Roundelay or shepherd-song.
Paint me next, if painting may   55
Such a theme as this portray,
All the earthly heaven of love
These delighted mortals prove.

IV

Vulcan! hear your glorious task;
I do not from your labors ask   60
In gorgeous panoply to shine,
For war was ne'er a sport of mine.
No—let me have a silver bowl,
Where I may cradle all my soul;
But mind that, o'er its simple frame   65
No mimic constellations flame;
Nor grave upon the swelling side,
Orion, scowling o'er the tide.
I care not for the glittering wain,
Nor yet the weeping sister train.   70
But let the vine luxuriant roll
Its blushing tendrils round the bowl,
While many a rose-lipped bacchant maid
Is culling clusters in their shade.
Let sylvan gods, in antic shapes,   75
Wildly press the gushing grapes,
And flights of Loves, in wanton play,
Wing through the air their winding way;
While Venus, from her arbor green,
Looks laughing at the joyous scene,   84

Odes of Anacreon. Translated by Thomas Moore. Anacreon (563-478 B.C.) passed most of his life at the courts of Greek tyrants for whom he composed graceful verses celebrating their pleasures. Later imitations of his work are called Anacreontics.

And young Lyæus by her side
Sits, worthy of so bright a bride.

V

Sculptor, wouldst thou glad my soul,
Grave for me an ample bowl,
Worthy to shine in hall or bower,   85
When spring-time brings the reveler's hour.
Grave it with themes of chaste design,
Fit for a simple board like mine.
Display not there the barbarous rites
In which religious zeal delights;   90
Nor any tale of tragic fate
Which History shudders to relate.
No—cull thy fancies from above,
Themes of heaven and themes of love;
Let Bacchus, Jove's ambrosial boy,   95
Distill the grape in drops of joy,
And while he smiles at every tear,
Let warm-eyed Venus, dancing near,
With spirits of the genial bed,
The dewy herbage deftly tread.   100
Let Love be there, without his arms,
In timid nakedness of charms;
And all the Graces, linked with Love,
Stray, laughing, through the shadowy grove;
While rosy boys disporting round,   105
In circlets trip the velvet ground.
But ah! if there Apollo toys,
I tremble for the rosy boys.

VI

As late I sought the spangled bowers,
To cull a wreath of matin flowers,   110
Where many an early rose was weeping,
I found the urchin Cupid sleeping.
I caught the boy, a goblet's tide
Was richly mantling by my side,
I caught him by his downy wing,   115
And whelmed him in the racy spring.
Then drank I down the poisoned bowl,
And Love now nestles in my soul.
Oh, yes, my soul is Cupid's nest,
I feel him fluttering in my breast.   120

VII

The women tell me every day
That all my bloom has past away.
"Behold," the pretty wantons cry,
"Behold this mirror with a sigh;
The locks upon thy brow are few,   125

And like the rest, they're withering too!"
Whether decline has thinned my hair,
I'm sure I neither know nor care;
But this I know, and this I feel,
As onward to the tomb I steal,   130
That still as death approaches nearer,
The joys of life are sweeter, dearer;
And had I but an hour to live,
That little hour to bliss I'd give.

VIII

I care not for the idle state   135
Of Persia's king, the rich, the great:
I envy not the monarch's throne,
Nor wish the treasured gold my own.
But oh! be mine the rosy wreath,
Its freshness o'er my brow to breathe;   140
Be mine the rich perfumes that flow,
To cool and scent my locks of snow.
Today I'll haste to quaff my wine,
As if tomorrow comes, why then—
I'll haste to quaff my wine again.   145
And thus while all our days are bright,
Let us the festal hours beguile
With mantling cup and cordial smile;
And shed from each new bowl of wine
The richest drop on Bacchus' shrine.   150
For Death may come, with brow unpleasant,
May come, when least we wish him present,
And beckon to the sable shore,
And grimly bid us—drink no more!

ANACREONTICS

The Bard of Love

I wish to tune my quivering lyre
To deeds of fame and notes of fire;
To echo, from its rising swell,
How heroes fought and nations fell,
When Atreus' sons advanced to war,   5
Or Tyrian Cadmus roved afar;
But still, to martial strains unknown,
My lyre recurs to love alone.
Fired with the hope of future fame,
I seek some nobler hero's name;   10
The dying chords are strung anew,
To war, to war, my harp is due:
With glowing strings, the epic strain
To Jove's great son I raise again;
Alcides and his glorious deeds,   15

Beneath whose arms the Hydra bleeds,
All, all in vain; my wayward lyre
Wakes silver notes of soft desire.
Adieu, ye chiefs renowned in arms!
Adieu the clang of war's alarms!   20
To other deeds my soul is strung,
And sweeter notes shall now be sung;
My harp shall all its powers reveal,
To tell the tale my heart must feel;
Love, love alone my lyre shall claim,   25
In songs of bliss and sighs of flame.

                  —*tr. by Byron*

The Cicada

On your verdant throne elate,
Lovely insect, here in state,
Nectared dew you sip, and sing,
Like a little happy king.
All thou seest so blooming fine,   5
Lovely insect, all is thine,
Which the painted fields produce,
Or the soft-wing hours profuse.
Swains adore thy guiltless charms;
None thy blissful revel harms;   10
Thee, sweet prophet, all revere;

Thou foretellst the ripening year.
Thou by Muses art caressed,
Thou by golden Phœbus blessed;
He inspired thy tuneful voice;   15
Age ne'er interrupts thy joys.
Wisest offspring of the earth,
Thou for nothing car'st but mirth;
Free from pain, and flesh, and blood,
Thou'rt almost a little god.   20

                  —*tr. by Addison*

Stung

Love a bee, that lurked among
Roses, saw not, and was stung;
Who for his hurt finger crying,
Running sometimes, sometimes flying,
Did to his fair mother hie;   5
And "Help," cried he, "ere I die;
A snake winged has bitten me,
Called by country-folks a bee."
On which Venus—"If such smart
Little sting of bee impart,   10
How much greater is the pain
Which, whom thou hast stung, sustain."

                  —*tr. by T. Stanley*

CATULLUS

Home to Sirmio

Dear Sirmio, that art the very eye
Of islands and peninsulas, that lie
Deeply embosomed in calm inland lake,
Or where the waves of the vast ocean break;
Joy of all joys, to gaze on thee once more!   5
I scarce believe that I have left the shore
Of Thynia, and Bithynia's parching plain,
And gaze on thee in safety once again!
Oh, what more sweet than when, from care set
     free,
The spirit lays its burden down, and we,   10
With distant travel spent, come home and spread
Our limbs to rest along the wished-for bed!
This, this alone, repays such toils as these!

Smile, then, fair Sirmio, and thy master please,—
And you, ye dancing waters of the lake,   15
Rejoice; and every smile of home awake!

Love Is All

Let us, Lesbia darling, still
Live our life, and love our fill;
Heeding not a jot, howe'er
Churlish dotards chide or stare!
Suns go down, but 'tis to rise   5
Brighter in the morning skies;
But when sets our little light,
We must sleep in endless night.
A thousand kisses grant me sweet;
With a hundred these complete;   10

Catullus, *Home to Sirmio*. Translated by Theodore Martin. Gaius Valerius Catullus (c. 87-54 B.C.)
divided his life between his native Verona and Rome. His poems reflect the life of a gentleman of leisure
and an unhappy lover of a cruel mistress.
     Catullus, *Love Is All*. Translated by Theodore Martin.

Lip me a thousand more, and then
Another hundred give again.
A thousand add to these, anon
A hundred more, then hurry one
Kiss after kiss without cessation,   15
Until we lose all calculation;
So envy shall not mar our blisses
By numbering up our tale of kisses.

The Dead Sparrow

Ye Cupids, droop each little head,
Nor let your wings with joy be spread;
My Lesbia's favorite bird is dead,
    Whom dearer than her eyes she loved.
For he was gentle, and so true,   5
Obedient to her call he flew,
No fear, no wild alarm he knew,
    But lightly o'er her bosom moved:

And softly fluttering here and there,
He never sought to clear the air,   10
But chirruped oft, and, free from care,
    Tuned to her ear his grateful strain.
Now having passed the gloomy bourne
From whence he never can return,
His death and Lesbia's grief I mourn,   15
    Who sighs, alas! but sighs in vain.

Oh! curst be thou, devouring grave!
Whose jaws eternal victims crave,
From whom no earthly power can save;
    For thou hast ta'en the bird away: 20
From thee my Lesbia's eyes o'erflow,
Her swollen cheeks with weeping glow;
Thou art the cause of all her woe,
    Receptacle of life's decay.

Love's Unreason

I hate and love—the why I cannot tell,
But by my tortures know the fact too well.

True or False

None could ever say that she,
Lesbia! was so loved by me.

Never all the world around
Faith so true as mine was found.
If no longer it endures   5
(Would it did!) the fault is yours.
I can never think again
Well of you: I try in vain.
But . . . be false . . . do what you will.—
Lesbia! I must love you still.   10

On the Burial of His Brother

By ways remote and distant waters sped,
    Brother, to thy sad graveside am I come
That I may give the last gifts to the dead,
    And vainly parley with thine ashes dumb;
Since She who now bestows and now denies   5
    Hath ta'en thee, hopeless brother, from mine
        eyes.
But lo! these gifts, the heirlooms of past years,
    Are made sad things to grace thy coffin-shell;
Take them, all drenched with a brother's tears,
    And, brother, for all time, hail and farewell. 10

Farewell to Bithynia

A balmy warmth comes wafted o'er the seas,
    The savage howl of wintry tempests drear
In the sweet whispers of the western breeze
    Has died away; the spring, the spring is here!

Now quit, Catullus, quit the Phrygian plain,   5
    Where days of sweltering sunshine soon shall
        crown
Nicæa's fields with wealth of golden grain,
    And fly to Asia's cities of renown!

Already through each nerve a flutter runs
    Of eager hope, that longs to be away;   10
Already 'neath the light of other suns
    My feet, new-winged for travel, yearn to stray.

And you, ye band of comrades tried and true,
    Who side by side went forth from home, fare-
        well!
How far apart the paths shall carry you   15
    Back to your native shore, ah, who can tell?

Catullus, *The Dead Sparrow*. Translated by Lord Byron.
Catullus, *True or False*. Translated by Walter Savage Landor.
Catullus, *On the Burial of His Brother*. Translated by Aubrey Beardsley.
Catullus, *Farewell to Bithynia*. Translated by Theodore Martin.

HORACE

Ode I, 4. To Lucius Sestius

As biting Winter flies, lo, Spring with sunny skies
  And balmy airs! and barks long dry put out
    again from shore;
Now the ox forsakes his byre, and the husband-
    man his fire,
  And daisy-dappled meadows bloom where win-
    ter frosts lay hoar.

By Cytherea led, while the moon shines overhead,
  The Nymphs and Graces, hand in hand, with
    alternating feet   6
Shake the ground, while swinking Vulcan strikes
    the sparkles fierce and red
  From the forges of the Cyclops, with reiterated
    beat.

'T is the time with myrtle green to bind our glis-
    tening locks,
  Or with flowers wherein the loosened earth her-
    self hath newly dressed,   10
And to sacrifice to Faunus in some glade amidst
    the rocks
  A yearling lamb, or else a kid, if such delight
    him best.

Death comes alike to all—to the monarch's lordly
    hall,
  Or the hovel of the beggar, and his summons
    none shall stay.
O Sestius, happy Sestius! use the moments as they
    pass;   15
  Far-reaching hopes are not for us, the creatures
    of a day.

Thee soon shall night enshroud, and the Manes'
    phantom crowd,
  And the starveling house unbeautiful of Pluto
    shut thee in;
And thou shalt not banish care by the ruddy wine-
    cup there,
  Nor woo the gentle Lycidas, whom all are mad
    to win.   20

Ode I, 5. To Pyrrha

What slender youth, with perfumed locks,
In some sweet nook beneath the rocks,
Pyrrha, where clustering roses grow,
Bends to thy fatal beauty now?
For whom is now that golden hair   5
Wreathed in a band so simply fair?
How often will he weep to find
Thy pledges frail, Love's power unkind?
And start to see the tempest sweep
With angry blast the darkening deep;   10
Though sunned by thy entrancing smile,
He fears no change, suspects no guile.
A sailor on bright summer seas,
He wots not of the fickle breeze.
For me—yon votive tablet scan;   15
It tells that I, a shipwrecked man,
Hung my dank weeds in Neptune's fane,
And ne'er will tempt those seas again.

Ode I, 14. The Ship of State

Ship of State, beware!
Hold fast the port. Cling to the friendly shore
Lest sudden storms and whirling eddies bear
Thy shattered hull to faithless seas once more.

See how the rower faints upon his oar!   5
  Hark to the groaning of the mast,
  Sore stricken by the Libyan blast!
  Thy shrouds are burst; thy sails are torn;
  And through thy gaping ribs forlorn
    The floods remorseless pour.   10
Dare not to call for aid on powers divine;
  Dishonored once they hear no more:
    Nor boast, majestic pine,
Daughter of Pontic forests, thy great name,
  Old lineage, well-earned fame,   15
  The honors of thy sculptured prow—
Sport of the mocking winds, nor feared nor trusted
    now!

Alas! my country, long my anxious care,
Source now of bitter pain and fond regret!

Horace, *To Lucius Sestius*. Translated by Theodore Martin. Quintus Horatius Flaccus (65-8 B.C.),
educated in the best schools of Rome and Athens, was a close friend of important men in a most interesting period of Roman history. His patron, the wealthy Mæcenas, enabled him to live a pleasant life on
his Sabine Farm.
  Horace, *To Pyrrha*. Translated by Goldwin Smith.
  Horace, *The Ship of State*. Translated by Sir Stephen E. De Vere.

Thy stars obscured, thy course beset   20
   By rocks unseen, beware!
Trust not soft winds and treacherous seas
Or the false glitter of the Cyclades.

Ode I, 22. To Aristius Fuscus

Fuscus, the man of life upright and pure,
Needeth nor javelin, nor bow of Moor,
Nor arrows tipped with venom deadly sure,
   Loading his quiver;

Whether o'er Afric's burning sands he rides,   5
Or frosty Caucasus' bleak mountain-sides,
Or wanders lonely where Hydaspes glides,
   That storied river.

For as I strayed along the Sabine wood
Singing my Lalage in careless mood,   10
Lo, all at once a wolf before me stood,
   Then turned and fled:

Creature so huge did warlike Daunia ne'er
Engender in her forests' wildest lair,
Not Juba's land, parched nurse of lions, e'er   15
   Such monster bred.

Place me where no life-laden summer breeze
Freshens the meads, or murmurs 'mongst the trees,
Where clouds oppress and withering tempests
    freeze
   From shore to shore.   20

Place me beneath the sunbeams' fiercest glare,
On arid sands, no dwelling anywhere;
Still Lalage's sweet smile, sweet voice even there
   I will adore.

Ode I, 23. To Chloe

Chloe, thou fliest me like a fawn
That on some lonely upland lawn,
Seeking its dam, in winds and trees
Imaginary dangers sees.
Does Spring's fresh breeze the foliage shake   5
Or lizard rustle in the brake?
At once it quakes in heart and limb.
Yet I, sweet girl, no tiger grim,
No fierce Gætulian lion am.
Then, no more, fawn-like, seek thy dam,   10
But bury all thy fond alarms—
'T is time thou should'st—in true love's arms.

Ode I, 37. The Death of Cleopatra

Drink, comrades, drink; give loose to mirth!
  With joyous footstep beat the earth,
  And spread before the War-God's shrine
The Salian feast, the sacrificial wine.

  Bring forth from each ancestral hoard   5
  Strong draughts of Cæcuban long stored,
   Till now forbidden. Fill the bowl!
For she is fallen, that great Egyptian Queen,
With all her crew contaminate and obscene,
  Who, mad with triumph, in her pride,   10
   The manly might of Rome defied,
And vowed destruction to the Capitol.

As the swift falcon stooping from above
  With beak unerring strikes the dove,
  Or as the hunter tracks the deer   15
  Over Hæmonian plains of snow,
Thus Cæsar came. Then on her royal State
With Mareotic fumes inebriate,
  A shadow fell of fate and fear,
   And thro' the lurid glow   20
  From all her burning galleys shed
She turned her last surviving bark, and fled.

  She sought no refuge on a foreign shore.
  She sought her doom: far nobler 't was to die
Than like a panther caged in Roman bonds to lie.
  The sword she feared not. In her realm once
    more,   26
   Serene amongst deserted fanes,
   Unmoved 'mid vacant halls she stood;
  Then to the aspic gave her darkening veins,
   And sucked the death into her blood.   30

Deliberately she died: fiercely disdained
To bow her haughty head to Roman scorn,
Discrowned, and yet a Queen; a captive chained;
  A woman desolate and forlorn.

Ode I, 38. To His Cup-Bearer

  Persia's pomp, my boy, I hate;
   No coronals of flowerets rare
  For me on bark of linden plait,
   Nor seek thou to discover where
  The lush rose lingers late.   5

  With unpretending myrtle twine
   Naught else! It fits your brows

Horace, *To Aristius Fuscus*. Translated by Theodore Martin.
Horace, *To Chloe*. Translated by Goldwin Smith.
Horace, *The Death of Cleopatra*. Translated by Sir Stephen E. De Vere.
Horace, *To His Cup-Bearer*. Translated by Theodore Martin.

Attending me; it graces mine
As I in happy ease carouse
Beneath the thick-leaved vine. 10

Ode II, 3. To Quintus Dellius

When dangers press, a mind sustain
Unshaken by the storms of fate,
And when delight succeeds to pain
With no glad insolence elate;
For death will end the various toys 5
Of hopes, and fears, and cares, and joys.

Mortal alike, if sadly grave
You pass life's melancholy day,
Or in some green, retired cave,
Wearing the idle hours away, 10
Give to the Muses all your soul,
And pledge them in the flowing bowl,

Where the broad pine, and poplar white,
To join their hospitable shade
With intertwisted boughs delight, 15
And, o'er its pebbly bed conveyed,
Labors the winding stream to run,
Trembling and glittering to the sun.

Thy generous wine, and rich perfume,
And fragrant roses hither bring, 20
That with the early zephyrs bloom,
And wither with declining spring.
While joy and youth not yet have fled,
And Fate still holds th' uncertain thread.

You soon must leave your verdant bowers 25
And groves yourself had taught to grow,
Your soft retreats from sultry hours,
Where Tiber's gentle waters flow,
Soon leave; and all you call your own
Be squandered by an heir unknown. 30

Whether of wealth and lineage proud,
A high patrician name you bear,
Or pass ignoble in the crowd,
Unsheltered from the midnight air,
'T is all alike; no age or state 35
Is spared by unrelenting Fate.

To the same port our barks are bound;
One final doom is fixed for all;
The universal wheel goes round,
And, soon or late, each lot must fall, 40

When all together shall be sent
To one eternal banishment.

Ode II, 10. To Licinius Murena

Receive, dear friend, the truths I teach;
So shalt thou live beyond the reach
Of adverse Fortune's power:
Not always tempt the distant deep,
Nor always timorously creep 5
Along the treach'rous shore.

He that holds fast the golden mean,
And lives contentedly between
The little and the great,
Feels not the wants that pinch the poor, 10
Nor plagues that haunt the rich man's door,
Embittering all his state.

The tallest pines feel most the power
Of wintry blasts; the loftiest tower
Comes heaviest to the ground; 15
The bolts that spare the mountain's side,
His cloud-capt eminence divide,
And spread the ruin round.

The well-informed philosopher
Rejoices, with a wholesome fear, 20
And hopes in spite of pain;
If winter bellows from the north,
Soon the sweet spring comes dancing forth,
And nature laughs again.

What if thine heaven be overcast? 25
The dark appearance will not last;
Expect a brighter sky!
The god that strings the silver bow
Awakes sometimes the Muses too,
And lays his arrows by. 30

If hindrances obstruct thy way,
Thy magnanimity display,
And let thy strength be seen;
But oh! if Fortune fill thy sail
With more than a propitious gale, 35
Take half thy canvas in.

Ode II, 14. To Postumus

Alas, my Postumus, our years
Glide silently away. No tears,

Horace, *To Quintus Dellius*. Translated by John Herman Merivale.
Horace, *To Licinius Murena*. Translated by William Cowper.
Horace, *To Postumus*. Translated by Sir Stephen E. De Vere.

No loving orisons repair
The wrinkled cheek, the whitening hair
That drop forgotten to the tomb. 5
Pluto's inexorable doom
Mocks at thy daily sacrifice.
Around his dreary kingdom lies
That fatal stream whose arms infold
The giant race accurst of old: 10
All, all alike must cross its wave,
The kind, the noble, and the slave.
In vain we shun the battle's roar,
And breakers dashed on Adria's shore;
Vainly we flee in terror blind 15
The plague that walketh on the wind;
The sluggish river of the dead,
Cocytus, must be visited,
The Danaïds' detested brood,
Foul with their murdered husbands' blood, 20
And Sisyphus with ghastly smile
Pointing to his eternal toil.
All must be left; thy gentle wife,
Thy home, the joys of rural life:
And when thy fleeting days are gone 25
Th' ill-omened cypresses alone
Of all thy fondly cherished trees
Shall grace thy funeral obsequies.
Cling to thy loved remains, and wave
Their mournful shadows o'er thy grave. 30
A lavish but a nobler heir
Thy hoarded Cæcuban shall share,
And on the tessellated floor
The purple nectar madly pour—
Nectar more worthy of the halls 35
Where pontiffs hold high festivals.

Ode III, 9. The Reconciliation

HORACE

Whilst I was dear and thou wert kind,
  And I, and I alone, might lie
Upon thy snowy breast reclined,
  Not Persia's king so blest as I.

LYDIA

Whilst I to thee was all in all, 5
  Nor Chloe might with Lydia vie,
Renowned in ode or madrigal,
  Not Roman Ilia famed as I.

HORACE

I now am Thracian Chloe's slave,
  With hand and voice that charms the air, 10
For whom even death itself I'd brave,
  So fate the darling girl would spare!

LYDIA

I dote on Calais—and I
  Am all his passion, all his care,
For whom a double death I'd die, 15
  So fate the darling boy would spare!

HORACE

What if our ancient love return,
  And bind us with a closer tie,
If I the fair-haired Chloe spurn,
  And as of old for Lydia sigh. 20

LYDIA

Though lovelier than yon star is he,
  Thou fickle as an April sky,
More churlish, too, than Adria's sea,
  With thee I'd live, with thee I'd die!

Ode III, 13. The Fountain of Bandusia

O babbling Spring, than glass more clear,
Worthy of wreath and cup sincere,
  Tomorrow shall a kid be thine
  With swelled and sprouting brows for sign—
Sure sign!—of loves and battles near. 5

Child of the race that butt and rear!
Not less, alas! his life-blood dear
  Shall tinge thy cold wave crystalline,
    O babbling Spring!

Thee Sirius knows not. Thou dost cheer 10
With pleasant cool the plow-worn steer,
  The wandering flock. This verse of mine
  Shall rank thee one with founts divine;
Men shall thy rock and tree revere,
    O babbling Spring! 15

Horace, *The Reconciliation*. Translated by Theodore Martin.
Horace, *The Fountain of Bandusia*. Translated by Austin Dobson.

VIRGIL

Eclogue IV: "The Messiah"

Sicilian Muse, begin a loftier strain!
Tho' lowly shrubs, and trees that shade the plain,
Delight not all; Sicilian Muse, prepare
To make the vocal woods deserve a consul's care.
The last great age, foretold by sacred rhymes, 5
Renews its finished course: Saturnian times
Roll round again; and mighty years, begun
From their first orb, in radiant circles run.
The base degenerate iron offspring ends;
A golden progeny from heaven descends. 10
O chaste Lucina,[1] speed the mother's pains,
And haste the glorious birth! thy own Apollo
        reigns!
The lovely boy, with his auspicious face,
Shall Pollio's consulship and triumph grace;
Majestic months set out with him to their appointed
        race. 15
The father banished virtue shall restore,
And crimes shall threat the guilty world no more.
The son shall lead the life of gods, and be
By gods and heroes seen, and gods and heroes see.
The jarring nations he in peace shall bind, 20
And with paternal virtues rule mankind.
Unbidden Earth shall wreathing ivy bring,
And fragrant herbs (the promises of spring),
As her first offerings to her infant king.
The goats with strutting dugs shall homeward
        speed, 25
And lowing herds secure from lions feed.
His cradle shall with rising flowers be crowned:
The serpent's brood shall die; the sacred ground
Shall weeds and poisonous plants refuse to bear;
Each common bush shall Syrian roses wear. 30
But when heroic verse his youth shall raise,
And form it to hereditary praise,
Unlabored harvests shall the fields adorn,
And clustered grapes shall blush on every thorn;
The knotted oaks shall showers of honey weep, 35
And thro' the matted grass the liquid gold shall
        creep.
Yet of old fraud some footsteps shall remain:
The merchant still shall plow the deep for gain;
Great cities shall with walls be compassed round,
And sharpened shares shall vex the fruitful ground;
Another Tiphys[2] shall new seas explore; 41

Another Argo[3] land the chiefs upon the Iberian
        shore;
Another Helen other wars create,
And great Achilles urge the Trojan fate.
But when to ripened manhood he shall grow, 45
The greedy sailor shall the seas forego;
No keel shall cut the waves for foreign ware,
For every soil shall every product bear.
The laboring hind his oxen shall disjoin;
No plow shall hurt the glebe, no pruning hook the
        vine; 50
Nor wool shall in dissembled colors shine.
But the luxurious father of the fold,
With native purple, or unborrowed gold,
Beneath his pompous fleece shall proudly sweat;
And under Tyrian robes the lamb shall bleat. 55
The Fates, when they this happy web have spun,
Shall bless the sacred clew, and bid it smoothly
        run.
Mature in years, to ready honors move,
O of celestial seed! O foster son of Jove!
See, laboring Nature calls thee to sustain 60
The nodding frame of heaven, and earth, and
        main!
See to their base restored, earth, seas, and air;
And joyful ages, from behind, in crowding ranks
        appear.
To sing thy praise, would Heaven my breath
        prolong,
Infusing spirits worthy such a song, 65
Not Thracian Orpheus should transcend my lays,
Nor Linus[4] crowned with never-fading bays;
Tho' each his heavenly parent should inspire;
The Muse instruct the voice, and Phœbus tune the
        lyre.
Should Pan contend in verse, and thou my theme,
Arcadian judges should their god condemn. 71
Begin, auspicious boy, to cast about
Thy infant eyes, and, with a smile, thy mother
        single out:
Thy mother well deserves that short delight,
The nauseous qualms of ten long months and
        travel to requite. 75
Then smile: the frowning infant's doom is read;
No god shall crown the board, nor goddess bless
        the bed.[5]

Virgil (Publius Virgilius Maro, 70-19 B.C.), translated by John Dryden. [1] goddess of childbirth.
[2] pilot of the Argo. [3] ship in which Jason sailed. [4] singer who taught music to Hercules. [5] Actually:
"Of them who have not smiled on a parent, never was one honored at a god's feast or on a goddess'
couch." Dryden's last line predicts the end of the pagan gods, in accordance with medieval Christian
interpretations of this Eclogue.

THE VIGIL OF VENUS

Love he to-morrow, who loved never;
To-morrow, who hath loved, persever.

The spring appears, in which the earth
Receives a new harmonious birth;
When all things mutual love unites;   5
When birds perform their nuptial rites;
And fruitful by her watery lover,
Each grove its tresses doth recover.
Love's Queen to-morrow, in the shade,
Which by these verdant trees is made,   10
Their sprouting tops in wreaths shall bind,
And myrtles into arbors wind;
To-morrow, raised on a high throne,
Dione[1] shall her laws make known.

    Love he to-morrow, who loved never;   15
    To-morrow, who hath loved, persever.

Then the round ocean's foaming flood
Immingled with celestial blood,
'Mongst the blue purple of the main,
And horses whom two feet sustain,   20
Rising Dione did beget
With fruitful waters dropping wet.

    Love he to-morrow, who loved never;
    To-morrow, who hath loved, persever.

With flowery jewels everywhere   25
She paints the purple-color'd year;
She, when the rising bud receives
Favonius'[2] breath, thrusts forth the leaves,
The naked roof with these t' adorn;
She the transparent dew o' th' morn,   30
Which the thick air of night still uses
To leave behind, in rain diffuses;
These tears with orient brightness shine,
Whilst they with trembling weight decline,
Whose every drop, into a small   35
Clear orb distill'd, sustains its fall.
Pregnant with these the bashful rose
Her purple blushes doth disclose.
The drops of falling dew that are
Shed in calm nights by every star,   40
She in her humid mantle holds,
And then her virgin leaves unfolds.
I' th' morn, by her command, each maid
With dewy roses is array'd;
Which from Cythera's[3] crimson blood,   45

From the soft kisses Love bestow'd,
From jewels, from the radiant flame,
And the sun's purple luster, came.
She to her spouse shall married be
To-morrow; not ashamed that he   50
Should with a single knot untie
Her fiery garment's purple dye.

    Love he to-morrow, who loved never;
    To-morrow, who hath loved, persever.

The goddess bade the nymphs remove   55
Unto the shady myrtle grove;
The boy goes with the maids, yet none
Will trust, or think Love tame is grown,
If they perceive that anywhere
He arrows doth about him bear.   60
Go fearless, nymphs, for Love hath laid
Aside his arms, and tame is made.
His weapons by command resign'd,
Naked to go he is enjoin'd,
Lest he hurt any by his craft,   65
Either with flame, or bow, or shaft.
But yet take heed, young nymphs, beware
You trust him not, for Cupid's fair,
Lest by his beauty you be harm'd;
Love naked is completely arm'd.   70

    Love he to-morrow, who loved never;
    To-morrow, who hath loved, persever.

Fair Venus virgins sends to thee,
Indued with equal modesty:
One only thing we thee desire,   75
Chaste Delia,[4] for a while retire;
That the wide forest, that the wood,
May be unstain'd with savage blood.
She would with prayers herself attend thee,
But that she knew she could not bend thee;   80
She would thyself to come have pray'd,
Did these delights beseem a maid.
Now might'st thou see with solemn rites
The Chorus celebrate three nights;
'Mongst troops whom equal pleasure crowns,   85
To play and sport upon thy downs;
'Mongst garlands made of various flowers,
'Mongst ever-verdant myrtle bowers.
Ceres nor Bacchus[5] absent be,
Nor yet the poet's deity.   90
All night we wholly must employ

Translated by Thomas Stanley. An address to Venus commending a night devoted to her, this song —or dance song, possibly—is related to spring rites intended to induce the fertility of nature by glorifying the fecundating power of Venus. [1] poetic name of Venus taken from her mother's name. [2] the west wind, favorable to vegetation. [3] poetic name of Venus, from the island to which Venus was wafted in a shell. [4] name for Diana, goddess of the moon, the hunt, and chastity. [5] Ceres: goddess of agriculture; Bacchus, god of wine.

In vigils, and in songs of joy;
None but Dione must bear sway
Amongst the woods; Delia, give way.

> *Love he to-morrow, who loved never;*   95
> *To-morrow, who hath loved, persever.*

She the tribunal did command
Deck'd with Hyblæan flowers should stand;
She will in judgment sit; the Graces
On either side shall have their places;   100
Hybla, the flowers pour forth, whate'er
Was brought thee by the welcome year;
Hybla, thy flowery garment spread,
Wide as is Enna's⁶ fruitful mead;
Maids of the country here will be;   105
Maids of the mountain come to see;
Hither resort all such as dwell
Either in grove, or wood, or well.
The wing'd boy's mother every one
Commands in order to sit down;   110
Charging the virgins that they must
In nothing Love, though naked, trust.

> *Love he to-morrow, who loved never;*
> *To-morrow, who hath loved, persever.*

Let the fresh covert of a shade   115
Be by these early flowers display'd,
To-morrow (which with sports and play
We keep) was Æther's⁷ wedding day;
When first the father of the spring
Did out of clouds the young year bring.   120
The husband Shower⁸ then courts his spouse,
And in her sacred bosom flows,
That all which that vast body bred
By this defluxion may be fed:
Produced within, she all there sways   125
By a hid spirit, which by ways
Unknown diffused through soul and veins,
All things both governs and sustains.
Piercing through the unsounded sea,
And earth, and highest heaven, she   130
All places with her power doth fill,
Which through each part she doth distil;
And to the world the mystic ways
Of all production open lays.

> *Love he to-morrow, who loved never;*   135
> *To-morrow, who hath loved, persever.*

She to the Latins did transfer
The Trojan nephews; and by her
Was the Laurentian virgin won,

And join'd in marriage to her son.   140
By her assistance did Mars gain
A votaress from Vesta's⁹ fane.
To marriage Romulus detray'd
The Sabine women, by her aid,
(Of Romans the wide-spreading stem,)   145
And in the long descent of them
In whom that offspring was dilated,
Cæsar her nephew she created.

> *Love he to-morrow, who loved never;*
> *To-morrow, who hath loved, persever.*   150

The fields are fruitful made by pleasure;
The fields are rich in Venus' treasure;
And Love, Dione's son, fame yields
For truth, his birth had in the fields;
As soon as born the field reliev'd him,   155
Into its bosom first receiv'd him;
She bred him from his infant hours
With the sweet kisses of the flowers.

> *Love he to-morrow, who loved never;*
> *To-morrow, who hath loved, persever.*   160

See how the bulls their sides distend,
And broom-stalks with the burthen bend;
Now every one doth safely lie
Confined within his marriage tie;
See, with their husbands here are laid   165
The bleating flocks beneath the shade.
The warbling birds on every tree
The goddess wills not silent be.
The vocal swans on every lake,
With their hoarse voice a harsh sound make;   170
And Tereus'¹⁰ hapless maid beneath
The poplar's shade her song doth breathe;
Such as might well persuade thee love
Doth in those trembling accents move,
Not that the sister in those strains   175
Of the inhuman spouse complains.
We silent are whilst she doth sing,
How long in coming is my spring?
When will the time arrive, that I
May swallow-like my voice untie?   180
My muse for being silent flies me,
And Phœbus¹¹ will no longer prize me:
So did Amiclæ once, whilst all
Silence observed, through silence fall.

> *Love he to-morrow, who loved never;*   185
> *To-morrow, who hath loved, persever.*

---

⁶ where there is perpetual springtime. ⁷ Zeus or Jupiter, god of the sky and all its phenomena; here, the gatherer of the clouds that dispense the fertilizing rain. ⁸ rain pouring on the earth and fructifying it. ⁹ Roman goddess of the hearth and its fire. Six virgins called Vestals served her. ¹⁰ Tereus married Procne but fell in love with her sister Philomela. When the latter rejected him, he cut out her tongue. Procne avenged herself by killing her child Itys and feeding him to Tereus. Itys was turned into a pheasant, Procne into a swallow, Tereus into a hawk or vulture, and Philomela into a nightingale. ¹¹ Phœbus Apollo, god of poetry as well as god of the sun

LATIN EPIC POETRY

It would have been strange if the Romans, whose course of empire-making was so resolute and far-reaching, had failed to produce epic poems. The material was at hand, from the early wars against neighboring towns to the Punic Wars that brought the Roman legions to campaigns as distant as northern Africa. The latter ended in the destruction of the Phœnician capital of Carthage. This was a war of empires, involving not only a vast battlefield, not only such memorable deeds as the crossing of the Alps by the Carthaginians, but heroic leaders like Hannibal and Scipio Africanus whose accomplishments captured the imaginations of mankind. Nor was this followed by an easy lapse into contentment and mere colonization, for there were still wars to be fought in Asia Minor, Egypt, and Greece. Finally, Julius Cæsar carried the Roman standards to all Gaul and, across the Channel, to sea-girt England.

When this was concluded, Roman patriots in the golden age of Augustus Cæsar could look back upon a record of world conquest unparalleled in history, regard the present as the ripe harvest of a glorious seed-time, and look forward to æons of rulership by the master-race of which they were proud members. That all this would pass away because there can be no survival for a community half-slave and half-free—or rather one-tenth fabulously rich and nine-tenths incredibly poor and oppressed—could not occur to those who enjoyed a sinecure in the Queen of Cities.

However, the writing of folk epics requires two conditions—creativity and an exuberant people happy in the enjoyment of its strength and its share in the fruits thereof. Neither condition existed. On the one hand, the Roman people were essentially hard-headed and unimaginative, and drew upon the culture of the Greeks, deriving both instruction and early literature from Greek slaves.

On the other, the profits of victory went to a few plutocrats, while the poor only became poorer when the acquisition of rich granaries in Northern Africa began to make a homeless proletariat out of the agricultural population of Italy. Yet epic writing was inevitable after the triumphal march of the Roman standard over three continents, and the rise and progress of national glory soon found expression in the *Annals* of Ennius (239-169 B.C.), whom a later poet, Horace, called "Father Ennius" and revered as the creator of Latin literature. Unhappily, only fragments of his work survive, and those do not suggest a folk epic. The one memorable epic poem of the Romans comes later, during the transiently stable regime of Augustus; and this work, the *Æneid* of Virgil, is inevitably something different from the *Iliad*. It is based on a model belonging to another nation—namely, the Homeric poems. It is not the genuine balladry and heroic songs of a people created during the epic ages from which the subject of the poem is taken. It is written by a poet whose authorship is beyond dispute, in an artificial age, and in an atmosphere of urban cultivation and refinements. Its polished and carefully ordered language is that of a literary set, and its epic devices are borrowed. It is, in short, a supreme example of another type of composition, for which a suitable name is the "literary epic."

The author of this work, already known to his time for his polished pastoral poetry, was a man of culture. Publius Virgilius Maro, or simply Virgil, was born in 70 B.C. in Mantua. His well-to-do father provided him with a liberal education under slave-tutors and in schools in Cremona, Milan, and Naples. He studied Greek literature, pursued philosophy under the most expert tutelage, and even dabbled in the sciences. Of delicate health and disposed to tuberculosis, he could only be a spectator in the whirl of Roman history. Losing his estate during the civil war, he became dependent upon the patronage of the governor of the province. His property was restored to him, but from this time on he was a protégé of the men in power. Mæcenas took him under his wing, and Octavian, now Augustus Cæsar, made him virtually a court poet.

Beginning in his fortieth year, Virgil devoted about a decade to his task, and he would have continued polishing his poem if death had not interfered. The literary circle watched his progress with intense interest, expecting a work that would eclipse the *Iliad*. Augustus himself asked to see the work in progress. Only the poet had grave misgivings about it, continued to revise conscientiously, and on his death-bed, in 19 B.C., asked his friends to destroy the manuscript as unworthy of its great theme. It was Augustus who released them of the obligation of fulfilling Virgil's request, and he had good grounds. Apart from the poem's literary merits, as Alexander Pope surmised, this epic had political importance in strengthening the popularity of the first of the emperors.

Virgil chose for the central character of the *Æneid* the Trojan hero Æneas, who is also the son of Venus. Since Æneas becomes the mythical founder of Rome, Virgil gave his city firm roots in remotest antiquity. Æneas' wanderings take him to Africa, where he starts the historic cleavage between the two rival imperial cities of Rome and Carthage by abandoning Dido, Queen of Carthage, and departing to fulfil his divinely appointed task of founding Rome. Thus Virgil makes legend the handmaid of the commercial and imperialistic conflict that gave empire to the Cæsars. It is noteworthy, too, that his hero's descent from Trojan royalty emphasizes the political antagonism between the Greeks and their Roman conquerors. Virgil's patriotism led him to force upon his material every parallelism that would give the sanction of legend to historical fact.

Virgil had no hesitation in linking his poem to Homeric tradition, thereby adding the final period to the story of Rome's dependence on Greek art. The *Æneid* takes up where the Homeric account ends—the imminent fall of Troy. It is Virgil who writes the tale of the actual fall of Troy, thus supplementing the *Iliad*. Since the first half of his poem concerns the wanderings of his hero before the establishment of Rome, the analogy with the wanderings of Odysseus in the *Odyssey* is also apparent. Dido is a lovely passionate woman like Helen of Troy, and Æneas is in danger of falling into her hands like Paris, until his mother Venus (who also befriended Paris) orders him to Italy. There Æneas engages in a protracted conflict with the native inhabitants led by the hero Turnus, whom he finally defeats. The parallel with Achilles and Hector, and with the long struggle on the fields of Troy, is also evident.

The *Æneid* is, nevertheless, Roman to the core. No one could confuse Virgil's stately, orotund style and slow measures with Homer's simple loveliness and swift, limpid lines. The recital of Æneas' wars has a matter-of-fact, rather tedious, quality, suggestive of the Roman's more literal, business-like view of war. The characterizations of the *Æneid* reveal little of the humanization of the Greek epics, though Virgil follows Homer's example in making his hero's antagonist, Turnus, relatively sympathetic. Dido is well realized, and is a superb achievement, but her passion, too, reflects the Roman concept of love. It reminds us of the carnal intensities of the matrons who gave poets like Catullus so much trouble, and who soon degenerated into the torrid women of Rome's decay. And Æneas is a Roman gentleman, whose repeatedly stressed "piety" is devoid of spirituality, and is tinged with the so-called Babbittism of the self-made man.

If it were not for compensating qualities, the *Æneid* would not be entitled to its high estate in the field of letters. Notable among the compensations are Virgil's superb descriptive faculty, the noble music of his lines, the felicitous phrasing, the words that seem so apt. It is these qualities that have made the poem so quotable, and its isolated passages so adaptable for many occasions. And, above all, it is the inherent grandeur of the work that engages the reader; one derives from the poem a sense of man's dignity which is so tonic to the spirit in a world of petty concerns and commonplaces.

The *Æneid* begins in the usual epic fashion, with an invocation to the muse and a short declaration of his purpose in writing. We are then shown Æneas and his companions sailing on their way from Troy. A remarkable description of a storm and of the eventual arrival of Æneas at Carthage complete the first book.

In the second, the hero tells the assembled court of his adventures, especially of the tragic fall of Troy and his dramatic escape. This is one of the most vivid books in the epic.

After the relatively quiet third book we are taken into the midst of one of the world's great love stories—that of Dido and Æneas. The tragedy of love here is as great as is the tragedy of war and catastrophe in Book II. For the average reader, these two books, because of their universality of emotional appeal, will always be more vital than the rest of the poem, in which we follow Æneas to Italy and see him conquer his foes. Yet the casual reader must not forget that those who really know Virgil find much of his greatest poetry in the latter part of the epic.

VIRGIL

The Æneid

Book II

Every tongue was hushed,[1] and every eye fixed intently, when, from his high couch, father Æneas began thus:—

"Too cruel to be told, great queen, is the sorrow you bid me revive—how the power of Troy and its empire met with piteous overthrow from the Danaans—the heartrending sights which my own eyes saw, and the scenes where I had a large part to play. Who, in such recital—be he of the Myrmidons or the Dolopes,[2] or a soldier of ruthless Ulysses's band—would refrain from tears? And now, too, night is rushing dews down the steep of heaven, and the setting stars counsel repose. Still, if so great be your longing to acquaint yourself with our disasters, and hear the brief tale of Troy's last agony, though my mind shudders at the remembrance, and starts back in sudden anguish, I will essay the task.

"Broken by war and foiled by destiny, the chiefs of the Danaans, now that the flying years were numbering so many, build a horse of mountain size, by the inspiration of Pallas's skill, and interlace its ribs with planks of fir. A vow for their safe journey home is the pretext: such the fame that spreads. In this they secretly enclose chosen men of sinew, picked out by lot, in the depth of its sides, and fill every corner of those mighty caverns, the belly of the monster, with armed warriors.

"In sight of Troy lies Tenedos, an island of wide-spread renown, powerful and rich while Priam's empire yet was, now a mere bay, a treacherous roadstead for ships. Thus far they sail out, and hide themselves on the forsaken coast. We thought them gone off with a fair wind for Mycenæ. And so all Trojan land shakes off the agony of years. Open fly the gates; what pleasure to go and see the Dorian camp, and the places deserted, and the shore forsaken! Yes, here were the troops of the Dolopes; here the tent of that savage Achilles; here the ships were drawn up; here they use to set the battle in array. Some of us are standing agaze at the fatal offering to the virgin goddess,[3] and wondering at the hugeness of the horse; and Thymœtes takes the lead, urging to have it dragged within the walls, and lodged in the citadel, either with treasonable intent, or that the fate of Troy had begun to set that way. But Capys, and the men of saner judgment, bid us send this snare of the Danaans, this suspicious present, headlong into the sea, or light a fire under and burn it; or, if not that, to pierce and probe that hollow womb that might hide so much. The populace, unstable as ever, divides off into opposite factions.

"Throwing himself before all, with a great crowd at his back, Laocoon,[4] all on fire, comes running down the steep of the citadel, crying in the distance, 'What strange madness is this, my unhappy countrymen? Think you that the enemy has sailed off, or that a Danaan could ever make a present that had no treachery in it? Is this your knowledge of Ulysses? Either the Achæans are shut up and hiding in this piece of wood, or it is an engine framed against our walls, to command the houses and come down on the city from above, or there

Virgil, *The Æneid*. Translated by John Conington. Publius Virgilius Maro (70-19 B.C.) was born near Mantua in northern Italy. When he was about fifteen he came to Rome to complete his education. He secured the friendship of the Emperor Augustus, who sponsored his greatest poem.
[1] Æneas is speaking before an assembly at the court of Queen Dido of Carthage.
[2] Myrmidons and Dolopes were tribes of Greeks in the Trojan War, the former being under the rule of Achilles.
[3] Pallas.
[4] Pronounce La-o-co-on.

is some other secret trick. Men of Troy, put no faith in the horse. Whatever it be, I fear a Greek even with a gift in his hand.' With these words he hurled a mighty spear with all his force against the beast's side, the jointed arch of its belly. It lodged, and stood quivering; the womb shook again, and an echo and a groan rang hollow from its caverns; and then, had but heaven's destiny and man's judgment been unwarped, he had led us to carry sword and havoc into the Argive lurking-place, and Troy would now be standing, and thou, Priam's tall fortress, still in being.

"Meanwhile, see! some Dardan shepherds are dragging with loud shouts before the king a young man with his hands tied behind him, who had thrown himself, a stranger, across their way, to compass this very thing, and thus let the Achæans into Troy—bold of heart, and ready for either issue, either to play off his stratagem, or to meet inevitable death. From all sides, in eager curiosity, the Trojan youth come streaming round, vying in their insults to the prisoner. Now then, listen to the tale of Danaan fraud, and from one act of guilt learn what the whole nation is. There as he stood, with all eyes bent on him, bewildered, defenseless, and looked round on the Phrygian bands, 'Alas,' he cries, 'where is there a spot of earth or sea that will give me shelter now? or what last resource is left for a wretch like me—one who has no place among the Danaans to hide my head—while the children of Dardanus no less are in arms against me, crying for bloody vengeance?' At that piteous cry our mood was changed, and every outrage checked. We encourage him to speak—to tell us what his parentage is; what his business; what he has to rest on as a prisoner. 'All, my lord, shall be avowed to you truly, whatever be the issue. I will not deny that I am an Argive by nation; this to begin with. Nor if Fortune has made a miserable man out of Sinon, shall her base schooling make him deceiver and liar as well. If haply in talk your ears ever caught the name of Palamedes,[5] of the house of Belus, and his wide-spread renown—his, whom under false accusation, an innocent man, charged by the blackest calumny, all because his voice was against the war, the Pelasgians sent down to death, and now, when he is laid in darkness, lament him too late—know that it was as his comrade and near kinsman I was sent by a needy father to a soldier's life in earliest youth. While he stood with his royal state unimpaired, an honored member of the kingly council, I, too, enjoyed my measure of name and dignity; but after the jealousy of false Ulysses—you know the tale—removed him from this upper clime—dashed him from my height, I dragged on life in darkness and sorrow, and vented to my own heart my rage at the disaster of my innocent friend. Nor did I keep silence—madman that I was! No, if ever the chance were given me—if ever I came back with glory to my native Argos—I vowed myself his avenger, and my words stirred up bitter enmity. From that time my ruin began; from that time Ulysses was ever threatening me with some new charge, ever scattering abroad words of mystery, and looking for allies to plot with. Nor did he rest till by Calchas's agency—but why recall this unwelcome story with no end to gain? Why waste your time, if you hold all Achæans alike, and to hear *that* is to hear enough? Take the vengeance you should have taken long ago. It is just what would please the Ithacan, and earn a large reward from the sons of Atreus!'

"This makes us burn, indeed, to explore and inquire into the reason of his tale, not knowing that crime could be so monstrous, and Pelasgian art so cunning. He resumes, in faltering tones, spoken from his false heart:—

"'Often have the Danaans designed to turn their back on Troy and accomplish a retreat, and abandon the war that had wearied them so long; and would they had done it! As often has the fierce inclemency of the deep barred their purpose, and the south wind frightened them from sailing. Especially, when this horse was set up at last, a compacted mass of maple planks, the thunder of the storm-clouds was heard the whole firmament over. In our perplexity we send Eurypylus to inquire of the Phœbus's oracle, and this is the gloomy message that he brings from the shrine: "With blood it was ye appeased the winds, even with a maiden's slaughter,[6] when first ye came, Danaans, to the shore of Ilion. With blood it is ye must buy your return, and propitiate heaven by the life of an Argive!" Soon as the news reached the public ear, every mind was cowed, and a cold shudder thrilled the depths of every heart. For whom has Fate a summons? Whom does Apollo demand as his prey? And now the Ithacan, with boisterous vehemence, drags forward the prophet Calchas, insists on knowing what that announcement of heaven's will may mean; and many even then

---

[5] Palamedes, who disclosed Ulysses' feigned madness. See p. 40 above.
[6] For Iphigenia at Aulis, see p. 41 above.

were the prophetic mouths that warned me of the trickster's cruel villainy, and many the eyes that silently foresaw the future. Ten days the seer holds his peace, and keeps his tent, refusing to utter a word that should disclose any name or sacrifice any life. At last, goaded by the Ithacan's vehement clamor, he breaks into a concerted utterance, and dooms me to the altar. All assented, well content that the danger which each feared for himself should be directed to the extinction of one poor wretch. And now the day of horror was come; all was being ready for my sacrifice—the salt cakes for the fire, and the fillet to crown my brow— when I escaped, I own it, from death, and broke my bonds, and hid myself that night in a muddy marsh in the covert of the rushes, while they should be sailing, in the faint hope that they had sailed. My old country, I never expect to see it again, nor my darling children, and the father I have longed so for! No! they are likely to visit them with vengeance for my escape, and expiate this guilt of mine by taking their poor lives. O! by the gods above, and the powers that know when truth is spoken, if there is yet abiding anywhere among men such a thing as unsullied faith, I conjure you, have pity on this weight of suffering, have pity on a soul that is unworthily borne down!'

"Such a tearful appeal gains him his life, and our compassion too. Priam himself is first to bid them relieve the man of his manacles and the chains that bound him, and addresses him in words of kindness, 'Whoever you are, from this time forth have done with the Greeks, and forget them. I make you my man, and bid you answer truly the questions I shall put. What do they mean by setting up this huge mountain of a horse? Who was the prompter of it? What is their object? Some religious offering, or some engine of war?'

"Thus Priam: the prisoner, with all his Pelasgian craft and cunning about him, raised his unfettered hands to the stars:—

"'You, eternal fires, with your inviolable majesty, be my witnesses; you, altars and impious swords, from which I fled; and you, hallowed fillets, which I wore for the sacrifice! I am free to break all the sacred ties that bound me to the Greeks. I am free to treat them as my foes, and disclose all their secrets to the light of day, all the claims of the land of my birth notwithstanding. Only do thou abide by thy plighted word, and preserve faith with thy preserver, land of Troy, if he tells thee true, and makes thee large returns.

"'The strength of the Danaan hopes, and the soul of their confidence in the war they plunged into, has ever been the aid of Pallas. From the time when Tydeus's impious son and Ulysses, that coiner of villainy, dared to drag away from her hallowed temple the fateful Palladium,[7] slaughtering the guards who watched the citadel's height, thenceforth there was an ebb and a backsliding in the Danaan hopes, their forces shattered, the goddess estranged. Nor were the portents dubious that betokened Tritonia's[8] change of mood. Scarce was the image lodged in the camp, when flashing fire glowed in her uplifted eyes, and salt sweat trickled over her frame, and thrice of herself she leaped from the ground, marvelous to relate, shield and quivering lance and all. Forthwith Calchas sounds the note for flight over the perilous deep, for that Pergamus can never be razed by Argive steel, unless they go to Argos for fresh omens, and bring back the divine aid which their crooked keels bore with them aforetime over the sea. And now this their voyage home to Mycenæ is to get new forces and gods to sail with them; they will recross the deep and come upon you unforeseen. Such is Calchas's scanning of the omens. As for this image, he warned them to set it up in exchange for the Palladium, and, in expiation of injured deity, to atone for their fatal crime. Calchas, however, bade them raise it to the vast height you see, knitting plank to plank, till it was brought near to heaven, that it might not be admitted at the gates or dragged within the walls, and thus restore to the people the bulwark of their old worship. For if your hand should profane Minerva's offering, then (said he) a mighty destruction—may the gods turn the omen on his head ere it falls on yours!— would come on the empire of Priam and the Phrygian nation; but if these hands of yours should help it to scale your city's height, Asia would roll the mighty tide of invasion on the walls of Pelops, and our posterity would have to meet the fate he threatened.'

"Such was the stratagem—the cursed art of perjured Sinon—that gained credence for the tale; and such the victory won over us by wiles and constrained tears—over us, whom not Tydeus's son, nor Achilles of Larissa, nor ten years of war subdued, nor a fleet of a thousand sail.

---

[7] The Palladium was a wooden image of Athena holding a spear in one hand and a distaff in the other. It was supposed to have fallen from heaven when Troy was founded. Troy was thought unconquerable as long as it was safe.

[8] Pallas.

"And now another object, greater and far more terrible, is forced on my poor countrymen, to the confusion of their unprophetic souls. Laocoon, drawn by lot as Neptune's priest, was sacrificing a mighty bull at the wonted altar—when behold from Tenedos, over the still deep—I shudder as I recount the tale—two serpents coiled in vast circles are seen breasting the sea, and moving side by side towards the shore. Their breasts rise erect among the waves; their manes, of blood-red hue, tower over the water; the rest of them floats behind on the main, trailing a huge undulating length; the brine foams and dashes about them; they are already on shore, in the plain—with their glowing eyes bloodshot and fiery, and their forked tongues playing in their hissing mouths. We fly all ways in pale terror: they, in an unswerving column, make for Laocoon, and first each serpent folds round one of his two sons, clasping the youthful body, and greedily devouring the poor limbs. Afterwards, as the father comes to the rescue, weapon in hand, they fasten on him and lash their enormous spires tight round him—and now twice folded round his middle, twice embracing his neck with their scaly length, they tower over him with uplifted head and crest. He is straining with agonizing clutch to pull the knots asunder, his priestly fillets all bedewed with gore and black poison, and raising all the while dreadful cries to heaven—like the bellowing, when a wounded bull darts away from the altar, dashing off from his neck the ill-aimed ax. But the two serpents escape glidingly to the temple top, making for the height where ruthless Tritonia is enthroned, and there shelter themselves under the goddess's feet and the round of her shield. Then, indeed, every breast is cowed and thrilled through by a new and strange terror—every voice cries that Laocoon has been duly punished for his crime, profaning the sacred wood with his weapon's point, and hurling his guilty lance against the back of the steed. Let the image be drawn to her temple, and let prayer be made to the goddess, is the general cry—we break through the walls and open the town within. All gird them to the work, putting wheels to run easily under its feet, and throwing lengths of hempen tie round its neck. It scales the walls, that fateful engine, with its armed brood—boys and unwedded girls, standing about it, chant sacred hymns, delighted to touch the rope. In it moves, rolling with threatening brow into the heart of the city. O my country! O Ilion, home of the gods! O ye, Dardan towers, with your martial fame! Yes—four times on the gateway's very threshold it stopped, four times the arms rattled in its womb. On, however, we press, unheeding, in the blindness of our frenzy, and lodge the ill-starred portent in our hallowed citadel. Even then Cassandra [9] unseals to speak of future fate those lips which by the god's command no Trojan ever believed—while we, alas! we, spend the day that was to be our last in crowning the temples of the gods with festal boughs the whole city through.

"Meantime round rolls the sky, and on comes night from the ocean, wrapping in its mighty shade earth and heaven and Myrmidon wiles: through the city the Trojans are hushed in careless repose, their tired limbs in the arms of sleep. Already was the Argive host on its way from Tenedos, through the friendly stillness of the quiet moon, making for the well-known shore, when see! the royal ship mounts its fire signal, and Sinon, sheltered by heaven's partial decree, stealthily sets at large the Danaans, hid in that treacherous womb, and opens the pine-wood door: they as the horse opens are restored to upper air, and leap forth with joy from the hollow timber, Thessander and Sthenelus leading the way, and the dreaded Ulysses, gliding down the lowered rope, and Achamas and Thoas, and Neoptolemus of Peleus's line, and first Machaon, and Menelaus, and the framer of the cheat himself, Epeus. They rush on the town as it lies drowned in sleep and revelry. The watchers are put to the sword, the gates thrown open, and all are welcoming their comrades, and uniting with the conspiring bands.

"It was just the time when first slumber comes to heal human suffering, stealing on men by heaven's blessing with balmiest influence. Lo! as I slept, before my eyes Hector, in deepest sorrow, seemed to be standing by me, shedding rivers of tears—mangled from dragging at the car, as I remember him of old, and black with gory dust, and with his swollen feet bored by the thong. Aye me! what a sight was there! what a change from that Hector of ours, who comes back to us clad in the spoils of Achilles, or from hurling Phrygian fire on Danaan vessels! with stiffened beard and hair matted with blood, and those wounds fresh about him, which fell on him so thickly round his country's walls. Methought I addressed him first with tears like his own, fetching from my breast the accents of

9 This daughter of Priam was loved by Apollo, who gave her the power of prophecy. Later, in anger, he decreed that she should never be believed. We meet her in Æschylus' *Agamemnon*, p. 151 above.

sorrow—'O light of Dardan land, surest hope that Trojans ever had! What delay has kept you so long? From what clime is the Hector of our longings returned to us at last? O the eyes with which, after long months of death among your people, months of manifold suffering to Troy and her sons, spent and weary, we look upon you now! What unworthy cause has marred the clear beauty of those features, or why do I behold these wounds?' He answers nought, and gives no idle heed to my vain inquiries, but with a deep sigh, heaved from the bottom of his heart—'Ah! fly, goddess-born!' cries he, 'and escape from these flames—the walls are in the enemy's hand—Troy is tumbling from its summit—the claims of country and king are satisfied—if Pergamus could be defended by force of hand, it would have been defended by mine, in my day. Your country's worship and her gods are what she entrusts to you now—take them to share your destiny—seek for them a mighty city, which you shall one day build when you have wandered the ocean over.' With these words he brings out Queen Vesta with her fillets and the ever-burning fire from the secret shrine.

"Meanwhile the city in its various quarters is being convulsed with agony—and ever more and more, though my father Anchises's palace was retired in the privacy of embosoming trees, the sounds deepen, and the alarm of battle swells. I start up from sleep, mount the sloping roof, and stand intently listening—even as, when among standing corn a spark falls with a fierce south wind to fan it, or the impetuous stream of a mountain torrent sweeps the fields, sweeps the joyous crops and the bullocks' toil, and drives the woods headlong before it, in perplexed amazement a shepherd takes in the crash from a rock's tall summit. Then, indeed, all doubt was over, and the wiles of the Danaans stood confessed. Already Deiphobus's palace has fallen with a mighty overthrow before the mastering fire-god—already his neighbor Ucalegon is in flames—the expanse of the Sigean sea shines again with the blaze. Up rises at once the shouting of men and the braying of trumpets. To arms I rush in frenzy—not that good cause is shown for arms—but to muster a troop for fight, and run to the citadel with my comrades is my first burning impulse—madness and rage drive my mind headlong, and I think how glorious to die with arms in my hand.

"But see! Panthus, escaped from an Achæan volley, Panthus, Othrys's son, priest of Phœbus in the citadel, comes dragging along with his own hand the vanquished gods of his worship and his young grandchild, and making distractedly for my door. 'How goes the day, Panthus? What hold have we of the citadel?' The words were scarcely uttered when with a groan he replies, 'It is come, the last day, the inevitable hour—on Dardan land no more Trojans; no more of Ilion, and the great renown of the sons of Teucer; Jove, in his cruelty, has carried all over to Argos; the town is on fire, and the Danaans are its masters. There, planted high in the heart of the city, the horse is pouring out armed men, and Sinon is flinging about fire in the insolence of conquest; some are crowding into the unfolded gates—thousands, many as ever came from huge Mycenæ; some are blocking up the narrow streets, with weapons pointed at all comers; the sharp steel with its gleaming blade stands drawn, ready for slaughter; hardly, even on the threshold, the sentinels of the gates are attempting resistance, in a struggle where the powers of war are blind.'

"At these words of the son of Othrys, and heaven's will thus expressed, I plunge into the fire and the battle, following the war fiend's yell, the din of strife, and the shout that rose to the sky. There join me Rhipeus and Epytus, bravest in fight, crossing my way in the moonlight, as also Hypanis and Dymas, and form at my side; young Corœbus, too, Mygodon's son; he happened to be just then come to Troy, with a frantic passion for Cassandra, and was bringing a son-in-law's aid to Priam and his Phrygians—poor boy! to have given no heed to the warnings of his heaven-struck bride! Seeing them gathered in a mass and nerved for battle, I begin thereon:—'Young hearts, full of unavailing valor, if your desire is set to follow a desperate man, you see what the plight of our affairs is—gone in a body from shrine and altar are the gods who upheld this our empire—the city you succor is a blazing ruin; choose we then death, and rush we into the thick of the fight. The one safety for vanquished men is to hope for none.' These words stirred their young spirits to madness: then, like ravenous wolves in night's dark cloud, driven abroad by the blind rage of lawless hunger, with their cubs left at home waiting their return with parched jaws, among javelins, among foemen, on we go with no uncertain fate before us, keeping our way through the heart of the town, while night flaps over us its dark, overshadowing wings. Who could unfold in speech the carnage, the horrors of that night, or make his tears keep pace with our suffering? It is an ancient city, falling from the height where she queened it many a year; and heaps of unresisting bodies are lying confusedly in the streets, in the houses, on the hallowed steps of temples. Nor is it on Teucer's sons alone that bloody vengeance lights. There are times when even the vanquished feel courage rushing back to their hearts, and the conquering Danaans fall. Everywhere is relentless agony; everywhere terror, and the vision of death in many a manifestation.

"First of the Danaans, with a large band at his back, Androgeos crosses our way, taking us for a troop of his friends in his ignorance, and hails us at once in words of fellowship: 'Come, my men, be quick. Why, what sloth is keeping you so late? Pergamus is on fire, and the rest of us are spoiling and sacking it, and here are you, but just disembarked from your tall ships.' He said, and instantly, for no reply was forthcoming to reassure him, saw that he had fallen into the thick of the enemy. Struck with consternation, he drew back foot and tongue. Just as a man who at unawares has trodden on a snake among thorns and briers in his walk, and recoils at once in sudden alarm from the angry uplifted crest and the black swelling neck, so Androgeos, appalled at the sight, was retiring. But we rush on him, and close round, weapons in hand; and, in their ignorance of the ground, and the surprise of their terror, they fall before us everywhere. Fortune smiles on our first encounter. Hereon Corœbus, flushed with success and daring, 'Come, my friends,' he cries, 'where Fortune at starting directs us to the path of safety, and reveals herself as our ally, be it ours to follow on. Let us change shields, and see if Danaan decorations will fit us. Trick or strength of hand, who, in dealing with an enemy, asks which? They shall arm us against themselves.' So saying, he puts on Androgeos's crested helm, and his shield with its goodly device, and fastens to his side an Argive sword. So does Rhipeus, so Dymas too, and all our company, with youthful exultation, each arming himself out of the new-won spoils. On we go, mixing with the Greeks, under auspices not our own, and many are the combats in which we engage in the blindness of night, many the Danaans whom we send down to the shades. They fly on all hands: some to the ships, making at full speed for safety on the shore; others, in the debasement of terror, climb once more the horse's huge sides, and hide themselves in the womb they knew so well.

"Alas! it is not for man to throw himself on the gods against their will!

"Lo! there was a princess of Priam's house being dragged by her disheveled hair from the temple, from the very shrine of Minerva, Cassandra, straining her flashing eyes to heaven in vain—her eyes—for those delicate hands were confined by manacles. The sight was too much for the infuriate mind of Corœbus: rushing to his doom, he flung himself into the middle of the hostile force. One and all, we follow, close our ranks, and fall on. And now, first from the temple's lofty top we are overwhelmed by a shower of our own countrymen's darts, and a most piteous carnage ensues, all along of the appearance of our arms and our mistaken Grecian crests. Then the Danaans, groaning and enraged at the rescue of the maiden, rally from all sides, and fall on us. Ajax, in all his fury, and the two sons of Atreus, and the whole array of the Dolopes—even as one day when the tempest is broken loose, and wind meets wind—west, and south, and east exulting in his orient steeds—there is crashing in the woods, and Nereus, in a cloud of foam, is plying his ruthless trident, and stirring up the sea from its very bottom. Such of the foe, moreover, as in the darkness of night we had driven routed through the gloom —thanks to our stratagem—and scattered the whole city over, rally again: they are the first to recognize the imposture of shield and weapon, and to mark the different sound of our speech. All is over—we are overwhelmed by numbers: first of all, Corœbus is stretched low; his slayer Peneleos, his place of death the altar of the Goddess of Arms; slain, too, is Rhipeus, the justest and most righteous man in Troy—but heaven's will is not ours—down go Hypanis and Dymas both, shot by their friends; nor could all your acts of piety, good Panthus, shield you in your fall; no, nor the fillet of Apollo on your brow. Ye ashes of Ilion, and thou, funeral fire of those I loved, witness ye that in your day of doom I shrank from no Danaan dart, no hand-to-hand encounter; nay, that had my fate been to fall, my hand had earned it well. We are parted from the rest, Iphitus, Pelias, and I. Iphitus, a man on whom years were already pressing; Pelias, crippled by a wound from Ulysses—all three summoned by the shouting to Priam's palace.

"Here, indeed, the conflict was gigantic—just as if the rest of the war were nowhere—as if none were dying in the whole city beside: even such was the sight we saw—the war-god raging untamed, the Danaans streaming up to the roof, the door blockaded by a long penthouse of shields. The scaling ladders are clasping the walls; close to the very door men are climbing, with their left hands presenting the buckler to shelter them from darts, while with their right they are clasping the battlements. The Dardans, on their part, are tearing up from the palace turret and roof—such the weapons with which, in their dire extremity, in the last death-struggle, they make ready for their defense—gilded rafters, the stately ornaments of [10] elder days, they are hurling down; while others, their swords drawn, are stationed at the doors at the bottom, and guarding them in close array. The fire revived within me, to bring succor to the royal roof, and relieve those brave men, and breathe new daring into the vanquished.

"A door there was, a hidden entrance, a thoroughfare through Priam's palace, a postern which you leave in the rear; by it the hapless Andromache, while yet the throne was standing, used [20] often to repair unattended to her husband's parents, and pull the boy Astyanax into his grandsire's presence. Through it I make my way to the summit of the roof, whence the wretched Teucrians were hurling darts without avail. There was a tower standing precipitous, its roof reared high to the stars, whence could be seen all Troy, and the Danaan fleet, and the Achæan camp; to this we applied our weapons, just where the lofty flooring made the joining insecure; we wrench it from its [30] eminence, we have toppled it over—down it falls at once, a huge crashing ruin, and tumbles far and wide over the Danaan ranks. But others fill their place; while stones and every kind of missile keep raining unabated.

"There in the entry, at the very gate, is Pyrrhus in his glory, gleaming with spear and sword, and with all the brilliance of steel. Even as against the daylight a serpent gorged with baleful herbage, whom winter's cold of late was keeping swollen [40] underground, now, his skin shed, in new life and in the beauty of youth, rears his breast erect, and wreathes his shining scales, towering to the sun, and flashes in his mouth his three-forked tongue. With him gigantic Periphas and Automedon, his armor-bearer, once Achilles's charioteer, with him the whole chivalry of Scyros press to the walls, and hurl up fire to the roof. Himself among the foremost, a two-edged ax in hand, is bursting through the stubborn door and forcing from their [50] hinges the valves copper-sheathed; see! now he has cut out a plank and delved into that stout heart of oak, and made a wide gaping window in the

middle. There is seen the house within, and the long vista of the hall; there is seen the august retirement of Priam and the monarchs of past days, and armed warriors are disclosed standing in the entrance.

"But the palace within is a confused scene of shrieking and piteous disorder; the vaulted chambers wail from their hollow depths with female lamentation; the noise strikes the golden stars above. The terror-stricken matrons are running to and fro through the spacious courts, clinging claspingly to the gates and printing them with kisses. On presses Pyrrhus with all his father's might; neither barrier of oak nor yet living guard can resist him; the door gives way under the thick strokes of the battery, and the valves are torn from their hinges and brought down. Force finds its way; the Danaans burst a passage, rush in, and slaughter those they meet, and the whole wide space is flooded with soldiers. With far less fury, when the river, all foam, has broken the prison of its banks and streamed with triumphant tide over the barriers set to check it, down it comes tumbling along the corn-fields, and along the whole country sweeps away herd and stall. With my own eyes I saw Neoptolemus, mad with carnage, and the two Atridæ on the palace-floor. I saw Hecuba and her hundred daughters-in-law, and Priam at the altar, polluting with his blood the flames he had himself made holy. Those fifty marriage-chambers, the splendid promise of children's children, doors gorgeous with barbaric gold and plundered treasure, all sank in dust. Where the fire flags, the Danaans are masters.

"Perhaps, too, you may be curious to hear the fate of Priam. When he saw his city fallen and captured, the doors of his palace burst open, the foe in the heart of his home's sanctuary, poor old man! helplessly and hopelessly he puts about his shoulders, trembling with age, his armor, long disused, and girds on his unavailing sword, and is going to his doom among the thick of the foe. In the midst of the palace, under the naked height of the sky, stood a great altar, and by it a bay tree of age untold, leaning over the altar and enfolding the household gods in its shade. Here about the altar Hecuba and her daughters, all helpless, like doves driven headlong down by a murky tempest, huddled together and clinging to the statues of the gods, were sitting. But when she saw Priam—yes, Priam—wearing the arms of his youth—'What monstrous thought,' cries she, 'my most wretched spouse, has moved you to gird on these weapons?

or to what are you hurrying? It is not help like this, not protections like those you wear, that the crisis needs. No, not even if my lost Hector were now at our side. Come, join us here at last; this altar shall be a defense for us all, or we will die together.' With these words she took him to where she was, and lodged his aged frame in the hallowed resting-place.

"But, see! here is Polites, one of Priam's sons escaped from Pyrrhus's murderous hand, through showers of darts and masses of foemen, flying down the long corridors and traversing the empty courts, sore and wounded, while Pyrrhus, all on fire, is pursuing him with a deadly stroke, his hand all but grasping him, his spear close upon him. Just as at last he won his way into the view and presence of his parents, down he fell and poured out his life in a gush of blood. Hereon Priam, though hemmed in by death on all sides, could not restrain himself, or control voice and passion. 'Aye,' cries he, 'for a crime, for an outrage like this, may the gods, if there is any sense of right in heaven to take cognizance of such deeds, give you the full thanks you merit, and pay you your due reward; you, who have made me look with my own eyes on my son's death, and stained a father's presence with the sight of blood. But he whom your lying tongue calls your sire, Achilles, dealt not thus with Priam his foe—he had a cheek that could crimson at a suppliant's rights, a suppliant's honor. Hector's lifeless body he gave back to the tomb, and sent me home to my realms in peace.' So said the poor old man, and hurled at him a dart unwarlike, unwounding, which the ringing brass at once shook off, and left hanging helplessly from the end of the shield's boss. Pyrrhus retorts: 'You shall take your complaint, then, and carry your news to my father, Pelides. Tell him about my shocking deeds, about his degenerate Neoptolemus, and do not forget. Now die.' With these words he dragged him to the very altar, palsied and sliding in a pool of his son's blood, wreathed his left hand in his hair, and with his right flashed forth and sheathed in his side the sword to the hilt. Such was the end of Priam's fortunes, such the fatal lot that fell upon him, with Troy blazing and Pergamus in ruins before his eyes—upon him, once the haughty ruler of those many nations and kingdoms, the sovereign lord of Asia! There he lies on the shore, a gigantic trunk, a head severed from the shoulders, a body without a name.

"Now, for the first time grim horror prisoned me round—I was wildered—there rose up the image of my dear father, as I saw the king, his fellow in age, breathing out his life through that ghastly wound. There rose up Creusa unprotected, my house, now plundered, and the chance to which I had left my little Iulus. I cast my eyes back and look about to see what strength there is round me. All had forsaken me, too tired to stay; they had leapt to the ground, or dropped helplessly into the flames. And now I was there alone. When lodged in the temple of Vesta, and crouching mutely in its darkest recess, the daughter of Tyndareus meets my eye; the brilliant blaze gives light to my wandering feet and ranging glance. Yes, she in her guilty fears, dreading at once the Teucrians whom the overthrow of Pergamus had made her foes, and the vengeance of the Danaans, and the wrath of the husband she abandoned— she, the common fiend of Troy and of her country, had hid herself away, and was sitting in hateful solitude at the altar. My spirit kindled into flame —a fury seized me to avenge my country in its fall, and to do justice on a wretch. 'So she is to see Sparta and her native Mycenæ again in safety, and is to move as a queen in a triumph of her own? She is to look upon her lord and her old home, her children and her parents, with a crowd of our Trojan ladies and Phrygian captives to wait on her? Shall it be for this that Priam has died by the sword, that Troy has been burnt with fire, that the Dardan shore has gushed so oft with the sweat of blood? No, never—for though there are no proud memories to be won by vengeance on a woman, no laurels to be reaped from a conquest like this, yet the extinction of so base a life and the exaction of vengeance so merited will count as a praise, and it will be a joy to have glutted my spirit with the flame of revenge and slaked the thirsty ashes of those I love.' Such were the wild words I was uttering, such the impulse of my infuriate heart, when suddenly there appeared to me, brighter than I had ever seen her before, and shone forth in clear radiance through the night, my gracious mother, all her deity confessed, with the same mien and stature by which she is known to the dwellers in heaven. She seized me by the hand and stayed me, seconding her action with these words from her roseate lips: 'My son, what mighty agony is it that stirs up this untamed passion? What means your frenzy? or whither has fled your care for me? Will you not first see where you have left your father Anchises, spent with age as he is? whether your wife, Creusa, be yet alive, and your child, Ascanius? All about them the Grecian armies are ranging to and fro, and were not my care exerted to rescue them, ere this they had been snatched by the flame, devoured by the foeman's sword. It is not the hated beauty of the daughter of Tyndareus, the Spartan woman—not the reviled Paris. No, it is heaven, unpitying heaven that is overturning this great empire and leveling Troy from its summit. See here—for I will take away wholly the cloud whose veil, cast over your eyes, dulls your mortal vision and darkles round you damp and thick—do you on your part shrink in naught from your mother's commands, nor refuse to obey the instructions she gives. Here, where you see huge masses rent asunder, and stones wrenched from stones, and blended torrents of smoke and dust, is Neptune with his mighty trident shaking the walls and up-heaving the very foundations; here is Juno, cruelest of foes, posted at the entry of the Scæan gate, and summoning in tones of fury from the ships her confederate band, herself girt with steel like them. Look behind you—there is Tritonian Pallas, seated already on the summit of our towers, in the lurid glare of her storm-cloud and grim Gorgon's head. The great Father himself is nerving the Danaans with courage and strength for victory—himself leading the gods against our Dardan forces. Come, my son, catch at flight while you may and bring the struggle to an end. I will not leave you, till I have set you in safety at your father's door.' She had ceased, and veiled herself at once in night's thickest shadows. I see a vision of awful shapes—mighty presences of gods arrayed against Troy.

"Then, indeed, I beheld all Ilion sinking into flame, and Neptune's city, Troy, overturned from its base. Even as an ancient ash on the mountain-top, which woodmen have hacked with steel and repeated hatchet strokes, and are trying might and main to dislodge—it keeps nodding menacingly, its leafy head palsied and shaken, till at last, gradually overborne by wound after wound, it has given its death-groan, and fallen uprooted in ruined length along the hill. I come down, and, following my heavenly guide, thread my way through flames and foemen, while weapons glance aside and flames retire.

"Now when at last I had reached the door of my father's house, that old house I knew so well, my sire, whom it was my first resolve to carry away high up the hills—who was the first object I sought—refuses to survive the razing of Troy and submit to banishment. 'You, whose young blood is untainted, whose strength is firmly based and self-sustained, it is for you to think of flight. For me, had the dwellers in heaven willed me to pro-long my life, they would have preserved for me my home. It is enough and more than enough to have witnessed one sack, to have once outlived the capture of my city. Here, O here as I lie, bid farewell to my corpse and begone. I will find me a warrior's death. The enemy will have mercy on me, and my spoils will tempt him. The loss of a tomb will fall on me lightly. Long, long have I been a clog on time, hated of heaven and useless to earth, from the day when the father of gods and sovereign of men blasted me with the wind of his lightning, and laid on me the finger of flame.'

"Such the words he kept on repeating and con-tinued unshaken, while we were shedding our hearts in tears—Creusa, my wife, and Ascanius and my whole house, imploring my father not to be bent on dragging all with him to ruin, and lending his weight to the avalanche of destiny. But he refuses, and will not be moved from his purpose or his home. Once more I am plunging into battle, and choosing death in the agony of my wretchedness—for what could wisdom or fortune do for me now? What, my father? that I could stir a step to escape, leaving you behind? was this your expectation? could aught so shocking fall from a parent's lips? No—if it is the will of heaven that naught of this mighty city should be spared—if your purpose is fixed, and you find pleasure in throwing yourself and yours on Troy's blazing pile, the door stands open for the death you crave. Pyrrhus will be here in a moment, fresh from bathing in Priam's blood—Pyrrhus, who butchers the son before the father's face, who butchers the father at the altar. Gracious mother! was it for this that thou rescuest me from fire and sword—all that I may see the foe in the heart of my home's sanctuary—may see my Ascanius, and my father, and my Creusa by them sacrificed in a pool of each other's blood? My arms, friends, bring me my arms! the call of the day of death rings in the ears of the conquered. Give me back to the Dan-aans, let me return and renew the combat. Never shall this day see us all slaughtered unresisting.

"Now I gird on my sword again, and was buck-ling and fitting my shield to my left arm, and making my way out of the house—when lo! my wife on the threshold began to clasp and cling to my feet, holding out my little Iulus to his father. 'If it is to death you are going, then carry us with you to death and all, but if experience gives you any hope in the arms you are resuming, let your first stand be made at your home. To whom, think you, are you leaving your little Iulus—your father, and me who was once styled your wife?'

"Thus she was crying, while her moaning filled the house, when a portent appears, sudden and marvelous to relate. Even while the hands and eyes of his grieving parents were upon him, lo, a flickering tongue of flame on the top of Iulus's head was seen to shoot out light, playing round his soft curly locks with innocuous contact and pasturing about his temples. We are all hurry and alarm, shaking out his blazing hair and quenching the sacred fire with water from the spring—but Anchises my father raised his eyes in ecstasy to heaven, directing hand and voice to the stars: 'Almighty Jove, if any prayer can bow thy will, look down on us,—'tis all I crave—and if our piety have earned requital, grant us thy succor, father, and ratify the omen we now see.' Scarce had the old man spoken, when there came a sudden peal of thunder on the left, and a star fell from heaven and swept through the gloom with a torchlike train and a blaze of light. Over the top of the house we see it pass, and mark its course along the sky till it buries itself lustrously in Ida's wood —then comes a long furrowed line of light, and a sulphurous smoke fills the space all about. Then it length overcome, my father raises himself towards the sky, addresses the gods, and does reverence to the sacred meteor: 'No more, no more delay from me. I follow your guidance, and am already in the way by which you would lead me. Gods of my country! preserve my house, preserve my grandchild. Yours is this augury—your shield is stretched over Troy. Yes, my son, I give way, and shrink not from accompanying your flight.' He said—and by this the blaze is heard louder and louder through the streets, and the flames roll their hot volumes nearer. 'Come then, dear father, take your seat on my back, my shoulders shall support you, nor shall I feel the task a burden. Fall things as they may, we twain will share the peril, share the deliverance. Let my little Iulus walk by my side, while my wife follows our steps at a distance. You, our servants, attend to what I now say. As you leave the city there is a mound, where stands an ancient temple of Ceres all alone, and by it an old cypress, observed these many years by the reverence of our sires. This shall be our point of meeting in one place from many quarters. You, my father, take in your hand these sacred things, our country's household gods. For me, just emerged from this mighty war, with the stains of carnage fresh upon me, it were sacrilege to touch them, till I have cleansed me in the running stream.'

"So saying, I spread out my shoulders, bow my neck, cover them with a robe, a lion's tawny hide, and take up the precious burden. My little Iulus has fastened his hand in mine, and is following his father with ill-matched steps, my wife comes on behind. On we go, keeping in the shade—and I, who erewhile quailed not for a moment at the darts that rained upon me or at the masses of Greeks that barred my path, now am scared by every breath of air, startled by every sound, fluttered as I am, and fearing alike for him who holds my hand and him I carry. And now I was nearing the gates, and the whole journey seemed accomplished, when suddenly the noise of thick trampling feet came to my ear, and my father looks onward through the darkness. 'Son, son,' he cries, 'fly: they are upon us. I distinguish the flashing of their shields and the gleam of their steel.' In this alarm some unfriendly power perplexed and took away my judgment. For, while I was tracking places where no track was, and swerving from the wonted line of road, woe is me! destiny tore from me my wife Creusa. Whether she stopped, or strayed from the road, or sat down fatigued, I never knew—nor was she ever restored to my eyes in life. Nay, I did not look back to discover my loss, or turn my thoughts that way till we had come to the mound and temple of ancient Ceres; then, at last, when all were mustered, she alone was missing, and failed those who should have traveled with her, her son and husband both. Whom of gods or men did my upbraiding voice spare? what sight in all the ruin of the city made my heart bleed more? Ascanius and Anchises my father and the Teucrian household gods I give to my comrades' care, and lodge them in the winding glade. I repair again to the city and don my shining armor. My mind is set to try every hazard again, and retrace my path through the whole of Troy, and expose my life to peril once more. First I repair again to the city walls, and the gate's dark entry by which I had passed out. I track and follow my footsteps back through the night, and traverse the ground with my eye. Everywhere my sense is scared by the horror, scared by the very stillness. Next I betake me home, in the hope, the faint hope that she may have turned her steps thither. The Danaans had broken in and were lodged in every chamber. All is over—the greedy flame is wafted by the wind to the roof, the fire towers triumphant—the glow streams madly heavenwards. I pass on, and look again at Priam's palace and the citadel. There already in the empty cloisters, yes, in Juno's sanctuary, chosen guards, Phœnix and Ulysses the terrible, were watching the spoil. Here are gathered the treasures of Troy torn from blazing shrines, tables of gods, bowls of solid gold, and captive vestments in one great heap. Boys and mothers stand trembling all about in long array. 10

"Nay, I was emboldened even to fling random cries through the darkness. I filled the streets with shouts, and in my agony called again and again on my Creusa with unavailing iteration. As I was thus making my search and raving unceasingly the whole city through, the hapless shade, the specter of my own Creusa appeared in my presence—a likeness larger than the life. I was aghast, my hair stood erect, my tongue clove to my mouth, 20 while she began to address me thus, and relieve my trouble with words like these: 'Whence this strange pleasure in indulging frantic grief, my darling husband? It is not without Heaven's will that these things are happening: that you should carry your Creusa with you on your journey is forbidden by fate, forbidden by the mighty ruler of heaven above. You have long years of exile, a vast expanse of ocean to traverse—and then you will arrive at the land of Hesperia, where Tiber, 30 Lydia's river, rolls his gentle volumes through rich and cultured plains. There you have a smiling future, a kingdom, and a royal bride waiting your coming. Dry your tears for Creusa, your heart's choice though she be. I am not to see the face of Myrmidons or Dolopes in their haughty homes, or to enter the service of some Grecian matron—I, a Dardan princess, daughter by marriage of Venus the immortal. No, I am kept in this country by heaven's mighty mother. And now farewell, and 40 continue to love your son and mine.' Thus having spoken, in spite of my tears, spite of the thousand things I longed to say, she left me and vanished into unsubstantial air. Thrice, as I stood, I essayed to fling my arms round her neck—thrice the phantom escaped the hands that caught at it in vain—impalpable as the wind, fleeting as the wings of sleep.

"So passed my night, and such was my return to my comrades. Arrived there, I find with wonder 50 their band swelled by a vast multitude of new companions, matrons and warriors both, an army mustered for exile, a crowd of the wretched. From every side they were met, prepared in heart as in fortune to follow me over the sea to any land where I might take them to settle. And now the morning star was rising over Ida's loftiest ridge with the day in its train—Danaan sentinels were blocking up the entry of the gates, and no hope of succor appeared. I retired at last, took up my father, and made for the mountains."

Book IV

But the queen, pierced long since by love's cruel shaft, is feeding the wound with her life-blood, and wasting under a hidden fire. Many times the hero's own worth comes back to her mind, many times the glory of his race; his every look remains imprinted on her breast, and his every word, nor will trouble let soothing sleep have access to her frame.

The dawn-goddess of the morrow was surveying the earth with Phœbus's torch in her hand, and had already withdrawn the dewy shadow from the sky, when she, sick of soul, thus bespoke the sister whose heart was one with hers:—"Anna, my sister, what dreams are these that confound and appall me! Who is this new guest that has entered our door! What a face and carriage! What strength of breast and shoulders! I do believe—it is no mere fancy—that he has the blood of gods in his veins. An ignoble soul is known by the coward's brand. Ah! by what fates he has been tossed! What wars he was recounting, every pang of them borne by himself! Were it not the fixed, immovable purpose of my mind never to consent to join myself with any in wedlock's bands, since my first love played me false and made me the dupe of death—had I not been weary of bridal bed and nuptial torch, perchance I might have stooped to this one reproach. Anna—for I will own the truth—since the fate of Sychæus, my poor husband—since the sprinkling of the gods of my home with the blood my brother shed, he and he only has touched my heart and shaken my resolution till it totters. I recognize the traces of the old flame. But first I would pray that earth may yawn for me from her foundations, or the all-powerful sire hurl me thunder-stricken to the shades, to the wan shades of Erebus and abysmal night, ere I violate thee, my woman's honor, or unknit the bonds thou tiest. He who first wedded me, he has carried off my heart—let him keep it all his own, and retain it in his grave." Thus having said, she deluged her bosom with a burst of tears.

Anna replies:—"Sweet love, dearer than the light to your sister's eye, are you to pine and grieve in loneliness through life's long spring, nor know aught of a mother's joy in her children, nor of the prizes Venus gives? Think you that dead ashes and ghosts low in the grave take this to heart? Grant that no husbands have touched your bleeding heart in times gone by, none now in Libya, none before in Tyre; yes, Iarbas has been slighted, and the other chieftains whom Afric, rich in 10 triumphs, rears as its own—will you fight against a welcome, no less than an unwelcome passion? Nor does it cross your mind in whose territories you are settled? On one side the cities of the Gætulians, a race invincible in war, and the Numidians environ you, unbridled as their steeds, and the inhospitable Syrtis; on another, a region unpeopled by drought, and the widespread barbarism of the nation of Barce. What need to talk of the war-cloud threatening from Tyre, and the 20 menaces of our brother? It is under Heaven's auspices, I deem, and by Juno's blessing, that the vessels of Ilion have made this voyage hither. What a city, my sister, will ours become before your eyes! what an empire will grow out of a marriage like this! With the arms of the Teucrians at its back, to what a height will the glory of Carthage soar! Only be it yours to implore the favor of Heaven, and having won its acceptance, give free course to hospitality and weave a chain 30 of pleas for delay, while the tempest is raging its full on the sea, and Orion, the star of rain, while his ships are still battered, and the rigor of the sky still unyielding." By these words she added fresh fuel to the fire of love, gave confidence to her wavering mind, and loosed the ties of woman's honor.

First they approach the temples and inquire for pardon from altar to altar; duly they slaughter chosen sheep to Ceres the lawgiver, to Phœbus, 40 and to father Lyæus—above all to Juno, who makes marriage bonds her care. Dido herself, in all her beauty, takes a goblet in her hand, and pours it out full between the horns of a heifer of gleaming white, or moves majestic in the presence of the gods towards the richly-laden altars, and solemnizes the day with offerings, and gazing greedily on the victims' open breasts, consults the entrails yet quivering with life. Alas! how blind are the eyes of seers! What can vows, what can 50 temples do for the madness of love? All the while a flame is preying on the very marrow of her bones, and deep in her breast a wound keeps noiselessly alive. She is on fire, the ill-fated Dido, and in her madness ranges the whole city through, like a doe from an arrow-shot, whom, unguarded in the thick of the Cretan woods, a shepherd, chasing her with his darts, has pierced from a distance, and left the flying steel in the wound, unknowing of his prize; she at full speed scours the forests and lawns of Dicte; the deadly reed still sticks in her side. Now she leads Æneas with her through the heart of the town, and displays the wealth of Sidon, and the city built to dwell in. She begins to speak, and stops midway in the utterance. Now, as the day fades, she seeks again the banquet of yesterday, and once more in frenzy asks to hear of the agonies of Troy, and hangs once more on his lips as he tells the tale. Afterwards, when the guests are gone, and the dim moon in turn is hiding her light, and the setting stars invite to slumber, alone she mourns in the empty hall, and presses the couch he has just left; him far away she sees and hears, herself far away; or holds Ascanius long in her lap, spellbound by his father's image, to cheat, if she can, her ungovernable passion. The towers that were rising rise no longer; the youth ceases to practice arms, or to make ready havens and bulwarks for safety in war; the works are broken and suspended, the giant frowning of the walls, and the engine level with the sky.

Soon as Jove's loved wife saw that she was so mastered by the plague, and that good name could not stand in the face of passion, she, the daughter of Saturn, bespeaks Venus thus:—"Brilliant truly is the praise, ample the spoils you are carrying off, you and your boy—great and memorable the fame, if the plots of two gods have really conquered one woman. No; I am not so blind either to your fears of my city, to your suspicions of the open doors of my stately Carthage. But when is this to end? or what calls now for such terrible contention? Suppose for a change we establish perpetual peace and a firm marriage bond. You have gained what your whole heart went to seek. Dido is ablaze with love, and the madness is coursing through her frame. Jointly then let us rule this nation, each with full sovereignty; let her stoop to be the slave of a Phrygian husband, and make over her Tyrians in place of dowry to your control."

To her—for she saw that she had spoken with a feigned intent, meaning to divert the Italian empire to the coast of Libya—Venus thus replied:— "Who would be so mad as to spurn offers like these, and prefer your enmity to your friendship, were it but certain that the issue you name would bring good fortune in its train? But I am groping blindly after destiny—whether it be Jupiter's will that the Tyrians and the voyagers from Troy should have one city—whether he would have the two nations blended and a league made between them. You are his wife; it is your place to approach him by entreaty. Go on, I will follow." Imperial Juno rejoined thus:—"That task shall rest with me. Now, in what way our present purpose can be contrived, lend me your attention, and I will explain in brief. Æneas and Dido, poor sufferer! are proposing to go hunting in the forest, when first tomorrow's sun displays his rising, and with his beams uncurtains the globe. On them I will pour from above a black storm of mingled rain and hail, just when the horsemen are all astir, and spreading their toils before the wood-walks, and the whole heaven shall be convulsed with thunder. The train shall fly here and there, and be lost in the thick darkness. Dido and the Trojan chief shall find themselves in the same cave. I will be there, and, if I may count on your sanction, will unite her to him in lasting wedlock, and consecrate her his for life. Thus shall Hymen give us his presence." The Queen of Cythera makes no demur, but nods assent, smiling at the trick she has found out.

Meanwhile Aurora has risen, and left the ocean. Rising with the day-star, the chivalry of Carthage streams through the gates, their woven toils, and nets, and hunting-spears tipped with broad iron, and Massylian horsemen hurry along, and a force of keen-scented hounds. There are the Punic princes, waiting for the queen, who still lingers in her chamber; there stands her palfrey, conspicuous in purple and gold, fiercely champing the foaming bit. At length she comes forth, with a mighty train attending, a Tyrian scarf round her, itself surrounded by an embroidered border; her quiver of gold, her hair knotted up with gold, her purple robe fastened with a golden clasp. The Phrygian train, too, are in motion, and Iulus, all exultation. Æneas himself, comely beyond all the rest, adds his presence to theirs, and joins the procession; like Apollo, when he leaves his Lycian winter-seat and the stream of Xanthus, and visits Delos, his mother's isle, and renews the dance; while with mingled voices round the altar shout Cretans and Dryopians, and tattooed Agathyrsians. The god in majesty walks on the heights of Cynthus, training his luxuriant hair with the soft pressure of a wreath of leaves, and twining it with gold; his arrows rattle on his shoulders. Not with less ease than he moves Æneas; such the beauty that sparkles in that peerless countenance. When they reach the high mountains and the pathless coverts, see! the wild goats, dropping from the tops of the crags, have run down the slopes; in another quarter the deer are scouring the open plains, massing their herds as they fly in a whirlwind of dust, and leaving the mountains. But young Ascanius is in the heart of the glens, exulting in his fiery courser. Now he passes one, now another of his comrades at full speed, and prays that in the midst of such spiritless game he may be blest with the sight of a foaming boar, or that a tawny lion may come down the hill. Meantime the sky begins to be convulsed with a mighty turmoil; a storm-cloud follows of mingled rain and hail. The Tyrian train, all in confusion, and the chivalry of Troy, and the hope of Dardania, Venus's grandson, have sought shelter in their terror up and down the country, some here, some there. The streams run in torrents down the hills. Dido and the Trojan chief find themselves in the same cave. Earth, the mother of all, and Juno give the sign.

Lightnings blaze, and heaven flashes in sympathy with the bridal; and from mountain-tops the nymphs give the nuptial shout. That day was the birthday of death, the birthday of woe. Henceforth she has no thought for the common eye or the common tongue; it is not a stolen passion that Dido has now in her mind—no, she calls it marriage; that name is the screen of her sin.

Instantly Fame takes her journey through Libya's great cities—Fame, a monster surpassed in speed by none; her nimbleness lends her life, and she gains strength as she goes. At first fear keeps her low; soon she rears herself skyward, and treads on the ground, while her head is hidden among the clouds. Earth, her parent, provoked to anger against the gods, brought her forth, they say, the youngest of the family of Cœus and Enceladus—swift of foot and untiring of wing, a portent terrible and vast—who, for every feather on her body has an ever-wakeful eye beneath, marvelous to tell, for every eye a loud tongue and mouth, and a pricked-up ear. At night she flies midway between heaven and earth, hissing through the darkness, nor ever yields her eyes to the sweets of sleep. In the daylight she sits sentinel on a high housetop, or on a lofty turret, and makes great cities afraid; as apt to cling to falsehood and wrong as to proclaim the truth. So then she was filling the public ear with a thousand tales—things done and things never done alike the burden of her song—how that Æneas, a prince of Trojan blood, had arrived at Carthage, a hero whom lovely Dido deigned to make her husband, and now in luxurious ease they were wearing away the length of winter together, forgetful of the crowns they wore or hoped to wear, and enthralled by unworthy passion. Such are the tales the fiendlike goddess spreads from tongue to tongue. Then, in due course, she turns her steps to King Iarbas, and inflames him with her rumors, and piles his indignation high. He, the son of Ammon, from the ravished embrace of a Garamantian nymph, built within his broad realms a hundred temples to Jove, and in each temple an altar; there he had consecrated an ever-wakeful fire, the god's unsleeping sentry, a floor thick with victim's blood, and doors wreathed with parti-colored garlands. And he, frenzied in soul, and stung by the bitter tidings, is said, as he stood before the altars, with the majesty of Heaven all around him, to have prayed long and earnestly to Jove with upturned hands:—"Jove, the Almighty, to whom in this my reign the Moorish race, feasting on embroidered couches, pour out the offering of the vintage, seest thou this? or is our dread of thee, Father, when thou hurlest thy lightnings, an idle panic? are those aimless fires in the clouds that appall us? have their confused rumblings no meaning? See here: a woman, who, wandering in our territories, bought leave to build a petty town, to whom we made over a strip of land for tillage, with its rights of lordship, she has rejected an alliance with us, and received Æneas into her kingdom, to be its lord and hers. And now that second Paris, with his emasculate following, a Mæonian cap supporting his chin and his essenced hair, is enjoying his prize, while we, forsooth, are making offerings to temples of thine, and keeping alive an idle rumor."

Thus as he prayed, his hands grasping the altar, the almighty one heard him, and turned his eyes to the queenly city and the guilty pair, lost to their better fame. Then thus he bespeaks Mercury, and gives him a charge like this:—"Go, haste, my son, summon the Zephyrs, and float on thy wings; address the Dardan chief, who is now dallying in Tyrian Carthage, and giving no thought to the city which Destiny makes his own; carry him my commands through the flying air. It was not a man like that whom his beauteous mother promised us in him, and on the strength of her word twice rescued him from the sword of Greece. No,

he was to be one who should govern Italy—Italy with its brood of unborn empires, and the war-cry bursting from its heart—who should carry down a line sprung from the grand fountain-head of Teucer's blood, and should force the whole world to bow to the laws he makes. If he is fired by no spark of ambition for greatness like this, and will not rear a toilsome fabric for his own praise, is it a father's heart that grudges Ascanius the hills of Rome? What is he building? What does he look to in lingering on among a nation of enemies, with no thought for the great Ausonian family, or for the fields of Lavinium? Away with him to sea! This is our sentence; thus far be our messenger."

Jove had spoken, and Mercury was preparing to execute the great sire's command: first he binds to his feet his sandals, all of gold, which carry him, uplifted by their pinions, over sea no less than land, with the swiftness of the wind that wafts him. Then he takes his rod—the rod with which he is wont to call up pale specters from the place of death, to send others on their melancholy way to Tartarus, to give sleep or take it away, and to open the eyes when death is past. With this in hand, he drives the winds before him, and makes a path through the sea of clouds. And now in his flight he espies the crest and the tall sides of Atlas the rugged, who with his top supports the sky—Atlas, whose pine-crowned head, everwreathed with dark clouds, is buffeted by wind and rain. A mantle of snow wraps his shoulders; rivers tumble from his hoary chin, and his grisly beard is stiff with ice. Here first Cyllene's god poised himself on his wings and rested; then from his stand stooping his whole body, he sent himself headlong to the sea, like a bird which haunting the coast and the fishy rocks flies low, close to the water. Even so was he flying between earth and heaven, between Libya's sandy coast and the winds that swept it, leaving his mother's father behind, himself Cyllene's progeny.

Soon as his winged feet alit among the huts of Carthage, he sees Æneas founding towers and making houses new. A sword was at his side, starred with yellow jaspers, and a mantle drooped from his shoulders, ablaze with Tyrian purple—a costly gift which Dido had made, varying the web with threads of gold. Instantly he assails him:—"And are you at a time like this laying the foundations of stately Carthage, and building, like a fond husband, your wife's goodly city, forgetting, alas! your own kingdom and the cares that should be yours? It is no less than the ruler of the gods who sends me down to you from his bright Olympus—he whose nod sways heaven and earth; it is he that bids me carry his commands through the flying air. What are you building? what do you look to in squandering your leisure in Libyan land? If you are fired by no spark of ambition for the greatness in your view, and will not rear a toilsome fabric for your own praise, think of Ascanius rising into youth, think of Iulus, your heir and your hope, to whom you owe the crown of Italy and the realm of Rome." With these words Cyllene's god quitted mortal sight ere he had well ceased to speak, and vanished away from the eye into unsubstantial air.

The sight left Æneas dumb and aghast indeed; his hair stood shudderingly erect; his speech clave to his throat. He burns to take flight and leave the land of pleasure, as his ears ring with the thunder of Heaven's imperious warning. What—ah! what is he to do? with what address can he now dare to approach the impassioned queen? what first advances can he employ? And thus he dispatches his rapid thought hither and thither, hurrying it east and west, and sweeping every corner of the field. So balancing, at last he thought this judgment the best. He calls Mnestheus and Sergestus and brave Serestus; bids them quietly get ready the fleet, muster the crews on the shore, with their arms in their hands, hiding the reason for so sudden a change. Meantime he, while Dido, kindest of friends, is in ignorance, deeming love's chain too strong to be snapped, will feel his way, and find what are the happiest moments for speech, what the right hold to take of circumstance. At once all gladly obey his command, and are busy on the tasks enjoined.

But the queen (who can cheat a lover's senses?) scented the plot, and caught the first sound of the coming stir, alive to fear in the midst of safety. Fame, as before, the same baleful fiend, whispered in her frenzied ear that the fleet was being equipped and the voyage got ready. She storms in impotence of soul, and, all on fire, goes raving through the city, like a Mænad starting up at the rattle of the sacred emblems, when the triennial orgies lash her with the cry of Bacchus, and Cithæron's yell calls her into the night. At length she thus bespeaks Æneas, unaddressed by him:—

"To hide, yes, hide your enormous crime, perfidious wretch, did you hope *that* might be done— to steal away in silence from my realm? Has our love no power to keep you? has our troth, once plighted, none, nor she whom you doom to a cruel death, your Dido? Nay, are you fitting out your fleet with winter's sky overhead, and hastening to cross the deep in the face of all the northern winds, hard-hearted as you are? Why, suppose you were not seeking a strange clime and a home you know not—suppose old Troy were still standing—would even Troy draw you to seek her across a billowy sea? Flying, and from me! By the tears I shed, and by your plighted hand, since my own act, alas! has left me nought else to plead—by our union—by the nuptial rites thus prefaced—if I have ever deserved well of you, or aught of mine ever gave you pleasure—have pity on a falling house, and strip off, I conjure you, if prayer be not too late, the mind that clothes you. It is owing to you that the Libyan tribes and the Nomad chiefs hate me, that my own Tyrians are estranged; owing to you, yes, you, that my woman's honor has been put out, and that which was my one passport to immortality, my former fame. To whom are you abandoning a dying woman, my guest?—since the name of husband has dwindled to that. Why do I live any longer?—to give my brother Pygmalion time to batter down my walls, or Iarbas the Moor to carry me away captive? Had I but borne any offspring of you before your flight, were there some tiny Æneas to play in my hall, and remind me of you, though but in look, I should not then feel utterly captive and forlorn."

She ceased. He all the while, at Jove's command, was keeping his eyes unmoved, and shutting up in his heart his great love. At length he answers in brief:—"Fair queen, name all the claims to gratitude you can. I shall never gainsay one, nor will the thought of Elissa ever be unwelcome while memory lasts, while breath animates this frame. A few words I will say, as the case admits. I never counted—do not dream it—on stealthily concealing my flight. I never came with a bridegroom's torch in my hand, nor was this the alliance to which I agreed. For me, were the Fates to suffer me to live under a star of my own choosing, and to make with care the terms I would, the city of Troy, first of all the dear remains of what was mine, would claim my tendance. Priam's tall roof-tree would still be standing, and my hand would have built a restored Pergamus, to solace the vanquished. But now to princely Italy Grynean Apollo, to Italy his Lycian oracles bid me repair. There is my heart, there my fatherland. If you are riveted here by the sight of your stately Carthage, a daughter of Phœnicia by a Libyan town, why, I would ask, should jealousy forbid Teucrians to settle in Ausonian land? We, like you, have the right of looking for a foreign realm. There is my father Anchises, oft as night's dewy shades invest the earth, oft as the fiery stars arise, warning me in dreams and appalling me by his troubled presence. There is my son Ascanius, and the wrongs heaped on his dear head every day that I rob him of the crown of Hesperia, and of the land that fate makes his. Now, too, the messenger of the gods, sent down from Jove himself (I swear by both our lives) has brought me orders through the flying air. With my own eyes I saw the god in clear daylight entering the walls, and took in his words with the ears that hear you now. Cease then to harrow up both our souls by your reproaches: my quest of Italy is not of my own motion."

Long ere he had done this speech she was glaring at him askance, rolling her eyes this way and that, and scanning the whole man with her silent glances, and thus she bursts forth all ablaze:— "No goddess was mother of yours, no Dardanus the head of your line, perfidious wretch!—no, your parent was Caucasus, rugged and craggy, and Hyracanian tigresses put their breasts to your lips. For why should I suppress aught? or for what worse evil hold myself in reserve? Did he groan when I wept? did he move those hard eyes? did he yield and shed tears, or pity her that loved him? What first? what last? Now, neither Juno, queen of all, nor Jove, the almighty Father, eyes us with impartial regard. Nowhere is there aught to trust— nowhere. A shipwrecked beggar, I welcomed him, and madly gave him a share of my realm; his lost fleet, his crews, I brought back from death's door. Ah! Fury sets me on fire, and whirls me round! Now, prophet Apollo, now the Lycian oracles. Now the messenger of the gods, sent down by Jove himself, bears his grim bidding through the air! Aye, of course, that is the employment of the powers above, those the cares that break their repose! I retain not your person, nor refute your talk. Go, chase Italy with the winds at your back; look for realms with the whole sea between you. I have hope that on the rocks midway, if the gods are as powerful as they are good, you will drain the cup of punishment, with Dido's name ever on your lips. I will follow you with murky fires when I am far away; and when cold death shall have parted soul and body, my shade shall haunt you everywhere. Yes, wretch, you shall suffer. I shall hear it—the news will reach me down among

the dead." So saying, she snaps short her speech, and flies with loathing from the daylight, and breaks and rushes from his sight, leaving him hesitating, and fearing, and thinking of a thousand things to say. Her maidens support her, and carry her sinking frame into her marble chamber, and lay her on her bed.

But good Æneas, though yearning to solace and soothe her agonized spirit, and by his words to check the onset of sorrow, with many a groan, his whole soul upheaved by the force of love, goes nevertheless about the commands of Heaven, and repairs to his fleet. The Teucrians redouble their efforts, and along the whole range of the shore drag their tall ships down. The keels are careened and floated. They carry oars with their leaves still on, and timber unfashioned as it stood in the woods, so strong their eagerness to fly. You may see them all in motion, streaming from every part of the city. Even as ants when they are sacking a huge heap of wheat, provident of winter days, and laying up the plunder in their stores; a black column is seen moving through the plain, and they convey their booty along the grass in a narrow path: some are putting their shoulders to the big grains, and pushing them along; others are rallying the force and punishing the stragglers; the whole track is in a glow of work. What were your feelings then, poor Dido, at a sight like this! How deep the groans you heaved, when you looked out from your lofty tower on a beach all seething and swarming, and saw the whole sea before you deafened with that hubbub of voices! Tyrant love! what force dost thou not put on human hearts? Again she has to condescend to tears, again to use the weapons of entreaty, and bow her spirit in suppliance under love's yoke, lest she should have left aught untried, and be rushing on a needless death.

"Anna, you see there is hurrying all over the shore—they are met from every side; the canvas is already wooing the gale, and the joyful sailors have wreathed the sterns. If I have had the foresight to anticipate so heavy a blow, I shall have the power to bear it too, my sister. Yet, Anna, in my misery, perform me this one service. You, and you only, the perfidious man was wont to make his friend—aye, even to trust you with his secret thoughts. You, and you only, know the subtle approaches to his heart, and the times of essaying them. Go, then, my sister, and supplicate our haughty foe. Tell him I was no party to the Danaan league at Aulis to destroy the Trojan nation; I sent no ships to Pergamus; I never disinterred his father Anchises, his dust or his spirit. Why will he not let my words sink down into his obdurate ears? Whither is he hurrying? Let him grant this last boon to her who loves him so wildly; let him wait till the way is smoothed for his flight, and there are winds to waft him. I am not asking him now to renew our old vows which he has forsworn. I am not asking him to forego his fair Latium, and resign his crown. I entreat but a few vacant hours, a respite and breathing-space for my passion, till my fortune shall have taught baffled love how to grieve. This is my last request of you—oh, pity your poor sister!—a request which when granted shall be returned with interest in death."

Such was her appeal—such the wailing which her afflicted sister bears to him, and bears again; but no wailing moves him, no words find him a gentle listener. Fate bars the way, and Heaven closes the hero's unrelenting ears. Even as an aged oak, still hale and strong, which Alpine winds, blowing now here, now there, strive emulously to uproot—a loud noise is heard, and, as the stem rocks, heaps of leaves pile the ground; but the tree cleaves firmly to the cliff; high as its head strikes into the air, so deep its root strikes down to the abyss—even thus the hero is assailed on all sides by a storm of words: his mighty breast thrills through and through with agony; but his mind is unshaken, and tears are showered in vain.

Then at last, maddened by her destiny, poor Dido prays for death: heaven's vault is a weariness to look on. To confirm her in pursuing her intent, and closing her eyes on the sun, she saw, as she was laying her offerings on the incense-steaming altars—horrible to tell—the sacred liquor turn black, and the streams of wine curdle into loathly gore. This appearance she told to none, not even to her sister. Moreover, there was in her palace a marble chapel to her former husband, to which she used to pay singular honors, wreathing it with snowy fillets and festal boughs; from it she thought she heard a voice, the accents of the dead man calling her, when the darkness of night was shrouding the earth; and on the roof a lonely owl in funereal tones kept complaining again and again, and drawing out wailingly its protracted notes; and a thousand predictions of seers of other days come back on her, terrifying her with their awful warnings. When she dreams, there is Æneas himself driving her in furious chase: she seems always being left alone to herself, always pacing companionless on a never-ending road, and looking for her Tyrians in a realm without inhabitants—like Pentheus, when in frenzy he sees troops of Furies, and two suns, and a double Thebes rising round him; or Agamemnon's Orestes rushing over the stage, as he flies from his mother, who is armed with torches and deadly snakes, while the avenging fiends sit couched on the threshold.

So when, spent with agony, she gave conception to the demon, and resolved on death, she settled with herself time and means, and thus bespoke her grieving sister, her face disguising her intent, and hope smiling on her brow:—"Dearest, I have found a way—wish me joy, as a sister should—to bring him back to me, or to loose me from the love which binds me to him. Hard by the bound of ocean and the setting sun lies the extreme Ethiopian clime, where mighty Atlas turns round on his shoulders the pole, studded with burning stars. From that clime, I have heard of a priestess of the Massylian race, once guardian of the temple of the Hesperides, who used to give the dragon his food, and so preserve the sacred boughs on the tree, sprinkling for him moist honey and drowsy poppy-seed. She, by her spells, undertakes to release souls at her pleasure, while into others she shoots cruel pangs; she stops the water in the river-bed, and turns back the stars in their courses, and calls ghosts from realms of night. You will see the earth bellowing under you, and the ashes coming down from the mountain-top. By the gods I swear, dearest sister, by you and your dear life, that unwillingly I gird on the weapons of magic. Do you, in the privacy of the inner court, build a pile to the open sky; lay on it the arms which that godless man left hanging in the chamber, and all his doffed apparel, and the nuptial bed which was my undoing. To destroy every memorial of the hateful wretch is my pleasure, and the priestess's bidding." This said, she is silent—paleness overspreads her face. Yet Anna does not dream that these strange rites are a veil to hide her sister's death: she cannot grasp frenzy like that; she fears no darker day than that of their mourning for Sychæus, and so she does her bidding.

But the queen, when the pile had been built in the heart of the palace to the open sky, a giant mass of pine-wood and hewn oak, spans the place with garlands, and crowns it with funeral boughs. High above it on the couch she sets the doffed apparel, and the sword that had been left, and the image of the false lover, knowing too well what was to come. Altars rise here and there; the priest ess, with hair disheveled, thunders out the roll of three hundred gods, Erebus and Chaos, and Hecate with her triple form—the three faces borne by maiden Dian. See! she has sprinkled water, brought, so she feigns, from Avernus's spring, and she is getting green downy herbs, cropped by moonlight with brazen shears, whose sap is the milk of deadly poison, and the love-charm, torn from the brow of the new-born foal, ere the mother could snatch it. Dido herself, with salted cake and pure hands at the altars, one foot unshod, her vest ungirdled, makes her dying appeal to the gods and to the stars who share Fate's counsels, begging the powers, if any there be, that watch, righteous and unforgetting, over ill-yoked lovers, to hear her prayer.

It was night, and overtoiled mortality throughout the earth was enjoying peaceful slumber; the woods were at rest, and the raging waves—the hour when the stars are rolling midway in their smooth courses, when all the land is hushed, cattle, and gay-plumed birds, haunters far and wide of clear waters and rough forest-ground, lapped in sleep with stilly night overhead, their troubles assuaged, their hearts dead to care. Not so the vexed spirit of Phœnicia's daughter; she never relaxes into slumber, or welcomes the night to eye or bosom; sorrow doubles peal on peal; once more love swells, and storms, and surges, with a mighty tempest of passion. Thus, then, she plunges into speech, and whirls her thoughts about thus in the depth of her soul:—"What am I about? Am I to make fresh proof of my former suitors, with scorn before me? Must I stoop to court Nomad bridegrooms, whose offered hand I have spurned so often? Well, then, shall I follow the fleet of Ilion, and be at the beck and call of Teucrian masters? Is it that they think with pleasure on the succor once rendered them? that gratitude for past kindness yet lives in their memory? But even if I wished it, who will give me leave, or admit the unwelcome guest to his haughty ships? Are you so ignorant, poor wretch? Do you not yet understand the perjury of the race of Laomedon? What then? Shall I fly alone, and swell the triumph of their crews? or shall I put to sea, with the Tyrians and whole force of my people at my back, dragging those whom it was so hard to uproot from their Sidonian home again into the deep, and bidding them spread sail to the winds? No!—die the death you have merited, and let the sword put your sorrow to flight. You, sister, are the cause; overmastered by my tears, you heap this

deadly fuel on my flame, and fling me upon my enemy. Why could I not forswear wedlock, and live an unblamed life in savage freedom, nor meddle with troubles like these? Why did I not keep the faith I vowed to the ashes of Sychæus?" Such were the reproaches that broke from that bursting heart.

Meanwhile Æneas, resolved on his journey, was slumbering in his vessel's tall stern, all being now in readiness. To him a vision of the god, appearing again with the same countenance, presented itself as he slept, and seemed to give this second warning—the perfect picture of Mercury, his voice, his blooming hue, his yellow locks, and the youthful grace of his frame:—"Goddess-born, at a crisis like this can you slumber on? Do you not see the wall of danger which is fast rising round you, infatuate that you are, nor hear the favoring whisper of the western gale? She is revolving in her bosom thoughts of craft and cruelty, resolved on death, and surging with a changeful tempest of passion. Will you not haste away while haste is in your power? you will look on a sea convulsed with ships, an array of fierce torch-fires, a coast glowing with flame, if the dawn-goddess shall have found you loitering here on land. Quick!—burst through delay. A thing of moods and changes is woman ever." He said, and was lost in the darkness of night.

At once Æneas, scared by the sudden apparition, springs up from his sleep, and rouses his comrades, "Wake in a moment, my friends, and seat you on the benches. Unfurl the sails with all speed. See! here is a god sent down from heaven on high, urging us again to hasten our flight, and cut the twisted cables. Yes! sacred power, we follow thee, whoever thou art, and a second time with joy obey thy behest. Be thou with us, and graciously aid us, and let propitious stars be ascendant in the sky." So saying, he snatches from the scabbard his flashing sword, and with the drawn blade cuts the hawsers. The spark flies from man to man; they scour, they scud; they have left the shore behind; you cannot see the water for ships. With strong strokes they dash the foam, and sweep the blue.

And now Aurora was beginning to sprinkle the earth with fresh light, rising from Tithonus's saffron couch. Soon as the queen from her watch-tower saw the gray dawn brighten, and the fleet moving on with even canvas, and coast and haven forsaken, with never an oar left, thrice and again smiting her beauteous breast with her hands, and rending her golden locks. "Great Jupiter!" cries one, "shall he go? Shall a chance-comer boast of having flouted our realm? Will they not get their arms at once, and give chase from all the town, and pull, some of them, the ships from the docks? Away! bring fire; quick! get darts, ply oars! What am I saying? Where am I? What madness turns my brain? Wretched Dido! do your sins sting you now? They should have done so then, when you were giving your crown away. What truth! what fealty!—the man who, they say, carries about with him the gods of his country, and took up on his shoulders his old worn-out father! Might I not have caught and torn him piecemeal, and scattered him to the waves?—destroyed his friends, aye, and his own Ascanius, and served up the boy for his father's meal? But the chance of a battle would have been doubtful. Let it have been. I was to die, and whom had I to fear? I would have flung torches into his camp, filled his decks with flame, consumed son and sire and the whole line, and leapt myself upon the pile. Sun, whose torch show thee all that is done on earth, and thou, Juno, revealer and witness of these stirrings of the heart, and Hecate, whose name is yelled in civic crossways by night, avenging fiends, and gods of dying Elissa, listen to this! Let your power stoop to ills that call for it, and hear what I now pray! If it must needs be that the accursed wretch gain the haven and float to shore—if such the requirement of Jove's destiny, such the fixed goal—yet grant that, harassed by the sword and battle of a warlike nation, a wanderer from his own confines, torn from his Iulus's arms, he may pray for succor, and see his friends dying miserably round him! Nor when he has yielded to the terms of an unjust peace, may he enjoy his crown, or the life he loves; but may he fall before his time, and lie unburied in the midst of the plain! This is my prayer—these the last accents that flow from me with my life-blood. And you, my Tyrians, let your hatred persecute the race and people for all time to come. Be this the offering you send down to my ashes: never be there love or league between nation and nation. Arise from my bones, my unknown avenger, destined with fire and sword to pursue the Dardanian settlers, now or in afterdays, whenever strength shall be given! Let coast be at war with coast, water with wave, army with army; fight they, and their sons, and their sons' sons!"

Thus she said, as she whirled her thought to this side and that, seeking at once to cut short the life she now abhorred. Then briefly she spoke to Barce,

Sychæus's nurse, for her own was left in her old country, in the black ashes of the grave:—"Fetch me here, dear nurse, my sister Anna. Bid her hasten to sprinkle herself with water from the stream, and bring with her the cattle and the atoning offerings prescribed. Let her come with these; and do you cover your brow with the holy fillet. The sacrifice to Stygian Jove, which I have duly commenced and made ready, I wish now to accomplish, and with it the end of my sorrows, giving to the flame the pile that pillows the Dardan head!" She said: the nurse began to quicken her pace with an old wife's zeal.

But Dido, wildered and maddened by her enormous resolve, rolling her bloodshot eye, her quivering cheeks stained with fiery streaks, and pale with the shadow of death, bursts the door of the inner palace, and frantically climbs the tall pile, and unsheaths the Dardan sword, a gift procured for a far different end. Then, after surveying the Trojan garments and the bed, too well known, and pausing awhile to weep and think, she pressed her bosom to the couch, and uttered her last words:—

"Relics, once darlings of mine, while Fate and Heaven gave leave, receive this my soul, and release me from these my sorrows. I have lived my life—the course assigned me by Fortune is run, and now the august phantom of Dido shall pass underground. I have built a splendid city. I have seen my walls completed. In vengeance for a husband, I have punished a brother that hated me—blest, ah! blest beyond human bliss, if only Dardan ships had never touched coast of ours!" She spoke—and kissing the couch: "Is it to be death without revenge? But be it death," she cries —"this, this is the road by which I love to pass to the shades. Let the heartless Dardanian's eyes drink in this flame from the deep, and let him carry with him the presage of my death."

She spoke, and even while she was yet speaking, her attendants see her fallen on the sword, the blade spouting blood, and her hands dabbled in it. Their shrieks rise to the lofty roof; Fame runs wild through the convulsed city. With wailing and groaning, and screams of women cries palace rings; the sky resounds with ... were to and beating of breasts—even a ... Carthage or burst the gates and to the dwellings of men ancient Tyre, and ... were leaping from roof ... Breathless and frantic, with and god...

wild speed, disfiguring her cheeks with her nails, her bosom with her fists, she bursts through the press, and calls by name on the dying queen:— "Was this your secret, sister? Were you plotting to cheat me? Was this what your pile was preparing for me, your fires, and your altars? What should a lone heart grieve for first? Did you disdain your sister's company in death? You should have called me to share your fate—the same keen sword-pang, the same hour, should have been the end of both. And did these hands build the pile, this voice call on the gods of our house, that you might lie there, while I, hard-hearted wretch, was away? Yes, sister, you have destroyed yourself and me, the people and the elders of Sidon, and your own fair city. Let in the water to the wounds; let me cleanse them, and if any remains of breath be still flickering, catch them in my mouth!" As she thus spoke, she was at the top of the lofty steps, and was embracing and fondling in her bosom her dying sister, and stanching with her robe the black streams of blood. Dido strives to raise her heavy eyes, and sinks down again, the deep stab gurgles in her breast. Thrice, with an effort, she lifted and reared herself up on her elbow; thrice, she fell back on the couch, and with helpless wandering eyes aloft in the sky, sought for the light and groaned when she found it.

Then Juno almighty, in compassion for her lengthened agony and her trouble in dying, sent down Iris from Olympus to part the struggling soul and its prison of flesh. For, as she was dying, not in the course of fate, nor for any crime of hers, but in mere misery, before her time, the victim of sudden frenzy, not yet had Proserpine carried off a lock of her yellow hair, and thus doomed her head to Styx and the place of death. So then Iris glides down the sky with saffron wings dew-besprent, trailing a thousand various colors in the face of the sun, and alights above her head. "This I am bidden to bear away as an offering to Pluto, and hereby set you free from the body." So saying, she stretches her hand and cuts the lock: at once all heat parts from the frame, and the life has passed into air.

ROMAN HISTORIANS

A nation that made history as arduously as Rome did was bound to write it, too, and Roman historians have contributed many vivid pages to our heritage. The practical inclinations of Roman character and the rhetorical tendencies of Latin writers lowered the level of their inspiration. But the historical writings of Julius Cæsar, Sallust, Livy, and Tacitus possess a variety of virtues and a great deal of interest. Many of their stories and comments passed into the cultural stream of Europe.

Although the *Commentaries* of Julius Cæsar (100-44 B.C.) are merely records of his campaigns, his book is notable for simplicity and directness, though his complacency is somewhat offensive. His graphic descriptions of battles and conquests have never been forgotten. Sallust (86-34 B.C.), author of the *Jugurthine War* and *The War of Catiline*, an account of the famous conspiracy that was scotched by Cicero, was an ostentatious writer. Yet he managed to create vivid pictures of Roman society, to analyze the motivations of his chief actors, and to draw thoughtful conclusions from his narrative. Sallust, in fact, initiated the writing of formal history in Rome. He was succeeded by the two Latin masters of historical prose, Livy and Tacitus.

Livy (59 B.C.-A.D. 17) was not a careful historian, but he became a superb narrator. Born in Padua, but making Rome his home, he was the proud chronicler of its ascent to power from the obscure beginnings to 9 B.C. He conceived his *Annals* almost as an epic of Rome's early grandeur, and glorified its past by tracing its heroic spirit from struggle to struggle, from hero to hero.

Livy was primarily interested in watching Roman character in action. This gives his *Annals* a lavish procession of personages and exciting events. It was not accuracy that Livy sought but vitality; therefore, though acknowledging that his earliest material bears "the semblance rather of poetic fictions than of authentic records," he made no serious attempt to distinguish between legend and historical fact. The battles he describes may be topographically vague, but they never fail to be rousing. His biographical sketches are open to suspicion on the grounds of uncritical glorification or simplification, and there is certainly no profundity in his observations, but they are remarkably vivid. Livy selected the most striking details of his characters and events, and then strung them together into a flowing narrative, noble and stately. The world is under deep obligation to him for many household portraits and stories.

Livy, who had been a partisan of the Pompey faction during the civil war in which Cæsar triumphed, gave evidence of dissatisfaction with the trends of his day. In fact, his professed object was to set an example to his contemporaries. The Preface to the *Annals* states this clearly.

If Livy found it necessary to instruct his age, his successor Tacitus had even better reason to look for didactic possibilities in the writing of history. Born about A.D. 55, he grew up in a turbulent world. If, as is believed, he lived until about A.D. 126, he spanned some extremely significant decades of Roman history. He held offices under the Emperors Vespasian, Titus, Domitian, and Nerva, serving as consul under the latter. In 78, he married the daughter of the famous Agricola, governor of Britain, whom Tacitus later made the subject of an excellent biography. His political appointments apparently took him to various parts of the empire. Such a career and such connections provided ideal opportunities for observation and reflection upon the times. Directly and by implication Tacitus followed a didactic purpose—the inculcation of virtue. Fortunately this did not vitiate his writings and actually gave them a singular nobility of style.

In the *Agricola,* Tacitus wrote a memorable biography of his father-in-law and set him up as a model for Roman gentlemen. In the *Germania,* in which he provided the first substantial description of the Germanic tribes that were beginning to challenge the Roman empire, he not only produced a remarkable ethnographic work, but implied a criticism of Roman decadence through the sheer contrast between the life of the Romans and the vigorous customs of the still unspoiled Teutons, whom he probably idealized. His greatest works, the *Annales* (*Annals*) and the *Historiæ* (*Histories*), both very incompletely preserved, include the best historical writing of the Romans. The former spans the period between the death of Augustus (A.D. 14) and the inglorious end of Nero (A.D. 68). It contains some of the most vivid accounts of a nation moving toward dissolution.

Tacitus is an engaging, though formal and moralistic, writer. Uncorrupted by his age, he set down his liberal thoughts and his facts with becoming gravity and striking suggestiveness, implying more than he stated. He could also be vividly descriptive and dramatic, and at times he attained poetic elevation. The suitability of the Latin language for dignified and compact expression is excellently exemplified in his style. At its worst, this kind of writing could be vitiated by sententiousness or pomposity. But Tacitus generally avoided this defect, and poured into his rounded sentences provocative and often universally apt observations.

Comments like the following, taken from his biographical sketch of Agricola, abound in his work: "By the very nature of human imperfection the remedy is slower than the ill; and as our bodies take years to grow, and perish in a moment, so too it is easier to suppress genius and industry than it is to revive them . . . Courage and liberty perished together . . . Gradually the Britons yielded to the seduction of our Roman vices, and took to lounges and baths and elegant banquets. This was all part of their slavery. The ignorant called it 'civilization.' . . . To robbery, murder, and pillage they give the false name of Empire, and when they make a wilderness they call it Peace . . . It is but human nature to hate the man whom you have hurt . . . I would have all such know that even under bad rulers men may be great . . . Men's statues, like the faces they depict, are weak and crumbling." Men write like this only out of the fullness of reflection, and such classic definiteness outlasts many subtleties and graces. No one can read lines like these without becoming aware of their application to one's own times.

LIVY

Hannibal's March Across the Alps

In about three days after Hannibal's moving from the bank of the Rhone, the consul Publius Cornelius had come with his forces in order of battle to the camp of the enemy, intending to fight them without delay. But finding the fortifications abandoned, and concluding that, as they had got the start of him so far, it would be difficult to overtake them, he marched back to the sea where his ships lay; for he judged that he might thus with greater ease and safety meet Hannibal on his descent from the Alps. However, not to leave Spain, the province which the lots had assigned to his care, destitute of the aid of the Roman troops, he sent his brother Cneius Scipio with the greater part of his forces against Hasdrubal,[1] with the expectation of not merely protecting old allies, and acquiring new, but of driving him out of Spain. He himself, with a very small force, repaired to Genoa, proposing, with the army which was stationed on the Po, to provide for the security of Italy. From the Druentia, Hannibal, passing through a tract in general level, without any molestation from the Gauls inhabiting those regions, arrived at the Alps. And now, notwithstanding that the men had already conceived notions from the reports, which in cases capable of misrepresentation generally go beyond the truth, yet the present view exhibited such objects as renewed all their terrors: the height of the mountains, the snow almost touching the sky, the wretched huts standing on cliffs, the cattle and

---

[1] Hannibal's brother.

Livy (59 B.C.–A.D. 17) Translation by George Baker.

beasts shivering with the cold, the natives squalid and in uncouth dress, all things, in short, animate and inanimate, stiffened with frost, besides other circumstances more shocking to the sight than can be represented in words. As they marched up the first acclivities, they beheld the eminences which hung over them covered with parties of the mountaineers, who, if they had posted themselves in the valleys out of view, and, rushing out suddenly, had made an unexpected attack, must have occasioned the most terrible havoc and dismay. Hannibal commanded the troops to halt, and having discovered from some Gauls whom he sent forward to examine the ground that there was no passage on that side, encamped in the widest valley which he could find, where the whole circuit around consisted of rocks and precipices. Then having gained intelligence by means of the same Gauls (who differed not much from the others in language and manners, and who had entered into conversation with them) that the pass was blocked up only by day, and that at night they separated to their several dwellings, he advanced at the first dawn to the eminences, as if with the design of forcing his way through the pass. This feint he carried on through the whole day, his men at the same time fortifying a camp in the spot where they were drawn up. As soon as he understood that the mountaineers had retired from the heights and withdrawn their guards, he made, for a show, a greater number of fires than was proportioned to the troops who remained in the camp, and leaving behind the baggage with the cavalry and the greater part of the infantry, he himself, with a light-armed band composed of the most daring men in the army, pushed rapidly through the pass, and took post on those very eminences of which the enemy had been in possession.

At the first dawn of the next day the rest of the army began to march forward. By this time the mountaineers, on a given signal, were coming together out of their fortresses to their usual station; when on a sudden they perceived a part of the enemy over their heads in possession of their own strong post, and the rest passing along the road. Both these circumstances striking them at once, they were for some time incapable of thought, or of turning their eyes to any other object. Afterwards, when they observed the confusion in the pass, and that the body of the enemy was disordered on their march by the hurry among themselves, and particularly by the unruliness of the affrighted horses, they thought that if they could

augment in any degree the terror under which the army already labored, they could destroy it. They therefore ran down the rocks in an oblique direction through pathless and circuitous ways which habitual practice rendered easy to them. And now the Carthaginians had to contend at once with the Gauls and the disadvantage of the ground, and there was a greater struggle among themselves than with the enemy, for every one strove to get first out of danger. But the greatest disorder was occasioned by the horses, which, affrighted at the dissonant clamors, multiplied by the echoes from the woods and valleys, became nearly unmanageable; and when they happened to receive a stroke or a wound, grew so unruly as to overthrow numbers of men and heaps of baggage of all sorts; and as there were abrupt passages on each side of the pass, their violence cast down many to an immense depth, so that the fall of such great masses caused a dreadful effect. Although these were shocking sights to Hannibal, yet he kept his place for a while, and restrained the troops that were with him, lest he should increase the tumult and confusion. Afterwards, seeing the line of the army broken, and that there was danger of their being wholly deprived of their baggage, in which case the effecting of their passage would answer no purpose, he hastened down from the higher ground; and while by the mere rapidity of his motion he dispersed the forces of the enemy, he at the same time increased the confusion among his own. But this, when the roads were cleared by the flight of the mountaineers, was instantly remedied, and the whole army was soon brought through the pass not only without disturbance, but almost without any noise. He then seized a fort, which was the capital of that district, and several villages that lay around it, and fed his army for three days with cattle taken from the fugitives. During these three days, as he was not incommoded by the mountaineers, nor much by the nature of the ground, he made a considerable progress in his march.

He then reached the territory of another state, which was thickly inhabited for a mountainous country: there he was very near suffering a defeat, not only by open force, but by his own arts, treachery, and ambush. Some men of advanced age, governors of their forts, came to the Carthaginian as ambassadors, with humble representations that "as the calamities of others had afforded them a profitable lesson, they wished to make trial of the friendship rather than of the strength of the Carthaginians. That they were therefore resolved to yield obedience to all his commands, and requested him to accept provisions and guides on his march, and hostages to insure the performance of their engagements." Hannibal neither hastily crediting, nor yet slighting their offers, lest, if rejected, they might declare openly against him, after returning a favorable answer, accepted the hostages, and made use of the provisions which they had, of their own accord, brought to the road; but followed the guides, not as through a friendly country, but with the strictest order in his march. The elephants and cavalry composed the van, and he himself followed with the main body of the infantry, carefully inspecting every particular. On their coming into a road narrower than the rest, confined on one side by an impending hill, the barbarians rising up on all sides from places where they had lain concealed, assailed them in front and rear, in close and in distant fight, rolling down also huge rocks on the troops. The most numerous body pressed on the rear. There the main force of infantry was ready to oppose them; but had not that been very strong, it must undoubtedly, in such a difficult pass, have suffered very great loss: even as the case stood, it was brought to the extremity of danger, and almost to destruction: for whilst Hannibal hesitated to lead his horsemen into the narrower road, though he had left no kind of support at the back of the infantry, the mountaineers, rushing across and breaking through between the two divisions of the army, took possession of the pass, and Hannibal spent one night separated from his cavalry and his baggage.

Next day, the barbarians having relaxed the violence of their attacks in the centre, the troops were reunited, and carried through the defile, but not without loss; the destruction was greater however among the beasts of burden than among the men. Thenceforward the mountaineers made their attacks in smaller parties, more like robbers than an army; at one time on the van, at another on the rear, just as the ground happened to afford them an advantage, or as stragglers advancing before the rest, or staying behind, gave them an opportunity. Although the driving of the elephants through the narrow roads, even with all the haste that could be made, occasioned much loss of time, yet wherever they went they effectually secured the troops from the enemy; who, being unaccustomed to such creatures, dared not to come near them. On the ninth day the army completed the ascent to the summit of the Alps, mostly through path-

less tracts and wrong roads; into which they had been led either by the treachery of their guides, or when these were not trusted, rashly, on the strength of their own conjectures, following the courses of the valleys. On the summit they remained encamped two days, in order to refresh the soldiers, who were spent with toil and fighting; and in this time several of the beasts which had fallen among the rocks, following the tracks of the army, came into camp. Tired as the troops were of struggling so long with hardships, they found their terrors very much increased by a fall of snow, this being the season of the setting of the constellation Pleiades.[2] The troops were put in motion with the first light; and as they marched slowly over ground which was entirely covered with snow, dejection and despair being strongly marked in every face, Hannibal went forward before the standards, and ordering the soldiers to halt on a projecting eminence, from which there was a wide extended prospect, made them take a view of Italy, and of the plains about the Po, stretching along the foot of the mountains; then told them that "they were now scaling the walls, not only of Italy, but of the city of Rome: that all the rest would be plain and smooth; and after one or at most a second battle, they would have the bulwark and capital of Italy in their power and disposal." The army then began to advance, the enemy now desisting from any farther attempts on them except by trifling parties for pillaging, as opportunity offered. But the way was much more difficult than it had been in the ascent, the declivity on the Italian side of the Alps being in most places shorter, and consequently more perpendicular; while the whole way was narrow and slippery, so that the soldiers could not prevent their feet from sliding, nor, if they made the least false step, could they, on falling, stop themselves: and thus men and beasts tumbled promiscuously over one another.

Then they came to a ridge much narrower than the others, and composed of rock so upright that a light-armed soldier, making the trial, could with difficulty by laying hold of bushes and roots, which appeared here and there, accomplish the descent. In this place the precipice, originally great, had by a late falling away of the earth been increased to the depth of at least one thousand feet. Here the cavalry stopped, as if at the end of their journey, and Hannibal, wondering what could be the cause of the troops' halting, was told that the cliff was impassable. Then going up himself to view the

[2] The beginning of November.

place, it seemed clear to him that he must lead his army in a circuit, though ever so great, and through tracks never trodden before. That way, however, was found to be impracticable. The old snow indeed had become hard, and being covered with the new of a moderate depth, the men found good footing as they walked through it; but when that was dissolved by the treading of so many men and beasts, they then trod on the naked ice below. Here they were much impeded, because the foot could take no hold on the smooth ice, and was besides more apt to slip on account of the declivity of the ground; and whenever they attempted to rise, either by aid of the hands or knees, they fell again. Add to this that there were neither stumps nor roots within reach, on which they could lean for support; so that they wallowed in the melted snow on one entire surface of slippery ice. This the cattle sometimes penetrated as soon as their feet reached the lower bed; and sometimes, when they lost their footing, by striking more strongly with their hoofs in striving to keep themselves up, they broke it entirely through; so that the greatest part of them, as if caught in traps, stuck fast in the hard, deep ice.

At length, after men and beasts were heartily fatigued to no purpose, they fixed a camp on the summit, having with very great difficulty cleared even the ground which that required, so great was the quantity of snow to be dug and carried off. The soldiers were then employed to make a way down the steep, through which alone it was possible to effect a passage; and as it was necessary to break the mass, they felled and lopped a number of huge trees which stood near, which they raised into a vast pile, and as soon as a smart wind arose, to forward the kindling of it, set it on fire; and then, when the stone was violently heated, made it crumble to pieces by pouring on vinegar. When the rock was thus disjointed by the power of the heat, they opened a way through it with iron instruments, and inclined the descents with it in such a manner, that not only the beasts of burden, but even the elephants could be brought down. Four days were spent about this rock, during which the cattle were nearly destroyed by hunger; for the summits are for the most part bare, and whatever little pasture there might have been was covered with snow. In the lower parts are valleys and some hills, which, enjoying the benefit of the sun, with rivulets at the side of the woods, are better suited to become the residence of human beings. There

the horses were sent out to pasture, and the men, fatigued with the labor on the road, allowed to rest for three days. They then descended into the plains, where the climate, like the character of the inhabitants, was of a milder cast.

In this manner, as nearly as can be ascertained, they accomplished their passage into Italy, in the fifth month, according to some authors, after leaving New Carthage, having spent fifteen days in crossing the Alps. As to what number of forces Hannibal had when he arrived in Italy, writers by no means agree. Those who state them at the highest make them amount to one hundred thousand foot and twenty thousand horse; while those who state them at the lowest say twenty thousand foot and six of horse. The authority of Lucius Cincius Alimentus, who writes that he was taken prisoner by Hannibal, would have the greatest weight with me, did he not confound the number by adding the Gauls and Ligurians. He says that, including these (who, it is more probable, however, flocked to him afterwards, and so some writers assert), there were brought into Italy eighty thousand foot and ten thousand horse; and that he heard from Hannibal himself, that from the time of his passing the Rhone he had lost thirty-six thousand men, together with a vast number of horses and other beasts of burden, before he left the country of the Taurinians,[3] the next nation to the Gauls as he went down into Italy. That he came to this state is agreed by all. I am therefore the more surprised at its remaining doubtful by what road he crossed the Alps, and that the opinion should commonly prevail that he passed over the Pennine Hill, and that from thence that summit of these mountains got its name.[4] Coelius says that he passed over the hill of Cremo. Either of these passes would have led him not in the territory of the Taurinians, but through that of the mountaineers, called Salluvians, to the Libyan Gauls. Nor is it probable that those roads into Hither Gaul should at that time have been open: those, especially, which led to the Pennine Hill would have been blocked up by nations half German. And besides, if the assertions of the inhabitants be admitted as an argument of any weight, it must be allowed that the Veragrians, the inhabitants of that very hill, deny that the name was given to these mountains from any passage of the Carthaginians, and allege that it was so named from a person, called by the mountaineers Penninus, worshipped as a divinity on the highest peak.

[3] Modern Turin, in northern Italy.
[4] The Carthaginians were called *Poeni*, owing to their Phoenician origin.

TACITUS

Customs of the Germans

The Germans, it is well known, have no regular cities; nor do they allow a continuity of houses. They dwell in separate habitations, dispersed up and down as a grove, a meadow, or a fountain happens to invite. They have villages, but not with a series of connected buildings. Every tenement stands detached, with a vacant piece of ground round it, either to prevent accidents by fire, or for want of skill in the art of building. They do not know the use of mortar or of tiles. They build with rude materials, regardless of beauty, order, and proportion. Particular parts are covered over with a kind of earth so smooth and shining that the natural veins have some resemblance to the lights and shades of painting. Besides these habitations they have a number of subterranean caves, dug by their own labor and carefully covered over with dung: in winter their retreat from cold and the repository of their corn. In those recesses they not only find a shelter from the rigor of the season, but in times of foreign invasion their effects are safely concealed. The enemy lays waste the open country, but the hidden treasure escapes the general ravage; safe in its obscurity, or because the search would be attended with too much trouble.

The clothing in use is a loose mantle, made fast with a clasp, or, when that cannot be had, with a thorn. With only this on they loiter away whole days by the fire-side. The rich wear a more pretentious garment, not however displayed and flowing like the Parthians or the people of Sarmatia, but drawn so tight that the form of the limbs is palpably expressed. The skins of wild animals are also much in use. Near the frontier, on the borders of the Rhine, the inhabitants wear them, but are wholly indifferent as to the choice. The people who live in the more remote regions near the northern seas, and who have not acquired by commerce a taste for new-fashioned apparel, are more careful in their selection. They choose particular beasts, and having stripped off the furs clothe themselves with the spoil, decorated with particolored spots, or fragments taken from the skins of fish that swim the ocean as yet unexplored by the Romans. In point of dress there is no distinction between the sexes, except that the garment of the women is frequently made of linen, adorned with purple spots, but without sleeves, leaving the arms and part of the bosom uncovered.

Marriage is considered as a strict and sacred institution. In the national character there is nothing so truly commendable. To be contented with one wife is peculiar to the Germans. They differ in this respect from all other savage nations. There are indeed a few instances of polygamy; not however the effect of loose desire, but occasioned by the ambition of various families, who court the alliance of a chief distinguished by the nobility of his rank and character. The bride brings no portion, but receives a dowry from her husband. In the presence of her parents and relations he makes a tender of part of his wealth; if accepted, the match is approved. In the choice of the presents female vanity is not consulted. There are no frivolous trinkets to adorn the future bride. The whole fortune consists of oxen, a caparisoned horse, a shield, a spear, and a sword. She in return delivers a present of arms, and by this exchange of gifts the marriage is concluded. This is the nuptial ceremony; this the bond of union; these their hymeneal gods. Lest the wife should think that her sex exempts her from the rigor of the severest virtue and the toils of war, she is informed of her duty by the marriage ceremony; and thence she learns that she is received by her husband to be his partner in toil and danger, to dare with him in war, and suffer with him in peace. The oxen yoked, the horse accoutred, and the arms given on the occasion inculcate this lesson; and thus she is prepared to live, and thus to die. These are the terms of their union: she receives her armor as a sacred treasure, to be preserved inviolate, and transmitted with honor to her sons, a portion for their wives, and from them going down to her grandchildren.

In consequence of these manners the married state is a life of affection and female constancy. The virtue of the woman is guarded from seduction: no public spectacles to seduce her, no banquets to inflame her passions, no baits of pleasure to disarm her virtue. The art of intriguing by clandestine letters is unknown to both sexes. Populous as the country is, adultery is rarely heard of; when detected, the punishment is instant, and inflicted by the husband. He cuts off the hair of his guilty

Tacitus (A.D. 55-120). Translation by Arthur Murphy.

wife, and having assembled her relations expels her naked from his house, pursuing her with stripes through the village. To public loss of honor no favor is shown. She may possess beauty, youth, and riches; but a husband she can never obtain. Vice is not treated by the Germans as a subject of raillery, nor is the profligacy of corrupting and being corrupted called the fashion of the age. By the practice of some [German] states, female virtue is advanced to still higher perfection: with them none but virgins marry. When the bride has fixed her choice, her hopes of matrimony are closed for life. With one husband, as with one life, one mind, one body, every woman is satisfied. In him her happiness is centred, her desires find their limit, and the result is not only affection for the husband's person, but reverence for the married state. To set limits to population by rearing up only a certain number of children, and destroying the rest, is accounted a scandalous crime. Among the savages of Germany virtuous manners operate more than good laws in other countries.

In every family the children are reared in filth. They run about naked, and in time grow up to that strength and size of limb which we behold with wonder. The infant is nourished at the mother's breast, not turned over to nurses and to servants. No distinction is made between the future chieftain and the infant son of a common slave. On the same ground and mixed with the same cattle they pass their days, till the age of manhood draws the line of separation, and early valor shows the person of free birth. It is generally late before their young men come to manhood, nor are the virgins married too soon. Both parties wait to attain their full growth. In due time the match is made, and the children of the marriage have the constitution of their parents. The uncle by the mother's side regards his nephews with an affection not at all inferior to that of their father. With some the relation of the sister's children to their maternal uncle is held to be the strongest tie of consanguinity, so that in demanding hostages that line of kindred is preferred as the most endearing objects of the family and, consequently, the most tender pledges. The son is always heir to his father. Last wills and testaments are not in use. In case of failure of issue, the brothers of the deceased are next in succession, or else the paternal or maternal uncles. A numerous train of relations is the comfort and honor of old age. To live without raising heirs to yourself is no advantage in Germany.

To adopt the quarrels as well as the friendships of your parents and relations is held to be an indispensable duty. In their resentments, however, they are not implacable. Injuries are adjusted by a settled measure of compensation. Atonement is made for homicide by a certain number of cattle, and by that satisfaction the whole family is appeased; a happy regulation and conducive to the public interest, since it serves to curb that spirit of revenge which is the natural result of liberty in the excess. Hospitality and convivial pleasure are nowhere else so liberally enjoyed. To refuse admittance to a guest were an outrage against humanity. The master of the house welcomes every stranger, and regales him to the best of his ability. If his stock falls short, he becomes a visitor to his neighbor, and conducts his new acquaintance to a more plentiful table. They do not wait to be invited, nor is this of any consequence, since a cordial reception is always certain. Between an intimate and an entire stranger no distinction is made. The law of hospitality is the same. The departing guest receives as a present whatever he desires, and the host retaliates by asking with the same freedom. A German delights in the gifts which he receives, yet by bestowing he imputes nothing to you as a favor, and for what he receives he acknowledges no obligation.

In this manner the Germans pride themselves on their frankness and generosity. Their hours of rest are protracted to broad daylight. As soon as they rise, they bathe, generally, on account of the intense severity of the climate, in warm water. They then betake themselves to their meal, each on a separate seat and at his own table. Having finished their repast they proceed completely armed to the despatch of business, and frequently to a convivial meeting. To devote both day and night to deep drinking is a disgrace to no man. Disputes, as will be the case with people in liquor, frequently arise, and are seldom confined to opprobrious language. The quarrel generally ends in a scene of blood. Important subjects, such as the reconciliation of enemies, the forming of family alliances, the election of chiefs, and even peace and war, are generally canvassed in their carousing festivals. The convivial moment, according to their notion, is the true season for business, when the mind opens itself in plain simplicity, or grows warm with bold and noble ideas. Strangers to artifice and knowing no refinement, they tell their sentiments without disguise. The pleasure of the table expands their hearts and calls forth every secret. On the following day the subject of debate is again taken into consideration, and thus two different periods of time have their distinct uses: when warm, they debate; when cool, they decide.

Their beverage is a liquor drawn from barley or from wheat, and, like the juice of the grape, fermented to a spirit. The settlers on the banks of the Rhine provide themselves with wine. Their food is of the simplest kind: wild apples, the flesh of an animal recently killed, or coagulated milk. Without skill in cookery, or without seasoning to stimulate the palate, they eat to satisfy nature. But they do not drink merely to quench their thirst. Indulge their love of liquor to the excess which they require, and you need not employ the terror of your arms; their own vices will subdue them.

Their public spectacles boast of no variety. They have but one sort, and that they repeat at all their meetings. A band of young men make it their pastime to dance entirely naked amidst pointed swords and javelins. By constant exercise this kind of exhibition has become an art, and art has taught them to perform with grace and elegance. Their talents, however, are not let out for hire. Though some danger attends the practice, the pleasure of the spectator is their only recompense. In the character of a German there is nothing so remarkable as his passion for play. Without the excuse of liquor, strange as it may seem, in their cool and sober moments they have recourse to dice, as to a serious and regular business, with the most desperate spirit committing their whole substance to chance, and when they have lost their all, putting their liberty and even their persons on the last hazard of the die! The loser yields himself to slavery. Young, robust, and valiant, he submits to be chained, and even exposed to sale. Such is the effect of a ruinous and inveterate habit. They are victims to folly, and they call themselves men of honor. The winner is always in a hurry to barter away the slaves acquired by success at play; he is ashamed of his victory, and therefore puts away the remembrance of it as soon as possible.

The slaves in general are not arranged at their several employments in the household affairs, as is the practice at Rome. Each has his separate habitation, and his own establishment to manage. The master considers him as an agrarian dependent, who is obliged to furnish a certain quantity of grain, cattle, or wearing apparel. The slave obeys, and the state of servitude extends no further. All domestic affairs are managed by the master's wife and children. To punish a slave with stripes, to load him with chains or condemn him to hard labor is unusual. It is true that slaves are sometimes put to death, not under color of justice, or of any authority vested in the master, but in transport of passion, in a fit of rage, as is often the case in a sudden affray; but it is also true that this species of homicide passes with impunity. The freedmen are not of much higher consideration than the actual slaves; they obtain no rank in the master's family, and, if we except the parts of Germany where monarchy is established, they never figure on the stage of public business. In despotic governments they rise above the men of ingenuous birth, and even eclipse the whole body of the nobles. In other states the subordination of the freedmen is a proof of public liberty.

The practice of placing money at interest and reaping the profits of usury is unknown in Germany; and that happy ignorance is a better preventive of the evil than a code of prohibitory laws. In cultivating the soil they do not settle on one spot, but shift from place to place. The state or community takes possession of a certain tract proportioned to its number of hands; allotments are afterwards made to individuals according to their rank and dignity. In so extensive a country, where there is no want of land, the partition is easily made. The ground tilled in one year lies fallow the next, and a sufficient quantity always remains, the labor of the people being by no means adequate to the extent or fertility of the soil. Nor have they the skill to make orchard plantations, to enclose the meadow grounds, or to lay out and water gardens. From the earth they demand nothing but grain. Hence their year is not, as with the Romans, divided into four seasons. They have distinct ideas of winter, spring, and summer, and their language has terms for each; but they neither know the blessings nor the name of autumn.

Their funerals have neither pomp nor vain ambition. When the bodies of illustrious men are to be burned, they choose a particular kind of wood for the purpose, and have no other attention. The funeral pile is neither strewed with garments nor enriched with fragrant spices. The arms of the deceased are committed to the flames, and sometimes his horse. A mound of turf is raised to his memory; and this, in their opinion, is a better sepulchre than those structures of labored grandeur which display the weakness of human vanity, and are at best a burden to the dead. Tears and lamentations are soon at an end, but their regret does not so easily wear away. To grieve for the departed is comely in the softer sex. The women weep for their friends; the men remember them.

ROMAN STORY-TELLERS

Story-telling is one of the oldest forms of literary activity; it cannot be regarded as the monopoly or invention of any single nation. The folktales of the Greeks found their way into the Homeric epics, lyric poetry, and drama, and were variously transformed; that is, they did not retain the form of folktales. An interesting minor achievement of Roman literature was the retelling of these stories in a manner so graceful and engaging that they achieve a place in our literary heritage.

The name of Ovid (43 B.C.-A.D. 17) is inseparable from many of the tales and myths of the Greco-Roman world. Perhaps he acquired his narrative gift at his native hearth, for he was born at Sulmo in the mountains more than a hundred miles east of Rome, where no doubt the love of yarn-spinning was as strong as in other outlying provinces. Plunging into the social whirl after his education at Rome and Athens, Ovid (Publius Ovidius Naso) wrote fashionable love poetry. His early *Amores* were erotic lyrics, his *Heroides* a series of imaginary letters from deserted women to their lovers, and his *Art of Love* an amusing and sophisticated treatise. These vivacious verses earned him prosperity and social success. Finally, his reputation as a lyricist was strengthened by a book of laments, *Tristitia,* written while he lived in exile on the shores of the Black Sea, to which he had been banished by Augustus for some scandalous affair.

He was at his best, however, as a story-teller, and it is his series of short narrative poems, known as the *Metamorphoses,* that ultimately assured him a niche in literature's Hall of Fame. In this book, Ovid brings together the stories from the old myths in which persons or objects change their form and substance. His descriptive and imaginative powers, rich figures of speech, fluency, and clever transitions make this work a remarkable feat, beguiling both as narration and poetry. In the case of many ancient myths, Ovid's versions became the standard ones for the literary world of later times, and the *Metamorphoses* remained a source for European poets from the Renaissance to the nineteenth century. Ovid exerted a vast influence on them as a fabulist and as an erotic poet. Both Marlowe and Shakespeare became his debtors.

What we have in Apuleius, who wrote around A.D. 150, is the elaboration of folktales rather than myths. These tales are common to many countries and some are world-wide. There is no doubt that those he used were as current in the Italy of his day as they are in ours. In such a story as *Cupid and Psyche,* Apuleius has taken an ordinary folktale of a girl with a supernatural husband and has connected it with Greek mythology, so that his hero and heroine have relation to the gods. The folklore that produced the story has been greatly sophisticated here and made a part of a long, elaborate tale called *The Golden Ass.* In this work, a late product of classic culture, we meet a prose romance, a type of writing found more abundantly in medieval than in classic literature. *The Golden Ass,* also known as *The Metamorphoses,* recounts the strange adventures of a certain Lucius, who was transformed into an ass by a magic potion, but who retained his human intelligence. In the course of his odd experiences, Lucius overhears the tale of Cupid and Psyche as it is told in a robbers' cave to a captive girl.

That Lucius Apuleius should have been an exotic writer, opulent in style and interested in magic, is not strange. He belonged to the Roman Empire rather than to Rome, for he was born in Northern Africa and educated at Carthage and Athens. Like Ovid's *Metamorphoses,* Apuleius' romance became a source-book for later generations.

OVID

Metamorphoses

Pygmalion and Galatea

When Pygmalion saw women spending their lives in criminal pursuits, shocked at the vices which Nature had *so* plentifully imparted to the female disposition, he lived a single life without a wife, and for a long time was without a partner of his bed. In the meantime, he ingeniously carved *a statue of* snow-white ivory with wondrous skill; and gave it a beauty with which no woman can be born; and *then* conceived a passion for his own workmanship. The appearance was that of a real virgin, whom you might suppose to be alive, and if modesty did not hinder her, to be desirous to move; so much did art lie concealed under his skill. Pygmalion admires it; and entertains, within his breast, a flame for this fictitious body.

Often does he apply his hands to the work, to try whether it is a *human* body, or whether it is ivory; and yet he does not own it to be ivory. He gives it kisses, and fancies that they are returned, and speaks to it, and takes hold of it, and thinks that his fingers make an impression on the limbs which they touch, and is fearful lest a livid mark should come on her limbs *when* pressed. And one while he employs soft expressions, at another time he brings her presents that are agreeable to maidens, *such as* shells, and smooth pebbles, and little birds, and flowers of a thousand tints, and lilies, and painted balls, and tears of the Heliades, that have fallen from the trees. He decks her limbs, too, with clothing, and puts jewels on her fingers; he puts, *too,* a long necklace on her neck. Smooth pendants hang from her ears, and bows from her breast. All things are becoming *to her;* and she does not seem less beautiful than when naked. He places her on coverings dyed with the Sidonian shell, and calls her the companion of his bed, and lays down her reclining neck upon soft feathers, as though it were sensible.

A festival of Venus, much celebrated throughout all Cyprus, had *now* come; and heifers, with snow-white necks, having their spreading horns tipped with gold, fell, struck *by the ax.* Frankincense, too, was smoking, when, having made his offering, Pygmalion stood before the altar, and timorously said, "If ye Gods can grant all things, let my wife be, I pray," *and* he did not dare to say "this ivory maid," *but* "like to this *statue* of ivory." The golden Venus, as she herself was present at her own festival, understood what that prayer meant; and as an omen of the Divinity being favorable, thrice was the flame kindled up, and it sent up a tapering flame into the air. Soon as he returned, he repaired to the image of his maiden, and, lying along the couch, he gave her kisses. She seems to grow warm. Again he applies his mouth; with his hands, too, he feels her breast. The pressed ivory becomes soft, and losing its hardness, yields to the fingers, and gives way, just as Hymettian wax grows soft in the sun, and being worked with the fingers is turned into many shapes, and becomes pliable by the very handling. While he is amazed, and is rejoicing, *though* with apprehension, and is fearing that he is deceived; the lover again and again touches the object of his desires with his hand. It is a *real* body; the veins throb, when touched with the thumb.

Then, indeed, the Paphian hero conceives *in his mind* the most lavish expressions, with which to give thanks to Venus, and at length presses lips, no *longer* fictitious, with his own lips. The maiden, too, feels the kisses given her, and blushes; and raising her timorous eyes towards the light *of day,* she sees at once her lover and the heavens. The Goddess was present at the marriage which she *thus* effected. And now, the horns of the moon having been nine times gathered into a full orb, she brought forth Paphos; from whom the island derived its name.

Pluto and Proserpine

Not far from the walls of Henna there is a lake of deep water, Pergus by name; Cayster does not hear more songs of swans, in his running streams, than

Ovid, *Pygmalion and Galatea.* Translated by H. T. Riley. Publius Ovidius Naso (43 B.C.-17 A.D.) was born at Sulmo in the mountains more than a hundred miles east of Rome. Educated in Rome he led a gay social life there until he was exiled to the wild country on the Black Sea, where he spent the last nine years of his life. Aside from his *Metamorphoses* his most famous work is *The Art of Love.*
Ovid, *Pluto and Proserpine.* Translated by H. T. Riley.

that. A wood skirts the lake, surrounding it on every side, and with its foliage, as though with an awning, keeps out the rays of the sun. The boughs produce a coolness, the moist ground flowers of Tyrian hue. *There* the spring is perpetual. In this grove, while Proserpine is amusing herself, and is plucking either violets or white lilies, and while, with child-like eagerness, she is filling her baskets and her bosom, and is striving to out-do *her companions* of the same age in gathering, almost at the same instant she is beheld, beloved, and seized by Pluto; in such great haste is love. The Goddess, affrighted, with lamenting lips calls both her mother and her companions, but more frequently her mother; and as she has torn her garment from the upper edge, the collected flowers fall from her loosened robes. So great, too, is the innocence of her childish years, this loss excites the maiden's grief as well. The ravisher drives on his chariot, and encourages his horses, called, each by his name, along whose necks and manes he shakes the reins, dyed with swarthy rust. He is borne through deep lakes, and the pools of the Palici, smelling strong of sulphur, *and* boiling fresh from out of the burst earth; and where the Bacchiadæ, a race sprung from Corinth, with its two seas, built a city between unequal harbors.

There is a stream in the middle, between Cyane and the Pisæan Arethusa, which is confined within itself, being enclosed by mountain ridges at a short distance *from each other.* Here was Cyane, the most celebrated among the Sicilian Nymphs, from whose name the pool also was called, who stood up from out of the midst of the water, as far as the higher part of her stomach, and recognized the God, and said, "No further shall you go. Thou mayst not be the son-in-law of Ceres against her will. *The girl* should have been asked *of her*

mother, not carried away. But if I may be allowed to compare little matters with great ones, Anapis also loved me. Yet I married him, courted, and not frightened *into it,* like her." She *thus* said, and stretching her arms on different sides, she stood in his way. The son of Saturn no longer restrained his rage; and encouraging his terrible steeds, he threw his royal scepter, hurled with a strong arm, into the lowest depths of the stream. The earth, *thus* struck, made a way down to Tartarus, and received the descending chariot in the middle of the yawning space. But Cyane, lamenting both the ravished Goddess, and the slighted privileges of her spring, carries in her silent mind an inconsolable wound, and is entirely dissolved into tears, and melts away into those waters, of which she had been but lately the great guardian Divinity. You might see her limbs soften, her bones become subjected to bending, her nails lay aside their hardness: each, too, of the smaller extremities of the whole of her body melts away; both her azure hair, her fingers, her legs, and her feet; for easy is the change of those small members into a cold stream. After that, her back, her shoulders, her side, and her breast dissolve, vanishing into thin rivulets. Lastly, pure water, instead of live blood, enters her corrupted veins, and nothing remains which you can grasp *in your hands.*

In the meantime, throughout all lands and in every sea, the daughter is sought in vain by her anxious mother. Aurora, coming with her ruddy locks, does not behold her taking any rest, neither does Hesperus. She, with her two hands, sets light to some pines at the flaming Ætna, and giving herself no rest, bears them through the frosty darkness. Again when the genial day has dulled the light of the stars, she seeks her daughter from the rising of the sun to the setting thereof.

Pyramus and Thisbe

In Babylon, where first her queen, for state,
Rais'd walls of brick magnificently great,
Liv'd Pyramus and Thisbe, lovely pair!
He found no eastern youth his equal there,
And she beyond the fairest nymph was fair.   5
A closer neighborhood was never known,
Though two the houses, yet the roof was one.
Acquaintance grew, th' acquaintance they improve
To friendship, friendship ripen'd into love:
Love had been crown'd, but impotently mad,   10
What parents could not hinder, they forbade.

For with fierce flames young Pyramus still burn'd;
Aloud in words their thoughts they dare not break,
But silent stand; and silent looks can speak.
The fire of love, the more it is supprest,   15
The more it glows, and rages in the breast.
When the division-wall was built, a chink
Was left, the cement unobserv'd to shrink.
So slight the cranny, that it still had been
For centuries unclos'd, because unseen.   20
But oh! what thing so small, so secret lies,
Which 'scapes, if form'd for love, a lover's eyes?
Ev'n in this narrow chink they quickly found
A friendly passage for a trackless sound.

Ovid, *Pyramus and Thisbe.* Translated by Laurence Eusden.

Safely they told their sorrows, and their joys,   25
In whisper'd murmurs, and a dying noise
By turns to catch each other's breath they strove,
And suck'd in all the balmy breeze of love.
Oft as on diff'rent sides they stood, they cry'd,
"Malicious wall, thus lovers to divide!   30
Suppose, thou should'st awhile to us give place
To lock, and fashion in a close embrace:
But if too much to grant so sweet a bliss,
Indulge at least the pleasure of a kiss.
We scorn ingratitude: to thee, we know,   35
This conveyance of our minds we owe."
    Thus they their vain petition did renew
Till night, and then they softly sigh'd adieu.
But first they strove to kiss, and that was all;
Their kisses died untasted on the wall.   40
Soon as the morn had o'er the stars prevail'd,
And, warm'd by Phœbus, flow'rs their dews ex-
    haled,
The lovers to their well-known place return,
Alike they suffer, and alike they mourn.
At last their parents they resolve to cheat   45
(If to deceive in love be called deceit),
To steal by night from home, and thence unknown
To seek the fields, and quit th' unfaithful town.
But, to prevent their wand'ring in the dark,
They both agree to fix upon a mark;   50
A mark, that could not their designs expose:
The tomb of Ninus was the mark they chose.
There they might rest secure beneath the shade,
Which boughs, with snowy fruit encumber'd,
    made:
A wide-spread mulberry its rise had took   55
Just on the margin of a gurgling brook.
Impatient for the friendly dusk they stay,
And chide the slowness of departing day;
In western seas down sunk at last the light.
From western seas uprose the shades of night.   60
The loving Thisbe ev'n prevents the hour,
With cautious silence she unlocks the door,
And veils her face, and marching thro' the gloom
Swiftly arrives at th' assignation-tomb.
For still the fearful sex can fearless prove;   65
Boldly they act, if spirited by love.
When lo! a lioness rush'd o'er the plain,
Grimly besmear'd with blood of oxen slain:
And what to the dire sight new horrors brought,
To slake her thirst the neighb'ring spring she
    sought,   70
Which, by the Moon, when trembling Thisbe
    spies,
Wing'd with her fear, swift as the wind, she flies;

And in a cave recovers from her fright,
But dropt her veil, confounded in her flight.
When sated with repeated draughts, again   75
The queen of beasts scour'd back along the plain,
She found the veil, and mouthing it all o'er,
With bloody jaws the lifeless prey she tore.
    The youth, who could not cheat his guards so
        soon,
Late came, and noted by the glimmering Moon
Some savage feet, now printed on the ground,   81
His cheeks turn'd pale, his limbs no vigor found:
But when advancing on, the veil he spy'd
Distain'd with blood, and ghastly torn, he cry'd,
"One night shall death to two young lovers give,
But she deserv'd unnumber'd years to live!   86
'Tis I am guilty, I have thee betray'd,
Who came not early, as my charming maid.
Whatever slew thee, I the cause remain;
I nam'd, and fix'd the place where thou wast slain.
Ye lions, from your neighb'ring dens repair,   91
Pity the wretch, this impious body tear!
But cowards thus for death can idly cry;
The brave still have it in their pow'r to die."
Then to the appointed tree he hastes away,   95
The veil first gather'd, though all rent it lay:
The veil all rent yet still endears,
He kiss'd and kissing, wash'd it with his tears.
"Tho' rich," he cry'd, "with many a precious stain,
Still from my blood a deeper tincture gain."   100
Then in his breast his shining sword he drown'd,
And fell supine, extended on the ground.
As out again the blade he dying drew,
Out spun the blood, and streaming upwards flew.
So if a conduit-pipe e'er burst you saw,   105
Swift spring the gushing waters thro' the flaw:
Then spouting in a bow, they rise on high,
And a new fountain plays amid the sky.
The berries, stain'd with blood, began to show
A dark complexion, and forgot their snow;   110
While fatten'd with the flowing gore, the root
Was doom'd for ever to a purple fruit.
    Meantime poor Thisbe fear'd, so long she stay'd,
Her lover might suspect a perjur'd maid.
Her fright scarce o'er, she strove the youth to find,
With ardent eyes, which spoke an ardent mind.
Already in his arms, she hears him sigh   117
At her destruction, which was once so nigh.
The tomb, the tree, but not the fruit she knew;
The fruit she doubted for its alter'd hue.   120
Still as she doubts, her eyes a body found
Quiv'ring in death, and gasping on the ground.
She started back, the red her cheeks forsook,
And ev'ry nerve with thrilling horrors shook.

So trembles the smooth surface of the seas,   125
If brush'd o'er gently with a rushing breeze.
But when her view her bleeding love confess'd,
She shriek'd, she tore her hair, she beat her breast.
She rais'd the body, and embrac'd it round,
And bath'd with tears unfeign'd the gaping
    wound.   130
Then her warm lips to the cold face apply'd;
"And is it thus, ah! thus we meet?" she cry'd:
"My Pyramus! whence sprung the cruel fate?
My Pyramus!—ah! speak, ere 'tis too late.
I, thy own Thisbe, but one word implore,   135
One word thy Thisbe never ask'd before."
At Thisbe's name, awak'd, he open'd wide
His dying eyes; with dying eyes he try'd
On her to dwell, but clos'd them slow, and died.
    The fatal cause was now at last explor'd,   140
Her veil she knew, she saw his sheathless sword:
"From thy own hand thy ruin thou hast found,"
She said; "but love first taught that hand to wound.
Ev'n I for thee as bold a hand can show,
And love, which shall as true direct the blow.   145
I will against the woman's weakness strive,

And never thee, lamented youth, survive.
The world may say, I caus'd, alas! thy death,
But saw thee breathless, and resign'd my breath
Fate, tho' it conquers, shall no triumph gain,   150
Fate, that divides us, still divides in vain.
Now, both our cruel parents, hear my pray'r;
My pray'r to offer for us both I dare;
Oh! see our ashes in one urn confin'd,
Whom Love at first, and Fate at last has join'd.
The bliss, you envy'd, is not our request;   156
Lovers when dead, may sure together rest.
Thou, tree, where now one lifeless lump is laid,
Ere long o'er two shalt cast a friendly shade.
Still let our loves from thee be understood,   160
Still witness in thy purple fruit our blood."
She spoke, and in her bosom plung'd the sword
All warm and reeking from its slaughter'd lord.
    The pray'r, which dying Thisbe had preferr'd,
Both gods, and parents, with compassion heard.
The whiteness of the mulberry soon fled,   166
And, ripening, sadden'd in a dusky red:
While both their parents their lost children mourn,
And mix their ashes in one golden urn.

APULEIUS

Cupid and Psyche

In a certain city lived a king and queen who had three daughters exceeding fair. But the beauty of the elder sisters, though pleasant to behold, yet passed not the measure of human praise, while such was the loveliness of the youngest that men's speech was too poor to commend it worthily and could express it not at all. Many of the citizens and of strangers, whom the fame of this excellent vision had gathered thither, confounded by that matchless beauty, could but kiss the finger-tips of their right hands at sight of her, as in adoration to the goddess Venus herself. And soon a rumor passed through the country that she whom the blue deep had borne, forbearing her divine dignity, was even then moving among men, or that by some fresh germination from the stars, not the

sea now, but the earth, had put forth a new Venus, endued with the flower of virginity.

This belief, with the fame of the maiden's loveliness, went daily further into distant lands, so that many people were drawn together to behold that glorious model of the age. Men sailed no longer to Paphos, to Cnidos or Cythera, to the presence of the goddess Venus: her sacred rites were neglected, her images stood uncrowned, the cold ashes were left to disfigure her forsaken altars. It was to a maiden that men's prayers were offered, to a human countenance they looked, in propitiating so great a godhead: when the girl went forth in the morning they strewed flowers on her way, and the victims proper to that unseen goddess were presented as she passed along. This conveyance of

Apuleius, *Cupid and Psyche*. Translated by Walter Pater. Lucius Apuleius was born about 125 A.D. in northern Africa and, aside from some years when he practiced law in Rome, lived his life there. The *Cupid and Psyche* is part of a longer work, the *Metamorphoses*, in which the hero, transformed to an ass, experiences many adventures.

divine worship to a mortal kindled meantime the anger of the true Venus. "Lo! now, the ancient parent of nature," she cried, "the fountain of all elements! Behold me, Venus, benign mother of the world, sharing my honors with a mortal maiden, while my name, built up in heaven, is profaned by the mean things of earth! Shall a perishable woman bear my image about with her? In vain did the shepherd of Ida prefer me! Yet shall she have little joy, whosoever she be, of her usurped and unlawful loveliness!" Thereupon she called to her that winged, bold boy, of evil ways, who wanders armed by night through men's houses, spoiling their marriages; and stirring yet more by her speech his inborn wantonness, she led him to the city, and showed him Psyche as she walked.

"I pray thee," she said, "give thy mother a full revenge. Let this maid become the slave of an unworthy love." Then, embracing him closely, she departed to the shore and took her throne upon the crest of the wave. And lo! at her unuttered will, her ocean-servants are in waiting: the daughters of Nereus are there singing their song, and Portunus, and Salacia, and the tiny charioteer of the dolphin, with a host of Tritons leaping through the billows. And one blows softly through his sounding sea-shell, another spreads a silken web against the sun, a third presents the mirror to the eyes of his mistress, while the others swim side by side below, drawing her chariot. Such was the escort of Venus as she went upon the sea.

Psyche meantime, aware of her loveliness, had no fruit thereof. All people regarded and admired, but none sought her in marriage. It was but as on the finished work of the craftsman that they gazed upon that divine likeness. Her sisters, less fair than she, were happily wedded. She, even as a widow, sitting at home, wept over her desolation, hating in her heart the beauty in which all men were pleased.

And the king, supposing the gods were angry, inquired of the oracle of Apollo, and Apollo answered him thus: "Let the damsel be placed on the top of a certain mountain, adorned as for the bed of marriage, and of death. Look not for a son-in-law of mortal birth; but for that evil serpent-thing, by reason of whom even the gods tremble and the shadows of Styx are afraid."

So the king returned home and made known the oracle to his wife. For many days she lamented, but at last the fulfillment of the divine precept is urgent upon her, and the company make ready to conduct the maiden to her deadly bridal. And now the nuptial torch gathers dark smoke and ashes: the pleasant sound of the pipe is changed into a cry: the marriage hymn concludes in a sorrowful wailing: below her yellow wedding-veil the bride shook away her tears; insomuch that the whole city was afflicted together at the ill-luck of the stricken house.

But the mandate of the god impelled the hapless Psyche to her fate, and, these solemnities being ended, the funeral of the living soul goes forth, all the people following. Psyche, bitterly weeping, assists not at her marriage but at her own obsequies, and while the parents hesitate to accomplish a thing so unholy the daughter cries to them: "Wherefore torment your luckless age by long weeping? This was the prize of my extraordinary beauty! When all people celebrated us with divine honors, and in one voice named the New Venus, it was then ye should have wept for me as one dead. Now at last I understand that that one name of Venus has been my ruin. Lead me and set me upon the appointed place. I am in haste to submit to that well-omened marriage, to behold that goodly spouse. Why delay the coming of him who was born for the destruction of the whole world?"

She was silent, and with firm step went on the way. And they proceeded to the appointed place on a steep mountain, and left there the maiden alone, and took their way homewards dejectedly. The wretched parents, in their close-shut house, yielded themselves to perpetual night; while to Psyche, fearful and trembling and weeping sore upon the mountain-top, comes the gentle Zephyrus. He lifts her mildly, and, with vesture afloat on either side, bears her by his own soft breathing over the windings of the hills, and sets her lightly among the flowers in the bosom of a valley below.

Psyche, in those delicate grassy places, lying sweetly on her dewy bed, rested from the agitation of her soul and arose in peace. And lo! a grove of mighty trees, with a fount of water, clear as glass, in the midst; and hard by the water, a dwelling-place, built not by human hands but by some divine cunning. One recognized, even at the entering, the delightful hostelry of a god. Golden pillars sustained the roof, arched most curiously in cedar-wood and ivory. The walls were hidden under wrought silver,—all tame and woodland creatures leaping forward to the visitor's gaze. Wonderful indeed was the craftsman, divine or half-divine, who by the subtlety of his art had breathed so wild a soul into the silver! The very pavement was distinct with pictures in goodly stones. In the glow of its precious metal the house is its own daylight, having no need of the sun. Well might it seem a place fashioned for the conversation of gods with men!

Psyche, drawn forward by the delight of it, came near, and, her courage growing, stood within the doorway. One by one, she admired the beautiful things she saw; and, most wonderful of all! no lock, no chain, nor living guardian protected that great treasure-house. But as she gazed there came a voice,—a voice, as it were, unclothed by bodily vesture. "Mistress!" it said, "all these things are thine. Lie down, and relieve thy weariness, and rise again for the bath when thou wilt. We thy servants, whose voice thou hearest, will be beforehand with our service, and a royal feast shall be ready."

And Psyche understood that some divine care was providing, and, refreshed with sleep and the bath, sat down to the feast. Still she saw no one: only she heard words falling here and there, and had voices alone to serve her. And the feast being ended, one entered the chamber and sang to her unseen, while another struck the chords of a harp, invisible with him who played on it. Afterwards the sound of a company singing together came to her, but still so that none was present to sight, yet it appeared that a great multitude of singers was there. . . .

One night the bridegroom spoke thus to his beloved, "O Psyche, most pleasant bride! Fortune is grown stern with us, and threatens thee with mortal peril. Thy sisters, troubled at the report of thy death and seeking some trace of thee, will come to the mountain's top. But if by chance their cries reach thee, answer not, neither look forth at all, lest thou bring sorrow upon me and destruction upon thyself." Then Psyche promised that she would do according to his will. But the bridegroom was fled away again with the night. And all that day she spent in tears, repeating that she was now dead indeed, shut up in that golden prison, powerless to console her sisters sorrowing after her, or to see their faces; and so went to rest weeping.

And after a while came the bridegroom again, and embracing her as she wept, complained, "Was this thy promise, my Psyche? What have I to hope from thee? Even in the arms of thy husband thou ceasest not from pain. Do now as thou wilt. Indulge thine own desire, though it seeks what will ruin thee. Yet wilt thou remember my warning, repentant too late." Then, protesting that she is like to die, she obtains from him that he suffer her to see her sisters, and present to them moreover what gifts she would of golden ornaments; but therewith he ofttimes advised her never at any time yielding to pernicious counsel, to inquire concerning his bodily form, lest she fall, through unholy curiosity, from so great a height of fortune, nor feel ever his embrace again. "I would die a hundred times," she said, cheerfully at last, "rather than be deprived of thy most sweet usage. I love thee as my own soul, beyond comparison even with Love himself. Only bid thy servant Zephyrus bring hither my sisters, as he brought me. My honeycomb! My Husband! Thy Psyche's breath of life!" So he promised; and ere the light appeared, vanished from the hands of his bride.

And the sisters, coming to the place where Psyche was abandoned, wept loudly among the rocks, and called upon her by name, so that the sound came down to her, and running out of the palace distraught, she cried, "Wherefore afflict your souls with lamentation? I whom you mourn am here." Then, summoning Zephyrus, she reminded him of her husband's bidding; and he bare them down with a gentle blast. "Enter now," she said, "into my house, and relieve your sorrow in the company of Psyche your sister."

And Psyche displayed to them all the treasures of the golden house, and its great family of ministering voices, nursing in them the malice which was already at their hearts. And at last one of them asks curiously who the lord of that celestial array may be, and what manner of man her husband. And Psyche answered dissemblingly, "A young man, handsome and mannerly, with a goodly beard. For the most part he hunts upon the mountains." And lest the secret should slip from her in the way of further speech, loading her sisters with gold and gems, she commanded Zephyrus to bear them away.

And they returned home, on fire with envy. "See now the injustice of fortune!" cried one. "We, the elder children, are given like servants to be the wives of strangers, while the youngest is possessed of so great riches, who scarcely knows how to use them. You saw, sister! what a hoard of wealth lies in the house; what glittering gowns; what splendor of precious gems, besides all that gold trodden under foot. If she indeed has, as she said, a bridegroom so goodly then no one in all the world is happier. And it may be that this husband, being of divine nature, will make her too a goddess. Nay, so in truth it is. It was even thus she bore herself. Already she looks aloft and breathes divinity, who, though but a woman, has voices for her handmaidens, and can command the winds." "Think," answered the other, "how arrogantly she dealt with us, grudging us these trifling gifts out of all that store, and when our company became a burden, causing us to be hissed and driven away from her through the air! But I am no woman if she keep her hold on this great fortune; and if the insult done us has touched thee too, take we counsel together. Meanwhile let us hold our peace, and know nought of her, alive or dead. For they are not truly happy of whose happiness other folk are unaware."

And the bridegroom, whom still she knows not, warns her thus a second time, as he talks with her by night: "Seest thou what peril besets thee? Those cunning wolves have made ready for thee their snares, of which the sum is that they persuade thee to search into the fashion of my countenance, the seeing of which, as I have told thee often, will be the seeing of it no more forever. But do thou neither listen nor make answer to ought regarding thy husband. Besides, we have sown also the seed of our race. Even now this bosom grows with a child to be born to us, a child, if thou but keep our secret, of divine quality; if thou profane it, subject to death." And Psyche was glad at the tidings, rejoicing in that solace of a divine seed, and in the glory of that pledge of love to be, and the dignity of the name of mother. Anxiously she notes the increase of the days, the waning months. And again, as he tarries briefly beside her, the bridegroom repeats his warning: "Even now the sword is drawn with which thy sisters seek thy life. Have pity on thyself, sweet wife, and upon our child, and see not those evil women again." But the sisters make their way into the palace once more, crying to her in wily tones, "O Psyche! and thou too wilt be a mother! How great will be the joy at home! Happy indeed shall we be to have the nursing of the golden child. Truly if he be answerable to the beauty of his parents, it will be a birth of Cupid himself."

So, little by little, they stole upon the heart of their sister. She, meanwhile, bids the lyre to sound for their delight, and the playing is heard: she bids the pipes to move, the quire to sing, and the music and the singing come invisibly, soothing the mind of the listener with sweetest modulation. Yet not even thereby was their malice put to sleep: once

more they seek to know what manner of husband she has, and whence that seed. And Psyche, simple over-much, forgetful of her first story, answers, "My husband comes from a far country, trading for great sums. He is already of middle age, with whitening locks." And therewith she dismisses them again.

And returning home upon the soft breath of Zephyrus one cried to the other, "What shall be said of so ugly a lie? He who was a young man with goodly beard is now in middle life. It must be that she told a false tale: else is she in very truth ignorant of what manner of man he is. Howsoever it be, let us destroy her quickly. For if she indeed knows not, be sure that her bridegroom is one of the gods: it is a god she bears in her womb. And let that be far from us! If she be called the mother of a god, then will life be more than I can bear."

So, full of rage against her, they returned to Psyche, and said to her craftily, "Thou livest in an ignorant bliss, all incurious of thy real danger. It is a deadly serpent, as we certainly know, that comes to sleep at thy side. Remember the words of the oracle, which declared thee destined to a cruel beast. There are those who have seen it at nightfall, coming back from its feeding. In no long time, they say, it will end its blandishments. It but waits for the babe to be formed in thee, that it may devour thee by so much the richer. If indeed the solitude of this musical place, or it may be the loathsome commerce of a hidden love, delight thee, we at least in sisterly piety have done our part." And at last the unhappy Psyche, simple and frail of soul, carried away by the terror of their words, losing memory of her husband's precepts and her own promise, brought upon herself a great calamity. Trembling and turning pale, she answers them, "And they who tell those things, it may be, speak the truth. For in very deed never have I seen the face of my husband, nor know I at all what manner of man he is. Always he frights me diligently from the sight of him, threatening some great evil should I too curiously look upon his face. Do ye, if ye can help your sister in her great peril, stand by her now."

Her sisters answered her, "The way of safety we have well considered, and will teach thee. Take a sharp knife, and hide it in that part of the couch where thou art wont to lie: take also a lamp filled with oil, and set it privily behind the curtain. And when he shall have drawn up his coils into the accustomed place, and thou hearest him breathe in sleep, slip then from his side and discover the lamp, and, knife in hand, put forth thy strength, and strike off the serpent's head." And so they departed in haste.

And Psyche left alone (alone but for the furies which beset her) is tossed up and down in her distress, like a wave of the sea; and though her will is firm, yet, in the moment of putting hand to the deed, she falters, and is torn asunder by various apprehensions of the great calamity upon her. She hastens and anon delays, now full of distrust, and now of angry courage: under one bodily form she loathes the monster and loves the bridegroom. But twilight ushers in the night; and at length in haste she makes ready for the terrible deed. Darkness came, and the bridegroom; and he first falls into a deep sleep.

And she, erewhile of no strength, the hard purpose of destiny assisting her, is confirmed in force. With lamp plucked forth, knife in hand, she put by her sex; and lo! as the secrets of the bed became manifest, the sweetest and most gentle of all creatures, Love himself, reclined there, in his own proper loveliness! At sight of him the very flame of the lamp kindled more gladly! But Psyche was afraid of the vision, and, faint of soul, trembled back upon her knees, and would have hidden the steel in her own bosom. But the knife slipped from her hand; and now, undone, yet ofttimes looking upon the beauty of that divine countenance, she lives again. She sees the locks of that golden head, pleasant with the unction of the gods, shed down in graceful entanglement behind and before, about the ruddy cheeks and white throat. The pinions of the winged god, yet fresh with the dew, are spotless upon his shoulders, the delicate plumage wavering over them as they lie at rest. Smooth he was, and touched with light, worthy of Venus his mother. At the foot of the couch lay his bow and arrows, the instruments of his power, propitious to men.

And Psyche, gazing hungrily thereon, draws an arrow from the quiver, and trying the point upon the thumb, tremulous still, drave in the barb, so that a drop of blood came forth. Thus fell she, by her own act, and unaware, into the love of Love. Falling upon the bridegroom, with indrawn breath, in a hurry of kisses from eager and open lips, she shuddered as she thought how brief that sleep might be. And it chanced that a drop of burning oil fell from the lamp upon the god's shoulder. Ah! maladroit minister of love, thus to wound him from whom all fire comes; though

'twas a lover, I trow, first devised thee, to have the fruit of his desire even in the darkness! At the touch of the fire the god started up, and beholding the overthrow of her faith, quietly took flight from her embraces.

And Psyche, as he rose upon the wing, laid hold on him with her two hands, hanging upon him in his passage through the air, till she sinks to the earth through weariness. And as she lay there, the divine lover, tarrying still, lighted upon a cypress tree which grew near, and, from the top of it, spake thus to her, in great emotion. "Foolish one! unmindful of the command of Venus, my mother, who had devoted thee to one of base degree, I fled to thee in his stead. Now know I that this was vainly done. Into mine own flesh pierced mine arrow, and I made thee my wife, only that I might seem a monster beside thee—that thou shouldst seek to wound the head wherein lay the eyes so full of love to thee! Again and again, I thought to put thee on thy guard concerning these things, and warned thee in loving-kindness. Now I would but punish thee by my flight hence." And therewith he winged his way into the deep sky.

Psyche, prostrate upon the earth, and following far as sight might reach the flight of the bridegroom, wept and lamented; and when the breadth of space had parted him wholly from her, cast herself down from the bank of a river which was nigh. But the stream, turning gentle in honor of the god, put her forth again unhurt upon its margin. And as it happened, Pan, the rustic god, was sitting just then by the waterside. Hard by, his flock of goats browsed at will. And the shaggy god called her, wounded and outworn, kindly to him and said, "I am but a rustic herdsman, pretty maiden, yet wise, by favor of my great age and long experience; and if I guess truly by those faltering steps, by thy sorrowful eyes and continual sighing, thou laborest with excess of love. Listen then to me, and seek not death again, in the stream or otherwise. Put aside thy woe, and turn thy prayers to Cupid. He is in truth a delicate youth: win him by the delicacy of thy service."

So the shepherd-god spoke, and Psyche, answering nothing, but with a reverence to this serviceable deity, went on her way. And while she, in her search after Cupid, wandered through many lands, he was lying in the chamber of his mother, heart-sick. And the white bird which floats over the waves plunged in haste into the sea, and approaching Venus, as she bathed, made known to her that her son lies afflicted with some grievous

hurt, doubtful of life. And Venus cried, angrily,
"My son, then, has a mistress! And it is Psyche,
who witched away my beauty and was the rival
of my godhead, whom he loves!"

Therewith she issued from the sea, and returning to her golden chamber, found there the lad,
sick, as she had heard, and cried from the doorway, "Well done, truly! to trample thy mother's
precepts under foot, to spare my enemy that cross
of an unworthy love; nay, unite her to thyself, 10
child as thou art, that I might have a daughter-in-
law who hates me! I will make thee repent of thy
sport, and the savor of thy marriage bitter. There
is one who shall chasten this body of thine, put
out thy torch and unstring thy bow. Not till she
has plucked forth that hair, into which so oft these
hands have smoothed the golden light, and sheared
away thy wings, shall I feel the injury done me
avenged." And with this she hastened in anger
from the doors.   20

And Ceres and Juno met her, and sought to
know the meaning of her troubled countenance.
"Ye come in season," she cried; "I pray you, find
for me Psyche. It must needs be that ye have heard
the disgrace of my house." And they, ignorant of
what was done, would have soothed her anger,
saying, "What fault, Mistress, hath thy son committed, that thou wouldst destroy the girl he loves?
Knowest thou not that he is now of age? Because
he wears his years so lightly must he seem to thee 30
ever but a child? Wilt thou forever thus pry into
the pastimes of thy son, always accusing his wantonness, and blaming in him those delicate wiles
which are all thine own?" Thus, in secret fear of
the boy's bow, did they seek to please him with
their gracious patronage. But Venus, angry at
their light taking of her wrongs, turned her back
upon them, and with hasty steps made her way
once more to the sea.

Meanwhile Psyche, tossed in soul, wandering 40
hither and thither, rested not night or day in the
pursuit of her husband, desiring, if she might not
soothe his anger by the endearments of a wife, at
the least to propitiate him with the prayers of a
handmaid. And seeing a certain temple on the top
of a high mountain, she said, "Who knows
whether yonder place be not the abode of my
lord?" Thither, therefore, she turned her steps,
hastening now the more because desire and hope
pressed her on, weary as she was with the labors 50
of the way, and so, painfully measuring out the
highest ridges of the mountain, drew near to the
sacred couches. She sees ears of wheat, in heaps or

twisted into chaplets; ears of barley also, with
sickles and all the instruments of harvest, lying
there in disorder, thrown at random from the
hands of the laborers in the great heat. These she
curiously sets apart, one by one, duly ordering
them; for she said within herself, "I may not neglect the shrines, nor the holy service, of any god
there be, but must rather win by supplication the
kindly mercy of them all."

And Ceres found her bending sadly upon her
task, and cried aloud, "Alas, Psyche! Venus, in the
furiousness of her anger, tracks thy footsteps
through the world, seeking for thee to pay her the
utmost penalty; and thou, thinking of anything
rather than thine own safety, hast taken on thee
the care of what belongs to me!" Then Psyche fell
down at her feet, and sweeping the floor with her
hair, washing the footsteps of the goddess in her
tears, besought her mercy, with many prayers:
"By the gladdening rites of harvest, by the lighted
lamps and mystic marches of the marriage and
mysterious invention of thy daughter Proserpine,
and by all beside that the holy place of Attica veils
in silence, minister, I pray thee, to the sorrowful
heart of Psyche! Suffer me to hide myself but for
a few days among the heaps of corn, till time have
softened the anger of the goddess, and my strength,
outworn in my long travail, be recovered by a little
rest."

But Ceres answered her, "Truly thy tears move
me, and I would fain help thee; only I dare not
incur the ill-will of my kinswoman. Depart hence
as quickly as may be." And Psyche, repelled
against hope, afflicted now with twofold sorrow,
making her way back again, beheld among the
half-lighted woods of the valley below a sanctuary
builded with cunning art. And that she might lose
no way of hope, howsoever doubtful, she drew
near to the sacred doors. She sees there gifts of
price, and garments fixed upon the door-posts and
to the branches of the trees, wrought with letters
of gold which told the name of the goddess to
whom they were dedicated, with thanksgiving for
that she had done. So, with bent knee and hands
laid about the glowing altar, she prayed, saying,
"Sister and spouse of Jupiter! be thou to these my
desperate fortunes Juno the Auspicious! I know that
thou dost willingly help those in travail with child;
deliver me from the peril that is upon me." And
as she prayed thus, Juno in the majesty of her
godhead was straightway present, and answered,
"Would that I might incline favorably to thee: but
against the will of Venus, whom I have ever loved

as a daughter, I may not, for very shame, grant thy prayer."

And Psyche, dismayed by this new shipwreck of her hope, communed thus with herself, "Whither, from the midst of the snares that beset me, shall I take my way once more? In what dark solitude shall I hide me from the all-seeing eye of Venus? What if I put on at length a man's courage, and yielding myself unto her as my mistress, soften by a humility not yet too late the fierceness of her purpose? Who knows but that I may find him also whom my soul seeketh after, in the abode of his mother?"

And Venus, renouncing all earthly aid in her search, prepared to return to heaven. She ordered the chariot to be made ready, wrought for her by Vulcan as a marriage-gift, with a cunning of hand which had left his work so much the richer by the weight of gold it lost under his tool. From the multitude which housed the bed-chamber of their mistress, white doves came forth, and with joyful motions bent their painted necks beneath the yoke. Behind it, with playful riot, the sparrows sped onward, and other birds sweet of song, making known by their soft notes the approach of the goddess. Eagle and cruel hawk alarmed not the quireful family of Venus. And the clouds broke away, as the uttermost ether opened to receive her, daughter and goddess, with great joy.

And Venus passed straightway to the house of Jupiter to beg from him the service of Mercury, the god of speech. And Jupiter refused not her prayer. And Venus and Mercury descended from heaven together; and as they went, the former said to the latter, "Thou knowest, my brother of Arcady, that never at any time have I done anything without thy help; for how long time, moreover, I have sought a certain maiden in vain. And now nought remains but that by thy heraldry, I proclaim a reward for whomsoever shall find her. Do thou my bidding quickly." And therewith she conveyed to him a little scrip, in the which was written the name of Psyche, with other things; and so returned home.

And Mercury failed not in his office; but departing into all lands, proclaimed that whosoever delivered up to Venus the fugitive girl should receive from herself seven kisses—one thereof full of the inmost honey of her throat. With that the doubt of Psyche was ended. And now, as she came near to the doors of Venus, one of the household, whose name was Use-and-Wont, ran out to her, crying, "Hast thou learned, Wicked Maid! now at last! that thou hast a mistress?" and seizing her roughly by the hair, drew her into the presence of Venus. And when Venus saw her, she cried out, saying, "Thou hast deigned, then, to make thy salutations to thy mother-in-law. Now will I in turn treat thee as becometh a dutiful daughter-in-law."

And she took barley and millet and poppyseed, every kind of grain and seed, and mixed them together, and laughed, and said to her: "Methinks so plain a maiden can earn lovers only by industrious ministry: now will I also make trial of thy service. Sort me this heap of seed, the one kind from the others, grain by grain; and get thy task done before the evening." And Psyche, stunned by the cruelty of her bidding, was silent, and moved not her hand to the inextricable heap. And there came forth a little ant, which had understanding of the difficulty of her task, and took pity upon the consort of the god of Love; and he ran deftly hither and thither, and called together the whole army of his fellows. "Have pity," he cried, "nimble scholars of the Earth, Mother of all things!—have pity upon the wife of Love, and hasten to help her in her perilous effort." Then, one upon the other, the hosts of the insect people hurried together; and they sorted asunder the whole heap of seed, separating every grain after its kind, and so departed quickly out of sight.

And at nightfall Venus returned, and seeing that task finished with so wonderful diligence, she cried, "The work is not thine, thou naughty maid, but his in whose eyes thou hast found favor." And calling her again in the morning, "See now the grove," she said, "beyond yonder torrent. Certain sheep feed there, whose fleeces shine with gold. Fetch me straightway a lock of that precious stuff, having gotten it as thou mayst."

And Psyche went forth willingly, not to obey the command of Venus, but even to seek a rest from her labor in the depths of the river. But from the river, the green reed, lowly mother of music, spake to her: "O Psyche! pollute not these waters by self-destruction, nor approach that terrible flock; for, as the heat groweth, they wax fierce. Lie down under yon planetree, till the quiet of the river's breath have soothed them. Thereafter thou mayst shake down the fleecy gold from the trees of the grove, for it holdeth by the leaves."

And Psyche, instructed thus by the simple reed, in the humanity of its heart, filled her bosom with the soft golden stuff, and returned to Venus. But the goddess smiled bitterly, and said to her, "Well know I who was the author of this thing also. I will make further trial of thy discretion, and the boldness of thy heart. Seest thou the utmost peak of yonder steep mountain? The dark stream which flows down thence waters the Stygian fields, and swells the flood of Cocytus. Bring me now, in this little urn, a draught from its innermost source." And therewith she put into her hands a vessel of wrought crystal.

And Psyche set forth in haste on her way to the mountain, looking there at last to find the end of her hapless life. But when she came to the region which borders on the cliff that was shown to her, she understood the deadly nature of her task. From a great rock, steep and slippery, a horrible river of water poured forth, falling straightway by a channel exceeding narrow into the unseen gulf below. And lo! creeping from the rocks on either hand, angry serpents, with their long necks and sleepless eyes. The very waters found a voice and bade her depart, in smothered cries of, "Depart hence!" and, "What doest thou here? Look around thee!" and, "Destruction is upon thee!" And then sense left her, in the immensity of her peril, as one changed to stone.

Yet not even then did the distress of this innocent soul escape the steady eye of a gentle providence. For the bird of Jupiter spread his wings and took flight to her, and asked her, "Didst thou think, simple one, even thou! that thou couldst steal one drop of that relentless stream, the holy river of Styx, terrible even to the gods? But give me thine urn." And the bird took the urn, and filled it at the source, and returned to her quickly from among the teeth of the serpents, bringing with him of the waters, all unwilling—nay! warning him to depart away and not molest them.

And she, receiving the urn with great joy, ran back quickly that she might deliver it to Venus, and yet again satisfied not the angry goddess. "My child!" she said, "in this one thing further must thou serve me. Take now this tiny casket, and get thee down even unto hell, and deliver it to Proserpine. Tell her that Venus would have of her beauty so much at least as may suffice for but one day's use, that beauty she possessed erewhile being forworn and spoiled, through her tendance upon the sick-bed of her son; and be not slow in returning."

And Psyche perceived there the last ebbing of her fortune—that she was now thrust openly upon death, who must go down, of her own motion, to Hades and the Shades. And straightway she climbed to the top of an exceeding high tower, thinking within herself, "I will cast myself down thence: so shall I descend most quickly into the kingdom of the dead." And the tower again broke forth into speech: "Wretched Maid! Wretched Maid! Wilt thou destroy thyself? If the breath quit thy body, then wilt thou indeed go down into Hades, but by no means return hither. Listen to me. Among the pathless wilds not far from this place lies a certain mountain, and therein one of hell's vent-holes. Through the breach a rough way lies open, following which thou wilt come, by straight course, to the castle of Orcus. And thou must not go empty-handed. Take in each hand a morsel of barley-bread, soaked in hydromel; and in thy mouth two pieces of money. And when thou shalt be now well onward in the way of death, then wilt thou overtake a lame ass laden with wood, and a lame driver, who will pray thee reach him certain cords to fasten the burden which is falling from the ass; but be thou cautious to pass on in silence. And soon as thou comest to the river of the dead, Charon, in that crazy bark he has, will put thee over upon the further side.

"There is greed even among the dead; and thou shalt deliver to him, for the ferrying, one of those two pieces of money, in such wise that he take it with his hand from between thy lips. And as thou passest over the stream, a dead old man, rising on the water, will put up to thee his moldering hands, and pray thee draw him into the ferry-boat. But beware thou yield not to unlawful pity.

"When thou shalt be come over, and art upon the causeway, certain aged women, spinning, will cry to thee to lend thy hand to their work; and beware again that thou take no part therein; for this also is the snare of Venus, whereby she would cause thee to cast away one at least of those cakes thou bearest in thy hands. And think not that a slight matter; for the loss of either one of them will be to thee the losing of the light of day. For a watch-dog exceeding fierce lies ever before the threshold of that lonely house of Proserpine. Close his mouth with one of thy cakes; so shalt thou pass by him, and enter straightway into the presence of Proserpine herself. Then do thou deliver thy message, and taking what she shall give thee, return back again; offering the watch-dog the other cake, and to the ferryman that other piece of money thou hast in thy mouth. After this manner mayst thou return again beneath the stars. But withal, I charge thee, think not to look into, nor open, the casket thou bearest, with that treasure of the beauty of the divine countenance hidden therein."

So spake the stones of the tower; and Psyche delayed not, but proceeding diligently after the manner enjoined, entered into the house of Proserpine, at whose feet she sat down humbly, and would have neither the delicate couch nor that divine food the goddess offered her, but did straightway the business of Venus. And Proserpine filled the casket secretly, and shut the lid, and delivered it to Psyche, who fled therewith from Hades with new strength. But coming back into the light of day, even as she hasted now to the ending of her service, she was seized by a rash curiosity. "Lo! now," she said within herself, "my simpleness! who bearing in my hands the divine loveliness, heed not to touch myself with a particle at least therefrom, that I may please the more, by the favor of it, my fair one, my beloved." Even as she spoke, she lifted the lid; and behold! within, neither beauty, nor anything beside, save sleep only, the sleep of the dead, which took hold upon her, filling all her members with its drowsy vapor, so that she lay down in the way and moved not, as in the slumber of death.

And Cupid being healed of his wound, because he would endure no longer the absence of her he loved, gliding through the narrow window of the chamber where he was holden, his pinions being now repaired by a little rest, fled forth swiftly upon them, and coming to the place where Psyche was, shook that sleep away from her, and set him in his prison again, awaking her with the innocent point of his arrow: "Lo! thine old error again," he said, "which had like once more to have destroyed thee! But do thou now what is lacking of the command to my mother: the rest shall be my care."

With these words, the lover rose upon the air; and being consumed inwardly with the greatness of his love, penetrated with vehement wing into the highest place of heaven, to lay his cause before the father of the gods. And the father of the gods took his hand in his, and kissed his face, and said to him, "At no time, my son, hast thou regarded me with due honor. Often hast thou vexed my bosom, wherein lies the disposition of the stars, with those busy darts of thine. Nevertheless, because thou hast grown up between these mine hands, I will accomplish thy desire." And straightway he bade Mercury call the gods together; and, the council-chamber being filled, sitting upon a high throne, "Ye gods," he said, "all ye whose names are in the white book of the Muses, ye know yonder lad. It seems good to me that his youthful heats should by some means be restrained. And that all occasion may be taken from him, I would even confine him in the bonds of marriage. He has chosen and embraced a mortal maiden. Let him have fruit of his love, and possess her forever."

Thereupon he bade Mercury produce Psyche in heaven; and holding out to her his ambrosial cup, "Take it," he said, "and live forever; nor shall Cupid ever depart from thee." And the gods sat down together to the marriage-feast. On the first couch lay the bridegroom, and Psyche in his bosom. His rustic serving-boy bare the wine to Jupiter; and Bacchus to the rest. The Seasons crimsoned all things with their roses. Apollo sang to the lyre, while a little Pan prattled on his reeds, and Venus danced very sweetly to the soft music. Thus—with due rites—did Psyche pass into the power of Cupid; and from them was born the daughter whom men call Voluptas.

GREEK AND LATIN LETTERS

Letter writing becomes an art and a fashion only in a high state of culture. It is an art of communication between the articulate, an exchange of random observations and reflections by means of which experience is recorded informally. What the good letter loses in comprehensiveness it compensates for by intimate information, personal revelation, or suggestiveness. With the familiar essay, it belongs to *belles lettres,* a field of literature written by and for the cultured who understand each other. An artificial elaboration of the epistolary form is the poetic epistle such as Horace and Alexander Pope wrote. The letter has also been used for didactic purposes, notable examples being the religious epistles written by St. Paul and the other apostles. Letter writing, therefore, possesses great diversity, as well as interest.

Essay writing became of special interest as early as the fourth century B.C., the most interesting examples being the *Characters* of Theophrastus (372?-287? B.C.), a philosopher and natural scientist who succeeded Aristotle as director of the Lyceum and made contributions to botany. His distinction lies in his composition of thumbnail sketches of familiar character types that are astute and charming not only as little essays on character, but as intimate observations on manners. Theophrastus was Menander's teacher and may have exerted an influence on this playwright's contribution to New Comedy, which abounds in character types. If that is true, Theophrastus left his imprint on the whole course of European comedy, since comic types abound in the plays of Plautus, Terence, Shakespeare, Ben Jonson, Molière, Congreve, and Sheridan. But Theophrastus exerted a more direct influence on European literature as the originator of the brief character essay or sketch, known as "the

Character," which was popular in the seventeenth century. It is best described as a short objective account of the qualities of a typical character. We find it in English in Ben Jonson's descriptions of the characters of *Every Man in His Humour,* Joseph Hall's *The Characters of Virtues and Vices,* Sir Thomas Overbury's *Characters,* Owen Feltham's *Resolves,* and John Earle's *Microcosmographie.* Since these writers contributed to the development of the modern novel, the influence of Theophrastus has had considerable importance. The essay also profited from the character sketch; this may be seen in Addison and Steele's *Spectator.*

The most remarkable of the classic letters were written by two Roman gentlemen, the politician and orator Marcus Tullius Cicero (106-43 B.C.) and Pliny the Younger (A.D. 62?-114?). They are strictly letters rather than essays like the character sketches of Theophrastus.

Cicero's work is a veritable compendium of Roman culture during the last period of the Republic, because he stood at its center as a political and literary leader. After an extensive education and exposure to Greek thought and literature, he became a leading figure in the political world, holding many important offices. As consul he was instrumental in exposing Catiline's conspiracy to overthrow the Republic. Later he supported Pompey against Cæsar during their struggle for pre-eminence in Rome. After the triumph of Cæsar's party, Cicero retired from political life and devoted himself to writing. However, he made the mistake of returning to the political arena after the assassination of Cæsar and became an opponent of Mark Anthony. This resulted in his proscription and murder.

In politics, Cicero was formidable, largely owing

to his ingenuity and his remarkable oratory. Catullus referred to him as the "most eloquent of all the descendants of Romulus." His vigorous and colorful speeches, though open to the charge of unfairness and sophistry, became the model for later oratory. But he was a man of letters in a much wider sense. His philosophical works, written during his retirement, merely restate Greek thought and interpret it for the Romans. But they not only cover a wide range of subjects; they also have literary value; cast largely in dialogue form, they are notable for their grace and interesting characterizations.

The greatest interest, however, pertains to his intimate letters, most of them addressed to his friend Atticus, others to members of his household, still others to such luminaries as Pompey, Brutus, and Julius Cæsar. An ingratiating personality, as well as much information about Roman life, emanates from this correspondence, and the informality of Cicero's style comes as a relief after his more ponderous periods.

Cicero's epistles, moreover, inspired the greater ones written by Pliny the Younger (Caius Plinius Cæcilius Secundus), nephew and adopted son of the famous Roman naturalist, Pliny the Elder. One of the leading lawyers of Rome and an office-holder under Emperor Trajan, he became governor of Bithynia. Rather pedantic, complacent, and irresolute, he was nevertheless a conscientious observer of important and unimportant matters. Being amiable and gentlemanly, he wrote gracefully and pleasantly. His letters are not only a veritable mine of casual information, but are vividly descriptive.

His account of the eruption of Vesuvius is a masterpiece of reporting. His report to Emperor Trajan on the early Christians is typical of a Roman gentleman's view of the new religion. Pliny tries to be fair and tolerant but evinces no profundity of thought or emotion. He remains in all things the urbane observer, on solid ground when he is describing, superficial when evaluations are in order.

THEOPHRASTUS

The Characters

Letter Dedicatory

I have often marveled, when I have given the matter my attention, and it may be I shall never cease to marvel, why it has come about that, albeit the whole of Greece lies in the same clime and all Greeks have a like upbringing, we have not the same constitution of character. I therefore, Polycles, having observed human nature a long time (for I have lived ninety years and nine and moreover 10 had converse with all sorts of dispositions and compared them with great diligence), have thought it incumbent upon me to write in a book the manners of each several kind of men both good and bad. And you shall have set down sort by sort the behavior proper to them and the fashion of their life; for I am persuaded, Polycles, that our sons will prove the better men if there be left them such memorials as will, if they imitate them, make them choose the friendship and converse of the 20 better sort, in the hope they may be as good as they. But now to my tale; and be it yours to follow with understanding and see if I speak true.

First, then, I shall dispense with all preface and with the saying of much that is beside the mark, and treat of those that have pursued the worser way of life, beginning with Dissembling and the definition of it, and without more ado recount the nature of the Dissembler and the ways to which he is come; and thereafter I shall endeavor, as I purposed to do, to make clear the other affections each in its own place.

Newsmaking

Newsmaking is the putting together of fictitious sayings and doings at a man's own caprice; and the Newsmaker is one that no sooner meets a friend than his face softens and he asks him with a smile, "Where do you come from? How do you? and Have you any news of this?" and throwing himself, so to speak, upon him, "Can there be any greater news? nay, and it is good news"; and without suffering him to answer, "What?" cries he, "have you heard nothing? methinks I can give you a rare feast." And it seems he has some sol-

Characters. Translated by J. M. Edmonds. By permission of The Harvard University Press.
Theophrastus (c. 372-287 B.C.) was born in Lesbos. He succeeded Aristotle as head of the Lyceum. Besides his *Characters* he wrote works on botany.

dier, or a servant of Asteius the flute-player's, or maybe Lycon the contractor, come straight from the battle-field, who has told him all about it. Thus his authorities are such as no man could lay hands on. Yet he recounts, with them for sponsors, how that Polyperchon and the King have won a battle, and Casander is taken. And if it be asked him, "Do you believe this?" he will reply that it is so indeed, 'tis common talk, and the report gains ground, and everyone says the same; all agree about the battle, and the butchers' bill is very long; he can tell it from the faces of the Government, they are all so changed. Moreover, he has been told in secret that they are keeping in close hiding one that came four days ago out of Macedonia who has seen it all. While this long tale is telling, you cannot think how true to life are his cries of woe: "Poor Casander! unhappy man! do you see how luck turns? Well, he was a strong man once, and now—!" and he ends with saying, "But mind you, this must go no further," albeit he has been running up to all the town to tell them of it.

Superstitiousness

Superstitiousness, I need hardly say, would seem to be a sort of cowardice with respect to the divine; and your Superstitious man such as will not sally forth for the day till he have washed his hands and sprinkled himself at the Nine Springs, and put a bit of bay-leaf from a temple in his mouth. And if a cat cross his path he will not proceed on his way till someone else be gone by, or he have cast three stones across the street. Should he espy a snake in his house, if it be one of the red sort he will call upon Sabazius, if of the sacred,

build a shrine then and there. When he passes one of the smooth stones set up at crossroads he anoints it with oil from his flask, and will not go his ways till he have knelt down and worshiped it. If a mouse gnaw a bag of his meal, he will off to the wizard's and ask what he must do, and if the answer be "send it to the cobbler's to be patched," he neglects the advice and frees himself of the ill by rites of aversion. He is for ever purifying his house on the plea that Hecate has been drawn thither. Should owls hoot when he is abroad, he is much put about, and will not on his way till he have cried, "Athena forfend!" Set foot on a tomb he will not, nor come nigh a dead body nor a woman in childbed; he must keep himself unpolluted. On the fourth and seventh days of every month he has wine mulled for his household, and goes out to buy myrtle-boughs, frankincense, and a holy picture, and then returning spends the livelong day doing sacrifice to the Hermaphrodites and putting garlands about them. He never has a dream but he flies to a diviner, or a soothsayer, or an interpreter of visions, to ask what God or Goddess he should appease; and when he is about to be initiated into the holy orders of Orpheus, he visits the priests every month and his wife with him, or if she have not the time, the nurse and children. He would seem to be one of those who are for ever going to the seaside to besprinkle themselves; and if ever he see one of the figures of Hecate at the crossroads wreathed with garlic, he is off home to wash his head and summon priestesses whom he bids purify him with the carrying around him of a squill or a puppy-dog. If he catch sight of a madman or an epilept, he shudders and spits in his bosom.

CICERO

Letters

To Lucceius

Antium, June, 56 B.C.

A certain sense of shame has often halted me when I have been minded to take up with you face to face the topic which I now will set forth more boldly in your absence; for a letter does not blush. I burn with a longing incredible but yet not reprehensible, as I believe, to have my name honored and celebrated in your writings. Although you

Cicero, *Letters*. Translated by A. P. McKinlay. By permission of Houghton Mifflin Co. Marcus Tullius Cicero (106-43 B.C.), though born at the inland town of Arpinum, was given a thorough education in Rome, where he became a leading orator and led an active and varied political life. In the troubles following the death of Julius Cæsar he was assassinated.

have often signified your intention of doing so, yet I would have you pardon my impatience; for although I always had the keenest expectations as to your work in hand, yet what I have already seen has so far surpassed my anticipations that I long to have my consulship written up by you as soon as possible. Not only am I seized with a hope of immortality in the praises of the ages to come, but I long while still alive to enjoy—if it so be—the authoritative expression of your judgment on my exploits, the proof of your kindly feeling toward me, or at least the charm of your native ability. I am, of course, not unaware how presuming I am not only in imposing on you the task of narrating my deeds—for you might make the excuse of being too busy—but also in demanding that you sound my praises. "What," someone might suggest, "if you should not deem my exploits worthy of commendation?" Still it becomes him who has overstepped the bounds of modesty to be wholly and thoroughly brazen; hence I ask you again and again to embellish that episode more than your opinion might warrant and in the process to put aside the rules of historical composition and grant a little more to your love for me than the truth might allow.

If I should induce you to undertake this task, you will find in it, I feel sure, a topic worthy of your eloquence and your powers; for covering the period from the beginning of the conspiracy to my exile, there can be got together, no doubt, a fair body of material which will allow you to display your well-known knowledge of the civil commotions either in explaining the causes of civic troubles or in setting forth their remedies. All the while, you will find fault with what should be blamed and will approve of what stands the test of reason, and if you should think that you should be as frank as you usually are, you will put the brand of infamy on many for their treachery toward me.

Also in your task my career with its variety of vicissitudes will furnish a certain pleasure which with you as author will intensely interest the reader; for nothing is more likely to please than diversity of events and change of fortune. Although these were not to be desired as matters of experience, they will be pleasing as subjects for reading; for there is pleasure when one in safety recalls past sorrow; and those who have never had any trouble upon beholding the misery of others take some pleasure in pity itself.

Mere chronicles furnish a degree of interest as do the data of an almanac; but the varying fortunes of a prominent man produce wonder, apprehension, joy, annoyance, expectation, and fear. Moreover, if the whole be summed up in a notable conclusion, the mind takes the greatest delight in the reading.

I do not fear that I may seem to be a flatterer in fishing, as it were, for your favor when I show myself as being very eager to be praised by you; you are not the one to be ignorant of your own worth nor, on the other hand, am I so foolish as to be willing to risk my reputation to one who would not himself gain honor in praising me. Therefore it will redound to my joy of soul and to the magnifying of my memory if you of all writers will put me into your pages; because I shall have the advantage not only of your intellect, just as Themistocles had of Herodotus', but also of the authoritative judgment of a gentleman most eminent in society, well versed in politics, and thoroughly approved of among his fellows; so that I shall seem to have had the advantage not merely of a trumpeter, as Alexander said was the case of Homer and Achilles, but also of the unimpeachable testimony of a great and famous man. I approve, to be sure, of the sentiment of Hector in a play of Nævius' when he said that he rejoiced not so much at being praised as at being praised by a praiseworthy man.

If I should fail to obtain this request of mine, I shall be compelled to do that which is often criticized—namely, write about myself. Although I have, to be sure, the example of many famous men as a warrant for my undertaking, yet the objections to an autobiography cannot escape you. One must write more modestly about one's self if there is anything to be praised, and one must pass by whatever is to be criticized. Furthermore, there is less of authority and credence in autobiographies. This awkwardness of situation we desire to avoid, and if you will take up our case, we shall be successful; hence I make this appeal to you.

If you wonder why I urge my request so at length although you have repeatedly assured me of your intention of writing a full and complete history of the critical events of my career, know you that I am fired, as I said in the beginning, with a feeling of impatience that, while I am still alive, I may be known to others through your books and that I myself may have a little pleasure in my own glory. Please let me know, if you are not too busy, what you will do about this matter. If you will undertake the case, I will furnish you with a compilation of my notes. If you put me off to another time, I shall talk with you face to face. In the meantime you will put the finishing touches on your present task and will keep on loving me.

To M. Marius (at Cumæ)

Rome, Fall, 55 B.C.

If it was ill health that kept you from the games, I congratulate you on your good fortune; but if it was your dislike for such diversions that detained you I rejoice doubly: that you are well and that you are sane enough in mind to scorn the silly admirations of the people. I say this, however, on the supposition that during the days of the games you were putting in your time profitably. You would withdraw, no doubt, to that den of yours, which looks out over the Bay of Naples, and in the seclusion of your charming retreat you would spend the morning hours in cursory reading; whereas we, who left you for the show were going to sleep over the performance; the rest of the day you were passing according to your fancy; whereas we had to put up with what could pass the Board of Censors.

In fact, the offerings were most elaborate but, to judge your taste by mine, not at all to your liking; for first, to do honor to the occasion those actors returned to the stage from which they had retired to do honor to themselves. Why, the voice of your particular favorite, Æsop, failed him in an especially impressive passage.

Why should I say more? Being familiar with such programs, you know what events came next. These did not have the charm even of ordinary shows, for the elaborateness of the spectacle took away all delight. I am sure you missed the display with perfect equanimity. How could one be pleased with six hundred mules in the *Clytemnestra,* or three thousand punch bowls in the *Trojan Horse,* or varied paraphernalia of cavalry and infantry in some battle scene! These spectacles won popular approval, but they would have pleased you not at all. If during the days of the games you had heard your slave Protogenes read anything whatsoever except my orations, you would have had more delight than any one of us.

As to the Greek and the Oscan shows, I am sure you did not miss them; for you can see the Oscans show off any day in your town council, and as for Greeks, you take to them so little that you will not take the Greek highway to your villa. Why should I suppose that you missed the athletic games when I know that you scorn gladiators? In these performances even Pompey acknowledges that he wasted his money and his pains. The final event consisted of hunting shows, two of them, continuing through five days, magnificent, to be sure; but what pleasure can a gentleman take in seeing a puny man torn to pieces by a monstrous beast or a beautiful animal pierced by a spear? The last was the day of the elephant-baiting, which brought the crowd much wonder, but little pleasure. Nay rather the beasts aroused some sense of pity as if there were some community of feeling between them and man (so that the crowd rose up and cursed Pompey).

I have written you a longer letter than usual out of an abundance, not of leisure, but of affection, because in a certain letter, if you but remember, you gave me a half-way invitation to write you something that would console you for having missed the games. If I have attained my object, I rejoice; if not, I comfort myself with the reflection that hereafter you will come to the show and visit me and not stake your hope of enjoyment on a letter from me.

To Atticus (at Rome)

Formlæ, 18 March, 49 B.C.

I seem to have been mad from the beginning, and I am tormented because in every vicissitude I did not, like a common private, follow Pompey as he was slipping, or rather rushing to destruction. January 17 I saw him in a panic. On that day I felt what he would do. Never after that did he please me, never cease making now one mistake, now another. Meanwhile not a line to me, not a thought except flight!

Why then should I go to him? As in the case of lovers traits of inelegance, insipidity, and indecency alienate the affections, so with me the unseemly spectacle of Pompey's flight and sloth estranged my love; for nothing that he did was such as to make me accompany him in his flight. Now my love emerges; now I cannot bear the separation; now my books, my literary pursuits, my learning avail me nought. And so day and night, like the halcyon looking out on the sea, I long to fly away.

Cicero, Jr., to Tiro

Athens, 44 B.C.

I had been looking for a letter when one finally came, forty-six days out. Its arrival brought me the keenest joy; for in addition to the pleasure I got from the kind words of my father your most delightful letter filled my cup of joy to overflowing. Accordingly, I was not sorry that there had been a break in our correspondence, but rather was I glad; for I profit greatly by your writing after my long silence. Therefore I rejoice exceedingly that you have accepted my excuses.

I don't doubt, my dearest Tiro, that you are deeply gratified over the rumors that are reaching your ears, and I will guarantee and strive that with the passing days this nascent good report may be increased two-fold. You may, therefore, keep your promise of being a trumpeter of my good repute, for the errors of my youth have brought me such pain and sorrow that not only does my soul recoil at the acts themselves but my ear shrinks from the very mention of them. I know full well that you shared in the anxiety and worry of this experience.

Since I then brought you sorrow, I'll warrant that now I will bring you joy in double measure. Let me tell you that I am associated with Cratippus not as a disciple but as a son, for not only do I listen to his lectures with pleasure but also I am greatly privileged to enjoy him in person. I am with him all day and very often a part of the night since by much pleading I often succeed in getting him to dine with me. Now that he has got used to this habit, he often drops in on me at dinner time, and, laying aside the severe demeanor of a college professor, he jokes with me like a human. See to it, therefore, that you embrace the earliest opportunity of meeting the eminent gentleman, of finding out what he is like, and of becoming acquainted with his merry disposition.

What now shall I say of Professor Bruttius? I keep him with me all the time. He is a regular stoic in his habits of life but a jolly good fellow withal, for he is very much of a wit both in his lectures and in his discussions. I have hired lodgings for him next door, and, as best I may, out of my slender purse I relieve him in his slender circumstances.

Besides, I am studying public speaking in Greek with Cassius. I am planning to do the same with Bruttius in Latin. On Cratippus' recommendation I am on very intimate terms with certain learned gentlemen whom he brought with him from Mytilene. I also spend a good deal of time with Epicrates, the chief Athenian, Dean Leonidas, and other men of that sort. So much for what I am doing. (Of course, I followed your suggestion as to getting rid of Gorgias, though to tell the truth he was a great help in my daily exercises.) Still I laid aside all considerations if only I might obey my father who had sent me unequivocal orders to dismiss him instanter.

I am deeply grateful to you for looking out for my commissions; please send me as soon as possible a secretary, by all means one who knows Greek; he will save me much labor in copying out my notes. Of all things, be sure to take care of yourself that we may be able to pursue our studies together. I commend to you Anterus (the postman).

PLINY THE YOUNGER

Letters

Prefatory

PLINY TO SULPICIUS [1]

You have frequently urged me to put together and publish the letters that I have written with especial care. I have done so, not keeping to the strict order of their dates (for I was not arranging a history), but as they came to hand one by one. I hope you may not regret your advice nor I my compliance. For in that case I will be hunting up others that still lie neglected and, if I add any more, will not suppress them. Farewell.

Recommending a Husband for a Young Lady

C. PLINIUS TO JUNIUS MAURICUS

You ask me to look out a husband for your brother's daughter; and it is eminently fitting that you ask this of me. For you know how I looked up to him and loved him; with what advice he watched over my youth; and how by his words of commendation he brought me to the point where I seemed to deserve commendation. You could not make a greater or a more welcome request of me than that I select a young man worthy to be the father of grandchildren of Arulenus Rusticus.

A long search would have to be made were not Minicius Acilianus at hand as if specially reared for this match. He is a few years younger than I am and loves me dearly as youth loves youth; yet he looks up to me as if I were old. For he is as eager to be guided and shaped by me as I used to be for the guidance of you and your brother.

He comes from Brixia in our section of Italy, which still retains and preserves much of the modesty, the thriftiness, and even the country ways of the older days. His father is Minicius Macrinus, a foremost man of the equestrian [2] order, only because he has not cared to go higher.

For having been given the standing of an expraetor by the deified Vespasian,[3] he has continued to prefer this honored quiet of private life to the ambition, shall I call it, or the dignity that we have sought. As grandmother he has Serrana Procula, of the municipality of Padua. You know the character of that town: but even the Paduans look on Serrana as a model of severity. He has the good fortune to have P. Acilius as his uncle, a man hard to match for solid worth, prudence, and conscientiousness. In short, there is nothing in the whole family that will not be as satisfactory to you as is your own.

Acilianus himself has great vigor and industry, and with it great modesty. He has quickly run through the quaestorship, the tribuneship, and the praetorship with excellent reputation. His face looks like that of a gentleman, with a vigorous ruddiness in it: his whole person has the comeliness of the high born, the distinguished look of a senator. For my part, I think these are points not

---

Pliny the Younger, *Letters*. Selected and translated for this volume by Selatie E. Stout. Caius Plinius Cæcilius Secundus (62-113 A.D.) was nephew of the elder Pliny, whose death he describes. He was born and lived on Lake Como in northern Italy. He held important political positions under the Emperor Trajan.

[1] All of the letters in the books of Pliny's Letters bear this simple style of address in their published form: *C. Plinius to his Sulpicius.* Another word lurks in "his," such as friend, buddy, colleague, wife, aunt, or an adjective, dear, etc. This other word may often have been expressed in the letters as they were originally written and sent. None of the letters is dated in the published form. There are other evidences that they were edited before they were published by their author, but the personal touch has not been removed in the editing. One reads them even now in their published form with a constantly growing sense of the genial, kindly spirit of their author. We feel instinctively that he was a gentleman, one whose friendship would have been prized in any age.

[2] The three orders in the Roman state were the senatorial class, made up of the families that had been honored by furnishing successful candidates for the higher offices of the state; the class of knights, chiefly the more important business men and financial agents of the government; and the plebeians, from which both the other orders drew recruits as men of character and ability were developed among the common people.

[3] When Vespasian was censor in 74 A.D. After this, Macrinus was eligible for election or appointment to the highest offices of the state in spite of the fact that he had never held office. Had he won or accepted such an office, he would have passed from the equestrian to the senatorial order. He was, however, not attracted to a political career by this recognition of his worth and ability by the emperor.

to be overlooked: young ladies have a right to demand them as a sort of reward for their chastity.

I hardly know whether I should mention that his father is quite well off. For when I think of you people for whom we are seeking a son-in-law, I think no mention should be made of money, but when I think of the demands of public life and even of the laws of the state, which make financial rating[4] the first thing to be examined, it becomes clear that consideration of finances may not be passed over. This is especially true when children, several of them, are desired.

You may think that my affection for him has let me extol him above what the simple facts justify. But I promise on my faith that you will find my statements conservative in every respect. I do love this young man most warmly, but one who loves keeps this also in view, not to praise more highly than can be lived up to. Farewell.

A Corinthian Bronze Statue

C. PLINIUS TO ANNIUS SEVERUS

From an inheritance which came my way, I purchased recently a Corinthian bronze, not a large one, but pleasing and with good lines, so far as my taste goes, which is scant enough perhaps in everything, certainly in this. But this statue even I appreciate. It is nude, and neither hides its faults, if there are any, nor fails to display its good points.

It represents an old man, standing; bones, muscles, tendons, veins, wrinkles look as if it could breathe; hair thin and receding, forehead broad, face weazened, neck thin, biceps flabby, breasts flat, waist receding. From the rear it gives the same impression of age, so far as a rear can. The bronze itself, so far as its untreated color shows, is old and antique. Such details can give pleasure to the novice even as they catch and hold the eyes of artists.

That is what tempted me, though a tiro, to buy it. I bought it, however, not to have at home (for up to now I have no Corinthian bronze at home), but to set it up in some much attended place in our home town, preferably in the temple of Jupiter. For it is worthy of a temple, a gift worthy of a God.

You always do everything I ask you, and I would like you now to have a base made of any marble you like to receive my name and offices, if you think these should be added. As soon as I find someone coming to whom it will not be a burden, I will send the statue itself, or, and this would please you more, I will bring it myself; for I am planning to run up there if the demands of my office will permit it. You are happy that I promise to come, but you will frown when I add "for a few days" for the same things that have not yet let me come prevent my being away long. Farewell.

A Busy Man Sighs for the Country

C. PLINIUS TO CANINIUS

Are you studying or fishing or hunting, or doing all of them at the same time? For they can all be done at our Larius.[5] For there are plenty of fish in the lake and game in the woods around it, and your high retreat is ideal for study. But whether you are doing them all or one of them, I cannot say, "I envy you." Though it does distress me that I have no chance at what I crave as sick people crave wine, baths, fountains. Shall I never break these tight tethers, if I can't unloose them? Never, I suppose. For new jobs pile up on the old ones, and the old ones not yet done. By so many interlacings, linked chains you might better call them, the line of things to be done grows longer day by day. Farewell.

A Good Crop

C. PLINIUS TO JULIUS NASO

My Tuscan farm was struck by hail. There is a good crop in the country across the Po, but the price is said to be very small; only my Laurentine place shows a profit. I have nothing there but a house and garden on the edge of the sands; still it is the only place that shows a profit. For there I write a great deal, and instead of land, which I do not have, I cultivate myself in studies. Just as I can show full cribs elsewhere, here I can show you a full desk.

And so, if you want estates that bear and do not disappoint, get something on this shore. Farewell.

The Guests of a Snob

C. PLINIUS TO AVITUS

It would be a long story, and it does not matter, how it happened that, though only slightly acquainted, I had dinner at the home of a man who

[4] A property rating of 400,000 sesterces was required for admission or retention in the senatorial order.
[5] The lake on which Pliny's ancestral estates were.

thought himself elegant and careful, but who seemed to me sordid and at the same time a spendthrift.

For himself and a few he set out rich servings; for the rest, cheap foods and small portions. The wine also in little flagons he had divided into three sorts, not to give opportunity for choice, but to take away the privilege of declining, one sort for himself and us, one for his lesser friends (for he grades his friends), one for his freedmen and ours.

The guest who was reclining[6] next to me noticed this and asked me whether I liked the idea. I said, "No." "Well," said he, "what is your custom?" "I serve the same to all; for I invite them to have dinner, not to be graded. Having made them equal at my table and couch, I make them equal in all things." "Freedmen too?" "Yes: I think of them as guests, not as freedmen." Then he said, "It costs you a lot." "Not at all." "How can that be?" "Why, because my freedmen do not drink the same as I, but I drink the same as they do." And really, if you control your palate, it is not burdensome to share with many what you use yourself. Your appetite must be curbed and told where to stand, so to speak, if you are limiting expenses. You will control expenses somewhat better by controlling yourself than by insulting others.

Why all this? You are a young man of excellent fiber, and I do not want some folks' luxury to impose on you by a show of frugality. It is a part of my love for you, when a thing like this happens, to forewarn you by an example of a thing that you should not be caught doing. Have in mind then that nothing is more to be avoided than this newfangled partnership of luxury and niggardliness. They are vile when they appear separately, more vile when they are combined. Farewell.

Good Heirs

C. PLINIUS TO STATIUS SABINUS

You write me that Sabina, who has made us her heirs, has nowhere ordered Modestus, her slave, to have his freedom, and yet in a codicil she left him a gift in these words: "To Modestus, whom I have ordered to be free." You ask how I feel about it.

I have talked with lawyers; they all agree that he cannot claim his freedom because it was not granted, nor the legacy, because she gave it to her slave. But to me it seems clearly an error, and for that reason I think we should do as if Sabina had written what she thought she had.

I am confident that you will join me in this view, since it is your custom to guard the wish of the dead so scrupulously. To good heirs, the will of the dead, when understood, is as law. Honesty has no less weight with us than necessity with others. Let him enjoy his liberty, then, with our consent, and let him have the legacy, as if she had used all diligence and precaution. For she did use ample precaution when she picked her heirs. Farewell.

A Country House for a Professor

C. PLINIUS TO BÆBIUS HISPANUS

Tranquillus,[7] a close friend of mine, wants to buy a patch of ground which your friend is said to have for sale. Please see that he gets it at a fair price. Then he will be happy in his purchase. For a bad purchase constantly irks one, especially because it is always reminding its owner of his poor judgment.

In this little plot of ground, if the price is right, there is much that appeals to the taste of my Tranquillus: its nearness to the city, its access to the highway, the moderate size of the house, the small amount of ground, enough for diversion without making it a burden. Teachers, such as he is, want only enough ground to rest their head, refresh their eyes, saunter along its borders, wearing a single path, know the history of every vine in the little vineyard, and the number of its trees.

I have told you all this to let you know how greatly he will feel indebted to me and I to you if this little farm, which has many attractions for him, is bought so reasonably that it will leave no room for regret. Farewell.

The Eruption of Vesuvius (I)

C. PLINIUS TO TACITUS

You ask me to write you of my uncle's death, that you may give posterity a truer account of it. I thank you; for I see that his death will have undying glory if it be spoken of with praise by you. In spite of the fact that he fell in the midst of the destruction of most beautiful regions and is destined, like these peoples and cities, to live always because of the unforgettable stroke of fortune, and

---

[6] Guests at Roman formal dinners reclined on couches at the table.

[7] C. Suetonius Tranquillus, who later became the author of an important historical work, *The Lives of the Cæsars.*

In spite of his having himself composed many enduring works, still the eternity of your writings will add to his perpetuity. I count those happy to whom by the gift of the gods it has been granted either to do things worth being written about or to write things worth reading, most happy those to whom it has been given to do both. My uncle will be among this number both because of his own books and because of yours. So I gladly undertake, even ask for, the task you put upon me.

He was at Misenum, in personal command of the fleet. On August 24th[8] about one o'clock in the afternoon, my mother called his attention to a cloud of unusual size and appearance that was becoming visible. He had had his sun bath and after that a cold bath, had taken a little food on his couch, and was studying. He called for his sandals and went up to a spot from which that marvel could best be observed. From a mountain (it was uncertain from the distance what one, but was afterwards learned to be Vesuvius)[9] was rising a cloud whose shape was like that of a tree, more like that of the umbrella pine than any other. For, lifted up on a sort of tall trunk, it spread out into branches. I suppose the material was first carried up by a fresh spurt, and then as that died down, it settled back of its own weight and drifted to the sides, sometimes bright, again dark and blotched, according as earth or ash had been carried up.

To a man of his great learning this seemed a marvelous thing, one deserving examination at closer range. He ordered a light boat to be made ready. He gave me a chance to go with him if I wished. I told him I preferred to study; and, as it happened, he had himself given me a subject to write upon. As he was leaving the house, a note was delivered to him from Rectina, the wife of Tascus. She was terrified at the impending danger. Their villa lay at the foot of the mountain, and there was no escape except by boats. She begged him to rescue her from this critical plight. He changed his plans. A situation that had attracted him first through his curiosity, he now met with greatest courage. He launched larger boats and went aboard, purposing to carry aid not to Rectina alone, but to many, for that pleasant shore was very populous. He hastened toward the place from which others were fleeing. He steered a direct course toward the point of danger, so free from fear that he gave dictation and noted down all the movements, all the figures of that calamitous phenomenon.

Soon ash was falling on the ships; hotter and thicker the nearer they came; now bits of pumice and stones, black, half-burned, broken by the fire; now a new shoal, and shore lines thrust out into the sea by the debris falling from the mountain.[10] He hesitated a bit, whether he should turn back; but to his pilot, who was urging him to do so, he said: "Fortune is on the side of the brave; make for Pomponianus." Pomponianus was at Stabiæ, across the middle of the bay; for the sea comes in upon shores that gradually curve around the bay. The danger had not yet reached there, though it was visible, and when it welled up seemed quite near. He had put his baggage on boats, resolved on flight if the strong adverse wind quieted. This wind was with my uncle coming in. He embraced and soothed and encouraged Pomponianus, who was in a panic. To allay his fear by his own nonchalance, he asked to be taken to a bath. After the bath he reclined at the table and had his dinner, jovial, or, an equal achievement, apparently so.

Meantime from Mount Vesuvius in several places broad flames and high-driven fires spread their light, the brightness heightened by the pitchy blackness of the night. To allay their fears he suggested that the farmers in their nervous haste had left their fires and that deserted, isolated farm houses were burning. Then he turned in to sleep, and he did sleep in most genuine slumber. The movement of his breath, which was unusually heavy and sonorous in him owing to the size of his body, was heard by those who were stationed at his door. But the open space which gave access to the chamber was now filling with ash and pumice and had risen so much that a longer stay would shut off exit. He was awakened, rose, and rejoined Pomponianus and the others who had remained awake. They discussed together whether they should remain in the house or move about outside. For the house was rocked by frequent earth tremors of great intensity and seemed to be moved from its foundations, now this way, now that, and then to settle back once more upon them. Outside in the open they feared the falling pumice

---

[8] 79 A.D.

[9] Vesuvius was not so high then as it has since become through materials which it has ejected, and within historical times it had not been active as a volcano.

[10] The new shoal and the change in the shore line were caused rather by a slight rising of the sea floor at this point under volcanic disturbance than by the discharge of materials into the sea from the mountain.

stones, though light and porous. But having compared the dangers, they chose this latter one. With him, the better reason prevailed over the worse; with others, the greater fear outweighed the lesser. As a protection against falling objects, they tied pillows upon their heads with strips of cloth.

Elsewhere it was now day, there darkness blacker and thicker than any night, which they relieved as best they could by numerous torches and various kinds of lights. They decided to go down to the shore and take a near-by look at the sea to determine whether it would permit any venture. It was still rough and running against them. He lay down there on a cast-off sail, and repeatedly called for cold water and drank it. Then flames and the ominous odor of sulphur set the others to flight. They aroused him. Leaning on two slaves, he got up, and immediately collapsed. I suppose the dense moisture obstructed his breath and closed his esophagus, which was weak and constricted in him, and frequently inflamed. When day returned, now the second from the last one he had seen, his body was found, unmutilated, unbruised, covered over, still clad as he had been. His appearance was more like one asleep than dead.

Meanwhile my mother and I at Misenum—but that has nothing to do with history, and you asked only about his death. I will, therefore, bring my account to a close. Let me add one more thing. I have run through all that I knew at first hand and all that I was told immediately after the event, when one is most likely to get the truth. You will take what you want. A letter and history are quite different things, and a matter is written differently for the eyes of a friend and for the general public. Farewell.

The Eruption of Vesuvius (II)

C. PLINIUS TO TACITUS

You say that the letter which I wrote you at your request about the death of my uncle has aroused in you a keen interest to learn of the alarms and the experiences I went through after being left at Misenum. I had started that subject when I broke off my letter.

"Although my heart-strings twitch at the memory"— Here it is!

After my uncle set off, I spent the remaining time at study. It was for that I had remained. Then followed the bath, dinner, sleep, though a restless and brief one. For many days there had been tremors of the earth, not alarming because they are common in Campania. But on that night they became so violent that everything seemed not to be shaken, but to be on the point of toppling. My mother burst into my room. She found me just getting up to wake her if she was asleep. We sat down in the open space that separates the buildings a little from the sea. I hardly know whether I should call it firmness or lack of prudence (I was then in my eighteenth year), but I called for a book of Titus Livy and read as if nothing were going on, and made notes as I had already begun. In comes a friend of my uncle who had recently arrived from Spain. When he saw my mother and me sitting there, he took her to task for her apathy and me for my unconcern. I kept right on none the less intent on my book.

The first hour of the day finally came, the light still indistinct and sickly, if I may use the term. Buildings in the neighborhood had been shaken down, and although we were in an open space, it was small and the danger from falling walls was great, and, in fact, certain. At last it seemed the best course to get out of the town. A terrified crowd of common folks followed. It preferred another's wisdom to its own, an approach to prudence in time of fear, and crowded and pushed in the long line of those who were leaving. When we had got past the buildings, we halted. We had many curious and alarming experiences there. The wagons which we had ordered brought up danced around this way and that, and even when chocked with stones would not keep to one place. We saw the sea, too, sucked back into itself, repelled as it were by the tremor of the land. At any rate the shore advanced and many sea animals were stranded on the exposed sands. On the other side the ominous black cloud, disrupted by twisting and darting tongues of fire, gaped open into long figures of flames; they were like flashes of lightning, but larger.

Then our friend from Spain got really excited and insistent. "If," says he, "your brother, your uncle is alive, he wants you to be safe; if he has perished, he wished you to survive him. So why do you delay getting away from here?" We told him that we would not think of plans for our own safety so long as we were uncertain about my uncle's. At this he delayed no longer but tore himself away and with all the speed he could command made his way from the danger.

Not much later the cloud of which I have spoken descended upon the land and covered the seas; it had encompassed Capreæ and hidden it, and had taken from our view the part of Misenum on the tip of the cape. Then mother began to beg, urge, order me to make my escape in whatever way I could. She said that I was young and could do it; that her body was heavy with years, and she would do well to die if she kept from being a cause of death to me. I told her that I would not save myself except with her; and then, taking her by the hand, I forced her to come along. She yielded reluctantly, blaming herself because she was delaying me.

Ashes were falling now, infrequent up to then. I looked behind; a thick mist, close behind us, poured down upon the ground and followed us like a torrent. "Let us turn aside," I said, "till we are sure that we shall not be knocked down in the road and trampled in the darkness by the crowd behind us." We had hardly sat down when there was night, not like a cloudy, moonless night, but like enclosed places when the light is put out. You could hear the shrieks of women, the wailing of infants, the shouting of men. Some were seeking parents, some children, some wives or husbands by calling to them, and would make them out by their voices. Here were some lamenting their own misfortune, there others lamenting the lot of their dear ones. Some were driven by the fear of death to pray for it. The hands of many were lifted to the gods; even more concluded that there were no longer gods anywhere and that that final, eternal night was enveloping the universe. And there were not lacking some who increased the real dangers by inventing fictitious ones. Some there were who gave out that a part of Misenum was sunk into the sea, part was in flames. It was false, but found believers. A glimmer of light appeared; this seemed to us not day, but a sign of the approach of fires. The fire stopped at a distance; darkness again; again a copious shower of heavy ashes. Repeatedly we get up and shake them off. If we had not done so we should have been covered up and crushed by the weight. I might boast of the fact that no moan, no unmanly word fell from me, if I had not taken such comfort at thought of death from the fact that I was perishing along with everything else, everything else with me.

Finally the fog thinned out, as if into smoke or a cloud, and left us. Soon real daylight again, but sallow, as it is during an eclipse. Covered with a deep layer of ash as with snow, everything seemed strange as it met our still confused eyes. We went back to Misenum, cared for our bodies the best we could, and spent a night of suspense, wavering between hope and fear. Fear predominated, for the trembling of the earth kept up, and many, distraught at terrifying predictions, were raving about their own hard lot and that of others. In spite of it all, however, though we had been through dangers and looked for more, we did not even then think of leaving until there was news of my uncle.

Do not read these details, unworthy of history, with the thought of writing them; and blame yourself, since you asked for them, if they do not measure up even to the proper dignity of a letter. Farewell.

The Early Christians

C. PLINIUS TO THE EMPEROR TRAJAN

It is my fixed policy, my lord, to refer every matter to you on which I have doubts. For who is better able to guide my uncertainty or to instruct my ignorance?

I have never been present at official investigations of the Christians. For that reason I do not know exactly what is sought to be determined nor the limitations upon the investigations or punishments directed against them. I have felt no little uncertainty as to whether any distinction should be made on the ground of age or whether those ever so young stand in no different case from those who are older; whether penitence should bring pardon or whether one who has been a Christian does not improve his situation by having ceased to be one; whether just the name with no proof of disgraceful conduct, or disgraceful acts connected with being a Christian should be punished.

Meanwhile I have proceeded as follows in the case of those who were brought before me on the charge of being Christians. I have asked them pointedly whether they were Christians. If they said they were I have put the question to them a second [11] and a third time threatening punishment. If they persisted, I have ordered them to be taken to execution; for I felt no doubt that their unyielding obstinacy at any rate deserved punishment, no matter what the nature of the thing they were confessing. There have been others of the same demented attitude whom I have ordered sent to Rome for trial because they were Roman citizens.

Lately, as generally happens when such a matter is being dealt with, the charge is spreading, and several new phases have arisen.

An unsigned document was brought before me

[11] Probably on their being brought back after having an interval of time to think it over in prison.

containing many names. When any stated that they were not Christians and had not been, and repeated after me a formula calling upon the gods and made supplication with incense and wine to your image, which I had for this purpose ordered to be brought with the statues of the gods, and when in addition they reviled Christ, I have thought that they should be dismissed. It is said that those who really are Christians can not be forced to do any one of these things. Others, after being named by a witness, stated that they were Christians, and later denied that they were; saying that they had been, but had ceased to be so, some of them three years, some a longer time before, and occasionally one even twenty years before. All of them worshiped your image and the statues of the gods, and reviled Christ.

They affirm moreover that the whole of their crime—or error—was this, that they had been accustomed to gather before daylight on a fixed day and each in turn in the presence of the others to say a formula of words to Christ as to a god and to bind themselves with an oath, not that they would do some crime, but that they would commit no theft or robbery or adultery, that they would not break a promise, nor deny having received a deposit when called upon to return it; that after doing these things it was their custom to separate, and again to come together to take food, but of an ordinary and innocent sort,[12] and that they had ceased doing even this after my edict forbidding clubs, which I issued in accordance with your instructions. In view of this, I believed it necessary, even by the use of torments, to find out what the truth was from two slave-women that they styled "deaconesses." I have found nothing but a superstition, though a perverse and extravagant one.

I have, therefore, deferred further investigation on this charge and hasten to seek your advice concerning it; for this matter has seemed one on which your counsel should be sought, especially because of the number of those who stand in peril of it. For many of every age, of every rank, of both sexes too, are being brought and will be brought into danger. The contagion of this superstition has pervaded not only the towns, but the villages, too, and the countryside. But it seems to have received a check and to be able to be corrected. At any rate it is common observation that temples which had almost become deserted have begun to be thronged, that regular rites are being renewed after a long intermission, and that food for sacrificial victims is again being sold, for which until now only a rare purchaser was found. From this it is easy to conjecture what a great number of persons can be cured of their folly if only there is a chance for repentance.

TRAJAN TO PLINY

You have done as you should, my Secundus, in investigating the charges against those who had been brought before you as Christians. No principle applicable to all cases can be set up to be followed as a fixed procedure.

They are not to be hunted out. If any are brought in and proved guilty, they must be punished; with this reservation, however, that if one denies that he is a Christian and makes this evident by his acts, that is, by making prayer to our gods, he shall win mercy by his change of heart regardless of suspicions as to his past.

Anonymous informations deserve no attention on any charge. It is exceedingly bad precedent and does not belong to our day.

---

[12] Reports had been spread that Christians at their love-feast drank the blood of a murdered child.

CLASSICAL SATIRISTS

There are good reasons why Greece and Rome
should have given birth to the art of satire.
Although mockery, in some form or other, may
be found in primitive societies and affords some
release from the tensions of primitive social organization, urbane social criticism is a rather late
development. A high state of civilization is the
most favorable condition for the rise of satirical
writing, which requires a critical faculty and thrives
on artificial manners. First Greece, then Rome developed such a civilization.

In Greece, early mock heroic epics like *The Battle of the Frogs and Mice*, burlesque satyr plays,
and other rudimentary farces were succeeded by
dramatic satire in fifth-century Athens. As we
have seen, Aristophanic comedy was essentially
satirical in content and style. The New Comedy
that appeared in the fourth century was mainly
romantic, but a degree of satire was never entirely
absent in its picture of manners or its portraits of
social types; and undoubtedly the staging of these
comedies, especially the exaggerated comic masks
worn by the actors, furthered the satiric intent.
Dramatic satire was indeed the special province
of the Greeks, and it lived on in Rome only while
Plautus and Terence continued the tradition of
Greek New Comedy with adaptations and imitations. It is significant that the very last examples
of Greek satire, in the work of Lucian, are cast
in the form of dialogues. That they are not plays
is undoubtedly explained by the fact that by the
second century A.D. the Greek theater was defunct.

Non-dramatic satire, however, is virtually a
Roman product. Roman writers had a strong
inclination toward criticism and decadent Roman
society provided them with many provocations.
Since the theater in Rome declined rapidly and
was soon supplanted by gladiatorial shows and
spectacles, satiric poetry and fiction became the
only possible outlets for social criticism.

Satirical poetry was introduced into Rome by the
early popular mockery of the so-called Fescennine
verses, which influenced Roman comedy, and by
Lucilius, a poet of the second century B.C. But it
was in the last decades of the Republic and during
the reigns of Augustus and his decadent successors that Roman satire became memorable. There
are traces of its animus in the sophisticated verses
of Catullus, and it attained the perfection of urbanity in the work of Horace. In his *Epodes,*
Horace addressed himself to such characters as
the parvenu who draws attention to himself by
his extravagant dress, the jealous *littérateur* who
libels his fellow-scribes, and the money-lender who
dreams of country pleasures but cannot resist "the
love of pelf." In his less vituperative *Satires* and
Epistles, this witty poet made charm and subtlety
his instrument. A poem like *The Bore* is apt and
brilliant; its suavity does not assuage the sting.

However, Horace's example brought little fruit
among the later poets of the Empire. Persius (A.D.
34-62), who emulated his delicacy, was a mild
satirist and Phædrus (1st century A.D.) generalized his satire by casting it in the form of fables,
as he himself explained:

"What from the founder Aesop fell,
In neat familiar verse I tell."

The irascible Juvenal (A.D. 60?-140?), on the
other hand, possessed vigor but lacked grace. He
delivered himself of telling assaults on decadent
ways, using a bludgeon instead of a rapier.
Abounding in his satires are toga-clad clients be-
sieging the doors of wealthy patrons at the crack
of dawn, flatterers, legacy hunters, revelers, adul-
terers, and criminals. His caustic forthrightness
made him indeed a potent model for writers during and after the Renaissance. Still, his diatribes
become wearisome owing to their sultry rhetoric.
Martial (A.D. 40-102?) alone among the versifiers

retains his salt for moderns owing to his ready and neat wit. Patronized by the rich, he set down their life, and the behavior of their protégés and parasites. Notable, too, are his cynical thoughts on the foibles of the age, which he reflects in his own sophistication and cynicism, as well as in occasional grossness. The medium he perfected is the short poem or epigram. He exploited the possibilities of this limited field so successfully that his name has become identified with epigrammatic poetry, and his translators and imitators have been numerous. The epigram saved him from fulsomeness and encouraged clever writing, though it also limited his importance.

When classic satire achieved true eminence after Horace, it was in prose and in semi-dramatic or dialogue form, the one written by a Roman, the other by a latter-day Greek.

The *Satyricon* (or *Satiræ*), which is technically a miscellany,[1] is our first example of a novel of manners. In its early form this was also known as the picaresque novel (after the Spanish word *picaro*, which denotes a rogue), because the story recounts the adventures of one or more roguish characters who are necessarily in contact with the unworthy aspects of society. (Famous English picaresque novels are Defoe's *Moll Flanders* and Fielding's *Tom Jones*; famous continental examples are the Spanish novel, *Lazarillo de Tormes,* and Le Sage's *Gil Blas.*)

The extant manuscript of the *Satyricon*, found in Dalmatia in 1663, is a fragment, consisting of a series of episodes connected by the fact that they relate the adventures of three young men: Encolpius, who tells the story, his friend Ascyltus, and their servant Gito. Penurious scholars, who live from hand to mouth and are not above stealing when hospitality fails them, they wander from place to place, get into various scrapes, and see the worst side of Roman life. The account of their wanderings becomes an objective record of social corruption, pretense, and fatuity, all the more satirical because presented without didactic commentary. The most vivid episode concerns a visit to the home of a Roman millionaire, the wealthy freedman and parvenu Trimalchio.[2] His fantastic display of luxury is the epitome of vulgarity. The descriptions of his behavior, his home, his guests, and his banquet comprise a satire on the grossness of an age in which men's heads were turned by sudden riches.

This novel, into which several poems are inserted, is attributed to Nero's arbiter of manners, Petronius. A more suitable author could not be found for this masterpiece of ironic realism. A contemporary description of the man, from the pen of the historian Tacitus, suggests a remarkable person who was both of his time and above it.

"His days he passed in sleep, his nights in the business and pleasures of life. Indolence had raised him to fame, as energy raises others, and he was reckoned not a debauchee and spendthrift, like most of those who squander their substance, but a man of refined luxury. And indeed his talk and his doings, the freer they were and the more show of carelessness they exhibited, were the better liked, for their look of a natural simplicity. Yet as proconsul of Bithynia and soon afterwards as consul, he showed himself a man of vigor, and equal to business. Then falling back into vice or affecting vice, he was chosen by Nero to be one of his few intimate associates, as a critic in matters of taste, while the emperor thought nothing charming or elegant in luxury unless Petronius had expressed to him his approval of it. Hence jealousy on the part of Tigellinus, who looked on him as a rival, and even his superior in the science of pleasure. And so he worked on the prince's cruelty, which dominated every other passion, charging Petronius with having been the friend of Scaevinus, bribing a slave to become informer, robbing him of the means of defence, and hurrying into prison the greater part of his domestics. . . .

"Yet he did not fling away life with precipitate haste, but having made an incision in his veins and then, according to his humor, bound them up, he again opened them, while he conversed with his friends, not in a serious strain or on topics that might win for him the glory of courage. And he listened to them as they repeated, not thoughts on the immortality of the soul or on the theories of philosophers, but light poetry and playful verses. To some of his slaves he gave liberal presents, a flogging to others. He dined, indulged himself in sleep, that death, though forced on him, might have a natural appearance. Even in his will he did not, as did many others in their last moments, flatter Nero or Tigellinus or any other of the men

---

[1] The title *Satyricon* (*Miscellany*) does not, strictly speaking, mean "satire," but this latter meaning may well have suggested itself to the author as a kind of play on words.

[2] The word is apparently compounded of Latin and Semitic words and may mean Thrice-Blessed.

in power. On the contrary, he described fully the prince's shameful excesses, with the names of his male and female companions, and their novelties in debauchery, and sent the account under seal to Nero."

The last master of classic satire, Lucian, was born about A.D. 125 near Antioch in Syria. He became a Greek by adoption and assumed the profession of a Sophist or teacher of rhetoric. After lecturing in Syria, Greece, Italy, and Romanized Gaul (France), he settled in Athens for a time. Here he tasted poverty, and became a humble law clerk out of necessity. He died in Egypt about A.D. 200. A large portion of the classic world was therefore known to this man, and what came to his knowledge was conducive to the skepticism that marks his work. Lucian had the best of training for a professional satirist.

His detestation of quackery and conceit sharpened his pen. He noted the "price of everything and the value of nothing" in his age, holding no fixed belief and ridiculing alike the polytheism of Greece and the rising faith of Christianity. He was no respecter of false reputations and fashionable doctrines and remained unawed by the purveyors of philosophy. At the heart of everything he detected vanity and self-interest. No doubt he identified himself with the subject of one of his most trenchant works *Timon of Athens*. Timon, whose generosity to all had been repaid with base ingratitude when he lost his wealth, is instantly surrounded by sycophants after he discovers gold in the desert to which he repaired in an access of misanthropy; he unmasks them one by one, and drives them away with blows.

Nevertheless, the bulk of Lucian's work is not weighted with invective, but possesses fantastication, humor, and wit. The spirit of Aristophanes lives on in this satirist's *Dialogues of the Dead*, which are replete with observations on humanity, and in his *Dialogues of the Gods*, which travesty Greek mythology. His gay and inventive ridicule reveals the Greek genius for blithe creativeness, by comparison with which the efforts of the Romans seem, for the most part, laborious. With Lucian we can take our departure from the classic world with an assurance that there was something undying in that civilization even while it was passing away.

The Greek view could not pre-empt the whole culture of the world, it could not exhaust the resources of the human mind and soul, and it could hardly cope with man's travail on the face of the earth, for there are limits to the potency of the worldly spirit and the amoral intellect. Classic philosophy came to realize this, and therefore ended in mysticism and was finally absorbed in the stream of Christian thought. Classic satire, as a whole, also highlights the impasse of the Greco-Roman world, revealing it in the process of disintegration. But Lucian's swan-song echoes, even in diminished measures, the imperishable part of this civilization. With Lucian we can almost take our departure from a great civilization. We cannot, however, do so without first considering the manner in which classic culture attempted to cope with the meaning of life, without discovering the questions it asked concerning man and the universe and the answers it found.

HORACE

The Bore

It chanced that I, the other day,
Was sauntering up the Sacred Way,
And musing, as my habit is,
Some trivial random fantasies,
That for the time absorbed me quite,   5
When there comes running up a wight,
Whom only by his name I knew;
"Ha, my dear fellow, how d'ye do?"
Grasping my hand, he shouted. "Why,
As times go, pretty well," said I;   10
"And you, I trust, can say the same."
But after me as still he came,
"Sir, is there anything," I cried,
"You want of me?" "Oh," he replied,
"I'm just the man you ought to know;—   15
A scholar, author!" "Is it so?
For this I'll like you all the more!"
Then, writhing to evade the bore,
I quicken now my pace, now stop,
And in my servant's ear let drop   20
Some words, and all the while I feel
Bathed in cold sweat from head to heel.
    "Oh for a touch," I moaned in pain,
"Bolanus, of thy slapdash vein,
To put this incubus to rout!"   25
As he went chattering on about
Whatever he descries or meets,
The crowds, the beauty of the streets,
The city's growth, its splendor, size.
"You're dying to be off," he cries;   30
For all the while I'd been struck dumb.
"I've noticed it some time. But come,
Let's clearly understand each other;
It's no use making all this pother.
My mind's made up to stick by you;   35
So where you go, there I go too."
    "Don't put yourself," I answered, "pray,
So very far out of your way.
I'm on the road to see a friend,
Whom you don't know, that's near his end,   40
Away beyond the Tiber far,
Close by where Cæsar's gardens are."
    "I've nothing in the world to do,
And what's a paltry mile or two?
I like it, so I'll follow you!"   45

Down dropped my ears on hearing this
Just like a vicious jackass's
That's loaded heavier than he likes;
But off anew my torment strikes,
"If well I know myself, you'll end   50
With making of me more a friend
Than Viscus, aye, or Varius; for
Of verses who can run off more,
Or run them off at such a pace?
Who dance with such distinguished grace?
And as for singing, zounds!" said he,   56
"Hermogenes might envy me!"
    Here was an opening to break in.
"Have you a mother, father, kin,
To whom your life is precious?" None;—   60
Oh happy they, I inly groan.
Now I am left, and I alone.
Quick, quick, despatch me where I stand!
Now is the direful doom at hand   65
Which erst the Sabine beldam old,
Shaking her magic urn, foretold
In days when I was yet a boy:—
"Him shall no poisons fell destroy,
Nor hostile sword in shock of war,   70
Nor gout, nor colic, nor catarrh.
In fullness of the time his thread
Shall by a prate-apace be shred;
So let him, when he's twenty-one,
If he be wise, all babblers shun."   75
    Now we were close to Vesta's fane.
'Twas hard on ten, and he, my bane,
Was bound to answer to his bail,
Or lose his cause, if he should fail.
"Do, if you love me, step aside   80
One moment with me here," he cried.
"Upon my life, indeed, I can't;
Of law I'm wholly ignorant;
And you know where I'm hurrying to."
"I'm fairly puzzled what to do.   85
Give you up, or my cause?" "Oh, me,
Me, by all means!" "I won't," quoth he;
And stalks on, holding by me tight.
As with your conqueror to fight
Is hard, I follow. "How," anon   90
He rambles off—"how get you on,

Horace, *The Bore*. Translated by Theodore Martin.

You and Mæcenas? To so few
He keeps himself. So clever, too!
No man more dexterous to seize
And use his opportunities.   95
Just introduce me, and you'll see,
We'll pull together famously;
And hang me, then, if with my backing,
You don't send all your rivals packing!"
  "Things in that quarter, sir, proceed   100
In very different style indeed.
No house more free from all that's base,
In none cabals more out of place.
It hurts me not, if there I see
Men richer, better read than me.   105
Each has his place!" "Amazing tact!
Scarce credible!" "But 'tis the fact."
"You quicken my desire to get
An introduction to his set."
  "With merit such as yours, you need   110
But wish it, and you must succeed.
He's to be won, and that is why
Of strangers he's so very shy."
  "I'll spare no pains, no arts, no shifts!
His servants I'll corrupt with gifts.   115
Today though driven from his gate,
What matter? I will lie in wait,
To catch some lucky chance; I'll meet,
Or overtake him in the street;
I'll haunt him like his shadow! Nought   120
In life without much toil is bought."
  Just at this moment who but my
Dear friend Aristius should come by?
My rattle-brain right well he knew.
We stop. "Whence, friends, and whither to?"

He asks and answers. Whilst we ran   125
The usual courtesies, I began
To pluck him by the sleeve, to pinch
His arms, that feel but will not flinch,
By nods and winks most plain to see   130
Imploring him to rescue me:
He, wickedly obtuse the while,
Meets all my signals with a smile.
I, choked with rage, said, "Was there not
Some business, I've forgotten what,   135
You mentioned, that you wished with me
To talk about, and privately?"
  "Oh, I remember! Never mind.
Some more convenient time I'll find.
The Thirtieth Sabbath this! Would you   140
Offend the circumcised Jew?"
  "Religious scruples I have none."
"Ah! But I have. I am but one
Of the canaille—a feeble brother.
Your pardon! Some fine day or other   145
I'll tell you what it was." Oh, day
Of woeful doom to me! Away
The rascal bolted like an arrow,
And left me underneath the harrow;
When by the rarest luck, we ran   150
At the next turn against the man
Who had the lawsuit with my bore.
"Ha, knave!" he cried with loud uproar,
"Where are you off to? Will you here
Stand witness?" I present my ear.   155
To court he hustles him along;
High words are bandied, high and strong,
A mob collects, the fray to see;
So did Apollo rescue me.

MARTIAL

Post-Obits and the Poets

He unto whom thou art so partial,
Oh, reader! is the well-known Martial,
The Epigrammatist: while living,
Give him the fame thou wouldst be giving;
So shall he hear, and feel, and know it—
  Post-obits rarely reach a poet.

A Hinted Wish

You told me, Maro, whilst you live
You'd not a single penny give,
But that, whene'er you chanct to die,
You'd leave a handsome legacy:
You must be mad beyond redress,
If my next wish you cannot guess!

Martial (40?-102?). Translations: "Post-Obits and the Poets," Lord Byron; "A Hinted Wish," Samuel
Johnson; "To Cloe," Thomas Moore; "Proscrastination," Abraham Cowley; "Bought Locks," Sir John
Harington.

To Cloe

I could resign that eye of blue
   Howe'er its splendor used to thrill me;
And even that cheek of roseate hue,—
   To lose it, Cloe, scarce would kill me.

That snowy neck I ne'er should miss,   5
   However much I've raved about it;
And sweetly as that lip can kiss,
   I *think* I could exist without it.

In short, so well I've learned to fast,
   That, sooth my love, I know not whether   10
I might not bring myself at last,
   To—do without you altogether.

Procrastination

To-morrow you will live, you always cry;
In what far country does this morrow lie,
That 'tis so mighty long ere it arrive?
Beyond the Indies does this morrow live?
'Tis so far fetched, this morrow, that I fear
'Twill be both very old and very dear.
To-morrow I will live, the fool does say;
To-day itself's too late: the wise lived yesterday.

Bought Locks

The golden hair that Gulla wears
   Is hers: who would have thought it?
She swears 'tis hers, and true she swears,
   For I know where she bought it.

PETRONIUS

Trimalchio's Dinner

Boy slaves from Alexandria poured iced water over our hands. Others knelt down at our feet and began, with remarkable skill, to pare our hangnails. Even this unpleasant operation did not silence them, but they sang during their work. I desired to learn whether the whole household was able to sing, so I asked for a drink. A slave repeated my request in a shrill chant. They did all things to the accompaniment of a tune. It was more like a comic opera than a gentleman's dining room.

But some rich and tasty *hors d'œuvres* were brought on in due course. Every one had now been seated except Trimalchio, who, being quite modern, had the first place reserved for him. A donkey of Corinthian bronze, on the sideboard, was laden with panniers holding olives, white in one tray, black in the other. Two dishes, engraved with Trimalchio's name and their weight in silver, also encumbered the donkey. There were also dormice steeped in honey and poppy seed, on iron frames that looked like little bridges. Then, on a silver grill, there were hot sausages, and beneath it were plums and sliced pomegranates.

While we were relishing these delicacies, Trimalchio was borne into the hall to the sound of music, propped on tiny cushions. A laugh escaped the surprised guests. His shaven head popped out of a scarlet cloak, and over his well-wrapped neck he had put a napkin with a broad stripe and fringes dangling all around. On the little finger of his left hand he wore a huge gilt ring, and on the last joint of the next finger was a smaller ring which appeared to me to be solid gold, but was really set with star-shaped bits of steel. And to show that this display of wealth was but part of his possession, he bared his right arm, encircled by a golden bracelet and an ivory bangle clasped with a plate of gleaming metal.

Then picking his teeth with a silver quill, he said, "It is inconvenient for me to appear at dinner so soon, my friends, but I did not like to stay away any longer and keep you from your enjoyment. But you will allow me to finish my game?"

A boy followed him, carrying a table of terebinth wood and crystal pieces, and I noticed a curious thing. Instead of black and white counters he used gold and silver coins. Trimalchio kept swearing as he played, and we were still occupied with the *hors d'œuvres*, when a tray was brought in with a basket on it, in which there was a wooden

Petronius died about A.D. 66. "Trimalchio's Dinner" is from *The Satyricon*.

hen with outspread wings as if in the act of laying an egg. While the music grew loud, two slaves came up to the tray and began to search in the straw. They pulled out peahen's eggs and distributed them to the guests. Trimalchio observed this procedure and said, "I have ordered, my friends, to put peahen's eggs under this hen. And upon my word I hope they are not yet hatched. But let us try them and see whether they are still fresh." We took our spoons, weighing at least half a pound, and beat the eggs, which were made of a fine paste. I was on the point of throwing away my share, believing that a chick had already formed. But hearing an experienced diner exclaim, "What dainty have we here?" I broke the shell and found a fat warbler smothered in yolk spiced with pepper.

Trimalchio had now finished his game, and began to partake of all the same dishes. In a loud voice he invited any of us who might so desire, to drink a second glass of mead. Suddenly the music crashed forth, and the appetizers were swept away by a host of chanting waiters. A dish happened to fall in the confusion, and a boy gathered it up from the floor. Trimalchio saw him, and had his ear boxed, and directed him to throw down the dish again. A litter man appeared and swept out the silver with the other wasted contents. Then entered two long-haired Ethiopians with small wine-skins, just like those used for scattering sand in an amphitheater, and poured wine on our hands, for no one thought of offering us common water.

We complimented our host on his excellent taste. "Mars loves fair play," said he, "and therefore I ordered that every one should have a separate table. This will give us room and these filthy slaves will not make us uncomfortable by pressing upon us."

While he was speaking, some glass jars carefully sealed were brought on, the necks of which were labeled

"FALERNIAN,

OPIMIUS'S VINTAGE,

ONE HUNDRED YEARS OLD."

As we were poring over the inscriptions, Trimalchio clapped his hands and cried, "Ah me, wine lives longer than miserable man. So let us be merry, for wine is life. I treat you to real wine of Opimius's year. I provided some inferior stuff yesterday, although there was a more distinguished set of people to dinner." As we drank and appreciated with gusto each luxury, a slave brought in a silver skeleton, so constructed that its limbs and spine could be moved at will. He put it down several times on the table so that the flexible joints flopped into various attitudes, and Trimalchio mused appropriately: "Alas for us poor mortals, our life is pretty mean and poor. So shall we be, after the world below takes us away. Let us then enjoy ourselves while we may."

After we had applauded this sentiment, another course was brought in, not quite as sumptuous as we expected; but its novelty attracted every eye. This was a round plate with the signs of the Zodiac circling the edge, and on each one the chef had placed some food in keeping with the symbol; over the Ram, ram's-head peas, a piece of beef on the Bull, kidneys over the Twins, over the Crab a crown, an African fig over the Lion, a barren sow's udder over Virgo, over Libra a pair of scales with a tart on one side and a cake on the other, over Scorpio a small sea-fish, over Sagittarius a bull's eye, over Capricornus a lobster, over Aquarius a goose, over Pisces two mullets. In the center lay a honeycomb on a bit of grassy turf. An Egyptian boy offered us bread kept hot in a silver chafing dish. Nor did he fail to amuse us with a song, excruciatingly rendered.

Such a poor course depressed our spirits. "Now," said Trimalchio, "let us begin. This is merely the beginning of the dinner." As he spoke, four slaves ran up keeping time with the music and removed the top part of the tray, revealing in its hollow fat fowls and sows' bellies, and in the middle a hare prepared with wings to resemble Pegasus. We also perceived figures of Marsyas at the corners of the dish, from which a spiced sauce ran over the fish, swimming about in a kind of canal. We all took up the applause which the slaves started and heartily assailed these viands. Trimalchio was delighted with this cunning dish, and said, "Now, Carver." Whereupon the man approached at once, and flourishing his instruments in time with the music, carved the dainty in pieces, like a gladiator in a chariot, fighting to the accompaniment of a barrel-organ. As Trimalchio kept repeating softly, "Oh, Carver, Carver," I pondered on the meaning of this word, believing it to be a jest, and I made bold to ask the man who sat on my left what it meant. (He had seen such performances before.) "Do you see the fellow carving the meat? Well, his name is Carver. So whenever Trimalchio says the words, he calls him by name, and gives him his orders."

When I had eaten my fill, I turned to my neighbor to get as much gossip as possible. I inquired who the woman was who kept running about the hall. "She is Trimalchio's wife Fortunata," he said, "and she counts her money by the bushel." "And what was she before?" I asked. "You will pardon me if I say that you would not have taken a piece of bread from her hand. Now, who knows why or wherefore, she is queen of heaven, and Trimalchio's all in all. Fact is, if she tells him that it is dark at midday, he will believe her. He is so enormously wealthy that he himself does not know all he possesses; but his lynx-eyed wife has a plan for everything, even where you least suspect it. She is temperate, sober, and thrifty, but she has a shrewish tongue, and henpecks him in his own home. Whom she likes, she likes; whom she dislikes, she dislikes. Trimalchio has estates greater than a kite can fly over in a day, and has uncounted millions. There is more plate in his steward's cupboard than other people have in the whole world. And his legion of slaves! My word! I really don't believe that one in ten knows his master by sight! Why, he can knock any of these young wretches into a cocked hat.

"You must not suppose that he buys anything. Everything is produced by him; wool, citrons, pepper; even pigeon's milk. Just to show you, his sheep were growing a poor quality of wool, so he bought rams from Tarentum to improve his flocks. He had bees consigned from Athens to give him Attic honey on the spot; the Roman bees incidentally will be improved by breeding with the Greeks. A few days ago he sent to India for a cargo of mushroom spawn. And every mule he has is the child of a wild ass. Note these cushions: every one has purple or scarlet stuffing. He is nothing if not extravagant.

"But do not be contemptuous of his fellow freedmen. They are saturated with money. Do you see that one lying at the bottom of the end sofa? Well, he has his eight hundred thousand. He was quite a nobody. He started by carrying loads of wood on his back. People do say—I can't vouch for it, but I have heard—that he pulled off a goblin's cap and found a hidden treasure. I am jealous of nobody receiving favors of Providence. He still shows the marks of his master's fingers, but he has an exalted opinion of himself. So he has just put up a sign on his door:

"THIS ATTIC,

THE PROPERTY OF GAIUS POMPEIUS DIOGENES,

TO LET FROM THE 1ST OF JULY,

THE OWNER HAVING PURCHASED A MANSION."

"As for that person sprawling with such a satisfied air in the freedman's place, he had money at one time. I do not blame him, poor fellow. He had his million in his hands, but he has had a bad shaking. I believe he cannot call his hair his own, and that through no fault of his. Here is a fine chap, but these damned freedmen pocketed everything he had. You know how it is: when the pot stops boiling, or business takes a bad turn your friends desert you. Now you see him in this reduced state. He was an undertaker. He used to dine like a prince; boars cooked in a cloth, wonderful pastry, game; chefs innumerable and confectioners! There used to be more wine spilt in his house than many a man has in his cellars. He was a fairy prince, not a mortal. When his business was falling to pieces, and he feared his creditors might suspect that he was going bankrupt, he advertised an auction:

"GAIUS JULIUS PROCULUS

WILL OFFER FOR SALE SOME SURPLUS STOCK."

Trimalchio interrupted this delightful chat, for the meat had now been removed, and the cheerful guests began to turn their attention to the wine and general conversation. He reclined on his couch and remarked: "Now you must sparkle as much as this wine. A fish must naturally swim. But say, did you suppose I would be content with the dinner you saw in the hollow of that dish—'Is this the old Ulysses whom ye knew—?' well, well, one must exhibit one's culture even at dinner. My patron, may God rest his soul, wanted me to be an equal among men. There is little one can teach me, as that last dish demonstrated. The sky where the twelve gods inhabit is divided into as many symbols. Let us take the Ram. Any one who is born under that sign has many flocks and abundance of wool; a hard head and brazen forehead and a fine brain. Many professors and young rams are born under this sign."

We applauded the cleverness of his astrological utterance, while he went on: "Men who kick with their heels, and oxherds and people who have to scout their own food, are born under the Bull. Under the Twins two-wheeled chariots are born, and oxen, and debauchees, and those who serve many masters. I was born under the Crab. Therefore I have many feet to stand on, and immense estates by sea and land; for either of these elements suits your crab. And that was why I put nothing on top of the Crab, for fear of weighing down my good star. Under the Lion gluttons and masterful men are born; under Virgo women, and runaway slaves, and criminals; under Libra butchers, and perfumers, and various tradesmen; poisoners and assassins under Scorpio; under Sagittarius cross-eyed men, who take the bacon while they look at the cabbage; under Capricornus the poor toilers whose troubles cause horns to sprout on them; under Aquarius, innkeepers and men with water on the brain; under Pisces chefs and orators. So the world turns round like a mill, and always brings evil in one form or another, causing the birth of men or their death. And you saw the green turf in the middle surmounted by the honeycomb? Even that has significance. Mother Earth lies in the world's midst rounded like an egg, within which all blessings are contained as in a honeycomb."

"Excellent!" we all cried, vowing with our hands uplifted that even Hipparchus and Aratus were inferior to him. Just then servants appeared and spread over the couches coverlets embroidered with scenes of nets and hunters lying in wait with spears, and all the instruments of the chase. We were still wondering what next to expect when a deafening shout arose outside the dining room and in rushed some Spartan hounds, leaping round the tables. A tray was brought in after them with a wild boar of huge proportions upon it, wearing a cap of freedom; two little baskets woven of palm twigs were hanging from its tusks, one full of dry dates and the other of fresh. Round it lay sucking pigs made of pastry, . . . thereby showing that we had a sow before us. These sucking pigs were for the guests to take away. Carver, who had dealt with the fowls, did not carve the boar, but a tall bearded man with

leggings round his legs, and a spangled silken hunting cape, who drew a hunting knife and plunged it hard into the boar's side. Whereupon a number of thrushes flew out and were immediately caught by fowlers standing with limed twigs. Trimalchio ordered each guest to be given one, and added: "Now you see what fine acorns our boar has been eating." Then boys came and took the baskets which hung from its tusks and distributed fresh and dry dates to the guests.

Meantime I had got a quiet corner to myself and had begun to ponder—why the pig had come in decorated with a cap of freedom. After speculating on the problem without arriving at a satisfactory conclusion, I ventured to put the question which was troubling me to my old informant. "Your humble servant can explain that too," he said. "There is no mystery, the thing is as clear as daylight. Yesterday when this animal was served as *pièce de résistance* at dinner, the guests turned him down; and so today he comes back to dinner as a freedman." I cursed my stupidity and determined to ask no more questions, for fear of showing that I had never dined among decent people.

As we were speaking, a lovely boy crowned with vine leaves and ivy impersonating Bacchus in ecstasy, Bacchus full of wine, Bacchus dreaming, brought round grapes in a little basket, and rendered one of Trimalchio's verses in a piercing voice. Trimalchio turned at the noise and said, "Dionysus, rise and be free." The boy clutched the cap of freedom off the boar and put it on his own head. Then Trimalchio continued: "I am sure you will agree that the god of liberation is my father." We applauded Trimalchio's phrase and kissed the boy heartily as he passed round.

LUCIAN

Dialogues of the Dead

X

CHARON   *Various Shades*
HERMES

CH. I'll tell you how things stand. Our craft, as you see, is small, and leaky, and three-parts rot-

ten; a single lurch, and she will capsize without more ado. And here are all you passengers, each with his luggage. If you come on board like that I am afraid you may have cause to repent it; especially those who have not learnt to swim.

HER. Then how are we to make a trip of it?

Lucian, *Dialogues of the Dead*. Translated by F. G. Fowler. Used by permission of The Oxford University Press. Lucian was a Greek who lived from about 120 to 180 A.D. Little is known of his life aside from the works which have survived.

CH. I'll tell you. They must leave all this non-sense behind them on shore, and come aboard in their skins. As it is, there will be no room to spare. And in future, Hermes, mind you admit no one till he has cleared himself of encumbrances, as I say. Stand by the gangway, and keep an eye on them, and make them strip before you let them pass.

HER. Very good. Well, Number One, who are you?

MEN. Menippus. Here are my wallet and staff; overboard with them. I had the sense not to bring my cloak.

HER. Pass on, Menippus; you're a good fellow; you shall have the seat of honor, up by the pilot, where you can see everyone.—Here is a handsome person; who is he?

CHAR. Charmoleos of Megara; the irresistible, whose kiss was worth a thousand pounds.

HER. That beauty must come off,—lips, kisses, and all; the flowing locks, the blushing cheeks, the skin entire. That's right. Now we're in better trim;—you may pass on.—And who is the stunning gentleman in the purple and the diadem?

LAM. I am Lampichus, tyrant of Gela.

HER. And what is all this splendor doing here, Lampichus?

LAM. How! would you have a tyrant come hither stripped?

HER. A tyrant! That would be too much to expect. But with a *shade* we must insist. Off with these things.

LAM. There, then: away goes my wealth.

HER. Pomp must go too, and pride; we shall be overfreighted else.

LAM. At least let me keep my diadem and robes.

HER. No, no; off they come!

LAM. Well? That is all, as you see for yourself.

HER. There is something more yet: cruelty, folly, insolence, hatred.

LAM. There then: I am bare.

HER. Pass on.—And who may you be, my bulky friend?

DAM. Damasias the athlete.

HER. To be sure; many is the time I have seen you in the gymnasium.

DAM. You have. Well, I have peeled; let me pass.

HER. Peeled! my dear sir, what, with all this fleshy encumbrance? Come, off with it; we should go to the bottom if you put one foot aboard. And those crowns, those victories, remove them.

DAM. There; no mistake about it this time; I am as light as any shade among them.

HER. That's more the kind of thing. On with you.—Crato, you can take off that wealth and luxury and effeminacy; and we can't have that funeral pomp here, nor those ancestral glories either; down with your rank and reputation, and any votes of thanks or inscriptions you have about you; and you need not tell us what size your tomb was; remarks of that kind come heavy.

CRA. Well, if I must, I must; there's no help for it.

HER. Hullo! in full armor? What does this mean? and why this trophy?

A GENERAL. I am a great conqueror; a valiant warrior; my country's pride.

HER. The trophy may stop behind; we are at peace; there is no demand for arms.—Whom have we here? Whose is this knitted brow, this flowing beard? 'Tis some reverend sage, if outside goes for anything; he mutters; he is wrapped in meditation.

MEN. That's a philosopher, Hermes; and an impudent quack into the bargain. Have him out of that cloak; you will find something to amuse you underneath it.

HER. Off with your clothes first; and then we will see to the rest. My goodness, what a bundle: quackery, ignorance, quarrelsomeness, vainglory; idle questionings, prickly arguments, intricate conceptions; humbug and gammon and wishy-washy hair-splittings without end; and hullo! why, here's avarice, and self-indulgence, and impudence! luxury, effeminacy and peevishness!—Yes, I see them all; you need not try to hide them. Away with falsehood and swagger and superciliousness; why, the three-decker is not built that would hold you with all this luggage.

A PHILOSOPHER. I resign them all, since such is your bidding.

MEN. Have his beard off too, Hermes; only look what a ponderous bush of a thing! There's a good five pounds' weight there.

HER. Yes; the beard must go.

PHIL. And who shall shave me?

HER. Menippus here shall take it off with the carpenter's ax; the gangway will serve for a block.

MEN. Oh, can't I have a saw, Hermes? It would be much better fun.

HER. The ax must serve.—Shrewdly chopped!—why, you look more like a man and less like a goat already.

MEN. A little off the eyebrows?

Her. Why, certainly; he has trained them up all over his forehead, for reasons best known to himself.—Worm! what, sniveling? afraid of death? Oh, get on board with you.

Men. He has still got the biggest thumper of all under his arm.

Her. What's that?

Men. Flattery; many is the good turn that has done him.

Phil. Oh, all right, Menippus; suppose you leave your independence behind you, and your plain-speaking, and your indifference, and your high spirit, and your jests!—No one else here has a jest about him.

Her. Don't you, Menippus! you stick to them; useful commodities, these, on shipboard; light and handy.—You rhetorician there, with your verbosities and your barbarisms, your antitheses and balances and periods, off with the whole pack of them.

Rhet. Away they go.

Her. All's ready. Loose the cable, and pull in the gangway; haul up the anchor; spread all sail; and, pilot, look to your helm. Good luck to our voyage!—What are you all whining about, you fools? You philosopher, late of the beard,—you're as bad as any of them.

Phil. Ah, Hermes: I had thought that the soul was immortal.

Men. He lies: that is not the cause of his distress.

Her. What is it, then?

Men. He knows that he will never have a good dinner again; never sneak about at night with his cloak over his head, going the round of the brothels; never spend his mornings in fooling boys out of their money, under the pretext of teaching them wisdom.

Phil. And pray are *you* content to be dead?

Men. It may be presumed so, as I sought death of my own accord.—By the way, I surely heard a noise, as if people were shouting on the earth?

Her. You did; and from more than one quarter.—There are people running in a body to the Town-hall, exulting over the death of Lampichus; the women have got hold of his wife; his infant children fare no better,—the boys are giving them a handsome pelting. Then again you hear the applause that greets the orator Diophantus, as he pronounces the funeral oration of our friend Crato. Ah yes, and that's Damasias's mother, with her women, striking up a dirge. No one has a tear for

you, Menippus; your remains are left in peace. Privileged person!

Men. Wait a bit: before long you will hear the mournful howl of dogs, and the beating of crows' wings, as they gather to perform my funeral rites.

Her. I like your spirit.—However, here we are in port. Away with you all to the judgment-seat; it is straight ahead. The ferryman and I must go back for a fresh load.

Men. Good voyage to you, Hermes.—Let us be getting on; what are you all waiting for? We have got to face the judge, sooner or later; and by all accounts his sentences are no joke; wheels, rocks, vultures are mentioned. Every detail of our lives will now come to light!

XII

ALEXANDER   MINOS
HANNIBAL   SCIPIO

Alex. Libyan, I claim precedence of you. I am the better man.

Han. Pardon me.

Alex. Then let Minos decide.

Mi. Who are you both?

Alex. This is Hannibal, the Carthaginian: I am Alexander, the son of Philip.

Mi. Bless me, a distinguished pair! And what is the quarrel about?

Alex. It is a question of precedence. He says he is the better general: and I maintain that neither Hannibal nor (I might almost add) any of my predecessors was my equal in strategy: all the world knows that.

Mi. Well, you shall each have your say in turn: the Libyan first.

Han. Fortunately for me, Minos, I have mastered Greek since I have been here; so that my adversary will not have even that advantage of me. Now I hold that the highest praise is due to those who have won their way to greatness from obscurity; who have clothed themselves in power, and shown themselves fit for dominion. I myself entered Spain with a handful of men, took service under my brother, and was found worthy of the supreme command. I conquered the Celtiberians, subdued Western Gaul, crossed the Alps, overran the valley of the Po, sacked town after town, made myself master of the plains, approached the bulwarks of the capital, and in one day slew such a host, that their finger-rings were measured by bushels, and the rivers were bridged by their bodies. And this I did, though I had never been called a son of Ammon; I never pretended to be a god, never related visions of my mother; I made no secret of the fact that I was mere flesh and blood. My rivals were the ablest generals in the world, commanding the best soldiers in the world; I warred not with Medes or Assyrians, who fly before they are pursued, and yield the victory to him that dares take it.

Alexander, on the other hand, in increasing and extending as he did the dominion which he had inherited from his father, was but following the impetus given to him by Fortune. And this conqueror had no sooner crushed his puny adversary by the victories of Issus and Arbela, than he forsook the traditions of his country, and lived the life of a Persian; accepting the prostrations of his subjects, assassinating his friends at his own table, or handing them over to the executioner. I in my command respected the freedom of my country, delayed not to obey her summons, when the enemy with their huge armament invaded Libya, laid aside the privileges of my office, and submitted to my sentence without a murmur. Yet I was a barbarian all unskilled in Greek culture; I could not recite Homer, nor had I enjoyed the advantages of Aristotle's instruction; I had to make a shift with such qualities as were mine by nature. —It is on these grounds that I claim the preeminence. My rival has indeed all the luster that attaches to the wearing of a diadem, and—I know not—for Macedonians such things may have charms: but I cannot think that this circumstance constitutes a higher claim than the courage and genius of one who owed nothing to Fortune, and everything to his own resolution.

Mɪ. Not bad, for a Libyan.—Well, Alexander, what do you say to that?

Alex. Silence, Minos, would be the best answer to such confident self-assertion. The tongue of Fame will suffice of itself to convince you that I was a great prince, and my opponent a petty adventurer. But I would have you consider the distance between us. Called to the throne while I was yet a boy, I quelled the disorders of my kingdom, and avenged my father's murder. By the destruction of Thebes, I inspired the Greeks with such awe, that they appointed me their commander-in-chief; and from that moment, scorning to confine myself to the kingdom that I inherited from my father, I extended my gaze over the entire face of the earth, and thought it shame if I should govern less than the whole. With a small force I invaded Asia, gained a great victory on the Granicus, took

Lydia, Ionia, Phrygia,—in short, subdued all that was within my reach, before I commenced my march for Issus, where Darius was waiting for me at the head of his myriads. You know the sequel: yourselves can best say what was the number of the dead whom on one day I dispatched hither. The ferryman tells me that his boat would not hold them; most of them had to come across on rafts of their own construction. In these enterprises, I was ever at the head of my troops, ever courted danger. To say nothing of Tyre and Arbela, I penetrated into India, and carried my empire to the shores of Ocean; I captured elephants; I conquered Porus; I crossed the Tanais, and worsted the Scythians—no mean enemies—in a tremendous cavalry engagement. I heaped benefits upon my friends: I made my enemies taste my resentment. If men took me for a god, I cannot blame them; the vastness of my undertakings might excuse such a belief. But to conclude. I died a king: Hannibal, a fugitive at the court of the Bithynian Prusias—fitting end for villainy and cruelty. Of his Italian victories I say nothing; they were the fruit not of honest legitimate warfare, but of treachery, craft, and dissimulation. He taunts me with self-indulgence: my illustrious friend has surely forgotten the pleasant time he spent in Capua among the ladies, while the precious moments fleeted by. Had I not scorned the Western world, and turned my attention to the East, what would it have cost me to make the bloodless conquest of Italy, and Libya, and all, as far West as Gades? But nations that already cowered beneath a master were unworthy of my sword.—I have finished, Minos, and await your decision; of the many arguments I might have used, these shall suffice.

Scı. First, Minos, let me speak.

Mɪ. And who are you, friend? and where do you come from?

Scı. I am Scipio, the Roman general, who destroyed Carthage, and gained great victories over the Libyans.

Mɪ. Well, and what have you to say?

Scı. That Alexander is my superior, and I am Hannibal's, having defeated him, and driven him to ignominious flight. What impudence is this, to contend with Alexander, to whom I, your conqueror, would not presume to compare myself!

Mɪ. Honestly spoken, Scipio, on my word! Very well, then: Alexander comes first, and you next; and I think we must say Hannibal third And a very creditable third, too.

Dialogues of the Gods

XX. The Judgment of Paris[1]

ZEUS	ATHENE
HERMES	APHRODITE
HERA	PARIS

ZEUS. Hermes, take this apple, and go with it to Phrygia; on the Gargaran peak of Ida you will find Priam's son, the herdsman. Give him this message: "Paris, because you are handsome, and wise in the things of love, Zeus commands you to judge between the Goddesses, and say which is the most beautiful. And the prize shall be this apple." —Now, you three, there is no time to be lost: away with you to your judge. I will have nothing to do with the matter: I love you all exactly alike, and I only wish you could all three win. If I were to give the prize to one of you, the other two would hate me, of course. In these circumstances, I am ill qualified to be your judge. But this young Phrygian to whom you are going is of the royal blood—a relation of Ganymede's,—and at the same time a simple countryman; so that we need have no hesitation in trusting his eyes.

APH. As far as I am concerned, Zeus, Momus himself might be our judge; I should not be afraid to show myself. What fault could he find with me? But the others must agree too.

HERA. Oh, we are under no alarm, thank you,— though your admirer Ares should be appointed. But Paris will do; whoever Paris is.

ZEUS. And my little Athene; have we her approval? Nay, never blush, nor hide your face. Well, well, maidens will be coy; 'tis a delicate subject. But there, she nods consent. Now, off with you; and mind, the beaten ones must not be cross with the judge; I will not have the poor lad harmed. The prize of beauty can be but one.

HERM. Now for Phrygia. I will show the way; keep close behind me, ladies, and don't be nervous. I know Paris well: he is a charming young man; a great gallant, and an admirable judge of beauty. Depend on it, he will make a good award.

APH. I am glad to hear that; I ask for nothing better than a just judge.—Has he a wife, Hermes, or is he a bachelor?

HERM. Not exactly a bachelor.

APH. What do you mean?

HERM. I believe there is wife, as it were; a good enough sort of girl—a native of those parts—but sadly countrified! I fancy he does not care very much about her.—Why do you ask?

APH. I just wanted to know.

ATH. Now, Hermes, that is not fair. No whispering with Aphrodite.

HERM. It was nothing, Athene; nothing about you. She only asked me whether Paris was a bachelor.

ATH. What business is that of hers?

HERM. None that I know of. She meant nothing by the question; she just wanted to know.

ATH. Well, and is he?

HERM. Why, no.

ATH. And does he care for military glory? has he ambition? or is he a *mere* neatherd?

HERM. I couldn't say for certain. But he is a young man, so it is to be presumed that distinction on the field of battle is among his desires.

APH. There, you see; *I* don't complain; I say nothing when you whisper with *her*. Aphrodite is not so particular as some people.

HERM. Athene asked me almost exactly the same as you did; so don't be cross. It will do you no harm, my answering a plain question.—Meanwhile, we have left the stars far behind us, and are almost over Phrygia. There is Ida: I can make out the peak of Gargarum quite plainly; and if I am not mistaken, there is Paris himself.

HERA. Where is he? I don't see him.

HERM. Look over there to the left, Hera: not on the top, but down the side, by that cave where you see the herd.

HERA. But I *don't* see the herd.

HERM. What, don't you see them coming out from between the rocks,—where I am pointing, look—and the man running down from the crag, and keeping them together with his staff?

HERA. I see him now; if he it is.

HERM. Oh, that is Paris. But we are getting near; it is time to alight and walk. He might be frightened, if we were to descend upon him so suddenly.

HERA. Yes; very well. And now that we are on

Lucian, *Dialogues of the Gods.* Translated by F. G. Fowler. By permission of The Oxford University Press.

[1] See the serious account of this scene in "Myths of the Trojan War," p. 40 above.

the earth, you might go on ahead, Aphrodite, and show us the way. You know the country, of course, having been here so often to see Anchises; or so I have heard.

APH. Your sneers are thrown away on me, Hera.

HERM. Come; I'll lead the way myself. I spent some time on Ida, while Zeus was courting Ganymede. Many is the time that I have been sent here to keep watch over the boy; and when at last the eagle came, I flew by his side, and helped him with his lovely burden. This is the very rock, if I remember; yes, Ganymede was piping to his sheep, when down swooped the eagle behind him, and tenderly, oh, so tenderly, caught him up in those talons, and with the turban in his beak bore him off, the frightened boy straining his neck the while to see his captor. I picked up his pipes—he had dropped them in his fright— and—ah! here is our umpire, close at hand. Let us accost him.—Good-morrow, herdsman!

PAR. Good-morrow, youngster. And who may you be, who come thus far afield? And these dames? They are over comely, to be wandering on the mountain-side.

HERM. "These dames," good Paris, are Hera, Athene, and Aphrodite; and I am Hermes, with a message from Zeus. Why so pale and tremulous? Compose yourself: there is nothing the matter. Zeus appoints you the judge of their beauty. "Because you are handsome, and wise in the things of love" (so runs the message), "I leave the decision to you; and for the prize,—read the inscription on the apple."

PAR. Let me see what it is about. *For the Fair,* it says. But, my lord Hermes, how shall a mortal and a rustic like myself be judge of such unparalleled beauty? This is no sight for a herdsman's eyes; let the fine city folk decide on such matters. As for me, I can tell you which of two goats is the fairer beast; or I can judge betwixt heifer and heifer;—'tis my trade. But here, where all are beautiful alike, I know not how a man may leave looking at one, to look upon another. Where my eyes fall, there they fasten,—for there is beauty: I move them, and what do I find? more loveliness! I am fixed again, yet distracted by neighboring charms. I bathe in beauty: I am enthralled: ah, why am I not *all* eyes like Argus? Methinks it were a fair award, to give the apple to all three. Then again: one is the wife and sister of Zeus; the others are his daughters. Take it where you will, 'tis a hard matter to judge.

HERM. So it is, Paris. At the same time—Zeus's orders. There is no way out of it.

PAR. Well, please point out to them, Hermes, that the losers must not be angry with me; the fault will be in my eyes only.

HERM. That is quite understood. And now to work.

PAR. I must do what I can; there is no help for it. But first let me ask,—am I just to look at them as they are, or must I go into the matter thoroughly?

HERM. That is for you to decide, in virtue of your office. You have only to give your orders; it is as you think best.

PAR. As I think best? Then I will be thorough.

HERM. Get ready, ladies. Now, Mr. Umpire.—I will look the other way.

HERA. I approve your decision, Paris. I will be the first to submit myself to your inspection. You shall see that I have more to boast of than white arms and large eyes: nought of me but is beautiful.

PAR. Aphrodite, will you also prepare?

ATH. Oh, Paris,—make her take off that girdle, first; there is magic in it; she will bewitch you. For that matter, she has no right to come thus tricked out and painted,—just like a courtesan! She ought to show herself unadorned.

PAR. They are right about the girdle, madam; it must go.

APH. Oh, very well, Athene: then take off that helmet, and show your head bare, instead of trying to intimidate the judge with that waving plume. I suppose you are afraid the color of your eyes may be noticed, without their formidable surroundings.

ATH. Oh, here is my helmet.

APH. And here is my girdle.

HERA. Now then.

PAR. God of wonders! What loveliness is here! Oh, rapture! How exquisite these maiden charms! How dazzling the majesty of Heaven's true queen! And oh, how sweet, how enthralling is Aphrodite's smile! 'Tis too much, too much of happiness.—But perhaps it would be well for me to view each in detail; for as yet I doubt, and know not where to look; my eyes are drawn all ways at once.

APH. Yes, that will be best.

PAR. Withdraw then, you and Athene; and let Hera remain.

HERA. So be it; and when you have finished your scrutiny, you have next to consider, how you would like the present which I offer you. Paris.

give me the prize of beauty, and you shall be lord of all Asia.

PAR. I will take no presents. Withdraw. I shall judge as I think right. Approach, Athene.

ATH. Behold. And, Paris, if you will say that I am the fairest, I will make you a great warrior and conqueror, and you shall always win, in every one of your battles.

PAR. But I have nothing to do with fighting, Athene. As you see, there is peace throughout all Lydia and Phrygia, and my father's dominion is uncontested. But never mind: I am not going to take your present, but you shall have fair play. You can robe again and put on your helmet; I have seen. And now for Aphrodite.

APH. Here I am; take your time, and examine carefully; let nothing escape your vigilance. And I have something else to say to you, handsome Paris. Yes, you handsome boy, I have long had an eye on you; I think you must be the handsomest young fellow in all Phrygia. But it is such a pity that you don't leave these rocks and crags, and live in a town: you will lose all your beauty in this desert. What have you to do with mountains? What satisfaction can your beauty give to a lot of cows? You ought to have been married long ago; not to any of these dowdy women hereabouts, but to some Greek girl; an Argive, perhaps, or a Corinthian, or a Spartan; Helen, now, is a Spartan, and such a pretty girl—quite as pretty as I am—and so susceptible! Why, if she once caught sight of *you*, she would give up everything, I am sure, to go with you, and a most devoted wife she would be. But you have heard of Helen, of course?

PAR. No, ma'am; but I should like to hear all about her now.

APH. Well, she is the daughter of Leda, the beautiful woman, you know, whom Zeus visited in the disguise of a swan.

PAR. And what is she like?

APH. She is fair, as might be expected from the swan, soft as down (she was hatched from an egg, you know), and such a lithe, graceful figure; and only think, she is so much admired, that there was a war because Theseus ran away with her; and she was a mere child then. And when she grew up, the very first men in Greece were suitors for her

hand, and she was given to Menelaus, who is descended from Pelops.—Now, if you like, she shall be your wife.

PAR. What, when she is married already?

APH. Tut, child, you are a simpleton: *I* understand these things.

PAR. I should like to understand them too.

APH. You will set out for Greece on a tour of inspection: and when you get to Sparta, Helen will see you; and for the rest—her falling in love, and going back with you—that will be my affair.

PAR. But that is what I cannot believe,—that she will forsake her husband to cross the seas with a stranger, a barbarian.

APH. Trust me for that. I have two beautiful children, Love and Desire. They shall be your guides. Love will assail her in all his might, and compel her to love you: Desire will encompass you about, and make you desirable and lovely as himself; and I will be there to help. I can get the Graces to come too, and between us we shall prevail.

PAR. How this will end, I know not. All I do know is, that I am in love with Helen already. I see her before me—I sail for Greece—I am in Sparta—I am on my homeward journey, with her at my side! Ah, why is none of it true?

APH. Wait. Do not fall in love yet. You have first to secure my interest with the bride, by your award. The union must be graced with my victorious presence: your marriage-feast shall be my feast of victory. Love, beauty, wedlock; all these you may purchase at the price of yonder apple.

PAR. But perhaps after the award you will forget all about *me*?

APH. Shall I swear?

PAR. No; but promise once more.

APH. I promise that you shall have Helen to wife; that she shall follow you, and make Troy her home; and I will be present with you, and help you in all.

PAR. And bring Love, and Desire, and the Graces?

APH. Assuredly; and Passion and Hymen as well.

PAR. Take the apple: it is yours.

GREEK AND LATIN PHILOSOPHY

One of the most remarkable achievements of the Greeks from the sixth century B.C. onwards was the development of philosophy. All Hellas shared this development and contributed to it; some philosophers came from the Italian colonies, some from Sicily, some from Thrace, before Athens became the intellectual center of Greece. Nowadays we are so used to the presence of speculative thinking among us that it is difficult to realize how late is its appearance among men and how extremely hard it is for such activity to flourish.

Although among savages and the early peoples of antiquity there were priests and sages who uttered the practical and proverbial wisdom of the tribe or race, these men made no attempt to reason things out systematically. The age-long beliefs which had come from the past compelled the early thinker to move within very narrow limits. He could not cast doubt on the gods or the other religious beliefs of his people and he must respect their superstitions. It was also very difficult for thought to be free so long as the thinkers were under the control of masters whom they ran the risk of offending.

The Greeks were the first who were able to shake off these shackles from their minds and to look clearly at the world about them and ask questions concerning it. Of course, they did not ask all questions at once, but began with one which is today as insistent as it was at first: Is there some fundamental substance out of which the whole universe is made? That the early answers (water, air, fire, and the like) seem foolish today shows only that the scientific technique of these Greeks was faulty. They were trying to solve a fundamental philosophical question.

Before beginning the consideration of the philosophers of Greece and Rome it may be well to remind ourselves of some of the main branches of philosophical inquiry, and to see some of the questions which have presented themselves to thinkers. In this way we may be able better to understand just what field a particular author is considering and what are some of the ways in which it has been treated by other philosophers.

THREE MAIN CONCERNS OF PHILOSOPHY: THE REAL, THE GOOD, THE BEAUTIFUL

Philosophy sets as its goal the attainment of truth about the nature of things. There are three principal divisions, directed toward the understanding of (a) the real (*metaphysics*), (b) the good (*ethics*), (c) the beautiful (*æsthetics*).

A few of the problems of metaphysics are these:

What is the nature of reality? Does the universe have an objective existence or is its existence dependent in some way on the mind that perceives it? How do we know things, anyway? Are there any truths about which one can be sure? These are some of the problems of *epistemology* (the science of understanding). The methods of arriving at truth are the concern of *logic*.

Is there a fundamental essence in the universe? —or a group of essences? The early Greeks' failure to find an answer was followed by a theory of atoms, which anticipated crudely the efforts of modern physics and chemistry to solve this problem.

How did the universe begin? In attempting to answer this, we come to the central problem of *theology*: is there a ruler of the universe? Various answers have been given: (1) *polytheism* (existence of many gods), (2) *pantheism* (god manifested in every part of the universe), (3) *monotheism* (one god controlling everything), (4) *atheism* (no god). *Monotheists* are either *theists* (God originated the universe and is still in active control and association with men), or *deists* (God established for the universe perfect laws with which he does not interfere). At this point should be mentioned *agnosticism*, which holds that such ultimate questions as those of God and Immortality constitute unsolvable problems about which there exists no reliable information.

What is the nature of personality? Are the traditional divisions—physical, mental, spiritual—valid? Is there a soul? If so, just what is it? Does the personality continue after death? Is there immortality of the soul? If so, what kind? Did the soul exist before birth (*pre-existence*)? May the soul return in other forms or other persons (*metempsychosis* or *transmigration*)? Does the soul (or personality) have rewards and punishments after death?

These are but a few of the questions the philosopher asks himself about the reality of things. Let us now see what are some of the fundamental questions of the student of *ethics*.

Ethics is primarily a study of conduct and is concerned with discovering what acts are good. The three most usual answers to the problem have been that the good is what one owes (a) to God, (b) to one's neighbor, or (c) to oneself.

The answer of religion has usually been that the good consists in acquitting oneself of one's duty to God. This introduces the question of how one is to know what is owed to God, which leads to the problem of how trustworthy are the words of books, priests, or sages professing to proclaim this duty.

Another answer to the problem of good is that an act is ethical when it is helpful to mankind as a whole. This principle is sometimes formulated as the pursuit of "the greatest good for the greatest number." Much of modern *humanitarianism* is based on this assumption.

A third attitude toward ethics is the *individualistic* approach. A good deed is whatever is best for oneself, so that the effect of an act on oneself is the principal consideration in ordering one's conduct. Among the ancients the two great philosophies of this type were the *Epicurean* and the *Stoic*. These were best exemplified in the classic world in the works of Lucretius, the Epicurean,

and Marcus Aurelius, the Stoic. For the Epicurean the greatest good is pleasure, the greatest evil pain. One should order one's life so as to derive from it all the pleasures possible. At its best, this philosophy promotes a fine and well-balanced life. A pleasurable old age, for example, can come only from a well-spent youth; and that it is more pleasant to be loved than hated suggests making ourselves congenial to others. But Epicureanism has nearly always led to abuse by those who made it a pretext for indulgence in all kinds of sensual gratifications. The modern world knows it largely from the description by one of its enemies: let us eat, drink, and be merry, for tomorrow we die.

Stoicism glorified the serene spirit above everything. Though all in the world may be wrong and though the heavens fall, the stoic preserves the integrity of his best self. The English poet Henley gave us pure Stoicism when he wrote:

> In the fell clutch of circumstance
> I have not winced nor cried aloud.
> Under the bludgeonings of chance
> My head is bloody, but unbowed.

The practical measure of what is good most frequently ascribed to the Greeks was set down by Aristotle in his *Ethics* when he developed the principle of "the golden mean." Nothing should be done in the extreme—"nothing too much."

The last main division of speculative thinking is *æsthetics*, the theory of the beautiful. Its problem concerns everything connected with artistic expression and enjoyment. A few of the questions of æsthetics are:

What is the urge toward artistic expression? Why, for example, does a painter paint? Some of the answers suggested are: (a) enjoyment of the art itself, and satisfaction in the successful expression of an idea, (b) enjoyment of appreciation by others because of (1) the enhancement of one's own personality through having one's work noticed, (2) the pleasure in being applauded, (3) practical rewards. There also enters here the special pleasure of communal art—that is, of artistic expression which is carried on with others at the same time. Is there more pleasure in dancing in a group than by oneself? If so, why? The joy in work songs and marching songs illustrates this kind of artistic urge.

A second question of æsthetics is why art is liked. Why do people listen to music, look at pictures, read poems? Some answers have been these:

(a) Art brings a relief from a tedious existence—a release from boredom. (b) Art acts as a hand-maiden for religion and stirs men to devotion. (c) Art is useful in teaching lessons of life and conduct (that is, it is *didactic*). (d) Art gives joy to all who appreciate artistic form and pattern and color and sound—a joy quite separate from any practical use (*art for art's sake*). (e) Art brings about a great increase in the pleasure of life by permitting us to share the observations, emotions, or thoughts of the artist—a peculiarly gifted person.

The hardest problem of æsthetics is the distinction between good and bad art. Is the beautiful good art and the ugly bad? The Greeks early discarded any such idea, if they ever entertained it. Is it necessarily good art if an artist has been able to carry out his aims? Are all aims equally valid for the artist?—These problems seem as far from final solution as ever. Only a careful study of the whole product of literature and the arts will help us approach a satisfactory answer.

Philosophy is not strictly confined to such problems as have been outlined here—but perhaps enough has been suggested to show the extensiveness of the field speculative thinkers have been cultivating for the past twenty-five centuries.

GREEK PHILOSOPHY BEFORE SOCRATES

As has been already mentioned, the earliest problems attacked by the Greeks concerned the essential nature of the universe. Was it all originally water—which can become solid, liquid, or gas? Or was it made up of four elements—earth, fire, water, and air? From such speculation they proceeded to consider the origins of the universe, and the nature of time and space. They put forward some of the fundamental problems of thought.

Many of the early Greek philosophers are little more than names to us, for we now possess but fragmentary accounts of what they believed. The activities of Thales began in the seventh century before Christ with speculations about the constitution of the universe. For two centuries before Socrates and Plato, with whom most of us begin our knowledge of philosophy, there were continual attempts to state and to solve basic problems. One of Thales' disciples thought that living creatures came from the moist element (water) as it was evaporated by the sun and that man at first was like a fish. A generation later Pythagoras (582-507? B.C.) interested himself in speculations about the transmigration of the soul and in the significance of relationship between numbers. With

Xenophanes, who lived at the same time, the Greeks began to reason about the existence of God. In this philosopher's ideas we also find a God who neither toils nor moves but rules everything by his thought. In the next century Anaxagoras (500-428 B.C.) considered *Nous* (the Greek for "mind") as the arranger of the infinite number of seeds that make up the universe. From his time on, the idea of a Divine Will as creator continued to appear as an important problem in all philosophical thinking.

The two principal thinkers who were living around 500 B.C., Heraclitus and Parmenides, were concerned with the question of permanence or change. They came to opposite conclusions. Parmenides regarded all change as merely apparent and reality as changeless. Heraclitus, however, with his analogy of the river which is never the same from one time to the next, maintained that "all things flow." The world to him represented a strife of opposite and unresting forces.

The doctrines of Empedocles (500?-430? B.C.), in which the world seems to consist of four elements played upon by the forces of Love and Strife, do not seem nearly so important to the modern student as the teachings of the atomists who succeeded him. These men, Leucippus and Democritus (460-362 B.C.), advanced the theory that the universe is made up of atoms, objects so small that they cannot be divided. The atoms are of every shape, are separated by narrow fissures of space, and are in ceaseless motion.

SOCRATES (469-399 B.C.)

By the time Socrates appeared, a number of the great problems had already been stated. For his own work the speculations of Democritus on the mind were perhaps more important than those on physics, because Socrates' main interest was in logical processes. We shall see him in his *Apology* describing the way in which he strives to make logical analyses by means of persistent questioning. How to get beyond mere easy answers to conclusions that would bear the severest scrutiny and criticism: this was Socrates' problem. His greatest contribution to his age was perhaps not any one principle he discovered, but rather the passion for the pursuit of truth. This passion made him misunderstood, so that many men confused him with the Sophists and their easy-going contention that man is the measure of truth and that a search for anything more satisfactory than each man's idea of the truth is futile.

All who read the *Apology* and the *Crito* will wonder how such an admirable character as Socrates should have been put to death. It must, of course, be remembered that this death sentence took place at a time when Athens had just been defeated and when a new and tyrannical government had taken hold. Moreover, the conservatives were honestly alarmed. The hold he had over all the brilliant young men of his day, his disconcerting way of questioning all that these substantial citizens had implicitly trusted—these were enough to make many men, Aristophanes, for example, looked on Socrates and all speculative thinkers as nuisances who would some day bring them all to ruin. At the same time, moreover, Socrates was regarded with distrust by the democratic faction, for his connection with the oligarchs who oppressed the Athenians after their final defeat by Sparta.

Among the aristocratic young men who followed Socrates was one who was not willing that the teachings of his master should perish. Plato has so injected his own thinking into dialogues in which Socrates is speaking that it is now extremely hard to tell whether we are listening to the ideas of the master or the pupil.

PLATO (427-347 B.C.)

Of all philosophers perhaps Plato is the most pleasing writer. He has in him the talents of many men. His dramatic power is so great that we feel ourselves members of the group of rare souls he gathers together to discuss the weighty problems of life and death. In such a work as the *Crito* the philosophical problem of obedience to law is raised from mere colorless speculation into an absorbing interest. We see a man's philosophy being actually lived. And in the *Phædo* where Plato brings all his reasoning to bear on the question of the soul and the after life, the interest is heightened by that incomparable scene in which Socrates spends his last hour on earth talking of these matters with the young men he is so soon to leave behind. What a rare combination of emotional intensity and lucid thinking!

Of all Plato's works *The Republic* probably brings greatest reward to the inexperienced reader of philosophy. The delightful picture of the group gathering together and falling naturally into a discussion of some of the profoundest of questions immediately engages the interest of the reader. As he progresses, he sees a whole world of thought unrolling before him, yet he is not conscious that he is doing more than merely hearing simple ideas. And if his attention begins anywhere to lag, Plato is always ready with some interesting myth that he has invented to illustrate his point. *The Republic* is not short, and of course cannot be included in a collection like this, but a leisurely reading, in which for some hours or days we converse with Socrates and his friends, may well be one of the most memorable experiences of life.

Plato, moreover, was no mere echo of Socrates, whom indeed we see largely through Plato's eyes, and to whom he ascribed his own ideas, making of him a dramatic convenience and a mouthpiece. In Plato, we find the culmination of one of the main trends of Greek philosophical thought. He ignored and lowered the prestige of the scientific, materialistic school that brought Greece to the threshold of modern science. He also turned against the individualism, the enlightened skepticism, and relativism of the most progressive Sophists, although, like his master Socrates, he employed their dialectical method of argumentation. But he brought to perfection all the tentative speculations of the idealistic school that began with Pythagoras.

In metaphysics Plato rejected the senses as the criterion of truth, because these can only lead to disorder and confusion. Knowledge is possible only through what Plato called Ideas—classifications or concepts to which he appears to have attributed independent existence; indeed, he regarded them as the only reality, for they are "generalized images and forms that mold the chaos of sensation into the order of thought." "These Ideas are not objective to the senses but they are real to thought, for they remain, and are unchanged, even when all the sense objects to which they correspond are destroyed. Men are born to die, but man survives. Every individual triangle is only imperfectly a triangle, soon or later passes away, and therefore is relatively unreal; but triangle—the form and law of all triangles—is perfect and everlasting."[1] This is also true of goodness, beauty, and other abstractions; the highest of the Ideas is the Good. Philosophy deals with Ideas and not with particulars, and the philosopher's chief aim is the discovery of the Good. God orders the universe according to perfect and changeless ideas. The soul is not mate-

---

[1] *The Life of Greece* by Will Durant, pp. 515-16. The fable of the Cave in the *Republic* is an attempt to describe the common man's ignorance and the philosopher's knowledge of "Ideas" poetically.

rial, but the ordering or self-moving force in man; it cannot therefore die like the body. It existed before the body, it will exist after it in other incarnations. The Soul brings with it memories from preceding incarnations, and knowledge is merely a recovery of these memories by means of education. Truth, in short, is innate, and truth is order or harmony. To seek it in private and social behavior is the aim of ethics; that is the subject of *The Republic*, in which the nature of justice is subjected to investigation until Plato demonstrates that justice is harmony in the individual, even as it is harmony in the state. The soul has three levels—desire, will, and reason or thought; and the three must collaborate harmoniously under the rule of reason in any individual. In Plato's utopian state, the Republic, we find the same three levels, represented by the three classes of workers, soldiers, and rulers or philosopher-kings. Love, too, in Plato's *Symposium*, progresses through three stages —love of the body, love of the soul, and love of the truth—that is, philosophy; the last is "Platonic Love," a term that has been carelessly employed to denote sexually unconsummated love.

In all these matters, Plato's influence was far-reaching. His dream of a harmonious state ruled by reason is the first of the utopias or imaginary states (literal meaning, "nowhere") envisioned by idealists like Sir Thomas More, Campanella and William Morris, throughout the ages. His philosophy of Ideas became the basis of all later philosophical *idealism*. His philosophy of love found its way into Renaissance and Elizabethan poetry, from Petrarch's Sonnets to Laura to the sonnet sequences of Spencer, Sidney, and Shakespeare.

Not content with speculation, Plato tried to put his aristocratic political theories into practice in Sicily by influencing the ruler of Syracuse. But after some success, his efforts only got him sold into slavery, from which he had to be ransomed by his friends. His admirers then bought him a suburban place where he established his school, the Academy, named after the local god "Academus." His real triumphs remained in the speculative field, and these he owed not only to the greatness of his thought but to the superiority of his artistry. As a youth who won distinction in practically every physical and mental activity, he hesitated between poetry and philosophy. He did not cease to be a poet when he became a philosopher.

ARISTOTLE (384-322 B.C.)

Both Socrates and Plato were fortunate in having great disciples to carry philosophy on to a new generation. Aristotle was perhaps of all the ancients the most nearly universal in his interests. He discussed all the fundamental problems of philosophy. He worked out the principles of logic. He wrote on physics and astronomy (though he was fundamentally mistaken). He discussed the soul of man and its methods of apprehension. He classified living organisms and began work in comparative anatomy and embryology. His *Ethics* and his *Politics* show his interest in the practical life, and his *Rhetoric* and *Politics* in literature and art.

In another part of this volume we have already examined Aristotle's discussion of Tragedy. It had a profound influence on the writing of drama during the sixteenth and seventeenth centuries, and in some respects it is still affecting our practice and judgments. Any clear understanding of the principles of the Greek drama depends on a knowledge of this treatise although it is not easy reading. (Perhaps we have only Aristotle's lecture notes or a bare outline that he hoped at some time to work over into something more pleasing.)

Aristotle, a native of Thrace, absorbed everything he could from Plato and upon the latter's death removed to Atarneus in Asia Minor, to the court of a fellow-student, Hermeias, who had become the dictator of that city. Aristotle even married Hermeias' sister. But his patron was soon assassinated, and the philosopher found it expedient to flee to the island of Lesbos, where he devoted himself to the study of natural history. In 343 B.C. he was invited by Philip of Macedonia to educate his thirteen-year-old son Alexander. Philip also commissioned him to direct the re-establishment of a war-destroyed city and to draw up its laws. Aristotle returned to Athens nine years later, and in rivalry to the Academy of the deceased Plato opened a school in an Athenian gymnasium, the Lyceum, dedicated to Apollo Lyceus. There, characteristically, he turned his students into research workers, making them compile and organize all existing knowledge. For Aristotle was the most scientific of Greek philosophers.

Even in his metaphysics, derived from Plato, he reflected this inclination. Although agreeing with his master that true knowledge must deal with universals or concepts—that is, "Ideas"—Aristotle maintained that they have no separate existence. They are merely generalizations "formed from many perceptions of like objects"[2]—that is, they are concepts arrived at by discovering something common to various phenomena, like the "laws" of modern science. In all things, it is true, "there is a design, but it is less a guidance from without than an inner drive by which each thing is drawn to its natural fulfilment"—just as there is something dynamic or directive (some "final cause") in the acorn that makes it grow into an oak tree. In the universe, it is God who is the "final cause," the purposive, motive force. "God is not the creator of the material world, but its energizing form; he moves it not from behind, but as an inner direction or goal, as something beloved moves the lover. Finally, says Aristotle, God is pure thought, rational soul, contemplating itself in the eternal forms that constitute at once the essence of the world, and God."[3] This could and did lead to mysticism and non-rationalistic theology. But Aristotle himself remained a pure Greek rationalist. And this quality of cool, balanced thinking also appeared in his ethics. The good life, in his opinion, is the happy life, which is achieved by moderation after certain external conditions—like wealth, social position, health, good looks, and luck—are present. The best life, however, is the contemplative life, for thought or intelligence is the special excellence of humanity. In his sentence "the proper work of man is a working of the soul in accordance with reason," he also summed up the special excellence of Greek civilization.

Aristotle summed up the various philosophical trends of the pre-Socratic and Socratic schools of thought. That he should have left an imprint on both science and philosophy for more than two thousand years of European and Arabian civilization was inevitable. For what animated him was the accumulation of three centuries of intellectual speculation and observation in the cradle of Western civilization, the Greek world.

This is not the place to trace the decline of Greek philosophy. As time went on, the interest of philosophers turned more and more to ethics. In a world where it was growing ever more difficult for the individual to control his surroundings, the dreams of Plato's *Republic* faded away. The great question became how to live the satisfactory life. Two men in the generation after Aristotle

stated the principles of the two ethical systems that were to prevail in the Greco-Roman world for five hundred years.

EPICURUS AND LUCRETIUS

Epicurus (342-270 B.C.) was the beginner of *Epicureanism*, which found the greatest good in pleasure. But as we have stated above, he did not interpret pleasure in a narrow sense. Virtue, for example, is desirable because pleasant, and so are friendship and kindness. The other ethical philosophy was *Stoicism*, founded by Zeno (336?-264? B.C.). Based on a belief in the power of reason, Stoicism held that all conduct could be directed by the rationally controlled will. The Stoic would suppress all his emotions and pay no attention to sensations of pleasure or pain. Neither of these ethical systems was much concerned with duty either to God or to one's neighbor, but because of the identification of reason with God as the personification of law, the Stoic was much more receptive to an active belief in God.

The greatest literary product of Epicureanism is the majestic and forceful Latin poem of Lucretius, *Of the Nature of Things*. Yet it is not really the Epicurean ethics which interests us in this poem. It is rather the materialistic scientific background of the philosophy that is vital for us. Here we have the clear statement of the best that the thinkers of ancient times could do to explain the world about them. Many of the guesses—for they were hardly more than that—are extremely shrewd. And the observation, without modern instruments, is sometimes remarkable.

Besides, so great is the literary value of this work that it can be read as poetry as well as philosophy. A consuming passion for freedom from superstition pervades the poem. It is for this reason that Lucretius turns to a picture of a world determined by natural law rather than by the will of the gods, that he identifies soul with perishable matter and rejects a definition of spirit that would ensure a life after death and would give the priesthood power over people. He denounces pagan religion as the fabrication of priests and as a cult of barbarism. One of his greatest passages is his description of the sacrifice of Iphigenia by Agamemnon at the behest of the priest Calchas, which he presents as a horrible example of the effects of super-

[2] *Op. cit.*, p. 527. This makes Aristotle a "Nominalist," as opposed to a Platonic "Idealist"—that is, the "idea" is just a name for something held in common by like objects, instead of being a thing in itself.
[3] *Ibid.*, p. 532.

stition. A materialistic, atomic interpretation of the universe is necessary, in Lucretius' opinion, if man is to achieve freedom and happiness, as well as human dignity. He writes like a man possessed of a great and noble purpose. His hexameters may be a trifle stiff, for Titus Lucretius Carus (about 96-55 B.C.) lived before the Latin epic had attained the flexibility of Virgil's poetry. But the poem is enriched by magnificent descriptive passages and superb rhapsodies. *Of the Nature of Things* is, in the last analysis, a pæan to the life of reason. Its author was heartily disliked by the early Christians; and this may explain St. Jerome's report in his *Chronicle* that Lucretius became insane after drinking a love potion and wrote his works during some lucid intervals. But he was a singularly pure-minded thinker and poet.

MARCUS AURELIUS (A.D. 121-180)

Of the three principal Stoic writers, Nero's tutor Seneca (4 B.C.-65 A.D.), the sublime Phrygian slave Epictetus (60-120 A.D.), and Marcus Aurelius, the last effectively represents his predecessors. The reader will surely wish at some time to read the works of Epictetus, in which so many men have found guidance in the conduct of life. But it is in the *Meditations* of the great Roman Emperor that Stoicism seems most glowing and persuasive.

Marcus Aurelius was a philosopher only by avocation. He lived in the midst of the greatest responsibilities and the most unfortunate personal difficulties. He was Emperor of the Roman Empire when it was at the apex of its glory, so that Gibbon begins his *Decline and Fall of the Roman Empire* with this reign. But on all sides the empire was pressed by the forces of barbarism and the peace-loving philosophical Emperor was compelled to spend his days at war. This would be enough to make demands on all his stoical calm, even if he had not been compelled to suffer from a dissolute wife and a disgraceful son. Through all these troubles the Emperor retained his serene spirit and insisted that life's greatest battles are not fought with barbarians but within one's own soul.

A broad philosophical outlook underlay stoicism. Although it held that everything was material (that is, consists of matter), it maintained that God is, at once, the creator of the universe and its Soul; he diffuses himself through the universe; or God and the world are the same reality. This is the doctrine of *pantheism* that one encounters in later European thought, as in the philosophy of Spinoza, who inspired Goethe and other great writers. However, the Stoics looked upon philosophy as a matter of practical application, and developed their view of the universe only in order to find a basis for ethical principles. Time and again, Marcus Aurelius considers diametrically opposed metaphysical theories only to conclude that his code of conduct is valid regardless of which theory one adopts. If he favors pantheism it is basically because it enables him to exalt the law of necessity, the acceptance of whatever befalls a man, which is the core of stoic ethics. The soul within us is a part of the universal soul; therefore we cannot escape the necessity which divine law imposes on all things. Our merit and reward come from perfect acquiescence in the rule of divine destiny, from letting reason tell us that this is best. This alone can spare us suffering, for suffering is a mental state, and what we do not consider painful, regardless of what happens to us, cannot cause us anguish. Stoicism, then, is ultimately an austere defense against pain.

With Marcus Aurelius the ethical systems of the ancient world came to a close. The day was ready for something warmer and more vital than his rather tired moral precepts. New forces of thought had been at work for two centuries and more, and now were to affect men's thinking for all time to come.

These forces were all from the East, and their effect was to diminish the rational and increase the irrational in men's thought. To consider the play and interplay of these philosophies is always to come to the conclusion that men had abandoned the attempt to reason things out. They wanted to go beyond reason. If they often ended with mere emotional solutions for intellectual problems, they nevertheless thought that they were making an advance. Known as neo-Platonists, they adopted the irrational part of Plato's philosophy—his picture of an ideal otherworld, and they changed his philosophy so radically that he would never have recognized it. Investigation of the facts of the world ceased. Demons and spirits and incantations—all that would establish contact with this otherworld—became the chief end of man.

In short, the ancient world, tired of a pursuit of reason, was ready for a philosophy that depended not on reason but on revelation. It was tired also of a code of conduct having individual satisfaction as its goal, and responded increasingly, generation after generation, to the new preaching of the Kingdom of Heaven. As the old culture with all that it had of good or bad, gradually failed and the old world passed, something new took its place. The new world was uncouth, barbaric, unappreciative of the great civilization it overran. But the new religion of Christ, an outgrowth of Hebraism, came to the people and stirred their minds and hearts. From the beginning of the fourth century onwards the barbarians were in real control of the world. During all the dark and discouraging centuries that were to come, however, there were some of these men who thought long thoughts and tried to reason clearly about life and the world. No longer in the old free manner of the Greeks were they to think. For in their new religion they had gained peace and certainty of mind and direction of effort, but they had lost their freedom of philosophical speculation. For a thousand years and more, men of western Europe were to direct their thoughts in patterns prescribed by the Christian Church.

PLATO

The Apology of Socrates

How you have felt, O men of Athens, at hearing the speeches of my accusers, I cannot tell; but I know that their persuasive words almost made me forget who I was, such was the effect of them; and yet they have hardly spoken a word of truth. But many as their falsehoods were, there was one of them which quite amazed me: I mean when they told you to be upon your guard, and not to let yourself be deceived by the force of my eloquence. They ought to have been ashamed of saying this, because they were sure to be detected as soon as I opened my lips and displayed my deficiency; they certainly did appear to be most shameless in saying this, unless by the force of eloquence they mean the force of truth: for then I do indeed admit that I am eloquent. But in how different a way from theirs! Well, as I was saying, they have hardly uttered a word, or not more than a word, of truth; but you shall hear from me the whole truth: not, however, delivered after their manner, in a set oration duly ornamented with words and phrases. No, indeed! but I shall use the words and arguments which occur to me at the moment; for I am certain that this is right, and that at my time of life I ought not to be appearing before you, O men of Athens, in the character of a juvenile orator: let no one expect this of me. And I must beg of you to grant me one favor, which is this—if you hear me using the same words in my defense which I have been in the habit of using, and which most of you may have heard in the *agora*, and at the tables of the money changers, or anywhere else, I would ask you not to be surprised at this, and not to interrupt me. For I am more than seventy years of age, and this is the first time that I have ever appeared in a court of law, and I am quite a stranger to the ways of the place; and therefore I would have you regard me as if I were really a stranger, whom you would excuse if he spoke in his native tongue, and after the fashion of his country: that I think is not an unfair request. Never mind the manner, which may or may not be good; but think only of the justice of my cause, and give heed to that: let the judge decide justly and the speaker speak truly.

And first, I have to reply to the older charges and to my first accusers, and then I will go to the later ones. For I have had many accusers, who accused me of old, and their false charges have continued during many years; and I am more afraid of them than of Anytus and his associates, who are dangerous, too, in their own way. But far more dangerous are these, who began when you were

Plato, *The Apology of Socrates.* Translated by Benjamin Jowett. Plato (c. 427-347 B.C.) was one of the aristocratic young men of Athens who fell under the spell of Socrates. Later he gave us the best account of his master and expounded a remarkable philosophical system of his own, which he first taught for forty years at his school, The Academy.

children, and took possession of your minds with their falsehoods, telling of one Socrates, a wise man, who speculated about the heaven above, and searched into the earth beneath, and made the worse appear the better cause. These are the accusers whom I dread; for they are the circulators of this rumor, and their hearers are too apt to fancy that speculators of this sort do not believe in the gods. And they are many, and their charges against me are of ancient date, and they made them in days when you were impressible—in childhood, or perhaps in youth—and the cause when heard went by default, for there was none to answer. And, hardest of all, their names I do not know and cannot tell; unless in the chance of a comic poet. But the main body of these slanderers who from envy and malice have wrought upon you—and there are some of them who are convinced themselves, and impart their convictions to others—all these, I say, are most difficult to deal with; for I cannot have them up here, and examine them, and therefore I must simply fight with shadows in my own defense, and examine when there is no one who answers. I will ask you then to assume with me, as I was saying, that my opponents are of two kinds—one recent, the other ancient; and I hope that you will see the propriety of my answering the latter first, for these accusations you heard long before the others, and much oftener.

Well, then, I will make my defense, and I will endeavor in the short time which is allowed to do away with this evil opinion of me which you have held for such a long time; and I hope I may succeed, if this be well for you and me, and that my words may find favor with you. But I know that to accomplish this is not easy—I quite see the nature of the task. Let the event be as God wills: in obedience to the law I make my defense.

I will begin at the beginning, and ask what the accusation is which has given rise to this slander of me, and which has encouraged Meletus to proceed against me. What do the slanderers say? They shall be my prosecutors, and I will sum up their words in an affidavit: "Socrates is an evil-doer, and a curious person, who searches into things under the earth and in heaven, and he makes the worse appear the better cause; and he teaches the aforesaid doctrines to others." That is the nature of the accusation, and that is what you have seen yourselves in the comedy of Aristophanes; who has introduced a man whom he calls Socrates, going about and saying that he can walk in the air, and talking a deal of nonsense concerning matters of which I do not pretend to know either much or little—not that I mean to say anything disparaging of anyone who is a student of natural philosophy. I should be very sorry if Meletus could lay that to my charge. But the simple truth is, O Athenians, that I have nothing to do with these studies. Very many of those here present are witnesses to the truth of this, and to them I appeal. Speak then, you who have heard me, and tell your neighbors whether any of you have ever known me hold forth in few words or in many upon matters of this sort. . . . You hear their answer. And from what they say of this you will be able to judge of the truth of the rest.

As little foundation is there for the report that I am a teacher, and take money; that is no more true than the other. Although, if a man is able to teach, I honor him for being paid. There is Gorgias of Leontium, and Prodicus of Ceos, and Hippias of Elis, who go the round of the cities, and are able to persuade the young men to leave their own citizens, by whom they might be taught for nothing, and come to them, whom they not only pay, but are thankful if they may be allowed to pay them. There is actually a Parian philosopher residing in Athens, of whom I have heard; and I came to hear of him in this way: I met a man who has spent a world of money on the Sophists, Callias the son of Hipponicus, and knowing that he had sons, I asked him: "Callias," I said, "if your two sons were foals or calves, there would be no difficulty in finding someone to put over them; we should hire a trainer of horses or a farmer probably who would improve and perfect them in their own proper virtue and excellence; but as they are human beings, whom are you thinking of placing over them? Is there anyone who understands human and political virtue? You must have thought about this as you have sons; is there anyone?" "There is," he said. "Who is he?" said I, "and of what country? and what does he charge?" "Evenus the Parian," he replied; "he is the man, and his charge is five minæ." Happy is Evenus, I said to myself, if he really has this wisdom, and teaches at such a modest charge. Had I the same, I should have been very proud and conceited; but the truth is that I have no knowledge of the kind, O Athenians.

I dare say that someone will ask the question, "Why is this, Socrates, and what is the origin of these accusations of you: for there must have been something strange which you have been doing? All this great fame and talk about you would never have arisen if you had been like other men: tell us, then, why this is, as we should be sorry to judge hastily of you." Now I regard this as a fair challenge, and I will endeavor to explain to you the origin of this name of "wise," and of this evil fame. Please to attend them. And although some of you may think I am joking, I declare that I will tell you the entire truth. Men of Athens, this reputation of mine has come of a certain sort of wisdom which I possess. If you ask me what kind of wisdom, I reply, such wisdom as is attainable by man, for to that extent I am inclined to believe that I am wise; whereas the persons of whom I was speaking have a superhuman wisdom, which I may fail to describe, because I have it not myself; and he who says that I have, speaks falsely, and is taking away my character. And here, O men of Athens, I must beg you not to interrupt me, even if I seem to say something extravagant. For the word which I will speak is not mine. I will refer you to a witness who is worthy of credit, and will tell you about my wisdom—whether I have any, and of what sort—and that witness shall be the god of Delphi. You must have known Chærephon; he was early a friend of mine, and also a friend of yours, for he shared in the exile of the people, and returned with you. Well, Chærephon, as you know, was very impetuous in all his doings, and he went to Delphi and boldly asked the oracle to tell him whether—as I was saying, I must beg you not to interrupt—he asked the oracle to tell him whether there was anyone wiser than I was, and the Pythian prophetess answered that there was no man wiser. Chærephon is dead himself, but his brother, who is in court, will confirm the truth of this story.

Why do I mention this? Because I am going to explain to you why I have such an evil name. When I heard the answer, I said to myself, What can the god mean? and what is the interpretation of this riddle? for I know that I have no wisdom, small or great. What can he mean when he says that I am the wisest of men? And yet he is a god and cannot lie; that would be against his nature. After a long consideration, I at last thought of a method of trying the question. I reflected that if I could only find a man wiser than myself, then I might go to the god with a refutation in my hand. I should say to him, "Here is a man who is wiser than I am; but you said that I was the wisest." Accordingly I went to one who had the reputation of wisdom, and observed to him—his name I need not mention; he was a politician whom I selected for examination—and the result was as follows:

When I began to talk with him, I could not help thinking that he was not really wise, although he was thought wise by many, and wiser still by himself; and I went and tried to explain to him that he thought himself wise, but was not really wise; and the consequence was that he hated me, and his enmity was shared by several who were present and heard me. So I left him, saying to myself, as I went away: Well, although I do not suppose that either of us knows anything really beautiful and good, I am better off than he is—for he knows nothing, and thinks that he knows. I neither know nor think that I know. In this latter particular, then, I seem to have slightly the advantage of him. Then I went to another, who had still higher philosophical pretensions, and my conclusion was exactly the same. I made another enemy of him, and of many others besides him.

After this I went to one man after another, being not unconscious of the enmity which I provoked, and I lamented and feared this: but necessity was laid upon me—the word of God, I thought, ought to be considered first. And I said to myself, Go I must to all who appear to know, and find out the meaning of the oracle. And I swear to you, Athenians, by the dog I swear!—for I must tell you the truth—the result of my mission was just this: I found that the men most in repute were all but the most foolish; and that some inferior men were really wiser and better. I will tell you the tale of my wanderings and of the "Herculean" labors, as I may call them, which I endured only to find at last the oracle irrefutable. When I left the politicians, I went to the poets; tragic, dithyrambic, and all sorts. And there, I said to myself, you will be detected; now you will find out that you are more ignorant than they are. Accordingly, I took them some of the most elaborate passages in their own writings, and asked what was the meaning of them—thinking that they would teach me something. Will you believe me? I am almost ashamed to speak of this, but still I must say that there is hardly a person present who would not have talked better about their poetry than they did themselves. That showed me in an instant that not by wisdom do poets write poetry, but by a sort of genius and inspiration; they are like diviners or soothsayers who also say many fine things, but do not understand the meaning of them. And the poets appeared to me to be much in the same case; and I further observed that upon the strength of their poetry they believed themselves to be the wisest of men in other things in which they were not wise

So I departed, conceiving myself to be superior to them for the same reason that I was superior to the politicians.

At last I went to the artisans, for I was conscious that I knew nothing at all, as I may say, and I was sure that they knew many fine things; and in this I was not mistaken, for they did know many things of which I was ignorant, and in this they certainly were wiser than I was. But I observed that even the good artisans fell into the same error as the poets; because they were good workmen they thought that they also knew all sorts of high matters, and this defect in them overshadowed their wisdom—therefore I asked myself on behalf of the oracle, whether I would like to be as I was, neither having their knowledge nor their ignorance, or like them in both; and I made answer to myself and the oracle that I was better off as I was.

This investigation has led to my having many enemies of the worst and most dangerous kind, and has given occasion also to many calumnies, and I am called wise, for my hearers always imagine that I myself possess the wisdom which I find wanting in others: but the truth is, O men of Athens, that God only is wise; and in this oracle he means to say that the wisdom of men is little or nothing; he is not speaking of Socrates, he is only using my name as an illustration, as if he said, He, O men, is the wisest, who, like Socrates, knows that his wisdom is in truth worth nothing. And so I go my way, obedient to the god, and make inquisition into the wisdom of anyone, whether citizen or stranger, who appears to be wise; and if he is not wise, then in vindication of the oracle I show him that he is not wise; and this occupation quite absorbs me, and I have no time to give either to any public matter of interest or to any concern of my own, but I am in utter poverty by reason of my devotion to the god.

There is another thing:—young men of the richer classes, who have not much to do, come about me of their own accord; they like to hear the pretenders examined, and they often imitate me, and examine others themselves; there are plenty of persons, as they soon enough discover, who think that they know something, but really know little or nothing: and then those who are examined by them instead of being angry with themselves are angry with me: This confounded Socrates, they say; this villainous misleader of youth!—and then if somebody asks them, Why, what evil does he practice or teach? they do not know, and cannot tell: but in order that they may not appear to be at a loss, they repeat the ready-made charges which are used against all philosophers about teaching things up in the clouds and under the earth, and having no gods, and making the worse appear the better cause; for they do not like to confess that their pretense of knowledge has been detected—which is the truth: and as they are numerous and ambitious and energetic, and are all in battle array and have persuasive tongues, they have filled your ears with their loud and inveterate calumnies. And this is the reason why my three accusers, Meletus and Anytus and Lycon, have set upon me: Meletus, who has a quarrel with me on behalf of the poets; Anytus, on behalf of the craftsmen; Lycon, on behalf of the rhetoricians; and as I said at the beginning, I cannot expect to get rid of this mass of calumny all in a moment. And this, O men of Athens, is the truth and the whole truth; I have concealed nothing, I have dissembled nothing. And yet I know that this plainness of speech makes them hate me, and what is their hatred but a proof that I am speaking the truth?—this is the occasion and reason of their slander of me, as you will find out either in this or in any future inquiry.

I have said enough in my defense against the first class of my accusers; I turn to the second class, who are headed by Meletus, that good and patriotic man, as he calls himself. And now I will try to defend myself against them: these new accusers must also have their affidavit read. What do they say? Something of this sort: That Socrates is a doer of evil, and corrupter of the youth, and he does not believe in the gods of the State, and has other new divinities of his own. That is the sort of charge; and now let us examine the particular counts. He says that I am a doer of evil, who corrupts the youth; but I say, O men of Athens, that Meletus is a doer of evil, and the evil is that he makes a joke of a serious matter, and is too ready at bringing other men to trial from a pretended zeal and interest about matters in which he really never had the smallest interest. And the truth of this I will endeavor to prove.

Come hither, Meletus, and let me ask a question of you. You think a great deal about the improvement of youth?

Yes, I do.

Tell the judges, then, who is their improver; for you must know, as you have taken the pains to discover their corrupter, and are citing and accusing me before them. Speak, then, and tell the judges who their improver is. Observe, Meletus, that you are silent, and have nothing to say. But is not this rather disgraceful, and a very considerable proof of what I was saying, that you have no interest in the matter? Speak up, friend, and tell us who their improver is.

The laws.

But that, my good sir, is not my meaning. I want to know who the person is, who, in the first place, knows the laws.

The judges, Socrates, who are present in court.

What do you mean to say, Meletus, that they are able to instruct and improve youth?

Certainly they are.

What, all of them, or some only and not others?

All of them.

By the goddess Here, that is good news! There are plenty of improvers, then. And what do you say of the audience—do they improve them?

Yes, they do.

And the Senators?

Yes, the Senators improve them.

But perhaps the ecclesiasts corrupt them?—or do they too improve them?

They improve them.

Then every Athenian improves and elevates them; all with the exception of myself; and I alone am their corrupter? Is that what you affirm?

That is what I stoutly affirm.

I am very unfortunate if that is true. But suppose I ask you a question: Would you say that this also holds true in the case of horses? Does one man do them harm and all the world good? Is not the exact opposite of this true? One man is able to do them good, or at least not many; the trainer of horses, that is to say, does them good, and others who have to do with them rather injure them? Is not that true, Meletus, of horses, or any other animals? Yes, certainly. Whether you and Anytus say yes or no, that is no matter. Happy indeed would be the condition of youth if they had one corrupter only, and all the rest of the world were their improvers. And you, Meletus, have sufficiently shown that you never had a thought about the young: your carelessness is seen in your not caring about matters spoken of in this very indictment.

And now, Meletus, I must ask you another question: Which is better, to live among bad citizens, or among good ones? Answer, friend, I say; for that is a question which may be easily answered. Do not the good do their neighbors good, and the bad do them evil?

Certainly.

And is there anyone who would rather be injured than benefited by those who live with him?

Answer, my good friend; the law requires you to answer—does anyone like to be injured?

Certainly not.

And when you accuse me of corrupting and deteriorating the youth, do you allege that I corrupt them intentionally or unintentionally?

Intentionally, I say.

But you have just admitted that the good do their neighbors good, and the evil do them evil. Now is that a truth which your superior wisdom has recognized thus early in life, and am I, at my age, in such darkness and ignorance as not to know that if a man with whom I have to live is corrupted by me, I am very likely to be harmed by him, and yet I corrupt him, and intentionally, too? that is what you are saying, and of that you will never persuade me or any other human being. But either I do not corrupt them, or I corrupt them unintentionally, so that on either view of the case you lie. If my offense is unintentional, the law has no cognizance of unintentional offenses: you ought to have taken me privately, and warned and admonished me; for if I had been better advised, I should have left off doing what I only did unintentionally—no doubt I should; whereas you hated to converse with me or teach me, but you indicted me in this court, which is a place not of instruction, but of punishment.

I have shown, Athenians, as I was saying, that Meletus has no care at all, great or small, about the matter. But still I should like to know, Meletus, in what I am affirmed to corrupt the young. I suppose you mean, as I infer from your indictment, that I teach them not to acknowledge the gods which the State acknowledges, but some other new divinities or spiritual agencies in their stead. These are the lessons which corrupt the youth, as you say.

Yes, that I say emphatically.

Then, by the gods, Meletus, of whom we are speaking, tell me and the court, in somewhat plainer terms, what you mean! for I do not as yet understand whether you affirm that I teach others to acknowledge some gods, and therefore do believe in gods and am not an entire atheist—this you do not lay to my charge; but only that they are not the same gods which the city recognizes—the charge is that they are different gods. Or, do you mean to say that I am an atheist simply, and a teacher of atheism?

I mean the latter—that you are a complete atheist.

That is an extraordinary statement, Meletus. Why do you say that? Do you mean that I do not believe in the god-head of the sun or moon, which is the common creed of all men?

I assure you, judges, that he does not believe in them; for he says that the sun is stone, and the moon earth.

Friend Meletus, you think that you are accusing Anaxagoras; and you have but a bad opinion of the judges, if you fancy them ignorant to such a degree as not to know that these doctrines are found in the books of Anaxagoras the Clazomenian, who is full of them. And these are the doctrines which the youth are said to learn of Socrates, when there are not unfrequently exhibitions of them at the theater (price of admission one drachma at the most); and they might cheaply purchase them, and laugh at Socrates if he pretends to father such eccentricities. And so, Meletus, you really think that I do not believe in any god?

I swear by Zeus that you believe absolutely in none at all.

You are a liar, Meletus, not believed even by yourself. For I cannot help thinking, O men of Athens, that Meletus is reckless and impudent, and that he has written this indictment in a spirit of mere wantonness and youthful bravado. Has he not compounded a riddle, thinking to try me? He said to himself: I shall see whether this wise Socrates will discover my ingenious contradiction, or whether I shall be able to deceive him and the rest of them. For he certainly does appear to me to contradict himself in the indictment as much as if he said that Socrates is guilty of not believing in the gods, and yet of believing in them—but this surely is a piece of fun.

I should like you, O men of Athens, to join me in examining what I conceive to be his inconsistency; and do you, Meletus, answer. And I must remind you that you are not to interrupt me if I speak in my accustomed manner.

Did ever man, Meletus, believe in the existence of human things, and not of human beings? . . . I wish, men of Athens, that he would answer, and not be always trying to get up an interruption. Did ever any man believe in horsemanship, and not in horses? or in flute-playing and not in flute-players? No, my friend; I will answer to you and to the court, as you refuse to answer for yourself. There is no man who ever did. But now please to answer the next question: Can a man believe in spiritual and divine agencies, and not in spirits or demigods?

He cannot.

I am glad that I have extracted that answer, by the assistance of the court; nevertheless you swear in the indictment that I teach and believe in divine or spiritual agencies (new or old, no matter for that); at any rate, I believe in spiritual agencies, as you say and swear in the affidavit; but if I believe in divine beings, I must believe in spirits or demigods; is not that true? Yes, that is true, for I may assume that your silence gives assent to that. Now what are spirits or demigods? are they not either gods or the sons of gods? Is that true?

Yes, that is true.

But this is just the ingenious riddle of which I was speaking: the demigods or spirits are gods, and you say first that I don't believe in gods, and then again that I do believe in gods; that is, if I believe in demigods. For if the demigods are the illegitimate sons of gods, whether by the Nymphs or by any other mothers, as is thought, that, as all men will allow, necessarily implies the existence of their parents. You might as well affirm the existence of mules, and deny that of horses and asses. Such nonsense, Meletus, could only have been intended by you as a trial of me. You have put this into the indictment because you had nothing real of which to accuse me. But no one who has a particle of understanding will ever be convinced by you that the same man can believe in divine and superhuman things, and yet not believe that there are gods and demigods and heroes.

I have said enough in answer to the charge of Meletus: any elaborate defense is unnecessary; but as I was saying before, I certainly have many enemies, and this is what will be my destruction if I am destroyed; of that I am certain; not Meletus, nor yet Anytus, but the envy and detraction of the world, which has been the death of many good men, and will probably be the death of many more; there is no danger of my being the last of them.

Someone will say: And are you not ashamed, Socrates, of a course of life which is likely to bring you to an untimely end? To him I may fairly answer: There you are mistaken: a man who is good for anything ought not to calculate the chance of living or dying; he ought only to consider whether in doing anything he is doing right or wrong—acting the part of a good man or of a bad. Whereas, according to your view, the heroes who fell at Troy were not good for much, and the son of Thetis above all, who altogether despised danger in comparison with disgrace; and when his goddess mother said to him, in his eagerness to slay Hector, that if he avenged his companion Patroclus, and slew Hector, he would die himself—"Fate," as she said, "waits upon you next after Hector"; he, hearing this, utterly despised danger and death, and instead of fearing them, feared rather to live in dishonor, and not to avenge his friend. "Let me die next," he replies, "and be avenged of my enemy, rather than abide here by the beaked ships, a scorn and a burden of the earth." Had Achilles any thought of death and danger? For wherever a man's place is, whether the place which he has chosen or that in which he has been placed by a commander, there he ought to remain in the hour of danger; he should not think of death or of anything, but of disgrace. And this, O men of Athens, is a true saying.

Strange, indeed, would be my conduct, O men of Athens, if I who, when I was ordered by the generals whom you chose to command me at Potidæa and Amphipolis and Delium, remained where they placed me, like any other man, facing death—if, I say, now, when, as I conceive and imagine, God orders me to fulfill the philosopher's mission of searching into myself and other men, I were to desert my post through fear of death, or any other fear; that would indeed be strange, and I might justly be arraigned in court for denying the existence of the gods, if I disobeyed the oracle because I was afraid of death: then I should be fancying that I was wise when I was not wise. For this fear of death is indeed the pretense of wisdom, and not real wisdom, being the appearance of knowing the unknown; since no one knows whether death, which they in their fear apprehend to be the greatest evil, may not be the greatest good. Is there not here conceit of knowledge, which is a disgraceful sort of ignorance? And this is the point in which, as I think, I am superior to men in general, and in which I might perhaps fancy myself wiser than other men—that whereas I know but little of the world below, I do not suppose that I know: but I do know that injustice and disobedience to a better, whether God or man, is evil and dishonorable, and I will never fear or avoid a possible good rather than a certain evil. And therefore if you let me go now, and reject the counsels of Anytus, who said that if I were not put to death I ought not to have been prosecuted, and that if I escape now, your sons will all be utterly ruined by listening to my words—if you say to me, Socrates, this time we will not mind Anytus, and will let you off, but upon one condition, that you are not to inquire and speculate in this way any more, and that if you are caught doing this again you shall die—if this was the condition on which you let me go, I should reply: Men of Athens, I honor and love you; but I shall obey God rather than you, and while I have life and strength I shall never cease from the practice and teaching of philosophy, exhorting anyone whom I meet after my manner, and convincing him, saying: O my friend, why do you who are a citizen of the great and mighty and wise city of Athens, care so much about laying up the greatest amount of money and honor and reputation, and so little about wisdom and truth and the greatest improvement of the soul, which you never regard or heed at all? Are you not ashamed of this? And if the person with whom I am arguing says: Yes, but I do care; I do not depart or let him go at once; I interrogate and examine and cross-examine him, and if I think that he has no virtue, but only says that he has, I reproach him with undervaluing the greater, and overvaluing the less. And this I should say to everyone whom I meet, young and old, citizen and alien, but especially to the citizens, inasmuch as they are my brethren. For this is the command of God, as I would have you know; and I believe that to this day no greater good has ever happened in the State than my service to the God. For I do nothing but go about persuading you all, old and young alike, not to take thought for your persons and your properties, but first and chiefly to care about the greatest improvement of the soul. I tell you that virtue is not given by money, but that from virtue come money and every other good of man, public as well as private. This is my teaching, and if this is the doctrine which corrupts the youth, my influence is ruinous indeed. But if anyone says that this is not my teaching, he is speaking an untruth. Wherefore, O men of Athens, I say to you, do as Anytus bids or not as Anytus bids, and either acquit me or not; but whatever you do, know that I shall never alter my ways, not even if I have to die many times.

Men of Athens, do not interrupt, but hear me; there was an agreement between us that you should hear me out. And I think that what I am going to say will do you good: for I have something more to say, at which you may be inclined to cry out; but I beg that you will not do this. I would have you know that, if you kill such a one as I am, you will injure yourselves more than you will injure me. Meletus and Anytus will not injure me: they cannot; for it is not in the nature of things that a bad man should injure a better than himself. I do not deny that he may, perhaps, kill him, or drive him into exile, or deprive him of civil rights; and he may imagine, and others may imagine, that he is doing him a great injury: but in that I do not agree with him; for the evil of doing as Anytus is doing—of unjustly taking away another man's life—is greater far. And now, Athenians, I am not going to argue for my own sake, as you may think, but for yours, that you may not sin against the God, or lightly reject his boon by condemning me. For if you kill me you will not easily find another like me, who, if I may use such a ludicrous figure of speech, am a sort of gadfly, given to the State by the God; and the State is like a great and noble steed who is tardy in his motions owing to his very size, and requires to be stirred into life. I am that gadfly which God has given the State and all day long and in all places am always fastening upon you, arousing and persuading and reproaching you. And as you will not easily find another like me, I would advise you to spare me. I dare say that you may feel irritated at being suddenly awakened when you are caught napping; and you may think that if you were to strike me dead, as Anytus advises, which you easily might, then you would sleep on for the remainder of your lives, unless God in his care of you gives you another gadfly. And that I am given to you by God is proved by this: that if I had been like other men, I should not have neglected all my own concerns, or patiently seen the neglect of them during all these years, and have been doing yours, coming to you individually, like a father or elder brother, exhorting you to regard virtue; this, I say, would not be like human nature. And had I gained anything, or if my exhortations had been paid, there would have been some sense in that: but now, as you will perceive, not even the impudence of my accusers dares to say that I have ever exacted or sought pay of anyone; they have no witness of that. And I have a witness of the truth of what I say; my poverty is a sufficient witness.

Someone may wonder why I go about in private, giving advice and busying myself with the concerns of others, but do not venture to come forward in public and advise the State. I will tell you the reason of this. You have often heard me speak of an oracle or sign which comes to me, and is the divinity which Meletus ridicules in the indictment. This sign I have had ever since I was a child. The sign is a voice which comes to me and always forbids me to do something which I am going to do, but never commands me to do anything, and this is what stands in the way of my being a politician.

And rightly, as I think. For I am certain, O men of Athens, that if I had engaged in politics, I should have perished long ago and done no good either to you or to myself. And don't be offended at my telling you the truth: for the truth is that no man who goes to war with you or any other multitude, honestly struggling against the commission of unrighteousness and wrong in the State, will save his life; he who will really fight for the right, if he would live even for a little while, must have a private station and not a public one.

I can give you as proofs of this, not words only, but deeds, which you value more than words. Let me tell you a passage of my own life, which will prove to you that I should never have yielded to injustice from any fear of death, and that if I had not yielded I should have died at once. I will tell you a story—tasteless, perhaps, and commonplace, but nevertheless true. The only office of State which I ever held, O men of Athens, was that of Senator; the tribe of Antiochis, which is my tribe, had the presidency at the trial of the generals who had not taken up the bodies of the slain after the battle of Arginusæ; and you proposed to try them all together, which was illegal, as you all thought afterwards; but at the time I was the only one of the Prytanes who was opposed to the illegality, and I gave my vote against you; and when the orators threatened to impeach and arrest me, and have me taken away, and you called and shouted, I made up my mind that I would run the risk, having law and justice with me, rather than take part in your injustice because I feared imprisonment and death. This happened in the days of the democracy. But when the oligarchy of the Thirty was in power, they sent for me and four others into the rotunda, and bade us bring Leon the Salaminian from Salamis, as they wanted to execute him. This was a specimen of the sort of commands which they were always giving with the view of implicating as many as possible in their crimes; and then I showed, not in words only, but in deed, that, if I may be allowed to use such an expression, I cared not a straw for death, and that my only fear was the fear of doing an unrighteous or unholy thing. For the strong arm of that oppressive power did not frighten me into doing wrong; and when we came out of the rotunda the other four went to Salamis and fetched Leon, but I went quietly home. For which I might have lost my life, had not the power of the Thirty shortly afterwards come to an end. And to this many will witness.

Now do you really imagine that I could have

survived all these years, if I had led a public life, supposing that like a good man I had always supported the right and had made justice, as I ought, the first thing? No, indeed, men of Athens, neither I nor any other. But if I have been always the same in all my actions, public as well as private, and never have I yielded any base compliance to those who are slanderously termed my disciples or to any other. For the truth is that I have no regular disciples: but if anyone likes to come and hear me while I am pursuing my mission, whether he be young or old, he may freely come. Nor do I converse with those who pay only, and not with those who do not pay; but anyone, whether he be rich or poor, may ask and answer me and listen to my words; and whether he turns out to be a bad man or a good one; that cannot be justly laid to my charge, as I never taught him anything. And if anyone says that he has ever learned or heard anything from me in private which all the world has not heard, I should like you to know that he is speaking an untruth.

But I shall be asked, Why do people delight in continually conversing with you? I have told you already, Athenians, the whole truth about this: they like to hear the cross examination of the pretenders to wisdom; there is amusement in this. And this is a duty which the God has imposed upon me, as I am assured by oracles, visions, and in every sort of way in which the will of divine power was ever signified to anyone. This is true, O Athenians; or, if not true, would be soon refuted. For if I am really corrupting the youth, and have corrupted some of them already, those of them who have grown up and have become sensible that I gave them bad advice in the days of their youth should come forward as accusers and take their revenge; and if they do not like to come themselves, some of their relatives, fathers, brothers, or other kinsmen, should say what evil their families suffered at my hands. Now is their time. Many of them I see in the court. There is Crito, who is of the same age and of the same *deme* with myself; and there is Critobulus his son, whom I also see. Then again there is Lysanias of Sphettus, who is the father of Æschines—he is present; and also there is Antiphon of Cephisus, who is the father of Epignes; and there are the brothers of several who have associated with me. There is Nicostratus the son of Theosdotides, and the brother of Theodotus (now Theodotus himself is dead, and therefore he, at any rate, will not seek to stop him); and there is Paralus the son of Demodocus, who had a brother Theages; and Adeimantus the son of Ariston, whose brother Plato is present; and Æantodorus, who is the brother of Apollodorus, whom I also see. I might mention a great many others, any of whom Meletus should have produced as witnesses in the course of his speech; and let him still produce them, if he has forgotten; I will make way for him. And let him say, if he has any testimony of the sort which he can produce. Nay, Athenians, the very opposite is the truth. For all these are ready to witness on behalf of the corrupter, of the destroyer of their kindred, as Meletus and Anytus call me; not the corrupted youth only —there might have been a motive for that—but their uncorrupted elder relatives. Why should they too support me with their testimony? Why, indeed, except for the sake of truth and justice, and because they know that I am speaking the truth, and that Meletus is lying.

Well, Athenians, this and the like of this is nearly all the defense which I have to offer. Yet a word more. Perhaps there may be someone who is offended at me, when he calls to mind how he himself, on a similar or even a less serious occasion, had recourse to prayers and supplications with many tears, and how he produced his children in court, which was a moving spectacle, together with a posse of his relations and friends; whereas I, who am probably in danger of my life, will do none of these things. Perhaps this may come into his mind, and he may be set against me, and vote in anger because he is displeased at this. Now if there be such a person among you, which I am far from affirming, I may fairly reply to him: My friend, I am a man, and like other men, a creature of flesh and blood, and not of wood or stone, as Homer says; and I have a family, yes, and sons, O Athenians, three in number, one of whom is growing up, and the two others are still young; and yet I will not bring any of them hither in order to petition you for an acquittal. And why not? Not from any self-will or disregard of you. Whether I am or am not afraid of death is another question, of which I will not now speak. But my reason simply is that I feel such conduct to be discreditable to myself, and you, and the whole State. One who has reached my years, and who has a name for wisdom, whether deserved or not, ought not to debase himself. At any rate, the world has decided that Socrates is in some way superior to other men. And if those among you who are said to be superior in wisdom and courage, and any other virtue, demean themselves in this way, how shameful is their conduct! I have seen men of reputation, when they have been condemned, behaving in the strangest manner: they seemed to fancy that they were going to suffer something dreadful if they died, and that they could be immortal if you only allowed them to live; and I think that they were a dishonor to the State, and that any stranger coming in would say of them that the most eminent men of Athens, to whom the Athenians themselves give honor and command, are no better than women. And I say that these things ought not to be done by those of us who are of reputation; and if they are done, you ought not to permit them; you ought rather to show that you are more inclined to condemn, not the man who is quiet, but the man who gets up a doleful scene, and makes the city ridiculous.

But, setting aside the question of dishonor, there seems to be something wrong in petitioning a judge, and thus procuring an acquittal instead of informing and convincing him. For his duty is, not to make a present of justice, but to give judgment; and he has sworn that he will judge according to the laws, and not according to his own good pleasure; and neither he nor we should get into the habit of perjuring ourselves—there can be no piety in that. Do not then require me to do what I consider dishonorable and impious and wrong, especially now, when I am being tried for impiety on the indictment of Meletus. For if, O men of Athens, by force of persuasion and entreaty, I could overpower your oaths, then I should be teaching you to believe that there are no gods, and convict myself, in my own defense, of not believing in them. But that is not the case; for I do believe that there are gods, and in a far higher sense than that in which any of my accusers believe in them. And to you and to God I commit my cause, to be determined by you as is best for you and me.

There are many reasons why I am not grieved, O men of Athens, at the vote of condemnation. I expected this, and am only surprised that the votes are so nearly equal; for I had thought that the majority against me would have been far larger; but now, had thirty votes gone over to the other side, I should have been acquitted. And I may say that I have escaped Meletus. And I may say more; for without the assistance of Anytus and Lycon, he would not have had a fifth part of the votes, as the law requires, in which case he would have incurred a fine of a thousand drachmæ, as is evident.

And so he proposes death as the penalty. And what shall I propose on my part, O men of Athens? Clearly that which is my due. And what is that which I ought to pay or to receive? What shall be done to the man who has never had the wit to be idle during his whole life; but has been careless of what the many care about—wealth and family interests, and military offices, and speaking in the assembly, and magistracies, and plots, and parties. Reflecting that I was really too honest a man to follow in this way and live, I did not go where I could do no good to you or to myself; but where I could do the greatest good privately to every one of you, thither I went, and sought to persuade every man among you that he must look to himself, and seek virtue and wisdom before he looks to his private interests, and look to the State before he looks to the interests of the State; and that this should be the order which he observes in all his actions. What shall be done to such a one? Doubtless some good thing, O men of Athens, if he has his reward; and the good should be of a kind suitable to him. What would be a reward suitable to a poor man who is your benefactor, who desires leisure that he may instruct you? There can be no more fitting reward than maintenance in the Prytaneum, O men of Athens, a reward which he deserves far more than the citizen who has won the prize at Olympia in the horse or chariot race, whether the chariots were drawn by two horses or by many. For I am in want, and he has enough; and he only gives you the appearance of happiness, and I give you the reality. And if I am to estimate the penalty justly, I say that maintenance in the Prytaneum is the just return.

Perhaps you may think that I am braving you in saying this, as in what I said before about the tears and prayers. But that is not the case. I speak rather because I am convinced that I never intentionally wronged anyone, although I cannot convince you of that—for we have had a short conversation only; but if there were a law at Athens, such as there is in other cities, that a capital cause should not be decided in one day, then I believe that I should have convinced you; but now the time is too short. I cannot in a moment refute great slanders; and, as I am convinced that I never wronged another, I will assuredly not wrong myself. I will not say of myself that I deserve any evil, or propose any penalty. Why should I? Because I am afraid of the penalty of death which Meletus proposes? When I do not know whether death is a good or an evil, why should I propose a penalty which would certainly be an evil? Shall I say imprisonment? And why should I live in prison, and be the slave of the magistrates of the year—of the Eleven? Or shall the penalty be a fine, and imprisonment until the fine is paid? There is the same objection. I should have to lie in prison, for money I have none, and I cannot pay. And if I say exile (and this may possibly be the penalty which you will affix), I must indeed be blinded by the love of life if I were to consider that when you, who are my own citizens, cannot endure my discourses and words, and have found them so grievous and odious that you would fain have done with them, others are likely to endure me. No, indeed, men of Athens, that is not very likely. And what a life should I lead, at my age, wandering from city to city, living in ever-changing exile, and always being driven out! For I am quite sure that into whatever place I go, as here so also there, the young men will come to me; and if I drive them away, their elders will drive me out at their desire: and if I let them come, their fathers and friends will drive me out for their sakes.

Someone will say: Yes, Socrates, but cannot you hold your tongue, and then you may go into a foreign city, and no one will interfere with you? Now I have great difficulty in making you understand my answer to this. For if I tell you that this would be a disobedience to a divine command, and therefore that I cannot hold my tongue, you will not believe that I am serious; and if I say again that the greatest good of man is daily to converse about virtue, and all that concerning which you hear me examining myself and others, and that the life which is unexamined is not worth living—that you are still less likely to believe. And yet what I say is true, although a thing of which it is hard for me to persuade you. Moreover, I am not accustomed to think that I deserve any punishment. Had I money I might have proposed to give you what I had, and have been none the worse. But you see that I have none, and can only ask you to proportion the fine to my means. However, I think that I could afford a mina, and therefore, I propose that penalty: Plato, Crito, Critobulus, and Apollodorus, my friends here, bid me say thirty minæ, and they will be the sureties. Well then, say thirty minæ, let that be the penalty; for that they will be ample security to you.

Not much time will be gained, O Athenians, in return for the evil name which you will get from the detractors of the city, who will say that you killed Socrates, a wise man; for they will call me wise even although I am not wise when they want to reproach you. If you had waited a little while, your desire would have been fulfilled in the course of nature. For I am far advanced in years, as you may perceive and not far from death. I am speaking now only to those of you who have condemned me to death. And I have another thing to say to them: You think that I was convinced through deficiency of words—I mean, that if I had thought fit to leave nothing undone, nothing unsaid, I might have gained an acquittal. Not so; the deficiency which led to my conviction was not of words—certainly not. But I had not the boldness or impudence or inclination to address you, weeping and wailing and lamenting, and saying and doing many things which you have been accustomed to hear from others, and which, as I say, are unworthy of me. But I thought that I ought not to do anything common or mean in the hour of danger: nor do I now repent of the manner of my defense, and I would rather die having spoken after my manner, than speak in your manner and live. For neither in war nor yet at law ought any man to use every way of escaping death. For often in battle there is no doubt that if a man will throw away his arms, and fall on his knees before his pursuers, he may escape death; and in other dangers there are other ways of escaping death, if a man is willing to say and do anything. The difficulty, my friends, is not in avoiding death, but in avoiding unrighteousness; for that runs faster than death. I am old and move slowly, and the slower runner has overtaken me, and my accusers are keen and quick, and the faster runner, who is unrighteousness, has overtaken them. And now I depart hence condemned by you to suffer the penalty of death, and they, too, go their ways condemned by the truth to suffer the penalty of villainy and wrong; and I must abide by my award—let them abide by theirs. I suppose that these things may be regarded as fated—and I think that they are well.

And now, O men who have condemned me, I would fain prophesy to you; for I am about to die, and that is the hour in which men are gifted with prophetic power. And I prophesy to you who are my murderers, that immediately after my death punishment far heavier than you have inflicted on me will surely await you. Me you have killed because you wanted to escape the accuser, and not to give an account of your lives. But that will not be as you suppose: far otherwise. For I say that there will be more accusers of you than there are now; accusers whom hitherto I have restrained: and as they are younger they will be more severe with you, and you will be more offended at them. For if you think that by killing men you can avoid the accuser censuring your lives, you are mistaken; that is not a way of escape which is either possible or honorable; the easiest and noblest way is not to be crushing others, but to be improving yourselves. This is the prophecy which I utter before my departure, to the judges who have condemned me.

Friends, who would have acquitted me, I would like also to talk with you about this thing which has happened, while the magistrates are busy, and before I go to the place at which I must die. Stay then awhile, for we may as well talk with one another while there is time. You are my friends, and I should like to show you the meaning of this event which has happened to me. O my judges—for you I may truly call judges—I should like to tell you of a wonderful circumstance. Hitherto the familiar oracle within me has constantly been in the habit of opposing me even about trifles, if I was going to make a slip or error about anything; and now as you see there has come upon me that which may be thought, and is generally believed to be, the last and worst evil. But the oracle made no sign of opposition, either as I was leaving my house and going out in the morning, or when I was going up into this court, or while I was speaking, at anything which I was going to say; and yet I have often been stopped in the middle of a speech; but now in nothing I either said or did touching this matter has the oracle opposed me. What do I take to be the explanation of this? I will tell you. I regard this as a proof that what has happened to me is a good, and that those of us who think that death is an evil are in error. This is a great proof to me of what I am saying, for the customary sign would surely have opposed me had I been going to evil and not to good.

Let us reflect in another way, and we shall see that there is great reason to hope that death is a good, for one of two things: either death is a state of nothingness and utter unconsciousness, or, as men say, there is a change and migration of the soul from this world to another. Now if you suppose that there is no consciousness, but a sleep like the sleep of him who is undisturbed even by the sight of dreams, death will be an unspeakable gain. For if a person were to select the night in which his sleep was undisturbed even by dreams, and were to compare with this the other days and nights of his life, and then were to tell us how many days and nights he had passed in the course of his life better and more pleasantly than this one, I think that any man, I will not say a private man, but even the great king, will not find many such days or nights, when compared with the others. Now if death is like this, I say that to die, is gain; for eternity is then only a single night. But if death is the journey to another place, and there, as men say, all the dead are, what good, O my friends and judges, can be greater than this? If indeed when the pilgrim arrives in the world below, he is delivered from the professors of justice in this world, and finds the true judges who are said to give judgment there, Minos and Rhadamanthus and Æacus and Triptolemus, and other sons of God who were righteous in their own life, that pilgrimage will be worth making. What would not a man give if he might converse with Orpheus and Musæus and Hesiod and Homer? Nay, if this be true, let me die again and again. I, too, shall have a wonderful interest in a place where I can converse with Palamedes, and Ajax the son of Telamon, and other heroes of old, who have suffered death through an unjust judgment; and there will be no small pleasure, as I think, in comparing my own sufferings with theirs. Above all, I shall be able to continue my search into true and false knowledge; as in this world, so also in that; I shall find out who is wise, and who pretends to be wise, and is not. What would not a man give, O judges, to be able to examine the leader of the great Trojan expedition; or Odysseus or Sisyphus, or numberless others, men and women too! What infinite delight would there be in conversing with them and asking them questions! For in that world they do not put a man to death for this; certainly not. For besides being happier in that world than in this, they will be immortal, if what is said is true.

Wherefore, O judges, be of good cheer about death, and know this of a truth—that no evil can happen to a good man, either in life or after death. He and his are not neglected by the gods; nor has my own approaching end happened by mere chance. But I see clearly that to die and be released was better for me; and therefore the oracle gave no sign. For which reason also, I am not angry with my accusers, or my condemners; they have done me no harm, although neither of them meant to do me any good; and for this I may gently blame them.

Still I have a favor to ask of them. When my

sons are grown up, I would ask you, O my friends, to punish them; and I would have you trouble them, as I have troubled you, if they seem to care about riches, or anything, more than about virtue; or if they pretend to be something when they are really nothing—then reprove them, as I have reproved you, for not caring about that for which they ought to care, and thinking that they are something when they are really nothing. And if you do this, I and my sons will have received justice at your hands.

The hour of departure has arrived, and we go our ways—I to die, and you to live. Which is better, God only knows.

Phædo

PERSONS OF THE DIALOGUE

PHÆDO, *who is the narrator of the Dialogue to Echecrates of Phlius*
SOCRATES
Attendant of the Prison
APOLLODORUS
SIMMIAS
CEBES
CRITO

SCENE:—*The Prison of Socrates*

PLACE OF THE NARRATION:—*Phlius*

ECH. Were you yourself, Phædo, in the prison with Socrates on the day when he drank the poison?

PHÆD. Yes, Echecrates, I was.

ECH. I should so like to hear about his death. What did he say in his last hours? We were informed that he died by taking poison, but no one knew anything more; for no Phliasian ever goes to Athens now, and it is a long time since any stranger from Athens has found his way hither; so that we had no clear account.

PHÆD. Did you not hear of the proceedings at the trial?

ECH. Yes; someone told us about the trial, and we could not understand why, having been condemned, he should have been put to death, not at the time, but long afterwards. What was the reason of this?

PHÆD. An accident, Echecrates: the stern of the ship which the Athenians send to Delos happened to have been crowned on the day before he was tried.

ECH. What is this ship?

PHÆD. It is the ship in which, according to Athenian tradition, Theseus went to Crete when he took with him the fourteen youths, and was the savior of them and of himself. And they are said to have vowed to Apollo at the time, that if they were saved they would send a yearly mission to Delos. Now this custom still continues, and the whole period of the voyage to and from Delos, beginning when the priest of Apollo crowns the stern of the ship, is a holy season, during which the city is not allowed to be polluted by public executions; and when the vessel is detained by contrary winds, the time spent in going and returning is very considerable. As I was saying, the ship was crowned on the day before the trial, and this was the reason why Socrates lay in prison and was not put to death until long after he was condemned.

ECH. What was the manner of his death, Phædo? What was said or done? And which of his friends were with him? Or did the authorities forbid them to be present—so that he had no friends near him when he died?

PHÆD. No; there were several of them with him.

ECH. If you have nothing to do, I wish that you would tell me what passed, as exactly as you can.

PHÆD. I have nothing at all to do, and will try to gratify your wish. To be reminded of Socrates is always the greatest delight to me, whether I speak myself or hear another speak of him.

ECH. You will have listeners who are of the same mind with you, and I hope that you will be as exact as you can.

PHÆD. I had a singular feeling at being in his company. For I could hardly believe that I was present at the death of a friend, and therefore I did not pity him, Echecrates; he died so fearlessly, and his words and bearing were so noble and gra-

Plato. *Phædo*. Translated by Benjamin Jowett.

cious, that to me he appeared blessed. I thought that in going to the other world he could not be without a divine call, and that he would be happy, if any man ever was, when he arrived there; and therefore I did not pity him as might have seemed natural at such an hour. But I had not the pleasure which I usually feel in philosophical discourse (for philosophy was the theme of which we spoke). I was pleased, but in the pleasure there was also a strange admixture of pain; for I reflected that he was soon to die, and this double feeling was shared by us all; we were laughing and weeping by turns, especially the excitable Apollodorus—you know the sort of man?

Ech. Yes.

Phæd. He was quite beside himself; and I and all of us were greatly moved.

Ech. Who were present?

Phæd. Of native Athenians there were, besides Apollodorus, Critobulus and his father Crito, Hermogenes, Epigenes, Æschines, Antisthenes; likewise Ctesippus of the deme of Pæania, Menexenus, and some others; Plato, if I am not mistaken, was ill.

Ech. Were there any strangers?

Phæd. Yes, there were; Simmias the Theban, and Cebes, and Phædondes; Euclid and Terpsion, who came from Megara.

Ech. And was Aristippus there, and Cleombrotus?

Phæd. No, they were said to be in Ægina.

Ech. Anyone else?

Phæd. I think that these were nearly all.

Ech. Well, and what did you talk about?

Phæd. I will begin at the beginning, and endeavor to repeat the entire conversation. On the previous days we had been in the habit of assembling early in the morning at the court in which the trial took place, and which is not far from the prison. There we used to wait talking with one another until the opening of the doors (for they were not opened very early); then we went in and generally passed the day with Socrates. On the last morning we assembled sooner than usual, having heard on the day before when we quitted the prison in the evening that the sacred ship had come from Delos; and so we arranged to meet very early at the accustomed place. On our arrival the jailer who answered the door, instead of admitting us, came out and told us to stay until he called us. "For the Eleven," he said, "are now with Socrates; they are taking off his chains, and giving orders that he is to die today." He soon returned and said

that we might come in. On entering we found Socrates just released from chains, and Xanthippè, whom you know, sitting by him, and holding his child in her arms. When she saw us she uttered a cry and said, as women will: "O Socrates, this is the last time that either you will converse with your friends, or they with you." Socrates turned to Crito and said: "Crito, let someone take her home." Some of Crito's people accordingly led her away, crying out and beating herself. And when she was gone, Socrates, sitting up on the couch, bent and rubbed his leg, saying, as he was rubbing: How singular is the thing called pleasure, and how curiously related to pain, which might be thought to be the opposite of it; for they are never present to a man at the same instant, and yet he who pursues either is generally compelled to take the other; their bodies are two, but they are joined by a single head. And I cannot help thinking that if Æsop had remembered them, he would have made a fable about God trying to reconcile their strife, and how, when he could not, he fastened their heads together; and this is the reason why when one comes the other follows: as I know by my own experience now, when after the pain in my leg which was caused by the chain pleasure appears to succeed.

Upon this Cebes said: I am glad, Socrates, that you have mentioned the name of Æsop. For it reminds me of a question which has been asked by many, and was asked of me only the day before yesterday by Evenus the poet—he will be sure to ask it again, and therefore if you would like me to have an answer ready for him, you may as well tell me what I should say to him:—he wanted to know why you, who never before wrote a line of poetry, now that you are in prison are turning Æsop's fables into verse, and also composing that hymn in honor of Apollo.

Tell him, Cebes, he replied, what is the truth— that I had no idea of rivaling him or his poems; to do so, as I knew, would be no easy task. But I wanted to see whether I could purge away a scruple which I felt about the meaning of certain dreams. In the course of my life I have often had intimations in dreams "that I should compose music." The same dream came to me sometimes in one form, and sometimes in another, but always saying the same or nearly the same words: "Cultivate and make music," said the dream. And hitherto I had imagined that this was only intended to exhort and encourage me in the study of philosophy, which has been the pursuit of my life, and is the noblest and best of music. The dream was bidding me do what I was already doing, in the same way that the competitor in a race is bidden by the spectators to run when he is already running. But I was not certain of this; for the dream might have meant music in the popular sense of the word, and being under sentence of death, and the festival giving me a respite, I thought that it would be safer for me to satisfy the scruple, and, in obedience to the dream, to compose a few verses before I departed. And first I made a hymn in honor of the god of the festival, and then considering that a poet, if he is really to be a poet, should not only put together words, but should invent stories, and that I have no invention, I took some fables of Æsop, which I had ready at hand and which I knew—they were the first I came upon—and turned them into verse. Tell this to Evenus, Cebes, and bid him be of good cheer; say that I would have him come after me if he be a wise man, and not tarry; and that today I am likely to be going, for the Athenians say that I must.

Simmias said: What a message for such a man! having been a frequent companion of his I should say that, as far as I know him, he will never take your advice unless he is obliged.

Why, said Socrates,—is not Evenus a philosopher?

I think that he is, said Simmias.

Then he, or any man who has the spirit of philosophy, will be willing to die; but he will not take his own life, for that is held to be unlawful.

Here he changed his position, and put his legs off the couch on to the ground, and during the rest of the conversation he remained sitting.

Why do you say, enquired Cebes, that a man ought not to take his own life, but that the philosopher will be ready to follow the dying?

Socrates replied: And have you, Cebes and Simmias, who are the disciples of Philolaus, never heard him speak of this?

Yes, but his language was obscure, Socrates.

My words, too, are only an echo; but there is no reason why I should not repeat what I have heard: and indeed, as I am going to another place, it is very meet for me to be thinking and talking of the nature of the pilgrimage which I am about to make. What can I do better in the interval between this and the setting of the sun?

Then tell me, Socrates, why is suicide held to be unlawful? as I have certainly heard Philolaus, about whom you were just now asking, affirm when he was staying with us at Thebes; and there

are others who say the same, although I have never understood what was meant by any of them.

Do not lose heart, replied Socrates, and the day may come when you will understand. I suppose that you wonder why, when other things which are evil may be good at certain times and to certain persons, death is to be the only exception, and why, when a man is better dead, he is not permitted to be his own benefactor, but must wait for the hand of another.

Very true, said Cebes, laughing gently and speaking in his native Bœotian.

I admit the appearance of inconsistency in what I am saying; but there may not be any real inconsistency after all. There is a doctrine whispered in secret that man is a prisoner who has no right to open the door and run away; this is a great mystery which I do not quite understand. Yet I too believe that the gods are our guardians, and that we men are a possession of theirs. Do you not agree?

Yes, I quite agree, said Cebes.

And if one of your own possessions, an ox or an ass, for example, took the liberty of putting himself out of the way when you had given no intimation of your wish that he should die, would you not be angry with him, and would you not punish him if you could?

Certainly, replied Cebes.

Then, if we look at the matter thus, there may be reason in saying that a man should wait, and not take his own life until God summons him, as he is now summoning me.

Yes, Socrates, said Cebes, there seems to be truth in what you say. And yet how can you reconcile this seemingly true belief that God is our guardian and we his possessions, with the willingness to die which you were just now attributing to the philosopher? That the wisest of men should be willing to leave a service in which they are ruled by the gods who are the best of rulers, is not reasonable; for surely no wise man thinks that when set at liberty he can take better care of himself than the gods take of him. A fool may perhaps think so—he may argue that he had better run away from his master, not considering that his duty is to remain to the end, and not to run away from the good, and that there would be no sense in his running away. The wise man will want to be ever with him who is better than himself. Now this, Socrates, is the reverse of what was just now said; for upon this view the wise man should sorrow and the fool rejoice at passing out of life.

The earnestness of Cebes seemed to please Socrates. Here, said he, turning to us, is a man who is always enquiring, and is not so easily convinced by the first thing which he hears.

And certainly, added Simmias, the objection which he is now making does appear to me to have some force. For what can be the meaning of a truly wise man wanting to fly away and lightly leave a master who is better than himself? And I rather imagine that Cebes is referring to you; he thinks that you are too ready to leave us, and too ready to leave the gods whom you acknowledge to be our good masters.

Yes, replied Socrates; there is reason in what you say. And so you think that I ought to answer your indictment as if I were in a court?

We should like you to do so, said Simmias.

Then I must try to make a more successful defense before you than I did before the judges. For I am quite ready to admit, Simmias and Cebes, that I ought to be grieved at death, if I were not persuaded in the first place that I am going to other gods who are wise and good (of which I am as certain as I can be of any such matters), and secondly (though I am not so sure of this last) to men departed, better than those whom I leave behind; and therefore I do not grieve as I might have done, for I have good hope that there is yet something remaining for the dead, and as has been said of old, some far better thing for the good than for the evil.

But do you mean to take away your thoughts with you, Socrates? said Simmias. Will you not impart them to us?—for they are a benefit in which we too are entitled to share. Moreover, if you succeed in convincing us, that will be an answer to the charge against yourself.

I will do my best, replied Socrates. But you must first let me hear what Crito wants; he has long been wishing to say something to me.

Only this, Socrates, replied Crito:—the attendant who is to give you the poison has been telling me, and he wants me to tell you, that you are not to talk much; talking, he says, increases heat, and this is apt to interfere with the action of the poison; persons who excite themselves are sometimes obliged to take a second or even a third dose.

Then, said Socrates, let him mind his business and be prepared to give the poison twice or even thrice if necessary; that is all.

I knew quite well what you would say, replied Crito; but I was obliged to satisfy him.

Never mind him, he said.

And now, O my judges, I desire to prove to you that the real philosopher has reason to be of good cheer when he is about to die, and that after death he may hope to obtain the greatest good in the other world. And how this may be, Simmias and Cebes, I will endeavor to explain. For I deem that the true votary of philosophy is likely to be misunderstood by other men; they do not perceive that he is always pursuing death and dying; and if this be so, and he has had the desire of death all his life long, why when his time comes should he repine at that which he has been always pursuing and desiring?

Simmias said laughingly: Though not in a laughing humor, you have made me laugh, Socrates; for I cannot help thinking that the many when they hear your words will say how truly you have described philosophers, and our people at home will likewise say that the life which philosophers desire is in reality death, and that they have found them out to be deserving of the death which they desire.

And they are right, Simmias, in thinking so, with the exception of the words "they have found them out"; for they have not found out either what is the nature of that death which the true philosopher deserves, or how he deserves or desires death. But enough of them:—let us discuss the matter among ourselves. Do we believe that there is such a thing as death?

To be sure, replied Simmias.

Is it not the separation of soul and body? And to be dead is the completion of this; when the soul exists in herself, and is released from the body and the body is released from the soul, what is this but death?

Just so, he replied.

There is another question, which will probably throw light on our present enquiry if you and I can agree about it:—Ought the philosopher to care about the pleasures—if they are to be called pleasures—of eating and drinking?

Certainly not, answered Simmias.

And what about the pleasures of love—should he care for them?

By no means.

And will he think much of the other ways of indulging the body, for example, the acquisition of costly raiment, or sandals, or other adornments of the body? Instead of caring about them, does he not rather despise anything more than nature needs? What do you say?

I should say that the true philosopher would despise them.

Would you not say that he is entirely concerned with the soul and not with the body? He would like, as far as he can, to get away from the body and to turn to the soul.

Quite true.

In matters of this sort philosophers, above all other men, may be observed in every sort of way to dissever the soul from the communion of the body.

Very true.

Whereas, Simmias, the rest of the world are of opinion that to him who has no sense of pleasure and no part in bodily pleasure, life is not worth having; and that he who is indifferent about them is as good as dead.

That is also true.

What again shall we say of the actual acquirement of knowledge?—is the body, if invited to share in the enquiry, a hinderer or a helper? I mean to say, have sight and hearing any truth in them? Are they not, as the poets are always telling us, inaccurate witnesses? and yet, if even they are inaccurate and indistinct, what is to be said of the other senses?—for you will allow that they are the best of them?

Certainly, he replied.

Then when does the soul attain truth?—for in attempting to consider anything in company with the body she is obviously deceived.

True.

Then must not true existence be revealed to her in thought, if at all?

Yes.

And thought is best when the mind is gathered into herself and none of these things trouble her—neither sounds nor sights nor pain nor any pleasure,—when she takes leave of the body, and has as little as possible to do with it, when she has no bodily sense or desire, but is aspiring after true being?

Certainly.

And in this the philosopher dishonors the body; his soul runs away from his body and desires to be alone and by herself?

That is true.

Well, but there is another thing, Simmias: Is there or is there not an absolute justice?

Assuredly there is.

And an absolute beauty and absolute good?

Of course.

But did you ever behold any of them with your eyes?

Certainly not.

Or did you ever reach them with any other bodily sense?—and I speak not of these alone, but of absolute greatness, and health, and strength, and of the essence or true nature of everything. Has the reality of them ever been perceived by you through the bodily organs? or rather, is not the nearest approach to the knowledge of their several natures made by him who so orders his intellectual vision as to have the most exact conception of the essence of each thing which he considers?

Certainly.

And he attains to the purest knowledge of them who goes to each with the mind alone, not introducing or intruding in the act of thought sight or any other sense together with reason, but with the very light of the mind in her own clearness searches into the very truth of each; he who has got rid, as far as he can, of eyes and ears and, so to speak, of the whole body, these being in his opinion distracting elements which when they infect the soul hinder her from acquiring truth and knowledge—who, if not he, is likely to attain to the knowledge of true being?

What you say has a wonderful truth in it, Socrates, replied Simmias.

And when real philosophers consider all these things, will they not be led to make a reflection which they will express in words something like the following? "Have we not found," they will say, "a path of thought which seems to bring us and our argument to the conclusion, that while we are in the body, and while the soul is infected with the evils of the body, our desire will not be satisfied? and our desire is of the truth. For the body is a source of endless trouble to us by reason of the mere requirement of food; and is liable also to diseases which overtake and impede us in the search after true being: it fills us full of loves, and lusts, and fears, and fancies of all kinds, and endless foolery, and in fact, as men say, takes away from us the power of thinking at all. Whence come wars, and fightings, and factions? whence but from the body and the lusts of the body? Wars are occasioned by the love of money, and money has to be acquired for the sake and in the service of the body; and by reason of all these impediments we have no time to give to philosophy; and, last and worst of all, even if we are at leisure and betake ourselves to some speculation, the body is always breaking in upon us, causing turmoil and confusion in our enquiries, and so amazing us that we are prevented from seeing the truth. It has been proved to us by experience that if we would have pure knowledge of anything we must be quit of the body—the soul in herself must behold things in themselves: and then we shall attain the wisdom which we desire, and of which we say that we are lovers; not while we live, but after death; for if while in company with the body, the soul cannot have pure knowledge, one of two things follows—either knowledge is not to be attained at all, or, if at all, after death. For then, and not till then, the soul will be parted from the body and exist in herself alone. In this present life, I reckon that we make the nearest approach to knowledge when we have the least possible intercourse or communion with the body, and are not surfeited with the bodily nature, but keep ourselves pure until the hour when God himself is pleased to release us. And thus having got rid of the foolishness of the body we shall be pure and hold converse with the pure, and know of ourselves the clear light everywhere, which is no other than the light of truth." For the impure are not permitted to approach the pure. These are the sort of words, Simmias, which the true lovers of knowledge cannot help saying to one another, and thinking. You would agree; would you not?

Undoubtedly, Socrates.

But, O my friend, if this be true, there is great reason to hope that, going whither I go, when I have come to the end of my journey, I shall attain that which has been the pursuit of my life. And therefore I go on my way rejoicing, and not I only, but every other man who believes that his mind has been made ready and that he is in a manner purified.

Certainly, replied Simmias.

And what is purification but the separation of the soul from the body, as I was saying before; the habit of the soul gathering and collecting herself into herself from all sides out of the body; the dwelling in her own place alone, as in another life, so also in this, as far as she can;—the release of the soul from the chains of the body?

Very true, he said.

And this separation and release of the soul from the body is termed death?

To be sure, he said.

And the true philosophers, and they only, are ever seeking to release the soul. Is not the separation and release of the soul from the body their especial study?

That is true.

And, as I was saying at first, there would be a ridiculous contradiction in men studying to live as nearly as they can in a state of death, and yet repining when it comes upon them.

Clearly.

And the true philosophers, Simmias, are always occupied in the practice of dying, wherefore also to them least of all men is death terrible. Look at the matter thus:—if they have been in every way the enemies of the body, and are wanting to be alone with the soul, when this desire of theirs is granted, how inconsistent would they be if they trembled and repined, instead of rejoicing at their departure to that place where, when they arrive, they hope to gain that which in life they desired— and this was wisdom—and at the same time to be rid of the company of their enemy. Many a man has been willing to go to the world below animated by the hope of seeing there an earthly love, or wife, or son, and conversing with them. And will he who is a true lover of wisdom, and is strongly persuaded in like manner that only in the world below he can worthily enjoy her, still repine at death? Will he not depart with joy? Surely he will, O my friend, if he be a true philosopher. For he will have a firm conviction that there, and there only, he can find wisdom in her purity. And if this be true, he would be very absurd, as I was saying, if he were afraid of death.

He would indeed, replied Simmias.

And when you see a man who is repining at the approach of death, is not his reluctance a sufficient proof that he is not a lover of wisdom, but a lover of the body, and probably at the same time a lover of either money or power, or both?

Quite so, he replied.

And is not courage, Simmias, a quality which is specially characteristic of the philosopher?

Certainly.

There is temperance again, which even by the vulgar is supposed to consist in the control and regulation of the passions, and in the sense of superiority to them—is not temperance a virtue belonging to those only who despise the body, and who pass their lives in philosophy?

Most assuredly.

For the courage and temperance of other men, if you will consider them, are really a contradiction.

How so?

Well, he said, you are aware that death is regarded by men in general as a great evil.

Very true, he said.

And do not courageous men face death because they are afraid of yet greater evils?

That is quite true.

Then all but the philosophers are courageous only from fear, and because they are afraid; and yet that a man should be courageous from fear, and because he is a coward, is surely a strange thing.

Very true.

And are not the temperate exactly in the same case? They are temperate because they are intemperate—which might seem to be a contradiction, but is nevertheless the sort of thing which happens with this foolish temperance. For there are pleasures which they are afraid of losing; and in their desire to keep them, they abstain from some pleasures, because they are overcome by others; and although to be conquered by pleasure is called by men intemperance, to them the conquest of pleasure consists in being conquered by pleasure. And that is what I mean by saying that, in a sense, they are made temperate through intemperance.

Such appears to be the case.

Yet the exchange of one fear or pleasure or pain for another fear or pleasure or pain, and of the greater for the less, as if they were coins, is not the exchange of virtue. O my blessed Simmias, is there not one true coin for which all things ought to be exchanged?—and that is wisdom; and only in exchange for this, and in company with this, is anything truly bought or sold, whether courage or temperance or justice. And is not all true virtue the companion of wisdom, no matter what fears or pleasures or other similar goods or evils may or may not attend her? But the virtue which is made up of these goods, when they are severed from wisdom and exchanged with one another, is a shadow of virtue only, nor is there any freedom or health or truth in her; but in the true exchange there is a purging away of all these things, and temperance, and justice, and courage, and wisdom herself are the purgation of them. The founders of the mysteries would appear to have had a real meaning, and were not talking nonsense when they intimated in a figure long ago that he who passes unsanctified and uninitiated into the world below will lie in a slough, but that he who arrives there after initiation and purification will dwell with the gods. For "many," as they say in the mysteries, "are the thyrsus-bearers, but few are the mystics,"—meaning, as I interpret the words, "the true philosophers." In the number of whom, during my whole life, I have been seeking, according

to my ability, to find a place;—whether I have sought in a right way or not, and whether I have succeeded or not, I shall truly know in a little while, if God will, when I myself arrive in the other world—such is my belief. And therefore I maintain that I am right, Simmias and Cebes, in not grieving or repining at parting from you and my masters in this world, for I believe that I shall equally find good masters and friends in another world. But most men do not believe this saying; if then I succeed in convincing you by my defense better than I did the Athenian judges, it will be well.

Cebes answered: I agree, Socrates, in the greater part of what you say. But in what concerns the soul, men are apt to be incredulous; they fear that when she has left the body her place may be nowhere, and that on the very day of death she may perish and come to an end—immediately on her release from the body, issuing forth dispersed like smoke or air and in her flight vanishing away into nothingness. If she could only be collected into herself after she has obtained release from the evils of which you were speaking, there would be good reason to hope, Socrates, that what you say is true. But surely it requires a great deal of argument and many proofs to show that when the man is dead his soul yet exists, and has any force or intelligence.

True, Cebes, said Socrates; and shall I suggest that we converse a little of the probabilities of these things?

I am sure, said Cebes, that I should greatly like to know your opinion about them.

I reckon, said Socrates, that no one who heard me now, not even if he were one of my old enemies, the Comic poets, could accuse me of idle talking about matters in which I have no concern:—If you please, then, we will proceed with the enquiry.

Suppose we consider the question whether the souls of men after death are or are not in the world below. There comes into my mind an ancient doctrine which affirms that they go from hence into the other world, and returning hither, are born again from the dead. Now if it be true that the living come from the dead, then our souls must exist in the other world, for if not, how could they have been born again? And this would be conclusive, if there were any real evidence that the living are only born from the dead; but if this is not so, then other arguments will have to be adduced.

Very true, replied Cebes.

Then let us consider the whole question, not in relation to man only, but in relation to animals generally, and to plants, and to everything of which there is generation, and the proof will be easier. Are not all things which have opposites generated out of their opposites? I mean such things as good and evil, just and unjust—and there are innumerable other opposites which are generated out of opposites. And I want to show that in all opposites there is of necessity a similar alternation; I mean to say, for example, that anything which becomes greater must become greater after being less.

True.

And that which becomes less must have been once greater and then have become less.

Yes.

And the weaker is generated from the stronger, and the swifter from the slower.

Very true.

And the worse is from the better, and the more just is from the more unjust.

Of course.

And is this true of all opposites? and are we convinced that all of them are generated out of opposites?

Yes.

And in this universal opposition of all things, are there not also two intermediate processes which are ever going on, from one to the other opposite, and back again; where there is a greater and a less there is also an intermediate process of increase and diminution, and that which grows is said to wax, and that which decays to wane?

Yes, he said.

And there are many other processes, such as division and composition, cooling and heating, which equally involve a passage into and out of one another. And this necessarily holds of all opposites, even though not always expressed in words—they are really generated out of one another, and there is a passing or process from one to the other of them?

Very true, he replied.

Well, and is there not an opposite of life, as sleep is the opposite of waking?

True, he said.

And what is it?

Death, he answered.

And these, if they are opposites, are generated the one from the other, and have their two intermediate processes also?

Of course.

Now, said Socrates, I will analyze one of the two pairs of opposites which I have mentioned to you, and also its intermediate processes, and you shall analyze the other to me. One of them I term sleep, the other waking. The state of sleep is opposed to the state of waking, and out of sleeping waking is generated, and out of waking, sleeping; and the process of generation is in the one case falling asleep, and in the other waking up. Do you agree?

I entirely agree.

Then, suppose that you analyze life and death to me in the same manner. Is not death opposed to life?

Yes.

And they are generated one from the other?

Yes.

What is generated from the living?

The dead.

And what from the dead?

I can only say in answer—the living.

Then the living, whether things or persons, Cebes, are generated from the dead?

That is clear, he replied.

Then the inference is that our souls exist in the world below?

That is true.

And one of the two processes or generations is visible—for surely the act of dying is visible?

Surely, he said.

What then is to be the result? Shall we exclude the opposite process? and shall we suppose nature to walk on one leg only? Must we not rather assign to death some corresponding process of generation?

Certainly, he replied.

And what is that process?

Return to life.

And return to life, if there be such a thing, is the birth of the dead into the world of the living?

Quite true.

Then here is a new way by which we arrive at the conclusion that the living come from the dead, just as the dead come from the living; and this, if true, affords a most certain proof that the souls of the dead exist in some place out of which they come again.

Yes, Socrates, he said; the conclusion seems to flow necessarily out of our previous admissions.

And that these admissions were not unfair, Cebes, he said, may be shown, I think, as follows: If generation were in a straight line only, and there were no compensation or circle in nature, no turn or return of elements into their opposites, then you know that all things would at last have the same form and pass into the same state, and there would be no more generation of them.

What do you mean? he said.

A simple thing enough, which I will illustrate by the case of sleep, he replied. You know that if there were no alternation of sleeping and waking, the tale of the sleeping Endymion would in the end have no meaning, because all other things would be asleep too, and he would not be distinguishable from the rest. Or if there were composition only, and no division of substances, then the chaos of Anaxagoras would come again. And in like manner, my dear Cebes, if all things which partook of life were to die, and after they were dead remained in the form of death, and did not come to life again, all would at last die, and nothing would be alive—what other result could there be? For if the living spring from any other things, and they too die, must not all things at last be swallowed up in death?

There is no escape, Socrates, said Cebes; and to me your argument seems to be absolutely true.

Yes, he said, Cebes, it is and must be so, in my opinion; and we have not been deluded in making these admissions; but I am confident that there truly is such a thing as living again, and that the living spring from the dead, and that the souls of the dead are in existence, and that the good souls have a better portion than the evil.

Cebes added: Your favorite doctrine, Socrates, that knowledge is simply recollection, if true, also necessarily implies a previous time in which we have learned that which we now recollect. But this would be impossible unless our soul had been in some place before existing in the form of man; here then is another proof of the soul's immortality.

But tell me, Cebes, said Simmias, interposing, what arguments are urged in favor of this doctrine of recollection. I am not very sure at the moment that I remember them.

One excellent proof, said Cebes, is afforded by questions. If you put a question to a person in a right way, he will give a true answer of himself, but how could he do this unless there were knowledge and right reason already in him? And this is most clearly shown when he is taken to a diagram or to anything of that sort.

But if, said Socrates, you are still incredulous, Simmias, I would ask you whether you may not agree with me when you look at the matter in another way;—I mean, if you are still incredulous as to whether knowledge is recollection?

Incredulous I am not, said Simmias; but I want to have this doctrine of recollection brought to my own recollection, and, from what Cebes has said, I am beginning to recollect and be convinced: but I should still like to hear what you were going to say.

This is what I would say, he replied:—We should agree, if I am not mistaken, that what a man recollects he must have known at some previous time.

Very true.

And what is the nature of this knowledge or recollection? I mean to ask, Whether a person who, having seen or heard or in any way perceived anything, knows not only that, but has a conception of something else which is the subject, not of the same but of some other kind of knowledge, may not be fairly said to recollect that of which he has the conception?

What do you mean?

I mean what I may illustrate by the following instance:—The knowledge of a lyre is not the same as the knowledge of a man?

True.

And yet what is the feeling of lovers when they recognize a lyre, or a garment, or anything else which the beloved has been in the habit of using? Do not they, from knowing the lyre, form in the mind's eye an image of the youth to whom the lyre belongs? And this is recollection. In like manner anyone who sees Simmias may remember Cebes; and there are endless examples of the same thing.

Endless, indeed, replied Simmias.

And recollection is most commonly a process of recovering that which has been already forgotten through time and inattention.

Very true, he said.

Well; and may you not also from seeing the picture of a house or a lyre remember a man? and from the picture of Simmias, you may be led to remember Cebes?

True.

Or you may also be led to the recollection of Simmias himself?

Quite so.

And in all these cases, the recollection may be derived from things either like or unlike?

It may be.

And when the recollection is derived from like things, then another consideration is sure to arise, which is—whether the likeness in any degree falls short or not of that which is recollected?

Very true, he said.

And shall we proceed a step further, and affirm that there is such a thing as equality, not of one piece of wood or stone with another, but that, over and above this, there is absolute equality? Shall we say so?

Say so, yes, replied Simmias, and swear to it, with all the confidence in life.

And do we know the nature of this absolute essence?

To be sure, he said.

And whence did we obtain our knowledge? Did we not see equalities of material things, such as pieces of wood and stones, and gather from them the idea of an equality which is different from them? For you will acknowledge that there is a difference. Or look at the matter in another way:—Do not the same pieces of wood or stone appear at one time equal, and at another time unequal?

That is certain.

But are real equals ever equal? or is the idea of equality the same as of inequality?

Impossible, Socrates.

Then these (so-called) equals are not the same with the idea of equality?

I should say, clearly not, Socrates.

And yet from these equals, although differing from the idea of equality, you conceived and attained that idea?

Very true, he said.

Which might be like, or might be unlike them?

Yes.

But that makes no difference: whenever from seeing one thing you conceived another, whether like or unlike, there must surely have been an act of recollection?

Very true.

But what would you say of equal portions of wood and stone, or other material equals? and what is the impression produced by them? Are they equals in the same sense in which absolute equality is equal? or do they fall short of this perfect equality in a measure?

Yes, he said, in a very great measure too.

And must we not allow, that when I or anyone, looking at any object, observes that the thing which he sees aims at being some other thing, but falls short of, and cannot be, that other thing, but is inferior, he who makes this observation must have had a previous knowledge of that to which the other, although similar, was inferior.

Certainly.

And has not this been our own case in the matter of equals and of absolute equality?

Precisely.

Then we must have known equality previously to the time when we first saw the material equals, and reflected that all these apparent equals strive to attain absolute equality, but fall short of it?

Very true.

And we recognize also that this absolute equality has only been known, and can only be known, through the medium of sight or touch, or of some other of the senses, which are all alike in this respect?

Yes, Socrates, as far as the argument is concerned, one of them is the same as the other.

From the senses then is derived the knowledge that all sensible things aim at an absolute equality of which they fall short?

Yes.

Then before we began to see or hear or perceive in any way, we must have had a knowledge of absolute equality, or we could not have referred to that standard the equals which are derived from the senses?—for to that they all aspire, and of that they fall short.

No other inference can be drawn from the previous statements.

And did we not see and hear and have the use of our other senses as soon as we were born?

Certainly.

Then we must have acquired the knowledge of equality at some previous time?

Yes.

That is to say, before we were born, I suppose?

True.

And if we acquired this knowledge before we were born, and were born having the use of it, then we also knew before we were born and at the instant of birth not only the equal or the greater or the less, but all other ideas; for we are not speaking only of equality, but of beauty, goodness, justice, holiness, and of all which we stamp with the name of essence in the dialectical process, both when we ask and when we answer questions. Of all this we may certainly affirm that we acquired the knowledge before birth?

We may.

But if, after having acquired, we have not forgotten what in each case we acquired, then we must always have come into life having knowledge, and shall always continue to know as long as life lasts—for knowing is the acquiring and retaining knowledge and not forgetting. Is not forgetting, Simmias, just the losing of knowledge?

Quite true, Socrates.

But if the knowledge which we acquired before birth was lost by us at birth, and if afterwards by the use of the senses we recovered what we previously knew, will not the process which we call learning be a recovering of the knowledge which is natural to us, and may not this be rightly termed recollection?

Very true.

So much is clear—that when we perceive something, either by the help of sight, or hearing, or some other sense, from that perception we are able to obtain a notion of some other thing like or unlike which is associated with it but has been forgotten. Whence, as I was saying, one of two alternatives follows:—either we had this knowledge at birth, and continued to know through life; or, after birth, those who are said to learn only remember, and learning is simply recollection.

Yes, that is quite true, Socrates.

And which alternative, Simmias, do you prefer? Had we the knowledge at our birth, or did we recollect the things which we knew previously to our birth?

I cannot decide at the moment.

At any rate you can decide whether he who has knowledge will or will not be able to render an account of his knowledge? What do you say?

Certainly, he will.

But do you think that every man is able to give an account of these very matters about which we are speaking?

Would that they could, Socrates, but I rather fear that tomorrow, at this time, there will no longer be anyone alive who is able to give an account of them such as ought to be given.

Then you are not of opinion, Simmias, that all men know these things?

Certainly not.

They are in process of recollecting that which they learned before?

Certainly.

But when did our souls acquire this knowledge? —not since we were born as men?

Certainly not.

And therefore, previously?

Yes.

Then, Simmias, our souls must also have existed without bodies before they were in the form of man, and must have had intelligence.

Unless indeed you suppose, Socrates, that these notions are given us at the very moment of birth; for this is the only time which remains.

Yes, my friend, but if so, when do we lose them? for they are not in us when we are born— that is admitted. Do we lose them at the moment of receiving them, or if not at what other time?

No, Socrates, I perceive that I was unconsciously talking nonsense.

Then may we not say, Simmias, that if, as we are always repeating, there is an absolute beauty, and goodness, and an absolute essence of all things; and if to this, which is now discovered to have existed in our former state, we refer all our sensations, and with this compare them, finding these ideas to be pre-existent and our inborn possession —then our souls must have had a prior existence, but if not, there would be no force in the argument? There is the same proof that these ideas must have existed before we were born, as that our souls existed before we were born; and if not the ideas, then not the souls.

Yes, Socrates; I am convinced that there is precisely the same necessity for the one as for the other; and the argument retreats successfully to the position that the existence of the soul before birth cannot be separated from the existence of the essence of which you speak. For there is nothing which to my mind is so patent as that beauty, goodness, and the other notions of which you were just now speaking, have a most real and absolute existence; and I am satisfied with the proof.

Well, but is Cebes equally satisfied? for I must convince him too.

I think, said Simmias, that Cebes is satisfied: although he is the most incredulous of mortals, yet I believe that he is sufficiently convinced of the existence of the soul before birth. But that after death the soul will continue to exist is not yet proven even to my own satisfaction. I cannot get rid of the feeling of the many to which Cebes was referring—the feeling that when the man dies the soul will be dispersed, and that this may be the extinction of her. For admitting that she may have been born elsewhere, and framed out of other elements, and was in existence before entering the human body, why after having entered in and gone out again may she not herself be destroyed and come to an end?

Very true, Simmias, said Cebes; about half of what was required has been proven; to wit, that our souls existed before we were born:—that the soul will exist after death as well as before birth is the other half of which the proof is still wanting.

and has to be supplied; when that is given the demonstration will be complete.

But that proof, Simmias and Cebes, has been already given, said Socrates, if you put the two arguments together—I mean this and the former one, in which we admitted that everything living is born of the dead. For if the soul exists before birth, and in coming to life and being born can be born only from death and dying, must she not after death continue to exist, since she has to be born again?—Surely the proof which you desire has been already furnished. Still I suspect that you and Simmias would be glad to probe the argument further. Like children, you are haunted with a fear that when the soul leaves the body, the wind may really blow her away and scatter her; especially if a man should happen to die in a great storm and not when the sky is calm.

Cebes answered with a smile: Then, Socrates, you must argue us out of our fears—and yet, strictly speaking, they are not our fears, but there is a child within us to whom death is a sort of hobgoblin: him too we must persuade not to be afraid when he is alone in the dark.

Socrates said: Let the voice of the charmer be applied daily until you have charmed away the fear.

And where shall we find a good charmer of our fears, Socrates, when you are gone?

Hellas, he replied, is a large place, Cebes, and has many good men, and there are barbarous races not a few: seek for him among them all, far and wide, sparing neither pains nor money; for there is no better way of spending your money. And you must seek among yourselves too; for you will not find others better able to make the search.

The search, replied Cebes, shall certainly be made. And now, if you please, let us return to the point of the argument at which we digressed.

By all means, replied Socrates; what else should I please?

Very good.

Must we not, said Socrates, ask ourselves what that is which, as we imagine, is liable to be scattered, and about which we fear? and what again is that about which we have no fear? And then we may proceed further to enquire whether that which suffers dispersion is or is not of the nature of soul—our hopes and fears as to our own souls will turn upon the answers to these questions.

Very true, he said.

Now the compound or composite may be supposed to be naturally capable, as of being compounded, so also of being dissolved; but that which is uncompounded, and that only, must be, if anything is, indissoluble.

Yes; I should imagine so, said Cebes.

And the uncompounded may be assumed to be the same and unchanging, whereas the compound is always changing and never the same.

I agree, he said.

Then now let us return to the previous discussion. Is that idea or essence, which in the dialectical process we define as essence or true existence—whether essence of equality, beauty, or anything else—are these essences, I say, liable at times to some degree of change? or are they each of them always what they are, having the same simple self-existent and unchanging forms, not admitting of variation at all, or in any way, or at any time?

They must be always the same, Socrates, replied Cebes.

And what would you say of the many beautiful —whether men or horses or garments or any other things which are named by the same names and may be called equal or beautiful,—are they all unchanging and the same always, or quite the reverse? May they not rather be described as almost always changing and hardly ever the same, either with themselves or with one another?

The latter, replied Cebes; they are always in a state of change.

And these you can touch and see and perceive with the senses, but the unchanging things you can only perceive with the mind—they are invisible and are not seen?

That is very true, he said.

Well then, added Socrates, let us suppose that there are two sorts of existences—one seen, the other unseen.

Let us suppose them.

The seen is the changing, and the unseen is the unchanging?

That may be also supposed.

And, further, is not one part of us body, another part soul?

To be sure.

And to which class is the body more alike and akin?

Clearly to the seen—no one can doubt that.

And is the soul seen or not seen?

Not by man, Socrates.

And what we mean by "seen" and "not seen" is that which is or is not visible to the eye of man?

Yes, to the eye of man.

And is the soul seen or not seen?

Not seen.

Unseen then?

Yes.

Then the soul is more like to the unseen, and the body to the seen?

That follows necessarily, Socrates.

And were we not saying long ago that the soul when using the body as an instrument of perception, that is to say, when using the sense of sight or hearing or some other sense (for the meaning of perceiving through the body is perceiving through the senses)—were we not saying that the soul too is then dragged by the body into the region of the changeable, and wanders and is confused; the world spins round her, and she is like a drunkard, when she touches change?

Very true.

But when returning into herself she reflects, then she passes into the other world, the region of purity, and eternity, and immortality, and unchangeableness, which are her kindred, and with them she ever lives, when she is by herself and is not let or hindered; then she ceases from her erring ways, and being in communion with the unchanging is unchanging. And this state of the soul is called wisdom?

That is well and truly said, Socrates, he replied.

And to which class is the soul more nearly alike and akin, as far as may be inferred from this argument, as well as from the preceding one?

I think, Socrates, that, in the opinion of everyone who follows the argument, the soul will be infinitely more like the unchangeable—even the most stupid person will not deny that.

And the body is more like the changing?

Yes.

Yet once more consider the matter in another light: When the soul and the body are united, then nature orders the soul to rule and govern, and the body to obey and serve. Now which of these two functions is akin to the divine? and which to the mortal? Does not the divine appear to you to be that which naturally orders and rules, and the mortal to be that which is subject and servant?

True.

And which does the soul resemble?

The soul resembles the divine, and the body the mortal—there can be no doubt of that, Socrates.

Then reflect, Cebes: of all which has been said is not this the conclusion?—that the soul is in the very likeness of the divine, and immortal, and intellectual, and uniform, and indissoluble, and unchangeable; and that the body is in the very likeness of the human, and mortal, and unintellectual, and multiform, and dissoluble, and changeable. Can this, my dear Cebes, be denied?

It cannot.

But if it be true, then is not the body liable to speedy dissolution? and is not the soul almost or altogether indissoluble?

Certainly.

And do you further observe, that after a man is dead, the body, or visible part of him, which is lying in the visible world, and is called a corpse, and would naturally be dissolved and decomposed and dissipated, is not dissolved or decomposed at once, but may remain for some time, nay even for a long time, if the constitution be sound at the time of death, and the season of the year favorable? For the body when shrunk and embalmed, as the manner is in Egypt, may remain almost entire through infinite ages; and even in decay, there are still some portions, such as the bones and ligaments, which are practically indestructible:—Do you agree?

Yes.

And is it likely that the soul, which is invisible, in passing to the place of the true Hades, which like her is invisible, and pure, and noble, and on her way to the good and wise God, whither, if God will, my soul is also soon to go,—that the soul, I repeat, if this be her nature and origin, will be blown away and destroyed immediately on quitting the body, as the many say? That can never be, my dear Simmias and Cebes. The truth rather is, that the soul which is pure at departing and draws after her no bodily taint, having never voluntarily during life had connection with the body, which she is ever avoiding, herself gathered into herself;—and making such abstraction her perpetual study—which means that she has been a true disciple of philosophy; and therefore has in fact been always engaged in the practice of dying? For is not philosophy the study of death?—

Certainly—

That soul, I say, herself invisible, departs to the invisible world—to the divine and immortal and rational; thither arriving, she is secure of bliss and is released from the error and folly of men, their fears and wild passions and all other human ills, and for ever dwells, as they say of the initiated, in company with the gods. Is not this true, Cebes?

Yes, said Cebes, beyond a doubt.

But the soul which has been polluted, and is impure at the time of her departure, and is the companion and servant of the body always, and is in love with and fascinated by the body and by the desires and pleasures of the body, until she is led to believe that the truth only exists in a bodily form, which a man may touch and see and taste, and use for the purposes of his lusts,—the soul, I mean, accustomed to hate and fear and avoid the intellectual principle, which to the bodily eye is dark and invisible, and can be attained only by philosophy;—do you suppose that such a soul will depart pure and unalloyed?

Impossible, he replied.

She is held fast by the corporeal, which the continual association and constant care of the body have wrought into her nature.

Very true.

And this corporeal element, my friend, is heavy and weighty and earthy, and is that element of sight by which a soul is depressed and dragged down again into the visible world, because she is afraid of the invisible and of the world below—prowling about tombs and sepulchers, near which, as they tell us, are seen certain ghostly apparitions of souls which have not departed pure, but are cloyed with sight and therefore visible.

That is very likely, Socrates.

Yes, that is very likely, Cebes; and these must be the souls, not of the good, but of the evil, which are compelled to wander about such places in payment of the penalty of their former evil way of life; and they continue to wander until through the craving after the corporeal which never leaves them, they are imprisoned finally in another body. And they may be supposed to find their prisons in the same natures which they have had in their former lives.

What natures do you mean, Socrates?

What I mean is that men who have followed after gluttony, and wantonness, and drunkenness, and have had no thought of avoiding them, would pass into asses and animals of that sort. What do you think?

I think such an opinion to be exceedingly probable.

And those who have chosen the portion of injustice, and tyranny, and violence, will pass into wolves, or into hawks and kites;—whither else can we suppose them to go?

Yes, said Cebes; with such natures, beyond question.

And there is no difficulty, he said, in assigning to all of them places answering to their several natures and propensities?

There is not, he said.

Some are happier than others; and the happiest both in themselves and in the place to which they go are those who have practiced the civil and social virtues which are called temperance and justice, and are acquired by habit and attention without philosophy and mind.

Why are they the happiest?

Because they may be expected to pass into some gentle and social kind which is like their own, such as bees or wasps or ants, or back again into the form of man, and just and moderate men may be supposed to spring from them.

Very likely.

No one who has not studied philosophy and who is not entirely pure at the time of his departure is allowed to enter the company of the Gods, but the lover of knowledge only. And this is the reason, Simmias and Cebes, why the true votaries of philosophy abstain from all fleshly lusts, and hold out against them and refuse to give themselves up to them,—not because they fear poverty or the ruin of their families, like the lovers of money, and the world in general; nor like the lovers of power and honor, because they dread the dishonor or disgrace of evil deeds.

No, Socrates, that would not become them, said Cebes.

No indeed, he replied; and therefore they who have any care of their own souls, and do not merely live molding and fashioning the body, say farewell to all this; they will not walk in the ways of the blind: and when philosophy offers them purification and release from evil, they feel that they ought not to resist her influence, and whither she leads they turn and follow.

What do you mean, Socrates?

I will tell you, he said. The lovers of knowledge are conscious that the soul was simply fastened and glued to the body—until philosophy received her, she could only view real existence through the bars of a prison, not in and through herself; she was wallowing in the mire of every sort of ignorance, and by reason of lust had become the principal accomplice in her own captivity. This was her original state; and then, as I was saying, and as the lovers of knowledge are well aware, philosophy, seeing how terrible was her confinement, of which she was to herself the cause, received and gently comforted her and sought to release her, pointing out that the eye and the ear and the other senses are full of deception, and persuading her to retire from them, and abstain from all but the necessary use of them, and be gathered up and collected into herself, bidding her trust in herself and her own pure apprehension of pure existence, and to mistrust whatever comes to her through other channels and is subject to variation; for such things are visible and tangible, but what she sees in her own nature is intelligible and invisible. And the soul of the true philosopher thinks that she ought not to resist this deliverance, and therefore abstains from pleasures and desires and pains and fears, as far as she is able; reflecting that when a man has great joys or sorrows or fears or desires, he suffers from them, not merely the sort of evil which might be anticipated—as for example, the loss of his health or property which he has sacrificed to his lusts—but an evil greater far, which is the greatest and worst of all evils, and one of which he never thinks.

What is it, Socrates? said Cebes.

The evil is that when the feeling of pleasure or pain is most intense, every soul of man imagines the objects of this intense feeling to be then plainest and truest: but this is not so, they are really the things of sight.

Very true.

And is not this the state in which the soul is most enthralled by the body?

How so?

Why, because each pleasure and pain is a sort of nail which nails and rivets the soul to the body, until she becomes like the body, and believes that to be true which the body affirms to be true; and from agreeing with the body and having the same delights she is obliged to have the same habits and haunts, and is not likely ever to be pure at her departure to the world below, but is always infected by the body; and so she sinks into another body and there germinates and grows, and has therefore no part in the communion of the divine and pure and simple.

Most true, Socrates, answered Cebes.

And this, Cebes, is the reason why the true lovers of knowledge are temperate and brave; and not for the reason which the world gives.

Certainly not.

Certainly not! The soul of a philosopher will reason in quite another way; she will not ask philosophy to release her in order that when released she may deliver herself up again to the thraldom of pleasures and pains, doing a work only to be undone again, weaving instead of unweaving her Penelope's web. But she will calm passion, and follow reason, and dwell in the contemplation of her, beholding the true and divine (which is not matter of opinion), and thence deriving nourishment. Thus she seeks to live while she lives, and after death she hopes to go to her own kindred and to that which is like her, and to be freed from human ills. Never fear, Simmias and Cebes, that a soul which has been thus nurtured and has had these pursuits, will at her departure from the body be scattered and blown away by the winds and be nowhere and nothing.

When Socrates had done speaking, for a considerable time there was silence; he himself appeared to be meditating, as most of us were, on what had been said; only Cebes and Simmias spoke a few words to one another. And Socrates observing them asked what they thought of the argument, and whether there was anything wanting? For, said he, there are many points still open to suspicion and attack, if anyone were disposed to sift the matter thoroughly. Should you be considering some other matter I say no more, but if you are still in doubt do not hesitate to say exactly what you think, and let us have anything better which you can suggest; and if you think that I can be of any use, allow me to help you.

A man of sense ought not to say, nor will I be very confident, that the description which I have given of the soul and her mansions is exactly true. But I do say that, inasmuch as the soul is shown to be immortal, he may venture to think, not improperly or unworthily, that something of the kind is true. The venture is a glorious one, and he ought to comfort himself with words like these, which is the reason why I lengthen out the tale. Wherefore, I say, let a man be of good cheer about his soul, who having cast away the pleasures and ornaments of the body as alien to him and working harm rather than good, has sought after the pleasures of knowledge; and has arrayed the soul, not in some foreign attire, but in her own proper jewels, temperance, and justice, and courage, and nobility, and truth—in these adorned she is ready to go on her journey to the world below, when her hour comes. You, Simmias and Cebes, and all other men, will depart at some time or other. Me already, as a tragic poet would say, the voice of fate calls. Soon I must drink the poison; and I think that I had better repair to the bath first, in order that the women may not have the trouble of washing my body after I am dead.

When he had done speaking, Crito said: And have you any commands for us, Socrates—anything to say about your children, or any other matter in which we can serve you?

Nothing particular, Crito, he replied: only, as I have always told you, take care of yourselves; that is a service which you may be ever rendering to me and mine and to all of us, whether you promise to do so or not. But if you have no thought for yourselves, and care not to walk according to the rule which I have prescribed for you, not now for the first time, however much you may profess or promise at the moment, it will be of no avail.

We will do our best, said Crito: And in what way shall we bury you?

In any way that you like; but you must get hold of me, and take care that I do not run away from you. Then he turned to us, and added with a smile:—I cannot make Crito believe that I am the same Socrates who have been talking and conducting the argument; he fancies that I am the other Socrates whom he will soon see, a dead body—and he asks, How shall he bury me? And though I have spoken many words in the endeavor to show that when I have drunk the poison I shall leave you and go to the joys of the blessed,—these words of mine, with which I was comforting you and myself, have had, as I perceive, no effect upon Crito. And therefore I want you to be surety for me to him now, as at the trial he was surety to the judges for me: but let the promise be of another sort; for he was surety for me to the judges that I would remain, and you must be my surety to him that I shall not remain, but go away and depart; and then he will suffer less at my death, and not be grieved when he sees my body being burned or buried. I would not have him sorrow at my hard lot, or say at the burial, Thus we lay out Socrates, or, Thus we follow him to the grave or bury him; for false words are not only evil in themselves, but they infect the soul with evil. Be of good cheer then, my dear Crito, and say that you are burying my body only, and do with that whatever is usual, and what you think best.

When he had spoken these words, he arose and went into a chamber to bathe; Crito followed him and told us to wait. So we remained behind, talking and thinking of the subject of discourse, and also of the greatness of our sorrow; he was like a father of whom we were being bereaved, and we were about to pass the rest of our lives as orphans. When he had taken the bath his children were brought to him—(he had two young sons and an elder one); and the women of his family also came, and he talked to them and gave them a few directions in the presence of Crito; then he dismissed them and returned to us.

Now the hour of sunset was near, for a good deal of time had passed while he was within. When he came out, he sat down with us again after his bath, but not much was said. Soon the jailer, who was the servant of the Eleven, entered and stood by him, saying:—To you, Socrates, whom I know to be the noblest and gentlest and best of all who ever came to this place, I will not impute the angry feelings of other men, who rage and swear at me, when, in obedience to the authorities, I bid them drink the poison—indeed, I am sure that you will not be angry with me; for others, as you are aware, and not I, are to blame. And so fare you well, and try to bear lightly what must needs be—you know my errand. Then bursting into tears he turned away and went out.

Socrates looked at him and said: I return your good wishes, and will do as you bid. Then turning to us, he said, How charming the man is: since I have been in prison he has always been coming to see me, and at times he would talk to me, and was as good to me as could be, and now see how generously he sorrows on my account. We must do as he says, Crito; and therefore let the cup be brought, if the poison is prepared: if not, let the attendant prepare some.

Yet, said Crito, the sun is still upon the hill-tops, and I know that many a one has taken the draught late, and after the announcement has been made to him, he has eaten and drunk, and enjoyed the society of his beloved; do not hurry—there is time enough.

Socrates said: Yes, Crito, and they of whom you speak are right in so acting, for they think that they will be gainers by the delay; but I am right in not following their example, for I do not think that I should gain anything by drinking the poison a little later; I should only be ridiculous in my own eyes for sparing and saving a life which is already forfeit. Please then to do as I say, and not to refuse me.

Crito made a sign to the servant, who was standing by; and he went out, and having been absent for some time, returned with the jailer carrying the cup of poison. Socrates said: You, my good friend, who are experienced in these matters, shall give me directions how I am to proceed. The man answered: You have only to walk about until your legs are heavy, and then to lie down, and the poison will act. At the same time he handed the cup to Socrates, who in the easiest and gentlest manner, without the least fear or change of color or feature, looking at the man with all his eyes, Echecrates, as his manner was, took the cup and said: What do you say about making a libation out of this cup to any god? May I, or not? The man answered: We only prepare, Socrates, just so much as we deem enough. I understand, he said: but I may and must ask the gods to prosper my journey from this to the other world—even so—and so be it according to my prayer. Then raising the cup to his lips, quite readily and cheerfully he drank off the poison. And hitherto most of us had been able to control our sorrow; but now when we saw him drinking, and saw too that he had finished the draught, we could no longer forbear, and in spite of myself my own tears were flowing fast; so that I covered my face and wept, not for him, but at the thought of my own calamity in having to part from such a friend. Nor was I the first; for Crito, when he found himself unable to restrain his tears, had got up, and I followed; and at that moment, Apollodorus, who had been weeping all the time, broke out in a loud and passionate cry which made cowards of us all. Socrates alone retained his calmness: What is this strange outcry? he said. I sent away the women mainly in order that they might not misbehave in this way, for I have been told that a man should die in peace. Be quiet then, and have patience. When we heard his words we were ashamed, and refrained our tears; and he walked about until, as he said, his legs began to fail, and then he lay on his back, according to the directions, and the man who gave him the poison now and then looked at his feet and legs; and after a while he pressed his foot hard, and asked him if he could feel; and he said, No; and then his leg, and so upwards and upwards, and showed us that he was cold and stiff. And he felt them himself, and said: When the poison reaches the heart, that will be the end. He was beginning to grow cold about the groin, when he uncovered his face, for he had covered himself up, and said—they were his last words—he said: Crito, I owe a cock to Asclepius; will you remember to pay the debt? The debt shall be paid, said Crito; is there anything else? There was no answer to this question; but in a minute or two a movement was heard, and the attendants uncovered him; his eyes were set, and Crito closed his eyes and mouth.

Such was the end, Echecrates, of our friend; concerning whom I may truly say, that of all the men of his time whom I have known, he was the wisest and justest and best.

The Republic

Book VII

And now, I said, let me show in a figure how far our nature is enlightened or unenlightened:— Behold! human beings living in an underground den, which has a mouth open towards the light and reaching all along the den; here they have been from their childhood, and have their legs and necks chained so that they cannot move, and can only see before them, being prevented by the chains from turning round their heads. Above and behind them a fire is blazing at a distance, and between the fire and the prisoners there is a raised way; and you will see, if you look, a low wall built along the way, like the screen which marionette players have in front of them, over which they show the puppets.

I see.

And do you see, I said, men passing along the wall carrying all sorts of vessels, and statues and figures of animals made of wood and stone and various materials, which appear over the wall? Some of them are talking, others silent.

You have shown me a strange image, and they are strange prisoners.

Like ourselves, I replied; and they see only their own shadows, or the shadows of one another, which the fire throws on the opposite wall of the cave?

True, he said; how could they see anything but the shadows if they were never allowed to move their heads?

And of the objects which are being carried in like manner they would only see the shadows?

Yes, he said.

And if they were able to converse with one another, would they not suppose that they were naming what was actually before them?

Very true.

And suppose further that the prison had an echo which came from the other side, would they not be sure to fancy when one of the passers-by spoke that the voice which they heard came from the passing shadow?

No question, he replied.

To them, I said, the truth would be literally nothing but the shadows of the images.

That is certain.

And now look again, and see what will naturally follow if the prisoners are released and disabused of their error. At first, when any of them is liberated and compelled suddenly to stand up and turn his neck round and walk and look towards the light, he will suffer sharp pains; the glare will distress him, and he will be unable to see the realities of which in his former state he had seen the shadows; and then conceive someone saying to him, that what he saw before was an illusion, but that now, when he is approaching nearer to being and his eye is turned towards more real existence, he has a clearer vision,—what will be his reply? And you may further imagine that his instructor is pointing to the objects as they pass and requiring him to name them,—will he not be perplexed? Will he not fancy that the shadows which he formerly saw are truer than the objects which are now shown to him?

Far truer.

And if he is compelled to look straight at the light, will he not have a pain in his eyes which will make him turn away to take refuge in the objects of vision which he can see, and which he will conceive to be in reality clearer than the things which are now being shown to him?

True, he said.

And suppose once more, that he is reluctantly dragged up a steep and rugged ascent, and held fast until he is forced into the presence of the sun himself, is he not likely to be pained and irritated? When he approaches the light his eyes will be dazzled, and he will not be able to see anything at all of what are now called realities.

Not all in a moment, he said.

He will require to grow accustomed to the sight of the upper world. And first he will see the shadows best, next the reflections of men and other objects in the water, and then the objects themselves; then he will gaze upon the light of the moon and the stars and the spangled heaven; and he will see the sky and the stars by night better than the sun or the light of the sun by day?

Certainly.

Last of all he will be able to see the sun, and not mere reflections of him in the water, but he will see him in his own proper place, and not in another; and he will contemplate him as he is.

Certainly.

He will then proceed to argue that this is he who gives the season and the years, and is the guardian of all that is in the visible world, and in a certain way the cause of all things which he and his fellows have been accustomed to behold?

Clearly, he said, he would first see the sun and then reason about him.

And when he remembered his old habitation, and the wisdom of the den and his fellow-prisoners, do you not suppose that he would felicitate himself on the change, and pity them?

Certainly, he would.

And if they were in the habit of conferring honors among themselves on those who were quickest to observe the passing shadows and to remark which of them went before, and which followed after, and which were together; and who were therefore best able to draw conclusions as to the future, do you think that he would care for such honors and glories, or envy the possessors of them? Would he not say with Homer,

Better to be the poor servant of a poor master

and to endure anything, rather than think as they do and live after their manner?

Yes, he said, I think that he would rather suffer anything than entertain these false notions and live in this miserable manner.

Imagine once more, I said, such an one coming suddenly out of the sun to be replaced in his old situation; would he not be certain to have his eyes full of darkness?

To be sure, he said.

And if there were a contest, and he had to compete in measuring the shadows with the prisoners who had never moved out of the den, while his sight was still weak, and before his eyes had become steady (and the time which would be needed to acquire this new habit of sight might be very considerable), would he not be ridiculous? Men would say of him that up he went and down he came without his eyes; and that it was better not even to think of ascending; and if anyone tried to loose another and lead him up to the light, let them only catch the offender, and they would put him to death.

No question, he said.

This entire allegory, I said, you may now append, dear Glaucon, to the previous argument; the prison-house is the world of sight, the light of the fire is the sun, and you will not misapprehend me if you interpret the journey upwards to be the ascent of the soul into the intellectual world according to my poor belief, which, at your desire, I have expressed—whether rightly or wrongly God knows. But, whether true or false, my opinion is that in the world of knowledge the idea of good appears last of all, and is seen only with an effort; and, when seen, is also inferred to be the universal author of all things beautiful and right, parent of light and of the lord of light in this visible world, and the immediate source of reason and truth in the intellectual; and that this is the power upon which he who would act rationally either in public or private life must have his eye fixed.

I agree, he said, as far as I am able to understand you.

Moreover, I said, you must not wonder that those who attain to this beatific vision are unwilling to descend to human affairs; for their souls are ever hastening into the upper world where they desire to dwell; which desire of theirs is very natural, if our allegory may be trusted.

Yes, very natural.

And is there anything surprising in one who passes from divine contemplations to the evil state of man, misbehaving himself in a ridiculous manner; if, while his eyes are blinking and before he has become accustomed to the surrounding darkness, he is compelled to fight in courts of law, or in other places, about the images or the shadows of images of justice, and is endeavoring to meet the conceptions of those who have never yet seen absolute justice?

Anything but surprising, he replied.

Anyone who has common sense will remember that the bewilderments of the eyes are of two kinds, and arise from two causes, either from coming out of the light or from going into the light, which is true of the mind's eye, quite as much as of the bodily eye; and he who remembers this when he sees anyone whose vision is perplexed and weak, will not be too ready to laugh; he will first ask whether that soul of man has come out of the brighter life, and is unable to see because unaccustomed to the dark, or having turned from darkness to the day is dazzled by excess of light. And he will count the one happy in his condition and state of being, and he will pity the other; or, if he have a mind to laugh at the soul which comes from below into the light, there will be more reason in this than in the laugh which greets him who returns from above out of the light into the den.

That, he said, is a very just distinction.

But then, if I am right, certain professors of education must be wrong when they say that they can put a knowledge into the soul which was not there before, like sight into blind eyes.

They undoubtedly say this, he replied.

Whereas, our argument shows that the power and capacity of learning exists in the soul already; and that just as the eye was unable to turn from darkness to light without the whole body, so too the instrument of knowledge can only by the movement of the whole soul be turned from the world of becoming into that of being, and learn by degrees to endure the sight of being, and of the brightest and best of being, or in other words, of the good.

Very true.

ARISTOTLE

The Nicomachean Ethics

Book II

THE GOLDEN MEAN

Well: human Excellence is of two kinds, Intellectual and Moral: now the Intellectual springs originally, and is increased subsequently, from teaching (for the most part that is), and needs therefore experience and time; whereas the Moral comes from custom, and so the Greek term denoting it is but a slight deflection from the term denoting custom in that language.

From this fact it is plain that not one of the

Moral Virtues comes to be in us merely by nature: because of such things as exist by nature, none can be changed by custom: a stone, for instance, by nature gravitating downwards, could never by custom be brought to ascend, not even if one were to try and accustom it by throwing it up ten thousand times; nor could fire again be brought to descend, nor in fact could anything whose nature is in one way be brought by custom to be in another. The Virtues then come to be in us neither by nature, nor in despite of nature, but we are furnished by nature with a capacity for receiving them, and are perfected in them through custom.

Again, in whatever cases we get things by nature, we get the faculties first and perform the acts of working afterwards; an illustration of which is afforded by the case of our bodily senses, for it was not from having often seen or heard that we got these senses, but just the reverse: we had them and so exercised them, but did not have them because we had exercised them. But the Virtues we get by first performing single acts of working, which, again, is the case of other things, as the arts for instance; for what we have to make when we have learned how, these we learn how to make by making: men come to be builders, for instance, by building; harp-players, by playing on the harp: exactly so, by doing just actions we come to be just; by doing the actions of self-mastery we come to be perfected in self-mastery; and by doing brave actions brave.

And to the truth of this testimony is borne by what takes place in communities: because the law-givers make the individual members good men by habituation, and this is the intention certainly of every law-giver, and all who do not effect it well fail of their intent; and herein consists the difference between a good Constitution and a bad.

Again, every Virtue is either produced or destroyed from and by the very same circumstances: art too in like manner; I mean it is by playing the harp that both the good and the bad harp-players are formed: and similarly builders and all the rest; by building well men will become good builders; by doing it badly bad ones: in fact, if this had not been so, there would have been no need of instructors, but all men would have been at once good or bad in their several arts without them.

So too then is it with the Virtues: for by acting in the various relations in which we are thrown with our fellow men, we come to be, some just, some unjust: and by acting in dangerous positions and being habituated to feel fear or confidence, we come to be, some brave, others cowards.

Similarly is it also with respect to the occasions of lust and anger: for some men come to be perfected in self-mastery and mild, others destitute of all self-control and passionate; the one class by behaving in one way under them, the other by behaving in another. Or, in one word, the habits are produced from the acts of working like to them: and so what we have to do is to give a certain character to these particular acts, because the habits formed correspond to the differences of these.

So then, whether we are accustomed this way or that straight from childhood, makes not a small but an important difference, or rather I would say it makes all the difference.

Since then the object of the present treatise is not mere speculation, as it is of some others (for we are inquiring not merely that we may know what virtue is but that we may become virtuous, else it would have been useless), we must consider as to the particular actions how we are to do them, because, as we have just said, the quality of the habits that shall be formed depends on these.

Now, that we are to act in accordance with Right Reason is a general maxim, and may for the present be taken for granted: we will speak of it hereafter, and say both what Right Reason is, and what are its relations to the other virtues.

But let this point be first thoroughly understood between us, that all which can be said on moral action must be said in outline, as it were, and not exactly: for as we remarked at the commencement, such reasoning only must be required as the nature of the subject-matter admits of, and matters of moral action and expediency have no fixedness any more than matters of health. And if the subject in its general maxims is such, still less in its application to particular cases is exactness attainable: because these fall not under any art or system of rules, but it must be left in each instance to the individual agents to look to the exigencies of the particular case, as it is in the art of healing, or that of navigating a ship. Still, though the present subject is confessedly such, we must try and do what we can for it.

First then this must be noted, that it is the nature of such things to be spoiled by defect and excess; as we see in the case of health and strength (since for the illustration of things which cannot be seen we must use those that can), for excessive training impairs the strength as well as deficient: meat and drink, in like manner, in too great or too small quantities, impair the health: while in due proportion they cause, increase, and preserve it.

Thus it is therefore with the habits of perfected Self-Mastery and Courage and the rest of the Virtues: for the man who flies from and fears all things, and never stands up against anything, comes to be a coward; and he who fears nothing, but goes at everything, comes to be rash. In like manner too, he that tastes of every pleasure and abstains from none comes to lose all self-control; while he who avoids all, as do the dull and clownish, comes as it were to lose his faculties of perception: that is to say, the habits of perfected Self-Mastery and Courage are spoiled by the excess and defect, but by the mean state are preserved.

Furthermore, not only do the origination, growth, and marring of the habits come from and by the same circumstances, but also the acts of working after the habits are formed will be exercised on the same: for so it is also with those other things which are more directly matters of sight, strength for instance: for this comes by taking plenty of food and doing plenty of work, and the man who has attained strength is best able to do these: and so it is with the Virtues, for not only do we by abstaining from pleasures come to be perfected in Self-Mastery, but when we have come to be so we can best abstain from them: similarly too with Courage: for it is by accustoming ourselves to despise objects of fear and stand up against them that we come to be brave; and after we have come to be so we shall be best able to stand up against such objects.

And for a test of the formation of the habits we must take the pleasure or pain which succeeds the acts; for he is perfected in Self-Mastery who not only abstains from the bodily pleasures but is glad to do so; whereas he who abstains but is sorry to do it has not Self-Mastery: he again is brave who stands up against danger, either with positive pleasure or at least without any pain; whereas he who does it with pain is not brave.

For Moral Virtue has for its object-matter pleasures and pains, because by reason of pleasure we do what is bad, and by reason of pain decline doing what is right (for which cause, as Plato observes, men should have been trained straight from their childhood to receive pleasure and pain from proper objects, for this is the right education). Again: since Virtues have to do with actions and feelings, and on every feeling and every action pleasure and pain follow, here again is another proof that Virtue has for its object-matter pleasure and pain. The same is shown also by the fact that punishments are effected through the instrumentality of these; because they are of the nature of remedies, and it is the nature of remedies to be the contraries of the ills they cure. Again, to quote what we said before: every habit of the Soul by its very nature has relation to, and exerts itself upon, things of the same kind as those by which it is naturally deteriorated or improved: now such habits do come to be vicious by reason of pleasures and pains, that is, by men pursuing or avoiding respectively, either such as they ought not, or at wrong times, or in wrong manner, and so forth (for which reason, by the way, some people define the Virtues as certain states of impassibility and utter quietude, but they are wrong because they speak without modification, instead of adding, "as they ought," "as they ought not," and "when," and so on). Virtue then is assumed to be that habit which is such, in relation to pleasures and pains, as to effect the best results, and Vice the contrary.

The following considerations may also serve to set this in a clear light. There are principally three things moving us to choice and three to avoidance, the honorable, the expedient, the pleasant; and their three contraries, the dishonorable, the hurtful, and the painful: now the good man is apt to go right, and the bad man wrong, with respect to all these of course, but most specially with respect to pleasure: because not only is this common to him with all animals but also it is a concomitant of all those things which move to choice, since both the honorable and the expedient give an impression of pleasure.

Again, it grows up with us all from infancy, and so it is a hard matter to remove from ourselves this feeling, engrained as it is into our very life.

Again, we adopt pleasure and pain (some of us more, and some less) as the measure even of actions: for this cause then our whole business must be with them, since to receive right or wrong impressions of pleasure and pain is a thing of no little importance in respect of the actions. Once more; it is harder, as Heraclitus says, to fight against pleasure than against anger: now it is about that which is more than commonly difficult that art comes into being, and virtue too, because in that which is difficult the good is of a higher order: and so for this reason too both virtue and moral philosophy generally must wholly busy themselves respecting pleasures and pains, because he that uses these well will be good, he that does so ill will be bad.

Let us then be understood to have stated, that Virtue has for its object-matter pleasures and pains, and that it is either increased or marred by the same circumstances (differently used) by which it is originally generated, and that it exerts itself on the same circumstances out of which it was generated.

Now I can conceive a person perplexed as to the meaning of our statement, that men must do just actions to become just, and those of self-mastery to acquire the habit of self-mastery; "for," he would say, "if men are doing the actions they have the respective virtues already, just as men are grammarians or musicians when they do the actions of either art." May we not reply by saying that it is not so even in the case of the arts referred to: because a man may produce something grammatical either by chance or the suggestion of another; but then only will he be a grammarian when he not only produces something grammatical but does so grammarian-wise, i.e., in virtue of the grammatical knowledge he himself possesses.

Again, the cases of the arts and the virtues are not parallel: because those things which are produced by the arts have their excellence in themselves, and it is sufficient therefore that these when produced should be in a certain state: but those which are produced in the way of the virtues, are, strictly speaking, actions of a certain kind (say of Justice or perfected Self-Mastery), not merely if in themselves they are in a certain state but if also he who does them does them being himself in a certain state, first if knowing what he is doing, next if with deliberate preference, and with such preference for the things' own sake; and thirdly if being himself stable and unapt to change. Now to constitute possession of the arts these requisites are not reckoned in, excepting the one point of knowledge: whereas for possession of the virtues knowledge avails little or nothing, but the other requisites avail not a little, but, in fact, are all in all, and these requisites as a matter of fact do come from oftentimes doing the actions of Justice and perfected Self-Mastery.

The facts, it is true, are called by the names of these habits when they are such as the just or perfectly self-mastering man would do; but he is not in possession of the virtues who merely does these facts, but he who also so does them as the just and self-mastering do them.

We are right then in saying, that these virtues are formed in a man by his doing the actions; but no one, if he should leave them undone, would be even in the way to become a good man. Yet people in general do not perform these actions, but taking refuge in talk they flatter themselves they are philosophizing, and that they will so be good men: acting in truth very like those sick people who listen to the doctor with great attention but do nothing that he tells them: just as these then cannot be well bodily under such a course of treatment, so neither can those be mentally by such philosophizing.

Next, we must examine what Virtue is. Well, since the things which come to be in the mind are, in all, of three kinds, Feelings, Capacities, States, Virtue of course must belong to one of the three classes.

By Feelings, I mean such as lust, anger, fear, confidence, envy, joy, friendship, hatred, longing, emulation, compassion, in short all such as are followed by pleasure or pain: by Capacities, those in right of which we are said to be capable of these feelings; as by virtue of which we are able to have been made angry, or grieved, or to have compassionated; by States, those in right of which we are in a certain relation good or bad to the aforementioned feelings; to having been made angry, for instance, we are in a wrong relation if in our anger we were too violent or too slack, but if we were in the happy medium we are in a right relation to the feeling. And so on of the rest.

Now Feelings neither the virtues nor vices are, because in right of the Feelings we are not denominated either good or bad, but in right of the virtues and vices we are.

Again, in right of the Feelings we are neither praised nor blamed (for a man is not commended for being afraid or being angry, nor blamed for being angry merely but for being so in a particular way), but in right of the virtues and vices we are.

Again, both anger and fear we feel without moral choice, whereas the virtues are acts of moral choice, or at least certainly not independent of it.

Moreover, in right of the Feelings we are said to be moved, but in right of the virtues and vices not to be moved, but disposed, in a certain way.

And for these same reasons they are not Capacities, for we are not called good or bad merely because we are able to feel, nor are we praised or blamed.

And again, Capacities we have by nature, but

we do not come to be good or bad by nature, as we have said before.

Since then the virtues are neither Feelings nor Capacities, it remains that they must be States.

Now what the genus of Virtue is has been said; but we must not merely speak of it thus, that it is a state but say also what kind of a state it is.

We must observe then that all excellence makes that whereof it is the excellence both to be itself in a good state and to perform its work well. The excellence of the eye, for instance, makes both the eye good and its work also: for by the excellence of the eye we see well. So too the excellence of the horse makes a horse good, and good in speed, and in carrying his rider, and standing up against the enemy. If then this is universally the case, the excellence of Man, i.e., Virtue, must be a state whereby Man comes to be good and whereby he will perform well his proper work. Now how this shall be it is true we have said already, but still perhaps it may throw light on the subject to see what is its characteristic nature.

In all quantity then, whether continuous or discrete, one may take the greater part, the less, or the exactly equal, and these either with reference to the thing itself, or relatively to us: and the exactly equal is a mean between excess and defect. Now by the mean of the thing, i.e., absolute mean, I denote that which is equidistant from either extreme (which of course is one and the same to all), and by the mean relatively to ourselves, that which is neither too much nor too little for the particular individual. This of course is not one nor the same to all: for instance, suppose ten is too much and two too little, people take six for the absolute mean; because it exceeds the smaller sum by exactly as much as it is itself exceeded by the larger, and this mean is according to arithmetical proportion.

But the mean relatively to ourselves must not be so found; for it does not follow, supposing ten minæ is too large a quantity to eat and two too small, that the trainer will order his man six; because for the person who is to take it this also may be too much or too little: for Milo it would be too little, for a man just commencing his athletic exercises too much: similarly too of the exercises themselves, as running or wrestling.

So then it seems everyone possessed of skill avoids excess and defect, but seeks for and chooses the mean, not the absolute but the relative.

Now if all the skill thus accomplishes well its work by keeping an eye on the mean, and bringing the works to this point (whence it is common enough to say of such works as are in a good state, "one cannot add to or take ought from them," under the notion of excess or defect destroying goodness but the mean state preserving it), and good artisans, as we say, work with their eye on this, and excellence, like nature, is more exact and better than any art in the world, it must have an aptitude to aim at the mean.

It is moral excellence, i.e., Virtue, of course which I mean, because this it is which is concerned with feelings and actions, and in these there can be excess and defect and the mean: it is possible, for instance, to feel the emotions of fear, confidence, lust, anger, compassion, and pleasure and pain generally, too much or too little, and in either case wrongly; but to feel them when we ought, on what occasions, towards whom, why, and as, we should do, is the mean, or in other words the best state, and this is the property of Virtue.

In like manner too with respect to the actions, there may be excess and defect and the mean. Now Virtue is concerned with feelings and actions, in which the excess is wrong and the defect is blamed but the mean is praised and goes right; and both these circumstances belong to Virtue. Virtue then is in a sense a mean state, since it certainly has an aptitude for aiming at the mean.

Again, one may go wrong in many different ways (because, as the Pythagoreans expressed it, evil is of the class of the infinite, good of the finite), but right only in one; and so the former is easy, the latter difficult; easy to miss the mark, but hard to hit it: and for these reasons, therefore, both the excess and defect belong to Vice, and the mean state to Virtue; for, as the poet has it,

> Men may be bad in many ways,
> But good in one alone.

Virtue then is "a state apt to exercise deliberate choice, being in the relative mean, determined by reason, and as the man of practical wisdom would determine."

It is a middle state between too faulty ones, in the way of excess on one side and of defect on the other: and it is so moreover, because the faulty states on one side fall short of, and those on the other exceed, what is right, both in the case of the feelings and the actions; but Virtue finds, and when found adopts, the mean.

And so, viewing it in respect of its essence and definition, Virtue is a mean state; but in reference to the chief good and to excellence it is the highest state possible.

But it must not be supposed that every action or every feeling is capable of subsisting in this mean state, because some there are which are so named as immediately to convey the notion of badness, as malevolence, shamelessness, envy; or, to instance in actions, adultery, theft, homicide; for all these and suchlike are blamed because they are in themselves bad, not the having too much or too little of them.

In these then you never can go right, but must always be wrong: nor in such does the right or wrong depend on the selection of a proper person, time, or manner (take adultery for instance), but simply doing any one soever of those things is being wrong.

You might as well require that there should be determined a mean state, an excess and a defect in respect of acting unjustly, being cowardly, or giving up all control of the passions: for at this rate there will be of excess and defect a mean state; of excess, excess; and of defect, defect.

But just as of perfected self-mastery and courage there is no excess and defect, because the mean is in one point of view the highest possible state, so in neither of those faulty states can you have a mean state, excess, or defect, but howsoever done they are wrong: you cannot, in short, have of excess and defect a mean state, nor of a mean state excess and defect.

It is not enough, however, to state this in general terms, we must also apply it to particular instances, because in treatises on moral conduct general statements have an air of vagueness, but those which go into detail one of greater reality: for the actions after all must be in detail, and the general statements, to be worth anything, must hold good here.

We must take these details then from the Table.

I. In respect of fears and confidence or boldness:

The mean state is Courage: men may exceed, of course, either in absence of fear or in positive confidence: the former has no name (which is a common case), the latter is called rash: again, the man who has too much fear and too little confidence is called a coward.

II. In respect of pleasures and pains (but not all, and perhaps fewer pains than pleasures):

The mean state here is perfected Self-Mastery, the defect total absence of Self-control. As for defect in respect of pleasure, there are really no people who are chargeable with it, so, of course,

there is really no name for such characters, but, as they are conceivable, we will give them one and call them insensible.

III. In respect of giving and taking wealth (a):

The mean state is Liberality, the excess Prodigality, the defect Stinginess: here each of the extremes involves really an excess and defect contrary to each other: I mean, the prodigal gives out too much and takes in too little, while the stingy man takes in too much and gives out too little. (It must be understood that we are now giving merely an outline and summary, intentionally: and we will, in a later part of the treatise, draw out the distinctions with greater exactness.)

IV. In respect of wealth (b):

There are other dispositions besides these just mentioned; a mean state called Munificence (for the munificent man differs from the liberal, the former having necessarily to do with great wealth, the latter with but small); the excess called by the names either of Want of taste or Vulgar Profusion, and the defect Paltriness (these also differ from the extremes connected with liberality, and the manner of their difference shall also be spoken of later).

V. In respect of honor and dishonor (a):

The mean state Greatness of Soul, the excess which may be called braggadocio, and the defect Littleness of Soul.

VI. In respect of honor and dishonor (b):

Now there is a state bearing the same relation to Greatness of Soul as we said just now Liberality does to Munificence, with the difference that is of being about a small amount of the same thing: this state having reference to small honor, as Greatness of Soul to great honor; a man may, of course, grasp at honor either more than he should or less; now he that exceeds in his grasping at it is called ambitious, he that falls short unambitious, he that is just as he should be has no proper name: nor in fact have the states, except that the disposition of the ambitious man is called ambition. For this reason those who are in either extreme lay claim to the mean, as a debatable land, and we call the virtuous character sometimes by the name ambitious, sometimes by that of unambitious, and we commend sometimes the one and sometimes the other. Why we do it shall be said in the subsequent part of the treatise; but now we will go on with the rest of the virtues after the plan we have laid down.

VII. In respect of anger:

Here too there is excess, defect, and a mean

state; but since they may be said to have really no proper names, as we call the virtuous character Meek, we will call the mean state Meekness, and of the extremes, let the man who is excessive be denominated Passionate, and the faulty state Passionateness, and him who is deficient Angerless, and the defect Angerlessness.

There are also three other mean states, having some mutual resemblance, but still with differences: they are alike in that they all have for their object-matter intercourse of words and deeds, and they differ in that one has respect to truth herein, the other two to what is pleasant; and this in two ways, the one in relaxation and amusement, the other in all things which occur in daily life. We must say a word or two about these also, that we may the better see that in all matters the mean is praiseworthy, while the extremes are neither right nor worthy of praise but of blame.

Now of these, it is true, the majority have really no proper names, but still we must try, as in the other cases, to coin some for them for the sake of clearness and intelligibleness.

I. In respect of truth:

The man who is in the mean state we will call Truthful, and his state Truthfulness, and as to the disguise of truth, if it be on the side of exaggeration, Braggadocio, and him that has it a Braggadocio; if on that of diminution, Reserve and Reserved shall be the terms.

II. In respect of what is pleasant in the way of relaxation or amusement:

The mean state shall be called Easy-pleasantry, and the character accordingly a man of Easy-pleasantry; the excess Buffoonery, and the man a Buffoon; the man deficient herein a Clown, and his state Clownishness.

III. In respect of what is pleasant in daily life:

He that is as he should be may be called Friendly, and his mean state Friendliness: he that exceeds, if it be without any interested motive, somewhat too Complaisant, if with such motive, a Flatterer: he that is deficient and in all instances unpleasant, Quarrelsome and Cross.

There are mean states likewise in feelings and matters concerning them. Shamefacedness, for instance, is no virtue, still a man is praised for being shamefaced: for in these too the one is denominated the man in the mean state, the other in the excess; the Dumbfoundered, for instance, who is overwhelmed with shame on all and any occasion: the man who is in the defect, i.e., who has no

shame at all in his composition, is called Shameless: but the right character Shamefaced.

Indignation against successful vice, again, is a state in the mean between Envy and Malevolence: they all three have respect to pleasure and pain produced by what happens to one's neighbor: for the man who has this right feeling is annoyed at undeserved success of others, while the envious man goes beyond him and is annoyed at all success of others, and the malevolent falls so far short of feeling annoyance that he even rejoices [at misfortune of others].

But for the discussion of these also there will be another opportunity, as of Justice too, because the term is used in more senses than one. So after this we will go accurately into each and say how they are mean states: and in like manner also with respect to the Intellectual Excellences.

Now as there are three states in each case, two faulty either in the way of excess or defect, and one right, which is the mean state, of course all are in a way opposed to one another; the extremes, for instance, not only to the mean but also to one another, and the mean to the extremes: for just as the half is greater if compared with the less portion, and less if compared with the greater, so the mean states, compared with the defects, exceed, whether in feelings or actions, and *vice versa*. The brave man, for instance, shows as rash when compared with the coward, and cowardly when compared with the rash; similarly too the man of perfected self-mastery, viewed in comparison with the man destitute of all perception, shows like a man of no self-control, but in comparison with the man who really has no self-control, he looks like one destitute of all perception: and the liberal man compared with the stingy seems prodigal, and by the side of the prodigal, stingy.

And so the extreme characters push away, so to speak, towards each other the man in the mean state; the brave man is called a rash man by the coward, and a coward by the rash man, and in the other cases accordingly. And there being this mutual opposition, the contrariety between the extremes is greater than between either and the mean, because they are further from one another than from the mean, just as the greater or less portion differ more from each other than either from the exact half.

Again, in some cases an extreme will bear a resemblance to the mean; rashness, for instance, to courage, and prodigality to liberality; but between the extremes there is the greatest dissimilarity.

Now things which are furthest from one another are defined to be contrary, and so the further off the more contrary will they be.

Further: of the extremes in some cases the excess, and in others the defect, is most opposed to the mean: to courage, for instance, not rashness which is the excess, but cowardice which is the defect; whereas to perfected self-mastery not insensibility which is the defect but absence of all self-control which is the excess.

And for this there are two reasons to be given; one from the nature of the thing itself, because from the one extreme being nearer and more like the mean, we do not put this against it, but the other; as, for instance, since rashness is thought to be nearer to courage than cowardice is, and to resemble it more, we put cowardice against courage rather than rashness, because those things which are further from the mean are thought to be more contrary to it. This then is one reason arising from the thing itself; there is another arising from our own constitution and make: for in each man's own case those things give the impression of being more contrary to the mean to which we individually have a natural bias. Thus we have a natural bias towards pleasures, for which reason we are much more inclined to the rejection of all self-control, than to self-discipline.

These things then to which the bias is, we call more contrary, and so total want of self-control (the excess) is more contrary than the defect is to perfected self-mastery.

Now that Moral Virtue is a mean state, and how it is so, and that it lies between two faulty states, one in the way of excess and another in the way of defect, and that it is so because it has an aptitude to aim at the mean both in feelings and actions, all this has been set forth fully and sufficiently.

And so it is hard to be good: for surely hard it is in each instance to find the mean, just as to find the mean point or center of a circle is not what any man can do, but only he who knows how: just so to be angry, to give money, and be expansive, is what any man can do, and easy: but to do these to the right person, in due proportion, at the right time, with a right object, and in the right manner, this is not as before what any man can do, nor is it easy; and for this cause goodness is rare, and praiseworthy, and noble.

Therefore he who aims at the mean should make it his first care to keep away from that extreme which is more contrary than the other to the mean; just as Calypso in Homer advises Ulysses,

Clear of this smoke and surge thy barque direct;

because of the two extremes the one is always more, and the other less, erroneous; and, therefore, since to hit exactly on the mean is difficult, one must take the least of the evils as the safest plan; and this a man will be doing, if he follows this method.

We ought also to take into consideration our own natural bias; which varies in each man's case, and will be ascertained from the pleasure and pain arising in us. Furthermore, we should force ourselves off in the contrary direction, because we shall find ourselves in the mean after we have removed ourselves far from the wrong side, exactly as men do in straightening bent timber.

But in all cases we must guard most carefully against what is pleasant, and pleasure itself, because we are not impartial judges of it.

We ought to feel in fact towards pleasure as did the old counselors towards Helen, and in all cases pronounce a similar sentence; for so by sending it away from us, we shall err the less.

Well, to speak very briefly, these are the precautions by adopting which we shall be best able to attain the mean.

Still, perhaps, after all it is a matter of difficulty, and specially in the particular instances: it is not easy, for instance, to determine exactly in what manner, with what persons, for what causes, and for what length of time, one ought to feel anger: for we ourselves sometimes praise those who are defective in this feeling, and we call them meek; at another, we term the hot-tempered manly and spirited.

Then, again, he who makes a small deflection from what is right, be it on the side of too much or too little, is not blamed, only he who makes a considerable one; for he cannot escape observation. But to what point or degree a man must err in order to incur blame, it is not easy to determine exactly in words: nor in fact any of those points which are matters of perception by the Moral Sense: such questions are matters of detail, and the decision of them rests with the Moral Sense.

At all events thus much is plain, that the mean state is in all things praiseworthy, and that practically we must deflect sometimes towards excess, sometimes towards defect, because this will be the easiest method of hitting on the mean, that is, on what is right.

LUCRETIUS

Of the Nature of Things

Origins of Vegetable and Animal Life

And now to what remains!—Since I've resolved
By what arrangements all things come to pass
Through the blue regions of the mighty world,—
How we can know what energy and cause
Started the various courses of the sun   5
And the moon's goings, and by what far means
They can succumb, the while with thwarted light,
And veil with shade the unsuspecting lands,
When, as it were, they blink, and then again
With open eye survey all regions wide,   10
Resplendent with white radiance—I do now
Return unto the world's primeval age
And tell what first the soft young fields of earth
With earliest parturition had decreed
To raise in air unto the shores of light   15
And to entrust unto the wayward winds.

In the beginning, earth gave forth, around
The hills and over all the length of plains,
The race of grasses and the shining green;
The flowery meadows sparkled all aglow   20
With greening color, and thereafter, lo,
Unto the divers kinds of trees was given
An emulous impulse mightily to shoot,
With a free rein, aloft into the air.
As feathers and hairs and bristles are begot   25
The first on members of the four-foot breeds
And on the bodies of the strong-y-winged,
Thus then the new Earth first of all put forth
Grasses and shrubs, and afterward begat
The mortal generations, there upsprung—   30
Innumerable in modes innumerable—
After diverging fashions. For from sky
These breathing-creatures never can have dropped,
Nor the land-dwellers ever have come up
Out of sea-pools of salt. How true remains,   35
How merited is that adopted name
Of earth—"The Mother!"—since from out the
  earth
Are all begotten. And even now arise
From out the loams how many living things—
Concreted by the rains and heat of the sun.   40
Wherefore 'tis less a marvel, if they sprang

In Long Ago more many, and more big,
Matured of those days in the fresh young years
Of earth and ether. First of all, the race
Of the wingèd ones and parti-colored birds,   45
Hatched out in spring-time, left their eggs behind;
As now-a-days in summer tree-crickets
Do leave their shiny husks of own accord,
Seeking their food and living. Then it was
This earth of thine first gave unto the day   50
The mortal generations; for prevailed
Among the fields abounding hot and wet.
And hence, where any fitting spot was given,
There 'gan to grow womb-cavities, by roots
Affixed to earth. And when in ripened time   55
The age of the young within (that sought the air
And fled earth's damps) had burst these wombs, O
  then
Would Nature thither turn the pores of earth
And make her spurt from open veins a juice
Like unto milk; even as a woman now   60
Is filled, at child-bearing, with the sweet milk,
Because all that swift stream of aliment
Is thither turned unto the mother-breasts.
There earth would furnish to the children food;
Warmth was their swaddling cloth, the grass their
  bed   65
Abounding in soft down. Earth's newness then
Would rouse no dour spells of the bitter cold,
Nor éxtreme heats nor winds of mighty powers—
For all things grow and gather strength through
  time
In like proportions; and then earth was young.   70
  Wherefore, again, again, how merited
Is that adopted name of Earth—the Mother!—
Since she herself begat the human race,
And at one well-nigh fixèd time brought forth
Each beast that ranges raving round about   75
Upon the mighty mountains and all birds
Aerial with many a varied shape.
But, lo, because her bearing years must end,
She ceased, like to a woman worn by eld.
For lapsing æons change the nature of   80

Lucretius, *Of the Nature of Things* (Book V, lines 769-1455). Translated by William Ellery Leonard and published by E. P. Dutton and Co. in Everyman's Library. Used by permission. Titus Lucretius Carus (c. 96-55 B.C.) lived in Rome. His long poem expounds the Epicurean philosophy.

The whole wide world, and all things needs must
    take
One status after other, nor aught persists
Forever like itself. All things depart;
Nature she changeth all, compelleth all
To transformation. Lo, *this* molders down,   85
A-slack with weary eld, and *that,* again,
Prospers in glory, issuing from contempt.
In suchwise, then, the lapsing æons change
The nature of the whole wide world, and earth
Taketh one status after other. And what   90
She bore of old, she now can bear no longer,
And what she never bore, she can today.

    In those days also the telluric world
Strove to beget the monsters that upsprung
With their astounding visages and limbs—   95
The Man-woman—a thing betwixt the twain,
Yet neither, and from either sex remote—
Some gruesome Boggles orphaned of the feet,
Some widowed of the hands, dumb Horrors too
Without a mouth, or blind Ones of no eye,   100
Or Bulks all shackled by their legs and arms
Cleaving unto the body fore and aft,
Thuswise, that never could they do or go,
Nor shun disaster, nor take the good they would.
And other prodigies and monsters earth   105
Was then begetting of this sort—in vain,
Since Nature banned with horror their increase,
And powerless were they to reach unto
The coveted flower of fair maturity,
Or to find aliment, or to intertwine   110
In works of Venus. For we see there must
Concur in life conditions manifold,
If life is ever by begetting life
To forge the generations one by one:
First, foods must be; and, next, a path whereby
The seeds of impregnation in the frame   116
May ooze, releasèd from the members all;
Last, the possession of those instruments
Whereby the male with female can unite,
The one with other in mutual ravishments.   120

    And in the ages after monsters died,
Perforce there perished many a stock, unable
By propagation to forge a progeny.
For whatsoever creatures thou beholdest
Breathing the breath of life, the same have been
Even from their earliest age preserved alive   126
By cunning, or by valor, or at least
By speed of foot or wing. And many a stock
Remaineth yet, because of use to man,
And so committed to man's guardianship.   130
Valor hath saved alive fierce lion-breeds
And many another terrorizing race,

Cunning the foxes, flight the antlered stags.
Light-sleeping dogs with faithful heart in breasts,
However, and every kind begot from seed   135
Of beasts of draft, as, too, the woolly flocks
And hornèd cattle, all, my Memmius,
Have been committed to guardianship of men.
For anxiously they fled the savage beasts,
And peace they sought and their abundant foods,
Obtained with never labors of their own,   141
Which we secure to them as fit rewards
For their good service. But those beasts to whom
Nature has granted naught of these same things—
Beasts quite unfit by own free will to thrive   145
And vain for any service unto us
In thanks for which we should permit their kind
To feed and be in our protection safe—
Those, of a truth, were wont to be exposed,
Enshackled in the gruesome bonds of doom,   150
As prey and booty for the rest, until
Nature reduced that stock to utter death.

    But Centaurs ne'er have been, nor can there be
Creatures of twofold stock and double frame,
Compact of members alien in kind,   155
Yet formed with equal function, equal force
In every bodily part—a fact thou mayst,
However dull thy wits, well learn from this:
The horse, when his three years have rolled away,
Flowers in his prime of vigor; but the boy   160
Not so, for oft even then he gropes in sleep
After the milky nipples of the breasts,
An infant still. And later, when at last
The lusty powers of horses and stout limbs,
Now weak through lapsing life, do fail with age,
Lo, only then doth youth with flowering years   166
Begin for boys, and clothe their ruddy cheeks
With the soft down. So never deem, percase,
That from a man and from the seed of horse,
The beast of draft, can Centaurs be composed   170
Or e'er exist alive, nor Scyllas be—
The half-fish bodies girdled with mad dogs—
Nor others of this sort, in whom we mark
Members discordant each with each; for ne'er   174
At one same time they reach their flower of age
Or gain and lose full vigor of their frame,
And never burn with one same lust of love,
And never in their habits they agree,
Nor find the same foods equally delightsome—
Sooth, as one oft may see the bearded goats   180
Batten upon the hemlock which to man
Is violent poison. Once again, since flame
Is wont to scorch and burn the tawny bulks
Of the great lions as much as other kinds
Of flesh and blood existing in the lands,   185

How could it be that she, Chimæra lone,
With triple body,—fore, a lion she;
And aft, a dragon; and betwixt, a goat—
Might at the mouth from out the body belch 189
Infuriate flame? Wherefore, the man who feigns
Such beings could have been engenderèd
When earth was new and the young sky was fresh
(Basing his empty argument on *new*)
May babble with like reason many whims
Into our ears: he'll say, perhaps, that then 195
Rivers of gold through every landscape flowed,
That trees were wont with precious stones to
    flower,
Or that in those far æons man was born
With such gigantic length and lift of limbs
As to be able, based upon his feet, 200
Deep oceans to bestride; or with his hands
To whirl the firmament around his head.
For though in earth were many seeds of things
In the old time when this telluric world
First poured the breeds of animals abroad, 205
Still that is nothing of a sign that then
Such hybrid creatures could have been begot
And limbs of all beasts heterogeneous
Have been together knit; because, indeed,
The divers kinds of grasses and the grains 210
And the delightsome trees—which even now
Spring up abounding from within the earth—
Can still ne'er be begotten with their stems
Begrafted into one; but each sole thing
Proceeds according to its proper wont 215
And all conserve their own distinctions based
In nature's fixed decree.

Origins and Savage Period of Mankind

              But mortal man
Was then far hardier in the old champaign,
As well he should be, since a hardier earth
Had him begotten; builded too was he 220
Of bigger and more solid bones within,
And knit with stalwart sinews through the flesh,
Nor easily seized by either heat or cold,
Or alien food or any ail or irk.
And whilst so many lustrums of the sun 225
Rolled on across the sky, men led a life
After the roving habit of wild beasts.
Not then were sturdy guiders of curvèd plows,
And none knew then to work the fields with iron,
Or plant young shoots in holes of delvèd loam, 230
Or lop with hookèd knives from off high trees
The boughs of yester-year. What sun and rains
To them had given, what earth of own accord

Created then, was boon enough to glad
Their simple hearts. Mid acorn-laden oaks 235
Would they refresh their bodies for the nonce;
And the wild berries of the arbute-tree,
Which now thou seest to ripen purple-red
In winter time, the old telluric soil
Would bear then more abundant and more big.
And many coarse foods, too, in long ago 241
The blooming freshness of the rank young world
Produced, enough for those poor wretches there.
And rivers and springs would summon them of
    old
To slake the thirst, as now from the great hills
The water's down-rush calls aloud and far 246
The thirsty generations of the wild.
So, too, they sought the grottos of the Nymphs—
The woodland haunts discovered as they ranged—
From forth of which they knew that gliding
    rills 250
With gush and splash abounding laved the rocks,
The dripping rocks, and trickled from above
Over the verdant moss; and here and there
Welled up and burst across the open flats.
As yet they knew not to enkindle fire 255
Against the cold, nor hairy pelts to use
And clothe their bodies with the spoils of beasts;
But huddled in groves, and mountain-caves, and
    woods,
And 'mongst the thickets hid their squalid backs,
When driven to flee the lashings of the winds 260
And the big rains. Nor could they then regard
The general good, nor did they know to use
In common any customs, any laws:
Whatever of booty fortune unto each
Had proffered, each alone would bear away, 265
By instinct trained for self to thrive and live.
And Venus in the forests then would link
The lovers' bodies; for the woman yielded
Either from mutual flame, or from the man's
Impetuous fury and insatiate lust, 270
Or from a bribe—as acorn-nuts, choice pears,
Or the wild berries of the arbute-tree.
And trusting wondrous strength of hands and legs,
They'd chase the forest-wanderers, the beasts; 274
And many they'd conquer, but some few they fled,
A-skulk into their hiding-places . . .

         .   .   .   .   .

With the flung stones and with the ponderous heft
Of gnarlèd branch. And by the time of night
O'ertaken, they would throw, like bristly boars,
Their wildman's limbs naked upon the earth, 280
Rolling themselves in leaves and fronded boughs.

Nor would they call with lamentations loud
Around the fields for daylight and the sun,
Quaking and wand'ring in shadows of the night;
But, silent and buried in a sleep, they'd wait   285
Until the sun with rosy flambeau brought
The glory to the sky. From childhood wont
Ever to see the dark and day begot
In times alternate, never might they be
Wildered by wild misgiving, lest a night   290
Eternal should possess the lands, with light
Of sun withdrawn forever. But their care
Was rather that the clans of savage beasts
Would often make their sleep-time horrible
For those poor wretches; and, from home y-driven,
They'd flee their rocky shelters at approach   296
Of boar, the spumy-lipped, or lion strong,
And in the midnight yield with terror up
To those fierce guests their beds of out-spread
    leaves.

  And yet in those days not much more than now
Would generations of mortality   301
Leave the sweet light of fading life behind.
Indeed, in those days here and there a man,
More oftener snatched upon, and gulped by fangs,
Afforded the beasts a food that roared alive,   305
Echoing through groves and hills and forest-trees,
Even as he viewed his living flesh entombed
Within a living grave; whilst those whom flight
Had saved, with bone and body bitten, shrieked,
Pressing their quivering palms to loathsome sores,
With horrible voices for eternal death—   311
Until, forlorn of help, and witless what
Might medicine their wounds, the writhing pangs
Took them from life. But not in those far times
Would one lone day give over unto doom   315
A soldiery in thousands marching on
Beneath the battle-banners, nor would then
The ramping breakers of the main seas dash
Whole argosies and crews upon the rocks.
But ocean uprisen would often rave in vain   320
Without all end or outcome, and give up
Its empty menacings as lightly too;
Nor soft seductions of a sérene sea
Could lure by laughing billows any man
Out to disaster: for the science bold   325
Of ship-sailing lay dark in those far times.
Again, 'twas *then* that lack of food gave o'er
Men's fainting limbs to dissolution: now
'Tis plenty overwhelms. Unwary, they
Oft for themselves themselves would then outpour
The poison; now, with nicer art, themselves   331
They give the drafts to others.

Beginnings of Civilization

                  Afterwards,
When huts they had procured and pelts and fire,
And when the woman, joined unto the man,
Withdrew with him into one dwelling place,   335

    .   .   .   .   .

Were known; and when they saw an offspring
    born
From out themselves, then first the human race
Began to soften. For 'twas now that fire
Rendered their shivering frames less staunch to
    bear,
Under the canopy of the sky, the cold;   340
And Love reduced their shaggy hardiness;
And children, with the prattle and the kiss,
Soon broke the parents' haughty temper down.
Then, too, did neighbors 'gin to league as friends,
Eager to wrong no more or suffer wrong,   345
And urged for children and the womankind
Mercy, of fathers, whilst with cries and gestures
They stammered hints how meet it was that all
Should have compassion on the weak. And still,
Though concord not in every wise could then   350
Begotten be, a good, a goodly part
Kept faith inviolate—or else mankind
Long since had been unutterably cut off,
And propagation never could have brought
The species down the ages.

                  Lest, perchance,   355
Concerning these affairs thou ponderest
In silent meditation, let me say
'Twas lightning brought primevally to earth
The fire for mortals, and from thence hath spread
O'er all the lands the flames of heat. For thus   360
Even now we see so many objects, touched
By the celestial flames, to flash aglow,
When thunderbolt has dowered them with heat.
Yet also when a many-branchèd tree,
Beaten by winds, writhes swaying to and fro,   365
Pressing 'gainst branches of a neighbor tree,
There by the power of mighty rub and rub
Is fire engendered; and at times out-flares
The scorching heat of flame, when boughs do chafe
Against the trunks. And of these causes, either
May well have given to mortal men the fire.   371
Next, food to cook and soften in the flame
The sun instructed, since so oft they saw
How objects mellowed, when subdued by warmth
And by the raining blows of fiery beams,   375
Through all the fields.

           And more and more each day

Would men more strong in sense, more wise in
heyt,
Teach 'iem to change their earlier mode and life
By fire ind new devices. Kings began
Cities o found and citadels to set, 380
As stro igholds and asylums for themselves,
And flocks and fields to portion for each man
After the beauty, strength, and sense of each—
For beauty then imported much, and strength 384
Had its own rights supreme. Thereafter, wealth
Discovered was, and gold was brought to light,
Which soon of honor stripped both strong and
fair;
For men, however beautiful in form
Or valorous, will follow in the main
The rich man's party. Yet were man to steer 390
His life by sounder reasoning, he'd own
Abounding riches, if with mind content
He lived by thrift; for never, as I guess,
Is there a lack of little in the world. 394
But men wished glory for themselves and power
Even that their fortunes on foundations firm
Might rest forever, and that they themselves,
The opulent, might pass a quiet life—
In vain, in vain; since, in the strife to climb
On to the heights of honor, men do make 400
Their pathway terrible; and even when once
They reach them, envy like the thunderbolt
At times will smite, O hurling headlong down
To murkiest Tartarus, in scorn; for, lo,
All summits, all regions loftier than the rest, 405
Smoke, blasted as by envy's thunderbolts;
So better far in quiet to obey,
Than to desire chief mastery of affairs
And ownership of empires. Be it so;
And let the weary sweat their life-blood out 410
All to no end, battling in hate along
The narrow path of man's ambition;
Since all their wisdom is from others' lips,
And all they seek is known from what they've
heard
And less from what they've thought. Nor is this
folly 415
Greater today, nor greater soon to be,
Than 'twas of old.

And therefore kings were slain,
And pristine majesty of golden thrones
And haughty scepters lay o'erturned in dust;
And crowns, so splendid on the sovereign heads,
Soon bloody under the proletarian feet, 421
Groaned for their glories gone—for erst o'er-much
Dreaded, thereafter with more greedy zest
Trampled beneath the rabble heel. Thus things

Down to the vilest lees of brawling mobs 425
Succumbed, whilst each man sought unto himself
Dominion and supremacy. So next
Some wiser heads instructed men to found
The magisterial office, and did frame
Codes that they might consent to follow laws. 430
For humankind, o'erwearied with a life
Fostered by force, was ailing from its feuds;
And so the sooner of its own free will
Yielded to laws and strictest codes. For since
Each hand made ready in its wrath to take 435
A vengeance fiercer than by man's fair laws
Is now conceded, men on this account
Loathed the old life fostered by force. 'Tis thence
That fear of punishments defiles each prize
Of wicked days; for force and fraud ensnare 440
Each man around, and in the main recoil
On him from whence they sprung. Not easy 'tis
For one who violates by ugly deeds
The bonds of common peace to pass a life
Composed and tranquil. For albeit he 'scape 445
The race of gods and men, he yet must dread
'Twill not be hid forever—since, indeed,
So many, oft babbling on amid their dreams
Or raving in sickness, have betrayed themselves
(As stories tell) and publishèd at last 450
Old secrets and the sins.

But nature 'twas
Urged men to utter various sounds of tongue
And need and use did mold the names of things,
About in same wise as the lack-speech years
Compel young children unto gesturings, 455
Making them point with finger here and there
At what's before them. For each creature feels
By instinct to what use to put his powers.
Ere yet the bull-calf's scarce begotten horns
Project above his brows, with them he 'gins 460
Enraged to butt and savagely to thrust.
But whelps of panthers and the lion's cubs
With claws and paws and bites are at the fray
Already, when their teeth and claws be scarce
As yet engendered. So again, we see 465
All breeds of wingèd creatures trust to wings
And from their fledgling pinions seek to get
A fluttering assistance. Thus, to think
That in those days some man apportioned round
To things their names, and that from him men
learned 470
Their first nomenclature, is foolery.
For why could *he* mark everything by words
And utter the various sounds of tongue, what time
The rest may be supposèd powerless
To do the same? And, if the rest had not 475

Already one with other usèd words,
Whence was implanted in the teacher, then,
Fore-knowledge of their use, and whence was
      given
To him alone primordial faculty
To know and see in mind what 'twas he willed?
Besides, one only man could scarce subdue   481
An overmastered multitude to choose
To get by heart *his* names of things. A task
Not easy 'tis in any wise to teach
And to persuade the deaf concerning what   485
'Tis needful for to do. For ne'er would they
Allow, nor ne'er in anywise endure
Perpetual vain dingdong in their ears
Of spoken sounds unheard before. And what,
At last, in this affair so wondrous is,   490
That human race (in whom a voice and tongue
Were now in vigor) should by divers words
Denote its objects, as each divers sense
Might prompt?—since even the speechless herds,
      aye, since
The very generations of wild beasts   495
Are wont dissimilar and divers sounds
To rouse from in them, when there's fear or pain,
And when they burst with joys. And this, forsooth,
'Tis thine to know from plainest facts: when first
Huge flabby jowls of mad Molossian hounds,   500
Baring their hard white teeth, begin to snarl,
They threaten, with infuriate lips peeled back,
In sounds far other than with which they bark
And fill with voices all the regions round.
And when with fondling tongue they start to
      lick   505
Their puppies, or do toss them round with paws,
Feigning with gentle bites to gape and snap,
They fawn with yelps of voice far other then
Than when, alone within the house, they bay,
Or whimpering slink with cringing sides from
      blows.   510
Again the neighing of the horse, is that
Not seen to differ likewise, when the stud
In buoyant flower of his young years raves,
Goaded by wingèd Love, amongst the mares,
And when with widening nostrils out he snorts
The call to battle, and when haply he   516
Whinnies at times with terror-quaking limbs?
Lastly, the flying race, the dappled birds,
Hawks, ospreys, sea-gulls, searching food and life
Amid the ocean billows in the brine,   520
Utter at other times far other cries
Than when they fight for food, or with their prey
Struggle and strain. And birds there are which
      change

With changing weather their own raucous songs—
As long-lived generations of the crows   525
Or flocks of rooks, when they be said to cry
For rain and water and to call at times
For winds and gales. Ergo, if divers moods
Compel the brutes, though speechless evermore,
To send forth divers sounds, O truly then   530
How much more likely 'twere that mortal men
In those days could with many a different sound
Denote each separate thing.
                              And now what cause
Hath spread divinities of gods abroad
Through mighty nations, and filled the cities full
Of the high altars, and led to practices   536
Of solemn rites in season—rites which still
Flourish in midst of great affairs of state
And midst great centers of man's civic life,
The rites whence still in poor mortality   540
Is grafted that quaking awe which rears aloft
Still the new temples of gods from land to land
And drives mankind to visit them in throngs
On holy days—'tis not so hard to give
Reason thereof in speech. Because, in sooth,   545
Even in those days would the race of man
Be seeing excelling visages of gods
With mind awake; and in his sleeps, yet more,—
Bodies of wondrous growth. And, thus, to these   549
Would men attribute sense, because they seemed
To move their limbs and speak pronouncements
      high,
Befitting glorious visage and vast powers.
And men would give them an eternal life,
Because their visages forevermore
Were there before them, and their shapes re-
      mained,   555
And chiefly, however, because men would not
      think
Beings augmented with such mighty powers
Could well by any force o'ermastered be.
And men would think them in their happiness
Excelling far, because the fear of death   560
Vexèd no one of them at all, and since
At same time in men's sleeps men saw them do
So many wonders, and yet feel therefrom
Themselves no weariness. Besides, men marked
How in a fixèd order rolled around   565
The systems of the sky, and changèd times
Of annual seasons, nor were able then
To know thereof the causes. Therefore 'twas
Men would take refuge in consigning all
Unto divinities, and in feigning all   570
Was guided by their nod. And in the sky
They set the seats and vaults of gods, because

Across the sky night and the moon are seen
To roll along—moon, day, and night, and night's
Old awesome constellations evermore,   575
And the night-wandering fireballs of the sky,
And flying flames, clouds, and the sun, the rains,
Snow and the winds, the lightnings, and the hail,
And the swift rumblings, and the hollow roar
Of mighty menacings forevermore.   580
   O humankind unhappy!—when it ascribed
Unto divinities such awesome deeds,
And coupled thereto rigors of fierce wrath!
What groans did men on that sad day beget
Even for themselves, and O what wounds for
   us,   585
What tears for our children's children! Nor, O
   man,
Is thy true piety in this: with head
Under the veil, still to be seen to turn
Fronting a stone, and ever to approach
Unto all altars; nor so prone on earth   590
Forward to fall, to spread upturnèd palms
Before the shrines of gods, nor yet to dew
Altars with prófuse blood of four-foot beasts,
Nor vows with vows to link. But rather this:
To look on all things with a master eye   595
And mind at peace. For when we gaze aloft
Upon the skiey vaults of yon great world
And ether, fixèd high o'er twinkling stars,
And into our thought there come the journeyings
Of sun and moon, O then into our breasts,   600
O'erburdened already with their other ills,
Begins forthwith to rear its sudden head
One more misgiving: lest o'er us, percase,
It be the gods' immeasurable power
That rolls, with varied motion, round and round
The far white constellations. For the lack   606
Of aught of reasons tries the puzzled mind:
Whether was ever a birth-time of the world,
And whether, likewise, any end shall be
How far the ramparts of the world can still   610
Outstand this strain of ever-rousèd motion,
Or whether, divinely with eternal weal
Endowed, they can through endless tracts of age
Glide on, defying the o'er-mighty powers
Of the immeasurable ages. Lo,   615
What man is there whose mind with dread of gods
Cringes not close, whose limbs with terror-spell
Crouch not together, when the parchèd earth
Quakes with the horrible thunderbolt amain,
And across the mighty sky the rumblings run?   620
Do not the peoples and the nations shake,
And haughty kings do they not hug their limbs,
Strook through with fear of the divinities,

Lest for aught foully done or madly said
The heavy time be now at hand to pay?   625
When, too, fierce force of fury-winds at sea
Sweepeth a navy's admiral down the main
With his stout legions and his elephants,
Doth he not seek the peace of gods with vows,
And beg in prayer, a-tremble, lullèd winds   630
And friendly gales?—in vain, since, often up-
   caught
In fury-cyclones, is he borne along,
For all his mouthings, to the shoals of doom.
Ah, so irrevocably some hidden power
Betramples forevermore affairs of men,   635
And visibly grindeth with its heel in mire
The lictors' glorious rods and axes dire,
Having them in derision! Again, when earth
From end to end is rocking under foot,
And shaken cities ruin down, or threaten   640
Upon the verge, what wonder is it then
That mortal generations abase themselves,
And unto gods in all affairs of earth
Assign as last resort almighty powers
And wondrous energies to govern all?   645
   Now for the rest: copper and gold and iron
Discovered were, and with them silver's weight
And power of lead, when with prodigious heat
The conflagrations burned the forest trees
Among the mighty mountains, by a bolt   650
Of lightning from the sky, or else because
Men, warring in the woodlands, on their foes
Had hurlèd fire to frighten and dismay,
Or yet because, by goodness of the soil
Invited, men desired to clear rich fields   655
And turn the countryside to pasture-lands,
Or slay the wild and thrive upon the spoils.
(For hunting by pit-fall and by fire arose
Before the art of hedging the covert round
With net or stirring it with dogs of chase.)   660
Howso the fact, and from what cause soever
The flamy heat with awful crack and roar
Had there devourèd to their deepest roots
The forest trees and baked the earth with fire,
Then from the boiling veins began to ooze   665
O rivulets of silver and of gold,
Of lead and copper too, collecting soon
Into the hollow places of the ground.
And when men saw the coolèd lumps anon   669
To shine with splendor-sheen upon the ground,
Much taken with that lustrous smooth delight,
They 'gan to pry them out, and saw how each
Had got a shape like to its earthy mold.
Then would it enter their heads how these same
   lumps,

If melted by heat, could into any form   675
Or figure of things be run, and how, again,
If hammered out, they could be nicely drawn
To sharpest point or finest edge, and thus
Yield to the forgers tools and give them power
To chop the forest down, to hew the logs,   680
To shave the beams and planks, besides to bore
And punch and drill. And men began such work
At first as much with tools of silver and gold
As with the impetuous strength of the stout
    copper;
But vainly—since their over-mastered power   685
Would soon give way, unable to endure,
Like copper, such hard labor. In those days
Copper it was that was the thing of price;
And gold lay useless, blunted with dull edge.
Now lies the copper low, and gold hath come   690
Unto the loftiest honors. Thus it is
That rolling ages change the times of things:
What erst was of a price, becomes at last
A discard of no honor; whilst another
Succeeds to glory, issuing from contempt,   695
And day by day is sought for more and more,
And, when 'tis found, doth flower in men's praise,
Object of wondrous honor.
                    Now, Memmius,
How nature of iron discovered was, thou mayst
Of thine own self divine. Man's ancient arms   700
Were hands, and nails and teeth, stones too and
    boughs—
Breakage of forest trees—and flame and fire,
As soon as known. Thereafter force of iron
And copper discovered was; and copper's use
Was known ere iron's, since more tractable   705
Its nature is and its abundance more.
With copper men to work the soil began,
With copper to rouse the hurly waves of war,
To straw the monstrous wounds, and seize away
Another's flocks and fields. For unto them,   710
Thus armèd, all things naked of defense
Readily yielded. Then by slow degrees
The sword of iron succeeded, and the shape
Of brazen sickle into scorn was turned:
With iron to cleave the soil of earth they 'gan, 715
And the contentions of uncertain war
Were rendered equal.
                    And, lo, man was wont
Armèd to mount upon the ribs of horse
And guide him with the rein, and play about
With right hand free, of times before he tried 720
Perils of war in yokèd chariot;
And yokèd pairs abreast came earlier
Than yokes of four, or scythèd chariots

Whereinto clomb the men-at-arms. And next
The Punic folk did train the elephants—   725
Those curst Lucanian oxen, hideous,
The serpent-handed, with turrets on their bulks
To dure the wounds of war and panic-strike
The mighty troops of Mars. Thus Discord sad
Begat the one Thing after other, to be   730
The terror of the nations under arms,
And day by day to horrors of old war
She added an increase.
                    Bulls, too, they tried
In war's grim business; and essayed to send
Outrageous boars against the foes. And some   735
Sent on before their ranks puissant lions
With armèd trainers and with masters fierce
To guide and hold in chains—and yet in vain,
Since fleshed with pell-mell slaughter, fierce they
    flew,   739
And blindly through the squadrons havoc wrought,
Shaking the frightful crests upon their heads,
Now here, now there. Nor could the horsemen
    calm
Their horses, panic-breasted at the roar,
And rein them round to front the foe. With spring
The infuriate she-lions would up-leap   745
Now here, now there; and whoso came apace
Against them, these they'd rend across the face;
And others unwitting from behind they'd tear
Down from their mounts, and twinging round
    them, bring
Tumbling to earth, o'ermastered by the wound,   750
And with those powerful fangs and hookèd claws
Fasten upon them. Bulls would toss their friends,
And trample under foot, and from beneath
Rip flanks and bellies of horses with their horns,
And with a threat'ning forehead jam the sod;   755
And boars would gore with stout tusks their allies,
Splashing in fury their own blood on spears
Splintered in their own bodies, and would fell
In rout and ruin infantry and horse.
For there the beasts-of-saddle tried to scape   760
The savage thrusts of tusk by shying off,
Or rearing up with hoofs a-paw in air.
In vain—since there thou mightest see them sink,
Their sinews severed, and with heavy fall
Bestrew the ground. And such of these as men   766
Were in the thick of action seen to foam
In fury, from the wounds, the shrieks, the flight,
The panic, and the tumult; nor could men
Aught of their numbers rally. For each breed   770
And various of the wild beasts fled apart
Hither or thither, as often in wars today

Flee those Lucanian oxen, by the steel
Grievously mangled, after they have wrought
Upon their friends so many a dreadful doom.   775
(If 'twas, indeed, that thus they did at all:
But scarcely I'll believe that men could not
With mind foreknow and see, as sure to come,
Such foul and general disaster.—This
We, then, may hold as true in the great All,   780
In divers worlds on divers plan create,—
Somewhere afar more likely than upon
One certain earth.) But men chose this to do
Less in the hope of conquering than to give
Their enemies a goodly cause of woe,   785
Even though thereby they perishèd themselves,
Since weak in numbers and since wanting arms.
    Now, clothes of roughly inter-plaited strands
Were earlier than loom-wove coverings;
The loom-wove later than man's iron is,   790
Since iron is needful in the weaving art,
Nor by no other means can there be wrought
Such polished tools—the treadles, spindles, shuttles,
And sounding yarn-beams. And nature forced the
    men,
Before the woman kind, to work the wool: 795
For all the male kind far excels in skill,
And cleverer is by much—until at last
The rugged farmer folk jeered at such tasks,
And so were eager soon to give them o'er
To women's hands, and in more hardy toil   800
To harden arms and hands.
                            But nature herself,
Mother of things, was the first seed-sower
And primal grafter; since the berries and acorns,
Dropping from off the trees, would there beneath
Put forth in season swarms of little shoots;   805
Hence too men's fondness for ingrafting slips
Upon the boughs and setting out in holes
The young shrubs o'er the fields. Then would they
    try
Ever new modes of tilling their loved crofts,
And mark they would how earth improved the
    taste   810
Of the wild fruits by fond and fostering care.
And day by day they'd force the woods to move
Still higher up the mountain, and to yield
The place below for tilth, that there they might,
On plains and uplands, have their meadow-
    plats,   815
Cisterns and runnels, crops of standing grain,
And happy vineyards, and that all along
O'er hillocks, intervales, and plains might run
The silvery-green belt of olive-trees,
Marking the plotted landscape; even as now   820

Thou seest so marked with varied loveliness
All the terrain which men adorn and plant
With rows of goodly fruit-trees and hedge round
With thriving shrubberies sown.
                            But by the mouth,
To imitate the liquid notes of the birds   825
Was earlier far 'mongst men than power to make,
By measured song, melodious verse and give
Delight to ears. And whistlings of the wind
Athrough the hollows of the reeds first taught
The peasantry to blow into the stalks   830
Of hollow hemlock-herb. Then bit by bit
They learned sweet plainings, such as pipe out-
    pours,
Beaten by finger-tips of singing men,
When heard through unpathed groves and forest
    deeps
And woodsy meadows, through the untrod haunts
Of shepherd folk and spots divinely still.   836
Thus time draws forward each and everything
Little by little unto the midst of men,
And reason uplifts it to the shores of light.
These tunes would soothe and glad the minds of
    mortals   840
When sated with food,—for songs are welcome
    then.
And often, lounging with friends in the soft grass
Beside a river of water, underneath
A big tree's branches, merrily they'd refresh
Their frames, with no vast outlay—most of all   845
If the weather were smiling and the times of the
    year
Were painting the green of the grass around with
    flowers.
Then jokes, then talk, then peals of jollity
Would circle round; for then the rustic muse
Was in her glory; then would antic Mirth   850
Prompt them to garland head and shoulders about
With chaplets of intertwinèd flowers and leaves,
And to dance onward, out of tune, with limbs
Clownishly swaying, and with clownish foot
To beat our mother earth—from whence arose   855
Laughter and peals of jollity, for, lo,
Such frolic acts were in their glory then,
Being more new and strange. And wakeful men
Found solaces for their unsleeping hours
In drawing forth variety of notes,   860
In modulating melodies, in running
With puckered lips along the tunèd reeds,
Whence, even in our day do the watchmen guard
These old traditions, and have learnèd well
To keep true measure. And yet they no whit   865

Do get a larger fruit of gladsomeness
Than got the woodland aborigines
In olden times. For *what* we have at hand—
If theretofore naught sweeter we have known—
That chiefly pleases and seems best of all;   870
But then some later, likely better, find
Destroys its worth and changes our desires
Regarding good of yesterday.
                              And thus
Began the loathing of the acorn; thus
Abandoned were those beds with grasses strewn
And with the leaves beladen. Thus, again,   876
Fell into new contempt the pelts of beasts—
Erstwhile a robe of honor, which, I guess,
Aroused in those days envy so malign
That the first wearer went to woeful death   880
By ambuscades,—and yet that hairy prize,
Rent into rags by greedy foemen there
And splashed by blood, was ruined utterly
Beyond all use or vantage. Thus of old
'Twas pelts, and of today 'tis purple and gold   885
That cark men's lives with cares and weary with
        war.
Wherefore, methinks, resides the greater blame
With us vain men today: for cold would rack,
Without their pelts, the naked sons of earth;
But us it nothing hurts to do without   890
The purple vestment, broiderèd with gold
And with imposing figures, if we still
Make shift with some mean garment of the Plebs.
So man in vain futilities toils on
Forever and wastes in idle cares his years—   895
Because, of very truth, he hath not learnt
What the true end of getting is, nor yet
At all how far true pleasure may increase.

And 'tis desire for better and for more
Hath carried by degrees mortality   900
Out onward to the deep, and rousèd up
From the far bottom mighty waves of war.
    But sun and moon, those watchmen of the
        world,
With their own lanterns traversing around
The mighty, the revolving vault, have taught   905
Unto mankind that seasons of the years
Return again, and that the Thing takes place
After a fixèd plan and order fixed.
    Already would they pass their life, hedged round
By the strong towers; and cultivate an earth   910
All portioned out and boundaried; already
Would the sea flower with sail-wingèd ships;
Already men had, under treaty pacts,
Confederates and allies, when poets began
To hand heroic actions down in verse;   915
Nor long ere this had letters been devised—
Hence is our age unable to look back
On what has gone before, except where reason
Shows us a footprint.
                    Sailings on the seas,
Tillings of fields, walls, laws, and arms, and roads,
Dress and the like, all prizes, all delights   921
Of finer life, poems, pictures, chiseled shapes
Of polished sculptures—all these arts were learned
By practice and the mind's experience,
As men walked forward step by eager step.   925
Thus time draws forward each and everything
Little by little into the midst of men,
And reason uplifts it to the shores of light.
For one thing after other did men see
Grow clear by intellect, till with their arts   930
They've now achieved the súpreme pinnacle.

MARCUS AURELIUS

Meditations

Begin the morning by saying to thyself, I shall meet with the busybody, the ungrateful, arrogant, deceitful, envious, unsocial. All these things happen to them by reason of their ignorance of what is good and evil. But I who have seen the nature of

the good that it is beautiful and of the bad that it is ugly, and the nature of him who does wrong, that it is akin to me, not [only] of the same blood or seed, but that it participates in [the same] intelligence and [the same] portion of the divinity,

Marcus Aurelius, *Meditations*. Translated by George Long. Marcus Aurelius Antoninus (121-180 A.D.) was an adopted son of his grandfather and succeeded his uncle Antoninus Pius as emperor. He is recognized as one of the world's greatest rulers.

I can neither be injured by any of them, for no one can fix on me what is ugly, nor can I be angry with my kinsman, nor hate him. For we are made for co-operation, like feet, like hands, like eyelids, like the rows of the upper and lower teeth. To act against one another then is contrary to nature; and it is acting against one another to be vexed and to turn away.

Whatever this is that I am, it is a little flesh and breath, and the ruling part. Throw away thy books; no longer distract thyself: it is not allowed; but as if thou wast now dying, despise the flesh, it is blood and bones and a network, a contexture of nerves, veins and arteries. See the breath also, what kind of a thing it is; air, and not always the same, but every moment sent out and again sucked in. The third then is the ruling part: consider thus: Thou art an old man; no longer let this be a slave, no longer be pulled by the strings like a puppet to unsocial movements, no longer be either dissatis- fied with thy present lot, or shrink from the future.

All that is from the gods is full of providence. That which is from fortune is not separated from nature or without an interweaving and involution with the things which are ordered by Providence. From thence all things flow; and there is besides necessity, and that which is for the advantage of the whole universe, of which thou art a part. But that is good for every part of nature which the na- ture of the whole brings, and what serves to main- tain this nature. Now the universe is preserved, as by the changes of the elements so by the changes of things compounded of the elements. Let these principles be enough for thee; let them always be fixed opinions. But cast away the thirst after books, that thou mayest not die murmuring, but cheer- fully, truly, and from thy heart thankful to the gods.

Remember how long thou hast been putting off these things, and how often thou hast received an opportunity from the gods, and yet dost not use it. Thou must now at last perceive of what universe thou art a part, and of what administrator of the universe thy existence is an efflux, and that a limit of time is fixed for thee, which if thou dost not use for clearing away the clouds from thy mind, it will go and thou wilt go, and it will never return.

Every moment think steadily as a Roman and a man to do what thou hast in hand with perfect and simple dignity, and feeling of affection, and free- dom, and justice; and to give thyself relief from all other thoughts. And thou wilt give thyself relief, if thou doest every act of thy life as if it were the last, laying aside all carelessness and passionate aversion from the commands of reason, and all hypocrisy, and self-love, and discontent with the portion which has been given to thee. Thou seest how few the things are, the which if a man lays hold of, he is able to live a life which flows in quiet, and is like the existence of the gods; for the gods on their part will require nothing more from him who observes these things.

Do wrong to thyself, do wrong to thyself, my soul; but thou wilt no longer have the opportunity of honoring thyself. Every man's life is sufficient. But thine is nearly finished, though thy soul rev- erences not itself, but places thy felicity in the souls of others.

Do the things external which fall upon thee dis- tract thee? Give thyself time to learn something new and good, and cease to be whirled around. But then thou must also avoid being carried about the other way. For those too are triflers who have wearied themselves in life by their activity, and yet have no object to which to direct every move- ment, and, in a word, all their thoughts.

Through not observing what is in the mind of another a man has seldom been seen to be un- happy; but those who do not observe the move- ments of their own minds must of necessity be unhappy.

This thou must always bear in mind, what is the nature of the whole, and what is my nature, and how this is related to that, and what kind of a part it is of what kind of a whole; and that there is no one who hinders thee from always doing and say- ing the things which are according to the nature of which thou art a part.

Theophrastus, in his comparison of bad acts— such a comparison as one would make in accord- ance with the common notions of mankind—says, like a true philosopher, that the offenses which are committed through desire are more blamable than those which are committed through anger. For he who is excited by anger seems to turn away from reason with a certain pain and unconscious con- traction; but he who offends through desire, being overpowered by pleasure, seems to be in a manner more intemperate and more womanish in his of- fenses. Rightly then, and in a way worthy of philos- ophy, he said that the offense which is committed with pleasure is more blamable than that which is committed with pain; and on the whole the one is more like a person who has been first wronged and through pain is compelled to be angry; but the other is moved by his own impulse to do wrong, being carried toward doing something by desire.

Since it is possible that thou mayest depart from life this very moment, regulate every act and thought accordingly. But to go away from among men, if there are gods, is not a thing to be afraid of, for the gods will not involve thee in evil; but if indeed they do not exist, or if they have no concern about human affairs, what is it to me to live in a universe devoid of gods or devoid of providence? But in truth they do exist, and they do care for human things, and they have put all the means in man's power to enable him not to fall into real evils. And as to the rest, if there was anything evil, they would have provided for this also, that it should be altogether in a man's power not to fall into it. Now, that which does not make a man worse, how can it make a man's life worse? But neither through ignorance, nor having the knowledge, but not the power to guard against or correct these things, is it possible that the nature of the universe has overlooked them; nor is it possible that it has made so great a mistake, either through want of power or want of skill, that good and evil should happen indiscriminately to the good and the bad. But death certainly, and life, honor and dishonor, pain and pleasure, all these things equally happen to good men and bad, being things which make us neither better nor worse. Therefore they are neither good nor evil.

How quickly all these things disappear, in the universe the bodies themselves, but in time the remembrance of them; what is the nature of all sensible things, and particularly whose which attract with the bait of pleasure or terrify by pain, or are noised about by vapory fame; how worthless, and contemptible, and sordid and perishable, and dead they are—all this it is the part of the intellectual faculty to observe. To observe too who these are whose opinions and voices give reputation; what death is, and the fact that, if a man looks at it in itself, and by the abstractive power of reflection resolves into their parts all the things which present themselves to the imagination in it, he will then consider it to be nothing else than an operation of nature; and if anyone is afraid of an operation of nature he is a child. This, however, is not only an operation of nature, but it is also a thing which conduces to the purposes of nature. To observe, too, how man comes near to the Deity, and by what part of him, and when this part of man is so disposed.

Nothing is more wretched than a man who traverses everything in a round, and pries into things beneath the earth, as the poet says, and seeks by conjecture what is in the minds of his neighbors, without perceiving that it is sufficient to attend to the dæmon within him, and to reverence it sincerely. And reverence of the dæmon consists in keeping it pure from passion and thoughtlessness, and dissatisfaction with what comes from gods and men. For the things from the gods merit veneration for their excellence; and the things from men should be dear to us by reason of kinship; and sometimes even, in a manner, they move our pity by reason of men's ignorance of good and bad; this defect being not less than that which deprives us of the power of distinguishing things that are white and black.

Though thou shouldest be going to live three thousand years, and as many times ten thousand years, still remember that no man loses any other life than this which he now lives, nor lives any other than this which he now loses. The longest and shortest are thus brought to the same. For the present is the same to all, though that which perishes is not the same; and so that which is lost appears to be a mere moment. For a man cannot lose either the past or the future: for what a man has not, how can anyone take this from him? These two things then thou must bear in mind: the one, that all things from eternity are of like forms and come round in a circle, and that it makes no difference whether a man shall see the same things during a hundred years or two hundred, or an infinite time; and the second, that the longest liver and he who will die soonest lose just the same. For the present is the only thing of which a man can be deprived, if it is true that this is the only thing which he has, and that a man cannot lose a thing if he has it not.

Remember that all is opinion. For what was said by the Cynic Monimus is manifest: and manifest too is the use of what was said, if a man receives what may be got out of it as far as it is true.

The soul of man does violence to itself, first of all when it becomes an abscess and, as it were, a tumor on the universe, so far as it can. For to be vexed at anything which happens is a separation of ourselves from nature, in some part of which the natures of all other things are contained. In the next place, the soul does violence to itself when it turns away from any man, or even moves towards him with the intention of injuring, such as are the souls of those who are angry. In the third place, the soul does violence to itself when it is overpowered by pleasure or by pain. Fourthly, when it plays a part, and does or says anything insincerely and untruly. Fifthly, when it allows any act of its own and any movement to be without an aim, and does anything thoughtlessly and without considering what it is, it being right that even the smallest things be done with reference to an end; and the end of rational animals is to follow the reason and the law of the most ancient city and polity.

Of the human life the time is a point, and the substance is in a flux, and the perception dull, and the composition of the whole body subject to putrefaction, and the soul of a whirl, and fortune hard to divine, and fame a thing devoid of judgment. And, to say all in a word, everything which belongs to the body is a stream, and what belongs to the soul is a dream and vapor, and life is a warfare and a stranger's sojourn, and after-fame is oblivion. What, then, is that which is able to conduct a man? One thing, and only one—philosophy. But this consists in keeping the dæmon within a man free from violence and unharmed, superior to pains and pleasures, doing nothing without a purpose, nor yet falsely and with hypocrisy, not feeling the need of another man's doing or not doing anything; and besides, accepting all that happens, and all that is allotted, as coming from thence, wherever it is, from whence he himself came; and, finally, waiting for death with a cheerful mind, as being nothing else than a dissolution of the elements of which every living being is compounded. But if there is no harm to the elements themselves in each continually changing into another, why should a man have any apprehension about the change and dissolution of all the elements? For it is according to nature, and nothing is evil which is according to nature.

We ought to consider not only that our life is daily wasting away and a smaller part of it is left, but another thing also must be taken into the account, that if a man should live longer it is quite uncertain whether the understanding will still continue sufficient for the comprehension of things, and retain the power of contemplation which strives to acquire the knowledge of the divine and the human. For if he shall begin to fall into dotage, perspiration and nutrition and imagination and appetite, and whatever else there is of the kind, will not fail; but the power of making use of ourselves, and filling up the measure of our duty, and clearly separating all appearances, and considering whether a man should now depart from life, and whatever else of the kind absolutely requires a disciplined reason, all this is already extinguished. We must make haste then, not only because we are daily nearer to death, but also because the conception of things and the understanding of them cease first.

We ought to observe also that even the things which follow after the things which are produced according to nature contain something pleasing and attractive. For instance, when bread is baked some parts are split at the surface, and these parts which thus open, and have a certain fashion contrary to the purpose of the baker's art, are beautiful in a manner, and in a peculiar way excite a desire for eating. And again, figs, when they are quite ripe, gape open, and in the ripe olives the very circumstance of their being near to rottenness adds a peculiar beauty to the fruit. And the ears of corn bending down, and the lion's eyebrows, and the foam which flows from the mouth of wild boars, and many other things—though they are far from being beautiful, if a man should examine them severally—still, because they are consequent upon the things which are formed by nature, help to adorn them, and they please the mind; so that if a man should have a feeling and deeper insight with respect to the things which are produced in the universe, there is hardly one of those which follow by way of consequence which will not seem to him to be in a manner disposed so as to give pleasure. And so he will see even the real gaping jaws of wild beasts with no less pleasure than those which painters and sculptors show by imitation; and in an old woman and an old man he will be able to see a certain maturity and comeliness; and the attractive loveliness of young persons he will be able to look on with chaste eyes; and many such things will present themselves, not pleasing to every man, but to him only who has become truly familiar with nature and her works.

Hippocrates after curing many diseases himself fell sick and died. The Chaldæi foretold the deaths of many, and then fate caught them too. Alexander, and Pompeius, and Caius Cæsar, after so often completely destroying whole cities, and in battle cutting to pieces many ten thousands of cavalry and infantry, themselves too at last departed from life. Heraclitus, after so many speculations on the conflagration of the universe, was filled with water internally and died smeared all over with mud. And lice destroyed Democritus; and other lice killed Socrates. What means all this? Thou hast embarked, thou hast made the voyage, thou art come to shore; get out. If indeed to another life, there is no want of gods, not even there. But if to a state without sensation, thou wilt cease to be held by pains and pleasures, and to be a slave to the vessel, which is as much inferior as that which serves it is superior; for the one is intelligence and deity; the other is earth and corruption.

Do not waste the remainder of thy life in thoughts about others, when thou dost not refer thy thoughts to some object of common utility. For thou losest the opportunity of doing something else when thou hast such thoughts as these, What is such a person doing, and why, and what is he saying, and what is he thinking of, and what is he contriving, and whatever else of the kind makes us wander away from the observation of our own ruling power. We ought then to check in the series of our thoughts everything that is without a purpose and useless, but most of all the over-curious feeling and the malignant; and a man should use himself to think of those things only about which if one should suddenly ask, What hast thou now in thy thoughts? with perfect openness thou mightest immediately answer, This or That; so that from thy words it should be plain that everything in thee is simple and benevolent, and such as befits a social animal, one that cares not for thoughts about pleasure or sensual enjoyments at all, nor has any rivalry or envy and suspicion, or anything else for which thou wouldest blush if thou shouldst say that thou hadst it in thy mind. For the man who is such and no longer delays being among the number of the best, is like a priest and minister of the gods, using too the [deity] which is planted within him, which makes the man uncontaminated by pleasure, unharmed by any pain, untouched by any insult, feeling no wrong, a fighter in the noblest fight, one who cannot be overpowered by any passion, dyed deep with justice, accepting with all his soul everything which happens and is assigned to him as his portion; and not often, nor yet without great necessity and for the general interest, imagining what another says, or does, or thinks. For it is only what belongs to himself that he makes the matter for his activity; and he constantly thinks of that which is allotted to himself out of the sum total of things, and he makes his own acts fair, and he is persuaded that his own portion is good. For the lot which is assigned to each man is carried along with him and carries him along with it. And he remembers also that every rational animal is his

kinsman, and that to care for all men is according to man's nature; and a man should hold on to the opinion not of all but of those only who confessedly live according to nature. But as to those who live not so, he always bears in mind what kind of men they are both at home and from home, both by night and by day, and what they are, and with what men they live an impure life. Accordingly, he does not value at all the praise which comes from such men, since they are not even satisfied with themselves.

Labor not unwillingly, nor without regard to the common interest, nor without due consideration, nor with distraction; nor let studied ornament set off thy thoughts, and be not either a man of many words, or busy about too many things. And further, let the deity which is in thee be the guardian of a living being, manly and of ripe age, and engaged in matter political, and a Roman, and a ruler, who has taken his post like a man waiting for the signal which summons him from life, and ready to go, having need neither of oath nor of any man's testimony. Be cheerful also, and seek not external help nor the tranquillity which others give. A man then must stand erect, not be kept erect by others.

If thou findest in human life anything better than justice, truth, temperance, fortitude, and, in a word, anything better than thy own mind's self-satisfaction in the things which it enables thee to do according to right reason, and in the condition that is assigned to thee without thy own choice; if, I say, thou seest anything better than this, turn to it with all thy soul, and enjoy that which thou hast found to be the best. But if nothing appears to be better than the deity which is planted in thee, which has subjected to itself all thy appetites, and carefully examines all the impressions, and as Socrates said, has detached itself from the persuasions of sense, and has submitted itself to the gods, and cares for mankind; if thou findest everything else smaller and of less value than this, give place to nothing else, for if thou dost once diverge and incline to it, thou wilt no longer without distraction be able to give the preference to that good thing which is thy proper possession and thy own; for it is not right that anything of any other kind, such as praise from the many, or power, or enjoyment of pleasure, should come into competition with that which is rationally and politically [or, practically] good. All these things, even though they may seem to adapt themselves [to the better things] in a small degree, obtain the superiority all at once, and carry us away. But do thou, I say, simply and freely choose the better, and hold to it.—But that which is useful is the better.—Well then, if it is only useful to thee as a rational being, keep to it; but if it is only useful to thee as an animal, say so, and maintain thy judgment without arrogance; only take care that thou makest the inquiry by a sure method.

Never value anything as profitable to thyself which shall compel thee to break thy promise, to lose thy self-respect, to hate any man, to suspect, to curse, to act the hypocrite, to desire anything which needs walls and curtains: for he who has preferred to everything else his own intelligence and dæmon and the worship of its excellence, acts no tragic part, does not groan, will not need either solitude or much company; and, what is chief of all, he will live without either pursuing or flying from [death]; but whether for a longer or a shorter time he shall have the soul inclosed in the body, he cares not at all; for even if he must depart immediately, he will go as readily as if he were going to do anything else which can be done with decency and order; taking care of this only all through life, that his thoughts turn not away from anything which belongs to an intelligent animal and a member of a civil community.

In the mind of one who is chastened and purified thou wilt find no corrupt matter, nor impurity, nor any sore skinned over. Nor is his life incomplete when fate overtakes him, as one may say of an actor who leaves the stage before ending and finishing the play. Besides, there is in him nothing servile, nor affected, nor too closely bound [to other things], nor yet detached [from other things], nothing worthy of blame, nothing which seeks a hiding-place.

Reverence the faculty which produces opinion. On this faculty it entirely depends whether there shall exist in thy ruling part any opinion inconsistent with nature and the constitution of the rational animal. And this faculty promises freedom from hasty judgment, and friendship towards men, and obedience to the gods.

Throwing away, then, all things, hold to these only which are few; and besides bear in mind that every man lives only this present time, which is an indivisible point, and that all the rest of his life is either past or it is uncertain. Short then is the time which every man lives, and small the nook of the earth where he lives; and short too the longest posthumous fame, and even this only continued by a succession of poor human beings, who will very soon die, and who know not even themselves, much less him who died long ago.

To the aids which have been mentioned let this one still be added:—Make for thyself a definition or description of the thing which is presented to thee, so as to see distinctly what kind of a thing it is in its substance, in its nudity, in its complete entirety, and tell thyself its proper name, and the names of the things of which it has been compounded, and into which it will be resolved. For nothing is so productive of elevation of mind as to be able to examine methodically and truly every object which is presented to thee in life, and always to look at things so as to see at the same time what kind of universe this is, and what kind of use everything performs in it, and what value everything has with reference to the whole, and what with reference to man, who is a citizen of the highest city, of which all other cities are like families; what each thing is, and of what it is composed, and how long it is the nature of this thing to endure which now makes an impression on me, and what virtue I have need of with respect to it, such as gentleness, manliness, truth, fidelity, simplicity, contentment, and the rest. Wherefore, on every occasion a man should say: This comes from God; and this is according to the apportionment and spinning of the thread of destiny, and such-like coincidence and chance; and this is from one of the same stock and a kinsman and partner, one who knows not however what is according to his nature. But I know; for this reason I behave towards him according to the natural law of fellowship with benevolence and justice. At the same time however in things indifferent I attempt to ascertain the value of each.

If thou workest at that which is before thee, following right reason seriously, vigorously, calmly, without allowing anything else to distract thee, but keeping thy divine part pure, as if thou shouldst be bound to give it back immediately; if thou holdest to this, expecting nothing, fearing nothing, but satisfied with thy present activity according to nature, and with heroic truth in every word and sound which thou utterest, thou wilt live happy. And there is no man who is able to prevent this.

As physicians have always their instruments and knives ready for cases which suddenly require their skill, so do thou have principles ready for the understanding of things divine and human, and doing everything, even the smallest, with a recollection of the bond which unites the divine and human to one another. For neither wilt thou do anything well which pertains to man without at the same time having a reference to things divine; nor the contrary.

No longer wander at hazard; for neither wilt thou read thy own memoirs, nor the acts of the ancient Romans and Hellenes, and the selections from books which thou wast reserving for thy old age. Hasten then to the end which thou hast before thee, and, throwing away idle hopes, come to thy own aid, if thou carest at all for thyself, while it is in thy power.

They know not how many things are signified by the words stealing, sowing, buying, keeping quiet, seeing what ought to be done; for this is not effected by the eyes, but by another kind of vision.

Body, soul, intelligence: to the body belong sensations, to the soul appetites, to the intelligence principles. To receive the impressions of forms by means of appearances belongs even to animals; to be pulled by the strings of desire belongs both to wild beasts and to men who have made themselves into women, and to a Phalaris and a Nero: and to have the intelligence that guides to the things which appear suitable belongs also to those who do not believe in the gods, and who betray their country, and do their impure deeds when they have shut the doors. If then everything else is common to all that I have mentioned, there remains that which is peculiar to the good man, to be pleased and content with what happens, and with the thread which is spun for him; and not to defile the divinity which is planted in his breast, nor disturb it by a crowd of images, but to preserve it tranquil, following it obediently as a god, neither saying anything contrary to the truth, nor doing anything contrary to justice. And if all men refuse to believe that he lives a simple, modest, and contented life, he is neither angry with any of them, nor does he deviate from the way which leads to the end of life, to which a man ought to come pure, tranquil, ready to depart, and without any compulsion perfectly reconciled to his lot.

THE BIBLE

"Vicisti Galilæ."—Thou hast conquered, O Galilean!—These words, uttered by Julian the Apostate, the ill-fated emperor who failed to restore paganism in the Greek world, sum up the most momentous event in European history. Julian and his world were conquered by the ideals of a tiny nation occupying a strip of land in Syria about one hundred and fifty miles long and only half as broad at its widest point. Geographically, Palestine lay midway between the capitals of the two mightiest centers of Near Eastern civilization, situated respectively in the valley of the Nile and in Mesopotamia between the Tigris and Euphrates rivers. Geographically, then, it lay between two of the most ancient oriental worlds, the two that faced Europe most directly.

Its culture belonged to both these civilizations, and yet only in part. In everything that ultimately mattered, Judea became something apart from them, and something above them, too. Politically the pawn of two powerful empires, Palestine's people underwent the travail of centuries of insecurity and struggle, of conquest and captivity. Out of their sufferings arose longings, visions, and ideals that were destined to change the face of the world. They lost their own land, but their spirit took over nations larger than any dreamt of by their conquerors. They created for themselves and for others a "portable country" in the form of an imperishable book, the Bible. Its supreme prose and poetry determine in a large measure the pattern in which Jews, Christians, and Mohammedans have expressed their views of God, man's destiny, and man's duties.

The Hebrew peoples came of the Semitic stock and were closely related to the Arabs and the ancient Assyrians. Early in their history they settled in Palestine, at the eastern end of the Mediterranean. The Bible tells of this settlement under Abraham, who came from Chaldea. After several generations they probably went to Egypt, where they remained for many years. After a tedious and painful return, they lived for a long time under judges, who were their religious leaders but were also active in conducting war against their many enemies. They were not very successful in these wars, and finally established kings over themselves. The most famous of these were David (about 990 B.C.), known for his music and sacred songs, and his son Solomon (about 960 B.C.), who became proverbially famous for his wisdom. Though the exploits of these two kings were exaggerated by succeeding ages, there is no doubt that their reigns were the highest point of political importance reached by the old Hebrew people.

After the days of Solomon the kingdom split in two—Israel in the north, and Judah around Jerusalem in the south. For several centuries the people fought a losing battle with all their neighbors. In 721 B.C. the population of Israel was carried off into captivity and was in time entirely lost to history. The southern kingdom survived for more than a century longer, but at last in 586 B.C. most of its inhabitants were taken as captives to Babylon.

The seventy years which the Jews spent in Babylon were by no means an unmixed calamity. In many ways it was a liberal education to them. For two generations they were in close contact with a highly civilized people, from whom they absorbed much culture and learning. The captivity served to make them strongly conscious of their identity as a separate people and desirous of making records of their history and religious life. On their return to Jerusalem they restored their temple and brought together much of the older Scriptures.

For the student of literature the most important fact about the Hebrews during the last centuries before the Christian era is the presence of the prophets. These men felt themselves called by God to lead the people into the proper paths. Their influence was both political and religious. Ezekiel, Isaiah, Jeremiah, and Amos, and a group of lesser men, by their preaching not only helped to clarify for the Jews their idea of God and of the peculiar destiny of the people, but also put forward the promise of an eventual Messiah who should come to succor them and establish his kingdom.

Along with the rest of the eastern Mediterranean World the Jews came under the influence of Greek culture, so that by the time of Christ the language of a great number of the most cultivated of them was Greek. Politically also they shared the fortunes of their neighbors, and when the New Testament story opens at the time of the birth of Jesus, Judea is a part of a Roman province. Greek culture, therefore, and Roman rule must be understood as the background for the life of Christ.

The gulf between the East and the West was thus bridged. The little Hebrew sect of the Nazarenes began to affect the Greco-Roman world at a time when the latter civilization began to crumble under the weight of its social contradictions, when its people needed a solace and guidance which paganism could not provide, when the oppressed lower classes and degenerate upper classes were ready for a new dispensation. After resolute missionary work and martyrdom, the followers of Christ conquered the Roman Empire with their ideals. Christianity became the official religion of the eastern and western parts of the Empire, absorbed its culture, and took over its languages— Greek in the eastern Empire, and Latin in the west. When the western Roman Empire fell under the assault of the Teutonic tribes who infiltrated and invaded it, only the Church remained intact. Then the Church militant turned its attention to the barbarian conquerors, converted and tamed them, and imposed divine law and conscience upon them. Under its leadership, Europe began slowly to emerge from its age of darkness. It began laboriously to build a new post-classic civilization whose achievements have been the most remarkable in human history.

The Old Testament reveals Hebraism in the process of development. In a variety of literary works, cast in various molds and written at different times in response to different phases of national development and conflict, we see a people emerging from a primitive outlook and painfully ascending the heights of religious, ethical, and social vision.

This ascent, as traced in the Bible, constitutes an epic of such richness of event and meaning that it easily overshadows the *Iliad* and the *Odyssey*. Read in the light of modern knowledge, moreover, it traces an illuminating history, the most significant aspect of which is the evolution of the idea of God. At first the nomadic Hebrews entertained many superstitions and, like other primitive peoples, worshiped serpents as phallic symbols, cattle, rocks, and the spirits of hills and caves. They were polytheists—one of the names for God was *Elohim*, a noun in the plural number. Polytheism, in fact, never quite vanished in Palestine and was a constant cause of irritation and conflict in the community. In time, the Jews arrived at the concept of a national god, Yahweh,[1] who was regarded as not the only god but merely the most powerful one, who was jealous of his rivals and ordered his people to destroy their images. He was not omniscient; he made mistakes and regretted them; he was petulant, vengeful, and bloodthirsty; above all, he was war-like, literally a "Lord of Hosts" and a "man of war." His worship at first merely brought the Hebrews closer to monotheism than were the surrounding nations, but this god of a conquering race was then transformed in the course of centuries of war, military disaster, captivity, and moral and intellectual development. He became the champion of the poor and oppressed, the guarantor of social justice, and the relentless judge of evil. His wrath overtook all transgressors and caused all private and national calamities, for Israel, so conscious of sin, had not yet developed a consciousness of another life. (Both the good and the wicked were consigned after death to *Sheol*, the pit underground, the "land of darkness." The belief in an after-life and resurrection was adopted, probably from Persia and Egypt, only after Yahweh's flock lost hope in triumphant vindication in this world; it became established only with the advent of Christianity in Judea.) Finally, He became the God of mercy and Messianic promise.

The spiritualization of God is the work of the Prophets, religious radicals who brought social criticism and pity into Hebrew religion and politics. Beginning as more or less primitive diviners and frenzied dervishes, the Prophets became socially conscious spiritual leaders, whose concept of

---

[1] Probably the name was taken from the Canaanite god Yahu, a god of thunder, whose image was excavated in 1931.

God grew increasingly refined. One of the earliest of them, the shepherd Amos, came to the city of Beth-El, discovered its corruption, and started the tradition of social criticism.

The siege of Jerusalem in 733 B.C., which resulted in the withdrawal of the plague-stricken Assyrian hosts under Sennacherib, brought to the fore Isaiah, who became King Hezekiah's counselor. Assyria he considered the whip of God, who used that great power for his punitive purposes but would ultimately destroy it along with other oppressive worldly powers. The Hebrews must merely look to their conduct and ensure justice, which alone would satisfy Yahweh and make his people find favor in his eyes. Isaiah's words were charged with such denunciations as "What mean ye that ye beat my people to pieces, and grind the faces of the poor," and with injunctions to put away evil and relieve the oppressed. And his great dream is that of the coming of a Redeemer filled with the spirit of the Lord, who shall ensure social justice, bring "equity for the meek of the earth," and international peace. In *Isaiah*, God becomes completely the guarantor of a good society, and his social gospel strikes a new note in the religions of the ancient world.

Under the impact of prophetic thought, the priests "discovered" a new covenant, probably the one that is set forth in *Deuteronomy*, and inaugurated a series of religious reforms. New disasters ensued, Jerusalem was conquered by Nebuchadnezzar, large numbers of Jews were carried into slavery, and a revolt by the remnant resulted in the complete destruction of the city and the dispersion of its people into Babylon. This was the cue for the bitterest of the prophets, the pacifistic Jeremiah, whose denunciations of the evil ways of his people and whose prophecies of appropriate punishment reaffirmed the new doctrine that disaster is God's punishment of wickedness. The same thought appears in the *Lamentations*, a series of fiercely poetic dirges, attributed to him. Like his predecessors, Jeremiah demanded an active religion, a religion of ethical behavior rather than of ritualistic observance dear to the priesthood.

In Babylon, Ezekiel continued the denunciation of evil but added a new thought to prophetic idealism—the comforting doctrine of individual responsibility, the idea that the sons would no longer suffer for the sins of their fathers. An anonymous prophet, restating the Book of *Isaiah*, nowadays called the Second Isaiah or the Unknown Prophet,[2] refined the first Isaiah's Yahweh and brought good tidings of healing to the brokenhearted and the promise of liberty to the captives. Yahweh is no longer vengeful but is merciful; he is the kind Father who was to be proclaimed centuries later by Christ. God will send his "Servant," the Messiah, who will expiate the sins of mankind through his own sufferings, "a man of sorrows" upon whom will be laid "the iniquity of us all." And, as if in answer to this prophecy of forgiveness, Cyrus conquered Babylon and enabled the Jews to return to their homeland and rebuild their city. It was probably at this time, too, that the Pentateuch was compiled by the priesthood out of existent material and with priestly additions.[3] The later history of Hebrew prophecy blends in time with the gospel of Christ, which is too well known to require any description at this point. This, in brief, is the history of the evolution of Hebraism in the Bible.

THE BIBLE AS LITERATURE

This remarkable book, however, is not devoted to a single species of writing; it is best described as an anthology comprising nearly every form of literature. Reviewing it as a compilation of great histories, poems, stories, law books, rhapsodies, and visions fills one with wonder.

Historical Writings

Large portions of the Bible comprise a fairly continuous national history, though it is also a kind of universal history, in the sense that its authors view events as the unfolding of a purpose in the whole world.

The first subdivision of this history consists of six books—from *Genesis* to *Joshua*—and covers events from the creation of the world to the conquest of Canaan by the Hebrews. It was welded out of ninth- and eighth-century materials in the fourth century B.C.[4] The first eleven chapters of

[2] According to modern scholarship, he is the author of chapters XL–LV of the Book of *Isaiah*.

[3] According to modern scholarship the Pentateuch represents a fourth-century B.C. amalgamation of several texts. The oldest are the portions of *Genesis* marked "J" and "E" because they refer to God as Jehova or Yahweh and Elohim, respectively. A third text, called "D," contains the more advanced code of Deuteronomy. Other sections, "P," are those inserted by the later priests.

[4] The names by which we know the first five of these books (the *Pentateuch*) were given to them by the Alexandrian Jews who translated the Bible into Greek: *Genesis* (Beginning), *Exodus* (Going Out), *Leviticus* (the Book of Levites), *Numbers* (the Census), *Deuteronomy* (The Second Giving of the Law).

Genesis (the stories of the Creation, the Garden of Eden, and the Tower of Babel) constitute a mythology whose spiritual meaning contains deeper truths than mere historical documentation. They exemplify divine purpose, the appearance of human evil and travail, and the beginning of nations and their conflicts. The rest of *Genesis* includes three cycles of superbly humanized legends, those revolving around Abraham, Jacob, and Joseph, respectively. *Exodus* is closer to historical fact. It is a dramatic epic of national liberation, revolving around the personality of the spiritual hero Moses. *Leviticus* is a priestly product. It presents a legal system and a stabilization of regulations and ritual. Passionately peremptory, it orders men to avoid oppression and exploitation and to be generous to the poor and the stranger. *Numbers* opens with a census of the people that is of no literary interest, but its narratives are enlivened with miracles and fables. This book is notable for its dramatic recital of the wanderings of the Jews, climaxed by conflicts between a naïve polytheistic people only recently emancipated and their leader Moses, who struggles manfully to lead them in the ways of God. *Deuteronomy* is the best example of a body of statutes that is also great literature. The thought is simple but passionately and majestically wrought, and despite its simplicity the basic idea is a stupendous revelation. A nation, in this book, "is not a collection of independent individuals, but a moral person, having a conscience, a will, a unity of spirit which joins together the generations. A nation has a soul . . ."[5]

Joshua is a military epic, a story of the conquest of Canaan touched with fancy, as in the staying of the sun in the Vale of Ajalon. *Judges* recounts the dark ages of early Jewish history, a critical period of struggles against the Canaanite tribes. It is one of the oldest works of literature; some of its stories and the Song of Deborah, a ringing military ballad, belong to the twelfth century B.C. It also contains the primitive tale of Samson. Written in a vigorous and vivid style, *Judges* is really saga literature which has been colored by later religious idealism. The two books of *Samuel*, for the most part also very ancient, recount the rise of a monarchy among the Jews under Saul, the revolt of

David against him, and the court history of David's reign. It is history composed of three remarkable biographies, whose subjects are the puritanical Samuel, the tragically disordered Saul, and the talented and impassioned David. The two books of *Kings* support the thesis that the proper worship of God promotes national success and that apostasy produces political disaster. The facts are warped from time to time, but the result is an exciting chronicle of the Jews from 970 to 586 B.C., beginning with the reign of Solomon and ending with the Babylonian captivity. After *Kings*, Hebrew historical writing falls under the spell of the priesthood, and *Chronicles* is a feeble book. But the short personal memoirs of Nehemiah and Ezra achieve literary effectiveness, and the Alexandrian Jews who developed the *Apocrypha* continued to enrich the art of historical narrative in the books of *Esdras* and *Maccabees*. The latter closes biblical history with an account of the successful second-century B.C. rebellion of Simon and Judas Maccabeus against Antiochus Epiphanes, the Greek ruler of Palestine after Alexander the Great's conquest.

Prophetic Writings

Biblical history is supplemented by biblical prophecy. The historical works are a composite product, written, as it were, by the race. The books of prophecy are the utterances of distinct individuals whose passion and visions led them to create poetry of the highest rank, as well as magnificent prose. Their work has already been reviewed in relation to the evolution of Hebraism. As poets they availed themselves of many devices—prophecy, exhortation, rhapsody, and dramatic symbolism. Like all Hebrew poetry, this verse consists of glowing parallelisms of phrase instead of uniformity of meter. Related to the prophetic books are also many works like the prudential *Book of Proverbs*, the *Lamentations*, a series of dirges on the fall of Jerusalem,[6] and such a work of didactic fiction as the *Book of Jonah*, whose hero is a prophet and whose moral is internationalism. (Even the inhabitants of Nineveh are God's children, and the nationalistically vindictive prophet is punished for refusing to try to save them.) In a sense, even the lovely idyll *Ruth* is related to the

---

[5] Charles Allen Dinsmore, *The English Bible as Literature*, p. 159.
[6] The *Lamentations* is an artificial literary product, written in couplets and triplets. It constitutes an acrostic, each line beginning with a different letter of the alphabet. The King James translation gives slight indication of the literary elaborateness of this work.

prophetic writings; it is a protest in story form against the prohibition of mixed marriages between Jews and the neighboring races.

Related, also, are the two late products of skepticism, *The Book of Job* and *Ecclesiastes*, that question the principles promulgated by the prophets, although the challenge was toned down and sometimes cancelled by the scribes who gave them a place among the canonical scriptures. Stripped of apparently interpolated pious phrases, the second century B.C. *Ecclesiastes* is seen to be a pessimistic answer to the God-intoxicated prophets. Success or disaster has no relation to virtue or evil but both are the product of "time and chance." The past was no better than the present, and the future holds no millennial promises. Everything is vanity; for man is subject to the same final fate as the beasts—"all go unto one place; all are of the dust, and turn to dust." However, the religious adjurations, possibly interpolated, draw this series of essays back into the circle of religious literature; only the love of God is not vanity.

Dramatic Writings

The philosophical drama or dramatic symposium, *The Book of Job,* one of the world's supreme works of art, aims its questions more forcefully and suggests an answer so grand that it dazzles the understanding. Job's great question, uttered with fiery passionateness when he is afflicted by disaster to his family and himself, is Why do the innocent suffer? Job's friends provide the conventional explanation when they maintain that suffering is punishment for sin, and they bid him confess that he has transgressed. Job scornfully rejects their insinuations and their commonplace consolations. Instead, he presents his case directly to God, and it is the Lord who answers him out of the whirlwind, in a torrent of poetry whose majesty and inspiration are unequalled in any language. God rebukes Job's friends for their moralistic platitudes. His answer is simply that divine benevolence is not to be sought in the particular but in the general; and that man, who is not the whole of creation, must not exaggerate his personal problems. Jehovah describes himself pantheistically as the generative and living force in nature. It is in the contemplation of the universe as a whole, with its wonders and multiplicity of forms, that Job loses his sense of personal suffering and injustice. Man, faced by unmerited suffering, is not pacified by an easy answer. He is simply shown God through his wondrous manifestations in the natural world, whereupon all personal complaints seem insignificant to the enraptured, god-intoxicated man. The epilogue, a pious interpolation in which Job recovers his health and possessions, is a bromide by comparison with the great answer, Job's fierce questionings and deep pathos, and the exciting argumentation so aptly assigned to different speakers. Thus out of an old folktale of the patient man Job, retained in the prose prologue and epilogue, the latter-day Hebrews of the fourth century B.C. created a masterpiece both of skepticism with respect to established beliefs and of ineffable faith. Above all, *The Book of Job* is great dramatic poetry, regardless of anyone's interpretation of its meaning.

Lyric Poetry

The Bible also contains some of the world's greatest lyric verse, in two of the most divergent collections possible—the fervid religious lyrics known as the *Psalms* and the sensuous love poems that comprise the *Song of Songs*. The fourth-century *Song of Songs* may be regarded as a collection of wedding songs fused into a consecutive narrative with dramatic possibilities. It suggests an idyll arranged for a wedding celebration, in which the bride and groom appear as king and queen; and it may have been acted out with music, dances, choral song, and dialogue. Its ecstatic realization of earthly love, its idyllic imagery, and its opulent language provide a rare poetic experience. Its spiritual counterpart, *The Psalms,* is an even more remarkable compilation of poetry, of religious lyrics written over a period of more than a thousand years. Some of the *Psalms* are so vindictive in spirit that they reflect a fairly primitive world; others are so enlightened and spiritual that they clearly reveal the influence of the noblest prophets. They were intended to be sung by the priesthood on religious occasions and are therefore pure lyrics. Many of them are liturgical and are antiphonal in character.

Prose Fiction and Biography

Some notable examples of prose fiction are found in the Bible: the *Book of Ruth,* the *Book of Esther,* a vivid historical romance, *Daniel,* and the *Book of Jonah.* As the ancient Hebrews had a remarkable talent for narrative writing, their literature must have included many other tales; and indeed the *Apocrypha* supplies a number of them: the patriotic story of *Judith*, the delightful fairy-tale *Tobit*, and the superb satirical short story *Susanna and the Elders*.[7]

The New Testament added to the Bible four biographies. These are the four gospels of Mark, Matthew, Luke, and John, written in that order.[8] Accounts of Christ's life and ministry are presented as the most effective announcement of a new faith. The same basic story is told through the temperament and outlook of four different narrators, who compile a variety of reminiscences and opinions in them. Mark stresses the miraculous deeds of Christ; Matthew, the fulfillment of Hebraic prophecy in Christ's mission; Luke, his humanitarianism; and John, his mystic and universal significance. They are simple, often crude, compositions rather than the products of literary genius. But their reverence has fervor, and their pathos is genuine; there is much unconscious art in their narratives. They are illumined by the great sayings of the Master, which comprise a beautiful form of literature by themselves, and they present a composite portrait of Christ that is indelible. The *Book of Acts* is propagandist history, tracing the advance of Christianity from Jerusalem to Rome, and resembles the historical writings of the Old Testament. It lacks great sentences, but it is a graphic account. Then, too, St. Paul's propagandizing letters to various Christian congregations, though often written with sharpness or in haste, have passionate power. They may lack charm and sometimes even cohesion, but they reveal a gift for condensing ideas in such memorable sentences as "O death, where is thy sting? O grave, where is thy victory?" "The letter killeth, the spirit giveth life," and "Whatsoever a man soweth, that shall he also reap." Their figures of speech reveal imagination of a high order, and they burst into lyric flame, now and then, as in his Gospel of Love in *First Corinthians*. "In all Paul's greatest passages intellect, heart, and imagination work in unison."[9] A man with his endowment was a poet, as well as thinker, though poetry was furthest from his intention.

Finally, from the periods of persecution under Nero and Domitian (about A.D. 93), the early Christians drew the intoxicating vision of *The Book of Revelation*. It belongs to the genre of apocalyptical writings cultivated by the Hebrews, an example of which is the *Book of Daniel*.

SELECTIONS FROM THE BIBLE

The Garden of Eden

Genesis 2:4-3:24

These are the generations of the heavens and of the earth when they were created, in the day that the Lord God made the earth and the heavens, and every plant of the field before it was in the earth, and every herb of the field before it grew: for the Lord God had not caused it to rain upon the earth, and there was not a man to till the ground. But there went up a mist from the earth, and watered the whole face of the ground.

And the Lord God formed man of the dust of the ground, and breathed into his nostrils the breath of life; and man became a living soul. And the Lord God planted a garden eastward in Eden; and there he put the man whom he had formed. And out of the ground made the Lord God to grow every tree that is pleasant to the sight, and good for food; the tree of life also in the midst of the garden, and the tree of knowledge of good and evil. And a river went out of Eden to water the garden; and from thence it was parted, and became into four heads.

And the Lord God took the man, and put him into the garden of Eden to dress it and to keep it. And the Lord God commanded the man, saying, of every tree of the garden thou mayest freely eat: but of the tree of the knowledge of good and evil, thou shalt not eat of it: for in the day that thou eatest thereof thou shalt surely die.

And the Lord God said, it is not good that the

---

[7] The *Apocrypha* has a variety of writings, including the wisdom literature of *Ecclesiasticus* and *The Wisdom of Solomon*, not admitted into the Palestinian canon but highly regarded by the Alexandrian Jews who included them in their Greek translation of the Bible known as the *Septuagint*. The Roman Catholic Church admitted the *Apocrypha* into its canon at the Council of Trent, the Anglican Church gave it a subordinate place, the Protestant Bibles omit it.

[8] Authorities disagree as to the dates: A.D. 70-100 and A.D. 40-70 have been suggested.

[9] Dinsmore, *op. cit.*, p. 289.

man should be alone; I will make him an help meet for him.

And out of the ground the Lord God formed every beast of the field, and every fowl of the air; and brought them unto Adam to see what he would call them: and whatsoever Adam called every living creature, that was the name thereof. And Adam gave names to all cattle, and to the fowl of the air, and to every beast of the field; but for Adam there was not found an help meet for 10 him.

And the Lord God caused a deep sleep to fall upon Adam, and he slept: and he took one of his ribs, and closed up the flesh instead thereof; and the rib, which the Lord God had taken from man, made he a woman, and brought her unto the man. And Adam said, This is now bone of my bones, and flesh of my flesh: she shall be called Woman, because she was taken out of Man. Therefore shall a man leave his father and his mother, and shall 20 cleave unto his wife: and they shall be one flesh. And they were both naked, the man and his wife, and were not ashamed.

Now the serpent was more subtil than any beast of the field which the Lord God had made. And he said unto the woman, Yea, hath God said, Ye shall not eat of every tree of the garden?

And the woman said unto the serpent, We may eat of the fruit of the trees of the garden: but of the fruit of the tree which is in the midst of the 30 garden, God hath said, Ye shall not eat of it, neither shall ye touch it, lest ye die.

And the serpent said unto the woman, Ye shall not surely die: for God doth know that in the day ye eat thereof, then your eyes shall be opened, and ye shall be as gods, knowing good and evil.

And when the woman saw that the tree was good for food, and that it was pleasant to the eyes, and a tree to be desired to make one wise, she took of the fruit thereof, and did eat, and gave also unto 40 her husband with her; and he did eat. And the eyes of them both were opened, and they knew that they were naked; and they sewed fig leaves together, and made themselves aprons. And they heard the voice of the Lord God walking in the garden in the cool of the day: and Adam and his wife hid themselves from the presence of the Lord God amongst the trees of the garden.

And the Lord God called unto Adam, and said unto him, Where art thou? 50

And he said, I heard thy voice in the garden, and I was afraid, because I was naked; and I hid myself.

And he said, Who told thee that thou wast naked? Hast thou eaten of the tree, whereof I commanded thee that thou shouldest not eat?

And the man said, The woman whom thou gavest to be with me, she gave me of the tree, and I did eat.

And the Lord God said unto the woman, What is this that thou hast done? And the woman said, The serpent beguiled me, and I did eat.

And the Lord God said unto the serpent, Because thou hast done this, thou art cursed above all cattle, and above every beast of the field; upon thy belly shalt thou go, and dust shalt thou eat all the days of thy life: and I will put enmity between thee and the woman, and between thy seed and her seed; it shall bruise thy head, and thou shalt bruise his heel.

Unto the woman he said, I will greatly multiply thy sorrow and thy conception; in sorrow thou shalt bring forth children; and thy desire shall be to thy husband, and he shall rule over thee.

And unto Adam he said, Because thou hast hearkened unto the voice of thy wife, and hast eaten of the tree, of which I commanded thee, saying, Thou shalt not eat of it: cursed is the ground for thy sake; in sorrow shalt thou eat of it all the days of thy life; thorns also and thistles shall it bring forth to thee; and thou shalt eat the herb of the field; in the sweat of thy face shalt thou eat bread, till thou return unto the ground; for out of it wast thou taken: for dust thou art, and unto dust shalt thou return.

And Adam called his wife's name Eve; because she was the mother of all living. Unto Adam also and to his wife did the Lord God make coats of skins, and clothed them.

And the Lord God said, Behold, the man is become as one of us, to know good and evil: and now, lest he put forth his hand, and take also of the tree of life, and eat, and live for ever: therefore the Lord God sent him forth from the garden of Eden, to till the ground from whence he was taken. So he drove out the man; and he placed at the east of the garden of Eden Cherubims, and a flaming sword which turned every way, to keep the way of the tree of life.

Noah and the Flood

Genesis 6: 5-8: 22

And God saw that the wickedness of man was great in the earth, and that every imagination of the thoughts of his heart was only evil continually. And it repented the Lord that he had made man on the earth, and it grieved him at his heart. And the Lord said, I will destroy man whom I have created from the face of the earth; both man, and beast, and the creeping thing, and the fowls of the air; for it repenteth me that I have made them.

But Noah found grace in the eyes of the Lord. And God said unto Noah, The end of all flesh is come before me; for the earth is filled with vio- 10 lence through them; and, behold, I will destroy them with the earth. Make thee an ark of gopher wood; rooms shalt thou make in the ark, and shalt pitch it within and without with pitch. . . .

And the Lord said unto Noah, Come thou and all thy house into the ark; for thee have I seen righteous before me in this generation. Of every clean beast thou shalt take to thee by sevens, the male and his female: and of beasts that are not clean by two, the male and his female. Of fowls 20 also of the air by sevens, the male and the female; to keep seed alive upon the face of all the earth. For yet seven days, and I will cause it to rain upon the earth forty days and forty nights; and every living substance that I have made will I destroy from off the face of the earth.

And Noah did according unto all that the Lord commanded him. And Noah was six hundred years old when the flood of waters was upon the earth. And Noah went in, and his sons, and his 30 wife, and his sons' wives with him, into the ark, because of the waters of the flood. Of clean beasts, and of beasts that are not clean, and of fowls, and of every thing that creepeth upon the earth, there went in two and two unto Noah into the ark, the male and the female, as God had commanded Noah.

And it came to pass after seven days, that the waters of the flood were upon the earth. In the six hundredth year of Noah's life, in the second 40 month, the seventeenth day of the month, the same day were all the fountains of the great deep broken up, and the windows of heaven were opened. And the rain was upon the earth forty days and forty nights. In the selfsame day entered Noah, and Shem, and Ham, and Japheth, the sons of Noah, and Noah's wife, and the three wives of his sons with them, into the ark; they, and every beast after his kind, and all the cattle after their kind, and every creeping thing that creepeth upon the earth 50 after his kind, and every fowl after his kind, every bird of every sort. And they went in unto Noah into the ark, two and two of all flesh, wherein is the breath of life. And they that went in, went in male and female of all flesh, as God had commanded him: and the Lord shut him in.

And the flood was forty days upon the earth; and the waters increased, and bare up the ark, and it was lift up above the earth. And the waters prevailed, and were increased greatly upon the earth; and the ark went upon the face of the waters. And the water prevailed exceedingly upon the earth; and all the high hills, that were under the whole heaven, were covered. Fifteen cubits upward did the waters prevail; and the mountains were covered. And all flesh died that moved upon the earth, both of fowl, and of cattle, and of beast, and of every creeping thing that creepeth upon the earth, and every man: all in whose nostrils was the breath of life, of all that was in the dry land, died. And every living substance was destroyed which was upon the face of the ground, both man, and cattle, and the creeping things, and the fowl of the heaven; and they were destroyed from the earth: and Noah only remained alive, and they that were with him in the ark. And the waters prevailed upon the earth an hundred and fifty days.

And God remembered Noah, and every living thing, and all the cattle that was with him in the ark: and God made a wind to pass over the earth, and the waters assuaged; the fountains also of the deep and the windows of heaven were stopped, and the rain from heaven was restrained; and the waters returned from off the earth continually: and after the end of the hundred and fifty days the waters were abated. And the ark rested in the seventh month, on the seventeenth day of the month, upon the mountains of Ararat. And the waters decreased continually until the tenth month: in the tenth month, on the first day of the month, were the tops of the mountains seen.

And it came to pass at the end of forty days, that Noah opened the window of the ark which he had made: and he sent forth a raven, which went forth to and fro, until the waters were dried up from off the earth. Also he sent forth a dove from him, to see if the waters were abated from off the face of the ground; but the dove found no rest for the sole of her foot, and she returned unto him into the ark, for the waters were on the face of the whole earth: then he put forth his hand, and took her, and pulled her in unto him into the ark. And he stayed yet other seven days; and again he sent forth the dove out of the ark; and the dove came in to him in the evening; and, lo, in her mouth was an olive leaf pluckt off: so Noah knew that the waters were abated from off the earth. And he stayed yet other seven days; and sent forth the dove; which returned not again unto him any more. And Noah removed the covering of the ark, and looked, and, behold, the face of the ground was dry.

And Noah builded an altar unto the Lord; and took of every clean beast, and of every clean fowl, and offered burnt-offerings on the altar. And the Lord smelled a sweet savor; and the Lord said in his heart, I will not again curse the ground any more for man's sake; for the imagination of man's heart is evil from his youth; neither will I again smite any more every thing living, as I have done. While the earth remaineth, seedtime and harvest, and cold and heat, and summer and winter, and day and night shall not cease.

Abraham and Isaac
Genesis 22: 1-22: 13

And it came to pass after these things, that God did tempt Abraham, and said unto him, Abraham.

And he said, Behold, here I am.

And he said, Take now thy son, thine only son Isaac, whom thou lovest, and get thee into the land of Moriah; and offer him there for a burnt-offering upon one of the mountains which I will tell thee of.

And Abraham rose up early in the morning, and saddled his ass, and took two of his young men with him, and Isaac his son, and clave the wood for the burnt-offering, and rose up, and went unto the place of which God had told him. Then on the third day Abraham lifted up his eyes, and saw the place afar off. And Abraham said unto his young men, Abide ye here with the ass; and I and the lad will go yonder and worship, and come again to you. And Abraham took the wood of the burnt-offering, and laid it upon Isaac his son; and he took the fire in his hand, and a knife; and they went both of them together.

And Isaac spake unto Abraham his father, and said, My father: and he said, Here am I, my son. And he said, Behold the fire and the wood: but where is the lamb for a burnt-offering?

And Abraham said, My son, God will provide himself a lamb for a burnt-offering.

So they went both of them together. And they came to the place which God had told him of; and Abraham built an altar there, and laid the wood in order, and bound Isaac his son, and laid him on the altar upon the wood. And Abraham stretched forth his hand, and took the knife to slay his son. And the angel of the Lord called unto him out of heaven, and said, Abraham, Abraham: and he said, Here am I. And he said, Lay not thine hand upon the lad, neither do thou any thing unto him: for now I know that thou fearest God, seeing thou hast not withheld thy son, thine only son from me.

And Abraham lifted up his eyes, and looked, and behold behind him a ram caught in a thicket by his horns: and Abraham went and took the ram, and offered him up for a burnt-offering in the stead of his son.

Joseph and His Brethren
Genesis 37: 3-37: 36; 39: 1-46: 30

Now Israel loved Joseph more than all his children, because he was the son of his old age: and he made him a coat of many colors. And when his brethren saw that their father loved him more than all his brethren, they hated him, and could not speak peaceably unto him.

And Joseph dreamed a dream, and he told it his brethren: and they hated him yet the more. And he said unto them, Hear, I pray you, this dream which I have dreamed: For, behold, we were binding sheaves in the field, and, lo, my sheaf arose, and also stood upright; and, behold, your sheaves stood round about, and made obeisance to my sheaf.

And his brethren said to him, Shalt thou indeed reign over us? or shalt thou indeed have dominion over us? And they hated him yet the more for his dreams, and for his words.

And he dreamed yet another dream, and told it his brethren, and said, Behold, I have dreamed a dream more; and, behold, the sun and the moon and the eleven stars made obeisance to me. And he told it to his father, and to his brethren: and his father rebuked him, and said unto him, What is this dream that thou hast dreamed? Shall I and thy mother and thy brethren indeed come to bow down ourselves to thee to the earth?

And his brethren envied him; but his father observed the saying. And his brethren went to feed their father's flock in Shechem.

And Israel said unto Joseph, Do not thy brethren feed the flock in Shechem? come, and I will send thee unto them. And he said to him, Here am I. And he said to him, Go, I pray thee, see whether it be well with thy brethren, and well with the flocks; and bring me word again. So he sent him out of the vale of Hebron, and he came to Shechem.

And a certain man found him, and, behold, he was wandering in the field: and the man asked him, saying, What seekest thou? And he said, I seek my brethren: tell me, I pray thee, where they feed their flocks. And the man said, They are departed hence; for I heard them say, Let us go to Dothan. And Joseph went after his brethren, and 10 found them in Dothan.

And when they saw him afar off, even before he came near unto them, they conspired against him to slay him. And they said one to another, Behold, this dreamer cometh. Come now therefore, and let us slay him, and cast him into some pit, and we will say, Some evil beast hath devoured him: and we shall see what will become of his dreams.

And Reuben heard it, and he delivered him out of their hands; and said, Let us not kill him. And 20 Reuben said unto them, Shed no blood, but cast him into this pit that is in the wilderness, and lay no hand upon him; that he might rid him out of their hands, to deliver him to his father again.

And it came to pass, when Joseph was come unto his brethren, that they stript Joseph out of his coat, his coat of many colors that was on him; and they took him, and cast him into a pit: and the pit was empty, there was no water in it.

And they sat down to eat bread: and they lifted 30 up their eyes and looked, and, behold, a company of Ishmeelites came from Gilead with their camels bearing spicery and balm and myrrh, going to carry it down to Egypt. And Judah said unto his brethren, What profit is it if we slay our brother, and conceal his blood? Come, and let us sell him to the Ishmeelites, and let not our hand be upon him; for he is our brother and our flesh. And his brethren were content. Then there passed by Midianites merchantmen; and they drew and lifted up 40 Joseph out of the pit, and sold Joseph to the Ishmeelites for twenty pieces of silver: and they brought Joseph into Egypt.

And Reuben returned unto the pit; and, behold, Joseph was not in the pit; and he rent his clothes. And he returned unto his brethren, and said, The child is not; and I, whither shall I go? And they took Joseph's coat, and killed a kid of the goats, and dipped the coat in the blood; and they sent the coat of many colors, and they brought it to their 50 father; and said, This have we found: know now whether it be thy son's coat or no. And he knew it, and said, It is my son's coat; an evil beast hath devoured him; Joseph is without doubt rent in pieces. And Jacob rent his clothes, and put sackcloth upon his loins, and mourned for his son many days. And all his sons and all his daughters rose up to comfort him; but he refused to be comforted; and he said, For I will go down into the grave unto my son mourning. Thus his father wept for him. And the Midianites sold him into Egypt unto Potiphar, an officer of Pharaoh's, and captain 10 of the guard.

And Joseph was brought down to Egypt; and Potiphar, an officer of Pharaoh, captain of the guard, an Egyptian, bought him of the hands of the Ishmeelites, which had brought him down thither. And the Lord was with Joseph, and he was a prosperous man; and he was in the house of his master the Egyptian. And his master saw that the Lord was with him, and that the Lord made all that he did to prosper in his hand. And Joseph 20 found grace in his sight, and he served him: and he made him overseer over his house, and all that he had he put into his hand. And it came to pass from the time that he had made him overseer in his house, and over all that he had, that the Lord blessed the Egyptian's house for Joseph's sake; and the blessing of the Lord was upon all that he had in the house, and in the field. And he left all that he had in Joseph's hand; and he knew not ought he had, save the bread which he did eat. And 30 Joseph was a goodly person, and well favored.

And it came to pass after these things, that his master's wife cast her eyes upon Joseph; and she said, Lie with me. But he refused, and said unto his master's wife, Behold, my master wotteth not what is with me in the house, and he hath committed all that he hath to my hand; there is none greater in this house than I; neither hath he kept back any thing from me but thee, because thou art his wife: how then can I do this great wicked- 40 ness, and sin against God? And it came to pass, as she spake to Joseph day by day, that he hearkened not unto her, to lie by her, or to be with her.

And it came to pass about this time, that Joseph went into the house to do his business; and there was none of the men of the house there within. And she caught him by his garment, saying, Lie with me: and he left his garment in her hand, and fled, and got him out. And it came to pass, when she saw that he had left his garment in her hand, and was fled forth, That she called unto the men 50 of her house, and spake unto them, saying, See, he hath brought in an Hebrew unto us to mock us; he came in unto me to lie with me, and I cried with a loud voice: and it came to pass, when he heard that I lifted up my voice and cried, that he left his garment with me, and fled, and got him out.

And she laid up his garment by her, until his lord came home. And she spake unto him according to these words, saying, The Hebrew servant, which thou hast brought unto us, came in unto me to mock me: and it came to pass, as I lifted up my voice and cried, that he left his garment with me, and fled out. And it came to pass, when his master heard the words of his wife, which she spake unto him, saying, After this manner did thy servant to me; that his wrath was kindled. And Joseph's master took him, and put him into the prison, a place where the king's prisoners were bound: and he was there in the prison. But the Lord was with Joseph, and shewed him mercy, and gave him favor in the sight of the keeper of the prison. And the keeper of the prison committed to Joseph's hand all the prisoners that were in the prison; and whatsoever they did there, he was the doer of it. The keeper of the prison looked not to any thing that was under his hand; because the Lord was with him, and that which he did, the Lord made it to prosper.

And it came to pass after these things, that the butler of the king of Egypt and his baker had offended their lord the king of Egypt. And Pharaoh was wroth against two of his officers, against the chief of the butlers, and against the chief of the bakers. And he put them in ward in the house of the captain of the guard, into the prison, the place where Joseph was bound. And the captain of the guard charged Joseph with them, and he served them: and they continued a season in ward. And they dreamed a dream both of them, each man his dream in one night, each man according to the interpretation of his dream, the butler and the baker of the king of Egypt, which were bound in the prison.

And Joseph came in unto them in the morning, and looked upon them, and, behold, they were sad. And he asked Pharaoh's officers that were with him in the ward of his lord's house, saying, Wherefore look ye so sadly today? And they said unto him, We have dreamed a dream, and there is no interpreter of it. And Joseph said unto them, Do not interpretations belong to God? tell me them, I pray you.

And the chief butler told his dream to Joseph, and said to him, In my dream, behold, a vine was before me; and in the vine were three branches: and it was as though it budded, and her blossoms shot forth; and the clusters thereof brought forth ripe grapes: and Pharaoh's cup was in my hand: and I took the grapes, and pressed them into Pharaoh's cup, and I gave the cup into Pharaoh's hand. And Joseph said unto him, This is the interpretation of it: The three branches are three days: yet within three days shall Pharaoh lift up thine head, and restore thee unto thy place: and thou shalt deliver Pharaoh's cup into his hand, after the former manner when thou wast his butler. But think on me when it shall be well with thee, and shew kindness, I pray thee, unto me, and make mention of me unto Pharaoh, and bring me out of this house: for indeed I was stolen away out of the land of the Hebrews: and here also have I done nothing that they should put me into the dungeon.

When the chief baker saw that the interpretation was good, he said unto Joseph, I also was in my dream, and, behold, I had three white baskets on my head: and in the uppermost basket there was of all manner of bakemeats for Pharaoh; and the birds did eat them out of the basket upon my head. And Joseph answered and said, This is the interpretation thereof: The three baskets are three days: yet within three days shall Pharaoh lift up thy head from off thee, and shall hang thee on a tree; and the birds shall eat thy flesh from off thee. And it came to pass the third day, which was Pharaoh's birthday, that he made a feast unto all his servants: and he lifted up the head of the chief butler and of the chief baker among his servants. And he restored the chief butler unto his butlership again; and he gave the cup into Pharaoh's hand: but he hanged the chief baker: as Joseph had interpreted to them. Yet did not the chief butler remember Joseph, but forgat him.

And it came to pass at the end of two full years, that Pharaoh dreamed: and, behold, he stood by the river. And, behold, there came up out of the river seven well favored kine and fatfleshed; and they fed in a meadow. And, behold, seven other kine came up after them out of the river, ill favored and leanfleshed; and stood by the other kine upon the brink of the river. And the ill favored and leanfleshed kine did eat up the seven well favored and fat kine. So Pharaoh awoke. And he slept and dreamed the second time: and, behold, seven ears of corn came up upon one stalk, rank and good. And, behold, seven thin ears and blasted with the east wind sprung up after them. And the seven thin ears devoured the seven rank and full ears. And Pharaoh awoke, and, behold, it was a dream

And it came to pass in the morning that his spirit was troubled; and he sent and called for all the magicians of Egypt, and all the wise men thereof: and Pharaoh told them his dream; but there was none that could interpret them unto Pharaoh. Then spake the chief butler unto Pharaoh, saying, I do remember my faults this day: Pharaoh was wroth with his servants, and put me in ward in the captain of the guard's house, both me and the chief baker: and we dreamed a dream in one night, I and he; we dreamed each man according to the interpretation of his dream. And there was there with us a young man, an Hebrew, servant to the captain of the guard; and we told him, and he interpreted to us our dreams; to each man according to his dream he did interpret. And it came to pass, as he interpreted to us, so it was; me he restored unto mine office, and him he hanged.

Then Pharaoh sent and called Joseph, and they brought him hastily out of the dungeon: and he shaved himself, and changed his raiment, and came in unto Pharaoh. And Pharaoh said unto Joseph, I have dreamed a dream, and there is none that can interpret it: and I have heard say of thee, that thou canst understand a dream to interpret it. And Joseph answered Pharaoh, saying, It is not in me: God shall give Pharaoh an answer of peace. And Pharaoh said unto Joseph, In my dream, behold, I stood upon the bank of the river: and, behold, there came up out of the river seven kine, fat-fleshed and well favored; and they fed in a meadow: and, behold, seven other kine came up after them, poor and very ill favored and lean-fleshed, such as I never saw in all the land of Egypt for badness: and the lean and the ill favored kine did eat up the first seven fat kine: and when they had eaten them up, it could not be known that they had eaten them; but they were still ill favored, as at the beginning. So I awoke. And I saw in my dream, and, behold, seven ears came up in one stalk, full and good: and, behold, seven ears, withered, thin, and blasted with the east wind, sprung up after them: and the thin ears devoured the seven good ears: and I told this unto the magicians; but there was none that could declare it to me.

And Joseph said unto Pharaoh, The dream of Pharaoh is one: God hath shewed Pharaoh what he is about to do. The seven good kine are seven years; and the seven good ears are seven years: the dream is one. And the seven thin and ill favored kine that came up after them are seven years; and seven empty ears blasted with the east wind shall be seven years of famine. This is the thing which I have spoken unto Pharaoh: What God is about to do he sheweth unto Pharaoh. Behold, there come seven years of great plenty throughout all the land of Egypt: and there shall arise after them seven years of famine; and all the plenty shall be forgotten in the land of Egypt; and the famine shall consume the land; and the plenty shall not be known in the land by reason of that famine following; for it shall be very grievous. And for that the dream was doubled unto Pharaoh twice; it is because the thing is established by God, and God will shortly bring it to pass. Now therefore let Pharaoh look out a man discreet and wise, and set him over the land of Egypt. Let Pharaoh do this, and let him appoint officers over the land, and take up the fifth part of the land of Egypt in the seven plenteous years. And let them gather all the food of those good years that come, and lay up corn under the hand of Pharaoh, and let them keep food in the cities. And that food shall be for store to the land against the seven years of famine, which shall be in the land of Egypt; that the land perish not through the famine.

And the thing was good in the eyes of Pharaoh, and in the eyes of all his servants. And Pharaoh said unto his servants, Can we find such a one as this is, a man in whom the Spirit of God is? And Pharaoh said unto Joseph, Forasmuch as God hath shewed thee all this, there is none so discreet and wise as thou art: thou shalt be over my house, and according unto thy word shall all my people be ruled: only in the throne will I be greater than thou. And Pharaoh said unto Joseph, See I have set thee over all the land of Egypt. And Pharaoh took off his ring from his hand, and put it upon Joseph's hand, and arrayed him in vestures of fine linen, and put a gold chain about his neck; and he made him to ride in the second chariot which he had; and they cried before him, Bow the knee: and he made him ruler over all the land of Egypt. And Pharaoh said unto Joseph, I am Pharaoh, and without thee shall no man lift up his hand or foot in all the land of Egypt.

And Joseph was thirty years old when he stood before Pharaoh king of Egypt. And Joseph went out from the presence of Pharaoh, and went throughout all the land of Egypt. And in the seven plenteous years the earth brought forth by handfuls. And he gathered up all the food of the seven years, which were in the land of Egypt, and laid up the food in the cities: the food of the field, which was round about every city, laid he up in the same. And Joseph gathered corn as the sand of the sea, very much, until he left numbering; for it was without number.

And the seven years of plenteousness, that was in the land of Egypt, were ended. And the seven years of dearth began to come, according as Joseph had said: and the dearth was in all lands; but in all the land of Egypt there was bread. And when all the land of Egypt was famished, the people cried to Pharaoh for bread: and Pharaoh said unto 10 all the Egyptians, Go unto Joseph; what he saith to you, do. And the famine was over all the face of the earth: And Joseph opened all the storehouses, and sold unto the Egyptians; and the famine waxed sore in the land of Egypt. And all countries came into Egypt to Joseph for to buy corn; because that the famine was so sore in all lands.

Now when Jacob saw that there was corn in Egypt, Jacob said unto his sons, Why do ye look 20 one upon another? And he said, Behold, I have heard that there is corn in Egypt: get you down thither, and buy for us from thence; that we may live, and not die. And Joseph's ten brethren went down to buy corn in Egypt. But Benjamin, Joseph's brother, Jacob sent not with his brethren; for he said, Lest peradventure mischief befall him. And the sons of Israel came to buy corn among those that come: for the famine was in the land of Canaan.

And Joseph was the governor over the land, and he it was that sold to all the people of the land: and Joseph's brethren came, and bowed down themselves before him with their faces to the earth. And Joseph saw his brethren, and he knew them, but made himself strange unto them, and spake roughly unto them; and he said unto them, Whence come ye? And they said, From the land of Canaan to buy food. And Joseph knew his brethren, but they knew not him. And Joseph re- 40 membered the dreams which he dreamed of them, and said unto them, Ye are spies; to see the nakedness of the land ye are come. And they said unto him, Nay, my lord, but to buy food are thy servants come. We are all one man's sons; we are true men, thy servants are no spies. And he said unto them, Nay, but to see the nakedness of the land ye are come. And they said, Thy servants are twelve brethren, the sons of one man in the land of Canaan; and, behold, the youngest is this day 50 with our father, and one is not.

And Joseph said unto them, That is it that I spake unto you, saying, Ye are spies: hereby ye shall be proved: By the life of Pharaoh ye shall not go forth hence, except your youngest brother come hither. Send one of you, and let him fetch your brother, and ye shall be kept in prison, that your words may be proved, whether there be any truth in you: or else by the life of Pharaoh surely ye are spies. And he put them all together into ward three days. And Joseph said unto them the third day, This do, and live; for I fear God: if ye be true men, let one of your brethren be bound in the house of your prison: go ye, carry corn for the famine of your houses: but bring your youngest brother unto me; so shall your words be verified, and ye shall not die. And they did so.

And they said one to another, We are verily guilty concerning our brother, in that we saw the anguish of his soul, when he besought us, and we would not hear; therefore is this distress come upon us. And Reuben answered them, saying, Spake I not unto you, saying, Do not sin against the child; and ye would not hear? therefore, behold, also his blood is required. And they knew not that Joseph understood them, for he spake unto them by an interpreter. And he turned himself about from them, and wept; and returned to them again, and communed with them, and took from them Simeon, and bound him before their eyes.

Then Joseph commanded to fill their sacks with corn, and to restore every man's money into his sack, and to give them provision for the way: and thus did he unto them. And they laded their asses with the corn, and departed thence. And as one of them opened his sack to give his ass provender in the inn, he espied his money; for, behold, it was in his sack's mouth. And he said unto his brethren, My money is restored; and, lo, it is even in my sack: and their heart failed them, and they were afraid, saying one to another, What is this that God hath done unto us?

And they came unto Jacob their father unto the land of Canaan, and told him all that befell unto them; saying, The man, who is the lord of the land, spake roughly to us, and took us for spies of the country. And we said unto him, We are true men; we are no spies: We be twelve brethren, sons of our father; one is not, and the youngest is this day with our father in the land of Canaan. And the man, the lord of the country, said unto us, Hereby shall I know that ye are true men; leave one of your brethren here with me, and take food for the famine of your households, and be gone: and bring your youngest brother unto me: then shall I know that ye are no spies, but that ye are true men: so will I deliver you your brother, and ye shall traffick in the land.

And it came to pass as they emptied their sacks, that, behold, every man's bundle of money was in his sack: and when both they and their father saw the bundles of money, they were afraid. And Jacob their father said unto them, Me have ye bereaved of my children: Joseph is not, and Simeon is not, and ye will take Benjamin away: all these things are against me. And Reuben spake unto his father, saying, Slay my two sons, if I bring him not to thee: deliver him into my hand, and I will bring him to thee again. And he said, My son shall not go down with you; for his brother is dead, and he is left alone: if mischief befall him by the way in the which ye go, then shall ye bring down my gray hairs with sorrow to the grave.

And the famine was sore in the land. And it came to pass, when they had eaten up the corn which they had brought out of Egypt, their father said unto them, Go again, buy us a little food. And Judah spake unto him, saying, The man did solemnly protest unto us, saying, Ye shall not see my face, except your brother be with you. If thou wilt send our brother with us, we will go down and buy thee food: But if thou wilt not send him, we will not go down: for the man said unto us, Ye shall not see my face, except your brother be with you. And Israel said, Wherefore dealt ye so ill with me, as to tell the man whether ye had yet a brother?

And they said, The man asked us straitly of our state, and of our kindred, saying, Is your father yet alive? have ye another brother? and we told him according to the tenor of these words: could we certainly know that he would say, Bring your brother down? And Judah said unto Israel his father, Send the lad with me, and we will arise and go; that we may live, and not die, both we, and thou, and also our little ones. I will be surety for him; of my hand shalt thou require him: if I bring him not unto thee, and set him before thee, then let me bear the blame for ever: for except we had lingered, surely now we had returned this second time.

And their father Israel said unto them, If it must be so now, do this; take of the best fruits in the land in your vessels, and carry down the man a present, a little balm, and a little honey, spices, and myrrh, nuts, and almonds: and take double money in your hand; and the money that was brought again in the mouth of your sacks, carry it again in your hand; peradventure it was an oversight: take also your brother, and arise, go again unto the man: and God Almighty give you mercy before the man, that he may send away your other brother, and Benjamin. If I be bereaved of my children, I am bereaved. And the men took that present, and they took double money in their hand, and Benjamin; and rose up, and went down to Egypt, and stood before Joseph.

And when Joseph saw Benjamin with them, he said to the ruler of his house, Bring these men home, and slay, and make ready; for these men shall dine with me at noon. And the man did as Joseph bade; and the man brought the men into Joseph's house. And the men were afraid, because they were brought into Joseph's house; and they said, Because of the money that was returned in our sacks at the first time are we brought in; that he may seek occasion against us, and fall upon us, and take us for bondmen, and our asses. And they came near to the steward of Joseph's house, and they communed with him at the door of the house, and said, O sir, we came indeed down at the first time to buy food: and it came to pass, when we came to the inn, that we opened our sacks, and, behold, every man's money was in the mouth of his sack, our money in full weight: and we have brought it again in our hand. And other money have we brought down in our hands to buy food: we cannot tell who put our money in our sacks. And he said, Peace be to you, fear not: your God, and the God of your father, hath given you treasure in your sacks: I had your money. And he brought Simeon out unto them.

And the man brought the men into Joseph's house, and gave them water, and they washed their feet; and he gave their asses provender. And they made ready the present against Joseph came at noon: for they heard that they should eat bread there. And when Joseph came home, they brought him the present which was in their hand into the house, and bowed themselves to him to the earth. And he asked them of their welfare, and said, Is your father well, the old man of whom ye spake? Is he yet alive? And they answered, Thy servant our father is in good health, he is yet alive. And they bowed down their heads, and made obeisance. And he lifted up his eyes, and saw his brother Benjamin, his mother's son, and said, Is this your younger brother, of whom ye spake unto me? And he said, God be gracious unto thee, my son. And Joseph made haste; for his bowels did yearn upon his brother: and he sought where to weep; and he entered into his chamber, and wept there. And he washed his face, and went out, and refrained himself, and said, Set on bread. And they set on for him by himself, and for them by themselves, and for the Egyptians, which did not eat with him, by themselves: because the Egyptians might not eat bread with the Hebrews; for that is an abomination unto the Egyptians. And they sat before him, the firstborn according to his birthright, and the youngest according to his youth: and the men marveled one at another. And he took and sent messes unto them from before him: but Benjamin's mess was five times so much as any of theirs. And they drank, and were merry with him.

And he commanded the steward of his house, saying, Fill the men's sacks with food, as much as they can carry, and put every man's money in his sack's mouth. And put my cup, the silver cup, in the sack's mouth of the youngest, and his corn money. And he did according to the word that Joseph had spoken. As soon as the morning was light, the men were sent away, they and their asses. And when they were gone out of the city, and not yet far off, Joseph said unto his steward, Up, follow after the men; and when thou dost overtake them, say unto them, Wherefore have ye rewarded evil for good? Is not this it in which my lord drinketh, and whereby indeed he divineth? ye have done evil in so doing.

And he overtook them, and he spake unto them these same words. And they said unto him, Wherefore saith my lord these words? God forbid that thy servants should do according to this thing: Behold, the money, which we found in our sacks' mouths, we brought again unto thee out of the land of Canaan: how then should we steal out of thy lord's house silver or gold? With whomsoever of thy servants it be found, both let him die, and we also will be my lord's bondmen. And he said, Now also let it be according unto your words: he with whom it is found shall be my servant; and ye shall be blameless. Then they speedily took down every man his sack to the ground, and opened every man his sack. And he searched, and began at the eldest, and left at the youngest: and the cup was found in Benjamin's sack.

Then they rent their clothes, and laded every man his ass, and returned to the city. And Judah and his brethren came to Joseph's house; for he was yet there: and they fell before him on the ground. And Joseph said unto them, What deed is this that ye have done? wot ye not that such a man as I can certainly divine? And Judah said, What shall we say unto my lord? what shall we speak? or how shall we clear ourselves? God hath found out the iniquity of thy servants: behold, we are my lord's servants, both we, and he also with whom the cup is found. And he said, God forbid that I should do so: but the man in whose hand the cup is found, he shall be my servant; and as for you, get you up in peace unto your father. Then Judah came near unto him, and said, Oh my lord, let thy servant, I pray thee, speak a word in my lord's ears, and let not thine anger burn against thy servant: for thou art even as Pharaoh. My lord asked his servants, saying, Have ye a father, or a brother? And we said unto my lord, We have a father, an old man, and a child of his old age, a little one; and his brother is dead, and he alone is left of his mother, and his father loveth him. And thou saidst unto thy servants, Bring him down unto me, that I may set mine eyes upon him. And we said unto my lord, The lad cannot leave his father: for if he should leave his father, his father would die. And thou saidst unto thy servants, Except your youngest brother come down with you, ye shall see my face no more. And it came to pass when we came up unto thy servant my father, we told him the words of my lord. And our father said, Go again, and buy us a little food. And we said, We cannot go down: if our youngest brother be with us, then will we go down: for we may not see the man's face, except our youngest brother be with us. And thy servant my father said unto us, Ye know that my wife bare me two sons: and the one went out from me, and I said, Surely he is torn in pieces; and I saw him not since: and if ye take this also from me, and mischief befall him, ye shall bring down my gray hairs with sorrow to the grave. Now therefore when I come to thy servant my father, and the lad be not with us; seeing that his life is bound up in the lad's life; it shall come to pass, when he seeth that the lad is not with us, that he will die: and thy servants shall bring down the gray hairs of thy servant our father with sorrow to the grave. For thy servant became surety for the lad unto my father, saying, If I bring him not unto thee, then I shall bear the blame to my father for ever. Now therefore, I pray thee, let thy servant abide instead of the lad a bondman to my lord; and let the lad go up with his brethren. For how shall I go up to my father, and the lad be not with me? lest peradventure I see the evil that shall come on my father.

Then Joseph could not refrain himself before all them that stood by him; and he cried, Cause every man to go out from me. And there stood no man with him, while Joseph made himself known unto his brethren. And he wept aloud: and the Egyptians and the house of Pharaoh heard. And Joseph said unto his brethren, I am Joseph; doth my father yet live? And his brethren could not answer him; for they were troubled at his presence.

And Joseph said unto his brethren, Come near to me, I pray you. And they came near. And he said, I am Joseph, your brother, whom ye sold into Egypt. Now therefore be not grieved, nor angry with yourselves, that ye sold me hither: for God did send me before you to preserve life. For these two years hath the famine been in the land: and yet there are five years, in the which there shall neither be earing nor harvest. And God sent me before you to preserve you a posterity in the earth, and to save your lives by a great deliverance. So now it was not you that sent me hither, but God: and he hath made me a father to Pharaoh, and lord of all his house, and a ruler throughout all the land of Egypt. Haste ye, and go up to my father, and say unto him, Thus saith thy son Joseph, God hath made me lord of all Egypt: come down unto me, tarry not: and thou shalt dwell in the land of Goshen, and thou shalt be near unto me, thou, and thy children, and thy children's children, and thy flocks, and thy herds, and all that thou hast: and there will I nourish thee; for yet there are five years of famine; lest thou, and thy household, and all that thou hast, come to poverty. And, behold, your eyes see, and the eyes of my brother Benjamin, that it is my mouth that speaketh unto you. And ye shall tell my father of all my glory in Egypt, and of all that ye have seen; and ye shall haste and bring down my father hither. And he fell upon his brother Benjamin's neck, and wept; and Benjamin wept upon his neck. Moreover he kissed all his brethren, and wept upon them: and after that his brethren talked with him.

And the fame thereof was heard in Pharaoh's house, saying, Joseph's brethren are come: and it pleased Pharaoh well, and his servants. And Pharaoh said unto Joseph, Say unto thy brethren, This do ye; lade your beasts, and go, get you unto the land of Canaan; and take your father and your households, and come unto me: and I will give you the good of the land of Egypt, and ye shall eat the fat of the land. Now thou art commanded, this do ye; take you wagons out of the land of Egypt for your little ones, and for your wives, and bring your father, and come. Also regard not your stuff; for the good of all the land of Egypt is yours.

And the children of Israel did so: and Joseph gave them wagons, according to the commandment of Pharaoh, and gave them provision for the way.

To all of them he gave each man changes of raiment; but to Benjamin he gave three hundred pieces of silver, and five changes of raiment. And to his father he sent after this manner: ten asses laden with the good things of Egypt, and ten she asses laden with corn and bread and meat for his father by the way. So he sent his brethren away, and they departed: and he said unto them, See that ye fall not out by the way. And they went up out of Egypt, and came into the land of Canaan unto Jacob their father, and told him, saying, Joseph is yet alive, and he is governor over all the land of Egypt. And Jacob's heart fainted, for he believed them not. And they told him all the words of Joseph, which he had said unto them: and when he saw the wagons which Joseph had sent to carry him, the spirit of Jacob their father revived: and Israel said, It is enough; Joseph my son is yet alive: I will go and see him before I die.

And Israel took his journey with all that he had, and came to Beer-sheba, and offered sacrifices unto the God of his father Isaac. And God spake unto Israel in the visions of the night, and said, Jacob, Jacob. And he said, Here am I. And he said, I am God, the God of thy father: fear not to go down into Egypt; for I will there make of thee a great nation: I will go down with thee into Egypt; and I will also surely bring thee up again: and Joseph shall put his hand upon thine eyes. And Jacob rose up from Beer-sheba: and the sons of Israel carried Jacob their father, and their little ones, and their wives, in the wagons which Pharaoh had sent to carry him. And they took their cattle, and their goods, which they had gotten in the land of Canaan, and came into Egypt, Jacob, and all his seed with him.

And he sent Judah before him unto Joseph, to direct his face unto Goshen; and they came into the land of Goshen. And Joseph made ready his chariot, and went up to meet Israel his father, to Goshen, and presented himself unto him; and he fell on his neck, and wept on his neck a good while. And Israel said unto Joseph, now let me die, since I have seen thy face, because thou art yet alive.

The Child Moses

Exodus 1:7-2:15

And the children of Israel were fruitful, and increased abundantly, and multiplied, and waxed exceeding mighty; and the land was filled with them. Now there arose up a new king over Egypt, which knew not Joseph. And he said unto his people, Behold, the people of the children of Israel are more and mightier than we: come on, let us deal wisely with them; lest they multiply, and it come to pass, that, when there falleth out any war, they join also unto our enemies, and fight against us, and so get them up out of the land. Therefore they did set over them taskmasters to afflict them with their burdens. And they built for Pharaoh treasure cities, Pithom and Raamses. But the more they afflicted them, the more they multiplied and grew. And they were grieved because of the children of Israel. And the Egyptians made the children of Israel to serve with rigor: and they made their lives bitter with hard bondage, in mortar, and in brick, and in all manner of service in the field: all their service, wherein they made them serve, was with rigor.

And Pharaoh charged all his people, saying, Every son that is born ye shall cast into the river, and every daughter ye shall save alive. And there went a man of the house of Levi, and took to wife a daughter of Levi. And the woman conceived, and bare a son: and when she saw him that he was a goodly child, she hid him three months.

And when she could not longer hide him, she took for him an ark of bulrushes, and daubed it with slime and with pitch, and put the child therein; and she laid it in the flags by the river's brink. And his sister stood afar off, to wit what would be done to him.

And the daughter of Pharaoh came down to wash herself at the river; and her maidens walked along by the river's side; and when she saw the ark among the flags, she sent her maid to fetch it. And when she had opened it, she saw the child: and, behold, the babe wept. And she had compassion on him, and said, This is one of the Hebrew's children. Then said his sister to Pharaoh's daughter, Shall I go and call to thee a nurse of the Hebrew women, that she may nurse the child for thee? And Pharaoh's daughter said to her, Go. And the maid went and called the child's mother. And Pharaoh's daughter said unto her, Take this child away, and nurse it for me, and I will give thee thy wages. And the woman took the child, and nursed it. And the child grew, and she brought him unto Pharaoh's daughter, and he became her son. And she called his name Moses: and she said, Because I drew him out of the water.

And it came to pass in those days, when Moses was grown, that he went out unto his brethren, and looked on their burdens: and he spied an Egyptian smiting an Hebrew, one of his brethren.

And he looked this way and that way, and when he saw that there was no man, he slew the Egyptian, and hid him in the sand. And when he went out the second day, behold, two men of the Hebrews strove together: and he said to him that did the wrong, Wherefore smitest thou thy fellow? And he said, Who made thee a prince and a judge over us? intendest thou to kill me, as thou killedst the Egyptian? And Moses feared, and said, Surely this thing is known. Now when Pharaoh heard this thing, he sought to slay Moses. But Moses fled from the face of Pharaoh, and dwelt in the land of Midian: and he sat down by a well.

Jephthah's Daughter
Judges 11:30-11:40

And Jephthah vowed a vow unto the Lord, and said, If thou shalt without fail deliver the children of Ammon into mine hands, then it shall be, that whatsoever cometh forth of the doors of my house to meet me, when I return in peace from the children of Ammon, shall surely be the Lord's, and I will offer it up for a burnt-offering.

So Jephthah passed over unto the children of Ammon to fight against them; and the Lord delivered them into his hands. And he smote them from Aroer, even till thou come to Minnith, even twenty cities, and unto the plain of the vineyards, with a very great slaughter. Thus the children of Ammon were subdued before the children of Israel.

And Jephthah came to Mizpeh unto his house, and, behold, his daughter came out to meet him with timbrels and with dances: and she was his only child; beside her he had neither son nor daughter. And it came to pass, when he saw her, that he rent his clothes, and said, Alas, my daughter! thou hast brought me very low, and thou art one of them that trouble me: for I have opened my mouth unto the Lord, and I cannot go back.

And she said unto him, My father, if thou hast opened thy mouth unto the Lord, do to me according to that which hath proceeded out of thy mouth; forasmuch as the Lord hath taken vengeance for thee of thine enemies, even of the children of Ammon. And she said unto her father, Let this thing be done for me: let me alone two months, that I may go up and down upon the mountains and bewail my virginity, I and my fellows. And he said, Go. And he sent her away for two months: and she went with her companions, and bewailed her virginity upon the mountains. And it came to pass at the end of two months, that she returned unto her father, who did with her according to his vow which he had vowed: and she knew no man. And it was a custom in Israel, that the daughters of Israel went yearly to lament the daughter of Jephthah the Gileadite four days in a year.

David and Bathsheba
II Samuel 11:2-12:18

And it came to pass in an eveningtide, that David arose from off his bed, and walked upon the roof of the king's house: and from the roof he saw a woman washing herself; and the woman was very beautiful to look upon. And David sent and enquired after the woman. And one said, Is not this Bathsheba, the daughter of Eliam, the wife of Uriah the Hittite? And David sent messengers, and took her; and she came in unto him, and he lay with her; for she was purified from her uncleanness: and she returned unto her house.

And the woman conceived, and sent and told David, and said, I am with child. And David sent to Joab, saying, Send me Uriah the Hittite. And Joab sent Uriah to David. And when Uriah was come unto him, David demanded of him how Joab did, and how the people did, and how the war prospered. And David said to Uriah, Go down to thy house, and wash thy feet. And Uriah departed out of the king's house, and there followed him a mess of meat from the king. But Uriah slept at the door of the king's house with all the servants of his lord, and went not down to his house.

And when they had told David, saying, Uriah went not down unto his house, David said unto Uriah, Camest thou not from thy journey? why then didst thou not go down unto thine house? And Uriah said unto David, The ark, and Israel, and Judah, abide in tents; and my lord Joab, and the servants of my lord, are encamped in the open fields; shall I then go into mine house, to eat and to drink, and to lie with my wife? as thou livest, and as thy soul liveth, I will not do this thing.

And David said to Uriah, tarry here today also, and tomorrow I will let thee depart. So Uriah abode in Jerusalem that day, and the morrow. And when David had called him, he did eat and drink before him; and he made him drunk: and at even he went out to lie on his bed with the servants of his lord, but went not down to his house.

And it came to pass in the morning, that David wrote a letter to Joab, and sent it by the hand of Uriah. And he wrote in the letter, saying, Set ye Uriah in the forefront of the hottest battle, and retire ye from him, that he may be smitten and die. And it came to pass, when Joab observed the city, that he assigned Uriah unto a place where he knew valiant men were. And the men of the city went out, and fought with Joab: and there fell some of the people of the servants of David; and Uriah the Hittite died also.

And when the wife of Uriah heard that Uriah her husband was dead, she mourned for her husband. And when the mourning was past, David sent and fetched her to his house, and she became his wife, and bare him a son. But the thing that David had done displeased the Lord.

And the Lord sent Nathan unto David. And he came unto him, and said unto him, There were two men in one city; the one rich, and the other poor. The rich man had exceeding many flocks and herds: but the poor man had nothing, save one little ewe lamb, which he had bought and nourished up: and it grew up together with him, and with his children; it did eat of his own meat, and drank of his own cup, and lay in his bosom, and was unto him as a daughter. And there came a traveler unto the rich man, and he spared to take of his own flock and of his own herd, to dress for the wayfaring man that was come unto him; but took the poor man's lamb, and dressed it for the man that was come to him.

And David's anger was greatly kindled against the man; and he said to Nathan, As the Lord liveth, the man that hath done this thing shall surely die: and he shall restore the lamb fourfold, because he did this thing, and because he had no pity.

And Nathan said to David, Thou art the man. Thus saith the Lord God of Israel, I anointed thee king over Israel, and I delivered thee out of the hand of Saul; And I gave thee thy master's house, and thy master's wives into thy bosom, and gave thee the house of Israel and of Judah; and if that had been too little, I would moreover have given unto thee such and such things. Wherefore hast thou despised the commandment of the Lord, to do evil in his sight? thou has killed Uriah the Hittite with the sword, and hast taken his wife to be thy wife, and hast slain him with the sword of the children of Ammon. Now therefore the sword shall never depart from thine house; because thou hast despised me, and hast taken the wife of Uriah the Hittite to be thy wife.

And David said unto Nathan, I have sinned

against the Lord. And Nathan said unto David, The Lord also hath put away thy sin; thou shalt not die. Howbeit, because by this deed thou hast given great occasion to the enemies of the Lord to blaspheme, the child also that is born unto thee shall surely die. And Nathan departed unto his house.

And the Lord struck the child that Uriah's wife bare unto David, and it was very sick. David therefore besought God for the child; and David fasted, and went in, and lay all night upon the earth. And the elders of his house arose, and went to him, to raise him up from the earth: but he would not, neither did he eat bread with them. And it came to pass on the seventh day, that the child died.

Hymns of Praise

PSALM 8

O Lord our Lord,
How excellent is thy name in all the earth!
Who hast set thy glory above the heavens.
Out of the mouth of babes and sucklings hast thou
  ordained strength because of thine enemies,
That thou mightest still the enemy and the
  avenger.
When I consider thy heavens, the work of thy
  fingers,
The moon and the stars, which thou hast ordained;
What is man, that thou art mindful of him?
And the son of man, that thou visitest him?
For thou hast made him a little lower than the
  angels,
And hast crowned him with glory and honor.
Thou madest him to have dominion
Over the works of thy hands;
Thou hast put all things under his feet:
All sheep and oxen,
Yea, and the beasts of the field;
The fowl of the air, and the fish of the sea,
And whatsoever passeth through the paths of the
  seas.
O Lord our Lord,
How excellent is thy name in all the earth!

PSALM 15

Lord, who shall abide in thy tabernacle?
Who shall dwell in thy holy hill?
He that walketh uprightly, and worketh righteous-
  ness,
And speaketh the truth in his heart.
He that backbiteth not with his tongue,
Nor doeth evil to his neighbor,
Nor taketh up a reproach against his neighbor.
In whose eyes a vile person is contemned;
But he honoreth them that fear the Lord.
He that sweareth to his own hurt, and changeth
  not.

He that putteth not out his money to usury,
Nor taketh reward against the innocent.
He that doeth these things shall never be moved.

PSALM 19

The heavens declare the glory of God;
And the firmament sheweth his handywork.
Day unto day uttereth speech,
And night unto night sheweth knowledge.
There is no speech nor language,
Where their voice is not heard.
Their line is gone out through all the earth,
And their words to the end of the world.
In them hath he set a tabernacle for the sun,
Which is as a bridegroom coming out of his
  chamber,
And rejoiceth as a strong man to run a race.
His going forth is from the end of the heaven,
And his circuit unto the ends of it:
And there is nothing hid from the heat thereof.
The law of the Lord is perfect, converting the
  soul:
The testimony of the Lord is sure, making wise
  the simple.
The statutes of the Lord are right, rejoicing the
  heart:
The commandment of the Lord is pure, enlighten-
  ing the eyes.
The fear of the Lord is clean, enduring for ever:
The judgments of the Lord are true and righteous
  altogether.
More to be desired are they than gold,
Yea, than much fine gold:
Sweeter also than honey and the honeycomb.
Moreover by them is thy servant warned:
And in keeping of them there is great reward.
Who can understand his errors?
Cleanse thou me from secret faults.
Keep back thy servant also from presumptuous
  sins;
Let them not have dominion over me:

Then shall I be upright, and I shall be innocent
   from the great transgression.
Let the words of my mouth, and the meditation of
   my heart,
Be acceptable in thy sight, O Lord, my strength,
   and my redeemer.

PSALM 23

The Lord is my shepherd;
I shall not want.
He maketh me to lie down in green pastures:
He leadeth me beside the still waters.
He restoreth my soul:
He leadeth me in the paths of righteousness for his
   name's sake.
Yea, though I walk through the valley of the
   shadow of death,
I will fear no evil: for thou art with me;
Thy rod and thy staff they comfort me.
Thou preparest a table before me in the presence
   of mine enemies:
Thou anointest my head with oil; my cup run-
   neth over.
Surely goodness and mercy shall follow me all the
   days of my life:
And I will dwell in the house of the Lord for ever.

PSALM 24

The earth is the Lord's, and the fullness thereof;
The world, and they that dwell therein.
For he hath founded it upon the seas,
And established it upon the floods.
Who shall ascend into the hill of the Lord?
Or who shall stand in his holy place?
He that hath clean hands, and a pure heart;
Who hath not lifted up his soul unto vanity, nor
   sworn deceitfully.
He shall receive the blessing from the Lord,
And righteousness from the God of his salvation.
This is the generation of them that seek him,
That seek thy face, O Jacob.
Lift up your heads, O ye gates;
And be ye lift up, ye everlasting doors; and the
   King of glory shall come in.
Who is this King of glory?
The Lord strong and mighty, the Lord mighty in
   battle.
Lift up your heads, O ye gates;
Even lift them up, ye everlasting doors; and the
   King of glory shall come in.
Who is this King of glory? The Lord of hosts,
   he is the King of glory.

PSALM 95

O come, let us sing unto the Lord:
Let us make a joyful noise to the rock of our sal-
   vation.
Let us come before his presence with thanksgiving,
And make a joyful noise unto him with psalms.
For the Lord is a great God,
And a great King above all gods.
In his hand are the deep places of the earth:
The strength of the hills is his also.
The sea is his, and he made it:
And his hands formed the dry land.
O come, let us worship and bow down:
Let us kneel before the Lord our maker.
For he is our God;
And we are the people of his pasture, and the
   sheep of his hand.
Today if ye will hear his voice,
Harden not your heart, as in the provocation,
And as in the day of temptation in the wilderness:
When your fathers tempted me,
Proved me, and saw my work.
Forty years long was I grieved with this genera-
   tion,
And said, It is a people that do err in their heart,
And they have not known my ways:
Unto whom I sware in my wrath that they should
   not enter into my rest.

PSALM 121

I will lift up mine eyes unto the hills,
From whence cometh my help.
My help cometh from the Lord,
Which made heaven and earth.
He will not suffer thy foot to be moved:
He that keepeth thee will not slumber.
Behold, he that keepeth Israel
Shall neither slumber nor sleep.
The Lord is thy keeper:
The Lord is thy shade upon thy right hand.
The sun shall not smite thee by day,
Nor the moon by night.
The Lord shall preserve thee from all evil:
He shall preserve thy soul.
The Lord shall preserve thy going out and thy
   coming in from this time forth,
And even for evermore.

Youth and Age

Ecclesiastes 11: 1-12: 7.

Cast thy bread upon the waters:
For thou shalt find it after many days.

Give a portion to seven, and also to eight;
For thou knowest not what evil shall be upon the
earth.
If the clouds be full of rain, they empty them-
selves upon the earth:
And if the tree fall toward the south, or toward
the north,
In the place where the tree falleth,
There it shall be.
He that observeth the wind shall not sow;
And he that regardeth the clouds shall not reap.
As thou knowest not what is the way of the spirit,
Nor how the bones do grow in the womb of her
that is with child:
Even so thou knowest not the works of God who
maketh all.
In the morning sow thy seed,
And in the evening withhold not thine hand:
For thou knowest not whether shall prosper,
either this or that,
Or whether they both shall be alike good.
Truly the light is sweet,
And a pleasant thing it is for the eyes to behold
the sun:
But if a man live many years, and rejoice in them
all;
Yet let him remember the days of darkness;
For they shall be many.
All that cometh is vanity.
Rejoice, O young man, in thy youth;
And let thy heart cheer thee in the days of thy
youth,
And walk in the ways of thine heart,
And in the sight of thine eyes:
But know thou, that for all these things God will
bring thee into judgment.
Therefore remove sorrow from thy heart,
And put away evil from thy flesh:
For childhood and youth are vanity.
Remember now thy Creator in the days of thy
youth,
While the evil days come not,
Nor the years draw nigh, when thou shalt say,
I have no pleasure in them;
While the sun, or the light, or the moon, or the
stars, be not darkened,
Nor the clouds return after the rain:
In the day when the keepers of the house shall
tremble,
And the strong men shall bow themselves,
And the grinders cease because they are few,

And those that look out of the windows be dark-
ened,
And the doors shall be shut in the streets,
When the sound of the grinding is low,
And he shall rise up at the voice of the bird,
And all the daughters of music shall be brought
low;
Also when they shall be afraid of that which is
high,
And fears shall be in the way,
And the almond tree shall flourish,
And the grasshopper shall be a burden,
And desire shall fail:
Because man goeth to his long home,
And the mourners go about the streets:
Or ever the silver cord be loosed,
Or the golden bowl be broken,
Or the pitcher be broken at the fountain,
Or the wheel broken at the cistern.
Then shall the dust return to the earth as it was:
And the spirit shall return unto God who gave it.

Love Lyrics

SONG OF SOLOMON 2:8-2:14.

The voice of my beloved!
Behold, he cometh
Leaping upon the mountains,
Skipping upon the hills.
My beloved is like a roe or a young hart:
Behold, he standeth behind our wall,
He looketh forth at the windows,
Shewing himself through the lattice.
My beloved spake, and said unto me,
Rise up, my love,
My fair one, and come away.
For, lo, the winter is past,
The rain is over and gone;
The flowers appear on the earth;
The time of the singing of birds is come,
And the voice of the turtle is heard in our land;
The fig tree putteth forth her green figs,
And the vines with the tender grape
Give a good smell. Arise, my love,
My fair one, and come away.
O my dove, that art in the clefts of the rock,
In the secret places of the stairs,
Let me see thy countenance,
Let me hear thy voice;
For sweet is thy voice,
And thy countenance is comely.

The Story of Ruth

Now it came to pass in the days when the judges ruled that there was a famine in the land. And a certain man of Bethlehem-judah went to sojourn in the country of Moab, he, and his wife, and his two sons. And the name of the man was Elimelech, and the name of his wife Naomi, and the name of his two sons Mahlon and Chilion, Ephrathites of Bethlehem-judah. And they came into the country of Moab, and continued there. And Elimelech Naomi's husband died; and she was left, and her two sons. And they took them wives of the women of Moab; the name of the one was Orpah, and the name of the other Ruth: and they dwelled there about ten years. And Mahlon and Chilion died also both of them; and the woman was left of her two sons and her husband.

Then she arose with her daughters-in-law, that she might return from the country of Moab: for she had heard in the country of Moab how that the Lord had visited his people in giving them bread. Wherefore she went forth out of the place where she was, and her two daughters-in-law with her; and they went on the way to return unto the land of Judah.

And Naomi said unto her two daughters-in-law, Go, return each to her mother's house: the Lord deal kindly with you, as ye have dealt with the dead, and with me. The Lord grant you that ye may find rest, each of you in the house of her husband. Then she kissed them; and they lifted up their voice, and wept. And they said unto her, Surely we will return with thee unto thy people. And Naomi said, Turn again, my daughters: why will ye go with me? are there yet any more sons in my womb, that they may be your husbands? And they lifted up their voice, and wept again: and Orpah kissed her mother-in-law; but Ruth clave unto her.

And she said, Behold, thy sister-in-law is gone back unto her people, and unto her gods: return thou after thy sister-in-law.

And Ruth said, Intreat me not to leave thee, or to return from following after thee: for whither thou goest, I will go; and where thou lodgest, I will lodge: thy people shall be my people, and thy God my God: where thou diest, will I die, and there will I be buried: the Lord do so to me, and more also, if ought but death part thee and me.

When she saw that she was stedfastly minded to go with her, then she left speaking unto her.

So they two went until they came to Bethlehem. And it came to pass, when they were come to Bethlehem, that all the city was moved about them, and they said, Is this Naomi? And she said unto them, call me not Naomi, call me Mara: for the Almighty hath dealt very bitterly with me. I went out full, and the Lord hath brought me home again empty: why then call ye me Naomi, seeing the Lord hath testified against me, and the Almighty hath afflicted me? So Naomi returned, and Ruth the Moabitess, her daughter-in-law, with her, which returned out of the country of Moab: and they came to Bethlehem in the beginning of barley harvest.

And Naomi had a kinsman of her husband's, a mighty man of wealth, of the family of Elimelech; and his name was Boaz. And Ruth the Moabitess said unto Naomi, Let me now go to the field, and glean ears of corn after him in whose sight I shall find grace. And she said unto her, Go, my daughter. And she went, and came, and gleaned in the field after the reapers: and her hap was to light on a part of the field belonging unto Boaz, who was of the kindred of Elimelech.

And, behold, Boaz came from Bethlehem, and said unto the reapers, The Lord be with you. And they answered him, The Lord bless thee. Then said Boaz unto his servant that was set over the reapers, Whose damsel is this? And the servant that was set over the reapers answered and said, It is the Moabitish damsel that came back with Naomi out of the country of Moab: and she said, I pray you, let me glean and gather after the reapers among the sheaves: so she came, and hath continued even from the morning until now, that she tarried a little in the house.

Then said Boaz unto Ruth, Hearest thou not, my daughter? Go not to glean in another field, neither go from hence, but abide here fast by my maidens: let thine eyes be on the field that they do reap, and go thou after them: have I not charged the young men that they shall not touch thee? and when thou art athirst, go unto the vessels, and drink of that which the young men have drawn.

Then she fell on her face, and bowed herself to the ground, and said unto him, Why have I found grace in thine eyes, that thou shouldest take knowledge of me, seeing I am a stranger?

And Boaz answered and said unto her, It hath fully been shewed me, all that thou hast done unto thy mother-in-law since the death of thine husband: and how thou hast left thy father and thy mother, and the land of thy nativity, and art come unto a people which thou knewest not heretofore. The Lord recompense thy work, and a full reward be given thee of the Lord God of Israel, under whose wings thou art come to trust. Then she said, Let me find favor in thy sight, my lord; for that thou hast comforted me, and for that thou hast spoken friendly unto thine handmaid, though I be not like unto one of thine handmaidens. And Boaz said unto her, At mealtime come thou hither, and eat of the bread, and dip thy morsel in the vinegar. And she sat beside the reapers: and he reached her parched corn, and she did eat, and was sufficed, and left.

And when she was risen up to glean, Boaz commanded his young men, saying, Let her glean even among the sheaves, and reproach her not: and let fall also some of the handfuls of purpose for her, and leave them, that she may glean them, and rebuke her not. So she gleaned in the field until even, and beat out that she had gleaned: and it was about an ephah of barley.

And she took it up, and went into the city: and her mother-in-law saw what she had gleaned: and she brought forth, and gave to her that she had reserved after she had sufficed. And her mother-in-law said unto her, Where hast thou gleaned today? and where wroughtest thou? blessed be he that did take knowledge of thee. And she shewed her mother-in-law with whom she had wrought, and said, The man's name with whom I wrought today is Boaz.

And Naomi said unto her daughter-in-law, blessed be he of the Lord, who hath not left off his kindness to the living and to the dead. And Naomi said unto her, the man is near kin unto us, one of our next kinsmen. And Ruth the Moabitess said, he said unto me also, Thou shalt keep fast by my young men, until they have ended all my harvest. And Naomi said unto Ruth her daughter in law, It is good, my daughter, that thou go out with his maidens, that they meet thee not in any other field. So she kept fast by the maidens of Boaz to glean unto the end of barley harvest and of wheat harvest; and dwelt with her mother-in-law.

Then Naomi her mother-in-law said unto her, My daughter, shall I not seek rest for thee, that it may be well with thee? And now is not Boaz of our kindred, with whose maidens thou wast? Behold, he winnoweth barley tonight in the threshingfloor. Wash thyself therefore, and anoint thee, and put thy raiment upon thee, and get thee down to the floor: but make not thyself known unto the man, until he shall have done eating and drinking. And it shall be, when he lieth down, that thou shalt mark the place where he shall lie, and thou shalt go in, and uncover his feet, and lay thee down; and he will tell thee what thou shalt do. And she said unto her, All that thou sayest unto me I will do.

And she went down unto the floor, and did according to all that her mother-in-law bade her. And when Boaz had eaten and drunk, and his heart was merry, he went to lie down at the end of the heap of corn: and she came softly, and uncovered his feet, and laid her down. And it came to pass at midnight, that the man was afraid, and turned himself: and, behold, a woman lay at his feet. And he said, Who art thou? And she answered, I am Ruth thine handmaid: spread therefore thy skirt over thine handmaid; for thou art a near kinsman. And he said, Blessed be thou of the Lord, my daughter: for thou hast shewed more kindness in the latter end than at the beginning, inasmuch as thou followedst not young men, whether poor or rich. And now, my daughter, fear not; I will do to thee all that thou requirest: for all the city of my people doth know that thou art a virtuous woman. And now it is true that I am thy near kinsman: howbeit there is a kinsman nearer than I. Tarry this night, and it shall be in the morning, that if he will perform unto thee the part of a kinsman, well; let him do the kinsman's part: but if he will not do the part of a kinsman to thee, then will I do the part of a kinsman to thee, as the Lord liveth: lie down until the morning.

And she lay at his feet until the morning: and she rose up before one could know another. And he said, Let it not be known that a woman came into the floor. Also he said, Bring the vail that thou hast upon thee, and hold it. And when she held it, he measured six measures of barley, and laid it on her: and she went into the city. And when she came to her mother-in-law, she said, Who art thou, my daughter? And she told her all that the man had done to her. And she said, These six measures of barley gave he me; for he said to me, Go not empty unto thy mother-in-law. Then said she, Sit still, my daughter, until thou know how the matter will fall: for the man will not be in rest, until he have finished the thing this day.

Then went Boaz up to the gate, and sat him down there: and, behold, the kinsman of whom Boaz spake came by; unto whom he said, Ho, such a one! turn aside, sit down here. And he turned aside, and sat down. And he took ten men of the elders of the city, and said, Sit ye down here. And they sat down.

And he said unto the kinsman, Naomi, that is come again out of the country of Moab, selleth a parcel of land, which was our brother Elimelech's: and I thought to advertise thee, saying, Buy it before the inhabitants, and before the elders of my people. If thou wilt redeem it, redeem it: but if thou wilt not redeem it, then tell me, that I may know: for there is none to redeem it beside thee; and I am after thee. And he said, I will redeem it. Then said Boaz, What day thou buyest the field of the hand of Naomi, thou must buy it also of Ruth the Moabitess, the wife of the dead, to raise up the name of the dead upon his inheritance.

And the kinsman said, I cannot redeem it for myself, lest I mar mine own inheritance: redeem thou my right to thyself; for I cannot redeem it. Now this was the manner in former time in Israel concerning redeeming and concerning changing, for to confirm all things; a man plucked off his shoe, and gave it to his neighbor: and this was a testimony in Israel. Therefore the kinsman said unto Boaz, Buy it for thee. So he drew off his shoe.

And Boaz said unto the elders, and unto all the people, Ye are witnesses this day, that I have bought all that was Elimelech's, and all that was Chilion's and Mahlon's, of the hand of Naomi. Moreover Ruth the Moabitess, the wife of Mahlon, have I purchased to be my wife, to raise up the name of the dead upon his inheritance, that the name of the dead be not cut off from among his brethren, and from the gate of his place ye are witnesses this day. So Boaz took Ruth, and she was his wife.

Susanna and the Elders

There dwelt a man in Babylon, called Joacim: and he took a wife, whose name was Susanna, the daughter of Chelcias, a very fair woman, and one that feared the Lord. Her parents also were righteous, and taught their daughter according to the law of Moses.

Now Joacim was a great rich man, and had a fair garden joining unto his house: and to him resorted the Jews; because he was more honorable than all others.

The same year were appointed two of the ancients of the people to be judges, such as the Lord spoke of, that wickedness came from Babylon from ancient judges, who seemed to govern the people. These kept much at Joacim's house: and all that had any suits in law came unto them.

Now when the people departed away at noon, Susanna went into her husband's garden to walk. And the two elders saw her going in every day, and walking; so that their lust was inflamed toward her. And they perverted their own mind, and turned away their eyes, that they might not look unto heaven, nor remember just judgments.

And albeit they both were wounded with her love, yet durst not one show another his grief. For they were ashamed to declare their lust, that they desired to have to do with her. Yet they watched diligently from day to day to see her. And the one said to the other, "Let us now go home: for it is dinner time."

So when they were gone out, they parted the one from the other, and turning back again they came to the same place; and after that they had asked one another the cause, they acknowledged their lust: then appointed they a time both together, when they might find her alone.

And it fell out, as they watched a fit time, she went in as before with two maids only, and she was desirous to wash herself in the garden: for it was hot. And there was nobody there save the two elders, that had hid themselves, and watched her.

Then she said to her maids, "Bring me oil and washing balls, and shut the garden doors, that I may wash me."

And they did as she bade them, and shut the garden doors, and went out themselves at privy doors to fetch the things that she had commanded them: but they saw not the elders, because they were hid.

Now when the maids were gone forth, the two elders rose up, and ran unto her, saying, "Behold, the garden doors are shut, that no man can see us, and we are in love with thee; therefore consent unto us, and lie with us. If thou wilt not, we will bear witness against thee, that a young man was with thee: and therefore thou didst send away thy maids from thee."

Then Susanna sighed, and said, "I am straitened on every side: for if I do this thing, it is death unto me: and if I do it not, I cannot escape your hands. It is better for me to fall into your hands, and not do it, than to sin in the sight of the Lord."

With that Susanna cried with a loud voice: and the two elders cried out against her.

Then ran the one, and opened the garden door.

So when the servants of the house heard the cry in the garden, they rushed in at a privy door, to see what was done unto her. But when the elders had declared their matter, the servants were greatly ashamed: for there was never such a report made of Susanna.

And it came to pass the next day, when the people were assembled to her husband Joacim, the two elders came also full of mischievous imagina- 10 tion against Susanna to put her to death; and said before the people, "Send for Susanna, the daughter of Chelcias, Joacim's wife."

And so they sent. So she came with her father and mother, her children, and all her kindred. Now Susanna was a very delicate woman, and beauteous to behold. And these wicked men commanded to uncover her face (for she was covered), that they might be filled with her beauty. Therefore her friends and all that saw her wept.

Then the two elders stood up in the midst of the people, and laid their hands upon her head. And she weeping looked up toward heaven: for her heart trusted in the Lord. And the elders said, "As we walked in the garden alone, this woman came in with two maids, and shut the garden doors, and sent the maids away. Then a young man, who there was hid, came unto her, and lay with her. Then we that stood in a corner of the garden, seeing this wickedness, ran unto them. And when 30 we saw them together, the man we could not hold: for he was stronger than we, and opened the door, and leaped out. But having taken this woman, we asked who the young man was, but she would not tell us: these things do we testify."

Then the assembly believed them, as those that were the elders and judges of the people: so they condemned her to death.

Then Susanna cried out with a loud voice, and said, "O everlasting God, that knowest the secrets, 40 and knowest all things before they be: thou knowest that they have borne false witness against me, and, behold, I must die; whereas I never did such things as these men have maliciously invented against me."

And the Lord heard her voice.

Therefore when she was led to be put to death, the Lord raised up the holy spirit of a young youth, whose name was Daniel: who cried with a loud voice, "I am clear from the blood of this woman."

Then all the people turned them toward him, and said, "What mean these words that thou hast spoken?"

So he standing in the midst of them said, "Are ye such fools, ye sons of Israel, that without examination or knowledge of the truth ye have condemned a daughter of Israel? Return again to the place of judgment: for they have borne false witness against her."

Wherefore all the people turned again in haste, and the elders said unto him, "Come, sit down among us, and show it us, seeing God hath given thee the honor of an elder."

Then said Daniel unto them, "Put these two aside one far from another, and I will examine them."

So when they were put asunder one from another, he called one of them, and said unto him, "O thou that art waxed old in wickedness, now thy sins which thou hast committed aforetime are come to light: for thou hast pronounced false judgment, and hast condemned the innocent, and hast let the guilty go free; albeit the Lord saith, 'The 20 innocent and righteous shalt thou not slay.' Now then, if thou hast seen her, tell me under what tree sawest thou them companying together?"

Who answered, "Under the mastic tree."

And Daniel said, "Very well; thou hast lied against thine own head; for even now the angel of God hath received the sentence of God to cut thee in two."

So he put him aside, and commanded to bring the other, and said unto him, "O thou seed of 30 Chanaan, and not of Juda, beauty hath deceived thee, and lust hath perverted thine heart. Thus have ye dealt with the daughters of Israel, and they for fear companied with you: but the daughter of Juda would not abide your wickedness. Now therefore tell me under what tree didst thou take them companying together?"

Who answered, "Under a holm tree."

Then said Daniel unto him, "Well; thou hast also lied against thine own head: for the angel of 40 God waiteth with the sword to cut thee in two, that he may destroy you."

With that all the assembly cried out with a loud voice, and praised God, who saveth them that trust in him. And they arose against the two elders, for Daniel had convicted them of false witness by their own mouth: and according to the law of Moses they did unto them in such sort as they maliciously intended to do to their neighbor: and they put them to death. Thus the innocent blood 50 was saved the same day.

Therefore Chelcias and his wife praised God for their daughter Susanna, with Joacim her husband, and all the kindred, because there was no dishonesty found in her.

The Rod of Jesse

And there shall come forth a rod out of the stem
of Jesse,
And a Branch shall grow out of his roots.
And the spirit of the Lord shall rest upon him,
The spirit of wisdom and understanding,
The spirit of counsel and might,　　　　　5
The spirit of knowledge and of the fear of the
Lord;
And shall make him of quick understanding in the
fear of the Lord:
And he shall not judge after the sight of his eyes,
Neither reprove after the hearing of his ears;
But with righteousness shall he judge the poor,　10
And reprove with equity for the meek of the earth;
And he shall smite the earth with the rod of his
mouth,
And with the breath of his lips shall he slay the
wicked.
And righteousness shall be the girdle of his loins,
And faithfulness the girdle of his reins.　　15
The wolf also shall dwell with the lamb,
And the leopard shall lie down with the kid;
And the calf and the young lion and the fatling
together;
And a little child shall lead them.
And the cow and the bear shall feed;　　20
Their young ones shall lie down together:
And the lion shall eat straw like the ox.
And the sucking child shall play on the hole of the
asp,
And the weaned child shall put his hand on the
cockatrice's den.
They shall not hurt nor destroy　　　25
In all my holy mountain:
For the earth shall be full of the knowledge of the
Lord,
As the waters cover the sea.
Yet it pleased the Lord to bruise him;
He hath put him to grief:　　　　30
When thou shalt make his soul an offering for
sin,
The pleasure of the Lord shall prosper in his hand.
He shall see of the travail of his soul, and shall be
satisfied:
By his knowledge shall my righteous servant jus-
tify many;
For he shall bear their iniquities.　　　35
Therefore will I divide him a portion with the
great,
And he shall divide the spoil with the strong;
Because he hath poured out his soul unto death:

And he was numbered with the transgressors;
And he bore the sin of many,　　　　40
And made intercession for the transgressors.

Behold, My Servant

Behold, my servant shall deal prudently,
He shall be exalted and extolled, and be very high
As many were astonished at thee;
His visage was so marred more than any man,
And his form more like the sons of men:　　5
So shall he sprinkle many nations;
The kings shall shut their mouths at him:
For that which had not been told them shall they
see;
And that which they had not heard shall they con-
sider.
Who hath believed our report?　　　10
And to whom is the arm of the Lord revealed?
For he shall grow up before him as a tender plant,
And as a root out of a dry ground:
He hath no form nor comeliness;
And when we shall see him, there is no beauty that
we should desire him.　　　　15
He is despised and rejected of men;
A man of sorrows, and acquainted with grief:
And we hid as it were our faces from him;
He was despised, and we esteemed him not.
Surely he hath borne our griefs,　　　20
And carried our sorrows:
Yet we did esteem him stricken,
Smitten of God, and afflicted.
But he was wounded for our transgressions,
He was bruised for our iniquities:　　　25
The chastisement of our peace was upon him;
And with his stripes we are healed.
All we like sheep have gone astray;
We have turned every one to his own way;
And the Lord hath laid on him　　　30
The iniquity of us all.
He was oppressed, and he was afflicted,
Yet he opened not his mouth:
He is brought as a lamb to the slaughter,
And as a sheep before her shearers is dumb,　35
So he openeth not his mouth.
He was taken from prison and from judgment:
And who shall declare his generation?
For he was cut off out of the land of the living:
For the transgression of my people was he stricken.
And he made his grave with the wicked,　41
And with the rich in his death;
Because he had done no violence,
Neither was any deceit in his mouth.

Job's Questions

Man that is born of a woman
Is of few days, and full of trouble.
He cometh forth like a flower, and is cut down:
He fleeth also as a shadow, and continueth not.
And dost thou open thine eyes upon such a one,   5
And bringest me into judgment with thee?
Who can bring a clean thing out of an unclean?
     not one.
Seeing his days are determined, the number of his
     months is with thee,
And thou hast appointed his bounds that he cannot
     pass;
Look away from him, that he may rest,   10
Till he shall accomplish, as a hireling, his day.
For there is hope of a tree, if it be cut down, that
     it will sprout again,
And that the tender branch thereof will not cease.
Though the root thereof wax old in the earth,
And the stock thereof die in the ground;   15
Yet through the scent of water it will bud,
And put forth boughs like a plant.
But man dieth, and wasteth away:
Yea, man giveth up the ghost, and where is he?
As the waters fail from the sea,   20
And the river decayeth and drieth up;
So man lieth down and riseth not:
Till the heavens be no more, they shall not awake,
Nor be roused out of their sleep.
Oh that thou wouldest hide me in Sheol,   25
That thou wouldest keep me secret, until thy wrath
     be past,
That thou wouldest appoint me a set time, and
     remember me!
If a man die, shall he live again?
All the days of my warfare would I wait,
Till my release should come.   30
Thou shouldest call, and I would answer thee:
Thou wouldest have a desire to the work of thine
     hands.
But now thou numberest my steps:
Dost thou not watch over my sin?
My transgression is sealed up in a bag,   35
And thou fastenest up mine iniquity.
And surely the mountain falling cometh to nought,
And the rock is removed out of its place;
The waters wear the stones;
The overflowings thereof wash away the dust of the
     earth: 40
And thou destroyest the hope of man.
Thou prevailest for ever against him, and he
     passeth;

Thou changest his countenance, and sendest him
     away.
His sons come to honor, and he knoweth it not;
And they are brought low, but he perceiveth it not
     of them.   45
But his flesh upon him hath pain,
And his soul within him mourneth.

The Voice Out of the Whirlwind

Who is this that darkeneth counsel
By words without knowledge?
Gird up now thy loins like a man;
For I will demand of thee, and declare thou unto
     me.
Where wast thou when I laid the foundations of
     the earth?   5
Declare, if thou hast understanding.
Who determined the measures thereof, if thou
     knowest?
Or who stretched the line upon it?
Whereupon were the foundations thereof fastened?
Or who laid the corner stone thereof;   10
When the morning stars sang together,
And all the sons of God shouted for joy?
Or who shut up the sea with doors,
When it broke forth, as if it had issued out of the
     womb;
When I made the cloud the garment thereof,   15
And thick darkness a swaddlingband for it,
And prescribed for it my decree,
And set bars and doors,
And said, "Hitherto shalt thou come, but no fur-
     ther;
And here shall thy proud waves be stayed"?   20
Hast thou commanded the morning since thy days
     began,
And caused the dayspring to know its place;
That it might take hold of the ends of the earth,
And the wicked be shaken out of it?
It is changed as clay under the seal;   25
And all things stand forth as a garment:
And from the wicked their light is withheld,
And the high arm is broken.
Hast thou entered into the springs of the sea?
Or hast thou walked in the recesses of the deep?   30
Have the gates of death been revealed unto thee?
Or hast thou seen the gates of the shadow of
     death?
Hast thou comprehended the breadth of the earth?
Declare, if thou knowest it all.
Where is the way to the dwelling of light,   35
And as for darkness, where is the place thereof;

That thou shouldest take it to the bound thereof,
And that thou shouldest discern the paths to the
house thereof?
Doubtless, thou knowest, for thou wast then born,
And the number of thy days is great!   40
Hast thou entered the treasuries of the snow,
Or hast thou seen the treasuries of the hail,
Which I have reserved against the time of trouble,
Against the day of battle and war?
By what way is the light parted,   45
Or the east wind scattered upon the earth?
Who hath cleft a channel for the waterflood,
Or a way for the lightning of the thunder;
To cause it to rain on a land where no man is;
On the wilderness, wherein there is no man;   50
To satisfy the waste and desolate ground;
And to cause the tender grass to spring forth?
Hath the rain a father?
Or who hath begotten the drops of dew?
Out of whose womb came the ice?   55
And the hoary frost of heaven, who hath gendered
it?
The waters are hidden as with stone,
And the face of the deep is frozen.
Canst thou bind the cluster of the Pleiades,
Or loose the bands of Orion?   60
Canst thou lead forth the Mazzaroth in their
season?
Or canst thou guide the Bear with her train?
Knowest thou the ordinances of the heavens?
Canst thou establish the dominion thereof in the
earth?
Canst thou lift up thy voice to the clouds,   65
That abundance of waters may cover thee?
Canst thou send forth lightnings, that they may go,
And say unto thee, "Here we are"?
Who hath put wisdom in the inward parts?
Or who hath given understanding to the mind? 70
Who can number the clouds by wisdom?
Or who can pour out the bottles of heaven,
When the dust runneth into a mass,
And the clods cleave fast together?
Wilt thou hunt the prey for the lioness?   75
Or satisfy the appetite of the young lions,
When they couch in their dens,
And abide in the covert to lie in wait?
Who provideth for the raven his food,
When his young ones cry unto God,   80
And wander for lack of meat?

Knowest thou the time when the wild goats of
the rock bring forth?
Or canst thou mark when the hinds do calve?

Canst thou number the months that they fulfil? 84
Or knowest thou the time when they bring forth?
They bow themselves, they bring forth their young,
They cast out their sorrows.
Their young ones are in good liking, they grow up
in the open field;
They go forth, and return not again.
Who hath sent out the wild ass free?   90
Or who hath loosed the bands of the wild ass?
Whose house I have made the wilderness,
And the salt land his dwelling place.
He scorneth the tumult of the city,
Neither heareth he the shoutings of the driver. 95
The range of the mountains is his pasture,
And he searcheth after every green thing.
Will the wild ox be content to serve thee?
Or will he abide by thy crib?
Canst thou bind the wild ox with his band in the
furrow?   100
Or will he harrow the valleys after thee?
Wilt thou trust him, because his strength is great?
Or wilt thou leave to him thy labor?
Wilt thou confide in him, that he will bring home
thy seed,
And gather the corn of thy threshing-floor? 105
The wing of the ostrich rejoiceth;
But are her pinions and feathers kindly?
For she leaveth her eggs on the earth,
And warmeth them in the dust,
And forgetteth that the foot may crush them, 110
Or that the wild beast may trample them.
She is hardened against her young ones, as if they
were not hers:
Though her labor be in vain, she is without fear;
Because God hath deprived her of wisdom,
Neither hath he imparted to her understanding.
What time she lifteth up herself on high,   116
She scorneth the horse and his rider.
Hast thou given the horse his might?
Hast thou clothed his neck with the quivering
mane?
Hast thou made him to leap as a locust?   120
The glory of his snorting is terrible.
He paweth in the valley, and rejoiceth in his
strength:
He goeth out to meet the armed men.
He mocketh at fear, and is not dismayed;
Neither turneth he back from the sword.   125
The quiver rattleth against him,
The flashing spear and the javelin.
He swalloweth the ground with fierceness and rage;
Neither believeth he that it is the voice of the
trumpet.

As oft as the trumpet soundeth he saith, "Aha!"
And he smelleth the battle afar off,   131
The thunder of the captains, and the shouting.
   Doth the hawk soar by thy wisdom,
And stretch her wings toward the south?
Doth the eagle mount up at thy command,   135
And make her nest on high?
She dwelleth on the rock, and hath her lodging
   there,
Upon the crag of the rock, and the strong hold
From thence she spieth out the prey;
Her eyes behold it afar off.   140
Her young ones also suck up blood:
And where the slain are, there is she.
Shall he that cavilleth contend with the Almighty?
He that argueth with God, let him answer it.

Job. Behold, I am of small account; what shall I
   answer thee?   145
I lay mine hand upon my mouth.
Once have I spoken, and I will not answer;
Yea twice, but I will proceed no further.

Voice out of the Whirlwind. Gird up thy loins
   now like a man: 149
I will demand of thee, and declare thou unto me.
Wilt thou even disannul my judgment?
Wilt thou condemn me, that thou mayest be justi-
   fied?
Or hast thou an arm like God?
And canst thou thunder with a voice like him?
Deck thyself now with excellency and dignity;   155
And array thyself with honor and majesty.
Pour forth the overflowings of thine anger:
And look upon every one that is proud, and abase
   him.
Look on every one that is proud, and bring him
   low;
And tread down the wicked where they stand.   160
Hide them in the dust together;
Bind their faces in the hidden place.
Then will I also confess of thee
That thine own right hand can save thee.
   Behold now Behemoth, which I made with thee;
He eateth grass as an ox.   166
Lo now, his strength is in his loins,
And his force is in the muscles of his belly.
He moveth his tail like a cedar:
The sinews of his thighs are knit together.   170
His bones are as tubes of brass;
His limbs are like bars of iron.
He is the chief of the ways of God:
He only that made him can make his sword to
   approach unto him.

Surely the mountains bring him forth food;   175
Where all the beasts of the field do play.
He lieth under the lotus trees,
In the covert of the reed, and the fen.
The lotus trees cover him with their shadow;
The willows of the brook compass him about. 180
Behold, if a river overflow, he trembleth not:
He is confident, though Jordan swell even to his
   mouth.
Shall any take him when he is on the watch,
Or pierce through his nose with a snare?

   Canst thou draw out Leviathan with a fishhook?
Or press down his tongue with a cord?   186
Canst thou put a rope into his nose?
Or pierce his jaw through with a hook?
Will he make many supplications unto thee?
Or will he speak soft words unto thee?   190
Will he make a covenant with thee,
That thou shouldest take him for a servant for
   ever?
Wilt thou play with him as with a bird?
Or wilt thou bind him for thy maidens?
Shall the bands of fishermen make traffic of him?
Shall they part him among the merchants?   196
Canst thou fill his skin with barbed irons,
Or his head with fish spears?
Lay thine hand upon him;
Remember the battle, and do so no more.   200
Behold, the hope of him is in vain:
Shall not one be cast down even at the sight of
   him?
None is so fierce that he dare stir him up:
Who then is he that can stand before me?
Who hath first given unto me, that I should repay
   him?   205
Whatsoever is under the whole heaven is mine.
I will not keep silence concerning his limbs,
Nor his mighty strength, nor his comely propor-
   tion.
Who can strip off his outer garment?
Who shall come within his double bridle?   210
Who can open the doors of his face?
Round about his teeth is terror.
His strong scales are his pride,
Shut up together as with a close seal.
One is so near to another,   215
That no air can come between them.
They are joined one to another;
They stick together, that they cannot be sundered.
His sneezings flash forth light,
And his eyes are like the eyelids of the morning
Out of his mouth go burning torches.   221

And sparks of fire leap forth.
Out of his nostrils a smoke goeth,
As of a seething pot and burning rushes.
His breath kindleth coals, 225
And a flame goeth forth from his mouth.
In his neck abideth strength,
And terror danceth before him.
The flakes of his flesh are joined together:
They are firm upon him; they cannot be moved.
His heart is as firm as a stone; 231
Yea, firm as the nether millstone.
When he raiseth himself up, the mighty are afraid:
By reason of consternation they are beside them-
    selves. 234
If one lay at him with his sword, it cannot avail;
Nor the spear, the dart, nor the pointed shaft.
He counteth iron as straw,
And brass as rotten wood.
The arrow cannot make him flee:
Slingstones are turned with him into stubble. 240
Clubs are counted as stubble:
He laugheth at the rushing of the javelin.
His underparts are like sharp potsherds:
He spreadeth as it were a threshing wain upon the
    mire.
He maketh the deep to boil like a pot: 245
He maketh the sea like ointment.
He maketh a path to shine after him;
One would think the deep to be hoary.
Upon earth there is not his like,
That is made without fear. 250
He beholdeth every thing that is high:
He is king over all the sons of pride.

Job. I know that thou canst do all things,
And that no purpose of thine can be restrained.
"Who is this that hideth counsel without knowl-
    edge?" 255
Therefore have I uttered that which I understood
    not,
Things too wonderful for me, which I knew not.
Hear, I beseech thee, and I will speak;
I will demand of thee, and declare thou unto me.
I had heard of thee by the hearing of the ear; 260
But now mine eye seeth thee,
Wherefore I abhor myself, and repent
In dust and ashes.

Vanity

I the Preacher was king over Israel in Jerusalem.
And I applied my heart to seek and to search out
by wisdom concerning all that is done under
heaven: it is a sore travail that God hath given to
the sons of men to be exercised therewith. I have
seen all the works that are done under the sun;
and, behold, all is vanity and a striving after wind.
That which is crooked cannot be made straight:
and that which is wanting cannot be numbered.
I communed with mine own heart, saying, "Lo, I
have gotten me great wisdom above all that were
before me in Jerusalem: yea, my heart hath had
great experience of wisdom and knowledge." And
I applied my heart to know wisdom, and to know
madness and folly: I perceived that this also was
a striving after wind: For in much wisdom is much
grief: and he that increaseth knowledge increaseth
sorrow.

I said in mine heart, "Go to now, I will prove
thee with mirth; therefore enjoy pleasure": and,
behold, this also was vanity. I said of laughter, "It
is mad": and of mirth, "What doeth it?" I searched
in mine heart how to cheer my flesh with wine,
mine heart yet guiding me with wisdom, and how
to lay hold on folly, till I might see what it was
good for the sons of men that they should do under
the heaven all the days of their life. I made me
great works; I builded me houses; I planted me
vineyards; I made me gardens and parks, and I
planted trees in them of all kinds of fruit: I made
me pools of water, to water therefrom the forest
where trees were reared. I bought menservants and
maidens, and had servants born in my house; also
I had great possessions of herds and flocks, above
all that were before me in Jerusalem: I gathered
me also silver and gold, and the peculiar treasure
of kings and of the provinces. I got me men singers
and women singers, and the delights of the sons of
men, concubines very many. So I was great, and
increased more than all that were before me in
Jerusalem: also my wisdom remained with me.
And whatsoever mine eyes desired I kept not from
them: I withheld not my heart from any joy, for
my heart rejoiced because of all my labor; and
this was my portion from all my labor. Then I
looked on all the works that my hands had
wrought, and on the labor that I had labored to
do: and, behold, all was vanity and a striving after
wind, and there was no profit under the sun.

And I turned myself to behold wisdom, and
madness and folly: for what can the man do that
cometh after the king? even that which hath been
already done. Then I saw that wisdom excelleth
folly, as far as light excelleth darkness. The wise
man's eyes are in his head, and the fool walketh
in darkness: and yet I perceived that one event
happeneth to them all. Then said I in my heart,

"As it happeneth to the fool, so will it happen even to me"; and why was I then more wise? Then I said in my heart, that this also was vanity. For of the wise man, even as of the fool, there is no remembrance for ever; seeing that in the days to come all will have been already forgotten. And how doth the wise man die even as the fool! So I hated life; because the work that is wrought under the sun was grievous unto me: for all is vanity and a striving after wind.

And I hated all my labor wherein I labored under the sun: seeing that I must leave it unto the man that shall be after me. And who knoweth whether he shall be a wise man or a fool? yet shall he have rule over all my labor wherein I have labored, and wherein I have showed wisdom under the sun. This also is vanity. Therefore I turned about to cause my heart to despair concerning all the labor wherein I had labored under the sun. For there is a man whose labor is with wisdom, and with knowledge, and with skilfulness; yet to a man that hath not labored therein shall he leave it for his portion. This also is vanity and a great evil. For what hath a man of all his labor, and of the striving of his heart, wherein he laboreth under the sun? For all his days are but sorrows, and his travail is grief; yea, even in the night his heart taketh no rest. This also is vanity.

There is nothing better for a man than that he should eat and drink, and make his soul enjoy good in his labor. This also I saw, that it is from the hand of God. For who can eat, or who can have enjoyment, more than I? For to the man that pleaseth him God giveth wisdom, and knowledge, and joy: but to the sinner he giveth travail, to gather and to heap up, that he may give to him that pleaseth God. This also is vanity and a striving after wind.

The Sermon on the Mount
St. Matthew 5: 1-7: 29.

And seeing the multitudes, he went up into a mountain: and when he was set, his disciples came unto him: and he opened his mouth, and taught them, saying,

Blessed are the poor in spirit; for theirs is the kingdom of heaven.

Blessed are they that mourn: for they shall be comforted.

Blessed are the meek: for they shall inherit the earth.

Blessed are they which do hunger and thirst after righteousness: for they shall be filled.

Blessed are the merciful: for they shall obtain mercy.

Blessed are the pure in heart: for they shall see God.

Blessed are the peacemakers: for they shall be called the children of God.

Blessed are they which are persecuted for righteousness' sake: for theirs is the kingdom of heaven.

Blessed are ye, when men shall revile you, and persecute you, and shall say all manner of evil against you falsely, for my sake.

Rejoice, and be exceeding glad: for great is your reward in heaven: for so persecuted they the prophets which were before you.

Ye are the salt of the earth: but if the salt have lost his savor, wherewith shall it be salted? it is thenceforth good for nothing, but to be cast out, and to be trodden under foot of men. Ye are the light of the world. A city that is set on an hill cannot be hid. Neither do men light a candle, and put it under a bushel, but on a candlestick; and it giveth light unto all that are in the house. Let your light so shine before men, that they may see your good works, and glorify your Father which is in heaven.

Think not that I am come to destroy the law, or the prophets: I am not come to destroy, but to fulfill. For verily I say unto you, Till heaven and earth pass, one jot or one tittle shall in no wise pass from the law, till all be fulfilled. Whosoever therefore shall break one of these least commandments, and shall teach men so, he shall be called the least in the kingdom of heaven: but whosoever shall do and teach them, the same shall be called great in the kingdom of heaven. For I say unto you, That except your righteousness shall exceed the righteousness of the scribes and Pharisees, ye shall in no case enter into the kingdom of heaven.

Ye have heard that it was said by them of old time, Thou shalt not kill; and whosoever shall kill shall be in danger of the judgment: But I say unto you, That whosoever is angry with his brother without a cause shall be in danger of the judgment: and whosoever shall say to his brother, Raca, shall be in danger of the council: but whosoever shall say, thou fool, shall be in danger of hell fire. Therefore if thou bring thy gift to the altar, and there rememberest that thy brother hath ought against thee; Leave there thy gift before the altar, and go thy way; first be reconciled to thy brother and then come and offer thy gift.

Agree with thine adversary quickly, whiles thou art in the way with him; lest at any time the adversary deliver thee to the judge, and the judge deliver thee to the officer, and thou be cast into prison. Verily I say unto thee, Thou shalt by no means come out thence, till thou hast paid the uttermost farthing.

Ye have heard that it was said by them of old time, Thou shalt not commit adultery: but I say unto you, That whosoever looketh on a woman to lust after her hath committed adultery with her already in his heart.

And if thy right eye offend thee, pluck it out, and cast it from thee: for it is profitable for thee that one of thy members should perish, and not that thy whole body should be cast into hell. And if thy right hand offend thee, cut it off, and cast it from thee: for it is profitable for thee that one of thy members should perish, and not that thy whole body should be cast into hell.

It hath been said, Whosoever shall put away his wife, let him give her a writing of divorcement: but I say unto you, That whosoever shall put away his wife, saving for the cause of fornication, causeth her to commit adultery: and whosoever shall marry her that is divorced committeth adultery.

Again, ye have heard that it hath been said by them of old time, Thou shalt not forswear thyself, but shalt perform unto the Lord thine oaths: but I say unto you, Swear not at all; neither by heaven; for it is God's throne: nor by the earth; for it is his footstool: neither by Jerusalem; for it is the city of the great King. Neither shalt thou swear by thy head, because thou canst not make one hair white or black. But let your communication be, Yea, yea; Nay, nay; for whatsoever is more than these cometh of evil.

Ye have heard that it hath been said, An eye for an eye, and a tooth for a tooth: but I say unto you, That ye resist not evil: but whosoever shall smite thee on thy right cheek, turn to him the other also. And if any man will sue thee at the law, and take away thy coat, let him have thy cloke also. And whosoever shall compel thee to go a mile, go with him twain. Give to him that asketh thee, and from him that would borrow of thee turn not thou away.

Ye have heard that it hath been said, Thou shalt love thy neighbor, and hate thine enemy: But I say unto you, Love your enemies, bless them that curse you, do good to them that hate you, and pray for them which despitefully use you, and persecute you; that ye may be the children of your Father which is in heaven: for he maketh his sun to rise on the evil and on the good, and sendeth rain on the just and on the unjust. For if ye love them which love you, what reward have ye? do not even the publicans the same? And if ye salute your brethren only, what do ye more than others? do not even the publicans so? Be ye therefore perfect, even as your Father which is in heaven is perfect.

Take heed that ye do not your alms before men, to be seen of them: otherwise ye have no reward of your Father which is in heaven. Therefore, when thou doest thine alms, do not sound a trumpet before thee, as the hypocrites do in the synagogues and in the streets, that they may have glory of men. Verily I say unto you, They have their reward. But when thou doest alms, let not thy left hand know what thy right hand doeth: that thine alms may be in secret: and thy Father which seeth in secret himself shall reward thee openly. And when thou prayest, thou shalt not be as the hypocrites are: for they love to pray standing in the synagogues and in the corners of the streets, that they may be seen of men. Verily I say unto you, They have their reward. But thou, when thou prayest, enter into thy closet, and when thou hast shut thy door, pray to thy Father which is in secret; and thy Father which seeth in secret shall reward thee openly. But when ye pray, use not vain repetitions, as the heathen do: for they think that they shall be heard for their much speaking. Be not ye therefore like unto them: for your Father knoweth what things ye have need of before ye ask him.

After this manner therefore pray ye: Our Father, which art in heaven, Hallowed be thy name. Thy kingdom come. Thy will be done in earth, as it is in heaven. Give us this day our daily bread. And forgive us our debts, as we forgive our debtors. And lead us not into temptation, but deliver us from evil: For thine is the kingdom, and the power, and the glory, for ever. Amen. For if ye forgive men their trespasses, your heavenly Father will also forgive you: but if ye forgive not men their trespasses, neither will your Father forgive your trespasses.

Moreover when ye fast, be not, as the hypocrites, of a sad countenance: for they disfigure their faces, that they may appear unto men to fast. Verily I say unto you, They have their reward. But thou, when thou fastest, anoint thine head, and wash thy face; that thou appear not unto men to fast, but unto thy Father which is in secret: and thy

Father which seeth in secret, shall reward thee openly.

Lay not up for yourselves treasures upon earth, where moth and rust doth corrupt, and where thieves break through and steal: but lay up for yourselves treasures in heaven, where neither moth nor rust doth corrupt, and where thieves do not break through and steal: for where your treasure is, there will your heart be also. The light of the body is the eye: if therefore thine eye be single, thy whole body shall be full of light. But if thine eye be evil, thy whole body shall be full of darkness. If therefore the light that is in thee be darkness, how great is that darkness! No man can serve two masters: for either he will hate the one, and love the other; or else he will hold to the one, and despise the other. Ye cannot serve God and mammon.

Therefore, I say unto you, Take no thought for your life, what ye shall eat, or what ye shall drink; nor yet for your body, what ye shall put on. Is not the life more than meat, and the body than raiment? Behold the fowls of the air: for they sow not, neither do they reap, nor gather into barns; yet your heavenly Father feedeth them. Are ye not much better than they? Which of you by taking thought can add one cubit unto his stature? And why take ye thought for raiment? Consider the lilies of the field, how they grow; they toil not, neither do they spin: and yet I say unto you, That even Solomon in all his glory was not arrayed like one of these. Wherefore, if God so clothe the grass of the field, which today is, and tomorrow is cast into the oven, shall he not much more clothe you, O ye of little faith? Therefore take no thought, saying, What shall we eat? or, What shall we drink? or, Wherewithal shall we be clothed? (For after all these things do the Gentiles seek:) for your heavenly Father knoweth that ye have need of all these things. But seek ye first the kingdom of God, and his righteousness; and all these things shall be added unto you. Take therefore no thought for the morrow: for the morrow shall take thought for the things of itself. Sufficient unto the day is the evil thereof.

Judge not, that ye be not judged. For with what judgment ye judge, ye shall be judged: and with what measure ye mete, it shall be measured to you again. And why beholdest thou the mote that is in thy brother's eye, but considerest not the beam that is in thine own eye? Or how wilt thou say to thy brother, Let me pull out the mote out of thine eye; and, behold, a beam is in thine own eye?

Thou hypocrite, first cast out the beam out of thine own eye; and then shalt thou see clearly to cast out the mote out of thy brother's eye. Give not that which is holy unto the dogs, neither cast ye your pearls before swine, lest they trample them under their feet, and turn again and rend you.

Ask, and it shall be given you; seek, and ye shall find; knock, and it shall be opened unto you: for everyone that asketh receiveth; and he that seeketh findeth; and to him that knocketh it shall be opened. Or what man is there of you, whom if his son ask bread, will he give him a stone? Or if he ask a fish, will he give him a serpent? If ye then, being evil, know how to give good gifts unto your children, how much more shall your Father which is in heaven give good things to them that ask him? Therefore all things whatsoever ye would that men should do to you, do ye even so to them: for this is the law and the prophets.

Enter ye in at the strait gate: for wide is the gate, and broad is the way, that leadeth to destruction, and many there be which go in thereat: because strait is the gate, and narrow is the way, which leadeth unto life, and few there be that find it.

Beware of false prophets, which come to you in sheep's clothing, but inwardly they are ravening wolves. Ye shall know them by their fruits. Do men gather grapes of thorns, or figs of thistles? Even so every good tree bringeth forth good fruit; but a corrupt tree bringeth forth evil fruit. A good tree cannot bring forth evil fruit, neither can a corrupt tree bring forth good fruit. Every tree that bringeth not forth good fruit is hewn down, and cast into the fire. Wherefore by their fruits ye shall know them.

Not everyone that saith unto me, Lord, Lord, shall enter into the kingdom of heaven; but he that doeth the will of my Father which is in heaven. Many will say to me in that day, Lord, Lord, have we not prophesied in thy name? And in thy name have cast out devils? and in thy name done many wonderful works? And then will I profess unto them, I never knew you: depart from me, ye that work iniquity.

Therefore whosoever heareth these sayings of mine, and doeth them, I will liken him unto a wise man, which built his house upon a rock: And the rain descended, and the floods came, and the winds blew, and beat upon that house; and it fell not: for it was founded upon a rock. And everyone that heareth these sayings of mine, and doeth them not, shall be likened unto a foolish man, which built his house upon the sand: And the rain descended, and the floods came, and the winds blew, and beat upon that house; and it fell: and great was the fall of it. And it came to pass, when Jesus had ended these sayings, the people were astonished at his doctrine: For he taught them as one having authority, and not as the scribes.

The Last Supper

Now before the feast of the passover, when Jesus knew that his hour was come that he should depart out of this world unto the Father, having loved his own which were in the world, he loved them unto the end. And supper being ended, the devil having now put into the heart of Judas Iscariot, Simon's son, to betray him, Jesus, knowing that the Father had given all things into his hands, and that he was come from God, and went to God, riseth from supper, and laid aside his garments; and took a towel, and girded himself. After that, he poureth water into a basin, and began to wash the disciples' feet, and to wipe them with the towel wherewith he was girded. Then cometh he to Simon Peter: and Peter saith unto him, "Lord, dost thou wash my feet?" Jesus answered and said unto him, "What I do thou knowest not now; but thou shalt know hereafter." Peter saith unto him, "Thou shalt never wash my feet." Jesus answered him, "If I wash thee not, thou hast no part with me." Simon Peter saith unto him, "Lord, not my feet only, but also my hands and my head." Jesus saith to him, "He that is washed needeth not save to wash his feet, but is clean every whit: and ye are clean, but not all." For he knew who should betray him; therefore said he, "Ye are not all clean." So after he had washed their feet, and had taken his garments, and was set down again, he said unto them, "Know ye what I have done to you? Ye call me Master and Lord: and ye say well; for so I am. If I then, your Lord and Master, have washed your feet; ye also ought to wash one another's feet. For I have given you an example, that ye should do as I have done to you. Verily, verily, I say unto you, 'The servant is not greater than his lord; neither he that is sent greater than he that sent him.' If ye know these things, happy are ye if ye do them. I speak not of you all: I know whom I have chosen: but that the scripture may be fulfilled, 'He that eateth bread with me hath lifted up his heel against me.' Now I tell you before it come, that, when it is come to pass, ye may believe that I am he. Verily, verily, I say unto you, 'He that receiveth

whomsoever I send receiveth me; and he that receiveth me receiveth him that sent me.'"

When Jesus had thus said, he was troubled in spirit, and testified, and said, "Verily, verily, I say unto you that one of you shall betray me."

Then the disciples looked one on another, doubting of whom he spoke. Now there was leaning on Jesus' bosom one of his disciples, whom Jesus loved. Simon Peter therefore beckoned to him, that he should ask who it should be of whom he spoke. He then lying on Jesus' breast saith unto him, "Lord, who is it?"

Jesus answered, "He it is, to whom I shall give a sop, when I have dipped it." And when he had dipped the sop, he gave it to Judas Iscariot, the son of Simon. And after the sop Satan entered into him. Then said Jesus unto him, "That thou doest, do quickly." Now no man at the table knew for what intent he spoke this unto him. For some of them thought, because Judas had the bag, that Jesus had said unto him, "Buy those things that we have need of against the feast"; or, that he should give something to the poor. He then having received the sop went immediately out: and it was night.

Therefore, when he was gone out, Jesus said, "Now is the Son of Man glorified, and God is glorified in him. If God be glorified in him, God shall also glorify him in himself, and shall straightway glorify him. Little children, yet a little while I am with you. Ye shall seek me: and as I said unto the Jews, 'Whither I go, ye cannot come'; so now I say to you. A new commandment I give unto you: that ye love one another; as I have loved you, that ye also love one another. By this shall all men know that ye are my disciples, if ye have love one to another."

Simon Peter said unto him, "Lord, whither goest thou?"

Jesus answered him, "Whither I go, thou canst not follow me now; but thou shalt follow me afterwards."

Peter said unto him, "Lord, why cannot I follow thee now? I will lay down my life for thy sake."

Jesus answered him, "Wilt thou lay down thy life for my sake? Verily, verily, I say unto thee, 'The cock shall not crow, till thou hast denied me thrice.'

"Let not your heart be troubled: ye believe in God, believe also in me. In my Father's house are many mansions: if it were not so, I would have told you. I go to prepare a place for you. And if I go and prepare a place for you, I will come again, and receive you unto myself; that where I am, there ye may be also. And whither I go ye know, and the way ye know."

Thomas saith unto him, "Lord, we know not whither thou goest; and how can we know the way?"

Jesus saith unto him, "I am the way, the truth, and the life: no man cometh unto the Father, but by me. If ye had known me, ye should have known my Father also: and from henceforth ye know him, and have seen him." 10

Philip saith unto him, "Lord, show us the Father, and it sufficeth us."

Jesus saith unto him, "Have I been so long time with you, and yet hast thou not known me, Philip? he that hath seen me hath seen the Father; and how sayest thou then, 'Show us the Father'? Believest thou not that I am in the Father, and the Father in me? the words that I speak unto you I speak not of myself: but the Father that dwelleth 20 in me, he doeth the works. Believe me that I am in the Father, and the Father in me: or else believe me for the very works' sake. Verily, verily, I say unto you, 'He that believeth on me, the works that I do shall he do also; and greater works than these shall he do; because I go unto my Father.' And whatsoever ye shall ask in my name, that will I do, that the Father may be glorified in the Son. If ye shall ask any thing in my name, I will do it.

"If ye love me, keep my commandments. And 30 I will pray the Father, and he shall give you another Comforter, that he may abide with you for ever; even the Spirit of truth; whom the world cannot receive, because it seeth him not, neither knoweth him: but ye know him; for he dwelleth with you, and shall be in you. I will not leave you comfortless: I will come to you. Yet a little while, and the world seeth me no more; but ye see me: because I live, ye shall live also. At that day ye shall know that I am in my Father, and ye in me, 40 and I in you. He that hath my commandments, and keepeth them, he it is that loveth me: and he that loveth me shall be loved of my Father, and I will love him, and will manifest myself to him."

Judas (not Iscariot) saith unto him, "Lord, how is it that thou wilt manifest thyself unto us, and not unto the world?"

Jesus answered and said unto him, "If a man love me, he will keep my words: and my Father will love him, and we will come unto him, and 50 make our abode with him. He that loveth me not keepeth not my sayings: and the word which ye hear is not mine, but the Father's which sent me.

"These things have I spoken unto you, being yet present with you. But the Comforter, which is the Holy Ghost, whom the Father will send in my name, he shall teach you all things, and bring all things to your remembrance, whatsoever I have said unto you. Peace I leave with you, my peace I give unto you: not as the world giveth, give I unto you. Let not your heart be troubled, neither let it be afraid. Ye have heard how I said unto you, 'I go away, and come again unto you.' If ye loved me, ye would rejoice because I said, 'I go unto the Father': for my Father is greater than I. And now I have told you before it come to pass that, when it is come to pass, ye might believe. Hereafter I will not talk much with you: for the prince of this world cometh, and hath nothing in me. But that the world may know that I love the Father; and as the Father gave me commandment, even so I do.

"I am the true vine, and my Father is the husbandman. Every branch in me that beareth not fruit he taketh away: and every branch that beareth fruit, he purgeth it, that it may bring forth more fruit. Now ye are clean through the word which I have spoken unto you. Abide in me, and I in you. As the branch cannot bear fruit of itself, except it abide in the vine; no more can ye, except ye abide in me. I am the vine, ye are the branches: he that abideth in me, and I in him, the same bringeth forth much fruit: for without me ye can do nothing. If a man abide not in me, he is cast forth as a branch, and is withered; and men gather them, and cast them into the fire, and they are burned. If ye abide in me, and my words abide in you, ye shall ask what ye will, and it shall be done unto you. Herein is my Father glorified, that ye bear much fruit; so shall ye be my disciples. As the Father hath loved me, so have I loved you: continue ye in my love. If ye keep my commandments, ye shall abide in my love; even as I have kept my Father's commandments, and abide in his love. These things have I spoken unto you, that my joy might remain in you, and that your joy might be full. This is my commandment: that ye love one another, as I have loved you. Greater love hath no man than this, that a man lay down his life for his friends. Ye are my friends, if ye do whatsoever I command you. Henceforth I call you not servants; for the servant knoweth not what his lord doeth: but I have called you friends; for all things that I have heard of my Father I have made known unto you. Ye have not chosen me, but I have chosen you, and ordained you, that ye should go and bring forth fruit, and that your fruit should remain: that whatsoever ye shall ask of the Father in my name he may give it you.

"These things I command you, that ye love one another. If the world hate you, ye know that it hated me before it hated you. If ye were of the world, the world would love his own: but because ye are not of the world, but I have chosen you out of the world, therefore the world hateth you. Remember the word that I said unto you, 'The servant is not greater than his lord.' If they have persecuted me, they will also persecute you; if they have kept my saying, they will keep yours also. But all these things will they do unto you for my name's sake, because they know not him that sent me. If I had not come and spoken unto them, they had not had sin: but now they have no cloak for their sin. He that hateth me hateth my Father also. If I had not done among them the works which none other man did, they had not had sin: but now have they both seen and hated both me and my Father. But this cometh to pass that the word might be fulfilled that is written in their law, 'They hated me without a cause.' But when the Comforter is come, whom I will send unto you from the Father, even the Spirit of truth, which proceedeth from the Father, he shall testify of me: and ye also shall bear witness, because ye have been with me from the beginning.

"These things have I spoken unto you, that ye should not be offended. They shall put you out of the synagogues: yea, the time cometh that whosoever killeth you will think that he doeth God service. And these things will they do unto you, because they have not known the Father, nor me. But these things have I told you, that when the time shall come, ye may remember that I told you of them. And these things I said not unto you at the beginning, because I was with you. But now I go my way to him that sent me; and none of you asketh me, 'Whither goest thou?' But because I have said these things unto you, sorrow hath filled your heart. Nevertheless I tell you the truth: 'It is expedient for you that I go away: for if I go not away, the Comforter will not come unto you; but if I depart, I will send him unto you. And when he is come, he will reprove the world of sin, and of righteousness, and of judgment: of sin, because they believe not on me; of righteousness, because I go to my Father, and ye see me no more; of judgment, because the prince of this world is

judged.' I have yet many things to say unto you, but ye cannot bear them now. Howbeit when he, the Spirit of truth, is come, he will guide you into all truth: for he shall not speak of himself; but whatsoever he shall hear, that shall he speak: and he will show you things to come. He shall glorify me: for he shall receive of mine, and shall show it unto you. All things that the Father hath are mine: therefore said I, that he shall take of mine, and shall show it unto you. A little while, and ye shall not see me: and again, a little while, and ye shall see me, because I go to the Father."

The Gospel of Love

I Corinthians 13.

Though I speak with the tongues of men and of angels, and have not charity, I am become as sounding brass, or a tinkling cymbal. And though I have the gift of prophecy, and understand all mysteries, and all knowledge; and though I have all faith, so that I could remove mountains, and have not charity, I am nothing. And though I bestow all my goods to feed the poor, and though I give my body to be burned, and have not charity, it profiteth me nothing.

Charity suffereth long, and is kind; charity envieth not; charity vaunteth not itself, is not puffed up, doth not behave itself unseemly, seeketh not her own, is not easily provoked, thinketh no evil; rejoiceth not in iniquity, but rejoiceth in the truth; beareth all things, believeth all things, hopeth all things, endureth all things.

Charity never faileth: but whether there be prophecies, they shall fail; whether there be tongues, they shall cease; whether there be knowledge, it shall vanish away. For we know in part, and we prophesy in part. But when that which is perfect is come, then that which is in part shall be done away.

When I was a child, I spake as a child, I understood as a child, I thought as a child: but when I became a man, I put away childish things. For now we see through a glass, darkly; but then face to face: now I know in part; but then shall I know even as also I am known.

And now abideth faith, hope, charity, these three; but the greatest of these is charity.

THE CHRISTIAN CHURCH

To Hebraism in its final form belong many of the writings of the Church. Although not written by Hebrews, the religious literature of Christianity is permeated by the spirit of the Bible. This is true even of those philosophical writings that tried to link Christianity with Platonic and Aristotelian thought, for these merely sought a rational basis for faith. This literature begins to be written in the second century A.D. and it extends to the present day. It was produced in Greek, Latin, and later in the vernaculars; by both the Greek Orthodox and Roman Catholic religions; and by both Catholics and Protestants. Here, however, we are concerned only with the literature of the Church during Roman and medieval times, which represents the progress of the Church after the composition of the New Testament. It is a vast body of writing, moralistic, philosophical, and liturgical. The few examples in this section represent only the nontheological, emotional elements.

As an institution, the Church began modestly in the form of Christian communities in the Near East and the Roman provinces, and its activities were missionary work and local organization. The first important step was taken when, under Paul's leadership, the Christians differentiated their worship more and more from the synagogue; rejected those elements of Hebraic ritual (such as circumcision and dietary prohibitions) that stood in the way of converting the Gentiles;[1] and developed the idea of a universal Church as contrasted with the nationalistic faith favored by the Jews and by many early Christians in Palestine. This transformation made it possible for the little Christian sect to spread its teachings over the world. Paul, aptly named the "Apostle of the Gentiles," laid the foundations of this Church by both preachment and missionary practice. After this, no amount of persecution by Roman emperors and governors could stem the tide of conversion. By the fourth century, Christianity, which hitherto had been merely one among several oriental faiths in Rome, became the chief political force in the Empire. In A.D. 313, Emperor Constantine gave the Christian Church a privileged position, and his successors gradually made it the state religion of the Empire. By the end of the century, paganism retained adherents only among the aristocrats, the teachers of philosophy, and the natives of the remote countryside.[2] Heathen sacrifices were forbidden and temples closed toward the end of the fourth century by Theodosius. In 408, pagans were disqualified from any public office. A few years later, they were actively persecuted, and thereafter paganism existed only furtively in the Empire. All that remained was for the Church to cement its power, to clarify its doctrine, to adapt it to the customs of the world which it had mastered, and to convert the Teutonic tribes that had not yet been Romanized.[3]

In organization, the Church, taking Rome for its capital, became a spiritual replica of the dying Roman Empire, and for many centuries, it played

[1] The non-Hebraic peoples.

[2] The term for country people, *pagani*, supplied the term *pagan* with which to designate polytheism. The English word "heathen" is derived from "heath"—that is, the people of the heath.

[3] The tribes that conquered Rome directly "were all or nearly all half Romanized before entering on the work of conquest." E. B. Osborn's *The Middle Ages*, p. 4

the same role of unifying western Europe and giving its peoples a central authority "The material Empire decayed, lost province after province, fell into complete ruin. Yet, as it wasted and vanished, the Church, enthroned in the ancient city, waxed stronger and more stately, century after century extending her spiritual conquests."[4]

What remained of Roman culture became the possession of this spiritual empire. Latin remained the language of the Church. The Bible was read in the august translation ("the Vulgate") prepared by St. Jerome. A mastery of the classic tongue was also apparent in the writings of the founder of ecclesiastical philosophy, St. Augustine; and it was in the same language that Christian philosophers like St. Anselm and St. Thomas Aquinas continued to expound Christian thought. It is indeed true that in the Middle Ages Latin underwent changes and acquired some inaccuracies of grammar and diction. But the organ-music of classic speech continued to be heard in the noble prayers and hymns composed through the centuries. The simplifications, moreover, introduced a fresh charm and emotional coloring, not classic, but still admirable, in such works as the *De Imitatione Christi* (*The Imitation of Christ*) of Thomas à Kempis and the letters of Abelard and Heloise. Chronicles and romances, and compilations of tales like the *Gesta Romanorum*, also found a serviceable language in medieval Latin. The pure Ciceronian style might have actually proved too formal for many of the stories of wonder and the legends of the saints.

All learning passed into the Church. Its monasteries afforded a haven for scholarly men during the shipwreck of the political state. Here they found an outlet, no matter how limited, for their intellect and their literary talents. Here they gave utterance to their faith in God, their longing for a better life, their belief in a just and humane world. They wrote chronicles like Eginhard's *Life of Charlemagne* and the Venerable Bede's account of the *Ecclesiastical History of the English Nation.* They could meticulously copy and thus preserve classic writings as well as works in the vernaculars.

They created a hymnology that ranks high as poetry. They also began a new age of the drama by introducing, in the ninth century, short dramatic passages, known as *tropes*, in the wordless sequences of the Mass, and later by composing short liturgical plays based on biblical episodes, as well as dramatizations of legends of the Virgin and the saints.

Finally, the medieval Church helped to stabilize European life, acting as a check upon the continual wars of the barons, glorifying labor, and leveling social inequalities by opening ecclesiastical offices to common men and assuring them equality before God. Moreover, in organizing religion as an institution, in achieving a fixed dogma and in developing a rational basis for faith, the Church stabilized the faith of European man. It kept the religious impulse from degenerating into spiritual anarchy.

The fathers of the Church followed both common sense and the example of the Roman Empire in stabilizing ritual and theology and rejecting the extremism of many early sects by denouncing them as heresies. The methods may frequently have been ruthless, but the aim of the early Christian organizers was sound; the intention was moderation in all things, even in faith. Many proponents of the heresies may have been noble men maligned by their opponents, but a list of their beliefs reveals a welter of confusions.[5] The theological theories multiplied rapidly, and if the Church had accepted all of them, the result would have been utter confusion. Instead its leaders, men who excelled as organizers, adopted a middle-of-the-ground attitude and crystallized the faith in a series of councils, beginning with the Council of Nicæa in 325 A.D.

St. Augustine (A.D. 350-430), the leading intellectual figure of the early Church, summed up in his life many of the tendencies and conflicts of the formative period. These he recorded in his remarkable autobiography, the *Confessions*, a personal history of his search for certainty and stability. Born in Numidia, Aurelius Augustinus, was the typical offspring of a mixed marriage. His father, Patricius, was a pagan; his mother, Monica, a

---

[4] *Ibid.,* p. 7.

[5] Certain so-called Gnostics, for example, wanted to deprive Christianity of its valuable Old Testament basis, by representing the Hebrew God as a demon who created the world but was the enemy of mankind. Others the Montanists, exaggerated the importance of asceticism. Still others, known as Manicheists (after the founder of their belief, the third-century Persian teacher Manes), maintained that the world was ruled by two principles,—a power of good identified with God and a power of evil— instead of simply by God; all matter, according to them, was evil,—a thought that is foreign to practical, activist Western civilization, and that orthodox Christianity had to reject since it was, after all, God who created matter.

pious Christian. After the usual pagan education, he led the dissolute life of a Roman youth, delighting, as he later wrote, in "the muddy concupiscence of the flesh." A devoted father supplied him with all means for study and worldly gratifications, but had no concern for the lad's spiritual welfare. Even his Christian mother did not, he complains in the *Confessions*, interfere with his amours, out of fear that marriage would hinder his career. He went to Carthage to complete his education. There, he tells us, he pursued studies which "had a view to excelling in the courts of litigation; the more bepraised, the craftier," in rhetoric and eloquence, "out of a damnable and vainglorious end." Cicero's philosophical work *Hortensius*, however, made him long for "the immortality of wisdom," though the "name of Christ was not in it." He turned, indeed, to the Scriptures at this time, but they seemed unworthy compared to the stateliness of Cicero's literary work. He began instead to teach rhetoric at Carthage and Rome.

In his struggle toward faith he next became attracted to the doctrines of the Manicheans, who called upon men to fight the power of darkness in their souls and foretold the ultimate triumph of the principle of the goodness or light. But he abandoned Manicheism because "a piety, such as it was," constrained him to believe "that the good God never created any evil nature." Going to Milan in this crisis, he was moved by the eloquence of its bishop, St. Ambrose, to become a catechumen of the Church. In this approach to the Christian faith St. Augustine was ardently supported by his pious mother, to whom his attachment was strong. At the same time, he found himself strongly attracted to Platonism, becoming morally inspired by Plato and "taught to search for incorporeal truth," but rejecting the worship of spirits favored by the mystical neo-Platonists. Finally, after great mental and spiritual agony, being troubled by the fact that "the unlearned start up and take heaven by force" while his learning could not bring him peace, he heard a voice "as of a boy or a girl, I know not, chanting, and oft repeating, 'Take up and read; take up and read.'" He opened the New Testament at random and read "put ye on the Lord Jesus Christ." Instantly he decided to become converted, renounced his profession of rhetoric, and retired to the country to prepare himself to receive baptism. This occurred in his thirty-second year.

The nine chapters of the *Confessions* which recount St. Augustine's development comprise one of the great autobiographies of literature. The rest of the book reveals what contribution he was able to bring the Church. Early Christian apologists such as Tertullian (155?-222?) had tried to show that Christianity could be harmonized with classic philosophy. Augustine brought to this problem, in his capacity of bishop of Hippo, in Africa, a keen intellect. He revealed a remarkable faculty for giving Catholic Christianity something more than an apology—a systematic philosophical basis. His philosophy fused important elements of Platonism and Christian belief, making philosophical knowledge the handmaiden of faith as it was summed up in the two propositions of the later Christian philosophers or Scholastics: "I believe in order to understand" and "I understand in order to believe." In his notable *City of God* (*De Civitate Dei*), moreover, he set down a philosophy of history for the Church and its believers. There is a law of progress that governs the history of humanity, bringing the fulfillment of divine purpose,—a law "of which even those who fight against it become instruments in the hands of Providence according to the Divine plan."

St. Augustine was followed by numerous Christian thinkers, such as John Scotus Erigena, Roscelin, St. Anselm, St. Thomas of Aquinas, and that master of dialectics or argumentation Peter Abelard. They created Scholastic philosophy, which reached its peak in the thirteenth century after the works of Aristotle became known to the medieval world through the translations and teachings of Arabian and Jewish philosophers.

The student of literature, however, is more interested in the writings of those who found emotional expression for the Christian Church. He is impressed first of all by the great Latin hymns. Begun by St. Ambrose in the fourth century, these poems took on the charms of the new versification.[6] The authorship of many of the hymns is unknown or uncertain, although the names of Prudentius, Fortunatus, Bernard of Clairvaux, Adam of Saint Victor, Jacopone (author of *Stabat mater dolorosa*), and Thomas of Celano (author of the *Dies Iræ*) have come down to us. The twelfth and thirteenth centuries witnessed a simul-

[6] Meter based on accented syllables instead of on quantity, and rhyme, which had been used sparingly in Classic Latin verse as a special ornament.

taneous flowering of Gothic architecture and Latin hymnology. And like the former, the hymns expressed an intense aspiration and a loving elaboration of rhythmic pattern. They became the inspiration of some of the best music of medieval and modern times.

Notable also was the nonliturgical inspirational prose and verse of the devout. The first important example, the treatise on the *Consolations of Philosophy*, was cast in dialogue form by the sixth-century Roman Bœthius while he languished in prison, awaiting execution. Philosophy visits him there and consoles him with the knowledge that nothing happens without divine providence. This work became one of the favorite classics of the Middle Ages and attracted such distinguished translators as King Alfred the Great, Chaucer, and Queen Elizabeth. Later, the most important religious literature was written by men like St. Francis of Assisi and St. Thomas à Kempis, who did not try to rationalize faith but exemplified it in their life and expressed it rhapsodically.

The most appealing of these figures was St. Francis of Assisi (1182-1226), founder of the Franciscan order and a mystic who revived the idealism of early Christianity by leading a life of voluntary poverty and setting forth lessons of brotherly love and of consideration even for the animal world. Legends and miracles grew around him, and the mendicant brotherhood that he founded ushered in, for a time, a revival of simple faith at a period when the Church had become an increasingly worldly institution. The record of his life and teachings as set forth in *The Little Flowers, The Mirror of Perfection,* Saint Bonaventura's *Life,* and *The Legend of Saint Francis by the Three Companions* is an oasis in the literary desert of Scholasticism. His lovely song, *The Canticle of the Sun,* expresses all the sweetness of this poet of religion.

A kindred spirit was the German monk St. Thomas à Kempis (*circa* 1380-1471[7]), a peasant's son who led the life of a recluse and busied himself copying pious manuscripts. He expressed his mysticism in *The Imitation of Christ.*[8] This devotional work, consisting of strands of beautiful thoughts, became one of the treasured possessions of the Christian world. Its approach to religion is entirely through individual feeling and faith, and its simplicity came as a great relief to those who were beginning to tire of the controversial subtleties of latter-day, decadent Scholasticism.

---

[7] Thomas of Kempen, a place near Düsseldorf. His name was Thomas Hemerken or Hammerchen. The authorship of the book has been disputed, but most opinions have held it to be his.

SAINT AUGUSTINE

Confessions

In boyhood itself, however, (so much less dreaded for me than youth,) I loved not study, and hated to be forced to it. Yet I was forced; and this was well done towards me, but I did not well; for, unless forced, I had not learnt. But no one doth well against his will, even though what he doth, be well. Yet neither did they well who forced me, but what was well came to me from Thee, my God. For they were regardless how I should employ what they forced me to learn, except to satiate the insatiate desires of a wealthy beggary, and a shameful glory. But Thou, *by whom the very hairs of our head are numbered,* didst use for my good the error of all who urged me to learn; and my own, who would not learn, Thou didst use for my punishment—a fit penalty for one, so small a boy and so great a sinner. So by those who did not well, Thou didst well for me; and by my own sin Thou didst justly punish me. For Thou hast commanded, and so it is, that every inordinate affection should be its own punishment.

But why did I so much hate the Greek, which I studied as a boy? I do not yet fully know. For the Latin I loved; not what my first masters, but what the so-called grammarians taught me. For those first lessons, reading, writing, and arithmetic, I thought as great a burden and penalty as any Greek. And yet whence was this too, but from the sin and vanity of this life, because *I was flesh, and a breath that passeth away and cometh not again?* For those first lessons were better certainly, because more certain; by them I obtained, and still retain, the power of reading what I find written, and myself writing what I will; whereas in the others, I was forced to learn the wanderings of one Æneas, forgetful of my own, and to weep for dead Dido, because she killed herself for love; the while, with dry eyes, I endured my miserable self dying among these things, far from Thee, O God my life.

For what more miserable than a miserable being who commiserates not himself; weeping the death of Dido for love to Æneas, but weeping not his own death for want of love to Thee, O God. Thou light of my heart, Thou bread of my inmost soul, Thou Power who givest vigor to my mind, who quickenest my thoughts, I loved Thee not. . . . And all this I wept not, I who wept for Dido slain, and "seeking by the sword a stroke and wound extreme," myself seeking the while a worse extreme, the extremest and lowest of Thy creatures, having forsaken Thee, earth passing into the earth. And if forbid to read all this, I was grieved that I might not read what grieved me. Madness like this is thought a higher and a richer learning, than that by which I learned to read and write.

But now, my God, cry Thou aloud in my soul; and let Thy truth tell me, "Not so, not so. Far better was that first study." For, lo, I would readily forget the wanderings of Æneas and all the rest, rather than how to read and write. But over the entrance of the Grammar School is a vail drawn! true; yet is this not so much an emblem of aught recondite, as a cloke of error. Let not those, whom I no longer fear, cry out against me, while I confess to Thee, my God, whatever my soul will, and acquiesce in the condemnation of my evil ways, that I may love Thy good ways. Let not either buyers or sellers of grammar-learning cry out against me. For if I question them whether it be true, that Æneas came on a time to Carthage, as the Poet tells, the less learned will reply that they know not, the more learned that he never did. But should I ask with what letters the name "Æneas" is written, everyone who has learnt this will answer me aright, as to the signs which men have conventionally settled. If, again, I should ask, which might be forgotten with least detriment to the concerns of life, reading and writing or these poetic fictions? who does not foresee, what all must answer who have not wholly forgotten themselves? I sinned, then, when as a boy I preferred those empty to those more profitable studies, or rather loved the one and hated the other. "One and one, two"; "two and two, four;" this was to me a hateful sing-song: "the wooden horse lined

Confessions. Selections. Translated by E. B. Pusey. Lucius Aurelius Augustinus (354-430) was born in Numidia. He was educated at Madaura and Carthage and later moved to Rome. He was converted to orthodox Christianity through the influence of his mother. He was Bishop of Hippo in Numidia.

with armed men," and "the burning of Troy," and "Creusa's shade and sad similitude," were the choice spectacle of my vanity.

Why then did I hate the Greek classics, which have the like tales? For Homer also curiously wove the like fictions, and is most sweetly-vain, yet was he bitter to my boyish taste. And so I suppose would Virgil be to Grecian children, when forced to learn him as I was Homer. Difficulty, in truth, the difficulty of a foreign tongue, dashed, as it were, with gall all the sweetness of Grecian fable. For not one word of it did I understand, and to make me understand I was urged vehemently with cruel threats and punishments. Time was also, (as an infant,) I knew no Latin; but this I learned without fear of suffering, by mere observation, amid the caresses of my nursery and jests of friends, smiling and sportively encouraging me. This I learned without any pressure of punishment to urge me on, for my heart urged me to give birth to its conceptions, which I could only do by learning words not of those who taught, but of those who talked with me; in whose ears also I gave birth to the thoughts, whatever I conceived. No doubt then, that a free curiosity has more force in our learning these things, than a frightful enforcement. Only this enforcement restrains the rovings of that freedom, through Thy laws, O my God, Thy laws, from the master's cane to the martyr's trials, being able to temper for us a wholesome bitter, recalling us to Thyself from that deadly pleasure which lures us from Thee.

Hear, Lord, my prayer; let not my soul faint under Thy discipline, nor let me faint in confessing unto Thee all Thy mercies, whereby Thou hast drawn me out of all my most evil ways, that Thou mightest become a delight to me above all the allurements which I once pursued; that I may most entirely love Thee, and clasp Thy hand with all my affections, and Thou mayest yet rescue me from every temptation, even unto the end. For, lo, O Lord, my King and my God, for Thy service be whatever useful thing my childhood learned; for Thy service, that I speak—write—read—reckon. For Thou didst grant me Thy discipline, while I was learning vanities; and my sin of delighting in those vanities Thou hast forgiven. In them, indeed, I learnt many a useful word, but these may as well be learned in things not vain; and that is the safe path for the steps of youth.

But woe is thee, thou torrent of human custom! Who shall stand against thee? How long shalt thou not be dried up? How long roll the sons of Eve into that huge and hideous ocean, which even they scarcely overpass who climb the cross? Did not I read in thee of Jove the thunderer and the adulterer? Both, doubtless, he could not be; but so the feigned thunder might countenance and pander to real adultery. And now which of our gowned masters, lends a sober ear to one who from their own school cries out, "These were Homer's fictions, transferring things human to the gods; would he had brought down things divine to us!" Yet more truly had he said, "These are indeed his fictions; but attributing a divine nature to wicked men, that crimes might be no longer crimes, and whoso commits them might seem to imitate not abandoned men, but the celestial gods." . . .

Bear with me, my God, while I say somewhat of my wit, Thy gift, and on what dotages I wasted it. For a task was set me, troublesome enough to my soul, upon terms of praise or shame, and fear of stripes, to speak the words of Juno, as she raged and mourned that she could not

This Trojan prince from Latium turn.

Which words I had heard that Juno never uttered; but we were forced to go astray in the footsteps of these poetic fictions, and to say in prose much what he expressed in verse. And his speaking was most applauded, in whom the passions of rage and grief were most pre-eminent, and clothed in the most fitting language, maintaining the dignity of the character. What is it to me, O my true life, my God, that my declamation was applauded above so many of my own age and class? Is not all this smoke and wind? And was there nothing else whereon to exercise my wit and tongue? Thy praises, Lord, Thy praises might have stayed the yet tender shoot of my heart by the prop of Thy Scriptures; so had it not trailed away amid these empty trifles, a defiled prey for the fowls of the air. For in more ways than one do men sacrifice to the rebellious angels. . . .

This was the world at whose gate unhappy I lay in my boyhood; this the stage, where I had feared more to commit a barbarism, than having committed one, to envy those who had not. These things I speak and confess to Thee, my God; for which I had praise from them, whom I then thought it all virtue to please. For I saw not the abyss of vileness, wherein *I was cast away from Thine eyes.* Before them what more foul than I was already, displeasing even such as myself? with innumerable lies deceiving my tutor, my masters.

my parents, from love of play, eagerness to see vain shows, and restlessness to imitate them! Thefts also I committed, from my parents' cellar and table, enslaved by greediness, or that I might have to give to boys, who sold me their play, which all the while they liked no less than I. In this play, too, I often sought unfair conquests, conquered myself meanwhile by vain desire of preeminence. And what could I so ill endure, or, when I detected it, upbraided I so fiercely, as that I was doing to others? and for which if, detected, I was upbraided, I chose rather to quarrel, than to yield. And is this the innocence of boyhood? Not so, Lord, not so; I cry Thy mercy, O my God. For these very sins, as riper years succeed, these very sins are transferred from tutors and masters, from nuts and balls and sparrows, to magistrates and kings, to gold and manors and slaves, just as severer punishments displace the cane. It was the low stature then of childhood, which Thou our King didst commend as an emblem of lowliness, when Thou saidst, *Of such is the kingdom of heaven.*

Yet, Lord, to Thee, the Creator and Governor of the universe, most excellent and most good, thanks were due to Thee our God, even hadst Thou destined for me boyhood only. For even then I was, I lived, and felt; and had an implanted providence over my own well-being,—a trace of that mysterious Unity, whence I was derived;—I guarded by the inward sense the entireness of my senses, and in these minute pursuits, and in my thoughts on things minute, I learnt to delight in truth, I hated to be deceived, had a vigorous memory, was gifted with speech, was soothed by friendship, avoided pain, baseness, ignorance. In so small a creature, what was not wonderful, not admirable? But all are gifts of my God; it was not I, who gave them me; and good these are, and these together are myself. Good, then, is He that made me, and He is my good, and before Him will I exult for every good which of a boy I had For it was my sin, that not in Him, but in His creatures—myself and others—I sought for pleasures, sublimities, truths, and so fell headlong into sorrows, confusions, errors. Thanks be to Thee, my joy and my glory and my confidence, my God, thanks be to Thee for Thy gifts; but do Thou preserve them to me. For so wilt Thou preserve me, and those things shall be enlarged and perfected, which Thou hast given me, and I myself shall be with Thee, since even to be Thou hast given me

LATIN HYMNS

Veni Creator Spiritus

Creator Spirit, by whose aid
The world's foundations first were laid,
Come visit ev'ry pious mind;
Come pour thy joys on humankind;
From sin and sorrow set us free,
And make thy temples worthy thee.
 O source of uncreated light,
The Father's promis'd Paraclete![1]
Thrice holy fount, thrice holy fire,
Our hearts with heav'nly love inspire;
Come, and thy sacred unction bring
To sanctify us, while we sing!
 Plenteous of grace, descend from high,
Rich in thy sev'nfold energy,
Thou strength of his almighty hand,
Whose pow'r does heav'n and earth command!
Proceeding Spirit, our defense,
Who dost the gifts of tongues dispense,
And crown'st thy gift with eloquence!

Refine and purge our earthy parts;
But, O, inflame and fire our hearts!
Our frailties help, our vice control,
Submit the senses to the soul;
And when rebellious they are grown,
Then lay thy hand, and hold 'em down.
 Chase from our minds th' infernal foe,
And peace, the fruit of love, bestow;
And lest our feet should step astray,
Protect and guide us in the way.
 Make us eternal truths receive,
And practice all that we believe:
Give us thyself, that we may see
The Father and the Son, by thee.
 Immortal honor, endless fame,
Attend th' Almighty Father's name:
The Savior Son be glorified,
Who for lost man's redemption died;
And equal adoration be,
Eternal Paraclete, to thee.

Latin Hymns. *Veni Creator Spiritus* (Come, Creator Spirit) and *The Te Deum* (We Praise Thee, God) translated by John Dryden; *Dies Iræ* (Day of Wrath), by Richard Crashaw.
[1] The Holy Spirit as the Helper or Comforter of man

The Te Deum

Thee, Sovereign God, our grateful accents praise;
We own thee Lord, and bless thy wondrous ways;
To thee, Eternal Father, earth's whole frame,
With loudest trumpets, sounds immortal fame.
Lord God of Hosts! for thee the heavenly powers
With sounding anthems fill the vaulted towers.
Thy Cherubims thrice, Holy, Holy, Holy, cry;
Thrice, Holy, all the Seraphims reply,
And thrice returning echoes endless songs supply.
Both heaven and earth thy majesty display;
They owe their beauty to thy glorious ray.
Thy praises fill the loud apostles' choir;
The train of prophets in the song conspire.
Legions of martyrs in the chorus shine,
And vocal blood with vocal music join.
By these thy church, inspir'd by heavenly art,
Around the world maintains a second part;
And tunes her sweetest notes, O God, to thee,
The Father of unbounded majesty;
The Son, ador'd copartner of thy seat,
And equal everlasting Paraclete.
Thou King of Glory, Christ, of the most high,
Thou coeternal filial Deity;
Thou who, to save the world's impending doom,
Vouchsaf'dst to dwell within a Virgin's womb;
Old tyrant Death disarm'd, before thee flew
The bolts of heaven, and back the foldings drew,
To give access, and make thy faithful way;
From God's right hand thy filial beams display.
Thou art to judge the living and the dead;
Then spare those souls for whom thy veins have
     bled.
O take us up amongst thy blest above,
To share with them thy everlasting love.
Preserve, O Lord, thy people, and enhance
Thy blessing on thine own inheritance.
For ever raise their hearts, and rule their ways;
Each day we bless thee, and proclaim thy praise:
No age shall fail to celebrate thy name,
No hour neglect thy everlasting fame.
Preserve our souls, O Lord, this day from ill;
Have mercy on us, Lord, have mercy still:
As we have hop'd, do thou reward our pain;
We've hop'd in thee—let not our hope be vain.

Dies Iræ

Hear'st thou, my soul, what serious things
Both the Psalm and Sibyl sings
Of a sure Judge, from whose sharp ray
The world in flames shall fly away!

O that Fire! before whose face   5
Heaven and earth shall find no place:
O those Eyes! whose angry light
Must be the day of that dread night.

O that Trump! whose blast shall run
An even round with th' circling Sun,   10
And urge the murmuring graves to bring
Pale mankind forth to meet his King.

Horror of Nature, Hell, and Death!
When a deep groan from beneath
Shall cry, "We come, we come!" and all   15
The caves of night answer one call.

O that book! whose leaves so bright
Will set the world in severe light.
O that Judge! whose hand, whose eye
None can endure, yet none can fly.   20

Ah then, poor soul! what wilt thou say?
And to what patron choose to pray,
When stars themselves shall stagger, and
The most firm foot no more shall stand?

But Thou giv'st leave, dread Lord, that we   25
Take shelter from Thyself in Thee;
And with the wings of Thine own dove
Fly to Thy scepter of soft love!

Dear [LORD], remember in that day
Who was the cause Thou cam'st this way;   30
Thy sheep was strayed, and Thou wouldst be
Even lost Thyself in seeking me!

Shall all that labor, all that cost
Of love, and even that loss, be lost?
And this loved soul judged worth no less   35
Than all that way and weariness?

Just mercy, then, Thy reck'ning be
With my price, and not with me;
'Twas paid at first with too much pain
To be paid twice, or once in vain.   40

Mercy, my Judge, mercy I cry,
With blushing cheek and bleeding eye;
The conscious colors of my sin
Are red without, and pale within.

O let Thine own soft bowels pay   45
Thyself, and so discharge that day!
If Sin can sigh, Love can forgive,
O, say the word, my soul shall live!

Those mercies which Thy Mary found,
Or who Thy cross confess'd and crowned, 50
Hope tells my heart the same loves be
Still alive, and still for me.

Though both my prayers and tears combine,
Both worthless are, for they are mine;
But Thou Thy bounteous self still be, 55
And show Thou art by saving me.

O when Thy last frown shall proclaim
The flocks of goats to folds of flame,

And all Thy lost sheep found shall be,
Let "Come ye blessed" then call me! 60

When the dread *"ITE"*[1] shall divide
Those limbs of death from Thy left side,
Let those life-speaking lips command
That I inherit Thy right hand!

O, hear a suppliant heart all crush'd, 65
And crumbled into contrite dust!
My hope, my fear—my Judge, my Friend!
Take charge of me, and of my end!

ST. FRANCIS OF ASSISI

Canticle of the Sun

O most high, almighty, good Lord God, to thee belong praise, glory, honor, and all blessing!

Praised be my Lord God with all his creatures; and specially our brother the sun, who brings us the day, and who brings us the light; fair is he, and shining with a very great splendor: O Lord, he signifies to us thee!

Praised be my Lord for our sister the moon, and 10 for the stars, the which he has set clear and lovely in heaven.

Praised be my Lord for our brother the wind, and for air and cloud, calms and all weather, by the which thou upholdest in life all creatures.

Praised be my Lord for our sister water, who is very serviceable unto us, and humble, and precious, and clean.

Praised be my Lord for our brother fire, through whom thou givest us light in the darkness; and he 20 is bright, and pleasant, and very mighty, and strong.

Praised be my Lord for our mother the earth, the which doth sustain us and keep us, and bringeth forth divers fruits, and flowers of many colors, and grass.

Praised be my Lord for all those who pardon one another for his love's sake, and who endure weakness and tribulation; blessed are they who peaceably shall endure, for thou, O most Highest, shall give them a crown!

Praised be my Lord for our sister, the death of the body, from whom no man escapeth. Woe to him who dieth in mortal sin! Blessed are they who are found walking by thy most holy will, for the second death shall have no power to do them harm.

Praise ye, and bless ye the Lord, and give thanks unto him, and serve him with great humility.

Sermon to the Birds

When St. Francis drew nigh unto Bevagna he came unto a spot wherein a great multitude of birds of divers species were gathered together. When the holy man of God perceived them, he ran with all speed unto the place and greeted them as if they shared in human understanding. They on their part all awaited him and turned toward him, those that were perched on bushes bending their heads as he drew nigh them, and looking on him in unwonted wise, while he came right among them, and diligently exhorted them all to hear the word of God, saying: "My brothers the birds, much ought ye to praise your Creator, Who hath clothed you with feathers and given you wings to fly, and hath made over unto you the pure air, and careth for you without your taking thought for yourselves." While he was speaking unto them these

---

[1] "Go!" (Latin).

St. Francis, *Canticle of the Sun*. Translated by Matthew Arnold. St. Francis of Assisi (1182-1226) turned from a life of ease to one of ascetic devotion and founded the order of Franciscan Friars. He passed nearly all his life in Italy.

and other like words, the little birds—behaving themselves in wondrous wise—began to stretch their necks, to spread their wings, to open their beaks, and to look intently on him. He, with wondrous fervor of spirit, passed in and out among them, touching them with his habit, nor did one of them move from the spot until he had made the

sign of the Cross over them and given them leave; then, with the blessing of the man of God, they all flew away together. All these things were witnessed by his companions that stood awaiting him by the way. Returning unto them, the simple and holy man began to blame himself for neglect in that he had not afore then preached unto the birds.

THOMAS À KEMPIS

Of the Imitation of Christ

The Thoughts of Death

1. Very quickly will it be over with thee here; see then how matters stand with thee. A man is here to-day, and to-morrow he is no longer seen.

And when he is taken away from the sight, he is also quickly out of mind.

Oh! the dulness and hardness of the human heart, which thinks only of what is present and does not look rather forward to things to come.

Thou oughtest in every action and thought so to order thyself, as if thou wert immediately to die.

If thou hadst a good conscience, thou wouldst not much fear death.

It were better for thee to avoid sin, than to escape death.

If thou are not prepared to-day, how wilt thou be to-morrow?

To-morrow is an uncertain day; and how dost thou know that thou shalt be alive to-morrow?

2. What good is it to live long, when we advance so little?

Ah! long life does not always make us better, but often rather adds to our guilt.

Would that we had behaved ourselves well in this world, even for one day!

Many reckon up the years of their conversion; but oftentimes the fruit of amendment is but small.

If it be frightful to die, perhaps it will be more dangerous to live longer.

Blessed is he that has always the hour of his

death before his eyes, and every day prepares himself to die.

If thou hast at any time seen a man die, think that thou also must traverse the same path.

3. In the morning, think that thou mayest not live till night; and when evening comes, presume not to promise thyself the next morning.

Be therefore always prepared, and live in such a manner, that death may never find thee unprepared.

Many die suddenly, and when they little think of it: For in such an hour as ye think not the Son of Man will come.

When that last hour shall come, thou wilt begin to have quite other thoughts of thy whole past life, and be exceeding sorry that thou hast been so negligent and remiss.

4. How happy and prudent is he who strives now to be such in this life, as he desires to be found at his death.

A perfect contempt of the world, a fervent desire to advance in virtue, a love of discipline, labor in penitence, readiness in obedience, self-denial, and patience in affliction for the love of Christ, will give us great assurance of dying happily.

Thou mayest do many good things whilst thou art well; but when thou art sick, I know not what thou wilt be able to do.

Few are improved by sickness; so they also that rove about much, seldom become holy.

5. Trust not in thy friends and kinsfolk, nor put

Thomas à Kempis (1380-1471).

off the welfare of thy soul to hereafter; for men will forget thee sooner than thou thinkest.

It is better now to provide in time, and send some good before thee, than to depend upon the help of others.

If thou art not now careful for thyself, who will be careful for thee hereafter?

The present time is very precious. Now is the acceptable time; now is the day of salvation.

But oh, the sorrow that thou dost not spend this time more profitably, wherein thou mayest earn life for ever! The time will come, when thou wilt wish for one day or hour to amend; and I know not whether thou wilt obtain it.

6. O dearly beloved, from how great a danger mayest thou deliver thyself, from how great a fear mayest thou rescue thyself, if thou wilt but now be always fearful, and looking for death!

Strive now so to live, that in the hour of thy death thou mayest be able to rejoice rather than fear.

Learn now to die to the world, that thou mayest then begin to live with Christ.

Learn now to despise all things, that thou mayest then freely go to Christ.

Chasten thy body now by penitence, that thou mayest then have a sure confidence.

7. Ah, fool! why dost thou think to live long, when thou art not sure of one day?

How many thinking to live long have been deceived, and snatched unexpectedly away?

How often hast thou heard related, that such a one was slain by the sword; another drowned; another, from a height, broke his neck; one died eating, another playing?

Some have perished by fire; some by the sword; some by pestilence; and some by robbers.

And so death is the end of all; and man's life suddenly passeth away like a shadow.

8. Who will remember thee when thou art dead? and who will pray for thee?

Do now, beloved, do now all thou canst, because thou knowest not when thou shalt die, nor dost thou know what shall befall thee after death.

Whilst thou hast time, gather up for thyself everlasting riches; think of nothing but thy salvation; care for nothing but the things of God.

Make now to thyself friends, by honoring the saints of God, and imitating their actions; that when thou failest, they may receive thee into everlasting habitations.

9. Keep thyself as a pilgrim and a stranger upon earth, whom none of the affairs of this world concern.

Keep thy heart free, and raised upwards to God; for here thou hast no continuing city.

Send thither thy daily prayers with sighs and with tears; that after death thy spirit may be worthy happily to pass to our Lord. Amen.

PART TWO
THE ORIENTAL WORLD

Although Hellenism and Hebraism contributed the main ferment of European culture and bulk largest in our literary heritage, we cannot entirely overlook the ancient contributions of Egypt, India, and China, as well as of the Mohammedan peoples of the Near East who matured later than other oriental nations. From Egypt came the Western World's strong concern with the survival of the soul; from India, mystic teachings and charming fables; from China, admirable ethical precepts and excellent lyric poetry. During the last century Europeans and Americans became increasingly aware of the literature of these countries, poets and thinkers reflected its influence, and cultivated readers began to find in it novel pleasure and stimulation.

EGYPT

We know that Egypt enjoyed one of the oldest civilizations, if not indeed the oldest. The ancient Egyptians' great architectural feats, their temples and pyramids, are appreciated today; so are their sculpture, their development of writing, their use of papyrus, and their advances in early science and mathematics, especially geometry. Most of their literature has been lost, but what we now possess has much interest.

From Egypt has been recovered the earliest of all books of folktales, dating from about 1300 B.C., and some of the stories are still popular in Europe. This literature includes royal romances, ghost stories, fables, and an ancient version of the Cinderella story. Whether such a delightful tale as *The Two Brothers* started in Egypt or was already far along in its history when an Egyptian scribe recorded it 3200 years ago is a moot point. The Egyptians appear to have been the first masters of the short-story form.

From papyrus manuscripts found along the Nile we have also acquired a very ancient wisdom literature in the form of maxims or sayings, belonging to the twenty-ninth century B.C.—2300 years before Confucius, Socrates, and Buddha. In addition, the Egyptians left considerable love poetry, celebrating the attachment between brothers and sisters who, in the upper classes, often married each other. Finally, there are religious writings, which are the most important. The people of the Nile were consumed with a fierce passion for permanence. Their religion, their pyramids, their inimitable embalming process, their tombs, and their fondness for recording events all revolved around their desire to cancel death. They became the first poets of the belief in immortality.

This faith centered in the personality of Egypt's chief divinity, Osiris, the god of the Nile, who in overflowing irrigated their fields, made vegetation possible, and assured their food supply. He was supposed to have been resurrected by his sister and wife Isis after being killed and dismembered by his enemy Set, the god of darkness, evil, and death. In the myth told about Osiris and in the Passion Play that celebrated his story annually, his worshipers represented the fall and rise of the Nile and symbolized the death and resurrection of the soul. He became the Lord of Life, the power that could grant the dead man life eternal if he observed the rites prescribed by the priests and addressed himself to the god seated on the judgment throne with appropriate prayers, charms, and formulas. These were found inscribed on some two thousand papyrus rolls entitled *Coming Forth by Day*, better known to us under the title of *The Book of the Dead*.

The Book of the Dead exonerates the soul with numerous expressions like "I have not laid labor upon any free man beyond that which he wrote for himself. . . . I have not defaulted, I have not committed that which is an abomination to the gods. . . . I have not caused the slave to be ill-

..reated of his master," although there is no evidence of agreement between these professions and actual practice in Egypt. Some poems are also full of penitence for wickedness and for transgression. But the most remarkable feature of the poems is the lyric exaltation distilled from persistent assertions of the eternity of life; of "eternal life through eternal living forms," as one translator, Robert Hillyer, puts it. For all the solemnity of Egyptian ritual, the poems reflect a nation that exulted in animation and pleasure. The dead man arises and sings a hymn to the sun: its priests "go forth at dawn; they wash their hearts with laughter; divine winds move in music across thy golden strings." Time is limitless, the dead man assures himself:

"Millions of years have passed—we cannot count
    their number—
Millions of years shall come. Thou art above the
    years!"[1]

Limitless, too, is the dead man's wishful triumph. He has traversed the tomb, "Like the Hawk I went in; I came forth like the Phoenix, Star of the Dawn"; and he makes himself one with the God Rā (the Sun)—"I am the Lord of Light, the self-begotten youth. . . . The Prince of Years . . . my body is Eternity; my form is Everlastingness that trampleth down the darkness. . . . I am Yesterday, Today, and Tomorrow. . . ." The repetitiousness of the original poems and their confusing mythological references can become wearisome to the modern reader. But Egypt's psalmody of resurrection is a memorable testimony to the aspirations of the human spirit which found their ultimate gratification in the West in Christianity.

INDIA

Moving East, we meet a very ancient civilization and literature in India, although all Hindu chronology is exceedingly speculative before the fourth century B.C. India is a conglomeration of nations and customs, and its literary work is multifarious. It contains religious and philosophical poetry, beast fables and didactic pieces, great legends that reflect both primitive culture and the refined religion of Buddhism, two notable epics, and a number of charmingly romantic plays. All these are the products of an Aryan-speaking race that conquered and enslaved the aboriginal population that appears to have achieved a highly developed civilization of its own in some regions. This literature, which appeared in various cultural centers of a chronically disorganized country, is written largely in Sanskrit, the oldest surviving Aryan language.[2]

The mythology of the Hindus, which corresponds with that of Greece and Rome,[3] forms the subject matter of early hymns and later, highly elaborated, tales, plays, and philosophical writings. The oldest sacred literature is found in the four books called *Vedas*; *veda* means knowledge, and the *Vedas* are "Books of Knowledge." Of these, the *Rig-veda* (*circa* 1400 B.C.) is both the most ancient and the most notable. It is an anthology of 1028 hymns of simple praise to a variety of gods who have not yet been entirely personalized or humanized—gods of the sky, sun, moon, stars, rain, wind, fire, the forest, and dawn. The one highly personalized god is Indra, god of the thunder who was the warrior god of the Aryan tribes and may have been originally a human leader. Many of these hymns are beautiful descriptions of nature and some, probably of later origin, contain spiritual concepts of a high order. The noblest of them is the Creation Hymn, with its pantheistic conception of God and the world as one and the same, which permeates most Hindu thought. The latter appears in full blossom in commentaries that the learned priests (Brahmans) added to the primitive myths after coming to regard them as poetic fictions. First the priesthood added the *Brahmanas*, theological appendages to the Vedic hymns; then the *Sutras*, strings of pithy sentences about ritual practices; then the *Upanishads*,[4] a collection of opinions and observations. The one hundred and eight discourses of the *Upanishads*, composed between 800 and 500 B.C., do not develop a systematic philosophy. But they repeat and embroider the same broad concepts. They regard the world as illusion (*maya*), consider birth in the body a fall from grace, and maintain that the highest bliss (*Nirvana*) is loss of personal identity and absorption of the individual in the soul of the universe.

Buddha, the Luther and St. Francis of Brahmanism (563-483 B.C.), reformed the official creed. Rejecting its ritualistic and metaphysical refinements as vain and wasteful, he gave religion

[1] The Robert Hillyer translation is used here and in the other quotations.
[2] The word *Arya* means "noble"; no doubt the conquerors considered themselves nature's noblemen.
[3] The sky-god Dyaus, for instance, corresponds in function and etymology, with the Greek Zeus. The fire-god Hephæstus has a Hindu forerunner in Agni; the goddess Eos in Ushas.
[4] From *upa* (near) and *shad* (to sit)—*i.e.*, "sitting near" the teacher, or knowledge imparted to the student directly by the master.

a noble ethical superstructure: "Saintliness and content lie not in knowledge of the universe and God, but simply in selfless and beneficent living."[5] Suffering is universal, and it is caused by a desire that is never gratified. *Nirvana,* for Buddha, meant "the extinction of all individual desire" or selflessness, the reward for which would be release from painful rebirth or captivity in the flesh, and from never gratified desire: "When we have learned to love not our separate life, but all men and all living things, then at last we shall find peace." Early Buddhism, then, was less a philosophy than an ethical movement; it insisted on the most humane individual and social idealism and disregarded the caste system. As a result, Buddha's religion won a vast number of adherents. After Buddhism became corrupted, the Brahmans recovered their influence, and Buddhist teachers had to seek refuge in Tibet, China, and Japan.

In India both Buddhism and resurgent Brahmanism became increasingly overladen with superstition and ceremonial pomp. But not before leaving a heritage to which Western thinkers like Emerson and Schopenhauer returned, and not before leaving a remarkable literature of spiritual philosophy, poetry, maxims, and legends.

India's two epics were colored and deepened by Hindu religion and philosophy. The older and greater of the two is the *Mahabharata,* begun about 500 B.C. The subject of numerous additions for many centuries, it became seven times as long as the *Iliad* and *Odyssey* combined. Its original portions deal with the conflict between two sets of warrior cousins, the Kurus and the Pandavas, for the rule of the country around Delhi. This part of the work constitutes a colorful, vigorous war poem like the *Iliad*, and reflects the life and ideals of the warrior caste. But the *Mahabharata*, owing to the fact that the priests imbedded in it many moral disquisitions and "philosophical ideas," also became a repository of Hindu wisdom literature. This made the complete poem cumbersome and occasionally dull. Nevertheless, we must be grateful for the addition of some charming romances and for one of the loftiest spiritual poems of the world, the *Bhagavat Gita* or *Divine Song.*

This work is a series of discussions between the hero Arjun and the god Krishna, who is acting as his charioteer and inspirer. Arjun, loath to shed the blood of his kinsmen, is answered by Krishna, who justifies activism. Krishna interprets the quietist doctrines and practices of the Brahmans in such a manner that a man could engage in the struggles and responsibilities of life without renouncing religion. If death does not exist because the soul cannot be slain, then Arjun need have no hesitation in fighting for his just cause. Nor need anyone refrain from engaging in any activity, provided he works "without attachment": that is, provided he acts without selfish desire, does not lose sight of ultimate spiritual reality, and realizes the underlying unity of the varied phenomena or aspects of the world. Here activism and spirituality are reconciled. But the poem never loses sight of the ultimate goal—union with the immortal and infinite soul of the world which is present in all things and in all forms. The most ecstatic and imaginative section of the *Bhagava. Gita* expresses this thought in the vision of the god Krishna, manifesting himself in myriad shapes and persons, including the warring princes themselves.

The later epic, the *Ramayana*, briefer and less burdened than the *Mahabharata*, is the *Odyssey* of the Hindus. It is a romance of the hero Rama's wanderings and adventure, of his wife Sita's faithfulness and of a Golden Age in India.

India's dramatic masterpieces are the anonymous ten-act *Little Clay Cart* attributed to King Shudraka and Kalidasa's seven-act *Shakuntala*, as well as other plays by this sophisticated romantic poet (*circa* A.D. 500), who was succeeded a century late, by the even more romantic Bhavahabhuti. The length of these pieces precludes their inclusion here, but their charm has won them a place in the cultivated Western man's heritage.

The intricate plots of the plays reflect one of the best attributes of Hindu writers, namely, their talent for story-telling. Hindu literature is especially rich in embroidered tales, such as the *Jatakas*, fanciful legends of Buddha's birth and youth. When stories, moreover, were combined with moralization and maxims of practical wisdom, they led to the literary form of the *fable*. In this art the Hindus were supreme. According to one scholar, Sir William Jones, the first translator of the *Shakuntala*, the Hindus claimed that they gave the world three inventions—chess, the decimal system, and instruction by means of fables.

The *Panchatantra (Five Headings)*, written or collected *circa* A.D. 500, may not be, as claimed, the source of many of the world's fables, but it is one of the world's most important collections of stories. The European Middle Ages knew these tales in Latin translations, and many of them have been woven into the texture of European literature. This book and an adaptation called the *Hito-padesha* (*Good Advice*) were classified by the Hindus as instruction in politics and morals. The characters are beasts whose behavior exemplifies human conduct, and whose experiences point some moral of private or political significance. The *Panchatantra* is a "frame-story," like *The Arabian Nights*; one anecdote leads to another until there are stories within stories, sometimes four or five deep. This work consists of five parts, each containing fables bearing on the acquisition of wisdom. The best known of these books is the first, "The Loss of Friends," from which our selection is taken.

One cannot depart from ancient India, however, without noting that, unlike Egypt, its people did not lose their identity and capacity for creating culture in modern times. They have in our own century brought forth renowned scientists, political and religious leaders, painters, and one delicate poet and playwright who wrote both in English and the Bengali dialect, Rabindranath Tagore, recipient of the Nobel Prize in 1913.

THE FAR EAST

Early in European history—as early as 1295 when Marco Polo returned to Venice from his travels—Western man began to appreciate the achievements of his most distant cousins, the Chinese people who had created a civilization thousands of years before Europe emerged from barbarism. Isolated from the rest of the world by a great ocean, steep mountains, and vast deserts, China developed an indigenous culture, though borrowings may have been made in remote antiquity from Mesopotamia.[6] The complicated history of the Chinese is a long account of discords, chaos, and invasions. But China had long intervals of comparative stability and great culture out of which arose a profound courtliness, the cult of education which gave scholars a place in the government, and a humane, non-theological philosophy of which Confucius became the great proponent. Marked advances were made in science, art, and literature, until China achieved one of the world's greatest civilizations.

As might be expected, Chinese literature is extensive and includes practically every form of writing. It contains many books of history, political and philosophical disquisitions, tales of marvels, and plays, as well as beautiful examples of letter writing and some of the world's loveliest lyrics.

Some of this literature is only for the specialist, and the drama, written for a highly stylized form of theater,[7] possesses only moderate distinction. But the teachings of Confucius or Kung-fu-tze (551-478 B.C.) collected in his *Analects*, have been widely disseminated in the West. This master of wise and discreet behavior and champion of good government ("Oppressive government," he declared, "is fiercer than a tiger"), rejected the passive mysticism of earlier thinkers. For four years he governed a province, reformed its laws, and devoted himself to the guidance of an important prince. When the latter failed him, Confucius, who continued seeking opportunities to put his reforms into operation, gave his doctrine to all China. He assembled many students, collected and edited the best in Chinese literature and history, and left to his people the example of a life richly spent. His maxims, the *Analects*,[8] are masterpieces of serene wisdom and insight; they are free of metaphysical muddlement and mythological esotericism, and are readily comprehensible. A charming personality shines through them. He did not exhaust Chinese philosophy, which was rich in many schools of thought from mysticism, known as Taoism, to sophism and socialism. But he was the most catholic and persuasive Chinese thinker, and his influence never disappeared.

Confucius also provided a strong stimulus to the creation and enjoyment of Chinese poetry through his collection of ancient lyrics, the *Shi-Shing* or *Book of Odes*. Through them he taught his generation to cherish the thoughts and sentiments of their forebears, reverence for whom became the stabilizing force of this vast nation, as well as a barrier to progress in later centuries.

Poetry, indeed, became China's major literary achievement. The Chinese poets celebrated the delights of nature and simple pleasures. They were partial to peaceful pursuits far from ambitious strife, to the sentiment of domestic affection, and to the edifications of cultivated friendship. They were eminently reflective writers, and their ironic or sober comments on government and war penetrate deeply. In short, they were graceful devotees of the civilized approach to living.

This temper is evident exuberantly in the work

---

[6] Latest researches have unearthed a civilization in Mongolia as far back as 20,000 B.C.

[7] The Chinese style of staging is most familiar to those who saw Thornton Wilder's stage play, *Our Town*.

[8] The original title, *Lun Yu*, means *Discourses and Dialogues*. It was the translator Legge who called this book *Analects*. *i.e.*. collected fragments.

of China's most popular master, the shiftless Li Po or Li T'ai-Po (701-762 A.D.). He simply could not have enough of either life or wine, and he was drowned, according to legend, in a state of intoxication while trying to embrace the moon in the Yellow River. One of the world's most genial lyricists, he was followed by Tu Fu (712-770 A.D.), a more restrained and refined poet who was the scholars' favorite, and by Po Chü-i (772-846 A.D.), a man of great simplicity, humor, and tenderness who found repose and serenity even in an active political career. Most of the poets sought shelter from the heat of the political race, tried to win content in simple things, and never thought of storming heaven and hell. One of the finest of

them, T'ao Ch'ien (365-427 A.D.), retiring from public life because he could no longer "crook the hinges of the back for five pecks of rice a day," expressed their general sense of relief when he wrote: "For a long time I have lived in a cage; now I have returned."

Subtlety and purity of expression are the main characteristics of Chinese poetry. It does not resort to figures of speech, metaphors, comparisons, and other devices of Western poetry but presents the thing itself. Passion is set down without exaggeration or excitement in phrasing or form; the strongest feeling is given with restraint and scrupulous taste; and the lyric flight is generally brief and to the point.

BOOK OF THE DEAD

Hymn to Rā

A hymn of praise to Rā when he riseth in the Eastern part of heaven. Those who are in his train rejoice, and lo! Osiris Ani, victorious, saith:

"Hail, thou Disk, thou lord of days, who risest on the horizon day by day! Shine thou with thy beams of light upon the face of Osiris Ani, who is victorious; for he singeth hyms of praise unto thee at dawn, and he maketh thee to set at eventide with words of adoration. May the soul of Osiris Ani, the triumphant one, come forth with thee into heaven. May he come into port, and may he cleave his path among the never-resting stars in the heavens."

Osiris Ani, being in peace and in triumph, adoreth his lord, the lord of eternity, saying: "Homage to thee, O Herukhuti, who art the god Khepera, the self-created; when thou risest on the horizon and sheddest thy beams of light upon the lands of the North and of the South, thou art beautiful, yea beautiful, and all the gods rejoice when they behold thee, the King of heaven. The goddess Nebt-Unnut is stablished upon thy head; and her uræi[1] of the South and of the North are upon thy brow; she taketh up her place before thee. The god Thoth is stablished in the bows of thy boat to

destroy utterly all thy foes. Those who are in the Tuat (underworld) come forth to meet thee, and they bow in homage as they come toward thee, to behold thy beautiful Image. And I have come before thee that I may be with thee to behold thy Disk every day. May I not be shut up in the tomb, may I not be turned back, may the limbs of my body be made new again when I view thy beauties, even as are those of all thy favored ones, because I am one of those who worshiped thee whilst I lived upon earth. May I come in unto the land of eternity, may I come even unto the everlasting land, for behold, O my lord, this hast thou ordained for me."

And lo, Osiris Ani triumphant in peace, the triumphant one, saith: "Homage to thee, O thou who risest in thy horizon as Rā, thou reposest upon law which changeth not nor can it be altered. Thou passest over the sky, and every face watcheth thee and thy course, for thou hast been hidden from their gaze. Thou dost show thyself at dawn and at eventide day by day. The boat wherein is thy Majesty goeth forth with might; thy beams shine upon all faces; the number of thy red and yellow rays cannot be known, nor can

Hymn to Rā. Translated by E. A. Wallis Budge.
[1] Asps which rise from the sun, a detail which occurs in all representations of Rā.

thy bright beams be told. The lands of the gods, and the eastern lands of Punt[2] must be seen, ere that which is hidden in thee may be measured. Alone and by thyself thou dost manifest thyself when thou comest into being above the sky. May Ani advance, even as thou dost advance; may he never cease to go forward, even as thy Majesty ceaseth not to go forward, even though it be for a moment; for with strides dost thou in one little moment pass over the spaces which would need hundreds of thousands and millions of years for man to pass over; this thou doest, and then dost thou sink to rest. Thou puttest an end to the hours of the night, and thou dost count them, even thou; thou endest them in thine own appointed season, and the earth becometh light. Thou settest thyself before thy handiwork in the likeness of Rā; thou risest in the horizon."

Osiris, the scribe Ani, triumphant, declareth his praise of thee when thou shinest, and when thou risest at dawn he crieth in his joy at thy birth: "Thou art crowned with the majesty of thy beauties; thou moldest thy limbs as thou dost advance, and thou bringest them forth without birth-pangs in the form of Rā, as thou dost rise up into the upper air. Grant thou that I may come unto the heaven which is everlasting, and unto the mountain where dwell thy favored ones. May I be joined unto those shining beings, holy and perfect, who are in the underworld; and may I come forth with them to behold thy beauties when thou shinest at eventide and goest to thy mother Nu. Thou dost place thyself in the west, and my two hands are raised in adoration of thee when thou settest as a living being. Behold, thou art the maker of eternity, and thou art adored when thou settest in the heavens. I have given my heart unto thee without wavering, O thou who art mightier than the gods."

Osiris Ani, triumphant, saith: "A hymn of praise to thee, O thou who risest like unto gold, and who dost flood the world with light on the day of thy birth. Thy mother giveth thee birth upon her hand, and thou dost give light unto the course of the Disk. O thou great Light, who shinest in the heavens, thou dost strengthen the generations of men with the Nile-flood, and thou dost cause gladness in all lands, and in all cities, and in all the temples. Make thou glorious Osiris Ani with victory in the underworld; grant thou that in the netherworld he may be without evil. I pray thee to put away his faults behind thee: grant thou that he may be one of thy venerable servants who are with the shining ones.

And the god saith:

"Thou shalt come forth into heaven, thou shalt pass over the sky, thou shalt be joined into the starry deities. Praises shall be offered unto thee in thy boat, thou shalt be hymned in the *Atet* boat, thou shalt behold Rā within his shrine, thou shalt set together with his Disk day by day, thou shalt see the *Ant* fish when it springeth into being in the waters of turquoise, and thou shalt see the *Abtu* fish in his hour. It shall come to pass that the Evil One shall fall when he layeth a snare to destroy thee, and the joints of his neck and of his back shall be hacked asunder. Rā saileth with a fair wind, and the *Sektet* boat draweth on and cometh into port. The mariners of Rā rejoice, and the heart of Nebt-ānkh is glad, for the enemy of her lord hath fallen to the ground. Thou shalt behold Horus on the standing-place of the pilot of the boat, and Thoth and Maāt shall stand one upon each side of him. All the gods shall rejoice when they behold Rā coming in peace to make the hearts of the shining ones to live, and Osiris Ani, victorious, the scribe of the divine offerings of the lords of Thebes, shall be along with them!"

THE TWO BROTHERS

Once there were two brethren, of one mother and one father; Anpu was the name of the elder, and Bata was the name of the younger. Now, as for Anpu he had a house, and he had a wife. But his little brother was to him as it were a son; he it was who made for him his clothes; he it was who followed behind his oxen to the fields; he it was who did the plowing; he it was who harvested the corn; he it was who did for him all the matters that were in the field. Behold, his younger brother

[2] The land on each side of the Red Sea and on the coast of Africa.
The Two Brothers is found in a papyrus of about 1300 B.C. Translated by E. A. Wallis Budge.

grew to be an excellent worker, there was not his
equal in the whole land; behold, the spirit of a
god was in him.

Now after this the younger brother followed his
oxen in his daily manner; and every evening he
turned again to the house, laden with all the herbs
of the field, with milk and with wood, and with
all things of the field. And he put them down before his elder brother, who was sitting with his
wife; and he drank and ate, and he lay down 10
in his stable with the cattle. And at the dawn of
day he took bread which he had baked, and laid
it before his elder brother; and he took with him
his bread to the field, and he drave his cattle to
pasture in the fields. And as he walked behind his
cattle, they said to him, "Good is the herbage
which is in that place"; and he listened to all that
they said, and he took them to the good place
which they desired. And the cattle which were
before him became exceeding excellent, and they 20
multiplied greatly.

Now at the time of plowing his elder brother said unto him: "Let us make ready for ourselves a goodly yoke of oxen for plowing, for
the land has come out from the water, it is fit
for plowing. Moreover, do thou come to the
field with corn, for we will begin the plowing in the morrow morning." Thus said he to
him; and his younger brother did all things as
his elder brother had spoken unto him to do 30
them.

And when the morn was come, they went to the
fields with their things; and their hearts were
pleased exceedingly with their task in the beginning of their work. And it came to pass after this
that as they were in the field they stopped for
corn, and he sent his younger brother, saying,
"Haste thou, bring to us corn from the farm." And
the younger brother found the wife of his elder
brother, as she was sitting tying her hair. He said 40
to her: "Get up, and give to me corn, that I may
run to the field, for my elder brother hastened me;
do not delay." She said to him: "Go, open the
bin, and thou shalt take to thyself according to thy
will, that I may not drop my locks of hair while
I dress them."

The youth went into the stable; he took a large
measure, for he desired to take much corn; he
loaded it with wheat and barley; and he went out
carrying it. She said to him, "How much of the 50
corn that is wanted, is that which is on thy shoulder?" He said to her: "Three bushels of barley,
and two of wheat, in all five; these are what are

upon my shoulder." Thus said he to her. And
she conversed with him, saying, "There is great
strength in thee, for I see thy might every day."
And her heart knew him with the knowledge of
youth. And she arose and came to him, and conversed with him, saying, "Come, stay with me, and
it shall be well for thee, and I will make for thee
beautiful garments." Then the youth became like
a panther of the south with fury at the evil speech
which she had made to him; and she feared
greatly. And he spake unto her, saying: "Behold
thou art to me as a mother, thy husband is to me
as a father, for he who is elder than I has brought
me up. What is this wickedness that thou hast said
to me? Say it not to me again. For I will not tell
it to any man, for I will not let it be uttered by
the mouth of any man." He lifted up his burden,
and he went to the field and came to his elder
brother; and they took up their work, to labor
at their task.

Now afterward, at eventime, his elder brother
was returning to his house; and the younger
brother was following after his oxen, and he
loaded himself with all the things of the field; and
he brought his oxen before him, to make them lie
down in their stable which was in the farm. And
behold the wife of the elder brother was afraid for
the words which she had said. She took a parcel of
fat, she became like one who is evilly beaten, desiring to say to her husband, "It is thy younger
brother who has done this wrong." Her husband
returned in the even, as was his wont of every day;
he came unto his house; he found his wife ill of
violence; she did not give him water upon his
hands as he used to have, she did not make a light
before him, his house was in darkness, and she was
lying very sick. Her husband said to her, "Who
has spoken with thee?" Behold she said: "No one
has spoken with me except thy younger brother.
When he came to take for thee corn he found me
sitting alone; he said to me, 'Come, let us stay together, tie up thy hair.' Thus spake he to me. I
did not listen to him, but thus spake I to him:
'Behold, am I not thy mother, is not thy elder
brother to thee as a father?' And he feared, and
he beat me to stop me from making report to thee,
and if thou lettest him live I shall die. Now behold
he is coming in the evening; and I complain of
these wicked words, for he would have done this
even in daylight."

And the elder brother became as a panther of
the south; he sharpened his knife; he took it in his
hand; he stood behind the door of his stable to

slay his younger brother as he came in the evening to bring his cattle into the stable.

Now the sun went down, and he loaded himself with herbs in his daily manner. He came, and his foremost cow entered the stable, and she said to her keeper, "Behold thou thy elder brother standing before thee with his knife to slay thee; flee from before him." He heard what his first cow had said; and the next entering, she also said likewise. He looked beneath the door of the stable; he saw the feet of his elder brother; he was standing behind the door, and his knife was in his hand. He cast down his load to the ground, and betook himself to flee swiftly; and his elder brother pursued after him with his knife. Then the younger brother cried out unto Ra Harakhti, saying, "My good Lord! Thou art he who divides the evil from the good." And Ra stood and heard all his cry; and Ra made a wide water between him and his elder brother, and it was full of crocodiles; and the one brother was on one bank, and the other on the other bank; and the elder brother smote twice on his hands at not slaying him. Thus did he. And the younger brother called to the elder on the bank, saying: "Stand still until the dawn of day; and when Ra ariseth, I shall judge with thee before him, and he discerneth between the good and the evil. For I shall not be with thee any more forever; I shall not be in the place in which thou art; I shall go to the valley of the acacia."

Now when the land was lightened, and the next day appeared, Ra Harakhti arose, and one looked unto the other. And the youth spake with his elder brother, saying: "Wherefore camest thou after me to slay me in craftiness, when thou didst not hear the words of my mouth? For I am thy brother in truth, and thou art to me as a father, and thy wife even as a mother: is it not so? Verily, when I was sent to bring for us corn, thy wife said to me, 'Come, stay with me'; for behold this has been turned over unto thee into another wise." And he caused him to understand of all that happened with him and his wife. And he swore an oath by Ra Harakhti, saying, "Thy coming to slay me by deceit with thy knife was an abomination." Then the youth took a knife, and cut off of his flesh, and cast it into the water, and the fish swallowed it. He failed; he became faint; and his elder brother cursed his own heart greatly; he stood weeping for him afar off; he knew not how to pass over to where his younger brother was, because of the crocodiles. And the younger brother called unto him, saying: "Whereas thou hast devised an evil thing, wilt thou not also devise a good thing, even like that which I would do unto thee? When thou goest to thy house thou must look to thy cattle, for I shall not stay in the place where thou art; I am going to the valley of the acacia. And now as to what thou shalt do for me; it is even that thou shalt come to seek after me, if thou perceivest a matter, namely, that there are things happening unto me. And this is what shall come to pass, that I shall draw out my soul, and I shall put it upon the top of the flowers of the acacia, and when the acacia is cut down, and it falls to the ground, and thou comest to seek for it, if thou searchest for it seven years do not let thy heart be wearied. For thou wilt find it, and thou must put it in a cup of cold water, and expect that I shall live again, that I may make answer to what has been done wrong. And thou shalt know of this, that is to say, that things are happening to me, when one shall give to thee a cup of beer in thy hand, and it shall be troubled; stay not then, for verily it shall come to pass with thee."

And the youth went to the valley of the acacia; and his elder brother went unto his house; his hand was laid on his head, and he cast dust on his head; he came to his house, and he slew his wife, he cast her to the dogs, and he sat in mourning for his younger brother.

Now many days after these things, the younger brother was in the valley of the acacia; there was none with him; he spent his time in hunting the beasts of the desert, and he came back in the even to lie down under the acacia, which bore his soul upon the topmost flower. And after this he built himself a tower with his own hands, in the valley of the acacia; it was full of all good things, that he might provide for himself a home.

And he went out from his tower, and he met the Nine Gods, who were walking forth to look upon the whole land. The Nine Gods talked one with another, and they said unto him: "Ho! Bata, bull of the Nine Gods, art thou remaining alone? Thou hast left thy village for the wife of Anpu, thy elder brother. Behold his wife is slain. Thou hast given him an answer to all that was transgressed against thee." And their hearts were vexed for him exceedingly. And Ra Harakhti said to Khnumu, "Behold, frame thou a woman for Bata, that he may not remain alive alone." And Khnumu made for him a mate to dwell with him. She was more beautiful in her limbs than any woman who is in the whole land. The essence of every god was in her. The seven Hathors came to see her: they said with one mouth, "She will die a sharp death."

And Bata loved her very exceedingly, and she dwelt in his house; he passed his time in hunting the beasts of the desert, and brought and laid them before her. He said: "Go not outside, lest the sea seize thee; for I cannot rescue thee from it, for I am a woman like thee; my soul is placed on the head of the flower of the acacia; and if another find it, I must fight with him." And he opened unto her his heart in all its nature.

Now after these things Bata went to hunt in his daily manner. And the young girl went to walk under the acacia which was by the side of her house. Then the sea saw her, and cast its waves up after her. She betook herself to flee from before it. She entered her house. And the sea called unto the acacia, saying, "Oh, would that I could seize her!" And the acacia brought a lock from her hair, and the sea carried it to Egypt, and dropped it in the place of the fullers of Pharaoh's linen. The smell of the lock of hair entered into the clothes of Pharaoh; and they were wroth with the fullers of Pharaoh, saying, "The smell of ointment is in the clothes of Pharaoh." And the people were rebuked every day, they knew not what they should do. And the chief fuller of Pharaoh walked by the bank, and his heart was very evil within him after the daily quarrel with him. He stood still, he stood upon the sand opposite to the lock of hair, which was in the water, and he made one enter into the water and bring it to him; and there was found in it a smell, exceeding sweet. He took it to Pharaoh; and they brought the scribes and the wise men, and they said unto Pharaoh: "This lock of hair belongs to a daughter of Ra Harakhti: the essence of every god is in her, and it is a tribute to thee from another land. Let messengers go to every strange land to seek her: and as for the messenger who shall go to the valley of the acacia, let many men go with him to bring her." Then said his Majesty, "Excellent exceedingly is what has been said to us"; and they sent them. And many days after these things the people who were sent to strange lands came to give report unto the King: but there came not those who went to the valley of the acacia, for Bata had slain them, but let one of them return to give a report to the King. His Majesty sent many men and soldiers, as well as horsemen, to bring her back. And there was a woman among them, and to her had been given in her hand beautiful ornaments

of a woman. And the girl came back with her, and they rejoiced over her in the whole land.

And his Majesty loved her exceedingly, and raised her to high estate; and he spake unto her that she should tell him concerning her husband. And she said, "Let the acacia be cut down, and let one chop it up." And they sent men and soldiers with their weapons to cut down the acacia; and they came to the acacia, and they cut the flower upon which was the soul of Bata, and he fell dead suddenly.

And when the next day came, and the earth was lightened, the acacia was cut down. And Anpu, the elder brother of Bata, entered his house, and washed his hands; and one gave him a cup of beer, and it became troubled; and one gave him another of wine, and the smell of it was evil. Then he took his staff, and his sandals, and likewise his clothes, with his weapons of war; and he betook himself forth to the valley of the acacia. He entered the tower of his younger brother, and he found him lying upon his mat; he was dead. And he wept when he saw his younger brother verily lying dead. And he went out to seek the soul of his younger brother under the acacia tree, under which his younger brother lay in the evening. He spent three years in seeking for it, but found it not. And when he began the fourth year, he desired in his heart to return into Egypt; he said, "I will go tomorrow morn." Thus spake he in his heart.

Now when the land lightened, and the next day appeared, he was walking under the acacia; he was spending his time in seeking it. And he returned in the evening, and labored at seeking it again. He found a seed. He returned with it. Behold this was the soul of his younger brother. He brought a cup of cold water, and he cast the seed into it: and he sat down, as he was wont. Now when the night came his soul sucked up the water; Bata shuddered in all his limbs, and he looked on his elder brother; his soul was in the cup. Then Anpu took the cup of cold water, in which the soul of his younger brother was; Bata drank it, his soul stood again in its place, and he became as he had been. They embraced each other, and they conversed together.

And Bata said to his elder brother: "Behold I am to become as a great bull, which bears every good mark; no one knoweth its history, and thou must sit upon my back. When the sun arises I shall be in the place where my wife is, that I may return answer to her; and thou must take me to the place where the King is. For all good things shall be done for thee; for one shall lade thee with silver and gold, because thou bringest me to Pharaoh, for I become a great marvel, and they shall rejoice for me in all the land. And thou shalt go to thy village."

And when the land was lightened, and the next day appeared, Bata became in the form which he had told to his elder brother. And Anpu sat upon his back until the dawn. He came to the place where the King was, and they made his Majesty to know of him; he saw him, and he was exceeding joyful with him. He made for him great offerings, saying, "This is a great wonder which has come to pass." There were rejoicings over him in the whole land. They presented unto him silver and gold for his elder brother, who went and stayed in his village. They gave to the bull many men and many things, and Pharaoh loved him exceedingly above all that is in this land.

And after many days after these things, the bull entered the purified place; he stood in the place where the princess was; he began to speak with her, saying, "Behold, I am alive indeed." And she said to him, "And, pray, who art thou?" He said to her, "I am Bata. I perceived when thou causedst that they should destroy the acacia of Pharaoh, which was my abode, that I might not be suffered to live. Behold, I am alive indeed, I am as an ox." Then the princess feared exceedingly for the words that her husband had spoken to her. And he went out from the purified place.

And his Majesty was sitting, making a good day with her: she was at the table of his Majesty, and the King was exceeding pleased with her. And she said to his Majesty, "Swear to me by God, saying, 'What thou shalt say, I will obey it for thy sake.'" He hearkened unto all that she said, even this. "Let me eat of the liver of the ox, because he is fit for naught." Thus spake she to him. And the King was exceeding sad at her words, the heart of Pharaoh grieved him greatly. And after the land was lightened, and the next day appeared, they proclaimed a great feast with offerings to the ox. And the King sent one of the chief butchers of his Majesty, to cause the ox to be sacrificed. And when he was sacrificed, as he was upon the shoulders of the people, he shook his neck, and he threw two drops of blood over against the two doors of his Majesty. The one fell upon the one side, on the great door of Pharaoh, and the other upon the other door. They grew as two great Persea trees, and each of them was excellent.

And one went to tell unto his Majesty, "Two great Persea trees have grown, as a great marvel of his Majesty, in the night by the side of the great gate of his Majesty." And there was rejoicing for them in all the land, and there were offerings made to them.

And when the days were multiplied after these things, his Majesty was adorned with the blue crown, with garlands of flowers on his neck, and he was upon the chariot of pale gold, and he went out from the palace to behold the Persea trees: the princess also was going out with horses behind his Majesty. And his Majesty sat beneath one of the Persea trees, and it spake thus with his wife: "Oh, thou deceitful one, I am Bata, I am alive, though I have been evilly entreated. I knew who caused the acacia to be cut down by Pharaoh at my dwelling. I then became an ox, and thou causedst that I should be killed."

And many days after these things the princess stood at the table of Pharaoh, and the King was pleased with her. And she said to his Majesty, "Swear to me by God, saying, 'That which the princess shall say to me I will obey it for her.'" And he hearkened unto all she said. And he commanded, "Let these two Persea trees be cut down, and let them be made into goodly planks." And he hearkened unto all she said. And after this his Majesty sent skillful craftsmen, and they cut down the Persea trees of Pharaoh; and the princess, the royal wife, was standing looking on, and they did all that was in her heart unto the trees. But a chip flew up, and it entered into the mouth of the princess; she swallowed it, and after many days she bore a son. And one went to tell his Majesty, "There is born to thee a son." And they brought him, and gave to him a nurse and servants; and there were rejoicings in the whole land. And the King sat making a merry day, as they were about the naming of him, and his Majesty loved him exceedingly at that moment, and the King raised him to be the royal son of Kush.

Now after the days had multiplied after these things, his Majesty made him heir of all the land. And many days after that, when he had fulfilled many years as heir, his Majesty flew up to heaven. And the heir said, "Let my great nobles of his Majesty be brought before me, that I may make them to know all that has happened to me." And they brought also before him his wife, and he judged with her before him, and they agreed with him. They brought to him his elder brother; he made him hereditary prince in all his land. He was thirty years King of Egypt, and he died, and his elder brother stood in his place on the day of burial.

Excellently finished in peace, for the ka of the scribe of the treasury Kagabu, of the treasury of Pharaoh, and for the scribe Hora, and the scribe Meremapt. Written by the scribe Anena, the owner of this roll. He who speaks against this roll, may Tahuti smite him.

INDIA

THE RIG-VEDA

The Creation Hymn

BOOK X.—HYMN 129

1. Then was not non-existent nor existent: there was no realm of air, no sky beyond it.
   What covered in, and where and what gave shelter? Was water there, unfathomed depth of water?
2. Death was not then, nor was there aught immortal: no sign was there, the day's and night's divider.
   That One Thing, breathless, breathed by its own nature: apart from it was nothing whatsoever.
3. Darkness there was: at first concealed in darkness this All was indiscriminated chaos.
   All that existed then was void and formless: by the great power of Warmth was born that Unit.
4. Thereafter rose Desire in the beginning—Desire, the primal seed and germ of Spirit
   Sages who searched with their heart's thought discovered the existent's kinship in the non-existent.
5. Transversely was their severing line extended: what was above it then, and what below it?
   There were begetters, there were mighty forces, free action here and energy up yonder.
6. Who verily knows and who can here declare it, whence it was born and whence comes this creation?
   The Gods are later than this world's production.

Who knows then whence it first came into being?
7. He, the first origin of this creation, whether he formed it all or did not form it,
   Whose eye controls this world in highest heaven, he verily knows it, or perhaps he knows not.

To the Unknown God

BOOK X.—HYMN 121

1. In the beginning there arose the Golden Child (Hiranya-garbha); as soon as born, he alone was the lord of all that is. He established the earth and this heaven: Who is the God to whom we shall offer sacrifice?
2. He who gives breath, he who gives strength, whose command all the bright gods revere, whose shadow is immortality, whose shadow is death: Who is the God to whom we shall offer sacrifice?
3. He who through his might became the sole king of the breathing and twinkling world, who governs all this, man and beast: Who is the God to whom we shall offer sacrifice?
4. He through whose might these snowy mountains are, and the sea, they say, with the distant river (the Rasa), he of whom these regions are indeed the two arms: Who is the God to whom we shall offer sacrifice?
5. He through whom the awful heaven and the earth were made fast, he through whom the ether was established, and the firmament; he who meas-

The Rig Veda (fourth century B.C.). "The Creation Hymn" translated by R. T. H. Griffith, "To the Unknown God," by F. Max Müller.

ured the air in the sky: Who is the God to whom we shall offer sacrifice?

6. He to whom heaven and earth, standing firm by his will, look up, trembling in their mind; he over whom the risen sun shines forth: Who is the God to whom we shall offer sacrifice?

7. When the great waters went everywhere, holding the germ (Hiranya-garbha), and generating light, then there arose from them the sole breath of the gods: Who is the God to whom we shall offer sacrifice?

8. He who by his might looked even over the waters which held power (the germ) and gen-

erated the sacrifice (light), he who alone is God above all gods: Who is the God to whom we shall offer sacrifice?

9. May he not hurt us, he who is the begetter of the earth, or he, the righteous, who begat the heaven; he who also begat the bright and mighty waters: Who is the God to whom we shall offer sacrifice?

10. Pragâpati, no other than thou embraces all these created things. May that be ours which we desire when sacrificing to thee: may we be lords of wealth![1]

BHAGAVAT GITA

The Transfiguration

ARJUNA. This, for my soul's peace, have I heard
    from thee,
The unfolding of the Mystery Supreme
Named Adhyâtman; comprehending which,
My darkness is dispelled; for now I know—
O Lotus-eyed!—whence is the birth of men,   5
And whence their death, and what the majesties
Of thine immortal rule. Fain would I see,
As thou thyself declar'st it, Sovereign Lord!
The likeness of that glory of thy form
Wholly revealed. O thou Divinest One!   10
If this can be, if I may bear the sight,
Make thyself visible, Lord of all prayers!
Show me thy very self, the Eternal God!
   KRISHNA: Gaze, then, thou Son of Prithâ! I mani-
    fest for thee
Those hundred thousand thousand shapes that
    clothe my Mystery: 15
I show thee all my semblances, infinite, rich, di-
    vine,
My changeful hues, my countless forms. See! in
    this face of mine,
Adityas, Vasus, Rudras, Aswins, and Maruts; see
Wonders unnumbered, Indian Prince! revealed to
    none save thee.
Behold! this is the Universe!—Look! what is live
    and dead   20
I gather all in one—in me! Gaze, as thy lips have
    said,

On God Eternal, Very God! See me! see what thou
    prayest!
. . . .
Thou canst not!—nor, with human eyes, Arjuna!
    ever mayest!
Therefore I give thee sense divine. Have other eyes,
    new light!
And, look! This is my glory, unveiled to mortal
    sight!   25
   SANJAYA: Then, O King! the God, so saying,
    Stood, to Prithâ's Son displaying
    All the splendor, wonder, dread
    Of his vast Almighty-head.
    Out of countless eyes beholding,   30
    Out of countless mouths commanding,
    Countless mystic forms enfolding
    In one form: supremely standing
    Countless radiant glories wearing,
    Countless heavenly weapons bearing,   35
    Crowned with garlands of star-clusters,
    Robed in garb of woven lusters,
    Breathing from his perfect Presence
    Breaths of every subtle essence
    Of all heavenly odors; shedding   40
    Blinding brilliance; overspreading—
    Boundless, beautiful—all spaces
    With his all-regarding faces;
    So he showed! If there should rise
    Suddenly within the skies   45
    Sunburst of a thousand suns
    Flooding earth with beams undeemed-of

[1] This last verse, identifying the "Unknown God" with Pragâpati, is generally regarded as a later addition.
   Bhagavat Gita. Translation by Sir Edward Arnold.

Then might be that Holy One's
Majesty and radiance dreamed of!

So did Pandu's Son behold   50
All this universe enfold
All its huge diversity
Into one vast shape, and be
Visible, and viewed, and blended
In one Body—subtle, splendid,   55
Nameless—th' All-comprehending
God of Gods, the Never-Ending
Deity!

But, sore amazed,
Thrilled, o'erfilled, dazzled, and dazed,
Arjuna knelt; and bowed his head,   60
And clasped his palms; and cried, and said:
ARJUNA: Yea! I have seen! I see!
Lord! all is wrapped in thee!
The gods are in thy glorious frame! the creatures
Of earth, and heaven, and hell   65
In thy Divine form dwell,
And in thy countenance shine all the features

Of Bráhmâ, sitting lone
Upon his lotus-throne;
Of saints and sages, and the serpent races   70
Ananta, Vâsuki;
Yea! mightiest Lord! I see
Thy thousand thousand arms, and breasts, and
faces,

And eyes—on every side
Perfect, diversified;   75
And nowhere end of thee, nowhere beginning,
Nowhere a center! Shifts—
Wherever a soul's gaze lifts—
Thy central Self, all-wielding, and all-winning!

Infinite King! I see   80
The anadem on thee
The club, the shell, the discus; see thee burning
In beams insufferable,
Lighting earth, heaven, and hell
With brilliance blazing, glowing, flashing; turn-
ing   85

Darkness to dazzling day,
Look I whichever way;
Ah, Lord! worship thee, the Undivided,
The Uttermost of thought,
The Treasure-Palace wrought   90
To hold the wealth of the worlds; the Shield pro-
vided

To shelter Virtue's laws;
The Fount whence Life's stream draws
All waters of all rivers of all being:
The One Unborn, Unending: 95
Unchanging and Unbending!
With might and majesty, past thought, past seeing!

Silver of moon and gold
Of sun are glories rolled
From thy great eyes; thy visage, beaming tender
Throughout the stars and skies,   101
Doth to warm life surprise
Thy Universe. The worlds are filled with wonder

Of thy perfections! Space
Star-sprinkled, and void place   105
From pole to pole of the Blue, from bound to
bound,
Hath thee in every spot,
Thee, thee!—Where thou art not,
O Holy, Marvelous Form! is nowhere found!

O Mystic, Awful One!   110
At sight of thee, made known,
The Three Worlds quake; the lower gods draw
nigh thee;
They fold their palms, and bow
Body, and breast, and brow,
And, whispering worship, laud and magnify thee!

Rishis and Siddhas cry   116
"Hail! Highest Majesty!"
From sage and singer breaks the hymn of glory
In dulcet harmony,
Sounding the praise of thee;   120
While countless companies take up the story . . .

These see thee, and revere
In sudden-stricken fear;
Yea! the Worlds—seeing thee with form stupen-
dous,   130
With faces manifold,
With eyes which all behold,
Unnumbered eyes, vast arms, members tremen-
dous,

Flanks, lit with sun and star,
Feet planted near and far,   135
Tushes of terror, mouths wrathful and tender—
The Three wide Worlds before thee
Adore, as I adore thee,
Quake, as I quake, to witness so much splendor!

I mark thee strike the skies   140
    With front, in wondrous wise
Huge, rainbow-painted, glittering; and thy mouth
    Opened, and orbs which see
    All things, whatever be
In all thy worlds, east, west, and north and south.

    O Eyes of God! O Head!   146
    My strength of soul is fled,
Gone is heart's force, rebuked is mind's desire!
    When I behold thee so,
    With awful brows a-glow,   150
With burning glance, and lips lighted by fire

    Fierce as those flames which shall
    Consume, at close of all,
Earth, Heaven! Ah me! I see no Earth and
    Heaven!
    Thee, Lord of Lords! I see,   155
    Thee only—only thee!
Now let thy mercy unto me be given,

    Thou Refuge of the World!
    Lo! to the cavern hurled
Of thy wide-opened throat, and lips white-tushed,
    I see our noblest ones,   161
    Great Dhritarashtra's sons,
Bhishma, Drona, and Karna, caught and crushed!

    The Kings and Chiefs drawn in,
    That gaping gorge within;   165
The best of both these armies torn and riven!
    Between thy jaws they lie,
    Mangled full bloodily,
Ground into dust and death! Like streams down-
    driven

    With helpless haste, which go   170
    In headlong furious flow
Straight to the gulfing deeps of th' unfilled ocean,
    So to that flaming cave
    Those heroes great and brave
Pour, in unending streams, with helpless motion!

    Like moths which in the night   176
    Flutter toward a light,
Drawn to their fiery doom, flying and dying,
    So to their death still throng,
    Blind, dazzled, borne along   180
Ceaselessly, all those multitudes, wild flying!

    Thou, that hast fashioned men,
    Devourest them again,
One with another, great and small, alike!

    The creatures whom thou mak'st,   185
    With flaming jaws thou tak'st,
Lapping them up! Lord God! Thy terrors strike

    From end to end of earth,
    Filling life full, from birth
To death, with deadly, burning, lurid dread!   190
    Ah, Vishnu! make me know
    Why is thy visage so?
Who art thou, feasting thus upon thy dead?

    Who? awful Deity!
    I bow myself to thee,   195
Nâmostu Tê, Devavara! Prasîd![1]
    O Mightiest Lord! rehearse
    Why hast thou face so fierce?
Whence doth this aspect horrible proceed?
    KRISHNA: Thou seest me as Time who kills, Time
        who brings all to doom,   200
The Slayer Time, Ancient of Days, come hither to
    consume;
Excepting thee, of all these hosts of hostile chiefs
    arrayed,
There stands not one shall leave alive the battle-
    field! Dismayed
No longer be! Arise! obtain renown! destroy thy
    foes
Fight for the kingdom waiting thee when thou
    hast vanquished those.   205
By me they fall—not thee! the stroke of death is
    dealt them now,
Even as they show thus gallantly; my instrument
    art thou!
Strike, strong-armed Prince, at Drona! at Bhishma
    strike! deal death
On Karna, Jyadratha; stay all their warlike breath!
'Tis I who bid them perish! Thou wilt but slay the
    slain;   210
Fight! they must fall, and thou must live, victor
    upon this plain!
    SANJAYA: Hearing mighty Keshav's word,
    Tremblingly that helmèd Lord
    Clasped his lifted palms, and praying
    Grace of Krishna—stood there, saying,   215
    With bowed brow and accents broken,
    These words, timorously spoken:

    ARJUNA: Worthily, Lord of Might!
    The whole world hath delight
In thy surpassing power, obeying thee;   220
    The Rakshasas, in dread
    At sight of thee, are sped
To all four quarters; and the company

[1] "Hail to thee, God of Gods! Be favorable!"

Of Siddhas sound thy name.
How should they not proclaim   225
Thy Majesties, Divinest, Mightiest?
Thou Brahm, than Bráhmá greater!
Thou Infinite Creator!
Thou God of gods, Life's Dwelling-place and Rest.

Thou, of all souls the Soul!   230
The Comprehending Whole!
Of being formed, and formless being the Framer;
O Utmost One! O Lord!
Older than eld, who stored
The worlds with wealth of life! O Treasure-
        Claimer,   235
Who wottest all, and art
Wisdom thyself! O Part
In all, and All; for all from thee have risen
Numberless now I see
The aspects are of thee! . . .   240
Hail to thee! Praise to thee! Thou One in all;

For thou art All! Yea, thou!   260
Ah! if in anger now
Thou shouldst remember I did think thee Friend,
Speaking with easy speech,
As men use each to each;
Did call thee "Krishna," "Prince," nor compre-
        hend   265

Thy hidden Majesty,
The might, the awe of thee;
Did, in my heedlessness, or in my love,
On journey, or in jest,
Or when we lay at rest,   270
Sitting at council, straying in the grove,

Alone, or in the throng,
Do thee, most Holy! wrong,
Be thy grace granted for that witless sin
For thou art, now I know,   275
Father of all below,
Of all above, of all the worlds within

Garu of Gurus; more
To reverence and adore
Than all which is adorable and high!   280
How, in the wide worlds three
Should any equal be?
Should any other share thy Majesty?

Therefore, with body bent
And reverent intent,   285
I praise, and serve, and seek thee, asking grace.
As father to a son,
As friend to friend, as one
Who loveth to his lover, turn thy face

In gentleness on me!   290
Good is it I did see
This unknown marvel of thy Form! But fear
Mingles with joy! Retake,
Dear Lord! for pity's sake
Thine earthly shape, which earthly eyes may bear;

Be merciful, and show   296
The visage that I know;
Let me regard thee, as of yore, arrayed
With disk and forehead-gem,
With mace and anadem,   300
Thou that sustainest all things! Undismayed

Let me once more behold
The form I loved of old,
Thou of the thousand arms and countless eyes!
This frightened heart is fain   305
To see restored again
My Charioteer, in Krishna's kind disguise.
    KRISHNA: Yea! thou hast seen, Arjuna! because
        I loved thee well,
The secret countenance of me, revealed by mystic
        spell,
Shining, and wonderful, and vast, majestic, mani-
        fold,   310
Which none save thou in all the years had favor
        to behold;
For not by Vedas cometh this, nor sacrifice, nor
        alms,
Nor works well-done, nor penance long, nor
        prayers, nor chanted psalms,
That mortal eyes should bear to view the Immortal
        Soul unclad,
Prince of the Kurus! This was kept for thee alone!
        Be glad!   315
Let no more trouble shake thy heart, because thine
        eyes have seen
My terror with my glory. As I before have been
So will I be again for thee; with lightened heart
        behold!
Once more I am thy Krishna, the form thou
        knew'st of old!
    SANJAYA: These words to Arjuna spake   320
        Vâsudev, and straight did take
        Back again the semblance dear
        Of the well-loved charioteer;
        Peace and joy it did restore
        When the Prince beheld once more   325
        Mighty Bráhmá's form and face
        Clothed in Krishna's gentle grace
    ARJUNA: Now that I see come back, Janârdana!

This friendly human frame, my mind can think
Calm thoughts once more; my heart beats still
    again!   330
  KRISHNA: Yea! it was wonderful and terrible
To view me as thou didst, dear Prince! The gods
Dread and desire continually to view!
Yet not by Vedas, nor from sacrifice,
Nor penance, nor gift-giving, nor with prayer 335

Shall any so behold, as thou hast seen!
Only by fullest service, perfect faith,
And uttermost surrender am I known
And seen, and entered into, Indian Prince!
Who doeth all for me; who findeth me   340
In all; adoreth always; loveth all
Which I have made, and me, for Love's sole end,
That man, Arjuna! unto me doth wend.

THE PANCHATANTRA

How the Crow-Hen Killed the Black Snake

In a certain region grew a great banyan tree. In it
lived a crow and his wife, occupying the nest which
they had built. But a black snake crawled through
the hollow trunk and ate their chicks as fast as
they were born, even before baptism. Yet for all
his sorrow over this violence, the poor crow could
not desert the old familiar banyan and seek another tree. For

> Three cannot be induced to go—
> The deer, the cowardly man, the crow:
> Three go when insult makes them pant—
> The lion, hero, elephant.

At last the crow-hen fell at her husband's feet
and said: "My dear lord, a great many children of
mine have been eaten by that awful snake. And
grief for my loved and lost haunts me until I think
of moving. Let us make our home in some other
tree. For

> No friend like health abounding;
>   And like disease, no foe;
> No love like love of children;
>   Like hunger-pangs, no woe.

And again:

> With fields o'erhanging rivers,
>   With wife on flirting bent,
> Or in a house with serpents,
>   No man can be content.

We are living in deadly peril."
  At this the crow was dreadfully depressed, and
he said: "We have lived in this tree a long time,
my dear. We cannot desert it. For

> Where water may be sipped, and grass
>   Be cropped, a deer might live content;
> Yet insult will not drive him from
>   The wood where all his life was spent.

Moreover, by some shrewd device I will bring
death upon this villainous and mighty foe."
  "But," said his wife, "this is a terribly venomous
snake. How will you hurt him?" And he replied:
"My dear, even if I have not the power to hurt
him, still I have friends who possess learning, who
have mastered the works on ethics. I will go and
get from them some shrewd device of such nature
that the villain—curse him!—will soon meet his
doom."
  After this indignant speech he went at once to
another tree, under which lived a dear friend, a
jackal. He courteously called the jackal forth, related all his sorrow, then said: "My friend, what
do you consider opportune under the circumstances? The killing of our children is sheer death
to my wife and me."
  "My friend," said the jackal, "I have thought the
matter through. You need not put yourself out.
That villainous black snake is near his doom by
reason of his heartless cruelty. For

> Of means to injure brutal foes
>   You do not need to think,
> Since of themselves they fall, like trees
>   Upon the river's brink.

And there is a story:

> A heron ate what fish he could,
>   The bad, indifferent, and good;
> His greed was never satisfied
> Till, strangled by a crab, he died."

  "How was that?" asked the crow. And the
jackal told the story of

The Heron That Liked Crab-meat

  There was once a heron in a certain place on the
edge of a pond. Being old, he sought an easy way

The Panchatantra. Translated by Arthur W. Ryder. By permission of The University of Chicago Press.

of catching fish on which to live. He began by lingering at the edge of his pond, pretending to be quite irresolute, not eating even the fish within his reach.

Now among the fish lived a crab. He drew near and said: "Uncle, why do you neglect today your usual meals and amusements?" And the heron replied: "So long as I kept fat and flourishing by eating fish, I spent my time pleasantly, enjoying the taste of you. But a great disaster will soon befall you. And as I am old, this will cut short the pleasant course of my life. For this reason I feel depressed."

"Uncle," said the crab, "of what nature is the disaster?" And the heron continued: "Today I overheard the talk of a number of fishermen as they passed near the pond. 'This is a big pond,' they were saying, 'full of fish. We will try a cast of the net tomorrow or the day after. But today we will go to the lake near the city.' This being so, you are lost, my food supply is cut off, I too am lost, and in grief at the thought, I am indifferent to food today."

Now when the water-dwellers heard the trickster's report, they all feared for their lives and implored the heron, saying: "Uncle! Father! Brother! Friend! Thinker! Since you are informed of the calamity, you also know the remedy. Pray save us from the jaws of this death."

Then the heron said: "I am a bird, not competent to contend with men. This, however, I can do. I can transfer you from this pond to another, a bottomless one." By this artful speech they were so led astray that they said: "Uncle! Friend! Unselfish kinsman! Take me first! Me first! Did you never hear this?

> Stout hearts delight to pay the price
> Of merciful self-sacrifice,
> Count life as nothing, if it end
> In gentle service to a friend."

Then the old rascal laughed in his heart, and took counsel with his mind, thus: "My shrewdness has brought these fishes into my power. They ought to be eaten very comfortably." Having thus thought it through, he promised what the thronging fish implored, lifted some in his bill, carried them a certain distance to a slab of stone, and ate them there. Day after day he made the trip with supreme delight and satisfaction, and meeting the fish, kept their confidence by ever new inventions.

One day the crab, disturbed by the fear of death, importuned him with the words: "Uncle, pray save me, too, from the jaws of death." And the heron reflected: "I am quite tired of this unvarying fish diet. I should like to taste him. He is different, and choice." So he picked up the crab and flew through the air.

But since he avoided all bodies of water and seemed planning to alight on the sun-scorched rock, the crab asked him: "Uncle, where is that pond without any bottom?" And the heron laughed and said: "Do you see that broad, sun-scorched rock? All the water-dwellers have found repose there. Your turn has now come to find repose."

Then the crab looked down and saw a great rock of sacrifice, made horrible by heaps of fish-skeletons. And he thought: "Ah me!

> Friends are foes and foes are friends
> As they mar or serve your ends;
> Few discern where profit tends.

Again:

> If you will, with serpents play;
> Dwell with foemen who betray:
> Shun your false and foolish friends,
> Fickle, seeking vicious ends.

Why, he has already eaten these fish whose skeletons are scattered in heaps. So what might be an opportune course of action for me? Yet why do I need to consider?

> Man is bidden to chastise
> Even elders who devise
> Devious courses, arrogant,
> Of their duty ignorant.

Again:

> Fear fearful things, while yet
>   No fearful thing appears;
> When danger must be met,
>   Strike, and forget your fears.

So, before he drops me there, I will catch his neck with all four claws."

When he did so, the heron tried to escape, but being a fool, he found no parry to the grip of the crab's nippers, and had his head cut off.

Then the crab painfully made his way back to the pond, dragging the heron's neck as if it had been a lotus-stalk. And when he came among the fish, they said: "Brother, why come back?" Thereupon he showed the head as his credentials and said: "He enticed the water-dwellers from every quarter, deceived them with his prevarications, dropped them on a slab of rock not far away, and ate them. But I—further life being predestined—perceived that he destroyed the trustful, and I have brought back his neck. Forget your worries. All the water-dwellers shall live in peace."

"And that is why I say:

A heron ate what fish he could, . . .

and the rest of it."

"My friend," said the crow, "tell me how this villainous snake is to meet his doom." And the jackal answered: "Go to some spot frequented by a great monarch. There seize a golden chain or a necklace from some wealthy man who guards it carelessly. Deposit this in such a place that when it is recovered, the snake may be killed."

So the crow and his wife straightway flew off at random, and the wife came upon a certain pond. As she looked about, she saw the women of a king's court playing in the water, and on the bank they had laid golden chains, pearl necklaces, garments, and gems. One chain of gold the crow-hen seized and started for the tree where she lived.

But when the chamberlains and the eunuchs saw the theft, they picked up clubs and ran in pursuit. Meanwhile, the crow-hen dropped the golden chain in the snake's hole and waited at a safe distance.

Now when the king's men climbed the tree, they found a hole and in it a black snake with swelling hood. So they killed him with their clubs, recovered the golden chain, and went their way. Thereafter the crow and his wife lived in peace.

Leap and Creep

In the palace of a certain king stood an incomparable bed, blessed with every cubiculary virtue. In a corner of its coverlet lived a female louse named Creep. Surrounded by a thriving family of sons and daughters, with the sons and daughters of sons and daughters, and with more remote descendants, she drank the king's blood as he slept. On this diet she grew plump and handsome.

While she was living there in this manner, a flea named Leap drifted in on the wind and dropped on the bed. This flea felt supreme satisfaction on examining the bed—the wonderful delicacy of its coverlet, its double pillow, its exceptional softness like that of a broad, Gangetic sandbank, its delicious perfume. Charmed by the sheer delight of touching it, he hopped this way and that until—fate willed it so—he chanced to meet Creep,

who said to him: "Where do *you* come from? This is a dwelling fit for a king. Begone, and lose no time about it." "Madam," said he, "you should not say such things. For

The Brahman reverences fire,
Himself the lower castes' desire;
The wife reveres her husband dear;
But all the world must guests revere.

Now I am your guest. I have of late sampled the various blood of Brahmans, warriors, business men, and serfs, but found it acid, slimy, quite unwholesome. On the contrary, he who reposes on this bed must have a delightful vital fluid, just like nectar. It must be free from morbidity, since wind, bile, and phlegm are kept in harmony by constant and heedful use of potions prepared by physicians. It must be enriched by viands unctuous, tender, melting in the mouth; viands prepared from the flesh of the choicest creatures of land, water, and air, seasoned furthermore with sugar, pomegranate, ginger, and pepper. To me it seems an elixir of life. Therefore, with your kind permission, I plan to taste this sweet and fragrant substance, thus combining pleasure and profit."

"No," said she. "For fiery-mouthed stingers like you, it is out of the question. Leave this bed. You know the proverb:

The fool who does not know
His own resource, his foe,
His duty, time, and place,
Who sets a reckless pace,
Will by the wayside fall,
Will reap no fruit at all."

Thereupon he fell at her feet, repeating his request. And she agreed, since courtesy was her hobby, and since, when the story of that prince of sharpers, Muladeva, was being repeated to the king while she lay on a corner of the coverlet, she had heard how Muladeva quoted this verse in answer to the question of a certain damsel:

Whoever, angry though he be,
Has spurned a suppliant enemy,
In Shiva, Vishnu, Brahma, he
Has scorned the Holy Trinity.

Recalling this, she agreed, but added: "However, you must not come to dinner at a wrong place or time." "What is the right place and what is the right time?" he asked. "Being a newcomer, I am not *au courant*." And she replied: "When the king's body is mastered by wine, fatigue, or sleep, then you may quietly bite him on the feet. This is the right place and the right time." To these conditions he gave his assent.

In spite of this arrangement, the famished bungler, when the king had just dozed off in the early evening, bit him on the back. And the poor king, as if burned by a firebrand, as if stung by a scorpion, as if touched by a torch, bounded to his feet, scratched his back, and cried to a servant: "Rascal! Somebody bit me. You must hunt through this bed until you find the insect."

Now Leap heard the king's command and in terrified haste crept into a crevice in the bed. Then the king's servants entered, and following their master's orders, brought a lamp and made a minute inspection. As fate would have it, they came upon Creep as she crouched in the nap of the fabric, and killed her with her family.

The Mice That Ate Iron

In a certain town lived a merchant named Naduk, who lost his money and determined to travel abroad. For

> The meanest of mankind is he
> Who, having lost his money, can
> Inhabit lands or towns where once
> He spent it like a gentleman.

And again:

> The neighbor gossips blame
> His poverty as shame
> Who long was wont to play
> Among them, proud and gay.

In his house was an iron balance-beam inherited from his ancestors, and it weighed a thousand *pals*. This he put in pawn with Merchant Lakshman before he departed for foreign countries.

Now after he had long traveled wherever business led him through foreign lands, he returned to his native city and said to Merchant Lakshman: "Friend Lakshman, return my deposit, the balance-beam." And Lakshman said: "Friend Naduk, your balance-beam has been eaten by mice."

To this Naduk replied: "Lakshman, you are in no way to blame, if it has been eaten by mice. Such is life. Nothing in the universe has any permanence. However, I am going to the river for a bath. Please send your boy Money-God with me, to carry my bathing things."

Since Lakshman was conscience-stricken at his own theft, he said to his son Money-God: "My dear boy, let me introduce Uncle Naduk, who is going to the river to bathe. You must go with him and carry his bathing things." Ah, there is too much truth in the saying:

> There is no purely loving deed
> Without a pinch of fear or greed
> Or service of a selfish need.

And again:

> Wherever there is fond attention
> That does not seek a service pension,
> Was there no timid apprehension?

So Lakshman's son took the bathing things and delightedly accompanied Naduk to the river. After Naduk had taken his bath, he thrust Lakshman's son Money-God into a mountain cave, blocked the entrance with a great rock, and returned to Lakshman's house. And when Lakshman said: "Friend Naduk, tell me what has become of my son Money-God who went with you," Naduk answered: "My good Lakshman, a hawk carried him off from the river-bank."

"Oh, Naduk!" cried Lakshman. "You liar! How could a hawk possibly carry off a big boy like Money-God?" "But, Lakshman," retorted Naduk, "the mice could eat a balance-beam made of iron. Give me my balance-beam, if you want your son."

Finally, they carried their dispute to the palace gate, where Lakshman cried in a piercing tone: "Help! Help! A ghastly deed! This Naduk person has carried off my son—his name is Money-God."

Thereupon the magistrates said to Naduk: "Sir, restore the boy to Lakshman." But Naduk pleaded: "What am I to do? Before my eyes a hawk carried him from the river-bank." "Come, Naduk!" said they, "you are not telling the truth. How can a hawk carry off a fifteen-year-old boy?" Then Naduk laughed outright and said: "Gentlemen, listen to my words.

> Where mice eat balance-beams of iron
> A thousand *pals* in weight,
> A hawk might steal an elephant;
> A boy is trifling freight."

"How was that?" they asked, and Naduk told them the story of the balance-beam. At this they laughed and caused the restoration of balance-beam and boy to the respective owners.

CHINA

CONFUCIUS

Analects

The Master said: "In governing, cleave to good; as the north star holds his place, and the multitude of stars revolve upon him."

The Master said: "To sum up the three hundred songs in a word, they are free from evil thought."

The Master said: "Guide the people by law, subdue them by punishment; they may shun crime, but will be void of shame. Guide them by example, subdue them by courtesy; they will learn shame, and come to be good."

The Master said: "At fifteen, I was bent on study; at thirty, I could stand; at forty, doubts ceased; at fifty, I understood the laws of Heaven; at sixty, my ears obeyed me; at seventy, I could do as my heart lusted, and never swerve from right."

Meng Yi asked the duty of a son.

The Master said: "Obedience."

As Fan Ch'ih was driving him, the Master said: "Meng-sun asked me the duty of a son; I answered 'Obedience.'"

"What did ye mean?" said Fan Ch'ih.

"To serve our parents with courtesy whilst they live," said the Master; "to bury them with all courtesy when they die; and to worship them with all courtesy."

Meng Wu asked the duty of a son.

The Master said: "What weighs on your father and mother is concern for your health."

Tzu-yu asked the duty of a son.

The Master said: "To-day a man is called dutiful if he keep both our dogs and horses, and unless we honor parents, is it not all one?"

Tzu-hsia asked the duty of a son.

The Master said: "Our manner is the hard part. For the young to be a stay in toil, and leave the wine and cakes to their elders, is this to fulfil their duty?"

The Master said: "If I talk all day to Hui, like a dullard, he never stops me. But when he is gone, if I pry into his life, I find he can do what I say. No, Hui is no dullard."

The Master said: "Look at a man's acts; watch his motives; find out what pleases him: can the man evade you? Can the man evade you?"

The Master said: "Who keeps the old akindle and adds new knowledge is fitted to be a teacher."

The Master said: "A gentleman is not a vessel."

Tzu-kung asked, What is a gentleman?

The Master said: "He puts words into deeds first, and sorts what he says to the deed."

The Master said: "A gentleman is broad and fair: the vulgar are biassed and petty."

The Master said: *"Study without thought is vain: thought without study is dangerous."*

The Master said: "Work on strange doctrines does harm."

The Master said: "Yu, shall I teach thee what is understanding? *To know what we know, and know what we do not know, that is understanding."*

Tzu-chang studied with an eye to pay.

The Master said: "Listen much, keep silent when in doubt, and always take heed of the tongue; thou wilt make few mistakes. See much, beware of pitfalls, and always give heed to thy walk; thou wilt have little to rue. If thy words are seldom wrong, thy deeds leave little to rue, pay will follow."

Duke Ai asked, What should be done to make the people loyal?

Confucius answered: "Exalt the straight, set aside the crooked, the people will be loyal. Exalt the crooked, set aside the straight, the people will be disloyal."

Chi K'ang asked how to make the people lowly, faithful, and willing.

The Master said: "Behave with dignity, they will be lowly: be pious and merciful, they will be faithful: exalt the good, teach the unskilful, they will grow willing."

One said to Confucius: "Why are ye not in power, Sir?"

Confucius (551-478 B.C.).

The Master answered: "What does the book say of a good son? 'An always dutiful son, who is a friend to his brothers, showeth the way to rule.' This also is to rule. What need to be in power?"

The Master said: "Without truth I know not how man can live. A cart without a crosspole, a carriage without harness, how could they be moved?"

Tzu-chang asked whether we can know what is to be ten generations hence.

The Master said: "The Yin inherited the manners of the Hsia; the harm and the good that they wrought them is known. The Chou inherited the manners of the Yin; the harm and the good that they wrought them is known. And we may know what is to be, even an hundred generations hence, when others follow Chou."

The Master said: "To worship the ghosts of strangers is fawning. To see the right and not do it is want of courage."

The Master said: "Love makes a spot beautiful: who chooses not to dwell in love, has he got wisdom?"

The Master said: *"Loveless men cannot bear need long, they cannot bear fortune long.* Loving hearts find peace in love; clever heads find profit in it."

The Master said: "A man and his faults are of a piece. By watching his faults we learn whether love be his."

The Master said: "To learn the truth at daybreak and die at eve were enough."

The Master said: "A scholar in search of truth who is ashamed of poor clothes and poor food it is idle talking to."

The Master said: "A gentleman has no likes and no dislikes below heaven. He follows right."

The Master said: "Gentlemen cherish worth; the vulgar cherish dirt. Gentlemen trust in justice; the vulgar trust in favour."

The Master said: *"The chase of gain is rich in hate."*

The Master said: "Be not concerned at want of place; be concerned that thou stand thyself. Sorrow not at being unknown, but seek to be worthy of note."

The Master said: "Who contains himself goes seldom wrong."

The Master said: "A gentleman wishes to be slow to speak and quick to act."

The Master said: "Good is no hermit. It has ever neighbours."

The Master said: "One thread, Shen, runs through all my teaching."

"Yes," said Tseng-tzu.

After the Master had left, the disciples asked what was meant.

Tseng-tzu said: "The Master's teaching all hangs on faithfulness and fellow-feeling."

CHINESE POEMS

Home

Great trees in the south
Give me no shelter,
And women loitering by the Han
Leave me cold.

O Han too deep for diving,   5
O Kiang too long for poling!

Faggots, brambles,
I cut them with a will—
But those girls facing home,
I should like to feed their horses.   10

O Han too deep for diving,
O Kiang too long for poling!

Faggots, artemisia,
I cut them with a will—
But those girls facing home,   15
I should like to feed their colts.

O Han too deep for diving,
O Kiang too long for poling!

—AUTHOR UNKNOWN

Bringing in the Wine

See how the Yellow River's waters move from
  heaven,
Entering the ocean, never to return!
See how lovely locks in bright mirrors in high
  chambers,
Though silken black at morning, have turned by
  night to snow!
O let a man of spirit venture where he pleases 5
And never tip his golden cup empty towards the
  moon!
Since heaven gave the talent, let it be employed!
Spin a thousand pieces of silver, all of them come
  back!
Cook a sheep, kill a cow, whet the appetite,
And make me, of three hundred bowls, one long
  drink!   10

To old Master Ts'en
And young Tan-ch'iu
Bring in the wine!
Let your cups never rest!
Let me sing you a song!   15
Let your ears attend!
What are bell and drum, rare dishes and treasure?
Let me be forever drunk and never come to
  reason!
Sober men of older days and sages are forgotten,
And only the great drinkers are famous for all
  time.   20
Prince Ch'en paid at a banquet in the Palace of
  Perfection,
Ten thousand coins for a bucket of wine, with
  many a laugh and quip . . .
Why say, my host, that your money is gone?
Go and buy wine and we'll drink it together!
My flower-spotted horse,   25
My furs worth a thousand,
Hand them to the boy to exchange for good wine,
And we'll drown away the woe of ten thousand
  generations!

—LI PO

Answering Vice-Prefect Chang

As the years go by, give me but peace,
Freedom from ten thousand matters.
I ask myself and always answer,
What can be better than coming home?
A wind from the pine-trees blows my sash,
And my lute is bright with the mountain-moon.
You ask me about good and evil? . . .
Hark, on the lake there's a fisherman singing!

WANG WEI

What Should a Man Want?

"Tell me now, what should a man want
But to sit alone sipping his cup of wine?"
I should like to have visitors come to discuss
  philosophy
And not to have tax-collectors coming to collect
  taxes;

Chinese Poems. The following poems taken from *The Jade Mountain* by Witter Bynner and Kiang Kang-hu and from *170 Chinese Poems* by Arthur Waley are used by permission of Alfred A. Knopf, Inc.
Home. Translated by Witter Bynner and Kiang Kang-hu.
Bringing in the Wine. Li Po (705-762). Translated by Witter Bynner and Kiang Kang-hu.
Wang Wei (699-759). Translations by Witter Bynner and Kiang Kang-hu.

My three sons married into good families,
My five daughters provided with steady husbands;
Then I could jog through a happy five score years,
Craving no cloud-ascent, no resurrection.

—WANG CHI

The Beautiful Hsi-Shih

Since beauty is honored all over the empire,
How could Hsi-shih remain humbly at home?
At dawn washing clothes by a lake in Yueh;
At dusk in the palace of Wu, a great lady!
Poor, no rarer than the others—   5
Exalted, everyone praising her rareness.
But above all honors, the honor was hers
Of blinding with passion an emperor's reason.
Girls who had once washed silk beside her
Now were ordered away from her carriage . . .
Ask them, in her neighbors' houses,   11
If by wrinkling their brows they can copy her
  beauty.

—WANG WEI

Anxiety of a Young Lady to Get Married

Ripe, the plums fall from the bough:
Only seven tenths left there now!
Ye whose hearts on me are set,
Now the time is fortunate!

Ripe, the plums fall from the bough;   5
Only three tenths left there now!
Ye who wish my love to gain,
Will not now apply in vain!

No more plums upon the bough!
All are in my basket now!   10
Ye who me with ardor seek,
Need the word but freely speak!

—AUTHOR UNKNOWN

A Complaint

The wind blows from the north.
He looks and his eyes are cold.
He looks and smiles and then goes forth,
My grief grows old.

The wind blows and the dust.   5
Tomorrow he swears he will come.
His words are kind, but he breaks his trust,
My heart is numb.

All day the wind blew strong,
The sun was buried deep.   10
I have thought of him so long, so long,
I cannot sleep.

The clouds are black with night,
The thunder brings no rain.
I wake and there is no light,   15
I bear my pain.

—LADY CHWANG KËANG

A View of T'ai-Shan

What shall I say of the Great Peak?
The ancient Dukedoms are everywhere green,
Inspired and stirred by the breath of Creation;
With the Twin Forces balancing day and night,
I open my breast toward widening clouds,
And I strain my sight after birds flying home . . .
When shall I climb to the top and hold
All mountains in a single glance!

—TU FU

With Her Beauty

Lovelier than all the rest,
But living alone in an empty valley,
She says that she came from an excellent clan
Which is humbled now among grasses and tree-
  trunks . . .
When trouble arose in the Küan district,   5
Her brothers and close kin were killed.
What use were their high offices,
Not even saving their own lives!
The world has but scorn for adversity;
And hope goes out, like the light of a candle.   10
Her husband, with a vagrant heart,
Finds a new love like a new piece of jade;
And when morning-glories furl at night
And mandarin-ducks lie side by side,
All he can see is the smile of the new love   15
While the old love weeps unheard.
Pure was the spring in its mountain-source,
But away from the mountain its waters are
  roiled . . .
Waiting for her maid to come from selling pearls
For straw to cover the roof again,   20
She breaks off flowers, not now for her hair,
And absently fills up her hand with pine needles
And, forgetting her worn silk sleeve, and the cold,
Leans in the sunset by a tall bamboo.

—TU FU

Wang Chi. About 700 A.D. Translated by Arthur Waley.
Anxiety of a Young Lady . . . Translated by James Legge.
A Complaint. 718 B.C. Translated by James Legge; revised by Helen Waddell.
A View of T'ai-Shan and *With Her Beauty.* Tu Fu (712-770). Translated by Witter Bynner and
Kiang Kang-hu.

In Absence

White gleam the gulls across the darkling tide,
On the green hills the red flowers seem to burn;
Alas! I see another spring has died . . .
When will it come—the day of my return?

—TU FU

The Red Cockatoo

Sent as a present from Annam—
A red cockatoo.
Colored like the peach-tree blossom,
Speaking with the speech of men.

And they did to it what is always done
To the learned and eloquent.
They took a cage with stout bars
And shut it up inside.

—PO CHÜ-I

Madly Singing in the Mountains

There is no one among men that has not a special
    failing:
And my failing consists in writing verses.
I have broken away from the thousand ties of life:
But this infirmity still remains behind.
Each time that I look at a fine landscape: 5
Each time that I meet a loved friend,
I raise my voice and recite a stanza of poetry
And am glad as though a god had crossed my
    path.

Ever since the day I was banished to Hsün-yang
Half my time I have lived among the hills.   10
And often, when I have finished a new poem,
Alone I climb the road to the Eastern Rock.
I lean my body on the banks of white stone:
I pull down with my hands a green cassia branch.
My mad singing startles the valleys and hills: 15
The apes and birds all come to peep.
Fearing to become a laughing-stock to the world,
I choose a place that is unfrequented by men.

—PO CHÜ-I

A Cicada

Pure of heart and therefore hungry,
All night long you cry in vain
With a final, broken, indrawn breath.
Among the green, indifferent trees . . .
Knocking about like a piece of driftwood,
Letting my garden fill with weeds,
I bless you for your true advice
To purify my life again.

—LI SHANG-YIN

Homeward

No letters to the frontier come,
The winter softens into spring . . .
I tremble as I draw near home,
And dare not ask what news you bring.

—LI PIN

In Absence. Tu Fu. Translated by Herbert A. Giles.
Po Chü-I (772-846). Translated by Arthur Waley.
Li Shang-Yin (813-858). Translated by Witter Bynner and Kiang Kang-hu.
Li Pin. About 854 A.D. Translated by Herbert A. Giles.

THE MOHAMMEDAN WORLD

Although the areas occupied by the Mohammedan cultures of the Near East—Persia and Arabia—had pre-Mohammedan civilizations, they attained literary importance largely after the triumph of the prophet Mahomet and his successors. For several centuries the people of this faith outshone medieval European man in everything cultural, and contributed to his development more than ancient Greece and Rome.

From time immemorial, Arabia, homeland of Mohammedanism, had been populated by nomads of the Semitic race, continually warring against one another and frequently drifting into Egypt, the Mediterranean coast of Asia Minor, and Mesopotamia. In Arabia proper, there were no world-shaking events, and its literature, rich in impassioned love poetry, was unknown to the outside world. Even in the seventh century A.D. the mass of the population was poor and undeveloped, and only along the main caravan routes of the south did two cities, Mecca and Medina, enjoy some prosperity and cultivation. Except for Jewish colonists and proselytes, the people were pagans, and their worship centered in a Meccan sanctuary known as the Kaaba, the chief feature of which was a meteorite; it was regarded as a god superior to the many minor tribal deities. This was the spiritual condition of the Arabs when an unlettered man, born in 570, began to ruminate on religious matters and came to regard himself as the sole prophet of a new faith.

In his fortieth year, Mahomet (Mohammed or Muhammad), probably influenced by both Judaism and Christianity during his travels, began to preach monotheism. As his influence spread, his native city became alarmed for it had subsisted on the polytheistic cult that brought numerous pilgrims to the Kaaba. At last he had to flee for his life, but he found a ready following in the rival city of Medina. This flight (the *Hegira*), in 622 A.D., proved a memorable event and, after some fighting, the prophet's faction triumphed. Mecca accepted his religion under the terms of a compromise requiring all Mohammedans to turn toward Mecca while praying. Before he died in 632 Mahomet was master of all Arabia.

There was little originality in his teachings, which amalgamated Judaism and Christianity and ranked both Moses and Jesus as prophets next in importance to Mahomet. There was as little sublimity in his religion as in his life, which was marred by cruelty and sensuality. Nevertheless, the new faith of Islam swept over Asia Minor and northern Africa, and was ultimately carried into Spain. Its tenets were simple and unmetaphysical. It appealed to an uncritical imagination with its clear-cut division between paradise and hell, its ornate fancifulness, and its promise of happiness to the believer who, upon passing *Al Sirat* (the Bridge of Judgment), would be permanently settled in a luxurious garden tended by beautiful nymphs (the Houris), and would receive seventy-two wives and eighty thousand servants. A multitude of angels, demons, *peris* (fairies), and *devs* (giants) peopled the Mohammedan world, and ensured a life of perpetual wonder and excitement.[1] So at-

---

[1] Three Mohammedan names have become familiar to the reader of English literature: *Israfel*, the trumpeter of the Last Judgment and the angel of music (see Poe's poem, *Israfel*); *Azrael*, the angel of death; *Eblis*, the prince of darkness, the chief demon of the fallen angels.

480

tractive was Arabian mythology that it entered Europe in the eleventh century and became an element in medieval and Renaissance romances. During the romantic movement of the late eighteenth and early nineteenth centuries, this fanciful world also attracted much attention. Goethe, Robert Southey, Thomas Moore, Byron, and others used Mohammedan themes and backgrounds.

The ethics of this faith, moreover, "established in the world a great tradition of dignified fair dealing, they breathe a spirit of generosity, and they are human and workable."[2] The faithful are ordered to observe considerate treatment of women and slaves, kindliness in daily conduct, and the brotherhood of all members of the faith. The book which contains Mahomet's teachings, the *Koran*,[3] is one of the Bibles of the world. It presents in rhythmical prose the revelations of the one god Allah to his prophet. Though undistinguished as a whole and confusingly arranged, it nevertheless has ethical fervor and some exalted passages.

Under the leadership of the Prophet's friend, Abu Bekr, who became the first *Caliph* (Successor), the Arabs began their attempted subjugation of the world. The worship of Allah was carried by the sword to the very gates of Constantinople, throughout the eastern Mediterranean countries, through Persia, into parts of India, and beyond. Mohammedanism overran all of northern Africa and Spain, and was turned back in the eighth century only in southern France. Religious dissension, intrigue in the harems of rulers, and oriental luxury began to corrode the Arab world, but it was some centuries before it crumbled. It was strong enough to resist successive European invasions. Although the Crusaders succeeded in capturing and holding Jerusalem for a time, they could not prevail against the Arabs in Palestine, and Christian Spain could not drive them out until the end of the fifteenth century, shortly before Columbus started on his voyage of discovery. When, moreover, the Arabs were conquered by the Mongol Turks, Mohammedanism continued to spread over the world, for the Turks, who had adopted the faith, captured Constantinople and conquered all of the Balkans.

Although the conquests brought much misery to Christian Europe (reflected in many slurs on the character and religion of the Arabs), it remains true that, until the thirteenth century and even later, Mohammedan culture was higher than anything Europe could show. The Arab world, coming into contact with Greek, Jewish, and Hindu civilization, flowered magnificently in science, art, and literature. Great universities arose in Bagdad, Cairo, and Spanish Cordoba. Their scientists devoted themselves to important research and invention. In mathematics, building on Greek foundations, the Arabs developed algebra, spherical trigonometry, and the decimal system of notation; they also gave the world the useful Arabic system of numerals, and invented the zero. They modernized medicine, discovered new chemical substances, constructed astronomical instruments, and made important astronomical calculations. Their philosophers, Avicenna, Averroës, and the Spanish Jew Maimonides, preserved and developed Aristotelian thought. The Arabs brought much of the learning of Greece and the ancient East to fruition and passed it on to the crude new nations of the West during the Middle Ages.

Europe went to school to Arabian civilization for its medicine, mathematics, and philosophy. Southern France was in continual contact with the Arabs in Spain, who were known as the Moors; Christian scholars attended the Moslem universities; and the Crusaders who went to the Near East with the intention of crushing a barbaric people were filled with wonder and learned much from them.[4] This also led to a strong infiltration of tales and legends that the Mohammedans had brought from the East, and undoubtedly stimulated the rise of European love poetry, a field in which the Arabs had been supreme as early as the sixth century A.D. Of this poetry immediately before the advent of Mahomet, the great student of Arabic culture Wilfrid Scawen Blunt wrote, that it is "the most delightful wild flower of literature the Eastern world can show." It is perhaps too torrid for Western taste (the Arabs considered Greek poetry lukewarm), but its manly feeling and imaginative intensity entitled it to be better known than it is.

In spite of these powerful influences on the Western World, the actual literary works of the Arabs known to Europeans and assimilated by them are very few. But one of their collections of stories, *The Thousand and One Nights* (usually

[2] H. G. Wells, *Outline of History*, p. 580.
[3] The *Koran* means the Reading.
[4] There were six Crusades for the recovery of the Holy Land from the Moslems; the first began in 1096, the last in 1229.

known as *The Arabian Nights*), became a household article in the West. The time of these tales is the reign of Haroun al Raschid (766?-809), whose love of letters was exceeded only by that of his son Al Mamoun, who made Bagdad a center of all learning he could gather from different parts of the world. In *The Arabian Nights* the Sultan of India is entertained with a seemingly endless string of tales by his queen Scheherezade in a desperate effort to postpone her execution night after night. As each tale is only half told, she keeps him interested for a thousand and one nights until he finally relents.

Although the work is of unknown authorship, the date of composition uncertain,[5] and its literary history vague, *The Arabian Nights* is a distillation of oriental story-telling. Their spirit is romantic but not war-like; they reflect the interests of a mercantile, far-traveling people, and must have been developed after the Arabs settled down to enjoy the fruits of their conquest. The tales were undoubtedly collected with great catholicity from various times and places; many of them had their origin in India. Included are some excellent short poems, revealing a love for nature and filled with passion and a pained sense of the transitoriness of life and glory. Great delicacy appears in the verses. But it is the stories that have captured the imagination of the world with their exuberant fantastication and escape into the world of the marvelous. They were given to European readers in 1704 in the French translation of Galland, and immediately became known throughout the West.

This does not, however, exhaust the Mohammedan world's legacy to us, for some of the finest oriental literature came to us from Persia after its conquest by the followers of Mahomet.

Persia had, of course, enjoyed a powerful civilization from very early times, even before Cyrus the Great started its Aryan-speaking people on the road to conquest in the sixth century B.C. Its major literary composition, which may have been begun in the eighth century B.C., if not earlier, was the *Zendavesta* (*The Living Word*), a sacred book containing the doctrines of Persia's religious and moral teacher Zarathustra, known to the West as Zoroaster. The chief feature of its teaching, an effort to explain the world and to guide mankind, is the doctrine that attributes everything to the conflict between two principles—*Ormuzd*, the principle of the good as represented by light, and *Ahriman*, the principle of evil as represented by darkness. Both born from eternity, they contend for the dominion of the world and of man's soul until the time when Ormuzd will conquer Ahriman. Men are either servants of the one or the other, and this can be determined by their adhering to or turning from the moral code. This religion penetrated deeply into Western thought, filtered into Greek philosophy, and into Christianity in the form of Manicheism.[6] It lingered on as late as the twelfth century in southern France, where it was fused with Christianity by the heretical Albigensian sect. This dualistic interpretation of divine providence enabled its believers and the much earlier Gnostic sect, to explain the presence of evil in the world. They maintained that the god of the Old Testament was evil and that Jesus, the good principle, was actually his opponent.

However, nothing produced by ancient Persia, not even the *Zendavesta*, has struck the West as possessing literary distinction. Work of this quality began to appear only in Mohammedan Persia from the tenth to the thirteenth centuries of our era. This was largely inspired by the rise of a pantheistic sect of mystics called the Sufis, from which most of the poets drew their ideas and imagery. Probably deriving their thought from India, the Sufis taught that worldly attachments are worthless and that the object of life should be identification with the permeating spirit of the world. Love, wine, and intoxication were some of the symbols representing the feeling of rapture upon union with the spirit. At the same time, the growth of luxury fostered the development of intensely romantic sentiment. Philosophical and worldly feelings, contempt for the world and enjoyment of its pleasures, mystic faith and sophisticated skepticism, existed side by side in the golden age of Persian literature.

Three love stories served many poets: *Khosru and Shireen*, a tale of idyllic love; *Mejnoun the Arabian*, a romance of unhappy love that drove its victim to madness; and *Yussuf and Zuleika*, the passion of Potiphar's wife for the biblical Joseph and the triumph of holiness over carnal desire. These tales inspired long romances highly regarded in the East and occasionally favored by writers of the West. But it is the Persian lyrics and epigrams that impressed themselves most strongly on the latter, except for the epic *Shah Nameh* (*Book of Kings*) by Firdausi (about 940-1020), from which

---

[5] The thirteenth century has been suggested as the probable date.
[6] See p. 445, Introduction to *The Christian Church*.

Matthew Arnold took the matter of his long poem *Sohrab and Rustum*.[7]

The first of the poets to impress the West, Omar Khayyam (died about 1123), was in a sense unique among the Persian writers. A redoubtable scientist who contributed to the development of astronomy, reformed the Persian calendar, and made it almost as accurate as the Gregorian Calendar, he was in philosophy a skeptic and an epicurean. Having no faith in the ecstasies of the mystics, he satirized their beliefs freely. Since life is transient, it is the better part of wisdom not to burden oneself with fruitless speculation, love of power, and a sense of sin, but to enjoy one's worldly existence as far as possible. Omar, who avoided political office and led a pleasant scholarly life, expressed his thought in his *Rubaiyat* in disconnected quatrains that are remarkably epigrammatic. They consist of four lines of equal length linked by a single rhyme, with the third line (generally unrhymed) suspending the movement and carrying it over into the last line.

Omar was not a great descriptive poet, and his poetic flights are very short; he could not, or did not care to, write a developed, organic poem. He has, in fact, been overrated in the English-speaking world because his stanzas appear in a superb translation. But an appealing personality glows in the quatrains. These often alternate between grave and gay feelings. The poet is alternately depressed and playful, argumentative and serene, pessimistic and ecstatic, though he leaves the final impression of pessimism on anyone accustomed to the consolations of Christianity. As Edward Fitzgerald noted, what especially distinguishes Omar is that in his verses we have the Man Omar himself "with all his humors and passions, as frankly before us as if we were really at Table with him, after the Wine had gone around."

The poem was introduced to the English-speaking world by Edward Fitzgerald in 1859. His translation is a very free reworking of the original. Its popularity for fifty years was enormous, not only because of the sheer beauty of the poetry but because the best-known quatrains expressed ideas that were in the minds of many of the readers, chiefly the pessimism and determinism that Victorians derived from the advancing science of the period. Here they read of the shortness of life, the impossibility of knowing certainly anything about such questions as God or immortality, and the

conclusion of the whole matter in a philosophy of "eat, drink and be merry, for tomorrow we die." Nowhere has that doctrine been expressed more enticingly than in the lines of Omar Khayyam.

As a poet Omar had his peers in at least two Persian writers who have been abundantly translated into English: Sa'di (1184-1291) and Hafiz (who died in 1389).

Sa'di, acclaimed by the Persians as "the nightingale of the groves of Shiraz," the city in which he was born, spent part of a long life in travel, and then enjoyed the remainder in philosophical retirement. He was a man of simple devotion, a believer in plain living and high thinking. "I never complained of my condition but once, when my feet were bare and I had not money to buy shoes. But I met a man without feet, and I became contented with my lot." His most famous books, the *Bustan* (*Fruit Garden*) and the *Gulistan* (*Rose Garden*), consist of short philosophic and moralistic poems, exceedingly apt and well-turned in their epigrammatic incisiveness. His favorite style reveals his simplicity and tenderness, his sensitivity and knowledge of human nature. At worst he lapsed into platitudes.

The prince of Persian lyricists is Hafiz, another native of Shiraz, who deserves to be placed in the company of the world's greatest lyricists. Disdaining the courts to which he was frequently invited and preferring a life of proud independence and easy companionship, he spent his life in poverty without any dampening of his natural exuberance. Whether he celebrated conviviality and love or mystic ecstasy, he remained a pure poet. This contemporary of Dante is so revered in Persia that his tomb near Shiraz is a shrine. Every year the maidens of Shiraz bring him bouquets of roses, tied together with brightly colored silken handkerchiefs, and try to tell their futures by consulting his odes. His reflective and religious poems are permeated with a fine ecstasy, but it is as the great poet of love that he is venerated. These verses are odes (*gazels*) and, in accordance with convention, weave in the poet's name in the final couplet. He is also the rhapsodist of wine and conviviality, and is deservedly known as the "Anacreon of the East." Among his admiring English translators have been Sir William Jones, Gertrude Lowthian Bell, Richard Le Gallienne, Ralph Waldo Emerson.

[7] Arnold's style is, however, in conscious imitation of Homer, and therefore not Persian at all.

RUBAIYAT OF OMAR KHAYYAM

I

Wake! For the Sun, who scatter'd into flight
The Stars before him from the Field of Night,
  Drives Night along with them from Heav'n, and strikes
The Sultan's Turret with a Shaft of Light.

II

Before the phantom of False morning died,   5
Methought a Voice within the Tavern cried,
  "When all the Temple is prepared within,
Why nods the drowsy Worshiper outside?"

III

And, as the Cock crew, those who stood before
The Tavern shouted—"Open then the Door!   10
  You know how little while we have to stay,
And, once departed, may return no more."

IV

Now the New Year reviving old Desires,
The thoughtful Soul to Solitude retires,   14
  Where the WHITE HAND OF MOSES on the Bough
Puts out,[1] and Jesus from the Ground suspires.

V

Iram indeed is gone with all his Rose,
And Jamshyd's Sev'n-ring'd Cup where no one knows;
  But still a Ruby kindles in the Vine,
And many a Garden by the Water blows.   20

VI

And David's lips are lockt; but in divine
High-piping Pehlevi,[2] with "Wine! Wine! Wine!
  Red Wine!"—the Nightingale cries to the Rose
That sallow cheek of hers to incarnadine.

VII

Come, fill the Cup, and in the fire of Spring   25
Your Winter-garment of Repentance fling:

The Bird of Time has but a little way
To flutter—and the Bird is on the Wing.

VIII

Whether at Naishapur [3] or Babylon,
Whether the Cup with sweet or bitter run,   30
  The Wine of Life keeps oozing drop by drop,
The Leaves of Life keep falling one by one.

IX

Each Morn a thousand Roses brings, you say;
Yes, but where leaves the Rose of Yesterday?
  And this first Summer month that brings the Rose   35
Shall take Jamshyd and Kaikobad away.

X

Well, let it take them! What have we to do
With Kaikobad the Great, or Kaikhosru?
  Let Zal and Rustum bluster as they will,
Or Hatim [4] call to Supper—heed not you.   40

XI

With me along the strip of Herbage strown
That just divides the desert from the sown,
  Where name of Slave and Sultan is forgot—
And Peace to Mahmud [5] on his golden Throne!

XII

A Book of Verses underneath the Bough,   45
A jug of Wine, a Loaf of Bread—and Thou
  Beside me singing in the Wilderness—
Oh, Wilderness were Paradise enow!

XIII

Some for the Glories of This World; and some
Sigh for the Prophet's Paradise to come;   50
  Ah, take the Cash, and let the Credit go,
Nor heed the rumble of a distant Drum!

Rubaiyat of Omar Khayyam. Translated by Edward Fitzgerald. Omar Khayyam was born at Naishapur in Persia, son of a tent-maker. He was a mathematician and astronomer. He died about 1123 A.D. His rubaiyat (or four-line stanzas) were quite unconnected. The semblance of order is due to Fitzgerald's rearrangement.

[1] See *Exodus IV, 6*, where Moses draws forth his hand white with leprosy. Here the reference is to the white blossoms on the trees in spring, the Mohammedan New Year.
[2] The ancient heroic language of Persia; therefore any heroic strain.
[3] Naishapur, the small town, or Babylon, the metropolis.
[4] Like all the names just given, a famous man of old.
[5] Mohammed.

XIV

Look to the blowing Rose about us—"Lo,
Laughing," she says, "into the world I blow.
  At once the silken tassel of my Purse 55
Tear, and its Treasure on the Garden throw."

XV

And those who husbanded the Golden grain,
And those who flung it to the winds like Rain,
  Alike to no such aureate Earth are turn'd
As, buried once, Men want dug up again. 60

XVI

The Worldly Hope men set their Hearts upon
Turns Ashes—or it prospers; and anon,
  Like Snow upon the Desert's dusty Face,
Lighting a little hour or two—is gone.

XVII

Think, in this batter'd Caravanserai 65
Whose Portals are alternate Night and Day,
  How Sultan after Sultan with his Pomp
Abode his destined Hour, and went his way.

XVIII

They say the Lion and the Lizard keep
The Courts where Jamshyd gloried and drank
    deep: 70
  And Bahram, that great Hunter—the Wild Ass
Stamps o'er his Head, but cannot break his Sleep.

XIX

I sometimes think that never blows so red
The Rose as where some buried Cæsar bled;
  That every Hyacinth the Garden wears 75
Dropt in her Lap from some once lovely Head.

XX

And this reviving Herb whose tender Green
Fledges the River-Lip on which we lean—
  Ah, lean upon it lightly! for who knows
From what once lovely Lip it springs unseen! 80

XXI

Ah, my Beloved, fill the Cup that clears
TODAY of past Regrets and Future Fears:
  Tomorrow!—Why, Tomorrow I may be
Myself with Yesterday's Sev'n thousand Years.

XXII

For some we loved, the loveliest and the best 85
That from his Vintage rolling Time hath prest
Have drunk their Cup a Round or two before,
And one by one crept silently to rest.

XXIII

And we, that now make merry in the Room
They left, and Summer dresses in new bloom, 90
  Ourselves must we beneath the Couch of Earth
Descend—ourselves to make a Couch—for whom?

XXIV

Ah, make the most of what we yet may spend,
Before we too into the Dust descend;
  Dust into Dust, and under Dust to lie 95
Sans Wine, sans Song, sans Singer, and—sans
    End!

XXV

Alike for those who for TODAY prepare,
And those that after some TOMORROW stare,
  A Muezzin from the Tower of Darkness cries, 99
"Fools! your Reward is neither Here nor There."

XXVI

Why, all the Saints and Sages who discuss'd
Of the Two Worlds so wisely—they are thrust
  Like foolish Prophets forth; their Words to
    Scorn
Are scatter'd, and their Mouths are stopt with
    Dust.

XXVII

Myself when young did eagerly frequent 105
Doctor and Saint, and heard great argument
  About it and about: but evermore
Came out by the same door where in I went.

XXVIII

With them the seed of Wisdom did I sow,
And with mine own hand wrought to make it
    grow; 110
  And this was all the Harvest that I reap'd—
"I came like Water, and like Wind I go."

XXIX

Into this Universe, and *Why* not knowing
Nor *Whence*, like Water willy-nilly flowing;
  And out of it, as Wind along the Waste, 115
I know not *Whither*, willy-nilly blowing.

XXX

What, without asking, hither hurried *Whence?*
And, without asking, *Whither* hurried hence!
  Oh, many a Cup of this forbidden Wine
Must drown the memory of that insolence! 120

XXXI

Up from Earth's Center through the Seventh Gate
I rose, and on the Throne of Saturn [6] sate;
    And many a Knot unravel'd by the Road;
But not the Master-knot of Human Fate.

XXXII

There was the Door to which I found no Key: 125
There was the Veil through which I might not see:
    Some little talk awhile of ME and THEE
There was—and then no more of THEE and ME.

XXXIII

Earth could not answer; nor the Seas that mourn
In flowing Purple, of their Lord forlorn;   130
    Nor rolling Heaven, with all his Signs reveal'd
And hidden by the sleeve of Night and Morn.

XXXIV

Then of the THEE IN ME who works behind
The Veil, I lifted up my hands to find
    A Lamp amid the Darkness; and I heard,   135
As from Without—"THE ME WITHIN THEE BLIND!"

XXXV

Then to the lip of this poor earthen Urn
I lean'd, the Secret of my Life to learn:
    And Lip to Lip it murmur'd—"While you live,
Drink!—for, once dead, you never shall re-
    turn."   140

XXXVI

I think the Vessel, that with fugitive
Articulation answer'd, once did live,
    And drink; and Ah! the passive Lip I kiss'd.
How many Kisses might it take—and give!

XXXVII

For I remember stopping by the way   145
To watch a Potter thumping his wet Clay:
    And with its all-obliterated Tongue
It murmur'd—"Gently, Brother, gently, pray!"

XXXVIII

And has not such a Story from of Old
Down Man's successive generations roll'd   150
    Of such a clod of saturated Earth
Cast by the Maker into Human mold?

XXXIX

And not a drop that from our Cups we throw
For Earth to drink of, but may steal below

To quench the fire of Anguish in some Eye   155
There hidden—far beneath, and long ago.

XL

As then the Tulip for her morning sup
Of Heav'nly Vintage from the soil looks up,
    Do you devoutly do the like, till Heav'n
To Earth invert you—like an empty Cup.   160

XLI

Perplext no more with Human or Divine,
Tomorrow's tangle to the winds resign,
    And lose your fingers in the tresses of
The Cypress-slender Minister of Wine.

XLII

And if the Wine you drink, the Lip you press,   165
End in what All begins and ends in—Yes;
    Think then you are TODAY what YESTERDAY
You were—TOMORROW you shall not be less.

XLIII

So when that Angel of the darker Drink
At last shall find you by the river-brink,   170
    And, offering his Cup, invite your Soul
Forth to your Lips to quaff—you shall not shrink.

XLIV

Why, if the Soul can fling the Dust aside,
And naked on the Air of Heaven ride,
    Were't not a Shame—were't not a Shame for
    him   175
In this clay carcase crippled to abide?

XLV

'Tis but a Tent where takes his one day's rest
A Sultan to the realm of Death addrest;
    The Sultan rises, and the dark Ferrash
Strikes, and prepares it for another Guest.   180

XLVI

And fear not lest Existence closing your
Account, and mine, should know the like no more;
    The Eternal Saki from that Bowl has pour'd
Millions of Bubbles like us, and will pour.

XLVII

When You and I behind the Veil are past,   185
Oh, but the long, long while the World shall last,
    Which of our Coming and Departure heeds
As the Sea's self should heed a pebble-cast.

---

⁶ Saturn was lord of the seventh heaven.

XLVIII

A Moment's Halt—a momentary taste
Of BEING from the Well amid the Waste—   190
  And Lo!—the phantom Caravan has reach'd
The NOTHING it set out from—Oh, make haste!

XLIX

Would you that spangle of Existence spend
About the SECRET—quick about it, Friend!
  A Hair perhaps divides the False and True—
And upon what, prithee, may life depend?   196

L

A Hair perhaps divides the False and True;
Yes; and a single Alif were the clue—
  Could you but find it—to the Treasure-house,
And peradventure to THE MASTER too;   200

LI

Whose secret Presence, through Creation's veins
Running Quicksilver-like eludes your pains;
  Taking all shapes from Mah to Mahi; and
They change and perish all—but He remains;

LII

A moment guess'd—then back behind the Fold   205
Immerst of Darkness round the Drama roll'd
  Which, for the Pastime of Eternity,
He doth Himself contrive, enact, behold.

LIII

But if in vain, down on the stubborn floor   209
Of Earth, and up to Heav'n's unopening Door,
  You gaze TODAY while You are You—how then
TOMORROW, You when shall be You no more?

LIV

Waste not your Hour, nor in the vain pursuit
Of This and That endeavor and dispute;
  Better be jocund with the fruitful Grape   215
Than sadden after none, or bitter, Fruit.

LV

You know, my Friends, with what a brave Carouse
I made a Second Marriage in my house;
  Divorced old barren Reason from my Bed,
And took the Daughter of the Vine to Spouse.   220

LVI

For "IS" and "IS-NOT" though with Rule and Line
And "UP-AND-DOWN" by Logic I define,
  Of all that one should care to fathom, I
Was never deep in anything but—Wine.

LVII

Ah, but my Computations, People say,   225
Reduced the Year to better reckoning?—Nay,
  'Twas only striking from the Calendar
Unborn Tomorrow, and dead Yesterday.

LVIII

And lately, by the Tavern Door agape,
Came shining through the Dusk an Angel Shape
  Bearing a Vessel on his Shoulder; and   231
He bid me taste of it; and 'twas—the Grape!

LIX

The Grape that can with Logic absolute
The Two-and-Seventy jarring Sects confute:
  The sovereign Alchemist that in a trice   235
Life's leaden metal into Gold transmute:

LX

The mighty Mahmud, Allah-breathing Lord,
That all the misbelieving and black Horde
  Of Fears and Sorrows that infest the Soul
Scatters before him with his whirlwind Sword.   240

LXI

Why, be this Juice the growth of God, who dare
Blaspheme the twisted tendril as a Snare?
  A Blessing, we should use it, should we not?
And if a Curse—why, then, Who set it there?

LXII

I must abjure the Balm of Life, I must,   245
Scared by some After-reckoning ta'en on trust,
  Or lured with Hope of some Diviner Drink,
To fill the Cup—when crumbled into Dust!

LXIII

Oh threats of Hell and Hopes of Paradise!
One thing at least is certain—*This* Life flies;   250
  One thing is certain and the rest is Lies;
The Flower that once has blown forever dies.

LXIV

Strange, is it not? that of the myriads who
Before us pass'd the door of Darkness through,
  Not one returns to tell us of the Road,   255
Which to discover we must travel too.

LXV

The Revelations of Devout and Learn'd
Who rose before us, and as Prophets burn'd,
  Are all but Stories, which, awoke from Sleep
They told their comrades, and to Sleep return'd.   260

LXVI

I sent my Soul through the Invisible,
Some letter of that After-life to spell:
   And by and by my Soul return'd to me,
And answered "I Myself am Heav'n and Hell:"

LXVII

Heav'n but the Vision of fulfill'd Desire,   265
And Hell the Shadow from a Soul on fire,
   Cast on the Darkness into which Ourselves,
So late emerged from, shall so soon expire.

LXVIII

We are no other than a moving row
Of Magic Shadow-shapes that come and go   270
   Round with the Sun-illumined Lantern held
In Midnight by the Master of the Show;

LXIX

But helpless Pieces of the Game He plays
Upon his Chequer-board of Nights and Days;
   Hither and thither moves, and checks, and slays,
And one by one back in the Closet lays.   276

LXX

The Ball no question makes of Ayes and Noes,
But Here or There as strikes the Player goes;
   And He that toss'd you down into the Field,
He knows about it all—HE knows—HE knows!   280

LXXI

The Moving Finger writes; and, having writ,
Moves on: nor all your Piety nor Wit
   Shall lure it back to cancel half a Line,
Nor all your Tears wash out a Word of it.

LXXII

And that inverted Bowl they call the Sky,   285
Whereunder crawling coop'd we live and die,
   Lift not your hands to *It* for help—for It
As impotently moves as you or I.

LXXIII

With Earth's first Clay They did the Last Man
   knead,   289
And there of the Last Harvest sow'd the Seed:
   And the first Morning of Creation wrote
What the Last Dawn of Reckoning shall read.

LXXIV

YESTERDAY *This* Day's Madness did prepare;
TOMORROW's Silence, Triumph, or Despair:

Drink! for you know not whence you came, nor
   why: 295
Drink! for you know not why you go, nor where.

LXXV

I tell you this—When, started from the Goal,
Over the flaming shoulders of the Foal
   Of Heav'n Parwin and Mushtari[7] they flung,
In my predestined Plot of Dust and Soul   300

LXXVI

The Vine had struck a fiber: which about
If clings my being—let the Dervish flout;
   Of my Base metal may be filed a Key,
That shall unlock the Door he howls without.

LXXVII

And this I know: whether the one True Light
Kindle to Love, or Wrath-consume me quite,   306
   One Flash of It within the Tavern caught
Better than in the Temple lost outright.

LXXVIII

What! out of senseless Nothing to provoke
A conscious Something to resent the yoke   310
   Of unpermitted Pleasure, under pain
Of Everlasting Penalties, if broke!

LXXIX

What! from his helpless Creature be repaid
Pure Gold for what he lent him dross-allay'd—
   Sue for a Debt he never did contract,   315
And cannot answer—Oh the sorry trade!

LXXX

Oh Thou, who didst with pitfall and with gin
Beset the Road I was to wander in,
   Thou wilt not with Predestined Evil round
Enmesh, and then impute my Fall to Sin!   320

LXXXI

Oh Thou, who Man of baser Earth didst make,
And ev'n with Paradise devise the Snake:
   For all the Sin wherewith the Face of Man
Is blacken'd—Man's forgiveness give—and take!

   ·   ·   ·   ·

LXXXII

As under cover of departing Day   325
Slunk hunger-stricken Ramazan[8] away,
   Once more within the Potter's house alone
I stood, surrounded by the Shapes of Clay.

---

[7] The Pleiades and Jupiter.   [8] The month of fasting.

LXXXIII

Shapes of all Sorts and Sizes, great and small,
That stood along the floor and by the wall;   330
  And some loquacious Vessels were; and some
Listen'd perhaps, but never talk'd at all.

LXXXIV

Said one among them—"Surely not in vain
My substance of the common Earth was ta'en
  And to this Figure molded, to be broke,   335
Or trampled back to shapeless Earth again."

LXXXV

Then said a Second—"Ne'er a peevish Boy
Would break the Bowl from which he drank in
    joy;
  And He that with his hand the Vessel made
Will surely not in after Wrath destroy."   340

LXXXVI

After a momentary silence spake
Some Vessel of a more ungainly Make;
  "They sneer at me for leaning all awry:
What! did the Hand then of the Potter shake?"

LXXXVII

Whereat someone of the loquacious Lot—   345
I think a Sufi pipkin—waxing hot—
  "All this of Pot and Potter—Tell me then,
Who is the Potter, pray, and who the Pot?"

LXXXVIII

"Why," said another, "Some there are who tell
Of one who threatens he will toss to Hell   350
  The luckless Pots he marr'd in making—Pish!
He's a Good Fellow, and 'twill all be well."

LXXXIX

"Well," murmur'd one, "Let whoso make or buy,
My Clay with long Oblivion is gone dry:
  But fill me with the old familiar Juice,   355
Methinks I might recover by and by."

XC

So while the Vessels one by one were speaking,
The little Moon [9] look'd in that all were seeking:
  And then they jogg'd each other, "Brother!
    Brother!   359
Now for the Porter's shoulder-knot a-creaking!"

   .   .   .   .   .

[9] Indicating the close of the month of fasting.

XCI

Ah, with the Grape my fading Life provide,
And wash the Body whence the Life has died,
  And lay me, shrouded in the living Leaf,
By some not unfrequented Garden-side.

XCII

That ev'n my buried Ashes such a snare   365
Of Vintage shall fling up into the Air
  As not a True-believer passing by
But shall be overtaken unaware.

XCIII

Indeed the Idols I have loved so long
Have done my credit in this World much wrong:
  Have drowned my Glory in a shallow Cup   371
And sold my Reputation for a Song.

XCIV

Indeed, indeed, Repentance oft before
I swore—but was I sober when I swore?
  And then and then came Spring, and Rose-in-
    hand   375
My thread-bare Penitence apieces tore.

XCV

And much as Wine has play'd the Infidel,
And robb'd me of my Robe of Honor—Well,
  I wonder often what the Vintners buy
One half so precious as the stuff they sell.   380

XCVI

Yet Ah, that Spring should vanish with the Rose!
That Youth's sweet-scented manuscript should
    close!
  The Nightingale that in the branches sang,
Ah whence, and whither flown again, who knows!

XCVII

Would but the Desert of the Fountain yield   385
One glimpse—if dimly, yet indeed, reveal'd,
  To which the fainting Traveler might spring,
As springs the trampled herbage of the field!

XCVIII

Would but some winged Angel ere too late
Arrest the yet unfolded Roll of Fate,   390
  And make the stern Recorder otherwise
Enregister, or quite obliterate!

XCIX

Ah Love! could you and I with Him conspire
To grasp this sorry Scheme of Things entire,
   Would not we shatter it to bits—and then   395
Re-mold it nearer to the Heart's Desire!

.   .   .   .   .

C

Yon rising Moon that looks for us again—
How oft hereafter will she wax and wane;

How oft hereafter rising look for us   399
Through this same Garden—and for *one* in vain!

CI

And when like her, oh Saki, you shall pass
Among the Guests Star-scatter'd on the Grass,
   And in your joyous errand reach the spot
Where I made One—turn down an empty Glass!

TAMAM

SA'DI

The Gulistan

Purgatory May Be Paradise

A king was embarked along with a Persian slave on board a ship. The boy had never been at sea, nor experienced the inconvenience of a ship. He set up a weeping and wailing, and all his limbs were in a state of trepidation; and, however much they soothed him, he was not to be pacified. The king's pleasure-party was disconcerted by him; but they had no help. On board that ship there was a physician. He said to the king: "If you will order it, I can manage to silence him." The king replied: "It will be an act of great favor." The physician so directed that they threw the boy into the sea, and after he had plunged repeatedly, they seized him by the hair of the head and drew him close to the ship, when he clung with both hands by the rudder, and, scrambling upon the deck, slunk into a corner and sat down quiet. The king, pleased with what he saw, said: "What art is there in this?" The physician replied: "Originally he had not experienced the danger of being drowned, and undervalued the safety of being in a ship; in like manner as a person is aware of the preciousness of health when he is overtaken with the calamity of sickness. *A barley loaf of bread has, O epicure, no relish for thee. That is my mistress who appears so ugly to thy eye.—To the houris, or nymphs of paradise, purgatory would be a hell; ask the inmates of hell whether purgatory is not paradise.— There is a distinction between the man that folds his mistress in his arms and him whose two eyes are fixed on the door expecting her.*"

The Wrestler

A person had become a master in the art of wrestling; he knew three hundred and sixty sleights in this art, and could exhibit a fresh trick for every day throughout the year. Perhaps owing to a liking that a corner of his heart took for the handsome person of one of his scholars, he taught him three hundred and fifty-nine of those feats, but he was putting off the last one, and under some pretence deferring it.

In short, the youth became such a proficient in the art and talent of wrestling that none of his contemporaries had ability to cope with him, till he at length had one day boasted before the reigning sovereign, saying: "To any superiority my master possesses over me, he is beholden to my reverence of his seniority, and in virtue of his tutorage; otherwise I am not inferior in power, and am his equal in skill." This want of respect displeased the king. He ordered a wrestling match to be held, and a spacious field to be fenced in for the occasion. The ministers of state, nobles of the court, and gallant men of the realm were assembled, and the ceremonials of the combat marshalled. Like a huge and lusty elephant, the youth rushed into the ring with such a crash that had a brazen mountain opposed him he would have moved it from its base. The master being aware that the youth was his superior in strength, engaged him in that strange feat of which he had kept him ignorant. The youth was unacquainted with its guard. Advancing, nevertheless, the master seized him with both hands, and,

Sa'di (1184-1291). Translations by Sir Edwin Arnold. By permission of Harper & Brothers, publishers.

lifting him bodily from the ground, raised him above his head and flung him on the earth. The crowd set up a shout. The king ordered them to give the master an honorary dress and handsome largess, and the youth he addressed with reproach and asperity, saying: "You played the traitor with your own patron, and failed in your presumption of opposing him." He replied: "O sire! my master did not overcome me by strength and ability, but one cunning trick in the art of wrestling was left which he was reserved in teaching me, and by that little feat had today the upper hand of me." The master said: "I reserved myself for such a day as this. As the wise have told us, put not so much into a friend's power that, if hostilely disposed, he can do you an injury. Have you not heard what that man said who was treacherously dealt with by his own pupil: *'Either in fact there was no good faith in this world, or nobody has perhaps practised it in our days. No person learned the art of archery from me who did not in the end make me his butt.'* "

From Slavery to Slavery

Having taken offence with the society of my friends at Damascus, I retired into the wilderness of the Holy Land, or Jerusalem, and sought the company of brutes till such time as I was made a prisoner by the Franks, and employed by them, along with some Jews, in digging earth in the ditches of Tripoli. At length one of the chiefs of Aleppo, between whom and me an intimacy had of old subsisted, happening to pass that way, recognized me, and said: "How is this? and how came you to be thus occupied?" I replied: "What can I say? *I was flying from mankind into the forests and mountains, for my resource was in God and in none else. Fancy to thyself what my condition must now be, when forced to associate with a tribe scarcely human?—To be linked in a chain with a company of acquaintance were pleasanter than to walk in a garden with strangers."*

He took pity on my situation; and, having for ten dinars redeemed me from captivity with the Franks, carried me along with him to Aleppo. Here he had a daughter, and her he gave me in marriage, with a dower of a hundred dinars. Soon after this damsel turned out a termagant and vixen, and discovered such a perverse spirit and virulent tongue as quite unhinged all my domestic comfort. *A scolding wife in the dwelling of a peaceable man is his hell even in this world. Protect and guard us against a wicked inmate. Save us, O Lord, and preserve us from the fiery, or hell, torture.*

Having on one occasion given a liberty to the tongue of reproach, she was saying: "Are you not the fellow whom my father redeemed from the captivity of the Franks for ten dinars?" I replied: "Yes, I am that same he delivered from captivity for ten dinars, and enslaved me with you for a hundred!" *I have heard that a reverend and mighty man released a sheep from the paws and jaws of a wolf. That same night he was sticking a knife into its throat, when the spirit of the sheep reproached him, saying: "Thou didst deliver me from the clutches of a wolf, when I at length saw that thou didst prove a wolf to me thyself."*

Wealth

He that owns wealth, in mountain, wold, or waste,
Plays master—pitches tent at his own taste;
Whilst he who lacks that which the world commends
Must pace a stranger, e'en in his own lands.

The Bustan

The Great Physician

A tumult in a Syrian town had place:
They seized an old man there of wit and grace;
   Still in my ear lingers his noble saying,
When, fettered fast, they smote him in the face.

Quotha: "If of all Sultans the Sultàn
Gives not the word for plunder, who else can?
   Who, save upon His bidding, would be bold
To do such deeds? Therefore I hold the man

That wrongs me not mine enemy but friend;
God hath appointed him unto this end!
   If there fall scorn or honor, gifts or shackles,
'Tis God—not Zayd or Omar—who doth send."

Right, Sheykh! no griefs the wise heart will annoy;
The Great Physician sharp drugs doth employ!
   A sick man's not more skillful than his Hâkim;
Take what the Friend gives as a bliss and joy.

The Dancer

I heard how, to the beat of some quick tune,
There rose and danced a Damsel like the moon,
  Flower-mouthed and Pâri-faced; and all around
    her
Neck-stretching Lovers gathered close; but, soon

A flickering lamp-flame caught her skirt, and set 5
Fire to the flying gauze. Fear did beget
  Trouble in that light heart! She cried amain.

Quoth one among her worshipers, "Why fret,
Tulip of Love? Th' extinguished fire hath burned
Only one leaf of thee; but I am turned   10
  To ashes—leaf and stalk, and flower and root—
By lamp-flash of thine eyes!"—"Ah, Soul concerned

"Solely with self!"—she answered, laughing low,
"If thou wert Lover thou hadst not said so.
  Who speaks of the Belov'd's woe as not his 15
Speaks infidelity, true Lovers know!"

HAFIZ

A Persian Song

Sweet maid, if thou wouldst charm my sight,
And bid these arms thy neck infold;
That rosy cheek, that lily hand,
Would give thy poet more delight
Than all Bocara's vaunted gold, 5
Than all the gems of Samarcand.

Boy, let yon liquid ruby flow,
And bid thy pensive heart be glad,
Whate'er the frowning zealots say:
Tell them, their Eden cannot show 10
A stream so clear as Rocnabad,
A bow'r so sweet as Mosellay.

Oh! when these fair perfidious maids,
Whose eyes our secret haunts infest,
Their dear destructive charms display, 15
Each glance my tender heart invades,
And robs my wounded soul of rest,
As Tartars seize their destined prey.

In vain with love our bosoms glow:
Can all our tears, can all our sighs, 20
New luster to those charms impart?
Can cheeks, where living roses blow,
Where Nature spreads her richest dyes,
Require the borrowed gloss of art?

Speak not of fate:—ah! change the theme, 25
And talk of odors, talk of wine,

Talk of the flow'rs that round us bloom:
'Tis all a cloud, 'tis all a dream;
To love and joy thy thoughts confine,
Nor hope to pierce the sacred gloom. 30

Beauty has such resistless pow'r,
That ev'n the chaste Egyptian dame
Sighed for the blooming Hebrew boy:
For her how fatal was the hour
When to the banks of Nilus came 35
A youth so lovely and so coy!

But ah! sweet maid, my counsel hear
(Youth should attend when those advise
Whom long experience renders sage)
While music charms the ravished ear, 40
While sparkling cups delight our eyes,
Be gay, and scorn the frowns of age.

What cruel answer have I heard?
And yet, by Heav'n, I love thee still
Can aught be cruel from thy lips? 45
Yet say, how fell that bitter word
From lips which streams of sweetness fill,
Which nought but drops of honey sip?

Go boldly forth, my simple lay,
Whose accents flow with artless ease, 50
Like orient pearls at random strung;
Thy notes are sweet, the damsels say,
But oh, far sweeter, if they please
The Nymph for whom these notes are sung.

Hafiz (?-1389). "A Persian Song" translated by Sir William Jones; "Ode 11," by John Hindley; "Ode 12" and "Ode 13," by Ralph Waldo Emerson, reprinted by permission of Houghton Mifflin Company.

Ode 11

I have borne the anguish of love, which ask me not
    to describe:
I have tasted the poison of absence, which ask me
    not to relate.

Far through the world have I roved, and at length
    I have chosen
A sweet creature (a ravisher of hearts), whose
    name ask me not to disclose.

The flowing of my tears bedews her footsteps   5
In such a manner as ask me not to utter.

On yesternight from her own mouth with my own
    ears I heard
Such words as pray ask me not to repeat.

Why dost you bite thy lip at me? What dost thou
    not hint (*that I may have told*)?
I have devoured a lip like a ruby: but whose, ask
    me not to mention.   10

Absent from thee, and the sole tenant of my cot-
    tage,
I have endured such tortures, as ask me not to
    enumerate.

Thus am I, HAFIZ, arrived at extremity in the
    ways of Love,
Which, alas! ask me not to explain.

Ode 12

I said to heaven that glowed above,
O hide yon sun-filled zone,
Hide all the stars you boast;
For, in the world of love
And estimation true,   5
The heaped-up harvest of the moon
Is worth one barley-corn at most,
The Pleiads' sheaf but two.

If my darling should depart,
And search the skies for prouder friends,   10
God forbid my angry heart
In other love should seek amends.

When the blue horizon's hoop
Me a little pinches here,
Instant to my grave I stoop,   15
And go find thee in the sphere.

Ode 13

Oft have I said, I say it once more,
I, a wanderer, do not stray from myself.
I am a kind of parrot; the mirror is holden to me:
What the Eternal says, I stammering say again.

Give me what you will; I eat thistles as roses,
And according to my food I grow and I give.
Scorn me not, but know I have the pearl,
And am only seeking one to receive it.

THE ARABIAN NIGHTS

The First Voyage of Es-Sindibad of the Sea

Know, O masters, O noble persons, that I had a father; a merchant, who was one of the first in rank among the people and the merchants, and who possessed abundant wealth and ample fortune. He died when I was a young child, leaving to me wealth and buildings and fields; and when I grew up, I put my hand upon the whole of the property, ate well and drank well, associated with the young men, wore handsome apparel, and passed my life with my friends and companions, [10] feeling confident that this course would continue and profit me; and I ceased not to live in this manner for a length of time. I then returned to my reason, and recovered from my heedlessness, and found that my wealth had passed away, and my condition had changed, and all [the money] that I had possessed had gone. I recovered not to see my situation but in a state of fear and confusion of mind, and remembered a tale that I had heard before, the tale of our lord Suleyman the son of Da'ud [1] (on both of whom be peace!), respecting his saying, Three things are better than three: the day of death is better than the day of birth; and a living dog is better than a dead lion; and the

---

[1] The Solomon and David of The Bible.

grave is better than the palace. Then I arose, and collected what I had, of effects and apparel, and sold them; after which I sold my buildings and all that my hand possessed, and amassed three thousand pieces of silver; and it occurred to my mind to travel to the countries of other people.

Upon this, I resolved, and arose, and bought for myself goods and commodities and merchandise, with such other things as were required for travel; and my mind had consented to my performing a sea-voyage. So I embarked in a ship, and it descended to the city of El-Basrah, with a company of merchants; and we traversed the sea for many days and nights. We had passed by island after island, and from sea to sea, and from land to land, and in every place by which we passed we sold and bought, and exchanged merchandise. We continued our voyage until we arrived at an island like one of the gardens of Paradise, and at that island the master of the ship brought her to anchor with us. He cast the anchor, and put forth the landing-plank, and all who were in the ship landed upon that island. They had prepared for themselves fire-pots, and they lighted the fires in them; and their occupations were various: some cooked; others washed; and others amused themselves. I was among those who were amusing themselves upon the shores of the island, and the passengers were assembled to eat and drink and play and sport. But while we were thus engaged, lo, the master of the ship, standing upon its side, called out with his loudest voice, O ye passengers, whom may God preserve! come up quickly into the ship, hasten to embark, and leave your merchandise, and flee with your lives, and save yourselves from destruction; for this apparent island, upon which ye are, is not really an island, but it is a great fish that hath become stationary in the midst of the sea, and the sand hath accumulated upon it, so that it hath become like an island, and trees have grown upon it since times of old; and when ye lighted the fire upon it, the fish felt the heat, and put itself in motion, and now it will descend with you into the sea, and ye will all be drowned: then seek for yourselves escape before destruction, and leave the merchandise.—The passengers, therefore, hearing the words of the master of the ship, hastened to go up into the vessel, leaving the merchandise, and their other goods, and their copper cooking-pots, and their fire-pots; and some reached the ship, and others reached it not. The island had moved, and descended to the bottom of the sea, with all that were upon it, and the roaring sea, agitated with waves, closed over it.

I was among the number of those who remained behind upon the island; so I sank in the sea with the rest who sank. But God (whose name be exalted!) delivered me and saved me from drowning and supplied me with a great wooden bowl, of the bowls in which the passengers had been washing, and I laid hold upon it and got into it, induced by the sweetness of life, and beat the water with my feet as with oars, while the waves sported with me, tossing me to the right and left. The master of the vessel had caused her sails to be spread, and pursued his voyage with those who had embarked, not regarding such as had been submerged; and I ceased not to look at that vessel until it was concealed from my eye. I made sure of destruction, and night came upon me while I was in this state; but I remained so a day and a night, and the wind and the waves aided me until the bowl came to a stoppage with me under a high island, whereon were trees overhanging the sea. So I laid hold upon a branch of a lofty tree, and clung to it, after I had been at the point of destruction; and I kept hold upon it until I landed on the island, when I found my legs benumbed, and saw marks of the nibbling of fish upon their hams, of which I had been insensible by reason of the violence of the anguish and fatigue that I was suffering.

I threw myself upon the island like one dead, and was unconscious of my existence, and drowned in my stupefaction; and I ceased not to remain in this condition until the next day. The sun having then risen upon me, I awoke upon the island, and found that my feet were swollen, and that I had become reduced to the state in which I then was. Awhile I dragged myself along in a sitting posture, and then I crawled upon my knees. And there were in the island fruits in abundance, and springs of sweet water: therefore I ate of those fruits; and I ceased not to continue in this state for many days and nights. My spirit had then revived, my soul had returned to me, and my power of motion was renewed; and I began to meditate, and to walk along the shore of the island, amusing myself among the trees with the sight of the things that God (whose name be exalted!) had created; and I had made for myself a staff from those trees, to lean upon it. Thus I remained until I walked, one day, upon the shore of the island, and there appeared unto me an indistinct object in the distance. I imagined that it was a wild beast, or one of the beasts of the sea; and I walked towards it ceasing not to gaze at it; and, lo, it was a mare, of superb appearance, tethered in a part of the island by the sea-shore. I approached her; but she cried out against me with a great cry, and I trembled with fear of her, and was about to return, when, behold, a man came forth from beneath the earth, and he called to me and pursued me, saying to me, Who art thou, and whence hast thou come, and what is the cause of thine arrival in this place? So I answered him, O my master, know that I am a stranger, and I was in a ship, and was submerged in the sea with certain others of the passengers; but God supplied me with a wooden bowl, and I got into it, and it bore me along until the waves cast me upon this island. And when he heard my words, he laid hold of my hand and said to me, Come with me. I therefore went with him, and he descended with me into a grotto beneath the earth, and conducted me into a large subterranean chamber, and, having seated me at the upper end of that chamber, brought me some food. I was hungry; so I ate until I was satiated and contented, and my soul became at ease. Then he asked me respecting my case, and what had happened to me; wherefore I acquainted him with my whole affair from beginning to end; and he wondered at my story.

And when I had finished my tale, I said, I conjure thee by Allah, O my master, that thou be not displeased with me: I have acquainted thee with the truth of my case and of what hath happened to me, and I desire of thee that thou inform me who thou art, and what is the cause of thy dwelling in this chamber that is beneath the earth, and what is the reason of thy tethering this mare by the sea-side. So he replied, Know that we are a party dispersed in this island, upon its shores, and we are the grooms of the King El-Mihraj, having under our care all his horses; and every month, when moonlight commenceth, we bring the swift mares, and tether them in this island, every mare that has not foaled, and conceal ourselves in this chamber beneath the earth, that they may attract the sea-horses. This is the time of the coming forth of the sea-horse; and afterwards, if it be the will of God (whose name be exalted!), I will take thee with me to the King El-Mihraj, and divert thee with the sight of our country. Know, moreover, that if thou hadst not met with us, thou hadst not seen anyone in this place, and wouldst have died in misery, none knowing of thee. But I will be the means of the preservation of thy life, and of thy return to thy country.—I therefore prayed for him, and thanked him for his kindness and beneficence; and while we were thus talking, the horse came forth from the sea, as he had said. And shortly after, his companions came each leading a mare; and, seeing me with him, they inquired of me my story, and I told them what I had related to him. They then drew near to me, and spread the table, and ate, and invited me: so I ate with them, after which, they arose, and mounted the horses, taking me with them, having mounted me on a mare.

We commenced our journey, and proceeded without ceasing until we arrived at the city of the King El-Mihraj, and they went in to him and acquainted him with my story. He therefore desired my presence, and they took me in to him, and stationed me before him; whereupon I saluted him, and he returned my salutation, and welcomed me, greeting me in an honorable manner, and inquired of me respecting my case. So I informed him of all that had happened to me, and of all that I had seen, from beginning to end; and he wondered at that which had befallen me and happened to me, and said to me, O my son, by Allah, thou hast experienced an extraordinary preservation, and had it not been for the predestined length of thy life, thou hadst not escaped from these difficulties; but praise be to God for thy safety! Then he treated me with beneficence and honor, caused me to draw near to him, and began to cheer me with conversation and courtesy; and he made me his superintendent of the sea-port, and registrar of every vessel that came to the coast. I stood in his presence to transact his affairs, and he favored me and benefited me in every respect; he invested me with a handsome and costly dress, and I became a person high in credit with him in intercessions, and in accomplishing the affairs of the people. I ceased not to remain in his service for a long time; and whenever I went to the shore of the sea, I used to inquire of the merchants and travelers and sailors respecting the direction of the city of Baghdad, that perchance someone might inform me of it, and I might go with him thither and return to my country; but none knew it, nor knew anyone who went to it. At this I was perplexed, and I was weary of the length of my absence from home; and in this state I continued for a length of time, until I went in one day to the King El-Mihraj, and found with him a party of Indians. I saluted them, and they returned my salutation and welcomed me, and asked me respecting my country; after which, I questioned them as to their country, and they told me that they consisted of various races. Among them are the Shakiriyeh, who are the most noble of their races, who oppress no one, nor offer violence to any. And among them are a class called the Brahmans, a people who never drink wine; but they are persons of pleasure and joy and sport and merriment, and possessed of camels and horses and cattle. They informed me also that the Indians are divided into seventy-two classes; and I wondered at this extremely. And I saw, in the dominions of the King El-Mihraj, an island, among others, which is called Kasil, in which is heard the beating of tambourines and drums throughout the night, and the islanders and travelers informed us that Ed-Dejjal is in it. I saw too, in the sea in which is that island, a fish two hundred cubits long, and the fishermen fear it; wherefore they knock some pieces of wood, and it fleeth from them; and I saw a fish whose face was like that of the owl. I likewise saw during that voyage many wonderful and strange things, such that, if I related them to you, the description would be too long.

I continued to amuse myself with the sight of those islands and the things they contained, until I stood one day upon the shore of the sea, with a staff in my hand, as was my custom, and lo, a great vessel approached, wherein were many merchants; and when it arrived at the harbor of the city and its place of anchoring, the master furled its sails, brought it to an anchor by the shore, and put forth the landing-plank; and the sailors brought out everything that was in that vessel to the shore. They were slow in taking forth the goods, while I stood writing their account, and I said to the master of the ship, Doth aught remain in thy vessel? He answered, Yes, O my master; I have some goods in the hold of the ship; but their owner was drowned in the sea at one of the islands during our voyage hither, and his goods are in our charge; so we desire to sell them, and to take a note of their price, in order to convey it to his family in the city of Baghdad, the Abode of Peace. I therefore said to the master, What was the name of that man, the owner of the goods? He answered, His name was Es-Sindibad of the Sea, and he was drowned on his voyage with us in the sea. And when I heard his words, I looked at him with a scrutinizing eye, and recognized him; and I cried out at him with a great cry, and said, O master, know that I am the owner of the goods which thou hast mentioned, and I am Es-Sindibad

of the Sea, who descended upon the island from the ship, with the other merchants who descended; and when the fish that we were upon moved, and thou calledst out to us, some got into the vessel, and the rest sank, and I was among those who sank. But God (whose name be exalted!) preserved me and saved me from drowning by means of a large wooden bowl, of those in which passengers were washing, and I got into it, and began to beat the water with my feet, and the wind and the waves aided me until I arrived at this island, when I landed on it, and God (whose name be exalted!) assisted me, and I met the grooms of the King El-Mihraj, who took me with them and brought me to this city. They then led me into the King El-Mihraj, and I acquainted him with my story; whereupon he bestowed benefits upon me, and appointed me clerk of the harbor of this city, and I obtained profit in his service, and favor with him. Therefore these goods that thou hast are my goods and my portion.

But the master said, There is no strength nor power but in God, the High, the Great! There is no longer faith nor conscience in anyone!—Wherefore, O master, said I, when thou hast heard me tell thee my story? He answered, Because thou heardest me say that I had goods whose owner was drowned: therefore thou desirest to take them without price; and this is unlawful to thee; for we saw him when he sank, and there were with him many of the passengers, not one of whom escaped. How then dost thou pretend that thou art the owner of the goods?—So I said to him, O master, hear my story, and understand my words, and my veracity will become manifest to thee; for falsehood is a characteristic of the hypocrites. Then I related to him all that I had done from the time that I went forth with him from the city of Baghdad until we arrived at that island upon which we were submerged in the sea, and I mentioned to him some circumstances that had occurred between me and him. Upon this, therefore, the master and the merchants were convinced of my veracity, and recognized me; and they congratulated me on my safety, all of them saying, By Allah, we believed not that thou hadst escaped drowning; but God hath granted thee a new life. They then gave me the goods, and I found my name written upon them, and nought of them was missing. So I opened them, and took forth from them something precious and costly; the sailors of the ship carried it with me, and I went up with it to the King to offer it as a present, and inform him that this ship was the one in which I was a passenger. I told him also that my goods had arrived all entire, and that this present was a part of them. And the King wondered at this affair extremely; my veracity in all that I had said became manifest to him, and he loved me greatly, and treated me with exceeding honor, giving me a large present in return for mine.

Then I sold my bales, as well as the other goods that I had, and gained upon them abundantly; and I purchased other goods and merchandise and commodities of that city. And when the merchants of the ship desired to set forth on their voyage, I stowed all that I had in the vessel, and, going in to the King, thanked him for his beneficence and kindness; after which I begged him to grant me permission to depart on my voyage to my country and my family. So he bade me farewell, and gave me an abundance of things at my departure, of the commodities of that city; and when I had taken leave of him, I embarked in the ship, and we set sail by the permission of God, whose name

be exalted! Fortune served us, and destiny aided us, and we ceased not to prosecute our voyage night and day until we arrived in safety at the city of El-Basrah. There we landed and remained a short time; and I rejoiced at my safety, and my return to my country; and after that, I repaired to the city of Baghdad, the Abode of Peace, with abundance of bales and goods and merchandise of great value. Then I went to my quarter, and entered my house, and all my family and companions came to me. I procured for myself servants and other dependants, and memluks and concubines and male black slaves, so that I had a large establishment; and I purchased houses and other immovable possessions, more than I had at first. I enjoyed the society of my companions and friends, exceeding my former habits, and forgot all that I had suffered from fatigue, and absence from my native country, and difficulty, and the terrors of travel. I occupied myself with delights and pleasures, and delicious meats and exquisite drinks, and continued in this state.

PART THREE

THE MEDIEVAL WORLD

In conventional chronology the period of European history from about 450 to 1450 is known as the Middle Ages. The term is significant, for it was introduced by leaders of the Renaissance and by eighteenth-century intellectuals who considered everything between classic times and their own as "middle." According to them, it was an age of barbarism and darkness in which mankind had retrogressed.

This view of the age recalls the famous description of chaotic society by the seventeenth-century English philosopher Thomas Hobbes, in his *Leviathan*: "In such condition, there is no place for industry, because the fruit thereof is uncertain, and consequently no culture of the earth; no navigation nor use of the commodities that must be imported by sea; no commodious building; no instruments of moving and removing such things as require much force; no account of time; no arts; no letters; no society; and what is worst of all, continual fear and danger of violent death; and the life of man, solitary, poor, nasty and short." This depressing picture is supported by many facts, but these apply only to two or three centuries—from the sixth to the ninth. And even then, conditions were not uniform throughout Europe: In the southeastern part, the Byzantine, or Eastern Roman Empire, held its own, although it was steeped in decadence; in southwest Europe, vestiges of Roman civilization stood out like oases in the desert; everywhere the Church kept some order and maintained outposts of culture; and the Teutonic tribes that conquered the Roman world were either partially Romanized or had some orderly native customs.

After the tenth century, moreover, Europe began to move toward notable achievements. A world that produced the wonderful Gothic cathedrals, epics, romances, lyric poetry, medieval drama, and the philosophy of St. Thomas Aquinas, can hardly be called primitive. By the thirteenth century, in fact, Europe had experienced an early renaissance.

The literature that is most strictly medieval in spirit is that which emanated from medieval institutions. These were the medieval Church (which we have already considered); the world of the Celtic peoples of Ireland, Wales, and Brittany in northern France; the religious and warlike traditions of the Germanic peoples before and during their mastery of Europe; and the institutions of feudalism and chivalry. It is a literature that, in one sense, requires no introduction. We respond directly to its tales of heroism, to its wonder and magic, and to its chivalry and romance. However, we shall understand it better and shall be able to place it more intelligently in the stream of world literature, if we are familiar with its background. The history of this period consists largely of the conquests of the Germanic peoples, their adoption of Christianity, the mingling of the Germanic races with the older populations of the Roman empire, the establishment of a social pattern which we call feudalism, and the rise of those kingdoms and empires that laid the foundations for the states of modern Europe.

When in A.D. 493 Theodoric, a Gothic chieftain, became King of Rome, the classic empire in the West was split into numerous petty, unstable kingdoms. It was, in the sixth century, a "shattered civilization, without law, without administration, with roads destroyed and education disorganized."[1] It was an age of pillage and brigandage, with one group of invaders harrying the other.

A new organization became necessary if men were to survive at all, and it arose from the instinct for banding together and from the residue of civilized ideas and habits that many people retained. The freemen of towns or villages and the rulers of tiny communities began to align themselves with some comparatively powerful lord. They placed themselves under his protection, and thus arose the feudal system, which acquired a legal status as well as the traditions and customs now preserved only in the literature of romance. This form of association was partly inherited from the Roman economic and social system under which clients congregated around some wealthy patron, and partly from the Germanic military grouping of many warriors around some chieftain.

The system was pyramidal, in the sense that one lord would owe allegiance to a higher lord, who in turn was the vassal of a still more powerful leader; finally, a king stood on the apex of this pyramid of allegiances. It was even possible for one king to be the vassal of another; thus, for some time, the kings of England were supposed to be vassals of the kings of France. The relationships were often confused and loose; there was little uniformity of practice; and the system was frequently, in the words of H. G. Wells, little better than "confusion roughly organized."

Such a "system" obviously needed the cement of customs and ideals. "The foundation of the feudal relationship proper was the *fief*, which was usually land. . . . In return for the fief, the man became the *vassal* of his lord; he knelt before him, and, with his hands between the lord's hands, promised him fealty and service. . . . In the ceremony of homage[2] and investiture, which is the creative contract of feudalism, the obligations assumed by the two parties were, as a rule, not specified in exact terms. They were determined by local custom. . . . We may say, however, that they fall into classes, general and specific. The general included all that might come under the idea of loyalty, seeking the lord's interests, keeping his secrets, betraying the plans of his enemies, protecting his family, etc. The specific services . . . usually re- ceived exact definition in custom and sometimes in written documents. The most characteristic of these was the military service, which included appearance in the field on summons with a certain force, often armed in a specific way, and remaining a specified length of time." It was largely a private obligation, entered into voluntarily or forced upon the vassal by war. It always needed reaffirmation by custom, ceremony, or threat, or a show of force. But where this system was effectively enforced, under a strong ruler, stable kingdoms could actually flourish for a time.

The first real state to emerge was the Frankish kingdom in France, founded by Clovis (465-511), who extended his frontiers from Belgium to the Pyrenees. After his death, the kingdom split into two parts—Austrasia or the Rhineland, which retained the Low German speech, and Neurasia, the land of the Western Franks who had become more Romanized in culture and race, and who spoke the corrupted Latin of the conquered population, which later became the French tongue.[3] The court leaders of the successors of Clovis took over the government. It was one of these mayors, Charles Martel, who stopped the Moslems in the decisive battle of Poitiers in 732. His grandson, Charlemagne, actually established an empire that, during his lifetime, took the place of the one the Cæsars had lost to the Germanic invaders. He subjugated the Saxons and Bavarians, conquered northern Italy (Lombardy), and on Christmas Day in 800 was crowned Emperor of Rome by Pope Leo III.

More lasting than his empire-building and campaigns was Charlemagne's effort to introduce learning into his kingdom by attracting teachers to his court. From England, where the monasteries already had excellent scholars, he brought the learned Alcuin, and he established in his palace a school engaged in literary and theological discussion. He collected the war-songs and tales of the early Teutons. He encouraged architecture, importing architects from Italy; built numerous cathedrals, and founded monastic schools.

These beginnings were not fated to develop as rapidly as Charlemagne expected, and his empire fell apart. Europe began to be harassed by new invasions from the north. The seafaring Vikings, whose destructiveness became proverbial, pushed into England, invaded northern France, and estab-

---

[1] H. G. Wells, *Outline of Civilization*, p. 607.

[2] That is, of becoming somebody's *man* (*homme*).

[3] Where the Franks were not Latinized, they became the Flemings of Belgium, and the Dutch of southern Holland.

lished the kingdom of Normandy, in 885. Nevertheless, Europe recovered from these fresh onslaughts within a century. The Danes in England were assimilated, and in Wessex, Alfred the Great inaugurated a veritable revival of learning. In Normandy, the Northmen or Normans (who lent their name to this province) quickly adopted Frankish customs, intermarried with the French, and developed feudalism to a high degree. When they invaded England in 1066, they brought with them a culture manifestly superior to that of the Anglo-Saxons.

Throughout this early period, the Church was making itself a powerful center of culture. Its first medieval leader, Gregory I (540-604), started missions that Christianized and civilized the barbaric tribes. It was with his sanction that his friend St. Benedict was able to establish the civilizing Benedictine monasteries that took the place of the Roman schools. The Benedictine monks served God actively with their minds and hands, in accordance with the Benedictine formula that to work was to pray (*laborare est orare*). They were pioneers in agriculture, not disdaining to soil their hands with common toil and thus raising labor to some dignity in the eyes of warriors who considered fighting the only manly occupation. These monks also became craftsmen, and busy towns grew up around their monasteries; they even started medieval architecture, some of them working as master masons. In addition, they preserved, copied, and illustrated manuscripts. Although the Benedictine monasteries were ultimately corrupted by wealth, they were unassailable outposts of culture for centuries.

In the eleventh century a strong cleric, Pope Gregory VII (1020-1085), reformed the Church, making it powerful enough to curb emperors and to give Europe some sorely needed spiritual and moral guidance. His successor Urban II (1042-1099) introduced a new spiritual ferment by inspiring the first Crusade. This brought the many warring feudal lords together; and although they never ceased quarreling, their meeting as allies was beneficial. Contact with Moslem civilization proved particularly enriching, and European culture began to flower again.

Meanwhile, in southern France (the Provence), during the eleventh and twelfth centuries, industry started to flourish; universities, at which Jewish scholars taught, arose in Narbonne and Montpellier; and feudal chivalry began to express itself in refined manners and a new literature based not on Teutonic mythology and war stories, but on tales of pleasure and love. The poetry of its *troubadours* spread into Italy, northern France, and Germany. From Germany, moreover, came the half-Italian, autocratic Emperor Frederick II, who gathered Jewish, Mohammedan, and Christian scholars at his court in Sicily. Arabic numerals and algebra were introduced there, and Aristotle was studied in translations and in Arabian-Jewish commentaries. Frederick established the University of Naples and expanded the ancient medical school at Salermo. Himself a writer of Italian poetry, he could point with some pride to the *minnesingers*, in the German part of his realm, writers of love poetry, whose lyrics and romances are a memorable portion of medieval literature. The greatest of them, Walther von der Vogelweide, expressed the same liberal opinions as the emperor, and the same revolt against too much priestly authority. In northern France, too, a succession of rulers encouraged the development of culture; they patronized poets known as *trouvères*. A great university arose in Paris, and its most brilliant twelfth-century teacher Peter Abelard shaped theological disputation into a fine instrument for intellectual analysis.

The gradual elevation of woman's social position was another powerful ferment. Woman had been maligned by the zealous celibates of the early Church, considered the greatest obstacle to salvation, and blamed for causing Adam to be driven out of Paradise. This attitude was summarized by a monk who declared that at the beginning "There was but one woman; yet she had no rest until she succeeded in banishing her husband from the garden of delights and in condemning Christ to the torture of the Cross"—that is, by making it necessary for God to redeem mankind. In practice, however, this attitude could not be maintained, nor was it conducive to morality. The sexual behavior of the new noblemen and kings of Europe was often immoral, if not bestial; and the Church was not unwilling to foster the cult of the Virgin, which arose out of people's need for a gentle intermediary between themselves and Christ. The worship of Mary was expressed in pious poems, in tender legends, and in an entire cycle of French plays, *The Miracles of the Virgin*.

The later Middle Ages witnessed a marked improvement in woman's status. She was now respected and idealized, and from her new eminence she could exert a wholesome influence. Manners improved, and the entire etiquette of chivalry arose; it may have been excessive and artificial, but it served to counteract barbarism.

Even more important, however, was the social development that arose out of the economic organization of the Middle Ages. In time prosperous trading towns arose on the Baltic, North Sea, and Mediterranean coasts, and these were augmented by cities given over to both trade and industry in northern Italy, France, Flanders, and England. Large urban populations arose in the thirteenth century: Paris had 240,000 people; London 50,000; Florence, Venice, and Milan each had over 100,000. Many merchants were wealthier than the barons and indulged in luxuries envied by the aristocracy. Craftsmen, organized in craft associations known as *guilds*, became increasingly ingenious and prosperous, acquired pride of class, and struggled successfully with feudal overlords. A new middle class was born, a class that enlarged rapidly and was destined in time to substitute modern capitalist economy and democracy for feudalism. It was in these towns that the medieval theater became a notable institution, popularizing the Bible and secularizing its stories to such a degree that the biblical heroes were represented on the stage as medieval peasants and merchants.

In the twelfth century the medieval institution of serfdom began to collapse. Rumblings of protest stirred, for the serfs' lords were often capricious and selfish, and no allowances were made for bad seasons. Peasant revolts were so frequent that "Beware of the villein"[4] became a common saying, and so this formerly innocent name for a serf assumed its modern meaning. Great estates were crumbling, for many barons died in the Crusades or bankrupted themselves with their incessant fighting and sold their land to merchants, or allowed serfs to purchase their freedom. Kings, who were beginning to count on commoners for support against the feudal aristocracy, and sympathetic townspeople helped the peasantry win its freedom, with the result that by the close of the thirteenth century large sections of the rural population enjoyed true independence. Within a generation, as a result of dynastic and national conflicts, many freemen were pushed back into serfdom by indebtedness and legalistic trickery. But the leaven of freedom continued to rise. Even when the peasants suffered such disasters as the brutal crushing of Wat Tyler's revolt in England and of the fierce revolt of the French peasantry known as the *Jac-*

querie, their protest and their dream of human freedom and self-respect could not be suppressed. Democratic forces were released and made themselves felt in an increasing middle class and in a class of free farmers. Even in a military sense, the old feudal aristocracy could no longer remain unchallenged after the long-bow of the English yeoman overthrew the panoplied pomp of the French nobility during the Hundred Years War. What remained after the fifteenth century were feudal privileges, but political power passed into the hands of strong monarchs like the Tudors, and economic power into the shops and savings-accounts of the middle class.

This, in brief, is the story of the formative centuries of modern Europe; their literature reflects their diversified and complex life. The main trends of this literature fall into five classifications:

1. The literature of the Church, written in medieval Latin. This we have already considered in *The Christian Church.*

2. The myths and sagas of the Germanic tribes. These are of remote antiquity; they stem from the pre-Christian stage of the Germanic tribes, although they were written down largely during the Christian period. Much of this literature therefore has Christian elements, but these are largely superficial, and pagan customs and beliefs predominate. The zeal of Christian copyists preserved only a part of this literature; however, this remainder possesses a primitive directness and an epic force.

3. The myths and tales of the Celts, whose exotic literature was later incorporated into the romances of chivalry and transformed in the process. In its pure state, it is pagan and magical.

4. The literature of feudalism and chivalry. Its chief forms are: refined poetry written by courtly poets chiefly on love and woman-worship; such epics of chivalry (*chansons de geste*) as *The Song of Roland;* and romances like the numerous stories written about King Arthur and his knights.

5. The literature of the people, consisting of simple songs, ballads, and tales. The latter fall into two classes: pious stories or legends and *fabliaux* or humorous verse tales, mostly of roguery, which reflect the life of the peasant and merchant. The legends satisfied the hard-pressed commoner's need for religious consolation; the *fabliaux,* his desire for humor and the kind of release one finds in

___
[4] This name for the serf was derived from the Roman word for an estate—*villa.* From this also came the word *village.*

mockery. The legends were, in a sense, the romances of the downtrodden; the *fabliaux,* their literature of social protest.

Typical of the legends are the story of St. Hugh, the murdered Christian child who was pieced together and made whole by the Virgin, and the lovely tale of *Our Lady's Tumbler.* In this legend, a minstrel-acrobat enters a monastery; unable, because of ignorance, to recite the Latin prayers, the simple monk goes into the crypt and leaps and dances in honor of the Virgin, thereby winning sainthood.

Good *fabliaux* are: *The Three Thieves,* in which each thief outwits the other; *The Divided Horsecloth,* in which an ungrateful son who drives off his aged father is promised similar treatment by his own son who has watched his behavior; and *The Ass's Last Will and Testament,* written by the French minstrel Rutebeuf who mocks the greed of the clergy.

Fairy tales and the story of *Reynard the Fox,* showing how cunning and craft may prevail against brute strength such as the nobles possessed, also belong to the literature of the people In *Reynard the Fox,* we find the same spirit that animates the democratic *fabliaux.* Indeed, the demo-cratic spirit even found its way into one of the episodes of so delicate a romance as *Aucassin and Nicolete.* In another romance of the eleventh century (*Roman de Rose*) the rebellious peasants who killed the bishop of Laon and burned the castles of their masters, declare: "We are men, we are men even as they are; such limbs as they have we have; as great bodies have we; and we can endure as much. Nothing fails us and we can endure as much. Nothing fails us but heart alone. Let us ally ourselves by oath. Let us defend our own and ourselves. Let us keep together, and if they wish to fight, we have against one knight thirty or forty peasants, vigorous and strong to fight."

Still another form of popular literature is the drama of the Middle Ages, which began in the Church and ended in the market-place. As it emerged out of an early liturgical form and began to be written in the vernaculars, the entire body of miracle plays about saints and the Virgin and "mystery plays" about biblical episodes became permeated with popular elements.

It is necessary to remember that the Middle Ages were no less complex than other eras, and that saga and romance are merely the wild and the cultivated flowers of a vast terrain.

GERMANIC MYTH AND SAGA

The character of the medieval world was formed by the fusion of three racial elements—the Roman, the Celtic, and Germanic, of which the last was the most vigorous. It is true that the older non-Germanic population in many cases absorbed and transformed the Germanic invaders in western Europe, and that the Church modified their outlook and way of life. However, they did not lose their identity in Germany and Scandinavia, and they continued to harass the rest of Europe and to shape medieval history for many centuries.

Their warlike spirit permeated European life and literature. Their grim humor, violent passions, and glorification of brute courage retreated into the background only after chivalry had completely captivated the nobility, and after the rising middle class had thrust into the foreground the peaceful interests of trade and industry. Even the Teutonic superstitions and pagan rites held their own, in one form or another. They were retained in folk customs such as sword-dances, Christmas mummings, and Maypole dancing; in the widespread belief in demons during the Middle Ages; and in the Church itself, after it had accommodated itself to the traditions of the pagans it had converted. Thus, "the Christian commemoration of the tremendous drama of Calvary took even its name from Eastre, the gracious goddess of spring so well loved that her converted votaries would not have her degraded to the rank of a demon."[1]

Germanic mythology managed to survive intact in Scandinavia and Iceland because it was there that Germanic culture remained least modified. Here the myths were regarded by the Christian converts as a great allegory of nature.

We may be grateful that this mythology was not destroyed with the advent of Christianity, for it has given us magnificent stories. The rugged poems that include these tales have the loftiness of the Northern mountain ridges; not merely a "greatness of mere body and gigantic bulk," as Carlyle says, "but a rude greatness of soul." European chivalry may have ignored or even forgotten them, but they remained intact throughout the Middle Ages. They were added to our heritage in the eighteenth century by romanticists like the compiler of British ballads, Bishop Percy, and the poet Thomas Gray.

The myths, so important to the understanding of the Germanic peoples that we include Bulfinch's account of them, were the common property of all the early German nations.

Linguistic scholars divide the Germanic stock into three large groups. The East Germanic or Gothic tribes were important during the final contest with the Roman Empire, but soon ceased to be an active force and eventually lost their identity.

North and west of the Goths were the West Germanic peoples. Of these the High Germanic branch has continued to occupy southern Germany, and its language has gradually spread over the whole of the present German Empire. The Low Germanic peoples are the Low Germans who live in northern Germany;[2] the old tribes of Angles, Saxons, and Jutes, who migrated to England in the fifth and sixth centuries; the Frisians and Dutch of Holland; and the Flemish inhabitants of Belgium. It should be noted that our English language belongs to this low Germanic branch.

The North Germanic, Norse, or Scandinavian group, consists of the Norwegians, Danes, Swedes, and Icelanders.

From about 900 to 1300, and even somewhat later, the Scandinavians evinced great industry in writing and produced the best Germanic poetry, especially in Iceland, which maintained close cultural contact with Scandinavia. These people, as early as the eighth century, had begun to disturb the peace of Europe. In several great waves of invasion covering some three centuries, they subdued large parts of England and Ireland and left an indelible imprint on Scotland. They settled Normandy in northern France and, after several generations in which they had become good Frenchmen, conquered the Anglo-Saxons in 1066 and took possession of England. Meantime they had occupied Iceland and had begun the development of a vigorous colony in that remote island. By 1000 they were exploring the shores of North America.

The literature produced by the Norse peoples is remarkable for vigor and intensity. It reflects a strong and adventurous race, superstitious, filled with thoughts of doom, and fond of their bard's (or *skald's*) recitals of actual adventures, to which were added numerous legendary details. They celebrate passion and heroism, are frequently cruel, and describe a world as hard as the northern winter.

Most characteristic of Norse writing are the poems of the *Elder Edda*[3] (*circa* 900-1250). The *Elder* or *Poetic Edda*, which was recovered by an Icelandic bishop in 1643, is a collection of numerous poems, heroic legends, and moralistic statements. The poems must have been composed in different periods, since they vary in style and spirit; and many of them have come down to us in a fragmentary state. But they are invariably dignified and exalted, and the verses have one characteristic common to early Germanic poetry, namely, *alliteration*. There is a correspondence between the sound of words in the two halves of many of the lines, though rhyme is also used. Each line is divided into two halves by a pause (or cæsura), and contains two accented syllables, beginning with the same letter, and three or four unaccented ones.

The *Elder Edda* appears to have been created between 800 and 1100. It opens with the *Völuspá* or

---

[1] E. B. Osborne, *The Middle Ages,* p. 22. An interesting example of popular medieval mythology combining classic and Teutonic elements is to be found in the Tannhauser story, celebrated in opera by Richard Wagner. The Germanic goddess Hulda was identified with Venus, who was degraded by medieval Christianity to the rank of a witch or enchantress. It is in this capacity that she seduced the minstrel and knight Tannhauser.

[2] Called Low Germans because they occupied the countries downstream. "Middle" High German, the literary language of much medieval literature, bears to modern German the same relationship that Chaucer's English (called "Middle English") bears to modern English.

[3] The word *Edda,* which means great-grandmother, suggests the antiquity of the stories.

The Vision of the Prophetess, a kind of Norse Genesis, which describes the beginnings of the world and its doom. Another group of poems, *Hávamál* or *The Sayings of the High One,* is a book of proverbs concerning social conduct and morals. A whole cycle of heroic poems contains the old Norse version of the Siegfried story which later appeared in the German poem the *Nibelungenlied* and in Wagner's operatic cycle, *The Ring of the Nibelungs.* These are vividly descriptive and show remarkable penetration into human feeling and motivation. Our selections, *The Short Lay of Sigurd* and *The Hell-Ride of Brynhild,* correspond to the story told in Wagner's opera *Götterdämmerung (The Dusk of the Gods).*

A somewhat later type of writing is the court poetry of the *skalds* or court minstrels. It differs in a number of respects from Eddic verse. It is not anonymous but the work of known poets. The Eddic poems present Norse mythology, heroic love, and ethics; skaldic poetry celebrates kings and chieftains. The former is simple, the other, intricate and full of poetic diction, abounding in far-fetched metaphorical expressions (known as *kennings*). In the original, the form of the poems is elaborate and complicated, for the skalds were not only master narrators but skilled versifiers.

A third form of Norse literature is the great body of Icelandic *sagas* (stories), historical and biographical prose narratives, mingled with fiction or entirely fictitious. Written between the twelfth and fifteenth centuries, the sagas were the outgrowth of a long oral tradition. Story-tellers or "saga-men" were popular in Iceland because they furnished the chief form of entertainment, but they did not, as a rule, attach their names to their tales. The sagas are sheer narrative writing, objective instead of moralizing, and admirably concise. The stories are carefully constructed, the characters sharply etched, being revealed through action and speech. Most of the stories are intensely tragic, although one of the best (*the Bandamanna*) is a rollicking satire on Icelandic political leaders.

Poets in Germany also enriched medieval literature, but their contributions were in no case as original as those made by the Scandinavians. After 1150, German literature began to flourish under the influence of Christianity, chivalry, and French lyricism and romance. Its outstanding epic, the *Nibelungenlied* (c. 1200), retells the old Norse tale of Sigurd, with Christian and chivalric coloring. The Norse warrior, Sigurd, is here the medieval knight, Sir Siegfried; the Valkyrie Brunhilde (Brynhild in the Norse poems), whom he wooed and abandoned and who encompassed his destruction, is considerably tamed in the German version, and is deprived of all supernatural qualities except her strength. Siegfried's wife Kriemhilde, before his murder makes her vengeful, is a courtly lady.

When these epics came to be written down, Germany was also witnessing the flowering of some folk poetry and of excellent lyric poetry known as *Minnesong,* written under the influence of the poetry of southern France. This movement produced many lyric poets, among whom there were some who brought freshness and depth to love poetry. Still, it is the epic writings of Germanic peoples that made the greatest impression on English literature, and their pristine spirit is best exemplified by the Norse heroic poems. They are not only the original storehouse of Germanic myth, but a universal poetry, revealing elemental conceptions and passions never wholly absent in man.

STORIES FROM NORSE MYTHOLOGY

Thor's Visit to Jotunheim

One day the god Thor, with his servant Thialfi, and accompanied by Loki, set out on a journey to the giant's country. Thialfi was of all men the swiftest of foot. He bore Thor's wallet, containing their provisions. When night came on they found themselves in an immense forest, and searched on all sides for a place where they might pass the night, and at last came to a very large hall, with an entrance that took the whole breadth of one end of the building. Here they lay down to sleep, but towards midnight were alarmed by an earthquake which shook the whole edifice. Thor, rising up, called on his companions to seek with him a place of safety. On the right they found an adjoining chamber, into which the others entered, but Thor remained at the doorway with his mallet in his hand, prepared to defend himself, whatever might happen. A terrible groaning was heard dur-

Stories from Norse Mythology. From Bulfinch, *The Age of Fable.*

ing the night, and at dawn of day Thor went out and found lying near him a huge giant, who slept and snored in the way that had alarmed them so. It is said that for once Thor was afraid to use his mallet, and as the giant soon waked up, Thor contented himself with simply asking his name.

"My name is Skrymir," said the giant, "but I need not ask thy name, for I know that thou art the god Thor. But what has become of my glove?" Thor then perceived that what they had taken overnight for a hall was the giant's glove, and the chamber where his two companions had sought refuge was the thumb. Skrymir then proposed that they should travel in company, and Thor consenting, they sat down to eat their breakfast, and when they had done, Skrymir packed all the provisions into one wallet, threw it over his shoulder, and strode on before them, taking such tremendous strides that they were hard put to it to keep up with him. So they traveled the whole day, and at dusk Skrymir chose a place for them to pass the night in under a large oak tree. Skrymir then told them he would lie down to sleep. "But take ye the wallet," he added, "and prepare your supper."

Skrymir soon fell asleep and began to snore strongly; but when Thor tried to open the wallet, he found the giant had tied it up so tight he could not untie a single knot. At last Thor became wroth, and grasping his mallet with both hands he struck a furious blow on the giant's head. Skrymir, awakening, merely asked whether a leaf had not fallen on his head, and whether they had supped and were ready to go to sleep. Thor answered that they were just going to sleep, and so saying went and laid himself down under another tree. But sleep came not that night to Thor, and when Skrymir snored again so loud that the forest re-echoed with the noise, he arose, and grasping his mallet launched it with such force at the giant's skull that it make a deep dint in it. Skrymir, awakening, cried out, "What's the matter? Are there any birds perched on this tree? I felt some moss from the branches fall on my head. How fares it with thee, Thor?" But Thor went away hastily, saying that he had just then awoke, and that it was only midnight, there was still time for sleep. He, however, resolved that if he had an opportunity of striking a third blow, it should settle all matters between them. A little before daybreak he perceived that Skrymir was again fast asleep, and again grasping his mallet, he dashed it with such violence that it forced its way into the giant's skull

up to the handle. But Skrymir sat up, and stroking his cheek said, "An acorn fell on my head. What! Art thou awake, Thor? Methinks it is time for us to get up and dress ourselves; but you have not now a long way before you to the city called Utgard. I have heard you whispering to one another that I am not a man of small dimensions; but if you come to Utgard you will see there many men much taller than I. Wherefore I advise you, when you come there, not to make too much of yourselves, for the followers of Utgard-Loki will not brook the boasting of such little fellows as you are. You must take the road that leads eastward, mine lies northward, so we must part here."

Hereupon he threw his wallet over his shoulders and turned away from them into the forest, and Thor had no wish to stop him or to ask for any more of his company.

Thor and his companions proceeded on their way, and towards noon descried a city standing in the middle of a plain. It was so lofty that they were obliged to bend their necks quite far back on their shoulders in order to see to the top of it. On arriving they entered the city, and seeing a large palace before them with the door wide open, they went in, and found a number of men of prodigious stature, sitting on benches in the hall. Going further, they came before the king, Utgard-Loki, whom they saluted with great respect. The king, regarding them with a scornful smile, said, "If I do not mistake me, that stripling yonder must be the god Thor." Then addressing himself to Thor, he said, "Perhaps thou mayst be more than thou appearest to be. What are the feats that thou and thy fellows deem yourselves skilled in, for no one is permitted to remain here who does not, in some feat or other, excel all other men?"

"The feat that I know," said Loki, "is to eat quicker than anyone else, and in this I am ready to give a proof against anyone here who may choose to compete with me."

"That will indeed be a feat," said Utgard-Loki, "if thou performest what thou promisest, and it shall be tried forthwith."

He then ordered one of his men who was sitting at the farther end of the bench, and whose name was Logi, to come forward and try his skill with Loki. A trough filled with meat having been set on the hall floor, Loki placed himself at one end, and Logi at the other, and each of them began to eat as fast as he could, until they met in the middle of the trough. But it was found that Loki had only eaten the flesh, while his adversary had devoured both flesh and bone, and the trough to boot. All the company therefore adjudged that Loki was vanquished.

Utgard-Loki then asked what feat the young man who accompanied Thor could perform. Thialfi answered that he would run a race with anyone who might be matched against him. The king observed that skill in running was something to boast of, but if the youth would win the match he must display great agility. He then arose and went with all who were present to a plain where there was good ground for running on, and calling a young man named Hugi, bade him run a match with Thialfi. In the first course Hugi so much outstripped his competitor that he turned back and met him not far from the starting place. Then they ran a second and a third time, but Thialfi met with no better success.

Utgard-Loki then asked Thor in what feats he would choose to give proofs of that prowess for which he was so famous. Thor answered that he would try a drinking-match with anyone. Utgard-Loki bade his cupbearer bring the large horn which his followers were obliged to empty when they had trespassed in any way against the law of the feast. The cupbearer having presented it to Thor, Utgard-Loki said, "Whoever is a good drinker will empty that horn at a single draught, though most men make two of it, but the most puny drinker can do it in three."

Thor looked at the horn, which seemed of no extraordinary size though somewhat long; however, as he was very thirsty, he set it to his lips, and without drawing breath, pulled as long and as deeply as he could, that he might not be obliged to make a second draught of it; but when he set the horn down and looked in, he could scarcely perceive that the liquor was diminished.

After taking breath, Thor went to it again with all his might, but when he took the horn from his mouth, it seemed to him that he had drunk rather less than before, although the horn could now be carried without spilling.

"How now, Thor?" said Utgard-Loki; "thou must not spare thyself; if thou meanest to drain the horn at the third draught thou must pull deeply; and I must needs say that thou wilt not be called so mighty a man here as thou art at home if thou showest no greater prowess in other feats than methinks will be shown in this."

Thor, full of wrath, again set the horn to his lips, and did his best to empty it; but on looking in found the liquor was only a little lower, so he resolved to make no further attempt, but gave back the horn to the cupbearer.

"I now see plainly," said Utgard-Loki, "that thou art not quite so stout as we thought thee: but wilt thou try any other feat, though methinks thou art not likely to bear any prize away with thee hence."

"What new trial hast thou to propose?" said Thor.

"We have a very trifling game here," answered Utgard-Loki, "in which we exercise none but children. It consists in merely lifting my cat from the ground; nor should I have dared to mention such a feat to the great Thor if I had not already observed that thou art by no means what we took thee for."

As he finished speaking, a large gray cat sprang on the hall floor. Thor put his hand under the cat's belly and did his utmost to raise him from the floor, but the cat, bending his back, had, notwithstanding all Thor's efforts, only one of his feet lifted up, seeing which Thor made no further attempt.

"This trial has turned out," said Utgard-Loki, "just as I imagined it would. The cat is large, but Thor is little in comparison to our men."

"Little as ye call me," answered Thor, "let me see who among you will come hither now I am in wrath and wrestle with me."

"I see no one here," said Utgard-Loki, looking at the men sitting on the benches, "who would not think it beneath him to wrestle with thee; let somebody, however, call hither that old crone, my nurse Elli, and let Thor wrestle with her if he will. She has thrown to the ground many a man not less strong than this Thor is."

A toothless old woman then entered the hall, and was told by Utgard-Loki to take hold of Thor. The tale is shortly told. The more Thor tightened his hold on the crone the firmer she stood. At length after a very violent struggle Thor began to lose his footing, and was finally brought down upon one knee. Utgard-Loki then told them to desist, adding that Thor had now no occasion to ask anyone else in the hall to wrestle with him, and it was also getting late; so he showed Thor and his companions to their seats, and they passed the night there in good cheer.

The next morning, at break of day, Thor and his companions dressed themselves and prepared for their departure. Utgard-Loki ordered a table to be set for them, on which there was no lack of victuals or drink. After the repast Utgard-Loki led them to the gate of the city, and on parting asked Thor how he thought his journey had turned out, and whether he had met with any men stronger than himself. Thor told him that he could not deny but that he had brought great shame on himself. "And what grieves me most," he added, "is that ye will call me a person of little worth."

"Nay," said Utgard-Loki, "it behooves me to tell thee the truth, now thou art out of the city, which so long as I live and have my way thou shalt never enter again. And, by my troth, had I known beforehand that thou hadst so much strength in thee, and wouldst have brought me so near to a great mishap, I would not have suffered thee to enter this time. Know then that I have all along deceived thee by my illusions; first in the forest, where I tied up the wallet with iron wire so that thou couldst not untie it. After this thou gavest me three blows with thy mallet; the first, though the least, would have ended my days had it fallen on me, but I slipped aside and thy blows fell on the mountain, where thou wilt find three glens, one of them remarkably deep. These are the dints made by thy mallet. I have made use of similar illusions in the contests you have had with my followers. In the first, Loki, like hunger itself, devoured all that was set before him, but Logi was in reality nothing else than Fire, and therefore consumed not only the meat, but the trough which held it. Hugi, with whom Thialfi contended in running, was Thought, and it was impossible for Thialfi to keep pace with that. When thou in thy turn didst attempt to empty the horn, thou didst perform, by my troth, a deed so marvelous that had I not seen it myself I should never have believed it. For one end of that horn reached the sea, which thou wast not aware of, but when thou comest to the shore thou wilt perceive how much the sea has sunk by thy draughts. Thou didst perform a feat no less wonderful by lifting up the cat, and to tell thee the truth, when we saw that one of his paws was off the floor, we were all of us terror-stricken, for what thou tookest for a cat was in reality the Midgard serpent that encompasseth the earth, and he was so stretched by thee that he was barely long enough to enclose it between his head and tail. Thy wrestling with Elli was also a most astonishing feat, for there was never yet a man, nor ever will be, whom Old Age, for such in fact was Elli, will not sooner or later lay low. But now, as we are going to part, let me tell thee that it will be better for both of us if thou never come

near me again, for shouldst thou do so, I shall again defend myself by other illusions, so that thou wilt only lose thy labor and get no fame from the contest with me."

On hearing these words Thor in a rage laid hold of his mallet and would have launched it at him, but Utgard-Loki had disappeared, and when Thor would have returned to the city to destroy it, he found nothing around him but a verdant plain.

The Death of Baldur

Baldur the Good, having been tormented with terrible dreams indicating that his life was in peril, told them to the assembled gods, who resolved to conjure all things to avert from him the threatened danger. Then Frigga, the wife of Odin, exacted an oath from fire and water, from iron and all other metals, from stones, trees, diseases, beasts, birds, poisons, and creeping things, that none of them would do any harm to Baldur. Odin, not satisfied with all this, and feeling alarmed for the fate of his son, determined to consult the prophetess Angerbode, a giantess, mother of Fenris, Hela, and the Midhard serpent. She was dead, and Odin was forced to seek her in Hela's dominions. This Descent of Odin forms the subject of Gray's fine ode beginning:

> Uprose the king of men with speed
> And saddled straight his coal-black steed.

But the other gods, feeling that what Frigga had done was quite sufficient, amused themselves with using Baldur as a mark, some hurling darts at him, some stones, while others hewed at him with their swords and battle-axes; for do what they would, none of them could harm him. And this became a favorite pastime with them and was regarded as an honor shown to Baldur. But when Loki beheld the scene he was sorely vexed that Baldur was not hurt. Assuming, therefore, the shape of a woman, he went to Fensalir, the mansion of Frigga. That goddess, when she saw the pretended woman, inquired of her if she knew what the gods were doing at their meetings. She replied that they were throwing darts and stones at Baldur, without being able to hurt him. "Aye," said Frigga, "neither stones, nor sticks, nor anything else can hurt Baldur, for I have exacted an oath from all of them." "What," exclaimed the woman, "have all things sworn to spare Baldur?" "All things," replied Frigga, "except one little shrub that grows on the eastern side of Valhalla, and is called Mistletoe, and which I thought too young and feeble to crave an oath from."

As soon as Loki heard this he went away, and resuming his natural shape, cut off the mistletoe, and repaired to the place where the gods were assembled. There he found Hodur standing apart, without partaking of the sports, on account of his blindness, and going up to him, said, "Why dost thou not also throw something at Baldur?"

"Because I am blind," answered Hodur, "and see not where Baldur is, and have, moreover, nothing to throw."

"Come, then," said Loki, "do like the rest, and show honor to Baldur by throwing this twig at him, and I will direct thy arm towards the place where he stands."

Hodur then took the mistletoe, and under the guidance of Loki, darted it at Baldur, who, pierced through and through, fell down lifeless. Surely never was there witnessed, either among gods or men, a more atrocious deed than this. When Baldur fell, the gods were struck speechless with horror, and then they looked at each other, and all were of one mind to lay hands on him who had done the deed, but they were obliged to delay their vengeance out of respect for the sacred place where they were assembled. They gave vent to their grief by loud lamentations. When the gods came to themselves, Frigga asked who among them wished to gain all her love and good will. "For this," said she, "shall he have who will ride to Hel and offer Hela a ransom if she will let Baldur return to Asgard." Whereupon Hermod, surnamed the Nimble, the son of Odin, offered to undertake the journey. Odin's horse, Sleipnir, which has eight legs and can outrun the wind, was then led forth, on which Hermod mounted and galloped away on his mission. For the space of nine days and as many nights he rode through deep glens so dark that he could not discern anything, until he arrived at the river Gyoll, which he passed over on a bridge covered with glittering gold. The maiden who kept the bridge asked him his name and lineage, telling him that the day before five bands of dead persons had ridden over the bridge, and did not shake it as much as he alone. "But," she added, "thou hast not death's hue on thee; why then ridest thou here on the way to Hel?"

"I ride to Hel," answered Hermod, "to seek Baldur. Hast thou perchance seen him pass this way?"

She replied, "Baldur hath ridden over Gyoll's bridge, and yonder lieth the way he took to the abodes of death."

Hermod pursued his journey until he came to the barred gates of Hel. Here he alighted, girthed his saddle tighter, and remounting clapped both spurs to his horse, who cleared the gate by a tremendous leap without touching it. Hermod then rode on to the palace, where he found his brother Baldur occupying the most distinguished seat in the hall, and passed the night in his company. The next morning he besought Hela to let Baldur ride home with him, assuring her that nothing but lamentations were to be heard among the gods. Hela answered that it should now be tried whether Baldur was so beloved as he was said to be. "If, therefore," she added, "all things in the world, both living and lifeless, weep for him, then shall he return to life; but if any one thing speak against him or refuse to weep, he shall be kept in Hel."

Hermod then rode back to Asgard and gave an account of all he had heard and witnessed.

The gods upon this despatched messengers throughout the world to beg everything to weep in order that Baldur might be delivered from Hel. All things very willingly complied with this request, both men and every other living being, as well as earths, and stones, and trees, and metals, just as we have all seen these things weep when they are brought from a cold place into a hot one. As the messengers were returning they found an old hag named Thaukt sitting in a cavern, and begged her to weep Baldur out of Hel. But she answered:

> Thaukt will wail
> With dry tears
> Baldur's bale-fire.
> Let Hela keep her own.

It was strongly suspected that this hag was no other than Loki himself, who never ceased to work evil among gods and men. So Baldur was prevented from coming back to Asgard.

The Funeral of Baldur

The gods took up the dead body and bore it to the seashore where stood Baldur's ship *Hringham,* which passed for the largest in the world. Baldur's dead body was put on the funeral pile, on board the ship, and his wife Nanna was so struck with grief at the sight that she broke her heart, and her body was burned on the same pile with her husband's. There was a vast concourse of various kinds of people at Baldur's obsequies. First came Odin accompanied by Frigga, the Valkyrior, and his ravens; then Frey in his car drawn by Gullinbursti, the boar; Heimdall rode his horse Gulltopp, and Freya drove in her chariot drawn by cats. There were also a great many Frost giants and giants of the mountain present. Baldur's horse was led to the pile fully caparisoned and consumed in the same flames with his master.

But Loki did not escape his deserved punishment. When he saw how angry the gods were, he fled to the mountain, and there built himself a hut with four doors, so that he could see every approaching danger. He invented a net to catch the fishes, such as fishermen have used since his time. But Odin found out his hiding-place and the gods assembled to take him. He, seeing this, changed himself into a salmon, and lay hid among the stones of the brook. But the gods took his net and dragged the brook, and Loki, finding he must be caught, tried to leap over the net; but Thor caught him by the tail and compressed it, so that salmons ever since have had that part remarkably fine and thin. They bound him with chains and suspended a serpent over his head, whose venom falls upon his face drop by drop. His wife Siguna sits by his side and catches the drops as they fall, in a cup; but when she carries it away to empty it, the venom falls upon Loki, which makes him howl with horror, and twist his body about so violently that the whole earth shakes, and this produces what men call earthquakes.

The Elves

The Edda mentions another class of beings, inferior to the gods, but still possessed of great power; these were called Elves. The white spirits, or Elves of Light, were exceedingly fair, more brilliant than the sun, and clad in garments of a delicate and transparent texture. They loved the light, were kindly disposed to mankind, and generally appeared as fair and lovely children. Their country was called Alfheim, and was the domain of Freyr, the god of the sun, in whose light they were always sporting.

The black or Night Elves were a different kind of creatures. Ugly, long-nosed dwarfs, of a dirty brown color, they appeared only at night, for they avoided the sun as their most deadly enemy, because whenever his beams fell upon any of them they changed them immediately into stones. Their language was the echo of solitudes, and their dwelling-places subterranean caves and clefts. They were supposed to have come into existence as maggots produced by the decaying flesh of Ymir's body, and were afterwards endowed by the gods with a human form and great understanding. They were particularly distinguished for a knowledge of the mysterious powers of nature, and for the runes which they carved and explained. They were the most skillful artificers of all created beings, and worked in metals and in wood. Among their most noted works were Thor's hammer, and the ship *Skidbladnir,* which they gave to Freyr, and which was so large that it could contain all the deities with their war and household implements, but so skillfully was it wrought that when folded together it could be put into a side pocket.

Ragnarok, the Twilight of the Gods

It was a firm belief of the northern nations that a time would come when all the visible creation, the gods of Valhalla and Niffleheim, the inhabitants of Jotunheim, Alfheim, and Midgard, together with their habitations, would be destroyed. The fearful day of destruction will not, however, be without its forerunners. First will come a triple winter, during which snow will fall from the four corners of the heavens, the frost be very severe, the wind piercing, the weather tempestuous, and the sun impart no gladness. Three such winters will pass away without being tempered by a single summer. Three other similar winters will then follow, during which war and discord will spread over the universe. The earth itself will be frightened and begin to tremble, the sea leave its basin, the heavens tear asunder, and men perish in great numbers, and the eagles of the air feast upon their still quivering bodies. The wolf Fenris will now break his bands, the Midgard serpent rise out of her bed in the sea, and Loki, released from his bonds, will join the enemies of the gods. Amidst the general devastation the sons of Muspelheim will rush forth under their leader Surtur, before and behind whom are flames and burning fire. Onward they ride over Bifrost, the rainbow bridge, which breaks under the horses' hoofs. But they, disregarding its fall, direct their course to the battlefield called Vigrid. Thither also repair the wolf Fenris, the Midgard serpent, Loki with all the followers of Hela, and the Frost giants.

Heimdall now stands up and sounds the Giallar horn to assemble the gods and heroes for the contest. The gods advance, led on by Odin, who engages the wolf Fenris, but falls a victim to the monster, who is, however, slain by Vidar, Odin's son. Thor gains great renown by killing the Midgard serpent, but recoils and falls dead, suffocated with the venom which the dying monster vomits over him. Loki and Heimdall meet and fight till they are both slain. The gods and their enemies having fallen in battle, Surtur, who has killed Freyr, darts fire and flames over the world, and the whole universe is burned up. The sun becomes dim, the earth sinks into the ocean, the stars fall from heaven, and time is no more.

After this Alfadur (the Almighty) will cause a new heaven and a new earth to arise out of the sea. The new earth filled with abundant supplies will spontaneously produce its fruits without labor or care. Wickedness and misery will no more be known, but the gods and men will live happily together.

Miscellaneous Norse Mythology

According to the Eddas there was once no heaven above nor earth beneath, but only a bottomless deep, and a world of mist in which flowed a fountain. Twelve rivers issued from this fountain, and when they had flowed far from their source, they froze into ice, and one layer accumulating over another, the great deep was filled up.

Southward from the world of mist was the world of light. From this flowed a warm wind upon the ice and melted it. The vapors rose in the air and formed clouds, from which sprang Ymir, the Frost giant and his progeny, and the cow Audhumbla, whose milk afforded nourishment and food to the giant. The cow got nourishment by licking the hoar frost and salt from the ice. While she was one day licking the salt stones there appeared at first the hair of a man, on the second day the whole head, and on the third the entire form endowed with beauty, agility, and power. This new being was a god, from whom and his wife, a daughter of the giant race, sprang the three brothers Odin, Vili, and Ve. They slew the giant Ymir, and out of his body formed the earth, of his blood the seas, of his bones the mountains, of his hair the trees, of his skull the heavens, and of his brain clouds, charged with hail and snow. Of Ymir's eyebrows the gods formed Midgard (mid earth), destined to become the abode of man.

Odin then regulated the periods of day and night and the seasons by placing in the heavens the sun and moon, and appointing to them their respective courses. As soon as the sun began to shed its rays upon the earth, it caused the vegetable world to bud and sprout. Shortly after the gods had created the world they walked by the side of the sea, pleased with their new work, but found that it was still incomplete, for it was without human beings. They therefore took an ash tree and made a man out of it, and they made a woman out of an alder, and called the man Aske and the woman Embla. Odin then gave them life and soul, Vili reason and motion, and Ve bestowed upon them the senses, expressive features, and speech. Midgard was then given them as their residence, and they became the progenitors of the human race.

The mighty ash tree Ygdrasill was supposed to support the whole universe. It sprang from the body of Ymir, and had three immense roots, extending one into Asgard (the dwelling of the gods), the other into Jotunheim (the abode of the giants), and the third to Niffleheim (the regions of darkness and cold). By the side of each of these roots is a spring, from which it is watered. The root that extends into Asgard is carefully tended by the three Norns, goddesses, who are regarded as the dispensers of fate. They are Urdur (the past), Verdandi (the present), Skuld (the future). The spring at the Jotunheim side is Ymir's well, in which wisdom and wit lie hidden, but that of Niffleheim feeds the adder Nidhogge (darkness), which perpetually gnaws at the root. Four harts run across the branches of the tree and bite the buds; they represent the four winds. Under the tree lies Ymir, and when he tries to shake off its weight the earth quakes.

Asgard is the name of the abode of the gods, access to which is only gained by crossing the bridge Bifrost (the rainbow). Asgard consists of golden and silver palaces, the dwellings of the gods, but the most beautiful of these is Valhalla, the residence of Odin. When seated on his throne he overlooks all heaven and earth. Upon his shoulders are the ravens Hugin and Munin, who fly every day over the whole world, and on their return report to him all they have seen and heard. At his feet lie his two wolves, Geri and Freki, to whom

Odin gives all the meat that is set before him, for he himself stands in no need of food. Mead is for him both food and drink. He invented the Runic characters, and it is the business of the Norns to engrave the runes of fate upon a metal shield. From Odin's name, spelt Woden, as it sometimes is, came Wednesday, the name of the fourth day of the week.

Odin is frequently called Alfdaur (All-father), but this name is sometimes used in a way that shows that the Scandinavians had an idea of a deity superior to Odin, uncreated and eternal.

Of the Joys of Valhalla

Valhalla is the great hall of Odin, wherein he feasts with his chosen heroes, all those who have fallen bravely in battle, for all who die a peaceful death are excluded. The flesh of the boar Schrimnir is served up to them, and is abundant for all. For although this boar is cooked every morning, he becomes whole again every night. For drink the heroes are supplied abundantly with mead from the she-goat Heidrum. When the heroes are not feasting they amuse themselves with fighting. Every day they ride out into the court or field and fight until they cut each other in pieces. This is their pastime; but when meal time comes they recover from their wounds and return to feast in Valhalla.

The Valkyrior

The Valkyrior are warlike virgins, mounted upon horses and armed with helmets and spears. Odin, who is desirous to collect a great many heroes in Valhalla, to be able to meet the giants in a day when the final contest must come, sends down to every battlefield to make choice of those who shall be slain. The Valkyrior are his messengers, and their name means "Choosers of the slain." When they ride forth on their errand, their armor sheds a strange flickering light, which flashes up over the northern skies, making what men call the "Aurora Borealis," or "Northern Lights."[1]

Of Thor and the Other Gods

Thor, the thunderer, Odin's eldest son, is the strongest of gods and men, and possesses three very precious things. The first is a hammer, which both the Frost and the Mountain giants know to their cost, when they see it hurled against them in the air, for it has split many a skull of their fathers

and kindred. When thrown, it returns to his hand of its own accord. The second rare thing he possesses is called the belt of strength. When he girds it about him his divine might is doubled. The third, also very precious, is his iron gloves, which he puts on whenever he would use his mallet efficiently. From Thor's name is derived our word Thursday.

Frey is one of the most celebrated of the gods. He presides over rain and sunshine and all the fruits of the earth. His sister Freya is the most propitious of the goddesses. She loves music, spring, and flowers, and is particularly fond of the Elves (fairies). She is very fond of love ditties, and all lovers would do well to invoke her.

Bragi is the god of poetry, and his song records the deeds of warriors. His wife, Iduna, keeps in a box the apples which the gods, when they feel old age approaching, have only to taste of to become young again.

Heimdall is the watchman of the gods, and is therefore placed on the borders of heaven to prevent the giants from forcing their way over the bridge Bifrost (the rainbow). He requires less sleep than a bird, and sees by night as well as by day a hundred miles around him. So acute is his ear that no sound escapes him, for he can even hear the grass grow and the wool on a sheep's back.

Of Loki and His Progeny

There is another deity who is described as the calumniator of the gods and the contriver of all fraud and mischief. His name is Loki. He is handsome and well made, but of a very fickle mood and most evil disposition. He is of the giant race, but forced himself into the company of the gods, and seems to take pleasure in bringing them into difficulties, and in extricating them out of the danger by his cunning, wit and skill. Loki has three children. The first is the wolf Fenris, the second the Midgard serpent, the third Hela (Death). The gods were not ignorant that these monsters were growing up, and that they would one day bring much evil upon gods and men. So Odin deemed it advisable to send one to bring them to him. When they came he threw the serpent into that deep ocean by which the earth is surrounded. But the monster had grown to such an enormous size that holding his tail in his mouth he encircles the whole earth. Hela he cast into Niffleheim, and gave her power over nine worlds or regions, into which she distributes those who are sent to her; that is, all who die of sickness or old age. Her hall is called

[1] Gray's ode, "The Fatal Sisters," is founded on this superstition.

Elvidner. Hunger is her table, Starvation her knife, Delay her man, Slowness her maid, Precipice her threshold, Care her bed, and Burning Anguish forms the hangings of the apartments. She may easily be recognized, for her body is half flesh color and half blue, and she has a dreadfully stern and forbidding countenance.

The wolf Fenris gave the gods a great deal of trouble before they succeeded in chaining him. He broke the strongest fetters as if they were made of cobwebs. Finally the gods sent a messenger to the mountain spirits, who made for them the chain called Gleipnir. It is fashioned of six things, viz., the noise made by the footfall of a cat, the beards of women, the roots of stones, the breath of fishes, the nerves (sensibilities) of bears, and the spittle of birds. When finished it was as smooth and soft as a silken string. But when the gods asked the wolf to suffer himself to be bound with this apparently slight ribbon, he suspected their design, fearing that it was made by enchantment. He therefore only consented to be bound with it upon condition that one of the gods put his hand in his (Fenris's) mouth as a pledge that the band was to be removed again. Tyr (the god of battles) alone had courage enough to do this. But when the wolf found that he could not break his fetters, and that the gods would not release him, he bit off Tyr's hand, and he has ever since remained one-handed.

THE LAY CALLED THE SHORT LAY OF SIGURD

Sigurd of yore,
Sought the dwelling of Giuki,
As he fared, the young Volsung,[1]
After fight won;[2]
Troth he took
From the two brethren;
Oath swore they betwixt them,
Those bold ones of deed.

A may[3] they gave to him
And wealth manifold,
Gudrun the young,
Giuki's daughter:
They drank and gave doom[4]
Many days together,
Sigurd the young,
And the sons of Giuki.

Until they wended
For Brynhild's wooing,
Sigurd a-riding
Amidst their rout;
The wise young Volsung
Who knew of all ways—
Ah! he had wed her,
Had fate so willed it.

Southlander Sigurd
A naked sword,
Bright, well grinded,
Laid betwixt them;
No kiss he won
From the fair woman,

Nor in arms of his
Did the Hun King[5] hold her,
Since he gat the young maid
For the son of Giuki.

No lack in her life
She wotted[6] of now,
And at her death-day
No dreadful thing
For a shame indeed
Or a shame in seeming;
But about and betwixt
Went baleful fate.

Alone, abroad,
She sat of an evening,
Of full many things
She fell a-talking:
"O for my Sigurd!
I shall have death,
Or my fair, my lovely,
Laid in mine arms.

"For the word once spoken,
I sorrow sorely—
His queen is Gudrun,
I am wed to Gunnar;
The dread Norns wrought for us
A long while of woe."

Oft with heart deep
In dreadful thoughts,
O'er ice-fields and ice-hills
She fared a-night time,

When he and Gudrun
Were gone to their fair bed,
And Sigurd wrapped
The bed-gear round her.

"Ah! now the Hun King
His queen in arms holdeth,
While love I go lacking,
And all things longed for
With no delight
But in dreadful thought."

These dreadful things
Thrust her toward murder:
—"Listen, Gunnar,
For thou shalt lose
My wide lands,
Yea, me myself!
Never love I my life,
With thee for my lord—

"I will fare back thither
From whence I came,
To my nighest kin
And those that know me
There shall I sit
Sleeping my life away,
Unless thou slayest
Sigurd the Hun King,
Making thy might more
E'en than his might was!

"Yea, let the son fare
After the father,

Translated by William Morris and Eirikr Magnusson.   [1] Sigurd's grandfather was Volsung.
[2] the fight with the dragon Fafnir.   [3] maid.   [4] judgment.   [5] Sigurd.   [6] knew.

And no young wolf
A long while nourish!
For on each man lieth
Vengeance lighter,
And peace shall be surer
If the son live not."

Adrad[7] was Gunnar,
Heavy-hearted was he,
And in doubtful mood
Day-long he sat.
For naught he wotted,
Nor might see clearly
What was the seemliest
Of deeds to set hand to;
What of all deeds
Was best to be done:
For he minded the vows
Sworn to the Volsung,
And the sore wrong
To be wrought against Sigurd.

Wavered his mind
A weary while,
No wont it was
Of those days worn by,
That queens should flee
From the realms of their kings.

"Brynhild to me
Is better than all,
The child of Budli
Is the best of women.
Yea, and my life
Will I lay down,
Ere I am twinned[8]
From that woman's treasure."

He bade call Hogni
To the place where he bided;
With all the trust that might be,
Trowed[9] he in him.

"Wilt thou bewray Sigurd
For his wealth's sake?—
Good it is to rule
O'er the Rhine's metal;
And well content
Great wealth to wield,
Biding in peace
And blissful days."

One thing alone Hogni
Had for an answer:

"Such doings for us
Are naught seemly to do;
To rend with sword
Oaths once sworn,
Oaths once sworn,
And troth once plighted.

"Nor know we on mould,
Men of happier days,
The while we four
Rule over the folk;
While the bold in battle,
The Hun King, bides living.

"And no nobler kin
Shall be known afield,
If our five sons
We long may foster;
Yea, a goodly stem
Shall surely wax.
—But I clearly see
In what wise it standeth,
Brynhild's sore urging
O'ermuch on thee beareth.

"Guttorm shall we
Get for the slaying,
Our younger brother
Bare of wisdom;
For he was out of
All the oaths sworn,
All the oaths sworn,
And the plighted troth."

Easy to rouse him
Who of naught recketh!
—Deep stood the sword
In the heart of Sigurd.
There, in the hall,
Gat the high-hearted vengeance;
For he cast his sword
At the reckless slayer:
Out at Guttorm
Flew Gram the mighty,
The gleaming steel
From Sigurd's hand.

Down fell the slayer
Smitten asunder;
The heavy head
And the hands fell one way,
But the feet and such like
Aback where they stood.

Gudrun was sleeping
Soft in the bed,

Empty of sorrow
By the side of Sigurd:
When she awoke
With all pleasure gone,
Swimming in blood
Of Frey's beloved.

So sore her hands
She smote together,
That the great-hearted
Gat raised in bed;
—"O Gudrun, weep not
So woefully,
Sweet lovely bride,
For thy brethren live for thee!

"A young child have I
For heritor;
Too young to win forth
From the house of his foes.—
Black deeds and ill
Have they been a-doing,
Evil rede[10]
Have they wrought at last.

"Late, late, rideth with them
Unto the Thing,[11]
Such sister's son,
Though seven thou bear,—
—But well I wot
Which way all goeth;
Alone wrought Brynhild
This bale against us.

"That maiden loved me
Far before all men,
Yet wrong to Gunnar
I never wrought;
Brotherhood I heeded
And all bounden oaths,
That none should deem me
His queen's darling."

Weary sighed Gudrun,
As the king gat ending,
And so sore her hands
She smote together,
That the cups arow
Rang out therewith,
And the geese cried on high
That were in the homefield.

Then laughed Brynhild
Budli's daughter,
Once, once only,

From out her heart;
When to her bed
Was borne the sound
Of the sore greeting
Of Giuki's daughter.

Then, quoth Gunnar,
The king, the hawk-bearer,
"Whereas, thou laughest,
O hateful woman,
Glad on thy bed,
No good it betokeneth:
Why lackest thou else
Thy lovely hue?
Feeder of foul deeds,
Fey[12] do I deem thee,

"Well worthy art thou
Before all women,
That thine eyes should see
Atli[13] slain of us;
That thy brother's wounds
Thou shouldst see a-bleeding,
That his bloody hurts
Thine hands should bind."

"No man blameth thee, Gunnar,
Thou hast fulfilled death's measure
But naught Atli feareth
All thine ill will;
Life shall he lay down
Later than ye,
And still bear more might
Aloft than thy might.

"I shall tell thee, Gunnar,
Though well the tale thou knowest,
In what early days
Ye dealt abroad your wrong:
Young was I then,
Worn with no woe,
Good wealth I had
In the house of my brother!

"No mind had I
That a man should have me,
Or ever ye Giukings,
Rode into our garth;[14]
There ye sat on your steeds
Three kings of the people—
—Ah! that that faring[15]
Had never befallen!

"Then spake Atli
To me apart,

And said that no wealth
He would give unto me,
Neither gold nor lands
If I would not be wedded;
Nay, and no part
Of the wealth apportioned,
Which in my first days
He gave me duly;
Which in my first days
He counted down.

"Wavered the mind
Within me then,
If to fight I should fall
And the felling of folk,
Bold in byrny[16]
Because of my brother;
A deed of fame
Had that been to all folk,
But to many a man
Sorrow of mind.

"So I let all sink
Into peace at the last:
More grew I minded
For the mighty treasure,
The red-shining rings
Of Sigmund's son;
For no man's wealth else
Would I take unto me.

"For myself had I given
To that great king
Who sat amid gold
On the back of Grani;[17]
Nought were his eyen
Like to your eyen,
Nor in any wise
Went his visage with yours;
Though ye might deem you
Due kings of men.

"One I loved,
One, and none other,
The gold-decked may
Had no doubtful mind;
Thereof shall Atli
Wot full surely,
When he getteth to know
I am gone to the dead.

"Far be it from me,
Feeble and wavering,
Ever to love

Another's love—
—Yet shall my woe
Be well avenged."

Up rose Gunnar,
The great men's leader,
And cast his arms
About the queen's neck;
And all went nigh
One after other,
With their whole hearts
Her heart to turn.
But then all these
From her neck she thrust,
Of her long journey
No man should let her.

Then called he Hogni
To have talk with him:
"Let all folk go
Forth into the hall,
Thine with mine—
—O need sore and mighty!—
To wot if we yet
My wife's parting may stay.
Till with time's wearing
Some hindrance wax."

One answer Hogni
Had for all;
"Nay, let hard need
Have rule thereover,
And no man let[18] her
Of her long journey!
Never born again,
May she come back thence!

"Luckless she came
To the lap of her mother,
Born into the world
For utter woe,
To many a man
For heart-whole mourning."

Upraised he turned
From the talk and the trouble
To where the gem-field
Dealt out goodly treasure;
As she looked and beheld
All the wealth that she had,
And the hungry bondmaids,
And maids of the hall.

With no good in her heart

---

[12] fated.   [13] who contrived the marriage of Gunnar and Brynhild.   [14] home.
[15] adventure, experience.   [16] coat of mail.   [17] Sigurd's horse.   [18] prevent.

She donned her gold byrny,
Ere she thrust the sword-point
Through the midst of her body:
On the bolster's far side
Sank she adown,
And, smitten with sword,
Still bethought her of redes.[19]

"Let all come forth
Who are fain[20] the red gold,
Or things less worthy
To win from my hands;
To each one I give
A necklace gilt over,
Wrought hangings and bed-gear,
And bright woven weed."[21]

All they kept silence,
And thought what to speak,
Then all at once
Answer gave:
"Full enow are death-doomed,
Fain are we to live yet,
Maids of the hall
All meet work winning."

From her wise heart at last
The linen-clad damsel,
The one of few years
Gave forth the word:
"I will that none driven
By hand or by word,
For our sake should lose
Well-loved life.

"Thou on the bones of you
Surely shall burn,
Less dear treasure
At your departing
Nor with Menia's Meal[22]
Shall ye come to see me."

"Sit thee down, Gunnar,
A word must I say to thee
Of the life's ruin
Of thy lightsome bride—
—Nor shall thy ship
Swim soft and sweetly
For all that I
Lay life adown.

"Sooner than ye might deem
Shall ye make peace with Gudrun,
For the wise woman

Shall lull in the young wife
The hard memory
Of her dead husband.

"There is a may born
Reared by her mother,
Whiter and brighter
Than is the bright day;
She shall be Swanhild[23]
She shall be Sunbeam.

"Thou shalt give Gudrun
Unto a great one,
Noble, well-praised
Of the world's folk;
Not with her goodwill,
Or love shalt thou give her;
Yet will Atli
Come to win her,
My very brother,
Born of Budli.

—"Ah! many a memory
Of how ye dealt with me,
How sorely, how evilly
Ye ever beguiled me,
How all pleasure left me
The while my life lasted!—

"Fain wilt thou be
Oddrun to win,
But thy good liking
Shall Atli let;
But in secret wise
Shall ye win together,
And she shall love thee
As I had loved thee,
If in such wise
Fate had willed it.

"But with all ill
Shall Atli sting thee,
Into the strait worm-close[24]
Shall he cast thee.

"But no long space
Shall slip away
Ere Atli too
All life shall lose.
Yea, all his weal
With the life of his sons,
For a dreadful bed
Dights Gudrun for him,

From a heart sore laden,
With the sword's sharp edge.

"More seemly for Gudrun,
Your very sister,
In death to wend after
Her love first wed;
Had but good rede
To her been given,
Or if her heart
Had been like to my heart.

—"Faint my speech groweth—
But for our sake
Ne'er shall she lose
Her life beloved;
The sea shall have her,
High billows bear her
Forth unto Jonakr's[25]
Fair land of his fathers.

"There shall she bear sons,
Stays of a heritage,
Stays of a heritage,
Jonakr's sons;
And Swanhild shall she
Send from the land,
That may born of her,
The may born of Sigurd.

"Her shall bite
The rede of Bikki,[26]
Whereas for no good
Wins Jormunrek life;
And so is clean perished
All the kin of Sigurd,
Yea, and more greeting,
And more for Gudrun.

"And now one prayer
Yet pray I of thee—
The last word of mine
Here in the world—
So broad on the field
Be the burg of the dead
That fair space may be left
For us all to lie down,
All those that died
At Sigurd's death!

"Hang round that burg
Fair hangings and shields,
Web by Gauls woven,

---

[19] counsels.   [20] desirous of.   [21] clothes.   [22] gold.   [23] daughter of Sigurd and Gudrun.
[24] the grave.   [25] Gudrun's third husband.   [26] After Swanhild marries the aged Ermanarich,
Bikki accuses her of infidelity and she is punished by being torn to pieces by wild horses.

And folk of the Gauls:
There burn the Hun King
Lying beside me.

"But on the other side
Burn by the Hun King
Those who served me
Strewn with treasure;
Two at the head,
And two at the feet,
Two hounds therewith,
And two hawks moreover:
Then is all dealt
With even dealing.

"Lay there amidst us
The ring-dight metal,

The sharp-edged steel,
That so lay erst;
When we both together
Into one bed went,
And were called by the name
Of man and wife.

"Never, then, belike
Shall clash behind him
Valhall's bright door
With rings bedight:
And if my fellowship
Followeth after,
In no wretched wise
Then shall we wend.

"For him shall follow

My five bondmaids,
My eight bondsmen,
No borel[27] folk:
Yea, and my fosterer,
And my father's dower
That Budli of old days
Gave to his dear child.

"Much have I spoken,
More would I speak,
If the sword would give me
Space for speech;
But my words are waning,
My wounds are swelling—
Naught but truth have I told-—
—And now make I ending."

THE HELL-RIDE OF BRYNHILD

After the death of Brynhild were made two bales, one for Sigurd, and that was first burned; but Brynhild was burned on the other, and she was in a chariot hung about with goodly hangings.

And so folk say that Brynhild drave in her chariot down along the way to Hell, and passed by an abode where dwelt a certain giantess, and the giantess spake:—

"Nay, with my goodwill
Never goest thou
Through this stone-pillared
Stead of mine!
More seemly for thee
To sit sewing the cloth,
Than to go look on
The love of another.

"What dost thou, going
From the land of the Gauls,
O restless head,
To this mine house?
Golden girl, hast thou not,
If thou listest to hearken,
In sweet wise from thy hands
The blood of men washen?"

BRYNHILD

"Nay, blame me naught,
Bride of the rock-hall,
Though I roved a warring
In the days that were;
The higher of us twain
Shall I ever be holden
When of our kind
Men make account."

THE GIANT-WOMAN

"Thou, O Brynhild,
Budli's daughter,
Wert the worst ever born
Into the world:
For Giuki's children
Death hast thou gotten,
And turned to destruction
Their goodly dwelling."

BRYNHILD

"I shall tell thee
True tale from my chariot,
O thou who naught wottest,
If thou listest to wot;
How for me they have gotten
Those heirs of Giuki,
A loveless life,
A life of lies.

"Hild under helm,
The Hlymdale people,
E'en those who knew me,
Ever would call me.

"The changeful shapes
Of us eight sisters,

The wise king bade
Under oak-tree to bear:
Of twelve winters was I,
If thou listest to wot,
When I sware to the young lord
Oaths of love.

"Thereafter gat I
Mid the folk of the Goths,
For Helmgunnar the old,
Swift journey to Hell,
And gave to Aud's brother
The young, gain and glory;
Whereof overwrath
Waxed Odin with me.

"So he shut me in shield-wall
In Skata grove,
Red shields and white
Close set around me;
And bade him alone
My slumber to break
Who in no land
Knew how to fear.

"He set round my hall,
Toward the south quarter,

---

[27] low-born. *The Hell-Ride of Brynhild*, translated by William Morris and Eirikr Magnusson.

The Bane of all trees
Burning aloft;
And ruled that he only
Thereover should ride
Who should bring me the gold
O'er which Fafnir brooded.

"Then upon Grani rode
The goodly gold-strewer
To where my fosterer
Ruled his fair dwelling.
He who alone there
Was deemed best of all,

The War-lord of the Danes,
Well worthy of men.

"In peace did we sleep
Soft in one bed,
As though he had been
Naught but my brother:
There as we lay
Through eight nights wearing,
No hand in love
On each other we laid.

"Yet thence blamed me, Gudrun,
Giuki's daughter,
That I had slept

In the arms of Sigurd;
And then I wotted
As I fain had not wotted,
That they had bewrayed me
In my betrothals.

"Ah! for unrest
All too long
Are men and women
Made alive!
Yet we twain together
Shall wear through the ages,
Sigurd and I.—
—Sink adown, O giant-wife!"

THE LAY OF THRYM

1. Wild was Vingthor [1]   when he awoke,
And when his mighty   hammer he missed;
He shook his beard,   his hair was bristling
As the son of Jorth   about him sought.

2. Hear now the speech   that first he spake: 5
"Harken, Loki,   and heed my words,
Nowhere on earth   is it known to man,
Nor in heaven above: our hammer is stolen."

3. To the dwelling fair   of Freyja [2] went they,
Hear now the speech   that first he spake: 10
"Wilt thou, Freyja,   thy feather-dress lend me,
That so my hammer   I may seek?"

Freyja spake:
4. "Thine should it be   though of silver bright,
And I would give it   though 'twere of gold."
Then Loki flew,   and the feather-dress whirred,   15
Till he left behind him   the home of the gods,
And reached at last   the realm of the giants.

5. Thrym sat on a mound,   the giants' master,
Leashes of gold   he laid for his dogs,
And stroked and smoothed   the manes of his steeds.   20

Thrym spake:
6. "How fare the gods,   how fare the elves?
Why comest thou alone   to the giants' land?"

Loki spake:
"Ill fare the gods,   ill fare the elves!
Hast thou hidden   Hlorrithi's hammer?"

Thrym spake:
7. "I have hidden   Hlorrithi's hammer,   25
Eight miles down   deep in the earth;
And back again   shall no man bring it
If Freyja I win not   to be my wife."

8. Then Loki flew,   and the feather-dress whirred,
Till he left behind him   the home of the giants,   30
And reached at last   the realm of the gods.
There in the courtyard   Thor he met:
Hear now the speech   that first he spake:

9. "Hast thou found tidings   as well as trouble?
Thy news in the air   shalt thou utter now;
Oft doth the sitter   his story forget,   36
And lies he speaks   who lays himself down."

Loki spake:
10. "Trouble I have,   and tidings as well:
Thrym, king of the giants,   keeps thy hammer,
And back again   shall no man bring it   40
If Freyja he wins not   to be his wife."

11. Freyja the fair   then went they to find;
Hear now the speech   that first he spake:

The Lay of Thrym. Translated by Henry Adams Bellows. By permission of The American Scandinavian Foundation.
[1] Thor, the thunder-god.
[2] Norse goddess of Love.

"Bind on, Freyja,   the bridal veil,
For we two must haste   to the giants'
     home."   45

12. Wrathful was Freyja,   and fiercely she
        snorted,
And the dwelling great   of the gods was
        shaken
And burst was the mighty   Brisings' neck-
        lace:
"Most lustful indeed   should I look to all
If I journeyed with thee   to the giants'
        home."   50

13. Then were the gods   together met,
And the goddesses came   and council held,
And the far-famed ones   a plan would find,
How they might Hlorrithi's   hammer win.

14. Then Heimdall spake,   whitest of the gods,
Like the Wanes he knew   the future well:
"Bind we on Thor   the bridal veil,   57
Let him bear the mighty   Brisings' necklace;

15. Keys around him   let there rattle,
And down to his knees   hang woman's
        dress;   60
With gems full broad   upon his breast,
And a pretty cap   to crown his head."

16. Then Thor the mighty   his answer made:
"Me would the gods   unmanly call
If I let bind   the bridal veil."   65

17. Then Loki spake,   the son of Laufey:
"Be silent, Thor,   and speak not thus;
Else will the giants   in Asgarth [3] dwell
If thy hammer is brought not   home to
        thee."

18. Then bound they on Thor   the bridal veil,
And next the mighty   Brisings' necklace. 71

19. Keys around him   let they rattle,
And down to his knees   hung woman's
        dress;
With gems full broad   upon his breast,
And a pretty cap   to crown his head.   75

20. Then Loki spake,   the son of Laufey:
"As thy maid-servant thither   I go with thee;
We two shall haste   to the giants' home."

21. Then home the goats   to the hall were
        driven,

They wrenched at the halters,   swift were
        they to run;   80
The mountains burst,   earth burned with
        fire,
And Othin's son   sought Jotunheim. [4]

22. Then loud spake Thrym,   the giants' leader:
"Bestir ye, giants,   put straw on the benches;
Now Freyja they bring   to be my bride,   85
The daughter of Njorth   out of Noatun.

23. "Gold-horned cattle   go to my stables,
Jet-black oxen,   the giant's joy;
Many my gems,   and many my jewels,
Freyja alone   did I lack, methinks."   90

24. Early it was   to evening come,
And forth was borne   the beer for the giants;
Thor alone ate an ox,   and eight salmon,
All the dainties as well   that were set for the
        women;
And drank Sif's mate   three tuns of mead. 95

25. Then loud spake Thrym,   the giants' leader:
"Who ever saw bride   more keenly bite?
I ne'er saw bride   with a broader bite,
Nor a maiden who drank   more mead than
        this!"

26. Hard by there sat   the serving-maid wise,
So well she answered   the giant's words: 101
"From food has Freyja   eight nights fasted,
So hot was her longing   for Jotunheim."

27. Thrym looked 'neath the veil,   for he longed
        to kiss,
But back he leaped   the length of the hall:
"Why are so fearful   the eyes of Freyja? 106
Fire, methinks,   from her eyes burns forth."

28. Hard by there sat   the serving-maid wise,
So well she answered   the giant's words:
"No sleep has Freyja   for eight nights
        found,   110
So hot was her longing   for Jotunheim."

29. Soon came the giant's   luckless sister,
Who feared not to ask   the bridal fee:
"From thy hands the rings   of red gold take,
If thou wouldst win   my willing love, 115
(My willing love   and welcome glad.)"

[3] Home of the gods.   [4] Home of the giants.

30. Then loud spake Thrym,   the giants'
       leader:
    "Bring in the hammer   to hallow the
       bride;
    On the maiden's knees   let Mjollnir lie, 119
    That us both the hand   of Vor may bless."

31. The heart in the breast   of Hlorrithi laughed
    When the hard-souled one   his hammer be-
       held;

First Thrym, the king   of the giants, he
   killed,
Then all the folk   of the giants he felled.

32. The giant's sister   old he slew,   125
    She who had begged   the bridal fee;
    A stroke she got   in the shilling's stead,
    And for many rings   the might of the ham-
       mer.

33. And so his hammer   got Othin's son.

CELTIC MYTH
AND ROMANCE

The Teutonic poetry of war and passion is a hardy plant, but its appearance is somewhat forbidding, and its nature is essentially premedieval; it reflects a way of life that existed before the Christian and chivalric Middle Ages. The true flower of the medieval world is *romance*.

In general, romance denotes the literature of chivalry. But it not only represents the customs and ideals of the feudal gentry; it evokes a world of wonder and magic. It is because the medieval tales of knightly love and adventure are steeped in this spirit that they are romances. Knighthood and the unscientific outlook of the Middle Ages favored the development of romance. But it came from much deeper well-springs—from the imagination of the peoples that preceded the Teutons in occupying western Europe—namely, the Celts. Although they had the usual interest in war and heroism, their outlook was magical.

The world they saw was full of marvels; it was exquisite and playful. It was a world not of grim conquerors but of a people who worshiped the loveliness of nature, loved life, and loved love. Sensibility, high spirits, and a romantic temperament characterized these Celts. They were not made to rule the world but to enjoy it. No wonder that, unlike both the Romans and the Teutons, they established no empire and enslaved no nations. No wonder, too, that wherever they were exposed to conquest-bent hordes, they would fight gallantly and recklessly but would be unable in the end to withstand the shock of assault. The juggernaut of the unimaginative, well-organized Roman legions rolled over them. The fury of the Teutonic tribes battered them until they found protection in mountain fastnesses and other areas where nature was their defense.

By A. D. 500 the culture of the classic world was at an end. Surrounded by barbarians, it eventually gave way before the superior weight of the enemy. Besides, it had already decayed. When Emperor Justinian in the sixth century closed the schools of Athens, all life had gone from them. Although in Constantinople the Eastern Roman Empire lived on for a thousand years, it was devoid of vitality and maintained itself precariously. This vestige of the classical world preserved precious manuscripts and works of art, maintained many of the antique forms of grandeur, and served as a bridge between the modern world and the ancient, but it looked only backward and created no new culture. The future lay with the crude but vigorous Germanic barbarians, who were gradually to become civilized. However, there was vitality in the Celtic peoples wherever they were able to maintain their independence. For a period of several centuries, it was their high destiny to carry the torch of culture while the rest of Europe was plunged in darkness, and the torch was especially bright in Ireland.

At the beginning of the Christian era the Celts

were an important and numerous people, already well settled in western Europe, probably since the seventh century B.C. They occupied much of France, as every school boy who has read his Cæsar remembers. These Celts of Gaul were entirely absorbed by the Romans and Germans, so that the Gallic language disappeared. In Cæsar's time all the other Celts were in the British Isles. The Britons were in England and Wales, the Picts in Scotland, and the Gaels, or Irish, in Ireland. When in the fifth and sixth centuries the Britons were overcome by the Anglo-Saxons, the Celts moved westward into Wales and Cornwall or crossed the sea to Brittany in northern France. This whole group, the ancient British, the Welsh, the Cornish, and the Breton, is known as Brythonic. The Irish Celts sent out expeditions and settled the Highlands and islands of Scotland. Though this branch of the Celts is considerably mixed with the Brythonic, we speak of both the Irish and the Highland Scotch as Goidelic Celts and their language as Gaelic. The English-speaking person may be interested in a few differences in these languages. For example, the common word for mountain in Gaelic is *ben* (Ben Nevis), in Welsh it is *pen* (Penryth). The patronymic ("son of") is *Mac* in Gaelic, but *Map* or *Ap* in Welsh. It is from Wales and Ireland that the artistic and cultural influences have come.

The period of greatest Welsh literary activity came several centuries later than that of Ireland. We cannot date exactly the collection of stories known as the Mabinogion, but it was certainly current in the twelfth century and influenced several of the great romantic legends, like those of King Arthur and Tristram. The Welsh accounts of Arthur and his knights are primitive and grotesque, but they are clearly recognizable as the heroes of continental romance. Before they were courtly knights in the latter, they were characters in Celtic folklore and myth. To the student of European literary tradition, therefore, Welsh literature is of great importance, even though in artistic form it is inferior to the Irish.

Since Ireland was so far removed from the center of the wars of Europe during the unsettled centuries (from the third to the eighth or ninth), while the Roman Empire was tottering and the new nations were being formed, it had the best chance to develop a culture of its own. It also proved a haven for Celtic refugees from Wales and Gaul during the Teutonic invasions, and among these were scholars of Roman culture.

Christianity came into Ireland in the early fifth century with St. Patrick, and during the next two centuries, Ireland was one of the principal centers from which missionaries were sent to convert the rest of Europe. The conversion of Germany and Switzerland and of northern England was primarily a result of their efforts. When in the ninth century Charlemagne gathered about him learned monks to help him revive learning and culture in Europe, one of the most brilliant of these was the Irish philosopher Scotus Erigena.

But before Christianity, Ireland had had a heroic age when the old gods were still in honor. This period, which the later bards and story-tellers celebrated with a profusion of fairy-tale and folklore, probably belongs to the first centuries of the Christian era. The stories of pre-Christian Irish civilization are usually woven about the court of King Conchubar (pronounced Conachoor) at Emain Macha, the ancient capital of Ulster in northern Ireland. One of the most interesting tales is *The Feast of Bricriu*. It contains the Celtic source for *Sir Gawain and the Green Knight*, the most famous English romance in verse. (See p. 1021.)

Many of these legends were written down from the eighth to the tenth centuries, and in the last generation were arranged and translated by Lady Gregory in her *Cuchulain of Muirthemne*. Cuchulain (pronounced Cu-hoolin) is the epic hero of the Irish. His exploits, which began at the age of seven, are fabulous, but he remains a very human character. Perhaps the most famous of these stories is that of Deirdre, which we include in this book. Deirdre and the heroes of her cycle have remained a living tradition among the Irish. These tales are still to be heard from old men in remote parts of western Ireland who have learned them from other story-tellers. Seated about their turf fires on long winter evenings, these old men vie with one another in recounting the adventures of the ancient heroes and demigods. After hearing them, one can no longer have any doubt that the charm of style which Arnold, whose famous essay on Celtic literature is appended as an introduction to the selections, finds in Celtic literature is real; and that it is not confined to learned men or poets, but is the common possession of hundreds of humbler narrators. In late years Irish authors have written much about the story of Deirdre. Indeed, the Irish legends proved an important influence twice in our literature; once in the second half of the eighteenth century, and again in the recent movement led by W. B. Yeats, Lady Gregory, and J. M. Synge, which is known as the Celtic Renaissance.

MATTHEW ARNOLD

On the Study of Celtic Literature

The Celt's quick feeling for what is noble and distinguished gave his poetry style; his indomitable personality gave it pride and passion; his sensibility and nervous exaltation gave it a better gift still, the gift of rendering with wonderful felicity the magical charm of nature. The forest solitude, the bubbling spring, the wild flowers, are everywhere in romance. They have a mysterious life and grace there; they are Nature's own children, and utter her secret in a way which makes them something quite different from the woods, waters, and plants of Greek and Latin poetry. Now of this delicate magic, Celtic romance is so pre-eminent a mistress, that it seems impossible to believe the power did not come into romance from the Celts. Magic is just the word for it,—the magic of nature; not merely the beauty of nature,—that the Greeks and Latins had; not merely an honest smack of the soil, a faithful realism,—that the Germans had; but the intimate life of Nature, her weird power and her fairy charm. As the Saxon names of places, with the pleasant wholesome smack of the soil in them,—Weathersfield, Thaxted, Shalford,—are to the Celtic names of places, with their penetrating, lofty beauty,—Velindra, Tyntagel, Caernarvon,—so is the homely realism of German and Norse nature to the fairy-like loveliness of Celtic nature. Gwydion wants a wife for his pupil: "Well," says Math, "we will seek, I and thou, by charms and illusions, to form a wife for him out of flowers. So they took the blossoms of the oak, and the blossoms of the broom, and the blossoms of the meadow-sweet, and produced from them a maiden, the fairest and most graceful that man ever saw. And they baptized her, and gave her the name of Flower-Aspect." Celtic romance is full of exquisite touches like that, showing the delicacy of the Celt's feeling in these matters, and how deeply Nature lets him come into her secrets. The quick dropping of blood is called "faster than the fall of the dewdrop from the blade of reed-grass upon the earth, when the dew of June is at the heaviest."

And thus is Olwen described: "More yellow was her hair than the flower of the broom, and her skin was whiter than the foam of the wave, and fairer were her hands and her fingers than the blossoms of the wood-anemony amidst the spray of the meadow fountains." For loveliness it would be hard to beat that; and for magical clearness and nearness take the following:—

"And in the evening Peredur entered a valley, and at the head of the valley he came to a hermit's cell, and the hermit welcomed him gladly, and there he spent the night. And in the morning he arose, and when he went forth, behold, a shower of snow had fallen the night before, and a hawk had killed a wild-fowl in front of the cell. And the noise of the horse scared the hawk away, and a raven alighted upon the bird. And Peredur stood and compared the blackness of the raven, and the whiteness of the snow, and the redness of the blood, to the hair of the lady whom best he loved, which was blacker than the raven, and to her skin, which was whiter than the snow, and to her two cheeks, which were redder than the blood upon the snow appeared to be."

And this, which is perhaps less striking, is not less beautiful:—

"And early in the day Geraint and Enid left the wood, and they came to an open country, with meadows on one hand and mowers mowing the meadows. And there was a river before them, and the horses bent down and drank the water. And they went up out of the river by a steep bank, and there they met a slender stripling with a satchel about his neck; and he had a small blue pitcher in his hand, and a bowl on the mouth of the pitcher."

And here the landscape, up to this point so Greek in its clear beauty, is suddenly magicalized by the romance touch:—

"And they saw a tall tree by the side of the river, one-half of which was in flames from the root to the top, and the other half was green and in full leaf."

Arnold, *On the Study of Celtic Literature.* Selections.

Magic is the word to insist upon,—a magically vivid and near interpretation of nature; since it is this which constitutes the special charm and power of the effect I am calling attention to, and it is for this that the Celt's sensibility gives him a peculiar aptitude. But the matter needs rather fine handling, and it is easy to make mistakes here in our criticism. In the first place, Europe tends constantly to become more and more one community, and we tend to become Europeans instead of merely Englishmen, Frenchmen, Germans, Italians; so whatever aptitude or felicity one people imparts into spiritual work, gets imitated by the others, and thus tends to become the common property of all. Therefore anything so beautiful and attractive as the natural magic I am speaking of, is sure, nowadays, if it appears in the productions of the Celts, or of the English, or of the French, to appear in the productions of the Germans also, or in the productions of the Italians: but there will be a stamp of perfectness and inimitableness about it in the literatures where it is native, which it will not have in the literatures where it is not native. Novalis or Rückert, for instance, have their eye fixed on nature, and have undoubtedly a feeling for natural magic; a rough-and-ready critic easily credits them and the Germans with the Celtic fineness of tact, the Celtic nearness to Nature and her secret; but the question is whether the strokes in the German's picture of nature have ever the indefinable delicacy, charm, and perfection of the Celt's touch in the pieces I just now quoted, or of Shakspeare's touch in his daffodil, Wordsworth's in his cuckoo, Keats's in his Autumn, Obermann's in his mountain birch-tree or his Easter-daisy among the Swiss farms. To decide where the gift for natural magic originally lies, whether it is properly Celtic or Germanic, we must decide this question.

In the second place, there are many ways of handling nature, and we are here only concerned with one of them; but a rough-and-ready critic imagines that it is all the same so long as nature is handled at all, and fails to draw the needful distinction between modes of handling her. But these modes are many; I will mention four of them now: there is the conventional way of handling nature, there is the faithful way of handling nature, there is the Greek way of handling nature, there is the magical way of handling nature. In all these three last the eye is on the object, but with a difference; in the faithful way of handling nature, the eye is on the object, and that is all you can say; in the Greek, the eye is on the object, but lightness and brightness are added; in the magical, the eye is on the object, but charm and magic are added. In the conventional way of handling nature, the eye is not on the object; what that means we all know, we have only to think of our eighteenth-century poetry:—

As when the moon, refulgent lamp of night—

to call up any number of instances. Latin poetry supplies plenty of instances too; if we put this from Propertius's *Hylas:*—

. . . manus heroum . . .
Mollia composita litora fronde tegit—

side by side the line of Theocritus by which it was suggested:—

λειμων γαρ σφιν εκειτο μεγας, στιβαδεσσιν ονειαρ [1]

we get at the same moment a good specimen both of the conventional and of the Greek way of handling nature. But from our own poetry we may get specimens of the Greek way of handling nature, as well as of the conventional: for instance, Keats's:—

What little town, by river or seashore,
Or mountain-built with quiet citadel,
Is emptied of its folk, this pious morn?

is Greek, as Greek as a thing from Homer or Theocritus; it is composed with the eye on the object, a radiancy and light clearness being added. German poetry abounds in specimens of the faithful way of handling nature; an excellent example is to be found in the stanzas called *Zueignung*, prefixed to Goethe's poems; the morning walk, the mist, the dew, the sun, are as faithful as they can be, they are given with the eye on the object, but there the merit of the work, as a handling of nature, stops; neither Greek radiance nor Celtic magic is added; the power of these is not what gives the poem in question its merit, but a power of quite another kind, a power of moral and spiritual emotion. But the power of Greek radiance Goethe could give to his handling of nature, and nobly too, as anyone who will read his *Wanderer*, —the poem in which a wanderer falls in with a peasant woman and her child by their hut, built out of the ruins of a temple near Cuma,—may see.

[1] "For a great meadow lies before them, good for beds."—Theocritus: *Idylls*, xiii, 34.

Only the power of natural magic Goethe does not, I think, give; whereas Keats passes at will from the Greek power to that power which is, as I say, Celtic; from his:—

> What little town, by river or seashore—

to his:—

> White hawthorn and the pastoral eglantine,
> Fast-fading violets cover'd up in leaves—

or his:—

> . . . magic casements, opening on the foam
> Of perilous seas, in faery lands forlorn—

in which the very same note is struck as in those extracts which I quoted from Celtic romance, and struck with authentic and unmistakable power.

Shakspeare, in handling nature, touches this Celtic note so exquisitely, that perhaps one is inclined to be always looking for the Celtic note in him, and not to recognize his Greek note when it comes. But if one attends well to the difference between the two notes, and bears in mind, to guide one, such things as Virgil's "moss-grown springs and grass softer than sleep:"—

> Muscosi fontes et somno mollior herba—

as his charming flower-gatherer, who:—

> Pallentes violas et summa papavera carpens
> Narcissum et florem jungit bene olentis anethi—

as his quinces and chestnuts:—

> . . . cana legam tenera lanugine mala
> Castaneasque nuces . . .

then, I think, we shall be disposed to say that in Shakspeare's:—

I know a bank where the wild thyme blows,
Where oxlips and the nodding violet grows,
Quite over-canopied with luscious woodbine,
With sweet musk-roses and with eglantine—

it is mainly a Greek note which is struck. Then, again in his:—

> . . . look how the floor of heaven
> Is thick inlaid with patines of bright gold!

we are at the very point of transition from the Greek note to the Celtic; there is the Greek clearness and brightness, with the Celtic aërialness and magic coming in. Then we have the sheer, inimitable Celtic note in passages like this:—

> Met we on hill, in dale, forest or mead,
> By paved fountain or by rushy brook,
> Or in the beached margent of the sea—

or this, the last I will quote:—

> The moon shines bright. In such a night as this,
> When the sweet wind did gently kiss the trees,
> And they did make no noise, in such a night
> Troilus, methinks mounted the Trojan walls—

> . . . in such a night
> Did Thisbe fearfully o'ertrip the dew—

> . . . in such a night
> *Stood Dido, with a willow in her hand,*
> *Upon the wild sea-banks, and waved her love*
> *To come again to Carthage.*

And those last lines of all are so drenched and intoxicated with the fairy-dew of that natural magic which is our theme, that I cannot do better than end with them.

DEIRDRE

The Fate of the Sons of Usnach

Now it was one Fedlimid, son of Doll, was harper to King Conchubar, and he had but one child, and this is the story of her birth.

Cathbad the Druid was at Fedlimid's house one day. "Have you got knowledge of the future?" said Fedlimid. "I have a little," said Cathbad. "What is it you are wanting to know?"

"I was not asking to know anything," said

Deirdre. From Lady Gregory's *Cuchulain of Muirthemne.* Used by permission of Charles Scribner's Sons

Fedlimid, "but if you know of anything that may be going to happen me, it is as well for you to tell me."

Cathbad went out of the house for a while, and when he came back he said:

"Had you ever any children?" "I never had," said Fedlimid, "and the wife I have had none, and we have no hope ever to have any; there is no one with us but only myself and my wife."

"That puts wonder on me," said Cathbad, "for I see by Druid signs that it is on account of a daughter belonging to you that more blood will be shed than ever was shed in Ireland since time and race began. And great heroes and bright candles of the Gael will lose their lives because of her."

"Is that the foretelling you have made for me?" said Fedlimid, and there was anger on him, for he thought the Druid was mocking him; "if that is all you can say, you can keep it for yourself; it is little I think of your share of knowledge." "For all that," said Cathbad, "I am certain of its truth, for I can see it all clearly in my own mind."

The Druid went away, but he was not long gone when Fedlimid's wife was found to be with child. And as her time went on, his vexation went on growing, that he had not asked more questions of Cathbad at the time he was talking to him, and he was under a smoldering care by day and by night, for it is what he was thinking, that neither his own sense and understanding, nor the share of friends he had, would be able to save him, or to make a back against the world, if this misfortune should come upon him, that would bring such great shedding of blood upon the earth; and it is the thought that came, that if this child should be born, what he had to do was to put her far away, where no eye would see her, and no ear hear word of her.

The time of the delivery of Fedlimid's wife came on, and it was a girl-child she gave birth to. Fedlimid did not allow any living person to come to the house, or to see his wife but himself alone.

But just after the child was born, Cathbad the Druid came in again, and there was shame on Fedlimid when he saw him, and when he remembered how he would not believe his words. But the Druid looked at the child and he said: "Let Deirdre be her name; harm will come through her. She will be fair, comely, bright-haired; heroes will fight for her, and kings go seeking for her."

And then he took the child in his arms, and it is what he said: "O Deirdre, on whose account many shall weep, on whose account many women shall be envious, there will be trouble on Ulster for your sake, O fair daughter of Fedlimid.

"Many will be jealous of your face, O flame of beauty. For your sake heroes shall go to exile; for your sake deeds of anger shall be done in Emain. There is harm in your face, for it will bring banishment and death on the sons of kings.

"In your fate, O beautiful child, are wounds, and ill-doings, and shedding of blood.

"You will have a little grave apart to yourself; you will be a tale of wonder forever, Deirdre."

Cathbad went away then, and he sent Levarcham, daughter of Aedh, to the house; and Fedlimid asked her would she take the venture of bringing up the child, far away where no eye would see her, and no ear hear of her. Levarcham said she would do that, and that she would do her best to keep her the way he wished.

So Fedlimid got his men, and brought them away with him to a mountain, wide and waste, and there he bade them to make a little house, by the side of a round green hillock, and to make a garden of apple-trees behind it, with a wall about it. And he bade them put a roof of green sods over the house, the way a little company might live in it, without notice being taken of them.

Then he sent Levarcham and the child there, that no eye might see, and no ear hear of, Deirdre. He put all in good order before them, and he gave them provisions, and he told Levarcham that food and all she wanted would be sent from year to year as long as she lived.

And so Deirdre and her foster-mother lived in the lonely place among the hills, without the knowledge or the notice of any strange person, until Deirdre was fourteen years of age. And Deirdre grew straight and clean like a rush on the bog, and she was comely beyond comparison of all the women of the world, and her movements were like the swan on the wave, or the deer on the hill. She was the young girl of the greatest beauty and of the gentlest nature of all the women of Ireland.

Levarcham, that had charge of her, used to be giving Deirdre every knowledge and skill that she had herself. There was not a blade of grass growing from root, or a bird singing in the wood, or a star shining from heaven, but Deirdre had the name of it. But there was one thing she would not have her know—she would not let her have friendship with any living person of the rest of the world outside their own house.

But one dark night of winter, with black clouds overhead, a hunter came walking the hills, and it

Is what happened; he missed the track of the hunt, and lost his way and his comrades.

And a heaviness came upon him, and he lay down on the side of the green hillock by Deirdre's house. He was weak with hunger and going, and perished with cold, and a deep sleep came upon him. While he was lying there, a dream came to the hunter, and he thought that he was near the warmth of a house of the Sidhe,[1] and the Sidhe inside making music, and he called out in his dream, "If there is anyone inside, let them bring me in, in the name of the sun and the moon." Deirdre heard the voice, and she said to Levarcham, "Mother, mother, what is that?" But Levarcham said, "It is nothing that matters; it is the birds of the air gone astray, and trying to find one another. But let them go back to the branches of the wood."

Another troubled dream came on the hunter, and he cried out a second time. "What is that?" asked Deirdre again. "It is nothing that matters," said Levarcham. "The birds of the air are looking for one another; let them go past to the branches of the wood."

Then a third dream came to the hunter, and he cried out a third time, if there was anyone in the hill to let him in for the sake of the elements, for he was perished with cold and overcome with hunger. "Oh! what is that, Levarcham?" said Deirdre. "There is nothing there for you to see, my child, but only the birds of the air, and they lost to one another; but let them go past us to the branches of the wood. There is no place or shelter for them here tonight." "Oh, mother," said Deirdre, "the bird asked to come in for the sake of the sun and the moon, and it is what you yourself told me, that anything that is asked like that, it is right for us to give it. If you will not let in the bird that is perished with cold and overcome with hunger, I myself will let it in."

So Deirdre rose up and drew the bolt from the leaf of the door, and let in the hunter. She put a seat in the place for sitting, food in the place for eating, and drink in the place for drinking, for the man who had come into the house. "Come now and eat food, for you are in want of it," said Deirdre. "Indeed it is I was in want of food and drink and warmth when I came into this house; but by my word, I have forgotten that since I saw yourself," said the hunter.

"How little you are able to curb your tongue," said Levarcham. "It is not a great thing for you to keep your tongue quiet when you get the shelter of a house and the warmth of a hearth on a dark winter night." "That is so," said the hunter, "I may do that much, to keep my mouth shut; but I swear by the oath my people swear by, if some others of the people of the world saw this great beauty that is hidden away here, they would not leave her long with you."

"What people are those?" said Deirdre. "I will tell you that," said the hunter; "they are Naoise, son of Usnach, and Ainnle and Ardan, his two brothers."[2] "What is the appearance of these men, if we should ever see them?" said Deirdre. "This is the appearance that is on those three men," said the hunter: "the color of the raven is on their hair, their skin is like the swan on the wave, their cheeks like the blood of the speckled red calf, and their swiftness and their leap are like the salmon of the stream and like the deer of the gray mountain; and the head and shoulders of Naoise are above all the other men of Ireland." "However they may be," said Levarcham, "get you out from here, and take another road; and by my word, little is my thankfulness to yourself, or to her that let you in." "You need not send him out for telling me that," said Deirdre, "for as to those three men, I myself saw them last night in a dream, and they hunting upon a hill."

The hunter went away, but in a little time after he began to think to himself how Conchubar, High King of Ulster, was used to lie down at night and to rise up in the morning by himself, without a wife or anyone to speak to; and that if he could see this great beauty it was likely he would bring her home to Emain, and that he himself would get the good-will of the king for telling him there was such a queen to be found on the face of the world.

So he went straight to King Conchubar at Emain Macha, and he sent word in to the King that he had news for him, if he would hear it. The King sent for him to come in. "What is the reason of your journey?" he said. "It is what I have to tell you, King," said the hunter, "that I have seen the greatest beauty that ever was born in Ireland, and I am come to tell you of it."

"Who is this great beauty, and in what place is she to be seen, when she was never seen before you saw her, if you did see her?" "I did see her, indeed," said the hunter, "but no other man can

---

[1] Pronounced "she." Fairies who live underground, usually in a hill.
[2] These sons of Usnach are also nephews of King Conchubar through their mother.

see her, unless he knows from me the place where she is living." "Will you bring me to the place where she is, and you will have a good reward?" said the King. "I will bring you there," said the hunter. "Let you stay with my household tonight," said Conchubar, "and I myself and my people will go with you early on the morning of tomorrow." "I will stay," said the hunter, and he stayed that night in the household of King Conchubar.

Then Conchubar sent to Fergus and to the other chief men of Ulster, and he told them of what he was about to do. Though it was early when the songs and the music of the birds began in the woods, it was earlier yet when Conchubar, king of Ulster, rose up with his little company of near friends, in the fresh spring morning of the fresh and pleasant month of May, and the dew was heavy on every bush and flower as they went out toward the green hill where Deirdre was living.

But many a young man of them that had a light, glad, leaping step when they set out, had but a tired, slow, failing step before the end, because of the length and the roughness of the way. "It is down there below," said the hunter, "in the house in that valley, the woman is living, but I myself will not go nearer it than this."

Conchubar and his troop went down then to the green hillock where Deirdre was, and they knocked at the door of the house. Levarcham called out that neither answer nor opening would be given to anyone at all, and that she did not want disturbance put on herself or her house. "Open," said Conchubar, "in the name of the High King of Ulster." When Levarcham heard Conchubar's voice, she knew there was no use trying to keep Deirdre out of sight any longer, and she rose up in haste and let in the King, and as many of his people as could follow him.

When the King saw Deirdre before him, he thought in himself that he never saw in the course of the day, or in the dreams of the night, a creature so beautiful, and he gave her his full heart's weight of love there and then. It is what he did; he put Deirdre up on the shoulders of his men, and she herself and Levarcham were brought away to Emain Macha.

With the love that Conchubar had for Deirdre, he wanted to marry her with no delay, but when her leave was asked, she would not give it, for she was young yet, and she had no knowledge of the duties of a wife, or the ways of a king's house. And when Conchubar was pressing her hard, she asked him to give her a delay of a year and a day. He said he would give her that, though it was hard for him, if she would give him her certain promise to marry him at the year's end. She did that, and Conchubar got a woman teacher for her, and nice, fine, pleasant, modest maidens to be with her at her lying down and at her rising up, to be companions to her. And Deirdre grew wise in the works of a young girl, and in the understanding of a woman; and if anyone at all looked at her face, whatever color she was before that, she would blush crimson red. And it is what Conchubar thought, that he never saw with the eyes of his body a creature that pleased him so well.

One day Deirdre and her companions were out on a hill near Emain Macha, looking around them in the pleasant sunshine, and they saw three men walking together. Deirdre was looking at the men and wondering at them, and when they came near, she remembered the talk of the hunter, and the three men she saw in her dream, and she thought to herself that these were the three sons of Usnach, and that this was Naoise, that had his head and shoulders above all the men of Ireland. The three brothers went by without turning their eyes at all upon the young girls on the hillside, and they were singing as they went, and whoever heard the low singing of the sons of Usnach, it was enchantment and music to them, and every cow that was being milked and heard it, gave two-thirds more of milk. And it is what happened, that love for Naoise came into the heart of Deirdre, so that she could not but follow him. She gathered up her skirt and went after the three men that had gone past the foot of the hill, leaving her companions there after her.

But Ainnle and Ardan had heard talk of the young girl that was at Conchubar's court, and it is what they thought, that if Naoise their brother would see her, it is for himself he would have her, for she was not yet married to the King. So when they saw Deirdre coming after them, they said to one another to hasten their steps, for they had a long road to travel, and the dusk of night coming on. They did so, and Deirdre saw it, and she cried out after them, "Naoise, son of Usnach, are you going to leave me?" "What cry was that came to my ears, that it is not well for me to answer, and not easy for me to refuse?" said Naoise. "It was nothing but the cry of Conchubar's wild ducks," said his brothers; "but let us quicken our steps and hasten our feet, for we have a long road to travel, and the dusk of the evening coming on."

They did so, and they were widening the distance between themselves and her.

Then Deirdre cried, "Naoise! Naoise! son of Usnach, are you going to leave me?" "What cry was it that came to my ears and struck my heart, that it is not well for me to answer, or easy for me to refuse?" said Naoise. "Nothing but the cry of Conchubar's wild geese," said his brothers; "but let us quicken our steps and hasten our feet, for the darkness of night is coming on." They did so, and were widening the distance between themselves and her.

Then Deirdre cried the third time, "Naoise! Naoise! Naoise! son of Usnach, are you going to leave me?" "What sharp, clear cry was that, the sweetest that ever came to my ears, and the sharpest that ever struck my heart, of all the cries I ever heard?" said Naoise. "What is it but the scream of Conchubar's lake swans," said his brothers. "That was the third cry of some person beyond there," said Naoise, "and I swear by my hand of valor," he said, "I will go no farther until I see where the cry comes from." So Naoise turned back and met Deirdre, and Deirdre and Naoise kissed one another three times, and she gave a kiss to each of his brothers. And with the confusion that was on her, a blaze of red fire came upon her, and her color came and went as quickly as the aspen by the stream. And it is what Naoise thought to himself, that he never saw a woman so beautiful in his life; and he gave Deirdre, there and then, the love that he never gave to living thing, to vision, or to creature, but to herself alone.

Then he lifted her high on his shoulder, and he said to his brothers to hasten their steps; and they hastened them.

"Harm will come of this," said the young men. "Although there should harm come," said Naoise, "I am willing to be in disgrace while I live. We will go with her to another province, and there is not in Ireland a king who will not give us a welcome." So they called their people, and that night they set out with three times fifty men, and three times fifty women, and three times fifty greyhounds, and Deirdre in their midst.

They were a long time after that shifting from one place to another all around Ireland, from Essruadh in the South, to Beinn Etair in the East again, and it is often they were in danger of being destroyed by Conchubar's devices. And one time the Druids raised a wood before them, but Naoise and his brothers cut their way through it. But at last they got out of Ulster and sailed to the country of Alban,[3] and settled in a lonely place; and when hunting on the mountains failed them, they fell upon the cattle of the men of Alban, so that these gathered together to make an end of them. But the sons of Usnach called to the King of Scotland, and he took them into his friendship, and they gave him their help when he went out into battles or to war.

But all this time they had never spoken to the King of Deirdre, and they kept her with themselves, not to let anyone see her, for they were afraid they might get their death on account of her, she being so beautiful.

But it chanced very early, one morning, the King's steward came to visit them, and he found his way into the house where Naoise and Deirdre were, and there he saw them asleep beside one another. He went back then to the King, and he said: "Up to this time there has never been found a woman that would be a fitting wife for you; but there is a woman on the shore of Loch Ness now, is well worthy of you, King of the East. And what you have to do is to make an end of Naoise, for it is of his wife I am speaking." "I will not do that," said the King; "but go to her," he said, "and bid her to come and see me secretly." The steward brought her that message, but Deirdre sent him away, and all that he had said to her, she told it to Naoise afterwards. Then when she would not come to him, the King sent the sons of Usnach into every hard fight, hoping they would get their death, but they won every battle, and came back safe again.

And after a while they went to Loch Eitche, near the sea, and they were left to themselves there for a while in peace and quietness. And they settled and made a dwelling-house for themselves by the side of Loch Ness, and they could kill the salmon of the stream from out their own door, and the deer of the gray hills from out their window. But when Naoise went to the court of the King, his clothes were splendid among the great men of the army of Scotland: a cloak of bright purple, rightly shaped, with a fringe of bright gold; a coat of satin with fifty hooks of silver; a brooch on which were a hundred polished gems; a gold-hilted sword in his hand, two blue-green spears of bright points, a dagger with the color of yellow gold on it, and a hilt of silver. But the two children they had, Gaiar and Aebgreine, they gave into the care of Manannan, Son of the Sea. And he cared

[3] In the Highlands of Scotland.

them well in Emhain of the Apple Trees, and he brought Bobaras the poet to give learning to Gaiar. And Aebgreine of the Sunny Face he gave in marriage afterwards to Rinn, son of Eochaidh Juil of the Land of Promise.

Now it happened, after a time, that a very great feast was made by Conchubar, in Emain Macha, for all the great among his nobles, so that the whole company were easy and pleasant together. The musicians stood up to play their songs and to give poems, and they gave out the branches of relationship and of kindred. These are the names of the poets that were in Emain at the time: Cathbad the Druid, son of Conall, son of Rudraige; Geanann of the Bright Face, son of Cathbad; Ferceirtne, and Geanann Black-Knee, and many others, and Sencha, son of Ailell.

They were all drinking and making merry until Conchubar, the King, raised his voice and spoke aloud, and it is what he said: "I desire to know from you, did you ever see a better house than this house of Emain, or a hearth better than my hearth in any place you were ever in?" "We did not," they said. "If that is so," said Conchubar, "do you know of anything at all that is wanting to you?" "We know of nothing," said they. "That is not so with me," said Conchubar. "I know of a great want that is on you, the want of the three best candles of the Gael, the three noble sons of Usnach, that ought not to be away from us for the sake of any woman in the world, Naoise, Ainnle, and Ardan; for surely they are the sons of a king, and they would defend the High Kingship against the best men of Ireland."

"If we had dared," said they, "it is long ago we would have said it, and more than that, the province of Ulster would be equal to any other province in Ireland, if there was no Ulsterman in it but those three alone, for it is lions they are in hardness and in bravery."

"If that is so," said Conchubar, "let us send word by a messenger to Alban, and to the dwelling-place of the sons of Usnach, to ask them back again." "Who will go there with the message?" said they all. "I cannot know that," said Conchubar, "for there is geasa,[4] that is, bonds, on Naoise not to come back with any man only one of the three, Conall Cearnach, or Fergus, or Cuchulain, and I will know now," said he, "which one of those three loves me best."

Then he called Conall to one side, and he asked him, "What would you do with me if I should send you for the sons of Usnach, and if they were destroyed through me—a thing I do not mean to do?" "As I am not going to undertake it," said Conall, "I will say that it is not one alone I would kill, but any Ulsterman I would lay hold of that had harmed them would get shortening of life from me and the sorrow of death." "I see well," said Conchubar, "you are no friend of mine," and he put Conall away from him.

Then he called Cuchulain to him, and asked him the same as he did the other. "I give my word, as I am not going," said Cuchulain, "if you want that of me, and that you think to kill them when they come, it is not one person alone that would die for it, but every Ulsterman I could lay hold of would get shortening of life from me and the sorrow of death." "I see well," said Conchubar, "that you are no friend of mine." And he put Cuchulain from him.

And then he called Fergus to him, and asked him the same question, and Fergus said, "Whatever may happen, I promise your blood will be safe from me, but besides yourself there is no Ulsterman that would try to harm them, and that I would lay hold of, but I would give him shortening of life and the sorrow of. death." "I see well," said Conchubar, "is it yourself must go for them, and it is tomorrow you must set out, for it is with you they will come, and when you are coming back to us westward, I put you under bonds to go first to the fort of Borach, son of Cainte, and give me your word now that as soon as you get there, you will send on the sons of Usnach to Emain, whether it be day or night at the time." After that the two of them went in together, and Fergus told all the company how it was under his charge they were to be put.

Then Conchubar went to Borach and asked had he a feast ready prepared for him. "I have," said Borach, "but although I was able to make it ready, I was not able to bring it to Emain." "If that is so," said Conchubar, "give it to Fergus when he comes back to Ireland, for it is geasa on him not to refuse your feast." Borach promised he would do that, and so they wore away that night.

So Fergus set out in the morning, and he brought no guard nor helpers with him, but himself and his two sons, Fair-Haired Iollan, and Rough-Red Buinne, and Cuillean, the shield-bearer, and the shield itself. They went on till they got to the dwelling-place of the sons of Usnach

---

[4] An absolute compulsion which, if disregarded, will bring great disaster.

and to Loch Eitche in Alba. It is how the sons of Usnach lived: they had three houses; and the house where they made ready the food, it is not there they would eat it, and the house where they would eat it, it is not there they would sleep.

When Fergus came to the harbor he let a great shout out of him. And it is how Naoise and Deirdre were: they had a chessboard between them, and they playing on it. Naoise heard the shout, and he said, "That is the shout of a man of Ireland." "It is not, but the cry of a man of Alban," said Deirdre. She knew at the first it was Fergus gave the shout, but she denied it. Then Fergus let another shout out of him. "That is an Irish shout," said Naoise again. "It is not, indeed," said Deirdre; "let us go on playing." Then Fergus gave the third shout, and the sons of Usnach knew this time it was the shout of Fergus, and Naoise said to Ardan to go out and meet him. Then Deirdre told him that she herself knew at the first shout that it was Fergus. "Why did you deny it, then, Queen?" said Naoise. "Because of a vision I saw last night," said Deirdre. "Three birds I saw coming to us from Emain Macha, and three drops of honey in their mouths, and they left them with us, and three drops of our blood they brought away with them." "What meaning do you put on that, Queen?" said Naoise. "It is," said Deirdre, "Fergus that is coming to us with a message of peace from Conchubar, for honey is not sweeter than a message of peace sent by a lying man." "Let that pass," said Naoise. "Is there anything in it but troubled sleep and the melancholy of woman? And it is a long time Fergus is in the harbor. Rise up, Ardan, to be before him, and bring him with you here."

And Ardan went down to meet him, and gave a fond kiss to himself and to his two sons. And it is what he said: "My love to you, dear comrades." After that he asked news of Ireland, and they gave it to him, and then they came to where Naoise and Ainnle and Deirdre were, and they kissed Fergus and his two sons, and they asked news of Ireland from them. "It is the best news I have for you," said Fergus, "that Conchubar, King of Ulster, has sworn by the earth beneath him, by the high heaven above him, and by the sun that travels to the west, that he will have no rest by day nor sleep by night if the sons of Usnach, his own foster-brothers, will not come back to the land of their home and the country of their birth; and he has sent us to ask you there." "It is better for them to stop here," said Deirdre, "for they have a greater sway in Scotland than Conchubar himself has in Ireland." "One's own country is better than any other thing," said Fergus, "for no man can have any pleasure, however great his good luck and his way of living, if he does not see his own country every day." "That is true," said Naoise, "for Ireland is dearer to myself than Alban, though I would get more in Alban than in Ireland." "It will be safe for you to come with me," said Fergus. "It will be safe indeed," said Naoise, "and we will go with you to Ireland; and though there were no trouble beneath the sun, but a man to be far from his own land, there is little delight in peace and a long sleep to a man that is an exile. It is a pity for the man that is an exile; it is little his honor, it is great his grief, for it is he will have his share of wandering."

It was not with Deirdre's will Naoise said that, and she was greatly against going with Fergus. And she said: "I had a dream last night of the three sons of Usnach, and they bound and put in the grave by Conchubar of the Red Branch." But Naoise said: "Lay down your dream, Deirdre, on the heights of the hills, lay down your dream on the sailors of the sea, lay down your dream on the rough gray stones, for we will give peace and we will get it from the king of the world and from Conchubar." But Deirdre spoke again, and it is what she said: "There is the howling of dogs in my ears; a vision of the night is before my eyes; I see Fergus away from us; I see Conchubar without mercy in his dun; I see Naoise without strength in battle; I see Ainnle without his loud-sounding shield; I see Ardan without shield or breastplate, and the Hill of Atha without delight. I see Conchubar asking for blood; I see Fergus caught with hidden lies; I see Deirdre crying with tears. I see Deirdre crying with tears."

"A thing that is unpleasing to me, and that I would never give in to," said Fergus, "is to listen to the howling of dogs and to the dreams of women; and since Conchubar, the High King, has sent a message of friendship, it would not be right for you to refuse it." "It would not be right, indeed," said Naoise, "and we will go with you to-morrow." And Fergus gave his word, and he said, "If all the men of Ireland were against you, it would not profit them, for neither shield nor sword nor a helmet itself would be any help or protection to them against you, and I myself to be with you." "That is true," said Naoise, "and we will go with you to Ireland."

They spent the night there until morning, and then they went where the ships were, and they went on the sea, and a good many of their people with them, and Deirdre looked back on the land of Alban, and it is what she said:

"My love to you, O land to the east, and it goes ill with me to leave you; for it is pleasant are your bays and your harbors and your wide, flowery plains and your green-sided hills; and little need was there for us to leave you." And she made this complaint:

"Dear to me is that land, that land to the east, Alban, with its wonders; I would not have come from it hither but that I came with Naoise.

"Dear to me Dun Fiodhaigh [5] and Dun Fionn; dear is the dun above them; dear to me Inis Droignach; dear to me Dun Suibhne.

"O Coill Cuan! Ochone! Coil Cuan! where Ainnle used to come. My grief! it was short I thought his stay there with Naoise in Western Alban. Glen Laoi, O Glen Laoi, where I used to sleep under soft coverings; fish and venison and badger's flesh, that was my portion in Glen Laoi.

"Glen Masan, my grief! Glen Masan! high its hart's-tongue, bright its stalks; we were rocked to pleasant sleep over the wooded harbor of Masan.

"Glen Archan, my grief! Glen Archan, the straight valley of the pleasant ridge; never was there a young man more light-hearted than my Naoise used to be in Glen Archan.

"Glen Eitche, my grief! Glen Eitche, it was there I built my first house; beautiful were the woods on our rising; the home of the sun is Glen Eitche.

"Glen-da-Rua, my grief! Glen-da-Rua, my love to every man that belongs to it; sweet is the voice of the cuckoo on the bending branch on the hill above Glen-da-Rua.

"Dear to me is Droighin over the fierce strand; dear are its waters over the clean sand. I would never have come out from it at all but that I came with my beloved!"

After she had made that complaint they came to Dun Borach, and Borach gave three fond kisses to Fergus and to the sons of Usnach along with him. It was then Borach said he had a feast laid out for Fergus, and that it was *geasa* for him to leave it until he would have eaten it. But Fergus reddened with anger from head to foot, and it is what he said: "It is a bad thing you have done, Borach, laying out a feast for me, and Conchubar to have made me give my word that as soon as I would come to Ireland, whether it would be by day or in the nighttime, I would send on the sons

of Usnach to Emain Macha." "I hold you under bonds," said Borach, "to stop and use the feast."

Then Fergus asked Naoise what should he do about the feast. "You must choose," said Deirdre, "whether you will forsake the children of Usnach or the feast, and it would be better for you to refuse the feast than to forsake the sons of Usnach." "I will not forsake them," said he, "for I will send my two sons, Fair-Haired Iollan and Rough-Red Buinne, with them, to Emain Macha." "On my word," said Naoise, "that is a great deal to do for us; for up to this no other person ever protected us but ourselves." And he went out of the place in great anger; and Ainnle, and Ardan, and Deirdre, and the two sons of Fergus followed him, and they left Fergus dark and sorrowful after them. But for all that, Fergus was full sure that if all the provinces of Ireland would go into one council, they would not consent to break the pledge he had given.

As for the sons of Usnach, they went on their way by every short road, and Deirdre said to them, "I will give you a good advice, Sons of Usnach, though you may not follow it." "What is that advice, Queen?" said Naoise. "It is," said she, "to go to Rechrainn, between Ireland and Scotland, and to wait there until Fergus has done with the feast; and that will be the keeping of his word to Fergus, and it will be the lengthening of your lives to you." "We will not follow that advice," said Naoise; and the children of Fergus said it was little trust she had in them, when she thought they would not protect her, though their hands might not be so strong as the hands of the sons of Usnach; and besides that, Fergus had given them his word. "Alas! it is sorrow came on us with the word of Fergus," said Deirdre, "and he to forsake us for a feast"; and she made this complaint:

"It is grief to me that ever I came from the east on the word of the unthinking son of Rogh.[6] It is only lamentations I will make. Och! it is very sorrowful my heart is!

"My heart is heaped up with sorrow; it is tonight my great hurt is. My grief! my dear companions, the end of your days is come."

And it is what Naoise answered her: "Do not say that in your haste, Deirdre, more beautiful than the sun. Fergus would never have come for us eastward to bring us back to be destroyed."

And Deirdre said, "My grief! I think it too far for you, beautiful sons of Usnach, to have come

[5] The places named in the lament are all in Scotland.
[6] Fergus, the son of Rogh.

from Alban of the rough grass; it is lasting will be its lifelong sorrow."

After that they went forward to Finncairn of the watch-tower on sharp-peaked Slieve Fuad, and Deirdre stayed after them in the valley, and sleep fell on her there.

When Naoise saw that Deirdre was left after them, he turned back as she was rising out of her sleep, and he said, "What made you wait after us, Queen?" "Sleep that was on me," said Deirdre; "and I saw a vision in it." "What vision was that?" said Naoise. "It was," she said, "Fair-Haired Iollan that I saw without his head on him, and Rough-Red Buinne with his head on him; and it is without help of Rough-Red Buinne you were, and it is with the help of Fair-Haired Iollan you were." And she made this complaint:

"It is a sad vision has been shown to me, of my four tall, fair, bright companions; the head of each has been taken from him, and no help to be had one from another."

But when Naoise heard this he reproached her, and said, "O fair, beautiful woman, nothing does your mouth speak but evil. Do not let the sharpness and the great misfortune that come from it fall on your friends." And Deirdre answered him with kind, gentle words, and it is what she said: "It would be better to me to see harm come on any other person than upon any one of you three, with whom I have traveled over the seas and over the wide plains; but when I look on you, it is only Buinne I can see safe and whole, and I know that his life will be longest among you; and indeed it is I that am sorrowful tonight."

After that they came forward to the high willows, and it was then Deirdre said: "I see a cloud in the air, and it is a cloud of blood; and I would give you a good advice, Sons of Usnach," she said. "What is that advice?" said Naoise. "To go to Dundealgan where Cuchulain is, until Fergus has done with the feast, and to be under the protection of Cuchulain, for fear of the treachery of Conchubar." "Since there is no fear on us, we will not follow that advice," said Naoise. And Deirdre complained, and it is what she said:

"O Naoise, look at the cloud I see above us in the air; I see a cloud over green Macha, cold and deep red like blood. I am startled by the cloud that I see here in the air; a thin, dreadful cloud that is like a clot of blood. I give a right advice to the beautiful sons of Usnach not to go to Emain tonight, because of the danger that is over them.

We will go to Dundealgan, where the Hound of the Smith [7] is; we will come tomorrow from the south along with the Hound, Cuchulain."

But Naoise said in his anger to Deirdre, "Since there is no fear on us, we will not follow your advice." And Deirdre turned to the grandsons of Rogh, and it is what she said: "It is seldom until now, Naoise, that yourself and myself were not of the one mind. And I say to you, Naoise, that you would not have gone against me like this the day Manannan gave me the cup in the time of his great victory."

After that they went on to Emain Macha. "Sons of Usnach," said Deirdre, "I have a sign by which you will know if Conchubar is going to do treachery on you." "What sign is that?" said Naoise. "If you are let come into the house where Conchubar is, and the nobles of Ulster, then Conchubar is not going to do treachery on you. But if it is in the House of the Red Branch you are put, then he is going to do treachery on you."

After that they came to Emain Macha, and they took the handwood and struck the door, and the doorkeeper asked who was there. They told him that it was the sons of Usnach, and Deirdre, and the two sons of Fergus were there.

When Conchubar heard that, he called his stewards and serving men to him, and he asked them how was the House of the Red Branch for food and for drink. They said that if all the seven armies of Ulster would come there, they would find what would satisfy them. "If that is so," said Conchubar, "bring the sons of Usnach into it."

It was then Deirdre said, "It would have been better for you to follow my advice, and never to have come to Emain, and it would be right for you to leave it, even at this time." "We will not," said Fair-Haired Iollan, "for it is not fear or cowardliness was ever seen on us, but we will go to the house." So they went on to the House of the Red Branch, and the stewards and the serving-men with them, and well-tasting food was served to them, and pleasant drinks, till they were all glad and merry, except only Deirdre and the sons of Usnach; for they did not use much food or drink, because of the length and the greatness of their journey from Dun Borach to Emain Macha. Then Naoise said, "Give the chessboard to us till we go playing." So they gave them the chessboard and they began to play.

It was just at that time Conchubar was asking, "Who will I send that will bring me word of

[7] The literal meaning of Cuchulain, Irish god and hero.

Deirdre, and that will tell me if she has the same appearance and the same shape she had before, for if she has, there is not a woman in the world has a more beautiful shape or appearance than she has, and I will bring her out with edge of blade and point of sword in spite of the sons of Usnach, good though they be. But if not, let Naoise have her for himself." "I myself will go there," said Levarcham, "and I will bring you word of that." And it is how it was, Deirdre was dearer to her than any other person in the world; for it was often she went through the world looking for Deirdre and bringing news to her and from her. So Levarcham went over to the House of the Red Branch, and near it she saw a great troop of armed men, and she spoke to them, but they made her no answer, and she knew by that it was none of the men of Ulster were in it, but men from some strange country that Conchubar's messengers had brought to Emain.

And then she went in where Naoise and Deirdre were, and it is how she found them, the polished chessboard between them, and they playing on it; and she gave them fond kisses, and she said: "You are not doing well to be playing; and it is to bring Conchubar word if Deirdre has the same shape and appearance she used to have that he sent me here now; and there is grief on me for the deed that will be done in Emain tonight, treachery that will be done, and the killing of kindred, and the three bright candles of the Gael to be quenched, and Emain will not be the better of it to the end of life and time"; and she made this complaint sadly and wearily:

"My heart is heavy for the treachery that is being done in Emain this night; on account of this treachery, Emain will never be at peace from this out.

"The three that are most king-like today under the sun; the three best of all that live on the earth, it is grief to me tonight they to die for the sake of any woman. Naoise and Ainnle, whose deeds are known, and Ardan, their brother; treachery is to be done on the young, bright-faced three; it is not I that am not sorrowful tonight."

When she had made this complaint, Levarcham said to the sons of Usnach and to the children of Fergus to shut close the doors and the windows of the house and to do bravery. "And, oh, sons of Fergus," she said, "defend your charge and your care bravely till Fergus comes, and you will have praise and a blessing for it." And she cried with many tears, and she went back to where Conchu-

bar was, and he asked news of Deirdre of her. And Levarcham said, "It is good news and bad news I have for you." "What news is that?" said Conchubar. "It is the good news," she said, "the three sons of Usnach to have come to you and to be over there, and they are the three that are bravest and mightiest in form and in looks and in countenance, of all in the world; and Ireland will be yours from this out, since the sons of Usnach are with you; and the news that is worst with me is, the woman that was best of the women of the world in form and in looks, going out of Emain, is without the form and without the appearance she used to have."

When Conchubar heard that, much of his jealousy went backward, and he was drinking and making merry for a while, until he thought on Deirdre again the second time, and on that he asked, "Who will I get to bring me word of Deirdre?" But he did not find anyone would go there. And then he said to Gelban, the merry, pleasant son of the King of Lochlann: "Go over and bring me word if Deirdre has the same shape and the same appearance she used to have, for if she has, there is not on the ridge of the world or on the waves of the earth a woman more beautiful than herself."

So Gelban went to the House of the Red Branch, and he found the doors and the windows of the fort shut, and fear came on him. And it is what he said: "It is not an easy road for anyone that would get to the sons of Usnach, for I think there is very great anger on them." And after that he found a window that was left open by forgetfulness in the house, and he was looking in. Then Deirdre saw him through the window, and when she saw him looking at her, she went into a red blaze of blushes, and Naoise knew that someone was looking at her from the window, and she told him that she saw a young man looking in at them. It is how Naoise was at that time, with a man of the chessmen in his hand, and he made a fair throw over his shoulder at the young man, that put the eye out of his head. The young man went back to where Conchubar was. "You were merry and pleasant going out," said Conchubar, "but you are sad and cheerless coming back." And then Gelban told him the story from beginning to end. "I see well," said Conchubar, "the man that made that throw will be king of the world, unless he has his life shortened. And what appearance is there on Deirdre?" he said. "It is this," said Gelban: "although Naoise put out my eye, I would have wished to stay there looking at her with the other eye, but for the haste you put on me; for there is not in the world a woman is better of shape or of form than herself."

When Conchubar heard that, he was filled with jealousy and with envy, and he bade the men of his army that were with him, and that had been drinking at the feast, to go and attack the place where the sons of Usnach were. So they went forward to the House of the Red Branch, and they gave three great shouts around it, and they put fires and red flames to it. When the sons of Usnach heard the shouts, they asked who those men were that were about the house. "Conchubar and the men of Ulster," they all said together. "Is it the pledge of Fergus you would break?" said Fair-Haired Iollan. "On my word," said Conchubar, "there will be sorrow on the sons of Usnach, Deirdre to be with them." "That is true," said Deirdre; "Fergus has deceived you." "By my oath," said Rough-Red Buinne, "if he betrayed, we will not betray."

It was then Buinne went out and killed three-fifths of the fighting men outside, and put great disturbance on the rest; and Conchubar asked who was there, and who was doing destruction on his men like that. "It is I, myself, Rough-Red Buinne, son of Fergus," said he. "I will give you a good gift if you will leave off," said Conchubar. "What gift is that?" said Rough-Red Buinne. "A hundred of land," said Conchubar. "What besides?" said Rough-Red Buinne. "My own friendship and my counsel," said Conchubar. "I will take that," said Rough-Red Buinne. It was a good mountain that was given him as a reward, but it turned barren in the same night, and no green grew on it again forever, and it used to be called the Mountain of the Share of Buinne.

Deirdre heard what they were saying. "By my word," she said, "Rough-Red Buinne has forsaken you, and, in my opinion, it is like the father the son is." "I give my word," says Fair-Haired Iollan, "that is not so with me; as long as this narrow, straight sword stays in my hand, I will not forsake the sons of Usnach."

After that Fair-Haired Iollan went out, and made three courses around the house, and killed three-fifths of the heroes outside, and he came in again where Naoise was, and he playing chess, and Ainnle with him. So Iollan went out the second time, and made three other courses round the fort, and he brought a lighted torch with him on the

lawn, and he went destroying the hosts, so that they dared not come to attack the house. And he was a good son, Fair-Haired Iollan, for he never refused any person on the ridge of the world anything that he had, and he never took wages from any person but only Fergus.

It was then Conchubar said: "What place is my own son, Fiacra the Fair?" "I am here, High Prince," said Fiacra. "By my word," said Conchubar, "it is on the one night yourself and Iollan were born, and as it is the arms of his father he has with him, let you take my arms with you, that is, my shield, the Ochain[8] my two spears, and my great sword, the Gorm Glas, the Blue Green—and do bravery and great deeds with them."

Then Fiacra took Conchubar's arms, and he and Fair-Haired Iollan attacked one another, and they made a stout fight, one against the other. But however it was, Fair-Haired Iollan put down Fiacra, so that he made him lie under the shelter of his shield, till it roared for the greatness of the strait he was in; for it was the way with the Ochain, the shield of Conchubar, to roar when the person on whom it would be was in danger; and the three chief waves of Ireland, the Wave of Tuagh, the Wave of Cliodna, and the Wave of Rudraige, roared in answer to it.

It was at that time Conall Cearnach was at Dun Sobairce, and he heard the Wave of Tuagh. "True it is," said Conall, "Conchubar is in some danger, and it is not right for me to be here listening to him."

Conall rose up on that, and he put his arms and his armor on him, and came forward to where Conchubar was at Emain Macha, and he found the fight going on on the lawn, and Fiacra, the son of Conchubar, greatly pressed by Fair-Haired Iollan, and neither the King of Ulster nor any other person dared to go between them. But Conall went aside, behind Fair-Haired Iollan, and thrust his sword through him. "Who is it has wounded me behind my back?" said Fair-Haired Iollan. "Whoever did it, by my hand of valor, he would have got a fair fight, face to face, from myself." "Who are you yourself?" said Conall. "I am Iollan, son of Fergus, and are you yourself Conall?" "It is I," said Conall. "It is evil and it is heavy the work you have done," said Iollan, "and the sons of Usnach under my protection." "Is that true?" said Conall. "It is true, indeed," said Iollan. "By my hand of valor," said Conall, "Conchubar will not get his

[8] This magic shield had been received from the queen of the sea. It would roar whenever its owner was hard pressed.

own son alive from me to avenge it," and he gave a stroke of the sword to Fiacra, so that he struck his head off, and he left them so. The clouds of death came upon Fair-Haired Iollan then, and he threw his arms toward the fortress, and called out to Naoise to do bravery, and after that he died.

It is then Conchubar himself came out and nineteen hundred men with him, and Conall said to him: "Go up now to the doorway of the fort, and see where your sister's children are lying on a bed of trouble." And when Conchubar saw them he said: "You are not sister's children to me; it is not the deed of sister's children you have done me, but you have done harm to me with treachery in the sight of all the men of Ireland." And it is what Ainnle said to him: "Although we took well-shaped, soft-handed Deirdre from you, yet we did a little kindness to you at another time, and this is the time to remember it. That day your ship was breaking up on the sea, and it full of gold and silver, we gave you up our own ship, and ourselves went swimming to the harbor."

But Conchubar said: "If you did fifty good deeds to me, surely this would be my thanks: I would not give you peace, and you in distress, but every great want I could put on you."

And then Ardan said: "We did another little kindness to you, and this is the time to remember it; the day the speckled horse failed you on the green of Dundealgan, it was we gave you the gray horse that would bring you fast on your road."

But Conchubar said: "If you had done fifty good deeds to me, surely this would be my thanks: I would not give you peace, and you in distress, but every great want I could put on you."

And then Naoise said: "We did you another good deed, and this is the time to remember it; we have put you under many benefits; it is strong our right is to your protection.

"The time when Murcael, son of Brian, fought the seven battles at Beinn Etair, we brought you, without fail, the heads of the sons of the King of the Southeast."

But Conchubar said: "If you had done me fifty good deeds, surely this is my thanks: I would not give you peace in your distress, but every great want I could put upon you.

"Your death is not a death to me now, young sons of Usnach, since he that was innocent fell by you, the third best of the horsemen of Ireland."

Then Deirdre said: "Rise up, Naoise, take your sword, good son of a king, mind yourself well, for it is not long that life will be left in your fair body."

It is then all Conchubar's men came about the house, and they put fires and burning to it. Ardan went out then, and his men, and put out the fires and killed three hundred men. And Ainnle went out in the third part of the night, and he killed three hundred, and did slaughter and destruction on them.

And Naoise went out in the last quarter of the night, and drove away all the army from the house.

He came into the house after that, and it is then Deirdre rose up and said to him: "By my word, it is well you won your way; and do bravery and valor from this out; and it was bad advice you took when you ever trusted Conchubar."

As for the sons of Usnach, after that they made a good protection with their shields, and they put Deirdre in the middle and linked the shields around her, and they gave three leaps out over the walls of Emain, and they killed three hundred men in that sally.

When Conchubar saw that, he went to Cathbad the Druid, and said to him: "Go, Cathbad, to the sons of Usnach, and work enchantment on them; for unless they are hindered they will destroy the men of Ulster forever if they go away in spite of them; and I give the word of a true hero, they will get no harm from me, but let them only make agreement with me."

When Cathbad heard that, he agreed, believing him, and he went to the end of his arts and his knowledge to hinder the sons of Usnach, and he worked enchantment on them, so that he put the likeness of a dark sea about them, with hindering waves. And when Naoise saw the waves rising he put up Deirdre on his shoulder, and it is how the sons of Usnach were, swimming on the ground as they were going out of Emain; yet the men of Ulster did not dare to come near them until their swords had fallen from their hands. But after their swords fell from their hands, the sons of Usnach were taken. And when they were taken, Conchubar asked of the children of Durthacht to kill them. But the children of Durthacht said they would not do that. There was a young man with Conchubar whose name was Maine, and his surname Rough-Hand, son of the king of the fair Norwegians, and it is Naoise had killed his father and his two brothers; Athrac and Triathrach were their names. And he said he himself would kill the sons of Usnach. "If that is so," said Ardan, "kill me the first, for I am younger than my brothers, so that I will not see my brothers killed." "Let him not be killed but myself," said Ainnle. "Let that not be done," said Naoise, "for I have a sword that Manannan, son of Lir, gave me, and the stroke of it leaves nothing after it, track nor trace; and strike the three of us together, and we will die at the one time." "That is well," said they all, "and let you lay down your heads," they said. They did that, and Maine gave a strong quick blow of the sword on the three necks together on the block, and struck the three heads off them with one stroke; and the men of Ulster gave three loud sorrowful shouts, and cried aloud about them there.

As for Deirdre, she cried pitifully, wearily, and tore her fair hair, and she was talking on the sons of Usnach and on Alban, and it is what she said:

"A blessing eastward to Alban from me. Good is the sight of her bays and valleys; pleasant was it to sit on the slopes of her hills, where the sons of Usnach used to be hunting.

"One day, when the nobles of Scotland were drinking with the sons of Usnach, to whom they owed their affection, Naoise gave a kiss secretly to the daughter of the lord of Duntreon. He sent her a frightened deer, wild, and a fawn at its foot; and he went to visit her coming home from the host of Inverness. When myself heard that, my head filled full of jealousy; I put my boat on the waves; it was the same to me to live or to die. They followed me swimming, Ainnle and Ardan, that never said a lie; they turned me back again, two that would give battle to a hundred; Naoise gave me his true word, he swore three times, with his arms as witness, he would never put vexation on me again, until he would go from me to the hosts of the dead.

"Och! if she knew tonight, Naoise to be under a covering of clay, it is she would cry her fill, and it is I would cry along with her."

After she had made this complaint, seeing they were all taken up with one another, Deirdre came forward on the lawn, and she was running round and round, up and down, from one to another, and Cuchulain met her, and she told him the story from first to last, how it had happened to the sons of Usnach. It is sorrowful Cuchulain was for that, for there was not in the world a man was dearer to him than Naoise. And he asked who killed him. "Maine Rough-Hand," said Deirdre. Then Cuchulain went away, sad and sorrowful, to Dundealgan.

After that Deirdre lay down by the grave, and they were digging earth from it, and she made this lament after the sons of Usnach:

"Long is the day without the sons of Usnach; it was never wearisome to be in their company; sons of a king that entertained exiles; three lions of the Hill of the Cave.

"Three darlings of the women of Britain; three hawks of Slieve Cuilenn; sons of a king served by valor, to whom warriors did obedience. The three mighty bears; three lions of the fort of Conrach; three sons of a king who thought well of their praise; three nurslings of the men of Ulster.

"Three heroes not good at homage; their fall is a cause of sorrow; three sons of the sister of a king; three props of the army of Cuailgne.

"Three dragons of Dun Monad, the three valiant men from the Red Branch; I myself will not be living after them, the three that broke hard battles.

"Three that were brought up by Aoife, to whom lands were under tribute; three pillars in the breach of battle; three pupils that were with Scathach.

"Three pupils that were with Uathach; three champions that were lasting in might; three shining sons of Usnach; it is weariness to be without them.

"The High King of Ulster, my first betrothed, I forsook for love of Naoise; short my life will be after him; I will make keening [9] at their burial.

"That I would live after Naoise let no one think on the earth; I will not go on living after Ainnle and after Ardan.

"After them I myself will not live; three that would leap through the midst of battle; since my beloved is gone from me I will cry my fill over his grave.

"O young man, digging the new grave, do not make the grave narrow; I will be along with them in the grave, making lamentation and ochones.

"Many the hardship I met with along with the three heroes. I suffered want of house, want of fire; it is myself that used not to be troubled.

"Their three shields and their spears made a bed for me often. O young man, put their three swords close over their grave.

"Their three hounds, their three hawks, will be from this time without huntsmen; three helpers of every battle; three pupils of Conall Cearnach.

"The three leashes of those three hounds have brought a sigh from my heart. It is I had the care of them; the sight of them is a cause of grief.

"I was never one day alone to the day of the making of this grave, though it is often that myself and yourselves were in loneliness.

"My sight is gone from me with looking at the grave of Naoise; it is short till my life will leave

[9] Lamentations at the funeral

me, and those who would have keened me do not live.

"Since it is through me they were betrayed I will be tired out with sorrow; it is a pity I was not in the earth before the sons of Usnach were killed.

"Sorrowful was my journey with Fergus, betraying me to the Red Branch; we were deceived all together with his sweet, flowery words. I left the delights of Ulster for the three heroes that were bravest; my life will not be long, I myself am alone after them.

"I am Deirdre without gladness, and I at the end of my life; since it is grief to be without them, I myself will not be long after them."

After that complaint Deirdre loosed out her hair, and threw herself on the body of Naoise before it was put into the grave and gave three kisses to him, and when her mouth touched his blood, the color of burning sods came into her cheeks, and she rose up like one that had lost her wits, and she went on through the night till she came to where the waves were breaking on the strand. And a fisherman was there and his wife, and they brought her into their cabin and sheltered her, and she neither smiled nor laughed, nor took food, drink, or sleep, nor raised her head from her knees, but was crying always after the sons of Usnach.

But when she could not be found at Emain, Conchubar sent Levarcham to look for her, and to bring her back to his palace, that he might make her his wife. And Levarcham found her in the fisherman's cabin, and she bade her come back to Emain, where she would have protection and riches and all that she would ask. And she gave her this message she brought from Conchubar: "Come up to my house, O branch with the dark eyelashes, and there need be no fear on your fair face, of hatred or of jealousy or of reproach." And Deirdre said: "I will not go up to his house, for it is not land or earth or food I am wanting, or gold or silver or horses, but leave to go to the grave where the sons of Usnach are lying, till I give the three honey kisses to their three white, beautiful bodies." And she made this complaint:

"Make keening for the heroes that were killed on their coming to Ireland; stately they used to be, coming to the house, the three great sons of Usnach.

"The sons of Usnach fell in the fight like three branches that were growing straight and nice, and they destroyed in a heavy storm that left neither bud nor twig of them.

"Naoise, my gentle, well-learned comrade, make no delay in crying him with me; cry for Ardan that killed the wild boars; cry for Ainnle whose strength was great.

"It was Naoise that would kiss my lips, my first man and my first sweetheart; it was Ainnle would pour out my drink; and it was Ardan would lay my pillow.

"Though sweet to you is the mead that is drunk by the soft-living son of Ness,[10] the food of the sons of Usnach was sweeter to me all through my lifetime.

"Whenever Naoise would go out to hunt through the woods or the wide plains, all the meat he would bring back was better to me than honey.

"Though sweet to you are the sounds of pipes and of trumpets, it is truly, I say to the King, I have heard music that is sweeter.

"Delightful to Conchubar, the king, are pipes and trumpets; but the singing of the sons of Usnach was more delightful to me.

"It was Naoise had the deep sound of the waves in his voice; it was the song of Ardan that was good, and the voice of Ainnle toward their green dwelling-place.

"Their birth was beautiful and their blossoming, as they grew to the strength of manhood; sad is the end today, the sons of Usnach to be cut down.

"Dear were their pleasant words, dear their young, high strength; in their going through the plains of Ireland there was a welcome before the coming of their strength.

"Dear their gray eyes that were loved by women; many looked on them as they went. When they went freely searching through the woods, their steps were pleasant on the dark mountain.

"I do not sleep at any time, and the color is gone from my face; there is no sound can give me delight since the sons of Usnach do not come.

"I do not sleep through the night; my senses are scattered away from me; I do not care for food or drink. I have no welcome today for the pleasant drink of nobles, or ease, or comfort, or delight, or a great house, or the palace of a king.

"Do not break the strings of my heart as you took hold of my young youth, Conchubar; though my darling is dead, my love is strong to live. What is country to me, or land, or lordship? What are swift horses? What are jewels and gold? Och! it is I will be lying tonight on the strand like the beautiful sons of Usnach."

So Levarcham went back to Conchubar to tell

10 Conchubar.

him what way Deirdre was, and that she would not come with her to Emain Macha.

And when she was gone, Deirdre went out on the strand, and she found a carpenter making an oar for a boat, and making a mast for it, clean and straight, to put up a sail to the wind. And when she saw him making it, she said: "It is a sharp knife you have, to cut the oar so clean and so straight, and if you will give it to me," she said, "I will give you a ring of the best gold in Ireland for it, the ring that belonged to Naoise, and that was with him through the battle and through the fight; he thought much of it in his lifetime; it is pure gold, through and through." So the carpenter took the ring in his hand, and the knife in the other hand, and he looked at them together, and he gave her the knife for the ring, and for her asking and her tears. Then Deirdre went close to the waves, and she said: "Since the other is not with me now, I will spend no more of my lifetime without him." And with that she drove the black knife into her side, but she drew it out again and threw it in the sea to her right hand, the way no one would be blamed for her death.

Then Conchubar came down to the strand and five hundred men along with him, to bring Deirdre away to Emain Macha, but all he found before him was her white body on the ground, and it without life. And it is what he said: "A thousand deaths on the time I brought death on my sister's children; now I am myself without Deirdre, and they themselves are without life.

"They were my sister's children, the three brothers I vexed with blows, Naoise, and Ainnle, and Ardan; they have died along with Deirdre."

And they took her white, beautiful body, and laid it in a grave, and a flagstone was raised over her grave, and over the grave of the sons of Usnach, and their names were written in Ogham, and keening was made for their burial.

And as to Fergus, son of Rogh, he came on the day after the children of Usnach were killed, to Emain Macha. And when he found they had been killed and his pledge to them broken, he himself, and Cormac Conloingeas, Conchubar's own son, and Dubthach, the Beetle of Ulster, with their men, made an attack on Conchubar's house and men, and a great many were killed by them, and Emain Macha was burned and destroyed.

And after doing that, they went into Connaught, to Ailell and to Maeve at Cruachan, and they were made welcome there, and they took service with them and fought with them against Ulster because of the treachery that was done by Conchubar. And that is the way Fergus and the others came to be on the side of the men of Connaught in the war for the Brown Bull of Cuailgne.

And Cathbad laid a curse on Emain Macha, on account of that great wrong. And it is what he said, that none of the race of Conchubar should have the kingdom, to the end of life and time.

And that came true, for the most of Conchubar's sons died in his own lifetime, and when he was near his death, he bade the men of Ulster bring back Cormac Conloingeas out of Cruachan, and give him the kingdom.

So they sent messengers to Cormac, and he set out and his three troops of men with him, and he left his blessing with Ailell and with Maeve, and he promised them a good return for all the kind treatment they had given him. And they crossed the river at Athluain, and there they saw a red woman at the edge of the ford, and she washing her chariot and her harness. And after that they met a young girl coming toward them, and a light-green cloak about her, and a brooch of precious stones at her breast. And Cormac asked her was she coming with them, and she said she was not, and it would be better for himself to turn back, for the ruin of his life was come.

And he stopped for the night at the House of the Two Smiths on the hill of Bruighean Mor, the great dwelling-place.

But a troop of the men of Connaught came about the house in the night, for they were on the way home after destroying and robbing a district of Ulster, and they thought to make an end of Cormac before he would get to Emain.

And it chanced there was a great harper, Craiftine, living close by, and his wife, Sceanb, daughter of Scethern, a Druid of Connaught, loved Cormac Conloingeas, and three times she had gone to meet him at Athluain, and she planted three trees there —Grief, and Dark, and Dumbness.

And there was great hatred and jealousy of Cormac on Craiftine, so when he knew the men of Connaught were going to make an attack on him, he went outside the house with his harp, and played a soft, sleepy tune to him, the way he had not the strength to rouse himself up, and himself and the most of his people were killed. And Amergin, that had gone with the message to him, made his grave and his mound, and the place is called Cluain Duma, the Lawn of the Mound.

SEUMAS MACMANUS

The Amadan of the Dough

There was a king once on a time that had a son that was an Amadan [half-foolish fellow]. The Amadan's mother died, and the king married again.

The Amadan's step-mother was always afraid of him beating her children, he was growing so big and strong. So to keep him from growing and to weaken him, she had him fed on dough made of raw meal and water, and for that he was called "The Amadan of the Dough." But instead of get- 10 ting weaker, it was getting stronger the Amadan was on this fare, and he was able to thrash all of his step-brothers together.

At length his step-mother told his father that he would have to drive the Amadan away. The father consented to put him away; but the Amadan refused to go till his father would give him a sword so sharp that it would cut a pack of wool falling on it.

After a great deal of time and trouble the father 20 got such a sword and gave it to the Amadan; and when the Amadan had tried it and found it what he wanted, he bade them all good-by and set off.

For seven days and seven nights he traveled away before him without meeting anything wonderful, but on the seventh night he came up to a great castle. He went in and found no one there, but he found a great dinner spread on the table in the hall. So to be making the most of his time, down the Amadan sat at the table and whacked 30 away.

When he had finished with his dinner, up to the castle came three young princes, stout, strong, able fellows, but very, very tired, and bleeding from wounds all over them.

They struck the castle with a flint, and all at once the whole castle shone as if it were on fire.

The Amadan sprang at the three of them to kill them. He said, "What do you mean by putting the castle on fire?"

"O Amadan," they said, "don't interfere with us, for we are nearly killed as it is. The castle isn't on fire. Every day we have to go out to fight three giants—Slat Mor, Slat Marr, and Slat Beag. We fight them all day long, and just as night is falling we have them killed. But however it comes, in the night they always come to life again, and if they didn't see this castle lit up, they'd come in on top of us and murder us while we slept. So every night, when we come back from the fight, we light up the castle. Then we can sleep in peace until 10 morning, and in the morning go off and fight the giants again."

When the Amadan heard this, he wondered; and he said he would very much like to help them kill the giants. They said they would be very glad to have such a fine fellow's help; and so it was agreed that the Amadan should go with them to the fight next day.

Then the three princes washed themselves and took their supper, and they and the Amadan went 20 to bed.

In the morning all four of them set off, and traveled to the Glen of the Echoes, where they met the three giants.

"Now," says the Amadan, "if you three will engage the two smaller giants, Slat Marr and Slat Beag, I'll engage Slat Mor myself and kill him."

They agreed to this.

Now the smallest of the giants was far bigger and more terrible than anything ever the Amadan 30 had seen or heard of in his life before, so you can fancy what Slat Mor must have been like.

But the Amadan was little concerned at this. He went to meet Slat Mor, and the two of them fell to the fight, and a great, great fight they had. They made the hard ground into soft,[1] and the soft into spring wells; they made the rock into pebbles, and the pebbles into gravel, and the gravel fell over the country like hailstones. All the birds of the air from the lower end of the world to the upper end 40 of the world, and all the wild beasts and tame from the four ends of the earth, came flocking to see the fight; and in the end the Amadan ran Slat Mor

[1] This passage, which is several times repeated word for word, is an example of what the Irish storytellers call a "run." When they reach these passages they change the tone of their voice and speak very rapidly.

through with his sword and laid him down dead.

Then he turned to help the three princes, and very soon he laid the other two giants down dead for them also.

Then the three princes said they would all go home. The Amadan told them to go, but warned them not to light up the castle this night, and said he would sit by the giants' corpses and watch if they came to life again.

The three princes begged of him not to do this, for the three giants would come to life, and then he, having no help, would be killed.

The Amadan was angry with them, and ordered them off instantly. Then he sat down by the giants' corpses to watch. But he was so tired from his great day's fighting that by and by he fell asleep.

After twelve o'clock at night, when the Amadan was sleeping soundly, up comes a cailliach [old hag] and four badachs [unwieldy big fellows], and the cailliach carried with her a feather and a bottle of iocshlainte [ointment of health], with which she began to rub the giants' wounds.

Two of the giants were already alive when the Amadan awoke, and the third was just opening his eyes. Up sprang the Amadan, and at him leaped them all—Slat Mor, Slat Marr, Slat Beag, the cailliach, and the four badachs.

If the Amadan had had a hard fight during the day, this one was surely ten times harder. But a brave and a bold fellow he was, and not to be daunted by numbers or showers of blows. They fought for long and long. They made the hard ground into soft, and the soft into spring wells; they made the rocks into pebbles, and the pebbles into gravel, and the gravel fell over the country like hailstones. All the birds of the air from the lower end of the world to the upper end of the world, and all the wild beasts and tame from the four ends of the earth, came flocking to see the fight; and one after the other of them the Amadan ran his sword through, until he had every one of them stretched on the ground, dying or dead.

And when the old cailliach was dying, she called the Amadan to her and put him under geasa [an obligation that he could not shirk] to lose the power of his feet, of his strength, of his sight, and of his memory if he did not go to meet and fight the Black Bull of the Brown Wood.

When the old hag died outright, the Amadan rubbed some of the iocshlainte to his wounds with the feather, and at once he was as hale and as fresh as when the fight began. Then he took the feather and the bottle of iocshlainte, buckled on his sword, and started away before him to fulfill his geasa.

He traveled for the length of all that lee-long day, and when night was falling, he came to a little hut on the edge of a wood; and the hut had no shelter inside or out but one feather over it, and there was a rough, red woman standing in the door.

"You're welcome," says she, "Amadan of the Dough, the King of Ireland's son. What have you been doing or where are you going?"

"Last night," says the Amadan, "I fought a great fight, and killed Slat Mor, Slat Marr, Slat Beag, the Cailliach of the Rocks, and four badachs. Now I'm under geasa to meet and to fight the Black Bull of the Brown Wood. Can you tell me where to find him?"

"I can that," says she, "but it's now night. Come in and eat and sleep."

So she spread for the Amadan a fine supper, and made a soft bed, and he ate heartily and slept heartily that night.

In the morning she called him early, and she directed him on his way to meet the Black Bull of the Brown Wood. "But my poor Amadan," she said, "no one has ever yet met that bull and come back alive."

She told him that when he reached the place of meeting, the bull would come tearing down the hill like a hurricane. "Here's a cloak," says she, "to throw upon the rock that is standing there. You hide yourself behind the rock, and when the bull comes tearing down, he will dash at the cloak, and blind himself with the crash against the rock. Then you jump on the bull's back and fight for life. If, after the fight, you are living, come back and see me; and if you are dead, I'll go and see you."

The Amadan took the cloak, thanked her, and set off, and traveled on and on until he came to the place of meeting.

When the Amadan came there, he saw the Bull of the Brown Wood come tearing down the hill like a hurricane, and he threw the cloak on the rock and hid behind it, and with the fury of his dash against the cloak the bull blinded himself, and the roar of his fury split the rock.

The Amadan lost no time jumping on his back, and with his sword began hacking and slashing him; but he was no easy bull to conquer, and a great fight the Amadan had. They made the hard ground into soft, and the soft into spring wells; they made the rocks into pebbles, and the pebbles into gravel, and the gravel fell over the country like hailstones. All the birds of the air from the lower end of the world to the upper end of the world, and all the wild beasts and tame from the four ends of the earth, came flocking to see the fight; at length, after a long time, the Amadan ran his sword right through the bull's heart, and the bull fell down dead. But before he died he put the Amadan under geasa to meet and to fight the White Wether of the Hill of the Waterfalls.

Then the Amadan rubbed his own wounds with the iocshlainte, and he was as fresh and hale as when he went into the fight. Then he set out and traveled back again to the little hut that had no shelter without or within, only one feather over it, and the rough, red woman was standing in the door, and she welcomed the Amadan and asked him the news.

He told her all about the fight, and that the Black Bull of the Wood had put him under geasa to meet and to fight the White Wether of the Hill of the Waterfalls.

"I'm sorry for you, my poor Amadan," says she, "for no one ever before met that White Wether and came back alive. But come in and eat and rest anyhow, for you must be both hungry and sleepy."

So she spread him a hearty meal and made him a soft bed, and the Amadan ate and slept heartily; and in the morning she directed him to where he would meet the White Wether of the Hill of the Waterfalls. And she told him that no steel was tougher than the hide of the White Wether, that a sword was never yet made that could go through it, and that there was only one place—a little white spot just over the wether's heart—where he could be killed or sword could cut through. And she told the Amadan that his only chance was to hit this spot.

The Amadan thanked her, and set out. He traveled away and away before him until he came to the Hill of the Waterfalls, and as soon as he reached it he saw the White Wether coming tearing toward him in a furious rage, and the earth he was throwing up with his horns was shutting out the sun.

And when the wether came up and asked the Amadan what great feats he had done that made him impudent enough to dare to come there, the Amadan said: "With this sword I have killed Slat Mor, Slat Marr, Slat Beag, the Cailliach of the Rocks and her four badachs, and likewise the Black Bull of the Brown Wood."

"Then," said the White Wether, "you'll never kill any other." And at the Amadan he sprang.

The Amadan struck at him with his sword, and the sword glanced off as if it might off steel. Both of them fell to the fight with all their hearts, and such a fight never was before or since. They made the hard ground into soft, and the soft into spring wells; they made the rocks into pebbles, and the pebbles into gravel, and the gravel fell over the country like hailstones. All the birds of the air from the lower end of the world to the upper end of the world, and all the wild beasts and tame from the four ends of the earth, came flocking to see the fight. But at length and at last, after a long and terrible fight, the Amadan seeing the little spot above the heart that the red woman had told him of, struck for it and hit it, and drove his sword through the White Wether's heart, and he fell down. And when he was dying, he called the Amadan and put him under a geasa to meet and fight the Beggarman of the King of Sweden.

The Amadan took out his bottle of iocshlainte and rubbed himself with the iocshlainte, and he was as fresh and hale as when he began the fight. Then he set out again, and when night was falling, he reached the hut that had no shelter within or without, only one feather over it, and the rough, red woman was standing in the door.

Right glad she was to see the Amadan coming back alive, and she welcomed him heartily and asked him the news.

He told her of the wonderful fight he had had, and that he was now under geasa to meet and fight the Beggarman of the King of Sweden.

She made him come in and eat and sleep, for he was tired and hungry. And heartily the Amadan ate and heartily he slept; and in the morning she called him early, and directed him on his way to meet the Beggarman of the King of Sweden.

She told him that when he reached a certain hill, the beggarman would come down from the sky in a cloud; and that he would see the whole world between the beggarman's legs and nothing above his head. "If ever he finds himself beaten," she said, "he goes up into the sky in a mist, and stays there to refresh himself. You may let him go up once; but if you let him go up the second time, he will surely kill you when he comes down. Remember that. If you are alive when the fight is over, come to see me. If you are dead, I will go to see you."

The Amadan thanked her, parted with her, and traveled away and away before him until he reached the hill which she had told him of. And when he came there, he saw a great cloud that shot out of the sky, descending on the hill, and when it came down on the hill and melted away, there it left the Beggarman of the King of Sweden standing, and between his legs the Amadan saw the whole world and nothing over his head.

And with a roar and a run the beggarman made for the Amadan, and the roar of him rattled the stars in the sky. He asked the Amadan who he was, and what he had done to have the impudence to come there and meet him.

The Amadan said: "They call me the Amadan of the Dough, and I have killed Slat Mor, Slat Marr, Slat Beag, the Cailliach of the Rocks and her four badachs, the Black Bull of the Brown Wood, and the White Wether of the Hill of the Waterfalls, and before night I'll have killed the Beggarman of the King of Sweden."

"That you never will, you miserable object," says the beggarman. "You're going to die now, and I'll give you your choice to die either by a hard squeeze of wrestling or a stroke of the sword."

"Well," says the Amadan, "if I have to die, I'd sooner die by a stroke of the sword."

"All right," says the beggarman, and drew his sword.

But the Amadan drew his sword at the same time, and both went to it. And if his fights before had been hard, this one was harder and greater and more terrible than the others put together. They made the hard ground into soft, and the soft into spring wells; they made the rocks into pebbles, and the pebbles into gravel, and the gravel fell over the country like hailstones. All the birds of the air from the lower end of the world to the upper end of the world, and all the wild beasts and tame from the four ends of the earth, came flocking to see the fight. And at length the fight was putting so hard upon the beggarman, and he was getting so weak, that he whistled, and the mist came around him, and he went up into the sky before the Amadan knew. He remained there until he refreshed himself, and then came down again, and at it again he went for the Amadan, and fought harder and harder than before, and again it was putting too hard on him, and he whistled as before for the mist to come down and take him up.

But the Amadan remembered what the red woman had warned him; he gave one leap into the air, and coming down, drove the sword through the beggarman's heart, and the beggarman fell dead. But before he died he put geasa on the Amadan to meet and fight the Silver Cat of the Seven Glens.

The Amadan rubbed his wounds with the iocshlainte, and he was as fresh and hale as when he began the fight; and then he set out, and when night was falling, he reached the hut that had no shelter within or without, only one feather over it, and the rough, red woman was standing in the door.

Right glad she was to see the Amadan coming back alive, and she welcomed him right heartily, and asked him the news.

He told her that he had killed the beggarman, and said he was now under geasa to meet and fight the Silver Cat of the Seven Glens.

"Well," she said, "I'm sorry for you, for no one ever before went to meet the Silver Cat and came back alive. But," she says, "you're both tired and hungry; come in and rest and sleep."

So in the Amadan went, and had a hearty supper and a soft bed; and in the morning she called him up early, and she gave him directions where to meet the cat and how to find it, and she told him there was only one vital spot on that cat, and it was a black speck on the bottom of the cat's stomach, and unless he could happen to run his sword right through this, the cat would surely kill him. She said:

"My poor Amadan, I'm very much afraid you'll not come back alive. I cannot go to help you myself or I would; but there is a well in my garden, and by watching that well I will know how the fight goes with you. While there is honey on top of the well, I will know you are getting the better of the cat; but if the blood comes on top, then the cat is getting the better of you; and if the blood stays there, I will know, my poor Amadan, that you are dead."

The Amadan bade her good-by, and set out to travel to where the Seven Glens met at the Sea. Here there was a precipice, and under the precipice a cave. In this cave the Silver Cat lived, and once a day she came out to sun herself on the rocks.

The Amadan let himself down over the precipice by a rope, and he waited until the cat came out to sun herself.

When the cat came out at twelve o'clock and saw the Amadan, she let a roar out of her that drove back the waters of the sea and piled them up a quarter of a mile high, and she asked him who he was and how he had the impudence to come there to meet her.

The Amadan said: "They call me the Amadan of the Dough, and I have killed Slat Mor, Slat Marr, Slat Beag, the Cailliach of the Rocks and her four badachs, the Black Bull of the Brown Woods, the White Wether of the Hill of the Waterfalls, and the Beggarman of the King of Sweden, and before night I will have killed the Silver Cat of the Seven Glens."

"That you never will," says she, "for a dead man you will be yourself." And at him she sprang.

But the Amadan raised his sword and struck at her, and both of them fell to the fight, and a great, great fight they had. They made the hard ground into soft, and the soft into spring wells; they made the rocks into pebbles, and the pebbles into gravel, and the gravel fell over the country like hailstones. All the birds of the air from the lower end of the world to the upper end of the world, and all the wild beasts and tame from the four ends of the earth, came flocking to see the fight; and if the fights that the Amadan had had on the other days were great and terrible, this one was far greater and far more terrible than all the others put to-gether, and the poor Amadan sorely feared that before night fell he would be a dead man.

The red woman was watching at the well in her garden, and she sorely distressed, for though at one time the honey was uppermost, at another time it was all blood, and again the blood and the honey mixed; so she felt bad for the poor Amadan.

At length the blood and the honey got mixed again, and it remained that way until night; so she cried, for she believed the Amadan himself was dead as well as the Silver Cat.

And so he was. For when the fight had gone on for long and long, the cat, with a great long nail which she had in the end of her tail, tore him open from mouth to his toes; and as she tore the Amadan open and he was about to fall, she opened her mouth so wide that the Amadan saw down to the very bottom of her stomach, and there he saw the black speck that the red woman had told him of. And just before he dropped he drove his sword through this spot, and the Silver Cat, too, fell over dead.

It was not long now till the red woman arrived at the place and found both the Amadan and the cat lying side by side dead. At this the poor woman was frantic with sorrow, but suddenly she saw by the Amadan's side the bottle of iocshlainte and the feather. She took them up and rubbed the Amadan with the iocshlainte, and he jumped to his feet alive and well, and fresh as when he began the fight.

He smothered her with kisses and drowned her with tears. He took the red woman with him, and set out on his journey back, and traveled and traveled on and on till he came to the Castle of Fire.

Here he met the three young princes, who were now living happily with no giants to molest them. They had one sister, the most beautiful young maiden that the Amadan had ever beheld. They gave her to the Amadan in marriage, and gave her half of all they owned for fortune.

The marriage lasted nine days and nine nights. There were nine hundred fiddlers, nine hundred fluters, and nine hundred pipers, and the last day and night of the wedding were better than the first.

FRENCH AND SPANISH ROMANCE

The country in which romance reached full bloom and acquired its characteristic form and style was France. There chivalry first became fashionable, and developed a system of customs, formalities, and obligations. Chivalry gave the nobility self-confidence and an exalted sense of its position; and the vigorous training of aspirants to knighthood and the tournaments in which the knights engaged ensured a "physically fit" ruling class. But chivalry was not regarded as simply utilitarian. It was a code of social behavior that cemented feudal relationships by investing a vassal's loyalty to his lord with dignity and idealism; that raised woman's status in medieval society and gave her an opportunity to exert a civilizing influence on manners; and that gave worldly love, refined of brutish sensuality, a place in the bleak fortresses of the feudal nobility.

Marriage in feudal society was a business affair concerned with joining land to land and matters of inheritance. Romantic feeling found its outlet, not in these marriages of convenience but in the fashionable system of courtly love, under which women could enjoy the attentions of men other than their husbands, and men could form attachments for women other than their wives. These were often innocent, and may be described as a highly formal kind of flirtation, though the formalities could also serve as a cover for genuine passion or actual adultery. But even when entirely "platonic," the idealization of women introduced an element of romantic gratification into the relations of the sexes.

The cultural and literary effect of courtly love can hardly be overestimated. It left an indelible mark on nearly a thousand years of Western civilization. The literature that grew up around romantic love in the age of chivalry virtually began modern literature. Its spirit is found in the many modern poems, plays, stories, and novels that treat the pleasantries or the passions of love, whether the treatment be romantic or realistic, superficial or psychological.

This literature arose in southern France or the Provence. It is called "romance" because it was first composed in the romance languages of France and Italy. The fact that these became a literary medium proved to be of the greatest importance. If we owed nothing more to medieval romance than that it started literature in the new languages of Europe, our debt would be enormous.

Classical Latin is a precise tongue, hemmed in with many grammatical rules and syntactical constructions. But when the Roman legions invaded Gaul and Spain, settled there and intermarried with the natives, the "low Latin" they brought with them was not the Latin of Cicero but Latin dialect. In time accents were shifted and case endings were dropped; the word order, so carefully balanced and so formal, was changed and simplified; words assumed new meanings, and new words were added from Celtic, Germanic, and even Arabic. As a result, the romance languages were born. At first they were little more than a profusion of local dialects; then in each country one dialect became dominant as some province or city became socially and politically supreme. Modern Italian is the dialect of Florence or its province Tuscany, the dialect spoken by Dante; modern French grew out of the dialect of the northern French and their capital, Paris; modern Spanish is derived from the dialect of the kingdom of

Castile. (Modern English—not a romance language—comes from the dialect of London.)

The first of the romance tongues to become a literary vehicle was the dialect of Provence. During medieval time two main languages could be distinguished, those of southern and northern France, corresponding to two political and cultural divisions. The former was called *langue d'oc*, because it used the word *oc* for "yes," from the Latin word *hoc*. The latter was called *langue d'œil*, because the word for "yes" was *œil*, which ultimately became the modern French *oui*. Provençal was spoken in France south of the Loire River, and extended into northern Italy and northeastern Spain.

A new civilization, after the fall of Rome, first appeared in the sunny regions of the south—in the Spanish, French, and Italian Riviera—and its center was Provence, so called because it had been the first province conquered by Rome outside Italy. Here, during the Germanic invasions, Roman civilization suffered less destruction than anywhere else. The land was protected by mountains, but was not isolated because it bordered on the Mediterranean, and Marseilles became a thriving seaport. The countryside was fertile and the towns plied many crafts, making leather, cloth, soap and jewelry. Wealth and luxury increased, and with them leisure; and consequently culture could thrive as nowhere else. Contact with Arabian civilization augmented it, and the customary tolerance of a folk engaged in commerce and travel enabled the people of the Provence to assimilate other cultures. The Arabs, then at the peak of their civilization, contributed valuable knowledge, and the Jews actually maintained a university in Montpellier, where they taught philosophy and medicine. The aristocracy was less warlike and caste-conscious than in the North, and even admitted wealthy merchants into its ranks; and both the nobles and the magnates were zealous patrons of art.

Courtly love was the creation of the Provence. As the historian Osborne notes, "It was natural that the conception of love as an art to be practiced for art's sake, should grow up and flourish in this luxurious and leisured society." Courtly love was full of conceits and pleasurable extravagances, with a touch of oriental warmth and luxuriance such as characterized Arabian poetry. A knight, who was conceived to be a man of great spirit, was expected to respond fully to the tender passion; a knight without love was "a husk without grain," according to a poet from Auvergne. A virtual Code became fashionable, and decisions were given on questions of love by arbiters of elegance, mostly ladies of rank, who constituted so-called Courts of Love.

The poets of the Provence, who were called *troubadours*[1] were courtly singers. Many of them were the friends of princes and had social rank; some were princes and kings, like William, the Duke of Anjou, and Richard-the-Lion-Hearted. Some of them had a smattering of Latin literature, particularly of Ovid's verses, but most of them probably could not read or write. They transmitted their songs orally to professional minstrels, known as *jongleurs*, who spread them from place to place. The troubadours often composed both the words and the music, singing their compositions themselves, or hiring professional singers. They were the first to bring poetic composition to the level of a craft, since they went far beyond the simple, though lovely, lyrics of the common folk, creating elaborate stanzas and making rhyme a characteristic of European lyric verse. Their poems have been called "a fascinating jingle of cunningly disposed rhymes, fleet as the feet of dancing youths, tinkling as silver bells." No wonder that they received many honors, and that their number multiplied so rapidly that more than five hundred poets' names have come down to us. They were the singers of a "gay science" (*gaya scienza*) for a society that was in its day the least medieval and closest in spirit to the worldly renaissance of the fourteenth and fifteenth centuries.

In time, the Provence became decadent, and began to be troubled by civil and religious dissension. Many people in southern France belonged to the Albigensian sect[2] which held Manichean beliefs. The Church of Rome called a crusade against them, and northern knights took the opportunity to plunder the rich province. The Provence never recovered.

Provençal poetry, however, could not be extinguished, for by now it was the common possession of France, Italy, Germany, and England. Its forms became standard modes of poetic expression. Among these were the *chanzo* or *canso* (*chanson*, in northern France), whose theme was love; the *tenso*, a witty debate in dialogue; the *alba* (in northern France *aubade*), a song of dawn in which secret lovers are compelled to separate by the ap-

---

[1] The word means "finders" (*cf.* the French word *trouver*) of treasure.
[2] Named after the district of Albi where this heresy was most strongly held.

proach of day;[3] the *sirvente*, a satire or a comment on political or moral matters; and the *planh*, a lament for the poet's patron or his lady-love. Greater love poets than the rather superficial troubadours were to come—Dante, Petrarch, Shakespeare, and Heine. Indeed, there was no limit to the variations that were to be played on the Provençal singers' themes, though theirs is the credit for having planted the seed. And in northern France, their fellow-minstrels, the *trouvères*, began very soon to create romances that had greater scope and interest. The trouvères considered themselves more professional than the troubadours, and were less interested in song than in narration. They started the French toward mastery of the field of fiction.

One of the trouvères, Jean Bodel, divided his fellow-narrators' subject material into three parts —the matter (*matière*) of France, Bretaigne or Britain, and Rome. This does not mean that three main plots were repeated by the minstrels, but that their greatly varied stories fell into one of three cycles or types.

The "matter of Rome" consisted of tales about Alexander the Great and Virgil's and Homer's heroes, to whom were attributed the most fabulous characteristics and events. Everything was treated anachronistically, the poets attributing romantic and feudal details to classic material without the slightest realization that these were ridiculously inappropriate. Most of these romances were inferior to other narratives, but they had a great vogue. (The first book Caxton printed in English was a *History of Troy*.) They revived some interest in classical tradition, thus preparing the way somewhat for the Renaissance, and they gave to Boccaccio and Chaucer the unstable heroine Cressida. More interesting and productive of better literary work were the "matter of France," which revolved around Charlemagne, and the "matter of Britain," whose central figure was Arthur.

Charlemagne captured the imagination because he was the hero-king of France. By the eleventh century he had become a supernatural figure. Fabulous deeds were attributed to him, and the story-tellers surrounded him with a group of followers, known as paladins, whose accomplishments in war and love were in all respects marvelous. The tales spun around Charlemagne and his circle, known as *chansons de geste*,[4] multiplied until there were over seventy of them. They reflect not Charlemagne's times but the age of the poets, being steeped in feudalism, and in crusading zeal against the Mohammedans (called the Saracens). However, they lack the complete trappings of romance. The love element in the most genuine *chansons de geste* is comparatively simple and unartificial, their spirit and matter are largely epic and patriotic.

These qualities are most pronounced in the best of the poems, the stirring *Song of Roland*, based on a historical event but romantically elaborated. In an attack on Charlemagne's rearguard by the Basques in a Pyrenean mountain pass, the entire force was wiped out, and among the dead was a certain *Hruodlandus*. Out of these simple facts later poets created the hero Roland, who became the ideal knight by virtue of his courage and loyalty to king and country. Roland is a far more patriotic, vigorous, and far less ornate figure than the heroes of the true romances; he belongs more to epic literature. It is only later that the "matter of France" became true romance.

In style and verse form, too, the *Song of Roland* has a hardy quality that distinguishes it from the later romances, which were written in rhymed lines or in ornate prose. It consists of stanzas (called *laisses*) composed in lines of ten syllables, and the same vowel sound appears in the final stressed syllable of each line in the stanza, a device known as *assonance*. Assonance, which was soon supplanted by rhyme, has been recently brought back into favor by ultra-modern English poets as a means of avoiding jingling effects. But in all except the most inspired kind of writing, assonance still seems crude, and the translation used in our selection from the poem employs rhyme.

If *The Song of Roland* is an epic colored by romance, the "matter of Britain" is romance in full bloom. Originally national in its roots, in so far as the historical Arthur was a Celtic chieftain who fought the Anglo-Saxon invaders of England, the Arthurian theme was quickly transformed into legend by the Celtic imagination.

The Arthurian poets aimed at artistic perfection, grace, and delicacy, and their poems were intended for the most cultivated medieval audiences. The twelfth-century French masters of Arthurian romance, who were followed by writers in other

---

[3] The *alba* usually has a refrain, as will be seen in the selection given on page 552. Scene 5, Act III of Shakespeare's *Romeo and Juliet* opens with a lovely *alba*, in which the lovers are warned by the lark's song.

[4] Songs of deeds; *geste* comes from *gesta*, the Latin word for deeds.

countries, were Marie de France and Chrétien de Troyes.

Marie de France, a well-born lady, was the ablest author of short narrative poems know as *lais* or lays. Though she lived and wrote in England, she was French by birth and composed in French. Marie de France wrote on a variety of subjects, but the perfection she gave to her treatment of Arthurian tales made her important in the development of "the matter of Britain."

Chrétien (or Chrestien) de Troyes treated the Celtic tales at more length, and gave them their greatest popularity at the medieval courts. It is with good reason that his work served as a foundation for later prose romances, which were finally incorporated in Malory's compilation of Arthurian matter, *Le Morte d'Arthur* (see page 1052). Chrétien lived at the court of Champagne in the second half of the twelfth century. Basing his work on older French versions, he took from the Celtic matter only that which could be interpreted in terms of medieval feudalism. However, the English reader does not have to turn to him when he has in his own language the delightful anonymous metrical romance *Sir Gawain and the Green Knight* (see page 1021) and Malory's fascinating *Le Morte d'Arthur*. The Arthurian "matter" indeed constitutes a vast literature, and it has been increased in modern times by the composer Wagner and by such poets as Tennyson (*Idylls of the King*), Swinburne, and E. A. Robinson.

Medieval romance also found expression in other tales. Some of them are crude, but one of them, the twelfth-century *Aucassin and Nicolete*, is a masterpiece of fragile charm. Its story belongs to a special class of romances in which the Orient figures in some way. In them we generally find a Christian knight in love with a Saracen maiden, although in *Aucassin and Nicolete* the heroine turns out to be a Christian girl. This work is, moreover, interesting as an example of a unique literary form, the *cante-fable* or "song-story," in which the tale is told in prose but is embroidered with passages of verse sung by the minstrel.

Aucassin and Nicolete is a plainly naïve narrative. Its author even introduced folklore, in the episode of the king who took to his bed because he fancied himself with child—a custom familiar to students of primitive peoples. The story concerns moonstruck adolescents, and the young lovers are indeed the Romeo and Juliet of medieval romance. However, it is in this delicate and fanciful

tale that we are unexpectedly reminded that a critical spirit was beginning to intrude into the medieval world and its romantic outlook. Whether because the author stemmed from the common people or felt sympathy for them, he allowed them to have their say in the memorable conversation between the love-sick Aucassin, who pretends to be weeping because he has lost a white hound, and a hard-pressed, coarsely dressed peasant who is outraged at the triviality of the youth's complaint and proceeds to tell him of his own bitter plight.

The intellectual spirit was most evident in the brilliant Abelard (died 1142) who was both a bold philosopher and an ardent lover. Although a medieval thinker in the sense that he expended his mental endowment on religious dogma, he anticipated the intellectual awakening of Europe by several centuries. He contended that unquestioning faith is an impediment to the discovery of truth, that doubt was actually a means whereby the truth could be ascertained—a thought that seemed so radical that he was forbidden to teach it. He began early to challenge the teachings of his masters in Paris, and attracted hundreds of students when he became a lecturer. His method was to demonstrate the illogicality and inconsistencies of the authorities of his time, and his dialectic skill in these demonstrations was remarkable.

Abelard, however, is best remembered for the stormy passion to which he succumbed. In the opinion of the noted scholar H. O. Taylor, "There has never been a passion between a man and woman more famous than that which brought happiness and sorrow to the lives of Abelard and Heloise."[5] Centuries after their death, flowers and wreaths were still being laid on the tomb of the lovers in the Père-Lachaise cemetery in Paris. The great intellectual of his day, it is well to remember, was a native of Brittany, one of the fountainheads of medieval romance. When he was thirty-eight he met the beautiful and intelligent girl, who was then seventeen. Her uncle, Canon Fulbert, engaged Abelard as tutor, gave him a place in his home, and authorized him to punish his pupil whenever necessary. Before long the learned man, then occupying the highest academic position in Europe as professor in the Episcopal School or university in Paris, found himself madly in love with Heloise. Their love had none of the trappings of the courts of love, but it was more truly a distillation of the spirit of romance than any courtly affair.

"I saw," he wrote, "that she possessed every at-

[5] H. O. Taylor, *The Mediæval Mind*, Volume II, p. 29.

traction that lovers seek; nor did I regard my success as doubtful, when I considered my fame and my goodly person, and also her love of letters. Our hours of study were given to love. The books lay open, but our words were of love rather than philosophy; there were more kisses than aphorisms. To avert suspicion I struck her occasionally—very gentle blows of love."

Tragedy came in the wake of their passion. They were discovered, and they fled to Brittany where a child was born to them. Heloise denied having married Abelard because she feared that it would hinder his advancement in the clerical world. Her uncle became so furious at the shame to his honor that he hired ruffians to invade Abelard's apartment and emasculate him. Abelard entered a monastery, and Heloise became a nun. After many years she sent him a letter, to which he replied. Their meager correspondence in Latin is the tragic climax to the Middle Ages' most famous and most authentic romance; it also contains some of the greatest letters of all time.

In culture, Christian Spain was a part of France, and there were many correspondences between Spanish and French writing. There were troubadours in the northern part of the Spanish peninsula, among them being a king, Alfonso, known as the "Learned." Corresponding to the *Song of Roland*, the Spaniards had their long heroic *Poem of the Cid*, based on the life of a doughty eleventh-century warrior, Ruy Diaz de Bivar, whose title "Cid" is the Arabic word for "Lord." Banished in 1081 from Castile, he became an outlaw, found refuge among the Moors in Spain, captured Valencia in 1094, and won control over a small state. In time extravagant exploits were attributed to him in numerous ballads and tales. The *Poem of the Cid*, which was based on them, is a spirited work, but less polished and appealing than the work of the best French writers.

The Spanish poets, moreover, turned their talent to the composition of ballads. These are remarkably vivacious, and though some of them are doggerel the Spanish ballads evoke a vivid and strenuous world, a world in which Christians and Saracens lived in adjacent territories and engaged in rivalries and bitter struggles. Since, moreover, the Spaniards loved gallantry and sentiment, and the wealth and splendor of the Moorish cities evoked wonder, Spanish balladry was exuberantly romantic. The ballads included in this section are examples of a truly profuse balladry, popular among the common people as well as the aristocracy.

THE SONG OF ROLAND

[The most important Old French epic poem, *The Song of Roland,* is based on a song in celebration of an engagement between Charlemagne and the Basques in 778. By the eleventh century the story has assumed epic proportions. The hero, Roland, has come to be typical for his bravery, his friend Olivier for his wisdom, and Ganelon for his treachery. In the epic, Roland is attacked by the Saracen king on the advice of Ganelon. Roland refuses to summon aid until too late to save himself and his army. Then he blows his horn and Charlemagne comes to the rescue and punishes Ganelon and the Moors. The passage below is the conclusion of Part II of the poem.]

When Roland saw that life had fled,
And with face to earth his comrade dead,
He thus bewept him, soft and still:
"Ah, friend, thy prowess wrought thee ill!

So many days and years gone by   5
We lived together, thou and I:
And thou hast never done me wrong,
Nor I to thee, our lifetime long.
Since thou art dead, to live is pain."
He swooned on Veillantif again,   10
Yet may not unto earth be cast,
His golden stirrups held him fast.

When passed away had Roland's swoon,
With sense restored, he saw full soon
What ruin lay beneath his view.   15
His Franks have perished all save two—
The archbishop and Walter of Hum alone.
From the mountain-side hath Walter flown,
Where he met in battle the bands of Spain,
And the heathen won and his men were slain   20

The Song of Roland. Translated by John O'Hagan.

In his own despite to the vale he came;
Called unto Roland, his aid to claim.
"Ah, count! brave gentleman, gallant peer!
Where art thou? With thee I know not fear.
I am Walter, who vanquished Maelgut of yore,
Nephew to Drouin, the old and hoar.　　　26
For knightly deeds I was once thy friend.
I fought the Saracen to the end;
My lance is shivered, my shield is cleft,
Of my broken mail are but fragments left.　　30
I bear in my body eight thrusts of spear;
I die, but I sold my life right dear."
Count Roland heard as he spake the word,
Pricked his steed, and anear him spurred.

"Walter," said Roland, "thou hadst affray　　35
With the Saracen foe on the heights today.
Thou wert wont a valorous knight to be:
A thousand horsemen gave I thee;
Render them back, for my need is sore."
"Alas, thou seest them never more!　　　40
Stretched they lie on the dolorous ground,
Where myriad Saracen swarms we found,—
Armenians, Turks, and the giant brood
Of Balisa, famous for hardihood,
Bestriding their Arab Coursers fleet,　　45
Such host in battle 'twas ours to meet;
Nor vaunting thence shall the heathen go,—
Full sixty thousand on earth lie low.
With our brands of steel we avenged us well,
But every Frank by the foeman fell.　　　50
My hauberk plates are riven wide,
And I bear such wounds in flank and side,
That from every part the bright blood flows,
And feebler ever my body grows.
I am dying fast, I am well aware:　　　55
Thy liegeman I, and claim thy care.
If I fled perforce, thou wilt forgive,
And yield me succor while thou dost live."
Roland sweated with wrath and pain,
Tore the skirts of his vest in twain,　　　60
Bound Walter's every bleeding vein.

In Roland's sorrow his wrath arose,
Hotly he struck at the heathen foes,
Nor left he one of a score alive;
Walter slew six, the archbishop five.　　65
The heathens cry, "What a felon three!
Look to it, lords, that they shall not flee.
Dastard is he who confronts them not;
Craven, who lets them depart this spot."
Their cries and shoutings begin once more,　70
And from every side on the Franks they pour.

Count Roland in sooth is a noble peer;
Count Walter, a valorous cavalier;
The archbishop, in battle proved and tried,
Each struck as if knight there were none beside.
From their steeds a thousand Saracens leap,　76
Yet forty thousand their saddles keep;
I trow they dare not approach them near,
But they hurl against them lance and spear,
Pike and javelin, shaft and dart.　　　80
Walter is slain as the missiles part;
The archbishop's shield in pieces shred,
Riven his helm, and pierced his head;
His corselet of steel they rent and tore;
Wounded his body with lances four;　　85
His steed beneath him dropped withal:
What woe to see the archbishop fall!

When Turpin felt him flung to ground,
And four lance wounds within him found,
He swiftly rose, the dauntless man,　　90
To Roland looked, and nigh him ran.
Spake but, "I am not overthrown—
Brave warrior yields with life alone."
He drew Almace's burnished steel,
A thousand ruthless blows to deal.　　95
In after time, the Emperor said
He found four hundred round him spread,—
Some wounded, others cleft in twain;
Some lying headless on the plain.
So Giles the saint, who saw it, tells,　　100
For whom High God wrought miracles.
In Laon cell the scroll he wrote;
He little weets who knows it not.

Count Roland combateth nobly yet,
His body burning and bathed in sweat;　105
In his brow a mighty pain, since first,
When his horn he sounded, his temple burst;
But he yearns of Karl's approach to know,
And lifts his horn once more—but oh!
How faint and feeble a note to blow!　110
The Emperor listened, and stood full still.
"My lords," he said, "we are faring ill.
This day is Roland my nephew's last;
Like dying man he winds that blast.
On! Who would aid, for life must press.　115
Sound every trump our ranks possess."
Peal sixty thousand clarions high,
The hills re-echo, the vales reply.
It is now no jest for the heathen band.
"Karl!" they cry, "it is Karl at hand!"　120

They said, " 'Tis the Emperor's advance,
We hear the trumpets resound of France.

If he assail us, hope in vain;
If Roland live, 'tis war again,
And we lose for aye the land of Spain." 125
Four hundred in arms together drew,
The bravest of the heathen crew;
With serried power they on him press,
And dire in sooth is the count's distress.

When Roland saw his coming foes, 130
All proud and stern his spirit rose;
Alive he shall never be brought to yield:
Veillantif spurred he across the field,
With golden spurs he pricked him well,
To break the ranks of the infidel; 135
Archbishop Turpin by his side.
"Let us flee, and save us," the heathen cried;
"These are the trumpets of France we hear—
It is Karl, the mighty Emperor, near."

Count Roland never hath loved the base, 140
Nor the proud of heart, nor the dastard race,—
Nor knight, but if he were vassal good,—
And he spake to Turpin, as there he stood;
"On foot are you, on horseback I;
For your love I halt, and stand you by. 145
Together for good and ill we hold;
I will not leave you for man of mold.
We will pay the heathen their onset back,
Nor shall Durindana of blows be slack."
"Base," said Turpin, "who spares to smite: 150
When the Emperor comes, he will all requite."

The heathens said, "We were born to shame.
This day for our disaster came:
Our lords and leaders in battle lost,
And Karl at hand with his marshaled host; 155
We hear the trumpets of France ring out,
And the cry 'Montjoie!' their rallying shout.
Roland's pride is of such a height,
Not to be vanquished by mortal wight;
Hurl we our missiles, and hold aloof." 160
And the word they spake, they put in proof,—
They flung, with all their strength and craft,
Javelin, barb, and plumed shaft.
Roland's buckler was torn and frayed,
His cuirass broken and disarrayed, 165
Yet entrance none to his flesh they made.
From thirty wounds Veillantif bled,
Beneath his rider they cast him, dead;
Then from the field have the heathen flown:
Roland remaineth, on foot, alone. 170

The heathens fly in rage and dread;
To the land of Spain have their footsteps sped;

Nor can Count Roland make pursuit—
Slain is his steed, and he rests afoot;
To succor Turpin he turned in haste, 175
The golden helm from his head unlaced,
Ungirt the corselet from his breast,
In stripes divided his silken vest;
The archbishop's wounds hath he staunched and bound,
His arms around him softly wound; 180
On the green sward gently his body laid,
And, with tender greeting, thus him prayed:
"For a little space, let me take farewell;
Our dear companions, who round us fell,
I go to seek; if I haply find, 185
I will place them at thy feet reclined."
"Go," said Turpin; "the field is thine—
To God the glory, 'tis thine and mine."

Alone seeks Roland the field of fight,
He searcheth vale, he searcheth height. 190
Ivon and Ivor he found, laid low,
And the Gascon Engelier of Bordeaux,
Gerein and his fellow in arms, Gerier;
Otho he found, and Berengier;
Samson the duke, and Anseis bold, 195
Gerard of Roussillon, the old.
Their bodies, one after one, he bore,
And laid them Turpin's feet before.
The archbishop saw them stretched arow,
Nor can he hinder the tears that flow; 200
In benediction his hands he spread:
"Alas! for your doom, my lords," he said,
"That God in mercy your souls may give,
On the flowers of Paradise to live;
Mine own death comes, with anguish sore 205
That I see mine Emperor never more."

Once more to the field doth Roland wend,
Till he findeth Olivier, his friend;
The lifeless form to his heart he strained,
Bore him back with what strength remained, 210
On a buckler laid him, beside the rest,
The archbishop assoiled them all, and blessed.
Their dole and pity anew find vent,
And Roland maketh his fond lament:
"My Olivier, my chosen one, 215
Thou wert the noble Duke Renier's son,
Lord of the March unto River vale.
To shiver lance and shatter mail,
The brave in council to guide and cheer,
To smite the miscreant foe with fear,— 220
Was never on earth such cavalier."

Dead around him his peers to see,
And the man he loved so tenderly,
Fast the tears of Count Roland ran,
His visage discolored became, and wan,   225
He swooned for sorrow beyond control.
"Alas," said Turpin, "how great thy dole!"

To look on Roland swooning there,
Surpassed all sorrow he ever bare;
He stretched his hand, the horn he took,—   230
Through Roncesvalles there flowed a brook,—
A draught to Roland he thought to bring;
But his steps were feeble and tottering,
Spent his strength, from waste of blood,—
He struggled on for scarce a rood,   235
When sank his heart, and drooped his frame,
And his mortal anguish on him came.

Roland revived from his swoon again;
On his feet he rose, but in deadly pain;
He looked on high, and he looked below,   240
Till, a space his other companions fro,
He beheld the baron, stretched on sward,
The archbishop, vicar of God our Lord.
Mea Culpa was Turpin's cry,
While he raised his hands to heaven on high,   245
Imploring Paradise to gain.
So died the soldier of Carlemaine,—
With word or weapon, to preach or fight,
A champion ever of Christian right,
And a deadly foe of the infidel.   250
God's benediction within him dwell!

When Roland saw him stark on earth
(His very vitals were bursting forth,
And his brain was oozing from out his head),
He took the fair white hands outspread,   255
Crossed and clasped them upon his breast,
And thus plaint to the dead addressed,—
So did his country's law ordain:—
"Ah, gentleman of noble strain,
I trust thee unto God the True,   260
Whose service never man shall do
With more devoted heart and mind:
To guard the faith, to win mankind,
From the apostles' day till now,
Such prophet never rose as thou.   265
Nor pain or torment thy soul await,
But of Paradise the open gate."

Roland feeleth his death is near,
His brain is oozing by either ear.
For his peers he prayed—God keep them well;
Invoked the angel Gabriel   271

That none reproach him, his horn he clasped;
His other hand Durindana grasped;
Then, far as quarrel from crossbow sent,
Across the march of Spain he went,   275
Where, on a mound, two trees between,
Four flights of marble steps were seen;
Backward he fell, on the field to lie;
And he swooned anon, for the end was nigh.

High were the mountains and high the trees,   280
Bright shone the marble terraces;
On the green grass Roland hath swooned away.
A Saracen spied him where he lay:
Stretched with the rest he had feigned him dead,
His face and body with blood bespread.   285
To his feet he sprang, and in haste he hied,—
In pride and wrath he was overbold,—
And on Roland, body and arms, laid hold.
"The nephew of Karl is overthrown!
To Araby bear I this sword, mine own."   290
He stooped to grasp it, but as he drew,
Roland returned to his sense anew.

He saw the Saracen seize his sword;
His eyes he oped, and he spake one word—
"Thou art not one of our band, I trow,"   295
And he clutched the horn he would ne'er forego;
On the golden crest he smote him full,
Shattering steel and bone and skull,
Forth from his head his eyes he beat,
And cast him lifeless before his feet.   300
"Miscreant, makest thou then so free,
As, right or wrong, to lay hold on me?
Who hears it will deem thee a madman born;
Behold the mouth of mine ivory horn
Broken for thee, and the gems and gold   305
Around its rim to earth are rolled."

Roland feeleth his eyesight reft,
Yet he stands erect with what strength is left;
From his bloodless cheek is the hue dispelled,
But his Durindana all bare he held.   310
In front a dark brown rock arose—
He smote upon it ten grievous blows.
Grated the steel as it struck the flint,
Yet it brake not, nor bore its edge one dint.
"Mary, Mother, be thou mine aid!   315
Ah, Durindana, my ill-starred blade,
I may no longer thy guardian be!
What fields of battle I won with thee!
What realms and regions 'twas ours to gain,
Now the lordship of Carlemaine!   320
Never shalt thou possessor know
Who would turn from face of mortal foe;

A gallant vassal so long thee bore,
Such as France the free shall know no more."

He smote anew on the marble stair.   325
It grated, but breach nor notch was there.
When Roland found that it would not break,
Thus began he his plaint to make.
"Ah, Durindana, how fair and bright
Thou sparklest, flaming against the light!   330
When Karl in Maurienne valley lay,
God sent his angel from heaven to say—
'This sword shall a valorous captain's be,'
And he girt it, the gentle king, on me.
With it I vanquished Poitou and Maine,   335
Provence I conquered and Aquitaine;
I conquered Normandy the free,
Anjou, and the marches of Brittany;
Romagna I won, and Lombardy,
Bavaris, Flanders from side to side,   340
And Burgundy, and Poland wide;
Constantinople affiance vowed,
And the Saxon soil to his bidding bowed;
Scotia, and Wales, and Ireland's plain,
Of England made he his own domain.   345
What mighty regions I won of old,
For the hoary-headed Karl to hold!
But there presses on me a grievous pain,
Lest thou in heathen hands remain.
O God our Father, keep France from stain!"   350

His strokes once more on the brown rock fell,
And the steel was bent past words to tell;
Yet it brake not, nor was notched the grain,
Erect it leaped to the sky again.
When he failed at the last to break his blade,   355
His lamentation he inly made.
"Oh, fair and holy, my peerless sword,
What relics lie in thy pommel stored!
Tooth of Saint Peter, Saint Basil's blood,
Hair of Saint Denis beside them strewed,   360
Fragment of holy Mary's vest.
'Twere shame that thou with the heathen rest;
Thee should the hand of a Christian serve
One who would never in battle swerve.
What regions won I with thee of yore,   365
The empire now of Karl the hoar!
Rich and mighty is he therefore."

That death was on him he knew full well;
Down from his head to his heart it fell.
On the grass beneath a pine-tree's shade,   370
With face to earth, his form he laid,
Beneath him placed he his horn and sword,
And turned his face to the heathen horde.
Thus hath he done the sooth to show,
That Karl and his warriors all may know,   375
That the gentle count a conqueror died.
Mea Culpa full oft he cried;
And, for all his sins, unto God above,
In sign of penance, he raised his glove.

Roland feeleth his hour at hand;   380
On a knoll he lies towards the Spanish land.
With one hand beats he upon his breast:
"In thy sight, O God, be my sins confessed.
From my hour of birth, both the great and small,
Down to this day, I repent of all."   385
As his glove he raised to God on high,
Angels of heaven descend him nigh.

Beneath a pine was his resting-place,
To the land of Spain hath he turned his face,
On his memory rose full many a thought—   390
Of the lands he won and the fields he fought;
Of his gentle France, of his kin and line;
Of his nursing father, King Karl benign;—
He may not the tear and sob control,
Nor yet forgets he his parting soul.   395
To God's compassion he makes his cry:
"O Father true, who canst not lie,
Who didst Lazarus raise unto life agen,
And Daniel shield in the lions' den;
Shield my soul from its peril, due   400
For the sins I sinned my lifetime through."
He did his right-hand glove uplift—
Saint Gabriel took from his hand the gift;
Then drooped his head upon his breast,
And with clasped hands he went to rest.   405
God from on high sent down to him
One of his angel Cherubim—
Saint Michael of Peril of the sea,
Saint Gabriel in company—
From heaven they came for that soul of price,   410
And they bore it with them to Paradise.

FRENCH TROUBADOUR SONGS

BERNARD DE VENTADOUR

No Marvel Is It

No marvel is it if I sing
Better than other minstrels all:
For more than they I am Love's thrall,
And all myself therein I fling,—
Knowledge and sense, body and soul,   5
And whatso power I have beside;
The rein that doth my being guide
Impels me to this only goal.

His heart is dead whence did not spring
Love's odor, sweet and magical;   10
His life doth ever on him pall
Who knoweth not that blessed thing;
Yea! God, who doth my life control,
Were cruel did he bid me bide
A month, or even a day, denied   15
The love whose rapture I extol.

How keen, how exquisite the sting
Of that sweet odor! At its call
An hundred times a day I fall
And faint, an hundred rise and sing.   20
So fair the semblance of my dole,
'Tis lovelier than another's pride:
If such the ill doth me betide,
Good hap were more than I could thole.

Yet haste, kind heaven! the sundering   25
True swains from false, great hearts from small!
The traitor in the dust bid crawl!
The faithless to confession bring!
Ah! if I were the master sole
Of all earth's treasures multiplied,   30
To see my Lady satisfied
Of my pure faith, I'd give the whole.

GUILLAUME DE POITIERS

Behold the Meads

Behold, the meads are green again,
The orchard-bloom is seen again,
Of sky and stream the mien again
   Is mild, is bright!

Now should each heart that loves obtain   5
   Its own delight.

But I will say no ill of Love,
However slight my guerdon prove:
Repining doth not me behove:
   And yet—to know   10
How lightly she I fain would move
   Might bliss bestow!

There are who hold my folly great,
Because with little hope I wait;
But one old saw doth animate   15
   And me assure:
Their hearts are high, their might is great,
   Who will endure.

Anonymous Alba

Sheltered beneath white hawthorn boughs,
A lady held her loved one close
In her arms, till the watchman cried abroad:
God! It is dawn! How soon it's come!

"How wildly have I wished that the night   5
Would never end, and that my love
Could stay, and the watchman never cry
God! It is dawn! How soon it's come!

"My gentle love, let us kiss once more
Here in this field where the small birds sing;   10
Let us defy their jealous throats—
God! It is dawn! How soon it's come!

"Still one more touch, my tender love,
Here in our field where the small birds sing,
Till the watchman blow his reedy strain—   15
God! It is dawn! How soon it's come!

"From the wind from below where my love has
   gone
Thoughtful and happy, I have drunk
A long sweet draught of his breath—O God,
God! It is dawn! How soon it's come!"   20

Envoi

Flowing with grace and charm is she;
Her loveliness draws many eyes,
Whose full heart throbs with a true love:
God! It is dawn! How soon it's come!

French Troubadour Songs. The first two are translated by Harriet Waters Preston, the last by Stanley Burnshaw

MARIE DE FRANCE

Would I Might Go Far Over Sea

Would I might go far over sea,
My Love, or high above the air,
And come to land or heaven with thee,
Where no law is, and none shall be.
Against beholding the most rare
Strange beauty that thou hast for me.
Alas, for, in this bitter land,
Full many a written curse doth stand
Against the kiss thy lips should bear;
Against the sweet gift of thy hands;
Against the knowing that thou art fair,
And too fond loving of thy hair.

The Lay of the Honeysuckle

With a glad heart and right good mind will I tell the Lay that men call Honeysuckle; and that the truth may be known of all it shall be told as many a minstrel has sung it to my ear, and as the scribe hath written it for our delight. It is of Tristan and Isoude, the Queen. It is of a love which passed all other love, from whence came wondrous sorrow, and whereof they died together the selfsame day.

King Mark was sorely wroth with Tristan, his sister's son, and bade him avoid his realm, by reason of the love he bore the Queen. So Tristan repaired to his own land, and dwelt for a full year in South Wales, where he was born. Then since he might not come where he would be, Tristan took no heed to his ways, but let his life run waste to Death. Marvel not overmuch thereat, for he who loves beyond measure must ever be sick in heart and hope, when he may not win according to his wish. So sick in heart and mind was Tristan that he left his kingdom, and returned straight to the realm of his banishment, because that in Cornwall dwelt the Queen. There he hid privily in the deep forest, withdrawn from the eyes of men; only when the evening was come, and all things sought their rest, he prayed the peasant and other mean folk of that country, of their charity to grant him shelter for the night. From the serfs he gathered tidings of the King. These gave again to him what they, in turn, had taken from some outlawed knight. Thus Tristan learned that when Pentecost was come King Mark purposed to hold high court at Tintagel; moreover that thither would ride Isoude, the Queen. When Tristan heard this thing he rejoiced greatly, since the Queen might not adventure through the forest, except he saw her with his eyes.

After the King had gone his way, Tristan entered within the wood, and sought the path by which the Queen must come. There he cut a wand from out a certain hazel-tree, and having trimmed and peeled it of its bark, with his dagger he carved his name upon the wood. This he placed upon her road, for well he knew that should the Queen but mark his name she would bethink her of her friend. Thus had it chanced before. For this was the sum of the writing set upon the wand, for Queen Isoude's heart alone: how that in this wild place Tristan had lurked and waited long, so that he might look upon her face, since without her he was already dead. Was it not with them as with the Honeysuckle and the Hazel tree she was passing by! So sweetly laced were they in one close embrace, that thus they might remain whilst life endured. But should rough hands part so fond a clasping, the hazel would wither at the root, and the honeysuckle must fail. Fair friend, thus is the case with us, nor you without me, nor I without you.

Now the Queen fared at adventure down the forest path. She spied the hazel wand set upon her road, and well she remembered the letters and the name. She bade the knights of her company to draw rein, and dismount from their palfreys, so that they might refresh themselves a little. When her commandment was done she withdrew from them a space, and called to her Brangwaine, her maiden, and own familiar friend. Then she hastened within the wood, to come on him whom more she loved than any living soul. How great the joy between these twain, that once more they might speak together softly, face to face. Isoude showed him her delight. She showed in what fashion she strove to bring peace and concord betwixt Tristan and the King, and how grievously his banishment had weighed upon her heart. Thus sped the hour, till it was time for them to part; but when these lovers freed them from the other's arms, the tears were wet upon their cheeks. So Tristan returned to Wales, his own realm, even as his uncle bade. But for the joy that he had had of her, his friend, for her sweet face, and for the tender words that she had spoken, yea, and for that writing upon the wand, to remember all these things, Tristan, that cunning harper, wrought a new Lay, as shortly I have told you. Goatleaf, men call this song in English. Chèvrefeuille it is named in French; but Goatleaf or Honeysuckle, here you have the very truth in the Lay that I have spoken.

"Would I Might Go Far Over Sea" translated by Arthur O'Shaughnessy: "The Lay of the Honeysuckle," by Eugene Mason.

AUCASSIN AND NICOLETE

'Tis of Aucassin and Nicolete.
Who would list to the good lay
Gladness of the captive gray?
'Tis how two young lovers met,
Aucassin and Nicolete,
Of the pains the lover bore
And the sorrows he outwore,
For the goodness and the grace,
Of his love, so fair of face.

Sweet the song, the story sweet,
There is no man hearkens it,
No man living 'neath the sun,
So outwearied, so foredone,
Sick and woeful, worn and sad,
But is healed, but is glad,
   'Tis so sweet.

So say they, speak they, tell they the Tale:

How the Count Bougars de Valence made war on Count Garin de Biaucaire, war so great, and so marvelous, and so mortal that never a day dawned but alway he was there, by the gates and walls, and barriers of the town with a hundred knights, and ten thousand men at arms, horsemen and footmen: so burned he the Count's land, and spoiled his country, and slew his men. Now the Count Garin de Biaucaire was old and frail, and his good days were gone over. No heir had he, neither son nor daughter, save one young man only; such an one as I shall tell you. Aucassin was the name of the damoiseau: fair was he, goodly, and great, and featly fashioned of his body, and limbs. His hair was yellow, in little curls, his eyes blue and laughing, his face beautiful and shapely, his nose high and well set, and so richly seen was he in all things good, that in him was none evil at all. But so suddenly overtaken was he of Love, who is a great master, that he would not, of his will, be dubbed knight, nor take arms, nor follow tourneys, nor do whatsoever him beseemed. Therefore his father and mother said to him:

"Son, go take thine arms, mount thy horse, and hold thy land, and help thy men, for if they see thee among them, more stoutly will they keep in battle their lives, and lands, and thine, and mine."

"Father," said Aucassin, "I marvel that you will be speaking. Never may God give me aught of my desire if I be made knight, or mount my horse, or

face stour and battle wherein knights smite and are smitten again, unless thou give me Nicolete, my true love, that I love so well."

"Son," said the father, "this may not be. Let Nicolete go, a slave girl she is, out of a strange land, and the captain of this town bought her of the Saracens, and carried her hither, and hath reared her and let christen the maid, and took her for his daughter in God, and one day will find a young man for her, to win her bread honorably. Herein hast thou nought to make or mend, but if a wife thou wilt have, I will give thee the daughter of a King, or a Count. There is no man so rich in France, but if thou desire his daughter, thou shalt have her."

"Faith! my father," said Aucassin, "tell me where is the place so high in all the world, that Nicolete, my sweet lady and love, would not grace it well? If she were Empress of Constantinople or of Germany, or Queen of France or England, it were little enough for her; so gentle is she and courteous, and debonaire, and compact of all good qualities."

Here singeth one:

Aucassin was of Biaucaire
Of a goodly castle there,
But from Nicolete the fair
None might win his heart away
Though his father, many a day,
And his mother said him nay,
"Ha! fond child, what wouldest thou?
Nicolete is glad enow!
Was from Carthage cast away,
Paynims sold her on a day!
Wouldst thou win a lady fair
Choose a maid of high degree
Such an one is meet for thee."
"Nay of these I have no care,
Nicolete is debonaire,
Her body sweet and the face of her
Take my heart as in a snare,
Loyal love is but her share
   That is so sweet."

Then speak they, say they, tell they the Tale:

When the Count Garin de Biaucaire knew that he would avail not to withdraw Aucassin his son from the love of Nicolete, he went to the Captain

Aucassin and Nicolete. Translated by Andrew Lang.

of the city, who was his man, and spake to him saying:

"Sir Count; away with Nicolete thy daughter in God; cursed be the land whence she was brought into this country, for by reason of her do I lose Aucassin, that will neither be dubbed knight, nor do aught of the things that fall to him to be done. And wit ye well," he said, "that if I might have her at my will, I would burn her in a fire, and yourself might well be sore adread."

"Sir," said the Captain, "this is grievous to me that he comes and goes and hath speech with her. I had bought the maiden at mine own charges, and nourished her, and baptized, and made her my daughter in God. Yea, I would have given her to a young man that should win her bread honorably. With this had Aucassin thy son nought to make or mend. But, sith it is thy will and thy pleasure, I will send her into that land and that country where never will he see her with his eyes."

"Have a heed to thyself," said the Count Garin, "thence might great evil come on thee."

So parted they from each other. Now the Captain was a right rich man: so had he a rich palace with a garden in face of it; in an upper chamber thereof he let place Nicolete with one old woman to keep her company, and in that chamber put bread and meat and wine and such things as were needful. Then he let seal the door, that none might come in or go forth, save that there was one window, over against the garden, and strait enough, where through came to them a little air.

Here singeth one:

Nicolete as ye heard tell
Prisoned is within a cell
That is painted wondrously
With colors of a far countrie,
And the window of marble wrought,
There the maiden stood in thought,
With straight brows and yellow hair
Never saw ye fairer fair!
On the wood she gazed below,
And she saw the roses blow,
Heard the birds sing loud and low,
Therefore spoke she woefully:
"Ah me, wherefore do I lie
Here in prison wrongfully:
Aucassin, my love, my knight,
Am I not thy heart's delight,
Thou that lovest me aright!
'Tis for thee that I must dwell
In the vaulted chamber cell,
Hard beset and all alone!

By our Lady Mary's Son
Here no longer will I wonn,
If I may flee!"

Then speak they, say they, tell they the Tale:

Nicolete was in prison, as ye have heard soothly, in the chamber. And the noise and bruit of it went through all the country and all the land, how that Nicolete was lost. Some said she had fled the country, and some that the Count Garin de Biaucaire had let slay her. Whosoever had joy thereof, Aucassin had none, so he went to the Captain of the town and spoke to him, saying:

"Sir Captain, what hast thou made of Nicolete, my sweet lady and love, the thing that best I love in all the world? Hast thou carried her off or ravished her away from me? Know well that if I die of it, the price shall be demanded of thee, and that will be well done, for it shall be even as if thou hadst slain me with thy two hands, for thou hast taken from me the thing that in this world I loved the best."

"Fair Sir," said the Captain, "let these things be. Nicolete is a captive that I did bring from a strange country. Yea, I bought her at my own charges of the Saracens, and I bred her up and baptized her, and made her my daughter in God. And I have cherished her, and one of these days I would have given her a young man, to win her bread honorably. With this thou hast naught to make, but do thou take the daughter of a King or a Count. Nay more, what wouldst thou deem thee to have gained, hadst thou made her thy leman, and taken her to thy bed? Plentiful lack of comfort hadst thou got thereby, for in Hell would thy soul have lain while the world endures, and into Paradise wouldst thou have entered never."

"In Paradise what have I to win? Therein I seek not to enter, but only to have Nicolete, my sweet lady that I love so well. For into Paradise go none but such folk as I shall tell thee now. Thither go these same old priests, and halt old men and maimed, who all day and night cower continually before the altars, and in the crypts; and such folk as wear old amices and old clouted frocks, and naked folk and shoeless, and covered with sores, perishing of hunger and thirst, and of cold, and of little ease. These be they that go into Paradise, with them have I naught to make. But into Hell would I fain go; for into Hell fare the goodly clerks, and goodly knights that fall in tourneys and great wars, and stout men at arms, and all men noble. With these would I liefly go. And thither

pass the sweet ladies and courteous that have two
lovers, or three, and their lords also thereto.
Thither goes the gold, and the silver, and cloth of
vair, and cloth of gris, and harpers, and makers,
and the princes of this world. With these I would
gladly go, let me but have with me Nicolete, my
sweetest lady."

"Certes," quoth the Captain, "in vain wilt thou
speak thereof, for never shalt thou see her; and if
thou hadst word with her, and thy father knew it,
he would let burn in a fire both her and me, and
thyself might well be sore adread."

"That is even what irketh me," quoth Aucassin.
So he went from the Captain sorrowing.

Here singeth one:

Aucassin did so depart
Much in dole and heavy at heart
For his love so bright and dear,
None might bring him any cheer,
None might give good words to hear.
To the palace doth he fare
Climbeth up the palace-stair,
Passeth to a chamber there,
Thus great sorrow doth he bear,
For his lady and love so fair.
"Nicolete how fair art thou,
Sweet thy foot-fall, sweet thine eyes,
Sweet the mirth of thy replies,
Sweet thy laughter, sweet thy face,
Sweet thy lips and sweet thy brow,
And the touch of thine embrace,
All for thee I sorrow now,
Captive in an evil place,
Whence I ne'er may go my ways
Sister, sweet friend!"

So say they, speak they, tell they the Tale:

While Aucassin was in the chamber sorrowing
for Nicolete his love, even then the Count Bougars
de Valence, that had his war to wage, forgat it no
wit, but had called up his horsemen and his footmen, so made he for the castle to storm it. And
the cry of battle arose, and the din, and knights
and men at arms busked them, and ran to walls
and gates to hold the keep. And the townsfolk
mounted to the battlements, and cast down bolts
and pikes. Then while the assault was great and
even at its height, the Count Garin de Biaucaire
came into the chamber where Aucassin was making lament, sorrowing for Nicolete, his sweet lady
that he loved so well.

"Ha! son," quoth he, "how caitiff art thou, and
cowardly, that canst see men assail thy goodliest
castle and strongest. Know thou that if thou lose

it, thou losest all. Son, go to, take arms, and mount
thy horse, and defend thy land, and help thy men
and fare into the stour. Thou needst not smite nor
be smitten. If they do but see thee among them,
better will they guard their substance, and their
lives, and thy land and mine. And thou art so
great, and hardy of thy hands, that well mightst
thou do this thing, and to do it is thy devoir."

"Father," said Aucassin, "what is this thou sayest now? God grant me never aught of my desire,
if I be dubbed knight, or mount steed, or go into
the stour where knights do smite and are smitten,
if thou givest me not Nicolete, my sweet lady,
whom I love so well."

"Son," quoth his father, "this may never be:
rather would I be quite disinherited and lose all
that is mine, than that thou shouldst have her to
thy wife, or to love *par amours.*"

So he turned him about. But when Aucassin saw
him going he called to him again saying,

"Father, go to now, I will make with thee fair
covenant."

"What covenant, fair son?"

"I will take up arms, and go into the stour, on
this covenant, that, if God bring me back sound
and safe, thou wilt let me see Nicolete my sweet
lady, even so long that I may have of her two
words or three, and one kiss."

"That will I grant," said his father.

At this was Aucassin glad.

Here one singeth:

Of the kiss heard Aucassin
That returning he shall win.
None so glad would he have been
Of a myriad marks of gold
Of a hundred thousand told.
Called for raiment brave of steel,
Then they clad him, head to heel,
Twyfold hauberk doth he don,
Firmly braced the helmet on.
Girt the sword with hilt of gold,
Horse doth mount, and lance doth wield,
Looks to stirrups and to shield,
Wondrous brave he rode to field.
Dreaming of his lady dear
Setteth spurs to the destrere,
Rideth forward without fear,
Through the gate and forth away
    To the fray.

So speak they, say they, tell they the Tale:

Aucassin was armed and mounted as ye have
heard tell. God! how goodly sat the shield on his

shoulder, the helm on his head, and the baldric on his left haunch! And the damoiseau was tall, fair, featly fashioned, and hardy of his hands, and the horse whereon he rode swift and keen, and straight had he spurred him forth of the gate. Now believe ye not that his mind was on kine, nor cattle of the booty, nor thought he how he might strike a knight, nor be stricken again: nor no such thing. Nay, no memory had Aucassin of aught of these; rather he so dreamed of Nicolete, his sweet lady, that he dropped his reins, forgetting all there was to do, and his horse that had felt the spur, bore him into the press and hurled among the foe, and they laid hands on him all about, and took him captive, and seized away his spear and shield, and straightway they led him off a prisoner, and were even now discoursing of what death he should die.

And when Aucassin heard them,

"Ha! God," said he, "sweet Savior. Be these my deadly enemies that have taken me, and will soon cut off my head? And once my head is off, no more shall I speak with Nicolete, my sweet lady, that I love so well. Natheless have I here a good sword, and sit a good horse unwearied. If now I keep not my head for her sake, God help her never, if she love me more!"

The damoiseau was tall and strong, and the horse whereon he sat was right eager. And he laid hand to sword, and fell a-smiting to right and left, and smote through helm and *nasal,* and arm and clenched hand, making a murder about him, like a wild boar when hounds fall on him in the forest, even till he struck down ten knights, and seven he hurt, and straightway he hurled out of the press, and rode back again at full speed, sword in hand. The Count Bougars de Valence heard say they were about hanging Aucassin, his enemy, so he came into that place and Aucassin was ware of him, and gat his sword into his hand, and lashed at his helm with such a stroke that he drave it down on his head, and he being stunned, fell groveling. And Aucassin laid hands on him, and caught him by the *nasal* of his helmet, and gave him to his father.

"Father," quoth Aucassin, "lo here is your mortal foe, who hath so warred on you with all malengin. Full twenty years did this war endure, and might not be ended by man."

"Fair son," said his father, "thy feats of youth shouldst thou do, and not seek after folly."

"Father," said Aucassin, "sermon me no sermons, but fulfill my covenant."

"Ha! what covenant, fair son?"

"What, father, hast thou forgotten it? By mine own head, whosoever forgets, will I not forget it, so much it hath me at heart. Didst thou not covenant with me when I took up arms, and went into the stour, that if God brought me back safe and sound, thou wouldst let me see Nicolete, my sweet lady, even so long that I may have of her two words or three, and one kiss? So didst thou covenant, and my mind is that thou keep thy word."

"I!" quoth the father, "God forsake me when I keep this covenant! Nay, if she were here I would let her burn in the fire, and thyself shouldst be sore adread."

"Is this thy last word?" quoth Aucassin.

"So help me God," quoth his father, "yea!"

"Certes," quoth Aucassin, "this is a sorry thing meseems, when a man of thine age lies!"

"Count of Valence," quoth Aucassin, "I took thee?"

"In sooth, Sir, didst thou," saith the Count.

"Give me thy hand," saith Aucassin.

"Sir, with good will."

So he set his hand in the other's.

"Now givest thou me thy word," saith Aucassin, "that never whiles thou art living man wilt thou avail to do my father dishonor, or harm him in body, or in goods, but do it thou wilt?"

"Sir, in God's name," saith he, "mock me not, but put me to my ransom; ye cannot ask of me gold nor silver, horses nor palfreys, *vair* nor *gris,* hawks nor hounds, but I will give you them."

"What?" quoth Aucassin. "Ha, knowest thou not it was I that took thee?"

"Yea, sir," quoth the Count Bougars.

"God help me never, but I will make thy head fly from thy shoulders, if thou makest not truth," said Aucassin.

"In God's name," said he, "I make what promise thou wilt."

So they did the oath, and Aucassin let mount him on a horse, and took another and so led him back till he was all in safety.

Here one singeth:

When the Count Garin doth know
That his child would ne'er forego
Love of her that loved him so,
Nicolete, the bright of brow,
In a dungeon deep below
Childe Aucassin did he throw.
Even there the Childe must dwell
In a dun-walled marble cell.
There he waileth in his woe

Crying thus as ye shall know.
"Nicolete, thou lily white,
My sweet lady, bright of brow,
Sweeter than the grape art thou,
Sweeter than sack posset good
In a cup of maple wood!
Was it not but yesterday
That a palmer came this way,
Out of Limousin came he,
And at ease he might not be,
For a passion him possessed
That upon his bed he lay,
Lay, and tossed, and knew not rest
In his pain discomforted.
But thou camest by the bed,
Where he tossed amid his pain,
Holding high thy sweeping train,
And thy kirtle of ermine,
And thy smock of linen fine,
Then these fair white limbs of thine,
Did he look on, and it fell
That the palmer straight was well,
Straight was hale—and comforted,
And he rose up from his bed,
And went back to his own place,
Sound and strong, and full of face!
My sweet lady, lily white,
Sweet thy footfall, sweet thine eyes,
And the mirth of thy replies.
Sweet thy laughter, sweet thy face,
Sweet thy lips and sweet thy brow,
And the touch of thine embrace.
Who but doth in thee delight?
I for love of thee am bound
In this dungeon underground,
All for loving thee must lie
Here where loud on thee I cry,
Here for loving thee must die
    For thee, my love."

Then say they, speak they, tell they the Tale:

Aucassin was cast into prison as ye have heard
tell, and Nicolete, of her part, was in the chamber.
Now it was summer time, the month of May, 40
when days are warm, and long, and clear, and the
night still and serene. Nicolete lay one night on
her bed, and saw the moon shine clear through a
window, yea, and heard the nightingale sing in the
garden, so she minded her of Aucassin her lover
whom she loved so well. Then fell she to thoughts
of Count Garin de Biaucaire, that hated her to the
death; therefore deemed she that there she would
no longer abide, for that, if she were told of, and
the Count knew whereas she lay, an ill death 50
would he make her die. Now she knew that the
old woman slept who held her company. Then she
arose, and clad her in a mantle of silk she had by

her, very goodly, and took napkins, and sheets of
the bed, and knotted one to the other, and made
therewith a cord as long as she might, so knitted
it to a pillar in the window, and let herself slip
down into the garden, then caught up her raiment
in both hands, behind and before, and kilted up
her kirtle, because of dew that she saw lying deep
on the grass, and so went her way down through
the garden.

10   Her locks were yellow and curled, her eyes blue
and smiling, her face featly fashioned, the nose
high and fairly set, the lips more red than cherry
or rose in time of summer, her teeth white and
small; her breasts so firm that they bore up the
folds of her bodice as they had been two apples;
so slim she was in the waist that your two hands
might have clipped her, and the daisy flowers that
brake beneath her as she went tip-toe, and that
bent above her instep, seemed black against her
20 feet, so white was the maiden. She came to the
postern gate, and unbarred it, and went out
through the streets of Biaucaire, keeping always on
the shadowy side, for the moon was shining right
clear, and so wandered she till she came to the
tower where her lover lay. The tower was flanked
with buttresses, and she cowered under one of
them, wrapped in her mantle. Then thrust she her
head through a crevice of the tower that was
old and worn, and so heard she Aucassin wailing
30 within, and making dole and lament for the sweet
lady he loved so well. And when she had listened
to him she began to say:

Here one singeth:

Nicolete the bright of brow
On a pillar leanest thou,
All Aucassin's wail dost hear
For his love that is so dear,
Then thou spakest, shrill and clear,
"Gentle knight withouten fear
Little good befalleth thee,
Little help of sigh or tear,
Ne'er shalt thou have joy of me.
Never shalt thou win me; still
Am I held in evil will
Of thy father and thy kin,
Therefore must I cross the sea,
And another land must win."
Then she cut her curls of gold,
Cast them in the dungeon hold,
Aucassin doth clasp them there,
Kissed the curls that were so fair,
Them doth in his bosom bear,
Then he wept, even as of old,
    All for his love!

Then say they, speak they, tell they the Tale:

When Aucassin heard Nicolete say that she would pass into a far country, he was all in wrath.

"Fair sweet friend," quoth he, "thou shalt not go, for then wouldst thou be my death. And the first man that saw thee and had the might withal, would take thee straightway into his bed to be his leman. And once thou camest into a man's bed and that bed not mine, wit ye well that I would not tarry till I had found a knife to pierce my heart and slay myself. Nay, verily, wait so long I would not; but would hurl myself on it so soon as I could find a wall, or a black stone, thereon would I dash my head so mightily, that the eyes would start, and my brain burst. Rather would I die even such a death, than know thou hadst lain in a man's bed, and that bed not mine."

"Aucassin," she said, "I trow thou lovest me not as much as thou sayest, but I love thee more than thou lovest me."

"Ah, fair sweet friend," said Aucassin, "it may not be that thou shouldst love me even as I love thee. Woman may not love man as man loves woman, for a woman's love lies in the glance of her eye, and the bud of her breast, and her foot's tip-toe, but the love of man is in his heart planted, whence it can never issue forth and pass away."

Now while Aucassin and Nicolete held this parley together, the town's guards came down a street, with swords drawn beneath their cloaks, for the Count Garin had charged them that if they could take her they should slay her. But the sentinel that was on the tower saw them coming, and heard them speaking of Nicolete as they went, and threatening to slay her.

"God!" quoth he, "this were great pity to slay so fair a maid! Right great charity it were if I could say aught to her, and they perceive it not, and she should be on her guard against them, for if they slay her, then were Aucassin, my damoiseau, dead, and that were great pity."

Here one singeth:

Valiant was the sentinel,
Courteous, kind, and practiced well,
So a song did sing and tell
Of the peril that befell.
"Maiden fair that lingerest here,
Gentle maid of merry cheer,
Hair of gold, and eyes as clear
As the water in a mere,
Thou, meseems, hast spoken word
To thy lover and thy lord,

That would die for thee, his dear;
Now beware the ill accord,
Of the cloaked men of the sword,
These have sworn and keep their word,
They will put thee to the sword
Save thou take heed!"

Then speak they, say they, tell they the Tale:

"Ha!" quoth Nicolete, "be the soul of thy father and the soul of thy mother in the rest of Paradise, so fairly and so courteously hast thou spoken me! Please God, I will be right ware of them, God keep me out of their hands."

So she shrank under her mantle into the shadow of the pillar till they had passed by, and then took she farewell of Aucassin, and so fared till she came unto the castle wall. Now that wall was wasted and broken, and some deal mended, so she clomb thereon till she came between wall and fosse, and so looked down, and saw that the fosse was deep and steep, whereat she was sore adread.

"Ah, God," saith she, "sweet Savior! If I let myself fall hence, I shall break my neck, and if here I abide, tomorrow they will take me and burn me in a fire. Yet liefer would I perish here than that tomorrow the folk should stare on me for a gazing-stock."

Then she crossed herself, and so let herself slip into the fosse, and when she had come to the bottom, her fair feet, and fair hands that had not custom thereof, were bruised and frayed, and the blood springing from a dozen places, yet felt she no pain nor hurt, by reason of the great dread wherein she went. But if she were in cumber to win there, in worse was she to win out. But she deemed that there to abide was of none avail, and she found a pike sharpened, that they of the city had thrown out to keep the hold. Therewith made she one stepping place after another, till, with much travail, she climbed the wall. Now the forest lay within two crossbow shots, and the forest was of thirty leagues this way and that. Therein also were wild beasts, and beasts serpentine, and she feared that if she entered there they would slay her. But anon she deemed that if men found her there they would hale her back into the town to burn her.

Here one singeth:

Nicolete, the fair of face,
Climbed upon the coping stone,
There made she lament and moan
Calling on our Lord alone
For his mercy and his grace.

"Father, king of Majesty,
Listen, for I nothing know
Where to flee or whither go.
If within the wood I fare,
Lo, the wolves will slay me there,
Boars and lions terrible,
Many in the wild wood dwell,
But if I abide the day,
Surely worse will come of it,
Surely will the fire be lit
That shall burn my body away,
Jesus, lord of Majesty,
Better seemeth it to me,
That within the wood I fare,
Though the wolves devour me there
Than within the town to go,
Ne'er be it so!"

Then speak they, say they, tell they the Tale:

Nicolete made great moan, as ye have heard;
then commended she herself to God, and anon
fared till she came unto the forest. But to go deep
in it she dared not, by reason of the wild beasts,
and beasts serpentine. Anon crept she into a little
thicket, where sleep came upon her, and she slept
till prime next day, when the shepherds issued
forth from the town and drove their bestial between wood and water. Anon came they all into
one place by a fair fountain which was on the
fringe of the forest, thereby spread they a mantle,
and thereon set bread. So while they were eating,
Nicolete wakened, with the sound of the singing
birds, and the shepherds, and she went unto them,
saying, "Fair boys, our Lord keep you!"

"God bless thee," quoth he that had more words
to his tongue than the rest.

"Fair boys," quoth she, "know ye Aucassin, the
son of Count Garin de Biaucaire?"

"Yea, well we know him."

"So may God help you, fair boys," quoth she,
"tell him there is a beast in this forest, and bid
him come chase it, and if he can take it, he would
not give one limb thereof for a hundred marks of
gold, nay, nor for five hundred, nor for any ransom."

Then looked they on her, and saw her so fair
that they were all astonished.

"Will I tell him thereof?" quoth he that had
more words to his tongue than the rest; "foul fall
him who speaks of the thing or tells him the tidings. These are but visions ye tell of, for there is
no beast so great in this forest, stag, nor lion, nor
boar, that one of his limbs is worth more than two
deniers, or three at the most, and ye speak of such

great ransom. Foul fall him that believes your
word, and him that telleth Aucassin. Ye be a
Fairy, and we have none liking for your company
nay, hold on your road."

"Nay, fair boys," quoth she, "nay, ye will do my
bidding. For this beast is so mighty of medicine
that thereby will Aucassin be healed of his torment. And lo! I have five sols in my purse, take
them, and tell him: for within three days must he
come hunting it hither, and if within three days
he find it not, never will he be healed of his
torment."

"My faith," quoth he, "the money will we take,
and if he come hither we will tell him, but seek
him we will not."

"In God's name," quoth she; and so took farewell of the shepherds, and went her way.

Here one singeth:

Nicolete the bright of brow
From the shepherds doth she pass
All below the blossomed bough
Where an ancient way there was,
Overgrown and choked with grass,
Till she found the cross-roads where
Seven paths do all way fare,
Then she deemeth she will try,
Should her lover pass thereby,
If he love her loyally.
So she gathered white lilies,
Oak-leaf, that in green wood is,
Leaves of many a branch I wis,
Therewith built a lodge of green,
Goodlier was never seen,
Swore by God who may not lie,
"If my love the lodge should spy,
He will rest awhile thereby
If he love me loyally."
Thus his faith she deemed to try,
"Or I love him not, not I,
Nor he loves me!"

Then speak they, say they, tell they the Tale:

Nicolete built her lodge, of boughs, as ye have
heard, right fair and featously, and wove it well,
within and without, of flowers and leaves. So lay
she hard by the lodge in a deep coppice to know
what Aucassin will do. And the cry and the bruit
went abroad through all the country and all the
land, that Nicolete was lost. Some told that she
had fled, and some that the Count Garin had let
slay her. Whosoever had joy thereof, no joy had
Aucassin. And the Count Garin, his father, had
taken him out of prison, and had sent for the
knights of that land, and the ladies, and let make

a right great feast, for the comforting of Aucassin his son. Now at the high time of the feast, was Aucassin leaning from the gallery, all woeful and discomforted. Whatsoever men might devise of mirth, Aucassin had no joy thereof, nor no desire, for he saw not her that he loved. Then a knight looked on him, and came to him, and said:

"Aucassin, of that sickness of thine have I been sick, and good counsel will I give thee, if thou wilt hearken to me—"

"Sir," said Aucassin, "gramercy, good counsel would I fain hear."

"Mount thy horse," quoth he, "and go take thy pastime in yonder forest, there wilt thou see the good flowers and grass, and hear the sweet birds sing. Perchance thou shalt hear some word, whereby thou shalt be the better."

"Sir," quoth Aucassin, "gramercy, that will I do."

He passed out of the hall, and went down the stairs, and came to the stable where his horse was. He let saddle and bridle him, and mounted, and rode forth from the castle, and wandered till he came to the forest, so rode till he came to the fountain and found the shepherds at point of noon. And they had a mantle stretched on the grass, and were eating bread, and making great joy.

Here singeth one:

There were gathered shepherds all,
Martin, Esmeric, and Hal,
Aubrey, Robin, great and small.
Saith the one, "Good fellows all,
God keep Aucassin the fair,
And the maid with yellow hair,
Bright of brow and eyes of vair.
She that gave us gold to ware.
Cakes therewith to buy ye know,
Goodly knives and sheaths also.
Flutes to play, and pipes to blow,
May God him heal!"

Here speak they, say they, tell they the Tale:

When Aucassin heard the shepherds, anon he bethought him of Nicolete, his sweet lady he loved so well, and he deemed that she had passed thereby; then set he spurs to his horse, and so came to the shepherds.

"Fair boys, God be with you."

"God bless you," quoth he that had more words to his tongue than the rest.

"Fair boys," quoth Aucassin, "say the song again that anon ye sang."

"Say it we will not," quoth he that had more words to his tongue than the rest, "foul fall him who will sing it again for you, fair sir!"

"Fair boys," quoth Aucassin, "know ye me not?"

"Yea, we know well that you are Aucassin, our damoiseau, natheless we be not your men, but the Count's."

"Fair boys, yet sing it again, I pray you."

"Hearken! by the Holy Heart," quoth he, "wherefore should I sing for you, if it likes me not? Lo, there is no such rich man in this country, saving the body of Garin the Count, that dare drive forth my oxen, or my cows, or my sheep, if he finds them in his fields, or his corn, lest he lose his eyes for it, and wherefore should I sing for you, if it likes me not?"

"God be your aid, fair boys, sing it ye will, and take ye these ten sols I have here in a purse."

"Sir, the money will we take, but never a note will I sing, for I have given my oath, but I will tell thee a plain tale, if thou wilt."

"By God," saith Aucassin, "I love a plain tale better than naught."

"Sir, we were in this place, a little time agone, between prime and tierce, and were eating our bread by this fountain, even as now we do, and a maid came past, the fairest thing in the world, whereby we deemed that she should be a fay, and all the wood shone round about her. Anon she gave us of that she had, whereby we made covenant with her, that if ye came hither we would bid you hunt in this forest, wherein is such a beast that, an ye might take him, ye would not give one limb of him for five hundred marks of silver, nor for no ransom; for this beast is so mighty of medicine, that, an ye could take him, ye should be healed of your torment, and within three days must ye take him, and if ye take him not then, never will ye look on him. So chase ye the beast, an ye will, or an ye will let be, for my promise have I kept with her."

"Fair boys," quoth Aucassin, "ye have said enough. God grant me to find this quarry."

Here singeth one:

Aucassin when he had heard,
Sore within his heart was stirred,
Left the shepherds on that word,
Far into the forest spurred
Rode into the wood; and fleet
Fled his horse through paths of it,
Three words spake he of his sweet,
"Nicolete the fair, the dear,
'Tis for thee I follow here

Track of boar, nor slot of deer,
But thy sweet body and eyes so clear,
All thy mirth and merry cheer,
That my very heart have slain,
So please God to me maintain
I shall see my love again,
 Sweet sister, friend!"

Then speak they, say they, tell they the Tale:

Aucassin fared through the forest from path to path after Nicolete, and his horse bare him furiously. Think ye not that the thorns him spared, nor the briars, nay, not so, but tare his raiment, that scarce a knot might be tied with the soundest part thereof, and the blood sprang from his arms, and flanks, and legs, in forty places, or thirty, so that behind the Childe men might follow on the track of his blood in the grass. But so much he went in thoughts of Nicolete, his lady sweet, that he felt no pain nor torment, and all the day hurled through the forest in this fashion nor heard no word of her. And when he saw Vespers draw nigh, he began to weep for that he found her not. All down an old road, and grassgrown he fared, when anon, looking along the way before him, he saw such an one as I shall tell you. Tall was he, and great of growth, laidly and marvelous to look upon: his head huge, and black as charcoal, and more than the breadth of a hand between his two eyes, and great cheeks, and a big nose and broad, big nostrils and ugly, and thick lips redder than a collop, and great teeth yellow and ugly, and he was shod with hosen and shoon of bull's hide, bound with cords of bark over the knee, and all about him a great cloak twyfold, and he leaned on a grievous cudgel, and Aucassin came unto him, and was afraid when he beheld him.

"Fair brother, God aid thee."

"God bless you," quoth he.

"As God he helpeth thee, what makest thou here?"

"What is that to thee?"

"Nay, naught, naught," saith Aucassin, "I ask but out of courtesy."

"But for whom weepest thou," quoth he, "and makest such heavy lament? Certes, were I as rich a man as thou, the whole world should not make me weep."

"Ha! know ye me?" saith Aucassin.

"Yea, I know well that ye be Aucassin, the son of the Count, and if ye tell me for why ye weep, then will I tell you what I make here."

"Certes," quoth Aucassin, "I will tell you right gladly. Hither came I this morning to hunt in this forest; and with me a white hound, the fairest in the world; him have I lost, and for him I weep."

"By the Heart our Lord bare in his breast," quoth he, "are ye weeping for a stinking hound? Foul fall him that holds thee high henceforth! for there is no such rich man in the land, but if thy father asked it of him, he would give thee ten, or fifteen, or twenty, and be the gladder for it. But I have cause to weep and make dole."

"Wherefore so, brother?"

"Sir, I will tell thee. I was hireling to a rich villain, and drove his plow; four oxen had he. But three days since came on me great misadventure, whereby I lost the best of mine oxen, Roger, the best of my team. Him go I seeking, and have neither eaten nor drunken these three days, nor may I go to the town, lest they cast me into prison, seeing that I have not wherewithal to pay. Out of all the wealth of the world have I no more than ye see on my body. A poor mother bare me, that had no more but one wretched bed; this have they taken from under her, and she lies in the very straw. This ails me more than mine own case, for wealth comes and goes; if now I have lost, another tide will I gain, and will pay for mine ox whenas I may; never for that will I weep. But you weep for a stinking hound. Foul fall whoso thinks well of thee!"

"Certes thou art a good comforter, brother, blessed be thou! And of what price was thine ox?"

"Sir, they ask me twenty sols for him, whereof I cannot abate one doit."

"Nay, then," quoth Aucassin, "take these twenty sols I have in my purse, and pay for thine ox."

"Sir," saith he, "gramercy. And God give thee to find that thou seekest."

So they parted each from other, and Aucassin rode on: the night was fair and still, and so long he went that he came to the lodge of boughs, that Nicolete had builded and woven within and without, over and under, with flowers, and it was the fairest lodge that might be seen. When Aucassin was ware of it, he stopped suddenly, and the light of the moon fell therein.

"God!" quoth Aucassin, "here was Nicolete, my sweet lady, and this lodge builded she with her fair hands. For the sweetness of it, and for love of her, will I alight, and rest here this night long."

He drew forth his foot from the stirrup to alight, and the steed was great and tall He dreamed so much on Nicolete his right sweet lady, that he slipped on a stone, and drave his shoulder out of its place. Then knew he that he was hurt sore, natheless he bore him with what force he might, and fastened with the other hand the mare's son to a thorn. Then turned he on his side, and crept backwise into the lodge of boughs. And he looked through a gap in the lodge and saw the stars in heaven, and one that was brighter than the rest; so began he to say:

Here one singeth:

"Star, that I from far behold,
Star, the Moon calls to her fold,
Nicolete with thee doth dwell,
My sweet love with locks of gold,
God would have her dwell afar,
Dwell with him for evening star,
Would to God, whate'er befell,
Would that with her I might dwell.
I would clip her close and strait,
Nay, were I of much estate,
Some king's son desirable,
Worthy she to be my mate,
Me to kiss and clip me well,
   Sister, sweet friend!"

So speak they, say they, tell they the Tale:

When Nicolete heard Aucassin, right so came she unto him, for she was not far away. She passed within the lodge, and threw her arms about his neck, and clipped and kissed him.

"Fair sweet friend, welcome be thou."

"And thou, fair sweet love, be thou welcome."

So either kissed and clipped the other, and fair joy was them between.

"Ha! sweet love," quoth Aucassin, "but now was I sore hurt, and my shoulder wried, but I take no force of it, nor have no hurt therefrom since I have thee."

Right so felt she his shoulder and found it was wried from its place. And she so handled it with her white hands, and so wrought in her surgery, that by God's will who loveth lovers, it went back into its place. Then took she flowers, and fresh grass, and leaves green, and bound these herbs on the hurt with a strip of her smock, and he was all healed.

"Aucassin," saith she, "fair sweet love, take counsel what thou wilt do. If thy father let search this forest tomorrow, and men find me here, they will slay me, come to thee what will."

"Certes, fair sweet love, therefore should I sorrow heavily, but, an if I may, never shall they take thee."

Anon gat he on his horse, and his lady before him, kissing and clipping her, and so rode they at adventure.

Here one singeth:

Aucassin the frank, the fair,
Aucassin of the yellow hair,
Gentle knight, and true lover,
From the forest doth he fare,
Holds his love before him there,
Kissing cheek, and chin, and eyes,
But she spake in sober wise,
"Aucassin, true love and fair,
To what land do we repair?"
Sweet my love, I take no care,
Thou art with me everywhere!
So they pass the woods and downs,
Pass the villages and towns,
Hills and dales and open land,
Came at dawn to the sea sand,
Lighted down upon the strand,
   Beside the sea.

Then say they, speak they, tell they the Tale:

Aucassin lighted down and his love, as ye have heard sing. He held his horse by the bridle, and his lady by the hands; so went they along the sea shore, and on the sea they saw a ship, and he called unto the sailors, and they came to him. Then held he such speech with them, that he and his lady were brought aboard that ship, and when they were on the high sea, behold a mighty wind and tyrannous arose, marvelous and great, and drave them from land to land, till they came unto a strange country, and won the haven of the castle of Torelore. Then asked they what this land might be, and men told them that it was the country of the King of Torelore. Then he asked what manner of man was he, and was there war afoot, and men said,

"Yea, and mighty!"

Therewith took he farewell of the merchants, and they commended him to God. Anon Aucassin mounted his horse, with his sword girt, and his lady before him, and rode at adventure till he was come to the castle. Then asked he where the King was, and they said that he was in childbed.

"Then where is his wife?"

And they told him she was with the host, and had led with her all the force of that country.

Now when Aucassin heard that saying, he made great marvel, and came into the castle, and lighted down, he and his lady, and his lady held his horse. Right so went he up into the castle, with his sword girt, and fared hither and thither till he came to the chamber where the King was lying.

Here one singeth:

Aucassin the courteous knight
To the chamber went forthright,
To the bed with linen dight
Even where the King was laid.
There he stood by him and said:
"Fool, what makst thou here abed?"
Quoth the King: "I am brought to bed
Of a fair son, and anon
When my month is over and gone,
And my healing fairly done,
To the Minister will I fare
And will do my churching there,
As my father did repair.
Then will sally forth to war,
Then will drive my foes afar
　From my countrie!"

Then speak they, say they, tell they the Tale:

When Aucassin heard the King speak on this wise, he took all the sheets that covered him, and threw them all abroad about the chamber. Then saw he behind him a cudgel, and caught it into his hand, and turned, and took the King, and beat him till he was well-nigh dead.

"Ha! fair sir," quoth the King, "what would you with me? Art thou beside thyself, that beatest me in mine own house?"

"By God's heart," quoth Aucassin, "thou ill son of an ill wench, I will slay thee if thou swear not that never shall any man in all thy land lie in of child henceforth for ever."

So he did that oath, and when he had done it, "Sir," said Aucassin, "bring me now where thy wife is with the host."

"Sir, with good will," quoth the King.

He mounted his horse, and Aucassin gat on his own, and Nicolete abode in the Queen's chamber. Anon rode Aucassin and the King even till they came to that place where the Queen was, and lo! men were warring with baked apples, and with eggs, and with fresh cheeses, and Aucassin began to look on them, and made great marvel.

Here singeth one:

Aucassin his horse doth stay,
From the saddle watched the fray,
All the stour and fierce array;
Right fresh cheeses carried they,
Apples baked, and mushrooms gray,
Whoso splasheth most the ford

He is master called and lord.
Aucassin doth gaze awhile,
Then began to laugh and smile
　And made game.

Then speak they, say they, tell they the Tale:

When Aucassin beheld these marvels, he came to the King, and said, "Sir, be these thine enemies?"

"Yea, Sir," quoth the King.

"And will ye that I should avenge you of them?"

"Yea," quoth he, "with all my heart."

Then Aucassin put hand to sword, and hurled among them, and began to smite to the right hand and the left, and slew many of them. And when the King saw that he slew them, he caught at his bridle and said,

"Ha! fair sir, slay them not in such wise."

"How," quoth Aucassin, "will ye not that I should avenge you of them?"

"Sir," quoth the King, "over-much already hast thou avenged me. It is nowise our custom to slay each other."

Anon turned they and fled. Then the King and Aucassin betook them again to the castle of Torelore, and the folk of that land counseled the King to put Aucassin forth, and keep Nicolete for his son's wife, for that she seemed a lady high of lineage. And Nicolete heard them and had no joy of it, so began to say:

Here singeth one:

Thus she spake the bright of brow:
"Lord of Torelore and king,
Thy folk deem me a light thing,
When my love doth me embrace,
Fair he finds me, in good case,
Then am I in such derray,
Neither harp, nor lyre, nor lay,
Dance nor game, nor rebeck play
　Were so sweet."

Then speak they, say they, tell they the Tale:

Aucassin dwelt in the castle of Torelore, in great ease and great delight, for that he had with him Nicolete his sweet love, whom he loved so well. Now while he was in such pleasure and such delight, came a troop of Saracens by sea, and laid siege to the castle and took it by main strength. Anon took they the substance that was therein and carried off the men and maidens captives. They seized Nicolete and Aucassin, and bound Aucassin hand and foot, and cast him into one ship, and Nicolete into another. Then rose there a mighty wind over sea, and scattered the ships. Now that ship wherein was Aucassin, went wandering on the sea, till it came to the castle of Biaucaire, and the folk of the country ran together to wreck her, and there found they Aucassin, and they knew him again. So when they of Biaucaire saw their damoiseau, they made great joy of him, for Aucassin had dwelt full three years in the castle of Torelore, and his father and mother were dead. So the people took him to the castle of Biaucaire, and there were they all his men. And he held the land in peace.

. . . . . .

Now leave we Aucassin, and speak we of Nicolete. The ship wherein she was cast pertained to the King of Carthage, and he was her father, and she had twelve brothers, all princes or kings. When they beheld Nicolete, how fair she was, they did her great worship, and made much joy of her, and many times asked her who she was, for surely seemed she a lady of noble line and high parentry. But she might not tell them of her lineage, for she was but a child when men stole her away. So sailed they till they won the City of Carthage, and when Nicolete saw the walls of the castle, and the country-side, she knew that there had she been nourished and thence stolen away, being but a child. Yet was she not so young a child but that well she knew she had been daughter of the King of Carthage; and of her nurture in that City.

Here one singeth:

Nicolete the good and true
To the land hath come anew,
Sees the palaces and walls,
And the houses and the halls!
Then she spake and said, "Alas!
That of birth so great I was,
Cousin of the Amiral
And the very child of him
Carthage counts King of Paynim,
Wild folk hold me here withal;
Nay, Aucassin, love of thee
Gentle knight, and true, and free,
Burns and wastes the heart of me.
Ah, God grant it of his grace,
That thou hold me, and embrace,
That thou kiss me on the face
  Love and lord!"

Then speak they, say they, tell they the Tale:

When the King of Carthage heard Nicolete speak in this wise, he cast his arms about her neck.

"Fair sweet love," saith he, "tell me who thou art, and be not adread of me."

"Sir," said she, "I am daughter to the King of Carthage, and was taken, being then a little child, it is now fifteen years gone."

When all they of the court heard her speak thus, they knew well that she spake sooth: so made they great joy of her, and led her to the castle in great honor, as the King's daughter. And they would have given her to her lord a King of Paynim, but she had no mind to marry. There dwelt she three days or four. And she considered by that means she might seek for Aucassin. Then she got her a viol, and learned to play on it, till they would have married her on a day to a great King of Paynim, and she stole forth by night, and came to the seaport, and dwelt with a poor woman thereby. Then took she a certain herb, and therewith smeared her head and her face, till she was all brown and stained. And she let make coat, and mantle, and smock, and hose, and attired herself as if she had been a harper. So took she the viol and went to a mariner, and so wrought on him that he took her aboard his vessel. Then hoisted they sail, and fared on the high seas even till they came to the land of Provence. And Nicolete went forth and took the viol, and went playing through all that country, even till she came to the castle of Biaucaire, where Aucassin lay.

Here one singeth:

At Biaucaire below the tower
Sat Aucassin, on an hour,
Heard the bird, and watched the flower,
With his barons him beside,
Then came on him in that tide,
The sweet influence of love
And the memory thereof;
Thought of Nicolete the fair,
And the dainty face of her
He had loved so many years,
Then was he in dule and tears!
Even then came Nicolete
On the stair a foot she set,
And she drew the viol bow
Through the strings and chanted so;
"Listen, lords and knights, to me,
Lords of high or low degree,
To my story list will ye
All of Aucassin and her
That was Nicolete the fair?
And their love was long to tell
Deep woods through he sought her well,
Paynims took them on a day
In Torelore and bound they lay.

Of Aucassin naught know we,
But fair Nicolete the free
Now in Carthage doth she dwell,
There her father loves her well,
Who is king of that countrie.
Her a husband hath he found,
Paynim lord that serves Mahound!
Ne'er with him the maid will go,
For she loves a damoiseau,
Aucassin, that ye may know,
Swears to God that never mo
With a lover she will go
Save with him she loveth so
    In long desire."

So speak they, say they, tell they the Tale:

When Aucassin heard Nicolete speak in this wise, he was right joyful, and drew her on one side, and spoke, saying:

"Sweet fair friend, know ye nothing of this Nicolete, of whom ye have thus sung?"

"Yea, Sir, I know her for the noblest creature, and the most gentle, and the best that ever was born on ground. She is daughter to the King of Carthage that took her there where Aucassin was taken, and brought her into the city of Carthage, till he knew that verily she was his own daughter, whereon he made right great mirth. Anon wished he to give her for her lord one of the greatest kings of all Spain, but she would rather let herself be hanged or burned, than take any lord. how great soever."

"Ha! fair sweet friend," quoth the Count Aucassin, "if thou wilt go into that land again, and bid her come and speak to me, I will give thee of my substance, more than thou wouldst dare to ask or take. And know ye, that for the sake of her, I have no will to take a wife, howsoever high her lineage. So wait I for her, and never will I have a wife, but her only. And if I knew where to find her, no need would I have to seek her."

"Sir," quoth she, "if ye promise me that, I will go in quest of her for your sake, and for hers, that I love much."

So he sware to her, and anon let give her twenty livres, and she departed from him, and he wept for the sweetness of Nicolete. And when she saw him weeping, she said:

"Sir, trouble not thyself so much withal. For in a little while shall I have brought her into this city, and ye shall see her."

When Aucassin heard that, he was right glad thereof. And she departed from him, and went into the city to the house of the Captain's wife, for the Captain her father in God was dead. So she dwelt there, and told all her tale; and the Captain's wife knew her, and knew well that she was Nicolete that she herself had nourished. Then she let wash and bathe her, and there rested she eight full days. Then took she an herb that was named *Eyebright* and anointed herself therewith, and was as fair as ever she had been all the days of her life. Then she clothed herself in rich robes of silk whereof the lady had great store, and then sat herself in the chamber on a silken coverlet, and called the lady and bade her go and bring Aucassin her love, and she did even so. And when she came to the Palace she found Aucassin weeping, and making lament for Nicolete his love, for that she delayed so long. And the lady spake unto him and said:

"Aucassin, sorrow no more, but come thou on with me, and I will shew thee the thing in the world that thou lovest best; even Nicolete thy dear love, who from far lands hath come to seek of thee." And Aucassin was right glad.

Here singeth one:

When Aucassin heareth now
That his lady bright of brow
Dwelleth in his own countrie,
Never man was glad as he.
To her castle doth he hie
With the lady speedily,
Passeth to the chamber high,
Findeth Nicolete thereby.
Of her true love found again
Never maid was half so fain.
Straight she leaped upon her feet;
When his love he saw at last,
Arms about her did he cast,
Kissed her often, kissed her sweet
Kissed her lips and brows and eyes.
Thus all night do they devise,
Even till the morning white.
Then Aucassin wedded her,
Made her Lady of Biaucaire.
Many years abode they there,
Many years in shade or sun,
In great gladness and delight.
Ne'er hath Aucassin regret
Nor his lady Nicolete.
Now my story all is done,
    Said and sung!

ABELARD AND HELOISE

Heloise to Abelard

To her Lord, her Father, her Husband, her Brother; his Servant, his Child, his Wife, his Sister, and to express all that is humble, respectful and loving to her Abelard, Heloise writes this.

A consolatory letter of yours to a friend happened some days since to fall into my hands; my knowledge of the writing and my love of the hand gave me the curiosity to open it. In justification of the liberty I took, I flattered myself I might claim a sovereign privilege over everything which came from you. Nor was I scrupulous to break through the rules of good breeding when I was to hear news of Abelard. But how dear did my curiosity cost me! What disturbance did it occasion, and how surprised I was to find the whole letter filled with a particular and melancholy account of our misfortunes! I met with my name a hundred times; I never saw it without fear—some heavy calamity always followed it. I saw yours too, equally unhappy.

These mournful but dear remembrances put my heart into such violent motion that I thought it was too much to offer comfort to a friend for a few slight disgraces, but such extraordinary means as the representation of our sufferings and revolutions. What reflections did I not make! I began to consider the whole afresh, and perceived myself pressed with the same weight of grief as when we first began to be miserable. Though length of time ought to have closed up my wounds, yet the seeing them described by your hand was sufficient to make them all open and bleed afresh. . . .

My tears, which I could not restrain, have blotted half your letter; I wish they had effaced the whole, and that I had returned it to you in that condition; I should then have been satisfied with the little time I kept it; but it was demanded of me too soon.

I must confess I was much easier in my mind before I read your letter. Surely all the misfortunes of lovers are conveyed to them through the eyes: upon reading your letter I feel all mine renewed. I reproached myself for having been so long without venting my sorrows, when the rage of our unrelenting enemies still burns with the same fury.

Since length of time, which disarms the strongest hatred, seems but to aggravate theirs; since it is decreed that your virtue shall be persecuted till it takes refuge in the grave—and even then, perhaps, your ashes will not be allowed to rest in peace!—let me always meditate on your calamities, let me publish them through all the world, if possible, to shame an age that has not known how to value you. . . .

Let me have a faithful account of all that concerns you; I would know everything, be it ever so unfortunate. Perhaps by mingling my sighs with yours I may make your sufferings less, for it is said that all sorrows divided are made lighter.

Tell me not by way of excuse you will spare me tears; the tears of women shut up in a melancholy place and devoted to penitence are not to be spared. And if you wait for an opportunity to write pleasant and agreeable things to us, you will delay writing too long. Prosperity seldom chooses the side of the virtuous, and fortune is so blind that in a crowd in which there is perhaps but one wise and brave man it is not to be expected that she should single him out. Write to me then immediately and wait not for miracles; they are too scarce, and we too much accustomed to misfortunes to expect a happy turn. I shall always have this, if you please, and this will always be agreeable to me, that when I receive any letter from you I shall know you still remember me. . . .

I have your picture in my room; I never pass it without stopping to look at it; and yet when you are present with me I scarce ever cast my eyes on it. If a picture, which is but a mute representation of an object, can give such pleasure, what cannot letters inspire? They have souls; they can speak; they have in them all that force which expresses the transports of the heart; they have all the fire of our passions, they can raise them as much as if the persons themselves were present; they have all the tenderness and the delicacy of speech, and sometimes even a boldness of expression beyond it.

We may write to each other; so innocent a pleasure is not denied us. Let us not lose through negligence the only happiness which is left us, and the only one perhaps which the malice of our enemies can never ravish from us. I shall read that you are my husband and you shall see me sign myself your wife. In spite of all our misfortunes

Abelard (1079-1142), Heloise (1101?-1164?).

you may be what you please in your letter. Letters were first invented for consoling such solitary wretches as myself. Having lost the substantial pleasures of seeing and possessing you, I shall in some measure compensate this loss by the satisfaction I shall find in your writing. There I shall read your most sacred thoughts; I shall carry them always about with me, I shall kiss them every moment; if you can be capable of any jealousy let it be for the fond caresses I shall bestow upon your letters, and envy only the happiness of those rivals.

That writing may be no trouble to you, write always to me carelessly and without study; I had rather read the dictates of the heart than of the brain. I cannot live if you will not tell me that you still love me; but that language ought to be so natural to you, that I believe you cannot speak otherwise to me without violence to yourself. And since by this melancholy relation to your friend you have awakened all my sorrows, 'tis but reasonable you should allay them by some tokens of your unchanging love. . . .

You cannot but remember (for lovers cannot forget) with what pleasure I have passed whole days in hearing your discourse. How when you were absent I shut myself from everyone to write to you; how uneasy I was till my letter had come to your hands; what artful management it required to engage messengers. This detail perhaps surprises you, and you are in pain for what may follow. But I am no longer ashamed that my passion had no bounds for you, for I have done more than all this. I have hated myself that I might love you. I came hither to ruin myself in a perpetual imprisonment that I might make you live quietly and at ease.

Nothing but virtue, joined to a love perfectly disengaged from the senses, could have produced such effects. Vice never inspires anything like this: it is too much enslaved to the body. When we love pleasures we love the living and not the dead. We leave off burning with desire for those who can no longer burn for us. This was my cruel uncle's notion; he measured my virtue by the frailty of my sex, and thought it was the man and not the person I loved. But he has been guilty to no purpose. I love you more than ever; and so revenge myself on him. I will still love you with all the tenderness of my soul till the last moment of my life. If, formerly, my affection for you was not so pure, if in those days both mind and body loved you, I often told you even then that I was more pleased with possessing your heart than with any other happi-

ness, and the man was the thing I least valued in you.

You cannot but be entirely persuaded of this by the extreme unwillingness I showed to marry you, though I knew that the name of wife was honorable in the world and holy in religion; yet the name of your mistress had greater charms because it was more free. The bonds of matrimony, however honorable, still bear with them a necessary engagement, and I was very unwilling to be necessitated to love always a man who would perhaps not always love me. I despised the name of wife that I might live happy with that of mistress; and I find by your letter to your friend you have not forgot that delicacy of passion which loved you always with the utmost tenderness—and yet wished to love you more!

You have very justly observed in your letter that I esteemed those public engagements insipid which form alliances only to be dissolved by death, and which put life and love under the same unhappy necessity. But you have not added how often I have protested that it was infinitely preferable to me to live with Abelard as his mistress than with any other as Empress of the World. I was more happy in obeying you than I should have been as lawful spouse of the King of the Earth. Riches and pomp are not the charm of love. True tenderness makes us separate the lover from all that is external to him, and setting aside his position, fortune, or employments, consider him merely as himself. . . .

It is not love, but the desire of riches and position which makes a woman run into the embraces of an indolent husband. Ambition, and not affection, forms such marriages. I believe indeed they may be followed with some honors and advantages, but I can never think that this is the way to experience the pleasures of affectionate union, nor to feel those subtle and charming joys when hearts long parted are at last united. These martyrs of marriage pine always for larger fortunes which they think they have missed. The wife sees husbands richer than her own, and the husband wives better portioned than his. Their mercenary vows occasion regret, and regret produces hatred. Soon they part—or else desire to. This restless and tormenting passion for gold punishes them for aiming at other advantages by love than love itself.

If there is anything that may properly be called happiness here below, I am persuaded it is the union of two persons who love each other with perfect liberty, who are united by a secret inclination, and satisfied with each other's merits. Their hearts are full and leave no vacancy for any other passion; they enjoy perpetual tranquillity because they enjoy content. . . .

What rivalries did your gallantries of this kind occasion me! How many ladies lay claim to them? 'Twas a tribute their self-love paid to their beauty. How many have I seen with sighs declare their passion for you when, after some common visit you had made them, they chanced to be complimented for the Sylvia of your poems. Others in despair and envy have reproached me that I had no charms but what your wit bestowed on me, nor in anything the advantage over them but in being beloved by you. Can you believe me if I tell you, that notwithstanding my sex, I thought myself peculiarly happy in having a lover to whom I was obliged for my charms; and took a secret pleasure in being admired by a man who, when he pleased, could raise his mistress to the character of a goddess. Pleased with your glory only, I read with delight all those praises you offered me, and without reflecting how little I deserved, I believed myself such as you described, that I might be more certain that I pleased you.

But oh! where is that happy time? I now lament my lover, and of all my joys have nothing but the painful memory that they are past. Now learn, all you my rivals who once viewed my happiness with jealous eyes, that he you once envied me can never more be mine. I loved him; my love was his crime and the cause of his punishment. My beauty once charmed him; pleased with each other, we passed our brightest days in tranquillity and happiness. If that were a crime, 'tis a crime I am yet fond of, and I have no other regret save that against my will I must now be innocent.

But what do I say? My misfortune was to have cruel relatives whose malice destroyed the calm we enjoyed; had they been reasonable I had now been happy in the enjoyment of my dear husband. Oh! how cruel were they when their blind fury urged a villain to surprise you in your sleep! Where was I—where was your Heloise then? What joy should I have had in defending my lover; I would have guarded you from violence at the expense of my life. Oh! whither does this excess of passion hurry me? Here love is shocked and modesty deprives me of words.

But tell me whence proceeds your neglect of me since my being professed? You know nothing moved me to it but your disgrace, nor did I give my consent, but yours. Let me hear what is the occasion of your coldness, or give me leave to tell you now my opinion. Was it not the sole thought of pleasure which engaged you to me? And has not my tenderness, by leaving you nothing to wish for, extinguished your desires?

Wretched Heloise! you could please when you wished to avoid it; you merited incense when you could remove to a distance the hand that offered it: but since your heart has been softened and has yielded, since you have devoted and sacrificed yourself, you are deserted and forgotten!

I am convinced by a sad experience that it is natural to avoid those to whom we have been too much obliged, and that uncommon generosity causes neglect rather than gratitude. My heart surrendered too soon to gain the esteem of the conqueror; you took it without difficulty and threw it aside with ease. But ungrateful as you are I am no consenting party to this, and though I ought not to retain a wish of my own, yet I still preserve secretly the desire to be loved by you.

When I pronounced my sad vow I then had about me your last letters in which you protested your whole being wholly mine, and would never live but to love me. It is to you therefore I have offered myself; you had my heart and I had yours; do not demand anything back. You must bear with my passion as a thing which of right belongs to you, and from which you can be no ways disengaged.

Alas! what folly it is to talk in this way! I see nothing here but marks of the Deity, and I speak of nothing but man! You have been the cruel occasion of this by your conduct, unfaithful one! Ought you at once to break off loving me! Why did you not deceive me for a while rather than immediately abandon me? If you had given me at least some faint signs of a dying passion I would have favored the deception. But in vain do I flatter myself that you could be constant; you have left no vestige of an excuse for you. I am earnestly desirous to see you, but if that be impossible I will content myself with a few lines from your hand.

Is it so hard for one who loves to write? I ask for none of your letters filled with learning and writ for your reputation; all I desire is such letters as the heart dictates, and which the hand cannot transcribe fast enough. How did I deceive myself with hopes that you would be wholly mine when I took the veil, and engaged myself to live forever under your laws? For in being professed I vowed no more than to be yours only, and I forced myself voluntarily to a confinement which you desired for me. Death only then can make me leave the cloister where you have placed me; and then my ashes shall rest here and wait for yours in order to show to the very last my obedience and devotion to you.

Why should I conceal from you the secret of my call? You know it was neither zeal nor devotion that brought me here. Your conscience is too faithful a witness to permit you to disown it. Yet here I am, and here I will remain; to this place an unfortunate love and a cruel relation have condemned me. But if you do not continue your concern for me, if I lose your affection, what have I gained by my imprisonment? What recompense can I hope for? The unhappy consequences of our love and your disgrace have made me put on the habit of chastity, but I am not penitent of the past. Thus I strive and labor in vain. Among those who are wedded to God I am wedded to a man; among the heroic supporters of the Cross I am the slave of a human desire; at the head of a religious community I am devoted to Abelard alone.

What a monster am I! Enlighten me, O Lord, for I know not if my despair of Thy grace draws these words from me! I am, I confess, a sinner, but one who, far from weeping for her sins, weeps only for her lover; far from abhorring her crimes, longs only to add to them; and who, with a weakness unbecoming my state, please myself continually with the remembrance of past delights when it is impossible to renew them.

Good God! What is all this? I reproach myself for my own faults, I accuse you for yours, and to what purpose? Veiled as I am, behold in what a disorder you have plunged me! How difficult it is to fight for duty against inclination. I know what obligations this veil lays upon me, but I feel more strongly what power an old passion has over my heart. . . .

Oh, for pity's sake help a wretch to renounce her desires—her self—and if possible even to renounce you! If you are a lover—a father, help a mistress, comfort a child! These tender names must surely move you; yield either to pity or to love. If you gratify my request I shall continue a religious, and without longer profaning my calling.

I am ready to humble myself with you to the wonderful goodness of God, who does all things for our sanctification, who by His grace purifies all that is vicious and corrupt, and by the great riches of His mercy draws us against our wishes, and by degrees opens our eyes to behold His bounty which at first we could not perceive. . . .

A heart which has loved as mine cannot soon be indifferent. We fluctuate long between love and hatred before we can arrive at tranquillity, and we always flatter ourselves with some forlorn hope that we shall not be utterly forgotten.

Yes, Abelard, I conjure you by the chains I bear here to ease the weight of them, and make them as agreeable as I would they were to me. Teach me the maxims of Divine Love; since you have forsaken me I would glory in being wedded to Heaven. My heart adores that title and disdains any other; tell me how this Divine Love is nourished, how it works, how it purifies.

When we were tossed on the ocean of the world we could hear of nothing but your verses, which published everywhere our joys and pleasures. Now we are in the haven of grace is it not fit you should discourse to me of this new happiness, and teach me everything that might heighten or improve it? Show me the same complaisance in my present condition as you did when we were in the world. Without changing the ardor of our affections let us change their objects; let us leave our songs and sing hymns; let us lift up our hearts to God and have no transports but for His glory!

I expect this from you as a thing you cannot refuse me. God has a peculiar right over the hearts of great men He has created. When He pleases to touch them He ravishes them, and lets them not speak nor breathe but for His glory. Till that moment of grace arrives, O think of me—do not forget me—remember my love and fidelity and constancy: love me as your mistress, cherish me as your child, your sister, your wife! Remember I still love you, and yet strive to avoid loving you. What a terrible saying is this! I shake with horror, and my heart revolts against what I say. I shall blot all my paper with tears. I end my long letter wishing you, if you desire it (would to Heaven I could!), forever adieu!

Abelard to Heloise

Could I have imagined that a letter not written to yourself would fall into your hands, I had been more cautious not to have inserted anything in it which might awaken the memory of our past misfortunes. I described with boldness the series of my disgraces to a friend, in order to make him less sensible to a loss he had sustained.

If by this well-meaning device I have disturbed you, I purpose now to dry up those tears which the sad description occasioned you to shed; I intend to mix my grief with yours, and pour out my heart before you: in short, to lay open before your eyes all my trouble, and the secret of my soul, which my vanity has hitherto made me conceal from the rest of the world, and which you now force from me, in spite of my resolutions to the contrary.

It is true, that in a sense of the afflictions which have befallen us, and observing that no change of our condition could be expected; that those prosperous days which had seduced us were now past, and there remained nothing but to erase from our minds, by painful endeavors, all marks and remembrances of them. I had wished to find in philosophy and religion a remedy for my disgrace; I searched out an asylum to secure me from love. I was come to the sad experiment of making vows to harden my heart.

But what have I gained by this? If my passion has been put under a restraint my thoughts yet run free. I promise myself that I will forget you, and yet cannot think of it without loving you. My love is not at all lessened by those reflections I make in order to free myself. The silence I am surrounded by makes me more sensible to its impressions, and while I am unemployed with any other things, this makes itself the business of my whole vocation. Till after a multitude of useless endeavors I begin to persuade myself that it is a superfluous trouble to strive to free myself; and that it is sufficient wisdom to conceal from all but you how confused and weak I am.

I remove to a distance from your person with an intention of avoiding you as an enemy; and yet I incessantly seek for you in my mind; I recall your image in my memory, and in different disquietudes I betray and contradict myself. I hate you! I love you! Shame presses me on all sides.

I am at this moment afraid I should seem more indifferent than you fare, and yet I am ashamed to discover my trouble. How weak are we in ourselves if we do not support ourselves on the Cross of Christ. Shall we have so little courage, and shall that uncertainty of serving two masters which afflicts your heart affect mine too? You see the confusion I am in, how I blame myself and how I suffer.

Religion commands me to pursue virtue since I have nothing to hope for from love. But love still preserves its dominion over my fancies and entertains itself with past pleasures. Memory supplies the place of a mistress. Piety and duty are not always the fruits of retirement; even in deserts, when the dew of heaven falls not on us, we love what we ought no longer to love.

The passions, stirred up by solitude, fill these regions of death and silence; it is very seldom that what ought to be is truly followed here and that God only is loved and served. Had I known this before, I had instructed you better. You call me your master; it is true you were entrusted to my care. I saw you, I was earnest to teach you vain sciences; it cost you your innocence and me my liberty.

Your uncle, who was fond of you, became my enemy and revenged himself on me. If now having lost the power of satisfying my passion I had also lost that of loving you, I should have some consolation. My enemies would have given me that tranquillity which Origen[1] purchased with a crime. How miserable am I! I find myself much more guilty in my thoughts of you, even amidst my tears, than in possessing you when I was in full liberty. I continually think of you; I continually call to mind your tenderness.

In this condition, O Lord! if I run to prostrate myself before your altar, if I beseech you to pity me, why does not the pure flame of the Spirit consume the sacrifice that is offered? Cannot this habit of penitence which I wear interest Heaven to treat me more favorably? But Heaven is still inexorable, because my passion still lives in me; the fire is only covered over with deceitful ashes, and cannot be extinguished but by extraordinary grace. We deceive men, but nothing is hid from God.

You tell me that it is for me you live under that veil which covers you; why do you profane your vocation with such words? Why provoke a jealous God with a blasphemy? I hoped after our separation you would have changed your sentiments; I hoped too that God would have delivered me from the tumult of my senses. We commonly die to the affections of those we see no more, and they to ours; absence is the tomb of love. But to me absence is an unquiet remembrance of what I once loved which continually torments me. I flattered myself that when I should see you no more you would rest in my memory without troubling my mind; that Brittany and the sea would suggest other thoughts; that my fasts and studies would by degrees delete you from my heart. But in spite of severe fasts and redoubled studies, in spite of the distance of three hundred miles which separates us, your image, as you describe yourself in your veil, appears to me and confounds all my resolutions.

What means have I not used! I have armed my hands against myself; I have exhausted my strength in constant exercises; I comment upon Saint Paul; I contend with Aristotle: in short, I do all I used

[1] Origen (185-254), philosopher of Alexandria, whose views gave rise to bitter theological struggles.

to do before I loved you, but all in vain; nothing can be successful that opposes you. Oh! do not add to my miseries by your constancy. . . Why use your eloquence to reproach me for my flight and for my silence? Spare the recital of our assignations and your constant exactness to them; without calling up such disturbing thoughts I have enough to suffer. What great advantages would philosophy give us over other men, if by studying it we could learn to govern our passions? What efforts, what relapses, what agitations do we undergo! And how long are we lost in this confusion, unable to exert our reason, to possess our souls, or to rule our affections? . . .

How can I separate from the person I love, the passion I should detest? Will the tears I shed be sufficient to render it odious to me? I know not how it happens, there is always a pleasure in weeping for a beloved object. It is difficult in our sorrow to distinguish penitence from love. The memory of the crime and the memory of the object which has charmed us are too nearly related to be immediately separated. And the love of God in its beginning does not wholly annihilate the love of the creature.

But what excuses could I not find in you if the crime were excusable? Unprofitable honor, troublesome riches, could never tempt me: but those charms, that beauty, that air, which I yet behold at this instant, have occasioned my fall. Your looks were the beginning of my guilt; your eyes, your discourse, pierced my heart; and in spite of that ambition and glory which tried to make a defense, love was soon the master.

God, in order to punish me, forsook me. You are no longer of the world; you have renounced it: I am a religious devoted to solitude; shall we not take advantage of our condition? Would you destroy my piety in its infant state? Would you have me forsake the abbey into which I am but newly entered? Must I renounce my vows? I have made them in the presence of God; whither shall I fly from His wrath should I violate them? Suffer me to seek ease in my duty. . . .

Regard me no more, I entreat you, as a founder or any great personage; your praises ill agree with my many weaknesses. I am a miserable sinner, prostrate before my Judge, and with my face pressed to the earth I mix my tears with the earth. Can you see me in this posture and solicit me to love you? Come, if you think fit, and in your holy habit thrust yourself between my God and me, and be a wall of separation. Come and force from me

those sighs and thoughts and vows I owe to Him alone. Assist the evil spirits and be the instrument of their malice. What cannot you induce a heart to do whose weakness you so perfectly know?

Nay, withdraw yourself and contribute to my salvation. Suffer me to avoid destruction, I entreat you by our former tender affection and by our now common misfortune. It will always be the highest love to show none; I here release you from all your oaths and engagements. Be God's wholly, to whom you are appropriated; I will never oppose so pious a design. How happy shall I be if I thus lose you! Then shall I indeed be a religious and you a perfect example of an abbess.

Make yourself amends by so glorious a choice; make your virtue a spectacle worthy of men and angels. Be humble among your children, assiduous in your choir, exact in your discipline, diligent in your reading; make even your recreations useful.

Have you purchased your vocation at so light a rate that you should not turn it to the best advantage? Since you have permitted yourself to be abused by false doctrine and criminal instruction, resist not those good counsels which grace and religion inspire me with.

I will confess to you I have thought myself hitherto an abler master to instill vice than to teach virtue. My false eloquence has only set off false good. My heart, drunk with voluptuousness, could only suggest terms proper and moving to recommend that. The cup of sinners overflows with so enchanting a sweetness, and we are naturally so much inclined to taste it, that it needs only to be offered to us.

On the other hand the chalice of saints is filled with a bitter draught and nature starts from it. And yet you reproach me with cowardice for giving it to you first. I willingly submit to these accusations. I cannot enough admire the readiness you showed to accept the religious habit; bear therefore with courage the Cross you so resolutely took up. Drink of the chalice of saints, even to the bottom, without turning your eyes with uncertainty upon me; let me remove far from you and obey the Apostle who hath said "Fly!"

You entreat me to return under a pretense of devotion. Your earnestness in this point creates a suspicion in me and makes me doubtful how to answer you. Should I commit an error here my words would blush, if I may say so, after the history of our misfortunes. The Church is jealous of its honor, and commands that her children should be induced to the practice of virtue by virtuous means. When we approach God in a blameless manner then we may with boldness invite others to Him.

But to forget Heloise, to see her no more, is what Heaven demands of Abelard; and to expect nothing from Abelard, to forget him even as an idea, is what Heaven enjoins on Heloise. To forget, in the case of love, is the most necessary penance, and the most difficult. It is easy to recount our faults; how many, through indiscretion, have made themselves a second pleasure of this instead of confessing them with humility. The only way to return to God is by neglecting the creature we have adored, and adoring the God whom we have neglected. This may appear harsh, but it must be done if we would be saved.

To make it more easy consider why I pressed you to your vow before I took mine; and pardon my sincerity and the design I have of meriting your neglect and hatred if I conceal nothing from you. When I saw myself oppressed by my misfortune I was furiously jealous, and regarded all men as my rivals. Love has more of distrust than assurance. I was apprehensive of many things because of my many defects, and being tormented with fear because of my own example I imagined your heart so accustomed to love that it could not be long without entering on a new engagement. Jealousy can easily believe the most terrible things.

I was desirous to make it impossible for me to doubt you. I was very urgent to persuade you that propriety demanded your withdrawal from the eyes of the world; that modesty and our friendship required it; and that your own safety obliged it. After such a revenge taken on me you could expect to be secure nowhere but in a convent.

I will do you justice, you were very easily persuaded. My jealousy secretly rejoiced in your innocent compliance; and yet, triumphant as I was, I yielded you up to God with an unwilling heart. I still kept my gift as much as was possible, and only parted with it in order to keep it out of the power of other men. I did not persuade you to religion out of any regard to your happiness, but condemned you to it like an enemy who destroys what he cannot carry off. And yet you heard my discourses with kindness, you sometimes interrupted me with tears, and pressed me to acquaint you with those convents I held in the highest esteem. What a comfort I felt in seeing you shut up. I was now at ease and took a satisfaction in considering that you continued no longer in the world after my disgrace, and that you would return to it no more.

But still I was doubtful. I imagined women were incapable of steadfast resolutions unless they were forced by the necessity of vows. I wanted those vows, and Heaven itself for your security, that I might no longer distrust you. Ye holy mansions and impenetrable retreats! from what innumerable apprehensions have ye freed me? Religion and piety keep a strict guard around your grates and walls. What a haven of rest this is to a jealous mind! And with what impatience did I endeavor after it!

I went every day trembling to exhort you to this sacrifice; I admired, without daring to mention it then, a brightness in your beauty which I had never observed before. Whether it was the bloom of a rising virtue, or an anticipation of the great loss I was to suffer, I was not curious in examining the cause, but only hastened your being professed. I engaged your prioress in my guilt by a criminal bribe with which I purchased the right of burying you. The professed of the house were alike bribed and concealed from you, at my directions, all their scruples and disgusts. I omitted nothing, either little or great; and if you had escaped my snares I myself would not have retired; I was resolved to follow you everywhere. The shadow of myself would always have pursued your steps and continually have occasioned either your confusion or your fear, which would have been a sensible gratification to me.

But, thanks to Heaven, you resolved to take the vows. I accompanied you to the foot of the altar, and while you stretched out your hand to touch the sacred cloth I heard you distinctly pronounce those fatal words that forever separated you from man. Till then I thought your youth and beauty would foil my design and force your return to the world. Might not a small temptation have changed you? Is it possible to renounce oneself entirely at the age of two-and-twenty? At an age which claims the utmost liberty could you think the world no longer worth your regard? How much did I wrong you, and what weakness did I impute to you? You were in my imagination both light and inconstant. Would not a woman at the noise of the flames and the fall of Sodom involuntarily look back in pity on some person? I watched your eyes, your every movement, your air; I trembled at everything. You may call such self-interested conduct treachery, perfidy, murder. A love so like to hatred should provoke the utmost contempt and anger.

It is fit you should know that the very moment when I was convinced of your being entirely devoted to me, when I saw you were infinitely worthy of all my love, I imagined I could love you no more. I thought it time to leave off giving you marks of my affection, and I considered that by your Holy Espousals you were now the peculiar care of Heaven, and no longer a charge on me as my wife. My jealousy seemed to be extinguished. When God only is our rival we have nothing to fear; and being in greater tranquillity than ever before I even dared to pray to Him to take you away from my eyes.

But it was not a time to make rash prayers, and my faith did not warrant them being heard. Necessity and despair were at the root of my proceedings, and thus I offered an insult to Heaven rather than a sacrifice. God rejected my offering and my prayer, and continued my punishment by suffering me to continue my love. Thus I bear alike the guilt of your vows and of the passion that preceded them, and must be tormented the rest of my life.

If God spoke to your heart as to that of a religious whose innocence had first asked Him for favors, I should have matter of comfort; but to see both of us the victims of a guilty love, to see this love insult us in our very habits and spoil our devotions, fills me with horror and trembling. Is this a state of reprobation? Or are these the consequences of a long drunkenness in profane love?

We cannot say love is a poison and a drunkenness till we are illuminated by grace; in the meantime it is an evil we dote on. When we are under such a mistake, the knowledge of our misery is the first step towards amendment. Who does not know that 'tis for the glory of God to find no other reason in man for His mercy than man's very weakness? When He has shown us this weakness and we have bewailed it, He is ready to put forth His omnipotence and assist us. Let us say for our comfort that what we suffer is one of those terrible temptations which have sometimes disturbed the vocations of the most holy.

God can grant His presence to men in order to soften their calamities whenever He shall think fit. It was His pleasure when you took the veil to draw you to Him by His grace. I saw your eyes, when you spoke your last farewell, fixed upon the Cross. It was more than six months before you wrote me a letter, nor during all that time did I receive a message from you. I admired this silence, which I durst not blame, but could not imitate. I wrote to you, and you returned me no answer: your heart was then shut, but this garden of the spouse is now opened; He is withdrawn from it and has left you alone.

By removing from you He has made trial of you; call Him back and strive to regain Him. We must have the assistance of God, that we may break our chains; we are too deeply in love to free ourselves.

Our follies have penetrated into the sacred places; our amours have been a scandal to the whole kingdom. They are read and admired; love which produced them has caused them to be described. We shall be a consolation to the failings of youth forever; those who offend after us will think themselves less guilty. We are criminals whose repentance is late; oh, let it be sincere! Let us repair as far as is possible the evils we have done, and let France, which has been the witness of our crimes, be amazed at our repentance. Let us confound all who would imitate our guilt; let us take the side of God against ourselves, and by so doing prevent His judgment.

Our former lapses require tears, shame, and sorrow to expiate them. Let us offer up these sacrifices from our hearts, let us blush and let us weep. If in these feeble beginnings, O Lord, our hearts are not entirely Thine, let them at least feel that they ought to be so.

Deliver yourself, Heloise, from the shameful remains of a passion which has taken too deep root. Remember that the least thought for any other than God is an adultery. If you could see me here with my meager face and melancholy air, surrounded with numbers of persecuting monks, who are alarmed at my reputation for learning and offended at my lean visage, as if I threatened them with a reformation, what would you say of my base sighs and of those unprofitable tears which deceive these credulous men? Alas! I am humbled under love, and not under the Cross. Pity me and free yourself. If your vocation be, as you say, my work, deprive me not of the merit of it by your continual inquietudes.

Tell me you will be true to the habit which covers you by an inward retirement. Fear God, that you may be delivered from your frailties; love Him that you may advance in virtue. Be not restless in the cloister, for it is the peace of saints. Embrace your bands, they are the chains of Christ Jesus; He will lighten them and bear them with you, if you will but accept them with humility.

Without growing severe to a passion that still possesses you, learn from your misery to succor your weak sisters; pity them upon consideration of your own faults. And if any thoughts too natural should importune you, fly to the foot of the Cross and there beg for mercy.

At the head of a religious society be not a slave, and having rule over queens, begin to govern yourself. Blush at the least revolt of your senses. Remember that even at the foot of the altar we often sacrifice to lying spirits, and that no incense can be more agreeable to them than the earthly passion that still burns in the heart of a religious.

If during your abode in the world your soul has acquired a habit of loving, feel it now no more save for Jesus Christ. Repent of all the moments of your life which you have wasted in the world and on pleasure; demand them of me, 'tis a robbery of which I am guilty; take courage and boldly reproach me with it.

I have been indeed your master, but it was only to teach sin. You call me your father; before I had any claim to the title, I deserved that of parricide. I am your brother, but it is the affinity of sin that brings me that distinction. I am called your husband, but it is after a public scandal.

If you have abused the sanctity of so many holy terms in the superscription of your letter to do me honor and flatter your own passion, blot them out and replace them with those of murderer, villain, and enemy, who has conspired against your honor, troubled your quiet, and betrayed your innocence. You would have perished through my means but for an extraordinary act of grace, which, that you might be saved, has thrown me down in the middle of my course.

This is the thought you ought to have of a fugitive who desires to deprive you of the hope of ever seeing him again. But when love has once been sincere how difficult it is to determine to love no more! 'Tis a thousand times more easy to renounce the world than love. I hate this deceitful, faithless world; I think no more of it; but my wandering heart still eternally seeks you, and is filled with anguish at having lost you, in spite of all the powers of my reason. In the meantime, though I should be so cowardly as to retract what you have read, do not suffer me to offer myself to your thoughts save in this last fashion.

Remember my last worldly endeavors were to seduce your heart; you perished by my means and I with you: the same waves swallowed us up. We waited for death with indifference, and the same death had carried us headlong to the same punishments. But Providence warded off the blow, and our shipwreck has thrown us into a haven.

There are some whom God saves by suffering. Let my salvation be the fruit of your prayers; let me owe it to your tears and your exemplary holiness. Though my heart, Lord, be filled with the love of Thy creature, Thy hand can, when it pleases, empty me of all love save for Thee.

To love Heloise truly is to leave her to that quiet which retirement and virtue afford. I have resolved it: this letter shall be my last fault. Adieu.

If I die here I will give orders that my body be carried to the house of the Paraclete. You shall see me in that condition, not to demand tears from you, for it will be too late; weep rather for me now and extinguish the fire which burns me.

You shall see me in order that your piety may be strengthened by horror of this carcass, and my death be eloquent to tell you what you brave when you love a man. I hope you will be willing, when you have finished this mortal life, to be buried near me. Your cold ashes need then fear nothing, and my tomb shall be the more rich and renowned.

SPANISH BALLADS

Abenamar, Abenamar

O thou Moor of *Morería*,
There were mighty signs and aspects
On the day when thou wert born,
Calm and lovely was the ocean,
Bright and full the moon above.   5
Moor, the child of such an aspect
Never ought to answer falsely.
Then replied the Moorish captive,
(You shall hear the Moor's reply):

Nor will I untruly answer,   10
Though I died for saying truth.
I am son of Moorish sire.

My mother was a Christian slave.
In my childhood, in my boyhood,
Often would my mother bid me   15
Never know the liar's shame.
Ask thou, therefore, King, thy question.
Truly will I answer thee.

Thank thee, thank thee, Abenamar,
For thy gentle answer, thanks.   20
What are yonder lofty castles,
Those that shine so bright on high?

That, O King, is the Alhambra,
Yonder is the Mosque of God.

"Abenamar, Abenamar," translated by Robert Southey; "The Lamentation for Celin," by J. G. Lockhart

There you see the Alixares,   25
Works of skill and wonder they;
Ten times ten doubloons the builder
Daily for his hire received;
If an idle day he wasted
Ten times ten doubloons he paid.   30
Farther is the Generalife,
Peerless are its garden groves.
Those are the Vermilion Towers,
Far and wide their fame is known.

Then spake up the King Don Juan   35
(You shall hear the Monarch's speech):
Wouldst thou marry me Granada,
Gladly would I for thy dowry
Cordoba and Seville give.

I am married, King Don Juan.   40
King, I am not yet a widow.
Well I love my noble husband.
Well my wedded Lord loves me.

The Lamentation for Celin

At the gate of old Granada, when all its bolts are
    barred,
At twilight, at the Vega-gate, there is a trampling
    heard;
There is a trampling heard, as of horses treading
    slow,
And a weeping voice of women, and a heavy
    sound of woe!—
"What tower is fallen? what star is set; what chief
    come these bewailing?"   5
"A tower is fallen! a star is set!—Alas! alas for
    Celin!"

Three times they knock, three times they cry,—and
    wide the doors they throw;
Dejectedly they enter, and mournfully they go;
In gloomy lines they mustering stand beneath the
    hollow porch,
Each horseman grasping in his hand a black and
    flaming torch;   10
Wet is each eye as they go by, and all around is
    wailing,—
For all have heard the misery,—"Alas! alas for
    Celin!"

Him yesterday a Moor did slay, of Bencerrage's
    blood,—
'Twas at the solemn jousting,—around the nobles
    stood;
The nobles of the land were by, and ladies bright
    and fair   15

Looked from their latticed windows, the haughty
    sight to share:
But now the nobles all lament,—the ladies are be-
    wailing,—
For he was Granada's darling knight,—"Alas! alas
    for Celin!"

Before him ride his vassals, in order two by two,
With ashes on their turbans spread, most pitiful
    to view;   20
Behind him his four sisters, each wrapped in sable
    veil,
Between the tambour's dismal strokes take up their
    doleful tale;
When stops the muffled drum, ye hear their
    brotherless bewailing,
And all the people, far and near, cry,—"Alas! alas
    for Celin!"

O, lovely lies he on the bier, above the purple pall,
The flower of all Granada's youth, the loveliest of
    them all!   26
His dark, dark eyes are closed, his rosy lip is pale,
The crust of blood lies black and dim upon his
    burnished mail;
And evermore the hoarse tambour breaks in upon
    their wailing,—
Its sound is like no earthly sound,—"Alas! alas for
    Celin!"   30

The Moorish maid at the lattice stands,—the Moor
    stands at his door;
One maid is wringing of her hands, and one is
    weeping sore;
Down to the dust men bow their heads, and ashes
    black they strew
Upon their broidered garments, of crimson, green,
    and blue;
Before each gate the bier stands still,—then bursts
    the loud bewailing,   35
From door and lattice, high and low,—"Alas! alas
    for Celin!"

An old, old woman cometh forth, when she hears
    the people cry,—
Her hair is white as silver, like horn her glazed
    eye;
'Twas she that nursed him at her breast,—that
    nursed him long ago:
She knows not whom they all lament, but soon she
    well shall know!   40
With one deep shriek, she through doth break,
    when her ears receive their wailing,—
"Let me kiss my Celin, ere I die!—Alas! alas for
    Celin!"

PART FOUR

THE RENAISSANCE
AND MODERN WORLD

ITALY AND THE RENAISSANCE

It is not too much to say that the modern world was born in Italy. For three hundred years, from about 1300 to 1600, an intellectually awakened Italy exercised a powerful influence on the rest of Europe in thought, art, and literature, shaping modern outlooks in each of these fields. This period, which we call the Renaissance, has been aptly defined by John Addington Symonds, author of the monumental *Renaissance in Italy*, as "the Middle Ages in dissolution," for the age was transitional. Feudalism was giving way to the modern capitalistic system of free labor, trade, banking, and industrialism. The medieval Church was beginning to lose its hold on the people. As an institution, it was becoming the object of criticism, until even its dogmas were defiantly questioned and large sections of Europe adopted Protestantism. Worldliness replaced the other-worldliness fostered by medieval Catholicism, so that even the papacy was permeated with individualism, the love of splendor, and tolerance of free inquiry. Only when put on the defensive by the Protestant reformation did the Church adopt the policy of reaction and suppression as part of its Counter-Reformation. Men came to be consumed with a passion for self-realization, self-advancement, comfort, luxury, pleasure in themselves, and love of beauty in behavior, costume, art, and literature.

In this spirit, men started to expand the boundaries of the knowable; as early as the thirteenth century travelers to the East, like the famous Marco Polo, began bringing knowledge of remote civilizations, and in the fifteenth century discoverers and conquerors like Columbus and Cortez began annexing a new world to the old. By the fourteenth century, moreover, the men of the Renaissance were turning to classic culture as the repository of the worldly outlook and the free intellect. A new continent of the mind and spirit was zealously recovered by scholars appropriately called Humanists because the literature they explored dealt with human rather than other-worldly experience and aspiration.

The land in which these developments first occurred was politically bewildering. It was divided into numerous principalities and cities, many of them ruled by upstart despots, some of them republics dominated by a mercantile or financial aristocracy like the Medicis of Florence. It was an age of continual struggles and numerous contradictions. But it was essentially favorable to the expansion of the human spirit. The Italian states grew rapidly in wealth and came in frequent contact with the Byzantine world and the East. The political struggles of the period encouraged enterprise and individual self-assertion, the rewards for which were power and wealth. An unstable world could no longer keep men in their place, could no longer fix behavior and thought in a rigid mold, so that new ideas and ventures in art and science began to run riot. Finally, the upstart despots' thirst for fame and desire to display their wealth, along with their effort to publicize themselves, made them patrons of the arts. They built magnificent palaces, commissioned sculptors to glorify them in stone, and painters to immortalize them on canvas, and they attracted scholars and poets to their courts. The leaders of the republics of Venice and Florence, as well as the Popes, were equally affected by this interest in art as a means of enriching life and gratifying the senses.

There arose a cosmopolitan outlook which was well expressed by Dante when he wrote, "My country is the whole world," and by a sixteenth-century minor humanist who declared "Wherever a learned man fixes his seat, there is his home." The idea of progress became a driving force, and the belief in the perfectibility of man filled men with optimism and self-confidence. Men considered themselves capable of unlimited development, and of mastery over every subject: "Men can do all things if they will." Thus was born the "all-sided man" or *l'uomo universale* of Italy so brilliantly exemplified by Leonardo da Vinci, who made all knowledge his province and anticipated many of the achievements of modern science. The age began to recognize a new aristocracy of the intellect, an aristocracy of men whose claim to prominence was not noble birth or piety but good manners and varied accomplishments.

The ferment of this Renaissance was felt in all fields. All the arts began to flourish mightily, until Italy's architects, sculptors, painters, goldsmiths, and musicians took first rank in the modern world. In the history of art few names are as memorable as those of Giotto, Botticelli, Leonardo da Vinci, Michelangelo, Raphael, Titian, and many others. But the men of the age were also remarkably articulate, and created a powerful literature which in turn left its mark on all the modern literatures.

At the crossroads of the medieval and the Renaissance worlds stands the imposing figure of the Florentine poet Dante Alighieri (1265-1321). He was, first and foremost, the child of the medieval world, its greatest poet, and the one writer in whom we find a synthesis of its outlook. In reading his greatest work, *The Divine Comedy,* we take our farewell from the Middle Ages when they are at the peak of their spiritual and creative possibilities. Although he is sensible of the greatness of the classic poets and thinkers, in so far as medieval knowledge enabled him to know their work, he reluctantly relegates them to his *Inferno* or Hell because they did not die in the true faith. Because they were good men, Homer, Horace, Virgil, Plato, Aristotle, Cicero, and the rest live on without torment in the nether regions, but because they lived before the coming of Christianity they are lost through all eternity. Even less enviable is the fate of those Christians who indulged in worldly gratifications; even the pathetic lovers Paolo and Francesca, to whom a modern poet would be very indulgent, are doomed because their passion was illicit. In Dante's lyric verse, the beautiful *Vita Nuova (New Life)*, he continues the troubadour tradition of love poetry and indeed brings it to its ultimate perfection. Although, too, the object of his love is a real person, Bice (Beatrice) Portinari, whom he first met at the age of nine and who died in 1290, his earthly passion is sublimated in a mystic, medieval longing of the soul. He turns from worldly love to "the Love which moves the sun and the other stars." This is Dante's point of view in his *Vita Nuova*, and it is the keystone of the stupendous arch of his major work, *The Divine Comedy,* in which Beatrice leads him through *Purgatory* and *Paradiso* to the highest heaven and the presence of God. Dante finds the final happiness of love in heaven, whereas his successors were to seek it on earth.

Dante's theology is thoroughly medieval. His *Divine Comedy* is an allegory of man's struggle for salvation, which is still for Dante the primary purpose of the human race. The sense of sin and the necessity for purgation weigh heavily upon his soul, and he considers all human conduct with reference to man's life in another world. According to man's conduct and faith during his brief interlude on earth he reaches Hell, Purgatory, or Paradise, and God's justice is terrible to sinners.

The journey that the poet takes is also typically medieval in its cosmology. The world consists of concentric spheres. The earth is the center of the universe, and around it move nine spheres or heavens at increasing speeds in proportion to their distance. Man is thus the center of the created world and of the divine scheme. The ninth sphere, the *Primum Mobile*, is a crystalline sphere and imparts movement to the other spheres. Encircling them all is the motionless, timeless, and infinite Empyrean, which is the seat of God. The fall of Lucifer produced a cone-shaped cavity in the earth with its apex at the center of the planet. This is Hell, divided into nine circles, each reserved for different types of sinners, who are nearer to Satan at the apex in proportion to the gravity of their sins. When Hell was created, the displaced mass of earth formed a mountain—the mountain of Purgatory, arranged in seven circles, on top of which is the Earthly Paradise that Adam and Eve inhabited before their fall. On this mountain penitent sinners, who have been spared the fires of Hell, are cleansed of their sins by the fires of Purgatory until they are ready to enter Heaven, which is divided into various spheres of ascending sublimity until one reaches the Empyrean.

In its literary form, too, the *Divine Comedy* belongs to the Middle Ages. It is an allegorical poem, making use of such medieval devices as the dream vision, symbolical figures, and mystic number. The work consists of one hundred cantos or chapters, thirty-four in the *Inferno* and thirty-three in both the *Purgatorio* and the *Paradiso*. Since the first canto of the *Inferno* is an introduction to the entire work, there are ninety-nine cantos for the three divisions. Ninety-nine is a multiple of the two mystic numbers, nine and three. Dante's verse form, too, has a mystic attribute; the poem is written in a meter of three linked lines, known as *terza rima*. The Middle Ages are, thus, commemorated in a Christian epic, august, severe, and mystical. *The Divine Comedy* takes one's breath away with its solemn and remote majesty.

However, Dante stood at the dividing of the ways and was a dual personality. In the very process of immortalizing the medieval outlook, he could not avoid reflecting the slowly rising new world. Dante, the son of a noble family, received an excellent worldly education, mastered the accomplishments of a gentleman, and led the life of a gallant rather than an ascetic, even succumbing to debauchery that he regretted in later years. He lived in the most thriving and progressive of the Italian states, and the Florence he knew was replete with worldly interests and political struggles. So was the whole of Italy, then torn between the faction known as the Neri, or Blacks, which defended the temporal power of the Pope, and the Bianchi, or Whites, who championed the rule of a strong emperor. The poet of the transitional worldview joined the Bianchi, and became so involved in his cause, fighting in two crucial battles, that he was exiled from Florence in 1301 when his party was defeated. He spent the rest of his life wandering from city to city, eating, as he said, the bread of strangers, but being treated with honor especially by the ruler of Ravenna, who even sent him on an embassy to Venice. Dante therefore saw a great deal of a life remote from both medieval monasticism and romantic chivalry. It was this life, refracted by his intensely partisan temperament, that he poured into his *Divine Comedy*, especially into the *Inferno*, dooming the politicians and popes he disliked to perdition and describing countless personalities and worldly conduct with vivid power.

For a mystic poem, Dante's masterpiece is remarkably full of the business and passions of the world. These may be condemned by the author, but he is deeply involved with them. No poet was more sensible of the struggle for worldly power and for personal gratification, and he draws not types but individuals in his gallery of sinners. His interest in the world even led him to write a Latin book on the nature of government, *De Monarchia*, in which he proposed to limit the power of the papacy to the spiritual sphere. It is also significant that he paid such reverence to a classic, pagan author when he called Virgil his master and made him his guide in the *Inferno*.

The beginnings of the Renaissance are also strongly present in Dante's attitude toward literary language and style. At a time when Latin was still regarded as the only proper language for dignified letters, he became the champion and leading exponent of the Italian language. He defended its use for all important literary work in his Latin treatise *De Vulgari Eloquentia*, and set his fellow-writers the all-important example of writing a work of such high seriousness as *The Divine Comedy* in Italian. By devoting himself to the creation of a pleasurable, sweet new style, he foreshadowed, in addition, the Renaissance love of fine artistry.

When Dante died in exile and a professorship was established in Florence for the study of his work, a post first held by none other than Boccaccio, he was honored not as a medieval figure but as the father of Italian literature. Moreover, the two men who were his immediate successors, Petrarch and Boccaccio, quickly made themselves leaders of the new age.

Francesco Petrarca, or Petrarch (1304-1374), became the first Humanist. His father was one of the men who were exiled from Florence when Dante was banished, and moved to Avignon in Southern France. Petrarch grew up in Southern France and studied at Montpellier and Bologna. Later, finding himself penniless he entered the Church, but this was a formality rather than an act of piety. He became a man of affairs, went on diplomatic missions, and later was involved in patriotic activities. His interest in the classic world and pagan culture made him dream of the resurrection of Rome.

Petrarch turned hungrily to the classics, and his uniqueness lay in his seeking in them esthetic gratifications and human values instead of material for theological disputation; it is this attitude that distinguishes him from medieval scholars. He began a search for Greek and Latin manuscripts, making frequent and arduous journeys for this purpose. Cicero was his special delight, and he actually recovered some of the letters to Atticus. Moreover, he was the first to realize the importance of Greece, to recognize fully that Greek culture underlay Roman. He bought a copy of the *Iliad* from a Greek traveler, but was unable to read it, and was distressed to find that there were no grammars and dictionaries to which one could resort. Thereupon he prevailed upon his wealthy friend Boccaccio to take a Greek into his household in Florence and employ him to translate the *Iliad* into Latin. It was a very poor translation, but it was a move toward the recovery of Hellenic culture, and Petrarch became indefatigable in promoting humanist studies and prevailing upon Italian princes to foster them. Numerous Greek and Roman manuscripts were gradually recovered and edited after his death. Soon, too, classic scholarship was vastly improved by Greek scholars who found hospitality in Italy and refuge there after Constantinople fell to the Turks in 1453. It was not long before many Italians set themselves up as missionaries of the recovered culture.

Petrarch overrated his Latin epic *Africa* and wished to be remembered as a humanist and scholar. He attached less importance to his writings in Italian, but it is these that ensure him his lasting fame. At the age of twenty-three, in Avignon he fell in love with a young married woman, immortalized by him under the name of Laura. His absorption in this attachment became a veritable obsession, and he continued to nurse an unrequited passion for her for many years, always returning to Avignon from his numerous travels during Laura's lifetime. The gain to all literature was considerable, for Laura became the subject of over three hundred Italian sonnets of remarkable purity and perfection, as well as other short lyrics and one long poem written by Petrarch in imitation of *The Divine Comedy*.

The sonnet form which Petrarch perfected and popularized became the chief lyric form of the Renaissance in Europe. In Shakespeare's England it was altered, but in its new shape it became the mold for the finest lyric expression of the Elizabethan poets.[1] Petrarch's uses of conceits and his idealization of an unapproachable married woman belonged to the medieval convention. But the frequent naturalness of his expression was a new quality, and he used Laura as the focus of a great delight in beauty.

Even more typically a man of the Renaissance was Petrarch's friend Boccaccio (1313-1375). Petrarch sought seclusion, retiring in his last years, dreaming of a humanist monastery, and becoming religious after the death of Laura. He did not take wholeheartedly to the creation of a literature in the vernacular, and treated love with fervid idealization as did Dante. Boccaccio was wholly of this world. The love-child of a French mother and a Florentine banker-father who tried to dissuade him from the pursuit of letters, Boccaccio became a gay and reckless youth, and won the love of the married woman and natural daughter of King Robert of Naples whom he celebrated under the name of Fiammeta.

After his father's death in the plague of 1348, Boccaccio began to write steadily and freely and threw himself into the humanist movement, joining his friend Petrarch in the zealous search for manuscripts and the promotion of Greek studies.

Boccaccio's literary work expressed his exuberance, his enjoyment of pleasure and love, and the insight he acquired into the manners and character of men and women. In his writings we can observe medieval interests receding steadily. His first work, the prose tale *Filicopo*, was a knightly romance, and his next, the *Teseide*, the story of Palamon and Arcite which Chaucer imitated in *The Knight's Tale*, is still essentially medieval. Although his poem *Filostrato*, which recounts the story of Troilus and Cressida, is more modern in spirit, it is fairly conventional, and is best remembered as Chaucer's source for Chaucer's *Troilus and Criseyde*. But Boccaccio's *Fiammeta*, in which he tells the story of his very mundane love, has been properly called "the first novel of psychology ever written in Europe"; and climaxing Boccaccio's development, his *Decameron*, which appeared in

---

[1] See p. 1139 for a discussion of the two principal sonnet forms, the Italian, or Petrarchan, and the Shakespearean. All sonnets have 14 lines of iambic pentameter. The Italian has a rhyme scheme of *a b b a a b b a* for the first 8 lines (octave) and a variety of orders for the last 6. Usually there is a thought division at the end of the octave.

1353, is Europe's first truly modern prose narrative.

This collection of one hundred stories is tied together by a frame, such as Chaucer employed in *The Canterbury Tales*. To escape the plague in Florence, three young men and seven young women seclude themselves in a villa in the country, and entertain themselves for ten days by telling stories. Drawn from a variety of sources, from the realistic and satirical *fabliaux*, folk material, and current anecdotes, the work is a veritable panorama of life. Whether the stories deal with love, philandering, or adventure, they are invariably well turned and full of keen observation. Many of them are light-hearted, mocking, and irreverent, reflecting a young world that is taking flight from the Middle Ages. Although there is pathos in some of the tales, there is no medieval gloom in them. The spirit of the whole work is fresh, kindly, and genial.

The influence of this book cannot be overestimated. It made its way into France, Germany, Spain, and England; and many Italian writers followed Boccaccio in composing and grouping short stories. These were called *novellas*, from which we derived the word "novel." Some fifty writers of *novellas* appeared in Italy after Boccaccio. Many Elizabethan playwrights, including Shakespeare, became indebted to them for their plots.

About a century of humanist activity had to be consumed by the literati before important literary figures again arose in Italy, and indeed even the fifteenth and the sixteenth centuries brought forth no writers of such world-wide significance as Dante, Petrarch, and Boccaccio. The two excellent poets Ludovico Ariosto (1474-1533), author of the knightly romance *Orlando Furioso*, and Torquato Tasso (1544-1595), author of a romance about the Crusades, *Jerusalem Delivered,* did not reflect the vital aspects of their period. The latter part of the Italian Renaissance was given over largely to politics, the fine arts, and scientific beginnings.

Niccolò Machiavelli (1469-1527), being a rounded personality, wrote verses, a *History of Florence*, a brilliant satirical story *Belphagor*, and several plays, including the clever and obscene *Mandragola* which is the best comedy of the Italian Renaissance. But it is as a political theorist that he shone most brightly and exerted the greatest influence. He served the republic of Florence for eight years until he was dismissed from office when the Medicis returned to power in 1512. An ardent patriot, he dreamed of the unification of all Italy

under a strong leader. He thought he found such a man in the notorious Cesare Borgia, whose ruthless methods were for a time effective in unifying portions of Italy.

Cesare's methods did not appall Machiavelli, because like most men of his time he believed that the end justified the means, and because he prided himself on his realism. In *The Prince*, Machiavelli set himself the task of recording with complete objectivity the political policies that got the best results. He recommended nothing that was not being practiced in Italy. Unfortunately, there have been leaders since his day who have applied his theories only too literally, without intending or achieving the benefits he expected. The truth is that his range of observation was too narrow to enable him to find other methods than those he recorded. Moreover, in the *Prince*, as the liberal historian Macaulay noted, "The great principle, that societies and laws exist only for the purpose of increasing the sum of private happiness, is not recognized with sufficient clearness." Machiavelli was so devoted to the ideal of stability in society that he made stability an end in itself and thought only of the welfare of the state. Macaulay wisely comments: "Of all political fallacies, this has had the widest and the most mischievous operation."

However, the *Prince* and another political study by Machiavelli, the *Discourses,* mark the beginning of modern political science. He took the study of politics out of the realm of moral preachment and abstruse speculation. Henceforth this study was to concentrate on social realities, on the factors that operate in political life because men are what they are, follow certain motives, and respond in certain ways. *The Prince,* moreover, deserves the high place it holds in literature because it gives vivid expression to its age and is written with brilliant realism. At the same time, those who read it in its entirety will find in it passages of eloquent nobility and keen analyses of human conduct.

Benvenuto Cellini (1500-1571) reflected the artistic and personal side of the Italian Renaissance in his naïvely frank *Autobiography*. His was by no means the only or even the important record of Italy's absorption in the arts. For a contemporary account of the painters of the times we would have to turn to Vasari's famous, if inadequate, *Lives of the Painters*. Besides, Cellini himself was only a minor artist. But in reading the autobiography of this Florentine master goldsmith and sculptor we get the most vivid eye-witness report on the behavior and spirit of his times. He was a man of inflammable temperament, an egotist, a ruffian, an immoral adventurer—and an artist, with an artist's pride in his work and interest in the details of his craft. He was twice banished from Florence before he was eighteen for duelling and brawling, and twice imprisoned by Pope Paul III for appropriating some gold from the papal jewelry. His *Autobiography* reads like a novel of adventure, and Cellini appears in it as a character who sums up the best and worst features of Renaissance man's individualism.

Since the modern world to which the Renaissance gave birth cannot be separated from modern science, it is fitting to conclude our account with Giordano Bruno, the poet of modern science. Science does not often express itself in great literature, and the selection from Bruno is given primarily as background material for the student. Giordano Bruno (1548-1600), who was burned at the stake by the Church, became the spokesman of a new view of the world. The Middle Ages considered the earth the center of the universe. The new science of cosmology begun by Copernicus and later developed by the German Johann Kepler and the Italian Galileo Galilei (1564-1642) destroyed this notion. It held that our solar system revolves around the sun, that the world is infinite and has no center, and that there is a plurality of universes. This view contradicted the teachings of the Church, which did not come to terms with the scientists until the nineteenth century, and it made man a very insignificant atom in boundless space. Bruno was entranced with this new cosmology, and the world revealed by science filled him with wonder instead of fear. There was even an unorthodox piety in his ecstasy, for this limitless world only made God's creation more marvellous and exalted His glory. The little world of the Middle Ages was gone. Man had to make himself at home in a different world and adjust his thought and feeling to it. Bruno was the first to do this in his book, *The Infinity of the Universe.*

DANTE ALIGHIERI

Inferno

Canto I

ARGUMENT

The writer, having lost his way in a gloomy forest, and being hindered by certain wild beasts from ascending a mountain, is met by Virgil, who promises to show him the punishments of Hell, and afterwards of Purgatory; and that he shall then be conducted by Beatrice into Paradise. He follows the Roman poet.

In the midway of this our mortal life,[1]
I found me in a gloomy wood, astray
Gone from the path direct: and e'en to tell,
It were no easy task, how savage wild

That forest, how robust and rough its growth,   5
Which to remember only, my dismay
Renews, in bitterness not far from death.
Yet, to discourse of what there good befell,
All else will I relate discover'd there.

How first I enter'd it I scarce can say,   10
Such sleepy dullness in that instant weigh'd
My senses down, when the true path I left;
But when a mountain's foot I reach'd, where closed
The valley that had pierced my heart with dread,
I look'd aloft, and saw his shoulders broad   15
Already vested with that planet's[2] beam,
Who leads all wanderers safe through every way.

Then was a little respite to the fear,
That in my heart's recesses deep had lain

Dante, *Inferno.* Translated by Henry F. Cary. Dante Alighieri (1265-1321) took a prominent part in the political life of his native city of Florence. Banished in middle life, he lived in Verona, Bologna, Padua, and Ravenna, never returning to Florence.
[1] Middle of the life-span of seventy years. This was Good Friday of the year 1300, when Dante was thirty-five years old.
[2] The sun's.

All of that night, so pitifully past: 20
And as a man, with difficult short breath,
Forespent with toiling, 'scaped from sea to shore,
Turns to the perilous wide waste, and stands
At gaze; e'en so my spirit, that yet fail'd,   24
Struggling with terror, turn'd to view the straits
That none hath past and lived. My weary frame
After short pause recomforted, again
I journey'd on over that lonely steep,
The hinder foot still firmer. Scarce the ascent
Began, when, lo! a panther,[3] nimble, light,   30
And cover'd with a speckled skin, appear'd;
Nor, when it saw me, vanish'd; rather strove
To check my onward going; that oft-times,
With purpose to retrace my steps, I turn'd.

The hour was morning's prime, and on his way
Aloft the sun ascended with those stars,   36
That with him rose when Love Divine first moved
Those its fair works: so that with joyous hope
All things conspired to fill me, the gay skin
Of that swift animal, the matin dawn,   40
And the sweet season. Soon that joy was chased,
And by new dread succeeded, when in view
A lion came, 'gainst me as it appear'd,
With his head held aloft and hunger-mad,
That e'en the air was fear-struck. A she-wolf   45
Was at his heels, who in her leanness seem'd
Full of all wants, and many a land hath made
Disconsolate ere now. She with such fear
O'erwhelm'd me, at the sight of her appall'd,
That of the height all hope I lost. As one,   50
Who, with his gain elated, sees the time
When all unwares is gone, he inwardly
Mourns with heart-griping anguish; such was I,
Haunted by that fell beast, never at peace,
Who coming o'er against me, by degrees   55
Impell'd me where the sun in silence rests.

While to the lower space with backward step
I fell, my ken discern'd the form of one
Whose voice seem'd faint through long disuse of
    speech.
When him in that great desert I espied,   60
"Have mercy on me," cried I out aloud,
"Spirit! or living man! whate'er thou be."
He answer'd: "Now not man, man once I was,
And born of Lombard parents, Mantuans both
By country, when the power of Julius yet   65
Was scarcely firm. At Rome my life was past,
Beneath the mild Augustus, in the time

Of fabled deities and false. A bard
Was I, and made Anchises' upright son
The subject of my song, who came from Troy,   70
When the flames prey'd on Ilium's haughty towers.
But thou, say wherefore to such perils past
Return'st thou? wherefore not this pleasant mount
Ascendest, cause and source of all delight?"
"And art thou then that Virgil, that well-spring,
From which such copious floods of eloquence   76
Have issued?" I with front abash'd replied.
"Glory and light of all the tuneful train!
May it avail me, that I long with zeal   79
Have sought thy volume, and with love immense
Have conn'd it o'er. My master thou, and guide!
Thou he from whom alone I have derived
That style, which for its beauty into fame
Exalts me. See the beast, from whom I fled.
O save me from her, thou illustrious sage!   85
For every vein and pulse throughout my frame
She hath made tremble." He, soon as he saw
That I was weeping, answer'd, "Thou must needs
Another way pursue, if thou wouldst 'scape
From out that savage wilderness. This beast,   90
At whom thou criest, her way will suffer none
To pass, and no less hindrance makes than death:
So bad and so accursed in her kind,
That never sated is her ravenous will,
Still after food more craving than before.   95
To many an animal in wedlock vile
She fastens, and shall yet to many more,
Until that Greyhound[4] come, who shall destroy
Her with sharp pain. He will not life support
By earth nor its base metals, but by love,   100
Wisdom, and virtue; and his land shall be
The land 'twixt either Feltro. In his might
Shall safety to Italia's plains arise,
For whose fair realm, Camilla, virgin pure,
Nisus, Euryalus, and Turnus fell.[5]   105
He, with incessant chase, through every town
Shall worry, until he to Hell at length
Restore her, thence by envy first let loose.
I, for thy profit pondering, now devise
That thou mayst follow me; and I, thy guide,   110
Will lead thee hence through an eternal space,
Where thou shalt hear despairing shrieks, and see
Spirits of old tormented, who invoke
A second death; and those next view, who dwell
Content in fire, for that they hope to come,   115
Whene'er the time may be, among the blest,

[3] The three animals are: panther (sensuality), lion (pride of ambition), she-wolf (avarice).
[4] The greyhound, who will be a savior from the she-wolf, has had many interpretations. No one knows what Dante had in mind.
[5] Persons prominent in the latter part of Virgil's _Æneid_.

Into whose regions if thou then desire
To ascend, a spirit worthier than I
Must lead thee, in whose charge, when I depart,
Thou shalt be left: for that Almighty King,   120
Who reigns above, a rebel to His law
Adjudges me; and therefore hath decreed
That, to His city, none through me should come.[6]
He in all parts hath sway; there rules, there holds
His citadel and throne. O happy those,   125
Whom there He chooses!" I to him in few:
"Bard! by that God, whom thou didst not adore,
I do beseech thee (that this ill and worse
I may escape) to lead me where thou said'st,
That I Saint Peter's gate may view, and those   130
Who, as thou tell'st, are in such dismal plight."
Onward he moved, I close his steps pursued.

Canto II

ARGUMENT

After the invocation, which poets are used to
prefix to their works, he shows, that, on a consideration of his own strength, he doubted
whether it sufficed for the journey proposed to
him, but that, being comforted by Virgil, he at
last took courage, and followed him as his
guide and master.

Now was the day departing, and the air,
Imbrown'd with shadows, from their toils released
All animals on earth; and I alone   135
Prepared myself the conflict to sustain,
Both of sad pity, and that perilous road,
Which my unerring memory shall retrace.
    O Muses! O high genius! now vouchsafe
Your aid. O mind! that all I saw hast kept   140
Safe in a written record, here thy worth
And eminent endowments come to proof.
    I thus began: "Bard! thou who art my guide,
Consider well, if virtue be in me
Sufficient, ere to this high enterprise   145
Thou trust me. Thou hast told that Silvius' sire,
Yet clothed in corruptible flesh, among
The immortal tribes had entrance, and was there
Sensibly present. Yet if Heaven's great Lord,
Almighty foe to ill, such favor show'd   150
In contemplation of the high effect,
Both what and who from him should issue forth,
It seems in reason's judgment well deserved;

Sith he of Rome and of Rome's empire wide,
In Heaven's empyreal height was chosen sire: 155
Both which, if truth be spoken, were ordain'd
And stablish'd for the holy place, where sits
Who to great Peter's sacred chair succeeds.
He from this journey, in thy song renown'd,
Learn'd things, that to his victory gave rise   160
And to the papal robe. In after-times
The Chosen Vessel also travel'd there,
To bring us back assurance in that faith
Which is the entrance to salvation's way.
But I, why should I there presume? or who   165
Permits it? not Æneas I, nor Paul.
My self I deem not worthy, and none else
Will deem me. I, if on this voyage then
I venture, fear it will in folly end.
Thou, who art wise, better my meaning know'st,
Than I can speak." As one, who unresolves   171
What he hath late resolved, and with new thoughts
Changes his purpose, from his first intent
Remov'd; e'en such was I on that dun coast,
Wasting in thought my enterprise, at first   175
So eagerly embraced. "If right thy words
I scan," replied that shade magnanimous,
"Thy soul is by vile fear assail'd, which oft
So overcasts a man, that he recoils
From noblest resolution, like a beast   180
At some false semblance in the twilight gloom.
That from this terror thou mayst free thyself,
I will instruct thee why I came, and what
I heard in that same instant, when for thee
Grief touch'd me first. I was among the tribe   185
Who rest suspended,[7] when a dame,[8] so blest
And lovely I besought her to command,
Call'd me; her eyes were brighter than the star
Of day; and she, with gentle voice and soft,
Angelically tuned, her speech address'd: 190
'O courteous shade of Mantua! thou whose fame
'Yet lives, and shall live long as nature lasts!
'A friend, not of my fortune but myself,
'On the wide desert in his road has met
'Hindrance so great, that he through fear has
        turn'd.   195
'Now much I dread lest he past help have stray'd,
'And I be risen too late for his relief,
'From what in heaven of him I heard. Speed now,
'And by thy eloquent persuasive tongue,
'And by all means for his deliverance meet,   200
'Assist him. So to me will comfort spring.

---

[6] Virgil, not being a Christian, is not admitted into Paradise.

[7] In limbo; cf. line 400 below.

[8] Beatrice, the lady of Dante's idealistic love. She represents Theology, which leads man to the contemplation of God.

'I, who now bid thee on this errand forth,
'Am Beatrice; from a place I come
'Revisited with joy. Love brought me thence,
'Who prompts my speech. When in my Master's
    sight   205
'I stand, thy praise to him I oft will tell.'
   "She then was silent, and I thus began:
'O Lady! by whose influence alone
'Mankind excels whatever is contain'd
'Within that heaven which hath the smallest orb,[9]
'So thy command delights me, that to obey,   211
'If it were done already, would seem late.
'No need hast thou farther to speak thy will:
'Yet tell the reason, why thou art not loth
'To leave that ample space, where to return   215
'Thou burnest, for this center here beneath.'
   "She then: 'Since thou so deeply wouldst in-
    quire,
'I will instruct thee briefly why no dread
'Hinders my entrance here. Those things alone
'Are to be fear'd whence evil may proceed;   220
'None else, for none are terrible beside.
'I am so framed by God, thanks to his grace!
'That any sufferance of your misery
'Touches me not, nor flame of that fierce fire
'Assails me. In high Heaven a blessed Dame   225
'Resides, who mourns with such effectual grief
'That hindrance, which I send thee to remove,
'That God's stern judgment to her will inclines.
'To Lucia calling, her she thus bespake:
"Now doth thy faithful servant need thy aid,   230
"And I commend him to thee." At her word
'Sped Lucia, of all cruelty the foe,
'And coming to the place, where I abode
'Seated with Rachel, her of ancient days,   234
'She thus address'd me: "Thou true praise of God!
"Beatrice! why is not thy succor lent
"To him, who so much loved thee, as to leave
"For thy sake all the multitude admires?
"Dost thou not hear how pitiful his wail,   239
"Nor mark the death, which in the torrent flood,
"Swoln mightier than a sea, him struggling holds?"
'Ne'er among men did any with such speed
'Haste to their profit, flee from their annoy,
'As, when these words were spoken, I came here,
'Down from my blessed seat, trusting the force
'Of thy pure eloquence, which thee, and all   246
'Who well have mark'd it, into honor brings.'
   "When she had ended, her bright beaming eyes
Tearful she turn'd aside; whereat I felt
Redoubled zeal to serve thee. As she will'd,   250
Thus am I come: I saved thee from the beast,

Who thy near way across the goodly mount
Prevented. What is this comes o'er thee then?
Why, why dost thou hang back? why in thy
    breast
Harbor vile fear? why hast not courage there,
And noble daring; since three maids, so blest,   256
Thy safety plan, e'en in the court of Heaven;
And so much certain good my words forebode?"
   As florets, by the frosty air of night
Bent down and closed, when day has blanch'd
    their leaves,   260
Rise all unfolded on their spiry stems;
So was my fainting vigor new restored,
And to my heart such kindly courage ran,
That I as one undaunted soon replied:
"O full of pity she, who undertook   265
My succor! and thou kind, who didst perform
So soon her true behest! With such desire
Thou hast disposed me to renew my voyage,
That my first purpose fully is resumed.
Lead on: one only will is in us both.   270
Thou art my guide, my master thou, and lord."
   So spake I; and when he had onward moved,
I enter'd on the deep and woody way.

Canto III

ARGUMENT

Dante, following Virgil, comes to the gate of Hell;
   where, after having read the dreadful words that
   are written thereon, they both enter. Here, as he
   understands from Virgil, those were punished
   who had passed their time (for living it could
   not be called) in a state of apathy and indifference both to good and evil. Then pursuing their
   way, they arrive at the river Acheron; and there
   find the old ferryman Charon, who takes the
   spirits over to the opposite shore; which as soon
   as Dante reaches, he is seized with terror, and
   falls into a trance.

"Through me you pass into the city of woe:
Through me you pass into eternal pain: 275
Through me among the people lost for aye.
Justice the founder of my fabric moved:
To rear me was the task of Power divine,
Supremest Wisdom, and primeval Love.
Before me things create were none, save things
Eternal, and eternal I endure.   281
All hope abandon, ye who enter here."
   Such characters, in color dim, I mark'd
Over a portal's lofty arch inscribed.

---

[9] The moon.

Whereat I thus: "Master, these words import   285
Hard meaning." He as one prepared replied:
"Here thou must all distrust behind thee leave;
Here be vile fear extinguish'd. We are come
Where I have told thee we shall see the souls
To misery doom'd, who intellectual good   290
Have lost." And when his hand he had stretch'd
    forth
To mine, with pleasant looks, whence I was
    cheer'd,
Into that secret place he led me on.
    Here sighs, with lamentations and loud moans,
Resounded through the air pierced by no star,   295
That e'en I wept at entering. Various tongues,
Horrible languages, outcries of woe,
Accents of anger, voices deep and hoarse,
With hands together smote that swell'd the sounds,
Made up a tumult, that for ever whirls   300
Round through that air with solid darkness
    stain'd,
Like to the sand that in the whirlwind flies.
    I then, with terror yet encompast, cried:
"O master! what is this I hear? What race
Are these, who seem so overcome with woe?"
    He thus to me: "This miserable fate   306
Suffer the wretched souls of those, who lived
Without or praise or blame, with that ill band
Of angels mix'd, who nor rebellious proved,
Nor yet were true to God, but for themselves   310
Were only. From his bounds Heaven drove them
    forth,
Not to impair his luster; nor the depth
Of Hell receives them, lest the accursed tribe
Should glory thence with exultation vain."   314
    I then: "Master! what doth aggrieve them thus,
That they lament so loud?" He straight replied:
"That will I tell thee briefly. These of death
No hope may entertain: and their blind life
So meanly passes, that all other lots   319
They envy. Fame of them the world hath none,
Nor suffers; Mercy and Justice scorn them both.
Speak not of them, but look, and pass them by."
    And I, who straightway look'd, beheld a flag,
Which whirling ran around so rapidly,
That it no pause obtain'd: and following came   325
Such a long train of spirits, I should ne'er
Have thought that death so many had despoil'd.
    When some of these I recognized, I saw
And knew the shade of him, who to base fear
Yielding, abjured his high estate. Forthwith   330
I understood, for certain, this the tribe
Of those ill spirits both to God displeasing
And to His foes. These wretches, who ne'er lived,

Went on in nakedness, and sorely stung
By wasps and hornets, which bedew'd their cheeks
With blood, that, mix'd with tears, dropp'd to
    their feet,   336
And by disgustful worms was gather'd there.
    Then looking further onwards, I beheld
A throng upon the shore of a great stream:
Whereat I thus: "Sir! grant me now to know   340
Whom here we view, and whence impell'd they
    seem
So eager to pass o'er, as I discern
Through the blear light?" He thus to me in few:
"This shalt thou know, soon as our steps arrive
Beside the woeful tide of Acheron."   345
    Then with eyes downward cast, and fill'd with
    shame,
Fearing my words offensive to his ear,
Till we had reach'd the river, I from speech
Abstained. And lo! toward us in a bark
Comes on an old man, hoary white with eld,   350
Crying, "Woe to you, wicked spirits! hope not
Ever to see the sky again. I come
To take you to the other shore across,
Into eternal darkness, there to dwell
In fierce heat and in ice. And thou, who there   355
Standest, live spirit! get thee hence, and leave
These who are dead." But soon as he beheld
I left them not, "By other way," said he,
"By other haven shalt thou come to shore,
Not by this passage; thee a nimbler boat   360
Must carry." Then to him thus spake my guide:
"Charon! thyself torment not: so 'tis will'd,
Where will and power are one: ask thou no
    more."
    Straightway in silence fell the shaggy cheeks
Of him, the boatman o'er the livid lake,   365
Around whose eyes glared wheeling flames. Mean-
    while
Those spirits, faint and naked, color changed,
And gnash'd their teeth, soon as the cruel words
They heard. God and their parents they blas-
    phemed,   369
The human kind, the place, the time, and seed,
That did engender them and give them birth.
    Then all together sorely wailing drew
To the curst strand, that every man must pass
Who fears not God. Charon, demoniac form,
With eyes of burning coal, collects them all,   375
Beckoning, and each, that lingers, with his oar
Strikes. As fall off the light autumnal leaves,
One still another following, till the bough
Strews all its honors on the earth beneath;
E'en in like manner Adam's evil brood   380

Cast themselves, one by one, down from the shore,
Each at a beck, as falcon at his call.

Thus go they over through the umber'd wave;
And ever they on the opposing bank
Be landed, on this side another throng   385
Still gathers. "Son," thus spake the courteous
    guide,
"Those who die subject to the wrath of God
All here together come from every clime,
And to o'erpass the river are not loth:
For so Heaven's justice goads them on, that fear
Is turn'd into desire. Hence ne'er hath past   391
Good spirit. If of thee Charon complain,
Now mayst thou know the import of his words."

This said, the gloomy region trembling shook
So terribly, that yet with clammy dews   395
Fear chills my brow. The sad earth gave a blast,
That, lightening, shot forth a vermilion flame,
Which all my senses conquer'd quite, and I
Down dropp'd, as one with sudden slumber seized.

Canto IV

ARGUMENT

The Poet, being roused by a clap of thunder, and
following his guide onwards, descends into
Limbo, which is the first circle of Hell, where
he finds the souls of those, who, although they
have lived virtuously and have not to suffer for
great sins, nevertheless, through lack of baptism,
merit not the bliss of Paradise. Hence he is led
on by Virgil to descend into the second circle.

Broke the deep slumber in my brain a crash   400
Of heavy thunder, that I shook myself,
As one by main force roused. Risen upright,
My rested eyes I moved around, and search'd,
With fixed ken, to know what place it was
Wherein I stood. For certain, on the brink   405
I found me of the lamentable vale,
The dread abyss, that joins a thundrous sound
Of plaints innumerable. Dark and deep,
And thick with clouds o'erspread, mine eye in vain
Explored its bottom, nor could aught discern.   410

"Now let us to the blind world there beneath
Descend," the bard again, all pale of look:
"I go the first, and thou shalt follow next."

Then I, his alter'd hue perceiving, thus:
"How may I speed, if thou yieldest to dread,   415
Who still art wont to comfort me in doubt?"

He then: "The anguish of that race below

With pity stains my cheek, which thou for fear
Mistakest. Let us on. Our length of way
Urges to haste." Onward, this said, he moved;   420
And entering led me with him, on the bounds
Of the first circle that surrounds the abyss.

Here, as mine ear could note, no plaint was
    heard
Except of sighs, that made the eternal air
Tremble, not caused by tortures, but from grief
Felt by those multitudes, many and vast,   426
Of men, women, and infants. Then to me
The gentle guide: "Inquirest thou not what spirits
Are these which thou beholdest? Ere thou pass
Farther, I would thou know, that these of sin
Were blameless; and if aught they merited,   431
It profits not, since baptism was not theirs,
The portal to thy faith. If they before
The Gospel lived, they served not God aright;
And among such am I. For these defects,   435
And for no other evil, we are lost;
Only so far afflicted, that we live
Desiring without hope." Sore grief assail'd
My heart at hearing this, for well I knew
Suspended in that Limbo many a soul   440
Of mighty worth. "O tell me, sire revered!
Tell me, my master!" I began, through wish
Of full assurance in that holy faith
Which vanquishes all error; "say, did e'er
Any, or through his own or other's merit,   445
Come forth from thence, who afterward was
    blest?"

Piercing the secret purport of my speech,
He answer'd: "I was new to that estate,[10]
When I beheld a puissant one arrive
Amongst us, with victorious trophy crown'd.   450
He forth the shade of our first parent drew,
Abel his child, and Noah righteous man,
Of Moses lawgiver for faith approved,
Of Patriarch Abraham, and David king,
Israel with his sire and with his sons,   455
Nor without Rachel whom so hard he won,
And others many more, whom He to bliss
Exalted. Before these, be thou assured,
No spirit of human kind was ever saved."

We, while he spake, ceased not our onward
    road,   460
Still passing through the wood; for so I name
Those spirits thick beset. We were not far
On this side from the summit, when I kenn'd
A flame, that o'er the darken'd hemisphere
Prevailing shined. Yet we a little space   465

[10] Virgil has been dead but a short time when Christ comes to hell and rescues the good men and women of the Old Testament story.

Were distant, not so far but I in part
Discover'd that a tribe in honor high
That place possess'd. "O thou, who every art
And science valuest! who are these, that boast
Such honor, separate from all the rest?"   470
He answer'd: "The renown of their great names,
That echoes through your world above, acquires
Favor in Heaven, which holds them thus advanced."
Meantime a voice I heard: "Honor the bard
Sublime! his shade returns, that left us late!"   475
No sooner ceased the sound, than I beheld
Four mighty spirits toward us bend their steps,
Of semblance neither sorrowful nor glad.
When thus my master kind began: "Mark him,
Who in his right hand bears that falchion keen,
The other three preceding, as their lord.   481
This is that Homer, of all bards supreme:
Flaccus[11] the next, in satire's vein excelling:
The third is Naso; Lucan is the last.
Because they all that appellation own,   485
With which the voice singly accosted me,
Honoring they greet me thus, and well they
      judge."
So I beheld united the bright school
Of him the monarch of sublimest song,
That o'er the others like an eagle soars.   490
When they together short discourse had held,
They turn'd to me, with salutation kind
Beckoning me; at the which my master smiled:
Nor was this all; but greater honor still
They gave me, for they made me of their tribe;
And I was sixth amid so learn'd a band.   496
Far as the luminous beacon on we pass'd,
Speaking of matters, then befitting well
To speak, now fitter left untold. At foot
Of a magnificent castle we arrived,   500
Seven times with lofty walls begirt, and round
Defended by a pleasant stream. O'er this
As o'er dry land we pass'd. Next, through seven
      gates,
I with those sages enter'd, and we came
Into a mead with lively verdure fresh.   505
There dwelt a race, who slow their eyes around
Majestically moved, and in their port
Bore eminent authority: they spake

Seldom, but all their words were tuneful sweet.
We to one side retired, into a place   510
Open and bright and lofty, whence each one
Stood manifest to view. Incontinent,
There on the green enamel of the plain
Were shown me the great spirits, by whose sight
I am exalted in my own esteem.   515
Electra[12] there I saw accompanied
By many, among whom Hector I knew,
Anchises' pious son, and with hawk's eye
Cæsar alarm'd, and by Camilla there
Penthesilea. On the other side,   520
Old king Latinus seated by his child
Lavinia, and that Brutus I beheld
Who Tarquin chased, Lucretia, Cato's wife
Marcia, with Julia and Cornelia there;
And sole apart retired, the Soldan[13] fierce.   525
Then when a little more I raised my brow
I spied the master of the sapient throng,[14]
Seated amid the philosophic train.
Him all admire, all pay him reverence due.
There Socrates and Plato both I mark'd   530
Nearest to him in rank, Democritus,
Who sets the world at chance, Diogenes,
With Heraclitus, and Empedocles,
And Anaxagoras, and Thales sage,
Zeno, and Dioscorides well read   535
In nature's secret lore. Orpheus I mark'd
And Linus, Tully and moral Seneca,
Euclid and Ptolemy, Hippocrates,
Galenus, Avicen, and him who made
That commentary vast, Averroës.   540
Of all to speak at full were vain attempt;
For my wide theme so urges, that oft-times
My words fall short of what bechanced. In two
The six associates part. Another way
My sage guide leads me, from that air serene,   545
Into a climate ever vex'd with storms:
And to a part I come, where no light shines.

Canto V

ARGUMENT

Coming into the second circle of Hell, Dante at
the entrance beholds Minos the Infernal Judge,
by whom he is admonished to beware how he

---

[11] Flaccus is Horace; Naso, Ovid.
[12] The persons mentioned in the following lines, all important in the history of Rome, are: Electra,
whose son Dardanus founded Troy; Hector, the defender of Troy; Æneas, the supposed founder of
Rome; Cæsar, who founded the Roman Empire; Camilla, who died fighting for Latium; Penthesilea,
who defended Troy; Latinus, king of Latium, and his daughter, Lavinia, who married Æneas. Lucius
Junius Brutus delivered Rome from its tyrants. Lucretia, Marcia, Julia, and Cornelia were famous
Roman women.
[13] Saladin.
[14] Aristotle.

enters those regions. Here he witnesses the punishment of carnal sinners, who are tost about
ceaselessly in the dark air by the most furious
winds. Among these, he meets with Francesca
of Rimini, through pity at whose sad tale he
falls fainting to the ground.

From the first circle I descended thus
Down to the second, which, a lesser space
Embracing, so much more of grief contains,   550
Provoking bitter moans. There Minos stands,
Grinning with ghastly feature: he, of all
Who enter, strict examining the crimes,
Gives sentence, and dismisses them beneath,
According as he foldeth him around: 555
For when before him comes the ill-fated soul,
It all confesses; and that judge severe
Of sins, considering what place in Hell
Suits the transgression, with his tail so oft
Himself encircles, as degrees beneath   560
He dooms it to descend. Before him stand
Alway a numerous throng: and in his turn
Each one to judgment passing, speaks, and hears
His fate, thence downward to his dwelling hurl'd.
    "O thou! who to this residence of woe   565
Approachest!" when he saw me coming, cried
Minos, relinquishing his dread employ,
"Look how thou enter here; beware in whom
Thou place thy trust; let not the entrance broad
Deceive thee to thy harm." To him my guide:
"Wherefore exclaimest? Hinder not his way   571
By destiny appointed; so 'tis will'd,
Where will and power are one. Ask thou no
    more."
    Now 'gin the rueful wailings to be heard.
Now am I come where many a plaining voice
Smites on mine ear. Into a place I came   576
Where light was silent all. Bellowing there
    groan'd
A noise, as of a sea in tempest torn
By warring winds. The stormy blast of Hell
With restless fury drives the spirits on,   580
Whirl'd round and dash'd amain with sore annoy.
When they arrive before the ruinous sweep,
There shrieks are heard, there lamentations, moans,
And blasphemies 'gainst the good Power in
    Heaven.
    I understood, that to this torment sad   585
The carnal sinners are condemn'd, in whom
Reason by lust is swayed. As in large troops
And multitudinous, when winter reigns,
The starlings on their wings are borne abroad;
So bears the tyrannous gust those evil souls.   590

On this side and on that, above, below,
It drives them: hope of rest to solace them
Is none, nor e'en of milder pang. As cranes,
Chanting their dolorous notes, traverse the sky,
Stretch'd out in long array; so I beheld   595
Spirits, who came loud wailing, hurried on
By their dire doom. Then I: "Instructor! who
Are these, by the black air so scourged?"—"The
    first
'Mong those, of whom thou question'st," he re-
    plied,
"O'er many tongues was empress. She in vice   600
Of luxury was so shameless, that she made
Liking be lawful by promulged decree,
To clear the blame she had herself incurr'd.
This is Semiramis, of whom 'tis writ,
That she succeeded Ninus her espoused;   605
And held the land, which now the Soldan rules.
The next in amorous fury slew herself,
And to Sicheus' ashes broke her faith:
Then follows Cleopatra, lustful queen."   609
    There mark'd I Helen, for whose sake so long
The time was fraught with evil; there the great
Achilles, who with love fought to the end.
Paris I saw, and Tristan; and beside,
A thousand more he show'd me, and by name
Pointed them out, whom love bereaved of life.   615
    When I had heard my sage instructor name
Those dames and knights of antique days, o'er-
    power'd
By pity, well-nigh in amaze my mind
Was lost; and I began: "Bard! willingly
I would address those two together coming,   620
Which seem so light before the wind." He thus:
"Note thou, when nearer they to us approach.
Then by that love which carries them along,
Entreat; and they will come." Soon as the wind
Sway'd them towards us, I thus framed my speech:
"O wearied spirits! come, and hold discourse   626
With us, if by none else restrain'd." As doves
By fond desire invited, on wide wings
And firm, to their sweet nest returning home,
Cleave the air, wafted by their will along;   630
Thus issued, from that troop where Dido ranks,
They, through the ill air speeding: with such force
My cry prevail'd, by strong affection urged
"O gracious creature and benign! who go'st
Visiting, through this element obscure,   635
Us, who the world with bloody stain imbrued;
If, for a friend, the King of all, we own'd,
Our prayer to him should for thy peace arise,
Since thou hast pity on our evil plight.
Of whatsoe'er to hear or to discourse   640

It pleases thee, that will we hear, of that
Freely with thee discourse, while e'er the wind,
As now, is mute. The land, that gave me birth.
Is situate on the coast, where Po descends
To rest in ocean with his sequent streams.   645

  "Love, that in gentle heart is quickly learnt,
Entangled him by that fair form, from me
Ta'en in such cruel sort, as grieves me still:
Love, that denial takes from none beloved,
Caught me with pleasing him so passing well,   650
That, as thou seest, he yet deserts me not.
Love brought us to one death: Caïna waits
The soul, who spilt our life." Such were their
     words;
At hearing which, downward I bent my looks,
And held them there so long, that the bard cried:
"What art thou pondering?" I in answer thus: 656
"Alas! by what sweet thoughts, what fond desire,
Must they at length to that ill pass have reach'd!"

  Then turning, I to them my speech address'd,
And thus began: "Francesca! your sad fate   660
Even to tears my grief and pity moves.
But tell me; in the time of your sweet sighs,
By what, and how Love granted, that ye knew
Your yet uncertain wishes?" She replied:
"No greater grief than to remember days   665
Of joy, when misery is at hand. Then kens
Thy learn'd instructor. Yet so eagerly
If thou art bent to know the primal root,
From whence our love gat being, I will do
As one, who weeps and tells his tale. One day,
For our delight we read of Lancelot,   671
How him love thrall'd. Alone we were, and no
Suspicion near us. Oft-times by that reading
Our eyes were drawn together, and the hue
Fled from our alter'd cheek. But at one point   675
Alone we fell. When of that smile we read,
The wished smile, so rapturously kiss'd
By one so deep in love, than he, who ne'er
From me shall separate, at once my lips   679
All trembling kiss'd. The book and writer both
Were love's purveyors. In its leaves that day
We read no more." While thus one spirit spake,
The other wail'd so sorely, that heart-struck
I, through compassion fainting, seem'd not far   684
From death, and like a corse fell to the ground.

[*Canto VI.* On his recovery, the Poet finds himself in the third circle, where the gluttonous are punished. Their torment is, to lie in the mire, under a continual and heavy storm of hail, snow, and discolored water; Cerberus meanwhile barking over them with his threefold throat, and rending them piecemeal. One of these, who on earth was named Ciacco, foretells the divisions with which Florence is about to be distracted. Dante proposes a question to his guide, who solves it; and they proceed towards the fourth circle.

Canto VII. In the present Canto, Dante describes his descent into the fourth circle, at the beginning of which he sees Plutus stationed. Here one like doom awaits the prodigal and the avaricious; which is, to meet in direful conflict, rolling great weights against each other with mutual upbraidings. From hence Virgil takes occasion to show how vain the goods that are committed into the charge of Fortune; and this moves our author to inquire what being that Fortune is, of whom he speaks: which question being resolved, they go down into the fifth circle, where they find the wrathful and gloomy tormented in the Stygian lake. Having made a compass round great part of this lake, they come at last to the base of a lofty tower.

Canto VIII. A signal having been made from the tower, Phlegyas, the ferryman of the lake, speedily crosses it, and conveys Virgil and Dante to the other side. On their passage, they meet with Filippo Argenti, whose fury and torment are described. They then arrive at the city of Dis, the entrance whereto is denied, and the portals closed against them by many Demons.

Canto IX. After some hindrances, and having seen the hellish furies and other monsters, the Poet, by the help of an angel, enters the city of Dis, wherein he discovers that the heretics are punished in tombs burning with intense fire: and he, together with Virgil, passes onwards between the sepulchers and the walls of the city.

Canto X. Dante, having obtained permission from his guide, holds discourse with Farinata degli Uberti and Cavalcante Cavalcanti, who lie in their fiery tombs that are yet open, and not to be closed up till after the last judgment. Farinata predicts the Poet's exile from Florence; and shows him that the condemned have knowledge of future things, but are ignorant of what is at present passing, unless it be revealed by some newcomer from earth.

Canto XI. Dante arrives at the verge of a rocky precipice which encloses the seventh circle, where he sees the sepulcher of Anastasius the Heretic; behind the lid of which, pausing a little, to make himself capable by degrees of enduring the fetid smell that steamed upward from the abyss, he is instructed by Virgil concerning the manner in which the three following circles are disposed, and what description of sinners is punished in each.

He then inquires the reason why the carnal, the gluttonous, the avaricious and prodigal, the wrathful and gloomy suffer not their punishments within the city of Dis. He next asks how the crime of usury is an offense against God; and at length the two Poets go towards the place from whence a passage leads down to the seventh circle.

Canto XII. Descending by a very rugged way into the seventh circle, where the violent are punished, Dante and his leader find it guarded by the Minotaur; whose fury being pacified by Virgil, they step downwards from crag to crag; till, drawing near the bottom, they descry a river of blood, wherein are tormented such as have committed violence against their neighbor. At these, when they strive to emerge from the blood, a troop of Centaurs, running along the side of the river, aim their arrows; and three of their band opposing our travelers at the foot of the steep, Virgil prevails so far, that one consents to carry them both across the stream; and on their passage, Dante is informed by him of the course of the river, and of those that are punished therein.

Canto XIII. Still in the seventh circle, Dante enters its second compartment, which contains both those who have done violence on their own persons and those who have violently consumed their goods; the first changed into rough and knotted trees whereon the harpies build their nests, the latter chased and torn by black female mastiffs. Among the former, Piero delle Vigne is one who tells him the cause of his having committed suicide, and moreover in what manner the souls are transformed into those trunks. Of the latter crew, he recognizes Lano, a Sienese, and Giacomo, a Paduan; and lastly, a Florentine, who had hung himself from his own roof, speaks to him of the calamities of his countrymen.

Canto XIV. They arrive at the beginning of the third of those compartments into which this seventh circle is divided. It is a plain of dry and hot sand, where three kinds of violence are punished; namely, against God, against Nature, and against Art; and those who have thus sinned, are tormented by flakes of fire, which are eternally showering down upon them. Among the violent against God is found Capaneus, whose blasphemies they hear. Next, turning to the left along the forest of self-slayers, and having journeyed a little onwards, they meet with a streamlet of blood that issues from the forest and traverses the sandy plain. Here Virgil speaks to our Poet of a huge ancient statue that stands within Mount Ida in Crete, from a fis-

sure in which statue there is a dripping of tears, from which the said streamlet, together with the three other infernal rivers, are formed.

Canto XV. Taking their way upon one of the mounds by which the streamlet, spoken of in the last Canto, was embanked, and having gone so far that they could no longer have discerned the forest if they had turned round to look for it, they meet a troop of spirits that come along the sand by the side of the pier. These are they who have done violence to Nature; and amongst them Dante distinguishes Brunetto Latini, who had been formerly his master; with whom, turning a little backward, he holds a discourse which occupies the remainder of this Canto.

Canto XVI. Journeying along the pier, which crosses the sand, they are now so near the end of it as to hear the noise of the stream falling into the eighth circle, when they meet the spirits of three military men; who judging Dante, from his dress, to be a countryman of theirs, entreat him to stop. He complies, and speaks with them. The two Poets then reach the place where the water descends, being the termination of this third compartment in the seventh circle; and here Virgil having thrown down into the hollow a cord, wherewith Dante was girt, they behold at that signal a monstrous and horrible figure come swimming up to them.

Canto XVII. The monster Geryon is described; to whom while Virgil is speaking in order that he may carry them both down to the next circle, Dante, by permission, goes a little farther along the edge of the void, to descry the third species of sinners contained in this compartment, namely, those who have done violence to Art; and then returning to his master, they both descend, seated on the back of Geryon.

Canto XVIII. The Poet describes the situation and form of the eighth circle, divided into ten gulfs, which contain as many different descriptions of fraudulent sinners; but in the present Canto he treats only of two sorts: the first is of those who, either for their own pleasure, or for that of another, have seduced any woman from her duty; and these are scourged of demons in the first gulf: the other sort is of flatterers, who in the second gulf are condemned to remain immersed in filth.

Canto XIX. They come to the third gulf, wherein are punished those who have been guilty of simony. These are fixed with the head downwards in certain apertures, so that no more of them than the legs appears without, and on the soles of their feet are seen burning flames. Dante is taken down by his guide into the bottom of the gulf; and there finds Pope Nicholas the Third, whose evil deeds, together with those of other pontiffs, are bitterly reprehended. Virgil then carries him up again to the arch, which affords them a passage over the following gulf.

Canto XX. The Poet relates the punishment of such as presumed, while living, to predict future events. It is to have their faces reversed and set the contrary way on their limbs, so that, being deprived of the power to see before them, they are constrained ever to walk backwards. Among these Virgil points out to him Amphiaraüs, Tiresias, Aruns, and Manto (from the mention of whom he takes occasion to speak of the origin of Mantua), together with several others, who had practiced the arts of divination and astrology.

Canto XXI. Still in the eighth circle, which bears the name of Malebolge, they look down from the bridge that passes over its fifth gulf, upon the barterers or public peculators. These are plunged in a lake of boiling pitch, and guarded by demons, to whom Virgil, leaving Dante apart, presents himself; and license being obtained to pass onward, both pursue their way.

Canto XXII. Virgil and Dante proceed, accompanied by the demons, and see other sinners of the same description in the same gulf. The device of Ciampolo, one of these, to escape from the demons, who had laid hold on him.

Canto XXIII. The enraged demons pursue Dante, but he is preserved from them by Virgil. On reaching the sixth gulf he beholds the punishment of the hypocrites; which is, to pace continually round the gulf under the pressure of caps and hoods, that are gilt on the outside, but leaden within. He is addressed by two of these, Catalano and Loderingo, Knights of Saint Mary, otherwise called Joyous Friars of Bologna. Caïaphas is seen fixed to a cross on the ground, and lies so stretched along the way, that all tread on him in passing.

Canto XXIV. Under the escort of his faithful master, Dante not without difficulty makes his way out of the sixth gulf; and in the seventh, sees the robbers tormented by venomous and pestilent serpents. The soul of Vanni Fucci, who had pillaged the sacristy of Saint James in Pistoia, predicts some calamities that impended over that city, and over the Florentines.

Canto XXV. The sacrilegious Fucci vents his fury in blasphemy, is seized by serpents, and flying

is pursued by Cacus in the form of a Centaur, who is described with a swarm of serpents on his haunch, and a dragon on his shoulders breathing forth fire. Our Poet then meets with the spirits of three of his countrymen, two of whom undergo a marvelous transformation in his presence.

Canto XXVI. Remounting by the steps, down which they had descended to the seventh gulf, they go forward to the arch that stretches over the eighth, and from thence behold numberless flames wherein are punished the evil counselors, each flame containing a sinner, save one, in which were Diomede and Ulysses, the latter of whom relates the manner of his death.

Canto XXVII. The Poet, treating of the same punishment as in the last Canto, relates that he turned towards a flame in which was the Count Guido da Montefeltro, whose inquiries respecting the state of Romagna he answers; and Guido is thereby induced to declare who he is, and why condemned to that torment.

Canto XXVIII. They arrive in the ninth gulf, where the sowers of scandal, schismatics, and heretics, are seen with their limbs miserably maimed or divided in different ways. Among these the Poet finds Mahomet, Piero da Medicina, Curio, Mosca, and Bertrand de Born.

Canto XXIX. Dante, at the desire of Virgil, proceeds onward to the bridge that crosses the tenth gulf, from whence he hears the cries of the alchemists and forgers, who are tormented therein; but not being able to discern anything on account of the darkness, they descend the rock, that bounds this the last of the compartments in which the eighth circle is divided, and then behold the spirits who are afflicted by divers plagues and diseases. Two of them, namely, Grifolino of Arezzo and Capocchio of Siena, are introduced speaking.

Canto XXX. In the same gulf, other kinds of impostors, as those who have counterfeited the persons of others, or debased the current coin, or deceived by speech under false pretenses, are described as suffering various diseases. Sinon of Troy and Adamo of Brescia mutually reproach each other with their several impostures.

Canto XXXI. The poets, following the sound of a loud horn, are led by it to the ninth circle, in which there are four rounds, one enclosed within the other, and containing as many sorts of Traitors; but the present Canto shows only that the circle is encompassed with Giants, one of whom, Antæus, takes them both in his arms and places them at the bottom of the circle.

Canto XXXII. This Canto treats of the first, and, in part, of the second of those rounds, into which the ninth and last, or frozen circle, is divided. In the former, called Caïna, Dante finds Camiccione de' Pazzi, who gives him an account of other sinners who are there punished; and in the next, named Antenora, he hears in like manner from Bocca degli Abbati who his fellow-sufferers are.

Canto XXXIII. The Poet is told by Count Ugolino de' Gherardeschi of the cruel manner in which he and his children were famished in the tower at Pisa, by command of the Archbishop Ruggieri. He next discourses of the third round, called Ptolomea, wherein those are punished who have betrayed others under the semblance of kindness; and among these he finds the Friar Alberigo de' Manfredi, who tells him of one whose soul was already tormented in that place, though his body appeared still to be alive upon the earth, being yielded up to the governance of a fiend.

Canto XXXIV. In the fourth and last round of the ninth circle, those who have betrayed their benefactors are wholly covered with ice. And in the midst is Lucifer, at whose back Dante and Virgil ascend, till by a secret path they reach the surface of the other hemisphere of the earth, and once more obtain sight of the stars.]

Purgatory

Canto I

ARGUMENT

The Poet describes the delight he experienced at issuing a little before dawn from the infernal regions, into the pure air that surrounds the isle of Purgatory; and then relates how, turning to the right, he beheld four stars never seen before but by our first parents, and met on his left the shade of Cato of Utica, who, having warned him and Virgil what is needful to be done before they proceed on their way through Purgatory, disappears; and the two poets go towards the shore, where Virgil cleanses Dante's face with the dew, and girds him with a reed, as Cato had commanded.

O'er better waves to speed her rapid course
The light bark of my genius lifts the sail,
Well pleased to leave so cruel sea behind;
And of that second region will I sing,
In which the human spirit from sinful blot   5
Is purged, and for ascent to Heaven prepares.
　Here, O ye hallow'd Nine! for in your train
I follow, here the deaden'd strain revive;
Nor let Calliope refuse to sound
A somewhat higher song, of that loud tone   10

Which when the wretched birds of chattering
　　note [1]
Had heard, they of forgiveness lost all hope.
　Sweet hue of eastern sapphire, that was spread
O'er the serene aspect of the pure air,
High up as the first circle, to mine eyes   15
Unwonted joy renew'd, soon as I 'scaped
Forth from the atmosphere of deadly gloom,
That had mine eyes and bosom fill'd with grief,
The radiant planet, that to love invites,
Made all the orient laugh, and veil'd beneath   20
The Pisces' light, [2] that in his escort came.
　To the right hand I turn'd, and fix'd my mind
On the other pole attentive, where I saw
Four stars [3] ne'er seen before save by the ken
Of our first parents. Heaven of their rays   25
Seem'd joyous. O thou northern site! bereft
Indeed, and widow'd, since of these deprived.
　As from this view I had desisted, straight
Turning a little towards the other pole,
There from whence now the wain had disappear'd,
I saw an old man [4] standing by my side   31
Alone, so worthy of reverence in his look,
That ne'er from son to father more was owed.
Low down his beard, and mix'd with hoary white,
Descended, like his locks, which, parting, fell   35
Upon his breast in double fold. The beams

[1] The daughters of Pierus, who challenged the Muses to sing, and were by them changed into magpies.
[2] The constellation of the Fish veiled by the more luminous body of Venus, then a morning star.
[3] Symbolical of the four cardinal virtues, Prudence, Justice, Fortitude, and Temperance.
[4] Cato.

Of those four luminaries on his face
So brightly shone, and with such radiance clear
Deck'd it, that I beheld him as the sun.
　"Say who are ye, that stemming the blind
　　stream,　　　　　　　　　　　　　　　40
Forth from the eternal prison-house have fled?"
He spoke and moved those venerable plumes.
"Who hath conducted, or with lantern sure
Lights you emerging from the depth of night,
That makes the infernal valley ever black?　　45
Are the firm statutes of the dread abyss
Broken, or in high heaven new laws ordain'd,
That thus, condemn'd, ye to my caves approach?"
　My guide, then laying hold on me, by words
And intimations given with hand and head,　　50
Made my bent knees and eye submissive pay
Due reverence; then thus to him replied:
　"Not of myself I come; a Dame from heaven [5]
Descending, him besought me in my charge
To bring. But since thy will implies, that more
Our true condition I unfold at large,　　　　56
Mine is not to deny thee thy request.
This mortal ne'er hath seen the furthest gloom;
But erring by his folly had approach'd
So near, that little space was left to turn.　　60
Then, as before I told, I was dispatch'd
To work his rescue; and no way remain'd
Save this which I have ta'en. I have display'd
Before him all the regions of the bad;
And purpose now those spirits to display,　　65
That under thy command are purged from sin.
How I have brought him would be long to say.
From high descends the virtue, by whose aid
I to thy sight and hearing him have led.
Now may our coming please thee. In the search　70
Of liberty he journeys: that how dear,
They know who for her sake have life refused.
Thou knowest, to whom death for her was sweet
In Utica, where thou didst leave those weeds,
That in the last great day will shine so bright.　75
For us the eternal edicts are unmoved:
He breathes, and I of Minos am not bound,
Abiding in that circle, where the eyes
Of thy chaste Marcia [6] beam, who still in look
Prays thee, O hallow'd spirit! to own her thine.
Then by her love we implore thee, let us pass　81
Through thy seven regions; [7] for which, best
　　thanks
I for thy favor will to her return,

If mention there below thou not disdain."
　"Marcia so pleasing in my sight was found,"　85
He then to him rejoin'd, "while I was there,
That all she ask'd me I was fain to grant.
Now that beyond the accursed stream she dwells,
She may no longer move me, by that law, [8]
Which was ordain'd me, when I issued thence.　90
Not so, if Dame from heaven, as thou sayst,
Moves and directs thee; then no flattery needs.
Enough for me that in her name thou ask.
Go therefore now: and with a slender reed
See that thou duly gird him, and his face　　95
Lave, till all sordid stain thou wipe from thence.
For not with eye, by any cloud obscured,
Would it be seemly before Him to come,
Who stands the foremost minister in heaven.
This islet all around, there far beneath,　　100
Where the wave beats it, on the oozy bed
Produces store of reeds. No other plant,
Cover'd with leaves, or harden'd in its stalk,
There lives, not bending to the water's sway.
After, this way return not; but the sun　　105
Will show you, that now rises, where to take
The mountain in its easiest ascent."
　He disappear'd; and I myself upraised
Speechless, and to my guide retiring close,
Toward him turn'd mine eyes. He thus began:
"My son! observant thou my steps pursue.　111
We must retreat to rereward; for that way
The champain to its low extreme declines."
　The dawn had chased the matin hour of prime,
Which fled before it, so that from afar　　115
I spied the trembling of the ocean stream.
　We traversed the deserted plain, as one
Who, wander'd from his track, thinks every step
Trodden in vain till he regain the path.
　When we had come, where yet the tender dew
Strove with the sun, and in a place where fresh　121
The wind breathed o'er it, while it slowly dried;
Both hands extended on the watery grass
My master placed, in graceful act and kind.
Whence I of his intent before apprized,　　125
Stretch'd out to him my cheeks suffused with tears.
There to my visage he anew restored
That hue which the dun shades of hell conceal'd.
　Then on the solitary shore arrived,
That never sailing on its waters saw　　130
Man that could after measure back his course,
He girt me in such manner as had pleased

[5] Beatrice.
[6] The wife of Cato.
[7] The seven rounds of Purgatory, in which the seven capital sins are punished.
[8] When he was delivered by Christ from limbo, a change of affections accompanied his change of
place.

Him who instructed; and O, strange to tell!
As he selected every humble plant,
Wherever one was pluck'd another there   135
Resembling, straightway in its place arose.

Canto II

ARGUMENT

They behold a vessel under conduct of an angel,
coming over the waves with spirits to Purgatory,
among whom, when the passengers have landed,
Dante recognizes his friend Casella; but, while
they are entertained by him with a song, they
hear Cato exclaiming against their negligent
loitering, and at that rebuke hasten forwards to
the mountain.

Now had the sun to that horizon reach'd,
That covers, with the most exalted point
Of its meridian circle, Salem's walls;
And night, that opposite to him her orb   140
Rounds, from the stream of Ganges issued forth,
Holding the scales,[9] that from her hands are dropt
When she reigns highest: so that where I was,
Aurora's white and vermeil-tinctured cheek
To orange turn'd as she in age increased.   145
  Meanwhile we linger'd by the water's brink,
Like men who, musing on their road, in thought
Journey, while motionless the body rests.
When lo! as, near upon the hour of dawn,
Through the thick vapors Mars with fiery beam
Glares down in west, over the ocean floor;   151
So seem'd, what once again I hope to view,
A light, so swiftly coming through the sea,
No winged course might equal its career.
From which when for a space I had withdrawn
Mine eyes, to make inquiry of my guide,   156
Again I look'd, and saw it grown in size
And brightness: then on either side appear'd
Something, but what I knew not, of bright hue,
And by degrees from underneath it came   160
Another. My preceptor silent yet
Stood, while the brightness, that we first discern'd,
Open'd the form of wings: then when he knew
The pilot, cried aloud, "Down, down; bend low
Thy knees; behold God's angel: fold thy hands:
Now shalt thou see true ministers indeed.   166
Lo! how all human means he sets at nought;
So that nor oar he needs, nor other sail
Except his wings, between such distant shores.
Lo! how straight up to heaven he holds them
    rear'd,   170

Winnowing the air with those eternal plumes,
That not like mortal hairs fall off or change."
  As more and more toward us came, more bright
Appear'd the bird of God, nor could the eye
Endure his splendor near: I mine bent down.   175
He drove ashore in a small bark so swift
And light, that in its course no wave it drank.
The heavenly steersman at the prow was seen,
Visibly written Blessed in his looks.
Within, a hundred spirits and more there sat.   180
  "In Exitu[10] Israel de Egypto,"
All with one voice together sang, with what
In the remainder of that hymn is writ.
Then soon as with the sign of holy cross
He bless'd them, they at once leap'd out on land:
He, swiftly as he came, return'd. The crew,   186
There left, appear'd astounded with the place,
Gazing around, as one who sees new sights.
  From every side the sun darted his beams,
And with his arrowy radiance from mid heaven
Had chased the Capricorn, when that strange
    tribe,   191
Lifting their eyes toward us: "If ye know,
Declare what path will lead us to the mount."
  Them Virgil answer'd: "Ye suppose, perchance,
Us well acquainted with this place: but here,   195
We, as yourselves, are strangers. Not long erst
We came, before you but a little space,
By other road so rough and hard, that now
The ascent will seem to us as play." The spirits,
Who from my breathing had perceived I lived,
Grew pale with wonder. As the multitude   201
Flock round a herald sent with olive branch,
To hear what news he brings, and in their haste
Tread one another down; e'en so at sight
Of me those happy spirits were fix'd, each one
Forgetful of its errand to depart   206
Where, cleansed from sin, it might be made all
    fair.
  Then one I saw darting before the rest
With such fond ardor to embrace me, I
To do the like was moved. O shadows vain!   210
Except in outward semblance: thrice my hands
I clasp'd behind it, they as oft return'd
Empty into my breast again. Surprise
I need must think was painted in my looks,
For that the shadow smiled and backward drew.
To follow it I hasten'd, but with voice   216
Of sweetness it enjoin'd me to desist.
Then who it was I knew, and pray'd of it,
To talk with me it would a little pause.

[9] The constellation Libra.   [10] "When Israel came out of Egypt." *Psalms* cxiv.

It answer'd: "Thee as in my mortal frame   220
I loved, so loosed from it I love thee still,
And therefore pause: but why walkest thou here?"

"Not without purpose once more to return,
Thou find'st me, my Casella,[11] where I am,[12]
Journeying this way"; I said: "but how of thee
Hath so much time been lost?" He answer'd
     straight: 226

"No outrage hath been done to me, if he,[13]
Who when and whom he chooses takes, hath oft
Denied me passage here; since of just will
His will he makes. These three months past [14] in-
     deed,   230
He, whoso chose to enter, with free leave
Hath taken; whence I wandering by the shore [15]
Where Tiber's wave grows salt, of him gain'd kind
Admittance, at that river's mouth, toward which
His wings are pointed; for there always throng
All such as not to Acheron descend."   236

Then I: "If new law taketh not from thee
Memory or custom of love-tuned song,
That whilom all my cares had power to 'swage;
Please thee therewith a little to console   240
My spirit, that encumber'd with its frame,
Traveling so far, of pain is overcome."

"Love, that discourses in my thoughts," he then
Began in such soft accents, that within
The sweetness thrills me yet. My gentle guide,   245
And all who came with him, so well were pleased,
That seem'd nought else might in their thoughts
     have room.

Fast fix'd in mute attention to his notes
We stood, when lo! that old man venerable
Exclaiming, "How is this, ye tardy spirits?   250
What negligence detains you loitering here?
Run to the mountain to cast off those scales,
That from your eyes the sight of God conceal."

As a wild flock of pigeons, to their food
Collected, blade or tares, without their pride   255
Accustom'd, and in still and quiet sort,
If aught alarm them, suddenly desert
Their meal, assail'd by more important care;
So I that new-come troop beheld, the song
Deserting, hasten to the mountain's side,   260
As one who goes, yet, where he tends, knows not.
     Nor with less hurried step did we depart.

[*Canto III.* Our Poet, perceiving no shadow except that cast by his own body, is fearful that Virgil has deserted him; but he is freed from that
error, and both arrive together at the foot of the
mountain: on finding it too steep to climb, they inquire the way from a troop of spirits that are coming towards them, and are by them shown which
is the easiest ascent. Manfredi, King of Naples,
who is one of these spirits, bids Dante inform his
daughter Costanza, Queen of Arragon, of the
manner in which he had died.

Canto IV. Dante and Virgil ascend the mountain of Purgatory, by a steep and narrow path pent
in on each side by rock, till they reach a part of it
that opens into a ledge or cornice. There seating
themselves, and turning to the east, Dante wonders at seeing the sun on their left, the cause of
which is explained to him by Virgil; and while
they continue their discourse, a voice addresses
them, at which they turn, and find several spirits
behind the rock, and amongst the rest one named
Belacqua, who had been known to our Poet on
earth, and who tells that he is doomed to linger
there on account of his having delayed his repentance to the last.

Canto V. They meet with others, who had deferred their repentance till they were overtaken by
a violent death, when sufficient space being allowed them, they were then saved; and amongst
these, Giacopo del Cassero, Buonconte da Montefeltro, and Pia, a lady of Siena.

Canto VI. Many besides, who are in like case
with those spoken of in the last Canto, beseech our
Poet to obtain for them the prayers of their friends,
when he shall be returned to this world. This
moves him to express a doubt to his guide, how
the dead can be profited by the prayers of the living; for the solution of which doubt he is referred
to Beatrice. Afterwards he meets with Sordello the
Mantuan, whose affection, shown to Virgil his
countryman, leads Dante to break forth into an
invective against the unnatural divisions with
which Italy, and more especially Florence, was
distracted.

Canto VII. The approach of night hindering
further ascent, Sordello conducts our Poets apart
to an eminence, from whence they behold a pleas-

---

[11] A Florentine, celebrated for his skill in music.

[12] Cary has not made this passage clear. Dante means that he has undertaken this journey in order
to save his soul, so that after death he may be numbered among the holy spirits in Purgatory.

[13] The conducting angel.

[14] Since the time of the Jubilee, during which all spirits not condemned to eternal punishment were
supposed to pass over to Purgatory as soon as they pleased.

[15] Ostia.

ant recess, in form of a flowery valley, scooped out of the mountain; where are many famous spirits, and among them the Emperor Rodolph, Ottocar, King of Bohemia, Philip III of France, Henry of Navarre, Peter III of Arragon, Charles I of Naples, Henry III of England, and William, Marquis of Montferrat.

Canto VIII. Two angels, with flaming swords broken at the points, descend to keep watch over the valley, into which Virgil and Dante entering by desire of Sordello, our Poet meets with joy the spirit of Nino, the judge of Gallura, one who was well known to him. Meantime three exceedingly bright stars appear near the pole, and a serpent creeps subtly into the valley, but flees at hearing the approach of those angelic guards. Lastly, Conrad Malaspina predicts to our Poet his future banishment.

Canto IX. Dante is carried up the mountain, asleep and dreaming, by Lucia; and, on wakening, finds himself, two hours after sunrise, with Virgil, near the gate of Purgatory, through which they are admitted by the angel deputed by Saint Peter to keep it.

Canto X. Being admitted at the gate of Purgatory, our Poets ascend a winding path up the rock, till they reach an open and level space that extends each way round the mountain. On the side that rises, and which is of white marble, are seen artfully engraven many stories of humility, which whilst they are contemplating, there approach the souls of those who expiate the sin of pride, and who are bent down beneath the weight of heavy stones.

Canto XI. After a prayer uttered by the spirits, who were spoken of in the last Canto, Virgil inquires the way upwards, and is answered by one, who declares himself to have been Omberto, son of the Count of Santafiore. Next our Poet distinguishes Oderigi, the illuminator, who discourses on the vanity of worldly fame, and points out to him the soul of Provenzano Salvani.

Canto XII. Dante being desired by Virgil to look down on the ground which they are treading, observes that it is wrought over with imagery exhibiting various instances of pride recorded in history and fable. They leave the first cornice, and are ushered to the next by an angel who points out the way.

Canto XIII. They gain the second cornice, where the sin of envy is purged; and having proceeded a little to the right, they hear voices uttered by invisible spirits recounting famous examples of char-

ity, and next behold the shades, or souls, of the envious clad in sackcloth, and having their eyes sewed up with an iron thread. Amongst these Dante finds Sapia, a Sienese lady, from whom he learns the cause of her being there.

Canto XIV. Our Poet on this second cornice finds also the souls of Guido del Duca of Brettinoro, and Rinieri da Calboli of Romagna; the latter of whom, hearing that he comes from the banks of the Arno, inveighs against the degeneracy of all those who dwell in the cities visited by that stream; and the former, in like manner, against the inhabitants of Romagna. On leaving these, our Poets hear voices recording noted instances of envy.

Canto XV. An angel invites them to ascend the next steep. On their way Dante suggests certain doubts, which are resolved by Virgil; and, when they reach the third cornice, where the sin of anger is purged, our Poet, in a kind of waking dream, beholds remarkable instances of patience; and soon after they are enveloped in a dense fog.

Canto XVI. As they proceed through the mist, they hear the voices of spirits praying. Marco Lombardo, one of these, points out to Dante the error of such as impute our actions to necessity; explains to him that man is endued with free will; and shows that much of human depravity results from the undue mixture of spiritual and temporal authority in rulers.

Canto XVII. The Poet issues from that thick vapor; and soon after his fancy represents to him in lively portraiture some noted examples of anger. This imagination is dissipated by the appearance of an angel, who marshals them onward to the fourth cornice, on which the sin of gloominess or indifference is purged; and here Virgil shows him that this vice proceeds from a defect of love, and that all love can be only of two sorts, either natural, or of the soul; of which sorts the former is always right, but the latter may err either in respect of object or of degree.

Canto XVIII. Virgil discourses further concerning the nature of love. Then a multitude of spirits rush by; two of whom in van of the rest, record instances of zeal and fervent affection, and another, who was abbot of San Zeno in Verona, declares himself to Virgil and Dante; and lastly follow other spirits, shouting forth memorable examples of the sin for which they suffer. The Poet, pursuing his meditations, falls into a dreamy slumber.

Canto XIX. The Poet, after describing his dream, relates how, at the summoning of an angel, he ascends with Virgil to the fifth cornice, where the sin of avarice is cleansed, and where he finds Pope Adrian the fifth.

Canto XX. Among those on the fifth cornice, Hugh Capet records illustrious examples of voluntary poverty and of bounty; then tells who himself is, and speaks of his descendants on the French throne; and, lastly, adds some noted instances of avarice. When he has ended, the mountain shakes, and all the spirits sing "Glory to God."

Canto XXI. The two Poets are overtaken by the spirit of Statius, who, being cleansed, is on his way to Paradise, and who explains the cause of the mountain shaking, and of the hymn; his joy at beholding Virgil.

Canto XXII. Dante, Virgil, and Statius mount to the sixth cornice, where the sin of gluttony is cleansed, the two Latin Poets discoursing by the way. Turning to the right, they find a tree hung with sweet-smelling fruit, and watered by a shower that issues from the rock. Voices are heard to proceed from among the leaves, recording examples of temperance.

Canto XXIII. They are overtaken by the spirit of Forese, who had been a friend of our Poet's on earth, and who now inveighs against the immodest dress of their countrywomen at Florence.

Canto XXIV. Forese points out several others by name who are here, like himself, purifying themselves from the vice of gluttony; and amongst the rest, Buonaggiunta of Lucca, with whom our Poet converses. Forese then predicts the violent end of Dante's political enemy, Corso Donati; and, when he has quitted them, the Poet, in company with Statius and Virgil, arrives at another tree, from whence issue voices that record ancient examples of gluttony; and proceeding forwards, they are directed by an angel which way to ascend to the next cornice of the mountain.

Canto XXV. Virgil and Statius resolve some doubts that have arisen in the mind of Dante from what he had just seen. They all arrive on the seventh and last cornice, where the sin of incontinence is purged in fire; and the spirits of those suffering therein are heard to record illustrious instances of chastity.

Canto XXVI. The spirits wonder at seeing the shadow cast by the body of Dante on the flame as he passes it. This moves one of them to address him. It proves to be Guido Guinicelli, the Italian poet, who points out to him the spirit of Arnault Daniel, the Provençal, with whom he also speaks.

Canto XXVII. An angel sends them forward through the fire to the last ascent, which leads to the terrestrial Paradise, situated on the summit of the mountain. They have not proceeded many steps on their way upward, when the fall of night hinders them from going farther; and our Poet, who has lain down with Virgil and Statius to rest, beholds in a dream two females, figuring the active and contemplative life. With the return of morning, they reach the height; and here Virgil gives Dante full liberty to use his own pleasure and judgment in the choice of his way, till he shall meet with Beatrice.

Canto XXVIII. Dante wanders through the forest of the terrestrial Paradise, till he is stopped by a stream, on the other side of which he beholds a fair lady, culling flowers. He speaks to her; and she, in reply, explains to him certain things touching the nature of that place, and tells that the water, which flows between them, is here called Lethe, and in another place has the name of Eunoe.

Canto XXIX. The lady, who in a following Canto is called Matilda, moves along the side of the stream in a contrary direction to the current, and Dante keeps equal pace with her on the opposite bank. A marvelous sight, preceded by music, appears in view.]

Canto XXX

ARGUMENT

Beatrice descends from heaven, and rebukes the Poet.

Soon as that polar light,[16] fair ornament
Of the first heaven, which hath never known
Setting nor rising, nor the shadowy veil   265
Of other cloud than sin, to duty there
Each one convoying, as that lower doth
The steersman to his port, stood firmly fix'd;
Forthwith the saintly tribe, who in the van
Between the Gryphon and its radiance came,   270
Did turn them to the car, as to their rest:
And one, as if commission'd from above,
In holy chant thrice shouted forth aloud;
"Come,[17] spouse! from Libanus": and all the rest
Took up the song.—At the last audit, so   273

---

[16] The seven candlesticks of gold, which he calls the polar light of heaven itself, because they perform the same office for Christians that the polar star does for mariners, in guiding them to their port.
[17] "Come with me from Lebanon, my spouse, with me, from Lebanon." *Song of Solomon* iv. 8.

The blest shalt rise, from forth his cavern each
Uplifting lightly his new-vested flesh;
As, on the sacred litter, at the voice
Authoritative of that elder, sprang
A hundred ministers and messengers   280
Of life eternal. "Blessed [18] thou, who comest!"
And, "Oh!" they cried, "from full hands scatter ye
Unwithering lilies": and, so saying, cast
Flowers over head and round them on all sides.

    I have beheld, ere now, at break of day,   285
The eastern clime all roseate; and the sky
Opposed, one deep and beautiful serene;
And the sun's face so shaded, and with mists
Attemper'd, at his rising, that the eye
Long while endured the sight: thus, in a cloud   290
Of flowers, that from those hands angelic rose,
And down within and outside of the car
Fell showering, in white veil with olive wreathed,
A virgin in my view appear'd, beneath
Green mantle, robed in hue of living flame: 295
And o'er my spirit, that so long a time
Had from her presence felt no shuddering dread,
Albeit mine eyes discern'd her not, there moved
A hidden virtue from her, at whose touch
The power of ancient love was strong within me.

    No sooner on my vision streaming, smote   301
The heavenly influence, which, years past, and e'en
In childhood, thrill'd me, than towards Virgil I
Turn'd me to leftward; panting, like a babe,
That flees for refuge to his mother's breast,   305
If aught have terrified or work'd him woe:
And would have cried, "There is no dram of
    blood,
That doth not quiver in me. The old flame
Throws out clear tokens of reviving fire."
But Virgil had bereaved us of himself;   310
Virgil, my best loved father; Virgil, he
To whom I gave me up for safety: nor
All, our prime mother lost, avail'd to save
My undew'd cheeks from blur of soiling tears.
    "Dante! weep not that Virgil leaves thee; nay,
Weep thou not yet: behoves thee feel the edge   316
Of other sword; and thou shalt weep for that."

    As to the prow or stern, some admiral
Paces the deck, inspiriting his crew,
When 'mid the sail-yards all hands ply aloof;   320
Thus, on the left side of the car, I saw
(Turning me at the sound of mine own name,
Which here I am compell'd to register)
The virgin station'd, who before appear'd
Veil'd in that festive shower angelical.   325

Towards me, across the stream, she bent her
    eyes;
Though from her brow the veil descending, bound
With foliage of Minerva, suffer'd not
That I beheld her clearly: then with act
Full royal, still insulting o'er her thrall,   330
Added, as one who, speaking, keepeth back
The bitterest saying, to conclude the speech:
"Observe me well. I am, in sooth, I am
Beatrice. What! and hast thou deign'd at last
Approach the mountain? Knewest not, O man!
Thy happiness is here?" Down fell mine eyes   336
On the clear fount; but there, myself espying,
Recoil'd, and sought the greens_werd; such a
    weight
Of shame was on my forehead. With a mien
Of that stern majesty, which doth surround   340
A mother's presence to her awe-struck child,
She look'd; a flavor of such bitterness
Was mingled in her pity. There her words
Brake off; and suddenly the angels sang,   344
"In thee, O gracious Lord! my hope hath been":
But went no further than, "Thou, Lord! hast set
My feet in ample room." As snow, that lies,
Amidst the living rafters [19] on the back
Of Italy, congeal'd, when drifted high
And closely piled by rough Sclavonian blasts;   350
Breathe but the land whereon no shadow falls,
And straightway melting it distils away,
Like a fire-wasted taper: thus was I,
Without a sigh or tear, or ever these
Did sing, that, with the chiming of heaven's
    sphere,   355
Still in their warbling chime: but when the strain
Of dulcet symphony express'd for me
Their soft compassion, more than could the words,
"Virgin! why so consumest him?" then, the ice
Congeal'd about my bosom, turn'd itself   360
To spirit and water; and with anguish forth
Gush'd, through the lips and eyelids, from the
    heart.
    Upon the chariot's same edge till she stood,
Immoveable; and thus address'd her words
To those bright semblances with pity touch'd:
"Ye in the eternal day your vigils keep;   366
So that nor night nor slumber, with close stealth,
Conveys from you a single step, in all
The goings on of time: thence, with more heed
I shape mine answer, for his ear intended,   370
Who there stands weeping; that the sorrow now
May equal the transgression. Not alone

---

[18] "Blessed is he that cometh in the name of the Lord." *Matt.* xxi. 9.
[19] The leafless woods on the Apennine.

Through operation of the mighty orbs,
That mark each seed to some predestined aim,
As with aspect or fortunate or ill   375
The constellations meet; but through benign
Largess of heavenly graces, which rain down
From such a height as mocks our vision, this man
Was, in the freshness of his being, such,
So gifted virtually, that in him   380
All better habits wonderously had thrived.
The more of kindly strength is in the soil,
So much doth evil seed and lack of culture
Mar it the more, and make it run to wildness.
These looks sometime upheld him; for I show'd
My youthful eyes, and led him by their light   386
In upright walking. Soon as I had reach'd
The threshold of my second age, and changed
My mortal for immortal; then he left me,
And gave himself to others. When from flesh   390
To spirit I had risen, and increase
Of beauty and of virtue circled me,
I was less dear to him, and valued less.
His steps were turn'd into deceitful ways,
Following false images of good, that make   395
No promise perfect. Nor avail'd me aught
To sue for inspirations, with the which,
I, both in dreams of night, and otherwise,
Did call him back; of them, so little reck'd him.
Such depth he fell, that all device was short   400
Of his preserving, save that he should view
The children of perdition. To this end
I visited the purlieus of the dead:
And one, who hath conducted him thus high,
Received my supplications urged with weeping.
It were a breaking of God's high decree,   406
If Lethe should be past, and such food [20] tasted,
Without the cost of some repentant tear."

Canto XXXI

ARGUMENT

Beatrice continues her reprehension of Dante, who
confesses his error, and falls to the ground: coming to himself again, he is by Matilda drawn
through the waters of Lethe, and presented first
to the four virgins who figure the cardinal virtues; these in their turn lead him to the
Gryphon, a symbol of our Saviour; and the three
virgins, representing the evangelical virtues, in-

tercede for him with Beatrice, that she would
display to him her second beauty.

"O thou!" her words she thus without delay
Resuming, turn'd their point on me, to whom   410
They, but with lateral edge, [21] seem'd harsh before:
"Say thou, who stand'st beyond the holy stream,
If this be true. A charge, so grievous, needs
Thine own avowal." On my faculty
Such strange amazement hung, the voice expired
Imperfect, ere its organs gave it birth.   416
A little space refraining, then she spake:
"What dost thou muse on? Answer me. The wave
On thy remembrances of evil yet
Hath done no injury." A mingled sense   420
Of fear and of confusion, from my lips
Did such a "Yea" produce, as needed help
Of vision to interpret. As when breaks,
In act to be discharged, a cross-bow bent
Beyond its pitch, both nerve and bow o'erstretch'd;
The flagging weapon feebly hits the mark: 426
Thus, tears and sighs forth gushing, did I burst,
Beneath the heavy load: and thus my voice
Was slacken'd on its way. She straight began:
"When my desire invited thee to love   430
The good, which sets a bound to our aspirings;
What bar of thwarting foss or linked chain
Did meet thee, that thou so shouldst quit the hope
Of further progress? or what bait of ease,
Or promise of allurement, led thee on   435
Elsewhere, that thou elsewhere shouldst rather
     wait?"
A bitter sigh I drew, then scarce found voice
To answer; hardly to these sounds my lips
Gave utterance, wailing: "Thy fair looks with-
     drawn,
Things present, with deceitful pleasures, turn'd
My steps aside." She answering spake: "Hadst
     thou   441
Been silent, or denied what thou avow'st,
Thou hadst not hid thy sin the more; such eye
Observes it. But whene'er the sinner's cheek
Breaks forth into the precious-streaming tears   445
Of self-accusing, in our court the wheel
Of justice doth run counter to the edge. [22]
Howe'er, that thou mayst profit by thy shame
For errors past, and that henceforth more strength
May arm thee, when thou hear'st the Syren-voice;
Lay thou aside the motive to this grief,   451
And lend attentive ear, while I unfold

[20] The oblivion of sins.
[21] The words of Beatrice, when not addressed directly to himself, but spoken to the angel of him,
Dante had thought sufficiently harsh.
[22] "The weapons of divine justice are blunted by the confession and sorrow of the offender."

How opposite a way my buried flesh
Should have impell'd thee. Never didst thou spy,
In art or nature, aught so passing sweet, 455
As were the limbs that in their beauteous frame
Enclosed me, and are scatter'd now in dust.
If sweetest thing thus fail'd thee with my death,
What, afterward, of mortal, should thy wish
Have tempted? When thou first hadst felt the dart
Of perishable things, in my departing 461
For better realms, thy wing thou shouldst have
    pruned
To follow me; and never stoop'd again,
To 'bide a second blow, for a slight girl,
Or other gaud as transient and as vain.[23] 465
The new and inexperienced bird awaits,
Twice it may be, or thrice, the fowler's aim;
But in the sight of one whose plumes are full,
In vain the net is spread, the arrow wing'd."
    I stood, as children silent and ashamed 470
Stand, listening, with their eyes upon the earth,
Acknowledging their fault, and self-condemn'd.
And she resumed: "If, but to hear, thus pains thee;
Raise thou thy beard, and lo! what sight shall do."
    With less reluctance yields a sturdy holm, 475
Rent from its fibers by a blast, that blows
From off the pole, or from Iarbas' land,[24]
Than I at her behest my visage raised:
And thus the face denoting by the beard,
I mark'd the secret sting her words convey'd. 480
    No sooner lifted I mine aspect up,
Than I perceived those primal creatures cease
Their flowery sprinkling; and mine eyes beheld
(Yet unassured and wavering in their view)
Beatrice; she, who towards the mystic shape, 485
That joins two natures in one form, had turn'd:
And, even under shadow of her veil,
And parted by the verdant rill that flow'd
Between, in loveliness she seem'd as much
Her former self surpassing, as on earth 490
All others she surpass'd. Remorseful goads
Shot sudden through me. Each thing else, the
    more
Its love had late beguiled me, now the more
Was loathsome. On my heart so keenly smote
The bitter consciousness, that on the ground 495
O'erpower'd I fell: and what my state was then,
She knows, who was the cause. When now my
    strength

Flow'd back, returning outward from the heart,
The lady,[25] whom alone I first had seen,
I found above me. "Loose me not," she cried: 500
"Lose not thy hold": and lo! had dragg'd me high
As to my neck into the stream; while she,
Still as she drew me after, swept along,
Swift as a shuttle, bounding o'er the wave.
    The blessed shore approaching, then was heard
So sweetly "Tu asperges me,"[26] that I 506
May not remember, much less tell the sound.
    The beauteous dame, her arms expanding,
    clasp'd
My temples, and immerged me where 'twas fit
The wave should drench me: and, thence raising
    up, 510
Within the fourfold dance of lovely nymphs
Presented me so laved; and with their arm
They each did cover me. "Here are we nymphs,
And in the heaven are stars. Or ever earth
Was visited of Beatrice, we, 515
Appointed for her handmaids, tended on her.
We to her eyes will lead thee: but the light
Of gladness, that is in them, well to scan,
Those yonder three,[27] of deeper ken than ours,
Thy sight shall quicken." Thus began their song:
And then they led me to the Gryphon's breast, 521
Where, turn'd toward us, Beatrice stood.
"Spare not thy vision. We have station'd thee
Before the emeralds,[28] whence love, erewhile,
Hath drawn his weapons on thee." As they spake,
A thousand fervent wishes riveted 526
Mine eyes upon her beaming eyes, that stood,
Still fix'd toward the Gryphon, motionless.
As the sun strikes a mirror, even thus
Within those orbs the twyfold being shone; 530
For ever varying, in one figure now
Reflected, now in other. Reader! muse
How wondrous in my sight it seem'd, to mark
A thing, albeit stedfast in itself,
Yet in its imaged semblance mutable. 535
    Full of amaze, and joyous, while my soul
Fed on the viand, whereof still desire
Grows with satiety; the other three,
With gesture that declared a loftier line,
Advanced: to their own carol, on they came 540
Dancing, in festive ring angelical.
    "Turn, Beatrice!" was their song: "Oh! turn
Thy saintly sight on this thy faithful one,

[23] Beatrice alludes to Dante's unworthy life after her death.
[24] The south.
[25] Matilda.
[26] "Purge me with hyssop, and I shall be clean; wash me, and I shall be whiter than snow." *Psalms* li. 7.
[27] Faith, hope, and charity.
[28] The eyes of Beatrice.

Who, to behold thee, many a wearisome pace
Hath measured. Gracious at our prayer, vouchsafe
Unveil to him thy cheeks; that he may mark   546
Thy second beauty, now conceal'd." O splendor!
O sacred light eternal! who is he,
So pale with musing in Pierian shades,
Or with that fount so lavishly imbued,   550
Whose spirit should not fail him in the essay
To represent thee such as thou didst seem,
When under cope of the still-chiming heaven
Thou gavest to open air thy charms reveal'd?

Canto XXXII

ARGUMENT

Dante is warned not to gaze too fixedly on Beatrice. The procession moves on, accompanied by
Matilda, Statius, and Dante, till they reach an
exceeding lofty tree, where divers strange
chances befall.

Mine eyes with such an eager coveting   555
Were bent to rid them of their ten years' thirst,[29]
No other sense was waking: and e'en they
Were fenced on either side from heed of aught;
So tangled, in its custom'd toils, that smile
Of saintly brightness drew me to itself: 560
When forcibly, toward the left, my sight
The sacred virgins turn'd; for from their lips
I heard the warning sounds: "Too fix'd a gaze!"
  Awhile my vision labor'd; as when late
Upon the o'erstrained eyes the sun hath smote:
But soon, to lesser object, as the view   566
Was now recover'd (lesser in respect
To that excess of sensible, whence late
I had perforce been sunder'd), on their right
I mark'd that glorious army wheel, and turn, 570
Against the sun and sevenfold lights, their front.
As when, their bucklers for protection raised,
A well-ranged troop, with portly banners curl'd,
Wheel circling, ere the whole can change their
      ground;
E'en thus the goodly regiment of heaven,   575
Proceeding, all did pass us ere the car
Had sloped his beam. Attendant at the wheels
The damsels turn'd; and on the Gryphon moved
The sacred burden, with a pace so smooth,
No feather on him trembled. The fair dame,   580
Who through the wave had drawn me, companied

By Statius and myself, pursued the wheel,
Whose orbit, rolling, mark'd a lesser arch.
  Through the high wood, now void (the more
      her blame,
Who by the serpent was beguiled), I pass'd,   585
With step in cadence to the harmony
Angelic. Onward had we moved, as far,
Perchance, as arrow at three several flights
Full wing'd had sped, when from her station down
Descended Beatrice. With one voice   590
All murmur'd "Adam"; circling next a plant
Despoil'd of flowers and leaf, on every bough.
Its tresses, spreading more as more they rose,
Were such, as 'midst their forest wilds, for height,
The Indians might have gazed at. "Blessed thou,
Gryphon![30] whose beak hath never pluck'd that
      tree   596
Pleasant to taste: for hence the appetite
Was warp'd to evil." Round the stately trunk
Thus shouted forth the rest, to whom return'd
The animal twice-gender'd: "Yea! for so   600
The generation of the just are saved."
And turning to the chariot-pole, to foot
He drew it of the widow'd branch, and bound
There, left unto the stock whereon it grew.
  As when large floods of radiance from above 605
Stream, with that radiance mingled, which ascends
Next after setting of the scaly sign,
Our plants then burgein, and each wears anew
His wonted colors, ere the sun have yoked
Beneath another star his flamy steeds;   610
Thus putting forth a hue more faint than rose,
And deeper than the violet, was renew'd
The plant, erewhile in all its branches bare.
Unearthly was the hymn, which then arose.
I understood it not, nor to the end   615
Endured the harmony. Had I the skill
To pencil forth how closed the unpitying eyes
Slumbering, when Syrinx warbled (eyes that paid
So dearly for their watching), then, like painter,
That with a model paints, I might design   620
The manner of my falling into sleep.
But feign who will the slumber cunningly,
I pass it by to when I waked; and tell,
How suddenly a flash of splendor rent
The curtain of my sleep, and one cries out,   625
"Arise: what dost thou?" As the chosen three,
On Tabor's mount, admitted to behold
The blossoming of that fair tree,[31] whose fruit

---

[29] Beatrice had been dead ten years.
[30] Our Saviour's submission to the Roman empire appears to be intended, and particularly His in-
junction, "to render unto Cæsar the things that are Cæsar's."
[31] Our Saviour's transfiguration. "As the apple-tree among the trees of the wood, so is my beloved
among the sons." *Song of Solomon* ii. 3.

Is coveted of angels, and doth make
Perpetual feast in heaven; to themselves   630
Returning, at the word whence deeper sleeps [32]
Were broken, they their tribe diminish'd saw;
Both Moses and Elias gone, and changed
The stole their master wore; thus to myself
Returning, over me beheld I stand   635
The piteous one,[33] who, cross the stream, had brought
My steps. "And where," all doubting, I exclaim'd,
"Is Beatrice?"—"See her," she replied,
"Beneath the fresh leaf, seated on its root.
Behold the associate choir, that circles her.   640
The others, with a melody more sweet
And more profound, journeying to higher realms,
Upon the Gryphon tend." If there her words
Were closed, I know not; but mine eyes had now
Ta'en view of her, by whom all other thoughts
Were barr'd admittance. On the very ground   646
Alone she sat, as she had there been left
A guard upon the wain, which I beheld
Bound to the twyform beast. The seven nymphs
Did make themselves a cloister round about her;
And, in their hands, upheld those lights [34] secure
From blast septentrion and the gusty south.   652
    "A little while thou shalt be forester here;
And citizen shalt be, for ever with me,
Of that true Rome,[35] wherein Christ dwells a Roman   655
To profit the misguided world, keep now
Thine eyes upon the car; and what thou seest,
Take heed thou write, returning to that place." [36]
    Thus Beatrice: at whose feet inclined
Devout, at her behest, my thought and eyes   660
I, as she bade, directed. Never fire,
With so swift motion, forth a stormy cloud
Leap'd downward from the welkin's furthest bound,
As I beheld the bird of Jove descend
Down through the tree; and, as he rush'd, the rind
Disparting crush beneath him; buds much more,
And leaflets. On the car, with all his might   667
He struck; whence, staggering, like a ship it reel'd,

At random driven, to starboard now, o'ercome,
And now to larboard, by the vaulting waves.   670
    Next, springing up into the chariot's womb,
A fox [37] I saw, with hunger seeming pined
Of all good food. But, for his ugly sins
The saintly maid rebuking him, away
Scampering he turn'd, fast as his hide-bound corpse   675
Would bear him. Next, from whence before he came,
I saw the eagle dart into the hull
O' the car, and leave it with his feathers lined: [38]
And then a voice, like that which issues forth
From heart with sorrow rived, did issue forth   680
From heaven, and "O poor bark of mine!" it cried,
"How badly art thou freighted." Then it seem'd
That the earth open'd, between either wheel;
And I beheld a dragon [39] issue thence,   684
That through the chariot fix'd his forked train;
And like a wasp, that draggeth back the sting,
So drawing forth his baleful train, he dragg'd
Part of the bottom forth; and went his way,
Exulting. What remain'd, as lively turf   689
With green herb, so did clothe itself with plumes,[40]
Which haply had, with purpose chaste and kind,
Been offer'd; and therewith were clothed the wheels,
Both one and other, and the beam, so quickly,
A sigh were not breathed sooner. Thus transform'd,
The holy structure, through its several parts,   695
Did put forth heads; [41] three on the beam, and one
On every side: the first like oxen horn'd;
But with a single horn upon their front,
The four. Like monster, sight hath never seen.
O'er it [42] methought there sat, secure as rock   700
On mountain's lofty top, a shameless whore,
Whose ken roved loosely round her. At her side,
As 'twere that none might bear her off, I saw
A giant stand; and ever and anon
They mingled kisses. But, her lustful eyes   705
Chancing on me to wander, that fell minion
Scourged her from head to foot all o'er; then full
Of jealousy, and fierce with rage, unloosed

[32] The sleep of death, in the instance of the ruler of the synagogue's daughter and of Lazarus.
[33] Matilda.
[34] The tapers of gold.
[35] Of heaven.
[36] To the earth.
[37] By the fox probably is represented the treachery of the heretics.
[38] In allusion to the donations made by Constantine to the Church.
[39] Probably Mahomet.
[40] The increase of wealth and temporal dominion, which followed the supposed gift of Constantine.
[41] By the seven heads, it is supposed with sufficient probability, are meant the seven capital sins.
[42] The harlot is thought to represent the state of the Church under Boniface VIII and the giant to figure Philip IV of France.

The monster, and dragg'd on,[43] so far across
The forest, that from me its shades alone   710
Shielded the harlot and the new-form'd brute.

Canto XXXIII

ARGUMENT

After a hymn sung, Beatrice leaves the tree, and takes with her the seven virgins, Matilda, Statius, and Dante. She then darkly predicts to our Poets some future events. Lastly, the whole band arrive at the fountain, from whence the two streams, Lethe and Eunoe, separating, flow different ways; and Matilda, at the desire of Beatrice, causes our Poet to drink of the latter stream.

"The heathen,[44] Lord! are come": responsive thus,
The trinal now, and now the virgin band
Quaternion, their sweet psalmody began,
Weeping; and Beatrice listen'd, sad   715
And sighing, to the song, in such a mood,
That Mary, as she stood beside the cross,
Was scarce more changed. But when they gave her place
To speak, then, risen upright on her feet,
She, with a color glowing bright as fire,   720
Did answer: "Yet a little while, and ye
Shall see me not; and, my beloved sisters!
Again a little while, and ye shall see me."
  Before her then she marshal'd all the seven;
And, beckoning only, motion'd me, the dame,
And that remaining sage,[45] to follow her.   726
  So on she pass'd; and had not set, I ween,
Her tenth step to the ground, when, with mine eyes,
Her eyes encounter'd; and, with visage mild,
"So mend thy pace," she cried, "that if my words
Address thee, thou mayst still be aptly placed   731
To hear them." Soon as duly to her side
I now had hasten'd: "Brother!" she began,
"Why makest thou no attempt at questioning,
As thus we walk together?" Like to those   735
Who, speaking with too reverent an awe

Before their betters, draw not forth the voice
Alive unto their lips, befell me then
That I in sounds imperfect thus began: 739
"Lady! what I have need of, that thou know'st;
And what will suit my need." She answering thus:
"Of fearfulness and shame, I will that thou
Henceforth do rid thee; that thou speak no more,
As one who dreams. Thus far be taught of me:
The vessel which thou saw'st the serpent break,
Was, and is not: let him, who hath the blame,   746
Hope not to scare God's vengance with a sop.[46]
Without an heir for ever shall not be
That eagle,[47] he, who left the chariot plumed,
Which monster made it first and next a prey.   750
Plainly I view, and therefore speak, the stars
E'en now approaching, whose conjunction, free
From all impediment and bar, brings on
A season, in the which, one sent from God   754
(Five hundred, five, and ten, do mark him out),
That foul one, and the accomplice of her guilt,
The giant, both, shall slay. And if perchance
My saying, dark as Themis or as Sphinx,
Fail to persuade thee (since like them it foils
The intellect with blindness), yet erelong   760
Events shall be the Naïads, that will solve
This knotty riddle; and no damage light
On flock or field. Take heed; and as these words
By me are utter'd, teach them even so
To those who live that life, which is a race   765
To death: and when thou writest them, keep in mind
Not to conceal how thou hast seen the plant,
That twice [48] hath now been spoil'd. This whoso robs,
This whoso plucks, with blasphemy of deed
Sins against God, who for His use alone   770
Creating hallow'd it. For taste of this,
In pain and in desire, five thousand years
And upward, the first soul did yearn for Him
Who punish'd in Himself the fatal gust.
  "Thy reason slumbers, if it deem this height,
And summit thus inverted, of the plant,   776
Without due cause: and were not vainer thoughts,

---

[43] The removal of the Pope's residence from Rome to Avignon is pointed at.

[44] "O God, the heathen are come into Thine inheritance." *Psalms* lxxix. 1.

[45] Statius.

[46] "Let not him who hath occasioned the destruction of the Church, that vessel which the serpent brake, hope to appease the anger of the Deity by any outward acts of religious, or rather superstitious ceremony; such as was that, in our Poet's time, performed by a murderer at Florence, who imagined himself secure from vengeance, if he ate a sop of bread in wine upon the grave of the person murdered, within the space of nine days."

[47] He prognosticates that the Emperor of Germany will not always continue to submit to the usurpations of the Pope, and foretells the coming of Henry VII, Duke of Luxemburg, signified by the numerical figures DVX; or, as Lombardi supposes, of Can Grande della Scala, appointed the leader of the Ghibelline forces.

[48] First by the eagle and next by the giant.

As Elsa's numbing waters,[49] to thy soul.
And their fond pleasures had not dyed it dark
As Pyramus the mulberry; thou hadst seen,   780
In such momentous circumstances alone,
God's equal justice morally implied
In the forbidden tree. But since I mark thee,
In understanding, harden'd into stone,
And, to that hardness, spotted too and stain'd,
So that thine eye is dazzled at my word;   786
I will, that, if not written, yet at least
Painted thou take it in thee, for the cause,
That one brings home his staff inwreathed with
    palm."
    I thus: "As wax by seal, that changeth not   790
Its impress, now is stamp'd my brain by thee.
But wherefore soars thy wish'd-for speech so high
Beyond my sight, that loses it the more,
The more it strains to reach it?"—"To the end
That thou mayst know," she answer'd straight,
    "the school,   795
That thou hast follow'd; and how far behind,
When following my discourse, its learning halts:
And mayst behold your art, from the divine
As distant, as the disagreement is
'Twixt earth and heaven's most high and raptur-
    ous orb."   800
    "I not remember," I replied, "that e'er
I was estranged from thee; nor for such fault
Doth conscience chide me." Smiling she return'd:
"If thou canst not remember, call to mind
How lately thou hast drunk of Lethe's wave;   805
And, sure as smoke doth indicate a flame,
In that forgetfulness itself conclude
Blame from thy alienated will incurr'd.
From henceforth, verily, my words shall be
As naked, as will suit them to appear   810
In thy unpracticed view." More sparkling now,
And with retarded course, the sun possess'd
The circle of mid-day, that varies still
As the aspect varies of each several clime;

When, as one, sent in vaward of a troop   815
For escort, pauses, if perchance he spy
Vestige of somewhat strange and rare; so paused
The sevenfold band, arriving at the verge
Of a dun umbrage hoar, such as is seen,
Beneath green leaves and gloomy branches, oft
To overbrow a bleak and alpine cliff.   821
And, where they stood, before them, as it seem'd,
I, Tigris and Euphrates both, beheld
Forth from one fountain issue; and, like friends,
Linger at parting. "O enlightening beam!   825
O glory of our kind! beseech thee say
What water this, which, from one source derived,
Itself removes to distance from itself?"
    To such entreaty answer thus was made:
"Entreat Matilda, that she teach thee this."   830
And here, as one who clears himself of blame
Imputed, the fair dame return'd: "Of me
He this and more hath learnt; and I am safe
That Lethe's water hath not hid it from him."
    And Beatrice: "Some more pressing care,   835
That oft the memory 'reaves, perchance hath made
His mind's eye dark. But lo, where Eunoe flows!
Lead thither; and, as thou art wont, revive
His fainting virtue." As a courteous spirit,
That proffers no excuses, but as soon   840
As he hath token of another's will,
Makes it his own; when she had ta'en me, thus
The lovely maiden moved her on, and call'd
To Statius, with an air most lady-like:
"Come thou with him." Were further space
    allow'd,   845
Then, Reader! might I sing, though but in part,
That beverage, with whose sweetness I had ne'er
Been sated. But, since all the leaves are full,
Appointed for this second strain, mine art
With warning bridle checks me. I return'd   850
From the most holy wave, regenerate,
E'en as new plants renew'd with foliage new.
Pure and made apt for mounting to the stars

[49] The Elsa, a little stream, which flows into the Arno about twenty miles below Florence, is said to possess a petrifying quality.

Paradise

Canto I

ARGUMENT

The Poet ascends with Beatrice towards the first heaven; and is by her resolved of certain doubts which arise in his mind.

His glory, by whose might all things are moved,
Pierces the universe, and in one part
Sheds more resplendence, elsewhere less. In heaven,
That largeliest of his light partakes, was I,
Witness of things, which, to relate again,   5
Surpasseth power of him who comes from thence;
For that, so near approaching its desire,
Our intellect is to such depth absorb'd,
That memory cannot follow. Nathless all,
That in my thoughts I of that sacred realm   10
Could store, shall now be matter of my song.
    Benign Apollo! this last labor aid;
And make me such a vessel of thy worth,
As thy own laurel claims, of me beloved.
Thus far [1] hath one of steep Parnassus' brows   15
Sufficed me; henceforth, there is need of both
For my remaining enterprise. Do thou [2]
Enter into my bosom, and there breathe
So, as when Marsyas by thy hand was dragg'd
Forth from his limbs, unsheathed. O power divine!   20
If thou to me of thine impart so much,
That of that happy realm the shadow'd form
Traced in my thoughts I may set forth to view;
Thou shalt behold me of thy favor'd tree
Come to the foot, and crown myself with leaves:
For to that honor thou, and my high theme   26
Will fit me. If but seldom, mighty Sire!
To grace his triumph, gathers thence a wreath
Cæsar, or bard (more shame for human wills
Depraved), joy to the Delphic god must spring
From the Peneian foliage, when one breast   31
Is with such thirst inspired. From a small spark
Great flame hath risen: after me, perchance,
Others with better voice may pray, and gain,
From the Cyrrhæan city, answer kind.   35

Through divers passages, the world's bright lamp
Rises to mortals; but through that [3] which joins
Four circles with the threefold cross, in best
Course, and in happiest constellation [4] set,
He comes; and, to the worldly wax, best gives   40
Its temper and impression. Morning there,
Here eve was well nigh by such passage made;
And whiteness had o'erspread that hemisphere,
Blackness the other part: when to the left
I saw Beatrice turn'd, and on the sun   45
Gazing, as never eagle fix'd his ken.
As from the first a second beam is wont
To issue, and reflected upwards rise,
Even as a pilgrim bent on his return;
So of her act, that through the eyesight pass'd   50
Into my fancy, mine was form'd: and straight,
Beyond our mortal wont, I fix'd mine eyes
Upon the sun. Much is allow'd us there,
That here exceeds our power; thanks to the place
Made for the dwelling of the human kind.   55
    I suffer'd it not long; and yet so long,
That I beheld it bickering sparks around,
As iron that comes boiling from the fire.
And suddenly upon the day appear'd
A day new-risen; as he, who hath the power,   60
Had with another sun bedeck'd the sky.
    Her eyes fast fix'd on the eternal wheels,
Beatrice stood unmoved; and I with ken
Fix'd upon her, from upward gaze removed,
At her aspect, such inwardly became   65
As Glaucus, when he tasted of the herb
That made him peer among the ocean gods:
Words may not tell of that transhuman change;
And therefore let the example serve, though weak,
For those whom grace hath better proof in store.
    If I were only what thou didst create,   71
Then newly, Love! by whom the heaven is ruled;
Thou know'st, who by thy light didst bear me up.
Whenas the wheel which thou dost ever guide,
Desired Spirit! with its harmony,   75
Temper'd of thee and measured, charm'd mine ear
Then seem'd to me so much of heaven to blaze

---

[1] He appears to mean nothing more than that this part of his poem will require a greater exertion of his powers than the former.

[2] Make me thine instrument; and, through me, utter such sound as when thou didst contend with Marsyas.

[3] "Where the four circles, the horizon, the zodiac, the equator, and equinoctial colure join; the last three intersecting each other so as to form three crosses, as may be seen in the armillary sphere."

[4] Aries. Some understand the planet Venus by the "miglior stella."

With the sun's flame, that rain or flood ne'er made
A lake so broad. The newness of the sound,
And that great light, inflamed me with desire, 80
Keener than e'er was felt, to know their cause.

Whence she, who saw me, clearly as myself,
To calm my troubled mind, before I ask'd,
Open'd her lips, and gracious thus began:
"With false imagination thou thyself 85
Makest dull; so that thou seest not the thing,
Which thou hadst seen, had that been shaken off.
Thou art not on the earth as thou believest;
For lightning, scaped from its own proper place,
Ne'er ran, as thou hast hither now return'd." 90

Although divested of my first-raised doubt
By those brief words accompanied with smiles,
Yet in new doubt was I entangled more,
And said: "Already satisfied, I rest
From admiration deep; but now admire 95
How I above those lighter bodies rise."

Whence, after utterance of a piteous sigh,
She towards me bent her eyes, with such a look,
As on her frenzied child a mother casts;
Then thus began: "Among themselves all things
Have order; and from hence the form,[5] which makes 101
The universe resemble God. In this
The higher creatures see the printed steps
Of that eternal worth, which is the end
Whither the line is drawn.[6] All natures lean, 105
In this their order, diversly; some more,
Some less approaching to their primal source.
Thus they to different havens are moved on
Through the vast sea of being, and each one
With instinct given, that bears it in its course:
This to the lunar sphere directs the fire; 111
This moves the hearts of mortal animals;
This the brute earth together knits, and binds.
Nor only creatures, void of intellect,
Are aim'd at by this bow; but even those, 115
That have intelligence and love, are pierced.
That Providence, who so well orders all,
With her own light makes ever calm the heaven,[7]
In which the substance, that hath greatest speed,[8]
Is turn'd: and thither now, as to our seat 120
Predestined, we are carried by the force
Of that strong cord, that never looses dart
But at fair aim and glad. Yet it is true,
That as, oft-times, but ill accords the form
To the design of art, through sluggishness 125

Or unreplying matter; so this course
Is sometimes quitted by the creature, who
Hath power, directed thus, to bend elsewhere;
As from a cloud the fire is seen to fall,
From its original impulse warp'd to earth, 130
By vitious fondness. Thou no more admire
Thy soaring (if I rightly deem), than lapse
Of torrent downwards from a mountain's height.
There would in thee for wonder be more cause,
If, free of hindrance, thou hadst stay'd below,
As living fire unmoved upon the earth." 136

So said, she turn'd toward the heaven her face.

[*Canto II*. Dante and his celestial guide enter the moon. The cause of the spots or shadows, which appear in that body, is explained to him.

Canto III. In the moon Dante meets with Piccarda, the sister of Forese, who tells him that this planet is allotted to those, who, after having made profession of chastity and a religious life, had been compelled to violate their vows; and she then points out to him the spirit of the Empress Costanza.

Canto IV. While they still continue in the moon, Beatrice removes certain doubts which Dante had conceived respecting the place assigned to the blessed, and respecting the will absolute or conditional. He inquires whether it is possible to make satisfaction for a vow broken.

Canto V. The question proposed in the last Canto is answered. Dante ascends with Beatrice to the planet Mercury, which is the second heaven; and here he finds a multitude of spirits, one of whom offers to satisfy him of anything he may desire to know from them.

Canto VI. The spirit, who had offered to satisfy the inquiries of Dante, declares himself to be the Emperor Justinian; and after speaking of his own actions, recounts the victories, before him, obtained under the Roman Eagle. He then informs our Poet that the soul of Romeo the pilgrim, is in the same star.

Canto VII. In consequence of what had been said by Justinian, who together with the other spirits have now disappeared, some doubts arise in the mind of Dante respecting the human redemption. These difficulties are fully explained by Beatrice.

Canto VIII. The Poet ascends with Beatrice to the third heaven, which is the planet Venus; and

---

[5] This order it is, that gives to the universe the form of unity, and therefore of resemblance to God.
[6] All things, as they have their beginning from the Supreme Being, so are they referred to Him again.
[7] The empyrean, which is always motionless.
[8] The primum mobile.

here finds the soul of Charles Martel, King of Hungary, who had been Dante's friend on earth, and who now, after speaking of the realms to which he was heir, unfolds the cause why children differ in disposition from their parents.

Canto IX. The next spirit, who converses with our Poet in the planet Venus, is the amorous Cunizza. To her succeeds Folco, or Folques, the Provençal bard, who declares that the soul of Rahab the harlot is there also; and then, blaming the Pope for his neglect of the holy land, prognosticates some reverse to the papal power.

Canto X. Their next ascent carries them into the sun, which is the fourth heaven. Here they are encompassed with a wreath of blessed spirits, twelve in number. Thomas Aquinas, who is one of these, declares the names and endowments of the rest.

Canto XI. Thomas Aquinas enters at large into the life and character of St. Francis; and then solves one of two difficulties, which he perceived to have risen in Dante's mind from what he had heard in the last Canto.

Canto XII. A second circle of glorified souls encompasses the first. Buonaventura, who is one of them, celebrates the praises of St. Dominic, and informs Dante who the other eleven are, that are in this second circle or garland.

Canto XIII. Thomas Aquinas resumes his speech. He solves the other of those doubts which he discerned in the mind of Dante, and warns him earnestly against assenting to any proposition without having duly examined it.

Canto XIV. Solomon, who is one of the spirits in the inner circle, declares what the appearance of the blest will be after the resurrection of the body. Beatrice and Dante are translated into the fifth heaven, which is that of Mars; and here behold the souls of those who had died fighting for the true faith, ranged in the sign of a cross, athwart which the spirits move to the sound of a melodious hymn.

Canto XV. The spirit of Cacciaguida, our Poet's ancestor, glides rapidly to the foot of the cross; tells who he is; and speaks of the simplicity of the Florentines in his days, since then much corrupted.

Canto XVI. Cacciaguida relates the time of his birth; and, describing the extent of Florence when he lived there, recounts the names of the chief families who then inhabited it. Its degeneracy, and subsequent disgrace, he attributes to the introduction of families from the neighboring country and villages, and to their mixture with the primitive citizens.

Canto XVII. Cacciaguida predicts to our Poet his exile and the calamities he had to suffer; and, lastly, exhorts him to write the present poem.

Canto XVIII. Dante sees the souls of many renowned warriors and crusaders in the planet Mars; and then ascends with Beatrice to Jupiter, the sixth heaven, in which he finds the souls of those who had administered justice rightly in the world, so disposed, as to form the figure of an eagle. The Canto concludes with an invective against the avarice of the clergy, and especially of the pope.

Canto XIX. The eagle speaks as with one voice proceeding from a multitude of spirits, that compose it; and declares the cause for which it is exalted to that state of glory. It then solves a doubt, which our Poet had entertained, respecting the possibility of salvation without belief in Christ; exposes the inefficacy of a mere profession of such belief; and prophesies the evil appearance that many Christian potentates will make at the day of judgment.

Canto XX. The eagle celebrates the praise of certain kings, whose glorified spirits form the eye of the bird. In the pupil is David; and, in the circle round it, Trajan, Hezekiah, Constantine, William II of Sicily, and Ripheus. It explains to our Poet, how the souls of those whom he supposed to have had no means of believing in Christ, came to be in heaven; and concludes with an admonition against presuming to fathom the counsels of God.

Canto XXI. Dante ascends with Beatrice to the seventh heaven, which is the planet Saturn; wherein is placed a ladder, so lofty, that the top of it is out of his sight. Here are the souls of those who had passed their life in holy retirement and contemplation. Piero Damiano comes near them, and answers questions put to him by Dante; then declares who he was on earth; and ends by declaiming against the luxury of pastors and prelates in those times.

Canto XXII. He beholds many other spirits of the devout and contemplative; and amongst these is addressed by St. Benedict, who, after disclosing his own name and the names of certain of his companions in bliss, replies to the request made by our Poet that he might look on the form of the saint, without that covering of splendor, which then invested it; and then proceeds, lastly, to inveigh against the corruption of the monks. Next Dante mounts with his heavenly conductress to the eighth heaven, or that of the fixed stars, which he enters at the constellation of the Twins; and thence looking back, reviews all the space he has past between his present station and the earth.

Canto XXIII. He sees Christ triumphing with His church. The Saviour ascends, followed by His Virgin Mother. The others remain with St. Peter.

Canto XXIV. St. Peter examines Dante touching Faith, and is contented with his answers.

Canto XXV. St. James questions our Poet concerning Hope. Next St. John appears; and, on perceiving that Dante looks intently on him, informs him that he, St. John, had left his body resolved into earth, upon the earth, and that Christ and the Virgin alone had come with their bodies into heaven.

Canto XXVI. St. John examines our Poet touching Charity. Afterwards Adam tells when he was created, and placed in the terrestrial Paradise; how long he remained in that state; what was the occasion of his fall; when he was admitted into heaven; and what language he spake.

Canto XXVII. St. Peter bitterly rebukes the covetousness of his successors in the apostolic see, while all the heavenly host sympathize in his indignation: they then vanish upwards. Beatrice bids Dante again cast his view below. Afterwards they are borne into the ninth heaven, of which she shows him the nature and properties; blaming the perverseness of man, who places his will on low and perishable things.]

Canto XXVIII

ARGUMENT

Still in the ninth heaven, our Poet is permitted to behold the divine essence; and then sees, in three hierarchies, the nine choirs of angels. Beatrice clears some difficulties which occur to him on this occasion.

So she, who doth imparadise my soul,
Had drawn the veil from off our present life,
And bared the truth of poor mortality;   140
When lo! as one who, in a mirror, spies
The shining of a flambeau at his back,
Lit sudden ere he deem of its approach,
And turneth to resolve him, if the glass
Have told him true, and sees the record faithful
As note is to its meter; even thus,   146
I well remember, did befall to me,
Looking upon the beauteous eyes, whence love
Had made the leash to take me. As I turn'd:
And that which none, who in that volume looks,
Can miss of, in itself apparent, struck   151
My view; a point I saw, that darted light

So sharp, no lid, unclosing, may bear up
Against its keenness. The least star we ken
From hence, had seem'd a moon; set by its side,
As star by side of star. And so far off,   156
Perchance, as is the halo from the light
Which paints it, when most dense the vapor spreads;
There wheel'd about the point a circle of fire,
More rapid than the motion which surrounds,   160
Speediest, the world. Another this enring'd;
And that a third; the third a fourth, and that
A fifth encompass'd; which a sixth next bound;
And over this, a seventh, following, reach'd
Circumference so ample, that its bow,   165
Within the span of Juno's messenger,[9]
Had scarce been held entire. Beyond the seventh,
Ensued yet other two. And every one,
As more in number distant from the first,
Was tardier in motion: and that glow'd   170
With flame most pure, that to the sparkle of truth,
Was nearest; as partaking most, methinks,
Of its reality. The guide beloved
Saw me in anxious thought suspense, and spake:
"Heaven, and all nature, hangs upon that point
The circle thereto most conjoin'd observe;   176
And know, that by intenser love its course
Is, to this swiftness, wing'd." To whom I thus:
"It were enough; nor should I further seek,
Had I but witness'd order, in the world   180
Appointed, such as in these wheels is seen.
But in the sensible world such difference is,
That in each round shows more divinity,
As each is wider from the center. Hence,
If in this wondrous and angelic temple,   185
That hath, for confine, only light and love,
My wish may have completion, I must know,
Wherefore such disagreement is between
The exemplar and its copy: for myself,
Contemplating, I fail to pierce the cause."   190
"It is no marvel, if thy fingers foil'd
Do leave the knot untied: so hard 'tis grown
For want of tenting." Thus she said: "But take,"
She added, "if thou wish thy cure, my words,
And entertain them subtly. Every orb,   195
Corporeal, doth proportion its extent
Unto the virtue through its parts diffused.
The greater blessedness preserves the more.
The greater is the body (if all parts
Share equally) the more is to preserve.   200
Therefore the circle, whose swift course enwheels
The universal frame, answers to that
Which is supreme in knowledge and in love.

[9] Iris. the rainbow.

Thus by the virtue, not the seeming breadth
Of substance, measuring, thou shalt see the
    heavens,   205
Each to the intelligence that ruleth it,
Greater to more, and smaller unto less,
Suited in strict and wondrous harmony."

   As when the north blows from his milder cheek
A blast, that scours the sky, forthwith our air, 210
Clear'd of the rack that hung on it before,
Glitters; and, with his beauties all unveil'd,
The firmament looks forth serene, and smiles:
Such was my cheer, when Beatrice drove
With clear reply the shadows back, and truth 215
Was manifested, as a star in heaven.
And when the words were ended, not unlike
To iron in the furnace, every cirque,
Ebullient, shot forth scintillating fires:
And every sparkle shivering to new blaze, 220
In number [10] did outmillion the account
Reduplicate upon the checker'd board.
Then heard I echoing on, from choir to choir,
"Hosanna," to the fixed point, that holds,
And shall for ever hold them to their place, 225
From everlasting, irremovable.

   Musing awhile I stood: and she, who saw
My inward meditations, thus began:
"In the first circles, they, whom thou beheld'st
Are seraphim and cherubim. Thus swift 230
Follow their hoops, in likeness to the point,
Near as they can, approaching; and they can
The more, the loftier their vision. Those
That round them fleet, gazing the Godhead next,
Are thrones; in whom the first trine ends. And all
Are blessed, even as their sight descends 236
Deeper into the truth, wherein rest is
For every mind. Thus happiness hath root
In seeing, not in loving, which of sight
Is aftergrowth. And of the seeing such 240
The meed, as unto each, in due degree,
Grace and good-will their measure have assign'd.
The other trine, that with still opening buds
In this eternal springtide blossom fair,
Fearless of bruising from the nightly ram, [11] 245
Breathe up in warbled melodies threefold

Hosannas, blending ever; from the three,
Transmitted, hierarchy of gods, for aye
Rejoicing; dominations first; next them, 249
Virtues; and powers the third; the next to whom
Are princedoms and archangels, with glad round
To tread their festal ring; and last, the band
Angelical, disporting in their sphere.
All as they circle in their orders, look
Aloft; and, downward, with such sway prevail,
That all with mutual impulse tend to God. 256
These once a mortal view beheld. Desire,
In Dionysius, [12] so intensely wrought,
That he, as I have done, ranged them; and named
Their orders, marshal'd in his thought. From him,
Dissentient, one refused his sacred rede. 261
But soon as in this heaven his doubting eyes
Were open'd, Gregory [13] at his error smiled.
Nor marvel, that a denizen of earth
Should scan such secret truth; for he had learnt [14]
Both this and much beside of these our orbs, 266
From an eye-witness to heaven's mysteries."

   [*Canto XXIX*. Beatrice beholds, in the mirror of
divine truth, some doubts which had entered the
mind of Dante. These she resolves; and then di-
gresses into a vehement reprehension of certain
theologians and preachers in those days, whose
ignorance or avarice induced them to substitute
their own inventions for the pure word of the
Gospel.]

Canto XXX

ARGUMENT

Dante is taken up with Beatrice into the empy-
    rean; and there having his sight strengthened by
    her aid, and by the virtue derived from looking
    on the river of light, he sees the triumph of the
    angels and of the souls of the blessed.

Noon's fervid hour perchance six thousand miles [15]
From hence is distant; and the shadowy cone
Almost to level on our earth declines; 270
When, from the midmost of this blue abyss,
By turns some star is to our vision lost.
And straightway as the handmaid of the sun

---

[10] The sparkles exceeded the number which would be produced by the sixty-four squares of a chess-board, if for the first we reckoned one; for the next, two; for the third, four; and so went on doubling to the end of the account.

[11] Not injured, like the productions of our spring, by the influence of autumn, when the constellation Aries rises at sunset.

[12] The Areopagite, in his book *De Cœlesti Hierarchiâ*.

[13] Gregory the Great.

[14] Dionysius, he says, had learnt from St. Paul.

[15] He compares the vanishing of the vision to the fading away of the stars at dawn, when it is noon-day six thousand miles off, and the shadow, formed by the earth over the part of it inhabited by the Poet, is about to disappear.

Puts forth her radiant brow, all, light by light,
Fade; and the spangled firmament shuts in, 275
E'en to the loveliest of the glittering throng.
Thus vanish'd gradually from my sight
The triumph, which plays ever round the point,
That overcame me, seeming (for it did)
Engirt [16] by that it girdeth. Wherefore love, 280
With loss of other object, forced me bend
Mine eyes on Beatrice once again.
   If all, that hitherto is told of her,
Were in one praise concluded, 'twere too weak
To furnish out this turn. Mine eyes did look 285
On beauty, such, as I believe in sooth,
Not merely to exceed our human; but,
That save its Maker, none can to the full
Enjoy it. At this point o'erpower'd I fail;
Unequal to my theme; as never bard 290
Of buskin or of sock hath fail'd before.
For as the sun doth to the feeblest sight,
E'en so remembrance of that witching smile
Hath dispossesst my spirit of itself.
Not from that day, when on this earth I first 295
Beheld her charms, up to that view of them,
Have I with song applausive ever ceased
To follow; but now follow them no more;
My course here bounded, as each artist's is,
When it doth touch the limit of his skill. 300
   She (such as I bequeath her to the bruit
Of louder trump than mine, which hasteneth on
Urging its arduous matter to the close)
Her words resumed, in gesture and in voice
Resembling one accustom'd to command: 305
"Forth [17] from the last corporeal are we come
Into the heaven, that is unbodied light;
Light intellectual, replete with love,
Love of true happiness, replete with joy;
Joy, that transcends all sweetness of delight. 310
Here shalt thou look on either mighty host [18]
Of Paradise; and one in that array,
Which in the final judgment thou shalt see."
   As when the lightning, in a sudden spleen
Unfolded, dashes from the blinding eyes 315
The visive spirits, dazzled and bedimm'd;
So, round about me, fulminating streams
Of living radiance play'd, and left me swathed
And veil'd in dense impenetrable blaze.
Such weal is in the love, that stills this heaven;
For its own flame the torch thus fitting ever. 321
   No sooner to my listening ear had come

The brief assurance, than I understood
New virtue into me infused, and sight
Kindled afresh, with vigor to sustain 325
Excess of light however pure. I look'd;
And, in the likeness of a river, saw
Light flowing, from whose amber-seeming waves
Flash'd up effulgence, as they glided on
'Twixt banks, on either side, painted with spring,
Incredible how fair: and, from the tide, 331
There ever and anon, outstarting, flew
Sparkles instinct with life; and in the flowers
Did set them, like to rubies chased in gold:
Then, as if drunk with odors, plunged again 335
Into the wondrous flood; from which, as one
Re-enter'd, still another rose. "The thirst
Of knowledge high, whereby thou art inflamed,
To search the meaning of what here thou seest,
The more it warms thee, pleases me the more.
But first behoves thee of this water drink, 341
Or e'er that longing be allay'd." So spake
The day-star of mine eyes: then thus subjoin'd:
"This stream; and these, forth issuing from its gulf,
And diving back, a living topaz each; 345
With all this laughter on its bloomy shores;
Are but a preface, shadowy of the truth
They emblem: not that, in themselves, the things
Are crude; but on thy part is the defect,
For that thy views not yet aspire so high." 350
   Never did babe that had outslept his wont,
Rush, with such eager straining, to the milk,
As I toward the water; bending me,
To make the better mirrors of mine eyes
In the refining wave: and as the eaves 355
Of mine eyelids did drink of it, forthwith
Seem'd it unto me turn'd from length to round.
Then as a troop of maskers, when they put
Their vizors off, look other than before;
The counterfeited semblance thrown aside: 360
So into greater jubilee were changed
Those flowers and sparkles; and distinct I saw,
Before me, either court of heaven display'd.
   O prime enlightener! thou who gavest me strength
On the high triumph of thy realm to gaze; 365
Grant virtue now to utter what I kenn'd.
   There is in heaven a light, whose goodly shine
Makes the Creator visible to all
Created, that in seeing Him alone

[16] "Appearing to be encompassed by these angelic bands, which are in reality encompassed by it."
[17] From the ninth sphere to the empyrean, which is mere light.
[18] Of angels, that remained faithful, and of beautified souls; the latter in that shape which they will have at the last day.

Have peace; and in a circle spreads so far,   370
That the circumference were too loose a zone
To girdle in the sun. All is one beam,
Reflected from the summit of the first,
That moves, which being hence and vigor takes.
And as some cliff, that from the bottom eyes   375
His image mirror'd in the crystal flood,
As if to admire his brave appareling
Of verdure and of flowers; so, round about,
Eying the light, on more than million thrones,
Stood, eminent, whatever from our earth   380
Has to the skies return'd. How wide the leaves,
Extended to their utmost, of this rose,
Whose lowest step embosoms such a space
Of ample radiance! Yet, nor amplitude
Nor height impeded, but my view with ease   385
Took in the full dimensions of that joy.
Near or remote, what there avails, where God
Immediate rules, and Nature, awed, suspends
Her sway? Into the yellow of the rose
Perennial, which, in bright expansiveness,   390
Lays forth its gradual blooming, redolent
Of praises to the never-wintering sun,
As one, who fain would speak yet holds his peace,
Beatrice led me; and, "Behold," she said,
"This fair assemblage; stoles of snowy white,   395
How numberless. The city, where we dwell,
Behold how vast; and these our seats so throng'd,
Few now are wanting here. In that proud stall,
On which, the crown, already o'er its state
Suspended, holds thine eyes—or e'er thyself   400
Mayst at the wedding sup,—shall rest the soul
Of the great Harry,[19] he who, by the world
Augustus hail'd, to Italy must come,
Before her day be ripe. But ye are sick,
And in your tetchy wantonness as blind,   405
As is the bantling, that of hunger dies,
And drives away the nurse. Nor may it be,
That he,[20] who in the sacred forum sways,
Openly or in secret, shall with him
Accordant walk: whom God will not endure   410
I' the holy office long; but thrust him down
To Simon Magus, where Alagna's priest[21]
Will sink beneath him: such will be his meed."

[Canto XXXI. The Poet expatiates further on
the glorious vision described in the last Canto. On
looking round for Beatrice, he finds that she has

left him, and that an old man is at his side. This
proves to be St. Bernard, who shows him that
Beatrice has returned to her throne, and then
points out to him the blessedness of the Virgin
Mother.]

Canto XXXII
ARGUMENT

St. Bernard shows him, on their several thrones,
the other blessed souls, both of the Old and New
Testament; explains to him that their places are
assigned them by grace, and not according to
merit; and lastly, tells him that if he would
obtain power to descry what remained of the
heaven-vision, he must unite with him in supplication to Mary.

Freely the sage, though wrapt in musings high,
Assumed the teacher's part, and mild began: 415
"The wound, that Mary closed, she[22] open'd first,
Who sits so beautiful at Mary's feet.
The third in order, underneath her, lo!
Rachel with Beatrice: Sarah next;
Judith; Rebecca; and the gleaner-maid,   420
Meek ancestress[23] of him, who sang the songs
Of sore repentance in his sorrowful mood.
All, as I name them, down from leaf to leaf,
Are, in gradation, throned on the rose.
And from the seventh step, successively,   425
Adown the breathing tresses of the flower,
Still doth the file of Hebrew dames proceed.
For these are a partition wall, whereby
The sacred stairs are sever'd, as the faith
In Christ divides them. On this part, where blooms
Each leaf in full maturity, are set   431
Such as in Christ, or e'er He came, believed.
On the other, where an intersected space
Yet shows the semicircle void, abide
All they, who look'd to Christ already come.   435
And as our Lady on her glorious stool,
And they who on their stools beneath her sit,
This way distinction make; e'en so on his,
The mighty Baptist, that way marks the line,
(He who endured the desert, and the pains   440
Of martyrdom, and, for two years,[24] of hell,
Yet still continued holy), and beneath,
Augustine;[25] Francis; Benedict; and the rest,

---

[19] The Emperor Henry VII, who died in 1313.
[20] Pope Clement V.
[21] Pope Boniface VIII.
[22] Eve.
[23] Ruth, the ancestress of David.
[24] The time that elapsed between the death of the Baptist and his redemption by the death of Christ.
[25] Bishop of Hippo, in the fourth century.

Thus far from round to round. So heaven's decree
Forecasts, this garden equally to fill, 445
With faith in either view, past or to come.
Learn too, that downward from the step, which cleaves,
Midway, the twain compartments, none there are
Who place obtain for merit of their own,
But have through others' merit been advanced,
On set conditions; spirits all released, 451
Ere for themselves they had the power to choose.
And, if thou mark and listen to them well,
Their childish looks and voice declare as much.

   "Here, silent as thou art, I know thy doubt; 455
And gladly will I loose the knot, wherein
Thy subtile thoughts have bound thee. From this realm
Excluded, chance no entrance here may find;
No more than hunger, thirst, or sorrow can.
A law immutable hath stablish'd all; 460
Nor is there aught thou seest, that doth not fit,
Exactly, as the finger to the ring.
It is not, therefore, without cause, that these,
O'erspeedy comers to immortal life,
Are different in their shares of excellence. 465
Our Sovran Lord, that settleth this estate
In love and in delight so absolute,
That wish can dare no further, every soul,
Created in His joyous sight to dwell,
With grace, at pleasure, variously endows. 470
And for a proof the effect may well suffice.
And 'tis moreover most expressly mark'd
In holy Scripture, where the twins are said
To have struggled in the womb. Therefore, as grace
Inweaves the coronet, so every brow 475
Weareth its proper hue of orient light.
And merely in respect to His prime gift,
Not in reward of meritorious deed,
Hath each his several degree assign'd.
In early times with their own innocence 480
More was not wanting, than the parents' faith,
To save them: those first ages past, behoved
That circumcision in the males should imp
The flight of innocent wings: but since the day
Of grace hath come, without baptismal rites 485
In Christ accomplish'd, innocence herself
Must linger yet below. Now raise thy view
Unto the visage most resembling Christ:
For, in her splendor only, shalt thou win
The power to look on Him." Forthwith I saw 490
Such floods of gladness on her visage shower'd,
From holy spirits, winging that profound;

That, whatsoever I had yet beheld,
Had not so much suspended me with wonder,
Or shown me such similitude of God. 495
And he, who had to her descended, once,
On earth, now hail'd in heaven; and on poised wing,
"Ave, Maria, Gratia Plena," sang:
To whose sweet anthem all the blissful court,
From all parts answering, rang: that holier joy
Brooded the deep serene. "Father revered! 501
Who deign'st, for me, to quit the pleasant place
Wherein thou sittest, by eternal lot;
Say, who that angel is, that with such glee
Beholds our queen, and so enamor'd glows 505
Of her high beauty, that all fire he seems."
   So I again resorted to the lore
Of my wise teacher, he, whom Mary's charms
Embellish'd, as the sun the morning star;
Who thus in answer spake: "In him are summ'd,
Whate'er of buxomness and free delight 510
May be in spirit, or in angel, met:
And so beseems: for that he bare the palm
Down unto Mary, when the Son of God
Vouchsafed to clothe him in terrestrial weeds. 515
Now let thine eyes wait heedful on my words;
And note thou of this just and pious realm
The chiefest nobles. Those, highest in bliss,
The twain, on each hand next our empress throned,
Are as it were two roots unto this rose: 520
He to the left, the parent, whose rash taste
Proves bitter to his seed; and, on the right,
That ancient father of the holy church,
Into whose keeping Christ did give the keys
Of this sweet flower; near whom behold the seer,[26]
That, ere he died, saw all the grievous times 526
Of the fair bride, who with the lance and nails
Was won. And, near unto the other, rests
The leader, under whom, on manna, fed
The ungrateful nation, fickle and perverse. 530
On the other part, facing to Peter, lo!
Where Anna sits, so well content to look
On her loved daughter, that with moveless eye
She chants the loud hosanna: while, opposed
To the first father of your mortal kind, 535
Is Lucia, at whose hest thy lady sped,
When on the edge of ruin closed thine eye.
   "But (for the vision hasteneth to an end)
Here break we off, as the good workman doth,
That shapes the cloak according to the cloth; 540
And to the primal love our ken shall rise;
That thou mayst penetrate the brightness, far

[26] St. John.

As sight can bear thee. Yet, alas! in sooth
Beating thy pennons, thinking to advance,
Thou backward fall'st. Grace then must first be
    gain'd,   545
Her grace, whose might can help thee. Thou in
    prayer
Seek her: and, with affection, whilst I sue,
Attend, and yield me all thy heart." He said;
And thus the saintly orison began.

Canto XXXIII

ARGUMENT

St. Bernard supplicates the Virgin Mary that
    Dante may have grace given him to contemplate
    the brightness of the Divine Majesty, which is
    accordingly granted; and Dante then himself
    prays to God for ability to show forth some part
    of the celestial glory in his writings. Lastly, he is
    admitted to a glimpse of the great mystery; the
    Trinity, and the Union of Man with God.

"O virgin mother, daughter of thy Son!   550
Created beings all in lowliness
Surpassing, as in height above them all;
Term by the eternal counsel pre-ordain'd;
Ennobler of thy nature, so advanced
In thee, that its great Maker did not scorn,   555
To make Himself His own creation,
For in thy womb rekindling shone the love
Reveal'd, whose genial influence makes now
This flower to germin in eternal peace:
Here thou to us, of charity and love,   560
Art, as the noon-day torch; and art, beneath,
To mortal men, of hope a living spring.
So mighty art thou, lady, and so great,
That he, who grace desireth, and comes not
To thee for aidance, fain would have desire   565
Fly without wings. Not only him, who asks,
Thy bounty succors; but doth freely oft
Forerun the asking. Whatsoe'er may be
Of excellence in creature, pity mild,
Relenting mercy, large munificence,   570
Are all combined in thee. Here kneeleth one,
Who of all spirits hath review'd the state,
From the world's lowest gap unto this height.
Suppliant to thee he kneels, imploring grace
For virtue yet more high, to lift his ken   575
Toward the bliss supreme. And I, who ne'er
Coveted sight, more fondly, for myself,
Than now for him, my prayers to thee prefer,
(And pray they be not scant), that thou wouldst
    drive

Each cloud of his mortality away,   580
Through thine own prayers, that on the sovran joy
Unveil'd he gaze. This yet, I pray thee, Queen,
Who canst do what thou wilt; that in him thou
Wouldst, after all he hath beheld, preserve
Affection sound, and human passions quell.   585
Lo! where, with Beatrice, many a saint
Stretch their clasp'd hands, in furtherance of my
    suit."
    The eyes, that heaven with love and awe regards,
Fix'd on the suitor, witness'd, how benign
She looks on pious prayers: then fasten'd they   590
On the everlasting light, wherein no eye
Of creature, as may well be thought, so far
Can travel inward. I, meanwhile, who drew
Near to the limit, where all wishes end,
The ardor of my wish (for so behoved)   595
Ended within me. Beckoning smiled the sage,
That I should look aloft: but, ere he bade,
Already of myself aloft I look'd;
For visual strength, refining more and more
Bare me into the ray authentical   600
Of sovran light. Thenceforward, what I saw,
Was not for words to speak, nor memory's self
To stand against such outrage on her skill.
    As one, who from a dream awaken'd, straight,
All he hath seen forgets; yet still retains   605
Impression of the feeling in his dream;
E'en such am I: for all the vision dies,
As 'twere, away; and yet the sense of sweet,
That sprang from it, still trickles in my heart.
Thus in the sun-thaw is the snow unseal'd;   610
Thus in the winds on flitting leaves was lost
The Sibyl's sentence. O eternal beam!
(Whose height what reach of mortal thought may
    soar?)
Yield me again some little particle
Of what thou then appearedst; give my tongue
Power, but to leave one sparkle of thy glory,   616
Unto the race to come, that shall not lose
Thy triumph wholly, if thou waken aught
Of memory in me, and endure to hear
The record sound in this unequal strain.   620
    Such keenness from the living ray I met,
That, if mine eyes had turn'd away, methinks,
I had been lost; but, so embolden'd, on
I pass'd, as I remember, till my view
Hover'd the brink of dread infinitude.   625
    O grace, unenvying of thy boon! that gavest
Boldness to fix so earnestly my ken
On the everlasting splendor, that I look'd,
While sight was unconsumed; and, in that depth,

Saw in one volume clasp'd of love, whate'er   630
The universe unfolds; all properties
Of substance and of accident, beheld,
Compounded, yet one individual light
The whole. And of such bond methinks I saw
The universal form; for that whene'er   635
I do but speak of it, my soul dilates
Beyond her proper self; and, till I speak,
One moment seems a longer lethargy,
Than five-and-twenty ages had appear'd
To that emprize, that first made Neptune wonder
At Argo's shadow darkening on his flood.   641
  With fixed heed, suspense and motionless,
Wondering I gazed; and admiration still
Was kindled as I gazed. It may not be,
That one, who looks upon that light, can turn
To other object, willingly, his view,   646
For all the good, that will may covet, there
Is summ'd; and all, elsewhere defective found,
Complete. My tongue shall utter now, no more
E'en what remembrance keeps, than could the babe's   650
That yet is moisten'd at his mother's breast.
Not that the semblance of the living light
Was changed (that ever as at first remain'd),
But that my vision quickening, in that sole
Appearance, still new miracles descried,   655
And toil'd me with the change. In that abyss

Of radiance, clear and lofty, seem'd, methought,
Three orbs of triple hue, clipt in one bound: [27]
And, from another, one reflected seem'd,
As rainbow is from rainbow: and the third   660
Seem'd fire, breathed equally from both. O speech!
How feeble and how faint art thou, to give
Conception birth. Yet this to what I saw
Is less than little. O eternal light!
Sole in thyself that dwell'st; and of thyself   665
Sole understood, past, present, or to come;
Thou smiledst, on that circling, [28] which in thee
Seem'd as reflected splendor, while I mused;
For I therein, methought, in its own hue
Beheld our image painted: stedfastly   670
I therefore pored upon the view. As one,
Who versed in geometric lore, would fain
Measure the circle; and though pondering long
And deeply, that beginning, which he needs,
Finds not: e'en such was I, intent to scan   675
The novel wonder, and trace out the form,
How to the circle fitted, and therein
How placed: but the flight was not for my wing;
Had not a flash darted athwart my mind,
And, in the spleen, unfolded what it sought.   680
  Here vigor fail'd the towering fantasy:
But yet the will roll'd onward, like a wheel,
In even motion, by the love impell'd,
That moves the sun in heaven and all the stars.

La Vita Nuova

10

Ladies that have intelligence in love,
  Of mine own lady I would speak with you;
  Not that I hope to count her praises through,
    But telling what I may, to ease my mind.
And I declare that when I speak thereof,   5
Love sheds such perfect sweetness over me
That if my courage failed not, certainly
  To him my listeners must be all resign'd.
  Wherefore I will not speak in such large kind
That mine own speech should foil me, which were base;   10
But only will discourse of her high grace
  In these poor words, the best that I can find,
With you alone, dear dames and damozels:
'Twere ill to speak thereof with any else.

An angel, of his blessed knowledge, saith   15
  To God: "Lord, in the world that Thou hast made,
  A miracle in action is display'd,
    By reason of a soul whose splendors fare
Even hither: and since Heaven requireth
  Nought saving her, for her it prayeth Thee,   20
  Thy Saints crying aloud continually."
    Yet Pity still defends our earthly share
  In that sweet soul; God answering thus the prayer:
"My well-belovèd, suffer that in peace
Your hope remain, while so My pleasure is,   25
  There where one dwells who dreads the loss of her:
And who in Hell unto the doomed shall say,

[27] The Trinity.
[28] The second of the circles, "Light of Light," in which he dimly beheld the mystery of the incarnation.
  La Vita Nuova, translated by D. G. Rossetti.

'I have looked on that for which God's chosen
   pray.' "

My lady is desired in the high Heaven:
   Wherefore, it now behoveth me to tell,   30
   Saying: Let any maid that would be well
      Esteemed keep with her: for as she goes by,
Into foul hearts a deathly chill is driven
By Love, that makes ill thought to perish there:
While any who endures to gaze on her   35
      Must either be ennobled, or else die.
   When one deserving to be raised so high
Is found, 'tis then her power attains its proof,
Making his heart strong for his soul's behoof
      With the full strength of meek humility.   40
Also this virtue owns she, by God's will:
Who speaks with her can never come to ill.

Love saith concerning her: "How chanceth it
   That flesh, which is of dust, should be thus
      pure?"
   Then, gazing always, he makes oath: "Forsure, 45
      This is a creature of God till now unknown."
She hath that paleness of the pearl that's fit
In a fair woman, so much and not more;
She is as high as Nature's skill can soar;
      Beauty is tried by her comparison.   50
   Whatever her sweet eyes are turned upon,
Spirits of love do issue thence in flame,
Which through their eyes who then may look on
      them
      Pierce to the heart's deep chamber every one.
And in her smile Love's image you may see;   55
Whence none can gaze upon her steadfastly.

Dear Song, I know thou wilt hold gentle speech
   With many ladies, when I send thee forth:
   Wherefore (being mindful that thou hadst thy
      birth
      From Love, and art a modest, simple child,) 60
Whomso thou meetest, say thou this to each:
"Give me good speed! To her I went along
In whose much strength my weakness is made
      strong."
      And if, i' the end, thou wouldst not be beguiled
      Of all thy labor seek not the defiled   65
And common sort; but rather choose to be
Where man and woman dwell in courtesy.
   So to the road thou shalt be reconciled,
And find the Lady, and with the lady, Love.
Commend thou me to each, as doth behove.   70

II

Love and the gentle heart are one same thing,
   Even as the wise man in his ditty saith:
   Each, of itself, would be such life in death
As rational soul bereft of reasoning.
'Tis Nature makes them when she loves: a king
   Love is, whose palace where he sojourneth
   Is called the Heart; there draws he quiet breath
At first, with brief or longer slumbering.
Then beauty seen in virtuous womankind
   Will make the eyes desire, and through the heart
      Send the desiring of the eyes again;
Where often it abides so long enshrin'd
   That Love at length out of his sleep will start
      And women feel the same for worthy men.

18

Love hath so long possessed me for his own
   And made his lordship so familiar
That he, who at first irked me, is now grown
   Unto my heart as its best secrets are.
   And thus, when he is such sore wise doth mar
My life that all its strength seems gone from it,
   Mine inmost being then feels thoroughly quit
   Of anguish, and all evil keeps afar.
Love also gathers to such power in me
   That my sighs speak, each one a grievous thing,
   Always soliciting
My lady's salutation piteously.
Whenever she beholds me, it is so,
Who is more sweet than any words can show.

19

The eyes that weep for pity of the heart
   Have wept so long that their grief languisheth,
      And they have no more tears to weep withal:
And now, if I would ease me of a part
   Of what, little by little, leads to death,   5
      It must be done by speech, or not at all.
      And because often, thinking, I recall
How it was pleasant, ere she went afar,
   To talk of her with you, kind damozels,
   I talk with no one else,   10
But only with such hearts as women's are.
   And I will say,—still sobbing as speech fails,—
That she hath gone to Heaven suddenly,
And hath left Love below, to mourn with me.

Beatrice is gone up into high Heaven,   15
   The kingdom where the angels are at peace;

And lives with them: and to her friends is
dead.
Not by the frost of winter was she driven
  Away, like others; nor by summer-heats;
    But through a perfect gentleness, instead. 20
    For from the lamp of her meek lowlihead
Such an exceeding glory went up hence
  That it woke wonder in the Eternal Sire,
  Until a sweet desire
Entered Him for that lovely excellence, 25
  So that He bade her to Himself aspire;
Counting this weary and most evil place
Unworthy of a thing so full of grace.

Wonderfully out of the beautiful form
  Soared her clear spirit, waxing glad the while; 30
  And is in its first home, there where it is.
Who speaks thereof, and feels not the tears warm
  Upon his face, must have become so vile
    As to be dead to all sweet sympathies.
    Out upon him! an abject wretch like this 35
May not imagine anything of her,—
  He needs no bitter tears for his relief.
  But sighing comes, and grief,
And the desire to find no comforter,
  (Save only Death, who makes all sorrow brief,)
To him who for a while turns in his thought 41
How she hath been among us, and is not.

With sighs my bosom always laboreth
  In thinking, as I do continually,
    Of her for whom my heart now breaks apace;
And very often when I think of death, 46
  Such a great inward longing comes to me
    That it will change the color of my face;
    And, if the idea settles in its place,
All my limbs shake as with an ague-fit: 50
  Till, starting up in wild bewilderment,
  I do become so shent
That I go forth, lest folk misdoubt of it.
  Afterward, calling with a sore lament
On Beatrice, I ask, "Canst thou be dead?" 55
And calling on her, I am comforted.

Grief with its tears, and anguish with its sighs,
  Come to me now whene'er I am alone;
    So that I think the sight of me gives pain.
And what my life hath been, that living dies, 60
  Since for my lady the New Birth's begun,
    I have not any language to explain.

And so, dear ladies, though my heart were
    fain,
I scarce could tell indeed how I am thus.
All joy is with my bitter life at war; 65
  Yea, I am fallen so far
That all men seem to say, "Go out from us,"
  Eyeing my cold white lips, how dead they are.
But she, though I be bowed unto the dust,
Watches me; and will guerdon me, I trust. 70

Weep, pitiful Song of mine, upon thy way,
  To the dames going and the damozels
  For whom and for none else
Thy sisters have made music many a day.
Thou, that art very sad and not as they, 75
  Go dwell thou with them as a mourner dwells.

26

A gentle thought there is will often start,
  Within my secret self, to speech of thee:
  Also of Love it speaks so tenderly
That much in me consents and takes its part.
"And what is this," the soul saith to the heart,
  "That cometh thus to comfort thee and me,
  And thence where it would dwell, thus potently
Can drive all other thoughts by its strange art?"
And the heart answers: "Be no more at strife
  'Twixt doubt and doubt: this is Love's messenger
    And speaketh but his words, from him
    received;
And all the strength it owns and all the life
  It draweth from the gentle eyes of her
    Who, looking on our grief, hath often grieved."

29

Beyond the sphere which spreads to widest space
    Now soars the sigh that my heart sends above;
  A new perception born of grieving Love
Guideth it upward the untrodden ways.
When it hath reached unto the end, and stays,
  It sees a lady round whom splendors move
  In homage; till, by the great light thereof
Abashed, the pilgrim spirit stands at gaze.
It sees her such, that when it tells me this
  Which it hath seen, I understand it not,
    It hath a speech so subtle and so fine.
And yet I know its voice within my thought
Often remembereth me of Beatrice:
  So that I understand it, ladies mine.

PETRARCH

Love's Inconsistency

I find no peace, and all my war is done;
  I fear and hope, I burn and freeze likewise;
  I fly above the wind, yet cannot rise;
  And nought I have, yet all the world I seize on;
That looseth, nor locketh, holdeth me in prison, 5
  And holds me not, yet can I 'scape no wise;
  Nor lets me live, nor die, at my devise,
  And yet of death it giveth none occasion.
Without eyes I see, and without tongue I plain;
  I wish to perish, yet I ask for health;   10
  I love another, and yet I hate myself;
I feed in sorrow, and laugh in all my pain;
  Lo, thus displeaseth me both death and life,
  And my delight is causer of my grief.

Summer Is Come

The soote season, that bud and bloom forth brings
With green hath clad the hill, and eke the vale.
The nightingale with feathers new she sings;
The turtle to her mate hath told her tale.
Summer is come, for every spray now springs;   5
The hart has hung his old head on the pale;
The buck in brake his winter coat he flings;
The fishes flete with new repairèd scale;
The adder all her slough away she slings;
The swift swallow pursueth the flies smale;   10
The busy bee her honey now she mings.
Winter is worn that was the flowers' bale,
And thus I see among these pleasant things
Each care decays, and yet my sorrow springs!

A Complaint by Night of the Lover Not Beloved

Alas, so all things now do hold their peace!
  Heaven and earth disturbèd in no thing;
The beasts, the air, the birds their song do cease,
  The nightès car the stars about doth bring;
Calm is the sea; the waves work less and less: 5
  So am not I, whom love, alas! doth wring,
Bringing before my face the great increase
  Of my desires, whereat I weep and sing,
In joy and woe, as in a doubtful case.
  For my sweet thoughts sometime do pleasure
    bring;   10
But by and by, the cause of my disease
  Gives me a pang that inwardly doth sting,
When that I think what grief it is again
To live and lack the thing should rid my pain.

Sonnet VI

Of His Foolish Passion for Laura

My tameless will doth recklessly pursue
Her, who, unshackled by love's heavy chain,
Flies swiftly from its chase, whilst I in vain
My fetter'd journey pantingly renew;
The safer track I offer to its view,   5
But hopeless is my power to restrain,
It rides regardless of the spur or rein;
Love makes it scorn the hand that would subdue.
The triumph won, the bridle all its own,
Without one curb I stand within its power,   10
And my destruction helplessly presage:
It guides me to that laurel, ever known,
To all who seek the healing of its flower,
To aggravate the wound it should assuage.

Petrarch (Francesco Petrarcha, 1304-1374). Translations: "Love's Inconsistency," by Sir Thomas Wyatt; "A Complaint by Night . . ." and "Summer Is Come," by the Earl of Surrey; "Sonnet VI," by Miss Wollaston.

Sonnet XI

He Hopes That Time Will Render Her More Merciful

Lady, if grace to me so long be lent
From love's sharp tyranny and trials keen,
Ere my last days, in life's far vale, are seen,
To know of thy bright eyes the luster spent,
The fine gold of thy hair with silver sprent,   5
Neglected the gay wreaths and robes of green,
Pale, too, and thin the face which made me, e'en
'Gainst injury, slow and timid to lament:
Then will I, for such boldness love would give,
Lay bare my secret heart, in martyr's fire   10
Years, days, and hours that yet has known to live;
And, though the time then suit not fair desire,
At least there may arrive to my long grief,
Too late of tender sighs the poor relief.

Sonnet XVIII

The Praises of Laura Transcend His Poetic Power

Ashamed at times that I am silent, yet,
Lady, though your rare beauties prompt my
  rhyme,
When first I saw thee I recall the time
Such as again no other can be met.
But, with such burthen on my shoulders set.   5
My mind, its frailty feeling, cannot climb,
And shrinks alike from polish'd and sublime,
While my vain utterance frozen terrors let.
Often already have I sought to sing,
But midway in my breast the voice was stay'd,   10
For ah! so high what praise may ever spring?
And oft have I the tender verse essay'd,
But still in vain; pen, hand, and intellect
In the first effort conquer'd are and check'd.

BOCCACCIO

The Decameron

Introduction

In 1348 in the illustrious city of Florence, the fairest of all the cities of Italy, there made its appearance that deadly pestilence, which, whether disseminated by the influence of the celestial bodies, or sent upon us mortals by God in His just wrath by way of retribution for our iniquities, had had its origin some years before in the East, whence, after destroying an innumerable multitude of living beings, it had propagated itself without respite from place to place, and so, calamitously, had spread into the West.

In Florence, despite all that human wisdom and forethought could devise to avert it, as the cleansing of the city from many impurities by officials appointed for the purpose, the refusal of entrance to all sick folk, and the adoption of many precautions for the preservation of health; despite also humble supplications addressed to God, and often repeated both in public procession and otherwise, by the devout; towards the beginning of the spring of the said year the doleful effects of the pestilence began to be horribly apparent by symptoms that showed as if miraculous.

Not such were they as in the East, where an issue of blood from the nose was a manifest sign of inevitable death; but in men and women alike it first betrayed itself by the emergence of certain tumors in the groin or the armpits, some of which grew as large as a common apple, others as an egg, some more, some less, which the common folk called *gavoccioli*. From the two said parts of the body this deadly *gavoccioli* soon began to propagate and spread itself in all directions indifferently; after which the form of the malady began to change, black spots or livid making their appearance in many cases on the arm or the thigh or elsewhere, now few and large, now minute and numerous. And as the *gavocciolo* had been and

Petrarch, *Sonnets XI and XVIII*. Translated by Major Macgregor.

Boccaccio, *The Decameron*. Translated by J. M. Rigg. Giovanni Boccaccio (1313-1375) was born in Paris of a French mother and Florentine father but soon went to Italy, where he had a notable literary career in Naples and Florence. Though all his poems were well received in his own day, his fame rests on his *Decameron*, with its setting of the plague which carried off more than half the population in 1348.

still was an infallible token of approaching death, such also were these spots on whomsoever they showed themselves. . . .

Irksome it is to myself to rehearse in detail so sorrowful a history. Wherefore, being minded to pass over so much thereof as I fairly can, I say, that our city being thus well-nigh depopulated, it so happened, as I afterwards learned from one worthy of credit, that on a Tuesday morning after Divine Service the venerable church of Santa Maria Novella was almost deserted save for the presence of seven young ladies habited sadly in keeping with the season. All were connected either by blood or at least as friends or neighbors; and fair and of good understanding were they all, as also of noble birth, gentle manners, and a modest sprightliness. In age none exceeded twenty-eight, or fell short of eighteen years. Their names I would set down in due form, had I not good reason to withhold them, being solicitous lest the matters which here ensue, as told and heard by them, should in after-time be occasion of reproach to any of them, in view of the ample indulgence which was then, for the reasons heretofore set forth, accorded to the lighter hours of persons of much riper years than they, but which the manners of today have somewhat restricted; nor would I furnish material to detractors, ever ready to bestow their bite where praise is due, to cast by invidious speech the least slur upon the honor of these noble ladies. Wherefore, that what each says may be apprehended without confusion, I intend to give them names more or less appropriate to the character of each. The first, then, being the eldest of the seven, we will call Pampinea, the second Fiammetta, the third Filomena, the fourth Emilia, the fifth we will distinguish as Lauretta, the sixth as Neifile, and the last, not without reason, shall be named Elisa.

'Twas not of set purpose but by mere chance that these ladies met in the same part of the church; but at length grouping themselves into a sort of circle, after heaving a few sighs, they gave up saying paternosters, and began to converse (among other topics) on the times.

So they continued for a while, and then Pampinea, the rest listening in silent attention, thus began:—"Dear ladies mine, often have I heard it said, and you doubtless as well as I, that wrong is done to none by whoso but honestly uses his reason. And to fortify, preserve, and defend his life to the utmost of his power is the dictate of natural reason in everyone that is born. Which right is accorded in such measure that in defense thereof men have been held blameless in taking life. And if this be allowed by the laws, albeit on their stringency depends the well-being of every mortal, how much more exempt from censure should we, and all other honest folk, be in taking such means as we may for the preservation of our life? As often as I bethink me how we have been occupied this morning, and not this morning only, and what has been the tenor of our conversation, I perceive—and you will readily do the like—that each of us is apprehensive on her own account; nor threat do I marvel, but at this I do marvel greatly, that, though none of us lacks a woman's wit, yet none of us has recourse to any means to avert that which we all justly fear. Here we tarry, as if, methinks, for no other purpose than to bear witness to the number of the corpses that are brought hither for interment, or to hearken if the brothers there within, whose number is now almost reduced to nought, chant their offices at the canonical hours, or, by our weeds of woe, to obtrude on the attention of everyone that enters, the nature and degree of our sufferings.

"And if we quit the church, we see dead or sick folk carried about, or we see those, who for their crimes were of late condemned to exile by the outraged majesty of the public laws, but who now, in contempt of those laws, well knowing that their ministers are a prey to death or disease, have returned, and traverse the city in packs, making it hideous with their riotous antics; or else we see the refuse of the people, fostered on our blood, *becchini,* as they call themselves, who for our torment go prancing about here and there and everywhere, making mock of our miseries in scurrilous songs. Nor hear we aught but:—Such and such are dead; or, Such and such are dying; and should hear dolorous wailing on every hand, were there but any to wail. Or go we home, what see we there? I know not if you are in like case with me; but there, where once were servants in plenty, I find none left but my maid, and shudder with terror, and feel the very hairs of my head to stand on end; and turn or tarry where I may, I encounter the ghosts of the departed, not with their wonted mien, but with something horrible in their aspect that appalls me. For which reasons church and street and home are alike distressful to me, and the more so that none, methinks, having means and place of retirement as we have, abides here save only we; or if any such there be, they are of those, as my senses too often have borne witness, who make no distinction between things honorable and their opposites, so they but answer the cravings of appetite, and, alone or in company, do daily and nightly what things soever give promise of most gratification. Nor are these secular persons alone; but such as live recluse in monasteries break their rule, and give themselves up to carnal pleasures, persuading themselves that they are permissible to them, and only forbidden to others, and, thereby thinking to escape, are become unchaste and dissolute. If such be our circumstances —and such most manifestly they are—what do we here? what wait we for? what dream we of? why are we less prompt to provide for our own safety than the rest of the citizens? Is life less dear to us than to all other women? or think we that the bond which unites Soul and body in us is stronger than in others, so that there is no blow that may light upon it, of which we need be apprehensive? If so, we err, we are deceived. What insensate folly were it in us so to believe! We have but to call to mind the number and condition of those, young as we, and of both sexes, who have succumbed to this cruel pestilence, to find therein conclusive evidence to the contrary. And lest from lethargy or indolence we fall into the vain imagination that by some lucky accident we may in some way or another, when we would, escape—I know not if your opinion accord with mine—I should deem it most wise in us, our case being what it is, if, as many others have done before us, and are still doing, we were to quit this place, and, shunning like death the evil example of others, betake ourselves to the country, and there live as honorable women on one of the estates, of which none of us has any lack, with all cheer of festal gathering and other delights, so long as in no particular we overstep the bounds of reason. There we shall hear the chant of birds, have sight of verdant hills and plains, of cornfields undulating like the sea, of trees of a thousand sorts; there also we shall have a larger view of the heavens, which, however harsh to usward, yet deny not their eternal beauty; things fairer far for eye to rest on than the desolate walls of our city. Moreover, we shall there breathe a fresher air, find ampler store of things meet for such as live in these times, have fewer causes of annoy. For, though the husbandmen die there, even as here the citizens, they are dispersed in scattered homesteads, and 'tis thus less painful to witness. Nor, so far as I can see, is there a soul here whom we shall desert; rather we may truly say, that we are ourselves deserted; for, our kinsfolk being either dead or fled in fear of death, no more regardful of us than if we were strangers, we are left alone in our great affliction. No censure, then, can fall on us if we do as I propose; and otherwise grievous suffering, perhaps death, may ensue. Wherefore, if you agree, 'tis my advice, that, attended by our maids with all things needful, we sojourn, now on this, now on the other estate, and in such way of life continue, until we see—if death should not first overtake us—the end which Heaven reserves for these events. And I remind you that it will be at least as seemly in us to leave with honor, as in others, of whom there are not a few, to stay with dishonor."

The other ladies praised Pampinea's plan, and indeed were so prompt to follow it that they had already begun to discuss the manner in some detail, as if they were forthwith to rise from their seats and take the road, when Filomena, whose judgment was excellent, interposed, saying:—"Ladies, though Pampinea has spoken to most excellent effect, yet it were not well to be so precipitate as you seem disposed to be. Bethink you that we are all women; nor is there any here so young, but she is of years to understand how women are minded towards one another, when they are alone together, and how ill they are able to rule themselves without the guidance of some man. We are sensitive, perverse, suspicious, pusillanimous and timid; wherefore I much misdoubt, that, if we find no other guidance than our own, this company is like to break up sooner, and with less credit to us, than it should. Against which it were well to provide at the outset." Said then Elisa:— "Without doubt man is woman's head, and, without man's governance, it is seldom that aught that we do is brought to a commendable conclusion. But how are we to come by the men? Every one of us here knows that her kinsmen are for the most part dead, and that the survivors are dispersed, one here, one there, we know not where, bent each on escaping the same fate as ourselves; nor were it seemly to seek the aid of strangers; for, as we are in quest of health, we must find some means so to order matters that, wherever we seek diversion or repose, trouble and scandal do not follow us."

While the ladies were thus conversing, there came into the church three young men, young, I say, but not so young that the age of the youngest was less than twenty-five years; in whom neither the sinister course of events, nor the loss of friends or kinsfolk, nor fear for their own safety, had availed to quench, or even temper, the ardor of their love. The first was called Pamfilo, the second Filostrato, and the third Dioneo. Very debonair and chivalrous were they all; and in this troublesome time they were seeking if haply, to their exceeding great solace, they might have sight of their fair friends, all three of whom chanced to be among the said seven ladies, besides some that were of kin to the young men. At one and the same moment they recognized the ladies and were recognized by them: wherefore, with a gracious smile, Pampinea thus began:—"Lo, fortune is propitious to our enterprise, having vouchsafed us the good offices of these young men, who are as gallant as they are discreet, and will gladly give us their guidance and escort, so we but take them into our service." Whereupon Neifile, crimson from brow to neck with the blush of modesty, being one of those that had a lover among the young men, said:—"For God's sake, Pampinea, have a care what you say. Well assured am I that nought but good can be said of any of them, and I deem them fit for office far more onerous than this which you propose for them, and their good and honorable company worthy of ladies fairer by far and more tenderly to be cherished than such as we. But 'tis no secret that they love some of us here; wherefore I misdoubt that, if we take them with us, we may thereby give occasion for scandal and censure merited neither by us nor by them." "That," said Filomena, "is of no consequence; so I but live honestly, my conscience gives me no disquietude; if other asperse me, God and the truth will take arms in my defense. Now, should they be disposed to attend us, of a truth we might say with Pampinea, that fortune favors our enterprise." The silence which followed betokened consent on the part of the other ladies, who then with one accord resolved to call the young men, and acquaint them with their purpose, and pray them to be of their company. So without further parley Pampinea, who had kinsman among the young men, rose and approached them where they stood intently regarding them; and greeting them gaily, she opened to them their plan, and besought them on the part of herself and her friends to join their company on terms of honorable and fraternal comradeship. At first the young men thought she did but trifle with them; but when they saw that she was in earnest, they answered with alacrity that they were ready, and promptly, even before they left the church, set matters in train for their departure. So all things meet being first sent forward

in due order to their intended place or sojourn, the ladies with some of their maids, and the three young men, each attended by a man-servant, sallied forth of the city on the morrow, being Wednesday, about daybreak, and took the road; nor had they journeyed more than two short miles when they arrived at their destination. The estate lay upon a little hill some distance from the nearest highway, and, embowered in shrubberies of divers hues, and other greenery, afforded the eye a pleasant prospect. On the summit of the hill was a palace with galleries, halls and chambers, disposed around a fair and spacious court, each very fair in itself, and the goodlier to see for the gladsome pictures with which it was adorned; the whole set amidst meads and gardens laid out with marvelous art, wells of the coolest water, and the vaults of the finest wines, things more suited to dainty drinkers than to sober and honorable women. On their arrival the company, to their no small delight, found their beds already made, the rooms well swept and garnished with flowers of every sort that the season could afford, and the floors carpeted with rushes. When they were seated, Dioneo, a gallant who had not his match for courtesy and wit, spoke thus:—"My ladies, 'tis not our forethought so much as your own motherwit that has guided us hither. How you mean to dispose of your cares I know not; mine I left behind me within the city-gate when I issued thence with you a brief while ago. Wherefore, I pray you, either address yourselves to make merry, to laugh and sing with me (so far, I mean, as may consist with your dignity), or give me leave to hie me back to the stricken city, there to abide with my cares." To whom blithely Pampinea replied, as if she too had cast off all her cares:—"Well sayest thou, Dioneo, excellent well; gaily we mean to live; 'twas a refuge from sorrow that here we sought, nor had we other cause to come hither. But, as no anarchy can long endure, I who initiated the deliberations of which this fair company is the fruit, do now, to the end that our joy may be lasting, deem it expedient, that there be one among us in chief authority, honored and obeyed by us as our superior, whose exclusive care it shall be to devise how we may pass our time blithely. And that each in turn may prove the weight of the care, as well as enjoy the pleasure, of sovereignty, and, no distinction being made of sex, envy be felt by none by reason of exclusion from the office; I propose, that the weight and honor be borne by each one for a day; and let the first to bear sway be chosen by us all, those that follow to be appointed towards the vesper hour by him or her who shall have had the signory for that day; and let each holder of the signory be, for the time, sole arbiter of the place and manner in which we are to pass our time."

Pampinea's speech was received with the utmost applause, and with one accord she was chosen queen for the first day. Whereupon Filomena hied her lightly to a bay tree, having often heard of the great honor in which its leaves, and such as were deservedly crowned therewith, were worthy to be holden; and having gathered a few sprays, she made thereof a goodly wreath of honor, and set it on Pampinea's head; which wreath was thenceforth, while their company endured, the visible sign of the wearer's sway and sovereignty.

No sooner was Queen Pampinea crowned than she bade all be silent. She then caused summon to her presence their four maids, and the servants of the three young men, and, all keeping silence, said to them:—"That I may show you all at once, how, well still giving place to better, our company may flourish and endure, as long as it shall pleasure us, with order meet and assured delight and without reproach, I first of all constitute Dioneo's man Parmeno, my seneschal, and intrust him with the care and control of all our household, and all that belongs to the service of the hall. Pamfilo's man, Sirisco, I appoint treasurer and chancellor of our exchequer; and be he ever answerable to Parmeno. While Parmeno and Sirisco are too busy about their duties to serve their masters, let Filostrato's man, Tindaro, have charge of the chambers of all three. My maid, Missia, and Filomena's maid, Licisca, will keep in the kitchen, and with all due diligence prepare such dishes as Parmeno shall bid them. Lauretta's maid, Chimera, and Fiammetta's maid, Stratilia, we make answerable for the ladies' chambers, and wherever we may take up our quarters, let them see that all is spotless. And now we enjoin you, one and all alike, as you value our favor, that none of you, go where you may, return whence you may, hear or see what you may, bring us any tidings but such as be cheerful." These orders thus succinctly given were received with universal approval. Whereupon Pampinea rose, and said gaily:—"Here are gardens, meads, and other places delightsome enough, where you may wander at will, and take your pleasure; but on the stroke of tierce, let all be here to breakfast in the shade."

Thus dismissed by their new queen the gay company sauntered gently through a garden, the young men saying sweet things to the fair ladies, who wove fair garlands of divers sorts of leaves and sang love-songs.

Having thus spent the time allowed them by the queen, they returned to the house, where they found that Parmeno had entered on his office with zeal; for in a hall on the ground-floor they saw tables covered with the whitest of cloths, and beakers that shone like silver, and sprays of broom scattered everywhere. So, at the bidding of the queen, they washed their hands, and all took their places as marshaled by Parmeno. Dishes, daintily prepared, were served, and the finest wines were at hand; the three serving men did their office noiselessly; in a word all was fair and ordered in a seemly manner; whereby the spirits of the company rose, and they seasoned their viands with pleasant jests and sprightly sallies. Breakfast done, the tables were removed, and the queen bade fetch instruments of music; for all, ladies and young men alike, knew how to tread a measure, and some of them played and sang with great skill: so, at her command, Dioneo having taken a lute, and Fiammetta a viol, they struck up a dance in sweet concert; and, the servants being dismissed to their repast, the queen, attended by the other ladies and the two young men, led off a stately carol; which ended they fell to singing ditties dainty and gay. Thus they diverted themselves until the queen, deeming it time to retire to rest, dismissed them all for the night. So the three young men and the ladies withdrew to their several quarters, which were in different parts of the palace. There they found the beds well made, and abundance of flowers, as in the hall; and so they undressed, and went to bed. Shortly after nine the queen rose, and roused the rest of the ladies, as also the young men, averring that it was injurious to the health to sleep long in the daytime. They therefore hied them to a meadow, where the grass grew green and luxuriant, being nowhere scorched by the sun, and a light breeze gently fanned them. So at the queen's command they all ranged themselves in a circle on the grass, and hearkened while she thus spoke:—

"You mark that the sun is high, the heat intense, and the silence unbroken save by the cicadas among the olive trees. It were therefore the height of folly to quit this spot at present. Here the air is cool and the prospect fair, and here, observe, are dice and chess. Take, then, your pleasure as you may be severally minded; but, if you take my

advice, you will find pastime for the hot hours before us, not in play, in which the loser must needs
be vexed, and neither the winner nor the onlooker
much the better pleased, but in telling of stories,
in which the invention of one may afford solace
to all the company of his hearers. You will not
each have told a story before the sun will be low,
and the heat abated, so that we shall be able to go
and severally take our pleasure where it may seem
best to each. Wherefore, if my proposal meet with
your approval—for in this I am disposed to consult
your pleasure—let us adopt it; if not, divert yourselves as best you may, until the vesper hour."

The queen's proposal being approved by all, ladies and men alike, she added:—"So please you,
then, I ordain, that, for this first day, we be free to
discourse of such matters as most commend themselves to each in turn." She then addressed Pamfilo, who sat on her right hand, bidding him with
a gracious air to lead off with one of his stories.

The Falcon of Sir Federigo

There was of yore in Florence a gallant named
Federigo di Messer Filippo Alberighi, who for
feats of arms and courtesy had not his peer in
Tuscany; who, as is the common lot of gentlemen,
became enamored of a lady named Monna Giovanna, who in her day held rank among the fairest
and most elegant ladies of Florence; to gain whose
love he jousted, tilted, gave entertainments, scattered largess, and in short set no bounds to his
expenditure. However, the lady, no less virtuous
than fair, cared not a jot for what he did for her
sake, nor yet for him.

Spending thus greatly beyond his means, and
making nothing, Federigo could hardly fail to come
to lack, and was at length reduced to such poverty
that he had nothing left but a little estate, on the
rents of which he lived very straitly, and a single
falcon, the best in the world. The estate was at
Campi, and thither, deeming it no longer possible
for him to live in the city as he desired, he repaired,
more in love than ever before; and there, in complete seclusion, diverting himself with hawking,
he bore his poverty as patiently as he might.

Now, Federigo being thus reduced to extreme
poverty, it so happened that one day Monna Giovanna's husband, who was very rich, fell ill, and
seeing that he was nearing his end, made his will,
whereby he left his estate to his son, who was now
growing up, and in the event of his death without
lawful heir named Monna Giovanna, whom he

dearly loved, heir in his stead; and having made
these dispositions he died.

Monna Giovanna, being thus left a widow, did
as our ladies are wont, and repaired in the summer
to one of her estates in the country which lay very
near to that of Federigo. And so it befell that the
urchin began to make friends with Federigo, and
to shew a fondness for hawks and dogs, and having seen Federigo's falcon fly not a few times, took
a singular fancy to him, and greatly longed to
have him for his own, but still did not dare to ask
him of Federigo, knowing that Federigo prized
him so much. So the matter stood when by chance
the boy fell sick; whereby the mother was sore
distressed, for he was her only son, and she loved
him as much as might be, insomuch that all day
long she was beside him, and ceased not to comfort him, and again and again asked him if there
were aught that he wished for, imploring him to
say the word, and, if it might by any means be had,
she would assuredly do her utmost to procure it
for him. Thus repeatedly exhorted, the boy said:—
"Mother mine, do but get me Federigo's falcon,
and I doubt not I shall soon be well." Whereupon
the lady was silent for a while, bethinking her
what she should do. She knew that Federigo had
long loved her, and had never had so much as a
single kind look from her: wherefore she said to
herself:—How can I send or go to beg of him this
falcon, which by what I hear is the best that ever
flew, and moreover is his sole comfort? And how
could I be so unfeeling as to seek to deprive a
gentleman of the one solace that is now left him?
And so, albeit she very well knew that she might
have the falcon for the asking, she was perplexed,
and knew not what to say, and gave her son no
answer. At length, however, the love she bore the
boy carried the day, and she made up her mind
for his contentment, come what might, not to send,
but to go herself and fetch him the falcon. So:—
"Be of good cheer, my son," she said, "and doubt
not thou wilt soon be well; for I promise thee that
the very first thing that I shall do tomorrow morning will be to go and fetch thee the falcon."
Whereat the child was so pleased that he began
to mend that very day

On the morrow the lady, as if for pleasure, hied
her with another lady to Federigo's little house,
and asked to see him. 'Twas still, as for some days
past, no weather for hawking, and Federigo was
in his garden, busy about some small matters
which needed to be set right there. When he heard
that Monna Giovanna was at the door, asking to

see him, he was not a little surprised and pleased, and hied him to her with all speed. As soon as she saw him, she came forward to meet him with womanly grace, and having received his respectful salutation, said to him:—"Good morrow, Federigo," and continued:—"I am come to requite thee for what thou hast lost by loving me more than thou shouldst: which compensation is this, that I with this lady that accompanies me will breakfast with thee without ceremony this morning." "Madam," Federigo replied with all humility, "I mind not ever to have lost aught by loving you, but rather to have been so much profited that, if I ever deserved well in aught, 'twas to your merit that I owed it, and to the love that I bore you. And of a surety had I still as much to spend as I have spent in the past, I should not prize it so much as this visit you so frankly pay me, come as you are to one who can afford you but a sorry sort of hospitality." Which said, with some confusion, he bade her welcome to his house, and then led her into his garden, where, having none else to present to her by way of companion, he said:—"Madam, as there is none other here, this good woman, wife of this husbandman, will bear you company, while I go to have the table set." Now, albeit his poverty was extreme, yet he had not known as yet how sore was the need to which his extravagance had reduced him; but this morning 'twas brought home to him, for that he could find nought wherewith to do honor to the lady, for love of whom he had done the honors of his house to men without number: wherefore, distressed beyond measure, and inwardly cursing his evil fortune, he sped hither and thither like one beside himself, but never a coin found he, nor yet aught to pledge. Meanwhile it grew late, and sorely he longed that the lady might not leave his house altogether unhonored, and yet to crave help of his own husbandman was more than his pride could brook. In these desperate straits his glance happened to fall on his brave falcon on his perch in his little parlor. And so, as a last resource, he took him, and finding him plump, deemed that he would make a dish meet for such a lady. Wherefore, without thinking twice about it, he wrung the bird's neck, and caused his maid forthwith to pluck him and set him on a spit, and roast him carefully; and having still some spotless table-linen, he had the table laid therewith, and with a cheerful countenance hied him back to his lady in the garden, and told her that such breakfast as he could give her was ready. So the lady and her companion rose and came to table, and there, with Federigo, who waited on them most faithfully, ate the brave falcon, knowing not what they ate.

When they were risen from table, and had dallied a while in gay converse with him, the lady deemed it time to tell the reason of her visit: wherefore, graciously addressing Federigo, thus began she:—"Federigo, by what thou rememberest of thy past life and my virtue, which, perchance thou hast deemed harshness and cruelty, I doubt not thou must marvel at my presumption, when thou hearest the main purpose of my visit; but if thou hadst sons, or hadst had them, so that thou mightest know the full force of the love that is borne them, I should make no doubt that thou wouldst hold me in part excused. Nor, having a son, may I, for that thou hast none, claim exemption from the laws to which all other mothers are subject, and, being thus bound to own their sway, I must, though fain were I not, and though 'tis neither meet nor right, crave of thee that which I know thou dost of all things and with justice prize most highly, seeing that this extremity of thy adverse fortune has left thee nought else wherewith to delight, divert and console thee; which gift is no other than thy falcon, on which my boy has so set his heart that, if I bring him it not, I fear lest he grow so much worse of the malady that he has, that thereby it may come to pass that I lose him. And so, not for the love which thou dost bear me, and which may nowise bind thee, but for that nobleness of temper, whereof in courtesy more conspicuously than in aught else thou hast given proof, I implore thee that thou be pleased to give me the bird, that thereby I may say that I have kept my son alive, and thus made him for aye thy debtor."

No sooner had Federigo apprehended what the lady wanted, than, for grief that 'twas not in his power to serve her, because he had given her the falcon to eat, he fell a-weeping in her presence, before he could so much as utter a word. At first the lady supposed that 'twas only because he was loath to part with the brave falcon that he wept, and as good as made up her mind that he would refuse her: however, she awaited with patience Federigo's answer, which was on this wise:—"Madam, since it pleased God that I should set my affections upon you there have been matters not a few, in which to my sorrow I have deemed Fortune adverse to me; but they have all been trifles in comparison of the trick that she now plays me: the which I shall never forgive her, seeing that you are come here to my poor house, where, while I was rich, you deigned not to come, and ask a trifling favor of me, which she has put it out of my power to grant: how 'tis so, I will briefly tell you. When I learned that you, of your grace, were minded to breakfast with me, having respect to your high dignity and desert, I deemed it due and seemly that in your honor I should regale you, to the best of my power, with fare of a more excellent quality than is commonly set before others; and, calling to mind the falcon which you now ask of me, and his excellence, I judged him meet food for you, and so you have had him roasted on the trencher this morning; and well indeed I thought I had bestowed him; but, as now I see that you would fain have had him in another guise, so mortified am I that I am not able to serve you, that I doubt I shall never know peace of mind more." In witness whereof he had the feathers and feet and beak of the bird brought in and laid before her.

The first thing the lady did, when she had heard Federigo's story, and seen the relics of the bird, was to chide him that he had killed so fine a falcon to furnish a woman with a breakfast; after which the magnanimity of her host, which poverty had been and was powerless to impair, elicited no small share of inward commendation. Then, frustrate of her hope of possessing the falcon, and doubting of her son's recovery, she took her leave with the heaviest of hearts, and hied her back to the boy: who, whether for fretting, that he might not have the falcon, or by the unaided energy of his disorder, departed this life not many days after, to the exceeding great grief of his mother. For a while she would do nought but weep and bitterly bewail herself; but being still young, and left very wealthy, she was often urged by her brothers to marry again, and though she would rather have not done so, yet being importuned, and remembering Federigo's high desert, and the magnificent generosity with which he had finally killed his falcon to do her honor, she said to her brothers:—"Gladly, with your consent, would I remain a widow, but if you will not be satisfied except I take a husband, rest assured that none other will I ever take save Federigo degli Alberighi." Whereupon her brothers derided her, saying:—"Foolish woman, what is't thou sayst? How wouldst thou want Federigo, who has not a thing in the world?" To whom she answered:—"My brothers, well wot I that 'tis as you say; but I had rather have a man without wealth than wealth without a man." The brothers, perceiving that her mind was made up, and knowing Federigo for a good man and true, poor though he was, gave her to him with all her wealth. And so Federigo, being mated with such a wife, and one that he had so much loved, and being very wealthy to boot, lived happily, keeping more exact accounts, to the end of his days.

NICCOLÒ MACHIAVELLI

The Prince

The Conduct of a Successful Ruler

Ch. XV. *Of Such Things as Render Men (Especially Princes) Worthy of Blame or Applause.*

It remains now that we see in what manner a prince ought to comport with his subjects and friends; and because many have written of this subject before, it may perhaps seem arrogant in me, especially considering that in my discourse I shall deviate from the opinion of other men. But my intention being to write for the benefit and advantage of him who understands, I thought it more convenient to respect the essential verity, rather than an imaginary view, of the subject; for many have framed imaginary commonwealths and governments to themselves which never were seen nor had any real existence. And the present manner of living is so different from the way that ought to be taken, that he who neglects what is done to follow what ought to be done, will sooner learn how to ruin than how to preserve himself; for a tender man, and one that desires to be honest

The Prince. Translated by Henry Morley. Niccolò Machiavelli (1469-1527), a Florentine statesman and politician, spent his life in the midst of political intrigues, in which he gained the experience necessary for writing *The Prince.*

in everything, must needs run a great hazard among so many of a contrary principle. Wherefore it is necessary for a prince who is willing to subsist to harden himself, and learn to be good or otherwise according to the exigence of his affairs. Laying aside, therefore, all imaginary notions of a prince, and discoursing of nothing but what is actually true, I say that all men when they are spoken of, and especially princes, who are in a higher and more eminent station, are remarkable for some quality or other that makes them either honorable or contemptible. Hence it is that some are counted liberal, others miserly; . . . some munificent, others rapacious; some cruel, others merciful; some faithless, others precise; one poor-spirited and effeminate, another fierce and ambitious; one courteous, another haughty; one modest, another libidinous; one sincere, another cunning; one rugged and morose, another accessible and easy; one grave, another giddy; one devout, another an atheist.

No man, I am sure, will deny but that it would be an admirable thing and highly to be commended to have a prince endued with all the good qualities aforesaid; but because it is impossible to have, much less to exercise, them all by reason of the frailty and grossness of our nature, it is convenient that he be so well instructed as to know how to avoid the scandal of those vices which may deprive him of his state, and be very cautious of the rest, though their consequence be not so pernicious but that where they are unavoidable he need trouble himself the less. Again, he is not to concern himself if he incur the infamy of those vices without which his dominion is not to be preserved; for if we consider things impartially we shall find some things are virtuous in appearance, and yet, if pursued, would bring certain destruction; while others, seemingly bad, yet, if followed by a prince, procure his peace and security.

Ch. XVI. *Of Liberality and Parsimony.*

To begin, then, with the first of the above-mentioned qualities, I say, it would be advantageous to be accounted liberal; nevertheless, liberality so used as not to render you formidable does but injure you; for if it be used virtuously as it ought to be it will not be known, nor secure you from the imputation of its contrary. To keep up, therefore, the name of liberal amongst men, it is necessary that no kind of luxury be omitted, so that a prince of that disposition will consume his revenue in that kind of expenses, and be obliged at last, if he

would preserve that reputation, to become grievous, and a great exactor upon the people, and do whatever is practicable for the getting of money, which will cause him to be hated of his subjects and despised by everybody else when he once comes to be poor, so that offending many with his liberality and rewarding but few, he becomes sensible of the first disaster, and runs great hazard of being ruined the first time he is in danger; which, when afterward he discovers, and desires to remedy, he runs into the other extreme, and grows as odious for his avarice. So, then, if a prince cannot exercise this virtue of liberality so as to be publicly known, without detriment to himself, he ought, if he be wise, not to dread the imputation of being covetous, for in time he shall be esteemed liberal when it is discovered that by his parsimony he has increased his revenue to a condition of defending himself against invasion and of engaging in enterprises upon other people without oppressing his subjects; so that he shall be accounted noble to all from whom he takes nothing away, which are an infinite number, and near and parsimonious only to such few as he gives nothing to.

In our days we have seen no great action done but by those who were accounted miserly; others have failed always. Pope Julius II made use of his bounty to get into the Chair, but to enable himself to make war with the King of France he never practiced it afterwards, and by his frugality he maintained several wars without any tax or imposition upon the people, his long parsimony having furnished him for his extraordinary expenses. The present King of Spain, if he had affected to be thought liberal, could never have undertaken so many great designs nor obtained so many great victories. A prince, therefore, ought not to be much concerned over being accounted covetous—so long as he is enabled thereby to forbear from burdening his subjects, to defend himself, and to keep himself from becoming poor and despicable; covetousness is one of those vices which fortify his dominion. If anyone objects that Cæsar by his liberality made his way to the empire, and many others upon the same score of reputation have made themselves great, I answer: "Either you are actually a prince, or you are in a fair way to be made one. In the first case, liberality is hurtful; in the second, it is necessary; Cæsar aspired to the sovereignty of Rome; when he was arrived at that dignity, if he had lived, and had not retrenched his expenses, he would have ruined that empire." If anyone replies that many have been princes, and with their armies performed great matters, who have been reputed liberal, I rejoin that a prince spends either of his own, or his subjects', or other people's. In the first case he is to be frugal; in the second, he may be as profuse as he pleases, and balk no point of liberality. But that prince whose army is to be maintained with free quarter and plunder and exactions from other people, is obliged to be liberal, or his army will desert him; and well he may be prodigal of what neither belongs to him nor his subjects, as was the case with Cæsar, and Cyrus, and Alexander; for to spend upon another's stock rather adds to than subtracts from his reputation; it is spending of his own that is so mortal and pernicious. Nor is there anything that destroys itself like liberality; for in practicing it you lose the means whereby it can be practiced, and you become poor and contemptible, or, to avoid that poverty, you make yourself odious and a tyrant; and there is nothing of so much importance to a prince to avoid as to be either contemptible or odious, both of which depend much upon the prudent exercise of your liberality. Upon these considerations it is more wisdom to lie under the scandal of being miserly, which is an imputation rather infamous than odious, than to be thought liberal and run yourself into a necessity of playing the tyrant, which is infamous and odious both.

Ch. XVII. *Of Cruelty and Clemency, and Whether it is Best for a Prince to be Beloved or Feared.*

To come now to the other qualities proposed, I say every prince is to desire to be esteemed rather merciful than cruel, but with great caution that his mercy be not abused; Cæsar Borgia was counted cruel, yet that cruelty reduced Romagna, united it, settled it in peace, and rendered it faithful: so that if well considered, he will appear much more merciful than the Florentines, who rather than be thought cruel suffered Pistoia to be destroyed. A prince, therefore, is not to regard the reproach of being cruel, if thereby he keeps his subjects in their allegiance and united, seeing that by some few examples of justice he may be more merciful than they who by a universal exercise of pity permit several disorders to follow, which occasion rapine and murder; and the reason is, because that exorbitant mercy has an ill effect upon the whole community, whereas particular executions extend only to particular persons. But among all princes a new prince has the hardest task to avoid the scandal of being cruel by reason of the newness of

his government, and the dangers which attend it: hence Virgil in the person of Dido excused the inhospitality of her government.

> Res dura, et regni novitas, me talia cogunt
> Moliri, et late fines Custode tueri.

> My new dominion and my harder fate
> Constrains me to't, and I must guard my state.

Nevertheless, he is not to be too credulous of reports, too hasty in his motions, nor create fears and jealousies to himself, but so to temper his administrations with prudence and humanity that neither too much confidence may make him careless, nor too much diffidence intolerable. And hence arises a new question, Whether it be better to be beloved than feared, or feared than beloved? It is answered, both would be convenient, but because that is hard to attain, it is better and more secure, if one must be wanting, to be feared than beloved; for in general men are ungrateful, inconstant, hypocritical, fearful of danger, and covetous of gain; while they receive any benefit by you, and the danger is at a distance, they are absolutely yours, and their blood, their estates, their lives and their children, as I said before, are all at your service; but when mischief is at hand, and you have present need of their help, they make no scruple to revolt; and that prince who leaves himself naked of other preparations, and relies wholly upon their professions, is sure to be ruined; for amity contracted by price, and not by the greatness and generosity of the mind, may seem a good pennyworth; yet when you have occasion to make use of it, you will find no such thing. Moreover, men do with less remorse offend against those who desire to be beloved than against those who are ambitious of being feared; the reason is that love is fastened only by a ligament of obligation, which the ill-nature of man breaks upon every occasion that is presented to his profit; but fear depends upon an apprehension of punishment, which is never to be dispelled. Yet a prince is to render himself awful in such sort that, if he gains not his subjects' love, he may escape their hatred; for to be feared and not hated are compatible enough, and he may be always in that condition if he offers no violence to their estates, nor attempts anything upon the honor of their wives, and when he has occasion to take away any man's life, if he takes his time when the cause is manifest, and he has good matter for his justification; but above all things he is to have a care of intrenching upon their estates, for men do sooner forget the death of their father than the loss of their patrimony; besides, occasions of confiscation never fail, and he that once gives way to that humor or rapine shall never want temptation to ruin his neighbor. But, on the contrary, provocations to blood are more rare, and do sooner evaporate; but when a prince is at the head of his army, and has a multitude of soldiers to govern, then it is absolutely necessary not to value the epithet of cruel, for without that no army can be kept in unity, nor in disposition for any great act.

Among the several instances of Hannibal's great conduct, it is one that, having a vast army constituted out of several nations, and conducted to make war in an enemy's country, there never happened any sedition among them, or any mutiny against their general, either in his adversity or prosperity. This can only be attributed to his great cruelty, which, added to his infinite virtues, rendered him both awful and terrible to his soldiers; without that all his virtues would have signified nothing. Some writers there are, but of little consideration, who admire his great exploits and condemn the true causes of them. But to prove that his other virtues would never have carried him through, let us reflect upon Scipio, a person honorable not only in his own time, but in all history whatever; nevertheless his army mutinied in Spain, and the true cause of it was his too much gentleness and lenity, which gave his soldiers more liberty than was suitable or consistent with military discipline. Fabius Maximus upbraided him for it in the senate, and called him corrupter of the Roman Militia; the inhabitants of Locris having been plundered and destroyed by one of Scipio's lieutenants, they were never redressed, nor the legate's insolence corrected, all proceeding from the mildness of Scipio's nature, which was so eminent in him, that a person undertaking to excuse him in the senate declared that there were many who knew better how to avoid doing ill themselves than to punish it in other people; which temper would doubtless in time have eclipsed the glory and reputation of Scipio, had that authority been continued in him; but receiving orders and living under the direction of the senate, that ill quality was not only not discovered in him, but turned to his renown. I conclude, therefore, according to what I have said about being feared or beloved, that forasmuch as men do love at their own discretion, but fear at their prince's, a wise prince is obliged to lay his foundation upon that which is in his own power, not that which depends on other people, but, as I said before, with great caution that he does not make himself odious.

Ch. XVIII. *How Far a Prince is Obliged by His Promise.*

How honorable it is for a prince to keep his word, and act rather with integrity than collusion, I suppose everybody understands: nevertheless, experience has shown in our times that those princes who have not pinned themselves up to that punctuality and preciseness have done great things, and by their cunning and subtilty have not only circumvented those with whom they had to deal, but have overcome and been too hard for those who have been so superstitiously exact. For further explanation you must understand there are two ways of contending—by law and by force: the first is proper to men; the second to beasts; but because many times the first is insufficient, recourse must be had to the second. It belongs, therefore, to a prince to understand both—when to make use of the rational and when of the brutal way; and this is recommended to princes, though abstrusely, by ancient writers, who tell them how Achilles and several other princes were committed for education to Chiron the Centaur, who was half man and half beast—thus showing how necessary it is for a prince to be acquainted with both natures for one without the other will be of little duration. Seeing, therefore, it is of such importance to a prince to take upon him the nature and disposition of a beast, of all the whole flock he ought to imitate the lion and the fox; for the lion is in danger of toils and snares, and the fox of the wolf; so that he must be a fox to find out the snares, and a lion to fight away the wolves, but they who keep wholly to the lion have no true notion of themselves. A prince, therefore, who is wise and prudent, cannot or ought not to keep his word, when the keeping of it is to his prejudice, and the causes for which he promised removed. Were men all good this doctrine would not be taught, but because they are wicked and not likely to be punctual with you, you are not obliged to any such strictness with them; nor was there ever any prince that lacked lawful pretense to justify his breach of promise. I might give many modern examples, and show how many confederations, and peaces, and promises have been broken by the infidelity of princes, and how he that best personated the fox had the better success. Nevertheless, it is of great consequence to disguise your inclination, and to play the hypocrite well; and men are so simple in their temper and so submissive to their present necessities that he that is neat and cleanly in his collusions shall never want people to practice them upon. I cannot forbear one example which is still fresh in our memory. Alexander VI never did, nor thought of, anything but cheating, and never wanted matter to work upon; and though no man promised a thing with greater asseveration, nor confirmed it with more oaths and imprecations, and observed them less, yet understanding the world well he never miscarried.

A prince, therefore, is not obliged to have all the forementioned good qualities in reality, but it is necessary he have them in appearance; nay, I will be bold to affirm that, having them actually, and employing them upon all occasions, they are extremely prejudicial, whereas, having them only in appearance, they turn to better account; it is honorable to seem mild, and merciful, and courteous, and religious, and sincere, and indeed to be so, provided your mind be so rectified and prepared that you can act quite contrary upon occasion. And this must be premised, that a prince, especially if come but lately to the throne, cannot observe all those things exactly which cause men to be esteemed virtuous, being oftentimes necessitated, for the preservation of his state, to do things inhuman, uncharitable, and irreligious; and, therefore, it is convenient for his mind to be at his command, and flexible to all the puffs and variations of fortune; not forbearing to be good while it is in his choice, but knowing how to be evil when there is a necessity. A prince, then, is to have particular care that nothing falls from his mouth but what is full of the five qualities aforesaid, and that to see and hear him he appears all goodness, integrity, humanity, and religion, which last he ought to pretend to more than ordinarily, because more men do judge by the eye than by the touch; for everybody sees but few understand; everybody sees how you appear, but few know what in reality you are, and those few dare not oppose the opinion of the multitude, who have the majesty of their prince to defend them; and in the actions of all men, especially princes, where no man has power to judge, everyone looks to the end. Let a prince, therefore, do what he can to preserve his life, and continue his supremacy, the means which he uses shall be thought honorable, and be commended by everybody; because the people are always taken with the appearance and event of things, and the greatest part of the world consists of the people; those few who are wise taking place when the multitude has nothing else to rely upon. There is a prince at this time in being (but his name I shall conceal) who has nothing in his mouth but fidelity and peace; and yet had he exercised either the one or the other, they had robbed him before this both of his power and reputation.

Ch. XIX. *That Princes Ought to be Cautious of Becoming either Odious or Contemptible.*

Since in our discourse of the qualifications of a prince we have hitherto spoken only of those which are of greatest importance, we shall now speak briefly of the rest, with the general statements that a prince should make it his business (as is partly hinted before) to avoid such things as may make him odious or contemptible, and that as often as he does that he plays his part very well, and shall meet no danger or inconveniences by the rest of his vices. Nothing, as I said before, makes a prince so insufferably odious as usurping his subjects' estates and debauching their wives, which are two things he ought studiously to forbear; for while the generality of the world live quietly upon their estates and unprejudiced in their honor, they live peaceably enough, and all his contention is only with the pride and ambition of some few persons who can in many ways and with great ease be restrained.

But a prince is contemptible when he is counted effeminate, light, inconstant, pusillanimous, and irresolute; and of this he ought to be as careful as of a rock in the sea; and he should strive that in all his actions there may appear magnanimity, courage, gravity, and fortitude, desiring that in the private affairs of his subjects his sentence and determination may be irrevocable, and that he himself may stand so in their opinion that none may think it possible either to delude or divert him. The prince who causes himself to be esteemed in that manner shall be highly feared, and if he be feared, people will not easily conspire against him, nor readily invade him, because he is known to be an excellent person and formidable to his subjects; for a prince ought to be terrible in two places— at home to his subjects, and abroad to his equals, from whom he defends himself by good arms and good allies; for, if his power be good, his friends will not be wanting, and while his affairs are fixed at home, there will be no danger from abroad, unless they be disturbed by some former conspiracy; and upon any commotion *ab extra,* if he be composed at home, has lived as I prescribe, and not deserted himself, he will be able to bear up against any attack, according to the example of Nabis the Spartan.

When things are well abroad his affairs at home will be safe enough, unless they be perplexed by some secret conspiracy, against which the prince sufficiently provides if he keeps himself from being hated or despised, and the people remain satisfied of him, which is a thing very necessary, as I have shown at length before. And one of the best remedies a prince can use against conspiracy is to keep himself from being hated or despised by the multitude; for nobody plots but expects by the death of the prince to gratify the people, and the thought of offending them will deter him from any such enterprise, because in conspiracies the difficulties are infinite. By experience we find that many conspiracies have been on foot, but few have succeeded, because no man can conspire alone, nor choose a confederate but out of those who are discontented; and no sooner shall you impart your mind to a malcontent but you give him opportunity to reconcile himself, because there is no advantage which he seeks but what he may hope to gain by betraying you. So that the gain being certain on that side, and hazardous and uncertain on the other, he must be either an extraordinary friend to you or an implacable enemy to the prince if he does not betray you; in short, on the side of the conspirators there is nothing but fear and jealousy, and apprehension of punishment; but, on the prince's side, there is the majesty of the government, the laws, the assistance of his friends and state, which defend him so effectually that, if the affections of the people be added to them, no man can be so rash and precipitate as to conspire; for if, before the execution of his design, the conspirator has reason to be afraid, in this case he has much more afterwards, having offended the people in the execution and left himself no refuge to fly to. Of this many examples may be produced, but I shall content myself with one which happened in the memory of our fathers. Hannibal Bentivoglio, grandfather to this present Hannibal, was Prince of Bologna, and was killed by the Canneschi who conspired against him, none of his race being left behind but John, who was then in his cradle; the murder was no sooner committed but the people took arms and slew all the Canneschi, which proceeded only from the affection that the house of Bentivoglio had at that time among the populace in Bologna, which was then so great that when Hannibal was dead, there being none of that family remaining in a capacity for the government of the state, upon information that at Florence there was a natural son of the said Bentivoglio's, who till that time had passed only for the son of a smith, they sent ambassadors for him, and having conducted him honorably to that city, they gave him the government, which he executed very well till the said John came of age. I conclude, therefore, a prince need not be much apprehensive of conspiracies while the people are his friends; but when they are dissatisfied, and have taken prejudice against him, there is nothing nor no person which he ought not to fear.

It has been the constant care of all wise princes and all well-governed states not to reduce the nobility to despair nor the people to discontent, which is one of the most material things a prince is to prevent. Among the best-ordered monarchies of our times France is one, in which there are many good laws and constitutions tending to the liberty and preservation of the king. The first of them is the Parliament and the authority wherewith it is vested; for he who was the founder of that monarchy, was sensible of the ambition and insolence of the nobles, and judged it convenient to have them bridled and restrained; he knew, on the other side, the hatred of the people against the nobility, and that it proceeded from fear, and he desired to protect the people; but in order to save himself from the displeasure of the nobles if he sided with the people, or from the malice of the people if he inclined to the nobles, he established a third party to be arbitrator, who, without any reflection upon the king, should keep the nobility under, and protect the people; nor could there be a better order, wiser, nor of greater security to the king and the kingdom, whence we may deduce another observation—That princes are to leave things of injustice and envy to the ministry and execution of others, but acts of favor and grace are to be performed by themselves. . . .

Ch. XXI. *How a Prince is to Demean Himself to Gain Reputation.*

Nothing recommends a prince so highly to the world as great enterprises and noble expressions of his own valor and conduct. We have in our days Ferdinand, King of Aragon—the present King of Spain—who may, and not improperly, be called a new prince, since from one of the smallest and weakest he has become for fame and renown the greatest monarch in Christendom; and if his exploits be considered you will find them all brave, but some of them extraordinary. In the beginning of his reign he invaded the kingdom of Granada, and that enterprise was the foundation of his grandeur. He began it leisurely, and without suspicion of impediment, holding the barons of Castile employed in that service, and so intent upon that war that they dreamt not of any innovation, while in the meantime, before they were aware, he got reputation and authority over them. He found out a way of maintaining his army at the expense of the church and the people; and by the length of that war he established such order and discipline among his soldiers, that afterwards they gained him many honorable victories. Besides this, to adapt him for greater enterprises (always making religion his pretense), by a kind of devout cruelty he destroyed and exterminated the Moors, than which nothing could be more strange or deplorable. Under the same cloak of religion he invaded Africa, made his expedition into Italy, assaulted France, and began many great things which always kept the minds of his subjects in admiration and suspense, wondering what the event of his machinations would be. And these enterprises had so sudden a spring and result one from the other that they gave no leisure to any man to be at quiet, or to continue anything against him. It is likewise of great advantage to a prince to give some rare example of his own administration at home whenever the actions, good or bad, of someone in civil life give him opportunity to reward or punish such actions in such a way as to make himself much talked of in the world. Above all, a prince is to have a care in all his actions to behave himself so as to give himself the reputation of being excellent as well as great.

A prince is likewise much esteemed when he shows himself a sincere friend or a generous enemy—that is, when without any hesitation he declares himself in favor of one against another, which, as it is more frank and princely, so it is more profitable than to stand neutral; for if two of your potent neighbors be at war, they are either of such condition that you are to be afraid of the victor or not; in either of which cases it will be always more for your benefit to discover yourself freely, and make a fair war. For in the first case, if you do not declare, you shall be a prey to him who overcomes, and it will be a pleasure and satisfaction to him that is conquered to see you his fellow-sufferer; nor will anybody either defend or receive you, and the reason is because the conqueror will never understand them to be his friends who would not assist him in his distress; and he that is worsted will not receive you because you neglected to share his fortune with your arms in your hands. . . . And those princes who are ill-advised to avoid some present danger by following the neutral way are most commonly ruined; but when you pronounce yourself courageously in favor of one party, if he with whom you join overcome, though he be very powerful, and you seem to remain at his discretion, yet he is obliged to you, and must needs have a respect for you; and men are not so wicked with signal and exemplary ingratitude as to oppress you after you have helped them. Besides, victories are never so clear and complete as to leave the conqueror without all sparks of reflection, and especially upon what is just. But if your confederate comes by the worst, you are received by him, and assisted while he is able, and you become a companion of his fortune, which may possibly restore you. In the second place, if they who contend be of such condition that they have no occasion to fear, let which will overcome, you are in prudence to declare yourself the sooner, because by assisting the one you contribute to the ruin of the other, whom, if your confederate had been wise, he ought rather to have preserved; if he whom you help overcomes, he remains wholly in your power, and by your assistance he must of necessity overcome. And here it is to be noted, if he can avoid it, a prince is never to league himself with another more powerful than himself in an offensive war; because in that case if the latter overcomes the former remains at his mercy, and princes ought to be as cautious as possible of falling under the discretion of other people. The Venetians, when there was no necessity for it, associated with France against the Duke of Milan, and that association was the cause of their ruin. But where it is not to be avoided, as happened to the Florentines when the Pope and the Spaniard sent their armies against Lombardy, then a prince is to adhere for the reasons aforesaid. Nor is any prince or government to imagine that in those cases any certain counsel can be taken, because the affairs of this world are so ordered that in avoiding one mischief we fall commonly into another. But a man's wisdom is most conspicuous where he is able to distinguish of dangers and make choice of the least.

Moreover, it is a prince's wisdom to show himself a virtuoso, and honorer of all that is excellent in any art whatsoever. He is likewise to encourage and assure his subjects that they may live quietly in peace, and exercise themselves in their several vocations, whether merchandise, agriculture, or any other employment whatever, to the end that no one may forbear improving or embellishing his estate for fear it should be taken from him, or forbear advancing his trade in apprehension of taxes; but the prince is rather to excite them by propositions of reward and immunities to all such as shall [10] any way amplify his territory or power. He is obliged, likewise, at convenient times in the year to entertain the people by feastings and plays, and spectacles of recreation; and, because all cities are divided into companies or wards, he ought to have respect to those societies, be merry with them sometimes, and give them some instance of his humanity and magnificence, but always retaining the majesty of his degree, which is never to be debased in any case whatever.

BENVENUTO CELLINI

The Casting of the Perseus

As I had been particularly successful in casting my Medusa, I made a model of my Perseus in wax, and flattered myself that I should have the same success in casting the latter in bronze, as I had had with the former. Upon its appearing to such advantage, and looking so beautiful in wax, the duke, whether somebody else put it into his head, or whether it was a notion of his own, as he came to my house oftener than usual, once took occasion to say to me, "Benvenuto, this statue cannot be [10] cast in bronze; it is not in the power of your art to compass it." Hearing him express himself in that manner, I discovered great vexation, and said, "My lord, I know that your excellency places very little confidence in me, and that you have but too good an opinion of those who speak ill of me; or else you do not understand things of this nature." Scarce did he suffer me to utter these words, when he answered, "I profess to understand them, and I do understand them perfectly." I replied, "You [20] may understand them as a prince, but not as an artist; for if you had that skill in these matters, which you think you have, you would believe me upon account of the fine bronze head which I cast for your excellency, and which was sent to the Elbe; as also for having restored the beautiful figure of Ganymede, a work that gave me infinite trouble, insomuch that it would have been easier for me to have made a new one; likewise for having cast the Medusa, which stands here before your [30] excellency, a performance of immense difficulty, in which I have done what no other man has done before me in this most laborious art. Consider, my lord, I have constructed a new sort of a furnace, in a manner unknown to other artists; for besides many other particulars and curious inventions to be seen in it, I have made two issues for the bronze; for otherwise that difficult and distorted figure could never come out, and it was only by [10] means of my skill and invention that it came out as well as it did; and do not imagine that every common artist could have done as much. Know likewise, my lord, that all the great and difficult undertakings that I have been employed in by the renowned King Francis, were attended with admirable success, purely on account of that king's generous encouragement of my labors, in providing me with everything I wanted, and allowing me as many hands as I required. At certain times I had [20] under me above forty journeymen, all of my own choosing; and this was the reason that I finished so many undertakings in so short a time. Therefore, my lord, take my advice, and afford me the assistance I want, for I have great hopes of producing a work that will please you; whereas, if your excellency discourages me, and does not supply me with the necessary helps, it is impossible that either I or any man living can produce any thing worth notice."

The duke scarcely had patience to hear me out,

The Casting of the Perseus from Cellini's *Autobiography*. Translated by Thomas Roscoe. Benvenuto Cellini (1501-1571) was born at Florence. He was a great artist in metal as well as an indefatigable adventurer.

but sometimes turned one way, sometimes another; and I was quite in despair when I recollected the circumstances in which I had lived in France. At last he all on a sudden said, "Tell me, Benvenuto, how is it possible that this fine head of Medusa, which Perseus holds aloft in his hand, should ever come out cleverly?" I immediately answered, "It is clear, my lord, that you are no connoisseur in statuary, as your excellency boasts yourself; for if you had any skill in the art, you would not be afraid of that fine head not coming out, but would express your apprehensions concerning that right foot, which is at such a distance below." The duke, half angry, addressing himself to some noblemen who were with him, said, "I really believe it is a practice of Benvenuto's to contradict and oppose everything he hears advanced"; then turning to me, as it were in derision, in which he was imitated by all present, he expressed himself thus: "I am willing to have patience to hear what reason you can allege, that can possibly induce me to believe what you affirm." I answered, "I will give your excellency a reason so satisfactory, that you will be able to conceive the full force of it." I thereupon began in these terms: "You know, my lord, that the nature of fire is to fly upwards; I therefore assure you that the head of Medusa will come out perfectly well. But as it is not the property of fire to descend, and it is necessary to force it down six cubits by art, hence, I affirm that it is impossible that yon foot should ever come out; but it will be an easy matter for me to make a new one. The duke thereupon said, "Why did you not think of contriving to make that foot come out as well as the head?" "I must then," answered I, "have made the furnace much bigger, to be able to cast a piece of brass as thick as my leg, and with that weight of hot metal I should have made it come out by force; whereas, my brass, which goes down to the feet six cubits, as I mentioned before, is not above two inches thick. Therefore, it was not worth your notice, for it can soon be rectified; but when my mold is something more than half full, I have good hopes that from that half upwards, the fire mounting, by its natural property, the heads of Perseus and Medusa will come out admirably; and this you may depend upon." When I had laid before the duke all these reasons, with many more, which I for the sake of brevity omit, he shook his head, and departed.

I now took courage, resolving to depend on myself, and banished all those thoughts which from time to time occasioned me great inquietude, and made me sorely repent my ever having quitted France, with a view of assisting six poor nieces at Florence; which good intention proved the source and origin of all the misfortunes that afterwards befell me. However, I still flattered myself that if I could but finish my statue of Perseus, all my labors would be converted to delight, and meet with a glorious and happy reward. Thus, having recovered my vigor of mind, I exerted all my strength of body and of purse, though indeed I had but little money left, and began to purchase several loads of pine-wood from the pine-grove of the Serristori, hard by Monte Lupo; and whilst I was waiting for it, I covered my Perseus with the earth which I had prepared several months beforehand, that it might have its proper seasoning. After I had made its coat of earth, covered it well, and bound it properly with irons, I began by means of a slow fire to draw off the wax, which melted away by many vent-holes; for the more of these are made, the better the molds are filled: and when I had entirely stripped off the wax, I made a sort of fence round my Perseus, that is, round the mold above-mentioned, of bricks, piling them one upon another, and leaving several vacuities for the fire to exhale at. I next began gradually to put on the wood, and kept a constant fire for two days and two nights, till, the wax being quite off, and the mold well baked, I began to dig a hole to bury my mold in, and observed all those fine methods of proceeding that are prescribed by our art. When I had completely dug my hole, I took my mold, and by means of levers and strong cables directed it with care, and suspended it a cubit above the level of the furnace, so that it hung exactly in the middle of the hole. I then let it gently down to the very bottom of the furnace, and placed it with all the care and exactness I possibly could. After I had finished this part of my task, I began to make a covering of the very earth I had taken off, and in proportion as I raised the earth, I made vents for it, which are a sort of tubes of baked earth, generally used for conduits, and other things of a similar nature. As soon as I saw that I had placed it properly, and that this manner of covering it, by putting on these small tubes in their proper places, was likely to answer, as also that my journeymen thoroughly understood my plan, which was very different from that of all other masters, and I was sure that I could depend upon them, I turned my thoughts to my furnace. I had caused it to be filled with several pieces of brass and bronze, and heaped them upon one another in the manner taught us by our art, taking particular care to leave a passage for the flames, that the metal might the sooner assume its color and dissolve into a fluid. Thus, I with great alacrity, excited my men to lay on the pine-wood, which, because of the oiliness of the resinous matter that oozes from the pine-tree, and that my furnace was admirably well made, burned at such a rate, that I was continually obliged to run to and fro, which greatly fatigued me. I, however, bore the hardship; but to add to my misfortune, the shop took fire, and we were all very much afraid that the roof would fall in and crush us. From another quarter, that is, from the garden, the sky poured in so much rain and wind, that it cooled my furnace.

Thus did I continue to struggle with these cross accidents for several hours, and exerted myself to such a degree that my constitution, though robust, could no longer bear such severe hardship, and I was suddenly attacked by a most violent intermitting fever: in short, I was so ill that I found myself under a necessity of lying down upon my bed. This gave me great concern, but it was unavoidable. I thereupon addressed myself to my assistants, who were about ten in number, consisting of masters who melted bronze, helpers, men from the country, and the journeymen that worked in the shop, amongst whom was Bernardino Manellini di Mugello, who had lived with me several years. After having recommended it to them all to take proper care of my business, I said to Bernardino, "My friend, be careful to observe the method which I have shown you, and use all possible expedition, for the metal will soon be ready. You cannot mistake: these two worthy men here will quickly make the tubes; with two such directors you can certainly contrive to pour out the hot metal by means of the mandriani or iron crooks; and I have no doubt but my mold will be filled completely. I find myself extremely ill, and really believe that in a few hours this severe disorder will put an end to my life." Thus I left them in great sorrow, and went to bed. I then ordered the maids to carry victuals and drink into the shop for all the men, and told them I did not expect to live till the next morning. They encouraged me notwithstanding, assuring me that my disorder would not last, as it was only the effect of over-fatigue. In this manner did I continue for two hours in a violent fever, which I every moment perceived to increase; and I was incessantly crying out, "I am dying, I am dying."

My housekeeper, whose name was Mona Fiore da Castel del Rio, was one of the most sensible and affectionate women in the world: she rebuked me for giving way to vain fears, and at the same time attended me with the greatest kindness and care imaginable: however, seeing me so very ill, and terrified to such a degree, she could not contain herself, but shed a flood of tears, which she endeavored to conceal from me. Whilst we were both in this deep affliction, I perceived a man enter the room, who in his person appeared to be as crooked and distorted as a great S, and began to express himself in these terms, with a tone of voice as dismal and melancholy as those who exhort and pray with persons who are going to be executed: "Alas! poor Benvenuto, your work is spoiled, and the misfortune admits of no remedy."

No sooner had I heard the words uttered by this messenger of evil, but I cried out so loud that my voice might be heard to the skies, and got out of bed. I began immediately to dress, and giving plenty of kicks and cuffs to the maidservants and the boy as they offered to help me on with my clothes, I complained bitterly in these terms: "O you envious and treacherous wretches, this is a piece of villainy contrived on purpose; but I swear by the living God that I will sift it to the bottom, and before I die, give such proofs who I am as shall not fail to astonish the whole world." Having huddled on my clothes, I went with a mind boding evil to the shop, where I found all those whom I had left so alert, and in such high spirits, standing in the utmost confusion and astonishment. I thereupon addressed them thus: "Listen all of you to what I am going to say; and since you either would not or could not follow the method I pointed out, obey me now that I am present: my work is before us, and let none of you offer to oppose or contradict me, for such cases as this require activity and not counsel." Hereupon one Alessandro Lastricati had the assurance to say to me, "Look you, Benvenuto, you have undertaken a work which our art cannot compass, and which is not to be effected by human power."

Hearing these words I turned round in such a passion, and seemed so bent upon mischief, that both he and all the rest unanimously cried out to me, "Give your orders, and we will all second you in whatever you command: we will assist you as long as we have breath in our bodies." These kind and affectionate words they uttered, as I firmly believe, in a persuasion that I was upon the point of expiring. I went directly to examine the furnace, and saw all the metal in it concreted. I thereupon ordered two of the helpers to step over the way to Capretta, a butcher, for a load of young oak, which had been above a year drying, and been offered me by Maria Ginevera, wife to the said Capretta.

Upon his bringing me the first bundles of it, I began to fill the grate. This sort of oak makes a brisker fire than any other wood whatever; but the wood of elder-trees and pine-trees is used in casting artillery, because it makes a mild and gentle fire. As soon as the concreted metal felt the power of this violent fire, it began to brighten and glitter. In another quarter I made them hurry the tubes with all possible expedition, and sent some of them to the roof of the house to take care of the fire, which through the great violence of the wind had acquired new force; and towards the garden I had caused some tables with pieces of tapestry and old clothes to be placed, in order to shelter me from the rain. As soon as I had applied the proper remedy to each evil, I with a loud voice cried out to my men to bestir themselves and lend a helping hand; so that when they saw that the concreted metal began to melt again, the whole body obeyed me with such zeal and alacrity, that every man did the work of three. Then I caused a mass of pewter weighing about sixty pounds to be thrown upon the metal in the furnace, which with the other helps, as the brisk wood fire, and stirring it sometimes with iron, and sometimes with long poles, soon became completely dissolved. Finding that, contrary to the opinion of my ignorant assistants, I had effected what seemed as difficult as to raise the dead, I recovered my vigor to such a degree, that I no longer perceived whether I had any fever, nor had I the least apprehension of death. Suddenly a loud noise was heard, and a glittering of fire flashed before our eyes, as if it had been the darting of a thunderbolt. Upon the appearance of this extraordinary phenomenon, terror seized on all present, and on none more than myself. This tremendous noise being over, we began to stare at each other, and perceived that the cover of the furnace had burst and flown off, so that the bronze began to run.

I immediately caused the mouths of my mold to be opened; but finding that the metal did not run with its usual velocity, and apprehending that the cause of it was that the fusibility of the metal was injured by the violence of the fire, I ordered all my dishes and porringers, which were in number about two hundred, to be placed one by one before my tubes, and part of them to be thrown into the furnace; upon which all present perceived that my bronze was completely dissolved, and that my mold was filling; they now with joy and alacrity assisted and obeyed me. I for my part was sometimes in one place, sometimes in another, giving my directions and assisting my men, before whom I offered up this prayer: "O God, I address myself to thee, who, of thy divine power, didst rise from the dead, and ascend in glory to heaven. I acknowledge in gratitude this mercy that my mold has been filled: I fall prostrate before thee, and with my whole heart return thanks to thy divine majesty." My prayer being over, I took a plate of meat which stood upon a little bench, and ate with a great appetite. I then drank with all my journeymen and assistants, and went joyful and in good health to bed; for there were still two hours of night; and I rested as well as if I had been troubled with no manner of disorder.

My good housekeeper, without my having given any orders, had provided a young capon for my dinner. When I arose, which was not till about noon, she accosted me in high spirits, and said merrily, "Is this the man that thought himself dying? It is my firm belief that the cuffs and kicks which you gave us last night, when you were quite frantic and possessed, frightened away your fever, which, apprehending lest you should fall upon it in the same manner, took to flight." So my whole poor family, having got over such panics and hardships, without delay procured earthen vessels to supply the place of the pewter dishes and porringers, and we all dined together very cheerfully; indeed, I do not remember having ever in my life eaten a meal with greater satisfaction, or with a better appetite. After dinner, all those who had assisted me in my work came and congratulated me upon what had happened, returned thanks to the Divine Being, for having interposed so mercifully in our behalf, and declared that they had in theory and practice learnt such things as were judged impossible by other masters. I thereupon thought it allowable to boast a little of my knowledge and skill in this fine art, and, pulling out my purse, satisfied all my workmen for their labor.

My mortal enemy, Pier Francesco Ricci, the duke's steward, was very eager to know how the affair had turned out; so that the two whom I suspected of being the cause of my metal's concreting in the manner above related, told him that I was not a man, but rather a downright devil, for I had compassed that which was not in the power of art to effect; with many other surprising things which would have been too much even for the infernal powers. As they greatly exaggerated what had passed, perhaps with a view of excusing themselves, the steward wrote to the duke, who was then at Pisa, an account still more pompous, and more replete with the marvelous than that which the workingmen had given him.

Having left my work to cool during two days after it was cast, I began gradually to uncover it. I first of all found the Medusa's head, which had come out admirably by the assistance of the vents, as I had observed to the duke that the property of fire was to fly upwards. I proceeded to uncover the rest, and found that the other head, I mean that of Perseus, was likewise come out perfectly well. This occasioned me still greater surprise, because, as it is seen in the statue, it is much lower than that of Medusa, the mouth of that figure being placed over the head and shoulders of Perseus. I found that where the head of Perseus ends, all the bronze was exhausted which I had in my furnace. This surprised me very much, that there should not be any thing over and above what is necessary in casting. My astonishment, indeed, was raised to such a degree, that I looked upon it as a miracle immediately wrought by the Almighty. I went on uncovering it with great success, and found every part turn out to admiration, till I reached the foot of the right leg, which supports the figure, where I found the heel come out: so proceeding to examine it, and thinking that the whole was filled up, in one respect I was glad, in another sorry, because I had told the duke it would not have that effect. Continuing, however, to uncover it, I found that not only the toes were wanting, but part of the foot itself, so that there was almost one half deficient. This occasioned me some new trouble; but I was not displeased at it, because I could thereby convince the duke that I understood my business thoroughly; and though there had come out a great deal more of that foot than I thought there would, the reason was, that in consequence of the several accidents that had happened, it was heated much more than it could have been in the regular course of business; especially as the pewter plates had been thrown into the furnace, a thing never done before.

I was highly pleased that my work had succeeded so well, and went to Pisa to pay my respects to the duke, who received me in the most gracious manner imaginable. The duchess vied with him in kindness to me; and though the steward had written them an account of the affair, it appeared to them much more wonderful and extraordinary when I related it myself. Upon my speaking to him of the foot of Perseus, which had not come out (a circumstance of which I had apprised his excellency), I perceived that he was filled with the utmost astonishment, and told the affair to the duchess in the same terms that I had before related to him. Finding that these great personages were become so favorable to me, I availed myself of the opportunity to request the duke's permission to go to Rome: he granted it in the most obliging terms, and desired me to return speedily, in order to finish my statue of Perseus. He at the same time gave me letters of recommendation to his ambassador Averardo Serristori. This happened in the beginning of the pontificate of Pope Julio de Monti.

GIORDANO BRUNO

A Philosophy of the Infinite Universe

These are the doubts, difficulties and motives, about the solution whereof I have said enough in our dialogues to expose the intimate and radicated errors of the common philosophy, and to show the weight and worth of our own. Here you will meet with the reasons why we should not fear that any part of this Universe should fall or fly off, that the least particle should be lost in empty space, or be truly annihilated. Here you will perceive the reason of that vicissitude which may be observed in the constant change of all things, whereby it happens, that there is nothing so ill but may befall us or be prevented, nor anything so good but may be lost or obtained by us; since in this infinite field the parts and modes do perpetually vary, though the substance and the whole do eternally persevere the same.

From this contemplation (if we do but rightly consider), it will follow that we ought never to be dispirited by any strange accidents through excess of fear or pain, nor ever be elated by any prosperous event through excess of hope or pleasure; whence we have the way to true morality, and, following it, we would become the magnanimous despisers of what men of childish thoughts do fondly esteem, and the wise judges of the history of nature which is written in our minds, and the strict executioners of those divine laws which are engraven in the centre of our hearts. We would know that it is no harder thing to fly from hence up into heaven, than to fly from heaven back again to the earth, that ascending thither and ascending hither are all one; that we are no more circumferential to the other globes than they are to us, nor they more central to us than we are to them, and that none of them is more above the stars than we, as they are no less than we covered over or comprehended by the sky. Behold us therefore free from envying them! behold us delivered from the vain anxiety and foolish care of desiring to enjoy that good afar off, which in as great a degree we may possess so near hand, and even at home! Behold us freed from the terror that they should fall upon us, any more than we should hope that we might fall upon them; since every one as well as all of these globes are sustained by infinite ether, in which this our animal freely runs, and keeps to his prescribed course, as the rest of the planets do to theirs. . . .

We fear not, therefore, that what is accumulated in this world, should, by the malice of some wandering spirit, or by the wrath of some evil genius, be shook and scattered, as it were, into smoke or dust, out of this cupola of the sky, and beyond the starry mantle of the firmament; nor that the nature of things can otherwise come to be annihilated in substance, than, as it seems to our eyes, that the air contained in the concavity of a bubble is become nothing when that bubble is burst; because we know that in the world one thing ever succeeds another, *there being no utmost bottom,* whence, as by the hand of some artificer, things are irreparably struck into nothing. There are no ends, limits, margins, or walls, that keep back or subtract any parcel of the infinite abundance of things. Thence it is that the earth and sea are ever equally fertile, and thence the perpetual brightness of the sun, eternal fuel circulating to those devouring fires, and a supply of waters being eternally furnished to the evaporated seas, from the infinite and ever renewing magazine of matter: so that Democritus and Epicurus, who asserted the infinity of things with their perpetual variableness and restoration were so far more in the right than he who endeavored to account for the eternally same appearance of the Universe, by making homogeneous particles of matter ever and numerically to succeed one another.

Thus the excellency of God is magnified, and the grandeur of his Empire made manifest; he is not glorified in one, but in numberless suns, not in one earth nor in one world, but in ten hundred thousand, of infinite globes: so that this faculty of the intellect is not vain or arbitrary, that ever will or can add space to space, quantity to quantity, unity to unity, member to member. By this science we are loosened from the chains of a most narrow dungeon, and set at liberty to rove in a most august empire; we are removed from conceited boundaries and poverty, to the innumerable riches of an infinite space, of so worthy a field, and of such beautiful worlds: this science does not, in a word, make a horizontal circle feigned by the eye on earth, and imagined by the fancy in the spacious sky.

Giordano Bruno (1548-1600). Translation by John Toland.

THE GOLDEN AGE
OF SPAIN

The Renaissance faced various conditions and experienced various developments in different countries. Spain, the next country after Italy to be ready for the transition to modern times, first accepted and then rejected modernism, so that its life and literature reflected violent contrasts.

By the end of the fifteenth century had come the unification of Spain under Ferdinand and Isabella, the fall of Granada (which doomed the Moorish empire in Spain), and the voyages of Columbus. Within a generation or so after this, in the reign of Emperor Charles V, Spain was the greatest power in Europe, controlling large sections of the continent and acquiring the land and treasures of the greater portion of the New World. A people hardened by many centuries of conflict with the Moors now enjoyed the full release of its energies and became a master class, to which nothing seemed impossible when one considers the staggering conquests of the small bands of *conquistadores* in the Western hemisphere. Wealth pouring into Spain, moreover, made luxury and cultural gratifications possible. That medievalism would give way to modern enlightenment seemed, therefore, inevitable, and signs of this were not wanting in the literature that emerged.

As early as the fourteenth century, a rich lyric poetry appeared in Castille, and the later composition of pastoral romances expressed the gaiety and pleasure-seeking of the Renaissance. Bubbling plays of love-making and adventure, known as "cloak and sword" drama, were turned out by numerous writers for Spain's popular theaters. Tirso de Molina gave the stage the dashing worldly and cynical character Don Juan in his *Burlador de*

Sevilla; and Lope de Vega, the world's most prolific playwright, made "love and honor" the theme of about five hundred extant plays. Lope even composed a few dramas like *Fuente Ovejuna* (*The Sheep-Well*) in which the peasantry was endowed with a strong sense of its own worth and readiness to revolt against its feudal overlords. Realism appeared intermingled with the grossest obscenity in the famous prose play *Celestina*, which was intended to be read rather than staged. Prose, indeed, began to express contemporary reality with great vigor and satirical incisiveness. A veritable literature of roguery developed in such sixteenth-century novels as *Lazarillo de Tormes* and Aleman's *Guzman de Alfarache*. These are called *picaresque* novels after the word *picaro*, the Spanish name for a low-class adventurer or rogue. Seen through the eyes of the *picaro*, society revealed its corrupt and unromantic aspects. The modern novel of manners, represented in England by such masterpieces as *Tom Jones* and *Peregrine Pickle*, owes its beginnings to these picaresque tales. Cervantes' great *Don Quixote* successfully contrasted knightly adventure with everyday reality, and burlesqued the former. Gracián's *Worldly Wisdom* expressed the materialistic outlook of the times and spoke for the men who had to function in the business and official worlds of the empire. Finally, the Spain of the discoveries and conquests became articulate in histories and prose accounts.

Nevertheless, the Spanish Golden Age also revealed an exactly opposite tendency: to hold on to medievalism. Nowhere did the Church have such a strong grip on the people and put up such resistance to the critical spirit of the Renaissance

The lower clergy and the activist Dominican Order fought resolutely and drew the high clergy and the monarchs of Spain away from whatever concessions they were willing to make to the new forces. The Jews and the Moors, whose economic and intellectual activity favored the rise of the modern world, were driven out; Spain refused to accept modern economic and social life. The Inquisition crushed intellectual inquiry and stamped out the beginnings of protestantism. Mysticism, piety, and fanaticism counteracted worldliness and the cult of reason. Spain, in short, drew away from the Renaissance at the very time when it was drawn toward it.

This conflict in Spain between the medieval and Renaissance spirits divided the soul of her Golden Age. Even so effervescent and vital a person as the playwright, Lope de Vega, gave himself up to seizures of penitence and piety, flogged himself in a cell, and served as an officer of the Inquisition. Nevertheless, memorable poetic work came out of this "anguish" of the Spanish soul, to use the term of the Spanish scholar, Professor Américo Castro.

The selections that follow present some of the fluctuations of the two attitudes of Spain during her greatest epoch. In Cervantes we find a critical view of medievalism, a realization of the incongruity of unbridled chivalric romanticism, to which Spanish taste was particularly partial, and yet a respect for spiritual and chivalric ideals. *The Obscure Night of the Soul* by St. John of the Cross (1549-1591) reveals the pure flame of Spanish mysticism, which also burned in the poetry of Fray Luis de Leon and in the prose and verse of Saint Teresa. The epic spirit appears in *La Araucana*, written in 1569 by Alonso de Ercilla y Zúñiga (1533-1599?) a member of Philip II's court. As a captain in one of the armies sent to conquer Chile, Ercilla participated in the struggle against the Araucanian Indians, the only tribe that successfully resisted the Spaniards. In *La Araucana*, the first important European poem written in America, Ercilla described this war, as well as the customs and methods of warfare of the Araucanians. This epic of some eight thousand lines is noteworthy for its unbiased portrayal of Indian chieftains and its respect for the natives. Contrary to our general impression, some of the conquistadors discovered that the Indians were not contemptible and benighted by comparison with Europeans. This discovery was made not without some anguish by men who had been reared in the belief that Christianity made men better than the rest of mankind.

In the plays of Calderón de la Barca we encounter the reflectiveness and other-worldliness that invaded even the theater, which had been a generation earlier the breeziest and most active in the world. Calderón (1600-1681) was educated in a Jesuit college in Madrid and then studied law at the University of Salamanca. He won popularity with ingeniously contrived plays about love and honor but he achieved even greater distinction with his numerous philosophical and religious plays. In *La Vida es Sueño (Life Is a Dream)*, a philosophical play, a prince's evil disposition is cured by his realization that life is only a dream. In the body of Calderón's religious work there are about eighty, generally allegorical, short religious pieces (*autos*) and some long plays, among which the mystical *Devotion of the Cross* is the best. Its brigand hero Eusebio retains his devotion to the cross of Christ, at the foot of which he was born, even when he becomes a murderer, and thus achieves salvation after being restored to life long enough to confess his sins to a saint. The poems taken from *Life Is a Dream* and *Devotion to the Cross* represent the best of Calderón, his reflective and religious spirit.

The Art of Worldly Wisdom by Baltasar Gracián (1601-1658) represents the practical spirit that existed alongside the mystical one. The two often appeared in the same person; thus Saint Teresa was an energetic administrator as well as an enraptured nun and poetess. In Gracián we see the pragmatic side alone. His reflections are astute and admirably stated. But they reveal a narrow, compromising, and somewhat timid manner of approaching reality, like Spain's own policy when decadence made the country lackadaisical even in the struggle for political power.

Not many works of the Golden Age entered directly into our heritage. But there was one glorious exception: Cervantes' *Don Quixote*, which was translated into English as early as 1612, suggested the theme for Beaumont and Fletcher's charming Elizabethan play *The Knight of the Burning Pestle*, and was made an English masterpiece in 1701 by the Motteux translation.

Miguel de Cervantes (1547-1616) participated as a soldier in the famous naval victory of Lepanto over the Turks in 1571. Here he lost his left hand but remained in the service until three years later when he was captured by Algerian pirates while on his way home. After enduring many years of slavery in Algiers he was ransomed by his family and rejoined his regiment. Then he settled down to civilian life, marrying and becoming a clerk in the naval office, in which capacity he helped to equip the Spanish Armada. At this time, too, he resumed writing, realizing an ambition that had seized him in his youth.

He wrote about thirty plays but did not succeed in the theater. Following one Renaissance fashion, he composed an unsuccessful pastoral romance, *Galatea;* following another, he wrote two collections of novels, one of which, *Novelas Exemplares (Exemplary Novels)*, contained interesting stories and proved immensely successful. It was a special circumstance, however, that launched him on the road to immortality. In 1597, when he was collector of revenue for the city of Granada, he was accused of withholding money from the treasury and was sent to prison. Here he conceived *Don Quixote*, the first part of which was completed in 1604 and published a year later. The book achieved instant popularity. In 1615, aroused when another author wrote a sequel to it, Cervantes returned to the exploits of Don Quixote and wrote a second part, which was even more delightful than the first. With *Don Quixote* and the *Exemplary Novels* Cervantes became Spain's greatest writer.

Cervantes wrote his book as an extravaganza to put an end forever to medieval romances, which were becoming increasingly extravagant as medieval knighthood vanished from the world. Recalling over one hundred and thirty books of this kind, and realizing the absurdity of this fashion, he showed the effect of the romances on an impressionable gentleman, Don Quixote, who goes out into the everyday world as a knight errant and becomes the victim of his illusions. The result is one of the most amusing masterpieces of all time. But the author of this work was a man of generous feeling and profound understanding. He, therefore, made Don Quixote a deeply pathetic figure and a symbol of idealism tilting against the practical world represented by his delightfully realistic peasant squire Sancho Panza and by the people he encounters on his travels. Don Quixote's generosity, sense of justice, and fidelity to his principles in a mocking and often brutal world, exalt him above most men despite his aberrations. He has "a higher reason and a nobler sanity" than the men and women who laugh at his absurd conduct.

Many writers have pondered on the meaning that *Don Quixote* acquired as it grew beyond Cervantes' original intention of composing a travesty. One of them, the contemporary Spanish philosopher Miguel de Unamuno, concludes that *Don Quixote* teaches us to place warmth of sympathy before the cold light of reason, to regard nothing as impossible, and to have the courage to defy the grubbing, materialistic world in the name of true humanity. This interpretation need not, however, detract from our enjoyment of Cervantes' glorious humor, his realistic pictures of life, and his narrative interest. In the last analysis, Cervantes was not a philosopher but a great humorist and storyteller.

MIGUEL DE CERVANTES

Don Quixote

Chapter I

WHICH TREATS OF THE CONDITION AND PURSUITS OF
THE FAMOUS DON QUIXOTE DE LA MANCHA

In a village of la Mancha, the name of which I have no desire to recollect, there lived, not long ago, one of those gentlemen who usually keep a lance upon a rack, an old buckler, a lean horse, and a coursing greyhound. Soup, composed of some-
what more beef than mutton, salmagundy at night, lentils on Fridays, and a pigeon, by way of addition, on Sundays, consumed three-fourths of his income; the remainder of it supplied him with a cloak of fine cloth, velvet breeches, with slippers of the same for holidays, and a suit of the best homespun, in which he adorned himself on week days. His establishment consisted of a housekeeper above forty, a niece not quite twenty, and a lad

Cervantes, *Don Quixote*. Translated by Peter Motteux. Miguel de Cervantes Saavedra (1547-1616) was born and died in Madrid. He led an active life as a soldier before turning to writing. His *Don Quixote* was composed between 1603 and 1614.

who served him both in the field and at home, who could saddle the horse or handle the pruning hook. The age of our gentleman bordered upon fifty years; he was of a strong constitution, spare-bodied, of a meager visage, a very early riser, and a lover of the chase. Some pretend to say that he had the surname of Quixada, or Quesada, for on this point his historians differ: but, from very plausible conjectures, we may conclude that his name was Quixada. That is, however, of little importance to our history: let it suffice that in relating it, we swerve not a jot from the truth.

Be it known, then, that the above-mentioned gentleman, in his leisure moments, which composed the greater part of the year, applied himself with so much ardor and relish to the perusal of books of chivalry, that he almost wholly neglected the exercise of the chase, and even the regulation of his domestic affairs; indeed, so extravagant was his zeal in this pursuit that he sold many acres of arable land to purchase books of knight-errantry: collecting as many as he could possibly obtain. Among these, there were none he admired so much as those written by the famous Feliciano de Silva, whose brilliant prose and intricate style were, in his opinion, infinitely precious; especially those amorous speeches and challenges in which they so abound; such as: "the reason of unreasonable treatment of my reason so enfeebles my reason that with reason I complain of your beauty." And again: "the high heavens that, with your divinity, divinely fortify you with the stars, rendering you meritorious of the merit merited by your greatness." These and similar rhapsodies distracted the poor gentleman; for he labored to comprehend and unravel their meaning, which was more than Aristotle himself could do, were he to rise from the dead expressly for that purpose. He was not quite satisfied as to the wounds which Don Belianis gave and received; for he could not help thinking that, however skillful the professors who healed them, his face and whole body must infallibly have been covered with seams and scars. Nevertheless, he commended his author for concluding his book with the promise of that interminable adventure; and he often felt an inclination to seize the pen himself and conclude it, literally as it is there promised: this he would doubtless have done, and with success, had he not been diverted from it by meditations of greater moment, on which his mind was incessantly employed.

He often debated with the curate of the village, a man of learning, and a graduate of Siguenza, which of the two was the best knight, Palmerin of England,[1] or Amadis de Gaul; but master Nicholas, barber of the same place, declared that none ever equaled the knight of the sun; if, indeed, anyone could be compared to him, it was Don Galaor, brother of Amadis de Gaul, for he had a genius suited to everything: he was no effeminate knight, no whimperer, like his brother; and in point of courage, he was by no means his inferior. In short, he became so infatuated with this kind of study that he passed whole days and nights over these books: and thus, with little sleeping and much reading, his brains were dried up and his intellects deranged. His imagination was full of all that he had read; of enchantments, contests, battles, challenges, wounds, blandishments, amours, tortures, and impossible absurdities; and so firmly was he persuaded of the truth of the whole tissue of visionary fiction that, in his mind, no history in the world was more authentic. The Cid Ruy Diaz, he asserted, was a very good knight, but not to be compared with the knight of the flaming sword, who, with a single back-stroke, cleft asunder two fierce and monstrous giants. He was better pleased with Bernardo del Carpio, because, at Roncesvalles, he slew Roland the enchanted, by availing himself of the stratagem employed by Hercules upon Anteus, whom he squeezed to death within his arms. He spoke very favorably of the giant Morganti, for, although of that monstrous brood who are always proud and insolent, he alone was courteous and well-bred. Above all, he admired Rinaldo de Montalvan, particularly when he saw him sallying forth from his castle to plunder all he encountered; and when, moreover, he seized upon that image of Mahomet which according to history, was of massive gold. But he would have given his housekeeper, and even his niece into the bargain, for a fair opportunity of kicking the traitor, Ganelon.

In fine, his judgment being completely obscured, he was seized with one of the strangest fancies that ever entered the head of a madman; this was a persuasion that it behooved him, as well for the advancement of his glory as the service of his country, to become a knight-errant, and traverse the world, armed and mounted, in quest of adventures, and to practice all that had been performed by the knights-errant, of whom he had read; redressing every species of grievance, and exposing himself to dangers which, being surmounted, might

---

[1] These are all characters in Romances of Chivalry.

secure to him eternal glory and renown. The poor gentleman imagined himself at least crowned Emperor of Trapisonda, by the valor of his arm: and thus indulging in these agreeable meditations, and borne away by the extraordinary pleasure he found in them, he hastened to put his designs into execution.

The first thing he did was to scour up some rusty armor, which belonged to his great-grandfather, and had lain many years neglected in a corner. These he cleaned and adjusted as well as he could, but he found one grand defect; the helmet was incomplete; having only the morion: this deficiency, however, he ingeniously supplied, by making a kind of vizor of pasteboard, which, being fixed to the morion, gave the appearance of an entire helmet. True it is that, in order to prove its strength, he drew his sword and gave it two strokes, the first of which instantly demolished the labor of a week; but not altogether approving of the facility with which it was destroyed, and in order to secure himself against a similar misfortune, he made another vizor, which, having fenced in the inside with small bars of iron, he felt assured of its strength, and without making any more experiments, held it to be a most excellent helmet.

In the next place, he visited his steed; and although this animal had more blemishes than the horse of Gonela, which "tantum pellis et ossa fuit," [2] yet, in his eyes, neither the Bucephalus of Alexander, nor the Cid's Babicca, could be compared with him. Four days was he deliberating upon what name he should give him; for, as he said to himself, it would be very improper that a horse so excellent, appertaining to a knight so famous, should be without an appropriate name: he therefore endeavored to find one that should express what he had been before he belonged to a knight-errant, and also what he now was: nothing could, indeed, be more reasonable than that, when the master changed his state, the horse should likewise change his name and assume one, pompous and high-sounding as became the new order he now professed. So after having devised, altered, lengthened, curtailed, rejected, and again framed in his imagination a variety of names, he finally determined upon Rozinante, a name, in his opinion, lofty, sonorous, and full of meaning; importing that he had been only a *Rozin,* a drudge-horse, *before* his present condition, and that now he was *before* all the *Rozins* in the world.

Having given his horse a name so much to his satisfaction, he resolved to fix upon one for himself. This consideration employed him eight more days, which at length he determined to call himself Don Quixote; whence some of the historians of this most true history have concluded that his name was certainly Quixada, and not Quesada, as others would have it. Then recollecting that the valorous Amadis, not content with the simple appellation of Amadis, added thereto the name of his kingdom, and native country, in order to render it famous, styling himself Amadis de Gaul; so he, like a good knight, also added the name of his province, and called himself Don Quixote de la Mancha; whereby, in his opinion, he fully proclaimed his lineage and country, which, at the same time, he honored, by taking its name.

His armor being now furbished, his helmet made perfect, his horse and himself provided with names, he found nothing wanting but a lady to be in love with: for a knight-errant without the tender passion was a tree without leaves and fruit—a body without a soul. If, said he, for my sins, or rather, through my good fortune, I encounter some giant —an ordinary occurrence to knights-errant—and overthrow him at the first onset, or cleave him in twain, or, in short, vanquish him and force him to surrender, must I not have some lady, to whom I may send him, as a present? that when he enters into the presence of my charming mistress, he may throw himself upon his knees before her, and in a submissive, humble voice, say: "Madam, in me you behold the giant Caraculiambro, lord of the island Malendrania, who, being vanquished in single combat by the never-enough-to-be-praised Don Quixote de la Mancha, am by him commanded to present myself before you, to be disposed of according to the will and pleasure of your highness." How happy was our good knight after this harangue! How much more so when he found a mistress! It is said that, in a neighboring village, a good-looking peasant girl resided, of whom he had formerly been enamored, although it does not appear that she ever knew or cared about it; and this was the lady whom he chose to nominate mistress of his heart. He then sought a name for her, which, without entirely departing from her own, should incline and approach towards that of a princess, or great lady, and determined upon Dulcinea del Toboso (for she was a native of that village), a name, he thought, harmonious, uncommon, and expressive—like all the others which he had adopted.

[2] Was all skin and bones.

Chapter II

WHICH TREATS OF THE FIRST SALLY THAT DON QUIXOTE
MADE FROM HIS NATIVE ABODE

These arrangements being made, he would no longer defer the execution of his project, which he hastened from a consideration of what the world suffered by his delay: so many were the grievances he intended to redress, the wrongs to rectify, errors to amend, abuses to reform, and debts to discharge! Therefore, without communicating his intentions to any individual, and wholly unobserved, one morning before day, being one of the most sultry in the month of July, he armed himself cap-a-pie, mounted Rozinante, placed the helmet on his head, braced on his target, took his lance, and, through the private gate of his back yard, issued forth into the open plain, in a transport of joy to think he had met with no obstacles to the commencement of his honorable enterprise. But scarcely had he found himself on the plain when he was assailed by a recollection so terrible as almost to make him abandon the undertaking: for it just then occurred to him, that he was not yet a knight; therefore, in conformity to the laws of chivalry, he neither could nor ought to enter the lists against any of that order; and, even if he had been actually dubbed, he should, as a new knight, have worn white armor, without any device on his shield, until he had gained one by force of arms. These considerations made him irresolute whether to proceed; but frenzy prevailing over reason, he determined to get himself made a knight by the first one he should meet, like many others, of whom he had read. As to white armor, he resolved, when he had an opportunity, to scour his own, so that it should be whiter than ermine. Having now composed his mind, he proceeded, taking whatever road his horse pleased; for therein, he believed, consisted the true spirit of adventure.

Our new adventurer, thus pursuing his way, conversed within himself, saying: "Who doubts but that in future times, when the true history of my famous achievements is brought to light, the sage who records them will, in this manner, describe my first sally! 'Scarcely had ruddy Phœbus extended over the face of this wide and spacious earth the golden filaments of his beautiful hair, and scarcely had the little painted birds, with their forked tongues, hailed, in soft and mellifluous harmony, the approach of the rosy harbinger of morn, who, leaving the soft couch of her jealous consort, had just disclosed herself to mortals through the gates and balconies of the Manchegan horizon, when the renowned knight, Don Quixote de la Mancha, quitting the slothful down, mounted Rozinante, his famous steed, and proceeded over the ancient memorable plain of Montiel (which was indeed the truth).' O happy era, happy age," he continued, "when my glorious deeds shall be revealed to the world! deeds worthy of being engraven on brass, sculptured in marble, and recorded by the pencil! And thou, O sage enchanter, whosoever thou mayest be, destined to chronicle this extraordinary history! forget not, I beseech thee, my good Rozinante, the inseparable companion of all my toils!" Then again, as if really enamored, he exclaimed, "O Dulcinea, my princess! sovereign of this captive heart! greatly do you wrong me by a cruel adherence to your decree, forbidding me to appear in the presence of your beauty! Deign, O lady, to think on this enslaved heart, which, for love of you, endures so many pangs!"

In this wild strain he continued, imitating the style of his books as nearly as he could, and proceeding slowly on, while the sun arose with such intense heat that it was enough to dissolve his brains, if any had been left. He traveled almost the whole of that day without encountering any thing worthy of recital, which caused him much vexation, for he was impatient for an opportunity to prove the valor of his powerful arm.

Some author says his first adventure was that of the straits of Lapice; others affirm it to have been that of the wind-mills; but, from what I have been able to ascertain of this matter, and have found written in the annals of La Mancha, the fact is that he traveled all that day, and as night approached, both he and his horse were wearied and dying of hunger; and in this state, as he looked around him, in hopes of discovering some castle, or shepherd's cot, where he might repose and find refreshment, he descried, not far from the road, an inn, which to him was a star conducting him to the portals, if not the palaces, of his redemption. He made all the haste he could, and reached it at night-fall. There chanced to stand at the door two young women, ladies of pleasure (as they are called), on their journey to Seville, in the company of some carriers who rested there that night. Now as every thing that our adventurer saw and conceived was, by his imagination, molded to what he had read, so, in his eyes, the inn appeared to be a castle, with its four turrets, and pinnacles of shining silver, together with its draw-bridge, deep moat, and all the appurtenances with which such castles are usually described. When he had advanced within a short distance of it, he checked Rozinante, expecting some dwarf would mount the battlements, to announce, by sound of trumpet, the arrival of a knight-errant at the castle; but finding them tardy, and Rozinante impatient for the stable, he approached the inn-door, and there saw the two strolling girls, who to him appeared to be beautiful damsels or lovely dames, enjoying themselves before the gate of their castle.

It happened that just at this time a swineherd collecting his hogs (I make no apology, for so they are called) from an adjoining stubble field, blew the horn which assembles them together, and instantly Don Quixote was satisfied, for he imagined it was a dwarf who had given the signal of his arrival. With extraordinary satisfaction, therefore, he went up to the inn; upon which the ladies, being startled at the sight of a man armed in that manner, with lance and buckler, were retreating into the house; but Don Quixote, perceiving their alarm, raised his pasteboard vizor, thereby partly discovering his meager dusty visage, and, with gentle demeanor and placid voice, thus addressed them: "Fly not, ladies, nor fear any discourtesy, for it would be wholly inconsistent with the order of knighthood which I profess to offer insult to any person, much less to virgins of that exalted rank which your appearance indicates." The girls stared at him, and were endeavoring to find out his face, which was almost concealed by the sorry vizor; but hearing themselves called virgins, a thing so much out of the way of their profession, they could not forbear laughing, and to such a degree that Don Quixote was displeased, and said to them: "Modesty well becomes beauty, and excessive laughter, proceeding from a slight cause, is folly; but I say not this to humble or distress you, for my part is no other than to do you service." This language, so unintelligible to the ladies, added to the uncouth figure of our knight, increased their laughter; consequently he grew more indignant, and would have proceeded further, but for the timely appearance of the inn-keeper, a very corpulent, and therefore a very pacific, man, who, upon seeing so ludicrous an object, armed, and with accouterments so ill-sorted as were the bridle, lance, buckler, and corslet, felt disposed to join the damsels in demonstrations of mirth; but, in truth, apprehending some danger from a form thus strongly fortified, he resolved to behave with civility, and therefore said, "If, Sir Knight, you are seeking for a lodging, you will here find, excepting a bed (for there are none in this inn) every thing in abundance." Don Quixote, perceiving the humility of the governor of the fortress, for such to him appeared the inn-keeper, answered: "For me, Señor Castellano, any thing will suffice: since arms are my ornaments, warfare my repose." The host thought he called him Castellano, because he took him for a sound Castilian, whereas he was an Andalusian, of the coast of St. Lucar, as great a thief as Cacus, and not less mischievous than a collegian or a page: and he replied, "If so, your worship's beds must be hard rocks, and your sleep continual watching; and, that being the case, you may dismount with a certainty of finding here sufficient cause for keeping awake the whole year, much more a single night." So saying, he laid hold of Don Quixote's stirrup, who alighted with much difficulty and pain, for he had fasted the whole of the day. He then desired the host to take especial care of his steed, for it was the finest creature that ever fed; the inn-keeper examined him, but thought him not so good by half as his master had represented him. Having led the horse to the stable, he returned to receive the orders of his guest, whom the damsels, being now reconciled to him, were disarming; they had taken off the back and breast-plates, but endeavored in vain to disengage the gorget, or take off the counterfeit beaver, which he had fastened with green ribbons, in such a manner that they could not be untied, and he would upon no account allow them to be cut; therefore he remained all that night with his helmet on, making the strangest and most ridiculous figure imaginable.

While these light girls, whom he still conceived to be persons of quality and ladies of the castle, were disarming him, he said to them with infinite grace, "Never before was Knight so honored by ladies as Don Quixote, after his departure from his native village! damsels attended upon him; princesses took charge of his steed! O Rozinante,—for that, ladies, is the name of my horse, and Don Quixote de la Mancha my own; although it was not my intention to have discovered myself, until deeds, performed in your service, should have proclaimed me; but impelled to make so just an application of the ancient romance of Lanzarote, to my present situation, I have thus prematurely disclosed my name: yet the time shall come when your ladyships may command, and I obey; when the valor of my arm shall make manifest the desire I have to serve you." The girls, unaccustomed to such rhetorical flourishes, made no reply, but asked him whether he would please to eat anything. "I shall willingly take some food," answered Don Quixote, "for I apprehend it would be of much service to me." That day happened to be Friday, and there was nothing in the house but some fish, of that kind which in Castile is called Abadexo, in Andalusia, Bacallao, in some parts Curadillo, and in others Truchuela. They asked if his worship would like some truchuela, for they had no other fish to offer him. "If there be many troutlings," replied Don Quixote, "they will supply the place of one trout; for it is the same to me whether I receive eight single rials or one piece of eight. Moreover, these troutlings may be preferable, as veal is better than beef, and kid superior to goat; be that as it may, let it come immediately, for the toil and weight of arms cannot be sustained by the body unless the interior be supplied with aliments." For the benefit of the cool air, they placed the table at the door of the inn, and the landlord produced some of his ill-soaked, and worse-cooked, bacallao, with bread as foul and black as the Knight's armor: but it was a spectacle highly risible to see him eat; for his hands being engaged in holding his helmet on, and raising the beaver, he could not feed himself, therefore one of the ladies performed this office for him; but to drink would have been utterly impossible had not the inn-keeper bored a reed, and, placing one end into his mouth, at the other poured in the wine; and all this he patiently endured rather than cut the lacings of his helmet.

In the mean time there came to the inn a sow-gelder, who, as soon as he arrived, blew his pipe of reeds four or five times, which finally convinced Don Quixote that he was now in some famous castle, where he was regaled with music; that the poor jack was trout, the bread of the purest white, the strolling wenches ladies of distinction, and the inn-keeper governor of the castle; consequently he remained satisfied with his enterprise and first sally, though it troubled him to reflect that he was not yet a knight, being persuaded that he could not lawfully engage in any adventure until he had been invested with the order of knighthood.

Chapter III

IN WHICH IS DESCRIBED THE DIVERTING CEREMONY OF KNIGHTING DON QUIXOTE

Tormented by this idea, he abruptly finished his scanty meal, called the inn-keeper, and, shutting himself up with him in the stable, he fell on his knees before him, and said, "Never will I rise from this place, valorous knight, until your courtesy shall vouchsafe to grant a boon which it is my intention to request: a boon that will redound to your glory and to the benefit of all mankind." The inn-keeper, seeing his guest at his feet, and hearing such language, stood confounded, and stared at him, without knowing what to do or say; he entreated him to rise, but in vain, until he had promised to grant the boon he requested. "I expected no less, signor, from your great magnificence," replied Don Quixote; "know, therefore, that the boon I have demanded, and which your liberality has conceded, is that, on the morrow, you will confer upon me the honor of knighthood. This night I will watch my arms in the chapel of your castle, in order that, in the morning, my earnest desire may be fulfilled, and I may with propriety traverse the four quarters of the world, in quest of adventures, for the relief of the distressed; conformable to the duties of chivalry and of knights-errant, who, like myself, are devoted to such pursuits."

The host, who, as we have said, was a shrewd fellow, and had entertained some doubts respecting the wits of his guest, was now confirmed in his suspicions; and, to make sport for the night, determined to follow his humor. He told him therefore that his desire was very reasonable, and that such pursuits were natural and suitable to knights so illustrious as he appeared to be, and as his gallant demeanor fully testified; that he had himself in the days of his youth followed that honorable profession, and traveled over various parts of the world in search of adventures; failing not to visit the suburbs of Malaga, the isles of Riaran, the compass of Seville, the market place of Segovia, the olive field of Valencia, the rondilla of Granada, the coast of St. Lucar, the fountain of Cordova, the taverns of Toledo, and divers other parts, where he had exercised the agility of his heels and the dexterity of his hands; committing sundry wrongs, soliciting widows, seducing damsels, cheating youths; in short, making himself known to most of the tribunals in Spain; and that finally he had retired to this castle, where he lived upon his own revenue and that of others; entertaining therein all knights-errant of every quality and degree, solely for the great affection he bore them, and that they might share their fortune with him, in return for his good will. He further told him that in his castle there was no chapel wherein he could watch his armor, for it had been pulled down, in order to be rebuilt; but that, in cases of necessity, he knew it might be done wherever he pleased: therefore he might watch it that night in a court of the castle, and the following morning, if it pleased God, the requisite ceremonies should be performed, and he should be dubbed so effectually that the world would not be able to produce a more perfect knight. He then enquired if he had any money about him? Don Quixote told him he had none: having never read in their histories that knights-errant provided themselves with money. The inn-keeper assured him he was mistaken, for, admitting that it was not mentioned in their history, the authors deeming it unnecessary to specify things so obviously requisite as money and clean shirts, yet was it not, therefore, to be inferred that they had none; but, on the contrary, he might consider it as an established fact that all the knights-errant, of whose history so many volumes are filled, carried their purses well provided against accidents; that they were also supplied with shirts, and a small casket full of ointments, to heal the wounds they might receive; for, in plains and deserts, where they fought and were wounded, no aid was near, unless they had some sage enchanter for their friend, who could give them immediate assistance, by conveying in a cloud through the air some damsel or dwarf, with a vial of water, possessed of such virtue that, upon tasting a single drop of it, they should instantly become as sound as if they had received no injury. But when the knights of former times were without such a friend, they always took care that their esquires should be provided with money, and such necessary articles as lint and salves; and when they had no esquires, which very rarely happened, they carried these things themselves, upon the crupper of their horse, in wallets so small as to be scarcely visible, that they might seem to be something of more importance: for, except in such cases, the custom of carrying wallets was not tolerated among knights-errant. He therefore advised, though, as his godson (which he was soon to be), he might command him, never henceforth to travel without money and the aforesaid provisions; and he would find them serviceable when he least expected it. Don Quixote promised to follow his advice with punctuality; and an order was now given for performing the watch of the armor, in a large yard adjoining the inn. Don Quixote, having collected it together, placed it on a cistern which was close to a well; then, bracing on his target and grasping his lance, with graceful demeanor, he paced to and fro, before the pile, beginning his parade as soon as it was dark.

The inn-keeper informed all who were in the inn of the frenzy of his guest, the watching of his armor, and of the intended knighting. They were surprised at so singular a kind of madness, and went out to observe him at a distance. They perceived him sometimes quietly pacing along, and sometimes leaning upon his lance with his eyes fixed upon his armor, for a considerable time. It was now night, but the moon shone with a splendor which might vie even with that whence it was borrowed; so that every motion of our new knight might be distinctly seen.

At this time, it happened that one of the carriers wanted to give his mules some water; for which purpose it was necessary to remove Don Quixote's armor from the cistern, who, seeing him advance, exclaimed with a loud voice, "O thou, whosoever thou art, rash knight! who approachest the armor of the most valiant adventurer that ever girded sword, beware of what thou dost, and touch it not, unless thou wouldst yield thy life as the forfeit of thy temerity." The carrier heeded not this admonition (though better would it have been for him if he had) but, seizing hold of the straps, he threw the armor some distance from him, which Don Quixote perceiving, he raised his eyes to heaven, and addressing his thoughts, apparently, to his lady Dulcinea, said: "Assist me, O lady, to avenge this first insult offered to your vassal's breast; nor let your favor and protection fail me in this my first perilous encounter!" Having uttered these and similar ejaculations, he let slip his target, and, raising his lance with both hands, he gave the carrier such a stroke upon the head that he fell to the ground in so grievous a plight that, had the stroke been repeated, there would have been no need of a surgeon. This done, he replaced his armor, and continued his parade with the same tranquillity as before.

Soon after another carrier, not knowing what had passed, for the first yet lay stunned, came out with the same intention of watering his mules; and, as he approached to take away the armor from the cistern, Don Quixote, without saying a word or imploring any protection, again let slip his target, raised his lance, and, with no less effect than before, smote the head of the second carrier. The noise brought out all the people in the inn, and the landlord among the rest; upon which Don Quixote braced on his target, and, laying his hand upon his sword, said: "O lady of beauty! strength and vigor of my enfeebled heart! Now is the time for thee to turn thy illustrious eyes upon this thy captive knight, whom so mighty an encounter awaits!" This address had, he conceived, animated him with so much courage that, were all the carriers in the world to have assailed him, he would not have retreated one step.

The comrades of the wounded, upon discovering the situation of their friends, began at a distance to discharge a shower of stones upon Don Quixote, who sheltered himself as well as he could with his target, without daring to quit the cistern, because he would not abandon his armor. The inn-keeper called aloud to them, begging they would desist, for he had already told them he was insane, and that, as a madman, he would be acquitted, though he were to kill them all. Don Quixote, in a voice still louder, called them infamous traitors, and the lord of the castle a cowardly, base-born knight, for allowing knight-errant to be treated in that manner; declaring that, had he received the order of knighthood, he would have made him sensible of his perfidy. "But as for you, ye vile and worthless rabble, I utterly despise ye! Advance! Come on, molest me as far as ye are able, for quickly shall ye receive the reward of your folly and insolence!" This he uttered with so much spirit and intrepidity that the assailants were struck with terror; which, in addition to the landlord's persuasions, made them cease their attack; he then permitted the wounded to be carried off, and, with the same gravity and composure, resumed the watch of his armor.

The host, not relishing these pranks of his guest, determined to put an end to them, before any further mischief ensued, by immediately investing him with the luckless order of chivalry; approaching him, therefore, he disclaimed any concurrence, on his part, in the insolent conduct of those low people, who were, he observed, well chastised for their presumption. He repeated to him that there was no chapel in the castle, nor was it by any means necessary for what remained to be done; that the stroke of knighting consisted in blows on the neck and shoulders, according to the ceremonial of the order, which might be effectually performed in the middle of a field; that the duty of watching his armor he had now completely fulfilled, for he had watched more than four hours, though only two were required. All this Don Quixote believed, and said that he was there ready to obey him, requesting him, at the same time, to perform the deed as soon as possible; because, should he be assaulted again when he found himself knighted, he was resolved not to leave one

person alive in the castle, excepting those whom, out of request, he might be induced to spare.

The constable, thus warned and alarmed, immediately brought forth a book in which he kept his account of the straw and oats he furnished to the carriers, and, attended by a boy, who carried an end of candle, and the two damsels beforementioned, went towards Don Quixote, whom he commanded to kneel down; he then began reading in his manual, as if it were some devout prayer, in the course of which he raised his hand and gave him a good blow on the neck, and, after that, a handsome stroke over the shoulders, with his own sword, still muttering between his teeth, as if in prayer. This being done, he commanded one of the ladies to gird on his sword, an office she performed with much alacrity, as well as discretion, no small portion of which was necessary to avoid bursting with laughter at every part of the ceremony; but indeed the prowess they had seen displayed by the new knight kept their mirth within bounds. At girding on the sword, the good lady said: "God grant you may be a fortunate knight, and successful in battle." Don Quixote enquired her name, that he might thenceforward know to whom he was indebted for the favor received, as it was his intentions to bestow upon her some share of the honor he should acquire by the valor of his arm. She replied, with much humility, that her name was Tolosa, and that she was the daughter of a cobbler at Toledo, who lived at the stalls of Sanchobienaya; and that, wherever she was, she would serve and honor him as her lord. Don Quixote, in reply, requested her, for his sake, to do him the favor henceforth to add to her name the title of Don, and call herself Donna Tolosa, which she promised to do. The other girl now buckled on his spur, and with her he held nearly the same conference as with the lady of the sword; having enquired her name, she told him it was Molinera, and that she was daughter to an honest miller of Antiquera; he then requested her likewise to assume the Don, and style herself Donna Molinera, renewing his proffers of service and thanks.

These never-till-then-seen ceremonies being thus speedily performed, Don Quixote was impatient to find himself on horseback, in quest of adventures: he therefore instantly saddled Rozinante, mounted him, and, embracing his host, made his acknowledgments for the favor he had conferred, by knighting him, in terms so extraordinary that it would be in vain to attempt to repeat them. The host, in order to get rid of him the sooner, replied with no less flourish, but with more brevity; and, without making any demand for his lodging, wished him a good journey.

Chapter VIII

OF THE VALOROUS DON QUIXOTE'S SUCCESS IN THE DREADFUL AND NEVER-BEFORE-IMAGINED ADVENTURE OF THE WIND-MILLS; WITH OTHER EVENTS WORTHY TO BE RECORDED

As they were thus discoursing, they came in sight of thirty or forty wind-mills, which are in that plain; and, as soon as Don Quixote espied them, he said to his squire: "Fortune disposes our affairs better than we ourselves could have desired: look yonder, friend Sancho Panza, where thou mayest discover somewhat more than thirty monstrous giants, whom I intend to encounter and slay; and with their spoils we will begin to enrich ourselves: for it is lawful war, and doing God good service to remove so wicked a generation from off the face of the earth." "What giants?" said Sancho Panza. "Those thou seest yonder," answered his master, "with their long arms; for some are wont to have them almost of the length of two leagues." "Look, sir," answered Sancho, "those, which appear yonder are not giants, but wind-mills; and what seem to be arms are the sails, which, whirled about by the wind, make the mill-stone go." "It is very evident," answered Don Quixote, "that thou art not versed in the business of adventures: they are giants: and, if thou art afraid, get thee aside and pray, whilst I engage with them in fierce and unequal combat." So saying, he clapped spurs to his steed, notwithstanding the cries his squire sent after him, assuring him that they were certainly wind-mills, and not giants. But he was so fully possessed that they were giants that he neither heard the outcries of his squire Sancho, nor yet discerned what they were, though he was very near them, but went on crying out aloud: "Fly not, ye cowards and vile caitiffs; for it is a single knight who assaults you." The wind now rising a little, the great sails began to move: upon which Don Quixote called out: "Although ye should move more arms than the giant Briareus, ye shall pay for it."

Then recommending himself devoutly to his lady Dulcinea, beseeching her to succor him in the present danger, being well covered with his buckler, and setting his lance in the rest, he rushed on as fast as Rozinante could gallop, and attacked the first mill before him; when, running his lance into the sail, the wind whirled it about with so much violence that it broke the lance to shivers, dragging horse and rider after it, and tumbling them over and over on the plain, in very evil plight. Sancho Panza hastened to his assistance, as fast as the ass could carry him; and when he came up to his master, he found him unable to stir, so violent was the blow which he and Rozinante had received in their fall. "God save me!" quoth Sancho, "did I not warn you to have a care of what you did, for that they were nothing but wind-mills? And nobody could mistake them, but one that had the like in his head." "Peace, friend Sancho," answered Don Quixote: "for matters of war are, of all others, most subject to continual change. Now I verily believe, and it is most certainly the fact, that the sage Freston, who stole away my chamber and books, has metamorphosed those giants into wind-mills, on purpose to deprive me of the glory of vanquishing them, so great is the enmity he bears me! But his wicked arts will finally avail but little against the goodness of my sword." "God grant it!" answered Sancho Panza; then helping him to rise, he mounted him again upon his steed, which was almost disjointed.

Conversing upon the late adventure, they followed the road that led to the pass of Lapice; because there, Don Quixote said, they could not fail to meet with many and various adventures, as it was much frequented. He was, however, concerned at the loss of his lance; and, speaking of it to his squire, he said: "I remember to have read that a certain Spanish knight, called Diego Perez de Vargas, having broken his sword in fight, tore off a huge branch or limb from an oak, and performed such wonders with it that day, and dashed out the brains of so many Moors, that he was surnamed Machuca; and, from that day forward, he and his descendants bore the names of Vargas and Machuca. I now speak of this, because from the first oak we meet, I mean to tear a limb, at least as good as that; with which I purpose and resolve to perform such feats that thou shalt deem thyself most fortunate in having been thought worthy to behold them, and to be an eye-witness of things which will scarcely be credited." "God's will be done!" quoth Sancho; "I believe all just as you say, sir. But, pray set yourself more upright in your saddle: for you seem to me to ride sideling, owing, perhaps, to bruises received by your fall." "It is certainly so," said Don Quixote; "and, if I do not complain of pain, it is because knights-errant are not allowed to complain of any wound whatever, even though their entrails should issue from it." "If so, I have nothing more to say;" quoth Sancho; "but God knows I should be glad to hear your worship complain when any thing ails you. As for myself, I must complain of the least pain I feel, unless this business of not complaining extend also to the squires of knights-errant." Don Quixote could not forbear smiling at the simplicity of his squire, and told him he might complain whenever and as much as he pleased, either with or without cause, having never yet read any thing to the contrary in the laws of chivalry.

Sancho put him in mind that it was time to dine. His master answered that at present he had no need of food, but that he might eat whenever he thought proper. With this license, Sancho adjusted himself as well as he could upon his beast; and, taking out the contents of his wallet, he jogged on behind his master, very leisurely, eating, and ever anon raising the bottle to his mouth, with so much relish that the best fed victualer of Malaga might have envied him. And whilst he went on in this manner, repeating his draughts, he thought no more of the promises his master had made him; nor did he think it any toil, but rather a recreation, to go in quest of adventures, however perilous they might be. In fine, they passed that night under the shelter of some trees; and from one of them the knight tore a withered branch, to serve him in some sort as a lance, after fixing upon it the iron head of the one that had been broken. All that night Don Quixote slept not, but ruminated on his lady Dulcinea; comformably to the practice of knights-errant, who, as their histories told him, were wont to pass many successive nights in woods and deserts, without closing their eyes, indulging the sweet remembrance of their mistresses. Not so did Sancho spend the night; for, his stomach being full, and not of succory water, he made but one sleep of it; and, had not his master roused him, neither the beams of the sun, that darted full in his face, nor the melody of the birds, which, in great numbers, cheerfully saluted the approach of the new day, could have awaked him. At his uprising he applied again to his bottle, and found it much lighter than the evening before; which grieved him to the heart, for he did not think they were in the way soon to remedy that defect. Don Quixote would not yet break his fast; resolving, as we have said, still to subsist upon savory remembrances.

They now turned again into the road they had entered upon the day before, leading to the pass of Lapice, which they discovered about three in the afternoon. "Here, friend Sancho," said Don Quixote upon seeing it, "we may plunge our arms up to the elbows in what are termed adventures. But attend to this caution, that, even shouldst thou see me in the greatest peril in the world, thou must not lay hand to thy sword to defend me, unless thou perceivest that my assailants are vulgar and low people; in that case thou mayest assist me: but should they be knights, it is no wise agreeable to the laws of chivalry that thou shouldst interfere, until thou art thyself dubbed a knight." "Your worship," answered Sancho, "shall be obeyed most punctually therein, and the rather as I am naturally very peaceable, and an enemy to thrusting myself into brawls and squabbles; but, for all that, as to what regards the defense of my own person, I shall make no great account of those same laws, since both divine and human law allows every man to defend himself against whoever would wrong him." "That I grant," answered Don Quixote; "but with respect to giving me aid against knights, thou must refrain and keep within bounds thy natural impetuosity." "I say, I will do so," answered Sancho; "and I will observe this precept as religiously as the Lord's-day."

As they were thus discoursing, there appeared on the road two monks of the order of St. Benedict, mounted upon dromedaries; for the mules whereon they rode were not much less. They wore traveling masks, and carried umbrellas. Behind them came a coach, accompanied by four or five men on horseback, and two muleteers on foot. Within the coach, as it afterwards appeared, was a Biscaine lady on her way to join her husband at Seville, who was there waiting to embark for India, where he was appointed to a very honorable post. The monks were not in her company, but were only traveling the same road. Scarcely had Don Quixote espied them, when he said to his squire: "Either I am deceived, or this will prove the most famous adventure that ever happened; for those black figures that appear yonder must undoubtedly be enchanters, who are carrying off, in that coach, some princess, whom they have stolen; which wrong I am bound to use my utmost endeavors to redress." "This may prove a worse business than the windmills," said Sancho: "pray, sir, take notice that those are Benedictine monks, and the coach must belong to some travelers. Hearken to my advice, sir; have a care what you do, and let not the devil deceive you." "I have already told thee, Sancho," answered Don Quixote, "that thou knowest little concerning adventures: what I say is true, as thou wilt presently see." So saying, he advanced forward, and planted himself in the midst of the highway, by which the monks were to pass; and when they were so near that he supposed they could hear what he said, he cried out, with a loud voice: "Diabolical and monstrous race! Either instantly release the high-born princesses whom ye are carrying away perforce in that coach, or prepare for instant death, as the just chastisement of your wicked deeds." The monks stopped their mules, and stood amazed, as much at the figure of Don Quixote, as at his expressions; to which they answered: "Signor cavalier, we are neither diabolical nor monstrous, but monks of the Benedictine order, traveling on our own business, and entirely ignorant whether any princesses are carried away in that coach, by force, or not." "No fair speeches to me: for I know ye, treacherous scoundrels!" said Don Quixote: and, without waiting for a reply, he clapped spurs to Rozinante, and, with his lance couched, ran at the foremost monk, with such fury and resolution that, if he had not slid down from his mule, he would certainly have been thrown to the ground, and wounded too, if not killed outright. The second monk, on observing how his comrade was treated, clapped spurs to the sides of his good mule, and began to scour along the plain, lighter than the wind itself.

Sancho Panza, seeing the monk on the ground, leaped nimbly from his ass, and running up to him, began to disrobe him. While he was thus employed, the two lackeys came up and asked him why he was stripping their master. Sancho told them that they were his lawful perquisites, being the spoils of the battle, which his Lord Don Quixote had just won. The lackeys, who did not understand the jest, nor what was meant by spoils or battles, seeing that Don Quixote was at a distance, speaking with those in the coach, fell upon Sancho, threw him down, and, besides leaving him not a hair in his beard, gave him a hearty kicking, and left him stretched on the ground, deprived of sense and motion. Without losing a moment, the monk now got upon his mule again, trembling, terrified, and pale as death; and was no sooner mounted than he spurred after his companion, who stood at some distance, to observe the issue of this strange encounter: but, being unwilling to wait, they pursued their way, crossing themselves as often as if the devil had been at their heels. In the meantime Don Quixote, as it hath been already mentioned, addressing the lady in the coach, "Your

beauteous ladyship may now," said he, "dispose of your person as pleaseth you best; for the pride of your ravishers lies humbled in the dust, overthrown by my invincible arm; and, that you may be at no trouble to learn the name of your deliverer, know that I am called Don Quixote de la Mancha, knight-errant and adventurer, and captive to the peerless and beauteous Dulcinea del Toboso; and, in requital of the benefit you have received at my hands, all that I desire is that you would return to Toboso, and, in my name, present yourselves before that lady, and tell her what I have done to obtain your liberty."

All that Don Quixote said was overheard by a certain squire, who accompanied the coach, a Biscainer, who, finding he would not let it proceed, but talked of their immediately returning to Toboso, flew at Don Quixote, and, taking hold of his lance, addressed him, in bad Castilian and worse Biscaine, after this manner: "Cavalier, begone! and the devil go with thee! I swear, by the God that made me, if thou dost not quit the coach, thou forfeitest thy life, as I am a Biscainer."

Don Quixote understood him very well, and with great calmness answered: "If thou wert a gentleman, as thou art not, I would before now have chastised thy folly and presumption, thou pitiful slave." "I no gentleman!" said the Biscainer; "I swear by the great God, thou lyest, as I am a Christian; if thou wilt throw away thy lance, and draw thy sword, thou shalt see how soon the cat will get into the water: Biscainer by land, gentleman by sea, gentleman for the devil and thou lyest! Now what hast thou to say?" "Thou shalt see that presently, as said Agrages," answered Don Quixote; then, throwing down his lance, he drew his sword, grasped his buckler, and set upon the Biscainer, with a resolution to take his life. The Biscainer, seeing him come on in that manner, would fain have alighted, knowing that his mule, a wretched hackney, was not to be trusted, but he had only time to draw his sword. Fortunately for him he was so near the coach as to be able to snatch from it a cushion, that served him for a shield; whereupon, they immediately fell to, as if they had been mortal enemies. The rest of the company would have made peace between them, but it was impossible; for the Biscainer swore, in his jargon, that, if they would not let him finish the combat, he would murder his mistress, or whoever attempted to prevent him. The lady of the coach, amazed and affrighted at what she saw, ordered the coachman to remove a little out of the way, and sat at a distance, beholding the rigorous conflict; in the progress of which, the Biscainer gave Don Quixote so mighty a stroke on one of his shoulders, and above his buckler, that, had it not been for his armor, he had cleft him down to the girdle. Don Quixote, feeling the weight of that unmeasurable blow, cried out aloud, saying: "O lady of my soul! Dulcinea, flower of all beauty! Succor this thy knight, who, to satisfy thy great goodness, exposes himself to this perilous extremity!" This invocation, the drawing his sword, the covering himself well with his buckler, and rushing with fury on the Biscainer, was the work of an instant—resolving to venture all on the fortune of a single blow. The Biscainer, perceiving his determination, resolved to do the same, and therefore waited for him, covering himself well with his cushion; but he was unable to turn his mule either to the right, or the left, for, being already jaded, and unaccustomed to such sport, the creature would not move a step.

Don Quixote, as we before said, now advanced against the wary Biscainer, with his uplifted sword, fully determined to cleave him asunder; and the Biscainer awaited him, with his sword also raised, and guarded by his cushion. All the bystanders were in fearful suspense as to the event of those prodigious blows with which they threatened each other; and the lady of the coach and her attendants were making a thousand vows, and promises of offerings, to all the images and places of devotion in Spain, that God might deliver them and their squire from this great peril. But the misfortune is that the author of the history, at that very crisis, leaves the combat unfinished, pleading, in excuse, that he could find no more written of the exploits of Don Quixote than what he has already related. It is true, indeed, that the second undertaker of this work could not believe that so curious a history should have been consigned to oblivion; or that the wits of La Mancha should have so little curiosity as not to preserve in their archives, or cabinets, some memorials of this famous knight; and, under that persuasion, he did not despair of finding the conclusion of this delectable history; which, through the favor of heaven, actually came to pass, and in the manner that shall be faithfully recounted in the following chapter.

ST. JOHN OF THE CROSS

The Obscure Night of the Soul

Upon an obscure night
Fevered with love in love's anxiety
(O hapless-happy plight!)
I went, none seeing me,
Forth from my house where all things be.   5

By night, secure from sight,
And by the secret stair, disguisedly,
(O hapless-happy plight!)
By night, and privily,
Forth from my house where all things quiet be.   10

Blest night of wandering,
In secret, where by none might I be spied,
Nor I see anything;
Without a light or guide,
Save that which in my heart burnt in my side.   15

That light did lead me on,
More surely than the shining of noontide,
Where well I knew that one
Did for my coming bide;
Where He abode, might none but He abide.   20

O night that didst lead thus,
O night more lovely than the dawn of light,
O night that broughtest us,
Lover to lover's sight,
Lover with loved in marriage of delight!   25

Upon my flowery breast
Wholly for Him, and save Himself for none,
There did I give sweet rest
To my belovèd one;
The fanning of the cedars breathed thereon.   30

When the first moving air
Blew from the tower and waved His locks aside,
His hand, with gentle care,
Did wound me in the side,
And in my body all my senses died.   35

All things I then forgot,
My cheek on Him who for my coming came;
All ceased, and I was not,
Leaving my cares and shame
Among the lilies, and forgetting them.   40

St. John of the Cross (San Juan de la Cruz, 1549-1591). Translation by Arthur Symons. Reprinted by permission of Dodd Mead and Company, Publishers.

ALONSO DE ERCILLA

La Araucana

Not of ladies, love, or graces
Do I sing, nor knights enamored,
Nor of gifts and shows of feeling,
Cares of love, or love's affections;
But the valiant acts and prowess
Of those never-daunted Spaniards
Who with sword placed yoke of bondage
On the neck of untamed Indian.

Chile, fertile province, famous
In the vast Antarctic region,   10
Known to far-flung mighty nations
For its princely strength and courage,
Has produced a race so noble,
Proud and brave, illustrious, warlike,
That by king it ne'er was humbled,
Nor to foreign sway submitted. . . .

'Tis Arauco self-sufficient
That with wisdom, fame and glory
Holds the soil in far dominion
From the one Pole to the other,   20
Set the Spaniard in such hazard
As my writing soon will picture.
Twenty leagues contain its landmarks,
Sixteen Toqui[1] chiefs possess it.

Each brave has one weapon only,
Which he skills himself to handle,
One to which since early childhood
He has shown fond predilection.
He attempts with this one solely,
To win mastery; the archer   30
Is untrammelled by the pikestaff;
Pikeman spurns the bow and arrows. . . .

Beardless men, robust of gesture,
Theirs are full-grown, shapely bodies,
Lofty chests and massive shoulders,
Stalwart limbs and steely sinews;
They are confident, emboldened,
Dauntless, gallant, and audacious,
Firm inured to work, and suffering
Mortal cold, and heat, and hunger.   40

Never has a king subjected
Such fierce people proud of freedom,
Nor has alien nation boasted
E'er of having trod their borders;
Ne'er has dared a neighboring country
Raise the sword and move against them;
Always were they feared, unshackled,
Free of laws, with necks unbending.

[It was decreed in tribal council that the supreme
command should fall to him who could longest
bear a heavy tree trunk. Lincoya had borne the
log of leadership longer than all the contestants.
Then Caupolicán gave the best performance of all:]
Briskly walked the proud barbarian
Who was more than most outstanding,   50
When Caupolicán, sans escort,
Nimbly entered the arena.
Since his birth his eye was sightless,
Like a precious blood-red garnet;
But deficiency of vision
He offset by strength and effort.

This young blade was tall of stature,
Masculine, authoritative,
Grave, severe, and loving justice,
Harsh, and rigorous, and righteous,   60
Large of body, chest uplifted,
Skillful, passing strong, and agile,
Wise and resolute, sagacious,
E'er eschewing rash behavior.

With what happy signs they greeted
Him, though in their hearts they quavered!
To him they revealed the matter
Pithily from start to finish.
Seeing now Apollo plunging
Down the sea-lanes, they determined   70
That his testing wait the morrow,
Till the longed-for light had risen.

Night was passed in great contention
Which arose with his arrival.
Some upheld Lincoya; others
Claimed Caupolicán the stronger.
Pro and con the bets were posted.
Others, doubtful, waived their wagers,
Waiting with their eyes turned eastward
For a glimpse of Phoebus' horses.   80

Alonso de Ercilla y Zúñiga (1533-1599?), La Araucana. Translated by Paul Thomas Manchester and
Charles Maxwell Lancaster by whose permission these lines are reprinted.
[1] The ranking chieftains of the Araucanians were called *Ulmens, Apo-Ulmens,* and *Toquis.*

Rosy dawn had just embroidered
Cloudlets with a thousand stitches,
And the wretched folk and tillers
Wakened to accustomed labor,
Dawn already was restoring
Freshened hues to withered gardens;
New-born light suffused that valley
As Caupolicán came striding.

With disdain and haughty bearing,
Seizing hard the knotty tree-trunk,   90
As if 'twere a dainty yardstick,
On his sturdy back he laid it.
Silence hushed the crowd in wonder,
Seeing frame so strong of sinew;
Color changed for fell Lincoya;
Hope of victory had faded.

Slowly paced the prudent savage
In the daybreak's hastening brightness.
Sun cut down the lengthened shadows,
But he never shrank in purpose,   100
In the West the light was waning,
But his heart's flame never flickered.
Stars appeared in myriad radiance,
Gleaming on that tireless hero.

Peering moonbeams lamped the tourney
From their dampened lodge of shadows,
Ridding somber field and forest
Of their murky veil of darkness.
Still Caupolicán ne'er wavered
From his wager; but renewing   110
Strength, he stood and bore his burden,
As if by no weight afflicted.

'Twixt two towering Andean ridges
Loomed afar Tithonus'[2] lady,
With her golden hair disheveled,
Shaken free from dewy hoar-frost,
And she greened the languid meadows
Blossoming with cool-sprayed moisture,
And like pearls 'midst gems of colors
Lovely, lay enchased in flowers.   120

Phaeton's chariot came coursing
From the sea, o'er road long travelled;
Shadows plucked the peaks of mountains
From the sun's gaze; and the warrior,
Stout, though freighted down with burden,
Tottered back and forth, unwearied,
Though again the dense, black curtain
Swiftly fell, the day immersing.

[The burning and sacking of Concepción by the
Indians is the most graphic scene of Canto VII:]
Villagers in sight of houses
Spread about in all directions,   130
That the pillage of their city
Furnish booty nothing human.
On the signal of departure,
Like a darkened flock of starlings
Swooping on the whitened wheat stacks,
Hostile armies sacked the village. . . .

Some climbed stairs, and some descended,
Others rushed to clothes and coffers,
Opening or bursting hinges,
Leaving not one bag or trinket;   140
Some contended, others shuffled;
Some brought loot for fair division;
Through the turrets, roofs, and attics,
Burdened down, appeared the savage.

Savage hearts broke forth in madness
And their war-cries loud resounded,
Seeing flames respecting nothing,
Carvings, pillars, roofs, nor stables;
Not a man in all that rabble
Grieved, beholding such destruction;   150
But they groaned and muttered, sighing
For the things to fire resistant.

Then again the tongues Plutonian
Flicked the clouds with darting radiance;
Northern gales loosed violent swirlings,
Shook the trees and bent their branches:
Vulcan with his lusty bellows
Blew his smutty breath in anger,
Giving life to dying embers
Till in flames all things were leveled.   160

Nero fiddled, sang his ballads
As alone he laughed and gloated
O'er the crumbling gates of Caesar,
Rome, reduced to smoke and ashes.
Nero never laughed so raucous
As those loathsome base barbarians
Roared to see the blazes ravage
Opulence of magic cities.

[In Canto VIII, Caupolicán holds a powwow to
discuss a fresh attack:]
"We shall test these folks' divineness.
If they drop from skies of crystal,   170
As they claim, our steel will hew them
And will devastate their lineage . . .

---

[2] Eos, in Greek mythology; "rosy-fingered dawn"; Aurora to the Romans, who brought her lover,
Tithonus, the gift of immortality and bore him a son.

Flicked no eyelash, and their nostrils
Scarcely breathed upon their spirits
During this harangue so haughty
Which Caupolicán delivered.
Complimentary responses,
Courteous speech flowed. Prince Lautaro
Smiled, excused himself from speaking,
And Lincoya stood in answer: 180

"Lord, in token of my fealty
Where you lead I swear I'll follow,
Nor will chance adverse and horrid
Turn my bleeding bosom homeward.
Sire, of this you may be certain:
All will fail and all be blasted
Ere the vouchsafed word and promise
Of a man like me betray you."

Thus he spake, and when requested,
Old Curaca Peteguelen,   190
Stern and stolid in annoyance,
But in peacetime, soft and human,
Shrivelled, but of wiry structure,
Lord of that lush beauteous plainland,
Vast of voice and grave of gesture,
Rasped in accents philosophic:

"Warrior strong and perfect captain,
I'm not loath to be the first one
To assay my breastplate's texture.
If my axe breaks through its lining   200
I can pledge you as an expert
That much work remains unfinished
Ere the Spaniard quit our country,
Ere we dream of Spain invaded."

This chief hushed, strode Tucapelo
Scowling with inflamed demeanor,
And without respect he bellowed
In a tone of rage contemptuous,
Saying: "Spain does not affright me,
And I'll doff my cloak of manhood,   210
If alone I do not ruin
Christians, be they gods or earthlings.

By my dexterous arm I vow you,
If two years my stick sustains me,
Flouting Heaven with pure iron
I'll discharge this dire commission,
Let no wall of Spain stand upright.
Passion puffs me with ambition,
For when alien soil is leveled,
War I'll wage on Heaven's portals.   220

Fates exist not; silly twaddle,
Mouthed to clog us, and to hamper!
Witless is belief in Fortune.
Destiny is might of muscle.
Sooner will the skyland's fortress
Crumble in explosive fragments
Than will Tucapel's sworn promise
Fail or flag one jot or tittle."

[Colocolo again soothes their angry hearts:]
"Verdant age, oh sons, provokes you
To insanity. We old ones   230
Bring the world no other profit
Than the winds of wholesome counsel.
Smoky vapors do not blind us,
Nor the surging saps of springtime.
Free of fervor, young no longer,
We can plumb the depths of wisdom.

You, O captains, plucky, dauntless,
Swollen with a single triumph,
Bawl and stretch your toes and fingers
Like papooses born but lately.   240
Moderate your ire ungoverned.
Mitigate your breasts' upheaval.
Do not let your scorn of Spaniards
Sell away your lives too cheaply." . . .

After him, the necromancer,
Wizened weasel, aged Curaca,
Self-styled augur Puchecalco,
Held a sage prognosticator,
Heaving sighs of deep hysteria,
Thus began to rave in sorrow: 250
"Eponamon,[3] Prince of midnight,
Supplement my wails prophetic! . . .

Full of portents are the breezes;
Screeching birds flap wings nocturnal,
Fouling day's serenest glamor,
Boding fatal ills prodigious.
Plants with earthy humors laden.
Wither, starve, and vanish, fruitless.
Moon, sun, stars confirm this havoc,
Omens by the hundred thousands . . .   260

Death, irreparable and furious,
With a baleful mien looms on us.
Lady Luck, once bright and friendly,
Stares and frowns upon us outcasts.
Eponamon, grim, horrendous,
In warm blood of ours enveloped,
Hooks his claws and scours the desert,
Leading us to what oasis?"

[3] The war-god of the Araucanians.

[As the Spaniards rebuild Concepción, they are attacked by Lautaro's braves:]
When the sun had reached the zenith
Of the brazen vault celestial,   270
And the cricket shrill was chirring
With a counterpoint discordant,
Then Lautaro's camp was lifted,
Then marched off the close-packed squadron
In the din of rhythmic treading
Toward the site of Spanish sconces.

Those withdrawn within the fortress
Warded off the assault like tigers,
Prizing death above submission,
Treasuring a glorious sunset;   280
Powered with such aspiration,
Lunged they without hope of living,
Butchering their adversaries,
Loosening blood-lakes on the plaza.

In that citadel, Lautaro,
Flouting arms and men, first entered,
Tomahawked and scalped two soldiers,
Which that morning's chance had flung him.
Smiting, slashing went Lincoya.
Who can tell of Tucapelo   290
Who would brave celestial portals,
If he could but find a ladder?

Scarcely had the headstrong savage
Landed firmly in the plaza,
When he swung his bulky cudgel,
And dispersed his lurking foemen;
Fine-meshed mail, stout armor-plating,
Helmets were not worth a copper;
Raining blows they could not suffer;
Skulls and brains were mashed and mangled.   300

Some fell bruised and badly crippled;
Others swooned from life-long damage;
Through their chests he drove their neck-bones,
And their ribs and backs he fractured.
As if all their bones were beeswax,
They were twisted, crushed, and molded,
As he forced his way unflinching,
Through the armored human thicket. . . .

[Lautaro, surprised by the Spanish foe as he languishes in the arms of his beautiful wife, Guacolda:]
Their retreat had one lane only
Occupied with hawk-eyed sentries.   310
Other paths lacked trails or footprints
Since the land was almost barren.
On that night the savage slumbered
In the arms of fair Guacolda

Whom he loved with flaming passion,
Who for him felt equal ardor.

The Araucan was divested
Of his cumbrous martial trappings.
That night only fate disposed him
To repose and sweet caresses.   320
Heavy nightmares pressed his eyelids.
He awoke distressed and anxious,
And Guacolda, taut and breathless,
Asked him why he seemed so startled.

"Dear beloved," Lautaro answered,
"Just this instant I was dreaming
That a scowling Spaniard faced me
With ferocity depicted
In his mien. With hands of violence
He squeezed out my heart and robbed me   330
Of my manliness. I woke then
Overcome with rage and sorrow."
In a troubled tone she murmured:
"I, alas, have dreamed this, also.
Happiness I e'er distrusted. . . .

Spectral visions, soon unveiling,
Will attempt to mar love's banquet,
Leave our bridal bed forsaken.
Never shall they separate us.
Such a blow I cannot suffer.   340
But in other blows there's solace.
When cold earth received your body,
Mine shall lie in death above you."

Great Pillano's son embraced her;
Arms about her neck, he clasped her,
Bathed with tears her swan-white bosom;
And with reallumed love-longing
He responded: "Fret not, lady,
Nor becloud my joy with omens.
Let delight preside, for freely   350
In these arms I'll e'er possess you.

Who restored to Araucan people
Self-esteem, lost reputation,
After necks, untamed and stately,
To domestic yokes fell victim.
I, the man who ripped asunder
Spanish tyranny's dominions!
In this land my name suffices
Sans the sword to waken war-lust.

All the less, with you beside me   360
Should I fear or slink from damage;
Let not dreams harass you, lady,
For reality is tearless.
From more slippery crags abysmal

Has my fortune been left dangling.
I have looked on direr dangers,
Always thwarting them with honor."

She, less sure and still more plaintive
To Lautaro's neck was hanging,
And with piteous eyes she conjured   370
What her lips had failed to wheedle:
"If that purest love I gave you
Freely, when I had most freedom
If, as Heaven is my witness
It prevails, sweet lord and lover,

By it now, I swear, by torment
That I felt when you forsook me,
By that troth the wind has spared us,
That you pledged me with great weeping,
Give at least this one contentment,   380
If through me it has caressed you,
Don your war-gear, Do not tarry.
Lead your warriors to the rampart."

He responded: "All too clearly
Is your little faith depicted.
Is Lautaro held so feeble;
And do you despise his warclub
Cherished for the folk's redemption
Which has shown itself so worthy?
You accredit me a hero   390
Since forsooth you weep my passing."

"Lackaday," exclaimed Guacolda;
'I am satisfied, but worried.
Your strong arm can bring what profit,
If my woe is dire and stronger?
Now that qualms I have stand naked,
That same love I hold assures me
Since the sword that separates us
Sends me too to dog your traces.

Since necessity and hazard   400
Menace me with bitter downfall,
And I needs must bear such evil
As to see you parted from me,
Let the little life that's left me
Sip some sweetness ere I perish.
They who sense no ill are proven
To derive small bliss from blessings." . . .

As we may presume, Lautaro
Reasoned long with sweet Guacolda,
With assurances and chidings   410
For the little faith she offered;

Spurning reason, and offended,
She endured far greater sorrow
As the sound of drums and trumpets
Interrupted tender wranglings.

Never leaps the wretched miser
Pondering on his hoard of riches
With such sprightliness when startled
By the noise of thieves and robbers;
Never did a mother hasten   420
To the cries of son beloved,
Fearing some wild beast's encroachment,
As Lautaro met this summons.

On his arm was draped his mantle,
Bare his body, bare his rapier.
Ran the savage to the portal,
For he had no time for arming,
Oh perfidious, fickle Fortune,
With what cruelty art thou smirking,
For the goodness of the ages   430
Thus with one fell blow thou stealest!

Friends and neighboring troops four hundred
By one flank attacked the stronghold,
Who to aid, abet the Christians,
Hastened with their painted quivers;
Ready hands and nimble forces
Loosed the shafts in countless volleys;
From their midst Pillano's offspring
Stepped to meet the dart that sought him.

On the left, oh luck accursed!   440
Tore the arrow so directed
That it pierced the heart most noble
E'er contained in human bosom.
Death was proud of such a target,
Seeing in one blow its laurels,
And usurping murderous glory,
Death proclaimed this wound its guerdon.

Tragedy was the arrow's mission,
For the fierce one bit the gravel,
Opening wide a copious spigot,   450
Pouring blood in black abundance;
From his face the color vanished;
Eyes he walled; from mortal body
Rushed his soul in rapid anguish
Downward to the abode infernal.

[Book II continues with descriptions of battles between the Araucanians and the Spaniards.]

PEDRO CALDERÓN DE LA BARCA

The Dream Called Life

A dream it was in which I found myself.
And you that hail me now, then hailed me king,
In a brave palace that was all my own,
Within, and all without it, mine; until,
Drunk with excess of majesty and pride, 5
Methought I towered so big and swelled so wide
That of myself I burst the glittering bubble
Which my ambition had about me blown
And all again was darkness. Such a dream
As this, in which I may be walking now, 10
Dispensing solemn justice to you shadows,
Who make believe to listen; but anon
Kings, princes, captains, warriors, plume and steel,
Ay, even with all your airy theater,
May flit into the air you seem to rend 15
With acclamations, leaving me to wake
In the dark tower; or dreaming that I wake
From this that waking is; or this and that,
Both waking and both dreaming; such a doubt
Confounds and clouds our mortal life about. 20
But whether wake or dreaming, this I know
How dreamwise human glories come and go;
Whose momentary tenure not to break,
Walking as one who knows he soon may wake,
So fairly carry the full cup, so well 25
Disordered insolence and passion quell,
That there be nothing after to upbraid
Dreamer or doer in the part he played;
Whether to-morrow's dawn shall break the spell,
Or the last trumpet of the Eternal Day, 30
When dreaming, with the night, shall pass away.

The Dying Eusebio's Address to the Cross

Tree, whereon the pitying skies
Hang the true fruit love doth sweeten,
Antidote of that first eaten,
Flower of man's new paradise,
Rainbow, that to tearful eyes 5
Sin's receding flood discloses—
Pledge that earth in peace reposes,
Beauteous plant, all fruitful vine.
A newer David's harp divine,
Table of a second Moses;— 10
Sinner am I, therefore I
Claim thine aid as all mine own,
Since for sinful man alone,
God came down on thee to die:
Praise through me thou hast won thereby,
Since for me would God have died, 16
If the world held none beside.
Then, O Cross! thou 'rt all for me,
Since God had not died on thee
If sin's depths I had not tried. 20
Ever for thy intercession
Hath my faith implored, O Cross!
That thou wouldst not to my loss
Let me die without confession.
I, repenting my transgression, 25
Will not the first robber be
Who on thee confessed to God;
Since we two the same path trod,
And repent, deny not me
The redemption wrought on thee. 30

BALTASAR GRACIÁN

Worldly Wisdom

A MAN OF THE AGE

The rarest individuals depend on their age. It is not every one that finds the age he deserves, and even when he finds it he does not always know how to utilise it. Some men have been worthy of a better century, for every species of good does not always triumph. Things have their period; even excellences are subject to fashion. The sage has one advantage: he is immortal. If *this* is not his century many others will be.

SYMPATHY WITH GREAT MINDS

It is an heroic quality to agree with heroes. 'Tis like a miracle of nature for mystery and for use. There is a natural kinship of hearts and minds: its effects are such that vulgar ignorance scents witchcraft. Esteem established, goodwill follows, which at times reaches affection. It persuades without words and obtains without earning. This sympathy is sometimes active, sometimes passive, both alike felicific; the more so, the more sublime. 'Tis a great

Pedro Calderón de la Barca (1600-1681). "The Dream Called Life," translated by Edward Fitzgerald;
"The Dying Eusebio . . . " by D. F. MacCarthy.
Baltasar Gracián (1601-1658). Translated by Joseph Jacobs.

art to recognise, to distinguish and to utilise this gift. No amount of energy suffices without that favour of nature.

SEE THAT THINGS END WELL

Some regard more the rigour of the game than the winning of it, but to the world the discredit of the final failure does away with any recognition of the previous care The victor need not explain. The world does not notice the details of the measures employed, but only the good or ill result. You lose nothing if you gain your end. A good end gilds everything, however unsatisfactory the means. Thus at times it is part of the art of life to transgress the rules of the art, if you cannot end well otherwise.

DO AND BE SEEN DOING

Things do not pass for what they are but for what they seem. To be of use and to know how to show yourself of use, is to be twice as useful. What is not seen is as if it was not. Even the Right does not receive proper consideration if it does not seem right. The observant are far fewer in number than those who are deceived by appearances. Deceit rules the roost, and things are judged by their jackets, and many things are other than they seem. A good exterior is the best recommendation of the inner perfection.

BETTER MAD WITH THE REST OF THE WORLD THAN WISE ALONE

So say politicians. If all are so, one is no worse off than the rest, whereas solitary wisdom passes for folly. So important is it to sail with the stream. The greatest wisdom often consists in ignorance, or the pretence of it. One has to live with others, and others are mostly ignorant. "To live entirely alone one must be very like a god or quite like a wild beast," but I would turn the aphorism by saying: Better be wise with the many than a fool all alone. There be some too who seek to be original by seeking chimeras.

DO NOT SHOW YOUR WOUNDED FINGER,

for everything will knock up against it; nor complain about it, for malice always aims where weakness can be injured. It is no use to be vexed: being the butt of the talk will only vex you the more. Ill-will searches for wounds to irritate, aims darts to try the temper, and tries a thousand ways to sting to the quick. The wise never own to being hit, or disclose any evil, whether personal or hereditary. For even Fate sometimes likes to wound us where we are most tender. It always mortifies wounded flesh. Never therefore disclose the source of mortification or of joy, if you wish the one to cease, the other to endure.

LIVE FOR THE MOMENT

Our acts and thoughts and all must be determined by circumstances. Will when you may, for time and tide wait for no man. Do not live by certain fixed rules, except those that relate to the cardinal virtues. Nor let your will subscribe fixed conditions, for you may have to drink the water to-morrow which you cast away to-day. There be some so absurdly paradoxical that they expect all the circumstances of an action should bend to their eccentric whims and not *vice versa*. The wise man knows that the very polestar of prudence lies in steering by the wind.

ALWAYS ACT AS IF YOUR ACTS WERE SEEN

He must see all round who sees that men see him or will see him. He knows that walls have ears and that ill deeds rebound back. Even when alone he acts as if the eyes of the whole world were upon him. For as he knows that sooner or later all will be known, so he considers those to be present as witnesses who must afterwards hear of the deed. He that wished the whole world might always see him did not mind that his neighbours could see him over their walls.

IN ONE WORD, BE A SAINT

So is all said at once. Virtue is the link of all perfections, the centre of all the felicities. She it is that makes a man prudent, discreet, sagacious, cautious, wise, courageous, thoughtful, trustworthy, happy, honoured, truthful, and a universal Hero. Three HHH's make a man happy—Health, Holiness, and a Headpiece. Virtue is the sun of the microcosm, and has for hemisphere a good conscience. She is so beautiful that she finds favour with both God and man. Nothing is lovable but virtue, nothing detestable but vice. Virtue alone is serious, all else is but jest. A man's capacity and greatness are to be measured by his virtue and not by his fortune. She alone is all-sufficient. She makes men lovable in life, memorable after death.

THE FRENCH SPIRIT

The cultural supremacy of France on the European continent has been universally recognized. The cardinal fact to be remembered is that French culture remained uninterrupted during four fruitful centuries between its sixteenth-century Renaissance and our own day. No other land except England enjoyed such good fortune.

French literature revealed elements of modernism as early as the thirteenth century. In 1357 began the Hundred Years War with England over problems of vassalage and claims to the throne. The resulting misery and chaos pushed back the wheel of progress, and French writing stagnated. But by the middle of the fifteenth century the French nation began to recover, and even in the last years of the war a democratic spirit was making itself felt and was being harnessed to a strong monarchy.

VILLON AND MODERN BEGINNINGS

The new age appeared in the poetry of François Villon (1431-c.1484). By contrast with other poets of the period, like Alain Chartier and Charles, Duke of Orleans, Villon was exceptional. Medieval in his verse forms (the ballade, rondeau, etc.) and in his brooding on death, Villon was nevertheless modern in his realistic evocation of common life and in his satirical incisiveness. The child of a transitional era during which the social equilibrium of France was virtually destroyed, he led one of the most disorderly lives ever recorded of a poet. A scholar destined for the clergy, after receiving a Master's degree from the University of Paris, he fell into bad company, became a member of a thieving and robbing fraternity, committed murders in the course of unsavory brawls, and got into scrapes that caused his imprisonment and brought him within the shadow of the gallows in 1463. The sentence of death was commuted to banishment, but he appears to have died shortly thereafter, his health having been undermined by dissipation and prison.

Out of Villon's knowledge of the depths came a new poetry of democratic realism. His poems are filled with portraits of thieves, harlots, commoners, officials, and himself. Even the grossest people in his poems speak to us of their desires and pathos. Thus a horribly aged harlot evokes the tragedy of growing old and ugly that is the common lot of humanity; and elsewhere the poet reflects that the grave annihilates all social distinctions. Villon was also an autobiographical poet who made his feelings the center of his verse. Torn between evil and remorse, mocking and defiant but deeply sensible of his degradation and embittered by it, he is the lyricist of a complex and authentic personality. French wit keeps his lines spirited and vivid, but sorrow and passion give them depth and a dark turbulence.

The bulk of Villon's verse consists of two "testaments," a Little Testament and a later Great Testament, a long mocking death-bed bequest to his companions, friends, and enemies, mingled with superb lyrics mostly in *ballade* form. The Great Testament thus holds in solution all the elements of his inspiration—his realistic view of life, his personal story and self-evaluation, and his lyricism.

THE FRENCH RENAISSANCE

The fifteenth century prepared the ground for the Renaissance that came to full bloom in France in the next century. Under Francis I, who ascended the throne in 1515, French unification through a central monarchy was virtually completed. Feudal life was dissolved, and the fractious nobility flocked to the royal court where it became politically weakened and devoted itself to courtly graces and literary dilettantism. Humanist scholarship came to the foreground, liberal thought won many adherents, and even the Protestant Reformation advocated by Calvin in Geneva made its impression, giving rise to the powerful Huguenot sect and to Catholic critics of the Church.

The greatest singer of the French Renaissance was Pierre de Ronsard (1524-1585), court poet, traveler to other lands and courts, and a favorite of both Mary Stuart and her enemy Queen Elizabeth. Veering away from medieval verse forms, he adopted the Petrarchan sonnet and developed the ode and the heroic epic. In all this, Ronsard and the circle of seven learned poets (the Pleiad[1]), of which he was the brightest star, were consciously classical. Their chief manifesto, *The Defense and Illustration of the French Language* (1549), by the fine poet Du Bellay, asked "Are we inferior to the Greeks and Romans?" and outlined a program for epics, Pindaric odes, Anacreontic verses, and classic drama. If new words were needed, writers were to invent them by resorting to the classic tongues, a custom that in time overburdened the French language although enriching it at first. Literature, the manifesto also insisted, was to be gay and bright, instead of crabbed and somber. Ronsard fulfilled these requirements by virtue of a lively, charming character and a genuine lyric talent.

Still, for the world at large the French Renaissance is most memorably represented by two commanding prose writers, Rabelais and Montaigne, who became two of the most influential and delightful figures in world literature.

François Rabelais (1490?-1553) epitomized in his life and work the exuberance, the earnest and purposeful light-heartedness, and the intellectual curiosity and breadth of the dawning modern spirit. At first a monk in a Franciscan monastery, he gratified his passion for learning by studying Greek, Hebrew, and Arabic in addition to Latin, as well as mathematics and the sciences. His ability attracted a powerful clerical patron but aroused the Franciscans against him. Thereupon he deserted his monastery, won permission to leave the order, and joined the learned Benedictine monks. After staying with his patron, the Bishop Maillezais, for six years and traveling to various universities in search of knowledge, he began the study of medicine at the University of Montpellier. Following this he became resident physician at a hospital in Lyons, then an intellectual center. Here he began to write, publishing the first part of his book, *The Great and Inestimable Chronicles of the Grand and Enormous Giant Gargantua,* in 1532. Then followed its sequel, *Pantagruel.* In 1534 and 1536, after new editions of his books, he accompanied the liberal Cardinal du Bellay to Rome, and was greatly favored, receiving permission to hold ecclesiastical offices and to practice medicine. In 1537

he received his doctor's degree, taught at the University of Montpellier until 1539, and engaged in botanical hobbies which led him to introduce the melon, the carnation, and the artichoke into France.

A few years later Rabelais had his first two books read to Francis I, who was so greatly pleased that he granted him a license for a third book. But when Francis died, the clergy began to assail Rabelais' writings for their impieties, so that he found it expedient to escape to Metz in Lorraine, where he resumed the practice of medicine. Fortunately, he found powerful protectors, was allowed to return to France, and was made *curé* of Meudon and Jainbet. Demands for the destruction of his writings, however, continued, compelling him to discontinue writing further additions to his great rambling tale.

His book, a bulky and loosely organized tale about good and wise giants and their companions, is an extravaganza calculated to dispel the mists of the Middle Ages with enormous gusts of laughter and derision. Rabelais coined the sentence *"le rire est le propre de l'homme"*—(laughter is the attribute of man). Some of his laughter was outrageously obscene, but there was a sober purpose in it. It affirmed the right of man to happiness and self-realization. It was, moreover, an exuberant assault on the Middle Ages wrapped up and camouflaged by verbal fire, buffoonery, and fantasy.

His first and best book, *Gargantua,* starts as a mocking account of the young giant's medieval schooling that makes a colossal dunce of him. Then his father Grandgousier places him under a humanist teacher whose progressive methods make a modern man of Gargantua. This is followed by Gargantua's participation in Grandgousier's war against the neighboring state of Picrochole, an extravaganza that is still one of the best satires on war-making and ends with an enlightened peace-treaty far in advance of anything that Europe has yet witnessed. After the victory and the generous peace, Gargantua rewards his valiant colleague, the valiant Friar John, with the kind of abbey the lively monk desires. Thus arises the Abbey of Theleme, the which is the exact reverse of a medieval monastery, since it encourages the full savoring of life and the enjoyment of complete freedom in preparation for a career of enlightened self-realization.

The second book, *Pantagruel,* describes the adventures of Gargantua's son Pantagruel in the company of a devil-may-care, infinitely ingenious companion, Panurge, whose character sums up the

[1] Named after a Greek literary circle in Hellenic Alexandria.

gay abandon of the Renaissance. Here, too, musty ideas and practices are the object of ridicule. The rest of Rabelais' work revolves around adventures entailed by Panurge's search for an oracle that will tell him whether he can marry without danger of being betrayed. Hypocritical monks, mercenary lawyers, indifferent judges, and other corrupt representatives of medieval institutions come under the flail of Rabelais' mockery. This immoderate work blasts all aspects of the old world with the intention of clearing the way for a new spirit. Its strenuous modernity is still unshared by the bulk of mankind.

Even more modern was Michel Eyquem de Montaigne (1533-1592), the son of a devout, progressive father and a Protestant mother of Spanish-Jewish descent. By birth and by virtue of a humanist education under the supervision of his father, he became the most broad-minded of men. A brilliant student whose erudition at the age of ten awed his masters at the college of Bordeaux, he also studied law and entered public life. He saw military service, became Gentleman-in-Ordinary to the king, who entrusted him with important duties, and was Mayor of Bordeaux for four years. But he continued to be an ardent scholar, used his considerable means to acquire a large library, retired to his estate, and gave himself up to the contemplation of all life and knowledge. His informal *Essays*, written at different times, became the record of a remarkable personality, for at the center of all of Montaigne's reflections was the man himself. "Reader, thou hast here an honest book," Montaigne declared with every justification. "Cut these words," Emerson said of the *Essays*, "and they would bleed,"—because Montaigne is so alive in them.

Montaigne was the model of a truly civilized person. Never dogmatic but always curious, he merely asked questions and arrived at tentative answers ever qualified by his sense of the impossibility of certainty, as expressed in his favorite sentence "Que sçais-je?"—"What do I know?" Although he cautiously refrained from fighting tradition, he riddled it with questions like tracer-bullets. His position was that of a relativist who was impressed by the diversity of human customs revealed by the age of discoverers and explorers. Our reason, our study of the greatly varied customs of mankind, and our realization that all "contrarieties" or contradictory habits are found in every individual, should teach us that we cannot force mankind into a single mold; that we cannot establish a rigid and final truth or dogma which may be imposed on everyone. Tolerance, intellectual detachment, and

constant investigation comprise the trinity of this modern gospel. It was inevitable that Montaigne's views on such matters as the unity of soul and body, religion, and above all, education should have become blueprints for modernity.

THE NEO-CLASSIC AGE

In the next century, pursuant with the policies of centralized absolutism in France under Louis XIII and Louis XIV, there arose a marked reaction to the exuberant individual of Rabelais, Montaigne, and their fellow-writers. A new discipline was propounded by influential critics like Malherbe and Boileau in the name of classicism, and this was sanctioned by the establishment of the French Academy in 1635 under the protection of Cardinal Richelieu, Louis XIII's minister of state. Wayward individualism in manners, thought, and literature were banned, and the cult of order and grace invaded all corners from the *salon* of the fashionable blue-stocking Madame de Rambouillet to the secluded study of philosophers like Descartes and Pascal.

For the drama the age prescribed orderliness of a special sort. Harking back to statements in Aristotle's *Poetics* as misinterpreted by humanist critics, French academicians insisted on rigid adherence to the unities of time, place, and action. Henceforth the scene was to remain unchanged throughout the play, the duration of the action was not to exceed the length of time consumed by the presentation of the play, and there were to be no secondary plots. The difficulty of shifting scenery made these rules practical, and further support for them was found in the French ideal of *bon sens* (common sense); for, after all, these regulations appeared eminently reasonable. Above all, however, they were sanctioned by the fact that they were in accord with classic precepts, for this was an age in which classicism was venerated as the supreme model of reasonableness and good taste; hence the name for the period *neo-classicism* or (new classicism). The first important French playwright, Pierre Corneille, struggled valiantly against the rules, for the author of *The Cid* and *Horace* was a rugged dramatist partial to heroic themes. When he surrendered to the law of the unities, under pressure from Cardinal Richelieu and his circle, the battle was over.

The rules proved least hampering to comedy because it is not easy to suppress the freedom and effervescence of laughter, and because comedy of manners generally does not need an elaborate plot and many changes of scene. For this type of comedy, moreover, this age of artificial manners and social pretensions provided an ideal subject. The greatest writer of comedies in France, Molière, found everything his genius needed—everything but freedom for political discussion. George Meredith described this comic world brilliantly in his famous *Essay on Comedy*: "Politically it is accounted a misfortune for France that her nobles thronged to the Court of Louis Quatorze [XIV]. It was a boon to the comic poet. He had that lively, quicksilver world of the animalcule passions, the huge pretensions, the placid absurdities, under his eyes in full activity; vociferous quacks and snapping dupes, hypocrites, posturers, extravagants, pedants, rose-pinked ladies and mad grammarians, sonneteering marquises, high-flying mistresses, plain-minded maids, interthreading as in a loom, noisy as at a fair."

Jean Baptiste Poquelin (1622-1673), who assumed the pen-name Molière, had every qualification for recording that "quicksilver world." The son of the king's upholsterer, he received an excellent education in a Jesuit college and developed a skeptical intellect by observation and by discussion with the scientific philosopher Gassendi at a rich friend's home. Joining an unsuccessful company, he started touring, wrote plays for it, managed it, became its leading comedian, and brought it back to Paris in triumph. His success was so great that he became a favorite of the king and a friend of important noblemen and literary men, although he made enemies in the social set and aroused the clergy, which kept his satire on a religious hypocrite *Tartuffe* off the stage for many years. His later years were clouded by illness and by an unhappy marriage to a flirtatious young woman twenty years his junior. But throughout all difficulties he maintained a judicious and inventive spirit, a fine critical mind, and an unflagging sense of humor.

Molière wrote all kinds of plays in prose and in verse, from ballets and trivial farces to brilliant comedies like *Tartuffe* and *The Misanthrope*. In his best work, the predominant element is social satire. His shafts were aimed at affected manners (*Les Précieuses Ridicules, The Affected Misses*), pretentious learning (*The Learned Women*), religious hypocrisy (*Tartuffe*), social climbing (*The Would-Be Gentleman*), charlatanism in the medical profession (*The Imaginary Invalid*), and many other extravagances and corruptions. In *The Misanthrope*, these are collected into a single play, which is virtually a cross-section of French society.

The *Miser* has a double edge to its satire, for it is directed both at the growing greed of a society in which the middle-class was becoming rich and powerful, and at the excessive power of parents over their children. At the same time, the play exemplifies one of Molière's most appealing qualities—his tolerance and sympathy for natural impulses and wholesome, young love. If Molière became a satirist, it was chiefly because he was on the side of common sense, reasonableness, and naturalness. He set an example that the best writers of comedy have followed since his time in all countries.

His younger contemporary Jean Racine (1639-1699), whom he helped to launch on his career by giving him his first production, won equal triumphs in the field of neo-classic tragedy. Racine's perfect dramatic poetry, fine sensibility, and intense temperament enabled him to write tragedies of great beauty and power. This was an age in which women dominated the fashionable world, and Racine, most of whose plays deal with feminine passions and are named after classic heroines, had an unusual faculty for understanding women. Moreover, having been reared in the Jansenist faith, which regarded the majority of mankind as naturally evil owing to "original sin," he was partial to stories of guilty passion and perverse behavior. A French critic has said of Racine's heroines that they are "fair women full of Attic grace but lacking the grace of God." His plays have been ideal vehicles for prominent French actresses up to our own day. One historian has aptly declared that "the empire of women in [French] literature dates from Racine." *Phædra,* for which Racine found models in Euripides' *Hippolytus* and Seneca's *Phædra*, exemplifies all these qualities, including his polished use of Alexandrine (twelve-syllable, rhymed) verse.

Tiring of court intrigues aimed at this play, Racine retired to Port Royal. The erstwhile lover of popular actresses married a pious wife who never read a line of his plays. The only tragedies he wrote thereafter were *Esther* and the powerful *Athalie* (*Athaliah*), biblical tragedies composed at the request of Louis XIV's religious mistress, Madame de Maintenon, for performance at a girl's school.

The great age of the French theater was also the age of *belles-lettres*. It produced brilliant letters. memoirs, epigrams, and essays, in which keen observation was combined with wit and literary precision.

The genial Jean de La Fontaine (1621-1695) was called the "butterfly of Parnassus" because he led such a carefree life and followed all fashionable circles. Largely for amusement, he took the ori

ental beast fables that had long ago become associated in Europe with the name of Æsop, and
turned them into delightful verse. His *Fables* are
excellent examples of the new witty style and of
the sophisticated outlook of Louis XIV society.
Although a critical spirit is evident in such lines
as "The strongest reasons always yield to reasons
of the strongest," La Fontaine was content with
the society and government he knew, regarding
them as the normal state of affairs.

Accommodation to a world, appraised with complete freedom from idealization, also appeared in
the famous *Maxims* of François, the Duc de La
Rochefoucauld (1613-1680), who at first fought the
growing power of the throne like a medieval baron.
After plotting against Cardinal Richelieu, the king's
minister, and being imprisoned in the Bastille, La
Rochefoucauld retired and set down his observations on human nature in his *Maxims*. If, as Dean
Swift remarked, these scintillating aphorisms stress
self-interest as the driving force in human conduct,
the fault was not in their author but in mankind.
Still it must be remembered that La Rochefoucauld
was himself a product of the age and saw only what
he was inclined to see. Nevertheless, the one side of
the truth that he did record is observed with remarkable incisiveness and is etched into endurable
prose. In the epigrams we see the clearest examples
of the logic, lucidity, and urbane skepticism that has
distinguished so much of French literature and life.

The most important products of seventeenth-century thought, however, are to be found, not in the
casual writings of dilettantes like La Fontaine and
La Rochefoucauld, but in the mathematicians and
philosophers Pascal and his predecessor René
Descartes who made doubt the springboard for all
discovery of truth, and whose ideal of Reason was
summed up in the Latin sentence "cogito, ergo
sum" ("I think, therefore I am"). Blaise Pascal
(1623-1662) was one of the world's great mathematicians but he was also a man of strong and
deep feelings. A devout person, he became in his
Provincial Letters the ablest champion of the
Jansenist sect at Port Royal against the then dominant Jesuit order. Illness and excessive study filled
him with melancholia, and he felt uncomfortable in
the mechanical universe that science was discovering, a universe without moral purpose. "The eternal
silence of these infinite spaces frightens me," he
wrote. Nevertheless, he was at one with his age in
his reasonable approach to life and his love of
order, which is reflected not only in his lucid and
elegant prose style but even in his religious cravings
for a world well-ordered by God. In his beautiful

Pensées (*Thoughts*), scattered reflections jotted
down during his fatal illness, it is primarily the
man of reason who speaks.

THE FRENCH ENLIGHTENMENT

With Descartes, Pascal was indeed the father of
eighteenth-century rationalism. The difference lies
only in the fact that in the next century, owing
to the decadence of the monarchy and the growing
strength of the common people, the rationalists became socially and politically militant. They challenged the State and the Church, and riddled
superstition and tyranny with ridicule while making an effort to enlighten the people. They advocated religious tolerance, humanitarianism, and
progress in all directions, all this to be achieved
by free inquiry and the rule of Reason. Whether
their unlimited faith in the power of Reason was
misplaced is still a matter of debate. But it is indisputable that their teachings changed the face of
Europe for at least a century, bringing in their
wake the French Revolution, nineteenth-century
democracy, and the separation of the Church from
the State.

Many brilliant men pooled their talents to promote the "Enlightenment," as this movement is
called. Diderot, D'Alembert, Montesquieu, Condorcet, and others compiled a critical *Encyclopedia*
of all available knowledge that became the bible
of the age, and they made important contributions
to the study of sociology, government, science, and
philosophy. But two men, Voltaire and Rousseau,
stood foremost in the field of letters and added most
to our literary heritage.

François Marie Arouet, who became famous
under the pen-name of Voltaire (1694-1778), the
son of a Parisian lawyer, was studying for the law
himself when he turned instead to literature. He
soon found himself in difficulties owing to his
satirical and critical spirit. Louis XV had him confined in the Bastille for eleven months in 1717, and
he was again in prison over a quarrel with a nobleman seven years later. After his release he was
banished from France. He spent the next three
years in England, where he developed a strong
enthusiasm for British democracy and recommended it to his country in his *English Letters*.
Their publication in 1734 resulted in the imprisonment of his printer and made it expedient for
Voltaire to leave Paris and spend six years on the
estate of his admirer and friend, Madame de
Chatelet. His fame as a champion of liberty and
progressive thought, however, mounted so high
that his return to Paris became the occasion for

a public demonstration; he was even appointed royal historiographer and made a member of the French Academy. Between 1750 and 1752 he was an honored guest at the court of Frederick the Great in Potsdam, and his writings and pronouncements continued to influence Europe during the rest of his long life. His name became synonymous with liberalism and the cult of progressive and militant reason. "Let there be light and Voltaire arose," a later writer said of him; "this light is Reason, and from it was born the modern world."

A versatile writer whose writings filled one hundred volumes of poems, plays, histories, and philosophical treatises like his famous *Philosophical Dictionary*, Voltaire is best remembered today for his brilliant *contes* (tales). The most important of these is *Candide* (1759), a work inspired by religious persecutions in Lisbon after a disastrous earthquake in that city. It is a travesty on the optimistic opinion of the philosopher Leibniz that this is the best of all possible worlds, and of the eighteenth-century belief popularized by Alexander Pope in England that "whatever is, is right." Voltaire's opinion is the very opposite, and he also uses his philosophical argument as a peg on which to hang his satire on superstition, militarism, and other social evils.

Voltaire made men dissatisfied with existing institutions by means of satire. His chief contemporary, Jean-Jacques Rousseau (1712-1778), achieved the same effect by positive arguments for liberty, by asserting the rights of man, and by calling for a return to the life of nature as opposed to a socially stratified artificial world.

Rousseau, whose mother died at his birth and whose father abandoned him at the age of ten, was endowed with an unstable and rebellious temperament. He ran away from the home of his employer at the age of sixteen, wandered from place to place, and finally came under the influence of an attractive widow, Madame de Warens, with whom he lived for nine years and studied philosophy, literature, and music. The friendship of another woman got him the post of secretary to the French ambassador in Venice and saved him from penury. Returning to Paris, he led an impoverished life as a copyist of music and formed a connection with a hotel servant, Thérèse le Vaseur, whom he married many years later. He had no sense of responsibility and placed his five illegitimate children in a public institution because, as he said, this seemed to him "reasonable and good." At this time he became a friend of Diderot and other liberal thinkers, and began to write. His first effort, an essay published in 1749 on the subject "Has the progress of science and art contributed to corrupt or purify morals?" won him first prize in a public competition. He took the negative view, and he returned to this subject in his epoch-making *Discourse on the Origin and Basis of Inequality* in 1755. This he followed in time with other unconventional works: *The New Heloise,* a novel on free human relations; *Émile,* a plea for a new kind of education favorable to natural development and to natural religion independent of creeds or churches; and *The Social Contract* (1762) an argument to the effect that a contract exists between the people and their rulers, who lose all claim to obedience when they disregard the interests of the governed.

On the one hand, Rousseau's writings inspired the French Revolution and created the eighteenth-century doctrine of the natural rights of man which found its way into our *Declaration of Independence.* On the other hand, his books, to which must be added his utterly candid posthumously published *Confessions,* laid the foundations for the "back to nature" movement and the glorification of self-expression at all costs, which characterized the romantic movement in literature. Both political democracy and romanticism will be found in his *Discourse on the Origin and Basis of Inequality Among Men.*

THE NINETEENTH CENTURY

With Rousseau was born the Romantic movement in all of Europe, the movement represented in England by Coleridge, Wordsworth, Shelley, Keats, and Byron. It was natural that France should assume the leadership of romanticism, and the names of many once prominent French writers are associated with it. Among them were Chateaubriand who stressed the return to nature, Alexandre Dumas who wrote such popular romantic novels as *The Three Musketeers* and *The Count of Monte Cristo,* and Victor Hugo. The latter is remembered for his stirring poems, exciting and sentimental novels like *Les Misérables* and *Notre Dame de Paris,* and for his destruction of neo-classicism in the theater. However, the greatest contribution latter-day France made to world literature was the development and perfection of the modern realistic novel.

The greatest of the novelists was Honoré Balzac (1799-1850) a man of indefatigable energy who summed up an entire age, the first third of the nineteenth century, in nearly a hundred novels and short stories collectively called by him *La Comédie*

Humaine (*The Human Comedy*). The son of prosperous middle-class parents who suffered financial reverses, Balzac first attempted to study law, but soon launched himself on a literary career with a dogged resolve that no amount of failure and poverty could break. He was romantic in his philosophical speculations, his politics (which were anti-republican and monarchist), and his long attachment to a Polish lady, Madame de Hanska, whom he married only three months before his death. But Balzac was remarkably sensitive to the new age of business, large-scale finance, and other middle-class pursuits. Although he did not approve of the new world of cut-throat competition and devotion to money-making, he recorded it faithfully, though critically, in his novels, and even succumbed to the business spirit with ambitious, though unsuccessful, financial schemes.

Novels like his famous *Father Goriot*, the King Lear story of a vermicelli merchant who is abandoned by his socially ambitious daughters, and *Eugénie Grandet*, the tragedy of the daughter of a middle-class miser, are typical of Balzac's exhaustive exploration of the modern materialistic world. Two typical characters who appear in a number of his works are Vautrin, a criminal whose behavior and philosophy sum up the "dog-eat-dog" attitude of a money-minded age, and Rastignac, an ambitious young law student whose experiences in society convince him that one must be resourceful and hard if one is to survive. The short story *Gold*, included in this chapter, is a brief but dramatic representation of the driving force of greed that Balzac found in the soul of the nineteenth century.

Balzac was often an extravagant writer, a titan who did not always possess the gift of perfection and whose painstaking recording of reality was often personal and filled with his own comments. It remained for Gustave Flaubert (1821-1880) to perfect the realistic novel that Balzac and another, insufficiently read, master, Stendhal, had introduced. Flaubert, the son of a surgeon at Rouen, maintained a scientific detachment toward his characters and subject matter. Illness and a retiring disposition, aggravated by aversion to the materialistic age and by distress over the defeat of France in the Franco-Prussian War, also affected his writing. He became a perfectionist in his search for the precise shade of meaning, and an absolutely objective reporter of people's feelings and behavior. He followed this method regardless of his themes, so that his psychological fantasy *The Temptation of St. Antony* and his historical novel of Carthage, *Sa-*

lammbo, to which he devoted laborious research, are as meticulously set down as the treatment of his own times in *Madame Bovary*. Among his novels, these three are the most remarkable. The first is a study of the desires and repressions of an ascetic, set against a background of early Christianity. The second is a novel of lustful passion in an oriental world so wonderfully authenticated that each detail seems as real as a modern street scene. The third, *Madame Bovary* (1857), describes the tragedy of an unhappy, cheaply romantic wife of a provincial doctor; it is so relentlessly truthful that it is considered the masterpiece of modern realism.

Flaubert's long story *A Simple Heart* published in 1877 with two other superb stories, reveals all the attributes of his style and approach, including his ability to capture even the most inconspicuous details of an inconspicuous life. It is characteristic of realistic fiction, as exemplified in *A Simple Heart*, that it could treat commonplace characters and the lowest social levels with the same care that writers had hitherto bestowed only on the upper classes. This is also true of most contemporary writers of novels and stories, such as Sinclair Lewis, Theodore Dreiser, Ernest Hemingway, and William Faulkner.

Flaubert had many followers in France, but none so renowned as his protégé Guy de Maupassant (1850-1893), another native of Normandy and another tormented soul who finally went insane. The son of a Paris stock-broker, he became a clerk in the government service. Here he learned to understand the commonplace life of the "white-collar" worker that appears in a story like *The Diamond Necklace* which nearly everybody has read, as well as the higher political world of journalism and intrigue that he recorded in several novels. In addition, he knew the habits of the peasants in his native Normandy, and this gave him the material for some of his best short stories, among them his well-known *Piece of String* and his painful peasant sketch *The Christening*. Like Flaubert he also wrote a powerful novel about an ordinary woman's unhappiness, entitled *A Life*, and explored psychological aberrations in a number of stories, the most famous of which, *Le Horla*, is a gripping study of his approaching madness.

It was Flaubert who, taking Maupassant under his wing for seven years, introduced him to the literary world and guided him in his early writings. But Maupassant also fell under the influence of a general movement, an extension and intensification of realism known as *naturalism*. This appears in his frequent choice of unpleasant subjects and in his clinical manner of treating them without varnishing their sordidness.

The leader of the naturalistic movement was Émile Zola (1840-1902), the son of an Italian father and a French mother, who picked up an education informally while he acquainted himself with common realities by experience. He made his first connection with literature in a Parisian publishing house where he served as a clerk, and his first efforts at writing were newspaper articles of a political and critical nature. He threw himself completely into the struggle for a form of realism that would present life with the same painstaking documentation that he found in the natural sciences; hence his name for this style—"naturalism." His first novel, *Thérèse Raquin,* which he turned into a play and presented as an example of "naturalistic drama," was a sordid account of adultery, murder, and remorse among the lower classes. Then, resolving to study this life in terms of sociology and genetics, Zola wrote his Rougon-Macquart series of twenty novels about two families, which he aptly subtitled *A Physiological History of a Family under the Second Empire.* His main theme he described when he wrote in his essay *The Experimental Novel*: "We are, in a word, experimental moralists, showing by experiment in what way a passion acts in a certain social condition." His claims were extravagant and his writing was often crude and brutal. But in championing naturalism and exploring the lowest depths of society Zola extended the scope of the novel, and he taught novelists to pay close attention to social problems. It was as a socially conscious writer that Zola threw himself into the Dreyfus case and made justice prevail with his pen. The best known of Zola's novels is the lurid *Nana,* the story of a courtesan's career. The best of them are his novel of the Franco-Prussian War, *La Débâcle,* and *Germinal* (1889), his bleak picture of the lives of the miners.

Although Zola's example was not followed to any marked degree by important French novelists of the present century, they have all excelled in the realistic vein opened by Flaubert and Balzac. Nevertheless, other trends existed side by side with the dominant realistic one. Poets like Charles Baudelaire and Paul Verlaine and their so-called "symbolist" colleagues, to whom sufficient justice cannot be done in translation, developed an "art for art's sake" movement based on perfection of form and vague suggestiveness; and the Belgian dramatist Maurice Maeterlinck and Edmond Rostand, author of the famous *Cyrano de Bergerac,* wrote successful poetic and romantic plays. Finally, we must note that the spirit of refined skepticism continued to hover over French writers and expressed itself in many civilized and witty essays and narratives.

The strongest evidence of the enduring wit and skeptical wisdom of French literature appeared in the work of Anatole France (1884-1924), born Jacques Anatole Thibault. The extremely studious son of a bookseller, he became a remarkably erudite man. But he bore his learning lightly and gracefully like a true Frenchman, and extracted a wealth of humor from it. Nor did his scholarly interests prevent him from becoming politically embroiled as a street-corner speaker and publicist for the socialist movement, though in the last analysis he regarded the state in any form with skepticism. After publishing two books of poems, he turned to fiction, writing many stories and novels into which he poured his gentle cynicism with great charm and humor. Best known among his books are his novel about a delightful antiquarian, *The Crime of Sylvestre Bonnard*; his psychological story of an ascetic's downfall, *Thais*; his whimsical glorification of Satan as the eternal questioner and rebel, *Revolt of the Angels*; and his *Penguin Island.* He made the latter a particularly incisive travesty on the high spots of European history, satirizing superstition, government founded on property and the rights of the strongest, dictatorship, and militarism. It closes with a prediction of the collapse of civilization and an even more pessimistic inference that after the cataclysm man will begin making the same mistakes all over again. The same pessimism appeared in his powerful serious novel about the reign of terror in the French Revolution, *The Gods Are Athirst.*

His urbanity and sophistication, however, never forsook him. His shorter works exemplify the same spirit; his *Crainquebille* does this in a brilliant account of the growth of a legend, and his short story, *The Procurator of Judea,* in a skeptical comment on history. Its main point is that we often fail to understand the momentousness of events when we are too close to them, and that even Christ may have had no special significance to the man who condemned him to the cross. Anatole France was indeed the spiritual son of Montaigne and Voltaire, and our brief survey of all but recent French literature may appropriately end with him.

FRANÇOIS VILLON

The Little Testament

This year of fourteen fifty-six
I Francis Villon, man of letters,
With might and main, full speed, prefix
Advice to all in Fortune's fetters,
To take the judgment of your betters   5
About your work, the truth to know;
Vegece has made us all his debtors,
The sage of Rome, by saying so.

This winter, as was said before,
Near Christmas, season deathly old,   10
When wolves eat wind and nothing more,
And men are held indoors by cold
Where hearthstones glowing faggots hold,
The will I won to break a way
From Love's sweet gaol, whose walls enfold   15
My breaking heart this many a day.

This way I take to end my anguish,
For She is there, before my eyes,
Quite satisfied to see me languish,
No happier in any wise: 20
My sorrows and complainings rise
Demanding vengeance from above
From amorous gods of every guise
And cure for all my pangs of love.

As I believe, she showed me favor   25
With soft regrets and fine deceit
To lend duplicity more savor
And make my overthrow complete;
But as a horse of four white feet
What seemed so fair but brought displeasure:
I must replant this pleasaunce sweet   31
And go to dig for other treasure.

Full harsh and hard was her oppression;
For she who cast a spell on me,
Though I am guiltless of transgression,   35
Has doomed me die, and her decree
Is fixed that I shall cease to be.
I find no safety but in flight.
She means to break my life, I see,
Nor will take pity on my plight.   40

This danger to escape, I trow,
The best plan is to run away.
Adieu! I'm off to Angers now,
Since she ungraciously says nay,
Nor will a shred of ruth display.   45
Though free from bodily complaints,
I die Love's martyr, I might say,
Thus numbered with his band of saints.

Although departing brings despair,
Needs must, in truth, that I should fly,   50
As I conceive of the affair:
She loves another on the sly.
No kipper of Boulogne so dry
And tasteless as my wretched fate!
May God in mercy hear my cry: 55
For I am in a piteous state.

Well then, since go away I must,
And of return uncertain feel:
(Since I'm a being formed of dust,
No more than others brass or steel;   60
Unstable is all human weal
And death cannot be scared away:)
So setting out, I now reveal
My will, these presents, in this lay.

Then first, in His our Father dear,   65
The Son, and Holy Spirit's name,
Our Lady's too, whom we revere,
Whose grace keeps all of us from shame,
I leave, God helping me, my fame
To Guillaume Villon, foster sire,   70
My goods and chattels, and proclaim
The honor that those names inspire.

To her who harried me so hard
And banished, as you'll call to mind,
From every joy in life debarred,   75
All pleasure being left behind,
To her I leave my heart enshrined,
Pale, piteous, shriveled up and thin;
It perished by her deeds unkind,
May God forgive her this her sin!   80

The Little Testament. Translated by John Heron Lepper. By permission of the Liveright Publishing Corporation. François Villon (1431-c. 1484), born in Paris, somehow managed to acquire a good education. His own poems give us pictures of his life as thief and vagabond.

And Ythier Marchant shall get,
Joint heir with Master Cuckold John,
To both of whom I'm much in debt,
My trenchant sword of steel; undrawn,
Because, by chance, it lies in pawn   85
For some small trifle, which when paid,
I order that mine host anon
Shall hand them back the trusty blade.

Item, the White Horse tavern sign
To Saint Amant and Mule as well.   90
Blaru, that diamond of mine
And balking Ass with Brindled Fell.
The bull, whose opening letters spell
Omnis utriusque sexus,
That with the Carmelites played hell,   95
To parish priests for present use.

To Jehan Trouvé, the butcher chap,
A sheep that's young and fat be brought,
Thereto a feather whisk to flap
The flies that taint his ox unbought   100
Or cow; and when the villain's caught
Who lifts her by the neck to thieve her,
Let him receive a collar taut
And perish of a gallows fever.

To Master Robert Vallée now,   105
A clerk of Parliament, sans riches,
No hill or dale is his I trow.
He'll have a noble keepsake, which is
A special pair of under breeches,
That also lie in pawn, the stuff   110
To make a hood, with darns and stitches,
For Jehanneton, his bit of fluff.

Because he holds a decent post
He needs more pay, and might be led
Entirely by the Holy Ghost,   115
Because a trifle cracked, 'tis said;
The "Art of Memory" be read
To cure him, taken from Tom Fool;
For no more wisdom's in his head
Than lies within a wooden stool.   120

And furthermore, I will bestow
Said Robert's livelihood, and tell,
(No need to let your envy grow!)
You friends of mine, that you must sell
My hauberk, spend the money well,   125
Some house near St. Jacques' steeple seek,
Wherein this popinjay may dwell
And copy deeds all Easter Week.

To friend Jacques Cardon my bequest
Both absolute is and profuse: 130
To wit, my gloves and silken vest;
With willow acorns for his use,
And, every day, a fatted goose,
A capon bursting through its skin,
Ten tots of milk-white vineyard juice,   135
And lawsuits two, to keep him thin.

René de Montigny, three hounds,
As nobly born, I dedicate;
And Jehan Raguyer shall have three pounds
As charge upon my whole estate;   140
Yet stay! I can't anticipate
How rich I may become ere long:
To friends be too considerate
And rob my heirs, were surely wrong.

Item, I leave my lord of Grigny   145
Bicêtre in need of overhauling,
And six hounds more than to Montigny,
With Nygon tower that's near to falling;
And to that bastard caterwauling,
Mouton, who summonses his betters,   150
I fain would give a proper mauling
And place for slumber, bound in fetters.

To James Raguyer the Popin Fountain,
With chickens and blancmange and brill,
In short, of food a very mountain;   155
A rabbit cooked with choicest skill,
The Fir-Cone cellar at his will
To ope and shut, with feet to fire
And hooded gown to guard from chill;
And tarlets too, should he desire.   160

To Master Jehan Mautaint and Peter
Bassenier, for jointly sharing,
The Provost's favor, none is fleeter
To fine and punish without sparing;
To Proctor Fournier for his wearing   165
Light caps and shoes with toes embossed,
All of my cobbler's own preparing,
Meet fashion for this time of frost.

Item, the Captain of the Guard
Shall with the Helmet be bedight;   170
His men who keep their watch and ward
And stumble over stalls at night,
I leave to them the Lantern's light
And rubies two; they are requested
With their best dungeon to requite   175
The donor, if he be arrested.

To Perrenet Marchant I give,
The Bastard de la Barre renowned,
(No better dealer e'er did live)
Of straw three trusses, sweet and sound,   180
To spread as mattress on the ground
His amorous calling to pursue,
Whereby his living must be found,
The only trade he ever knew.

Then to the Wolf and Chollet falls   185
As legacy the ducklings which
Are snatched at dusk, beneath the walls,
As is their custom, from a ditch;
A mantle long and wide to hitch
About their prey, nor aught disclose,   190
Wood, charcoal, peas and gammon-flitch,
And my old waders lacking toes.

I leave, in pity of their cases,
To three young boys by Fate derided,
All mentioned in their proper places,   195
Three orphans wholly unprovided,
All barefoot, all three hollow-sided,
And wormlike naked altogether,
My order is that they be tided
At least o'er all this wintry weather.   200

Colin Laurens the first, the others
Girart Goussouyn and Jehan Marceau,
Devoid of goods and sires and mothers,
To each, who is not worth a row
Of pins, a slice of land shall go,   205
Or nimble fourpence paid in gold.
Good eating all these boys will know
In time to come, when I've grown old.

I here surrender and resign,
Two poor clerks from poverty to free,   210
Those high collegiate rights of mine,
The claim to be a nominee
Acquired on taking my degree;
Their names are here below included:
'Tis Charity that works in me   215
And Nature, seeing them denuded.

They're Guillaume Cotin, I declare,
And Thibault de Vitry, for each
Is Latin scholar, poor and bare,
Not quarrelsome, of peaceful speech,   220
And fit in any church to preach.
For Guillot Gueuldry's house-rent yet
Incontinent their hands shall reach,
While waiting something more to get.

St. Antoine's Cross that all may view,   225
The tavern sign that hangs so plain,
I leave them too, with billiard cue
And daily draughts from out the Seine:
To those poor pigeons laws constrain
In cages barred to spend their life,   230
My mirror bright without a stain,
And favors from the gaoler's wife.

Item, I leave the hospitals
My windows hung with cobweb-stuff;
To outcasts under butchers' stalls,   235
To each of them a hearty cuff,
To tremble at a visage gruff,
To go unshaven, starve and shiver,
Coat tattered, breeches scant enough,
Pinched, frozen, wet as any river.   240

My barber shall have this concession,
The shreds and clippings of my hair,
The whole in undisturbed possession;
My cobbler, shoes that need repair;
The ragman, clothes with many a tear;   245
And they shall have the residue
Of things that I have ceased to wear
For less than what they cost when new.

Item, I leave the begging friars
And nuns and tenders of the shrines,   250
All dainties that a man desires,
Flawns, capons and fat jellied chines;
Then let them preach the Fifteen Signs,
And keep on piling up the platter.
The Carmelites make concubines   255
Of our friends' wives, which doesn't matter.

Jehan de la Garde, who's spiced too much,
The Golden Mortar sign shall claim,
From St. Mor church a votive crutch
To crush his mustard in the same.   260
But he who plays the lawyers' game
And threatens to begin a suit,
Saint Anthony set him aflame!
That's my bequest to him, the brute!

To Merebeuf be handed down   265
And Nicolas de Louviers old,
An eggshell stuffed with many a crown
And franc, as full as it will hold.
While to the Gouvieulx porter bold,
Pierre Rousseville, without delay,   270
A larger sum of cash in gold,
Such crowns as princes give away.

At last, while sitting at my writing
Tonight, alone, in humor prime,
This lay composing and enditing,   275
I heard the Sorbonne belfry chime
At nine o'clock, its proper time,
The Angelus rang through the air;
And so an end was made, for I'm
Accustomed then to say a prayer.   280

Thereat, I fell into a doze,
But not from wine I swear to you,
My wits went wandering I suppose;
I saw Dame Memory review
Her shelves, collect in order due   285
Concurrent mental operations,
Opinions either false or true,
And other psychic ideations.

Thereto our estimative motions,
Whereby prosperity we gain,   290
Cognition and conceptive notions,
Whence, when disturbed, arises plain
A like disorder in the brain
And, monthly, men demented grow;
I read it, and the sense retain,   295
In Aristotle long ago.

My sensifacient system drove
The loom Imagination plied
Which divers paradoxes wove,
My sovereign part was quite defied,   300
Suspended, even might have died,
Forgetful of all moods and tenses,
While I in Schoolmen's jargon tried
To prove th' alliance of the senses.

Since now my senses were at rest   305
And I had found the matter out,
I thought to finish my bequest;
My ink was frozen round about,
The wind had blown my candle out,
There was no fire to light it at,   310
So wrapped up in my mantle stout
I fell asleep, and that was that.

By Francis Villon, name renowned,
On date aforesaid made and writ,
No figs or dates with him abound.   315
Of all his chattels not one whit,
Though black as scrubbing-brush with grit,
But for some special friend is meant;

Some coppers make his only bit
Of cash, and they will soon be spent.   320

The Ballad of Dead Ladies

Tell me now in what hidden way is
    Lady Flora the lovely Roman?
Where's Hipparchia, and where is Thais,
    Neither of them the fairer woman?
    Where is Echo, beheld of no man,   5
Only heard on river and mere,—
    She whose beauty was more than human? . . .
But where are the snows of yester-year?

Where's Héloise, the learned nun,
    For whose sake Abeillard, I ween,   10
Lost manhood and put priesthood on?
    (From Love he won such dule and teen!)
    And where, I pray you. is the Queen
Who willed that Buridan should steer
    Sewed in a sack's mouth down the Seine? . . .
But where are the snows of yester-year?   16

White Queen Blanche, like a queen of lilies,
    With a voice like any mermaiden,—
Bertha Broadfoot, Beatrice, Alice,
    And Ermengarde the lady of Maine,—   20
    And that good Joan whom Englishmen
At Rouen doomed and burned her there,—
    Mother of God, where are they then? . . .
But where are the snows of yester-year?

Nay, never ask this week, fair lord,   25
    Where they are gone, nor yet this year,
Save with this much for an overword,—
    But where are the snows of yester-year?

To Death of His Lady

Death, of thee do I make my moan,
    Who hadst my lady away from me,
    Nor wilt assuage thine enmity
Till with her life thou hast mine own;
For since that hour my strength has flown. 5
    Lo! what wrong was her life to thee,
                        Death?

Two we were, and the heart was one;
    Which now being dead, dead I must be,
    Or seem alive as lifelessly
As in the choir the painted stone,
                        Death!   10

The Ballad of Dead Ladies. Translated by D. G. Rossetti.
To Death of His Lady. Translated by D. G. Rossetti.

Fragment on Death

And Paris be it or Helen dying,
  Who dies soever, dies with pain.
He that lacks breath and wind for sighing,
  His gall bursts on his heart; and then
  He sweats, God knows what sweat! again,   5
No man may ease him of his grief;
  Child, brother, sister, none were fain
To bail him thence for his relief.

Death makes him shudder, swoon, wax pale,
  Nose bend, veins stretch, and breath surrender,
Neck swell, flesh soften, joints that fail   11
  Crack their strained nerves and arteries slender.
  O woman's body found so tender,
Smooth, sweet, so precious in men's eyes,
  Must thou too bear such count to render   15
Yes; or pass quick into the skies.

Ballad of the Women of Paris

Albeit the Venice girls get praise
  For their sweet speech and tender air,
And though the old women have wise ways
  Of chaffering for amorous ware,
  Yet at my peril dare I swear,   5
Search Rome, where God's grace mainly tarries,
  Florence and Savoy, everywhere,
There's no good girl's lip out of Paris.

The Naples women, as folk prattle,
  Are sweetly spoken and subtle enough: 10
German girls are good at tattle,
  And Prussians make their boast thereof;
  Take Egypt for the next remove,
Or that waste land the Tartar harries,
  Spain or Greece, for the matter of love,   15
There's no good girl's lip out of Paris.

Breton and Swiss know nought of the matter,
  Gascony girls or girls of Toulouse;
Two fishwomen with a half-hour's chatter
  Would shut them up by threes and twos;   20
  Calais, Lorraine, and all their crews,
(Names enow the mad song marries)
  England and Picardy, search them and choose,
There's no good girl's lip out of Paris.

Prince, give praise to our French ladies   25
  For the sweet sound their speaking carries;

'Twixt Rome and Cadiz many a maid is,
  But no good girl's lip out of Paris.

Epistle in Form of a Ballad to His Friends

Have pity, pity, friends, have pity on me,
  Thus much at least, may it please you, of your
    grace!
I lie not under hazel or hawthorn-tree
  Down in this dungeon ditch, mine exile's place
  By leave of God and fortune's foul disgrace.   5
Girls, lovers, glad young folk and newly wed,
Jumpers and jugglers, tumbling heel o'er head,
  Swift as a dart, and sharp as needle-ware,
Throats clear as bells that ring the kine to shed,
  Your poor old friend, what, will you leave him
    there?   10

Singers that sing at pleasure, lawlessly,
  Light, laughing, gay of word and deed, that race
And run like folk light-witted as ye be
  And have in hand nor current coin nor base,
  Ye wait too long, for now he's dying apace.   15
Rhymers of lays and roundels sung and read,
Ye'll brew him broth too late when he lies dead.
  Nor wind nor lightning, sunbeam nor fresh air,
May pierce the thick wall's bound where lies his
    bed;
  Your poor old friend, what, will you leave him
    there?   20

O noble folk from tithes and taxes free,
  Come and behold him in this piteous case,
Ye that nor king nor emperor holds in fee,
  But only God in heaven; behold his face
  Who needs must fast, Sundays and holidays,   25
Which makes his teeth like rakes; and when he
    hath fed
With never a cake for banquet but dry bread,
  Must drench his bowels with much cold watery
    fare,
With board nor stool, but low on earth instead;
  Your poor old friend, what, will you leave him
    there?   30

Princes afore-named, old and young foresaid,
Get me the king's seal and my pardon sped,
  And hoist me in some basket up with care:
So swine will help each other ill bested,   34
For where one squeaks they run in heaps ahead.
  Your poor old friend, what, will you leave him
    there?

Fragment on Death. Translated by Swinburne.
Ballad of the Women of Paris. Translated by Swinburne.
Epistle in Form of a Ballad. Translated by Swinburne.

The Epitaph in Form of a Ballad

WHICH VILLON MADE FOR HIMSELF AND HIS COMRADES,
EXPECTING TO BE HANGED ALONG WITH THEM

Men, brother men, that after us yet live,
  Let not your hearts too hard against us be;
For if some pity of us poor men ye give,
  The sooner God shall take of you pity.
  Here are we five or six strung up, you see,   5
And here the flesh that all too well we fed
Bit by bit eaten and rotten, rent and shred,
  And we the bones grow dust and ash withal;
Let no man laugh at us discomforted,
  But pray to God that he forgive us all.   10

If we call on you, brothers, to forgive,
  Ye should not hold our prayer in scorn, though
   we
Were slain by law; ye know that all alive
  Have not wit alway to walk righteously;
  Make therefore intercession heartily   15
With him that of a virgin's womb was bred,

That his grace be not as a dry well-head
  For us, nor let hell's thunder on us fall!
We are dead, let no man harry or vex us dead,
  But pray to God that he forgive us all.   20

The rain has washed and laundered us all five,
  And the sun dried and blackened; yea, perdie,
Ravens and pies with beaks that rend and rive
  Have dug our eyes out, and plucked off for fee
  Our beards and eyebrows; never we are free,   25
Not once, to rest; but here and there still sped,
Drive at its wild will by the wind's change led,
  More pecked of birds than fruits on garden-
   wall;
Men, for God's love, let no gibe here be said,
  But pray to God that he forgive us all.   30

Prince Jesus, that of all art lord and head,
Keep us, that hell be not our bitter bed;
  We have nought to do in such a master's hall.
Be not ye therefore of our fellowhead,
  But pray to God that he forgive us all.   35

PIERRE DE RONSARD

Fragment of a Sonnet

Nature withheld Cassandra in the skies
For more adornment, a full thousand years;
She took their cream of Beauty, fairest dies,
And shaped and tinted her above all peers: 4
Meanwhile Love kept her dearly with his wings,
  And underneath their shadow fill'd her eyes
With such a richness that the cloudy Kings
  Of high Olympus utter'd slavish sighs.
When from the Heavens I saw her first descend,
  My heart took fire, and only burning pains—   10
They were my pleasures—they my Life's sad end
Love pour'd her beauty into my warm veins.

To Helen

When you are very old, at evening
You'll sit and spin beside the fire, and say,
Humming my songs, "Ah well, ah well-a-day!

When I was young, of me did Ronsard sing."
None of your maidens that doth hear the thing,   5
Albeit with her weary task foredone,
But wakens at my name, and calls you one
Blessed, to be held in long remembering.
I shall be low beneath the earth, and laid
On sleep, a phantom in the myrtle shade,   10
While you beside the fire, a grandame gray,
My love, your pride, remember and regret;
Ah, love me, love! we may be happy yet,
And gather roses, while 'tis called today.

To His Young Mistress

Fair flower of fifteen springs, that still
  Art scarcely blossomed from the bud,
Yet hast such store of evil will,
  A heart so full of hardihood,
  Seeking to hide in friendly wise   4
  The mischief of your mocking eyes.

Epitaph in Form of a Ballad. Translated by Swinburne.
  Fragment of a Sonnet, translated by John Keats. Pierre de Ronsard (1524-1585) passed his youth at
the French and Scotch courts, but at the age of eighteen became deaf. He spent the rest of his life in
study of the classics and in trying to make French a great literary language.
  To Helen. Translated by Andrew Lang.
  To His Young Mistress. Translated by Andrew Lang.

If you have pity, child, give o'er;
　Give back the heart you stole from me,
Pirate, setting so little store
　On this your captive from Love's sea,　　　10
　　Holding his misery for gain,
　　And making pleasure of his pain.

Another, not so fair of face,
　But far more pitiful than you,
Would take my heart, if of his grace,　　　15

My heart would give her of Love's due;
　And she shall have it, since I find
　That you are cruel and unkind.

Nay, I would rather that it died,
　Within your white hands prisoning,　　　20
Would rather that it still abide
In your ungentle comforting
　Than change its faith, and seek to her
　That is more kind, but not so fair.

FRANÇOIS RABELAIS

Gargantua

[War Between Gargantua and Picrochole]

The cake-bakers, being returned to Lerné, went presently, before they did either eat or drink, to the Capitol, and there before their king, called Picrochole, the third of that name, made their complaint, showing their panniers broken, their caps all crumpled, their coats torn, their cakes taken away, but, above all, Marquet most enormously wounded, saying that all that mischief was done [10] by the shepherds and herdsmen of Grangousier, near the broad highway beyond Seville. Picrochole incontinent grew angry and furious; and, without asking[1] any further what, how, why, or wherefore, commanded the ban and arriere ban to be sounded throughout all his country, that all his vassals of what condition soever should, upon pain of the halter, come, in the best arms they could, unto the great place before the castle, at the hour of noon, and, the better to strengthen his design, he caused [20] the drum to be beat about the town. Himself, whilst his dinner was making ready, went to see his artillery mounted upon the carriage, to display his colors, and set up the great royal standard, and loaded wains with store of ammunition both for the field and the belly, arms and victuals. At dinner he despatched his commissions, and by his express edict my Lord Shagrag was appointed to command the vanguard, wherein were numbered sixteen thousand and fourteen arquebusiers or firelocks, [30] together with thirty thousand and eleven volunteer adventurers. The great Touquedillon, master of the horse, had the charge of the ordnance, wherein were reckoned nine hundred and fourteen brazen pieces, in cannons, double cannons, basilisks, serpentines, culverins, bombards or murderers, falcons, bases or passevolins, spirols, and other sorts of great guns. The rearguard was committed to the Duke of Scrapegood. In the main battle was the king and the princes of his kingdom. Thus being hastily furnished, before they would set forward, they sent three hundred light horsemen, under the conduct of Captain Swillwind, to discover the country, clear the avenues, and see whether there was any ambush laid for them. But, after they had made diligent search, they found all the land round about in peace and quiet, without any meeting or convention at all; which Picrochole understanding, commanded that everyone should march speedily under his colors. Then immediately in all disorder, without keeping either rank or file, they took the fields one amongst another, wasting, spoiling, destroying, and making havoc of all wherever they went, not sparing poor nor rich, privileged or unprivileged places, church nor laity, drove away oxen and cows, bulls, calves, heifers, wethers, ewes, lambs, goats, kids, hens, capons, chickens, geese, ganders, goslings, hogs, swine, pigs, and such like; beating down the walnuts, plucking the grapes, tearing the hedges, shaking the fruit-trees, and committing such incomparable abuses, that the like abomination was never heard of. Nevertheless, they met with none to resist them, for everyone submitted to their mercy, beseeching

Rabelais (1490?-1553). *Gargantua* and *Pantagruel*, translated by Urquhart and Motteux.
[1] The shepherds of Gargantua, having been provoked by the cake-bakers of Lerné, struck back in self-defense.

them that they might be dealt with courteously in regard that they had always carried themselves as became good and loving neighbors, and that they had never been guilty of any wrong or outrage done upon them, to be thus suddenly surprised, troubled, and disquieted, and that, if they would not desist, God would punish them very shortly. To which expostulations and remonstrances no other answer was made, but that they would teach them to eat cakes.

Grangousier's Unwillingness and Aversion from the Undertaking of War

. . . But let us leave them there, and return to our good Gargantua, who is at Paris very assiduous and earnest at the study of good letters and athletical exercitations, and to the good old man Grangousier his father, who after supper warmeth [himself] by a good, clear, great fire, and, waiting upon the broiling of some chestnuts, is very serious in drawing scratches on the hearth, with a stick burnt at the one end, wherewith they did stir up the fire, telling to his wife and the rest of the family pleasant old stories and tales of former times.

Whilst he was thus employed one of the shepherds which did keep the vines, named Pillot, came towards him, and to the full related the enormous abuses which were committed, and the excessive spoil that was made by Picrochole, King of Lerné, upon his lands and territories, and how he had pillaged, wasted, and ransacked all the country, except the enclosure at Seville, which Friar John des Entoumeures to his great honor had preserved; and that at the same present time the said king was in the rock Clermond, and there, with great industry and circumspection, was strengthening himself and his whole army. "Halas, halas, alas!" said Grangousier, "what is this, good people? Do I dream, or is it true that they tell me? Picrochole, my ancient friend of old time, of my kindred and alliance, comes he to invade me? What moves him? What provokes him? What sets him on? What drives him to it? Who hath given him this counsel? Ho, ho, ho, ho, ho, my God, my Saviour, help me, inspire me, and advise me what I shall do! I protest, I swear before thee, so be thou favorable to me, if ever I did him or his subjects any damage or displeasure, or committed any the least robbery in his country; but, on the contrary, I have succored and supplied him with men, money, friendship, and counsel, upon any occasion wherein I could be serviceable for the improvement of his good. That he hath therefore at this nick of time so outraged and wronged me, it cannot be but the malevolent and wicked spirit. Good God, thou knowest my courage, for nothing can be hidden from thee. If perhaps he be grown mad, and that thou hast sent him hither to me for the better recovery and re-establishment of his brain, grant me power and wisdom to bring him to the yoke of thy holy will by good discipline. Ho, ho, ho, ho, my good people, my friends and my faithful servants, must I hinder you from helping me? Alas, my old age required henceforward nothing else but rest, and all the days of my life I have labored for nothing so much as peace; but now I must, I see it well, load with arms my poor weary, and feeble shoulders, and take in my trembling hands the lance and horseman's mace, to succor and protect my honest subjects. Reason will have it so; for by their labor am I entertained, and with their sweat am I nourished, I, my children and my family. This notwithstanding, I will not undertake war, until I have first tried all the ways and means of peace; that I resolve upon."

Then assembled he his council, and proposed the matter as it was indeed. Whereupon it was concluded that they should send some discreet man unto Picrochole to know wherefore he had thus suddenly broken the peace and invaded those lands unto which he had no right or title. Furthermore, that they should send for Gargantua, and those under his command, for the preservation of the country, and defence thereof now at need. |In the ensuing struggle Gargantua's army, aided by the monk, thoroughly defeat Picrochole.]

Gargantua's Speech to the Vanquished

Our forefathers and ancestors of all times have been of this nature and disposition, that, upon the winning of a battle, they have chosen rather, for a sign and memorial of their triumphs and victories, to erect trophies and monuments in the hearts of the vanquished by clemency than by architecture in the lands which they had conquered. For they did hold in greater estimation the lively remembrance of men purchased by liberality than the dumb inscription of arches, pillars and pyramids, subject to the injury of storms and tempests, and the envy of everyone. You may very well remember of the courtesy which by them was used towards the Bretons in the battle of St. Aubin of Cormier and the demolishing of Partenay. You have heard, and hearing admire, their gentle comportment towards those at the barriers [the barbarians] of Spaniola, who had plundered, wasted and ransacked the maritime borders of Olone and Thalmondois. All this hemisphere of the world was filled with the praises and congratulations which yourselves and your fathers made, when Alpharbal, King of Canarre, not satisfied with his own fortunes, did most furiously invade the land of Onyx, and with cruel piracies molest all the Armoric Islands and confine regions of Brittany. Yet was he in a set naval fight justly taken and vanquished by my father, whom God preserve and protect. But what? Whereas other kings and emperors, yea, those who entitle themselves Catholics, would have dealt roughly with him, kept him a close prisoner, and put him to an extreme high ransom, he entreated him very courteously, lodged him kindly with himself in his own palace, and out of his incredible mildness and gentle disposition sent him back with a safe conduct, laden with gifts, laden with favors, laden with all offices of friendship. What fell out upon it? Being returned into his country, he called a parliament, where all the princes and states of his kingdom being assembled, he showed them the humanity which he had found in us, and therefore wished them to take such course by way of compensation therein as that the whole world might be edified by the example, as well of their honest graciousness to us as of our gracious honesty towards them. The result hereof was, that it was voted and decreed by an unanimous consent, that they should offer up entirely their land, dominions and kingdoms, to be disposed of by us according to our pleasure.

Alpharbal in his own person presently returned with nine thousand and thirty-eight great ships of burden, bringing with him the treasures, not only of his house and royal lineage, but almost of all the country besides. For he embarking himself, to set sail with a west-northeast wind, everyone in heaps did cast into the ship gold, silver, rings, jewels, spices, drugs, and aromatical perfumes, parrots, pelicans, monkeys, civet cats, black-spotted weasels, porcupines, &c. He was accounted no good mother's son that did not cast in all the rare and precious things he had.

Being safely arrived, he came to my said father, and would have kissed his feet. That action was found too submissively low, and therefore was not permitted, but in exchange he was most cordially embraced. He offered his presents; they were not received, because they were too excessive: he yielded himself voluntarily a servant and vassal, and was content his whole posterity should be liable to the same bondage; this was not accepted of, because it seemed not equitable: he surrendered, by virtue of the decree of his great parliamentary council, his whole countries and kingdoms to him, offering the deed and conveyance, signed, sealed and ratified by all those that were concerned in it; this was altogether refused, and the parchments cast into the fire. In end, this free goodwill and simple meaning of the Canarians wrought such tenderness in my father's heart, that he could not abstain from shedding tears, and wept most profusely; then, by choice, words very congruously adapted, strove in what he could to diminish the estimation of the good offices which he had done them, saying, that any courtesy he had conferred upon them was not worth a rush, and what favor soever he had showed them he was bound to do it. But so much the more did Alpharbal augment the repute thereof. What was the issue? Whereas for his ransom, in the greatest extremity of rigor and most tyrannical dealing, could not have been exacted above twenty times a hundred thousand crowns, and his eldest sons detained as hostages till that sum had been paid, they made themselves perpetual tributaries, and obliged to give us every year two millions of gold at four and twenty carats fine. The first year we received the whole sum of two millions; the second year of their own accord they paid freely to us three and twenty hundred thousand crowns; the third year six and twenty hundred thousand; the fourth year, three millions, and do so increase it always out of their own goodwill that we shall be constrained to forbid them to bring us any more. This is the nature of gratitude and true thankfulness. For time, which gnaws and diminisheth all things else, augments and increaseth benefits; because a noble action of liberality, done to a man of reason, doth grow continually by his generous thinking of it and remembering it.

Being unwilling, therefore any way to degenerate from the hereditary mildness and clemency of my parents, I do now forgive you, deliver you from all fines and imprisonments, fully release you, set you at liberty, and every way make you as frank and free as ever you were before. Moreover, at your going out of the gate, you shall have every one of you three months' pay to bring you home into your houses and families, and shall have a safe convoy of six hundred cuirassiers and eight thousand foot under the conduct of Alexander, esquire of my body, that the clubmen of the country may not do you any injury. God be with you. I am sorry from my heart that Picrochole is not here; for I would have given him to understand that this war was undertaken against my will and without any hope to increase either my goods or my renown. But seeing he is lost, and that no man can tell where nor how he went away, it is my will that his kingdom remain entire to his son; who, because he is too young, he not being yet full five years old, shall be brought up and instructed by the ancient princes and learned men of the kingdom. And because a realm thus desolate may easily come to ruin, if the covetousness and avarice of those who by their places are obliged to administer justice in it be not curbed and restrained, I ordain and will have it so, that Ponocrates be overseer and superintendent above all his governors, with whatever power and authority is requisite thereto, and that he be continually with the child until he find him able and capable to rule and govern by himself.

Now I must tell you, that you are to understand how a too feeble and dissolute facility in pardoning evildoers giveth them occasion to commit wickedness afterwards more readily, upon this pernicious confidence of receiving favor. I consider that Moses, the meekest man that was in his time upon the earth, did severely punish the mutinous and seditious people of Israel. I consider likewise that Julius Cæsar, who was so gracious an emperor that Cicero said of him that his fortune had nothing more excellent than that he could, and his virtue nothing better than that he would always save and pardon every man, he, notwithstanding all this, did in certain places most rigorously punish the authors of rebellion. After the example of these good men, it is my will and pleasure that you deliver over unto me before you depart hence, first, that fine fellow Marquet, who was the prime cause, origin, and groundwork of this war by his vain presumption and overweening; secondly, his fellow cake-bakers, who were neglective in checking and reprehending his idle hare-brained humor in the instant time; and lastly all the counsellors, captains, officers, and domestics of Picrochole, who had been incendiaries or fomenters of the war by provoking, praising, or counselling him to come out of his limits thus to trouble us.

How Gargantua Caused to Be Built for the Monk the Abbey of Theleme

There was left only the monk to provide for, whom Gargantua would have made abbot of Seville, but he refused it. He would have given him the abbey of Bourgueil, or of Sanct Florent, which was better, or both if it pleased him. But the monk gave him a very peremptory answer, that he would never take upon him the charge nor government of monks. . . . "If you think I have done you, or may hereafter do you any acceptable service, give me leave to found an abbey after my own mind and fancy." The motion pleased Gargantua very well, who thereupon offered him all the country of Theleme by the river of Loire, till within two leagues of the great forest of Porthuaut. The monk then requested Gargantua to institute his religious order contrary to all others. "First then," said Gargantua, "you must not build a wall about your convent, for all other abbeys are strongly walled and mured about." "See," said the monk, "and without cause, where there is mur before, and mur behind, there is store of murmur, envy, and mutual conspiracy."

Moreover, seeing there are certain convents in the world, whereof the custom is, if any woman come (I mean chaste and honest women) they immediately sweep the ground which they have trod upon. Therefore was it ordained, that if any man or woman, entered into religious orders, should by chance come within this new abbey, all the rooms should be thoroughly washed and cleansed, through which they had passed. And because in all other monasteries and nunneries all is compassed, limited, and regulated by hours, it was decreed, that in this new structure there should be neither clock nor dial, but that, according to the opportunities and incident occasions, all their hours should be disposed of. "For," said Gargantua, "the greatest loss of time that I know, is, to count the hours. What good comes of it? Nor can there be any greater dotage in the world, than for one to guide and direct his courses by the sound of a bell, and not by his own judgment and discretion."

Item, because at that time they put no women into nunneries but such as were either purblind, blinkards, lame, crooked, ill-favored, mis-shapen, fools, senseless, spoiled, or corrupt; nor encloistered any men, but those that were either sickly, subject to defluxions, ill-bred louts, simple sots, or peevish trouble-houses. "But to the purpose," said the monk: "a woman that is neither fair nor good, to what use serves she?" "To make a nun of," said Gargantua. "Yea," said the monk, "and to make shirts and smocks." Therefore was it ordained, that into this religious order should be admitted no women that were not fair, well featured, and of a sweet disposition; nor men that were not comely, personable, and well-conditioned.

Item, because in the convents of women, men

come not but underhand, privily, and by stealth; it was therefore enacted, that in this house there shall be no women in case there be not men, nor men in case there be not women.

Item, because both men and women that are received into religious orders, after the expiring of their novitiat, or probation year, were constrained and forced perpetually to stay there all the days of their life; it was therefore ordered, that all whatever, men or women, admitted within this abbey, should have full leave to depart with peace and contentment, whensoever it should seem good to them to do so.

Item, for that the religious men and women did ordinarily make three vows, to wit, those of chastity, poverty, and obedience; it was therefore constituted and appointed, that in this convent they might be honorably married, that they might be rich, and live at liberty. In regard of the legitimate time of the persons to be initiated, and years under and above which they were not capable of reception, the women were to be admitted from ten till fifteen, and the men from twelve to eighteen.

How the Abbey of the Thelemites Was Built and Endowed

For the fabric and furniture of the abbey Gargantua caused to be delivered out, in ready money, seven and twenty hundred thousand eight hundred and one, and thirty of those golden rams of Berrie, which have a sheep stamped on the one side, and a flowered cross on the other. And for every year, until the whole work were completed, he allotted three score and nine thousand crowns of the sun, and as many of the seven stars, to be charged all upon the receipt of the custom. For the foundation and maintenance thereof forever, he settled a perpetual fee-farm-rent of three and twenty hundred, threescore and nine thousand, five hundred and fourteen rose-nobles, exempt from all homage, fealty, service, or burden whatsoever, and payable every year at the gate of the abbey; and of this, by letters patent, passed a very good grant. The architecture was in a figure hexagonal, and in such a fashion that every one of the six corners there was built a great round tower of threescore feet in diameter; and were all of a like form and bigness. Upon the north side ran along the river of Loire, on the bank whereof was situated the tower called Arctic. Going towards the east, there was another called Calare; the next

following, Anatole; the next, Mesembrine; the next, Hesperia, and the last, Criere. Every tower was distant from the other the space of three hundred and twelve paces. The whole edifice was everywhere six stories high, reckoning the cellars underground for one. The second was arched after the fashion of a basket-handle. The rest was ceiled with pure wainscot, flourished with Flanders fretwork, in the form of the foot of a lamp; and covered above with fine slates, with an indorsement of lead, carrying the antique figures of little puppets, and animals of all sorts, notably well suited to one another, and gilt, together with the gutters, which jetting without the walls, from betwixt the cross bars in a diagonal figure, painted with gold and azure, reached to the very ground, where they ended into great conduit pipes, which carried all away unto the river from under the house.

This same building was a hundred times more sumptuous and magnificent than ever was Bonnivet, Chambourg, or Chantilly. For there were in it nine thousand, three hundred, and two and thirty chambers; every one whereof had a withdrawing room, a handsome closet, a wardrobe, an oratory, and neat passage, leading into a great and spacious hall. Between every tower, in the midst of the said body of building, there was a pair of winding stairs, whereof the steps were part of porphyry, part of Numidian stone, and part of serpentine marble; each of those steps being two and twenty feet in length, and three fingers thick, and the just number of twelve betwixt every rest or landing-place. In every resting-place were two fair antique arches, where the light came in; and by those they went into a cabinet (closet), made even with, and of the breadth of the said winding, and the re-ascending above the roofs of the house ending conically in a pavilion. By that vize, or winding, they entered on every side into a great hall, and from the halls into the chambers. From the Arctic tower unto the Criere, were the fair great libraries in Greek, Latin, Hebrew, French, Italian, and Spanish, respectively distributed in their several cantons, according to the diversity of these languages. In the midst there was a wonderful winding stair, the entry whereof was without the house, in a vault or arch, six fathoms broad. It was made in such symmetry and largeness that six men-at-arms, with their lances in their rests, might together in a breast ride all up to the very top of all the palace. From the tower Anatole to the Mesembrine were spacious galleries, all colored over and painted with the ancient prowesses, histories, and descriptions of the world. In the midst thereof there was likewise such another ascent and gate, as we said there was on the river side. Upon that gate was written, in great antique letters, that which followeth.

How the Thelemites Were Governed, and of Their Manner of Living

All their life was spent not in laws, statutes, or rules, but according to their own free will and pleasure. They rose out of their beds when they thought good; they did eat, drink, labor, sleep when they had a mind to it, and were disposed for it. None did awake them, none did offer to constrain them to eat, drink, nor do any other thing; for so had Gargantua established it. In all their rule and strictest tie of their order, there was but this one clause to be observed:

DO WHAT THOU WILT

Because men that are free, well-bred, and conversant in honest companies, have naturally an instinct and spur that prompteth them unto virtuous actions, and withdraws them from vice, which is called honor. Those same men, when by base subjection and constraint they are brought under and kept down, turn aside from that noble disposition, by which they formerly were inclined to virtue, to shake off that bond of servitude, wherein they are so tyrannously inslaved; for it is agreeable to the nature of man to long after things forbidden, and to desire what is denied us. By this liberty they entered into a very laudable emulation, to do all of them what they saw did please one.

If any of the gallants or ladies should say, "Let us drink," they would all drink. If any one of them said, "Let us play," they all played. If one said, "Let us go a-walking into the fields," they went all. If it were to go a-hawking, or a-hunting, the ladies mounted upon dainty well-paced nags, seated in a stately palfrey saddle, carried on their lovely fists miniardly begloved every one of them, either a sparhawk, or a laneret, or a marlin, and the young gallants carried the other kinds of hawks. So nobly were they taught, that there was neither he nor she amongst them, but could read, write, sing, play upon several musical instruments, speak five or six several languages, and compose in them all very quaintly, both in verse and prose. Never were seen so valiant knights, so noble and worthy, so dexterous and skillful both on foot and horseback, more brisk and lively, more nimble and quick, or better handling all manner of weapons, than were there. Never were seen ladies so proper and handsome, so miniard and dainty, less froward, or more ready with their hand, and with their needle, in every honest and free action belonging to that sex, than were there. For this reason, when the time came that any man of the said abbey, either at the request of his parents, or for some other cause, had a mind to go out of it, he carried along with him one of the ladies, namely, her, whom he had before that chosen for his mistress, and they were married together. And if they had formerly in Theleme lived in good devotion and amity, they did continue therein, and increase it to a greater height in their state of matrimony; and did entertain that mutual love till the very last day of their life, in no less vigor and fervency than at the very day of their wedding.

Pantagruel

[Gargantua has a son Pantagruel, who surpasses his father. In the following letter the giant gives the son advice concerning his education.]

How Pantagruel, Being at Paris, Received Letters from His Father Gargantua, and the Copy of Them

Pantagruel studied very hard, as you may well conceive, and profited accordingly; for he had an excellent understanding, and notable wit, together with a capacity in memory, equal to the measure of twelve oil budgets, or butts of olives. And, as he was there abiding one day, he received a letter from his father in manner as followeth:

Most dear Son,—Amongst the gifts, graces, and prerogatives with which the sovereign plasmator God Almighty hath endowed and adorned human nature at the beginning, that seems to me most singular and excellent, by which we may in a moral estate attain to a kind of immortality, and in the course of this transitory life perpetuate our name and seed, which is done by a progeny issued from us in the lawful bonds of matrimony. Whereby that in some measure is restored unto us, which was taken from us by the sin of our first parents, to whom it was said, that, because they had not obeyed the commandment of God their Creator, they should die; and by death should be brought to nought that so stately frame and plasmature, wherein the man at first had been created.

But by this means of seminal propagation, there continueth in the children what was lost in the parents; and in the grand-children that which perished in their fathers, and so successively until the day of the last judgment, when Jesus Christ shall have rendered up to God the Father his kingdom in a peaceable condition, out of all danger and contamination of sin; for then shall cease all generations and corruptions, and the elements leave off their continual transmutations, seeing the so much desired peace shall be attained unto and enjoyed, and that all things shall be brought to their end and period. And, therefore, not without just and reasonable cause do I give thanks to God my Savior and Preserver, for that he hath enabled me to see my bald old age reflourish in thy youth; for when, at his good pleasure, who rules and governs all things, my soul shall leave this mortal habitation, I shall not account myself wholly to die, but to pass from one place unto another, considering that, in and by thee, I continue in my visible image living in the world, visiting and conversing with people of honor, and other my good friends, as I was wont to do. Which conversation of mine, although it was not without sin, (because we are all of us trespassers, and therefore ought continually to beseech his divine majesty to blot our transgressions out of his memory,) yet was it by the help and grace of God, without all manner of reproach before men.

Wherefore, if those qualities of the mind but shine in thee, wherewith I am endowed, as in thee remaineth the perfect image of my body, thou wilt be esteemed by all men to be the perfect guardian and treasure of the immortality of our name. But, if otherwise, I shall truly take but small pleasure to see it, considering that the lesser part of me, which is the body, would abide in thee, and the best, to wit, that which is the soul, and by which our name continues blessed amongst men, would be degenerate and abastardized. This I do not speak out of any distrust that I have of thy virtue, which I have heretofore already tried, but to encourage thee yet more earnestly to proceed from good to better. And that which I now write unto thee is not so much that thou shouldst live in this virtuous course, as that thou shouldst rejoice in so living and having lived, and cheer up thyself with the like resolution in time to come; to the prosecution and accomplishment of which enterprise and generous undertaking thou mayest easily remember how that I have spared nothing, but have so helped thee as if I had no other treasure in this world, but to see thee once in my life completely well bred and accomplished, as well in virtue, honesty, and valor, as in all liberal knowledge and civility, and so to leave thee after my death as a mirror representing the person of me thy father, and if not so excellent, and such indeed as I do wish thee, yet such is my desire.

But although my deceased father of happy memory, Grandgousier, had bent his best endeavors to make me profit in all perfection and political knowledge, and that my labor and study was fully correspondent to, yea, went beyond his desire, nevertheless, as thou mayest well understand, the time then was not so proper and fit for learning as it is at present, neither had I plenty of such good masters as thou hast had. For that time was darksome, obscured with clouds of ignorance, and savoring a little of the infelicity and calamity of the Goths, who had, wherever they set footing, destroyed all good literature, which in my age hath by the divine goodness been restored unto its former light and dignity, and that with such amendment and increase of knowledge, that now hardly should I be admitted unto the first form of the little grammar-school boys. I say, I, who in my youthful days was, and that justly, reputed the most learned of that age. Which I do not speak in vain boasting, although I might lawfully do it in writing unto thee,—in verification whereof thou hast the authority of Marcus Tullius in his book of old age, and the sentence of Plutarch, in the book intituled, How a man may praise himself without envy:—but to give thee an emulous encouragement to strive yet further.

Now it is, that the minds of men are qualified with all manner of discipline and the old sciences revived, which for many ages were extinct. Now it is, that the learned languages are to their pristine purity restored, viz., Greek, without which a man may be ashamed to account himself a scholar, Hebrew, Arabic, Chaldæan, and Latin. Printing likewise is now in use, so elegant and so correct, that better cannot be imagined, although it was found out but in my time by divine inspiration, as by a diabolical suggestion on the other side, was the invention of ordnance. All the world is full of knowing men, of most learned schoolmasters, and vast libraries; and it appears to me as a truth, that neither in Plato's time, nor Cicero's, nor Papinian's, there was ever such conveniency for studying, as we see at this day there is. Nor must any adventure henceforward to come in public or present himself in company, that hath not been pretty well polished in the shop of Minerva. I see robbers, hangmen, free-booters, tapsters, ostlers, and such like, of the very rubbish of the people, more learned now than the doctors and preachers were in my time.

What shall I say? The very women and children have aspired to this praise and celestial manna of good learning. Yet so it is, that at the age I am now of, I have been constrained to learn the Greek tongue,—which I contemned not like Cato, but had not the leisure in my younger years to attend the study of it,—and I take much delight in the reading of Plutarch's Morals, the pleasant Dialogues of Plato, the Monuments of Pausanias, and the Antiquities of Athenæus, in waiting on the hour wherein God my Creator shall call me, and command me to depart from this earth and transitory pilgrimage. Wherefore, my son, I admonish thee to employ thy youth to profit as well as thou canst, both in thy studies and in virtue. Thou art at Paris, where the laudable examples of many brave men may stir up thy mind to gallant actions, and hast likewise, for thy tutor and pedagogue the learned Epistemon, who by his lively and vocal documents may instruct thee in the arts and sciences.

I intend, and will have it so, that thou learn the languages perfectly; first of all, the Greek, as Quintilian will have it; secondly, the Latin; and then the Hebrew, for the Holy Scripture-sake; and then the Chaldee and Arabic likewise, and that thou frame thy style in Greek in imitation of Plato; and for the Latin, after Cicero. Let there be no history which thou shalt not have ready in thy memory;—unto the prosecuting of which design, books of cosmography will be very conducible, and help thee much. Of the liberal arts of geometry, arithmetic, and music, I gave thee some taste when thou wert yet little, and not above five or six years old. Proceed further in them, and learn the remainder if thou canst. As for astronomy, study all the rules thereof. Let pass, nevertheless, the divining and judicial astrology, and the art of Lullius, as being nothing else but plain abuses and vanities. As for the civil law, of that I would have thee to know the texts by heart, and then to confer them with philosophy.

Now, in matter of the knowledge of the works of nature, I would have thee to study that exactly; that so there be no sea, river, nor fountain, of which thou dost not know the fishes; all the fowls of the air; all the several kinds of shrubs and trees, whether in forest or orchards; all the sort of herbs and flowers that grow upon the ground; all the various metals that are hid within the bowels of the earth; together with all the diversity of precious stones, that are to be seen, in the orient and south parts of the world. Let nothing of all these be hidden from thee. Then fail not most carefully to peruse the books of the Greek, Arabian, and Latin physicians, not despising the Talmudists and Cabalists; and by frequent anatomies get thee the perfect knowledge of that other world, called the microcosm, which is man. And at some of the hours of the day apply thy mind to the study of the Holy Scriptures; first, in Greek, the New Testament, with the Epistles of the Apostles; and then the Old Testament in Hebrew. In brief, let me see thee an abyss, and bottomless pit of knowledge: for from henceforward, as thou growest great and becomest a man, thou must part from this tranquillity and rest of study, thou must learn chivalry, warfare, and the exercises of the field, the better thereby to defend my house and our friends, and to succor and protect them at all their needs, against the invasion and assaults of evil doers.

Furthermore, I will that very shortly thou try how much thou hast profited, which thou canst not better do, than by maintaining publicly theses and conclusions in all arts, against all persons whatsoever, and by haunting the company of learned men, both at Paris and otherwhere. But because, as the wise man Solomon saith, Wisdom entereth not into a malicious mind, and that knowledge without conscience is but the ruin of the soul; it behoveth thee to serve, to love, to fear God, and on him to cast all thy thoughts and all thy hope, and, by faith formed in charity, to cleave unto him, so that thou mayst never be separated from him by thy sins. Suspect the abuses of the world. Set not thy heart upon vanity, for this life is transitory, but the Word of the Lord endureth for ever. Be serviceable to all thy neighbors, and love them as thyself. Reverence thy preceptors: shun the conversation of those whom thou desirest not to resemble; and receive not in vain the graces which God hath bestowed upon thee. And, when thou shalt see that thou hast attained to all the knowledge that is to be acquired in that part, return unto me, that I may see thee, and give thee my blessing before I die. My son, the peace and grace of our Lord be with thee, Amen.

Thy father, Gargantua.

From Utopia the 17th day of the month of March.

These letters being received and read, Pantagruel plucked up his heart, took a fresh courage to him, and was inflamed with a desire to profit in his studies more than ever, so that if you had seen him, how he took pains, and how he advanced in learning, you would have said that the vivacity of his spirit amidst the books was like a great fire amongst dry wood, so active it was, vigorous, and 10 indefatigable.

MICHEL DE MONTAIGNE

Essays

Of the Education of Children

To Madame Diane de Foix, Comtesse de Gurson
. . . A friend of mine, then, having read the preceding chapter, the other day told me, that I should a little farther have extended my discourse on the education of children. Now, madame, if I had any sufficiency in this subject, I could not possibly better employ it, than to present my best instructions to the little gentleman that threatens you shortly with a happy birth (for you are too generous to begin otherwise than with a male); for having had so great a hand in the treaty of your marriage, I have a certain particular right and interest in the greatness and prosperity of the issue that shall spring from it; besides that, your having had the best of my services so long in possession, sufficiently obliges me to desire the honor and advantage of all wherein you shall be concerned. But, in truth, all I understand as to that particular is only this, that the greatest and most important difficulty of human science is the education of children. . . .

For a boy of quality then, who pretends to letters not upon the account of profit (for so mean an object as that is unworthy of the grace and favor of the Muses, and moreover, in it a man directs his service to and depends upon others), nor so much for outward ornament, as for his own proper and peculiar use, and to fur-

nish and enrich himself within, having rather a desire to come out an accomplished cavalier than a mere scholar or learned man; for such a one, I say, I would, also, have his friends solicitous to find him out a tutor, who has rather a well-made than a well-filled head; seeking, indeed, both the one and the other, but rather of the two to prefer manners and judgment to mere learning, and that this man should exercise his charge after a 10 new method.

'Tis the custom of pedagogues to be eternally thundering in their pupils' ears, as they were pouring into a funnel, while the business of the pupil is only to repeat what the others have said: now I would have a tutor to correct this error, and, that at the very first, he should, according to the capacity he has to deal with, put it to the test, permitting his pupil himself to taste things, and of himself to discern and choose them, some- 20 times opening the way to him, and sometimes leaving him to open it for himself; that is, I would not have him alone to invent and speak, but that he should also hear his pupil speak in turn. Socrates, and since him Arcesilaus, made first their scholars speak, and then they spoke to them. It is good to make him, like a young horse, trot before him that he may judge of his going and how much he is to abate of his own speed, to accommodate himself to the vigor and capacity 30 of the other. For want of which due proportion we spoil all; which also to know how to adjust,

Montaigne, *Essays*. Translated by Charles Cotton. Michel Eyquem de Montaigne (1533-1592), aristo-crat and magistrate, lived the life of a country gentleman and scholar in his château near Bordeaux.

and to keep within an exact and due measure, is one of the hardest things I know, and 'tis the effect of a high and well-tempered soul to know how to condescend to such puerile motions and to govern and direct them. I walk firmer and more secure up hill than down.

Such as, according to our common way of teaching, undertake, with one and the same lesson, and the same measure of direction, to instruct several boys of differing and unequal capacities, are infinitely mistaken; and 'tis no wonder, if in a whole multitude of scholars, there are not found above two or three who bring away any good account of their time and discipline. Let the master not only examine him about the grammatical construction of the bare words of his lesson, but about the sense and substance of them, and let him judge of the profit he has made, not by the testimony of his memory, but by that of his life. Let him make him put what he has learned into a hundred several forms, and accommodate it to so many several subjects, to see if he yet rightly comprehends it, and has made it his own, taking instruction of his progress by the pedagogic institutions of Plato. 'Tis a sign of crudity and indigestion to disgorge what we eat in the same condition it was swallowed; the stomach has not performed its office unless it has altered the form and condition of what was committed to it to concoct. Our minds work only upon trust, when bound and compelled to follow the appetite of another's fancy, and slaved and captivated under the authority of another's instruction; we have been so subjected to the trammel, that we have no free, nor natural pace of our own; our own vigor and liberty are extinct and gone. . . .

Let him make him examine and thoroughly sift everything he reads, and lodge nothing in his fancy upon simple authority and upon trust. Aristotle's principles will then be no more principles to him, than those of Epicurus and the Stoics: let this diversity of opinions be propounded to, and laid before him; he will himself choose, if he be able; if not, he will remain in doubt. For, if he embrace the opinions of Xenophon and Plato, by his own reason, they will no more be theirs, but become his own. Who follows another, follows nothing, finds nothing, nay, is inquisitive after nothing.

Let him at least, know that he knows. It will be necessary that he imbibe their knowledge, not that he be corrupted with their precepts; and no matter if he forgot where he had his learning,

provided he know how to apply it to his own use. Truth and reason are common to every one, and are no more his who spake them first, than his who speaks them after: 'tis no more according to Plato, than according to me, since both he and I equally see and understand them. Bees cull their several sweets from this flower and that blossom, here and there where they find them, but themselves afterward make the honey, which is all and purely their own, and no more thyme and marjoram: so the several fragments he borrows from others, he will transform and shuffle together to compile a work that shall be absolutely his own; that is to say, his judgment: his instruction, labor and study, tend to nothing else but to form that. He is not obliged to discover whence he got the materials that have assisted him, but only to produce what he has himself done with them. Men that live upon pillage and borrowing, expose their purchases and buildings to every one's view: but do not proclaim how they came by the money. We do not see the fees and perquisites of a gentleman of the long robe; but we see the alliances wherewith he fortifies himself and his family, and the titles and honors he has obtained for him and his. No man divulges his revenue; or at least, which way it comes in: but every one publishes his acquisitions. The advantages of our study are to become better and more wise. 'Tis, says Epicharmus,[1] the understanding that sees and hears, 'tis the understanding that improves everything, that orders everything, and that acts, rules, and reigns: all other faculties are blind, and deaf, and without soul. And certainly we render it timorous and servile, in not allowing it the liberty and privilege to do anything of itself. Whoever asked his pupil what he thought of grammar or rhetoric, and of such and such a sentence of Cicero? Our masters stick them, full feathered, in our memories, and there establish them like oracles, of which the letters and syllables are of the substance of the thing. To know by rote, is no knowledge, and signifies no more but only to retain what one has intrusted to our memory. That which a man rightly knows and understands, he is the free disposer of at his own full liberty, without any regard to the author from whence he had it or fumbling over the leaves of his book. A mere bookish learning is a poor, paltry learning; it may serve for ornament, but there is yet no foundation for any superstructure to be built upon it, according to the opinion of Plato, who says that

[1] Greek comic poet (c. 540-450 B.C.).

constancy, faith, and sincerity, are the true philosophy, and the other sciences, that are directed to other ends, mere adulterate paint. I could wish that Paluel or Pompey, those two noted dancers of my time, could have taught us to cut capers, by only seeing them do it, without stirring from our places, as these men pretend to inform the understanding, without ever setting it to work; or that we could learn to ride, handle a pike, touch a lute, or sing, without the trouble of practice, as these attempt to make us judge and speak well, without exercising us in judging or speaking. Now in this initiation of our studies and in their progress, whatsoever presents itself before us is book sufficient; a roguish trick of a page, a sottish mistake of a servant, a jest at the table, are so many new subjects.

And for this reason, conversation with men is of very great use, and travel into foreign countries; not to bring back (as most of our young monsieurs do) an account only of how many paces Santa Rotonda[1] is in circuit; or of the richness of Signora Livia's petticoats; or, as some others, how much Nero's face, in a statue in such an old ruin, is longer and broader than that made for him on some medal; but to be able chiefly to give an account of the humors, manners, customs and laws of those nations where he has been, and that we may whet and sharpen our wits by rubbing them against those of others. I would that a boy should be sent abroad very young, and first, so as to kill two birds with one stone, into those neighboring nations whose language is most differing from our own, and to which, if it be not formed betimes, the tongue will grow too stiff to bend.

And also 'tis the general opinion of all, that a child should not be brought up in his mother's lap. Mothers are too tender, and their natural affection is apt to make the most discreet of them all so overfond, that they can neither find in their hearts to give them due correction for the faults they commit, nor suffer them to be inured to hardships and hazards, as they ought to be. They will not endure to see them return all dust and sweat from their exercise, to drink cold drink when they are hot, nor see them mount an unruly horse, nor take a foil in hand against a rude fencer, or so much as to discharge a carbine. And yet there is no remedy; whoever will breed a boy to be good for anything when he comes to be a man, must by no means spare him when young, and must very often transgress the rules of physic. It

is not enough to fortify his soul; you are also to make his sinews strong; for the soul will be oppressed if not assisted by the members, and would have too hard a task to discharge two offices alone. I know very well, to my cost, how much mine groans under the burden, from being accommodated with a body so tender and indisposed, as eternally leans and presses upon her; and often in my reading perceive that our masters, in their writings, make examples pass for magnanimity and fortitude of mind, which really are rather toughness of skin and hardness of bones; for I have seen men, women, and children, naturally born of so hard and insensible a constitution of body, that a sound cudgeling has been less to them than a flirt with a finger would have been to me, and that would neither cry out, wince, nor shrink, for a good swinging beating; and when wrestlers counterfeit the philosophers in patience, 'tis rather strength of nerves than stoutness of heart. Now to be inured to undergo labor, is to be accustomed to endure pain. A boy is to be broken into the toil and roughness of exercise, so as to be trained up to the pain and suffering of dislocations, cholics, cauteries, and even imprisonment and the rack itself; for he may come, by misfortune, to be reduced to the worst of these, which (as this world goes) is sometimes inflicted on the good as well as the bad.

And, moreover, by living at home, the authority of this governor which ought to be sovereign over the boy he has received into his charge, is often checked and hindered by the presence of parents; to which may also be added, that the respect the whole family pay him, as their master's son, and the knowledge he has of the estate and greatness he is heir to, are, in my opinion, no small inconveniences in these tender years.

And yet, even in this conversing with men I spoke of but now, I have observed this vice, that instead of gathering observations from others, we make it our whole business to lay ourselves upon them, and are more concerned how to expose and set out our own commodities, than how to increase our stock by acquiring new. Silence, therefore, and modesty are very advantageous qualities in conversation. One should, therefore, train up this boy to be sparing and a husband of his knowledge when he has acquired it; and to forbear taking exceptions at or reproving every idle saying or ridiculous story that is said or told in his presence; for it is a very unbecoming rudeness to carp at everything that is not agreeable to our own palate.

[1] The Pantheon of Agrippa.

Let him be satisfied with correcting himself, and not seem to condemn everything in another he would not do himself, nor dispute it as against common customs. Let him avoid these vain and uncivil images of authority, this childish ambition of coveting to appear better bred and more accomplished, than he really will, by such carriage, discover himself to be. And, as if opportunities of interrupting and reprehending were not to be omitted, to desire thence to derive the reputation of something more than ordinary. For as it becomes none but great poets to make use of the poetical license, so it is intolerable for any but men of great and illustrious souls to assume privilege above the authority of custom. Let him be instructed not to engage in discourse or dispute but with a champion worthy of him, and, even there, not to make use of all the little subtleties that may seem pat for his purpose, but only such arguments as may best serve him. Let him be taught to be curious in the election and choice of his reasons, to abominate impertinence, and, consequently, to affect brevity; but, above all, let him be lessoned to acquiesce and submit to truth so soon as ever he shall discover it, whether in his opponent's argument, or upon better consideration of his own; for he shall never be preferred to the chair for a mere clatter of words and syllogisms, and is no further engaged to any argument whatever, than as he shall in his own judgment approve it: nor yet is arguing a trade, where the liberty of recantation and getting off upon better thoughts, are to be sold for ready money.

If his governor be of my humor, he will form his will to be a very good and loyal subject to his prince, very affectionate to his person, and very stout in his quarrel; but withal he will cool in him the desire of having any other tie to his service than public duty. Besides several other inconveniences that are inconsistent with the liberty every honest man ought to have, a man's judgment, being bribed and prepossessed by these particular obligations, is either blinded and less free to exercise its function, or is blemished with ingratitude and indiscretion. A man that is purely a courtier, can neither have power nor will to speak or think otherwise than favorably and well of a master, who, among so many millions of other subjects, has picked out him with his own hand to nourish and advance; this favor, and the profit flowing from it, must needs, and not without some show of reason, corrupt his freedom and dazzle him; and we commonly see these people speak in another kind of phrase than is ordinarily spoken by others of the same nation, though what they say in that courtly language is not much to be believed.

Let his conscience and virtue be eminently manifest in his speaking, and have only reason for their guide. Make him understand, that to acknowledge the error he shall discover in his own argument, though only found out by himself, is an effect of judgment and sincerity, which are the principal things he is to seek after; that obstinacy and contention are common qualities, most appearing in mean souls; that to revise and correct himself, to forsake an unjust argument in the height and heat of dispute, are rare, great, and philosophical qualities. Let him be advised; being in company, to have his eye and ear in every corner, for I find that the places of greatest honor are commonly seized upon by men that have least in them, and that the greatest fortunes are seldom accompanied with the ablest parts. I have been present when, while they at the upper end of the chamber have only been commending the beauty of the arras, or the flavor of the wine, many things that have been very finely said at the lower end of the table have been lost or thrown away. Let him examine every man's talent; a peasant, a bricklayer, a passenger: one may learn something from every one of these in their several capacities, and something will be picked out of their discourse whereof some use may be made at one time or another; nay, even the folly and impertinence of others will contribute to his instruction. By observing the graces and manners of all he sees, he will create to himself an emulation of the good, and a contempt of the bad.

Let an honest curiosity be suggested to his fancy of being inquisitive after everything; whatever there is singular and rare near the place where he is, let him go and see it; a fine house, a noble fountain, an eminent man, the place where a battle has been anciently fought, the passages of Cæsar and Charlemagne.

Let him inquire into the manners, revenues and alliances of princes, things in themselves very pleasant to learn, and very useful to know.

In this conversing with men, I mean also, and principally, those who only live in the records of history; he shall, by reading those books, converse with the great and heroic souls of the best ages. 'Tis an idle and vain study to those who make it by so doing it after a negligent manner, but to those who do it with care and observation, 'tis a study of inestimable fruit and value; and the only study, as Plato reports, that the Lacedæmonians reserved to themselves. What profit shall he not reap as to the business of men, by reading the lives of Plutarch? But, withal, let my governor remember to what end his instructions are principally directed, and that he do not so much imprint in his pupil's memory the date of the ruin of Carthage, as the manners of Hannibal and Scipio; nor so much where Marcellus died, as why it was unworthy of his duty that he died there. Let him not teach him so much the narrative parts of history as to judge them; the reading of them, in my opinion, is a thing that of all others we apply ourselves unto with the most differing measure. I have read a hundred things in Livy that another has not, or not taken notice of at least; and Plutarch has read a hundred more there than ever I could find, or than, peradventure, that author ever wrote; to some it is merely a grammar study, to others the very anatomy of philosophy, by which the most abstruse parts of our human nature penetrate. There are in Plutarch many long discourses very worthy to be carefully read and observed, for he is, in my opinion, of all others the greatest master in that kind of writing; but there are a thousand others which he has only touched and glanced upon, where he only points with his finger to direct us which way we may go if we will, and contents himself sometimes with giving only one brisk hit in the nicest article of the question, whence we are to grope out the rest. As, for example, where he says that the inhabitants of Asia came to be vassals to one only, for not having been able to pronounce one syllable, which is No. Which saying of his gave perhaps matter and occasion to La Boetie [1530-1563] to write his "Voluntary Servitude." Only to see him pick out a light action in a man's life, or a mere word that does not seem to amount even to that, is itself a whole discourse. 'Tis to our prejudice that men of understanding should so immoderately affect brevity; no doubt their reputation is the better by it, but in the meantime we are the worse. Plutarch had rather we should applaud his judgment than commend his knowledge, and had rather leave us with an appetite to read more, than glutted with that we have already read. He knew very well, that a man may say too much even upon the best subjects, and that Alexandridas justly reproached him who made very good but too long speeches to the Ephori, when he said: "Oh stranger! thou speakest the things thou shouldst speak, but not as thou shouldst speak them." Such as have lean and spare bodies stuff themselves out with clothes; so they who are defective in matter, endeavor to make amends with words.

Human understanding is marvelously enlightened by daily conversation with men, for we are, otherwise, compressed and heaped up in ourselves, and have our sight limited to the length of our own noses. One asking Socrates of what country he was, he did not make answer, of Athens, but of the world. He whose imagination was fuller and wider, embraced the whole world for his country, and extended his society and friendship to all mankind; not as we do, who look no further than our feet. When the vines of my village are nipped with the frost, my parish priest presently concludes, that the indignation of God is gone out against all the human race, and that the cannibals have already got the pip. Who is it, that seeing the havoc of these civil wars of ours, does not cry out, that the machine of the world is near dissolution, and that the day of judgment is at hand; without considering, that many worse things have been seen, and that, in the meantime, people are very merry in a thousand other parts of the earth for all this? For my part, considering the license and impunity that always attend such commotions, I wonder they are so moderate, and that there is no more mischief done. To him who feels the hailstones patter about his ears, the whole hemisphere appears to be in storm and tempest . . . And, in truth, we are all of us, insensibly, in this error, an error of a very great weight and very pernicious consequence. But whoever shall represent to his fancy, as in a picture, that great image of our mother Nature, in her full majesty and lustre, whoever in her face shall read so general and so constant a variety, whoever shall observe himself in that figure, and not himself but a whole kingdom, no bigger than the least touch or prick of a pencil in comparison of the whole, that man alone is able to value things according to their true estimate and grandeur.

This great world which some do yet multiply as several species under one genus, is the mirror wherein we are to behold ourselves, to be able to know ourselves as we ought to do in the true bias. In short, I would have this to be the book my young gentleman should study with the most attention. So many humors, so many sects, so many judgments, opinions, laws and customs, teach us to judge aright of our own, and inform our understanding to discover its imperfection and natural infirmity, which is no trivial speculation. So many mutations of states and kingdoms, and so many turns and revolutions of public fortune, will make us wise enough to make no great wonder of our own. So many great names, so many famous victories and conquests drowned and swallowed in oblivion, render our hopes ridiculous of eternizing our names. . . . The pride and arrogance of so many foreign pomps and ceremonies, the tumorous majesty of so many courts and grandeurs, accustom and fortify our sight without astonishment or winking to behold the lustre of our own; so many millions of men, buried before us, encourage us not to fear to go seek such good company in the other world: and so of all the rest. Pythagoras[1] was wont to say, that our life resembles the great and populous assembly of the Olympic games, wherein some exercise the body, that they may carry away the glory of the prize; others bring merchandise to sell for profit; there are, also, some (and those none of the worst sort) who pursue no other advantage than only to look on, and consider how and why everything is done, and to be spectators of the lives of other men, thereby the better to judge of and regulate their own.

To examples may fitly be applied all the profitable discourses of philosophy, to which all human actions, as to their best rule, ought to be especially directed: a scholar shall be taught to know what it is to know, and what to be ignorant; what ought to be the end and design of study; what valor, temperance and justice are; the difference between ambition and avarice, servitude and subjection, license and liberty; by what token a man may know true and solid contentment; how far death, affliction, and disgrace are to be apprehended, by what secret springs we move, and the reason of our various agitations and irresolutions: for, methinks, the first doctrine with which one should season his understanding, ought to be that which regulates his manners and his sense; that teaches him to know himself, and how both well to die and well to live. Among the liberal sciences, let us begin with that which makes us free; not that they do not all serve in some measure to the instruction and use of life, as all other things in some sort also do; but let us make choice of that which directly and professedly serves to that end. If we are once able to restrain the offices of human life within their just and natural limits, we shall find that most of the sciences in use are of no great use to us, and even in those that are, that there are many very unnecessary cavities and dilatations which we had better let alone, and following

Socrates' direction, limit the course of our studies to those things only where is a true and real utility.

'Tis a great foolery to teach our children the knowledge of the stars and the motion of the eighth sphere, before their own.

Anaximenes[2] writing to Pythagoras, "To what purpose," said he, "should I trouble myself in searching out the secrets of the stars, having death or slavery continually before my eyes?" for the kings of Persia were at that time preparing to invade his country. Every one ought to say thus, "Being assaulted, as I am by ambition, avarice, temerity, superstition, and having within so many other enemies of life, shall I go cudgel my brains about the world's revolutions?"

After having taught him what will make him more wise and good, you may then entertain him with the elements of logic, physics, geometry, rhetoric, and the science which he shall then himself most incline to, his judgment being beforehand formed and fit to choose, he will quickly make his own. The way of instructing him ought to be sometimes by discourse, and sometimes by reading, sometimes his governor shall put the author himself, which he shall think most proper for him, into his hands, and sometimes only the marrow and substance of it; and if himself be not conversant enough in books to turn to all the fine discourses the books contain for his purpose, there may some man of learning be joined to him, that upon every occasion shall supply him with what he stands in need of, to furnish it to his pupil. . . .

The soul that lodges philosophy, ought to be of such a constitution of health, as to render the body in like manner healthful too; she ought to make her tranquillity and satisfaction shine so as to appear without, and her contentment ought to fashion the outward behavior to her own mold, and consequently to fortify it with a graceful confidence, an active and joyous carriage, and a serene and contented countenance. The most manifest sign of wisdom is a continual cheerfulness; her state is like that of things in the regions above the moon, always clear and serene. . . . It is she that calms and appeases the storms and tempests of the soul, and who teaches famine and fevers to laugh and sing; and that, not by certain imaginary epicycles, but by natural and manifest reasons. She has virtue for her end; which is not, as the schoolmen say, situate upon the summit of a perpendicular, rugged, inaccessible precipice: such as have approached her find her, quite on the contrary, to

[1] Greek philosopher (582 B.C.-507?).   [2] Greek philosopher (fl. 6th century B.C.)

be seated in a fair, fruitful, and flourishing plain, from whence she easily discovers all things below; to which place any one may, however, arrive, if he know but the way, through shady, green, and sweetly flourishing avenues, by a pleasant, easy, and smooth descent, like that of the celestial vault.

Such a tutor will make a pupil digest this new lesson, that the height and value of true virtue consists in the facility, utility, and pleasure of its exercise; so far from difficulty, that boys, as well as men, and the innocent as well as the subtle, may make it their own: it is by order, and not by force, that it is to be acquired. Socrates, her first minion, is so averse to all manner of violence, as totally to throw it aside, to slip into the more natural facility of her own progress: 'tis the nursing mother of all human pleasures, who in rendering them just, renders them also pure and permanent; in moderating them, keeps them in breath and appetite; in interdicting those which she herself refuses, whets our desire to those that she allows; and, like a kind and liberal mother, abundantly allows all that nature requires, even to satiety, if not to lassitude: unless we mean to say, that the regimen which stops the toper before he has drunk himself drunk, the glutton before he has eaten to a surfeit, and the lecher before he has got the pox, is an enemy to pleasure. If the ordinary fortune fail, she does without it, and forms another, wholly her own, not so fickle and unsteady as the other. She can be rich, be potent and wise, and knows how to lie upon soft perfumed beds: she loves life, beauty, glory, and health; but her proper and peculiar office is to know how to regulate the use of all these good things, and how to lose them without concern: an office much more noble than troublesome, and without which the whole course of life is unnatural, turbulent, and deformed, and there it is indeed, that men may justly represent those monsters upon rocks and precipices.

If this pupil shall happen to be of so contrary a disposition, that he had rather hear a tale of a tub than the true narrative of some noble expedition or some wise and learned discourse; who at the beat of drum, that excites the youthful ardor of his companions, leaves that to follow another that calls to a morris or the bears; who would not wish, and find it more delightful and more excellent, to return all dust and sweat victorious from a battle, than from tennis or from a ball, with the prize of those exercises; I see no other remedy, but that he be bound prentice in some good town to learn to make minced pies, though he were the son of a duke; according to Plato's precept, that children are to be placed out and disposed of, not according to the wealth, qualities, or condition of the father, but according to the faculties and the capacity of their own souls.

Since philosophy is that which instructs us to live and that infancy has there its lessons as well as other ages, why is it not communicated to children betimes?

They begin to teach us to live when we have almost done living. A hundred students have got the pox before they have to come to read Aristotle's lecture on temperance. Cicero said, that though he should live two men's ages, he should never find leisure to study the lyric poets; and I find these sophisters yet more deplorably unprofitable. The boy we would breed has a great deal less time to spare; he owes but the first fifteen or sixteen years of his life to education; the remainder is due to action. Let us, therefore, employ that short time in necessary instruction. Away with the thorny subtleties of dialectics; they are abuses, things by which our lives can never be amended: take the plain philosophical discourses, learn how rightly to choose, and then rightly to apply them; they are more easy to be understood than one of Boccaccio's novels; a child from nurse is much more capable of them, than of learning to read or to write. Philosophy has discourses proper for childhood, as well as for the decrepit age of men.

I am of Plutarch's mind, that Aristotle did not so much trouble his great disciple with the knack of forming syllogisms, or with the elements of geometry, as with infusing into him good precepts concerning valor, prowess, magnanimity, temperance, and the contempt of fear; and with this ammunition, sent him, while yet a boy, with no more than thirty thousand foot, four thousand horse, and but forty-two thousand crowns, to subjugate the empire of the whole earth. For the other arts and sciences, he says, Alexander highly indeed commended their excellence and charm, and had them in very great honor and esteem, but not ravished with them to that degree, as to be tempted to affect the practice of them in his own person.

Epicurus, in the beginning of his letter to Meniceus, says, "That neither the youngest should refuse to philosophize, nor the oldest grow weary of it." Who does otherwise, seems tacitly to imply, that either the time of living happily is not yet come, or that it is already past. And yet, for all that, I would not have this pupil of ours imprisoned and made a slave to his book: nor would

I have him give up to the morosity and melancholic humor of a sour, ill-natured pedant; I would not have his spirit cowed and subdued, by applying him to the rack, and tormenting him, as some do, fourteen or fifteen hours a day, and so make a pack-horse of him. Neither should I think it good, when, by reason of a solitary and melancholic complexion, he is discovered to be overmuch addicted to his book, to nourish that humor in him; for that renders him unfit for civil conversation, and diverts him from better employments. And how many have I seen in my time totally brutified by an immoderate thirst after knowledge? [One such] was so besotted with it, that he would not find time as so much as to comb his head or to pare his nails. . . .

But to our little monsieur, a closet, a garden, the table, his bed, solitude and company, morning and evening, all hours shall be the same, and all places to him a study; for philosophy, who, as the formatrix of judgment and manners, shall be his principal lesson, has that privilege to have a hand in everything. The orator Isocrates, being at a feast entreated to speak of his art, all the company were satisfied with and commended his answer: "It is not now a time," said he, "to do what I can do; and that which it is now time to do, I cannot do." For to make orations and rhetorical disputes in a company met together to laugh and make good cheer, had been very unseasonable and improper, and as much might have been said of all the other sciences. But as to what concerns philosophy, that part of it at least that treats of man, and of his offices and duties, it has been the common opinion of all wise men, that, out of respect to the sweetness of her conversation, she is ever to be admitted in all sports and entertainments. And Plato, having invited her to his feast, we see after how gentle and obliging a manner, accommodated both to time and place, she entertained the company, though in a discourse of the highest and most important nature. By this method of instruction, my young pupil will be much more and better employed than his fellows of the college are. But as the steps we take in walking to and fro in a gallery, though three times as many, do not tire a man so much as those we employ in a formal journey, so our lesson, as it were accidentally occurring, without any set obligation of time or place, and falling naturally into every action, will insensibly insinuate itself. By which means our very exercises and recreations, running, wrestling, music, dancing, hunting, riding, and fencing, will prove

to be a good part of our study. I would have his outward fashion and mien, and the disposition of his limbs, formed at the same time with his mind. 'Tis not a soul, 'tis not a body that we are training up, but a man, and we ought not to divide him. And, as Plato says, we are not to fashion one without the other, but make them draw together like two horses harnessed to a coach. By which saying of his, does he not seem to allow more time for, and to take more care of, exercises for the body, and to hold that the mind, in a good proportion, does her business at the same time too?

As to the rest, this method of education ought to be carried on with a severe sweetness, quite contrary to the practice of our pedants, who, instead of tempting and alluring children to letters by apt and gentle ways, do in truth present nothing before them but rods and ferules, horror and cruelty. Away with this violence! away with this compulsion! than which, I certainly believe nothing more dulls and degenerates a well-descended nature. If you would have him apprehend shame and chastisement, do not harden him to them: inure him to heat and cold, to wind and sun, and to dangers that he ought to despise; wean him from all effeminacy and delicacy in clothes and lodging, eating and drinking; accustom him to everything, that he may not be a Sir Paris, a carpet-knight, but a sinewy, hardy, and vigorous young man. I have ever from a child to the age wherein I now am, been of this opinion, and am still constant to it. But among other things, the strict government of most of our colleges has evermore displeased me; peradventure, they might have erred less perniciously on the indulgent side. 'Tis a real house of correction of imprisoned youth. They are made debauched, by being punished before they are so. Do but come in when they are about their lesson, and you shall hear nothing but the outcries of boys under execution, with the thundering noise of their pedagogues drunk with fury. A very pretty way this, to tempt these tender and timorous souls to love their book, with a furious countenance, and a rod in hand! A cursed and pernicious way of proceeding! Besides what Quintilian[1] has very well observed, that this imperious authority is often attended by very dangerous consequences, and particularly our way of chastising. How much more decent would it be to see their classes strewed with green leaves and fine flowers, than with the bloody stumps of birch and willows? Were it left to my ordering, I should paint the school with the pictures of joy and gladness. . . . Where their

[1] Roman rhetorician (?35-100).

profit is, let them there have their pleasure too. Such viands as are proper and wholesome for children, should be sweetened with sugar, and such as are dangerous to them, embittered with gall. 'Tis marvelous to see how solicitous Plato is in his Laws concerning the gayety and diversion of the youth of his city, and how much and often he enlarges upon their races, sports, songs, leaps, and dances: of which, he says, that antiquity has given the ordering and patronage particularly to the gods themselves, to Apollo, Minerva, and the Muses. He insists long upon, and is very particular in giving innumerable precepts for exercises; but as to the lettered sciences, says very little, and only seems particularly to recommend poetry upon the account of music.

All singularity in our manners and conditions is to be avoided as inconsistent with civil society. Who would not be astonished at so strange a constitution as that of Demophoon, steward to Alexander the Great, who sweated in the shade, and shivered in the sun? I have seen those who have run from the smell of a mellow apple with greater precipitation than from a harquebus shot, others afraid of a mouse; others vomit at the sight of cream; others ready to swoon at the making of a feather bed; Germanicus[1] could neither endure the sight nor the crowing of a cock. I will not deny, but that there may, peradventure, be some occult cause and natural aversion in these cases; but, in my opinion, a man might conquer it, if he took it in time. Precept has in this wrought so effectually upon me, though not without some pains on my part, I confess, that beer excepted, my appetite accommodates itself indifferently to all sorts of diet.

Young bodies are supple; one should, therefore, in that age bend and ply them to all fashions and customs: and provided a man can contain the appetite and the will within their due limits, let a young man, in God's name, be rendered fit for all nations and all companies, even to debauchery and excess, if need be; that is, where he shall do it out of complacency to the customs of the place. Let him be able to do everything, but love to do nothing but what is good. . . .

The lad will not so much get his lesson by heart as he will practice it: he will repeat it in his actions. We shall discover if there be prudence in his exercises, if there be sincerity and justice in his deportment, if there be grace and judgment in his speaking; if there be constancy in his sickness; if there be modesty in his mirth, temperance in his pleasures, order in his domestic economy, indifference in his palate, whether what he eats or

drinks be flesh or fish, wine or water. The conduct of our lives is the true mirror of our doctrine. Zeuxidamus, to one who asked him, why the Lacedæmonians did not commit their constitutions of chivalry to writing, and deliver them to their young men to read, made answer, that it was because they would inure them to action, and not amuse them with words. . . .

Going one day to Orleans, I met in the plain on this side Clery, two pedants traveling toward Bordeaux, about fifty paces distant from one another; and a good way further behind them, I discovered a troop of horse, with a gentleman at the head of them, who was the late Monsieur le Comte de la Rochefoucauld. One of my people inquired of the foremost of these dominies, who that gentleman was that came after him; he, having not seen the train that followed after, and thinking his companion was meant, pleasantly answered: "He is not a gentleman, he is a grammarian, and I am a logician." Now we who, quite contrary, do not here pretend to breed a grammarian or a logician, but a gentleman, let us leave them to throw away their time at their own fancy: our business lies elsewhere. Let but our pupil be well furnished with things, words will follow but too fast; he will pull them after him if they do not voluntarily follow. I have observed some to make excuses, that they cannot express themselves, and pretend to have their fancies full of a great many very fine things, which yet, for want of eloquence, they cannot utter; 'tis a mere shift, and nothing else. Will you know what I think of it? I think they are nothing but shadows of some imperfect images and conceptions that they know not what to make of within, nor consequently bring out: they do not yet themselves understand what they would be at, and if you but observe how they haggle and stammer upon the point of parturition, you will soon conclude, that their labor is not to delivery, but about conception, and that they are but licking their formless embryo. For my part, I hold, and Socrates commands it, that whoever has in his mind a sprightly and clear imagination, he will express it well enough in one kind of tongue or another. . . .

But what will become of our young gentleman, if he be attacked with the sophistic subtlety of some syllogism? "A Westphalia ham makes a man drink, drink quenches thirst; therefore, a Westphalia ham quenches thirst." Why, let him laugh at it; it will be more discretion to do so, than to go about to answer it: or let him borrow this pleasant evasion from Aristippus[2]: "Why should I trouble

---

[1] Roman general (15 B.C.-A.D. 19).   [2] Greek philosopher (c. 435-356 B.C.)

myself to untie that, which, bound as it is, gives me so much trouble?" One offering at this dialectic juggling against Cleanthes, Chrysippus[1] took him short, saying, "Reserve these baubles to play with children, and do not by such fooleries divert the serious thoughts of a man of years." If these ridiculous subtleties are designed to possess him with an untruth, they are dangerous; but if they signify no more than only to make him laugh, I do not see why a man need to be fortified against them. There are some so ridiculous, as to go a mile out of their way to hook in a fine word. I for my part rather bring in a fine sentence by head and shoulder to fit my purpose, than divert my designs to hunt after a sentence. On the contrary words are to serve, and to follow a man's purpose; and let Gascon come in play where French will not do. I would have things so excelling, and so wholly possessing the imagination of him that hears, that he should have something else to do, than to think of words. The way of speaking that I love, is natural and plain, the same in writing as in speaking, and a sinewy and muscular way of expressing a man's self, short and pithy, not so elegant and artificial as prompt and vehement—; rather hard than wearisome; free from affectation; irregular, incontinuous, and bold; where every piece makes up an entire body; not like a pedant, a preacher, or a pleader, but rather a soldier-like style, as Suetonius[2] calls that of Julius Cæsar. I have ever been ready to imitate the negligent garb, which is yet observable among the young men of our time, to wear my cloak on one shoulder, my cap on one side, a stocking in disorder, which seems to express a kind of haughty disdain of these exotic ornaments, and a contempt of the artificial; but I find this negligence of much better use in the form of speaking. All affectation, particularly in the French gayety and freedom, is ungraceful in a courtier, and in a monarchy every gentleman ought to be fashioned according to the court model; for which reason, an easy and natural negligence does well. . . . And as in our outward habit, 'tis a ridiculous effeminacy to distinguish ourselves by a particular and unusual garb or fashion; so in language, to study new phrases, and to affect words that are not of current use, proceeds from a puerile and scholastic ambition. May I be bound to speak no other language than what is spoken in the market places of Paris! . . . Not that fine speaking is not a very good and commendable quality; but not so excellent and so necessary as some would make it; and I am scandalized that our whole life should be spent in nothing else. I would first understand my own language, and that of my neighbors with whom most of my business and conversation lies.

No doubt but Greek and Latin are very great ornaments, and of very great use, but we buy them too dear. I will here discover one way, which has been experimented in my own person, by which they are to be had better cheap, and such may make use of it as will. My late father having made the most precise inquiry that any man could possibly make among men of the greatest learning and judgment, of an exact method of education, was by them cautioned of this inconvenience then in use, and made to believe, that the tedious time we applied to the learning of the tongues of them who had them for nothing, was the sole cause we could not arrive to the grandeur of soul and perfection of knowledge, of the ancient Greeks and Romans. I do not, however, believe that to be the only cause. However, the expedient my father found out for this was, that in my infancy, and before I began to speak, he committed me to the care of a German, who since died a famous physician in France, totally ignorant of our language, but very fluent, and a great critic in Latin. This man, whom he had fetched out of his own country, and whom he entertained with a very great salary for this only end, had me continually with him; to him there were also joined two others, of inferior learning, to attend me, and to relieve him; who all of them spoke to me in no other language but Latin. As to the rest of his family, it was an inviolable rule, that neither himself, nor my mother, man nor maid, should speak anything in my company, but such Latin words as every one had learned only to gabble with me. It is not to be imagined how great an advantage this proved to the whole family; my father and my mother by this means learned Latin enough to understand it perfectly well, and to speak it to such a degree as was sufficient for any necessary use; as also those of the servants did who were most frequently with me. In short, we Latined it at such a rate, that it overflowed to all the neighboring villages, where there yet remain, that have established themselves by custom, several Latin appellations of artisans and their tools. As for what concerns myself, I was above six years of age before I understood either French or Perigordin, any more than Arabic; and without art, book, grammar, or precept, whipping, or the expense of a tear, I had, by that time, learned to speak as pure Latin as my master himself, for I had no means of mixing it up with any other. . . .

[1] Stoic philosopher (about 280-206 B.C.). [2] Roman historian (fl. 100).

As to Greek, of which I have but a mere smattering, my father also designed to have it taught me by a device, but a new one, and by way of sport; tossing our declensions to and fro, after the manner of those who, by certain games at tables and chess, learn geometry and arithmetic. For he, among other rules, had been advised to make me relish science and duty by an unforced will, and of my own voluntary motion, and to educate my soul in all liberty and delight, without any severity or constraint; which he was an observer of to such a degree, even of superstition, if I may say so, that some being of opinion that it troubles and disturbs the brains of children suddenly to wake them in the morning, and to snatch them violently and over-hastily from sleep (wherein they are much more profoundly involved than we), he caused me to be wakened by the sound of some musical instrument, and was never unprovided of a musician for that purpose. By this example you may judge of the rest, this alone being sufficient to recommend both the prudence and the affection of so good a father, who is not to be blamed if he did not reap fruits answerable to so exquisite a culture. Of this, two things were the cause: first, a sterile and improper soil; for, though I was of a strong and healthful constitution, and of a disposition tolerably sweet and tractable, yet I was, withal, so heavy, idle, and indisposed, that they could not rouse me from my sloth, not even to get me out to play. What I saw, I saw clearly enough, and under this heavy complexion nourished a bold imagination, and opinions above my age. I had a slow wit, that would go no faster than it was led; a tardy understanding, a languishing invention, and above all, incredible defect of memory; so that, it is no wonder, if from all these nothing considerable could be extracted. Secondly, like those, who, impatient of a long and steady cure, submit to all sorts of prescriptions and recipes, the good man being extremely timorous of any way failing in a thing he had so wholly set his heart upon, suffered himself at last to be overruled by the common opinions; which always follow their leader as a flight of cranes, and complying with the method of the time, having no more those persons he had brought out of Italy, and who had given him the first model of education, about him, he sent me at six years of age to the College of Guienne, at that time the best and most flourishing in France. And there it was not possible to add anything to the care he had to provide me the most able tutors, with all other circumstances of education, reserving also several particular rules contrary to the college practice; but so it was, that with all these precautions it was a college still. My Latin immediately grew corrupt, of which also by discontinuance I have since lost all manner of use; so that this new way of education served me to no other end, than only at my first coming to prefer me to the first forms; for at thirteen years old, that I came out of the college, I had run through my whole course (as they call it), and, in truth, without any manner of advantage, that I can honestly brag of, in all this time.

The first thing that gave me any taste for books, was the pleasure I took in reading the fables of Ovid's *Metamorphoses*, and with them I was so taken, that being but seven or eight years old, I would steal from all other diversions to read them, both by reason that this was my own natural language, the easiest book that I was acquainted with, and for the subject, the most accommodated to the capacity of my age: for, as for Lancelot of the Lake, Amadis of Gaul, Huon of Bordeaux, and such trumpery, which children are most delighted with, I had never so much as heard their names, no more than I yet know what they contain; so exact was the discipline wherein I was brought up. But this was enough to make me neglect the other lessons that were prescribed me; and here it was infinitely to my advantage, to have to do with an understanding tutor, who very well knew discreetly to connive at this and other truantries of the same nature; for by this means I ran through Virgil's *Æneid*, and then Terence, and then Plautus, and then some Italian comedies, allured by the sweetness of the subject; whereas had he been so foolish as to have taken me off this diversion, I do really believe, I had brought nothing away from the college but a hatred of books, as almost all our young gentlemen do. But he carried himself very discreetly in that business, seeming to take no notice, and allowing me only such time as I could steal from my other regular studies, which whetted my appetite to devour those books. For the chief things my father expected from their endeavors to whom he had delivered me for education, were affability and good humor; and, to say the truth, my manners had no other vice but sloth and want of mettle. . . .

Yet for all this heavy disposition of mine, my mind, when retired into itself, was not altogether without strong movements, solid and clear judgments about those objects it could comprehend, and could also, without any helps, digest them; but, among other things, I do really believe, it had been totally impossible to have made it to submit by violence and force. Shall I here acquaint you with one faculty of my youth? I had great assurance of countenance, and flexibility of voice and gesture, in applying myself to any part I undertook to act: I played the chief parts in the Latin tragedies of Buchanan, Guerente, and Muret, that were presented in our College of Guienne with great dignity; now Andreas Goveanus, our principal, as in all other parts of his charge, was, without comparison, the best of that employment in France; and I was looked upon as one of the best actors. 'Tis an exercise that I do not disapprove in young people of condition; and I have since seen our princes, after the example of some of the ancients, in person handsomely and commendably perform these exercises; it was even allowed to persons of quality to make a profession of it in Greece. Nay, I have always taxed those with impertinence who condemn these entertainments, and with injustice those who refuse to admit such comedians as are worth seeing into our good towns, and grudge the people that public diversion. Well-governed corporations take care to assemble their citizens, not only to the solemn duties of devotion, but also to sports and spectacles. They find society and friendship augmented by it; and, besides, can there possibly be allowed a more orderly and regular diversion than what is performed in the sight of every one, and, very often, in the presence of the supreme magistrate himself? And I, for my part, should think it reasonable, that the prince should sometimes gratify his people at his own expense, out of paternal goodness and affection; and that in populous cities there should be theaters erected for such entertainments, if but to divert them from worse and private actions.

To return to my subject, there is nothing like alluring the appetite and affections; otherwise you make nothing but so many asses laden with books; by dint of the lash, you give them their pocketful of learning to keep; whereas, to do well, you should not only lodge it with them, but make them espouse it.

Of Democritus and Heraclitus

The judgment is an utensil proper for all subjects, and will have an oar in everything: which is the reason, that in these essays I take hold of all occasions where, though it happen to be a subject I do not very well understand, I try however, sounding it at a distance, and finding it too deep for my stature, I keep me on the shore; and this knowledge that a man can proceed no further, is one effect of its virtue, yea, one of those of which it is most proud. One while in an idle and frivolous subject, I try to find out matter whereof to compose a body, and then to prop and support it; another while, I employ it in a noble subject, one that has been tossed and tumbled by a thousand hands, wherein a man can scarce possibly introduce anything of his own, the way being so beaten on every side that he must of necessity walk in the steps of another: in such a case, 'tis the work of the judgment to take the way that seems best, and of a thousand paths, to determine that this or that is the best. I leave the choice of my arguments to fortune, and take that she first presents to me; they are all alike to me, I never design to go through any of them; for I never see all of anything: neither do they who so largely promise to show it to others. Of a hundred members and faces that everything has, I take one, one while to look it over only, another while to ripple up the skin, and sometimes to pinch it to the bones: I give a stab, not so wide but as deep as I can, and am for the most part tempted to take it in hand by some new light I discover in it. Did I know myself less, I might perhaps venture to handle something or other to the bottom, and to be deceived in my own inability; but sprinkling here one word and there another, patterns cut from several pieces and scattered without design and without engaging myself too far, I am not responsible for them, or obliged to keep close to my subject, without varying at my own liberty and pleasure, and giving up myself to doubt and uncertainty, and to my own governing method, ignorance.

All motion discovers us: the very same soul of Cæsar, that made itself so conspicuous in marshaling and commanding the battle of Pharsalia, was also seen as solicitous and busy in the softer affairs of love and leisure. A man makes a judgment of a horse, not only by seeing him when he is showing off his paces, but by his very walk, nay, and by seeing him stand in the stable.

Among the functions of the soul, there are some of a lower and meaner form; he who does not see her in those inferior offices as well as in those of nobler note, never fully discovers her; and, peradventure, she is best shown where she moves her simpler pace. The winds of passions take most hold of her in her highest flights; and the rather by reason that she wholly applies herself to, and exercises her whole virtue upon, every particular subject, and never handles more than one thing at a time, and that not according to it, but according to herself. Things in respect to themselves have, peradventure, their weight, measures and conditions; but when we once take them into us, the soul forms them as she pleases. Death is terrible to Cicero, coveted by Cato, indifferent to Socrates. Health, conscience, authority, knowledge, riches, beauty, and their contraries, all strip themselves at their entering into us, and receive a new robe, and of another fashion, from the soul; and of what color, brown, bright, green, dark, and of what quality, sharp, sweet, deep, or superficial, as best pleases each of them, for they are not agreed upon any common standard of forms, rules, or proceedings; every one is a queen in her own dominions. Let us, therefore, no more excuse ourselves upon the external qualities of things; it belongs to us to give ourselves an account of them. Our good or ill has no other dependence but on ourselves. 'Tis there that our offerings and our vows are due, and not to fortune: she has no power over our manners; on the contrary, they draw and make her follow in their train, and cast her in their own mold. Why should not I judge of Alexander at table, ranting and drinking at the prodigious rate he sometimes used to do? Or, if he played at chess? what string of his soul was not touched by this idle and childish game? I hate and avoid it, because it is not play enough, that it is too grave and serious a diversion, and I am ashamed to lay out as much thought and study upon it as would serve to much better uses. He did not more pump his brains about his glorious expedition into the Indies, nor than another in unraveling a passage upon which depends the safety of mankind. To what a degree does this ridiculous diversion molest the soul, when all her faculties are summoned together upon this trivial account! and how fair an opportunity she herein gives everyone to know and to make a right judgment of himself? I do not more thoroughly sift myself in any other posture than this: what passion are we exempted from in it? Anger, spite, malice, impatience, and a vehement desire of getting the better in a concern wherein it were more excusable to be ambitious of being overcome; for to be emi-

nent, to excel above the common rate in frivolous things, nowise befits a man of honor. What I say in this example may be said in all others. Every particle, every employment of man manifests him equally with any other.

Democritus and Heraclitus were two philosophers, of whom the first, finding human condition ridiculous and vain, never appeared abroad but with a jeering and laughing countenance; whereas Heraclitus commiserating that same condition of ours, appeared always with a sorrowful look, and tears in his eyes. I am clearly for the first humor: not because it is more pleasant to laugh than to weep, but because it expresses more contempt and condemnation than the other, and I think we can never be despised according to our full desert. Compassion and bewailing seem to imply some esteem of and value for the thing bemoaned; whereas the things we laugh at are by that expressed to be of no moment. I do not think that we are so unhappy as we are vain, or have in us so much malice as folly; we are not so full of mischief as inanity; nor so miserable as we are vile and mean. And therefore Diogenes, who passed away his time in rolling himself in his tub, and made nothing of the great Alexander esteeming us no better than flies, or bladders puffed up with wind, was a sharper and more penetrating, and, consequently in my opinion, a juster judge than Timon, surnamed the Man-hater; for what a man hates he lays to heart. This last was an enemy to all mankind, who passionately desired our ruin, and avoided our conversation as dangerous, proceeding from wicked and depraved natures: the other valued us so little that we could neither trouble nor infect him by our example; and left us to herd one with another, not out of fear, but from contempt of our society: concluding us as incapable of doing good as ill.

Of the same strain was Statilius' answer, when Brutus courted him into the conspiracy against Cæsar; he was satisfied that the enterprise was just, but he did not think mankind worthy of a wise man's concern; according to the doctrine of Hegasias, who said, that a wise man ought to do nothing but for himself, forasmuch as he only was worthy of it: and to the saying of Theodorus, that it was not reasonable a wise man should hazard himself for his country, and endanger wisdom for a company of fools. Our condition is as ridiculous as risible.

MOLIÈRE

The Miser

DRAMATIS PERSONÆ

HARPAGON, *father to Cléante and Elise, in love with Mariane*
CLÉANTE, *Harpagon's son, Mariane's lover*
VALÈRE, *son of Anselme, Elise's lover*
ANSELME, *father to Valère and Mariane*
MASTER SIMON, *agent*
MASTER JACQUES, *cook and coachman to Harpagon*
LA FLÈCHE, *Cléante's valet*
BRINDAVOINE } *Harpagon's lackeys*
LA MERLUCHE }
A Magistrate and his Clerk
ELISE, *Harpagon's daughter, Valère's sweetheart*
MARIANE, *Cléante's sweetheart, beloved by Harpagon*
FROSINE, *a designing woman*
MISTRESS CLAUDE, *Harpagon's servant*

The scene is in Paris, in Harpagon's House

ACT I

SCENE I:—VALÈRE, ELISE

VAL. Eh, what! charming Elise, you are growing melancholy, after the kind assurances which you were good enough to give me of your love! Alas! I see you sighing in the midst of my joy! Tell me, is it with regret at having made me happy? And do you repent of that engagement to which my affection has induced you?

ELISE. No, Valère, I cannot repent of anything that I do for you. I feel myself attracted to it by too sweet a power, and I have not even the will to wish that things were otherwise. But, to tell you the truth, our success causes me uneasiness; and I am very much afraid of loving you a little more than I ought.

VAL. Eh! what is there to fear, Elise, in the affection you have for me?

ELISE. Alas! a hundred things at once: the anger of a father, the reproaches of my family, the cen-sure of the world; but more than all, Valère, the change of your heart, and that criminal coolness with which those of your sex most frequently re-pay the too ardent proofs of an innocent love.

VAL. Ah! do not wrong me thus, to judge of me by others! Suspect me of anything, Elise, rather than of failing in my duty to you. I love you too well for that: and my affection for you will last as long as my life.

10 ELISE. Ah, Valère, everyone talks in the same strain! All men are alike in their words; their actions only show them to be different.

VAL. Since actions only can show what we are, wait then, at least, to judge of my heart by them; and do not search for crimes because you unjustly fear, and wrongly anticipate. Pray do not kill me with the poignant blows of an outrageous sus-picion; and give me time to convince you, by many thousand proofs, of the sincerity of my 20 affection.

ELISE. Alas, how easily we are persuaded by those we love! Yes, Valère, I hold your heart in-capable of deceiving me. I believe that you truly love me, and that you will be constant. I will no longer doubt of it, and I will confine my grief to the apprehensions of the blame which people may utter against me.

VAL. But why this uneasiness?

ELISE. I should have nothing to fear, if everyone 30 could see you with the eyes with which I look upon you; and in your own person I see sufficient to justify me in what I do for you. For its defense, my heart pleads all your merits, supported by the help of a gratitude with which Heaven has bound me to you. At every moment I call to mind that supreme danger which first made us acquainted with each other; that wonderful generosity which made you risk your life in order to snatch mine from the fury of the waves; those most tender 40 attentions which you lavished upon me, after having dragged me out of the water, and the assiduous homage of that ardent affection, which

Molière, *The Miser.* Translated by Henri van Laun. Molière's real name was Jean Baptiste Poquelin. He was born in 1622 and died in 1673. He had long experience as director of a theatrical company for whom he wrote his incomparable comedies. The patronage of King Louis XIV protected him from the enemies he had made by his biting satire.

neither time nor obstacles have been able to discourage, and which, causing you to neglect relatives and country, detains you in this spot, and keeps your position unrecognized all on my account, and has reduced you to assume the functions of servant to my father, in order to see me. All this produces, no doubt, a marvelous effect on me, and quite sufficient to justify, in my own eyes, the engagement to which I have consented; but it is not perhaps enough to justify it in that of others, and I am not certain that the world will enter into my sentiments.

VAL. Of all that you have mentioned, it is only by my love that I pretended to deserve anything from you; and as for the scruples which you have; your father himself takes but too good care to justify you before the world; and the excess of his avarice, and the austere way in which he treats his children, might authorize stranger things still. Pardon me, charming Elise, for speaking thus before you. You know that, on that subject, no good can be said. But in short, if I can, as I hope I shall, find my relatives again, we shall have very little difficulty in rendering them favorable to us. I am impatient to receive some tidings of them; and should they be delayed much longer, I will myself go in search of them.

ELISE. Ah! Valère, do not stir from this, I beseech you; and think only how to ingratiate yourself with my father.

VAL. You see how I go about it, and the artful wheedling which I have been obliged to make use of to enter his service; beneath what mask of sympathy and affinity of sentiments I disguise myself, in order to please him; and what part I daily play with him, that I may gain his affection. I am making admirable progress in it; and experience teaches me that to find favor with men, there is no better method than to invest ourselves in their eyes with their hobbies; than to act according to their maxims, to flatter their faults and to applaud their doings. One needs not fear to overdo this complaisance; the way in which one fools them may be as palpable as possible; even the sharpest are the greatest dupes when flattery is in the question; and there is nothing too impertinent or too ridiculous for them to swallow, if it be only seasoned with praises. Sincerity suffers somewhat by the trade which I follow; but, when we have need of people, we must suit ourselves to their tastes; and since they are to be gained over only in that way, it is not the fault of those who flatter, but of those who wish to be flattered.

ELISE. But why do you not try to gain the support of my brother, in case the servant should take it into her head to reveal our secret?

VAL. There is no managing them both at once; and the disposition of the father and that of the son are so opposed to each other, that it becomes difficult to arrange a confidence with both. But you, on your part, act upon your brother, and make use of the affection between you two, to bring him over to our interests. He is just coming. I go. Take this opportunity of speaking to him, and reveal our business to him, only when you judge the fit time come.

ELISE. I do not know whether I shall have the courage to intrust this confidence to him.

SCENE II:—CLÉANTE, ELISE

CLÉAN. I am very glad to find you alone, sister; I was dying to speak to you, to unburden myself to you of a secret.

ELISE. You find me quite ready to listen, brother. What have you to tell me?

CLÉAN. Many things, sister, all contained in one word. I am in love.

ELISE. You are in love?

CLÉAN. Yes, I am in love. But before going farther, I know that I am dependent on my father, and that the name of son subjects me to his will; that we ought not to pledge our affection without the consent of those to whom we owe our life; that Heaven has made them the masters of our affection, and that we are enjoined not to dispose of it but by their direction; that, not being biased by any foolish passion, they are less likely to deceive themselves than we are, and to see much better what is proper for us; that we ought rather to be guided by the light of their prudence than by the blindness of our passion; and that the ardor of our youth often drags us to dangerous precipices. I tell you all this, sister, that you may save yourself the trouble of telling it to me; for, frankly, my love will not listen to anything, and I pray you not to make any remonstrances.

ELISE. Have you pledged yourself, brother, with her whom you love?

CLÉAN. No; but I am determined to do so, and I implore you, once more, not to advance any reasons to dissuade me from it.

ELISE. Am I then so strange a person, brother?

CLÉAN. No, sister; but you are not in love; you are ignorant of the sweet empire which a tender passion exercises over our hearts; and I dread your wisdom.

ELISE. Alas! dear brother, let us not speak of my wisdom; there is no one who does not fail in it, at least once in his life; and were I to open my heart to you, perhaps I would appear less wise in your eyes than yourself.

CLÉAN. Ah! would to Heaven that your heart, like mine . . .

ELISE. Let us first finish your affair, and tell me who it is whom you love.

CLÉAN. A young person, who has lately come to live in this neighborhood, and who seems to be made to inspire love in all who behold her. Nature, sister, has created nothing more amiable; and I felt myself carried away the moment I saw her. Her name is Mariane, and she lives under the protection of a good motherly woman who is nearly always ill, and for whom this dear girl entertains feelings of friendship not to be imagined. She waits upon her, condoles with her, and cheers her with a tenderness that would touch you to the very soul. She does things with the most charming air in the world; a thousand graces shine through her every action, a gentleness full of attraction, a most prepossessing kindness, an adorable simplicity, a . . . Ah! sister, I wish you could have seen her!

ELISE. I see much, brother, in the things you tell me; and to understand what she really is, it is sufficient that you love her.

CLÉAN. I have learned, secretly, that they are not too well off; and that even their careful way of living has some difficulty in making both ends meet with the small means at their command. Imagine, dear sister, the pleasure it must be to improve the condition of her whom we love; to convey, delicately, some small assistance to the modest wants of a virtuous family; and then conceive how annoying it is to me to find myself, through the avarice of a father, powerless to taste that joy, and to be unable to show this fair one any proof of my love.

ELISE. Yes, I can conceive well enough, brother, what must be your grief.

CLÉAN. Ah! sister, it is greater than you can believe. For, in short, can anything be more cruel than this rigorous meanness that is exercised over us, this strange niggardliness in which we are made to languish? What good will it do us to have means, when we shall no longer be of an age to enjoy them, and if, to maintain myself, I am now obliged to run in debt on all sides; if I, as well as you, am obliged to crave daily the aid of tradesmen in order to wear decent clothes? In short, I

wished to speak to you to help me to sound my father upon my present feelings; and should I find him opposed to them, I am resolved to go elsewhere, with this dear girl, to enjoy whatever fortune providence may have in store for us. I have endeavored to raise money everywhere for this purpose, and if your affairs, sister, are similar to mine, and if our father runs counter to our wishes, we shall both leave him, and emancipate ourselves from that tyranny in which his insupportable avarice has so long held us.

ELISE. It is true enough that every day he gives us more cause to regret the death of our mother, and that . . .

CLÉAN. I hear his voice; let us go a little farther to finish our confidences; and afterwards we will join our forces to attack the ruggedness of his temper.

SCENE III:—HARPAGON, LA FLÈCHE

HARP. Clear out of this immediately, and let me have no reply! Get out of my house, you consummate cheat, you veritable gallow's bird!

LA FL. [aside]. I have never seen anything more vicious than this cursed old man; and I really think—I speak under correction—that he has got the devil in him.

HARP. You are muttering between your teeth!

LA FL. Why are you sending me away?

HARP. It well becomes you, you hangdog, to ask me my reasons. Out with you, quickly, that I may not knock you down.

LA FL. What have I done to you?

HARP. You have done so much to me that I wish you to get out.

LA FL. Your son, my master, has ordered me to wait.

HARP. Go and wait for him in the street, then; but do not remain in my house, planted bolt upright as a sentry, taking notice of everything that goes on, and making the best use of it. I will not have a spy over my concerns eternally before my eyes, a wretch, whose cursed eyes watch every one of my actions, covet all I have, and ferret about everywhere to see if there is nothing to pilfer.

LA FL. How the deuce could one manage to rob you? Are you a likely man to have aught stolen from you, when you lock up everything, and keep guard day and night?

HARP. I shall lock up whatever I think fit, and keep guard as long as I please. A nice pass it has come to with these spies, who take notice of everything one does. [*Softly, aside.*] I quake for fear he should suspect something about my money. [*Aloud.*] Ah! are you not just the fellow who would think nothing of bruiting the tale about that I have money hidden in my house?

LA FL. You have money hidden?

HARP. No, you scoundrel, I do not say that. [*To himself.*] I am bursting with rage. [*Aloud.*] I ask whether you would not, from sheer malice, bruit the story about that I have some.

LA FL. Eh! what does it matter to us whether you have any or not, as long as it comes to the same thing to us?

HARP. [*lifting up his hand, to slap La Flèche's face*]. You are arguing the matter! I will give you something for this reasoning on your ears. Once more, get out of this.

LA FL. Very well! I am going.

HARP. Wait: you are not taking anything away with you?

LA FL. What should I take from you?

HARP. I do not know until I look. Show me your hands?

LA FL. Here they are.

HARP. The others.

LA FL. The others?

HARP. Yes.

LA FL. Here they are.

HARP. [*pointing to the breeches of La Flèche*]. Have you put nothing in there?

LA FL. Look for yourself!

HARP. [*feeling the outside of La Flèche's pockets*]. Those wide breeches are just fit to become receivers for things purloined, and I wish one of them had been hanged at the gallows.

LA FL. [*aside*]. Ah, how a man like this well deserves the thing he fears! and how much pleasure I would have in robbing him!

HARP. Eh?

LA FL. What?

HARP. What are you muttering about robbing!

LA FL. I am saying that you feel carefully everywhere to see if I have robbed you.

HARP. That is what I mean to do. [HARPAGON *fumbles in La Flèche's pockets.*]

LA FL. [*aside*]. May the plague take avarice and all avaricious people!

HARP. What! what are you saying?

LA FL. What am I saying?

HARP. Yes; what are you saying about avarice and all avaricious people?

LA FL. I say may the plague take avarice and all avaricious people!

HARP. To whom are you alluding?

LA FL. To avaricious people.

HARP. And who are they, these avaricious people?

LA FL. Villains and curmudgeons.

HARP. But whom do you mean by that?

LA FL. What are you troubling yourself about?

HARP. I am troubling myself about what concerns me.

LA FL. Do you think that I am speaking of you?

HARP. I think what I think; but I wish you to tell me to whom you are addressing yourself when you say that.

LA FL. I am addressing myself . . . I am addressing myself to my cap.

HARP. And I might address myself to the head that is in it.

LA FL. Will you prevent me from cursing avaricious people?

HARP. No; but I will prevent you from jabbering, and from being insolent. Hold your tongue!

LA FL. I name no one.

HARP. I shall thrash you if you say another word.

LA FL. Whom the cap fits, let him wear it.

HARP. Will you hold your tongue?

LA FL. Yes, against my will.

HARP. Ah! Ah!

LA FL. [*showing* HARPAGON *a pocket in his doublet*]. Just look, there is another pocket; are you satisfied?

HARP. Come, you had better give it up without my searching you.

LA FL. What?

HARP. What you have taken from me.

LA FL. I have taken nothing at all from you.

HARP. Assuredly?

LA FL. Assuredly.

HARP. Good-by, then, and go to the devil.

LA FL. [*aside*]. That is a pretty dismissal.

HARP. I leave you to your own conscience, at least.

SCENE IV:—HARPAGON, *alone*

There is a hangdog of a valet who is very much in my way; I do not at all care to see this limping cur about the place. It is certainly no small trouble to keep such a large sum of money in one's house; and he is a happy man who has all his well laid out at interest, and keeps only so much by him as is necessary for his expenses. One is not a little puzzled to contrive, in the whole house, a safe hiding-place; for, as far as I am concerned, I distrust safes, and would never rely on them. I look upon them just as a distinct bait to burglars; for it is always the first thing which they attack.

SCENE V:—HARPAGON; ELISE *and* CLÉANTE *conversing together at the farther end of the stage*

HARP. [*still thinking himself alone*]. For all that, I am not quite sure if I have done right in burying in my garden these ten thousand crowns, which were paid to me yesterday. Ten thousand golden crowns in one's house is a sum sufficient. . . . [*Aside, perceiving* ELISE *and* CLÉANTE]. Oh, Heavens! I have betrayed myself! The excitement has carried me too far, and I verily believe I have spoken aloud, while arguing to myself. [*To* CLÉANTE *and* ELISE.] What is the matter?

CLÉAN. Nothing, father.

HARP. Have you been there long?

ELISE. We were just coming in.

HARP. You have heard . . .

CLÉAN. What, father?

HARP. There . . .

ELISE. What?

HARP. What I said just now.

CLÉAN. No.

HARP. Yes, you have.

ELISE. I beg your pardon.

HARP. I see well enough that you overheard some words. I was talking to myself about the difficulty one experiences nowadays in finding money, and I was saying how pleasant it must be to have ten thousand crowns in the house.

CLÉAN. We hesitated to speak to you, for fear of interrupting you.

HARP. I am very glad to tell you this, so that you may not take things the wrong way, and imagine that I said that I myself had ten thousand crowns.

CLÉAN. We have no wish to enter into your concerns.

HARP. Would to Heaven that I had them, ten thousand crowns!

CLÉAN. I do not think . .

HARP. It would be a capital affair for me.

ELISE. These are things . . .

HARP. I am greatly in need of them.

CLÉAN. I think . . .

HARP. That would suit me very well.

ELISE. You are . . .

HARP. And I should not have to complain as I do now, about the hard times.

CLÉAN. Good Heavens! father, you have no need to complain, and we know that you have wealth enough.

HARP. How! I wealth enough! Those who say so surely tell a lie. Nothing could be more false; and they are but a pack of rascals who spread all these reports about.

ELISE. Do not put yourself in a rage.

HARP. A strange thing, that my own children should betray me, and become my enemies.

CLÉAN. Is it becoming your enemy to say that you have wealth?

HARP. Yes. Such talk, and the expenses you indulge in will be the cause that one of these fine days people will come and cut my throat, in my own house, in the belief that I am stuffed with gold pieces.

CLÉAN. What great expenses do I indulge in?

HARP. Expenses? Can anything be more scandalous than this sumptuous attire, which you exhibit about the town? I scolded your sister yesterday; but this is much worse. This cries aloud to Heaven for vengeance; for, take you from top to toe, there is enough to ensure a handsome competency. I have told you twenty times, son, that all your manners displease me; you are furiously aping the aristocracy; and to go dressed as you do, you must rob me.

CLÉAN. Eh! how rob you?

HARP. How do I know? Where can you get the means of keeping up such an appearance?

CLÉAN. I, father? it is because I play; and, as I am very lucky, I put my winnings on my back.

HARP. That is very bad. If you are lucky at play, you should profit by it, and lay out the money you win at decent interest, that you may provide for a rainy day. I should much like to know, leaving all other things aside, what the good can be of all these ribbons with which you are decked out from head to foot, and if half-a-dozen tacks are not sufficient to fasten your breeches. Is it at all necessary to spend money upon wigs? when one can wear hair of home growth, which costs nothing! I would bet that your wig and ribbons cost far more than twenty pistoles. and twenty pistoles, at a little more than eight per cent, bring in eighteen livres, six pence, and eight groats a year.

CLÉAN. You are perfectly right.

HARP. Let us leave the subject, and talk of other things. [*Perceiving that* CLÉANTE *and* ELISE *interchange glances.*] Eh! [*Softly, aside.*] I believe that they are making signs to each other to rob me of my purse. [*Aloud.*] What mean those gestures?

ELISE. My brother and I are arguing who shall speak first. We have each something to say to you.

HARP. And I have something to say to you both.

CLÉAN. It is about marriage that we wish to speak to you, father.

HARP. And it is also about marriage that I wish to converse with you.

ELISE. Ah, father!

HARP. Why this cry? Is it the word, or the thing itself that frightens you, daughter?

CLÉAN. The way you may look at marriage may frighten us both; and we fear that your sentiments may not happen to chime in with our choice.

HARP. A little patience; do not alarm yourselves. I know what is good for you both, and neither the one nor the other shall have cause to complain of what I intend to do. To begin at one end of the story [to CLÉANTE], tell me, have you noticed a young person called Mariane, who lodges not far from here?

CLÉAN. Yes, father.

HARP. And you?

ELISE. I have heard her spoken of.

HARP. How do you like that girl, son?

CLÉAN. A very charming person.

HARP. What do you think of her countenance?

CLÉAN. Very genteel, and full of intelligence.

HARP. Her air and manner?

CLÉAN. Without doubt, admirable.

HARP. Do you not think that a girl like that deserves to be taken notice of?

CLÉAN. Yes, father.

HARP. That it would be a desirable match?

CLÉAN. Very desirable.

HARP. That she looks as if she would make a good wife?

CLÉAN. Undoubtedly.

HARP. And that a husband would have reason to be satisfied with her?

CLÉAN. Assuredly.

HARP. There is a slight difficulty. I fear that she has not as much money as one might reasonably pretend to.

CLÉAN. Ah! father, money is not worth considering when there is a question of marrying a respectable girl.

HARP. Not so, not so. But this much may be said, that if one finds not quite so much money as one might wish, there is a way of regaining it in other things.

CLÉAN. Of course.

HARP. Well, I am very glad to see that you share my sentiments; for her genteel behavior and her gentleness have quite gained my heart, and I have made up my mind to marry her, provided she has some dowry.

CLÉAN. Eh!

HARP. What now?

CLÉAN. You have made up your mind, you say . . .

HARP. To marry Mariane.

CLÉAN. Who? You, you?

HARP. Yes, I, I, I. What means this?

CLÉAN. I feel a sudden giddiness, and I had better go.

HARP. It will be nothing. Go quickly into the kitchen, and drink a large glassful of cold water.

SCENE VI:—HARPAGON, ELISE

HARP. A lot of flimsy sparks, with no more strength than chickens. Daughter, this is what I have resolved upon for myself. As for your brother, I intend him for a certain widow, of whom they spoke to me this morning; and you, I will give to M. Anselme.

ELISE. To M. Anselme?

HARP. Yes, a staid, prudent, and careful man, who is not above fifty, and whose wealth is spoken of everywhere.

ELISE [making a curtsey]. I have no wish to get married, father, if you please.

HARP. [imitating her]. And I, my dear girl, my pet, I wish you to get married, if you please.

ELISE [curtseying once more]. I beg your pardon, father.

HARP. [imitating ELISE]. I beg your pardon, daughter.

ELISE. I am M. Anselme's most humble servant [curtseying again]; but, with your leave, I shall not marry him.

HARP. I am your most humble slave, but [imitating ELISE], with your leave, you shall marry him not later than this evening.

ELISE. Not later than this evening?

HARP. Not later than this evening.

ELISE [curtseying again]. That shall not be, father.

HARP. [imitating her again]. This shall be, daughter.

ELISE. No.

HARP. Yes.

ELISE. No, I tell you.

HARP. Yes, I tell you.

ELISE. That is a thing you shall not drive me to.

HARP. That is a thing I shall drive you to.

ELISE. I will kill myself sooner than marry such a husband.

HARP. You shall not kill yourself, and you shall marry him. But has such boldness ever been seen!

Has ever a daughter been heard to speak to her father in this manner?

ELISE. But has anyone ever seen a father give away his daughter in marriage in this manner?

HARP. It is a match to which no one can object; and I bet that everyone will approve of my choice.

ELISE. And I bet that no reasonable being will approve of it.

HARP. [*perceiving* VALÈRE *in the distance*]. Here comes Valère. Shall we make him judge betwixt us in this matter?

ELISE. I consent to it.

HARP. Will you submit to his judgment?

ELISE. Yes; I will submit to what he shall decide.

HARP. That is agreed.

SCENE VII:—VALÈRE, HARPAGON, ELISE

HARP. Come here, Valère. We have elected you to tell us who is in the right, my daughter or I.

VAL. You, Sir, beyond gainsay.

HARP. Are you aware of what we are talking?

VAL. No. But you could not be in the wrong. You are made up of right.

HARP. I intend, this evening, to give her for a husband a man who is as rich as he is discreet; and the jade tells me to my face that she will not take him. What say you to this?

VAL. What do I say to it?

HARP. Yes.

VAL. Eh! eh!

HARP. What?

VAL. I say, that in the main, I am of your opinion; and you cannot but be right. But on the other side, she is not altogether wrong, and . . .

HARP. How is that? M. Anselme is a desirable match; he is a gentleman who is noble, kind, steady, discreet, and very well to do, and who has neither chick nor child left him from his first marriage. Could she meet with a better match?

VAL. That is true. But she might say to you that it is hurrying things a little too much, and that you should give her some time at least to see whether her inclinations would agree with . . .

HARP. This is an opportunity which should be taken by the forelock. I find in this marriage an advantage which I could not find elsewhere; and he agrees to take her without a dowry.

VAL. Without a dowry?

HARP. Yes.

VAL. In that case, I say no more. Do you see, this is altogether a convincing reason; one must yield to that.

HARP. It is a considerable saving to me.

VAL. Assuredly; it cannot be gainsaid. It is true that your daughter might represent to you that marriage is a more important matter than you think; that it involves a question of being happy or miserable all one's life; and that an engagement which must last till death ought never to be entered upon except with great precautions.

HARP. Without a dowry!

VAL. You are right. That decides it all, of course. There are people who might tell you that on such an occasion the wishes of a daughter are something, no doubt, that ought to be taken into consideration; and that this great disparity of age, of temper, and of feelings makes a marriage subject to very sad accidents.

HARP. Without a dowry!

VAL. Ah! there is no reply to that; I know that well enough. Who the deuce could say anything against that? Not that there are not many fathers who would prefer to humor the wishes of their daughters to the money they could give them; who would not sacrifice them to their own interests, and who would, above all things, try to infuse into marriage that sweet conformity, which, at all times, maintains honor, peace, and joy; and which . . .

HARP. Without a dowry!

VAL. It is true; that closes one's mouth at once. Without a dowry! There are no means of resisting an argument like that.

HARP. [*aside, looking towards the garden*]. Bless my soul! I think I hear a dog barking. Most likely it is someone with a design upon my money. [*To* VALÈRE.] Do not stir; I am coming back directly

SCENE VIII:—ELISE, VALÈRE

ELISE. Are you jesting, Valère, to speak to him in that manner?

VAL. It is in order not to sour his temper, and to gain my end the better. To run counter to his opinions is the way to spoil everything; and there are certain minds which cannot be dealt with in a straightforward manner; temperaments averse to all resistance; restive characters, whom the truth causes to rear, who always set their faces against the straight road of reason, and whom you cannot lead except by turning them with their back towards the goal. Pretend to consent to what he wishes, you will gain your end all the better; and . . .

ELISE. But this marriage, Valère!

VAL. We will find some pretext to break it off.

ELISE. But what to invent, if it is to be consummated this evening?

VAL. You must ask for a delay, and pretend to be ill.

ELISE. But the feint will be discovered, if they call in the doctors.

VAL. Are you jesting? What do they know about it? Come, come, with them you may have whatever illness you please; they will find you some reasons to tell you whence it proceeds.

SCENE IX:—HARPAGON, ELISE, VALÈRE

HARP. [*aside, at the further end of the stage*]. It is nothing, thank Heaven.

VAL. [*not seeing* HARPAGON]. In short, our last resource is flight, which will shelter us from everything; and if your love, fair Elise, be capable of acting with firmness . . . [*Perceiving* HARPAGON.] Yes, a daughter ought to obey her father. She ought not to look at the shape of a husband; and when the great argument of *without a dowry* is added to it, she must be ready to accept what is given to her.

HARP. Good: that is well spoken.

VAL. I crave your pardon, Sir, if I am a little warm, and take the liberty of speaking as I do.

HARP. How now! I am delighted with it, and I wish you to take an absolute control over her. [*To* ELISE.] Yes, you may run away as much as you like, I invest him with the authority which Heaven has given me over you, and I will have you do all that he tells you.

VAL. [*to* ELISE]. After that, resist my remonstrances.

SCENE X:—HARPAGON, VALÈRE

VAL. With your leave, Sir, I will follow her, to continue the advice which I was giving her.

HARP. Yes, you will oblige me. By all means . . .

VAL. It is as well to keep her tight in hand.

HARP. True. We must . . .

VAL. Do not be uneasy. I think that I shall succeed.

HARP. Do, do. I am going to take a little stroll in town, and I shall be back presently.

VAL. [*addressing himself to* ELISE, *leaving by the door, through which she went out*]. Yes, money is more precious than anything else in this world, and you ought to thank Heaven for having given you such an honest man for a father. He knows how to go through life. When anyone offers to take a girl without a dowry, one should look no farther. It sums up everything; and *with-out dowry* makes up for beauty, youth, birth, honor, wisdom, and probity.

HARP. Ah! the honest fellow! He speaks like an oracle. It is a rare piece of luck to have such a servant!

ACT II

SCENE I:—CLÉANTE, LA FLÈCHE

CLÉAN. Ah! wretch that you are! where have you been? Did I not give you the order . . .

LA FL. Yes, Sir; and I came here to wait for you without stirring: but your father, the most surly of men, ordered me out in spite of myself, at the risk of a thrashing.

CLÉAN. How is our affair getting on? Matters press more than ever, and since I have seen you, I have found out that my father is my rival.

LA FL. Your father in love?

CLÉAN. Yes; and I have had the utmost difficulty in concealing from him the trouble which these tidings have caused me.

LA FL. He meddle with love! What the devil put that in his head? Is he making fun of everyone? and has love been made for people like him?

CLÉAN. This passion must have got into his head to punish me for my sins.

LA FL. But for what reason do you keep your love a secret from him?

CLÉAN. In order to give him less suspicion, and to keep, if needs be, the means open for dissuading him from this marriage. What answer have they made to you?

LA FL. Upon my word, Sir, borrowers are very unlucky people; and one must put up with strange things, when one is compelled, like you, to pass through the hands of moneylenders.

CLÉAN. Will the affair fall through?

LA FL. I beg your pardon. Our Master Simon, the agent who has been recommended to us, an active and zealous man, says that he has done wonders for you, and he assures me that your face alone has won his heart.

CLÉAN. Shall I have the fifteen thousand francs which I want?

LA FL. Yes, but with some trifling conditions which you must accept, if you purpose that the affair should be carried through.

CLÉAN. Has he allowed you to speak to the person who is to lend the money?

LA FL. Ah! really, things are not managed in that way. He takes even more care to remain unknown than you do; and these things are much greater mysteries than you think. Simon would not tell me his name at all, and he will be confronted with you today in a house borrowed for the occasion, to be informed by you, personally, of your own substance and that of your family; and I have no doubt that the very name of your father may make things go smoothly.

CLÉAN. And above all our mother being dead, whose property cannot be alienated.

LA FL. Here are some clauses, which he has himself dictated to our go-between, to be shown to you before doing anything:—"Provided the lender see all his securities, and that the borrower be of age, and of a family whose estate is ample, solid, secure, and undoubted, and free from all encumbrance, a binding and correct bond shall be executed before a notary, the most honest man to be found, and who, for this purpose, shall be chosen by the borrower, to whom it is of the greatest importance that the instrument shall be regularly drawn up."

CLÉAN. There is nothing to object to that.

LA FL. "The lender, in order not to charge his conscience with the least scruple, will only lend his money at a little more than five and a half per cent."

CLÉAN. At a little more than five and a half per cent? Zounds! that is honest enough. There is no reason to complain.

LA FL. That is true. "But as the lender has not the sum in question by him, and as, to oblige the borrower, he is himself obliged to borrow it of someone at the rate of twenty per cent, it shall be agreed that the said first borrower shall pay this interest, without prejudice of the rest, seeing that it is only to oblige him that the said lender takes up the loan."

CLÉAN. What the devil! what Jew, what Arab is this? This is more than twenty-five per cent.

LA FL. It is true, that is what I have said. It is for you to see that.

CLÉAN. What can I see? I want the money, and I am bound to consent to everything.

LA FL. That is the answer which I made.

CLÉAN. There is something else still?

LA FL. Nothing but a small matter. "Of the fifteen thousand francs required, the lender can count down in cash only twelve thousand; and, for the remaining thousand crowns, the borrower will have to take them out in chattels, clothing, and jewelry, of which the following is the memorandum, and which the lender has set down honestly at the lowest possible price."

CLÉAN. What does this mean?

LA FL. Listen to the memorandum. "First, a four-post bed, elegantly adorned with Hungary-lace bands, with hangings of olive-colored cloth, with six chairs, and a counterpane of the same; the whole in very good condition, and lined with shot taffetas, red and blue. Item: a tester for this bed, of good Aumale, pale rose-colored serge, with large and small silk fringes."

CLÉAN. What does he want me to do with it?

LA FL. Wait. "Item: Tapestry hangings, representing the loves of Gombaud and Macée. Item: a large walnut wood table, with twelve columns or turned legs, which draws out at both sides, provided with six stools underneath it."

CLÉAN. What have I to do, egad! . . .

LA FL. Only have patience. "Item: three large muskets inlaid with mother-of-pearl, with the necessary rests. Item: a brick furnace, with two retorts, and three receivers very useful for those who have a turn for distilling."

CLÉAN. I am going mad.

LA FL. Gently. "Item: A Bologna lute with all its strings, or nearly all. Item: a troumadame table, a draughtboard, with the game of mother goose, restored from the Greeks, very agreeable to pass the time when one has nothing else to do. Item: a lizard's skin of three feet and a half, stuffed with hay: a very pretty curiosity to hang at the ceiling of a room. The whole of the above-mentioned, really worth more than four thousand five hundred francs, and brought down to the value of a thousand crowns, through the discretion of the lender."

CLÉAN. May the plague choke him with his discretion, the wretch, the cut-throat that he is! Has one ever heard of similar usury? Is he not satisfied with the tremendous interest which he demands, but must needs force me to take for the three thousand francs the old lumber which he picks up? I shall not get two hundred crowns for the whole of it; and nevertheless I must make up my mind to consent to what he wishes; for he has it in his power to make me accept anything: and the scoundrel holds me with a knife to my throat.

LA FL. Without offense, Sir, I see you exactly on the high road which Panurge took to ruin himself: taking money in advance, buying dear, selling cheap, and eating his corn whilst it was but grass.

CLÉAN. What am I to do? See to what young people are reduced by the cursed stinginess of their fathers, and then people are surprised when sons wish their fathers dead!

La Fl. One must confess that yours, with his stinginess, would incense the steadiest man in the world. I have, Heaven be praised, no very great inclination to be hanged; and, among my colleagues whom I see dabbling in many trifling things, I know well enough how to get cleverly out of a scrape, and to keep as clear as possible of those little amenities which savor more or less of the rope; but, to tell you the truth, he would, by his way of acting, give me the temptation to rob him; and I verily believe that, by doing so, I would commit a meritorious action.

Cléan. Give me this memorandum, that I may have another look at it.

Scene II:—Harpagon, Master Simon; Cléante and La Flèche *at the farther end of the stage*

Sim. Yes, Sir, it is a young man who is in want of money; his affairs compel him to find some, and he will consent to all that you dictate to him.

Harp. But think you, Master Simon, that there is no risk to run? and do you know the name, the property, and the family of him for whom you speak?

Sim. No. In reality I cannot well inform you about that, and it is only by chance that I have been recommended to him; but he will himself explain all these things to you, and his servant has assured me that you will be satisfied when you shall know him. All that I am able to tell you is that his family is very rich, that he has already lost his mother, and he will engage himself, if you wish it, that his father shall die before eight months are over.

Harp. That is something. Charity, Master Simon, enjoins us to be agreeable to people when we can.

Sim. That needs no comment.

La Fl. [*softly, to Cléante, recognizing Master Simon*]. Can anyone have told him who I am and are you perhaps betraying me?

Sim. [*to Cléante and La Flèche*]. Ah, ah! you are in a great hurry! Who told you that it was here? [*To Harpagon.*] It is not I, at least, Sir, who have given them your name and address; but, in my opinion, there is no great harm in this; they are discreet persons, and you can here come to an understanding with one another.

Harp. How?

Sim. [*pointing to Cléante*]. This gentleman is the party who wishes to borrow the fifteen thousand francs of which I spoke.

Harp. What, hangdog, it is you who abandon yourself to these culpable extravagances!

Cléan. What! it is you, father, who lend yourself to these shameful deeds!

Master Simon *runs away, and* La Flèche *hides himself.*

Scene III:—Harpagon, Cléante

Harp. It is you who wish to ruin yourself by such censurable loans?

Cléan. It is you who seek to enrich yourself by such criminal usury?

Harp. Can you dare, after this, to appear before me?

Cléan. Can you dare, after this, to show your face to the world?

Harp. Are you not ashamed, tell me, to practice this sort of excess, to rush into these dreadful expenses, and to dissipate so shamefully the property which your parents have amassed for you by the sweat of their brow?

Cléan. Do you not blush to dishonor your station by the trade you are engaged in; to sacrifice glory and reputation to the insatiable desire of piling crown upon crown, and to surpass, in matters of interest, the most infamous tricks that were ever invented by the most notorious usurers?

Harp. Begone out of my sight, scoundrel! begone out of my sight!

Cléan. Who, think you, is the more criminal—he who buys the money of which he is in need, or he who steals money for which he has no use?

Harp. Begone, I say, and do not break the drums of my ears. [*Alone.*] After all, I am not so vexed about this adventure; it will be a lesson to me to keep more than ever an eye upon his proceedings.

Scene IV:—Frosine, Harpagon

Fros. Sir.

Harp. Wait a moment: I shall be back directly to speak to you. [*Aside.*] I had better go and take a look at my money.

Scene V:—La Flèche, Frosine

La Fl. [*without seeing* Frosine]. The adventure is altogether funny! He must have somewhere a large store of furniture; for we could recognize nothing here from what is in the memorandum

Fros. Eh! is it you, my poor La Flèche! How comes this meeting?

La Fl. Ah! ah! it is you, Frosine! What brings you here?

Fros. The same that brings me everywhere else; to fetch and carry, to render myself serviceable to people, and to profit as much as possible by the small talents of which I am possessed. You know that in this world we must live by our wits, and that to persons like me, Heaven has given no other income than intrigue and industry.

La Fl. Have you any dealings with the master of this house?

Fros. Yes. I am arranging some small matter for him, for which I expect a reward.

La Fl. From him? Ah! you will have to be wide-awake enough if you get anything out of him; and I warn you that money is very scarce in this house.

Fros. There are certain services that touch to the quick marvelously.

La Fl. I am your humble servant. You do not know M. Harpagon yet. M. Harpagon is of all human beings the least human, of all mortals the hardest and most close-fisted. There is no service that touches his gratitude deeply enough to make him unloose his purse-strings. Praise, esteem, kindness in words, and friendship, as much as you like; but money, nothing of the kind. There is nothing drier and more arid than his good graces and his caresses; and *to give* is a word for which he has such an aversion that he never says: *I give you,* but *I lend you good day.*

Fros. Gad! I have the art of drawing something out of people; I have the secret of entering into their affections, of tickling their hearts, and of finding out their most sensitive spots.

La Fl. Of no avail here. I defy you to soften the man we are speaking of, so that he will give money. Upon this subject he is a Turk, but of a turkishness to cause the despair of everyone; and one might starve, and he would not budge. In one word, he loves money better than reputation, than honor, and than virtue; and the very sight of one who asks for it sends him into fits; it is touching him in his mortal part, it is piercing his heart, it is tearing out his very entrails; and if . . . But he is coming back; I am going.

Scene VI: Harpagon, Frosine

Harp. [*aside*]. Everything is going on right. [*Aloud.*] Well! what is it, Frosine?

Fros. Gad, how well you are looking; you are the very picture of health!

Harp. Who? I!

Fros. I never saw you with such a fresh and jolly complexion.

Harp. Really?

Fros. How? You never in your life looked so young as you do now; I see people of five-and-twenty who look older than you.

Harp. I am over sixty, nevertheless, Frosine.

Fros. Well! what does that signify, sixty years? that is nothing to speak of! It is the very flower of one's age, that is; and you are just entering the prime of manhood.

Harp. That is true; but twenty years less would do me no harm, I think.

Fros. Are you jesting? You have no need of that, and you are made of the stuff to live a hundred.

Harp. Do you think so?

Fros. Indeed I do. You show all the signs of it. Hold up your head a moment. Yes, it is there, well enough between your eyes, a sign of long life!

Harp. You are a judge of that sort of thing?

Fros. Undoubtedly I am. Show me your hand. Good heavens, what a line of life!

Harp. How?

Fros. Do you not see how far this line goes?

Harp. Well! what does it mean?

Fros. Upon my word, I said a hundred; but you shall pass six score.

Harp. Is it possible?

Fros. They will have to kill you, I tell you; and you shall bury your children, and your children's children.

Harp. So much the better! How is our affair getting on?

Fros. Need you ask? Does one ever see me meddle with anything that I do not bring to an issue? But for matchmaking, especially, I have a marvelous talent. There are not two people in the world whom I cannot manage, in a very short time, to couple together; and I believe that, if I took it into my head, I should marry the grand Turk to the republic of Venice. To be sure, there were no very great difficulties in this matter. As I am intimate with the ladies, I have often spoken of you to each of them; and I have told the mother of the design which you had upon Mariane, from seeing her pass in the street, and taking the fresh air at her window.

Harp. Who answered . . .

Fros. She has received your proposal with joy; and when I gave her to understand that you very much wished her daughter to be present this evening at the marriage-contract, which was to be signed for yours, she consented without difficulty, and has intrusted her to me for the purpose.

HARP. It is because I am obliged to offer a supper to M. Anselme; and I shall be glad that she share the treat.

FROS. You are right. She is to pay a visit after dinner to your daughter, whence she intends to take a turn in the fair, to come and sup here afterwards.

HARP. Well! they shall go together in my coach, which I will lend them.

FROS. That will do very nicely.

HARP. But, Frosine, have you spoken to the mother respecting the portion she can give her daughter? Have you told her that she must bestir herself a little; that she should make some effort; that she must even bleed herself a little on an occasion like that? For, after all, one does not marry a girl without her bringing something.

FROS. How something! She is a girl who brings you twelve thousand francs a year.

HARP. Twelve thousand francs!

FROS. Yes. To begin with; she has been brought up and accustomed to strict economy in feeding. She is a girl used to live on salad, milk, cheese, and apples; and who, in consequence, will neither want a well-appointed table, nor exquisite broths, nor peeled barley, at every turn, nor other delicacies which would be necessary to any other woman; and let these things cost ever so little, they always mount to about three thousand francs a year at the least. Besides this, she has no taste for anything but the utmost simplicity, and does not care for sumptuous dresses, or valuable jewels or magnificent furniture, to which other young ladies are so much given; and that comes to more than four thousand francs per annum. In addition, she has a terrible aversion to gambling, not a common thing in women of the present day; for I know one in our neighborhood who has lost more than twenty thousand francs this year at *trente-et-quarante*. But let us only estimate it at a fourth of that. Five thousand francs a year at play, and four thousand in jewelry and dresses, that makes nine thousand; and a thousand crowns, say, for the food: are there not your twelve thousand francs a year?

HARP. Yes: that is not so bad; but this reckoning contains, after all, nothing real.

FROS. Pardon me. Is it not something real to bring you for a marriage portion great sobriety, the inheritance of a great love for simplicity of dress, and the acquisition of a great hatred for gambling?

HARP. Surely it is a joke to wish to make up her

dowry to me out of expenses to which she will not go. I am not going to give a receipt for what I do not receive; and I shall have to get something down on the nail.

FROS. Good gracious! you shall get enough; and they have spoken to me of a certain country where they have some property, whereof you will become the master.

HARP. That remains to be seen. But, Frosine, there is something else still which makes me uneasy. The girl is young, as you can see; and young people ordinarily love only their equals, and seek only their society. I am afraid that a man of my age may not be to her taste, and that this might produce certain little troubles in my house, which would not at all suit me.

FROS. Ah! how little you know her! This is another peculiarity which I had to mention to you. She has a frightful aversion to young people, and cares for none except for old men.

HARP. She?

FROS. Yes, she. I should like you to have heard her speak upon that subject. She cannot at all bear the sight of a young man; but nothing gives her greater delight, she says, than to behold a handsome old man with a majestic beard. The oldest are the most charming to her; so I warn you beforehand not to make yourself look younger than you really are. She wishes one at least to be a sexagenarian; and it is not more than four months ago, that, on the point of being married, she flatly broke off the match, when it came out that her lover was but fifty-six years of age, and that he did not put spectacles on to sign the contract.

HARP. Only for that?

FROS. Yes. She says fifty-six will not do for her; and that above all things she cares for noses that wear spectacles.

HARP. You certainly tell me something new there.

FROS. She carries it farther than I could tell you. One may see some pictures and a few prints in her room; but what do you think they are? Portraits of Adonis, of Cephalus, of Paris, and of Apollo? Not at all. Beautiful likenesses of Saturn, of King Priam, of old Nestor, and of good father Anchises on his son's back.

HARP. This is admirable. That is what I should never have thought, and I am very glad to hear that she is of that disposition. In fact, had I been a woman, I should never have cared for young men.

FROS. I should think so. A nice lot they are, these

young men, to care for them! pretty beauties, indeed, these fine sparks to be enamored of! I should like to know what one can see in them!

HARP. As for me, I cannot understand it at all. I do not know how there are women who like them so much.

FROS. They must be downright fools. Does it sound like common sense to think youth amiable? Are they men at all, these young fops, and can one love such animals?

HARP. That is what I say every day; with their voices like chicken-hearted fellows, three small hairs in the beard twirled like a cat's whiskers; their tow-wigs, their breeches quite hanging down, and their open breasts!

FROS. Indeed! they are well built compared with a person like you! That is what I call a man; there is something there to please the sight; and that is the way to be made and dressed to inspire love.

HARP. Then you like my appearance?

FROS. Do I like your appearance! You are charming; your figure is worth painting. Turn round a little, if you please. Nothing could be better. Let me see you walk. That is a well-built body, free and easy as it ought to be, and without a sign of illness.

HARP. None to speak of, thank Heaven. Nothing but my cough, which worries me now and then.

FROS. That is nothing. It does not become you badly, seeing that you cough very gracefully.

HARP. Just tell me: has Mariane not seen me yet? She has not taken any notice of me in going past?

FROS. No; but we have spoken a great deal of you. I have tried to paint your person to her, and I have not failed to vaunt your merits, and the advantage which it would be to her to have a husband like you.

HARP. You have done well and I thank you for it.

FROS. I have, Sir, a slight request to make to you. I have a law-suit which I am on the point of losing for want of a little money [HARPAGON assumes a serious look]; and you might easily enable me to gain this suit by doing me a little kindness. You would not believe how delighted she will be to see you. [HARPAGON resumes his liveliness.] How you will charm her, and how this old-fashioned ruff will take her fancy! But above all things, she will like your breeches fastened to your doublet with tags; that will make her mad for

you; and a lover who wears tags will be most acceptable to her.

HARP. Certainly, I am delighted to hear you say so.

FROS. Really, Sir, this law-suit is of the utmost consequence to me. [HARPAGON resumes his serious air.] If I lose it, I am ruined; and some little assistance would set my affairs in order. . . . I should like you to have seen her delight at hearing me speak of you. [HARPAGON resumes his liveliness.] Joy shone in her eyes at the enumeration of your good qualities; and, in short, I have made her very anxious to have this match entirely concluded.

HARP. You have pleased me very much, Frosine; and I confess that I am extremely obliged to you.

FROS. I pray you, Sir, to give me the little assistance which I ask of you. [HARPAGON resumes his serious air.] It will put me on my legs again, and I shall be for ever grateful to you.

HARP. Good-by. I am going to finish my letters.

FROS. I assure you, Sir, that you could never come to my relief in a greater need.

HARP. I will give orders that my coach be ready to take you to the fair.

FROS. I would not trouble you, if I were not compelled to it from necessity.

HARP. And I will take care that the supper shall be served early, so as not to make you ill.

FROS. Do not refuse me the service which I ask of you. You would not believe, Sir, the pleasure which . . .

HARP. I must be gone. Someone is calling me. Till by-and-by.

FROS. [alone]. May ague seize you, and send you to the devil, you stingy cur! The rascal has resisted firmly all my attacks. But I must, for all that, not abandon the attempt; and I have got the other side, from whom, at any rate, I am certain to draw a good reward.

ACT III

SCENE I:—HARPAGON, CLÉANTE, ELISE, VALÈRE, MISTRESS CLAUDE *holding a broom*, MASTER JACQUES, LA MERLUCHE, BRINDAVOINE

HARP. Come here, all of you, that I may give you my orders for just now, and tell everyone what he has to do. Come here, Mistress Claude; let us begin with you. [*Looking at her broom.*] That is right, arms in hand. I trust to you for cleaning up everywhere: and above all, take care not to rub the furniture too hard, for fear of wearing it out. Besides this, I appoint you to look after the bottles during the supper; and, if one is missing, or if something gets broken, I shall hold you responsible, and deduct it from your wages.

JACQ. [*aside*]. There is policy in that punishment.

HARP. [*to* MISTRESS CLAUDE]. You can go.

SCENE II:—HARPAGON, CLÉANTE, ELISE, VALÈRE, MASTER JACQUES, BRINDAVOINE, LA MERLUCHE.

HARP. You, Brindavoine, and you, La Merluche, I confide to you the care of rinsing the glasses, and of serving out the drink, but only when the people are thirsty, and not in the manner of these impertinent lackeys who come and provoke them, and put drinking into their heads when they have no thought of such a thing. Wait till you are asked for it more than once, and bear in mind always to bring a good deal of water.

JACQ. [*aside*]. Yes. Wine undiluted mounts to the head.

LA M. Shall we throw off our smocks, Sir?

HARP. Yes, when you see the people coming; and take care not to spoil your clothes.

BRIND. You know, Sir, that the front of my doublet is covered with a large stain of oil from the lamp.

LA M. And I, Sir, I have a large hole in the seat of my breeches, and saving your presence, people can see . . .

HARP. Peace; keep it adroitly to the side of the wall, and always show your front to the world. [*To* BRINDAVOINE, *showing him how he is to keep his hat before his doublet, in order to hide the stain.*] And you, always hold your hat thus while you are waiting upon the guests.

SCENE III:—HARPAGON, CLÉANTE, ELISE, VALÈRE, MASTER JACQUES

HARP. As for you, daughter, you will keep an eye upon what goes away from the table, and take care that nothing be wasted. It becomes girls to do so. Meanwhile, get yourself ready to receive my intended properly. She is coming to visit you, and will take you to the fair with her. Do you hear what I say to you?

ELISE. Yes, father.

SCENE IV:—HARPAGON, CLÉANTE, VALÈRE, MASTER JACQUES

HARP. And you, my foppish son, to whom I have been good enough to forgive what has happened just now, do not take it into your head to show her a sour face.

CLÉAN. I, father? a sour face? And for what reason?

HARP. Egad! we know the ways of children whose fathers marry again, and with what sort of eyes they are in the habit of looking at their so-called stepmothers. But if you wish me to lose the recollection of this last escapade of yours, I recommend you, above all, to show this lady a friendly countenance, and to give her, in fact, the best possible reception.

CLÉAN. To tell you the truth, father, I cannot promise you to be glad that she is to become my stepmother. I should tell a lie if I said so to you; but as for receiving her well and showing her a friendly countenance, I promise to obey you punctually on this head.

HARP. Take care you do, at least.

CLÉAN. You shall see that you shall have no cause to complain.

HARP. You had better.

SCENE V:—HARPAGON, VALÈRE, MASTER JACQUES

HARP. You will have to help me in this, Valère. Now, Master Jacques, draw near, I have left you for the last.

JACQ. Is it to your coachman, Sir, or to your cook, that you wish to speak? For I am both the one and the other.

HARP. It is to both.

JACQ. But to which of the two first?

HARP. To the cook.

JACQ. Then wait a minute, if you please.

MASTER JACQUES *takes off his livery coat, and appears in a cook's dress.*

HARP. What the deuce does that ceremony mean?

JACQ. You have but to speak now.

HARP. I have promised, Master Jacques, to give a supper tonight.

JACQ. [*aside*]. Most miraculous!

HARP. Just tell me: will you dish us up something good?

JACQ. Yes, if you give me plenty of money.

HARP. The deuce, always money. It seems to me as if they could speak of nothing else; money, money, money! It is the only word they have got on their lips; money! they always speak of money. That is their chief argument, money.

VAL. I have never heard a more impertinent answer than that. A great wonder to dish up something good with plenty of money! It is the easiest thing in the world; any fool can do as much; but a clever man should speak of dishing up something good with little money.

JACQ. Something good with little money!

VAL. Yes.

JACQ. [to VALÈRE]. Upon my word, Master Steward, you would oblige us by showing us that secret, and by taking my place as cook; you that are meddling with everything in this house, and playing the factotum.

HARP. Hold your tongue. What shall we want?

JACQ. Apply to your steward here, who will dish you up something good for little money.

HARP. Enough! I wish you to answer me.

JACQ. How many people are to sit down?

HARP. We shall be eight or ten; but you must not count upon more than eight. If there is enough for eight, there is enough for ten.

VAL. That needs no comment.

JACQ. Very well! we must have four first-rate soups and five small dishes. Soups . . . Entrées . . .

HARP. What the devil! there is enough to feed a whole town.

JACQ. Roast . . .

HARP. [putting his hand over Jacques' mouth]. Hold! wretch, you will eat up all my substance.

JACQ. Side-dishes.

HARP [putting his hand over Jacques' mouth again]. What! more still?

VAL. [to JACQUES]. Do you intend to make everyone burst? and think you that master has invited people with the intention of killing them with food? Go and read a little the precepts of health, and ask the doctors whether there is aught more prejudicial to man than eating to excess.

HARP. He is right.

VAL. Learn, Master Jacques, you and the like of you, that a table overloaded with viands is a cutthroat business; that, to show one's self the friend of those whom one invites, frugality should reign in the meals which one offers; and that according to the saying of an ancient, *we must eat to live, and not live to eat.*

HARP. Ah! how well that is said! Come here, that I may embrace you for that saying. This is the finest sentence that I ever heard in my life; *one must live to eat, and not eat to li* . . . No, that is not it. How do you put it?

VAL. *That we must eat to live, and not live to eat.*

HARP. [to MASTER JACQUES]. That is it. Do you hear it? [To VALÈRE.] Who is the great man who has said that?

VAL. I do not recollect his name just now.

HARP. Just remember to write down these words for me: I wish to have them engraved in letters of gold on the mantel-piece of my dining-room.

VAL. I shall not forget it. And as for your supper, you have but to leave it to me; I shall manage everything right enough.

HARP. Do so.

JACQ. So much the better! I shall have less trouble.

HARP. [to VALÈRE]. We must have some of these things of which people eat very little, and which fill quickly; some good fat beans, with a potted pie, well stuffed with chestnuts. Let there be plenty of that.

VAL. Depend upon me.

HARP. And now, Master Jacques, you must clean my coach.

JACQ. Wait; that is a matter for the coachman. [Puts his livery coat on.] You were saying . . .

HARP. That you must clean my coach, and hold the horses in readiness to drive to the fair. . . .

JACQ. Your horses, Sir? Upon my word, they are not at all in a fit state to go. I will not tell you that they are on the straw; the poor beasts have not got even that much, and it would not be telling the truth; but you make them keep such austere fasts that they are no longer anything but ghosts or shadows, with horses' shapes.

HARP. They are very ill, and yet they are doing nothing!

JACQ. And because they do nothing, Sir, must they not eat? It would be far better to work the poor brutes much, and to feed them the same. It breaks my heart to see them in such a wretched condition; for, after all, I have got tender feeling for my horses; it seems to me it is myself, when I see them suffer. Not a day passes but I take the meat out of my own mouth to feed them; and, Sir, it is being too cruel to have no pity for one's neighbor.

HARP. The work will not be very hard to go as far as the fair.

JACQ. No, Sir, I have not the heart to drive them, and I would not have it on my conscience to give them the whip in the state they are in. How can you wish them to draw a coach when they can hardly drag themselves along?

VAL. Sir, I will make our neighbor, Picard, take charge of them and drive them; he will be at the same time needed to get the supper ready.

JACQ. Be it so; I prefer their dying under other people's than under mine.

VAL. Master Jacques is getting considerate!

JACQ. Sir Steward is getting indispensable!

HARP. Peace.

JACQ. I cannot bear flatterers, Sir; and I see what he makes of it; that his perpetual looking after the bread, the wine, the wood, the salt, the candles, is done only with the view of currying favor with you, and getting into your good books. This drives me mad, and I am sorry to hear every day what the world says of you; for, after all, I have some feeling for you; and, after my horses, you are the person whom I love most.

HARP. Might I know, Master Jacques, what people say of me?

JACQ. Yes, Sir, if I could be sure that it would not make you angry.

HARP. No, not in the least.

JACQ. I beg your pardon; I know full well that I shall put you in a rage.

HARP. Not at all. On the contrary, it will be obliging me, and I shall be glad to learn how people speak of me.

JACQ. Since you will have it, Sir, I shall tell you frankly that people everywhere make a jest of you, that they pelt us with a thousand jokes from every quarter on your account, and that they are never more delighted than when holding you up to ridicule, and continually relating stories of your meanness. One says that you have special almanacs printed, in which you double the ember weeks and vigils, in order to profit by the fast days, which you compel your people to keep; another that you have always a quarrel ready for your servants at New Year's day, or when they leave you, so that you may find a reason for not giving them anything. That one tells that you once sued one of your neighbor's cats for having eaten the remainder of a leg of mutton; this one again that you were surprised one night in purloining the hay of your own horses, and that your coachman, that is, the one who was here before me, dealt you I do not know how many blows in the dark, of which you never broached a word. In short, shall I tell you? one can go nowhere without hearing you hauled over the coals on all sides. You are the byword and laughing-stock of everyone; and you are never spoken of, except under the names of miser, curmudgeon, hunks, and usurer.

HARP. [thrashing MASTER JACQUES]. You are a numskull, a rascal, a scoundrel, and an impudent fellow.

JACQ. Well! did I not say so beforehand? You would not believe me. I told you well enough that I should make you angry by telling you the truth.

HARP. That will teach you how to speak.

SCENE VI:—VALÈRE, MASTER JACQUES

VAL. [laughing]. From what I can see, Master Jacques, your candor is ill rewarded.

JACQ. Zounds! Master Upstart, who assume the man of consequence, it is not your business. Laugh at your cudgel-blows when you shall receive them, but do not come here to laugh at mine.

VAL. Ah! Sir Master Jacques, do not get angry, I beg of you.

JACQ. [aside]. He is knuckling under. I shall bully him, and, if he is fool enough to be afraid of me, I shall give him a gentle drubbing. [Aloud.] Are you aware, Master Laughter, that I am not in a laughing humor, and that if you annoy me, I will make you laugh on the wrong side of your mouth? [MASTER JACQUES drives VALÈRE to the far end of the stage, threatening him.]

VAL. Eh! gently.

JACQ. How, gently? it does not suit me.

VAL. Pray.

JACQ. You are an impertinent fellow.

VAL. Sir Master Jacques . . .

JACQ. There is no Sir Master Jacques at all. If I had a stick, I would give you a good drubbing.

VAL. How, a stick! [VALÈRE makes MASTER JACQUES retreat in his turn.]

JACQ. Eh! I was not speaking of that.

VAL. Are you aware, Master Boaster, that I am the very man to give you a drubbing myself?

JACQ. I do not doubt it.

VAL. That you are, in all, nothing but a scrub of a cook?

JACQ. I am well aware of it.

VAL. And that you do not know me yet?

JACQ. I ask your pardon.

VAL. You will thrash me, say you?

JACQ. I said so only in jest.

VAL. And I say, that I do not relish your jests. [Thrashing him with a stick.] This will teach you, that you are but a sorry clown.

JACQ. [alone]. The plague take my candor! it is a bad business: I give it up for the future, and I will no more speak the truth. I might put up with it from my master; he has some right to thrash me; but as for this Master Steward, I will have my revenge if I can.

SCENE VII:—MARIANE, FROSINE, MASTER JACQUES

FROS. Do you know, Master Jacques, if your master is at home?

Jacq. Yes, indeed, he is; I know it but too well.

Fros. Tell him, pray, that we are here.

Scene VIII:—Mariane, Frosine

Mar. Ah! I feel very strange, Frosine! and, if I must tell you what I feel, I dread this interview!

Fros. But why, and whence this uneasiness?

Mar. Alas! can you ask me? and can you not imagine the alarms of anyone at the sight of the rack to which she is going to be tied?

Fros. I see well enough, that to die pleasantly, Harpagon is not exactly the rack which you would care to embrace; and I can see by your face, that this young spark, of whom you spoke to me, comes afresh into your head.

Mar. Yes! it is an accusation, Frosine, from which I shall not defend myself; and the respectful visits which he has paid us, have, I confess, made some impression on my heart.

Fros. But have you ascertained who he is?

Mar. No, I do not know who he is. But this I know, that he is made to be beloved: that, if things could be left to my choice, I would sooner have him than any other, and that he is the chief cause in making me feel that the husband whom they wish to give me is a terrible torment.

Fros. Egad, all these youngsters are agreeable, and play their part well enough, but most of them are as poor as church mice: it will be much better for you to take an old husband who will make you a good settlement. I grant you that the senses will not find their account so well on the side I speak of, and that there are some little distastes to overcome with such a spouse; but that cannot last, and his death, believe me, will soon put you in a position to take one who is more amiable, and who will mend all things.

Mar. Good gracious! Frosine, it is a strange thing that, to be happy, we should wish for or await the death of someone; the more so as death does not always accommodate itself to our projects.

Fros. Are you jesting? You marry him only on condition of soon leaving you a widow; and that must be one of the articles of the contract. It would be impertinent in him not to die within three months! Here he is himself!

Mar. Ah! Frosine, what a figure!

Scene IX:—Harpagon, Mariane, Frosine

Harp. [to Mariane]. Do not be offended, my beauty, that I come to you with my spectacles on. I know that your charms strike the eye sufficiently, are visible enough by themselves, and that there is no need of spectacles to perceive them; but after all, it is through them that we look at the stars, and I maintain and vouch for it that you are a star; but a star, the brightest in the land of stars. Frosine, she does not answer a word, and does not testify, from what I can perceive, the slightest joy in seeing me.

Fros. It is because she is as yet taken all aback; and besides, girls are always ashamed to show at first sight what passes in their hearts.

Harp. You are right. [To Mariane.] Here comes my daughter, sweet child, to welcome you.

Scene X:—Harpagon, Elise, Mariane, Frosine

Mar. I am much behind, Madam, in acquitting myself of such a visit.

Elise. You have done, Madam, what it was my duty to do, and it was my place to have been beforehand with you.

Harp. You see what a great girl she is; but ill weeds grow apace.

Mar. [in a whisper, to Frosine]. Oh! what an unpleasant man!

Harp. [in a whisper, to Frosine]. What says the fair one?

Fros. That she thinks you admirable.

Harp. You do me too much honor, adorable pet.

Mar. [aside]. What a brute!

Harp. I am much obliged to you for these sentiments.

Mar. [aside]. I can hold out no longer.

Scene XI:—Harpagon, Mariane, Elise, Cléante, Frosine, Brindavoine

Harp. There comes my son also, to pay his respects to you.

Mar. [in a whisper, to Frosine]. Ah! Frosine, what a meeting! It is the very person of whom I spoke to you.

Fros. [to Mariane]. The adventure is wonderful.

Harp. I see that you are surprised at my having such grown-up children; but I shall soon be rid of one and the other.

Cléan. [to Mariane]. Madam, to tell you the truth, this is an adventure, which no doubt, I did not expect; and my father has not a little astonished me, when, a short time ago, he communicated to me the plan which he had formed.

Mar. I may say the same thing. It is an unforeseen meeting which surprises me as much as it does you; and I was not at all prepared for such an adventure.

CLÉAN. It is true that my father, Madam, could not make a better choice, and that the honor of seeing you gives me unfeigned joy, but for all that, I cannot give you the assurance that I rejoice at the design which you may have of becoming my step-mother. I avow to you that it would be too much for me to pay you that compliment; and by your leave, it is a title which I do not wish you. This speech may become coarse to some; but I am sure that you will be the one to take it in the proper sense; that it is a marriage, Madam, for which, as you may well imagine, I can have only repugnance; that you are not unaware, knowing what I am, how it clashes with my interests; and that, in short, you will not take it amiss when I tell you, with the permission of my father, that, if matters depended upon me, this marriage would not take place.

HARP. This is a most impertinent compliment! What a pretty confession to make to her!

MAR. And I, in reply, must tell you, that things are pretty equal; and that, if you have any repugnance in seeing me your stepmother, I shall have, doubtless, no less in seeing you my step-son. Do not think, I pray you, that it is I who seek to give you that uneasiness. I should be very sorry to cause you any displeasure; and unless I see myself compelled to it by an absolute power, I give you my word that I shall not consent to a marriage that vexes you.

HARP. She is right. To a silly compliment, a similar retort is necessary. I beg your pardon, my dear, for the impertinence of my son; he is a young fool, who does not as yet know the consequence of what he says.

MAR. I promise you that what he has said has not at all offended me; on the contrary, he has pleased me by explaining thus his real feelings. I like such an avowal from his lips; and if he had spoken in any other way, I should have esteemed him the less for it.

HARP. It is too good of you to be willing thus to condone his faults. Time will make him wiser, and you shall see that he will alter his sentiments.

CLÉAN. No, father, I am incapable of changing upon that point, and I beg urgently of this lady to believe me.

HARP. But see what madness! he goes still more strongly.

CLÉAN. Do you wish me to go against my own heart?

HARP. Again! Perhaps you will be kind enough to change the conversation.

CLÉAN. Well! since you wish to speak in a different manner, allow me, Madam, to put myself in my father's place, and to confess to you that I have seen nothing in the world so charming as you; that I conceive nothing equal to the happiness of pleasing you, and that the title of your husband is a glory, a felicity which I would prefer to the destinies of the greatest princes on earth. Yes, Madam, the happiness of possessing you is, in my eyes, the best of all good fortunes; the whole of my ambition points to that. There is nothing which I would shrink from to make so precious a conquest; and the most powerful obstacles . . .

HARP. Gently, son, if you please.

CLÉAN. It is a compliment which I pay for you to this lady.

HARP. Good Heavens! I have a tongue to explain myself, and I have no need of an interpreter like you. Come, hand chairs.

FROS. No; it is better that we should go to the fair now, so that we may return the sooner, and have ample time afterwards to converse with you.

HARP. [to BRINDAVOINE]. Have the horses put to the carriage.

SCENE XII:—HARPAGON, MARIANE, ELISE, CLÉANTE, VALÈRE, FROSINE

HARP. [to MARIANE]. I pray you to excuse me, fair child, if I forgot to offer you some refreshments before going.

CLÉAN. I have provided for it, father, and have ordered some plates of China oranges, sweet citrons, and preserves, which I have sent for in your name.

HARP. [softly to VALÈRE]. Valère!

VAL. [to HARPAGON]. He has lost his senses.

CLÉAN. Do you think, father, that it is not sufficient? This lady will have the goodness to excuse that, if it please her.

MAR. It was not at all necessary.

CLÉAN. Have you ever seen, Madam, a diamond more sparkling than the one which you see on my father's finger?

MAR. It sparkles much indeed.

CLÉAN. [taking the diamond off his father's finger, and handing it to MARIANE]. You must see it close.

MAR. It is no doubt very beautiful, and throws out a deal of light.

CLÉAN. [placing himself before MARIANE, who is

about to return the diamond]. No, Madam, it is in hands too beautiful. It is a present which my father makes you.

HARP. I?

CLÉAN. Is it not true, father, that you wish this lady to keep it for your sake?

HARP. [*softly to his son*]. How?

CLÉAN. [*to* MARIANE]. A pretty request indeed! He has given me a sign to make you accept it.

MAR. I do not wish to . . .

CLÉAN. [*to* MARIANE]. Are you jesting? He does not care to take it back.

HARP. [*aside*]. I am bursting with rage!

MAR. It would be . . .

CLÉAN. [*preventing* MARIANE *from returning the diamond*]. No, I tell you; you would offend him.

MAR. Pray . . .

CLÉAN. Not at all.

HARP. [*aside*]. May the plague . . .

CLÉAN. He is getting angry at your refusal.

HARP. [*softly to his son*]. Ah! you wretch!

CLÉAN. [*to* MARIANE]. You see that he is getting desperate.

HARP. [*in a suppressed tone to his son, threatening him*]. Murderer that you are!

CLÉAN. It is not my fault, father. I am doing all that I can to make her keep it; but she is obstinate.

HARP. [*in a great passion, whispering to his son*]. Hangdog!

CLÉAN. You are the cause, Madam, of my father's upbraiding me.

HARP. [*same as before, to his son*]. The scoundrel!

CLÉAN. [*to* MARIANE]. You will make him ill. Pray, Madam, do not resist any longer.

FROS. [*to* MARIANE]. Good Heavens, what ceremonies! Keep the ring, since the gentleman wishes it.

MAR. [*to* HARPAGON]. Not to put you into a passion, I shall keep it now, and I shall take another opportunity of returning it to you.

SCENE XIII:—HARPAGON, MARIANE, ELISE, CLÉANTE, VALÈRE, FROSINE, BRINDAVOINE

BRIND. Sir, there is a man who wishes to speak to you.

HARP. Tell him that I am engaged, that he is to return at another time.

BRIND. He says that he brings you some money.

HARP. [*to* MARIANE]. I beg your pardon; I shall be back directly.

SCENE XIV:—HARPAGON, MARIANE, ELISE, CLÉANTE, VALÈRE, FROSINE, LA MERLUCHE

LA M. [*running against* HARPAGON, *whom he knocks down*]. Sir . . .

HARP. Oh! I am killed!

CLÉAN. What is it, father? have you hurt yourself?

HARP. The wretch has surely been bribed by my debtors to make me break my neck.

VAL. [*to* HARPAGON]. That will be nothing.

LA M. [*to* HARPAGON]. I beg your pardon, Sir; I thought I was doing well in running quickly.

HARP. What have you come here for, you hangdog?

LA M. To tell you that your two horses have lost their shoes.

HARP. Let them be taken to the farrier immediately.

CLÉAN. While waiting for their being shod, I will do the honors of your house for you, father, and conduct this lady into the garden, whither I shall have the refreshments brought.

SCENE XV:—HARPAGON, VALÈRE

HARP. Valère, keep your eye a little on this, and take care, I pray you, to save as much of it as you can, to send back to the tradespeople.

VAL. I know.

HARP. [*alone*]. Oh, impertinent son! do you mean to ruin me?

ACT IV

SCENE I:—CLÉANTE, MARIANE, ELISE, FROSINE

CLÉAN. Let us go in here; we shall be much better. There is no suspicious person near us now, and we can converse freely.

ELISE. Yes, Madam, my brother has confided to me the affection which he feels for you. I am aware of the grief and unpleasantness which such obstacles are capable of causing; and it is, I assure you, with the utmost tenderness that I interest myself in your adventure.

MAR. It is a sweet consolation to see someone like you in one's interest; and I implore you, Madam, always to reserve for me this generous friendship, so capable of alleviating the cruelties of fortune.

FROS. You are, upon my word, both unlucky people, in not having warned me before this of your affair. I would, no doubt, have warded off this uneasiness from you, and not have carried matters so far as they now are.

CLÉAN. Whose fault is it? It is my evil destiny that has willed it so. But fair Mariane, what have you resolved to do?

MAR. Alas! am I able to make any resolutions? And, in the dependent position in which you see me, can I form aught else than wishes?

CLÉAN. No other support in your heart for me than mere wishes? No strenuous pity? No helping kindness? No energetic affection?

MAR. What can I say to you? Put yourself in my place, and see what I can do. Advise, command yourself: I leave the matter to you; and I think you too reasonable to wish to exact from me aught but what may be consistent with honor and decency.

CLÉAN. Alas! to what straits do you reduce me by driving me back to what the annoying dictates of a rigorous honor and a scrupulous decency only will permit?

MAR. But what would you have me to do? Even if I could forego the many scruples to which my sex compels me, I have some consideration for my mother. She has always brought me up with the utmost tenderness, and I could not make up my mind to cause her any displeasure. Treat, transact with her; use all your means to gain her mind. You may say and do whatever you like, I give you full power; and if nothing is wanting but to declare myself in your favor, I am willing, myself, to make to her the avowal of all that I feel for you.

CLÉAN. Frosine, dear Frosine, will you try to serve us?

FROS. Upon my word, need you ask? I should like it with all my heart. You know that, naturally, I am kind-hearted enough. Heaven has not given me a heart of iron, and I have only too much inclination for rendering little services when I see people who love each other in all decency and honor. What can we do in this matter?

CLÉAN. Pray consider a little.

MAR. Give us some advice.

ELISE. Invent some means of undoing what you have done.

FROS. That is difficult enough. [*To* MARIANE.] As for your mother, she is not altogether unreasonable, and we might perhaps prevail upon her and induce her to transfer to the son the gift which she wished to make to the father. [*To* CLÉANTE.] But the mischief in it is that your father is your father.

CLÉAN. Of course.

FROS. I mean that he will bear malice if he finds that he is refused, and that he will not be of a mind afterwards to give his consent to your marriage. To do well, the refusal ought to come from himself, and she ought to try, by some means, to inspire him with a disgust towards her.

CLÉAN. You are right.

FROS. Yes, I am right; I know that well enough. That is what is wanted, but how the deuce can we find the means? Stop! Suppose we had some woman a little advanced in age who had my talent, and acted sufficiently well to counterfeit a lady of quality, by the help of a retinue made up in haste, and with an eccentric name of a marchioness or a viscountess, whom we will suppose to come from Lower Brittany, I would have skill enough to make your father believe that she was a person possessed of a hundred thousand crowns in ready money, besides her houses; that she was distractedly enamored of him, and had so set her mind upon being his wife, that she would make all her property over to him by marriage-contract. I do not doubt that he would lend an ear to this proposal. For, after all, he loves you much, I know it, but he loves money a little more; and when, dazzled with this bait, he had once given his consent in what concerns you, it would matter very little if he were afterwards disabused, when he wished to see more clearly into the property of our marchioness.

CLÉAN. All this is very well conceived.

FROS. Let me manage. I just recollect one of my friends who will suit us.

CLÉAN. Be assured of my gratitude, Frosine, if you carry out this matter. But, charming Mariane, let us begin, I pray you, by gaining over your mother; it is doing much, at any rate, to break off this match. Make every possible effort on your part, I entreat you. Employ all the power which her tenderness for you gives you over her. Show her unreserved, the eloquent graces, the all-powerful charms, with which Heaven has endowed your eyes and your lips; and please do not overlook any of these tender words, of these sweet prayers, and of these winning caresses to which, I am persuaded, nothing can be refused.

MAR. I will do my best, and forget nothing.

SCENE II:—HARPAGON, CLÉANTE, MARIANE, ELISE, FROSINE

HARP. [*aside, without being seen*]. Hey day! my son kisses the hand of his intended stepmother;

and his intended stepmother does not seem to take it much amiss! Can there be any mystery underneath this?

ELISE. Here is my father.

HARP. The carriage is quite ready; you can start as soon as you like.

CLÉAN. Since you are not going, father, permit me to escort them.

HARP. No: remain here. They will do well enough by themselves, and I want you.

SCENE III:—HARPAGON, CLÉANTE

HARP. Now, tell me, apart from becoming your stepmother, what think you of this lady?

CLÉAN. What do I think of her?

HARP. Yes, of her air, of her figure, of her beauty, of her mind?

CLÉAN. So, so.

HARP. That is no answer.

CLÉAN. To speak to you candidly, I have not found her what I expected. Her air is that of a downright coquette, her figure is sufficiently awkward, her beauty very so-so, and her mind quite ordinary. Do not think, father, that this is said to give you a distaste for her; for, stepmother for stepmother, I would as soon have her as any other.

HARP. You said to her just now, however . . .

CLÉAN. I have said some sweet nothings to her in your name, but it was to please you.

HARP. So much so, that you would not feel any inclination towards her?

CLÉAN. I? not at all.

HARP. I am sorry for it; for it does away with an idea that came into my head. In seeing her here, I have reflected upon my age; and I thought that people might find something to cavil at in seeing me marry so young a girl. This consideration has made me abandon the plan; and as I have made the demand of her hand, and am engaged to her by my word, I would have given her to you, had it not been for the aversion which you show.

CLÉAN. To me?

HARP. To you.

CLÉAN. In marriage?

HARP. In marriage.

CLÉAN. Listen. It is true that she is not much to my taste; but to please you, father, I would make up my mind to marry her, if you wish it.

HARP. I, I am more reasonable than you give me credit for. I will not force your inclination.

CLÉAN. Pardon me; I will make this effort for your sake.

HARP. No, no. No marriage can be happy where there is no inclination.

CLÉAN. Perhaps it will come afterwards, father; they say that love is often the fruit of wedlock.

HARP. No. From the side of the man, one must not risk such a thing; it generally brings grievous consequences, to which I do not care to commit myself. Had you felt any inclination for her, it would have been a different thing; I should have made you marry her instead of me; but, that not being the case, I will follow up my first plan, and marry her myself.

CLÉAN. Well! father, since matters are so, I must lay open my heart to you; I must reveal our secret to you. The truth is, I love her, since, on a certain day, I saw her walking; that my plan was, a short while ago, to ask her to become my wife, and that nothing restrained me but the declaration of your sentiments, and the fear of displeasing you.

HARP. Have you paid her any visits?

CLÉAN. Yes, father.

HARP. Many times?

CLÉAN. Just enough, considering the time of our acquaintance.

HARP. Have you been well received?

CLÉAN. Very well, indeed, but without her knowing who I was; and that is what just now caused the surprise of Mariane.

HARP. Have you declared your passion to her, and the design you had to marry her?

CLÉAN. Indeed yes; and I even made some overtures to her mother about it.

HARP. Has she listened to your proposal for her daughter?

CLÉAN. Yes, very civilly.

HARP. And does the girl much reciprocate your love?

CLÉAN. If I am to believe appearances, I flatter myself, father, that she has some affection for me.

HARP. [softly, to himself]. I am glad to have found out such a secret; that is just what I wished. [Aloud.] Hark you, my son, do you know what you will have to do? You must think, if you please, of getting rid of your love, of ceasing from all pursuits of a person whom I intend for myself, and of marrying shortly the one who has been destined for you.

CLÉAN. So, father; it is thus that you trick me! Well! since matters have come to this pass, I declare to you, that I will not get rid of my love for Mariane; that there is nothing from which I shall shrink to dispute with you her possession; and that, if you have the consent of a mother on your side, I have other resources, perhaps, which will combat on mine.

HARP. What, hang-dog, you have the audacity to poach on my preserves!

CLÉAN. It is you that are poaching on mine. I am the first comer.

HARP. Am I not your father, and do you not owe me respect?

CLÉAN. This is not a matter in which a child is obliged to defer to his father, and love is no respecter of persons.

HARP. I will make you respect me well enough with some sound cudgel-blows.

CLÉAN. All your threats will do nothing.

HARP. You shall renounce Mariane.

CLÉAN. I shall do nothing of the kind.

HARP. Give me a stick immediately.

SCENE IV:—HARPAGON, CLÉANTE, MASTER JACQUES

JACQ. Eh, eh, eh, gentlemen, what is all this? what are you thinking about?

CLÉAN. I do not care a straw.

JACQ. [to CLÉANTE]. Come, Sir, gently.

HARP. To speak to me with such impertinence!

JACQ. [to HARPAGON]. Pray, Sir, pray!

CLÉAN. I will not bate a jot.

JACQ. [to CLÉANTE]. Eh what! to your father?

HARP. Let me alone.

JACQ. [to HARPAGON]. What! to your son? I could overlook it to myself.

HARP. I will make yourself, Master Jacques, judge in this affair, to show you that I am in the right.

JACQ. I consent. [To CLÉANTE.] Get a little farther away.

HARP. I love a girl whom I wish to marry; and the hang-dog has the insolence to love her also, and to aspire to her hand in spite of my commands.

JACQ. He is wrong there.

HARP. Is it not a dreadful thing for a son to wish to enter into rivalry with his father? and ought he not, out of respect, to abstain from meddling with my inclinations?

JACQ. You are right. Let me speak to him, while you remain here.

CLÉAN. [to MASTER JACQUES, who is approaching him]. Well! yes, since he chooses you as judge, I shall not draw back; it matters not to me who it may be; and I am willing to refer to you, Master Jacques, in this our quarrel.

JACQ. You do me much honor.

CLÉAN. I am smitten with a young girl who re-
turns my affection, and tenderly accepts the offer of my love: and my father takes it into his head to come and trouble our passion, by asking for her hand.

JACQ. He is assuredly wrong.

CLÉAN. Is he not ashamed at his age to think of marrying? Does it still become him to be in love, and should he not leave this pastime to young people?

JACQ. You are right. He is only jesting. Let me speak a few words to him. [To HARPAGON.] Well! your son is not so strange as you make him out, and he is amenable to reason. He says that he knows the respect which he owes you, that he was only carried away by momentary warmth; and that he will not refuse to submit to your pleasure, provided you will treat him better than you do, and give him someone for a wife with whom he shall have reason to be satisfied.

HARP. Ah! tell him, Master Jacques, that, if he looks at it in that way, he may expect everything of me, and that, except Mariane, I leave him free to choose whom he likes.

JACQ. Let me manage it. [To CLÉANTE.] Well! your father is not so unreasonable as you make him out; and he has shown me that it was your violence that made him angry; that he objects only to your behavior; and that he will be very much disposed to grant you what you wish, provided you shall do things gently, and show him the deference, the respect, and the submission which a son owes to his father.

CLÉAN. Ah! Master Jacques, you may assure him that if he grants me Mariane, he will always find me the most submissive of beings, and that I never shall do anything except what he wishes.

JACQ. [to HARPAGON]. That is done. He consents to what you say.

HARP. Then things will go in the best possible way.

JACQ. [to CLÉANTE]. Everything is arranged; he is satisfied with your promises!

CLÉAN. Heaven be praised!

JACQ. Gentlemen, you have but to talk the matter over: you are agreed now, and you were going to quarrel for want of understanding each other.

CLÉAN. My dear Master Jacques, I shall be obliged to you all my life.

JACQ. Do not mention it, Sir.

HARP. You have given me great pleasure, Master Jacques; and that deserves a reward. [HARPAGON fumbles in his pockets; MASTER JACQUES holds out his hand, but HARPAGON only draws out his hand·

ᴋerchief.] Go now, I shall remember this, I assure you.

Jᴀᴄǫ. I kiss your hands.

Scene V:—Harpagon, Cléante

Cʟéᴀɴ. I ask your pardon, father, for the passion which I have displayed.

Hᴀʀᴘ. Never mind.

Cʟéᴀɴ. I assure you that I regret it exceedingly.

Hᴀʀᴘ. And I, I have the greatest delight in seeing you reasonable.

Cʟéᴀɴ. How good of you to forget my fault so quickly!

Hᴀʀᴘ. The faults of children are easily forgotten, when they return to their duty.

Cʟéᴀɴ. What! not retain any resentment for all my extravagance?

Hᴀʀᴘ. You compel me to it, by the submission and the respect to which you pledge yourself.

Cʟéᴀɴ. I promise you, father, that I shall carry the recollection of your goodness to my grave with me.

Hᴀʀᴘ. And I, I promise you, that you may obtain anything from me.

Cʟéᴀɴ. Ah! father, I ask for nothing more; you have given me enough by giving me Mariane.

Hᴀʀᴘ. How!

Cʟéᴀɴ. I say, father, that I am too well pleased with you, and that I find everything in your kindness in giving me Mariane.

Hᴀʀᴘ. Who says anything to you of giving you Mariane?

Cʟéᴀɴ. You, father.

Hᴀʀᴘ. I!

Cʟéᴀɴ. Undoubtedly.

Hᴀʀᴘ. What! it is you who have promised to renounce her.

Cʟéᴀɴ. I renounce her!

Hᴀʀᴘ. Yes.

Cʟéᴀɴ. Not at all.

Hᴀʀᴘ. You have not given up your pretensions to her?

Cʟéᴀɴ. On the contrary, I am more determined than ever upon them.

Hᴀʀᴘ. What! hang-dog, you begin afresh?

Cʟéᴀɴ. Nothing can change my mind.

Hᴀʀᴘ. Let me get at you, wretch.

Cʟéᴀɴ. Do what you like.

Hᴀʀᴘ. I forbid you ever to come within my sight.

Cʟéᴀɴ. All right.

Hᴀʀᴘ. I abandon you.

Cʟéᴀɴ. Abandon as much as you like.

Hᴀʀᴘ. I disown you as my son.

Cʟéᴀɴ. Be it so.

Hᴀʀᴘ. I disinherit you.

Cʟéᴀɴ. Whatever you please.

Hᴀʀᴘ. And I give you my malediction.

Cʟéᴀɴ. I want none of your gifts.

Scene VI:—Cléante, La Flèche

Lᴀ Fʟ. [coming from the garden with a casket under his arm]. Ah! Sir, I find you in the nick of time! Follow me quickly.

Cʟéᴀɴ. What is the matter?

Lᴀ Fʟ. Follow me, I tell you; we are all right.

Cʟéᴀɴ. How?

Lᴀ Fʟ. Here is your affair.

Cʟéᴀɴ. What?

Lᴀ Fʟ. I kept my eye upon this the whole day.

Cʟéᴀɴ. What is it?

Lᴀ Fʟ. Your father's treasure, which I have laid hands on.

Cʟéᴀɴ. How did you manage?

Lᴀ Fʟ. You shall know all. Let us fly; I hear his shouts.

Scene VII:—Harpagon, *aloud, shouting in the garden, rushing in without his hat*

Thieves! Thieves! Murder! Stop the murderers! Justice! just Heaven! I am lost! I am killed; they have cut my throat; they have stolen my money. Who can it be? What has become of him? Where is he? Where does he hide himself? What shall I do to find him? Where to run? Where not to run? Is he not there? Who is it? Stop! [*To himself, pressing his own arm.*] Give me back my money, scoundrel. . . . Ah, it is myself! My senses are wandering, and I do not know where I am, who I am, and what I am doing. Alas! my poor money! my poor money! my dearest friend, they have deprived me of you; and as you are taken from me, I have lost my support, my consolation, my joy: everything is at an end for me, and I have nothing more to do in this world. Without you, life becomes impossible. It is all over; I am utterly exhausted; I am dying; I am dead; I am buried. Is there no one who will resuscitate me by giving me back my beloved money, or by telling me who has taken it? Eh! what do you say? There is no one. Whoever he is who has done this, he must have carefully watched his hour; and he has just chosen the time when I was speaking to my wretch of a son. Let us go. I must inform the authorities, and have the whole of my household examined; female-servants, male-servants, son, daughter, and myself also. What an assembly! I do not look at anyone whom I do not suspect, and everyone seems to be my thief. Eh! what are they speaking of yonder? of him who has robbed me? What noise is that up there? Is it my thief who is there? For pity's sake, if you know any news of my thief, I implore you to tell me. Is he not hidden among you? They are all looking at me, and laughing in my face. You will see that they have, no doubt, a share in the robbery. Come quickly, magistrates, police-officers, provosts, judges, instruments of torture, gibbets, and executioners. I will have the whole world hanged; and if I do not recover my money, I will hang myself afterwards.

ACT V

Scene I:—Harpagon, *A Magistrate*

Mag. Let me manage it; I know my business, thank Heaven. Today is not the first time that I am engaged in discovering robberies; and I should like to have as many bags of a thousand francs as the number of people I have helped hang.

Harp. Every magistrate must have an interest in taking this matter in hand; and, if they do not enable me to find my money again, I shall demand justice upon the authorities themselves.

Mag. We must take all the needful steps. You said that there was in this box . . .

Harp. Ten thousand crowns in cash.

Mag. Ten thousand crowns!

Harp. [*crying*]. Ten thousand crowns.

Mag. The robbery is considerable!

Harp. There is no punishment great enough for the enormity of this crime; and, if it remain unpunished, the most sacred things are no longer safe.

Mag. And in what coin was this sum?

Harp. In good louis d'or and pistoles without a flaw.

Mag. Whom do you suspect of this robbery?

Harp. Everyone; and I wish you to arrest the town and the suburbs.

Mag. You must, if you will take my opinion, scare nobody, but endeavor gently to collect some proofs, in order to act afterwards, by severer process, to recover the coin which has been taken from you.

Scene II:—Harpagon, *A Magistrate*, Master Jacques

Jacq. [*at the far end of the stage, turning towards the door by which he entered*]. I am coming back directly. Let its throat be cut immediately; let them singe me its feet; let them put it in boiling water, and let them hang it from the ceiling.

Harp. Who? he who has robbed me?

Jacq. I am speaking of a sucking pig which your steward has just sent in, and I wish to dress it for you after my own fancy.

Harp. There is no question of that; and this is a gentleman to whom you must speak of something else.

Mag. [*to Master Jacques*]. Do not be alarmed. I am not the man to cause any scandal, and matters will be managed in a gentle way.

Jacq. Is this gentleman of the supper party?

Mag. In this case, dear friend, you must hide nothing from your master.

Jacq. Upon my word, Sir, I shall show all I know, and I shall treat you in the best possible way.

Harp. That is not the question.

Jacq. If I do not dish you up something as good as I could wish, it is the fault of your Master Steward, who has clipped my wings with the scissors of his economy.

Harp. You wretch! It concerns something else than the supper; and I wish you to give me some information respecting the money that has been stolen from me.

Jacq. They have stolen some money from you?

Harp. Yes, you scoundrel; and I shall have you hanged if you do not give it me back again.

Mag. [*to Harpagon*]. Good Heavens! do not ill-use him. I perceive by his face that he is an honest man, and that, without having him locked up, he will inform you of what you wish to know. Yes, my friend, if you confess the matter to me, no harm will come to you, and you will be suitably rewarded by your master. He has been robbed of his money today; and it is scarcely possible that you do not know something of the matter.

Jacq. [*aside to himself*]. This is just what I wish, in order to revenge myself on our steward. Since he has set foot in this house, he is the favorite; his counsels are the only ones listened to; and the cudgel-blows, just now received, are also sticking in my throat.

Harp. What are you muttering to yourself about?

Mag. [*to Harpagon*]. Leave him alone. He is preparing to give you satisfaction; and I told you that he was an honest man.

Jacq. If you wish me to tell you things as they

are, Sir, I believe that it is your dear steward who has done this.

HARP. Valère!

JACQ. Yes.

HARP. He! who seemed so faithful to me?

JACQ. Himself. I believe that he is the one who robbed you.

HARP. And upon what do you base your belief?

JACQ. Upon what?

HARP. Yes.

JACQ. I believe it . . . because I believe it.

MAG. But it is necessary to mention the evidence which you have.

HARP. Have you seen him hang about the spot where I had put my money?

JACQ. Yes, indeed. Where was your money?

HARP. In the garden.

JACQ. That is just where I have seen him hanging about, in the garden. And what was this money in?

HARP. In a cash-box.

JACQ. The very thing. I have seen him with a cash-box.

HARP. And this cash-box, how is it made? I shall soon see if it be mine.

JACQ. How is it made?

HARP. Yes.

JACQ. It is made . . . It is made like a cash-box.

MAG. Of course. But just describe it a little, that I may see.

JACQ. It is a large cash-box.

HARP. The one that has been stolen from me is a small one.

JACQ. Eh! Yes, it is small, if you take it in that way; but I call it large on account of its contents.

MAG. And what color is it?

JACQ. What color?

MAG. Yes.

JACQ. It is of a color . . . of a certain color. Could you not help me to say?

HARP. Ah!

JACQ. Is it not red?

HARP. No, gray.

JACQ. Yes, that is it, grayish-red; that is what I meant.

HARP. There is no longer any doubt; it is the one assuredly. Write down, Sir, write down his deposition. Heavens! whom is one to trust henceforth! One must no longer swear to anything; and I verily believe, after this, that I am the man to ⁵⁰ rob myself.

JACQ. [to HARPAGON]. He is just coming back, Sir. Do not tell him, at least, that it is I who have revealed all this.

SCENE III:—HARPAGON, *Magistrate,* VALÈRE, MASTER JACQUES

HARP. Come near, and confess to the blackest deed, the most horrible crime that ever was committed.

VAL. What do you wish, Sir?

HARP. How, wretch! you do not blush for your crime?

VAL. Of what crime are you talking?

HARP. Of what crime am I talking, infamous monster! as if you did not know what I mean! It is in vain that you attempt to disguise it; the thing has been discovered, and I have just learned all. How could you thus abuse my kindness, and introduce yourself into my house expressly to betray me, to play me a trick of that sort?

VAL. Since everything has been revealed to you, Sir, I will not prevaricate, and deny the matter to you.

JACQ. [aside]. Oh! Oh! Could I unconsciously have guessed aright!

VAL. It was my intention to speak to you about it, and I wished to wait for a favorable opportunity; but, since matters are so, I implore you not to be angry, and to be willing to listen to my motives.

HARP. And what pretty motives can you advance, infamous thief?

VAL. Ah! Sir, I have not deserved these names. It is true that I have committed an offense against you; but after all, the fault is pardonable.

HARP. How! pardonable? A trap, a murder like that?

VAL. For pity's sake, do not get angry. When you have heard me, you will see that the harm is not so great as you make it.

HARP. The harm is not so great as I make it! What! my blood, my very heart, hang-dog!

VAL. Your blood, Sir, has not fallen into bad hands. I am of a rank not to do it any injury; and there is nothing in all this but what I can easily repair.

HARP. That is what I intend, and that you should restore to me what you have robbed me of.

VAL. Your honor shall be amply satisfied, Sir.

HARP. There is no question of honor in it. But tell me, who has driven you to such a deed?

VAL. Alas! need you ask me?

HARP. Yes, indeed, I do ask you.

VAL. A god who carries his excuse for all he makes people do. Love.

HARP. Love?

VAL. Yes.

HARP. A pretty love, a pretty love, upon my word! the love for my gold pieces!

VAL. No, Sir, it is not your wealth that has tempted me; it is not that which has dazzled me; and I protest that I have not the slightest design upon your property, provided you leave me that which I have got.

HARP. No, by all the devils I shall not leave it to you. But see what insolence to wish to keep that of which he has robbed me!

VAL. Do you call that robbery?

HARP. If I call it a robbery? a treasure like that!

VAL. It is a treasure, that is true, and the most precious which you have got, no doubt; but it would not be losing it to leave it to me. I ask you for it on my knees, this treasure full of charms; and to do right, you should grant it to me.

HARP. I shall do nothing of the kind. What does it all mean?

VAL. We have pledged our faith to each other, and have sworn never to part.

HARP. The oath is admirable, and the promise rather funny.

VAL. Yes, we have bound ourselves to be all in all to each other for ever.

HARP. I shall hinder you from it, I assure you.

VAL. Nothing but death shall separate us.

HARP. It is being devilishly enamored of my money.

VAL. I have told you already, Sir, that interest did not urge me to do what I have done. My heart did not act from the motives which you imagine; a nobler one inspired me with this resolution.

HARP. You shall see that it is from Christian charity that he covets my property! But I shall look to that; and the law will give me satisfaction for all this, you bare-faced rogue.

VAL. You shall act as you like, and I am ready to bear all the violence you please; but I implore you to believe, at least, that if harm has been done, I only am to be blamed, and that in all this, your daughter is in nowise culpable.

HARP. Indeed, I believe you! it would be very strange if my daughter had had a part in this crime. But I will have my property back again, and I will have you confess where you have carried it away to.

VAL. I? I have not carried it away at all. It is still in your house.

HARP. [aside]. O! my beloved cash-box! [Aloud.] Then it has not gone out of my house?

VAL. No, Sir.

HARP. Just tell me that you have not made free with it?

VAL. I make free with it! Ah! you wrong us both; and it is with a wholly pure and respectable ardor that I burn.

HARP. [aside]. Burn for my cash-box!

VAL. I would sooner die than show her any offensive thought; she is too prudent and honorable for that.

HARP. [aside]. My cash-box too honorable!

VAL. All my wishes are confined to enjoy the sight of her; and nothing criminal has profaned the passion with which her beautiful eyes have inspired me.

HARP. [aside]. The beautiful eyes of my cash-box! He speaks of her as a lover speaks of his mistress.

VAL. Mistress Claude, Sir, knows the truth of this affair; and she can testify to it.

HARP. What! my servant is an accomplice in the matter?

VAL. Yes, Sir; she was a witness to our engagement; and it is after having known the honorable intent of my passion, that she has assisted me in persuading your daughter to plight her troth, and receive mine.

HARP. [aside]. He? Does the fear of justice make him rave? [To VALÈRE.] What means all this gibberish about my daughter?

VAL. I say, Sir, that I have had all the trouble in the world to bring her modesty to consent to what my love wished for.

HARP. The modesty of whom?

VAL. Of your daughter; and it is only yesterday that she could make up her mind to sign a mutual promise of marriage.

HARP. My daughter has signed you a promise of marriage?

VAL. Yes, Sir, as I have signed her one.

HARP. O Heaven! another disgrace!

JACQ. [to the Magistrate]. Write, Sir, write.

HARP. More harm! additional despair! [To the Magistrate.] Come, Sir, do the duty of your office, and draw up for him his indictment as a felon and a suborner.

JACQ. As a felon and a suborner.

VAL. These are names that do not belong to me; and when people shall know who I am . . .

SCENE IV:—HARPAGON, ELISE, MARIANE, VALÈRE, FROSINE, MASTER JACQUES, *A Magistrate*

HARP. Ah! graceless child! daughter unworthy of a father like me! it is thus that you carry out the lessons which I have given you? You allow yourself to become smitten with an infamous thief; and you pledge him your troth without my consent! But you shall both find out your mistake. [*To* ELISE.] Four strong walls will answer for your conduct; [*to* VALÈRE] and a good gibbet will give me satisfaction for your audacity.

VAL. It will not be your passion that shall judge this matter; and I shall get at least a hearing before being condemned.

HARP. I have made a mistake in saying a gibbet; you shall be broken alive on the wheel.

ELISE [*at Harpagon's knees*]. Ah! father, show a little more humanity in your feelings, I beseech you, and do not push matters with the utmost violence of paternal power. Do not give way to the first movements of your passion, and give yourself time to consider what you do. Take the trouble to know better him whom you believe to have offended you. He is quite different from what he appears in your eyes; and you will find it less strange that I have given myself to him, when you know that, had it not been for him, you would long ago have had me no longer. Yes, father, it is he who saved me from the great peril I was in when I fell into the water, and to whom you owe the life of that very daughter, who . . .

HARP. All that is nothing; and it would have been much better for me, had he allowed you to be drowned, than to do what he has done.

ELISE. I implore you, father, by your paternal love, to . . .

HARP. No, no; I will hear nothing, and justice must have its course.

JACQ. You shall pay me my cudgel-blows.

FROS. [*aside*]. What strange confusion is this!

SCENE V:—ANSELME, HARPAGON, ELISE, MARIANE, FROSINE, VALÈRE, *A Magistrate,* MASTER JACQUES

ANSEL. What is the matter, M. Harpagon? I find you quite upset.

HARP. Ah! M. Anselme, I am the most unfortunate of men; and there is a great deal of trouble and disorder connected with the contract which you have come to sign! I am attacked in my property, I am attacked in my honor; and behold a wretch, a scoundrel who has violated the most sacred rights; who has introduced himself into my house as a servant to rob me of my money, and to tamper with my daughter.

VAL. Who is thinking of your money, of which you make such a cock-and-bull story?

HARP. Yes, they have given each other a promise of marriage. This insult concerns you, M. Anselme, and it is you who ought to take up the cudgels against him, and employ all the rigors of the law, to revenge yourself upon him for his insolence.

ANSEL. It is not my intention to make anyone marry me by compulsion, and to lay claim to a heart which has already pledged itself; but, as far as your interests are concerned, I am ready to espouse them, as if they were my own.

HARP. This gentleman here is an honest magistrate who will forget nothing, from what he has said to me, of the duties of his office. [*To the Magistrate.*] Charge him, Sir, in the right fashion, and make matters very criminal.

VAL. I do not see what crime can be made out against me of the affection which I entertain for your daughter, and to what punishment you think I can be condemned on account of our engagement when it shall be known who I am. . . .

HARP. I do not care about any of these stories; in our days the world is full of these assumed noblemen; of these impostors, who take advantage of their obscurity, and with the greatest insolence adopt the first illustrious name which comes into their head.

VAL. I would have you to know that I am too upright to deck myself with anything that does not belong to me; and that all Naples can bear testimony to my birth.

ANSEL. Gently! take care what you are going to say. You run a greater risk in this than you think; you are speaking before a man to whom all Naples is known, and who can easily see through your story.

VAL. [*proudly putting his hat on*]. I am not the man to fear anything; and if you know Naples, you know who was Don Thomas d'Alburci.

ANSEL. No doubt, I know; and few people have known him better than I.

HARP. I do not care for Don Thomas nor Don Martin. [*Seeing two candles burning, blows one out.*]

ANSEL. Pray let him speak; we shall hear what he means to say about him.

VAL. I mean to say that to him I owe my birth.

ANSEL. To him?

VAL. Yes.

ANSEL. Come; you are jesting. Invent some other story which may succeed better, and do not attempt to save yourself by this imposture.

VAL. Learn to speak differently! It is not an imposture, and I advance nothing but what can be easily proved by me.

ANSEL. What! you dare call yourself the son of Don Thomas d'Alburci?

VAL. Yes, I dare; and I am prepared to maintain this truth against anyone.

ANSEL. The audacity is marvelous! Learn to your confusion, that it is sixteen years at least since the man you speak of perished at sea with his wife and children, while endeavoring to save their lives from the cruel persecutions which accompanied the troubles at Naples, and which caused the exile of several noble families.

VAL. Yes; but learn, to your confusion, you, that his son, seven years of age, with a servant, was saved from the wreck by a Spanish vessel, and that this son, who was saved, is the person who speaks to you. Learn that the captain of that ship, pitying my misfortune, conceived a friendship for me; that he had me educated as his own son, and that I was trained to the profession of arms ever since I was old enough; that I have learned lately that my father is not dead, as I always believed; that passing through here to go in search of him, an accident, arranged by Heaven, brought me into contact with the charming Elise; that the sight of her made me a slave to her beauty, and that the violence of my passion and the harshness of her father made me resolve to introduce myself into his house, and to send someone else in quest of my parents.

ANSEL. But what other proofs than your words can guarantee to us that this is not a fable based upon truth?

VAL. The Spanish captain; a ruby seal which belonged to my father; an agate bracelet which my mother had on her arm; old Pedro, the servant, who was saved with me from the wreck.

MAR. Alas! to your words I can answer, I, that you are not imposing, and all that you say shows me clearly that you are my brother.

VAL. You, my sister!

MAR. Yes. My heart was touched the moment you opened your lips; and our mother, who will be overjoyed at seeing you, has thousands of times related to me the misfortunes of our family. Heaven also permitted us not to perish in this dreadful shipwreck; but our lives were saved only at the cost of our liberty; and they were pirates that picked us up, my mother and me, on a plank of our vessel. After ten years of slavery, a happy accident regained for us our freedom; and we returned to Naples, where we found all our property sold, without being able to gather any news of our father. We then traveled to Genoa, whither my mother went to pick up some miserable remains of an inheritance of which she had been despoiled;

and thence, flying from the barbarous injustice of her relatives, she came hither, where she has barely been able to drag on her life.

ANSEL. O Heaven! how great is the evidence of thy power! and how well showest thou that it belongs only to thee to perform miracles? Embrace me, my children, and share your joys with those of your father.

VAL. You are our father?

MAR. It is you whom my mother has so much bewailed.

ANSEL. Yes, my daughter; yes, my son; I am Don Thomas d'Alburci, whom Heaven saved from the waves, with all the money which he carried with him, and who, believing you all dead during more than sixteen years, prepared, after long journeying, to seek, in the union with a gentle and discreet girl, the consolation of a new family. The little safety which I found for my life in Naples has made me for ever abandon the idea of returning; and having found means to sell all that I possessed there, I became used to this place, where, under the name of Anselme, I wished to get rid of the sorrows of this other name, which caused me so many misfortunes.

HARP. [to ANSELME]. Is this your son?

ANSEL. Yes.

HARP. Then I hold you responsible for paying me ten thousand crowns of which he has robbed me.

ANSEL. He has robbed you!

HARP. Himself.

VAL. Who tells you this?

HARP. Master Jacques.

VAL. [to MASTER JACQUES]. Is it you who say this?

JACQ. You see that I say nothing.

HARP. Yes. There is the Magistrate who has received his deposition.

VAL. Can you believe me capable of so base an action?

HARP. Capable or not capable, I want my money back again.

SCENE VI:—HARPAGON, ANSELME, ELISE, MARIANE, CLÉANTE, VALÈRE, FROSINE, *A Magistrate,* MASTER JACQUES, LA FLÈCHE

CLÉAN. Do not worry yourself any longer, father, and accuse no one. I have discovered tidings of your affair; and I have come to tell you, that if you will make up your mind to let me marry Mariane, your money shall be returned to you.

HARP. Where is it?

CLÉAN. Do not grieve about that. It is in a spot for which I answer; and everything depends upon me. It is for you to say what you resolve; and you can choose, either to give me Mariane, or to lose your cash-box.

HARP. Has nothing been taken out?

CLÉAN. Nothing at all. Now make up your mind whether you will subscribe to this marriage, and join your consent to that of her mother, who leaves her free to choose between us two.

MAR. [*to* CLÉANTE]. But you do not know that this consent is no longer sufficient; and that Heaven restores to me not only a brother [*pointing to* VALÈRE] but also [*pointing to* ANSELME] a father, from whom you must obtain me.

ANSEL. Heaven has not restored me to you, my children, to go contrary to your desires. M. Harpagon, you are well aware that the choice of a young girl will fall upon the son rather than upon the father; come, do not oblige people to say what it is not necessary to hear; and consent, as well as I do, to this double match.

HARP. To be well advised, I must see my cash-box.

CLÉAN. You shall see it safe and sound.

HARP. I have no money to give my children in marriage.

ANSEL. Well! I have some for them; do not let that trouble you.

HARP. Will you undertake to defray all the expenses of these two weddings?

ANSEL. Yes, I undertake it. Are you satisfied?

HARP. Yes, provided that you will order me a suit for the nuptials.

ANSEL. That is agreed. Let us go and rejoice in the happiness which this day brings us.

MAG. Hullo! gentlemen, hullo! Gently, if you please. Who is to pay for my writing?

HARP. We have nothing to do with your writings.

MAG. Yes! but I do not pretend to have written for nothing.

HARP. [*pointing to* MASTER JACQUES]. For your payment, there is a man of whom I make you a present; and you may hang him.

JACQ. Alas! how must one act? I get cudgel-blows for speaking the truth; and they wish to hang me for telling a lie!

ANSEL. M. Harpagon, you must forgive him this imposture.

HARP. Will you pay the magistrate, then?

ANSEL. Be it so. Come, let us go quickly to share our joy with your mother.

HARP. And I, to see my dear cash-box.

JEAN RACINE

Phædra

CHARACTERS

THESEUS, *son of Ægeus and King of Athens*
PHÆDRA, *wife of Theseus and daughter of Minos and Pasiphaë*
HIPPOLYTUS, *son of Theseus and Antiope, Queen of the Amazons*
ARICIA, *princess of the blood royal of Athens*
ŒNONE, *nurse of Phædra*
THERAMENES, *tutor of Hippolytus*
ISMENE, *friend of Aricia*
PANOPE, *waiting-woman of Phædra*
Guards

The scene is laid in Trœzen, a town of the Peloponnesus.

ACT I

Enter HIPPOLYTUS *and* THERAMENES.

HIPP. My mind is settled, dear Theramenes,
And I must stay no more in lovely Trœzen,
Racking my soul in doubt and mortal anguish.
I am ashamed of my long idleness.
Look you, my father gone six months and more—
One so dear gone,—and to what fate befallen
I do not know, nor do I know what corner

Racine, *Phædra*. Translated by Robert Henderson. Jean Racine, literary rival of Corneille, friend of Molière and La Fontaine, was born in 1639 and died in 1699. Previous to *Phædra* (*Phèdre*) he had written a number of tragic dramas, among them *Andromache* and *Britannicus*. Discouraged by the reception which *Phædra* received, Racine turned to sacred themes. *Esther* and *Athaliah* appeared in 1689 and 1691.

Of all the wide earth hides him!

THERA.   Ah, my prince,—
And where, then, would you seek him? I have
    sailed
Over the seas on either side of Corinth.   10
Where Acheron is lost among the Shades
I asked, indeed, if aught were known of Theseus!
And to content you, I have gone to Elis,
Rounded Tœnarus, sailed to the far waters
Where Icarus once fell. What newer hope . . . ?
Under what favored sky would you think now   16
To trace his footsteps? Who knows if your father
Wishes the secret of his absence known?
Perhaps while we are trembling for his life
The hero calmly plots a fresh intrigue,   20
And only waits till the deluded lady—

    HIPP. Peace, good Theramenes! Respect his
    name.
The waywardness of youth is his no longer,
And nothing so unworthy should detain him.
Now for a long time, Phædra has held that heart
Inconstant once, and she need fear no rival.   26
And if I seek him, it is but my duty.
I leave a place I dare no longer see!

    THERA. Indeed! When, prince, did you begin to
    dread
These peaceful haunts, so dear to happy child-
    hood,   30
Where I have often known you rather stay
Than face the tumult and the pomp of Athens?
What danger do you shun? Or is it grief?

    HIPP. All things are changed. That happy past
    is gone.
Since then, the gods sent Phædra!

    THERA.   Now I see!   35
It is the queen whose sight offends you. Yes,—
For with a step-dame's spite she schemed your
    exile
At her first sight of you. But then, her hatred
Is somewhat milder, if not wholly vanished.
A dying woman—one who longs for death!   40
What danger can she bring upon your head?
Weary of life, and weary of herself,—
Sick with some ill she will not ever speak of,—
Can Phædra then lay plots?—

    HIPP.   I do not fear
The hatred of the queen. There is another   45
From whom I fly, and that is young Aricia,
The sole survivor of an impious race.

    THERA. What! You become her persecutor, too?
The gentle sister of the cruel sons
Of Pallas, did not share their perfidy.   50
Why should you hate such charming innocence?

HIPP. If it were hate, I should not need to fly.

THERA. Then will you tell me what your flying
    means?
Is this the proud Hippolytus I see?
Love's fiercest foe alive?—the fiercest hater   55
Of Theseus' well-worn yoke?—Now can it be
That Venus, scorned, will justify your father?
And is Hippolytus, like other mortals,
To bow, perforce, and offer incense to her?—
And can he love? . . .

    HIPP.   My friend, you must not ask me.
You who have known my heart through all my
    life,   61
And known it to be proud and most disdainful,—
You will not ask that I should shame myself
By now disowning all that I professed.
My mother was an Amazon,—my wildness,   65
Which you think strange, I suckled at her breast,
And as I grew, why, Reason did approve
What Nature planted in me. Then you told me
The story of my father, and you know
How, often, when I listened to your voice   70
I kindled, hearing of his noble acts,—
And you would tell how he brought consolation
To mortals for the absence of Alcides,
And how he cleared the roads of monsters,—rob-
    bers,—
Procrustes, Cercyron, Sciro, Sinnis slain,   75
Scattered the Epidaurian giant's bones,
And how Crete ran with blood of the Minotaur!
But when you told me of less glorious deeds,—
Troth plighted here and there and everywhere,
Young Helen stolen from her home at Sparta,   80
And Peribœa's tears in Salamis,
And many other trusting ones deceived,
Whose very names he cannot now remember,—
Lone Ariadne, crying to the rocks,—
And last of all this Phædra, bound to him   85
By better ties,—You know that with regret
I heard, and urged that you cut short the tale.
I had been happier, could I erase
This one unworthy part of his bright story
Out of my memory. Must I in turn   90
Be made love's slave, and brought to bend so low?
It is the more contemptible in me,
For no such brilliance clings about my name
As to the name of Theseus,—no monsters quelled
Have given me the right to share his weakness.
And if I must be humbled for my pride,   96
Aricia should have been the last to tame me!
Was I not mad that I should have forgotten
Those barriers which must keep us far apart
Eternally? For by my father's order   100

Her brothers' blood must never flow again
In a child of hers. He dreads a single shoot
From any stock so guilty, and would bury
Their name with her; so even to the tomb
No torch of Hymen may be lit for her.   105
Shall I espouse her rights against my father,
Provoke his wrath, launch on a mad career?—
   THERA. But if your time has come, dear prince, the gods
Will care but little for your guiding reason.
Theseus would shut your eyes;—he but unseals them.   110
His hatred kindles you to burn, rebellious,
And only lends his enemy new charms.
Then, too, why should you fear a guiltless passion?
Do you not dare this once to try its sweetness,   114
Rather than follow such a hair-drawn scruple?—
Afraid to stray where Hercules has wandered?—
What heart so stout that Venus has not won it?
And you, so long her foe, where would you be
Had your own mother, always scorning love,
Never been moved with tenderness for Theseus?
What good to act a pride you do not feel?   121
If you are changed, confess it! For some time
You have been seldom seen urging the car
With wild delight, rapid, along the shore,
Or, skillful in the art that Neptune taught,   125
Making th' unbroken steed obey the bit.
The forest has flung back our shouts less often.
A secret burden, cast upon your spirits,
Has dimmed your eye.—Can I then doubt your love?
It is in vain that you conceal your hurt.   130
Tell me, has not Aricia touched your heart?
   HIPP. Theramenes, I go to find my father.
   THERA. Will you not see the queen before you leave?
   HIPP. So I intend. And you may tell her so.
Yes, I will see her, since it is my duty.   135
But what new ill vexes her dear Œnone?

Enter ŒNONE.

   ŒNONE. Alas, my lord, what grief was e'er like mine?
The queen has almost touched the gates of death.
It is in vain I watch her night and day,
In my very arms this secret malady   140
Is killing her—her mind is all disordered.
She rises from her bed, weary yet restless,
Pants for the outer air, yet she commands me
That none should see her in her misery.
She comes!   145

   HIPP. That is enough. I shall not vex her
Nor make her see the face of one she hates.
    [*Exeunt* HIPPOLYTUS *and* THERAMENES. *Enter*
     PHÆDRA.
   PHÆDRA. Yes, this is far enough. Stay here, Œnone.
My strength is failing. I must rest a little.
I am dazzled with the light; it has been long   150
Since I have seen it. Ah, and my trembling knees
Are failing me—
   ŒNONE. Dear Heaven, I would our tears
Might bring relief.
   PHÆDRA. And how these clumsy trinkets,   155
These veils oppress me! Whose officious hand
Tied up these knots, and gathered all these coils
Over my brow? All things conspire against me
And would distress me more!
   ŒNONE. That which you wish   160
This moment, frets you next! Did you not ask
A minute past, that we should deck you out,
Saying you felt your energy return,
Saying you sickened of your idleness,
And wished to go and see the light of day?   165
You sought the sun, and now you see it here,—
And now you would be hidden from its shining!
   PHÆDRA. O splendid author of a hapless race,—
You whom my mother boasted as her father,—
Well may you blush to see me in such plight.   170
For the last time I look on thee, O Sun!
   ŒNONE. So! And are you still in love with death?
Will you not ever make your peace with life,
And leave these cruel accents of despair?
   PHÆDRA. I wish that I were seated in the forest.
When may I follow with delighted eye,   176
Through glorious dust, flying in full career,—
A chariot?—
   ŒNONE. Madam?
   PHÆDRA. Have I lost my wits?   180
What did I say? Where am I? Ah, and where
Do my vain wishes wander? For the gods
Have made me mad! And now I blush, Œnone,—
I hide my face, for you have seen too clearly
The grief and shame, that, quite in spite of me,
Will overflow my eyes.   186
   ŒNONE. If you must blush,
Blush at the silence that inflames your grief.
Deaf to my voice, you will not have my care.
Then will you have no pity on yourself,   190
But let your life be ended in mid-course?
What evil spell has drained its fountains dry?
Night-shadows thrice have darkened all the heavens

Since sleep came to your eyes, and now three times
The dawn has chased the darkness back again
Since your pale lips knew food. You faint, are lan-
    guid,— 196
What awful purpose have you in your heart?
How do you dare attempt to lose your life
And so offend the gods who gave it you,—
And so prove false to Theseus and your mar-
    riage?— 200
Yes, and betray your most unhappy children,
Bending their necks yourself, beneath the yoke?
That day, be sure, which robs them of their mother
Will give his high hopes back to the stranger's
    son,—
To that proud enemy of you and yours, 205
Born of an Amazon,—Hippolytus!—
    PHÆDRA. You gods!
    ŒNONE. Ah, this is a reproach to move you!
    PHÆDRA. Unhappy one, what name have your
    lips spoken? 209
    ŒNONE. Your anger is most just, and it is well
That hated name can rouse such rage! Then live,
And hear again the claims of love and duty!
Live, then,—and stop this son of Scythia
From crushing down your children by his sway,
Ruling the noblest offspring of the gods,— 215
The purest blood of Greece! Never delay!
Death threatens every moment! Now restore
Your shattered strength, while the dim torch of life
Burns, and can yet be fanned into a flame.
    PHÆDRA. I have endured its guilt and shame too
    long. 220
    ŒNONE. Why? What remorse is gnawing at
    your heart?
What crime can have disturbed you so? Your
    hands
Have not been stained with the blood of inno-
    cence.
    PHÆDRA. No, I thank Heaven my hands are free
    from stain,—
I would my soul were innocent as they! 225
    ŒNONE. Why then, what awful plan have you
    been scheming,
At which your conscience still should be afraid?
    PHÆDRA. Have I not said enough? Spare me the
    rest!
I die to save myself a full confession.
    ŒNONE. Die, then,—and keep a silence more
    than human!— 230
But seek some other hand to close your eyes,
For I will go before you to the Shades.
There are a thousand highways always open,
And since you have so little faith in me.

I'll go the shortest! When has my love failed you?
Remember, in my arms you lay, new-born. 236
For you I left my country and my children,—
And is this payment for my service to you?
    PHÆDRA. What will you gain from words that are
    so bitter? 239
Were I to speak, horror would freeze your blood.
    ŒNONE. What can you say more terrible to me
Than to behold you die before my eyes?
    PHÆDRA. If you should know my sin, I still
    should die,
But with guilt added—
    ŒNONE. Oh, my dearest lady, 245
By all the tears that I have wept for you,
By these poor knees I clasp, now ease my mind
From doubt and torture!
    PHÆDRA. As you wish. Then rise.
    ŒNONE. I hear you. Speak. 250
    PHÆDRA. Ah, how shall I begin?
    ŒNONE. Leave off your fears,—you hurt me with
    distrust.
    PHÆDRA. O malice of great Venus! Into what
    madness,
What wild distractions, did she cast my mother!
    ŒNONE. Let them be blotted from all memory.
Buried in silence, for all times to come. 256
    PHÆDRA. My sister, Ariadne, what was the love
Which brought you death, forsaken on lone shores?
    ŒNONE. Madam, what deep pain is it prompts
    reproaches
Thus against all your kin—? 260
    PHÆDRA. It is her will—
It is the will of Venus, and I perish,
Last and least happy of a family
Where all were wretched!
    ŒNONE. Do you love? 265
    PHÆDRA. I feel
All of its fever—
    ŒNONE. Ah! For whom?
    PHÆDRA. Now hear
The final horror. Yes, I love. My lips 270
Tremble to name him.
    ŒNONE. Whom?
    PHÆDRA. And do you know him?—
He whom I tortured long,—the Amazon's son!
    ŒNONE. Hippolytus! Great gods! 275
    PHÆDRA. Yes, you have named him.
    ŒNONE. Blood freezes in my veins! O cursed
    race!
Ill-omened journey! Land of misery,
Why did we ever reach these dangerous shores?
    PHÆDRA. My wound is not a new one. Scarcely
    had I 280

Been bound to Theseus by our marriage tie,
With peace and happiness seeming so well secured,
Until at Athens I saw my enemy.
I looked, I first turned pale, then blushed to see
    him,
And all my soul was in the greatest turmoil;   285
A mist made dim my sight, and my voice faltered,
And now my blood ran cold, then burned like fire.
In all my fevered body I could feel
Venus, whose fury had pursued so many
Of my sad race. I sought to shun her torments
With fervent vows. I built a shrine for her,   291
And there, 'mid many victims did I seek
The reason I had lost; but all for nothing.
I found no remedy for pain of love!
I offered incense vainly on her altars,   295
I called upon her name, and while I called her,
I loved Hippolytus, always before me!
And when I made her altars smoke with victims,
'Twas for a god whose name I dared not utter,—
And still I fled his presence, only to find him—   300
(The worst of horrors)—in his father's features!
At last I raised revolt against myself,
And stirred my courage up to persecute
The enemy I loved. To banish him
I wore a harsh and jealous step-dame's manner,
And ceaselessly I clamored for his exile,   306
Till I had torn him from his father's arms!
I breathed once more, Œnone. In his absence
The days passed by less troubled than before—
Innocent days! I hid my bitter grief,   310
Submitted to my husband, cherished the fruits
Of our most fatal marriage,—and in vain!
Again I saw the one whom I had banished,
Brought here by my own husband, and again
The old wound bled. And now it is not love   315
Hid in my heart, but Venus in her might
Seizing her prey. Justly I fear my sin!
I hate my life, and hold my love in horror.
I die:—I would have kept my name unsullied,
Burying guilty passion in the grave;   320
But I have not been able to refuse you;
You weep and pray, and so I tell you all,
And I shall be content, if as I perish,
You do not vex me with unjust reproaches,
Nor vainly try to snatch away from death   325
The last faint sparks of life, yet lingering!

Enter PANOPE.

PANOPE. I wish that I might hide sad tidings
    from you,
But 'tis my duty, madam, to reveal them.
The hand of death has seized your peerless hus-
    band.
You are the last to hear it.   330
    ŒNONE. What is this?
    PANOPE. The queen begs Heaven for the safe
        return
Of Theseus, but she trusts, indeed, in vain—
She is deceived. Hippolytus, his son,
Has learned from vessels newly come to port   335
That Theseus is dead.
    PHÆDRA. Oh, gods!
    PANOPE. At Athens
Opinions are divided; some would have it
Your child should rule, and some, despite the law,
Are bold, and dare support the stranger's son,   341
While one presuming faction, it is said,
Would crown Aricia, and the house of Pallas.
I thought it well to warn you of this danger.
Hippolytus is ready, now, to start,   345
And if he chance to show himself in Athens,
The crowd, I fear, will follow in his lead.
    ŒNONE. It is enough. The queen has heard
        your message,
And she will not neglect your timely warning.
                    [Exit PANOPE.
Dear lady, I had almost ceased from urging   350
That you should wish to live. I thought to follow
My mistress to that tomb from which my pleading
Had failed to turn her,—but this new misfortune
Changes the aspect of affairs, and prompts us
To take fresh measures. Madam, Theseus is gone,
And you must fill his place. He leaves a son,—   356
Slave if you die, but if you live, a king!
Upon whom can he lean, but you, his mother?
There is no hand but yours to dry his tears.
Live then, for him, or else his guiltless weeping
Will move the gods to wrath against his mother.
Live, for no blame is in your passion now.   362
The king is dead, you bear the bonds no longer
Which made your love a thing of crime and hor-
    ror.
You need no longer dread Hippolytus,   365
For you may see him, now, without reproach.
Perhaps, if he is certain of your hatred,
He means to lead the rebels. Undeceive him!
Soften his callous heart, and bend his pride!
King of this fertile land, his portion lies   370
Here in his Trœzen, yet he knows the laws,—
They give your son these walls Minerva built,
Aye, and protects,—but if a common foe
Threatens you both, you had best be united.
For you must thwart Aricia!   375
    PHÆDRA. I consent.

Yes, I will live, if life can yet be mine,—
If my affection for a son has power
To rouse my sinking heart, at such a dangerous
      hour!   [*Exeunt.*

ACT II

Enter ARICIA *and* ISMENE.

ARICIA. Hippolytus has asked to see me here?
Hippolytus has asked to bid farewell?   381
'Tis true, Ismene? You are not deceived?

ISMENE. This is the first result of Theseus' death,
And you may look to see from every side
Hearts that he kept away, now turning to you. 385
Aricia soon shall find all Greece low-bending
To do her homage.

ARICIA. Then it is not only
An idle tale? Am I a slave no longer?
Have I no enemies?   390

ISMENE. The gods, Aricia,
Trouble your peace no more, for Theseus' soul
Is with your brothers, now.

ARICIA. Does rumor tell
How Theseus died?   395

ISMENE. Tales most incredible
Are spread. Some say, that, seizing a new bride,
The faithless man was swallowed by the waves.
Others have said, and this report prevails,
That he, together with Pirithous,   400
Went to the world below, seeking the shores
Of Cocytus, showing his living self
To the pale ghosts, but could not leave the gloom,
For they who enter there abide forever.

ARICIA. Can I believe a mortal may descend
Into that gulf before his destined hour?   406
What lure could ever overcome its terrors?

ISMENE. Nay, he is dead; 'tis only you who doubt
      it.
The men of Athens all bewail his loss.
Trœzen already hails Hippolytus,   410
And Phædra, fearing for her children's rights,
Asks counsel of such friends as share her troubles,
Here in this palace!

ARICIA. Will Hippolytus
Prove kinder than his father, make my chains
      light,   415
And pity my misfortunes?

ISMENE. Yes, I think so.

ARICIA. Indeed, I think you do not know him
      well,
Or you would not believe a heart so hard
Could ever pity, or could look on me   420
As one not sharing in the scorn he feels

For all our sex. Does he not still avoid
Whatever place we go?

ISMENE. I know the stories
Of proud Hippolytus, but I have seen him   425
When he was near to you, and watched to see
How one supposed so cold would bear himself.
I found his manners not at all like those
Which I had looked to see, for in his face
Was great confusion, at your slightest glance. 430
He could not turn his languid eyes away,
But still looked back again to gaze at you.
Love is a word that may offend his pride,
But though the tongue deny it, looks betray!

ARICIA. How eagerly my heart hears what you
      say,   435
Though it may be delusion, dear Ismene!
Did it seem possible to you, who know me,
That I, poor toy of unrelenting fate,
Fed upon bitter tears by night and day,
Could ever taste the maddening draught of love?
I am the last frail offspring of my race—   441
My royal race, the Children of the Earth,
And of them, I alone survive war's fury.
Yes, I have lost six brothers, in their youth,—
Mown by the sword, cut off in their first flower!
They were the hope of an illustrious house.   446
Earth drank their blood with sorrow; it was kin
To his whom she brought forth. And well you
      know,
Since then, no heart in Greece could sigh for me,
Lest, by a sister's flame, her brothers' ashes   450
Might chance to blaze again. And, too, you know
How I disdained the cautions of my captor,
His care, and his suspicion, and you know
How often I have thanked the king's injustice,
Since I had never loved the thought of love.   455
He happily confirmed my inclinations,—
But then, I never yet had seen his son!
It is not merely that my eye is caught,
And that I love him for his grace and beauty,—
Charms which he does not know, or seems to
      scorn,—   460
I love him for a kind of wealth that's rarer.
He has his father's virtues, not his faults.
I love, and I must grant it, that high pride
Which never stooped beneath the yoke of love.
Phædra gains little glory from a lover   465
Free of his sighs; I am too proud, I think,
To share devotion with a thousand others,
Or enter in a door that's never shut.
But to make one who never stooped before   469
Bend his proud neck,—to pierce a heart of stone,
And bind one captive, whom his chains astonish,

Who struggles vainly in his pleasant bonds,—
That takes my fancy, and I long for it.
The god of strength was easier disarmed
Than this Hippolytus, for Hercules   475
Yielded so often to the eyes of beauty
That he made triumph cheap. But, dear Ismene,
I take too little heed of a resistance
Which I may never quell. If I am humbled,
And if I find defeat, then you will hear me   480
Speak ill of that same pride I so admire!
What! can he love? And have I been so happy
That I have bent—?
ISMENE. He comes,—and you shall hear him.

Enter HIPPOLYTUS.

HIPP. Lady, before you go, it is my duty   485
To tell you of the changes of your fortune.
What I have feared is true; my sire is dead.
Yes, his long stay was what I had supposed it.
For only death, which came to end his labors,   489
Could keep him hidden from the world so long.
The gods at last have doomed Alcides' friend—
His friend, and his successor. Since your hatred
I think will grant his virtues, it can hear
Some praise for him, without resenting it,
Knowing that it is due. I have one hope   495
To soothe me in my sorrow. I can free you.
Now I revoke the laws, whose strictness moved me
To pity for you; you are your own mistress
Of heart and hand. Here in my heritage,
In Trœzen, here where Pittheus once reigned,   500
And where I now am king, by my own right,
I leave you free, free as myself,—and more.
ARICIA. Your kindness is too great; it overcomes
me.
A goodness which will pay disgrace with honor
Can give a greater force than you would think   505
To the harsh laws from which you would release
me.
HIPP. Athens, not knowing how to fill the
throne
Left empty, speaks of you, and then of me,
And then of Phædra's son.
ARICIA.   Of me, my lord?
HIPP. I know that by the law it is not mine,
For Greece reproaches me my foreign mother.   511
But if my brother were my only rival,
My rights are clearly truer ones than his,
So that I should not care for twists of the law.
There is a juster claim to check my boldness.   515
I yield my place to you, or rather, grant
That you should have it,—you should hold the
scepter,

Bequeathed to you from Earth's great son, Erec-
theus.
It came, then, to Ægeus, and the city
Which was protected and increased by him   520
Was glad to welcome such a king as Theseus,
Leaving your luckless brothers out of mind.
Now Athens calls you back within her walls.
Long strife has cost her groans enough already,
Her fields are glutted with your kinsmen's blood,
Fattening those same furrows whence it sprang.
I will rule here in Trœzen; Phædra's son   527
Has his rich kingdom waiting him in Crete.
Athens is yours, and I will do my best
To bring to you the votes which are divided   530
Between us two.
ARICIA.   I fear a dream deceives me.
For I am stunned, my lord, at what I hear.
Am I, indeed, awake? Can I believe
Such generosity as this? What god
Has put it in your heart? Well you deserve   535
That fame you have, yet it falls short of you.
For me, you will be traitor to yourself!
Was it not grace enough never to hate me,
To have been free so long from enmity,
Which some have harbored—
HIPP.   Hate you? I to hate you?
However darkly you have seen my pride,   541
Did you suppose a monster gave me birth?
What savagery, what hatred, full of venom
Would not become less evil, seeing you?
Could I resist this charm which caught my soul—
ARICIA. Why, what is this, sir?   546
HIPP. I have said too much
Not to say more. No prudence can resist
The violence of passion. Now, at last,
Silence is broken. I must tell you now   550
The secret that my heart can hold no longer.
You see before you an unhappy victim
Of hasty pride,—a prince who begs compassion.
For I was long the enemy of love.
I mocked his fetters, I despised his captives,   555
And while I pitied these poor, shipwrecked mor-
tals,
I watched the storms, and seemed quite safe on
land.
And now I find that I have such a fate,
And must be tossed upon a sea of troubles!
My boldness is defeated in a moment,   560
And all my boasted pride is humbleness.
For nearly six months past, ashamed, despairing,
Carrying with me always that sharp arrow
Which tears my heart, I struggle quite in vain
To free me, both from you and from myself.   565

I leave your presence;—leaving, I find you near,
And in the forest's darkness see your form.
Black night, no less than daylight brings the vision
Of charms that I avoid. All things conspire
To make Hippolytus your slave. The fruit   570
Of all my sighs is only that I cannot
Find my own self again. My bow, my spear,
Please me no longer. I have quite forgotten
My chariot, and the teaching of the Sea God.
The woods can only echo back my groans,   575
Instead of flinging back those joyous shouts
With which I urged my horses. Hearing this,
A tale of passion so uncouth, you blush
At your own handiwork. These are wild words
With which I offer you my heart, a captive   580
Held, strangely, by a silken jess. And yet
The off'ring should be dearer to your eyes,
Since such words come as strangers to my lips.
Nor do not scorn my vows, so poorly spoken   584
Since, but for you, they never had been formed.

Enter THERAMENES.

THERA. My lord, I came to tell you of the queen.
She comes to seek you.
      HIPP. Me?
      THERA. And what she wishes
I do not know. I speak at her request,   590
For she would talk with you before you go.
      HIPP. What shall I say to her? Can she expect—?
      ARICIA. You cannot, noble prince, refuse to hear
      her,
Though you are sure she is your enemy.
There is a shade of pity due her tears.   595
      HIPP. Shall we part so? And will you let me
      leave you
Not knowing if I have offended you,—
The goddess I adore,—with all this boldness?
Or if this heart, which I now leave with you—
      ARICIA. Go now, my prince, and do whatever
      deeds   600
Your generosity would have you do.
Make Athens own my scepter. All these gifts
I will accept. But the high throne of Empire
Is not the thing most precious to my eyes!
                    [*Exeunt* ARICIA *and* ISMENE.
      HIPP. Friend, are we ready?—But the queen is
      coming.   605
See that the ship is trimmed and fit to sail.
Hurry, gather the crew, and hoist the signal,
And then return, the sooner to release me
From a most irksome meeting.
            [*Exit* THERAMENES. *Enter* PHÆDRA *and*
            ŒNONE.

PHÆDRA [*to* ŒNONE]. Look, I see him!   610
My blood forgets to flow,—tongue will not speak
What I have come to say!
      ŒNONE. Think of your son.
And think that all his hopes depend on you.
      PHÆDRA. They tell me that you leave us, hastily.
I come to add my own tears to your sorrow,   616
And I would plead my fears for my young son.
He has no father, now; 'twill not be long
Until the day that he will see my death,
And even now, his youth is much imperiled   620
By a thousand foes. You only can defend him.
And in my inmost heart, remorse is stirring,—
Yes, and fear, too, lest I have shut your ears
Against his cries; I fear that your just anger
May, before long, visit on him that hatred   625
His mother earned.
      HIPP. Madam, you need not fear.
Such malice is not mine.
      PHÆDRA. I should not blame you
If you should hate me; I have injured you.   630
So much you know;—you could not read my
      heart.
Yes, I have tried to be your enemy,
For the same land could never hold us both.
In private and abroad I have declared it;—
I was your enemy! I found no peace   635
Till seas had parted us; and I forbade
Even your name to be pronounced to me.
And yet, if punishment be meted out
Justly, by the offense;—if only hatred
Deserves a hate, then never was there woman   640
Deserved more pity, and less enmity.
      HIPP. A mother who is jealous for her children
Will seldom love the children of a mother
Who came before her. Torments of suspicion
Will often follow on a second marriage.   645
Another would have felt that jealousy
No less than you; perhaps more violently.
      PHÆDRA. Ah, prince, but Heaven made me quite
      exempt
From what is usual, and I can call
That Heaven as my witness! 'Tis not this—   650
No, quite another ill devours my heart!
      HIPP. This is no time for self-reproaching,
      madam.
Perhaps your husband still beholds the light,
Perhaps he may be granted safe return
In answer to our prayers; his guarding god   655
Is Neptune, whom he never called in vain.
      PHÆDRA. He who has seen the mansions of the
      dead
Returns not thence. Since Theseus has gone

Once to those gloomy shores, we need not hope,
For Heaven will not send him back again. 660
Prince, there is no release from Acheron;—
It is a greedy maw,—and yet I think
He lives and breathes in you,—and still I see him
Before me here; I seem to speak to him—
My heart—! Oh, I am mad! Do what I will, 665
I cannot hide my passion.
    HIPP. Yes, I see
What strange things love will do, for Theseus,
    dead,
Seems present to your eyes, and in your soul
A constant flame is burning. 670
    PHÆDRA. Ah, for Theseus
I languish and I long, but not, indeed,
As the Shades have seen him, as the fickle lover
Of a thousand forms, the one who fain would rav-
    ish
The bride of Pluto;—but one faithful, proud, 675
Even to slight disdain,—the charm of youth
That draws all hearts, even as the gods are
    painted,—
Or as yourself. He had your eyes, your manner,—
He spoke like you, and he could blush like you,
And when he came across the waves to Crete, 680
My childhood home, worthy to win the love
Of Minos' daughters,—what were you doing then?
Why did my father gather all these men,
The flower of Greece, and leave Hippolytus? 684
Oh, why were you too young to have embarked
On board the ship that brought your father there?
The monster would have perished at your hands,
Despite the windings of his vast retreat.
My sister would have armed you with the clue 689
To guide your steps, doubtful within the maze.—
But no—for Phædra would have come before her,
And love would first have given me the thought,
And I it would have been, whose timely aid
Had taught you all the labyrinthine ways!
The care that such a dear life would have cost me!
No thread could satisfy my lover's fears. 696
I would have wished to lead the way myself,
And share the peril you were sure to face.
Yes, Phædra would have walked the maze with
    you,—
With you come out in safety, or have perished!
    HIPP. Gods! What is this I hear? Have you for-
    gotten 701
That Theseus is my father and your husband?
    PHÆDRA. Why should you fancy I have lost re-
    membrance
And that I am regardless of my honor?
    HIPP. Forgive me, madam! With a blush I own

That I mistook your words, quite innocent. 706
For very shame I cannot see you longer—
Now I will go—
    PHÆDRA. Ah, prince, you understood me,—
Too well, indeed! For I had said enough. 710
You could not well mistake. But do not think
That in those moments when I love you most
I do not feel my guilt. No easy yielding
Has helped the poison that infects my mind.
The sorry object of divine revenge, 715
I am not half so hateful to your sight
As to myself. The gods will bear me witness,—
They who have lit this fire within my veins,—
The gods who take their barbarous delight
In leading some poor mortal heart astray! 720
Nay, do you not remember, in the past,
How I was not content to fly?—I drove you
Out of the land, so that I might appear
Most odious—and to resist you better
I tried to make you hate me—and in vain! 725
You hated more, and I loved not the less,
While your misfortunes lent you newer charms.
I have been drowned in tears and scorched by fire!
Your own eyes might convince you of the truth
If you could look at me, but for a moment! 730
What do I say? You think this vile confession
That I have made, is what I meant to say?
I did not dare betray my son. For him
I feared,—and came to beg you not to hate him.
This was the purpose of a heart too full 735
Of love for you to speak of aught besides.
Take your revenge, and punish me my passion!
Prove yourself worthy of your valiant father,
And rid the world of an offensive monster!
Does Theseus' widow dare to love his son? 740
Monster indeed! Nay, let her not escape you!
Here is my heart! Here is the place to strike!
It is most eager to absolve itself!
It leaps impatiently to meet your blow!—
Strike deep! Or if, indeed, you find it shameful
To drench your hand in such polluted blood,—
If that be punishment too mild for you,— 747
Too easy for your hate,—if not your arm,
Then lend your sword to me.—Come! Give it
    now!—
    ŒNONE. What would you do, my lady? Oh, just
    gods! 750
But someone comes;—go quickly. Run from
    shame.
You cannot fly, if they should find you thus.
    [*Exeunt* PHÆDRA *and* ŒNONE. *Enter* THE-
    RAMENES.

THERA. Is that the form of Phædra that I see
Go hurrying? What are these signs of sorrow?
Where is your sword? Why are you pale and
    shaken?   755
    HIPP. Friend, let us fly. Indeed, I am confused
With greatest horror and astonishment.
Phædra—but no; gods, let this dreadful secret
Remain forever buried and unknown.
    THERA. The ship is ready if you wish to sail,
But Athens has already cast her vote.   761
Their leaders have consulted all the tribes.
Your brother is elected;—Phædra wins!
    HIPP. Phædra?
    THERA. A herald bringing a commission   765
Has come from Athens, placing the reins of power
In Phædra's hands. Her son is king.—
    HIPP. O gods,—
O ye who know her, is it thus, indeed,
That ye reward her virtue?   770
    THERA. Meanwhile rumor
Is whispering that Theseus is not dead,—
That there are those who saw him in Epirus,—
But I have searched, and I know all too well—
    HIPP. No matter. Let no chances be neglected.
This rumor must be hunted to its source,   776
And if it be not worthy of belief
Let us then sail, and at whatever cost,
We'll trust the scepter to deserving hands.
                                    [*Exeunt.*

ACT III

Enter PHÆDRA *and* ŒNONE.

    PHÆDRA. Ah, let them take away the worthless
    honors   780
They bring to me;—why urge that I should see
    them?
What flattery can soothe my wounded heart?
Far rather hide me. I have said too much.
My madness bursting like a stream in flood,   784
I spoke what never should have reached his ears.
Oh, gods! The way he heard me! How reluctant
To take my meaning,—dull and cold as marble,
And only eager for a quick retreat!
And how his blushes made my shame the deeper!
Why did you turn me from the death I sought?   790
Ah, when his sword was pointed at my breast,
Did he grow pale?—or try to snatch it from me?
That I had touched it was enough for him
To make it seem forever horrible,
And to defile whatever hand should hold it.   795
    ŒNONE. When you will brood upon your bitter
    grief.

You only fan a fire that must be quenched.
Would it not more become the blood of Minos
To find you peace in cares that are more noble?—
And in defiance of this wretch, who flies   800
From what he hates, reign on the throne you're
    offered?
    PHÆDRA. I reign?—And shall I hold the rod of
    empire,
When reason can no longer reign in me?
When I have lost control of mine own senses?
When I do gasp beneath a shameful yoke?   805
When I am dying?—
    ŒNONE. Fly!
    PHÆDRA. I cannot leave him.
    ŒNONE. You dare not fly from one you dared to
    banish?
    PHÆDRA. That time is past. He knows how I am
    frenzied,   810
For I have overstepped my modesty,
And blazoned out my shame before his eyes.
Against my will, hope crept into my heart.
Did you not call my failing powers to me?
Was it not you, yourself, called back my soul   815
Which fluttered on my lips, and with your counsel
Lent me new life? Who told me I might love
    him?
    ŒNONE. Blame me or blame me not for your
    misfortunes,—
What could I not have done if it would save you?
But if your anger ever was aroused   820
By insult, can you pardon him his scorn?
How cruel were his eyes, severe and fixed,
Surveying you, half prostrate at his feet!
How hateful, then, his savage pride appeared!
Why did not Phædra see as I saw then?   825
    PHÆDRA. This pride that you detest may yield to
    time.
The rudeness of the forest clings about him,
For he was bred there by the strictest laws.
Love is a word he never knew before.
Perhaps it was surprise that stunned him so;—
There was much vehemence in all I said.   831
    ŒNONE. Remember that his mother was bar-
    baric—
    PHÆDRA. She was a Scythian, but she learned to
    love.
    ŒNONE. He has a bitter hate for all our sex.
    PHÆDRA. Well, then no rival ever rules his heart.
Your counsel comes a little late, Œnone.   836
Now you must serve my madness, not my reason.
Love cannot find a way into his heart,
So let us take him where he has more feeling.   839
The lure of power seemed somewhat to touch him.

He could not hide that he was drawn to Athens,—
His vessels' prows were pointed there already,
With sails all set to run before the breeze.
Go, and on my behalf, touch his ambition,—
Dazzle his eyes with prospects of the crown. 845
The sacred diadem shall grace his brow,—
My highest honor is to set it there,
And he shall have the power I cannot keep.
He'll teach my son how men are ruled.—It may be
That he will deign to be a father to him. 850
He shall control both son and mother;—try him,—
Try every means to move him, for your words
Should meet more favor than my own could find.
Urge him with groans and tears,—say Phædra's
    dying,
Nor blush to speak in pleading terms with him.
My last hope is in you,—do what you will, 856
I'll sanction it,—the issue is my fate!

[*Exit* Œnone.

PHÆDRA [*alone*]. Venus implacable, thou seest
    me shamed,
And I am sore confounded. Have I not
Been humbled yet enough? Can cruelty 860
Stretch farther still? Thine arrows have struck
    home!
It is thy victory! Wouldst gain new triumphs?—
Then seek an enemy more obdurate,—
Hippolytus neglects thee, braves thine anger.
He never bows his knee before thine altars. 865
Thy name offends his proud, disdainful hearing.
Our interests are alike,—avenge thyself,
Force him to love— But what is this, Œnone?
Already back? Then it must be he hates me,
And will not hear you speak— 870

Enter Œnone.

ŒNONE. Yes, you must stifle
A love that's vain, and best call back your virtue.
The king we thought was dead will soon appear
Here to your eyes. Yes, Theseus will be here,
For he has come again. The eager people 875
Are hastening to see him. I had gone
As you commanded, seeking for the prince,
When all the air was torn,—a thousand shouts—
    PHÆDRA. My husband living! 'Tis enough,
    Œnone.
I owned a passion that dishonors him. 880
He is alive. I wish to know no more.
    ŒNONE. What is it?
    PHÆDRA. What I prophesied to you,—
What you refused to hear, while with your weep-
    ing
You overcame repentance. Had I died 885

I had deserved some pity, earlier.
I took your counsel, and I die dishonored.
    ŒNONE. You die?
    PHÆDRA. Just Heavens! What I have done today!
My husband comes, and with him comes his son,
And I shall see the witness of my passion, 891
The object of my most adulterous flame
Watch with what face I make his father welcome,
Knowing my heart is big with sighs he scorned,
And my eyes wet with tears that could not move
    him. 895
Will his respect for Theseus make him hide it?—
Conceal my madness?—not disgrace his father?
And do you think he can repress the horror
Which he must have for me? A fruitless silence!
I know my treason, and I lack the boldness 900
Of those abandoned women, who can feel
Tranquillity in crime,—can show a forehead
All unashamed. I know my madness well,
Recall it all. I think that these high roofs
And all these walls can speak. They will accuse
    me. 905
They only wait until my husband comes,
And then they will reveal my perfidy.
'Tis death alone can take away this horror.
Is it so great an ill to cease to live?
Death holds no fear for those in misery. 910
I tremble only for the name I leave,—
My son's sad heritage. The blood of Jove
Might justly swell the pride of those who boast it,
But what a heavy weight a mother's guilt
Leaves for her children! Yes, I dread that scorn
For my disgrace, which will be cast on them 916
With too much truth. I tremble when I think
How they will never dare to raise their heads,
Crushed with that curse.—
    ŒNONE. Nay, do not doubt my pity. 920
There never was a juster fear than yours.
Then why do you expose them to this shame?
And why must you accuse yourself, destroying
The one hope left. It will be said of Phædra
That she well knows of her own perfidy, 925
That she has fled from out her husband's sight,—
And proud Hippolytus may well rejoice
That, dying, you should lend his tale belief.
What answer can I make him? It will be
For him, a story easy to deny, 930
And I shall hear him, while triumphantly
He tells your shame to every open ear.
Why, I had sooner Heaven's fire consumed me!
Deceive me not! And do you love him still? 934
What think you now of this contemptuous prince?
    PHÆDRA. As of a monster fearful to mine eyes!

ŒNONE. Why do you give him easy victory?
You are afraid! Dare to accuse him first!
Say he is guilty of the charge he brings
This day against you. Who shall say it's false?   940
All things conspire against him. In your hands
His sword, which he most happily forgot,—
Your present trouble, and your past distress,—
Your warnings to his father,—and his exile
Which you accomplished with your earnest pray-
    ers—   945
    PHÆDRA. So! You would have me slander inno-
    cence!
    ŒNONE. My zeal asks nothing from you but
    your silence.
I also tremble. I am loath to do it.
I'd face a thousand deaths more willingly.
But since, without this bitter deed, I lose you,   950
And since, for me, your life outweighs all else,
Why, I will speak. Theseus, however angry,
Will do no worse than banish him again.
A father, punishing, remains a father.
His anger will be soothed with easy penance.   955
But even if some guiltless blood be spilt,
Is not your honor of a greater worth,—
A treasure far too precious to be risked?
You must submit, no matter what is needful,
For when your reputation is at stake,   960
Then you must sacrifice your very conscience.
But someone comes. 'Tis Theseus—
    PHÆDRA. Look, I see
Hippolytus most stern, and in his eyes
There is my ruin written. I am helpless.   965
My fate is yours. Do with it as you will.

Enter THESEUS, HIPPOLYTUS *and* THERAMENES.

    THESEUS. Fortune will fight no longer with my
    wishes,
But to your arms it brings me back—
    PHÆDRA. Wait, Theseus.
Nay, do not hurry to profane caresses   970
One time so sweet, which I am now not worthy
Even to taste of, for you have been wronged.
Fortune has proved most spiteful. In your absence
It has not spared your wife. I am not fit
To meet you tenderly, and from this time   975
I only care how I shall bear my shame.
    [*Exeunt* PHÆDRA *and* ŒNONE.
    THESEUS. Strange welcome for your father, is it
    not?
What does it mean, my son?
    HIPP. Why, only Phædra
Can solve that mystery. If I can move you   980
By any wish, then let me never see her.

Hippolytus begs leave to disappear,—
To leave the home that holds your wife, forever.
    THESEUS. You, my son! Leave me?
    HIPP. 'Twas not I who sought her.   985
You were the one to lead her to these shores!
My lord, at your departure you thought fit
To leave Aricia and the queen in Trœzen,
And I, myself, was charged with their protection.
But now, what cares will need to keep me here?
My idle youth has shown what skill it has   991
Over such petty foes as roam the woods.
May I not leave this life of little glory,—
Of ease—and dip my spear in nobler blood?
Before you reached my age, more than one tyrant,
More than one monster had already felt   996
The force of your good arm. You had succeeded
In whipping insolence; you had removed
All of the dangers lurking on our coasts.
The traveler no longer feared for outrage,   1000
And Hercules, himself, who knew your deeds,
Relied on you, and rested from his labors.
But I—the son of such a noble father,—
I am unknown, and I am far behind
Even my mother's footsteps. Let my courage   1005
Have scope to act. If there is yet some monster
Escaped from you, then let me seek for glory,
Bringing the spoils to you; or let it be
That memory of death well met with courage
Shall keep my name a living one,—shall prove
To all the world I am my father's son.   1011
    THESEUS. Why, what is this? What terror can
    have seized you?
What makes my kindred fly before my face?
If I return to find myself so feared,
To find so little welcome in my home,   1013
Then why did Heaven free me from my prison?
My only friend, misled by his own passion
Set out to rob the tyrant of Epirus,—
To rob him of his wife! Regretfully
I gave the lover aid. Fate blinded us,—   1020
Myself as well as him. The tyrant seized me,
Defenseless and unarmed. With tears I saw
Pirithous cast forth to be devoured
By savage beasts, that lapped the blood of men.
He shut me in a gloomy cave, far down,   1025
Deep in the earth, near to the realm of Pluto.
I lay six months, before the gods had pity,
Then I escaped the eyes that guarded me.
I purged the world of this, its enemy,
And he, himself has fed his monsters' hunger.
But when I come, with an expectant joy,   1031
When I draw close to all that is most precious
Of what the gods have left me,—when my soul

Looks for its happiness in these dear places,
Then I am welcome only with a shudder,   1035
With turning from me, and with hasty flight.
And since it seems that I inspire such terror,
Would I were still imprisoned in Epirus!
Phædra complains that I have suffered outrage.
Who has betrayed me? Speak! Was I avenged?
Why was I not? Has Greece, to whom mine
    arm   1041
Has often brought good help, sheltered my foe?
You do not answer. Is it that my son,—
My own son—has he joined mine enemies?
I'll enter, for I cannot bear to wonder.   1045
I'll learn at once the culprit and the crime,
And Phædra must explain her trouble to me.
                                         [*Exit.*

HIPP. What mean these words? They freeze my
    very blood!
Will Phædra, in her frenzy, blame herself,—
Make sure of her destruction? And the king,—
What will he say? O gods! The fatal poison   1051
That love has spread through all my father's
    house!
I burn with fires his hatred disapproves.
How changed he finds me from the son he knew!
My mind is much alarmed with dark forebodings,
But surely innocence need never fear.   1056
Come, let us go, and in some other place
Consider how I best may move my father
To make him tender, and to tell a love   1059
Troubled, but never vanquished, by his frown.
                                       [*Exeunt.*

ACT IV

Enter THESEUS AND ŒNONE.

THESEUS. Ah, what is this I hear? Presumptuous
    traitor!
And would he have disgraced his father's honor?
With what relentless footsteps Fate pursues me!
I know not where I go, nor where I am!
My kindest love, how very ill repaid!   1065
Bold scheme! Oh, most abominable thought!
A wretch who did not shrink from violence
To reach the object of his evil passion!
I know this sword,—it served to arm his fury,—
The sword I gave him for a nobler use!   1070
And could the sacred ties of blood not stop him?
And Phædra,—was she loath to have him pun-
    ished?
She held her silence. Was it to spare his guilt?

ŒNONE. Only to spare a most unhappy father.
She knew it shameful that her eyes had kindled

So infamous a love,—had prompted him   1076
To such a crime,—and Phædra would have died.
I saw her raise her arm, and ran to save her.
To me alone you owe it that she lives.
And since I pity her, and pity you   1080
I came, unwilling, to explain her tears.

THESEUS. The traitor! Well indeed might he
    turn pale!
It was for fear he trembled when he saw me!
I was amazed that he should show no gladness.
The coldness of his greeting chilled my love. 1085
But was this guilty passion that consumes him
Declared before I banished him from Athens?

ŒNONE. Remember, sire, how Phædra urged it
    on you.
It was illicit love that caused her hatred.

THESEUS. And then this flame burst out again at
    Trœzen?   1090

ŒNONE. Sire, I have told you all there is. The
    queen
Is left to bear her grief alone too long.
Let me now leave you. I will wait on her.
                          [*Exit. Enter* HIPPOLYTUS.

THESEUS. Ah, there he is! Great gods! That
    noble manner
Might well deceive an eye less fond than mine!
Why should the sacred mark of virtue shine   1096
Bright on the forehead of an evil wretch?
Why should the blackness of a traitor's heart
Not show itself by sure and certain signs?

HIPP. My father, may I ask what fatal cloud
Has troubled so the face of majesty?   1101
Dare you not trust this secret to your son?

THESEUS. Traitor, how dare you show yourself
    before me?
Monster, whom Heaven's bolts have spared too
    long!
A last survivor of that robber band   1105
Whereof I cleansed the earth, your brutal lust
Scorned to respect even my marriage bed!
And now you dare,—my hated foe,—to come
Here to my presence, here where all things are
    filled
And foul with infamy, instead of seeking   1110
Some unknown land, that never heard my name.
Fly, traitor, fly! Stay not to tempt my wrath!
I scarce restrain it. Do not brave my hatred.
I have been shamed forever; 'tis enough
To be the father of so vile a son,   1115
Without your death, to stain indelibly
The splendid record of my noble deeds.
Fly! And unless you yearn for punishment
To make you yet another villain slain.

Take heed that this sun, shining on us now   1120
Shall see your foot no more upon this soil.
I say it once again,—fly!—and in haste!
Rid all my realms of your detested person.
On thee,—on thee, great Neptune, do I call!
If once I cleared thy shores of murderers,   1125
Remember, then, thy promise to reward me
For these good deeds, by granting my first prayer.
I was held long in close captivity.
I did not then demand thy mighty aid,
For I have saved so great a privilege   1130
To use in greatest need. That time is come.
And now I ask,—avenge a wretched father!
I leave this traitor subject to thy wrath.
I ask that thou shouldst quench his fires in blood,
And by thy fury, I will judge thy favor!   1135
  HIPP. Phædra accuses me of wanton passion!
A final horror to confuse my soul!
Such blows, unlooked for, falling all at once,
Have crushed me, choked me, struck me into
    silence!
  THESEUS. Traitor, you thought that in a timid
    silence   1140
Phædra would cover your brutality.
But, though you fled, you still should not have left
    her
Holding the sword that seals your condemnation.
Or rather, to complete your perfidy,
You should have robbed her both of speech and
    life!   1145
  HIPP. Most justly angered at so black a lie,
I might be pardoned, should I speak the truth.
But it concerns your honor to conceal it.
Welcome that reverence which stops my tongue,
And, without seeking to increase your troubles,
Look closely at my life, as it has been.   1151
Great crimes come never singly; they are linked
To sins that went before. Who once has sinned,
May, at the last, do greater violence
To all that men hold sacred. Vice, like virtue,   1155
Grows in small steps, and no true innocence
Can ever fall at once to deepest guilt.
No man of virtue, in a single day,
Can turn himself to treason, murder, incest!
I am the son of one both chaste and brave.   1160
I have not proved unworthy of my birth.
Pittheus, one by all men reckoned wise,
Deigned to instruct me, when I left her keeping.
I do not wish to boast upon my merits,
But if I may lay claim to any virtue,   1165
I think I have displayed, beyond all else,
That I abhor those sins with which you charge me.
Look you, Hippolytus is known in Greece

As one so continent he's thought austere,
And all men know how I abstain, unbending.
The daylight is not purer than my heart.   1171
Then how could I, if burning so profanely,—
  THESEUS. Villain, it is that very pride condemns
    you!
I see the hateful reason for your coldness,
For only Phædra charmed your shameless eyes.
Your heart, quite cold to other witcheries,   1176
Refused the pure flame of a lawful love.
  HIPP. No, father, I have hidden it too long.
This heart has not disdained its sacred flame.
Here, at your feet, I'll tell my real offense.   1180
I love, and love, indeed, where you forbid it.
My heart's devotion binds me to Aricia,—
The child of Pallas has subdued your son!
Her I adore, rebellious to your laws.
For her alone I breathe my ardent sighs.   1185
  THESEUS. You love her? Gods! But no,—I see the
    truth.
You play this crime to justify yourself.
  HIPP. Sir, for six months I kept me from her
    presence,
And still I love her. I have come to tell it,—   1189
Trembling I come—! Can nothing free your mind
Of such an error? Can my oaths not soothe you?
By Heaven—Earth,—by all the powers of Nature—
  THESEUS. The wicked will not ever shrink from
    lying.
Be still, and spare me tiresome vows and pleadings,
Since your false virtue knows no other way.   1195
  HIPP. Although you think it false and insincere,
Phædra has cause enough to know it true.
  THESEUS. Ah, how your boldness rouses all my
    anger!
  HIPP. What is my term and place of banish-
    ment?   1199
  THESEUS. Were you beyond the Pillars of Alcides,
Your perjured presence still were far too near me!
  HIPP. What friends will pity me, if you forsake
    me
And think me guilty of so vile a crime?
  THESEUS. Go seek for friends who praise adul-
    tery,
And look for those who clap their hands at in-
    cest!—
Low traitors, lawless,—steeped in infamy,—   1206
Fit comforters for such an one as you!
  HIPP. Are incest and adultery the words
Which you will cast at me? I hold my peace.   1209
Yet think what mother Phædra had—remember
Her blood, not mine, is tainted with these horrors!

THESEUS. So then! Before my eyes your rage
  bursts out,
And loses all restraint. Go from my sight!—
This last time I will say it,—traitor, go!
And do not wait until a father's anger   1215
Drives you away in public execration!

[*Exit* HIPPOLYTUS.

THESEUS [*alone*]. Wretch! Thou must meet in-
  evitable ruin!
Neptune has sworn by Styx,—an oath most dread-
  ful
Even to gods,—and he will keep his promise.
Thou canst not ever flee from his revenge.   1220
I loved thee, and in spite of this offense
My heart is moved by what I see for thee.
Nay, but thy doom is but too fully earned.
Had father ever better cause for rage?
O you just gods, who see my crushing grief,   1225
Why was I cursed with such an evil son?

Enter PHÆDRA.

PHÆDRA. I come to you, my lord, in proper dread,
For I have heard your voice raised high in anger,
And much I fear that deeds have followed threats.
Oh, spare your child, if there is still some time! 1230
Respect your race, your blood, I do beseech you.
I would not hear that blood cry from the earth!
Save me the horror and the lasting shame
Of having caused his father's hand to shed it!
  THESEUS. No, madam, I am free from such a
    stain.   1235
But still the wretch has not escaped my vengeance.
The hand of an Immortal holds his doom,
And pledges his destruction. 'Tis a debt
That Neptune owes me. You shall be avenged.
  PHÆDRA. A debt to you? Prayers made in
    anger—   1240
  THESEUS. Fear not.
They will not fail. But join your prayers to mine,
And paint his crimes for me in all their blackness,
To fan my sluggish wrath to whitest heat.
You do not know of all his villainy.   1245
His rage against you feeds itself on slanders.
Your words, he says, are full of all deceit.
He says Aricia has his heart and soul,
That he loves only her—
  PHÆDRA. Aricia?—   1250
  THESEUS. Yes.
He said it to my face:—an idle pretext!
A trick I am not caught by. Let us hope
That Neptune does swift justice. I am going
Now to his altars, urging he keep his oath.   1255

[*Exit* THESEUS.

PHÆDRA [*alone*]. So he is gone! What words
  have struck mine ears?
What smothered fires are burning in my heart?
What fatal stroke falls like a thunder-bolt?
Stung with remorse that would not give me peace,
I tore myself from out Œnone's arms   1260
And hurried here to help Hippolytus,
With all my soul and strength. Who knows, in-
  deed,
But that new-found repentance might have moved
  me
To speak in accusation of myself?—
And if my voice had not been choked with shame,
Perhaps I might have told the frightful truth. 1266
Hippolytus can feel—but not for me!
Aricia has his heart, his plighted word!
You gods! I thought his heart could not be
  touched
By any love, when, deaf to all my tears,   1270
He armed his eye with scorn, his brow with
  threats.
I thought him strong against all other women,
And yet another has prevailed upon him!
She tamed his pride, and she has gained his favor!
Perhaps he has a heart that's quick to melt,   1275
And I alone am she he cannot bear!
Then shall I charge myself with his protection?

Enter ŒNONE.

PHÆDRA. Dear nurse, and do you know what I
  have learned?
  ŒNONE. No, but in truth I come with trembling
    limbs.
I dreaded what you planned when you went out,
And fear of fatal madness turned me pale.   1281
  PHÆDRA. Who would have thought it, nurse? I
    had a rival.
  ŒNONE. A rival?
  PHÆDRA. Yes, he loves. I cannot doubt it.
This wild Hippolytus I could not tame,—   1285
Who scorned to be admired, and who was wearied
With lovers' sighs,—this tiger whom I dreaded
Fawns on the hand of one who broke his pride.
Aricia found the entrance to his heart!
  ŒNONE. Aricia?   1290
  PHÆDRA. 'Tis a torture yet untried!
Now for what other pains am I reserved?
All I have suffered,—ecstasies of passion,
Longings and fears, the horrors of remorse,
The shame of being spurned with contumely,   1295
Were feeble tastes of what is now my torment.
They love each other! By what secret charm

Have they deceived me? When and where and
    how
Did they contrive to meet? You knew it all,—
And why, then, was I kept from knowing of it?
You never told me of their stolen hours   1301
Of love and of delight. Have they been seen
Talking together often?—did they seek
The forest shadows? Ah, they had full freedom
To be together. Heaven watched their sighs. 1305
They loved,—and never felt that they were guilty.
The morning sun shone always clear for them,
While I,—an outcast from the face of Nature,
Shunned the bright day, and would have hid my-
    self,—
Death the one god whom I dared ask for aid!
I waited for the freedom of the grave.   1311
My woe was fed with bitterness, and watered
With many tears. It was too closely watched.
I did not dare to weep without restraint,
And knowing it a solace perilous,   1315
I feared it, and I hid my mortal terror
Beneath a face most tranquil. Oftentimes
I stopped my tears, and made myself to smile—
    ŒNONE. What fruit can they desire from fruit-
    less love?
For they can meet no more.   1320
    PHÆDRA. That love will stay,
And it will stay forever. While I speak—
O dreadful thought—they laugh and scorn my
    madness
And my distracted heart. In spite of exile,
In spite of that which soon must come to part
    them,   1325
They make a thousand oaths to bind their union.
Œnone, can I bear this happiness
Which so insults me? I would have your pity.
Yes, she must be destroyed. My husband's fury
Against her hated race shall be renewed.   1330
The punishment must be a heavy one.
Her guilt outruns the guilt of all her brothers.
I'll plead with Theseus, in my jealousy,—
What do I say? Oh, have I lost my senses?
Is Phædra jealous? will she, then, go begging 1335
For Theseus' help? He lives,—and yet I burn.
For whom? Whose heart is this I claim as mine?
My hair stands up with horror at my words,
And from this time, my guilt has passed all
    bounds!
Hypocrisy and incest breathe at once   1340
Through all I do. My hands are ripe for murder,
To spill the guiltless blood of innocence.
Do I still live, a wretch, and dare to face
The holy Sun, from whom I have my being?

My father's father was the king of gods;   1345
My race is spread through all the universe.—
Where can I hide? In the dark realms of Pluto?
But there my father holds the fatal urn.
His hands award the doom irrevocable.—
Minos is judge of all the ghosts in hell.   1350
And how his awful shade will start and shudder
When he shall see his daughter brought before
    him,
And made confess such many-colored sins,
Such crimes, perhaps, as hell itself knows not!
O father, what will be thy words at seeing   1355
So dire a sight? I see thee drop the urn,
Turning to seek some punishment unheard of,—
To be, thyself, mine executioner!
O spare me! For a cruel deity
Destroys thy race. O look upon my madness, 1360
And in it see her wrath. This aching heart
Gathers no fruit of pleasure from its crime.
It is a shame which hounds me to the grave,
And ends a life of misery in torment.
    ŒNONE. Ah, madam, drive away this groundless
    fear.   1365
Look not so hard upon a little sin.
You love. We cannot conquer destiny.
Why, you were drawn as by a fatal charm;—
Is that a marvel we have never seen?
Has love, then, come to triumph over you,   1370
And no one else? By nature man is weak.
You are a mortal,—bow to mortal fortune.
You chafe against a yoke that many others
Have borne before you. They upon Olympus,—
The very gods themselves, who make us tremble
For our poor sins, have burned with lawless pas-
    sions.   1376
    PHÆDRA. What words are these? What counsels
    do you give me?
Why will you still pour poison in mine ears?
You have destroyed me. You have brought me
    back
When I should else have left the light of day.
You made me to forget my solemn duty,   1381
And see Hippolytus, whom I had shunned.
What have you done? Why did those wicked lips
Slander his faultless life with blackest lies?
It may be you have murdered him. By now   1385
The prayer unholy of a heartless father
May have been granted. I will have no words!
Go, monster! Leave me to my sorry fate.
May the just gods repay you properly,
And may your punishment remain forever   1390
To strike with fear, all such as you, who strive
To feed the frailty of the great with cunning,

To push them to the very brink of ruin
To which their feet incline,—to smooth the path
Of guilt. Such flatterers the gods, in anger,   1395
Bestow on kings as their most fatal gift!
                                    [*Exit* Phædra.
Œnone [*alone*]. O gods! What is there I've not
    done to serve her?
And this is the reward that I have won!   [*Exit*.

ACT V

Enter Hippolytus *and* Aricia.

Aricia. Can you keep silent in this mortal dan-
    ger?
Your father loves you. Will you leave him so—
When he is thus deceived? If you are cruel,—   1401
If, in your heart, you will not see my tears,
Why then, content,—and do not ever see me.
Abandon poor Aricia,—but at least
If you must go, make sure your life is safe.   1405
Defend your honor from a shameful stain,
And force your father to recall his prayers.
There still is time. Why, for a mere caprice,
Should you leave open way for Phædra's slanders?
Let Theseus know the truth.   1410
    Hipp. Could I say more
And not expose him to a great disgrace?
How should I dare, by speaking what I know,
To make my father's brow blush red with shame?
You only know the hateful mystery.   1415
I have not showed my heart to any other
But you and Heaven. Judge, then, if I love you,
Since you have seen I could not hide from you
All I would fain have hidden from myself!
Remember under what a seal I spoke.   1420
Forget what I have said, if that may be,
And never let so pure a mouth give voice
To such a secret. Let us trust to Heaven
To give me justice, for the gods are just.   1424
For their own honor they will clear the guiltless.
The time will come for Phædra to be punished.
She cannot always flee the shame she merits.
I ask no other favor than your silence.
In all besides, I give my wrath free scope.
Make your escape from this captivity,   1430
Be bold, and come with me upon my flight.
Oh, do not stay on this accursèd soil
Where virtue breathes the air of pestilence.
To hide your leaving, take the good advantage
Of all this turmoil, roused by my disgrace.   1435
I promise you the means of flight are ready.
You have, as yet, no other guards than mine.

Defenders of great strength will fight our quarrel.
Argos has open arms, and Sparta calls us.
Let us appeal for justice to our friends,   1440
And let us not stand by while Phædra joins us
Together in one ruin, driving us
Down from the throne,—and swells her son's pos-
    sessions
By robbing us. Come, take this happy chance.
What fear can hold you back? You seem to pause.
Only your better fortune makes me urge   1446
That we be bold. When I am all a-fire,
Why are you ice? Are you afraid to follow
One who is banished?
    Aricia. Ah, but such an exile   1450
Would be most dear to me. For with what joy
I'd live, if I could link my fate to yours,
And be forgot by all the world. But still
We are not bound by that sweet tie together.
Then how am I to steal away with you?   1455
I know the strictest honor need not stop me
From seeking freedom from your father's hands,
For this, indeed, is not my parents' home,
And flight is lawful, when one flies from tyrants.
But you, sir, love me, and my virtue shrinks—   1460
    Hipp. No, no! To me your honor is as dear
As it is to yourself. A nobler purpose
Brings me to you. I ask you leave your foes
And follow with your husband. That same Heaven
Which sends these woes, sets free the pledge be-
    tween us   1465
From human hands. There are not always torches
To light the face of Hymen. Come with me—
Beside the gates of Trœzen is a temple,
Amid the ancient tombs of princes, buried.
They who are false can never enter there,   1470
And there no mortal dares make perjured oaths,
For instant punishment will come on guilt.
There is not any stronger check to falsehood
Than what is present there,—fear of a death
That cannot be escaped. There we shall go,   1475
If you consent, and swear eternal love,
And call the god who watches there to witness
Our solemn vows, and ask his guarding care.
I will invoke the holiest of powers—   1479
The chaste Diana and the Queen of Heaven,—
Yes, all the gods, who know my inmost heart,
Will answer for my sacred promises.
    Aricia. Here is the king. Away—make no delay.
I linger yet a while to hide my flight.
Go you, and leave me with some trusted one
To lead my timid footsteps to your side.   1486
        [*Exit* Hippolytus. *Enter* Theseus *and*
        Ismene.

THESEUS. O gods, throw light upon my troubled mind!
Show me the truth which I am seeking here.

ARICIA [to ISMENE]. Be ready, dear Ismene, for our flight. [Exit ISMENE.

THESEUS. Your color changes, and you seem confused. 1490
Madam,—what dealing had my son with you?

ARICIA. Sire, he was bidding me his last farewell.

THESEUS. It seems your eyes can tame that stubborn pride,
And the first sighs he breathes are paid to you.

ARICIA. I cannot well deny the truth; he has not
Inherited your hatred and injustice,— 1496
He does not treat me as a criminal.

THESEUS. That is to say,—he swore eternal love.
Do not depend on such a fickle heart.
He swore as much to others, long before. 1500

ARICIA. He, Sire?

THESEUS. You stop the roving of his taste.
How should you bear so vile a partnership?

ARICIA. And how can you endure that wicked slanders
Should make so pure a life seem black as pitch?
How do you know so little of his heart? 1506
Do you so ill distinguish innocence
From the worst guilt? What mist before your eyes
Can make them blind to such an open virtue?
Ah! 'Tis too much to let false tongues defame him! 1510
Repent! Call back again your fatal prayers.
Oh, be afraid, lest Heaven in its justice
Hate you enough to hear your wish and grant it!
The gods, in anger, often take our victims,—
And oftentimes they punish us with gifts! 1515

THESEUS. No, it is vain to seek to hide his guilt.
Your love is blind to his depravity.
But I have witnesses beyond reproach,—
Tears I have seen,—true tears, that may be trusted.

ARICIA. Take heed, my lord. Although your mighty hand 1520
Has rid the world of many beasts and monsters,
You have not slain them all,—there's one alive!—
Your son, himself, forbids that I say more,
And since I know how much he still reveres you,
I know that I should cause him much distress
If I should dare to finish. I shall act 1526
Like reverence,—and to be silent,—leave you.
[Exit ARICIA.

THESEUS [alone]. What is there in her mind?
What hidden meaning
Lurks in a speech begun, then broken short?
Would both deceive me with a vain pretense? 1530
Have they conspired to put me to this torture?
And yet, for all that I am most severe,
What plaintive voice is crying in my heart?
I have a secret pity that disturbs me.
Œnone must be questioned, once again, 1535
For I must see this crime in clearer light.
Guards, bid Œnone come to me,—alone.

Enter PANOPE.

PANOPE. I do not know the purpose of the queen,
Yet, seeing her distress, I fear the worst;—
Despair most fatal, painted on her features,— 1540
Death's pallor is already in her face.
Œnone, shamed and driven from her sight,
Has thrown herself into the ocean's depths.
What moved her to so rash a deed, none knows,
And now the waves forever hide her from us. 1545

THESEUS. What is it that you say?

PANOPE. Her sad fate adds
New trouble to the queen's tempestuous soul.
Sometimes, to soothe her secret pain, she clasps
Her children to her, bathes them with her tears,—
Then suddenly forgets her mother's love, 1551
And thrusts them from her with a look of horror.
She wanders back and forth with doubtful steps,
Her eye looks vacantly, and will not know us.
She wrote three times, and thrice she changed her mind, 1555
And tore the letter when it scarce was started.
Be willing then to see her, Sire,—to help her.
[Exit PANOPE.

THESEUS. Œnone dead, and Phædra bent on dying?
Oh, call my son to me again, great Heaven!
Let him defend himself, for I am ready 1560
To hear him, now. Oh, haste not to bestow
Thy fatal bounty, Neptune. Rather my prayers
Should stay unheard forever. Far too soon
I raised too cruel hands, and I believed
Lips that may well have lied! Ah, what may follow? 1565

Enter THERAMENES.

THESEUS. 'Tis you, Theramenes? Where is my son?
I gave him to your keeping in his childhood,—
But why should tears be flowing from thine eyes?
How is it with my son—?

THERA. You worry late. 1570
It is a vain affection. He is dead.

THESEUS. O gods!

THERA. Yes, I have seen the very flower
Of all mankind cut down; and I am bold

To say that never man deserved it less.   1575
   THESEUS. My son! My son is dead! When I was
     reaching
My arms to him again, then why should Heaven
Hasten his doom? What sudden blow was this?
   THERA. When we had scarcely passed the gates
     of Trœzen,—
He, silent in his chariot, his guards   1580
Downcast and silent, too, all ranged around him,—
He turned his steeds to the Mycenian road,
And, lost in thought, allowed the reins to lie
Loose on their backs, and his high-mettled charg-
     ers,
One time so eager to obey his voice,   1585
Now seemed to know his sadness and to share it.
Then, coming from the sea, a frightful cry
Shatters the troubled air with sudden discord;
And groaning from the bosom of the earth
Answers the crying of that fearful voice.   1590
It froze the blood within our very hearts!
Our horses hear, and stand with bristling manes.
Meanwhile there rises on the watery plain
A mountain wave, mighty, with foaming crest.
It rolls upon the shore, and as it breaks   1595
It throws before our eyes a raging monster.
Its brow is armed with terrifying horns
And all its body clothed with yellow scales.
In front it is a bull, behind, a dragon,
Turning and twisting in impatient fury.   1600
It bellows till the very shores do tremble.
The sky is struck with horror at the sight.
The earth in terror quakes; breath of the beast
Poisons the air. The very wave that brought it
Runs back in fear. All fly, forgetting courage   1605
Which cannot help,—and in a nearby temple
Take refuge,—all but brave Hippolytus.
A hero's worthy son, he stays his horses,
Seizes his darts, and rushing forward, hurls   1609
A missile with sure aim, and wounds the beast
Deep in the flank. It springs, raging with pain,
Right to the horses' feet, and roaring, falls,
Writhes in the dust, shows them his fiery throat,
And covers them with flame and smoke and blood.
Fear lends them wings; deaf to his voice for once,
Heeding no curb, the horses race away.   1616
Their master tires himself in futile efforts.
Each courser's bit is red with blood and foam.
Some say a god, in all this wild disorder,
Is seen, pricking their dusty flanks with goads.   1620
They rush to jagged rocks, urged by this terror.
The axle crashes, and the hardy youth
Sees his car broken, shattered into bits.
He himself falls, entangled in the reins.—

Forgive my grief. That cruel sight will be   1625
For me, the source of never-ending tears.
I saw thy luckless son,—I saw him, Sire,
Dragged by those horses that his hands had fed.
He could not stop their fierce career,—his cries
But added to their terror. All his body   1630
Was soon a mass of wounds. Our anguished cries
Filled the whole plain. At length the horses slack-
     ened.
They stopped close by the ancient tombs which
     mark
The place where lie the ashes of his fathers.
I ran there panting, and behind me came   1635
His guard, along a track fresh-stained with blood,
Reddening all the rocks; locks of his hair
Hung dripping in the briers,—gory triumphs!
I came and called him. Stretching out his hand,
He opened dying eyes, soon to be closed.   1640
"The gods have robbed me of a guiltless life."
I heard him say, "Take care of sad Aricia,
When I am dead. Friend, if my father mourn
When he shall know his son's unhappy fate,—
One accused falsely,—then, to give me peace,
Tell him to treat his captive tenderly,   1646
And to restore—" The hero's breath had failed,
And in my arms there lay a mangled body,—
A thing most piteous, the bleeding spoil
Of Heaven's wrath,—his father could not know
     him.   1650
   THESEUS. Alas, my son:—my hope, now lost for-
     ever!
The gods are ruthless. They have served me well,
And I am left to live a life of anguish
And of a great remorse.
   THERA. And then Aricia,   1655
Flying from you, came timidly to take him
To be her husband, there, before the gods.
And coming close, she saw the grass, all reeking,
All bloody red, and (sad for a lover's eyes!)
She saw him, lying there, disfigured, pale,—   1660
And for a time she knew not her misfortune.
She did not know the hero she adores.
She looked and asked, "Where is Hippolytus?"
Only too sure, at last, that he was lying
Before her there, with sad eyes, silently   1665
Reproaching Heaven, she groaned, and shudder-
     ing
Fell fainting, all but lifeless, at his feet.
Ismene, all in tears, knelt down beside her,
And called her back to life, a life of nothing
But sense of pain. And I to whom the light   1670
Is only darkness, now, come to discharge
The duty he imposed on me: to tell you

His last desire,—a melancholy task.—
But here his mortal enemy is coming.

Enter PHÆDRA *and Guards.*

THESEUS. Madam, you've triumphed, and my
   son is killed!   1675
Ah, but what room have I for fear! How justly
Suspicion racks me that in blaming him
I erred! But he is dead; accept your victim,
Rightly or wrongly slain. Your heart may leap.
For me, my eyes shall be forever blind.   1680
Since you have said it, I'll believe him guilty.
His death is cause enough for me to weep.
It would be folly, should I seek a light
Which could not bring him back to soothe my
   grief,
And which might only make me more unhappy.
I will go far from you and from this shore, 1686
For here the vision of my mangled son
Would haunt my memory, and drive me mad.
I wish I might be banished from the world,
For all the world must rise in judgment on me.
Even my glory weights my punishment,   1691
For if I bore a name less known to men,
'Twere easier to hide me. Ah, I mourn
And hate all prayers the gods have granted me.
Nor will I ever go to them again   1695
With useless pleadings. All that they can give
Is far outweighed by what they took from me.
   PHÆDRA. My lord, I cannot hear you and be
   silent.
I must undo the wrong that he has suffered,—
Your son was innocent.   1700
   THESEUS. Unhappy father!
And I condemned him for a word of yours!
You think I can forgive such cruelty—?

   PHÆDRA. Moments are precious to me; let me
   speak.
'Twas I who cast an eye of lawless passion   1705
On chaste and dutiful Hippolytus.
The gods had lit a baleful fire in me,
And vile Œnone's cunning did the rest.
She feared Hippolytus,—who knew my madness,—
Would tell you of that passion which he hated.
And so she took advantage of my weakness   1711
And hastened, that she might accuse him first.
She has been punished now, but all too lightly.
She sought to flee my anger,—cast herself
Into the waves. The sword had long since cut
My thread of life, but still I heard the cry 1716
Of slandered innocence, and I determined
To die a slower way, and first confess
My penitence to you. There is a poison
Medea brought to Athens, in my veins.   1720
The venom works already in my heart.
A strange and fatal chill is spreading there.
I see already, through a gathering mist,
The husband whom I outrage with my presence.
Death veils the light of Heaven from mine eyes,
And gives it back its purity, defiled.   1726
   PANOPE. She dies, my lord.
   THESEUS. I would the memory
Of her disgraceful deed might perish with her!
Ah! I have learned too late! Come, let us go, 1730
And with the blood of mine unhappy son
Mingle our tears,—embrace his dear remains,
Repenting deeply for a hated prayer.
Let him have honor such as he deserves,
And, to appease his sore-offended spirit,   1735
No matter what her brothers' guilt has been,
From this day forth, Aricia is my daughter.
                      [*Exeunt.*

JEAN DE LA FONTAINE

Fables

The Two Doves

Two doves once cherished for each other
The love that brother hath for brother.

But one, of scenes domestic tiring,
To see the foreign world aspiring,
   Was fool enough to undertake   5
   A journey long, o'er land and lake.

Fables. Translated by E. Wright. Jean de La Fontaine (1621-1695) spent most of his life in Paris.
Though he studied for the church, he soon devoted himself to miscellaneous writing. Only his fables
are important.

"What plan is this?" the other cried;
"Wouldst quit so soon thy brother's side?
This absence is the worst of ills;
Thy heart may bear, but me it kills.   10
Pray, let the dangers, toil, and care,
  Of which all travelers tell,
  Your courage somewhat quell.
Still if the season later were—
O wait the zephyrs!—hasten not—"   15
  Just now the raven, on his oak,
  In hoarser tones than usual spoke:
"My heart forebodes the saddest lot,—
The falcons, nets— Alas, it rains!
My brother, are thy wants supplied?—   20
Provisions, shelter, pocket-guide,
And all that unto health pertains?"
These words occasioned some demur
In our imprudent traveler.
But restless curiosity   25
Prevailed at last; and so said he,—
"The matter is not worth a sigh;
Three days, at most, will satisfy,
And then returning, I shall tell
You all the wonders that befell,—   30
With scenes enchanting and sublime
Shall sweeten all our coming time.
Who seeth nought, hath nought to say.
My travel's course, from day to day,
Will be the source of great delight.   35
  A store of tales I shall relate,—
Say there I lodged at such a date,
And saw there such and such a sight.
You'll think it all occurred to you.
On this, both, weeping, bade adieu.   40
Away the lonely wanderer flew.
A thunder-cloud began to lower;
He sought, as shelter from the shower,
The only tree that graced the plain,
Whose leaves ill turned the pelting rain.   45
The sky once more serene above,
On flew our drenched and dripping dove,
And dried his plumage as he could.
Next, on the borders of a wood,
He spied some scattered grains of wheat,   50
Which one, he thought, might safely eat;
For there another dove he saw.
He felt the snare around him draw!
This wheat was but a treacherous bait
To lure poor pigeons to their fate.   55
The snare had been so long in use,
With beak and wings he struggled loose:
Some feathers perished while it stuck;
But, what was worst in point of luck,

A hawk, the cruelest of foes,   60
Perceived him clearly as he rose,
Off dragging, like a runaway,
A piece of string. The bird of prey
Had bound him, in a moment more,
Much faster than he was before,   65
But from the clouds an eagle came,
And made the hawk himself his game.
By war of robbers profiting,
The dove for safety plied the wing,
And, lighting on a ruined wall,   70
Believed his dangers ended all.
A roguish boy had there a sling,
  (Age pitiless!
We must confess)
And, by a most unlucky fling,   75
Half killed our hapless dove;
Who now, no more in love
  With foreign traveling,
  And lame in leg and wing,
Straight homeward urged his crippled flight,   80
Fatigued, but glad, arrived at night,
In truly sad and piteous plight.
The doves rejoined, I leave you all to say
What pleasure might their pains repay.
Ah, happy lovers, would you roam?   85
Pray, let it not be far from home.
To each the other ought to be
  A world of beauty ever new;
In each the other ought to see
  The whole of what is good and true.   90

Myself have loved; nor would I then,
For all the wealth of crownèd men,
Or arch celestial, paved with gold,
The presence of those woods have sold,
And fields, and banks, and hillocks, which   95
Were by the joyful steps made rich,
And smiled beneath the charming eyes
Of her who made my heart a prize—
To whom I pledged it nothing loath,
And sealed the pledge with virgin oath.   100
Ah, when will time such moments bring again?
To me are sweet and charming objects vain—
My soul forsaking to its restless mood?
O, did my withered heart but dare
  To kindle for the bright and good,   105
Should not I find the charm still there?
Is love, to me, with things that were?

The Oak and the Reed

The oak one day addressed the reed:—
"To you ungenerous indeed

Has nature been, my humble friend,
With weakness aye obliged to bend.
The smallest bird that flits in air   5
Is quite too much for you to bear;
The slightest wind that wreathes the lake
Your ever-trembling head doth shake.
    The while, my towering form
    Dares with the mountain top   10
    The solar blaze to stop,
    And wrestle with the storm.
What seems to you the blast of death,
To me is but a zephyr's breath.
Beneath my branches had you grown,   15
    That spread far round their friendly bower,
Less suffering would your life have known,
    Defended from the tempest's power.
Unhappily you oftenest show
    In open air your slender form,   20
Along the marshes wet and low,
    That fringe the kingdom of the storm.
    To you, declare I must,
    Dame Nature seems unjust."

Then modestly replied the reed: 25
"Your pity, sir, is kind indeed,
But wholly needless for my sake.
The wildest wind that ever blew
Is safe to me compared with you.
I bend, indeed, but never break.   30
Thus far, I own the hurricane
Has beat your sturdy back in vain;
But wait the end." Just at the word,
The tempest's hollow voice was heard.
The North sent forth her fiercest child,   35
Dark, jagged, pitiless, and wild.
The oak, erect, endured the blow;
The reed bowed gracefully and low.
But, gathering up its strength once more,
In greater fury than before,   40
    The savage blast
    O'erthrew, at last,
That proud, old, sky-encircled head,
Whose feet entwined the empire of the dead!

The Wolf and the Lamb

That innocence is not a shield,
A story teaches, not the longest.
The strongest reasons always yield
To reasons of the strongest.

A lamb her thirst was slaking,   5
Once, at a mountain rill.

A hungry wolf was taking
His hunt for sheep to kill,
When, spying on the streamlet's brink
This sheep of tender age,   10
He howled in tones of rage,
"How dare you roil my drink?"
Your impudence I shall chastise!"
"Let not your majesty," the lamb replies,
"Decide in haste or passion!   15
For sure 'tis difficult to think
In what respect or fashion
My drinking here could roil your drink
Since on the stream your majesty now faces
I'm lower down, full twenty paces."   20
    "You roil it," said the wolf; "and more I know,
    You cursed and slandered me a year ago."
"O no! how could I such a thing have done!
    A lamb that has not seen a year,
    A suckling of its mother dear?"   25
"Your brother then." "But brother I have none."
    "Well, well, what's all the same,
    'Twas someone of your name.
Sheep, men, and dogs of every nation,
Are wont to stab my reputation,   30
    As I have truly heard."

Without another word,
He made his vengeance good,—
Bore off the lambkin to the wood,
And there, without a jury,   35
Judged, slew, and ate her in his fury.

The Council Held by the Rats

Old Rodilard, a certain Cat,
    Such havoc of the Rats had made,
'Twas difficult to find a Rat
    With nature's debt unpaid.
The few that did remain,   5
    To leave their holes afraid,
From usual food abstain,
    Not eating half their fill.
    And wonder no one will
That one who made of Rats his revel,   10
With Rats pass'd not for Cat, but Devil.
Now, on a day, this dread Rat-eater,
Who had a wife, went out to meet her;
And while he held his caterwauling,
The unkill'd Rats, their chapter calling,   15
Discuss'd the point, in grave debate,
How they might shun impending fate.
    Their dean, a prudent Rat,
Thought best, and better soon than late,
    To bell the fatal Cat;   20

That, when he took his hunting round,
The Rats, well caution'd by the sound,
Might hide in safety under ground;
   Indeed he knew no other means.
      And all the rest   25
      At once confess'd
Their minds were with the dean's.
No better plan, they all believed,
Could possibly have been conceived,
No doubt the thing would work right well, 30
If anyone would hang the bell.
   But, one by one, said every Rat,
   "I'm not so big a fool as that."
The plan, knock'd up in this respect,
The council closed without effect.   35
     To argue or refute,
      Wise counselors abound;
     The man to execute
      Is harder to be found.

The Cobbler and the Rich Man

A Cobbler sang from morn till night;
   'Twas sweet and marvelous to hear;
   His trills and quavers told the ear
Of more contentment and delight,
   Enjoy'd by that laborious wight   5
Than e'er enjoy'd the sages seven,
Or any mortals short of heaven.
His neighbor, on the other hand,
With gold in plenty at command,
But little sang, and slumber'd less— 10
A Financier of great success.
If e'er he dozed, at break of day,
The Cobbler's song drove sleep away;
And much he wish'd that Heaven had made
Sleep a commodity of trade,   15
In market sold, like food and drink,
So much an hour, so much a wink.
At last, our songster did he call
To meet him in his princely hall.
Said he, "Now, honest Gregory,   20
What may your yearly earnings be?"

"My yearly earnings! faith, good sir,
I never go, at once, so far,"
The cheerful Cobbler said,
And queerly scratched his head,—   25
   "I never reckon in that way,
   But cobble on from day to day,
Content with daily bread."
"Indeed! Well, Gregory, pray,
What may your earnings be per day?" 30
"Why, sometimes more and sometimes less.
The worst of all, I must confess,
(And but for which our gains would be
A pretty sight, indeed, to see,)
Is that the days are made so many   35
In which we cannot earn a penny—
The sorest ill the poor man feels:
They tread upon each other's heels,
Those idle days of holy saints!
   And though the year is shingled o'er, 40
   The parson keeps a-finding more!"
With smiles provoked by these complaints,
Replied the lordly Financier,
   "I'll give you better cause to sing.
These hundred pounds I hand you here 43
   Will make you happy as a king.
Go, spend them with a frugal heed;
They'll long supply your every need."
The Cobbler thought the silver more
Than he had ever dream'd before,   50
The mines for ages could produce,
Or world, with all its people, use.
He took it home, and there did hide—
And with it laid his joy aside.
No more of song, no more of sleep,   55
   But cares, suspicions in their stead,
   And false alarms, by fancy fed.
His eyes and ears their vigils keep,
And not a cat can tread the floor
But seems a thief slipp'd through the door. 60
    At last, poor man!
   Up to the Financier he ran,—
Then in his morning nap profound:
"O, give me back my songs," cried he,
"And sleep, that used so sweet to be, 65
And take the money, every pound!"

LA ROCHEFOUCAULD

Reflections; or, Sentences and Moral Maxims

What we term virtue is often but a mass of various actions and divers interests, which fortune, or our own industry, manage to arrange; and it is not always from valor or from chastity that men are brave, and women chaste.

Self-love is the greatest of flatterers.

Passion often renders the most clever man a fool, and even sometimes renders the most foolish man clever.

Great and striking actions which dazzle the eyes are represented by politicians as the effect of great designs, instead of which they are commonly caused by the temper and the passions. Thus the war between Augustus and Antony, which is set down to the ambition they entertained of making themselves masters of the world, was probably but an effect of jealousy.

Passions often produce their contraries: avarice sometimes leads to prodigality, and prodigality to avarice; we are often obstinate through weakness and daring through timidity.

Whatever care we take to conceal our passions under the appearances of piety and honor, they are always to be seen through these veils.

The clemency of princes is often but policy to win the affections of the people.

This clemency, of which they make a merit, arises oftentimes from vanity, sometimes from idleness, oftentimes from fear, and almost always from all three combined.

We have all sufficient strength to support the misfortunes of others.

The constancy of the wise is only the talent of concealing the agitation of their hearts.

Those who are condemned to death affect sometimes a constancy and contempt for death which is only the fear of facing it; so that one may say that this constancy and contempt are to their mind what the bandage is to their eyes.

Few people know death, we only endure it, usually from determination, and even from stupidity and custom; and most men only die because they know not how to prevent dying.

We need greater virtues to sustain good than evil fortune.

Neither the sun nor death can be looked at without winking.

People are often vain of their passions, even of the worst, but envy is a passion so timid and shame-faced that no one ever dare avow her.

The evil that we do does not attract to us so much persecution and hatred as our good qualities.

Jealousy lives upon doubt; and comes to an end or becomes a fury as soon as it passes from doubt to certainty.

It would seem that nature, which has so wisely ordered the organs of our body for our happiness, has also given us pride to spare us the mortification of knowing our imperfections.

Those who apply themselves too closely to little things often become incapable of great things.

A man often believes himself leader when he is led; as his mind endeavors to reach one goal, his heart insensibly drags him towards another.

Whatever difference there appears in our fortunes, there is nevertheless a certain compensation of good and evil which renders them equal.

The contempt of riches in philosophers was only a hidden desire to avenge their merit upon the injustice of fortune, by despising the very goods of which fortune had deprived them; it was a secret to guard themselves against the degradation of poverty, it was a back way by which to arrive at that distinction which they could not gain by riches.

To establish ourselves in the world we do everything to appear as if we were established.

Although men flatter themselves with their great actions, they are not so often the result of a great design as of chance.

Happiness is in the taste, and not in the things themselves; we are happy from possessing what we like, not from possessing what others like.

We are never so happy or so unhappy as we suppose.

Reflections. François VI, Duc de la Rochefoucauld, Prince de Marsillac (1613-1680), was born in Paris and after a stormy and adventurous youth retired to a disillusioned but peaceful old age.

Nothing should so much diminish the satisfaction which we feel with ourselves as seeing that we disapprove at one time of that which we approve of at another.

There is no disguise which can long hide love where it exists, nor feign it, where it does not.

We may find women who have never indulged in an intrigue, but it is rare to find those who have intrigued but once.

There is only one sort of love, but there are a thousand different copies.

It is more disgraceful to distrust than to be deceived by our friends.

In the intercourse of life, we please more by our faults than by our good qualities.

To awaken a man who is deceived as to his own merit is to do him as bad a turn as that done to the Athenian madman, who was happy in believing that all the ships touching at that port belonged to him.

Ideas often flash across our minds more complete than we could make them after much labor.

If we never flattered ourselves we should have but scant pleasure.

We often boast that we are never bored, but yet we are so conceited that we do not perceive how often we bore others.

As it is the mark of great minds to say things in a few words, so it is that of little minds to use many words to say nothing.

Usually we only praise to be praised.

The refusal of praise is only the wish to be praised twice.

There are persons whose only merit consists in saying and doing stupid things at the right time, and who ruin all if they change their manners.

Avarice is more opposed to economy than to liberality.

However deceitful Hope may be, yet she carries us on pleasantly to the end of life.

It is far better to accustom our mind to bear the ills we have than to speculate on those which may befall us.

There are two kinds of constancy in love, one arising from incessantly finding in the loved one fresh objects to love, the other from regarding it as a point of honor to be constant.

Perseverance is not deserving of blame or praise, as it is merely the continuance of tastes and feelings which we can neither create nor destroy.

BLAISE PASCAL

Thoughts

Let man then contemplate nature as a whole, in all her exalted majesty; let him avert his eyes from the low objects that surround him; let him observe that brilliant light set as a lamp to illumine the universe eternally; let him see that the earth is but a point in comparison with the vast orbit of that star; and let him consider with amazement that this vast orbit itself is only a minute point when compared with those traversed by the stars which revolve in the firmament.

If our vision ends there, let imaginations pass beyond; it will exhaust its power of conception sooner than what nature offers it. The whole visible world is only an imperceptible speck in the wide bosom of nature. No idea approaches it. Expand our conception as we may beyond imaginable space, we beget only atoms in comparison with the reality of things. It is an infinite sphere whose center is everywhere, its circumference nowhere. In brief, it is the greatest sensible mark of the omnipotence of God, that our imagination loses itself in this thought.

Then, let man, having returned to himself, consider what he is in comparison with that which is; let him regard himself as astray in this remote district of nature, and from the little dungeon in

Thoughts. Blaise Pascal (1623-1662) was reared and educated in Paris. He did distinguished work in science and mathematics until, in 1654, he was converted to Christianity and renounced science. He joined the religious community of Port-Royal and passed the rest of his life in religious thought and writing.

which he finds himself lodged—I mean the universe—let him learn to rate at their true value the earth, kingdoms, cities, and himself.

What is man in the infinite?

But to exhibit to him another wonder quite as amazing, let him examine the most minute things he knows. A mite will show him, in its diminutive body, parts incomparably smaller—limbs with their joints, veins in these limbs, blood in the veins, humors in the blood, drops in the humors, vapors in the drops. Dividing these, again, let him exhaust his power of forming such conceptions, and then let us consider the last, least object at which he can arrive. Perhaps he will think that it is the limit of littleness in nature. But I will show him within this a new abyss. I will paint for him not only the visible universe, but all the immensity of nature that one can conceive, within the bounds of this epitome of an atom. He may see an infinity of universes, each with its firmament, its planets, its earth, in the same proportion as in the visible world; in the earth animals and finally mites in which he will find again what he found in the first; and finding in others yet the same things without end and without rest, let him lose himself in these wonders, as astonishing in their littleness as were the others from their magnitude. For who will not be amazed that our body, which just now was not perceptible in a universe itself imperceptible in the bosom of the all, has become a colossus, a world, or rather an all as compared with the nothing to which one cannot attain?

For what, in brief, is man in nature? A nothing in comparison with the infinite; an all in comparison with the nothing; a mean between nothing and all. Infinitely far from comprehending the extremes, the end of things and their first principle are for him absolutely hidden in impenetrable mystery: he is equally incapable of seeing the nothing whence he came and the infinite in which he is engulfed.

What can he do, then, except perceive a certain appearance of the midst of things, in eternal despair of knowing either their principle or their end? All things proceed from the nothing and are borne on to the infinite. Who can follow these amazing processes? The author of these wonders comprehends them; no one else can.

One naturally fancies that one is better able to get at the center of things than to embrace their circumference. The visible extent of the world stretches perceptibly beyond us; but since we ourselves surpass in the same way the minutest things, we imagine that we are more capable of grasping them; and yet it requires no less capacity to reach the nothing than to reach the all. One must be infinite to do either; and it seems to me that he who should comprehend the ultimate principles of things would be able also to attain to the knowledge of the infinite. The one depends upon the other, and the one leads to the other. The extremes touch and reunite by virtue of their very separation; but they meet in God, and in God alone.

Let us then recognize our scope; we are something, but not all. The being that we have deprives us of the knowledge of the first principles which arise from the nothing, and its littleness conceals from us the vision of the infinite.

Our intelligence holds in the order of intelligible things the same place that is held by our body in the extent of nature.

Our senses cannot perceive an extreme. Too much noise deafens us; too much light dazzles us; too great distance or proximity hinders vision; excessive prolixity or brevity in a discourse makes it obscure; too much truth amazes us. I know people who cannot comprehend that if one takes four from zero, zero is left. First principles are too evident for us. Too much pleasure disturbs; too many concords in music displease; too many benefits irritate; we wish to have the means of overpaying the debt.

In short, extremes are for us non-existent, and we are non-existent in relation to them; they escape us, or we them.

This, then, is our true state; this it is that renders us incapable of knowing with certainty and of being absolutely ignorant. We float over a vast middle region, always uncertain and tossed about, driven from one extreme to the other. If we think to attach ourselves and remain fixed at some point, it gives way and abandons us; and if we pursue it, it escapes our grasp, slips away from us, and flies from us forever. This is our natural state, and yet it is one that is most opposed to our inclinations. We burn with desire to find a firm resting-place—a fixed and final base—that we may build a tower that will reach the infinite; but our whole foundation cracks, and the earth yawns to the abyss.

If this is understood, one will, I think, remain quietly in the state in which nature has placed him. Since the mean which has fallen to our lot is always distant from the extremes, of what moment is it that a man has a little greater knowledge of things? If he has, he only grasps them a little higher up. Is he not always infinitely distant from the end, and is not the duration of our life just as infinitely far from eternity, even if it lasts ten years longer?

．　　．　　．　　．　　．

The pursuit of glory is man's greatest baseness; but it is also the greatest mark of his excellence. For whatever possessions he may have on earth, whatever degree of health and comfort, he is not satisfied if he does not possess the esteem of his fellow men. He values human reason so highly that whatever other advantages he may have in the world, if he is not also advantageously placed in the opinion of men, he is not content. That is the finest position in the world; nothing can turn him from this desire, this is the most ineffaceable characteristic of the human heart. Even those who despise men most, and think them to be no better than the brutes, wish to be admired and believed, and thus contradict themselves by their own feelings—their nature, which is stronger than all else, convincing them of the greatness of man more strongly than reason convinces them of his baseness.

．　　．　　．　　．　　．

God's justice must be as vast as his compassion; but justice toward the reprobate is less vast and should be less startling than compassion toward the elect.

We know that there is an infinite, but we are ignorant of its nature. Thus we know that it is false that numbers are finite; hence it is true that there is an infinite in number, but we do not know what it is. It is false that it is even; it is false that it is odd; for if unity be added to it, its nature is not changed. Yet it is a number, and every number is either even or odd; this is true, certainly, of all finite numbers. Thus we may know that there is a God without knowing what he is.

Let us speak now according to the light of nature. If there is a God, he is infinitely incomprehensible, since, having neither parts nor limits, he has no relation to us; we are then incapable of knowing either what he is or if he is. This being so, who will venture to undertake to solve this question? Not we, who have no relation to him.

Who, then, shall blame Christians for their inability to give a reason for their belief—blame those who profess a religion of which they cannot render a reason? They declare in exhibiting it to the world that it is foolishness, *stultitiam*. And yet you complain that they do not prove it! If they should prove it they would falsify their own words. Their lack of proofs shows that they do not lack sense. Yes; but while this excuses those who offer it as such, and removes from them the blame of setting it forth without reason, it does not excuse those who receive it.

Let us, then, examine this point and let us say: God either is, or is not. But to which side shall we incline? Reason cannot settle the matter. An infinite abyss separates us. At the extremity of this infinite distance a game is being played in which either heads or tails will turn up. What do you wager? You cannot rationally choose one or the other—there is no reason for fixing upon either.

Do not, then, accuse of error those who have made a choice, for you know nothing about it.— No, but I blame them for making not this choice, but any choice; for he who chooses "heads" and he who chooses "tails" commit the same error—they are both at fault: the proper thing is not to wager at all.

Yes, but you must wager; it is not a matter of volition; you are embarked. Which will you take, then? Let us see—since you cannot help choosing —let us see which interests you least. You have two things to lose, the true and the good; two things to stake, your reason and your will, your knowledge and your happiness; and your nature has two things to shun, error and misery. Since it is necessary to choose, your reason is no more hurt in taking one than in taking the other. That is one point settled—but your happiness?

Let us weigh the gain and the loss in choosing "heads"—that God is. Compare these two chances: if you win you win everything; if you lose you lose nothing. Wager, then, without hesitation, that he is.—This is admirable! Yes, I must wager, but perhaps I stake too much.—Let us see. Since there is an equal chance of winning and losing, if you had only to gain two lives for one you might still wager. But if there were three to be won, it would be necessary to play (since you are obliged to play whether you will or not), and you would use bad judgment (since you are forced to play) not to hazard your life to win three in a game in which the chances of gain and loss are even. But there is an eternity of life and happiness at stake; and since this is the case, if there were an infinity of chances of which one only was in your favor, you would still be right in wagering one for two, and you would act with the imprudent (since you are forced to play) to refuse to play one life against three in a game in which of an infinity of chances you have one, if there is an infinity of infinitely happy life to be won. But here there is an infinitely happy infinite life to be won; one chance of winning against a finite number of chances of loss; and what you stake is finite. That is fixed: where there is an infinite, and there is not an infinity of chances of loss against those of winning, there is no ground for deliberation—you must give all. And so, since one is obliged to play, it is irrational to guard one's life rather than risk it for an infinite gain which may as likely happen as a loss which is a loss of nothing.

For there is no sense in saying that it is uncertain that one will win, while it is certain that one risks; and that the infinite distance which separates the certainty that one risks for the uncertainty that one will win renders the finite good which one certainly stakes equal to the uncertain infinite. This is not so every player runs a certain risk, to win an uncertainty; and yet he risks a finite certainty to win a finite uncertainty without doing violence to his reason. There is not an infinite distance between the certainty of the risk and the uncertainty of winning; that statement is false. There is, in truth, an infinity between the certainty of winning and the certainty of losing. But the uncertainty of winning is proportioned to the certainty of the risk, according to the proportion of the chances of gain and loss; and hence if there are as many chances on one side as the other, the game is even; and then the certainty of the risk is equal to the uncertainty of winning: so far is it from being infinitely distant. And thus our proposition has an infinite force, when a finite is risked in a game in which the chances of winning and losing are equal and there is an infinite to be won. That is demonstrable; and if men are capable of grasping any truths, this is one of them.

I confess it, I grant it. But is there no way of seeing behind the game?—Yes, Scripture and the rest.

Yes, but my hands are bound and my mouth is dumb; I am forced to wager, and I am not free; no one releases me, and I am so constituted that I cannot believe. What, then, would you have me do?

That is true. But at least recognize your powerlessness to believe, since reason leads you to believe, and yet you cannot. Strive then to convince yourself, not by argumentation and proofs of the being of God, but by the lessoning of your passions. You wish to attain to faith, and you do not know the way; you desire to be cured of infidelity, and you ask for remedies. Learn of those who have been bound as you are, and who now are staking all that they possess: these are they who know the road that you would follow and have been cured of the disease of which you would be cured. Begin as they did—namely, acting as if they believed, taking holy water, having masses said, etc. This, naturally, will make you believe and dull you at the same time.—But that is just what I fear.—Why? What have you to lose?

"I would soon have given up pleasure," they say, "if I had had faith." I say to you, on the other hand: "You would soon have had faith if you had given up pleasure. But it is for you to begin. If I could, I would give you faith. This I cannot do, neither can I test the truth of what you say. But you can easily give up pleasure and prove that what you say is true."

If one ought not to act except upon a certainty, one ought not to do anything in religion; for it is not a certainty. But how many things one has to do on an uncertainty!—voyages, battles! I assert, accordingly, that in this case, nothing at all should be done, for nothing is certain, and that there is more certainty in religion than there is in the hope that we shall see the morrow; for it is not certain that we shall see the morrow, but it is certainly possible that we shall not see it. One cannot say the same of religion. It is not certain that it is, but who will venture to say that it is certainly possible that it is not? But when one labors for the morrow and the uncertain, one acts rationally.

This is what I see and what troubles me. I look on all sides, and everywhere see nothing but obscurity. Nature offers me nothing that is not a subject of doubt and disquietude. If I saw nothing there which indicated a Deity, I would decide not to believe in him. If I saw everywhere evidences of a Creator, I would rest peacefully in faith. But seeing too much for denial and too little for assurance, I am in a lamentable state, and have wished a hundred times that if there is a God behind nature he would indicate the fact unequivocally, and that if the evidences of him which nature gives are deceptive she would suppress them entirely—that she would tell all or nothing, so that I might see the course which I should follow. Instead of this, in my present state—ignorant of what I am and of what I ought to do—I know neither my condition nor my duty. My heart desires utterly to know where the true good is, that I may pursue it. Nothing would, for me, be too costly for eternity.

VOLTAIRE

Candide

[The first four chapters tell of Candide's rearing in a beautiful castle and of his being sent away from it; of his experiences in Bulgaria; and of his meeting with the learned Doctor Pangloss.]

V

TEMPEST, SHIPWRECK, EARTHQUAKE, AND WHAT BECAME OF DOCTOR PANGLOSS, CANDIDE, AND JAMES THE ANABAPTIST

Half dead of that inconceivable anguish which the rolling of a ship produces, one-half of the passengers were not even sensible of the danger. The other half shrieked and prayed. The sheets were rent, the masts broken, the vessel gaped. Work who would, no one heard, no one commanded. The Anabaptist being upon deck bore a hand; when a brutish sailor struck him roughly and laid him sprawling; but with the violence of the blow he himself tumbled head foremost overboard, and stuck upon a piece of the broken mast. Honest James ran to his assistance, hauled him up, and from the effort he made was precipitated into the sea in sight of the sailor, who left him to perish, without deigning to look at him. Candide drew near and saw his benefactor, who rose above the water one moment and was then swallowed up forever. He was just going to jump after him, but was prevented by the philosopher Pangloss, who demonstrated to him that the Bay of Lisbon had been made on purpose for the Anabaptist to be drowned. While he was proving this *a priori,* the ship foundered; all perished except Pangloss, Candide, and that brutal sailor who had drowned the good Anabaptist. The villain swam safely to the shore, while Pangloss and Candide were borne thither upon a plank.

As soon as they recovered themselves a little they walked toward Lisbon. They had some money left, with which they hoped to save themselves from starving, after they had escaped drowning. Scarcely had they reached the city, lamenting the death of their benefactor, when they felt the earth tremble under their feet. The sea swelled and foamed in the harbor, and beat to pieces the vessels riding at anchor. Whirlwinds of fire and ashes covered the streets and public places; houses fell, roofs were flung upon the pavements, and the pavements were scattered. Thirty thousand inhabitants of all ages and sexes were crushed under the ruins. The sailor, whistling and swearing, said there was booty to be gained here.

10 "What can be the *sufficient reason* of this phenomenon?" said Pangloss.

"This is the Last Day!" cried Candide.

The sailor ran among the ruins, facing death to find money; finding it, he took it, got drunk, and having slept himself sober, purchased the favors of the first good-natured wench whom he met on the ruins of the destroyed houses, and in the midst of the dying and the dead. Pangloss pulled him by the sleeve.

20 "My friend," said he, "this is not right. You sin against the *universal reason;* you choose your time badly."

"S'blood and fury!" answered the other; "I am a sailor and born at Batavia. Four times have I trampled upon the crucifix in four voyages to Japan; a fig for thy universal reason."

Some falling stones had wounded Candide. He lay stretched in the street covered with rubbish.

"Alas!" said he to Pangloss, "get me a little 30 wine and oil; I am dying."

"This concussion of the earth is no new thing," answered Pangloss. "The city of Lima, in America, experienced the same convulsions last year; the same cause, the same effects; there is certainly a train of sulphur under ground from Lima to Lisbon."

"Nothing more probable," said Candide; "but for the love of God a little oil and wine."

"How, probable?" replied the philosopher. "I 40 maintain that the point is capable of being demonstrated."

Candide fainted away, and Pangloss fetched him some water from a neighboring fountain. The

Voltaire, *Candide.* François Marie Arouet (1694-1778) was born and died in Paris. He assumed the name of Voltaire. He was celebrated as a writer of dramas, epic poetry, and satirical works. His last years were largely spent in Switzerland.

following day they rummaged among the ruins and found provisions, with which they repaired their exhausted strength. After this they joined with others in relieving those inhabitants who had escaped death. Some, whom they had succored, gave them as good a dinner as they could in such disastrous circumstances; true, the repast was mournful, and the company moistened their bread with tears; but Pangloss consoled them, assuring them that things could not be otherwise.

"For," said he, "all that is is for the best. If there is a volcano at Lisbon it cannot be elsewhere. It is impossible that things should be other than they are; for everything is right."

A little man dressed in black, Familiar of the Inquisition, who sat by him, politely took up his word and said:

"Apparently, then, sir, you do not believe in original sin; for if all is for the best there has then been neither Fall nor punishment."

"I humbly ask your Excellency's pardon," answered Pangloss, still more politely; "for the Fall and curse of man necessarily entered into the system of the best of worlds."

"Sir," said the Familiar, "you do not then believe in liberty?"

"Your Excellency will excuse me," said Pangloss; "liberty is consistent with absolute necessity, for it was necessary we should be free; for, in short, the determinate will—"

Pangloss was in the middle of his sentence, when the Familiar beckoned to his footman, who gave him a glass of wine from Porto or Opporto.

VI

HOW THE PORTUGUESE MADE A BEAUTIFUL AUTO-DA-FÉ, TO PREVENT ANY FURTHER EARTHQUAKES: AND HOW CANDIDE WAS PUBLICLY WHIPPED

After the earthquake had destroyed three-fourths of Lisbon, the sages of that country could think of no means more effectual to prevent utter ruin than to give the people a beautiful *auto-da-fé,* for it had been decided by the University of Coimbra, that the burning of a few people alive by a slow fire, and with great ceremony, is an infallible secret to hinder the earth from quaking.

In consequence hereof, they had seized on a Biscayner, convicted of having married his godmother, and on two Portuguese, for rejecting the bacon which larded a chicken they were eating; after dinner, they came and secured Dr. Pangloss, and his disciple Candide, the one for speaking his

mind, the other for having listened with an air of approbation. They were conducted to separate apartments, extremely cold, as they were never incommoded by the sun. Eight days after they were dressed in *san-benitos* and their heads ornamented with paper miters. The miter and *san-benito* belonging to Candide were painted with reversed flames and with devils that had neither tails nor claws; but Pangloss's devils had claws and tails and the flames were upright. They marched in procession thus habited and heard a very pathetic sermon, followed by fine church music. Candide was whipped in cadence while they were singing; the Biscayner, and the two men who had refused to eat bacon, were burnt; and Pangloss was hanged, though that was not the custom. The same day the earth sustained a most violent concussion.

Candide, terrified, amazed, desperate, all bloody, all palpitating, said to himself:

"If this is the best of possible worlds, what then are the others? Well, if I had been only whipped I could put up with it, for I experienced that among the Bulgarians; but oh, my dear Pangloss! thou greatest of philosophers, that I should have seen you hanged, without knowing for what! Oh, my dear Anabaptist, thou best of men, that thou should'st have been drowned in the very harbor! Oh, Miss Cunegonde, thou pearl of girls! that thou should'st have had thy belly ripped open!"

Thus he was musing, scarce able to stand, preached at, whipped, absolved, and blessed, when an old woman accosted him saying:

"My son, take courage and follow me."

VII

HOW THE OLD WOMAN TOOK CARE OF CANDIDE, AND HOW HE FOUND THE OBJECT HE LOVED

Candide did not take courage, but followed the old woman to a decayed house, where she gave him a pot of pomatum to anoint his sores, showed him a very neat little bed, with a suit of clothes hanging up, and left him something to eat and drink.

"Eat, drink, sleep," said she, "and may our lady of Atocha, the great St. Anthony of Padua, and the great St. James of Compostella, receive you under their protection. I shall be back tomorrow."

Candide, amazed at all he had suffered and still more with the charity of the old woman, wished to kiss her hand.

"It is not my hand you must kiss," said the old

woman; "I shall be back tomorrow. Anoint your-self with the pomatum, eat and sleep."

Candide, notwithstanding so many disasters, ate and slept. The next morning the old woman brought him his breakfast, looked at his back, and rubbed it herself with another ointment: in like manner she brought him his dinner; and at night she returned with his supper. The day following she went through the very same ceremonies.

"Who are you?" said Candide; "who has in-spired you with so much goodness? What return can I make you?"

The good woman made no answer; she returned in the evening, but brought no supper.

"Come with me," she said, "and say nothing."

She took him by the arm, and walked with him about a quarter of a mile into the country; they arrived at a lonely house, surrounded with gardens and canals. The old woman knocked at a little door, it opened, she led Candide up a private stair-case into a small apartment richly furnished. She left him on a brocaded sofa, shut the door and went away. Candide thought himself in a dream; indeed, that he had been dreaming unluckily all his life, and that the present moment was the only agreeable part of it all.

The old woman returned very soon, supporting with difficulty a trembling woman of a majestic figure, brilliant with jewels, and covered with a veil.

"Take off that veil," said the old woman to Candide.

The young man approaches, he raises the veil with a timid hand. Oh! what a moment! what surprise! he believes he beholds Miss Cunegonde! he really sees her! it is herself! His strength fails him, he cannot utter a word, but drops at her feet. Cunegonde falls upon the sofa. The old woman supplies a smelling bottle; they come to themselves and recover their speech. As they began with broken accents, with questions and answers inter-changeably interrupted with sighs, with tears, and cries. The old woman desired they would make less noise and then she left them to themselves.

"What, is it you?" said Candide, "you live? I find you again in Portugal? then you have not been ravished? then they did not rip open your belly as Doctor Pangloss informed me?"

"Yes, they did," said the beautiful Cunegonde; "but those two accidents are not always mortal."

"But were your father and mother killed?"

"It is but too true," answered Cunegonde, in tears.

"And your brother?"

"My brother also was killed."

"And why are you in Portugal? and how did you know of my being here? and by what strange adventure did you contrive to bring me to this house?"

"I will tell you all that," replied the lady, "but first of all let me know your history, since the in-nocent kiss you gave me and the kicks which you received."

Candide respectfully obeyed her, and though he was still in a surprise, though his voice was feeble and trembling, though his back still pained him, yet he gave her a most ingenuous account of everything that had befallen him since the moment of their separation. Cunegonde lifted up her eyes to heaven; shed tears upon hearing of the death of the good Anabaptist and of Pangloss; after which she spoke as follows to Candide, who did not lose a word and devoured her with his eyes.

[Chapters VIII-XII contain the history of Cune-gonde; the adventures of Cunegonde, Candide, the Grand Inquisitor, and a Jew; the arrival of Candide, Cunegonde, and the old woman at Cadiz; and the story told by the old woman.]

XIII

HOW CANDIDE WAS FORCED AWAY FROM FAIR CUNE-GONDE AND THE OLD WOMAN

The beautiful Cunegonde having heard the old woman's history, paid her all the civilities due to a person of her rank and merit. She likewise ac-cepted her proposal, and engaged all the passen-gers, one after the other, to relate their adventures; and then both she and Candide allowed that the old woman was in the right.

"It is a great pity," said Candide, "that the sage Pangloss was hanged contrary to custom at an *auto-da-fé;* he would tell us most amazing things in regard to the physical and moral evils that over-spread earth and sea, and I should be able, with due respect, to make a few objections."

While each passenger was recounting his story, the ship made her way. They landed at Buenos Ayres. Cunegonde, Captain Candide, and the old woman, waited on the Governor, Don Fernando d'Ibaraa, y Figueora, y Mascarenes, y Lampourdos, y Souza. This nobleman had a stateliness becom-ing a person who bore so many names. He spoke to men with so noble a disdain, carried his nose so loftily, raised his voice so unmercifully, assumed so imperious an air, and stalked with such intolerable pride, that those who saluted him were strongly inclined to give him a good drubbing. Cunegonde appeared to him the most beautiful he had ever met. The first thing he did was to ask whether she was not the captain's wife. The manner in which he asked the question alarmed Candide; he durst not say she was his wife, because indeed she was not; neither durst he say she was his sister, because it was not so; and although this obliging lie had been formerly much in favor among the ancients, and although it could be useful to the moderns, his soul was too pure to betray the truth.

"Miss Cunegonde," said he, "is to do me the honor to marry me, and we beseech your excellency to deign to sanction our marriage."

Don Fernando d'Ibaraa, y Figueora, y Mascarenes, y Lampourdos, y Souza, turning up his mustachios, smiled mockingly, and ordered Captain Candide to go and review his company. Candide obeyed, and the Governor remained alone with Miss Cunegonde. He declared his passion, protesting he would marry her the next day in the face of the church, or otherwise, just as should be agreeable to herself. Cunegonde asked a quarter of an hour to consider of it, to consult the old woman, and to take her resolution.

The old woman spoke thus to Cunegonde:

"Miss, you have seventy-two quarterings, and not a farthing; it is now in your power to be wife to the greatest lord in South America, who has very beautiful mustachios. Is it for you to pique yourself upon inviolable fidelity? You have been ravished by Bulgarians; a Jew and an Inquisitor have enjoyed your favors. Misfortune gives sufficient excuse. I own, that if I were in your place, I should have no scruple in marrying the Governor and in making the fortune of Captain Candide."

While the old woman spoke with all the prudence which age and experience gave, a small ship entered the port on board of which were an Alcalde and his alguazils, and this was what had happened.

As the old woman had shrewdly guessed, it was a Gray Friar who stole Cunegonde's money and jewels in the town of Badajos, when she and Candide were escaping. The Friar wanted to sell some of the diamonds to a jeweler; the jeweler knew them to be the Grand Inquisitor's. The Friar before he was hanged confessed he had stolen them. He described the persons, and the route they had taken. The flight of Cunegonde and Candide was already known. They were traced to Cadiz. A vessel was immediately sent in pursuit of them. The vessel was already in the port of Buenos Ayres. The report spread that the Alcalde was going to land, and that he was in pursuit of the murderers of my lord the Grand Inquisitor. The prudent old woman saw at once what was to be done.

"You cannot run away," said she to Cunegonde, "and you have nothing to fear, for it was not you that killed my lord; besides the Governor who loves you will not suffer you to be ill-treated; therefore stay."

Then she ran immediately to Candide.

"Fly," said she, "or in an hour you will be burnt."

There was not a moment to lose; but how could he part from Cunegonde, and where could he flee for shelter?

XIV

HOW CANDIDE AND CACAMBO WERE RECEIVED BY THE JESUITS OF PARAGUAY

Candide had brought such a valet with him from Cadiz, as one often meets with on the coasts of Spain and in the American colonies. He was a quarter Spaniard, born of a mongrel in Tucuman; he had been singing-boy, sacristan, sailor, monk, peddler, soldier, and lackey. His name was Cacambo, and he loved his master, because his master was a very good man. He quickly saddled the two Andalusian horses.

"Come, master, let us follow the old woman's advice; let us start, and run without looking behind us."

Candide shed tears.

"Oh! my dear Cunegonde! must I leave you just at a time when the Governor was going to sanction our nuptials? Cunegonde, brought to such a distance, what will become of you?"

"She will do as well as she can," said Cacambo; "the women are never at a loss; God provides for them. Let us run."

"Whither art thou carrying me? Where shall we go? What shall we do without Cunegonde?" said Candide.

"By St. James of Compostella," said Cacambo, "you were going to fight against the Jesuits; let us go to fight for them; I know the road well, I'll conduct you to their kingdom, where they will be charmed to have a captain that understands the Bulgarian exercise. You'll make a prodigious fortune; if we cannot find our account in one world, we shall in another. It is a great pleasure to see and do new things."

"You have before been in Paraguay, then?" said Candide.

"Aye, sure," answered Cacambo, "I was servant in the College of the Assumption, and am acquainted with the government of the good Fathers as well as I am with the streets of Cadiz. It is an admirable government. The kingdom is upwards of three hundred leagues in diameter, and divided into thirty provinces; there the Fathers possess all, and the people nothing; it is a masterpiece of reason and justice. For my part I see nothing so divine as the Fathers who here make war upon the kings of Spain and Portugal, and in Europe confess those kings; who here kill Spaniards, and in Madrid send them to heaven; this delights me, let us push forward. You are going to be the happiest of mortals. What pleasure will it be to those Fathers to hear that a captain who knows the Bulgarian exercise has come to them!"

As soon as they reached the first barrier, Cacambo told the advanced guard that a captain wanted to speak with my lord the Commandant. Notice was given to the main guard, and immediately a Paraguayan officer ran and laid himself at the feet of the Commandant, to impart this news to him. Candide and Cacambo were disarmed, and their two Andalusian horses seized. The strangers were introduced between two files of musketeers; the Commandant was at the further end, with the three-cornered cap on his head, his gown tucked up, a sword by his side, and a spontoon in his hand. He beckoned, and straightway the newcomers were encompassed by four-and-twenty soldiers. A sergeant told them they must wait, that the Commandant could not speak to them, and that the reverend Father Provincial does not suffer any Spaniard to open his mouth but in his presence, or to stay above three hours in the province.

"And where is the reverend Father Provincial?" said Cacambo.

"He is upon parade just after celebrating mass," answered the sergeant, "and you cannot kiss his spurs till three hours hence."

"However," said Cacambo, "the captain is not a Spaniard, but a German, he is ready to perish with hunger as well as myself; cannot we have something for breakfast, while we wait for his reverence?"

The sergeant went immediately to acquaint the Commandant with what he had heard.

"God be praised!" said the reverend Commandant, "since he is a German, I may speak to him; take him to my arbor."

Candide was at once conducted to a beautiful summerhouse, ornamented with a very pretty colonnade of green and gold marble, and with trellises, enclosing parraquets, humming-birds, fly-birds, guinea-hens, and all other rare birds. An excellent breakfast was provided in vessels of gold; and while the Paraguayans were eating maize out of wooden dishes, in the open fields and exposed to the heat of the sun, the reverend Father Commandant retired to his arbor.

He was a very handsome young man, with a full face, white skin but high in color; he had an arched eyebrow, a lively eye, red ears, vermilion lips, a bold air, but such a boldness as neither belonged to a Spaniard nor a Jesuit. They returned their arms to Candide and Cacambo, and also the two Andalusian horses; to whom Cacambo gave some oats to eat just by the arbor, having an eye upon them all the while for fear of a surprise.

Candide first kissed the hem of the Commandant's robe, then they sat down to table.

"You are, then, a German?" said the Jesuit to him in that language.

"Yes, reverend Father," answered Candide.

As they pronounced these words they looked at each other with great amazement, and with such an emotion as they could not conceal.

"And from what part of Germany do you come?" said the Jesuit.

"I am from the dirty province of Westphalia," answered Candide; "I was born in the Castle of Thunder-ten-Tronckh."

"Oh! Heavens! is it possible?" cried the Commandant.

"What a miracle!" cried Candide.

"Is it really you?" said the Commandant.

"It is not possible!" said Candide.

They drew back; they embraced; they shed rivulets of tears.

"What, is it you, reverend Father? You, the brother of the fair Cunegonde! You, that was slain by the Bulgarians! You, the Baron's son! You, a Jesuit in Paraguay! I must confess this is a strange world that we live in. Oh, Pangloss! Pangloss! how glad you would be if you had not been hanged!"

The Commandant sent away the negro slaves and the Paraguayans, who served them with liquors in goblets of rock-crystal. He thanked God and St. Ignatius a thousand times; he clasped Candide in his arms; and their faces were all bathed with tears.

"You will be more surprised, more affected, and transported," said Candide, "when I tell you that Cunegonde, your sister, whom you believe to have been ripped open, is in perfect health."

"Where?"

"In your neighborhood, with the Governor of Buenos Ayres; and I was going to fight against you."

Every word which they uttered in this long conversation but added wonder to wonder. Their souls fluttered on their tongues, listened in their ears, and sparkled in their eyes. As they were Germans, they sat a good while at table, waiting for the reverend Father Provincial, and the Commandant spoke to his dear Candide as follows.

XV

HOW CANDIDE KILLED THE BROTHER OF HIS DEAR CUNEGONDE

"I shall have ever present to my memory the dreadful day, on which I saw my father and mother killed, and my sister ravished. When the Bulgarians retired, my dear sister could not be found; but my mother, my father, and myself, with two maid-servants and three little boys all of whom had been slain, were put in a hearse, to be conveyed for interment to a chapel belonging to the Jesuits, within two leagues of our family seat. A Jesuit sprinkled us with some holy water; it was horribly salt; a few drops of it fell into my eyes; the father perceived that my eye-lids stirred a little; he put his hand upon my heart and felt it beat. I received assistance, and at the end of three weeks I recovered. You know, my dear Candide, I was pretty; but I grew much prettier, and the reverend Father Didrie, Superior of that House, conceived the tenderest friendship for me; he gave me the habit of the order, some years after I was sent to Rome. The Father-General needed new levies of young German-Jesuits. The sovereigns of Paraguay admit as few Spanish Jesuits as possible; they prefer those of other nations as being more subordinate to their commands. I was judged fit by the reverend Father-General to go and work in this vineyard. We set out—a Pole, a Tyrolese, and myself. Upon my arrival I was honored with a subdeaconship and a lieutenancy. I am today colonel and priest. We shall give a warm reception to the King of Spain's troops; I will answer for it that they shall be excommunicated and well beaten. Providence sends you here to assist us. But is it, indeed, true that my dear sister Cunegonde is in the neighborhood, with the Governor of Buenos Ayres?"

Candide assured him on oath that nothing was more true, and their tears began afresh.

The Baron could not refrain from embracing Candide; he called him his brother, his savior.

"Ah! perhaps," said he, "we shall together, my dear Candide, enter the town as conquerors, and recover my sister Cunegonde."

"That is all I want," said Candide, "for I intended to marry her, and I still hope to do so."

"You insolent!" replied the Baron, "would you have the impudence to marry my sister who has seventy-two quarterings! I find thou hast the most consummate effrontery to dare to mention so presumptuous a design!"

Candide, petrified at this speech, made answer:

"Reverend Father, all the quarterings in the world signify nothing; I rescued your sister from the arms of a Jew and of an Inquisitor; she has great obligations to me, she wishes to marry me; Master Pangloss always told me that all men are equal, and certainly I will marry her."

"We shall see that, thou scoundrel!" said the Jesuit Baron de Thunder-ten-Tronckh, and that instant struck him across the face with the flat of his sword. Candide in an instant drew his rapier, and plunged it up to the hilt in the Jesuit's belly; but in pulling it out reeking hot, he burst into tears.

"Good God!" said he, "I have killed my old master, my friend, my brother-in-law! I am the best-natured creature in the world, and yet I have already killed three men, and of these three two were priests."

Cacambo, who stood sentry by the door of the arbor, ran to him.

"We have nothing more for it than to sell our lives as dearly as we can," said his master to him, "without doubt someone will soon enter the arbor, and we must die sword in hand."

Cacambo, who had been in a great many scrapes in his lifetime, did not lose his head; he took the Baron's Jesuit habit, put it on Candide, gave him the square cap, and made him mount on horseback. All this was done in the twinkling of an eye.

"Let us gallop fast, master, everybody will take you for a Jesuit, going to give directions to your men, and we shall have passed the frontiers before they will be able to overtake us."

He flew as he spoke these words, crying out aloud in Spanish:

"Make way, make way, for the reverend Father Colonel."

XVII

ARRIVAL OF CANDIDE AND HIS VALET AT EL DORADO, AND WHAT THEY SAW THERE

"You see," said Cacambo to Candide, as soon as they had reached the frontiers of the Oreillons, "that this hemisphere is not better than the others—take my word for it; let us go back to Europe by the shortest way."

"How go back?" said Candide, "and where shall we go—to my own country? The Bulgarians and the Abares are slaying all; to Portugal? there I shall be burnt; and if we abide here we are every moment in danger of being spitted. But how can I resolve to quit a part of the world where my dear Cunegonde resides?"

"Let us turn toward Cayenne," said Cacambo, "there we shall find Frenchmen, who wander all over the world; they may assist us; God will perhaps have pity on us."

It was not easy to get to Cayenne; they knew vaguely in which direction to go, but rivers, precipices, robbers, savages, obstructed them all the way. Their horses died of fatigue. Their provisions were consumed; they fed a whole month upon wild fruits, and found themselves at last near a little river bordered with cocoa trees, which sustained their lives and their hopes.

Cacambo, who was as good a counselor as the old woman, said to Candide:

"We are able to hold out no longer; we have walked enough. I see an empty canoe near the river-side; let us fill it with cocoanuts, throw ourselves into it, and go with the current; a river always leads to some inhabited spot. If we do not find pleasant things we shall at least find new things."

"With all my heart," said Candide, "let us recommend ourselves to Providence."

They rowed a few leagues, between banks, in some places flowery, in others barren; in some parts smooth, in others rugged. The stream ever widened, and at length lost itself under an arch of frightful rocks which reached to the sky. The two travelers had the courage to commit themselves to the current. The river, suddenly contracting at this place, whirled them along with a dreadful noise and rapidity. At the end of four-and-twenty hours they saw daylight again, but their canoe was dashed to pieces against the rocks. For a league they had to creep from rock to rock, until at length

they discovered an extensive plain, bounded by inaccessible mountains. The country was cultivated as much for pleasure as for necessity. On all sides the useful was also the beautiful. The roads were covered, or rather adorned, with carriages of a glittering form and substance, in which were men and women of surprising beauty, drawn by large red sheep which surpassed in fleetness the finest coursers of Andalusia, Tetuan, and Mequinez.

"Here, however, is a country," said Candide, "which is better than Westphalia."

He stepped out with Cacambo toward the first village which he saw. Some children dressed in tattered brocades played at quoits on the outskirts. Our travelers from the outer world amused themselves by looking on. The quoits were large round pieces, yellow, red, and green, which cast a singular luster! The travelers picked a few of them off the ground; this was of gold, that of emeralds, the other of rubies—the least of them would have been the greatest ornament on the Mogul's throne.

"Without doubt," said Cacambo, "these children must be the king's sons that are playing at quoits!"

The village schoolmaster appeared at this moment and called them to school.

"There," said Candide, "is the preceptor of the royal family."

The little truants immediately quitted their game, leaving the quoits on the ground with all their other playthings. Candide gathered them up, ran to the master, and presented them to him in a most humble manner, giving him to understand by signs that their royal highnesses had forgotten their gold and jewels. The schoolmaster, smiling, flung them upon the ground; then, looking at Candide with a good deal of surprise, went about his business.

The travelers, however, took care to gather up the gold, the rubies, and the emeralds.

"Where are we?" cried Candide. "The king's children in this country must be well brought up, since they are taught to despise gold and precious stones."

Cacambo was as much surprised as Candide. At length they drew near the first house in the village. It was built like an European palace. A crowd of people pressed about the door, and there were still more in the house. They heard most agreeable music, and were aware of a delicious odor of cooking. Cacambo went up to the door and heard they were talking Peruvian; it was his mother tongue, for it is well known that Cacambo was born in Tucuman, in a village where no other language was spoken.

"I will be your interpreter here," said he to Candide; "let us go in, it is a public-house."

Immediately two waiters and two girls, dressed in cloth of gold, and their hair tied up with ribbons, invited them to sit down to table with the landlord. They served four dishes of soup, each garnished with two young parrots; a boiled condor which weighed two hundred pounds; two roasted monkeys, of excellent flavor; three hundred humming-birds in one dish, and six hundred fly-birds in another; exquisite ragouts; delicious pastries; the whole served up in dishes of a kind of rock-crystal. The waiters and girls poured out several liqueurs drawn from the sugar-cane.

Most of the company were chapmen and wagoners, all extremely polite; they asked Cacambo a few questions with the greatest circumspection, and answered his in the most obliging manner.

As soon as dinner was over, Cacambo believed as well as Candide that they might well pay their reckoning by laying down two of those large gold pieces which they had picked up. The landlord and landlady shouted with laughter and held their sides. When the fit was over:

"Gentlemen," said the landlord, "it is plain you are strangers, and such guests we are not accustomed to see; pardon us therefore for laughing when you offered us the pebbles from our high-roads in payment of your reckoning. You doubtless have not the money of the country; but it is not necessary to have any money at all to dine in this house. All hostelries established for the convenience of commerce are paid by the government. You have fared but very indifferently because this is a poor village; but everywhere else, you will be received as you deserve."

Cacambo explained this whole discourse with great astonishment to Candide, who was as greatly astonished to hear it.

"What sort of a country then is this," said they to one another; "a country unknown to all the rest of the world, and where nature is of a kind so different from ours? It is probably the country where all is well; for there absolutely must be one such place. And, whatever Master Pangloss might say, I often found that things went very ill in Westphalia."

XVIII

WHAT THEY SAW IN THE COUNTRY OF EL DORADO

Cacambo expressed his curiosity to the landlord, who made answer:

"I am very ignorant, but not the worse on that account. However, we have in this neighborhood an old man retired from the Court who is the most learned and most communicative person in the kingdom."

At once he took Cacambo to the old man. Candide acted now only a second character, and accompanied his valet. They entered a very plain house, for the door was only of silver, and the ceilings were only of gold, but wrought in so elegant a taste as to vie with the richest. The antechamber, indeed, was only encrusted with rubies and emeralds, but the order in which everything was arranged made amends for this great simplicity.

The old man received the strangers on his sofa, which was stuffed with humming-birds' feathers, and ordered his servants to present them with liqueurs in diamond goblets; after which he satisfied their curiosity in the following terms:

"I am now one hundred and seventy-two years old, and I learnt of my late father, Master of the Horse to the King, the amazing revolutions of Peru, of which he had been an eye-witness. The kingdom we now inhabit is the ancient country of the Incas, who quitted it very imprudently to conquer another part of the world, and were at length destroyed by the Spaniards.

"More wise by far were the princes of their family, who remained in their native country; and they ordained, with the consent of the whole nation, that none of the inhabitants should ever be permitted to quit this little kingdom; and this has preserved our innocence and happiness. The Spaniards have had a confused notion of this country, and have called it *El Dorado;* and an Englishman, whose name was Sir Walter Raleigh, came very near it about a hundred years ago; but being surrounded by inaccessible rocks and precipices, we have hitherto been sheltered from the rapaciousness of European nations, who have an inconceivable passion for the pebbles and dirt of our land, for the sake of which they would murder us to the last man."

The conversation was long: it turned chiefly on their form of government, their manners, their women, their public entertainments, and the arts. At length Candide, having always had a taste for metaphysics, made Cacambo ask whether there was any religion in that country.

The old man reddened a little.

"How then," said he, "can you doubt it? Do you take us for ungrateful wretches?"

Cacambo humbly asked, "What was the religion in El Dorado?"

The old man reddened again.

"Can there be two religions?" said he. "We have, I believe, the religion of all the world: we worship God night and morning."

"Do you worship but one God?" said Cacambo, who still acted as interpreter in representing Candide's doubts.

"Surely," said the old man, "there are not two, nor three, nor four. I must confess the people from your side of the world ask very extraordinary questions."

Candide was not yet tired of interrogating the good old man; he wanted to know in what manner they prayed to God in El Dorado.

"We do not pray to Him," said the worthy sage; "we have nothing to ask of Him; He has given us all we need, and we return Him thanks without ceasing."

Candide having a curiosity to see the priests asked where they were. The good old man smiled.

"My friend," said he, "we are all priests. The King and all the heads of families sing solemn canticles of thanksgiving every morning, accompanied by five or six thousand musicians."

"What! have you no monks who teach, who dispute, who govern, who cabal, and who burn people that are not of their opinion?"

"We must be mad, indeed, if that were the case," said the old man; "here we are all of one opinion, and we know not what you mean by monks."

During this whole discourse Candide was in raptures, and he said to himself:

"This is vastly different from Westphalia and the Baron's castle. Had our friend Pangloss seen El Dorado he would no longer have said that the castle of Thunder-ten-Tronckh was the finest upon earth. It is evident that one must travel."

After this long conversation the old man ordered a coach and six sheep to be got ready, and twelve of his domestics to conduct the travelers to Court.

"Excuse me," said he, "if my age deprives me of the honor of accompanying you. The King will receive you in a manner that cannot displease you; and no doubt you will make an allowance for the customs of the country, if some things should not be to your liking."

Candide and Cacambo got into the coach, the six sheep flew, and in less than four hours they reached the King's palace situated at the extremity of the capital. The portal was two hundred and twenty feet high, and one hundred wide; but words are wanting to express the materials of which it was built. It is plain such materials must have prodigious superiority over those pebbles and sand which we call gold and precious stones.

Twenty beautiful damsels of the King's guard received Candide and Cacambo as they alighted from the coach, conducted them to the bath, and dressed them in robes woven of the down of humming-birds; after which the great crown officers, of both sexes, led them to the King's apartment, between two files of musicians, a thousand on each side. When they drew near to the audience chamber Cacambo asked one of the great officers in what way he should pay his obeisance to his Majesty; whether they should throw themselves upon their knees or on their stomachs; whether they should put their hands upon their heads or behind their backs; whether they should lick the dust off the floor; in a word, what was the ceremony?

"The custom," said the great officer, "is to embrace the King, and to kiss him on each cheek."

Candide and Cacambo threw themselves round his Majesty's neck. He received them with all the goodness imaginable, and politely invited them to supper.

While waiting they were shown the city, and saw the public edifices raised as high as the clouds, the market places ornamented with a thousand columns, the fountains of spring water, those of rose water, those of liqueurs drawn from sugar-cane, incessantly flowing into the great squares, which were paved with a kind of precious stone, which gave off a delicious fragrance like that of cloves and cinnamon. Candide asked to see the court of justice, the parliament. They told him they had none, and that they were strangers to lawsuits. He asked if they had any prisons, and they answered no. But what surprised him most and gave him the greatest pleasure was the palace of sciences, where he saw a gallery two thousand feet long, and filled with instruments employed in mathematics and physics.

After rambling about the city the whole afternoon, and seeing but a thousandth part of it, they were reconducted to the royal palace, where Candide sat down to table with his Majesty, his valet Cacambo, and several ladies. Never was there a better entertainment, and never was more wit shown at a table than that which fell from his Majesty. Cacambo explained the King's *bon-mots* to Candide, and notwithstanding they were translated they still appeared to be *bon-mots*. Of all the things that surprised Candide this was not the least.

They spent a month in this hospitable place. Candide frequently said to Cacambo:

"I own, my friend, once more that the castle where I was born is nothing in comparison with this; but, after all, Miss Cunegonde is not here, and you have, without doubt, some mistress in Europe. If we abide here we shall only be upon a footing with the rest, whereas, if we return to our old world, only with twelve sheep laden with the pebbles of El Dorado, we shall be richer than all the kings of Europe. We shall have no more Inquisitors to fear, and we may easily recover Miss Cunegonde."

This speech was agreeable to Cacambo; mankind are so fond of roving, of making a figure in their own country, and of boasting of what they have seen in their travels, that the two happy ones resolved to be no longer so, but to ask his Majesty's leave to quit the country.

"You are foolish," said the King. "I am sensible that my kingdom is but a small place, but when a person is comfortably settled in any part he should abide there. I have not the right to detain strangers. It is a tyranny which neither our manners nor our laws permit. All men are free. Go when you wish, but the going will be very difficult. It is impossible to ascend that rapid river on which you came as by a miracle, and which runs under vaulted rocks. The mountains which surround my kingdom are ten thousand feet high, and as steep as walls; they are each over ten leagues in breadth, and there is no other way to descend them than by precipices. However, since you absolutely wish to depart, I shall give orders to my engineers to construct a machine that will convey you very safely. When we have conducted you over the mountains no one can accompany you further, for my subjects have made a vow never to quit the kingdom, and they are too wise to break it. Ask me besides anything that you please."

"We desire nothing of your Majesty," says Candide, "but a few sheep laden with provisions, pebbles, and the earth of this country."

The King laughed.

"I cannot conceive," said he, "what pleasure you Europeans find in our yellow clay, but take as much as you like, and great good may it do you."

At once he gave directions that his engineers should construct a machine to hoist up these two extraordinary men out of the kingdom. Three thousand good mathematicians went to work; it was ready in fifteen days, and did not cost more than twenty million sterling in the specie of that country. They placed Candide and Cacambo on the machine. There were two great red sheep saddled and bridled to ride upon as soon as they were beyond the mountains, twenty pack-sheep laden with provisions, thirty with presents of the curiosities of the country, and fifty with gold, diamonds, and precious stones. The King embraced the two wanderers very tenderly.

Their departure, with the ingenious manner in which they and their sheep were hoisted over the mountains, was a splendid spectacle. The mathematicians took their leave after conveying them to a place of safety, and Candide had no other desire, no other aim, than to present his sheep to Miss Cunegonde.

"Now," said he, "we are able to pay the Governor of Buenos Ayres if Miss Cunegonde can be ransomed. Let us journey toward Cayenne. Let us embark, and we will afterwards see what kingdom we shall be able to purchase."

[Chapters XIX–XXVIII tell of Candide's adventures in Surinam; on the voyage homeward; and on trips to France, England, Venice, and Constantinople.]

XXIX

HOW CANDIDE FOUND CUNEGONDE AND THE OLD WOMAN AGAIN

While Candide, the Baron, Pangloss, Martin, and Cacambo were relating their several adventures, were reasoning on the contingent or non-contingent events of the universe, disputing on effects and causes, on moral and physical evil, on liberty and necessity, and on the consolations a slave may feel even on a Turkish galley, they arrived at the house of the Transylvanian prince on the banks of the Propontis. The first object which met their sight were Cunegonde and the old woman hanging towels out to dry.

The Baron paled at this sight. The tender, loving Candide, seeing his beautiful Cunegonde embrowned, with blood-shot eyes, withered neck, wrinkled cheeks, and rough, red arms, recoiled three paces, seized with horror, and then advanced out of good manners. She embraced Candide and her brother; they embraced the old woman, and Candide ransomed them both.

There was a small farm in the neighborhood which the old woman proposed to Candide to make a shift with till the company could be provided for in a better manner. Cunegonde did not know she had grown ugly, for nobody had told her of it; and she reminded Candide of his promise in so positive a tone that the good man durst not refuse her. He therefore intimated to the Baron that he intended marrying his sister.

"I will not suffer," said the Baron, "such meanness on her part, and such insolence on yours; I will never be reproached with this scandalous thing; my sister's children would never be able to enter the church in Germany. No; my sister shall only marry a baron of the empire."

Cunegonde flung herself at his feet, and bathed them with her tears; still he was inflexible.

"Thou foolish fellow," said Candide; "I have delivered thee out of the galleys, I have paid thy ransom, and thy sister's also; she was a scullion, and is very ugly, yet I am so condescending as to marry her; and dost thou pretend to oppose the match? I should kill thee again, were I only to consult my anger."

"Thou mayest kill me again," said the Baron, "but thou shalt not marry my sister, at least whilst I am living."

XXX

THE CONCLUSION

At the bottom of his heart Candide had no wish to marry Cunegonde. But the extreme impertinence of the Baron determined him to conclude the match, and Cunegonde pressed him so strongly that he could not go from his word. He consulted Pangloss, Martin, and the faithful Cacambo. Pangloss drew up an excellent memorial, wherein he proved that the Baron had no right over his sister, and that according to all the laws of the empire, she might marry Candide with her left hand. Martin was for throwing the Baron into the sea; Cacambo decided that it would be better to deliver him up again to the captain of the galley, after which they sought to send him back to the General Father of the Order at Rome by the first ship. This advice was well received, the old woman approved it; they said not a word to his sister; the thing was executed for a little money, and they had the double pleasure of entrapping a Jesuit, and punishing the pride of a German baron.

It is natural to imagine that after so many disasters Candide married, and living with the philosopher Pangloss, the philosopher Martin, the prudent Cacambo, and the old woman, having besides brought so many diamonds from the country of the ancient Incas, must have led a very happy life. But he was so much imposed upon by the Jews that he had nothing left except his small farm; his wife became uglier every day, more peevish and unsupportable; the old woman was infirm and even more fretful than Cunegonde. Cacambo, who worked in the garden, and took vegetables for sale to Constantinople, was fatigued with hard work, and cursed his destiny. Pangloss was in despair at not shining in some German university. For Martin, he was firmly persuaded that he would be as badly off elsewhere, and therefore bore things patiently. Candide, Martin, and Pangloss sometimes disputed about morals and metaphysics. They often saw passing under the windows of their farm boats full of Effendis, Pashas, and Cadis, who were going into banishment to Lemnos, Mitylene, or Erzeroum. And they saw other Cadis, Pashas, and Effendis coming to supply the place of the exiles, and afterwards exiled in their turn. They saw heads decently impaled for presentation to the Sublime Porte. Such spectacles as these increased the number of their dissertations; and when they did not dispute time hung so heavily upon their hands, that one day the old woman ventured to say to them:

"I want to know which is the worse, to be ravished a hundred times by Negro pirates, to have a buttock cut off, to run the gauntlet among the Bulgarians, to be whipped and hanged at an auto-da-fé, to be dissected, to row in the galleys—in short, to go through all the miseries we have undergone, or to stay here and have nothing to do?"

"It is a great question," said Candide.

This discourse gave rise to new reflections, and Martin especially concluded that man was born to live either in a state of distracting inquietude or of lethargic disgust. Candide did not quite agree to that, but he affirmed nothing. Pangloss owned that he had always suffered horribly, but as he had once asserted that everything went wonderfully well, he asserted it still, though he no longer believed it.

· · · · ·

In the neighborhood there lived a very famous Dervish who was esteemed the best philosopher in all Turkey, and they went to consult him. Pangloss was the speaker.

"Master," said he, "we come to beg you to tell why so strange an animal as man was made."

"With what meddlest thou?" said the Dervish; "is it thy business?"

"But, reverend father," said Candide, "there is horrible evil in this world."

"What signifies it," said the Dervish, "whether there be evil or good? When his highness sends a ship to Egypt, does he trouble his head whether the mice on board are at their ease or not?"

"What, then, must we do?" said Pangloss.

"Hold your tongue," answered the Dervish.

"I was in hopes," said Pangloss, "that I should reason with you a little about causes and effects, about the best of possible worlds, the origin of evil, the nature of the soul, and the pre-established harmony."

At these words, the Dervish shut the door in their faces.

During this conversation, the news was spread that two Viziers and the Mufti had been strangled at Constantinople, and that several of their friends had been impaled. This catastrophe made a great noise for some hours. Pangloss, Candide, and Martin, returning to the little farm, saw a good old man taking the fresh air at his door under an orange bower. Pangloss, who was as inquisitive as he was argumentative, asked the old man what was the name of the strangled Mufti.

"I do not know," answered the worthy man, "and I have not known the name of any Mufti, nor of any Vizier. I am entirely ignorant of the event you mention; I presume in general that they who meddle with the administration of public affairs die sometimes miserably, and that they deserve it; but I never trouble my head about what is transacting at Constantinople; I content myself with sending there for sale the fruits of the garden which I cultivate."

Having said these words, he invited the strangers into his house; his two sons and two daughters presented them with several sorts of sherbet, which they made themselves, with Kaimak enriched with the candied-peel of citrons, with oranges, lemons, pineapples, pistachio-nuts, and Mocha coffee unadulterated with the bad coffee of Batavia or the American islands. After which the two daughters of the honest Mussulman perfumed the strangers' beards.

"You must have a vast and magnificent estate," said Candide to the Turk.

"I have only twenty acres," replied the old man; "I and my children cultivate them; our labor preserves us from three great evils—weariness, vice, and want."

Candide, on his way home, made profound reflections on the old man's conversation.

"This honest Turk," said he to Pangloss and Martin, "seems to be in a situation far preferable to that of the six kings with whom we had the honor of supping."

"Grandeur," said Pangloss, "is extremely dangerous according to the testimony of philosophers. For, in short, Eglon, King of Moab, was assassinated by Ehud; Absalom was hung by his hair, and pierced with three darts; King Nadab, the son of Jeroboam, was killed by Baasa; King Ela by Zimri; Ahaziah by Jehu; Athaliah by Jehoiada; the Kings Jehoiakim, Jeconiah, and Zedekiah, were led into captivity. You know how perished Crœsus, Astyages, Darius, Dionysius of Syracuse, Pyrrhus, Perseus, Hannibal, Jugurtha, Ariovistus, Cæsar, Pompey, Nero, Otho, Vitellius, Domitian, Richard II of England, Edward II, Henry VI, Richard III, Mary Stuart, Charles I, the three Henrys of France, the Emperor Henry IV! You know—"

"I know also," said Candide, "that we must cultivate our garden."

"You are right," said Pangloss, "for when man was first placed in the Garden of Eden, he was put there *ut operaretur eum,* that he might cultivate it; which shows that man was not born to be idle."

"Let us work," said Martin, "without disputing; it is the only way to render life tolerable."

The whole little society entered into this laudable design, according to their different abilities. Their little plot of land produced plentiful crops. Cunegonde was, indeed, very ugly, but she became an excellent pastry cook; Paquette worked at embroidery; the old woman looked after the linen. They were all, not excepting Friar Giroflée, of some service or other; for he made a good joiner, and became a very honest man.

Pangloss sometimes said to Candide:

"There is a concatenation of events in this best of all possible worlds: for, if you had not been kicked out of a magnificent castle for love of Miss Cunegonde: if you had not walked over America: if you had not stabbed the Baron: if you had not lost all your sheep from the fine country of El Dorado: you would not be here eating preserved citrons and pistachio-nuts."

"All that is very well," answered Candide, "but let us cultivate our garden."

JEAN-JACQUES ROUSSEAU

A Discourse on Inequality

The first man, who, after enclosing a piece of ground, took it into his head to say, "This is mine," and found people simple enough to believe him, was the true founder of civil society. How many crimes, how many wars, how many murders, how many misfortunes and horrors, would that man have saved the human species, who pulling up the stakes or filling up the ditches should have cried to his fellows: Be sure not to listen to this impostor; you are lost, if you forget that the fruits of the earth belong equally to us all, and the earth itself to nobody! But it is highly probable that things were now come to such a pass, that they could not continue much longer in the same way; for as this idea of property depends on several prior ideas which could only spring up gradually one after another, it was not formed all at once in the human mind: men must have made great progress; they must have acquired a great stock of industry and knowledge, and transmitted and increased it from age to age before they could arrive at this last term of the state of nature. Let us therefore take up things a little higher, and collect into one point of view, and in their most natural order, this slow succession of events and mental improvements.

The first sentiment of man was that of his existence, his first care that of preserving it. The production of the earth yielded him all the assistance he required; instinct prompted him to make use of them. Among the various appetites, which made him at different times experience different modes of existence, there was one that excited him to perpetuate his species; and this blind propensity, quite void of anything like pure love or affection, produced nothing but an act that was merely animal. The present heat once allayed, the sexes took no further notice of each other, and even the child ceased to have any tie in his mother, the moment he ceased to want her assistance.

Such was the condition of infant man; such was the life of an animal confined at first to pure sensations, and so far from harboring any thought of forcing her gifts from nature, that he scarcely availed himself of those which she offered to him of her own accord. But difficulties soon arose, and there was a necessity for learning how to surmount them: the height of some trees, which prevented his reaching their fruits; the competition of other animals equally fond of the same fruits; the fierceness of many that even aimed at his life; these were so many circumstances, which obliged him to apply to bodily exercise. There was a necessity for becoming active, swift-footed, and sturdy in battle. The natural arms, which are stones and the branches of trees, soon offered themselves to his assistance. He learned to surmount the obstacles of nature, to contend in case of necessity with other animals, to dispute his subsistence even with other men, or indemnify himself for the loss of whatever he found himself obliged to part with to the strongest.

In proportion as the human species grew more numerous, and extended itself, its pain likewise multiplied and increased. The difference of soils, climates and seasons, might have forced men to observe some differences in their way of living. Bad harvests, long and severe winters, and scorching summers, which parched up all the fruits of the earth, required extraordinary exertions of industry. On the sea shore, and the banks of rivers they invented the line and the hook, and became fishermen and ichthyophagous. In the forests they made themselves bows and arrows, and became huntsmen and warriors. In the cold countries they covered themselves with the skins of the beasts they had killed; thunder, a volcano, or some happy accident made them acquainted with fire, a new resource against the rigors of winter: they discovered the method of preserving this element, then that of reproducing it, and lastly the way of preparing with it the flesh of animals, which heretofore they devoured raw from the carcass.

This reiterated application of various beings to himself, and to one another, must have naturally engendered in the mind of man the idea of certain

Rousseau, *A Discourse on Inequality*. Selections. Jean-Jacques Rousseau (1712-1778), of Swiss birth, became the leader of the romantic movement which led to the French Revolution. By his own life he illustrated many of the principles of extreme freedom which he advocated.

relations. These relations, which we express by the words, great, little, strong, weak, swift, slow, fearful, bold, and the like, compared occasionally, and almost without thinking of it, produced in him some kind of reflection, or rather a mechanical prudence, which pointed out to him the precautions most essential to his preservation and safety.

The new lights resulting from this development increased his superiority over other animals, by making him sensible of it. He laid himself out to ensnare them; he played them a thousand tricks; and though several surpassed him in strength or in swiftness, he in time became the master of those that could be of any service to him, and a sore enemy to those that could do him any mischief. 'Tis thus, that the first look he gave into himself produced the first emotion of pride in him; 'tis thus that, at a time he scarce knew how to distinguish between the different ranks of existence, by attributing to his species the first rank among animals in general, he prepared himself at a distance to pretend to it as an individual among those of his own species in particular.

Though other men were not to him what they are to us, and he had scarce more intercourse with them than with other animals, they were not overlooked in his observations. The conformities, which in time he might discover between them, and between himself and his female, made him judge of those he did not perceive; and seeing that they all behaved as himself would have done in similar circumstances, he concluded that their manner of thinking and willing was quite conformable to his own; and this important truth, when once engraved deeply on his mind, made him follow, by a presentiment as sure as any logic, and withal much quicker, the best rules of conduct, which for the sake of his own safety and advantage it was proper he should observe towards them.

Instructed by experience that the love of happiness is the sole principle of all human actions, he found himself in a condition to distinguish the few cases, in which common interest might authorize him to build upon the assistance of his fellow, and those still fewer, in which a competition of interests might justly render it suspected. In the first case he united with them in the same flock, or at most by some kind of free association which obliged none of its members, and lasted no longer than the transitory necessity that had given birth to it. In the second case everyone aimed at his own private advantage, either by open force if he found himself strong enough, or by cunning and ad-

dress if he thought himself too weak to use violence.

Such was the manner in which men might have insensibly acquired some gross idea of their mutual engagements and the advantage of fulfilling them, but this only as far as their present and sensible interest required; for as to foresight they were utter strangers to it, and far from troubling their heads about a distant futurity, they scarce thought of the day following. Was a deer to be taken? Everyone saw that to succeed he must faithfully stand to his post; but suppose a hare to have slipped by within reach of any one of them, it is not to be doubted but he pursued it without scruple, and when he had seized his prey never reproached himself with having made his companions miss theirs.

We may easily conceive that such an intercourse scarce required a more refined language than that of crows and monkeys, which flock together almost in the same manner. Inarticulate exclamations, a great many gestures, and some imitative sounds, must have been for a long time the universal language of mankind, and by joining to these in every country some articulate and conventional sounds, of which, as I have already hinted, it is not very easy to explain the institution, there arose particular languages, but rude, imperfect, and such nearly as are to be found at this day among several savage nations. My pen straightened by the rapidity of time, the abundance of things I have to say, and the almost insensible progress of the first improvements, flies like an arrow over numberless ages, for the slower the succession of events, the quicker I may allow myself to be in relating them.

At length, these first improvements enabled man to improve at a greater rate. Industry grew perfect in proportion as the mind became more enlightened. Men soon ceasing to fall asleep under the first tree, or take shelter in the first cavern, lit upon some hard and sharp kinds of stone resembling spades or hatchets, and employed them to dig the ground, cut down trees, and with the branches build huts, which they afterwards bethought themselves of plastering over with clay or dirt. This was the epoch of a first revolution, which produced the establishment and distinction of families, and which introduced a species of property, and along with it perhaps a thousand quarrels and battles. As the strongest, however, were probably the first to make themselves cabins, which they knew they were able to defend, we may conclude that the weak found it much shorter and safer to imitate than to attempt to dislodge them: and as to those who were already provided with cabins, no one could have any great temptation to seize upon that of his neighbor, not so much because it did not belong to him, as because it could be of no service to him; and as besides to make himself master of it, he must expose himself to a very sharp conflict with the present occupiers.

The first developments of the heart were the effects of a new situation, which united husbands and wives, parents and children, under one roof; the habit of living together gave birth to the sweetest sentiments the human species is acquainted with, conjugal and paternal love. Every family became a little society, so much the more firmly united, as a mutual attachment and liberty were the only bonds of it; and it was now that the sexes, whose way of life had been hitherto the same, began to adopt different manners and customs. The women became more sedentary, and accustomed themselves to stay at home and look after the children, while the men rambled abroad in quest of subsistence for the whole family. The two sexes likewise by living a little more at their ease began to lose somewhat of their usual ferocity and sturdiness; but if on the one hand individuals became less able to engage separately with wild beasts, they on the other were more easily got together to make a common resistance against them.

In this new state of things, the simplicity and solitariness of man's life, the limitedness of his wants, and the instruments which he had invented to satisfy them, leaving him a great deal of leisure, he employed it to supply himself with several conveniences unknown to his ancestors; and this was the first yoke he inadvertently imposed upon himself, and the first source of mischief which he prepared for his children; for besides continuing in this manner to soften both body and mind, these conveniences having through use lost almost all their aptness to please, and even degenerated into real wants, the privation of them became far more intolerable than the possession of them had been agreeable; to lose them was a misfortune, to possess them no happiness.

Here we may a little better discover how the use of speech insensibly commences or improves in the bosom of every family, and may likewise from conjectures concerning the manner in which divers particular causes might have propagated language, and accelerated its progress by rendering it every day more and more necessary. Great inundations or earthquakes surrounded inhabited districts with water or precipices, portions of the continent were

by revolutions of the globe torn off and split into islands. It is obvious that among men thus collected, and forced to live together, a common idiom must have started up much sooner, than among those who freely wandered through the forests of the main land. Thus it is very possible that the inhabitants of the islands formed in this manner, after their first essays in navigation, brought among us the use of speech; and it is very probable at least that society and languages commenced in islands and even acquired perfection there, before the inhabitants of the continent knew anything of either.

Everything now begins to wear a new aspect. Those who heretofore wandered through the woods, by taking to a more settled way of life, gradually flock together, coalesce into several separate bodies, and at length form in every country distinct nations, united in character and manners, not by any laws or regulations, but by an uniform manner of life, a sameness of provisions, and the common influence of the climate. A permanent neighborhood must at last infallibly create some connection between different families. The transitory commerce required by nature soon produced, among the youth of both sexes living in contiguous cabins, another kind of commerce, which besides being equally agreeable is rendered more durable by mutual intercourse. Men begin to consider different objects, and to make comparisons; they insensibly acquire ideas of merit and beauty, and these soon produce sentiments of preference. By seeing each other often they contract a habit, which makes it painful not to see each other always. Tender and agreeable sentiments steal into the soul, and are by the smallest opposition wound up into the most impetuous fury: Jealousy kindles with love; discord triumphs; and the gentlest of passions requires sacrifices of human blood to appease it.

In proportion as ideas and sentiments succeed each other, and the head and the heart exercise themselves, men continue to shake off their original wildness, and their connections become more intimate and extensive. They now begin to assemble round a great tree: singing and dancing, the genuine offspring of love and leisure, become the amusement or rather the occupation of the men and women, free from care, thus gathered together. Everyone begins to survey the rest, and wishes to be surveyed himself; and public esteem acquires a value. He who sings or dances best; the handsomest, the strongest, the most dexterous, the most eloquent, comes to be the most respected: this was the first step towards inequality, and at the same time towards vice. From these first preferences there proceeded on one side vanity and contempt, on the other envy and shame; and the fermentation raised by these new leavens at length produced combinations fatal to happiness and innocence.

Men no sooner began to set a value upon each other, and know what esteem was, than each laid claim to it, and it was no longer safe for any man to refuse it to another. Hence the first duties of civility and politeness, even among savages; and hence every voluntary injury became an affront, as besides the mischief, which resulted from it as an injury, the party offended was sure to find in it a contempt for his person more intolerable than the mischief itself. It was thus that every man, punishing the contempt expressed for him by others in proportion to the value he set upon himself, the effects of revenge became terrible, and men learned to be sanguinary and cruel. Such precisely was the degree attained by most of the savage nations with whom we are acquainted. And it is for want of sufficiently distinguishing ideas, and observing at how great a distance these people were from the first state of nature, that so many authors have hastily concluded that man is naturally cruel, and requires a regular system of police to be reclaimed; whereas nothing can be more gentle than he in his primitive state, when placed by nature at an equal distance from the stupidity of brutes, and the pernicious good sense of civilized man; and equally confined by instinct and reason to the care of providing against the mischief which threatens him, he is withheld by natural compassion from doing any injury to others, so far from being ever so little prone even to return that which he has received. For according to the axiom of the wise Locke, Where there is no property, there can be no injury.

But we must take notice, that the society now formed and the relations now established among men required in them qualities different from those, which they derived from their primitive constitution; that as a sense of morality began to insinuate itself into human actions, and every man, before the enacting of laws, was the only judge and avenger of the injuries he had received, that goodness of heart suitable to the pure state of nature by no means suited infant society; that it was

necessary punishments should become severer in the same proportion that the opportunities of offending became more frequent, and the dread of vengeance add strength to the too weak curb of the law. Thus, though men were become less patient, and natural compassion had already suffered some alteration, this period of the development of the human faculties, holding a just mean between the indolence of the primitive state, and the petulant activity of self-love, must have been the happiest and most durable epoch. The more we reflect on this state, the more convinced we shall be, that it was the least subject of any to revolutions, the best for man, and that nothing could have drawn him out of it but some fatal accident, which, for the public good, should never have happened. The example of the savages, most of whom have been found in this condition, seems to confirm that mankind was formed ever to remain in it, that this condition is the real youth of the world, and that all ulterior improvements have been so many steps, in appearance towards the perfection of individuals, but in fact towards the decrepitness of the species.

As long as men remained satisfied with their rustic cabins; as long as they confined themselves to the use of clothes made of the skins of other animals, and the use of thorns and fish-bones, in putting these skins together; as long as they continued to consider feathers and shells as sufficient ornaments, and to paint their bodies of different colors, to improve or ornament their bows and arrows, to form and scoop out with sharp-edged stones some little fishing boats, or clumsy instruments of music; in a word, as long as they undertook such works only as a single person could finish, and stuck to such arts as did not require the joint endeavors of several hands, they lived free, healthy, honest and happy, as much as their nature would admit, and continued to enjoy with each other all the pleasures of an independent intercourse; but from the moment one man began to stand in need of another's assistance; from the moment it appeared an advantage for one man to possess the quantity of provisions requisite for two, all equality vanished; property started up; labor became necessary; and boundless forests became smiling fields, which it was found necessary to water with human sweat, and in which slavery and misery were soon seen to sprout out and grow with the fruits of the earth.

HONORÉ DE BALZAC

Gold

At this time I was living in a little street which no doubt you do not know, la rue de Lesdiguières; it begins in la rue Saint Antoine, opposite a fountain near la place de la Bastille, and ends in la rue de la Cerisaie. The love of science had thrown me into a garret where I worked all through the night; the day I spent at a neighboring library, la Bibliothèque de Monsieur. I lived frugally, accepting all the conditions of monastic life—conditions so necessary to men at work. When the weather was fine, the farthest I went was for a walk on le boulevard Bourdon. One passion alone drew me out of my studious habits; but even that was a study in itself. I used to go and watch the manners of the quarter, its inhabitants and their characters. As I was as ill-clad as the workmen and indifferent to appearances, I did not in any way put them on their guard against me; I was able to mix with them when they stood in groups, and watch them driving their bargains and disputing as they were leaving their work. With me observation had even then become intuitive; it did not neglect the body, but it penetrated further, into the soul, or rather, it grasped the exterior details so perfectly, that it at once passed beyond. It gave me the faculty of living the life of the individual upon whom it exercised itself, by allowing me to substitute myself for him, like the dervish in the Thousand-and-One Nights, who took possession of the body and soul of people over whom he pronounced certain words.

Between eleven and twelve o'clock at night I might fall in with a workman and his wife returning together from the Ambigu Comique; then I would amuse myself by following them from le boulevard du Pontaux-Choux to le boulevard Beaumarchais. First of all, the good people would talk about the piece they had seen; then, from the thread to the needle, they passed on to their own affairs. The mother would drag along her child by the hand without listening to his cries or his questions. Then the pair would count up the money to be paid them next day, and spend it in twenty different ways. Then there were details of housekeeping, grumblings about the enormous price of potatoes, or the length of the winter and the dearness of fuel: and then forcible representations as to what was owing to the baker; at last the discussion grew acrimonious, and each of them would betray his character in forcible expressions. As I listened to these people I was able to enter into their life; I felt their rags upon my back, and walked with my feet in their worn-out shoes; their desires, their wants—everything passed into my soul, or else it was my soul that passed into theirs. It was the dream of a man awake. I grew warm with them against some tyrannical foreman, or the bad customers who made them return many times without paying them. To be quit of one's own habits, to become another than oneself by an inebriation of the moral faculties, and to play this game at will—this formed my distraction.

To what do I owe this gift? Is it a kind of second sight? Is it one of those qualities which, if abused, induce madness? I have never sought to find the cause of this power; I possess it and I use it, that is all. It is enough to know that, at that time, I had decomposed the elements of the heterogeneous mass called the People—that I had analyzed it in such a way that I could set their proper value on its qualities, good and bad. I knew already the possible usefulness of the quarter, that seminary of Revolution which contains heroes, inventors, men of practical science, rogues, villains, virtues and vices, all oppressed by misery, stifled by poverty, drowned in wine, worn out by strong drink. You could not imagine how many unknown adventures, how many forgotten dramas, how many horrible and beautiful things lie hidden in this town of sorrow. Imagination will never reach the truth that lurks there, for no man can go to seek it out, the descent is too deep to discover its marvelous scenes of tragedy and comedy, its masterpieces which are born of chance.

I know not why I have kept the story I am about to relate so long without telling it; it is part of those strange tales stored in the bag whence memory draws them capriciously, like the numbers of a lottery. I have many more of them, as strange as this and as deeply buried; they will have their turn, I assure you.

One day my housekeeper, the wife of a workman, came to ask me to honor with my presence the marriage of one of her sisters. To make you

Honoré de Balzac (1799-1850).

understand what this marriage must have been like, I must tell you that I gave the poor creature forty *sous* a month; for this she came every morning to make my bed, clean my shoes, brush my clothes, sweep the room, and get ready my breakfast; the rest of her time she went to turn the handle of a machine, earning at this hard work ten *sous* a day. Her husband, a cabinet-maker, earned four *francs*. But as they had a family of three children, it was almost impossible for them to get an honest living. I never met with more thorough honesty than this man's and woman's. For five years after my leaving the district, *la mère Vaillant* used to come to congratulate me on my name day, and bring me a bouquet and some oranges,—and she was a woman who could never manage to save ten *sous*. Misery had drawn us together. I have never been able to give her more than ten *francs*, often borrowed on purpose. This may explain my promise to go to the wedding; I relied upon effacing myself in the poor creature's merriment.

The marriage feast, the ball, the whole entertainment took place on the first floor of a wine shop in la rue de Charenton. The room was large, papered up to the height of the tables with a filthy paper, and lit by lamps with tin reflectors; along the walls were wooden benches; in this room were twenty-four people, all dressed in their best, decked with large bouquets and ribands, their faces flushed, full of excitement, dancing as if the world were coming to an end. The bride and bridegroom were embracing to the general satisfaction, and certain hee-hees! and haw-haws! were heard, facetious, but really less indecent than the timid glances of girls who have been *well brought up*. The whole company expressed an animal contentment, which was somehow or other contagious. However, neither the physiognomies of the company, nor the wedding, nor in fact any of these people, have any connection with my story. Only bear in mind the strangeness of the frame. Picture to yourself the squalid, red shop, sniff the odor of the wine, listen to the howls of merriment, linger a while in this quarter, among those workmen and poor women and old men who had given themselves up to pleasure for a single night!

The orchestra was composed of three blind men from Les Quinze-Vingts; the first was violin, the second clarionet, and the third flageolet. They were paid seven *francs* for the night among the three. You may imagine they did not give Rossini or Beethoven at that price; they played what they chose or could; with charming delicacy, no one reproached them. Their music did such brutal violence to the drum of my ear, that, after glancing round at the company, I looked at the blind trio,—I was inclined to indulgence at once, when I recognized their uniform. The performers were in the embrasure of a window, so that you were obliged to be close to them to be able to distinguish their features; I did not go up immediately, but when I *did* get near them, I do not know how it was, but it was all over, the wedding party and the music disappeared; my curiosity was excited to the highest degree, for my soul passed into the body of the man who played the clarionet. The violin and the flageolet had both quite ordinary faces, the usual face of the blind, intense, attentive, and grave; but the clarionet's was a phenomenon such as arrests and absorbs the attention of a philosopher or an artist.

Imagine a plaster mask of Dante, lit up by the red glow of the lamp and crowned with a forest of silver-white hair. The bitter, sorrowful expression of this magnificent head was intensified by blindness, for thought gave a new life to the dead eyes; it was as if a scorching light came forth from them, the product of one single, incessant desire, itself inscribed in vigorous lines upon a prominent brow, scored with wrinkles, like the courses of stone in an old wall. The old man breathed into his instrument at random, without paying the least attention to the measure or the air; his fingers rose and fell as they moved the worn-out keys with mechanical unconsciousness; he did not trouble himself about making mistakes, but the dancers did not notice it any more than did my Italian's two acolytes; for I was determined he must be an Italian, and he *was* an Italian. There was something great and despotic in this old Homer keeping within himself an Odyssey doomed to oblivion. It was such real greatness that it still triumphed over its abject condition, a despotism so full of life that it dominated his poverty.

None of the violent passions which lead a man to good as well as to evil, and make of him a convict or a hero, were wanting in that grandly hewn, lividly Italian face. The whole was overshadowed by grizzled eyebrows which cast into shade the deep hollows beneath; one trembled lest one should see the light of thought reappear in them, as one fears to see brigands armed with torches and daggers come to the mouth of a cave. A lion dwelt within that cage of flesh, a lion whose rage was exhausted in vain against the iron of its bars. The flame of despair had sunk quenched into its ashes, the lava had grown cold; but its channels, its destructions, a little smoke, bore evidence to the violence of the eruption and the ravages of the fire. These ideas revealed in the man's appearance were as burning in his soul as they were cold upon his face.

Between dances the violin and the flageolet, gravely occupied with their bottle and glass, hung their instruments on to the button of their reddish-colored coats, stretched out their hands toward a little table placed in the embrasure of the window and on which was their canteen, and offered a full glass to the Italian;—he could not take it himself, as the table was always behind his chair;—he thanked them by a friendly gesture of the head. Their movements were accomplished with that precision which is always so astonishing in the blind of Les Quinze-Vingts, it almost makes you believe that they can see.

Presently I went up nearer to the three blind men, so as to be better able to listen to them; but when I was close to them they began to study me, and not, I suppose, recognizing a workman, they remained shy.

"What country do you come from, you who are playing the clarionet?"

"From Venice," replied the blind man, with a slight Italian accent.

"Were you born blind, or did you become blind from——"

"From an accident," he replied sharply; "it was a cursed cataract."

"Venice is a fine town; I have always had a longing to go there."

The old man's face lit up, his wrinkles worked, he was deeply moved.

"If I went there with you," he said, "you would not be losing your time."

"Don't talk to him about Venice," said the violin, "or you'll start our Doge off; especially as he has already put two bottles into his mouthpiece—that prince of ours!"

"Come, let's go on, old Quack," said the flageolet.

They all three began to play; but all the time they took to execute four country dances, the Venetian kept sniffing after me, he divined the excessive curiosity which I felt about him. His expression lost the cold, sad look; some hope—I know not what—enlivened all his features and ran like a blue flame through his wrinkles; he smiled and wiped his bold, terrible brow; in fact he grew cheerful, like a man getting on to his hobby.

"How old are you?" I asked.

"Eighty-two!"

"How long have you been blind?"

"Nearly fifty years," he replied, with an accent which showed that his regrets did not arise only from his loss of sight, but from some great power of which he must have been despoiled.

"Why is it they call you the Doge?" I asked.

"Oh, it's their joke," he said. "I am a patrician of Venice, and might have been Doge like the rest."

"What is your name then?"

"Here, le père Canet," he said. "My name could never be written on the registers different from that; but in Italian it is Marco Facino Cane, principe di Varese."

"Why! you are descended from the famous adventurer Facino Cane, whose conquests passed to the Duke of Milan?"

"True," said he. "In those days the son of Cane took refuge in Venice to avoid being killed by the Visconti, and got himself inscribed in the Golden Book. But now there is no Cane, any more than there is a book." And he made a terrible gesture of extinct patriotism and disgust for human affairs.

"But if you were a Senator of Venice, you must have been rich; how did you come to lose your fortune?"

At this question he raised his head toward me with a truly tragic movement as if to examine me, and answered, "By misfortune!"

He no longer thought of drinking, and refused by a sign the glass of wine which the old flageolet was just at that moment holding out to him, then his head sank. These details were not of a kind to extinguish my curiosity. While these three machines were playing a country dance, I watched the old Venetian noble with the feelings which devour a man of twenty. I saw Venice and the Adriatic; I saw her in ruins in the ruins of his face. I walked in that city that is so dear to its inhabitants. I went from the Rialto to the Grand Canal, from the Quay of the Slaves to the Lido; I came back to the unique, sublime Cathedral; I examined the casements of the Casa d'Oro, each with its different ornament; I gazed at the ancient palaces with all their wealth of marble; in a word, I saw all those marvels with which the savant sympathizes the more because he can color them to his liking, and does not rob his dreams of their poetry by the sight of the reality. I followed back the course of the life of this scion of the greatest of the *condottieri*, and sought to discover in him the traces of his misfortunes, and the causes of the physical and moral degradation which rendered yet more beautiful the sparks of greatness and nobleness that had just revived.

No doubt we shared the same thoughts, for I believe that blindness renders intellectual communications much more rapid, by preventing the attention from flitting away to exterior objects. The proof of our sympathy was not long in showing itself. Facino Cane stopped playing, rose from his seat, came to me, and said:

"Let us go outside!"

The effect it produced on me was like an electric douche. I gave him my arm and we went out.

When we were in the street, he said to me: "Will you take me to Venice, will you be my guide, will you have faith in me? You shall be richer than the ten richest houses in Amsterdam or London, richer than the Rothschilds, as rich as the Thousand-and-One Nights."

I thought the man was mad; but there was a power in his voice which I obeyed. I let him guide me; he led me toward the trenches of the Bastille, as if he had eyes. He sat down on a very lonely place, where the bridge connecting the Canal Saint Martin and the Seine has since been built. I placed myself on another stone in front of the old man; his white hair glistened like threads of silver in the moonlight. The silence, scarcely broken by the stormy sounds which reached us from the boulevards, the purity of the night—everything— combined to render the scene really fantastic.

"You speak of millions to a young man, and do you think he would hesitate to endure a thousand evils in order to obtain them! But you are not making fun of me?"

"May I die without confession," he said passionately, "if what I am going to tell you is not true. I was twenty—just as you are now—I was rich, handsome, and a noble. I began with the greatest of all madness—Love. I loved as men love no longer; I even hid in a chest at the risk of being stabbed to death in it, without having received anything more than the promise of a kiss. To die for *her* seemed to me life itself. In 1760 I became enamored of one of the Vendramini, a woman of eighteen, who was married to a Sagredo, one of the richest senators, a man of thirty, and mad about his wife. My mistress and I were as innocent as two cherubim when the husband surprised us as we were talking of love. I was unarmed; he missed me; I leaped upon him and strangled him with my two hands, wringing his neck like a chicken. I wanted to fly with Bianca, but she would not follow me. It was so like a woman! I went alone. I was condemned,

and my goods were confiscated to the benefit of my heirs; but I had rolled up and carried away with me five pictures by Titian, my diamonds, and all my gold. I went to Milan, where I was left in peace, as my affair did not concern the State."

"Just one remark before I go on," he said, after a pause. "Whether the fancies of a woman when she conceives, or while she is pregnant, influence her child or not, it is certain that my mother during her pregnancy had a passion for gold. I have a monomania for gold, the satisfaction of which is so necessary to my life that, in all situations I have found myself, I have never been without gold upon me. I have a constant mania for gold. When I was young I always wore jewelry, and always carried two or three hundred ducats about with me."

As he said these words he drew two ducats out of his pocket and showed them to me.

"I *feel* gold. Although I am blind, I stop before jewellers' shops. This passion ruined me. I became a gambler for the sake of gambling with *gold*. I was not a cheat, I was cheated; I ruined myself. When I had no fortune left I was seized by a mad longing to see Bianca; I returned to Venice in secret, found her again, and was happy for six months, hidden in her house and supported by her. I used to have delicious dreams of ending my life like this. She was courted by the *Provedittore*; he divined he had a rival. In Italy we have an instinct for them. The dastard played the spy upon us and caught us in bed. You may guess how fierce the fight was. I did not kill him, but I wounded him very severely. This event shattered our happiness; since then I have never found another Bianca. I have enjoyed great favors; I have lived at the Court of Louis XV among the most celebrated women; I have not found anywhere the noble qualities, the charms, the love, of my dear Venetian. The *Provedittore* had his servants with him; he called them; they surrounded the palace, and entered. I defended myself that I might die before Bianca's eyes—she helped me to kill the *Provedittore*. Before, this woman had refused to fly with me; but after six months of happiness she was ready to die on my body, and received several wounds. I was taken in a large mantle which they threw over me; they rolled me up in it, carried me away in a gondola, and put me into a cell in the dungeon. I was twenty-two. I held the stump of my sword so tight that they would have been obliged to cut off my wrist in order to take it away. By a strange chance, or rather inspired by some instinct of precaution, I hid this fragment of metal in a corner as a thing of possible use to me. My wounds were dressed, none of them was mortal; at twenty-two a man recovers from anything. I was to die by beheading. I feigned sickness to gain time. I believed I was in a cell bordering on the canal; my project was to escape by undermining the wall, and risk being drowned by swimming across the canal. My hopes were founded on the following calculations. Every time the jailer brought me food I read the notices fastened on the walls, such as—*The Palace; The Canal; The Subterranean Prisons.* Thus I succeeded in making out a plan which caused me some little apprehension, but was to be explained by the actual state of the ducal palace, which has never been finished. With that genius which the longing to recover one's liberty gives a man, I succeeded, by feeling the surface of a stone with the tips of my fingers, in deciphering an Arabic inscription, by which the author of the work warned his successors that he had dislodged two stones of the last course of masonry and dug eleven feet underground. To continue his work, it would be necessary to spread the fragments of stone and mortar caused by the work of excavation over the floor of the cell itself. Even if the jailers and the inquisitors had not felt satisfied, that, from the construction of the building, it only needed an external guard, the arrangement of the cells, in which was a descent of several steps, allowed the floor to be gradually raised without attracting the jailer's notice. This immense labor had been superfluous at least for the unknown person who had undertaken it; its incompletion was an evidence of his death. That his exertions might not be lost forever, it was necessary that a prisoner should know Arabic. Now I had studied the oriental languages at the Armenian monastery. A sentence written behind the stone told the unhappy man's fate; he had died a victim to his immense wealth, which was coveted and seized by Venice. It would require a month to arrive at any result. While I worked, and during those moments when I was prostrate with fatigue, I *heard* the sound of gold; I *saw* gold before me; I was dazzled by diamonds! Now, listen! One night my blunt sword touched wood. I sharpened the stump, and began to make a hole in the wood. In order to work, I used to crawl on my belly like a snake. I stripped myself and worked like a mole, with my hands in front, and using the rock itself as a fulcrum. Two nights before the day I was to appear before my judges, I determined to make one last effort during the night. I bored through the wood, and my sword touched nothing. You can imagine my amazement when I put my eye to the hole! I was in the panelled roof of a cellar, in which a dim light enabled me to see a heap of gold. In the cellar were the Doge and one of the Ten. I could hear their voices. I learned from their conversation that here was the secret treasure of the Republic, the gifts of the Doges and the reserves of booty called *The last hope of Venice,* a certain proportion of the spoils of all expeditions. I was saved! When the jailer came, I proposed to him to help me to escape and to fly with me, taking with us everything we could get. He had no cause to hesitate; he agreed. A ship was about to set sail for the Levant; every precaution was taken. I dictated a plan to my accomplice, and Bianca assisted in carrying it out. To avoid giving the alarm, Bianca was to join us at Smyrna. In one night we enlarged the hole and descended into the secret treasury of Venice. What a night it was! I saw four tons of pure gold. In the first chamber the silver was piled up in two even heaps, leaving a path between them by which to pass through the room; the coins formed banks, which covered the walls to the height of five feet. I thought the jailer would have gone mad; he sang, he leaped, he laughed, he gambolled about in the gold. I threatened to throttle him if he wasted the time or made a noise. In his delight he did not at first see a table where the diamonds were. I swooped down upon it so skillfully that I was able to fill my sailor's vest and the pockets of my pantaloons. My God! I did not take a third part. Under this table were ingots of gold. I persuaded my companion to fill as many sacks as we could carry with gold, pointing out to him that it was the only way to avoid being discovered in a foreign country. The pearls, jewelry, and diamonds, I told him, would lead to our being found out. In spite of our greed, we could not take more than two thousand *pounds* of gold, and this necessitated six journeys across the prison to the gondola. The sentinel at the water-gate had been bought with a bag containing ten *pounds* of gold; as for the two gondoliers, they believed they were serving the Republic. At daybreak we departed. When we were out at sea and I thought of that night, when I recalled the sensations which I had experienced, and seemed to see again that immense treasure, of which I calculated I must have left thirty millions in silver and twenty millions in gold, besides several millions in diamonds, pearls, and rubies; a feeling of madness rose within me: I had gold fever. We were landed at Smyrna; and immediately re-embarked for France. As we were going on board the French vessel, God did me the favor of relieving me of my accomplice. At the moment I did not think of all the bearings of this mishap; I was greatly rejoiced at it. We were so completely enervated that we remained in a state of torpor, without speaking, waiting until we were in a place of safety to play our parts at our ease. It is not to be wondered at that the fellow's head had been turned. You will see how God punished me. I did not consider myself safe until I had disposed of two-thirds of my diamonds in London and Amsterdam, and realized my gold dust in negotiable species. For five years I hid myself in Madrid; then in 1770 I came to Paris under a Spanish name, and lived in the most brilliant style.

"Bianca was dead.

"In the midst of my pleasures, when I was enjoying a fortune of six millions, I was struck with blindness. I concluded that this infirmity was the result of my sojourn in the prison and my labors in the dark, if indeed my faculty for seeing gold did not imply an abuse of the powers of vision and predestine me to lose my eyes. At this time I loved a woman to whom I had resolved to link my fate. I had told her the secret of my name; she belonged to a powerful family, and I had every hope from the favor shown me by Louis XV; she was a friend of Madame du Barry. I had put my trust in this woman; she advised me to consult a famous oculist in London; then, after staying in the town for some months, she deserted me in Hyde Park, robbing me of the whole of my fortune and leaving me without resources. I was obliged to conceal my name, for it would have exposed me to the vengeance of Venice. I could not invoke any one's help; I was afraid of Venice. The spies whom this woman had attached to my person had made capital out of my blindness. I spare you the history of adventures worthy of Gil Blas. Your Revolution came; I was obliged to enter at Les Quinze-Vingts; this creature got me admitted after having kept me for two years at Bicêtre as insane. I have never been able to kill her, I could not see to, and I was too poor to pay another hand. If, before I lost Benedetto Carpi, my jailer, I had consulted him on the situation of my cell, I should have been able to find the treasury again and return to Venice when the Republic was abolished by Napoleon. However, in spite of my blindness, let us go to Venice! I will find the door of the prison, I shall see the gold through the walls, I shall *feel* it where it lies buried beneath the waters; for the events which overturned the power of Venice are such that the secret of the treasury must

have died with Vendramino, the brother of Bianca, a Doge who, I hoped, would have made my peace with the Ten. I addressed notes to the First Consul, I proposed an agreement with the Emperor of Austria; every one treated me as a madman! Come, let us start for Venice, let us start beggars; we shall come back millionaires; we will buy back my property, and you shall be my heir, you shall be Prince of Varese."

I was thunderstruck at this confidence, at the sight of that white head; before the black waters of the trenches of the Bastille sleeping as still as the canals of Venice, it assumed in my imagination the proportions of a poem. I gave no answer. Facino Cane no doubt believed that I judged him, like all the rest, with disdainful pity; he made a gesture expressive of all the philosophy of despair. Perhaps his story had carried him back to those happy days at Venice; he seized his clarionet and played with the deepest pathos a Venetian song, a barcarolle in which he recovered all his first talent—the talent which was his when he was a patrician and in love. My eyes filled with tears.

If some belated passers-by chanced to be walking along le boulevard Bourdon, I dare say they stopped to listen to this last prayer of the exile, this last regret of a lost name, mingled with memories of Bianca. But gold soon got the mastery again, and its fatal passion quenched the glimmering of youth.

"That treasure!" he said; "I see it always, waking and in my dreams; I take my walks there, the diamonds sparkle, I am not so blind as you think; gold and diamonds lighten my night, the night of the last Facino Cane, for my title passes to the Memmi. Good God! the murderer's punishment has begun betimes! *Ave Maria!*" . . .

He recited some prayers which I could not hear.

"We will go to Venice," I exclaimed, as he was getting up.

"Then I have found my man," he cried, with a glow upon his face. I gave him my arm and led him back; at the door of Les Quinze-Vingts he pressed my hand; just then some of the people from the wedding were going home, shouting enough to blow one's head off.

"We will start to-morrow?" said the old man.

"As soon as we have got some money."

"But we can go on foot; I will ask alms—I am strong, and when a man sees gold before him he is young."

Facino Cane died during the winter after lingering for two months. The poor man had caught a chill.

GUSTAVE FLAUBERT

A Simple Heart

Madame Aubain's servant Félicité was the envy of the ladies of Pont-l'Évêque for half a century.

She received four pounds a year. For that she was cook and general servant, and did the sewing, washing, and ironing; she could bridle a horse, fatten poultry, and churn butter—and she remained faithful to her mistress, unamiable as the latter was.

Mme. Aubain had married a gay bachelor without money who died at the beginning of 1809, leaving her with two small children and a quantity of debts. She then sold all her property except the farms of Toucques and Geffosses, which brought in two hundred pounds a year at most, and left her house in Saint-Melaine for a less expensive one that had belonged to her family and was situated behind the market.

This house had a slate roof and stood between an alley and a lane that went down to the river. There was an unevenness in the levels of the rooms which made you stumble. A narrow hall divided the kitchen from the "parlour" where Mme. Aubain spent her day, sitting in a wicker easy chair by the window. Against the panels, which were painted white, was a row of eight mahogany chairs. On an old piano under the barometer a heap of wooden and cardboard boxes rose like a pyramid. A stuffed armchair stood on either side of the Louis-Quinze chimney-piece, which was in yellow marble with a clock in the middle of it modelled like a temple of Vesta. The whole room was a little musty, as the floor was lower than the garden.

The first floor began with "Madame's" room: very large, with a pale-flowered wall-paper and a portrait of "Monsieur" as a dandy of the period. It led to a smaller room, where there were two children's cots without mattresses. Next came the drawing-room, which was always shut up and full of furniture covered with sheets. Then there was a corridor leading to a study. The shelves of a large bookcase were respectably lined with books and papers, and its three wings surrounded a broad writing-table in darkwood. The two panels at the end of the room were covered with pen-drawings, water-colour landscapes, and engravings by Audran, all relics of better days and vanished splendour. Félicité's room on the top floor got its light from a dormer-window, which looked over the meadows.

She rose at daybreak to be in time for Mass, and worked till evening without stopping. Then, when dinner was over, the plates and dishes in order, and the door shut fast, she thrust the log under the ashes and went to sleep in front of the hearth with her rosary in her hand. Félicité was the stubbornest of all bargainers; and as for cleanness, the polish on her saucepans was the despair of other servants. Thrifty in all things, she ate slowly, gathering off the table in her fingers the crumbs of her loaf—a twelve-pound loaf expressly baked for her, which lasted for three weeks.

At all times of year she wore a print handkerchief fastened with a pin behind, a bonnet that covered her hair, grey stockings, a red skirt, and a bibbed apron—such as hospital nurses wear—over her jacket.

Her face was thin and her voice sharp. At twenty-five she looked like forty. From fifty onwards she seemed of no particular age; and with her silence, straight figure, and precise movements she was like a woman made of wood, and going by clockwork.

II

She had had her love-story like any other.

Her father, a mason, had been killed by falling off some scaffolding. Then her mother died, her sisters scattered, and a farmer took her in and employed her, while she was still quite little, to herd the cows at pasture. She shivered in rags and would lie flat on the ground to drink water from the ponds; she was beaten for nothing, and finally turned out for the theft of a shilling which she did not steal. She went to another farm, where she

Gustave Flaubert (1821-1880). Translation reprinted by permission of Alfred A. Knopf, Inc., Publishers. The translator, Arthur McDowall, follows the British style of spelling.

became dairy-maid; and as she was liked by her employers her companions were jealous of her.

One evening in August (she was then eighteen) they took her to the assembly at Colleville. She was dazed and stupefied in an instant by the noise of the fiddlers, the lights in the trees, the gay medley of dresses, the lace, the gold crosses, and the throng of people jigging all together. While she kept shyly apart a young man with a well-to-do air, who was leaning on the shaft of a cart and smoking his pipe, came up to ask her to dance. He treated her to cider, coffee, and cake, and bought her a silk handkerchief; and then, imagining she had guessed his meaning, offered to see her home. At the edge of a field of oats he pushed her roughly down. She was frightened and began to cry out; and he went off.

One evening later she was on the Beaumont road. A big hay-wagon was moving slowly along; she wanted to get in front of it, and as she brushed past the wheels she recognized Theodore. He greeted her quite calmly, saying she must excuse it all because it was "the fault of the drink." She could not think of any answer and wanted to run away.

He began at once to talk about the harvest and the worthies of the commune, for his father had left Colleville for the farm at Les Écots, so that now he and she were neighbours. "Ah!" she said. He added that they thought of settling him in life. Well, he was in no hurry; he was waiting for a wife to his fancy. She dropped her head; and then he asked her if she thought of marrying. She answered with a smile that it was mean to make fun of her.

"But I am not, I swear!"—and he passed his left hand round her waist. She walked in the support of his embrace; their steps grew slower. The wind was soft, the stars glittered, the huge wagon-load of hay swayed in front of them, and dust rose from the dragging steps of the four horses. Then, without a word of command, they turned to the right. He clasped her once more in his arms, and she disappeared into the shadow.

The week after Theodore secured some assignations with her.

They met at the end of farmyards, behind a wall, or under a solitary tree. She was not innocent as young ladies are—she had learned knowledge from the animals—but her reason and the instinct of her honour would not let her fall. Her resistance exasperated Theodore's passion; so much so that to satisfy it—or perhaps quite artlessly—he made her an offer of marriage. She was in doubt whether to trust him, but he swore great oaths of fidelity.

Soon he confessed to something troublesome; the year before his parents had bought him a substitute for the army, but any day he might be taken again, and the idea of serving was a terror to him. Félicité took this cowardice of his as a sign of affection, and it redoubled hers. She stole away at night to see him, and when she reached their meeting-place Theodore racked her with his anxieties and urgings.

At last he declared that he would go himself to the prefecture for information, and would tell her the result on the following Sunday, between eleven and midnight.

When the moment came she sped towards her lover. Instead of him she found one of his friends.

He told her that she would not see Theodore any more. To ensure himself against conscription he had married an old woman, Madame Lehoussais, of Toucques, who was very rich.

There was an uncontrollable burst of grief. She threw herself on the ground, screamed, called to the God of mercy, and moaned by herself in the fields till daylight came. Then she came back to the farm and announced that she was going to leave; and at the end of the month she received her wages, tied all her small belongings with a handkerchief, and went to Pont-l'Évêque.

In front of the inn there she made inquiries of a woman in a widow's cap, who, as it happened, was just looking for a cook. The girl did not know much, but her willingness seemed so great and her demands so small that Mme. Aubain ended by saying:

"Very well, then, I will take you."

A quarter of an hour afterwards Félicité was installed in her house.

She lived there at first in a tremble, as it were, at "the style of the house" and the memory of "Monsieur" floating over it all. Paul and Virginie, the first aged seven and the other hardly four, seemed to her beings of a precious substance; she carried them on her back like a horse; it was a sorrow to her that Mme. Aubain would not let her kiss them every minute. And yet she was happy there. Her grief had melted in the pleasantness of things all round.

Every Thursday regular visitors came in for a game of boston, and Félicité got the cards and foot-warmers ready beforehand. They arrived punctually at eight and left before the stroke of eleven.

On Monday mornings the dealer who lodged

in the covered passage spread out all his old iron on the ground. Then a hum of voices began to fill the town, mingled with the neighing of horses, bleating of lambs, grunting of pigs, and the sharp rattle of carts along the street. About noon, when the market was at its height, you might see a tall, hook-nosed old countryman with his cap pushed back making his appearance at the door. It was Robelin, the farmer of Geffosses. A little later came Liébard, the farmer from Toucques—short, red, and corpulent—in a grey jacket and gaiters shod with spurs.

Both had poultry or cheese to offer their landlord. Félicité was invariably a match for their cunning, and they went away filled with respect for her.

At vague intervals Mme. Aubain had a visit from the Marquis de Gremanville, one of her uncles, who had ruined himself by debauchery and now lived at Falaise on his last remaining morsel of land. He invariably came at the luncheon hour, with a dreadful poodle whose paws left all the furniture in a mess. In spite of efforts to show his breeding, which he carried to the point of raising his hat every time he mentioned "my late father," habit was too strong for him; he poured himself out glass after glass and fired off improper remarks. Félicité edged him politely out of the house —"You have had enough, Monsieur de Gremanville! Another time!"—and she shut the door on him.

She opened it with pleasure to M. Bourais, who had been a lawyer. His baldness, his white stock, frilled shirt, and roomy brown coat, his way of rounding the arm as he took snuff—his whole person, in fact, created that disturbance of mind which overtakes us at the sight of extraordinary men.

As he looked after the property of "Madame" he remained shut up with her for hours in "Monsieur's" study, though all the time he was afraid of compromising himself. He respected the magistracy immensely, and had some pretensions to Latin.

To combine instruction and amusement he gave the children a geography book made up of a series of prints. They represented scenes in different parts of the world: cannibals with feathers on their heads, a monkey carrying off a young lady, Bedouins in the desert, the harpooning of a whale, and so on. Paul explained these engravings to Félicité; and that, in fact, was the whole of her literary education. The children's education was undertaken by Guyot, a poor creature employed at the town hall,

who was famous for his beautiful hand and sharpened his penknife on his boots.

When the weather was bright the household set off early for a day at Geffosses Farm.

Its courtyard is on a slope, with the farmhouse in the middle, and the sea looks like a grey streak in the distance.

Félicité brought slices of cold meat out of her basket, and they breakfasted in a room adjoining the dairy. It was the only surviving fragment of a country house which was now no more. The wallpaper hung in tatters, and quivered in the draughts. Mme. Aubain sat with bowed head, overcome by her memories; the children became afraid to speak. "Why don't you play, then?" she would say, and off they went.

Paul climbed into the barn, caught birds, played at ducks and drakes over the pond, or hammered with his stick on the big casks which boomed like drums. Virginie fed the rabbits or dashed off to pick cornflowers, her quick legs showing their embroidered little drawers.

One autumn evening they went home by the fields. The moon was in its first quarter, lighting part of the sky; and mist floated like a scarf over the windings of the Toucques. Cattle, lying out in the middle of the grass, looked quietly at the four people as they passed. In the third meadow some of them got up and made a half-circle in front of the walkers. "There's nothing to be afraid of," said Félicité, as she stroked the nearest on the back with a kind of crooning song; he wheeled round and the others did the same. But when they crossed the next pasture there was a formidable bellow. It was a bull, hidden by the mist. Mme. Aubain was about to run. "No! no! don't go so fast!" They mended their pace, however, and heard a loud breathing behind them which came nearer. His hoofs thudded on the meadow grass like hammers; why, he was galloping now! Félicité turned round, and tore up clods of earth with both hands and threw them in his eyes. He lowered his muzzle, waved his horns, and quivered with fury, bellowing terribly. Mme. Aubain, now at the end of the pasture with her two little ones, was looking wildly for a place to get over the high bank. Félicité was retreating, still with her face to the bull, keeping up a shower of clods which blinded him, and crying all the time, "Be quick! be quick!"

Mme. Aubain went down into the ditch, pushed Virginie first and then Paul, fell several times as she tried to climb the bank, and managed it at last by dint of courage.

The bull had driven Félicité to bay against a rail-fence; his slaver was streaming into her face; another second, and he would have gored her. She had just time to slip between two of the rails, and the big animal stopped short in amazement.

This adventure was talked of at Pont-l'Évêque for many a year. Félicité did not pride herself on it in the least, not having the barest suspicion that she had done anything heroic.

Virginie was the sole object of her thoughts, for the child developed a nervous complaint as a result of her fright, and M. Poupart, the doctor, advised sea-bathing at Trouville. It was not a frequented place then. Mme. Aubain collected information, consulted Bourais, and made preparations as though for a long journey.

Her luggage started a day in advance, in Liébard's cart. The next day he brought round two horses, one of which had a lady's saddle with a velvet back to it, while a cloak was rolled up to make a kind of seat on the crupper of the other. Mme. Aubain rode on that, behind the farmer. Félicité took charge of Virginie, and Paul mounted M. Lechaptois' donkey, lent on condition that great care was taken of it.

The road was so bad that its five miles took two hours. The horses sank in the mud up to their pasterns, and their haunches jerked abruptly in the effort to get out; or else they stumbled in the ruts, and at other moments had to jump. In some places Liébard's mare came suddenly to a halt. He waited patiently until she went on again, talking about the people who had properties along the road, and adding moral reflections to their history. So it was that as they were in the middle of Toucques, and passed under some windows bowered with nasturtiums, he shrugged his shoulders and said: "There's a Mme. Lehoussais lives there; instead of taking a young man she . . ." Félicité did not hear the rest; the horses were trotting and the donkey galloping. They all turned down a bypath; a gate swung open and two boys appeared; and the party dismounted in front of a manure-heap at the very threshold of the farmhouse door.

When Mme. Liébard saw her mistress she gave lavish signs of joy. She served her a luncheon with a sirloin of beef, tripe, black-pudding, a fricassee of chicken, sparkling cider, a fruit tart, and brandied plums; seasoning it all with compliments to Madame, who seemed in better health; Mademoiselle, who was "splendid" now; and Monsieur Paul, who had "filled out" wonderfully. Nor did she forget their deceased grandparents, whom the Liébards had known, as they had been in the service of the family for several generations. The farm, like them, had the stamp of antiquity. The beams on the ceiling were worm-eaten, the walls blackened with smoke, and the window-panes grey with dust. There was an oak dresser laden with every sort of useful article—jugs, plates, pewter bowls, wolf-traps, and sheep-shears; and a huge syringe made the children laugh. There was not a tree in the three courtyards without mushrooms growing at the bottom of it or a tuft of mistletoe on its boughs. Several of them had been thrown down by the wind. They had taken root again at the middle; and all were bending under their wealth of apples. The thatched roofs, like brown velvet and of varying thickness, withstood the heaviest squalls. The cart-shed, however, was falling into ruin. Mme. Aubain said she would see about it, and ordered the animals to be saddled again.

It was another half-hour before they reached Trouville. The little caravan dismounted to pass Écores—it was an overhanging cliff with boats below it—and three minutes later they were at the end of the quay and entered the courtyard of the Golden Lamb, kept by good Mme. David.

From the first days of their stay Virginie began to feel less weak, thanks to the change of air and the effect of the sea-baths. These, for want of a bathing-dress, she took in her chemise; and her nurse dressed her afterwards in a coastguard's cabin which was used by the bathers.

In the afternoons they took the donkey and went off beyond the Black Rocks, in the direction of Hennequeville. The path climbed at first through ground with dells in it like the green sward of a park, and then reached a plateau where grass fields and arable lay side by side. Hollies rose stiffly out of the briary tangle at the edge of the road; and here and there a great withered tree made zigzags in the blue air with its branches.

They nearly always rested in a meadow, with Deauville on their left, Havre on their right, and the open sea in front. It glittered in the sunshine, smooth as a mirror and so quiet that its murmur was scarcely to be heard; sparrows chirped in hiding and the immense sky arched over it all. Mme. Aubain sat doing her needlework; Virginie plaited rushes by her side; Félicité pulled up lavender, and Paul was bored and anxious to start home.

Other days they crossed the Toucques in a boat and looked for shells. When the tide went out sea-urchins, starfish, and jelly-fish were left exposed; and the children ran in pursuit of the foam-flakes which scudded in the wind. The sleepy waves broke on the sand and unrolled all along the beach; it stretched away out of sight, bounded on the land-side by the dunes which parted it from the Marsh, a wide meadow shaped like an arena. As they came home that way, Trouville, on the hill-slope in the background, grew bigger at every step, and its miscellaneous throng of houses seemed to break into a gay disorder.

On days when it was too hot they did not leave their room. From the dazzling brilliance outside light fell in streaks between the laths of the blinds. There were no sounds in the village; and on the pavement below not a soul. This silence round them deepened the quietness of things. In the distance, where men were caulking, there was a tap of hammers as they plugged the hulls, and a sluggish breeze wafted up the smell of tar.

The chief amusement was the return of the fishing-boats. They began to tack as soon as they had passed the buoys. The sails came down on two of the three masts; and they drew on with the foresail swelling like a balloon, glided through the splash of the waves, and when they had reached the middle of the harbour suddenly dropped anchor. Then the boats drew up against the quay. The sailors threw quivering fish over the side; a row of carts was waiting, and women in cotton-bonnets darted out to take the baskets and give their men a kiss.

One of them came up to Félicité one day, and she entered the lodgings a little later in a state of delight. She had found a sister again—and then Nastasie Barette, "wife of Leroux," appeared, holding an infant at her breast and another child with her right hand, while on her left was a little cabin boy with his hands on his hips and a cap over his ear.

After a quarter of an hour Mme. Aubain sent them off; but they were always to be found hanging about the kitchen, or encountered in the course of a walk. The husband never appeared.

Félicité was seized with affection for them. She bought them a blanket, some shirts, and a stove; it was clear that they were making a good thing out of her. Mme. Aubain was annoyed by this weakness of hers, and she did not like the liberties taken by the nephew, who said "thee" and "thou" to Paul. So as Virginie was coughing and the fine weather gone, she returned to Pont-l'Évêque.

There M. Bourais enlightened her on the choice of a boys' school. The one at Caen was reputed to be the best, and Paul was sent to it. He said his good-byes bravely, content enough at going to live in a house where he would have companions.

Mme. Aubain resigned herself to her son's absence as a thing that had to be. Virginie thought about it less and less. Félicité missed the noise he made. But she found an occupation to distract her; from Christmas onward she took the little girl to catechism every day.

III

After making a genuflexion at the door she walked up between the double row of chairs under the lofty nave, opened Mme. Aubain's pew, sat down, and began to look about her. The choir stalls were filled with the boys on the right and the girls on the left, and the curé stood by the lectern. On a painted window in the apse the Holy Ghost looked down upon the Virgin. Another window showed her on her knees before the child Jesus, and a group carved in wood behind the altar-shrine represented St. Michael overthrowing the dragon.

The priest began with a sketch of sacred history. The Garden, the Flood, the Tower of Babel, cities in flames, dying nations, and overturned idols passed like a dream before her eyes; and the dizzying vision left her with reverence for the Most High and fear of his wrath. Then she wept at the story of the Passion. Why had they crucified Him, when He loved the children, fed the multitudes, healed the blind, and had willed, in His meekness, to be born among the poor, on the dung-heap of a stable? The sowings, harvests, wine-presses, all the familiar things the Gospel speaks of, were a part of her life. They had been made holy by God's passing; and she loved the lambs more tenderly for her love of the Lamb, and the doves because of the Holy Ghost.

She found it hard to imagine Him in person, for He was not merely a bird, but a flame as well, and a breath at other times. It may be His light, she thought, which flits at night about the edge of the marshes, His breathing which drives on the clouds, His voice which gives harmony to the bells; and she would sit rapt in adoration, enjoying the cool walls and the quiet of the church.

Of doctrines she understood nothing—did not even try to understand. The curé discoursed, the children repeated their lesson, and finally she went

778

THE FRENCH SPIRIT

to sleep, waking up with a start when their wooden shoes clattered on the flagstones as they went away.

It was thus that Félicité, whose religious education had been neglected in her youth, learned the catechism by dint of hearing it; and from that time she copied all Virginie's observances, fasting as she did and confessing with her. On Corpus Christi Day they made a festal altar together.

The first communion loomed distractingly ahead. She fussed over the shoes, the rosary, the book and gloves; and how she trembled as she helped Virginie's mother to dress her!

All through the mass she was racked with anxiety. She could not see one side of the choir because of M. Bourais; but straight in front of her was the flock of maidens, with white crowns above their hanging veils, making the impression of a field of snow; and she knew her dear child at a distance by her dainty neck and thoughtful air. The bell tinkled. The heads bowed, and there was silence. As the organ pealed, singers and congregation took up the "Agnus Dei"; then the procession of the boys began, and after them the girls rose. Step by step, with their hands joined in prayer, they went towards the lighted altar, knelt on the first step, received the sacrament in turn, and came back in the same order to their places. When Virginie's turn came Félicité leaned forward to see her; and with the imaginativeness of deep and tender feeling it seemed to her that she actually was the child; Virginie's face became hers, she was dressed in her clothes, it was her heart beating in her breast. As the moment came to open her mouth she closed her eyes and nearly fainted.

She appeared early in the sacristy next morning for Monsieur the curé to give her the communion. She took it with devotion, but it did not give her the same exquisite delight.

Mme. Aubain wanted to make her daughter into an accomplished person; and as Guyot could not teach her music or English she decided to place her in the Ursuline Convent at Honfleur as a boarder. The child made no objection. Félicité sighed and thought that Madame lacked feeling. Then she reflected that her mistress might be right; matters of this kind were beyond her.

So one day an old spring-van drew up at the door, and out of it stepped a nun to fetch the young lady. Félicité hoisted the luggage on to the top, admonished the driver, and put six pots of preserves, a dozen pears, and a bunch of violets under the seat.

At the last moment Virginie broke into a fit of sobbing; she threw her arms round her mother, who kissed her on the forehead, saying over and over "Come, be brave! be brave!" The step was raised, and the carriage drove off.

Then Mme. Aubain's strength gave way; and in the evening all her friends—the Lormeau family, Mme. Lechaptois, the Rochefeuille ladies, M. de Houppeville, and Bourais—came in to console her.

To be without her daughter was very painful for her at first. But she heard from Virginie three times a week, wrote to her on the other days, walked in the garden, and so filled up the empty hours.

From sheer habit Félicité went into Virginie's room in the mornings and gazed at the walls. It was boredom to her not to have to comb the child's hair now, lace up her boots, tuck her into bed—and not to see her charming face perpetually and hold her hand when they went out together. In this idle condition she tried making lace. But her fingers were too heavy and broke the threads; she could not attend to anything, she had lost her sleep, and was, in her own words, "destroyed."

To "divert herself" she asked leave to have visits from her nephew Victor.

He arrived on Sundays after Mass, rosy-cheeked, bare-chested, with the scent of the country he had walked through still about him. She laid her table promptly and they had lunch, sitting opposite each other. She ate as little as possible herself to save expense, but stuffed him with food so generously that at last he went to sleep. At the first stroke of vespers she woke him up, brushed his trousers, fastened his tie, and went to church, leaning on his arm with maternal pride.

Victor was always instructed by his parents to get something out of her—a packet of moist sugar, it might be, a cake of soap, spirits, or even money at times. He brought his things for her to mend and she took over the task, only too glad to have a reason for making him come back.

In August his father took him off on a coasting voyage. It was holiday time, and she was consoled by the arrival of the children. Paul, however, was getting selfish, and Virginie was too old to be called "thou" any longer; this put a constraint and barrier between them.

Victor went to Morlaix, Dunkirk, and Brighton in succession and made Félicité a present on his return from each voyage. It was a box made of shells the first time, a coffee cup the next, and on the third occasion a large gingerbread man. Victor was growing handsome. He was well made, had a hint of a moustache, good honest eyes, and a small leather hat pushed backwards like a pilot's. He entertained her by telling stories embroidered with nautical terms.

On a Monday, July 14, 1819 (she never forgot the date), he told her that he had signed on for the big voyage and next night but one he would take the Honfleur boat and join his schooner, which was to weigh anchor from Havre before long. Perhaps he would be gone two years.

The prospect of this long absence threw Félicité into deep distress; one more good-bye she must have, and on the Wednesday evening, when Madame's dinner was finished, she put on her clogs and made short work of the twelve miles between Pont-l'Évêque and Honfleur.

When she arrived in front of the Calvary she took the turn to the right instead of the left, got lost in the timber-yards, and retraced her steps; some people to whom she spoke advised her to be quick. She went all round the harbour basin, full of ships, and knocked against hawsers; then the ground fell away, lights flashed across each other, and she thought her wits had left her, for she saw horses up in the sky.

Others were neighing by the quay-side, frightened at the sea. They were lifted by a tackle and deposited in a boat, where passengers jostled each other among cider casks, cheese baskets, and sacks of grain; fowls could be heard clucking, the captain swore; and a cabin-boy stood leaning over the bows, indifferent to it all. Félicité, who had not recognized him, called "Victor!" and he raised his head; all at once, as she was darting forwards, the gangway was drawn back.

The Honfleur packet, women singing as they hauled it, passed out of harbour. Its framework creaked and the heavy waves whipped its bows. The canvas had swung round, no one could be seen on board now; and on the moon-silvered sea the boat made a black speck which paled gradually, dipped, and vanished.

As Félicité passed by the Calvary she had a wish to commend to God what she cherished most, and she stood there praying a long time with her face bathed in tears and her eyes towards the clouds. The town was asleep, coastguards were walking to and fro; and water poured without cessation through the holes in the sluice, with the noise of a torrent. The clocks struck two.

The convent parlour would not be open before day. If Félicité were late Madame would most certainly be annoyed; and in spite of her desire to kiss the other child she turned home. The maids at the inn were waking up as she came in to Pont-l'Évêque.

So the poor slip of a boy was going to toss for months and months at sea! She had not been frightened by his previous voyages. From England or Brittany you came back safe enough; but America, the colonies, the islands—these were lost in a dim region at the other end of the world.

Félicité's thoughts from that moment ran entirely on her nephew. On sunny days she was harassed by the idea of thirst; when there was a storm she was afraid of the lightning on his account. As she listened to the wind growling in the chimney or carrying off the slates she pictured him lashed by that same tempest, at the top of a shattered mast, with his body thrown backwards under a sheet of foam; or else (with a reminiscence of the illustrated geography) he was being eaten by savages, captured in a wood by monkeys, or dying on a desert shore. And never did she mention her anxieties.

Mme. Aubain had anxieties of her own, about her daughter. The good sisters found her an affectionate but delicate child. The slightest emotion unnerved her. She had to give up the piano.

Her mother stipulated for regular letters from the convent. She lost patience one morning when the postman did not come, and walked to and fro in the parlour from her armchair to the window. It was really amazing; not a word for four days!

To console Mme. Aubain by her own example Félicité remarked:

"As for me, Madame, it's six months since I heard . . ."

"From whom, pray?"

"Why . . . from my nephew," the servant answered gently.

"Oh! your nephew!" And Mme. Aubain resumed her walk with a shrug of the shoulders, as much as to say: "I was not thinking of him! And what is more, it's absurd! A scamp of a cabin-boy—what does he matter? . . . whereas my daughter . . . why, just think!"

Félicité, though she had been brought up on harshness, felt indignant with Madame—and then forgot. It seemed the simplest thing in the world to her to lose one's head over the little girl. For her the two children were equally important; a bond in her heart made them one, and their destinies must be the same.

She heard from the chemist that Victor's ship

had arrived at Havana. He had read this piece of news in a gazette.

Cigars—they made her imagine Havana as a place where no one does anything but smoke, and there was Victor moving among the negroes in a cloud of tobacco. Could you, she wondered, "in case you needed," return by land? What was the distance from Pont-l'Évêque? She questioned M. Bourais to find out.

He reached for his atlas and began explaining the longitudes; Félicité's consternation provoked a fine pedantic smile. Finally he marked with his pencil a black, imperceptible point in the indentations of an oval spot, and said as he did so, "Here it is." She bent over the map; the maze of coloured lines wearied her eyes without conveying anything; and on an invitation from Bourais to tell him her difficulty she begged him to show her the house where Victor was living. Bourais threw up his arms, sneezed, and laughed immensely: a simplicity like hers was a positive joy. And Félicité did not understand the reason; how could she when she expected, very likely, to see the actual image of her nephew—so stunted was her mind!

A fortnight afterwards Liébard came into the kitchen at market-time as usual and handed her a letter from her brother-in-law. As neither of them could read she took it to her mistress.

Mme. Aubain, who was counting the stitches in her knitting, put the work down by her side, broke the seal of the letter, started, and said in a low voice, with a look of meaning:

"It is bad news . . . that they have to tell you. Your nephew . . ."

He was dead. The letter said no more.

Félicité fell on to a chair, leaning her head against the wainscot; and she closed her eyelids, which suddenly flushed pink. Then with bent forehead, hands hanging, and fixed eyes, she said at intervals:

"Poor little lad! poor little lad!"

Liébard watched her and heaved sighs. Mme. Aubain trembled a little.

She suggested that Félicité should go to see her sister at Trouville. Félicité answered by a gesture that she had no need.

There was a silence. The worthy Liébard thought it was time for them to withdraw.

Then Félicité said:

"They don't care, not they!"

Her head dropped again; and she took up mechanically, from time to time, the long needles on her work-table.

Women passed in the yard with a barrow of dripping linen.

As she saw them through the window-panes she remembered her washing; she had put it to soak the day before, to-day she must wring it out; and she left the room.

Her plank and tub were at the edge of the Touques. She threw a pile of linen on the bank, rolled up her sleeves, and taking her wooden beater dealt lusty blows whose sound carried to the neighbouring gardens. The meadows were empty, the river stirred in the wind; and down below long grasses wavered, like the hair of corpses floating in the water. She kept her grief down and was very brave until the evening; but once in her room she surrendered to it utterly, lying stretched on the mattress with her face in the pillow and her hands clenched against her temples.

Much later she heard, from the captain himself, the circumstances of Victor's end. They had bled him too much at the hospital for yellow fever. Four doctors held him at once. He had died instantly, and the chief had said:

"Bah! there goes another!"

His parents had always been brutal to him. She preferred not to see them again; and they made no advances, either because they forgot her or from the callousness of the wretchedly poor.

Virginie began to grow weaker.

Tightness in her chest, coughing, continual fever, and veinings on her cheek-bones betrayed some deep-seated complaint. M. Poupart had advised a stay in Provence. Mme. Aubain determined on it, and would have brought her daughter home at once but for the climate of Pont-l'Évêque.

She made an arrangement with a job-master, and he drove her to the convent every Tuesday. There is a terrace in the garden, with a view over the Seine. Virginie took walks there over the fallen vine-leaves, on her mother's arm. A shaft of sunlight through the clouds made her blink sometimes, as she gazed at the sails in the distance and the whole horizon from the castle of Tancarville to the lighthouses at Havre. Afterwards they rested in the arbour. Her mother had secured a little cask of excellent Malaga; and Virginie, laughing at the idea of getting tipsy, drank a thimble-full of it, no more.

Her strength came back visibly. The autumn glided gently away. Félicité reassured Mme. Aubain. But one evening, when she had been out on a commission in the neighbourhood, she found

M. Poupart's gig at the door. He was in the hall, and Mme. Aubain was tying her bonnet.

"Give me my foot-warmer, purse, gloves! Quicker, come!"

Virginie had inflammation of the lungs; perhaps it was hopeless.

"Not yet!" said the doctor, and they both got into the carriage under whirling flakes of snow. Night was coming on and it was very cold.

Félicité rushed into the church to light a taper. Then she ran after the gig, came up with it in an hour, and jumped lightly in behind. As she hung on by the fringes a thought came into her mind: "The courtyard has not been shut up; supposing burglars got in!" And she jumped down.

At dawn next day she presented herself at the doctor's. He had come in and started for the country again. Then she waited in the inn, thinking that a letter would come by some hand or other. Finally, when it was twilight, she took the Lisieux coach.

The convent was at the end of a steep lane. When she was about half-way up it she heard strange sounds—a death-bell tolling. "It is for someone else," thought Félicité, and she pulled the knocker violently.

After some minutes there was a sound of trailing slippers, the door opened ajar, and a nun appeared.

The good sister, with an air of compunction, said that "she had just passed away." On the instant the bell of St. Leonard's tolled twice as fast.

Félicité went up to the second floor.

From the doorway she saw Virginie stretched on her back, with her hands joined, her mouth open, and head thrown back under a black crucifix that leaned towards her, between curtains that hung stiffly, less pale than was her face. Mme. Aubain, at the foot of the bed which she clasped with her arms, was choking with sobs of agony. The mother superior stood on the right. Three candlesticks on the chest of drawers made spots of red, and the mist came whitely through the windows. Nuns came and took Mme. Aubain away.

For two nights Félicité never left the dead child. She repeated the same prayers, sprinkled holy water over the sheets, came and sat down again, and watched her. At the end of the first vigil she noticed that the face had grown yellow, the lips turned blue, the nose was sharper, and the eyes sunk in. She kissed them several times, and would not have been immensely surprised if Virginie had opened them again; to minds like hers the supernatural is quite simple. She made the girl's toilette, wrapped her in her shroud, lifted her down into her bier, put a garland on her head, and spread out her hair. It was fair, and extraordinarily long for her age. Félicité cut off a big lock and slipped half of it into her bosom, determined that she should never part with it.

The body was brought back to Pont-l'Évêque, as Mme. Aubain intended; she followed the hearse in a closed carriage.

It took another three-quarters of an hour after the mass to reach the cemetery. Paul walked in front, sobbing. M. Bourais was behind, and then came the chief residents, the women shrouded in black mantles, and Félicité. She thought of her nephew; and because she had not been able to pay these honours to him her grief was doubled, as though the one were being buried with the other.

Mme. Aubain's despair was boundless. It was against God that she first rebelled, thinking it unjust of Him to have taken her daughter from her—she had never done evil and her conscience was so clear! Ah, no!—she ought to have taken Virginie off to the south. Other doctors would have saved her. She accused herself now, wanted to join her child, and broke into cries of distress in the middle of her dreams. One dream haunted her above all. Her husband, dressed as a sailor, was returning from a long voyage, and shedding tears he told her that he had been ordered to take Virginie away. Then they consulted how to hide her somewhere.

She came in once from the garden quite upset. A moment ago—and she pointed out the place—the father and daughter had appeared to her, standing side by side, and they did nothing, but they looked at her.

For several months after this she stayed inertly in her room. Félicité lectured her gently; she must live for her son's sake, and for the other, in remembrance of "her."

"Her?" answered Mme. Aubain, as though she were just waking up. "Ah, yes! . . . yes! . . . You do not forget her!" This was an allusion to the cemetery, where she was strictly forbidden to go.

Félicité went there every day.

Precisely at four she skirted the houses, climbed the hill, opened the gate, and came to Virginie's grave. It was a little column of pink marble with a stone underneath and a garden plot enclosed by chains. The beds were hidden under a coverlet of flowers. She watered their leaves, freshened the gravel, and knelt down to break up the earth better. When Mme. Aubain was able to come there she felt a relief and a sort of consolation.

Then years slipped away, one like another, and their only episodes were the great festivals as they recurred—Easter, the Assumption, All Saints' Day. Household occurrences marked dates that were referred to afterwards. In 1825, for instance, two glaziers whitewashed the hall; in 1827 a piece of the roof fell into the courtyard and nearly killed a man. In the summer of 1828 it was Madame's turn to offer the consecrated bread; Bourais, about this time, mysteriously absented himself; and one by one the old acquaintances passed away: Guyot, Liébard, Mme. Lechaptois, Robelin, and Uncle Gremanville, who had been paralysed for a long time.

One night the driver of the mail-coach announced the Revolution of July in Pont-l'Évêque. A new sub-prefect was appointed a few days later—Baron de Larsonnière, who had been consul in America, and brought with him, besides his wife, a sister-in-law and three young ladies, already growing up. They were to be seen about on their lawn, in loose blouses, and they had a negro and a parrot. They paid a call on Mme. Aubain which she did not fail to return. The moment they were seen in the distance Félicité ran to let her mistress know. But only one thing could really move her feelings—the letters from her son.

He was swallowed up in a tavern life and could follow no career. She paid his debts, he made new ones; and the sighs that Mme. Aubain uttered as she sat knitting by the window reached Félicité at her spinning-wheel in the kitchen.

They took walks together along the espaliered wall, always talking of Virginie and wondering if such and such a thing would have pleased her and what, on some occasion, she would have been likely to say.

All her small belongings filled a cupboard in the two-bedded room. Mme. Aubain inspected them as seldom as she could. One summer day she made up her mind to it—and some moths flew out of the wardrobe.

Virginie's dresses were in a row underneath a shelf, on which there were three dolls, some hoops, a set of toy pots and pans, and the basin that she used. They took out her petticoats as well, and the stockings and handkerchiefs, and laid them out on the two beds before folding them up again. The sunshine lit up these poor things, bringing out their stains and the creases made by the body's movements. The air was warm and blue, a black-bird warbled, life seemed bathed in a deep sweet-ness. They found a little plush hat with thick, chestnut-coloured pile; but it was eaten all over by moth. Félicité begged it for her own. Their eyes met fixedly and filled with tears; at last the mistress opened her arms, the servant threw herself into them, and they embraced each other, satisfying their grief in a kiss that made them equal.

It was the first time in their lives, Mme. Aubain's nature not being expansive. Félicité was as grateful as though she had received a favour, and cherished her mistress from that moment with the devotion of an animal and a religious worship.

The kindness of her heart unfolded.

When she heard the drums of a marching regiment in the street she posted herself at the door with a pitcher of cider and asked the soldiers to drink. She nursed cholera patients and protected the Polish refugees; one of these even declared that he wished to marry her. They quarrelled, however; for when she came back from the Angelus one morning she found that he had got into her kitchen and made himself a vinegar salad which he was quietly eating.

After the Poles came Father Colmiche, an old man who was supposed to have committed atrocities in '93. He lived by the side of the river in the ruins of a pigsty. The little boys watched him through the cracks in the wall, and threw pebbles at him which fell on the pallet where he lay constantly shaken by a catarrh; his hair was very long, his eyes inflamed, and there was a tumour on his arm bigger than his head. She got him some linen and tried to clean up his miserable hole; her dream was to establish him in the bakehouse, without letting him annoy Madame. When the tumour burst she dressed it every day; sometimes she brought him cake, and would put him in the sunshine on a truss of straw. The poor old man, slobbering and trembling, thanked her in his worn-out voice, was terrified that he might lose her, and stretched out his hands when he saw her go away. He died; and she had a mass said for the repose of his soul.

That very day a great happiness befell her; just at dinner-time appeared Mme. de Larsonnière's negro, carrying the parrot in its cage, with perch, chain, and padlock. A note from the baroness informed Mme. Aubain that her husband had been raised to a prefecture and they were starting that evening; she begged her to accept the bird as a memento and mark of her regard.

For a long time he had absorbed Félicité's imagination, because he came from America; and that name reminded her of Victor, so much so that she made inquiries of the negro. She had once gone so far as to say "How Madame would enjoy having him!"

The negro repeated the remark to his mistress; and as she could not take the bird away with her she chose this way of getting rid of him.

IV

His name was Loulou. His body was green and the tips of his wings rose-pink; his forehead was blue and his throat golden.

But he had the tiresome habits of biting his perch, tearing out his feathers, sprinkling his dirt about, and spattering the water of his tub. He annoyed Mme. Aubain, and she gave him to Félicité for good.

She endeavoured to train him; soon he could repeat "Nice boy! Your servant, sir! Good morning, Marie!" He was placed by the side of the door, and astonished several people by not answering to the name Jacquot, for all parrots are called Jacquot. People compared him to a turkey and a log of wood, and stabbed Félicité to the heart each time. Strange obstinacy on Loulou's part!—directly you looked at him he refused to speak.

None the less he was eager for society; for on Sundays, while the Rochefeuille ladies, M. de Houppeville, and new familiars—Onfroy the apothecary, Monsieur Varin, and Captain Mathieu—were playing their game of cards, he beat the windows with his wings and threw himself about so frantically that they could not hear each other speak.

Bourais' face, undoubtedly, struck him as extremely droll. Directly he saw it he began to laugh—and laugh with all his might. His peals rang through the courtyard and were repeated by the echo; the neighbours came to their windows and laughed too; while M. Bourais, gliding along under the wall to escape the parrot's eye, and hiding his profile with his hat, got to the river and then entered by the garden gate. There was a lack of tenderness in the looks which he darted at the bird.

Loulou had been slapped by the butcher-boy for making so free as to plunge his head into his basket; and since then he was always trying to nip him through his shirt. Fabu threatened to wring his neck, although he was not cruel, for all his tattooed arms and large whiskers. Far from it; he really rather liked the parrot, and in a jovial humour even wanted to teach him to swear. Félicité, who was alarmed by such proceedings, put the bird in the kitchen. His little chain was taken off and he roamed about the house.

His way of going downstairs was to lean on each step with the curve of his beak, raise the right foot, and then the left; and Félicité was afraid that these gymnastics brought on fits of giddiness. He fell ill and could not talk or eat any longer. There was a growth under his tongue, such as fowls have sometimes. She cured him by tearing the pellicle off with her finger-nails. Mr. Paul was thoughtless enough one day to blow some cigar smoke into his nostrils, and another time when Mme. Lormeau was teasing him with the end of her umbrella he snapped at the ferrule. Finally he got lost.

Félicité had put him on the grass to refresh him, and gone away for a minute, and when she came back—no sign of the parrot! She began by looking for him in the shrubs, by the waterside, and over the roofs, without listening to her mistress's cries of "Take care, do! You are out of your wits!" Then she investigated all the gardens in Pont-l'Évêque, and stopped the passers-by. "You don't ever happen to have seen my parrot, by any chance, do you?" And she gave a description of the parrot to those who did not know him. Suddenly, behind the mills at the foot of the hill she thought she could make out something green that fluttered. But on the top of the hill there was nothing. A hawker assured her that he had come across the parrot just before, at Saint-Melaine, in Mère Simon's shop. She rushed there; they had no idea of what she meant. At last she came home exhausted, with her slippers in shreds and despair in her soul; and as she was sitting in the middle of the garden-seat at Madame's side, telling the whole story of her efforts, a light weight dropped on to her shoulder—it was Loulou! What on earth had he been doing? Taking a walk in the neighbourhood, perhaps!

She had some trouble in recovering from this, or rather never did recover. As the result of a chill she had an attack of quinsy, and soon afterwards an earache. Three years later she was deaf; and she spoke very loud, even in church. Though Félicité's sins might have been published in every corner of the diocese without dishonour to her or scandal to anybody, his Reverence the priest thought it right now to hear her confession in the sacristy only.

Imaginary noises in the head completed her upset.

Her mistress often said to her, "Heavens! how stupid you are!" "Yes, Madame," she replied, and looked about for something.

Her little circle of ideas grew still narrower; the peal of church-bells and the lowing of cattle ceased to exist for her. All living beings moved as silently as ghosts. One sound only reached her ears now—the parrot's voice.

Loulou, as though to amuse her, reproduced the click-clack of the turn-spit, the shrill call of a man selling fish, and the noise of the saw in the joiner's house opposite; when the bell rang he imitated Mme. Aubain's "Félicité! the door! the door!"

They carried on conversations, he endlessly reciting the three phrases in his repertory, to which she replied with words that were just as disconnected but uttered what was in her heart. Loulou was almost a son and a lover to her in her isolated state. He climbed up her fingers, nibbled at her lips, and clung to her kerchief; and when she bent her forehead and shook her head gently to and fro, as nurses do, the great wings of her bonnet and the bird's wings quivered together.

When the clouds massed and the thunder rumbled Loulou broke into cries, perhaps remembering the downpours in his native forests. The streaming rain made him absolutely mad; he fluttered wildly about, dashed up to the ceiling, upset everything, and went out through the window to dabble in the garden; but he was back quickly to perch on one of the fire-dogs and hopped about to dry himself, exhibiting his tail and his beak in turn.

One morning in the terrible winter of 1837 she had put him in front of the fireplace because of the cold. She found him dead, in the middle of his cage: head downwards, with his claws in the wires. He had died from congestion, no doubt. But Félicité thought he had been poisoned with parsley, and though there was no proof of any kind her suspicions inclined to Fabu.

She wept so piteously that her mistress said to her, "Well, then, have him stuffed!"

She asked advice from the chemist, who had always been kind to the parrot. He wrote to Havre, and a person called Fellacher undertook the business. But as parcels sometimes got lost in the coach she decided to take the parrot as far as Honfleur herself.

Along the sides of the road were leafless appletrees, one after the other. Ice covered the ditches. Dogs barked about the farms; and Félicité, with her hands under her cloak, her little black sabots and her basket, walked briskly in the middle of the road.

She crossed the forest, passed High Oak, and reached St. Gatien.

A cloud of dust rose behind her, and in it a mail-coach, carried away by the steep hill, rushed down at full gallop like a hurricane. Seeing this woman who would not get out of the way, the driver stood up in front and the postilion shouted too. He could not hold in his four horses, which increased their pace, and the two leaders were grazing her when he threw them to one side with a jerk of the reins. But he was wild with rage, and lifting his arm as he passed at full speed, gave her such a lash from waist to neck with his big whip that she fell on her back.

Her first act, when she recovered consciousness, was to open her basket. Loulou was happily none the worse. She felt a burn in her right cheek, and when she put her hands against it they were red; the blood was flowing.

She sat down on a heap of stones and bound up her face with her handkerchief. Then she ate a crust of bread which she had put in the basket as a precaution, and found a consolation for her wound in gazing at the bird.

When she reached the crest of Ecquemauville she saw the Honfleur lights sparkling in the night sky like a company of stars; beyond, the sea stretched dimly. Then a faintness overtook her and she stopped; her wretched childhood, the disillusion of her first love, her nephew's going away, and Virginie's death all came back to her at once like the waves of an oncoming tide, rose to her throat, and choked her.

Afterwards, at the boat, she made a point of speaking to the captain, begging him to take care of the parcel, though she did not tell him what was in it.

Fellacher kept the parrot a long time. He was always promising it for the following week. After six months he announced that a packing-case had started, and then nothing more was heard of it. It really seemed as though Loulou was never coming back. "Ah, they have stolen him!" she thought.

He arrived at last, and looked superb. There he was, erect upon a branch which screwed into a mahogany socket, with a foot in the air and his head on one side, biting a nut which the bird-stuffer—with a taste for impressiveness—had gilded.

Félicité shut him up in her room. It was a place to which few people were admitted, and held so many religious objects and miscellaneous things that it looked like a chapel and bazaar in one.

A big cupboard impeded you as you opened the door. Opposite the window commanding the garden a little round one looked into the court; there was a table by the folding-bed with a water-jug, two combs, and a cube of blue soap in a chipped plate. On the walls hung rosaries, medals, several benign Virgins, and a holy water vessel made out of cocoa-nut; on the chest of drawers, which was covered with a cloth like an altar, was the shell box that Victor had given her, and after that a watering-can, a toy-balloon, exercise-books, the illustrated geography, and a pair of young lady's boots; and, fastened by its ribbons to the nail of the looking-glass, hung the little plush hat! Félicité carried observances of this kind so far as to keep one of Monsieur's frock-coats. All the old rubbish which Mme. Aubain did not want any longer she laid hands on for her room. That was why there were artificial flowers along the edge of the chest of drawers and a portrait of the Comte d'Artois in the little window recess.

With the aid of a bracket Loulou was established over the chimney, which jutted into the room. Every morning when she woke up she saw him there in the dawning light, and recalled old days and the smallest details of insignificant acts in a deep quietness which knew no pain.

Holding, as she did, no communication with anyone, Félicité lived as insensibly as if she were walking in her sleep. The Corpus Christi processions roused her to life again. Then she went round begging mats and candlesticks from the neighbours to decorate the altar they put up in the street.

In church she was always gazing at the Holy Ghost in the window, and observed that there was something of the parrot in him. The likeness was still clearer, she thought, on a crude colour-print representing the baptism of Our Lord. With his purple wings and emerald body he was the very image of Loulou.

She bought him, and hung him up instead of the Comte d'Artois, so that she could see them both together in one glance. They were linked in her thoughts; and the parrot was consecrated by his association with the Holy Ghost, which became more vivid to her eye and more intelligible. The Father could not have chosen to express Himself through a dove, for such creatures cannot speak; it must have been one of Loulou's ancestors, surely. And though Félicité looked at the picture while she said her prayers she swerved a little from time to time towards the parrot.

She wanted to join the Ladies of the Virgin, but Mme. Aubain dissuaded her.

And then a great event loomed up before them—Paul's marriage.

He had been a solicitor's clerk to begin with, and then tried business, the Customs, the Inland Revenue, and made efforts, even, to get into the Rivers and Forests. By an inspiration from heaven he had suddenly, at thirty-six, discovered his real line—the Registrar's Office. And there he showed such marked capacity that an inspector had offered him his daughter's hand and promised him his influence.

So Paul, grown serious, brought the lady to see his mother.

She sniffed at the ways of Pont-l'Évêque, gave herself great airs, and wounded Félicité's feelings. Mme. Aubain was relieved at her departure.

The week after came news of M. Bourais' death in an inn in Lower Brittany. The rumour of suicide was confirmed, and doubts arose as to his honesty. Mme. Aubain studied his accounts, and soon found out the whole tale of his misdoings—embezzled arrears, secret sales of wood, forged receipts, etc. Besides that he had an illegitimate child, and "relations with a person at Dozulé."

These shameful facts distressed her greatly. In March 1853 she was seized with a pain in the chest; her tongue seemed to be covered with film, and leeches did not ease the difficult breathing. On the ninth evening of her illness she died, just at seventy-two.

She passed as being younger, owing to the bands of brown hair which framed her pale, pock-marked face. There were few friends to regret her, for she had a stiffness of manner which kept people at a distance.

But Félicité mourned for her as one seldom mourns for a master. It upset her ideas and seemed contrary to the order of things, impossible and monstrous, that Madame should die before her.

Ten days afterwards, which was the time it took to hurry there from Besançon, the heirs arrived. The daughter-in-law ransacked the drawers, chose some furniture, and sold the rest; and then they went back to their registering.

Madame's armchair, her small round table, her foot-warmer, and the eight chairs were gone! Yellow patches in the middle of the panels showed where the engravings had hung. They had carried off the two little beds and the mattresses, and all Virginie's belongings had disappeared from the cupboard. Félicité went from floor to floor dazed with sorrow.

The next day there was a notice on the door, and the apothecary shouted in her ear that the house was for sale.

She tottered, and was obliged to sit down. What distressed her most of all was to give up her room, so suitable as it was for poor Loulou. She enveloped him with a look of anguish when she was imploring the Holy Ghost, and formed the idolatrous habit of kneeling in front of the parrot to say her prayers. Sometimes the sun shone in at the attic window and caught his glass eye, and a great luminous ray shot out of it and put her in an ecstasy.

She had a pension of fifteen pounds a year which her mistress had left her. The garden gave her a supply of vegetables. As for clothes, she had enough to last her to the end of her days, and she economized in candles by going to bed at dusk.

She hardly ever went out, as she did not like passing the dealer's shop, where some of the old furniture was exposed for sale. Since her fit of giddiness she dragged one leg; and as her strength was failing Mère Simon, whose grocery business had collapsed, came every morning to split the wood and pump water for her.

Her eyes grew feeble. The shutters ceased to be thrown open. Years and years passed, and the house was neither let nor sold.

Félicité never asked for repairs because she was afraid of being sent away. The boards on the roof rotted; her bolster was wet for a whole winter. After Easter she spat blood.

Then Mère Simon called in a doctor. Félicité wanted to know what was the matter with her. But she was too deaf to hear, and the only word which reached her was "pneumonia." It was a word she knew, and she answered softly "Ah! like Madame," thinking it natural that she should follow her mistress.

The time for the festal shrines was coming near. The first one was always at the bottom of the hill, the second in front of the post-office, and the third towards the middle of the street. There was some rivalry in the matter of this one, and the women of the parish ended by choosing Mme. Aubain's courtyard.

The hard breathing and fever increased. Félicité was vexed at doing nothing for the altar. If only she could at least have put something there! Then she thought of the parrot. The neighbours objected that it would not be decent. But the priest gave her permission, which so intensely delighted her that she begged him to accept Loulou, her sole possession, when she died.

From Tuesday to Saturday, the eve of the festival, she coughed more often. By the evening her face had shrivelled, her lips stuck to her gums, and she had vomitings; and at twilight next morning, feeling herself very low, she sent for a priest.

Three kindly women were round her during the extreme unction. Then she announced that she must speak to Fabu. He arrived in his Sunday clothes, by no means at his ease in the funereal atmosphere.

"Forgive me," she said, with an effort to stretch out her arm; "I thought it was you who had killed him."

What did she mean by such stories? She suspected him of murder—a man like him! He waxed indignant, and was on the point of making a row. "There," said the women, "she is no longer in her senses, you can see it well enough!"

Félicité spoke to shadows of her own from time to time. The women went away, and Mère Simon had breakfast. A little later she took Loulou and brought him close to Félicité with the words:

"Come, now, say good-bye to him!"

Loulou was not a corpse, but the worms devoured him; one of his wings was broken, and the tow was coming out of his stomach. But she was blind now; she kissed him on the forehead and kept him close against her cheek. Mère Simon took him back from her to put him on the altar.

V

Summer scents came up from the meadows; flies buzzed; the sun made the river glitter and heated the slates. Mère Simon came back into the room and fell softly asleep.

She woke at the noise of bells; the people were coming out from vespers. Félicité's delirium subsided. She thought of the procession and saw it as if she had been there.

All the school children, the church-singers, and the firemen walked on the pavement, while in the middle of the road the verger armed with his hallebard and the beadle with a large cross advanced in front. Then came the schoolmaster, with an eye on the boys, and the sister, anxious about her little girls; three of the daintiest, with angelic curls, scattered rose-petals in the air; the deacon controlled the band with outstretched arms; and two censer-bearers turned back at every step towards the Holy Sacrament, which was borne by Monsieur the curé, wearing his beautiful chasuble, under a canopy of dark-red velvet held up by four churchwardens. A crowd of people pressed behind, between the white cloths covering the house walls, and they reached the bottom of the hill.

A cold sweat moistened Félicité's temples. Mère Simon sponged her with a piece of linen, saying to herself that one day she would have to go that way.

The hum of the crowd increased, was very loud for an instant, and then went further away.

A fusillade shook the window-panes. It was the postilions saluting the monstrance. Félicité rolled her eyes and said as audibly as she could: "Does he look well?" The parrot was weighing on her mind.

Her agony began. A death-rattle that grew more and more convulsed made her sides heave. Bubbles of froth came at the corners of her mouth and her whole body trembled.

Soon the booming of the ophicleides,[1] the high voices of the children, and the deep voices of the men were distinguishable. At intervals all was silent, and the tread of feet, deadened by the flowers they walked on, sounded like a flock pattering on grass.

The clergy appeared in the courtyard. Mère Simon clambered on to a chair to reach the attic window, and so looked down straight upon the shrine. Green garlands hung over the altar, which was decked with a flounce of English lace. In the middle was a small frame with relics in it; there were two orange-trees at the corners, and all along stood silver candlesticks and china vases, with sunflowers, lilies, peonies, foxgloves, and tufts of hortensia. This heap of blazing colour slanted from the level of the altar to the carpet which went on over the pavement; and some rare objects caught the eye. There was a silver-gilt sugar-basin with a crown of violets; pendants of Alençon stone glittered on the moss, and two Chinese screens displayed their landscapes. Loulou was hidden under roses, and showed nothing but his blue forehead, like a plaque of lapis lazuli.

The churchwardens, singers, and children took their places round the three sides of the court. The priest went slowly up the steps, and placed his great, radiant golden sun upon the lace. Everyone knelt down. There was a deep silence; and the censers glided to and fro on the full swing of their chains.

An azure vapour rose up into Félicité's room. Her nostrils met it; she inhaled it sensuously, mystically; and then closed her eyes. Her lips smiled. The beats of her heart lessened one by one, vaguer each time and softer, as a fountain sinks, an echo disappears; and when she sighed her last breath she thought she saw an opening in the heavens, and a gigantic parrot hovering above her head.

GUY DE MAUPASSANT

Christening

"Come doctor, a little more cognac." "With pleasure." The old navy doctor watched the golden liquid flow into his glass, held it up to the light, took a sip and kept it in his mouth a long while before swallowing it and said:

"What a delicious poison! I should say, what a captivating destroyer of humanity! You do not know it as I know it. You may have read that

remarkable book called *L'Assommoir*, but you have not seen a whole tribe of savages exterminated by this same poison. I have seen with my own eyes a strange and terrible drama which was the result of too much alcohol. It happened not very far from here, in a little village near Pont-l'Abbé in Brittany. I was on a vacation and was living in the little country house which my father

[1] powerful organ-reed instrument.

Guy de Maupassant (1850-1893).

had left me. You all know that wild country surrounded by the sea—that wicked sea, always lying in wait for some new victim! The poor fishermen go out day and night in their little boats, and the wicked sea upsets their boats and swallows them! Fearlessly they go out, yet feeling uneasy as to their safety, but half of the time they are intoxicated. 'When the bottle is full we feel safe, but when it is empty we feel lost;' they say. If you got into their huts you will never find the father and if you ask the woman what has become of her man, she will answer, pointing to the raging sea: 'He stayed there one night when he had too much drink, and my eldest son too.' She has still four strong boys; it will be their turn soon!

"Well, as I have said, I was living at my little country house with one servant, an old sailor and the Breton family who took care of the place during my absence, which consisted of two sisters and the husband of one of them, who was also my gardener.

"Toward Christmas of that year the gardener's wife gave birth to a boy, and he asked me to be godfather. I could not very well refuse, and on the strength of it he borrowed ten francs from me, for the 'church expenses,' he said.

"The christening was to take place on the second of January. For the past week the ground had been covered with snow and it was bitter cold. At nine o'clock of the morning designated, Kerandec and his sister-in-law arrived in front of my door with a nurse carrying the baby wrapped up in a blanket, and we started for the church. The cold was terrific, and I wondered how the poor little child could stand such cold. These Bretons must be made of iron, I thought, if they can stand going out in such weather at their birth!

"When we arrived at the church the door was closed. The priest had not come yet. The nurse sat on the steps and began to undress the child. I thought at first that she only wanted to arrange his clothes, but to my horror I saw that she was taking every stitch of clothing off his back! I was horrified at such imprudence and I went toward her, saying:

"'What in the world are you doing? Are you crazy? Do you want to kill him?'

"'Oh no, master,' she answered placidly, 'but he must present himself before God naked.' His father and aunt looked on calmly. It was the custom in Brittany, and if they had not done this, they said, something would happen to the child.

"I got furiously angry. I called the father all kinds of names; I threatened to leave them and tried to cover the child by force, but in vain. The nurse ran away from me with the poor little naked body, which was fast becoming blue with the biting cold. I had made up my mind to leave these brutes to their ignorance, when I saw the priest coming along, followed by the sexton and an altar boy. I ran toward him and told him in a few words what these brutes had done, but he was not a bit surprised; nor did he hurry.

"'What can I do, my dear sir? It is the custom; they all do it.'

"'But for goodness sake, hurry up,' I cried impatiently.

"'I cannot go any faster,' he answered, and at last he entered the vestry. We waited outside the church door, and I suffered terribly at hearing that poor little wretch crying with pain. At last the door opened and we went in, but the child had to remain naked during the whole ceremony. It seemed to me as if it would never come to an end. The priest crawled along like a turtle, muttered his Latin words slowly, as if he took pleasure in torturing the poor little baby. At last the torture came to an end, and the nurse wrapped the child in his blanket again. By that time the poor little thing was chilled through and was crying piteously.

"'Will you come in and sign your name to the register?' asked the priest.

"I turned to the gardener and urged him to go home immediately and warm the child up, so as to avoid pneumonia if there was still time. He promised to follow my advice and left with his sister-in-law and the nurse. I followed the priest into the vestry, and when I had signed the register he demanded five francs. As I had given ten francs to the father, I refused. The priest threatened to tear up the certificate and to annul the ceremony, and I, in my turn, threatened to prosecute him. We quarreled for a long time, but at last I paid the five francs.

"As soon as I got home I ran to Kerandec's house, but neither he nor his sister-in-law nor the nurse had come home. The mother was in bed shivering with cold, and she was hungry, not having eaten anything since the day before.

"'Where on earth did they go?' I asked. She did not seem the least bit surprised and answered calmly:

"'They went to have a drink in honor of the christening.' That also was the custom, and I thought of my ten francs which I had given the father and which would pay for the drinks, no doubt. I sent some beef tea to the mother and her a good fire made in her room. I was so angry at those brutes that I made up my mind to discharge them when they came back, but what worried me most was the poor little baby. What would become of him?

"At six o'clock they had not come back. I ordered my servant to wait for them and I went to bed.

"I slept soundly, as a sailor will sleep, until day-break and did not wake until my servant brought me some hot water. As soon as I opened my eyes I asked him about Kerandec. The old sailor hesitated then finally answered:

"'He came home past midnight as drunk as a fool; the Kermagan woman and the nurse too. I think they slept in a ditch, and the poor little baby died without their even noticing it.'

"'Dead!' I cried, jumping to my feet.

"'Yes sir, they brought it to the mother, and when she saw it she cried terribly, but they made her drink to forget her sorrow.'

"'What do you mean by "they made her drink"?'

"'This, sir. I only found out this morning. Kerandec had no more liquor and no more money to buy any, so he took the wood alcohol that you gave him for the lamp, and they drank that until they had finished the bottle, and now the Kerandec woman is very sick.'

"I dressed in haste, seized a cane with the firm intention of chastising those human brutes and ran to the gardener's house. The mother lay help-less, dying from the effects of the alcohol, with the discolored corpse of her baby lying near her, while Kerandec and the Kermagan woman lay snoring on the floor.

"I did everything in my power to save the woman, but she died at noon."

The old doctor, having concluded his narra-tive, took the bottle of cognac, poured out a glass for himself and, having held it up to the light, swallowed the golden liquid and smacked his lips.

ÉMILE ZOLA

Germinal

The day before, at a meeting held at Rasseneur's house, Etienne and a few of his comrades had chosen the delegates to go to the superintendent's house the following day. In the evening, when Maheude found out that her man was one of them, she grew desperate, and she asked him if he wanted them to be thrown out into the street. Maheu had agreed to go with no little reluctance. Despite the injustice of their wretchedness, when the time came to act they both fell back into the resignation of their race, trembling before the mor-row, and choosing rather to bend their backs in submission. Maheu usually deferred to his wife in the management of their daily affairs, for her judgment was sound. This time, however, he ended by getting angry, all the more so because secretly he shared her fears.

"Aw, cut it out, will you!" he said, going to bed and turning his back. "It would be a fine thing to go back on the comrades now! I'm doing my duty!"

She too went to bed. Neither of them spoke. Then, after a long silence, she replied:

"You're right. Go ahead. Just the same, old fel-low, we're done for."

The meeting was set for one o'clock at the Avantage, from where they would proceed to M. Hennebeau's. Twelve o'clock struck while they were at lunch. There were potatoes on the table; but since there was only a small piece of butter left, no one touched it. That evening they would have bread and butter.

"We're counting on you to do the talking, you know," Etienne suddenly said to Maheu.

Maheu was so overcome with emotion that he could say nothing. But Maheude exclaimed:

"No, no! That's carrying things too far! I'm willing to have him go, but I won't have him be the leader. Why do you choose him rather than someone else?"

Etienne turned his fiery eloquence on Maheude Maheu was the best worker in the pit, the mos

Zola, *Germinal*. Translated by Joseph C. Palamountain. Emile Zola was born in Paris in 1840 and died in 1902. Chief of the school of Naturalism, Zola produced a series of novels on contemporary French themes, of which *Germinal* (1885) is an outstanding example. The present selections are from Parts IV, VI, and VII. Zola's pamphlet, *J'Accuse*, written in behalf of Captain Dreyfus, played a signifi-cant part in the final outcome of the Dreyfus Affaire.

popular, the most respected, the one whose good sense was a byword. Coming from his mouth the miners' demands would carry more weight. At first, Etienne was to have done the talking; but he had not worked at Montsou long enough. A man who had lived in the place a long time would get a better hearing. In short, the comrades were entrusting their interests to the most deserving one. And he could not refuse—that would be cowardly.

Maheude made a gesture of despair.

"Go ahead, my man! Go get yourself killed for the others. What can I do about it, anyhow?"

"But I won't know how to talk," stammered Maheu. "I'll say something foolish."

Etienne, happy to have won him over, patted him on the shoulder.

"Say the things that you feel, and everything will be all right."

His mouth full, old Bonnemort, listened and shook his head. While the group at the table ate the potatoes in silence, and the children were on good behavior. After swallowing a mouthful, the old man muttered slowly:

"No matter what you say, it will be just as if you hadn't said anything. . . . I've seen this kind of thing, I've seen it before! Forty years ago they kicked us out of the superintendent's house, and they used sabers too! Maybe they'll let you in this time, but you might as well be talking to a wall. Good God! They've got money; a lot they care about us!"

There was another silence. Maheu and Etienne got up and left the gloomy family sitting before their empty plates. They took Pierron and Levaque with them, then all four went to Rasseneur's. The delegates from the four neighboring coal patches kept arriving in small groups. Once the twenty members of the delegation were together, they agreed on the demands which they would put up against the Company's; and they set out for Montsou. A sharp wind from the northeast swept the street. Just as they arrived the clock struck two.

First the servant told them to wait, and shut the door in their faces; then, returning, he led them into the drawing-room and drew aside the curtains. A soft light sifted through the lace. Left alone, the miners in their embarrassment did not dare to sit down. They fairly glistened, with their yellow hair and mustaches, dressed in their best clothes, and freshly shaven. They twisted their caps between their fingers; they cast sidewise glances at the furniture, which was a confusion of all the styles that the taste for antiques had brought into fashion: Henri II armchairs, Louis XV chairs, a seventeenth-century Italian cabinet, a fifteenth-century Spanish contador, an altar-front serving as a chimney-piece, and ancient chasuble trimmings appliquéd to the curtains. This old gold, these old silks in tawny tones, all this luxurious chapel furniture, had filled them with an uneasy respect. The long wool of the Oriental rugs seemed to bind their feet. The heat stifled them, the even heat of a furnace. Its enveloping power surprised them as they felt it glow on their wind-chilled cheeks. Five minutes passed by. Their embarrassment increased in the comfort of this rich room which was so pleasantly warm.

At last M. Hennebeau entered, buttoned up in a military fashion, wearing on his frock coat the correct little knot of his decoration. He was the first to speak.

"Ah! Here you are! You are rebelling, it seems . . ."

He interrupted himself only to add with stiff politeness:

"Sit down. I would like nothing better than to talk things over."

The miners looked around for places to sit. A few ventured to sit down on the chairs while the others, made uneasy by the embroidered silks, chose to remain standing.

There was a silence. M. Hennebeau, who had drawn his easy chair up to the fireplace, quickly looked them over and tried to recall their faces. He had just recognized Pierron, hidden in the last row, when his eyes rested on Etienne, seated in front of him.

"Come now," he began. "What have you to say to me?"

He expected to hear the young man do the talking, and he was so surprised to see Maheu come forward that he could not keep from adding:

"What! You, a good workman who has always shown himself to be so sensible, one of the old Montsou people whose family has been working in the mines ever since the first pickax was driven into the ground! Ah! This is bad! I am sorry that you are at the head of the malcontents!"

Maheu listened with his eyes cast down. Then he began, his voice at first hesitant and low.

"Sir, it's just because I am a quiet man, a man no one can say anything against, that my comrades have chosen me. That ought to prove to you that this is not just a revolt of loud mouths, of malicious men trying to create disorder. We only want justice. We are tired of starving, and it seems to us that it is about time to fix things so that at least we'll have bread to eat every day."

His voice grew stronger. He raised his eyes and went on, fixing them on the superintendent.

"You know very well that we can't accept your new system. They accuse us of bad timbering. It's true we don't give the necessary time to that part of the work. But if we did, our day's pay would be even more reduced; and since it doesn't give us enough to eat now, why, that would be the end of everything—yes, the swish of the broom that would sweep away all your men. Pay us more and we'll timber better; we'll spend the necessary time in timbering, instead of putting all our strength into digging coal—the only job that pays anything. There's no other arrangement possible. If work is done, it must be paid for. And what have you invented as a substitute? A thing we can't get into our heads, don't you see? You lower the price of each carload, then you claim to make up for this reduction by paying separately for the timbering. If that was true, we'd still be getting robbed just as much, because the timbering would still take us more time. But what makes us mad is that it isn't even true. The Company is offering no compensation at all. It simply puts two centimes for every carload in its pocket, that's all!"

"Yes, yes, that's the truth," muttered the other delegates when they saw M. Hennebeau make a violent gesture as if to interrupt.

But Maheu cut short the superintendent before he had a chance to speak. Now that he was started, Maheu's words came all by themselves. At times he listened to himself with surprise as though it were a stranger within him speaking. There were things stored up inside himself, things he never knew were there, things which came out in this overflowing of his heart. He spoke of the wretchedness that was their common lot, the grinding toil, the brutal life, the wives and little ones at home crying from hunger. He cited the recent disastrous wages, the absurdly meager fortnightly wages, eaten up by fines and idle days and brought home to families in tears. Had it been decided that the workers must be destroyed?

"Then, sir," he concluded, "we have come to tell you that if we've got to starve we'd rather die doing nothing. It would be that much less trouble. We have left the coal mines and we shall not go down again unless the Company accepts our conditions. The Company wants to lower the price on carloads and pay for the timbering separately. As for us, we want things to stay as they were, and in addition we want to be given five centimes more for each carload. Now it's up to you to see whether you are on the side of justice and work!"

Voices rose among the miners.

"That's it. . . . He said what we all think. . . . We only ask what is right."

Others silently nodded their approval. The luxurious room disappeared with its gold and embroideries, its mysterious jumble of antiques, and the men no longer even felt the rug crushed beneath their heavy boots.

"Well, let me give my answer," finally exclaimed M. Hennebeau, who was getting angry. "First of all, it is not true that the Company is gaining two centimes per carload. Let us look at the figures."

A confused discussion followed. In order to try to divide them, the superintendent called upon Pierron, who, stammering, evaded giving an answer. Levaque on the other hand was at the head of the more aggressive group, muddling things up, stating facts of which he was ignorant. The loud hum of their voices was stifled beneath the hangings in the hothouse atmosphere.

"If you all talk at the same time," M. Hennebeau went on, "we shall never come to an agreement."

Displaying no ill humor, he had regained the calmness, the blunt politeness, of a superintendent who has received instructions and who means to see that they are respected. From the very first words he never took his eyes off Etienne. He maneuvered to draw the young man out of his obstinate silence. Therefore, abandoning the discussion about the two centimes, he abruptly broadened the question.

"No, confess the truth! You are responding to vicious agitation. It is a plague which is infecting all workers and corrupting the best of them. Oh, no one need confess. I can see perfectly well that something has changed you—you who used to be so orderly. Isn't that true? You've been promised more butter than bread. You've been told that your turn has come to be the masters. . . . Finally, you are being regimented into that famous International, that army of brigands whose dream is the destruction of society. . . ."

Then Etienne interrupted him.

"You are mistaken, sir. Not one single Montsou coal-digger has joined yet. But if they are driven to it, all the coal pits will join. That depends on the Company."

From that moment the struggle went on between M. Hennebeau and Etienne, as if the other miners were no longer there.

"The Company is a Providence for its men: you are wrong to threaten it. This year it has spent 300,000 francs building mining patches, which don't even bring in two per cent, and I'm not saying anything about the pensions it pays or the coal or medicines it gives away. You who seem intelligent, you who have become in a few months one of our most skillful workmen, wouldn't you be doing better to spread these truths than to ruin yourself by associating with people of bad reputation? Yes, I mean Rasseneur, whom we had to get rid of in order to save our coal pits from socialistic corruption. You are constantly seen at his house, and he is certainly the one who has induced you to create that Provident Fund, which we should be perfectly willing to tolerate if it were merely a means of saving, but which we regard as a weapon turned against us, a reserve fund to pay the expenses of a war. And, in that connection, I must add that the Company means to exert control over that fund."

Etienne allowed him to go on, his eyes fixed on the superintendent, his lips quivering nervously. He smiled at the last sentence. He answered simply:

"Then that is a new demand, for until now, sir, you have neglected to demand that control. . . . Our wish, unfortunately, is that the Company pay less attention to us, and that instead of playing the part of Providence it show itself merely fair to us by giving us what is coming to us: our profits which it is appropriating. Is it honest whenever a depression occurs to let the workers die of hunger in order to preserve the stockholders' dividends? . . . Say what you will, sir, the new system is a disguised lowering of wages, and that's what makes us indignant, for if the Company has to economize, it's acting in bad faith when it economizes on the men alone."

"Ah! So that's it!" cried M. Hennebeau. "I was waiting for that, that accusation of starving the people and of living by the sweat of their brows. How can you talk such nonsense, you who ought to know the enormous risks that capital runs in industry—in mines for example? A completely equipped coal-pit today costs from 1,500,000 to 2,000,000 francs; and then think of the trouble you have before you can get a moderate return on the sum you've sunk into it! Almost half of the mining companies in France go bankrupt. . . . Besides it is stupid to accuse the successful companies of cruelty. . . . When their workers suffer, they suffer too. Do you think the Company hasn't as much to lose as you in the present depression? The Company isn't the master of the wages it pays. It obeys the laws of competition, under penalty of ruin. Blame the facts, not the Company! . . . But you don't want to listen, you don't want to understand!"

"Yes," said the young man, "we understand very well that there is no improvement possible for us so long as things go on as they do, and it's just because of that that one of these days the workers will finally see to it that things go differently."

This sentence, so mild in form, was uttered in a low voice tremulous with its threat and with such conviction that a long silence followed. A constraint, a breath of fear, passed through the quietness of the drawing-room. The other delegates, who did not completely understand, felt, however, that the comrade had just demanded their share in those comforts which surrounded them; and they began to cast sidewise glances at the warm hangings, the comfortable chairs, all this luxury, the least knick-knack of which could pay for their food for a month.

At last M. Hennebeau, who had been reflecting a moment, rose as a signal for them to leave. They stood up too. Etienne had nudged Maheu; and the latter, his speech once more thick and clumsy, resumed:

"Then, sir, is that your final answer? We'll tell the rest that you reject our demands."

"I, my good fellow?" exclaimed the superintendent, "why, I'm rejecting nothing! . . . I am a wage earner just like yourselves. I have no more power here than the smallest of your trappers. I am given orders and my only job is to see that they are properly carried out. I have told you what I thought I ought to tell you, but far be it from me to make any decisions. . . . You bring me your demands; I shall make them known to the Directors; then I shall transmit the answer to you."

He spoke with the formal air of a high official who avoids getting stirred up about matters, with the polite curtness of a simple instrument of authority. And the miners now looked at him with distrust, wondering what interest he might have in lying, what he was to get out of putting himself between them and the real bosses. A tricky fellow perhaps, a man who was paid like a worker, and who lived so well!

Etienne ventured to intervene again.

"You see, sir, how regrettable it is that we cannot plead our cause in person. We would explain many things, we would find reasons which necessarily escape you. . . . If we only knew where we must go to see the right person."

M. Hennebeau did not get angry. He even smiled.

"Ah! Since you have no confidence in me, the matter gets complicated. . . . You will have to go over there."

The delegates had followed his vague gesture, his hand stretched out toward one of the windows. Where was "over there"? Paris, probably. But they didn't know for sure. "Over there" seemed to fall back into a terrifying distance, into an inaccessible and holy country where the unknown god crouched on his throne in the far recesses of his tabernacle. Never would they see him. They merely felt him as a force which from afar weighed heavily on the ten thousand coal miners of Montsou. And when the superintendent spoke it was this force that was hidden behind him, delivering oracles.

Discouragement overwhelmed them. Etienne himself shrugged his shoulders as if to tell them that the best thing to do was to go away. At the same time M. Hennebeau gave Maheu a friendly pat on the arm and asked him for news from Jeanlin.

"It certainly is a hard lesson for you, and you are the ones who are defending bad timbering! . . . You will think things over, my friends, you will come to see that a strike would be a disaster for everyone. Within a week you will die of hunger. What will you do? . . . Anyhow, I count on your good behavior, and I am convinced that you will go down into the mines on Monday at the latest."

The miners trooped out of the drawing-room like a herd, their backs bowed, without making any reply to the superintendent's hope that they would submit. The superintendent, accompanying them, felt it necessary to sum up their conversation: the Company on the one hand with its new tariff, the workers on the other with their demand for an increase of five centimes per carload. In order to leave them no illusion he felt it proper to warn them that their conditions would certainly be rejected by the Directors.

"Think it over before you do anything rash," he repeated, disturbed at their silence.

In the entry way Pierron bowed very low while Levaque pretended to put on his cap. Maheu was groping for some parting word when Etienne again nudged him. And they all left enveloped in this threatening silence. The door closed with a loud bang.

When M. Hennebeau returned to the dining room he found his guests motionless and mute before their liqueurs. In a few words he told his story to Deneulin, whose face grew even gloomier. Then, while M. Hennebeau drank his cold coffee, the guests tried to talk of other things. But the Grégoires themselves returned to the subject of the strike. They were amazed that there were no laws to forbid workers to leave their work. Paul quieted Cécile's fears, and said that they were expecting the police.

Finally Madame Hennebeau called the servant.

"Hippolyte, before we go into the drawing room, open the windows and let in some fresh air."

•   •   •   •   •

All the entrances to the Voreux had just been closed. The sixty soldiers, with grounded arms, barred the door leading to the receiving room, the foremen's room, and the shed. The captain had lined up the soldiers in two rows against the brick wall, so that they could not be attacked from the rear.

At first the band of miners who had come down from the patch kept at a distance. There were some thirty of them at most, and they talked to one another in confused and violent words.

Maheude, the first to arrive, her hair disheveled beneath a handkerchief hastily tied over it and holding Estelle asleep in her arms, kept repeating in feverish tones:

"Don't let anyone in or out! We've got to shut them all in there!"

Maheu nodded approval, and just then old Mouque arrived from Réquillart. The miners tried to stop him from going through. But he argued; he said that after all his horses had to have their oats to eat and they didn't give a hang about the revolution. Besides, there was a dead horse down there, and they were waiting for him to get it out. Etienne let Mouque through and the soldiers allowed him to go to the shaft. A quarter of an hour later, the band of strikers, gradually swelling in numbers, began to look threatening. A wide door opened on the surface of the ground, and men came out of it, carting the dead beast fastened in a rope net. They left the pitiful mass of flesh in the puddles of melting snow. The shock was so great that no one kept the men from returning and barricading the door anew. They had all recognized the horse, with his head bent back and stiff against his flank. Whispers ran about:

"It's Trompette, isn't it? It's Trompette."

It was indeed Trompette. Never since he had first gone down into the mine had he become acclimatized. He remained melancholy, without taste for his work, as though tortured with longing for the light. Vainly Bateille, the veteran horse of the mine, would rub his ribs against him in his friendly way, and softly bite his neck to give him a little of the resignation learned in his ten years in the mines. These caresses increased Trompette's melancholy, his skin quivered under the confidences of the comrade who had grown old in the darkness. And both of them, every time they met and snorted together, seemed to be grieving; the old one that he could no longer remember, the young one that he could never forget. At the stable they were neighbors at the manger, and they lived with lowered heads, breathing in each other's nostrils, exchanging their continual dreams of daylight, visions of green grass, white roads, endless yellow light. Then when Trompette, soaked in sweat, lay in death agony on his litter, Bateille sniffed at him despairingly—sniffs that were almost like sobs. He felt that Trompette was growing cold; the mine was taking from him his last joy, this friend fallen from above, fresh with pleasant odors which reminded him of his youth in the open air. And he broke his tether, neighing with fright, when he sensed that his friend no longer stirred.

Mouque had indeed warned the head foreman a week before. But a lot they cared about a sick horse at a time like this! The gentlemen were not very fond of removing the horses. Now, however, they had to make up their minds to take him out. The evening before, the groom with two other men had spent an hour tying up Trompette. They harnessed Bateille to bring Trompette to the shaft. Slowly the old horse pulled, dragging his dead comrade through a gallery so narrow that he had to jog along at the risk of scraping his skin off; and weary, his head shook as he listened to the long rustling of that shapeless mass which the men were waiting to slaughter. At the foot of the shaft when he had been unharnessed, he followed with a gloomy eye the preparations for the ascent; the body pushed onto crossbars above the sump, the net being fastened beneath a cage. At last the loaders called for the carcass. He lifted his head to watch the body go up, at first slowly, then sud-

denly lost in the darkness, flown up forever to the top of that black hole. And he remained with his neck outstretched, his vague animal memory perhaps recalling the things of the earth. But it was all over. The comrade would never see anything any more. He himself would also be tied up in a pitiful bundle the day that he would go up there. His legs began to tremble. The fresh gusts of wind from the distant countryside choked him; and he felt as if intoxicated when he plodded back to the stable.

At the surface the coal miners stood gloomily before Trompette's carcass. A woman said in a low voice:

"It's different with a man; a man goes down into the mines if he wants to!"

A new crowd was arriving from the coal patch, and Levaque at the head, followed by his wife and Bouteloup, shouted:

"Kill them, those Borains! We don't want any scabs around here! Kill them! Kill them!"

They all rushed forward—Etienne simply had to stop them. He was already talking to the captain, a tall slender young man hardly twenty-eight years old, whose face looked desperate and resolute. Etienne began to explain matters to him. He tried to win him over and watched the effect of his words. What was the good of risking a useless massacre? Wasn't justice on the side of the miners? We're all brothers, we ought to come to an understanding! At the word "republic," the captain had made a nervous gesture. He preserved his military stiffness and said abruptly:

"Get away from here! Don't force me to do my duty."

Three times Etienne tried. Behind him his comrades were growling. It was bruited about that M. Hennebeau was at the pit, and they talked of letting him down by the neck to see if he would dig his coal himself. But it was a false rumor for only Négrel and Dansaert were there. Both showed themselves for a moment at a window in the receiving room: the head foreman stood in the background while the engineer bravely looked around at the crowd with his bright little eyes, smiling with the sneering contempt he had for men and things. The miners hooted and the heads at the window disappeared. In their place nothing could be seen but Souvarine's pale face. As luck would have it he was on duty. He hadn't left his engine for a single day since the beginning of the strike. He no longer talked to anyone. He was being gradually penetrated by a fixed idea which glittered like a steel nail in the depths of his pale eyes.

"Get out of here!" shouted the captain. "I wish to hear nothing. I have orders to guard the shaft. I shall guard it. . . . And don't rush us, or I shall know how to make you get back."

Despite his firm voice, a mounting anxiety made him blanch at the sight of the ever-swelling flood of miners. He was to be relieved at noon; but, fearing he would be unable to hold out until then, he had just sent a trapper from the pit to Montsou to ask for reinforcements.

He had been answered by shouts.

"Kill the scabs! Kill the Borains! . . . We mean to be the masters in our own place!"

Etienne drew back in despair. The end had come; there was nothing left to do but fight and die. And he stopped holding back his comrades. The mob moved up to the little troop. There were nearly four hundred miners, and the nearby patches were emptying as more people arrived on the run. They all shouted one cry. Maheu and Levaque raged at the soldiers:

"Get out of here! We've got nothing against you! But get out of here!"

"This is none of your business," said Maheude. "Let us attend to our own affairs."

And, behind her, Levaque's wife added, more violently:

"Do we have to eat you to get through? Get the hell out of here!"

Even Lydie's shrill voice was heard. Having jammed herself into the thick of it with Bébert, she said in a sharp voice:

"There's a pack of scurvy soldier-dogs for you!"

Catherine, a few paces away, was gazing and listening, stupefied by these new scenes of violence, into the midst of which bad luck was always pushing her. Wasn't she suffering more than enough already? What fault could she have committed that misfortune would never let her rest? Only yesterday she could not understand the strikers' wrath. She thought when one has one's share of blows, there's no use looking for more. And now her heart was swelling with a gnawing hatred. She remembered what Etienne used to tell her in the evening, and she tried to hear what he was saying to the soldiers now. He called them comrades; he reminded them that they belonged to the people too; that they ought to be on the side of the people against those who exploited the people's misery.

A long shudder ran through the crowd and an old woman scurried forward. It was Mother Brûlé, terrifyingly scrawny, her neck and arms outstretched, rushing up so wildly that wisps of gray hair got in her eyes and blinded her.

"Ah! by God, here I am!" she stammered, breathless. "That traitor of a Pierron shut me up in the cellar!"

And without waiting, she fell onto the armed troops, her mouth livid, belching abuse.

"You pack of scoundrels! You dirty scum! These guys that lick their masters' boots and are only brave against poor people!"

Then the others joined her, and there were volleys of insults. Some of them shouted: "Hurrah for the soldiers! Throw the officer down the shaft!" Soon there was but the single roar: "Down with the red breeches!" The soldiers, having listened with mute and motionless faces to all these calls for brotherhood, and to the friendly attempts to win them over, preserved their passive stiffness beneath this hail of abusive words. Behind them the captain had drawn his sword; and, as the crowd pressed toward them ever closer, threatening to crush them against the wall, he ordered the soldiers to cross bayonets. They obeyed. A double row of steel blades pointed at the strikers' chests.

"Ah! The swine!" howled Mother Brûlé, drawing back.

The miners moved forward again in an exalted contempt for death. Women dashed forward. Maheude and Levaque's wife shouted:

"Kill us! Go ahead and kill us! We want our rights!"

Levaque, at risk of cutting himself, seized a bunch of bayonets with both hands. He shook them and he dragged them toward him in an effort to snatch them away; and he twisted them in the tenfold strength of his wrath. Bouteloup, sorry he had followed Levaque, stood aside and quietly watched him.

"Go ahead, get into it," Maheu kept shouting, "get into it, if you're real men!"

Levaque opened his jacket. Pulling his shirt apart, he showed his naked chest with its hairy skin tattooed with coal. He moved on toward the bayonet points; he forced them to draw back, terrible in his insolent bravado. One of the points pricked him in the chest, and he became like a madman, trying to make it enter so deep that he might hear his ribs crack.

"Cowards! You don't dare! . . . There are ten thousand behind us. Yes, you can kill us—but there will be ten thousand more to kill."

The position of the soldiers was becoming critical, for they had received strict orders not to use their arms, except as a last resort. And how were they to keep these furious people from impaling themselves? Moreover, the space was growing smaller; they were being driven against the wall, and they could not retreat any farther. The troop, a handful of men, face to face with the rising sea of miners still held its own, however; and calmly executed the brief orders given by the captain. The latter, with eyes clear and lips nervously compressed, feared only one thing: that his men would lose their tempers under the taunts. Already a young sergeant, a tall thin fellow, his scant mustache beginning to bristle, moved his eyelids in a disquieting way. Near him an old soldier, his skin tanned by twenty campaigns, grew pale when he saw his bayonet twisted like a piece of straw.

Another, probably a recruit still smelling of the plow, flushed every time he heard himself called "scum" and "riffraff." And the violent outbursts did not cease—the raised fists, the hateful words, the shovelfuls of accusations and threats which buffeted their faces. It required all the force of the orders they had received to keep them thus, with silent faces, in the morose and haughty silence of military discipline.

A collision seemed inevitable when from behind the soldiers Richomme appeared, the white-haired foreman, overcome with emotion. He shouted:

"Good God! This is all too stupid! Such damn fool nonsense can't go on!"

And he threw himself between the bayonets and the miners.

"Comrades, listen to me! . . . You know that I am an old worker and that I have never stopped being one of you. Well, good God, I promise you that if they are not fair to you I'll tell the bosses myself how things stand. But this is too much! It doesn't get you anywhere to yell ugly names at these good fellows and to want to have a hole drilled through your bellies!"

They listened, they hesitated. Up above, unfortunately, little Négrel's sharp profile reappeared. He feared, no doubt, that they would accuse him of sending a foreman instead of risking his own life; and he tried to speak. But his voice was lost in a tumult so frightful that he was obliged to leave the window again with merely a shrug of the shoulders. From that moment on Richomme vainly pleaded with them in his own name. He repeated that the miners must settle their own affairs and leave the soldiers alone. Now they repelled him; they suspected him. But he was obstinate and remained among them.

"Good God! Let them break my head as well as yours, but I won't desert you as long as you are so foolish!"

Etienne, whom he implored to help him make them listen to reason, made a helpless gesture. It was too late. Their number had now risen to more than five hundred. And in addition to the enraged men who had come to drive the Borains away, idle onlookers and banterers were enjoying the battle. In the midst of one group a little distance away, Zacharie and Philomène looked on as if this were a show. They were so unperturbed that they had brought along their two children, Achille and Désirée. A new stream of people poured in from Réquillart, among them Mouquet and his wife. The former with a grin on his face, walked up to his friend Zacharie and slapped him on the shoulder; while his wife excitedly dashed into the first row of hotheads.

Every minute, however, the captain kept turning his eyes toward the Montsou road. The reinforcements he had asked for had not arrived; his sixty men could not hold back any longer. Suddenly he was struck with the idea of kindling the crowd's imagination, and he ordered his men to load their rifles. The soldiers executed the order, but the excitement mounted—and the swaggering and the jeering.

"Look! Those good-for-nothings are going off to target practice!" jeered the women, the Brûlé woman, Levaque's wife, and the rest.

Maheude, holding against her breast the little body of Estelle, who had awakened and was crying, came so near that the sergeant asked her what she was doing there with that poor kid.

"What's that to you?" she replied. "Fire at us if you dare!"

Contemptuously the miners shook their heads. None of them thought that anyone could fire on them.

"They've got blank cartridges." said Levaque.

"Are we Cossacks?" cried Maheu. "You don't fire on Frenchmen, by God!"

Others exclaimed that in the Crimean campaign people were not afraid of lead. And they all continued to press against the rifles. If the soldiers had fired at that moment the crowd would have been mowed down.

In the front row Mouquet's wife was choking with fury at the thought that soldiers wanted to drill holes in women's flesh. She spat out all her ugly words at them. She found no vulgarity base enough, when, suddenly, having nothing left but that mortal offense to flaunt in the soldiers' faces, she exhibited her backside. With both hands she lifted her skirts, bent her back, and displayed the enormous rotundity.

"Take that, it's for you! And even at that it's too clean for you, you bunch of filthy rats!"

She plunged, bent, and turned so that everyone might get his share of the insult, repeating at each thrust she made:

"And this for the officer! And this for the sergeant! And this for the soldiers!"

A storm of laughter arose. Bébert and Lydie were in convulsions. Etienne himself, even though he was expecting dismal things to happen, applauded this insulting nakedness. All of them, the banterers as well as the infuriated, hooted the soldiers, as if they had seen them splashed by filth. Catherine, with blood in her throat, stood alone on an old plank. She remained speechless, her body boiling with hate.

There was a sudden commotion. In order to calm the excitement of his men, the captain decided to take some prisoners. With one leap, Mouquet's wife escaped between her comrades' legs. Three miners, Levaque and two others, were seized from among the more violent ones, and were closely guarded at the far end of the foremen's room. From above, Négrel and Dansaert shouted to the captain to come in and take refuge with them. He refused, feeling that these buildings, with their doors without locks, could be carried in an assault, and that he would be put to the shame of being disarmed. His little troop was already growling with impatience: it was impossible to flee before these wretches in wooden shoes. The sixty, with their backs to the wall and rifles loaded, once more faced the mob.

At first there was a recoil and a deep silence. The strikers were astonished at this energetic stroke. Then someone shouted a demand for the prisoners, calling for their immediate release. Some cried out that their throats were being cut in there. Without any attempt at concerted action and carried away by the same impulse, by the same need for revenge, all ran to the nearby piles of bricks— those bricks made from this very soil and baked on the spot. The children carried them one by one; women filled their skirts with them. Soon, every-

one had ammunition at his feet, and the battle of brick-throwing began.

It was Mother Brûlé who set to work first. She broke the bricks on the sharp edge of her knee, and first with her right hand and then her left hand, she hurled the two pieces. Levaque's wife almost threw her shoulder out; she was so fat, so soft that she had to move very close to get her aim, in spite of the pleading of Bouteloup, who pulled her back, in the hope of dragging her away, now that her husband had been taken away. All the women were frantic, and Mouquet's wife, tired of making herself bleed by breaking the bricks on her too fat thighs, preferred to throw them whole. Even the youngsters entered the combat. Bébert showed Lydie how the bricks should be thrown underhand. It was a storm of huge hailstones; one could hear the dull thuds. Suddenly in the midst of this fury Catherine seized some bricks and hurled them with all the strength of her little arms. She could not have said why; she was choking, she was longing to kill everyone. Would it not be over soon, this cursed life? She had had enough of it, beaten and driven out by her man, wandering about like a lost dog in the mud of the roads, being unable to get anything to eat even from her father—himself starving. Things never seemed to get better; they had always got worse ever since she could remember. And she broke bricks and threw them forward, with the one idea of sweeping everything away. Her eyes were so blinded that she did not even see whose jaws she might be smashing.

Etienne, still standing in front of the soldiers, almost had his skull broken. His ear swelled; he turned around; he started when he saw that the brick had come from Catherine's feverish hands. At the risk of being killed, he remained where he was, gazing at her. Many others also forgot themselves, excited by the battle, and remained with their arms dangling. Mouquet appraised the throws as if this were a game of *bouchon*: oh! that was a good shot! And that other one, no luck! He was having a good time. He nudged Zacharie, who was quarreling with Philomène because he had boxed Achille's and Désirée's ears, refusing to put them up on his shoulders so that they could see. There were spectators, massed all along the road. And at the top of the slope, at the entrance to the coal patch, old Bonnemort appeared, dragging himself along on his stick, motionless now, standing against the rust-colored sky.

From the moment the first brick had been thrown Richomme, the foreman, had placed himself between the soldiers and the miners. He pleaded with the soldiers; he exhorted the miners, ignoring the danger, and so desperate that big tears streamed from his eyes. No one could hear his words in the midst of the uproar; but one could see his big gray mustaches trembling.

The hail of bricks grew thicker; the men followed the women's example.

Then Maheude noticed that Maheu was standing in the rear. His hands were empty, and he looked gloomy.

"Say, what's the matter with you?" she shouted. "Are you a coward? Are you going to let them take your comrades to prison? Ah! If I didn't have this child, I'd show you!"

Estelle, clinging to her neck and screaming, kept her from joining the Brûlé woman and the others. And, as her man did not seem to hear, she kicked some bricks against his legs.

"Good God! There, take that! Must I spit in your face before everyone to give you courage?"

Turning very red, he broke bricks and threw them. She lashed him on, she stunned him, she yelped cries of death behind him. At the same time she crushed her daughter against her breast, holding her convulsively. Maheu kept moving forward until he was face to face with the rifles.

The little troop recoiled beneath the shower of bricks. Fortunately the women, aiming too high, were riddling the wall. What should the soldiers do? The idea of going inside, of turning their backs, made the captain's pale face flush for an instant; but that was no longer even possible: they would be cut to pieces at the slightest movement. A brick had just broken the visor of his military cap. Drops of blood trickled from his forehead. Several of his men were hurt; and he felt that they were losing self-control in that unbridled instinct of self-defense when obedience to leaders ceases. The sergeant had let out a "By God!" for his left shoulder was half out of its socket, his flesh bruised in a dull impact like the blow of a washerwoman's paddle on her linens. Grazed twice, the recruit was incensed by a smashed thumb, and a bruise on his right knee: were they going to let themselves be provoked much longer? A rebounding stone hit the old veteran in the belly and his cheeks turned green. His rifle trembled as he held it before him. Three times the captain was on the point of ordering his men to fire. He was choked by anguish; an interminable struggle of a few seconds jumbled within him ideas, duties, all his beliefs as a man and a soldier. The rain of bricks

redoubled, and he opened his mouth. He was just about to shout: "Fire!" when the rifles went off by themselves, three shots at first, then five, then the roll of a volley. In the great silence that followed there came a lone shot.

Stupor reigned. They had fired. The gaping crowd stood motionless, not yet believing their eyes. But heart-rending cries pierced the air at the same time that the bugler sounded the signal to cease firing. There was a mad panic,—the rush of cattle filled with grapeshot, a wild flight through the mud.

At the first three shots Bébert and Lydie had fallen one on top of the other, the girl struck in the face, the boy wounded beneath the left shoulder. Knocked to the ground, she lay motionless. But he moved and seized her with both his arms, in the convulsions of a death agony. And Jeanlin, who had run all the way from Réquillart, still half asleep, groping his way through the smoke, arrived to see Bébert die, holding his little wife tightly in his arms.

The other five shots had brought down Mother Brûlé and Richomme, the foreman. Hit in the back just as he was pleading with his comrades, he had fallen to his knees; and, slipping onto one hip, there he lay on the ground in the throes of the death rattle, his face still wet with the tears he had wept. The old woman, her throat slit open, fell stiff and crackling like a bundle of dry faggots. She stammered one last oath in the gurgling of blood.

But then the volley of bullets swept the field and mowed down the groups of bystanders laughing at the battle from their vantage point a hundred paces away. A bullet entered Mouquet's mouth and knocked him down, shattered his head at the feet of Zacharie and Philomène, whose two youngsters were splashed with red drops. At the same moment Mouquet's wife received two bullets in the stomach. She had seen the soldiers shoulder arms, and, being game, she had instinctively thrown herself in front of Catherine, shouting to her to look out for herself. She uttered a great shriek and fell on her back, overturned by the shock. Etienne ran up, tried to lift her, and carry her away; but she motioned to him that it was all over. Then the death rattle rolled in her throat, but she kept smiling at both Catherine and Etienne, as if she were happy to see them together, now that she was going away.

Everything seemed to be over. The hurricane of bullets had been lost in the distance as far even as the house fronts in the mining patch when the last shot, isolated and delayed, was fired.

Maheu, struck in the heart, pivoted and fell face forward into a puddle of water, black with coal dust.

Stupefied, Maheude leaned over him.

"Come, old man, get up. It isn't anything, is it?"

Since both her arms were taken up with Estelle, she had to put the child under one arm, so that with the other she could turn her man's head over.

"Say something! Where does it hurt you?"

His eyes were empty, his mouth drooled with a bloody froth. She realized he was dead. Then she remained sitting in the mud, her daughter like a bundle under her arm, looking at her man with a besotted expression on her face.

The pit was free. With a nervous gesture the captain had taken off his cap which had been cut by a piece of brick, then had put it right on again. In the face of the disaster of his life he preserved his pallid stiffness, while his men, with mute faces, reloaded their rifles. The terrified faces of Négrel and Dansaert could be seen at the window of the receiving room. Souvarine was behind them, his forehead lined with a deep wrinkle, as if his fixed idea were imprinted there, menacing. On the other side of the horizon, on the edge of the plain, Bonnemort had not stirred. Bracing himself with one hand on his stick, with the other he cupped his eyes to get a better view of the murder of his own people down there. The wounded howled. The dead were growing cold in their twisted postures, muddy with the liquid mud of the thaw. Here and there inky patches of coal shone through the soiled tatters of snow. And, in the midst of those human corpses, so small, so pitiful in their scrawny misery, lay the carcass of Trompette, a monstrous, harrowing mass of dead flesh.

Etienne had not been killed. He was still waiting near Catherine who had fallen from weariness and anguish, when a vibrant voice made him start. It was Abbé Ranvier, on his way back from saying Mass. His two arms upraised in the fury of a prophet, he called down the wrath of God upon the assassins! He heralded the era of justice, the approaching extermination by fire from heaven of the middle class which now was putting the crowning touch on its crimes by massacring the toilers and the disinherited of the world.

It was four o'clock in the morning. The cool April night was growing warmer as day approached. Stars shimmered in the limpid sky while the light of dawn threw a reddish haze over the east. And the drowsy black countryside had scarcely shuddered with that vague rumble that precedes waking.

Etienne was striding down the road to Vandame. He had just spent six weeks at Montsou in a hospital bed. Still sallow and very thin, he nevertheless had felt strong enough to leave, and he left. The Company, still trembling for its pits and constantly firing men, had notified him that it could not keep him on. The Company offered him a compensation of one hundred francs with the paternal advice to give up work in the mines since it would be too hard for him from now on. But he had refused the hundred francs. . . . He got up early in the morning. There was only one thing more that he wanted to do before going to take the eight o'clock train at Marchiennes—say good-by to his comrades.

Etienne stopped for a moment on the road which was bathed in rosy light. It was good to breathe this pure air of early spring. The morning promised to be beautiful. The sun was slowly rising and the life of the earth was rising with it. He continued walking, striking the ground vigorously with his briar stick, gazing off in the distance at the plain rising out of the mists of night. He had seen no one since leaving the mine save Maheude who had come only once to the hospital, then had doubtless been unable to return. But he knew that the whole patch was now going down to work in the Jean-Bart mine and that Maheude had gone back to work there too.

Little by little people appeared on the deserted roads, silent charcoal-burners kept passing Etienne, their faces wan. It was said that the Company was taking unfair advantage of its triumph. After the strike had been on for two-and-a-half months the miners, beaten by hunger, had returned to the pits. They had been obliged to accept the tariff on timbering—that disguised lowering of wages, now all the more hateful because it was stained with the blood of their comrades. The Company was stealing an hour of work from them. They were forced to go back on their oath never to submit, and that imposed perjury was like bitter gall in their throats. Work was being resumed everywhere, at Mirou, at Madeleine, at Crèvecœur, at La Victoire. Everywhere in the morning haze, along the roads still drowned in shadow, the herd tramped on, rows of men walking with heads bowed down, like cattle led to the slaughterhouse. They shivered under their thin clothing. And when one saw these men, mute black shadows, returning to work in a body, without a laugh, without a sidewise glance, one felt that their teeth were gritting with anger, that their hearts were swelling with hatred, and that all this was simply a resignation to the needs of the belly.

Etienne took the road to the left, to Joiselle. In the distance, in the clear sunlight, he could see the tipples of several mines—Mirou on the right, Madeleine and Crèvecœur side by side. Work was roaring on every hand. He thought he heard the blows of the pickax at the bottom of the earth resounding now from one end of the plain to the other. One blow, and another blow, and yet more blows, under the fields, the roads, and the villages which were smiling at the daylight. The sound of the dark toil in the subterranean dungeon was so crushed by the enormous mass of rock that one had to know it was buried there to feel its great sorrowful sigh. And now he mused that violence perhaps did not hasten things. Severed cables, torn-up rails, broken lamps—what useless tasks! . . . Vaguely he divined that lawful methods might one day be more terrible. . . . Yes, Maheude with her good sense had said the right thing: that this would be the final blow: to organize quietly, to learn to know one another, to join unions when the law would permit; and then, one day when they would feel their united strength, when they would number millions of workers against a few thousand idlers, let them then take the power, let them then be the masters! Ah! What an awakening of truth and justice! The sated and crouching god would instantly be destroyed, that monstrous idol hidden in the deep recesses of his tabernacle, in that faraway unknown place where the poor toiling wretches who had never even seen him, fed him on their flesh.

Etienne, leaving the road to Vandame, now came onto the paved street. To the right he saw Montsou fading in the distance. Opposite were the ruins of Voreux, the cursed hole where three pumps worked relentlessly. Then, there were the other pits against the horizon, La Victoire, Saint-Thomas, Feutry-Cantel; while, toward the north, the tall chimneys of the blast furnaces and the batteries of coke kilns stood smoking in the transparent air of the morning. If he did not want to miss the eight o'clock train, he would have to hurry, for he still had six kilometers to go.

Beneath his feet the deep blows, the stubborn blows, of the pickaxes continued. The comrades were all there; at every stride he could hear them following him. Wasn't that Maheude far down under that bed of beets, dragging her twisted spine? Wasn't that her raucous breathing mingled with the rumble of the ventilator? He thought he recognized others, to the left, to the right, farther on, under the wheatfields, the hedges, and the young trees. Overhead the April sun shone in all its glory, warming the pregnant earth. Life was gushing forth from its fertile soil; buds burst into green leaves; the fields were quivering with the growing of the grass. Everywhere seeds swelled, reached upward, and broke through the plain, throbbing with a great need for warmth and light. Sap overflowed in whispering voices; the sound of seeds burst forth into a great kiss. Again, again, and ever more distinctly, as if they had drawn nearer the surface, the comrades were wielding their pickaxes. And the country was pregnant with the rumbling beneath the flaming rays of the sun in the young morning. Men were pushing through the ground, a black avenging army, springing up slowly in the furrows, growing for the harvests of the future century—and this germination would soon make the whole earth burst

ANATOLE FRANCE

The Procurator of Judæa

Ælius Lamia, born in Italy of illustrious parents, had not yet discarded the *toga prœtexta* when he set out for the schools of Athens to study philosophy. Subsequently he took up his residence at Rome, and in his house on the Esquiline, amid a circle of youthful wastrels, abandoned himself to licentious courses. But, being accused of engaging in criminal relations with Lepida, the wife of Suipicius Quirinus, a man of consular rank, and being found guilty, he was exiled by Tiberius Cæsar. At

Anatole France (Jacques Anatole Thibault, 1844-1924). Translated by Frederic Chapman and reprinted by permission of Dodd, Mead and Company. Translator uses British style of spelling.

that time he was just entering his twenty-fourth year. During the eighteen years that his exile lasted he traversed Syria, Palestine, Cappadocia, and Armenia, and made prolonged visits to Antioch, Cæsarea, and Jerusalem. When, after the death of Tiberius, Caius was raised to the purple, Lamia obtained permission to return to Rome. He even regained a portion of his possessions. Adversity had taught him wisdom.

He avoided all intercourse with the wives and daughters of Roman citizens, made no efforts toward obtaining office, held aloof from public honours, and lived a secluded life in his house on the Esquiline. Occupying himself with the task of recording all the remarkable things he had seen during his distant travels, he turned, as he said, the vicissitudes of his years of expiation into a diversion for his hours of rest. In the midst of these calm enjoyments, alternating with assiduous study of the works of Epicurus, he recognized with a mixture of surprise and vexation that age was stealing upon him. In his sixty-second year, being afflicted with an illness which proved in no slight degree troublesome, he decided to have recourse to the waters at Baiæ. The coast at that point, once frequented by the halcyon, was at this date the resort of the wealthy Roman, greedy of pleasure. For a week Lamia lived alone, without a friend in the brilliant crowd. Then one day, after dinner, an inclination to which he yielded urged him to ascend the inclines which, covered with vines that resembled bacchantes, looked out upon the waves.

Having reached the summit, he seated himself by the side of a path beneath a terebinth and let his glances wander over the lovely landscape. To his left, livid and bare, the Phlegræan plain stretched out towards the ruins of Cumæ. On his right, Cape Misenum plunged its abrupt spur beneath the Tyrrhenian sea. Beneath his feet luxurious Baiæ, following the graceful outline of the coast, displayed its gardens, its villas thronged with statues, its porticos, its marble terraces along the shores of the blue ocean where the dolphins sported. Before him, on the other side of the bay, on the Campanian coast, gilded by the already sinking sun, gleamed the temples which far away rose above the laurels of Posilippo, whilst on the extreme horizon Vesuvius looked forth smiling.

Lamia drew from a fold of his toga a scroll containing the *Treatise upon Nature*, extended himself upon the ground, and began to read. But the warning cries of a slave necessitated his rising to allow of the passage of a litter which was being carried along the narrow pathway through the vineyards. The litter, being uncurtained, permitted Lamia to see stretched upon the cushions as it was borne nearer to him the figure of an elderly man of immense bulk who, supporting his head on his hand, gazed out with a gloomy and disdainful expression. His nose, which was aquiline, and his chin, which was prominent, seemed desirous of meeting across his lips, and his jaws were powerful.

From the first moment Lamia was convinced that the face was familiar to him. He hesitated a moment before the name came to him. Then suddenly hastening towards the litter with a display of surprise and delight—

"Pontius Pilate!" he cried. "The gods be praised who have permitted me to see you once again!"

The old man gave a signal to the slaves to stop, and cast a keen glance upon the stranger who had addressed him.

"Pontius, my dear host," resumed the latter, "have twenty years so far whitened my hair and hollowed my cheeks that you no longer recognise your friend Ælius Lamia?"

At this name Pontius Pilate dismounted from the litter as actively as the weight of his years and the heaviness of his gait permitted him, and embraced Ælius Lamia again and again.

"Gods! what a treat it is to me to see you once more! But, alas, you call up memories of those long-vanished days when I was Procurator of Judæa, in the province of Syria. Why, it must be thirty years ago that I first met you. It was at Cæsarea, whither you came to drag out your weary term of exile. I was fortunate enough to alleviate it a little, and out of friendship, Lamia, you followed me to that depressing place Jerusalem, where the Jews filled me with bitterness and disgust. You remained for more than ten years my guest and my companion, and in converse about Rome and things Roman we both of us managed to find consolation—you for your misfortunes, and I for my burdens of State."

Lamia embraced him afresh.

"You forget two things, Pontius; you are overlooking the facts that you used your influence on my behalf with Herod Antipas, and that your purse was freely open to me."

"Let us not talk of that," replied Pontius, "since after your return to Rome you sent me by one of your freedmen a sum of money which repaid me with usury."

"Pontius, I could never consider myself out of your debt by the mere payment of money. But tell me, have the gods fulfilled your desires? Are you in the enjoyment of all the happiness you deserve?

Tell me about your family, your fortunes, your health."

"I have withdrawn to Sicily, where I possess estates, and where I cultivate wheat for the market. My eldest daughter, my best-beloved Pontia, who has been left a widow, lives with me and directs my household. The gods be praised, I have preserved my mental vigour; my memory is not in the least degree enfeebled. But old age always brings in its train a long procession of griefs and infirmities. I am cruelly tormented with gout. And at this very moment you find me on my way to the Phlegræan plain in search of a remedy for my sufferings. From that burning soil, whence at night flames burst forth, proceed acrid exhalations of sulphur which, so they say, ease the pains and restore suppleness to the stiffened joints. At least, the physicians assure me that it is so."

"May you find it so in your case, Pontius! But, despite the gout and its burning torments, you scarcely look as old as myself, although in reality you must be my senior by ten years. Unmistakably you have retained a greater degree of vigour than I ever possessed, and I am overjoyed to find you looking so hale. Why, dear friend, did you retire from the public service before the customary age? Why, on resigning your governorship in Judæa, did you withdraw to a voluntary exile on your Sicilian estates? Give me an account of your doings from the moment that I ceased to be a witness of them. You were preparing to suppress a Samaritan rising when I set out for Cappadocia, where I hoped to draw some profit from the breeding of horses and mules. I have not seen you since then. How did that expedition succeed? Pray tell me. Everything interests me that concerns you in any way."

Pontius Pilate sadly shook his head.

"My natural disposition," he said, "as well as a sense of duty, impelled me to fulfil my public responsibilities, not merely with diligence, but even with ardour. But I was pursued by unrelenting hatred. Intrigues and calumnies cut short my career in its prime, and the fruit it should have looked to bear has withered away. You ask me about the Samaritan insurrection. Let us sit down on this hillock. I shall be able to give you an answer in few words. These occurrences are as vividly present to me as if they had happened yesterday.

"A man of the people, of persuasive speech— there are many such to be met with in Syria— induced the Samaritans to gather together in arms on Mount Gerizim (which in that country is looked upon as a holy place) under the promise that he would disclose to their sight the sacred vessels which in the ancient days of Evander and our father, Æneas, had been hidden away by an eponymous hero, or rather a tribal deity, named Moses. Upon this assurance the Samaritans rose in rebellion; but, having been warned in time to forestall them, I dispatched detachments of infantry to occupy the mountain and stationed cavalry to keep the approaches to it under observation.

"These measures of prudence were urgent. The rebels were already laying siege to the town of Tyrathaba, situated at the foot of Mount Gerizim. I easily dispersed them and stifled the as yet scarcely organized revolt. Then, in order to give a forcible example with as few victims as possible, I handed over to execution the leaders of the rebellion. But you are aware, Lamia, in what strait dependence I was kept by the proconsul Vitellius, who governed Syria not in, but against, the interests of Rome, and looked upon the provinces of the empire as territories which could be farmed out to tetrarchs. The head men among the Samaritans, in their resentment against me, came and fell at his feet lamenting. To listen to them, nothing had been further from their thoughts than to disobey Cæsar. It was I who had provoked the rising, and it was purely in order to withstand my violence that they had gathered together around Tyrathaba. Vitellius listened to their complaints and, handing over the affairs of Judæa to his friend Marcellus, commanded me to go and justify my proceedings before the Emperor himself. With a heart overflowing with grief and resentment I took ship. Just as I approached the shores of Italy, Tiberius, worn out with age and the cares of empire, died suddenly on the self-same Cape Misenum whose peak we see from this very spot magnified in the mists of evening. I demanded justice of Caius, his successor, whose perception was naturally acute, and who was acquainted with Syrian affairs. But marvel with me, Lamia, at the maliciousness of fortune, resolved on my discomfiture. Caius then had in his suite at Rome the Jew Agrippa, his companion, the friend of his childhood, whom he cherished as his own eyes. Now Agrippa favoured Vitellius, inasmuch as Vitellius was the enemy of Antipas, whom Agrippa pursued with his hatred. The Emperor adopted the prejudices of his beloved Asiatic, and refused even to listen to me. There was nothing for me to do but bow beneath the stroke of unmerited misfortune. With tears for my meat and gall for my portion, I withdrew to my estates in Sicily, where I should have died of grief if my sweet Pontia had not come to console her father. I have cultivated wheat, and succeeded in producing the fullest ears in the whole province. But now my life is ended; the future will judge between Vitellius and me."

"Pontius," replied Lamia, "I am persuaded that you acted towards the Samaritans according to the rectitude of your character, and solely in the interests of Rome. But were you not perchance on that occasion a trifle too much influenced by that impetuous courage which has always swayed you? You will remember that in Judæa it often happened that I who, younger than you, should naturally have been more impetuous than you, was obliged to urge you to clemency and suavity."

"Suavity towards the Jews!" cried Pontius Pilate. "Although you have lived amongst them, it seems clear that you ill understand those enemies of the human race. Haughty and at the same time base, combining an invincible obstinacy with a despicably mean spirit, they weary alike your love and your hatred. My character, Lamia, was formed upon the maxims of the divine Augustus. When I was appointed Procurator of Judæa, the world was already penetrated with the majestic ideal of the *pax romana*. No longer, as in the days of our internecine strife, were we witnesses to the sack of a province for the aggrandisement of a proconsul. I knew where my duty lay. I was careful that my actions should be governed by prudence and moderation. The gods are my witnesses that I was resolved upon mildness, and upon mildness only. Yet what did my benevolent intentions avail me? You were at my side, Lamia, when, at the outset of my career as ruler, the first rebellion came to a head. Is there any need for me to recall the details to you? The garrison had been transferred from Cæsarea to take up its winter quarters at Jerusalem. Upon the ensigns of the legionaries appeared the presentment of Cæsar. The inhabitants of Jerusalem, who did not recognize the indwelling divinity of the Emperor, were scandalized at this, as though, when obedience is compulsory, it were not less abject to obey a god than a man. The priests of their nation appeared before my tribunal imploring me with supercilious humility to have the ensigns removed from within the holy city. Out of reverence for the divine nature of Cæsar and the majesty of the empire, I refused to comply. Then the rabble made common cause with the priests, and all around the pretorium portentous cries of supplication arose. I ordered the soldiers to stack their spears in front of the tower of Antonia, and to proceed, armed only with sticks like lictors, to disperse the insolent crowd. But, heedless of blows, the Jews continued their entreaties, and the more obstinate amongst them threw themselves on the ground and, exposing their throats to the rods, deliberately courted death. You were a witness of my humiliation on that occasion, Lamia. By the order of Vitellius I was forced to send the insignia back to Cæsarea. That disgrace I had certainly not merited. Before the immortal gods I swear that never once during my term of office did I flout justice and the laws. But I am grown old. My enemies and detractors are dead. I shall die unavenged. Who will now retrieve my character?"

He moaned and lapsed into silence. Lamia replied:

"That man is prudent who neither hopes nor fears anything from the uncertain events of the future. Does it matter in the least what estimate men may form of us hereafter? We ourselves are after all our own witnesses, and our own judges. You must rely, Pontius Pilate, on the testimony you yourself bear to your own rectitude. Be content with your own personal respect and that of your friends. For the rest, we know that mildness by itself will not suffice for the work of government. There is but little room in the actions of public men for that indulgence of human frailty which the philosophers recommend."

"We'll say no more at present," said Pontius. "The sulphurous fumes which rise from the Phlegræan plain are more powerful when the ground which exhales them is still warm beneath the sun's rays. I must hasten on. Adieu! But now that I have rediscovered a friend, I should wish to take advantage of my good fortune. Do me the favour, Ælius Lamia, to give me your company at supper at my house to-morrow. My house stands on the seashore, at the extreme end of the town in the direction of Misenum. You will easily recognize it by the porch, which bears a painting representing Orpheus surrounded by tigers and lions, whom he is charming with the strains from his lyre.

"Till to-morrow, Lamia," he repeated, as he climbed once more into his litter. "To-morrow we will talk about Judæa."

The following day at the supper hour Lamia presented himself at the house of Pontius Pilate. Two couches only were in readiness for occupants. Creditable but simply equipped, the table held a silver service in which were set out beccaficos in honey, thrushes, oysters from the Lucrine lake, and lampreys from Sicily. As they proceeded with their repast, Pontius and Lamia interchanged inquiries with one another about their ailments, the symptoms of which they described at considerable length, mutually emulous of communicating the various remedies which had been recommended to them. Then, congratulating themselves on being thrown together once more at Baiæ, they vied with one another in praise of the beauty of that enchanting coast and the mildness of the climate they enjoyed. Lamia was enthusiastic about the charms of the courtesans who frequented the sea- 10 shore laden with golden ornaments and trailing draperies of barbaric broidery. But the aged Procurator deplored the ostentation with which by means of trumpery jewels and filmy garments foreigners and even enemies of the empire beguiled the Romans of their gold. After a time they turned to the subject of the great engineering feats that had been accomplished in the country; the prodigious bridge constructed by Caius between Puteoli and Baiæ, and the canals which Augustus exca- 20 vated to convey the waters of the ocean to Lake Avernus and the Lucrine lake.

"I also," said Pontius, with a sigh, "I also wished to set afoot public works of great utility. When, for my sins, I was appointed Governor of Judæa, I conceived the idea of furnishing Jerusalem with an abundant supply of pure water by means of an aqueduct. The elevation of the levels, the proportionate capacity of the various parts, the gradient for the brazen reservoirs to which the distribution 30 pipes were to be fixed—I had gone into every detail and decided everything for myself with the assistance of mechanical experts. I had drawn up regulations for the superintendents so as to prevent individuals from making unauthorized depredations. The architects and the workmen had their instructions. I gave orders for the commencement of operations. But, far from viewing with satisfaction the construction of that conduit which was intended to carry to their town upon its massive 40 arches not only water but health, the inhabitants of Jerusalem gave vent to lamentable outcries. They gathered tumultuously together, exclaiming against the sacrilege and impiousness, and, hurling themselves upon the workmen, scattered the very foundation stones. Can you picture to yourself, Lamia, a filthier set of barbarians? Nevertheless, Vitellius decided in their favour, and I received orders to put a stop to the work."

"It is a knotty point," said Lamia, "how far one 50 is justified in devising things for the commonweal against the will of the populace."

Pontius Pilate continued as though he had not heard this interruption.

"Refuse an aqueduct! What madness! But whatever is of Roman origin is distasteful to the Jews. In their eyes we are an unclean race, and our very presence appears a profanation to them. You will remember that they would never venture to enter the pretorium for fear of defiling themselves, and that I was consequently obliged to discharge my magisterial functions in an open-air tribunal on that marble pavement your feet so often trod.

"They fear us and they despise us. Yet is not Rome the mother and warden of all these peoples who nestle smiling upon her venerable bosom? With her eagles in the van, peace and liberty have been carried to the very confines of the universe. Those whom we have subdued we look on as our friends, and we leave those conquered races, nay, we secure to them the permanence of their customs and their laws. Did Syria, aforetime rent asunder by its rabble of petty kings, ever even begin to taste of peace and prosperity until it submitted to the armies of Pompey? And when Rome might have reaped a golden harvest as the price of her goodwill, did she lay hands on the hoards that swell the treasuries of barbaric temples? Did she despoil the shrine of Cybele at Pessinus, or the Morimene and Cilician sanctuaries of Jupiter, or the temple of the Jewish god at Jerusalem? Antioch, Palmyra, and Apamea, secure despite their wealth, and no longer in dread of the wandering Arab of the desert, have erected temples to the genius of Rome and the divine Cæsar. The Jews alone hate and withstand us. They withhold their tribute till it is wrested from them, and obstinately rebel against military service."

"The Jews," replied Lamia, "are profoundly attached to their ancient customs. They suspected you, unreasonably I admit, of a desire to abolish their laws and change their usages. Do not resent it, Pontius, if I say that you did not always act in such a way as to disperse their unfortunate illusion. It gratified you, despite your habitual selfrestraint, to play upon their fears, and more than once have I seen you betray in their presence the contempt with which their beliefs and religious ceremonies inspired you. You irritated them particularly by giving instructions for the sacerdotal garments and ornaments of their high priest to be kept in ward by your legionaries in the Antonine tower. One must admit that though they have never risen like us to an appreciation of things divine, the Jews celebrate rites which their very antiquity renders venerable."

Pontius Pilate shrugged his shoulders.

"They have very little exact knowledge of the

nature of the gods," he said. "They worship Jupiter, yet they abstain from naming him or erecting a statue of him. They do not even adore him under the semblance of a rude stone, as certain of the Asiatic peoples are wont to do. They know nothing of Apollo, of Neptune, of Mars, nor of Pluto, nor of any goddess. At the same time, I am convinced that in days gone by they worshipped Venus. For even to this day their women bring doves to the altar as victims; and you know as well as I that the dealers who trade beneath the arcades of their temple supply those birds in couples for sacrifice. I have even been told that on one occasion some madman proceeded to overturn the stalls bearing these offerings, and their owners with them. The priests raised an outcry about it, and looked on it as a case of sacrilege. I am of opinion that their custom of sacrificing turtle-doves was instituted in honour of Venus. Why are you laughing, Lamia?"

"I was laughing," said Lamia, "at an amusing idea which, I hardly know how, just occurred to me. I was thinking that perchance some day the Jupiter of the Jews might come to Rome and vent his fury upon you. Why should he not? Asia and Africa have already enriched us with a considerable number of gods. We have seen temples in honour of Isis and the dog-faced Anubis erected in Rome. In the public squares, and even on the race-courses, you may run across the Bona Dea of the Syrians mounted on an ass. And did you never hear how, in the reign of Tiberius, a young patrician passed himself off as the horned Jupiter of the Egyptians, Jupiter Ammon, and in this disguise procured the favours of an illustrious lady who was too virtuous to deny anything to a god? Beware, Pontius, lest the invisible Jupiter of the Jews disembark some day on the quay at Ostia!"

At the idea of a god coming out of Judæa, a fleeting smile played over the severe countenance of the Procurator. Then he replied gravely:

"How would the Jews manage to impose their sacred law on outside peoples when they are in a perpetual state of tumult amongst themselves as to the interpretation of that law? You have seen them yourself, Lamia, in the public squares, split up into twenty rival parties, with staves in their hands, abusing each other and clutching one another by the beard. You have seen them on the steps of the temple, tearing their filthy garments as a symbol of lamentation, with some wretched creature in a frenzy of prophetic exaltation in their midst. They have never realized that it is possible to discuss peacefully and with an even mind those matters concerning the divine which yet are hidden from the profane and wrapped in uncertainty. For the nature of the immortal gods remains hidden from us, and we cannot arrive at a knowledge of it. Though I am of opinion, none the less, that it is a prudent thing to believe in the providence of the gods. But the Jews are devoid of philosophy, and cannot tolerate any diversity of opinions. On the contrary, they judge worthy of the extreme penalty all those who on divine subjects profess opinions opposed to their law. And as, since the genius of Rome has towered over them, capital sentences pronounced by their own tribunals can only be carried out with the sanction of the proconsul or the procurator, they harry the Roman magistrate at any hour to procure his signature to their baleful decrees, they besiege the pretorium with their cries of Death! A hundred times, at least, have I known them, mustered, rich and poor together, all united under their priests, make a furious onslaught on my ivory chair, seizing me by the skirts of my robe, by the thongs of my sandals, and all to demand of me—nay, to exact from me—the death sentence on some unfortunate whose guilt I failed to perceive, and as to whom I could only pronounce that he was as mad as his accusers. A hundred times, do I say! Not a hundred, but every day and all day. Yet it was my duty to execute their law as if it were ours, since I was appointed by Rome not for the destruction but for the upholding of their customs, and over them I had the power of the rod and the axe. At the outset of my term of office I endeavoured to persuade them to hear reason. I attempted to snatch their miserable victims from death. But this show of mildness only irritated them the more; they demanded their prey, fighting around me like a horde of vultures with wing and beak. Their priests reported to Cæsar that I was violating their law, and their appeals, supported by Vitellius, drew down upon me a severe reprimand. How many times did I long, as the Greeks used to say, to dispatch accusers and accused in one convoy to the crows!

"Do not imagine, Lamia, that I nourish the rancour of the discomfited, the wrath of the superannuated, against a people which in my person has prevailed against both Rome and tranquillity. But I foresee the extremity to which sooner or later they will reduce us. Since we cannot govern them, we shall be driven to destroy them. Never doubt it. Always in a state of insubordination, brewing rebellion in their inflammatory minds, they will one day burst forth upon us with a fury beside which the wrath of the Numidians and the mutterings of the Parthians are mere child's play. They are secretly nourishing preposterous hopes, and madly premeditating our ruin. How can it be otherwise, when, on the strength of an oracle, they are living in expectation of the coming of a prince of their own blood whose kingdom shall extend over the whole earth? There are no half measures with such a people. They must be exterminated. Jerusalem must be laid waste to the very foundation. Perchance, old as I am, it may be granted me to behold the day when her walls shall fall and the flames shall envelop her houses, when her inhabitants shall pass under the edge of the sword, when salt shall be strewn on the place where once the temple stood. And in that day I shall at length be justified."

Lamia exerted himself to lead the conversation back to a less acrimonious note.

"Pontius," he said, "it is not difficult for me to understand both your long-standing resentment and your sinister forebodings. Truly, what you have experienced of the character of the Jews is nothing to their advantage. But I lived in Jerusalem as an interested onlooker, and mingled freely with the people, and I succeeded in detecting certain obscure virtues in these rude folk which were altogether hidden from you. I have met Jews who were all mildness, whose simple manners and faithfulness of heart recalled to me what our poets have related concerning the Spartan lawgiver. And you yourself, Pontius, have seen perish beneath the cudgels of your legionaries simple-minded men who have died for a cause they believed to be just without revealing their names. Such men do not deserve our contempt. I am saying this because it is desirable in all things to preserve moderation and an even mind. But I own that I never experienced any lively sympathy for the Jews. The Jewesses, on the contrary, I found extremely pleasing. I was young, then, and the Syrian women stirred all my senses to response. Their ruddy lips, their liquid eyes that shone in the shade, their sleepy gaze pierced me to the very marrow. Painted and stained, smelling of nard and myrrh, steeped in odours, their physical attractions are both rare and delightful."

Pontius listened impatiently to these praises.

"I was not the kind of man to fall into the snares of the Jewish women," he said; "and since you have opened the subject yourself, Lamia, I was never able to approve of your laxity. If I did not express with sufficient emphasis formerly how culpable I held you for having intrigued at Rome with the wife of a man of consular rank, it was because you were then enduring heavy penance for your misdoings. Marriage from the patrician point of view is a sacred tie; it is one of the institutions which are the support of Rome. As to foreign women and slaves, such relations as one may enter into with them would be of little account were it not that they habituate the body to a humiliating effeminacy. Let me tell you that you have been too liberal in your offerings to the Venus of the Marketplace; and what, above all, I blame in you is that you have not married in compliance with the law and given children to the Republic, as every good citizen is bound to do."

But the man who had suffered exile under Tiberius was no longer listening to the venerable magistrate. Having tossed off his cup of Falernian, he was smiling at some image visible to his eye alone.

After a moment's silence he resumed in a very deep voice, which rose in pitch by little and little:

"With what languorous grace they dance, those Syrian women! I knew a Jewess at Jersualem who used to dance in a pokey little room, on a threadbare carpet, by the light of one smoky little lamp, waving her arms as she clanged her cymbals. Her loins arched, her head thrown back, and, as it were, dragged down by the weight of her heavy red hair, her eyes swimming with voluptuousness, eager, languishing, compliant, she would have made Cleopatra herself grow pale with envy. I was in love with her barbaric dances, her voice—a little raucous and yet so sweet—her atmosphere of incense, the semi-somnolescent state in which she seemed to live. I followed her everywhere. I mixed with the vile rabble of soldiers, conjurers, and extortioners with which she was surrounded. One day, however, she disappeared, and I saw her no more. Long did I seek her in disreputable alleys and taverns. It was more difficult to learn to do without her than to lose the taste for Greek wine. Some months after I lost sight of her, I learned by chance that she had attached herself to a small company of men and women who were followers of a young Galilean thaumaturgist.

"His name was Jesus; he came from Nazareth, and he was crucified for some crime, I don't quite know what. Pontius, do you remember anything about the man?"

Pontius Pilate contracted his brows, and his hand rose to his forehead in the attitude of one who probes the deeps of memory. Then after a silence of some seconds:

"Jesus?" he murmured, "Jesus—of Nazareth? I cannot call him to mind."

THE GERMANIC LANDS

The modern Germanic literatures have been rich and distinguished, but their most remarkable feature has been a tendency toward excess and explosiveness. Long placid stretches of Germanic culture and literature (especially in Germany) have now and then been followed by violent upheavals. On the one hand, this has led to extravagance and appalling sins against good taste and common sense; on the other, to works of remarkable power and, occasionally, world-shaking importance.

Germany responded avidly at first to the ferment of the Renaissance in the fifteenth century. Indeed in neighboring Holland arose one of the chief figures of modernism, Desiderius Erasmus (1466-1536), whose criticism of the medieval Church in his delightful *Praise of Folly* and *Colloquies* paved the way for Protestantism, and who promoted the study of Greek and Hebrew. But in Germany proper the Renaissance was quickly transformed into the Protestant Reformation under the leadership of Martin Luther (1483-1546). A long period of stagnation set in as a result of heated religious controversie, and the devastating Thirty Years War (1618-1648). Not until the middle of the eighteenth century did German literature begin to recover, under the leadership of a great critic and champion of enlightenment, Gotthold Ephraim Lessing (1729-1781).

Lessing, the son of a Saxon pastor, entered the University of Leipzig as a theological student but turned to philosophy and letters. These twin interests made him one of those versatile men who led the "Enlightenment" throughout Europe. He became one of the greatest critics of all time, one of the foremost proponents of liberal thought, and Germany's first important playwright. As critic, he wrote the brilliant analysis of the comparative functions of poetry and painting, *Laocoön,* and the *Hamburg Dramaturgy,* a collection of dramatic criticism that challenged French neoclassicism, denounced its stultifying influence on the German theater, and recognized Shakespeare as the king of dramatists. In this work he paved the way for the romantic and realistic drama by proclaiming that a playwright does not have to abide by any regulations, classic or otherwise.

As a philosopher, Lessing ranged himself on the side of the rationalists, subjecting dogma to severe criticism, calling for a "natural religion" of the heart, and preaching and practicing religious tolerance. His important plays were all related to his championing of liberalism. Thus his *Miss Sarah Sampson* and *Emilia Galotti* were "bourgeois tragedies," for along with Diderot in France and Lillo in England he regarded the common people as a suitable subject for tragedy. His comedy *Minna von Barnhelm* was intended to reconcile the German states after Frederick the Great's Seven Years War, with a romance between a humane Prussian officer and a sprightly girl from a conquered German state.

An even more explicit statement of liberalism appeared in his noble *Nathan the Wise.* He came to it after having concluded a bitter theological battle in favor of "natural religion." The plot, which concerns the noble Jew, Nathan, who reared a Christian girl-child after losing his own children in a religious massacre, is slowed up by many discussions, and is snarled when a Crusader falls in love with her only to discover that she is his sister. But no European play gave such eloquent expression to the ideal of religious tolerance. Nathan's profound parable of the Three Rings can be read separately as a lesson in tolerance and ethics that the eighteenth-century idealists strove to impress on the world.

After Lessing and a fellow-critic, Herder, had cleared the way for the free development of German literature, there arose a so-called "Storm and Stress" movement of frantic romanticism and of frothing against all restrictions. Most of the "Storm and Stress" writers are insignificant, but the poet, dramatist, and historian Frederich von Schiller is remembered for high-spirited philosophic poems and noble, if no longer highly valued plays, like *William Tell* and *Wallenstein*. And Goethe, who fired the first rounds of the German romantic revolt in his play *Götz von Berlichingen* (1771), became one of the supreme poets and intellects of Europe.

Johann Wolfgang von Goethe (1749-1832) was one of the universal and Olympian men of European culture. He is the Leonardo da Vinci of the literary world. The son of a well-to-do Frankfort lawyer, he received every opportunity, mastered many languages, learned how to paint, familiarized himself with architecture and science, and studied law and philosophy. He came under the influence of Rousseau, and became entranced with Shakespeare and with folk-poetry. Depressions and stormy love affairs at first made him an intense romanticist whose highly subjective lyrics would have alone gained him a reputation. His tragedy, *Götz von Berlichingen,* glorified a medieval baron who defied the growing materialism of the world. A later play, *Egmont,* treated the revolt of the Netherlands against Spanish tyranny with much feeling. His youthful *Sorrows of Werther* (1774), the story of an unhappy love affair, was rich in sentimental self-torments ending in the suicide. It gave him an international reputation at the age of twenty-four.

A year later, in 1775, the young Duke of Saxe-Weimar, who had become his admirer, invited him to his court at Weimar. Goethe became the intellectual monarch of the little state. In Weimar, Goethe also experienced a great change. His early romanticism left him, and he steeped himself in practical activities as a minister of state, regulating Weimar's transportation and finance and directing the state theater. At the same time he also applied himself to scientific research, studying the evolution of plants and discovering evidence for the theory of evolution.

Acquiring moderation and practical wisdom, summed up in his thought that everybody must learn renunciation, he began to examine his life and the development of the human personality in his long novels *Wilhelm Meister's Apprenticeship* and *Wilhelm Meister's Travels,* and in his autobiography *Poetry and Truth.* Indeed all his writing, as he once declared, was autobiographical. Out of his realization of the wisdom of moderation he arrived at the conclusion that "classicism is health, romanticism is disease." He therefore wrote two noble classic plays, *Iphigenia in Tauris* and *Torquato Tasso,* the latter a tragedy about the Italian poet whose madness is exhibited in the play as a lesson in restraint; Tasso's great mistake, according to Goethe, was his failure to realize that poetry was not the only important accomplishment in society.

Throughout his entire adult life, Goethe was occupied with one major work, his *Faust,* based on the medieval legend of the scholar who sold his soul to the devil. Goethe, who had seen a puppet-play on Faust in childhood, found in this story a symbol of humanity's consuming passion for knowledge and self-realization. He conceived the idea for a Faust drama as early as 1769. Part One was published in 1802, thirty-nine years later. Part Two, which he fashioned for the next thirty years, was finished on his last birthday, shortly before his death in 1832. *Faust* thus grew slowly and became one man's record of his life-long development. In Part II, a fascinating but somewhat chaotic work, Faust's long journey, which led him into many mistakes and by-paths and destroyed a sweet girl's happiness, comes to an end with the realization that although his vague strivings for the infinite have not been crowned with success, he has found the highest self-realization in actively serving mankind. Moreover, man's endless striving is the secret of his true strength and humanity.

The critic, John Macy, has well stated the meaning of *Faust*: "The road itself is the goal, life is its own end and must justify itself from within; perfection is beyond our reach; we do not know what it is and, indeed, to the human mind, it seems akin to stagnation and to death. Thus our highest achievement is a noble striving, a tireless creative living. That it is which saves Faust and defeats Mephistopheles [the devil to whom he sells his soul]; it is with an affirmation of this truth that the eternal armies welcome Faust."

This glorification of striving Goethe found in his own life. But he also found it in the whole history of modern Europe—in the progressive ideals of the Enlightenment, in the romantic movement, and in the ceaseless experimentation that characterized the nineteenth century. *Faust* is something bigger than a play. It is a dramatic poem of epic proportions setting forth Renaissance-inspired modern man's gospel of creative evolution.

Goethe also belonged to an age in which lyric poetry attained new heights, and he was himself one of the world's great lyricists. This may be seen in the songs he inserted into *Faust*. The modern German lyric, however, entered our heritage primarily through the work of one superb poet, Heinrich Heine (1797-1856).

Heine was born at Düsseldorf, in Rhenish Prussia, of Jewish parentage, but he was educated by Jesuits, and his mother even entertained the possibility of his becoming a priest. Although he was later primed by his family for a business career, his unstable, romantic nature was wholly unsuited for a sedate, practical life. Like other young romanticists he was attracted to medieval legends and to weird experiences, and his imagination was heightened by secret visits to a woman who was reputed to be a witch and to her niece, who was the daughter of a hangman. His earliest poems were steeped in this eerie atmosphere. Having an extremely susceptible heart, he also fell in love frequently, and his unrequited passion for his rich cousin Amalie exerted a powerful influence on his poetry. His rich uncle Solomon set him up in the dry-goods business in Hamburg. But this son of an impractical father and of an intellectual mother quickly became bankrupt, and his patient uncle, whom Heine was not above satirizing as a *bourgeois*, made it possible for him to enter the University of Bonn in 1819. Instead of pursuing the study of law, he became immersed in the activities of the democratic student organization known as the *Burschenshaft* and fell under the influence of the romantic critic and philosopher August Wilhelm Schlegel. From Bonn he went to the University of Göttingen, where he found the pedantic and conservative atmosphere repellent and got into a quarrel that resulted in his being advised to leave. In the spring of 1821 he enrolled at the University in Berlin, where he found congenial literary companionship and became known as a promising young writer. His first volume *Gedichte* (*Poems*) was published there in 1821.

Uncle Solomon, although pleased at his erratic nephew's growing reputation, insisted that Heine complete his law studies. Dutifully the young poet returned to Göttingen, taking his degree of Doctor of Laws in 1825 and becoming baptized in the Lutheran Church in order to obtain the right to practice his profession. Both his conversion and his preparation for a legal career, however, were mere formalities. He went to Norderney for a vacation where his love for the North Sea, celebrated in superb poems, became deepened. He visited the Hartz Mountains and responded to the region with an enthusiasm that he shared with many romanticists. He traveled to England, whose materialism depressed him, and then to Italy. The result of these travels was his fascinating and witty book of prose descriptions and verses, *Pictures of Travel*, published in four parts between 1826 and 1831. In 1827 Heine also collected most of his poems under the title *Buch der Lieder* (*Book of Songs*).

Political reaction in his native land and the Parisian Revolution of 1830 led Heine to go to Paris toward the end of May, 1831, and Paris remained his home until his death a quarter of a century later. Here he became attached to a charming but ignorant woman Mathilde, to whom he was deeply devoted, and earned a slender livelihood with his pen by contributing to various French and German publications. In 1837 he also began to receive a pension of 4,800 francs from the French government, which continued until 1848. Here he also wrote his last books of poems, *New Songs, Germany, Atta Troll,* and *Romanzero* (1851), in which he included biting satires aimed at the extravagances of romanticism and at anti-democratic German forces. Germany regarded him as a renegade, but this did not deter him from writing brilliant studies of German literature and political satires intended to promote a democratic change in that country. Indeed he came to regard himself as a soldier in the war for the liberation of Germany and the entire world. His last ten years were a painful conclusion to his fiery and zestful life. He was stricken with a disease of the spine, and was bedridden during his last five years.

The best known of Heine's lyric poems communicate their magic readily, though some of it necessarily disappears in translation. They express, in the words of Professor Charles Harvey Genung, "the tenderness, the gaiety, and the pained humor of the human heart." Other poems, no less distinguished but less popular, reveal him as a satirist who does not hesitate to resort to Rabelaisian grossness but possesses the spirit of French wit. Heine, in addition, was one of the most brilliant essayists of the nineteenth century. He had, as Professor Genung noted, a "Byronic power to blend satire, criticism, and unbridled imagination with poetic elements and impassioned expression." And well he might, for he was in spirit related both to the revolutionary enlightenment of France and the romantic movement. He was both a poet and a revolutionary journalist, and in temperament both gay and morbid, both a passionate lover and a humorist and cynic. "To be born with diverse souls," wrote the critic Edward Dowden, "is embarrassing, but it was Heine's distinction. It signifies that life is to be no steady progress, directed by some guiding light, but a wavering advance through a countless series of attractions and repulsions, and of repulsions transformed into attractions." Moreover, he had a sensibility so quivering that it needed the protective armor of laughter.

The restlessness of Heine marked the later course of German literature. Some of the romanticists represented morbid psychology, and one of them, Friedrich Hebbel, took a step in the direction of realism in his powerful middle-class tragedy, *Maria Magdalena* (1844), which anticipated Ibsen's realistic dramas. In the field of economic and social thought Karl Marx (1818-1883) and his followers gave birth to the revolutionary movement of socialism that has profoundly influenced the course of the world. Marx and his collaborator Engels possessed literary talent, and their *Communist Manifesto* (1847) is a challenging essay. In the field of philosophy, Arthur Schopenhauer (1788-1860) set forth his philosophy of pessimism in essays of great literary distinction.

Schopenhauer's disciple, Friedrich Wilhelm Nietzsche (1844-1900), was a tortured and extremist genius who never developed a systematic philosophy but delivered himself of forceful philosophic ideas. These echoed many tendencies of the time—Darwinism, atheism, and rising Prussianism, which he consciously detested. He also represented a reaction to other trends: to materialism, middle-class complacency, utilitarianism (the principle of the greatest good for the greatest number, as propounded by John Stuart Mill and other English social thinkers), and socialism. Central in Nietzsche's thought was the glorification of man's *"will to power,"* of unhampered self-realization and self-assertion by the individual. He condemned both Christianity and socialism as "slave philosophies" which opposed the superior individual's full development and mastery over the mediocre and weak. Schopenhauer believed that the Will brought misery. Nietzsche, on the contrary, regarded the Will as the source of all noble achievement leading, through the assertion of life and tireless striving, to the evolutionary development of superior people or "supermen." Above all, Nietzsche fulminated against human pettiness, against a dull life of pampering and complacency. The real goal of man is, not ease, but greatness. And for this, courage is needed —the courage to struggle incessantly and to pass beyond social and religious conventions—"beyond good and evil."

In all things Nietzsche expressed himself with unbridled extremism, for he was an impassioned and suffering man. He was born in Prussia, though of Polish descent, and was the son of a clergyman, which may explain his constant struggle against Christianity. A precocious student, he became a professor of philology at the University of Basel, Switzerland, when he was only twenty-five. In the same year, 1870, he joined the Prussian army, and the privations he endured during the Franco-Prussian War undermined his already delicate health. Returning to his professorship after the war, he held his post until 1889, with occasional interruptions of illness, until he was struck down with paralysis of the brain. He spent the last five years of his life in an insane asylum, suffering from delusions.

He started writing in 1871. Among his books were *The Birth of Tragedy*, a brilliant speculation on Greek drama; *Ecce Homo*, a unique apology for his life; *The Genealogy of Morals*, an attack on Christianity for its "slave morality" and sense of sin; *Beyond Good and Evil*, a plea for freedom from moral conventions; and the uncompleted *The Will to Power*.

His greatest book is *Thus Spake Zarathustra*, a collection of rhapsodies on the glory of life, freedom from sentimentality and convention, and the will to power, which Nietzsche put into the mouth of the Persian sage Zarathustra or Zoroaster. In this work we see Nietzsche for what he really was —a poet rather than a systematic philosopher. It has always been a mistake to interpret Nietzsche practically; he would have shuddered at some of Germany's political policies associated with his name. It is as a literary artist, a rhapsodist of life and individuality, and an erratically but also brilliantly intuitive critic and idealist that Nietzsche can be expected to survive.

It was, nevertheless, in Scandinavia—in the work of the dramatist Ibsen (1828-1906)—that the nineteenth century expressed the most telling criticism of middle-class society and the most influential promulgation of modern ideas of liberation from convention in the name of individual self-realization. Through the powerful social instrument of the theater, Ibsen's challenge was trumpeted throughout the Western world. Moreover, Ibsen radically transformed the style and purpose of the theater. The drama that deals with social ideas and that represents the conditions and issues of the real world virtually began with him.

Born in 1828 in a small Norwegian town, of a conservative merchant family that became insolvent and experienced poverty, Henrik Ibsen had sufficient provocation to chafe under the restraints and prejudices he subsequently fought in his plays. He spent seven years of drudgery as an apothecary's asistant and then engaged in a long struggle for recognition as a playwright. Failing to receive a poet's pension from the government, and embittered by the failure of such early plays as *The Vikings* and *The Pretenders*, Ibsen left Norway in 1863. His self-imposed exile for more than a quarter of a century was mostly spent in Rome and in Germany, and it was there that he composed many of his masterpieces. The first of these, *Brand,* an attack on the spirit of compromise, was published with enviable success in 1865, the coveted poet's pension followed a year later, and in time sturdy champions like William Archer and Bernard Shaw arose to argue his cause with the world. But his plays, which became increasingly incisive, continued to be received with hostility. Recognition came to him at last on his seventieth birthday, which was publicly celebrated in Norway. Before he died, in 1906, his work was already the most potent force in the modern theater.

Ibsen began his literary career as a romanticist, whose earnestness and probing into character could only strike the theater of his time and place as strange and incongruous. His later plays faced the world squarely on a platform of realism that shook the stage to its foundations. The transition to realism was a natural development in his work: There were modern characters in his medieval saga dramas *The Vikings* and *The Pretenders*; as early as 1862 his rhymed play, *Love's Comedy,* discussed conventionality in the relation of the sexes; his powerful poetic dramas, *Brand* and *Peer Gynt,* crossed swords with philistinism; and his satirical *League of Youth,* was a political comedy. Eight years later, in 1877, Ibsen definitely inaugurated his realistic period with the composition of *The Pillars of Society,* an exposé of hypocritical small-town respectability.

A Doll's House, in 1879, challenged the conventions of marriage which deprived woman of access to experience and limited her individuality. The conclusion, in which Nora leaves her husband, became a subject of heated debate throughout Europe. In 1881 Ibsen went even further in *Ghosts,* a tragedy that denounced its heroine Mrs. Alving's conformity to the social traditions that sanctioned a loveless marriage to a debauched husband who gave her a son doomed to hereditary venereal disease. As late as 1913 Ibsen was still being accused by the American critic William Winter of "mental astigmatism," "purblind censoriousness, gross falsehood, and ignominious censure." Both the thesis of *Ghosts* and the presentation of the tabooed subject of venereal disease were revolutionary in their day and resulted in pitched battles between conservatives and radicals. The author answered his critics with a stinging indictment of corrupt society a year later in *An Enemy of the People.*

After this explosion Ibsen seems to have been shaken in his reformer's faith, and he grew less aggressive. After voicing his doubts concerning the "call of the ideal" in *The Wild Duck* (1884), he became more an observer and recorder of realities than a champion of causes. In realistic plays, such as *Rosmersholm* (1886), *Hedda Gabler* (1890), and *John Gabriel Borkman* (1896), as well as in symbolical dramas, such as *The Lady from the Sea* (1888) and *The Master Builder* (1892), he continued his analysis of modern characters and problems, but without strenuous preachment on the whole.

A Doll's House is not his best realistic play, but no student can afford to be unfamiliar with it. It is with this work that Ibsen inaugurated dramatic realism and his championing of women's right to equality with men. It made him known as the iconoclast and rebel of modern literature, and it set an example in social criticism for the many important continental and English playwrights who arose after 1880.

It was Germany that first responded to Ibsen's call after giving him the best hearing. Realistic social dramas appeared on the German stage after 1890 in great profusion, and realism was intensified there in the manner of Zola. Naturalistic drama, as this extreme form of realism was called, went beyond Ibsen in using the most colloquial speech, including dialect; in recording facts and observing people with scientific objectivity; in touching many tabooed subjects, representing the sexual instinct in its most bestial forms, treating alcoholism and disease, and dramatizing explosions of protest and violence on the part of the most submerged groups in society—namely, the working class. The most potent of the naturalist dramatists, Gerhart Hauptmann (1862-   ), summed up all these tendencies.

Hauptmann, the son of a Silesian innkeeper, was a poet who was early exposed to the scientific, practical world, to socialist agitation, and to the literary program of the naturalists. In 1889 he fired the first shot for naturalism in his first play *Before Sunrise*, a somber picture of degeneration, incest, and alcoholism among the Silesian peasantry, as well as a warning against hereditary disease and a plea for eugenics. Another unrelieved representation of drab and hopeless life appeared in his *Lonely Lives* two years later, and in 1893 he delivered himself of his masterpiece, *The Weavers,* a powerful account of the sufferings and rebellion of the Silesian weavers in 1844. This epoch-making work gave voice to the protests and aspirations of the working class, and was indeed the first modern "proletarian" play. Permission to perform it was won only after years of litigation, and it cost the leading *Deutsches Theater* the Emperor's patronage. It set an example in militantly social-minded playwriting that has been followed by numerous twentieth-century dramatists.

Hauptmann continued to consolidate his position as a commanding realist with many other plays, such as his naturalistic fantasy *The Assumption of Hannele,* his study of a girl caught in the net of men's bestial sexuality, *Rose Bernd,* and his two naturalistic comedies *The Beaver Coat* and *The Conflagration,* for which the nearest equivalent in America is *Tobacco Road*. Responding to a romantic reaction against the excessive unpleasantness of much naturalistic drama—a reaction that produced Rostand's beautiful romantic play *Cyrano de Bergerac* in France—Hauptmann wrote a number of romantic plays distinguished for their poetry. Among these *The Sunken Bell* enjoyed a vogue. But Hauptmann will be remembered longest for his realistic work, and our survey of German literature before the twentieth century may be properly concluded with *The Weavers,* which brings us to the threshold of the contemporary world. As a representation of the conflict between capital and labor it foreshadowed the most far-reaching and still unresolved problem of our century.

GOTTHOLD EPHRAIM LESSING

Nathan the Wise

NATHAN. A man, many years ago, received from a beloved hand a ring of priceless worth. The stone, an opal, radiant with a hundred hues and shades, possessed a certain secret power—a secret power to make whoever wore it pleasing alike to God and men. Is there a wonder that the man would never take it off?

SALADIN. No wonder. Where is this ring?

NATHAN. In his will the man declared that it should stay forever in his family.

Translated and adapted by Ferdinand Bruckner. Upon being requested by Sultan Saladin to tell which of the three faiths—the Christian, Jewish, and Mohammedan—is the best, Nathan answers with this parable.

SALADIN. He died?

NATHAN. And left it to the dearest of his sons, ordaining that he in turn should leave it to the son he loved the most and that in every age the dearest, not the first-born son—by virtue of the magic ring alone—should be the family head.

SALADIN. They all had sons?

NATHAN. They had.

SALADIN. And the magic ring?

NATHAN. —came down from son to son.

SALADIN. Where is it now?

NATHAN. You'll see. It reached a father of three sons. All three were equally obedient to his word, all three an equal pleasure to his eyes, and thus he loved all three as one. Whenever one or another was alone with him, he thought that one the dearest of the three and promised him the ring. Thus, by and by, the tender weakness of his overflowing heart led him to swear the ring in turn to each of them. But when he was about to die, his heart faced painfully the thought that two of his beloved sons, who'd trusted him so well, should be deceived.

SALADIN. What could he do?

NATHAN. What could he do? A man when faced with death—as if some thought has reached him from the eternal world he's nearing—often surprises us with a solution which we'd seek in vain. But be that as it may: at once this man sent for an artisan and ordered him in strictest secrecy to make at any cost and pain two other rings precisely like the first. The artisan had wrought so well that when at last he brought the rings even the father could not tell the genuine one. With joy he summoned his three sons, on separate calls, of course, bestowed on each his blessing and his ring and died.

SALADIN. And died. And then?

NATHAN. I'm at the end. The genuine ring could never be discovered. After the father's death each son at once produced his ring and claimed to be the dearest son. They investigated, began proceedings one against the other, quarreled and fought—in vain. Which was the one and genuine ring remained still unrevealed almost as much as now the one and true belief.

SALADIN. You didn't mean a tale of rings should be the answer to my question?

NATHAN. Almost, sir.

SALADIN. That's preposterous.

NATHAN. How could I dare distinguish the three rings when the father himself with purpose had them made the same?

SALADIN. You cannot put me off with tales of rings. I asked you about religions, unlike in all respects, even to their ways of dressing, eating, drinking.

NATHAN. But not to ways of feeling, which are the same for all mankind. Our feeling is the soil from which all trees arise, divide themselves in branches, twigs, and leaves. Millions of leaves we are, but nurtured by one soil.

SALADIN. Why then do we so hate our fellows?

NATHAN. For better air, for better place to catch the sun, another ray or two. Besides a leaf sticks to its branch, the branch to the tree. Could I then love my father less than you do yours?

SALADIN. My father was the most heroic man on earth. He killed four thousand Christians. At Heaven's table his place is close to Mahomet himself.

NATHAN. Let's turn again to the rings. Each of the sons swore he received his ring straight from his father's hand and therefore charged the others with fraudulence and greed, determined to protect his own, the genuine ring.

SALADIN. And the judge? Now all depends on him.

NATHAN. How would you judge, O Sultan, in such a case?

SALADIN. I never could.

NATHAN. I bow before this word of yours.

SALADIN. Go on. What did the judge pronounce?

NATHAN. The judge pronounced the case dismissed.

SALADIN. Dismissed?

NATHAN. The genuine ring, he said, contains the secret power to make its bearer the most beloved in sight of God and men. You three put on your rings and let me see which one of you is most beloved by his brothers.

SALADIN. And did the secret power work?

NATHAN. It didn't. The brothers went on looking at one another, their hate unchanged. I see, said then the judge, each ring works only for his owner and makes him fall in love with him alone.

SALADIN. That's good. Oh, what a judge!

NATHAN. Well, then, he said, all three of you—you're nothing but deceived deceivers, and all your rings are false. Your father might have had them made to replace the genuine one which doubtless he had lost.

SALADIN. The genuine one is lost?

NATHAN. That's what the judge assumed.

SALADIN. Oh, what a shame!

NATHAN. But let me tell you how the case was ended. The fact, he said, that each of you received his ring straight from his father's hand entitles each of you to think his own the genuine ring. He loved you all, and loved you all alike. If only each of you believes in him and his bequest, then all three rings are genuine alike. Vie now each with the other to prove the secret powers of the rings you wear, and after they have worked, these secret powers—humility, forbearance, tolerance and love—

SALADIN. I see!

NATHAN. —have worked for a thousand years within your children's children; then let them be called once more before this seat whereon a wiser judge than I shall sit and give his verdict.

SALADIN. Listening to you, I feel that they're not only words.

NATHAN. Perhaps that thousand years have passed. Could you but be the wiser judge!

SALADIN. Stupid warrior that I am? Oh, no!

NATHAN. You must. At every dawn, as Sultan and victorious warrior, you have to be the wiser judge. Right now you must decide on armistice or not.

SALADIN. I have already. Why should I punish with the death of thousands a childish charge by some fanatic templars? Who knows if in their place I had not done the same?

NATHAN. He is the wisest judge who sets himself on the defendant bench. If God held the final truth enclosed in his right hand and in his left only our longing for it, and he should say to me: "Come, choose!" I would bow humbly to his left and say: "This hand, my Father, for the final truth belongs to Thee alone."

J. W. VON GOETHE

Faust

THE STUDY

FAUST   MEPHISTOPHELES

FAUST. A knock? Come in! Who now would break my rest?

MEPH. 'Tis I!

FAUST. Come in!

MEPH. Thrice be the words express'd.

FAUST. Then I repeat, Come in!

MEPH.   'Tis well,   5
I hope that we shall soon agree!
For now your fancies to expel,
Here, as a youth of high degree,
I come in gold-lac'd scarlet vest,
And stiff-silk mantle richly dress'd,   10
A cock's gay feather for a plume,
A long and pointed rapier, too;
And briefly I would counsel you
To don at once the same costume,
And, free from trammels, speed away,   15
That what life is you may essay.

FAUST. In every garb I needs must feel oppress'd,

My heart to earth's low cares a prey.
Too old the trifler's part to play,
Too young to live by no desire possess'd.   20
What can the world to me afford?
Renounce! renounce! is still the word;
This is the everlasting song
In every ear that ceaseless rings,
And which, alas, our whole life long,   25
Hoarsely each passing moment sings.
But to new horror I awake each morn,
And I could weep hot tears, to see the sun
Dawn on another day, whose round forlorn
Accomplishes no wish of mine—not one.   30
Which still, with froward captiousness, impairs
E'en the presentiment of every joy,
While low realities and paltry cares
The spirit's fond imaginings destroy.
Then must I too, when falls the veil of night,   35
Stretch'd on my pallet languish in despair:
Appalling dreams my soul affright;
No rest vouchsafed me even there.
The god, who throned within my breast resides,

Goethe, *Faust*. Translated by Miss Swanwick. Johann Wolfgang von Goethe (1749-1832), Germany's greatest poet and critic, was born at Frankfort, but after he had achieved his fame spent much of his romantic life at Weimar.

Deep in my soul can stir the springs;   40
With sovereign sway my energies he guides,
He cannot move external things;
And so existence is to me a weight,
Death fondly I desire, and life I hate.
   MEPH. And yet, methinks, by most 'twill be
     confess'd   45
That Death is never quite a welcome guest.
   FAUST. Happy the man around whose brow he
     binds
The bloodstain'd wreath in conquest's dazzling
     hour;
Or whom, excited by the dance, he finds
Dissolv'd in bliss, in love's delicious bower!   50
O that before the lofty spirit's might,
Enraptured, I had rendered up my soul!
   MEPH. Yet did a certain man refrain one night,
Of its brown juice to drain the crystal bowl.
   FAUST. To play the spy diverts you then?
   MEPH.   I own,   55
Though not omniscient, much to me is known.
   FAUST. If o'er my soul the tone familiar, stealing,
Drew me from harrowing thought's bewild'ring
     maze,
Touching the ling'ring chords of childlike feeling,
With the sweet harmonies of happier days: 60
So curse I all, around the soul that windeth
Its magic and alluring spell,
And with delusive flattery bindeth
Its victim to this dreary cell!
Curs'd before all things be the high opinion,   65
Wherewith the spirit girds itself around!
Of shows delusive curs'd be the dominion,
Within whose mocking sphere our sense is bound!
Accurs'd of dreams the treacherous wiles.
The cheat of glory, deathless fame!   70
Accurs'd what each as property beguiles,
Wife, child, slave, plow, whate'er its name!
Accurs'd be mammon, when with treasure
He doth to daring deeds incite:
Or when to steep the soul in pleasure,   75
He spreads the couch of soft delight!
Curs'd be the grape's balsamic juice!
Accurs'd love's dream, of joys the first!
Accurs'd be hope! accurs'd be faith!
And more than all, be patience curs'd!   80
   CHOR. OF SPIRITS [*invisible*]. Woe! woe!
Thou hast destroy'd
The beautiful world
With violent blow;
'Tis shiver'd! 'tis shatter'd!   85
The fragments abroad by a demigod scatter'd!
Now we sweep

The wrecks into nothingness!
Fondly we weep
The beauty that's gone!   90
Thou, 'mongst the sons of earth,
Lofty and mighty one,
Build it once more!
In thine own bosom the lost world restore!
Now with unclouded sense   95
Enter a new career;
Songs shall salute thine ear,
Ne'er heard before!
   MEPH. My little ones these spirits be.
Hark! with shrewd intelligence,   100
How they recommend to thee
Action, and the joys of sense!
In the busy world to dwell,
Fain they would allure thee hence:
For within this lonely cell,   105
Stagnate sap of life and sense.
Forbear to trifle longer with thy grief,
Which, vulture-like, consumes thee in this den.
The worst society is some relief,
Making thee feel thyself a man with men.   110
Nathless, it is not meant, I trow,
To thrust thee 'mid the vulgar throng.
I to the upper ranks do not belong;
Yet if, by me companion'd, thou
Thy steps through life forthwith wilt take,   115
Upon the spot myself I'll make
Thy comrade:—
Should it suit thy need,
I am thy servant, am thy slave indeed!
   FAUST. And how must I thy services repay? 120
   MEPH. Thereto thou lengthen'd respite hast!
   FAUST. No! no!
The devil is an egoist I know:
And, for Heaven's sake, 'tis not his way
Kindness to anyone to show.   125
Let the condition plainly be exprest!
Such a domestic is a dangerous guest.
   MEPH. I'll pledge myself to be thy servant *here,*
Still at thy back alert and prompt to be;
But when together *yonder* we appear,   130
Then shalt thou do the same for me.
   FAUST. But small concern I feel for yonder
     world;
Hast thou this system into ruin hurl'd,
Another may arise the void to fill.
This earth the fountain whence my pleasures
     flow,   135
This sun doth daily shine upon my woe,
And if this world I must forego,
Let happen then,—what can and will.

I to this theme will close mine ears,
If men hereafter hate and love,   140
And if there be in yonder spheres
A depth below or height above.

    MEPH. In this mood thou mayst venture it. But
    make
The compact! I at once will undertake
To charm thee with mine arts. I'll give thee more
Than mortal eye hath e'er beheld before.   146

    FAUST. What, sorry Devil, hast thou to bestow?
Was ever mortal spirit, in its high endeavor,
Fathom'd by Being such as thou?
Yet food thou hast which satisfieth never,   150
Hast ruddy gold, that still doth flow
Like restless quicksilver away,
A game thou hast, at which none win who play,
A girl who would, with amorous eyen,
E'en from my breast, a neighbor snare,   155
Lofty ambition's joy divine,
That, meteor-like, dissolves in air.
Show me the fruit that, ere 'tis pluck'd, doth rot,
And trees, whose verdure daily buds anew!

    MEPH. Such a commission scares me not,   160
I can provide such treasures, it is true;
But, my good friend, a season will come round,
When on what's good we may regale in peace.

    FAUST. If e'er upon my couch, stretched at my
    ease, I'm found,
Then may my life that instant cease!   165
Me canst thou cheat with glozing wile
Till self-reproach away I cast,—
Me with joy's lure canst thou beguile;—
Let that day be for me the last!
Be this our wager!

    MEPH.   Settled!

    FAUST.   Sure and fast!   170
When to the moment I shall say,
"Linger awhile! so fair thou art!"
Then mayst thou fetter me straightway,
Then to the abyss will I depart!
Then may the solemn death-bell sound,   175
Then from thy service thou art free,
The index then may cease its round,
And time be never more for me!

    MEPH. I shall remember: pause, ere 'tis too late.

    FAUST. Thereto a perfect right hast thou.   180
My strength I do not rashly overrate.
Slave am I here, at any rate,
If thine, or whose, it matters not, I trow.

    MEPH. At thine inaugural feast I will this day
Attend, my duties to commence.—   185
But one thing!—Accidents may happen, hence
A line or two in writing grant, I pray.

    FAUST. A writing, Pedant! dost demand from
    me?
Man, and man's plighted word, are these unknown
    to thee?
Is't not enough, that by the word I gave,   190
My doom for evermore is cast?
Doth not the world in all its currents rave,
And must a promise hold me fast?
Yet fixed is this delusion in our heart;   194
Who, of his own free will, therefrom would part?
How blest within whose breast truth reigneth
    pure!
No sacrifice will he repent when made!
A formal deed, with seal and signature,
A specter this from which all shrink afraid.
The word its life resigneth in the pen,   200
Leather and wax usurp the mastery then.
Spirits of evil! what dost thou require?
Brass, marble, parchment, paper, dost desire?
Shall I with chisel, pen, or graver write?
Thy choice is free; to me 'tis all the same.   205

    MEPH. Wherefore thy passion so excite,
And thus thine eloquence inflame?
A scrap is for our compact good.
Thou under-signest merely with a drop of blood.

    FAUST. If this will satisfy thy mind,   210
Thy whim I'll gratify, howe'er absurd.

    MEPH. Blood is a juice of very special kind.

    FAUST. Be not afraid that I shall break my word!
The scope of all my energy
Is in exact accordance with my vow.   215
Vainly I have aspired too high;
I'm on a level but with such as thou;
Me the great spirit scorn'd, defied;
Nature from me herself doth hide;
Rent is the web of thought; my mind   220
Doth knowledge loathe of every kind.
In depths of sensual pleasure drown'd,
Let us our fiery passions still!
Enwrapp'd in magic's veil profound,
Let wondrous charms our senses thrill!   225
Plunge we in time's tempestuous flow,
Stem we the rolling surge of chance!
There may alternate weal and woe,
Success and failure, as they can,
Mingle and shift in changeful dance!   230
Excitement is the sphere for man.

    MEPH. Nor goal, nor measure is prescrib'd to
    you,
If you desire to taste of every thing,
To snatch at joy while on the wing,
May your career amuse and profit too!   235
Only fall to and don't be over coy!

FAUST. Hearken! The end I aim at is not joy;
I crave excitement, agonizing bliss,
Enamor'd hatred, quickening vexation. 239
Purg'd from the love of knowledge, my vocation,
The scope of all my powers henceforth be this,
To bare my breast to every pang,—to know
In my heart's core all human weal and woe,
To grasp in thought the lofty and the deep,
Men's various fortunes on my breast to heap, 245
And thus to theirs dilate my individual mind,
And share at length with them the shipwreck of
 mankind.
MEPH. Oh, credit me, who still as ages roll,
Have chew'd this bitter fare from year to year,
No mortal, from the cradle to the bier, 250
Digests the ancient leaven! Know, this Whole
Doth for the Deity alone subsist!
He in eternal brightness doth exist,
Us unto darkness he hath brought, and here
Where day and night alternate, is your sphere.
FAUST. But 'tis my will! 256
MEPH. Well spoken, I admit!
But one thing puzzles me, my friend;
Time's short, art long; methinks 'twere fit
That you to friendly counsel should attend.
A poet choose as your ally! 260
Let him thought's wide dominion sweep,
Each good and noble quality,
Upon your honored brow to heap;
The lion's magnanimity,
The fleetness of the hind, 265
The fiery blood of Italy,
The Northern's stedfast mind.
Let him to you the mystery show
To blend high aims and cunning low;
And while youth's passions are aflame 270
To fall in love by rule and plan!
I fain would meet with such a man;
Would him Sir Microcosmus name.
FAUST. What then am I, if I aspire in vain
The crown of our humanity to gain, 275
Towards which my every sense doth strain?
MEPH. Thou'rt after all—just what thou art.
Put on thy head a wig with countless locks,
And to a cubit's height upraise thy socks,
Still thou remainest ever, what thou art. 280
FAUST. I feel it, I have heap'd upon my brain
The gather'd treasure of man's thought in vain;
And when at length from studious toil I rest,
No power, new-born, springs up within my breast;
A hair's breadth is not added to my height, 285
I am no nearer to the infinite.
MEPH. Good sir, these things you view indeed,

Just as by other men they're view'd;
We must more cleverly proceed,
Before life's joys our grasp elude. 290
The devil! thou hast hands and feet,
And head and heart are also thine;
What I enjoy with relish sweet,
Is it on that account less mine?
If for six stallions I can pay, 295
Do I not own their strength and speed?
A proper man I dash away,
As their two dozen legs were mine indeed.
Up then, from idle pondering free,
And forth into the world with me! 300
I tell you what;—your speculative churl
Is like a beast which some ill spirit leads,
On barren wilderness, in ceaseless whirl,
While all around lie fair and verdant meads.
FAUST. But how shall we begin?
MEPH. We will go hence with speed, 305
A place of torment this indeed!
A precious life, thyself to bore,
And some few youngsters evermore!
Leave that to neighbor Paunch!—withdraw,
Why wilt thou plague thyself with thrashing
 straw? 310
The very best that thou dost know
Thou dar'st not to the striplings show.
One in the passage now doth wait!
FAUST. I'm in no mood to see him now.
MEPH. Poor lad! He must be tired, I trow; 315
He must not go disconsolate.
Hand me thy cap and gown; the mask
Is for my purpose quite first rate.

He changes his dress.

Now leave it to my wit! I ask
But quarter of an hour; meanwhile equip, 320
And make all ready for our pleasant trip!
 [*Exit* FAUST.
MEPH. [*in Faust's long gown*]. Mortal! the
 loftiest attributes of men,
Reason and Knowledge, only thus contemn,
Still let the Prince of lies, without control,
With shows, and mocking charms delude thy soul,
I have thee unconditionally then!— 326
Fate hath endow'd him with an ardent mind,
Which unrestrain'd still presses on for ever,
And whose precipitate endeavor
Earth's joys o'erleaping, leaveth them behind. 330
Him will I drag through life's wild waste,
Through scenes of vapid dullness, where at last
Bewilder'd, he shall falter, and stick fast;
And, still to mock his greedy haste,

Viands and drink shall float his craving lips
    beyond—   335
Vainly he'll seek refreshment, anguish-tost,
And were he not the devil's by his bond,
Yet must his soul infallibly be lost!

A Student enters.

STUD. But recently I've quitted home,
Full of devotion am I come   340
A man to know and hear, whose name
With reverence is known to fame.
  MEPH. Your courtesy much flatters me!
A man like other men you see;
Pray have you yet applied elsewhere?   345
  STUD. I would entreat your friendly care!
I've youthful blood and courage high;
Of gold I bring a fair supply;
To let me go my mother was not fain;
But here I longed true knowledge to attain. 350
  MEPH. You've hit upon the very place.
  STUD. And yet my steps I would retrace.
These walls, this melancholy room,
O'erpower me with a sense of gloom;
The space is narrow, nothing green,   355
No friendly tree is to be seen:
And in these halls, with benches filled, distraught,
Sight, hearing, fail me, and the power of thought.
  MEPH. It all depends on habit. Thus at first
The infant takes not kindly to the breast, 360
But before long, its eager thirst
Is fain to slake with hearty zest:
Thus at the breasts of wisdom day by day
With keener relish you'll your thirst allay.
  STUD. Upon her neck I fain would hang with
    joy;
To reach it, say, what means must I employ? 365
  MEPH. Explain, ere further time we lose,
What special faculty you choose?
  STUD. Profoundly learned I would grow,
What heaven contains would comprehend, 370
O'er earth's wide realm my gaze extend,
Nature and science I desire to know.
  MEPH. You are upon the proper track, I find;
Take heed, let nothing dissipate your mind.
  STUD. My heart and soul are in the chase! 375
Though to be sure I fain would seize,
On pleasant summer holidays,
A little liberty and careless ease.
  MEPH. Use well your time, so rapidly it flies;
Method will teach you time to win;   380
Hence, my young friend, I would advise,
With college logic to begin!
Then will your mind be so well braced,

In Spanish boots so tightly laced,
That on 'twill circumspectly creep,   385
Thought's beaten track securely keep,
Nor will it, ignis-fatuus like,
Into the path of error strike.
Then many a day they'll teach you how
The mind's spontaneous acts, till now 390
As eating and as drinking free,
Require a process;—one! two! three!
In truth the subtle web of thought
Is like the weaver's fabric wrought:
One treadle moves a thousand lines, 395
Swift dart the shuttles to and fro,
Unseen the threads together flow,
A thousand knots one stroke combines.
Then forward steps your sage to show,
And prove to you, it must be so;   400
The first being so, and so the second,
The third and fourth deduc'd we see;
And if there were no first and second,
Nor third nor fourth would ever be.
This, scholars of all countries prize,— 405
Yet 'mong themselves no weavers rise.
He who would know and treat of aught alive,
Seeks first the living spirit thence to drive:
Then are the lifeless fragments in his hand,
There only fails, alas! the spirit-band. 410
This process, chemists name, in learned thesis,
Mocking themselves, *Naturæ encheiresis.*
  STUD. Your words I cannot fully comprehend.
  MEPH. In a short time you will improve, my
    friend,
When of scholastic forms you learn the use; 415
And how by method all things to reduce.
  STUD. So doth all this my brain confound,
As if a mill-wheel there were turning round.
  MEPH. And next, before aught else you learn,
You must with zeal to metaphysics turn! 420
There see that you profoundly comprehend,
What doth the limit of man's brains transcend;
For that which is or is not in the head
A sounding phrase will serve you in good stead.
But before all strive this half year   425
From one fix'd order ne'er to swerve!
Five lectures daily you must hear;
The hour still punctually observe!
Yourself with studious zeal prepare,
And closely in your manual look,   430
Hereby may you be quite aware
That all he utters standeth in the book;
Yet write away without cessation,
As at the Holy Ghost's dictation!

STUD. This, Sir, a second time you need not say! 435
Your counsel I appreciate quite;
What we possess in black and white,
We can in peace and comfort bear away.
  MEPH. A faculty I pray you name.
  STUD. For jurisprudence some distaste I own. 440
  MEPH. To me this branch of science is well known,
And hence I cannot your repugnance blame.
Customs and laws in every place,
Like a disease, an heir-loom dread,
Still trail their curse from race to race, 445
And furtively abroad they spread.
To nonsense, reason's self they turn;
Beneficence becomes a pest;
Woe unto thee, that thou'rt a grandson born!
As for the law born with us, unexpressed;— 450
That law, alas, none careth to discern.
  STUD. You deepen my dislike. The youth
Whom you instruct, is blest in sooth!
To try theology I feel inclined.
  MEPH. I would not lead you willingly astray,
But as regards this science, you will find 456
So hard it is to shun the erring way,
And so much hidden poison lies therein,
Which scarce can you discern from medicine.
Here too it is the best, to listen but to one, 460
And by the master's words to swear alone.
To sum up all—To words hold fast!
Then the safe gate securely pass'd,
You'll reach the fane of certainty at last.
  STUD. But then some meaning must the words convey. 465
  MEPH. Right! But o'er-anxious thought, you'll find of no avail,
For there precisely where ideas fail,
A word comes opportunely into play
Most admirable weapons words are found,
On words a system we securely ground, 470
In words we can conveniently believe,
Nor of a single jot can we a word bereave.
  STUD. Your pardon for my importunity;
Yet once more must I trouble you:
On medicine, I'll thank you to supply 475
A pregnant utterance or two!
Three years! how brief the appointed tide!
The field, heaven knows, is all too wide!
If but a friendly hint be thrown,
'Tis easier then to feel one's way. 480
  MEPH. [aside]. I'm weary of the dry pedantic tone,

And must again the genuine devil play. [Aloud.]
Of medicine the spirit's caught with ease,
The great and little world you study through,
That things may then their course pursue, 485
As heaven may please.
In vain abroad you range through science' ample space,
Each man learns only that which learn he can;
Who knows the moment to embrace,
He is your proper man. 490
In person you are tolerably made,
Nor in assurance will you be deficient:
Self-confidence acquire, be not afraid,
Others will then esteem you a proficient.
Learn chiefly with the sex to deal! 495
Their thousand ahs and ohs,
These the sage doctor knows,
He only from one point can heal.
Assume a decent tone of courteous ease,
You have them then to humor as you please. 500
First a diploma must belief infuse,
That you in your profession take the lead:
You then at once those easy freedoms use
For which another many a year must plead;
Learn how to feel with nice address 505
The dainty wrist;—and how to press,
With ardent furtive glance, the slender waist,
To feel how tightly it is laced.
  STUD. There is some sense in that! one sees the how and why.
  MEPH. Gray is, young friend, all theory: 510
And green of life the golden tree.
  STUD. I swear it seemeth like a dream to me.
May I some future time repeat my visit,
To hear on what your wisdom grounds your views?
  MEPH. Command my humble service when you choose. 515
  STUD. Ere I retire, one boon I must solicit:
Here is my album, do not, Sir. deny
This token of your favor!
  MEPH.   Willingly!

He writes and returns the book.

STUD. [reads]. ERITIS SICUT DEUS, SCIENTES BONUM ET MALUM.[1]

He reverently closes the book and retires.

MEPH. Let but this ancient proverb be your rule, 520
My cousin follow still, the wily snake,
And with your likeness to the gods, poor fool,

[1] Ye shall be as gods, knowing good and evil (*Genesis* 3:5).

Ere long be sure your poor sick heart will quake!
FAUST [*enters*]. Whither away?
MEPH. 'Tis thine our course to steer.   525
The little world, and then the great we'll view.
With what delight, what profit too,
Thou'lt revel through thy gay career!
    FAUST. Despite my length of beard I need
The easy manners that insure success;   530
Th' attempt I fear can ne'er succeed;
To mingle in the world I want address;
I still have an embarrass'd air, and then
I feel myself so small with other men.
    MEPH. Time, my good friend, will all that's
        needful give;   535
Be only self-possessed, and thou hast learn'd to
    live.
    FAUST. But how are we to start, I pray?
Steeds, servants, carriage, where are they?
    MEPH. We've but to spread this mantle wide,
'Twill serve whereon through air to ride,   540
No heavy baggage need you take,
When we our bold excursion make,
A little gas, which I will soon prepare,
Lifts us from earth; aloft through air,
Light laden, we shall swiftly steer;—   545
I wish you joy of your new life-career.

A STREET

FAUST   MARGARET *passing by*

    FAUST. Fair lady, may I thus make free
To offer you my arm and company?
    MARG. I am no lady, am not fair,
Can without escort home repair.   550
            [*She disengages herself and exit.*
    FAUST. By heaven! This girl is fair indeed!
No form like hers can I recall.
Virtue she hath, and modest heed,
Is piquant too, and sharp withal.
Her cheek's soft light, her rosy lips,   555
No length of time will e'er eclipse!
Her downward glance in passing by,
Deep in my heart is stamp'd for aye;
How curt and sharp her answer too,
To ecstasy the feeling grew!   560

MEPHISTOPHELES *enters.*

    FAUST. This girl must win for me! Dost hear?
    MEPH. Which?
    FAUST. She who but now passed.
    MEPH.   What! She?
She from confession cometh here.

From every sin absolved and free;   565
I crept near the confessor's chair.
All innocence her virgin soul,
For next to nothing went she there;
O'er such as she I've no control!
    FAUST. She's past fourteen.
    MEPH.   You really talk   570
Like any gay Lothario,
Who every floweret from its stalk
Would pluck, and deems nor grace, nor truth,
Secure against his arts, forsooth!
This ne'er the less won't always do.   575
    FAUST. Sir Moralizer, prithee, pause;
Nor plague me with your tiresome laws!
To cut the matter short, my friend,
She must this very night be mine,—
And if to help me you decline,   580
Midnight shall see our compact end.
    MEPH. What may occur just bear in mind!
A fortnight's space, at least, I need,
A fit occasion but to find.
    FAUST. With but seven hours I could succeed;
Nor should I want the devil's wile,   586
So young a creature to beguile.
    MEPH. Like any Frenchman now you speak,
But do not fret, I pray; why seek
To hurry to enjoyment straight?   590
The pleasure is not half so great,
As when at first, around, above,
With all the fooleries of love,
The puppet you can knead and mold
As in Italian story oft is told.   595
    FAUST. No such incentives do I need.
    MEPH. But now, without offense or jest!
You cannot quickly, I protest,
In winning this sweet child succeed.
By storm we cannot take the fort,   600
To stratagem we must resort.
    FAUST. Conduct me to her place of rest!
Some token of the angel bring!
A kerchief from her snowy breast,
A garter bring me,—any thing!   605
    MEPH. That I my anxious zeal may prove,
Your pangs to soothe and aid your love,
A single moment will we not delay,
Will lead you to her room this very day.
    FAUST. And shall I see her?—Have her?
    MEPH.   No!   610
She to a neighbor's house will go;
But in her atmosphere alone,
The tedious hours meanwhile you may employ,
In blissful dreams of future joy.
    FAUST. Can we go now?

MEPH.   'Tis yet too soon. 615
FAUST. Some present for my love procure! [*Exit.*
MEPH. Presents so soon! 'tis well! success is sure!
Full many a goodly place I know,
And treasures buried long ago;   619
I must a bit o'erlook them now.   [*Exit.*

EVENING

A small and neat room.

MARG. [*braiding and binding up her hair*]. I
    would give something now to know,
Who yonder gentleman could be!
He had a gallant air, I trow,
And doubtless was of high degree:
That written on his brow was seen—   625
Nor else would he so bold have been.   [*Exit.*
MEPH. Come in! tread softly! be discreet!
FAUST [*after a pause*]. Begone and leave me, I
    entreat!
MEPH. [*looking round*]. Not every maiden is so
    neat.   [*Exit.*
FAUST [*gazing round*]. Welcome sweet twilight,
    calm and blest,   630
That in this hallow'd precinct reigns!
Fond yearning love, inspire my breast,
Feeding on hope's sweet dew thy blissful pains!
What stillness here environs me!
Content and order brood around.   635
What fullness in this poverty!
In this small cell what bliss profound!

*He throws himself on the leather arm-chair beside
the bed.*

Receive me thou, who hast in thine embrace,
Welcom'd in joy and grief the ages flown!
How oft the children of a by-gone race   640
Have cluster'd round this patriarchal throne!
Haply she, also, whom I hold so dear,
For Christmas gift, with grateful joy possess'd,
Hath with the full round cheek of childhood, here,
Her grandsire's wither'd hand devoutly press'd.
Maiden! I feel thy spirit haunt the place, 646
Breathing of order and abounding grace.
As with a mother's voice it prompteth thee,
The pure white cover o'er the board to spread,
To strew the crisping sand beneath thy tread. 650
Dear hand! so godlike in its ministry!
The hut becomes a paradise through thee!
And here— [*He raises the bed-curtain.*]
How thrills my pulse with strange delight!
Here could I linger hours untold;   655

Thou, Nature, didst in vision bright,
The embryo angel here unfold.
Here lay the child, her bosom warm
With life; while steeped in slumber's dew,
To perfect grace, her godlike form,   660
With pure and hallow'd weavings grew!
And thou! ah here what seekest thou?
How quails mine inmost being now!
What wouldst thou here? what makes thy heart so
    sore?
Unhappy Faust! I know thee now no more.   665
Do I a magic atmosphere inhale?
Erewhile, my passion would not brook delay!
Now in a pure love-dream I melt away.
Are we the sport of every passing gale?
Should she return and enter now,   670
How wouldst thou rue thy guilty flame!
Proud vaunter—thou wouldst hide thy brow,—
And at her feet sink down with shame.
MEPH. Quick! quick! below I see her there.
FAUST. Away! I will return no more!   675
MEPH. Here is a casket, with a store
Of jewels, which I got elsewhere.
Just lay it in the press; make haste!
I swear to you, 'twill turn her brain;
Therein some trifles I have placed,   680
Wherewith another to obtain.
But child is child, and play is play.
FAUST. I know not—shall I?
MEPH.   Do you ask?
Perchance you would retain the treasure?
If such your wish, why then, I say,   685
Henceforth absolve me from my task,
Nor longer waste your hours of leisure.
I trust you're not by avarice led!
I rub my hands, I scratch my head,—

*He places the casket in the press and closes the
lock.*

Now quick! Away!   690
That soon the sweet young creature may
The wish and purpose of your heart obey;
Yet stand you there
As would you to the lecture-room repair,
As if before you stood,   695
Arrayed in flesh and blood,
Physics and metaphysics weird and gray!—
Away!   [*Exeunt.*

MARGARET *enters with a lamp.*

MARG. Here 'tis so close, so sultry now,

She opens the window.

Yet out of doors 'tis not so warm. 700
I feel so strange, I know not how—
I wish my mother would come home.
Through me there runs a shuddering—
I'm but a foolish timid thing!

While undressing herself she begins to sing.

There was a king in Thule, 705
True even to the grave;
To whom his dying mistress
A golden beaker gave.

At every feast he drained it,
Naught was to him so dear, 710
And often as he drained it,
Gush'd from his eyes the tear.

When death came, unrepining
His cities o'er he told;
All to his heir resigning, 715
Except his cup of gold.

With many a knightly vassal
At a royal feast sat he,
In yon proud hall ancestral,
In his castle o'er the sea. 720

Up stood the jovial monarch,
And quaff'd his last life's glow,
Then hurled the hallow'd goblet
Into the flood below.

He saw it splashing, drinking, 725
And plunging in the sea;
His eyes meanwhile were sinking,
And never again drank he.

*She opens the press to put away her clothes, and
perceives the casket.*

How comes this lovely casket here? The press
I locked, of that I'm confident. 730
'Tis very wonderful! What's in it I can't guess;
Perhaps 'twas brought by someone in distress,
And left in pledge for loan my mother lent.
Here by a ribbon hangs a little key!
I have a mind to open it and see! 735
Heavens! only look! what have we here!
In all my days ne'er saw I such a sight!
Jewels! which any noble dame might wear,
For some high pageant richly dight!
This chain—how would it look on me! 740
These splendid gems, whose may they be?

She puts them on and steps before the glass.

Were but the ear-rings only mine!
Thus one has quite another air.
What boots it to be young and fair?
It doubtless may be very fine; 745
But then, alas, none cares for you,
And praise sounds half like pity too.

Gold all doth lure,
Gold doth secure
All things. Alas, we poor! 750

PROMENADE

FAUST *walking thoughtfully up and down. To him*
MEPHISTOPHELES:

MEPH. By all rejected love! By hellish fire I
curse,
Would I knew aught to make my imprecation
worse!
FAUST. What aileth thee? what chafes thee now
so sore?
A face like that I never saw before!
MEPH. I'd yield me to the devil instantly, 755
Did it not happen that myself am he!
FAUST. There must be some disorder in thy wit!
To rave thus like a madman, is it fit?
MEPH. Think! only think! The gems for
Gretchen brought,
Them hath a priest now made his own!— 760
A glimpse of them the mother caught,
And 'gan with secret fear to groan.
The woman's scent is keen enough;
Doth ever in the prayer-book snuff;
Smells every article to ascertain 765
Whether the thing is holy or profane,
And scented in the jewels rare,
That there was not much blessing there.
"My child," she cries, "ill-gotten good
Ensnares the soul, consumes the blood; 770
With them we'll deck our Lady's shrine,
She'll cheer our souls with bread divine!"
At this poor Gretchen 'gan to pout;
'Tis a gift-horse, at least, she thought,
And sure, he godless cannot be, 775
Who brought them here so cleverly.
Straight for a priest the mother sent,
Who, when he understood the jest,
With what he saw was well content.
"This shows a pious mind!" Quoth he: 780
"Self-conquest is true victory.
The Church hath a good stomach, she, with zest,
Whole countries hath swallow'd down,
And never yet a surfeit known.

The Church alone, be it confessed,   785
Daughters, can ill-got wealth digest."
  FAUST. It is a general custom, too,
Practiced alike by king and Jew.
  MEPH. With that, clasp, chain, and ring, he
    swept
As they were mushrooms; and the casket,   790
Without one word of thanks, he kept,
As if of nuts it were a basket.
Promised reward in heaven, then forth he hied—
And greatly they were edified.
  FAUST. And Gretchen!
  MEPH.   In unquiet mood   795
Knows neither what she would or should;
The trinkets night and day thinks o'er,
On him who brought them, dwells still more.
  FAUST. The darling's sorrow grieves me, bring
Another set without delay!   800
The first, methinks, was no great thing.
  MEPH. All's to my gentleman child's play!
  FAUST. Plan all things to achieve my end!
Engage the attention of her friend!
No milk-and-water devil be,   805
And bring fresh jewels instantly!
  MEPH. Aye, sir! Most gladly I'll obey.
                  [FAUST exit.
  MEPH. Your doting love-sick fool, with ease,
Merely his lady-love to please,   809
Sun, moon, and stars in sport would puff away.
                  [Exit.

THE NEIGHBOR'S HOUSE

  MARTH. [alone]. God pardon my dear husband,
    he
Doth not in truth act well by me!
Forth in the world abroad to roam,
And leave me on the straw at home.
And yet his will I ne'er did thwart,   815
God knows, I lov'd him from my heart. [She
    weeps.]
Perchance he's dead!—oh wretched state!—
Had I but a certificate!

MARGARET enters.

  MARG. Dame Martha!
  MARTH.   Gretchen?
  MARG.   Only think!
My knees beneath me well-nigh sink!   820
Within my press I've found today,
Another case, of ebony.
And things—magnificent they are,
More costly than the first, by far.

  MARTH. You must not name it to your mother;
It would to shrift, just like the other.   826
  MARG. Nay look at them! now only see!
  MARTH. [dresses her up]. Thou happy creature!
  MARG.   Woe is me!
Them in the street I cannot wear,
Or in the church, or any where.   830
  MARTH. Come often over here to me,
The gems put on quite privately;
And then before the mirror walk an hour or so,
Thus we shall have our pleasure too.
Then suitable occasions we must seize,   835
As at a feast, to show them by degrees:
A chain at first, pearl ear-drops then,—your
    mother
Won't see them, or we'll coin some tale or other.
  MARG. But, who, I wonder, could the caskets
    bring?   839
I fear there's something wrong about the thing!
    [A knock.]
Good heavens! can that my mother be?
  MARTH. [peering through the blind]. 'Tis a
    strange gentleman, I see.
Come in!

MEPHISTOPHELES enters.

  MEPH. I've ventur'd to intrude today.
Ladies, excuse the liberty, I pray.   845

He steps back respectfully before MARGARET.

After dame Martha Schwerdtlein I inquire!
  MARTH. 'Tis I. Pray what have you to say to me?
  MEPH. [aside to her]. I know you now,—and
    therefore will retire;
At present you've distinguished company.
Pardon the freedom, Madam, with your leave,   850
I will make free to call again at eve.
  MARTH. [aloud]. Why, child, of all strange
    notions, he
For some grand lady taketh thee!
  MARG. I am, in truth, of humble blood—
The gentleman is far too good—   855
Nor gems nor trinkets are my own.
  MEPH. Oh 'tis not the mere ornaments alone;
Her glance and mien far more betray.
Rejoiced I am that I may stay.   859
  MARTH. Your business, Sir? I long to know—
  MEPH. Would I could happier tidings show!
I trust mine errand you'll not let me rue;
Your husband's dead, and greeteth you.
  MARTH. Is dead? True heart! Oh misery!
My husband dead! Oh, I shall die!   865
  MARG. Alas! good Martha! don't despair!

MEPH. Now listen to the sad affair!
MARG. I for this cause should fear to love.
The loss my certain death would prove.   869
MEPH. Joy still must sorrow, sorrow joy attend.
MARTH. Proceed, and tell the story of his end!
MEPH. At Padua, in St. Anthony's,
In holy ground his body lies;
Quiet and cool his place of rest,
With pious ceremonials blest.   875
MARTH. And had you naught besides to bring?
MEPH. Oh yes! one grave and solemn prayer;
Let them for him three hundred masses sing!
But in my pockets, I have nothing there.
MARTH. No trinket! no love-token did he send!
What every journeyman safe in his pouch will
    hoard   881
There for remembrance fondly stored,
And rather hungers, rather begs than spend!
MEPH. Madam, in truth, it grieves me sore,
But he his gold not lavishly hath spent.   885
His failings too he deeply did repent,
Aye! and his evil plight bewail'd still more.
    MARG. Alas! That men should thus be doomed
        to woe!
I for his soul will many a requiem pray.
    MEPH. A husband you deserve this very day;   890
A child so worthy to be loved.
    MARG.   Ah no,
That time hath not yet come for me.
    MEPH. If not a spouse, a gallant let it be.
Among heaven's choicest gifts, I place,
So sweet a darling to embrace.   895
    MARG. Our land doth no such usage know.
    MEPH. Usage or not, it happens so.
    MARTH. Go on, I pray!
    MEPH.   I stood by his bedside.
Something less foul it was than dung;
'Twas straw half rotten; yet, he as a Christian
    died.   900
And sorely hath remorse his conscience wrung.
"Wretch that I was," quoth he, with parting
    breath,
"So to forsake my business and my wife!
Ah! the remembrance is my death.
Could I but have her pardon in this life!"—   905
    MARTH. [weeping]. Dear soul! I've long forgiven
        him, indeed!
    MEPH. "Though she, God knows, was more to
        blame than I."
    MARTH. He lied! What, on the brink of death to
        lie!
    MEPH. If I am skill'd the countenance to read,
He doubtless fabled as he parted hence.—   910

"No time had I to gape, or take my ease," he said,
"First to get children, and then get them bread;
And bread, too, in the very widest sense;
Nor could I eat in peace even my proper share."
    MARTH. What, all my truth, my love forgotten
        quite?   915
My weary drudgery by day and night!
    MEPH. Not so! He thought of you with tender
        care.
Quoth he: "Heaven knows how fervently I prayed,
For wife and children when from Malta bound;—
The prayer hath heaven with favor crowned;   920
We took a Turkish vessel which conveyed
Rich store of treasure for the Sultan's court;
Its own reward our gallant action brought;
The captur'd prize was shared among the crew,
And of the treasure I received my due."   925
    MARTH. How? Where? The treasure hath he
        buried, pray?
    MEPH. Where the four winds have blown it,
        who can say?
In Naples as he stroll'd, a stranger there,—
A comely maid took pity on my friend;
And gave such tokens of her love and care,   930
That he retained them to his blessed end.
    MARTH. Scoundrel! to rob his children of their
        bread!
And all this misery, this bitter need,
Could not his course of recklessness impede!
    MEPH. Well, he hath paid the forfeit, and is
        dead.   935
Now were I in your place, my counsel hear;
My weeds I'd wear for one chaste year,
And for another love meanwhile would look out.
    MARTH. Alas, I might search far and near,
Not quickly should I find another like my first!
There could not be a fonder fool than mine,   941
Only he loved too well abroad to roam;
Loved foreign women too, and foreign wine,
And loved besides the dice accurs'd.
    MEPH. All had gone swimmingly, no doubt,   945
Had he but given you at home,
On his side, just as wide a range.
Upon such terms, to you I swear,
Myself with you would gladly rings exchange!   949
    MARTH. The gentleman is surely pleas'd to jest!
    MEPH. [aside]. Now to be off in time, were best!
She'd make the very devil marry her.
[To MARGARET.] How fares it with your heart?
    MARG. How mean you, sir?
    MEPH. [aside]. The sweet young innocent!
                    [Aloud.] Ladies, farewell!
    MARG. Farewell!   956

MARTH. But ere you leave us, quickly tell!
I from a witness fain had heard,
Where, how, and when my husband died and was
    interr'd.
To forms I've always been attached indeed,   960
His death I fain would in the journals read.
    MEPH. Aye, madam, what two witnesses declare
Is held as valid everywhere;
A gallant friend I have, not far from here,
Who will for you before the judge appear.   965
I'll bring him straight.
    MARTH.   I pray you do!
    MEPH. And this young lady, we shall find her
    too?
A noble youth, far traveled, he
Shows to the sex all courtesy.
    MARG. I in his presence needs must blush for
    shame.   970
    MEPH. Not in the presence of a crowned king!
    MARTH. The garden, then, behind my house,
    we'll name,
There we'll await you both this evening.

A STREET

FAUST   MEPHISTOPHELES

    FAUST. How is it now? How speeds it? Is't in
    train?
    MEPH. Bravo! I find you all aflame!   975
Gretchen full soon your own you'll name.
This eve, at neighbor Martha's, her you'll meet
    again;
The woman seems expressly made
To drive the pimp and gypsy's trade.
    FAUST. Good.   980
    MEPH. But from us she something would re-
    quest.
    FAUST. A favor claims return as this world goes.
    MEPH. We have on oath but duly to attest,
That her dead husband's limbs, outstretch'd, repose
In holy ground at Padua.
    FAUST.   Sage indeed!   985
So I suppose we straight must journey there!
    MEPH. *Sancta simplicitas!* For that no need!
Without much knowledge we have but to swear.
    FAUST. If you have nothing better to suggest,
Against your plan I must at once protest.   990
    MEPH. Oh, holy man! methinks I have you there!
In all your life say, have you ne'er
False witness borne, until this hour?
Have you of God, the world, and all it doth con-
    tain,

Of man, and that which worketh in his heart and
    brain,   995
Not definitions given, in words of weight and
    power,
With front unblushing, and a dauntless breast?
Yet, if into the depth of things you go,
Touching these matters, it must be confess'd,
As much as of Herr Schwerdtlein's death you
    know!   1000
    FAUST. Thou art and dost remain liar and sophist
    too.
    MEPH. Aye, if one did not take a somewhat
    deeper view!
Tomorrow, in all honor, thou
Poor Gretchen wilt befool, and vow
Thy soul's deep love, in lover's fashion.   1005
    FAUST. And from my heart.
    MEPH.   All good and fair!
Then deathless constancy thou'lt swear;
Speak of one all o'ermastering passion,—
Will that too issue from the heart?
    FAUST.   Forbear!
When passion sways me, and I seek to frame   1010
Fit utterance for feeling, deep, intense,
And for my frenzy finding no fit name,
Sweep round the ample world with every sense,
Grasp at the loftiest words to speak my flame,
And call the glow, wherewith I burn,   1015
Quenchless, eternal, yea, eterne—
Is that of sophistry a devilish play?
    MEPH. Yet am I right!
    FAUST. Mark this, my friend,
And spare my lungs; who would the right main-
    tain,   1020
And hath a tongue wherewith his point to gain,
Will gain it in the end.
But come, of gossip I am weary quite;
Because I've no resource, thou'rt in the right.

A GARDEN

MARGARET *on* FAUST's *arm.* MARTHA *with* MEPHIS-
    TOPHELES *walking up and down.*

    MARG. I feel it, you but spare my ignorance,   1025
The gentleman to shame me stoops thus low.
A traveler from complaisance,
Still makes the best of things; I know
Too well, my humble prattle never can
Have power to entertain so wise a man.   1030
    FAUST. One glance, one word from thee doth
    charm me more,
Than the world's wisdom or the sage's lore.

    He kisses her hand.

MARG. Nay; trouble not yourself! A hand so coarse,
So rude as mine, how can you kiss!
What constant work at home must I not do perforce!   1035
My mother too exacting is.   [*They pass on.*
   MARTH. Thus, sir, unceasing travel is your lot?
   MEPH. Traffic and duty urge us! With what pain
Are we compelled to leave full many a spot,
Where yet we dare not once remain!   1040
   MARTH. In youth's wild years, with vigor crown'd,
'Tis not amiss thus through the world to sweep;
But ah, the evil days come round!
And to a lonely grave as bachelor to creep,
A pleasant thing has no one found.   1045
   MEPH. The prospect fills me with dismay.
   MARTH. Therefore in time, dear sir, reflect, I pray.   [*They pass on.*
   MARG. Aye, out of sight, is out of mind!
Politeness easy is to you;
Friends everywhere, and not a few,   1050
Wiser than I am, you will find.
   FAUST. O dearest, trust me, what doth pass for sense
Full oft is self-conceit and blindness!
   MARG.   How?
   FAUST. Simplicity and holy innocence,—
When will ye learn your hallow'd worth to know!
Ah, when will meekness and humility,   1056
Kind and all-bounteous nature's loftiest dower—
   MARG. Only one little moment think of me!
To think of you I shall have many an hour.
   FAUST. You are perhaps much alone?   1060
   MARG. Yes, small our household is, I own,
Yet must I see to it. No maid we keep,
And I must cook, sew, knit, and sweep,
Still early on my feet and late;
My mother is in all things, great and small,   1065
So accurate!
Not that for thrift there is such pressing need;
Than others we might make more show indeed;
My father left behind a small estate,
A house and garden near the city-wall.   1070
But fairly quiet now my days, I own;
As soldier is my brother gone;
My little sister's dead; the babe to rear
Occasion'd me some care and fond annoy;
But I would go through all again with joy,   1075
The darling was to me so dear.
   FAUST. An angel, sweet, if it resembled thee!
   MARG. I reared it up, and it grew fond of me.

After my father's death it saw the day;
We gave my mother up for lost, she lay   1080
In such a wretched plight, and then at length
So very slowly she regain'd her strength.
Weak as she was, 'twas vain for her to try
Herself to suckle the poor babe, so I
Reared it on milk and water all alone;   1085
And thus the child became as 'twere my own;
Within my arms it stretched itself and grew,
And smiling, nestled in my bosom too.
   FAUST. Doubtless the purest happiness was thine.
   MARG. But many weary hours, in sooth, were also mine.   1090
At night its little cradle stood
Close to my bed; so was I wide awake
If it but stirred;
One while I was obliged to give it food,
Or to my arms the darling take;   1095
From bed full oft must rise, whene'er its cry I heard,
And, dancing it, must pace the chamber to and fro;
Stand at the wash-tub early; forthwith go
To market, and then mind the cooking too—
Tomorrow like today, the whole year through.
Ah, sir, thus living, it must be confess'd   1101
One's spirits are not always of the best;
Yet it a relish gives to food and rest.
                     [*They pass on.*
   MARTH. Poor women! we are badly off, I own;
A bachelor's conversion's hard, indeed!   1105
   MEPH. Madam, with one like you it rests alone,
To tutor me a better course to lead.
   MARTH. Speak frankly, sir, none is there you have met?
Has your heart ne'er attach'd itself as yet?
   MEPH. One's own fireside and a good wife are gold   1110
And pearls of price, so says the proverb old.
   MARTH. I mean, has passion never stirred your breast?
   MEPH. I've everywhere been well received, I own.
   MARTH. Yet hath your heart no earnest preference known?
   MEPH. With ladies one should ne'er presume to jest.   1115
   MARTH. Ah! you mistake!
   MEPH. I'm sorry I'm so blind!
But this I know—that you are very kind.
                     [*They pass on.*
   FAUST. Me, little angel, didst thou recognize,
When in the garden first I came?   1120

Marg. Did you not see it? I cast down my eyes.

Faust. Thou dost forgive my boldness, dost not blame

The liberty I took that day,

When thou from church didst lately wend thy way?

Marg. I was confused. So had it never been; 1126
No one of me could any evil say.

Alas, thought I, he doubtless in thy mien,

Something unmaidenly or bold hath seen?

It seemed as if it struck him suddenly,

Here's just a girl with whom one may make free!

Yet I must own that then I scarcely knew 1131
What in your favor here began at once to plead;

Yet I was angry with myself indeed,

That I more angry could not feel with you.

 Faust. Sweet love. 1135

 Marg. Just wait awhile!

She gathers a star-flower and plucks off the leaves one after another.

Faust. A nosegay may that be?

Marg. No! It is but a game.

Faust. How?

Marg. Go, you'll laugh at me! 1140

She plucks off the leaves and murmurs to herself.

Faust. What murmurest thou?

Marg. [*half aloud*]. He loves me,—loves me not.

Faust. Sweet angel, with thy face of heavenly bliss!

Marg. [*continues*]. He loves me—not—he loves me—not— [*Plucking off the last leaf with fond joy.*] He loves me!

Faust.   Yes!

And this flower-language, darling, let it be, 1145
A heavenly oracle! He loveth thee!

Know'st thou the meaning of, He loveth thee?

He seizes both her hands.

Marg. I tremble so!

Faust. Nay! do not tremble, love!

Let this hand-pressure, let this glance reveal 1150
Feelings, all power of speech above;

To give oneself up wholly and to feel

A joy that must eternal prove!

Eternal!—Yes, its end would be despair.

No end!—It cannot end! 1155

Margaret presses his hand, extricates herself, and runs away. He stands a moment in thought, and then follows her.

Marth. [*approaching*]. Night's closing.

Meph. Yes, we'll presently away.

Marth. I would entreat you longer yet to stay;

But 'tis a wicked place, just here about;

It is as if the folk had nothing else to do, 1160
Nothing to think of too,

But gaping watch their neighbors, who goes in and out;

And scandal's busy still, do whatso'er one may.

And our young couple?

 Meph.   They have flown up there.

The wanton butterflies!

 Marth.   He seems to take to her.

Meph. And she to him. 'Tis of the world the way! 1166

A SUMMER-HOUSE

Margaret *runs in, hides behind the door, holds the tip of her finger to her lip, and peeps through the crevice.*

Marg. He comes!

Faust.   Ah, little rogue, so thou
Think'st to provoke me! I have caught thee now!

He kisses her.

Marg. [*embracing him, and returning the kiss*]. Dearest of men! I love thee from my heart!

Mephistopheles *knocks*.

Faust [*stamping*]. Who's there?

Meph.   A friend!

Faust.   A brute!

Meph.   'Tis time to part.

Marth. [*comes*]. Aye, it is late, good sir. 1171

Faust. Mayn't I attend you, then?

Marg. Oh no—my mother would—adieu, adieu!

Faust. And must I really then take leave of you? Farewell! 1175

Marth. Good-by!

Marg. Ere long to meet again!

    [*Exeunt* Faust *and* Mephistopheles.

Marg. Good heavens! How all things far and near

Must fill his mind,—a man like this!

Abash'd before him I appear, 1180
And say to all things only, yes.

Poor simple child, I cannot see,

What 'tis that he can find in me.   [*Exit.*

FOREST AND CAVERN

Faust [*alone*]. Spirit sublime! Thou gav'st me, gav'st me all

For which I pray'd! Not vainly hast thou turn'd

To me thy countenance in flaming fire: 1186

Gavest me glorious nature for my realm,
And also power to feel her and enjoy;
Not merely with a cold and wondering glance,
Thou dost permit me in her depths profound,   1190
As in the bosom of a friend to gaze.
Before me thou dost lead her living tribes,
And dost in silent grove, in air and stream
Teach me to know my kindred. And when roars
The howling storm-blast through the groaning
    wood,   1195
Wrenching the giant pine, which in its fall
Crashing sweeps down its neighbor trunks and
    boughs,
While hollow thunder from the hill resounds;
Then thou dost lead me to some shelter'd cave,
Dost there reveal me to myself, and show   1200
Of my own bosom the mysterious depths.
And when with soothing beam, the moon's pale
    orb
Full in my view climbs up the pathless sky,
From crag and dewy grove, the silvery forms
Of by-gone ages hover, and assuage   1205
The joy austere of contemplative thought.

Oh, that naught perfect is assign'd to man,
I feel, alas! With this exalted joy,
Which lifts me near and nearer to the gods,
Thou gav'st me this companion, unto whom   1210
I needs must cling, though cold and insolent,
He still degrades me to myself, and turns
Thy glorious gifts to nothing, with a breath.
He in my bosom with malicious zeal
For that fair image fans a raging fire;   1215
From craving to enjoyment thus I reel,
And in enjoyment languish for desire.

MEPHISTOPHELES *enters.*

MEPH. Of this lone life have you not had your
    fill?
How for so long can it have charms for you?
'Tis well enough to try it if you will;   1220
But then away again to something new!
    FAUST. Would you could better occupy your
    leisure,
Than in disturbing thus my hours of joy.
    MEPH. Well! Well! I'll leave you to yourself
    with pleasure,
A serious tone you hardly dare employ.   1225
To part from one so crazy, harsh, and cross,
Were not in truth a grievous loss.
The live-long day, for you I toil and fret;
Ne'er from his worship's face a hint I get,
What pleases him, or what to let alone.   1230

FAUST. Aye truly! that is just the proper tone!
He wearies me, and would with thanks be paid!
    MEPH. Poor Son of Earth, without my aid,
How would thy weary days have flown?
Thee of thy foolish whims I've cured,   1235
Thy vain imaginations banished.
And but for me, be well assured,
Thou from this sphere must soon have vanished.
In rocky hollows and in caverns drear,
Why like an owl sit moping here?   1240
Wherefore from dripping stones and moss with
    ooze embued,
Dost suck, like any toad, thy food?
A rare, sweet pastime. Verily!
The doctor cleaveth still to thee.
    FAUST. Dost comprehend what bliss without
    alloy   1245
From this wild wand'ring in the desert springs?—
Couldst thou but guess the new life-power it
    brings,
Thou wouldst be fiend enough to envy me my joy.
    MEPH. What super-earthly ecstasy! at night,
To lie in darkness on the dewy height,   1250
Embracing heaven and earth in rapture high,
The soul dilating to a deity;
With prescient yearnings pierce the core of earth,
Feel in your laboring breast the six-days' birth,
Enjoy, in proud delight what no one knows,   1255
While your love-rapture o'er creation flows,—
The earthly lost in beatific vision,
And then the lofty intuition— [*With a gesture.*]
I need not tell you how—to close!
    FAUST. Fie on you!   1260
    MEPH. This displeases you? "For shame!"
You are forsooth entitled to exclaim;
We to chaste ears it seems must not pronounce
What, nathless, the chaste heart cannot renounce.
Well, to be brief, the joy as fit occasions rise,   1265
I grudge you not, of specious lies.
But long this mood thou'lt not retain.
Already thou'rt again outworn,
And should this last, thou wilt be torn
By frenzy or remorse and pain.   1270
Enough of this! Thy true love dwells apart,
And all to her seems flat and tame;
Alone thine image fills her heart,
She loves thee with an all-devouring flame.   1274
First came thy passion with o'erpowering rush,
Like mountain torrent, swollen by the melted
    snow;
Full in her heart didst pour the sudden gush,
Now has thy brooklet ceased to flow.
Instead of sitting throned midst forests wild,

It would become so great a lord   1286
To comfort the enamor'd child,
And the young monkey for her love reward.
To her the hours seem miserably long;
She from the window sees the clouds float by
As o'er the lofty city-walls they fly.   1285
"If I a birdie were!" so runs her song,
Half through the night and all day long.
Cheerful sometimes, more oft at heart full sore;
Fairly outwept seem now her tears,
Anon she tranquil is, or so appears,   1290
And love-sick evermore.

   FAUST. Snake! Serpent vile!

   MEPH. [aside]. Good! If I catch thee with my
     guile!

   FAUST. Vile reprobate! go get thee hence;
Forbear the lovely girl to name!   1295
Nor in my half-distracted sense,
Kindle anew the smoldering flame!

   MEPH. What wouldest thou! She thinks you've
     taken flight;
It seems, she's partly in the right.

   FAUST. I'm near her still—and should I distant
     rove,   1300
Her I can ne'er forget, ne'er lose her love;
And all things touch'd by those sweet lips of hers,
Even the very Host, my envy stirs.

   MEPH. 'Tis well! I oft have envied you indeed,
The twin-pair that among the roses feed.   1305

   FAUST. Pander, avaunt!

   MEPH. Go to! I laugh, the while you rail.
The power which fashion'd youth and maid,
Well understood the noble trade;
So neither shall occasion fail.   1310
But hence!—A mighty grief I trow!
Unto thy lov'd one's chamber thou
And not to death shouldst go.

   FAUST. What is to me heaven's joy within her
     arms?
What though my life her bosom warms!—   1315
Do I not ever feel her woe?
The outcast am I not, unhoused, unblest,
Inhuman monster, without aim or rest,
Who, like the greedy surge, from rock to rock,
Sweeps down the dread abyss with desperate
     shock?   1320
While she, within her lowly cot, which graced
The Alpine slope, beside the waters wild,
Her homely cares in that small world embraced,
Secluded lived, a simple artless child.
Was't not enough, in thy delirious whirl   1325
To blast the steadfast rocks;
Her, and her peace as well,

Must I, God-hated one, to ruin hurl!
Dost claim this holocaust, remorseless Hell!
Fiend, help me to cut short the hours of dread!
Let what must happen, happen speedily!   1331
Her direful doom fall crushing on my head,
And into ruin let her plunge with me!

   MEPH. Why how again it seethes and glows!
Away, thou fool! Her torment ease!   1335
When such a head no issue sees,
It pictures straight the final close.
Long life to him who boldly dares!
A devil's pluck thou'rt wont to show;
As for a devil who despairs,   1340
Nothing I find so mawkish here below.

MARGARET'S ROOM

   MARG. [alone at her spinning wheel].

     My peace is gone,
       My heart is sore,
     I find it never,
       And nevermore!   1345

     Where him I have not,
       Is the grave; and all
     The world to me
       Is turned to gall.

     My wilder'd brain   1350
       Is overwrought;
     My feeble senses
       Are distraught.

     My peace is gone,
       My heart is sore,   1355
     I find it never,
       And nevermore!

     For him from the window
       I gaze, at home;
     For him and him only   1360
       Abroad I roam.

     His lofty step,
       His bearing high,
     The smile of his lip,
       The power of his eye,   1365

     His witching words,
       Their tones of bliss,
     His hand's fond pressure,
       And ah—his kiss!

     My peace is gone,   1370
       My heart is sore,

I find it never,
And nevermore.

My bosom aches
   To feel him near;   1375
Ah, could I clasp
   And fold him here!

Kiss him and kiss him
   Again would I,
And on his kisses   1380
   I fain would die!

MARTHA'S GARDEN

MARGARET *and* FAUST

MARG. Promise me, Henry!
FAUST.   What I can!
MARG. How thy religion fares, I fain would hear.
Thou art a good kind-hearted man,
Only that way not well-disposed, I fear.   1385
   FAUST. Forbear, my child! Thou feelest thee I
      love;
My heart, my blood, I'd give, my love to prove,
And none would of their faith or church bereave.
   MARG. That's not enough, we must ourselves
      believe!
FAUST. Must we?   1390
MARG. Ah, could I but thy soul inspire!
Thou honorest not the sacraments, alas!
   FAUST. I honor them.
MARG. But yet without desire;
'Tis long since thou hast been either to shrift or
      mass.   1395
Dost thou believe in God?
   FAUST. My darling, who dares say,
Yes, I in God believe?
Question or priest or sage, and they
Seem, in the answer you receive,   1400
To mock the questioner.
   MARG. Then thou dost not believe?
   FAUST. Sweet one! my meaning do not miscon-
      ceive!
Him who dare name?
And who proclaim,   1405
Him I believe?
Who that can feel,
His heart can steel,
To say: I believe him not?
The All-embracer,   1410
All-sustainer,
Holds and sustains he not
Thee, me, himself?

Lifts not the Heaven its dome above?
Doth not the firm-set earth beneath us lie?   1415
And beaming tenderly with looks of love,
Climb not the everlasting stars on high?
Do we not gaze into each other's eyes?
Nature's impenetrable agencies,
Are they not thronging on thy heart and brain,
Viewless, or visible to mortal ken,   1421
Around thee weaving their mysterious chain?
Fill thence thy heart, how large soe'er it be;
And in the feeling when thou utterly art blest,
Then call it, what thou wilt,—   1425
Call it Bliss! Heart! Love! God!
I have no name for it!
'Tis feeling all;
Name is but sound and smoke
Shrouding the glow of heaven.   1430
   MARG. All this is doubtless good and fair;
Almost the same the parson says,
Only in slightly different phrase.
   FAUST. Beneath Heaven's sunshine, everywhere,
This is the utterance of the human heart;   1435
Each in his language doth the like impart;
Then why not I in mine?
   MARG.   What thus I hear
Sounds plausible, yet I'm not reconciled;
There's something wrong about it; much I fear
That thou art not a Christian.
   FAUST.   My sweet child!   1440
   MARG. Alas! it long hath sorely troubled me,
To see thee in such odious company.
   FAUST. How so?
   MARG. The man who comes with thee, I hate,
Yea, in my spirit's inmost depths abhor;   1445
As his loath'd visage, in my life before,
Naught to my heart e'er gave a pang so great.
   FAUST. Him fear not, my sweet love!
   MARG. His presence chills my blood.
Towards all beside I have a kindly mood;   1450
Yet, though I yearn to gaze on thee, I feel
At sight of him strange horror o'er me steal;
That he's a villain my conviction's strong.
May Heaven forgive me, if I do him wrong!
   FAUST. Yet such strange fellows in the world
      must be!   1455
   MARG. I would not live with such an one as he.
If for a moment he but enter here,
He looks around him with a mocking sneer,
And malice ill-conceal'd;
That he with naught on earth can sympathize is
      clear;   1460
Upon his brow 'tis legibly revealed,
That to his heart no living soul is dear.

So blest I feel, within thine arms,
So warm and happy,—free from all alarms;
And still my heart doth close when he comes near.

    FAUST. Foreboding angel! check thy fear!   1466
    MARG. It so o'ermasters me, that when,
Or wheresoe'er, his step I hear,
I almost think, no more I love thee then.
Besides, when he is near, I ne'er could pray.   1470
This eats into my heart; with thee
The same, my Henry, it must be.

    FAUST. This is antipathy!
    MARG.   I must away.
    FAUST. For one brief hour then may I never rest,
And heart to heart, and soul to soul be pressed?

    MARG. Ah, if I slept alone! Tonight   1476
The bolt I fain would leave undrawn for thee;
But then my mother's sleep is light,
Were we surprised by her, ah me!
Upon the spot I should be dead.   1480

    FAUST. Dear angel! there's no cause for dread.
Here is a little phial,—if she take
Mixed in her drink three drops, 'twill steep
Her nature in a deep and soothing sleep.

    MARG. What do I not for thy dear sake!   1485
To her it will not harmful prove?

    FAUST. Should I advise it else, sweet love?
    MARG. I know not, dearest, when thy face I see,
What doth my spirit to thy will constrain;
Already I have done so much for thee,   1490
That scarcely more to do doth now remain. [*Exit.*

MEPHISTOPHELES *enters.*

    MEPH. The monkey! Is she gone?
    FAUST. Again hast played the spy?
    MEPH. Of all that pass'd I'm well apprized,
I heard the doctor catechized,   1495
And trust he'll profit much thereby!
Fain would the girls inquire indeed
Touching their lover's faith and creed,
And whether pious in the good old way;   1499
They think, if pliant there, us too he will obey.

    FAUST. Thou monster, dost not see that this
Pure soul, possessed by ardent love,
Full of the living faith,
To her of bliss
The only pledge, must holy anguish prove,   1505
Holding the man she loves, fore-doomed to end-
    less death!

    MEPH. Most sensual, supersensualist? The while
A damsel leads thee by the nose!

    FAUST. Of filth and fire abortion vile!
    MEPH. In physiognomy strange skill she shows;
She in my presence feels she knows not how;   1511

My mask it seems a hidden sense reveals;
That I'm a genius she must needs allow,
That I'm the very devil perhaps she feels.
So then tonight—

    FAUST.   What's that to you?   1515
    MEPH. I've my amusement in it too!

AT THE WELL

MARGARET *and* BESSY, *with pitchers*

    BESSY. Of Barbara hast nothing heard?
    MARG. I rarely go from home,—no, not a word.
    BESSY. 'Tis true: Sybilla told me so today!
That comes of being proud, methinks;   1520
She played the fool at last.

    MARG.   How so?
    BESSY.   They say
That two she feedeth when she eats and drinks.
    MARG. Alas!
    BESSY. She's rightly served, in sooth.
How long she hung upon the youth!   1525
What promenades, what jaunts there were,
To dancing booth and village fair!
The first she everywhere must shine,
He always treating her to pastry and to wine.
Of her good looks she was so vain,   1530
So shameless too, that to retain
His presents, she did not disdain;
Sweet words and kisses came anon—
And then the virgin flower was gone.

    MARG. Poor thing!   1535
    BESSY. Forsooth dost pity her?
At night, when at our wheels we sat,
Abroad our mothers ne'er would let us stir.
Then with her lover she must chat,
Or on the bench, or in the dusky walk,   1540
Thinking the hours too brief for their sweet talk;
Her proud head she will have to bow,
And in white sheet do penance now!

    MARG. But he will surely marry her?
    BESSY.   Not he!
He won't be such a fool! a gallant lad   1545
Like him, can roam o'er land and sea,
Besides, he's off.

    MARG.   That is not fair!
    BESSY. If she should get him, 'twere almost as
    bad!
Her myrtle wreath the boys would tear;
And then we girls would plague her too,   1550
For we chopp'd straw before her door would
    strew!   [*Exit.*
    MARG. [*walking towards home*]. How stoutly
    once I could inveigh,

If a poor maiden went astray;
Not words enough my tongue could find,
'Gainst others' sin to speak my mind! 1555
Black as it seemed, I blacken'd it still more,
And strove to make it blacker than before.
And did myself securely bless—
Now my own trespass doth appear!
Yet ah!—what urg'd me to transgress, 1560
God knows, it was so sweet, so dear!

ZWINGER

*Enclosure between the city-wall and the gate. In
the niche of the wall a devotional image of the
Mater dolorosa, with flower-pots before it.*

MARG. [*putting fresh flowers in the pots*].
Ah, rich in sorrow, thou,
Stoop thy maternal brow,
And mark with pitying eye my misery!
The sword in thy pierced heart, 1565
Thou dost with bitter smart,
Gaze upwards on thy Son's death agony.
To the dear God on high,
Ascends thy piteous sigh,
Pleading for his and thy sore misery. 1570

Ah, who can know
The torturing woe,
The pangs that rack me to the bone?
How my poor heart, without relief,
Trembles and throbs, its yearning grief 1575
Thou knowest, thou alone!

Ah, wheresoe'er I go,
With woe, with woe, with woe,
My anguish'd breast is aching!
When all alone I creep, 1580
I weep, I weep, I weep,
Alas! my heart is breaking!
The flower-pots at my window
Were wet with tears of mine,
The while I pluck'd these blossoms, 1585
At dawn to deck thy shrine!

When early in my chamber
Shone bright the rising morn,
I sat there on my pallet,
My heart with anguish torn. 1590
Help! from disgrace and death deliver me!
Ah! rich in sorrow, thou,
Stoop thy maternal brow,
And mark with pitying eye my misery!

NIGHT

A street before Margaret's door

VALENTINE [*a soldier, Margaret's brother*].
When seated 'mong the jovial crowd, 1595
Where merry comrades boasting loud
Each named with pride his favorite lass,
And in her honor drain'd his glass;
Upon my elbows I would lean,
With easy quiet view the scene; 1600
Nor give my tongue the rein, until
Each swaggering blade had talked his fill.
Then smiling I my beard would stroke,
The while, with brimming glass, I spoke;
"Each to his taste!—but to my mind, 1605
Where in the country will you find,
A maid, as my dear Gretchen fair,
Who with my sister can compare?"
Cling! Clang! so rang the jovial sound!
Shouts of assent went circling round; 1610
Pride of her sex is she!—cried some;
Then were the noisy boasters dumb.

And now!—I could tear out my hair,
Or dash my brains out in despair!—
Me every scurvy knave may twit, 1615
With stinging jest and taunting sneer!
Like skulking debtor I must sit,
And sweat each casual word to hear!
And though I smash'd them one and all,—
Yet them I could not liars call. 1620
    Who comes this way? who's sneaking here?
    If I mistake not, two draw near.
    If he be one, have at him;—well I wot
    Alive he shall not leave this spot!

FAUST *and* MEPHISTOPHELES *enter.*

FAUST. How from yon sacristy, athwart the
    night, 1625
Its beams the ever-burning taper throws,
While ever waning, fades the glimmering light,
As gathering darkness doth around it close!
So night-like gloom doth in my bosom reign.
    MEPH. I'm like a tom-cat in a thievish vein,
That up fire-ladders tall and steep, 1631
And round the walls doth slyly creep;
Virtuous withal, I feel, with, I confess,
A touch of thievish joy and wantonness.
Thus through my limbs already burns 1635
The glorious Walpurgis night!
After tomorrow it returns,
Then why one wakes, one knows aright!

FAUST. Meanwhile, the treasure I see glimmer-
    ing there,
Will it ascend into the open air?   1640
   MEPH. Ere long thou wilt proceed with pleasure,
To raise the casket with its treasure;
I took a peep, therein are stored,
Of lion-dollars a rich hoard.
   FAUST. And not a trinket? not a ring?   1645
Wherewith my lovely girl to deck?
   MEPH. I saw among them some such thing,
A string of pearls to grace her neck.
   FAUST. 'Tis well! I'm always loath to go,
Without some gift my love to show.   1650
   MEPH. Some pleasures gratis to enjoy,
Should surely cause you no annoy.
While bright with stars the heavens appear,
I'll sing a masterpiece of art:
A moral song shall charm her ear,   1655
More surely to beguile her heart.
[Sings to the guitar.]

     Kathrina say,
     Why lingering stay
     At dawn of day
     Before your lover's door?   1660
     Maiden, beware,
     Nor enter there,
     Lest forth you fare,
     A maiden never more.

     Maiden take heed!   1665
     Reck well my rede!
     Is't done, the deed?
     Good night, you poor, poor thing!
     The spoiler's lies,
     His arts despise,   1670
     Nor yield your prize,
     Without the marriage ring!

   VAL. [steps forward]. Whom are you luring
    here? I'll give it you!
Accursed rat-catchers, your strains I'll end!
First, to the devil the guitar I'll send!   1675
Then to the devil with the singer too!
   MEPH. The poor guitar! 'tis done for now.
   VAL. Your skull shall follow next, I trow!
   MEPH. [to FAUST]. Doctor, stand fast! your
    strength collect!
Be prompt, and do as I direct.   1680
Out with your whisk! keep close, I pray,
I'll parry! do you thrust away!
   VAL. Then parry that!
   MEPH.   Why not?

   VAL.   That too!
   MEPH. With ease!
   VAL. The devil fights for you!   1685
Why how is this? my hand's already lamed!
   MEPH. [to FAUST]. Thrust home!
   VAL. [falls]. Alas!
   MEPH. There! Now the lubber's tamed!
But quick, away! We must at once take wing;
A cry of murder strikes upon the ear;   1691
With the police I know my course to steer,
But with the blood-ban 'tis another thing.
   MARTH. [at the window]. Without! without!
   MARG. [at the window]. Quick, bring a light!
   MARTH. [as above]. They rail and scuffle, scream
    and fight!   1696
   PEOPLE. One lieth here already dead!
   MARTH. [coming out]. Where are the murder-
    ers? are they fled?
   MARG. [coming out]. Who lieth here?
   PEOPLE.   Thy mother's son.
   MARG. Almighty God! I am undone!   1700
   VAL. I'm dying—'tis a soon-told tale,
And sooner done the deed.
Why, women, do ye howl and wail?
To my last words give heed! [All gather round
    him.]
My Gretchen, see! still young art thou,   1705
Art not discreet enough, I trow,
Thou dost thy matters ill;
Let this in confidence be said:
Since thou the path of shame dost tread,
Tread it with right good will!   1710
   MARG. My brother! God! what can this mean?
   VAL. Abstain,
Nor dare God's holy name profane!
What's done, alas, is done and past!
Matters will take their course at last;   1715
By stealth thou dost begin with one,
Others will follow him anon;
And when a dozen thee have known,
Thou'lt common be to all the town.
When infamy is newly born,   1720
In secret she is brought to light,
And the mysterious veil of night
O'er head and ears is drawn;
The loathsome birth men fain would slay;
But soon, full grown, she waxes bold,   1725
And though not fairer to behold,
With brazen front insults the day:
The more abhorrent to the sight,
The more she courts the day's pure light,
The time already I discern,   1730
When thee all honest folk will spurn,

And shun thy hated form to meet,
As when a corpse infects the street.
Thy heart will sink in blank despair,
When they shall look thee in the face!   1735
A golden chain no more thou'lt wear!
Nor near the altar take in church thy place!
In fair lace collar simply dight
Thou'lt dance no more with spirits light!
In darksome corners thou wilt bide,   1740
Where beggars vile and cripples hide,
And e'en though God thy crime forgive,
On earth, a thing accursed, thou'lt live!

   MARTH. Your parting soul to God commend!
Your dying breath in slander will you spend?   1745

   VAL. Could I but reach thy wither'd frame,
Thou wretched beldame, void of shame!
Full measure I might hope to win
Of pardon then for every sin.

   MARG. Brother! what agonizing pain!   1750

   VAL. I tell thee, from vain tears abstain!
'Twas thy dishonor pierced my heart,
Thy fall the fatal death-stab gave.
Through the death-sleep I now depart   1754
To God, a soldier true and brave.   [*Dies.*

CATHEDRAL

Service, organ, and anthem

MARGARET *amongst a number of people.* EVIL-SPIRIT *behind* MARGARET.

   EVIL-SPIRIT. How different, Gretchen, was it
    once with thee,
When thou, still full of innocence,
Here to the altar camest,
And from the small and well-conn'd book
Didst lisp thy prayer,   1760
Half childish sport,
Half God in thy young heart!
Gretchen!
What thoughts are thine?
What deed of shame   1765
Lurks in thy sinful heart?
Is thy prayer utter'd for thy mother's soul,
Who into long, long torment slept through thee?
Whose blood is on thy threshold?
--And stirs there not already 'neath thy heart   1770
Another quick'ning pulse, that even now
Tortures itself and thee
With its foreboding presence?

   MARG. Woe! Woe!
Oh could I free me from the thoughts   1775

That hither, thither, crowd upon my brain,
Against my will!

   CHOR.   *Dies iræ, dies illa,*
      Solvet sæclum in favilla.[2]

     The organ sounds.

   EVIL-SPIRIT. Grim horror seizes thee!   1780
     The trumpet sounds!
     The graves are shaken!
     And thy heart
     From ashy rest
     For torturing flames   1785
     Anew created,
     Trembles into life!

   MARG.   Would I were hence!
     It is as if the organ
     Choked my breath,   1790
     As if the choir
     Melted my inmost heart!

   CHOR.   *Judex ergo cum sedebit,*
      Quidquid latet adparebit,
      Nil inultum remanebit.   1795

   MARG. I feel oppressed!
     The pillars of the wall
     Imprison me!
     The vaulted roof
     Weighs down upon me!—air!   1800

   EVIL-SPIRIT. Wouldst hide thee? sin and shame
     Remain not hidden!
     Air! light!
     Woe's thee!

   CHOR. *Quid sum miser tunc dicturus?*   1805
     Quem patronum rogaturus!
     Cum vix justus sit securus.

   EVIL-SPIRIT. The glorified their faces turn
     Away from thee!
     Shudder the pure to reach   1810
     Their hands to thee!
     Woe!

   CHOR. *Quid sum miser tunc dicturus—*

   MARG. Neighbor! your smelling bottle!
            [*She swoons away.*

A GLOOMY DAY

A plain

FAUST *and* MEPHISTOPHELES *enter.*

   FAUST. In misery! despairing! long wandering pitifully on the face of the earth and now imprisoned! This gentle hapless creature, immured in the dungeon as a malefactor and reserved for

---

[2] The ominous church hymn of the *Day of Doom*, by Thomas of Celano, "Day of wrath, that dreadful day."

horrid tortures! That it should come to this! To this!—Perfidious, worthless spirit, and this thou hast concealed from me!—Stand, aye, stand! roll in malicious rage thy fiendish eyes! Stand and brave me with thine insupportable presence! Imprisoned! In hopeless misery! Delivered over to the power of evil spirits and the judgment of unpitying humanity!—And me, the while, thou wert lulling with tasteless dissipations, concealing from me her growing anguish, and leaving her to perish without help!   1829

MEPH. She is not the first.

FAUST. Hound! Execrable monster!—Back with him, oh thou infinite spirit! back with the reptile into his dog's shape, in which it was his wont to scamper before me at eventide, to roll before the feet of the harmless wanderer, and to fasten on his shoulders when he fell! Change him again into his favorite shape, that he may crouch on his belly before me in the dust, whilst I spurn him with my foot, the reprobate!—Not the first!— Woe! Woe! By no human soul is it conceivable, that more than one human creature has ever sunk into a depth of wretchedness like this, or that the first in her writhing death-agony should not have atoned in the sight of all-pardoning Heaven for the guilt of all the rest! The misery of this one pierces me to the very marrow, and harrows up my soul; thou art grinning calmly over the doom of thousands!   1848

MEPH. Now we are once again at our wit's end, just where the reason of you mortals snaps! Why dost thou seek our fellowship, if thou canst not go through with it? Wilt fly, and art not proof against dizziness? Did we force ourselves on thee, or thou on us?

FAUST. Cease thus to gnash thy ravenous fangs at me! I loathe thee!—Great and glorious spirit, thou who didst vouchsafe to reveal thyself unto me, thou who dost know my very heart and soul, why hast thou linked me with this base associate, who feeds on mischief and revels in destruction?

MEPH. Hast done?   1861

FAUST. Save her!—or woe to thee! The direst of curses on thee for thousands of years!

MEPH. I cannot loose the bands of the avenger, nor withdraw his bolts.—Save her!—Who was it plunged her into perdition? I or thou? [FAUST looks wildly around.]

MEPH. Would'st grasp the thunder? Well for you, poor mortals, that 'tis not yours to wield! To smite to atoms the being however innocent, who obstructs his path, such is the tyrant's fashion of relieving himself in difficulties!   1872

FAUST. Convey me thither! She shall be free!

MEPH. And the danger to which thou dost expose thyself? Know, the guilt of blood, shed by thy hand, lies yet upon the town. Over the place where fell the murdered one, avenging spirits hover and watch for the returning murderer.

FAUST. This too from thee? The death and downfall of a world be on thee, monster! Conduct me thither, I say, and set her free!   1881

MEPH. I will conduct thee. And what I can do, —hear! Have I all power in heaven and upon earth? I'll cloud the senses of the warder,—do thou possess thyself of the keys and lead her forth with human hand! I will keep watch! The magic steeds are waiting, I bear thee off. Thus much is in my power.

FAUST. Up and away!

NIGHT

Open country

FAUST and MEPHISTOPHELES *rushing along on black horses.*

FAUST. What weave they yonder round the Ravenstone?   1891

MEPH. I know not what they shape and brew.

FAUST. They're soaring, swooping, bending, stooping.

MEPH. A witches' pack.

FAUST. They charm, they strew.

MEPH.   On! On!

DUNGEON

FAUST [*with a bunch of keys and a lamp before a small iron door*]. A fear unwonted o'er my spirit falls;
Man's concentrated woe o'erwhelms me here!
She dwells immur'd within these dripping walls;
Her only trespass a delusion dear!
Thou lingerest at the fatal door?   1900
Thou dread'st to see her face once more?
On! While thou dalliest, draws her death-hour near.

He seizes the lock.

MARG. [*singing within*].
   My mother, the harlot,
   She took me and slew!
   My father, the scoundrel,   1905
   Hath eaten me too!
   My sweet little sister

Hath all my bones laid,
Where soft breezes whisper
All in the cool shade! 1910
Then became I a wood-bird, and sang on
 the spray,
Fly away! little bird, fly away! fly away![3]

FAUST [opening the lock]. Ah! she forebodes
 not that her lover's near,
The clanking chains, the rustling straw, to hear.

He enters.

MARG. [hiding her face in the bed of straw].
 Woe! woe! they come! oh bitter 'tis to die! 1915

FAUST [softly]. Hush! hush! be still! I come to
 set thee free?

MARG. [throwing herself at his feet]. If thou art
 human, feel my misery!

FAUST. Thou wilt awake the jailor with thy
 cry!

He grasps the chains to unlock them.

MARG. [on her knees]. Who, headsman, unto
 thee this power
O'er me could give? 1920
Thou com'st for me at midnight-hour.
Be merciful, and let me live!
Is morrow's dawn not time enough? [She stands
 up.]
I'm still so young, so young—
And must so early die! 1925
Fair was I too, and that was my undoing.
My love is now afar, he then was nigh;
Torn lies the garland, the fair blossoms strew'd.
Nay, seize me not with hand so rude!
Spare me! What harm have I e'er done to thee?
Oh let me not in vain implore! 1931
I ne'er have seen thee in my life before!

 FAUST. Can I endure this bitter agony?

 MARG. I now am at thy mercy quite.
Let me my babe but suckle once again! 1935
I fondled it the live-long night;
They took it from me but to give me pain,
And now, they say that I my child have slain.
Gladness I ne'er again shall know.
Then they sing songs about me,—'tis wicked of
 the throng— 1940
An ancient ballad endeth so;
Who bade them thus apply the song?

 FAUST [throwing himself on the ground]. A
 lover at thy feet bends low,
To loose the bonds of wretchedness and woe.

MARG. [throws herself beside him]. Oh, let us
 kneel and move the saints by prayer! 1945
Look! look! yon stairs below,
Under the threshold there,
Hell's flames are all aglow!
Beneath the floor,
The devils roar! 1950

FAUST [aloud]. Gretchen! Gretchen!

MARG. [listening]. That was my lov'd one's
 voice! [She springs up, the chains fall off.]
Where is he? I heard him calling me.
Free am I! There's none shall hinder me.
To his neck will I fly, 1955
On his bosom will lie!
Gretchen, he called!—On yon threshold he stood;
Amidst all the howling of hell's fiery flood,
The scoff and the scorn of its devilish crew,
The tones of his voice, sweet and loving, I knew.

FAUST. 'Tis I! 1961

MARG. 'Tis thou! O say so once more again!
 [Embracing him.]
'Tis he! 'Tis he! where's now the torturing pain?
Where are the fetters? where the dungeon's
 gloom?
'Tis thou! To save me thou art come! 1965
And I am sav'd!—
Already now the street I see
Where the first time I caught a glimpse of thee.
There too the pleasant garden shade,
Where I and Martha for thy coming stay'd. 1970

FAUST [endeavoring to lead her away]. Come!
 come away!

MARG.   Oh do not haste!
I love to linger where thou stayest. [Caressing
 him.]

FAUST. Ah haste! For if thou still delayest,
Our lingering we shall both deplore.

 MARG. How, dearest? canst thou kiss no more!
So short a time away from me, and yet, 1976
To kiss thou couldst so soon forget!
Why on thy neck so anxious do I feel—
When formerly a perfect heaven of bliss
From thy dear looks and words would o'er me
 steal? 1980
As thou wouldst stifle me thou then didst kiss!—
Kiss me!
Or I'll kiss thee! [She embraces him.]
Woe! woe! Thy lips are cold,—
Are dumb! 1985
Thy love where hast thou left?

---

[3] A song from the well-known German folktale of "The Juniper Tree" (No. 49 of the Grimm Collection).

Who hath me of thy love bereft? [*She turns away
    from him.*]

FAUST. Come! Follow me, my dearest love, be
    bold!
I'll cherish thee with ardor thousand-fold;
I but entreat thee now to follow me!   1990
    MARG. [*turning towards him*]. And art thou he?
    and art thou really he?
    FAUST. 'Tis I! Oh come!
    MARG. Thou wilt strike off my chain,
And thou wilt take me to thine arms again.
How comes it that thou dost not shrink from
    me?—   1995
And dost thou know, love, whom thou wouldst
    set free?
    FAUST. Come! come! already night begins to
    wane.
    MARG. I sent my mother to her grave,
I drown'd my child beneath the wave.
Was it not given to thee and me—thee too?   2000
'Tis thou thyself! I scarce believe it yet.
Give me thy hand! It is no dream! 'Tis true!
Thine own dear hand!—But how is this? 'Tis
    wet!
Quick, wipe it off! Meseems that yet
There's blood thereon.   2005
Ah God! what hast thou done?
Put up thy sword,
I beg of thee!
    FAUST. Oh, dearest, let the past forgotten be!
Death is in every word.   2010
    MARG. No, thou must linger here in sorrow!
The graves I will describe to thee,
And thou to them must see
Tomorrow:
The best place give to my mother,   2015
Close at her side my brother,
Me at some distance lay—
But not too far away!
And the little one place on my right breast.
Nobody else will near me lie!   2020
To nestle beside thee so lovingly,
That was a rapture, gracious and sweet!
A rapture I never again shall prove;
Methinks I would force myself on thee, love,
And thou dost spurn me, and back retreat—   2025
Yet 'tis thyself, thy fond kind looks I see.
    FAUST. If thou dost feel 'tis I, then come with
    me!
    MARG. What, there? without?
    FAUST. Yes, forth in the free air.
    MARG. Aye, if the grave's without,—if death lurk
    there!   2030

Hence to the everlasting resting-place,
And not one step beyond!—Thou'rt leaving me?
Oh Henry! would that I could go with thee!
    FAUST. Thou canst! But will it! Open stands the
    door.
    MARG. I dare not go! I've naught to hope for
    more!   2035
What boots it to escape? They lurk for me!
'Tis wretched to beg, as I must do,
And with an evil conscience thereto!
'Tis wretched, in foreign lands to stray;
And me they will catch, do what I may!   2040
    FAUST. With thee will I abide.
    MARG. Quick! Quick!
Save thy poor child!
Keep to the path
The brook along,   2045
Over the bridge
To the wood beyond,
To the left, where the plank is,
In the pond.
Seize it at once!   2050
It fain would rise,
It struggles still!
Save it. Oh save!
    FAUST. Dear Gretchen, more collected be!
One little step, and thou art free!   2055
    MARG. Were we but only past the hill!
There sits my mother upon a stone—
My brain, alas, is cold with dread!—
There sits my mother upon a stone,
And to and fro she shakes her head;   2060
She winks not, she nods not, her head it droops
    sore;
She slept so long, she waked no more;
She slept, that we might taste of bliss:
Ah! those were happy times, I wis!
    FAUST. Since here avails nor argument nor
    prayer,   2065
Thee hence by force I needs must bear.
    MARG. Loose me! I will not suffer violence!
With murderous hand hold not so fast!
I have done all to please thee in the past! 2069
    FAUST. Day dawns! My love! My love!
    MARG.   Yes! day draws near,
The day of judgment too will soon appear!
It should have been my bridal! No one tell,
That thy poor Gretchen thou hast known too well.
Woe to my garland!
Its bloom is o'er!   2075
Though not at the dance—
We shall meet once more.

The crowd doth gather, in silence it rolls;
The squares, the streets,
Scarce hold the throng. 2080
The staff is broken,—the death-bell tolls,—
They bind and seize me! I'm hurried along,
To the seat of blood already I'm bound!
Quivers each neck as the naked steel
Quivers on mine the blow to deal— 2085
The silence of the grave now broods around!
  Faust. Would I had ne'er been born!
  Meph. [*appears without*]. Up! or you're lost.
Vain hesitation! Babbling, quaking!
My steeds are shivering, 2090
Morn is breaking.
  Marg. What from the floor ascendeth like a
    ghost?
'Tis he! 'Tis he! Him from my presence chase!

What would he in this holy place?
It is for me he cometh!
  Faust.   Thou shalt live! 2095
  Marg. Judgment of God! To thee my soul I
    give!
  Meph. [*to* Faust]. Come, come! With her I'll
    else abandon thee!
  Marg. Father, I'm thine! Do thou deliver me!
Ye angels! Ye angelic hosts! descend,
Encamp around to guard me and defend!— 2100
Henry! I shudder now to look on thee!
  Meph. She now is judged!
  Voices [*from above*]. Is saved!
  Meph. [*to* Faust]. Come thou with me!
    [*Vanishes with* Faust.
  Voice [*from within, dying away*]. Henry!
  Henry! 2105

HEINRICH HEINE

Ein Fichtenbaum Steht Einsam

A pine tree standeth lonely
  In the North on an upland bare;
It standeth whitely shrouded
  With snow, and sleepeth there.

It dreameth of a Palm Tree
  Which far in the East alone,
In mournful silence standeth
  On its ridge of burning stone.

Der Mond Ist Aufgegangen

The moon is fully risen,
  And shineth o'er the sea;
And I embrace my darling,
  Our hearts are swelling free.

In the arms of the lovely maiden 5
  I lie alone on the strand;—
"What sounds in the breezes sighing?
  Why trembles your white hand?"

"That is no breeze's sighing,
  That is the mermaiden's song, 10
The singing of my sisters
  Whom the sea hath drowned so long."

Sag', Wo Ist Dein Schönes Liebchen

"Say, where is the maiden sweet,
  Whom you once so sweetly sung,
When the flames of mighty heat
  Filled your heart and fired your tongue?"

Ah, those flames no longer burn,
  Cold and drear the heart that fed;
And this book is but the urn
  Of the ashes of love dead.

The Grenadiers

For France two grenadiers held their way,
  Had prisoners been in Russia;
And sorrowful men they were, when they
  The frontier reached of Prussia.

For there they heard of a dire event,— 5
  How the world 'gainst France had risen, her
Grande armée had shattered and shent,
  And taken her Emperor prisoner.

They mingled their tears, these two grenadiers,
  To the sad tale ever returning; 10
"Oh would," said one, "that my days were done!
  My old wounds, how they're burning!"

Heinrich Heine (1796-1856). The first three translations are by James Thomson; the fourth, fifth, sixth, seventh, and ninth, by Theodore Martin; the eighth by Henry Wadsworth Longfellow; the tenth by Lord Houghton.

"All's up!" said the other; "and sooner than not
    I would die like you, never doubt me;
But a wife and child at home I've got,   15
    And they must be starved without me!"

"Hang wife and child! It is something more,
    And better far, that I pant for;
My Emperor prisoner! My Emperor!
    Let them go beg what they want for!   20

"If I die just now, as 'tis like I may,
    Then, comrade, this boon grant me,
Take my body with you to France away,
    And in France's dear earth plant me.

"The *Croix d'Honneur,* with its crimson band,
    On my heart see that you place it;   26
Then give me my rifle in my hand,
    And my sword, around me brace it.

"So will I lie, and listen all ear,
    Like a sentinel, low in my bed there,   30
Till the roar of the cannon some day I hear,
    And the chargers' neigh and their tread there.

"Then I'll know 'tis my Emperor riding by;
    The sabers flash high that attend him,
And out from my grave full-armed spring I,   35
    The Emperor! to shield and defend him!"

Wenn Ich in Deine Augen Seh'

Whene'er I look into thine eyes,
Then every fear that haunts me flies;
But when I kiss thy mouth, oh then
I feel a giant's strength again.

Whene'er I couch me on thy breast,
I know what heaven is to the blest;
But when thou sayest, "I love thee!"
Then must I weep, and bitterly.

Loreley

I cannot tell what's coming o'er me,
    That makes me so eerie and low:
An old-world legend before me,
    Keeps rising, and will not go.

The air chills, day is declining,   5
    And smoothly Rhine's waters run,
And the peaks of the mountains are shining
    Aloft in the setting sun.

A maiden of wondrous seeming,
    Most beautiful, sits up there,   10
Her jewels in gold are gleaming,
    She combs out her golden hair.

With a comb of red gold she parts it,
    And still as she combs it, she sings;
Her song pierces home to our hearts, it   15
    Has tones of a sweetness that stings.

The boatman, he thrills as he hears it
    Out there in his little skiff:
He sees not the reef as he nears it,
    He only looks up to the cliff.   20

The waters will sweep, I am thinking,
    O'er skiff, and o'er boatman ere long;
And this is, when daylight is sinking,
    What Loreley did with her song.

Du Schönes Fischer-Mädchen

My bonnie blithe fisher-maiden,
    Row in your boat to the strand;
Come here and sit down beside me,
    And chat with me hand in hand.

Rest your dear little head on my bosom,   5
    And be not so frightened, child;
Every day you trust without thinking
    Yourself to the ocean wild.

My heart is quite like the ocean,
    It has tempests, and ebb, and flow;   10
And fine pearls lie there a-many,
    Down, down in its depths below.

The Sea Hath Its Pearls

The sea hath its pearls,
    The heaven hath its stars;
But my heart, my heart,
    My heart hath its love.

Great are the sea and the heaven;   5
    Yet greater is my heart,
And fairer than pearls and stars
    Flashes and beams my love.

Thou little, youthful maiden,
    Come unto my great heart;   10
My heart, and the sea, and the heaven
    Are melting away with love!

Du Bist Wie Eine Blume

Thou art even as a flower is,
  So gentle, and pure, and fair;
I gaze on thee, and sadness
  Comes over my heart unaware.

I feel as though I should lay, sweet,   5
  My hands on thy head, with a prayer
That God may keep thee alway, sweet,
  As gentle, and pure, and fair!

Lost Child—Enfant Perdu

In Freedom's War, of "Thirty Years" and more,
  A lonely outpost have I held—in vain!
With no triumphant hope or prize in store,
  Without a thought to see my home again.

I watched both day and night: I could not sleep   5
  Like my well-tented comrades far behind,
Though near enough to let their snoring keep
  A friend awake, if e'er to doze inclined.

And thus, when solitude my spirits shook,
  Or fear—for all but fools know fear sometimes,—
To rouse myself and them, I piped and took   11
  A gay revenge in all my wanton rhymes.

Yes! there I stood, my musket always ready,
  And when some sneaking rascal showed his head,
My eye was vigilant, my aim was steady,   15
  And gave his brains an extra dose of lead.

But war and justice have far different laws,
  And worthless acts are often done right well;
The rascals' shots were better than their cause,
  And I was hit—and hit again, and fell!   20

That outpost was abandoned: while the one
  Lies in the dust, the rest in troops depart;
Unconquered—I have done what could be done,
  With sword unbroken, and with broken heart.

Last Words

It was a depressed, an arrested time in Germany when I wrote the second volume of the *Reisebilder*,[1] and had it printed as I wrote. But before it appeared something was whispered about it; it was said that my book would awaken and encourage the cowed spirit of freedom, and that measures were being taken to suppress it. When such rumors were afloat, it was advisable to advance the book as quickly as possible, and to hurry it through the press. As it was necessary, too, that it should contain a certain number of leaves, to escape the requisitions of the estimable censorship, I followed the example of Benvenuto Cellini, who, in founding his Perseus, was short of bronze, and to fill up the mould threw into the molten metal all the tin plates he could lay his hands on. It was certainly easy to distinguish between the tin—especially the tin termination of the book—and the better bronze; anyone, however, who understands the craft will not betray the workman.

But as everything in this world is likely to turn up again, so it came to pass that, in this very volume, I found myself again in the same scrape, and I have been obliged to again throw some tin into the mould—let me hope that this renewed melting of baser metal will simply be attributed to the pressure of the times.

Alas! the whole book sprang from the pressure of the times, as well as the earlier writings of similar tendency. The more intimate friends of the writer, who are acquainted with his private circumstances, know well how little his own vanity forced him to the tribune, and how great were the sacrifices which he was obliged to make for every independent word which he has spoken since then and—if God will!—which he still means to speak. Now-a-days, a word is a deed whose consequences cannot be measured, and no one knows whether he may not in the end appear as witness to his words in blood.

For many years I have waited in vain for the words of those bold orators, who once in the meetings of the German Burschenschaft[2] so often claimed a hearing, who so often overwhelmed me with their rhetorical talent, and spoke a language spoken so oft before; they were then so forward in noise—they are now so backward in silence. How they then reviled the French and the foreign Babel, and the un-German frivolous betrayers of the Fatherland, who praised French-dom. That praise verified itself in the great week![3]

Ah, the great week of Paris! The spirit of freedom, which was wafted thence over Germany, has certainly upset the night-lamps here and there, so that the red curtains of several thrones took fire, and golden crowns grew hot under blazing night-

---

[1] Pictures of Travel; vol. 1, 1826, vol. 2, 1827.   [2] liberal student organizations.
[3] During the French revolution of 1830 that removed the Bourbons and installed Louis Philippe.

caps; but the old catch-polls, in whom the royal police trusted, are already bringing out the fire-buckets, and now scent around all the more suspiciously, and forge all the more firmly their secret chains, and I mark well that a still thicker prison vault is being invisibly arched over the German people.

Poor imprisoned people! be not cast down in your need. Oh, that I could speak catapults! Oh, that I could shoot falarica from my heart!

The distinguished ice-rind of reserve melts from my heart, a strange sorrow steals over me—is it love, and love for the German people? Or is it sickness?—my soul quivers and my eyes burn, and that is an unfortunate occurrence for a writer, who should command his material, and remain charmingly objective, as the art school requires, and as Goethe has done—he has grown to be eighty years old in so doing, and a minister, and portly—poor German people! that is thy greatest man!

I still have a few octavo pages to fill, and I will therefore tell a story—it has been floating in my head since yesterday—a story from the life of Charles the Fifth.[4] But it is now a long time since I heard it, and I no longer remember its details exactly. Such things are easily forgotten, if one does not receive a regular salary for reading them every half-year from his lecture books. But what does it matter if places and dates are forgotten, so long as one holds their significance, their moral meaning, in his memory. It is this which stirs my soul and moves me even to tears. I fear I am getting ill.

The poor emperor was taken prisoner by his enemies, and lay in strict imprisonment. I believe it was in Tyrol. There he sat in solitary sorrow, forsaken by all his knights and courtiers, and no one came to his help. I know not if he had even in those days that cheese-yellow complexion with which Holbein painted him. But the misanthropic under-lip certainly protruded, even more then than in his portraits. He must have despised the people who fawned around him in the sunshine of prosperity, and who left him alone in his bitter need. Suddenly the prison door opened, and there entered a man wrapped in a cloak, and as he cast it aside, the emperor recognised his trusty Kunz von der Rosen, the court-fool. One brought him consolation and counsel—and it was the court-fool.

My German Fatherland! dear German people! I am thy Kunz von der Rosen. The man whose real office was pastime, and who should only make thee merry in happy days, forces his way into thy prison, in time of need; here, beneath my mantle, I bring thee thy strong sceptre and the beautiful crown—dost thou not remember me, my emperor? If I cannot free thee, I will at least console thee, and thou shalt have some one by thee who will talk with thee about thy most pressing oppressions, and will speak courage to thee, and who loves thee, and whose best jokes and best blood are ever at thy service. For thou, my people, art the true emperor, the true lord of the land—thy will is sovereign and more legitimate than that purple *Tel est notre plaisir*,[5] which grounds itself upon divine right, without any better guarantee than the quackery of shaven jugglers—thy will, my people, is the only righteous source of all power. Even though thou liest down there in fetters, thy good right will arise in the end, the day of freedom draws near, a new time begins—my emperor, the night is over, and the dawn shines outside.

"Kunz von der Rosen, my Fool, thou errest. Thou hast perhaps mistaken a bright axe for the sun, and the dawn is nothing but blood."

"No, my Emperor, it is the sun, though it rises in the west—for six thousand years men have always seen it rise in the east—it is high time that it for once made a change in its course."

"Kunz von der Rosen, my Fool, thou hast lost the bells from thy red cap, and it now has such a strange look, that red cap!"

"Ah, my Emperor, I have shaken my head in such mad earnest over your distress that the fool's bell fell from my cap; but it is none the worse for that!"

"Kunz von der Rosen, my Fool, what is that breaking and cracking outside there?"

"Hush! it is the saw and the carpenter's axe; the doors of your prison will soon be broken in, and you will be free, my Emperor!"

"Am I then really Emperor? Alas! it is only the Fool who tells me so!"

"Oh, do not sigh, my dear lord, it is the air of the dungeon which so dispirits you; when you have once regained your power, you will feel the bold imperial blood in your veins, and you will be proud as an emperor, and arrogant, and gracious, and unjust, and smiling, and ungrateful as princes are."

"Kunz von der Rosen, my Fool, when I am free again, what wilt thou be doing?"

"I shall sew new bells on my cap."

"And how shall I reward thy fidelity?"

"Ah! dear master—do not let me be put to death!"

[4] Actually the Emperor in this legend was Maximilian.
[5] "Such is our pleasure"—the arbitrary comments of a typical autocracy

FRIEDRICH NIETZSCHE
Thus Spake Zarathustra

Before Sunrise

O heaven above me, thou pure, thou deep heaven!
Thou abyss of light! Gazing on thee, I tremble
with divine desires.

Up to thy height to toss myself—that is my depth!
In thy purity to hide myself—that is mine innocence!

The God veileth his beauty: thus hidest thou thy
stars. Thou speakest not: thus proclaimest thou thy 10
wisdom unto me.

Mute o'er the raging sea hast thou risen for me
to-day; thy love and thy modesty make a revelation
unto my raging soul.

In that thou camest unto me beautiful, veiled in
thy beauty, in that thou spakest unto me mutely,
obvious in thy wisdom:

Oh, how could I fail to divine all the modesty of
thy soul! Before the sun didst thou come unto me
—the lonesomest one.   20

We have been friends from the beginning: to us
are grief, gruesomeness, and ground common; even
the sun is common to us.

We do not speak to each other, because we know
too much—: we keep silent to each other, we smile
our knowledge to each other.

Art thou not the light of my fire? Hast thou
not the sister-soul of mine insight?

Together did we learn everything; together did
we learn to ascend beyond ourselves, and to smile 30
uncloudedly:—

Uncloudedly to smile down out of luminous eyes
and out of miles of distance, when under us constraint and purpose and guilt steam like rain.

And wandered I alone, for what did my soul
hunger by night and in labyrinthine paths? And
climbed I mountains, whom did I ever seek, if not
thee, upon mountains?

And all my wandering and mountain climbing: 40
a necessity was it merely, and a makeshift of the
unhandy one:—to fly only, wanteth mine entire
will, to fly into thee!

And what have I hated more than passing clouds,
and whatever tainteth thee? And mine own hatred
have I even hated, because it tainted thee!

The passing clouds I detest—those stealthy cats
of prey: they take from thee and me what is common to us—the vast unbounded Yea- and Amen-
saying.

These mediators and mixers we detest—the passing clouds: those half-and-half ones, that have
neither learned to bless nor to curse from the heart.

Rather will I sit in a tub under a closed heaven,
rather will I sit in the abyss without heaven, than
see thee, thou luminous heaven, tainted with passing clouds!

And oft have I longed to pin them fast with the
jagged gold-wires of lightning, that I might, like
the thunder, beat the drum upon their kettle-
bellies:—

—An angry drummer, because they rob me of
thy Yea and Amen!—thou heaven above me, thou
pure, thou luminous heaven! Thou abyss of light!
—because they rob thee of my Yea and Amen.

For rather will I have noise and thunders and
tempest-blasts, than this discreet, doubting cat-
repose; and also amongst men do I hate most of
all the soft-treaders, and half-and-half ones, and the
doubting, hesitating, passing clouds.

And "he who cannot bless shall learn to curse!"—
this clear teaching dropt unto me from the clear
heaven; this star standeth in my heaven even in
dark nights.

I, however, am a blesser and a Yea-sayer, if thou
be but around me, thou pure, thou luminous
heaven! Thou abyss of light!—into all abysses do I
then carry my beneficent Yea-saying.

A blesser have I become and a Yea-sayer: and
therefore strove I long and was a striver, that I
might one day get my hands free for blessing.

This, however, is my blessing: to stand above
everything as its own heaven, its round roof, its
azure bell and eternal security: and blessed is he
who thus blesseth!

For all things are baptized at the font of eternity,
and beyond good and evil; good and evil themselves, however, are but fugitive shadows and
damp afflictions and passing clouds.

Verily, it is a blessing and not a blasphemy when
I teach that "above all things there standeth the
heaven of chance, the heaven of innocence, the
heaven of hazard, the heaven of wantonness."

"Of Hazard"—that is the oldest nobility in the

Friedrich Nietzsche (1844–1900). Translation by Thomas Common.

world; that gave I back to all things; I emancipated them from bondage under purpose.

This freedom and celestial serenity did I put like an azure bell above all things, when I taught that over them and through them, no "eternal Will"—willeth.

This wantonness and folly did I put in place of that Will, when I taught that "In everything there is one thing impossible—rationality!"

A little reason, to be sure, a germ of wisdom scattered from star to star—this leaven is mixed in all things: for the sake of folly, wisdom is mixed in all things!

A little wisdom is indeed possible; but this blessed security have I found in all things, that they prefer—to dance on the feet of chance.

O heaven above me! thou pure, thou lofty heaven! This is now thy purity unto me, that there is no eternal reason-spider and reason-cobweb:—

—That thou art to me a dancing-floor for divine chances, that thou art to me a table of the Gods, for divine dice and dice-players!—

But thou blushest? Have I spoken unspeakable things? Have I abused, when I meant to bless thee?

Or is it the shame of being two of us that maketh thee blush!—Dost thou bid me go and be silent, because now—day cometh?

The world is deep—: and deeper than e'er the day could read. Not everything may be uttered in presence of day. But day cometh: so let us part!

O heaven above me, thou modest one! thou glowing one! O thou, my happiness before sunrise! The day cometh: so let us part!—

Thus spake Zarathustra.

Old and New Tables

When the water hath planks, when gangways and railings o'erspan the stream, verily, he is not believed who then saith: "All is in flux."

But even the simpletons contradict him. "What?" say the simpletons, "all in flux? Planks and railings are still over the stream!"

"Over the stream all is stable, all the values of things, the bridges and bearings, all 'good' and 'evil': these are all stable!" —

Cometh, however, the hard winter, the stream-tamer, then learn even the wittiest distrust, and verily, not only the simpletons then say: "Should not everything—stand still?"

"Fundamentally standeth everything still"—that is an appropriate winter doctrine, good cheer for an unproductive period, a great comfort for winter-sleepers and fireside-loungers.

"Fundamentally standeth everything still"—: but contrary thereto, preacheth the thawing wind!

The thawing wind, a bullock, which is no ploughing bullock—a furious bullock, a destroyer, which with angry horns breaketh the ice! The ice however—breaketh gangways!

O my brethren, is not everything at present in flux? Have not all railings and gangways fallen into the water? Who would still hold on to "good" and "evil"?

"Woe to us! Hail to us! The thawing wind bloweth!"—Thus preach, my brethren, through all the streets!

. . . . .

There is an old illusion—it is called good and evil. Around soothsayers and astrologers hath hitherto revolved the orbit of this illusion.

Once did one believe in soothsayers and astrologers; and therefore did one believe, "Everything is fate: thou shalt, for thou must!"

Then again did one distrust all soothsayers and astrologers; and therefore did one believe, "Everything is freedom: thou canst, for thou willest!"

O my brethren, concerning the stars and the future there hath hitherto been only illusion, and not knowledge; and therefore concerning good and evil there hath hitherto been only illusion and not knowledge!

. . . . .

"Thou shalt not rob! Thou shalt not slay!"—such precepts were once called holy; before them did one bow the knee and the head, and took off one's shoes.

But I ask you: Where have there ever been better robbers and slayers in the world than such holy precepts?

Is there not even in all life—robbing and slaying? And for such precepts to be called holy, was not truth itself thereby—slain?

—Or was it a sermon of death that called holy what contradicted and dissuaded from life?—O my brethren, break up, break up for me the old tables!

. . . . .

It is my sympathy with all the past that I see it is abandoned,—

—Abandoned to the favor, the spirit and the madness of every generation that cometh, and reinterpreteth all that hath been as its bridge!

A great potentate might arise, an artful prodigy, who with approval and disapproval could strain and constrain all the past, until it became for him a bridge, a harbinger, a herald, and a cock-crowing.

This however is the other danger, and mine other sympathy:—he who is of the populace, his thoughts go back to his grandfather,—with his grandfather, however, doth time cease.

Thus is all the past abandoned: for it might some day happen for the populace to become master, and drown all time in shallow waters.

Therefore, O my brethren, a new nobility is needed, which shall be the adversary of all populace and potentate rule, and shall inscribe anew the word "noble" on new tables.

For many noble ones are needed, and many kinds of noble ones, for a new nobility! Or, as I once said in parable: "That is just divinity, that there are Gods, but no God!"

HENRIK IBSEN

A Doll's House

CHARACTERS

TORVALD HELMER	ANNA } Servants
NORA HELMER	ELLEN }
DR. RANK	IVAR } The Helmers'
NILS KROGSTAD	EMMY } Children
MRS. LINDEN	BOB }

SCENE:—*Sitting-room in Helmer's House (a flat) in Christiania.*

TIME:—*The Present Day; Christmastide.*

The action takes place on three consecutive days.

ACT I

A room comfortably and tastefully, but not expensively, furnished. In the background, to the right, a door leads to the hall; to the left, another door leads to Helmer's study. Between the two doors a pianoforte. In the middle of the left wall, a door, and nearer the front a window. Near the window a round table with armchairs and a small sofa. In the right wall, somewhat to the back, a door; and against the same wall, farther forward, a porcelain stove; in front of it a couple of armchairs and a rocking-chair. Between the stove and the side door a small table. Engravings on the walls. A whatnot with china and bric-à-brac. A small book-case of showily bound books. Carpet. A fire in the stove. A winter day. A bell rings in the hall outside. Presently the outer door is heard to open. Then NORA enters, hum-

ming contentedly. She is in out-door dress, and carries several parcels, which she lays on the right-hand table. She leaves the door into the hall open behind her, and a Porter is seen outside, carrying a Christmas-tree and a basket, which he gives to the maid-servant who has opened the door.

NORA. Hide the Christmas-tree carefully, Ellen; the children mustn't see it before this evening, when it's lighted up. [*To the Porter, taking out her purse.*] How much?

PORTER. Fifty öre.[1]

NORA. There's a crown. No, keep the change. [*The Porter thanks her and goes. NORA shuts the door. She continues smiling in quiet glee as she takes off her walking things. Then she takes from her pocket a bag of macaroons, and eats one or two. As she does so, she goes on tip-toe to her husband's door and listens.*]

NORA. Yes; he is at home. [*She begins humming again, going to the table on the right.*]

HELM. [*in his room*]. Is that my lark twittering there?

NORA [*busy opening some of her parcels*]. Yes, it is.

HELM. Is it the squirrel skipping about?

NORA. Yes!

HELM. When did the squirrel get home?

NORA. Just this minute. [*Hides the bag of macaroons in her pocket and wipes her mouth.*] Come here, Torvald, and see what I've bought.

Henrik Ibsen, *A Doll's House.* Translated by William Archer. Henrik Ibsen (1828-1906), born in a village of southern Norway, had practical experience in stage production and play revision at Bergen. After achieving success he spent much of his life in Germany and Italy, though in his later years he returned to Norway.

[1] Half a Norwegian crown, or about thirteen cents.

HELM. Don't disturb me. [*A little later he opens the door and looks in, pen in hand.*] "Bought," did you say? What! all that? Has my little spendthrift been making the money fly again?

NORA. Why, Torvald, surely we can afford to launch out a little now! It's the first Christmas we haven't had to pinch.

HELM. Come, come; we can't afford to squander money.

NORA. Oh, yes, Torvald, do let us squander a little—just the least little bit, won't you? You know you'll soon be earning heaps of money.

HELM. Yes, from New Year's Day. But there's a whole quarter before my first salary is due.

NORA. Never mind; we can borrow in the meantime.

HELM. Nora! [*He goes up to her and takes her playfully by the ear.*] Thoughtless as ever! Supposing I borrowed a thousand crowns today, and you spent it during Christmas week, and that on New Year's Eve a tile blew off the roof and knocked my brains out—

NORA [*laying her hand on his mouth*]. Hush! How can you talk so horridly?

HELM. But, supposing it were to happen—what then?

NORA. If anything so dreadful happened, I shouldn't care whether I was in debt or not.

HELM. But what about the creditors?

NORA. They! Who cares for them? They're only strangers.

HELM. Nora, Nora! What a woman you are! But seriously, Nora, you know my ideas on these points. No debts! No credit! Home-life ceases to be free and beautiful as soon as it is founded on borrowing and debt. We two have held out bravely till now, and we won't give in at the last.

NORA [*going to the fireplace*]. Very well—as you like, Torvald.

HELM. [*following her*]. Come, come; my little lark mustn't let her wings droop like that. What? Is the squirrel pouting there? [*Takes out his purse.*] Nora, what do you think I've got here?

NORA [*turning round quickly*]. Money!

HELM. There! [*Gives her some notes.*] Of course I know all sorts of things are wanted at Christmas.

NORA [*counting*]. Ten, twenty, thirty, forty. Oh! thank you, thank you, Torvald. This will go a long way.

HELM. I should hope so.

NORA. Yes, indeed, a long way! But come here, and see all I've been buying. And so cheap! Look, here is a new suit for Ivar, and a little sword. Here are a horse and a trumpet for Bob. And here are a doll and a cradle for Emmy. They're only common; but she'll soon pull them all to pieces. And dresses and neckties for the servants; only I should have got something better for dear old Anna.

HELM. And what's in that other parcel?

NORA [*crying out*]. No, Torvald, you're not to see that until this evening.

HELM. Oh! ah! But now tell me, you little rogue, what have you got for yourself?

NORA. For myself? Oh, I don't want anything.

HELM. Nonsense. Just tell me something sensible you would like to have.

NORA. No. Really I want nothing. . . . Well, listen, Torvald—

HELM. Well?

NORA [*playing with his coat buttons, without looking him in the face*]. If you really want to give me something, you might, you know, you might—

HELM. Well, well? Out with it!

NORA [*quickly*]. You might give me money, Torvald. Only just what you think you can spare; then I can buy myself something with it later.

HELM. But, Nora—

NORA. Oh, please do, dear Torvald, please do! Then I would hang the money in lovely gilt paper on the Christmas-tree. Wouldn't that be fun?

HELM. What do they call the birds that are always making the money fly?

NORA. Yes, I know—spendthrifts, of course. But please do as I say, Torvald. Then I shall have time to think what I want most. Isn't that very sensible, now?

HELM. [*smiling*]. Certainly; that is to say, if you really kept the money I gave you, and really bought yourself something with it. But it all goes in housekeeping, and for all sorts of useless things, and then I have to find more.

NORA. But, Torvald—

HELM. Can you deny it, Nora dear? [*He puts his arm round her.*] It's a sweet little lark; but it gets through a lot of money. No one would believe how much it costs a man to keep such a little bird as you.

NORA. For shame! how can you say so? Why, I save as much as ever I can.

HELM. [*laughing*]. Very true—as much as you can—but you can't.

NORA [*hums and smiles in quiet satisfaction*]. H'm!—you should just know, Torvald, what expenses we larks and squirrels have.

HELM. You're a strange little being! Just like your father—always eager to get hold of money;

but the moment you have it, it seems to slip through your fingers; you never know what becomes of it. Well, one must take you as you are. It's in the blood. Yes, Nora, that sort of thing is inherited.

NORA. I wish I had inherited many of my father's qualities.

HELM. And I don't wish you anything but just what you are—my own, sweet little song-bird. But, I say—it strikes me—you look so, so—what shall I call it?—so suspicious today—

NORA. Do I?

HELM. You do, indeed. Look me full in the face.

NORA [looking at him]. Well?

HELM. [threatening with his finger]. Hasn't the little sweet-tooth been breaking the rules today?

NORA. No; how can you think of such a thing!

HELM. Didn't she just look in at the confectioner's?

NORA. No, Torvald, really—

HELM. Not to sip a little jelly?

NORA. No; certainly not.

HELM. Hasn't she even nibbled a macaroon or two?

NORA. No, Torvald, indeed, indeed!

HELM. Well, well, well; of course I'm only joking.

NORA [goes to the table on the right]. I shouldn't think of doing what you disapprove of.

HELM. No, I'm sure of that; and, besides, you've given me your word. [Going toward her.] Well, keep your little Christmas secrets to yourself, Nora darling. The Christmas-tree will bring them all to light, I daresay.

NORA. Have you remembered to ask Doctor Rank?

HELM. No. But it's not necessary; he'll come as a matter of course. Besides, I shall invite him when he looks in today. I've ordered some capital wine. Nora, you can't think how I look forward to this evening!

NORA. And I too. How the children will enjoy themselves, Torvald!

HELM. Ah! it's glorious to feel that one has an assured position and ample means. Isn't it delightful to think of?

NORA. Oh, it's wonderful!

HELM. Do you remember last Christmas? For three whole weeks beforehand you shut yourself up till long past midnight to make flowers for the Christmas-tree, and all sorts of other marvels that were to have astonished us. I was never so bored in my life.

NORA. I did not bore myself at all.

HELM. [smiling]. And it came to so little after all, Nora.

NORA. Oh! are you going to tease me about that again? How could I help the cat getting in and spoiling it all?

HELM. To be sure you couldn't, my poor little Nora. You did your best to amuse us all, and that's the main thing. But, all the same, it's a good thing the hard times are over.

NORA. Oh, isn't it wonderful!

HELM. Now, I needn't sit here boring myself all alone; and you needn't tire your dear eyes and your delicate little fingers—

NORA [clapping her hands]. No, I needn't, need I, Torvald? Oh! it's wonderful to think of! [Takes his arm.] And now I'll tell you how I think we ought to manage, Torvald. As soon as Christmas is over— [The hall-door bell rings.] Oh, there's a ring! [Arranging the room.] That's somebody to call. How vexing!

HELM. I am "not at home" to callers; remember that.

ELLEN [in the doorway]. A lady to see you, ma'am.

NORA. Show her in.

ELLEN [to HELMER]. And the Doctor is just come, sir.

HELM. Has he gone into my study?

ELLEN. Yes, sir.

HELMER goes into his study. ELLEN ushers in MRS. LINDEN in traveling costume, and shuts the door behind her.

MRS. L. [timidly and hesitatingly]. How do you do, Nora?

NORA [doubtfully]. How do you do?

MRS. L. I daresay you don't recognize me?

NORA. No, I don't think—oh, yes!—I believe— [Effusively.] What! Christina! Is it really you?

MRS. L. Yes, really I!

NORA. Christina! and to think I didn't know you! But how could I— [More softly.] How changed you are, Christina!

MRS. L. Yes, no doubt. In nine or ten years—

NORA. Is it really so long since we met? Yes, so it is. Oh! the last eight years have been a happy time, I can tell you. And now you have come to town? All that long journey in mid-winter! How brave of you.

MRS. L. I arrived by this morning's steamer.

NORA. To keep Christmas, of course. Oh, how delightful! What fun we shall have! Take your things off. Aren't you frozen? [*Helping her.*] There, now we'll sit down here cozily by the fire. No, you take the arm-chair; I'll sit in this rocking-chair. [*Seizes her hand.*] Yes, now I can see the dear old face again. It was only at the first glance— But you're a little paler, Christina, and perhaps a little thinner.

MRS. L. And much, much older, Nora.

NORA. Yes, perhaps a little older—not much— ever so little. [*She suddenly stops; seriously.*] Oh! what a thoughtless wretch I am! Here I sit chattering on, and— Dear, dear Christina, can you forgive me?

MRS. L. What do you mean, Nora?

NORA [*softly*]. Poor Christina! I forgot, you are a widow?

MRS. L. Yes; my husband died three years ago.

NORA. I know, I know, I saw it in the papers. Oh! believe me, Christina, I did mean to write to you; but I kept putting it off, and something always came in the way.

MRS. L. I can quite understand that, Nora dear.

NORA. No, Christina; it was horrid of me. Oh, you poor darling! how much you must have gone through!—and he left you nothing?

MRS. L. Nothing.

NORA. And no children?

MRS. L. None.

NORA. Nothing, nothing at all?

MRS. L. Not even a sorrow or a longing to dwell upon.

NORA [*looking at her incredulously*]. My dear Christina, how is that possible?

MRS. L. [*smiling sadly and stroking her hair*]. Oh, it happens sometimes, Nora.

NORA. So utterly alone. How dreadful that must be! I have three of the loveliest children. I can't show them to you just now; they're out with their nurse. But now you must tell me everything.

MRS. L. No, no, I want you to tell me—

NORA. No, you must begin; I won't be egotistical today. Today, I will think of you only. Oh! I must tell you one thing; but perhaps you've heard of our great stroke of fortune?

MRS. L. No. What is it?

NORA. Only think! my husband has been made Manager of the Joint Stock Bank.

MRS. L. Your husband! Oh, how fortunate!

NORA. Yes, isn't it? A lawyer's position is so uncertain, you see, especially when he won't touch any business that's the least bit . . . shady, as of course Torvald won't; and in that I quite agree with him. Oh! you can imagine how glad we are.

He is to enter on his new position at the New Year, and then he will have a large salary, and percentages. In future we shall be able to live quite differently—just as we please, in fact. Oh, Christina, I feel so light and happy! It's splendid to have lots of money, and no need to worry about things, isn't it?

MRS. L. Yes; it must be delightful to have what you need.

NORA. No, not only what you need, but heaps of money—heaps!

MRS. L. [*smiling*]. Nora, Nora, haven't you learnt reason yet? In our schooldays you were a shocking little spendthrift!

NORA [*quietly smiling*]. Yes; Torvald says I am still. [*Threatens with her finger.*] But "Nora, Nora," is not so silly as you all think. Oh! I haven't had the chance to be much of a spendthrift. We have both had to work.

MRS. L. You too?

NORA. Yes, light fancy work; crochet, and embroidery, and things of that sort, [*significantly*] and other work too. You know, of course, that Torvald left the Government service when we were married. He had little chance of promotion, and of course he was required to make more money. But in the first year of our marriage he overworked himself terribly. He had to undertake all sorts of odd jobs, you know, and to work early and late. He couldn't stand it, and fell dangerously ill. Then the doctors declared he must go to the South.

MRS. L. Yes; you spent a whole year in Italy, didn't you?

NORA. We did. It wasn't easy to manage, I can tell you. It was just after Ivar's birth. But of course we had to go. Oh, it was a delicious journey! And it saved Torvald's life. But it cost a frightful lot of money, Christina.

MRS. L. So I should think.

NORA. Twelve hundred dollars! Four thousand eight hundred crowns! Isn't that a lot of money?

MRS. L. How lucky you had the money to spend!

NORA. I must tell you we got it from father.

MRS. L. Ah, I see. He died just about that time, didn't he?

NORA. Yes, Christina, just then. And only think! I couldn't go and nurse him! I was expecting little Ivar's birth daily. And then I had my Torvald to attend to. Dear, kind old father! I never saw him again, Christina. Oh! that's the hardest thing I've had to bear since my marriage.

MRS. L. I know how fond you were of him. And then you went to Italy?

NORA. Yes; we had the money, and the doctors insisted. We started a month later.

MRS. L. And your husband returned completely cured?

NORA. Sound as a bell.

MRS. L. But—the doctor?

NORA. What about him?

MRS. L. I thought as I came in your servant announced the Doctor—

NORA. Oh, yes; Doctor Rank. But he doesn't come as a doctor. He's our best friend, and never lets a day pass without looking in. No, Torvald hasn't had an hour's illness since that time. And the children are so healthy and well, and so am I. [*Jumps up and claps her hands.*] Oh, Christina, Christina, it's so lovely to live and to be happy!— Oh! but it's really too horrid of me!—Here am I talking about nothing but my own concerns. [*Sits down upon a footstool close to her and lays her arms on Christina's lap.*] Oh! don't be angry with me!—Now just tell me, is it really true that you didn't love your husband? What made you take him?

MRS. L. My mother was then alive, bedridden and helpless; and I had my two younger brothers to think of. I thought it my duty to accept him.

NORA. Perhaps it was. I suppose he was rich then?

MRS. L. Very well off, I believe. But his business was uncertain. It fell to pieces at his death, and there was nothing left.

NORA. And then—?

MRS. L. Then I had to fight my way by keeping a shop, a little school, anything I could turn my hand to. The last three years have been one long struggle for me. But now it's over, Nora. My poor mother no longer needs me; she is at rest. And the boys are in business, and can look after themselves.

NORA. How free your life must feel!

MRS. L. No, Nora; only inexpressibly empty. No one to live for. [*Stands up restlessly.*] That is why I couldn't bear to stay any longer in that out-of-the-way corner. Here it must be easier to find something really worth doing—something to occupy one's thoughts. If I could only get some settled employment—some office-work.

NORA. But, Christina, that's so tiring, and you look worn out already. You should rather go to some watering-place and rest.

MRS. L. [*going to the window*]. I have no father to give me the money, Nora.

NORA [*rising*]. Oh! don't be vexed with me.

MRS. L. [*going toward her*]. My dear Nora, don't you be vexed with me. The worst of a position like mine is that it makes one bitter. You have no one to work for, yet you have to be always on the strain. You must live; and so you become selfish. When I heard of the happy change in your circumstances—can you believe it?—I rejoiced more on my own account than on yours.

NORA. How do you mean? Ah! I see. You mean Torvald could perhaps do something for you.

MRS. L. Yes; I thought so.

NORA. And so he shall, Christina. Just you leave it all to me. I shall lead up to it beautifully, and think of something pleasant to put him in a good humor! Oh! I should so love to do something for you.

MRS. L. How good of you, Nora! And doubly good in you, who know so little of the troubles of life.

NORA. I? I know so little of—?

MRS. L. [*smiling*]. Ah, well! a little fancy-work, and so forth. You're a mere child, Nora.

NORA [*tosses her head and paces the room*]. Oh, come, you mustn't be so patronizing!

MRS. L. No?

NORA. You're like the rest. You all think I'm fit for nothing really serious—

MRS. L. Well—

NORA. You think I've had no troubles in this weary world.

MRS. L. My dear Nora, you've just told me all your troubles.

NORA. Pooh—these trifles. [*Softly.*] I haven't told you the great thing.

MRS. L. The great thing? What do you mean?

NORA. I know you look down upon me, Christina; but you've no right to. You're proud of having worked so hard and so long for your mother?

MRS. L. I'm sure I don't look down upon anyone; but it's true I'm both proud and glad when I remember that I was able to make my mother's last days free from care.

NORA. And you're proud to think of what you have done for your brothers?

MRS. L. Have I not the right to be?

NORA. Yes, surely. But now let me tell you, Christina—I, too, have something to be proud and glad of.

MRS. L. I don't doubt it. But what do you mean?

NORA. Hush! Not so loud. Only think, if Torvald were to hear! He mustn't—not for worlds! No one must know about it, Christina—no one but you.

Mrs. L. What can it be?

Nora. Come over here. [*Draws her beside her on the sofa.*] Yes—I, too, have something to be proud and glad of. *I* saved Torvald's life.

Mrs. L. Saved his life? How?

Nora. I told you about our going to Italy. Torvald would have died but for that.

Mrs. L. Yes—and your father gave you the money.

Nora [*smiling*]. Yes, so Torvald and everyone believes; but—

Mrs. L. But—?

Nora. Father didn't give us one penny. *I* found the money.

Mrs. L. You? All that money?

Nora. Twelve hundred dollars. Four thousand eight hundred crowns. What do you say to that?

Mrs. L. My dear Nora, how did you manage it? Did you win it in the lottery?

Nora [*contemptuously*]. In the lottery? Pooh! Any fool could have done that!

Mrs. L. Then wherever did you get it from?

Nora [*hums and smiles mysteriously*]. H'm; tra-la-la-la!

Mrs. L. Of course you couldn't borrow it.

Nora. No? Why not?

Mrs. L. Why, a wife can't borrow without her husband's consent.

Nora [*tossing her head*]. Oh! when the wife knows a little of business, and how to set about things, then—

Mrs. L. But, Nora, I don't understand—

Nora. Well you needn't. I never said I borrowed the money. Perhaps I got it another way. [*Throws herself back on the sofa.*] I may have got it from some admirer. When one is so—attractive as I am—

Mrs. L. You're too silly, Nora.

Nora. Now, I'm sure you're dying of curiosity, Christina—

Mrs. L. Listen to me, Nora dear. Haven't you been a little rash?

Nora [*sitting upright again*]. Is it rash to save one's husband's life?

Mrs. L. I think it was rash of you, without his knowledge—

Nora. But it would have been fatal for him to know! Can't you understand that? He was never to suspect how ill he was. The doctors came to me privately and told me that his life was in danger—that nothing could save him but a trip to the South. Do you think I didn't try diplomacy first? I told him how I longed to have a trip abroad, like other young wives; I wept and prayed; I said

he ought to think of my condition, and not thwart me; and then I hinted that he could borrow the money. But then, Christina, he got almost angry. He said I was frivolous, and that it was his duty as a husband not to yield to my whims and fancies —so he called them. Very well, thought I, but saved you must be; and then I found the way to do it.

Mrs. L. And did your husband never learn from your father that the money was not from him?

Nora. No; never. Father died at that very time. I meant to have told him all about it, and begged him to say nothing. But he was so ill—unhappily, it was not necessary.

Mrs. L. And you have never confessed to your husband?

Nora. Good Heavens! What can you be thinking of? Tell him, when he has such a loathing of debt? And besides—how painful and humiliating it would be for Torvald, with his manly self-reliance, to know that he owed anything to me! It would utterly upset the relation between us; our beautiful, happy home would never again be what it is.

Mrs. L. Will you never tell him?

Nora [*thoughtfully, half-smiling*]. Yes, some time perhaps—after many years, when I'm—not so pretty. You mustn't laugh at me. Of course I mean when Torvald is not so much in love with me as he is now; when it doesn't amuse him any longer to see me skipping about, and dressing up and acting. Then it might be well to have something in reserve. [*Breaking off.*] Nonsense! nonsense! That time will never come. Now, what do you say to my grand secret, Christina? Am I fit for nothing now? You may believe it has cost me a lot of anxiety. It has been no joke to meet my engagements punctually. You must know, Christina, that in business there are things called installments and quarterly interest, that are terribly hard to meet. So I had to pinch a little here and there, wherever I could. I could not save anything out of the housekeeping, for of course Torvald had to live well. And I couldn't let the children go about badly dressed; all I got for them, I spent on them, the darlings.

Mrs. L. Poor Nora! So it had to come out of your own pocket-money.

Nora. Yes, of course. After all, the whole thing was my doing. When Torvald gave me money for clothes and so on, I never used more than half of it; I always bought the simplest things. It's a mercy everything suits me so well; Torvald never noticed anything. But it was often very hard, Christina dear. For it's nice to be beautifully dressed. Now, isn't it?

Mrs. L. Indeed it is.

Nora. Well, and besides that, I made money in other ways. Last winter I was so lucky—I got a heap of copying to do. I shut myself up every evening and wrote far on into the night. Oh, sometimes I was so tired, so tired. And yet it was splendid to work in that way and earn money. I almost felt as if I was a man.

Mrs. L. Then how much have you been able to pay off?

Nora. Well, I can't precisely say. It's difficult to keep that sort of business clear. I only know that I paid off everything I could scrape together. Sometimes I really didn't know where to turn. [*Smiles.*] Then I used to imagine that a rich old gentleman was in love with me—

Mrs. L. What! What gentleman?

Nora. Oh! nobody—that he was now dead, and that when his will was opened, there stood in large letters: Pay over at once everything of which I die possessed to that charming person, Mrs. Nora Helmer.

Mrs. L. But, dear Nora, what gentleman do you mean?

Nora. Dear, dear, can't you understand? There wasn't any old gentleman: it was only what I used to dream, and dream when I was at my wit's end for money. But it's all over now—the tiresome old creature may stay where he is for me; I care nothing for him or his will; for now my troubles are over. [*Springing up.*] Oh, Christina, how glorious it is to think of! Free from cares! Free, quite free. To be able to play and romp about with the children; to have things tasteful and pretty in the house, exactly as Torvald likes it! And then the spring is coming, with the great blue sky. Perhaps then we shall have a short holiday. Perhaps I shall see the sea again. Oh, what a wonderful thing it is to live and to be happy! [*The hall door-bell rings.*]

Mrs. L. [*rising*]. There is a ring. Perhaps I had better go.

Nora. No; do stay. It's sure to be someone for Torvald.

Ellen [*in the doorway*]. If you please, ma'am, there's a gentleman to speak to Mr. Helmer.

Nora. Who is the gentleman?

Krog. [*in the doorway to the hall*]. It is I, Mrs. Helmer. [Ellen *goes.* Mrs. Linden *starts and turns away to the window.*]

Nora [*goes a step toward him, anxiously, half aloud*]. You? What is it? What do you want with my husband?

Krog. Bank business—in a way. I hold a small post in the Joint Stock Bank, and your husband is to be our new chief, I hear.

Nora. Then it is—?

Krog. Only tiresome business, Mrs. Helmer; nothing more.

Nora. Then will you please go to his study. [Krogstad *goes. She bows indifferently while she closes the door into the hall. Then she goes to the fireplace and looks to the fire.*]

Mrs. L. Nora—who was that man?

Nora. A Mr. Krogstad. Do you know him?

Mrs. L. I used to know him—many years ago. He was in a lawyer's office in our town.

Nora. Yes, so he was.

Mrs. L. How he has changed!

Nora. I believe his marriage was unhappy.

Mrs. L. And he is now a widower?

Nora. With a lot of children. There! now it'll burn up. [*She closes the stove, and pushes the rocking-chair a little aside.*]

Mrs. L. His business is not of the most creditable, they say.

Nora. Isn't it? I daresay not. I don't know— But don't let us think of business—it's so tiresome.

Dr. Rank *comes out of Helmer's room.*

Rank [*still in the doorway*]. No, no; I won't keep you. I'll just go and have a chat with your wife. [*Shuts the door and sees* Mrs. Linden.] Oh, I beg your pardon. I am *de trop* here too.

Nora. No, not in the least. [*Introduces them.*] Doctor Rank—Mrs. Linden.

Rank. Oh, indeed; I've often heard Mrs. Linden's name. I think I passed you on the stairs as we came up.

Mrs. L. Yes; I go so very slowly. Stairs try me so much.

Rank. You're not very strong?

Mrs. L. Only overworked.

Rank. Ah! Then you have come to town to find rest in a round of dissipation.

Mrs. L. I have come to look for employment.

Rank. Is that an approved remedy for over-work?

Mrs. L. One must live, Doctor Rank.

Rank. Yes, that seems to be the general opinion.

Nora. Come, Doctor Rank, you yourself want to live.

Rank. To be sure I do. However wretched I may be, I want to drag on as long as possible. And my patients have all the same mania. It's just the same with people whose complaint is moral. At this very moment Helmer is talking to such a wreck as I mean.

MRS. L. [softly]. Ah!

NORA. Whom do you mean?

RANK. Oh, a fellow named Krogstad, a man you know nothing about—corrupt to the very core of his character. But even he began by announcing solemnly that he must live.

NORA. Indeed? Then what did he want with Torvald?

RANK. I really don't know; I only gathered that it was some Bank business.

NORA. I didn't know that Krog—that this Mr. Krogstad had anything to do with the Bank?

RANK. He has some sort of place there. [To Mrs. LINDEN.] I don't know whether, in your part of the country, you have people who go wriggling and snuffing around in search of moral rottenness —whose policy it is to fill good places with men of tainted character whom they can keep under their eye and in their power? The honest men they leave out in the cold.

MRS. L. Well, I suppose the—delicate characters require most care.

RANK [shrugs his shoulders]. There we have it! It's that notion that makes society a hospital. [NORA, deep in her own thoughts, breaks into half-stifled laughter and claps her hands.] What are you laughing at? Have you any idea what society is?

NORA. What do I care for your tiresome society. I was laughing at something else—something awfully amusing. Tell me, Doctor Rank, are all the employees at the Bank dependent on Torvald now?

RANK. Is that what strikes you as awfully amusing?

NORA [smiles and hums]. Never mind, never mind! [Walks about the room.] Yes, it is amusing to think that we—that Torvald has such power over so many people. [Takes the box from her pocket.] Doctor Rank, will you have a macaroon?

RANK. Oh, dear, dear—macaroons! I thought they were contraband here.

NORA. Yes; but Christina brought me these.

MRS. L. What! I?

NORA. Oh, well! Don't be frightened. You couldn't possibly know that Torvald had forbidden them. The fact is, he is afraid of me spoiling my teeth. But, oh, bother, just for once. That's for you, Doctor Rank! [Puts a macaroon into his mouth.]

And you, too, Christina. And I will have one at the same time—only a tiny one, or at most two. [Walks about again.] Oh, dear, I am happy! There is only one thing in the world that I really want.

RANK. Well; what's that?

NORA. There's something I should so like to say —in Torvald's hearing.

RANK. Then why don't you say it?

NORA. Because I daren't, it's so ugly.

MRS. L. Ugly?

RANK. In that case you'd better not. But to us you might. What is it you would so like to say in Helmer's hearing?

NORA. I should so love to say—"Damn!"

RANK. Are you out of your mind?

MRS. L. Good gracious, Nora!

RANK. Say it. There he is!

NORA [hides the macaroons]. Hush-sh-sh.

HELMER comes out of his room, hat in hand, with his overcoat on his arm.

[Going toward him.] Well, Torvald, dear, have you got rid of him?

HELM. Yes; he's just gone.

NORA. May I introduce you?—This is Christina, who has come to town—

HELM. Christina? Pardon me, but I don't know—?

NORA. Mrs. Linden, Torvald dear—Christina Linden.

HELM. [to Mrs. LINDEN]. A school-friend of my wife's, no doubt?

MRS. L. Yes; we knew each other as girls.

NORA. And only think! She has taken this long journey on purpose to speak to you.

HELM. To speak to me!

MRS. L. Well, not quite—

NORA. You see Christina is tremendously clever at accounts, and she is so anxious to work under a first-rate man of business in order to learn still more—

HELM. Very sensible indeed.

NORA. And when she heard you were appointed Manager—it was telegraphed, you know—she started off at once, and—Torvald dear, for my sake, you must do something for Christina. Now can't you?

HELM. It's not impossible. I presume you are a widow?

MRS. L. Yes.

HELM. And have already had some experience in office-work?

MRS. L. A good deal.

HELM. Well then, it is very likely I may find a place for you.

NORA [clapping her hands]. There now! there now!

HELM. You have come at a lucky moment, Mrs. Linden.

MRS. L. Oh! how can I thank you—?

HELM. [smiling]. There's no occasion. [Puts his overcoat on.] But for the present you must excuse me.

RANK. Wait; I'll go with you [fetches his fur coat from the hall and warms it at the fire].

NORA. Don't be long, dear Torvald.

HELM. Only an hour; not more.

NORA. Are you going too, Christina?

MRS. L. [putting on her walking things]. Yes; I must set about looking for lodgings.

HELM. Then perhaps we can go together?

NORA [helping her]. What a pity we haven't a spare room for you; but I'm afraid—

MRS. L. I shouldn't think of troubling you. Good-by, dear Nora, and thank you for all your kindness.

NORA. Good-by for a little while. Of course you come back this evening. And you too, Doctor Rank. What! if you're well enough? Of course you'll be well enough. Only wrap up warmly. [They go out into the hall, talking. Outside on the stairs are heard children's voices.] There they are! there they are! [She runs to the door and opens it. The nurse ANNA enters with the children.] Come in! come in! [Bends down and kisses the children.] Oh! my sweet darlings! Do you see them, Christina? Aren't they lovely?

RANK. Don't let's stand here chattering in the draught.

HELM. Come, Mrs. Linden; only mothers can stand such a temperature. [DR. RANK, HELMER, and MRS. LINDEN go down the stairs; ANNA enters the room with the children; NORA also, shutting the door.]

NORA. How fresh and bright you look! And what red cheeks you have!—like apples and roses. [The children talk low to her during the following.] Have you had great fun? That's splendid. Oh, really! you've been giving Emmy and Bob a ride on your sledge!—Both at once, only think! Why, you're quite a man, Ivar. Oh, give her to me a little, Anna. My sweet little dolly! [Takes the smallest from the nurse and dances with her.] Yes, yes; mother will dance with Bob too. What! did you have a game of snowballs? Oh! I wish I'd been there. No; leave them, Anna; I'll take their things off. Oh, yes, let me do it; it's such fun. Go to the nursery; you look frozen. You'll find some hot coffee on the stove. [The nurse goes into the room on the left. NORA takes off the children's things, and throws them down anywhere, while the children talk to each other and to her.] Really! A big dog ran after you all the way home? But he didn't bite you? No; dogs don't bite dear little dolly children. Don't peep into those parcels, Ivar. What is it? Wouldn't you like to know? Oh, take care—it'll bite? What! shall we have a game? What shall we play at? Hide-and-seek? Yes, let's play hide-and-seek. Bob shall hide first. Am I to? Yes, let me hide first. [She and the children play, with laughter and shouting, in the room and the adjacent one to the right. At last NORA hides under the table; the children come rushing in, look for her, but cannot find her, hear her half-choked laughter, rush to the table, lift up the cover, and see her. Loud shouts. She creeps out, as though to frighten them. Fresh shouts. Meanwhile there has been a knock at the door leading into the hall. No one has heard it. Now the door is half opened and KROGSTAD is seen. He waits a little; the game is renewed.]

KROG. I beg your pardon, Mrs. Helmer—

NORA [with a suppressed cry, turns round and half jumps up]. Ah! What do you want?

KROG. Excuse me; the outer door was ajar—somebody must have forgotten to shut it—

NORA [standing up]. My husband is not at home, Mr. Krogstad.

KROG. I know it.

NORA. Then—what do you want here?

KROG. To say a few words to you.

NORA. To me? [To the children, softly.] Go in to Anna. What? No, the strange man won't hurt mamma. When he's gone we'll go on playing. [She leads the children into the left-hand room, and shuts the door behind them. Uneasy, with suspense.] It's with me you wish to speak?

KROG. Yes.

NORA. Today? But it's not the first yet—

KROG. No; today is Christmas Eve. It will depend upon yourself whether you have a merry Christmas.

NORA. What do you want? I certainly can't today—

KROG. Never mind that just now. It's about another matter. You have a minute to spare?

NORA. Oh, yes, I suppose so; although—

KROG. Good. I was sitting in the restaurant opposite, and I saw your husband go down the street.

Nora. Well!

Krog. With a lady.

Nora. What then?

Krog. May I ask if the lady was a Mrs. Linden?

Nora. Yes.

Krog. Who has just come to town?

Nora. Yes. Today.

Krog. I believe she's an intimate friend of yours?

Nora. Certainly. But I don't understand—

Krog. I used to know her too.

Nora. I know you did.

Krog. Ah! you know all about it. I thought as much. Now, frankly, is Mrs. Linden to have a place in the bank?

Nora. How dare you catechise me in this way, Mr. Krogstad, you, a subordinate of my husband's? But since you ask you shall know. Yes, Mrs. Linden is to be employed. And it's I who recommended her, Mr. Krogstad. Now you know.

Krog. Then my guess was right.

Nora [walking up and down]. You see one has a little wee bit of influence. It doesn't follow because one's only a woman that— When one is in a subordinate position, Mr. Krogstad, one ought really to take care not to offend anybody who— h'm—

Krog. Who has influence?

Nora. Exactly!

Krog. [taking another tone]. Mrs. Helmer, will you have the kindness to employ your influence on my behalf?

Nora. What? How do you mean?

Krog. Will you be so good as to see that I retain my subordinate position in the bank?

Nora. What do you mean? Who wants to take it from you?

Krog. Oh, you needn't pretend ignorance. I can very well understand that it cannot be pleasant for your friend to meet me; and I can also understand now for whose sake I am to be hounded out.

Nora. But I assure you—

Krog. Come now, once for all: there is time yet, and I advise you to use your influence to prevent it.

Nora. But, Mr. Krogstad, I have absolutely no influence.

Krog. None? I thought you just said—

Nora. Of course not in that sense—I! How should I have such influence over my husband?

Krog. Oh! I know your husband from our college days. I don't think he's firmer than other husbands.

Nora. If you talk disrespectfully of my husband, I must request you to go.

Krog. You are bold, madam.

Nora. I am afraid of you no longer. When New Year's Day is over, I shall be out of the whole business.

Krog. [controlling himself]. Listen to me, Mrs. Helmer. If need be, I shall fight as though for my life to keep my little place in the bank.

Nora. Yes, so it seems.

Krog. It's not only for the money: that matters least to me. It's something else. Well, I'd better make a clean breast of it. Of course you know, like everyone else, that some years ago I—got into trouble.

Nora. I think I've heard something of the sort.

Krog. The matter never came into court; but from that moment all paths were barred to me. Then I took up the business you know about. I was obliged to grasp at something; and I don't think I've been one of the worst. But now I must clear out of it all. My sons are growing up; for their sake I must try to win back as much respectability as I can. This place in the bank was the first step, and now your husband wants to kick me off the ladder, back into the mire.

Nora. But I assure you, Mr. Krogstad, I haven't the power to help you.

Krog. You have not the will; but I can compel you.

Nora. You won't tell my husband that I owe you money!

Krog. H'm; suppose I were to?

Nora. It would be shameful of you! [With tears in her voice.] This secret which is my joy and my pride—that he should learn it in such an ugly, coarse way—and from you! It would involve me in all sorts of unpleasantness.

Krog. Only unpleasantness?

Nora [hotly]. But just do it. It will be worst for you, for then my husband will see what a bad man you are, and then you certainly won't keep your place.

Krog. I asked if it was only domestic unpleasantness you feared?

Nora. If my husband gets to know about it, he will of course pay you off at once, and then we'll have nothing more to do with you.

Krog. [stepping a pace nearer]. Listen, Mrs. Helmer. Either you have a weak memory, or you don't know much about business. I must make your position clearer to you.

Nora. How so?

Krog. When your husband was ill, you came to me to borrow twelve hundred dollars.

Nora. I knew nobody else.

Krog. I promised to find you the money—

Nora. And you did find it.

Krog. I promised to find you the money under certain conditions. You were then so much taken up about your husband's illness, and so eager to have the money for your journey, that you probably did not give much thought to the details. Let me remind you of them. I promised to find you the amount in exchange for a note of hand which 10 I drew up.

Nora. Yes, and I signed it.

Krog. Quite right. But then I added a few lines, making your father a security for the debt. Your father was to sign this.

Nora. Was to? He did sign it!

Krog. I had left the date blank. That is to say, your father was himself to date his signature. Do you recollect that?

Nora. Yes, I believe—

Krog. Then I gave you the paper to send to your father. Is not that so?

Nora. Yes.

Krog. And of course you did so at once? For within five or six days, you brought me back the paper, signed by your father, and I gave you the money.

Nora. Well! Haven't I made my payments punctually?

Krog. Fairly—yes. But to return to the point. 30 You were in great trouble at the time, Mrs. Helmer.

Nora. I was indeed!

Krog. Your father was very ill, I believe?

Nora. He was on his death-bed.

Krog. And died soon after?

Nora. Yes.

Krog. Tell me, Mrs. Helmer: do you happen to recollect the day of his death? The day of the month, I mean?

Nora. Father died on the 29th of September.   40

Krog. Quite correct. I have made inquiries, and here comes in the remarkable point—[produces a paper] which I cannot explain.

Nora. What remarkable point? I don't know—

Krog. The remarkable point, madam, that your father signed this paper three days after his death!

Nora. What! I don't understand—

Krog. Your father died on the 29th of September. But look here, he has dated his signature October 2d! Is not that remarkable, Mrs. Helmer? [Nora is 50 silent.] Can you explain it? [Nora continues silent.] It is noteworthy too that the words "October 2d" and the year are not in your father's handwrit-

ing, but in one which I believe I know. Well, this may be explained; your father may have forgotten to date his signature, and somebody may have added the date at random before the fact of his death was known. There is nothing wrong in that. Everything depends on the signature. Of course it is genuine, Mrs. Helmer? It was really your father who with his own hand wrote his name here?

Nora [after a short silence throws her head back and looks defiantly at him]. No; I wrote father's name there.

Krog. Ah! Are you aware, madam, that that is a dangerous admission?

Nora. Why? You'll soon get your money.

Krog. May I ask you one more question? Why did you not send the paper to your father?

Nora. It was impossible. Father was ill. If I had asked him for his signature I should have had to tell him why I wanted the money; but he was so ill I really could not tell him that my husband's life was in danger. It was impossible.

Krog. Then it would have been better to have given up your tour.

Nora. No, I couldn't do that; my husband's life depended on that journey. I couldn't give it up.

Krog. And did you not consider that you were playing me false?

Nora. That was nothing to me. I didn't care in the least about you. I couldn't endure you for all the cruel difficulties you made, although you knew how ill my husband was.

Krog. Mrs. Helmer, you have evidently no clear idea what you have really done. But I can assure you it was nothing more and nothing worse that made me an outcast from society.

Nora. You! You want me to believe that you did a brave thing to save your wife's life?

Krog. The law takes no account of motives.

Nora. Then it must be a very bad law.

Krog. Bad or not, if I lay this document before a court of law you will be condemned according to law.

Nora. I don't believe that. Do you mean to tell me that a daughter has no right to spare her dying father anxiety?—that a wife has no right to save her husband's life? I don't know much about the law, but I'm sure that, somewhere or another, you will find that that is allowed. And you don't know that—you, a lawyer! You must be a bad one, Mr. Krogstad.

Krog. Possibly. But business—such business as ours—I do understand. You believe that? Very well; now do as you please. But this I may tell you, that if I'm flung into the gutter a second time, you shall keep me company. [*Bows and goes out through hall.*]

NORA [*stands awhile thinking, then throws her head back*]. Never! He wants to frighten me. I'm not so foolish as that. [*Begins folding the children's clothes. Pauses.*] But—? No, it's impossible. I did it for love!

CHILDREN [*at the door, left*]. Mamma, the strange man is gone now.

NORA. Yes, yes, I know. But don't tell anyone about the strange man. Do you hear? Not even papa!

CHILDREN. No, mamma; and now will you play with us again?

NORA. No, no, not now.

CHILDREN. Oh, do, mamma; you know you promised.

NORA. Yes, but I can't just now. Run to the nursery; I've so much to do. Run along, run along, and be good, my darlings! [*She pushes them gently into the inner room, and closes the door behind them. Sits on the sofa, embroiders a few stitches, but soon pauses.*] No! [*Throws down work, rises, goes to the hall-door and calls out.*] Ellen, bring in the Christmas-tree! [*Goes to table, left, and opens the drawer; again pauses.*] No, it's quite impossible!

ELLEN [*with the Christmas-tree*]. Where shall I stand it, ma'am?

NORA. There, in the middle of the room.

ELLEN. Shall I bring in anything else?

NORA. No, thank you, I have all I want.

[ELLEN, *having put down the tree, goes out.*]

NORA [*busy dressing the tree*]. There must be a candle here, and flowers there.—The horrid man! Nonsense, nonsense! there's nothing in it. The Christmas-tree shall be beautiful. I will do everything to please you, Torvald; I'll sing and dance, and—

Enter HELMER *by the hall-door, with bundle of documents.*

NORA. Oh! you're back already?

HELM. Yes. Has anybody been here?

NORA. Here? No.

HELM. Curious! I saw Krogstad come out of the house.

NORA. Did you? Oh, yes, by the bye, he was here for a minute.

HELM. Nora, I can see by your manner that he has been asking you to put in a good word for him.

NORA. Yes.

HELM. And you were to do it as if of your own accord? You were to say nothing to me of his having been here! Didn't he suggest that too?

NORA. Yes, Torvald; but—

HELM. Nora, Nora! and you could condescend to that! To speak to such a man, to make him a promise! And then to tell me an untruth about it!

NORA. An untruth!

HELM. Didn't you say nobody had been here? [*Threatens with his finger.*] My little bird must never do that again! A song-bird must never sing false notes. [*Puts his arm round her.*] That's so, isn't it? Yes, I was sure of it. [*Lets her go.*] And now we'll say no more about it. [*Sits down before the fire.*] Oh, how cozy and quiet it is here. [*Glances into his documents.*]

NORA [*busy with the tree, after a short silence*]. Torvald.

HELM. Yes.

NORA. I'm looking forward so much to the Stenborgs' fancy ball the day after tomorrow.

HELM. And I'm on tenterhooks to see what surprise you have in store for me.

NORA. Oh, it's too tiresome!

HELM. What is?

NORA. I can't think of anything good. Everything seems so foolish and meaningless.

HELM. Has little Nora made that discovery?

NORA [*behind his chair, with her arms on the back*]. Are you very busy, Torvald?

HELM. Well—

NORA. What sort of papers are those?

HELM. Bank business.

NORA. Already?

HELM. I got the retiring manager to let me make some changes in the staff, and so forth. This will occupy Christmas week. Everything will be straight by the New Year.

NORA. Then that's why that poor Krogstad—

HELM. H'm.

NORA [*still leaning over the chair-back, and slowly stroking his hair*]. If you hadn't been so very busy, I should have asked you a great, great favor, Torvald.

HELM. What can it be? Let's hear it.

NORA. Nobody has such exquisite taste as you. Now, I should so love to look well at the fancy ball. Torvald dear, couldn't you take me in hand, and settle what I'm to be, and arrange my costume for me?

HELM. Aha! so my willful little woman's at a loss, and making signals of distress.

NORA. Yes, *please,* Torvald. I can't get on without you.

HELM. Well, well, I'll think it over, and we'll soon hit upon something.

NORA. Oh, how good that is of you! [*Goes to the tree again; pause.*] How well the red flowers show. Tell me, was it anything so very dreadful this Krogstad got into trouble about?

HELM. Forgery, that's all. Don't you know what that means?

NORA. Mayn't he have been driven to it by need?

HELM. Yes, or like so many others, done it out of heedlessness. I'm not so hard-hearted as to condemn a man absolutely for a single fault.

NORA. No, surely not, Torvald.

HELM. Many a man can retrieve his character if he owns his crime and takes the punishment.

NORA. Crime?

HELM. But Krogstad didn't do that; he resorted to tricks and dodges, and it's that that has corrupted him.

NORA. Do you think that—?

HELM. Just think how a man with that on his conscience must be always lying and canting and shamming. Think of the mask he must wear even toward his own wife and children. It's worst for the children, Nora!

NORA. Why?

HELM. Because such a dust-cloud of lies poisons and contaminates the whole air of home. Every breath the children draw contains some germ of evil.

NORA [*closer behind him*]. Are you sure of that!

HELM. As a lawyer, my dear, I've seen it often enough. Nearly all cases of early corruption may be traced to lying mothers.

NORA. Why—mothers?

HELM. It generally comes from the mother's side, but of course the father's influence may act in the same way. And this Krogstad has been poisoning his own children for years past by a life of lies and hypocrisy—that's why I call him morally ruined. [*Stretches out his hands toward her.*] So my sweet little Nora must promise not to plead his cause. Shake hands upon it. Come, come, what's this? Give me your hand. That's right. Then it's a bargain. I assure you it would have been impossible for me to work with him. It gives me a positive sense of physical discomfort to come in contact with such people. [*Nora snatches her hand away, and moves to the other side of the Christmas-tree.*]

NORA. How warm it is here; and I have so much to do.

HELM. Yes, and I must try to get some of these papers looked through before dinner; and I'll think over your costume, too. And perhaps I may even find something to hang in gilt paper on the Christmas-tree! [*Lays his hand on her head.*] My precious little song-bird. [*He goes into his room and shuts the door behind him.*]

NORA [*softly, after a pause*]. It can't be— It's impossible! It must be impossible!

ANNA [*at the door, left*]. The little ones are begging so prettily to come to mamma.

NORA. No, no, don't let them come to me! Keep them with you, Anna.

ANNA. Very well, ma'am. [*Shuts the door.*]

NORA [*pale with terror*]. Corrupt my children!— Poison my home! [*Short pause. She raises her head.*] It's not true. It can never, never be true.

ACT II

The same room. In the corner, beside the piano, stands the Christmas-tree, stripped, and the candles burnt out. Nora's walking things lie on the sofa. NORA discovered walking about restlessly. She stops by sofa, takes up cloak, then lays it down again.

NORA. There's somebody coming. [*Goes to hall door; listens.*] Nobody; nobody is likely to come today, Christmas Day! nor tomorrow either. But perhaps— [*Opens the door and looks out.*] No, nothing in the letter box; quite empty. [*Comes forward.*] Stuff and nonsense! Of course he only meant to frighten me. There's no fear of any such thing. It's impossible! Why, I have three little children.

Enter ANNA, from the left with a large cardboard box.

ANNA. At last I've found the box with the fancy dress.

NORA. Thanks; put it down on the table.

ANNA [*does so*]. But it is very much out of order.

NORA. Oh, I wish I could tear it into a hundred thousand pieces.

ANNA. Oh, no. It can easily be put to rights—just a little patience.

NORA. I'll go and get Mrs. Linden to help me.

ANNA. Going out again! In such weather as this! You'll catch cold, ma'am, and be ill.

NORA. Worse things might happen— What are the children doing?

ANNA. They're playing with their Christmas presents, poor little dears; but—

NORA. Do they often ask for me?

ANNA. You see they've been so used to having their mamma with them.

NORA. Yes; but, Anna, in future I can't have them so much with me.

ANNA. Well, little children get used to anything.

NORA. Do you think they do? Do you believe they would forget their mother if she went quite away?

ANNA. Gracious me! Quite away?

NORA. Tell me, Anna—I've so often wondered about it—how could you bring yourself to give your child up to strangers?

ANNA. I had to when I came as nurse to my little Miss Nora.

NORA. But how could you make up your mind to it?

ANNA. When I had the chance of such a good place? A poor girl who's been in trouble must take what comes. That wicked man did nothing for me.

NORA. But your daughter must have forgotten you.

ANNA. Oh, no, ma'am, that she hasn't. She wrote to me both when she was confirmed and when she was married.

NORA [embracing her]. Dear old Anna—you were a good mother to me when I was little.

ANNA. My poor little Nora had no mother but me.

NORA. And if my little ones had nobody else, I'm sure you would—nonsense, nonsense! [Opens the box.] Go in to the children. Now I must— Tomorrow you shall see how beautiful I'll be.

ANNA. I'm sure there will be no one at the ball so beautiful as my Miss Nora. [She goes into the room on the left.]

NORA [takes the costume out of the box, but soon throws it down again]. Oh, if I dared go out. If only nobody would come. If only nothing would happen here in the meantime. Rubbish; nobody will come. Only not to think. What a delicious muff! Beautiful gloves, beautiful gloves! Away with it all—away with it all! One, two, three, four, five, six— [With a scream.] Ah, there they come— [Goes toward the door, then stands undecidedly.]

MRS. LINDEN enters from hall where she has taken off her things.

NORA. Oh, it's you, Christina. Is nobody else there? How delightful of you to come.

MRS. L. I hear you called at my lodgings.

NORA. Yes, I was just passing. I do so want you to help me. Let us sit here on the sofa—so. Tomorrow evening there's to be a fancy ball at Consul Stenborg's overhead, and Torvald wants me to appear as a Neapolitan fisher girl, and dance the tarantella; I learnt it at Capri.

MRS. L. I see—quite a performance!

NORA. Yes, Torvald wishes me to. Look, this is the costume. Torvald had it made for me in Italy; but now it is all so torn, I don't know—

MRS. L. Oh! we'll soon set that to rights. It's only the trimming that's got loose here and there. Have you a needle and thread? Ah! here's the very thing.

NORA. Oh, how kind of you.

MRS. L. So you're to be in costume, tomorrow, Nora? I'll tell you what—I shall come in for a moment to see you in all your glory. But I've quite forgotten to thank you for the pleasant evening yesterday.

NORA [rises and walks across room]. Oh! yesterday, it didn't seem so pleasant as usual. You should have come a little sooner, Christina. Torvald has certainly the art of making home bright and beautiful.

MRS. L. You, too, I should think, or you wouldn't be your father's daughter. But tell me— is Doctor Rank always so depressed as he was yesterday?

NORA. No; yesterday it was particularly striking. You see he has a terrible illness. He has spinal consumption, poor fellow. They say his father led a terrible life—kept mistresses and all sorts of things —so the son has been sickly from his childhood, you understand.

MRS. L. [lets her sewing fall into her lap]. Why, my darling Nora, how do you learn such things?

NORA [walking]. Oh! when one has three children one has visits from women who know something of medicine—and they talk of this and that.

MRS. L. [goes on sewing—a short pause]. Does Doctor Rank come here every day?

NORA. Every day. He's been Torvald's friend from boyhood, and he's a good friend of mine too. Doctor Rank is quite one of the family.

MRS. L. But tell me—is he quite sincere? I mean, doesn't he like to say flattering things to people?

NORA. On the contrary. Why should you think so?

MRS. L. When you introduced us yesterday he declared he had often heard my name; but I noticed your husband had no notion who I was. How could Doctor Rank—?

NORA. Yes, he was quite right, Christina. You see, Torvald loves me so indescribably he wants to have me all to himself, as he says. When we were first married he was almost jealous if I even mentioned one of the people at home! so I naturally let it alone. But I often talk to Doctor Rank about the old times, for he likes to hear about them.

MRS. L. Listen to me, Nora! You're still a child in many ways. I am older than you, and have more experience. I'll tell you something: you ought to get clear of the whole affair with Doctor Rank.

NORA. What affair?

MRS. L. You were talking yesterday of a rich admirer who was to find you money—

NORA. Yes, one who never existed, worse luck. What then?

MRS. L. Has Doctor Rank money?

NORA. Yes, he has.

MRS. L. And nobody to provide for?

NORA. Nobody. But—?

MRS. L. And he comes here every day?

NORA. Yes, every day.

MRS. L. I should have thought he'd have had better taste.

NORA. I don't understand you.

MRS. L. Don't pretend, Nora. Do you suppose I don't guess who lent you the twelve hundred dollars?

NORA. Are you out of your senses? You think *that!* A friend who comes here every day! How painful that would be!

MRS. L. Then it really is not he?

NORA. No, I assure you. It never for a moment occurred to me. Besides, at that time he had nothing to lend; he came into his property afterward.

MRS. L. Well, I believe that was lucky for you, Nora dear.

NORA. No, really, it would never have struck me to ask Doctor Rank. But I'm certain that if I did—

MRS. L. But of course you never would?

NORA. Of course not. It's inconceivable that it should ever be necessary. But I'm quite sure that if I spoke to Doctor Rank—

MRS. L. Behind your husband's back?

NORA. I must get out of the other thing; that's behind his back too. I must get out of that.

MRS. L. Yes, yes, I told you so yesterday; but—

NORA [*walking up and down*]. A man can manage these things much better than a woman.

MRS. L. One's own husband, yes.

NORA. Nonsense. [*Stands still.*] When everything is paid, one gets back the paper?

MRS. L. Of course.

NORA. And can tear it into a hundred thousand pieces, and burn it, the nasty, filthy thing!

MRS. L. [*looks at her fixedly, lays down her work, and rises slowly*]. Nora, you're hiding something from me.

NORA. Can you see that in my face?

MRS. L. Something has happened since yesterday morning. Nora, what is it?

NORA [*going toward her*]. Christina [*listens*]— Hush! There's Torvald coming home. Here, go into the nursery. Torvald cannot bear to see dressmaking. Let Anna help you.

MRS. L. [*gathers some of the things together*]. Very well, but I shan't go away until you've told me all about it. [*She goes out to the left as* HELMER *enters from hall.*]

NORA [*runs to meet him*]. Oh! how I've been longing for you to come, Torvald dear.

HELM. Was the dressmaker here?

NORA. No, Christina. She is helping me with my costume. You'll see how well I shall look.

HELM. Yes, wasn't that a lucky thought of mine?

NORA. Splendid. But isn't it good of me, too, to have given in to you?

HELM. [*takes her under the chin*]. Good of you! To give in to your own husband? Well, well, you little madcap, I know you don't mean it. But I won't disturb you. I dare say you want to be "trying on."

NORA. And you're going to work, I suppose?

HELM. Yes. [*Shows her bundle of papers.*] Look here. [*Goes toward his room.*] I've just come from the Bank.

NORA. Torvald.

HELM. [*stopping*]. Yes?

NORA. If your little squirrel were to beg you for something so prettily—

HELM. Well?

NORA. Would you do it?

HELM. I must know first what it is.

NORA. The squirrel would jump about and play all sorts of tricks if you would only be nice and kind.

HELM. Come, then, out with it.

NORA. Your lark would twitter from morning till night—

HELM. Oh, that she does in any case.

NORA. I'll be an elf and dance in the moonlight for you, Torvald.

HELM. Nora—you can't mean what you were hinting at this morning?

NORA [coming nearer]. Yes, Torvald, I beg and implore you.

HELM. Have you really the courage to begin that again?

NORA. Yes, yes; for my sake, you must let Krogstad keep his place in the bank.

HELM. My dear Nora, it's his place I intend for Mrs. Linden.

NORA. Yes, that's so good of you. But instead of Krogstad, you could dismiss some other clerk.

HELM. Why, this is incredible obstinacy! Because you thoughtlessly promised to put in a word for him, I am to—

NORA. It's not that, Torvald. It's for your own sake. This man writes for the most scurrilous newspapers; you said so yourself. He can do you such a lot of harm. I'm terribly afraid of him.

HELM. Oh, I understand; it's old recollections that are frightening you.

NORA. What do you mean?

HELM. Of course you're thinking of your father.

NORA. Yes, of course. Only think of the shameful things wicked people used to write about father. I believe they'd have got him dismissed if you hadn't been sent to look into the thing and been kind to him and helped him.

HELM. My dear Nora, between your father and me there is all the difference in the world. Your father was not altogether unimpeachable. I am; and I hope to remain so.

NORA. Oh, no one knows what wicked men can hit upon. We could live so happily now, in our cozy, quiet home, you and I and the children, Torvald! That's why I beg and implore you—

HELM. And it's just by pleading his cause that you make it impossible for me to keep him. It's already known at the bank that I intend to dismiss Krogstad. If it were now reported that the new manager let himself be turned round his wife's little finger—

NORA. What then?

HELM. Oh, nothing! So long as a willful woman can have her way I am to make myself the laughing-stock of everyone, and set people saying I am under petticoat government? Take my word for it, I should soon feel the consequences. And besides, there's one thing that makes Krogstad impossible for me to work with.

NORA. What thing?

HELM. I could perhaps have overlooked his shady character at a pinch—

NORA. Yes, couldn't you, Torvald?

HELM. And I hear he is good at his work. But the fact is, he was a college chum of mine—there was one of those rash friendships between us that one so often repents of later. I don't mind confessing it—he calls me by my Christian name; and he insists on doing it even when others are present. He delights in putting on airs of familiarity—Torvald here, Torvald there! I assure you it's most painful to me. He would make my position at the Bank perfectly unendurable.

NORA. Torvald, you're not serious?

HELM. No? Why not?

NORA. That's such a petty reason.

HELM. What! Petty! Do you consider me petty?

NORA. No, on the contrary, Torvald dear; and that's just why—

HELM. Never mind, you call my motives petty; then I must be petty too. Petty! Very well. Now we'll put an end to this once for all. [Goes to the door into the hall and calls.] Ellen!

NORA. What do you want?

HELM. [searching among his papers]. To settle the thing. [ELLEN enters.] There, take this letter, give it to a messenger. See that he takes it at once. The address is on it. Here is the money.

ELLEN. Very well. [Goes with the letter.]

HELM. [arranging papers]. There, Madame Obstinacy!

NORA [breathless]. Torvald—what was in that letter?

HELM. Krogstad's dismissal.

NORA. Call it back again, Torvald! There is still time. Oh, Torvald, get it back again! For my sake, for your own, for the children's sake! Do you hear, Torvald? Do it. You don't know what that letter may bring upon us all.

HELM. Too late.

NORA. Yes, too late.

HELM. My dear Nora, I forgive your anxiety, though it's anything but flattering to me. Why should I be afraid of a blackguard scribbler's spite? But I forgive you all the same, for it's a proof of your great love for me. [Takes her in his arms.] That's how it should be, my own dear Nora. Let what will happen—when the time comes, I shall have strength and courage enough. You shall see, my shoulders are broad enough to bear the whole burden.

NORA [terror-struck]. What do you mean by that?

HELM. The whole burden, I say.

NORA [firmly]. That you shall never, never do.

HELM. Very well; then we'll share it, Nora, as man and wife. [*Petting her.*] Are you satisfied now? Come, come, come, don't look like a scared dove. It is all nothing—fancy. Now you must play the tarantella through, and practice the tambourine. I shall sit in my inner room and shut both doors, so that I shall hear nothing. You can make as much noise as you please. [*Turns round in doorway.*] And when Rank comes, just tell him where I'm to be found. [*He nods to her and goes with his papers into his room, closing the door.*]

NORA [*bewildered with terror, stands as though rooted to the ground, and whispers*]. He would do it. Yes, he would do it. He would do it, in spite of all the world. No, never that, never, never! Anything rather than that! Oh, for some way of escape! What to do! [*Hall bell rings.*] Anything rather than that—anything, anything! [*Nora draws her hands over her face, pulls herself together, goes to the door and opens it. Rank stands outside, hanging up his greatcoat. During the following, it grows dark.*]

NORA. Good afternoon, Doctor Rank. I knew you by your ring. But you mustn't go to Torvald now. I believe he's busy.

RANK. And you?

NORA. Oh, you know very well I've always time for you.

RANK. Thank you. I shall avail myself of your kindness as long as I can!

NORA. What do you mean? As long as you can?

RANK. Yes. Does that frighten you?

NORA. I think it's an odd expression. Do you expect anything to happen?

RANK. Something I've long been prepared for; but I didn't think it would come so soon.

NORA [*seizing his arm*]. What is it, Doctor Rank? You must tell me.

RANK [*sitting down by the stove*]. I am running down hill. There's no help for it.

NORA [*draws a long breath of relief*]. It's you?

RANK. Who else should it be? Why lie to one's self? I'm the most wretched of all my patients, Mrs. Helmer. I have been auditing my life-account —bankrupt! Before a month is over I shall lie rotting in the churchyard.

NORA. Oh! What an ugly way to talk!

RANK. The thing itself is so confoundedly ugly, you see. But the worst of it is, so many other ugly things have to be gone through first. There is one last investigation to be made, and when that is over I shall know exactly when the break-up will begin. There's one thing I want to say to you.

Helmer's delicate nature shrinks so from all that is horrible; I will not have him in my sick room.

NORA. But, Doctor Rank—

RANK. I won't have him, I say—not on any account! I shall lock my door against him. As soon as I have ascertained the worst, I shall send you my visiting card with a black cross on it; and then you will know that the horror has begun.

NORA. Why, you're perfectly unreasonable today. And I did so want you to be in a really good humor.

RANK. With death staring me in the face? And to suffer thus for another's sin! Where's the justice of it? And in every family you can see some such inexorable retribution—

NORA [*stopping her ears*]. Nonsense, nonsense; now cheer up.

RANK. Well, after all, the whole thing's only worth laughing at. My poor innocent spine must do penance for my father's wild oats.

NORA [*at table, left*]. I suppose he was too fond of asparagus and Strasbourg pâté, wasn't he?

RANK. Yes; and truffles.

NORA. Yes, truffles, to be sure. And oysters, I believe?

RANK. Yes, oysters; oysters of course.

NORA. And then all the port and champagne. It's sad all these good things should attack the spine.

RANK. Especially when the spine attacked never had the good of them.

NORA. Yes, that's the worst of it.

RANK [*looks at her searchingly*]. H'm—

NORA [*a moment later*]. Why did you smile?

RANK. No; it was you that laughed.

NORA. No; it was you that smiled, Doctor Rank.

RANK [*standing up*]. You're deeper than I thought.

NORA. I'm in such a crazy mood today.

RANK. So it seems.

NORA [*with her hands on his shoulders*]. Dear, dear Doctor Rank, death shall not take you away from Torvald and me.

RANK. Oh, you'll easily get over the loss. The absent are soon forgotten.

NORA [*looks at him anxiously*]. Do you think so?

RANK. People make fresh ties, and then—

NORA. Who make fresh ties?

RANK. You and Helmer will, when I'm gone. You yourself are taking time by the forelock, it seems to me. What was that Mrs. Linden doing here yesterday?

NORA. Oh! You're surely not jealous of Christina?

RANK. Yes, I am. She will be my successor in this house. When I'm gone, this woman will perhaps—

NORA. Hush! Not so loud; she is in there.

RANK. Today as well? You see!

NORA. Only to put my costume in order—how unreasonable you are! [*Sits on sofa.*] Now do be good, Doctor Rank. Tomorrow you shall see how beautifully I dance; and then you may fancy that I am doing it all to please you—and of course Torvald as well. [*Takes various things out of box.*] Doctor Rank, sit here, and I'll show you something.

RANK [*sitting*]. What is it?

NORA. Look here. Look!

RANK. Silk stockings.

NORA. Flesh-colored. Aren't they lovely? Oh, it's so dark here now; but tomorrow— No, no, no, you must only look at the feet. Oh, well, I suppose you may look at the rest too.

RANK. H'm—

NORA. What are you looking so critical about? Do you think they won't fit me?

RANK. I can't possibly have any valid opinion on that point.

NORA [*looking at him a moment*]. For shame! [*Hits him lightly on the ear with the stockings.*] Take that. [*Rolls them up again.*]

RANK. And what other wonders am I to see?

NORA. You shan't see any more, for you don't behave nicely. [*She hums a little and searches among the things.*]

RANK [*after a short silence*]. When I sit here gossiping with you, I simply can't imagine what would have become of me if I had never entered this house.

NORA [*smiling*]. Yes, I think you do feel at home with us.

RANK [*more softly—looking straight before him*]. And now to have to leave it all—

NORA. Nonsense. You shan't leave us.

RANK [*in the same tone*]. And not to be able to leave behind the slightest token of gratitude; scarcely even a passing regret—nothing but an empty place, that can be filled by the first comer.

NORA. And if I were to ask for—? No—

RANK. For what?

NORA. For a great proof of your friendship.

RANK. Yes?—Yes?

NORA. No, I mean—for a very, very great service.

RANK. Would you really for once make me so happy?

NORA. Oh! you don't know what it is.

RANK. Then tell me.

NORA. No, I really can't; it's far, far too much—not only a service, but help and advice besides—

RANK. So much the better. I can't think what you can mean. But go on. Don't you trust me?

NORA. As I trust no one else. I know you are my best and truest friend. So I will tell you. Well, then, Doctor Rank, you must help me to prevent something. You know how deeply, how wonderfully Torvald loves me; he would not hesitate a moment to give his very life for my sake.

RANK [*bending toward her*]. Nora, do you think he is the only one who—

NORA [*with a slight start*]. Who—?

RANK. Who would gladly give his life for you?

NORA [*sadly*]. Oh!

RANK. I have sworn that you shall know it before I—go. I should never find a better opportunity— Yes, Nora, now you know it, and now you know too that you can trust me as you can no one else.

NORA [*standing up, simply and calmly*]. Let me pass, please.

RANK [*makes way for her, but remains sitting*]. Nora—

NORA [*in the doorway*]. Ellen, bring the lamp. [*Crosses to the stove.*] Oh, dear, Doctor Rank, that was too bad of you.

RANK [*rising*]. That I have loved you as deeply as—anyone else? Was that too bad of me?

NORA. No, but that you should tell me so. It was so unnecessary—

RANK. What do you mean? Did you know—?

ELLEN *enters with the lamp; sets it on table and goes out again.*

RANK. Nora—Mrs. Helmer—I ask you, did you know?

NORA. Oh, how can I tell what I knew or didn't know. I really can't say— How could you be so clumsy, Doctor Rank? It was all so nice!

RANK. Well, at any rate, you know now that I am yours, soul and body. And now, go on.

NORA [*looking at him*]. Go on—now?

RANK. I beg you to tell what you want.

NORA. I can tell you nothing now.

RANK. Yes, yes! You mustn't punish me in that way. Let me do for you whatever a man can.

NORA. You can really do nothing for me now. Besides, I really want no help. You'll see it was only my fancy. Yes, it must be so. Of course! [*Sits *in the rocking-chair smiling at him.*] You're a nice one, Doctor Rank. Aren't you ashamed of yourself now the lamp's on the table?

RANK. No, not exactly. But perhaps I ought to go—forever.

NORA. No, indeed you mustn't. Of course you must come and go as you've always done. You know very well that Torvald can't do without you.

RANK. Yes, but you?

NORA. Oh, you know I always like to have you here.

RANK. That's just what led me astray. You're a riddle to me. It has often seemed to me as if you liked being with me almost as much as being with Helmer.

NORA. Yes, don't you see?—there are some people one loves, and others one likes to talk to.

RANK. Yes—there's something in that.

NORA. When I was a girl I naturally loved papa best. But it always delighted me to steal into the servants' room. In the first place they never lectured me, and in the second it was such fun to hear them talk.

RANK. Oh, I see; then it's their place I have taken?

NORA [*jumps up and hurries toward him*]. Oh, my dear Doctor Rank, I don't mean that. But you understand, with Torvald it's the same as with papa—

ELLEN *enters from the hall.*

ELLEN. Please, ma'am— [*Whispers to* NORA *and gives her a card.*]

NORA [*glances at the card*]. Ah! [*Puts it in her pocket.*]

RANK. Anything wrong?

NORA. No, not in the least. It's only—it's my new costume—

RANK. Why, it's there.

NORA. Oh, that one, yes. But it's another that— I ordered it—Torvald mustn't know—

RANK. Aha! so that's the great secret.

NORA. Yes, of course. Do just go to him; he's in the inner room; do keep him as long as you can.

RANK. Make yourself easy; he shan't escape. [*Goes into Helmer's room.*]

NORA [*to* ELLEN]. Is he waiting in the kitchen?

ELLEN. Yes, he came up the back stair—

NORA. Didn't you tell him I was engaged?

ELLEN. Yes, but it was no use.

NORA. He won't go away?

ELLEN. No, ma'am, not until he has spoken with you.

NORA. Then let him come in; but quietly. And, Ellen—say nothing about it; it's a surprise for my husband.

ELLEN. Oh, yes, ma'am, I understand—
[*She goes out.*

NORA. It's coming. It's coming after all. No, no, no, it can never be; it shall not! [*She goes to Helmer's door and slips the bolt.* ELLEN *opens the hall-door for* KROGSTAD, *and shuts it after him. He wears a traveling coat, high boots, and a fur cap.*]

NORA. Speak quietly; my husband is at home.

KROG. All right. I don't care.

NORA. What do you want?

KROG. A little information.

NORA. Be quick then. What is it?

KROG. You know I've got my dismissal.

NORA. I could not prevent it, Mr. Krogstad. I fought for you to the last, but it was no good.

KROG. Does your husband care for you so little? He knows what I can bring upon you, and yet he dares—

NORA. How can you think I should tell him?

KROG. I knew very well you hadn't. It wasn't like my friend Torvald Helmer to show so much courage—

NORA. Mr. Krogstad, be good enough to speak respectfully of my husband.

KROG. Certainly, with all due respect. But since you're so anxious to keep the matter secret, I suppose you're a little clearer than yesterday as to what you have done.

NORA. Clearer than you could ever make me.

KROG. Yes, such a bad lawyer as I—

NORA. What is it you want?

KROG. Only to see how you're getting on, Mrs. Helmer. I've been thinking about you all day. A mere money-lender, a penny-a-liner, a—in short, a creature like me—has a little bit of what people call "heart."

NORA. Then show it; think of my little children.

KROG. Did you and your husband think of mine? But enough of that. I only wanted to tell you that you needn't take this matter too seriously. I shan't lodge any information for the present.

NORA. No, surely not. I knew you would not.

KROG. The whole thing can be settled quite quietly. Nobody need know. It can remain among us three.

NORA. My husband must never know.

KROG. How can you prevent it? Can you pay off the debt?

NORA. No, not at once.

Krog. Or have you any means of raising the money in the next few days?

Nora. None that I will make use of.

Krog. And if you had it would be no good to you now. If you offered me ever so much ready money you should not get back your I O U.

Nora. Tell me what you want to do with it.

Krog. I only want to keep it, to have it in my possession. No outsider shall hear anything of it. So, if you've got any desperate scheme in your head—

Nora. What if I have?

Krog. If you should think of leaving your husband and children—

Nora. What if I do?

Krog. Or if you should think of—something worse—

Nora. How do you know that?

Krog. Put all that out of your head.

Nora. How did you know what I had in my mind?

Krog. Most of us think of *that* at first. I thought of it, too; but I had not the courage—

Nora [voicelessly]. Nor I.

Krog. [relieved]. No one has. You haven't the courage either, have you?

Nora. I haven't, I haven't.

Krog. Besides, it would be very silly—when the first storm is over— I have a letter in my pocket for your husband—

Nora. Telling him everything?

Krog. Sparing you as much as possible.

Nora [quickly]. He must never have that letter. Tear it up. I will get the money somehow.

Krog. Pardon me, Mrs. Helmer, but I believe I told you—

Nora. Oh, I'm not talking about the money I owe you. Tell me how much you demand from my husband—I'll get it.

Krog. I demand no money from your husband.

Nora. What *do* you demand then?

Krog. I'll tell you. I want to regain my footing in the world. I want to rise; and your husband shall help me to do it. For the last eighteen months my record has been spotless; I've been in bitter need all the time; but I was content to fight my way up, step by step. Now, I've been thrust down, and I won't be satisfied with merely being allowed to sneak back again. I want to rise, I tell you. I must get into the bank again, in a higher position than before. Your husband shall create a place on purpose for me—

Nora. He will never do that!

Krog. He will do it; I know him—he won't dare to refuse! And when I'm in, you'll soon see! I shall be the manager's right hand. It won't be Torvald Helmer, but Nils Krogstad, that manages the Joint Stock Bank.

Nora. That will never be.

Krog. Perhaps you'll—?

Nora. *Now* I have the courage for it.

Krog. Oh, you don't frighten me. A sensitive, petted creature like you—

Nora. You shall see, you shall see!

Krog. Under the ice, perhaps? Down in the cold, black water? And next spring to come up again, ugly, hairless, unrecognizable—

Nora. You can't terrify me.

Krog. Nor you me. People don't do that sort of thing, Mrs. Helmer. And, after all, what good would it be? I have your husband in my pocket all the same.

Nora. Afterward? When I am no longer—

Krog. You forget, your reputation remains in my hands! [Nora *stands speechless and looks at him.*] Well, now you are prepared. Do nothing foolish. So soon as Helmer has received my letter I shall expect to hear from him. And remember that it is your husband himself who has forced me back again into such paths. That I will never forgive him. Good-by, Mrs. Helmer. [*Goes through hall.* Nora *hurries to the door, opens it a little, and listens.*]

Nora. He's going. He is not putting the letter into the box. No, no, it would be impossible. [*Opens the door farther and farther.*] What's that? He's standing still; not going downstairs. Is he changing his mind? Is he—? [*A letter falls into the box. Krogstad's footsteps are heard gradually receding down the stair.* Nora *utters suppressed shriek; pause.*] In the letter box. [*Slips shrinkingly up to the door.*] There it lies—Torvald, Torvald—now we are lost!

Mrs. Linden *enters from the left with the costume.*

Mrs. L. There, I think it's all right now. Shall we just try it on?

Nora [hoarsely and softly]. Christina, come here.

Mrs. L. [throws dress on sofa]. What's the matter? You look quite aghast.

Nora. Come here. Do you see that letter? There, see—through the glass of the letter-box.

Mrs. L. Yes, yes, I see it.

Nora. That letter is from Krogstad—

Mrs. L. Nora—it was Krogstad who lent you the money!

Nora. Yes, and now Torvald will know everything.

Mrs. L. Believe me, Nora, it's the best thing for you both.

Nora. You don't know all yet. I have forged a name—

Mrs. L. Good heavens!

Nora. Now listen to me, Christina, you shall bear me witness.

Mrs. L. How "witness"? What am I to—?

Nora. If I should go out of my mind—it might easily happen—

Mrs. L. Nora!

Nora. Or if anything else should happen to me —so that I couldn't be here myself—

Mrs. L. Now, Nora, you're quite beside yourself!

Nora. In case anyone wanted to take it all upon himself—the whole blame, you understand—

Mrs. L. Yes, but how can you think—

Nora. You shall bear witness that it's not true, Christina. I'm not out of my mind at all; I know quite well what I'm saying; and I tell you nobody else knew anything about it; I did the whole thing, I myself. Don't forget that.

Mrs. L. I won't forget. But I don't understand what you mean—

Nora. Oh, how should you? It's the miracle coming to pass.

Mrs. L. The miracle?

Nora. Yes, the miracle. But it's so terrible, Christina;—it mustn't happen for anything in the world.

Mrs. L. I will go straight to Krogstad and talk to him.

Nora. Don't; he will do you some harm.

Mrs. L. Once he would have done anything for me.

Nora. He?

Mrs. L. Where does he live?

Nora. Oh, how can I tell—? Yes; [feels in her pocket] here's his card. But the letter, the letter—!

Helm. [knocking outside]. Nora.

Nora [shrieks in terror]. What is it? What do you want?

Helm. Don't be frightened, we're not coming in; you've bolted the door. Are you trying on your dress?

Nora. Yes, yes, I'm trying it on. It suits me so well, Torvald.

Mrs. L. [who has read the card]. Then he lives close by here?

Nora. Yes, but it's no use now. The letter is actually in the box.

Mrs. L. And your husband has the key?

Nora. Always.

Mrs. L. Krogstad must demand his letter back, unread. He must make some excuse—

Nora. But this is the very time when Torvald generally—

Mrs. L. Prevent him. Keep him occupied. I'll come back as quickly as I can.

[She goes out quickly through the hall door.

Nora [opens Helmer's door and peeps in]. Torvald!

Helm. Well, now may one come back into one's own room? Come, Rank, we'll have a look— [In the doorway.] But how's this?

Nora. What, Torvald dear?

Helm. Rank led me to expect a grand dressing-up.

Rank [in the doorway]. So I understood. I suppose I was mistaken.

Nora. No, no one shall see me in my glory till tomorrow evening.

Helm. Why, Nora dear, you look so tired. Have you been practicing too hard?

Nora. No, I haven't practiced at all yet.

Helm. But you'll have to—

Nora. Yes, it's absolutely necessary. But, Torvald, I can't get on without your help. I've forgotten everything.

Helm. Oh, we'll soon freshen it up again.

Nora. Yes, do help me, Torvald. You must promise— Oh, I'm so nervous about it. Before so many people—this evening you must give yourself up entirely to me. You mustn't do a stroke of work! Now promise, Torvald dear!

Helm. I promise. All this evening I will be your slave. Little helpless thing!—But, by the by, I must first— [Going to hall door.]

Nora. What do you want there?

Helm. Only to see if there are any letters.

Nora. No, no, don't do that, Torvald.

Helm. Why not?

Nora. Torvald, I beg you not to. There are none there.

Helm. Let me just see. [Is going. Nora, at the piano, plays the first bars of the tarantella.]

Helm. [at the door, stops]. Aha!

Nora. I can't dance tomorrow if I don't rehearse with you first.

Helm. [going to her]. Are you really so nervous, dear Nora?

Nora. Yes, dreadfully! Let me rehearse at once. We have time before dinner. Oh! do sit down and accompany me, Torvald dear; direct me as you used to do.

HELM. With all the pleasure in life, if you wish it. [*Sits at piano.* NORA *snatches the tambourine out of the box, and hurriedly drapes herself in a long parti-colored shawl; then, with a bound, stands in the middle of the floor.*]

NORA. Now play for me! Now I'll dance! [HELMER *plays and* NORA *dances.* RANK *stands at the piano behind* HELMER *and looks on.*]

HELM. [*playing*]. Slower! Slower!

NORA. Can't do it slower.

HELM. Not so violently, Nora.

NORA. I must! I must!

HELM. [*stops*]. Nora—that'll never do.

NORA [*laughs and swings her tambourine*]. Didn't I tell you so?

RANK. Let me accompany her.

HELM. [*rising*]. Yes, do—then I can direct her better. [RANK *sits down to the piano.* NORA *dances more and more wildly.* HELMER *stands by the stove and addresses frequent corrections to her. She seems not to hear. Her hair breaks loose and falls over her shoulders. She does not notice it, but goes on dancing.* MRS. LINDEN *enters and stands spellbound in the doorway.*]

MRS. L. Ah!

NORA [*dancing*]. We're having such fun here, Christina!

HELM. Why, Nora dear, you're dancing as if it were a matter of life and death.

NORA. So it is.

HELM. Rank, stop! this is the merest madness. Stop, I say! [RANK *stops playing, and* NORA *comes to a sudden standstill,* HELMER *going toward her.*] I couldn't have believed it. You've positively forgotten all I taught you.

NORA [*throws tambourine away*]. You see for yourself.

HELM. You really do want teaching.

NORA. Yes, you see how much I need it. You must practice with me up to the last moment. Will you promise me, Torvald?

HELM. Certainly, certainly.

NORA. Neither today nor tomorrow you think of anything but me. You mustn't open a single letter—mustn't look at the letter-box!

HELM. Ah, you're still afraid of that man—

NORA. Oh, yes, yes, I am.

HELM. Nora, I can see it in your face—there's a letter from him in the box.

NORA. I don't know, I believe so. But you're not to read anything now; nothing must come between us until all is over.

RANK [*softly to* HELMER]. You mustn't contradict her.

HELM. [*putting his arm around her*]. The child shall have her own way. But tomorrow night, when the dance is over—

NORA. Then you will be free.

ELLEN *appears in doorway, right.*

ELLEN. Dinner is ready, ma'am.

NORA. We'll have some champagne, Ellen!

ELLEN. Yes, ma'am. [*Goes out.*

HELM. Dear me! Quite a feast.

NORA. Yes, and we'll keep it up till morning. [*Calling out.*] And macaroons, Ellen—plenty—just this once.

HELM. [*seizing her hands*]. Come, come, don't let's have this wild excitement! Be my own little lark again.

NORA. Oh, yes I will. But now go into the dining-room; and you too, Doctor Rank. Christina, you must help me to do up my hair.

RANK [*softly as they go*]. There is nothing in the wind? Nothing— I mean—

HELM. Oh, no, nothing of the kind. It's merely this babyish anxiety I was telling you about. [*They go out to the right.*]

NORA. Well?

MRS. L. He's gone out of town.

NORA. I saw it in your face.

MRS. L. He comes back tomorrow evening. I left a note for him.

NORA. You shouldn't have done that. Things must take their course. After all, there's something glorious in waiting for the miracle.

MRS. L. What are you waiting for?

NORA. Oh, you can't understand. Go to them in the dining-room; I'll come in a moment. [MRS. LINDEN *goes into dining-room;* NORA *stands for a moment as though collecting her thoughts; then looks at her watch.*] Five. Seven hours till midnight. Then twenty-four hours till the next midnight. Then the tarantella will be over. Twenty-four and seven? Still thirty-one hours to live.

HELMER *appears at door, right.*

HELM. What's become of my little lark?

NORA [*runs to him with open arms*]. Here she is!

ACT III

The same room. The table with the chairs around it is in the middle. A lamp lit on the table. The door to the hall stands open. Dance music is heard from the floor above. MRS. LINDEN *sits by the table, and turns the pages of a book absently. She tries to read, but seems unable to fix her attention; she frequently listens and looks anxiously toward the hall door.*

Mrs. L. [*looks at her watch*]. Still not here; and the time's nearly up. If only he hasn't— [*Listens again.*] Ah, there he is— [*She goes into the hall and opens the outer door; soft footsteps are heard on the stairs; she whispers:*] Come in; there's no one here.

Krog. [*in the doorway*]. I found a note from you at my house. What does it mean?

Mrs. L. I must speak with you.

Krog. Indeed? And in this house?

Mrs. L. I could not see you at my rooms. They have no separate entrance. Come in; we are quite alone. The servants are asleep and the Helmers are at the ball upstairs.

Krog. [*coming into room*]. Ah! So the Helmers are dancing this evening. Really?

Mrs. L. Yes. Why not?

Krog. Quite right. Why not?

Mrs. L. And now let us talk a little.

Krog. Have we anything to say to each other?

Mrs. L. A great deal.

Krog. I should not have thought so.

Mrs. L. Because you have never really understood me.

Krog. What was there to understand? The most natural thing in the world—a heartless woman throws a man over when a better match offers.

Mrs. L. Do you really think me so heartless? Do you think I broke with you lightly?

Krog. Did you not?

Mrs. L. Do you really think so?

Krog. If not, why did you write me that letter?

Mrs. L. Was it not best? Since I had to break with you, was it not right that I should try to put an end to your love for me?

Krog. [*pressing his hands together*]. So that was it? And all this—for the sake of money.

Mrs. L. You ought not to forget that I had a helpless mother and two little brothers. We could not wait for you, as your prospects then stood.

Krog. Did that give you the right to discard me for another?

Mrs. L. I don't know. I've often asked myself whether I did right.

Krog. [*more softly*]. When I had lost you the very ground seemed to sink from under my feet. Look at me now. I am a shipwrecked man clinging to a spar.

Mrs. L. Rescue may be at hand.

Krog. It was at hand; but then you stood in the way.

Mrs. L. Without my knowledge, Nils. I did not know till today that it was you I was to replace in the bank.

Krog. Well, I take your word for it. But now you do know, do you mean to give way?

Mrs. L. No, for that would not help you.

Krog. Oh, help, help—! I should do it whether or no.

Mrs. L. I have learnt prudence. Life and bitter necessity have schooled me.

Krog. And life has taught me not to trust fine speeches.

Mrs. L. Then life has taught you a very sensible thing. But deeds you will trust?

Krog. What do you mean?

Mrs. L. You said you were a shipwrecked man, clinging to a spar.

Krog. I have good reason to say so.

Mrs. L. I am a shipwrecked woman clinging to a spar. I have no one to care for.

Krog. You made your own choice.

Mrs. L. I had no choice.

Krog. Well, what then?

Mrs. L. How if we two shipwrecked people could join hands?

Krog. What!

Mrs. L. Suppose we lashed the spars together?

Krog. Christina!

Mrs. L. What do you think brought me to town?

Krog. Had you any thought of me?

Mrs. L. I must have work, or I can't live. All my life, as long as I can remember, I have worked; work has been my one great joy. Now I stand quite alone in the world, so terribly aimless and forsaken. There is no happiness in working for one's self. Nils, give me somebody and something to work for.

Krog. No, no, that can never be. It's simply a woman's romantic notion of self-sacrifice.

Mrs. L. Have you ever found me romantic?

Krog. Would you really—? Tell me, do you know my past?

Mrs. L. Yes.

Krog. And do you know what people say of me?

Mrs. L. Did not you say just now that with me you would have been another man?

Krog. I am sure of it.

Mrs. L. Is it too late?

Krog. Christina, do you know what you are

doing? Yes, you do; I see it in your face. Have you the courage?

Mrs. L. I need someone to tend, and your children need a mother. You need me, and I—I need you. Nils, I believe in your better self. With you I fear nothing.

Krog. [seizing her hands]. Thank you—thank you, Christina. Now I shall make others see me as you do. Ah, I forgot—

Mrs. L. [listening]. Hush! The tarantella! Go, go!

Krog. Why? What is it?

Mrs. L. Don't you hear the dancing overhead? As soon as that is over they will be here.

Krog. Oh, yes, I'll go. But it's too late now. Of course you don't know the step I have taken against the Helmers?

Mrs. L. Yes, Nils, I do know.

Krog. And yet you have the courage to—

Mrs. L. I know what lengths despair can drive a man to.

Krog. Oh, if I could only undo it!

Mrs. L. You can—. Your letter is still in the box.

Krog. Are you sure?

Mrs. L. Yes, but—

Krog. [looking at her searchingly]. Ah, now I understand. You want to save your friend at any price. Say it out—is that your idea?

Mrs. L. Nils, a woman who has once sold herself for the sake of others does not do so again.

Krog. I will demand my letter back again.

Mrs. L. No, no.

Krog. Yes, of course; I'll wait till Helmer comes; I'll tell him to give it back to me—that it's only about my dismissal—that I don't want it read.

Mrs. L. No, Nils, you must not recall the letter.

Krog. But tell me, wasn't that just why you got me to come here?

Mrs. L. Yes, in my first terror. But a day has passed since then, and in that day I have seen incredible things in this house. Helmer must know everything; there must be an end to this unhappy secret. These two must come to a full understanding. They can't possibly go on with all these shifts and concealments.

Krog. Very well, if you like to risk it. But one thing I can do, and at once—

Mrs. L. [listening]. Make haste. Go, go! The dance is over; we are not safe another moment.

Krog. I'll wait for you in the street.

Mrs. L. Yes, do; you must take me home.

Krog. I never was so happy in all my life!

[Krogstad goes, by the outer door. The door between the room and hall remains open.]

Mrs. L. [setting furniture straight and getting her out-door things together]. What a change! What a change! To have someone to work for; a home to make happy. I shall have to set to work in earnest. I wish they would come. [Listens.] Ah, here they are! I must get my things on. [Takes bonnet and cloak. Helmer's and Nora's voices are heard outside; a key is turned in the lock, and Helmer drags Nora almost by force into the hall. She wears the Italian costume with a large black shawl over it. He is in evening dress and wears a black domino.]

Nora [still struggling with him in the doorway]. No, no, no; I won't go in! I want to go up-stairs again; I don't want to leave so early!

Helm. But, my dearest girl—!

Nora. Oh, please, please, Torvald, only one hour more.

Helm. Not one minute more, Nora dear; you know what we agreed! Come, come in; you are catching cold here! [He leads her gently into the room in spite of her resistance.]

Mrs. L. Good evening.

Nora. Christina!

Helm. What, Mrs. Linden, you here so late!

Mrs. L. Yes, pardon me! I did so want to see Nora in her costume!

Nora. Have you been sitting here waiting for me?

Mrs. L. Yes, unfortunately I came too late. You had already gone up-stairs, and I couldn't go away without seeing you.

Helm. [taking Nora's shawl off]. Well then, just look at her! I think she's worth looking at. Isn't she lovely, Mrs. Linden?

Mrs. L. Yes, I must say—

Helm. Isn't she exquisite? Everyone said so. But she is dreadfully obstinate, dear little creature. What's to be done with her? Just think, I had almost to force her away.

Nora. Oh, Torvald, you'll be sorry some day you didn't let me stop, if only for one half hour.

Helm. There! You hear her, Mrs. Linden? She dances her tarantella with wild applause, and well she deserved it, I must say—though there was, perhaps, a little too much nature in her rendering of the idea—more than was, strictly speaking, artistic. But never mind—she made a great success, and that's the main thing. Ought I to let her stop after that—to weaken the impression? Not if I know it. I took my sweet little Capri girl—my capricious little Capri girl, I might say—under my arm; a rapid turn round the room, a courtesy to all sides, and—as they say in novels—the lovely apparition vanished! An exit should always be effective, Mrs. Linden; but I can't get Nora to see it. By Jove, it's warm here. [*Throws his domino on a chair, and opens the door to his room.*] What! No light here? Oh, of course! Excuse me— [*Goes in and lights candles.*]

NORA [*whispers breathlessly*]. Well?

MRS. L. [*softly*]. I have spoken to him.

NORA. And—?

MRS. L. Nora—you must tell your husband everything—

NORA [*almost voiceless*]. I knew it!

MRS. L. You have nothing to fear from Krogstad; but you must speak out.

NORA. I shall not speak!

MRS. L. Then the letter will.

NORA. Thank you, Christina. Now I know what I have to do. Hush!

HELM. [*coming back*]. Well, Mrs. Linden, have you admired her?

MRS. L. Yes; and now I'll say good-night.

HELM. What, already? Does this knitting belong to you?

MRS. L. [*takes it*]. Yes, thanks; I was nearly forgetting it.

HELM. Then you do knit?

MRS. L. Yes.

HELM. Do you know, you ought to embroider instead?

MRS. L. Indeed! Why?

HELM. Because it's so much prettier. Look now! You hold the embroidery in the left hand so, and then work the needle with the right hand, in a long, easy curve, don't you?

MRS. L. Yes, I suppose so.

HELM. But knitting is always ugly. Look now, your arms close to your sides, and the needles going up and down—there's something Chinese about it.—They really gave us splendid champagne tonight.

MRS. L. Well, good-night, Nora, and don't be obstinate any more.

HELM. Well said, Mrs. Linden!

MRS. L. Good-night, Mr. Helmer.

HELM. [*going with her to the door*]. Good-night, good-night; I hope you'll get safely home. I should be glad to—but really you haven't far to go. Good-night, good-night! [*She goes;* HELMER *shuts the door after her and comes down again.*] At last we've got rid of her; she's an awful bore.

NORA. Aren't you very tired, Torvald?

HELM. No, not in the least.

NORA. Nor sleepy?

HELM. Not a bit. I feel particularly lively. But you? You do look tired and sleepy.

NORA. Yes, very tired. I shall soon sleep now.

HELM. There, you see. I was right after all not to let you stop longer.

NORA. Oh, everything you do is right.

HELM. [*kissing her forehead*]. Now my lark is speaking like a reasonable being. Did you notice how jolly Rank was this evening?

NORA. Was he? I had no chance of speaking to him.

HELM. Nor I, much; but I haven't seen him in such good spirits for a long time. [*Looks at* NORA *a little, then comes nearer her.*] It's splendid to be back in our own home, to be quite alone together! Oh, you enchanting creature!

NORA. Don't look at me in that way, Torvald.

HELM. I am not to look at my dearest treasure?—at the loveliness that is mine, mine only, wholly and entirely mine?

NORA [*goes to the other side of the table*]. You mustn't say these things to me this evening.

HELM. [*following*]. I see you have the tarantella still in your blood—and that makes you all the more enticing. Listen! the other people are going now. [*More softly.*] Nora—soon the whole house will be still.

NORA. I hope so.

HELM. Yes, don't you, Nora darling? When we're among strangers do you know why I speak so little to you, and keep so far away, and only steal a glance at you now and then—do you know why I do it? Because I am fancying that we love each other in secret, that I am secretly betrothed to you, and that no one guesses there is anything between us.

NORA. Yes, yes, yes. I know all your thoughts are with me.

HELM. And then, when we have to go, and I put the shawl about your smooth, soft shoulders, and this glorious neck of yours, I imagine you are my bride, that our marriage is just over, that I am bringing you for the first time to my home, and that I am alone with you for the first time, quite alone with you, in your quivering loveliness. All this evening I was longing for you, and you only. When I watched you swaying and whirling in the tarantella—my blood boiled—I could endure it no longer; and that's why I made you come home with me so early.

NORA. Go now, Torvald. Go away from me. I won't have all this.

Helm. What do you mean? Ah! I see you're teasing me! Won't! won't! Am I not your husband? [*A knock at the outer door.*]

Nora [*starts*]. Did you hear?

Helm. [*going toward the hall*]. Who's there?

Rank [*outside*]. It's I; may I come in a moment?

Helm. [*in a low tone, annoyed*]. Oh! what can he want? [*Aloud.*] Wait a moment. [*Opens door.*] Come, it's nice of you to give us a look in.

Rank. I thought I heard your voice, and that put it into my head. [*Looks around.*] Ah! this dear old place! How cozy you two are here!

Helm. You seemed to find it pleasant enough upstairs, too.

Rank. Exceedingly. Why not? Why shouldn't one get all one can out of the world? All one can for as long as one can. The wine was splendid—

Helm. Especially the champagne.

Rank. Did you notice it? It's incredible the quantity I contrived to get down.

Nora. Torvald drank plenty of champagne too.

Rank. Did he?

Nora. Yes, and it always puts him in such spirits.

Rank. Well, why shouldn't one have a jolly evening after a well-spent day?

Helm. Well spent! Well, I haven't much to boast of.

Rank [*slapping him on the shoulder*]. But I have, don't you see?

Nora. I suppose you've been engaged in a scientific investigation, Doctor Rank?

Rank. Quite right.

Helm. Bless me! Little Nora talking about scientific investigations!

Nora. Am I to congratulate you on the result?

Rank. By all means.

Nora. It was good then?

Rank. The best possible, both for doctor and patient—certainty.

Nora [*quickly and searchingly*]. Certainty?

Rank. Absolute certainty. Wasn't I right to enjoy myself after it?

Nora. Yes, quite right, Doctor Rank.

Helm. And so say I, provided you don't have to pay for it tomorrow.

Rank. Well, in this life nothing's to be had for nothing.

Nora. Doctor Rank, aren't you very fond of masquerades?

Rank. Yes, when there are plenty of comical disguises.

Nora. Tell me, what shall we two be at our next masquerade?

Helm. Little insatiable! Thinking of your next already!

Rank. We two? I'll tell you. You must go as a good fairy.

Helm. Oh, but what costume would indicate that?

Rank. She has simply to wear her every-day dress.

Helm. Capital! But don't you know what you yourself will be?

Rank. Yes, my dear friend, I'm perfectly clear upon that point.

Helm. Well?

Rank. At the next masquerade I shall be invisible.

Helm. What a comical idea!

Rank. There's a big, black hat—haven't you heard of the invisible hat? It comes down all over you, and then no one can see you.

Helm. [*with a suppressed smile*]. No, you're right there.

Rank. But I'm quite forgetting what I came for. Helmer, give me a cigar, one of the dark Havanas.

Helm. With the greatest pleasure. [*Hands case.*]

Rank [*takes one and cuts the end off*]. Thanks.

Nora [*striking a wax match*]. Let me give you a light.

Rank. A thousand thanks. [*She holds match. He lights his cigar at it.*] And now, good-by.

Helm. Good-by, good-by, my dear fellow.

Nora. Sleep well, Doctor Rank.

Rank. Thanks for the wish.

Nora. Wish me the same.

Rank. You? Very well, since you ask me—sleep well. And thanks for the light.

[*He nods to them both and goes out.*]

Helm. [*in an undertone*]. He's been drinking a good deal.

Nora [*absently*]. I dare say. [Helmer *takes his bunch of keys from his pocket and goes into the hall.*] Torvald, what are you doing there?

Helm. I must empty the letter-box, it's quite full; there will be no room for the newspapers tomorrow morning.

Nora. Are you going to work tonight?

Helm. Not very likely! Why, what's this? Someone's been at the lock.

Nora. The lock—?

Helm. I'm sure of it. What does it mean? I can't think that the servants—? Here's a broken hairpin. Nora, it's one of yours.

Nora [*quickly*]. It must have been the children.

Helm. Then you must break them of such tricks. H'm, h'm! There! at last I've got it open. [*Takes* contents out and calls into the kitchen.] Ellen, Ellen, just put the hall-door lamp out. [He returns with letters in his hand, and shuts the inner door.] Just see how they've accumulated. [Turning them over.] Why, what's this?

NORA [at the window]. The letter! Oh, no, no, Torvald!

HELM. Two visiting cards—from Rank.

NORA. From Doctor Rank?

HELM. [looking at them]. Doctor Rank. They were on the top. He must just have put them in.

NORA. Is there anything on them?

HELM. There's a black cross over the name. Look at it. What a horrid idea! It looks just as if he were announcing his own death.

NORA. So he is.

HELM. What! Do you know anything? Has he told you anything?

NORA. Yes. These cards mean that he has taken his last leave of us. He intends to shut himself up and die.

HELM. Poor fellow! Of course I knew we couldn't hope to keep him long. But so soon—and then to go and creep into his lair like a wounded animal—

NORA. What must be, must be, and the fewer words the better. Don't you think so, Torvald?

HELM. [walking up and down]. He had so grown into our lives. I can't realize that he's gone. He and his sufferings and his loneliness formed a sort of cloudy background to the sunshine of our happiness. Well, perhaps it's best so—at any rate for him. [Stands still.] And perhaps for us, too, Nora. Now we two are thrown entirely upon each other. [Puts his arm round her.] My darling wife! I feel as if I could never hold you close enough. Do you know, Nora, I often wish some danger might threaten you, that I might risk body and soul, and everything, everything, for your dear sake.

NORA [tears herself from him and says firmly]. Now you shall read your letters, Torvald.

HELM. No, no; not tonight. I want to be with you, sweet wife.

NORA. With the thought of your dying friend?

HELM. You are right. This has shaken us both. Unloveliness has come between us—thoughts of death and decay. We must seek to cast them off. Till then we will remain apart.

NORA [her arms round his neck]. Torvald! good-night, good-night.

HELM. [kissing her forehead]. Good-night, my little bird. Sleep well, Nora. Now I'll go and read my letters. [He goes into his room and shuts the door.]

NORA [with wild eyes, gropes about her, seizes Helmer's domino, throws it round her, and whispers quickly, hoarsely, and brokenly]. Never to see him again. Never, never, never. [Throws her shawl over her head.] Never to see the children again. Never, never. Oh, that black icy water! Oh, that bottomless— If it were only over! Now he has it; he's reading it. Oh, no, no, no, not yet. Torvald, good-by. Good-by, my little ones—! [She is rushing out by the hall; at the same moment HELMER tears his door open, and stands with an open letter in his hand.]

HELM. Nora!

NORA [shrieking]. Ah—!

HELM. What is this? Do you know what is in this letter.

NORA. Yes, I know. Let me go! Let me pass!

HELM. [holds her back]. Where do you want to go?

NORA [tries to get free]. You sha'n't save me, Torvald.

HELM. [falling back]. True! Is it true what he writes? No, no, it cannot be true.

NORA. It is true. I have loved you beyond all else in the world.

HELM. Pshaw—no silly evasions.

NORA [a step nearer him]. Torvald—!

HELM. Wretched woman! what have you done?

NORA. Let me go—you shall not save me. You shall not take my guilt upon yourself.

HELM. I don't want any melodramatic airs. [Locks the door.] Here you shall stay and give an account of yourself. Do you understand what you have done? Answer. Do you understand it?

NORA [looks at him fixedly, and says with a stiffening expression]. Yes; now I begin fully to understand it.

HELM. [walking up and down]. Oh, what an awful awakening! During all these eight years— she who was my pride and my joy—a hypocrite, a liar—worse, worse—a criminal. Oh! the hideousness of it! Ugh! Ugh! [NORA is silent, and continues to look fixedly at him.] I ought to have foreseen something of the kind. All your father's dishonesty—be silent! I say all your father's dishonesty you have inherited—no religion, no morality, no sense of duty. How I am punished for shielding him! I did it for your sake, and you reward me like this.

NORA. Yes—like this!

HELM. You have destroyed my whole happiness.

You have ruined my future. Oh! it's frightful to think of! I am in the power of a scoundrel; he can do whatever he pleases with me, demand whatever he chooses, and I must submit. And all this disaster is brought upon me by an unprincipled woman.

NORA. When I'm gone, you will be free.

HELM. Oh, no fine phrases. Your father, too, was always ready with them. What good would it do to me if you were "gone" as you say? No good in the world! He can publish the story all the same; I might even be suspected of collusion. People will think I was at the bottom of it all and egged you on. And for all this I have you to thank—you whom I have done nothing but pet and spoil during our whole married life. Do you understand now what you have done to me?

NORA [*with cold calmness*]. Yes.

HELM. It's incredible. I can't grasp it. But we must come to an understanding. Take that shawl off. Take it off, I say. I must try to pacify him in one way or other—the secret must be kept, cost what it may. As for ourselves, we must live as we have always done; but of course only in the eyes of the world. Of course you will continue to live here. But the children cannot be left in your care. I dare not trust them to you— Oh, to have to say this to one I have loved so tenderly—whom I still—but that must be a thing of the past. Henceforward there can be no question of happiness, but merely of saving the ruins, the shreds, the show of it! [*A ring;* HELMER *starts.*] What's that? So late! Can it be the worst? Can he—? Hide yourself, Nora; say you are ill. [NORA *stands motionless.* HELMER *goes to the door and opens it.*]

ELLEN [*half dressed, in the hall*]. Here is a letter for you, ma'am.

HELM. Give it to me. [*Seizes letter and shuts the door.*] Yes, from him. You shall not have it. I shall read it.

NORA. Read it!

HELM. [*by the lamp*]. I have hardly courage to. We may be lost, both you and I. Ah! I must know. [*Tears the letter hastily open; reads a few lines, looks at an enclosure; a cry of joy.*] Nora. [NORA *looks interrogatively at him.*] Nora! Oh! I must read it again. Yes, yes, it is so. I am saved! Nora, I am saved!

NORA. And I?

HELM. You too, of course; we are both saved, both of us. Look here, he sends you back your promissory note. He writes that he regrets and apologizes—that a happy turn in his life— Oh, what matter what he writes. We are saved, Nora! No one can harm you. Oh! Nora, Nora—; no, first to get rid of this hateful thing. I'll just see— [*Glances at the I O U.*] No, I won't look at it; the whole thing shall be nothing but a dream to me. [*Tears the I O U and both letters in pieces, throws them into the fire and watches them burn.*] There, it's gone. He wrote that ever since Christmas Eve— Oh, Nora, they must have been three awful days for you!

NORA. I have fought a hard fight for the last three days.

HELM. And in your agony you saw no other outlet but—no; we won't think of that horror. We will only rejoice and repeat—it's over, all over. Don't you hear, Nora? You don't seem to be able to grasp it. Yes, it's over. What is this set look on your face? Oh, my poor Nora, I understand; you can't believe that I have forgiven you. But I have, Nora; I swear it. I have forgiven everything. I know that what you did was all for love of me.

NORA. That's true.

HELM. You loved me as a wife should love her husband. It was only the means you misjudged. But do you think I love you the less for your helplessness? No, no, only lean on me. I will counsel and guide you. I should be no true man if this very womanly helplessness did not make you doubly dear in my eyes. You mustn't think of the hard things I said in my first moment of terror, when the world seemed to be tumbling about my ears. I have forgiven you, Nora—I swear I have forgiven you.

NORA. I thank you for your forgiveness. [*Goes out, right.*]

HELM. No, stay. [*Looks in.*] What are you going to do?

NORA [*inside*]. To take off my doll's dress.

HELM. [*in doorway*]. Yes, do, dear. Try to calm down, and recover your balance, my scared little song-bird. You may rest secure, I have broad wings to shield you. [*Walking up and down near the door.*] Oh, how lovely—how cozy our home is, Nora. Here you are safe; here I can shelter you like a hunted dove, whom I have saved from the claws of the hawk. I shall soon bring your poor beating heart to rest, believe me, Nora, I will. Tomorrow all this will seem quite different—everything will be as before; I shall not need to tell you again that I forgive you; you will feel for yourself that it is true. How could I find it in my heart to drive you away, or even so much as to reproach you? Oh, you don't know a true man's heart, Nora. There is something indescribably sweet and soothing to a man in having forgiven his wife—honestly forgiven her from the bottom of his heart. She becomes his property in a double sense. She is as though born again; she has become, so to speak, at once his wife and his child. That is what you shall henceforth be to me, my bewildered, helpless darling. Don't worry about anything, Nora; only open your heart to me, and I will be both will and conscience to you. [Nora *enters, crossing to table in* 10 *everyday dress.*] Why, what's this? Not gone to bed? You have changed your dress.

Nora. Yes, Torvald; now I have changed my dress.

Helm. But why now so late?

Nora. I shall not sleep tonight.

Helm. But, Nora dear—

Nora [*looking at her watch*]. It's not so late yet. Sit down, Torvald, you and I have much to say to each other. [*She sits on one side of the table.*]

Helm. Nora, what does this mean; your cold, set face—

Nora. Sit down. It will take some time; I have much to talk over with you. [Helmer *sits at the other side of the table.*]

Helm. You alarm me; I don't understand you.

Nora. No, that's just it. You don't understand me; and I have never understood you—till tonight. No, don't interrupt. Only listen to what I say. We must come to a final settlement, Torvald!   30

Helm. How do you mean?

Nora [*after a short silence*]. Does not one thing strike you as we sit here?

Helm. What should strike me?

Nora. We have been married eight years. Does it not strike you that this is the first time we two, you and I, man and wife, have talked together seriously?

Helm. Seriously! Well, what do you call seriously?

Nora. During eight whole years and more— ever since the day we first met—we have never exchanged one serious word about serious things.

Helm. Was I always to trouble you with the cares you could not help me to bear?

Nora. I am not talking of cares. I say that we have never yet set ourselves seriously to get to the bottom of anything.

Helm. Why, my dear Nora, what have you to do with serious things?

Nora. There we have it! You have never understood me. I have had great injustice done me, Torvald. First by my father and then by you.

Helm. What! by your father and me?—by us

who have loved you more than all the world?

Nora [*shaking her head*]. You have never loved me. You only thought it amusing to be in love with me.

Helm. Why, Nora, what a thing to say!

Nora. Yes, it is so, Torvald. While I was at home with father he used to tell me all his opinions and I held the same opinions. If I had others I concealed them, because he would not have liked it. He used to call me his doll child, and play with me as I played with my dolls. Then I came to live in your house—

Helm. What an expression to use about our marriage!

Nora [*undisturbed*]. I mean I passed from father's hands into yours. You settled everything according to your taste; and I got the same tastes as you; or I pretended to—I don't know which— both ways perhaps. When I look back on it now, 20 I seem to have been living here like a beggar, from hand to mouth. I lived by performing tricks for you, Torvald. But you would have it so. You and father have done me a great wrong. It's your fault that my life has been wasted.

Helm. Why, Nora, how unreasonable and ungrateful you are. Haven't you been happy here?

Nora. No, never; I thought I was, but I never was.

Helm. Not—not happy?

Nora. No, only merry. And you have always   30 been so kind to me. But our house has been nothing but play-room. Here I have been your doll-wife, just as at home I used to be papa's doll-child. And the children in their turn have been my dolls. I thought it fun when you played with me, just as the children did when I played with them. That has been our marriage, Torvald.

Helm. There is some truth in what you say, exaggerated and overstrained though it be. But 40 henceforth it shall be different. Playtime is over; now comes the time for education.

Nora. Whose education? Mine, or the children's.

Helm. Both, my dear Nora.

Nora. Oh, Torvald, you can't teach me to be a fit wife for you.

Helm. And you say that?

Nora. And I—am I fit to educate the children?

Helm. Nora!

Nora. Did you not say yourself a few minutes 50 ago you dared not trust them to me?

Helm. In the excitement of the moment! Why should you dwell upon that?

Nora. No—you are perfectly right. That problem is beyond me. There's another to be solved first—I must try to educate myself. You are not the man to help me in that. I must set about it alone. And that is why I am now leaving you!

HELM. [*jumping up*]. What—do you mean to say—

NORA. I must stand quite alone to know myself and my surroundings; so I cannot stay with you.

HELM. Nora! Nora!

NORA. I am going at once. Christina will take me in for tonight—

HELM. You are mad. I shall not allow it. I forbid it.

NORA. It's no use your forbidding me anything now. I shall take with me what belongs to me. From you I will accept nothing, either now or afterward.

HELM. What madness!

NORA. Tomorrow I shall go home.

HELM. Home!

NORA. I mean to what was my home. It will be easier for me to find some opening there.

HELM. Oh, in your blind experience—

NORA. I must try to gain experience, Torvald.

HELM. To forsake your home, your husband, and your children! You don't consider what the world will say.

NORA. I can pay no heed to that! I only know that I must do it.

HELM. It's exasperating! Can you forsake your holiest duties in this way?

NORA. What do you call my holiest duties?

HELM. Do you ask me that? Your duties to your husband and your children.

NORA. I have other duties equally sacred.

HELM. Impossible! What duties do you mean?

NORA. My duties toward myself.

HELM. Before all else you are a wife and a mother.

NORA. That I no longer believe. I think that before all else I am a human being, just as much as you are—or, at least, I will try to become one. I know that most people agree with you, Torvald, and that they say so in books. But henceforth I can't be satisfied with what most people say, and what is in books. I must think things out for myself and try to get clear about them.

HELM. Are you not clear about your place in your own home? Have you not an infallible guide in questions like these? Have you not religion?

NORA. Oh, Torvald, I don't know properly what religion is.

HELM. What do you mean?

NORA. I know nothing but what our clergyman told me when I was confirmed. He explained that religion was this and that. When I get away from here and stand alone I will look into that matter too. I will see whether what he taught me is true, or, at any rate, whether it is true for me.

HELM. Oh, this is unheard of! But if religion cannot keep you right, let me appeal to your conscience—I suppose you have some moral feeling? Or, answer me, perhaps you have none?

NORA. Well, Torvald, it's not easy to say. I really don't know—I am all at sea about these things. I only know that I think quite differently from you about them. I hear, too, that the laws are different from what I thought; but I can't believe that they are right. It appears that a woman has no right to spare her dying father, or to save her husband's life. I don't believe that.

HELM. You talk like a child. You don't understand the society in which you live.

NORA. No, I don't. But I shall try to. I must make up my mind which is right—society or I.

HELM. Nora, you are ill, you are feverish. I almost think you are out of your senses.

NORA. I never felt so much clearness and certainty as tonight.

HELM. You are clear and certain enough to forsake husband and children?

NORA. Yes, I am.

HELM. Then there is only one explanation possible.

NORA. What is that?

HELM. You no longer love me.

NORA. No, that is just it.

HELM. Nora! Can you say so?

NORA. Oh, I'm so sorry, Torvald; for you've always been so kind to me. But I can't help it. I do not love you any longer.

HELM. [*keeping his composure with difficulty*]. Are you clear and certain on this point too?

NORA. Yes, quite. That is why I won't stay here any longer.

HELM. And can you also make clear to me, how I have forfeited your love?

NORA. Yes, I can. It was this evening, when the miracle did not happen. For then I saw you were not the man I had taken you for.

HELM. Explain yourself more clearly; I don't understand.

NORA. I have waited so patiently all these eight years; for, of course, I saw clearly enough that miracles do not happen every day. When this crushing blow threatened me, I said to myself, confidently, "Now comes the miracle!" When Krogstad's letter lay in the box, it never occurred to me that you would think of submitting to that man's conditions. I was convinced that you would say to him, "Make it known to all the world," and that then—

HELM. Well? When I had given my own wife's name up to disgrace and shame—?

NORA. Then I firmly believed that you would come forward, take everything upon yourself, and say, "I am the guilty one."

HELM. Nora!

NORA. You mean I would never have accepted such a sacrifice? No, certainly not. But what would my assertions have been worth in opposition to yours? That was the miracle that I hoped for and dreaded. And it was to hinder that that I wanted to die.

HELM. I would gladly work for you day and night, Nora—bear sorrow and want for your sake —but no man sacrifices his honor, even for one he loves.

NORA. Millions of women have done so.

HELM. Oh, you think and talk like a silly child.

NORA. Very likely. But you neither think nor talk like the man I can share my life with. When your terror was over—not for me, but for yourself —when there was nothing more to fear,—then it was to you as though nothing had happened. I was your lark again, your doll—whom you would take twice as much care of in the future, because she was so weak and fragile. [Stands up.] Torvald, in that moment it burst upon me, that I had been living here these eight years with a strange man, and had borne him three children— Oh! I can't bear to think of it—I could tear myself to pieces!

HELM. [sadly]. I see it, I see it; an abyss has opened between us— But, Nora, can it never be filled up?

NORA. As I now am, I am no wife for you.

HELM. I have strength to become another man.

NORA. Perhaps—when your doll is taken away from you.

HELM. To part—to part from you! No, Nora, no; I can't grasp the thought.

NORA [going into room, right]. The more reason for the thing to happen. [She comes back with outdoor things and a small traveling bag, which she puts on a chair.]

HELM. Nora, Nora, not now! Wait till tomorrow.

NORA [putting on cloak]. I can't spend the night in a strange man's house.

HELM. But can't we live here as brother and sister?

NORA [fastening her hat]. You know very well that would not last long. Good-by, Torvald. No, I won't go to the children. I know they are in better hands than mine. As I now am, I can be nothing to them.

HELM. But some time, Nora—some time—

NORA. How can I tell? I have no idea what will become of me.

HELM. But you are my wife, now and always?

NORA. Listen, Torvald—when a wife leaves her husband's house, as I am doing, I have heard that in the eyes of the law he is free from all the duties toward her. At any rate I release you from all duties. You must not feel yourself bound any more than I shall. There must be perfect freedom on both sides. There, there is your ring back. Give me mine.

HELM. That too?

NORA. That too.

HELM. Here it is.

NORA. Very well. Now it is all over. Here are the keys. The servants know about everything in the house, better than I do. Tomorrow, when I have started, Christina will come to pack up my things. I will have them sent after me.

HELM. All over! All over! Nora, will you never think of me again?

NORA. Oh, I shall often think of you, and the children—and this house.

HELM. May I write to you, Nora?

NORA. No, never. You must not.

HELM. But I must send you—

NORA. Nothing, nothing.

HELM. I must help you if you need it.

NORA. No, I say. I take nothing from strangers.

HELM. Nora, can I never be more than a stranger to you?

NORA [taking her traveling bag]. Oh, Torvald, then the miracle of miracles would have to happen.

HELM. What is the miracle of miracles?

NORA. Both of us would have to change so that— Oh, Torvald, I no longer believe in miracles.

HELM. But I will believe. We must so change that—?

NORA. That communion between us shall be a marriage. Good-by.   [She goes out.

HELM. [sinks in a chair by the door with his face in his hands.] Nora! Nora! [He looks around and stands up.] Empty. She's gone! [A hope inspires him.] Ah! The miracle of miracles—?! [From below is heard the reverberation of a heavy door closing.]

GERHART HAUPTMANN

The Weavers

CHARACTERS

DREISSIGER, *fustian manufacturer*
MRS. DREISSIGER
PFEIFER, *manager*
NEUMANN, *cashier*
AN APPRENTICE
JOHN, *coachman*
A MAID } *in* DREISSIGER'S *employment*
WEINHOLD, *tutor to* DREISSIGER'S *sons*
PASTOR KITTELHAUS
MRS. KITTELHAUS
HEIDE, *Police Superintendent*
KUTSCHE, *policeman*
WELZEL, *publican*
MRS. WELZEL
ANNA WELZEL
WIEGAND, *joiner*
A COMMERCIAL TRAVELER
A PEASANT
A FORESTER
SCHMIDT, *surgeon*
HORNIG, *rag-dealer*
WITTIG, *smith*

WEAVERS

BECKER
MORITZ JAEGER
OLD BAUMERT
MOTHER BAUMERT
BERTHA } BAUMERT
EMMA
FRITZ, EMMA'S *son (four years old)*
AUGUST BAUMERT
OLD ANSORGE
MRS. HEINRICH
OLD HILSE
MOTHER HILSE
GOTTLIEB HILSE
LUISE, GOTTLIEB'S *wife*
MIELCHEN, *their daughter (six years old)*
REIMANN, *weaver*
HEIBER, *weaver*
A WEAVER'S WIFE

A number of weavers, young and old, of both sexes

The action passes in the forties, at Kaschbach, Peterswaldau and Langenbielau, in the Eulengebirge

ACT I

A large whitewashed room on the ground floor of DREISSIGER'S *house at Peterswaldau, where the weavers deliver their finished webs and the fustian is stored. To the left are uncurtained windows, in the back wall there is a glass door, and to the right another glass door, through which weavers, male and female, and children, are passing in and out. All three walls are lined with shelves for the storing of the fustian. Against the right wall stands a long bench, on which a number of weavers have already spread out their cloth. In the order of arrival each presents his piece to be examined by* PFEIFER, DREISSIGER'S *manager, who stands, with compass and magnifying-glass, behind a large table, on which the web to be inspected is laid. When* PFEIFER *has satisfied himself, the weaver lays the fustian on the scale, and an office apprentice tests its weight. The same boy stores the accepted pieces on the shelves.* PFEIFER *calls out the payment due in each case to* NEUMANN, *the cashier, who is seated at a small table.*

It is a sultry day toward the end of May. The clock is on the stroke of twelve. Most of the waiting work-people have the air of standing before the bar of justice, in torturing expectation of a decision that means life or death to them. They are marked, too, by the anxious timidity characteristic of the receiver of charity, who has suffered many humiliations, and, conscious that he is barely tolerated, has acquired the habit of self-effacement. Add to this an expression on every face that tells of constant, fruitless brooding. There is a general resemblance among the men. They have something about them of the dwarf, something of the schoolmaster. The majority are flat-breasted, short-winded, sallow, and poor-looking—creatures of the loom, their knees bent with much sitting. At a first glance the women show fewer typical traits. They look

Gerhart Hauptmann (1862-   ). From the Dramatic Works of Gerhart Hauptmann, Vol. I, copyright 1912 by B. W. Huebsch. By permission of The Viking Press.

over-driven, worried, reckless, whereas the men still make some show of a pitiful self-respect; and their clothes are ragged, while the men's are patched and mended. Some of the young girls are not without a certain charm, consisting in a wax-like pallor, a slender figure, and large, projecting, melancholy eyes.

NEUMANN [*counting out money*]. Comes to one and sevenpence halfpenny.

WEAVER'S WIFE [*about thirty, emaciated, takes up the money with trembling fingers*]. Thank you, sir.

NEUMANN [*seeing that she does not move on*]. Well, something wrong this time, too?

WEAVER'S WIFE [*agitated, imploringly*]. Do you think I might have a few pence in advance, sir? I need it that bad.

NEUMANN. And I need a few pounds. If it was only a question of needing it—! [*Already occupied in counting out another weaver's money, shortly.*] It's Mr. Dreissiger who settles about pay in advance.

WEAVER'S WIFE. Couldn't I speak to Mr. Dreissiger himself, then, sir?

PFEIFER [*Now manager, formerly weaver. The type is unmistakable, only he is well fed, well dressed, clean-shaven; also takes snuff copiously. He calls out roughly.*] Mr. Dreissiger would have enough to do if he had to attend to every trifle himself. That's what we are here for. [*He measures, and then examines through the magnifying-glass.*] Mercy on us! what a draught! [*Puts a thick muffler round his neck.*] Shut the door, whoever comes in.

APPRENTICE [*loudly to* PFEIFER]. You might as well talk to stocks and stones.

PFEIFER. That's done!—Weigh! [*The weaver places his web on the scales.*] If you only understood your business a little better! Full of lumps again. . . . I hardly need to look at the cloth to see them. Call yourself a weaver, and "draw as long a bow" as you've done there!

BECKER *has entered. A young, exceptionally powerfully-built weaver; offhand, almost bold in manner.* PFEIFER, NEUMANN, *and the* APPRENTICE *exchange looks of mutual understanding as he comes in.*

BECKER. Devil take it! This is a sweating job, and no mistake.

FIRST WEAVER [*in a low voice*]. This blazing heat means rain.

OLD BAUMERT *forces his way in at the glass door on the right, through which the crowd of weavers*

can be seen, standing shoulder to shoulder, waiting their turn. The old man stumbles forward and lays his bundle on the bench, beside BECKER'S. *He sits down by it, and wipes the sweat from his face.*

OLD BAUMERT. A man has a right to a rest after that.

BECKER. Rest's better than money.

OLD BAUMERT. Yes, but we *needs* the money, too. Good-mornin' to you, Becker!

BECKER. Morning, Father Baumert! Goodness knows how long we'll have to stand here again.

FIRST WEAVER. And what does that matter? What's to hinder a weaver waitin' for an hour, or for a day if need be? What else is he there for?

PFEIFER. Silence there! We can't hear our own voices.

BECKER [*in a low voice*]. This is one of his bad days.

PFEIFER [*to the weaver standing before him*]. How often have I told you that you must bring cleaner cloth? What sort of mess is this? Knots, and straw, and all kinds of dirt.

REIMANN. It's for want of a new picker, sir.

APPRENTICE [*has weighed the piece*]. Short weight, too.

PFEIFER. I never saw such weavers. I hate to give out the yarn to them. It was another story in my day! I'd have caught it finely from my master for work like that. The business was carried on in different style then. A man had to know his trade—that's the last thing that's thought of nowadays. Reimann, one shilling.

REIMANN. But there's always a pound allowed for waste.

PFEIFER. I've no time. Next man!—What have you to show?

HEIBER [*Lays his web on the table. While* PFEIFER *is examining it, he goes close up to him; eagerly in a low tone.*] Beg pardon, Mr. Pfeifer, but I wanted to ask you, sir, if you would perhaps be so very kind as do me the favor an' not take my advance money off this week's pay.

PFEIFER [*measuring and examining the texture; jeeringly*]. Well! What next, I wonder? This looks very much as if half the weft had stuck to the bobbins again.

HEIBER [*continues*]. I'll be sure to make it all right next week, sir. But this last week I've had to put in two days' work on the estate. And my missus is ill in bed. . . .

PFEIFER [*giving the web to be weighed*]. Another

piece of real slop-work. [*Already examining a new web.*] What a selvage! Here it's broad, there it's narrow; here it's drawn in by the wefts goodness knows how tight, and there's it's torn out again by the temples. And hardly seventy threads weft to the inch. What's come of the rest? Do you call this honest work? I never saw anything like it.

HEIBER, *repressing tears, stands humiliated and helpless.*

BECKER [*in a low voice to* BAUMERT]. To please that brute you would have to pay for extra yarn out of your own pocket.

The WEAVER'S WIFE, *who has remained standing near the cashier's table, from time to time looking round appealingly, takes courage and once more comes forward.*

WEAVER'S WIFE [*to cashier imploringly*]. I don't know what's to come of me, sir, if you won't give me a little advance this time—O Lord, O Lord!

PFEIFER [*calls across*]. It's no good whining, or dragging the Lord's name into the matter. You're not so anxious about Him at other times. You look after your husband and see that he's not to be found so often lounging in the public house. We can give no pay in advance. We have to account for every penny. It's not our money. People that are industrious, and understand their work, and do it in the fear of God, never need their pay in advance. So now you know.

NEUMANN. If a Bielau weaver got four times as much pay, he would squander it four times over and be in debt into the bargain.

WEAVER'S WIFE [*in a loud voice, as if appealing to the general sense of justice*]. No one can't call me idle, but I'm not fit now for what I once was. I've twice had a miscarriage. And as to John, he's but a poor creature. He's been to the shepherd at Zerlau, but he couldn't do him no good, and . . . you can't do more than you've strength for. . . . We works as hard as ever we can. This many a week I've been at it till far on into the night. An' we'll keep our heads above water right enough if I can just get a bit of strength into me. But you must have pity on us, Mr. Pfeifer, sir. [*Eagerly, coaxingly.*] You'll please be so very kind as to let me have a few pence on the next job, sir?

PFEIFER [*paying no attention*]. Fiedler, one and twopence.

WEAVER'S WIFE. Only a few pence, to buy bread with. We can't get no more credit. We've a lot of little ones.

NEUMANN [*half aside to the* APPRENTICE, *in a serio-comic tone*]. "Every year brings a child to

the linen-weaver's wife, heigh-ho, heigh-ho, heigh."

APPRENTICE [*takes up the rhyme, half singing*]. "And the little brat it's blind the first weeks of its life, heigh-ho, heigh-ho, heigh."

REIMANN [*not touching the money which the cashier has counted out to him*]. We've always got one and fourpence for the web.

PFEIFER [*calls across*]. If our terms don't suit you, Reimann, you have only to say so. There's no scarcity of weavers—especially of your sort. For full weight we give full pay.

REIMANN. How anything can be wrong with the weight is past . . .

PFEIFER. You bring a piece of fustian with no faults in it, and there will be no fault in the pay.

REIMANN. It's not possible that there's too many knots in this web.

PFEIFER [*examining*]. If you want to live well, then be sure you weave well.

HEIBER [*Has remained standing near* PFEIFER, *so as to seize on any favorable opportunity. He laughs at* PFEIFER's *little witticism, then steps forward and again addresses him.*] I wanted to ask you, sir, if you would perhaps have the great kindness not to take my advance of sixpence off to-day's pay? My missus has been bedridden since February. She can't do a hand's turn for me, and I've to pay a bobbin girl. And so . . .

PFEIFER [*takes a pinch of snuff*]. Heiber, do you think I have no one to attend to but you? The others must have their turn.

REIMANN. As the warp was given me I took it home and fastened it to the beam. I can't bring back better yarn than I get.

PFEIFER. If you are not satisfied, you need come for no more. There are plenty ready to tramp the soles off their shoes to get it.

NEUMANN [*to* REIMANN]. Do you not want your money?

REIMANN. I can't bring myself to take such pay.

NEUMANN [*paying no further attention to* REIMANN]. Heiber, one shilling. Deduct sixpence for pay in advance. Leave sixpence.

HEIBER [*goes up to the table, looks at the money, stands shaking his head as if unable to believe his eyes, then slowly takes it up*]. Well, I never!— [*Sighing.*] Oh, dear, oh, dear!

OLD BAUMERT [*looking into* HEIBER's *face*]. Yes, Franz, that's so! There's matter enough for sighing.

HEIBER [*speaking with difficulty*]. I've a girl lying sick at home, too, an' she needs a bottle of medicine.

OLD BAUMERT. What's wrong with her?

HEIBER. Well, you see, she's always been a sickly bit of a thing. I don't know. . . . I needn't mind tellin' you—she brought her trouble with her. It's in her blood, and it breaks out here, there, and everywhere.

OLD BAUMERT. It's always the way. Let folks be poor, and one trouble comes to them on the top of another. There's no help for it and there's no end to it.

HEIBER. What are you carryin' in that cloth, Father Baumert?

OLD BAUMERT. We haven't so much as a bite in the house, and so I've had the little dog killed. There's not much on him, for the poor beast was half starved. A nice little dog he was! I couldn't kill him myself. I hadn't the heart to do it.

PFEIFER [has inspected BECKER's web—calls]. Becker, one and threepence.

BECKER. That's what you might give to a beggar: it's not pay.

PFEIFER. Every one who has been attended to must clear out. We haven't room to turn round in.

BECKER [to those standing near, without lowering his voice]. It's a beggarly pittance, nothing else. A man works his treadle from early morning till late at night, an' when he has bent over his loom for days an' days, tired to death every evening, sick with the dust and the heat, he finds he's made a beggarly one and threepence!

PFEIFER. No impudence allowed here.

BECKER. If you think I'll hold my tongue for your telling, you're much mistaken.

PFEIFER [exclaims]. We'll see about that! [Rushes to the glass door and calls into the office.] Mr. Dreissiger, Mr. Dreissiger, will you be good enough to come here?

Enter DREISSIGER. About forty, full-bodied, asthmatic. Looks severe.

DREISSIGER. What is it, Pfeifer?

PFEIFER [spitefully]. Becker says he won't be told to hold his tongue.

DREISSIGER [draws himself up, throws back his head, stares at BECKER; his nostrils tremble]. Oh, indeed!—Becker. [To PFEIFER.] Is he the man? . . . [The clerks nod.]

BECKER [insolently]. Yes, Mr. Dreissiger, yes! [Pointing to himself.] This is the man. [Pointing to DREISSIGER.] And that's a man, too!

DREISSIGER [angrily]. Fellow, how dare you?

PFEIFER. He's too well off. He'll go dancing on the ice once too often, though.

BECKER [recklessly]. You shut up, you Jack-in-the-box. Your mother must have gone dancing once too often with Satan to have got such a devil for a son.

DREISSIGER [now in a violent passion, roars]. Hold your tongue this moment, sir, or . . .

He trembles and takes a few steps forward.

BECKER [holding his ground steadily]. I'm not deaf. My hearing's quite good yet.

DREISSIGER [controls himself, asks in an apparently cool business tone]. Was this fellow not one of the pack? . . .

PFEIFER. He's a Bielau weaver. When there's any mischief going, they are sure to be in it.

DREISSIGER [trembling]. Well, I give you all warning: if the same thing happens again as last night—a troop of half-drunken cubs marching past my windows singing that low song . . .

BECKER. Is it "Bloody Justice" you mean?

DREISSIGER. You know well enough what I mean. I tell you that if I hear it again I'll get hold of one of you, and—mind, I'm not joking—before the justice he shall go. And if I can find out who it was that made up that vile doggerel . . .

BECKER. It's a beautiful song, that's what it is!

DREISSIGER. Another word and I send for the police on the spot, without more ado. I'll make short work with you young fellows. I've got the better of very different men before now.

BECKER. I believe you there. A real thoroughbred manufacturer will get the better of two or three hundred weavers in the time it takes you to turn round—swallow them up, and not leave as much as a bone. He's got four stomachs like a cow, and teeth like a wolf. That's nothing to him at all!

DREISSIGER [to his clerks]. That man gets no more work from us.

BECKER. It's all the same to me whether I starve at my loom or by the roadside.

DREISSIGER. Out you go, then, this moment! . . .

BECKER [determinedly]. Not without my pay.

DREISSIGER. How much is owing to the fellow, Neumann?

NEUMANN. One and threepence.

DREISSIGER [takes the money hurriedly out of the cashier's hand, and flings it on the table, so that some of the coins roll off on to the floor]. There you are, then; and now, out of my sight with you!

BECKER. Not without my pay.

DREISSIGER. Do you not see it lying there? If you don't take it and go . . . It's exactly twelve now . . . The dyers are coming out for their dinner. . . .

BECKER. I get my pay into my hand—here.

Points with the fingers of his right hand at the palm of his left.

DREISSIGER [*to the* APPRENTICE]. Pick up the money, Tilgner.

The APPRENTICE *lifts the money and puts it into* BECKER'S *hand.*

BECKER. Everything in proper order.

Deliberately takes an old purse out of his pocket and puts the money into it.

DREISSIGER [*as* BECKER *still does not move away*]. Well? Do you want me to come and help you?

Signs of agitation are observable among the crowd of weavers. A long, loud sigh is heard, and then a fall. General interest is at once diverted to this new event.

DREISSIGER. What's the matter there?

CHORUS OF WEAVERS AND WOMEN. "Some one's fainted."—"It's a little sickly boy."—"Is it a fit, or what?"

DREISSIGER. What do you say? Fainted? [*He goes nearer.*]

OLD WEAVER. There he lies, any way.

They make room. A boy of about eight is seen lying on the floor as if dead.

DREISSIGER. Does any one know the boy?

OLD WEAVER. He's not from our village.

OLD BAUMERT. He's like one of Weaver Heinrich's boys. [*Looks at him more closely.*] Yes, that's Heinrich's little Philip.

DREISSIGER. Where do they live?

OLD BAUMERT. Up near us in Kaschbach, sir. He goes round playin' music in the evenings, and all day he's at the loom. They've nine children an' a tenth a-coming.

CHORUS OF WEAVERS AND WOMEN. "They're terrible put to it."—"The rain comes through their roof."—"The woman hasn't two shirts among the nine."

OLD BAUMERT [*taking the boy by the arm*]. Now then, lad, what's wrong with you? Wake up, lad.

DREISSIGER. Some of you help me, and we'll get him up. It's disgraceful to send a sickly child this distance. Bring some water, Pfeifer.

WOMAN [*helping to lift the boy*]. Surely you're not going to die, lad!

DREISSIGER. Brandy, Pfeifer, brandy will be better.

BECKER [*Forgotten by all, has stood looking on. With his hand on the door-latch, he now calls loudly and tauntingly.*] Give him something to eat, an' he'll soon be all right. [*Goes out.*]

DREISSIGER. That fellow will come to a bad end. —Take him under the arm, Neumann. Easy now, easy, we'll get him into my room. What?

NEUMANN. He said something, Mr. Dreissiger. His lips are moving.

DREISSIGER. What—what is it, boy?

BOY [*whispers*]. I'm h—hungry.

WOMAN. I think he says . . .

DREISSIGER. We'll find out. Don't stop. Let us get him into my room. He can lie on the sofa there. We'll hear what the doctor says.

DREISSIGER, NEUMANN, *and the woman lead the boy into the office. The weavers begin to behave like school-children when their master has left the classroom. They stretch themselves, whisper, move from one foot to the other, and in the course of a few moments are conversing loudly.*

OLD BAUMERT. I believe as how Becker was right.

CHORUS OF WOMEN AND WEAVERS. "He did say something like that."—"It's nothing new here to fall down from hunger."—"God knows what's to come of them in winter if this cutting down of wages goes on."—"An' this winter the potatoes aren't no good at all."—"Things'll get worse and worse till we're all done for together."

OLD BAUMERT. The best thing a man could do would be put a rope round his neck and hang hisself on his own loom, like Weaver Nentwich. [*To another old weaver.*] Here, take a pinch. I was at Neurode yesterday. My brother-in-law, he works in the snuff factory there, and he give me a grain or two. Have you anything good in your handkercher?

OLD WEAVER. Only a little pearl barley. I was coming along behind Ulbrich the miller's cart, and there was a slit in one of the sacks. I can tell you we'll be glad of it.

OLD BAUMERT. There's twenty-two mills in Peterswaldau, but of all they grind, there's never nothing comes our way.

OLD WEAVER. We must keep up heart. There's always something comes to help us on again.

HEIBER. Yes, when we're hungry, we can pray to all the saints to help us, and if that don't fill our bellies we can put a pebble in our mouths and suck it. Eh, Baumert?

Reënter DREISSIGER, PFEIFER, *and* NEUMANN.

DREISSIGER. It was nothing serious. The boy is all right again. [*Walks about excitedly, panting.*] But all the same it's a disgrace. The child's so weak that a puff of wind would blow him over. How people, how any parents can be so thoughtless is what passes my comprehension. Loading him with two heavy pieces of fustian to carry a good six miles! No one would believe it that hadn't seen it. It simply means that I shall have to make a rule that no goods brought by children will be taken over. [*He walks up and down silently for a few moments.*] I sincerely trust such a thing will not occur again.—Who gets all the blame for it? Why, of course the manufacturer. It's entirely our fault. If some poor little fellow sticks in the snow in winter and goes to sleep, a special correspondent arrives posthaste, and in two days w have a blood-curdling story served up in all the papers. Is any blame laid on the father, the parents, that send such a child?—not a bit of it. How should they be to blame? It's all the manufacturer's fault—he's made the scapegoat. They flatter the weaver, and give the manufacturer nothing but abuse—he's a cruel man, with a heart like a stone, a wicked fellow, at whose calves every cur of a journalist may take a bite. He lives on the fat of the land, and pays the poor weavers starvation wages. In the flow of his eloquence the writer forgets to mention that such a man has his cares too and his sleepless nights; that he runs risks of which the workman never dreams; that he is often driven distracted by all the calculations he has to make, and all the different things he has to take into account; that he has to struggle for his very life against competitio. ; and that no day passes without some annoyance or some loss. And think of the manufacturer's responsibilities, think of the numbers that depend on him, that look to him for their daily bread. No, no! none of you need wish yourselves in my shoes —you would soon have enough of it. [*After a moment's reflection.*] You all saw how that fellow, that scoundrel Becker, behaved. Now he'll go and spread about all sorts of tales of my hard-heartedness, of how my weavers are turned off for a mere trifle, without a moment's notice. Is that true? Am I so very unmerciful?

CHORUS OF VOICES. No, sir.

DREISSIGER. It doesn't seem to me that I am. And yet these ne'er-do-wells come round singing low songs about us manufacturers—prating about hunger, with enough in their pockets to pay for quarts of bad brandy. If they would like to know what want is, let them go and ask the linen-weavers: they can tell something about it. But you here, you fustian-weavers, have every reason to thank God that things are no worse than they are. And I put it to all the old, industrious weavers present: Is a good workman able to gain a living in my employment, or is he not?

MANY VOICES. Yes, sir; he is, sir.

DREISSIGER. There now! You see! Of course such a fellow as that Becker can't. I advise you to keep these young lads in check. If there's much more of this sort of thing, I'll shut up shop—give up the business altogether, and then you can shift for yourselves, get work where you like—perhaps Mr. Becker will provide it.

FIRST WEAVER'S WIFE [*has come close to* DREISSIGER, *obsequiously removes a little dust from his coat*]. You've been an' rubbed ag'in' something, sir.

DREISSIGER. Business is as bad as it can be just now, you know that yourselves. Instead of making money, I am losing it every day. If, in spite of this, I take care that my weavers are kept in work, I look for some little gratitude from them. I have thousands of pieces of cloth in stock, and don't know if I'll ever be able to sell them. Well, now, I've heard how many weavers hereabouts are out of work, and—I'll leave Pfeifer to give the particulars—but this much I'll tell you, just to show you my good will. . . . I can't deal out charity all round; I'm not rich enough for that; but I can give the people who are out of work the chance of earning at any rate a little. It's a great business risk I run by doing it, but that's my affair. I say to myself: Better that a man should work for a bite of bread than that he should starve altogether. Am I not right?

CHORUS OF VOICES. Yes, yes, sir.

DREISSIGER. And therefore I am ready to give employment to two hundred more weavers. Pfeifer will tell you on what conditions. [*He turns to go.*]

FIRST WEAVER'S WIFE [*comes between him and the door, speaks hurriedly, eagerly, imploringly*]. Oh, if you please, sir, will you let me ask you if you'll be so good . . . I've been twice laid up for . . .

DREISSIGER [*hastily*]. Speak to Pfeifer, good woman. I'm too late as it is. [*Passes on, leaving her standing.*]

REIMANN [*Stops him again. In an injured, complaining tone.*] I have a complaint to make, if you please, sir. Mr. Pfeifer refuses to . . . I've always got one and twopence for a web . . .

DREISSIGER [*interrupts him*]. Mr. Pfeifer's my manager. There he is. Apply to him.

HEIBER [*detaining* DREISSIGER; *hurriedly and confusedly*]. O sir, I wanted to ask if you would p'r'aps, if I might p'r'aps . . . if Mr. Pfeifer might . . . might . . .

DREISSIGER. What is it you want?

HEIBER. That advance pay I had last time, sir; I thought p'r'aps you would kindly . . .

DREISSIGER. I have no idea what you are talking about.

HEIBER. I'm awful hard up, sir, because . . .

DREISSIGER. These are things Pfeifer must look into—I really have not the time. Arrange the matter with Pfeifer.

He escapes into the office. The supplicants look helplessly at one another, sigh, and take their places again among the others.

PFEIFER [*resuming his task of inspection*]. Well, Annie, let us see what yours is like.

OLD BAUMERT. How much are we to get for the web, then, Mr. Pfeifer?

HEIBER. One shilling a web.

OLD BAUMERT. Has it come to that!

Excited whispering and murmuring among the weavers.

ACT II

A small room in the house of WILHELM ANSORGE, *weaver and house-owner in the village of Kaschbach, in the Eulengebirge.*

In this room, which does not measure six feet from the dilapidated wooden floor to the smoke-blackened rafters, sit four people. Two young girls, EMMA *and* BERTHA BAUMERT, *are working at their looms;* MOTHER BAUMERT, *a decrepit old woman, sits on a stool beside the bed, with a winding-wheel in front of her; her idiot son* AUGUST *sits on a footstool, also winding. He is twenty, has a small body and head, and long, spider-like legs and arms.*

Faint, rosy evening light makes its way through two small windows in the right wall, which have their broken panes pasted over with paper or stuffed with straw. It lights up the flaxen hair of the girls, which falls loose on their slender white necks and thin bare shoulders, and their coarse chemises. These, with a short petticoat of the roughest linen, form their whole attire. The warm glow falls on the old woman's face, neck, and breast—a face worn away to a skeleton, with shriveled skin and sunken eyes, red and watery with smoke, dust, and working by lamplight; a long goitre neck, wrinkled and sinewy; a hollow breast covered with faded, ragged shawls.

Part of the right wall is also lighted up, with stove, stove-bench, bedstead, and one or two gaudily colored sacred prints. On the stove-rail rags are hanging to dry, and behind the stove is a collection of worthless lumber. On the bench stand some old pots and cooking-utensils, and potato-parings are laid out on it, on paper, to dry. Hanks of yarn and reels hang from the rafters; baskets of bobbins stand beside the looms. In the backwall there is a low door without fastening. Beside it a bundle of willow wands is set up against the wall, and beyond them lie some damaged quarter-bushel baskets.

The room is full of sound—the rhythmic thud of the looms, shaking floor and walls, the click and rattle of the shuttles passing back and forward, and the steady whirr of the winding-wheels, like the hum of gigantic bees.

MOTHER BAUMERT [*in a querulous, feeble voice, as the girls stop weaving and bend over their webs*]. Got to make knots again already, have you?

EMMA [*the elder of the two girls, about twenty-two, tying a broken thread*]. It's the plagueyest web, this!

BERTHA [*fifteen*]. Yes, it's real bad yarn they've given us this time.

EMMA. What can have happened to father? He's been away since nine.

MOTHER BAUMERT. You may well ask. Where in the wide world can he be?

BERTHA. Don't you worry yourself, mother.

MOTHER BAUMERT. I can't help it, Bertha lass.

EMMA *begins to weave again.*

BERTHA. Stop a minute, Emma!

EMMA. What is it!

BERTHA. I thought I heard some one.

EMMA. It'll be Ansorge coming home.

Enter FRITZ, *a little, barefooted, ragged boy of four.*

FRITZ [*whimpering*]. I'm hungry, mother.

EMMA. Wait, Fritzel, wait a bit! Gran'father will be here very soon, an' he's bringin' bread along with him, an' coffee, too.

FRITZ. But I'm awful hungry, mother.

EMMA. Be a good boy now, Fritz. Listen to what I'm tellin' you. He'll be here this minute. He's bringin' nice bread an' nice corn-coffee; an' when we stop working mother'll take the tater peelin's and carry them to the farmer, and the farmer'll give her a drop o' good skim milk for her little boy.

FRITZ. Where's grandfather gone?

EMMA. To the manufacturer, Fritz, with a web.

FRITZ. To the manufacturer?

EMMA. Yes, yes, Fritz; down to Dreissiger's at Peterswaldau.

FRITZ. Is it there he gets the bread?

EMMA. Yes; Dreissiger gives him money, and then he buys the bread.

FRITZ. Does he give him a heap of money?

EMMA [*impatiently*]. Oh, stop that chatter, boy

She and BERTHA *go on weaving for a time, and then both stop again.*

BERTHA. August, go and ask Ansorge if he'll give us a light.

AUGUST *goes out accompanied by* FRITZ.

MOTHER BAUMERT [*overcome by her childish apprehension, whimpers*]. Emma! Bertha! where can father be?

BERTHA. He'll have looked in to see Hauffen.

MOTHER BAUMERT [*crying*]. What if he's sittin' drinkin' in the public house?

EMMA. Don't cry, mother! You know well enough father's not the man to do that.

MOTHER BAUMERT [*half distracted by a multitude of gloomy forebodings*]. What . . . what . . . what's to become of us if he doesn't come home?—if he drinks the money, and brings us nothin' at all? There's not so much as a handful of salt in the house—not a bite o' bread, nor a bit o' wood for the fire.

BERTHA. Wait a bit, mother! It's moonlight just now. We'll take August with us and go into the wood and get some sticks.

MOTHER BAUMERT. Yes, an' be caught by the forester.

ANSORGE, *an old weaver of gigantic stature, who has to bend down to get into the room, puts his head and shoulders in at the door. Long, unkempt hair and beard.*

ANSORGE. What's wanted?

BERTHA. Light, if you please.

ANSORGE [*in a muffled voice, as if speaking in a sick-room*]. There's good daylight yet.

MOTHER BAUMERT. Are we to sit in the dark next?

ANSORGE. I've to do the same myself. [*Goes out.*]

BERTHA. It's easy to see that he's a miser.

EMMA. Well, there's nothin' for it but to sit an' wait his pleasure.

Enter MRS. HEINRICH, *a woman of thirty, enceinte; an expression of torturing anxiety and apprehension on her worn face.*

MRS. HEINRICH. Good-evenin' t' you all.

MOTHER BAUMERT. Well, Jenny, and what's your news?

MRS. HEINRICH [*who limps*]. I've got a piece o' glass into my foot.

BERTHA. Come an' sit down, then, an' I'll see if I can get it out.

MRS. HEINRICH *seats herself.* BERTHA *kneels down in front of her, and examines her foot.*

MOTHER BAUMERT. How are you all at home, Jenny?

MRS. HEINRICH [*breaks out despairingly*]. Things is in a terrible way with us!

She struggles in vain against a rush of tears, then weeps silently.

MOTHER BAUMERT. The best thing as could happen to the likes of us, Jenny, would be if God had pity on us an' took us away out o' this weary world.

MRS. HEINRICH [*no longer able to control herself, screams, still crying*]. My children's starvin'. [*Sobs and moans.*] I'm at my wits' ends. Let me work till I fall down—I'm more dead than alive—it's all no use. Am I able to fill nine hungry mouths? We got a bit o' bread last night, but it wasn't enough even for the two smallest ones. Who was I to give it to, eh? They all cried: Me, me, mother! give it to me! . . . An' if it's like this while I'm still on my feet, what'll it be when I've to take to bed? Our few taters was washed away. We haven't a thing to put in our mouths.

BERTHA [*has removed the bit of glass and washed the wound*]. We'll put a rag around it. Emma, see if you can find one.

MOTHER BAUMERT. We're no better off than you, Jenny.

MRS. HEINRICH. You have your girls, anyway. You've a husband as can work. Mine was taken with one of his fits last week again—so bad that I didn't know what to do with him, and was half out o' my mind with fright. And when he's had a turn like that, he can't stir out of bed under a week.

MOTHER BAUMERT. Mine's no better. His breathin''s bad now as well as his back. An' there's not a farthin' nor a farthin's worth in the house. If he don't bring a few pence with him to-day, I don't know what we're to do.

EMMA. It's the truth she's tellin' you, Jenny. We had to let father take the little dog with him to-day, to have him killed, that we might get a bite into our stomachs again!

MRS. HEINRICH. Have you not got as much as a handful of flour to spare?

MOTHER BAUMERT. And that we have not, Jenny. There's not as much as a grain of salt in the house.

MRS. HEINRICH. Oh, whatever am I to do? [*Rises, stands still, brooding.*] I don't know what'll be the end of this! It's more nor I can bear. [*Screams in rage and despair.*] I would be contented if it was nothin' but pigs' food!—But I can't go home again empty-handed—that I can't. God forgive me, I see no other way out of it. [*She limps quickly out.*]

MOTHER BAUMERT [*calls after her in a warning voice*]. Jenny, Jenny! don't you be doin' anything foolish, now!

BERTHA. She'll do herself no harm, mother. You needn't be afraid.

EMMA. That's the way she always goes on. [*Seats herself at the loom and weaves for a few seconds.*]

AUGUST *enters, carrying a tallow candle, and lighting his father,* OLD BAUMERT, *who follows close behind him, staggering under a heavy bundle of yarn.*

MOTHER BAUMERT. Oh, father, where have you been all this long time? Where have you been?

OLD BAUMERT. Come now, mother, don't fall on a man like that. Give me time get my breath first. An' look who I've brought with me.

MORITZ JAEGER *comes stooping in at the low door. Reserve soldier, newly discharged. Middle height, rosy-cheeked, military carriage. His cap on the side of his head, hussar fashion, whole clothes and shoes, a clean shirt without collar. Draws himself up and salutes.*

JAEGER [*in a hearty voice*]. Good evening, Auntie Baumert!

MOTHER BAUMERT. Well, well, now! And to think you've got back! An' you've not forgotten us? Take a chair, then, lad.

EMMA [*wiping a wooden chair with her apron, and pushing it toward* MORITZ]. An' so you've come to see what poor folks are like again, Moritz?

JAEGER. I say, Emma, is it true that you've got a boy nearly old enough to be a soldier? Where did you get hold of him, eh?

BERTHA, *having taken the small supply of provisions which her father has brought, puts meat into a saucepan, and shoves it into the oven, while* AUGUST *lights the fire.*

BERTHA. You knew Weaver Finger, didn't you?

MOTHER BAUMERT. We had him here in the house with us. He was ready enough to marry her; but he was too far gone in consumption; he was as good as a dead man. It didn't happen for want of warning from me. But do you think she would listen? Not she. Now he's dead an' forgotten long ago, an' she's left with the boy to provide for as best she can. But now tell us how you've been gettin' on, Moritz.

OLD BAUMERT. You've only to look at him, mother, to know that. He's had luck. It'll be about as much as he can do to speak to the likes of us. He's got clothes like a prince, an' a silver watch, an' thirty shillings in his pocket into the bargain.

JAEGER [*stretching himself consequentially, a knowing smile on his face*]. I can't complain. I didn't get on at all badly in the regiment.

OLD BAUMERT. He was the major's own servant. Just listen to him—he speaks like a gentleman.

JAEGER. I've got so accustomed to it that I can't help it.

MOTHER BAUMERT. Well, now, to think that such a good-for-nothing as you were should have come to be a rich man. For there wasn't nothing to be made of you. You would never sit still to wind more than a hank of yarn at a time, that you wouldn't. Off you went to your tom-tit boxes an' your robin redbreast snares—they was all you cared about. Is it not the truth I'm telling?

JAEGER. Yes, yes, auntie, it's true enough. It wasn't only redbreasts. I went after swallows, too.

EMMA. Though we were always tellin' you that swallows were poison.

JAEGER. What did I care?—But how have you all been getting on, Auntie Baumert?

MOTHER BAUMERT. Oh, badly, lad, badly these last four years. I've had the rheumatics—just look at them hands. And it's more than likely as I've had a stroke o' some kind, too, I'm that helpless. I can hardly move a limb, an' nobody knows the pains I suffers.

OLD BAUMERT. She's in a bad way, she is. She'll not hold out long.

BERTHA. We've to dress her in the mornin' an' undress her at night, an' to feed her like a baby.

MOTHER BAUMERT [*speaking in a complaining, tearful voice*]. Not a thing can I do for myself. It's far worse than bein' ill. For it's not only a burden to myself I am, but to every one else. Often and often do I pray to God to take me. For oh! mine's a weary life. I don't know . . . p'r'aps they think . . . but I'm one that's been a hard worker all my days. An' I've always been able to do my turn, too; but now, all at once [*she vainly attempts to rise*], I can't do nothing.—I've a good husband an' good children, but to have to sit here and see them! . . . Look at the girls! There's hardly any blood left in them—faces the color of a sheet. But on they must work at these weary looms whether they earn enough to keep themselves or not. What sort o' life is it they lead? Their feet never off the treadle from year's end to year's end. An' with it all they can't scrape together as much as'll buy them clothes that they can let theirselves be seen in; never a step can they go to church, to hear a word of comfort. They're liker scarecrows than young girls of fifteen and twenty.

BERTHA [*at the stove*]. It's beginnin' to smoke again!

OLD BAUMERT. There now; look at that smoke. And we can't do nothin' for it. The whole stove's goin' to pieces. We must let it fall, and swallow the soot. We're coughin' already, one worse than the other. We may cough till we choke, or till we cough our lungs up—nobody cares.

JAEGER. But this here is Ansorge's business; he must see to the stove.

BERTHA. He'll see us out of the house first; he has plenty against us without that.

MOTHER BAUMERT. We've only been in his way this long time past.

OLD BAUMERT. One word of complaint an' out we go. He's had no rent from us this last half-year.

MOTHER BAUMERT. A well-off man like him needn't be so hard.

OLD BAUMERT. He's no better off than we are, mother. He's hard put to it, too, for all he holds his tongue about it.

MOTHER BAUMERT. He's got his house.

OLD BAUMERT. What are you talkin' about, mother? Not one stone in the wall is the man's own.

JAEGER [*has seated himself, and taken a short pipe with gay tassels out of one coat-pocket, and a quart bottle of brandy out of another*]. Things can't go on like this. I'm dumbfoundered when I see the life the people live here. The very dogs in the towns live better.

OLD BAUMERT [*eagerly*]. That's what I say! Eh? eh? You know it, too! But if you say that here, they'll tell you that it's only bad times.

Enter ANSORGE, *an earthenware pan with soup in one hand, in the other a half-finished quarter-bushel basket.*

ANSORGE. Glad to see you again, Moritz!

JAEGER. Thank you, Father Ansorge—same to you!

ANSORGE [*shoving his pan into the oven*]. Why, lad, you look like a duke!

OLD BAUMERT. Show him your watch, Moritz! An' he's got a new suit of clothes besides them he's on, an' thirty shillings in his purse.

ANSORGE [*shaking his head*]. Is that so? Well, well!

EMMA [*puts the potato-parings into a bag*]. I must be off; I'll maybe get a drop o' skim milk for these. [*Goes out.*]

JAEGER [*the others hanging on his words*]. You know how you all used to be down on me. It was always: Wait, Moritz, till your soldiering time comes—you'll catch it then. But you see how well I've got on. At the end of the first half-year I had got my good conduct stripes. You've got to be willing—that's where the secret lies. I brushed the sergeant's boots; I groomed his horse; I fetched his

beer. I was as sharp as a needle. Always ready, accoutrements clean and shining—first at stables, first at roll-call, first in the saddle. And when the bugle sounded to the assault—why, then, blood and thunder, and ride to the devil with you! I was as keen as a pointer. Says I to myself: There's no help for it now, my boy, it's got to be done; and I set my mind to it and did it. Till at last the major said before the whole squadron: There's a hussar now that shows you what a hussar should be!

Silence. He lights his pipe.

ANSORGE [*shaking his head*]. Well, well, well! You had luck with you, Moritz.

Sits down on the floor, with his willow twigs beside him, and continues mending the basket, which he holds between his legs.

OLD BAUMERT. Let's hope you've brought some of it to us.—Are we to have a drop to drink your health in?

JAEGER. Of course you are, Father Baumert. And when this bottle's done, we'll send for more. [*He flings a coin on the table.*]

ANSORGE [*open-mouthed with amazement*]. Oh, my! Oh, my! What goings on to be sure! Roast meat frizzlin' in the oven! A bottle o' brandy on the table! [*He drinks out of the bottle.*] Here's to you, Moritz!—Well, well, well!

The bottle circulates freely after this.

OLD BAUMERT. If we could anyway have a bit o' meat on Sundays and holidays, instead of never seein' the sight of it from year's end to year's end! Now we'll have to wait till another poor little dog find its way into the house like this one did four weeks gone by—an' that's not likely to happen soon again.

ANSORGE. Have you killed the little dog?

OLD BAUMERT. We had to do that or starve.

ANSORGE. Well, well!

MOTHER BAUMERT. A nice, kind little beast he was, too!

JAEGER. Are you as keen as ever on roast dog hereabouts?

OLD BAUMERT. My word, if we could only get enough of it!

MOTHER BAUMERT. A nice little bit o' meat like that does you a lot o' good.

OLD BAUMERT. Have you lost the taste for it, Moritz? Stay with us a bit, and it'll soon come back to you.

ANSORGE [*sniffing*]. Yes, yes! That will be a tasty bite—what a good smell it has!

OLD BAUMERT [*sniffing*]. Splendid!

ANSORGE. Come, then, Moritz, tell us your opinion, you that's been out and seen the world. Are things at all like improving for us weavers, eh?

JAEGER. They would need to.

ANSORGE. We're in an awful state here. It's not livin' an' it's not dyin'. A man fights to the bitter end, but he's bound to be beat at last—to be left without a roof over his head, you may say without ground under his feet. As long as he can work at the loom he can earn some sort o' poor, miserable livin'. But it's many a day since I've been able to get that sort o' job. Now I tries to put a bite into my mouth with this here basket-makin'. I sits at it late into the night, and by the time I tumbles into bed I've earned three-halfpence. I put it to you if a man can live on that, when everything's so dear? Nine shillin' goes in one lump for house tax, three shillin' for land tax, nine shillin' for mortgage interest—that makes one pound one. I may reckon my year's earnin' at just double that money, and that leaves me twenty-one shillin' for a whole year's food, an' fire, an' clothes, an' shoes; and I've got to keep up some sort of a place to live in. Is it any wonder if I'm behind-hand with my interest payments?

OLD BAUMERT. Some one would need to go to Berlin and tell the King how hard put to it we are.

JAEGER. Little good that would do, Father Baumert. There's been plenty written about it in the newspapers. But the rich people, they can turn and twist things round . . . as cunning as the devil himself.

OLD BAUMERT [shaking his head]. To think they've no more sense than that in Berlin!

ANSORGE. And is it really true, Moritz? Is there no law to help us? If a man hasn't been able to scrape together enough to pay his mortgage interest, though he's worked the very skin off his hands, must his house be taken from him? The peasant that's lent the money on it, he wants his rights— what else can you look for from him? But what's to be the end of it all, I don't know.—If I'm put out o' the house. . . . [In a voice choked by tears.] I was born here, and here my father sat at his loom for more than forty year. Many was the time he said to mother: Mother, when I'm gone, the house'll still be here. I've worked hard for it. Every nail means a night's weaving, every plank a year's dry bread. A man would think that . . .

JAEGER. They're quite fit to take the last bite out of your mouth—that's what they are.

ANSORGE. Well, well, well! I would rather be carried out than have to walk out now in my old days. Who minds dyin'? My father, he was glad to die. At the very end he got frightened, but I crept into bed beside him, an' he quieted down again. I was a lad of thirteen then. I was tired and fell asleep beside him—I knew no better—and when I woke he was quite cold.

MOTHER BAUMERT [after a pause]. Give Ansorge his soup out o' the oven, Bertha.

BERTHA. Here, Father Ansorge, it'll do you good.

ANSORGE [eating and shedding tears]. Well, well!

OLD BAUMERT has begun to eat the meat out of the saucepan.

MOTHER BAUMERT. Father, father, can't you have patience an' let Bertha serve it up properly?

OLD BAUMERT [chewing]. It's two years now since I took the Sacrament. I went straight after that an' sold my Sunday coat, an' we bought a good bit o' pork, an' since then never a mouthful of meat has passed my lips till to-night.

JAEGER. How should we need meat? The manufacturers eat it for us. It's the fat of the land they live on. Whoever doesn't believe that has only to go down to Bielau and Peterswaldau. He'll see fine things there—palace upon palace, with towers and iron railings and plate-glass windows. Who do they all belong to? Why, of course, the manufacturers! No signs of bad times there! Baked and boiled and fried—horses and carriages and governesses— they've money to pay for all that and goodness knows how much more. They're swelled out to bursting with pride and good living.

ANSORGE. Things was different in my young days. Then the manufacturers let the weaver have his share. Now they keep everything to theirselves. An' would you like to know what's at the bottom of it all? It's that the fine folks nowadays believes neither in God nor devil. What do they care about commandments or punishments? And so they steal our last scrap o' bread, an' leave us no chance of earnin' the barest living. For it's their fault. If our manufacturers was good men, there would be no bad times for us.

JAEGER. Listen, then, and I'll read you something that will please you. [He takes one or two loose papers from his pocket.] I say, August, run and fetch another quart from the public-house. Eh, boy, do you laugh all day long?

MOTHER BAUMERT. No one knows why, but our August's always happy—grins an' laughs, come what may. Off with you, then, quick! [Exit AUGUST with the empty brandy-bottle.] You've got something good now, eh, father?

OLD BAUMERT [still chewing; spirits rising from

the effect of food and drink]. Moritz, you're the very man we want. You can read an' write. You understand the weavin' trade, and you've a heart to feel for the poor weavers' sufferin's. You should stand up for us here.

JAEGER. I'd do that quick enough! There's nothing I'd like better than to give the manufacturers round here a bit of a fright—dogs that they are! I'm an easy-going fellow, but let me once get worked up into a real rage, and I'll take Dreissiger in the one hand and Dittrich in the other, and knock their heads together till the sparks fly out of their eyes.—If we could only arrange all to join together, we'd soon give the manufacturers a proper lesson . . . without help from King or Government . . . all we'd have to do would be to say: We want this and that, and we don't want the other thing. There would be a change of days then. As soon as they see that there's some pluck in us, they'll cave in. I know the rascals; they're a pack of cowardly hounds.

MOTHER BAUMERT. There's some truth in what you say. I'm not an ill-natured woman. I've always been the one to say as how there must be rich folks as well as poor. But when things come to such a pass as this. . . .

JAEGER. The devil may take them all, for what I care. It would be no more than they deserve.

OLD BAUMERT *has quietly gone out.*

BERTHA. Where's father?

MOTHER BAUMERT. I don't know where he can have gone.

BERTHA. Do you think he's not been able to stomach the meat, with not gettin' none for so long?

MOTHER BAUMERT [*in distress, crying*]. There, now, there! He's not even able to keep it down when he's got it. Up it comes again, the only bite o' good food as he's tasted this many a day.

Reënter OLD BAUMERT, *crying with rage.*

OLD BAUMERT. It's no good! I'm too far gone! Now that I've at last got hold of somethin' with a taste in it, my stomach won't keep it.

He sits down on the bench by the stove crying.

JAEGER [*with a sudden violent ebullition of rage*]. And yet there are people not far from here, justices they call themselves too, over-fed brutes, that have nothing to do all the year round but invent new ways of wasting their time. And these people say that the weavers would be quite well off if only they weren't so lazy.

ANSORGE. The men as say that are no men at all, they're monsters.

JAEGER. Never mind, Father Ansorge: we're mak-ing the place hot for 'em. Becker and I have been and given Dreissiger a piece of our mind, and before we came away we sang him "Bloody Justice."

ANSORGE. Good Lord! Is that the song?

JAEGER. Yes; I have it here.

ANSORGE. They call it Dreissiger's song, don't they?

JAEGER. I'll read it to you.

MOTHER BAUMERT. Who wrote it?

JAEGER. That's what nobody knows. Now listen. *He reads, hesitating like a schoolboy, with incorrect accentuation, but unmistakably strong feeling Despair, suffering, rage, hatred, thirst for revenge, all find utterance.*

> The justice to us weavers dealt
>   Is bloody, cruel, and hateful;
> Our life's one torture, long drawn out:
>   For Lynch law we'd be grateful.
> Stretched on the rack day after day,
>   Hearts sick and bodies aching,
> Our heavy sighs their witness bear
>   To spirits slowly breaking.

The words of the song make a strong impression on OLD BAUMERT. *Deeply agitated, he struggles against the temptation to interrupt* JAEGER. *At last he can keep quiet no longer.*

OLD BAUMERT [*to his wife, half laughing, half crying, stammering*]. Stretched on the rack day after day. Whoever wrote that, mother, wrote the truth. You can bear witness . . . eh, how does it go? "Our heavy sighs their witness bear" . . . what's the rest?

JAEGER. "To spirits slowly breaking."

OLD BAUMERT. You know the way we sigh, mother, day and night, sleepin' and wakin'.

ANSORGE *has stopped working, and cowers on the floor, strongly agitated.* MOTHER BAUMERT *and* BERTHA *wipe their eyes frequently during the course of the reading.*

JAEGER [*continues to read*].

> The Dreissigers true hangmen are,
>   Servants no whit behind them;
> Masters and men with one accord
>   Set on the poor to grind them.
>
> You villains all, you brood of hell . . .

OLD BAUMERT [*trembling with rage, stamping on the floor*]. Yes, brood of hell!!!

JAEGER [*reads*].

> You fiends in fashion human,
>   A curse will fall on all like you,
>   Who prey on man and woman.

ANSORGE. Yes, yes, a curse upon them!

OLD BAUMERT [*clenching his fist threateningly*]. You prey on man and woman.

JAEGER [*reads*].

  The suppliant knows he asks in vain,
    Vain every word that's spoken.
  "If not content, then go and starve—
    Our rules cannot be broken."

OLD BAUMERT. What is it? "The suppliant knows he asks in vain"? Every word of it's true . . . every word . . . as true as the Bible. He knows he asks in vain.

ANSORGE. Yes, yes! It's all no good.

JAEGER [*reads*].

  Then think of all our woe and want,
    O ye who hear this ditty!
  Our struggle vain for daily bread
    Hard hearts would move to pity.
  But pity's what *you've* never known,—
    You'd take both skin and clothing,
  You cannibals, whose cruel deeds
    Fill all good men with loathing.

OLD BAUMERT [*jumps up, beside himself with excitement*]. Both skin and clothing. It's true, it's all true! Here I stand, Robert Baumert, master-weaver of Kaschbach. Who can bring up anything against me? I've been an honest, hard-working man all my life long, an' look at me now! What have I to show for it? Look at me! See what they've made of me! Stretched on the rack day after day. [*He holds out his arms.*] Feel that! Skin and bone! "You villains all, you brood of hell!!" *He sinks down on a chair, weeping with rage and despair.*

ANSORGE [*flings his basket from him into a corner, rises, his whole body trembling with rage, gasps*]. And the time's come now for a change, I say. We'll stand it no longer! We'll stand it no longer! Come what may!

ACT III

The common room of the principal public house in Peterswaldau. A large room with a raftered roof supported by a central wooden pillar, round which a table runs. In the back wall, a little to the right of the pillar, is the entrance door, through the opening of which the spacious lobby or outer room is seen, with barrels and brewing utensils. To the right of this door, in the corner, is the bar—a high wooden counter with receptacles for beer-mugs, glasses, etc.; a cupboard with rows of brandy and liqueur bottles on the wall behind, and between counter and cupboard a narrow space for the barkeeper. In front of the bar stands a table with a gay-colored cover, a pretty lamp hanging above it, and several cane chairs placed around it. Not far off, in the right wall, is a door with the inscription: Bar Parlor. Nearer the front on the same side an old eight-day clock stands ticking. At the back, to the left of the entrance door, is a table with bottles and glasses, and beyond this, in the corner, is the great stove. In the left wall there are three small windows. Below them runs a long bench; and in front of each stands a large oblong wooden table, with the end towards the wall. There are benches with backs along the sides of these tables, and at the end of each facing the window stands a wooden chair. The walls are washed blue and decorated with advertisements, colored prints and oleographs, among the latter a portrait of Frederick William III.

WELZEL, *the publican, a good-natured giant, upwards of fifty, stands behind the counter, letting beer run from a barrel into a glass.*

MRS. WELZEL *is ironing by the stove. She is a handsome, tidily dressed woman in her thirty-fifth year.*

ANNA WELZEL, *a good-looking girl of seventeen, with a quantity of beautiful, fair, reddish hair, sits, nicely dressed, with her embroidery, at the table with the colored cover. She looks up from her work for a moment and listens, as the sound of a funeral hymn sung by school-children is heard in the distance.*

WIEGAND, *the joiner, in his working clothes, is sitting at the same table, with a glass of Bavarian beer before him. His face shows that he understands what the world requires of a man if he is to attain his ends—namely, craftiness, sharpness, and relentless determination.*

A COMMERCIAL TRAVELER *is seated at the pillar-table, vigorously masticating a beefsteak. He is of middle height, stout and thriving-looking, inclined to jocosity, lively, and impudent. He is dressed in the fashion of the day, and his portmanteau, pattern-case, umbrella, overcoat, and traveling-rug lie on chairs beside him.*

WELZEL [*carrying a glass of beer to the* TRAVELER, *but addressing* WIEGAND]. The devil's loose in Peterswaldau to-day.

WIEGAND [*in a sharp, shrill voice*]. That's because it's delivery day at Dreissiger's.

MRS. WELZEL. But they don't generally make such an awful row.

WIEGAND. It's maybe because of the two hundred new weavers that he's going to take on.

MRS. WELZEL [at her ironing]. Yes, yes, that'll be it. If he wants two hundred, six hundred's sure to have come. There's no lack of *them*.

WIEGAND. You may well say that. There's no fear of their dying out, let them be ever so badly off. They bring more children into the world than we know what do with. [*The strains of the funeral hymn are suddenly heard more distinctly*.] There's a funeral to-day, too. Weaver Nentwich is dead, as no doubt you know.

WELZEL. He's been long enough about it. He's been goin' about like a livin' ghost this many a day.

WIEGAND. You never saw such a little coffin, Welzel; it was the tiniest, miserablest little thing I ever glued together. And what a corpse! It didn't weigh ninety pounds.

TRAVELER [*his mouth full*]. What I don't understand's this. . . . Take up whatever paper you like and you'll find the most heartrending accounts of the destitution among the weavers. You get the impression that three-quarters of the people in this neighborhood are starving. Then you come and see a funeral like what's going on just now. I met it as I came into the village. Brass band, schoolmaster, school-children, pastor, and such a procession behind them that you would think it was the Emperor of China that was getting buried. If the people have money to spend on this sort of thing, well! . . . [*He takes a drink of beer; puts down the glass; suddenly and jocosely*.] What do you say to it, miss? Don't you agree with me?

ANNA *gives an embarrassed laugh, and goes on working busily.*

TRAVELER. Now, I'll take a bet that these are slippers for papa.

WELZEL. You're wrong, then; I wouldn't put such things on my feet.

TRAVELER. You don't say so! Now, I would give half of what I'm worth if these slippers were for me.

MRS. WELZEL. Oh, you don't know nothing about such things.

WIEGAND [*has coughed once or twice, moved his chair, and prepared himself to speak*]. You were saying, sir, that you wondered to see such a funeral as this. I tell you, and Mrs. Welzel here will bear me out, that it's quite a small funeral.

TRAVELER. But, my good man . . . what a monstrous lot of money it must cost! Where does that all come from?

WIEGAND. If you'll excuse me for saying so, sir, there's a deal of foolishness among the poorer working-people hereabouts. They have a kind of inordinate idea, if I may say so, of the respect an' duty an' honor they're bound to show to such as are taken from their midst. And when it comes to be a case of parents, then there's no bounds whatever to their superstitiousness. The children and the nearest family scrapes together every farthing they can call their own, an' what's still wanting, that they borrow from some rich man. They run themselves into debt over head and ears; they're owing money to the pastor, to the sexton, and to all concerned. Then there's the victuals an' the drink, an' such like. No, sir, I'm far from speaking against dutifulness to parents; but it's too much when it goes the length of the mourners having to bear the weight of it for the rest of their lives.

TRAVELER. But surely the pastor might reason them out of such foolishness.

WIEGAND. Begging your pardon, sir, but I must mention that every little place hereabouts has its church an' its respected pastor to support. These honorable gentlemen has their advantages from big funerals. The larger the attendance is, the larger the offertory is bound to be. Whoever knows the circumstances connected with the working classes here, sir, will assure you that the pastors are strong against quiet funerals.

Enter HORNIG, *the rag-dealer, a little bandy-legged old man, with a strap round his chest.*

HORNIG. Good-mornin', ladies and gentlemen! A glass of schnapps, if you please, Mr. Welzel. Has the young mistress anything for me to-day? I've got beautiful ribbons in my cart, Miss Anna, an' tapes, an' garters, an' the very best of pins an' hairpins an' hooks an' eyes. An' all in exchange for a few rags. [*He changes his voice*.] An' out of them rags fine white paper's to be made, for your sweetheart to write you a letter on.

ANNA. Thank you, but I've nothing to do with sweethearts.

MRS. WELZEL [*putting a bolt into her iron*]. No, she's not that kind. She'll not hear of marrying.

TRAVELER [*jumps up, affecting delighted surprise, goes forward to* ANNA'S *table, and holds out his hand to her across it*]. That's right, miss. You and I think alike in this matter. Give me your hand on it. We'll both remain single.

ANNA [*blushing scarlet, gives him her hand*]. But you are married already!

TRAVELER. Not a bit of it. I only pretend to be. You think so because I wear a ring. I only have it on my finger to protect my charms against shameless attacks. I'm not afraid of you, though. [*He puts the ring into his pocket.*] But tell me, truly, miss, are you quite determined never, never, never, to marry?

ANNA [*shakes her head*]. Oh, get along with you!

MRS. WELZEL. You may trust her to remain single unless something very extra good turns up.

TRAVELER. And why should it not? I know of a rich Silesian proprietor who married his mother's lady's maid. And there's Dreissiger, the rich manufacturer, his wife is an innkeeper's daughter, too, and not half so pretty as you, miss, though she rides in her carriage now, with servants in livery. And why not? [*He marches about, stretching himself, and stamping his feet.*] Let me have a cup of coffee, please.

Enter ANSORGE *and* OLD BAUMERT, *each with a bundle. They seat themselves meekly and silently beside* HORNIG, *at front table to left.*

WELZEL. How are you, Father Ansorge? Glad to see you once again.

HORNIG. Yes, it's not often as you crawl down from that smoky old nest.

ANSORGE [*visibly embarrassed, mumbles*]. I've been fetchin' myself a web again.

BAUMERT. He's goin' to work at a shilling the web.

ANSORGE. I wouldn't have done it, but there's no more to be made now by basket-weavin'.

WIEGAND. It's always better than nothing. He does it only to give you employment. I know Dreissiger very well. When I was up there taking out his double windows last week we were talking about it, him and me. It's out of pity he does it.

ANSORGE. Well, well, well! That may be so.

WELZEL [*setting a glass of schnapps on the table before each of the weavers*]. Here you are, then. I say, Ansorge, how long is it since you had a shave? The gentleman over there would like to know.

TRAVELER [*calls across*]. Now, Mr. Welzel, you know I didn't say that. I was only struck by the venerable appearance of the master-weaver. It isn't often one sees such a gigantic figure.

ANSORGE [*scratching his head, embarrassed*]. Well, well!

TRAVELER. Such specimens of primitive strength are rare nowadays. We're all rubbed smooth by civilization . . . but I can still take pleasure in nature untampered with. . . . These bushy eyebrows! That tangled length of beard!

HORNIG. Let me tell you, sir, that these people haven't the money to pay a barber, and as to a razor for themselves, that's altogether beyond them. What grows, grows. They haven't nothing to throw away on their outsides.

TRAVELER. My good friend, you surely don't imagine that I would. . . . [*Aside to* WELZEL.] Do you think I might offer the hairy one a beer?

WELZEL. No, no; you mustn't do that. He wouldn't take it. He's got some queer ideas in that head of his.

TRAVELER. All right, then, I won't. With your permission, miss. [*He seats himself at* ANNA'S *table.*] I declare, miss, that I've not been able to take my eyes off your hair since I came in—such glossy softness, such a splendid quantity! [*Ecstatically kisses his finger-tips.*] And what a color! . . . like ripe wheat. Come to Berlin with that hair and you'll create no end of a sensation. On my honor, with hair like that you may go to Court. . . . [*Leans back, looking at it.*] Glorious, simply glorious!

WIEGAND. They've given her a name because of it.

TRAVELER. And what may that be?

HORNIG. The chestnut filly, isn't it?

WELZEL. Come, now, we've had enough o' this. I'm not goin' to have the girl's head turned altogether. She's had a-plenty of silly notions put into it already. She'll hear of nothing under a count to-day, and to-morrow it'll be a prince.

MRS. WELZEL. You let her alone, father. There's no harm in wantin' to rise in the world. It's as well that people don't all think as you do, or nobody would get on at all. If Dreissiger's grandfather had been of your way of thinkin', they would be poor weavers still. And now they're rollin' in wealth. An' look at old Tromtra. He was nothing but a weaver, too, and now he owns twelve estates, an' he's been made a nobleman into the bargain.

WIEGAND. Yes, Welzel, you must look at the thing fairly. Your wife's in the right this time. I can answer for that. I'd never be where I am, with seven workmen under me, if I had thought like you.

HORNIG. Yes, you understand the way to get on; that your worst enemy must allow. Before the weaver has taken to bed, you're gettin' his coffin ready.

WIEGAND. A man must attend to his business if he's to make anything of it.

HORNIG. No fear of you for that. You know before the doctor when death's on the way to knock at a weaver's door.

WIEGAND [*attempting to laugh, suddenly furi-*

ous]. And you know better than the police where the thieves are among the weavers, that keep back two or three bobbins full every week. It's rags you ask for, but you don't say No, if there's a little yarn among them.

HORNIG. An' your corn grows in the churchyard. The more that are bedded on the sawdust, the better for you. When you see the rows of little children's graves, you pats yourself on the belly, and says you: This has been a good year; the little brats have fallen like cockchafers off the trees. I can allow myself a quart extra in the week again.

WIEGAND. And supposing this is all true, it still doesn't make me a receiver of stolen goods.

HORNIG. No; perhaps the worst you do is to send in an account twice to the rich fustian manufacturers, or to help yourself to a plank or two at Dreissiger's when there's building goin' on and the moon happens not to be shinin'.

WIEGAND [turning his back]. Talk to any one you like, but not to me. [Then suddenly.] Hornig the liar!

HORNIG. Wiegand the coffin-jobber!

WIEGAND [to the rest of the company]. He knows charms for bewitching cattle.

HORNIG. If you don't look out, I'll try one on you.

WIEGAND turns pale.

MRS. WELZEL [had gone out; now returns with the TRAVELER's coffee; in the act of putting it on the table]. Perhaps you would rather have it in the parlor, sir?

TRAVELER. Most certainly not! [With a languishing look at ANNA.] I could sit here till I die.

Enter a YOUNG FORESTER and a PEASANT, the latter carrying a whip. They wish the others "Good-Morning," and remain standing at the counter.

PEASANT. Two brandies, if you please.

WELZEL. Good-morning to you, gentlemen.

He pours out their beverage; the two touch glasses, take a mouthful, and then set the glasses down on the counter.

TRAVELER [to FORESTER]. Come far this morning, sir?

FORESTER. From Steinseiffersdorf—that's a good step.

Two old WEAVERS enter, and seat themselves beside ANSORGE, BAUMERT, and HORNIG.

TRAVELER. Excuse me asking, but are you in Count Hochheim's service?

FORESTER. No, I'm in Count Keil's.

TRAVELER. Yes, yes, of course—that was what I meant. One gets confused here among all the counts and barons and other gentlemen. It would

take a giant's memory to remember them all. Why do you carry an ax, if I may ask?

FORESTER. I've just taken this one from a man who was stealing wood.

OLD BAUMERT. Yes, their lordships are mighty strict with us about a few sticks for the fire.

TRAVELER. You must allow that if every one were to help himself to what he wanted. . . .

OLD BAUMERT. By your leave, sir, but there's a difference made here as elsewhere between the big an' the little thieves. There's some here as deals in stolen wood wholesale, and grows rich on it. But if a poor weaver . . .

FIRST OLD WEAVER [interrupts BAUMERT]. We're forbid to take a single branch; but their lordships, they take the very skin off of us—we've assurance money to pay, an' spinning-money, an' charges in kind—we must go here an' go there, an' do so an' so much field work, all willy-nilly.

ANSORGE. That's just how it is—what the manufacturer leaves us, their lordships takes from us.

SECOND OLD WEAVER [has taken a seat at the next table]. I've said it to his lordship himself. By your leave, my lord, says I, it's not possible for me to work on the estate so many days this year. For why—my own bit of ground, my lord, it's been next to carried away by the rains. I've to work both night and day if I'm to live at all. For oh, what a flood that was! . . . There I stood an' wrung my hands, an' watched the good soil come pourin' down the hill, into the very house! And all that dear, fine seed! . . . I could do nothing but roar an' cry until I couldn't see out o' my eyes for a week. And then I had to start an' wheel eighty heavy barrow-loads of earth up that hill, till my back was all but broken.

PEASANT [roughly]. You weavers here make such an awful outcry. As if we hadn't all to put up with what Heaven sends us. An' if you are badly off just now, whose fault is it but your own? What did you do when trade was good? Drank an' squandered all you made. If you had saved a bit then, you'd have it to fall back on now when times is bad, and not need to be goin' stealin' yarn and wood.

FIRST YOUNG WEAVER [standing with several comrades in the lobby or outer room, calls in at the door]. What's a peasant but a peasant, though he lies in bed till nine?

FIRST OLD WEAVER. The peasant an' the count, it's the same story with 'em both. Says the peasant when a weaver wants a house: I'll give you a little bit of a hole to live in, an' you'll pay me so much rent in money, an' the rest of it you'll make up by helpin' me to get in my hay an' my corn—an' if that doesn't please you, why, then you may go elsewhere. He tries another, and the second he says the same as the first.

BAUMERT [angrily]. The weaver's like a bone that every dog takes a gnaw at.

PEASANT [furious]. You starving curs, you're no good for anything. Can you yoke a plough? Can you draw a straight furrow or throw a bundle of sheaves on to a cart. You're fit for nothing but to idle about an' go after the women. A pack of scoundrelly ne'er-do-wells!

He has paid and now goes out. The FORESTER follows, laughing. WELZEL, the JOINER, and MRS. WELZEL laugh aloud; the TRAVELER laughs to himself. Then there is a moment's silence.

HORNIG. A peasant like that's as stupid as his own ox. As if I didn't know all about the distress in the villages round here. Sad sights I've seen! Four and five lyin' naked on one sack of straw.

TRAVELER [in a mildly remonstrative tone]. Allow me to remark, my good man, that there's a great difference of opinion as to the amount of distress here in the Eulengebirge. If you can read . . .

HORNIG. I can read straight off, as well as you. An' I know what I've seen with my own eyes. It would be queer if a man that's traveled the country with a pack on his back these forty years an' more didn't know something about it. There was Fullern, now. You saw the children scraping about among the dung-heaps with the peasants' geese. The people up there died naked, on the bare stone floors. In their sore need they ate the stinking weavers' glue. Hunger carried them off by the hundred.

TRAVELER. You must be aware, since you are able to read, that strict investigation has been made by the Government, and that . . .

HORNIG. Yes, yes, we all know what that means. They send a gentleman that knows all about it already better nor if he had seen it, an' he goes about a bit in the village, at the lower end, where the best houses are. He doesn't want to dirty his shining boots. Thinks he to himself: All the rest'll be the same as this. An' so he steps into his carriage, an' drives away home again, an' then writes to Berlin that there's no distress in the place at all. If he had but taken the trouble to go higher up into a village like that, to where the stream comes in, or across the stream on to the narrow side—or, better still, if he'd gone up to the little out-o'-the-way hovels on the hill above, some of 'em that black an' tumbledown as it would be the waste of a good match to set fire to 'em—it's another kind of

report he'd have sent to Berlin. They should have come to me, these government gentlemen that wouldn't believe there was no distress here. I would have shown them something. I'd have opened their eyes for 'em in some of these starvation holes.

The strains of the WEAVERS' SONG are heard, sung outside.

WELZEL. There they are, roaring at that devil's song again.

WIEGAND. They're turning the whole place upside down.

MRS. WELZEL. You'd think there was something in the air.

JAEGER and BECKER arm in arm, at the head of a troop of young weavers, march noisily through the outer room and enter the bar.

JAEGER. Halt! To your places!

The new arrivals sit down at the various tables, and begin to talk to other weavers already seated.

HORNIG [calls out to BECKER]. What's up now, Becker, that you've got together a crowd like this?

BECKER [significantly]. Who knows but something may be going to happen? Eh, Moritz?

HORNIG. Come, come, lads. Don't you be a-gettin' of yourselves into mischief.

BECKER. Blood's flowed already. Would you like to see it?

He pulls up his sleeve and shows bleeding tattoo-marks on the upper part of his arm. Many of the other young weavers do the same.

BECKER. We've been at Father Schmidt's gettin' ourselves vaccinated.

HORNIG. Now the thing's explained. Little wonder there's such an uproar in the place, with a band of young rapscallions like you paradin' round.

JAEGER [consequentially, in a loud voice]. You may bring two quarts at once, Welzel! I pay. Perhaps you think I haven't got the needful. You're wrong, then. If we wanted we could sit an' drink your best brandy an' swill coffee till to-morrow morning with any bagman in the land.

Laughter among the young weavers.

TRAVELER [affecting comic surprise]. Is the young gentleman kind enough to take notice of me?

Host, hostess, and their daughter, WIEGAND, and the TRAVELER all laugh.

JAEGER. If the cap fits wear it.

TRAVELER. Your affairs seem to be in a thriving condition, young man, if I may be allowed to say so.

JAEGER. I can't complain. I'm a traveler in made-up goods. I go shares with the manufacturers.

The nearer starvation the weaver is, the better I fare. His want butters my bread.

BECKER. Well done, Moritz! You gave it to him that time. Here's to you!

WELZEL *has brought the corn-brandy. On his way back to the counter he stops, turns round slowly, and stands, an embodiment of phlegmatic strength, facing the weavers.*

WELZEL [*calmly but emphatically*]. You let the gentleman alone. He's done you no harm.

YOUNG WEAVERS. And we're doing him no harm.

MRS. WELZEL *has exchanged a few words with the TRAVELER. She takes the cup with the remains of his coffee and carries it into the parlor. The TRAVELER follows her amidst the laughter of the weavers.*

YOUNG WEAVERS [*singing*].
"The Dreissigers the hangmen are,
Servants no whit behind them."

WELZEL. Hush-sh! Sing that song anywhere else you like, but not in my house.

FIRST OLD WEAVER. He's quite right. Stop that singin', lads.

BECKER [*roars*]. But we must march past Dreissiger's, boys, and let them hear it once more.

WIEGAND. You'd better take care—you may march once too often.

Laughter and cries of Ho, ho!

WITTIG *has entered; a gray-haired old smith, bareheaded, with leather apron and wooden shoes, sooty from the smithy. He is standing at the counter waiting for his schnapps.*

YOUNG WEAVER. Wittig, Wittig!

WITTIG. Here he is. What do you want with him?

YOUNG WEAVERS. "It's Wittig!"—"Wittig, Wittig!"—"Come here, Wittig."—"Sit beside us, Wittig."

WITTIG. Do you think I would sit beside a set of rascals like you?

JAEGER. Come and take a glass with us.

WITTIG. Keep your brandy to yourselves. I pay for my own drink. [*Takes his glass and sits down beside* BAUMERT *and* ANSORGE. *Clapping the latter on the stomach.*] What's the weavers' food so nice? Sauerkraut and roasted lice!

OLD BAUMERT [*excitedly*]. But what would you say now if they'd made up their minds as how they would put up with it no longer.

WITTIG [*with pretended astonishment, staring open-mouthed at the old weaver*]. Heinerle! you don't mean to tell me that that's you? [*Laughs immoderately.*] O Lord, O Lord! I could laugh myself to death. Old Baumert risin' in rebellion! We'll have the tailors at it next, and then there'll be a rebellion among the baa-lambs, and the rats and the mice. Damn it all, but we'll see some sport. [*He nearly splits with laughter.*]

OLD BAUMERT. You needn't go on like that, Wittig. I'm the same man I've always been. I still say 't would be better if things could be put right peaceably.

WITTIG. Peaceably! How could it be done peaceably? Did they do it peaceably in France? Did Robespeer tickle the rich men's palms? No! It was: Away with them, everyone! To the gilyoteen with them! Allongs onfong! You've got your work before you. The geese'll not fly ready roasted into your mouths.

OLD BAUMERT. If I could make even half a livin'—

FIRST OLD WEAVER. The water's up to our chins now, Wittig.

SECOND OLD WEAVER. We're afraid to go home. It's all the same whether we works or whether we lies abed; it's starvation both ways.

FIRST OLD WEAVER. A man's like to go mad at home.

OLD ANSORGE. It's that length with me now that I don't care how things go.

OLD WEAVERS [*with increasing excitement*]. "We've no peace anywhere."—"We've no spirit left to work."—"Up with us in Steenkunzendorf you can see a weaver sittin' by the stream washin' hisself the whole day long, naked as God made him. It's driven him clean out of his mind."

THIRD OLD WEAVER [*moved by the spirit, stands up and begins to "speak with tongues," stretching out his hand threateningly*]. Judgment is at hand! Have no dealings with the rich and the great! Judgment is at hand! The Lord God of Sabaoth . . .

Some of the weavers laugh. He is pulled down on to his seat.

WELZEL. That's a chap that can't stand a single glass—he gets wild at once.

THIRD OLD WEAVER [*jumps up again*]. But they —they believe not in God, not in hell, not in heaven. They mock at religion . . .

FIRST OLD WEAVER. Come, come now, that's enough!

BECKER. You let him do his little bit o' preaching. There's many a one would be the better for taking it to heart.

VOICES [*in excited confusion*]. "Let him alone!" —"Let him speak!"

THIRD OLD WEAVER [*raising his voice*]. But hell is opened, saith the Lord; its jaws are gaping wide, to swallow up all those that oppress the afflicted and pervert judgment in the cause of the poor.

Wild excitement.

THIRD OLD WEAVER [*suddenly declaiming, school-boy fashion*].

When one has thought upon it well,
It's still more difficult to tell
Why they the linen-weaver's work despise.

BECKER. But we're fustian-weavers, man.

Laughter.

HORNIG. The linen-weavers is ever so much worse off than you. They're wandering about among the hills like ghosts. You people here have still got the pluck left in you to kick up a row.

WITTIG. Do you suppose the worst's over here? It won't be long till the manufacturers drain away that little bit of strength they still have left in their bodies.

BECKER. You know what he said: It will come to the weavers working for a bite of bread.

Uproar.

SEVERAL OLD AND YOUNG WEAVERS. Who said that?

BECKER. Dreissiger said it.

A YOUNG WEAVER. The damned rascal should be hung up by the heels.

JAEGER. Look here, Wittig. You've always jawed such a lot about the French revolution, and a good deal too about your own doings. A time may be coming, and that before long, when every one will have a chance to show whether he's a braggart or a true man.

WITTIG [*flaring up angrily*]. Say another word if you dare! Have you heard the whistle of bullets? Have you done outpost duty in an enemy's country?

JAEGER. You needn't get angry about it. We're comrades. I meant no harm.

WITTIG. None of your comradeship for me, you impudent young fool.

Enter KUTSCHE, the policeman.

SEVERAL VOICES. Hush—sh! Police!

This calling goes on for some time, till at last there is complete silence, amidst which KUTSCHE takes his place at the central pillar-table.

KUTSCHE. A small brandy, please.

Again complete silence.

WITTIG. I suppose you've come to see if we're all behaving ourselves, Kutsche?

KUTSCHE [*paying no attention to WITTIG*]. Good-morning, Mr. Wiegand.

WIEGAND [*still in the corner in front of the counter*]. Good-morning t' you, sir.

KUTSCHE. How's trade?

WIEGAND. Thank you, much as usual.

BECKER. The chief constable's sent him to see if we're spoiling our stomach on these big wages we're getting.

Laughter.

JAEGER. I say, Welzel, you will tell him how we've been feasting on roast pork an' sauce an' dumplings and sauerkraut, and now we're sitting at our champagne wine.

Laughter.

WELZEL. The world's upside down with them to-day.

KUTSCHE. An' even if you had the champagne wine and the roast meat, you wouldn't be satisfied. I've to get on without champagne wine as well as you.

BECKER [*referring to KUTSCHE's nose*]. He waters his beet-root with brandy and gin. An' it thrives upon it, too.

Laughter.

WITTIG. A p'liceman like that has a hard life. Now it's a starving beggar boy he has to lock up, then it's a pretty weaver girl he has to lead astray; then he has to get roarin' drunk an' beat his wife till she goes screamin' to the neighbors for help; and there's the ridin' about on horseback and the lyin' in bed till nine—nay, faith, but it's no easy job!

KUTSCHE. Jaw away; you'll jaw a rope round your neck in time. It's long been known what sort of a fellow you are. The magistrates know all about that dangerous tongue of yours. I know who'll drink wife and child into the poorhouse an' himself into jail before long, who it is that'll go on agitatin' and agitatin' till he brings down judgment on himself and all concerned.

WITTIG [*laughs bitterly*]. It's true enough—no one knows what'll be the end of it. You may be right yet. [*Bursts out in fury.*] But if it does come to that, I know who I've got to thank for it, who it is that's blabbed to the manufacturers an' all the gentlemen round, an' blackened my character to that extent that they never give me a hand's turn of work to do—an' set the peasants an' the millers against me, so that I'm often a whole week without a horse to shoe or a wheel to put a tire on. I know who's done it. I once pulled the damned brute off his horse, because he was givin' a little stupid boy the most awful flogging for stealin' a few unripe pears. But I tell you this, Kutsche, and you know me—if you get me put into prison, you may make your own will. If I hear as much as a whisper of it, I'll take the first thing as comes handy, whether it's a horseshoe or a hammer, a wheel-spoke or a pail; I'll get hold of you if I've to drag you out of bed from beside your wife, and I'll beat in your brains, as sure as my name's Wittig. [*He has jumped up and is going to rush at* KUTSCHE.]

OLD AND YOUNG WEAVERS [*holding him back*]. 10 Wittig, Wittig! Don't lose your head!

KUTSCHE [*has risen involuntarily, his face pale. He backs toward the door while speaking. The nearer the door the higher his courage rises. He speaks the last words on the threshold, and then instantly disappears.*] What are you goin' on at me about? I didn't meddle with you. I came to say something to the weavers. My business is with them an' not with you, and I've done nothing to you. But I've this to say to you weavers: The Super- 20 intendent of Police herewith forbids the singing of that song—Dreissiger's song, or whatever it is you call it. And if the yelling of it on the streets isn't stopped at once, he'll provide you with plenty of time and leisure for going on with it in jail. You may sing there, on bread and water, to your hearts' content. [*Goes out.*]

WITTIG [*roars after him*]. He's no right to forbid it—not if we were to roar till the windows shook an' they could hear us at Reichenbach—not 30 if we sang till the manufacturers' houses tumbled about their ears an' all the Superintendents' helmets danced on the top of their heads. It's nobody's business but our own.

BECKER *has in the meantime got up, made a signal for singing, and now leads off, the others joining in.*

    The justice to us weavers dealt
      Is bloody, cruel, and hateful;
    Our life's one torture, long drawn out;   40
      For Lynch law we'd be grateful.

WELZEL *attempts to quiet them but they pay no attention to him.* WIEGAND *puts his hands to his ears and rushes off. During the singing of the next verse the weavers rise and form into procession behind* BECKER *and* WITTIG, *who have given pantomimic signs for a general break-up.*

    Stretched on the rack, day after day,
      Hearts sick and bodies aching,
    Our heavy sighs their witness bear   50
      To spirit slowly breaking.

Most of the weavers sing the following verse out on the street, only a few young fellows, who are paying, being still in the bar. At the conclusion

of the verse no one is left in the room except WELZEL *and his wife and daughter,* HORNIG, *and* OLD BAUMERT.

    You villains all, you brood of hell,
      You fiends in fashion human,
    A curse will fall on all like you
      Who prey on man and woman.

WELZEL [*phlegmatically collecting the glasses*]. Their backs are up to-day, and no mistake.

HORNIG [*to* OLD BAUMERT, *who is preparing to go*]. What in the name of Heaven are they up to, Baumert?

BAUMERT. They're goin' to Dreissiger's to make him add something on to the pay.

WELZEL. And are you joining in these foolish goings-on?

OLD BAUMERT. I've no choice, Welzel. The young men may an' the old men must. [*Goes out rather shamefacedly.*]

HORNIG. It'll not surprise me if this ends badly.

WELZEL. To think that even old fellows like him are goin' right off their heads!

HORNIG. We all set our hearts on something!

ACT IV

Peterswaldau. Private room of DREISSIGER, *the fustian manufacturer—luxuriously furnished in the chilly taste of the first half of this century. Ceiling, doors, and stove are white, and the wall paper, with its small, straight-lined floral pattern, is dull and cold in tone. The furniture is mahogany, richly-carved, and upholstered in red. On the right, between two windows with crimson damask curtains, stands the writing-table, a high bureau with falling flap. Directly opposite to this is the sofa, with the strong-box beside it; in front of the sofa a table, with chairs and easy-chairs arranged about it. Against the back wall is a gun-cupboard. All three walls are decorated with bad pictures in gilt frames. Above the sofa is a mirror with a heavily gilt rococo frame. On the left an ordinary door leads into the hall. An open folding-door at the back shows the drawing-room, over-furnished in the same style of comfortless splendor. Two ladies,* MRS. DREISSIGER *and* MRS. KITTELHAUS, *the Pastor's wife, are seen in the drawing-room, looking at pictures.* PASTOR KITTELHAUS *is there too, engaged in conversation with* WEINHOLD, *the tutor, a theological graduate.*

KITTELHAUS [*a kindly little elderly man, enters the front room, smoking and talking to the tutor, who is also smoking; he looks round and shakes his head in surprise at finding the room empty*]

You are young, Mr. Weinhold, which explains everything. At your age we old fellows held—well, I won't say the same opinions—but certainly opinions of the same tendency. And there's something fine about youth—youth with its grand ideals. But unfortunately, Mr. Weinhold, they don't last; they are as fleeting as April sunshine. Wait till you are my age. When a man has said his say from the pulpit for thirty years—fifty-two times every year, not including saints' days—he has inevitably calmed down. Think of me, Mr. Weinhold, when you come that length.

WEINHOLD [*nineteen, pale, thin, tall, with lanky fair hair; restless and nervous in his movements*]. With all due respect, Mr. Kittelhaus—I can't think —people have such different natures.

KITTELHAUS. My dear Mr. Weinhold, however restless-minded and unsettled a man may be—[*in a tone of reproof*]—and you are a case in point— however violently and wantonly he may attack the existing order of things, he calms down in the end. I grant you, certainly, that among our professional brethren individuals are to be found, who, at a fairly advanced age, still play youthful pranks. One preaches against the drink evil and founds temperance societies, another publishes appeals which undoubtedly read most effectively. But what good do they do? The distress among the weavers, where it does exist, is in no way lessened—but the peace of society is undermined. No, no; one feels inclined in such cases to say: Cobbler, stick to your last; don't take to caring for the belly, you who have the care of souls. Preach the pure Word of God, and leave all else to Him who provides shelter and food for the birds, and clothes the lilies of the field. But I should like to know where our good host, Mr. Dreissiger, has suddenly disappeared to. MRS. DREISSIGER, *followed by* MRS. KITTELHAUS, *now comes forward. She is a pretty woman of thirty, of a healthy, florid type. A certain discordance is noticeable between her deportment and way of expressing herself and her rich, elegant toilette.*

MRS. DREISSIGER. That's what I want to know, too, Mr. Kittelhaus. But it's what William always does. No sooner does a thing come into his head than off he goes and leaves me in the lurch. I've said enough about it, but it does no good.

KITTELHAUS. It's always the way with business men, my dear Mrs. Dreissiger.

WEINHOLD. I'm almost certain that something has happened downstairs.

DREISSIGER *enters, hot and excited.*

DREISSIGER. Well, Rosa, is coffee served?

MRS. DREISSIGER [*sulkily*]. Fancy your needing to run away again!

DREISSIGER [*carelessly*]. Ah! these are things you don't understand.

KITTELHAUS. Excuse me—has anything happened to annoy you, Mr. Dreissiger?

DREISSIGER. Never a day passes without that, my dear sir. I am accustomed to it. What about that coffee, Rosa?

MRS. DREISSIGER *goes ill-humoredly and gives one or two violent tugs at the broad embroidered bell-pull.*

DREISSIGER. I wish you had been down stairs just now, Mr. Weinhold. You'd have gained a little experience. Besides . . . But now let us have our game of whist.

KITTELHAUS. By all means, sir. Shake off the dust and burden of the day, Mr. Dreissiger; forget it in our company.

DREISSIGER [*has gone to the window, pushed aside a curtain, and is looking out*]. Vile rabble!! Come here, Rosa! [*She goes to the window.*] Look . . . that tall red-haired fellow there! . . .

KITTELHAUS. That's the man they call Red Becker.

DREISSIGER. Is he the man that insulted you the day before yesterday? You remember what you told me—when John was helping you into the carriage?

MRS. DREISSIGER [*pouting, carelessly*]. I'm sure I don't know.

DREISSIGER. Come now, what's the use of being cross? I must know. If he's the man, I mean to have him arrested. [*The strains of the Weavers' Song are heard.*] Listen to that! Just listen!

KITTELHAUS [*highly incensed*]. Is there to be no end to this nuisance? I must acknowledge now that it is time for the police to interfere. Permit me. [*He goes forward to the window.*] See, see, Mr. Weinhold! These are not only young people. There are numbers of steady-going old weavers among them, men whom I have known for years and looked upon as most deserving and God-fearing. There they are, taking part in this intolerable uproar, trampling God's law under foot. Do you mean to tell me that you still defend these people?

WEINHOLD. Certainly not, Mr. Kittelhaus. That is, sir . . . *cum grano salis*. For after all, they are hungry and they are ignorant. They are giving expression to their dissatisfaction in the only way they understand. I don't expect that such people . . .

MRS. KITTELHAUS [*short, thin, faded, more like*

an old maid than a married woman]. Mr. Weinhold, Mr. Weinhold, how can you?

DREISSIGER. Mr. Weinhold, I am sorry to be obliged to . . . I didn't bring you into my house to give me lectures on philanthropy, and I must request that you will confine yourself to the education of my boys, and leave my other affairs entirely to me—entirely! Do you understand?

WEINHOLD [*stands for a moment rigid and deathly pale, then bows, with a strained smile. In a low voice.*] Certainly, of course I understand. I have seen this coming. It is my wish too. [*Goes out.*]

DREISSIGER [*rudely*]. As soon as possible then, please. We require the room.

MRS. DREISSIGER. William, William!

DREISSIGER. Have you lost your senses, Rosa, that you're taking the part of a man who defends a low, blackguardly libel like that song?

MRS. DREISSIGER. But, William, he didn't defend it.

DREISSIGER. Mr. Kittelhaus, did he defend it or did he not?

KITTELHAUS. His youth must be his excuse, Mr. Dreissiger.

MRS. KITTELHAUS. I can't understand it. The young man comes of such a good, respectable family. His father held a public appointment for forty years, without a breath on his reputation. His mother was overjoyed at his getting this good situation here. And now . . . he himself shows so little appreciation of it.

PFEIFER [*suddenly opens the door leading from the hall and shouts in*]. Mr. Dreissiger, Mr. Dreissiger! they've got him! Will you come, please? They've caught one of them.

DREISSIGER [*hastily*]. Has some one gone for the police?

PFEIFER. The Superintendent's on his way upstairs.

DREISSIGER [*at the door*]. Glad to see you, sir. We want you here.

KITTELHAUS *makes signs to the ladies that it will be better for them to retire. He, his wife, and* MRS. DREISSIGER *disappear into the drawing-room.*

DREISSIGER [*exasperated, to the* POLICE SUPERINTENDENT, *who has now entered*]. I have at last had one of the ringleaders seized by my dyers. I could stand it no longer—their insolence was beyond all bounds—quite unbearable. I have visitors in my house, and these blackguards dare to . . . They insult my wife whenever she shows herself; my boys' lives are not safe. My visitors run the risk of being jostled and cuffed. Is it possible that in a well-ordered community incessant public insult offered to unoffending people like myself and my family should pass unpunished? If so . . . then . . . then I must confess that I have other ideas of law and order.

SUPERINTENDENT [*A man of fifty, middle height, corpulent, full-blooded. He wears cavalry uniform with a long sword and spurs.*] No, no, Mr. Dreissiger . . . certainly not! I am entirely at your disposal. Make your mind easy on the subject. Dispose of me as you will. What you have done is quite right. I am delighted that you have had one of the ringleaders arrested. I am very glad indeed that a settling day has come. There are a few disturbers of the peace here whom I have long had my eye on.

DREISSIGER. Yes, one or two raw lads, lazy vagabonds, that shirk every kind of work, and lead a life of low dissipation, hanging about the publichouses until they've sent their last halfpenny down their throats. But I'm determined to put a stop to the trade of these professional blackguards once and for all. It's in the public interest to do so, not only my private interest.

SUPERINTENDENT. Of course it is! Most undoubtedly, Mr. Dreissiger! No one can possibly blame you. And everything that lies in my power . . .

DREISSIGER. The cat-o'-nine tails is what should be taken to the beggarly pack.

SUPERINTENDENT. You're right, quite right. We must make an example.

KUTSCHE, *the policeman, enters and salutes. The door is open, and the sound of heavy steps stumbling up the stair is heard.*

KUTSCHE. I have to inform you, sir, that we have arrested a man.

DREISSIGER [*to* SUPERINTENDENT]. Do you wish to see the fellow?

SUPERINTENDENT. Certainly, most certainly. We must begin by having a look at him at close quarters. Oblige me, Mr. Dreissiger, by not speaking to him at present. I'll see to it that you get complete satisfaction, or my name's not Heide.

DREISSIGER. That's not enough for me, though. He goes before the magistrates. My mind's made up.

JAEGER *is led in by five dyers, who have come straight from their work—faces, hands, and clothes stained with dye. The prisoner, his cap set jauntily on the side of his head, presents an appearance of impudent gayety; he is excited by the brandy he has just drunk.*

JAEGER. Hounds that you are!—Call yourselves workingmen!—Pretend to be comrades! Before I would do such a thing as lay my hands on a mate, I'd see my hand rot off my arm!

At a sign from the SUPERINTENDENT, KUTSCHE *orders the dyers to let go their victim.* JAEGER *straightens himself up, quite free and easy. Both doors are guarded.*

SUPERINTENDENT [*shouts to* JAEGER]. Off with your cap, sir. [JAEGER *takes it off, but very slowly, still with an impudent grin on his face.*] What's your name!

JAEGER. What's yours? I'm not your swine-herd. *Great excitement is produced among the audience by this reply.*

DREISSIGER. This is too much of a good thing.

SUPERINTENDENT [*changes color, is on the point of breaking out furiously, but controls his rage*]. We'll see about this afterwards.—Once more, what's your name? [*Receiving no answer, furiously.*] If you don't answer at once, fellow, I'll have you flogged on the spot.

JAEGER [*perfectly cheerful, not showing by so much as the twitch of an eyelid that he has heard the* SUPERINTENDENT'S *angry words, calls over the heads of those around him to a pretty servant girl, who has brought in the coffee and is standing open-mouthed with astonishment at the unexpected sight*]. Hullo, Emmy, do you belong to this company now? The sooner you find your way out of it, then, the better. A wind may begin to blow here, an' blow everything away overnight. *The girl stares at* JAEGER, *and as soon as she comprehends that it is to her he is speaking, blushes with shame, covers her eyes with her hands, and rushes out, leaving the coffee things in confusion. Renewed excitement among those present.*

SUPERINTENDENT [*half beside himself, to* DREISSIGER]. Never in all my long service . . . such a case of shameless effrontery . . .

JAEGER *spits on the floor.*

DREISSIGER. I'll thank you to remember that this is not a stable.

SUPERINTENDENT. My patience is at an end now. For the last time: What's your name?

KITTELHAUS, *who has been peering out at the partly opened drawing-room door, listening to what has been going on, can no longer refrain from coming forward to interfere. He is trembling with excitement.*

KITTELHAUS. His name is Jaeger, sir. Moritz . . . is it not? Moritz Jaeger. [*To* JAEGER.] And, Jaeger, you know me.

JAEGER [*seriously*]. You are Pastor Kittelhaus.

KITTELHAUS. Yes, I am your pastor, Jaeger! It was I who received you, a babe in swaddling clothes, into the Church of Christ. From my hands you took for the first time the body of the Lord.

Do you remember that, and how I toiled and strove to bring God's Word home to your heart? Is this your gratitude?

JAEGER [*like a scolded schoolboy, in a surly voice*]. I paid my half-crown like the rest.

KITTELHAUS. Money, money . . . Do you imagine that the miserable little bit of money . . . Such utter nonsense! I'd much rather you kept your money. Be a good man, be a Christian! Think of what you promised. Keep God's law. Money, money! . . .

JAEGER. I'm a Quaker now, sir. I don't believe in anything.

KITTELHAUS. Quaker! What are you talking about? Try to behave yourself, and don't use words you don't understand. Quaker, indeed! They are good Christian people, and not heathens like you.

SUPERINTENDENT. Mr. Kittelhaus, I must ask you . . . [*He comes between the* PASTOR *and* JAEGER.] Kutsche! tie his hands!

Wild yelling outside: "Jaeger, Jaeger! come out!"

DREISSIGER [*like the others, slightly startled, goes instinctively to the window*]. What's the meaning of this next?

SUPERINTENDENT. Oh, I understand well enough. It means that they want to have the blackguard out among them again. But we're not going to oblige them. Kutsche, you have your orders. He goes to the lock-up.

KUTSCHE [*with the rope in his hand, hesitating*]. By your leave, sir, but it'll not be an easy job. There's a confounded big crowd out there—a pack of raging devils. They've got Becker with them, and the smith . . .

KITTELHAUS. Allow me one more word!—So as not to rouse still worse feeling, would it not be better if we tried to arrange things peaceably? Perhaps Jaeger will give his word to go with us quietly, or . . .

SUPERINTENDENT. Quite impossible! Think of my responsibility. I couldn't allow such a thing. Come, Kutsche! lose no more time.

JAEGER [*putting his hands together, and holding them out*]. Tight, tight, as tight as ever you can! It's not for long.

KUTSCHE, *assisted by the workmen, ties his hands.*

SUPERINTENDENT. Now, off with you, march [*to* DREISSIGER]. If you feel anxious, let six of the weavers go with them. They can walk on each side of him, I'll ride in front, and Kutsche will bring up the rear. Whoever blocks the way will be cut down.

Cries from below: "Cock-a-doodle-doo-oo-oo! or wow, wow!"

SUPERINTENDENT [*with a threatening gesture in the direction of the window*]. You rascals, I'll cock-a-doodle-doo and bow-wow you! Forward! March! *He marches out first, with drawn sword; the others, with* JAEGER, *follow.*

JAEGER [*shouts as he goes*]. An' Mrs. Dreissiger there may play the lady as proud as she likes, but for all that she's no better than us. Many a hundred times she's served my father with a half pennyworth of schnapps. Left wheel—march! [*Exit laughing.*]

DREISSIGER [*after a pause, with apparent calmness*]. Well, Mr. Kittelhaus, shall we have our game now? I think there will be no further interruption. [*He lights a cigar, giving short laughs as he does so; when it is lighted, bursts into a regular fit of laughing.*] I'm beginning now to think the whole thing very funny. That fellow! [*Still laughing nervously.*] It really is too comical: first came the dispute at dinner with Weinhold—five minutes after that he takes leave—off to the other end of the world; then this affair crops up—and now we'll proceed with our whist.

KITTELHAUS. Yes, but . . . [*Roaring is heard outside.*] Yes, but . . . that's a terrible uproar they're making outside.

DREISSIGER. All we have to do is to go into the other room; it won't disturb us in the least there.

KITTELHAUS [*shaking his head*]. I wish I knew what has come over these people. In so far I must agree with Mr. Weinhold, or at least till quite lately I was of his opinion, that the weavers were a patient, humble, easily-led class. Was it not your idea of them, too, Mr. Dreissiger?

DREISSIGER. Most certainly that is what they used to be—patient, easily managed, peaceable people. They were that as long as these so-called humanitarians let them alone. But for ever so long now they've had the awful misery of their condition held up to them. Think of all the societies and associations for the alleviation of the distress among the weavers. At last the weaver believes in it himself, and his head's turned. Some of them had better come and turn it back again, for now he's fairly set a-going there's no end to his complaining. This doesn't please him, and that doesn't please him. He must have everything of the best.

A loud roar of "Hurrah!" is heard from the crowd.

KITTELHAUS. So that with all their humanitarianism they have only succeeded in almost literally turning lambs into wolves.

DREISSIGER. I won't say that, sir. When you take time to think of the matter cooly, it's possible that some good may come of it yet. Such occurrences as this will not pass unnoticed by those in authority, and may lead them to see that things can't be allowed to go on as they are doing—that means must be taken to prevent the utter ruin of our home industries.

KITTELHAUS. Possibly. But what is the cause, then, of this terrible falling off of trade?

DREISSIGER. Our best markets have been closed to us by the heavy import duties foreign countries have laid on our goods. At home the competition is terrible, for we have no protection, none whatever.

PFEIFER [*staggers in, pale and breathless*]. Mr. Dreissiger, Mr. Dreissiger!

DREISSIGER [*in the act of walking into the drawing-room, turns round, annoyed*]. Well, Pfeifer, what now?

PFEIFER. Oh, sir! Oh, sir! . . . It's worse than ever!

DREISSIGER. What are they up to next?

KITTELHAUS. You're really alarming us—what is it?

PFEIFER [*still confused*]. I never saw the like. Good Lord!—The Superintendent himself . . . they'll catch it for this yet.

DREISSIGER. What's the matter with you, in the devil's name? Is any one's neck broken?

PFEIFER [*almost crying with fear, screams*]. They've set Moritz Jaeger free—they've thrashed the Superintendent and driven him away—they've thrashed the policeman and sent him off to—without his helmet . . . his sword broken . . . Oh dear, oh dear!

DREISSIGER. I think you've gone crazy, Pfeifer.

KITTELHAUS. This is actual riot.

PFEIFER [*sitting on a chair, his whole body trembling*]. It's turning serious, Mr. Dreissiger! Mr. Dreissiger, it's serious now!

DREISSIGER. Well, if that's all the police . . .

PFEIFER. Mr. Dreissiger, it's serious now!

DREISSIGER. Damn it all, Pfeifer, will you hold your tongue?

MRS. DREISSIGER [*coming out of the drawing-room with* MRS. KITTELHAUS]. This is really too bad, William. Our whole evening's being spoiled. Here's Mrs. Kittlehaus saying that she'd better go home.

KITTELHAUS. You mustn't take it amiss, dear Mrs. Dreissiger, but perhaps, under the circumstances, it *would* be better . . .

MRS. DREISSIGER. But, William, why in the world don't you go out and put a stop to it?

DREISSIGER. Go you and try if you can do it. Try! Go and speak to them! [*Standing helplessly in front of the* PASTOR.] Am I such a tyrant? Am I a cruel master?

Enter JOHN *the coachman.*

JOHN. If you please, m'm, I've put to the horses. Mr. Weinhold's put Georgie and Charlie into the carriage. If it comes to the worst, we're ready to be off.

MRS. DREISSIGER. If what comes to the worst?

JOHN. I'm sure I don't know, m'm. But the crowd's gettin' bigger and bigger, an' they've sent the Superintendent an' the p'liceman to the right-about.

PFEIFER. It's serious now, Mr. Dreissiger! It's serious!

MRS. DREISSIGER [*with increasing alarm*]. What's going to happen?—What do the people want?—They're never going to attack us, John?

JOHN. There's some rascally hounds among 'em, ma'am.

PFEIFER. It's serious now! serious!

DREISSIGER. Hold your tongue, fool!—Are the doors barred?

KITTELHAUS. I ask you as a favor, Mr. Dreissiger . . . as a favor . . . I am determined to . . . I ask you as a favor . . . [*To* JOHN.] What demands are the people making?

JOHN [*awkwardly*]. It's higher wages they're after, the blackguards.

KITTELHAUS. Good, good!—I shall go out and do my duty. I shall speak seriously to these people.

JOHN. Oh, sir, please, sir, don't do any such thing. Words is quite useless.

KITTELHAUS. One little favor, Mr. Dreissiger. May I ask you to post men behind the door, and to have it closed at once after me?

MRS. KITTELHAUS. O Joseph, Joseph! you're not really going out?

KITTELHAUS. I am. Indeed I am. I know what I'm doing. Don't be afraid. God will protect me.

MRS. KITTELHAUS *presses his hand, draws back, and wipes tears from her eyes.*

KITTELHAUS [*while the murmur of a great, excited crowd is heard uninterruptedly outside*]. I'll go . . . I'll go out as if I were simply on my way home. I shall see if my sacred office . . . if the people have not sufficient respect for me left to . . . I shall try . . . [*He takes his hat and stick.*] Forward, then, in God's name!

Goes out accompanied by DREISSIGER, PFEIFER, *and* JOHN.

MRS. KITTELHAUS. Oh, dear Mrs. Dreissiger! [*She bursts into tears and embraces her.*] I do trust nothing will happen to him.

MRS. DREISSIGER [*absently*]. I don't know how it is, Mrs. Kittelhaus, but I . . . I can't tell you how I feel. I didn't think such a thing was possible.

It's . . . it's as if it was a sin to be rich. If I had been told about all this beforehand, Mrs. Kittelhaus, I don't know but what I would rather have been left in my own humble position.

MRS. KITTELHAUS. There are troubles and disappointments in every condition of life, Mrs. Dreissiger.

MRS. DREISSIGER. True, true, I can well believe that. And suppose we have more than other people . . . goodness me! we didn't steal it. It's been honestly got, every penny of it. It's not possible that the people can be going to attack us! If trade's bad, that's not William's fault, is it?

Loud, confused yelling is heard outside. While the two women stand gazing at each other, pale and startled, DREISSIGER *rushes in.*

DREISSIGER. Quick, Rosa—put on something, and get into the carriage. I'll be after you this moment.

He rushes to the strong box, and takes out papers and various articles of value.

Enter JOHN.

JOHN. We're ready to start. But come quickly, before they get round to the back door.

MRS. DREISSIGER [*in a transport of fear, throwing her arms around* JOHN'S *neck*]. John, John, dear, good John! Save us, John. Save my boys! Oh, what is to become of us?

DREISSIGER. Rosa, try to keep your head. Let John go.

JOHN. Yes, yes, ma'am! Don't you be frightened. Our good horses'll soon leave them all behind; an' whoever doesn't get out of the way'll be driven over.

MRS. KITTELHAUS [*in helpless anxiety*]. But my husband . . . my husband? But, Mr. Dreissiger, my husband?

DREISSIGER. He's in safety now, Mrs. Kittelhaus. Don't alarm yourself; he's all right.

MRS. KITTELHAUS. Something dreadful has happened to him. I know it. You needn't try to keep it from me.

DREISSIGER. You mustn't take it to heart—they'll be sorry for it yet. I know exactly whose fault it was. Such a detestable, shameful outrage will not go unpunished. A community laying hands on its own pastor and maltreating him—abominable! Mad dogs they are—raging brutes—and they'll be treated as such. [*To his wife who still stands petrified.*] Go, for my sake, Rosa, go quickly! [*The clatter of window panes being smashed on the ground floor is heard.*] They've gone quite mad. There's nothing for it but to get away as fast as we can.

Cries of "Pfeifer, come out!"—"We want Pfeifer!"
—"Pfeifer, come out!" are heard.

MRS. DREISSIGER. Pfeifer, Pfeifer, they want Pfeifer!

PFEIFER [*dashes in*]. Mr. Dreissiger, there are people at the back gate already, and the house door won't hold much longer. The smith's battering it in with a stable pail.

The cry sounds louder and clearer: "Pfeifer! Pfeifer! Pfeifer! come out!" MRS. DREISSIGER rushes 10 *off as if pursued. MRS. KITTELHAUS follows. PFEIFER listens, and changes color as he hears what the cry is. A perfect panic of fear seizes him; he weeps, entreats, whimpers, writhes, all at the same moment. He overwhelms DREISSIGER with childish caresses, strokes his cheeks and arms, kisses his hands, and at last, like a drowning man, throws his arms round him and prevents him moving.*

PFEIFER. Dear, good, kind Mr. Dreissiger, don't 20 leave me behind. I've always served you faithfully. I've always treated the people well. I couldn't give them more wages than the fixed rate. Don't leave me here—they'll do for me! If they find me, they'll kill me. O God! O God! My wife, my children!

DREISSIGER [*making his way out, vainly endeavoring to free himself from PFEIFER's clutch*]. Can't you let me go, fellow? It'll be all right; it'll be all right.

For a few seconds the room is empty. Windows 30 *are broken in the drawing-room. A loud crash resounds through the house, followed by shouts of "Hurrah!" For an instant there is silence. Then gentle, cautious steps are heard on the stair, then timid, hushed ejaculations: "To the left!"—"Up with you!"—"Hush!"—"Slow, slow!" —"Don't shove like that!"—"It's a wedding we're goin' to!"—"Stop that crowding!"—"You go first!"—"No, you go!"*
40
Young weavers and weaver girls appear at the door leading from the hall, not daring to enter, but each trying to shove the other in. In the course of a few moments their timidity is overcome, and the poor, thin, ragged or patched figures, many of them sickly-looking, disperse themselves through DREISSIGER's room and the drawing-room, first gazing timidly and curiously at everything, then beginning to touch things. Girls sit down on the sofas, whole groups admire them- 50 *selves in the mirrors, men stand up on chairs, examine the pictures and take them down. There is a steady influx of miserable-looking creatures from the hall.*

FIRST OLD WEAVER [*entering*]. No, no, this is carryin' it too far. They've started smashing things downstairs. There's no sense nor reason in that. There'll be a bad end to it. No man in his wits would do that. I'll keep clear of such goings-on.

JAEGER, BECKER, WITTIG *carrying a wooden pail,* BAUMERT, *and a number of other old and young weavers, rush in as if in pursuit of something, shouting hoarsely.*

JAEGER. Where has he gone?

BECKER. Where's the cruel brute?

BAUMERT. If we can eat grass, he may eat sawdust.

WITTIG. We'll hang him whenever we catch him.

FIRST YOUNG WEAVER. We'll take him by the legs and fling him out at the window, onto the stones. He'll never get up again.

SECOND YOUNG WEAVER [*enters*]. He's off!

ALL. Who?

SECOND YOUNG WEAVER. Dreissiger.

BECKER. Pfeifer too?

VOICES. Let's get hold of Pfeifer. Look for Pfeifer!

BAUMERT. Yes, yes! Pfeifer! Tell him there's a weaver here for him to starve.

Laughter.

JAEGER. If we can't lay hands on that brute Dreissiger himself . . . we'll at any rate make a poor man of him.

BAUMERT. As poor as a church mouse . . . we'll see to that!

All, bent on the work of destruction, rush towards the drawing-room door.

BECKER [*who is leading, turns round and stops the others*]. Halt! Listen to me! This is nothing but a beginning. When we're done here, we'll go straight to Bielau, to Dittrich's, where the steam power-looms are. The whole mischief's done by these factories.

OLD ANSORGE [*Enters from hall. Takes a few steps, then stops and looks round, bewildered; shakes his head, taps his forehead.*] Who am I? Weaver Anton Ansorge. Has he gone mad, Old Ansorge? My head's goin' round like a humming-top, sure enough. What's he doing here? He'll do whatever he's a mind to. Where is Ansorge? [*He taps his forehead repeatedly.*] Something's wrong! I'm not answerable! I'm off my head! Off with you, off with you, rioters that you are! Heads off, legs off, hands off! If you take my house, I take your house. Forward, forward!

Goes yelling into the drawing-room, followed by a yelling, laughing mob.

ACT V

Langenbielau. OLD WEAVER HILSE'S workroom. On the left a small window, in front of which stands the loom. On the right a bed, with a table pushed close to it. Stove, with stove-bench, in the right-hand corner. Family worship is going on. HILSE, his old, blind, and almost deaf wife, his son GOTTLIEB, and LUISE, GOTTLIEB's wife, are sitting at the table, on the bed and wooden stools. A winding-wheel and bobbins on the floor between table and loom. Old spinning, weaving, and winding implements are disposed of on the smoky rafters; hanks of yarn are hanging down. There is much useless lumber in the low narrow room. The door, which is in the back wall, and leads into the big outer passage, or entry-room of the house, stands open. Through another open door on the opposite side of the passage, a second, in most respects similar weaver's room is seen. The large passage, or entry-room of the house, is paved with stone, has damaged plaster, and a tumble-down wooden staircase leading to the attics; a washing-tub on a stool is partly visible; dirty linen of the most miserable description and poor household utensils lie about untidily. The light falls from the left into all three apartments.

OLD HILSE *is a bearded man of strong build, but bent and wasted with age, toil, sickness, and hardship. He is an old soldier, and has lost an arm. His nose is sharp, his complexion ashen-gray, and he shakes; he is nothing but skin and bone, and has the deep-set, sore weaver's eyes.*

OLD HILSE [*stands up, as do his son and daughter-in-law; prays*]. O Lord, we know not how to be thankful enough to Thee, for that Thou hast spared us this night again in thy goodness . . . an' hast had pity on us . . . an' hast suffered us to take no harm. Thou art the All-Merciful, an' we are poor, sinful children of men—that bad that we are not worthy to be trampled under thy feet. Yet Thou art our loving Father, an' Thou will look upon us an' accept us for the sake of thy dear Son, our Lord and Savior Jesus Christ. "Jesus' blood and righteousness, Our covering is and glorious dress." An' if we're sometimes too sore cast down under thy chastening—when the fire of thy purification burns too raging hot—oh, lay it not to our charge; forgive us our sin. Give us patience, heavenly Father, that after all these sufferin's we may be made partakers of thy eternal blessedness. Amen.

MOTHER HILSE [*who has been bending forward, trying hard to hear*]. What a beautiful prayer you do say, father!

LUISE *goes off to the wash-tub*, GOTTLIEB *to the room on the other side of the passage.*

OLD HILSE. Where's the little lass?

LUISE. She's gone to Peterswaldau, to Dreissiger's. She finished all she had to wind last night.

OLD HILSE [*speaking very loud*]. You'd like the wheel now, mother, eh?

MOTHER HILSE. Yes, father, I'm quite ready.

OLD HILSE [*setting it down before her*]. I wish I could do the work for you.

MOTHER HILSE. An' what would be the good of that, father? There would I be, sittin' not knowin' what to do.

OLD HILSE. I'll give your fingers a wipe, then, so that they'll not grease the yarn. [*He wipes her hands with a rag.*]

LUISE [*at her tub*]. If there's grease on her hands, it's not from what she's eaten.

OLD HILSE. If we've no butter, we can eat dry bread—when we've no bread, we can eat potatoes—when there's no potatoes left, we can eat bran.

LUISE [*saucily*]. An' when that's all eaten, we'll do as the Wenglers did—we'll find out where the skinner's buried some stinking old horse, an' we'll dig it up an' live for a week or two on rotten carrion—how nice that'll be!

GOTTLIEB [*from the other room*]. There you are, letting that tongue of yours run away with you again.

OLD HILSE. You should think twice, lass, before you talk that godless way. [*He goes to his loom, calls.*] Can you give me a hand, Gottlieb?—there's a few threads to pull through.

LUISE [*from her tub*]. Gottlieb, you're wanted to help father.

GOTTLIEB *comes in, and he and his father set themselves to the troublesome task of "drawing and slaying," that is, pulling the strands of the warp through the "heddles" and "reed" of the loom. They have hardly begun to do this when HORNIG appears in the outer room.*

HORNIG [*at the door*]. Good luck to your work!

HILSE AND HIS SON. Thank you, Hornig.

GOTTLIEB. I say, Hornig, when do you take your sleep? You're on your rounds all day, and on watch all night.

HORNIG. Sleep's gone from me nowadays.

LUISE. Glad to see you, Hornig!

OLD HILSE. And what's the news?

HORNIG. It's queer news this mornin'. The weavers at Peterswaldau have taken the law into their own hands, an' chased Dreissiger an' his whole family out of the place.

LUISE [*perceptibly agitated*]. Hornig's at his lies again.

HORNIG. No, missus, not this time, not to-day.— I've some beautiful pinafores in my cart.—No, it's God's truth I'm telling you. They've sent him to the right-about. He came down to Reichenbach last night, but, Lord love you! they daren't take him in there, for fear of the weavers—off he had to go again, all the way to Schweidnitz.

OLD HILSE [*has been carefully lifting threads of the web and approaching them to the holes, through which, from the other side,* GOTTLIEB *pushes a wire hook, with which he catches them and draws them through*]. It's about time you were stopping now, Hornig!

HORNIG. It's as sure as I'm a livin' man. Every child in the place'll soon tell you the same story.

OLD HILSE. Either your wits are a-wool-gatherin' or mine are.

HORNIG. Not mine. What I'm telling you's as true as the Bible. I wouldn't believe it myself if I hadn't stood there an' seen it with my own eyes— as I see you now, Gottlieb. They've wrecked his house from the cellar to the roof. The good china came flyin' out at the garret windows, rattlin' down the roof. God only knows how many pieces of fustian are lying soakin' in the river! The water can't get away for them—it's running over the banks, the color of washin'-blue with all the indigo they've poured out at the windows—it was flyin' like clouds of sky-blue dust. Oh, it's a terrible destruction they've worked! And it's not only the house—it's the dyeworks, too—an' the stores! They've broken the stair rails, they've torn up the fine flooring—smashed the lookin'-glasses—cut an' hacked an' torn an' smashed the sofas an' the chairs.—It's awful—it's worse than war.

OLD HILSE. An' you would have me believe that my fellow weavers did all that?

He shakes his head incredulously. Other tenants of the house have collected at the door and are listening eagerly.

HORNIG. Who else, I'd like to know? I could put names to every one of 'em. It was me took the sheriff through the house, an' I spoke to a whole lot of 'em, an' they answered me back quite friendly like. They did their business with little noise, but my word! they did it well. The sheriff spoke to them, and they answered him mannerly, as they always do. But there wasn't no stoppin' of them. They hacked on at the beautiful furniture as if they were workin' for wages.

OLD HILSE. *You* took the sheriff through the house?

HORNIG. An' what would I be frightened of? Every one knows me. I'm always turning up, like a bad penny. But no one has anything agin' me. They're all glad to see me. Yes, I went the rounds with him, as sure as my name's Hornig. An' you may believe me or not as you like, but my heart's sore yet from the sight—an' I could see by the sheriff's face that he felt queer enough, too. Not a living word did we hear—they were doin' their work and holdin' their tongues. It was a solemn an' a woeful sight to see the poor starving creatures for once in a way takin' their revenge.

LUISE [*with irrepressible excitement, trembling, wiping her eyes with her apron*]. An' right they are! It's only what should be!

VOICES AMONG THE CROWD AT THE DOOR. "There's some of the same sort here."—"There's one no farther away than across the river."—"He's got four horses in his stable an' six carriages, an' he starves his weavers to keep them."

OLD HILSE [*still incredulous*]. What was it set them off?

HORNIG. Who knows? Who knows? One says this, another says that.

OLD HILSE. What do they say?

HORNIG. The story as most of them tells is that it began with Dreissiger sayin' that if the weavers were hungry they might eat grass.

Excitement at the door, as one person repeats this to the other, with signs of indignation.

OLD HILSE. Well, now, Hornig—if you was to say to me: Father Hilse, says you, you'll die to-morrow, I would answer back: That may be— an' why not? You might even go to the length of saying: You'll have a visit to-morrow from the King of Prussia. But to tell me that weavers, men like me an' my son, have done such things as that —never! I'll never in this world believe it.

MIELCHEN [*a pretty girl of seven, with long, loose flaxen hair, carrying a basket on her arm, comes running in, holding out a silver spoon to her mother*]. Mammy, mammy! look what I've got! An' you're to buy me a new frock with it.

LUISE. What d'you come tearing in like that for, girl? [*With increased excitement and curiosity.*] An' what's that you've got hold of now? You've been runnin' yourself out o' breath, an' there—if the bobbins aren't in her basket yet? What's all this about?

OLD HILSE. Mielchen, where did that spoon come from?

LUISE. She found it, maybe.

HORNIG. It's worth is seven or eight shillin's at least.

OLD HILSE [*in distressed excitement*]. Off with you, lass—out of the house this moment—unless you want a lickin'! Take that spoon back where you got it from. Out you go! Do you want to make thieves of us all, eh? I'll soon drive that out of you. [*He looks round for something to beat her with.*]

MIELCHEN [*clinging to her mother's skirts, crying*]. No, grandfather, no! don't lick me! We—we did find them. All the other bob—bobbin . . . girls has . . . has them, too.

LUISE [*half frightened, half excited*]. I was right, you see. She found it. Where did you find it, Mielchen?

MIELCHEN [*sobbing*]. At—at Peterswaldau. We—we found them in front of—in front of Drei—Dreissiger's house.

OLD HILSE. This is worse an' worse! Get off with you this moment, unless you would like me to help you.

MOTHER HILSE. What's all the to-do about?

HORNIG. I'll tell you what, Father Hilse. The best way'll be for Gottlieb to put on his coat an' take the spoon to the police office.

OLD HILSE. Gottlieb, put on your coat.

GOTTLIEB [*pulling it on, eagerly*]. Yes, an' I'll go right in to the office an' say they're not to blame us for it, for what can a child like that understand about it? an' I brought the spoon back at once. Stop your crying now, Mielchen!

The crying child is taken into the opposite room by her mother, who shuts her in and comes back.

HORNIG. I believe it's worth as much as nine shillin's.

GOTTLIEB. Give us a cloth to wrap it in, Luise, so that it'll take no harm. To think of the thing bein' worth all that money!

Tears come into his eyes while he is wrapping up the spoon.

LUISE. If it was only ours, we could live on it for many a day.

OLD HILSE. Hurry up, now! Look sharp! As quick as ever you can. A fine state o' matters, this! Get that devil's spoon out o' the house.

GOTTLIEB *goes off with the spoon.*

HORNIG. I must be off now, too.

He goes, is seen talking to the people in the entry-room before he leaves the house.

SURGEON SCHMIDT [*a jerky little ball of a man, with a red, knowing face, comes into the entry-room*]. Good-morning, all! These are fine goings on! Take care! Take care! [*Threatening with his finger.*] You're a sly lot—that's what you are. [*At HILSE's door without coming in.*] Morning, Father Hilse. [*To a woman in the outer room.*] And how are the pains, mother? Better, eh? Well, well. And how's all with you, Father Hilse? [*Enters.*] Why the deuce! what's the matter with mother?

LUISE. It's the eye veins, sir—they've dried up, so as she can't see at all now.

SURGEON SCHMIDT. That's from the dust and weaving by candle-light. Will you tell me what it means that all Peterswaldau's on the way here? I set off on my rounds this morning as usual, thinking no harm; but it wasn't long till I had my eyes opened. Strange doings, these! What in the devil's name has taken possession of them, Hilse? They're like a pack of raging wolves. Riot—why, it's revolution! they're plundering and laying waste right and left . . . Mielchen! where's Mielchen? [*MIELCHEN, her face red with crying, is pushed in by her mother.*] Here, Mielchen, put your hand into my coat pocket. [*MIELCHEN does so.*] The ginger-bread nuts are for you. Not all at once, though, you baggage! And a song first! The fox jumped up on a . . . come, now . . . The fox jumped up . . . on a moonlight . . . Mind, I've heard what you did. You called the sparrows on the churchyard hedge a nasty name, and they're gone and told the pastor. Did any one ever hear the like? Fifteen hundred of them agog—men, women, and children. [*Distant bells are heard.*] That's at Reichenbach—alarm-bells! Fifteen hundred people! Uncomfortably like the world coming to an end!

OLD HILSE. An' is it true that they're on their way to Bielau?

SURGEON SCHMIDT. That's just what I'm telling you. I've driven through the middle of the whole crowd. What I'd have liked to do would have been to get down and give each of them a pill there and then. They were following on each other's heels like grim death, and their singing was more than enough to turn a man's stomach. I was nearly sick, and Friedrich was shaking on the box like an old woman. We had to take a stiff glass at the first opportunity. I wouldn't be a manufacturer, not though I could drive my carriage and pair. [*Distant singing.*] Listen to that! It's for all the world as if they were beating at some broken old boiler. We'll have them here in five minutes, friends. Good-bye! Don't you be foolish. The troops will be upon them in no time. Keep your wits about you. The Peterswaldau people have lost theirs. [*Bells ring close at hand.*] Good gracious!

There are our bells ringing too! Every one's going mad. [*He goes upstairs.*]

GOTTLIEB [*Comes back. In the entry-room, out of breath.*] I've seen them, I've seen them! [*To a woman.*] They're here, auntie, they're here! [*At the door.*] They're here, father, they're here! They've got bean-poles, an' ox-goads, an' axes. They're standin' outside the upper Dittrich's kickin' up an awful row. I think he's payin' them money. O Lord! whatever's goin' to happen? What a crowd! Oh, you never saw such a crowd! Dash it all—if once they make a rush, our manufacturers'll be hard put to it.

OLD HILSE. What have you been runnin' like that for? You'll go racin' till you bring on your old trouble, and then we'll have you on your back again, strugglin' for breath.

GOTTLIEB [*almost joyously excited*]. I had to run, or they would have caught me an' kept me. They were all roarin' to me to join them. Father Baumert was there too, and says he to me: You come an' get your sixpence with the rest—you're a poor starving weaver, too. An' I was to tell you, father, from him, that you were to come an' help to pay out the manufacturers for their grindin' of us down. Other times is coming, he says. There's going to be a change of days for us weavers. An' we're all to come an' help to bring it about. We're to have our half-pound of meat on Sundays, and now and again on a holiday sausage with our cabbage. Yes, things is to be quite different, by what he tells me.

OLD HILSE [*with repressed indignation*]. An' that man calls himself your godfather! and he bids you take part in such works of wickedness? Have nothing to do with them, Gottlieb. They've let themselves be tempted by Satan, an' it's his works they're doin'.

LUISE [*no longer able to restrain her passionate excitement, vehemently*]. Yes, Gottlieb, get into the chimney corner, an' take a spoon in your hand, an' a dish of skim milk on your knee, an' put on a petticoat an' say your prayers, an' then father'll be pleased with you. And *he* sets up to be a man! *Laughter from the people in the entry-room.*

OLD HILSE [*quivering with suppressed rage*]. An' you set up to be a good wife, eh? You call yourself a mother, an' let your evil tongue run away with you like that? You think yourself fit to teach your girl, you that would egg on your husband to crime an' wickedness?

LUISE [*has lost all control of herself*]. You an' your piety an' religion—did they serve to keep the life in my poor children? In rags an' dirt they lay, all the four—it didn't as much as keep them

dry. Yes! I set up to be a mother, that's what I do—an' if you'd like to know it, that's why I would send all the manufacturers to hell—because I'm a mother!—Not one of the four could I keep in life! It was cryin' more than breathin' with me from the time each poor little thing came into the world till death took pity on it. The devil a bit you cared! You sat there prayin' and singin', and let me run about till my feet bled, tryin' to get one little drop o' skim milk. How many hundred nights have I lain an' racked my head to think what I could do to cheat the churchyard of my little one? What harm has a baby like that done that it must come to such a miserable end—eh? An' over there at Dittrich's they're bathed in wine an' washed in milk. No! you may talk as you like, but if they begin here, ten horses won't hold me back. An' what's more—if there's a rush on Dittrich's, you'll see me in the forefront of it—an' pity the man as tries to prevent me—I've stood it long enough, so now you know it.

OLD HILSE. You're a lost soul—there's no help for you.

LUISE [*frenzied*]. It's you that there's no help for! Tatter-breeched scarecrows—that's what you are—an' not men at all. Whey-faced gutter-scrapers that take to your heels at the sound of a child's rattle. Fellows that say "thank you" to the man as gives you a hidin'. They've not left that much blood in you as that you can turn red in the face. You should have the whip taken to you, an' a little pluck flogged into your rotten bones. [*She goes out quickly.*]

Embarrassed pause.

MOTHER HILSE. What's the matter with Liesl, father?

OLD HILSE. Nothin', mother! What should be the matter with her?

MOTHER HILSE. Father, is it only me that's thinkin' it, or are the bells ringin'?

OLD HILSE. It'll be a funeral, mother.

MOTHER HILSE. An' I've got to sit waitin' here yet. Why must I be so long a-dyin', father? *Pause.*

OLD HILSE [*leaves his work, holds himself up straight; solemnly*]. Gottlieb!—you heard all your wife said to us. Look here, Gottlieb! [*He bares his breast.*] Here they cut out a bullet as big as a thimble. The King knows where I lost my arm. It wasn't the mice as ate it. [*He walks up and down.*] Before that wife of yours was ever thought of, I had spilled my blood by the quart for King an' country. So let her call what names she likes —an' welcome! It does me no harm.—Frightened?

Me frightened? What would I be frightened of, will you tell me that? Of the few soldiers, maybe, that'll be comin' after the rioters? Good gracious me! That would be a lot to be frightened at! No, no, lad; I may be a bit stiff in the back, but there's some strength left in the old bones; I've got the stuff in me yet to make a stand against a few rubbishin' bay'nets.—An' if it came to the worst! Willin', willin' would I be to say good-bye to this weary world. Death would be welcome—welcomer to me to-day than to-morrow. For what is it we leave behind? That old bundle of aches an' pains we call our body, the care an' the oppression we call by the name of life. We may be glad to get away from it.—But there's something to come after, Gottlieb!—an' if we've done ourselves out of that too—why, then it's all over with us!

GOTTLIEB. Who knows what's to come after? Nobody's seen it.

OLD HILSE. Gottlieb! don't you be throwin' doubts on the one comfort us poor people have. Why have I sat here an' worked my treadle like a slave this forty year an' more?—sat still an' looked on at him over yonder livin' in pride an' wastefulness—why? Because I have a better hope, something as supports me in all my troubles. [Points out at the window.] You have your good things in this world—I'll have mine in the next. That's been my thought. An' I'm that certain of it—I'd let myself be torn in pieces. Have we not His promise? There's a Day of Judgment coming; but it's not us as are the judges—no: vengeance is mine, saith the Lord.

A cry of "Weavers, come out!" is heard outside the window.

OLD HILSE. Do what you will for me. [He seats himself at his loom.] I stay here.

GOTTLIEB [after a short struggle]. I'm going to work, too—come what may. [Goes out.]

The Weavers' Song is heard, sung by hundreds of voices quite close at hand; it sounds like a dull monotonous wail.

INMATES OF THE HOUSE [in the entry-room]. "Oh, mercy on us! there they come swarmin' like ants!"—"Where can all these weavers be from?"—"Don't shove like that, I want to see too."—"Look at that great maypole of a woman leadin' on in front!"—"Gracious! they're comin' thicker an' thicker."

HORNIG [comes into the entry-room from outside]. There's a theayter play for you now! That's what you don't see every day. But you should go up to the other Dittrich's an' look what they've done there. It's been no half work. He's got no house now, nor no factory, nor no wine-cellar, nor nothing. They're drinkin' out of the bottles—not so much as takin' the time to get out the corks. One, two, three, an' off with the neck, an' no matter whether they cut their mouths or not. There's some of them runnin' about bleedin' like stuck pigs.—Now they're goin' to do for this Dittrich.

The singing has stopped.

INMATES OF THE HOUSE. There's nothin' so very wicked-like about them.

HORNIG. You wait a bit! you'll soon see! All they're doin' just now is makin' up their minds where they'll begin. Look, they're inspectin' the palace from every side. Do you see that little stout man there, him with the stable pail? That's the smith from Peterswaldau—an' a dangerous little chap he is. He batters in the thickest doors as if they were made o' pie-crust. If a manufacturer was to fall into his hands it would be all over with him!

INMATES OF THE HOUSE. "That was a crack!"—"There went a stone through the window!"—"There's old Dittrich, shakin' with fright."—"He's hangin' out a board."—"Hangin' out a board?"—"What's written on it?"—"Can you not read?"—"It would be a bad job for me if I couldn't read!"—"Well, read it, then!"—"'You—shall have—full—satisfaction! You—shall have full satisfaction.'"

HORNIG. He might ha' spared himself the trouble—that won't help him. It's something else they've set their minds on here. It's the factories. They're goin' to smash up the power-looms. For it's them that are ruinin' the hand-loom weaver. Even a blind man might see that. No! the good folks know what they're after, an' no sheriff an' no p'lice superintendent'll bring them to reason—much less a bit of a board. Him as has seen them at work already knows what's comin'.

INMATES OF THE HOUSE. "Did any one ever see such a crowd?"—"What can these ones be wantin'?"—[Hastily.] "They're crossin' the bridge!"—[Anxiously.] "They're never comin' over on this side, are they?"—[In excitement and terror.] "It's to us they're comin'!"—"They're comin' to us!"—"They're comin' to fetch the weavers out of their houses!"

General flight. The entry-room is empty. A crowd of dirty, dustry rioters rush in, their faces scarlet with brandy and excitement; tattered, untidy-looking, as if they had been up all night. With the shout: "Weavers, come out!" they disperse themselves through the house. BECKER and several other young weavers, armed with cudgels and poles, come into OLD HILSE's room. When *they see the old man at his loom they start, and cool down a little.*

BECKER. Come, Father Hilse, stop that. Leave your work to them as wants to work. There's no need now for you to be doin' yourself harm. You'll be well taken care of.

FIRST YOUNG WEAVER. You'll never need to go hungry to bed again.

SECOND YOUNG WEAVER. The weaver's goin' to have a roof over his head and a shirt on his back once more.

OLD HILSE. An' what's the devil sendin' you to do now, with your poles an' axes?

BECKER. These are what we're goin' to break on Dittrich's back.

SECOND YOUNG WEAVER. We'll beat them red hot an' stick them down the manufacturers' throats, so as they'll feel for once what burnin' hunger tastes like.

THIRD YOUNG WEAVER. Come along, Father Hilse! We'll give no quarter.

SECOND YOUNG WEAVER. No one had mercy on us—neither God nor man. Now we're standin' up for our rights ourselves.

OLD BAUMERT *enters, somewhat shaky on the legs, a newly killed cock under his arm.*

OLD BAUMERT [*stretching out his arms*]. My brothers—we're all brothers! Come to my arms, brothers!

Laughter.

OLD HILSE. And that's the state you're in, Willem?

OLD BAUMERT. Gustav, is it you? My poor starvin' friend! Come to my arms, Gustav!

OLD HILSE [*mutters*]. Let me alone.

OLD BAUMERT. I'll tell you what, Gustav. It's nothin' but luck that's wanted. You look at me. What do I look like? Luck's what's wanted. Do I not look like a lord? [*Pats his stomach.*] Guess what's in there! There's food fit for a prince in that belly. When luck's with him a man gets roast hare to eat an' champagne wine to drink.—I'll tell you something: We've made a big mistake—we must help ourselves.

ALL [*speaking at once*]. We must help ourselves, hurrah!

OLD BAUMERT. As soon as we get the first good bite inside us we're different men. Damn it all! but you feel the power comin' into you till you're like an ox, an' that wild with strength that you hit out right an' left without as much as takin' time to look. Dash it, but it's grand!

JAEGER [*at the door, armed with an old cavalry sword*]. We've made one or two first-rate attacks.

BECKER. We know how to set about it now. One, two, three, an' we're inside the house. Then, at it like lightning—bang, crack, shiver! till the sparks are flyin' as if it was a smithy.

FIRST YOUNG WEAVER. It wouldn't be half bad to light a bit o' fire.

SECOND YOUNG WEAVER. Let's march to Reichenbach an' burn the rich folks' houses over their heads!

JAEGER. That would be nothing but butterin' their bread. Think of all the insurance money they'd get.

Laughter.

BECKER. No, from here we'll go to Freiburg, to Tromtra's.

JAEGER. What would you say to givin' all them as holds Government appointments a lesson? I've read somewhere as how all our troubles come from them birocrats, as they call them.

SECOND YOUNG WEAVER. Before long we'll go to Breslau, for more an' more'll be joining us.

OLD BAUMERT [*to* HILSE]. Won't you take a drop, Gustav?

OLD HILSE. I never touches it.

OLD BAUMERT. That was in the old world; we're in a new world to-day, Gustav.

FIRST YOUNG WEAVER. Christmas comes but once a year.

Laughter.

OLD HILSE [*impatiently*]. What is it you want in my house, you limbs of Satan?

OLD BAUMERT [*a little intimidated, coaxingly*]. I was bringin' you a chicken, Gustav. I thought it would make a drop o' soup for mother.

OLD HILSE [*embarrassed, almost friendly*]. Well, you can tell mother yourself.

MOTHER HILSE [*who has been making efforts to hear, her hand at her ear, motions them off*]. Let me alone. I don't want no chicken soup.

OLD HILSE. That's right, mother. An' I want none, an' least of all that sort. An' let me say this much to you, Baumert: The devil stands on his head for joy when he hears the old ones jabberin' and talkin' as if they was infants. An' to you all I say—to every one of you: Me and you, we've got nothing to do with each other. It's not with my will that you're here. In law an' justice you've no right to be in my house.

A VOICE. Him that's not with us is against us.

JAEGER [*roughly and threateningly*]. You're a cross-grained old chap, and I'd have you remember that we're not thieves.

A VOICE. We're hungry men, that's all.

FIRST YOUNG WEAVER. We want to *live*—that's

all. An' so we've cut the rope we were hung up with.

JAEGER. And we were in our right! [*Holding his fist in front of the old man's face.*] Say another word, and I'll give you one between the eyes.

BECKER. Come now, Jaeger, be quiet. Let the old man alone.—What we say to ourselves, Father Hilse, is this: Better dead than begin the old life again.

OLD HILSE. Have I not lived that life for sixty years an' more?

BECKER. That doesn't help us—there's got to be a change.

OLD HILSE. On the Judgment Day.

BECKER. What they'll not give us willingly we're going to take by force.

OLD HILSE. By force. [*Laughs.*] You may as well go an' dig your graves at once. They'll not be long showin' you where the force lies. Wait a bit, lad!

JAEGER. Is it the soldiers you're meaning? We've been soldiers, too. We'll soon do for a company or two of them.

OLD HILSE. With your tongues, maybe. But supposin' you did—for two that you'd beat off, ten'll come back.

VOICES [*call through the window*]. The soldiers are comin'! Look out!

General, sudden silence. For a moment a faint sound of fifes and drums is heard; in the ensuing silence a short, involuntary exclamation, "The devil! I'm off!" followed by general laughter.

BECKER. Who was that? Who speaks of running away?

JAEGER. Which of you is it that's afraid of a few paltry helmets? You have me to command you, and I've been in the trade. I know their tricks.

OLD HILSE. An' what are you goin' to shoot with? Your sticks, eh?

FIRST YOUNG WEAVER. Never mind that old chap; he's wrong in the upper story.

SECOND YOUNG WEAVER. Yes, he's a bit off his head.

GOTTLIEB [*has made his way unnoticed among the rioters; catches hold of the speaker*]. Would you give your impudence to an old man like him?

SECOND YOUNG WEAVER. Let me alone. 'Twasn't anything bad I said.

OLD HILSE [*interfering*]. Let him jaw, Gottlieb. What would you be meddlin' with him for? He'll soon see who it is that's been off his head to-day, him or me.

BECKER. Are you comin', Gottlieb?

OLD HILSE. No, he's goin' to do no such thing.

LUISE [*comes into the entry-room, calls*]. What are you puttin' off your time with prayin' hypocrites like them for? Come quick to where you're wanted! Quick! Father Baumert, run all you can! The Major's speakin' to the crowd from horseback. They're to go home. If you don't hurry up, it'll be all over.

JAEGER [*as he goes out*]. That's a brave husband of yours.

LUISE. Where is he? I've got no husband!

Some of the people in the entry-room sing.

> Once on a time a man so small,
>   Heigh-ho, heigh!
> Set his heart on a wife so tall,
>   Heigh diddle-di-dum-di!

WITTIG, THE SMITH [*comes downstairs, still carrying the stable pail; stops on his way through the entry-room*]. Come on! all of you that are not cowardly scoundrels!—hurrah!

He dashes out, followed by LUISE, JAEGER, *and others, all shouting "Hurrah!"*

BECKER. Good-bye, then, Father Hilse; we'll see each other again. [*Is going.*]

OLD HILSE. I doubt that. I've not five years to live, and that'll be the soonest you'll get out.

BECKER [*stops, not understanding*]. Out o' what, Father Hilse?

OLD HILSE. Out of prison—where else?

BECKER [*laughs wildly*]. Do you think I would mind that? There's bread to be had there anyhow! [*Goes out.*]

OLD BAUMERT [*has been cowering on a low stool, painfully beating his brains; he now gets up*]. It's true, Gustav, as I've had a drop too much. But for all that I know what I'm about. You think one way in this here matter; I think another. I say Becker's right: even if it ends in chains an' ropes —we'll be better off in prison than at home. You're cared for there, an you don't need to starve. I wouldn't have joined them, Gustav, if I could have let it be; but once in a lifetime a man's got to show what he feels. [*Goes slowly toward the door.*] Good-bye, Gustav. If anything happens, mind you put in a word for me in your prayers. [*Goes out.*]

The rioters are now all gone. The entry-room gradually fills again with curious onlookers from the different rooms of the house. OLD HILSE knots at his web. GOTTLIEB has taken an ax from behind the stove and is unconsciously feeling its edge. He and the old man are silently agitated. The hum and roar of a great crowd penetrate into the room.

MOTHER HILSE. The very boards is shakin', father —what's goin' on? What's goin' to happen to us?
Pause.
OLD HILSE. Gottlieb!
GOTTLIEB. What is it?
OLD HILSE. Let that ax alone.
GOTTLIEB. Who's to split the wood, then? [*He leans the ax against the stove.*]
Pause.
MOTHER HILSE. Gottlieb, you listen to what father says to you.
Some one sings outside the window.
Our little man does all that he can,
Heigh-ho, heigh!
At home he cleans the pots an' the pan,
Heigh-diddle-di-dum-di!
Passes on.
GOTTLIEB [*jumps up, shakes his clenched fist at the window*]. Brute that you are, would you drive me crazy?
A volley of musketry is heard.
MOTHER HILSE [*starts and trembles*]. Good Lord! is that thunder again?
OLD HILSE [*instinctively folding his hands*]. Oh, our Father in heaven! defend the poor weavers, protect my poor brothers!
A short pause ensues.
OLD HILSE [*to himself, painfully agitated*]. There's blood flowing now.
GOTTLIEB [*had started up and grasped the ax when the shooting was heard; deathly pale, almost beside himself with excitement*]. And am I to lie to heel like a dog still?
A GIRL [*calls from the entry-room*]. Father Hilse, Father Hilse! get away from the window. A bullet's just flown in at ours upstairs. [*Disappears.*]
MIELCHEN [*puts her head in at the window, laughing*]. Gran'father, gran'father, they've shot with their guns. Two or three's been knocked down, an' one of them's turnin' round and round like a top, an' one's twistin' himself like a sparrow when its head's bein' pulled of. An' oh, if you saw all the blood that came pourin'—! [*Disappears.*]
A WEAVER'S WIFE. Yes, there's two or three'll never get up again.
AN OLD WEAVER [*in the entry-room*]. Look out! They're goin' to make a rush on the soldiers.
A SECOND WEAVER [*wildly*]. Look, look, look at the women!—skirts up', an' spittin' in the soldiers' faces already!
A WEAVER'S WIFE [*calls in*]. Gottlieb, look at your wife. She's more pluck in her than you.

She's jumpin' about in front o' the bay'nets as if she was dancin' to music.
Four men carry a wounded rioter through the entry-room. Silence, which is broken by some one saying in a distinct voice, "It's Weaver Ulbrich." Once more silence for a few seconds, when the same voice is heard again: "It's all over with him; he's got a bullet in his ear." The men are heard climbing the wooden stair. Sudden shouting outside: "Hurrah, hurrah!"
VOICES IN THE ENTRY-ROOM. "Where did they get the stones from?"—"Yes, it's time you were off!"—"From the new road."—"Ta-ta, soldiers!"—"It's raining paving-stones."
Shrieks of terror and loud roaring outside, taken up by those in the entry-room. There is a cry of fear, and the house door is shut with a bang.
VOICES IN THE ENTRY-ROOM. "They're loading again."—"They'll fire another volley this minute."—"Father Hilse, get away from that window."
GOTTLIEB [*clutches the ax*]. What! are we mad dogs? Are we to eat powder an' shot now instead of bread? [*Hesitating an instant: to the old man.*] Would you have me sit here an' see my wife shot? Never! [*As he rushes out.*] Look out! I'm coming!
OLD HILSE. Gottlieb, Gottlieb!
MOTHER HILSE. Where's Gottlieb gone?
OLD HILSE. He's gone to the devil.
VOICES FROM THE ENTRY-ROOM. Go away from the window, Father Hilse.
OLD HILSE. Not I! Not if you all go crazy together! [*To MOTHER HILSE, with rapt excitement.*] My heavenly Father has placed me here. Isn't that so, mother? Here we'll sit, an' do our bounden duty—ay, though the snow was to go on fire. [*He begins to weave.*]
Rattle of another volley. OLD HILSE, mortally wounded, starts to his feet and then falls forward over the loom. At the same moment loud shouting of "Hurrah!" is heard. The people who till now have been standing in the entry-room dash out, joining in the cry. The old woman repeatedly asks: "Father, father, what's wrong with you?" The continued shouting dies away gradually in the distance. MIELCHEN rushes in.
MIELCHEN. Gran'father, gran'father, they're drivin' the soldiers out of the village; they've got into Dittrich's house, an' they're doin' what they did at Dreissiger's. Gran'father! [*The child grows frightened, notices that something has happened, puts her finger in her mouth, and goes up cautiously to the dead man.*] Gran'father!
MOTHER HILSE. Come now, father, can't you say something? You're frightenin' me.

THE RUSSIAN SOUL

It was only in the nineteenth century that Russia began to contribute to our literary heritage. It was then that Western liberalism and science invaded the land of the autocratic Tzars, that Napoleon was crushed by the powerful arms of the Russian giant, and that the latter began to rouse himself. Russia forged ahead and became one of the chief cultural and social forces of the world.

The most singular cultural contribution of the Russians was their development of realistic literature, for masters like Gogol, Turgenev, Tolstoy, Dostoyevsky, and Chekhov became second to none in the art of revealing life. The West has never been entirely able to understand Russia, a nation torn between the orient and the occident, and conditioned by insufficiently comprehended economic forces. "The Russian soul," a term employed by writers both in Russia and in Western Europe, may mean much or little; it is certainly another name for an enigma to the West. In literature, however, it means a unique combination of the most vigorous and candid realism with extreme sensitiveness, awareness of the pangs of the human heart, and aspiration toward the highest ideals. Above all, the well-spring of nineteenth-century Russian literature was sympathy with mankind, respect for its strivings, pity for its failures. Realism in the writings of a Flaubert or a Maupassant had a brain, but realism in the work of the Russian masters had a heart.

The peculiar nature of Russian literature became apparent early in the last century when the prevailing fashion was still romanticism and when Byron was the idol of the intellectuals. Russia's two great romantic poets, Alexander Pushkin (1799-1837) and Michael Lermontov (1814-1841), were realists in their treatment of character. The former's great verse novel *Eugene Onegin* was an incisive study of society and social types; the latter's prose novel, *A Hero of Our Times*, a thorough-going analysis of a restless and bedevilled personality. Moreover, they were quickly followed by one of the chief masters of early realism, Nikolay V. Gogol (1809-1852).

Gogol was a Ukrainian by birth and a descendant of Cossacks, on the paternal side. He wrote both plays and novels, and among the former is *Revizor* or *The Inspector-General*, a satire on bureaucratic corruption and one of the most trenchant of modern comedies. Even better known is his work in fiction, which he started with beautiful tales of Ukrainian folk life. To his Cossack ancestry he also paid the tribute of a stirring prose epic, *Taras Bulba*. But he attained full stature only when he began to write out of the pity and grief that overwhelmed him. As he looked around him, he saw a vast and potentially great nation sunk in a mire of corruption and listlessness, and in describing these conditions in his unique style—compounded of realism, laughter, and tears—he became a great realist.

His most ambitious work was the long adventure novel *Dead Souls*. His rogue, Chichikov, covers large stretches of the Russian land in an ingenious effort to collect collateral for a loan by buying up "dead souls"—that is, serfs who have died since the last census. The picture is terrifying: Most of the people are virtual slaves bound to their masters' estates and can be bought and sold. The rural gentry consists of downright boors, sharp horse-traders, refined people who subsist on charm and procrastinate for years, and intelligent men steeped in despair. It is slight wonder that Gogol should have found reality unendurable in the end. He sought escape in religious mysticism and died under a cloud of melancholy in 1852.

Dead Souls is one of the great novels of Europe. Gogol was also a master of the short story. The best of his stories is *The Cloak*, the tale of a poor government clerk's misadventures when he finally buys himself a new coat. It exemplifies this writer's talent for recording the paltry life of little people, his pity for the weak, and his wry humor and ironic fantastication.

"We have all emerged from Gogol's cloak," said one of his successors, Dostoyevsky, in a memorable eulogy on the father of Russian realism. Many writers followed him, all distinguished for their graphic descriptions of common reality. But the greatest of Gogol's immediate successors and the first to win international recognition was Ivan Sergyeevich Turgenev (1818-1883). He was the author of several plays, including a beautiful drama of unhappiness in the provinces, *A Month in the Country*, and of many works of fiction.

Born of an aristocratic family, and well educated in Moscow, St. Petersburg, and Berlin, Turgenev fell under the influence of Western ideas and became a liberal. A giant in size but one of the gentlest of men, he could not brook serfdom, and was depressed by political oppression and the listlessness of the educated classes. Inheriting considerable wealth after his mother's death, he freed the serfs on his estate and, chafing under Tzarist censorship, left his native land, following a famous singer throughout Europe in a fruitless pursuit. In Paris he won the friendship of Flaubert, and was looked up to by younger writers like Maupassant.

Among his novels, the most famous is *Fathers and Sons*, a moving and balanced study of a Russian intellectual or "nihilist," Bazarov, who challenges all conventions in the name of science but is destroyed by such natural forces as infatuation and disease. In his novels *Rudin* and *Virgin Soil*, he created other memorable intellectuals, and exposed their weakness—their inability to support their fine ideals with action, their contradictions and vacillations. At the same time, Turgenev evoked a new and vigorous generation that would grapple with the old order practically and scientifically. The pathos of his Russian Hamlets and the freshness of his heroines, combined with his simple prose lyricism, make him one of the most appealing of modern writers.

Some of his best work is to be found in his stories, and the most memorable of them appeared in his *Annals of a Sportsman* (1852). Here he sketched the various aspects of the Russian countryside, portraying characters in all walks of life, and evoking beauty and tenderness out of man and nature. These qualities are well exhibited in the sympathetic story *Biryuk*.

Turgenev was a perfect artist and a most temperate man. His successors, Dostoyevsky and Tolstoy, both artists in their own right, cared less for art and were intemperate. But they overshadowed him, for they were truly giants of the earth.

Perhaps the most tortured of all writers was Fiodor Mikhaylovitch Dostoyevsky (1821-1881), and his sufferings gave him uncanny penetration into the anguish of the soul. He was the sensitive and moody son of a tyrannical Lithuanian army surgeon, who sent him to an engineering school in St. Petersburg but kept him penniless there. Dostoyevsky's attitude toward his father was one of bitter enmity mingled with an acute sense of guilt because of this hatred. It was the murder of this parent by peasants he had oppressed that sent Dostoyevsky into his first epileptic fit. The memory of his father seems to be the undercurrent of Dostoyevsky's concern with murder and remorse in his writings.

The remainder of this writer's life only served to deepen his morbid inclinations and his comprehension of suffering. He scored an early success with *Poor People*, a novel of humble people's attachments and frustration that recalls Dickens, but followed this with many unsuccessful, imitative writings. He seemed stalemated when an unhappy event changed the course of his life. Dostoyevsky was arrested for participating in a conspiracy to overthrow the Tzarist regime, condemned to death, taken out at dawn with a halter around his neck, and saved from hanging only by a last-minute reprieve. This diabolical trick, ordered by the sadistic Nicholas I, shook Dostoyevsky's spirit; henceforth he was keenly sensible of death and felt like Lazarus risen from the grave. Then came experiences worse than death when Dostoyevsky's sentence was commuted to hard labor for life in Siberia. He was paroled after four years, and after some years of penal service in the army, completely released. His record of his years in the convict camp in *House of the Dead* is one of the most harrowing of all books. There followed an unhappy marriage with a frivolous woman who tortured him with her infidelity and hated him until the day she died of tuberculosis. (The experiences of a betrayed husband make painful but penetrative reading in his novel *The Eternal Husband*.) No more fortunate in his next affair, a comic-opera infatuation with a young woman student, he found understanding only late in life when he married his secretary, a long-suffering young woman who bore with his eccentricities. He had an inordinate passion for gambling, which often made him lose all his earnings; it was a disease in his case, and his long story *The Gambler* records it with searing intensity. Moreover he still had his epilepsy to contend with; it is the subject of his profound book, *The Idiot*.

Dostoyevsky wrote hastily and carelessly under excruciating conditions of poverty, illness, and suffering. But out of his writings came novels of superlative psychological insight and profound sympathy with suffering humanity. This son of devout Catholic parents knew all the stations of the Cross and followed them with loving-kindness and forgiveness. His work can be represented adequately only by his great novels: preferably by his study of guilt, *Crime and Punishment*; his analysis of demoniacal passion set against the gentle Christianity of an epileptic, *The Idiot*; and above all, his *The Brothers Karamazov*, a dramatic treatment of the grossly sensual, inordinately passionate, nihilistically intellectual, and altruistic types of personality that exist in society and are contained, at least potentially, in nearly every individual. The short story, *The Christmas Tree and the Wedding*, can convey only this titan's consummate pity in its less Promethean proportions.

Count Lev Nikolaevich Tolstoy (1828-1910) enjoyed the advantages of wealth, social connections, and a lusty body. But his entire life history was a restless struggle with himself and with the world. Reared by a pious aunt after losing his mother at an early age, he became filled with an intense sense of sin while remaining a man of strong passions, given to lust, debauchery, and gambling. His conscience and his animal self engaged in a long-drawn struggle that led Tolstoy to fill his diary with unsavory confessions, to enlist in a regiment of Cossacks in the Caucasus in order to find purgation in nature, to try to educate the peasantry and convert his estate into a village commune. After this period of restlessness he settled down to an at first very happy and fruitful marriage with the daughter of a Moscow court physician. In the midst of this marriage, however, and at the height of his fame, he succumbed to an agonizing depression, contemplated hanging himself, and became profoundly religious, adopting a primitive form of Christianity that became known as Tolstoyism. Denying all creeds and courting expulsion from the Russian Church, he expounded a doctrine of absolute pacifism and non-resistance, which gave rise to a religious sect persecuted in Russia for its refusal to serve in the army. He became the center of a cult, drawing to himself disciples from all parts of Europe. All this resulted in a protracted struggle with his wife, who did not share his beliefs, was

jealous of his followers, and refused to let him give away his wealth. The situation became so unbearable that Tolstoy ran away from home in his eighty-second year. He contracted pneumonia on the way and died on November 20, 1910.

Regardless of his feelings or convictions at any one time, Tolstoy invariably proved himself a superlative writer. His early work, before his marriage in 1862, included one of the best autobiographies, *Childhood, Boyhood, and Youth*; *The Cossacks*, a beautiful novel about life in the Caucasus, rich in descriptions of nature; his *Sebastopol* sketches of the Crimean War, notable as one of the first realistic pictures of the horrors of the battlefield; and some superb stories, such as *The Two Hussars*, *The Three Deaths*, *The Snow Storm*, and *Polikushka*, one of the tenderest studies of a hapless common man—a serf.

In the happy early years of his marriage Tolstoy turned out those two masterpieces of the modern novel: his epic of the Napoleonic age *War and Peace*, and his profoundly psychological tragedy of illicit passion *Anna Karenina*. Both are novels of tremendous scope, replete with wonderful portraits.

Although he passed the high-water mark of his creative output with the completion of *Anna Karenina*, the work of his long religious period revealed no reduction of his talent, even though it was now limited and often side-tracked by his didactic intentions. His *Confessions*, in which he announced his new-won faith, is worthy of being ranked with St. Augustine's *Confessions*. At this time he wrote a series of plays: *The Power of Darkness*, the strongest naturalistic peasant drama of the century; *Redemption*, an attack on Russian marriage laws combined with Tolstoy's gospel of self-sacrifice; *The Fruits of Enlightenment*, a delightful satire on the upper classes; and the uncompleted *The Light Shines in Darkness*, an autobiographical tragedy of an idealist at war with his wife and her world. His two late novels, *Hadji Murad* and *Resurrection*, a social study of the conversion of a worldly nobleman, are also impressive.

In this last period Tolstoy also wrote a number of little folk stories that have remained unsurpassed. To these he added several larger stories, *The Death of Ivan Ilyitch* and *Master and Man*, both dealing with the imminence of death and the transformation this effects in human beings. *The Death of Ivan Ilyitch* is one of the great short novels of the world by virtue of its realistic observation of the mental processes of a suffering man and its deep humanity.

The last important Russian writer before the present century, Anton Pavlovich Chekhov (1860-1904), was less Promethean than either Dostoyevsky or Tolstoy. He was a gentle person with a rich capacity for humor; his life was uneventful, though shattered by illness and saddened by the stagnation of the pre-revolutionary period in Russia. The son of an emancipated serf, he studied medicine while supporting himself and his large family by writing humorous stories that proved very successful. After receiving his degree in 1884, he practiced medicine for a while, and then achieved fame as a master of the short story and the drama. He married the famous actress, Madame Olga Knipper of the Moscow Art Theater, which alone understood how to stage his plays and made them successful. But he became the victim of tuberculosis at an early age, and he died shortly after the production of his masterpiece *The Cherry Orchard*.

After the success of two collections of amusing tales, Chekhov's artistry deepened. He no longer wrote cleverly contrived stories, but deep and somber records of life. Some of them are tender portraits of people, like *The Darling* and *The Kiss*; others are studies of the frustration in an oppressive and spiritually empty environment, like *A Tiresome Story* and the terrifying *Ward No. 6*; and still others are depressing pictures of the ignorant and brutalized peasantry, like *The Hollow*. His realistic and pessimistic stories resemble Maupassant's but are always suffused with sympathy and always free from cynicism.

These qualities also appear in his plays, which, though few in number, give him his greatest claim to immortality. The best of them, *The Sea-Gull,* *Uncle Vanya, The Three Sisters,* and *The Cherry Orchard,* are all studies in stagnation, heightened by the passionate longings of the characters and (in the last three plays) by their sense of the coming of a new world in which their tentative struggles would attain fulfillment. He gave to the realistic drama its final sublimation, avoiding all theatrical contrivances, creating a counterpoint of characters, and immersing them in their own thoughts and feelings as if they were often unaware of any external reality, though they are painfully conscious of it. The final tragedy in Chekhov's plays is the inability of people to act; theirs is the tragedy of attrition, of rusting away in the manner of so many people, and yet being aware of their failure and struggling against it.

The Cherry Orchard is the supreme achievement of this contrapuntal realistic technique and tragedy of frustration. But despite its superb characterizations, the play, produced one year before the unsuccessful revolution of 1905 which became a dress-rehearsal for the Marxist revolution of 1917, goes beyond personal drama in its representation of the social upheaval that Chekhov expected. Its nearest equivalents in our English heritage are Shaw's *Heartbreak House* and Odets' *Awake and Sing!* It is a wistful elegy on the decay of Russia's aristocracy and the futility of her unrealistic, inactive educated classes. At the same time, the play heralds the dawn of a new world, unpleasant to members of the old but strong and pregnant with new possibilities. *The Cherry Orchard*, in short, is the tragedy of the process of social transition as it affects people. This is peculiarly a problem of our own age, and may be traced through the whole fabric of our present life and thought.

NIKOLAY V. GOGOL

The Cloak

In the department of ——, but it is better not to mention the department. The touchiest things in the world are departments, regiments, courts of justice, in a word, all branches of public service. Each individual nowadays thinks all society insulted in his person. Quite recently, a complaint was received from a district chief of police in which he plainly demonstrated that all the imperial institutions were going to the dogs, and that the Czar's sacred name was being taken in vain; and in proof he appended to the complaint a romance, in which the district chief of police is made to appear about once in every ten pages, and sometimes in a downright drunken condition. Therefore, in order to avoid all unpleasantness, it will be better to designate the department in question, as a certain department.

So, in a certain department there was a certain

Nikolay V. Gogol (1809-1852). Translation from *Best Russian Short Stories*, by arrangement with Random House, Inc., publishers official—not a very notable one, it must be allowed —short of stature, somewhat pock-marked, red-haired, and mole-eyed, with a bald forehead, wrinkled cheeks, and a complexion of the kind known as sanguine. The St. Petersburg climate was responsible for this. As for his official rank—with us Russians the rank comes first—he was what is called a perpetual titular councillor, over which, as is well known, some writers make merry and crack their jokes, obeying the praiseworthy custom of attacking those who cannot bite back.

His family name was Bashmachkin. This name is evidently derived from bashmak (shoe); but, when, at what time, and in what manner, is not known. His father and grandfather, and all the Bashmachkins, always wore boots, which were re-soled two or three times a year. His name was Akaky Akakiyevich. It may strike the reader as rather singular and far-fetched; but he may rest assured that it was by no means far-fetched, and that the circumstances were such that it would have been impossible to give him any other.

This was how it came about.

Akaky Akakiyevich was born, if my memory fails me not, in the evening on the 23rd of March. His mother, the wife of a Government official, and a very fine woman, made all due arrangements for having the child baptised. She was lying on the bed opposite the door; on her right stood the godfather, Ivan Ivanovich Eroshkin, a most estimable man, who served as the head clerk of the senate; and the godmother, Arina Semyonovna Bielobrinshkova, the wife of an officer of the quarter, and a woman of rare virtues. They offered the mother her choice of three names, Mokiya, Sossiya, or that the child should be called after the martyr Khozdazat. "No," said the good woman, "all those names are poor." In order to please her, they opened the calendar at another place; three more names appeared, Triphily, Dula, and Varakhasy. "This is awful," said the old woman. "What names! I truly never heard the like. I might have put up with Varadat or Varukh, but not Triphily and Varakhasy!" They turned to another page and found Pavsikakhy and Vakhtisy. "Now I see," said the old woman, "that it is plainly fate. And since such is the case, it will be better to name him after his father. His father's name was Akaky, so let his son's name be Akaky too." In this manner he became Akaky Akakiyevich. They christened the child, whereat he wept, and made a grimace, as though he foresaw that he was to be a titular councillor.

In this manner did it all come about. We have mentioned it in order that the reader might see for himself that it was a case of necessity, and that it was utterly impossible to give him any other name.

When and how he entered the department, and who appointed him, no one could remember. However much the directors and chiefs of all kinds were changed, he was always to be seen in the same place, the same attitude, the same occupation —always the letter-copying clerk—so that it was afterwards affirmed that he had been born in uniform with a bald head. No respect was shown him in the department. The porter not only did not rise from his seat when he passed, but never even glanced at him, any more than if a fly had flown through the reception-room. His superiors treated him in coolly despotic fashion. Some insignificant assistant to the head clerk would thrust a paper under his nose without so much as saying, "Copy," or, "Here's an interesting little case," or anything else agreeable, as is customary amongst well-bred officials. And he took it, looking only at the paper, and not observing who handed it to him, or whether he had the right to do so; simply took it, and set about copying it.

The young officials laughed at and made fun of him, so far as their official wit permitted; told in his presence various stories concocted about him, and about his landlady, an old woman of seventy; declared that she beat him; asked when the wedding was to be; and strewed bits of paper over his head, calling them snow. But Akaky Akakiyevich answered not a word, any more than if there had been no one there besides himself. It even had no effect upon his work. Amid all these annoyances he never made a single mistake in a letter. But if the joking became wholly unbearable, as when they jogged his head, and prevented his attending to his work, he would exclaim:

"Leave me alone! Why do you insult me?"

And there was something strange in the words and the voice in which they were uttered. There was in it something which moved to pity; so much so that one young man, a newcomer, who, taking pattern by the others, had permitted himself to make sport of Akaky, suddenly stopped short, as though all about him had undergone a transformation, and presented itself in a different aspect. Some unseen force repelled him from the comrades whose acquaintance he had made, on the supposition that they were decent, well-bred men. Long afterwards, in his gayest moments, there recurred to his mind the little official with the bald forehead, with his heart-rending words, "Leave me alone! Why do you insult me?" In these moving words, other words resounded—"I am thy brother." And the young man covered his face with his hand; and many a time afterwards, in the course of his life, shuddered at seeing how much inhumanity there is in man, how much savage coarseness is concealed beneath refined, cultured, worldly refinement, and even, O God! in that man whom the world acknowledges as honourable and upright.

It would be difficult to find another man who lived so entirely for his duties. It is not enough to say that Akaky laboured with zeal; no, he laboured with love. In his copying, he found a varied and agreeable employment. Enjoyment was written on his face; some letters were even favourites with him; and when he encountered these, he smiled, winked, and worked with his lips, till it seemed as though each letter might be read in his face, as his pen traced it. If his pay had been in proportion to his zeal, he would, perhaps, to his great surprise, have been made even a councillor of state. But he worked, as his companions, the wits, put it, like a horse in a mill.

However, it would be untrue to say that no attention was paid to him. One director being a kindly man, and desirous of rewarding him for his long service, ordered him to be given something more important than mere copying. So he was ordered to make a report of an already concluded affair, to another department; the duty consisting simply in changing the heading and altering a few words from the first to the third person. This caused him so much toil, that he broke into a perspiration, rubbed his forehead, and finally said, "No, give me rather something to copy" After that they let him copy on forever.

Outside this copying, it appeared that nothing existed for him. He gave no thought to his clothes. His uniform was not green, but a sort of rusty-meal colour. The collar was low, so that his neck, in spite of the fact that it was not long, seemed inordinately so as it emerged from it, like the necks of the plaster cats which pedlars carry about on their heads. And something was always sticking to his uniform, either a bit of hay or some trifle. Moreover, he had a peculiar knack, as he walked along the street, of arriving beneath a window just as all sorts of rubbish was being flung out of it; hence he always bore about on his hat scraps of melon rinds, and other such articles. Never once in his life did he give heed to what was going on every day in the street; while it is well known that his young brother officials trained the range of their glances till they could see when any one's trouser-straps came undone upon the opposite sidewalk, which always brought a malicious smile to their faces. But Akaky Akakiyevich saw in all things the clean, even strokes of his written lines; and only when a horse thrust his nose, from some unknown quarter, over his shoulder, and sent a whole gust of wind down his neck from his nostrils, did he observe that he was not in the middle of a line, but in the middle of the street.

On reaching home, he sat down at once at the table, sipped his cabbage-soup up quickly, and swallowed a bit of beef with onions, never noticing their taste, and gulping down everything with flies and anything else which the Lord happened to send at the moment. When he saw that his stomach was beginning to swell, he rose from the table, and copied papers which he had brought home. If there happened to be none, he took copies for himself, for his own gratification, especially if the document was noteworthy, not on account of its style, but of its being addressed to some distinguished person.

Even at the hour when the grey St. Petersburg sky had quite disappeared, and all the official world had eaten or dined, each as he could, in accordance with the salary he received and his own fancy; when all were resting from the department jar of pens, running to and fro, for their own and other people's indispensable occupations, and from all the work that an uneasy man makes willingly for himself, rather than what is necessary; when officials hasten to dedicate to pleasure the time which is left to them, one bolder than the rest going to the theatre; another, into the street looking under the bonnets; another wasting his evening in compliments to some pretty girl, the star of a small official circle; another—and this is the common case of all—visiting his comrades on the third or fourth floor, in two small rooms with an anteroom or kitchen, and some pretensions to fashion, such as a lamp or some other trifle which has cost many a sacrifice of dinner or pleasure trip; in a word, at the hour when all officials disperse among the contracted quarters of their friends, to play whist, as they sip their tea from glasses with a kopek's worth of sugar, smoke long pipes, relate at time some bits of gossip which a Russian man can never, under any circumstances, refrain from, and when there is nothing else to talk of, repeat eternal anecdotes about the commandant to whom they had sent word that the tails of the horses on the Falconet Monument had been cut off; when all strive to divert themselves, Akaky Akakiyevich indulged in no kind of diversion. No one could even say that he had seen him at any kind of evening party. Having written to his heart's content, he lay down to sleep, smiling at the thought of the coming day—of what God might send him to copy on the morrow.

Thus flowed on the peaceful life of the man, who, with a salary of four hundred rubles, understood how to be content with his lot; and thus it would have continued to flow on, perhaps, to extreme old age, were it not that there are various ills strewn along the path of life for titular councillors as well as for private, actual, court, and every other species of councillor, even to those who never give any advice or take any themselves.

There exists in St. Petersburg a powerful foe of all who receive a salary of four hundred rubles a year, or thereabouts. This foe is no other than the Northern cold, although it is said to be very healthy. At nine o'clock in the morning, at the very hour when the streets are filled with men bound for the various official departments, it begins to bestow such powerful and piercing nips on all noses impartially, that the poor officials really do not know what to do with them. At an hour when the foreheads of even those who occupy exalted positions ache with the cold, and tears start to their eyes, the poor titular councillors are sometimes quite unprotected. Their only salvation lies in traversing as quickly as possible, in their thin little cloaks, five or six streets, and then warming their feet in the porter's room, and so thawing all their talents and qualifications for official service, which had become frozen on the way.

Akaky Akakiyevich had felt for some time that his back and shoulders were paining with peculiar poignancy, in spite of the fact that he tried to traverse the distance with all possible speed. He began finally to wonder whether the fault did not lie in his cloak. He examined it thoroughly at home, and discovered that in two places, namely, on the back and shoulders, it had become thin as gauze. The cloth was worn to such a degree that he could see through it, and the lining had fallen into pieces. You must know that Akaky Akakiyevich's cloak served as an object of ridicule to the officials. They even refused it the noble name of cloak, and called it a cape. In fact, it was of singular make, its collar diminishing year by year to serve to patch its other parts. The patching did not exhibit great skill on the part of the tailor, and was, in fact, baggy and ugly. Seeing how the matter stood, Akaky Akakiyevich decided that it would be necessary to take the cloak to Petrovich,

the tailor, who lived somewhere on the fourth floor up a dark staircase, and who, in spite of his having but one eye and pock-marks all over his face, busied himself with considerable success in repairing the trousers and coats of officials and others; that is to say, when he was sober and not nursing some other scheme in his head.

It is not necessary to say much about this tailor, but as it is the custom to have the character of each personage in a novel clearly defined there is no help for it, so here is Petrovich the tailor. At first he was called only Grigory, and was some gentleman's serf. He commenced calling himself Petrovich from the time when he received his free papers, and further began to drink heavily on all holidays, at first on the great ones, and then on all church festivals without discrimination, wherever a cross stood in the calendar. On this point he was faithful to ancestral custom; and when quarrelling with his wife, he called her a low female and a German. As we have mentioned his wife, it will be necessary to say a word or two about her. Unfortunately, little is known of her beyond the fact that Petrovich had a wife, who wore a cap and a dress, but could not lay claim to beauty, at least, no one but the soldiers of the guard even looked under her cap when they met her.

Ascending the staircase which led to Petrovich's room—which staircase was all soaked with dish-water and reeked with the smell of spirits which affects the eyes, and is an inevitable adjunct to all dark stairways in St. Petersburg houses—ascending the stairs, Akaky Akakiyevich pondered how much Petrovich would ask, and mentally resolved not to give more than two rubles. The door was open, for the mistress, in cooking some fish, had raised such a smoke in the kitchen that not even the beetles were visible. Akaky Akakiyevich passed through the kitchen unperceived, even by the housewife, and at length reached a room where he beheld Petrovich seated on a large unpainted table, with his legs tucked under him like a Turkish pasha. His feet were bare, after the fashion of tailors as they sit at work; and the first thing which caught the eye was his thumb, with a deformed nail thick and strong as a turtle's shell. About Petrovich's neck hung a skein of silk and thread, and upon his knees lay some old garment. He had been trying unsuccessfully for three minutes to thread his needle, and was enraged at the darkness and even at the thread, growling in a low voice, "It won't go through, you pricked me, you rascal!"

Akaky Akakiyevich was vexed at arriving at

the precise moment when Petrovich was angry. He liked to order something of Petrovich when he was a little downhearted, or, as his wife expressed it, "when he had settled himself with brandy, the one-eyed devil!" Under such circumstances Petrovich generally came down in his price very readily, and even bowed and returned thanks. Afterwards, to be sure, his wife would come, complaining that her husband had been drunk, and so had fixed the price too low; but, if only a tenkopek piece were added then the matter would be settled. But now it appeared that Petrovich was in a sober condition, and therefore rough, taciturn, and inclined to demand, Satan only knows what price. Akaky Akakiyevich felt this, and would gladly have beat a retreat, but he was in for it. Petrovich screwed up his one eye very intently at him, and Akaky Akakiyevich involuntarily said, "How do you do, Petrovich?"

"I wish you a good morning, sir," said Petrovich squinting at Akaky Akakiyevich's hands, to see what sort of booty he had brought.

"Ah! I—to you, Petrovich, this—" It must be known that Akaky Akakiyevich expressed himself chiefly by prepositions, adverbs, and scraps of phrases which had no meaning whatever. If the matter was a very difficult one, he had a habit of never completing his sentences, so that frequently, having begun a phrase with the words, "This, in fact, is quite—" he forgot to go on, thinking he had already finished it.

"What is it?" asked Petrovich, and with his one eye scanned Akaky Akakiyevich's whole uniform from the collar down to the cuffs, the back, the tails and the buttonholes, all of which were well known to him, since they were his own handiwork. Such is the habit of tailors; it is the first thing they do on meeting one.

"But I, here, this—Petrovich—a cloak, cloth— here you see, everywhere, in different places, it is quite strong—it is a little dusty and looks old, but it is new, only here in one place it is a little—on the back, and here on one of the shoulders, it is a little worn, yes, here on this shoulder it is a little —do you see? That is all. And a little work——"

Petrovich took the cloak, spread it out, to begin with, on the table, looked at it hard, shook his head, reached out his hand to the window-sill for his snuff-box, adorned with the portrait of some general, though what general is unknown, for the place where the face should have been had been rubbed through by the finger and a square bit of paper had been pasted over it. Having taken a pinch of snuff, Petrovich held up the cloak, and inspected it against the light, and again shook his head. Then he turned it, lining upwards, and shook his head once more. After which he again lifted the general-adorned lid with its bit of pasted paper, and having stuffed his nose with snuff, closed and put away the snuff-box, and said finally, "No, it is impossible to mend it. It is a wretched garment!"

Akaky Akakiyevich's heart sank at these words. "Why is it impossible, Petrovich?" he said, almost in the pleading voice of a child. "All that ails it is, that it is worn on the shoulders. You must have some pieces——"

"Yes, patches could be found, patches are easily found," said Petrovich, "but there's nothing to sew them to. The thing is completely rotten. If you put a needle to it—see, it will give way."

"Let it give way, and you can put on another patch at once."

"But there is nothing to put the patches on to. There's no use in strengthening it. It is too far gone. It's lucky that it's cloth, for, if the wind were to blow, it would fly away."

"Well, strengthen it again. How this, in fact——"

"No," said Petrovich decisively, "there is nothing to be done with it. It's a thoroughly bad job. You'd better, when the cold winter weather comes on, make yourself some gaiters out of it, because stockings are not warm. The Germans invented them in order to make more money." Petrovich loved on all occasions to have a fling at the Germans. "But it is plain you must have a new cloak."

At the word "new" all grew dark before Akaky Akakiyevich's eyes, and everything in the room began to whirl round. The only thing he saw clearly was the general with the paper face on the lid of Petrovich's snuff-box. "A new one?" said he, as if still in a dream. "Why, I have no money for that."

"Yes, a new one," said Petrovich, with barbarous composure.

"Well, if it came to a new one, how—it——"

"You mean how much would it cost?"

"Yes."

"Well, you would have to lay out a hundred and fifty or more," said Petrovich, and pursed up his lips significantly. He liked to produce powerful effects, liked to stun utterly and suddenly, and then to glance sideways to see what face the stunned person would put on the matter.

"A hundred and fifty rubles for a cloak!" shrieked poor Akaky Akakiyevich, perhaps for the first time in his life, for his voice had always been distinguished for softness.

"Yes, sir," said Petrovich, "for any kind of cloak. If you have a marten fur on the collar, or a silk-lined hood, it will mount up to two hundred."

"Petrovich, please," said Akaky Akakiyevich in a beseeching tone, not hearing, and not trying to hear, Petrovich's words, and disregarding all his "effects," "some repairs, in order that it may wear yet a little longer."

"No, it would only be a waste of time and money," said Petrovich. And Akaky Akakiyevich went away after these words, utterly discouraged. But Petrovich stood for some time after his departure, with significantly compressed lips, and without betaking himself to his work, satisfied that he would not be dropped, and an artistic tailor employed.

Akaky Akakiyevich went out into the street as if in a dream. "Such an affair!" he said to himself. "I did not think it had come to—" and then after a pause, he added, "Well, so it is! see what it has come to at last! and I never imagined that it was so!" Then followed a long silence, after which he exclaimed, "Well, so it is! see what already—nothing unexpected that—it would be nothing—what a strange circumstance!" So saying, instead of going home, he went in exactly the opposite direction without suspecting it. On the way, a chimney-sweep bumped up against him, and blackened his shoulder, and a whole hatful of rubbish landed on him from the top of a house which was being built. He did not notice it, and only when he ran against a watchman, who, having planted his halberd beside him, was shaking some snuff from his box into his horny hand, did he recover himself a little, and that because the watchman said, "Why are you poking yourself into a man's very face? Haven't you room enough?" This caused him to look about him, and turn towards home.

There only, he finally began to collect his thoughts, and to survey his position in its clear and actual light, and to argue with himself, sensibly and frankly, as with a reasonable friend, with whom one can discuss private and personal matters. "No," said Akaky Akakiyevich, "it is impossible to reason with Petrovich now. He is that—evidently, his wife has been beating him. I'd better go to him on Sunday morning. After Saturday night he will be a little cross-eyed and sleepy, for he will want to get drunk, and his wife won't give him any money, and at such a time, a ten-kopek piece

in his hand will—he will become more fit to reason with, and then the cloak and that——" Thus argued Akaky Akakiyevich with himself, regained his courage, and waited until the first Sunday, when, seeing from afar that Petrovich's wife had left the house, he went straight to him.

Petrovich's eye was indeed very much askew after Saturday. His head drooped, and he was very sleepy; but for all that, as soon as he knew what it was a question of, it seemed as though Satan jogged his memory. "Impossible," said he. "Please to order a new one." Thereupon Akaky Akakiyevich handed over the ten-kopek piece. "Thank you, sir. I will drink your good health," said Petrovich. "But as for the cloak, don't trouble yourself about it; it is good for nothing. I will make you a capital new one, so let us settle about it now."

Akaky Akakiyevich was still for mending it, but Petrovich would not hear of it, and said, "I shall certainly have to make you a new one, and you may depend upon it that I shall do my best. It may even be, as the fashion goes, that the collar can be fastened by silver hooks under a flap."

Then Akaky Akakiyevich saw that it was impossible to get along without a new cloak, and his spirit sank utterly. How, in fact, was it to be done? Where was the money to come from? He must have some new trousers, and pay a debt of long standing to the shoemaker for putting new tops to his old boots, and he must order three shirts from the seamstress, and a couple of pieces of linen. In short, all his money must be spent. And even if the director should be so kind as to order him to receive forty-five or even fifty rubles instead of forty, it would be a mere nothing, a mere drop in the ocean towards the funds necessary for a cloak, although he knew that Petrovich was often wrong-headed enough to blurt out some outrageous price, so that even his own wife could not refrain from exclaiming, "Have you lost your senses, you fool?" At one time he would not work at any price, and now it was quite likely that he had named a higher sum than the cloak would cost.

But although he knew that Petrovich would undertake to make a cloak for eighty rubles, still, where was he to get the eighty rubles from? He might possibly manage half. Yes, half might be procured, but where was the other half to come from? But the reader must first be told where the first half came from.

Akaky Akakiyevich had a habit of putting, for every ruble he spent, a groschen into a small box, fastened with lock and key, and with a slit in the top for the reception of money. At the end of every half-year he counted over the heap of coppers, and changed it for silver. This he had done for a long time, and in the course of years, the sum had mounted up to over forty rubles. Thus he had one half on hand. But where was he to find the other half? Where was he to get another forty rubles from? Akaky Akakiyevich thought and thought, and decided that it would be necessary to curtail his ordinary expenses, for the space of one year at least, to dispense with tea in the evening, to burn no candles, and, if there was anything which he must do, to go into his landlady's room, and work by her light. When he went into the street, he must walk as lightly as he could, and as cautiously, upon the stones, almost upon tiptoe, in order not to wear his heels down in too short a time. He must give the laundress as little to wash as possible; and, in order not to wear out his clothes, he must take them off as soon as he got home, and wear only his cotton dressing-gown, which had been long and carefully saved.

To tell the truth, it was a little hard for him at first to accustom himself to these deprivations. But he got used to them at length, after a fashion, and all went smoothly. He even got used to being hungry in the evening, but he made up for it by treating himself, so to say, in spirit, by bearing ever in mind the idea of his future cloak. From that time forth, his existence seemed to become, in some way, fuller, as if he were married, or as if some other man lived in him, as if, in fact, he were not alone, and some pleasant friend had consented to travel along life's path with him, the friend being no other than the cloak, with thick wadding and a strong lining incapable of wearing out. He became more lively, and even his character grew firmer, like that of a man who has made up his mind, and set himself a goal. From his face and gait, doubt and indecision, all hesitating and wavering disappeared of themselves. Fire gleamed in his eyes, and occasionally the boldest and most daring ideas flitted through his mind. Why not, for instance, have marten fur on the collar? The thought of this almost made him absent-minded. Once, in copying a letter, he nearly made a mistake, so that he exclaimed almost aloud, "Ugh!" and crossed himself. Once, in the course of every month, he had a conference with Petrovich on the subject of the cloak, where it would be better to buy the cloth, and the colour, and the price. He always returned home satisfied, though troubled,

reflecting that the time would come at last when it could all be bought, and then the cloak made.

The affair progressed more briskly than he had expected. For beyond all his hopes, the director awarded neither forty nor forty-five rubles for Akaky Akakiyevich's share, but sixty. Whether he suspected that Akaky Akakiyevich needed a cloak, or whether it was merely chance, at all events, twenty extra rubles were by this means provided. This circumstance hastened matters. Two or three months more of hunger and Akaky Akakiyevich had accumulated about eighty rubles. His heart, generally so quiet, began to throb. On the first possible day, he went shopping in company with Petrovich. They bought some very good cloth, and at a reasonable rate too, for they had been considering the matter for six months, and rarely let a month pass without their visiting the shops to enquire prices. Petrovich himself said that no better cloth could be had. For lining, they selected a cotton stuff, but so firm and thick, that Petrovich declared it to be better than silk, and even prettier and more glossy. They did not buy the marten fur, because it was, in fact, dear, but in its stead, they picked out the very best of cat-skin which could be found in the shop, and which might, indeed, be taken for marten at a distance.

Petrovich worked at the cloak two whole weeks, for there was a great deal of quilting; otherwise it would have been finished sooner. He charged twelve rubles for the job, it could not possibly have been done for less. It was all sewed with silk, in small, double seams, and Petrovich went over each seam afterwards with his own teeth, stamping in various patterns.

It was—it is difficult to say precisely on what day, but probably the most glorious one in Akaky Akakiyevich's life, when Petrovich at length brought home the cloak. He brought it in the morning, before the hour when it was necessary to start for the department. Never did a cloak arrive so exactly in the nick of time, for the severe cold had set in, and it seemed to threaten to increase. Petrovich brought the cloak himself as befits a good tailor. On his countenance was a significant expression, such as Akaky Akakiyevich had never beheld there. He seemed fully sensible that he had done no small deed, and crossed a gulf separating tailors who put in linings, and execute repairs, from those who make new things. He took the cloak out of the pocket-handkerchief in which he had brought it. The handkerchief was fresh from the laundress, and he put it in his pocket for use. Taking out the cloak, he gazed proudly at it, held it up with both hands, and flung it skilfully over the shoulders of Akaky Akakiyevich. Then he pulled it and fitted it down behind with his hand, and he draped it around Akaky Akakiyevich without buttoning it. Akaky Akakiyevich, like an experienced man, wished to try the sleeves. Petrovich helped him on with them, and it turned out that the sleeves were satisfactory also. In short, the cloak appeared to be perfect, and most seasonable. Petrovich did not neglect to observe that it was only because he lived in a narrow street, and had no signboard, and had known Akaky Akakiyevich so long, that he had made it so cheaply; but that if he had been in business on the Nevsky Prospect, he would have charged seventy-five rubles for the making alone. Akaky Akakiyevich did not care to argue this point with Petrovich. He paid him, thanked him, and set out at once in his new cloak for the department. Petrovich followed him, and pausing in the street, gazed long at the cloak in the distance, after which he went to one side expressly to run through a crooked alley, and emerge again into the street beyond to gaze once more upon the cloak from another point, namely, directly in front.

Meantime Akaky Akakiyevich went on in holiday mood. He was conscious every second of the time that he had a new cloak on his shoulders, and several times he laughed with internal satisfaction. In fact, there were two advantages, one was its warmth, the other its beauty. He saw nothing of the road, but suddenly found himself at the department. He took off his cloak in the ante-room, looked it over carefully, and confided it to the special care of the attendant. It is impossible to say precisely how it was that every one in the department knew at once that Akaky Akakiyevich had a new cloak, and that the "cape" no longer existed. All rushed at the same moment into the ante-room to inspect it. They congratulated him, and said pleasant things to him, so that he began at first to smile, and then to grow ashamed. When all surrounded him, and said that the new cloak must be "christened," and that he must at least give them all a party, Akaky Akakiyevich lost his head completely, and did not know where he stood, what to answer, or how to get out of it. He stood blushing all over for several minutes, trying to assure them with great simplicity that it was not a new cloak, that it was in fact the old "cape."

At length one of the officials, assistant to the head clerk, in order to show that he was not at all proud, and on good terms with his inferiors, said: "So be it, only I will give the party instead of Akaky Akakiyevich; I invite you all to tea with me to-night. It just happens to be my name-day too."

The officials naturally at once offered the assistant clerk their congratulations, and accepted the invitation with pleasure. Akaky Akakiyevich would have declined; but all declared that it was discourteous, that it was simply a sin and a shame, and that he could not possibly refuse. Besides, the notion became pleasant to him when he recollected that he should thereby have a chance of wearing his new cloak in the evening also.

That whole day was truly a most triumphant festival for Akaky Akakiyevich. He returned home in the most happy frame of mind, took off his cloak, and hung it carefully on the wall, admiring afresh the cloth and the lining. Then he brought out his old, worn-out cloak, for comparison. He looked at it, and laughed, so vast was the difference. And long after dinner he laughed again when the condition of the "cape" recurred to his mind. He dined cheerfully, and after dinner wrote nothing, but took his ease for a while on the bed, until it got dark. Then he dressed himself leisurely, put on his cloak, and stepped out into the street.

Where the host lived, unfortunately we cannot say. Our memory begins to fail us badly. The houses and streets in St. Petersburg have become so mixed up in our head that it is very difficult to get anything out of it again in proper form. This much is certain, that the official lived in the best part of the city; and therefore it must have been anything but near to Akaky Akakiyevich's residence. Akaky Akakiyevich was first obliged to traverse a kind of wilderness of deserted, dimly-lighted streets. But in proportion as he approached the official's quarter of the city, the streets became more lively, more populous, and more brilliantly illuminated. Pedestrians began to appear; handsomely dressed ladies were more frequently encountered; the men had otter skin collars to their coats; shabby sleigh-men with their wooden, railed sledges stuck over with brass-headed nails, became rarer; whilst on the other hand, more and more drivers in red velvet caps, lacquered sledges and bear-skin coats began to appear, and carriages with rich hammer-cloths flew swiftly through the streets, their wheels scrunching the snow.

Akaky Akakiyevich gazed upon all this as upon a novel sight. He had not been in the streets during the evening for years. He halted out of curiosity before a shop-window, to look at a picture representing a handsome woman, who had thrown off her shoe, thereby baring her whole foot in a very pretty way; whilst behind her the head of a man with whiskers and a handsome moustache peeped through the doorway of another room. Akaky Akakiyevich shook his head, and laughed, and then went on his way. Why did he laugh? Either because he had met with a thing utterly unknown, but for which every one cherishes, nevertheless, some sort of feeling, or else he thought, like many officials, "Well, those French! What is to be said? If they do go in for anything of that sort, why——" But possibly he did not think at all.

Akaky Akakiyevich at length reached the house in which the head clerk's assistant lodged. He lived in fine style. The staircase was lit by a lamp, his apartment being on the second floor. On entering the vestibule, Akaky Akakiyevich beheld a whole row of goloshes on the floor. Among them, in the centre of the room, stood a samovar, humming and emitting clouds of steam. On the walls hung all sorts of coats and cloaks, among which there were even some with beaver collars, or velvet facings. Beyond, the buzz of conversation was audible, and became clear and loud, when the servant came out with a trayful of empty glasses, cream-jugs and sugar-bowls. It was evident that the officials had arrived long before, and had already finished their first glass of tea.

Akaky Akakiyevich, having hung up his own cloak, entered the inner room. Before him all at once appeared lights, officials, pipes, and card-tables, and he was bewildered by a sound of rapid conversation rising from all the tables, and the noise of moving chairs. He halted very awkwardly in the middle of the room, wondering what he ought to do. But they had seen him. They received him with a shout, and all thronged at once into the ante-room, and there took another look at his cloak. Akaky Akakiyevich, although somewhat confused, was frank-hearted, and could not refrain from rejoicing when he saw how they praised his cloak. Then, of course, they all dropped him and his cloak, and returned, as was proper, to the tables set out for whist.

All this, the noise, the talk, and the throng of people, was rather overwhelming to Akaky Akakiyevich. He simply did not know where he stood, or where to put his hands, his feet, and his whole body. Finally he sat down by the players, looked at the cards, gazed at the face of one and another, and after a while began to gape, and to feel that it was wearisome, the more so, as the hour was already long past when he usually went to bed. He wanted to take leave of the host, but they would not let him go, saying that he must not fail to drink a glass of champagne, in honour of his new garment. In the course of an hour, supper, consisting of vegetable salad, cold veal, pastry, confectioner's pies, and champagne, was served. They made Akaky Akakiyevich drink two glasses of champagne, after which he felt things grow livelier.

Still, he could not forget that it was twelve o'clock, and that he should have been at home long ago. In order that the host might not think of some excuse for detaining him, he stole out of the room quickly, sought out, in the ante-room, his cloak, which, to his sorrow, he found lying on the floor, brushed it, picked off every speck upon it, put it on his shoulders, and descended the stairs to the street.

In the street all was still bright. Some petty shops, those permanent clubs of servants and all sorts of folks, were open. Others were shut, but, nevertheless, showed a streak of light the whole length of the door-crack, indicating that they were not yet free of company, and that probably some domestics, male and female, were finishing their stories and conversations, whilst leaving their masters in complete ignorance as to their whereabouts. Akaky Akakiyevich went on in a happy frame of mind. He even started to run, without knowing why, after some lady, who flew past like a flash of lightning. But he stopped short, and went on very quietly as before, wondering why he had quickened his pace. Soon there spread before him those deserted streets which are not cheerful in the daytime, to say nothing of the evening. Now they were even more dim and lonely. The lanterns began to grow rarer, oil, evidently, had been less liberally supplied. Then came wooden houses and fences. Not a soul anywhere; only the snow sparkled in the streets, and mournfully veiled the low-roofed cabins with their closed shutters. He approached the spot where the street crossed a vast square with houses barely visible on its farther side, a square which seemed a fearful desert.

Afar, a tiny spark glimmered from some watchman's-box, which seemed to stand on the edge of the world. Akaky Akakiyevich's cheerfulness diminished at this point in a marked degree. He entered the square, not without an involuntary sensation of fear, as though his heart warned him of some evil. He glanced back, and on both sides it was like a sea about him. "No, it is better not to look," he thought, and went on, closing his eyes.

When he opened them, to see whether he was near the end of the square, he suddenly beheld, standing just before his very nose, some bearded individuals of precisely what sort, he could not make out. All grew dark before his eyes, and his heart throbbed.

"Of course, the cloak is mine!" said one of them in a loud voice, seizing hold of his collar. Akaky Akakiyevich was about to shout "Help!" when the second man thrust a fist, about the size of an official's head, at his very mouth, muttering, "Just you dare to scream!"

Akaky Akakiyevich felt them strip off his cloak, and give him a kick. He fell headlong upon the snow, and felt no more.

In a few minutes he recovered consciousness, and rose to his feet, but no one was there. He felt that it was cold in the square, and that his cloak was gone. He began to shout, but his voice did not appear to reach the outskirts of the square. In despair, but without ceasing to shout, he started at a run across the square, straight towards the watch-box, beside which stood the watchman, leaning on his halberd, and apparently curious to know what kind of a customer was running towards him shouting. Akaky Akakiyevich ran up to him, and began in a sobbing voice to shout that he was asleep, and attended to nothing, and did not see when a man was robbed. The watchman replied that he had seen two men stop him in the middle of the square, but supposed that they were friends of his, and that, instead of scolding vainly, he had better go to the police on the morrow, so that they might make a search for whoever had stolen the cloak.

Akaky Akakiyevich ran home and arrived in a state of complete disorder, his hair which grew very thinly upon his temples and the back of his head all tousled, his body, arms and legs, covered with snow. The old woman, who was mistress of his lodgings, on hearing a terrible knocking, sprang hastily from her bed, and, with only one shoe on, ran to open the door, pressing the sleeve of her chemise to her bosom out of modesty. But when she had opened it, she fell back on beholding Akaky Akakiyevich in such a condition. When he told her about the affair, she clasped her hands, and said that he must go straight to the district chief of police, for his subordinate would turn up his nose, promise well, and drop the matter there. The very best thing to do, therefore, would be to go to the district chief, whom she knew, because Finnish Anna, her former cook, was now nurse at his house. She often saw him passing the house, and he was at church every Sunday, praying, but at the same time gazing cheerfully at everybody; so that he must be a good man, judging from all appearances. Having listened to this opinion, Akaky Akakiyevich betook himself sadly to his room. And how he spent the night there, any one who can put himself in another's place may readily imagine.

Early in the morning, he presented himself at the district chief's, but was told the official was asleep. He went again at ten and was again informed that he was asleep. At eleven, and they said, "The superintendent is not at home." At dinner time, and the clerks in the ante-room would not admit him on any terms, and insisted upon knowing his business. So that at last, for once in his life, Akaky Akakiyevich felt an inclination to show some spirit, and said curtly that he must see the chief in person, that they ought not to presume to refuse him entrance, that he came from the department of justice, and that when he complained of them, they would see.

The clerks dared make no reply to this, and one of them went to call the chief, who listened to the strange story of the theft of the coat. Instead of directing his attention to the principal points of the matter, he began to question Akaky Akakiyevich. Why was he going home so late? Was he in the habit of doing so, or had he been to some disorderly house? So that Akaky Akakiyevich got thoroughly confused, and left him, without knowing whether the affair of his cloak was in proper train or not.

All that day, for the first time in his life, he never went near the department. The next day he made his appearance, very pale, and in his old cape, which had become even more shabby. The news of the robbery of the cloak touched many, although there were some officials present who never lost an opportunity, even such a one as the present, of ridiculing Akaky Akakiyevich. They decided to make a collection for him on the spot, but the officials had already spent a great deal in subscribing for the director's portrait, and for some book, at the suggestion of the head of that division, who was a friend of the author; and so the sum was trifling.

One of them, moved by pity, resolved to help Akaky Akakiyevich with some good advice, at least, and told him that he ought not to go to the police, for although it might happen that a police-officer, wishing to win the approval of his superiors, might hunt up the cloak by some means, still, his cloak would remain in the possession of the police if he did not offer legal proof that it belonged to him. The best thing for him, therefore, would be to apply to a certain prominent personage; since this prominent personage, by entering into relation with the proper persons, could greatly expedite the matter.

As there was nothing else to be done, Akaky Akakiyevich decided to go to the prominent personage. What was the exact official position of the prominent personage, remains unknown to this day. The reader must know that the prominent personage had but recently become a prominent personage, having up to that time been only an insignificant person. Moreover, his present position was not considered prominent in comparison with others still more so. But there is always a circle of people to whom what is insignificant in the eyes of others, is important enough. Moreover, he strove to increase his importance by sundry devices. For instance, he managed to have the inferior officials meet him on the staircase when he entered upon his service; no one was to presume to come directly to him, but the strictest etiquette must be observed; the collegiate recorder must make a report to the government secretary, the government secretary to the titular councillor, or whatever other man was proper, and all business must come before him in this manner. In Holy Russia, all is thus contaminated with the love of imitation; every man imitates and copies his superior. They even say that a certain titular councillor, when promoted to the head of some small separate office, immediately partitioned off a private room for himself, called it the audience chamber, and posted at the door a lackey with red collar and braid, who grasped the handle of the door, and opened to all comers, though the audience chamber would hardly hold an ordinary writing table.

The manners and customs of the prominent personage were grand and imposing, but rather exaggerated. The main foundation of his system was strictness. "Strictness, strictness, and always strictness!" he generally said; and at the last word he looked significantly into the face of the person to whom he spoke. But there was no necessity for this, for the halfscore of subordinates, who formed the entire force of the office, were properly afraid. On catching sight of him afar off, they left their work, and waited, drawn up in line, until he had passed through the room. His ordinary converse with his inferiors smacked of sternness, and consisted chiefly of three phrases: "How dare you?" "Do you know whom you are speaking to?" "Do you realise who is standing before you?"

Otherwise he was a very kind-hearted man, good to his comrades, and ready to oblige. But the rank of general threw him completely off his balance. On receiving any one of that rank, he became confused, lost his way, as it were, and never knew what to do. If he chanced to be amongst his equals, he was still a very nice kind of man, a very good fellow in many respects, and not stupid, but the very moment that he found himself in the society of people but one rank lower than himself, he became silent. And his situation aroused sympathy, the more so, as he felt himself that he might have been making an incomparably better use of his time. In his eyes, there was sometimes visible a desire to join some interesting conversation or group, but he was kept back by the thought, "Would it not be a very great condescension on his part? Would it not be familiar? And would he not thereby lose his importance?" And in consequence of such reflections, he always remained in the same dumb state, uttering from time to time a few monosyllabic sounds, and thereby earning the name of the most wearisome of men.

To this prominent personage Akaky Akakiyevich presented himself, and this at the most unfavourable time for himself, though opportune for the prominent personage. The prominent personage was in his cabinet, conversing very gaily with an old acquaintance and companion of his childhood, whom he had not seen for several years, and who had just arrived, when it was announced to him that a person named Bashmachkin had come. He asked abruptly, "Who is he?"—"Some official," he was informed. "Ah, he can wait! This is no time for him to call," said the important man.

It must be remarked here that the important man lied outrageously. He had said all he had to say to his friend long before, and the conversation had been interspersed for some time with very long pauses, during which they merely slapped each other on the leg, and said, "You think so, Ivan Abramovich!" "Just so, Stepan Varlamovich!" Nevertheless, he ordered that the official should be kept waiting, in order to show his friend, a man who had not been in the service for a long time, but had lived at home in the country, how long officials had to wait in his ante-room.

At length, having talked himself completely out, and more than that, having had his fill of pauses, and smoked a cigar in a very comfortable armchair with reclining back, he suddenly seemed to recollect, and said to the secretary, who stood by the door with papers of reports, "So it seems that there is an official waiting to see me. Tell him that he may come in." On perceiving Akaky

Akakiyevich's modest mien and his worn uniform, he turned abruptly to him, and said, "What do you want?" in a curt hard voice, which he had practised in his room in private, and before the looking-glass, for a whole week before being raised to his present rank.

Akaky Akakiyevich, who was already imbued with a due amount of fear, became somewhat confused, and as well as his tongue would permit, explained, with a rather more frequent addition than usual of the word "that" that his cloak was quite new, and had been stolen in the most inhuman manner; that he had applied to him, in order that he might, in some way, by his intermediation—that he might enter into correspondence with the chief of police, and find the cloak.

For some inexplicable reason, this conduct seemed familiar to the prominent personage.

"What, my dear sir!" he said abruptly, "are you not acquainted with etiquette? To whom have you come? Don't you know how such matters are managed? You should first have presented a petition to the office. It would have gone to the head of the department, then to the chief of the division, then it would have been handed over to the secretary, and the secretary would have given it to me."

"But, your excellency," said Akaky Akakiyevich, trying to collect his small handful of wits, and conscious at the same time that he was perspiring terribly, "I, your excellency, presumed to trouble you because secretaries—are an untrustworthy race."

"What, what, what!" said the important personage. "Where did you get such courage? Where did you get such ideas? What impudence towards their chiefs and superiors has spread among the young generation!" The prominent personage apparently had not observed that Akaky Akakiyevich was already in the neighbourhood of fifty. If he could be called a young man, it must have been in comparison with some one who was seventy. "Do you know to whom you are speaking? Do you realise who is standing before you? Do you realise it? Do you realise it, I ask you!" Then he stamped his foot, and raised his voice to such a pitch that it would have frightened even a different man from Akaky Akakiyevich.

Akaky Akakiyevich's senses failed him. He staggered, trembled in every limb, and, if the porters had not run in to support him, would have fallen to the floor. They carried him out insensible. But the prominent personage, gratified that the effect should have surpassed his expectations, and quite intoxicated with the thought that his word could even deprive a man of his senses, glanced sideways at his friend in order to see how he looked upon this, and perceived, not without satisfaction, that his friend was in a most uneasy frame of mind, and even beginning on his part, to feel a trifle frightened.

Akaky Akakiyevich could not remember how he descended the stairs, and got into the street. He felt neither his hands nor feet. Never in his life had he been so rated by any high official, let alone a strange one. He went staggering on through the snow-storm, which was blowing in the streets, with his mouth wide open. The wind, in St. Petersburg fashion, darted upon him from all quarters, and down every cross-street. In a twinkling it had blown a quinsy into his throat, and he reached home unable to utter a word. His throat was swollen, and he lay down on his bed. So powerful is sometimes a good scolding!

The next day a violent fever developed. Thanks to the generous assistance of the St. Petersburg climate, the malady progressed more rapidly than could have been expected, and when the doctor arrived, he found, on feeling the sick man's pulse, that there was nothing to be done, except to prescribe a poultice, so that the patient might not be left entirely without the beneficent aid of medicine. But at the same time, he predicted his end in thirty-six hours. After this he turned to the landlady, and said, "And as for you, don't waste your time on him. Order his pine coffin now, for an oak one will be too expensive for him."

Did Akaky Akakiyevich hear these fatal words? And if he heard them, did they produce any overwhelming effect upon him? Did he lament the bitterness of his life?—We know not, for he continued in a delirious condition. Visions incessantly appeared to him, each stranger than the other. Now he saw Petrovich, and ordered him to make a cloak, with some traps for robbers, who seemed to him to be always under the bed; and he cried every moment to the landlady to pull one of them from under his coverlet. Then he enquired why his old mantle hung before him when he had a new cloak. Next he fancied that he was standing before the prominent person, listening to a thorough setting-down and saying, "Forgive me, your excellency!" but at last he began to curse, uttering the most horrible words, so that his aged landlady crossed herself, never in her life having heard anything of the kind from him, and more so, as these words followed directly after the words "your excellency." Later on he talked utter nonsense, of which nothing could be made, all that was evident being that these incoherent words and thoughts hovered ever about one thing, his cloak.

At length poor Akaky Akakiyevich breathed his last. They sealed up neither his room nor his effects, because, in the first place, there were no heirs, and, in the second, there was very little to inherit beyond a bundle of goose-quills, a quire of white official paper, three pairs of socks, two or three buttons which had burst off his trousers, and the mantle already known to the reader. To whom all this fell, God knows. I confess that the person who told me this tale took no interest in it. They carried Akaky Akakiyevich out, and buried him.

And St. Petersburg was left without Akaky Akakiyevich, as though he had never lived there. A being disappeared, who was protected by none, dear to none, interesting to none, and who never even attracted to himself the attention of those students of human nature who omit no opportunity of thrusting a pin through a common fly and examining it under the microscope. A being who bore meekly the jibes of the department, and went to his grave without having done one unusual deed, but to whom, nevertheless, at the close of his life, appeared a bright visitant in the form of a cloak, which momentarily cheered his poor life, and upon him, thereafter, an intolerable misfortune descended, just as it descends upon the heads of the mighty of this world!

Several days after his death, the porter was sent from the department to his lodgings, with an order for him to present himself there immediately, the chief commanding it. But the porter had to return unsuccessful, with the answer that he could not come; and to the question, "Why?" replied, "Well, because he is dead! he was buried four days ago." In this manner did they hear of Akaky Akakiyevich's death at the department. And the next day a new official sat in his place, with a handwriting by no means so upright, but more inclined and slanting.

But who could have imagined that this was not really the end of Akaky Akakiyevich, that he was destined to raise a commotion after death, as if in compensation for his utterly insignificant life? But so it happened, and our poor story unexpectedly gains a fantastic ending.

A rumour suddenly spread through St. Petersburg, that a dead man had taken to appearing on the Kalinkin Bridge, and its vicinity, at night in the form of an official seeking a stolen cloak, and that, under the pretext of its being the stolen cloak, he dragged, without regard to rank or calling,

every one's cloak from his shoulders, be it catskin, beaver, fox, bear, sable, in a word, every sort of fur and skin which men adopted for their covering. One of the department officials saw the dead man with his own eyes, and immediately recognised in him Akaky Akakiyevich. This, however, inspired him with such terror, that he ran off with all his might, and therefore did not scan the dead man closely, but only saw how the latter threatened him from afar with his finger. Constant complaints poured in from all quarters, that the backs and shoulders, not only of titular but even of court councillors, were exposed to the danger of a cold, on account of the frequent dragging off of their cloaks.

Arrangements were made by the police to catch the corpse, alive or dead, at any cost, and punish him as an example to others, in the most severe manner. In this they nearly succeeded, for a watchman, on guard in Kirinshkin Lane, caught the corpse by the collar on the very scene of his evil deeds, when attempting to pull off the frieze cloak of a retired musician. Having seized him by the collar, he summoned, with a shout, two of his comrades, whom he enjoined to hold him fast, while he himself felt for a moment in his boot, in order to draw out his snuff-box, and refresh his frozen nose. But the snuff was of a sort which even a corpse could not endure. The watchman having closed his right nostril with his finger, had no sooner succeeded in holding half a handful up to the left, than the corpse sneezed so violently that he completely filled the eyes of all three. While they raised their hands to wipe them, the dead man vanished completely, so that they positively did not know whether they had actually had him in their grip at all. Thereafter the watchmen conceived such a terror of dead men that they were afraid even to seize the living, and only screamed from a distance. "Hey, there! go your way!" So the dead official began to appear even beyond the Kalinkin Bridge, causing no little terror to all timid people.

But we have totally neglected that certain prominent personage who may really be considered as the cause of the fantastic turn taken by this true history. First of all, justice compels us to say, that after the departure of poor, annihilated Akaky Akakiyevich, he felt something like remorse. Suffering was unpleasant to him, for his heart was accessible to many good impulses, in spite of the fact that his rank often prevented his showing his true self. As soon as his friend had left his cabinet, he began to think about poor Akaky Akakiyevich. And from that day forth, poor Akaky Akakiyevich, who could not bear up under an official reprimand, recurred to his mind almost every day. The thought troubled him to such an extent, that a week later he even resolved to send an official to him, to learn whether he really could assist him. And when it was reported to him that Akaky Akakiyevich had died suddenly of fever, he was startled, hearkened to the reproaches of his conscience, and was out of sorts for the whole day.

Wishing to divert his mind in some way and drive away the disagreeable impression, he set out that evening for one of his friends' houses, where he found quite a large party assembled. What was better, nearly every one was of the same rank as himself, so that he need not feel in the least constrained. This had a marvellous effect upon his mental state. He grew expansive, made himself agreeable in conversation, in short, he passed a delightful evening. After supper he drank a couple of glasses of champagne—not a bad recipe for cheerfulness, as every one knows. The champagne inclined him to various adventures, and he determined not to return home, but to go and see a certain well-known lady, of German extraction, Karolina Ivanovna, a lady, it appears, with whom he was on a very friendly footing.

It must be mentioned that the prominent personage was no longer a young man, but a good husband and respected father of a family. Two sons, one of whom was already in the service, and a good-looking, sixteen-year-old daughter, with a slightly arched but pretty little nose, came every morning to kiss his hand and say, "*Bon jour,* papa." His wife, a still fresh and good-looking woman, first gave him her hand to kiss, and then, reversing the procedure, kissed his. But the prominent personage, though perfectly satisfied in his domestic relations, considered it stylish to have a friend in another quarter of the city. This friend was scarcely prettier or younger than his wife; but there are such puzzles in the world, and it is not our place to judge them. So the important personage descended the stairs, stepped into his sledge, said to the coachman, "To Karolina Ivanovna's," and, wrapping himself luxuriously in his warm cloak, found himself in that delightful frame of mind than which a Russian can conceive nothing better, namely, when you think of nothing yourself, yet when the thoughts creep into your mind of their own accord, each more agreeable than the other, giving you no trouble either to drive them away, or seek them. Fully satisfied, he recalled all the gay features of the evening just passed and all

the *mots* which had made the little circle laugh. Many of them he repeated in a low voice, and found them quite as funny as before; so it is not surprising that he should laugh heartily at them. Occasionally, however, he was interrupted by gusts of wind, which, coming suddenly, God knows whence or why, cut his face, drove masses of snow into it, filled out his cloak-collar like a sail, or suddenly blew it over his head with supernatural force, and thus caused him constant trouble to disentangle himself.

Suddenly the important personage felt some one clutch him firmly by the collar. Turning round, he perceived a man of short stature, in an old, worn uniform, and recognised, not without terror, Akaky Akakiyevich. The official's face was white as snow, and looked just like a corpse's. But the horror of the important personage transcended all bounds when he saw the dead man's mouth open, and heard it utter the following remarks, while it breathed upon him the terrible odour of the grave: "Ah, here you are at last! I have you, that—by the collar! I need your cloak. You took no trouble about mine, but reprimanded me. So now give up your own."

The pallid prominent personage almost died of fright. Brave as he was in the office and in the presence of inferiors generally, and although, at the sight of his manly form and appearance, every one said, "Ugh! how much character he has!" at this crisis, he, like many possessed of an heroic exterior, experienced such terror, that, not without cause, he began to fear an attack of illness. He flung his cloak hastily from his shoulders and shouted to his coachman in an unnatural voice, "Home at full speed!" The coachman, hearing the tone which is generally employed at critical moments, and even accompanied by something much more tangible, drew his head down between his shoulders in case of an emergency, flourished his whip, and flew on like an arrow. In a little more than six minutes the prominent personage was at the entrance of his own house. Pale, thoroughly scared, and cloakless, he went home instead of to Karolina Ivanovna's, reached his room somehow or other, and passed the night in the direst distress; so that the next morning over their tea, his daughter said, "You are very pale to-day, papa." But papa remained silent, and said not a word to any one of what had happened to him, where he had been, or where he had intended to go.

This occurrence made a deep impression upon him. He even began to say, "How dare you? Do you realise who is standing before you?" less frejuently to the under-officials, and, if he did utter the words, it was only after first having learned the bearings of the matter. But the most noteworthy point was, that from that day forward the apparition of the dead official ceased to be seen. Evidently the prominent personage's cloak just fitted his shoulders. At all events, no more instances of his dragging cloaks from people's shoulders were heard of. But many active and solicitous persons could by no means reassure themselves, and asserted that the dead official still showed himself in distant parts of the city.

In fact, one watchman in Kolomen saw with his own eyes the apparition come from behind a house. But the watchman was not a strong man, so he was afraid to arrest him, and followed him in the dark, until, at length, the apparition looked round, paused, and enquired, "What do you want?" at the same time showing such a fist as is never seen on living men. The watchman said, "Nothing," and turned back instantly. But the apparition was much too tall, wore huge moustaches, and, directing its steps apparently towards the Obukhov Bridge, disappeared in the darkness of the night.

IVAN SERGYEEVICH TURGENEV

Biryuk

I was coming back from hunting one evening alone in a racing droshky. I was six miles from home; my good trotting mare galloped bravely along the dusty road, pricking up her ears with an occasional snort; my weary dog stuck close to the hind-wheels, as though he were fastened there. A tempest was coming on. In front, a huge, purplish storm-cloud slowly rose from behind the forest; long gray rain-clouds flew over my head and to meet me; the willows stirred and whispered restlessly. The suffocating heat changed suddenly to a damp chillness; the darkness rapidly thickened. I gave the horse a lash with the reins, descended a steep slope, pushed across a dry water-course overgrown with brushwood, mounted the hill, and drove into the forest. The road ran before me, bending between thick hazel bushes, now enveloped in darkness; I advanced with difficulty. The droshky jumped up and down over the hard roots of the ancient oaks and limes, which were continually intersected by deep ruts—the tracks of cart wheels; my horse began to stumble. A violent wind suddenly began to roar overhead; the trees blustered; big drops of rain fell with slow tap and splash on the leaves; there came a flash of lightning and a clap of thunder. The rain fell in torrents. I went on a step or so, and soon was forced to stop; my horse foundered; I could not see an inch before me. I managed to take refuge somehow in a spreading bush. Crouching down and covering my face, I waited patiently for the storm to blow over, when suddenly, in a flash of lightning, I saw a tall figure on the road. I began to stare intently in that direction—the figure seemed to have sprung out of the ground near my droshky.

"Who's that?" inquired a ringing voice.

"Why, who are you?"

"I'm the forester here."

I mentioned my name.

"Oh, I know! Are you on your way home?"

"Yes. But, you see, in such a storm . . ."

"Yes, there is a storm," replied the voice.

A pale flash of lightning lit up the forester from head to foot; a brief crashing clap of thunder followed at once upon it. The rain lashed with redoubled force.

"It won't be over just directly," the forester went on.

"What's to be done?"

"I'll take you to my hut, if you like," he said abruptly.

"That would be a service."

"Please to take your seat."

He went up to the mare's head, took her by the bit, and pulled her up. We set off. I held on to the cushion of the droshky, which rocked "like a boat on the sea," and called my dog. My poor mare splashed with difficulty through the mud, slipped and stumbled; the forester hovered before the

Biryuk. Translated by Constance Garnett. By permission of the Macmillan Co. Ivan Sergyeevich Turgenev (1818-1883) was educated at Moscow and St. Petersburg, and occupied official posts until 1854, after which he lived in western Europe.

shafts to right and to left like a ghost. We drove rather a long while; at last my guide stopped. "Here we are home, sir," he observed in a quiet voice. The gate creaked; some puppies barked a welcome. I raised my head, and in a flash of lightning I made out a small hut in the middle of a large yard, fenced in with hurdles. From the one little window there was a dim light. The forester led his horse up to the steps and knocked at the door. "Coming, coming!" we heard in a little shrill voice; there was the patter of bare feet, the bolt creaked, and a girl of twelve, in a little old smock tied round the waist with list, appeared in the doorway with a lantern in her hand.

"Show the gentleman a light," he said to her, "and I will put your droshky in the shed."

The little girl glanced at me, and went into the hut. I followed her.

The forester's hut consisted of one room, smoky, low-pitched, and empty, without curtains or partition. A tattered sheepskin hung on the wall. On the bench lay a single-barreled gun; in the corner lay a heap of rags; two great pots stood near the oven. A pine splinter was burning on the table, flickering up and dying down mournfully. In the very middle of the hut hung a cradle, suspended from the end of a long horizontal pole. The little girl put out the lantern, sat down on a tiny stool, and with her right hand began swinging the cradle, while with her left she attended to the smoldering pine splinter. I looked round—my heart sank within me: it's not cheering to go into a peasant's hut at night. The baby in the cradle breathed hard and fast.

"Are you all alone here?" I asked the little girl.

"Yes," she uttered, hardly audibly.

"You're the forester's daughter?"

"Yes," she whispered.

The door creaked, and the forester, bending his head, stepped across the threshold. He lifted the lantern from the floor, went up to the table, and lighted a candle.

"I dare say you're not used to the splinter light?" said he, and he shook back his curls.

I looked at him. Rarely has it been my fortune to behold such a comely creature. He was tall, broad-shouldered, and in marvelous proportion. His powerful muscles stood out in strong relief under his wet homespun shirt. A curly, black beard hid half of his stern and manly face; small brown eyes looked out boldly from under broad eyebrows which met in the middle. He stood before me, his arms held lightly akimbo.

I thanked him, and asked his name.

"My name's Foma," he answered, "and my nickname's Biryuk" (i.e., Wolf).

"Oh, you're Biryuk."

I looked with redoubled curiosity at him. From my Yermolaï and others I had often heard stories about the forester Biryuk, whom all the peasants of the surrounding districts feared as they feared fire. According to them there had never been such a master of his business in the world before. "He won't let you carry off a handful of brushwood; he'll drop upon you like a fall of snow, whatever time it may be, even in the middle of the night, and you needn't think of resisting him—he's strong, and as cunning as the devil. . . . And there's no getting at him, anyhow; neither by brandy nor by money; there's no snare he'll walk into. More than once good folks have planned to put him out of the world, but no—it's never come off."

That was how the neighboring peasants spoke of Biryuk.

"So you're Biryuk," I repeated; "I've heard talk of you, brother. They say you show no mercy to anyone."

"I do my duty," he answered grimly; "it's not right to eat the master's bread for nothing."

He took an ax from his girdle and began splitting splinters.

"Have you no wife?" I asked him.

"No," he answered, with a vigorous sweep of the ax.

"She's dead, I suppose?"

"No . . . yes . . . she's dead," he added, and turned away. I was silent; he raised his eyes and looked at me.

"She ran away with a traveling peddler," he brought out with a bitter smile. The little girl hung her head; the baby waked up and began crying; the little girl went to the cradle. "There, give it him," said Biryuk, thrusting a dirty feeding-bottle into her hand. "Him, too, she abandoned," he went on in an undertone, pointing to the baby. He went up to the door, stopped, and turned round.

"A gentleman like you," he began, "wouldn't care for our bread, I dare say, and except bread, I've—"

"I'm not hungry."

"Well, that's for you to say. I would have heated the samovar, but I've no tea. . . . I'll go and see how your horse is getting on."

He went out and slammed the door. I looked

round again. The hut struck me as more melancholy than ever. The bitter smell of stale smoke choked my breathing unpleasantly. The little girl did not stir from her place, and did not raise her eyes; from time to time she jogged the cradle, and timidly pulled her slipping smock up on to her shoulder; her bare legs hung motionless.

"What's your name?" I asked her.

"Ulita," she said, her mournful little face drooping more than ever.

The forester came in and sat down on the bench.

"The storm's passing over," he observed, after a brief silence; "if you wish it, I will guide you out of the forest."

I got up; Biryuk took his gun and examined the firepan.

"What's that for?" I inquired.

"There's mischief in the forest. . . . They're cutting a tree down on Mares' Ravine," he added, in reply to my look of inquiry.

"Could you hear it from here?"

"I can hear it outside."

We went out together. The rain had ceased. Heavy masses of storm-cloud were still huddled in the distance; from time to time there were long flashes of lightning; but here and there overhead the dark blue sky was already visible; stars twinkled through the swiftly flying clouds. The outline of the trees, drenched with rain, and stirred by the wind, began to stand out in the darkness. We listened. The forester took off his cap and bent his head. . . . "Th— . . . there!" he said suddenly, and he stretched out his hand: "see what a night he's pitched on." I had heard nothing but the rustle of the leaves. Biryuk led the mare out of the shed. "But, perhaps," he added aloud, "this way I shall miss him." "I'll go with you . . . if you like?" "Certainly," he answered, and he backed the horse in again; "we'll catch him in a trice, and then I'll take you. Let's be off." We started, Biryuk in front, I following him. Heaven only knows how he found out his way, but he only stopped once or twice, and then merely to listen to the strokes of the ax. "There," he muttered, "do you hear? do you hear?" "Why, where?" Biryuk shrugged his shoulders. We went down into the ravine; the wind was still for an instant; the rhythmical strokes reached my hearing distinctly. Biryuk glanced at me and shook his head. We went farther through the wet bracken and nettles. A slow muffled crash was heard. . . .

"He's felled it," muttered Biryuk. Meantime the sky had grown clearer and clearer; there was a faint light in the forest. We clambered at last out of the ravine.

"Wait here a little," the forester whispered to me. He bent down, and, raising his gun above his head, vanished among the bushes. I began listening with strained attention. Across the continual roar of the wind faint sounds from close by reached me; there was a cautious blow of an ax on the brushwood, the crash of wheels, the snort of a horse. . . .

"Where are you off to? Stop!" the iron voice of Biryuk thundered suddenly. Another voice was heard in a pitiful shriek, like a trapped hare. . . . A struggle was beginning.

"No, no, you've made a mistake," Biryuk declared, panting; "you're not going to get off. . . ." I rushed in the direction of the noise, and ran up to the scene of the conflict, stumbling at every step. A felled tree lay on the ground, and near it Biryuk was busily engaged holding the thief down and binding his hands behind his back with a kerchief. I came closer. Biryuk got up and set him on his feet. I saw a peasant drenched with rain, in tatters, and with a long, disheveled beard. A sorry little nag, half covered with a stiff mat, was standing by, together with a rough cart. The forester did not utter a word; the peasant too was silent; his head was shaking.

"Let him go," I whispered in Biryuk's ears; "I'll pay for the tree."

Without a word Biryuk took the horse by the mane with his left hand; in his right he held the thief by the belt. "Now turn round, you rat!" he said grimly.

"The bit of an ax there, take it," muttered the peasant.

"No reason to lose it, certainly," said the forester, and he picked up the ax. We started. I walked behind. . . . The rain began sprinkling again, and soon fell in torrents. With difficulty we made our way to the hut. Biryuk pushed the captured horse into the middle of the yard, led the peasant into the room, loosened the knot in the kerchief, and made him sit down in a corner. The little girl, who had fallen asleep near the oven, jumped up and began staring at us in silent terror. I sat down on the locker.

"Ugh, what a downpour!" remarked the forester; "you will have to wait till it's over. Won't you lie down?"

"Thanks."

"I would have shut him in the store loft, on your

honor's account," he went on, indicating the peasant; "but you see the bolt—"

"Leave him here; don't touch him," I interrupted.

The peasant stole a glance at me from under his brows. I vowed inwardly to set the poor wretch free, come what might. He sat without stirring on the locker. By the light of the lantern I could make out his worn, wrinkled face, his overhanging yellow eyebrows, his restless eyes, his thin limbs. . . . The little girl lay down on the floor, just at his feet, and again dropped asleep. Biryuk sat at the table, his head in his hands. A cricket chirped in the corner . . . the rain pattered on the roof and streamed down the windows; we were all silent.

"Foma Kuzmitch," said the peasant suddenly in a thick, broken voice; "Foma Kuzmitch!"

"What is it?"

"Let me go."

Biryuk made no answer.

"Let me go . . . hunger drove me to it; let me go."

"I know you," retorted the forester severely; "your set's all alike—all thieves."

"Let me go," repeated the peasant. "Our manager . . . we're ruined, that's what it is—let me go!"

"Ruined, indeed! . . . Nobody need steal."

"Let me go, Foma Kuzmitch. . . . Don't destroy me. Your manager, you know yourself, will have no mercy on me; that's what it is."

Biryuk turned away. The peasant was shivering as though he were in the throes of fever. His head was shaking, and his breathing came in broken gasps.

"Let me go," he repeated with mournful desperation. "Let me go; by God, let me go! I'll pay; see, by God, I will! By God, it was through hunger! . . . the little ones are crying, you know yourself. It's hard for us, see."

"You needn't go stealing, for all that."

"My little horse," the peasant went on, "my poor little horse, at least . . . our only beast . . . let it go."

"I tell you, I can't. I'm not a free man; I'm made responsible. You oughtn't to be spoilt, either."

"Let me go! It's through want, Foma Kuzmitch, want—and nothing else—let me go!"

"I know you!"

"Oh, let me go!"

"Ugh, what's the use of talking to you! sit quiet, or else you'll catch it. Don't you see the gentleman, hey?"

The poor wretch hung his head. . . . Biryuk yawned and laid his head on the table. The rain still persisted. I was waiting to see what would happen.

Suddenly the peasant stood erect. His eyes were glittering, and his face flushed dark red. "Come, then, here; strike yourself, here," he began, his eyes puckering up and the corners of his mouth dropping; "come, cursed destroyer of men's souls! drink Christian blood, drink."

The forester turned round.

"I'm speaking to you, Asiatic, blood-sucker, you!"

"Are you drunk, or what, to set to being abusive?" began the forester, puzzled. "Are you out of your senses, hey?"

"Drunk! not at your expense, cursed destroyer of souls—brute, brute, brute!"

"Ah, you—I'll show you!"

"What's that to me? It's all one; I'm done for; what can I do without a home? Kill me—it's the same in the end; whether it's through hunger or like this—it's all one. Ruin us all—wife, children . . . kill us all at once. But, wait a bit, we'll get at you!"

Biryuk got up.

"Kill me, kill me," the peasant went on in savage tones; "kill me; come, come, kill me. . . ." (The little girl jumped up hastily from the ground and stared at him.) "Kill me, kill me!"

"Silence!" thundered the forester, and he took two steps forward.

"Stop, Foma, stop," I shouted; "let him go. . . . Peace be with him."

"I won't be silent," the luckless wretch went on. "It's all the same—ruin, anyway—you destroyer of souls, you brute; you've not come to ruin yet. . . . But wait a bit; you won't have long to boast of; they'll wring your neck; wait a bit!"

Biryuk clutched him by the shoulder. I rushed to help the peasant. . . .

"Don't touch him, master!" the forester shouted to me.

I should not have feared his threats, and already had my fist in the air; but to my intense amazement, with one pull he tugged the kerchief off the peasant's elbows, took him by the scruff of the neck, thrust his cap over his eyes, opened the door, and shoved him out.

"Go to the devil with your horse!" he shouted after him; "but mind, next time. . . ."

He came back into the hut and began rummaging in the corner.

"Well, Biryuk," I said at last, "you've astonished me; I see you're a splendid fellow."

"Oh, stop that, master," he cut me short with an air of vexation; "please don't speak of it. But I'd better see you on your way now," he added; "I suppose you won't wait for this little rain. . . ."

In the yard there was the rattle of the wheels of the peasant's cart.

"He's off, then!" he muttered; "but next time!"

Half an hour later he parted from me at the edge of the wood.

LEV NIKOLAEVICH TOLSTOY

The Death of Ivan Ilyitch

Inside the great building of the Law Courts, during the interval in the hearing of the Melvinsky case, the members of the judicial council and the public prosecutor were gathered together in the private room of Ivan Yegorovitch Shebek, and the conversation turned upon the celebrated Krasovsky case. Fyodor Vassilievitch hotly maintained that the case was not in the jurisdiction of the court. Yegor Ivanovitch stood up for his own view; but from the first Pyotr Ivanovitch, who had not entered into the discussion, took no interest in it, but was looking through the newspapers which had just been brought in.

"Gentlemen!" he said, "Ivan Ilyitch is dead!"

"You don't say so!"

"Here, read it," he said to Fyodor Vassilievitch, handing him the fresh still damp-smelling paper.

Within a black margin was printed: "Praskovya Fyodorovna Golovin with heartfelt affliction informs friends and relatives of the decease of her beloved husband, member of the Court of Justice, Ivan Ilyitch Golovin, who passed away on the 4th of February. The funeral will take place on Thursday at one o'clock."

Ivan Ilyitch was a colleague of the gentlemen present, and all liked him. It was some weeks now since he had been taken ill; his illness had been said to be incurable. His post had been kept open for him, but it had been thought that in case of his death Alexyeev might receive his appointment, and either Vinnikov or Shtabel would succeed to Alexyeev's. So that on hearing of Ivan Ilyitch's death, the first thought of each of the gentlemen in the room was of the effect this death might have on the transfer or promotion of themselves or their friends.

"Now I am sure of getting Shtabel's place or Vinnikov's," thought Fyodor Vassilievitch. "It was promised me long ago, and the promotion means eight hundred rubles additional income, besides the grants for office expenses."

"Now I shall have to petition for my brother-in-law to be transferred from Kaluga," thought Pyotr Ivanovitch. "My wife will be very glad. She won't be able to say now that I've never done anything for her family."

"I thought somehow that he'd never get up from his bed again," Pyotr Ivanovitch said aloud. "I'm sorry!"

"But what was it exactly was wrong with him?"

"The doctors could not decide. That's to say, they did decide, but differently. When I saw him last, I thought he would get over it."

"Well, I positively haven't called there ever since the holidays. I've kept meaning to go."

"Had he any property?"

"I think there's something, very small, of his wife's. But something quite trifling."

"Yes, one will have to go and call. They live such a terribly long way off."

"A long way from you, you mean. Everything's a long way from your place."

"There, he can never forgive me for living the other side of the river," said Pyotr Ivanovitch, smiling at Shebek. And they began to talk of the great distances between different parts of the town, and went back into the court.

Besides the reflections upon the changes and promotions in the service likely to ensue from this death, the very fact of the death of an intimate acquaintance excited in every one who heard of it, as such a fact always does, a feeling of relief that "it is he that is dead, and not I."

"Only think! he is dead, but here am I all right," each one thought or felt. The more intimate acquaintances, the so-called friends of Ivan Ilyitch, could not help thinking too that now they had the exceedingly tiresome social duties to perform

Lev Nikolaevich Tolstoy (1828–1910).

of going to the funeral service and paying the widow a visit of condolence.

The most intimately acquainted with their late colleague were Fyodor Vassilievitch and Pyotr Ivanovitch.

Pyotr Ivanovitch had been a comrade of his at the school of jurisprudence, and considered himself under obligations to Ivan Ilyitch.

Telling his wife at dinner of the news of Ivan Ilyitch's death and his reflections as to the possibility of getting her brother transferred into their circuit, Pyotr Ivanovitch, without lying down for his usual nap, put on his frockcoat and drove to Ivan Ilyitch's.

At the entrance before Ivan Ilyitch's flat stood a carriage and two hired flies. Downstairs in the entry near the hat-stand there was leaning against the wall a coffin-lid with tassels and braiding freshly rubbed up with pipeclay. Two ladies were taking off their cloaks. One of them he knew, the sister of Ivan Ilyitch; the other was a lady he did not know. Pyotr Ivanovitch's colleague, Shvarts, was coming down; and from the top stair, seeing who it was coming in, he stopped and winked at him, as though to say: "Ivan Ilyitch has made a mess of it; it's a very different matter with you and me."

Shvarts's face, with his English whiskers and all his thin figure in his frockcoat, had, as it always had, an air of elegant solemnity; and this solemnity, always such a contrast to Shvarts's playful character, had a special piquancy here. So thought Pyotr Ivanovitch.

Pyotr Ivanovitch let the ladies pass on in front of him, and walked slowly up the stairs after them. Shvarts had not come down, but was waiting at the top. Pyotr Ivanovitch knew what for; he wanted obviously to settle with him where their game of *vint*[1] was to be that evening. The ladies went up to the widow's room; while Shvarts, with his lips tightly and gravely shut and amusement in his eyes, with a twitch of his eyebrows motioned Pyotr Ivanovitch to the right, to the room where the dead man was.

Pyotr Ivanovitch went in, as people always do on such occasions, in uncertainty as to what he would have to do there. One thing he felt sure of —that crossing oneself never comes amiss on such occasions. As to whether it was necessary to bow down while doing so, he did not feel quite sure, and so chose a middle course. On entering the room he began crossing himself, and made a slight sort of bow. So far as the movements of his hands and head permitted him, he glanced while doing so about the room. Two young men, one a high school boy, nephews probably, were going out of the room, crossing themselves. An old lady was standing motionless; and a lady, with her eyebrows queerly lifted, was saying something to her in a whisper. A deacon in a frockcoat, resolute and hearty, was reading something aloud with an expression that precluded all possibility of contradiction. A young peasant who used to wait at table, Gerasim, walking with light footsteps in front of Pyotr Ivanovitch, was sprinkling something on the floor. Seeing this, Pyotr Ivanovitch was at once aware of the faint odour of the decomposing corpse. On his last visit to Ivan Ilyitch Pyotr Ivanovitch had seen this peasant in his room; he was performing the duties of a sicknurse, and Ivan Ilyitch liked him particularly. Pyotr Ivanovitch continued crossing himself and bowing in a direction intermediate between the coffin, the deacon, and the holy pictures on the table in the corner. Then when this action of making the sign of the cross with his hand seemed to him to have been unduly prolonged, he stood still and began to scrutinise the dead man.

The dead man lay, as dead men always do lie, in a peculiarly heavy dead way, his stiffened limbs sunk in the cushions of the coffin, and his head bent back forever on the pillow, and thrust up, as dead men always do, his yellow waxen forehead with bald spots on the sunken temples, and his nose that stood out sharply and, as it were, squeezed on the upper lip. He was much changed, even thinner since Pyotr Ivanovitch had seen him, but his face—as always with the dead—was more handsome, and, above all, more impressive than it had been when he was alive. On the face was an expression of what had to be done having been done, and rightly done. Besides this, there was too in that expression a reproach or a reminder for the living. This reminder seemed to Pyotr Ivanovitch uncalled for, or, at least, to have nothing to do with him. He felt something unpleasant; and so Pyotr Ivanovitch once more crossed himself hurriedly, and, as it struck him, too hurriedly, not quite in accordance with the proprieties, turned and went to the door. Shvarts was waiting for him in the adjoining room, standing with his legs apart and both hands behind his back playing with his top hat. A single glance at the playful, sleek, and elegant figure of Shvarts revived Pyotr Ivanovitch. He felt that he, Shvarts, was above it, and would not give way to depressing impressions.

[1] a card game resembling auction bridge.

The mere sight of him said plainly: the incident of the service over the body of Ivan Ilyitch cannot possibly constitute a sufficient ground for recognising the business of the session suspended,—in other words, in no way can it hinder us from shuffling and cutting a pack of cards this evening, while the footman sets four unsanctified candles on the table for us; in fact, there is no ground for supposing that this incident could prevent us from spending the evening agreeably. He said as much indeed to Pyotr Ivanovitch as he came out, proposing that the party should meet at Fyodor Vassilievitch's. But apparently it was Pyotr Ivanovitch's destiny not to play *vint* that evening. Praskovya Fyodorovna, a short, fat woman who, in spite of all efforts in a contrary direction, was steadily broader from her shoulders downwards, all in black, with lace on her head and her eyebrows as queerly arched as those of the lady standing beside the coffin, came out of her own apartments with some other ladies, and conducting them to the dead man's room, said: "The service will take place immediately; come in."

Shvarts, making an indefinite bow, stood still, obviously neither accepting nor declining this invitation. Praskovya Fyodorovna, recognising Pyotr Ivanovitch, sighed, went right up to him, took his hand, and said, "I know that you were a true friend of Ivan Ilyitch's . . ." and looked at him, expecting from him the suitable action in response to these words. Pyotr Ivanovitch knew that, just as before he had to cross himself, now what he had to do was to press her hand, to sigh and to say, "Ah, I was indeed!" And he did so. And as he did so, he felt that the desired result had been attained; that he was touched, and she was touched. "Come, since it's not begun yet, I have something I want to say to you," said the widow. "Give me your arm."

Pyotr Ivanovitch gave her his arm, and they moved towards the inner rooms, passing Shvarts, who winked gloomily at Pyotr Ivanovitch.

"So much for our *vint*! Don't complain if we find another partner. You can make a fifth when you do get away," said his humorous glance.

Pyotr Ivanovitch sighed still more deeply and despondently, and Praskovya Fyodorovna pressed his hand gratefully. Going into her drawing-room, which was upholstered with pink cretonne and lighted by a dismal-looking lamp, they sat down at the table, she on a sofa and Pyotr Ivanovitch on a low ottoman with deranged springs which yielded spasmodically under his weight. Praskovya Fyodorovna was about to warn him to sit on another seat, but felt such a recommendation out of keeping with her position, and changed her mind. Sitting down on the ottoman, Pyotr Ivanovitch remembered how Ivan Ilyitch had arranged this drawing-room, and had consulted him about this very pink cretonne with green leaves. Seating herself on the sofa, and pushing by the table (the whole drawing-room was crowded with furniture and things), the widow caught the lace of her black fichu in the carving of the table. Pyotr Ivanovitch got up to disentangle it for her; and the ottoman, freed from his weight, began bobbing up spasmodically under him. The widow began unhooking her lace herself, and Pyotr Ivanovitch again sat down, suppressing the mutinous ottoman springs under him. But the widow could not quite free herself, and Pyotr Ivanovitch rose again, and again the ottoman became mutinous and popped up with a positive snap. When this was all over, she took out a clean cambric handkerchief and began weeping. Pyotr Ivanovitch had been chilled off by the incident with the lace and the struggle with the ottoman springs, and he sat looking sullen. This awkward position was cut short by the entrance of Sokolov, Ivan Ilyitch's butler, who came in to announce that the place in the cemetery fixed on by Praskovya Fyodorovna would cost two hundred rubles. She left off weeping, and with the air of a victim glancing at Pyotr Ivanovitch, said in French that it was very terrible for her. Pyotr Ivanovitch made a silent gesture signifying his unhesitating conviction that it must indeed be so.

"Please, smoke," she said in a magnanimous, and at the same time, crushed voice, and she began discussing with Sokolov the question of the price of the site for the grave.

Pyotr Ivanovitch, lighting a cigarette, listened to her very circumstantial inquiries as to the various prices of sites and her decision as to the one to be selected. Having settled on the site for the grave, she made arrangements also about the choristers. Sokolov went away.

"I see to everything myself," she said to Pyotr Ivanovitch, moving on one side the albums that lay on the table; and noticing that the table was in danger from the cigarette-ash, she promptly passed an ash-tray to Pyotr Ivanovitch, and said: "I consider it affectation to pretend that my grief prevents me from looking after practical matters. On the contrary, if anything could—not console me . . . but distract me, it is seeing after everything for him." She took out her handkerchief again, as though preparing to weep again; and suddenly, as though struggling with herself, she shook herself, and began speaking calmly: "But I've business to talk about with you."

Pyotr Ivanovitch bowed, carefully keeping in check the springs of the ottoman, which had at once begun quivering under him.

"The last few days his sufferings were awful."

"Did he suffer very much?" asked Pyotr Ivanovitch.

"Oh, awfully! For the last moments, hours indeed, he never left off screaming. For three days and nights in succession he screamed incessantly. It was insufferable. I can't understand how I bore it; one could hear it through three closed doors. Ah, what I suffered!"

"And was he really conscious?" asked Pyotr Ivanovitch.

"Yes," she whispered, "up to the last minute. He said good-bye to us a quarter of an hour before his death, and asked Volodya to be taken away too."

The thought of the sufferings of a man he had known so intimately, at first as a light-hearted boy, a schoolboy, then grown up as a partner at whist, in spite of the unpleasant consciousness of his own and this woman's hypocrisy, suddenly horrified Pyotr Ivanovitch. He saw again that forehead, the nose that seemed squeezing the lip, and he felt frightened for himself. "Three days and nights of awful suffering and death. Why, that may at once, any minute, come upon me too," he thought, and he felt for an instant terrified. But immediately, he could not himself have said how, there came to his support the customary reflection that this had happened to Ivan Ilyitch and not to him, and that to him this must not and could not happen; that in thinking thus he was giving way to depression, which was not the right thing to do, as was evident from Shvarts's expression of face. And making these reflections, Pyotr Ivanovitch felt reassured, and began with interest inquiring details about Ivan Ilyitch's end, as though death were a mischance peculiar to Ivan Ilyitch, but not at all incidental to himself.

After various observations about the details of the truly awful physical sufferings endured by Ivan Ilyitch (these details Pyotr Ivanovitch learned only through the effect Ivan Ilyitch's agonies had had on the nerves of Praskovya Fyodorovna), the widow apparently thought it time to get to business.

"Ah, Pyotr Ivanovitch, how hard it is, how awfully, awfully hard!" and she began to cry again.

Pyotr Ivanovitch sighed, and waited for her to blow her nose. When she had done so, he said, "Indeed it is," and again she began to talk, and brought out what was evidently the business she wished to discuss with him; that business consisted in the inquiry as to how on the occasion of her husband's death she was to obtain a grant from the government. She made a show of asking Pyotr Ivanovitch's advice about a pension. But he perceived that she knew already to the minutest details, what he did not know himself indeed, everything that could be got out of the government on the ground of this death; but that what she wanted to find out was, whether there were not any means of obtaining a little more? Pyotr Ivanovitch tried to imagine such means; but after pondering a little, and out of politeness abusing the government for its stinginess, he said that he believed that it was impossible to obtain more. Then she sighed and began unmistakably looking about for an excuse for getting rid of her visitor. He perceived this, put out his cigarette, got up, pressed her hand, and went out into the passage.

In the dining-room, where was the bric-à-brac clock that Ivan Iyitch had been so delighted at buying, Pyotr Ivanovitch met the priest and several people he knew who had come to the service for the dead, and saw too Ivan Ilyitch's daughter, a handsome young lady. She was all in black. Her very slender figure looked even slenderer than usual. She had a gloomy, determined, almost wrathful expression. She bowed to Pyotr Ivanovitch as though he were to blame in some way. Behind the daughter, with the same offended air on his face, stood a rich young man, whom Pyotr Ivanovitch knew, too, an examining magistrate, the young lady's *fiancé*, as he had heard. He bowed dejectedly to him, and would have gone on into the dead man's room. when from the staircase there appeared the figure of the son, the high school boy, extraordinarily like Ivan Ilyitch. He was the little Ivan Ilyitch over again as Pyotr Ivanovitch remembered him at school. His eyes were red with crying, and had that look often seen in unclean boys of thirteen or fourteen. The boy, seeing Pyotr Ivanovitch, scowled morosely and bashfully. Pyotr Ivanovitch nodded to him and went into the dead man's room. The service for the dead began—candles, groans, incense, tears, sobs. Pyotr Ivanovitch stood frowning, staring at his feet in front of him. He did not once glance at the dead man, and right through to the end did not once give way to depressing influences, and was one of the first to walk out. In the hall there was no one. Gerasim, the young peasant, darted out of the dead man's room, tossed over with his strong hand all the fur cloaks to find Pyotr Ivanovitch's, and gave it him.

"Well, Gerasim, my boy?" said Pyotr Ivanovitch, so as to say something. "A sad business, isn't it?"

"It's God's will. We shall come to the same," said Gerasim, showing his white, even, peasant teeth in a smile, and, like a man in a rush of extra work, he briskly opened the door, called up the coachman, saw Pyotr Ivanovitch into the carriage, and darted back to the steps as though bethinking himself of what he had to do next.

Pyotr Ivanovitch had a special pleasure in the fresh air after the smell of incense, of the corpse, and of carbolic acid.

"Where to?" asked the coachman.

"It's not too late. I'll still go round to Fyodor Vassilievitch's."

And Pyotr Ivanovitch drove there. And he did, in fact, find them just finishing the first rubber, so that he came just at the right time to take a hand.

II

The previous history of Ivan Ilyitch was the simplest, the most ordinary, and the most awful.

Ivan Ilyitch died at the age of forty-five, a member of the Judicial Council. He was the son of an official, whose career in Petersburg through various ministries and departments had been such as leads people into that position in which, though it is distinctly obvious that they are unfit to perform any kind of real duty, they yet cannot, owing to their long past service and their official rank, be dismissed; and they therefore receive a specially created fictitious post, and by no means fictitious thousands—from six to ten—on which they go on living till extreme old age. Such was the privy councillor, the superfluous member of various superfluous institutions, Ilya Efimovitch Golovin.

He had three sons. Ivan Ilyitch was the second son. The eldest son's career was exactly like his father's, only in a different department, and he was by now close upon that stage in the service in which the same sinecure would be reached. The third son was the unsuccessful one. He had

in various positions always made a mess of things, and was now employed in the railway department. And his father and his brothers, and still more their wives, did not merely dislike meeting him, but avoided, except in extreme necessity, recollecting his existence. His sister had married Baron Greff, a Petersburg official of the same stamp as his father-in-law. Ivan Ilyitch was *le phénix de la famille*,[1] as people said. He was not so frigid and precise as the eldest son, nor so wild as the youngest. He was the happy mean between them—a shrewd, lively, pleasant, and well-bred man. He had been educated with his younger brother at the school of jurisprudence. The younger brother had not finished the school course, but was expelled when in the fifth class. Ivan Ilyitch completed the course successfully. At school he was just the same as he was later on all his life—an intelligent fellow, highly good-humoured and sociable, but strict in doing what he considered to be his duty. His duty he considered whatever was so considered by those persons who were set in authority over him. He was not a toady as a boy, nor later on as a grown-up person; but from his earliest years he was attracted, as a fly to the light, to persons of good standing in the world, assimilated their manners and their views of life, and established friendly relations with them. All the enthusiasms of childhood and youth passed, leaving no great traces in him; he gave way to sensuality and to vanity, and latterly when in the higher classes at school to liberalism, but always keeping within certain limits which were unfailingly marked out for him by his instincts.

At school he had committed actions which had struck him beforehand as great vileness, and gave him a feeling of loathing for himself at the very time he was committing them. But later on, perceiving that such actions were committed also by men of good position, and were not regarded by them as base, he was able, not to regard them as good, but to forget about them completely, and was never mortified by recollections of them.

Leaving the school of jurisprudence in the tenth class, and receiving from his father a sum of money for his outfit, Ivan Ilyitch ordered his clothes at Sharmer's, hung on his watchchain a medallion inscribed *respice finem*,[2] said good-bye to the prince who was the principal of his school, had a farewell dinner with his comrades at Donon's, and with all his new fashionable belongings—travelling trunk, linen, suits of clothes, shaving and toilet appurtenances, and travelling rug, all ordered

[1] the phœnix (the paragon) of the family.   [2] look to the end.

and purchased at the very best shops—set off to take the post of secretary on special commissions for the governor of a province, a post which had been obtained for him by his father.

In the province Ivan Ilyitch without loss of time made himself a position as easy and agreeable as his position had been in the school of jurisprudence. He did his work, made his career, and at the same time led a life of well-bred social gaiety. Occasionally he visited various districts on official duty, behaved with dignity both with his superiors and his inferiors; and with exactitude and an incorruptible honesty of which he could not help feeling proud, performed the duties with which he was intrusted, principally having to do with the dissenters. When engaged in official work he was, in spite of his youth and taste for frivolous amusement, exceedingly reserved, official, and even severe. But in social life he was often amusing and witty, and always good-natured, well-bred, and *bon enfant*,[1] as was said of him by his chief and his chief's wife, with whom he was like one of the family.

In the province there was, too, a connection with one of the ladies who obtruded their charms on the stylish young lawyer. There was a dressmaker, too, and there were drinking bouts with smart officers visiting the neighbourhood, and visits to a certain outlying street after supper; there was a rather cringing obsequiousness in his behaviour, too, with his chief, and even his chief's wife. But all this was accompanied with such a tone of the highest breeding, that it could not be called by harsh names; it all came under the rubric of the French saying, *Il faut que la jeunesse se passe*.[2] Everything was done with clean hands, in clean shirts, with French phrases, and, what was of most importance, in the highest society, and consequently with the approval of people of rank.

Such was Ivan Ilyitch's career for five years, and then came a change in his official life. New methods of judicial procedure were established; new men were wanted to carry them out. And Ivan Ilyitch became such a new man. Ivan Ilyitch was offered the post of examining magistrate, and he accepted it in spite of the fact that this post was in another province, and he would have to break off all the ties he had formed and form new ones. Ivan Ilyitch's friends met together to see him off, had their photographs taken in a group, presented him with a silver cigarette-case, and he set off to his new post.

As an examining magistrate, Ivan Ilyitch was as *comme il faut*,[3] as well-bred, as adroit in keeping official duties apart from private life, and as successful in gaining universal respect, as he had been as secretary of private commissions. The duties of his new office were in themselves of far greater interest and attractiveness for Ivan Ilyitch. In his former post it had been pleasant to pass in his smart uniform from Sharmer's through the crowd of petitioners and officials waiting timorously and envying him, and to march with his easy swagger straight into the governor's private room, there to sit down with him to tea and cigarettes. But the persons directly subject to his authority were few. The only such persons were the district police superintendents and the dissenters, when he was serving on special commissions. And he liked treating such persons affably, almost like comrades; liked to make them feel that he, able to annihilate them, was behaving in this simple, friendly way with them. But such people were then few in number. Now as an examining magistrate Ivan Ilyitch felt that every one —every one without exception—the most dignified, the most self-satisfied people, all were in his hands, and that he had but to write certain words on a sheet of paper with a printed heading, and this dignified self-satisfied person would be brought before him in the capacity of a defendant or a witness; and if he did not care to make him sit down, he would have to stand up before him and answer his questions. Ivan Ilyitch never abused this authority of his; on the contrary, he tried to soften the expression of it. But the consciousness of this power and the possibility of softening its effect constituted for him the chief interest and attractiveness of his new position. In the work itself, in the preliminary inquiries, that is, Ivan Ilyitch very rapidly acquired the art of setting aside every consideration irrelevant to the official aspect of the case, and of reducing every case, however complex, to that form in which it could in a purely external fashion be put on paper, completely excluding his personal view of the matter, and what was of paramount importance, observing all the necessary formalities. All this work was new. And he was one of the first men who put into practical working the reforms in judicial procedure enacted in 1864.

On settling in a new town in his position as examining magistrate, Ivan Ilyitch made new acquaintances, formed new ties, took up a new line, and adopted a rather different attitude. He took up an attitude of somewhat dignified aloofness to-

[1] Literally: good child.   [2] Literally: youth must pass.   [3] Literally: proper.

wards the provincial authorities, while he picked out the best circle among the legal gentlemen and wealthy gentry living in the town, and adopted a tone of slight dissatisfaction with the government, moderate liberalism, and lofty civic virtue. With this, while making no change in the elegance of his get-up, Ivan Ilyitch in his new office gave up shaving, and left his beard free to grow as it liked. Ivan Ilyitch's existence in the new town proved to be very agreeable; the society which took the line of opposition to the governor was friendly and good; his income was larger, and he found a source of increased enjoyment in whist, at which he began to play at this time; and having a faculty for playing cards good-humouredly, and being rapid and exact in his calculations, he was as a rule on the winning side.

After living two years in the new town, Ivan Ilyitch met his future wife. Praskovya Fyodorovna Mihel was the most attractive, clever, and brilliant girl in the set in which Ivan Ilyitch moved. Among other amusements and recreations after his labours as a magistrate, Ivan Ilyitch started a light, playful flirtation with Praskovya Fyodorovna.

Ivan Ilyitch when he was an assistant secretary had danced as a rule; as an examining magistrate he danced only as an exception. He danced now as it were under protest, as though to show "that though I am serving on the new reformed legal code, and am of the fifth class in official rank, still if it comes to a question of dancing, in that line, too, I can do better than others." In this spirit he danced now and then towards the end of the evening with Praskovya Fyodorovna, and it was principally during these dances that he won the heart of Praskovya Fyodorovna. She fell in love with him. Ivan Ilyitch had no clearly defined intention of marrying; but when the girl fell in love with him, he put the question to himself: "After all, why not get married?"

The young lady, Praskovya Fyodorovna, was of good family, nice-looking. There was a little bit of property. Ivan Ilyitch might have reckoned on a more brilliant match, but this was a good match. Ivan Ilyitch had his salary; she, he hoped, would have as much of her own. It was a good family; she was a sweet, pretty, and perfectly *comme il faut* young woman. To say that Ivan Ilyitch got married because he fell in love with his wife and found in her sympathy with his views of life, would be as untrue as to say that he got married because the people of his world approved of the match. Ivan Ilyitch was influenced by both considerations; he was doing what was agreeable to himself in securing such a wife, and at the same time doing what persons of higher standing looked upon as the correct thing.

And Ivan Ilyitch got married.

The process itself of getting married and the early period of married life, with the conjugal caresses, the new furniture, the new crockery, the new house linen, all up to the time of his wife's pregnancy, went off very well; so that Ivan Ilyitch had already begun to think that so far from marriage breaking up that kind of frivolous, agreeable, light-hearted life, always decorous and always approved by society, which he regarded as the normal life, it would even increase its agreeableness. But at that point, in the early months of his wife's pregnancy, there came in a new element, unexpected, unpleasant, tiresome and unseemly, which could never have been anticipated, and from which there was no escape.

His wife, without any kind of reason, it seemed to Ivan Ilyitch, *de gaieté de cœur*,[1] as he expressed it, began to disturb the agreeableness and decorum of their life. She began without any sort of justification to be jealous, exacting in her demands on his attention, squabbled over everything, and treated him to the coarsest and most unpleasant scenes.

At first Ivan Ilyitch hoped to escape from the unpleasantness of this position by taking up the same frivolous and well-bred line that had served him well on other occasions of difficulty. He endeavoured to ignore his wife's ill-humour, went on living light-heartedly and agreeably as before, invited friends to play cards, tried to get away himself to the club or to his friends. But his wife began on one occasion with such energy, abusing him in such coarse language, and so obstinately persisted in her abuse of him every time he failed in carrying out her demands, obviously having made up her mind firmly to persist till he gave way, that is, stayed at home and was as dull as she was, that Ivan Ilyitch took alarm. He perceived that matrimony, at least with his wife, was not invariably conducive to the pleasures and proprieties of life; but, on the contrary, often destructive of them; and that it was therefore essential to erect some barrier to protect himself from these disturbances. And Ivan Ilyitch began to look about for such means of protecting himself. His official duties were the only thing that impressed Praskovya Fyodorovna, and Ivan Ilyitch began to

---

[1] out of mere wantonness.

use his official position and the duties arising from it in his struggle with his wife to fence off his own independent world apart.

With the birth of the baby, the attempts at nursing it, and the various unsuccessful experiments with foods, with the illnesses, real and imaginary, of the infant and its mother, in which Ivan Ilyitch was expected to sympathise, though he never had the slightest idea about them, the need for him to fence off a world apart for himself outside his family life became still more imperative. As his wife grew more irritable and exacting, so did Ivan Ilyitch more and more transfer the centre of gravity of his life to his official work. He became fonder and fonder of official life, and more ambitious than he had been.

Very quickly, not more than a year after his wedding, Ivan Ilyitch had become aware that conjugal life, though providing certain comforts, was in reality a very intricate and difficult business towards which one must, if one is to do one's duty, that is, lead the decorous life approved by society, work out for oneself a definite line, just as in the government service.

And such a line Ivan Ilyitch did work out for himself in his married life. He expected from his home life only those comforts—of dinner at home, of housekeeper and bed which it could give him, and, above all, that perfect propriety in external observances required by public opinion. For the rest, he looked for good-humoured pleasantness, and if he found it he was very thankful. If he met with antagonism and querulousness, he promptly retreated into the separate world he had shut off for himself in his official life, and there he found solace.

Ivan Ilyitch was prized as a good official, and three years later he was made assistant public prosecutor. The new duties of this position, their dignity, the possibility of bringing any one to trial and putting any one in prison, the publicity of the speeches and the success Ivan Ilyitch had in that part of his work,—all this made his official work still more attractive to him.

Children were born to him. His wife became steadily more querulous and ill-tempered, but the line Ivan Ilyitch had taken up for himself in home life put him almost out of reach of her grumbling.

After seven years of service in the same town, Ivan Ilyitch was transferred to another province with the post of public prosecutor. They moved, money was short, and his wife did not like the place they had moved to. The salary was indeed a little higher than before, but their expenses were larger. Besides, a couple of children died, and home life consequently became even less agreeable for Ivan Ilyitch.

For every mischance that occurred in their new place of residence, Praskovya Fyodorovna blamed her husband. The greater number of subjects of conversation between husband and wife, especially the education of the children, led to questions which were associated with previous quarrels, and quarrels were ready to break out at every instant. There remained only those rare periods of being in love which did indeed come upon them, but never lasted long. These were the islands at which they put in for a time, but they soon set off again upon the ocean of concealed hostility, that was made manifest in their aloofness from one another. This aloofness might have distressed Ivan Ilyitch if he had believed that this ought not to be so, but by now he regarded this position as perfectly normal, and it was indeed the goal towards which he worked in his home life. His aim was to make himself more and more free from the unpleasant aspects of domestic life and to render them harmless and decorous. And he attained this aim by spending less and less time with his family; and when he was forced to be at home, he endeavoured to secure his tranquillity by the presence of outsiders. The great thing for Ivan Ilyitch was having his office. In the official world all the interest of life was concentrated for him. And this interest absorbed him. The sense of his own power, the consciousness of being able to ruin any one he wanted to ruin, even the external dignity of his office, when he made his entry into the court or met subordinate officials, his success in the eyes of his superiors and his subordinates, and, above all, his masterly handling of cases, of which he was conscious,—all this delighted him and, together with chats with his colleagues, dining out, and whist, filled his life. So that, on the whole, Ivan's life still went on in the way he thought it should go—agreeably, decorously.

So he lived for another seven years. His eldest daughter was already sixteen, another child had died, and there was left only one other, a boy at the high school, a subject of dissension. Ivan Ilyitch wanted to send him to the school of jurisprudence, while Praskovya Fyodorovna to spite him sent him to the high school. The daughter had been educated at home, and had turned out well; the boy too did fairly well at his lessons.

III

Such was Ivan Ilyitch's life for seventeen years after his marriage. He had been prosecutor a long while by now, and had refused several appointments offered him, looking out for a more desirable post, when there occurred an unexpected incident which utterly destroyed his peace of mind. Ivan Ilyitch had been expecting to be appointed presiding judge in a university town, but a certain Goppe somehow stole a march on him and secured the appointment. Ivan Ilyitch took offence, began upbraiding him, and quarrelled with him and with his own superiors. A coolness was felt towards him, and on the next appointment that was made he was again passed over.

This was in the year 1880. That year was the most painful one in Ivan Ilyitch's life. During that year it became evident on the one hand that his pay was insufficient for his expenses; on the other hand, that he had been forgotten by every one, and that what seemed to him the most monstrous, the cruelest injustice, appeared to other people as a quite commonplace fact. Even his father felt no obligation to assist him. He felt that every one had deserted him, and that every one regarded his position with an income of three thousand five hundred rubles as a quite normal and even fortunate one. He alone, with a sense of the injustice done him, and the everlasting nagging of his wife and the debts he had begun to accumulate, living beyond his means, knew that his position was far from being normal.

The summer of that year, to cut down his expenses, he took a holiday and went with his wife to spend the summer in the country at her brother's.

In the country, with no official duties to occupy him, Ivan Ilyitch was for the first time a prey not to simple boredom, but to intolerable depression; and he made up his mind that things could not go on like that, and that it was absolutely necessary to take some decisive steps.

After a sleepless night spent by Ivan Ilyitch walking up and down the terrace, he determined to go to Petersburg to take active steps and to get transferred to some other department, so as to revenge himself on *them*, the people, that is, who had not known how to appreciate him.

Next day, in spite of all the efforts of his wife and his mother-in-law to dissuade him, he set off to Petersburg.

He went with a single object before him—to obtain a post with an income of five thousand. He was ready now to be satisfied with a post in any department, of any tendency, with any kind of work. He must only have a post—a post with five thousand, in the executive department, the banks, the railways, the Empress Marya's institutions, even in the customs duties—what was essential was five thousand, and essential it was, too, to get out of the department in which they had failed to appreciate his value.

And, behold, this quest of Ivan Ilyitch's was crowned with wonderful, unexpected success. At Kursk there got into the same first-class carriage F. S. Ilyin, an acquaintance, who told him of a telegram just received by the governor of Kursk, announcing a change about to take place in the ministry—Pyotr Ivanovitch was to be superseded by Ivan Semyonovitch.

The proposed change, apart from its significance for Russia, had special significance for Ivan Ilyitch from the fact that by bringing to the front a new person, Pyotr Petrovitch, and obviously, therefore, his friend Zahar Ivanovitch, it was in the highest degree propitious to Ivan Ilyitch's own plans. Zahar Ivanovitch was a friend and schoolfellow of Ivan Ilyitch's.

At Moscow the news was confirmed. On arriving at Petersburg, Ivan Ilyitch looked up Zahar Ivanovitch, and received a positive promise of an appointment in his former department—that of justice.

A week later he telegraphed to his wife: *"Zahar Miller's place. At first report I receive appointment."*

Thanks to these changes, Ivan Ilyitch unexpectedly obtained, in the same department as before, an appointment which placed him two stages higher than his former colleagues, and gave him an income of five thousand, together with the official allowance of three thousand five hundred for travelling expenses. All his ill-humour with his former enemies and the whole department was forgotten, and Ivan Ilyitch was completely happy.

Ivan Ilyitch went back to the country more lighthearted and good-tempered than he had been for a very long while. Praskovya Fyodorovna was in better spirits, too, and peace was patched up between them. Ivan Ilyitch described what respect every one had shown him in Petersburg; how all those who had been his enemies had been put to shame, and were cringing now before him; how envious they were of his appointment, and still more of the high favour in which he stood at Petersburg.

Praskovya Fyodorovna listened to this, and pretended to believe it, and did not contradict him in anything, but confined herself to making plans for her new arrangements in the town to which they would be moving. And Ivan Ilyitch saw with delight that these plans were his plans; that they were agreed; and that his life after this disturbing hitch in its progress was about to regain its true, normal character of light-hearted agreeableness and propriety.

Ivan Ilyitch had come back to the country for a short stay only. He had to enter upon the duties of his new office on the 10th of September; and besides, he needed some time to settle in a new place, to move all his belongings from the other province, to purchase and order many things in addition; in short, to arrange things as settled in his own mind, and almost exactly as settled in the heart too of Praskovya Fyodorovna.

And now when everything was so successfully arranged, and when he and his wife were agreed in their aim, and were, besides, so little together, they got on with one another as they had not got on together since the early years of their married life. Ivan Ilyitch had thought of taking his family away with him at once; but his sister and his brother-in-law, who had suddenly become extremely cordial and intimate with him and his family, were so pressing in urging them to stay that he set off alone.

Ivan Ilyitch started off; and the light-hearted temper produced by his success, and his good understanding with his wife, one thing backing up another, did not desert him all the time. He found a charming set of apartments, the very thing both husband and wife had dreamed of. Spacious, lofty reception-rooms in the old style, a comfortable, dignified-looking study for him, rooms for his wife and daughter, a schoolroom for his son, everything as though planned on purpose for them. Ivan Ilyitch himself looked after the furnishing of them, chose the wall-papers, bought furniture, by preference antique furniture, which had a peculiar *comme-il-faut* style to his mind, and it all grew up and grew up, and really attained the ideal he had set before himself. When he had half finished arranging the house, his arrangement surpassed his own expectations. He saw the *comme-il-faut* character, elegant and free from vulgarity, that the whole would have when it was all ready. As he fell asleep he pictured to himself the reception-room as it would be. Looking at the drawing-room, not yet finished, he could see the hearth, the screen, the *étagère*, and the little chairs dotted here and there, the plates and dishes on the wall, and the bronzes as they would be when they were all put in their places. He was delighted with the thought of how he would impress Praskovya and Lizanka, who had taste too in this line. They would never expect anything like it. He was particularly successful in coming across and buying cheap old pieces of furniture, which gave a peculiarly aristocratic air to the whole. In his letters he purposely disparaged everything so as to surprise them. All this so absorbed him that the duties of his new office, though he was so fond of his official work, interested him less than he had expected. During sittings of the court he had moments of inattention; he pondered the question which sort of cornices to have on the window-blinds, straight or fluted. He was so interested in this business that he often set to work with his own hands, moved a piece of furniture, or hung up curtains himself. One day he went up a ladder to show a workman who did not understand, how he wanted some hangings draped, made a false step and slipped; but, like a strong and nimble person, he clung on, and only knocked his side against the corner of a frame. The bruised place ached, but it soon passed off. Ivan Ilyich felt all this time particularly good-humoured and well. He wrote: "I feel fifteen years younger." He thought his house-furnishing would be finished in September, but it dragged on to the middle of October. But then the effect was charming; not he only said so, but every one who saw it told him so too.

In reality, it was all just what is commonly seen in the houses of people who are not exactly wealthy but want to look like wealthy people, and so succeed only in being like one another—hangings, dark wood, flowers, rugs and bronzes, everything dark and highly polished, everything that all people of a certain class have so as to be like all people of a certain class. And in his case it was all so like that it made no impression at all; but it all seemed to him somehow special. When he met his family at the railway station and brought them to his newly furnished rooms, all lighted up in readiness, and a footman in a white tie opened the door into an entry decorated with flowers, and then they walked into the drawing-room and the study, uttering cries of delight, he was very happy, conducted them everywhere, eagerly drinking in their praises, and beaming with satisfaction. The same evening, while they talked about various things at tea, Praskovya Fyodorovna inquired about his fall, and he laughed and showed them how he had gone flying, and how he had frightened the upholsterer.

"It's as well I'm something of an athlete. Another man might have been killed, and I got nothing worse than a blow here; when it's touched it hurts, but it's going off already; just a bruise."

And they began to live in their new abode, which, as is always the case, when they had got thoroughly settled in they found to be short of just one room, and with their new income, which, as always, was only a little—some five hundred rubles—too little, and everything went very well. Things went particularly well at first, before everything was quite finally arranged, and there was still something to do to the place—something to buy, something to order, something to move, something to make to fit. Though there were indeed several disputes between husband and wife, both were so well satisfied, and there was so much to do, that it all went off without serious quarrels. When there was nothing left to arrange, it became a little dull, and something seemed to be lacking, but by then they were making acquaintances and forming habits, and life was filled up again.

Ivan Ilyitch, after spending the morning in the court, returned home to dinner, and at first he was generally in a good humour, although this was apt to be upset a little, and precisely on account of the new abode. Every spot on the table-cloth, on the hangings, the string of a window blind broken, irritated him. He had devoted so much trouble to the arrangement of the rooms that any disturbance of their order distressed him. But, on the whole, the life of Ivan Ilyitch ran its course as, according to his conviction, life ought to do— easily, agreeably, and decorously. He got up at nine, drank his coffee, read the newspaper, then put on his official uniform, and went to the court. There the routine of the daily work was ready mapped out for him, and he stepped into it at once. People with petitions, inquiries in the office, the office itself, the sittings—public and preliminary. In all this the great thing necessary was to exclude everything with the sap of life in it, which always disturbs the regular course of official business, not to admit any sort of relations with people except the official relations; the motive of all intercourse had to be simply the official motive, and the intercourse itself to be only official. A man would come, for instance, anxious for certain information. Ivan Ilyitch, not being the functionary on duty, would have nothing whatever to do with such a man. But if this man's relation to him as a member of the court is such as can be formulated on official stamped paper—within the limits of such a relation Ivan Ilyitch would do everything, positively everything he could, and in doing so would observe the semblance of human friendly relations, that is, the courtesies of social life. But where the official relation ended, there everything else stopped too. This art of keeping the official aspect of things apart from his real life, Ivan Ilyitch possessed in the highest degree; and through long practice and natural aptitude, he had brought it to such a pitch of perfection that he even permitted himself at times, like a skilled specialist as it were in jest, to let the human and official relations mingle. He allowed himself this liberty just because he felt he had the power at any moment if he wished it to take up the purely official line again and to drop the human relation. This thing was not simply easy, agreeable, and decorous; in Ivan Ilyitch's hands it attained a positively artistic character. In the intervals of business he smoked, drank tea, chatted a little about politics, a little about public affairs, a little about cards, but most of all about appointments in the service. And tired, but feeling like some artist who has skilfully played his part in the performance, one of the first violins in the orchestra, he returned home. At home his daughter and her mother had been paying calls somewhere, or else some one had been calling on them; the son had been at school, had been preparing his lessons with his teachers, and duly learning correctly what was taught at the high school. Everything was as it should be. After dinner, if there were no visitors, Ivan Ilyitch sometimes read some book of which people were talking, and in the evening sat down to work, that is, read official papers, compared them with the laws, sorted depositions, and put them under the laws. This he found neither tiresome nor entertaining. It was tiresome when he might have been playing *vint;* but if there were no *vint* going on, it was better anyway than sitting alone or with his wife. Ivan Ilyitch's pleasures were little dinners, to which he invited ladies and gentlemen of good social position, and such methods of passing the time with them as were usual with such persons, so that his drawing-room might be like all other drawing-rooms.

Once they even gave a party—a dance. And Ivan Ilyitch enjoyed it, and everything was very successful, except that it led to a violent quarrel with his wife over the tarts and sweetmeats. Praskovya Fyodorovna had her own plan; while Ivan Ilyitch insisted on getting everything from an expensive pastry-cook, and ordered a great many tarts, and the quarrel was because these tarts were left over and the pastry-cook's bill came to forty-five rubles. The quarrel was a violent and unpleasant one, so much so that Praskovya Fyodorovna called him, "Fool, imbecile." And he clutched at his head, and in his anger made some allusion to a divorce. But the party itself was enjoyable. There were all the best people, and Ivan Ilyitch danced with Princess Trufanov, the sister of the one so well known in connection with the charitable association called, "Bear my Burden." His official pleasures lay in the gratification of his pride; his social pleasures lay in the gratification of his vanity. But Ivan Ilyitch's most real pleasure was the pleasure of playing *vint*. He admitted to himself that, after all, after whatever unpleasant incidents there had been in his life, the pleasure which burned like a candle before all others was sitting with good players, and not noisy partners, at *vint*; and, of course, a four-hand game (playing with five was never a success, though one pretends to like it particularly), and with good cards, to play a shrewd, serious game, then supper and a glass of wine. And after *vint*, especially after winning some small stakes (winning large sums was unpleasant), Ivan Ilyitch went to bed in a particularly happy frame of mind.

So they lived. They moved in the very best circle, and were visited by people of consequence and young people.

In their views of their circle of acquaintances, the husband, the wife, and the daughter were in complete accord; and without any expressed agreement on the subject, they all acted alike in dropping and shaking off various friends and relations, shabby persons who swooped down upon them in their drawing-room with Japanese plates on the walls, and pressed their civilities on them. Soon these shabby persons ceased fluttering about them, and none but the very best society was seen at the Golovins. Young men began to pay attention to Lizanka; and Petrishtchev, the son of Dmitry Ivanovitch Petrishtchev, and the sole heir of his fortune, an examining magistrate, began to be so attentive to Lizanka, that Ivan Ilyitch had raised the question with his wife whether it would not be as well to arrange a sledge drive for them, or to get up some theatricals. So they lived. And everything went on in this way without change, and everything was very nice.

IV

All were in good health. One could not use the word ill-health in connection with the symptoms Ivan Ilyitch sometimes complained of, namely, a queer taste in his mouth and a sort of uncomfortable feeling on the left side of the stomach.

But it came to pass that this uncomfortable feeling kept increasing, and became not exactly a pain, but a continual sense of weight in his side and the cause of an irritable temper. This irritable temper continually growing, began at last to mar the agreeable easiness and decorum that had reigned in the Golovin household. Quarrels between the husband and wife became more and more frequent, and soon all the easiness and amenity of life had fallen away, and mere propriety was maintained with difficulty. Scenes became again more frequent. Again there were only islands in the sea of contention—and but few of these—at which the husband and wife could meet without an outbreak. And Praskovya Fyodorovna said now, not without grounds, that her husband had a trying temper. With her characteristic exaggeration, she said he had always had this awful temper, and she had needed all her sweetness to put up with it for twenty years. It was true that it was he now who began the quarrels. His gusts of temper always broke out just before dinner, and often just as he was beginning to eat, at the soup. He would notice that some piece of the crockery had been chipped, or that the food was not nice, or that his son put his elbow on the table, or his daughter's hair was not arranged as he liked it. And whatever it was, he laid the blame of it on Praskovya Fyodorovna. Praskovya Fyodorovna had at first retorted in the same strain, and said all sorts of horrid things to him; but on two occasions, just at the beginning of dinner, he had flown into such a frenzy that she perceived that it was due to physical derangement, and was brought on by taking food, and she controlled herself; she did not reply, but simply made haste to get dinner over. Praskovya Fyodorovna took great credit to herself for this exercise of self-control. Making up her mind that her husband had a fearful temper, and made her life miserable, she began to feel sorry for herself. And the more she felt for herself, the more she hated her husband. She began to wish he were dead; yet could not wish it, because then there would be no income. And this exasperated her against him even more. She considered herself dreadfully unfortunate, precisely because even his death could not save her, and she felt irritated and concealed it, and this hidden irritation on her side increased his irritability.

After one violent scene, in which Ivan Ilyitch had been particularly unjust, and after which he had said in explanation that he certainly was irritable, but that it was due to illness, she said that if he were ill he ought to take steps, and insisted on his going to see a celebrated doctor.

He went. Everything was as he had expected; everything was as it always is. The waiting and the assumption of dignity, that professional dignity he knew so well, exactly as he assumed it himself in court, and the sounding and listening and questions that called for answers that were foregone conclusions and obviously superfluous, and the significant air that seemed to insinuate— you only leave it all to us, and we will arrange everything, for us it is certain and incontestable how to arrange everything, everything in one way for every man of every sort. It was all exactly as in his court of justice. Exactly the same air as he put on in dealing with a man brought up for judgment, the doctor put on for him.

The doctor said: This and that proves that you have such-and-such a thing wrong inside you; but if that is not confirmed by analysis of this and that, then we must assume this and that. If we assume this and that, then—and so on. To Ivan Ilyitch there was only one question of consequence, Was his condition dangerous or not? But the doctor ignored that irrelevant inquiry. From the doctor's point of view this was a side issue, not the subject under consideration; the only real question was the balance of probabilities between a loose kidney, chronic catarrh, and appendicitis. It was not a question of the life of Ivan Ilyitch, but the question between the loose kidney and the intestinal appendix. And this question, as it seemed to Ivan Ilyitch, the doctor solved in a brilliant manner in favour of the appendix, with the reservation that analysis of the water might give a fresh clue, and that then the aspect of the case would be altered. All this was point for point identical with what Ivan Ilyitch had himself done in brilliant fashion a thousand times over in dealing with some man on his trial. Just as brilliantly the doctor made his summing-up, and trium-

phantly, gaily even, glanced over his spectacles at the prisoner in the dock. From the doctor's summing-up Ivan Ilyitch deduced the conclusion —that things looked bad, and that he, the doctor, and most likely every one else, did not care, but that things looked bad for him. And this conclusion impressed Ivan Ilyitch morbidly, arousing in him a great feeling of pity for himself, of great anger against this doctor who could be unconcerned about a matter of such importance.

But he said nothing of that. He got up, and, laying the fee on the table, he said, with a sigh, "We sick people probably often ask inconvenient questions. Tell me, is this generally a dangerous illness or not?"

The doctor glanced severely at him with one eye through his spectacles, as though to say: "Prisoner at the bar, if you will not keep within the limits of the questions allowed you, I shall be compelled to take measures for your removal from the precincts of the court." "I have told you what I thought necessary and suitable already," said the doctor; "the analysis will show anything further." And the doctor bowed him out.

Ivan Ilyitch went out slowly and dejectedly, got into his sledge, and drove home. All the way home he was incessantly going over all the doctor had said, trying to translate all these complicated, obscure, scientific phrases into simple language, and to read in them an answer to the question, Is it bad—is it very bad, or nothing much as yet? And it seemed to him that the upshot of all the doctor had said was that it was very bad. Everything seemed dismal to Ivan Ilyitch in the streets. The sledge-drivers were dismal, the houses were dismal, the people passing, and the shops were dismal. This ache, this dull gnawing ache, that never ceased for a second, seemed, when connected with the doctor's obscure utterances, to have gained a new, more serious significance. With a new sense of misery Ivan Ilyitch kept watch on it now.

He reached home and began to tell his wife about it. His wife listened; but in the middle of his account his daughter came in with her hat on, ready to go out with her mother. Reluctantly she half sat down to listen to these tedious details, but she could not stand it for long, and her mother did not hear his story to the end.

"Well, I'm very glad," said his wife; "now you must be sure and take the medicine regularly. Give me the prescription; I'll send Gerasim to the chemist's!" And she went to get ready to go out.

He had not taken breath while she was in the

room, and he heaved a deep sigh when she was gone.

"Well," he said, "may be it really is nothing as yet."

He began to take the medicine, to carry out the doctor's directions, which were changed after the analysis of the water. But it was just at this point that some confusion arose, either in the analysis or in what ought to have followed from it. The doctor himself, of course, could not be blamed for it, but it turned out that things had not gone as the doctor had told him. Either he had forgotten or told a lie, or was hiding something from him.

But Ivan Ilyitch still went on just as exactly carrying out the doctor's direction, and in doing so he found comfort at first.

From the time of his visit to the doctor Ivan Ilyitch's principal occupation became the exact observance of the doctor's prescriptions as regards hygiene and medicine and the careful observation of his ailment in all the functions of his organism. Ivan Ilyitch's principal interest came to be people's ailments and people's health. When anything was said in his presence about sick people, about deaths and recoveries, especially in the case of an illness resembling his own, he listened, trying to conceal his excitement, asked questions, and applied what he heard to his own trouble.

The ache did not grow less; but Ivan Ilyitch made great efforts to force himself to believe that he was better. And he succeeded in deceiving himself so long as nothing happened to disturb him. But as soon as he had a mischance, some unpleasant words with his wife, a failure in his official work, an unlucky hand at *vint*, he was at once acutely sensible of his illness. In former days he had borne with such mishaps, hoping soon to retrieve the mistake, to make a struggle, to reach success later, to have a lucky hand. But now he was cast down by every mischance and reduced to despair. He would say to himself: "Here I'm only just beginning to get better, and the medicine has begun to take effect, and now this mischance or disappointment." And he was furious against the mischance or the people who were causing him the disappointment and killing him, and he felt that this fury was killing him, but could not check it. One would have thought that it should have been clear to him that this exasperation against circumstances and people was aggravating his disease, and that therefore he ought not to pay attention to the unpleasant incidents. But his reasoning took quite the opposite direction. He said that he needed peace, and was on the watch for everything that disturbed his peace, and at the slightest disturbance of it he flew into a rage. What made his position worse was that he read medical books and consulted doctors. He got worse so gradually that he might have deceived himself, comparing one day with another, the difference was so slight. But when he consulted the doctors, then it seemed to him that he was getting worse, and very rapidly so indeed. And in spite of this, he was continually consulting the doctors.

That month he called on another celebrated doctor. The second celebrity said almost the same as the first, but put his questions differently; and the interview with this celebrity only redoubled the doubts and terrors of Ivan Ilyitch. A friend of a friend of his, a very good doctor, diagnosed the disease quite differently; and in spite of the fact that he guaranteed recovery, by his questions and his suppositions he confused Ivan Ilyitch even more and strengthened his suspicions. A homœopath gave yet another diagnosis of the complaint, and prescribed medicine, which Ivan Ilyitch took secretly for a week; but after a week of the homœopathic medicine he felt no relief, and losing faith both in the other doctor's treatment and in this, he fell into even deeper depression. One day a lady of his acquaintance talked to him of the healing wrought by the holy pictures. Ivan Ilyitch caught himself listening attentively and believing in the reality of the facts alleged. This incident alarmed him. "Can I have degenerated to such a point of intellectual feebleness?" he said to himself. "Nonsense! it's all rubbish. I must not give way to nervous fears, but fixing on one doctor, adhere strictly to his treatment. That's what I will do. Now it's settled. I won't think about it, but till next summer I will stick to the treatment, and then I shall see. Now I'll put a stop to this wavering!" It was easy to say this, but impossible to carry it out. The pain in his side was always dragging at him, seeming to grow more acute and ever more incessant; it seemed to him that the taste in his mouth was queerer, and there was a loathsome smell even from his breath, and his appetite and strength kept dwindling. There was no deceiving himself; something terrible, new, and so important that nothing more important had ever been in Ivan Ilyitch's life, was taking place in him, and he alone knew of it. All about him did not or would not understand, and believed that everything in the world was going on as before. This was what tortured Ivan Ilyitch more than anything. Those of his own household, most of all his wife and daughter, who were absorbed in a perfect whirl of visits, did not, he saw, comprehend it at all, and were annoyed that he was so depressed and exacting, as though he were to blame for it. Though they tried indeed to disguise it, he saw he was a nuisance to them; but that his wife had taken up a definite line of her own in regard to his illness, and stuck to it regardless of what he might say and do. This line was expressed thus: "You know," she would say to acquaintances, "Ivan Ilyitch cannot, like all other simple-hearted folks, keep to the treatment prescribed him. One day he'll take his drops and eat what he's ordered, and go to bed in good time; the next day, if I don't see to it, he'll suddenly forget to take his medicine, eat sturgeon (which is forbidden by the doctors), yes, and sit up at *vint* till past midnight."

"Why, when did I do that?" Ivan Ilyitch asked in vexation one day at Pyotr Ivanovitch's.

"Why, yesterday, with Shebek."

"It makes no difference. I couldn't sleep for pain."

"Well, it doesn't matter what you do it for, only you'll never get well like that, and you make us wretched."

Praskovya Fyodorovna's external attitude to her husband's illness, openly expressed to others and to himself, was that Ivan Ilyitch was to blame in the matter of his illness, and that the whole illness was another injury he was doing to his wife. Ivan Ilyitch felt that the expression of this dropped from her unconsciously, but that made it no easier for him.

In his official life, too, Ivan Ilyitch noticed, or fancied he noticed, a strange attitude to him. At one time it seemed to him that people were looking inquisitively at him, as a man who would shortly have to vacate his position; at another time his friends would suddenly begin chaffing him in a friendly way over his nervous fears, as though that awful and horrible, unheard-of thing that was going on within him, incessantly gnawing at him, and irresistibly dragging him away somewhere, were the most agreeable subject for joking. Shvarts especially, with his jocoseness, his liveliness, and his *comme-il-faut* tone, exasperated Ivan Ilyitch by reminding him of himself ten years ago.

Friends came sometimes to play cards. They sat down to the card-table; they shuffled and dealt the new cards. Diamonds were led and followed by diamonds, the seven. His partner said, "Can't trump," and played the two of diamonds. What then? Why, delightful, capital, it should have been —he had a trump hand. And suddenly Ivan Ilyitch feels that gnawing ache, that taste in his mouth, and it strikes him as something grotesque that with that he could be glad of a trump hand.

He looks at Mihail Mihailovitch, his partner, how he taps on the table with his red hand, and affably and indulgently abstains from snatching up the trick, and pushes the cards towards Ivan Ilyitch so as to give him the pleasure of taking them up, without any trouble, without even stretching out his hand. "What, does he suppose that I'm so weak that I can't stretch out my hand?" thinks Ivan Ilyitch, and he forgets the trumps, and trumps his partner's cards, and plays his trump hand without making three tricks; and what's the most awful thing of all is that he sees how upset Mihail Mihailovitch is about it, while he doesn't care a bit, and it's awful for him to think why he doesn't care.

They all see that he's in pain, and say to him, "We can stop if you're tired. You go and lie down." Lie down? No, he's not in the least tired; they will play the rubber. All are gloomy and silent. Ivan Ilyitch feels that it is he who has brought this gloom upon them, and he cannot disperse it. They have supper, and the party breaks up, and Ivan Ilyitch is left alone with the consciousness that his life is poisoned for him and poisons the life of others, and that this poison is not losing its force, but is continually penetrating more and more deeply into his whole existence.

And with the consciousness of this, and with the physical pain in addition, and the terror in addition to that, he must lie in his bed, often not able to sleep for pain the greater part of the night; and in the morning he must get up again, dress, go to the law-court, speak, write, or, if he does not go out, stay at home for all the four-and-twenty hours of the day and night, of which each one is a torture. And he had to live thus on the edge of the precipice alone, without one man who would understand and feel for him.

V

In this way one month, then a second, passed by. Just before the New Year his brother-in-law arrived in the town on a visit to them. Ivan Ilyitch was at the court when he arrived. Praskovya Fyodorovna had gone out shopping. Coming home and going into his study, he found there his brother-in-law, a healthy, florid man, engaged in unpacking his trunk. He raised his head, hearing Ivan Ilyitch's step, and for a second stared at him without a word. That stare told Ivan Ilyitch everything. His brother-in-law opened his mouth to utter an "Oh!" of surprise, but checked himself. That confirmed it all.

"What! have I changed?"

"Yes, there is a change."

And all Ivan Ilyitch's efforts to draw him into talking of his appearance his brother-in-law met with obstinate silence. Praskovya Fyodorovna came in; the brother-in-law went to see her. Ivan Ilyitch locked his door and began gazing at himself in the looking-glass, first full face, then in profile. He took up his photograph, taken with his wife, and compared the portrait with what he saw in the looking-glass. The change was immense. Then he bared his arm to the elbow, looked at it, pulled the sleeve down again, sat down on an ottoman and felt blacker than night.

"I mustn't, I mustn't," he said to himself, jumped up, went to the table, opened some official paper, tried to read it, but could not. He opened the door, went into the drawing-room. The door into the drawing-room was closed. He went up to it on tiptoe and listened.

"No, you're exaggerating," Praskovya Fyodorovna was saying.

"Exaggerating? You can't see it. Why, he's a dead man. Look at his eyes—there's no light in them. But what's wrong with him?"

"No one can tell. Nikolaev" (that was another doctor) "said something, but I don't know, Leshtchetitsky" (this was the celebrated doctor) "said the opposite."

Ivan Ilyitch walked away, went to his own room, lay down, and fell to musing. "A kidney—a loose kidney." He remembered all the doctors had told him, how it had been detached, and how it was loose; and by an effort of imagination he tried to catch that kidney and to stop it, to strengthen it. So little was needed, he fancied. "No, I'll go again to Pyotr Ivanovitch" (this was the friend who had a friend a doctor). He rang, ordered the horse to be put in, and got ready to go out.

"Where are you off too, Jean?"[1] asked his wife with a peculiarly melancholy and exceptionally kind expression.

This exceptionally kind expression exasperated him. He looked darkly at her.

"I want to see Pyotr Ivanovitch."

He went to the friend who had a friend a doctor. And with him to the doctor's. He found him in, and had a long conversation with him.

Reviewing the anatomical and physiological details of what, according to the doctor's view, was taking place within him, he understood it all. It was just one thing—a little thing wrong with the intestinal appendix. It might all come right. Only strengthen one sluggish organ, and decrease the undue activity of another, and absorption would take place, and all would be set right. He was a little late for dinner. He ate his dinner, talked cheerfully, but it was a long while before he could go to his own room to work. At last he went to his study, and at once sat down to work. He read his legal documents and did his work, but the consciousness never left him of having a matter of importance very near to his heart which he had put off, but would look into later. When he had finished his work, he remembered that the matter near his heart was thinking about the intestinal appendix. But he did not give himself up to it; he went into the drawing-room to tea. There were visitors; and there was talking, playing on the piano, and singing; there was the young examining magistrate, the desirable match for the daughter. Ivan Ilyitch spent the evening, as Praskovya Fyodorovna observed, in better spirits than any of them; but he never forgot for an instant that he had the important matter of the intestinal appendix put off for consideration later. At eleven o'clock he said good night and went to his own room. He had slept alone since his illness in a little room adjoining his study. He went in, undressed, and took up a novel of Zola, but did not read it; he fell to thinking. And in his imagination the desired recovery of the intestinal appendix had taken place. There had been absorption, rejection, re-establishment of the regular action.

"Why, it's all simply that," he said to himself. "One only wants to assist nature." He remembered the medicine, got up, took it, lay down on his back, watching for the medicine to act beneficially and overcome the pain. "It's only to take it regularly and avoid injurious influences; why, already I feel rather better, much better." He began to feel his side; it was not painful to the touch. "Yes, I don't feel it—really, much better already." He put out the candle and lay on his side. "The appendix is getting better, absorption." Suddenly he felt the familiar, old, dull, gnawing ache, persistent, quiet, in earnest. In his mouth the same familiar loathsome taste. His heart sank, and his brain felt dim, misty. "My God, my God!" he said, "again, again, and it will never cease." And suddenly the whole thing rose before him in quite a different aspect. "Intestinal appendix! kidney!" he said to himself. "It's not a question of the appendix, not a question of the kidney, but of life and . . . death. Yes, life has been and now it's going, going away, and I cannot stop it. Yes. Why deceive myself? Isn't it obvious to every one, except me, that I'm dying, and it's only a question of weeks, of days—at once perhaps. There was light, and now there is darkness. I was here, and now I am going! Where?" A cold chill ran over him, his breath stopped. He heard nothing but the throbbing of his heart.

"I shall be no more, then what will there be? There'll be nothing. Where then shall I be when I'm no more? Can this be dying? No; I don't want to!" He jumped up, tried to light the candle; and fumbling with trembling hands, he dropped the candle and the candlestick on the floor and fell back again on the pillow. "Why trouble? it doesn't matter," he said to himself, staring with open eyes into the darkness. "Death. Yes, death. And they—all of them—don't understand, and don't want to understand, and feel no pity. They are playing. (He caught through the closed doors the far-away cadence of a voice and the accompaniment.) They don't care, but they will die too. Fools! Me sooner and them later; but it will be the same for them. And they are merry. The beasts!" Anger stifled him. And he was agonisingly, insufferably miserable. "It cannot be that all men always have been doomed to this awful horror!" He raised himself.

"There is something wrong in it; I must be calm I must think it all over from the beginning." And then he began to consider. "Yes, the beginning of my illness. I knocked my side, and I was just the same, that day and the days after; it ached a little, then more, then doctors, then depression, misery, and again doctors; and I've gone on getting closer and closer to the abyss. Strength growing less. Nearer and nearer. And here I am, wasting away, no light in my eyes. I think of how to cure the appendix, but this is death. Can it be death?" Again a horror came over him; gasping for breath, he bent over, began feeling for the matches, and knocked his elbow against the bedside table. It was in his way and hurt him; he felt furious with it, in his anger knocked against it more violently, and upset it. And in despair, breathless, he fell back on his spine waiting for death to come that instant.

The visitors were leaving at that time. Praskovya Fyodorovna was seeing them out. She heard something fall, and came in.

"What is it?"

"Nothing. I dropped something by accident."

She went out, brought a candle. He was lying, breathing hard and fast, like a man who has run a mile, and staring with fixed eyes at her.

"What is it, Jean?"

"No—othing, I say. I dropped something."—"Why speak? She won't understand," he thought.

She certainly did not understand. She picked up the candle, lighted it for him, and went out hastily. She had to say good-bye to a departing guest. When she came back, he was lying in the same position on his back, looking upwards.

"How are you—worse?"

"Yes."

She shook her head, sat down.

"Do you know what, Jean? I wonder if we hadn't better send for Leshtchetitsky to see you here?"

This meant calling in the celebrated doctor, regardless of expense. He smiled malignantly, and said no. She sat a moment longer, went up to him, and kissed him on the forehead.

He hated her with all the force of his soul when she was kissing him, and had to make an effort not to push her away.

"Good night. Please God, you'll sleep."

"Yes."

VI

Ivan Ilyitch saw that he was dying, and was in continual despair.

At the bottom of his heart Ivan Ilyitch knew that he was dying; but so far from growing used to this idea, he simply did not grasp it—he was utterly unable to grasp it.

The example of the syllogism that he had learned in Kiseveter's logic—Caius is a man, men are mortal, therefore Caius is mortal—had seemed to him all his life correct only as regards Caius, but not at all as regards himself. In that case it was a question of Caius, a man, an abstract man, and it was perfectly true, but he was not Caius, and was not an abstract man; he had always been a creature quite, quite different from all others; he had been little Vanya with a mamma and papa, and Mitya and Volodya, with playthings and a coachman and a nurse; afterwards with Katenka, with all the joys and griefs and ecstasies of childhood, boyhood, and youth. What did Caius know of the smell of the leathern ball Vanya had been so fond of? Had Caius kissed his mother's hand like that? Caius had not heard the silk rustle of his mother's skirts. He had not made a riot at school over the pudding. Had Caius been in love like that? Could Caius preside over the sittings of the court?

And Caius certainly was mortal, and it was right for him to die; but for me, little Vanya, Ivan Ilyitch, with all my feelings and ideas—for me it's a different matter. And it cannot be that I ought to die. That would be too awful.

That was his feeling.

"If I had to die like Caius, I should have known it was so, some inner voice would have told me so. But there was nothing of the sort in me. And I and all my friends, we felt that it was not at all the same as with Caius. And now here it is!" he said to himself. "It can't be! It can't be, but it is! How is it? How's one to understand it?" And he could not conceive it, and tried to drive away this idea as false, incorrect, and morbid, and to supplant it by other, correct, healthy ideas. But this idea, not as an idea merely, but as it were an actual fact, came back again and stood confronting him.

And to replace this thought he called up other thoughts, one after another, in the hope of finding support in them. He tried to get back into former trains of thought, which in old days had screened off the thought of death. But, strange to say, all that had in old days covered up, obliterated the sense of death, could not now produce the same effect. Latterly, Ivan Ilyitch spent the greater part of his time in these efforts to restore his old trains of thought which had shut off death. At one time he would say to himself, "I'll put myself into my official work; why, I used to live in it." And he would go to the law-courts, banishing every doubt. He would enter into conversation with his colleagues, and would sit carelessly, as his old habit was, scanning the crowd below dreamily, and with both his wasted hands he would lean on the arms of the oak arm-chair just as he always did; and bending over to a colleague, pass the papers to him and whisper to him, then suddenly dropping his eyes and sitting up straight, he would pronounce the familiar words that opened the proceedings. But suddenly in the middle, the pain in

his side, utterly regardless of the stage he had reached in his conduct of the case, began its work. It riveted Ivan Ilyitch's attention. He drove away the thought of it, but it still did its work, and then It came and stood confronting him and looked at him, and he felt turned to stone, and the light died away in his eyes, and he began to ask himself again, "Can it be that It is the only truth?" And his colleagues and his subordinates saw with surprise and distress that he, the brilliant, subtle judge, was losing the thread of his speech, was making blunders. He shook himself, tried to regain his self-control, and got somehow to the end of the sitting, and went home with the painful sense that his judicial labours could not as of old hide from him what he wanted to hide; that he could not by means of his official work escape from It. And the worst of it was that It drew him to itself not for him to do anything in particular, but simply for him to look at It straight in the face, to look at It and, doing nothing, suffer unspeakably.

And to save himself from this, Ivan Ilyitch sought amusements, other screens, and these screens he found, and for a little while they did seem to save him; but soon again they were not so much broken down as let the light through, as though It pierced through everything, and there was nothing that could shut It off.

Sometimes during those days he would go into the drawing-room he had furnished, that drawing-room where he had fallen, for which—how bitterly ludicrous it was for him to think of it!—for the decoration of which he had sacrificed his life, for he knew that it was that bruise that had started his illness. He went in and saw that the polished table had been scratched by something. He looked for the cause, and found it in the bronze clasps of the album, which had been twisted on one side. He took up the album, a costly one, which he had himself arranged with loving care, and was vexed at the carelessness of his daughter and her friends. Here a page was torn, here the photographs had been shifted out of their places. He carefully put it to rights again and bent the clasp back.

Then the idea occurred to him to move all this setting up of the albums to another corner where the flowers stood. He called the footman; or his daughter or his wife came to help him. They did not agree with him, contradicted him; he argued, got angry. But all that was very well, since he did not think of It; It was not in sight.

But then his wife would say, as he moved some-

thing himself, "Do let the servants do it, you'll
hurt yourself again," and all at once It peeped
through the screen; he caught a glimpse of It. He
caught a glimpse of It, but still he hoped It would
hide itself. Involuntarily though, he kept watch
on his side; there it is just the same still, aching
still, and now he cannot forget it, and *It* is staring
openly at him from behind the flowers. What's the
use of it all?

"And it's the fact that here, at that curtain, as
if it had been storming a fort, I lost my life. Is it
possible? How awful and how silly! It cannot be!
It cannot be, and it is."

He went into his own room, lay down, and was
again alone with It. Face to face with It, and
nothing to be done with It. Nothing but to look
at It and shiver.

VII

How it came to pass during the third month of
Ivan Ilyitch's illness, it would be impossible to say,
for it happened little by little, imperceptibly, but
it had come to pass that his wife and his daughter
and his son and their servants and their acquaintances, and the doctors, and, most of all, he himself—all were aware that all interest in him for
other people consisted now in the question how
soon he would leave his place empty, free the
living from the constraint of his presence, and be
set free himself from his sufferings.

He slept less and less; they gave him opium,
and began to inject morphine. But this did not
relieve him. The dull pain he experienced in the
half-asleep condition at first only relieved him as
a change, but then it became as bad, or even more
agonising, than the open pain. He had special
things to eat prepared for him according to the
doctors' prescriptions; but these dishes became
more and more distasteful, more and more revolting to him.

Special arrangements, too, had to be made for
his other physical needs, and this was a continual
misery to him. Misery from the uncleanliness, the
unseemliness, and the stench, from the feeling of
another person having to assist in it.

But just from this most unpleasant side of his
illness there came comfort to Ivan Ilyitch. There
always came into his room on these occasions to
clear up for him the peasant who waited on table,
Gerasim.

Gerasim was a clean, fresh, young peasant, who
had grown stout and hearty on the good fare in
town. Always cheerful and bright. At first the sight

of this lad, always cleanly dressed in the Russian
style, engaged in this revolting task, embarrassed
Ivan Ilyitch.

One day, getting up from the night-stool, too
weak to replace his clothes, he dropped on to a
soft low chair and looked with horror at his bare,
powerless thighs, with the muscles so sharply
standing out on them.

Then there came in with light, strong steps
Gerasim, in his thick boots, diffusing a pleasant
smell of tar from his boots, and bringing in the
freshness of the winter air. Wearing a clean
hempen apron, and a clean cotton shirt, with
his sleeves tucked up on his strong, bare young
arms, without looking at Ivan Ilyitch, obviously
trying to check the radiant happiness in his face
so as not to hurt the sick man, he went up to the
night-stool.

"Gerasim," said Ivan Ilyitch faintly.

Gerasim started, clearly afraid that he had done
something amiss, and with a rapid movement
turned towards the sick man his fresh, good-
natured, simple young face, just beginning to be
downy with the first growth of beard.

"Yes, your honour."

"I'm afraid this is very disagreeable for you. You
must excuse me. I can't help it."

"Why, upon my word, sir!" And Gerasim's eyes
beamed, and he showed his white young teeth in
a smile. "What's a little trouble? It's a case of illness with you, sir."

And with his deft, strong arms he performed his
habitual task, and went out, stepping lightly. And
five minutes later, treading just as lightly, he came
back.

Ivan Ilyitch was still sitting in the same way in
the arm-chair.

"Gerasim," he said, when the latter had replaced
the night-stool all sweet and clean, "please help
me; come here." Gerasim went up to him. "Lift
me up. It's difficult for me alone, and I've sent
Dmitry away."

Gerasim went up to him; as lightly as he stepped
he put his strong arms round him, deftly and
gently lifted and supported him, with the other
hand pulled up his trousers, and would have set
him down again. But Ivan Ilyitch asked him to
carry him to the sofa. Gerasim, without effort,
carefully not squeezing him, led him, almost
carrying him, to the sofa, and settled him there.

"Thank you; how neatly and well . . . you do
everything."

Gerasim smiled again, and would have gone

away. But Ivan Ilyitch felt his presence such a comfort that he was reluctant to let him go.

"Oh, move that chair near me, please. No, that one, under my legs. I feel easier when my legs are higher."

Gerasim picked up the chair, and without letting it knock, set it gently down on the ground just at the right place, and lifted Ivan Ilyitch's legs on to it. It seemed to Ivan Ilyitch that he was easier just at the moment when Gerasim lifted his legs higher.

"I'm better when my legs are higher," said Ivan Ilyitch. "Put that cushion under me."

Gerasim did so. Again he lifted his legs to put the cushion under them. Again it seemed to Ivan Ilyitch that he was easier at that moment when Gerasim held his legs raised. When he laid them down again, he felt worse.

"Gerasim," he said to him, "are you busy just now?"

"Not at all, sir," said Gerasim, who had learned among the town-bred servants how to speak to gentlefolks.

"What have you left to do?"

"Why, what have I to do? I've done everything, there's only the wood to chop for to-morrow."

"Then hold my legs up like that—can you?"

"To be sure, I can." Gerasim lifted the legs up. And it seemed to Ivan Ilyitch that in that position he did not feel the pain at all.

"But how about the wood?"

"Don't you trouble about that, sir. We shall have time enough."

Ivan Ilyitch made Gerasim sit and hold his legs, and began to talk to him. And, strange to say, he fancied he felt better while Gerasim had hold of his legs.

From that time forward Ivan Ilyitch would sometimes call Gerasim, and get him to hold his legs on his shoulders, and he liked talking with him. Gerasim did this easily, readily, simply, and with a good-nature that touched Ivan Ilyitch. Health, strength, and heartiness in all other people were offensive to Ivan Ilyitch; but the strength and heartiness of Gerasim did not mortify him, but soothed him.

Ivan Ilyitch's great misery was due to the deception that for some reason or other every one kept up with him—that he was simply ill, and not dying, and that he need only keep quiet and follow the doctor's orders, and then some great change for the better would be the result. He knew that whatever they might do, there would be no result except more agonising sufferings and death. And he was made miserable by this lie, made miserable at their refusing to acknowledge what they all knew and he knew, by their persisting in lying to him about his awful position, and in forcing him too to take part in this lie. Lying, lying, this lying carried on over him on the eve of his death, and destined to bring that terrible, solemn act of his death down to the level of all their visits, curtains, sturgeons for dinner . . . was a horrible agony for Ivan Ilyitch. And, strange to say, many times when they had been going through the regular performance over him, he had been within a hair's-breadth of screaming at them: "Cease your lying! You know, and I know, that I'm dying; so do, at least, give over lying!" But he had never had the spirit to do this. The terrible, awful act of his dying was, he saw, by all those about him, brought down to the level of a casual, unpleasant, and to some extent indecorous, incident (somewhat as they would behave with a person who should enter a drawing-room smelling unpleasant). It was brought down to this level by that very decorum to which he had been enslaved all his life. He saw that no one felt for him, because no one would even grasp his position. Gerasim was the only person who recognised the position, and felt sorry for him. And that was why Ivan Ilyitch was only at ease with Gerasim. He felt comforted when Gerasim sometimes supported his legs for whole nights at a stretch, and would not go away to bed, saying, "Don't you worry yourself, Ivan Ilyitch, I'll get sleep enough yet," or when suddenly dropping into the familiar peasant forms of speech, he added: "If thou weren't sick, but as 'tis, 'twould be strange if I didn't wait on thee." Gerasim alone did not lie; everything showed clearly that he alone understood what it meant, and saw no necessity to disguise it, and simply felt sorry for his sick, wasting master. He even said this once straight out, when Ivan Ilyitch was sending him away.

"We shall all die. So what's a little trouble?" he said, meaning by this to express that he did not complain of the trouble just because he was taking this trouble for a dying man, and he hoped that for him too some one would be willing to take the same trouble when his time came.

Apart from this deception, or in consequence of it, what made the greatest misery for Ivan Ilyitch was that no one felt for him as he would have liked them to feel for him. At certain moments, after prolonged suffering, Ivan Ilyitch, ashamed as he would have been to own it, longed more than anything for some one to feel sorry for him, as for a sick child. He longed to be petted, kissed, and wept over, as children are petted and comforted. He knew that he was an important member of the law-courts, that he had a beard turning grey, and that therefore it was impossible. But still he longed for it. And in his relations with Gerasim there was something approaching to that. And that was why being with Gerasim was a comfort to him. Ivan Ilyitch longs to weep, longs to be petted and wept over, and then there comes in a colleague, Shebek; and instead of weeping and being petted, Ivan Ilyitch puts on his serious, severe, earnest face, and from mere inertia gives his views on the effect of the last decision in the Court of Appeal, and obstinately insists upon them. This falsity around him and within him did more than anything to poison Ivan Ilyitch's last days.

VIII

It was morning. All that made it morning for Ivan Ilyitch was that Gerasim had gone away, and Pyotr the footman had come in; he had put out the candles, opened one of the curtains, and begun surreptitiously setting the room to rights. Whether it were morning or evening, Friday or Sunday, it all made no difference; it was always just the same thing. Gnawing, agonising pain never ceasing for an instant; the hopeless sense of life always ebbing away, but still not yet gone; always swooping down on him that fearful, hated death, which was the only reality, and always the same falsity. What were days, or weeks, or hours of the day to him?

"Will you have tea, sir?"

"He wants things done in their regular order. In the morning the family should have tea," he thought, and only said—

"No."

"Would you care to move on to the sofa?"

"He wants to make the room tidy, and I'm in his way. I'm uncleanness, disorder," he thought, and only said—

"No, leave me alone."

The servant still moved busily about his work. Ivan Ilyitch stretched out his hand. Pyotr went up to offer his services.

"What can I get you?"

"My watch."

Pyotr got out the watch, which lay just under his hand, and gave it to him.

"Half-past eight. Are they up?"

"Not yet, sir. Vladimir Ivanovitch" (that was his son) "has gone to the high school, and Praskovya Fyodorovna gave orders that she was to be waked if you asked for her. Shall I send word?"

"No, no need. Should I try some tea?" he thought.

"Yes, tea . . . bring it."

Pyotr was on his way out. Ivan Ilyitch felt frightened of being left alone. "How keep him? Oh, the medicine. Pyotr, give me my medicine. Oh well, may be, medicine may still be some good." He took the spoon, drank it. "No, it does no good. It's all rubbish, deception," he decided, as soon as he tasted the familiar, mawkish, hopeless taste. "No, I can't believe it now. But the pain, why this pain; if it would only cease for a minute." And he groaned. Pyotr turned round. "No, go on. Bring the tea."

Pyotr went away. Ivan Ilyitch, left alone, moaned, not so much from the pain, awful as it was, as from misery. Always the same thing again and again, all these endless days and nights. If it would only be quicker. Quicker to what? Death, darkness. No, no. Anything better than death!

When Pyotr came in with the tea on a tray, Ivan Ilyitch stared for some time absent-mindedly at him, not grasping who he was and what he wanted. Pyotr was disconcerted by this stare. And when he showed he was disconcerted, Ivan Ilyitch came to himself.

"Oh yes," he said, "tea, good, set it down. Only help me to wash and put on a clean shirt."

And Ivan Ilyitch began his washing. He washed his hands slowly, and then his face, cleaned his teeth, combed his hair, and looked in the looking-glass. He felt frightened at what he saw, especially at the way his hair clung limply to his pale forehead. When his shirt was being changed, he knew he would be still more terrified if he glanced at his body, and he avoided looking at himself. But at last it was all over. He put on his dressing-gown, covered himself with a rug, and sat in the armchair to drink his tea. For one moment he felt refreshed; but as soon as he began to drink the tea, again there was the same taste, the same pain. He forced himself to finish it, and lay down, stretched out his legs. He lay down and dismissed Pyotr.

Always the same. A gleam of hope flashes for a moment, then again the sea of despair roars about him again, and always pain, always pain, always heartache, and always the same thing. Alone it is awfully dreary; he longs to call some one, but he knows beforehand that with others present it will be worse. "Morphine again—only to forget again.

I'll tell him, the doctor, that he must think of something else. It can't go on; it can't go on like this."

One hours, two hours pass like this. Then there is a ring at the front door. The doctor, perhaps. Yes, it is the doctor, fresh, hearty, fat, and cheerful, wearing that expression that seems to say. "You there are in a panic about something, but we'll soon set things right for you." The doctor is aware that this expression is hardly fitting here, but he has put it on once and for all, and can't take it off, like a man who has put on a frockcoat to pay a round of calls.

In a hearty, reassuring manner the doctor rubs his hands.

"I'm cold. It's a sharp frost. Just let me warm myself," he says with an expression, as though it's only a matter of waiting a little till he's warm, and as soon as he's warm he'll set everything to rights.

"Well, now, how are you?"

Ivan Ilyitch feels that the doctor would like to say, "How's the little trouble?" but that he feels that he can't talk like that, and says, "How did you pass the night?"

Ivan Ilyitch looks at the doctor with an expression that asks—

"Is it possible you're never ashamed of lying?"

But the doctor does not care to understand this look.

And Ivan Ilyitch says—

"It's always just as awful. The pain never leaves me, never ceases. If only there were something!"

"Ah, you're all like that, all sick people say that. Come, now, I do believe I'm thawed; even Praskovya Fyodorovna, who's so particular, could find no fault with my temperature. Well, now I can say good morning." And the doctor shakes hands.

And dropping his former levity, the doctor, with a serious face, proceeds to examine the patient, feeling his pulse, to take his temperature, and then the tappings and soundings begin.

Ivan Ilyitch knows positively and indubitably that it's all nonsense and empty deception; but when the doctor, kneeling down, stretches over him, putting his ear first higher, then lower, and goes through various gymnastic evolutions over him with a serious face, Ivan Ilyitch is affected by this, as he used sometimes to be affected by the speeches of the lawyers in court, though he was perfectly well aware that they were telling lies all the while and why they were telling lies.

The doctor, kneeling on the sofa, was still sounding him, when there was the rustle of Praskovya Fyodorovna's silk dress in the doorway, and she was heard scolding Pyotr for not having let her know that the doctor had come.

She comes in, kisses her husband, and at once begins to explain that she has been up a long while, and that it was only through a misunderstanding that she was not there when the doctor came.

Ivan Ilyitch looks at her, scans her all over, and sets down against her her whiteness and plumpness, and the cleanness of her hands and neck, and the glossiness of her hair, and the gleam full of life in her eyes. With all the force of his soul he hates her. And when she touches him it makes him suffer from the thrill of hatred he feels for her.

Her attitude to him and his illness is still the same. Just as the doctor had taken up a certain line with the patient which he was not now able to drop, so she too had taken up a line with him— that he was not doing something he ought to do, and was himself to blame, and she was lovingly reproaching him for his neglect, and she could not now get out of this attitude.

"Why, you know, he won't listen to me; he doesn't take his medicine at the right times. And what's worse still, he insists on lying in a position that surely must be bad for him—with his legs in the air."

She described how he made Gerasim hold his legs up.

The doctor smiled with kindly condescension that said, "Oh well, it can't be helped, these sick people do take up such foolish fancies; but we must forgive them."

When the examination was over, the doctor looked at his watch, and then Praskovya Fyodorovna informed Ivan Ilyitch that it must, of course, be as he liked, but she had sent to-day for a celebrated doctor, and that he would examine him, and have a consultation with Mihail Danilovitch (that was the name of their regular doctor).

"Don't oppose it now, please. This I'm doing entirely for my own sake," she said ironically, meaning it to be understood that she was doing it all for his sake, and was only saying this to give him no right to refuse her request. He lay silent, knitting his brows. He felt that he was hemmed in by such a tangle of falsity that it was hard to disentangle anything from it.

Everything she did for him was entirely for her own sake, and she told him she was doing for her own sake what she actually was doing for her own sake as something so incredible that he would take it as meaning the opposite.

At half-past eleven the celebrated doctor came. Again came the sounding, and then grave conversation in his presence and in the other room about the kidney and the appendix, and questions and answers, with such an air of significance, that again, instead of the real question of life and death, which was now the only one that confronted him, the question that came uppermost was of the kidney and the appendix, which were doing something not as they ought to do, and were for that reason being attacked by Mihail Danilovitch and the celebrated doctor, and forced to mend their ways.

The celebrated doctor took leave of him with a serious, but not a hopeless face. And to the timid question that Ivan Ilyitch addressed to him while he lifted his eyes, shining with terror and hope, up towards him, Was there a chance of recovery? he answered that he could not answer for it, but that there was a chance. The look of hope with which Ivan Ilyitch watched the doctor out was so piteous that, seeing it, Praskovya Fyodorovna positively burst into tears, as she went out of the door to hand the celebrated doctor his fee in the next room.

The gleam of hope kindled by the doctor's assurance did not last long. Again the same room, the same pictures, the curtains, the wall-paper, the medicine-bottles, and ever the same, his aching suffering body. And Ivan Ilyitch began to moan; they gave him injections, and he sank into oblivion. When he waked up it was getting dark; they brought him his dinner. He forced himself to eat some broth; and again everything the same, and again the coming night.

After dinner at seven o'clock, Praskovya Fyodorovna came into his room, dressed as though to go to a soirée,[1] with her full bosom laced in tight, and traces of powder on her face. She had in the morning mentioned to him that they were going to the theatre. Sarah Bernhardt was visiting the town, and they had a box, which he had insisted on their taking. By now he had forgotten about it, and her smart attire was an offence to him. But he concealed this feeling when he recollected that he had himself insisted on their taking a box and going, because it was an æsthetic pleasure, beneficial and instructive for the children.

Praskovya Fyodorovna came in satisfied with herself, but yet with something of a guilty air. She sat down, asked how he was, as he saw, simply for the sake of asking, and not for the sake of learning anything, knowing indeed that there was nothing to learn, and began telling him how absolutely necessary it was; how she would not have gone for anything, but the box had been taken, and Liza, their daughter, and Petrishtchev (the examining lawyer, the daughter's suitor) were going, and that it was out of the question to let them go alone. But that she would have liked much better to stay with him. If only he would be sure to follow the doctor's prescription while she was away.

"Oh, and Fyodor Dmitryevitch" (the suitor) "would like to come in. May he? And Liza?"

"Yes, let them come in."

The daughter came in, in evening clothes, her fresh young body showing, while his body made him suffer so. But she made a show of it; she was strong, healthy, obviously in love, and impatient of the illness, suffering, and death that hindered her happiness.

Fyodor Dmitryevitch came in too in evening dress, his hair curled à la Capoul,[2] with his long sinewy neck tightly fenced round by a white collar, with his vast expanse of white chest and strong thighs displayed in narrow black trousers, with one white glove in his hand and a crush opera hat.

Behind him crept in unnoticed the little high school boy in his new uniform, poor fellow, in gloves, and with those awful blue rings under his eyes that Ivan Ilyitch knew the meaning of.

He always felt sorry for his son. And pitiable indeed was his scared face of sympathetic suffering. Except Gerasim, Ivan Ilyitch fancied that Volodya was the only one that understood and was sorry.

They all sat down; again they asked how he was. A silence followed. Liza asked her mother about the opera-glass. An altercation ensued between the mother and daughter as to who had taken it, and where it had been put. It turned into an unpleasant squabble.

Fyodor Dmitryevitch asked Ivan Ilyitch whether he had seen Sarah Bernhardt? Ivan Ilyitch could not at first catch the question that was asked him, but then he said, "No, have you seen her before?"

"Yes, in *Adrienne Lecouvreur*."

Praskovya Fyodorovna observed that she was particularly good in that part. The daughter made some reply. A conversation sprang up about the art and naturalness of her acting, that conversation that is continually repeated and always the same.

In the middle of the conversation Fyodor Dmitryevitch glanced at Ivan Ilyitch and relapsed

[1] evening affair.　　[2] "à la Capoul," in the Capoul style.

into silence. The others looked at him and became mute, too. Ivan Ilyitch was staring with glittering eyes straight before him, obviously furious with them. This had to be set right, but it could not anyhow be set right. This silence had somehow to be broken. No one would venture on breaking it, and all began to feel alarmed that the decorous deception was somehow breaking down, and the facts would be exposed to all. Liza was the first to pluck up courage. She broke the silence. She tried to cover up what they were all feeling, but inadvertently she gave it utterance.

"*If we are going,* though, it's time to start," she said, glancing at her watch, a gift from her father; and with a scarcely perceptible meaning smile to the young man, referring to something only known to themselves, she got up with a rustle of her skirts.

They all got up, said good-bye, and went away. When they were gone, Ivan Ilyitch fancied he was easier; there was no falsity—that had gone away with them, but the pain remained. That continual pain, that continual terror, made nothing harder, nothing easier. It was always worse.

Again came minute after minute, hour after hour, still the same and still no end, and ever more terrible the inevitable end.

"Yes, send Gerasim," he said in answer to Pyotr's question.

IX

Late at night his wife came back. She came in on tiptoe, but he heard her, opened his eyes, and made haste to close them again. She wanted to send away Gerasim and sit up with him herself instead. He opened his eyes and said, "No, go away."

"Are you in great pain?"

"Always the same."

"Take some opium."

He agreed, and drank it. She went away.

Till three o'clock he slept a miserable sleep. It seemed to him that he and his pain were being thrust somewhere into a narrow, deep, black sack, and they kept pushing him further and further in, and still could not thrust him to the bottom. And this operation was awful to him, and was accompanied with agony. And he was afraid, and yet wanted to fall into it, and struggled and yet tried to get into it. And all of a sudden he slipped and fell and woke up. Gerasim, still the same, is sitting at the foot of the bed half-dozing peacefully, patient. And he is lying with his wasted legs

clad in stockings, raised on Gerasim's shoulders, the same candle burning in the alcove, and the same interminable pain.

"Go away, Gerasim," he whispered.

"It's all right, sir. I'll stay a bit longer."

"No, go away."

He took his legs down, lay sideways on his arm, and he felt very sorry for himself. He only waited till Gerasim had gone away into the next room; he could restrain himself no longer, and cried like a child. He cried at his own helplessness, at his awful loneliness, at the cruelty of people, at the cruelty of God, at the absence of God.

"Why hast Thou done all this? What brought me to this? Why, why torture me so horribly?"

He did not expect an answer, and wept indeed that there was and could be no answer. The pain grew more acute again, but he did not stir, did not call.

He said to himself, "Come, more then; come, strike me! But what for? What have I done to Thee? what for?"

Then he was still, ceased weeping, held his breath, and was all attention; he listened, as it were, not to a voice uttering sounds, but to the voice of his soul, to the current of thoughts that rose up within him.

"What is it you want?" was the first clear idea capable of putting into words that he grasped.

"What? Not to suffer, to live," he answered.

And again he was utterly plunged into attention so intense that even the pain did not distract him.

"To live? Live how?" the voice of his soul was asking.

"Why, live as I used to live before—happily and pleasantly."

"As you used to live before—happily and pleasantly?" queried the voice. And he began going over in his imagination the best moments of his pleasant life. But strange to say, all these best moments of his pleasant life seemed now not at all what they had seemed then. All—except the first memories of childhood—there, in his childhood there had been something really pleasant in which one could have lived if it had come back. But the creature who had this pleasant experience was no more; it was like a memory of some one else.

As soon as he reached the beginning of what had resulted in him as he was now, Ivan Ilyitch all that had seemed joys to him then now melted away before his eyes and were transformed into something trivial, and often disgusting.

And the further he went from childhood, the

nearer to the actual present, the more worthless and uncertain were the joys. It began with life at the school of jurisprudence. Then there had still been something genuinely good; then there had been gaiety; then there had been friendship; then there had been hopes. But in the higher classes these good moments were already becoming rarer. Later on, during the first period of his official life, at the governor's, good moments appeared; but it was all mixed, and less and less of it was good. And further on even less was good, and the further he went the less good there was.

His marriage . . . as gratuitous as the disillusion of it and the smell of his wife's breath and the sensuality, the hypocrisy! And that deadly official life, and anxiety about money, and so for one year, and two, and ten, and twenty, and always the same thing. And the further he went, the more deadly it became. "As though I had been going steadily downhill, imagining that I was going uphill. So it was in fact. In public opinion I was going uphill, and steadily as I got up it, life was ebbing away from me. . . . And now the work's done, there's nothing left but to die.

"But what is this? What for? It cannot be! It cannot be that life has been so senseless, so loathsome? And if it really was so loathsome and senseless, then why die, and die in agony? There's something wrong.

"Can it be I have not lived as one ought?" suddenly came into his head. "But how not so, when I've done everything as it should be done?" he said, and at once dismissed this only solution of all the enigma of life and death as something utterly out of the question.

"What do you want now? To live? Live how? Live as you live at the courts when the usher booms out: 'The Judge is coming!' . . . The judge is coming, the judge is coming," he repeated to himself. "Here he is, the judge! But I'm not to blame!" he shrieked in fury. "What's it for?" And he left off crying, and turning with his face to the wall, fell to pondering always on the same question, "What for, why all this horror?"

But however much he pondered, he could not find an answer. And whenever the idea struck him, as it often did, that it all came of his never having lived as he ought, he thought of all the correctness of his life and dismissed the strange idea.

X

Another fortnight had passed. Ivan Ilyitch could

not now get up from the sofa. He did not like lying in bed, and lay on the sofa. And lying almost all the time facing the wall, in loneliness he suffered all the inexplicable agonies, and in loneliness pondered always that inexplicable question, "What is it? Can it be true that it's death?" And an inner voice answered, "Yes, it is true." "Why these agonies?" and a voice answered, "For no reason." Beyond and besides this there was nothing.

From the very beginning of his illness, ever since Ivan Ilyitch first went to the doctor's, his life had been split up into two contradictory moods, which were continually alternating—one was despair and the anticipation of an uncomprehended and awful death; the other was hope and an absorbed watching over the actual condition of his body. First there was nothing confronting him but a kidney or intestine which had temporarily declined to perform its duties, then there was nothing but unknown awful death, which there was no escaping.

These two moods had alternated from the very beginning of the illness; but the further the illness progressed, the more doubtful and fantastic became the conception of the kidney, and the more real the sense of approaching death.

He had but to reflect on what he had been three months before and what he was now, to reflect how steadily he had been going downhill, for every possibility of hope to be shattered.

Of late, in the loneliness in which he found himself, lying with his face to the back of the sofa, a loneliness in the middle of a populous town and of his numerous acquaintances and his family, a loneliness than which none more complete could be found anywhere—not at the bottom of the sea, not deep down in the earth;—of late in this fearful loneliness Ivan Ilyitch had lived only in imagination in the past. One by one the pictures of his past rose up before him. It always began from what was nearest in time and went back to the most remote, to childhood, and rested there. If Ivan Ilyitch thought of the stewed prunes that had been offered him for dinner that day, his mind went back to the damp, wrinkled French plum of his childhood, of its peculiar taste and the flow of saliva when the stone was sucked; and along with this memory of a taste there rose up a whole series of memories of that period—his nurse, his brother, his playthings. "I mustn't . . . it's too painful," Ivan Ilyitch said to himself, and he brought himself back to the present. The button on the back of the sofa and the creases in the morocco. "Morocco's dear, and doesn't wear well; there was a quarrel over it. But the morocco was different, and different too the quarrel when we tore father's portfolio and were punished, and mamma bought us the tarts." And again his mind rested on his childhood, and again it was painful, and he tried to drive it away and think of something else.

And again at that point, together with that chain of associations, quite another chain of memories came into his heart, of how his illness had grown up and become more acute. It was the same there, the further back the more life there had been. There had been both more that was good in life and more of life itself. And the two began to melt into one. "Just as the pain goes on getting worse and worse, so has my whole life gone on getting worse and worse," he thought. One light spot was there at the back, at the beginning of life, and then it kept getting blacker and blacker, and going faster and faster. "In inverse ratio to the square of the distance from death," thought Ivan Ilyitch. And the image of a stone falling downwards with increasing velocity sank into his soul. Life, a series of increasing sufferings, falls more and more swiftly to the end, the most fearful sufferings. "I am falling." He shuddered, shifted himself, would have resisted, but he knew beforehand that he could not resist; and again, with eyes weary with gazing at it, but unable not to gaze at what was before him, he stared at the back of the sofa and waited, waited expecting that fearful fall and shock and dissolution. "Resistance is impossible," he said to himself. "But if one could at least comprehend what it's for? Even that's impossible. It could be explained if one were to say that I hadn't lived as I ought. But that can't be alleged," he said to himself, thinking of all the regularity, correctness, and propriety of his life. "That really can't be admitted," he said to himself, his lips smiling ironically as though some one could see his smile and be deceived by it. "No explanation! Agony, death. . . . What for?"

XI

So passed a fortnight. During that fortnight an event occurred that had been desired by Ivan Ilyitch and his wife. Petrishtchev made a formal proposal. This took place in the evening. Next day Praskovya Fyodorovna went in to her husband, resolving in her mind how to inform him of Fyodor Dmitryevitch's proposal, but that night there had been a change for the worse in Ivan Ilyitch. Praskovya Fyodorovna found him on the same sofa, but in a different position. He was lying on his face, groaning, and staring straight before him with a fixed gaze.

She began talking of remedies. He turned his stare on her. She did not finish what she had begun saying; such hatred of her in particular was expressed in that stare.

"For Christ's sake, let me die in peace," he said.

She would have gone away, but at that moment the daughter came in and went up to say good morning to him. He looked at his daughter just as at his wife, and to her inquiries how he was, he told her drily that they would soon all be rid of him. Both were silent, sat a little while, and went out.

"How are we to blame?" said Liza to her mother. "As though we had done it! I'm sorry for papa, but why punish us?"

At the usual hour the doctor came. Ivan Ilyitch answered, "Yes, no," never taking his exasperated stare from him, and towards the end he said, "Why, you know that you can do nothing, so let me be."

"We can relieve your suffering," said the doctor.

"Even that you can't do; let me be."

The doctor went into the drawing-room and told Praskovya Fyodorovna that it was very serious, and that the only resource left them was opium to relieve his sufferings, which must be terrible. The doctor said his physical sufferings were terrible, and that was true; but even more terrible than his physical sufferings were his mental sufferings, and in that lay his chief misery.

His moral sufferings were due to the fact that during that night, as he looked at the sleepy, good-natured, broad-cheeked face of Gerasim, the thought had suddenly come into his head, "What if in reality all my life, my conscious life, has been not the right thing?" The thought struck him that what he had regarded before as an utter impossibility, that he had spent his life not as he ought, might be the truth. It struck him that those scarcely detected impulses of struggle within him against what was considered good by persons of higher position, scarcely detected impulses which he had dismissed, that they might be the real thing, and everything else might be not the right thing. And his official work, and his ordering of his daily life and of his family, and these social and official interests,—all that might be not the right thing He tried to defend it all to himself. And suddenly he felt all the weakness of what he was defending And it was useless to defend it.

"But if it's so," he said to himself, "and I am leaving life with the consciousness that I have lost all that was given me, and there's no correcting it, then what?" He lay on his back and began going over his whole life entirely anew. When he saw the footman in the morning, then his wife, then his daughter, then the doctor, every movement they made, every word they uttered, confirmed for him the terrible truth that had been revealed to him in the night. In them he saw himself, saw all in which he had lived, and saw distinctly that it was all not the right thing; it was a horrible, vast deception that concealed both life and death. This consciousness intensified his physical agonies, multiplied them tenfold. He groaned and tossed from side to side and pulled at the covering over him. It seemed to him that it was stifling him and weighing him down. And for that he hated them.

They gave him a big dose of opium; he sank into unconsciousness; but at dinner-time the same thing began again. He drove them all away, and tossed from side to side.

His wife came to him and said, "Jean, darling, do this for my sake" (for my sake?). "It can't do harm, and it often does good. Why, it's nothing. And often in health people——"

He opened his eyes wide.

"What? Take the sacrament? What for? No. Besides . . ."

She began to cry.

"Yes, my dear. I'll send for our priest, he's so nice."

"All right, very well," he said.

When the priest came and confessed him he was softened, felt as it were a relief from his doubts, and consequently from his sufferings, and there came a moment of hope. He began once more thinking of the intestinal appendix and the possibility of curing it. He took the sacrament with tears in his eyes.

When they laid him down again after the sacrament for a minute, he felt comfortable, and again the hope of life sprang up. He began to think about the operation which had been suggested to him. "To live, I want to live," he said to himself. His wife came in to congratulate him; she uttered the customary words and added—

"It's quite true, isn't it, that you're better?"

Without looking at her, he said, "Yes."

Her dress, her figure, the expression of her face, the tone of her voice,—all told him the same: "Not the right thing. All that in which you lived and are living is lying, deceit, hiding life and death away from you." And as soon as he had formed that thought, hatred sprang up in him, and with that hatred agonising physical sufferings, and with these sufferings the sense of inevitable, approaching ruin. Something new was happening; there were screwing and shooting pains, and a tightness in his breathing.

The expression of his face as he uttered that "Yes" was terrible. After uttering that "Yes," looking her straight in the face, he turned on to his face, with a rapidity extraordinary in his weakness, and shrieked—

"Go away, go away, let me be!"

XII

From that moment there began the scream that never ceased for three days, and was so awful that through two closed doors one could not hear it without horror. At the moment when he answered his wife he grasped that he had fallen, that there was no return, that the end had come, quite the end, while doubt was still as unsolved, still remained doubt.

"Oo! Oo—o! Oo!" he screamed in varying intonations. He had begun screaming, "I don't want to!" and so had gone on screaming on the same vowel sound—oo!

All those three days, during which time did not exist for him, he was struggling in that black sack into which he was being thrust by an unseen resistless force. He struggled as the man condemned to death struggles in the hands of the executioner, knowing that he cannot save himself. And every moment he felt that in spite of all his efforts to struggle against it, he was getting nearer and nearer to what terrified him. He felt that his agony was due both to his being thrust into this black hole and still more to his not being able to get right into it. What hindered him from getting into it was the claim that his life had been good. That justification of his life held him fast and would not let him get forward, and it caused him more agony than all.

All at once some force struck him in the chest, in the side, and stifled his breathing more than ever; he rolled forward into the hole, and there at the end there was some sort of light. It had happened with him, as it had sometimes happened to him in a railway carriage, when he had thought he was going forward while he was going back, and all of a sudden recognised his real direction.

"Yes, it has all been not the right thing," he said to himself, "but that's no matter." He could, he could do the right thing. "What is the right thing?" he asked himself, and suddenly he became quiet.

This was at the end of the third day, two hours before his death. At that very moment the schoolboy had stealthily crept into his father's room and gone up to his bedside. The dying man was screaming and waving his arms. His hand fell on the schoolboy's head. The boy snatched it, pressed it to his lips, and burst into tears.

At that very moment Ivan Ilyitch had rolled into the hole, and caught sight of the light, and it was revealed to him that his life had not been what it ought to have been, but that that could still be set right. He asked himself, "What is the right thing?"—and became quiet, listening. Then he felt some one was kissing his hand. He opened his eyes and glanced at his son. He felt sorry for him. His wife went up to him. He glanced at her. She was gazing at him with open mouth, the tears unwiped streaming over her nose and cheeks, a look of despair on her face. He felt sorry for her.

"Yes, I'm making them miserable," he thought. "They're sorry, but it will be better for them when I die." He would have said this, but had not the strength to utter it. "Besides, why speak, I must act," he thought. With a glance to his wife he pointed to his son and said—

"Take away . . . sorry for him. . . . And you too . . ." He tried to say "forgive," but said "forgo" . . . and too weak to correct himself, shook his hand, knowing that He would understand Whose understanding mattered.

And all at once it became clear to him that what had tortured him and would not leave him was suddenly dropping away all at once on both sides and on ten sides and on all sides. He was sorry for them, must act so that they might not suffer. Set them free and be free himself of those agonies. "How right and how simple!" he thought. "And the pain?" he asked himself. "Where's it gone? Eh, where are you, pain?"

He began to watch for it.

"Yes, here it is. Well, what of it, let the pain be. "And death. Where is it?"

He looked for his old accustomed terror of death, and did not find it. "Where is it? What death?" There was no terror, because death was not either.

In the place of death there was light. "So this is it!" he suddenly exclaimed aloud. "What joy!"

To him all this passed in a single instant, and the meaning of that instant suffered no change after. For those present his agony lasted another two hours. There was a rattle in his throat, a twitching in his wasted body. Then the rattle and the gasping came at longer and longer intervals. "It is over!" some one said over him.

He caught those words and repeated them in his soul.

"Death is over," he said to himself. "It's no more."

He drew in a breath, stopped midway in the breath, stretched and died.

FIODOR M. DOSTOYEVSKY
The Christmas Tree and the Wedding

The other day I saw a wedding. . . . But no! I would rather tell you about a Christmas tree. The wedding was superb. I liked it immensely. But the other incident was still finer. I don't know why it is that the sight of the wedding reminded me of the Christmas tree. This is the way it happened:

Exactly five years ago, on New Year's Eve, I was invited to a children's ball by a man high up in the business world, who had his connections, his circle of acquaintances, and his intrigues. So it seemed as though the children's ball was merely a pretext for the parents to come together and discuss matters of interest to themselves, quite innocently and casually.

I was an outsider, and, as I had no special matters to air, I was able to spend the evening independently of the others. There was another gentleman present who like myself had just stumbled upon this affair of domestic bliss. He was the first to attract my attention. His appearance was not that of a man of birth or high family. He was tall, rather thin, very serious, and well dressed. Apparently he had no heart for the family festivities. The instant he went off into a corner by himself the smile disappeared from his face, and his thick dark brows knitted into a frown. He knew no one except the host and showed every sign of being bored to death, though bravely sustaining the rôle

Fiodor M. Dostoyevsky (1821-1881). Translation reprinted by arrangement with Random House, Inc.

of thorough enjoyment to the end. Later I learned that he was a provincial, had come to the capital on some important, brain-racking business, had brought a letter of recommendation to our host, and our host had taken him under his protection, not at all *con amore*. It was merely out of politeness that he had invited him to the children's ball.

They did not play cards with him, they did not offer him cigars. No one entered into conversation with him. Possibly they recognised the bird by its feathers from a distance. Thus, my gentleman, not knowing what to do with his hands, was compelled to spend the evening stroking his whiskers. His whiskers were really fine, but he stroked them so assiduously that one got the feeling that the whiskers had come into the world first and afterwards the man in order to stroke them.

There was another guest who interested me. But he was of quite a different order. He was a personage. They called him Julian Mastakovich. At first glance one could tell he was an honoured guest and stood in the same relation to the host as the host to the gentleman of the whiskers. The host and hostess said no end of amiable things to him, were most attentive, wining him, hovering over him, bringing guests up to be introduced, but never leading him to any one else. I noticed tears glisten in our host's eyes when Julian Mastakovich remarked that he had rarely spent such a pleasant evening. Somehow I began to feel uncomfortable in this personage's presence. So, after amusing myself with the children, five of whom, remarkably well-fed young persons, were our host's, I went into a little sitting-room, entirely unoccupied, and seated myself at the end that was a conservatory and took up almost half the room.

The children were charming. They absolutely refused to resemble their elders, notwithstanding the efforts of mothers and governesses. In a jiffy they had denuded the Christmas tree down to the very last sweet and had already succeeded in breaking half of their playthings before they even found out which belonged to whom.

One of them was a particularly handsome little lad, dark-eyed, curly-haired, who stubbornly persisted in aiming at me with his wooden gun. But the child that attracted the greatest attention was his sister, a girl of about eleven, lovely as a Cupid. She was quiet and thoughtful, with large, full, dreamy eyes. The children had somehow offended her, and she left them and walked into the same room that I had withdrawn into. There she seated herself with her doll in a corner.

"Her father is an immensely wealthy business man," the guests informed each other in tones of awe. "Three hundred thousand rubles set aside for her dowry already."

As I turned to look at the group from which I heard this news item issuing, my glance met Julian Mastakovich's. He stood listening to the insipid chatter in an attitude of concentrated attention, with his hands behind his back and his head inclined to one side.

All the while I was quite lost in admiration of the shrewdness our host displayed in the dispensing of the gifts. The little maid of the many-rubled dowry received the handsomest doll, and the rest of the gifts were graded in value according to the diminishing scale of the parents' stations in life. The last child, a tiny chap of ten, thin, red-haired, freckled, came into possession of a small book of nature stories without illustrations or even head and tail pieces. He was the governess's child. She was a poor widow, and her little boy, clad in a sorry-looking little nankeen jacket, looked thoroughly crushed and intimidated. He took the book of nature stories and circled slowly about the children's toys. He would have given anything to play with them. But he did not dare to. You could tell he already knew his place.

I like to observe children. It is fascinating to watch the individuality in them struggling for self-assertion. I could see that the other children's things had tremendous charm for the red-haired boy, especially a toy theatre, in which he was so anxious to take a part that he resolved to fawn upon the other children. He smiled and began to play with them. His one and only apple he handed over to a puffy urchin whose pockets were already crammed with sweets, and he even carried another youngster pickaback—all simply that he might be allowed to stay with the theatre.

But in a few moments an impudent young person fell on him and gave him a pummeling. He did not dare even to cry. The governess came and told him to leave off interfering with the other children's games, and he crept away to the same room the little girl and I were in. She let him sit down beside her, and the two set themselves busily to dressing the expensive doll.

Almost half an hour passed, and I was nearly dozing off, as I sat there in the conservatory half listening to the chatter of the red-haired boy and the dowered beauty, when Julian Mastakovich entered suddenly. He had slipped out of the drawing-room under cover of a noisy scene among the children. From my secluded corner it had not escaped my notice that a few moments before he had been eagerly conversing with the rich girl's father, to whom he had only just been introduced.

He stood still for a while reflecting and mumbling to himself, as if counting something on his fingers.

"Three hundred—three hundred—eleven—twelve—thirteen—sixteen—in five years! Let's say four per cent—five times twelve—sixty, and on these sixty——. Let us assume that in five years it will amount to—well, four hundred. Hm—hm! But the shrewd old fox isn't likely to be satisfied with four per cent. He gets eight or even ten, perhaps. Let's suppose five hundred, five hundred thousand, at least, that's sure. Anything above that for pocket money—hm—"

He blew his nose and was about to leave the room when he spied the girl and stood still. I, behind the plants, escaped his notice. He seemed to me to be quivering with excitement. It must have been his calculations that upset him so. He rubbed his hands and danced from place to place, and kept getting more and more excited. Finally, however, he conquered his emotions and came to a standstill. He cast a determined look at the future bride and wanted to move toward her, but glanced about first. Then, as if with a guilty conscience, he stepped over to the child on tip-toe, smiling, and bent down and kissed her head.

His coming was so unexpected that she uttered a shriek of alarm.

"What are you doing here, dear child?" he whispered, looking around and pinching her cheek.

"We're playing."

"What, with him?" said Julian Mastakovich with a look askance at the governess's child. "You should go into the drawing-room, my lad."

The boy remained silent and looked up at the man with wide-open eyes. Julian Mastakovich glanced round again cautiously and bent down over the girl.

"What have you got, a doll, my dear?"

"Yes, sir." The child quailed a little, and her brow wrinkled.

"A doll? And do you know, my dear, what dolls are made of?"

"No, sir," she said weakly, lowering her head.

"Out of rags, my dear. You, boy, you go back to the drawing-room, to the children," said Julian Mastakovich, looking at the boy sternly.

The two children frowned. They caught hold of each other and would not part.

"And do you know why they gave you the doll?" asked Julian Mastakovich, dropping his voice lower and lower. "No."

"Because you were a good, very good little girl the whole week."

Saying which, Julian Mastakovich was seized with a paroxysm of agitation. He looked round and said in a tone faint, almost inaudible with excitement and impatience:

"If I come to visit your parents will you love me, my dear?"

He tried to kiss the sweet little creature, but the red-haired boy saw that she was on the verge of tears, and he caught her hand and sobbed out loud in sympathy. That enraged the man.

"Go away! Go away! Go back to the other room, to your playmates."

"I don't want him to. I don't want him to! You go away!" cried the girl. "Let him alone! Let him alone!" She was almost weeping.

There was a sound of footsteps in the doorway. Julian Mastakovich started and straightened up his respectable body. The red-haired boy was even more alarmed. He let go the girl's hand, sidled along the wall, and escaped through the drawing-room into the dining-room.

Not to attract attention, Julian Mastakovich also made for the dining-room. He was red as a lobster. The sight of himself in a mirror seemed to embarrass him. Presumably he was annoyed at his own ardour and impatience. Without due respect to his importance and dignity, his calculations had lured and pricked him to the greedy eagerness of a boy, who makes straight for his object—though this was not as yet an object; it only would be so in five years' time. I followed the worthy man into the dining-room, where I saw a remarkable play.

Julian Mastakovich, all flushed with vexation, venom in his look, began to threaten the red-haired boy. The red-haired boy retreated farther and farther until there was no place left for him to retreat to, and he did not know where to turn in his fright.

"Get out of here! What are you doing here? Get out, I say, you good-for-nothing! Stealing fruit, are you? Oh, so, stealing fruit! Get out, you freckle face, go to your likes!"

The frightened child, as a last desperate resort, crawled quickly under the table. His persecutor, completely infuriated, pulled out his large linen handkerchief and used it as a lash to drive the boy out of his position.

Here I must remark that Julian Mastakovich was a somewhat corpulent man, heavy, well-fed, puffy-cheeked, with a paunch and ankles as round as nuts. He perspired and puffed and panted. So strong was his dislike (or was it jealousy?) of the child that he actually began to carry on like a madman.

I laughed heartily. Julian Mastakovich turned. He was utterly confused and for a moment, apparently, quite oblivious of his immense importance. At that moment our host appeared in the doorway opposite. The boy crawled out from under the table and wiped his knees and elbows. Julian Mastakovich hastened to carry his handkerchief, which he had been dangling by the corner, to his nose. Our host looked at the three of us rather suspiciously. But, like a man who knows the world and can readily adjust himself, he seized upon the opportunity to lay hold of his very valuable guest and get what he wanted out of him.

"Here's the boy I was talking to you about," he said, indicating the red-haired child. "I took the liberty of presuming on your goodness in his behalf."

"Oh," replied Julian Mastakovich, still not quite master of himself.

"He's my governess's son," our host continued in a beseeching tone. "She's a poor creature, the widow of an honest official. That's why, if it were possible for you—"

"Impossible, impossible!" Julian Mastakovich cried hastily. "You must excuse me, Philip Alexeyevich, I really cannot. I've made inquiries. There are no vacancies, and there is a waiting list of ten who have a greater right—I'm sorry."

"Too bad," said our host. "He's a quiet, unobtrusive child."

"A very naughty little rascal, I should say," said Julian Mastakovich, wryly. "Go away, boy. Why are you here still? Be off with you to the other children."

Unable to control himself, he gave me a sidelong glance. Nor could I control myself. I laughed straight in his face. He turned away and asked our host, in tones quite audible to me, who that odd young fellow was. They whispered to each other and left the room, disregarding me.

I shook with laughter. Then I, too, went to the drawing-room. There the great man, already surrounded by the fathers and mothers and the host and the hostess, had begun to talk eagerly with a lady to whom he had just been introduced. The lady held the rich little girl's hand. Julian Mastakovich went into fulsome praise of her. He waxed ecstatic over the dear child's beauty, her talents, her grace, her excellent breeding, plainly laying himself out to flatter the mother, who listened scarcely able to restrain tears of joy, while the father showed his delight by a very gratified smile.

The joy was contagious. Everybody shared in it. Even the children were obliged to stop playing so as not to disturb the conversation. The atmosphere was surcharged with awe. I heard the mother of the important little girl, touched to her profoundest depths, ask Julian Mastakovich in the choicest language of courtesy, whether he would honour them by coming to see them. I heard Julian Mastakovich accept the invitation with unfeigned enthusiasm. Then the guests scattered decorously to different parts of the room, and I heard them, with veneration in their tones, extol the business man, the business man's wife, the business man's daughter, and, especially, Julian Mastakovich.

"Is he married?" I asked out loud of an acquaintance of mine standing beside Julian Mastakovich.

Julian Mastakovich gave me a venomous look.

"No," answered my acquaintance, profoundly shocked by my—intentional—indiscretion.

*

Not long ago I passed the Church of ——. I was struck by the concourse of people gathered there to witness a wedding. It was a dreary day. A drizzling rain was beginning to come down. I made my way through the throng into the church. The bridegroom was a round, well-fed, pot-bellied little man, very much dressed up. He ran and fussed about and gave orders and arranged things. Finally word was passed that the bride was coming. I pushed through the crowd, and I beheld a marvellous beauty whose first spring was scarcely commencing. But the beauty was pale and sad. She looked distracted. It seemed to me even that her eyes were red from recent weeping. The classic severity of every line of her face imparted a peculiar significance and solemnity to her beauty. But through that severity and solemnity, through the sadness, shone the innocence of a child. There was something inexpressibly naïve, unsettled and young in her features, which, without words, seemed to plead for mercy.

They said she was just sixteen years old. I looked at the bridegroom carefully. Suddenly I recognised Julian Mastakovich, whom I had not seen again in all those five years. Then I looked at the bride again.—Good God! I made my way, as quickly as I could, out of the church. I heard gossiping in the crowd about the bride's wealth—about her dowry of five hundred thousand rubles—so and so much for pocket money.

"Then his calculations were correct," I thought, as I pressed out into the street.

ANTON CHEKHOV

The Cherry Orchard

DRAMATIS PERSONÆ

MADAME RANÉVSKY, *a landowner*
ÁNYA, *her daughter, aged seventeen*
BARBARA, *her adopted daughter, aged twenty-seven*
LEONÍD GÁYEF, *brother of Madame Ranévsky*
LOPÁKHIN, *a merchant*
PETER TROPHÍMOF, *a student*
SIMEÓNOF-PÍSHTCHIK, *a landowner*
CHARLOTTE, *a governess*
EPHIKHÓDOF, *a clerk*
DUNYÁSHA, *a housemaid*
FIRS, *man-servant, aged eighty-seven*
YÁSHA, *a young man-servant*
Tramp
Stationmaster, Post-Office Official, Guests, Servants, etc.

The action takes place on Madame Ranévsky's property

ACT I

A room which is still called the nursery. One door leads to Ánya's room. Dawn; the sun will soon rise. It is already May; the cherry trees are in blossom, but it is cold in the garden and there is a morning frost. The windows are closed.

Enter DUNYÁSHA *with a candle, and* LOPÁKHIN *with a book in his hand.*

LOPÁK. So the train has come in, thank Heaven. What is the time?

DUNY. Nearly two. [*Putting the candle out.*] It is light already.

LOPÁK. How late is the train? A couple of hours at least. [*Yawning and stretching.*] What do you think of me? A fine fool I have made of myself. I came on purpose to meet them at the station and then I went and fell asleep, fell asleep as I sat in my chair. What a nuisance it is! You might have woke me up anyway.

DUNY. I thought that you had gone. [*She listens.*] That sounds like them driving up.

LOPÁK. [*listening*]. No; they have got to get the luggage out and all that. [*A pause.*] Madame Ranévsky has been five years abroad. I wonder what she has become like. What a splendid creature she is! So easy and simple in her ways. I remember when I was a youngster of fifteen my old father (he used to keep the shop here in the village then) struck me in the face with his fist and set my nose bleeding. We had come, for some reason or other, I forget what, into the courtyard, and he had been drinking. Madame Ranévsky—I remember it like yesterday, still a young girl, and oh, so slender—brought me to the wash-hand stand, here, in this very room, in the nursery. "Don't cry, little peasant," she said, "it'll mend by your wedding." [*A pause.*] "Little peasant"! . . . My father, it is true, was a peasant, and here am I in a white waistcoat and brown boots; a silk purse out of a sow's ear, as you might say; just turned rich, with heaps of money, but when you come to look at it, still a peasant of the peasants. [*Turning over the pages of the book.*] Here's this book that I was reading and didn't understand a word of it; I just sat reading and fell asleep.

DUNY. The dogs never slept all night; they knew that their master and mistress were coming.

LOPÁK. What's the matter with you, Dunyásha? You're all . . .

DUNY. My hands are trembling; I feel quite faint.

LOPÁK. You are too refined, Dunyásha; that's what it is. You dress yourself like a young lady; and look at your hair! You ought not to do it; you ought to remember your place.

Enter EPHIKHÓDOF *with a nosegay. He is dressed in a short jacket and brightly polished boots which squeak noisily. As he comes in he drops the nosegay.*

EPHIK. [*picking it up*]. The gardener has sent this; he says it is to go in the dining-room. [*Handing it to* DUNYÁSHA.]

LOPÁK. And bring me some quass.

DUNY. Yes, sir. [*Exit* DUNYÁSHA.

The Cherry Orchard. Translated by George Calderon. Anton Chekhov (1860-1904) was born at Taganrog on the Black Sea. He became a physician but eventually turned to writing plays and short stories.

EPHIK. There's a frost this morning, three degrees, and the cherry trees all in blossom. I can't say I think much of our climate; [*sighing*] that is impossible. Our climate is not adapted to contribute; and I should like to add, with your permission, that only two days ago I bought myself a new pair of boots, and I venture to assure you they do squeak beyond all bearing. What am I to grease them with?

LOPÁK. Get out; I'm tired of you.

EPHIK. Every day some misfortune happens to me; but do I grumble? No; I am used to it; I can afford to smile.

Enter DUNYÁSHA, *and hands a glass of quass to* LOPÁKHIN.

EPHIK. I must be going. [*He knocks against a chair, which falls to the ground.*] There you are! [*In a voice of triumph.*] You see, if I may venture on the expression, the sort of incidents *inter alia*. It really is astonishing!   [*Exit* EPHIKHÓDOF.

DUNY. To tell you the truth, Yermolái Alexéyitch, Ephikhódof has made me a proposal.

LOPÁK. Hmph!

DUNY. I hardly know what to do. He is such a well-behaved young man, only so often when he talks one doesn't know what he means. It is all so nice and full of good feeling, but you can't make out what it means. I fancy I am rather fond of him. He adores me passionately. He is a most unfortunate man; every day something seems to happen to him. They call him "Twenty-two misfortunes," that's his nickname.

LOPÁK. [*listening*]. There, surely that is them coming!

DUNY. They're coming! Oh, what is the matter with me? I am all turning cold.

LOPÁK. Yes, there they are, and no mistake. Let's go and meet them. Will she know me again, I wonder? It is five years since we met.

DUNY. I am going to faint! . . . I am going to faint!

Two carriages are heard driving up to the house. LOPÁKHIN *and* DUNYÁSHA *exeunt quickly. The stage remains empty. A hubbub begins in the neighboring rooms.* FIRS *walks hastily across the stage, leaning on a walking-stick. He has been to meet them at the station. He is wearing an old-fashioned livery and a tall hat; he mumbles something to himself, but not a word is audible. The noise behind the scenes grows louder and louder. A voice says:* "Let's go this way." *Enter*

MADAME RANÉVSKY, ÁNYA, CHARLOTTE, *leading a little dog on a chain, all dressed in traveling-dresses;* BARBARA *in greatcoat, with a kerchief over her head,* GÁYEF, SIMEÓNOF-PÍSHTCHIK, LOPÁKHIN, DUNYÁSHA, *carrying parcel and umbrella, servants with luggage, all cross the stage.*

ÁNYA. Come through this way. Do you remember what room this is, mamma?

MME. R. [*joyfully, through her tears*]. The nursery.

BARB. How cold it is. My hands are simply frozen. [*To* MADAME RANÉVSKY.] Your two rooms, the white room and the violet room, are just the same as they were, mamma.

MME. R. My nursery, my dear, beautiful nursery! This is where I used to sleep when I was a little girl. [*Crying.*] I am like a little girl still. [*Kissing* GÁYEF *and* BARBARA *and then* GÁYEF *again.*] Barbara has not altered a bit; she is just like a nun; and I knew Dunyásha at once. [*Kissing* DUNYÁSHA.]

GÁYEF. Your train was two hours late. What do you think of that? There's punctuality for you!

CHARL. [*to* SIMEÓNOF-PÍSHTCHIK]. My little dog eats nuts.

PÍSHT. [*astonished*]. You don't say so! Well, I never!   [*Exeunt all but* ÁNYA *and* DUNYÁSHA.

DUNY. At last you've come! [*She takes off* ÁNYA's *overcoat and hat.*]

ÁNYA. I have not slept for four nights on the journey. I am frozen to death.

DUNY. It was Lent when you went away. There was snow on the ground; it was freezing; but now! Oh, my dear! [*Laughing and kissing her.*] How I have waited for you, my joy, my light! Oh, I must tell you something at once, I cannot wait another minute.

ÁNYA [*without interest*]. What, again?

DUNY. Ephikhódof, the clerk, proposed to me in Easter Week.

ÁNYA. Same old story. . . . [*Putting her hair straight.*] All my hairpins have dropped out. [*She is very tired, staggering with fatigue.*]

DUNY. I hardly know what to think of it. He loves me! Oh, how he loves me!

ÁNYA [*looking into her bedroom, affectionately*]. My room, my window, just as if I had never gone away! I am at home again! When I wake up in the morning I shall run out into the garden. . . . Oh, if only I could get to sleep! I have not slept the whole journey from Paris, I was so nervous and anxious.

DUNY. Monsieur Trophímof arrived the day before yesterday.

ÁNYA [*joyfully*]. Peter?

DUNY. He is sleeping outside in the bath-house; he is living there. He was afraid he might be in the way. [*Looking at her watch.*] I'd like to go and wake him, only Mamzelle Barbara told me not to. "Mind you don't wake him," she said.

Enter BARBARA *with bunch of keys hanging from her girdle.*

BARB. Dunyásha, go and get some coffee, quick. Mamma wants some coffee.

DUNY. In a minute! [*Exit* DUNYÁSHA.

BARB. Well, thank Heaven, you have come. Here you are at home again. [*Caressing her.*] My little darling is back! My pretty one is back!

ÁNYA. What I've had to go through!

BARB. I can believe you.

ÁNYA. I left here in Holy Week. How cold it was! Charlotte would talk the whole way and keep doing conjuring tricks. What on earth made you tie Charlotte round my neck?

BARB. Well, you couldn't travel alone, my pet. At seventeen!

ÁNYA. When we got to Paris, it was so cold! There was snow on the ground. I can't talk French a bit. Mamma was on the fifth floor of a big house. When I arrived there were a lot of Frenchmen with her, and ladies, and an old Catholic priest with a book, and it was very uncomfortable and full of tobacco smoke. I suddenly felt so sorry for mamma, oh, so sorry! I took her head in my arms and squeezed it and could not let it go, and then mamma kept kissing me and crying.

BARB. [*crying*]. Don't go on; don't go on!

ÁNYA. She's sold her villa near Mentone already. She's nothing left, absolutely nothing; and I hadn't a farthing either. We only just managed to get home. And mamma won't understand! We get out at a station to have some dinner, and she asks for all the most expensive things and gives the waiters a florin each for a tip; and Charlotte does the same. And Yásha wanted his portion, too. It was too awful! Yásha is mamma's new man-servant. We have brought him back with us.

BARB. I've seen the rascal.

ÁNYA. Come, tell me all about everything! Has the interest on the mortgage been paid?

BARB. How could it be?

ÁNYA. Oh, dear! Oh, dear!

BARB. The property will be sold in August.

ÁNYA. Oh, dear! Oh, dear!

LOPÁK. [*looking in at the door and mooing like a cow*]. Moo-oo! [*He goes away again.*]

BARB. [*laughing through her tears, and shaking her fist at the door*]. Oh, I should like to give him one!

ÁNYA [*embracing* BARBARA *softly*]. Barbara, has he proposed to you?

BARBARA *shakes her head.*

ÁNYA. And yet I am sure he loves you. Why don't you come to an understanding? What are you waiting for?

BARB. I don't think anything will come of it. He has so much to do; he can't be bothered with me; he hardly takes any notice. Confound the man, I can't bear to see him! Everyone talks about our marriage; everyone congratulates me; but, as a matter of fact, there is nothing in it; it's all a dream. [*Changing her tone.*] You've got on a brooch like a bee.

ÁNYA [*sadly*]. Mamma bought it me. [*Going into her room, talking gaily, like a child.*] When I was in Paris, I went up in a balloon!

BARB. How glad I am you are back, my little pet! My pretty one!

DUNYÁSHA *has already returned with a coffee-pot and begins to prepare the coffee.*

BARB. [*standing by the door*]. I trudge about all day looking after things, and I think and think. What are we to do? If only we could marry you to some rich man it would be a load off my mind. I would go into a retreat, and then to Kief, to Moscow; I would tramp about from one holy place to another, always tramping and tramping. What bliss!

ÁNYA. The birds are singing in the garden. What time is it now?

BARB. It must be past two. It is time to go to bed, my darling. [*Following* ÁNYA *into her room.*] What bliss!

Enter YÁSHA *with a shawl and a traveling-bag.*

YÁSHA [*crossing the stage, delicately*]. May I pass this way, mademoiselle?

DUNY. One would hardly know you, Yásha. How you've changed abroad!

YÁSHA. Ahem! And who may you be?

DUNY. When you left here I was a little thing like that [*indicating with her hand*]. My name is Dunyásha, Theodore Kozoyédof's daughter. Don't you remember me?

YÁSHA. Ahem! You little cucumber! [*He looks*

round cautiously, then embraces her. She screams and drops a saucer. Exit YÁSHA hastily.]

BARB. [in the doorway, crossly]. What's all this?

DUNY. [crying]. I've broken a saucer.

BARB. Well, it brings luck.

Enter ÁNYA from her room.

ÁNYA. We must tell mamma that Peter's here.

BARB. I've told them not to wake him.

ÁNYA [thoughtfully]. It's just six years since papa died. And only a month afterwards poor little Grisha was drowned in the river; my pretty little brother, only seven years old! It was too much for mamma; she ran away, ran away without looking back. [Shuddering.] How well I can understand her, if only she knew! [A pause.] Peter Trophímof was Grisha's tutor; he might remind her.

Enter FIRS in long coat and white waistcoat.

FIRS [going over to the coffee-pot, anxiously]. My mistress is going to take coffee here. [Putting on white gloves.] Is the coffee ready? [Sternly, to DUNYÁSHA.] Here, girl, where's the cream?

DUNY. Oh, dear! oh, dear!
                        [Exit DUNYÁSHA hastily.

FIRS [bustling about the coffee-pot]. Ah, you . . . job-lot! [Mumbling to himself.] She's come back from Paris. The master went to Paris once in a post-chaise. [Laughing.]

BARB. What is it, Firs?

FIRS. I beg your pardon? [Joyfully.] My mistress has come home; at last I've seen her. Now I'm ready to die. [He cries with joy.]

Enter MADAME RANÉVSKY, LOPÁKHIN, GÁYEF, and PÍSHTCHIK; PÍSHTCHIK in Russian breeches and coat of fine cloth. GÁYEF as he enters makes gestures as if playing billiards.

MME. R. What was the expression? Let me see. "I'll put the red in the corner pocket; double into the middle—"

GÁYEF. I'll chip the red in the righthand top. Once upon a time, Lyuba, when we were children, we used to sleep here side by side in two little cots, and now I'm fifty-one, and can't bring myself to believe it.

LOPÁK. Yes; time flies.

GÁYEF. Who's that?

LOPÁK. Time flies, I say.

GÁYEF. There's a smell of patchouli!

ÁNYA. I am going to bed. Good-night, mamma. [Kissing her mother.]

MME. R. My beloved little girl! [Kissing her hands.] Are you glad you're home again? I can't come to my right senses.

ÁNYA. Good-night, uncle.

GÁYEF [kissing her face and hands]. God bless you, little Ánya. How like your mother you are! [To MADAME RANÉVSKY.] You were just such another girl at her age, Lyuba.

ÁNYA shakes hands with LOPÁKHIN and SIMEÓNOF-PÍSHTCHIK, and exit, shutting her bedroom door behind her.

MME. R. She's very, very tired.

PÍSHT. It must have been a long journey.

BARB. [to LOPÁKHIN and PÍSHTCHIK]. Well, gentlemen, it's past two; time you were off.

MME. R. [laughing]. You haven't changed a bit, Barbara! [Drawing her to herself and kissing her.] I'll just finish my coffee, then we'll all go. [FIRS puts a footstool under her feet.] Thank you, friend. I'm used to my coffee. I drink it day and night. Thank you, you dear old man. [Kissing FIRS.]

BARB. I'll go and see if they've got all the luggage.   [Exit BARBARA.

MME. R. Can it be me that's sitting here? [Laughing.] I want to jump and wave my arms about. [Pausing and covering her face.] Surely I must be dreaming! God knows I love my country. I love it tenderly. I couldn't see out of the window from the train, I was crying so. [Crying.] However, I must drink my coffee. Thank you, Firs; thank you, you dear old man. I'm so glad to find you still alive.

FIRS. The day before yesterday.

GÁYEF. He's hard of hearing.

LOPÁK. I've got to be off for Kharkof by the five-o'clock train. Such a nuisance! I wanted to stay and look at you and talk to you. You're as splendid as you always were.

PÍSHT. [sighing heavily]. Handsomer than ever and dressed like a Parisian . . . Perish my wagon and all its wheels!

LOPÁK. Your brother, Leoníd Andréyitch, says I'm a snob, a money-grubber. He can say what he likes. I don't care a hang. Only I want you to believe in me as you used to; I want your wonderful, touching eyes to look at me as they used to. Merciful God in heaven! My father was your father's serf, and your grandfather's serf before him; but you, you did so much for me in the old days that I've forgotten everything, and I love you like a sister—more than a sister.

MME. R. I can't sit still! I can't do it! [Jumping

up and walking about in great agitation.] This happiness is more than I can bear. Laugh at me! I am a fool! [*Kissing a cupboard.*] My darling old cupboard! [*Caressing a table.*] My dear little table!

GÁYEF. Nurse is dead since you went away.

MME. R. [*sitting down and drinking coffee*]. Yes, Heaven rest her soul. They wrote and told me.

GÁYEF. And Anastási is dead. Squint-eyed Peter has left us and works in the town at the Police Inspector's now. [GÁYEF *takes out a box of sugar candy from his pocket, and begins to eat it.*]

PÍSHT. My daughter Dáshenka sent her compliments.

LOPÁK. I long to say something charming and delightful to you. [*Looking at his watch.*] I'm just off; there's no time to talk. Well, yes, I'll put it in two or three words. You know that your cherry orchard is going to be sold to pay the mortgage: the sale is fixed for the twenty-second of August; but don't you be uneasy, my dear lady; sleep peacefully; there's a way out of it. This is my plan. Listen to me carefully. Your property is only fifteen miles from the town; the railway runs close beside it; and if only you will cut up the cherry orchard and the land along the river into building lots and let it off on lease for villas, you will get at least two thousand five hundred pounds a year out of it.

GÁYEF. Come, come! What rubbish you're talking!

MME. R. I don't quite understand what you mean, Yermolái Alcxéyitch.

LOPÁK. You will get a pound a year at least for every acre from the tenants, and if you advertise the thing at once, I am ready to bet whatever you like, by the autumn you won't have a clod of that earth left on your hands. It'll all be snapped up. In two words, I congratulate you; you are saved. It's a first-class site, with a good deep river. Only, of course you will have to put it in order and clear the ground; you will have to pull down all the old buildings—this house, for instance, which is no longer fit for anything; you'll have to cut down the cherry orchard. . . .

MME. R. Cut down the cherry orchard! Excuse me, but you don't know what you are talking about. If there is one thing that's interesting, remarkable in fact, in the whole province, it's our cherry orchard.

LOPÁK. There's nothing remarkable about the orchard except that it's a very big one. It only bears once every two years, and then you don't know what to do with the fruit. Nobody wants to buy it.

GÁYEF. Our cherry orchard is mentioned in Andréyevsky's Encyclopædia.

LOPÁK. [*looking at his watch*]. If we don't make up our minds or think of any way, on the twenty-second of August the cherry orchard and the whole property will be sold by auction. Come, make up your mind! There's no other way out of it, I swear—absolutely none.

FIRS. In the old days, forty or fifty years ago, they used to dry the cherries and soak 'em and pickle 'em, and make jam of 'em; and the dried cherries . . .

GÁYEF. Shut up, Firs.

FIRS. The dried cherries used to be sent in wagons to Moscow and Kharkof. A heap of money! The dried cherries were soft and juicy and sweet and sweet-smelling then. They knew some way in those days.

MME. R. And why don't they do it now?

FIRS. They've forgotten. Nobody remembers how to do it.

PÍSHT. [*to* MADAME RANÉVSKY]. What about Paris? How did you get on? Did you eat frogs?

MME. R. Crocodiles.

PÍSHT. You don't say so! Well, I never!

LOPÁK. Until a little while ago there was nothing but gentry and peasants in the villages; but now villa residents have made their appearance. All the towns, even the little ones, are surrounded by villas now. In another twenty years the villa resident will have multiplied like anything. At present he only sits and drinks tea on his veranda, but it is quite likely that he will soon take to cultivating his three acres of land, and then your old cherry orchard will become fruitful, rich and happy. . . .

GÁYEF [*angry*]. What gibberish!

Enter BARBARA *and* YÁSHA.

BARB. [*taking out a key and noisily unlocking an old-fashioned cupboard*]. There are two telegrams for you, mamma. Here they are.

MME. R. [*tearing them up without reading them*]. They're from Paris. I've done with Paris.

GÁYEF. Do you know how old this cupboard is, Lyuba? A week ago I pulled out the bottom drawer and saw a date burnt in it. That cupboard was made exactly a hundred years ago. What do you think of that, eh? We might celebrate its jubilee. It's only an inanimate thing, but for all that it's a historic cupboard.

PÍSHT. [*astonished*]. A hundred years? Well, I never!

GÁYEF [*touching the cupboard*]. Yes, it's a wonderful thing. . . . Beloved and venerable cupboard; honor and glory to your existence, which for more than a hundred years has been directed to the noble ideals of justice and virtue. Your silent summons to profitable labor has never weakened in all these hundred years. [Crying.] You have upheld the courage of succeeding generations of our humankind; you have upheld faith in a better future and cherished in us ideals of goodness and social consciousness. [A pause.]

Lopák. Yes. . . .

Mme. R. You haven't changed, Leoníd.

Gáyef [embarrassed]. Off the white in the corner, chip the red in the middle pocket!

Lopák. [looking at his watch]. Well, I must be off.

Yásha [handing a box to Madame Ranévsky]. Perhaps you'll take your pills now.

Písht. You oughtn't to take medicine, dear lady. It does you neither good nor harm. Give them here, my friend. [He empties all the pills into the palm of his hand, blows on them, puts them in his mouth, and swallows them down with a draught of quass.] There!

Mme. R. [alarmed]. Have you gone off your head?

Písht. I've taken all the pills.

Lopák. Greedy feller!

Everyone laughs.

Firs [mumbling]. They were here in Easter Week and finished off a gallon of pickled gherkins.

Mme. R. What's he talking about?

Barb. He's been mumbling like that these three years. We've got used to it.

Yásha. Advancing age.

Charlotte crosses in a white frock, very thin, tightly laced, with a lorgnette at her waist.

Lopák. Excuse me, Charlotte Ivánovna, I've not paid my respects to you yet. [He prepares to kiss her hand.]

Charl. [drawing her hand away]. If one allows you to kiss one's hand, you will want to kiss one's elbow next, and then one's shoulder.

Lopák. I'm having no luck today. [All laugh.] Charlotte Ivánovna, do us a conjuring trick.

Mme. R. Charlotte, do do us a conjuring trick.

Charl. No, thank you. I'm going to bed.

[Exit Charlotte.

Lopák. We shall meet again in three weeks. [Kissing Madame Ranévsky's hand.] Meanwhile, good-by. I must be off. [To Gáyef.] So-long.

[Kissing Píshtchik.] Ta-ta. [Shaking hands with Barbara, then with Firs and Yásha.] I hate having to go. [To Madame Ranévsky.] If you make up your mind about the villas, let me know, and I'll raise you five thousand pounds at once. Think it over seriously.

Barb. [angrily]. For Heaven's sake, do go!

Lopák. I'm going, I'm going. [Exit Lopákhin.

Gáyef. Snob! . . . However, pardon! Barbara's going to marry him; he's Barbara's young man.

Barb. You talk too much, uncle.

Mme. R. Why, Barbara, I shall be very glad. He's a nice man.

Písht. Not a doubt of it. . . . A most worthy individual. My Dáshenka, she says . . . oh, she says . . . lots of things. [Snoring and waking up again at once.] By the by, dear lady, can you lend me twenty-five pounds? I've got to pay the interest on my mortgage tomorrow.

Barb. [alarmed]. We can't! We can't!

Mme. R. It really is a fact that I haven't any money.

Písht. I'll find it somewhere. [Laughing.] I never lose hope. Last time I thought, "Now I really am done for, I'm a ruined man," when behold, they ran a railway over my land and paid me compensation. And so it'll be again; something will happen, if not today, then tomorrow. Dáshenka may win the twenty-thousand-pound prize; she's got a ticket in the lottery.

Mme. R. The coffee's finished. Let's go to bed.

Firs [brushing Gáyef's clothes, admonishingly]. You've put on the wrong trousers again. Whatever am I to do with you?

Barb. [softly]. Ánya is asleep. [She opens the window quietly.] The sun's up already; it isn't cold now. Look, mamma, how lovely the trees are. Heavens! what a sweet air! The starlings are singing!

Gáyef [opening the other window]. The orchard is all white. You've not forgotten it, Lyuba? This long avenue going straight on, straight on, like a ribbon between the trees? It shines like silver on moonlight nights. Do you remember? You've not forgotten?

Mme. R. [looking out into the garden]. Oh, my childhood, my pure and happy childhood! I used to sleep in this nursery. I used to look out from here into the garden. Happiness awoke with me every morning; and the orchard was just the same then as it is now; nothing is altered. [Laughing with joy.] It is all white, all white! Oh, my cherry orchard! After the dark and stormy autumn and the frosts of winter you are young again and full of happiness; the angels of heaven have not abandoned you. Oh! if only I could free my neck and shoulders from the stone that weighs them down! If only I could forget my past!

GÁYEF. Yes; and this orchard will be sold to pay our debts, however impossible it may seem. . . .

MME. R. Look! There's mamma walking in the orchard . . . in a white frock! [*Laughing with joy.*] There she is!

GÁYEF. Where?

BARB. Heaven help you!

MME. R. There's no one there really. It only looked like it; there on the right where the path turns down to the summer-house; there's a white tree that leans over and looks like a woman.

Enter TROPHÍMOF *in a shabby student uniform and spectacles.*

MME. R. What a wonderful orchard, with its white masses of blossom and the blue sky above!

TROPH. Lyubóf Andréyevna! [*She looks round at him.*] I only want to say, "How do you do," and go away at once. [*Kissing her hand eagerly.*] I was told to wait till the morning, but I hadn't the patience.

MADAME RANÉVSKY *looks at him in astonishment.*

BARB. [*crying*]. This is Peter Trophímof.

TROPH. Peter Trophímof; I was Grisha's tutor, you know. Have I really altered so much?

MADAME RANÉVSKY *embraces him and cries softly.*

GÁYEF. Come, come, that's enough, Lyuba!

BARB. [*crying*]. I told you to wait till tomorrow, you know, Peter.

MME. R. My little Grisha! My little boy! Grisha . . . my son. . . .

BARB. It can't be helped, mamma. It was the will of God.

TROPH. [*gently, crying*]. There, there!

MME. R. [*crying*]. He was drowned. My little boy was drowned. Why? What was the use of that, my dear? [*In a softer voice.*] Ánya's asleep in there, and I am speaking so loud, and making a noise. . . . But tell me, Peter, why have you grown so ugly? Why have you grown so old?

TROPH. An old woman in the train called me a "moldy gentleman."

MME. R. You were quite a boy then, a dear little student, and now your hair's going and you wear spectacles. Are you really still a student? [*Going toward the door.*]

TROPH. Yes, I expect I shall be a perpetual student.

MME. R. [*kissing her brother and then BARBARA*]. Well, go to bed. You've grown old too, Leoníd.

PÍSHT. [*following her*]. Yes, yes; time for bed. Oh, oh, my gout! I'll stay the night here. Don't forget, Lyubóf Andréyevna, my angel, tomorrow morning . . . twenty-five.

GÁYEF. He's still on the same string.

PÍSHT. Twenty-five . . . to pay the interest on my mortgage.

MME. R. I haven't any money, my friend.

PÍSHT. I'll pay you back, dear lady. It's a trifling sum.

MME. R. Well, well, Leoníd will give it you. Let him have it, Leoníd.

GÁYEF [*ironical*]. I'll give it him right enough! Hold your pocket wide!

MME. R. It can't be helped. . . . He needs it. He'll pay it back.

[*Exeunt* MADAME RANÉVSKY, TROPHÍMOF, PÍSHTCHIK, *and* FIRS. GÁYEF, BARBARA, *and* YÁSHA *remain.*

GÁYEF. My sister hasn't lost her old habit of scattering the money. [*To* YÁSHA.] Go away, my lad! You smell of chicken.

YÁSHA [*laughing*]. You're just the same as you always were, Leoníd Andréyevitch!

GÁYEF. Who's that? [*To* BARBARA.] What does he say?

BARB. [*to* YÁSHA]. Your mother's come up from the village. She's been waiting for you since yesterday in the servants' hall. She wants to see you.

YÁSHA. What a nuisance she is!

BARB. You wicked, unnatural son!

YÁSHA. Well, what do I want with her? She might just as well have waited till tomorrow.

[*Exit* YÁSHA.

BARB. Mamma is just like she used to be; she hasn't changed a bit. If she had her way, she'd give away everything she has.

GÁYEF. Yes. [*A pause.*] If people recommend very many cures for an illness, that means that the illness is incurable. I think and think, I batter my brains; I know of many remedies, very many, and that means really that there is none. How nice it would be to get a fortune left one by somebody! How nice it would be if Ánya could marry a very rich man! How nice it would be to go to Yaroslav and try my luck with my aunt the Countess. My aunt is very, very rich, you know.

BARB. [*crying softly*]. If only God would help us!

GÁYEF. Don't howl! My aunt is very rich, but she does not like us. In the first place, my sister married a solicitor, not a nobleman. [ÁNYA *appears in the doorway.*] She married a man who was not a nobleman, and it's no good pretending that she has led a virtuous life. She's a dear, kind, charming creature, and I love her very much, but whatever mitigating circumstances one may find for her, there's no getting round it that she's a sinful woman. You can see it in her every gesture.

BARB. [*whispering*]. Ánya is standing in the door!

GÁYEF. Who's that? [*A pause.*] It's very odd, something's got into my right eye. I can't see properly out of it. Last Thursday when I was down at the District Court . . .

ÁNYA comes down.

BARB. Why aren't you asleep, Ánya?

ÁNYA. I can't sleep. It's no good trying.

GÁYEF. My little pet! [*Kissing Ánya's hands and face.*] My little girl! [*Crying.*] You're not my niece; you're my angel; you're my everything. Trust me, trust me. . . .

ÁNYA. I do trust you, uncle. Everyone loves you, everyone respects you; but, dear, dear uncle, you ought to hold your tongue, only to hold your tongue. What were you saying just now about mamma?—about your own sister? What was the good of saying that?

GÁYEF. Yes, yes. [*Covering his face with her hand.*] You're quite right; it was awful of me! Lord, Lord! Save me from myself! And a little while ago I made a speech over a cupboard. What a stupid thing to do! As soon as I had done it, I knew it was stupid.

BARB. Yes, really, uncle. You ought to hold your tongue. Say nothing; that's all that's wanted.

ÁNYA. If only you would hold your tongue, you'd be so much happier!

GÁYEF. I will! I will! [*Kissing Ánya's and Barbara's hands.*] I'll hold my tongue. But there's one thing I must say; it's business. Last Thursday, when I was down at the District Court, a lot of us were there together, we began to talk about this and that, one thing and another, and it seems I could arrange a loan on note of hand to pay the interest into the bank.

BARB. If only Heaven would help us!

GÁYEF. I'll go in on Tuesday and talk it over again. [*To* BARBARA.] Don't howl! [*To* ÁNYA.] Your mamma shall have a talk with Lopákhin. Of course he won't refuse her. And as soon as you are rested you must go to see your grandmother, the Countess, at Yaroslav. We'll operate from three points, and the trick is done. We'll pay the interest, I'm certain of it. [*Taking sugar candy.*] I swear on my honor, or whatever you will, the property shall not be sold. [*Excitedly.*] I swear by my hope of eternal happiness! There's my hand on it. Call me a base, dishonorable man if I let it go to auction. I swear by my whole being!

ÁNYA [*calm again and happy*]. What a dear you are, uncle, and how clever! [*Embraces him.*] Now I'm easy again. I'm easy again! I'm happy!

Enter FIRS.

FIRS [*reproachfully*]. Leoníd Andréyevitch, have you no fear of God? When are you going to bed?

GÁYEF. I'm just off—just off. You get along, Firs. I'll undress myself all right. Come, children, by-bye! Details tomorrow, but now let's go to bed. [*Kissing* ÁNYA *and* BARBARA.] I'm a good Liberal, a man of the eighties. People abuse the eighties, but I think that I may say I've suffered something for my convictions in my time. It's not for nothing that the peasants love me. We ought to know the peasants; we ought to know with what . . .

ÁNYA. You're at it again, uncle!

BARB. Why don't you hold your tongue, uncle?

FIRS [*angrily*]. Leoníd Andréyevitch!

GÁYEF. I'm coming; I'm coming. Now go to bed. Off two cushions in the middle pocket! I start another life! . . .

[*Exit, with* FIRS *hobbling after him.*

ÁNYA. Now my mind is at rest. I don't want to go to Yaroslav; I don't like grandmamma; but my mind is at rest, thanks to Uncle Leoníd. [*She sits down.*]

BARB. Time for bed. I'm off. Whilst you were away there's been a scandal. You know that nobody lives in the old servants' quarters except the old people, Ephim, Pauline, Evstignéy, and old Karp. Well, they took to having in all sorts of queer fish to sleep there with them. I didn't say a word. But at last I heard they had spread a report that I had given orders that they were to have nothing but peas to eat; out of stinginess, you understand? It was all Evstignéy's doing. "Very well," I said to myself, "you wait a bit." So I sent for Evstignéy. [*Yawning.*] He comes. "Now then, Evstignéy," I said, "you old imbecile, how do you dare . . ." [*Looking at* ÁNYA.] Ánya, Ánya! [*A pause.*] She's asleep. [*Taking* ÁNYA's *arm.*] Let's go to bed. Come along. [*Leading her away.*] Sleep on, my little one! Come along; come along! [*They go towards Ánya's room. In the distance beyond the orchard a shepherd plays his pipe.* TROPHÍMOF *crosses the stage and, seeing* BARBARA *and* ÁNYA, *stops.*] 'Sh! She's asleep, she's asleep! Come along, my love.

ÁNYA [*drowsily*]. I'm so tired! Listen to the bells! Uncle, dear uncle! Mamma! Uncle!

BARB. Come along, my love! Come along.

[*Exeunt* BARBARA *and* ÁNYA *to the bedroom.*

TROPH. [*with emotion*]. My sunshine! My spring!

ACT II

In the open fields; an old crooked half-ruined shrine. Near it a well; big stones, apparently old tombstones; an old bench. Road to the estate beyond. On one side rise dark poplar trees. Beyond them begins the cherry orchard. In the distance a row of telegraph poles, and, far away on the horizon, the dim outlines of a big town, visible only in fine, clear weather. It is near sunset.

CHARLOTTE, YÁSHA, *and* DUNYÁSHA *sit on the bench.* EPHIKHÓDOF *stands by them and plays on a guitar; they meditate.* CHARLOTTE *wears an old peaked cap. She has taken a gun from off her shoulders and is mending the buckle of the strap.*

CHARL. [*thoughtfully*]. I have no proper passport. I don't know how old I am; I always feel I am still young. When I was a little girl my father and mother used to go about from one country fair to another, giving performances, and very good ones, too. I used to do the *salto mortale* and all sorts of tricks. When papa and mamma died, an old German lady adopted me and educated me. Good! When I grew up I became a governess. But where I come from and who I am, I haven't a notion. Who my parents were—very likely they weren't married—I don't know. [*Taking a cucumber from her pocket and beginning to eat.*] I don't know anything about it. [*A pause.*] I long to talk so, and I have no one to talk to, I have no friends or relations.

EPHIK. [*playing on the guitar and singing*].
   "What is the noisy world to me?
   Oh, what are friends and foes?"
How sweet it is to play upon a mandolin!

DUNY. That's a guitar, not a mandolin. [*She looks at herself in a hand-glass and powders her face.*]

EPHIK. For the madman who loves, it is a mandolin. [*Singing.*]
   "Oh, that my heart were cheered
   By the warmth of requited love."

YÁSHA *joins in.*

CHARL. How badly these people do sing! Foo! Like jackals howling!

DUNY. [*to* YÁSHA]. What happiness it must be to live abroad!

YÁSHA. Of course it is; I quite agree with you. [*He yawns and lights a cigar.*]

EPHIK. It stands to reason. Everything abroad has attained a certain culnimation.[1]

YÁSHA. That's right.

EPHIK. I am a man of cultivation; I have studied various remarkable books, but I cannot fathom the direction of my preferences; do I want to live or do I want to shoot myself, so to speak? But in order to be ready for all contingencies, I always carry a revolver in my pocket. Here it is. [*Showing revolver.*]

CHARL. That's done. I'm off. [*Slinging the rifle over her shoulder.*] You're a clever fellow, Ephikhódof, and very alarming. Women must fall madly in love with you. Brrr! [*Going.*] These clever people are all so stupid; I have no one to talk to. I am always alone, always alone; I have no friends or relations, and who I am, or why I exist, is a mystery. [*Exit slowly.*

EPHIK. Strictly speaking, without touching upon other matters, I must protest *inter alia* that destiny treats me with the utmost rigor, as a tempest might treat a small ship. If I labor under a misapprehension, how is it that when I woke up this morning, behold, so to speak, I perceived sitting on my chest a spider of preternatural dimensions, like that? [*Indicating with both hands.*] And if I go to take a draught of quass, I am sure to find something of the most indelicate character, in the nature of a cockroach. [*A pause.*] Have you read Buckle? [*A pause.—To* DUNYÁSHA.] I should like to trouble you, Avdotya Fëdorovna,[2] for a momentary interview.

DUNY. Talk away.

EPHIK. I should prefer to conduct it *tête-à-tête* [*Sighing.*]

DUNY. [*confused*]. Very well, only first please

---

[1] This represents a similar blunder in the Russian.
[2] Pronounced: Fvodorovna.

fetch me my cloak. It's by the cupboard. It's rather damp here.

EPHIK. Very well, mademoiselle. I will go and fetch it, mademoiselle. Now I know what to do with my revolver.

[*Takes his guitar and exit, playing.*

YÁSHA. Twenty-two misfortunes! Between you and me, he's a stupid fellow. [*Yawning.*]

DUNY. Heaven help him, he'll shoot himself! [*A pause.*] I have grown so nervous, I am always in a twitter. I was quite a little girl when they took me into the household, and now I have got quite disused to common life, and my hands are as white as white, like a lady's. I have grown so refined, so delicate and genteel, I am afraid of of everything. I'm always frightened. And if you deceive me, Yásha, I don't know what will happen to my nerves.

YÁSHA [*kissing her*]. You little cucumber! Of course every girl ought to behave herself properly; there's nothing I dislike as much as when girls aren't proper in their behavior.

DUNY. I've fallen dreadfully in love with you. You're so educated; you can talk about anything! [*A pause.*]

YÁSHA [*yawning*]. Yes. . . . The way I look at it is this; if a girl falls in love with anybody, then I call her immoral. [*A pause.*] How pleasant it is to smoke one's cigar in the open air. [*Listening.*] There's someone coming. It's the missis and the rest of 'em. . . . [DUNYÁSHA *embraces him hastily.*] Go towards the house as if you'd just been for a bathe. Go by this path or else they'll meet you and think that I've been walking out with you. I can't stand that sort of thing.

DUNY. [*coughing softly*]. Your cigar has given me a headache.

[*Exit* DUNYÁSHA. YÁSHA *remains sitting by the shrine.*

Enter MADAME RANÉVSKY, GÁYEF, *and* LOPÁKHIN.

LOPÁK. You must make up your minds once and for all. Time waits for no man. The question is perfectly simple. Are you going to let off the land for villas or not? Answer in one way; yes or no? Only one word!

MME. R. Who's smoking horrible cigars here? [*She sits down.*]

GÁYEF. How handy it is now they've built that railway. [*Sitting.*] We've been into town for lunch and back again. . . . Red in the middle! I must just go up to the house and have a game.

MME. R. There's no hurry.

LOPÁK. Only one word—yes or no! [*Entreatingly.*] Come, answer the question!

GÁYEF [*yawning*]. Who's that?

MME. R. [*looking into her purse*]. I had a lot of money yesterday, but there's hardly any left now. Poor Barbara tries to save money by feeding us all on milk soup; the old people in the kitchen get nothing but peas, and yet I go squandering aimlessly. . . . [*Dropping her purse and scattering gold coins; vexed.*] There, I've dropped it all!

YÁSHA. Allow me, I'll pick it up. [*Collecting the coins.*]

MME. R. Yes, please do, Yásha! Whatever made me go into town for lunch? I hate your horrid restaurant with the organ, and the tablecloths all smelling of soap. Why do you drink so much, Leoníd? Why do you eat so much? Why do you talk so much? You talked too much at the restaurant again, and most unsuitably, about the seventies, and the decadents. And to whom? Fancy talking about decadents to the waiters!

LOPÁK. Quite true.

GÁYEF [*with a gesture*]. I'm incorrigible, that's plain. [*Irritably to* YÁSHA.] What do you keep dodging about in front of me for?

YÁSHA [*laughing*]. I can't hear your voice without laughing.

GÁYEF [*to* MADAME RANÉVSKY]. Either he or I . . .

MME. R. Go away, Yásha; run along.

YÁSHA [*handing* MADAME RANÉVSKY *her purse*]. I'll go at once. [*Restraining his laughter with difficulty.*] This very minute. [*Exit* YÁSHA.

LOPÁK. Derigánof, the millionaire, wants to buy your property. They say he'll come to the auction himself.

MME. R. How did you hear?

LOPÁK. I was told so in town.

GÁYEF. Our aunt at Yaroslav has promised to send something; but I don't know when, or how much.

LOPÁK. How much will she send? Ten thousand pounds? Twenty thousand pounds?

MME. R. Oh, come. . . . A thousand or fifteen hundred at the most.

LOPÁK. Excuse me, but in all my life I never met anybody so frivolous as you two, so crazy and unbusiness-like! I tell you in plain Russian your property is going to be sold, and you don't seem to understand what I say.

MME. R. Well, what are we to do? Tell us what you want us to do.

LOPÁK. Don't I tell you every day? Every day I

say the same thing over and over again. You must lease off the cherry orchard and the rest of the estate for villas; you must do it at once, this very moment; the auction will be on you in two twos! Try and understand. Once you make up your mind there are to be villas, you can get all the money you want, and you're saved.

MME. R. Villas and villa residents, oh, please, . . . it's so vulgar!

GÁYEF. I quite agree with you.

LOPÁK. I shall either cry, or scream, or faint. I can't stand it! You'll be the death of me. [*To* GÁYEF.] You're an old woman!

GÁYEF. Who's that?

LOPÁK. You're an old woman! [*Going.*]

MME. R. [*frightened*]. No, don't go. Stay here, there's a dear! Perhaps we shall think of some way.

LOPÁK. What's the good of thinking!

MME. R. Please don't go; I want you. At any rate, it's gayer when you're here. [*A pause.*] I keep expecting something to happen, as if the house were going to tumble down about our ears.

GÁYEF [*in deep abstraction*]. Off the cushion on the corner; double into the middle pocket. . . .

MME. R. We have been very, very sinful!

LOPÁK. You! What sins have you committed?

GÁYEF [*eating candy*]. They say I've devoured all my substance in sugar candy. [*Laughing.*]

MME. R. Oh, the sins that I have committed. . . . I've always squandered money at random like a mad-woman; I married a man who made nothing but debts. My husband drank himself to death on champagne; he was a fearful drinker. Then for my sins I fell in love and went off with another man; and immediately—that was my first punishment—a blow full on the head . . . here, in this very river . . . my little boy was drowned; and I went abroad, right, right away, never to come back any more, never to see this river again. . . . I shut my eyes and ran, like a mad thing, and *he* came after me, pitiless and cruel. I bought a villa at Mentone, because he fell ill there, and for three years I knew no rest day or night; the sick man tormented and wore down my soul. Then, last year, when my villa was sold to pay my debts, I went off to Paris, and he came and robbed me of everything, left me and took up with another woman, and I tried to poison myself. . . . It was all so stupid, so humiliating. . . . Then suddenly I longed to be back in Russia, in my own country, with my little girl. . . . [*Wiping away her tears.*] Lord, Lord, be merciful to me; forgive my sins!

Do not punish me any more! [*Taking a telegram from her pocket.*] I got this today from Paris. . . . He asks to be forgiven, begs me to go back. . . . [*Tearing up the telegram.*] Isn't that music that I hear? [*Listening.*]

GÁYEF. That's our famous Jewish band. You remember? Four fiddles, a flute, and a double bass.

MME. R. Does it still exist? We must make them come up sometime; we'll have a dance.

LOPÁK. [*listening*]. I don't hear anything. [*Singing softly.*]

"The Germans for a fee will turn
A Russ into a Frenchman."

[*Laughing.*] I saw a very funny piece at the theater last night; awfully funny!

MME. R. It probably wasn't a bit funny. You people oughtn't to go and see plays; you ought to try to see yourselves; to see what a dull life you lead, and how much too much you talk.

LOPÁK. Quite right. To tell the honest truth, our life's an imbecile affair. [*A pause.*] My papa was a peasant, an idiot; he understood nothing; he taught me nothing; all he did was to beat me, when he was drunk, with a walking-stick. As a matter of fact I'm just as big a blockhead and idiot as he was. I never did any lessons; my handwriting's abominable; I write so badly I'm ashamed before people; like a pig.

MME. R. You ought to get married.

LOPÁK. Yes, that's true.

MME. R. Why not marry Barbara? She's a nice girl.

LOPÁK. Yes.

MME. R. She's a nice straightforward creature; works all day; and what's most important, she loves you. You've been fond of her for a long time.

LOPÁK. Well, why not? I'm quite willing. She's a very nice girl. [*A pause.*]

GÁYEF. I've been offered a place in a bank. Six hundred pounds a year. Do you hear?

MME. R. You in a bank! Stay where you are.

Enter FIRS, *carrying an overcoat.*

FIRS [*to* GÁYEF]. Put this on, please, master; it's getting damp.

GÁYEF [*putting on the coat*]. What a plague you are, Firs!

FIRS. What's the use. . . . You went off and never told me. [*Examining his clothes.*]

MME. R. How old you've got, Firs!

FIRS. I beg your pardon?

LOPÁK. She says how old you've got!

FIRS. I've been alive a long time. When they

found me a wife, your father wasn't even born yet. [*Laughing.*] And when the Liberation came I was already chief valet. But I wouldn't have any Liberation then; I stayed with the master. [*A pause.*] I remember how happy everybody was, but why they were happy they didn't know themselves.

LOPÁK. It was fine before then. Anyway they used to flog 'em.

FIRS [*mishearing him*]. I should think so! The peasants minded the masters, and the masters minded the peasants, but now it's all higgledy-piggledy; you can't make head or tail of it.

GÁYEF. Shut up, Firs. I must go into town again tomorrow. I've been promised an introduction to a general who'll lend money on a bill.

LOPÁK. You'll do no good. You won't even pay the interest; set your mind at ease about that.

MME. R. [*to LOPÁKHIN*]. He's only talking nonsense. There's no such general at all.

Enter TROPHÍMOF, ÁNYA and BARBARA.

GÁYEF. Here come the others.

ÁNYA. Here's mamma.

MME. R. [*tenderly*]. Come along, come along . . . my little ones. . . . [*Embracing ÁNYA and BARBARA.*] If only you knew how much I love you both! Sit beside me . . . there, like that. [*Everyone sits.*]

LOPÁK. The Perpetual Student's always among the girls.

TROPH. It's no affair of yours.

LOPÁK. He's nearly fifty and still a student.

TROPH. Stop your idiotic jokes!

LOPÁK. What are you losing your temper for, silly?

TROPH. Why can't you leave me alone?

LOPÁK. [*laughing*]. I should like to know what your opinion is of me.

TROPH. My opinion of you, Yermolái Alexéyitch, is this. You're a rich man; you'll soon be a millionaire. Just as a beast of prey which devours everything that comes in its way is necessary for the conversion of matter, so you are necessary, too. [*All laugh.*]

BARB. Tell us something about the planets, Peter, instead.

MME. R. No. Let's go on with the conversation we were having yesterday.

TROPH. What about?

GÁYEF. About the proud man.

TROPH. We had a long talk yesterday, but we didn't come to any conclusion. There is something mystical in the proud man in the sense in which

you use the words. You may be right from your point of view, but, if we look at it simple-mindedly, what room is there for pride? Is there any sense in it, when man is so poorly constructed from the physiological point of view, when the vast majority of us are so gross and stupid and profoundly unhappy? We must give up admiring ourselves. The only thing to do is to work.

GÁYEF. We shall die all the same.

TROPH. Who knows? And what does it mean, to die? Perhaps man has a hundred senses, and when he dies only the five senses that we know perish with him, and the other ninety-five remain alive.

MME. R. How clever you are, Peter!

LOPÁK. [*ironically*]. Oh, extraordinary!

TROPH. Mankind marches forward, perfecting its strength. Everything that is unattainable for us now will one day be near and clear; but we must work; we must help with all our force those who seek for truth. At present only a few men work in Russia. The vast majority of the educated people that I know seek after nothing, do nothing, and are as yet incapable of work. They call themselves the "Intelligentsia," they say "thou" and "thee" to the servants, they treat the peasants like animals, learn nothing, read nothing serious, do absolutely nothing, only talk about science, and understand little or nothing about art. They are all serious; they all have solemn faces; they only discuss important subjects; they philosophize; but meanwhile the vast majority of us, ninety-nine per cent, live like savages; at the least thing they curse and punch people's heads; they eat like beasts and sleep in dirt and bad air; there are bugs everywhere, evil smells, damp and moral degradation. . . . It's plain that all our clever conversations are only meant to distract our own attention and other people's. Show me where those crèches are, that they're always talking so much about; or those reading-rooms. They are only things people write about in novels; they don't really exist at all. Nothing exists but dirt, vulgarity, and Asiatic ways. I am afraid of solemn faces; I dislike them; I am afraid of solemn conversations. Let us rather hold our tongues.

LOPÁK. Do you know, I get up at five every morning; I work from morning till night; I am always handling my own money or other people's, and I see the sort of men there are about me. One only has to begin to do anything to see how few honest and decent people there are. Sometimes, as I lie awake in bed, I think: "O Lord, you have given us mighty forests, boundless fields and immeasurable horizons, and, we living in their midst, ought really to be giants."

MME. R. Oh, dear, you want giants! They are all very well in fairy stories; but in real life they are rather alarming.

EPHIKHÓDOF *passes at the back of the scene, playing on his guitar.*

MME. R. [*pensively*]. There goes Ephikhódof.
ÁNYA [*pensively*]. There goes Ephikhódof.
GÁYEF. The sun has set.
TROPH. Yes.
GÁYEF [*as if declaiming, but not loud*]. O Nature, wonderful Nature, you glow with eternal light; beautiful and indifferent, you whom we call our mother, uniting in yourself both life and death, you animate and you destroy. . . .
BARB. [*entreatingly*]. Uncle!
ÁNYA. You're at it again, uncle.
TROPH. You'd far better double the red into the middle pocket.
GÁYEF. I'll hold my tongue! I'll hold my tongue!

They all sit pensively. Silence reigns, broken only by the mumbling of old FIRS. *Suddenly a distant sound is heard as if from the sky, the sound of a string breaking, dying away, melancholy.*

MME. R. What's that?
LOPÁK. I don't know. It's a lifting-tub given way somewhere away in the mines. It must be a long way off.
GÁYEF. Perhaps it's some sort of bird . . . a heron, or something.
TROPH. Or an owl. . . .
MME. R. [*shuddering*]. There is something uncanny about it!
FIRS. The same thing happened before the great misfortune: the owl screeched and the samovar kept humming.
GÁYEF. What great misfortune?
FIRS. The Liberation. [*A pause.*]
MME. R. Come, everyone, let's go in; it's getting late. [*To* ÁNYA.] You've tears in your eyes. What is it, little one? [*Embracing her.*]
ÁNYA. Nothing, mamma. I'm all right.
TROPH. There's someone coming.

A Tramp appears in a torn white peaked cap and overcoat. He is slightly drunk.

TRAMP. Excuse me, but can I go through this way straight to the station?
GÁYEF. Certainly. Follow this path.

TRAMP. I am uncommonly obliged to you, sir. [*Coughing.*] We're having lovely weather. [*Declaiming.*] "Brother, my suffering brother" . . . "Come forth to the Volga. Who moans?" . . . [*To* BARBARA.] Mademoiselle, please spare a sixpence for a hungry fellow-countryman.

BARBARA, *frightened, screams.*

LOPÁK. [*angrily*]. There's a decency for every indecency to observe!
MME. R. Take this; here you are. [*Fumbling in her purse.*] I haven't any silver. . . . Never mind, take this sovereign.
TRAMP. I am uncommonly obliged to you, madam. [*Exit Tramp. Laughter.*
BARB. [*frightened*]. I'm going! I'm going! Oh, mamma, there's nothing for the servants to eat at home, and you've gone and given this man a sovereign.
MME. R. What's to be done with your stupid old mother? I'll give you up everything I have when I get back. Yermolái Alexéyitch, lend me some more money.
LOPÁK. Very good.
MME. R. Come along, everyone; it's time to go in. We've settled all about your marriage between us, Barbara. I wish you joy.
BARB. [*through her tears*]. You mustn't joke about such things, mamma.
LOPÁK. Amelia, get thee to a nunnery, go!
GÁYEF. My hands are all trembling; it's ages since I had a game of billiards.
LOPÁK. Amelia, nymphlet, in thine orisons remember me.
MME. R. Come along. It's nearly supper-time.
BARB. How he frightened me! My heart is simply throbbing.
LOPÁK. Allow me to remind you, the cherry orchard is to be sold on the twenty-second of August. Bear that in mind; bear that in mind!
[*Exeunt Omnes except* TROPHÍMOF *and* ÁNYA.
ÁNYA [*laughing*]. Many thanks to the Tramp for frightening Barbara; at last we are alone.
TROPH. Barbara's afraid we shall go and fall in love with each other. Day after day she never leaves us alone. With her narrow mind she cannot understand that we are above love. To avoid everything petty, everything illusory, everything that prevents one from being free and happy, that is the whole meaning and purpose of our life. Forward! We march on irresistibly towards that bright star which burns far, far before us! Forward! Don't tarry, comrades!

ÁNYA [*clasping her hands*]. What beautiful things you say! [*A pause.*] Isn't it enchanting here today!

TROPH. Yes, it's wonderful weather.

ÁNYA. What have you done to me, Peter? Why is it that I no longer love the cherry orchard as I did? I used to love it so tenderly; I thought there was no better place on earth than our garden.

TROPH. All Russia is our garden. The earth is great and beautiful; it is full of wonderful places. [*A pause.*] Think, Ánya, your grandfather, your great-grandfather and all your ancestors were serf-owners, owners of living souls. Do not human spirits look out at you from every tree in the orchard, from every leaf and every stem? Do you not hear human voices? . . . Oh! it is terrible. Your orchard frightens me. When I walk through it in the evening or at night, the rugged bark on the trees glows with a dim light, and the cherry trees seem to see all that happened a hundred and two hundred years ago in painful and oppressive dreams. Well, well, we have fallen at least two hundred years behind the times. We have achieved nothing at all as yet; we have not made up our minds how we stand with the past; we only philosophize, complain of boredom, or drink vodka. It is so plain that, before we can live in the present, we must first redeem the past, and have done with it; and it is only by suffering that we can redeem it, only by strenuous, unremitting toil. Understand that, Ánya.

ÁNYA. The house we live in has long since ceased to be our house; and I shall go away, I give you my word.

TROPH. If you have the household keys, throw them in the well and go away. Be free, be free as the wind.

ÁNYA [*enthusiastically*]. How beautifully you put it!

TROPH. Believe what I say, Ánya; believe what I say. I'm not thirty yet; I am still young, still a student; but what I have been through! I am hungry as the winter; I am sick, anxious, poor as a beggar. Fate has tossed me hither and thither; I have been everywhere, everywhere. But wherever I have been, every minute, day and night, my soul has been full of mysterious anticipations. I feel the approach of happiness, Ánya; I see it coming. . . .

ÁNYA [*pensively*]. The moon is rising.

EPHIKHÓDOF *is heard still playing the same sad tune on his guitar. The moon rises. Somewhere beyond the poplar trees,* BARBARA *is heard calling for* ÁNYA: *"Ánya, where are you?"*

TROPH. Yes, the moon is rising. [*A pause.*] There it is, there is happiness; it is coming towards us, nearer and nearer; I can hear the sound of its footsteps. . . . And if we do not see it, if we do not know it, what does it matter? Others will see it.

BARB. [*without*]. Ánya? Where are you?

TROPH. There's Barbara again! [*Angrily.*] It really is too bad!

ÁNYA. Never mind. Let us go down to the river. It's lovely there.

TROPH. Come on!

[*Exeunt* ÁNYA *and* TROPHÍMOF.

BARB. [*without*]. Ánya! Ánya!

ACT III

A sitting-room separated by an arch from a big drawing-room behind. Chandelier lighted. The Jewish band mentioned in Act II is heard playing on the landing. Evening. In the drawing-room they are dancing the grand rond. SIMEÓNOF-PÍSHTCHIK *is heard crying, "Promenade à une paire!"*

The dancers come down into the sitting-room. The first pair consists of PÍSHTCHIK *and* CHARLOTTE; *the second of* TROPHÍMOF *and* MADAME RANÉVSKY; *the third of* ÁNYA *and the Post-Office Official; the fourth of* BARBARA *and the Stationmaster, etc., etc.* BARBARA *is crying softly and wipes away the tears as she dances. In the last pair comes* DUNYÁSHA. *They cross the sitting-room.*

PÍSHT. "Grand rond, balances. . . . Les cavaliers à genou et remerciez vos dames."

FIRS *in evening dress carries seltzer water across on a tray.* PÍSHTCHIK *and* TROPHÍMOF *come down into the sitting-room.*

PÍSHT. I am a full-blooded man; I've had two strokes already; it's hard work dancing, but, as the saying goes, "If you run with the pack, bark or no, but anyway wag your tail." I'm as strong as a horse. My old father, who was fond of his joke, rest his soul, used to say, talking of our pedigree, that the ancient stock of the Simeónof-Píshtchiks was descended from that very horse that Caligula made a senator. . . . [*Sitting.*] But the worst of it is, I've got no money. A hungry dog believes in nothing but meat. [*Snoring and waking up again at once.*] I'm just the same. . . . It's nothing but money, money, with me.

TROPH. Yes, it's quite true, there is something horse-like about your build.

PÍSHT. Well, well . . . a horse is a jolly creature . . . you can sell a horse.

A sound of billiards being played in the next room. BARBARA *appears in the drawing-room beyond the arch.*

TROPH. [*teasing her*]. Madame Lopákhin! Madame Lopákhin.

BARB. [*angrily*]. Moldy gentleman!

TROPH. Yes, I'm a moldy gentleman, and I'm proud of it.

BARB. [*bitterly*]. We've hired the band, but where's the money to pay for it? [*Exit* BARBARA.

TROPH. [*to* PÍSHTCHIK]. If the energy which you have spent in the course of your whole life in looking for money to pay the interest on your loans had been diverted to some other purpose, you would have had enough of it, I dare say, to turn the world upside down.

PÍSHT. Nietzsche the philosopher, a very remarkable man, very famous, a man of gigantic intellect, says in his works that it's quite right to forge bank notes.

TROPH. What, have you read Nietzsche?

PÍSHT. Well . . . Dáshenka told me. . . . But I'm in such a hole, I'd forge 'em for twopence. I've got to pay thirty-one pounds the day after tomorrow. . . . I've got thirteen pounds already. [*Feeling his pockets; alarmed.*] My money's gone! I've lost my money! [*Crying.*] Where's my money got to? [*Joyfully.*] Here it is, inside the lining. . . . It's thrown me all in a perspiration.

Enter MADAME RANÉVSKY *and* CHARLOTTE.

MME. R. [*humming a lezginka*]. Why is Leoníd so long? What can he be doing in the town? [*To* DUNYÁSHA.] Dunyásha, ask the musicians if they'll have some tea.

TROPH. The sale did not come off, in all probability.

MME. R. It was a stupid day for the musicians to come; it was a stupid day to have this dance. . . . Well, well, it doesn't matter. . . . [*She sits down and sings softly to herself.*]

CHARL. [*giving* PÍSHTCHIK *a pack of cards*]. Here is a pack of cards. Think of any card you like.

PÍSHT. I've thought of one.

CHARL. Now shuffle the pack. That's all right. Give them here, oh, most worthy Mr. Píshtchik.

Ein, zwei, drei! Now look and you'll find it in your side pocket.

PÍSHT. [*taking a card from his side pocket*]. The Eight of Spades! You're perfectly right. [*Astonished.*] Well, I never!

CHARL. [*holding the pack on the palm of her hand, to* TROPHÍMOF]. Say quickly, what's the top card?

TROPH. Well, say the Queen of Spades.

CHARL. Right! [*To* PÍSHTCHIK.] Now, then, what's the top card?

PÍSHT. Ace of Hearts.

CHARL. Right! [*She claps her hands; the pack of cards disappears.*] What a beautiful day we've been having.

A mysterious female voice answers her as if from under the floor: "Yes, indeed, a charming day, mademoiselle."

CHARL. You are my beautiful idea.

THE VOICE. *"I think you also ferry beautiful, mademoiselle."*

STATIONMASTER [*applauding*]. Bravo, Miss Ventriloquist!

PÍSHT. [*astonished*]. Well, I never! Bewitching Charlotte Ivánovna, I'm head over ears in love with you.

CHARL. In love! [*Shrugging her shoulders.*] Are you capable of love? Guter Mensch, aber schlechter Musikant!

TROPH. [*slapping* PÍSHTCHIK *on the shoulder*]. You old horse!

CHARL. Now, attention, please; one more trick [*Taking a shawl from a chair.*] Now here's a shawl, and a very pretty shawl; I'm going to sell this very pretty shawl. [*Shaking it.*] Who'll buy? who'll buy?

PÍSHT. [*astonished*]. Well, I never!

CHARL. Ein, zwei, drei! [*She lifts the shawl quickly; behind it stands* ÁNYA, *who drops a curtsy, runs to her mother, kisses her, then runs up into the drawing-room amid general applause.*]

MME. R. [*applauding*]. Bravo! bravo!

CHARL. Once more. Ein, zwei, drei! [*She lifts up the shawl; behind it stands* BARBARA, *bowing.*]

PÍSHT. [*astonished*]. Well, I never!

CHARL. That's all. [*She throws the shawl over* PÍSHTCHIK, *makes a curtsy and runs up into the drawing-room.*]

PÍSHT. [*hurrying after her*]. You little rascal . . . there's a girl for you, there's a girl. . . . [*Exit.*

MME. R. And still no sign of Leoníd. What he's doing in the town so long, I can't understand. It must be all over by now; the property's sold; or the auction never came off; why does he keep me in suspense so long?

BARB. [trying to soothe her]. Uncle has bought it, I am sure of that.

TROPH. [mockingly]. Of course he has.

BARB. Grannie sent him a power of attorney to buy it in her name and transfer the mortgage. She's done it for Ánya's sake. I'm perfectly sure that Heaven will help us and uncle will buy it.

MME. R. Your Yaroslav grannie sent fifteen hundred pounds to buy the property in her name—she doesn't trust us—but it wouldn't be enough even to pay the interest. [Covering her face with her hands.] My fate is being decided today, my fate . . .

TROPH. [teasing BARBARA]. Madame Lopákhin!

BARB. [angrily]. Perpetual Student! He's been sent down twice from the University.

MME. R. Why do you get angry, Barbara? He calls you Madame Lopákhin for fun. Why not? You can marry Lopákhin if you like; he's a nice, interesting man; you needn't if you don't; nobody wants to force you, my pet.

BARB. I take it very seriously, mamma, I must confess. He's a nice man and I like him.

MME. R. Then marry him. There's no good putting it off that I can see.

BARB. But, mamma, I can't propose to him myself. For two whole years everybody's been talking about him to me, everyone; but he either says nothing or makes a joke of it. I quite understand. He's making money; he's always busy; he can't be bothered with me. If I only had some money, even a little, even ten pounds, I would give everything up and go right away. I would go into a nunnery.

TROPH. [mocking]. What bliss!

BARB. [to TROPHÍMOF]. A student ought to be intelligent. [In a gentler voice, crying.] How ugly you've grown, Peter; how old you've grown! [She stops crying; to MADAME RANÉVSKY.] But I can't live without work, mamma. I must have something to do every minute of the day.

Enter YÁSHA.

YÁSHA [trying not to laugh]. Ephikhódof has broken a billiard cue. [Exit YÁSHA.

BARB. What's Ephikhódof doing here? Who gave him leave to play billiards? I don't understand these people. [Exit BARBARA.

MME. R. Don't tease her, Peter. Don't you see that she's unhappy enough already?

TROPH. I wish she wouldn't be so fussy, always meddling in other people's affairs. The whole summer she's given me and Ánya no peace; she is afraid we'll work up a romance between us. What business is it of hers? I'm sure I never gave her any ground; I'm not likely to be so commonplace. We are above love!

MME. R. Then I suppose I must be beneath love. [Deeply agitated.] Why doesn't Leoníd come? Oh, if only I knew whether the property's sold or not! It seems such an impossible disaster, that I don't know what to think. . . . I'm bewildered . . . I shall burst out screaming, I shall do something idiotic. Save me, Peter; say something to me, say something. . . .

TROPH. Whether the property is sold today or whether it's not sold, surely it's all one? It's all over with it long ago; there's no turning back; the path is overgrown. Be calm, dear Lyubóf Andréyevna. You mustn't deceive yourself any longer; for once you must look the truth straight in the face.

MME. R. What truth? You can see what's truth, and what's untruth, but I seem to have lost the power of vision; I see nothing. You settle every important question so boldly; but tell me, Peter, isn't that because you're young, because you have never solved any question of your own as yet by suffering? You look boldly ahead; isn't it only that you don't see or divine anything terrible in the future; because life is still hidden from your young eyes? You are bolder, honester, deeper than we are, but reflect, show me just a finger's breadth of consideration, take pity on me. Don't you see? I was born here, my father and mother lived here, and my grandfather; I love this house; without the cherry orchard my life has no meaning for me, and if it *must* be sold, then for Heaven's sake, sell me too! [Embracing TROPHÍMOF and kissing him on the forehead.] My little boy was drowned here. [Crying.] Be gentle with me, dear, kind Peter.

TROPH. You know I sympathize with all my heart.

MME. R. Yes, yes, but you ought to say it somehow differently. [Taking out her handkerchief and dropping a telegram.] I am so wretched today, you can't imagine! All this noise jars on me, my heart jumps at every sound. I tremble all over; but I can't shut myself up; I am afraid of the silence when I'm alone. Don't be hard on me, Peter; I love you like a son. I would gladly let Ánya marry you, I swear it; but you must work, Peter; you must get your degree. You do nothing; Fate tosses you about from place to place; and that's not right. It's true what I say, isn't it? And you must do something to your beard to make it grow better. [*Laughing.*] I can't help laughing at you.

TROPH. [*picking up the telegram*]. I don't wish to be an Adonis.

MME. R. It's a telegram from Paris. I get them every day. One came yesterday, another today. That savage is ill again; he's in a bad way. . . . He asks me to forgive him, he begs me to come; and I really ought to go to Paris and be with him. You look at me sternly; but what am I to do, Peter? What am I to do? He's ill, he's lonely, he's unhappy. Who is to look after him? Who is to keep him from doing stupid things? Who is to give him his medicine when it's time? After all, why should I be ashamed to say it? I love him, that's plain. I love him, I love him. . . . My love is like a stone tied round my neck; it's dragging me down to the bottom; but I love my stone. I can't live without it. [*Squeezing Trophimof's hand.*] Don't think ill of me, Peter; don't say anything! Don't say anything!

TROPH. [*crying*]. Forgive my bluntness, for Heaven's sake; but the man has simply robbed you.

MME. R. No, no, no! [*Stopping her ears.*] You mustn't say that!

TROPH. He's a rascal; everybody sees it but yourself; he's a petty rascal, a ne'er-do-well . . .

MME. R. [*angry but restrained*]. You're twenty-six or twenty-seven, and you're still a Lower School boy!

TROPH. Who cares?

MME. R. You ought to be a man by now; at your age you ought to understand people who love. You ought to love someone yourself, you ought to be in love! [*Angrily.*] Yes, yes! It's not purity with you; it's simply you're a smug, a figure of fun, a freak. . . .

TROPH. [*horrified*]. What does she say?

MME. R. "I am above love"! You're not above love; you're simply what Firs calls a "job-lot." At your age you ought to be ashamed not to have a mistress!

TROPH. [*aghast*]. This is awful! What does she say? [*Going quickly up into the drawing-room, clasping his head with his hands.*] This is something awful! I can't stand it; I'm off . . . [*Exit, but returns at once.*] All is over between us!
[*Exit to landing.*

MME. R. [*calling after him*]. Stop, Peter! Don't be ridiculous; I was only joking! Peter!

TROPHÍMOF *is heard on the landing going quickly down the stairs, and suddenly falling down them with a crash.* ÁNYA *and* BARBARA *scream. A moment later the sound of laughter.*

MME. R. What has happened?

ÁNYA *runs in.*

ÁNYA [*laughing*]. Peter's tumbled downstairs.
[*She runs out again.*

MME. R. What a ridiculous fellow he is! [*The Stationmaster stands in the middle of the drawing-room beyond the arch and recites Alexey Tolstoy's poem, "The Sinner." Everybody stops to listen, but after a few lines the sound of a waltz is heard from the landing and he breaks off. All dance.* TROPHÍMOF, ÁNYA, BARBARA, *and* MADAME RANÉVSKY *enter from the landing.*]

MME. R. Come, Peter, come, you pure spirit. . . . I beg your pardon. Let's have a dance. [*She dances with* TROPHÍMOF. ÁNYA *and* BARBARA *dance.*]

Enter FIRS, *and stands his walking-stick by the side door. Enter* YÁSHA *by the drawing-room; he stands looking at the dancers.*

YÁSHA. Well, grandfather?

FIRS. I'm not feeling well. In the old days it was generals and barons and admirals that danced at our dances, but now we send for the Postmaster and the Stationmaster, and even they make a favor of coming. I'm sort of weak all over. The old master, their grandfather, used to give us all sealing wax, when we had anything the matter. I've taken sealing wax every day for twenty years and more. Perhaps that's why I'm still alive.

YÁSHA. I'm sick of you, grandfather. [*Yawning.*] I wish you'd die and have done with it.

FIRS. Ah! you . . . job-lot. [*He mumbles to himself.*]

TROPHÍMOF *and* MADAME RANÉVSKY *dance beyond the arch and down into the sitting-room.*

MME. R. *Merci.* I'll sit down. [*Sitting.*] I'm tired.

Enter ÁNYA.

ÁNYA [*agitated*]. There was somebody in the kitchen just now saying that the cherry orchard was sold today.

MME. R. Sold? Who to?

ÁNYA. He didn't say who to. He's gone. [*She dances with* TROPHÍMOF. *Both dance up into the drawing-room.*]

YÁSHA. It was some old fellow chattering; a stranger.

FIRS. And still Leoníd Andréyitch doesn't come. He's wearing his light overcoat, *demi-saison;* he'll catch cold as like as not. Ah, young wood, green wood!

MME. R. This is killing me. Yásha, go and find out who it was sold to.

YÁSHA. Why, he's gone long ago, the old man. [*Laughs.*]

MME. R. [*vexed*]. What are you laughing at? What are you glad about?

YÁSHA. He's a ridiculous fellow is Ephikhódof. Nothing in him. Twenty-two misfortunes!

MME. R. Firs, if the property is sold, where will you go to?

FIRS. Wherever you tell me, there I'll go.

MME. R. Why do you look like that? Are you ill? You ought to be in bed.

FIRS [*ironically*]. Oh, yes, I'll go to bed, and who'll hand the things round, who'll give orders? I've the whole house on my hands.

YÁSHA. Lyubóf Andréyevna! Let me ask a favor of you; be so kind; if you go to Paris again, take me with you, I beseech you. It's absolutely impossible for me to stay here. [*Looking about; sotto voce.*] What's the use of talking? You can see for yourself this is a barbarous country; the people have no morals; and the boredom! The food in the kitchen is something shocking, and on the top of it old Firs going about mumbling irrelevant nonsense. Take me back with you; be so kind!

Enter PÍSHTCHIK.

PÍSHT. May I have the pleasure . . . a bit of a waltz, charming lady? [MADAME RANÉVSKY *takes his arm*.] All the same, enchanting lady, you must let me have eighteen pounds. [*Dancing.*] Let me have . . . eighteen pounds.

[*Exeunt dancing through the arch.*]

YÁSHA [*singing to himself*].
"Oh, wilt thou understand
The turmoil of my soul?"

Beyond the arch appears a figure in gray tall hat and check trousers, jumping and waving its arms. Cries of "Bravo, Charlotte Ivánovna."

DUNY. [*stopping to powder her face*]. Mamselle Ánya tells me I'm to dance; there are so many gentlemen and so few ladies. But dancing makes me giddy and makes my heart beat, Firs Nikoláyevitch; and just now the gentleman from the postoffice said something so nice to me, oh, so nice! It quite took my breath away. [*The music stops.*]

FIRS. What did he say to you?

DUNY. He said, "You are like a flower."

YÁSHA [*yawning*]. Cad!   [*Exit* YÁSHA.

DUNY. Like a flower! I am so ladylike and refined, I dote on compliments.

FIRS. You'll come to a bad end.

Enter EPHIKHÓDOF.

EPHIK. You are not pleased to see me, Avdótya Fyódorovna, no more than if I were some sort of insect. [*Sighing.*] Ah! Life! Life!

DUNY. What do you want?

EPHIK. Undoubtedly perhaps you are right. [*Sighing.*] But of course, if one regards it, so to speak, from the point of view, if I may allow myself the expression, and with apologies for my frankness, you have finally reduced me to a state of mind. I quite appreciate my destiny; every day some misfortune happens to me, and I have long since grown accustomed to it, and face my fortune with a smile. You have passed your work to me, and although I . . .

DUNY. Let us talk of this another time, if you please; but now leave me in peace. I am busy meditating. [*Playing with her fan.*]

EPHIK. Every day some misfortune befalls me, and yet if I may venture to say so, I meet them with smiles and even laughter.

Enter BARBARA *from the drawing-room.*

BARB. [*to* EPHIKHÓDOF]. Haven't you gone yet, Simeon? You seem to pay no attention to what you're told. [*To* DUNYÁSHA.] You get out of here, Dunyásha. [*To* EPHIKHÓDOF.] First you play billiards and break a cue, and then you march about the drawing-room as if you were a guest!

EPHIK. Allow me to inform you that it's not your place to call me to account.

BARB. I'm not calling you to account; I'm merely talking to you. All you can do is to walk about from one place to another, without ever doing a stroke of work; and why on earth we keep a clerk at all Heaven only knows.

EPHIK. [*offended*]. Whether I work, or whether I walk, or whether I eat, or whether I play billiards is a question to be decided only by my elders and people who understand.

BARB. [*furious*]. How dare you talk to me like that! How dare you! I don't understand things, don't I? You clear out of here this minute! Do you hear me? This minute!

EPHIK. [*flinching*]. I must beg you to express yourself in genteeler language.

BARB. [*beside herself*]. You clear out this instant second! Out you go! [*Following him as he retreats towards the door.*] Twenty-two misfortunes! Make yourself scarce! Get out of my sight!

[*Exit* EPHIKHÓDOF.

EPHIK. [*without*]. I shall lodge a complaint against you.

BARB. What! You're coming back, are you? [*Seizing the walking-stick left at the door by* FIRS.] Come on! Come on! Come on! I'll teach you! Are you coming? Are you coming? Then take that. [*She slashes with the stick.*]

Enter LOPÁKHIN.

LOPÁK. Many thanks; much obliged.

BARB. [*still angry, but ironical*]. Sorry!

LOPÁK. Don't mention it. I'm very grateful for your warm reception.

BARB. It's not worth thanking me for. [*She walks away, then looks round and asks in a gentle voice:*] I didn't hurt you?

LOPÁK. Oh, no, nothing to matter. I shall have a bump like a goose's egg, that's all.

Voices from the drawing-room: "Lopákhin has arrived! Yermolái Alexéyitch!"

PÍSHT. Let my eyes see him, let my ears hear him! [*He and* LOPÁKHIN *kiss.*] You smell of brandy, old man. We're having a high time, too.

Enter MADAME RANÉVSKY.

MME. R. Is it you, Yermolái Alexéyitch? Why have you been so long? Where is Leoníd?

LOPÁK. Leoníd Andréyitch came back with me. He's just coming.

MME. R. [*agitated*]. What happened? Did the sale come off? Tell me, tell me!

LOPÁK. [*embarrassed, afraid of showing his pleasure*]. The sale was all over by four o'clock. We missed the train and had to wait till half-past eight. [*Sighing heavily.*] Ouf! I'm rather giddy. . . .

Enter GÁYEF. *In one hand he carries parcels; with the other he wipes away his tears.*

MME. R. What happened, Lénya? Come, Lénya? [*Impatiently, crying.*] Be quick, be quick, for Heaven's sake!

GÁYEF [*answering her only with an up-and-down gesture of the hand; to* FIRS, *crying*]. Here, take these. . . . Here are some anchovies and Black Sea herrings. I've had nothing to eat all day. Lord, what I've been through! [*Through the open door of the billiard-room comes the click of the billiard balls and* YÁSHA's *voice: "Seven, eighteen!"* GÁYEF's *expression changes; he stops crying.*] I'm frightfully tired. Come and help me change, Firs. [*He goes up through the drawing-room,* FIRS *following.*]

PÍSHT. What about the sale? Come on, tell us all about it.

MME. R. Was the cherry orchard sold?

LOPÁK. Yes.

MME. R. Who bought it?

LOPÁK. I did. [*A pause.* MADAME RANÉVSKY *is overwhelmed at the news. She would fall to the ground but for the chair and table by her.* BARBARA *takes the keys from her belt, throws them on the floor in the middle of the sitting-room, and exit.*] I bought it. Wait a bit; don't hurry me; my head's in a whirl; I can't speak. . . . [*Laughing.*] When we got to the sale, Deriganof was there already. Leoníd Andréyitch had only fifteen hundred pounds, and Derigánof bid three thousand more than the mortgage right away. When I saw how things stood, I went for him and bid four thousand. He said four thousand five hundred. I said five thousand five hundred. He went up by five hundreds, you see, and I went up by thousands. . . . Well, it was soon over. I bid nine thousand more than the mortgage, and got it; and now the cherry orchard is mine! Mine! [*Laughing.*] Heavens alive! Just think of it! The cherry orchard is mine! Tell me that I'm drunk; tell me that I'm off my head; tell me that it's all a dream! . . . [*Stamping his feet.*] Don't laugh at me! If only my father and my grandfather could rise from their graves and see the whole affair, how their Yermolái, their flogged and ignorant Yermolái, who used to run about barefooted in the winter, how this same Yermolái had bought a property that hasn't its equal for beauty anywhere in the whole world! I have bought the property where my father and grandfather were slaves, where they weren't even allowed into the kitchen. I'm asleep, it's only a vision, it isn't real. . . . 'Tis the fruit of imagination, wrapped in the mists of ignorance. [*Picking up the keys and smiling affectionately.*] She's thrown down her keys; she wants to show that she's no longer mistress here. . . . [*Jingling them together.*] Well, well, what's the odds? [*The musicians are heard tuning up.*] Hey, musicians, play! I want to hear you. Come, everyone, and see Yermolái Lopákhin lay his ax to the cherry orchard, come and see the trees fall down! We'll fill the place with villas; our grandsons and great-grandsons shall see a new life here. . . . Strike up, music!

The band plays. MADAME RANÉVSKY *sinks into a chair and weeps bitterly.*

LOPÁK. [*reproachfully*]. Oh, why, why didn't you listen to me? You can't put the clock back now, poor dear. [*Crying.*] Oh, that all this were past and over! Oh, that our unhappy topsy-turvy life were changed!

PÍSHT. [*taking him by the arm, sotto voce*]. She's crying. Let's go into the drawing-room and leave her alone to . . . Come on. [*Taking him by the arm, and going up toward the drawing-room.*]

LOPÁK. What's up? Play your best, musicians! Let everything be as I want. [*Ironically.*] Here comes the new squire, the owner of the cherry orchard! [*Knocking up by accident against a table and nearly throwing down the candelabra.*] Never mind, I can pay for everything!

[*Exit with* PÍSHTCHIK. *Nobody remains in the drawing-room or sitting-room except* MADAME RANÉVSKY, *who sits huddled together, weeping bitterly. The band plays softly.*

Enter ÁNYA *and* TROPHÍMOF *quickly.* ÁNYA *goes to her mother and kneels before her.* TROPHÍMOF *stands in the entry to the drawing-room.*

ÁNYA. Mamma! Are you crying, mamma? My dear, good, sweet mamma! Darling, I love you! I bless you! The cherry orchard is sold; it's gone; it's quite true, it's quite true. But don't cry, mamma, you've still got life before you, you've still got your pure and lovely soul. Come with me, darling; come away from here. We'll plant a new garden, still lovelier than this. You will see it and understand, and happiness, deep, tranquil happiness will sink down on your soul, like the sun at eventide, and you'll smile, mamma. Come, darling, come with me!

ACT IV

Same scene as Act I. There are no window curtains, no pictures. The little furniture left is stacked in a corner, as if for sale. A feeling of emptiness. By the door to the hall and at the back of the scene are piled portmanteaux, bundles, etc. The door is open and the voices of BARBARA *and* ÁNYA *are audible.*

LOPÁKHIN *stands waiting.* YÁSHA *holds a tray with small tumblers full of champagne.* EPHIKHÓDOF *is tying up a box in the hall. A distant murmur of voices behind the scene; the Peasants have come to say good-by.*

GÁYEF [*without*]. Thank you, my lads, thank you.

YÁSHA. The common people have come to say good-by. I'll tell you what I think, Yermolái Alexéyitch; they're good fellows but rather stupid.

The murmur of voices dies away.

Enter MADAME RANÉVSKY *and* GÁYEF *from the hall. She is not crying, but she is pale, her face twitches, she cannot speak.*

GÁYEF. You gave them your purse, Lyuba. That was wrong, very wrong!

MME. R. I couldn't help it, I couldn't help it! [*Exeunt both.*

LOPÁK. [*calling after them through the doorway.*] Please come here! Won't you come here? Just a glass to say good-by. I forgot to bring any from the town, and could only raise one bottle at the station. Come along. [*A pause.*] What, won't you have any? [*Returning from the door.*] If I'd known, I wouldn't have bought it. I shan't have any either. [YÁSHA *sets the tray down carefully on a chair.*] Drink it yourself, Yásha.

YÁSHA. Here's to our departure! Good luck to them that stay! [*Drinking.*] This isn't real champagne, you take my word for it.

LOPÁK. Sixteen shillings a bottle. [*A pause.*] It's devilish cold in here.

YÁSHA. The fires weren't lighted today; we're all going away. [*He laughs.*]

LOPÁK. What are you laughing for?

YÁSHA. Just pleasure.

LOPÁK. Here we are in October, but it's as calm and sunny as summer. Good building weather. [*Looking at his watch and speaking off.*] Don't forget that there's only forty-seven minutes before the train goes. You must start for the station in twenty minutes. Make haste.

Enter TROPHÍMOF *in an overcoat, from out of doors.*

TROPH. I think it's time we were off. The carriages are round. What the deuce has become of my goloshes? I've lost 'em. [*Calling off.*] Ánya, my goloshes have disappeared. I can't find them anywhere!

LOPÁK. I've got to go to Kharkof. I'll start in the same train with you. I'm going to spend the winter at Kharkof. I've been loafing about all this time with you people, eating my head off for want of work. I can't live without work, I don't know what to do with my hands; they dangle about as if they didn't belong to me.

TROPH. Well, we're going now, and you'll be able to get back to your beneficent labors.

LOPÁK. Have a glass.

TROPH. Not for me.

LOPÁK. Well, so you're off to Moscow?

TROPH. Yes, I'll see them into the town, and go on to Moscow tomorrow.

LOPÁK. Well, well, . . . I suppose the professors haven't started their lectures yet; they're waiting till you arrive.

TROPH. It's no affair of yours.

LOPÁK. How many years have you been up at the University?

TROPH. Try and think of some new joke; this one's getting a bit flat. [*Looking for his goloshes.*] Look here, I dare say we shan't meet again, so let me give you a bit of advice as a keepsake: Don't flap your hands about! Get out of the habit of flapping. Building villas, prophesying that villa residents will turn into small freeholders, all that sort of thing is flapping, too. Well, when all's said and done, I like you. You have thin, delicate, artist fingers; you have a delicate artist soul.

LOPÁK. [*embracing him*]. Good-by, old chap. Thank you for everything. Take some money off me for the journey if you want it.

TROPH. What for? I don't want it.

LOPÁK. But you haven't got any.

TROPH. Yes, I have. Many thanks. I got some for a translation. Here it is, in my pocket. [*Anxiously.*] I can't find my goloshes anywhere!

BARB. [*from the next room*]. Here, take your garbage away! [*She throws a pair of goloshes on the stage.*]

TROPH. What are you so cross about, Barbara? Humph! . . . But those aren't *my* goloshes!

LOPÁK. In the spring I sowed three thousand acres of poppy and I have cleared four thousand pounds net profit. When my poppies were in flower, what a picture they made! So you see, I cleared four thousand pounds; and I wanted to lend you a bit because I've got it to spare. What's the good of being stuck up? I'm a peasant. . . . As man to man . . .

TROPH. Your father was a peasant; mine was a chemist; it doesn't prove anything. [LOPÁKHIN *takes out his pocketbook with paper money.*] Shut up, shut up. . . . If you offered me twenty thousand pounds I would not take it. I am a free man; nothing that you value so highly, all of you, rich and poor, has the smallest power over me; it's like thistledown floating on the wind. I can do without you; I can go past you; I'm strong and proud. Mankind marches forward to the highest truth, to the highest happiness possible on earth, and I march in the foremost ranks.

LOPÁK. Will you get there?

TROPH. Yes. [*A pause.*] I will get there myself, or I will show others the way.

The sound of axes hewing is heard in the distance.

LOPÁK. Well, good-by, old chap; it is time to start. Here we stand swaggering to each other, and life goes by all the time without heeding us. When I work for hours without getting tired, I get easy in my mind and I seem to know why I exist. But God alone knows what most of the people in Russia were born for. . . . Well, who cares? It doesn't affect the circulation of work. They say Leoníd Andréyitch has got a place; he's going to be in a bank and get six hundred pounds a year. . . . He won't sit it out, he's too lazy.

ÁNYA [*in the doorway*]. Mamma says, will you stop them cutting down the orchard till she has gone?

TROPH. Really, haven't you got tact enough for that?   [*Exit* TROPHÍMOF *by the hall.*]

LOPÁK. Of course, I'll stop them at once.—What fools they are!   [*Exit after* TROPHÍMOF.

ÁNYA. Has Firs been sent to the hospital?

YÁSHA. I told 'em this morning. They're sure to have sent him.

ÁNYA [*to* EPHIKHÓDOF, *who crosses*]. Simeon Pantaléyitch, please find out if Firs has been sent to the hospital.

YÁSHA [*offended*]. I told George this morning. What's the good of asking a dozen times?

EPHIK. Our centenarian friend, in my conclusive opinion, is hardly worth tinkering; it's time he was despatched to his forefathers. I can only say I envy him. [*Putting down a portmanteau on a bandbox and crushing it flat.*] There you are! I knew how it would be!   [*Exit.*

YÁSHA [*jeering*]. Twenty-two misfortunes!

BARB. [*without*]. Has Firs been sent to the hospital?

ÁNYA. Yes.

BARB. Why didn't they take the note to the doctor?

ÁNYA. We must send it after them.

                                          [*Exit* ÁNYA.

BARB. [*from the next room*]. Where's Yásha? Tell him his mother is here. She wants to say good-by to him.

YÁSHA [with a gesture of impatience]. It's enough to try the patience of a saint!

DUNYÁSHA has been busying herself with the luggage. Seeing YÁSHA alone, she approaches him.

DUNY. You might just look once at me, Yásha. You are going away, you are leaving me. [Crying and throwing her arms round his neck.]

YÁSHA. What's the good of crying? [Drinking champagne.] In six days I shall be back in Paris. Tomorrow we take the express, off we go, and that's the last of us! I can hardly believe it's true. Vive la France! This place don't suit me. I can't bear it . . . it can't be helped. I have had enough barbarism; I'm fed up. [Drinking champagne.] What's the good of crying? You be a good girl, and you'll have no call to cry.

DUNY. [powdering her face and looking into a glass]. Write me a letter from Paris. I've been so fond of you, Yásha, ever so fond! I am a delicate creature, Yásha.

YÁSHA. Here's somebody coming. [He busies himself with the luggage singing under his breath.]

Enter MADAME RANÉVSKY, GÁYEF, ÁNYA, and CHARLOTTE.

GÁYEF. We'll have to be off; it's nearly time. [Looking at YÁSHA.] Who is it smells of red herring?

MME. R. We must take our seats in ten minutes. [Looking round the room.] Good-by, dear old house; good-by, grandpapa! When winter is past and spring comes again, you will be here no more; they will have pulled you down. Oh, think of all these walls have seen! [Kissing ÁNYA passionately.] My treasure, you look radiant, your eyes flash like two diamonds. Are you happy?—very happy?

ÁNYA. Very, very happy. We're beginning a new life, mamma.

GÁYEF [gaily]. She's quite right; everything's all right now. Till the cherry orchard was sold we were all agitated and miserable; but once the thing was settled finally and irrevocably, we all calmed down and got jolly again. I'm a bank clerk now; I'm a financier . . . red in the middle! And you, Lyuba, whatever you may say, you're looking ever so much better, not a doubt about it.

MME. R. Yes, my nerves are better; it's quite true. [She is helped on with her hat and coat.] I sleep well now. Take my things out, Yásha. We must be off. [To ÁNYA.] We shall soon meet again, darling. . . . I'm off to Paris; I shall live on the money your grandmother sent from Yaroslav to buy the property. God bless your grandmother! I'm afraid it won't last long.

ÁNYA. You'll come back very, very soon, won't you, mamma? I'm going to work and pass the examination at the Gymnase and get a place and help you. We'll read all sorts of books together, won't we, mamma? [Kissing her mother's hands.] We'll read in the long autumn evenings, we'll read heaps of books, and a new, wonderful world will open up before us. [Meditating.] . . . Come back, mamma!

MME. R. I'll come back, my angel. [Embracing her.]

Enter LOPÁKHIN. CHARLOTTE sings softly.

GÁYEF. Happy Charlotte, she's singing.

CHARL. [taking a bundle of rags, like a swaddled baby]. Hush-a-by, baby, on the tree-top . . . [The baby answers, "Wah, wah."] Hush, my little one, hush, my pretty one! ["Wah, wah."] You'll break your mother's heart. [She throws the bundle down on the floor again.] Don't forget to find me a new place, please. I can't do without it.

LOPÁK. We'll find you a place, Charlotte Ivánovna, don't be afraid.

GÁYEF. Everybody's deserting us. Barbara's going. Nobody seems to want us.

CHARL. There's nowhere for me to live in the town. I'm obliged to go. [Hums a tune.] What's the odds?

Enter PÍSHTCHIK.

LOPÁK. Nature's masterpiece!

PÍSHT. [panting]. Oy, oy, let me get my breath again! . . . I'm done up! . . . My noble friends! . . . Give me some water.

GÁYEF. Wants some money, I suppose. No, thank you; I'll keep out of harm's way. [Exit.

PÍSHT. It's ages since I have been here, fairest lady. [To LOPÁKHIN.] You here? Glad to see you, you man of gigantic intellect. Take this; it's for you. [Giving LOPÁKHIN money.] Forty pounds! I still owe you eighty-four.

LOPÁK. [amazed, shrugging his shoulders]. It's like a thing in a dream! Where did you get it from?

PÍSHT. Wait a bit. . . . I'm hot. . . . A most remarkable thing! Some Englishmen came and found some sort of white clay on my land. [To MADAME RANÉVSKY.] And here's forty pounds for you, lovely, wonderful lady. [Giving her money.] The rest another time. [Drinking water.] Only just now a young man in the train was saying that some . . . some great philosopher advises us all to jump off roofs. . . . Jump, he says, and there's an end of it. [*With an astonished air.*] Just think of that! More water!

LOPÁK. Who were the Englishmen?

PÍSHT. I leased them the plot with the clay on it for twenty-four years. But I haven't any time now . . . I must be getting on. I must go to Znoikof's, to Kardamónof's. . . . I owe everybody money. [*Drinking.*] Good-by to everyone; I'll look in on Thursday.

MME. R. We're just moving into town, and to-morrow I go abroad.

PÍSHT. What! [*Alarmed.*] What are you going into town for? Why, what's happened to the furniture? . . . Trunks? . . . Oh, it's all right. [*Crying.*] It's all right. People of powerful intellect . . . those Englishmen. It's all right. Be happy . . . God be with you . . . It's all right. Everything in this world has to come to an end. [*Kissing Madame Ranévsky's hand.*] If ever the news reaches you that *I* have come to an end, give a thought to the old . . . horse, and say, "Once there lived a certain Simeónof-Píshtchik, Heaven rest his soul." . . . Remarkable weather we're having. . . . Yes. . . . [*Goes out deeply moved. Returns at once and says from the doorway:*] Dáshenka sent her compliments. [*Exit.*]

MME. R. Now we can go. I have only two things on my mind. One is poor old Firs. [*Looking at her watch.*] We can still stay five minutes.

ÁNYA. Firs has been sent to the hospital already, mamma. Yásha sent him off this morning.

MME. R. My second anxiety is Barbara. She's used to getting up early and working, and now that she has no work to do she's like a fish out of water. She has grown thin and pale and taken to crying, poor dear. . . . [*A pause.*] You know very well, Yermolái Alexéyitch, I always hoped . . . to see her married to you, and as far as I can see, you're looking out for a wife. [*She whispers to ÁNYA, who nods to CHARLOTTE, and both exeunt.*] She loves you; you like her; and I can't make out why you seem to fight shy of each other. I don't understand it.

LOPÁK. I don't understand it either, to tell you the truth. It all seems so odd. If there's still time I'll do it this moment. Let's get it over and have done with it; without you there, I feel as if I should never propose to her.

MME. R. A capital idea! After all, it doesn't take more than a minute. I'll call her at once.

LOPÁK. And here's the champagne all ready. [*Looking at the glasses.*] Empty; someone's drunk it. [YÁSHA *coughs.*] That's what they call lapping it up and no mistake!

MME. R. [*animated*]. Capital! We'll all go away. . . . *Allez,* Yásha. I'll call her. [*At the door.*] Barbara, leave all that and come here. Come along!

[*Exeunt* MADAME RANÉVSKY *and* YÁSHA.
LOPÁK. [*looking at his watch*]. Yes.

A pause. A stifled laugh behind the door; whispering; at last enter BARBARA.

BARB. [*examining the luggage*]. Very odd; I can't find it anywhere. . . .

LOPÁK. What are you looking for?

BARB. I packed it myself, and can't remember. [*A pause.*]

LOPÁK. Where are you going today, Varvára Mikháilovna?

BARB. Me? I'm going to the Ragulins. I'm engaged to go and keep house for them, to be housekeeper or whatever it is.

LOPÁK. Oh, at Yashnevo? That's about fifty miles from here. [*A pause.*] Well, so life in this house is over now.

BARB. [*looking at the luggage*]. Wherever can it be? Perhaps I put it in the trunk. . . . Yes, life here is over now; there won't be any more . . .

LOPÁK. And I'm off to Kharkof at once . . . by the same train. A lot of business to do. I'm leaving Ephikhódof to look after this place. I've taken him on.

BARB. Have you?

LOPÁK. At this time last year snow was falling already, if you remember; but now it's fine and sunny. Still, it's cold for all that. Three degrees of frost.

BARB. Were there? I didn't look. [*A pause.*] Besides, the thermometer's broken. [*A pause.*]

A VOICE [*at the outer door*]. Yermolái Alexéyitch!

LOPÁK. [*as if he had only been waiting to be called*]. I'm just coming! [*Exit* LOPÁKHIN *quickly.*

BARBARA *sits on the floor, puts her head on a bundle and sobs softly. The door opens and* MADAME RANÉVSKY *comes in cautiously.*

MME. R. Well? [*A pause.*] We must be off.

BARB. [*no longer crying, wiping her eyes*]. Yes, it's time, mamma. I shall get to the Ragulins all right today, so long as I don't miss the train.

MME. R. [*calling off*]. Put on your things, Ánya

Enter ÁNYA, *then* GÁYEF *and* CHARLOTTE. GÁYEF *wears a warm overcoat with a hood. The servants and drivers come in.* EPHIKHÓDOF *busies himself about the luggage.*

MME. R. Now we can start on our journey.

ÁNYA [*delighted*]. We can start on our journey!

GÁYEF. My friends, my dear, beloved friends! Now that I am leaving this house forever, can I keep silence? Can I refrain from expressing those emotions which fill my whole being at such a moment?

ÁNYA [*pleadingly*]. Uncle!

BARB. Uncle, what's the good?

GÁYEF [*sadly*]. Double the red in the middle pocket. I'll hold my tongue.

Enter TROPHÍMOF, *then* LOPÁKHIN.

TROPH. Come along, it's time to start.

LOPÁK. Ephikhódof, my coat.

MME. R. I must sit here another minute. It's just as if I had never noticed before what the walls and ceilings of the house were like. I look at them hungrily, with such tender love. . . .

GÁYEF. I remember, when I was six years old, how I sat in this window on Trinity Sunday, and watched father starting out for church.

MME. R. Has everything been cleared out?

LOPÁK. Apparently everything. [*To* EPHIKHÓDOF, *putting on his overcoat.*] See that everything's in order, Ephikhódof.

EPHIK. [*in a hoarse voice*]. You trust me, Yermolái Alexéyitch.

LOPÁK. What's up with your voice?

EPHIK. I was just having a drink of water. I swallowed something.

YÁSHA [*contemptuously*]. Cad!

MME. R. We're going, and not a soul will be left here.

LOPÁK. Until the spring.

BARBARA *pulls an umbrella out of a bundle of rugs, as if she were brandishing it to strike.* LOPÁKHIN *pretends to be frightened.*

BARB. Don't be so silly! I never thought of such a thing.

TROPH. Come, we'd better go and get in. It's time to start. The train will be in immediately.

BARB. There are your goloshes, Peter, by that portmanteau. [*Crying.*] What dirty old things they are!

TROPH. [*putting on his goloshes*]. Come along.

GÁYEF [*much moved, afraid of crying*]. The train . . . the station . . . double the red in the middle; doublette to pot the white in the corner. . . .

MME. R. Come on!

LOPÁK. Is everyone here? No one left in there? [*Locking the door.*] There are things stacked in there; I must lock them up. Come on!

ÁNYA. Good-by, house! Good-by, old life!

TROPH. Welcome new life!

[*Exit with* ÁNYA. BARBARA *looks round the room, and exit slowly. Exeunt* YÁSHA, *and* CHARLOTTE *with her dog.*

LOPÁK. Till the spring, then. Go on, everybody. So-long! [*Exit.*

MADAME RANÉVSKY *and* GÁYEF *remain alone. They seem to have been waiting for this, throw their arms round each other's necks and sob restrainedly and gently, afraid of being overheard.*

GÁYEF [*in despair*]. My sister! my sister!

MME. R. Oh, my dear, sweet, lovely orchard! My life, my youth, my happiness, farewell! Farewell!

ÁNYA [*calling gaily, without*]. Mamma!

TROPH. [*gay and excited*]. Aoo!

MME. R. One last look at the walls and the windows. . . . Our dear mother used to love to walk up and down this room.

GÁYEF. My sister! my sister!

ÁNYA [*without*]. Mamma!

TROPH. [*without*]. Aoo!

MME. R. We're coming.

[*Exeunt. The stage is empty. One hears all the doors being locked, and the carriages driving away. All is quiet. Amid the silence the thud of the axes on the trees echoes sad and lonely. The sound of footsteps.* FIRS *appears in the doorway, right. He is dressed, as always, in his long coat and white waistcoat; he wears slippers. He is ill.*

FIRS [*going to the door, left, and trying the handle*]. Locked. They've gone. [*Sitting on the sofa.*] They've forgotten me. Never mind! I'll sit here. Leoníd Andréyitch is sure to put on his cloth coat instead of his fur. [*He sighs anxiously.*] He hadn't me to see. Young wood, green wood! [*He mumbles something incomprehensible.*] Life has gone by as if I'd never lived. [*Lying down.*] I'll lie down. There's no strength left in you; there's nothing, nothing. Ah, you . . . job-lot! [*He lies motionless. A distant sound is heard, as if from the sky, the sound of a string breaking, dying away, melancholy. Silence ensues, broken only by the stroke of the ax on the trees far away in the cherry orchard.*]

BOOK TWO

OUR INHERITANCE FROM

LITERATURE IN OUR OWN TONGUE:

THE WELL OF ENGLISH

INTRODUCTION
TO BOOK TWO

The second half of this collection is devoted to the two important literatures which have been written in the English language since it assumed its present general form after the Norman Conquest. Already we have examined the beginnings of literature in England by the small migratory Anglo-Saxon tribes. The long history that has made their purely Germanic tongue, through a happy admixture of French and Latin elements and through more than a thousand years of stirring events, the most widely-used of all world languages has produced an extraordinarily vital literature. No one today comes into so rich an inheritance of great books as we who use the same speech as Wordsworth and Milton and Shakespeare.

Though somewhat detailed treatment of various periods is given elsewhere, let us see the chief directions in which history and literature have moved since the days of the Anglo-Saxons.

When we first meet the English people in the sixth century they have but recently arrived in the island of Britain from their older home in Northern Germany. They were of Low Germanic stock and language, closely related to the Dutch and Flemish of today. Their civilization was Germanic, and therefore in contrast with that of the Celtic peoples whom they combated in England and Scotland. Later they were to be influenced by a succession of impacts from Scandinavia. For a long time the Danes harried the English and eventually ruled England, and of course left their mark on its people.

The greatest single event in English history, however, was the Norman Conquest (1066). This brought about a change in society, in language, and in literature. On the rather grim, melancholy, provincial Anglo-Saxon civilization there was now superimposed a culture from France. Though these conquerors were originally from Scandinavia, they had already acquired the language and the cultivation of the French. Now these people were the rulers and the Anglo-Saxons the conquered. Three centuries of this relationship produced the characteristic Englishman and the English language, with its large admixture of French, as we know it today. During these centuries England began its imperial expansion by the conquests of Wales and Ireland. And it produced one great poet, Geoffrey Chaucer.

After almost destroying itself in the suicidal struggles of the fifteenth century England recovered remarkably, and by the beginning of the seventeenth century it was one of the strong powers of Europe. It had absorbed the culture of the Italian

Renaissance, it had begun an ambitious program of world exploration, it was about to add Scotland to the holdings of its crown, and it had successfully resisted the Spanish Armada. All this was part of one of the most brilliant reigns in European history, a high point in national life and literature. This was the age of Elizabeth and Shakespeare.

In the seventeenth century the English people engaged in such a series of internal religious and political conflicts that many of the most valuable and talented citizens went away in colonies to America. In England the whole century passed before the civil wars and revolutions ended in a settlement that has remained almost unchallenged until the present day. This century of conflict produced many charming poets in its early part, some masters of sonorous prose, some satirists, and a number of ribald comedy writers. But it also gave us Bacon, Pepys, Bunyan, and Dryden, not to speak of the great voice of Puritanism, John Milton.

The eighteenth century witnessed the phenomenal growth of the British Empire, which began to spread over the entire world. Its one setback was the loss of those American colonies that have become the United States. The literature of the early eighteenth century was highly influenced by French writings of the time and gained in logic and preciseness. If there was a tendency to get away from common life, this was remedied before the middle of the century by the new interest in democracy. Enthusiasm for nature, for the Middle Ages, for strange and faraway countries, and for emotional display paved the way for the great romantic writers who were to come at the beginning of the nineteenth century. The rise of the modern novel and its large reading public also helped to democratize literature. Pope, Addison, Steele, and Defoe illustrate the early part of the century; Goldsmith, Burns, and Blake, the latter part. At the end of the eighteenth century appeared a brilliant group of portrait painters—Reynolds, Gainsborough, Lawrence, and Romney.

By 1798 the Romantic movement in literature had arrived with the work of Wordsworth and Coleridge. This phase of English literature lasted until about 1830, when the writers we know as Victorians began. In the Romantic period there had been a brief enthusiasm for the French Revolution with its doctrine of the rights of man, but this was followed by a conservative reaction. The problems of the age of Victoria were not simply democracy. The expanded Empire brought its many complications. New inventions had caused an Industrial Revolution, and new scientific discoveries had aroused new conflicts in religious thought. There was a ferment of new ideas in economics, sociology, and world relations. All this resulted in an extraordinary intellectual and literary activity. Our present age tends to look back on the Victorian era with a touch of scorn. We have yet to show that we can equal its great thinkers and writers.

In America there were two centuries of colonization before any important literature began. A great difference between English and American literature is the fact that racially the English type has been well set ever since the Renaissance, whereas America has always been a melting pot, never more so than in the colonial days. American writers have always looked to England for their models and yet have always striven to be American. Some have gone to one extreme, others to the other. But a realization of this conflict of purpose helps much in an understanding of American literature.

ANGLO-SAXON POETRY

For the long centuries of the occupation of England by the Britons and the four or five centuries of Roman rule there remains not a line of literature. It is only after the Anglo-Saxons had come over from the Continent in the fifth and sixth centuries and conquered the Britons, and had been in possession of the land for some two hundred years that they began to write. Literature hardly existed in England before the eighth century, and even then for a long time it was to be written in a language as remote from Modern English as German or Swedish.

In our discussion of the Germanic peoples we have already observed that the tribes who came to England were closely related to the peoples who now live in Holland and Flanders. They were more remotely akin to the Germans and Scandinavians, and with the latter peoples had many elements of culture in common. When these Anglo-Saxons came to England they consisted of three groups: the Angles, who settled in the east, the center, and the north; the Saxons, who occupied the south and west; and the Jutes, who confined themselves to the southeastern county of Kent.

From the continent these invaders brought their Germanic customs and legends. They were still pagan and had many of the same religious practices and beliefs as the Norse, whose myths we have already examined. From the end of the sixth century onward they became Christianized and gradually dropped many of their older practices, though not a few lived on and assumed a Christian coloring. Through much of Old English poetry Christian and heathen elements appear side by side.

We have in several of the poems some excellent pictures of the life of these people. The king's court was the focus of the tribal activity and received much attention from the poet. In the oldest of the poems, *Widsith,* appears a picture of the minstrel wandering from one king to another and bringing entertainment to the group of warriors who surrounded the ruler. This scene is repeated in *Deor's Lament,* where we see the minstrel in misfortune, and also in the best of the poems, *Beowulf.* The Germanic legends which we find not only in this poem but also in *Waldhere* and *The Fight at Finnsburh* give us the very spirit of the heroic age which seems to lie not very far in the past. Here, centuries before it is told elsewhere, we find the story of Sigurd and the dragon.

The best way to enter into the life of these Old English is, of course, through the *Beowulf*. This poem, though not written before the eighth century, represents a tradition going back to the old life on the continent. The scenery is English, but the tale is of tribes in Scandinavia; and the culture reflected is best seen in the remains of these northern peoples. The traveler today at Uppsala in Sweden can observe the huge burial mounds of the ancient kings and feel that these men must have been like Hrothgar and Hygelac.

A study of *Beowulf* rewards us in many ways. The heroic legend is handled so vigorously that there are very few passages where the interest flags. The demonic enemies are made frightful to the reader, as they were to the hero who met them in battle. The fighting, the joy, and despair of those who waited the event, the bearing of the hero, the reception of foreign guests at court, the gracious queen sharing in their entertainment—all these live in the ringing lines of this epic.

The student will soon accustom himself to certain peculiar stylistic effects, which *Beowulf* shares with nearly all Old English poems. One of these is the use of "kennings." The sea is "the gannet's bath," the king is "the ring-giver." These epithets become conventional, so that we expect them rather than the plain name. Aside from these "kennings" many metaphors occur, but only a few similes.

Generally speaking, Old English poems are not written in stanza form. To this rule *Deor's Lament* is an exception. Here we have the scop, or minstrel, out of favor with his chief. He consoles himself by recalling tragic stories of the past—one of them a well-known Norse myth—and ending each stanza with the heartening refrain: "That has passed over, so this may depart." Old English has several other short lyrics reflecting different aspects of the life of the time. *The Wanderer* and *The Seafarer* express the English love of the sea—in spite of its cruelty. *The Ruined City* gives the melancholy reflection of the barbarously surrounded Anglo-Saxon poet as he views the decayed splendors of the old Roman baths.

From the Latin writings that they were fast mastering, the Old English became interested in the composing of riddles. Of these there are nearly a hundred. They are seldom hard to guess, but their interest is in their close description of objects and events of common life.

Christianity plays an ever-increasing part in Old English literature. A number of poems tell stories taken from the Bible. There are poetic retellings of Genesis, Exodus, and Daniel. In *The Christ* of Cynewulf we have parts of the New Testament story beautifully reworked. There are also a number of legends of the saints, such as Cynewulf's *Andreas* and *Elene*. From the book of Judith, of the Old Testament Apocrypha, one of the most pleasing of the Old English poems has been made. Though what we have is a fragment, it must be almost complete. The characterization of the heroine so that her beauty and gentleness are always remembered in spite of her bloody deed, is very skillful. She is, of course, pictured as an Anglo-Saxon heroine, in spite of the Jewish setting.

Perhaps the finest piece of devotional poetry in Old English is *The Dream of the Rood*. The telling of the story of the crucifixion by the cross itself gave the poet an opportunity to make the great event in Christian history a living memory. Many centuries were to pass before any greater poem was to be written in English.

Before beginning a study of Anglo-Saxon poetry, the student should realize that no matter what form of translation we may read, it was all written in the same metrical form, and one which we no longer use. It is imitated in the translations here given to the poems other than *Beowulf*. The lines have four accents divided into two half-lines of two accents each. Instead of rhyme, there is alliteration. That is, the beginning sounds of these accented syllables echo each other. The involved rules for these correspondences are not needed in order to get the effect. The italicized letters in the following lines from the *Judith* will make the plan clear.

> Then a *b*and of *b*old knights   *b*usily gathered,
> *K*een men at the *c*onflict;   with *c*ourage they stepped *f*orth
> *B*earing *b*anners,   *b*rave-hearted companions,
> And *f*ared to the *f*ight,   *f*orth in right order.

With an ear tuned to this peculiar metrical effect, the reader should be able to find in Old English poetry many things to stimulate his imagination. That much of the phraseology, the "kennings," the metaphors, the parallel constructions, is conventional does not change the fact that the writers of these poems expressed some of the darker moods with an extraordinary sincerity and power. They could also be tender and could write appealing descriptions of paradise. They had, of course, no humor in their poems, but they showed the serious qualities of the English race in their purity. The development that would round them out into the English that we know came only with their conquest and submergence by their Norman neighbors from the south. And the same mixture would create the English language as we know it today.

BEOWULF

PROLOGUE

Of the Danish kings, they who were ancestors to Hrothgar, and of the passing of Scyld.

Lo! we have learned of the glory of the kings who ruled the Spear-Danes in the olden time, how those princes wrought mighty deeds. Oft did Scyld[1] of the Sheaf wrest the mead-benches from bands of warriors, from many a tribe. The hero bred awe in them from the time when first he was found helpless and outcast; for this he met with comfort, waxed great beneath the sky and throve in honors, until all the neighboring tribes beyond the ocean-paths were brought to serve him and pay him tribute. That was a good king!

In after-time there was born to him in his hall, a young heir whom God sent for a comfort to that people. He saw their sore distress, how in time past[2] they had long suffered for lack of a chief. Therefore, the Lord of life, the King of glory, granted him honor in this world. Beowulf,[3] son of Scyld, was renowned in Danish lands; his fame was spread abroad. So ought a youth to win favor by giving gifts unto his father's friends, that afterwards willing companions may attend him in his age, and the people serve him in time of war.[4] It [10] is by noble deeds that a man shall prosper in any land.

When at length the fated hour was come, Scyld, the valiant, departed unto the keeping of the Lord. Then his dear companions bore him down to the ocean-flood, even as he himself had bidden them, while as yet the friend of the Scyldings ruled them with his words and long did reign over them, dear

Beowulf, translated by Chauncey B. Tinker. Used by permission of Henry Holt and Company. The footnotes are Professor Tinker's.

[1] That is, "Shield," the defense of his people. He had apparently been found, an outcast babe, adrift in an open boat, with a sheaf of wheat for bed. The term has here become a sort of patronymic.

[2] Before the coming of Scyld.

[3] Not the hero of the poem; nothing else is known of him.

[4] One of the hortatory sentences in which the *Beowulf* abounds. A wise young prince will not neglect to win the favor of his father's *Comitatus* by suitable largess.

prince of the land. There at the harbor stood a ship with curving prow, all icy, eager to be gone—meet for a prince. And in the ship's bosom, hard by the mast, they laid that famous hero, their dear lord, the giver of treasure. Many treasures were there, abundance of ornaments brought from afar. Never have I heard men tell of a ship more splendidly laden with battle-weapons and war-harness, with swords and coats of mail. Upon his breast lay many precious things which were to go far out 10 with him into the realm of the waters. Verily no fewer of their gifts and tribal treasures did this people bestow upon him than they who at his birth sent him forth alone over the wave, babe as he was. Moreover, they set up a golden banner, high above his head, and let the sea bear him away, giving him over to the deep. Sad at heart were they, sorrowful in spirit. No man can truly say—no lord of hall, or hero under heaven—into whose hands that burden fell.

PART I

BEOWULF AND GRENDEL

I

Of Hrothgar, son of Healfdene and king of the Scyldings, and how he built a fair mead-hall, which he named Heorot. How the merriment in the hall angered Grendel, an evil monster.

Then Beowulf [5] of the Scyldings, dear king of the nation, was long famous in the cities and among the peoples—the prince, his father, had departed from his home [6]—till high Healfdene was born to him in after-time. He, while he lived, old and fierce in war, ruled graciously over the Scyldings. To him there were born into the world four children after this order: Heorogar, leader of armies, Hrothgar, and Halga the Good; Queen Elan, I have heard, was the dear wife of Ongentheow, the 40 brave Scylfing. [7]

Then to Hrothgar was given success in battle, glory in warfare, so that his loyal kinsmen gladly obeyed him, until the young warriors were grown, a mighty band. It came into his heart to command his men to build a hall, a mead-hall greater than any that the children of men had ever heard of, and therein to give gifts of all kinds to old and young, as God had prospered him, save the people's land and the lives of men. [8]

And I heard men tell how the work of adorning the people's hall was allotted unto many a tribe, far and wide throughout this earth. After a season —quickly, as man's work prospereth—it came to pass that it was completed for him, this greatest of halls. And he fashioned for it the name of *Heorot*, [9] he whose word had power far and near. He broke not his promise; but gave out rings and treasure at the feast. High and pinnacled, the hall towered aloft. Yet it awaited the surging blaze of hostile fire; nor was it long thereafter that fatal hatred was destined to arise between father-in-law and son-in-law, after the deadly strife. [10]

Then that mighty spirit [11] who dwelt in darkness bore in his wrath for a season to hear each 20 day the merriment, loud in the hall. There was the sound of the harp, the clear song of the gleeman. He spoke, who could recount from of old the creation of men, told how the Almighty made the earth, [12] the fair-faced land, and the waters that compass it about; how, exultant in victory, He set the sun and moon as lights to lighten the dwellers in the land. He adorned all the regions of the earth with leaf and branch, and created life in every-30 thing that lives and moves.

Thus the king's men lived, blissful and happy, until a certain one, a fiend of hell, began to plot mischief. This grim foe was called Grendel, a mighty stalker of the marches, who haunted the moors, the fens, and fastnesses. The wretched being had long inhabited the abode of the monster kind, e'er since the Creator had condemned him. The Lord eternal wreaked vengeance upon the kindred of Cain, because of the murder—the 40 slaying of Abel. He got no pleasure in the feud, but for that wicked deed the Lord banished him far from mankind. From him there woke to life all evil broods—monsters and elves and sea-beasts, and giants too, who long time strove with God. He gave them their reward.

[5] Not the hero; cf. p. 992.
[6] Died.
[7] The rendering of this sentence is extremely uncertain, owing to the corruption of the MS. Nothing else is known of the people mentioned.
[8] He respected rights of property and personal liberty.
[9] "Hart"; probably so called from its decoration with antlers.
[10] Epic prophecy; a reference to some tale of the fate of Heorot, familiar to the audience.
[11] Grendel.
[12] Cf. *Psalms* 148: *Æneid* I. 742 ff.

II

Grendel falls upon Heorot and slays thirty heroes. Hrothgar and his men are helpless before the monster, and the destruction is continued for twelve winters.

As soon as night was come, he set out for the high-built hall, to see how the Ring-Danes were faring after the drinking of the mead. And he found therein a band of warrior-nobles sleeping after feast. They knew naught of sorrow, that wretched lot of all mankind. The creature of destruction, fierce and greedy, wild and furious, was ready straight. He seized thirty thanes upon their bed. Then back he returned to his abode, exulting in his booty, back to his lair with his fill of slaughter.

Then at dawn, with break of day, Grendel's deeds were manifest to men, and the voice of weeping was uplifted—a great cry at morn, after their feast. The great lord, the prince exceeding good, sat joyless, when they had looked upon the track of the monster, the accursed foe; the mighty hero suffered, sorrowing for his thanes. Too great was that strife, too loathsome and lasting.

It was no longer than a single night ere he wrought more deeds of murder; he recked not of the feud and the crime—he was too fixed in them. Then, when the hatred of that thane of hell was fully known to them, truly told by tokens manifest, it was easy to find the man who sought him out a resting-place elsewhere more at large, a bed among the bowers of the hall. He kept himself thereafter further aloof and more secure, whosoever escaped the fiend.

Thus he held sway, and alone against them all fought accursedly, until that best of houses stood empty. Long was the time: for twelve winters the friend of the Scyldings suffered distress, yea, every woe, uttermost sorrow. And so it became known to the children of men—sadly told in song—that Grendel had long been fighting against Hrothgar, and for many a season had waged a bitter war and wicked feud, an unending strife. He would not stay the waste of life out of compassion toward any of the Danish race, compounding with them for tribute, and none of the wise men could look

for a fair ransom from the destroyer's hands. The dread monster, like a dark shadow of death, kept pursuing warrior and youth; he trapped and ensnared them. Night after night he haunted the misty moors. Men know not whither hell's sorcerers wander in their rounds.

Thus the enemy of man, the terrible lone wanderer, oft wrought many a foul deed, much grievous affliction. In the dark of the night-tide he took up his abode in Heorot, the hall brightly adorned. Hrothgar could not approach the throne, precious in the sight of God, nor did he know His love.[13]

Mighty grief and heart-break was this for the kind lord of the Scyldings to bear. Many mighty men oft sat in council and deliberated together touching what it were best for great-hearted men to do against these sudden terrors. Sometimes they vowed sacrifices at their idol-fanes; the people prayed aloud that the Destroying Spirit[14] would aid them in the torment that had fallen upon them. Such was their custom,[15] such their heathen faith; the thoughts of their heart were turned on hell; they knew not the Creator, Judge of deeds; they wist not of the Lord God; verily, they knew naught of the worship of the Ruler of heaven, the King of glory.

Woe unto him who through deadly hate[16] is doomed to thrust his soul into the fiery abyss, to hope for no comfort, no change in anywise. But blessed is the man who at his death may go unto the Lord and find refuge in the Father's bosom.

III

In the far country of the Geats, Beowulf hears of Grendel's deeds, and resolves to go to the help of Hrothgar. He makes him ready a great ship and sails with his men to the country of the Danes. On landing he is accosted by the shore-guard.

So the son of Healfdene[17] kept ever brooding over his sorrow. The wise hero could not stay the suffering; too grievous, too long and heart-sickening, was the struggle which had come upon that people, a cruel plague, greatest of evils that walk by night.

A thane of Hygelac,[18] great among the Geats, heard of these deeds of Grendel in his native land.

[13] The subject of this sentence, not plainly indicated in the original, may perhaps be Grendel. One spot was inviolate. But no thoroughly satisfactory explanation has ever been given.
[14] The devil.
[15] The rest of the section is usually regarded as the interpolation of a Christian scribe.
[16] The notion is not clear; hatred of the new Christianity, perhaps.
[17] Hrothgar.
[18] Beowulf, hero of the poem.

In his strength he was the best of men in the day of this life, noble and mighty. He bade make ready for him a goodly ship, saying that he would go over the ocean-road unto that war-king, the great prince, since he had need of men. Little did his prudent thanes blame him for that journey, though he was dear to them; they encouraged him in his high purpose, and looked for good omens. The hero had warriors, chosen from among the Geats, the keenest he could find. Fifteen in all went down ¹⁰ unto the ship. A skilled mariner pointed out the land-marks unto them.

Time wore on. The ship was upon the waves, the boat under the cliff. The ready warriors mounted the prow. The ocean-streams dashed the waves upon the beach. The men bore rich armor into the bosom of the ship, splendid war-harness. The warriors pushed off their tight-fitted craft on the willing adventure. So, driven by the wind, the bark most like unto a bird, sped foamy-necked ²⁰ across the waves, until, about the same hour the second day, the curving prow had journeyed on so far that the sailors caught sight of land, saw gleaming cliffs and lofty hills, broad ocean-headlands. Thus the sea was crossed, and the voyage ended. Then the Weder people ¹⁹ went quickly up ashore, and made fast their ship, while their mail-coats and battle-raiment clashed. And they thanked God that their sea-paths had been easy.

The guard of the Scyldings, he who had been set ³⁰ to watch the headland, saw them from the cliff, bearing over the gangway their bright shields and ready weapons. His heart was spurred with longing to know who the men were. So the thane of Hrothgar went down to the shore, riding upon his horse. He shook his spear mightily with his hands, and asked in fitting words: "What warriors are ye, in coats of mail, who come hither, sailing your great ship over the sea, the ocean-paths? I have been warden of the coast and have kept watch by ⁴⁰ the sea that no foe with force of ships might do harm in the Danish land. No shield-bearers have ever tried more openly to land here, nor did ye know at all the password, the agreement of the warriors, our kinsmen. Never have I seen a mightier hero upon earth, a mightier man in armor, than is one of you. He is no common thane decked out with weapons, unless his face, his matchless countenance, belie him. But now I must know your lineage from you, ye false spies, ere ye go further ⁵⁰

in the land of the Danes. Now ye seafarers, strangers from afar, give ear to my plain counsel: it were best to make known forthwith whence ye are come."

IV

Beowulf makes answer touching the purpose of his coming, and is guided by the coast-warden to Heorot.

The chieftain, leader of the band, answered him again and unlocked the treasure of his speech: "We are men of the Geatish kin, and Hygelac's hearth-companions. My father was well known among the peoples, a noble prince named Ecgtheow.²⁰ He lived many winters ere, full of years, he went his way from home. Him well nigh every wise man remembers, the wide world over. With friendly purpose we are come to thy lord, the son of Healfdene, guardian of the people. Give us thy gracious counsel; we have a great errand to the mighty lord of the Danes. Naught secret shall there be in that which I intend. Thou knowest if it be, as we have heard for a truth, that some foe among the Scyldings, a secret destroyer, causes on dark nights by the terror of his coming unutterable evil, shame and slaughter. Now by my great mind I may perchance give counsel to Hrothgar, how he, the wise and good, can overcome the foe; if this burden of anguish be destined ever to leave him, release come once again, and the waves of care wax cooler; or else, ever after, shall he suffer seasons of affliction, wretched misery, long as the noblest of houses stands there in its lofty place."

The warden spoke, the fearless servant, there where he sat upon his horse: "A keen shield-warrior, he who judges well, must know the difference between words and deeds. I learn that this is a band friendly to the lord of the Scyldings. Go forth, then, with your weapons and your armor. I ⁴⁰ will guide you. Likewise, I will command the thanes, my kinsmen, to guard your ship with honor against every foe, the new-tarred boat there upon the strand, until the bark with curving prow bear the dear master back over the ocean-streams to Wedermark. Unto so brave a man be it granted to endure unharmed the shock of conflict."

Then they departed along their way; the boat lay quiet, the broad-bosomed ship rested on her moorings, fast at anchor. The boar-images above ⁵⁰ their golden cheek-guards glistened; ²¹ bright were

---

¹⁹ Another name for the Geats.
²⁰ Nothing further is known of the events here touched upon.
²¹ Carven figures worn as charms upon the helmet.

they, and hardened in the fire—there the boar kept guard. The men hurried on in warlike mood; they hastened, marching on together, till they caught sight of the well-built hall, stately and bright with gold. It was the greatest among the dwellings of men beneath the skies; in it dwelt the king, and its light shone over many lands. Then the bold chief [22] pointed out to them that radiant dwelling of brave men that they might straightway go to it. He—himself a warrior—turned his horse and spoke a word to them: "It is time for me to go. May the Almighty Father by his grace keep you safe in your adventures. I will down to the sea to keep watch against hostile bands."

V

Beowulf and his men come to Heorot. They are met by the herald, who tells their coming to King Hrothgar.

The street was brightly set with stones; [23] this path guided the band of men. The byrnie gleamed, hard and hand-locked, the bright iron rings sang in the armor, as they came marching to the hall in battle-harness. Weary of the sea, they placed their shields, bucklers wondrous hard, against the wall of the house; they sat down upon the benches. [24] Their byrnies rang, harness of heroes. Their ashen spears stood together, gray-shafted weapons of the seamen. This armored band was well adorned with weapons.

Then a proud warrior asked the heroes concerning their lineage: "Whence bring ye your plated shields, your gray war-shirts, and your visored helmets and this group of spears? I am Hrothgar's servant and herald. Never have I seen so great a band of strangers of more courageous mood. I think that ye have sought out Hrothgar nowise as exiles, but from valor and out of the greatness of your hearts."

And the proud lord of the Weder people, famed for his strength, answered him again; he spoke a word to him, bold under his helmet: "We are table-companions of Hygelac. Beowulf is my name. I will tell my errand to the son of Healfdene, the great king thy lord, if he will grant us to draw nigh to him who is so good."

Wulfgar spoke (he was a chief of the Wendels, his boldness was known to many, his wisdom and might): "I will ask the friend of the Danes, king of the Scyldings, giver of rings, the mighty lord, touching thy journey, as thou dost entreat, and will straightway make known to thee what answer the good king thinketh meet to give me."

And he went quickly to where Hrothgar was sitting, old and exceeding white-haired, with his company of thanes; the valiant man went until he stood before the face of the lord of the Danes—he knew the custom of the court. Wulfgar spoke to his friendly lord: "Hither are come across the sea-waves travelers, Geatish men from a far country. Warriors call their chieftain Beowulf. They beg to have speech with thee, my lord. Refuse not to converse with them, O gracious Hrothgar. In their equipment they seem worthy of the esteem of heroes, and verily the chief who led the warriors hither is a man of valor."

VI

Beowulf is graciously welcomed by the king, and thereupon tells how he will fight with Grendel.

Then spoke Hrothgar, defense of the Scyldings: "I knew him when he was a child; his aged father was called Ecgtheow, to whom at his home Hrethel the Geat gave his only daughter in marriage. His bold son is now come hither to a loyal friend. Moreover, seafarers, who carried thither rich gifts as good-will offerings to the Geats, have said that he, strong in battle, had in the grip of his hand the strength of thirty men. Him holy God hath sent us, as I hope, to be a gracious help to the West-Danes against the terror of Grendel. I shall proffer the hero gifts for his boldness. Make haste and bid all the band of kinsmen come in together unto us. Say to them, moreover, that they are welcome among the Danish people."

Then Wulfgar came to the door of the hall and announced the word from within: "My victorious lord, prince of the East-Danes, bids me say that he knows your noble lineage, and that ye, as men of stout courage, are welcome unto him hither over the billows of the sea. Now ye may go in unto Hrothgar in your war-array, under your helmets; but let your spears, shafts of slaughter, here await the issue of your words."

Then the mighty one arose with many a warrior round him—it was a noble group of thanes. Some remained and guarded the armor as the chief bade them. The heroes hastened, as the guide led them

---

[22] The coast-guard.
[23] Notice the poet's interest in a paved road.
[24] Outside the hall.

under the roof of Heorot. The great-hearted man, bold under his helmet, went on until he stood within the hall. Beowulf spoke—on him gleamed his byrnie, his coat of mail linked by the smith's craft: "Hail to thee, Hrothgar! I am Hygelac's kinsman and thane. Many an exploit have I undertaken in the days of my youth. In my native land I learned of Grendel's deeds; for seafarers say that this hall, this best of houses, stands empty and useless for all men, as soon as evening light is hidden [10] under the vault of heaven. And my people, even the best and wisest men among them, urged me, King Hrothgar, to come to thee, for they knew the strength of my might. They had themselves beheld when I came from the fight, stained with the blood of my foes. There had I bound five of my enemies, destroyed a giant race, and slain by night the seabeasts on the wave.[25] I endured great distress, avenged the affliction of the Weder people—they who had suffered woes. I ground the angry foe in [20] pieces. And now I alone will decide the fight with Grendel, the giant monster. One boon I beg of thee, prince of the Bright Danes, defense of the Scyldings:—Deny me not, thou shield of warriors, friend of the people, now I am come so far, that I alone, I and my band of thanes, this my brave company, may cleanse Heorot of the evil that has come upon it. I have learned, too, that the monster in his rashness recks not of weapons. Therefore, that the heart of Hygelac my lord may be glad- [30] dened because of me, I scorn to carry sword or broad shield, the yellow buckler, into the fight; but with my hands I will grapple the fiend and fight for life, foe against foe. He whom death taketh must rely upon the judgment of the Lord. I think that if he can prevail in the hall of war he will fearlessly devour the Geats even as he has often devoured the best of the Hrethmen.[26] Thou shalt have no need to bury my head if death take me, for he will have me, all red with gore; he will [40] bear away the corpse to feast upon it; the lone wanderer will pitilessly eat it, staining his moorhaunts; thou needst not then take more thought for the sustenance of my body. But send thou to Hygelac, if the fight take me, the matchless mail,

best of armors, that guards my breast; it is a relic of Hrethel,[27] and the work of Weland.[28] Wyrd[29] ever goeth her destined course."

VII

Hrothgar makes answer touching the deeds of Grendel. They feast in Heorot.

Then spoke Hrothgar, defense of the Scyldings: "With kindly help, my friend Beowulf, thou hast come to fight in our defense. Thy father fought the greatest of feuds, for he slew with his hand Heatholaf among the Wylfings; wherefore the Weder people, in dread of war, could not harbor him.[30] From there he fled over the rolling waves to the South-Danes, the honored Scyldings; at the time when I first ruled the Danish folk, and in my [20] youth held the wealthy city of heroes, rich in treasure, for Heorogar, Healfdene's son, was dead, my elder brother lifeless;—he was a better man than I. Afterwards I settled that feud with money; I sent olden treasures[31] to the Wylfings across the ocean's back; and Ecgtheow swore oaths to me.[32]

"Sorrowful am I in soul to tell to any man what shame and sudden mischief Grendel has wrought for me in Heorot out of his hateful thoughts. My hall-troop,[33] my warrior-band, is melted away. Wyrd hath swept them away into the horrid clutch of Grendel. God alone can easily check the deeds [30] of that mad foe. Full oft my warriors, after the drinking of the beer, have boastfully vowed over their ale-cups to await with their dread swords the onset of Grendel in the hall. Then in the morning, when shone the day, this mead-hall, this lordly house, was all stained with blood, the benches reeking with gore—the hall was drenched in blood. So, the fewer loyal men, beloved warriors, had I then because of those whom death did snatch away. Sit now to the feast, and unseal to men as [40] thy mind moveth thee, the thoughts of thy heart, and all thy confidence of victory."

Then in the mead-hall a bench was made ready for the Geatmen, one and all. Thither the stout-hearted men went to sit in the pride of their strength. A thane did service, who bore a chased

---

[25] Cf. the tale on p. 996.
[26] Danes.
[27] His grandfather, once king of the Geats.
[28] The mythical smith of English and Norse legend. Cf. *Deor's Lament*.
[29] The Germanic goddess of Fate.
[30] He had forfeited his tribal rights by the murder of Heatholaf. Nothing further is known of the incident.
[31] Weregild for Heatholaf.
[32] To serve him, or to keep the peace.
[33] Comitatus. For the whole subject of this important institution, see Tacitus. *Germania* 13-14.

ale-flagon in his hand, and poured out the bright mead. At times a bard sang, clear-voiced in Heorot. There was merriment among the heroes, no little company of Danes and Weders.

VIII AND IX

Unferth, a thane of Hrothgar, grows jealous of Beowulf and taunts him, raking up old tales of a swimming-match with Breca. Beowulf is angered and boastfully tells the truth touching that adventure, and puts Unferth to silence. Queen Wealhtheow passes the cup. Hrothgar commends Heorot to the care of Beowulf.

Unferth, the son of Ecglaf, who sat at the feet of the lord of the Scyldings, spoke, and stirred up a quarrel; the coming of Beowulf, the brave seafarer, vexed him sore, for he would not that any other man under heaven should ever win more glories in this world than he himself. "Art thou that Beowulf who didst strive with Breca on the broad sea and didst contend with him in swimming, when ye two, foolhardy, made trial of the waves and for a mad boast risked your lives in the deep water? None, friend or foe, could turn you from the sorry venture when ye two swam out upon the sea. But ye enfolded the ocean-streams with your arms, measured the sea-streets, buffeted the water with your hands, gliding over the deep. The ocean was tossing with waves, a winter's sea. Seven nights ye toiled in the power of the waters; and he overcame thee in the match, for he had the greater strength. Then at morning-tide the sea cast him up on the coast of the Heathoræmas, whence he, beloved of his people, went to his dear fatherland, the country of the Brondings, and his own fair city where he was lord of a stronghold, and of subjects and treasure. Verily the son of Beanstan made good all his boast against thee. Wherefore, though thou hast ever been valiant in the rush of battle, I look to a grim fight, yea, and a worse issue for thee, if thou darest for the space of one night abide near Grendel."

Beowulf, son of Ecgtheow, spoke: "Well! thou hast said a deal about Breca in thy drunkenness, Unferth my friend, and hast talked much of his adventure. The truth now I tell, that I had more sea strength, more battling with the waves, than any man else. We talked of this when boys, and boasted, being yet in the days of our youth, that we would venture our lives out at sea; and we performed it even so. Naked in our hands, we held our hard swords as we swam, purposing to defend us against the whales. He, nowise swifter on the flood, could not swim far from me through the waves, nor would I part from him. Thus we two were in the sea for the space of five nights,[34] till the flood, the tossing waves, coldest of weathers, and darkening night drove us apart, and a fierce north wind beat down upon us;—rough were the waves. The wrath of the sea-fish was roused; then my shirt of mail, hard and hand-wrought, was of help to me against the foes; my woven armor, gold-adorned, lay upon my breast. An evil monster dragged me to the bottom; the grim foe held me fast in its clutch; yet it was granted me to strike the creature with the point of my war-sword; the fierce struggle carried off the mighty sea-beast by my hand.[35]

"Thus did the evil creatures often press me hard, but as was meet, I served them well with my war-sword; they had no joyous fill, by eating me, wicked destroyers, sitting round their feast nigh the bottom of the sea; but on the morrow, wounded by my sword, slain by the dagger, they lay up along the sea-strand so that they could nevermore hinder seafarers on their course in the deep channel.

"Light came from the east, the bright beacon of the Lord; the waves were stilled, and I could descry the sea-headlands, those wind-swept walls. Wyrd often saveth the warrior not doomed to die, if he be of good courage. Howbeit, it was granted me to slay nine sea-beasts with the sword. Never yet have I heard of a more desperate nightly struggle under the vault of heaven, nor of a man more sore beset in ocean-streams; yet I escaped with my life from the clutch of my foes, though spent with my adventure. The sea, the current of the flood, bore me on to the land of the Finns.

"Naught have I heard of like exploits on thy part, naught of the terror of thy sword. Breca never yet, nay, nor either of you, hath wrought so boldly in the play of battle with blood-stained swords—I boast not much of that—though thou wast the slayer of thine own brethren, thy next of kin; for that thou shalt be damned in hell, good though thy wit may be. I say to thee truly, thou son of Ecglaf, that Grendel, the fell monster, had never wrought against thy lord so many awful deeds, this shame in Heorot, were thy mind and heart so fierce in battle as thou thyself sayest. But

---

[34] Is this to be understood as a correction of Unferth's extravagance in saying seven?
[35] This fight should be compared with the encounter with Grendel's mother, pages 1004 ff.

he has found that he need not greatly fear the enmity, the dread attack, of thy people, the Victor-Scyldings. He takes forced tribute from you; he spares none of the Danish people, but he preys at will upon you; he kills and feasts, and looks not for resistance from the Spear-Danes. I, however, will show him ere long the strength and courage of the Geats in fight. Thereafter let him who may, go proudly to the mead-drinking when the morn- [10] ing-light of another day, the sun in its radiance, shines from the south over the children of men."

Then rejoiced the giver of treasure, the gray-haired king, famous in battle; the prince of the Bright-Danes trusted in him for help; the shepherd of the people heard from Beowulf his firm resolve. And the laughter[36] of the thanes arose; loud rang the din and joyous were their words.

Wealhtheow, Hrothgar's queen, went forth, mindful of courtesies; in her gold array she greeted [20] the men in the hall. The noble lady first gave the cup to him who guarded the land of the East-Danes; she bade him, beloved of his people, be blithe at the beer-drinking. The victorious[37] king partook in gladness of the feast and the hall-cup. Then the lady of the Helmings moved about to old and young in every part of the hall, handing the costly cup, until the moment came when the diademed queen, noble of mind, bore the cup to Beowulf. She greeted the lord of the Geats, and [30] thanked God, discreet in her words, that the desire of her heart was brought to pass, that she might put her trust in some hero for relief from all her affliction. That warrior, fierce in strife, received the cup from Wealhtheow; and then, eager for the fight, Beowulf, son of Ecgtheow, spoke and said: "I made this vow when I put to sea and embarked with my band of men; that I would either wholly fulfill the desire of your people, or fall in struggle, fast in the grip of the fiend. I will bravely accom- [40] plish noble deeds or abide mine end in this mead-hall." These words, these boastings of the Geat, were well-pleasing to the lady; the noble queen, in her array of gold, went to sit by her lord.

Then again as of old[38] the great word was spoken in that hall; joyous was the company—there was the sound of a mighty people—until of a sudden the son of Healfdene was minded to go to his evening rest; for he knew that the monster

intended war upon the high hall, as soon as men could no more see the light of the sun, and shadowy creatures came gliding forth, wan beneath the clouds, night darkening over all.[39] The whole company arose. Hrothgar greeted Beowulf—hero greeted hero—and wished him well, wished him the mastery in the wine-hall, and spoke this word: "Never, since I could lift hand and shield, have I entrusted unto any man this royal hall of the Danes save now to thee. Have thou and hold this best of houses; bethink thee of thy mighty deeds, show forth thy valiant strength, be watchful against the foe. Thy desires shall not be unsatisfied, if thou escape with thy life from the great adventure."

X

They leave Beowulf and his men alone in the hall. Grendel draws nigh.

And Hrothgar, lord of the Scyldings, went out of the hall with his company of men; for the warrior-chief was minded to go unto Wealhtheow, his queen and consort. The glorious king,[40] as men have learned, had set a guardian in the hall to wait for Grendel; Beowulf did special service for the lord of the Danes, keeping watch against the coming of the monster. Verily, the chief of the Geats trusted surely in his mighty strength and in the favor of the Lord. Then he put off his iron byrnie and took the helmet from his head; his jeweled sword, choicest of weapons, he gave to his thane, bidding him take charge of his war-armor. Then, ere he mounted upon his bed, Beowulf, the great Geat, spoke a boastful word: "I deem myself nowise lesser than Grendel in my deeds of warfare; therefore, not with the sword will I quell him and take his life, though I am fully able. He knows not the use of good weapons—how to strike at me, and hew my shield—famed though he be in evil deeds; but we two this night will forego the sword if he dare come to the fight without a weapon. Thereafter let all-knowing God, the holy Lord, adjudge the victory to whichsoever it be, as seemeth meet to Him."

Then the brave warrior laid him down and the pillow received the face of the hero, and round about him many a bold seaman sank down upon his bed. None of them thought ever again to reach the home he loved, his kinsfolk, or the town where

[36] Perhaps at the discomfiture of Unferth.
[37] The epithet, as often, is purely formal.
[38] Before the coming of Grendel; or perhaps, before Wealhtheow's entry.
[39] Cf. *Macbeth* 3. 2, l. 50.
[40] Perhaps meaning God.

he was bred; for they had heard that a bloody death had already destroyed far too many of the Danish men in that wine-hall. But the Lord wove victory for them, granting unto the Weder people comfort and help, inasmuch as they were all to overcome their foe by one man's might and by his single strength. And thus the truth is manifest that Almighty God hath ruled mankind throughout all time.

In the gloom of the night came stalking that [10] ranger of the dark. The watchmen [41] slept, they who had been set to guard the horn-gabled hall— all slept, save one—for it was well known to men that the ruthless destroyer could not drag them beneath the shades when the Creator willed it not. But Beowulf, wrathfully watching for the foe, awaited in anger the issue of the fight.

XI

Grendel comes into Heorot and devours one of the men. Beowulf grapples the monster.

Then from the moorland, beneath the misty hillsides, came Grendel drawing near; and God's wrath was on him. The deadly foe was thinking to ensnare some man in that high hall. On he strode beneath the clouds, until he could see full well the wine-hall, the gilded house of men, all bright with gold. This was not the first time that he had sought out Hrothgar's home, but never in [30] all the days of his life, before or since, did he meet among hall-thanes, warriors more sturdy. So the creature, of all joys bereft, came roaming on unto the hall. The door, though fast in fire-hardened bands, sprang open straightway, soon as he touched it with his hands. Thus, plotting evil, he burst open the entrance to the hall, for he was swollen with rage. Quickly thereafter the fiend was treading the bright-paved floor, moving on in wrathful mood. Out of his eyes started a loathsome [40] light, most like to flame. He saw in the hall many warriors, a kindred band together, a group of clansmen all asleep. And he laughed in his heart. The cursèd monster thought to take the life from each body, ere the day broke; for the hope of a plenteous feast was come to him. But he was not fated to devour any more of the race of men after that night.

The mighty kinsman of Hygelac was watching to see how the deadly foe would go about his swift [50]

attacks. The monster thought not of tarrying, but on a sudden, for his first move, he seized upon a sleeping thane, rent him in pieces unawares, bit into the flesh, drank the blood from the veins, and swallowed him in huge pieces. In a moment he had devoured the whole corpse, even the hands and feet. He stepped on nearer and seized with his hands the great-hearted warrior on his bed. The fiend clutched at him with his claw, but Beowulf quickly grasped it with deadly purpose, fastening upon the arm. Straightway that master of evils discovered that never in this world in all the corners of the earth, had he met in any man a mightier hand-grip. He was troubled in heart and soul; but he could get away never the faster for that. He was eager to be off; he wished to flee away into the darkness, to rejoin the horde of devils. He was not faring there as in former days. Then the good kinsman of Hygelac bethought him of his speech at even; he stood upright and grappled him fast; his fingers burst and bled.[42] The giant was making off. The hero followed close. The monster was minded to fling loose, if he could, and flee away thence to the fen-hollows; but he knew that the strength of his arm was in the grasp of an angry foe. A dire journey had the destroyer made to Heorot.

Loud rang the lordly hall. All the Danes dwelling in that city, nobles and heroes every one, were struck with terror. Furious were both the maddened wrestlers. The house re-echoed. It was a great wonder that the wine-hall withstood these battling foemen, that the fair building fell not to the ground; save that all within and without it was so firmly strengthened by iron bands, cunningly forged. There, as I have heard men tell, many a mead-bench, gold-adorned, started from its base, where the fierce ones were struggling. The wise councilors of the Scyldings had thought that none among men would ever be able to wreck by force this goodly house, bedecked with bones, nor to destroy it by craft, unless perchance the fire's embrace should swallow it in smoke.[43]

A noise arose, oft renewed; a ghastly terror fell on all the North-Danes who heard the shrieking in the house, heard God's enemy yelling out his horrid song, chant of the vanquished—Hell's captive howling o'er his wound. He held him fast who in his strength was the mightiest of men in the day of this life.

[41] The Geats.
[42] Grendel's fingers burst as a result of Beowulf's grip.
[43] A hint of the subsequent fate of Heorot; see p. 991.

XII

Beowulf has the victory, and tears out Grendel's arm. The monster escapes to the fen with his death-wound.

The defense of heroes would by no means let the murderer escape alive—he counted his life of no avail to any of the people. There many a warrior of Beowulf's drew his old sword; they thought to protect the life of their lord, the great prince, if 10 so they might. They knew not, those brave warriors, when they plunged into the fight, thinking to hack the monster on every side and take his life, that not the choicest blade on earth nor battle-ax could graze that foul destroyer; for he had bound by a spell weapons of war and every edged sword. Yet he was doomed to die a wretched death in the day of this life; the outcast spirit must needs journey far away into the power of fiends. There found that foe to God, who oft ere now in mirthful mood 20 had wrought mischief for the children of men, that his wound-proof body availed him not, for the valiant kinsman of Hygelac had got him by the hand. Hateful to each was the life of the other. The evil beast endured sore pain of body. Upon his shoulder a gaping wound appeared; the sinews sprang asunder, the flesh was rent apart. The glory of the fight was given to Beowulf. Grendel, sick to death, was doomed to flee thence and find out his joyless abode beneath the fen-banks. Full well 30 he knew that the end of his life was come, the appointed number of his days. By that deadly fight the desire of all the Danes was satisfied.

Thus he who came from far, wise and valiant in spirit, had cleansed Hrothgar's hall and freed it from danger. He rejoiced in the night's work, in his heroic deeds. The lord of the Geats had made good his boast to the East-Danes, for he had saved them out of all their affliction, the harrowing torment, no little sorrow, which they had suffered 40 and were doomed to bear in sad necessity. A token of the fight was seen, when, beneath the spacious roof, the warrior flung down the hand and arm and shoulder—the whole limb and claw of Grendel.

XIII

The Danes rejoice. They go and look upon the mere whither Grendel escaped, and return to Heorot, racing their horses and listening to the tale of the bard.

In the morning, as I have heard, many warriors were about the gift-hall; chieftains came from far and near to gaze upon the wonder, the traces of the foe. Grievous seemed his death to none of those who beheld the tracks of the inglorious one; how he, weary at heart, vanquished in strife, doomed and hunted, took his last steps to the Nicors'[44] mere. There the waters were seething with blood, the awful surge of the waves welled up, all mingled with blood and hot gore. Death-doomed he discolored all the flood, when, in his joyless lair, he laid down his life, his heathen soul; there Hell got him.

Thence returned the thanes and many a youth from their glad journey, proudly riding from the mere upon their horses, heroes upon white steeds. 20 There was proclaimed the greatness of Beowulf. Full oft 'twas said that south or north, between the seas, o'er all the broad earth beneath the arch of heaven, none among shield-bearing warriors was of higher worth, none more worthy of kingdom. They did not in the least say aught against their own kind lord, gracious Hrothgar, for he was a good king.

At times the warriors made their yellow steeds gallop or run a race, where the ways seemed good 30 to them and known for their excellence.

At times one of the king's thanes, whose memory was full of songs,[45] laden with vaunting rimes, who knew old tales without number, invented a new story, a truthful tale; the man deftly narrated the adventure of Beowulf, and cunningly composed other skillful lays with interwoven words.

THE LAY OF SIGEMUND

The bard sings how Sigemund, the Volsung, slew a mighty dragon; and how Heremod, a Danish king, was a sore burden to his people, much unlike Beowulf.

He told everything that he had heard of the mighty exploits of Sigemund, much that had ne'er been told:—the battle-toil of the Wælsing,[46] distant journeyings, feuds and crimes, of which the children of men knew nothing, save Fitela,[47] the nephew who

[44] Sea-beasts'.
[45] Songs boasting of personal prowess, or of the might of national heroes.
[46] Volsung. See the Norse saga. This is one of the earliest extant references to the Volsung myth, centuries older than the Norse saga and the German poem.
[47] Sinfiötli. his sister's son.

was with his uncle when he would repeat aught touching these things; for they were comrades at need in every strife. They had slain with their swords many of the monster broods. Sigemund, after his death, attained no little glory, since, brave in battle, he had slain the dragon who kept guard over the treasure. Alone beneath the gray rock, the prince ventured the daring deed, nor was Fitela with him. Nevertheless, it was granted unto him that his sword, the noble iron, pierced the wondrous serpent and stood fast in the wall. The dragon died the death. The dread warrior had won by his valor the enjoyment of the treasure, all at his own will. The son of Wæls [48] loaded his sea-boat and bore the glittering treasures into the bosom of his ship. Heat consumed the serpent. In his daring exploits he was by far the most famed of adventurers among the nations, this defense of warriors; wherefore he throve in days gone by.

After Heremod's [49] war-strength waned, his power and might, he was betrayed into the hands of his enemies, the Eotens, [50] and sent speedily away. Overwhelming sorrows disabled him too long; be became a lifelong care to his people, to all his nobles. Oft had the hero's life been bewailed in former days by many a prudent man, who had trusted his lord for protection from harm—trusted that the prince would prosper, attain his father's lordship, guard the nation, the treasure and sheltering city, the realm of heroes, fatherland of the Scyldings. Beowulf, the kinsman of Hygelac, was more gracious to all the children of men and to his friends. Sorrow befell Heremod.

At times, in races with their steeds, they measured the yellow roads. And the morning-light was thrust forth and urged onwards. [51] Many a stouthearted warrior went to the high hall to see the great wonder. Likewise, the king himself, guardian of the treasure, famed for his virtues, walked forth in glory from the bower with a great company; and his queen with him, amidst a bevy of maidens, passed up the path to the mead-hall.

XIV

Hrothgar and his men look upon Grendel's arm in Heorot. The king and Beowulf speak touching the fight.

Hrothgar spoke:—he went to the hall, stood in the entrance, gazed on the high roof bright with gold, and on the arm of Grendel: "Now for this sight be thanks to God straightway! Much evil, many hardships, have I endured at the hands of Grendel; but God, the King of glory, can evermore work wonder upon wonder. It was but now that I thought never to be delivered from any of my woe, while this best of houses stood drenched with blood and gore. The affliction scattered all my wise men, who thought that they could nevermore defend this stronghold of the people from hated foes, from demons and devils. Now, through the might of the Lord, a man hath wrought a deed which all of us erewhile with our craft were unable to compass. Lo! the woman, whoe'er she be, that gave birth to this son among the tribes of men may say, if she be yet alive, that our God of old hath been gracious unto her in childbearing.

"Now, O Beowulf, thou best of men, I will love thee like a son within my heart. Hold fast henceforth this our new-made kinship. Thou shalt not lack any good thing of earth within my power. Full oft for lesser deeds have I given rich gifts of honor unto a meaner warrior, a weaker in the fight. By thy deeds thou hast attained that thy glory liveth for ever and ever. May the Almighty ever reward thee as now He hath."

Then spoke Beowulf, son of Ecgtheow: "Fighting with great good-will, we wrought that mighty deed; boldly we met the power of the unknown. But I would indeed that thou couldst have seen the creature himself in full gear, the fiend wearied nigh to fainting. Grappling him there, I thought to fix him fast on his death-bed so that he should lie struggling for life in my grip, unless his body vanished utterly away. [52] But I could not stop his going, for the Lord willed it not. I did not cleave well unto the mortal foe, for the fiend was too powerful upon his feet. Yet, in saving his life, he left his claw behind, his arm and shoulder, to mark his track. But the wretched creature has not bought him any solace thus, none the longer will the evildoer live, weighed down by sin. But pain has got him close in its deadly clasp, within its baleful bonds. There, stained with sin, shall he abide the Great Doom—how the glorious Judge shall assign him his portion."

---

[48] Volsung, Sigemund.

[49] This incident, so awkwardly introduced, is probably intended to contrast the craven with the hero. Sigemund is compared, Heremod contrasted, with Beowulf. Heremod was an old king of the Danes—Scyld's predecessor possibly.

[50] Finns.

[51] The metaphorical expression may be derived from the launching of a boat. Day advanced.

[52] By virtue of his magic power.

Then, in his boastful speech, that son of Ecglaf [53] kept more silent touching warlike deeds, after all the nobles had beheld the arm before them, there upon the lofty roof, the fiendish claw, won by the hero's might. Most like to steel were all the nails, the hand-spurs, horrible spikes of the heathen foe. All declared that no warrior's sword, albeit keen, could have grazed the monster so as to strike off that bloody talon.

XV

They adorn Heorot for the feast. Hrothgar bestows gifts upon Beowulf.

Straightway it was bidden that Heorot be adorned within by the hand of man. Many men there were and women to prepare that hall of feasting and of guests. Along the walls shone hangings wrought with gold, many wondrous sights for all who gaze upon such things. That bright house had been greatly shattered, though all within was fast with iron bands. The hinges had been torn away. The roof alone was saved unhurt, when the monster, stained with wicked deeds, despairing of life, turned him to flight.

Death is not easily escaped, try it who will; but every living soul among the children of men dwelling upon the earth goeth of necessity unto his destined place, where the body, fast in its narrow bed, sleepeth after feast.[54]

Now the time was come for the son of Healfdene to go into the hall; the king himself was minded to partake of the feast. Never have I heard that that people in greater company gathered more bravely about their king. Then those happy men sat them down upon the benches; they rejoiced in the feasting. Their great-hearted kinsmen, Hrothgar and Hrothulf,[55] with fair courtesy quaffed many a bowl of mead in the high hall. Heorot was filled with friends. In that day the Scylding people had done no deeds of guile.

Then the son of Healfdene gave to Beowulf, in reward of victory, a golden ensign, a broidered banner, a helmet, and a byrnie; many men saw a mighty treasure-sword borne to the hero. Beowulf quaffed the cup in the hall. He needed not to be ashamed before warriors of those sumptuous gifts. Few have I heard of at the ale-bench who gave to others in more friendly wise four treasures, gold-adorned. About the crown of the helmet there was a wreath all wrought with wires, which protected the head, so that the tempered sword could not greatly injure it, when the shielded warrior went out against his foe.

Moreover, the defense of heroes bade that eight horses with golden bridles be led into the hall [56] under the barriers. Upon one of them there was a saddle, cunningly wrought, adorned with jewels;— it had been the battle-seat of the high king, when the son of Healfdene was minded to take part in the play of swords; [57] the might of the far-famed hero failed never at the front, while the slain were falling. And then the prince of the Ingwines [58] gave over to Beowulf the possession of these, both the horses and the armor; bade him enjoy them well. Thus, like a true man, did the great lord, the guardian of treasure and heroes, repay the storm of the fight with horses and treasure, so that none can dispraise them, none who wills to speak the truth aright.

XVI AND XVII

Hrothgar bestows gifts upon Beowulf's men. The bard sings the lay of King Finn.

And moreover, the lord of heroes, at the mead-bench, bestowed a treasure, some heirloom, upon each of those who crossed the ocean-paths with Beowulf. And he bade that gold be paid for the man whom Grendel had wickedly slain,[59] as he would have slain more of them, had not all-knowing God and the hero's courage turned that fate from them; for the Lord ruled over all the children of men, even as now He doth; wherefore is understanding best in every place, and prudence of heart. He who long dwelleth in this world endureth much of good and evil in these days of strife.

There were singing and music blended together concerning Healfdene's battle-chieftain: [60] the harp

---

[53] Unferth.
[54] This impressive, but irrelevant, passage is probably a bit of interpolation.
[55] Hrothgar's nephew, the Hrolf Kraki of Norse literature. His later quarrel with his uncle is prophetically hinted in the following sentences.
[56] It is a common occurrence in old ballads and romances to ride a horse directly into the hall. Cf. Malory's *Morte d'Arthur*, 2. 3, *et passim*.
[57] War.
[58] Danes.
[59] So that Beowulf should not lose the weregild for his murdered man.
[60] Hnæf in the following tale.

was struck, a lay oft sung, when Hrothgar's bard was to awaken joy in hall along the mead-bench.

THE LAY OF KING FINN

How Hnæf of the Scyldings fell in an ancient feud with Finn, king of the Eotens, he who had carried off his sister, Hildeburh; and how Hengest, brother to Hnæf and Hildeburh, made a treaty with Finn, and dwelt with the Eotens for a season, until they feared him and slew him. And of the last great fight when Finn was slain; and how Queen Hildeburh was restored to her people.

Hnæf of the Scyldings, the hero of the Half-Danes, was doomed to fall upon the Frisian slaughter-field at the hands of the sons of Finn, what time the peril got hold on them. Nor in truth did Hildeburh need to praise the good faith of the Eotens; she, all blameless, was bereft of her dear sons and brothers in the battle; wounded by the spear they fell according to their fate—a sorrowful woman she. Not without cause did the daughter of Hoc [61] bewail Fate's decree when morn was come—when she beheld her murdered kinsmen beneath the sky, there where she had erstwhile had the greatest of earth's joys. War swept away all the thanes of Finn, save but a few, so that he could nowise give battle to Hengest upon the field, nor save by fighting the wretched remnant from the prince's thane. But the Frisians offered Hengest terms: that they would fully prepare for him another great building, a hall and high throne, so that he might have equal power with the sons of the Eotens, and that Finn, son of Folcwald, would daily, at the giving of the gifts, do honor to the Danes, would do honor to the troop of Hengest with rings, with even as much costly treasure of plated gold, as that wherewith he would rejoice the Frisians in the mead-hall. Then on both sides they made a fast-binding treaty of peace; Finn swore an oath unto Hengest, absolutely and unreservedly, that he would honorably rule the sad remnant according to the decree of his councilors, so that no man there by word or deed should break the pact, or ever do it violence by guileful craft, although they, lordless men, followed the slayer of their own prince, as they must do perforce; and if any of the Frisians should with taunting words recall that feud, then the edge of the sword was to avenge it. The oath was sworn and massive gold was brought up from the hoard.

The best of the warriors [62] among the Battle-Scyldings was ready at the funeral pile; upon the pyre were clearly to be seen the blood-stained sark, the swine of gold, the boar-helm iron-hard, and many a hero who had perished of his wounds—these had fallen in the struggle. And Hildeburh bade them commit her own son to the flames at Hnæf's pyre, burn the body, laying it on the pile. The hapless woman wept upon his shoulder, lamented him in song. Uprose the warrior in the flame; the greatest of funeral fires rolled upward to the clouds; it roared before the mound. The heads were melted, the gashes were burst open, the blood gushed forth from the wounds upon the body. Flame, that greediest of spirits, swallowed up all of both peoples whom war had snatched away. Gone was their glory.

Bereft of their friends, the warriors departed to their dwellings, to see Friesland, their homes, and high city. And Hengest dwelt with Finn all that blood-stained winter, wholly without strife; yet he was mindful of his native land, although he could not drive over the mere his ring-stemmed ship. The sea surged in the storm, fought with the wind. Winter locked the waves in its icy bond, till that a new year came unto the dwellings of earth, as still it doth, and the days gloriously bright which ever observe the season. Thus was the winter spent, and fair was the bosom of earth.

Then the exile [63] was minded to be gone; the guest departed from the courts. But he was thinking more of vengeance than of the sea-voyage, if haply he might bring to pass a deadly conflict and so commemorate the sons of the Eotens. Therefore he escaped not the lot of mortals when the son of Hunlaf thrust into his breast the flashing sword, best of blades; wherefore its edges were well known among the Eotens. Likewise, thereafter, dire death by the sword befell the brave-hearted Finn in his own home, when Guthlaf and Oslaf, after the sea-journey, mournfully lamented the fierce struggle—blamed him for their share of sorrow. He could not retain the wavering spirit within his breast.

And the hall was covered with the bodies of foemen, and King Finn, likewise, was slain in the midst of his guardsmen, and the queen was taken. The Scylding warriors bore to their ships all the possessions of the king of the land—whatever they could find in Finn's home of jewels and curious gems. They bore the noble lady over the sea-paths to the land of the Danes, led her to her people.

The lay was sung, the gleeman's tale was ended. Mirth rose high again, clear sounded the noise of revelry. The cup-bearers poured out wine from wondrous vessels. And Wealhtheow came forth with a crown of gold upon her head, and went to where were seated uncle and nephew, those two good friends;—as yet there was peace between them, each to the other true. [64] There also sat Unferth, the spokesman, at the feet of the lord of the Scyldings; every man of them trusted his spirit.

[61] Hildeburh.
[62] Hnæf.
[63] Hengest.
[64] See p. 991 and note.

yea, and that he had good courage, although he dealt not uprightly with his kinsmen in the play of swords.[65]

And the lady of the Scyldings spoke: "Take this cup, my sovereign lord, giver of treasure. Rejoice, thou prince of the people, and speak kind words unto the Geats, as is well-fitting. Be gracious toward the Geats and mindful of gifts; for now thou hast peace both far and near. It has been told me that thou wouldst gladly have this warrior for a son. Heorot, the bright gift-hall, is cleansed. Give, then, while thou mayst, many rewards, and bequeath people and realm to thy kinsmen, when thou must go hence unto the appointed doom. I know that my gracious Hrothulf will honorably rule the youth,[66] if thou, lord of the Scyldings, leave the world ere he. I think that he will requite our offspring well, if he bethink him of our benefits toward him in time past, when he was a child, of all that we did for his pleasure and honor."

Then she turned to where her sons were sitting, Hrethric and Hrothmund, and the offspring of heroes, all the youth together; and there by the two brothers sat that brave man, Beowulf the Geat.

XVIII

The queen giveth gifts to Beowulf, and a fair collar which King Hygelac wore in aftertime. They feast, and the heroes rest in Heorot.

A cup was borne to him, and friendly greeting offered, and twisted gold graciously presented him: two armlets, rings, and armor, and the goodliest of collars I have ever heard of upon earth. Never heard I of a fairer among the treasured jewels of heroes beneath the sky, ne'er since Hama bore away to the bright city the collar of the Brisings,[67] the fair gem and its casket; he fled the cunning snares of Eormanric, and chose everlasting gain.[68] This ring had Hygelac, the Geat, grandson of Swerting, on his last raid,[69] when, beneath his banner, he defended his treasure and guarded the plunder of battle. Wyrd took him away, when he, foolhardy, suffered woe in feud with the Frisians; for that mighty chieftain bore the jewel with its precious stones over the arching sea; and he fell beneath his shield. Then the body of the king came into the possession of the Franks, his breast-mail, and the jewel, too; meaner warriors stripped the body after the slaughter of battle; the corpses of the Geats were strewed upon the field.

The hall resounded. Wealhtheow spoke before the host and said: "Receive with joy this collar, dear Beowulf, beloved youth, and use this armor —treasures of our people—and prosper well; show thyself strong; and be kind in thy counsel to these youths. I will be mindful of thy reward. Thou hast brought it to pass that men shall give thee honor evermore, in all the earth, far as the sea encompasseth its windswept walls. Be, while thou livest, a prosperous prince; much treasure truly I wish thee. Be thou friendly to my son, guarding his happy state.[70] Here is each hero true to the other, gentle of spirit, and loyal to his lord; the thanes are obedient, the people ready at call. Ye warriors, cheered with wine, do as I bid ye."

Then she went to her seat. There was the choicest of feasts; the men drank wine. They knew not Wyrd, cruel destiny, as it had gone forth of old unto many a hero.

When even was come, and Hrothgar, the ruler, had departed to his lodge unto his evening rest, countless heroes guarded the house as they had oft of yore. They made bare the bench and spread upon it beds and pillows. Doomed and nigh unto death, one of the revelers laid him down to rest in the hall. At their heads they placed their battle-shields, bright bucklers. There upon the bench above each hero were clearly to be seen the towering helm, the ringèd coat of mail, the mighty spear. It was their wont to be ever ready for battle, whether at home or in the field, ready for either, even at the moment when their chief had need of them. That was a good people.

---

[65] See Beowulf's charge against him, p. 996.

[66] Act as regent.

[67] Beowulf's collar is compared to the famous Brising necklace, which, according to the *Elder Edda*, is the property of the goddess Freya; apparently it later came into the possession of Hermanric the Ostrogoth (Eormanric), from whom it was stolen by one Hama. The later history of Beowulf's jewel follows, somewhat after the manner of the Homeric account of Agamemnon's scepter.

[68] Probably entered a monastery.

[69] One of the few authentic historical allusions in the poem. The account of the raid of "Chochilaicus" (Hygelac) may be found in the *Historia Francorum* of Gregory of Tours. The event occurred about 512 A.D.

[70] Probably in case of his father's death, which she referred to a moment since.

PART II

BEOWULF AND GRENDEL'S MOTHER

XIX

Grendel's mother cometh to avenge her son. She seizes Æschere in Heorot.

Then they sank to sleep. But one paid dearly for his evening rest, as had often happened when Grendel haunted that gold-hall and wrought evil 10 till his end came, death for his sins. It now became evident to men that, though the foe was dead, there yet lived for a long time after the fierce combat, an avenger—Grendel's mother. The witch, woman-monster, brooded over her woes, she who was doomed to dwell among the terrors of the waters, in the cold streams, from the time when Cain slew with the sword his only brother, his own father's son; then he departed, banished, marked with mur-der, fleeing from the joys of men and dwelt in the 20 wilderness. From him there woke to life many Fate-sent demons. One of these was Grendel,[71] a fierce wolf, full of hatred. But he had found at Heorot a man on the watch, waiting to give him battle. Then the monster grappled with him, but Beowulf bethought him of his mighty strength, the gift of God, and in Him as the Almighty he trusted for favor, for help and succor; in this trust he overcame the fiend, laid low that spirit of hell. Then Grendel, enemy to mankind, went forth joy- 30 less to behold the abode of death. But his mother, still wroth and ravenous, determined to go a sad journey to avenge the death of her son; and she came to Heorot, where the Ring-Danes lay asleep about the hall. Straightway terror fell upon the heroes once again when Grendel's mother burst in upon them. But the fear was less than in the time of Grendel, even as the strength of maids, or a woman's rage in war, is less than an armed man's, what time the hilted sword, hammer-forged, stained 40 with blood, cleaves with keen blade the boar on foeman's helmet. There above the benches in the hall the hard-edged sword was drawn, and many a shield upreared, fast in the hand; none thought of helm or broad corslet when the terror got hold of him. She was in haste, for she was discovered; she wished to get thence with her life. Of a sudden she clutched one of the heroes, and was off to the fen. The mighty warrior, the famed hero whom the hag murdered in his sleep, was the dearest to Hrothgar of all the men in his band of comrades between the seas. Beowulf was not there; for an-other lodging-place had been assigned to the mighty Geat after the giving of treasure. A cry arose in Heorot. All in its gore she had taken the famous arm;[72] sorrow was renewed in the dwellings. No good exchange was that which cost both peoples the lives of friends.

Then the old king, the hoary warrior, was sad at heart when he learned that his chief thane had lost his life, that his dearest friend was dead. Straightway Beowulf, the hero blessed with victory, was brought to the bower; the prince, the noble warrior, went at daybreak with his comrades to where the prudent king was waiting to know if perchance the Almighty would ever work a happy change for him, after grievous tidings. And the hero, famed in war, strode up the hall with his band of thanes—while loud the room resounded—to greet the wise lord of the Ingwines; he asked if his night had been restful, as he had wished.

XX

Hrothgar lamenteth for Æschere. He tells Beowulf of the monster and her haunt.

Hrothgar, defense of the Scyldings, spoke: "Ask not after bliss,—sorrow in hall is renewed for the Danish folk. Æschere is dead, Yrmenlaf's elder brother, my councilor and my adviser, who stood by me, shoulder to shoulder, when we warded our heads in battle, while hosts rushed together and helmets crashed. Like Æschere should every noble be—an excellent hero. He was slain in Heorot by a restless destroyer.

"I know not whither the awful monster, exult-ing in her prey, has turned her homeward steps, rejoicing in her fill. She has avenged the strife in which thou slewest Grendel yesternight, grappling fiercely with him, for that he too long had wasted and destroyed my people. He fell in the fight, forfeiting his life, and now another is come, a mighty and a deadly foe, thinking to avenge her son. She has carried the feud further; wherefore it may well seem a heavy woe to many a thane who grieveth in spirit for his treasure-giver. Low lies the hand which did satisfy all your desires.

"I have heard the people dwelling in my land,

---

[71] This repetition of the events of the earlier part may serve to show that the author was conscious of his transition to a new subject. It is even possible that the recitation of the story may sometimes have begun at or near this point.

[72] Grendel's.

hall-rulers, say that they had often seen two such mighty stalkers of the marches, spirits of other-where, haunting the moors. One of them, as they could know full well, was like unto a woman; the other miscreated being, in the image of man wandered in exile (save that he was larger than any man), whom in the olden time the people named Grendel. They knew not if he ever had a father among the spirits of darkness. They dwell in a hidden land amid wolf-haunted slopes and savage fen-paths, the wind-swept cliffs where the mountain-stream falleth, shrouded in the mists of the headlands, its flood flowing underground. It is not far thence in measure of miles that the mere lieth. Over it hang groves in hoary whiteness; a forest with fixed roots bendeth over the waters. There in the night-tide is a dread wonder seen—a fire on the flood. There is none of the children of men so wise that he knoweth the depths thereof. Although hard pressed by hounds, the heath-ranging stag, with mighty horns, may seek out that forest, driven from afar, yet sooner will he yield up life and breath upon the bank than hide his head within its waters. Cheerless is the place. Thence the surge riseth, wan to the clouds, when the winds stir up foul weather, till the air thicken and the heavens weep.

"Now once again help rests with thee alone. Thou knowest not yet the spot, the savage place where thou mayst find the sinful creature. Seek it out, if thou dare. I will reward thee, as I did before, with olden treasures and with twisted gold, if thou get thence alive."

XXI

They track Grendel's mother to the mere. Beowulf slayeth a sea-monster.

Then spoke Beowulf, son of Ecgtheow: "Sorrow not, thou wise man. It is better for a man to avenge his friend than mourn exceedingly. Each of us must abide the end of the worldly life, wherefore let him who may, win glory ere he die; thus shall it be best for a warrior when life is past. Arise, O guardian of the kingdom, let us straightway go and look upon the tracks of Grendel's dam. I promise thee this: she shall not escape to the covert, neither into the bosom of the earth, nor to mountain-wood, nor to the bottom of the sea, go where she will. This day do thou bear in patience every woe of thine, as I expect of thee."

Then the old man leapt up and thanked God, the mighty Lord, for what that man had said. And they bridled Hrothgar's horse, a steed with curling mane. The wise prince rode stately forth, and with him fared a troop of shielded warriors. Footprints were clearly seen along the forest-path, her track across the land. She had gone forth, over the murky moor, and borne away lifeless that best of thanes, who with Hrothgar ruled the hall.

And the offspring of princes went over steep and rocky slopes and narrow ways, straight lonely passes, an unknown course; over sheer cliffs and many a sea-beast's haunt. He, with a few prudent men, went on before to view the spot, until he suddenly came upon mountain-trees o'erhanging the gray rock—a cheerless wood. Beneath it lay a water, bloody and troubled. All the Danes, all the friends of the Scyldings, each hero and many a thane, sad at heart then suffered sore distress; for there upon the sea-cliff they found the head of Æschere. The waters were seething with blood and hot gore—the people gazed.

At times the horn sang out an eager lay. All the troop sat down. They saw in the water many of the serpent kind, strange dragons swimming the deep. Likewise they saw sea-monsters lying along the headland-slopes, serpents and wild beasts, such as oft at morning-tide make a journey, fraught with sorrow, over the sail-road. They sped away, bitter and swollen with wrath, when they heard the sound, the song of the battle-horn. But the lord of the Geats with bow and arrow took the life of one of them, as it buffeted the waves, so that the hard shaft pierced the vitals; he was then the slower in swimming the sea, for death seized him. Straightway he was hard pressed with the sharp barbs of hookèd spears, fiercely attacked, and drawn up on the cliff, a wondrous wave-tosser. The men looked on the strange and grisly beast.

Then Beowulf girded him with noble armor; he took no thought for his life. His byrnie, hand-woven, broad, and of many colors, was to search out the deeps. This armor could well protect his body so that the grip of the foe could not harm his breast, nor the clutch of the angry beast do aught against his life. Moreover, the white helmet guarded his head, even that which was to plunge into the depths of the mere, passing through the tumult of the waters; it was all decked with gold, encircled with noble chains, as the weapon-smith wrought it in days of yore; wondrously he made it, and set it about with boar-figures so that no brand nor battle-sword could bite it.[73]

[73] See p. 993, note 21.

Nor was that the least of his mighty aids which Hrothgar's spokesman [74] lent him in his need—the name of the hilted sword was Hrunting, and it was one of the greatest among olden treasures; its blade was of iron, stained with poison-twigs, hardened with blood of battle; it had never failed any man whose hand had wielded it in fight, any who durst go on perilous adventures to the field of battle—it was not the first time that it had need to do high deeds. Surely when the son of Ecglaf, strong in his might, lent that weapon to a better swordsman, he did not remember what he had said when drunk with wine; as for him, he durst not risk his life beneath the warring waves and do a hero's deeds; there he lost the glory, the fame of valor. It was not so with the other when he had armed him for the fight.

XXII

Beowulf bids farewell to Hrothgar and plunges into the mere. The monster seizes upon him. They fight.

Then spoke Beowulf, son of Ecgtheow: "Remember, thou great son of Healfdene, wise chieftain, gracious friend of men, now that I am ready for this exploit, what we two spoke of aforetime; that, if I must needs lose my life for thee, thou wouldst ever be as a father to me when I was gone hence. Guard thou my thanes, my own comrades, if the fight take me, and do thou also send unto Hygelac the treasures that thou gavest me, beloved Hrothgar. Then, when the son of Hrethel, lord of the Geats, shall look upon that treasure, he may behold and see by the gold that I found a bountiful benefactor, and enjoyed these gifts while I might. And do thou let Unferth, that far-famed man, have the old heirloom, the wondrous wavy sword of tempered blade. I will win glory with Hrunting, or death shall take me."

After these words the lord of the Weder-Geats boldly made haste; he would await no answer, but the surging waters swallowed up the warrior. It was the space of a day ere he got sight of the bottom.

Soon the blood-thirsty creature, she who had lived for a hundred seasons, grim and greedy, in the waters' flow, found that one was there from above seeking out the abode of monsters. She seized upon the warrior and clutched him with her horrid claws; nevertheless she did no harm to his sound body, for the ringèd armor girt him round about, so that she could not pierce the byrnie, the linkèd coat of mail, with her hateful fingers.

Then the mere-wolf, when she came to the bottom, bore the ring-prince to her dwelling, so that he could nowise wield his weapons, brave though he was; for many monsters came at him, many a sea-beast with awful tusks broke his battle-sark—the evil creatures pressed him hard.

Then the hero saw that he was in some dreadful hall, where the water could not harm him a whit; the swift clutch of the current could not touch him, because of the roofed hall. He saw a fire-light, a gleaming flame brightly shining. Then the hero got sight of the mighty mere-woman—the she-wolf of the deep. He made at her fiercely with his war-sword. His hand did not refuse the blow, so that the ringèd blade sang out a greedy war-song on her head. But the stranger found that the gleaming sword would make no wound, nor harm her life; so the blade failed the prince at need. It had aforetime endured many a hard fight, had often cleft the helmet and the byrnie of the doomed; this was the first time that the precious treasure ever failed of its glory. Yet the kinsman of Hygelac, heedful of great deeds, was steadfast of purpose, not faltering in courage. Then the angry warrior threw from him the carved sword, strong and steel-edged, studded with jewels, and it lay upon the ground. He trusted to his strength, to the mighty grip of his hand. So must a brave man do when he thinketh to win lasting praise in war—he taketh no thought for his life.

Then the lord of the War-Geats, shrinking not from the fight, seized Grendel's mother by the shoulder, and full of wrath, the valiant in battle threw his deadly foe so that she fell to the floor. Speedily she paid him his reward again with fierce grapplings and clutched at him, and being wearied, he stumbled and fell, he, the champion, strongest of warriors. Then she leapt and sat upon him, and drew her dagger, broad and brown-edged, to avenge her son, her only offspring. But on his shoulder lay his woven coat of mail; it saved his life, barring the entrance against point and blade. Then the son of Ecgtheow, chief of the Geats, would have perished beneath the sea-bottom, had not his byrnie, his hard war-shirt aided him, and Holy God, the wise Lord, brought victory to pass, the King of heaven easily adjudging it aright. Thereafter he stood up again.

XXIII

Beowulf lays hold upon a giant sword and slays the evil beast. He finds Grendel's dead body and

---

[74] Unferth.

cuts off the head, and swims up to his thanes upon the shore. They go back to Heorot.

Then he saw among the armor a victorious blade, an old sword of the giant-age, keen-edged, the glory of warriors; it was the choicest of weapons— save that it was larger than any other man was able to carry into battle—good, and splendidly wrought, for it was the work of the giants. And the warrior of the Scyldings seized the belted hilt; savage and angry, he drew forth the ring-sword, and, hopeless of life, smote so fiercely that the hard sword caught her by the neck, breaking the ring-bones; the blade drove right through her doomed body, and she sank upon the floor. The sword was bloody; the hero exulted in his deed.

The flame burst forth; light filled the place, even as when the candle of heaven is shining brightly from the sky. He gazed about the place and turned him to the wall; the thane of Hygelac, angry and resolute, lifted the great weapon by the hilts. The blade was not worthless to the warrior, for he wished to repay Grendel straightway for the many attacks which he had made upon the West-Danes— oftener far than once—what time he slew Hrothgar's hearth-companions in their slumber and devoured fifteen of the sleeping Danes and carried off as many more, a horrid prey. The fierce warrior had given him his reward, so that he now saw Grendel lying lifeless in his resting-place, spent with his fight, so deadly had the combat been for him in Heorot. The body bounded far when it suffered a blow after death, a mighty sword-stroke. And thus he smote off the head.

Soon the prudent men who were watching the mere with Hrothgar saw that the surging waves were all troubled, and the water mingled with blood. The old men, white-haired, talked together of the hero, how they thought that the prince would never come again to their great lord, exultant in victory; for many believed that the sea-wolf had rent him in pieces.

Then came the ninth hour of the day. The bold Scyldings left the cliff, the bounteous friend of men departed to his home. But the strangers sat there, sick at heart, and gazed upon the mere; they longed but did not ever think to see their own dear lord again.

Meanwhile the sword, that war-blade, being drenched with blood, began to waste away in icicles of steel; it melted wondrously like ice when the Father looseneth the frost, unwindeth the ropes that bind the waves; He who ruleth the times and seasons, He is a God of righteousness. The lord of the Weder-Geats took no treasure from that hall, although he saw much there, none save the head, and the hilt bright with gold; the blade had melted, the graven sword had burned away, so hot had been the blood, so venomous the strange spirit that had perished there.

Soon he was swimming off, he who had survived the onset of his foes; he plunged up through the water. The surging waves were cleansed, the wide expanse where that strange spirit had laid down her life and the fleeting days of this world.

And the defense of seamen came to land, stoutly swimming; he rejoiced in his sea-spoil, the great burden that he bore with him. And his valiant band of thanes went unto him, giving thanks to God; they rejoiced in their chief, for that they could see him safe and sound. Then they quickly loosed helm and byrnie from the valiant man. The mere grew calm, but the water beneath the clouds was stained with the gore of battle.

They set forth along the foot path glad at heart; the men, kingly bold, measured the earth-ways, the well-known roads. They bore away the head from the sea-cliff—a hard task for all those men, great-hearted as they were; four of them must needs bear with toil that head of Grendel upon a spear to the gold-hall. And forthwith the fourteen Geats, bold and warlike, came to the hall, and their brave lord in their midst trod the meadows. And the chief of the thanes, the valiant man crowned with glory, the warrior brave in battle, went in to greet Hrothgar. And Grendel's head was borne by the hair into the hall where the men were drinking—a terror alike to heroes and to queen. The people gazed upon that wondrous sight.

XXIV AND XXV

Beowulf tells of his fight, and Hrothgar discourses. They feast in Heorot. In the morning the Geats make ready to depart.

Beowulf, son of Ecgtheow, spoke: "Behold, O son of Healfdene, lord of the Scyldings, we have joyfully brought thee this sea-spoil which here thou lookest on, a token of glory. Hardly did I escape with my life; painfully fighting under the waters, I ventured on the work. The struggle would have well-nigh failed me, had not God shielded me. Nor could I do aught with Hrunting in the fight, though that be a good weapon; but the Ruler of the people—full often hath He guided friendless men—granted that I saw an old and mighty sword hanging all beauteous on the wall; so I drew that weapon forth. And I slew in fight the keepers of that house, for occasion favored me. But the war-sword, the graven blade, burned away when the blood gushed forth, hottest of battle-gore. The hilt I bore away from the enemy, avenging, as was meet, their crimes, the slaughter of the Danes. I promise thee that thou, with a troop of thy men, mayst sleep in Heorot free from care, thou and all the thanes of thy people, young and old; thou needest not fear death for them from that quarter, as formerly thou didst, O lord of the Scyldings." 10

Then the golden hilt, the ancient work of giants, was given into the hands of the agèd warrior, the hoary leader in battle. After the fall of the devils, this work of cunning smiths came into the posses-sion of the lord of the Danes; when the fierce-hearted enemy of God, guilty of murder, quitted this world, he and his mother too, it passed into the keeping of the best of kings between the seas, the best of those who gave out gifts of money in the Danish land.

Hrothgar spoke; he looked upon the hilt, the old heirloom on which was graven the beginning of the ancient strife, what time the flood, the rushing ocean, destroyed the giant race.[75] They had be-haved frowardly. That people was estranged from the eternal Lord; wherefore the Ruler gave them their final reward in the flood of waters. And on the guard of shining gold was rightly graven, set forth and told in runic letters, for whom the sword had first been made, that best of blades, with its 30 twisted hilt brightly adorned with snakes.

Then the wise son of Healfdene spoke—silent were they all: "Lo! the agèd ruler who remem-bereth far-off days, he who doeth righteousness and truth among the people, may say that this hero was born of the nobler stock. The fame of thee, my friend Beowulf, is spread abroad among every peo-ple far and wide. Thou dost hold it all with meek-ness; yea, all thy might with prudence of mind. I will make good my compact with thee, even as 40 we did agree aforetime. Thou shalt be a lasting comfort to thy people, a help to warriors.

"Not so was Heremod[76] to the children of Ecgwela, the Honor-Scyldings. He throve not for their welfare, but became the destruction and the deadly plague of the Danish people; for in his rage he slew his table-companions, the friends of his bosom, until he, the great prince, went forth alone, far from the joys of men. Although mighty God advanced him and set him above all men in 50 strength and in the joys of power, yet there grew up a blood-thirsty spirit in his heart; he gave no treasure to the Danes, as was meet, so that he lived

joyless, suffering punishment for his hostility in the lasting wretchedness of his people. Learn thou from this; lay hold upon manly virtue. With the wisdom of many winters I have told this tale for thee.

"Wonderful it is to tell how mighty God, in His great spirit, giveth wisdom unto mankind and land and noble rank. He ruleth over all. But at times He letteth the thoughts of a man's heart stray toward the satisfaction of his own desires; He giveth him worldly joys in his fatherland, a fenced city of men to hold; He maketh whole regions of the earth subject unto him, a wide domain, so that in his blindness he considereth not his end. He dwelleth in plenty; no whit doth sickness or age beset him; sorrow darkeneth not his spirit; no-where doth strife appear, or deadly hate; but all the world moveth to his will.

"He knoweth no worse state, until at length much pride grows and flourishes within him, while the watchman is sleeping, the keeper of the soul. Too deep is that slumber, encompassed with sor-rows; the Adversary is at hand, who shooteth from his bow in evil wise; and the helmeted man is smitten in the breast with a bitter arrow, being unable to ward off the crooked counsels of the Accursèd Spirit. Too little seemeth that which he hath long possessed. He is covetous in his froward heart; he doth not gloryingly bestow the plated rings, and he forgetteth and despiseth the future, by reason of the bounteous honors which God, the King of glory, hath accorded him.

"But in the end it is brought to pass that the failing body wasteth away; and falleth doomed. Another succeedeth, one who giveth out the treas-ure, nothing loath, the prince's store of riches laid up of old—naught to fear hath he.

"Keep thee from deadly envy, then, beloved Beowulf, best of men, and choose thou the better course, everlasting gain. Incline thee not to pride, O mighty warrior. Now the flower of thy strength lasteth for a season, but soon sickness or sword shall cut thee off from thy strength, or the embrace of fire, or the surge of the flood, or the stab of the sword, or the flight of the spear, or wretched age; or else the light of thine eyes shall fail and grow dim, and forthwith death shall overcome thee, O noble hero.

"Thus I ruled over the Ring-Danes fifty years beneath the sky, and defended them in battle with spear and sword from many a tribe throughout the world; insomuch that I thought I had no foe beneath the breadth of heaven. Lo! all this was

[75] *Genesis* 4, 1.   [76] See p. 1000 and note 49

changed for me in my land; joy changed to sorrow, when Grendel, my foe of old, fell upon my home. Ever in my heart I suffered great sorrow because of this persecution. Wherefore thanks be to God, our everlasting Lord, that I have lived to see with mine eyes this gory head, now the old strife is over.

"Go now to thy seat, honored warrior, partake in the joy of the feasting. Thou and I will share full many treasures when morning is come."

The Geat was glad at heart, and went straightway to his seat, as the wise king bade him. Then once again a fair feast was made ready as before for those brave men in the hall.

The helm of night loured dark over the warriors. All the company arose; the agèd man, the grayhaired Scylding, was minded to go to his bed. And the Geat, the brave shield-warrior, had an exceeding great desire of rest. Forthwith the hall-thane, he who duly supplied all the warrior's needs, such as seafarers must have in that day, guided forth that traveler from afar, wearied with his venture. And the great-hearted hero rested him.

The hall towered aloft, vast and gold-adorned. The guest slept within, until the black raven, blithe of heart, announced the joy of heaven, and the bright sun came gliding over earth. The warriors hastened, the heroes longed to be returning to their people; the great-hearted guest wished to take ship and go far thence.

And the hero bade the son of Ecglaf [77] bear away Hrunting, bade him take the sword, belovèd weapon; he thanked him for lending it, said that he counted it a good war-friend, a mighty in battle; he uttered no word in blame of that edged sword— he was a great-hearted man!

And when the warriors, eager for the voyage, were ready armed, the chief, dear in the sight of the Danes, went to the throne where the other was; the hero, bold in battle, gave greeting to Hrothgar.

XXVI

Beowulf bids farewell to Hrothgar and the aged king weeps at his departure. He giveth him many treasures. The Geats go down to the sea.

Beowulf, son of Ecgtheow, spoke: "Now we seafarers, travelers from afar, would say that we purpose to return unto Hygelac. We have been well entertained here to our heart's desire: thou hast been good to us. If, then, O lord of men, I can win upon earth more of thy heart's love than I have yet done, I shall be ready at once for warlike deeds. If I learn beyond the course of the waters that thy neighbors beset thee sore, as did thine enemies in days gone by, I will bring a thousand thanes and warriors to help thee. I know that Hygelac, lord of the Geats, shepherd of the people, young though he be, will further me by word and deed that I may do honor to thee and bring to thine aid the shafted spear and the succor of my strength, when thou hast need of men. Moreover, if Hrethric, the king's son, take service at the Geatish court, he will find there many friends; far countries are best sought out by him who is strong within himself."

Hrothgar spoke and answered him again: "The all-knowing Lord hath sent these words into thy mind; I never heard one so young in life speak more wisely. Thou art strong in thy might, and prudent of mind, wise in thy discourse. I count it likely that, if ever the spear or fierce warfare or sickness or weapon take away thy lord, the heir of Hrethel, shepherd of the people, and if thou be yet alive, the Sea-Geats will have none better to choose as king, as guardian of treasure and heroes, if haply thou be willing to govern the kingdom of thy folk. Thy great heart delighteth me more and more, dear Beowulf. Thou hast brought it to pass that there shall be peace between our people, the Geat folk and the Spear-Danes; and strife shall cease, the evil feuds which they have endured in time past. We shall have treasure in common while I rule over this wide realm; many friends shall greet one another with good things across the gannet's bath; [78] the ringèd ship shall bring gifts and love-tokens over the sea. I know that the peoples are firmly united toward friend and toward foe, blameless in every way, after the olden customs."

And moreover the son of Healfdene, shelter of warriors, gave unto him twelve treasures within the hall; he bade him go in safety with these gifts unto his own dear people, and quickly come again. And the king of noble lineage, lord of the Scyldings, kissed that best of thanes and clasped him round the neck; tears fell from the gray-haired man. The wise and aged king looked for either thing,[79] but rather for the second, that they would never meet again, brave in the council. The hero was so dear to him that he could not contain his welling grief, for in his breast secret longing after the dear man, fast bound within his heart, burned through his blood.

Then Beowulf, the warrior proud of his gold, exulting in his treasure, went thence treading the grassy plain. The ship awaited her lord, riding at anchor. And, as they went, Hrothgar's gift was praised full oft. He was a king, blameless in every wise, until old age, which has often wasted many a man, took from him the joys of strength.

XXVII

Beowulf presents to the coast-warden a golden sword. The Geats return unto their land. They bear the treasures to the hall where dwells King Hygelac with his queen, Hygd. The tale of Thrytho told.

Then the band of brave retainers came to the sea; they wore ringèd armor, woven shirts of mail. The land-warden beheld the heroes when they came again, even as he had done before. But not with insult did he greet the guests from the peak of the cliff, but rode toward them, as they came unto their ship, saying that the Weder people, the bright-coated warriors, were welcome.

Then the spacious bark, the ring-stemmed ship upon the beach, was laden with the armor, with the horses and the treasures; the mast towered high over the wealth from Hrothgar's hoard. Beowulf gave to the boat-warden a sword all bound with gold, so that he was the more honored thereafter at the mead-bench because of that treasure and heirloom.

And he departed in his ship, driving the deep waters asunder; he left the Danish land. Then a sail, one of the sea-cloths, was fastened to the mast. The sea-craft groaned. The wind blowing over the waters did not drive the bark from her course; the ship sailed on: with wreathèd prow she floated forth, foamy-necked, over the waters of the sea, until the men could descry the Geatish cliffs, the well-known headlands. The keel, driven by the wind, bounded up, and stood ashore. Straightway the harbor-guard was ready at the water's edge, he who upon the beach had long been looking out afar, eager for the dear men. He bound the broad-bosomed ship with anchor-ropes fast to the shore, lest the force of the waves should drive the fair boat away.

And Beowulf bade them bear up ashore the princely treasure, the jewels and the beaten gold. It was not far thence for them to go unto the giver of treasure, Hygelac, son of Hrethel; there at home he dwells with his companions, nigh the sea-wall.

Fair was the house; its lord a brave king, great in hall. Hygd, daughter of Hæreth, was very young, was wise and well nurtured, although she had lived but few winters within the castle walls; yet she was not mean-spirited, and nowise sparing in gifts of precious treasures to the Geats.

THE TALE OF THRYTHO

Much unlike Hygd was a queen named Thrytho, proud and wrathful, until Offa subdued her.

Thrytho,[80] the fierce queen of the people, showed forth wrath and evil dire; no brave man among the dear comrades durst venture by day to look upon her with his eyes, none save her lord; else he might count on deadly bonds, hand-woven, being destined for him. Straightway after his seizure the sword was appointed for use, so that the carved weapon might decide it, and tell forth the baleful murder. Such is no queenly custom for a woman to practice, peerless though she be—that a weaver of peace [81] should attempt the life of a dear retainer because of pretended insult.

But the kinsman of Hemming [82] checked this. The ale-drinkers told another story, how that she wrought less evil to the people, fewer deeds of hate after she was given, all gold-adorned, to the young warrior of noble lineage, when she at her father's bidding, journeyed over the dark waters unto Offa's hall. There, while she lived, she enjoyed her destiny upon the throne, famed for her goodness. She held high love toward the prince of heroes who, as I have heard, was the best of all mankind between the seas, best of all the race of men on earth. Therefore Offa, bold with the spear, was honored far and wide for gifts and warfare. Wisely he ruled his native land. From him sprang Eomær, kinsman of Hemming, grandson of Garmund, skillful in warfare, for the help of heroes.

XXVIII

Beowulf is received by Hygelac, and telleth of his meeting with Grendel. Of Freawaru.

Then the brave chief went forth over the sands with his companions, treading the sea-beach, the wide-stretching shores. The candle of the world was shining, the sun in its course beaming from

---

[80] This account of Thrytho is apparently introduced to contrast her with Hygd; so Beowulf (p. 1008) was praised by contrast with Heremod.
[81] This kenning for a queen is significant in many ways.
[82] Offa.

the south. They went their ways; boldly betook them to where, as they had heard, the young and gracious war-king, shelter of heroes, slayer of Ongentheow,[83] was giving out rings within his city. Speedily Beowulf's coming was announced to Hygelac, how that the shelter of warriors, his shield-comrade, was come back alive to the hall, come back to the court, safe from combat. Straightway the hall within was made ready for the travelers, even as the ruler bade.

Then he who had scaped from the strife sat by the king himself, kinsman by kinsman, after his lord with courtly speech had greeted the loyal hero with mighty words. And Hæreth's daughter passed about the hall, pouring out the mead; for she loved the people; she bore the mead-cup to the hands of the heroes.

Then Hygelac began to question his companions full fairly in the lofty hall, for he was spurred with longing to know touching the adventures of the Sea-Geats: "How fared ye in your journeying, dear Beowulf, when thou on a sudden didst resolve to seek combat far away over the salt waters, battle in Heorot? Didst thou in aught lessen the well-known woe of Hrothgar, the mighty lord? I have nourished brooding care and sorrow in my heart, for I put no trust in the journey of my belovèd thane. Long did I entreat thee not to attack the deadly beast, but let the South-Danes themselves put an end to their strife with Grendel. I give thanks unto God that I am suffered to see thee safe."

Beowulf, son of Ecgtheow, spoke: "Known unto many, my lord Hygelac, is the famous meeting 'twixt Grendel and me, and our fighting there on the field where he had wrought much sorrow for the Victor-[84] Scyldings and misery evermore. All that I avenged, so that none of Grendel's kin on earth need boast of that fray at twilight, not even he of the loathèd race who shall live the longest in the midst of the moorland.

"When I came into that country, I went first into the ring-hall to greet Hrothgar. Straightway the great kinsman of Healfdene, when he knew my mind, gave me a seat with his own son. It was a joyous host; I have never seen greater joy at the mead among any hall-guests beneath the vault of heaven. At times the great queen, the peace and bond of peoples,[85] passed all about the hall, and cheered the hearts of the young retainers; oft-times she gave a ring to some warrior ere she went to her seat. At times Hrothgar's daughter bore the ale-cup before the nobles, unto the warriors in order. I heard those in the hall call her Freawaru as she gave studded treasure to the heroes."

FREAWARU [86]

How Freawaru, daughter to Hrothgar, is betrothed to Ingeld of the Heathobards, they who were Hrothgar's enemies of old. And how Ingeld will be provoked to the murder of a thane who attends on Freawaru; and how Ingeld's love for that lady will wane.

"Young and gold-adorned, she is promised to the glad son of Froda; this has seemed good to the lord of the Scyldings, defender of the kingdom, and he counts it a gain—by this marriage to allay many deadly feuds and strifes. Yet, oft and not rarely, in any place after a prince has fallen, it is but a little time that the deadly spear lies at rest, fair though the bride may be.

"Wherefore it may well displease the lord of the Heathobards and all the thanes of that people when he goes into hall with his lady, that his warriors attend on a noble scion of the Danes,[87] for on him gleam the heirlooms of their fathers, hard and ring-adorned, once the Heathobards' treasure, while they could still wield their weapons, until in an evil day they led astray into battle their dear companions and their own lives.

"Then speaks one over the beer, an old warrior who sees the heirloom and who remembers all the slaughter of the men; and his soul is wrathful; and, sore at heart, he begins to try the spirit of the young warrior by the thoughts of his breast, begins to waken war-fury, and speaks this word: 'Knowst thou the sword, my friend, the precious blade that thy father bore into battle, when he wore his helmet for the last time, and the Danes, the bold Scyldings, slew him, and held the battle-field, because Withergild [88] was laid low after the fall of heroes? Now some stripling, offspring of those murderers, walks our hall

---

[83] In Part III of the *Beowulf* we are told that Ongentheow was slain by Eofor, one of Hygelac's men. It is proper for the retainer to attribute his glory to his lord. See *Agricola* 8, and *Germania* 14.

[84] The epithet is here either purely formal (cf. p. 997), or touched with sarcasm.

[85] Cf. p. 1010, and note 81.

[86] This episode, a fine piece of epic prophecy, refers to a tale probably well known to the poet's audience—the fight of Ingeld and Hrothgar. Our knowledge of the story is derived chiefly from the *Widsith* (see lines 45 ff.), which is the only other Old English poem that contains mention of the more important characters of the *Beowulf*.

[87] Heathobards, that is, are obliged to serve some Dane who has come in attendance on Freawaru.

[88] Nothing is known of him.

exulting in the spoil, boasts of that slaughter, and wears the treasure which thou shouldst rightly have.'

"Thus he ever goads him and stirs his memory with galling words, until the hour comes that the lady's [89] thane, because of his father's deeds, sleeps in blood after the sword-stroke, forfeiting his life; but the other escapes thence alive, for well he knows the land. Thus the warrior's oaths on both sides are broken, for deadly hate wells up in Ingeld's heart, and the love of the woman grows cooler within him, because of overwhelming woe.

"Therefore I count not sincere the faith of the Heathobards nor their part in the peace with the Danes, nor do I count their friendship firm."

"I must say on and tell again of Grendel, that thou mayst fully know, O king, to what issue the grappling came. After the jewel of heaven had glided over earth, the furious monster, the dread night-foe, came to find us out, where we all unharmed were watching over the hall. There slaughter and an awful death befell Hondscio, for he was doomed; that girded warrior was the first to fall, for Grendel bit him and slew him, our great kinsman-thane; he devoured the whole body of the man we loved. Yet none the sooner would the bloody-toothed murderer, bent on destruction, get him from the hall with empty hands. But he made trial of me and seized upon me with his ready claw. His pouch, wondrous and large, was hanging, fast in cunning bonds; it was all curiously wrought with dragon-skins and strange device of fiends. The bold ill-doer thought to put me therein, me, all sinless, and many another; but he could not so, when I in wrath arose and stood upright. It is too long to recount how I paid the enemy of that people a reward for his every crime. There, O my lord, did I bring glory to thy people by my deeds. He escaped and fled away—a little while he enjoyed the delights of life; but his right arm he left in Heorot, marking his track, and humbled, in woeful mood, fell thence to the bottom of the mere.

"When morning was come and we had sat down to the feast, the lord of the Scyldings richly rewarded me for that great fight, with beaten gold and many a treasure. There was song and glee. The aged Scylding, when he had asked of many things, told of the days of yore. At times a brave warrior touched the joyous harp, that instrument of mirth; at times he told a tale, truthful and sad; at times the great-hearted king would relate aright some strange legend; at times the hoary warrior, stricken with age, would lament his youth and battle-strength; his heart swelled within him as, old in winters, he thought on all the number of his days.

"So all day long we took our pleasure there, until another night came unto men. And straight thereafter, Grendel's mother was ready for vengeance; sorrowful she journeyed, for death and the war-wrath of the Geats had taken her son. The she-monster avenged her child. Furiously she slew a warrior. Life went from Æschere, the agèd counselor. Nor could the Danes, when morning was come, burn the corpse with fire, nor lay the belovèd man upon the funeral pile, for in her fiendish clutch she had borne away the body beneath the mountain stream. That was the bitterest of all the griefs that had long befallen Hrothgar, prince of the people. Then the king, heavy-hearted, besought me by thy life to do a hero's deed, to venture my life and win glory in the rush of waters; he promised me reward.

"Then, as is well known, I found the grim and awful guardian of the deep. And there we fought for a time, hand to hand; the mere was welling with gore. With a mighty sword I smote off the head of Grendel's mother in that sea-hall. Hardly did I get thence with my life, but not yet was I doomed. Thereafter the son of Healfdene, defense of warriors, gave me many treasures.

XXXI [90]

Beowulf maketh an end of his story, and giveth Hygelac all the gifts which he had of Hrothgar. Hygelac rewardeth him again.

"So the king of that people lived in seemly wise. I lost not my reward, the meed of valor, for the son of Healfdene gave me gifts to use at mine own will, which I will bring and gladly offer thee, O hero-king. Every good thing comes from thee, and I have few blood-kinsmen saving thee, O Hygelac."

And he bade them bring in the boar head-crest, the helm towering in battle, the gray byrnie, and the splendid war-sword, and thereupon he uttered these words: "Hrothgar, the wise prince, gave me this battle-armor, bidding me with express words to give thee first his kindly greeting; and he said that King Heorogar,[91] lord of the Scyldings, long possessed it, nevertheless he would not give the

[89] Freawaru's.
[90] The numbers XXIX and XXX are wanting in the MS., but no part of the text is lost.
[91] Hrothgar's own brother.

breast-mail to his own son, bold Heoroward, gracious though he was to him. Do thou enjoy it well."

I have learned that four dappled horses, all alike, followed upon the gift of the armor; graciously he presented unto him the horses and the treasures. So should a kinsman do, and nowise weave a cunning snare for his fellow, and plot the death of his comrade with secret craft. Full loyal was that nephew to Hygelac, the battle-strong; each took thought for the other's joy.

I have heard that he gave to Hygd the necklace, the wondrous jewel curiously wrought, which Wealhtheow, a king's daughter, had given him, and three horses therewith, slender and brightly saddled. Thereafter was her breast adorned, even from the time when she received the circlet.

Thus the son of Ecgtheow behaved himself in glorious wise, he who was famed for his warfare and for his gracious deeds; full honorably he lived, nor did he slay his hearth-companions when they were drunken; [92] his heart was not cruel, but the brave warrior with the greatest care of all mankind held fast the bounteous gift which God had given him.

Long had he been despised, [93] so that the sons of the Geats had esteemed him not, nor would the leader of the war-hosts do him much honor at the mead-bench; oft had they deemed him slothful, an unwarlike prince. That glorious man was rewarded for his every sorrow.

Then the king, the defense of heroes, strong in battle, bade them bring in the heirloom of Hrethel, all decked with gold,—there was no dearer sword among the treasures of the Geats. [94] He laid it in Beowulf's lap; and he gave to him seven thousand pieces of money, and a hall and a princely seat. The twain, by right of birth, held land in the nation, a home and its rights, but Hygelac had the broad kingdom, and therein he was the greater man. [95]

[In Part III Beowulf has become king and has reigned fifty years. A great fire-dragon who has watched over a treasure hoard wastes the land. The poem describes the burning of Beowulf's hall and the great fight in which the king kills the dragon but receives his own death wound. The epic closes with the burning of Beowulf's body and the praise of the hero.]

OTHER ANGLO-SAXON POEMS

Deor's Lament

To Weland [1] came woes   and wearisome trial,
And cares oppressed   the constant earl;
His lifelong companions   were pain and sorrow,
And winter-cold weeping: his ways were oft hard,
After Nithhad had struck   the strong man low,
Cut the supple sinew-bands   of the sorrowful earl.   6
    That has passed over: so this may depart!

Beadohild bore   her brother's death
Less sorely in soul   than herself and her plight
When she clearly discovered   her cursed condition,   10
That unwed she should bear   a babe to the world.
She never could think   of the thing that must happen.
    That has passed over: so this may depart!

Much have we learned   of Mæthhild's life:
How the courtship of Geat   was crowned with grief,   15
How love and its sorrows   allowed him no sleep.
    That has passed over: so this may depart!

---

[92] This strange praise may be contrasted with the criticism of the evil Heremod, p. 1008.
[93] His youth, like that of Brutus, had given no promise of his later glory.
[94] Beowulf already possessed his coat of mail.
[95] The implication is merely that Beowulf is now the second man in the nation.
Other Anglo-Saxon Poems. Translated by Stith Thompson. Used by permission of Scott, Foresman and Company.
[1] Weland was the blacksmith of the Norse gods, corresponding to Vulcan of Roman myth. The crafty king Nithhad captured him, fettered and hamstrung him, and robbed him of his magic ring. By the help of Nithhad's daughter, Beadohild, he recovered the ring and his power to fly. Before leaving, he stupefied Beadohild with liquor and violated her. She later bore him a child (see stanza 2).

Theodoric held   for thirty winters
The town of the Mærings: that was told unto
   many.
   That has passed over: so this may depart!   20

We all have heard   of Eormanric[2]
Of the wolfish heart: a wide realm he had
Of the Gothic kingdom.   Grim was the king.
Many men sat   and bemoaned their sorrows,
Woefully watching   and wishing always   25
That the cruel king   might be conquered at last.
   That has passed over: so this may depart!

Sad in his soul   he sittith joyless,
Mournful in mood.   He many times thinks
That no end will e'er come   to the cares he
   endures.   30
Then must he think   how throughout the world
The gracious God   often gives his help
And manifold honors   to many an earl
And sends wide his fame;   but to some he gives
   woes.   34
Of myself and my sorrows   I may say in truth
That I was happy once   as the Heodenings' scop,
Dear to my Lord.   Deor was my name.
Many winters I found   a worthy following,
Held my lord's heart,   till Heorrenda came,   39
The skillful singer,   and received the land-right
That the proud helm of earls   had once prom-
   ised to me!
   That has passed over: so this may depart!

Riddles

A Storm   I

What man is so clever,   so crafty of mind,
As to say for a truth   who sends me a-traveling?
When I rise in my wrath,   raging at times,
Savage is my sound.   Sometimes I travel,   4
Go forth among the folk,   set fire to their homes
And ravage and rob them;   then rolls the smoke
Gray over the gables;   great is the noise,
The death-struggle of the stricken.   Then I stir
   up the woods
And the fruitful forests;   I fell the trees,
I, roofed over with rain,   on my reckless jour-
   ney,   10
Wandering widely   at the will of heaven.
I bear on my back   the bodily raiment,
The fortunes of folk,   their flesh and their spirits,
Together to sea.   Say who may cover me,   14
Or what I am called,   who carry this burden?

A Storm   II

At times I travel   in tracks undreamed of,
In vasty wave-depths   to visit the earth,
The floor of the ocean.   Fierce is the sea
. . . .   the foam rolls high;
The whale-pool roars   and rages loudly;   5
The streams beat the shores,   and they sling at
   times
Great stones and sand   on the steep cliffs,
With weeds and waves,   while wildly striving
Under the burden of billows   on the bottom of
   ocean
The sea-ground I shake.   My shield of waters
I leave not ere he lets me   who leads me always
In all my travels.   Tell me, wise man,   12
Who was it that drew me   from the depth of the
   ocean
When the streams again   became still and quiet,
Who before had forced me   in fury to rage?   15

A Storm   III

At times I am fast   confined by my Master,
Who sendeth forth   under the fertile plain
My broad bosom,   but bridles me in.
He drives in the dark   a dangerous power
To a narrow cave,   where crushing my back   5
Sits the weight of the world.   No way of escape
Can I find from the torment;   so I tumble about
The homes of heroes.   The halls with their
   gables,
The tribe-dwellings tremble;   the trusty walls
   shake,
Steep over the head.   Still seems the air   10
Over all the country   and calm the waters,
Till I press in my fury   from my prison below,
Obeying His bidding   who bound me fast
In fetters at first   when he fashioned the world,
In bonds and in chains,   with no chance of
   escape   15
From his power who points out   the paths I
   must follow.
   Downward at times   I drive the waves,
Stir up the streams;   to the strand I press
The flint-gray flood: the foamy wave
Lashes the wall.   A lurid mountain   20
Rises on the deep;   dark in its trail
Stirred up with the sea   a second one comes
And close to the coast   it clashes and strikes
On the lofty hills.   Loud soundeth the boat,
The shouting of shipmen.   Unshaken abide   25

[2] King of the Goths. Died about 375 A.D.

The stone cliffs steep   through the strife of the waters,
The dashing of waves,   when the deadly tumult
Crowds to the coast.   Of cruel strife
The sailors are certain   if the sea drive their craft
With its terrified guests   on the grim rolling tide;   30
They are sure that the ship   will be shorn of its power,
Be deprived of its rule,   and will ride foam-covered
On the ridge of the waves.   Then arises a panic,
Fear among folk   of the force that commands me,
Strong on my storm-track.   Who shall still that power?   35
    At times I drive   through the dark wave-vessels
That ride on my back,   and wrench them asunder
And lash them with sea-streams;   or let them again
Glide back together.   It is the greatest of noises,
Of clamoring crowds,   of crashes the loudest,   40
When clouds as they strive   in their courses shall strike
Edge against edge;   inky of hue
In flight o'er the folk   bright fire they sweat,
A stream of flame;   destruction they carry
Dark over men   with a mighty din.   45
Fighting they fare.   They let fall from their bosom
A deafening rain   of rattling liquid,
Of storm from their bellies.   In battle they strive,
The awful army;   anguish arises,
Terror of mind   to the tribes of men,   50
Distress in the strongholds,   when the stalking goblins,
The pale ghosts shoot   with their sharp weapons.
The fool alone fears not   their fatal spears;
But he perishes too   if the true God send
Straight from above   in streams of rain,   55
Whizzing and whistling   the whirlwind's arrows,
The flying death.   Few shall survive
Whom that violent guest   in his grimness shall visit.
I always stir up   that strife and commotion;   59
Then I bear my course   to the battle of clouds,
Powerfully strive   and press through the tumult,
Over the bosom of the billows;   bursteth loudly
The gathering of elements.   Then again I descend
In my helmet of air   and hover near the land,
And lift on my back   the load I must bear,   65
Minding the mandates   of the mighty Lord.
    So I, a tried servant,   sometimes contend:
Now under the earth;   now from over the waves
I drive to the depths;   now dropping from heaven,
I stir up the streams,   or strive to the skies,   70
Where I war with the welkin.   Wide do I travel,
Swift and noisily.   Say now my name,
Or who raises me up   when rest is denied me,
Or who stays my course   when stillness comes to me?

A Swan

My robe is noiseless   when I roam the earth,
Or stay in my home,   or stir up the water.
At times I am lifted   o'er the lodgings of men
By the aid of my trappings   and the air above.
The strength of the clouds   then carries me far,
Bears me on its bosom.   My beautiful ornament,
My raiment rustles   and raises a song,
Sings without tiring.   I touch not the earth
But wander a stranger   over stream and wood.

A Horn

I was once an armed warrior.   Now the worthy youth
Gorgeously gears me   with gold and silver,
Curiously twisted.   At times men kiss me.
Sometimes I sound   and summon to battle
The stalwart company.   A steed now carries me
Across the border.   The courser of the sea   6
Now bears me o'er the billows,   bright in my trappings.
Now a comely maiden   covered with jewels
Fills my bosom with beer.   On the board now I lie
Lidless and lonely   and lacking my trappings.   10
Now fair in my fretwork   at the feast I hang
In my place on the wall   while warriors drink.
Now brightened for battle,   on the back of a steed
A war-chief shall bear me.   Then the wind I shall breathe,   14
Shall swell with sound   from someone's bosom.
At times with my voice   I invite the heroes,
The warriors to wine;   or I watch for my master

And sound an alarm   and save his goods,
Put the robber to flight.   Now find out my name.

A Bible[1]

A stern destroyer   struck out my life,
Deprived me of power;   he put me to soak,
Dipped me in water,   dried me again,
And set me in the sun,   where I straightway lost
The hairs that I had.   Then the hard edge   5
Of the keen knife cut me   and cleansed me of soil;
Then fingers folded me.   The fleet quill of the bird
With speedy drops   spread tracks often
Over the brown surface,   swallowed the tree-dye,
A deal of the stream,   stepped again on me,   10
Traveled a black track.   With protecting boards
Then a crafty one covered me,   enclosed me with hide,
Made me gorgeous with gold.   Hence I am glad and rejoice
At the smith's fair work   with its wondrous adornments.
    Now may these rich trappings,   and the red dye's tracings,   15
And all works of wisdom   spread wide the fame
Of the Sovereign of nations!   Read me not as a penance!
If the children of men   will cherish and use me,
They shall be safer and sounder   and surer of victory,
More heroic of heart   and happier in spirit,   20
More unfailing in wisdom.   More friends shall they have,
Dear and trusty,   and true and good,
And faithful always,   whose honors and riches
Shall increase with their love,   and who cover their friends
With kindness and favors   and clasp them fast
With loving arms.   I ask how men call me   26
Who aid them in need.   My name is far famed.
I am helpful to men,   and am holy myself.

The Dream of the Rood

Lo, I shall tell you   the truest of visions,
A dream that I dreamt   in the dead of night
While people reposed   in peaceful sleep.

I seemed to see   the sacred tree
Lifted on high   in a halo of light,   5
The brightest of beams;   that beacon was wholly
Gorgeous with gold;   glorious gems stood
Fair at the foot;   and five were assembled,
At the crossing of the arms.   The angels of God looked on,
Fair through the firmament.   It was truly no foul sinner's cross,   10
For beholding his sufferings   were the holy spirits,
The men of earth   and all of creation.
Wondrous was that victory-wood,   and I wounded and stained
With sorrows and sins.   I saw the tree of glory
Blessed and bright   in brilliant adornments,   15
Made joyous with jewels.   Gems on all sides
Full rarely enriched   the rood of the Savior.
    Through the sight of that cross   I came to perceive
Its stiff struggle of old,   when it started first
To bleed on the right side.   I was broken and cast down with sorrow;   20
The fair sight inspired me with fear.   Before me the moving beacon
Changed its clothing and color.   At times it was covered with blood
Fearful and grimy with gore.   At times with gold 'twas adorned.
Then I lay and looked   for a long time
And saw the Savior's   sorrowful tree   25
Until I heard it   lift high its voice.
The worthiest of the wood-race   formed words and spoke:
    "It was ages ago   —I shall always remember
When first I was felled   at the forest's edge,
My strong trunk stricken.   Then strange enemies took me   30
And fashioned my frame to a cross;   and their felons I raised on high.
On their backs and shoulders they bore me   to the brow of the lofty hill.
There the hated ones solidly set me.   I saw there the Lord of Mankind
Struggling forward with courage   to climb my sturdy trunk.
I dared not then oppose   the purpose of the Lord,   35
So I bent not nor broke   when there burst forth a trembling

---

[1] A manuscript Bible written on vellum. The preparation of the skin is first described and then the writing.

From the ends of the earth.   Easily might I
Destroy the murderers,   but I stood unmoved.
    "The Young Hero unclothed him   —it was
        the holy God—
Strong and steadfast;   he stepped to the high
        gallows,   40
Not fearing the look of the fiends,   and there he
        freed mankind.
At his blessed embrace I trembled,   but bow to
        the earth I dared not,
Or forward to fall to the ground,   but fast and
        true I endured.
As a rood I was raised up;   a royal King I bore,
The Lord of heavenly legions.   I allowed myself
        never to bend.   45
Dark nails through me they drove;   so that das-
        tardly scars are upon me,
Wounds wide open;   but not one of them dared
        I to harm.
They cursed and reviled us together.   I was cov-
        ered all over with blood,
That flowed from the Savior's side   when his
        soul had left the flesh.
Sorrowful the sights   I have seen on that hill, 50
Grim-visaged grief: the God of mankind I saw
And his frightful death.   The forces of darkness
Covered with clouds   the corpse of the Lord,
The shining radiance;   the shadows darkened
Under the cover of clouds.   Creation all wept,
The king's fall bewailed.   Christ was on the
        rood.   56
    Finally from afar   came faithful comrades
To the Savior's side,   and I saw it all.
Bitter the grief that I bore,   but I bowed me low
        to their hands;
My travail was grievous and sore.   They took
        then God Almighty,   60
From loathsome torment they lifted him.   The
        warriors left me deserted,
To stand stained with blood.   I was stricken and
        wounded with nails.
Limb-weary they laid him there,   and at their
        Lord's head they stood.
They beheld there the Ruler of heaven;   and
        they halted a while to rest,
Tired after the terrible struggle.   A tomb then
        they began to make,   65
His friends in sight of his foes.   Of the fairest
        of stone they built it,
And set their Savior upon it.   A sorrowful dirge
        they chanted,
Lamented their Master at evening,   when they
        made their journey home,

Tired from their loved Lord's side.   And they
        left him with the guard.
We crosses stood there   streaming with blood,
And waited long   after the wailing ceased   71
Of the brave company.   The body grew cold,
The most precious of corpses.   Then they pulled
        us down,
All to the earth   —an awful fate!
They buried us low in a pit.   But the loved dis-
        ciples of Christ,   75
His faithful friends made search   and found me
        and brought me to light,
And gorgeously decked me   with gold and with
        silver.
    "Now mayst thou learn,   my beloved friend,
That the work of the wicked   I have worthily
        borne,
The most trying of torments.   The time is now
        come   80
When through the wide world   I am worshiped
        and honored,
That all manner of men,   and the mighty crea-
        tion,
Hold sacred this sign.   On me the Son of God
Death-pangs endured.   Hence, dauntless in
        glory,
I rise high under heaven,   and hold out salva-
        tion   85
To each and to all   who have awe in my pres-
        ence.
    "Long ago I was the greatest   and most griev-
        ous of torments,
Most painful of punishments,   till I pointed
        aright
The road of life   for the race of men.
    "Lo, a glory was given   by the God of Crea-
        tion   90
To the worthless wood   —by the Warden of
        heaven—
Just as Mary, his mother,   the maiden blessed,
Received grace and glory   from God Almighty,
And homage and worship   over other women.
    "And now I bid thee,   my best of comrades,
That thou reveal   this vision to men.   96
Tell them I am truly   the tree of glory,
That the Savior sorrowed   and suffered upon
        me
For the race of men   and its many sins,
And the ancient evil   that Adam wrought.   100
    "He there tasted of death;   but in triumph he
        rose,
The Lord in his might   and gave life unto men.
Then he ascended to heaven,   and hither agai

Shall the Savior descend   to seek mankind
On the day of doom,   the dreaded Ruler   105
Of highest heaven,   with his host of angels.
Then will he adjudge   with justice and firmness
Rewards to the worthy   whose works have de-
    served them,
Who loyally lived   their lives on the earth.
Then a feeling of fear   shall fill every heart   110
For the warning they had   in the words of their
    Master:
He shall demand of many   where the man may
    be found
To consent for the sake   of his Savior to taste
The bitter death   as He did on the cross.
They are filled with fear   and few of them
    think   115
What words they shall speak   in response to
    Christ.
Then no feeling of fright   or fear need he have
Who bears on his heart   the brightest of tokens,
But there shall come to the kingdom   through
    the cross and its power
All the souls of the saved   from the sorrows of
    earth,   120
Of the holy who hope   for a home with their
    Lord."
   Then I adored the cross   with undaunted
    courage,
With the warmest zeal,   while I watched alone
And saw it in secret.   My soul was eager
To depart on its path,   but I have passed
    through many   125
An hour of longing.   Through all my life
I shall seek the sight   of that sacred tree
Alone more often   than all other men
And worthily worship it.   My will for this serv-
    ice

Is steadfast and sturdy,   and my strength is ever
In the cross of Christ.   My comrades of old,   131
The friends of fortune,   all far from the earth
Have departed from the world and its pleas-
    ures   and have passed to the King of Glory,
And high in the heavens   with the holy God
Are living eternally.   And I long for the time
To arrive at last   when the rood of the Lord,   136
Which once so plainly   appeared to my sight,
Shall summon my soul   from this sorrowful life,
And bring me to that bourne   where bliss is un-
    ending   139
And happiness of heaven,   where the holy saints
All join in a banquet,   where joy is eternal.
May he set me where always   in after time
I shall dwell in glory   with God's chosen ones
In delights everlasting.   May the Lord be my
    friend,
Who came to earth   and of old on the cross   145
Suffered and sorrowed   for the sins of men.
He broke there our bonds   and bought for us
    life
And a heavenly home.   The hearts were now
    filled
With blessings and bliss,   which once burned
    with remorse.
To the Son was his journey   successful and joy-
    ful   150
And crowned with triumph,   when he came
    with his troops,
With his gladsome guests   into God's kingdom,
The Almighty Judge's,   and brought joy to the
    angels,
And the host of the holy   who in heaven before
Dwelt in glory   when their God arrived,   155
The Lord Most High,   at his home at last.

ENGLISH IN THE MAKING

When in 1066 William the Conqueror and his Norman warriors overcame the English, the purely Anglo-Saxon history of England closed. For two hundred years the older population occupied an inferior social and economic position. The English language became the speech of laborers and serfs. Nobles and gentry spoke French and probably few of them ever troubled to learn the speech of the lower classes. We still use the English *calf* for the animal in the field, but the French *veal* when it is served up for My Lord's table, and so with *cow* and *beef,* or *sheep* and *mutton.* This social stratification between the languages kept them apart, so that when Layamon wrote his long English poem, the *Brut,* about 1205, he used but a handful of French words. A number of causes, however, brought it about that in the following century the two languages mixed very readily. By 1340, when Chaucer appeared, English had assumed almost its present proportion of Anglo-Saxon and French. This peculiar mixture of the most favorable elements of a Germanic and a Romance tongue was a most fortunate vehicle of expression for our first great poet, as it has been for all his successors.

Meantime both for speaking and writing, the clergy were using Latin, just as were the churchmen and all learned men from one end of Europe to the other. These Englishmen were thus right in the main stream of European culture. Their efforts were by no means confined to the laborious writing of chronicles. Many of them had been wandering scholars and had perhaps composed naughty student songs to be sung on all the roads of the Continent. They carried on philosophical debates with other Schoolmen from all over Europe. They read and retold the great international tales. They kept up the interest in the Latin classics and copied the ancient manuscripts. And they wrote saints' legends and sermons and allegories without end, and beautiful hymns. In this one period of a real international language they did their part to keep England from becoming a mere island far removed from the vigorous culture of Europe.

The Norman nobility also kept England in close touch with those social refinements that by the twelfth century were becoming the chief concern of certain of the great courts in France. The ideas of courtesy and of chivalric love became ever more prominent, especially from the time of Henry II (1154-1189) and his French queen, Eleanor of Aquitaine. The great devotion to the Virgin Mary that rose to a climax in this period was carried over into a general glorification of womanhood. Knights, in the romances at least, began to perform deeds of valor in order to secure the favor of their ladies, who now treated them disdainfully. A whole code of chivalric conduct came into being—an absurd code in many ways, but in the long run it made for a more gracious social life.

Aside from ideals of courtesy the French undoubtedly added much to our literature during these formative twelfth and thirteenth centuries. English writing begins to display humor here and there, and a strong vein of satire. The frank French fabliaux with their extreme realism begin to appear in English. The florid imagination of the Orient, whether acquired through the Crusades or otherwise, also adds to the variety of literary possibilities ready for development by Geoffrey Chaucer. Moreover, the thirteenth century, through much trial and error, had evolved metrical forms that were suitable for the new composite language.

In the two centuries preceding Chaucer the most important literary products of England were the Romances. We have already seen in our discussion of French literature that for the most part France was the home of these tales of chivalry. But England played a large part in their development, especially in those centering in the Court of King Arthur.

Many different things are called Medieval Romances—not only long metrical tales of knights and their warfare, which is the most usual form, but also short poetic lays similar to fairy tales, and even long prose stories. The writers of the time recognized several "cycles" of romance: (1) Troy, (2) Alexander, (3) Charlemagne, (4) Arthur. Besides these main subjects there were many others; for instance, the oriental romances, of which we have seen a charming example in *Aucassin and Nicolete*.

In England the Arthurian is the most important cycle. Arthur himself was a British leader against the English invaders, but this fact became obscured with the centuries. He lived in the sixth century. By 1135 Geoffrey of Monmouth was making of him a great hero who should bring glory to England as Charlemagne had done to France. After Geoffrey's time the tales of Arthur received contributions from many sources, so that in the final development of the story which we see in Malory, about 1470, there are at least Celtic, French, and English elements. A careful study of the romances will show how this story has grown bit by bit. Each author has added a detail or an interpretation until at the end it is impossible to make a consistent story or show consistent characterization. Arthur is now the great world conqueror, now a weakling. Gawain is hero or villain.

In English the two finest products of Romance are *Sir Gawain and the Green Knight* and Malory's *Morte d'Arthur*. The Gawain poem was written somewhere in western England in the fourteenth century. It is in an alliterative meter much like the Old English poetry. Professor Banks has imitated this form with rare success in the version we use. The fine descriptive passages in the poem and the real dramatic interest have always been justly admired.

Malory wrote his long prose retelling of all the Arthurian romances at the very end of the Middle Ages. Indeed it was one of the first books to be issued in England from the newly-invented printing press. He used as the basis for his composition various poems and prose works. He speaks often of "the French book." But whatever his sources, he has succeeded in bringing the material all together into a rather unified whole and stamping it all with his characteristic style. To most English readers Malory's story of King Arthur—perhaps modified by Tennyson—seems the only possible account of these romantic events.

At the same time as the minstrels and court poets were writing romances, the common people were having their entertainments, as they had had for thousands of years. They told tales and jokes, they had feasts and ceremonies, they danced, and they sang songs. The history of the English and Scottish ballads that began to develop in the late Middle Ages is not very clear, but we know that there must have been a great deal of singing of narrative songs in both these countries down to the beginning of the nineteenth century. These narrative songs had in English a favorite metrical form—a four line stanza with four, three, four, and three feet to the line and with the second and fourth rhyming. In most of our ballads this form is found.

As finally collected in the nineteenth century there are some 305 of these ballads, representing the poetic enjoyment of the great unlettered masses who have sung them. They have their own power, which one must come to feel by hearing them sung. For they are not poems but songs.

SIR GAWAIN AND THE GREEN KNIGHT

When the siege and assault ceased at Troy,[1] and
   the city
Was broken, and burned all to brands and to
   ashes,
The warrior who wove there the web of his
   treachery
Tried was for treason, the truest on earth.
'T was Æneas, who later with lords of his lineage
Provinces quelled, and became the possessors   6
Of well-nigh the whole of the wealth of the West
   Isles.
Then swiftly to Rome rich Romulus journeyed,
And soon with great splendor builded that city,
Named with his own name, as now we still know
   it.   10
Ticius to Tuscany turns for his dwellings;
In Lombardy Langobard lifts up his homes;
And far o'er the French flood fortunate Brutus
With happiness Britain on hillsides full broad
            Doth found.   15
   War, waste, and wonder there
   Have dwelt within its bound;
   And bliss has changed to care
   In quick and shifting round.

And after this famous knight founded his
   Britain,   20
Bold lords were bred there, delighting in battle,

Who many times dealt in destruction. More mar-
   vels
Befell in those fields since the days of their finding
Than anywhere else upon earth that I know of.
Yet of all kings who came there was Arthur most
     comely;   25
My intention is, therefore, to tell an adventure
Strange and surprising, as some men consider,
A strange thing among all the marvels of Arthur.
And if you will list to the lay for a little,
Forthwith I shall tell it, as I in the town   30
            Heard it told
   As it doth fast endure
   In story brave and bold,
   Whose words are fixed and sure,
   Known in the land of old.   35

   In Camelot Arthur the King lay at Christmas,
With many a peerless lord princely companioned,
The whole noble number of knights of the Round
   Table;
Here right royally held his high revels,
Care-free and mirthful. Now much of the com-
   pany,   40
Knightly born gentlemen, joyously jousted,
Now came to the court to make caroles; so kept
   they
For full fifteen days this fashion of feasting,

Sir Gawain and the Green Knight. Translated into the original meter by Theodore Banks. Used by permission of F. S. Crofts and Company.

[1] The tradition was that Brutus, or Brut, the great-grandson of Æneas, who had settled in Britain, was ancestor of the British kings.

All meat and all mirth that a man might devise.
Glorious to hear was the glad-hearted gaiety,   45
Dancing at night, merry din in the daytime;
So found in the courts and the chambers the fortunate
Ladies and lords the delights they best loved.
In greatest well-being abode they together:
The knights whose renown was next to the Savior's,   50
The loveliest ladies who ever were living,
And he who held court, the most comely of kings.
For these fine folk were yet in their first flush of youth

                   Seated there,
        The happiest of their kind,   55
        With a king beyond compare.
        It would be hard to find
        A company so fair.

And now while the New Year was young were the nobles
Doubly served as they sat on the dais,   60
When Arthur had come to the hall with his court,
In the chapel had ceased the singing of mass;
Loud shouts were there uttered by priests and by others,
Anew praising Noel, naming it often.
Then hastened the lords to give handsel, cried loudly   65
These gifts of the New Year, and gave them in person;
Debated about them busily, briskly.
Even though they were losers, the ladies laughed loudly,
Nor wroth was the winner, as well ye may know.
All this manner of mirth they made till meat-time,   70
Then when they had washed, they went to be seated,
Were placed in the way that appeared most proper,
The best men above. And Guinevere, beautiful,
Was in the midst of the merriment seated
Upon the rich dais, adorned all about: 75
Fine silks on all sides, and spread as a canopy
Tapestries treasured of Tars and Toulouse,
Embroidered and set with stones most splendid—
They'd prove of great price if ye pence gave to buy them

                   Some day.   80
        The comeliest was the Queen,
        With dancing eyes of gray.
        That a fairer he had seen
        No man might truly say.

But Arthur would eat not till all were attended;
Youthfully mirthful and merry in manner,   86
He loved well his life, and little it pleased him
Or long to be seated, or long to lie down,
His young blood and wild brain were so busy and brisk.
Moreover, the King was moved by a custom   90
He once had assumed in a spirit of splendor:
Never to fall to his feast on a festival
Till a strange story of something eventful
Was told him, some marvel that merited credence
Of kings, or of arms, or all kinds of adventures;
Or someone besought him to send a true knight   96
To join him in proving the perils of jousting
Life against life, each leaving the other
To have, as fortune would help him, the fairer lot.
This, when the King held his court, was his custom   100
At every fine feast 'mid his followers, freemen,
                   In hall.
        And so with countenance clear
        He stands there strong and tall,
        Alert on that New Year,   105
        And makes much mirth with all.

At his place the strong King stands in person, full courtly
Talking of trifles before the high table.
There sat the good Gawain by Guinevere's side,
And Sir Agravain, he of the Hard Hand, also,   110
True knights, and sons of the sister of Arthur.
At the top, Bishop Baldwin the table begins,
And Ywain beside him ate, Urien's son.
On the dais these sat, and were served with distinction;
Then many a staunch, trusty man at the side tables.   115
The first course was served to the sharp sound of trumpets,
With numerous banners beneath hanging brightly.
Then newly the kettledrums sounded and noble pipes;
Wild and loud warbles awakened such echoes
That many a heart leaped on high at their melody.   120
Came then the choice meats, cates rare and costly,
Of fair and fresh food such profusion of dishes
'T was hard to find place to put by the people
The silver that carried the various stews
                   On the cloth.   125
        Each to his best loved fare
        Himself helps, nothing loth;

Each two, twelve dishes share,
Good beer and bright wine both.

And now I will say nothing more of their serv-
    ice,   130
For well one may know that naught there was
    wanted.
Now another new noise drew nigh of a sudden,
To let all the folk take their fill of the feast.
And scarcely the music had ceased for a moment,
The first course been suitably served in the court,
When a being most dreadful burst through the
    hall-door,   136
Among the most mighty of men in his measure.
From his throat to his thighs so thick were his
    sinews,
His loins and his limbs so large and so long,
That I hold him half-giant, the hugest of men, 140
And the handsomest, too, in his height, upon
    horseback.
Though stalwart in breast and in back was his
    body,
His waist and his belly were worthily small;
Fashioned fairly he was in his form, and in fea-
    tures
                Cut clean.   145
       Men wondered at the hue
       That in his face was seen.
       A splendid man to view
       He came, entirely green.

All green was the man, and green were his gar-
    ments: 150
A coat, straight and close, that clung to his sides,
A bright mantle on top of this, trimmed on the
    inside
With closely-cut fur, right fair, that showed clearly,
The lining with white fur most lovely, and hood
    too,
Caught back from his locks, and laid on his
    shoulders,   155
Neat stockings that clung to his calves, tightly
    stretched,
Of the same green, and under them spurs of gold
    shining
Brightly on bands of fine silk, richly barred;
And under his legs, where he rides, guards of
    leather.
His vesture was verily color of verdure: 160
Both bars of his belt and other stones, beautiful,
Richly arranged in his splendid array
On himself and his saddle, on silken designs.
'T would be truly too hard to tell half the trifles

Embroidered about it with birds and with flies 165
In gay, verdant green with gold in the middle;
The bit-studs, the crupper, the breast-trappings'
    pendants,
And everything metal enameled in emerald.
The stirrups he stood on the same way were col-
    ored,
His saddle-bows too, and the studded nails splen-
    did,   170
That all with green gems ever glimmered and
    glinted.
The horse he bestrode was in hue still the same,
                Indeed;
       Green, thick, and of great height,
       And hard to curb, a steed   175
       In broidered bridle bright
       That such a man would need.

This hero in green was habited gaily,
And likewise the hair on the head of his good
    horse;
Fair, flowing tresses enfolded his shoulders,   180
And big as a bush a beard hung on his breast.
This, and the hair from his head hanging splendid,
Was clipped off evenly over his elbows,
In cut like a king's hood, covering the neck,   184
So that half of his arms were held underneath it.
The mane of the mighty horse much this resem-
    bled,
Well curled and combed, and with many knots
    covered,
Braided with gold threads about the fair green,
Now a strand made of hair, now a second of gold.
The forelock and tail were twined in this fashion,
And both of them bound with a band of bright
    green.   191
For the dock's length the tail was decked with
    stones dearly,
And then was tied with a thong in a tight knot,
Where many bright bells of burnished gold rang.
In the hall not one single man's seen before this
Such a horse here on earth, such a hero as on
    him   196
                Goes.
       That his look was lightning bright
       Right certain were all those
       Who saw. It seemed none might   200
       Endure beneath his blows.

Yet the hero carried nor helmet nor hauberk,
But bare was of armor, breastplate or gorget,
Spear-shaft or shield, to thrust or to smite.   204
But in one hand he bore a bough of bright holly,

That grows most greenly when bare are the groves,
In the other an ax, gigantic, awful,
A terrible weapon, wondrous to tell of.
Large was the head, in length a whole ell-yard,
The blade of green steel and beaten gold both;   210
The bit had a broad edge, and brightly was bur-
   nished,
As suitably shaped as sharp razors for shearing.
This steel by its strong shaft the stern hero
   gripped:
With iron it was wound to the end of the wood,
And in work green and graceful was everywhere
   graven.   215
About it a fair thong was folded, made fast
At the head, and oft looped down the length of the
   handle.
To this were attached many splendid tassels,
On buttons of bright green richly embroidered.
Thus into the hall came the hero, and hastened
Direct to the dais, fearing no danger.   221
He gave no one greeting, but haughtily gazed,
And his first words were, "Where can I find him
   who governs
This goodly assemblage? for gladly that man
I would see and have speech with." So saying,
   from toe   225
               To crown
   On the knights his look he threw,
   And rolled it up and down;
   He stopped to take note who
   Had there the most renown.   230

There sat all the lords, looking long at the
   stranger,
Each man of them marveling what it might mean
For a horse and a hero to have such a hue.
It seemed to them green as the grown grass, or
   greener,
Gleaming more bright than on gold green enamel.
The nobles who stood there, astonished, drew
   nearer,   236
And deeply they wondered what deed he would
   do.
Since never a marvel they'd met with like this one,
The folk all felt it was magic or phantasy.   239
Many great lords then were loth to give answer,
And sat stone-still, at his speaking astounded,
In swooning silence that spread through the hall.
As their speech on a sudden was stilled, fast asleep
              They did seem.
   They felt not only fright   245
   But courtesy, I deem.

Let him address the knight,
Him whom they all esteem.

This happening the King, ever keen and cou-
   rageous,
Saw from on high, and saluted the stranger   250
Suitably, saying, "Sir, you are welcome.
I, the head of this household, am Arthur;
In courtesy light, and linger, I pray you,
And later, my lord, we shall learn your desire."
"Nay, so help me He seated on high," quoth the
   hero,   255
"My mission was not to remain here a moment;
But, sir, since thy name is so nobly renowned,
Since thy city the best is considered, thy barons
The stoutest in steel gear that ride upon steeds,
Of all men in the world the most worthy and
   brave,   260
Right valiant to play with in other pure pastimes,
Since here, I have heard, is the highest of cour-
   tesy—
Truly, all these things have brought me at this
   time.
Sure ye may be by this branch that I bear
That I pass as in peace, proposing no fight.   265
If I'd come with comrades, equipped for a quarrel,
I have at my home both hauberk and helmet,
Shield and sharp spear, brightly shining, and other
Weapons to wield, full well I know also.
Yet softer my weeds are, since warfare I wished
   not;   270
But art thou as bold as is bruited by all,
Thou wilt graciously grant me the game that I ask
   for
               By right."
   Arthur good answer gave,
   And said, "Sir courteous knight,   275
   If battle here you crave,
   You shall not lack a fight."

"Nay, I ask for no fight; in faith, now I tell thee
But beardless babes are about on this bench.
Were I hasped in my armor, and high on a horse,
Here is no man to match me, your might is so
   feeble.   281
So I crave but a Christmas game in this court;
Yule and New Year are come, and here men have
   courage;
If one in this house himself holds so hardy,
So bold in his blood, in his brain so unbalanced
To dare stiffly strike one stroke for another,   286
I give this gisarme, this rich ax, as a gift to him,
Heavy enough, to handle as pleases him;

Bare as I sit, I shall bide the first blow.
If a knight be so tough as to try what I tell,   290
Let him leap to me lightly; I leave him this weapon,
Quitclaim it forever, to keep as his own;
And his stroke here, firm on this floor, I shall suffer,
This boon if thou grant'st me, the blow with another
                      To pay;   295
      Yet let his respite be
      A twelvemonth and a day.
      Come, let us quickly see
      If one here aught dare say."

If at first he had startled them, stiller then sat there   300
The whole of the court, low and high, in the hall.
The knight on his steed turned himself in his saddle,
And fiercely his red eyes he rolled all around,
Bent his bristling brows, with green gleaming brightly,
And waved his beard, waiting for one there to rise.   305
And when none of the knights spoke, he coughed right noisily,
Straightened up proudly, and started to speak:
"What!" quoth the hero, "Is this Arthur's household,
The fame of whose fellowship fills many kingdoms?
Now where is your vainglory? Where are your victories?   310
Where is your grimness, your great words, your anger?
For now the Round Table's renown and its revel
Is worsted by one word of one person's speech,
For all shiver with fear before a stroke's shown."
Then so loudly he laughed that the lord was grieved greatly,   315
And into his fair face his blood shot up fiercely
                For shame.
      As wroth as wind he grew,
      And all there did the same.
      The King that no fear knew   320
      Then to that stout man came.

And said, "Sir, by heaven, strange thy request is;
As folly thou soughtest, so shouldest thou find it.
I know that not one of the knights is aghast
Of thy great words. Give me thy weapon, for God's sake,   325
And gladly the boon thou hast begged I shall grant thee."
He leaped to him quickly, caught at his hand,
And fiercely the other lord lights on his feet.
Now Arthur lays hold of the ax by the handle,
As if he would strike with it, swings it round sternly.   330
Before him the strong man stood, in stature
A head and more higher than all in the house.
Stroking his beard, he stood with stern bearing,
And with a calm countenance drew down his coat,
No more frightened or stunned by the ax Arthur flourished   335
Than if on the bench someone brought him a flagon
                Of wine.
      Gawain by Guinevere
      Did to the King incline:
      "I pray in accents clear   340
      To let this fray be mine."

"If you now, honored lord," said this knight to King Arthur,
"Would bid me to step from this bench, and to stand there
Beside you—so could I with courtesy quit then
The table, unless my liege lady disliked it—   345
I'd come to your aid before all your great court.
For truly I think it a thing most unseemly
So boldly to beg such a boon in your hall here,
Though you in person are pleased to fulfill it,
While here on the benches such brave ones are seated,   350
Than whom under heaven, I think, none are higher
In spirit, none better in body for battle.
I am weakest and feeblest in wit, I know well,
And my life, to say truth, would be least loss of any.
I only since you are my uncle have honor;   355
Your blood the sole virtue I bear in my body.
Unfit is this foolish affair for you. Give it
To me who soonest have sought it, and let
All this court if my speech is not seemly, decide
              Without blame."   360
      The nobles gather round,
      And all advise the same:
      To free the King that's crowned,
      And Gawain give the game.

The King then commanded his kinsman to rise,   365

And quickly he rose up and came to him courteously,
Kneeled by the King, and caught the weapon,
He left it graciously, lifted his hand,
And gave him God's blessing, and gladly bade him
Be sure that his heart and his hand both were hardy. 370
"Take care," quoth the King, "how you start, coz, your cutting,
And truly, I think, if rightly you treat him,
That blow you'll endure that he deals you after."
Weapon in hand, Gawain goes to the hero,
Who boldly remains there, dismayed none the more. 375
Then the knight in the green thus greeted Sir Gawain,
"Let us state our agreement again ere proceeding.
And now first, sir knight, what your name is I beg
That you truly will tell, so in that I may trust."
"In truth," said the good knight, "I'm called Sir Gawain, 380
Who fetch you this blow, whatsoever befalls,
And another will take in return, this time twelvemonth,
From you, with what weapon you will; with no other

             I'll go."
    The other made reply: 385
    "By my life here below,
    Gawain, right glad am I
    To have you strike this blow.

By God," said the Green Knight, "Sir Gawain, it pleases me—
Here, at thy hand, I shall have what I sought. 390
Thou hast rightly rehearsed to me, truly and readily,
All of the covenant asked of King Arthur;
Except that thou shalt, by thy troth, sir, assure me
Thyself and none other shalt seek me, wherever
Thou thinkest to find me, and fetch thee what wages 395
Are due for the stroke that today thou dost deal me
Before all this splendid assembly." "Where should I,"
Said Gawain, "go look for the land where thou livest?
The realm where thy home is, by Him who hath wrought me,
I know not, nor thee, sir, thy court nor thy name.
Truly tell me thy title, and teach me the road, 401

And I'll use all my wit to win my way thither.
And so by my sure word truly I swear."
" 'T is enough. No more now at New Year is needed,"
The knight in the green said to Gawain the courteous: 405
"If truly I tell when I've taken your tap
And softly you've struck me, if swiftly I tell you
My name and my house and my home, you may then
Of my conduct make trial, and your covenant keep; 409
And if no speech I speak, you speed all the better:
No longer need look, but may stay in your land.
             But ho!
    Take your grim tool with speed,
    And let us see your blow."
    Stroking his ax, "Indeed," 415
    Said Gawain, "gladly so."

With speed then the Green Knight took up his stand,
Inclined his head forward, uncovering the flesh,
And laid o'er his crown his locks long and lovely,
And bare left the nape of his neck for the business.
His ax Gawain seized, and swung it on high; 421
On the floor his left foot he planted before him,
And swiftly the naked flesh smote with his weapon.
The sharp edge severed the bones of the stranger,
Cut through the clear flesh and cleft it in twain,
So the blade of the brown steel bit the ground deeply. 426
The fair head fell from the neck to the floor,
So that where it rolled forth with their feet many spurned it.
The blood on the green glistened, burst from the body;
And yet neither fell nor faltered the hero, 430
But stoutly he started forth, strong in his stride;
Fiercely he rushed 'mid the ranks of the Round Table,
Seized and uplifted his lovely head straightway;
Then back to his horse went, laid hold of the bridle,
Stepped into the stirrup and strode up aloft, 435
His head holding fast in his hand by the hair.
And the man as soberly sat in his saddle
As if he unharmed were, although now headless,
             Instead.
    His trunk around he spun, 441
    That ugly body that bled.

Frightened was many a one
When he his words had said.

For upright he holds the head in his hand,
And confronts with the face the fine folk on the
    dais.   445
It lifted its lids, and looked forth directly,
Speaking this much with its mouth, as ye hear:
"Gawain, look that to go as agreed you are ready,
And seek for me faithfully, sir, till you find me,
As, heard by these heroes, you vowed in this hall.
To the Green Chapel go you, I charge you, to get
Such a stroke as you struck. You are surely deserv-
    ing,   452
Sir knight, to be promptly repaid at the New
    Year.
As Knight of the Green Chapel many men know
    me;
If therefore to find me you try, you will fail not;
Then come, or be recreant called as befits thee." 456
With furious wrench of the reins he turned round,
And rushed from the hall-door, his head in his
    hands,
So the fire of the flint flew out from the foal's
    hoofs.
Not one of the lords knew the land where he went
    to,   460
No more than the realm whence he rushed in
    among them.
                    What then?
       The King and Gawain there
       At the Green Knight laughed again;
       Yet this the name did bear   465
       Of wonder among men.

Though much in his mind did the courtly King
    marvel,
He let not a semblance be seen, but said loudly
With courteous speech to the Queen, most comely:
"Today, my dear lady, be never alarmed;   470
Such affairs are for Christmas well fitted to sing of
And gaily to laugh at when giving an interlude,
'Mid all the company's caroles, most courtly.
None the less I may go now to get my meat;
For I needs must admit I have met with a mar-
    vel."   475
He glanced at Sir Gawain, and gladsomely said:
"Now, sir, hang up thine ax; enough it has hewn."
O'er the dais 't was placed, to hang on the dosser,
That men might remark it there as a marvel,
And truly describing, might tell of the wonder.
Together these two then turned to the table, 481

The sovereign and good knight, and swiftly men
    served them
With dainties twofold, as indeed was most fitting,
All manner of meat and of minstrelsy both.
So the whole day in pleasure they passed till night
    fell   485
             O'er the land.
       Now take heed Gawain lest,
       Fearing the Green Knight's brand,
       Thou shrinkest from the quest
       That thou hast ta'en in hand.   490

II

This sample had Arthur of strange things right
    early,
When young was the year, for he yearned to hear
    boasts.
Though such words when they went to be seated
    were wanting,
Yet stocked are they now with hand-fulls of stern
    work.
In the hall glad was Gawain those games to begin,
But not strange it would seem if sad were the end-
    ing;   496
For though men having drunk much are merry in
    mind,
Full swift flies a year, never yielding the same,
The start and the close very seldom according.
So past went this Yule, and the year followed after,
Each season in turn succeeding the other.   501
There came after Christmas the crabbed Lenten,
With fish and with plainer food trying the flesh;
But then the world's weather with winter con-
    tends;
Down to earth shrinks the cold, the clouds are
    uplifted;   505
In showers full warm descends the bright rain,
And falls on the fair fields. Flowers unfold;
The ground and the groves are green in their gar-
    ments;
Birds hasten to build, blithesomely singing
For soft summer's solace ensuing on slopes   510
             Everywhere.
       The blossoms swell and blow,
       In hedge-rows rich and rare,
       And notes most lovely flow
       From out the forest fair.   515

After this comes the season of soft winds of
    summer,
When Zephyrus sighs on the seeds and the green
    plants.

The herb that then grows in the ground is right
    happy,
When down from the leaves drops the dampening
    dew   519
To abide the bright sun that is blissfully shining.
But autumn comes speeding, soon grows severe,
And warns it to wax full ripe for the winter.
With drought then the dust is driven to rise,
From the face of the fields to fly to the heaven.
With the sun the wild wind of the welkin is strug-
    gling;   525
The leaves from the limbs drop, and light on the
    ground;
And withers the grass that grew once so greenly.
Then all ripens that formerly flourished, and rots;
And thus passes the year in yesterdays many,
And winter, in truth, as the way of the world is,
                       Draws near,   531
      Till comes the Michaelmas moon
      With pledge of winter sere.
      Then thinks Sir Gawain soon
      Of his dread voyage drear.   535

   Till the tide of Allhallows with Arthur he tar-
    ried;
The King made ado on that day for his sake
With rich and rare revel of all of the Round Table,
Knights most courteous, comely ladies,
All of them heavy at heart for the hero.   540
Yet nothing but mirth was uttered, though many
Joyless made jests for that gentleman's sake.
After meat, with sorrow he speaks to his uncle,
And openly talks of his travel, saying:
"Liege lord of my life, now I ask of you leave. 545
You know my case and condition, nor care I
To tell of its troubles even a trifle.
I must, for the blow I am bound to, tomorrow
Go seek as God guides me the man in the green."
Then came there together the best in the castle:
Ywain, Eric, and others full many,   551
Sir Dodinel de Sauvage, the Duke of Clarence,
Lancelot, Lyonel, Lucan the good,
Sir Bors and Sir Bedevere, both of them big men,
Mador de la Port, and many more nobles.   555
All these knights of the court came near to the
    King
With care in their hearts to counsel the hero;
Heavy and deep was the dole in the hall
That one worthy as Gawain should go on that er-
    rand,
To suffer an onerous stroke, and his own sword
                     To stay.   561
      The knight was of good cheer:

      "Why should I shrink away
      From a fate stern and drear?
      A man can but essay."   565

   He remained there that day; in the morning
    made ready.
Early he asked for his arms; all were brought him.
And first a fine carpet was laid on the floor,
And much was the gilt gear that glittered upon it.
Thereon stepped the strong man, and handled the
    steel,   570
Dressed in a doublet of Tars that cost dearly,
A hood made craftily, closed at the top,
And about on the lining bound with a bright fur.
Then they set on his feet shoes fashioned of steel,
And with fine greaves of steel encircled his legs.
Knee-pieces to these were connected, well polished,
Secured round his knees with knots of gold.   577
Then came goodly cuisses, with cunning enclosing
His thick, brawny thighs; with thongs they at-
    tached them.
Then the man was encased in a coat of fine mail,
With rings of bright steel on a rich stuff woven,
Braces well burnished on both of his arms,   582
Elbow-pieces gay, good, and gloves of plate,
All the goodliest gear that would give him most
    succor
                    That tide: 585
      Coat armor richly made,
      His gold spurs fixed with pride,
      Girt his unfailing blade
      By a silk sash to his side.

   When in arms he was clasped, his costume was
    costly;   590
The least of the lacings or loops gleamed with
    gold.
And armed in this manner, the man heard mass,
At the altar adored and made offering, and after-
    ward
Came to the King and all of his courtiers,
Gently took leave of the ladies and lords;   595
Him they kissed and escorted, to Christ him com-
    mending.
Then was Gringolet ready, girt with a saddle
That gaily with many a gold fringe was gleaming,
With nails studded newly, prepared for the nonce.
The bridle was bound about, barred with bright
    gold;   600
With the bow of the saddle, the breastplate, the
    splendid skirts,
Crupper, and cloth in adornment accorded,
With gold nails arrayed on a groundwork of red,

That glittered and glinted like gleams of the sun.
Then he caught up his helm, and hastily kissed
  it;   605
It stoutly was stapled and stuffed well within,
High on his head, and hasped well behind,
With a light linen veil laid over the visor,
Embroidered and bound with the brightest of
  gems
On a silken border; with birds on the seams   610
Like painted parroquets preening; true love-knots
As thickly with turtle doves tangled as though
Many women had been at the work seven winters
                       In town.
          Great was the circle's price   615
          Encompassing his crown;
          Of diamonds its device,
          That were both bright and brown.

  Then they showed him his shield, sheer gules,
    whereon shone
The pentangle painted in pure golden hue.   620
On his baldric he caught, and about his neck cast
  it;
And fairly the hero's form it befitted.
And why that great prince the pentangle suited
Intend I to tell, in my tale though I tarry.
'T is a sign that Solomon formerly set   625
As a token, for so it doth symbol, of truth.
A figure it is that with five points is furnished;
Each line overlaps and locks in another,
Nor comes to an end; and Englishmen call it
Everywhere, hear I, the endless knot.   630
It became then the knight and his noble arms also,
In five ways, and five times each way still faithful.
Sir Gawain was known as the good, refined gold,
Graced with virtues of castle, of villainy void,
                       Made clean.   635
          So the pentangle new
          On shield and coat was seen,
          As man of speech most true,
          And gentlest knight of mien.

  First, in his five wits he faultless was found;
In his five fingers too the man never failed;   641
And on earth all his faith was fixed on the five
  wounds
That Christ, as the creed tells, endured on the
  cross.
Wheresoever this man was midmost in battle,
His thought above everything else was in this,
To draw all his fire from the fivefold joys   646
That the fair Queen of Heaven felt in her child.
And because of this fitly he carried her image

Displayed on his shield, on its larger part,
That whenever he saw it his spirit should sink not.
The fifth five the hero made use of, I find,   651
More than all were his liberalness, love of his fel-
  lows,
His courtesy, chasteness, unchangeable ever,
And pity, all further traits passing. These five
In this hero more surely were set than in any.   655
In truth now, fivefold they were fixed in the
  knight,
Linked each to the other without any end,
And all of them fastened on five points unfailing;
Each side they neither united nor sundered,
Evermore endless at every angle,   660
Where equally either they ended or started.
And so his fair shield was adorned with this sym-
  bol,
Thus richly with red gold wrought on red gules,
So by people the pentangle perfect 't was called
                       As it ought.   665
          Gawain in arms is gay;
          Right there his lance he caught,
          And gave them all good-day
          For ever, as he thought.

  He set spurs to his steed, and sprang on his way
So swiftly that sparks from the stone flew behind
  him.   671
All who saw him, so seemly, sighed, sad at heart;
The same thing, in sooth, each said to the other,
Concerned for that comely man: "Christ, 't is a
  shame
Thou, sir knight, must be lost whose life is so
  noble!   675
To find, faith! his equal on earth is not easy.
'T would wiser have been to have acted more
  warily,
Dubbed yonder dear one a duke. He seems clearly
To be in the land here a brilliant leader:
So better had been than brought thus to naught,
By an elf-man beheaded for haughty boasting.   681
Who e'er knew any king such counsel to take,
As foolish as one in a Christmas frolic?"
Much was the warm water welling from eyes
When the seemly hero set out from the city   685
                       That day.
          Nowhere he abode,
          But swiftly went his way;
          By devious paths he rode,
          As I the book heard say.   690

  Through the realm of Logres now rides this
    lord,

Sir Gawain, for God's sake, no game though he
    thought it.
Oft alone, uncompanioned he lodges at night
Where he finds not the fare that he likes set before
    him.
Save his foal, he'd no fellow by forests and hills;
On the way, no soul but the Savior to speak to.   696
At length he drew nigh unto North Wales, and
    leaving
To left of him all of the islands of Anglesey,
Fared by the forelands and over the fords
Near the Holy Head; hastening hence to the
    mainland,   700
In Wyral he went through the wilderness. There,
Lived but few who loved God or their fellows with
    good heart.
And always he asked of any he met,
As he journeyed, if nearby a giant they knew of,
A green knight, known as the Knight of the
    Green Chapel.   705
All denied it with nay, in their lives they had
    never
Once seen any hero who had such a hue
                    Of green.

       The knight takes roadways strange
       In many a wild terrene;   710
       Often his feelings change
       Before that chapel's seen.

   Over many cliffs climbed he in foreign coun-
    tries;
From friends far sundered, he fared as a stranger;
And wondrous it were, at each water or shore   715
That he passed, if he found not before him a foe,
So foul too and fell that to fight he could fail not.
The marvels he met with amount to so many
Too tedious were it to tell of the tenth part.
For sometimes with serpents he struggled and
    wolves too,   720
With wood-trolls sometimes in stony steeps dwell-
    ing,
And sometimes with bulls and with bears and with
    boars;
And giants from high fells hunted and harassed
    him.
If he'd been not enduring and doughty, and served
    God,
These doubtless would often have done him to
    death.   725
Though warfare was grievous, worse was the win-
    ter,
When cold, clear water was shed from the clouds
That froze ere it fell to the earth, all faded.

With sleet nearly slain, he slept in his armor
More nights than enough on the naked rocks,   730
Where splashing the cold stream sprang from the
    summit,
And hung in hard icicles high o'er his head.
Thus in peril and pain and desperate plights,
Till Christmas Eve wanders this wight through
    the country
                    Alone.   735

       Truly the knight that tide
       To Mary made his moan,
       That she direct his ride
       To where some hearth-fire shone.

   By a mount on the morn he merrily rides   740
To a wood dense and deep that was wondrously
    wild;
High hills on each hand, with forests of hoar oaks
Beneath them most huge, a hundred together.
Thickly the hazel and hawthorn were tangled,
Everywhere mantled with moss rough and ragged,
With many a bird on the bare twigs, mournful,
That piteously piped for pain of the cold.   747
Sir Gawain on Gringolet goes underneath them
Through many a marsh and many a mire,
Unfriended, fearing to fail in devotion,   750
And see not His service, that Sire's, on that very
    night
Born of a Virgin to vanquish our pain.
And so sighing he said: "Lord, I beseech Thee,
And Mary, the mildest mother so dear,
For some lodging wherein to hear mass full lowly,
And matins, meekly I ask it, tomorrow;   756
So promptly I pray my pater and ave
                    And creed."

       Thus rode he as he prayed,
       Lamenting each misdeed;   760
       Often the sign he made,
       And said, "Christ's cross me speed."

   He scarcely had signed himself thrice, ere he
    saw
In the wood on a mound a moated mansion,
Above a fair field, enfolded in branches   765
Of many a huge tree hard by the ditches:
The comeliest castle that knight ever kept.
In a meadow 't was placed, with a park all about,
And a palisade, spiked and pointed, set stoutly
Round many a tree for more than two miles.   770
The lord on that one side looked at the stronghold
That shimmered and shone through the shapely
    oak trees;

Then duly his helm doffed, and gave his thanks
    humbly
To Jesus and Julian, both of them gentle,
For showing him courtesy, hearing his cry.   775
"Now good lodging," quoth Gawain, "I beg you
    to grant me."
Then with spurs in his gilt heels he Gringolet
    strikes,
Who chooses the chief path by chance that con-
    ducted
The man to the bridge-end ere many a minute
              Had passed.   780
        The bridge secure was made,
        Upraised; the gates shut fast;
        The walls were well arrayed.
        It feared no tempest's blast.

The hero abode on his horse by the bank   785
Of the deep, double ditch that surrounded the
    dwelling.
The wall stood wonderfully deep in the water,
And again to a huge height sprang overhead;
Of hard, hewn rock that reached to the cornices,
Built up with outworks under the battlements   790
Finely; at intervals, turrets fair fashioned,
With many good loopholes that shut tight; this
    lord
Had ne'er looked at a barbican better than this
    one.
Further in he beheld the high hall; here and there
Towers were stationed set thickly with spires,   795
With finials wondrously long and fair fitting,
Whose points were cunningly carven, and craftily.
There numerous chalk-white chimneys he noticed
That bright from the tops of the towers were
    gleaming.
Such pinnacles painted, so placed about every-
    where,   800
Clustering so thick 'mid the crenels, the castle
Surely appeared to be shaped to cut paper.
The knight on his foal it fair enough fancies
If into the court he may manage to come,
In that lodging to live while the holiday lasts   805
              With delight.
        A porter came at call.
        His mission learned, and right
        Civilly from the wall
        Greeted the errant knight.   810

Quoth Gawain: "Good sir, will you go on my
    errand,
Harbor to crave of this house's high lord?"

"Yea, by Peter. I know well, sir knight," said the
    porter,
"You're welcome as long as you list here to tarry."
Then went the man quickly, and with him, to
    welcome   815
The knight to the castle, a courteous company.
Down the great drawbridge they dropped, and
    went eagerly
Forth; on the frozen earth fell on their knees
To welcome this knight in the way they thought
    worthy;
Threw wide the great gate for Gawain to enter.
He bid them rise promptly, and rode o'er the
    bridge.   821
His saddle several seized as he lighted,
And stout men in plenty stabled his steed.
And next there descended knights and esquires
To lead to the hall with delight this hero.   825
When he raised his helmet, many made haste
From his hand to catch it, to care for the courtly
    man.
Some of them took then his sword and his shield
    both.   828
Then Gawain graciously greeted each knight;
Many proud men pressing to honor that prince,
To the hall they led him, all hasped in his harness,
Where fiercely a fair fire flamed on the hearth.
Then came the lord of this land from his chamber
To fittingly meet the man on the floor,
And said: "You are welcome to do what your will
    is;   835
To hold as your own, you have all that is here
              In this place."
        "Thank you," said Gawain then
        "May Christ reward this grace."
        The two like joyful men   840
        Each other then embrace.

Gawain gazed at the man who so graciously
    greeted him;
Doughty he looked, the lord of that dwelling,
A hero indeed huge, hale, in his prime;   844
His beard broad and bright, its hue all of beaver;
Stern, and on stalwart shanks steadily standing;
Fell faced as the fire, in speech fair and free.
In sooth, well suited he seemed, thought Gawain,
To govern as prince of a goodly people.
To his steward the lord turned, and strictly com-
    manded   850
To send men to Gawain to give him good service;
And prompt at his bidding were people in plenty.
To a bright room they brought him, the bed nobly
    decked

With hangings of pure silk with clear golden
    hems.
And curious coverings with comely panels,   855
Embroidered with bright fur above at the edges;
On cords curtains running with rings of red gold;
From Tars and Toulouse were the tapestries cover-
    ing
The walls; under foot on the floor more to match.
There he soon, with mirthful speeches, was
    stripped   860
Of his coat of linked mail and his armor; and
    quickly
Men ran, and brought him rich robes, that the best
He might pick out and choose as his change of
    apparel.
When lapped was the lord in the one he selected,
That fitted him fairly with flowing skirts,   865
The fur by his face, in faith it seemed made,
To the company there, entirely of colors,
Glowing and lovely; beneath all his limbs were.
That never made Christ a comelier knight
                They thought.   870
      On earth, or far or near,
      It seemed as if he ought
      To be a prince sans peer
      In fields where fierce men fought.

   A chair by the chimney where charcoal was
    burning   875
For Gawain was fitted most finely with cloths,
Both cushions and coverlets, cunningly made.
Then a comely mantle was cast on the man,
Of a brown, silken fabric bravely embroidered,
Within fairly furred with the finest of skins,   880
Made lovely with ermine, his hood fashioned like-
    wise.
He sat on that settle in clothes rich and seemly;
His mood, when well he was warmed, quickly
    mended.
Soon was set up a table on trestles most fair;
With a clean cloth that showed a clear white it
    was covered,   885
With top-cloth and salt-cellar, spoons too of silver.
When he would the man washed, and went to his
    meat,
And seemly enough men served him with several
Excellent stews in the best manner seasoned,
Twofold as was fitting, and various fishes;   890
In bread some were baked, some broiled on the
    coals,
Some seethed, some in stews that were savored
    with spices;

And ever such subtly made sauces as pleased him
He freely and frequently called it a feast,
Most courtly; the company there all acclaimed him
                Well-bred.   896
      "But now this penance take,
      And soon 't will mend," they said.
      That man much mirth did make,
      As wine went to his head.   900

   They enquired then and queried in guarded
    questions
Tactfully put to the prince himself,
Till he courteously owned he came of the court
The lord Arthur, gracious and goodly, alone holds,
Who rich is and royal, the Round Table's King;
And that Gawain himself in that dwelling was
    seated,   906
For Christmas come, as the case had befallen.
When he learned that he had that hero, the lord
Laughed loudly thereat so delightful he thought it.
Much merriment made all the men in that castle
By promptly appearing then in his presence;   911
For all prowess and worth and pure polished man-
    ners
Pertain to his person. He ever is praised;
Of all heroes on earth his fame is the highest.
Each knight full softly said to his neighbor,   915
"We now shall see, happily, knightly behavior,
And faultless terms of talking most noble;
What profit 's in speech we may learn without
    seeking,
For nurture's fine father has found here a wel-
    come;
In truth God has graciously given His grace   920
Who grants us to have such a guest as Gawain
When men for His birth's sake sit merry and sing.
                 To each
      Of us this hero now
      Will noble manners teach;   925
      Who hear him will learn how
      To utter loving speech."

   When at length the dinner was done, and the
    lords
Had risen, the night-time nearly was come.
The chaplains went their way to the chapels   930
And rang right joyfully, just as they should do.
For evensong solemn this festival season.
To this goes the lord, and the lady likewise;
She comes in with grace to the pew closed and
    comely,
And straightway Gawain goes thither right gaily;

The lord by his robe took him, led to a seat, 936
Acknowledged him kindly and called him by
    name,
Saying none in the world was as welcome as he
    was.
He heartily thanked him; the heroes embraced,
And together they soberly sat through the service.
Then longed the lady to look on the knight, 941
And emerged from her pew with many fair
    maidens;
In face she was fairest of all, and in figure,
In skin and in color, all bodily qualities;
Lovelier, Gawain thought, even than Guinevere.
He goes through the chancel to greet her, so gra-
    cious. 946
By the left hand another was leading her, older
Than she, a lady who looked as if aged,
By heroes around her reverenced highly.
The ladies, however, unlike were to look on: 950
If fresh was the younger, the other was yellow;
Rich red on the one was rioting everywhere,
Rough wrinkled cheeks hung in rolls on the other;
One's kerchiefs, with clear pearls covered and
    many,
Displayed both her breast and her bright throat all
    bare, 955
Shining fairer than snow on the hillsides falling;
The second her neck in a neck-cloth enswathed,
That enveloped in chalk-white veils her black
    chin;
Her forehead in silk was wrapped and enfolded
Adorned and tricked with trifles about it 960
Till nothing was bare but the lady's black brows,
Her two eyes, her nose, and her lips, all naked,
And those were bleared strangely, and ugly to see.
A goodly lady, so men before God
                            Might decide! 965
        Her body thick and short
        Her hips were round and wide;
        One of more pleasant sort
        She led there by her side.

When Gawain had gazed on that gay one so
    gracious 970
In look, he took leave of the lord and went toward
    them,
Saluted the elder, bowing full lowly,
The lovelier lapped in his two arms a little,
And knightly and comely greeted and kissed her.
They craved his acquaintance, and quickly he
    asked 975
To be truly their servant if so they desired it.

They took him between them, and led him with
    talk
To the sitting-room's hearth; then straightway for
    spices
They called, which men sped to unsparingly bring,
And with them as well pleasant wine at each com-
    ing. 980
Up leaped right often the courteous lord,
Urged many a time that the men should make
    merry,
Snatched off his hood, on a spear gaily hung it,
And waved it, that one for a prize might win it
Who caused the most mirth on that Christmas
    season. 985
"I shall try, by my faith, to contend with the finest
Ere hoodless I find myself, helped by my friends."
Thus with laughing speeches the lord makes merry
That night, to gladden Sir Gawain with games.
                        So they spent 990
        The evening in the hall.
        The king for lights then sent,
        And taking leave of all
        To bed Sir Gawain went.

On the morn when the Lord, as men all remem-
    ber, 995
Was born, who would die for our doom, in each
    dwelling
On earth grows happiness greater for His sake;
So it did on that day there with many a dainty:
With dishes cunningly cooked at meal-times,
With doughty men dressed in their best on the
    dais. 1000
The old lady was seated the highest; beside her
Politely the lord took his place, I believe;
The gay lady and Gawain together sat, mid-most,
Where fitly the food came, and afterward fairly
Was served through the hall as beseemed them the
    best, 1005
Of the company each in accord with his station.
There was meat and mirth, there was much joy,
    too troublous
To tell, though I tried in detail to describe it;
Yet I know both the lovely lady and Gawain
So sweet found each other's society (pleasant 1010
And polished their converse, courtly and private;
Unfailing their courtesy, free from offense)
That surpassing, in truth, any play of a prince was
                            Their game.
        There trumpets, drums and airs 1015
        Of piping loudly came.
        Each minded his affairs,
        And those two did the same.

Much mirth was that day and the day after
    made,
And the third followed fast, as full of delight.
Sweet was the joy of St. John's day to hear of,   1021
The last, as the folk there believed, of the festival.
Guests were to go in the gray dawn, and therefore
They wondrously late were awake with their wine,
And danced delightful, long lasting caroles.   1025
At length when 't was late they took their leave,
Each strong man among them to start on his way.
Gawain gave him good-day; then the good man
    laid hold of him,
Led to the hearth in his own room the hero;
There took him aside, and gave suitable thanks
For the gracious distinction that Gawain had given
In honoring his house that holiday season,   1032
And gracing his castle with courteous company.
"I'll truly as long as I live be the better
That Gawain at God's own feast was my guest."
"Gramercy," said Gawain, "by God, sir, not mine
Is the worth, but your own; may the high King
    reward you.   1037
I am here at your will to work your behest,
As in high and low it behooves me to do
                    By right."   1040
        The lord intently tries
        Longer to hold the knight;
        Gawain to him replies
        That he in no way might.

Then the man with courteous question en-
    quired   1045
What dark deed that feast time had driven him
    forth,
From the King's court to journey alone with such
    courage,
Ere fully in homes was the festival finished.
"In sooth," said the knight, "sir, ye say but the
    truth;
From these hearths a high and a hasty task took
    me.   1050
Myself, I am summoned to seek such a place
As to find it I know not whither to fare.
I'd not fail to have reached it the first of the New
    Year,
So help me our Lord, for the whole land of
    Logres;
And therefore, I beg this boon of you here, sir;
Tell me, in truth, if you ever heard tale   1056
Of the Chapel of Green, of the ground where it
    stands,
And the knight, green colored, who keeps it. By
    solemn

Agreement a tryst was established between us,
That man at that landmark to meet if I lived.
And now there lacks of New Year but little;   1061
I'd look at that lord, if God would but let me,
More gladly than own any good thing, by God's
    Son.
And hence, by your leave, it behooves me to go;
I now have but barely three days to be busy.   1065
As fain would I fall dead as fail of my mission."
Then laughing the lord said: "You longer must
    stay,
For I'll point out the way to that place ere the
    time's end,
The ground of the Green Chapel. Grieve no fur-
    ther;   1069
For, sir, you shall be in your bed at your ease
Until late, and fare forth the first of the year,
To your meeting place come by mid-morning, to do
    there
                Your pleasure.
        Tarry till New Year's day,
        Then rise and go at leisure.   1075
        I'll set you on your way;
        Not two miles is the measure."

Then was Gawain right glad, and gleefully
    laughed.
"Now for this more than anything else, sir, I thank
    you.   1079
I have come to the end of my quest; at your will
I shall bide, and in all things act as you bid me."
The lord then seized him, and set him beside him,
And sent for the ladies to better delight him.
Seemly the pleasure among them in private.   1084
So gay were the speeches he spoke, and so friendly,
The host seemed a man well-nigh mad in behavior.
He called to the knight there, crying aloud:
"Ye have bound you to do the deed that I bid you.
Here, and at once, will you hold to your word,
    sir?"
"Yes, certainly, sir," the true hero said;   1090
"While I bide in your house I obey your behest."
"You have toiled," said the lord; "from afar have
    traveled,
And here have caroused, nor are wholly recovered
In sleep or in nourishment, know I for certain.
In your room you shall linger, and lie at your ease
Tomorrow till mass-time, and go to your meat   1096
When you will, and with you my wife to amuse
    you
With company, till to the court I return.
                You stay
        And I shall early rise,   1100

And hunting go my way."
Bowing in courteous wise,
Gawain grants all this play.

"And more," said the man, "let us make an
     agreement:
Whatever I win the wood shall be yours;   1105
And what chance you shall meet shall be mine in
     exchange.
Sir, let's so strike our bargain and swear to tell
     truly
Whate'er fortune brings, whether bad, sir, or bet-
     ter."
Quoth Gawain the good: "By God, I do grant it.
What pastime you please appears to me pleasant."
"On the beverage brought us the bargain is
     made,"   1111
So the lord of the land said. All of them laughed,
And drank, and light-heartedly reveled and dal-
     lied,
Those ladies and lords, as long as they liked.
Then they rose with elaborate politeness, and lin-
     gered,   1115
With many fair speeches spoke softly together,
Right lovingly kissed, and took leave of each other.
Gay troops of attendants with glimmering torches
In comfort escorted each man to his couch
               To rest.   1120
     Yet ere they left the board
     Their promise they professed
     Often. That people's lord
     Could well maintain a jest.

III

Betimes rose the folk ere the first of the day;
The guests that were going then summoned their
     grooms,   1126
Who hastily sprang up to saddle their horses,
Packed their bags and prepared all their gear.
The nobles made ready, to ride all arrayed;
And quickly they leaped and caught up their
     bridles,   1130
And started, each wight on the way that well
     pleased him.
The land's beloved lord not last was equipped
For riding, with many a man too. A morsel
He hurriedly ate when mass he had heard,
And promptly with horn to the hunting field has-
     tened.   1135
And ere any daylight had dawned upon earth,
Both he and his knights were high on their horses.
The dog-grooms, accomplished, the hounds then
     coupled,

The door of the kennel unclosed, called them out,
On the bugle mightily blew three single notes;   1140
Whereupon bayed with a wild noise the brachets,
And some they turned back that went straying,
     and punished.
The hunters, I heard, were a hundred. To station
               They go,
     The keepers of the hounds,   1145
     And off the leashes throw.
     With noise the wood resounds
     From the good blasts they blow.

At the first sound of questing, the wild creatures
     quaked;
The deer fled, foolish from fright, in the dale,
To the high ground hastened, but quickly were
     halted   1151
By beaters, loud shouting, stationed about
In a circle. The harts were let pass with their high
     heads,
And also the bucks, broad-antlered and bold;
For the generous lord by law had forbidden   1155
All men with the male deer to meddle in close
     season.
The hinds were hemmed in with hey! and ware!
The does to the deep valleys driven with great din.
You might see as they loosed them the shafts
     swiftly soar—
At each turn of the forest their feathers went fly-
     ing—   1160
That deep into brown hides bit with their broad
     heads;
Lo! they brayed on the hill-sides, bled there, and
     died,
And hounds, fleet-footed, followed them headlong
And hunters after them hastened with horns
So loud in their sharp burst of sound as to sunder
The cliffs. What creatures escaped from the shoot-
     ers,   1166
Hunted and harried from heights to the waters,
Were pulled down and rent at the places there
     ready;
Such skill the men showed at these low-lying sta-
     tions,
So great were the greyhounds that quickly they
     got them   1170
And dragged them down, fast as the folk there
     might look
               At the sight.
     Carried with bliss away,
     The lord did oft alight,
     Oft gallop; so that day   1175
     He passed till the dark night.

Thus frolicked the lord on the fringe of the
    forest,
And Gawain the good in his gay bed reposed,
Lying snugly, till sunlight shone on the walls,
'Neath a coverlet bright with curtains about it.
As softly he slumbered, a slight sound he heard
At his door, made with caution, and quickly it
    opened.   1182
The hero heaved up his head from the clothes;
By a corner he caught up the curtain a little,
And glanced out with heed to behold what had
    happened.   1185
The lady it was, most lovely to look at,
Who shut the door after her stealthily, slyly,
And turned toward the bed. Then the brave man,
    embarrassed,
Lay down again subtly to seem as if sleeping;
And stilly she stepped, and stole to his bed,   1190
There cast up the curtain, and creeping within it,
Seated herself on the bedside right softly,
And waited a long while to watch when he woke.
And the lord too, lurking, lay there a long while,
Wondering at heart what might come of this hap-
    pening,   1195
Or what it might mean—a marvel he thought it.
Yet he said to himself, "'T would be surely more
    seemly
By speaking at once to see what she wishes."
Then roused he from sleep, and stretching turned
    toward her,
His eyelids unlocked, made believe that he won-
    dered,   1200
And signed himself so by his prayers to be safer
             From fall.
         Right sweet in chin and cheek,
         Both white and red withal,
         Full fairly she did speak   1205
         With laughing lips and small.

"Good morrow, Sir Gawain," that gay lady said,
"You're a sleeper unwary, since so one may steal
    in.
In a trice you are ta'en! If we make not a truce,
In your bed, be you certain of this, I shall bind
    you."   1210
All laughing, the lady delivered those jests.
"Good morrow, fair lady," said Gawain the merry,
"You may do what you will, and well it doth
    please me,
For quickly I yield me, crying for mercy;
This method to me seems the best—for I must!"
So the lord in turn jested with laughter right joy-
    ous.   1216

"But if, lovely lady, you would, give me leave,
Your prisoner release and pray him to rise,
And I'd come from this bed and clothe myself bet-
    ter;
So could I converse with you then with more
    comfort."   1220
"Indeed no, fair sir," that sweet lady said,
"You'll not move from your bed; I shall manage
    you better;
For here—and on that side too—I shall hold you,
And next I shall talk with the knight I have taken.
For well do I know that your name is Sir Ga-
    wain,   1225
By everyone honored wherever you ride;
Most highly acclaimed is your courtly behavior
With lords and ladies and all who are living.
And now you're here, truly, and none but we two;
My lord and his followers far off have fared;   1230
Other men remain in their beds, and my maidens;
The door is closed, and secured with a strong
    hasp;
Since him who delights all I have in my house,
My time, as long as it lasts, I with talking
               Shall fill.   1235
         My body's gladly yours;
         Upon me work your will.
         Your servant I, perforce,
         And now, and shall be still."

"In faith," quoth Sir Gawain, "a favor I think
    it,   1240
Although I am now not the knight you speak of;
To reach to such fame as here you set forth,
I am one, as I well know myself, most unworthy.
By God, should you think it were good, I'd be
    glad
If I could or in word or action accomplish   1245
Your ladyship's pleasure—a pure joy 't would
    prove."
"In good faith, Sir Gawain," the gay lady said,
"Ill-bred I should be if I blamed or belittled
The worth and prowess that please all others.
There are ladies enough who'd be now more de-
    lighted   1250
To have you in thraldom, as here, sir, I have you,
To trifle gaily in talk most engaging,
To give themselves comfort and quiet their cares,
Than have much of the gold and the goods they
    command.   1254
But to Him I give praise that ruleth the heavens,
That wholly I have in my hand what all wish."
               So she
         Gave him good cheer that day,

She who was fair to see.
To what she chanced to say   1260
With pure speech answered he.

Quoth the merry man, "Madam, Mary reward
    you,
For noble, in faith, I've found you, and generous.
People by other pattern their actions,
But more than I merit to me they give praise;
'T is your courteous self who can show naught but
    kindness."   1266
"By Mary," said she, "to me it seems other!
Were I worth all the host of women now living,
And had I the wealth of the world in my hands,
Should I chaffer and choose to get me a champion,
Sir, from the signs I've seen in you here   1271
Of courtesy, merry demeanor, and beauty,
From what I have heard, and hold to be true,
Before you no lord now alive would be chosen."
"A better choice, madam, you truly have made;
Yet I'm proud of the value you put now upon
    me.   1276
Your servant as seemly, I hold you my sovereign,
Become your knight, and Christ give you quit-
    tance."
Thus of much they talked till mid-morning was
    past.
The lady behaved as if greatly she loved him,   1280
But Gawain, on guard, right gracefully acted.
"Though I were the most lovely of ladies," she
    thought,
"The less would he take with him love." He was
    seeking,

            With speed,
    Grief that must be: the stroke   1285
    That him should stun indeed.
    She then of leaving spoke,
    And promptly he agreed.

Then she gave him good-day, and glanced at
    him, laughing,
And startled him, speaking sharp words as she
    stood: 1290
"He who blesses all words reward this reception!
I doubt if indeed I may dub you Gawain."
"Wherefore?" he queried, quickly enquiring,
Afraid that he'd failed in his fashion of speech.
But the fair lady blesses him, speaking as fol-
    lows: 1295
"One as good as is Gawain the gracious considered,
(And courtly behavior's found wholly in him)
Not lightly so long could remain with a lady
Without, in courtesy, craving a kiss   1299

At some slight subtle hint at the end of a story."
"Let it be as you like, lovely lady," said Gawain;
"As a knight is so bound, I'll kiss at your bidding,
And lest he displease you, so plead no longer."
Then closer she comes, and catches the knight
In her arms, and salutes him, leaning down af-
    fably.   1305
Kindly each other to Christ they commend.
She goes forth at the door without further ado,
And he quickly makes ready to rise, and hastens,
Calls to his chamberlain, chooses his clothes,
And merrily marches, when ready, to mass.   1310
Then he fared to his meat, and fitly he feasted,
Made merry all day with amusements till moon-
    rise.

            None knew
    A knight to better fare
    With dames so worthy, two: 1315
    One old, one younger. There
    Much mirth did then ensue.

Still was absent the lord of that land on his
    pleasure,
To hunt barren hinds in wood and in heath.   1319
By the set of the sun he had slain such a number
Of does and different deer that 't was wondrous.
Eagerly flocked in the folk at the finish,
And quickly made of the killed deer a quarry;
To this went the nobles with numerous men;
The game whose flesh was the fattest they gath-
    ered;   1325
With care, as the case required, cut them open.
And some the deer searched at the spot of assay,
And two fingers of fat they found in the poorest.
They slit at the base of the throat, seized the
    stomach,   1329
Scraped it away with a sharp knife and sewed it;
Next slit the four limbs and stripped off the hide;
Then opened the belly and took out the bowels
And flesh of the knot, quickly flinging them out.
They laid hold of the throat, made haste to divide,
    then,   1334
The windpipe and gullet, and tossed out the guts;
With their sharp knives carved out the shoulders
    and carried them
Held through a small hole to have the sides per-
    fect.
The breast they sliced, and split it in two;
And then they began once again at the throat,
And quickly as far as its fork they cut it;   1340
Pulled out the pluck, and promptly thereafter
Beside the ribs swiftly severed the fillets,

Cleared them off readily right by the backbone,
Straight down to the haunch, all hanging together.
They heaved it up whole, and hewed it off there,
And the rest by the name of the numbles—and
rightly— 1346
> They knew.
> Then where divide the thighs,
> The folds behind they hew,
> Hasten to cut the prize 1350
> Along the spine in two.

And next both the head and the neck off they
hewed;
The sides from the backbone swiftly they sun-
dered;
The fee of the ravens they flung in the branches.
They ran through each thick side a hole by the
ribs, 1355
And hung up both by the hocks of the haunches,
Each fellow to have the fee that was fitting.
On the fair beast's hide, they fed their hounds
With the liver and lights and the paunch's lining,
Among which bread steeped in blood was min-
gled. 1360
They blew boldly the blast for the prize; the
hounds barked.
Then the venison took they and turned toward
home,
And stoutly many a shrill note they sounded.
Ere close of the daylight, the company came
To the comely castle where Gawain in comfort
> Sojourned. 1366
> And when he met the knight
> As thither he returned,
> Joy had they and delight,
> Where the fire brightly burned. 1370

In the hall the lord bade all his household to
gather,
And both of the dames to come down with their
damsels.
In the room there before all the folk he ordered
His followers, truly, to fetch him his venison.
Gawain he called with courteous gaiety, 1375
Asked him to notice the number of nimble beasts,
Showed him the fairness of flesh on the ribs.
"Are you pleased with this play? Have I won your
praise?
Have I thoroughly earned your thanks through
my cunning?"
"In faith," said Sir Gawain, "this game is the fair-
est 1380

I've seen in the season of winter these seven years."
"The whole of it, Gawain, I give you," the host
said;
"Because of our compact, as yours you may claim
it."
"That is true," the knight said, "and I tell you the
same:
That this I have worthily won within doors, 1385
And surely to you with as good will I yield it."
With both of his arms his fair neck he embraced,
And the hero as courteously kissed as he could.
"I give you my gains. I got nothing further;
I freely would grant it, although it were greater."
"It is good," said the good man; "I give you my
thanks. 1391
Yet things so may be that you'd think it better
To tell where you won this same wealth by your
wit."
" 'T was no part of our pact," said he; "press me
no more;
For trust entirely in this, that you've taken 1395
> Your due."
> With laughing merriment
> And knightly speech and true
> To supper soon they went
> With store of dainties new. 1400

In a chamber they sat, by the side of the chim-
ney,
Where men right frequently fetched them mulled
wine.
In their jesting, again they agreed on the morrow
To keep the same compact they came to before:
That whatever should chance, they'd exchange at
evening, 1405
When greeting again, the new things they had got-
ten.
Before all the court they agreed to the covenant;
Then was the beverage brought forth in jest.
At last they politely took leave of each other,
And quickly each hero made haste to his couch.
When the cock but three times had crowed and
cackled, 1411
The lord and his men had leaped from their beds.
So that duly their meal was dealt with, and mass,
And ere daylight they'd fared toward the forest, on
hunting
> Intent. 1415
> The huntsmen with loud horns
> Through level fields soon went,
> Uncoupling 'mid the thorns
> The hounds swift on the scent.

Soon they cry for a search by the side of a
    swamp.   1420
The huntsmen encourage the hounds that first
    catch there
The scent, and sharp words they shout at them
    loudly;
And thither the hounds that heard them hastened,
And fast to the trail fell, forty at once.
Then such clamor and din from the dogs that had
    come there   1425
Arose that the rocks all around them rang.
With horn and with mouth the hunters heartened
    them;
They gathered together then, all in a group,
'Twixt a pool in that copse and a crag most for-
    bidding,
At a stone heap, beside the swamp, by a cliff,   1430
Where the rough rock had fallen in rugged con-
    fusion,
They fared to the finding, the folk coming after.
Around both the crag and the rubble-heap searched
The hunters, sure that within them was hidden
The beast whose presence was bayed by the blood-
    hounds.   1435
Then they beat on the bushes, and bade him rise
    up,
And wildly he made for the men in his way,
Rushing suddenly forth, of swine the most splen-
    did.
Apart from the herd he'd grown hoary with age,
For fierce was the beast, the biggest of boars.   1440
Then many men grieved, full grim when he
    grunted,
For three at his first thrust he threw to the earth,
And then hurtled forth swiftly, no harm doing
    further.
They shrilly cried hi! and shouted hey! hey!
Put bugles to mouth, loudly blew the recall.   1445
The men and dogs merry in voice were and many;
With outcry they all hurry after this boar
             To slay.
       He maims the pack when, fell,
       He often stands at bay.   1450
       Loudly they howl and yell,
       Sore wounded in the fray.

Then to shoot at him came up the company
    quickly.
Arrows that hit him right often they aimed,
But their sharp points failed that fell on his shoul-
    ders'   1455
Tough skin, and the barbs would not bite in his
    flesh;

But the smooth-shaven shafts were shivered in
    pieces,
The heads wherever they hit him rebounding.
But when hurt by the strength of the strokes they
    struck,
Then mad for the fray he falls on the men,   1460
And deeply he wounds them as forward he dashes.
Then many were frightened, and drew back in
    fear;
But the lord galloped off on a light horse after
    him,
Blew like a huntsman right bold the recall
On his bugle, and rode through the thick of the
    bushes,   1465
Pursuing this swine till the sun shone clearly.
Thus the day they passed in doing these deeds,
While bides our gracious knight Gawain in bed,
With bed-clothes in color right rich, at the castle
             Behind.   1470
       The dame did not forget
       To give him greetings kind.
       She soon upon him set,
       To make him change his mind.

Approaching the curtain, she peeps at the prince
And at once Sir Gawain welcomes her worthily.
Promptly the lady makes her reply.   1477
By his side she seats herself softly, heartily
Laughs, and with lovely look these words delivers:
"If you, sir, are Gawain, greatly I wonder   1480
That one so given at all times to goodness
Should be not well versed in social conventions,
Or, made once to know, should dismiss them from
    mind.
You have promptly forgotten what I in the plain-
    est
Of talk that I knew of yesterday taught you."   1485
"What is that?" said the knight. "For truly I know
    not;
If it be as you say, I am surely to blame."
"Yet I taught you," quoth the fair lady, "of kiss-
    ing;
When clearly he's favored, quickly to claim one
Becomes each knight who practices courtesy."   1490
"Cease, dear lady, such speech," said the strong
    man;
"I dare not for fear of refusal do that.
'T would be wrong to proffer and then be re-
    pulsed."
"In faith, you may not be refused," said the fair
    one;
"Sir, if you pleased, you have strength to compel
    it,   1495

Should one be so rude as to wish to deny you."
"By God, yes," said Gawain, "good is your speech;
But unlucky is force in the land I live in,
And every gift that with good will's not given.
Your word I await to embrace when you wish;
You may start when you please, and stop at your
  pleasure."   1501
            With grace,
        The lady, bending low,
        Most sweetly kissed his face.
        Of joy in love and woe   1505
        They talked for a long space.

"I should like," said the lady, "from you, sir, to
  learn,
If I roused not your anger by asking, the reason
Why you, who are now so young and valiant,
So known far and wide as knightly and courteous
(And principally, picked from all knighthood, is
  praised   1511
The sport of true love and the science of arms;
For to tell of these true knights' toil, it is surely
The title inscribed and the text of their deeds,
How men their lives for their leal love adventured,
Endured for their passion doleful days,   1516
Then themselves with valor avenged, and their
  sorrow
Cast off, and brought bliss into bowers by their
  virtues),
Why you, thought the noblest knight of your time,
Whose renown and honor are everywhere noted,
Have so let me sit on two separate occasions   1521
Beside you, and hear proceed from your head
Not one word relating to love, less or more.
You so goodly in vowing your service and gracious
Ought gladly to give to a young thing your guid-
  ance,   1525
And show me some sign of the sleights of true
  love.
What! know you nothing, and have all renown?
Or else do you deem me too dull, for your talking
            Unfit?
        For shame! Alone I come;   1530
        To learn some sport I sit;
        My lord is far from home;
        Now, teach me by your wit."

"In good faith," said Gawain, "God you reward;
For great is the happiness, huge the gladness   1535
That one so worthy should want to come hither,
And pains for so poor a man take, as in play
With your knight with looks of regard; it delights
  me.

But to take up the task of telling of true love,
To touch on those themes, and on tales of arms
To you who've more skill in that art, I am certain,
By half than a hundred men have such as I,   1542
Or ever shall have while here upon earth,
By my faith, 't would be, madam, a manifold folly.
Your bidding I'll do, as in duty bound,   1545
To the height of my power, and will hold myself
  ever
Your ladyship's servant, so save me the Lord."
Thus the fair lady tempted and tested him often
To make the man sin—whate'er more she'd in
  mind;
But so fair his defense was, no fault was appar-
  ent,   1550
Nor evil on either side; each knew but joy
            On that day.
        At last she kissed him lightly,
        After long mirth and play,
        And took her leave politely,   1555
        And went upon her way.

The man bestirs himself, springs up for mass.
Then made ready and splendidly served was their
  dinner;
In sport with the ladies he spent all the day.
But the lord through fields oft dashed as he fol-
  lowed   1560
The savage swine, that sped o'er the slopes,
And in two bit the backs of the best of his hounds
Where he stood at bay; till 't was broken by bow-
  men,
Who made him, despite himself, move to the open,
The shafts flew so thick when the throng had as-
  sembled.   1565
Yet sometimes he forced the stoutest to flinch,
Till at last too weary he was to run longer,
But came with such haste as he could to a hole
In a mound, by a rock whence the rivulet runs
  out.   1569
He started to scrape the soil, backed by the slope,
While froth from his mouth's ugly corners came
  foaming.
White were the tushes he whetted. The bold men
Who stood round grew tired of trying from far
To annoy him, but dared not for danger draw
  nearer.
            Before,   1575
        So many he did pierce
        That all were loth a boar
        So frenzied and so fierce
        Should tear with tusks once more, 157º

Till the hero himself came, spurring his horse,
Saw him standing at bay, the hunters beside him.
He leaped down right lordly, leaving his courser,
Unsheathed a bright sword and strode forth
    stoutly,
Made haste through the ford where that fierce one
    was waiting.
Aware of the hero with weapon in hand,   1585
So savagely, bristling his back up, he snorted
All feared for the wight lest the worst befall him.
Then rushed out the boar directly upon him,
And man was mingled with beast in the midst
Of the wildest water. The boar had the worse,
For the man aimed a blow at the beast as he met
    him,   1591
And surely with sharp blade struck o'er his breast
    bone,
That smote to the hilt, and his heart cleft asunder.
He squealing gave way, and swift through the
    water
                        Went back.   1595
        By a hundred hounds he's caught,
        Who fiercely him attack;
        To open ground he's brought,
        And killed there by the pack.

The blast for the beast's death was blown on
    sharp horns,   1600
And the lords there loudly and clearly hallooed.
At the beast bayed the brachets, as bid by their
    masters,
The chief, in that hard, long chase, of the hunters.
Then one who was wise in woodcraft began
To slice up this swine in the seemliest manner. 1605
First he hews off his head, and sets it on high;
Then along the back roughly rends him apart.
He hales out the bowels, and broils them on hot
    coals,
With these mixed with bread, rewarding his
    brachets.
Then slices the flesh in fine, broad slabs,   1610
And pulls out the edible entrails properly.
Whole, though, he gathers the halves together,
And proudly upon a stout pole he places them.
Homeward they now with this very swine hasten,
Bearing in front of the hero the boar's head, 1615
Since him at the ford by the force of his strong
    hand
                        He slew.
        It seemed long till he met
        In hall Sir Gawain, who
        Hastened, when called, to get   1620
        The payment that was due.

The lord called out loudly, merrily laughed
When Gawain he saw, and gladsomely spoke.
The good ladies were sent for, the household as-
    sembled;   1624
He shows them the slices of flesh, and the story
He tells of his largeness and length, and how fierce
Was the war in the woods where the wild swine
    had fled.
Sir Gawain commended his deeds right graciously,
Praised them as giving a proof of great prowess.
Such brawn on a beast, the bold man declared,
And such sides on a swine he had ne'er before
    seen.   1631
Then they handled the huge head; the courteous
    hero
Praised it, horror-struck, honoring his host.
Quoth the goodman, "Now, Gawain, yours is this
    game
By our covenant, fast and firm, you know truly."
"It is so," said the knight; "and as certain and
    sure   1636
All I get I'll give you again as I pledged you."
He about the neck caught, with courtesy kissed
    him,
And soon a second time served him the same way.
Said Gawain, "We've fairly fulfilled the agree-
    ment   1640
This evening we entered on, each to the other
                        Most true."
        "I, by Saint Giles, have met
        None," said the lord, "like you.
        Riches you soon will get,   1645
        If you such business do."

And then the tables they raised upon trestles,
And laid on them cloths; the light leaped up
    clearly
Along by the walls, where the waxen torches   1649
Were set by the henchmen who served in the hall.
A great sound of sport and merriment sprang up
Close by the fire, and on frequent occasions
At supper and afterward, many a splendid song,
Conduits of Christmas, new carols, all kinds
Of mannerly mirth that a man may tell of.   1655
Our seemly knight ever sat at the side
Of the lady, who made so agreeable her manner,
With sly, secret glances to glad him, so stalwart,
That greatly astonished was Gawain, and wroth
With himself; he in courtesy could not refuse her,
But acted becomingly, courtly, whatever   1661
The end, good or bad, of his action might be.
                        When quite
        Done was their play at last,

The host called to the knight,   1665
And to his room they passed
To where the fire burned bright.

The men there make merry and drink, and once
     more
The same pact for New Year's Eve is proposed;
But the knight craved permission to mount on the
     morrow: 1670
The appointment approached where he had to ap-
     pear.
But the lord him persuaded to stay and linger,
And said, "On my word as a knight I assure you
You'll get to the Green Chapel, Gawain, on New
     Year's,
And far before prime, to finish your business. 1675
Remain in your room then, and take your rest.
I shall hunt in the wood and exchange with you
     winnings,
As bound by our bargain, when back I return,
For twice I've found you were faithful when tried:
In the morning 'best be the third time,' remember.
Let's be mindful of mirth while we may, and
     make merry,   1681
For care when one wants it is quickly encoun-
     tered."
At once this was granted, and Gawain is stayed;
Drink blithely was brought him; to bed they were
     lighted.
                    The guest   1685
          In quiet and comfort spent
          The night, and took his rest.
          On his affairs intent,
          The host was early dressed.

After mass a morsel he took with his men. 1690
The morning was merry; his mount he demanded.
The knights who'd ride in his train were in readi-
     ness,
Dressed and horsed at the door of the hall.
Wondrous fair were the fields, for the frost was
     clinging;
Bright red in the cloud-rack rises the sun, 1695
And full clear sails close past the clouds in the sky.
The hunters unleashed all the hounds by a wood-
     side:
The rocks with the blast of their bugles were ring-
     ing.
Some dogs there fall on the scent where the fox is,
And trail oft a traitoress using her tricks. 1700
A hound gives tongue at it; huntsmen call to him;
Hastens the pack to the hound sniffing hard,
And right on his track run off in a rabble,

He scampering before them. They started the fox
     soon;   1704
When finally they saw him, they followed fast,
Denouncing him clearly with clamorous anger.
Through many a dense grove he dodges and
     twists,
Doubling back and harkening at hedges right
     often;
At last by a little ditch leaps o'er a thorn-hedge,
Steals out stealthily, skirting a thicket 1710
In thought from the wood to escape by his wiles
From the hounds; then, unknowing, drew near to
     a hunting-stand.
There hurled themselves, three at once, on him
     strong hounds,
                    All gray.
          With quick swerve he doth start 1715
          Afresh without dismay.
          With great grief in his heart
          To the wood he goes away.

Huge was the joy then to hark to the hounds.
When the pack all met him, mingled together,
Such curses they heaped on his head at the sight
That the clustering cliffs seemed to clatter down
     round them   1722
In heaps. The men, when they met him, hailed
     him,
And loudly with chiding speeches hallooed him;
Threats were oft thrown at him, thief he was
     called;   1725
At his tail were the greyhounds, that tarry he
     might not.
They rushed at him oft when he raced for the
     open,
And ran to the wood again, reynard the wily.
Thus he led them, all muddied, the lord and his
     men,
In this manner along through the hills until mid-
     day.   1730
At home, the noble knight wholesomely slept
In the cold of the morn within comely curtains.
But the lady, for love, did not let herself sleep,
Or fail in the purpose fixed in her heart; 1734
But quickly she roused herself, came there quickly,
Arrayed in a gay robe that reached to the ground,
The skins of the splendid fur skillfully trimmed
     close.
On her head no colors save jewels, well-cut,
That were twined in her hair-fret in clusters of
     twenty.
Her fair face was completely exposed, and her
     throat;   1740

In front her breast too was bare, and her back.
She comes through the chamber-door, closes it
    after her,
Swings wide a window, speaks to the wight,
And rallies him soon in speech full of sport
                    And good cheer.   1745
        "Ah! man, how can you sleep?
        The morning is so clear."
        He was in sorrow deep,
        Yet her he then did hear.

    In a dream muttered Gawain, deep in its gloom,
Like a man by a throng of sad thoughts sorely
    moved   1751
Of how fate was to deal out his destiny to him
That morn, when he met the man at the Green
    Chapel,
Bound to abide his blow, unresisting.
But as soon as that comely one came to his senses,
Started from slumber and speedily answered,   1756
The lovely lady came near, sweetly laughing,
Bent down o'er his fair face and daintily kissed
    him.
And well, in a worthy manner, he welcomed her.
Seeing her glorious, gaily attired,   1760
Without fault in her features, most fine in her
    color,
Deep joy came welling up, warming his heart.
With sweet, gentle smiling they straightway grew
    merry;
So passed naught between them but pleasure, joy,
                    And delight.   1765
        Goodly was their debate,
        Nor was their gladness slight.
        Their peril had been great
        Had Mary quit her knight.

    For that noble princess pressed him so closely,
Brought him so near the last bound, that her love
He was forced to accept, or, offending, refuse
    her: 1772
Concerned for his courtesy not to prove caitiff,
And more for his ruin if wrong he committed,
Betraying the hero, the head of that house.   1775
"God forbid," said the knight; "that never shall
    be";
And lovingly laughing a little, he parried
The words of fondness that fell from her mouth.
She said to him, "Sir, you are surely to blame
If you love not the lady beside whom you're ly-
    ing,   1780
Of all the world's women most wounded in heart,
Unless you've one dearer, a lover you like more,

Your faith to her plighted, so firmly made fast
You desire not to loosen it—so I believe.
Now tell me truly I pray you; the truth.   1785
By all of the loves that in life are, conceal not
                    Through guile."
        The knight said, "By Saint John,"
        And pleasantly to smile
        Began, "In faith I've none,   1790
        Nor will have for a while."

    "Such words," said the lady, "the worst are of
    all;
But in sooth I am answered, and sad it seems to
    me.
Kiss me now kindly, and quickly I'll go;
I on earth may but mourn, as a much loving
    mortal."   1795
Sighing she stoops down, and kisses him seemly;
Then starting away from him, says as she stands,
"Now, my dear, at parting, do me this pleasure:
Give me some gift, thy glove if it might be,   1799
To bring you to mind, sir, my mourning to lessen."
"On my word," quoth the hero, "I would that I
    had here,
For thy sake, the thing that I think the dearest
I own, for in sooth you've deserved very often
A greater reward than one I could give.
But a pledge of love would profit but little;   1805
'T would help not your honor to have at this time
For a keepsake a glove, as a gift of Gawain.
I've come on a mission to countries most strange;
I've no servants with splendid things filling their
    sacks:
That displeases me, lady, for love's sake, at pres-
    ent;   1810
Yet each man without murmur must do what he
    may
                    Nor repine."
        "Nay, lord of honors high,
        Though I have naught of thine,"
        Quoth the lovely lady, "I   1815
        Shall give you gift of mine."

    She offered a rich ring, wrought in red gold,
With a blazing stone that stood out above it,
And shot forth brilliant rays bright as the sun;
Wit you well that wealth right huge it was worth.
But promptly the hero replied, refusing it,   1821
"Madam, I care not for gifts now to keep;
I have none to tender and naught will I take."
Thus he ever declined her offer right earnest,
And swore on his word that he would not accept
    it;   1825

And, sad he declined, she thereupon said,
"If my ring you refuse, since it seems too rich,
If you would not so highly to me be beholden,
My girdle, that profits you less, I'll give you."
She swiftly removed the belt circling her sides,
Round her tunic knotted, beneath her bright
    mantle;   1831
'T was fashioned of green silk, and fair made with
    gold,
With gold, too, the borders embellished and beau-
    tiful.
To Gawain she gave it, and gaily besought him
To take it, although he thought it but trifling.
He swore by no manner of means he'd accept   1836
Either gold or treasure ere God gave him grace
To attain the adventure he'd there undertaken.
"And, therefore, I pray, let it prove not displeasing,
But give up your suit, for to grant it I'll never
                    Agree.   1841
          I'm deeply in your debt
          For your kind ways to me.
          In hot and cold I yet
          Will your true servant be."   1845

  "Refuse ye this silk," the lady then said,
"As slight in itself? Truly it seems so.
Lo! it is little, and less is its worth;
But one knowing the nature knit up within it,
Would give it a value more great, peradventure;
For no man girt with this girdle of green,   1851
And bearing it fairly made fast about him,
Might ever be cut down by any on earth,
For his life in no way in the world could be
    taken."   1854
Then mused the man, and it came to his mind
In the peril appointed him precious 't would prove
When he'd found the chapel, to face there his for-
    tune.
The device, might he slaying evade, would be
    splendid.
Her suit then he suffered, and let her speak;
And the belt she offered him, earnestly urging it
(And Gawain consented), and gave it with good
    will,   1861
And prayed him for her sake ne'er to display it,
But, true, from her husband to hide it. The hero
Agreed that no one should know of it ever.
                  Then he   1865
          Thanked her with all his might
          Of heart and thought; and she
          By then to this stout knight
          Had given kisses three.

Then the lady departs, there leaving the lord,
For more pleasure she could not procure from that
    prince.   1871
When she's gone, then quickly Sir Gawain clothes
    himself,
Rises and dresses in noble array,
Lays by the love-lace the lady had left him,
Faithfully hides it where later he'd find it.   1875
At once then went on his way to the chapel,
Approached in private a priest, and prayed him
To make his life purer, more plainly him teach
How his soul, when he had to go hence, should be
    saved.
He declared his faults, confessing them fully,   1880
The more and the less, and mercy besought,
And then of the priest implored absolution.
He surely absolved him, and made him as spotless,
Indeed, as if doomsday were due on the morrow.
Then among the fair ladies he made more merry
With lovely caroles, all kinds of delights,   1886
That day than before, until darkness fell.
                All there
          Were treated courteously,
          "And never," they declare,   1890
          "Has Gawain shown such glee
          Since hither he did fare."

  In that nook where his lot may be love let him
    linger!
The lord's in the meadow still, leading his men.
He has slain this fox that he followed so long;   1895
As he vaulted a hedge to get view of the villain,
Hearing the hounds that hastened hard after him,
Reynard from out a rough thicket came running,
And right at his heels in a rush all the rabble.
He, seeing that wild thing, wary, awaits him,   1900
Unsheaths his bright brand and strikes at the
    beast.
And he swerved from its sharpness and back would
    have started;
A hound, ere he could, came hurrying up to him;
All of them fell on him fast by the horse's feet,
Worried that sly one with wrathful sound.   1905
And quickly the lord alights, and catches him,
Takes him in haste from the teeth of the hounds,
And over his head holds him high, loudly shout-
    ing,
Where brachets, many and fierce, at him barked.
Thither huntsmen made haste with many a horn,
The recall, till they saw him, sounding right
    clearly.   1911
As soon as his splendid troop had assembled,
All bearing a bugle blew them together,

The others having no horns all hallooed.
'T was the merriest baying that man ever heard
That was raised for the soul of reynard with
    sounding   1916
                    Din.
        They fondle each dog's head
        Who his reward did win.
        Then take they reynard dead   1920
        And strip him of his skin.

And now, since near was the night, they turned
    homeward,
Strongly and sturdily sounding their horns.
At last at his loved home the lord alighted,
A fire on the hearth found, the hero beside it,
Sir Gawain the good, who glad was withal,   1926
For he had 'mong the ladies in love much delight.
A blue robe that fell to the floor he was wearing;
His surcoat, that softly was furred, well beseemed
    him;
A hood of the same hue hung on his shoulders,
And both were bordered with white all about.   1931
He, mid-most, met the good man in the hall,
And greeted him gladly, graciously saying:
"Now shall I first fulfill our agreement
We struck to good purpose, when drink was not
    spared."   1935
Then Gawain embraced him, gave him three
    kisses,
The sweetest and soundest a man could bestow.
"By Christ, you'd great happiness," quoth then the
    host,
'In getting these wares, if good were your bar-
    gains."   1939
"Take no care for the cost," the other said quickly,
"Since plainly the debt that is due I have paid."
Said the other, "By Mary, mine's of less worth.
The whole of the day I have hunted, and gotten
The skin of this fox—the fiend take its foulness!—
Right poor to pay for things of such price   1945
As you've pressed on me here so heartily, kisses
             So good."
        "Say no more," Gawain saith;
        "I thank you, by the rood!"
        How the fox met his death   1950
        He told him as they stood.

With mirth and minstrelsy, meat at their pleas-
    ure
They made as merry as any men might
(With ladies' laughter, and launching of jests
Right glad were they both, the good man and
    Gawain)   1955

Unless they had doted or else had been drunken.
Both the man and the company make many jokes,
Till the time is come when the two must be
    parted,
When finally the knights are forced to go bedward.
And first of the lord his respectful leave   1960
This goodly man took, and graciously thanked
    him:
"May God you reward for the welcome you gave
    me
This high feast, the splendid sojourn I've had here.
I give you myself, if you'd like it, to serve you.
I must, as you know, on the morrow move on;
Give me someone to show me the path, as you
    said,   1966
To the Green Chapel, there, as God will allow me,
On New Year the fate that is fixed to perform."
"With a good will, indeed," said the good man;
    "whatever
I promised to do I deem myself ready."   1970
He a servant assigns on his way to set him,
To take him by hills that no trouble he'd have,
And through grove and wood by the way most
    direct
             Might repair.
        The lord he thanked again   1975
        For the honor done him there.
        The knight his farewell then
        Took of those ladies fair.

To them with sorrow and kissing he spoke,
And besought them his thanks most sincere to
    accept;   1980
And they, replying, promptly returned them,
With sighings full sore to the Savior commended
    him.
Then he with courtesy quitted the company,
Giving each man that he met his thanks
For kindness, for trouble he'd taken, for care   1985
Whereby each had sought to serve him right
    eagerly.
Pained was each person to part with him then,
As if long they in honor had lived with that
    noble.
With people and lights he was led to his chamber.
To bed gaily brought there to be at his rest;   1990
Yet I dare not say whether soundly he slept,
For much, if he would, on the morn to remember
             Had he.
        Let him lie stilly there
        Near what he sought to see.   1995
        What happened I'll declare,
        If you will silent be.

IV

The New Year draws near, and the nighttime
    now passes;
The day, as the Lord bids, drives on to darkness.
Outside, there sprang up wild storms in the
    world;   2000
The clouds cast keenly the cold to the earth
With enough of the north sting to trouble the
    naked;
Down shivered the snow, nipping sharply the wild
    beasts;
The wind from the heights, shrilly howling, came
    rushing,   2004
And heaped up each dale full of drifts right huge.
Full well the man listened who lay in his bed.
Though he shut tight his lids, he slept but a little;
He knew by each cock that crowed 't was the
    tryst time,
And swiftly ere dawn of the day he arose,
For there shone then the light of a lamp in his
    room;   2010
To his chamberlain called, who answered him
    quickly,
And bade him his saddle to bring and his mail-
    shirt.
The other man roused up and fetched him his rai-
    ment,
Arrayed then that knight in a fashion right noble.
First he clad him in clothes to ward off the cold,
Then his other equipment, carefully kept: 2016
His pieces of plate armor, polished right cleanly,
The rings of his rich mail burnished from rust.
All was fresh as at first; he was fain to give thanks
                  To the men.   2020
        He had on every piece
        Full brightly burnished then.
        He, gayest from here to Greece,
        Ordered his steed again.

He garbed himself there in the loveliest gar-
    ments   2025
(His coat had its blazon of beautiful needlework
Stitched upon velvet for show, its rich stones
Set about it and studded, its seams all embroi-
    dered,
Its lovely fur in the fairest of linings),
Yet he left not the lace, the gift of the lady: 2030
That, Gawain did not, for his own sake, forget.
When the brand on his rounded thighs he had
    belted,
He twisted the love-token two times about him.
That lord round his waist with delight quickly
    wound

The girdle of green silk, that seemed very gay
Upon royal red cloth that was rich to behold. 2036
But Gawain the girdle wore not for its great price,
Or pride in its pendants although they were pol-
    ished,
Though glittering gold there gleamed on the ends,
But himself to save when he needs must suffer
The death, nor could stroke then of sword or of
    knife   2041
                Him defend.
        Then was the bold man dressed;
        Quickly his way did wend;
        To all the court expressed   2045
        His great thanks without end.

Then was Gringolet ready that great was and
    huge,
Who had safely, as seemed to him pleasant, been
    stabled;
That proud horse pranced, in the pink of condi-
    tion.
The lord then comes to him, looks at his coat,
And soberly says, and swears on his word,   2051
"In this castle's a company mindful of courtesy,
Led by this hero. Delight may they have;
And may love the dear lady betide all her lifetime.
If they for charity cherish a guest,   2055
And give so great welcome, may God reward
    them,
Who rules the heaven on high, and the rest of you.
Might I for long live my life on the earth,
Some repayment with pleasure I'd make, if 't were
    possible."
He steps in the stirrup, strides into the saddle,
Receives on his shoulder the shield his man brings
    him,   2061
And spurs into Gringolet strikes with his gilt
    heels;
Who leaps on the stones and lingers no longer
                To prance.
        The knight on his horse sits,   2065
        Who bears his spear and lance,
        The house to Christ commits,
        And wishes it good chance.

Then down the drawbridge they dropped, the
    broad gates
Unbarred, and on both sides bore them wide open.
He blessed them quickly, and crossed o'er the
    planks there   2071
(He praises the porter, who knelt by the prince
Begging God to save Gawain, and gave him good-
    day),

And went on his way with but one man attended
To show him the turns to that sorrowful spot   2075
Where he must to that onerous onset submit.
By hillsides where branches were bare they both
   journeyed;
They climbed over cliffs where the cold was cling-
   ing.
The clouds hung aloft, but 't was lowering beneath
   them.
On the moor dripped the mist, on the mountains
   melted;   2080
Each hill had a hat, a mist-cloak right huge.
The brooks foamed and bubbled on hillsides about
   them,
And brightly broke on their banks as they rushed
   down.
Full wandering the way was they went through
   the wood,
Until soon it was time for the sun to be springing.

                         Then they   2086
           Were on a hill full high;
           White snow beside them lay.
           The servant who rode nigh
           Then bade his master stay.   2090

"I have led you hither, my lord, at this time,
And not far are you now from that famous place
You have sought for, and asked so especially after.
Yet, sir, to you surely I'll say, since I know you,
A man in this world whom I love right well,   2095
If you'd follow my judgment, the better you'd fare.
You make haste to a place that is held full of peril;
One dwells, the worst in the world, in that waste,
For he's strong and stern, and takes pleasure in
   striking.
No man on the earth can equal his might;   2100
He is bigger in body than four of the best men
In Arthur's own household, Hestor or others.
And thus he brings it about at the chapel:
That place no one passes so proud in his arms
That he smites him not dead with a stroke of his
   hand.   2105
He's a man most immoderate, showing no mercy;
Be it chaplain or churl that rides by the chapel,
Monk or priest, any manner of man,
Him to slay seems as sweet as to still live himself.
So I say, as sure as you sit in your saddle   2110
You're killed, should the knight so choose, if you
   come here;
That take as the truth, though you twenty lives
   had

                         To spend.
           He's lived in this place long

In battles without end.   2115
           Against his strokes right strong
           You cannot you defend.

"So let him alone, good Sir Gawain, and leave
By a different road, for God's sake, and ride
To some other country where Christ may reward
   you.   2120
And homeward again I will hie me, and promise
To swear by the Lord and all his good saints
(So help me the oaths on God's halidom sworn)
That I'll guard well your secret, and give out no
   story
You hastened to flee any hero I've heard of."   2125
"Thank you," said Gawain, and grudgingly added,
"Good fortune go with you for wishing me well.
And truly I think you'd not tell; yet though never
So surely you hid it, if hence I should hasten,
Fearful, to fly in the fashion you tell of,   2130
A coward I'd prove, and could not be pardoned.
The chapel I'll find whatsoever befalls,
And talk with that wight the way that I want to,
Let weal or woe follow as fate may wish.

                         Though the knave,   2135
           Hard to subdue and fell,
           Should stand there with a stave,
           Yet still the Lord knows well
           His servants how to save."

Quoth the man, "By Mary, you've said now this
   much: 2140
That you wish to bring down your own doom on
   your head.
Since you'd lose your life, I will stay you no longer.
Put your helm on your head, take your spear in
   your hand,
And ride down this road by the side of that rock
Till it brings you down to the dale's rugged bot-
   tom;   2145
Then look at the glade on the left hand a little:
You'll see in the valley that self-same chapel,
And near it the great-limbed knight who is guard-
   ing it.
Gawain the noble, farewell now, in God's name!
I would not go with thee for all the world's wealth,
Nor in fellowship ride one more foot through the
   forest."   2151
The man in the trees there then turns his bridle,
As hard as he can hits his horse with his heels,
And across the fields gallops, there leaving Sir
   Gawain

                         Alone.   2155
"By God," the knight said, "now

I'll neither weep nor groan.
Unto God's will I bow,
And make myself his own."

He strikes spurs into Gringolet, starts on the
     path;   2160
By a bank at the side of a small wood he pushes
     in,
Rides down the rugged slope right to the dale.
Then about him he looks, and the land seems
     wild,
And nowhere he sees any sign of a shelter,
But slopes on each side of him, high and steep,
And rocks, gnarled and rough, and stones right
     rugged.   2166
The clouds there seemed to him scraped by the
     crags.
Then he halted and held back his horse at that
     time,
And spied on all sides in search of the chapel;
Such nowhere he saw, but soon, what seemed
     strange,   2170
In the midst of a glade a mound, as it might be,
A smooth, swelling knoll by the side of the water,
The falls of a rivulet running close by;
In its banks the brook bubbled as though it were
     boiling.   2174
The knight urged on Gringolet, came to the glade,
There leaped down lightly and tied to the limb
Of a tree, right rugged, the reins of his noble steed,
Went to the mound, and walked all about it,
Debating what manner of thing it might be:
On the end and on each side an opening; every-
     where   2180
Over it grass was growing in patches,
All hollow inside, it seemed an old cave
Or a crag's old cleft: which, he could not decide.
               Said the knight,
          "Is this the chapel here?   2185
          Alas, dear Lord! here might
          The fiend, when midnight's near,
          His matin prayers recite.

"Of a truth," said Gawain, "the glade here is
     gloomy;   2189
The Green Chapel's ugly, with herbs overgrown.
It greatly becomes here that hero, green-clad,
To perform in the devil's own fashion his worship.
I feel in my five senses this is the fiend
Who has made me come to this meeting to kill me.
Destruction fall on this church of ill-fortune!   2195
The cursedest chapel that ever I came to!"
With helm on his head and lance in his hand

He went right to the rock of that rugged abode.
From that high hill he heard, from a hard rock
     over
The stream, on the hillside, a sound wondrous
     loud.   2200
Lo! it clattered on cliffs fit to cleave them, as
     though
A scythe on a grindstone someone were grinding.
It whirred, lo! and whizzed like a water-mill's
     wheel;
Lo! it ground and it grated, grievous to hear.   2204
"By God, this thing, as I think," then said Gawain,
"Is done now for me, since my due turn to meet it
                    Is near.
          God's will be done! 'Ah woe!'
          No whit doth aid me here.
          Though I my life forego   2210
          No sound shall make me fear."

And then the man there commenced to call
     loudly,
"Who here is the master, with me to hold tryst?
For Gawain the good now is going right near.
He who craves aught of me let him come hither
     quickly;   2215
'T is now or never; he needs to make haste."
Said somebody, "Stop," from the slope up above
     him,
"And promptly you'll get what I promised to give
     you."
Yet he kept up the whirring noise quickly a while,
Turned to finish his sharpening before he'd de-
     scend.   2220
Then he came by a crag, from a cavern emerging,
Whirled out of a den with a dreadful weapon,
A new Danish ax to answer the blow with;
Its blade right heavy, curved back to the handle,
Sharp filed with the filing tool, four feet in length,
'T was no less, by the reach of that lace gleaming
     brightly.   2226
The fellow in green was garbed as at first,
Both his face and his legs, his locks and his beard,
Save that fast o'er the earth on his feet he went
     fairly,
The shaft on the stone set, and stalked on beside
     it.   2230
On reaching the water, he would not wade it;
On his ax he hopped over, and hastily strode,
Very fierce, through the broad field filled all about
     him
               With snow.
          Sir Gawain met the man,   2235
          And bowed by no means low.

Who said, "Good sir, men can
Trust you to tryst to go."

Said the green man, "Gawain, may God you
  guard!
You are welcome indeed, sir knight, at my dwell-
  ing.   2240
Your travel you've timed as a true man should,
And you know the compact we came to between
  us;
A twelvemonth ago you took what chance gave,
And I promptly at New Year was pledged to repay
  you.
In truth, we are down in this dale all alone;   2245
Though we fight as we please, here there's no one
  to part us.
Put your helm from your head, and have here
  your payment;
Debate no further than I did before,
When you slashed off my head with a single
  stroke."
"Nay," quoth Gawain, "by God who gave me my
  spirit,   2250
I'll harbor no grudge whatever harm happens.
Exceed not one stroke and still I shall stand;
You may do as you please, I'll in no way oppose
          The blow."
          He left the flesh all bare,   2255
          Bending his neck down low
          As if he feared naught there,
          For fear he would not show.

Then the man in green raiment quickly made
  ready,
Uplifted his grim tool Sir Gawain to smite;   2260
With the whole of his strength he heaved it on
  high,
As threateningly swung it as though he would slay
  him.
Had it fallen again with the force he intended
That lord, ever-brave, from the blow had been
  lifeless.
But Gawain a side glance gave at the weapon   2265
As down it came gliding to do him to death;
With his shoulders shrank from the sharp iron a
  little.
The other with sudden jerk stayed the bright ax,
And reproved then that prince with proud words
  in plenty:
"Not Gawain thou art who so good is considered,
Ne'er daunted by host in hill or in dale;   2271
Now in fear, ere thou feelest a hurt, thou art
  flinching;

Such cowardice never I knew of that knight.
When you swung at me, sir, I fled not nor started;
No cavil I offered in King Arthur's castle.   2275
My head at my feet fell, yet never I flinched,
And thy heart is afraid ere a hurt thou feelest,
And therefore thy better I'm bound to be thought
          On that score."
          "I shrank once," Gawain said,   2280
          "And I will shrink no more;
          Yet cannot I my head,
          If it fall down, restore.

"But make ready, sir, quickly, and come to the
  point;
My destiny deal me, and do it forthwith;   2285
For a stroke I will suffer, and start no further
Till hit with thy weapon; have here my pledged
  word."
Quoth the other, heaving it high, "Have at thee!"
As fierce in his manner as if he were mad,
He mightily swung but struck not the man.   2290
Withheld on a sudden his hand ere it hurt him,
And firmly he waited and flinched in no member,
But stood there as still as a stone or a stump
In rocky ground held by a hundred roots.
Then the Green Knight again began to speak
  gaily: 2295
"It behooves me to hit, now that whole is thy
  heart.
Thy high hood that Arthur once gave you now
  hold back,
Take care that your neck at this cut may recover."
And Gawain full fiercely said in a fury,
"Come! lay on, thou dread man; too long thou art
  threatening.   2300
I think that afraid of your own self you feel."
"In sooth," said the other, "thy speech is so savage
No more will I hinder thy mission nor have it
          Delayed."
          With puckered lips and brow   2305
          He stands with ready blade.
          Not strange 't is hateful now
          To him past hope of aid.

He lifts his ax lightly, and lets it down deftly,
The blade's edge next to the naked neck.   2310
Though he mightily hammered he hurt him no
  more
Than to give him a slight nick that severed the
  skin there.
Through fair skin the keen ax so cut to the flesh
That shining blood shot to the earth o'er his shoul-
  ders.

As soon as he saw his blood gleam on the snow
He sprang forth in one leap, for more than a spear
    length;   2316
His helm fiercely caught up and clapped on his
    head;
With his shoulders his fair shield shot round in
    front of him,
Pulled out his bright sword, and said in a passion
(And since he was mortal man born of his mother
The hero was never so happy by half),   2321
"Cease thy violence, man; no more to me offer,
For here I've received, unresisting, a stroke.
If a second thou strikest I soon will requite thee,
And swiftly and fiercely, be certain of that,   2325
                Will repay.
      One stroke on me might fall
      By bargain struck that way,
      Arranged in Arthur's hall;
      Therefore, sir knight, now stay!"   2330

    The man turned away, on his weapon rested,
The shaft on the ground set, leaned on the sharp
    edge,
And gazed at Sir Gawain there in the glade;
Saw that bold man, unblenching, standing right
    bravely,
Full-harnessed and gallant; at heart he was glad.
Then gaily the Green Knight spoke in a great
    voice,   2336
And said to the man in speech that resounded,
"Now be not so savage, bold sir, for towards you
None here has acted unhandsomely, save
In accord with the compact arranged in the King's
    court.   2340
I promised the stroke you've received, so hold you
Well payed. I free you from all duties further.
If brisk I had been, peradventure a buffet
I'd harshly have dealt that harm would have done
    you.
In mirth, with a feint I menaced you first,   2345
With no direful wound rent you; right was my
    deed,
By the bargain that bound us both on the first
    night,
When, faithful and true, you fulfilled our agree-
    ment,
And gave me your gain as a good man ought to.
The second I struck at you, sir, for the morning
You kissed my fair wife and the kisses accorded
    me.   2351
Two mere feints for both times I made at you,
    man,

                Without woe.
    True men restore by right,
    One fears no danger so;   2355
    You failed the third time, knight,
    And therefore took that blow.

    " 'T is my garment you're wearing, that woven
    girdle,
Bestowed by my wife, as in truth I know well.
I know also your kisses and all of your acts   2360
And my wife's advances; myself, I devised them.
I sent her to try you, and truly you seem
The most faultless of men that e'er fared on his
    feet.
As a pearl compared to white peas is more pre-
    cious,
So next to the other gay knights is Sir Gawain.
But a little you lacked, and loyalty wanted,   2366
Yet truly 't was not for intrigue or for wooing,
But love of your life; the less do I blame you."
Sir Gawain stood in a study a great while,   2369
So sunk in disgrace that in spirit he groaned;
To his face all the blood in his body was flowing;
For shame, as the other was talking, he shrank.
And these were the first words that fell from his
    lips:
"Be cowardice cursed, and coveting! In you
Are vice and villainy, virtue destroying."   2375
The lace he then seized, and loosened the strands,
And fiercely the girdle flung at the Green Knight.
"Lo! there is faith-breaking! evil befall it.
To coveting came I, for cowardice caused me
From fear of your stroke to forsake in myself   2380
What belongs to a knight: munificence, loyalty.
I'm faulty and false, who've been ever afraid
Of untruth and treachery; sorrow betide both
                And care!
      Here I confess my sin;   2385
      All faulty did I fare.
      Your good will let me win,
      And then I will beware."

    Then the Green Knight laughed, and right gra-
    ciously said,   2389
"I am sure that the harm is healed that I suffered.
So clean you're confessed, so cleared of your faults,
Having had the point of my weapon's plain pen-
    ance,
I hold you now purged of offense, and as perfectly
Spotless as though you'd ne'er sinned in your life.
And I give to you, sir, the golden-hemmed girdle,
As green as my gown. Sir Gawain, when going
Forth on your way among famous princes,   2397

Think still of our strife and this token right splen-
did,
'Mid chivalrous knights, of the chapel's adventure.
This New Year you'll come to my castle again,
And the rest of this feast in revel most pleasant
                                Will go."   2402
            Then pressed him hard the lord:
            "My wife and you, I know
            We surely will accord,   2405
            Who was your bitter foe."

    "No indeed," quoth the hero, his helm seized
        and doffed it
Graciously, thanking the Green Knight; "I've
        stayed
Long enough. May good fortune befall you; may
        He
Who all fame doth confer give it fully to you, sir.
To your lady, gracious and lovely, commend me,
To her and that other, my honored ladies,   2412
That so with their sleights deceived their knight
        subtly.
But no marvel it is for a fool to act madly,
Through woman's wiles to be brought to woe.
So for certain was Adam deceived by some
        woman,   2416
By several Solomon, Samson besides;
Delilah dealt him his doom; and David
Was duped by Bath-sheba, enduring much sorrow.
Since these were grieved by their guile, 't would be
        great gain   2420
To love them yet never believe them, if knights
        could.
For formerly these were most noble and fortunate,
More than all others who lived on the earth;
            And these few
            By women's wiles were caught   2425
            With whom they had to do.
            Though I'm beguiled, I ought
            To be excused now too.

    "But your girdle," said Gawain, "may God you
        reward!   2429
With a good will I'll use it, yet not for the gold,
The sash or the silk, or the sweeping pendants,
Or fame, or its workmanship wondrous, or cost,
But in sign of my sin I shall see it oft.
When in glory I move, with remorse I'll remem-
ber
The frailty and fault of the stubborn flesh,   2435
How soon 't is infected with stains of defilement;
And thus when I'm proud of my prowess in arms,
The sight of this sash shall humble my spirit.

But one thing I pray, if it prove not displeasing;
Because you are lord of the land where I stayed
In your house with great worship (may He now
        reward you   2441
Who sitteth on high and upholdeth the heavens),
What name do you bear? No more would I
        know."
And then "That truly I'll tell," said the other;
"Bercilak de Hautdesert here am I called.   2445
Through her might who lives with me, Morgan le
        Fay,
Well-versed in the crafts and cunning of magic
(Many of Merlin's arts she has mastered,
For long since she dealt in the dalliance of love
With him whom your heroes at home know, that
        sage   2450
                Without blame.
            'Morgan the goddess,' so
            She's rightly known by name.
            No one so proud doth go
            That him she cannot tame).   2455

    "I was sent in this way to your splendid hall
To make trial of your pride, and to see if the
        people's
Tales were true of the Table's great glory.
This wonder she sent to unsettle your wits,   2459
And to daunt so the Queen as to cause her to die
From fear at the sight of that phantom speaker
Holding his head in his hand at the high table.
Lives she at home there, that ancient lady;
She's even thine aunt, King Arthur's half-sister,
Tyntagel's duchess's daughter, whom Uther   2465
Made later the mother of mighty Lord Arthur.
I beg thee, sir, therefore, come back to thine aunt;
In my castle make merry. My company love thee,
And I, sir, wish thee as well, on my word,
As any on earth for thy high sense of honor."   2470
He said to him, nay, this he'd never consent to.
The men kiss, embrace, and each other commend
To the Prince of Paradise; there they part
                In the cold.
            Gawain on his fair horse   2475
            To Arthur hastens bold;
            The bright Green Knight his course
            Doth at his pleasure hold.

    Through the wood now goes Sir Gawain by
        wild ways
On Gringolet, given by God's grace his life.   2480
Oft in houses, and oft in the open he lodged,
Met many adventures, won many a victory:
These I intend not to tell in this tale.

Now whole was the hurt he had in his neck,
And about it the glimmering belt he was bearing,
Bound to his side like a baldric obliquely,　　2486
Tied under his left arm, that lace, with a knot
As a sign that with stain of sin he'd been found.
And thus to the court he comes all securely.
Delight in that dwelling arose when its lord knew
That Gawain had come; a good thing he thought
　　it.　　　　　　　　　　　　　　　　　　2491
The King kissed the lord, and the Queen did like-
　　wise,
And next many knights drew near him to greet
　　him
And ask how he'd fared; and he wondrously an-
　　swered,
Confessed all the hardships that him had befallen,
The happenings at chapel, the hero's behavior,
The lady's love, and lastly the lace.　　2497
He showed them the nick in his neck all naked
The blow that the Green Knight gave for deceit
　　　　　　　　　　　Him to blame.　　2500
　　　In torment this he owned;
　　　Blood in his face did flame;
　　　With wrath and grief he groaned,
　　　When showing it with shame.

　　　Laying hold of the lace, quoth the hero, "Lo!
　　　lord!　　　　　　　　　　　　　　　2505
The band of this fault I bear on my neck;
And this is the scathe and damage I've suffered,

For cowardice caught there, and coveting also,
The badge of untruth in which I was taken.
And this for as long as I live I must wear,　　2510
For his fault none may hide without meeting mis-
　　fortune,
For once it is fixed, it can ne'er be unfastened."
To the knight then the King gave comfort; the
　　court too
Laughed greatly, and made this gracious agree-
　　ment:
That ladies and lords to the Table belonging,　　2515
All of the brotherhood, baldrics should bear
Obliquely about them, bands of bright green,
Thus following suit for the sake of the hero.
For the Round Table's glory was granted that lace,
And he held himself honored who had it there-
　　after,　　　　　　　　　　　　　　　2520
As told in the book, the best of romances.
In the days of King Arthur this deed was done
Whereof witness is borne by Brutus's book.
Since Brutus, that bold man, first came here to
　　Britain,
When ceased, indeed, had the siege and assault
　　　　　　　　　　　　At Troy's wall,　　2526
　　　Full many feats ere now
　　　Like this one did befall.
　　　May He with thorn-crowned brow
　　　To His bliss bring us all. Amen.　　2530

HONY SOYT QUI MAL PENCE.[2]

THOMAS MALORY

Le Morte d'Arthur

Book XVIII

CHAPTER I

Of the joy King Arthur and the queen had of the achievement of the Sangreal; and how Launcelot fell to his old love again.

So after the quest of the Sangreal[1] was fulfilled, and all knights that were left on live were come again unto the Table Round, as the book of the

Sangreal maketh mention, then was there great joy in the court; and in especial King Arthur and Queen Guenever made great joy of the remnant that were come home, and passing glad was the king and the queen of Sir Launcelot and of Sir Bors, for they had been passing long away in the quest of the Sangreal. Then, as the book saith, Sir Launcelot began to resort unto Queen Guenever again, and forgat the promise and the perfection that he made in the quest. For, as the book saith,

[2] The motto of the Knights of the Garter ("Evil be to him who evil thinks of it").
Malory, Le Morte d'Arthur. English modernized in spelling. The language is of about 1470. Practically nothing is known of the life of Sir Thomas Malory. He has been identified as a knight and it is believed that he wrote the Morte d'Arthur in prison.
[1] The Holy Grail: the cup used by Christ at the Last Supper.

had not Sir Launcelot been in his privy thoughts and in his mind so set inwardly to the queen as he was in seeming outward to God, there had no knight passed him in the quest of the Sangreal; but ever his thoughts were privily on the queen, and so they loved together more hotter than they did toforehand, and had such privy draughts together, that many in the court spake of it, and in especial Sir Agravaine, Sir Gawaine's brother, for he was ever open-mouthed. So befel that Sir 10 Launcelot had many resorts of ladies and damosels that daily resorted unto him, that besought him to be their champion, and in all such matters of right Sir Launcelot applied him daily to do for the pleasure of Our Lord, Jesu Christ. And ever as much as he might he withdrew him from the company and fellowship of Queen Guenever, for to eschew the slander and noise; wherefore the queen waxed wroth with Sir Launcelot. And upon a day she called Sir Launcelot unto her chamber, and 20 said thus: Sir Launcelot, I see and feel daily that thy love beginneth to slake, for thou hast no joy to be in my presence, but ever thou art out of this court, and quarrels and matters thou hast nowadays for ladies and gentlewomen more than ever thou were wont to have aforehand. Ah, madam, said Launcelot, in this ye must hold me excused for divers causes; one is, I was but late in the quest of the Sangreal; and I thank God of His great mercy, and never of my desert, that I saw in that 30 my quest as much as ever saw any sinful man, and so was it told me. And if I had not had my privy thoughts to return to your love again as I do, I had seen as great mysteries as ever saw my son Galahad, outher [2] Percivale, or Sir Bors; and therefore, madam, I was but late in that quest. Wit ye well, madam, it may not be yet lightly forgotten the high service in whom I did my diligent labour. Also, madam, wit ye well that there be many men speak of our love in this court, and have you and 40 me greatly in a wait, as Sir Agravaine and Sir Mordred; and, madam, wit ye well I dread them more for your sake than for any fear I have of them myself, for I may happen to escape and rid myself in a great need, where ye must abide all that will be said unto you. And then if that ye fall in any distress through wilful folly, then is there none other remedy or help but by me and my blood. And wit ye well, madam, the boldness of you and me will bring us to great shame and 50

slander; and that were me loth to see you dishonoured. And that is the cause I take upon me more for to do for damosels and maidens than ever I did tofore, that men should understand my joy and my delight is my pleasure to have ado for damosels and maidens.

CHAPTER II

How the queen commanded Sir Launcelot to avoid the court, and of the sorrow that Launcelot made.

All this while the queen stood still and let Sir Launcelot say what he would. And when he had all said she brast [3] out on weeping, and so she sobbed and wept a great while. And when she might speak she said: Launcelot, now I well understand that thou art a false recreant knight and a common lecher, and lovest and holdest other ladies, and by me thou hast disdain and scorn. For wit thou well, she said, now I understand thy falsehood, and therefore shall I never love thee no more. And never be thou so hardy to come in my sight; and right here I discharge thee this court, that thou never come within it; and I forfend thee my fellowship, and upon pain of thy head that thou see me no more. Right so Sir Launcelot departed with great heaviness, that unnethe [4] he might sustain himself for great dole-making. [5] Then he called Sir Bors, Sir Ector de Maris, and Sir Lionel, and told them how the queen had forfended [6] him the court, and so he was in will to depart into his own country. Fair sir, said Sir Bors de Ganis, ye shall not depart out of this land by mine advice. Ye must remember in what honour ye are renowned, and called the noblest knight of the world; and many great matters ye have in hand. And women in their hastiness will do ofttimes that sore repenteth them; and therefore by mine advice ye shall take your horse, and ride to the good hermitage here beside Windsor, that sometime was a good knight, his name is Sir Brasias, and there shall ye abide till I send you word of better tidings. Brother, said Sir Launcelot, wit ye well I am full loth to depart out of this realm, but the queen hath defended me so highly, that meseemeth she will never be my good lady as she hath been. Say ye never so, said Sir Bors, for many times or this time she hath been wroth with you, and after it she was the first that repented it. Ye say well, said Launcelot, for now will

---

[2] Or.
[3] Broke.
[4] Hardly.

[5] Grief-making.
[6] Forbidden.

I do by your counsel, and take mine horse and my harness, and ride to the hermit Sir Brasias, and there will I repose me until I hear some manner of tidings from you; but, fair brother, I pray you get me the love of my lady, Queen Guenever, an [7] ye may. Sir, said Sir Bors, ye need not to move me of such matters, for well ye wot [8] I will do what I may to please you. And then the noble knight, Sir Launcelot, departed with right heavy cheer suddenly, that none earthly creature wist of him, nor where he was become, but Sir Bors. So when Sir Launcelot was departed, the queen outward made no manner of sorrow in showing to none of his blood nor to none other. But wit ye well, inwardly, as the book saith, she took great thought, but she bare it out with a proud countenance as though she felt nothing nor danger.

[Chapters III-VII tell of a false accusation of murder made against the queen. Launcelot comes in disguise as her champion and is taken back into her good graces.]

CHAPTER VIII

How the truth was known by the maiden of the lake, and of divers other matters.

. . . . . .

Thus it passed on till Our Lady Day, Assumption. Within a fifteen days of that feast the king let cry a great jousts and a tournament that should be at that day at Camelot, that is Winchester; and the king let cry that he and the king of Scots would joust against all that would come against them. And when this cry was made, thither came many knights. So there came thither the king of Northgalis, and King Anguish of Ireland, and the King with the Hundred Knights, and Galahad, the haut [9] prince, and the king of Northumberland, and many other noble dukes and earls of divers countries. So King Arthur made him ready to depart to these jousts, and would have had the queen with him, but at that time she would not, she said, for she was sick and might not ride at that time. That me repenteth, said the king, for this seven year ye saw not such a noble fellowship together except at Whitsuntide when Galahad departed from the court. Truly, said the queen to the king, ye must hold me excused, I may not be there, and that me repenteth. And many deemed the queen would

not be there by cause of Sir Launcelot du Lake, for Sir Launcelot would not ride with the king, for he said that he was not whole of the wound the which Sir Mador had given him; wherefore the king was heavy and passing wroth. And so he departed toward Winchester with his fellowship; and so by the way the king lodged in a town called Astolat, that is now in English called Gilford, and there the king lay in the castle. So when the king was departed the queen called Sir Launcelot to her, and said thus: Sir Launcelot, ye are greatly to blame thus to hold you behind my lord; what trow ye what will your enemies and mine say and deem? nought else but, See how Sir Launcelot holdeth him ever behind the king, and so doth the queen, for that they would have their pleasure together. And thus will they say, said the queen to Sir Launcelot, have ye no doubt thereof.

CHAPTER IX

How Sir Launcelot rode to Astolat, and received a sleeve to wear upon his helm at the request of a maid.

Madam, said Sir Launcelot, I allow your wit, it is of late come syne [10] ye were wise. And therefore, madam, at this time I will be ruled by your counsel, and this night I will take my rest, and tomorrow by time I will take my way toward Winchester. But wit you well, said Sir Launcelot to the queen, that at that jousts I will be against the king, and against all his fellowship. Ye may there do as ye list, said the queen, but by my counsel ye shall not be against your king and your fellowship. For therein be full many hard knights of your blood, as ye wot well enough, it needeth not to rehearse them. Madam, said Sir Launcelot, I pray you that ye be not displeased with me, for I will take the adventure that God will send me. And so upon the morn early Sir Launcelot heard mass and brake his fast, and so took his leave of the queen and departed. And then he rode so much until he came to Astolat, that is Gilford; and there it happed him in the eventide he came to an old baron's place that hight [11] Sir Bernard of Astolat. And as Sir Launcelot entered into his lodging, King Arthur espied him as he did walk in a garden beside the castle, how he took his lodging, and knew him full well. It is well, said King Arthur unto the knights that were with him in that garden beside the castle, I

---

[7] If.
[8] Know.
[9] High.

[10] Since (it is only lately that you have been wise).
[11] Was called.

have now espied one knight that will play his play at the jousts to the which we be gone toward; I undertake he will do marvels. Who is that, we pray you tell us? said many knights that were there at that time. Ye shall not wit for me, said the king, as at this time. And so the king smiled, and went to his lodging. So when Sir Launcelot was in his lodging, and unarmed him in his chamber, the old baron and hermit came to him making his reverence, and welcomed him in the best manner; but the old knight knew not Sir Launcelot. Fair sir, said Sir Launcelot to his host, I would pray you to lend me a shield that were not openly known, for mine is well known. Sir, said his host, ye shall have your desire, for meseemeth ye be one of the likeliest knights of the world, and therefore I shall shew you friendship. Sir, wit you well I have two sons that were but late made knights, and the eldest hight Sir Tirre, and he was hurt that same day he was made knight, that he may not [20] ride, and his shield ye shall have; for that is not known I dare say but here, and in no place else. And my youngest son hight Lavaine, and if it please you, he shall ride with you unto that jousts; and he is of his age strong and wight,[12] for much my heart giveth unto you that ye should be a noble knight, therefore I pray you, tell me your name, said Sir Bernard. As for that, said Sir Launcelot, ye must hold me excused as at this time, and if God give me grace to speed well at the jousts I [30] shall come again and tell you. But I pray you, said Sir Launcelot, in any wise let me have your son, Sir Lavaine, with me, and that I may have his brother's shield. All this shall be done, said Sir Bernard. This old baron had a daughter that was called that time the fair maiden of Astolat. And ever she beheld Sir Launcelot wonderfully; and as the book saith, she cast such a love unto Sir Launcelot that she could never withdraw her love, wherefore she died, and her name was Elaine le Blank. [40] So thus as she came to and fro she was so hot in her love that she besought Sir Launcelot to wear upon him at the jousts a token of hers. Fair damosel, said Sir Launcelot, an if I grant you that, ye may say I do more for your love than ever I did for lady or damosel. Then he remembered him he would go to the jousts disguised. And by cause he had never fore that time borne no manner of token of no damosel, then he bethought him that he would bear one of her, that none of his blood [50] thereby might know him, and then he said: Fair

maiden, I will grant you to wear a token of yours upon mine helmet, and therefore what it is, shew it me. Sir, she said, it is a red sleeve of mine of scarlet, well embroidered with great pearls: and so she brought it him. So Sir Launcelot received it, and said: Never did I erst so much for no damosel. And then Sir Launcelot betook the fair maiden his shield in keeping, and prayed her to keep that until that he came again; and so that night he had merry [10] rest and great cheer, for ever the damosel Elaine was about Sir Launcelot all the while she might be suffered.

[Launcelot goes in disguise to the tournament with Elaine's brother. He performs great deeds there but is sorely wounded. He leaves the field still unrecognized except by King Arthur, and takes refuge with a hermit.]

CHAPTER XIII

How Launcelot was brought to an hermit to be healed of his wound, and of other matters.

And when the hermit beheld him, as he sat leaning upon his saddle bow ever bleeding piteously, and ever the knight-hermit thought that he should know him, but he could not bring him to knowledge by cause he was so pale for bleeding. What knight are ye, said the hermit, and where were ye born? My fair lord, said Sir Launcelot, I am a [30] stranger and a knight adventurous, that laboureth throughout many realms for to win worship. Then the hermit advised him better, and saw by a wound on his cheek that he was Sir Launcelot. Alas, said the hermit, mine own lord why layne [13] you your name from me? Forsooth I ought to know you of right, for ye are the most noblest knight of the world, and well I know you for Sir Launcelot. Sir, said he, sith [14] ye know me help me an [15] ye may, for God's sake, for I would be out of this pain at [40] once, either to death or to life. Have ye no doubt, said the hermit, ye shall live and fare right well. And so the hermit called to him two of his servants, and so he and his servants bare him into the hermitage, and lightly unarmed him, and laid him in his bed. And then anon the hermit staunched his blood, and made him to drink good wine, so that Sir Launcelot was well refreshed and knew himself; for in these days it was not the guise of hermits as is nowadays, for there were none hermits in those days but that they had been men of worship and of prowess; and those hermits held

---

12 Courageous.   14 Since.
13 Conceal.   15 If.

great household, and refreshed people that were in distress.

Now turn we unto King Arthur, and leave we Sir Launcelot in the hermitage. So when the kings were come together on both parties, and the great feast should be holden, King Arthur asked the King of Northgalis and their fellowship, where was that knight that bare the red sleeve: Bring him afore me that he may have his laud, and honour, and the prize, as it is right. Then spake Sir Galahad, the haut prince, and the King with the Hundred Knights: We suppose that knight is mischieved, and that he is never like to see you nor none of us all, and that is the greatest pity that ever we wist of any knight. Alas, said Arthur, how may this be, is he so hurt? What is his name? said King Arthur. Truly, said they all, we know not his name, nor from whence he came, nor whither he would. Alas, said the king, this be to me the worst tidings that came to me this seven year, for I would not for all the lands I welde to know and wit it were so that that noble knight were slain. Know ye him? said they all. As for that, said Arthur, whether I know him or know him not, ye shall not know for me what man he is, but Almighty Jesu send me good tidings of him. And so said they all. By my head, said Sir Gawaine, if it so be that the good knight be so sore hurt, it is great damage and pity to all this land, for he is one of the noblest knights that ever I saw in a field handle a spear or a sword; and if he may be found I shall find him, for I am sure he nys not far from this town. Bear you well, said King Arthur, an ye may find him, unless that he be in such a plight that he may not welde himself. Jesu defend,[16] said Sir Gawaine, but wit I shall what he is, an I may find him. Right so Sir Gawaine took a squire with him upon hackneys,[17] and rode all about Camelot within six or seven mile, but so he came again and could hear no word of him. Then within two days King Arthur and all the fellowship returned unto London again. And so as they rode by the way it happed Sir Gawaine at Astolat to lodge with Sir Bernard there as was Sir Launcelot lodged. And so as Sir Gawaine was in his chamber to repose him Sir Bernard, the old baron, came unto him, and his daughter Elaine, to cheer him and to ask him what tidings, and who did best at that tournament of Winchester. So God help, said Sir Gawaine, there were two knights that bare two white shields, but the one of them bare a red sleeve upon his head, and certainly he was one of the best knights that ever I saw joust in field. For I dare say, said Sir Gawaine, that one knight with the red sleeve smote down forty knights of the Table Round, and his fellow did right well and worshipfully. Now blessed be God, said the fair maiden of Astolat, that that knight sped so well, for he is the man in the world that I first loved, and truly he shall be last that ever I shall love. Now, fair maid, said Sir Gawaine, is that good knight your love? Certainly, sir, said she, wit ye well he is my love. Then know ye his name? said Sir Gawaine. Nay truly, said the damosel, I know not his name nor from whence he cometh, but to say that I love him, I promise you and God that I love him. How had ye knowledge of him first? said Sir Gawaine.

CHAPTER XIV

How Sir Gawaine was lodged with the Lord of Astolat, and there had knowledge that it was Sir Launcelot that bare the red sleeve.

Then she told him as ye have heard tofore, and how her father betook him her brother to do him service, and how her father lent him her brother's, Sir Tirre's, shield: And here with me he left his own shield. For what cause did he so? said Sir Gawaine. For this cause, said the damosel, for his shield was too well known among many noble knights. Ah, fair damosel, said Sir Gawaine, please it you let me have a sight of that shield. Sir, said she, it is in my chamber, covered with a case, and if ye will come with me ye shall see it. Not so, said Sir Bernard till his daughter, let send for it. So when the shield was come, Sir Gawaine took off the case, and when he beheld that shield he knew anon that it was Sir Launcelot's shield, and his own arms. Ah, Jesu mercy, said Sir Gawaine, now is my heart more heavier than ever it was tofore. Why? said Elaine. For I have great cause, said Sir Gawaine. Is that knight that oweth[18] this shield your love? Yea, truly, said she, my love he is, God would I were his love. So God me speed, said Sir Gawaine, fair damosel ye have right, for an he be your love ye love the most honourable knight of the world, and the man of most worship. So me thought ever, said the damosel, for never or[19] that time, for no knight that ever I saw, loved never none erst.[20] God grant, said Sir Gawaine, that

[16] Forbid.
[17] Riding horses.
[18] Owns.
[19] Before.
[20] Before.

either of you may rejoice other, but that is in a great adventure. But truly, said Sir Gawaine unto the damosel, ye may say ye have a fair grace, for why I have known that noble knight this four and twenty year, and never or that day, I nor none other knight, I dare made good, saw or heard say that ever he bare token or sign of no lady, gentlewoman, ne maiden, at no jousts nor tournament. And therefore, fair maiden, said Sir Gawaine, ye are much beholden to him to give him thanks. But 10 I dread me, said Sir Gawaine, that ye shall never see him in this world, and that is great pity that ever was of earthly knight. Alas, said she, how may this be, is he slain? I say not so, said Sir Gawaine, but wit ye well he is grievously wounded, by all manner of signs, and by men's sight more likelier to be dead than to be on live; and wit ye well he is the noble knight, Sir Launcelot, for by this shield I know him. Alas, said the fair maiden of Astolat, how may this be, and what was his 20 hurt? Truly, said Sir Gawaine, the man in the world that loved him best hurt him so; and I dare say, said Sir Gawaine, an that knight that hurt him knew the very certainty that he had hurt Sir Launcelot, it would be the most sorrow that ever came to his heart. Now, fair father, said then Elaine, I require you give me leave to ride and seek him, or else I wot well I shall go out of my mind, for I shall never stint till that I find him and my brother, Sir Lavaine. Do as it liketh 30 you, said her father, for me sore repenteth of the hurt of that noble knight. Right so they made her ready, and before Sir Gawaine, making great dole.

Then on the morn Sir Gawaine came to King Arthur, and told him how he had found Sir Launcelot's shield in the keeping of the fair maiden of Astolat. All that knew I aforehand, said King Arthur, and that caused me I would not suffer you to have ado at the great jousts, for I espied, 40 said King Arthur, when he came in till his lodging full late in the evening in Astolat. But marvel have I, said Arthur, that ever he would bear any sign of any damosel, for or now I never heard say nor knew that ever he bare any token of none earthly woman. By my head, said Sir Gawaine, the fair maiden of Astolat loveth him marvellously well; what it meaneth I cannot say, and she is ridden after to seek him. So the king and all came to London, and there Sir Gawaine openly disclosed 50 to all the court that it was Sir Launcelot that jousted best.

CHAPTER XV

Of the sorrow that Sir Bors had for the hurt of Launcelot; and of the anger that the queen had because Launcelot bare the sleeve.

And when Sir Bors heard that, wit ye well he was an heavy man, and so were all his kinsmen. But when Queen Guenever wist that Sir Launcelot bare the red sleeve of the fair maiden of Astolat she was nigh out of her mind for wrath. And then she sent for Sir Bors de Ganis in all the haste that might be. So when Sir Bors was come tofore the queen, then she said: Ah, Sir Bors, have ye heard say how falsely Sir Launcelot hath betrayed me? Alas, madam, said Sir Bors, I am afeared he hath betrayed himself and us all. No force, said the queen, though he be destroyed, for he is a false traitor knight. Madam, said Sir Bors, I pray you say ye not so, for wit you well I may not hear such language of him. Why, Sir Bors, said she, should I not call him traitor when he bare the red sleeve upon his head at Winchester, at the great jousts? Madam, said Sir Bors, that sleeve bearing repenteth me sore, but I dare say he did it to none evil intent, but for this cause he bare the red sleeve that none of his blood should know him. For or then we nor none of us all never knew that ever he bare token or sign of maid, lady, ne gentlewoman. Fie on him, said the queen, yet for all his pride and bobaunce [21] there ye proved yourself his better. Nay, madam, say ye never more so, for he beat me and my fellows, and might have slain us an he had would. Fie on him, said the queen, for I heard Sir Gawaine say before my lord Arthur that it were marvel to tell the great love that is between the fair maiden of Astolat and him. Madam, said Sir Bors, I may not warn Sir Gawaine to say what it pleased him; but I dare say, as for my lord, Sir Launcelot, that he loveth no lady, gentlewoman, nor maid, but all he loveth in like much. And therefore, madam, said Sir Bors, ye may say what ye will, but wit ye well I will haste me to seek him, and find him wheresomever he be, and God send me good tidings of him.

And so leave we them there, and speak we of Sir Launcelot that lay in great peril. So as fair Elaine came to Winchester she sought there all about, and by fortune Sir Lavaine was ridden to play him, to enchafe [22] his horse. And anon as Elaine saw him she knew him, and then she cried on loud until him. And when he heard her anon he came to her, and then she asked her brother

[21] Pomp.   [22] Warm up.

how did my lord, Sir Launcelot. Who told you, sister, that my lord's name was Sir Launcelot? Then she told him how Sir Gawaine by his shield knew him. So they rode together till that they came to the hermitage, and anon she alit. So Sir Lavaine brought her in to Sir Launcelot; and when she saw him lie so sick and pale in his bed she might not speak, but suddenly she fell to the earth down suddenly in a swoon, and there she lay a great while. And when she was relieved, she shrieked 10 and said: My lord, Sir Launcelot, alas why be ye in this plight? and then she swooned again. And then Sir Launcelot prayed Sir Lavaine to take her up: And bring her to me. And when she came to herself Sir Launcelot kissed her, and said: Fair maiden, why fare ye thus? ye put me to pain; wherefore make ye no more such cheer, for an ye be come to comfort me ye be right welcome; and of this little hurt that I have I shall be right hastily whole by the grace of God. But I marvel, said Sir 20 Launcelot, who told you my name? Then the fair maiden told him all how Sir Gawaine was lodged with her father: And there by your shield he discovered your name. Alas, said Sir Launcelot, that me repenteth that my name is known, for I am sure it will turn unto anger. And then Sir Launcelot compassed in his mind that Sir Gawaine would tell Queen Guenever how he bare the red sleeve, and for whom; that he wist well would turn into great anger. So this maiden Elaine never went 30 from Sir Launcelot, but watched him day and night, and did such attendance to him, that the French book saith there was never woman did more kindlier for man than she.

[They remain with the hermit until Launcelot's wound permits him to travel.]

CHAPTER XVIII

How Sir Bors returned and told tidings of Sir 40 Launcelot; and of the tourney, and to whom the prize was given.

And so upon a morn they took their horses and Elaine le Blank with them; and when they came to Astolat there were they well lodged, and had great cheer of Sir Bernard, the old baron, and of Sir Tirre, his son. And so upon this morn when Sir Launcelot should depart, fair Elaine brought her father with her, and Sir Lavaine, and Sir Tirre, 50 and thus she said:

CHAPTER XIX

Of the great lamentation of the fair maid of Astolat when Launcelot should depart, and how she died for his love.

My lord, Sir Launcelot, now I see ye will depart; now fair knight and courteous knight, have mercy upon me, and suffer me not to die for thy love. What would ye that I did? said Sir Launcelot. I would have you to my husband, said Elaine. Fair damosel, I thank you, said Sir Launcelot, but truly, said he, I cast [23] me never to be wedded man. Then, fair knight, said she, will ye be my paramour? Jesu defend me, said Sir Launcelot, for then I rewarded your father and your brother full evil for their great goodness. Alas, said she, then must I die for your love. Ye shall not so, said Sir Launcelot, for wit ye well, fair maiden, I might have been married an I had would, but I never applied me to be married yet; but by cause, fair damosel, that ye love me as ye say ye do, I will for your good will and kindness show you some goodness, and that is this, that wheresomever ye will beset your heart upon some good knight that will wed you, I shall give you together a thousand pound yearly to you and to your heirs; thus much will I give you, fair madam, for your kindness, and always while I live to be your own knight. Of all this, said the maiden, I will none, for but if ye will wed me, or else be my paramour at the least, wit you well, Sir Launcelot, my good days are done. Fair damosel, said Sir Launcelot, of these two things ye must pardon me. Then she shrieked shrilly, and fell down in a swoon; and then women bare her into her chamber, and there she made over much sorrow; and then Sir Launcelot would depart, and there he asked Sir Lavaine what he would do. What should I do, said Sir Lavaine, but follow you, but if ye drive me from you, or command me to go from you. Then came Sir Bernard to Sir Launcelot and said to him: I cannot see but that my daughter Elaine will die for your sake. I may not do withal, said Sir Launcelot, for that me sore repenteth, for I report me to yourself, that my proffer is fair; and me repenteth, said Sir Launcelot, that she loveth me as she doth; I was never the causer of it, for I report me to your son I early ne late proffered her bounte [24] nor fair behests; and as for me, said Sir Launcelot, I dare do all that a knight should do that she is a clene maiden for me,[25] both for deed and for will. And I am right

23 Plan.   25 As far as concerns me.
24 Reward.

heavy of her distress, for she is a full fair maiden, good and gentle, and well taught. Father, said Sir Lavaine, I dare make good she is a clene maiden as for my lord Sir Launcelot; but she doth as I do, for sithen I first saw my lord Sir Launcelot, I could never depart from him, nor nought I will an I may follow him.

Then Sir Launcelot took his leave, and so they departed, and came unto Winchester. And when Arthur wist that Sir Launcelot was come whole and sound the king made great joy of him, and so did Sir Gawaine and all the knights of the Round Table except Sir Agravaine and Sir Mordred. Also Queen Guenever was wood[26] wroth with Sir Launcelot, and would by no means speak with him but estranged herself from him; and Sir Launcelot made all the means that he might for to speak with the queen, but it would not be.

Now speak we of the fair maiden of Astolat that made such sorrow day and night that she never slept, ate, nor drank, and ever she made her complaint unto Sir Launcelot. So when she had thus endured a ten days, that she feebled so that she must needs pass out of this world, then she shrived her clene, and received her Creator. And ever she complained still upon Sir Launcelot. Then her ghostly father[27] bad her leave such thoughts. Then she said, why should I leave such thoughts? Am I not an earthly woman? And all the while the breath is in my body I may complain me, for my belief is I do none offence though I love an earthly man; and I take God to my record I loved never none but Sir Launcclot du Lake, nor never shall, and a clene maiden I am for him and for all other; and sithen it is the sufferance of God that I shall die for the love of so noble a knight, I beseech the High Father of Heaven to have mercy upon my soul, and upon mine innumerable pains that I suffered may be allegiance of part of my sins. For sweet Lord Jesu, said the fair maiden, I take Thee to record, on Thee I was never great offencer against thy laws; but that I loved this noble knight, Sir Launcelot, out of measure, and of myself, good Lord, I might not withstand the fervent love wherefore I have my death.

And then she called her father, Sir Bernard, and her brother, Sir Tirre, and heartily she prayed her father that her brother might write a letter like as she did indite it: and so her father granted her. And when the letter was written word by word like as she devised, then she prayed her father that she might be watched until she were dead. And while my body is hot let this letter be put in my right hand, and my hand bound fast with the letter until that I be cold; and let me be put in a fair bed with all the richest clothes that I have about me, and so let my bed and all my richest clothes be laid with me in a chariot unto the next place where Thames is; and there let me be put within a barget, and but one man with me, such as ye trust to steer me thither, and that my barget be covered with black samite over and over: thus, father, I beseech you let it be done. So her father granted it her faithfully, all things should be done like as she had devised. Then her father and her brother made great dole, for when this was done anon she died. And so when she was dead the corpse and the bed all was led the next way unto Thames, and there a man, and the corpse, and all, were put into Thames; and so the man steered the barget unto Westminster, and there he rowed a great while to and fro or any espied it.

CHAPTER XX

How the corpse of the maid of Astolat arrived tofore King Arthur, and of the burying, and how Sir Launcelot offered the mass-penny.

So by fortune King Arthur and the Queen Guenever were speaking together at a window, and so as they looked into Thames they espied this black barget, and had marvel what it meant. Then the king called Sir Kay, and showed it him. Sir, said Sir Kay, wit you well there is some new tidings. Go thither, said the king to Sir Kay, and take with you Sir Brandiles and Agravaine, and bring me ready word what is there. Then these four knights departed and came to the barget and went in; and there they found the fairest corpse lying in a rich bed, and a poor man sitting in the barget's end, and no word would he speak. So these four knights returned unto the king again, and told him what they found. That fair corpse will I see, said the king. And so then the king took the queen by the hand, and went thither. Then the king made the barget to be holden fast, and then the king and the queen entered with certain knights with them; and there he saw the fairest woman lie in a rich bed, covered unto her middle with many rich clothes, and all was of cloth of gold, and she lay as though she had smiled. Then the queen espied a letter in her right hand, and told it to the king. Then the king took it and said: Now am I sure this letter will tell what she was, and why she is

[26] Mad.   [27] Father confessor.

come hither. So then the king and the queen went out of the barget, and so commanded a certain man to wait upon the barget. And so when the king was come within his chamber, he called many knights about him, and said that he would wit openly what was written within that letter. Then the king brake it, and made a clerk to read it, and this was the intent of the letter. Most noble knight, Sir Launcelot, now hath death made us two at debate for your love. I was your lover, that men called the fair maiden of Astolat; therefore unto all ladies I make my moan, yet pray for my soul and bury me at least, and offer ye my mass-penny: this is my last request. And a clene maiden I died, I take God to witness: pray for my soul, Sir Launcelot, as thou art peerless. This was all the substance in the letter. And when it was read, the king, the queen, and all the knights wept for pity of the doleful complaints. Then was Sir Launcelot sent for; and when he was come King Arthur made the letter to be read to him. And when Sir Launcelot heard it word by word, he said: My lord Arthur, wit ye well I am right heavy of the death of this fair damosel: God know-eth I was never causer of her death by my willing, and that will I report me to her own brother: here he is, Sir Lavaine. I will not say nay, said Sir Launcelot, but that she was both fair and good, and much I was beholden unto her, but she loved me out of measure. Ye might have shewed her, said the queen, some bounty and gentleness that might have preserved her life. Madam, said Sir Launcelot, she would none other ways be answered but that she would be my wife, outher else my paramour; and of these two I would not grant her, but I proffered her, for her good love that she showed me, a thousand pound yearly to her, and to her heirs, and to wed any manner knight that she could find best to love in her heart. For, madam, said Sir Launcelot, I love not to be con-strained to love; for love must arise of the heart, and not by no constraint. That is truth, said the king, and many knight's love is free in himself, and never will be bounden, for where he is bounden he looseth himself. Then said the king unto Sir Launcelot: It will be your worship that ye oversee that she be interred worshipfully. Sir, said Sir Launcelot, that shall be done as I can best devise. And so many knights yede [28] thither to behold that fair maiden. And so upon the morn she was in-terred richly, and Sir Launcelot offered her mass-penny; and all the knights of the Table Round

that were there at that time offered with Sir Launcelot. And then the poor man went again with the barget. Then the queen sent for Sir Launcelot, and prayed him of mercy, for why that she had been wroth with him causeless. This is not the first time, said Sir Launcelot, that ye had been displeased with me causeless, but, madam, ever I must suffer you, but what sorrow I endure I take no force. So this passed on all that winter, with all manner of hunting and hawking, and jousts and tourneys were many betwixt many great lords, and ever in all places Sir Lavaine gat great wor-ship, so that he was nobly renowned among many knights of the Table Round. . . .

CHAPTER XXV

How true love is likened to summer.

And thus it passed on from Candlemass until after Easter, that the month of May was come, when every lusty heart beginneth to blossom, and to bring forth fruit; for like as herbs and trees bring forth fruit and flourish in May, in likewise every lusty heart that is in any manner a lover, springeth and flourisheth in lusty deeds. For it giveth unto all lovers courage, that lusty month of May, in something to constrain him to some manner of thing more in that month than in any other month, for diverse causes. For then all herbs and trees renew a man and woman, and in likewise lovers call again to their mind old gentleness and old service, and many kind deeds that were forgot-ten by negligence. For like as winter rasure [29] doth alway arase and deface green summer, so fareth it by unstable love in man and woman. For in many persons there is no stability; for we may see all day, for a little blast of winter's rasure, anon we shall deface and lay apart true love for little or nought, that cost much thing; this is no wisdom nor stability, but it is feebleness of nature and great disworship, whomsoever useth this. There-fore, like as May month flowereth and flourisheth in many gardens, so in likewise let every man of worship flourish his heart in this world, first unto God, and next unto the joy of them that he prom-ised his faith unto; for there was never worshipful man nor worshipful woman, but they loved one better than another; and worship in arms may never be foiled, but first reserve the honour to God, and secondly the quarrel must come of thy lady; and such love I call virtuous love. But now-adays men can not love seven night but they must

---

[28] Went.   [29] Cutting.

have all their desires: that love may not endure by reason; for where they be soon accorded, and hasty heat, soon it cooleth. Right so fareth love nowadays, soon hot soon cold: this is no stability. But the old love was not so; men and women could love together seven years, and no lycours[30] lusts were between them, and then was love, truth, and faithfulness: and lo, in likewise was used love in

King Arthur's days. Wherefore I liken love nowadays unto summer and winter; for like as the one is hot and the other cold, so fareth love nowadays; therefore all ye that be lovers call unto your remembrance the month of May, like as did Queen Guenever, for whom I make here a little mention, that while she lived she was a true lover, and therefore she had a good end.

ENGLISH AND SCOTTISH BALLADS

Edward

"Why dois your brand sae drap wi bluid,
      Edward, Edward?
Why dois your brand sae drap wi bluid,
  And why sae sad gang yee O?"
"O I hae killed my hauke sae guid,   5
      Mither, mither,
O I hae killed my hauke sae guid,
  And I had nae mair bot hee O."

"Your haukis bluid was nevir sae reid,
      Edward, Edward,
Your haukis bluid was never sae reid,   11
  My deir son I tell thee O."
"O I hae killed my reid-roan steid,
      Mither, mither,
O I hae killed my reid-roan steid,   15
  That erst was sae fair and frie O."

"Your steid was auld, and ye hae gat mair,
      Edward, Edward,
Your steid was auld, and ye hae gat mair;
  Sum other dule ye drie O."   20
"O I hae killed my fadir deir,
      Mither, mither,
O I hae killed my fadir deir,
  Alas, and wae is mee O!"

"And whatten penance wul ye drie for that,   25
      Edward, Edward?

And whatten penance wul ye drie, for that?
  My deir son, now tell me O."
"Ile set my feit in yonder boat,
      Mither, mither,
Ile set my feit in yonder boat,   31
  And Ile fare ovir the sea O."

"And what wul ye doe wi your towirs and your ha,
      Edward, Edward?
And what wul ye doe wi your towirs and your ha,
  That were sae fair to see O?"   36
"Ile let thame stand tul they doun fa,
      Mither, mither,
Ile let thame stand tul they doun fa,
  For here nevir mair maun I bee O."   40

"And what wul ye leive to your bairns and your wife,
      Edward, Edward?
And what wul ye leive to your bairns and your wife,
  Whan ye gang ovir the sea O?"
"The warldis room, late them beg thrae life,   45
      Mither, mither,
The warldis room, late them beg thrae life,
  For thame nevir mair wul I see O."

"And what wul ye leive to your ain mither deir,
      Edward, Edward?

---

[30] Lecherous.

Edward achieves its effect of great dramatic intensity by means of repetition and refrain. The device at the end, of bequeathing various things to father, mother, etc., is frequent in ballads. The dialect is not difficult, though the spelling may cause some confusion to the inexperienced reader. Note the following words: dois (does), brand (sword), bluid (blood), gang (go), hauke (hawk), guid (good), mair (more), bot (but), reid (red), steid (steed), auld (old), dule (grief), drie (suffer), fadir (father), flit (felt), ha (hall), maun (must), bairns (children), warldis (world's), late (let), thrae (through), ain (own).

And what wul ye leive to your ain mither deir?
    My deir son, now tell me O."   52
"The curse of hell frae me sall ye beir,
               Mither, mither,
The curse of hell frae me sall ye beir,   55
    Sic counseils ye gave to me O."

Lord Randal

"O where hae ye been, Lord Randal, my son?
O where hae ye been, my handsome young man?"
"I hae been to the wild wood; mother, make my
    bed soon,
For I'm weary wi hunting, and fain wald lie
    down."

"Where gat ye your dinner, Lord Randal, my
    son?   5
Where gat ye your dinner, my handsome young
    man?"
"I dined wi my true-love; mother, make my bed
    soon,
For I'm weary wi hunting, and fain wald lie
    down."

"What gat ye to your dinner, Lord Randal, my
    son?
What gat ye to your dinner, my handsome young
    man?"   10
"I gat eels[1] boiled in broo; mother, make my bed
    soon,
For I'm weary wi hunting, and fain wald lie
    down."

"What became of your bloodhounds, Lord Randal,
    my son?
What became of your bloodhounds, my handsome
    young man?"
"O they swelld and they died; mother, make my
    bed soon,   15
For I'm weary wi hunting, and fain wald lie
    down."

"O I fear ye are poisond, Lord Randal, my son!
O I fear ye are poisond, my handsome young
    man!"
"O yes! I am poisond; mother, make my bed soon,
For I'm sick at the heart, and I fain wald lie
    down."   20

Bonny Barbara Allan

It was in and about the Martinmas[2] time,
    When the green leaves were a falling,
That Sir John Graeme, in the West Country,
    Fell in love with Barbara Allan.

He sent his man down through the town   5
    To the place where she was dwelling:
"O haste and come to my master dear,
    Gin[3] ye be Barbara Allan."

O hooly, hooly rose she up,
    To the place where he was lying,   10
And when she drew the curtain by,
    "Young man, I think you're dying."

"O it's I'm sick, and very, very sick,
    And 'tis a' for Barbara Allan";
"O the better for me ye's never be,   15
    Tho your heart's blood were a spilling.

"O dinna ye mind, young man," said she,
    "When ye was in the tavern a drinking,
That ye made the healths gae round and round,
    And slighted Barbara Allan?"   20

He turned his face unto the wall,
    And death was with him dealing:
"Adieu, adieu, my dear friends all,
    And be kind to Barbara Allan."

And slowly, slowly raise she up,   25
    And slowly, slowly left him,
And sighing said she coud not stay,
    Since death of life had reft him.

She had not gane a mile but twa,
    When she heard the dead-bell ringing,   30
And every jow that the dead-bell geid,
    It cry'd, Woe to Barbara Allan!

"Oh mother, mother, make my bed!
    O make it saft and narrow!
Since my love died for me today,   35
    I'll die for him tomorrow."

The Twa Sisters

There was twa sisters in a bowr,
    Edinburgh, Edinburgh,[4]

---

[1] His sweetheart has served him poisonous snakes instead of eels.
[2] Feast of St. Martin, November 11.
[3] Gin (if), hooly (slowly), dinna (do not).
[4] This meaningless refrain was repeated with each stanza as it was sung. The tune is one of the best of all the ballads.

There was twa sisters in a bowr,
   Stirling for ay;
There was twa sisters in a bowr,   5
There came a knight to be their wooer.
   Bonny Saint Johnston stands upon Tay.

He courted the eldest wi glove an ring,
But he lovd the youngest above a' thing.

He courted the eldest wi brotch [1] an knife,   10
But he lovd the youngest as his life.

The eldest she was vexéd sair,
An much envied her sister fair.

Into her bowr she could not rest;
Wi grief an spite she almos brast.   15

Upon a morning fair an clear,
She cried upon her sister dear:

"O sister, come to yon sea stran,
An see our father's ships come to lan."

She's taen her by the milk-white han,   20
An led her down to yon sea stran.

The youngest stood upon a stane;
The eldest came an threw her in.

She tooke her by the middle sma,
And dashed her bonny back to the jaw.   25

"O sister, sister, tak my han,
An Ise mack you heir to a' my lan.

"O sister, sister, tak my middle,
An yes get my goud and my gouden girdle.

"O sister, sister, save my life,   30
An I swear Ise never be nae man's wife."

"Foul fa the han that I should tacke;
It twin'd me an my wardles make.

"Your cherry cheeks an yallow hair
Gars me gae maiden for evermair."   35

Sometimes she sank, an sometimes she swam,
Till she came down yon bonny mill-dam.

O out it came the miller's son,
An saw the fair maid swimmin in.

"O father, father, draw your dam;   40
Here's either a mermaid or a swan."

The miller quickly drew the dam,
An there he found a drownd woman.

You coudna see her yellow hair
For gold and pearle that were so rare.   45

You coudna see her middle sma
For gouden girdle that was sae braw.

You coudna see her fingers white,
For gouden rings that were sae gryte.

An by there came a harper fine,   50
That harpéd to the king at dine.

When he did look that lady upon,
He sighd and made a heavy moan.

He's taen three locks o her yallow hair,
And wi them strung his harp sae fair.   55

The first tune he did play and sing,
Was, "Farewell to my father the king."

The nextin tune that he playd syne,
Was, "Farewell to my mother the queen."

The lasten tune that he playd then,   60
Was, "Wae to my sister, fair Ellen."

The Wife of Usher's Well

There lived a wife [2] at Usher's Well,
   And a wealthy wife was she;
She had three stout and stalwart sons,
   And sent them oer the sea.

They hadna been a week from her,   5
   A week but barely ane,
Whan word came to the carline wife
   That her three sons were gane.

---

[1] Brotch (brooch), brast (burst), upon (unto), stane (stone), sma (small), jaw (wave), Ise mack (I shall make), yes get (you shall get), goud (gold), twined (separated), wardles (world's), make (mate), gars (makes), gouden (golden), braw (fine), gryte (great), dine (dinner), taen (taken).

[2] Wife (woman), hadna (had not), ane (one), gane (gone), fashes in the flood (storms on the sea), mirk (dark), birk (birch), syke (trench), sheugh (furrow), gin (if), sair (sore), maun bide (must endure), byre (stable).

They hadna been a week from her,
  A week but barely three,   10
Whan word came to the carline wife
  That her sons she'd never see.

"I wish the wind may never cease,
  Nor fashes in the flood,
Till my three sons come hame to me,   15
  In earthly flesh and blood."

It fell about the Martinmass,
  When nights are lang and mirk,
The carline wife's three sons came hame,
  And their hats were o the birk.   20

It neither grew in syke nor ditch,
  Nor yet in ony sheugh;
But at the gates o Paradise,
  That birk grew fair eneugh.

.   .   .   .   .

"Blow up the fire, my maidens,   25
  Bring water from the well;
For a' my house shall feast this night,
  Since my three sons are well."

And she has made to them a bed,
  She's made it large and wide,   30
And she's taen her mantle her about,
  Sat down at the bed-side.

.   .   .   .   .

Up then crew the red, red cock,
  And up and crew the gray;
The eldest to the youngest said,   35
  " 'Tis time we were away."

The cock he hadna crawd but once,
  And clappd his wings at a',
When the youngest to the eldest said,
  "Brother, we must awa.   40

"The cock doth craw, the day doth daw,
  The channerin worm doth chide;
Gin we be mist out o our place,
  A sair pain we maun bide.

"Fare ye weel, my mother dear!   45
  Fareweel to barn and byre!
And fare ye weel, the bonny lass
  That kindles my mother's fire!"

Sir Patrick Spens

The king sits in Dumferling toune,
  Drinking the blude-reid wine:

"O whar will I get guid sailor,
  To sail this schip of mine?"

Up and spak an eldern knicht,   5
  Sat at the kings richt kne:
"Sir Patrick Spens is the best sailor,
  That sails upon the se."

The king has written a braid letter,
  And signd it wi his hand,   10
And sent it to Sir Patrick Spens,
  Was walking on the sand.

The first line that Sir Patrick red,
  A loud lauch lauched he;
The next line that Sir Patrick red,   15
  The teir blinded his ee.

"O wha is this has don this deid,
  This ill deid don to me,
To send me out this time o' the yeir,
  To sail upon the se!   20

"Mak hast, mak haste, my mirry men all,
  Our guid schip sails the morne."
"O say na sae, my master deir,
  For I feir a deadlie storme.

"Late, late yestreen I saw the new moone, 25
  Wi the auld moone in hir arme,
And I feir, I feir, my deir master,
  That we will cum to harme."

O our Scots nobles wer richt laith
  To weet their cork-heild schoone;   30
Bot lang owre a' the play wer playd,
  Thair hats they swam aboone.

O lang, lang may their ladies sit,
  Wi thair fans into their hand,
Or eir they se Sir Patrick Spens   35
  Cum sailing to the land.

O lang, lang may the ladies stand,
  Wi thair gold kems in their hair,
Waiting for thair ain deir lords,
  For they'll se thame na mair.   40

Haf owre, haf owre to Aberdour,
  It's fiftie fadom deip,
And thair lies guid Sir Patrick Spens,
  Wi the Scots lords at his feit.

The Three Ravens

1. There were three ravens sat on a tree,
   Downe a downe, hay down, hay downe,
There were three ravens sat on a tree,
   With a downe,
There were three ravens sat on a tree, 5
They were as blacke as they might be.
   With a downe derrie, derrie, derrie, downe,
   downe.

2 The one of them said to his mate,
   "Where shall we our breakefast take?"

3. "Downe in yonder greene field, 10
   There lies a knight slain under his shield.

4. "His hounds they lie downe at his feete,
   So well they can their master keepe.

5. "His haukes they flie so eagerly,
   There's no fowle dare him come nie." 15

6. Downe there comes a fallow doe,
   As great with yong as she might goe.

7. She lift up his bloudy hed,
   And kist his wounds that were so red.

8. She got him up upon her backe, 20
   And carried him to earthen lake.

9. She buried him before the prime,
   She was dead herselfe ere even-song time.

10. God send every gentleman,
    Such haukes, such hounds, and such a leman.[1]

Mary Hamilton

Word's gane[2] to the kitchen,
   And word's gane to the ha,
That Marie Hamilton gangs wi bairn
   To the hichest Stewart of a'.

He's courted her in the kitchen, 5
   He's courted her in the ha,
He's courted her in the laigh cellar,
   And that was warst of a'.

She's tyed it in her apron
   And she's thrown it in the sea; 10
Says, Sink ye, swim ye, bonny wee babe!
   You'l neer get mair o me.

Down then cam the auld queen,
   Goud tassels tying her hair:
"O Marie, where's the bonny wee babe 15
   That I heard greet sae sair?"

"There was never a babe intill my room,
   As little designs to be;
It was but a touch o my sair side,
   Come oer my fair bodie." 20

"O Marie, put on your robes o black,
   Or else your robes o brown,
For ye maun gang wi me the night,
   To see fair Edinbro town."

"I winna put on my robes o black, 25
   Nor yet my robes o brown;
But I'll put on my robes o white,
   To shine through Edinbro town."

When she gaed up the Cannogate,
   She laughd loud laughters three; 30
But when she cam down the Cannogate
   The tear blinded her ee.

When she gaed up the Parliament stair,
   The heel cam aff her shee;
And lang or she cam down again 35
   She was condemned to dee.

When she cam down the Cannogate,
   The Cannogate sae free,
Many a ladie lookd oer her window,
   Weeping for this ladie. 40

"Ye need nae weep for me," she says,
   "Ye need nae weep for me;
For had I not slain mine own sweet babe,
   This death I wadna dee.

"Bring me a bottle of wine," she says, 45
   "The best that eer ye hae,
That I may drink to my weil-wishers,
   And they may drink to me.

[1] Leman (sweetheart).
[2] Gane (gone), gangs wi bairn (is with child), hichest (highest), laigh (low), warst (worst), greet (cry), maun gang wi me the night (must go with me tonight), gaed (went), shee (shoe).

"Here's a health to the jolly sailors,
    That sail upon the main;   50
Let them never let on to my father and mother
    But what I'm coming hame.

"Here's a health to the jolly sailors,
    That sail upon the sea;
Let them never let on to my father and mother
    That I cam here to dee.   56

"Oh little did my mother think,
    The day she cradled me,
What lands I was to travel through,
    What death I was to dee.   60

"Oh little did my father think,
    The day he held up me,
What lands I was to travel through,
    What death I was to dee.

"Last night I washd the queen's feet,   65
    And gently laid her down;
And a' the thanks I've gotten the nicht
    To be hangd in Edinbro town!

"Last nicht there was four Maries,
    The nicht there'l be but three;   70
There was Marie Seton, and Marie Beton,
    And Marie Carmichael, and me."

CHAUCER

Geoffrey Chaucer was born about 1340 in London and died in 1400. His sixty years were nearly all spent in the city, usually in some sort of connection with the royal court. He was a court page; he fought in the war in France, where he was captured and ransomed; later, in his twenties, he was associated with the king's sons, the Dukes of Clarence and Lancaster; in his thirties he went twice on official visits to Italy; and for the rest of his life he underwent the shifting fortunes of political office. He somehow escaped three epidemics of the Black Death, which carried off so many of his contemporaries. When we consider how much he was doing in the practical world we wonder that he should have found time to write.

And yet his literary production from his late twenties until his last years was large and constant. He began writing poems that are primarily based on French models of his day, filled with allegories and dreams. But not all the work of this period of French influence is merely imitative. He soon showed his mastery of the newly-evolved English language and his knowledge of human life. In his late thirties and early forties he was greatly affected by his two Italian journeys, and we observe a growing power. Indeed, it is during this period that he wrote what many consider his best work, *Troilus and Creseyde*. Here he shows not only great dramatic ability and understanding of emotions but extraordinary technical skill in handling a difficult stanza form. The English language has come into the hands of the first man who could make use of its range and beauty.

The last fifteen to twenty years of his life were devoted to work on *The Canterbury Tales*. These were written from time to time, and some of them never finished. Eventually they were brought together in a framework which is explained in the Prologue. This task permitted Chaucer to use all his talents, for the tales are of the greatest variety. From the portrait painting of the Prologue and its incidental humor and satire, he could move to the pure romance of the Knight's tale, the piety of the tale of Saint Cecelia, or the ribald humor of the Miller or the Reeve. Perhaps the best single tale, considered as a short story, is the Pardoner's account of the three treasure-finders who kill each other, but for most readers the favorite is the Nun's Priest's Tale of the Cock and the Fox. The student who is for the first time reading Chaucer can make no mistake in choosing this tale and the Prologue. This experience may well lead him to a further acquaintance with the old poet who was so full of the joy of living and the wisdom of life.

GEOFFREY CHAUCER
The Canterbury Tales

THE PROLOGUE

*Here begins the Book
of the Tales of Canterbury*

When April with his showers sweet with fruit
The drought of March has pierced unto the root
And bathed each vein with liquor that has power
To generate therein and sire the flower;
When Zephyr also has, with his sweet breath, 5
Quickened again, in every holt and heath,
The tender shoots and buds, and the young sun
Into the Ram one half his course has run,
And many little birds make melody
That sleep through all the night with open eye 10
(So Nature pricks them on to ramp and rage)—
Then do folk long to go on pilgrimage,
And palmers to go seeking out strange strands,
To distant shrines well known in sundry lands.
And specially from every shire's end 15
Of England they to Canterbury wend,
The holy blessed martyr [1] there to seek
Who helped them when they lay so ill and weak.
  Befell that, in that season, on a day
In Southwark, at the Tabard,[2] as I lay 20
Ready to start upon my pilgrimage
To Canterbury, full of devout homage,
There came at nightfall to that hostelry
Some nine and twenty in a company
Of sundry persons who had chanced to fall 25
In fellowship, and pilgrims were they all
That toward Canterbury town would ride.
The rooms and stables spacious were and wide,
And well we there were eased, and of the best.
And briefly, when the sun had gone to rest, 30
So had I spoken with them, every one,
That I was of their fellowship anon,
And made agreement that we'd early rise
To take the road, as you I will apprise.
  But none the less, whilst I have time and space,
Before yet farther in this tale I pace, 36

It seems to me accordant with reason
To inform you of the state of every one
Of all of these, as it appeared to me,
And who they were, and what was their degree,
And even how arrayed there at the inn; 41
And with a knight thus will I first begin.

THE KNIGHT

A knight there was, and he a worthy man,
Who, from the moment that he first began
To ride about the world, loved chivalry, 45
Truth, honor, freedom and all courtesy.
Full worthy was he in his liege-lord's war,
And therein had he ridden (none more far)
As well in Christendom as heathenesse,
And honored everywhere for worthiness. 50
  At Alexandria, he, when it was won;
Full oft the table's roster he'd begun
Above all nations' knights in Prussia.
In Latvia raided he, and Russia,
No christened man so oft of his degree. 55
In far Granada at the siege was he
Of Algeciras, and in Belmarie.
At Ayas was he and at Satalye
When they were won; and on the Middle Sea
At many a noble meeting chanced to be. 60
Of mortal battles he had fought fifteen,
And he'd fought for our faith at Tramissene
Three times in lists, and each time slain his foe.
This self-same worthy knight had been also
At one time with the lord of Palatye 65
Against another heathen in Turkey:
And always won he sovereign fame for prize.
Though so illustrious, he was very wise
And bore himself as meekly as a maid.
He never yet had any vileness said, 70
In all his life, to whatsoever wight.
He was a truly perfect, gentle knight.
But now, to tell you all of his array,
His steeds were good, but yet he was not gay.

The *Prologue* and *Nun's Priest's Tale* are translated by J. U. Nicolson. Reprinted by permission of Covici, Friede, Inc. Geoffrey Chaucer (c. 1340-1400) was born in London. He spent most of his life in public service. He lived for a period in Italy.

[1] Saint Thomas à Becket, who had been murdered in a dispute with the English King. His shrine was visited by sick people in order to be cured.

[2] An inn in Southwark, just across the river from central London.

Of simple fustian wore he a jupon   75
Sadly discolored by his habergeon;
For he had lately come from his voyage
And now was going on this pilgrimage.

THE SQUIRE

With him there was his son, a youthful squire,
A lover and a lusty bachelor,   80
With locks well curled, as if they'd laid in press.
Some twenty years of age he was, I guess.
In stature he was of an average length,
Wondrously active, aye, and great of strength.
He'd ridden sometime with the cavalry   85
In Flanders, in Artois, and Picardy,
And borne him well within that little space
In hope to win thereby his lady's grace.
Prinked out he was, as if he were a mead,
All full of fresh-cut flowers white and red.   90
Singing he was, or fluting, all the day;
He was as fresh as is the month of May.
Short was his gown, with sleeves both long and
    wide.
Well could he sit on horse, and fairly ride.
He could make songs and words thereto indite,
Joust, and dance too, as well as sketch and write.
So hot he loved that, while night told her tale, 97
He slept no more than does a nightingale.
Courteous he, and humble, willing and able,
And carved before his father at the table.   100

THE YEOMAN

A yeoman had he, nor more servants, no,
At that time, for he chose to travel so;
And he was clad in coat and hood of green.
A sheaf of peacock arrows bright and keen
Under his belt he bore right carefully   105
(Well could he keep his tackle yeomanly:
His arrows had no draggled feathers low),
And in his hand he bore a mighty bow.
A cropped head had he and a sun-browned face.
Of woodcraft knew he all the useful ways.   110
Upon his arm he bore a bracer gay,
And at one side a sword and buckler, yea,
And at the other side a dagger bright,
Well sheathed and sharp as spear point in the
    light;
On breast a Christopher of silver sheen.   115
He bore a horn in baldric all of green;
A forester he truly was, I guess.

THE PRIORESS

There was also a nun, a prioress,
Who, in her smiling, modest was and coy;
Her greatest oath was but "By Saint Eloy!"   120

And she was known as Madam Eglantine.
Full well she sang the services divine,
Intoning through her nose, becomingly;
And fair she spoke her French, and fluently,
After the school of Stratford-at-the-Bow,   125
For French of Paris was not hers to know.
At table she had been well taught withal,
And never from her lips let morsels fall,
Nor dipped her fingers deep in sauce, but ate
With so much care the food upon her plate   130
That never driblet fell upon her breast.
In courtesy she had delight and zest.
Her upper lip was always wiped so clean
That in her cup was no iota seen
Of grease, when she had drunk her draught of
    wine.   135
Becomingly she reached for meat to dine.
And certainly delighting in good sport,
She was right pleasant, amiable—in short.
She was at pains to counterfeit the look
Of courtliness, and stately manners took,   140
And would be held worthy of reverence.
    But, to say something of her moral sense,
She was so charitable and piteous
That she would weep if she but saw a mouse
Caught in a trap, though it were dead or bled.
She had some little dogs, too, that she fed   146
On roasted flesh, or milk and fine white bread.
But sore she'd weep if one of them were dead,
Or if men smote it with a rod to smart:
For pity ruled her, and her tender heart.   150
Right decorous her pleated wimple was;
Her nose was fine; her eyes were blue as glass;
Her mouth was small and therewith soft and red;
But certainly she had a fair forehead;
It was almost a full span broad, I own,   155
For, truth to tell, she was not undergrown.
Neat was her cloak, as I was well aware.
Of coral small about her arm she'd bear
A string of beads and gauded all with green;
And therefrom hung a brooch of golden sheen
Whereon there was first written a crowned "A,"
And under, *Amor vincit omnia.*   162

THE NUN

Another little nun with her had she,

THE THREE PRIESTS

Who was her chaplain; and of priests she'd three.

THE MONK

A monk there was, one made for mastery,   163
An outrider, who loved his venery;

A manly man, to be an abbot able.
Full many a blooded horse had he in stable:
And when he rode men might his bridle hear
A-jingling in the whistling wind as clear,   170
Aye, and as loud as does the chapel bell
Where this brave monk was master of the cell.
The rule of Maurus or Saint Benedict,
By reason it was old and somewhat strict,   174
This said monk let such old things slowly pace
And followed new-world manners in their place.
He cared not for that text a clean-plucked hen
Which holds that hunters are not holy men;
Nor that a monk, when he is cloisterless,
Is like unto a fish that's waterless;   180
That is to say, a monk out of his cloister.
But this same text he held not worth an oyster;
And I said his opinion was right good.
What? Should he study as a madman would
Upon a book in cloister cell? Or yet   185
Go labor with his hands and swink and sweat,
As Austin bids? How shall the world be served?
Let Austin have his toil to him reserved.
Therefore he was a rider day and night;
Greyhounds he had, as swift as bird in flight.   190
Since riding and the hunting of the hare
Were all his love, for no cost would he spare.
I saw his sleeves were purfled at the hand
With fur of gray, the finest in the land;
Also, to fasten hood beneath his chin,   195
He had of good wrought gold a curious pin:
A love-knot in the larger end there was.
His head was bald and shone like any glass,
And smooth as one anointed was his face.
Fat was this lord, he stood in goodly case.   200
His bulging eyes he rolled about, and hot
They gleamed and red, like fire beneath a pot;
His boots were soft; his horse of great estate.
Now certainly he was a fine prelate:
He was not pale as some poor wasted ghost.   205
A fat swan loved he best of any roast.
His palfrey was as brown as is a berry.

THE FRIAR

A friar there was, a wanton and a merry,
A limiter, a very festive man.
In all the Orders Four is none that can   210
Equal his gossip and his fair language.
He had arranged full many a marriage
Of women young, and this at his own cost.
Unto his order he was a noble post.
Well liked by all and intimate was he   215
With franklins everywhere in his country,

And with the worthy women of the town:
For at confessing he'd more power in gown
(As he himself said) than a good curate,
For of his order he was licentiate.   220
He heard confession gently, it was said,
Gently absolved too, leaving naught of dread.
He was an easy man to give penance
When knowing he should gain a good pittance;
For to a begging friar, money given   225
Is sign that any man has been well shriven.
For if one gave (he dared to boast of this),
He took the man's repentance not amiss.
For many a man there is so hard of heart
He cannot weep however pains may smart.   230
Therefore, instead of weeping and of prayer,
Men should give silver to poor friars all bare.
His tippet was stuck always full of knives
And pins, to give to young and pleasing wives.
And certainly he kept a merry note: 235
Well could he sing and play upon the rote.
At balladry he bore the prize away.
His throat was white as lily of the May;
Yet strong he was as ever champion.
In towns he knew the taverns, every one,   240
And every good host and each barmaid too—
Better than begging lepers, these he knew.
For unto no such solid man as he
Accorded it, as far as he could see,
To have sick lepers for acquaintances.   245
There is no honest advantageousness
In dealing with such poverty-stricken curs;
It's with the rich and with big victualers.
And so, wherever profit might arise
Courteous he was and humble in men's eyes.   250
There was no other man so virtuous.
He was the finest beggar of his house;
A certain district being farmed to him,
None of his brethren dared approach its rim;
For though a widow had no shoes to show,   255
So pleasant was his *In principio,*
He always got a farthing ere he went.
He lived by pickings, it is evident.
And he could romp as well as any whelp.
On love days could he be of mickle help.   260
For there he was not like a cloisterer,
With threadbare cope as is the poor scholar,
But he was like a lord or like a pope.
Of double worsted was his semi-cope,
That rounded like a bell, as you may guess.   265
He lisped a little, out of wantonness,
To make his English soft upon his tongue;
And in his harping, after he had sung,

His two eyes twinkled in his head as bright
As do the stars within the frosty night.   270
This worthy limiter was named Hubert.

THE MERCHANT

There was a merchant with forked beard, and girt
In motley gown, and high on horse he sat,
Upon his head a Flemish beaver hat;
His boots were fastened rather elegantly.   275
He spoke his notions out right pompously,
Stressing the times when he had won, not lost.
He would the sea were held at any cost
Across from Middleburgh to Orwell town.
At money-changing he could make a crown.   280
This worthy man kept all his wits well set;
There was no one could say he was in debt,
So well he governed all his trade affairs
With bargains and with borrowings and with
    shares.
Indeed, he was a worthy man withal,   285
But, sooth to say, his name I can't recall.

THE CLERK

A clerk from Oxford was with us also,
Who'd turned to getting knowledge, long ago.
As meager was his horse as is a rake,
Nor he himself too fat, I'll undertake,   290
But he looked hollow and went soberly.
Right threadbare was his overcoat; for he
Had got him yet no churchly benefice,
Nor was so worldly as to gain office.
For he would rather have at his bed's head   295
Some twenty books, all bound in black and red,
Of Aristotle and his philosophy
Than rich robes, fiddle, or gay psaltery.
Yet, and for all he was philosopher,
He had but little gold within his coffer;   300
But all that he might borrow from a friend
On books and learning he would swiftly spend,
And then he'd pray right busily for the souls
Of those who gave him wherewithal for schools.
Of study took he utmost care and heed.   305
Not one word spoke he more than was his need;
And that was said in fullest reverence
And short and quick and full of high good sense.
Pregnant of moral virtue was his speech;
And gladly would he learn and gladly teach.   310

THE LAWYER

A sergeant of the law, wary and wise,
Who'd often gone to Paul's walk to advise,
There was also, compact of excellence.
Discreet he was, and of great reverence;

At least he seemed so, his words were so wise.
Often he sat as justice in assize,   316
By patent or commission from the crown;
Because of learning and his high renown,
He took large fees and many robes could own.
So great a purchaser was never known.   320
All was fee simple to him, in effect,
Wherefore his claims could never be suspect.
Nowhere a man so busy of his class,
And yet he seemed much busier than he was.
All cases and all judgments could he cite   325
That from King William's time were apposite.
And he could draw a contract so explicit
Not any man could fault therefrom elicit;
And every statute he'd verbatim quote.
He rode but badly in a medley coat,   330
Belted in a silken sash, with little bars,
But of his dress no more particulars.

THE FRANKLIN

There was a franklin in his company;
White was his beard as is the white daisy.
Of sanguine temperament by every sign,   335
He loved right well his morning sop in wine.
Delightful living was the goal he'd won,
For he was Epicurus' very son,
That held opinion that a full delight
Was true felicity, perfect and right.   340
A householder, and that a great, was he;
Saint Julian he was in his own country.
His bread and ale were always right well done;
A man with better cellars there was none.
Baked meat was never wanting in his house,   345
Of fish and flesh, and that so plenteous
It seemed to snow therein both food and drink
Of every dainty that a man could think.
According to the season of the year
He changed his diet and his means of cheer.   350
Full many a fattened partridge did he mew,
And many a bream and pike in fish-pond too.
Woe to his cook, except the sauces were
Poignant and sharp, and ready all his gear.
His table, waiting in his hall alway,   355
Stood ready covered through the livelong day.
At county sessions was he lord and sire,
And often acted as a knight of shire.
A dagger and a trinket-bag of silk
Hung from his girdle, white as morning milk.
He had been sheriff and been auditor;   361
And nowhere was a worthier vavasor.

THE HABERDASHER AND THE CARPENTER

A haberdasher and a carpenter,

THE WEAVER, THE DYER,
AND THE ARRAS-MAKER

An arras-maker, dyer, and weaver
Were with us, clothed in similar livery,   365
All of one sober, great fraternity.
Their gear was new and well adorned it was;
Their weapons were not cheaply trimmed with
    brass,
But all with silver; chastely made and well
Their girdles and their pouches too, I tell.   370
Each man of them appeared a proper burgess
To sit in guildhall on a high dais.
And each of them, for wisdom he could span,
Was fitted to have been an alderman;
For chattels they'd enough, and, too, of rent;   375
To which their goodwives gave a free assent,
Or else for certain they had been to blame.
It's good to hear "Madam" before one's name,
And go to church when all the world may see,
Having one's mantle borne right royally.   380

THE COOK

A cook they had with them, just for the nonce,
To boil the chickens with the marrow-bones,
And flavor tartly and with galingale.
Well could he tell a draught of London ale.
And he could roast and seethe and broil and fry,
And make a good thick soup, and bake a pie.   386
But very ill it was, it seemed to me,
That on his shin a deadly sore had he;
For sweet blanc-mange, he made it with the best.

THE SAILOR

There was a sailor, living far out west;   390
For aught I know, he was of Dartmouth town.
He sadly rode a hackney, in a gown,
Of thick rough cloth falling to the knee.
A dagger hanging on a cord had he
About his neck, and under arm, and down.   395
The summer's heat had burned his visage brown;
And certainly he was a good fellow.
Full many a draught of wine he'd drawn, I trow,
Of Bordeaux vintage, while the trader slept.
Nice conscience was a thing he never kept.   400
If that he fought and got the upper hand,
By water he sent them home to every land.
But as for craft, to reckon well his tides,
His currents and the dangerous watersides,
His harbors, and his moon, his pilotage,   405
There was none such from Hull to far Carthage.
Hardy, and wise in all things undertaken,
By many a tempest had his beard been shaken.

He knew well all the havens, as they were,
From Gottland to the Cape of Finisterre,   410
And every creek in Brittany and Spain;
His vessel had been christened *Madeleine*.

THE PHYSICIAN

With us there was a doctor of physic;
In all this world was none like him to pick
For talk of medicine and surgery;   415
For he was grounded in astronomy.
He often kept a patient from the pall
By horoscopes and magic natural.
Well could he tell the fortune ascendent
Within the houses for his sick patient.   420
He knew the cause of every malady,
Were it of hot or cold, of moist or dry,
And where engendered, and of what humor;
He was a very good practitioner.
The cause being known, down to the deepest root,
Anon he gave to the sick man his boot.   426
Ready he was, with his apothecaries,
To send him drugs and all electuaries;
By mutual aid much gold they'd always won—
Their friendship was a thing not new begun.   430
Well read was he in Esculapius,
And Deiscorides, and in Rufus,
Hippocrates, and Hali, and Galen,
Serapion, Rhazes, and Avicen,
Averrhoes, Gilbert, and Constantine,   435
Bernard, and Gatisden, and John Damascene.
In diet he was measured as could be,
Including naught of superfluity,
But nourishing and easy. It's no libel
To say he read but little in the Bible.   440
In blue and scarlet he went clad, withal,
Lined with a taffeta and with sendal;
And yet he was right chary of expense;
He kept the gold he gained from pestilence.
For gold in physic is a fine cordial,   445
And therefore loved he gold exceeding all.

THE WIFE OF BATH

There was a housewife come from Bath, or near,
Who—sad to say—was deaf in either ear.
At making cloth she had so great a bent
She bettered those of Ypres and even of Ghent.
In all the parish there was no goodwife   451
Should offering make before her, on my life;
And if one did, indeed, so wroth was she
It put her out of all her charity.   454
Her kerchiefs were of finest weave and ground;
I dare swear that they weighed a full ten pound

Which, of a Sunday, she wore on her head.
Her hose were of the choicest scarlet red,
Close gartered, and her shoes were soft and new.
Bold was her face, and fair, and red of hue.   460
She'd been respectable throughout her life,
With five churched husbands bringing joy and
      strife,
Not counting other company in youth;
But thereof there's no need to speak, in truth.
Three times she'd journeyed to Jerusalem;   465
And many a foreign stream she'd had to stem;
At Rome she'd been, and she'd been in Boulogne,
In Spain at Santiago, and at Cologne.
She could tell much of wandering by the way:
Gap-toothed was she, it is no lie to say.   470
Upon an ambler easily she sat,
Well wimpled, aye, and over all a hat
As broad as is a buckler or a targe;
A rug was tucked around her buttocks large,
And on her feet a pair of sharpened spurs.   475
In company well could she laugh her slurs.
The remedies of love she knew, perchance,
For of that art she'd learned the old, old dance.

THE PARSON

There was a good man of religion, too,
A country parson, poor, I warrant you;   480
But rich he was in holy thought and work.
He was a learned man also, a clerk,
Who Christ's own gospel truly sought to preach;
Devoutly his parishioners would he teach.
Benign he was and wondrous diligent,   485
Patient in adverse times and well content,
As he was ofttimes proven; always blithe,
He was right loath to curse to get a tithe,
But rather would he give, in case of doubt,
Unto those poor parishioners about,   490
Part of his income, even of his goods.
Enough with little, colored all his moods.
Wide was his parish, houses far asunder,
But never did he fail, for rain or thunder,
In sickness, or in sin, or any state,   495
To visit to the farthest, small and great,
Going afoot, and in his hand a stave.
This fine example to his flock he gave,
That first he wrought and afterwards he taught;
Out of the gospel then that text he caught,   500
And this figure he added thereunto—
That, if gold rust, what shall poor iron do?
For if the priest be foul, in whom we trust,
What wonder if a layman yield to lust?
And shame it is, if priest take thought for keep,
A shitty shepherd, shepherding clean sheep.   506

Well ought a priest example good to give,
By his own cleanness, how his flock should live.
He never let his benefice for hire,
Leaving his flock to flounder in the mire,   510
And ran to London, up to old Saint Paul's
To get himself a chantry there for souls,
Nor in some brotherhood did he withhold;
But dwelt at home and kept so well the fold
That never wolf could make his plans miscarry;
He was a shepherd and not mercenary.   516
And holy though he was, and virtuous,
To sinners he was not impiteous,
Nor haughty in his speech, nor too divine,
But in all teaching prudent and benign.   520
To lead folk into Heaven but by stress
Of good example was his busyness.
But if some sinful one proved obstinate,
Be who it might, of high or low estate,
Him he reproved, and sharply, as I know.   525
There is nowhere a better priest, I trow.
He had no thirst for pomp or reverence,
Nor made himself a special, spiced conscience,
But Christ's own lore, and His apostles' twelve
He taught, but first he followed it himself.   530

THE PLOWMAN

With him there was a plowman, was his brother,
That many a load of dung, and many another
Had scattered, for a good true toiler, he,
Living in peace and perfect charity.   534
He loved God most, and that with his whole heart,
At all times, though he played or plied his art,
And next, his neighbor, even as himself.
He'd thresh and dig, with never thought of pelf,
For Christ's own sake, for every poor wight,
All without pay, if it lay in his might.   540
He paid his taxes, fully, fairly, well,
Both by his own toil and by stuff he'd sell.
In a tabard he rode upon a mare.
      There were also a reeve and miller there;
A summoner, manciple and pardoner,   545
And these, beside myself, made all there were.

THE MILLER

The miller was a stout churl, be it known,
Hardy and big of brawn and big of bone;
Which was well proved, for when he went on lam
At wrestling, never failed he of the ram.   550
He was a chunky fellow, broad of build;
He'd heave a door from hinges if he willed,
Or break it through, by running, with his head.
His beard, as any sow or fox, was red,

And broad it was as if it were a spade. 555
Upon the coping of his nose he had
A wart, and thereon stood a tuft of hairs,
Red as the bristles in an old sow's ears;
His nostrils they were black and very wide.
A sword and buckler bore he by his side. 560
His mouth was like a furnace door for size.
He was a jester and could poetize,
But mostly all of sin and ribaldries.
He could steal corn and full thrice charge his fees;
And yet he had a thumb of gold, begad. 565
A white coat and blue hood he wore, this lad.
A bagpipe he could blow well, be it known,
And with that same he brought us out of town.

THE MANCIPLE

There was a manciple from an inn of court,
To whom all buyers might quite well resort 570
To learn the art of buying food and drink;
For whether he paid cash or not, I think
That he so knew the markets, when to buy,
He never found himself left high and dry.
Now is it not of God a full fair grace 575
That such a vulgar man has wit to pace
The wisdom of a crowd of learned men?
Of masters had he more than three times ten,
Who were in law expert and curious;
Whereof there were a dozen in that house 580
Fit to be stewards of both rent and land
Of any lord in England who would stand
Upon his own and live in manner good,
In honor, debtless (save his head were wood),
Or live as frugally as he might desire; 585
These men were able to have helped a shire
In any case that ever might befall;
And yet this manciple outguessed them all.

THE REEVE

The reeve he was a slender, choleric man,
Who shaved his beard as close as razor can. 590
His hair was cut round even with his ears;
His top was tonsured like a pulpiteer's.
Long were his legs, and they were very lean,
And like a staff, with no calf to be seen.
Well could he manage granary and bin; 595
No auditor could ever on him win.
He could foretell, by drought and by the rain,
The yielding of his seed and of his grain.
His lord's sheep and his oxen and his dairy,
His swine and horses, all his stores, his poultry,
Were wholly in this steward's managing; 601
And, by agreement, he'd made reckoning

Since his young lord of age was twenty years;
Yet no man ever found him in arrears.
There was no agent, hind, or herd who'd cheat
But he knew well his cunning and deceit; 606
They were afraid of him as of the death.
His cottage was a good one, on a heath;
By green trees shaded was this dwelling-place.
Much better than his lord could he purchase. 610
Right rich he was in his own private right,
Seeing he'd pleased his lord, by day or night,
By giving him, or lending, of his goods,
And so got thanked—but yet got coats and hoods.
In youth he'd learned a good trade, and had been
A carpenter, as fine as could be seen. 616
This steward sat a horse that well could trot,
And was all dapple-gray, and was named Scot.
A long surcoat of blue did he parade,
And at his side he bore a rusty blade. 620
Of Norfolk was this reeve of whom I tell,
From near a town that men call Badeswell.
Bundled he was like friar from chin to croup,
And ever he rode hindmost of our troop.

THE SUMMONER

A summoner was with us in that place, 625
Who had a fiery-red, cherubic face,
For eczema he had; his eyes were narrow.
As hot he was, and lecherous, as a sparrow;
With black and scabby brows and scanty beard;
He had a face that little children feared. 630
There was no mercury, sulphur, or litharge,
No borax, ceruse, tartar, could discharge,
Nor ointment that could cleanse enough, or bite,
To free him of his boils and pimples white,
Nor of the bosses resting on his cheeks. 635
Well loved he garlic, onions, aye and leeks,
And drinking of strong wine as red as blood.
Then would he talk and shout as madman would.
And when a deal of wine he'd poured within,
Then would he utter no word save Latin. 640
Some phrases had he learned, say two or three,
Which he had garnered out of some decree;
No wonder, for he'd heard it all the day;
And all you know right well that even a jay
Can call out "Wat" as well as can the pope. 645
But when, for aught else, into him you'd grope,
'Twas found he'd spent his whole philosophy;
Just *"Questio quid juris"* would he cry.
He was a noble rascal, and a kind;
A better comrade 'twould be hard to find. 650
Why, he would suffer, for a quart of wine,
Some good fellow to have his concubine

A twelve-month, and excuse him to the full.
(Between ourselves, though, he could pluck a
     gull).
And if he chanced upon a good fellow,   655
He would instruct him never to have awe,
In such a case, of the archdeacon's curse,
Except a man's soul lie within his purse;
For in his purse the man should punished be.
"The purse is the archdeacon's Hell," said he.   660
But well I know he lied in what he said;
A curse ought every guilty man to dread
(For curse can kill, as absolution save),
And 'ware *significavit* to the grave.
In his own power had he, and at ease,   665
The boys and girls of all the diocese,
And knew their secrets, and by counsel led.
A garland had he set upon his head,
Large as a tavern's wine-bush on a stake;
A buckler had he made of bread they bake.   670

THE PARDONER

With him there rode a gentle pardoner
Of Rouncival, his friend and his compeer;
Straight from the court of Rome had journeyed he.
Loudly he sang "Come hither, love, to me,"
The summoner joining with a burden round;   675
Was never horn of half so great a sound.
This pardoner had hair as yellow as wax,
But lank it hung as does a strike of flax;
In wisps hung down such locks as he'd on head,
And with them he his shoulders overspread;   680
But thin they dropped, and stringy, one by one.
But as to hood, for sport of it, he'd none,
Though it was packed in wallet all the while.
It seemed to him he went in latest style,
Disheveled, save for cap, his head all bare.   685
As shiny eyes he had as has a hare.
He had a fine veronica sewed to cap.
His wallet lay before him in his lap,
Stuffed full of pardons brought from Rome all hot.
A voice he had that bleated like a goat.   690
No beard had he, nor ever should he have,
For smooth his face as he'd just had a shave;
I think he was a gelding or a mare.
But in his craft, from Berwick unto Ware,
Was no such pardoner in any place.   695
For in his bag he had a pillowcase
The which, he said, was Our True Lady's veil:
He said he had a piece of the very sail
That good Saint Peter had, what time he went
Upon the sea, till Jesus changed his bent.   700
He had a latten cross set full of stones,
And in a bottle had he some pig's bones.

But with these relics, when he came upon
Some simple parson, then this paragon
In that one day more money stood to gain   705
Than the poor dupe in two months could attain.
And thus, with flattery and suchlike japes,
He made the parson and the rest his apes.
But yet, to tell the whole truth at the last,
He was, in church, a fine ecclesiast.   710
Well could he read a lesson or a story,
But best of all he sang an offertory;
For well he knew that when that song was sung,
Then might he preach, and all with polished
     tongue,
To win some silver, as he right well could;   715
Therefore he sang so merrily and so loud.

Now have I told you briefly, in a clause,
The state, the array, the number, and the cause
Of the assembling of this company
In Southwark, at this noble hostelry   720
Known as the Tabard Inn, hard by the Bell.
But now the time is come wherein to tell
How all we bore ourselves that very night
When at the hostelry we did alight.
And afterward the story I engage   725
To tell you of our common pilgrimage.
But first, I pray you, of your courtesy,
You'll not ascribe it to vulgarity
Though I speak plainly of this matter here,
Retailing you their words and means of cheer;
Nor though I use their very terms, nor lie.   731
For this thing do you know as well as I:
When one repeats a tale told by a man,
He must report, as nearly as he can,
Every least word, if he remember it,   735
However rude it be, or how unfit;
Or else he may be telling what's untrue,
Embellishing and fictionizing too.
He may not spare, although it were his brother;
He must as well say one word as another.   740
Christ spoke right broadly out, in holy writ,
And, you know well, there's nothing low in it.
And Plato says, to those able to read:
"The word should be the cousin to the deed."
Also, I pray that you'll forgive it me   745
If I have not set folk, in their degree
Here in this tale, by rank as they should stand.
My wits are not the best, you'll understand.

Great cheer our host gave to us, every one,
And to the supper set us all anon;   750
And served us then with victuals of the best.
Strong was the wine and pleasant to each guest.

A seemly man our good host was, withal,
Fit to have been a marshal in some hall;
He was a large man, with protruding eyes,   755
As fine a burgher as in Cheapside lies;
Bold in his speech, and wise, and right well taught,
And as to manhood, lacking there in naught.
Also, he was a very merry man,
And after meat, at playing he began,   760
Speaking of mirth among some other things,
When all of us had paid our reckonings;
And saying thus: "Now, masters, verily
You are all welcome here, and heartily:
For by my truth, and telling you no lie,   765
I have not seen, this year, a company
Here in this inn, fitter for sport than now.
Fain would I make you happy, knew I how.
And of a game have I this moment thought
To give you joy, and it shall cost you naught. 770
  "You go to Canterbury; may God speed
And the blest martyr soon requite your meed.
And well I know, as you go on your way,
You'll tell good tales and shape yourselves to play;
For truly there's no mirth nor comfort, none, 775
Riding the roads as dumb as is a stone;
And therefore will I furnish you a sport,
As I just said, to give you some comfort.
And if you like it, all, by one assent,
And will be ruled by me, of my judgment,   780
And will so do as I'll proceed to say,
Tomorrow, when you ride upon your way,
Then, by my father's spirit, who is dead,
If you're not gay, I'll give you up my head.
Hold up your hands, nor more about it speak."
  Our full assenting was not far to seek;   786
We thought there was no reason to think twice,
And granted him his way without advice,
And bade him tell his verdict just and wise.
  "Masters," quoth he, "here now is my advice;
But take it not, I pray you, in disdain;   791
This is the point, to put it short and plain,
That each of you, beguiling the long day,
Shall tell two stories as you wend your way
To Canterbury town; and each of you   795
On coming home, shall tell another two,
All of adventures he has known befall.
And he who plays his part the best of all,
That is to say, who tells upon the road
Tales of best sense, in most amusing mode,   800
Shall have a supper at the others' cost
Here in this room and sitting by this post,
When we come back again from Canterbury.
And now, the more to warrant you'll be merry,

I will myself, and gladly, with you ride   805
At my own cost, and I will be your guide.
But whosoever shall my rule gainsay
Shall pay for all that's bought along the way.
And if you are agreed that it be so,
Tell me at once, or if not, tell me no,   810
And I will act accordingly. No more."
  This thing was granted, and our oaths we swore,
With right glad hearts, and prayed of him, also,
That he would take the office, nor forgo
The place of governor of all of us,   815
Judging our tales; and by his wisdom thus
Arrange that supper at a certain price,
We to be ruled, each one, by his advice
In things both great and small; by one assent,
We stood committed to his government.   820
And thereupon, the wine was fetched anon;
We drank, and then to rest went everyone,
And that without a longer tarrying.
  Next morning, when the day began to spring,
Up rose our host, and acting as our cock,   825
He gathered us together in a flock,
And forth we rode, a jog-trot being the pace,
Until we reached Saint Thomas' watering-place.
And there our host pulled horse up to a walk,
And said: "Now, masters, listen while I talk.   830
You know what you agreed at set of sun.
If even-song and morning-song are one,
Let's here decide who first shall tell a tale.
And as I hope to drink more wine and ale,
Whoso proves rebel to my government   835
Shall pay for all that by the way is spent.
Come now, draw cuts, before we farther win,
And he that draws the shortest shall begin.
Sir knight," said he, "my master and my lord,
You shall draw first as you have pledged your
    word.   840
Come near," quoth he, "my lady prioress:
And you, sir clerk, put by your bashfulness,
Nor ponder more; out hands, now, every man!"
  At once to draw a cut each one began,
And, to make short the matter, as it was,   845
Whether by chance or whatsoever cause,
The truth is, that the cut fell to the knight,
At which right happy then was every wight.
Thus that his story first of all he'd tell,
According to the compact, it befell,   850
As you have heard. Why argue to and fro?
And when this good man saw that it was so,
Being a wise man and obedient
To plighted word, given by free assent,
He said: "Since I must then begin the game,   855
Why, welcome be the cut, and in God's name!

Now let us ride, and hearken what I say."
And at that word we rode forth on our way;
And he began to speak, with right good cheer,
His tale anon, as it is written here.   860

HERE ENDS THE PROLOGUE OF THIS BOOK
AND HERE BEGINS THE FIRST TALE,
WHICH IS THE KNIGHT'S TALE

THE NUN'S PRIEST'S TALE

*Of the Cock and Hen, Chanticleer
and Pertelote*

A widow poor, somewhat advanced in age,
Lived, on a time, within a small cottage
Beside a grove and standing down a dale.
This widow, now, of whom I tell my tale,
Since that same day when she'd been last a wife 5
Had led, with patience, her strait simple life,
For she'd small goods and little income-rent;
By husbanding of such as God had sent
She kept herself and her young daughters twain.
Three large sows had she, and no more, 'tis plain,
Three cows and a lone sheep that she called Moll.
Righty sooty was her bedroom and her hall,   12
Wherein she'd eaten many a slender meal.
Of sharp sauce, why she needed no great deal,
For dainty morsel never passed her throat;   15
Her diet well accorded with her coat.
Repletion never made this woman sick;
A temperate diet was her whole physic,
And exercise, and her heart's sustenance.
The gout, it hindered her nowise to dance,   20
Nor apoplexy spun within her head;
And no wine drank she, either white or red;
Her board was mostly garnished, white and black,
With milk and brown bread, whereof she'd no
    lack,
Broiled bacon and sometimes an egg or two,   25
For a small dairy business did she do.
    A yard she had, enclosed all roundabout
With pales, and there was a dry ditch without,
And in the yard a cock called Chanticleer.
In all the land, for crowing, he'd no peer.   30
His voice was merrier than the organ gay
On Mass days, which in church begins to play;
More regular was his crowing in his lodge
Than is a clock or abbey horologe.
By instinct he'd marked each ascension down   35
Of equinoctial value in that town;
For when fifteen degrees had been ascended,
Then crew he so it might not be amended.
His comb was redder than a fine coral,

And battlemented like a castle wall.   40
His bill was black and just like jet it shone;
Like azure were his legs and toes, each one;
His spurs were whiter than the lily flower;
And plumage of the burnished gold his dower.
This noble cock had in his governance   45
Seven hens to give him pride and all pleasance,
Which were his sisters and his paramours
And wondrously like him as to colors,
Whereof the fairest hued upon her throat
Was called the winsome Mistress Pertelote.   50
Courteous she was, discreet and debonnaire,
Companionable, and she had been so fair
Since that same day when she was seven nights
    old,
That truly she had taken the heart to hold
Of Chanticleer, locked in her every limb;   55
He loved her so that all was well with him.
But such a joy it was to hear them sing,
Whenever the bright sun began to spring,
In sweet accord, "My love walks through the
    land."
For at that time, and as I understand,   60
The beasts and all the birds could speak and sing.
    So it befell that, in a bright dawning,
As Chanticleer 'midst wives and sisters all
Sat on his perch, the which was in the hall,
And next him sat the winsome Pertelote,   65
This Chanticleer he groaned within his throat
Like man that in his dreams is troubled sore.
And when fair Pertelote thus heard him roar,
She was aghast and said: "O sweetheart dear,
What ails you that you groan so? Do you hear?
You are a sleepy herald. Fie, for shame!"   71
    And he replied to her thus: "Ah, *madame*,
I pray you that you take it not in grief:
By God, I dreamed I'd come to such mischief,
Just now, my heart yet jumps with sore affright.
Now, God," cried he, "my vision read aright   76
And keep my body out of foul prison!
I dreamed, that while I wandered up and down
Within our yard, I saw there a strange beast
Was like a dog, and he'd have made a feast   80
Upon my body, and have had me dead.
His color yellow was and somewhat red;
And tipped his tail was, as were both his ears,
With black, unlike the rest, as it appears;
His snout was small and gleaming was each eye.
Remembering how he looked, almost I die;   86
And all this caused my groaning, I confess."
    "Aha," said she, "fie on you, spiritless!
Alas!" cried she, "for by that God above,
Now have you lost my heart and all my love;   90

I cannot love a coward, by my faith.
For truly, whatsoever woman saith,
We all desire, if only it may be,
To have a husband hardy, wise, and free,
And trustworthy, no niggard, and no fool,   95
Nor one that is afraid of every tool,
Nor yet a braggart, by that God above!
How dare you say, for shame, unto your love
That there is anything that you have feared?
Have you not man's heart, and yet have a beard?
Alas! And are you frightened by a vision?   101
Dreams are, God knows, a matter for derision.
Visions are generated by repletions
And vapors and the body's bad secretions
Of humors overabundant in a wight.   105
Surely this dream, which you have had tonight
Comes only of the superfluity
Of your bilious irascibility,
Which causes folk to shiver in their dreams
For arrows and for flames with long red gleams,
For great beasts in the fear that they will bite,   111
For quarrels and for wolf whelps great and slight;
Just as the humor of melancholy
Causes full many a man, in sleep, to cry,
For fear of black bears or of bulls all black,   115
Or lest black devils put them in a sack.
Of other humors could I tell also,
That bring, to many a sleeping man, great woe;
But I'll pass on as lightly as I can.
    "Lo, Cato, and he was a full wise man,   120
Said he not, we should trouble not for dreams?
Now, sir," said she, "when we fly from the beams,
For God's love go and take some laxative;
On peril of my soul, and as I live,
I counsel you the best, I will not lie,   125
That both for choler and for melancholy
You purge yourself; and since you shouldn't tarry,
And on this farm there's no apothecary,
I will myself go find some herbs for you
That will be good for health and pecker too;   130
And in our own yard all these herbs I'll find,
The which have properties of proper kind
To purge you underneath and up above.
Forget this not, now, for God's very love!
You are so very choleric of complexion.   135
Beware the mounting sun and all dejection,
Nor get yourself with sudden humors hot;
For if you do, I dare well lay a groat
That you shall have the tertian fever's pain,
Or some ague that may well be your bane.   140
A day or two you shall have digestives
Of worms before you take your laxatives

Of laurel, centuary, and fumitory,
Or else of hellebore purificatory,
Or caper spurge, or else of dogwood berry,   145
Or herb ivy, all in our yard so merry;
Peck them just as they grow and gulp them in.
Be merry, husband, for your father's kin!
Dread no more dreams. And I can say no more."
    "Madam," said he, "gramercy for your lore.   150
Nevertheless, not running Cato down,
Who had for wisdom such a high renown,
And though he says to hold no dreams in dread,
By God, men have, in many old books, read
Of many a man more an authority   155
Than ever Cato was, pray pardon me,
Who say just the reverse of his sentence,
And have found out by long experience
That dreams, indeed, are good significations,
As much of joys as of all tribulations   160
That folk endure here in this life present.
There is no need to make an argument;
The very proof of this is shown indeed.
    "One of the greatest authors that men read
Says thus: That on a time two comrades went   165
On pilgrimage, and all in good intent;
And it so chanced they came into a town
Where there was such a crowding, up and down,
Of people, and so little harborage,
That they found not so much as one cottage   170
Wherein the two of them might sheltered be.
Wherefore they must, as of necessity,
For that one night at least, part company;
And each went to a different hostelry
And took such lodgment as to him did fall.   175
Now one of them was lodged within a stall,
Far in a yard, with oxen of the plow;
That other man found shelter fair enow,
As was his luck, or was his good fortune,
Whatever 'tis that governs us, each one.   180
    "So it befell that, long ere it was day,
This last man dreamed in bed, as there he lay,
That his poor fellow did unto him call,
Saying: 'Alas! For in an ox's stall
This night shall I be murdered where I lie.   185
Now help me, brother dear, before I die.
Come in all haste to me.' 'Twas thus he said.
This man woke out of sleep, then, all afraid;
But when he'd wakened fully from his sleep,
He turned upon his pillow, yawning deep,   190
Thinking his dream was but a fantasy.
And then again, while sleeping, thus dreamed he.
And then a third time came a voice that said
(Or so he thought): 'Now, comrade, I am dead;

Behold my bloody wounds, so wide and deep! 195
Early arise tomorrow from your sleep,
And at the west gate of the town,' said he,
'A wagon full of dung there shall you see,
Wherein is hid my body craftily;
Do you arrest this wagon right boldly. 200
They killed me for what money they could gain.'
And told in every point how he'd been slain,
With a most pitiful face and pale of hue.
And trust me well, this dream did all come true;
For on the morrow, soon as it was day, 205
Unto his comrade's inn he took the way;
And when he'd come into that ox's stall,
Upon his fellow he began to call.
    "The keeper of the place replied anon,
And said he: 'Sir, your friend is up and gone; 210
As soon as day broke he went out of town.'
This man, then, felt suspicion in him grown,
Remembering the dream that he had had,
And forth he went, no longer tarrying, sad,
Unto the west gate of the town, and found 215
A dung-cart on its way to dumping-ground,
And it was just the same in every wise
As you have heard the dead man advertise;
And with a hardy heart he then did cry
Vengeance and justice on this felony: 220
'My comrade has been murdered in the night,
And in this very cart lies, face upright.
I cry to all the officers,' said he
'That ought to keep the peace in this city.
Alas, alas, here lies my comrade slain!' 225
    "Why should I longer with this tale detain?
The people rose and turned the cart to ground,
And in the center of the dung they found
The dead man, lately murdered in his sleep.
    "O Blessed God, Who art so true and deep! 230
Lo, how Thou dost turn murder out alway!
Murder will out, we see it every day.
Murder's so hateful and abominable
To God, Who is so just and reasonable,
That He'll not suffer that it hidden be; 235
Though it may skulk a year, or two, or three,
Murder will out, and I conclude thereon.
Immediately the rulers of that town,
They took the carter and so sore they racked
Him and the host, until their bones were cracked,
That they confessed their wickedness anon, 241
And hanged they both were by the neck, and
    soon.
    "Here may men see that dreams are things to
    dread.
And certainly, in that same book I read,

Right in the very chapter after this 245
(I spoof not, as I may have joy and bliss),
Of two men who would voyage oversea,
For some cause, and unto a far country,
If but the winds had not been all contrary,
Causing them both within a town to tarry, 250
Which town was builded near the haven-side.
But then, one day, along toward eventide,
The wind did change and blow as suited best.
Jolly and glad they went unto their rest.
And were prepared right early for to sail; 255
But unto one was told a marvelous tale.
For one of them, a-sleeping as he lay,
Did dream a wondrous dream ere it was day.
He thought a strange man stood by his bedside
And did command him, he should there abide,
And said to him: 'If you tomorrow wend, 261
You shall be drowned; my tale is at an end.'
He woke and told his fellow what he'd met
And prayed him quit the voyage and forget;
For just one day he prayed him there to bide. 265
His comrade, who was lying there beside,
Began to laugh and scorned him long and fast.
'No dream,' said he, 'may make my heart aghast,
So that I'll quit my business for such things.
I do not care a straw for your dreamings, 270
For visions are but fantasies and japes.
Men dream, why, every day, of owls and apes,
And many a wild phantasm therewithal;
Men dream of what has never been, nor shall.
But since I see that you will here abide, 275
And thus forgo this fair wind and this tide,
God knows I'm sorry; nevertheless, good day!'
    "And thus he took his leave and went his way.
But long before the half his course he'd sailed,
I know not why, nor what it was that failed, 280
But casually the vessel's bottom rent,
And ship and men under the water went,
In sight of other ships were there beside,
The which had sailed with that same wind and
    tide.
    "And therefore, pretty Pertelote, my dear, 285
By such old-time examples may you hear
And learn that no man should be too reckless
Of dreams, for I can tell you, fair mistress,
That many a dream is something well to dread.
    "Why in the 'Life' of Saint Kenelm I read 290
(Who was Kenelphus' son, the noble king
Of Mercia), how Kenelm dreamed a thing;
A while ere he was murdered, so they say,
His own death in a vision saw, one day.
His nurse interpreted, as records tell, 295
That vision, bidding him to guard him well

From treason; but he was but seven years old,
And therefore 'twas but little he'd been told
Of any dream, so holy was his heart.
By God! I'd rather than retain my shirt   300
That you had read this legend, as have I.
Dame Pertelote, I tell you verily,
Macrobius, who wrote of Scipio
The African a vision long ago,
He holds by dreams, saying that they have been
Warnings of things that men have later seen.   306
    "And furthermore, I pray you to look well
In the Old Testament at Daniel,
Whether he held dreams for mere vanity.
Read, too, of Joseph, and you there shall see   310
Where dreams have sometimes been (I say not all)
Warnings of things that after did befall.
Consider Egypt's king, Dan Pharaoh,
His baker and his butler, these also,
Whether they knew of no effect from dreams.   315
Whoso will read of sundry realms the themes
May learn of dreams full many a wondrous thing.
Lo, Crœsus, who was once of Lydia king,
Dreamed he not that he sat upon a tree,
Which signified that hanged high he should be?
Lo, how Andromache, great Hector's wife,   321
On that same day when Hector lost his life,
She dreamed upon the very night before
That Hector's life should be lost evermore,
If on that day he battled, without fail.   325
She warned him, but no warning could avail;
He went to fight, despite all auspices,
And so was shortly slain by Achilles.
But that same tale is all too long to tell,
And, too, it's nearly day, I must not dwell   330
Upon this; I but say, concluding here,
That from this vision I have cause to fear
Adversity; and I say, furthermore,
That I do set by laxatives no store,
For they are poisonous, I know it well.   335
Them I defy and love not, truth to tell.
    "But let us speak of mirth and stop all this;
My lady Pertelote, on hope of bliss,
In one respect God's given me much grace;
For when I see the beauty of your face,   340
You are so rosy-red beneath each eye,
It makes my dreadful terror wholly die.
For there is truth in *In principio*
Mulier est hominis confusio
(Madam, the meaning of this Latin is,   345
Woman is man's delight and all his bliss).
For when I feel at night your tender side,
Although I cannot then upon you ride,
Because our perch so narrow is, alas!

I am so full of joy and all solace   350
That I defy, then, vision, aye and dream."
    And with that word he flew down from the
        beam,
For it was day, and down went his hens all;
And with a cluck he then began to call,
For he had found some corn within the yard.   355
Regal he was, and fears he did discard.
He feathered Pertelote full many a time
And twenty times he trod her ere 'twas prime.
He looked as if he were a grim lion
As on his toes he strutted up and down;   360
He deigned not set his foot upon the ground.
He clucked when any grain of corn he found,
And all his wives came running at his call.
Thus regal, as a prince is in his hall,
I'll now leave busy Chanticleer to feed,   365
And with events that followed I'll proceed.
    When that same month wherein the world
        began,
Which is called March, wherein God first made
        man,
Was ended, and were passed of days also,
Since March began, full thirty days and two,   370
It fell that Chanticleer, in all his pride,
His seven wives a-walking by his side,
Cast up his two eyes toward the great bright sun
(Which through the sign of Taurus now had run
Twenty degrees and one, and somewhat more),
And knew by instinct and no other lore   376
That it was prime, and joyfully he crew,
"The sun, my love," he said, "has climbed anew
Forty degrees and one, and somewhat more.
My lady Pertelote, whom I adore,   380
Mark now these happy birds, hear how they sing.
And see all these fresh flowers, how they spring;
Full is my heart of revelry and grace."
    But suddenly he fell in grievous case;
For ever the latter end of joy is woe.   385
God knows that worldly joys do swiftly go;
And if a rhetorician could but write,
He in some chronicle might well indite
And mark it down as sovereign in degree.
Now every wise man, let him hark to me: 390
This tale is just as true, I undertake,
As is the book of *Launcelot of the Lake,*
Which women always hold in such esteem.
But now I must take up my proper theme.
    A brant-fox, full of sly iniquity,   395
That in the grove had lived two years, or three,
Now by a fine premeditated plot
That same night, breaking through the hedge, had
        got

Into the yard where Chanticleer the fair
Was wont, and all his wives too, to repair;   400
And in a bed of greenery still he lay
Till it was past the quarter of the day,
Waiting his chance on Chanticleer to fall,
As gladly do these killers one and all
Who lie in ambush for to murder men.   405
O murderer false, there lurking in your den!
O new Iscariot, O new Ganelon!
O false dissimulator, Greek Sinon
That brought down Troy all utterly to sorrow!
O Chanticleer, accursed be that morrow   410
When you into that yard flew from the beams!
You were well warned, and fully, by your dreams
That this day should hold peril damnably.
But that which God foreknows, it needs must be,
So says the best opinion of the clerks.   415
Witness some cleric perfect for his works,
That in the schools there's a great altercation
In this regard, and much high disputation
That has involved a hundred thousand men.
But I can't sift it to the bran with pen,   420
As can the holy Doctor Augustine,
Or Boethius, or Bishop Bradwardine,
Whether the fact of God's great foreknowing
Makes it right needful that I do a thing
(By needful, I mean, of necessity);   425
Or else, if a free choice be granted me,
To do that same thing, or to do it not,
Though God foreknew before the thing was
    wrought;
Or if His knowing constrains never at all,
Save by necessity conditional.   430
I have no part in matters so austere;
My tale is of a cock, as you shall hear,
That took the counsel of his wife, with sorrow,
To walk within the yard upon that morrow
After he'd had the dream whereof I told.   435
Now women's counsels oft are ill to hold;
A woman's counsel brought us first to woe,
And Adam caused from Paradise to go,
Wherein he was right merry and at ease,
But since I know not whom it may displease   440
If woman's counsel I hold up to blame,
Pass over, I but said it in my game.
Read authors where such matters do appear,
And what they say of women, you may hear.
These are the cock's words, they are none of mine;
No harm in women can I e'er divine.   446
   All in the sand, a-bathing merrily,
Lay Pertelote, with all her sisters by,
There in the sun; and Chanticleer so free
Sang merrier than a mermaid in the sea   450

(For Physiologus says certainly
That they *do* sing, both well and merrily).
And so befell that, as he cast his eye
Among the herbs and on a butterfly,
He saw this fox that lay there, crouching low.   455
Nothing of urge was in him, then, to crow;
But he cried "Cock-cock-cock" and did so start
As man who has a sudden fear at heart.
For naturally a beast desires to flee
From any enemy that he may see,   460
Though never yet he's clapped on such his eye.
   When Chanticleer the fox did then espy,
He would have fled but that the fox anon
Said: "Gentle sir, alas! Why be thus gone?
Are you afraid of me, who am your friend?   465
Now, surely, I were worse than any fiend
If I should do you harm or villainy.
I came not here upon your deeds to spy;
But, certainly, the cause of my coming
Was only just to listen to you sing.   470
For truly, you have quite as fine a voice
As angels have that Heaven's choirs rejoice;
Boethius to music could not bring
Such feeling, nor do others who can sing.
My lord your father (God his soul pray bless!)
And too your mother, of her gentleness,   476
Have been in my abode, to my great ease;
And truly, sir, right fain am I to please.
But since men speak of singing, I will say
(As I still have my eyesight day by day),   480
Save you, I never heard a man so sing
As did your father in the gray dawning;
Truly 'twas from the heart, his every song.
And that his voice might ever be more strong,
He took such pains that, with his either eye,   483
He had to blink, so loudly would he cry,
A-standing on his tiptoes therewithal,
Stretching his neck till it grew long and small.
And such discretion, too, by him was shown,
There was no man in any region known   490
That him in song or wisdom could surpass.
I have well read, in *Dan Burnell the Ass*,
Among his verses, how there was a cock,
Because a priest's son gave to him a knock
Upon the leg, while young and not yet wise,   495
He caused the boy to lose his benefice.
But, truly, there is no comparison
With the great wisdom and the discretion
Your father had, or with his subtlety.
Now sing, dear sir, for holy charity,   500
See if you can your father counterfeit."
   This Chanticleer his wings began to beat,

As one that could no treason there espy,
So was he ravished by this flattery.
Alas, you lords! Full many a flatterer   505
Is in your courts, and many a cozener,
That please your honors much more, by my fay,
Than he that truth and justice dares to say.
Go read the Ecclesiast on flattery;
Beware, my lords, of all their treachery!   510
   This Chanticleer stood high upon his toes,
Stretching his neck, and both his eyes did close,
And so did crow right loudly, for the nonce;
And Russel Fox, he started up at once,
And by the gorget grabbed our Chanticleer,   515
Flung him on back, and toward the wood did
      steer,
For there was no man who as yet pursued.
O destiny, you cannot be eschewed!
Alas, that Chanticleer flew from the beams!
Alas, his wife recked nothing of his dreams!   520
And on a Friday fell all this mischance.
O Venus, who art goddess of pleasance,
Since he did serve thee well, this Chanticleer,
And to the utmost of his power here,
More for delight than cocks to multiply,   525
Why would'st thou suffer him that day to die?
O Gaufred, my dear master sovereign,
Who, when King Richard Lionheart was slain
By arrow, sang his death with sorrow sore,
Why have I not your faculty and lore   530
To chide Friday, as you did worthily?
(For truly, on a Friday slain was he).
Then would I prove how well I could complain
For Chanticleer's great fear and all his pain.
   Certainly no such cry and lamentation   535
Were made by ladies at Troy's desolation,
When Pyrrhus with his terrible bared sword
Had taken old King Priam by the beard
And slain him (as the Æneid tells to us),
As made then all those hens in one chorus   540
When they had caught a sight of Chanticleer.
But fair Dame Pertelote assailed the ear
Far louder than did Hasdrubal's good wife
When that her husband bold had lost his life,
And Roman legionaries burned Carthage;   545
For she so full of torment was, and rage,
She voluntarily to the fire did start
And burned herself there with a steadfast heart.
And you, O woeful hens, just so you cried
As when base Nero burned the city wide   550
Of Rome, and wept the senators' stern wives
Because their husbands all had lost their lives,
For though not guilty, Nero had them slain.
Now will I turn back to my tale again.

This simple widow and her daughters two   555
Heard these hens cry and make so great ado,
And out of doors they started on the run
And saw the fox into the grove just gone,
Bearing upon his back the cock away.
And then they cried, "Alas, and welladay!   560
Oh, oh, the fox!" and after him they ran,
And after them, with staves, went many a man;
Ran Coll, our dog, ran Talbot and Garland,
And Malkin with a distaff in her hand;
Ran cow and calf and even the very hogs,   565
So were they scared by barking of the dogs
And shouting men and women all did make,
They all ran so they thought their hearts would
      break
They yelled as very fiends do down in Hell;
The ducks they cried as at the butcher fell;   570
The frightened geese flew up above the trees;
Out of the hive there came the swarm of bees;
So terrible was the noise, ah *ben'cite!*
Certainly old Jack Straw and his army
Never raised shouting half so loud and shrill 575
When they were chasing Flemings for to kill,
As on that day was raised upon the fox.
They brought forth trumpets made of brass, of
      box,
Of horn, of bone, wherein they blew and pooped,
And therewithal they screamed and shrieked and
      whooped;   580
It seemed as if the heaven itself would fall!
   And now, good men, I pray you hearken all.
Behold how Fortune turns all suddenly
The hope and pride of even her enemy!
This cock, which lay across the fox's back,   585
In all his fear unto the fox did clack
And say: "Sir, were I you, as I should be,
Then would I say (as God may now help me!),
'Turn back again, presumptuous peasants all!
A very pestilence upon you fall!   590
Now that I've gained here to this dark wood's side,
In spite of you this cock shall here abide.
I'll eat him, by my faith, and that anon!' "
   The fox replied: "In faith, it shall be done!"
And as he spoke that word, all suddenly   595
This cock broke from his mouth, full cleverly,
And high upon a tree he flew anon.
And when the fox saw well that he was gone,
"Alas," quoth he, "O Chanticleer, alas!
I have against you done a base trespass   600
In that I frightened you, my dear old pard,
When you I seized and brought from out that
      yard;

But, sir, I did it with no foul intent;
Come down, and I will tell you what I meant.
I'll tell the truth to you, God help me so!"   605
  "Nay then," said he, "beshrew us both, you
    know,
But first, beshrew myself, both blood and bones,
If you beguile me, having done so once,
You shall no more, with any flattery,
Cause me to sing and close up either eye.   610
For he who shuts his eyes when he should see,
And willfully, God let him ne'er be free!"
  "Nay," said the fox, "but God give him mis-
    chance
Who is so indiscreet in governance   614

He chatters when he ought to hold his peace."
  Lo, such it is when watch and ward do cease,
And one grows negligent with flattery.
But you that hold this tale a foolery,
As but about a fox, a cock, a hen,
Yet do not miss the moral, my good men.   620
For Saint Paul says that all that's written well
Is written down some useful truth to tell.
Then take the wheat and let the chaff lie still.
  And now, good God, and if it be Thy will,
As says Lord Christ, so make us all good men
And bring us into His high bliss. Amen.   626

HERE ENDS THE NUN'S PRIEST'S TALE

SHAKESPEARE
AND HIS DRAMA

The death of Chaucer in 1400 left England without an important writer for almost a century. Indeed, if Malory's *Morte d'Arthur* be excepted, one must go more than a hundred and fifty years before finding anything that gives evidence of literary power. The political conflicts of the fifteenth century, culminating in the bloody War of the Roses, came to an end in 1485 and England entered upon a fifty year peace. This breathing spell permitted the learned men of the universities to come into contact with the new currents of thought that were abroad. The Renaissance had at last reached England.

This great movement in European life and thought was no sudden outburst. For several centuries the forces had been gathering that were to result in a quickening of the artistic and intellectual life of western Europe. The renewed study of the classics from the time of Petrarch in the early fourteenth century had brought about the rediscovery of the ancient Greek writers who had been known only at second hand for a thousand years. By 1500 Greek was being studied in the great universities, and scholars were traveling abroad carrying the new learning. Such a man was Erasmus of Holland, who came to England at the moment when his great learning and wisdom were an inestimable spur to the sluggish intellectual life of the land so lately emerged from suicidal warfare.

Not only was the new attention to Greek valuable to the theologians who now pored over Erasmus's edition of the Greek New Testament. Less godly men—and even sometimes the godliest—luxuriated in all the old Greek authors. They began to see virtue in the Hellenic attitude toward life—that which Matthew Arnold calls Hellenism—and to feel the desirability of beauty and joy and rich experience. Man and his needs and wishes began to seem as important as the glory of God, and the search for truth as heroic an adventure as was ever any hermit's search for perfect holiness. Not all this movement was good, of course, and "Humanism" sometimes became mere godlessness.[1] But at its best, as with Erasmus and Sir Thomas More in England, the new attention to the capabilities of the human spirit was of the utmost importance as a preparation for the great age soon to come.

Several other events must be mentioned if we are to understand the crescendo of national energy that, in spite of twenty years of religious conflict, arose to its climax in the reign of Elizabeth. In the fifteenth century Constantinople had fallen to the

[1] See pp. 577 ff. for a discussion of this phase of the Renaissance in Italy.

Turks and whatever remained there of the old classical culture was scattered over Europe, to the great enrichment of the whole Continent. By the middle of the century printing was perfected and books began to be circulated in undreamed of numbers. This ability to send one's thoughts abroad so easily was an extraordinary stimulus to all thinkers and writers. Moreover, the dreams and imaginations of the men of the Renaissance were stirred by the unprecedented explorations of the earth that began in the late fifteenth century. Not only Columbus with his three ships, and Magellan and, in later days, Drake, but every poet and dreamer in Europe ranged the seven seas and built his castle, no longer in Spain, but in some magic island of the West.

In England the great outburst of creative energy was delayed until the reign of Elizabeth (1558-1603). During this period and extending for some years over into the next century there was an astonishing productivity of literature of many kinds. Of lyric poetry we shall speak in our next chapter. Except for the beautiful language of the successive English translations of the Bible which began in the 1530's and culminated in the King James version of 1611,[2] much of the prose of the period seems to the modern reader too unnatural to be interesting. It is likely to be either stilted, or pompous, or filled with strange conceits. But in spite of the difficult style of the prose, many interesting things were written. The great foreign authors were now being translated, some of them very adequately. Works on ideals of government and proper conduct and the chivalric virtues were sometimes in prose and sometimes in allegorical poetry. These are of great interest to students of the period but are usually hard reading for others. We will all, however, enjoy some of the realistic novels about rogues and low life in London, as shown in the books of such men as Robert Greene and Thomas Deloney.

Of one great product of the Elizabethan Age it is hard to speak in short space. The Faerie Queene of Edmund Spenser is one of the most influential poems in the language. Succeeding generations of poets have found inspiration in its exquisite poetic technique. Those who like allegory luxuriate in its hundreds of characters made up wholly of the poet's imagination. The discussion of the private virtues— holiness, courtesy, etc.—is so elaborate that, in spite of the beauty of the poem, the average reader finds his attention continually flagging. Few except professional literary scholars have persisted to the end.[3]

It is not with The Faerie Queene, nor the lyrics, nor the prose that the Age of Elizabeth makes claim to be one of the outstanding periods of world literature. Its great glory is the Elizabethan Drama. Since we must discuss this drama in connection with the plays of Shakespeare a word must be said as to the history of productions for the stage up to his time.

The writing of drama in Greece and Rome came to an end with the works of Seneca in the first century of our era. Thereafter a thousand years passed before anything that could be recognized as a play was written in Europe, and when a revival finally came it was quite independent of the classics. In this second birth it is interesting to see that just as in the first, sixteen hundred years earlier in Greece, drama developed out of religious ceremonial.

By the end of the tenth century we find the Christian Church of Western Europe enriching the service for the celebration of Easter by a short presentation of the scene

---

[2] See the selections from the Bible, p. 414.

[3] In accordance with the general principle of choice in this volume, we have entirely omitted The Faerie Queene rather than present a mere fragment.

at the tomb of Christ. Dialogue between the women seeking the body and the angel was performed by the clergy, who apparently made some effort at impersonation. The angel's first speech, "Quem queritis in sepulchro?" (Whom do you seek in the tomb?), has given this first of the church dramas its name, the *Quem Queritis*. It is not hard to imagine the way in which this successful innovation grew until there were not only longer dialogues on Easter but also similar performances for Christmas and other great feasts of the church year.

In the course of three centuries the germ of the Easter play had developed into a whole cycle of dramas based on biblical stories (mystery plays) or on the lives of saints (miracle plays). From being a part of the religious service, the performances were moved out of the church, and eventually the acting was done by laymen. At the height of the development—during the thirteenth to fifteenth centuries—a cycle might consist of forty or fifty plays covering the whole biblical story from the Creation to the Day of Judgment. These entertainments were usually produced in late spring. Each number was sponsored by one of the trade guilds, which prepared the moving wagon on which it was played and furnished the actors. These wagons, divided into three stories—heaven, earth, and hell—moved through the city, one after another taking their stands at various stations.

These cycle plays were important in paving the way for later drama. In a few instances the authors exercised some creative ability by making the action truly dramatic. Some really tragic scenes occur and occasionally an author has been able to give the predominantly somber material a comic twist. But these dramatic achievements may easily be exaggerated, and it must be admitted that most of these plays make dull reading. Their real importance is their training of the people to like drama and to go to see it. These cycles were still performed long after English literary drama began, and they doubtless did much to provide appreciative audiences.

Two other early forms of drama appeared somewhat later than the mystery cycles. A number of plays written mainly during the fifteenth and early sixteenth centuries are known as Moralities. Such a work is *Everyman,* in which Everyman is summoned by God to Death. He visits his various friends, Good Fellowship, Cousin, and others, asking for someone to go with him. Only Good Deeds stands by him in the fatal hour. If all the Moralities had been as good as the *Everyman,* their vogue might have lasted longer. As it was, both they and the shorter humorous Interludes, which were sometimes played with them, had outlived their usefulness by 1540. It was time to prepare drama for larger things.

We now know that before 1500 a play that we would now call a drama, *Fulgens and Lucrece,* had been written, but another half century passed before the new movement in playmaking began. It is natural that the Renaissance in England should have aroused an interest in the plays of Greece and Rome. It was the comedies of Plautus and Terence that first secured attention. Actual production of these plays at boys' schools was followed by plays in English in imitation, first close and later very loose.[4] Of this kind were the early comedies, *Ralph Roister Doister* and *Gammer Gurton's Needle,* both of which were written before the beginning of Elizabeth's reign in 1558. They are crude but have real dramatic interest.

It was Seneca who served as inspiration for tragedy in the early days of Elizabeth. The dramatists of the time admired his bombastic style, his sensationalism, with murder and bloodshed and ghosts crying for revenge. The most popular of

[4] See *The Captives* of Plautus, p. 234.

these dramas based on Seneca was Kyd's *Spanish Tragedy,* one of the cruelest and bloodiest of plays, which held the stage for many decades. Though Shakespeare tended to get away from the Senecan influence, it is seen clearly in the main action of *Hamlet.*

A careful student of Elizabethan drama will be able to trace accurately the various gains made by writers of plays in the period 1560-1590, so that when Shakespeare came on the scene about the latter year he had his vehicle ready for him. Kyd, Lyly, Peele, Greene, and Marlowe each contributed his genius to the development of a form worthy of the craftsmanship of our greatest dramatist.

That Shakespeare was born at Stratford on Avon, a village of Warwickshire, in 1564 is not so important for us to know as that by 1591 or 1592 he had already written poetry and was trying his hand with the production of plays. His career as a writer covers about twenty years, for he did little after 1610.

The rapid development of Shakespeare as a dramatist during the dozen years from 1590 until the time of his supreme achievement in his great tragedies cannot be traced here. Much of his early work appears to have been the improving of old plays and some of it was doubtless done in collaboration with other dramatists. There is no doubt that he learned much from Marlowe and Greene at this stage of his career. He rapidly surpassed his contemporaries. Almost every play shows improvement in his handling of plot, or exposition, or character. A considerable number of plays written during his first ten years were based on English history. In these he progressed far beyond the bare chronicle of a king's reign, and we have such creations as Sir John Falstaff, one of the supreme comedy characters of all literature. A group of comedies, *A Midsummer Night's Dream, The Merchant of Venice, Much Ado about Nothing, As You Like It, Twelfth Night,* and a tragedy, *Romeo and Juliet,* serve to perfect his discipline so that by 1600 or thereabouts he is a master of plot, of dialogue, and of characterization. From this point on we see him writing his incomparable tragedies, the greatest of them being *Hamlet, Macbeth, Othello,* and *King Lear.* The final work of the great dramatist was *The Tempest* and *A Winter's Tale,* delightful comedies both, and filled with romantic situations.

In our selection of plays we have represented Shakespeare by what many persons regard as his greatest drama. *Hamlet* is, of course, perfectly adequate in its plot, its suspense, and its adaptability to Shakespeare's theater. But it is in the presentation of character that the play is most distinguished. Hamlet has been discussed by generations of readers as if he were a real historical character. One reading of the play may be somewhat confusing. The twentieth reading will still find something new and interesting.

Shakespeare had many active contemporary dramatists, some of whom would probably be better known if he did not so completely overshadow them. Most readers would find enjoyment not only in some of the very beautifully poetic plays of Marlowe, such as *Doctor Faustus,* but in such realistic studies of London life as Dekker's *The Shoemaker's Holiday.* Readers of somewhat sophisticated taste may enjoy some of Ben Jonson's Comedies of Humors, such as *Every Man in His Humor.*

After Shakespeare's work closed, the drama became in general more and more romantic, especially in the hands of Beaumont and Fletcher. Though some worthy tragedy was written by John Webster (*The Duchess of Malfi*), some good comedy by Massinger and Middleton, the course of drama from 1610 onward for thirty years was toward sensationalism. The audience that had followed *Hamlet* in 1603 was no more. A new generation fed on romanticism or broad comedy were given plays to their taste. Few of us who have read plays written in the 1630's have the heart to blame the Puritans much when in 1642 they closed the theaters. When playgoing was revived in 1660 it was something new. Elizabethan Drama had spent its force and lay far in the past.

WILLIAM SHAKESPEARE

Hamlet

DRAMATIS PERSONÆ

HAMLET, *only son of the murdered King Hamlet*

CLAUDIUS, *brother of the murdered king; usurper of the throne*

GERTRUDE, *widow of the murdered king; now wife of Claudius*

GHOST *of the murdered king*

POLONIUS, *Lord High Chamberlain*

LAERTES, *son to Polonius*

OPHELIA, *daughter to Polonius; beloved by Prince Hamlet*

HORATIO, *loyal friend to Prince Hamlet*

ROSENCRANTZ } *false friends to Prince Hamlet*
GUILDENSTERN }

OSRIC, *a foolish courtier*

FORTINBRAS, *Prince of Norway*

VOLTIMAND } *Ambassadors to Norway*
CORNELIUS }

MARCELLUS }
BERNARDO } *sentinels*
FRANCISCO }

REYNALDO, *servant to Polonius*

TWO GRAVE-DIGGERS

TROUPE OF CITY PLAYERS, *on tour*

Lords, Ladies, Ambassadors, Priests, Captain, Soldiers, Sailors, a Mob of Danes, Messengers, and Attendants

THE SCENE:—ELSINORE.

ACT I

SCENE I:—*Midnight. The sentinel's platform before the royal castle.*

FRANCISCO, *a sentinel, with lantern in hand and partisan on shoulder, pacing back and forth. The* clock *in the castle slowly beats the hour of twelve. Upon the last stroke,* BERNARDO, *the relief-sentinel, enters, with lantern and partisan.*

BERN. Who's there?

FRAN. Nay, answer me. Stand, and unfold yourself!

BERN. "Long live the king."

FRAN. [*lifting his lantern*]. Bernardo?

BERN. He.   5

FRAN. You come most carefully upon your hour.

BERN. 'Tis now struck twelve. Get thee to bed, Francisco.

FRAN. For this relief much thanks. 'Tis bitter cold;

And I am sick at heart.

BERN. Have you had quiet guard?

FRAN.   Not a mouse stirring.   10

BERN. Well, good-night.

As FRANCISCO *reaches the door,* BERNARDO *calls after him.*

If you do meet Horatio and Marcellus,

The rivals of my watch, bid them make haste.

FRAN. I think I hear them.

Enter MARCELLUS, *a soldier, accompanied by* HORATIO, *a young gentleman in civilian garb.* FRANCISCO *halts them with the sentinel's challenge.*

     Stand, ho! [*Lifts his lantern.*] Who's there?

HORAT. Friends to this ground.

MARC.   And liegemen to the Dane.   15

FRAN. Give you good-night.

MARC. [*recognizing him*]. O!—Farewell, honest soldier.

Who hath reliev'd you?

Shakespeare, *Hamlet.* Text of the Riverside Literature Series. Reprinted by special arrangement with the holders of the copyright, Houghton Mifflin Company.

FRAN. Bernardo hath my place.
Give you good-night. [*Exit.*
MARC. [*advancing*]. Holla?—Bernardo?
BERN. [*lifting his lantern*]. Say,
What! is Horatio there?
HORAT. A piece of him.
BERN. Welcome, Horatio. Welcome, good Marcellus. 20
MARC. What! has this thing appear'd again tonight?
BERN. I have seen nothing.
MARC. Horatio says 'tis but our fantasy,
And will not let belief take hold of him
Touching this dreaded sight, twice seen of us: 25
Therefore I have entreated him along
With us to watch the minutes of this night,
That if again this apparition come
He may approve our eyes, and speak to it.
HORAT. Tush, tush! 'Twill not appear!
BERN. Sit down awhile, 30
And let us once again assail your ears,
That are so fortified against our story,
What we, two nights, have seen.
HORAT. Well, sit we down,
And let us hear Bernardo speak of this.

They seat themselves.

BERN. Last night of all, 35
When yond same star, that's westward from the pole,
Had made his course to illume that part of heaven
Where now it burns, Marcellus and myself,
The bell then beating one,—
MARC. [*grasping his arm*]. Peace! Break thee off!
Look, where it comes again! 40

Enter GHOST.

BERN. [*whispering*]. In the same figure, like the king that's dead.
MARC. [*whispering*]. Thou art a scholar; speak to it, Horatio.
BERN. Looks it not like the king—mark it!—Horatio?
HORAT. Most like. It harrows me with fear and wonder.
BERN. It would be spoke to.
MARC. Question it, Horatio. 45
HORAT. [*rising*]. What art thou that usurp'st this time of night,
Together with that fair and warlike form
In which the majesty of buried Denmark
Did sometimes march? By heaven I charge thee, speak!

MARC. It is offended.
BERN. See, it stalks away. 50
HORAT. Stay! Speak! Speak! I charge thee, speak! [*Exit* GHOST.
MARC. 'Tis gone, and will not answer.
BERN. How now, Horatio! You tremble and look pale!
Is not this something more than fantasy?
What think you on't? 55
HORAT. Before my God! I might not this believe
Without the sensible and true avouch
Of mine own eyes!
MARC. Is it not like the king?
HORAT. As thou art to thyself!
Such was the very armor he had on 60
When he the ambitious Norway combated.
So frown'd he once, when in an angry parle
He smote the sledded Polack on the ice.
'Tis strange!
MARC. Thus twice before, and jump at this dead hour, 65
With martial stalk hath he gone by our watch.
HORAT. In what particular thought to work I know not;
But in the gross and scope of my opinion,
This bodes some strange eruption to our state.
MARC. Good now, sit down; and tell me, he that knows, 70
Why this same strict and most observant watch
So nightly toils the subject of the land;
And why such daily cast of brazen cannon,
And foreign mart for implements of war;
Why such impress of shipwrights, whose sore task
Does not divide the Sunday from the week. 76
What might be toward that this sweaty haste
Doth make the night joint-laborer with the day?
Who is't that can inform me?
HORAT. That can I;
At least, the whisper goes so. Our last king— 80
Whose image even but now appear'd to us—
Was, as you know, by Fortinbras of Norway,
Thereto prick'd on by a most emulate pride,
Dar'd to the combat; in which our valiant Hamlet—
For so this side of our known world esteem'd him— 85
Did slay this Fortinbras; who, by a seal'd compact,
Well ratified by law and heraldry,
Did forfeit, with his life, all those his lands
Which he stood seiz'd of to the conqueror;
Against the which a moiety competent 90
Was gaged by our king, which had return'd
To the inheritance of Fortinbras,

Had he been vanquisher, as, by the same covenant
And carriage of the article design'd,
His fell to Hamlet. Now, sir, young Fortinbras,
Of unimproved mettle hot and full,   96
Hath in the skirts of Norway here and there
Shark'd up a list of lawless resolutes,
For food and diet, to some enterprise
That hath a stomach in't; which is no other,   100
As it doth well appear unto our state,
But to recover of us, by strong hand
And terms compulsative, those foresaid lands
So by his father lost. And this, I take it,
Is the main motive of our preparations,   105
The source of this our watch, and the chief head
Of this post-haste and romage in the land.

   BERN. I think it be no other but e'en so.
Well may it sort that this portentous figure
Comes armed through our watch, so like the king
That was, and is, the question of these wars.   111

   HORAT. A mote it is to trouble the mind's eye.
In the most high and palmy state of Rome,
A little ere the mightiest Julius fell,
The graves stood tenantless, and the sheeted dead
Did squeak and gibber in the Roman streets;   116
As stars with trains of fire, and dews of blood,
Disasters in the sun; and the moist star
Upon whose influence Neptune's empire stands
Was sick almost to doomsday with eclipse.   120
And even the like precurse of fierce events—
As harbingers preceding still the fates
And prologue to the omen coming on—
Have heaven and earth together demonstrated
Unto our climatures and countrymen.   125

   Re-enter the GHOST.

But, soft! Behold! Lo, where it comes again!
I'll cross it, though it blast me.

HORATIO *steps into the path of the* GHOST *and bars
its way.*

                          Stay, illusion!
If thou hast any sound, or use of voice,
Speak to me!
If there be any good thing to be done,   130
That may to thee do ease and grace to me,
Speak to me!
If thou art privy to thy country's fate,
Which happily foreknowing may avoid,
O, speak!   135
Or if thou hast uphoarded in thy life
Extorted treasure in the womb of earth—
For which, they say, you spirits oft walk in death—
Speak of it!

The GHOST *raises its arms and starts to speak; but
instantly the cock crows, and the* GHOST, *frightened, drops its arms, and hurries away.*

                  Stay, and speak!—Stop it, Marcellus.
   MARC. Shall I strike at it with my partisan?   140
   HORAT. Do, if it will not stand.
   BERN. [*striking*]. 'Tis here!
   HORAT. [*striking*].   'Tis here! [*Exit* GHOST.
   MARC. 'Tis gone!
We do it wrong, being so majestical,
To offer it the show of violence;
For it is, as the air, invulnerable,   145
And our vain blows malicious mockery.
   BERN. It was about to speak when the cock crew.
   HORAT. And then it started, like a guilty thing
Upon a fearful summons. I have heard,
The cock, that is the trumpet to the morn,   150
Doth with his lofty and shrill-sounding throat
Awake the god of day; and at his warning,
Whether in sea or fire, in earth or air,
The extravagant and erring spirit hies
To his confine; and of the truth herein   155
This present object made probation.
   MARC. It faded on the crowing of the cock.
Some say that ever 'gainst that season comes
Wherein our Saviour's birth is celebrated,
The bird of dawning singeth all night long;   160
And then, they say, no spirit dare walk abroad,
The nights are wholesome, then no planets strike,
No fairy takes, nor witch hath power to charm,
So hallow'd and so gracious is the time.
   HORAT. So have I heard, and do in part believe it.
But, look! the morn in russet mantle clad   166
Walks o'er the dew of yon high eastern hill.
Break we our watch up. And by my advice
Let us impart what we have seen tonight
Unto young Hamlet; for, upon my life,   170
This spirit, dumb to us, will speak to him.
Do you consent we shall acquaint him with it,
As needful in our loves, fitting our duty?
   MARC. Let's do't, I pray. And I this morning
      know
Where we shall find him most conveniently.   175
                                            [*Exeunt.*

SCENE II:—*The following morning. A room of
state in the castle.*

A flourish of trumpets. Enter KING CLAUDIUS,
QUEEN GERTRUDE, PRINCE HAMLET, POLONIUS,
LAERTES, CORNELIUS, VOLTIMAND, *Lords, Ladies,
Attendants. The* KING *and* QUEEN *take their
places on the throne.*

KING. Though yet of Hamlet our dear brother's death
The memory be green, and that it us befitted
To bear our hearts in grief, and our whole kingdom
To be contracted in one brow of woe,
Yet so far hath discretion fought with nature 180
That we with wisest sorrow think on him,
Together with remembrance of ourselves.
Therefore, our sometime sister, now our queen,
The imperial jointress of this warlike state,
Have we, as 'twere with a defeated joy, 185
With one auspicious and one dropping eye,
With mirth in funeral and with dirge in marriage,
In equal scale weighing delight and dole,
Taken to wife. [*Turning to the assembled Lords.*]
          Nor have we herein barr'd
Your better wisdoms, which have freely gone 190
With this affair along. For all, our thanks.
Now follows that you know: young Fortinbras,
Holding a weak supposal of our worth,
Or thinking by our late dear brother's death
Our state to be disjoint and out of frame, 195
Colleaguéd with this dream of his advantage,
He hath not fail'd to pester us with message
Importing the surrender of those lands
Lost by his father, with all bands of law,
To our most valiant brother. So much for him.
Now for ourself, and for this time of meeting; 201
Thus much the business is: we have here writ
To Norway, uncle of young Fortinbras—
Who, impotent and bed-rid, scarcely hears
Of this his nephew's purpose—to suppress 205
His further gait herein, in that the levies,
The lists, and full proportions, are all made
Out of his subject. And we here dispatch
You, good Cornelius, and you, Voltimand,
For bearers of this greeting to old Norway, 210
Giving to you no further personal power
To business with the king more than the scope
Of these delated articles allow.

Hands them papers.

Farewell, and let your haste commend your duty.
CORN.⎱ In that, and all things, will we show our
VOLT.⎰   duty. 215
KING. We doubt it nothing. Heartily farewell.
            [*Exeunt* CORNELIUS *and* VOLTIMAND.
And now, Laertes, what's the news with you?
You told us of some suit; what is't, Laertes?
You cannot speak of reason to the Dane,
And lose your voice. What wouldst thou beg,
      Laertes, 220

That shall not be my offer, not thy asking?
The head is not more native to the heart,
The hand more instrumental to the mouth,
Than is the throne of Denmark to thy father.
What wouldst thou have, Laertes?
      LAERT.   Dread my lord,
Your leave and favor to return to France; 226
From whence though willingly I came to Denmark
To show my duty in your coronation,
Yet now, I must confess, that duty done,
My thoughts and wishes bend again toward
      France, 230
And bow them to your gracious leave and pardon.
    KING. Have you your father's leave? What says
      Polonius?
    POLON. He hath, my lord, wrung from me my
      slow leave
By laborsome petition; and at last
Upon his will I seal'd my hard consent. 235
I do beseech you, give him leave to go.
    KING. Take thy fair hour, Laertes. Time be
      thine,
And thy best graces spend it at thy will.
        [LAERTES *withdraws. The* KING *turns to*
          HAMLET.
But now, my cousin Hamlet, and my son,—
    HAML. [*aside*]. A little more than kin, and less
      than kind. 240
    KING. How is it that the clouds still hang on
      you?
    HAML. Not so, my lord; I am too much i' the
      sun.
    QUEEN. Good Hamlet, cast thy nighted color
      off,
And let thine eye look like a friend on Denmark.
Do not for ever with thy vailed lids 245
Seek for thy noble father in the dust.
Thou know'st 'tis common; all that live must die,
Passing through nature to eternity.
    HAML. Aye, madam, it is—"common."
    QUEEN.   If it be,
Why seems it so particular with thee? 250
    HAML. "Seems," madam! Nay, it is. I know not
      "seems."
'Tis not alone my inky cloak, good mother,
Nor customary suits of solemn black,
Nor windy suspiration of forc'd breath,
No, nor the fruitful river in the eye, 255
Nor the dejected havior of the visage,
Together with all forms, modes, shows of grief,
That can denote me truly; these indeed "seem,"
For they are actions that a man might play:

But I have that within which passeth show;   260
These but the trappings and the suits of woe.
    KING. 'Tis sweet and commendable in your na-
    ture, Hamlet,
To give these mourning duties to your father.
But, you must know, your father lost a father;
That father lost, lost his; and the survivor bound
In filial obligation for some term   266
To do obsequious sorrow: but to persever
In obstinate condolement is a course
Of impious stubbornness. 'Tis unmanly grief.
It shows a will most incorrect to heaven,   270
A heart unfortified, a mind impatient,
An understanding simple and unschool'd:
For, what we know must be, and is as common
As any the most vulgar thing to sense,
Why should we, in our peevish opposition,   275
Take it to heart? Fie! 'Tis a fault to heaven,
A fault against the dead, a fault to nature,
To reason most absurd, whose common theme
Is "death of fathers," and who still hath cried,
From the first corse till he that died today,   280
"This must be so." We pray you, throw to earth
This unprevailing woe; and think of us
As of a father. For—let the world take note!—
You are the most immediate to our throne;
And with no less nobility of love   285
Than that which dearest father bears his son
Do I impart toward you. For your intent
In going back to school in Wittenberg,
It is most retrograde to our desire!
And, we beseech you, bend you to remain   290
Here, in the cheer and comfort of our eye,
Our chiefest courtier, cousin, and—our son.
    QUEEN. Let not thy mother lose her prayers,
    Hamlet:
I pray thee, stay with us. Go not to Wittenberg.
    HAML. I shall in all my best obey you, madam.
    KING. Why, 'tis a loving and a fair reply!   296
Be as ourself in Denmark. Madam, come;
This gentle and unforc'd accord of Hamlet
Sits smiling to my heart; in grace whereof,
No jocund health that Denmark drinks today,
But the great cannon to the clouds shall tell,   301
And the king's rouse the heavens shall bruit again,
Re-speaking earthly thunder. Come; away.
                [*Exeunt all except* HAMLET.
    HAML. O, that this too too solid flesh would
    melt,
Thaw, and resolve itself into a dew!   305
Or that the Everlasting had not fix'd
His canon 'gainst self-slaughter! O God! O God!
How weary, stale, flat, and unprofitable

Seem to me all the uses of this world!
Fie on't! O fie! 'Tis an unweeded garden,   310
That grows to seed; things rank and gross in
    nature
Possess it merely.—That it should come to this!
But two months dead! nay, not so much, not two!
So excellent a king; that was, to this,
Hyperion to a satyr! so loving to my mother   315
That he might not beteem the winds of heaven
Visit her face too roughly.—Heaven and earth!
Must I remember?—Why, she would hang on him
As if increase of appetite had grown
By what it fed on; and yet, within a month—
Let me not think on't!—Frailty, thy name is
    "woman."   321
A little month! or ere those shoes were old
With which she follow'd my poor father's body,
Like Niobe, all tears; why she, even she!—
O God! a beast, that wants discourse of reason,
Would have mourn'd longer—married with mine
    uncle,   326
My father's brother!—but no more like my father
Than I to Hercules.—Within a month!
Ere yet the salt of most unrighteous tears
Had left the flushing in her galled eyes,   330
She married. O, most wicked speed, to post
With such dexterity to incestuous sheets!
It is not nor it cannot come to good!
But break my heart, for I must hold my tongue.

Enter HORATIO *with the two sentinels* MARCELLUS
and BERNARDO.

    HORAT. Hail to your lordship!
    HAML.   I am glad to see you well—
Horatio! or I do forget myself.   336
    HORAT. The same, my lord, and your poor ser-
    vant ever.
    HAML. Sir, my good friend. I'll change that
    name with you.
And what make you from Wittenberg, Horatio?—
Marcellus?   340
    MARC. My good lord.
    HAML. I am very glad to see you. [*To* BER-
    NARDO.] Good even, sir.—
But what, in faith, make you from Wittenberg?
    HORAT. A truant disposition, good my lord.
    HAML. I would not hear your enemy say so;
Nor shall you do mine ear that violence   346
To make it truster of your own report
Against yourself; I know you are no truant.
But what is your affair in Elsinore?
We'll teach you to drink deep ere you depart!   350

HORAT. My lord, I came to see your father's
funeral.
HAML. I pray thee, do not mock me, fellow-
student;
I think it was to see—my mother's wedding.
HORAT. Indeed, my lord, it follow'd hard upon.
HAML. Thrift, thrift, Horatio! the funeral bak'd
meats   355
Did coldly furnish forth the marriage tables.
Would I had met my dearest foe in heaven
Ere I had ever seen that day, Horatio!
My father, methinks I see my father—
HORAT. O, where, my lord?
HAML.   In my mind's eye, Horatio.   360
HORAT. I saw him—once. He was a goodly king.
HAML. He was a man! Take him for all in all,
I shall not look upon his like again.
HORAT. My lord, I think I saw him yesternight.
HAML. Saw? Who?   365
HORAT. My lord, the king your father.
HAML.   The king my father!
HORAT. Season your admiration for a while
With an attent ear, till I may deliver,
Upon the witness of these gentlemen,
This marvel to you.
HAML.   For God's love, let me hear!
HORAT. Two nights together had these gentle-
men,   371
Marcellus and Bernardo, on their watch,
In the dead waste and middle of the night,
Been thus encounter'd: a figure, like your father,
Armed at points exactly, cap-a-pie,   375
Appears before them, and with solemn march
Goes slow and stately by them; thrice he walk'd
By their oppress'd and fear-surprised eyes,
Within his truncheon's length, whilst they, distill'd
Almost to jelly with the act of fear,   380
Stand dumb and speak not to him. This to me
In dreadful secrecy impart they did;
And I with them the third night kept the watch;
Where, as they had deliver'd, both in time,
Form of the thing, each word made true and good,
The apparition comes. I knew your father;   386
These hands are not more like.
HAML.   But where was this?
MARC. My lord, upon the platform where we
watch'd.
HAML. Did you not speak to it?
HORAT.   My lord, I did;
But answer made it none. Yet once methought
It lifted up its head and did address   391
Itself to motion like as it would speak;
But even then the morning cock crew loud,

And at the sound it shrunk in haste away
And vanish'd from our sight.
HAML.   'Tis very strange!   395
HORAT. As I do live, my honor'd lord, 'tis true
And we did think it writ down in our duty
To let you know of it.
HAML. Indeed, indeed, sirs, but this troubles me!
Hold you the watch tonight?
MARC. ⎫
BERN. ⎬   We do, my lord.   400
HAML. Arm'd, say you?
MARC. ⎫
BERN. ⎬   Arm'd, my lord.
HAML.   From top to toe?
MARC. ⎫
BERN. ⎬ My lord, from head to foot.
HAML. Then saw you not his face.
HORAT. O yes, my lord; he wore his beaver up.
HAML. What, look'd he frowningly?   405
HORAT. A countenance more in sorrow than in
anger.
HAML. Pale, or red?
HORAT. Nay, very pale.
HAML.   And fix'd his eyes upon you?
HORAT. Most constantly.
HAML.   I would I had been there!
HORAT. It would have much amaz'd you.   410
HAML. Very like; very like. Stay'd it long?
HORAT. While one with moderate haste might
tell a hundred.
MARC. ⎫
BERN. ⎬ Longer, longer.
HORAT. Not when I saw it.
HAML.   His beard was grizzled, no?
HORAT. It was, as I have seen it in his life,   415
A sable silver'd.
HAML.   I will watch tonight;
Perchance 'twill walk again.
HORAT.   I warrant it will.
HAML. If it assume my noble father's person,
I'll speak to it though hell itself should gape
And bid me hold my peace! I pray you all,   420
If you have hitherto conceal'd this sight,
Let it be tenable in your silence still;
And whatsoever else shall hap tonight,
Give it an understanding, but no tongue:
I will requite your loves. So, fare you well.   425
Upon the platform, 'twixt eleven and twelve,
I'll visit you.
ALL.   Our duty to your honor.
HAML. Your love, as mine to you. Farewell.
[*Exeunt* HORATIO, MARCELLUS, *and* BERNARDO.

My father's spirit—in arms! All is not well.
I doubt some foul play. Would the night were
    come!   430
Till then sit still, my soul. Foul deeds will rise,
Though all the earth o'erwhelm them, to men's
    eyes.   [*Exit.*

SCENE III:—*Later the same day. A room in Polonius' house. Enter* LAERTES *and* OPHELIA.

  LAERT. My necessaries are embark'd. Farewell.
And, sister, as the winds give benefit,
And convoy is assistant, do not sleep,   435
But let me hear from you.
  OPHEL.   Do you doubt that?
  LAERT. For Hamlet, and the trifling of his favor,
Hold it a fashion and a toy in blood,
A violet in the youth of primy nature,
Forward, not permanent; sweet, not lasting,   440
The perfume and suppliance of a minute,
No more.
  OPHEL. No more but so?
  LAERT.   Think it no more:
For nature, crescent, does not grow alone
In thews and bulk, but, as this temple waxes,
The inward service of the mind and soul   445
Grows wide withal. Perhaps he loves you now,
And now no soil nor cautel doth besmirch
The virtue of his will; but you must fear,
His greatness weigh'd, his will is not his own,
For he himself is subject to his birth;   450
He may not, as unvalu'd persons do,
Carve for himself; for on his choice depends
The safety and the health of the whole state,
And therefore must his choice be circumscrib'd
Unto the voice and yielding of that body   455
Whereof he is the head. Then, if he says he loves
    you,
It fits your wisdom so far to believe it
As he in his peculiar act and force
May give his saying deed; which is no further
Than the main voice of Denmark goes withal.   460
Then weigh what loss your honor may sustain
If with too credent ear you list his songs,
Or lose your heart, or your chaste treasure open
To his unmaster'd importunity.
Fear it, Ophelia! fear it, my dear sister!   465
And keep you in the rear of your affection,
Out of the shot and danger of desire.
The chariest maid is prodigal enough
If she unmask her beauty to the moon;
Virtue itself 'scapes not calumnious strokes;   470
The canker galls the infants of the spring
Too oft before their buttons be disclos'd;

And in the morn and liquid dew of youth
Contagious blastments are most imminent.
Be wary then. Best safety lies in fear: 475
Youth to itself rebels, though none else near.
  OPHEL. I shall the effect of this good lesson keep
As watchman to my heart. But, good my brother,
Do not, as some ungracious pastors do,
Show me the steep and thorny way to heaven,   480
Whilst, like a puff'd and reckless libertine,
Himself the primrose path of dalliance treads,
And recks not his own rede.
  LAERT.   O, fear me not.
I stay too long. But here my father comes.

Enter POLONIUS. LAERTES *kneels for a blessing.*

A double blessing is a double grace;   485
Occasion smiles upon a second leave.
  POLON. Yet here, Laertes! Aboard, aboard, for
    shame!
The wind sits in the shoulder of your sail,
And you are stay'd for! There—my blessing with
    thee.

Places his hand upon Laertes' head.

And these few precepts in thy memory   490
See thou character. Give thy thoughts no tongue,
Nor any unproportion'd thought his act.
Be thou familiar, but by no means vulgar.
The friends thou hast, and their adoption tried,
Grapple them to thy soul with hoops of steel;   495
But do not dull thy palm with entertainment
Of each new-hatch'd, unfledg'd comrade. Beware
Of entrance to a quarrel; but, being in,
Bear't that th' opposed may beware of thee,
Give every man thine ear, but few thy voice;   500
Take each man's censure, but reserve thy judgment.
Costly thy habit as thy purse can buy—
But not express'd in fancy; rich, not gaudy;
For the apparel oft proclaims the man,
And they in France of the best rank and station
Are most select and generous chief in that.   506
Neither a borrower nor a lender be;
For loan oft loses both itself and friend,
And borrowing dulls the edge of husbandry.
This above all: To thine own self be true;   510
And it must follow, as the night the day,
Thou canst not then be false to any man.
Farewell! My blessing season this in thee!
  LAERT. Most humbly do I take my leave, my lord.
  POLON. The time invites you; go. Your servants
    tend.   515
  LAERT. Farewell, Ophelia; and remember well
What I have said to you.

OPHEL.   'Tis in my memory lock'd,
And you yourself shall keep the key of it.
   LAERT. Farewell!   [*Exit.*
   POLON. What is't, Ophelia, he hath said to you?
   OPHEL. So please you, something touching the
      Lord Hamlet.   521
   POLON. Marry, well bethought!
'Tis told me he hath very oft of late
Given private time to you, and you yourself
Have of your audience been most free and bounte-
     ous.   525
If it be so—as so 'tis put on me,
And that in way of caution—I must tell you,
You do not understand yourself so clearly
As it behoves my daughter and your honor.
What is between you? Give me up the truth!   530
   OPHEL. He hath, my lord, of late made many
     tenders
Of his affection to me.
   POLON. Affection! Pooh! You speak like a green
     girl,
Unsifted in such perilous circumstance.
Do you believe his "tenders," as you call them?   535
   OPHEL. I do not know, my lord, what I should
     think.
   POLON. Marry, I'll teach you! think yourself a
     baby,
That you have ta'en his "tenders" for true pay,
Which are not sterling. "Tender" yourself more
     dearly;
Or—not to crack the wind of the poor phrase   540
Running it thus—you'll "tender" me a fool.
   OPHEL. My lord, he hath importun'd me with
     love
In honorable fashion—
   POLON. Aye, "fashion" you may call it. Go to!
     Go to!
   OPHEL. And hath given countenance to his
     speech, my lord,   545
With almost all the holy vows of heaven.
   POLON. Aye, springes to catch woodcocks! I do
     know,
When the blood burns, how prodigal the soul
Lends the tongue vows. These blazes, daughter,
Giving more light than heat—extinct in both,   550
Even in their promise as it is a-making—
You must not take for fire. From this time
Be somewhat scanter of your maiden presence;
Set your entreatments at a higher rate
Than a command to parley. For Lord Hamlet,   555
Believe so much in him, that he is young,
And with a larger tether may he walk
Than may be given you. In few, Ophelia,

Do not believe his vows; for they are brokers,
Not of that dye which their investments show,   560
But mere implorators of unholy suits,
Breathing like sanctified and pious bawds
The better to beguile. This is for all:
I would not, in plain terms, from this time forth
Have you so slander any moment's leisure   565
As to give words or talk with the Lord Hamlet.
Look to't, I charge you! Come your ways.
   OPHEL. I shall obey, my lord.   [*Exeunt.*

SCENE IV:—*Midnight of the same day. Before the
castle.*

HAMLET, HORATIO, *and* MARCELLUS *on the sentinel's
platform waiting for the visitation of the* GHOST.

   HAML. The air bites shrewdly; it is very cold.
   HORAT. It is a nipping and an eager air.   570
   HAML. What hour now?
   HORAT.   I think it lacks of twelve.
   MARC. No, it is struck.
   HORAT. Indeed? I heard it not. Then it draws
     near the season
Wherein the spirit held his wont to walk.

*The roll of kettle-drums, a flourish of trumpets,
and two cannon shot off within.*

What does this mean, my lord?   575
   HAML. The king doth wake tonight, and takes
     his rouse,
Keeps wassail, and the swaggering up-spring reels;
And, as he drains his draughts of Rhenish down,
The kettle-drum and trumpet thus bray out
The triumph of his pledge.
   HORAT.   Is it a custom?   580
   HAML. Aye, marry, is't:
But to my mind—though I am native here
And to the manner born—it is a custom
More honor'd in the breach than the observance.
This heavy-headed revel east and west   585
Makes us traduc'd and tax'd of other nations;
They clepe us drunkards, and with swinish phrase
Soil our addition; and, indeed, it takes
From our achievements, though perform'd at
     height,
The pith and marrow of our attribute: 590
So, oft it chances in particular men,
That for some vicious mole of nature in them,
As in their birth—wherein they are not guilty,
Since nature cannot choose his origin—
By the o'ergrowth of some complexion,   595
Oft breaking down the pales and forts of reason,
Or by some habit that too much o'er-leavens

The form of plausive manners, that these men,
Carrying, I say, the stamp of one defect—
Being nature's livery, or fortune's star—   600
Their virtues else, be they as pure as grace,
As infinite as man may undergo,
Shall, in the general censure, take corruption
From that particular fault: the dram of eale   605
Doth all the noble substance of a doubt
To his own scandal—

Enter GHOST.

HORAT.   Look, my lord! It comes!
HAML. Angels and ministers of grace defend
      us!—
Be thou a spirit of health, or goblin damn'd,
Bring with thee airs from heaven, or blasts from
      hell,
Be thy intents wicked, or charitable,   610
Thou comest in such a questionable shape
That I will speak to thee. I'll call thee "Hamlet,"
"King," "Father."—Royal Dane, O, answer me!
Let me not burst in ignorance; but tell
Why thy canonized bones, hearsed in death,   615
Have burst their cerements; why the sepulcher,
Wherein we saw thee quietly inurn'd,
Hath op'd his ponderous and marble jaws
To cast thee up again. What may this mean,
That thou, dead corse, again in complete steel   620
Revisit'st thus the glimpses of the moon,
Making night hideous, and we fools of nature
So horridly to shake our disposition
With thoughts beyond the reaches of our souls?
Say, why is this? Wherefore? What should we
      do?   625

The GHOST *beckons* HAMLET.

HORAT. It beckons you to go away with it,
As if it some impartment did desire
To you alone.

The GHOST *beckons again.*

MARC.   Look, with what courteous action
It waves you to a more removed ground.
But do not go with it!
      HORAT.   No! by no means!   630
HAML. It will not speak? then will I follow it.
HORAT. Do not, my lord!
HAML.   Why, what should be the fear?
I do not set my life at a pin's fee;
And for my soul, what can it do to that,
Being a thing immortal as itself?   635

The GHOST *beckons a third time.*

It waves me forth again. I'll follow it.
      HORAT. What if it tempt you toward the flood
      my lord?
Or to the dreadful summit of the cliff
That beetles o'er his base into the sea,
And there assume some other horrible form   640
Which might deprive your sovereignty of reason
And draw you into madness? Think of it.
The very place puts toys of desperation,
Without more motive, into every brain
That looks so many fathoms to the sea   645
And hears it roar beneath.

The GHOST *beckons again.*

HAML. It waves me still.—Go on; I'll follow thee.
MARC. You shall not go, my lord!

They seize him.

HAML.   Hold off your hands!
HORAT. Be rul'd. You shall not go!
HAML.   My fate cries out,
And makes each petty artery in this body   650
As hardy as the Nemean lion's nerve.

The GHOST *beckons again.*

Still am I call'd.—Unhand me, gentlemen!

Draws his sword.

By heaven, I'll make a ghost of him that lets me!
I say, away!

He breaks from them.

            Go on; I'll follow thee.
[*Exit the* GHOST, *followed by* HAMLET *with
      sword drawn.*
HORAT. He waxes desperate with imagination.
MARC. Let's follow; 'tis not fit thus to obey
      him.   656
HORAT. Have after. To what issue will this come?
MARC. Something is rotten in the state of Den-
      mark.
HORAT. Heaven will direct it.
MARC.   Nay, let's follow him.
                                    [*Exeunt.*

SCENE V:—*A few moments later. Another part of
            the platform.*

Enter GHOST *and* HAMLET.

HAML. Whither wilt thou lead me? Speak. I'll
      go no further.   660
GHOST. Mark me!
HAML.   I will.

GHOST.   My hour is almost come
When I to sulphurous and tormenting flames
Must render up myself.

HAML.   Alas! poor ghost!

GHOST. Pity me not, but lend thy serious hearing
To what I shall unfold.

HAML.   Speak; I am bound to hear.

GHOST. So art thou to revenge, when thou shalt
    hear!   666

HAML. What?

GHOST. I am thy father's spirit,
Doom'd for a certain term to walk the night,
And for the day confin'd to fast in fires,   670
Till the foul crimes done in my days of nature
Are burnt and purg'd away. But that I am forbid
To tell the secrets of my prison-house,
I could a tale unfold whose lightest word   674
Would harrow up thy soul, freeze thy young blood,
Make thy two eyes, like stars, start from their
       spheres,
Thy knotted and combined locks to part
And each particular hair to stand an end
Like quills upon the fretful porpentine.
But this eternal blazon must not be   680
To ears of flesh and blood. List, Hamlet! O, list!
If thou didst ever thy dear father love—

HAML. O God!

GHOST. Revenge his foul and most unnatural
    murder!

HAML. Murder!   685

GHOST. Murder—most foul, as in the best it is,
But this most foul, strange, and unnatural.

HAML. Haste me to know't, that I with wings as
    swift
As meditation or the thoughts of love
May sweep to my revenge!

GHOST.   I find thee apt.   690
And duller shouldst thou be than the fat weed
That roots itself in ease on Lethe wharf
Wouldst thou not stir in this! Now, Hamlet, hear:
'Tis given out that, sleeping in mine orchard,
A serpent stung me; so the whole ear of Denmark
Is by a forged process of my death   696
Rankly abus'd. But know, thou noble youth,
The serpent that did sting thy father's life
Now wears his crown.

HAML.   O my prophetic soul!
My uncle?   700

GHOST. Ay. That incestuous, that adulterate
    beast,
With witchcraft of his wit, with traitorous gifts—
O wicked wit and gifts, that have the power
So to seduce!—won to his shameful lust

The will of my most seeming-virtuous queen.   705
O, Hamlet! What a falling-off was there,
From me, whose love was of that dignity
That it went hand in hand even with the vow
I made to her in marriage; and to decline
Upon a wretch, whose natural gifts were poor   710
To those of mine!
But virtue, as it never will be mov'd,
Though lewdness court it in a shape of heaven,
So lust, though to a radiant angel link'd,
Will sate itself in a celestial bed,   715
And prey on garbage.—
But, soft! methinks I scent the morning air.
Brief let me be. Sleeping within mine orchard-
My custom always in the afternoon—
Upon my secure hour thy uncle stole,   720
With juice of cursed hebona in a vial,
And in the porches of mine ears did pour
The leperous distillment; whose effect
Holds such an enmity with blood of man
That swift as quicksilver it courses through   725
The natural gates and alleys of the body,
And with a sudden vigor it doth posset
And curd, like eager droppings into milk,
The thin and wholesome blood: so did it mine;
And a most instant tetter bark'd about,   730
Most lazar-like, with vile and loathsome crust,
All my smooth body.
Thus was I, sleeping, by a brother's hand,
Of life, of crown, of queen, at once dispatch'd;
Cut off even in the blossoms of my sin,   735
Unhousel'd, disappointed, unanel'd,
No reckoning made, but sent to my account
With all my imperfections on my head.
O, horrible! O, horrible! most horrible!
If thou hast nature in thee, bear it not!   740
Let not the royal bed of Denmark be
A couch for luxury and damned incest!—
But, howsoever thou pursuest this act,
Taint not thy mind, nor let thy soul contrive
Against thy mother aught; leave her to heaven,
And to those thorns that in her bosom lodge,   746
To prick and sting her.—Fare thee well at once!
The glow-worm shows the matin to be near,
And 'gins to pale his uneffectual fire.
Adieu!—Adieu!—Hamlet, remember me!   750

The GHOST *sinks beneath the stage.* HAMLET *for a
time stands dazed, then tremblingly sags to his
knees.*

HAML. O all you host of heaven!—O earth!—
    What else?

And shall I couple hell? O fie!—Hold, hold, my
    heart!
And you, my sinews, grow not instant old,
But bear me stiffly up! [*Rises.*] Remember thee?
Aye, thou poor ghost, while memory holds a seat
In this distracted globe. Remember thee?   756
Yea, from the table of my memory
I'll wipe away all trivial fond records,
All saws of books, all forms, all pressures past
That youth and observation copied there,   760
And thy commandment, all alone, shall live
Within the book and volume of my brain
Unmix'd with baser matter: yes, by heaven!—
O most pernicious woman!—
O villain! villain! smiling, damned villain!   765
My tables.

He takes out his memorandum-book.

         Meet it is I set it down,
That one may smile, and smile, and be a villain—
At least I'm sure it may be so in Denmark.
                     [*Writing.*]
So, uncle, there you are! Now to my word;
It is [*Writing.*] "Adieu, adieu! Remember me!"—
I have sworn't!   771
   HORAT. [*within*]. My lord! My lord!
   MARC. [*within*].   Lord Hamlet!
   HORAT. [*within*].   Heaven secure him.
   MARC. [*within*]. So be it!
   HORAT. [*within*]. Hillo! ho ho! My lord!
   HAML. Hillo, ho, ho, boy! come, bird, come!

Enter HORATIO *and* MARCELLUS.

   MARC. How is't, my noble lord?
   HORAT.   What news, my lord?
   HAML. O, wonderful!
   HORAT.   Good, my lord, tell it.   776
   HAML. No; you'll reveal it.
   HORAT. Not I, my lord, by heaven!
   MARC.   Nor I, my lord.
   HAML. How say you, then! Would heart of man
     once think it!
But, you'll be secret?
   HORAT. ⎫
   MARC.   ⎬   Aye, by heaven, my lord.   780
   HAML. There's ne'er a villain dwelling in all
     Denmark—
But he's an arrant knave.
    HORAT. There needs no ghost, my lord, come
     from the grave
To tell us this.

   HAML.   Why, right! you are i' the right!
And so, without more circumstance at all,   786
I hold it fit that we shake hands and part.

Shakes hands with them.

You, as your business and desire shall point you—
For every man hath business and desire,
Such as it is—and, for mine own poor part,   790
Look you, I'll go pray.
   HORAT. These are but wild and whirling words,
     my lord.
   HAML. I am sorry they offend you; heartily;
Yes, faith, heartily.
   HORAT.   There's no offense, my lord.
   HAML. Yes, by Saint Patrick, but there is, Ho-
     ratio!   795
And much offense, too. Touching this vision here,
It is an honest ghost, that let me tell you.
For your desire to know what is between us,
O'ermaster't as you may. And now, good friends,
As you are friends, scholars, and soldiers,   800
Give me one poor request.
   HORAT. What is't, my lord? we will.
   HAML. Never make known what you have seen
     tonight.
   HORAT. ⎫
   MARC. ⎬ My lord, we will not.
   HAML.   Nay, but swear't.
   HORAT.   In faith,
My lord, not I.
   MARC.   Nor I, my lord, in faith.   805
   HAML. [*holding up his sword*]. Upon my sword.
   MARC.   We have sworn, my lord, already.
   HAML. Indeed, upon my sword; indeed!
   GHOST [*beneath*]. Swear!
   HAML. Ah, ha, boy! say'st thou so? Art thou
     there, true-penny?—
Come on; you hear this fellow in the cellarage.   810

*He leads them to another place, and holds up his
sword.*

Consent to swear.
   HORAT.   Propose the oath, my lord.
   HAML. Never to speak of this that you have seen.
Swear by my sword.
   GHOST [*beneath*]. Swear!
   HAML. *Hic et ubique?* then we'll shift our
     ground.—   815
Come hither, gentlemen;

He leads them to another place.

And lay your hands again upon my sword.
Never to speak of this that you have heard;
Swear by my sword.

GHOST [*beneath*]. Swear! 820

HAML. Well said, old mole! Canst work i' the earth so fast?

A worthy pioner!—Once more remove, good friends.

He leads them to another place.

HORAT. O day and night, but this is wondrous strange!

HAML. And therefore as a stranger give it welcome.

There are more things in heaven and earth, Horatio, 825

Than are dreamt of in your philosophy.

But come.

He holds up his sword.

Here, as before, never, so help you mercy,

How strange or odd soe'er I bear myself—

As I perchance hereafter shall think meet 830

To put an antic disposition on—

That you, at such times seeing me, never shall,

With arms encumber'd thus, or this head-shake,

Or by pronouncing of some doubtful phrase

As "Well, well, we know," or, "We could, an if we would," 835

Or, "If we list to speak," or, "There be, an if they might,"

Or such ambiguous giving-out, to note

That you know aught of me. This not to do,

So grace and mercy at your most need help you.

Swear! 840

GHOST [*beneath*]. Swear!

HAML. Rest, rest, perturbed spirit!

They swear, touching their lips to the sword.

So, gentlemen,

With all my love I do commend me to you:

And what so poor a man as Hamlet is 844

May do to express his love and friending to you,

God willing, shall not lack. Let us go in together.

And still your fingers on your lips, I pray.

[*Aside.*] The time is out of joint; O cursed spite

That ever I was born to set it right! 849

[*Aloud.*] Nay, come; let's go together. [*Exeunt.*

ACT II

SCENE I:—*Two months later. A room in Polonius' house.*

Enter POLONIUS *and his servant* REYNALDO.

POLON. Give him this money, and these notes, Reynaldo.

REYN. I will, my lord.

POLON. You shall do marvelous wisely, good Reynaldo,

Before you visit him, to make inquiry

Of his behavior.

REYN. My lord, I did intend it. 855

POLON. Marry, well said! very well said! Look you, sir,

Inquire me first what Danskers are in Paris;

And how, and who; what means, and where they keep;

What company, at what expense: and, finding

By this encompassment and drift of question 860

That they do know my son, come you more nearer

Than your particular demands will touch it;

Take you, as 'twere, some distant knowledge of him,

As thus: "I know his father, and his friends;

And, in part, him."—Do you mark this, Reynaldo?

REYN. Aye, very well, my lord. 866

POLON. "And, in part, him; but," you may say, "not well:

But if't be he I mean, he's very wild,

Addicted"—so and so. And there put on him

What forgeries you please; marry, none so rank

As may dishonor him; take heed of that! 87?

But, sir, such wanton, wild, and usual slips

As are companions noted and most known

To youth and liberty.

REYN. As gaming, my lord?

POLON. Aye; or drinking, fencing, swearing, quarreling,— 875

Drabbing; you may go so far.

REYN. My lord! that would dishonor him.

POLON. Faith, no; as you may season it in the charge.

You must not put another scandal on him,

That he is open to incontinency; 880

That's not my meaning; but breathe his faults so quaintly

That they may seem the taints of liberty,

The flash and outbreak of a fiery mind,

A savageness in unreclaimed blood,

Of general assault.

REYN. But, my good lord,— 885

POLON. Wherefore should you do this?

REYN. Aye, my lord;

I would know that.

POLON. Marry, sir, here's my drift,

And, I believe, it is a fetch of warrant:

You laying these slight sullies on my son,

As 'twere a thing a little soil'd i' the working— 890

Mark you?

Your party in converse—him you would sound—
Having ever seen in the prenominate crimes
The youth you breathe of guilty, be assur'd
He closes with you in this consequence: 895
"Good sir," or so; or "Friend," or "Gentleman,"
According to the phrase or the addition.
Of man and country—
    REYN.   Very good, my lord.
    POLON. And then, sir—does he this—he docs—
What was I about to say? By the mass I was about
to say something. Where did I leave?   901
    REYN. At "closes in the consequence,"
At "friend or so," and "gentleman."
    POLON. At "closes in the consequence"? aye,
      marry!
He closes with you thus: "I know the gentleman;
I saw him yesterday, or t'other day,   906
Or then, or then, with such, or such; and, as you
    say,
There was he gaming; there, o'ertook in's rouse;
There, falling out at tennis";
See you now?   910
Your bait of falsehood takes this carp of truth.
And thus do we of wisdom and of reach,
With windlasses, and with assays of bias,
By indirections find directions out:
So, by my former lecture and advice,   915
Shall you my son. You have me, have you not?
    REYN. My lord, I have.
    POLON.   God be wi' you; fare you well!
    REYN. Good my lord.   [*Leaving.*
    POLON. Observe his inclination in yourself.
    REYN. I shall, my lord.   920
    POLON. And let him ply his music.
    REYN.   Well, my lord.
    POLON. Farewell!   [*Exit* REYNALDO.

    Enter OPHELIA *running in fright.*

        How now, Ophelia! What's the matter?
    OPHEL. Oh, my lord! my lord! I have been so
    affrighted!
    POLON. With what, in the name of God?
    OPHEL. My lord, as I was sewing in my closet,
Lord Hamlet, with his doublet all unbrac'd,   926
No hat upon his head, his stockings foul'd,
Ungarter'd, and down-gyved to his ankle,
Pale as his shirt, his knees knocking each other,
And with a look so piteous in purport   930
As if he had been loosed out of hell
To speak of horrors, he comes before me.
    POLON. Mad for thy love?
    OPHEL.   My lord, I do not know;
But, truly, I do fear it.

    POLON.   What said he?
    OPHEL. He took me by the wrist, and held me
    hard.   935
Then goes he to the length of all his arm;
And, with his other hand thus o'er his brow,
He falls to such perusal of my face
As he would draw it. Long stay'd he so.
At last, a little shaking of mine arm,   940
And thrice his head thus waving up and down,
He rais'd a sigh so piteous and profound
That it did seem to shatter all his bulk
And end his being. That done, he lets me go.
And, with his head over his shoulder turn'd,   945
He seem'd to find his way without his eyes;
For out o'doors he went without their help,
And to the last bended their light on me.
    POLON. Come! Go with me! I will go seek the
    king.
This is the very ecstasy of love,   950
Whose violent property fordoes itself
And leads the will to desperate undertakings
As oft as any passion under heaven
That does afflict our natures. I am sorry—
What! have you given him any hard words of
    late?   955
    OPHEL. No, my good lord; but—as you did com-
    mand—
I did repel his letters, and denied
His access to me.
    POLON.   That hath made him mad!
I am sorry that with better heed and judgment
I had not quoted him. I fear'd he did but trifle,
And meant to wrack thee. But, beshrew my
    jealousy!   961
It seems it is as proper to our age
To cast beyond ourselves in our opinions
As it is common for the younger sort
To lack discretion. Come, go we to the king.   965
This must be known; which, being kept close,
    might move
More grief to hide than hate to utter love.
Come!   [*Exeunt.*

SCENE II:—*Later the same day. A room in the
castle.*

Enter KING, QUEEN, ROSENCRANTZ, GUILDENSTERN,
and Attendants.

    KING Welcome, dear Rosencrantz and Guilden-
stern!
Moreover that we much did long to see you,   970
The need we have to use you did provoke
Our hasty sending. Something have you heard

Of Hamlet's transformation—so I call it,
Since nor the exterior nor the inward man
Resembles that it was. What it should be,   975
More than his father's death, that thus hath put
  him
So much from the understanding of himself,
I cannot dream of. I entreat you both,
That, being of so young days brought up with
  him,   979
And since so neighbor'd to his youth and humor,
That you vouchsafe your rest here in our court
Some little time; so by your companies
To draw him on to pleasures, and to gather,
So much as from occasion you may glean,
Whe'r aught to us unknown afflicts him thus,
That, open'd, lies within our remedy.   986
    QUEEN. Good gentlemen, he hath much talk'd of
      you;
And sure I am two men there are not living
To whom he more adheres. If it will please you
To show us so much gentry and good will   990
As to expend your time with us awhile
For the supply and profit of our hope,
Your visitation shall receive such thanks
As fits a king's remembrance.
    ROSENC.   Both your majesties
Might, by the sovereign power you have of us,
Put your dread pleasures more into command
Than to entreaty.
    GUILDEN.   But we both obey,   997
And here give up ourselves in the full bent,
To lay our service freely at your feet
To be commanded.   1000
    KING. Thanks, Rosencrantz and gentle Guilden-
      stern.
    QUEEN. Thanks, Guildenstern and gentle Rosen-
      crantz.
And I beseech you instantly to visit
My too much changed son.—Go, some of you,
And bring these gentlemen where Hamlet is.
    GUILDEN. Heavens make our presence and our
      practices   1006
Pleasant and helpful to him!
    QUEEN.   Aye, amen!
      [Exeunt ROSENCRANTZ, GUILDENSTERN, and
        Attendants.

                  Enter POLONIUS.

    POLON. The ambassadors from Norway, my good
      lord,
Are joyfully return'd.
    KING. Thou still hast been the father of good
      news.   1010

    POLON. Have I, my lord? Assure you, my good
      liege,
I hold my duty, as I hold my soul,
Both to my God and to my gracious king.
And I do think—or else this brain of mine
Hunts not the trail of policy so sure   1015
As it hath us'd to do—that I have found
The very cause of Hamlet's lunacy.
    KING. O, speak of that! that do I long to hear.
    POLON. Give first admittance to the ambassadors;
My news shall be the fruit to that great feast. 1020
    KING. Thyself do grace to them and bring them
      in.   [Exit POLONIUS.
He tells me, my sweet queen, that he hath found
The head and source of all your son's distemper.
    QUEEN. I doubt it is no other but the main—
His father's death, and our o'erhasty marriage.
    KING. Well, we shall sift him.

    Re-enter POLONIUS, with VOLTIMAND and
                CORNELIUS.

                          Welcome, my good friends!
Say, Voltimand, what from our brother Norway?
    VOLTI. Most fair return of greetings and desires.
Upon our first, he sent out to suppress   1029
His nephew's levies, which to him appear'd
To be a preparation 'gainst the Polack,
But, better look'd into, he truly found
It was against your highness; whereat griev'd
That so his sickness, age, and impotence
Was falsely borne in hand, sends out arrests   1035
On Fortinbras; which he, in brief, obeys,
Receives rebuke from Norway, and, in fine,
Makes vow before his uncle never more
To give the assay of arms against your majesty.
Whereon old Norway, overcome with joy,   1040
Gives him three thousand crowns in annual fee,
And his commission to employ those soldiers,
So levied as before, against the Polack;
With an entreaty, herein further shown, [Giving
  a paper.]
That it might please you to give quiet pass   1045
Through your dominions for this enterprise,
On such regards of safety and allowance
As therein are set down.
    KING.   It likes us well;
And at our more consider'd time we'll read,
Answer, and think upon this business: 1050
Meantime we thank you for your well-took labor.
Go to your rest; at night we'll feast together.
Most welcome home.
                      [Exeunt VOLTIMAND and CORNELIUS.

POLON.   This business is well ended.
My liege, and madam, to expostulate
What majesty should be, what duty is,   1055
Why day is day, night night, and time is time,
Were nothing but to waste night, day, and time.
Therefore, since brevity is the soul of wit,
And tediousness the limbs and outward flourishes,
I will be brief. Your noble son is mad.   1060
Mad call I it; for, to define true madness,
What is't but to be nothing else but mad?
But let that go.
     QUEEN.   More matter, with less art.
     POLON. Madam, I swear I use no art at all.
That he is mad, 'tis true; 'tis true 'tis pity;   1065
And, pity 'tis 'tis true. A foolish figure;
But farewell it, for I will use no art.
Mad let us grant him, then. And now remains
That we find out the cause of this effect—
Or rather say, the cause of this defect;   1070
For this effect-defective comes by cause.
Thus it remains, and the remainder thus.
Perpend!
I have a daughter—have while she is mine—
Who, in her duty and obedience,—mark!—   1075
Hath given me this.

                Holds up a letter.

                    Now, gather, and surmise!

          Reads the address on the outside.

*To the celestial, and my soul's idol, the most beau-
     tified Ophelia,—*
That's an ill phrase! a vile phrase! "beautified" is
a vile phrase. But you shall hear. Thus:
     in her excellent white bosom, these, &c.
     QUEEN [*reaching out for the letter*]. Came this
          from Hamlet to her?   1081
     POLON. Good madam, stay awhile. I will be faith-
ful.

               Unfolds the letter and reads.

          Doubt thou the stars are fire;
          Doubt that the sun doth move;
          Doubt truth to be a liar;   1085
          But never doubt I love.
*O dear Ophelia! I am ill at these numbers: I
have not art to reckon my groans; but that I love
thee, Best, O most Best! believe it. Adieu.*
          Thine evermore, most dear lady, whilst
               this machine is to him,
                         Hamlet.
This, in obedience, hath my daughter shown me;
And, more above, hath his solicitings,   1094

As they fell out by time, by means, and place,
All given to mine ear.
     KING.   But how hath she
Receiv'd his love?
     POLON. [*in an injured tone*].   What do you
          think of me?
     KING. As of a man faithful and honorable.
     POLON. I would fain prove so. But what might
          you think,
When I had seen this hot love on the wing—
As I perceiv'd it, I must tell you that,   1101
Before my daughter told me—what might you,
Or my dear majesty your queen here, think,
If I had play'd the desk or table-book,
Or given my heart a winking mute and dumb,
Or look'd upon this love with idle sight?   1106
What might you think? No! I went round to
     work,
And my young mistress thus I did bespeak:
"Lord Hamlet is a prince, out of thy star;
This must not be!" And then I precepts gave her,
That she should lock herself from his resort,   1111
Admit no messengers, receive no tokens.
Which done, she took the fruits of my advice;
And he, repulsed—a short tale to make—
Fell into a sadness; then into a fast;   1115
Thence to a watch; thence into a weakness;
Thence to a lightness; and, by this declension,
Into the madness wherein now he raves
And all we wail for!
     KING [*to* GERTRUDE].   Do you think 'tis this?
     QUEEN. It may be; very likely.   1120
     POLON. Hath there been such a time—I'd fain
          know that—
That I have positively said, " 'Tis so,"
When it prov'd otherwise?
     KING.   Not that I know.
     POLON. Take this from this, if this be otherwise.
          [*Pointing to his head and shoulder.*]
If circumstances lead me, I will find   1125
Where truth is hid, though it were hid indeed
Within the center!
     KING.   How may we try it further?
     POLON. You know sometimes he walks four
          hours together
Here in the lobby.
     QUEEN.   So he does indeed.
     POLON. At such a time I'll loose my daughter to
          him;   1130
Be you and I behind an arras then;
Mark the encounter. If he love her not,
And be not from his reason fallen thereon,

Let me be no assistant for a state,
But keep a farm and carters.

KING.   We will try it.   1135

QUEEN. But look, where sadly the poor wretch
comes reading.

POLON. Away, I do beseech you! both away!
I'll board him presently.

[*Exeunt* KING *and* QUEEN.

Enter HAMLET, *reading on a book.*
POLONIUS *steps before him.*

                         O, give me leave.
How does my good Lord Hamlet?

HAML. Well, God a-mercy.   1140

POLON. Do you know me, my lord?

HAML. Excellent well; you are a fishmonger.

POLON. Not I, my lord!

HAML. Then I would you were so honest a man.

POLON. "Honest," my lord?   1145

HAML. Aye, sir; to be honest, as this world goes,
is to be one man picked out of ten thousand.

POLON. That's very true, my lord.

HAML. For, if the sun breed maggots in a dead
dog, being a good kissing carrion— Have you a
daughter?

POLON. I have, my lord.   1152

HAML. Let her not walk i' the sun! Friend, look
to't!

POLON. [*aside*]. How say you by that? Still harping on my daughter! Yet he knew me not at first;
he said I was a fishmonger. He is far gone! far
gone! And, truly, in my youth I suffered much extremity for love; very near this. I'll speak to him
again.—What do you read, my lord?   1160

HAML. Words, words, words.

POLON. What is the matter, my lord?

HAML. Between who?

POLON. I mean the matter that you read, my
lord.   1165

HAML. Slanders, sir: for the satirical rogue says
here that old men have gray beards, that their faces
are wrinkled, their eyes purging thick amber or
plum-tree gum, and that they have a plentiful lack
of wit, together with most weak hams. All which,
sir, though I most powerfully and potently believe,
yet I hold it not honesty to have it thus set down;
for you yourself, sir, should be old, as I am—if, like
a crab, you could go backward.   1174

POLON. [*aside*]. Though this be madness, yet
there is method in't!—Will you walk out of the
air, my lord?

HAML. Into my grave?

POLON. Indeed, that is out o' the air. [*Aside.*]

How pregnant sometimes his replies are! a happiness that often madness hits on, which reason and
sanity could not so prosperously be delivered of. I
will leave him, and suddenly contrive the means of
meeting between him and my daughter.—My
honorable lord, I will most humbly take my leave
of you.   1186

HAML. You cannot, sir, take from me anything
that I will more willingly part withal—except my
life, except my life, except my life.

POLON. Fare you well, my lord. [*Leaving.*]

HAML. These tedious old fools!   1191

Enter ROSENCRANTZ *and* GUILDENSTERN. POLONIUS
meets them at the door.

POLON. You go to seek the Lord Hamlet? there
he is.

ROSENC. [*to* POLONIUS]. God save you, sir!

[*Exit* POLONIUS. GUILDENSTERN *and* ROSEN-
CRANTZ *rush forward to greet* HAMLET.

GUILDEN. Mine honored lord!   1195

ROSENC. My most dear lord!

HAML. My excellent good friends! How dost
thou, Guildenstern? Ah, Rosencrantz! Good lads,
how do ye both?

ROSENC. As the indifferent children of the earth.

GUILDEN. Happy in that we are not over happy;
on Fortune's cap we are not the very button.

HAML. Nor the soles of her shoe?

ROSENC. Neither, my lord.

HAML. What news?   1205

ROSENC. None, my lord, but that the world's
grown honest.

HAML. Then is doomsday near. But your news
is not true. Let me question more in particular.
What have you, my good friends, deserved at the
hands of Fortune, that she sends you to prison
hither?

GUILDEN. Prison, my lord!

HAML. Denmark's a prison.

ROSENC. Then is the world one.   1213

HAML. A goodly one; in which there are many
confines, wards, and dungeons, Denmark being
one o' the worst.

ROSENC. We think not so, my lord.

HAML. Why, then 'tis none to you; for there is
nothing either good or bad but thinking makes it
so. To me it is a prison.

ROSENC. Why, then your ambition makes it one.
'Tis too narrow for your mind.   1222

HAML. O God! I could be bounded in a nutshell
and count myself a king of infinite space, were it
not that I have bad dreams.

GUILDEN. Which dreams, indeed, are ambition; for the very substance of the ambitious is merely the shadow of a dream. 1230

HAML. A dream itself is but a shadow.

ROSENC. Truly; and I hold ambition of so airy and light a quality that it is but a shadow's shadow.

HAML. Then are our beggars bodies, and our monarchs and outstretched heroes the beggars' shadows. Shall we to the court? for, by my fay, I cannot reason. 1238

ROSENC. }
GUILDEN. } We'll wait upon you.

HAML. No such matter; I will not sort you with the rest of my servants; for, to speak to you like an honest man, I am most dreadfully attended.—But, in the beaten way of friendship, what make you at Elsinore? 1244

ROSENC. To visit you, my lord; no other occasion.

HAML. Beggar that I am, I am even poor in thanks! But, I thank you; and sure, dear friends, my thanks are too dear a halfpenny.—Were you not sent for? Is it your own inclining? Is it a free visitation? Come; come; deal justly with me. [*They hesitate.*] Come, come. Nay, speak. 1252

GUILDEN. What should we say, my lord?

HAML. Why anything, but to the purpose. You were sent for; and there is a kind of confession in your looks which your modesties have not craft enough to color. I know the good king and queen have sent for you. 1258

ROSENC. To what end, my lord?

HAML. That you must teach me.—But let me conjure you: By the rights of our fellowship, by the consonancy of our youth, by the obligation of our ever-preserved love, and by what more dear a better proposer could charge you withal, be even and direct with me, whether you were sent for or no! 1266

ROSENC. [*aside to* GUILDENSTERN]. What say you?

HAML. [*aside*]. Nay, then, I have an eye of you.—If you love me, hold not off.

GUILDEN. My lord, we were sent for. 1270

HAML. I will tell you why; so shall my anticipation prevent your discovery, and your secrecy to the king and queen molt no feather. I have of late—but wherefore I know not—lost all my mirth, forgone all custom of exercise; and indeed it goes so heavily with my disposition that this goodly frame, the earth, seems to me a sterile promontory; this most excellent canopy, the air—look you!—this brave o'erhanging firmament, this majestical

roof fretted with golden fire,—why, it appears no other thing to me but a foul and pestilent congregation of vapors. What a piece of work is a man! How noble in reason! how infinite in faculty! in form, in moving, how express and admirable! in action how like an angel! in apprehension how like a god! the beauty of the world! the paragon of animals! And yet to me, what is this quintessence of dust? man delights not me.—No, nor woman neither, though by your smiling you seem to say so. 1290

ROSENC. My lord, there was no such stuff in my thoughts.

HAML. Why did you laugh, then, when I said, "man delights not me"?

ROSENC. To think, my lord, if you delight not in man, what lenten entertainment the players shall receive from you. We coted them on the way, and hither are they coming to offer you service. 1298

HAML. He that plays the king shall be welcome, his majesty shall have tribute of me; the adventurous knight shall use his foil and target; the lover shall not sigh gratis; the humorous man shall end his part in peace; the clown shall make those laugh whose lungs are tickle o' the sere; and the lady shall say her mind freely, or the blank verse shall halt for't. What players are they? 1306

ROSENC. Even those you were wont to take such delight in, the tragedians of the city.

HAML. How chances it they travel? Their residence, both in reputation and profit, was better both ways.

ROSENC. I think their inhibition comes by the means of the late innovation. 1313

HAML. Do they hold the same estimation they did when I was in the city? Are they so followed?

ROSENC. No, indeed, are they not.

HAML. How comes it? Do they grow rusty?

ROSENC. Nay, their endeavor keeps in the wonted pace: but there is, sir, an aery of children, little eyases, that cry out on the top of question, and are most tyrannically clapped for't. These are now the fashion, and so berattle the "common stages"—so they call them—that many wearing rapiers are afraid of goose-quills, and dare scarce come thither. 1325

HAML. What! are they children? Who maintains 'em? How are they escoted? Will they pursue the quality no longer than they can sing? Will they not say afterwards, if they should grow themselves to "common" players—as it is most like if their means are no better—their writers do them wrong to make them exclaim against their own succession? 1333

ROSENC. Faith, there has been much to-do on both sides; and the nation holds it no sin to tarre them to controversy. There was, for a while, no money bid for argument unless the poet and the player went to cuffs in the question.

HAML. Is it possible!

GUILDEN. O! there has been much throwing about of brains.

HAML. Do the boys carry it away? 1341

ROSENC. Aye, that they do, my lord—Hercules and his load, too.

HAML. It is not very strange; for my uncle is King of Denmark, and those that would make mows at him while my father lived, give twenty, forty, fifty, an hundred ducats a-piece for his picture in little. 'Sblood, there is something in this more than natural, if philosophy could find it out.

A flourish within, announcing the arrival of the players at the outer castle gates.

GUILDEN. There are the players. 1351

HAML. Gentlemen, you are welcome to Elsinore. Your hands; come. The appurtenance of welcome is fashion and ceremony; let me comply with you in this garb, lest my extent to the players, which, I tell you, must show fairly outward, should more appear like entertainment than yours. You are welcome.—But my uncle-father and aunt-mother are deceived.

GUILDEN. In what, my dear lord? 1360

HAML. I am but mad north-north-west: when the wind is southerly I know a hawk from a handsaw.

Enter POLONIUS.

POLON. Well be with you, gentlemen!

HAML. Hark you, Guildenstern; and you, too: at each ear a hearer. [*They gather about him. He whispers.*] That great baby you see there is not yet out of his swaddling-clouts.

ROSENC. Happily he's the second time come to them; for, they say, an old man is twice a child.

HAML. I will prophesy he comes to tell me of the players; mark it. [*Aloud.*] You say right, sir; o' Monday morning; 'twas so, indeed. 1372

POLON. My lord, I have news to tell you.

HAML. My lord, I have news to tell you. When Roscius was an actor in Rome—

POLON. The actors are come hither, my lord!

HAML. Buzz, buzz!

POLON. Upon my honor!

HAML. Then came each actor on his ass. 1379

POLON. The best actors in the world, either for tragedy, comedy, history, pastoral, pastoral-comical, historical-pastoral, tragical-historical, tragical-comical-historical-pastoral, scene individable, or poem unlimited. Seneca cannot be too heavy, nor Plautus too light, for the law of writ and the liberty; these are the only men— 1386

HAML. O Jephthah, judge of Israel, what a treasure hadst thou!

POLON. What a treasure had he, my lord?

HAML. Why—

> One fair daughter and no more,
> The which he loved passing well.

POLON. [*aside*]. Still on my daughter!

HAML. Am I not i' the right, old Jephthah?

POLON. If you call me Jephthah, my lord, I have a daughter, that I love passing well. 1396

HAML. Nay, that follows not.

POLON. What follows, then, my lord?

HAML. Why—

> As by lot, God wot. 1400

And then, you know—

> It came to pass, as most like it was.

The first row of the pious chanson will show you more; for look where my abridgment comes.

Enter the Players.

You are welcome, masters! Welcome, all! I am glad to see thee well. Welcome, good friends! O, my old friend! [*Taking one by the hand.*] Why, thy face is valanced since I saw thee last: comest thou to beard me in Denmark? [*To the boy-actor.*] What! my young lady and mistress? By'r lady, your ladyship is nearer heaven than when I saw you last, by the altitude of a chopine. Pray God, your voice, like a piece of uncurrent gold, be not cracked within the ring.—Masters, you are all welcome! We'll e'en to't like French falconers, fly at any thing we see: we'll have a speech straight. [*To the First Player.*] Come, give us a taste of your quality. Come, a passionate speech. 1418

FIRST PLAY. What speech, my good lord?

HAML. I heard thee speak me a speech once, but it was never acted; or, if it was, not above once, for the play, I remember, pleased not the million; 'twas caviare to the general: but it was—as I received it, and others whose judgments in such matters cried in the top of mine—an excellent play, well digested in the scenes, set down with as much modesty as cunning. I remember one said there were no sallets in the lines to make the matter savory, nor no matter in the phrase that might indict the author of affectation, but called it an honest method, as wholesome as sweet, and by very much more handsome than fine. One speech in it I chiefly loved; 'twas Æneas' tale to Dido; and thereabout of it especially where he speaks of Priam's slaughter. If it live in your memory, begin at this line—let me see—let me see—   1436

The rugged Pyrrhus, like the Hyrcanian beast,—

'Tis not so.—It begins with Pyrrhus.—

The rugged Pyrrhus, he, whose sable arms,
Black as his purpose, did the night resemble
When he lay couched in the ominous horse,
Hath now this dread and black complexion smear'd
With heraldry more dismal; head to foot   1443
Now is he total gules, horridly trick'd
With blood of fathers, mothers, daughters, sons,
Bak'd and impasted with the parching streets
That lend a tyrannous and damned light
To their vile murders. Roasted in wrath and fire,
And thus o'er-sized with coagulate gore,
With eyes like carbuncles; the hellish Pyrrhus
Old grandsire Priam seeks.   1451

So proceed you.

POLON. 'Fore God, my lord, well spoken! with good accent, and good discretion!

FIRST PLAY.   *Anon he finds him*
Striking too short at Greeks; his antique sword,
Rebellious to his arm, lies where it falls,
Repugnant to command. Unequal match'd,
Pyrrhus at Priam drives; in rage strikes wide;
But with the whiff and wind of his fell sword
The unnerved father falls. Then senseless Ilium,
Seeming to feel this blow, with flaming top   1461
Stoops to his base, and with a hideous crash
Takes prisoner Pyrrhus' ear: for lo! his sword,
Which was declining on the milky head
Of reverend Priam, seem'd i' the air to stick.
So, as a painted tyrant, Pyrrhus stood,
And, like a neutral to his will and matter,
Did nothing.   1468
But, as we often see, against some storm,
A silence in the heavens, the rack stand still,
The bold winds speechless, and the orb below
As hush as death, anon the dreadful thunder
Doth rend the region; so, after Pyrrhus' pause,
A roused vengeance sets him new a-work.
And never did the Cyclops' hammers fall
On Mars' armor, forg'd for proof eterne,
With less remorse than Pyrrhus' bleeding sword
Now falls on Priam.

Out, out, thou strumpet, Fortune! All you gods,
Break all the spokes and fellies from her wheel,
In general synod take away her power,   1481
And bowl the round nave down the hill of heaven
As low as to the fiends!

POLON. This is too long.

HAML. It shall to the barber's, with your beard.— Prithee, say on: he's for a jig, or a tale of bawdry, or he sleeps. Say on. Come to Hecuba.   1487

FIRST PLAY. *But who, O! who had seen the*
mobled queen—

HAML. The "mobled queen"?

POLON. That's good! "mobled queen" is good!

FIRST PLAY. *Run barefoot up and down, threat-*
ening the flames
With bisson rheum, a clout upon that head
Where late the diadem stood, and, for a robe,
About her lank and all o'er-teemed loins
A blanket, in the alarm of fear caught up—   1495
Who this had seen, with tongue in venom steep'd,
'Gainst Fortune's state would treason have pro-
nounc'd!
But if the Gods themselves did see her then,
When she saw Pyrrhus make malicious sport
In mincing with his sword her husband's limbs,
The instant burst of clamor that she made—   1501
Unless things mortal move them not at all—
Would have made milch the burning eyes of
heaven,
And passion in the gods.

POLON. Look! wh'er he has not turned his color and has tears in's eyes! Prithee, no more.   1506

HAML. 'Tis well. I'll have thee speak out the rest soon. [*To* POLONIUS.] Good my lord, will you see the players well bestowed? Do you hear, let them be well used, for they are the abstracts and brief chronicles of the time: after your death you were better have a bad epitaph than their ill report while you live.   1513

POLON. My lord, I will use them according to their desert.

HAML. God's bodikins, man, much better! Use every man after his desert, and who should 'scape whipping? Use them after your own honor and dignity: the less they deserve, the more merit is in your bounty. Take them in.   1520

POLON. Come, sirs.

HAML. Follow him, friends. We'll hear a play tomorrow. [*Exit* POLONIUS, *followed by the players;* HAMLET *holds back the First Player.*] Dost thou hear me, old friend? can you play *The Murder of Gonzago?*   1526

FIRST PLAY. Aye, my lord.

HAML. We'll ha't tomorrow night. You could, for a need, study a speech of some dozen or sixteen lines which I would set down and insert in't, could you not?   1531

FIRST PLAY. Aye, my lord.

HAML. Very well. Follow that lord; and look you mock him not. [*Exit First Player.*] [*To* ROSEN-CRANTZ *and* GUILDENSTERN.] My good friends, I'll leave you till night. You are welcome to Elsinore.

ROSENC. Good my lord—   1537

HAMLET waves them away.

HAML. Aye, so; God be wi' ye!

[*Exeunt* ROSENCRANTZ *and* GUILDENSTERN.
                                    Now I am alone.
O, what a rogue and peasant slave am I!
Is it not monstrous that this player here,   1540
But in a fiction, in a dream of passion,
Could force his soul so to his own conceit
That from her working all his visage wann'd,
Tears in his eyes, distraction in's aspect,   1544
A broken voice, and his whole function suiting
With forms to his conceit? And all for nothing!
For Hecuba!
What's Hecuba to him, or he to Hecuba,
That he should weep for her? What would he do
Had he the motive and the cue for passion   1550
That I have! He would drown the stage with tears,
And cleave the general ear with horrid speech,
Make mad the guilty and appall the free,
Confound the ignorant, and amaze indeed
The very faculties of eyes and ears.   1555
Yet I—
A dull and muddy-mettled rascal, peak,
Like John-a-dreams, unpregnant of my cause,
And can say nothing! no, not for a king,
Upon whose property and most dear life   1560
A damn'd defeat was made! Am I a coward?
Who calls me villain? breaks my pate across?
Plucks off my beard and blows it in my face?
Tweaks me by the nose? gives me the lie i' the throat
As deep as to the lungs? Who does me this?   1565
Ha!—
Swounds, I should take it; for it cannot be
But I am pigeon-liver'd, and lack gall
To make oppression bitter—or ere this
I should have fatted all the region kites   1570
With this slave's offal! Bloody, bawdy villain!
Remorseless, treacherous, lecherous, kindless villain!
O, vengeance!—
Why, what an ass am I! This is most brave
That I, the son of a dear father murder'd,   1575

Prompted to my revenge by heaven and hell,
Must, like a whore, unpack my heart with words,
And fall a-cursing like a very drab,
A scullion!—Fie upon't! Foh!
About, my brain!—H'm—I have heard   1580
That guilty creatures sitting at a play
Have by the very cunning of the scene
Been struck so to the soul that presently
They have proclaim'd their malefactions;   1584
For murder, though it have no tongue, will speak
With most miraculous organ. I'll have these players
Play something like the murder of my father
Before mine uncle. I'll observe his looks.
I'll tent him to the quick. If he but blench   1589
I know my course! The spirit that I have seen
May be the devil: and the devil hath power
To assume a pleasing shape; yea, and perhaps
Out of my weakness, and my melancholy—
As he is very potent with such spirits—
Abuses me to damn me. I'll have grounds   1595
More relative than this. The play's the thing
Wherein I'll catch the conscience of the king.
                                            [*Exit*

ACT III

SCENE I:—*The following day. A room in the castle.*

Enter KING, QUEEN, POLONIUS, OPHELIA, ROSEN-
CRANTZ *and* GUILDENSTERN.

KING. And can you by no drift of circumstance
Get from him why he puts on this confusion,
Grating so harshly all his days of quiet   1600
With turbulent and dangerous lunacy?

ROSENC. He does confess he feels himself dis-
            tracted;
But from what cause he will by no means speak.

GUILDEN. Nor do we find him forward to be
            sounded;
But, with a crafty madness, keeps aloof   1605
When we would bring him on to some confession
Of his true state.

QUEEN.   Did he receive you well?

ROSENC. Most like a gentleman.

GUILDEN. But with much forcing of his disposi-
            tion.   1609

ROSENC. Niggard of question, but of our demands
Most free in his reply.

QUEEN.   Did you assay him
To any pastime?

ROSENC. Madam, it so fell out that certain players
We o'er-raught on the way; of these we told him,

And there did seem in him a kind of joy   1615
To hear of it. They are about the court,
And, as I think, they have already order
This night to play before him.
POLON.   'Tis most true;
And he beseech'd me to entreat your majesties
To hear and see the matter.   1620
    KING. With all my heart; and it doth much
        content me
To hear him so inclin'd.
Good gentlemen, give him a further edge,
And drive his purpose on to these delights.   1624
    ROSENC. We shall, my lord.
            [Exeunt ROSENCRANTZ and GUILDENSTERN.
    KING.   Sweet Gertrude, leave us too;
For we have closely sent for Hamlet hither,
That he, as 'twere by accident, may here
Affront Ophelia.
Her father and myself, lawful espials,
Will so bestow ourselves that, seeing, unseen, 1630
We may of their encounter frankly judge,
And gather by him, as he is behav'd,
If't be the affliction of his love or no
That thus he suffers for.
    QUEEN.   I shall obey you.—
And for your part, Ophelia, I do wish   1635
That your good beauties be the happy cause
Of Hamlet's wildness; so shall I hope your virtues
Will bring him to his wonted way again,
To both your honors.
    OPHEL.   Madam, I wish it may.
                              [Exit QUEEN.
POLON. Ophelia, walk you here.—Gracious, so
    please you,   1640
We will bestow ourselves. [Hands OPHELIA a
    prayer-book.] Read on this book,
That show of such an exercise may color
Your loneliness.—We are oft to blame in this,
'Tis too much prov'd, that with devotion's visage
And pious action we do sugar o'er   1645
The devil himself.
    KING [aside].   O, 'tis too true!
How smart a lash that speech doth give my con-
    science!
The harlot's cheek, beautied with plastering art,
Is not more ugly to the thing that helps it
Than is my deed to my most painted word.   1650
O heavy burden!
    POLON. I hear him coming; let's withdraw, my
    lord.
            [Exeunt KING and POLONIUS to the gallery
            above.

Enter HAMLET.

    HAML. To be, or not to be; that is the question:
Whether 'tis nobler in the mind to suffer
The slings and arrows of outrageous fortune,
Or to take arms against a sea of troubles,   1656
And, by opposing, end them.—To die, to sleep;
No more: and, by a sleep, to say we end
The heart-ache and the thousand natural shocks
That flesh is heir to—'tis a consummation   1660
Devoutly to be wish'd!—To die, to sleep.
To sleep? perchance to dream! Aye, there's the rub!
For in that sleep of death what dreams may come,
When we have shuffled off this mortal coil,
Must give us pause. There's the respect   1665
That makes calamity of so long life!
For who would bear the whips and scorns of time,
The oppressor's wrong, the proud man's con-
    tumely,
The pangs of dispriz'd love, the law's delay,
The insolence of office, and the spurns   1670
That patient merit of the unworthy takes,
When he himself might his quietus make
With a bare bodkin? Who would fardels bear,
To grunt and sweat under a weary life,
But that the dread of something after death,   1675
The undiscover'd country, from whose bourn
No traveler returns, puzzles the will,
And makes us rather bear those ills we have
Than fly to others that we know not of?
Thus conscience does make cowards of us all.
And thus the native hue of resolution   1681
Is sicklied o'er with the pale cast of thought,
And enterprises of great pith and moment,
With this regard, their currents turn awry,
And lose the name of action.—Soft you now!
The fair Ophelia? Nymph, in thy orisons   1686
Be all my sins remember'd.
    OPHEL. [in wounded voice].   Good my lord,
How does your honor for this many a day?
    HAML. I humbly thank you, well, well, well.
    OPHEL. My lord, I have remembrances of yours
That I have longed long to re-deliver;
I pray you, now receive them.   1691

            She holds out the jewels.

    HAML.   No, not I!
I never gave you aught.
    OPHEL. My honor'd lord, you know right well
    you did;
And, with them, words of so sweet breath compos'd
As made the things more rich. Their perfume lost,
Take these again; for to the noble mind   1697

Rich gifts wax poor when givers prove unkind.—
There, my lord.

Holding the jewels at arm's length, she looks at him reproachfully. POLONIUS, *in his eagerness to see, stirs the curtain of the gallery, and* HAMLET, *out of the corner of his eye, spies the eaves-droppers.*

HAML. [*aside*]. Ha! Ha!—Are you honest?
OPHEL. My lord!   1701
HAML. Are you fair?
OPHEL. What means your lordship?
HAML. That if you be honest and fair, your honesty should admit no discourse to your beauty.
OPHEL. Could beauty, my lord, have better commerce than with honesty?   1707
HAML. Aye, truly; for the power of beauty will sooner transform honesty from what it is to a bawd than the force of honesty can translate beauty into his likeness. This was sometime a paradox, but now the time gives it proof.—I did love you once.   1713
OPHEL. Indeed, my lord, you made me believe so.
HAML. You should not have believed me! for virtue cannot so inoculate our old stock but we shall relish of it. I loved you not.
OPHEL. I was the more deceived!   1718
HAML. Get thee to a nunnery. Why wouldst thou be a breeder of sinners? I am myself indifferent honest, but yet I could accuse me of such things that it were better my mother had not borne me. I am very proud, revengeful, ambitious; with more offenses at my beck than I have thoughts to put them in, imagination to give them shape, or time to act them in. What should such fellows as I do crawling between heaven and earth? We are arrant knaves, all. Believe none of us. Go thy ways to a nunnery.—Where's your father?   1729
OPHEL. At home, my lord.
HAML. Let the doors be shut upon him, that he may play the fool no where but in's own house. Farewell. [*Starts away.*]
OPHEL. O! help him, you sweet heavens!
HAML. [*returning*]. If thou dost marry, I'll give thee this plague for thy dowry: Be thou as chaste as ice, as pure as snow, thou shalt not escape calumny. Get thee to a nunnery, go! Farewell. [*Starts away. Returning.*] Or, if thou wilt needs marry, marry a fool; for wise men know well enough what monsters you make of them. To a nunnery, go; and quickly too! Farewell. [*Starts away.*]   1743
OPHEL. O heavenly powers, restore him!

HAML. [*returning*]. I have heard of your paintings, too. Well enough; God hath given you one face, and you make yourselves another. You jig, you amble, and you lisp, and nickname God's creatures, and make your wantonness your ignorance. Go to! I'll no more on't! it hath made me mad! I say, we will have no more marriages. Those that are married already [*Draws his sword half out*]— all but one—shall live [*Drives his sword back into the scabbard*]; the rest shall keep as they are. To a nunnery, go!   [*Exit.*
OPHEL. O, what a noble mind is here o'erthrown! The courtier's, soldier's, scholar's, eye, tongue, sword;   1757
The expectancy and rose of the fair state,
The glass of fashion, and the mold of form,
The observ'd of all observers, quite, quite down!
And I, of ladies most deject and wretched,
That suck'd the honey of his music vows,
Now see that noble and most sovereign reason,
Like sweet bells jangled, out of tune and harsh;
That unmatch'd form and feature of blown youth
Blasted with ecstasy. O! woe is me
To have seen what I have seen, see what I see!

Re-enter below KING *and* POLONIUS.

KING. Love! his affections do not that way tend! Nor what he spake, though it lack'd form a little, Was not like madness. There's something in his soul   1770
O'er which his melancholy sits on brood;
And I do doubt the hatch and the disclose
Will be some danger. Which for to prevent,
I have in quick determination
Thus set it down: he shall with speed to England,
For the demand of our neglected tribute.
Haply the seas, and countries different,
With variable objects, shall expel   1778
This something-settled matter in his heart,
Whereon his brains still beating puts him thus
From fashion of himself. What think you on't?
POLON. It shall do well; but yet do I believe
The origin and commencement of his grief
Sprung from neglected love.—How now, Ophelia!
You need not tell us what Lord Hamlet said;
We heard it all.—My lord, do as you please;
But, if you hold it fit, after the play   1787
Let his queen-mother all alone entreat him
To show his griefs: let her be round with him;
And I'll be plac'd, so please you, in the ear
Of all their conference. If she find him not, 1791
To England send him, or confine him where
Your wisdom best shall think.

KING.   It shall be so.
Madness in great ones must not unwatch'd go.
                                        [*Exeunt.*

SCENE II:—*The night of the same day. A hall in
                    the castle.*

Enter HAMLET, *and three of the players (dressed as*
PLAYER-KING, PLAYER-QUEEN, *and* LUCIANUS).
HAMLET *holds in his hand the manuscript of the
scene he had written.*

HAML. Speak the speech, I pray you, as I pronounced it to you, trippingly on the tongue; but if
you mouth it, as many of your players do, I had
as lief the town-crier spoke my lines. Nor do not
saw the air too much with your hand, thus; but
use all gently: for in the very torrent, tempest, and,
as I may say, whirlwind of passion, you must
acquire and beget a temperance that may give it
smoothness. O! it offends me to the soul to hear
a robustious periwig-pated fellow tear a passion to
tatters, to very rags, to split the ears of the ground-
lings, who for the most part are capable of nothing
but inexplicable dumb shows and noise. I would
have such a fellow whipped for o'er-doing Termagant. It out-herods Herod. Pray you, avoid it.

FIRST PLAY. I warrant your honor.   1810

HAML. Be not too tame neither; but let your
own discretion be your tutor. Suit the action to the
word, the word to the action; with this special
observance, that you o'erstep not the modesty of
nature; for anything so overdone is from the purpose of playing, whose end, both at the first and
now, was and is, to hold, as 'twere, the mirror up
to nature, to show virtue her own feature, scorn
her own image, and the very age and body of the
time his form and pressure. Now, this overdone,
or come tardy off, though it make the unskillful
laugh, cannot but make the judicious grieve; the
censure of which one must in your allowance o'er-
weigh a whole theater of others. O! there be players
that I have seen play—and heard others praise, and
that highly—not to speak it profanely, that, neither
having the accent of Christians, nor the gait of
Christian, pagan, nor man, have so strutted, and
bellowed, that I have thought some of nature's
journeymen had made men, and not made them
well, they imitated humanity so abominably.

FIRST PLAY. I hope we have reformed that indifferently with us.   1833

HAML. O, reform it altogether! And let those
that play your clowns speak no more than is set
down for them; for there be of them that will
themselves laugh to set on some quantity of barren
spectators to laugh too, though in the mean time
some necessary question of the play be then to be
considered. That's villainous, and shows a most
pitiful ambition in the fool that uses it. Go, make
you ready.   [*Exeunt Players.*

Enter POLONIUS, ROSENCRANTZ, *and* GUILDENSTERN.

How now, my lord? will the king hear this piece
    of work?   1843
POLON. And the queen too, and that presently.
HAML. Bid the players make haste.
                                   [*Exit* POLONIUS.
Will you two help to hasten them?   1846
ROSENC. }
GUILDEN. } We will, my lord.

        [*Exeunt* ROSENCRANTZ *and* GUILDENSTERN.
HAML. What, ho! Horatio!

            Enter HORATIO.

HORAT. Here, sweet lord, at your service.
HAML. Horatio, thou art e'en as just a man
As e'er my conversation cop'd withal.   1851
HORAT. O! my dear lord.
HAML.   Nay, do not think I flatter;
For what advancement may I hope from thee,
That no revenue hast but thy good spirits
To feed and clothe thee? Why should the poor be
    flatter'd?   1855
No; let the candied tongue lick absurd pomp,
And crook the pregnant hinges of the knee
Where thrift may follow fawning. Dost thou hear?
Since my dear soul was mistress of her choice
And could of men distinguish, her election   1860
Hath seal'd thee for herself; for thou hast been
As one, in suffering all, that suffers nothing;
A man that fortune's buffets and rewards
Hath ta'en with equal thanks; and bless'd are those
Whose blood and judgment are so well co-mingled
That they are not a pipe for Fortune's finger 1866
To sound what stop she please. Give me that man
That is not passion's slave, and I will wear him
In my heart's core, aye, in my heart of heart,
As I do thee.—Something too much of this.
There is a play tonight before the king.   1871
One scene of it comes near the circumstance
Which I have told thee of my father's death.
I prithee, when thou seest that act afoot,
Even with the very comment of thy soul   1875
Observe mine uncle! If his occulted guilt
Do not itself unkennel in one speech,
It is a damned ghost that we have seen,
And my imaginations are as foul

As Vulcan's stithy. Give him heedful note!   1880
For I mine eyes will rivet to his face;
And after we will both our judgments join
In censure of his seeming.

HORAT.   Well, my lord,
If he steal aught the whilst this play is playing,
And 'scape detecting, I will pay the theft.   1885

HAML. They are coming to the play; I must be idle.

Get you a place.

Danish march playing. Enter attendants carrying torches. To a flourish of trumpets, enter KING, QUEEN, POLONIUS, OPHELIA, ROSENCRANTZ, GUILDENSTERN, LORDS *and* LADIES *of the Court. The* KING *and* QUEEN *take their places in state on an elevated dais; the others group themselves on either side of the dais, the ladies seated on low stools, the gentlemen reclining at the feet of the ladies.*

KING. How fares our cousin Hamlet?

HAML. Excellent, i' faith, of the chameleon's dish: I eat the air, promise-crammed. You cannot feed capons so!   1891

KING. I have nothing with this answer, Hamlet; these words are not mine.

HAML. No, nor mine now. [*Turning to* POLONIUS.] My lord, you played once i' the university, you say?   1896

POLON. That did I, my lord, and was accounted a good actor.

HAML. And what did you enact?

POLON. I did enact Julius Cæsar. I was killed i' the Capitol. Brutus killed me.   1901

HAML. It was a brute part of him to kill so capital a calf there. [*To* ROSENCRANTZ.] Be the players ready?

ROSENC. Aye, my lord; they stay upon your patience.

QUEEN. Come hither, my dear Hamlet, sit by me.

HAML. No, good mother, here's metal more attractive.   1909

Walks over to where OPHELIA *is seated.*

POLON. [*to the* KING]. O ho! do you mark that?

HAML. Lady, shall I lie in your lap?

OPHEL. No, my lord!

HAML. I mean, my head upon your lap?

Sits at her feet, and rests his head upon her lap in such a way that he can look directly at the royal pair.

OPHEL. Aye, my lord. You are merry, my lord.

HAML. Who, I?   1915

OPHEL. Aye, my lord.

HAML. O God, your only jig-maker! What should a man do but be merry? for, look you [*Points with his finger at the* QUEEN] how cheerfully my mother looks, and my father died within 's two hours!   1921

OPHEL. Nay, 'tis twice two months, my lord.

HAML. So long! Nay, then, let the Devil wear black, for I'll have a suit of—sables. O heavens! die two months ago, and not forgotten yet! Then there's hope a great man's memory may outlive his life half a year—but, by 'r lady, he must build churches then, or else shall he suffer not thinking on, with the hobby-horse, whose epitaph is [*sings*]

  For, O! for, O! the hobby-horse is forgot.   1930

Trumpets sound for the Dumb Show. Hautboys play softly while the Dumb Show is being presented.

Enter a KING *and a* QUEEN, *very lovingly; the* QUEEN *embracing him. She kneels, and makes show of protestation unto him. He takes her up, and declines his head upon her neck; lays him down upon a bank of flowers. She, seeing him asleep, leaves him. Anon comes in a fellow, takes off his crown, kisses it, and pours poison in the* KING's *ears, and exit. The* QUEEN *returns, finds the* KING *dead, and makes passionate action. The Poisoner, with some two or three Mutes, comes in again, seeming to lament with her. The dead body is carried away. The Poisoner woos the* QUEEN *with gifts. She seems loath and unwilling awhile, but in the end accepts his love.*

          [*Exeunt; the music ceases.*

OPHEL. What means this, my lord?

HAML. Marry, this is miching mallecho; it means mischief.

OPHEL. Belike this show imports the argument of the play?   1935

Enter a PLAYER *as* PROLOGUE.

HAML. We shall know by this fellow. The players cannot keep counsel; they'll tell all.

OPHEL. Will he tell us what this show meant?

HAML. Aye, or any show that you'll show him.

PRO. *For us and for our tragedy,*   1940
  Here stooping to your clemency,
  We beg your hearing patiently.

          [*Bows, and goes out.*

HAML. Is this a prologue, or the posy of a ring?

OPHEL. 'Tis brief, my lord.
HAML. As woman's love!   1945

Enter two PLAYERS, KING *and* QUEEN, *very lovingly, the* QUEEN *embracing him.*

P. KING. *Full thirty times hath Phœbus' cart
    gone round
Neptune's salt wash and Tellus' orbed ground,
And thirty dozen moons with borrow'd sheen
About the world have times twelve thirties been,
Since love our hearts and Hymen did our hands
Unite commutual in most sacred bands.*   1951
    P. QUEEN. *So many journeys may the sun and
        moon
Make us again count o'er ere love be done!
But, woe is me! you are so sick of late,
So far from cheer and from your former state,
That I distrust you. Yet, though I distrust,*   1956
*Discomfort you, my lord, it nothing must;
For women's fear and love holds quantity—
In neither aught, or in extremity.
Now, what my love is, proof hath made you know;
And as my love is siz'd, my fear is so.*   1961
*Where love is great, the littlest doubts are fear;
Where little fears grow great, great love grows
    there.*
    P. KING. *Faith, I must leave thee, love, and
        shortly too;
My operant powers their functions leave to do:
And thou shalt live in this fair world behind,
Honor'd, belov'd; and, happy, one as kind*   1967
For husband shalt thou—
    P. QUEEN.   *O, confound the rest!
Such love must needs be treason in my breast.
In second husband let me be accurst!*   1970
None wed the second but who kill'd the first.
    HAML. [*aside*]. Wormwood, wormwood!
    P. QUEEN. *The instances that second marriage
        move
Are base respects of thrift but none of love.
A second time I kill my husband dead,*   1975
When second husband kisses me in bed!
    P. KING. *I do believe you think what now you
        speak;
But what we do determine oft we break.
Purpose is but the slave to memory,
Of violent birth, but poor validity;*   1980
*Which now, like fruit unripe, sticks on the tree,
But fall unshaken when they mellow be.
Most necessary 'tis that we forget
To pay ourselves what to ourselves is debt:
What to ourselves in passion we propose,*   1985
The passion ending, doth the purpose lose.

*The violence of either grief or joy
Their own enactures with themselves destroy;
Where joy most revels grief doth most lament;
Grief joys, joy grieves, on slender accident.*   1990
*This world is not for aye, nor 'tis not strange
That even our loves should with our fortunes
    change;
For 'tis a question left us yet to prove
Whe'r love lead fortune or else fortune love.
The great man down, you mark his favorites flies;
The poor advanc'd makes friends of enemies.*   1996
*And hitherto doth love on fortune tend,
For who not needs shall never lack a friend;
And who in want a hollow friend doth try
Directly seasons him his enemy.*   2000
*But—orderly to end where I begun—
Our wills and fates do so contrary run
That our devices still are overthrown;
Our thoughts are ours, their ends none of our own.
So think thou wilt no second husband wed;*   2005
But die thy thoughts when thy first lord is dead.
    P. QUEEN. *Nor earth to me give food, nor heaven
        light!
Sport and repose lock from me day and night!
To desperation turn my trust and hope!
An anchor's cheer in prison be my scope!*   2010
*Each opposite that blanks the face of joy
Meet what I would have well and it destroy!
Both here and hence pursue me lasting strife!
If, once a widow, ever I be wife!*
    HAML. If she should break it now!   2015
    P. KING. *'Tis deeply sworn! Sweet, leave me here
        awhile;
My spirits grow dull, and fain I would beguile
The tedious day with sleep.* [*Lies down.*]
    P. QUEEN.   *Sleep rock thy brain;
And never come mischance between us twain!*

                                            [*Exit.*
    HAML. Madam, how like you this play?   2020
    QUEEN. The lady doth protest too much, me-
thinks.
    HAML. O, but she'll keep her word!
    KING. Have you heard the argument? Is there
no offense in't?   2025
    HAML. No, no! They do but jest!—poison in jest.
No offense i' the world!
    KING. What do you call the play?
    HAML. "The Mouse-trap." Marry, how? Tropi-
cally. [*The* KING *shows alarm.*] This play is the
image of a murder done in Vienna: Gonzago is
the duke's name, his wife, Baptista. You shall see
anon 'tis a knavish piece of work; but what of
that? Your majesty, and we, that have free souls,

it touches us not. Let the galled jade wince! our withers are unwrung. 2036

Enter PLAYER *as* LUCIANUS.

This is one Lucianus, nephew to the king.

OPHEL. You are as good as a chorus, my lord.

HAML. I could interpret between you and your love, if I could see the puppets dallying. 2040

OPHEL. You are keen, my lord, you are keen.

HAML. Begin, murderer! Pox, leave thy damnable faces, and begin! Come; the croaking raven doth bellow for revenge!

LUC. *Thoughts black, hands apt, drugs fit, and time agreeing;* 2045
Confederate season, else no creature seeing.
Thou mixture rank, of midnight weeds collected,
With Hecate's ban thrice blasted, thrice infected,
Thy natural magic and dire property
On wholesome life usurp immediately. 2050

Pours the poison into the Sleeper's ears.

HAML. He poisons him—i' the garden—for's estate. [*The* KING *shows alarm.*] His name's Gonzago! The story is extant, and writ in very choice Italian. You shall see anon how the murderer gets the love of—Gonzago's wife. 2055

OPHEL. The king rises!

HAML. What! frighted with false fire?

QUEEN. How fares my lord?

POLON. Give o'er the play!

KING. Give me some light. Away! 2060

ALL. Lights! lights! lights!
[*Exeunt all except* HAMLET *and* HORATIO.

HAML. [*sings*].
Why, let the stricken deer go weep,
The hart ungalled play;
For some must watch, while some must sleep:
So runs the world away. 2065

Would not this, sir [*Waves the manuscript of the scene he had written*], and a forest of feathers, if the rest of my fortunes turn Turk with me, with two Provincial roses on my razed shoes, get me a fellowship in a cry of players, sir? 2070

HORAT. Half a share.

HAML. A whole one, I. [*Sings.*]
For thou dost know, O Damon dear,
This realm dismantled was
Of Jove himself; and now reigns here
A very, very—pajock. 2076

HORAT. You might have rimed.

HAML. O good Horatio! I'll take the ghost's word for a thousand pound! Didst perceive?

HORAT. Very well, my lord. 2080

HAML. Upon the talk of the poisoning?

HORAT. I did very well note him.

HAML. Ah, ha!—Come, some music! come, the recorders! [*Sings.*]
For if the king like not the comedy,
Why then, belike—he likes it not, perdy.
Come, some music! 2087

Re-enter ROSENCRANTZ *and* GUILDENSTERN.

GUILDEN. Good my lord, vouchsafe me a word with you.

HAML. Sir, a whole history! 2090

GUILDEN. The king, sir,—

HAML. Aye, sir, what of him?

GUILDEN. Is in his retirement marvelous distempered.

HAML. With drink, sir? 2095

GUILDEN. No, my lord, rather with choler.

HAML. Your wisdom should show itself more richer to signify this to his doctor; for, for me to put him to his purgation would perhaps plunge him into far more choler. 2100

GUILDEN. Good my lord, put your discourse into some frame, and start not so wildly from my affair.

HAML. I am tame, sir; pronounce.

GUILDEN. The queen your mother, in most great affliction of spirit, hath sent me to you— 2105

HAML. [*shaking him by the hand*]. You are welcome!

GUILDEN. Nay, good my lord, this courtesy is not of the right breed. If it shall please you to make me a wholesome answer, I will do your mother's commandment; if not, your pardon and my return shall be the end of my business. 2111

HAML. Sir, I cannot.

GUILDEN. What, my lord?

HAML. Make you a wholesome answer; my wit's diseased. But, sir, such answer as I can make, you shall command—or, rather, as you say, my mother. Therefore no more, but to the matter. My mother, you say,— 2119

ROSENC. Then, thus she says: your behavior hath struck her into amazement and admiration.

HAML. O wonderful son, that can so astonish a mother! But is there no sequel at the heels of this mother's admiration? Impart.

ROSENC. She desires to speak with you in her closet ere you go to bed. 2126

HAML. We shall obey, were she ten times our mother. Have you any further trade with us?

ROSENC. My lord, you once did love me.

HAML. So I do still, by these pickers and stealers.

ROSENC. Good my lord, what is your cause of distemper? You do surely bar the door upon your own liberty, if you deny your griefs to your friend.

HAML. Sir, I lack advancement.   2134

ROSENC. How can that be when you have the voice of the king himself for your succession in Denmark?

HAML. Aye, sir, but "While the grass grows"— the proverb is something musty.

Enter one with recorders.

O! the recorders: let me see one. [*To* ROSENCRANTZ *and* GUILDENSTERN.] To withdraw with you. [*Takes them aside.*] Why did you go about to recover the wind of me, as if you would drive me into a toil?   2144

GUILDEN. O! my lord, if my duty be too bold, my love is too unmannerly.

HAML. I do not well understand that. Will you play upon this pipe?

GUILDEN. My lord, I cannot.

HAML. I pray you!   2150

GUILDEN. Believe me, I cannot.

HAML. I do beseech you!

GUILDEN. I know no touch of it, my lord.

HAML. 'Tis as easy as lying. Govern these vantages with your finger and thumb, give it breath with your mouth, and it will discourse most eloquent music. Look you, these are the stops.   2157

GUILDEN. But these cannot I command to any utterance of harmony; I have not the skill.

HAML. Why, look you now, how unworthy a thing you make of me! You would play upon me; you would seem to know my stops; you would pluck out the heart of my mystery; you would sound me from my lowest note to the top of my compass. And there is much music, excellent voice, in this little organ, yet cannot you make it speak. 'Sblood! do you think I am easier to be played on than a pipe? Call me what instrument you will, though you can fret me, you cannot play upon me.—   2170

Enter POLONIUS.

God bless you, sir!

POLON. My lord, the queen would speak with you, and presently.

HAML. Do you see yonder cloud that's almost in shape of a camel?   2175

POLON. By the mass! and 'tis like a camel, indeed.

HAML. Methinks it is like a weasel.

POLON. It is backed like a weasel.

HAML. Or like a whale?

POLON. Very like a whale!   2180

HAML. Then I will come to my mother by and by. [*Aside.*] They fool me to the top of my bent. [*Aloud.*] I will come by and by.

POLON. I will say so.

HAML. "By and by" is easily said.—Leave me, friends.   [*Exeunt all but* HAMLET.

'Tis now the very witching time of night,   2187
When churchyards yawn, and hell itself breathes out
Contagion to this world. Now could I drink hot blood!
And do such bitter business as the day   2190
Would quake to look on!—Soft; now to my mother.
O heart, lose not thy nature! let not ever
The soul of Nero enter this firm bosom!
Let me be cruel, not unnatural;
I will speak daggers to her, but use none.   2195
My tongue and soul in this be hypocrites:
How in my words soever she be shent,
To give them seals never, my soul, consent!   [*Exit.*

SCENE III:—*Later the same night. A room in the castle.*

Enter KING, ROSENCRANTZ, *and* GUILDENSTERN.

KING. I like him not; nor stands it safe with us
To let his madness range. Therefore prepare you;
I your commission will forthwith dispatch,   2201
And he to England shall along with you.
The terms of our estate may not endure
Hazard so dangerous as doth hourly grow
Out of his lunacies.

GUILDEN.   We will ourselves provide.
Most holy and religious fear it is   2206
To keep those many many bodies safe
That live and feed upon your majesty.

ROSENC. The single and peculiar life is bound
With all the strength and armor of the mind
To keep itself from noyance; but much more
That spirit upon whose weal depend and rest
The lives of many. The cease of majesty   2213
Dies not alone, but like a gulf doth draw
What's near it with it; it is a massy wheel,
Fix'd on the summit of the highest mount,
To whose huge spokes ten thousand lesser things
Are mortis'd and adjoined; which, when it falls,
Each small annexment, petty consequence,
Attends the boisterous ruin. Never alone   2220
Did the king sigh, but with a general groan.

KING. Arm you, I pray you, to this speedy voy-age;

For we will fetters put upon this fear,
Which now goes too free-footed.

ROSENC. ⎫
GUILDEN. ⎭   We will haste us.

[*Exeunt* ROSENCRANTZ *and* GUILDENSTERN.

Enter POLONIUS.

POLON. My lord, he's going to his mother's closet:
Behind the arras I'll convey myself   2226
To hear the process. I'll warrant she'll tax him
   home!
And, as you said—and wisely was it said—
'Tis meet that some more audience than a mother—
Since nature makes them partial—should o'erhear
The speech, of vantage. Fare you well, my liege.
I'll call upon you ere you go to bed   2232
And tell you what I know.

KING.   Thanks, dear my lord.
                                   [*Exit* POLONIUS.
O, my offense is rank! it smells to heaven!
It hath the primal eldest curse upon't,   2235
A brother's murder!—Pray can I not:
Though inclination be as sharp as will,
My stronger guilt defeats my strong intent;
And, like a man to double business bound,
I stand in pause where I shall first begin,   2240
And both neglect.—What if this cursed hand
Were thicker than itself with brother's blood,
Is there not rain enough in the sweet heavens
To wash it white as snow? Whereto serves mercy
But to confront the visage of offense?   2245
And what's in prayer but this two-fold force,
To be forestalled ere we come to fall,
Or pardon'd, being down? Then, I'll look up;
My fault is past.—But, O! what form of prayer
Can serve my turn? "Forgive me my foul mur-
   der"?   2250
That cannot be, since I am still possess'd
Of those effects for which I did the murder,
My crown, mine own ambition, and my queen.
May one be pardon'd and retain the offense?
In the corrupted currents of this world   2255
Offense's gilded hand may shove by justice;
And oft 'tis seen the wicked prize itself
Buys out the law: but 'tis not so above;
There, is no shuffling; there, the action lies
In his true nature, and we ourselves compell'd 2260
Even to the teeth and forehead of our faults
To give in evidence.—What then? What rests?
Try what repentance can? What can it not?
Yet what can it, when one can not repent!—
O wretched state! O bosom black as death!   2265
O limed soul, that, struggling to be free,

Art more engaged! Help, angels!—Make assay;
Bow, stubborn knees! and heart with strings of
   steel
Be soft as sinews of the new-born babe!
All may be well. [*Kneels.*]   2270

Enter HAMLET, *behind.*

HAML. Now might I do it pat, now he is pray-
   ing.—
And now I'll do't. [*Slowly draws his sword.*] And
   so he goes to heaven;
And so am I reveng'd.—That would be scann'd:
A villain kills my father; and, for that,
I, his sole son, do this same villain send   2275
To heaven.—
Oh, this is hire and salary, not revenge!
He took my father grossly, full of bread,   2278
With all his crimes broad blown, as flush as May;
And how his audit stands, who knows save heaven?
But in our circumstance and course of thought
'Tis heavy with him. And am I, then, reveng'd,
To take him in the purging of his soul,
When he is fit and season'd for his passage?
No!— [*Sheathes his sword.*]   2285
Up, sword; and know thou a more horrid hent!
When he is drunk asleep, or in his rage,
Or in the incestuous pleasure of his bed,
At game a-swearing or about some act
That has no relish of salvation in't,   2290
Then trip him, that his heels may kick at heaven,
And that his soul may be as damn'd and black
As hell, whereto it goes!—My mother stays.—
This physic but prolongs thy sickly days! [*Exit.*
KING. [*rising*]. My words fly up, my thoughts
   remain below: 2295
Words without thoughts never to heaven go.
                                         [*Exit.*

SCENE IV:—*A few moments later. The Queen's
private apartment.*

Enter QUEEN *and* POLONIUS.

POLON. He will come straight. Look you lay
   home to him.
Tell him his pranks have been too broad to bear
   with;
And that your Grace hath screen'd and stood
   between   2299
Much heat and him. I'll silence me e'en here.
Pray you, be round with him!
HAML. [*within*]. Mother, mother, mother!
QUEEN.   I'll warrant you;
Fear me not. Withdraw; I hear him coming.

POLONIUS hides behind the arras.

Enter HAMLET.

HAML. Now, mother, what's the matter?
QUEEN. Hamlet, thou hast thy father much
     offended.   2305
HAML. Mother, you have my father much of-
     fended.
QUEEN. Come, come! you answer with an idle
     tongue.
HAML. Go, go! you question with a wicked
     tongue.
QUEEN. Why, how now—Hamlet!
HAML.   What's the matter now?
QUEEN. Have you forgot me?
HAML.   No, by the rood, not so.
You are "the Queen," your husband's brother's
     wife,   2311
And—would it were not so!—you are my mother!
QUEEN. Nay then, I'll set those to you that can
     speak.

*Starts toward the door. HAMLET seizes her, and
forces her into a chair.*

HAML. Come, come; and sit you down. You shall
     not budge!

She struggles.

You go not, till I set you up a glass   2315
Where you may see the inmost part of you.
QUEEN. What wilt thou do? Thou wilt not mur-
     der me? Help, help, ho!
POLON. [*behind*]. What, ho! Help! Help! Help!
HAML. [*draws*]. How now, a rat? Dead, for a
     ducat! dead!

Makes a pass through the arras.

POLON. [*behind*]. O, I am slain!   2320
QUEEN. O me! what hast thou done?
HAML. Nay, I know not.—Is it the king?
QUEEN. O! what a rash and bloody deed is this!
HAML. A bloody deed! almost as bad, good
     mother,
As kill a king and marry with his brother.   2325
QUEEN. As kill a king!
HAML.   Aye, lady, 'twas my word.

Lifts up the arras and discovers POLONIUS.

Thou wretched, rash, intruding fool! Farewell!
I took thee for thy better. Take thy fortune;
Thou find'st to be too busy is some danger.—
Leave wringing of your hands! Peace! Sit you
     down!   2330

He forces her again into the chair.

And let me wring your heart; for so I shall,
If it be made of penetrable stuff,
If damned custom have not brass'd it so
That it is proof and bulwark against sense.
QUEEN. What have I done, that thou dar'st wag
     thy tongue   2335
In noise so rude against me?
HAML.   Such an act
That blurs the grace and blush of modesty!
Calls virtue hypocrite! takes off the rose
From the fair forehead of an innocent love
And sets a blister there! makes marriage vows
As false as dicers' oaths! O, such a deed   2341
As from the body of contraction plucks
The very soul, and sweet religion makes
A rhapsody of words! Heaven's face doth glow;
Yea, this solidity and compound mass,   2345
With tristful visage, as against the doom,
Is thought-sick at the act!
QUEEN.   Ay me, what act,
That roars so loud and thunders in the index?
HAML. Look here, upon this picture, and on this,

He points to two portraits hanging on the wall.

The counterfeit presentment of two brothers.
See, what a grace was seated on this brow!   2351
Hyperion's curls, the front of Jove himself,
An eye like Mars, to threaten and command,
A station like the herald Mercury
New-lighted on a heaven-kissing hill: 2355
A combination and a form, indeed,
Where every god did seem to set his seal
To give the world assurance of a man.
This was your husband. Look you now, what
     follows.
Here is your husband, like a mildew'd ear   2360
Blasting his wholesome brother! Have you eyes?
Could you on this fair mountain leave to feed,
And batten on this moor? Ha! have you eyes?
You cannot call it love; for at your age
The hey-day in the blood is tame, it's humble,
And waits upon the judgment; and what judg-
     ment   2366
Would step from this to this? Sense, sure, you have,
Else could you not have motion; but, sure, that
     sense
Is apoplex'd: for madness would not err,
Nor sense to ecstasy was ne'er so thrall'd   2370
But it reserv'd some quantity of choice
To serve in such a difference! What devil was't
That thus hath cozen'd you at hoodman-blind?
Eyes without feeling, feeling without sight,
Ears without hands or eyes, smelling sans all,   2375

Or but a sickly part of one true sense
Could not so mope.
O shame! Where is thy blush? Rebellious hell,
If thou canst mutine in a matron's bones,
To flaming youth let virtue be as wax   2380
And melt in her own fire!

QUEEN.   O Hamlet, speak no more!
Thou turn'st mine eyes into my very soul;
And there I see such black and grained spots
As will not leave their tinct.

    O, speak to me no more!
These words like daggers enter in mine ears.
No more, sweet Hamlet!

HAML.   A murderer! and a villain!
A slave, that is not twentieth part the tithe   2387
Of your precedent lord! A vice of kings!
A cutpurse of the empire and the rule,
That from a shelf the precious diadem stole,
And put it in his pocket!—

QUEEN.   No more!   2391
HAML. A king of shreds and patches!—

Enter GHOST.

Save me, and hover o'er me with your wings,
You heavenly guards!—What would your gracious
    figure?

QUEEN. Alas, he's mad!   2395
HAML. Do you not come your tardy son to chide,
That, laps'd in time and passion, lets go by
The important acting of your dread command?
O, say!

GHOST.   Do not forget! This visitation   2399
Is but to whet thy almost blunted purpose.—
But, look; amazement on thy mother sits.
O, step between her and her fighting soul.
Conceit in weakest bodies strongest works.
Speak to her, Hamlet.

HAML.   How is it with you, lady?
QUEEN. Alas, how is't with you,   2405
That you do bend your eye on vacancy,
And with the incorporal air do hold discourse?
Forth at your eyes your spirits wildly peep;
And, as the sleeping soldiers in the alarm,
Your bedded hair, like life in excrements,   2410
Starts up and stands an end. O, gentle son,
Upon the heat and flame of thy distemper
Sprinkle cool patience.—Whereon do you look?

HAML. On him! on him! Look you, how pale he
    glares!   2414
His form and cause conjoin'd, preaching to stones,
Would make them capable. [*To the* GHOST.] Do
    not look upon me;
Lest with this piteous action you convert

My stern effects; then what I have to do   2418
Will want true color; tears perchance for blood.
QUEEN. To whom do you speak this?
HAML.   Do you see nothing there?
QUEEN. Nothing at all; yet all that is I see.
HAML. Nor did you nothing hear?
QUEEN.   No; nothing but ourselves.
HAML. Why, look you! there! Look, how it steals
    away!
My father, in his habit as he liv'd!   2424
Look! where he goes, even now, out at the portal.
    [*Exit* GHOST.
QUEEN. This is the very coinage of your brain.
This bodiless creation ecstasy
Is very cunning in.
HAML. Ecstasy!   2429
My pulse, as yours, doth temperately keep time,
And makes as healthful music. It is not madness
That I have utter'd. Bring me to the test,
And I the matter will re-word which madness
Would gambol from. Mother, for love of grace
Lay not that flattering unction to your soul,   2435
That not your trespass but my madness speaks;
It will but skin and film the ulcerous place,
Whiles rank corruption, mining all within,
Infects unseen. Confess yourself to heaven;
Repent what's past, avoid what is to come;   2440
And do not spread the compost on the weeds
To make them ranker. Forgive me this my virtue;
For in the fatness of these pursy times
Virtue itself of vice must pardon beg,   2444
Yea, curb and woo for leave to do him good.
QUEEN [*burying her face in her hands*]. O Ham-
    let! thou has cleft my heart in twain!
HAML. O, throw away the worser part of it,
And live the purer with the other half.

He stands looking down at her as she sits weeping.

Good-night. But go not to mine uncle's bed;
Assume a virtue, if you have it not.   2450
That monster, custom, who all sense doth eat,
Of habits devil, is angel yet in this,
That to the use of actions fair and good
He likewise gives a frock or livery
That aptly is put on. Refrain tonight;   2455
And that shall lend a kind of easiness
To the next abstinence; the next more easy:
For use almost can change the stamp of nature,
And either [master] the devil or throw him out
With wondrous potency.—Once more, good-night.
And when you are desirous to be bless'd,   2461
I'll blessing beg of you. For this same lord,
I do repent: but heaven hath pleas'd it so,

To punish me with this, and this with me,
That I must be their scourge and minister.   2465
I will bestow him, and will answer well
The death I gave him.—So, again, good-night.
[*Aside.*] I must be cruel only to be kind;
Thus bad begins, and worse remains behind.
[*Aloud.*] One word more, good lady.
  QUEEN [*looking up*].   What shall I do?
  HAML. Not this, by no means, that I bid you do:
Let the bloat king tempt you again to bed:
Make you to ravel all this matter out,
That I essentially am not in madness,   2474
But mad in craft. 'Twere good you let him know.
For who that's but a queen, fair, sober, wise,
Would from a paddock, from a bat, a gib,
Such dear concernings hide? who would do so?
No; in despite of sense and secrecy,
Unpeg the basket on the house's top,   2480
Let the birds fly; and, like the famous ape,
To try conclusions, in the basket creep,
And break your own neck down!
  QUEEN. Be thou assur'd, if words be made of
  breath,
And breath of life, I have no life to breathe   2485
What thou hast said to me!
  HAML. I must to England; you know that?
  QUEEN.   Alack!
I had forgot: 'tis so concluded on.
  HAML. There's letters seal'd; and my two school-
  fellows—
Whom I will trust as I will adders fang'd—   2490
They bear the mandate. They must sweep my
  way,
And marshal me to knavery. Let it work!
For 'tis the sport to have the enginer
Hoist with his own petar: and it shall go hard
But I will delve one yard below their mines,
And blow them at the moon. O! 'tis most sweet,
When in one line two crafts directly meet.   2497

   Looking at POLONIUS.

This man shall set me packing.
I'll lug the guts into the neighbor room.—
Mother, good-night.—Indeed this counselor
Is now most still, most secret, and most grave,
Who was in life a foolish prating knave.   2502

   Seizing the body.

Come, sir, to draw toward an end with you.—
Good-night, mother!
  [*Exeunt severally;* HAMLET *dragging in the
  body of* POLONIUS.

SCENE V:—*A few moments later. A room in the
     castle.*

  Enter QUEEN *to* KING, ROSENCRANTZ *and*
     GUILDENSTERN.

  KING [*to the* QUEEN]. There's matter in these
  sighs, these profound heaves.   2505
You must translate; 'tis fit we understand them.
Where is your son?
  QUEEN [*to* ROSENCRANTZ *and* GUILDENSTERN]. Be-
stow this place on us a little while.
  [*Exeunt* ROSENCRANTZ *and* GUILDENSTERN.
Ah, my good lord, what have I seen tonight!
  KING. What, Gertrude? How does Hamlet?
  QUEEN. Mad as the sea and wind when both
  contend   2511
Which is the mightier! In his lawless fit,
Behind the arras hearing something stir,
Whips out his rapier, cries, "A rat! a rat!"
And, in this brainish apprehension, kills   2515
The unseen good old man.
  KING.   O heavy deed!—
It had been so with us had we been there!
His liberty is full of threats to all,
To you yourself, to us, to everyone.   2519
Alas! how shall this bloody deed be answered?
It will be laid to us, whose providence
Should have kept short, restrain'd, and out of
  haunt,
This mad young man. But so much was our love,
We would not understand what was most fit,
But, like the owner of a foul disease,   2525
To keep it from divulging, let it feed
Even on the pith of life. Where is he gone?
  QUEEN. To draw apart the body he hath kill'd;
O'er whom his very madness, like some ore
Among a mineral of metals base,   2530
Shows itself pure: he weeps for what is done.
  KING. O Gertrude, come away!
The sun no sooner shall the mountains touch
But we will ship him hence; and this vile deed
We must, with all our majesty and skill,   2535
Both countenance and excuse.—Ho! Guildenstern!

  Re-enter ROSENCRANTZ *and* GUILDENSTERN.

Friends both, go join you with some further aid:
Hamlet in madness hath Polonius slain,
And from his mother's closet hath he dragg'd him.
Go seek him out; speak fair, and bring the body
Into the chapel. I pray you, haste in this.   2541
  [*Exeunt* ROSENCRANTZ *and* GUILDENSTERN.
Come, Gertrude; we'll call up our wisest friends,
And let them know both what we mean to do,

And what's untimely done: [so, haply, slander,]
Whose whisper o'er the world's diameter,   2545
As level as the cannon to his blank
Transports his poison'd shot, may miss our name
And hit the woundless air. O, come away!
My soul is full of discord and dismay.   [*Exeunt.*

SCENE VI:—*A few moments later. A hall in the castle.*

Enter HAMLET.

HAML. Safely stowed.   2550
ROSENC. } [*within*]. Hamlet! Lord Hamlet!
GUILDEN. }
HAML. What noise? Who calls on Hamlet?
O, here they come.

Enter ROSENCRANTZ, GUILDENSTERN, *and Attendants.*

ROSENC. What have you done, my lord, with the
dead body?   2555
HAML. Compounded it with dust, whereto 'tis
kin.
ROSENC. Tell us where 'tis, that we may take it
thence
And bear it to the chapel.
HAML. Do not believe it.
ROSENC. Believe what?   2560
HAML. That I can keep your counsel and not
mine own. Besides, to be demanded of a sponge!
what replication should be made by the son of a
king?   2564
ROSENC. Take you me for a sponge, my lord?
HAML. Aye, sir, that soaks up the king's countenance, his rewards, his authorities. But such officers
do the king best service in the end: he keeps them,
like an ape, in the corner of his jaw; first mouthed,
to be, last, swallowed: when he needs what you
have gleaned, it is but squeezing you—and,
sponge, you shall be dry again.   2572
ROSENC. I understand you not, my lord.
HAML. I am glad of it: "a knavish speech sleeps
in a foolish ear."   2575
ROSENC. My lord, you must tell us where the
body is, and go with us to the king.
HAML. The body is with the king, but the king
is not with the body. The king is a thing—
GUILDEN. A thing, my lord!   2580
HAML. Of nothing. Bring me to him. Hide fox,
and all after!

[*Exit* HAMLET *running,* ROSENCRANTZ, GUILD-
ENSTERN *and Attendants following.*

SCENE VII:—*A few moments later. A room in the castle.*

Enter KING, *attended.*

KING. I have sent to seek him, and to find the
body.
How dangerous is it that this man goes loose!
Yet must not we put the strong law on him: 2585
He's lov'd of the distracted multitude,
Who like not in their judgment, but their eyes;
And where 'tis so, the offender's scourge is
weigh'd,
But never the offense. To bear all smooth and
even,
This sudden sending him away must seem   2590
Deliberate pause. Diseases desperate grown
By desperate appliance are reliev'd,
Or not at all.

Enter ROSENCRANTZ.

                How now! what hath befall'n?
ROSENC. Where the dead body is bestow'd, my
lord,   2594
We cannot get from him.
KING.   But where is he?
ROSENC. Without, my lord, guarded, to know
your pleasure.
KING. Bring him before us.
ROSENC. Ho, Guildenstern! bring in my lord.

Enter GUILDENSTERN *with* HAMLET *guarded.*

KING. Now, Hamlet, where's Polonius?
HAML. At supper.   2600
KING. At supper! Where?
HAML. Not where he eats, but where he is eaten:
a certain convocation of politic worms are e'en at
him. Your worm is your only emperor for diet:
we fat all creatures else to fat us, and we fat ourselves for maggots. Your fat king and your lean
beggar is but variable service; two dishes, but to
one table: that's the end.   2608
KING. Alas, alas!
HAML. A man may fish with the worm that
hath eat of a king, and eat of the fish that hath fed
of that worm.
KING. What dost thou mean by this?
HAML. Nothing, but to show you how a king
may go a progress through the guts of a beggar.
KING. Where is Polonius?   2616
HAML. In heaven. Send thither to see; if your
messenger find him not there, seek him i' the other
place yourself. But, indeed, if you find him not

within this month, you shall nose him as you go
up the stairs into the lobby.   2621

   KING [*to some Attendants*]. Go seek him there.

   HAML. He will stay till you come!

                        [*Exeunt Attendants.*

   KING. Hamlet, this deed, for thine especial
      safety—
Which we do tender, as we dearly grieve   2625
For that which thou hast done—must send thee
      hence
With fiery quickness. Therefore prepare thyself;
The bark is ready, and the wind at help,
The associates tend, and everything is bent   2629
For England.

   HAML.   For England?

   KING.   Aye, Hamlet.

   HAML.   Good!

   KING. So is it, if thou knew'st our purposes.

   HAML. I see a cherub that sees them! [*To* ROSEN-
CRANTZ *and* GUILDENSTERN.] But, come; for England! [*To the* KING.] Farewell, dear mother.

   KING. Thy loving father, Hamlet.   2635

   HAML. My mother: father and mother is man
and wife, man and wife is one flesh, and so, my
mother. [*To* ROSENCRANTZ *and* GUILDENSTERN.]
Come; for England!   [*Exit.*

   KING. Follow him at foot. Tempt him with
      speed aboard.   2640
Delay it not; I'll have him hence tonight.
Away; for everything is seal'd and done
That else leans on the affair. Pray you, make haste.

       [*Exeunt* ROSENCRANTZ *and* GUILDENSTERN.
And, England, if my love thou hold'st at aught—
As my great power thereof may give thee sense,
Since yet thy cicatric looks raw and red   2646
After the Danish sword, and thy free awe
Pays homage to us—thou mayst not coldly set
Our sovereign process; which imports at full,
By letters conjuring to that effect,   2650
The present death of Hamlet. Do it, England!
For like the hectic in my blood he rages,
And thou must cure me. Till I know 'tis done,
Howe'er my haps, my joys were ne'er begun.

                             [*Exit.*

SCENE VIII:—*Early the following morning. The
    highway leading from the port.*

Enter FORTINBRAS, *a Captain, and a troop of sol-
    diers, with drums, marching.*

   FORTIN. Go, captain; from me greet the Danish
      king;   2655
Tell him that, by his license, Fortinbras

Claims the conveyance of a promis'd march
Over his kingdom. You know the rendezvous.
If that his majesty would aught with us,
We shall express our duty in his eye;   2660
And let him know so.

   CAP.   I will do't, my lord.

   FORTIN. [*to the soldiers*]. Go softly on.

As FORTINBRAS *and his troop of soldiers march out,
    enter* HAMLET, ROSENCRANTZ, GUILDENSTERN, *and
    Attendants bearing luggage, on their way to the
    port.* HAMLET *stops the Captain.*

   HAML. Good sir, whose powers are these?

   CAP. They are of Norway, sir.

   HAML. How purpos'd, sir, I pray you?   2665

   CAP. Against some part of Poland.

   HAML. Who commands them, sir?

   CAP. The nephew to old Norway, Fortinbras.

   HAML. Goes it against the main of Poland, sir,
Or for some frontier?   2670

   CAP. Truly to speak, and with no addition,
We go to gain a little patch of ground
That hath in it no profit but the name.
To pay five ducats, five, I would not farm it;
Nor will it yield to Norway or the Pole   2675
A ranker rate should it be sold in fee.

   HAML. Why, then the Polack never will defend
      it.

   CAP. Yes, 'tis already garrison'd.

   HAML. Two thousand souls and twenty thou-
      sand ducats
Will not debate the question of this straw!   2680
This is the imposthume of much wealth and peace,
That inward breaks, and shows no cause without
Why the man dies.—I humbly thank you, sir.

   CAP. God be wi' you, sir.   [*Exit.*

   ROSENC.   Will't please you go, my lord?

   HAML. I'll be with you straight. Go a little be-
      fore.   [*Exeunt all except* HAMLET.
How all occasions do inform against me,   2686
And spur my dull revenge! What is a man,
If his chief good and market of his time
Be but to sleep and feed? a beast, no more.
Sure He that made us with such large discourse,
Looking before and after, gave us not   2691
That capability and god-like reason
To fust in us unus'd. Now, whe'r it be
Bestial oblivion, or some craven scruple
Of thinking too precisely on the event—   2695
A thought which, quarter'd, hath but one part wis-
    dom
And ever three parts coward—I do not know
Why yet I live to say "This thing's to do."

Sith I have cause, and will, and strength, and
  means
To do't. Examples gross as earth exhort me. 2700
Witness this army of such mass and charge
Led by a delicate and tender prince,
Whose spirit, with divine ambition puff'd,
Makes mouths at the invisible event,
Exposing what is mortal and unsure 2705
To all that fortune, death, and danger dare—
Even for an egg-shell! Rightly to be great
Is not to stir without great argument,
But greatly to find quarrel in a straw 2709
When honor's at the stake. How stand I, then,
That have a father kill'd, a mother stain'd,
Excitements of my reason and my blood,
And let all sleep? while, to my shame, I see
The imminent death of twenty thousand men,
That, for a fantasy and trick of fame, 2715
Go to their graves like beds, fight for a plot
Whereon the numbers cannot try to cause,
Which is not tomb enough and continent
To hide the slain! O, from this time forth,
My thoughts be bloody, or be nothing worth!

                                    [*Exit.*

ACT IV

SCENE I:—*Several weeks later. A room in the
castle.*

Enter QUEEN, HORATIO, *and a Gentleman.*

QUEEN. I will not speak with her. 2721
  GENT. She is importunate; indeed, distract.
Her mood will needs be pitied.
  QUEEN.   What would she have?
  GENT. She speaks much of her father; says she
    hears
There's tricks i' the world; and hems, and beats
    her heart; 2725
Spurns enviously at straws; speaks things in doubt,
That carry but half sense. Her speech is nothing,
Yet the unshaped use of it doth move
The hearers to collection; they aim at it, 2729
And botch the words up fit to their own thoughts;
Which, as her winks and nods and gestures yield
    them,
Indeed would make one think there might be
    thought,
Though nothing sure, yet much unhappily.
  HORAT. 'Twere good she were spoken with, for
    she may strew
Dangerous conjectures in ill-breeding minds. 2735
  QUEEN. Let her come in.

                [*Exeunt* HORATIO *and Gentleman.*
To my sick soul—as sin's true nature is—
Each toy seems prologue to some great amiss.
So full of artless jealousy is guilt,
It spills itself in fearing to be spilt. 2740

Re-enter HORATIO *and Gentleman with* OPHELIA,
distracted, holding a lute, her hair down.

  OPHEL. Where is the beauteous majesty of Den-
    mark?
  QUEEN. How now, Ophelia!
  OPHEL. [*Sings.*]
    How should I your true love know
      From another one?
    By his cockle hat and staff, 2745
      And his sandal shoon.
  QUEEN. Alas, sweet lady, what imports this
    song?
  OPHEL. Say you? Nay, pray you, mark: [*Sings.*]
    He is dead and gone, lady,
      He is dead and gone; 2750
    At his head a grass-green turf,
      At his heels a stone.
O, ho!
  QUEEN. Nay, but, Ophelia,—
  OPHEL. Pray you, mark: [*Sings.*] 2755
    White his shroud as the mountain snow,

              Enter KING.

  QUEEN. [*Aside to him.*] Alas, look here, my
    lord!
  OPHEL.   *Larded with sweet flowers;*
    Which bewept to the grave did not go
      With true-love showers. 2760
  KING. How do you, pretty lady?
  OPHEL. Well, God 'ild you. They say the owl
was a baker's daughter. Lord! we know what we
are, but know not what we may be. God be at
your table! 2765
  KING. Conceit upon her father.
  OPHEL. Pray you, let's have no words of this;
but when they ask you what it means, say you
this:
[*Sings.*] *Tomorrow is Saint Valentine's day,*
    All in the morning betime,
    And I a maid at your window
      To be your Valentine. 2773
  KING. How long hath she been thus?
  OPHEL. I hope all will be well. We must be patient: but I cannot choose but weep to think they
should lay him i' the cold ground. My brother shall
know of it. And so, I thank you for your good

counsel.—Come; my coach!—Good-night, ladies.
Good-night, sweet ladies. Good-night! Good-night!
                                                    [*Exit.*

KING. Follow her close; give her good watch, I
    pray you.   2781
                    [*Exeunt* HORATIO *and Gentleman.*
O! this is the poison of deep grief; it springs
All from her father's death. O Gertrude, Gertrude!
When sorrows come, they come not single spies,
But in battalions. First, her father slain;   2785
Next, your son gone—and he most violent author
Of his own just remove; the people muddied,
Thick, and unwholesome in their thoughts and
    whispers
For good Polonius' death—and we have done but
    greenly   2789
In hugger-mugger to inter him; poor Ophelia
Divided from herself and her fair judgment,
Without the which we are pictures, or mere beasts;
Last, and as much containing as all these,
Her brother is in secret come from France,
Feeds on his wonder, keeps himself in clouds,
And wants not buzzers to infect his ear   2796
With pestilent speeches of his father's death,
Wherein necessity, of matter beggar'd,
Will nothing stick our person to arraign
In ear and ear. O, my dear Gertrude, this,   2800
Like to a murdering-piece, in many places
Gives me superfluous death.

A noise within of shouts and clashing swords.

QUEEN.   Alack! what noise is this?
KING. Where are my Switzers? Let them guard
the door!

Enter a Gentleman in haste.

What is the matter?
    GENT.   Save yourself, my lord!
The ocean, overpeering of his list,   2806
Eats not the flats with more impetuous haste
Than young Laertes, in a riotous head,
O'erbears your officers. The rabble call him lord,
And, as the world were now but to begin,   2810
Antiquity forgot, custom not known,
The ratifiers and props of every word,
They cry, "Choose we; Laertes shall be king!"
Caps, hands, and tongues applaud it to the clouds,
"Laertes shall be king! Laertes king!"   2815
    QUEEN. How cheerfully on the false trail they
        cry!
O, this is counter, you false Danish dogs!

Noise within of crashing doors.

KING. The doors are broke.

Enter LAERTES, *with drawn sword, a mob of Danes*
at his back.

LAERT. Where is the king?—Sirs, stand you all
    without.
DANES. No, let's come in!
LAERT.   I pray you, give me leave.
DANES. We will! we will!   2821
LAERT. I thank you. Keep the door.

The mob retires. LAERTES, *brandishing his sword,*
confronts the KING.

                            O thou vile king!
Give me my father!
QUEEN.   Calmly, good Laertes.
LAERT. That drop of blood that's calm proclaims
    me bastard!

The QUEEN *throws her arms about* LAERTES, *and*
tries to hold him.

KING.   What is the cause, Laertes,
That thy rebellion looks so giant-like?—   2825
Let him go, Gertrude; do not fear our person:
There's such divinity doth hedge a king,
That treason can but peep to what it would,
Acts little of his will.—Tell me, Laertes,
Why thou art thus incens'd.—Let him go, Ger-
    trude.—   2830
Speak, man.
    LAERT. Where's my father?
KING.   Dead.
QUEEN.   But not by him.
KING. Let him demand his fill.
LAERT. How came he dead? I'll not be juggled
    with!
To hell, allegiance! vows, to the blackest devil!
Conscience and grace, to the profoundest pit! 2836
I dare damnation! To this point I stand,
That both the worlds I give to negligence!
Let come what comes, only I'll be reveng'd,
Most throughly, for my father!
KING.   Who shall stay you?
LAERT. My will, not all the world!   2841
And for my means, I'll husband them so well
They shall go far with little.
KING.   Good Laertes,
If you desire to know the certainty
Of your dear father's death, is't writ in your re-
    venge   2845
That, swoopstake, you will draw both friend and
    foe,
Winner and loser?

LAERT. None but his enemies.

KING.   Will you know them then?

LAERT. To his good friends thus wide I'll ope my
        arms,
And, like the kind life-rendering pelican,   2850
Repast them with my blood.

KING.   Why, now you speak
Like a good child and a true gentleman.
That I am guiltless of your father's death,
And am most sensibly in grief for it,
It shall as level to your judgment pierce   2855
As day does to your eye.

DANES [within].   Let her come in.

LAERT. How now! what noise is that?

Re-enter OPHELIA, *as before.*

O heat, dry up my brains! Tears seven times salt
Burn out the sense and virtue of mine eye!   2859
By heaven, thy madness shall be paid by weight,
Till our scale turn the beam! O rose of May!
Dear maid, kind sister, sweet Ophelia!—
O heavens! is't possible a young maid's wits
Should be as mortal as an old man's life?
Nature is fine in love, and where 'tis fine   2865
It sends some precious instance of itself
After the thing it loves.

OPHEL. [*sings*].
    They bore him barefac'd on the bier;
    Hey non nonny, nonny, hey nonny;
    And in his grave rain'd many a tear.
    Fare you well, my dove!   2871

LAERT. Hadst thou thy wits, and didst persuade
        revenge,
It could not move thus.

OPHEL. You must sing, *"A-down a-down!"* and
you, *"Call him a-down-a!"* O how the wheel becomes it! It is the false steward that stole his master's daughter.   2877

LAERT. This nothing's more than matter.

OPHEL. [*to* LAERTES]. There's rosemary; that's
for remembrance: pray, love, remember. And
there is pansies; that's for thoughts.

LAERT. A document in madness—"thoughts" and
"remembrance" fitted.   2883

OPHEL. [*to the* KING]. There's fennel for you;
and columbines. [*To the* QUEEN.] There's rue for
you; and here's some for me; we may call it herb
of grace o' Sundays.—O! you must wear your rue
with a difference. There's a daisy. I would give
you some violets, but they withered all when my
father died. They say he made a good end. [*Sings.*]
For bonny sweet Robin is all my joy.

LAERT. Thought and affliction, passion, hell itself,
She turns to favor and to prettiness.   2893

OPHEL. [*sings*].
    And will he not come again?
    And will he not come again?
        No, no, he is dead!
        Go to thy death-bed,
    He never will come again!

    His beard was as white as snow,
    All flaxen was his poll;   2900
        He is gone, he is gone,
        And we cast away moan:
    God ha' mercy on his soul!

And of all Christian souls, I pray God. God be wi'
    ye!   [*Exit.*

LAERT. Do you see this, O God?   2905

KING. Laertes, I must commune with your grief,
Or you deny me right. Go but apart,
Make choice of whom your wisest friends you
    will,
And they shall hear and judge 'twixt you and me.
If by direct or by collateral hand   2910
They find us touch'd, we will our kingdom give,
Our crown, our life, and all that we call ours,
To you in satisfaction; but if not,
Be you content to lend your patience to us,
And we shall jointly labor with your soul   2915
To give it due content.

LAERT.   Let this be so.
His means of death, his obscure burial,
No trophy, sword, nor hatchment o'er his bones,
No noble rite nor formal ostentation,   2919
Cry to be heard, as 'twere from heaven to earth,
That I must call 't in question.

KING.   So you shall;
And where the offense is let the great ax fall!
I pray you go with me.   [*Exeunt.*

SCENE II:—*Later the same day. A room in the
castle.*

Enter HORATIO *and a Servant.*

HORAT. What are they that would speak with
    me?

SERV. Sailors, sir. They say they have letters for
    you.   2925

HORAT. Let them come in.   [*Exit Servant.*
I do not know from what part of the world
I should be greeted, if not from Lord Hamlet.

Enter Sailors.

FIRST SAIL. God bless you, sir.

HORAT. Let him bless thee too.   2930

FIRST SAIL. He shall, sir, an't please him. There's a letter for you, sir; it comes from the ambassador that was bound for England—if your name be Horatio, as I am let to know it is.

HORAT. [*opens the letter, and reads*].

Horatio,   2935

When thou shalt have overlooked this, give these fellows some means to the king; they have letters for him. Ere we were two days old at sea, a pirate of very warlike appointment gave us chase. Finding ourselves too slow of sail, we put on a compelled valor, and in the grapple I boarded them; on the instant they got clear of our ship, so I alone became their prisoner. They have dealt with me like thieves of mercy; but they knew what they did —I am to do a good turn for them. Let the king have the letters I have sent; and repair thou to me with as much haste as thou wouldst fly death. I have words to speak in thine ear will make thee dumb; yet are they much too light for the bore of the matter. These good fellows will bring thee where I am. Rosencrantz and Guildenstern hold their course for England: of them I have much to tell thee. Farewell.   2953

He that thou knowest thine,

Hamlet.

Come; I will give you way for these your letters,
And do't the speedier that you may direct me
To him from whom you brought them.   [*Exeunt.*

SCENE III:—*Later the same day. A room in the castle.*

Enter KING *and* LAERTES.

KING. Now must your conscience my acquittance seal,   2959
And you must put me in your heart for friend,
Sith you have heard, and with a knowing ear,
That he which hath your noble father slain
Pursu'd my life.

LAERT.   It well appears. But tell me
Why you proceeded not against these feats
So crimeful and so capital in nature,   2965
As by your safety, wisdom, all things else,
You mainly were stirr'd up.

KING.   O, for two special reasons;
Which may to you, perhaps, seem much unsinew'd,
And yet to me they are strong. The queen his mother
Lives almost by his looks; and for myself—   2970
My virtue or my plague, be it either which—
She's so conjunctive to my life and soul,

That, as the star moves not but in his sphere,
I could not but by her. The other motive
Why to a public count I might not go   2975
Is the great love the general gender bear him;
Who, dipping all his faults in their affection,
Would, like the spring that turneth wood to stone,
Convert his gyves to graces; so that my arrows,
Too slightly timber'd for so loud a wind,   2980
Would have reverted to my bow again,
And not where I had aim'd them.

LAERT. And so have I a noble father lost,
A sister driven into desperate terms,   2984
Whose worth—if praises may go back again—
Stood challenger-on-mount of all the age
For her perfections. But my revenge will come.

KING. Break not your sleeps for that! You must not think
That we are made of stuff so flat and dull   2989
That we can let our beard be shook with danger
And think it pastime. You shortly shall hear more.
I lov'd your father; and we love ourself,
And that, I hope, will teach you to imagine—

Enter a Messenger.

How now! what news?

MESS.   Letters, my lord, from Hamlet:
This to your majesty; this to the queen.   2995

KING. From Hamlet! Who brought them?

MESS. Sailors, my lord, they say; I saw them not:
They were given me by Claudio; he receiv'd them
Of him that brought them.

KING.   Laertes, you shall hear them.—
Leave us.   [*Exit Messenger.*

High and Mighty: 3001
You shall know I am set naked on your kingdom. Tomorrow shall I beg leave to see your kingly eyes; when I shall, first asking your pardon thereunto, recount the occasions of my sudden and more strange return.

Hamlet.

What should this mean? Are all the rest come back?   3008
Or is it some abuse, and no such thing?

LAERT. Know you the hand?

KING.   'Tis Hamlet's character.—"Naked!"
And in a postscript here, he says, "alone."
Can you advise me?

LAERT. I'm lost in it, my lord. But, let him come!
It warms the very sickness in my heart
That I shall live and tell him to his teeth,   3015
"Thus diddest thou!"

KING. If it be so, Laertes—
As how should it be so?—[*Glances at the letter.*]
How otherwise?—
Will you be rul'd by me?
LAERT. Aye, my lord,
So you will not o'errule me to a peace.
KING. To thine own peace. If he be now re-
turn'd, 3020
As checking at his voyage, and that he means
No more to undertake it, I will work him
To an exploit, now ripe in my device,
Under the which he shall not choose but fall;
And for his death no wind of blame shall breathe,
But even his mother shall uncharge the practice
And call it accident.
LAERT. My lord, I will be rul'd;
The rather, if you could devise it so 3028
That I might be the organ.
KING. It falls right.
You have been talk'd of since your travel much,
And that in Hamlet's hearing, for a quality
Wherein, they say, you shine. Your sum of parts
Did not, together, pluck such envy from him
As did that one, and that, in my regard, 3034
Of the unworthiest siege.
LAERT. What part is that, my lord?
KING. A very riband in the cap of youth,
Yet needful, too; for youth no less becomes
The light and careless livery that it wears
Than settled age his sables and his weeds
Importing health and graveness. Two months
since 3040
Here was a gentleman of Normandy.
I've seen myself, and serv'd against, the French,
And they can well on horseback; but this gallant
Had witchcraft in't! He grew unto his seat,
And to such wondrous doing brought his horse,
As he had been incorps'd and demi-natur'd 3046
With the brave beast. So far he topp'd my thought,
That I, in forgery of shapes and tricks,
Come short of what he did.
LAERT. A Norman was't?
KING. A Norman. 3050
LAERT. Upon my life, Lamord!
KING. The very same.
LAERT. I know him well. He is the brooch indeed
And gem of all the nation.
KING. He made confession of you;
And gave you such a masterly report 3055
For art and exercise in your defense—
And for your rapier most especially—
That he cried out, 'twould be a sight indeed

If one could match you. The scrimers of their na-
tion, 3059
He swore, had neither motion, guard, nor eye,
If you oppos'd them. Sir, this report of his
Did Hamlet so envenom with his envy
That he could nothing do but wish and beg
Your sudden coming o'er to play with him.
Now, out of this—
LAERT. What out of this, my lord?
KING. Laertes, was your father dear to you?
Or are you, like the painting of a sorrow, 3067
A face without a heart?
LAERT. Why ask you this?
KING. Not that I think you did not love your
father,
But that I know love is begun by time, 3070
And that I see, in passages of proof,
Time qualifies the spark and fire of it.
There lives within the very flame of love
A kind of wick or snuff that will abate it;
And nothing is at a like goodness still, 3075
For goodness, growing to a plurisy,
Dies in his own too-much. That we would do,
We should do when we would, for this "would"
changes,
And hath abatements and delays as many
As there are tongues, are hands, are accidents;
And then this "should" is like a spendthrift sigh,
That hurts by easing. But, to the quick o' the
ulcer: 3082
Hamlet comes back— What would you undertake
To show yourself your father's son in deed
More than in words?
LAERT. To cut his throat i' the church!
KING. No place, indeed, should murder sanctu-
arize;
Revenge should have no bounds. But, good
Laertes, 3087
Will you do this? keep close within your chamber;
Hamlet return'd shall know you are come home;
We'll put on those shall praise your excellence,
And set a double varnish on the fame 3091
The Frenchman gave you; bring you, in fine, to-
gether
And wager on your heads. He, being remiss,
Most generous, and free from all contriving,
Will not peruse the foils; so that with ease,
Or with a little shuffling, you may choose 3096
A sword unbated, and, in a pass of practice,
Requite him for your father.
LAERT. I will do't!
And for that purpose I'll anoint my sword.
I bought an unction of a mountebank, 3100

So mortal that, but dip a knife in it,
Where it draws blood no cataplasm so rare,
Collected from all simples that have virtue
Under the moon, can save the thing from death
That is but scratch'd withal. I'll touch my point
With this contagion, that, if I gall him slightly,
It may be death.
    KING.   Let's further think of this;
Weigh what convenience both of time and means
May fit us to our shape. If this should fail,
And that our drift look through our bad perform-
    ance,   3110
'Twere better not assay'd; therefore this project
Should have a back, or second, that might hold
If this should blast in proof. Soft!—let me see.—
We'll make a solemn wager on your cunnings—
I ha't!   3115
When in your motion you are hot and dry—
As make your bouts more violent to that end—
And that he calls for drink, I'll have prepar'd him
A chalice for the nonce, whereon but sipping,
If he by chance escape your venom'd stuck,   3120
Our purpose may hold there.—

    Enter QUEEN.

                How now, sweet queen!
    QUEEN. One woe doth tread upon another's heel,
So fast they follow.—Your sister's drown'd, Laer-
    tes.
    LAERT. Drown'd! O, where?   3124
    QUEEN. There is a willow grows aslant a brook,
That shows his hoar leaves in the glassy stream;
There with fantastic garlands did she come,
Of crow-flowers, nettles, daisies, and long purples,
That liberal shepherds give a grosser name,
But our cold maids do "dead men's fingers" call
    them: 3130
There, on the pendent boughs her coronet weeds
Clambering to hang, an envious sliver broke,
When down her weedy trophies and herself
Fell in the weeping brook. Her clothes spread
    wide,   3134
And, mermaid-like, awhile they bore her up;
Which time she chanted snatches of old tunes,
As one incapable of her own distress,
Or like a creature native and indu'd
Unto that element. But long it could not be
Till that her garments, heavy with their drink,
Pull'd the poor wretch from her melodious lay
To muddy death.
    LAERT.   Alas! Then, she is drown'd?
    QUEEN. Drown'd, drown'd.   3143

    LAERT. Too much of water hast thou, poor
    Ophelia,
And therefore I forbid my tears.—But yet
It is our trick; nature her custom holds,
Let shame say what it will.—When these are gone
The woman will be out.—Adieu, my lord!
I have a speech of fire that fain would blaze,
But that this folly douts it.   [*Exit.*
    KING.   Let's follow, Gertrude.
How much I had to do to calm his rage!   3151
Now fear I this will give it start again;
Therefore let's follow.   [*Exeunt.*

ACT V

    SCENE I:—*A day later. A churchyard.*

    Enter two Clowns, with spades and mattock.

    FIRST CLO. Is she to be buried in Christian burial
that willfully seeks her own salvation?   3155
    SECOND CLO. I tell thee she is; and therefore
make her grave straight: the crowner hath sat on
her, and finds it Christian burial.
    FIRST CLO. How can that be, unless she drowned
herself in her own defense?   3160
    SECOND CLO. Why, 'tis found so.
    FIRST CLO. It must be *se offendendo;* it cannot
be else. For here lies the point: if I drown myself
wittingly, it argues an act; and an act hath three
branches; it is—to act, to do, and to perform:
argal, she drowned herself wittingly.   3166
    SECOND CLO. Nay, but hear you, goodman
delver,—
    FIRST CLO. Give me leave.—Here lies the water;
good: here stands the man; good: if the man go
to this water, and drown himself, it is, will-he-nill-
he, he goes—mark you that! but if the water come
to him, and drown him, he drowns not himself:
argal, he that is not guilty of his own death
shortens not his own life.   3175
    SECOND CLO. But is this law?
    FIRST CLO. Aye, marry, is't; crowner's quest law.
    SECOND CLO. Will you ha' the truth on't? If this
had not been a gentlewoman, she should have
been buried out o' Christian burial.   3180
    FIRST CLO. Why, there thou sayest! And the
more pity that great folk should have countenance
in this world to drown or hang themselves more
than their even Christian.—Come; my spade.
[*Hands him a spade.*] There is no ancient gentlemen but gardeners, ditchers, and grave-makers;
they hold up Adam's profession.   3187
    SECOND CLO. Was he a gentleman?

FIRST CLO. A' was the first that ever bore arms.

SECOND CLO. Why, he had none.

FIRST CLO. What! art a heathen? How dost thou understand the Scripture? The Scripture says, "Adam digged." Could he dig without arms? I'll put another question to thee; if thou answerest me not to the purpose, confess thyself—   3195

SECOND CLO. Go to!

FIRST CLO. What is he that builds stronger than either the mason, the shipwright, or the carpenter?

SECOND CLO. The gallows-maker; for that frame outlives a thousand tenants.   3200

FIRST CLO. I like thy wit well, in good faith. The gallows does well. But how does it well? it does well to those that do ill; now thou dost ill to say the gallows is built stronger than the church: argal, the gallows may do well to thee. To't again; come!   3206

SECOND CLO. "Who builds stronger than a mason, a shipwright, or a carpenter?"

FIRST CLO. Aye, tell me that, and unyoke.

SECOND CLO. Marry, now I can tell!   3210

FIRST CLO. To't!

SECOND CLO. Mass, I cannot tell.

Enter at a distance HAMLET *and* HORATIO, *coming from the pirates' hiding-place.*

FIRST CLO. Cudgel thy brains no more about it, for your dull ass will not mend his pace with beating; and when you are asked this question next, say "a grave-maker"; the houses that he makes last till doomsday.—Go, get thee to Yaughan; fetch me a stoup of liquor.   [*Exit Second Clown.*

FIRST CLO. [*digs and sings*].

In youth, when I did love, did love,
    Methought it was very sweet,   3220
To contract (uh!) *the time for* (uh!) *my behove,*
    O! methought there (uh!) *was nothing meet.*

HAML. Has this fellow no feeling of his business, that he sings at grave-making?

HORAT. Custom hath made it in him a property of easiness.   3226

HAML. 'Tis e'en so; the hand of little employment hath the daintier sense.

FIRST CLO. [*sings*].

    But age, with his stealing steps,
        Hath claw'd me in his clutch,   3230
    And hath shipped me intil the land,
        As if I had never been such.

Throws up a skull.

HAML. That skull had a tongue in it, and could sing once. How the knave jowls it to the ground,

as if it were Cain's jaw-bone, that did the first murder! This might be the pate of a politician, which this ass now o'er-offices, one that would circumvent God, might it not?   3238

HORAT. It might, my lord.

HAML. Or of a courtier, which could say, "Good morrow, sweet lord! how dost thou, good lord?" This might be my Lord Such-a-one, that praised my Lord Such-a-one's horse, when he meant to beg it, might it not?

HORAT. Aye, my lord.   3245

HAML. Why, e'en so; and now my Lady Worm's! chapless, and knocked about the mazzard with a sexton's spade! Here's fine revolution, an we had the trick to see't. Did these bones cost no more the breeding but to play at loggats with 'em? Mine ache to think on't.   3251

FIRST CLO. [*sings*].

    A pick-ax, and a spade, a spade
        For and a shrouding sheet;
    O! a pit of clay for to be made
        For such a guest is meet.

Throws up another skull.

HAML. There's another. Why might not that be the skull of a lawyer? Where be his quiddities now? his quillets, his cases, his tenures, and his tricks? Why does he suffer this rude knave now to knock him about the sconce with a dirty shovel, and will not tell him of his action of battery? Hum! This fellow might be in's time a great buyer of land, with his statutes, his recognizances, his fines, his double vouchers, his recoveries. Is this the fine of his fines, and the recovery of his recoveries, to have his fine pate full of fine dirt? Will his vouchers vouch him no more of his purchases, and double ones too, than the length and breadth of a pair of indentures? The very conveyances of his lands will hardly lie in this box; and must the inheritor himself have no more, ha?   3271

HORAT. Not a jot more, my lord.

HAML. Is not parchment made of sheep-skins?

HORAT. Aye, my lord, and of calf-skins too.

HAML. They are sheep and calves which seek out assurance in that.—I will speak to this fellow. [*Advancing.*] Whose grave's this, sir?   3277

FIRST CLO. Mine, sir. [*Sings.*]

    O! a pit of clay for to be made
        For such a guest is meet.

HAML. I think it be thine, indeed; for thou liest in't.

FIRST CLO. You lie out on't sir, and therefore it

is not yours. For my part, I do not lie in't, and yet it is mine.   3285

HAML. Thou dost lie in't, to be in't and say it is thine: 'tis for the dead, not for the quick; therefore thou liest.

FIRST CLO. 'Tis a "quick" lie, sir! 'twill away again, from me to you.   3290

HAML. What man dost thou dig it for?

FIRST CLO. For no man, sir.

HAML. What woman, then?

FIRST CLO. For none, either.

HAML. Who is to be buried in't?   3295

FIRST CLO. One that was a woman, sir; but, rest her soul, she's dead.

HAML. How absolute the knave is! We must speak by the card, or equivocation will undo us. By the Lord, Horatio, these three years I have taken note of it; the age is grown so picked that the toe of the peasant comes so near the heel of the courtier he galls his kibe.—How long hast thou been a grave maker?   3304

FIRST CLO. Of all the days i' the year, I came to't that day that our last King Hamlet overcame Fortinbras.

HAML. How long is that since?

FIRST CLO. Cannot you tell that? Every fool can tell that! It was the very day that young Hamlet was born—he that is mad, and sent into England.

HAML. Aye, marry; why was he sent into England?   3313

FIRST CLO. Why, because a' was mad. A' shall recover his wits there; or, if a' do not, 'tis no great matter there.

HAML. Why?

FIRST CLO. 'Twill not be seen in him there; there the men are as mad as he.

HAML. How came he mad?   3320

FIRST CLO. Very strangely, they say.

HAML. How strangely?

FIRST CLO. Faith, e'en with losing his wits.

HAML. Upon what ground?

FIRST CLO. Why, here in Denmark. I have been sexton here, man and boy, thirty years.   3326

HAML. How long will a man lie i' the earth ere he rot?

FIRST CLO. Faith, if a' be not rotten before a' die —as we have many pocky corses now-a-days that will scarce hold the laying in—a' will last you some tight year, or nine year; a tanner will last you nine year.   3333

HAML. Why he more than another?

FIRST CLO. Why, sir, his hide is so tanned with his trade that a' will keep out water a great while;

and your water is a sore decayer of your whoreson dead body. Here's a skull now; this skull hath lain you i' the earth three-and-twenty years.

HAML. Whose was it?

FIRST CLO.   A whoreson mad fellow's it was! Whose do you think it was?

HAML. Nay, I know not.

FIRST CLO. A pestilence on him for a mad rogue! a' poured a flagon of Rhenish on my head once. This same skull, sir, was Yorick's skull, the king's jester.   3346

HAML. This!

FIRST CLO. E'en that.

HAML. Let me see.— [Takes the skull.]—Alas! poor Yorick!—I knew him, Horatio; a fellow of infinite jest, of most excellent fancy; he hath borne me on his back a thousand times; and now, how abhorred in my imagination it is! My gorge rises at it! Here hung those lips that I have kissed I know not how oft. Where be your gibes now? your gambols? your songs? your flashes of merriment that were wont to set the table on a roar? Not one now, to mock your own grinning? quite chapfallen? Now get you to my lady's chamber, and tell her, let her paint an inch thick, to this favor she must come. Make her laugh at that!— Prithee, Horatio, tell me one thing.   3362

HORAT. What's that, my lord?

HAML. Dost thou think Alexander looked o' this fashion i' the earth?

HORAT. E'en so.   3366

Throws down the skull.

HAML. And smelt so? pah!

HORAT. E'en so, my lord.

HAML. To what base uses we may return, Horatio! Why may not imagination trace the noble dust of Alexander, till he find it stopping a bunghole?   3372

HORAT. 'Twere to consider too curiously to consider so.

HAML. No, faith, not a jot! But to follow him thither, with modesty enough, and likelihood to lead it, as thus: Alexander died; Alexander was buried; Alexander returneth into dust; the dust is earth; of earth we make loam; and why of that loam whereto he was converted might they not stop a beer-barrel?   3381

"Imperious Cæsar, dead and turn'd to clay,
   Might stop a hole to keep the wind away:
O, that that earth, which kept the world in awe,
   Should patch a wall to expel the winter's flaw!"
But soft! but soft! Aside. Here comes the king.

Enter Priests, &c., in procession; bell tolling; the corpse of OPHELIA *borne in,* LAERTES, KING, QUEEN, *Lords, &c., following.*

The queen, the courtiers? Who is that they follow?
And with such maimed rites? This doth betoken
The corse they follow did with desperate hand
Fordo its own life. 'Twas of some estate.   3390
Couch we awhile and mark.
                                        [*Retiring with* HORATIO.
    LAERT. What ceremony else?
    HAML.   That is Laertes—
A very noble youth! Mark.
    LAERT. What ceremony else?
    FIRST PRIEST. Her obsequies have been as far
        enlarg'd
                                                        3395
As we have warrantise. Her death was doubtful,
And, but that great command o'ersways the order,
She should in ground unsanctified have lodg'd
Till the last trumpet; for charitable prayers,
Shards, flints, and pebbles should be thrown on her.
Yet here she is allow'd her virgin crants,   3401
Her maiden strewments, and the bringing home
Of bell and burial.
    LAERT. Must there no more be done?
    FIRST PRIEST.   No more be done.
We should profane the service of the dead
To sing a requiem and such rest to her   3406
As to peace-parted souls.
    LAERT.   Lay her i' the earth;
And from her fair and unpolluted flesh
May violets spring!—I tell thee, churlish priest,
A ministering angel shall my sister be,   3410
When thou liest howling.
    HAML.   What! the fair Ophelia?
    QUEEN [*scattering flowers*]. Sweets to the sweet.
        Farewell!
I hop'd thou shouldst have been my Hamlet's wife;
I thought thy bride-bed to have deck'd, sweet maid,
And not t'have strewed thy grave.
    LAERT.   O! treble woe
Fall ten times treble on that cursed head   3416
Whose wicked deed thy most ingenious sense
Depriv'd thee of!—Hold off the earth awhile,
Till I have caught her once more in mine arms.

                Leaps into the grave.

Now pile your dust upon the quick and dead,
Till of this flat a mountain you have made
To o'ertop old Pelion or the skyish head
Of blue Olympus!
    HAML. [*advancing*]. What is he, whose grief
Bears such an emphasis? whose phrase of sorrow

Conjures the wandering stars, and makes them
        stand   3425
Like wonder-wounded hearers? This is I,
Hamlet, the Dane!

                Leaps into the grave.

    LAERT. [*seizing him by the throat*]. The devil
        take thy soul!
    HAML. Thou pray'st not well.
I prithee, take thy fingers from my throat!
For though I am not splenetive and rash,   3430
Yet have I in me something dangerous,
Which let thy wiseness fear. Away thy hand!

            They struggle in the grave.

    KING. Pluck them asunder.
    QUEEN.   Hamlet! Hamlet!
    ALL. Gentlemen!

*The Attendants part them, and they come out of
                the grave.*

    HORAT.   Good my lord, be quiet.
    HAML. Why, I will fight with him upon this
        theme   3435
Until my eyelids will no longer wag.
    QUEEN. O, my son, what theme?
    HAML. I lov'd Ophelia. Forty thousand brothers
Could not, with all their quantity of love,
Make up my sum!—What wilt thou do for her?
    KING. O, he is mad, Laertes.   3441
    QUEEN. For love of God, forbear him.
    HAML. 'Swounds, show me what thou'lt do!
Woo't weep? woo't fight? woo't fast? woo't tear
        thyself?
Woo't drink up Esill? eat a crocodile?   3445
I'll do't! Dost thou come here to whine?
To outface me with leaping in her grave?
Be buried quick with her, and so will I!
And, if thou prate of mountains, let them throw
Millions of acres on us, till our ground,   3450
Singeing his pate against the burning zone,
Make Ossa like a wart! Nay, an thou'lt mouth,
I'll rant as well as thou!
    QUEEN.   This is mere madness:
And thus a while the fit will work on him;
Anon, as patient as the female dove   3455
When that her golden couplets are disclos'd,
His silence will sit drooping.
    HAML.   Hear you, sir:
What is the reason that you use me thus?
I lov'd you ever.—But it is no matter;

Let Hercules himself do what he may,　　　3460
The cat will mew and dog will have his day.
　　　　　　　　　　　　　　　　　　[*Exit.*

KING. I pray you, good Horatio, wait upon him.
　　　　　　　　　　　　　　　[*Exit* HORATIO.

[*Aside to* LAERTES.] Strengthen your patience in
　　our last night's speech;
We'll put the matter to the present push.—
Good Gertrude, set some watch over your son.
This grave shall have a living monument.　　3466
[*Aside to* LAERTES.] An hour of quiet shortly shall
　　we see;
Till then, in patience our proceeding be.　[*Exeunt.*

SCENE II:—*Later the same day. A hall in the castle.*

Enter HAMLET *and* HORATIO.

HAML. So much for this, sir: now shall you see
　　the other.
You do remember all the circumstance?　　3470
　　HORAT. Remember it, my lord!
　　HAML. Sir, in my heart there was a kind of fight-
　　ing
That would not let me sleep; methought I lay
Worse than the mutines in the bilboes. Rashly—
And prais'd be rashness for it; let us know,
Our indiscretion sometimes serves us well　　3476
When our deep plots do pall, and that should teach
　　us
There's a divinity that shapes our ends,
Rough-hew them how we will,—
　　HORAT.　　　　　　　　　That is most certain.
　　HAML. Up from my cabin,　　　　　　3480
My sea-gown scarf'd about me, in the dark
Grop'd I to find out them; had my desire;
Finger'd their packet; and, in fine, withdrew
To mine own room again, making so bold—
My fears forgetting manners—to unseal　　3485
Their grand commission. Where I found, Ho-
　　ratio,—
O royal knavery!—an exact command,
Larded with many several sorts of reasons
Importing Denmark's health, and England's too,
With, ho! such bugs and goblins in my life,
That, on the supervise, no leisure bated,　　3491
No, not to stay the grinding of the ax,
My head should be struck off!
　　HORAT.　　　　　　　　Is't possible!
　　HAML. Here's the commission: read it at more
　　leisure.

Hands him the letter.

But wilt thou hear me how I did proceed?　　3495
　　HORAT. I beseech you.
　　HAML. Being thus be-netted round with villainies,
Ere I could make a prologue to my brains
They had begun the play. I sat me down,
Devis'd a new commission, wrote it fair.　　3500
I once did hold it, as our statists do,
A baseness to write fair, and labor'd much
How to forget that learning; but, sir, now
It did me yeoman's service. Wilt thou know
The effect of what I wrote?
　　HORAT.　　　　　　　　Aye, good my lord.
　　HAML. An earnest conjuration from the king,
As England was his faithful tributary,
As love between them like the palm should flour-
　　ish,　　　　　　　　　　　　　3508
As peace should still her wheaten garland wear,
And stand a comma 'tween their amities,
And many such-like "As"es of great charge,
That, on the view and knowing of these contents,
Without debatement further more or less,
He should the bearers put to sudden death,　3514
Not shriving-time allow'd.
　　HORAT.　　　　　　　How was this seal'd?
　　HAML. Why, even in that was heaven ordinant.
I had my father's signet in my purse,
Which was the model of that Danish seal;
Folded the writ up in form of the other,　　3519
Subscrib'd it, gave't the impression, plac'd it safely,
The changeling never known. Now, the next day
Was our sea-fight; and what to this was sequent
Thou know'st already.
　　HORAT. So Guildenstern and Rosencrantz go to't.
　　HAML. Why, man, they did make love to this
　　employment!　　　　　　　　　3525
They are not near my conscience; their defeat
Does by their own insinuation grow.
'Tis dangerous when the baser nature comes
Between the pass and fell-incensed points
Of mighty opposites.
　　HORAT.　　　　　Why, what a king is this!
　　HAML. Does it not, thinks't thee, stand me now
　　upon—　　　　　　　　　　　3531
He that hath kill'd my king, and whor'd my
　　mother,
Popp'd in between the election and my hopes,
Thrown out his angle for my proper life,
And with such cozenage—is't not perfect con-
　　science　　　　　　　　　　　3535
To quit him with this arm? and is't not to be
　　damn'd
To let this canker of our nature come
In further evil?

HORAT. It must be shortly known to him from England
What is the issue of the business there.   3540

HAML. It will be short; the interim is mine:
And a man's life's no more than to say "One!"—
But I am very sorry, good Horatio,
That to Laertes I forgot myself;
For, by the image of my cause, I see   3545
The portraiture of his. I'll court his favors.
But, sure, the bravery of his grief did put me
Into a towering passion!—

HORAT.   Peace! Who comes here?

Enter OSRIC, *a dandified gallant.*

OSR. Your lordship is right welcome back to Denmark.   3550

HAML. I humbly thank you, sir. [*Aside to* HORATIO.] Dost know this water-fly?

HORAT. [*aside to* HAMLET]. No, my good lord.

HAML. [*aside to* HORATIO]. Thy state is the more gracious; for 'tis a vice to know him. He hath much land, and fertile: let a beast be lord of beasts, and his crib shall stand at the king's mess. 'Tis a chough—but, as I say, spacious in the possession of dirt.   3559

OSR. Sweet lord, if your lordship were at leisure, I should impart a thing to you from his majesty.

HAML. I will receive it, sir, with all diligence of spirit. Put your bonnet to his right use; 'tis for the head.   3564

OSR. I thank your lordship, 'tis very hot.

HAML. No, believe me, 'tis very cold; the wind is northerly.

OSR. It is indifferent cold—my lord—indeed—

HAML. But yet methinks it is very sultry and hot for my complexion.   3570

OSR. Exceedingly, my lord! it is very sultry—as 'twere—I cannot tell how. But, my lord, his majesty bade me signify to you that he has laid a great wager on your head. Sir, this is the matter—

HAML. I beseech you, remember.   3575

HAMLET *moves him to put on his hat.*

OSR. Nay, good my lord. [HAMLET *again moves him to put on his hat.*] For mine ease, in good faith. [HAMLET *insists, until* OSRIC *yields and puts on his hat.*] Sir, here is newly come to court Laertes. Believe me, an absolute gentleman! full of most excellent differences! of very soft society, and great showing! Indeed, to speak feelingly of him, he is the card or calendar of gentry; for you shall find in him the continent of what part a gentleman would see.   3585

HAML. Sir, his definement suffers no perdition in you, though I know to divide him inventorially would dizzy the arithmetic of memory and yet but yaw neither in respect of his quick sail, but, in the verity of extolment, I take him to be a soul of great article, and his infusion of such dearth and rareness, as, to make true diction of him, his semblable is his mirror, and who else would trace him, his umbrage, nothing more.   3594

OSR. Your lordship speaks most infallibly of him.

HAML. The concernancy, sir? Why do we wrap the gentleman in our more rawer breath?

OSR. Sir?

HORAT. Is't not possible to understand in another tongue? You will too't, sir, really?   3600

HAML. What imports the nomination of this gentleman?

OSR. Of Laertes?

HORAT. [*aside to* HAMLET]. His purse is empty already; all's golden words are spent.   3605

HAML. Of him, sir.

OSR. I know you are not ignorant—

HAML. I would you did, sir; yet, in faith, if you did, it would not much approve me. Well, sir?

OSR. You are not ignorant of what excellence Laertes is—   3611

HAML. I dare not confess that, lest I should compare with him in excellence; but, to know a man well, were to know himself.

OSR. I mean, sir, for his weapon. But in the imputation laid on him by them, in his meed he's unfellowed.   3617

HAML. What's his weapon?

OSR. Rapier and dagger.

HAML. That's two of his weapons.—But? Well?

OSR. The king, sir, hath wagered with him six Barbary horses; against the which he has imponed, as I take it, six French rapiers and poniards, with their assigns, as girdle, hangers, and so. Three of the carriages, in faith, are very dear to fancy, very responsive to the hilts, most delicate carriages, and of very liberal conceit.   3627

HAML. What call you the "carriages"?

HORAT. [*aside to* HAMLET]. I knew you must be edified by the margent, ere you had done.

OSR. The "carriages," sir, are the hangers.

HAML. The phrase would be more german to the matter if we could carry cannon by our sides; I would it might be "hangers" till then. But, on: six Barbary horses against six French swords, their assigns, and three liberal-conceited carriages; that's the French bet against the Danish. Why is this "imponed," as you call it?   3638

Osr. The king, sir, hath laid that in a dozen passes between yourself and him, he shall not exceed you three hits; he hath laid on twelve for nine. And it would come to immediate trial, if your lordship would vouchsafe the answer.

Haml. How if I answer "No"?   3644

Osr. I mean, my lord, the opposition of your person in trial.

Haml. Sir, I will walk here in the hall. If it please his majesty, 'tis the breathing time of day with me. Let the foils be brought, the gentleman willing, and the king hold his purpose. I will win for him if I can; if not, I will gain nothing but my shame and the odd hits.   3652

Osr. Shall I re-deliver you so?

Haml. To this effect, sir, after what flourish your nature will.

Osr. I commend my duty to your lordship.

Haml. Yours, yours. [*Exit* Osric.]—He does well to commend it himself; there are no tongues else for's turn.

Horat. This lapwing runs away with the shell on his head.   3661

Haml. He did comply with his dug before he sucked it. Thus has he—and many more of the same bevy that I know the drossy age dotes on—only got the tune of the time and outward habit of encounter, a kind of yesty collection which carries them through and through the most fond and winnowed opinions; and do but blow them to their trial, the bubbles are out.   3669

Enter a Lord.

Lord. My lord, his majesty commended him to you by young Osric, who brings back to him that you attend him in the hall. He sends to know if your pleasure hold to play with Laertes, or that you will take longer time.   3674

Haml. I am constant to my purposes; they follow the king's pleasure. If his fitness speaks, mine is ready, now, or whensoever, provided I be so able as now.

Lord. The king, and queen, and all are coming down.   3680

Haml. In happy time.

Lord. The queen desires you to use some gentle entertainment to Laertes before you fall to play.

Haml. She well instructs me.   [*Exit Lord.*

Horat. You will lose this wager, my lord.   3685

Haml. I do not think so. Since he went into France, I have been in continual practice; I shall win at the odds.—But thou wouldst not think how ill all's here about my heart. But, it is no matter.

Horat. Nay, good my lord.   3690

Haml. It is but foolery.—But, it is such a kind of gain-giving as would perhaps trouble a woman.

Horat. If your mind dislike any thing, obey it. I will forestal their repair hither, and say you are not fit.   3695

Haml. Not a whit! We defy augury. There's a special providence in the fall of a sparrow. If it be now, 'tis not to come; if it be not to come, it will be now; if it be not now, yet it will come: the readiness is all. Since no man has aught of what he leaves, what is't to leave betimes? Let be.   3701

Enter King, Queen, Laertes, Osric, *Lords, &c.; Attendants with table, foils, flagons of wine.*

King. Come, Hamlet; come, and take this hand from me.

    Hamlet *seizes the hand of* Laertes.

Haml. Give me your pardon, sir. I've done you wrong;
But pardon't, as you are a gentleman.
This presence knows,   3705
And you must needs have heard, how I am punish'd
With sore distraction. What I have done
That might your nature, honor, and exception
Roughly awake, I here proclaim was madness.
Was't Hamlet wrong'd Laertes? Never Hamlet!
If Hamlet from himself be ta'en away,   3711
And when he's not himself does wrong Laertes,
Then Hamlet does it not. Hamlet denies it.
Who does it then? His madness. If't be so,
Hamlet is of the faction that is wrong'd;   3715
His madness is poor Hamlet's enemy.
Sir, in this audience,
Let my disclaiming from a purpos'd evil
Free me so far in your most generous thoughts,
That I have shot mine arrow o'er the house
And hurt my brother.

Laert.   I am satisfied in nature,
Whose motive in this case should stir me most
To my revenge; but in my terms of honor
I stand aloof, and will no reconcilement   3724
Till by some elder masters, of known honor,
I have a voice and precedent of peace,
To keep my name ungor'd. But till that time
I do receive your offer'd love like love,
And will not wrong it.

Haml.   I embrace it freely;
And will this brother's wager frankly play.—
Give us the foils. [*To* Laertes.] Come on!

Laert.   Come; one for me.

HAML. I'll be your foil, Laertes. In mine igno-
rance   3732
Your skill shall, like a star i' the darkest night,
Stick fiery off indeed.

LAERT.   You mock me, sir.

HAML. No, by this hand.

KING.   Give them the foils, young Osric.

OSRIC *spreads the foils upon the table. The* KING
takes his seat by the QUEEN *upon a dais.* LAERTES
advances to select a foil; whereupon the KING
seeks to divert HAMLET's *attention.*

Cousin Hamlet!   3736

HAMLET *turns.*

You know the wager?

HAML.   Very well, my lord.
Your Grace hath laid the odds o' the weaker side.

KING. I do not fear it; I have seen you both:
But since he is better'd, we have therefore odds.

LAERT. This is too heavy; let me see another.

*Selects the unbaited rapier, and stands holding the
point concealed.* HAMLET *picks up a foil.*

HAML. This likes me well.—These foils have all
a length?   3742

OSR. Aye, my good lord.

KING. Set me the stoups of wine upon that table.
If Hamlet give the first, or second, hit,   3745
Or quit in answer of the third exchange,
Let all the battlements their ordnance fire;
The king shall drink to Hamlet's better breath.
And in the cup an union shall he throw,
Richer than that which four successive kings 3750
In Denmark's crown have worn. Give me the cups;
And let the kettle to the trumpets speak,
The trumpets to the cannoneer without,
The cannons to the heavens, the heavens to earth,
"Now the king drinks to Hamlet!"—Come, begin.
And you, the judges, bear a wary eye.   3756

The Judges, OSRIC *and* HORATIO, *take their stand.*
HAMLET *and* LAERTES *assume the dueling posture.*

HAML. Come on, sir.

LAERT.   Come, my lord.

They begin to play.

HAML.   One!

LAERT.   No.

HAML.   Judgment.

OSR. A hit, a very palpable hit.

LAERT.   Well; again.

*They resume play. Upon the expiration of the time
limit the Judges bring the first bout to an end.*

KING. Stay; give me drink.—Hamlet, this pearl
is thine.

*Holds up what seems to be a pearl of great beauty;
drops it into the cup, and crushes it with a pestle.*

Here's to thy health! [*Pretends to drink.*] Give
him the cup.   3760

The Attendant offers the cup to HAMLET. *The
kettle-drums roll, the trumpets sound, and the
cannons roar within. When the noise dies away,*
HAMLET *speaks.*

HAML. I'll play this bout first; set it by awhile.—
Come!

*The second bout is begun, and for some time
played in tense silence.*

Another hit; what say you?

LAERT. A touch, a touch, I do confess.   3764

KING. Our son shall win.

QUEEN.   He's fat, and scant of breath.

At last the Judges end the second bout. The QUEEN
descends to where HAMLET *stands by the table.*

Here, Hamlet, take my napkin, rub thy brows.

*While he is mopping his brow, she lifts the cup in
a health to him.*

The queen carouses to thy fortune, Hamlet.

HAML. Good madam!

KING [*rushing down*].   Gertrude, do not
drink!

QUEEN. I will, my lord! I pray you, pardon me.
[*Drinks.*]

KING [*aside*]. It is the poison'd cup: it is too
late!   3770

She offers the cup to HAMLET.

HAML. I dare not drink yet, madam; by and by.

QUEEN. Come, let me wipe thy face.

LAERT. [*to the* KING]. My lord, I'll hit him now.

KING [*to* LAERTES].   I do not think't.

LAERT. [*aside*]. And yet 'tis almost 'gainst my
conscience.

HAML. Come, for the third! Laertes, you but
dally;   3775
I pray you, pass with your best violence.
I am afeared you make a wanton of me.

LAERT. Say you so? come on.

*The third bout is begun. Neither player is able to
score a touch.*

Osr. [*ready to end the bout*]. Nothing, neither
way.   3779
Laert. Have at you—now!

Laertes, *abandoning all defense, rushes in upon*
Hamlet *and wounds him.* Hamlet *seizes Laertes' wrist,* Laertes *seizes Hamlet's wrist, and
in the scuffle they exchange weapons.* Hamlet
wounds Laertes.

King.   Part them! they are incens'd.

The Judges step between them.

Haml. Nay; come, again.

The Queen *falls.*

Osr.   Look to the queen there, ho!
Horat. They bleed on both sides. [*To* Hamlet.]
How is it, my lord?
Osr. How is it, Laertes?
Laert. Why, as a woodcock to mine own springe,
Osric;
I am justly kill'd with mine own treachery.   3785
Haml. How does the queen?

Kneels by her.

King.   She swounds to see them bleed.
Queen. No, no! the drink! the drink!—O my
dear Hamlet!—
The drink! the drink! I am poison'd.   [*Dies.*
Haml. O villainy! Ho, let the door be lock'd!

Horatio *leaps to the door and locks it.*

Treachery! Seek it out!   3790

Laertes *falls.*

Laert. It is here, Hamlet. Hamlet, thou art slain.
No medicine in the world can do thee good;
In thee there is not half an hour of life.
The treacherous instrument is in thy hand,
Unbated and envenom'd. The foul practice   3795
Hath turn'd itself on me. Lo! here I lie,
Never to rise again. Thy mother's poison'd.
I can no more. The king, the king's to blame!
Haml. The point envenom'd too!—
Then, venom, to thy work!   3800

Stabs the King.

All. Treason! treason!
King. O, yet defend me, friends! I am but hurt.
Haml. Here, thou incestuous, murderous, damned
Dane!
Drink off this potion!

*He forces the contents of the poisoned cup down
the throat of the* King.

Is thy "union" here?   3804
Follow my mother!

King *dies.*

Laert.   He is justly serv'd;
It is a poison temper'd by himself.
Exchange forgiveness with me, noble Hamlet.

Holds out his hand; Hamlet *takes it.*

Mine and my father's death come not upon thee,
Nor thine on me!   [*Dies.*
Haml. Heaven make thee free of it! I follow
thee.   3810

Seats himself upon the steps of the dais.

I am dead, Horatio.—Wretched queen, adieu!—
You that look pale and tremble at this chance,
That are but mutes or audience to this act,
Had I but time [*A paroxysm of pain interrupts
him.*]—as this fell sergeant, death,
Is strict in his arrest,—O, I could tell you—
But let it be.—Horatio, I am dead;   3816
Thou livest: report me and my cause aright
To the unsatisfied.
Horat.   Never believe it!
I am more an antique Roman than a Dane.
Here's yet some liquor left.

Lifts the poisoned cup.

Haml. [*leaping to him*].   As thou'rt a man,
Give me the cup!—Let go!—By heaven, I'll have't!

*He wrests the cup from Horatio's hands, and
dashes it to the floor; then sinks again to the dais.*

O God, Horatio, what a wounded name,   3822
Things standing thus unknown, shall live behind
me!
If thou didst ever hold me in thy heart,
Absent thee from felicity awhile,
And in this harsh world draw thy breath in pain,
To tell my story.

March afar off, and shot within.

What warlike noise is this?
Osr. Young Fortinbras, with conquest come from
Poland,   3830
To the ambassadors of England gives
This warlike volley.
Haml.   O, I die, Horatio!
The potent poison quite o'er-crows my spirit.

I cannot live to hear the news from England;
But I do prophesy the election lights   3835
On Fortinbras: he has my dying voice;
So tell him—with the occurrents, more and less,
Which have solicited— The rest is silence.   [*Dies.*

  HORAT. Now cracks a noble heart! Good-night,
    sweet prince,
And flights of angels sing thee to thy rest!—   3840

March within.

Why does the drum come hither?

Enter FORTINBRAS *with his army; the English Am-*
    bassadors, and others.

  FORTIN. Where is this sight?
  HORAT.   What is it ye would see?
If aught of woe or wonder, cease your search.
  FORTIN. This quarry cries on havoc. O proud
    Death!
What feast is toward in thine eternal cell   3845
That thou so many princes at a shot
So bloodily hast struck?
  FIRST AMB.   The sight is dismal!
And our affairs from England come too late;
The ears are senseless that should give us hearing,
To tell him his commandment is fulfill'd,   3850
That Rosencrantz and Guildenstern are dead.
Where should we have our thanks?
  HORAT.   Not from his mouth,
Had it the ability of life to thank you:
He never gave commandment for their death.
But since, so jump upon this bloody question,
You from the Polack wars, and you from England,

Are here arriv'd, give order that these bodies
High on a stage be placed to the view;   3858
And let me speak to the yet unknowing world
How these things came about: so shall you hear
Of carnal, bloody, and unnatural acts,
Of accidental judgments, casual slaughters,
Of deaths put on by cunning and forc'd cause,
And, in this upshot, purposes mistook   3864
Fall'n on the inventors' heads. All this can I
Truly deliver.
  FORTIN.   Let us haste to hear it;
And call the noblest to the audience.
For me, with sorrow I embrace my fortune;
I have some rights of memory in this kingdom,
Which now to claim my vantage doth invite me.
  HORAT. Of that I shall have also cause to speak,
And from his mouth whose voice will draw on
    more.
But let this same be presently perform'd
Even while men's minds are wild, lest more mis-
    chance   3874
On plots and errors happen.
  FORTIN.   Let four captains
Bear Hamlet, like a soldier, to the stage;
For he was likely, had he been put on,
To have prov'd most royally: and for his passage,
The soldiers' music and the rites of war
Speak loudly for him.   3880
Take up the bodies. Such a sight as this
Becomes the field, but here shows much amiss.—
Go, bid the soldiers shoot.
    [*A dead march. Exeunt, bearing off the*
      bodies; after which, a peal of ordnance is
      shot off within.

RENAISSANCE LYRICS

The Elizabethan Age was ushered in very shortly after the publication of *Tottel's Miscellany* had introduced a number of new lyric poets. From the appearance of this book in 1557 for about a hundred years there is a remarkable succession of poets writing songs and other lyric forms.

The Shepherd's Calender of Spenser (1579) began a long tradition in England of the old classical pastoral. This form, beginning with Theocritus,[1] had been used by Virgil, some of whose *Bucolics* have much beauty. Spenser uses the old machinery of shepherds and writes a poem for each month of the shepherd's year. With one or two exceptions they make dull reading, unless one is already interested in the matters—sometimes purely local or temporary—which he discusses in the shepherds' dialogues. On the whole the pastoral form has not been successful in English, though two of our great elegies, *Lycidas* and *Adonais,* belong to the pastoral tradition.

Much more significant for the history of literature of that time as well as for later periods is the large outpouring of sonnets that began with *Tottel's Miscellany.* This lyric form had been perfected by Petrarch[2] in the early fourteenth century and it was brought to England by two noblemen, Sir Thomas Wyatt and the Earl of Surrey, some twenty years before the appearance of the *Miscellany* in which their poems were printed. After the introduction of the sonnets the principal use made of them for a long time was the composition of "cycles of sonnets," frequently series of a hundred. These were most often written to the poet's lady and expressed in many varying ways his love for her. Good examples are Sir Philip Sidney's *Astrophel and Stella* and Spenser's *Amoretti.* Shakespeare composed a longer cycle, but only a portion of this concerns a lady: the larger and better part are sonnets of friendship addressed to a man. Except in the hands of Milton this fourteen line form fell out of use after the close of the Elizabethan era and was not revived for another century and more. But for the past hundred and fifty years it has been employed by nearly all important poets. Even the love sonnet cycle was revived in the nineteenth century.

The plays written during the Elizabethan period gave occasion for the writing of many beautiful songs. As is true with all songs, the structure of these poems is very simple, with much repetition and occasional refrain. Their purpose is usually to express some emotion, though it may be that only a clever turn of expression is designed by the poet. *Full Fathom Five Thy Father Lies* is a dirge lamenting simply the supposed death of the hero's father. But the interest in *Cupid and Campaspe* or "Drink to me only with thine eyes" is in the unusual "conceit," the clever if somewhat far-fetched way of declaring love.

[1] For some remarks on the classical pastoral, see pp. 253 ff.
[2] See p. 618

As the seventeenth century succeeded the Elizabethan period, the poetry with these "conceits" became more popular. John Donne, in particular, was fond of exercising his playful intellect in composing such poems. In *Love's Deity,* for example, he tries to imagine what love was like before the perverse God of Love was born. This "metaphysical" poetry, as it is often called, was cultivated by several of the poets who wrote in the period after 1620, such as Herbert, Vaughan, and Marvell. It takes a specially developed taste to appreciate their works, but they have been increasingly enjoyed and discussed within the past few years.

The political troubles of England in the seventeenth century divided authors as well as other citizens into opposing parties. The adherents of the king, the Cavaliers, had among them a group of gay, light-hearted singers, who wrote very graceful lyrics. We speak of them as the Cavalier poets. Suckling and Lovelace are typical of these. Belonging to them in many of his moods was Robert Herrick, the most interesting of the group. The Puritans also had their poet, one of the great authors of all time. John Milton's lyrics will receive attention in a later chapter.

In the lyric more than in other kinds of poetry, the author is concerned with form, or pattern. He is dealing with a small unit. The subject is usually very simple and the interest is not so much in *what* the poet says but *how* he says it. He must learn the devices the language has developed to give proper melody to his verses. He must know what the reader finds pleasing to the ear and the eye, and what are the most effective ways of marshaling his impressions, or emotions, or thoughts. That the poet may by long experience have made these patterns subconscious does not change the fact that he employs them and that he is much concerned that they be used with most effect.

The reader of lyrics must, therefore, cultivate an intelligent interest in poetic pattern if he is to make any attempt to appreciate the poetry. The rhyme scheme of a lyric and the way in which the poet retains this scheme in succeeding stanzas, the number of accents in the various lines, and the general movement of the lines—all these make up the poetic form, and all are very easy to recognize if only a little attention is given to them.

The types of poetic feet in English are very simple. The most popular are the iambic, consisting of an unaccented and an accented syllable (˘´), and the trochaic with the reverse pattern (´˘). The two other usual feet are the anapestic (˘˘´) and the dactylic (´˘˘). A poem need not be entirely in any one of these patterns, but it is usually possible to speak of the general movement as being one or the other. It will be good practice with some of the songs to divide the poem into feet and try to see the formal structure as well as the meaning.

A little practice will very soon accustom a reader to recognize the movement of a line of poetry. The greater part of poetry in the English language is *iambic.* The movement will be recognized in the following lines:

(1) My mind to me a kingdom is.
(2) My lady sweet, Arise!
(3) The man of life upright.

It will be noted that each unit has an unaccented, followed by an accented, syllable. The lines given above have from three to four of these feet.

The opposite of *iambic* is *trochaic,* in which the foot begins with the accent and has one unaccented syllable. Illustrations are:

(1) Who is Silvia? what is she?
(2) Youth is full of pleasance,
(3) Here they are, my fifty men and women.
(4) In the spring a young man's fancy lightly turns to thoughts of love.

Somewhat less usual than *iambic* and *trochaic* are the so-called triple meters, *dactylic* and *anapestic*. In the latter the pattern consists of two unaccented syllables followed by an accented. Some examples of *anapestic* lines are:

(1) Thou wouldst still be adored, as this moment thou art,
    Let thy loveliness fade as it will,
(2) All the wonder and wealth of the mine in the heart of one gem;
(3) Up the creeks we will hie

It will be noted that these anapestic lines vary in their number of feet; that is, in the number of times the pattern is repeated in a line. This, of course, is true with all other types of feet, but the student unfamiliar with poetic form may well see if he can recognize the number of feet in each of the lines given above.

The exact opposite of *anapestic* meter is *dactylic*. This foot consists of an accented syllable followed by two unaccented. The lines given below will illustrate various lengths of *dactylic* verse:

(1) Touch her not scornfully;
(2) Come from the hills where the hirsels are grazing,
    Come from the glen of the buck and the roe;
(3) This is the forest primeval, the murmuring pines and the hemlocks.

This last line, the *dactylic hexameter,* as it is called, has the same basic pattern as the verse used by Homer and Virgil. As was pointed out in a discussion of Homer's verse, the Greek poet depended upon the proper succession of long and short syllables, whereas in English we are concerned with accent, or the lack of it. The last line just quoted has a light, tripping movement, whereas the same pattern in Greek with its quantitative meter is sonorous and dignified.

For practical purposes the four types of foot which have been discussed will serve to identify the movement of any poem in English. But it must be borne in mind that many poems are written in a loose metrical structure and that in these there occur frequent substitutions and shifts in the pattern. Extremely usual is the employment of a trochaic foot at the beginning of an iambic line. The first lines of sonnets frequently illustrate this tendency. For example,

> When to the sessions of sweet silent thought
> I summon up remembrance of things past.

Iambic and anapestic feet are likely to be substituted for each other, and the same is true with the combination of dactylic and trochaic. Examples of the iambic and anapestic combination are:

> I bring fresh showers for the thirsting flowers,
>   From the seas and the streams;
> I bear light shade for the leaves when laid
>   In their noonday dreams.

The stanza below illustrates a happy mixture of dactylic and trochaic:

Sing me a song of a lad that is gone,
  Say, could that lad be I?
Merry of soul he sailed on a day
  Over the sea to Skye.

It should be remembered that movement in poetry is a matter of the ear and not of the eye. It is only by reading aloud or at least by imagining the sound of a line that one can feel the rhythm which lies at the foundation of all poetic patterns. The main purpose of giving attention to these patterns, after all, is to make the reader acutely conscious of rhythm.

Very early in childhood most of us have learned what rhymes are like. We have probably practiced composing lines which end in words with similar terminations. Until we give some study to it, however, we will hardly realize the care and attention poets have given to their arrangement of rhymed lines in definite patterns known as *stanzas*. In this hurried sketch we shall look at only two or three of the most usual of these forms.

By far the most important stanza form in English is the sonnet, which is especially interesting because of the strictness of its structure. There are two principal kinds, the Italian, or Petrarchan, and the Shakespearean. All sonnets have fourteen lines of iambic pentameter (that is five-foot iambics). The Italian has a rhyme scheme that can be indicated as follows: a b b a a b b a for the first eight lines (or octave), and a variety of orders for the last six (or sestet). Usually there is a thought division at the end of the eighth line. In the Shakespearean sonnet there are groups of 4, 4, 4, and 2 lines. The rhyme is a b a b c d c d e f e f g g. The last two lines usually serve to bring the sonnet to an effective conclusion. Of the two, the Italian sonnet has been the more popular in English. Good examples of it can be found in the sonnets of Elizabeth Barrett Browning (p. 1329 below). With the other form, however, Shakespeare wrote some of the greatest poems in our language.

There are several other terms which the student of poetry is likely to encounter, and it will be a convenience for him to understand these terms and to know how to use them.

Monometer: a line of one foot; *dimeter:* of two feet; *trimeter:* of three feet; *tetrameter:* of four feet; *pentameter:* of five feet; *hexameter:* of six feet; *heptameter:* of seven feet; *octameter:* of eight feet.

Blank verse: Unrhymed iambic pentameter. Example: *Paradise Lost.*

Heroic couplet: Rhymed pairs of iambic pentameter lines. This term is usually restricted to such couplets as are found in Pope's poems, where the meaning of the couplet is concluded at the end of the second line. In these typical heroic couplets there is usually a cæsura, or pause, about the middle of the line.

Spenserian stanza: A nine-line stanza, rhyming a b a b b c b c c. The first eight lines are iambic pentameter; the last line, iambic hexameter. The stanza was invented by Spenser for his *Faerie Queene* and has been frequently used by later English poets.

Terza rima: Groups of three iambic pentameter lines rhyming as follows: a b a b c b c d c d e d, etc. The series ends with a couplet. Its most important use is in Dante's *Divine Comedy.* In English it is found in Shelley's *Ode to the West Wind* (p. 1270, below).

Rubaiyat stanza: a quatrain (that is, four lines) of iambic pentameter rhyming a a b a. See *The Rubaiyat of Omar Khayyam* (p. 484, above).

In Memoriam stanza: A quatrain of iambic tetrameter (that is, four-foot iambic) rhyming a b b a. See Tennyson's *In Memoriam* (p. 1321, below).

Rhyme: The matching of words at the end of lines so that all the sounds, beginning with the last accented syllable, correspond. In modern English, words of identical sound are not considered rhymes.

Masculine rhyme: Masculine rhyme is rhyme involving only the last syllable. Thus: *defeat, repeat. Feminine rhyme* involves the last two syllables: *defeating, repeating.*

Assonance: A correspondence like rhyme, except that the final consonants are different. Thus: *make, fate.*

Alliteration: A correspondence within lines of poetry affecting the initial sounds of accented syllables. Thus: "The furrow followed free." For extended use of alliteration, see the selections from Old English poetry and also *Sir Gawain and the Green Knight* (pp. 988 and 1021, above).

Onomatopœia: A correspondence between the sound of the word and the thing expressed. For example, the words *bang* and *clang.*

Students interested in matters of poetic form will find much to engage their attention in the works of poets of our last generation. Especially important has been an increasing use of free verse. The poet does not confine himself to any one pattern, but attempts to vary the poetic form to suit the thought or feeling. No better free verse can be found than the translations of the Psalms (p. 427, above) and in the poems of Whitman (p. 1362, below).

RENAISSANCE LYRICS

JOHN LYLY

Apelles' Song

Cupid and my Campaspe played
At cards for kisses,—Cupid paid;
He stakes his quiver, bow and arrows,
His mother's doves, and team of sparrows:
Loses them too; then down he throws   5
The coral of his lip, the rose
Growing on's cheek (but none knows how);
With these the crystal of his brow,
And then the dimple of his chin:
All these did my Campaspe win.   10
At last he set [1] her both his eyes;
She won, and Cupid blind did rise.
O Love, has she done this to thee?
What shall, alas! become of me?

ROBERT GREENE

Song

Sweet are the thoughts that savor of content;
   The quiet mind is richer than a crown.
Sweet are the nights in careless slumber spent;
   The poor estate scorns fortune's angry frown.
Such sweet content, such minds, such sleep, such bliss,   5
Beggars enjoy, when princes oft do miss.

The homely house that harbors quiet rest;
   The cottage that affords no pride nor care;
The mean that 'grees with country music best;
   The sweet consort of mirth and music's fare;   10
Obscuréd life sets down a type of bliss—
A mind content both crown and kingdom is.

Lyly, *Apelles' Song.* John Lyly (c. 1554-1606) was born in Kent and educated at Oxford. He went to London, where he entered politics and wrote prose novels, dramas, and lyrics.
[1] Staked.
Greene, *Song.* Robert Greene (1560-1592) was born at Norwich and died in London. He was educated at Cambridge. He wrote dramas, tracts, novels, and poems.

CHRISTOPHER MARLOWE

The Passionate Shepherd to His Love

Come live with me and be my Love,
And we will all the pleasures prove
That hills and valleys, dales and fields,
Or woods or steepy mountain yields.

And we will sit upon the rocks,   5
And see the shepherds feed their flocks
By shallow rivers, to whose falls
Melodious birds sing madrigals.

And I will make thee beds of roses
And a thousand fragrant posies;   10
A cap of flowers, and a kirtle
Embroidered all with leaves of myrtle;

A gown made of the finest wool
Which from our pretty lambs we pull;
Fair-linéd slippers for the cold,   15
With buckles of the purest gold;

A belt of straw and ivy buds
With coral clasps and amber studs—
And if these pleasures may thee move,
Come live with me and be my Love.   20

The shepherd swains shall dance and sing
For thy delight each May morning—
If these delights thy mind may move,
Then live with me and be my Love.

EDWARD DYER

My Mind to Me a Kingdom Is

My mind to me a kingdom is;
  Such present joys therein I find
That it excels all other bliss
  That earth affords or grows by kind.
Though much I want which most would have,   5
Yet still my mind forbids to crave.

No princely pomp, no wealthy store,
  No force to win the victory,
No wily wit to salve a sore,
  No shape to feed a loving eye;   10
To none of these I yield as thrall—
For why? My mind doth serve for all.

I see how plenty surfeits oft,
  And hasty climbers soon do fall;
I see that those which are aloft   15
  Mishap doth threaten most of all;
They get with toil, they keep with fear—
Such cares my mind could never bear.

Content to live, this is my stay;
  I seek no more than may suffice;   20
I press to bear no haughty sway;
  Look, what I lack my mind supplies.
Lo, thus I triumph like a king,
Content with that my mind doth bring.

Some have too much, yet still do crave;   25
  I little have, and seek no more.
They are but poor, though much they have,
  And I am rich with little store.
They poor, I rich; they beg, I give;
They lack, I leave; they pine, I live.   30

I laugh not at another's loss;
  I grudge not at another's pain;
No worldly waves my mind can toss;
  My state at one doth still remain.
I fear no foe, I fawn no friend;   35
I loathe not life, nor dread my end.

Some weigh their pleasure by their lust,
  Their wisdom by their rage of will;
Their treasure is their only trust;
  A cloakéd craft their store of skill.   40
But all the pleasure that I find
Is to maintain a quiet mind.

My wealth is health and perfect ease;
  My conscience clear my chief defense;
I neither seek by bribes to please,   45
  Nor by deceit to breed offense.
Thus do I live; thus will I die;
Would all did so as well as I!

WALTER RALEIGH

The Nymph's Reply to the Shepherd

If all the world and love were young,
And truth in every shepherd's tongue,
These pretty pleasures might me move,
To live with thee and be thy love.

Marlowe, *The Passionate Shepherd*. Christopher Marlowe was born at Canterbury in 1564 and killed at Deptford in 1593. Educated at Cambridge, he came to London, where he wrote successful plays, among them *Dr. Faustus* and *The Jew of Malta*.

Dyer, *My Mind to Me a Kingdom Is*. Sir Edward Dyer was educated at Oxford. He was a courtier and diplomat and friend of Sidney and Leicester. He died in 1607.

Raleigh, *The Nymph's Reply to the Shepherd*. Sir Walter Raleigh was born in Devonshire in 1552 and was executed in London in 1618. He led an active and romantic life as soldier and explorer.

But time drives flocks from field to fold,   5
When rivers rage, and rocks grow cold;
And Philomel becometh dumb;
The rest complains of cares to come.

The flowers do fade, and wanton fields
To wayward Winter reckoning yields;   10
A honey tongue, a heart of gall,
Is fancy's spring, but sorrow's fall.

Thy gowns, thy shoes, thy beds of roses,
Thy cap, thy kirtle, and thy posies,
Soon break, soon wither, soon forgotten,   15
In folly ripe, in reason rotten.

Thy belt of straw and ivy buds,
Thy coral clasps and amber studs,
All these in me no means can move,
To come to thee and be thy love.   20

But could youth last, and love still breed,
Had joys no date, nor age no need,
Then these delights my mind might move,
To live with thee and be thy love.

MICHAEL DRAYTON

Sonnet from IDEA

Since there's no help, come, let us kiss and part!
Nay, I have done; you get no more of me!
And I am glad, yea, glad, with all my heart,
That thus so cleanly I myself can free.
   Shake hands forever! Cancel all our vows!   5
And when we meet at any time again,
Be it not seen in either of our brows
That we one jot of former love retain!
   Now at the last gasp of Love's latest breath
When, his pulse failing, Passion speechless lies,
When Faith is kneeling by his bed of death,   11
And Innocence is closing up his eyes—
   Now, if thou wouldst, when all have given him over,
From death to life thou might'st him yet recover!

EDMUND SPENSER

Prothalamion

Calm was the day, and through the trembling air
Sweet, breathing Zephyrus did softly play

A gentle spirit, that lightly did delay
Hot Titan's [1] beams, which then did glister fair;
When I (whom sullen care,   5
Through discontent of my long fruitless stay
In princes' court, and expectation vain
Of idle hopes, which still do fly away,
Like empty shadows, did afflict my brain)
Walked forth to ease my pain   10
Along the shore of silver streaming Thames;
Whose rutty bank, the which his river hems,
Was painted all with variable flowers,
And all the meads adorned with dainty gems
Fit to deck maidens' bowers,   15
And crown their paramours
Against the bridal day, which is not long—
   Sweet Thames! run softly, till I end my song.

There, in a meadow, by the river's side,
A flock of nymphs I chancéd to espy,   20
All lovely daughters of the flood thereby,
With goodly greenish locks, all loose untied,
As each had been a bride.
And each one had a little wicker basket,
Made of fine twigs, entailéd curiously,   25
In which they gathered flowers to fill their flasket,
And with fine fingers cropt full feateously
The tender stalks on high.
Of every sort, which in that meadow grew,
They gathered some: the violet, pallid blue,   30
The little daisy, that at evening closes,
The virgin lily, and the primrose true,
With store of vermeil roses,
To deck their bridegroom's posies
Against the bridal day, which was not long—   35
   Sweet Thames! run softly, till I end my song.

With that I saw two swans of goodly hue
Come softly swimming down along the Lee; [2]
Two fairer birds I yet did never see.
The snow, which doth the top of Pindus strew,
Did never whiter shew,   41
Nor Jove himself, when he a swan would be
For love of Leda, whiter did appear;
Yet Leda was, they say, as white as he,
Yet not so white as these, nor nothing near;   45
So purely white they were,
That even the gentle stream, the which them bare,

Drayton, *Sonnet from Idea*. Michael Drayton was born in Warwickshire in 1563 and died in London in 1631. He was a voluminous writer of epic and lyric poems.

Spenser, *Prothalamion*. Written in 1596 to celebrate the double marriage of two daughters of the Earl of Worcester. "Prothalamion" means an ode preceding the marriage ceremony. Edmund Spenser (1552-1599) was born and died in London. His *Shepherd's Calender* showed great promise, which was fulfilled by his long allegorical poem, *The Faerie Queene*.

[1] Titan's (the sun's), rutty (rooty).

[2] Lee (Lea) is a river which flows into the Thames.

Seemed foul to them, and bade his billows spare
To wet their silken feathers, lest they might
Soil their fair plumes with water not so fair,   50
And mar their beauties bright,
That shone as heaven's light,
Against their bridal day, which was not long—
  Sweet Thames! run softly, till I end my song.

Eftsoons the nymphs, which now had flowers their
    fill,   55
Ran all in haste to see that silver brood,
As they came floating on the crystal flood;
Whom when they saw, they stood amazéd still,
Their wondering eyes to fill;
Them seemed they never saw a sight so fair   60
Of fowls so lovely, that they sure did deem
Them heavenly born, or to be that same pair
Which through the sky draw Venus' silver team;
For sure they did not seem
To be begot of any earthly seed,   65
But rather angels, or of angel's breed;
Yet were they bred of summer's heat, they say,
In sweetest season, when each flower and weed
The earth did fresh array;
So fresh they seemed as day,   70
Even as their bridal day, which was not long—
  Sweet Thames! run softly, till I end my song.

Then forth they all out of their baskets drew
Great store of flowers, the honor of the field,
That to the sense did fragrant odors yield,   75
All which upon those goodly birds they threw
And all the waves did strew,
That like old Peneus' waters they did seem,
When down along by pleasant Tempe's shore,
Scattered with flowers, through Thessaly they
    stream,   80
That they appear, through lilies' plenteous store,
Like a bride's chamber floor.
Two of those nymphs meanwhile, two garlands
    bound
Of freshest flowers which in that mead they found,
The which presenting all in trim array,   85
Their snowy foreheads there withal they crowned,
Whilst one did sing this lay,
Prepared against that day,
Against their bridal day, which was not long—
  Sweet Thames! run softly till I end my song. 90

"Ye gentle birds! the world's fair ornament,
And heaven's glory, whom this happy hour

Doth lead unto your lover's blissful bower,
Joy may you have, and gentle hearts' content
Of your love's couplement;   95
And let fair Venus, that is queen of love,
With her heart-quelling son upon you smile,
Whose smile, they say, hath virtue to remove
All love's dislike, and friendship's faulty guile
Forever to assoil;   100
Let endless peace your steadfast hearts accord,
And blessed plenty wait upon your board;
And let your bed with pleasures chaste abound,
That fruitful issue may to you afford,
Which may your foes confound,   105
And make your joys redound
Upon your bridal day, which is not long—"
  Sweet Thames! run softly, till I end my song.

So ended she; and all the rest around
To her redoubled that her undersong,   110
Which said their bridal day should not be long.
And gentle Echo from the neighbor ground
Their accents did resound.
So forth those joyous birds did pass along,
Adown the Lee, that to them murmured low,   115
As he would speak, but that he lacked a tongue,
Yet did by signs his glad affection show,
Making his stream run slow.
And all the fowl which in his flood did dwell
'Gan flock about these twain, that did excel   120
The rest, so far as Cynthia doth shend [3]
The lesser stars. So they, enrangéd well,
Did on those two attend,
And their best service lend   124
Against their wedding day, which was not long—
  Sweet Thames! run softly, till I end my song.

At length they all to merry London came,
To merry London, my most kindly nurse,
That to me gave this life's first native source,
Though from another place [4] I take my name,
An house of ancient fame.   131
There when they came, whereas those bricky
    towers
The which on Thames' broad, aged back do ride,
Where now the studious lawyers [5] have their
    bowers,
There whilom wont the Templar Knights to bide
Till they decayed through pride.   136
Next whereunto there stands a stately place, [6]

[3] Shend (to put to shame, surpass).
[4] Lancashire, in northwestern England.
[5] The Temple, where law is still studied. It formerly belonged to the Knights Templars.
[6] The palace of the Earl of Leicester, Spenser's patron. But it was by that time occupied by the Earl of Essex (see line 145).

Where oft I gainéd gifts and goodly grace
Of that great lord, which therein wont to dwell,
Whose want too well now feels my friendless case;
But ah! here fits not well   141
Old woes, but joys, to tell
Against the bridal day, which is not long—
    Sweet Thames! run softly, till I end my song.

Yet therein now doth lodge a noble peer,   145
Great England's glory, and the world's wide won-
    der,
Whose dreadful name late through all Spain did
    thunder,
And Hercules' two pillars [7] standing near
Did make to quake and fear:
Fair branch of honor, flower of chivalry!   150
That fillest England with thy triumph's fame,
Joy have thou of thy noble victory,
And endless happiness of thine own name,
That promiseth the same;
That through thy prowess, and victorious arms, 155
Thy country may be freed from foreign harms;
And great Elisa's glorious name may ring
Through all the world, filled with thy wide alarms,
Which some brave muse may sing
To ages following,   160
Upon the bridal day, which is not long—
    Sweet Thames! run softly, till I end my song.

From those high towers this noble lord issuing,
Like radiant Hesper, when his golden hair
In th' ocean billows he hath bathéd fair,   165
Descended to the river's open viewing,
With a great train ensuing.
Above the rest were goodly to be seen
Two gentle knights of lovely face and feature
Beseeming well the bower of any queen,   170
With gifts of wit, and ornaments of nature,
Fit for so goodly stature,
That like the twins of Jove they seemed in sight,
Which deck the baldrick of the heavens bright;
They two, forth pacing to the river's side,   175
Received those two fair brides, their love's delight;
Which, at th' appointed tide,
Each one did make his bride
Against their bridal day, which is not long—
    Sweet Thames! run softly, till I end my
    song.   180

WILLIAM SHAKESPEARE
Songs from the Plays

[FROM "LOVE'S LABOR'S LOST"]

When icicles hang by the wall,
    And Dick the shepherd blows his nail,
And Tom bears logs into the hall,
    And milk comes frozen home in pail,
When blood is nipped and ways be foul,   5
Then nightly sings the staring owl,
Tu-whit, tu-who! a merry note,
While greasy Joan doth keel [1] the pot.

When all aloud the wind doth blow,
    And coughing drowns the parson's saw, 10
And birds sit brooding in the snow,
    And Marian's nose looks red and raw,
When roasted crabs hiss in the bowl,
Then nightly sings the staring owl,
Tu-whit, tu-who! a merry note,   15
While greasy Joan doth keel the pot.

[FROM "TWO GENTLEMEN OF VERONA"]

Who is Silvia? what is she,
    That all our swains commend her?
Holy, fair, and wise is she;
    The heaven such grace did lend her
That she might admiréd be.   5

Is she kind as she is fair?
    For beauty lives with kindness.
Love doth to her eyes repair
    To help him of his blindness,
And, being helped, inhabits there.   10

Then to Silvia let us sing
    That Silvia is excelling;
She excels each mortal thing
    Upon the dull earth dwelling—
To her let us garlands bring.   15

[FROM "AS YOU LIKE IT"]

Under the greenwood tree
Who loves to lie with me,
And turn his merry note
Unto the sweet bird's throat,
Come hither! come hither! come hither!   5

---

[7] The Pillars of Hercules are the cliffs in Spain and Morocco on each side of the western entrance to the Mediterranean.

Shakespeare, *Songs from the Plays.* William Shakespeare (1564-1616) was born and died at Stratford on Avon. His active life as a dramatist in London extended from about 1590-1610.

[1] Keel (to cool, as by skimming), saw (sermon), crabs (crab-apples).

Here shall he see
No enemy
But winter and rough weather.

Who doth ambition shun
And loves to live i' the sun,   10
Seeking the food he eats
And pleased with what he gets,
Come hither! come hither! come hither!
Here shall he see
No enemy   15
But winter and rough weather.

[FROM "AS YOU LIKE IT"]

Blow, blow, thou winter wind!
Thou art not so unkind
As man's ingratitude;
Thy tooth is not so keen,
Because thou art not seen,   5
Although thy breath be rude.

Heigh ho! sing, heigh ho! unto the green holly;
Most friendship is feigning, most loving mere folly.
Then, heigh ho, the holly!
This life is most jolly.   10

Freeze, freeze, thou bitter sky!
That dost not bite so nigh
As benefits forgot;
Though thou the waters warp,
Thy sting is not so sharp   15
As friend remembered not.
Heigh ho! sing, heigh ho! etc.

[FROM "TWELFTH NIGHT"]

O Mistress mine, where are you roaming?
Oh, stay and hear; your true love's coming,
That can sing both high and low.
Trip no further, pretty sweeting,
Journeys end in lovers meeting,   5
Every wise man's son doth know.

What is Love? 'tis not hereafter;
Present mirth hath present laughter;
What's to come is still unsure.
In delay there lies no plenty;   10
Then come kiss me, sweet and twenty;
Youth's a stuff will not endure.

[FROM "MEASURE FOR MEASURE"]

Take, O, take those lips away
That so sweetly were forsworn;
And those eyes, the break of day,
Lights that do mislead the morn.

But my kisses bring again,
Bring again;
Seals of love, but sealed in vain,
Sealed in vain!

[FROM "CYMBELINE"]

Hark, hark! the lark at heaven's gate sings
And Phœbus 'gins arise,
His steeds to water at those springs
On chaliced flowers that lies;
And winking Mary-buds begin
To ope their golden eyes.
With every thing that pretty is,
My lady sweet, arise!
Arise, arise!

[FROM "CYMBELINE"]

Fear no more the heat o' the sun,
Nor the furious winter's rages;
Thou thy worldly task hast done,
Home art gone, and ta'en thy wages.
Golden lads and girls all must,   5
As chimney-sweepers, come to dust.

Fear no more the frown o' the great;
Thou art past the tyrant's stroke;
Care no more to clothe and eat;
To thee the reed is as the oak.   10
The scepter, learning, physic must
All follow this, and come to dust.

Fear no more the lightning flash,
Nor th' all-dreaded thunder-stone;
Fear not slander, censure rash;   15
Thou hast finished joy and moan.
All lovers young, all lovers must
Consign to thee, and come to dust.

No exorciser harm thee!
Nor no witchcraft charm thee!   20
Ghost unlaid forbear thee!
Nothing ill come near thee!
Quiet consummation have;
And renownéd be thy grave!

[FROM "THE TEMPEST"]

Full fathom five thy father lies.
Of his bones are coral made;
Those are pearls that were his eyes;
Nothing of him that doth fade
But doth suffer a sea change
Into something rich and strange.
Sea-nymphs hourly ring his knell:
Ding-dong!
Hark! now I hear them—Ding-dong, bell!

Sonnets

XII

When I do count the clock that tells the time,
And see the brave day sunk in hideous night;
When I behold the violet past prime,
And sable curls all silver'd o'er with white;
When lofty trees I see barren of leaves,   5
Which erst from heat did canopy the herd,
And summer's green all girded up in sheaves,
Borne on the bier with white and bristly beard,
Then of thy beauty do I question make,
That thou among the wastes of time must go,   10
Since sweets and beauties do themselves forsake
And die as fast as they see others grow;
    And nothing 'gainst Time's scythe can make defense
    Save breed, to brave him when he takes thee hence.

XV

When I consider every thing that grows
Holds in perfection but a little moment,
That this huge stage presenteth nought but shows
Whereon the stars in secret influence comment;
When I perceive that men as plants increase,   5
Cheered and check'd even by the self-same sky,
Vaunt in their youthful sap, at height decrease,
And wear their brave state out of memory;
Then the conceit of this inconstant stay
Sets you most rich in youth before my sight,   10
Where wasteful Time debateth with Decay,
To change your day of youth to sullied night;
    And all in war with Time for love of you,
    As he takes from you, I engraft you new.

XVIII

Shall I compare thee to a summer's day?
Thou art more lovely and more temperate:
Rough winds do shake the darling buds of May,
And summer's lease hath all too short a date;
Sometime too hot the eye of heaven shines,   5
And often is his gold complexion dimm'd;
And every fair from fair sometime declines,
By chance or nature's changing course untrimm'd;
But thy eternal summer shall not fade,
Nor lose possession of that fair thou owest;   10
Nor shall Death brag thou wander'st in his shade,
When in eternal lines to time thou grow'st:
    So long as men can breathe, or eyes can see,
    So long lives this. and this gives life to thee.

XXIX

When, in disgrace with fortune and men's eyes,
I all alone beweep my outcast state
And trouble deaf heaven with my bootless cries
And look upon myself and curse my fate,
Wishing me like to one more rich in hope,   5
Featured like him, like him with friends possessed,
Desiring this man's art and that man's scope,
With what I most enjoy contented least;
Yet in these thoughts myself almost despising,
Haply I think on thee, and then my state,   10
Like to the lark at break of day arising
From sullen earth, sings hymns at heaven's gate;
    For thy sweet love remembered such wealth brings
    That then I scorn to change my state with kings.

XXX

When to the sessions of sweet silent thought
I summon up remembrance of things past,
I sigh the lack of many a thing I sought,
And with old woes new wail my dear time's waste.
Then can I drown an eye, unused to flow,   5
For precious friends hid in death's dateless night,
And weep afresh love's long since canceled woe,
And moan the expense of many a vanished sight—
Then can I grieve at grievances foregone,
And heavily from woe to woe tell o'er   10
The sad account of fore-bemoanéd moan,
Which I new pay as if not paid before.
    But if the while I think on thee, dear friend,
    All losses are restored and sorrows end.

XXXIII

Full many a glorious morning have I seen
Flatter the mountain-tops with sovereign eye,
Kissing with golden face the meadows green,
Gilding pale streams with heavenly alchemy;
Anon permit the basest clouds to ride   5
With ugly rack on his celestial face,
And from the forlorn world his visage hide,
Stealing unseen to west with this disgrace.
Even so my sun one early morn did shine
With all-triumphant splendor on my brow;   10
But out, alack! he was but one hour mine;
The region cloud hath masked him from me now.
    Yet him for this my love no whit disdaineth;
    Suns of the world may stain when heaven's sun staineth.

LV

Not marble, nor the gilded monuments
Of princes, shall outlive this powerful rhyme;
But you shall shine more bright in these contents
Than unswept stone, besmeared with sluttish time.
When wasteful war shall statues overturn,   5
And broils root out the work of masonry.

Nor Mars his sword nor war's quick fire shall
    burn
The living record of your memory.
'Gainst death and all-oblivious enmity
Shall you pace forth; your praise shall still find
    room   10
Even in the eyes of all posterity
That wear this world out to the ending doom.
    So, till the judgment that yourself arise,
    You live in this, and dwell in lovers' eyes.

LXIV

When I have seen by Time's fell hand defaced
The rich-proud cost of outworn buried age;
When sometime lofty towers I see down-razed
And brass eternal slave to mortal rage;
When I have seen the hungry ocean gain   5
Advantage on the kingdom of the shore,
And the firm soil win of the watery main,
Increasing store with loss and loss with store;
When I have seen such interchange of state,
Or state itself confounded to decay;   10
Ruin hath taught me thus to ruminate,
That Time will come and take my love away.
    This thought is as a death, which cannot choose
    But weep to have that which it fears to lose.

LXV

Since brass, nor stone, nor earth, nor boundless sea,
But sad mortality o'er-sways their power,
How with this rage shall beauty hold a plea,
Whose action is no stronger than a flower?
O, how shall summer's honey breath hold out   5
Against the wreckful siege of battering days,
When rocks impregnable are not so stout,
Nor gates of steel so strong, but Time decays?
O fearful meditation! where, alack,   9
Shall Time's best jewel from Time's chest lie hid?
Or what strong hand can hold his swift foot back?
Or who his spoil of beauty can forbid?
    O, none, unless this miracle have might,
    That in black ink my love may still shine bright.

LXXI

No longer mourn for me when I am dead
Than you shall hear the surly, sullen bell
Give warning to the world that I am fled
From this vile world, with vilest worms to dwell.
Nay, if you read this line, remember not   5
The hand that writ it; for I love you so
That I in your sweet thoughts would be forgot
If thinking on me then should make you woe.
Oh, if, I say, you look upon this verse

When I perhaps compounded am with clay,   10
Do not so much as my poor name rehearse,
But let your love even with my life decay,
    Lest the wise world should look into your moan
    And mock you with me after I am gone.

LXXIII

That time of year thou mayst in me behold
When yellow leaves, or none, or few, do hang
Upon those boughs which shake against the cold,
Bare ruined choirs, where late the sweet birds sang.
In me thou see'st the twilight of such day   5
As after sunset fadeth in the west,
Which by and by black night doth take away,
Death's second self, that seals up all in rest.
In me thou see'st the glowing of such fire
That on the ashes of his youth doth lie,   10
As the deathbed whereon it must expire,
Consumed with that which it was nourished by.
    This thou perceivest, which makes thy love more
        strong,
    To love that well which thou must leave ere
        long.

CVI

When in the chronicles of wasted time
I see descriptions of the fairest wights,
And beauty making beautiful old rhyme
In praise of ladies dead and lovely knights,
Then, in the blazon of sweet beauty's best,   5
Of hand, of foot, of lip, of eye, of brow,
I see their antique pen would have express'd
Even such a beauty as you master now.
So all their praises are but prophecies
Of this our time, all you prefiguring;   10
And, for they look'd but with divining eyes,
They had not skill enough your worth to sing:
    For we, which now behold these present days,
    Have eyes to wonder, but lack tongues to praise.

CVII

Not mine own fears, nor the prophetic soul
Of the wide world dreaming on things to come,
Can yet the lease of my true love control,
Supposed as forfeit to a confined doom.
The mortal moon hath her eclipse endured,   5
And the sad augurs mock their own presage;
Incertainties now crown themselves assured,
And peace proclaims olives of endless age.
Now with the drops of this most balmy time   9
My love looks fresh, and Death to me subscribes,
Since, spite of him, I'll live in this poor rhyme,
While he insults o'er dull and speechless tribes:

And thou in this shalt find thy monument,
When tyrants' crests and tombs of brass are
    spent.

CXVI

Let me not to the marriage of true minds
Admit impediments. Love is not love
Which alters when it alteration finds,
Or bends with the remover to remove.
Oh, no! it is an ever-fixéd mark   5
That looks on tempests and is never shaken;
It is the star to every wandering bark,
Whose worth's unknown, although his height be
    taken.
Love's not Time's fool, though rosy lips and
    cheeks
Within his bending sickle's compass come;   10
Love alters not with his brief hours and weeks,
But bears it out even to the edge of doom.
    If this be error and upon me proved,
    I never writ, nor no man ever loved.

BEN JONSON

To Celia

Drink to me only with thine eyes,
    And I will pledge with mine;
Or leave a kiss but in the cup
    And I'll not look for wine.
The thirst that from the soul doth rise   5
    Doth ask a drink divine;
But might I of Jove's nectar sup,
    I would not change for thine.

I sent thee late a rosy wreath,
    Not so much honoring thee   10
As giving it a hope that there
    It could not withered be;
But thou thereon didst only breathe,
    And sent'st it back to me;
Since when it grows, and smells, I swear,   15
    Not of itself but thee!

Still to Be Neat

Still to be neat, still to be dressed,
As you were going to a feast;
Still to be powdered, still perfumed;
Lady, it is to be presumed,
Though art's hid causes are not found,   5
All is not sweet, all is not sound.

Give me a look, give me a face,
That makes simplicity a grace;
Robes loosely flowing, hair as free:
Such sweet neglect more taketh me   10
Than all the adulteries of art;
They strike mine eyes, but not my heart.

GEORGE WITHER

Shall I, Wasting in Despair

Shall I, wasting in despair,
Die because a woman's fair?
Or make pale my cheeks with care,
'Cause another's rosy are?
Be she fairer than the day,   5
Or the flowery meads in May,
    If she think not well of me,
    What care I how fair she be?

Should my silly heart be pined,
'Cause I see a woman kind?   10
Or a well disposéd nature
Joinéd with a lovely feature?
Be she meeker, kinder, than
Turtle dove or pelican,
    If she be not so to me,   15
    What care I how kind she be?

Shall a woman's virtues move
Me to perish for her love?
Or her well deserving known,
Make me quite forget mine own?   20
Be she with that goodness blest
Which may gain her name of best,
    If she be not such to me,
    What care I how good she be?

'Cause her fortune seems too high,   25
Shall I play the fool, and die?
Those that bear a noble mind,
Where they want of riches find,
Think "What, with them, they would do
That, without them, dare to woo."   30
    And unless that mind I see,
    What care I though great she be?

Great, or good, or kind, or fair,
I will ne'er the more despair!
If she love me (this believe!)   35

    Jonson, To Celia. Ben Jonson (1573?-1637) was the author of many plays of "humor." His life as
a dramatist was punctuated by adventures in politics.
    Wither, Shall I, Wasting in Despair. George Wither (1588-1667) was born at Brentworth, Hampshire,
and died in London. He served successively in both the Cavalier and Puritan armies. He wrote many
lyrics.

I will die, ere she shall grieve.
If she slight me when I woo,
I can scorn, and let her go!
  For if she be not for me,
  What care I for whom she be?   40

EDMUND WALLER

Go, Lovely Rose

Go, lovely Rose—
Tell her that wastes her time and me
  That now she knows,
When I resemble her to thee,
How sweet and fair she seems to be.   5

  Tell her that's young,
And shuns to have her graces spied,
  That hadst thou sprung
In deserts where no men abide,
Thou must have uncommended died.   10

  Small is the worth
Of beauty from the light retired;
  Bid her come forth,
Suffer herself to be desired,
And not blush so to be admired,   15

  Then die—that she
The common fate of all things rare
  May read in thee;
How small a part of time they share
That are so wondrous sweet and fair!   20

JOHN DONNE

Song

Go and catch a falling star,
  Get with child a mandrake root,
Tell me where all past years are,
  Or who cleft the devil's foot;
Teach me to hear mermaids singing,   5
Or to keep off envy's stinging,
    And find
    What wind
Serves to advance an honest mind.

If thou be'st born to strange sights,   10
  Things invisible go see,
Ride ten thousand days and nights
  Till Age snow white hairs on thee;

Thou, when thou return'st, wilt tell me
All strange wonders that befell thee,   15
    And swear
    No where
Lives a woman true and fair.

If thou find'st one, let me know;
  Such a pilgrimage were sweet.   20
Yet do not; I would not go,
  Though at next door we might meet.
Though she were true when you met her,
And last till you write your letter,
    Yet she   25
    Will be
False, ere I come, to two or three.

The Indifferent

I can love both fair and brown;
Her whom abundance melts, and her whom want
  betrays;
Her who loves loneness best, and her who masks
  and plays;
Her whom the country formed, and whom the
  town;
Her who believes, and her who tries;   5
Her who still weeps with spongy eyes,
And her who is dry cork and never cries.
I can love her, and her, and you, and you;
I can love any, so she be not true.

Will no other vice content you?   10
Will it not serve your turn to do as did your
  mothers?
Or have you all old vices spent and now would
  find out others?
Or doth a fear that men are true torment you?
O we are not, be not you so;
Let me—and do you—twenty know;   15
Rob me, but bind me not, and let me go.
Must I, who came to travel thorough you,
Grow your fixed subject, because you are true?

Venus heard me sigh this song;
And by love's sweetest part, variety, she swore   20
She heard not this till now; it should be so no
  more.
She went, examined, and returned ere long,
And said, "Alas! some two or three
Poor heretics in love there be,
Which think to stablish dangerous constancy.   25

Waller, *Go, Lovely Rose.* Edmund Waller (1606-1687) passed an active life as parliamentarian during the Civil Wars. He managed to remain in favor with both sides and wrote poems in praise of both Cromwell and Charles II.
  Donne, *Song.* John Donne (1573-1631) first entered political life, but afterward took holy orders and became Dean of St. Paul's. He wrote many theological works as well as poems.

But I have told them, 'Since you will be true,
You shall be true to them who're false to you.' "

Love's Deity

I long to talk with some old lover's ghost
  Who died before the god of love was born.
I cannot think that he who then loved most
  Sunk so low as to love one which did scorn.
But since this god produced a destiny   5
And that vice-nature, custom, lets it be,
  I must love her that loves not me.

Sure, they which made him god, meant not so
    much,
  Nor he in his young godhead practiced it.
But when an even flame two hearts did touch, 10
  His office was indulgently to fit
Actives to passives. Correspondency
Only his subject was; it cannot be
  Love till I love her who loves me.

But every modern god will now extend   15
  His vast prerogative as far as Jove.
To rage, to lust, to write to, to commend,
  All is the purlieu of the god of love.
O! were we wakened by this tyranny
To ungod this child again, it could not be   20
  I should love her who loves not me.

Rebel and atheist too, why murmur I,
  As though I felt the worst that love could do?
Love may make me leave loving, or might try
  A deeper plague, to make her love me too;   25
Which, since she loves before, I'm loath to see.
Falsehood is worse than hate; and that must be,
  If she whom I love, should love me.

ROBERT HERRICK

Corinna's Going a-Maying

Get up, get up for shame! The blooming morn
Upon her wings presents the god [1] unshorn.
  See how Aurora throws her fair,
  Fresh-quilted colors through the air.
  Get up, sweet slug-a-bed, and see   5
  The dew bespangling herb and tree!
Each flower has wept and bowed toward the east
Above an hour since, yet you not drest;

Nay! not so much as out of bed?
When all the birds have matins said   10
And sung their thankful hymns, 'tis sin,
Nay, profanation, to keep in,
Whereas a thousand virgins on this day
Spring sooner than the lark, to fetch in May.

Rise and put on your foliage, and be seen   15
To come forth, like the springtime, fresh and
    green,
  And sweet as Flora. Take no care
  For jewels for your gown or hair.
  Fear not; the leaves will strew
  Gems in abundance upon you.   20
Besides, the childhood of the day has kept
Against you come, some orient pearls unwept.
  Come, and receive them while the light
  Hangs on the dew-locks of the night;
  And Titan on the eastern hill   25
  Retires himself, or else stands still
Till you come forth! Wash, dress, be brief in pray-
    ing;
Few beads are best when once we go a-Maying.

Come, my Corinna, come; and coming, mark
How each field turns a street, each street a park,
  Made green and trimmed with trees! see how 31
  Devotion gives each house a bough
  Or branch! each porch, each door, ere this,
  An ark, a tabernacle is,
Made up of whitethorn neatly interwove,   35
As if here were those cooler shades of love.
  Can such delights be in the street
  And open fields, and we not see't?
  Come, we'll abroad; and let's obey
  The proclamation made for May,   40
And sin no more, as we have done, by staying;
But, my Corinna, come, let's go a-Maying.

There's not a budding boy or girl this day
But is got up and gone to bring in May.
  A deal of youth ere this is come   45
  Back, and with whitethorn laden home.
  Some have dispatched their cakes and cream,
  Before that we have left to dream;
And some have wept and wooed, and plighted
    troth,
And chose their priest, ere we can cast off sloth.
  Many a green-gown has been given,   51

Herrick, *Corinna's Going a-Maying.* A song sung on the morning of the first of May, when the boys
and girls go out to gather flowers. Robert Herrick was born in London in 1591 and died at Dean Prior,
Devonshire, in 1674. He studied law, but later entered holy orders and wrote his lyrics from his country
parish.
  [1] The sun in his glory. His locks (rays) are not shorn.

Many a kiss, both odd and even;
Many a glance, too, has been sent
From out the eye, love's firmament;
Many a jest told of the keys betraying   55
This night, and locks picked; yet we're not a-May-
ing!

Come, let us go, while we are in our prime,
And take the harmless folly of the time!
  We shall grow old apace, and die
  Before we know our liberty.   60
  Our life is short, and our days run
  As fast away as does the sun.
And, as a vapor or a drop of rain,
Once lost, can ne'er be found again,
  So when or you or I are made   65
  A fable, song, or fleeting shade,
  All love, all liking, all delight
  Lies drowned with us in endless night.
Then, while time serves, and we are but decaying,
Come, my Corinna, come, let's go a-Maying.   70

Upon Julia's Clothes

Whenas in silks my Julia goes,
Then, then, methinks, how sweetly flows
That liquefaction of her clothes.

Next, when I cast mine eyes and see
That brave vibration each way free;
O, how that glittering taketh me!

To the Virgins, to Make Much of Time

  Gather ye rosebuds while ye may,
    Old Time is still a-flying,
  And this same flower that smiles today
    Tomorrow will be dying.

  The glorious lamp of heaven, the sun,   5
    The higher he's a-getting,
  The sooner will his race be run,
    And nearer he's to setting.

  That age is best which is the first,
    When youth and blood are warmer;   10
  But being spent, the worse, and worst
    Times still succeed the former.

  Then be not coy, but use your time,
    And while ye may, go marry;
  For having lost but once your prime,   15
    You may forever tarry.

To Daffodils

Fair daffodils, we weep to see
  You haste away so soon;
As yet the early-rising sun
  Has not attained his noon.
    Stay, stay   5
    Until the hasting day
      Has run
    But to the evensong;
And, having prayed together, we
  Will go with you along.   10

We have short time to stay, as you,
  We have as short a spring;
As quick a growth to meet decay,
  As you, or anything.
    We die   15
    As your hours do, and dry
      Away
    Like to the summer's rain;
Or as the pearls of morning's dew,
  Ne'er to be found again.   20

RICHARD LOVELACE

To Lucasta, Going to the Wars

Tell me not, Sweet, I am unkind,
  That from the nunnery
Of thy chaste breast and quiet mind
  To war and arms I fly.

True, a new mistress now I chase,   5
  The first foe in the field;
And with a stronger faith embrace
  A sword, a horse, a shield.

Yet this inconstancy is such
  As thou too shalt adore;   10
I could not love thee, Dear, so much,
  Loved I not honor more.

To Althea, from Prison

When Love with unconfinéd wings
  Hovers within my gates,
And my divine Althea brings
  To whisper at the grates;
When I lie tangled in her hair   5
  And fettered to her eye,
The birds that wanton in the air
  Know no such liberty.

Lovelace, *To Lucasta*. Richard Lovelace (1618-1658) was a very active royalist in the Civil Wars. He
was born in Kent, was educated at Oxford, and died in poverty in London.

When flowing cups run swiftly round
  With no allaying Thames,   10
Our careless heads with roses bound,
  Our hearts with loyal flames;
When thirsty grief in wine we steep,
  When healths and drafts go free—
Fishes that tipple in the deep   15
  Know no such liberty.

When, like committed linnets, I
  With shriller throat shall sing
The sweetness, mercy, majesty,
  And glories of my King;   20
When I shall voice aloud how good
  He is, how great should be,
Enlargéd winds, that curl the flood,
  Know no such liberty.

Stone walls do not a prison make,   25
  Nor iron bars a cage;
Minds innocent and quiet take
  That for an hermitage;
If I have freedom in my love
  And in my soul am free,   30
Angels alone, that soar above,
  Enjoy such liberty.

JOHN SUCKLING

Why So Pale and Wan, Fond Lover?

Why so pale and wan, fond lover?
  Prithee, why so pale?
Will, when looking well can't move her,
  Looking ill prevail?
  Prithee, why so pale?   5

Why so dull and mute, young sinner?
  Prithee, why so mute?
Will, when speaking well can't win her,
  Saying nothing do 't?
  Prithee, why so mute?   10

Quit, quit for shame! This will not move;
  This cannot take her.
If of herself she will not love,
  Nothing can make her.
  The devil take her!   15

The Constant Lover

Out upon it, I have loved
  Three whole days together!

And am like to love three more,
  If it prove fair weather.

Time shall molt away his wings   5
  Ere he shall discover
In the whole wide world again
  Such a constant lover.

But the spite on 't is, no praise
  Is due at all to me;   10
Love with me had made no stays,
  Had it any been but she.

Had it any been but she,
  And that very face,
There had been at least ere this   15
  A dozen dozen in her place.

THOMAS CAREW

Disdain Returned

He that loves a rosy cheek,
  Or a coral lip admires,
Or from star-like eyes doth seek
  Fuel to maintain his fires,
As old Time makes these decay,   5
So his flames must waste away.

But a smooth and steadfast mind,
  Gentle thoughts and calm desires,
Hearts, with equal love combined,
  Kindle never-dying fires;   10
Where these art not, I despise
Lovely cheeks or lips or eyes.

No tears, Celia, now shall win,
  My resolved heart to return;
I have searched thy soul within   15
  And find nought but pride and scorn;
I have learned thy arts, and now
Can disdain as much as thou!

The Protestation

No more shall meads be decked with flowers,
Nor sweetness dwell in rosy bowers,
Nor greenest buds on branches spring,
Nor warbling birds delight to sing,
Nor April violets paint the grove,   5
If I forsake my Celia's love.

Suckling, *Why So Pale.* Sir John Suckling (1609-c. 1642) was a man of fashion about the court of Charles I, a soldier of fortune, and a royalist supporter. He wrote masques and lyrics.
  Carew, *Disdain Returned.* Thomas Carew (c. 1598-1639) was educated at Oxford, led an idle and wandering life, part of it about the court of Charles I and as ambassador in Italy. He wrote masques and lyrics.

The fish shall in the ocean burn,
And fountains sweet shall bitter turn,
The humble oak no flood shall know
When floods shall highest hills o'erflow,   10
Black Lethe shall oblivion leave,
If e'er my Celia I deceive.

Love shall his bow and shaft lay by,
And Venus' doves want wings to fly
The Sun refuse to show his light,   15
And day shall then be turned to night,
And in that night no star appear,
If once I leave my Celia dear.

Love shall no more inhabit earth,
Nor lovers more shall love for worth,   20
Nor joy above in heaven dwell,
Nor pain torment poor souls in hell,
Grim death no more shall horrid prove,
If e'er I leave bright Celia's love.

GEORGE HERBERT

The Collar

I struck the board, and cry'd, "No more;
   I will abroad!
What, shall I ever sigh and pine?
My lines and life are free; free as the road,
   Loose as the wind, as large as store.   5
   Shall I be still in suit?
Have I no harvest but a thorn
To let me blood, and not restore
What I have lost with cordial fruit?
   Sure there was wine   10
  Before my sighs did dry it; there was corn
  Before my tears did drown it;
  Is the year only lost to me?
  Have I no bays to crown it,
No flowers, no garlands gay? all blasted,   15
  All wasted?
Not so, my heart; but there is fruit,
  And thou hast hands.
Recover all thy sigh-blown age
On double pleasures; leave thy cold dispute   20
Of what is fit and not; forsake thy cage,
  Thy rope of sands
Which petty thoughts have made; and made to thee
  Good cable, to enforce and draw,
  And be thy law,   25

While thou didst wink and wouldst not see.
  Away! take heed;
   I will abroad.
Call in thy death's-head there, tie up thy fears;
  He that forbears   30
To suit and serve his need
   Deserves his load."
But as I rav'd, and grew more fierce and wild
  At every word,
Methought I heard one calling, "Child";   35
  And I reply'd, "My Lord."

The Pulley

When God at first made man,
Having a glass of blessing standing by;
Let us (said he) pour on him all we can:
Let the world's riches which dispersed lie
  Contract into a span.   5

So strength first made a way;
Then beauty flow'd, then wisdom, honor, pleasure;
When almost all was out, God made a stay,
Perceiving that alone, of all his treasure,
  Rest in the bottom lay.   10

For if I should (said he)
Bestow this jewel also on my creature,
He would adore my gifts instead of me,
And rest in Nature, not the God of Nature;
  So both should losers be.   15

Yet let him keep the rest,
But keep them with repining restlessness:
Let him be rich and weary, that at least,
If goodness lead him not, yet weariness
  May toss him to my breast.   20

HENRY VAUGHAN

The World

I saw Eternity the other night,
Like a great ring of pure and endless light,
  All calm, as it was bright;
And round beneath it, Time, in hours, days, years,
  Driven by the spheres   5
Like a vast shadow moved; in which the world
  And all her train were hurled.
The doting lover in his quaintest strain
  Did there complain;

Herbert, *The Collar*. George Herbert was born in Wales in 1593, the brother of Lord Herbert of Cherbury. He was educated at Cambridge and enjoyed a brilliant career at court. His last years he spent as a country rector in Wiltshire. He died there in 1633.
    Vaughan, *The World*. Henry Vaughan (1621-1693) was a Welsh poet and mystic. He studied at Oxford and became a physician in Wales.

Near him, his lute, his fancy, and his flights,   10
  Wit's sour delights,
With gloves, and knots, the silly snares of pleas-
    ure,
  Yet his dear treasure,
All scattered lay, while he his eyes did pour
  Upon a flower.   15

The darksome statesman, hung with weights and
    woe,
Like a thick midnight-fog moved there so slow,
  He did not stay, nor go;
Condemning thoughts, like sad eclipses, scowl
  Upon his soul,   20
And clouds of crying witnesses without
  Pursued him with one shout.
Yet digged the mole, and lest his ways be found,
  Worked under ground,
Where he did clutch his prey; but one did see   25
  That policy;
Churches and altars fed him; perjuries
  Were gnats and flies;
It rained about him blood and tears, but he
  Drank them as free.   30

The fearful miser on a heap of rust
Sat pining all his life there, did scarce trust
  His own hands with the dust,
Yet would not place one piece above, but lives
  In fear of thieves.   35
Thousands there were as frantic as himself,
  And hugged each one his pelf;
The downright epicure placed heaven in sense,
  And scorned pretense;
While others, slipped into a wide excess,   40
  Said little less;
The weaker sort, slight, trivial wares enslave,
  Who think them brave;
And poor, despiséd Truth sat counting by
  Their victory.   45

Yet some, who all this while did weep and sing,
And sing and weep, soared up into the ring;
  But most would use no wing.
O fools, said I, thus to prefer dark night
  Before true light!   50
To live in grots and caves, and hate the day
  Because it shows the way,
The way, which from this dead and dark abode
  Leads up to God;

A way there you might tread the sun, and be   55
  More bright than he!
But, as I did their madness so discuss,
  One whispered thus
"This ring the Bridegroom did for none provide,
  But for his bride."   60

ANDREW MARVELL
On a Drop of Dew

See, how the orient dew,
Shed from the bosom of the morn,
  Into the blowing roses,
(Yet careless of its mansion new,
For the clear region where 'twas born)   5
  Round in its self incloses:
  And in its little globe's extent,
Frames as it can its native element.
  How it the purple flow'r does slight,
    Scarce touching where it lies,   10
  But gazing back upon the skies,
    Shines with a mournful light;
      Like its own tear,
Because so long divided from the sphere.
  Restless it rolls and unsecure,   15
    Trembling lest it grow impure:
    Till the warm sun pity its pain,
And to the skies exhale it back again.
    So the soul, that drop, that ray
Of the clear fountain of eternal day,   20
Could it within the human flow'r be seen,
    Rememb'ring still its former height,
    Shuns the sweet leaves and blossoms green;
    And, recollecting its own light,
Does, in its pure and circling thoughts, express   25
The greater heaven in an heaven less.
    In how coy a figure wound,
    Every way it turns away:
    So the world excluding round,
    Yet receiving in the day,   30
    Dark beneath, but bright above:
    Here disdaining, there in love.
  How loose and easy hence to go:
  How girt and ready to ascend.
  Moving but on a point below,   35
  It all about does upwards bend,
Such did the manna's sacred dew distill;
White, and entire, though congeal'd and chill.
Congeal'd on earth: but does, dissolving, run
Into the glories of th' Almighty Sun.   40

Marvell, *On a Drop of Dew.* Andrew Marvell (1621-1678) was educated at Cambridge. During the Commonwealth he assisted Milton as Latin Secretary. He wrote satires directed against the restored Stuarts.

The Garden

I

How vainly men themselves amaze
To win the palm, the oak, or bays;
And their incessant labors see
Crown'd from some single herb or tree.
Whose short and narrow vergéd shade   5
Does prudently their toils upbraid;
While all flow'rs and all trees do close
To weave the garlands of repose.

II

Fair quiet, have I found thee here,
And innocence, thy sister dear!   10
Mistaken long, I sought you then
In busy companies of men.
Your sacred plants, if here below,
Only among the plants will grow.
Society is all but rude,   15
To this delicious solitude.

III

No white nor red was ever seen
So am'rous as this lovely green.
Fond lovers, cruel as their flame,
Cut in these trees their mistress' name.   20
Little, alas, they know, or heed,
How far these beauties hers exceed!
Fair trees! where soe'er your barks I wound,
No name shall but your own be found.

IV

When we have run our passion's heat,   25
Love hither makes his best retreat.
The gods, that mortal beauty chase,
Still in a tree did end their race.
Apollo hunted Daphne so,
Only that she might laurel grow.   30
And Pan did after Syrinx speed,
Not as a nymph, but for a reed.

V

What wondrous life is this I lead!
Ripe apples drop about my head;
And luscious clusters of the vine   35

Upon my mouth do crush their wine;
The nectarine, and curious peach,
Into my hands themselves do reach;
Stumbling on melons, as I pass,
Ensnared with flowers, I fall on grass.   40

VI

Meanwhile the mind, from pleasure less,
Withdraws into its happiness:
The mind, that ocean where each kind
Does straight its own resemblance find;
Yet it creates, transcending these,   45
Far other worlds, and other seas;
Annihilating all that's made
To a green thought in a green shade.

VII

Here at the fountain's sliding foot,
Or at some fruit tree's mossy root,   50
Casting the body's vest aside,
My soul into the boughs does glide:
There like a bird it sits, and sings,
Then whets, and combs its silver wings;
And, till prepared for longer flight,   55
Waves in its plumes the various light.

VIII

Such was that happy garden-state,
While man there walked without a mate:
After a place so pure, and sweet,
What other help could yet be meet!   60
But 'twas beyond a mortal's share
To wander solitary there:
Two paradises 'twere in one
To live in Paradise alone.

IX

How well the skillful gardener drew   65
Of flowers and herbs this dial new;
Where from above the milder sun
Does through a fragrant Zodiac run;
And, as it works, the industrious bee
Computes its time as well as we.   70
How could such sweet and wholesome hours
Be reckoned but with herbs and flowers!

THE POETRY

OF MILTON

John Milton was born in London in 1608 of a well-to-do family. When he showed talent for poetry he was given every opportunity to prepare himself properly for a literary career. A careful education at Cambridge was shortly followed by some years of reading and quiet in the country and eventually by extensive travel in Italy. The rising conflict between the King and the Parliament brought Milton to the side of the latter. His poetic career was then interrupted, so that he wrote little except prose from 1640 to 1660. He served the government as Latin Secretary and in the 1650's gradually lost his sight. At the Restoration in 1660 Milton retired to the country and in the next years wrote his great epic poems, *Paradise Lost* and *Paradise Regained,* and the drama *Samson Agonistes.* He died in obscurity in 1674.

In the period of 1630-1640 we find that Milton had already learned to write great poetry. The large harmonies in the verse of *Paradise Lost* can already be heard in many parts of *Lycidas,* the pastoral elegy which Milton wrote on the death of Edward King.

In his companion poems, *L'Allegro* and *Il Penseroso,* he shows not only a facility with English verse but also an appreciation of a large variety of human experiences. Milton also wrote an important masque, *Comus,* in which he not only displays his ability with blank verse but writes some beautiful songs.

For the twenty years between 1640 and 1660 Milton was primarily a prose writer, but this poetic silence was occasionally broken by the appearance of a sonnet. Though the number of these sonnets is small, they are among the noblest in the language.

As soon as the duties of political office no longer pressed him, he devoted himself to his life-long ambition, the writing of a great epic poem. The result is *Paradise Lost* and its sequel, *Paradise Regained.* The sonorous powers of the English language have never been employed with as great mastery as Milton attains throughout these poems. *Paradise Lost* is the great expression of Protestant Christianity, just as Dante's *Divine Comedy* is the expression of Roman Catholicism.

In his last years Milton wrote a drama after the manner of the Greeks. In *Samson Agonistes* he gives the tragedy of the blind hero in which the sympathetic reader will not fail to see a reflection of the great trials of the blind poet.

JOHN MILTON

Lycidas

In this Monody the Author bewails a learned
Friend, unfortunately drowned in his passage from
Chester on the Irish Seas, 1637; and by occasion,
foretells the ruin of our corrupted Clergy, then in
their height.

Yet once more, O ye laurels, and once more,
Ye myrtles brown, with ivy never sear,
I come to pluck your berries harsh and crude,
And with forced fingers rude
Shatter your leaves before the mellowing year.   5
Bitter constraint and sad occasion dear
Compels me to disturb your season due;
For Lycidas is dead, dead ere his prime,
Young Lycidas, and hath not left his peer.
Who would not sing for Lycidas? He knew   10
Himself to sing, and build the lofty rime.
He must not float upon his watery bier
Unwept, and welter to the parching wind,
Without the meed of some melodious tear.
  Begin, then, Sisters of the sacred well,[1]   15
That from beneath the seat of Jove doth spring;
Begin, and somewhat loudly sweep the string.
Hence with denial vain and coy excuse;
So may some gentle muse
With lucky words favor my destined urn,   20
And as he passes turn
And bid fair peace be to my sable shroud!
  For we were nursed upon the selfsame hill,[2]
Fed the same flock, by fountain, shade, and rill;
Together both, ere the high lawns appeared   25
Under the opening eyelids of the Morn,
We drove afield, and both together heard
What time the gray-fly winds her sultry horn,
Battening our flocks with the fresh dews of night,
Oft till the star that rose at evening, bright,   30
Toward heaven's descent had sloped his westering
    wheel.
Meanwhile the rural ditties were not mute,
Tempered to the oaten flute;
Rough Satyrs danced, and Fauns with cloven heel
From the glad sound would not be absent long;
And old Damoetas loved to hear our song.   36

But, oh! the heavy change, now thou art gone,
Now thou art gone, and never must return!
Thee, Shepherd, thee the woods and desert caves,
With wild thyme and the gadding vine o'ergrown,
And all their echoes, mourn.   41
The willows, and the hazel copses green,
Shall now no more be seen
Fanning their joyous leaves to thy soft lays.
As killing as the canker to the rose,   45
Or taint-worm to the weanling herds that graze,
Or frost to flowers, that their gay wardrobe wear,
When first the white-thorn blows—
Such, Lycidas, thy loss to Shepherd's ear.
  Where were ye, Nymphs, when the remorseless
    deep   50
Closed o'er the head of your loved Lycidas?
For neither were ye playing on the steep
Where your old bards, the famous Druids, lie,
Nor on the shaggy top of Mona[3] high,
Nor yet where Deva spreads her wizard stream.
Aye me! I fondly dream   56
"Had ye been there"—for what could that have
    done?
What could the Muse herself that Orpheus bore,
The Muse herself, for her enchanting son,
Whom universal nature did lament,   60
When, by the rout that made the hideous roar,
His gory visage down the stream was sent,
Down the swift Hebrus to the Lesbian shore?
  Alas! what boots it with uncessant care
To tend the homely, slighted shepherd's trade,   65
And strictly meditate the thankless Muse?
Were it not better done as others use,
To sport with Amaryllis in the shade,
Or with the tangles of Neæra's hair?
Fame is the spur that the clear spirit doth raise
(That last infirmity of noble mind)   71
To scorn delights, and live laborious days;
But, the fair guerdon when we hope to find,
And think to burst out into sudden blaze,   74
Comes the blind Fury with the abhorréd shears,

[1] The Muses, who had their home in the Pierian Spring near Mt. Olympus.
[2] They went to college together at Cambridge. Here they are compared to shepherds in the usual
manner of the pastoral.
[3] Mona (the island of Anglesey), Deva (the River Dee).

And slits the thin-spun life. "But not the praise,"
Phœbus replied, and touched my trembling ears;
"Fame is no plant that grows on mortal soil,
Nor in the glistering foil
Set off to the world, nor in broad rumor lies,   80
But lives and spreads aloft by those pure eyes
And perfect witness of all-judging Jove;
As he pronounces lastly on each deed,
Of so much fame in heaven expect thy meed."   84
    O fountain Arethuse,[4] and thou honored flood,
Smooth-sliding Mincius, crowned with vocal reeds,
That strain I heard was of a higher mood.
But now my oat [5] proceeds,
And listens to the Herald of the Sea
That came in Neptune's plea.   90
He asked the waves, and asked the felon winds,
What hard mishap hath doomed this gentle swain!
And questioned every gust of rugged wings
That blows from off each beakéd promontory.
They knew not of his story;   95
And sage Hippotades [7] their answer brings,
That not a blast was from his dungeon strayed;
The air was calm, and on the level brine
Sleek Panope with all her sisters [8] played.
It was that fatal and perfidious bark,   100
Built in the eclipse, and rigged with curses dark,
That sunk so low that sacred head of thine.
    Next, Camus,[9] reverend sire, went footing slow,
His mantle hairy, and his bonnet sedge,
Inwrought with figures dim, and on the edge   105
Like to that sanguine flower inscribed with woe.
"Ah! who hath reft," quoth he, "my dearest
    pledge?"
Last came, and last did go,
The Pilot of the Galilean Lake; [10]
Two massy keys he bore of metals twain   110
(The golden opes, the iron shuts amain).
He shook his mitered locks, and stern bespake:
"How well could I have spared for thee, young
    swain,
Enow of such as, for their bellies' sake,
Creep, and intrude, and climb into the fold!   115
Of other care they little reckoning make
Than how to scramble at the shearers' feast,
And shove away the worthy bidden guest.

Blind mouths! that scarce themselves know how
    to hold
A sheep-hook, or have learned aught else the least
That to the faithful herdman's art belongs!   121
What recks it them? What need they? They are
    sped;
And, when they list, their lean and flashy songs
Grate on their scrannel pipes of wretched straw;
The hungry sheep look up, and are not fed,   125
But, swoln with wind and the rank mist they
    draw,
Rot inwardly, and foul contagion spread;
Besides what the grim wolf [11] with privy paw
Daily devours apace, and nothing said.
But that two-handed engine at the door   130
Stands ready to smite once, and smite no more."
    Return, Alpheus, the dread voice is past
That shrunk thy streams; return, Sicilian Muse,
And call the vales, and bid them hither cast
Their bells and flowerets of a thousand hues. 135
Ye valleys low, where the mild whispers use
Of shades, and wanton winds, and gushing brooks,
On whose fresh lap the swart star sparely looks,
Throw hither all your quaint enameled eyes,
That on the green turf suck the honeyed showers,
And purple all the ground with vernal flowers. 141
Bring the rathe primrose that forsaken dies,
The tufted crow-toe, and pale jessamine,
The white pink, and the pansy freaked with jet,
The glowing violet,   145
The musk-rose, and the well-attired woodbine,
With cowslips wan that hang the pensive head,
And every flower that sad embroidery wears;
Bid amaranthus all his beauty shed,
And daffadillies fill their cups with tears,   150
To strew the laureate hearse where Lycid lies.
For so, to interpose a little ease,
Let our frail thoughts dally with false surmise.
Aye me! Whilst thee the shores and sounding seas
Wash far away, where'er thy bones are hurled,
Whether beyond the stormy Hebrides,   156
Where thou perhaps under the whelming tide
Visit'st the bottom of the monstrous world;
Or whether thou, to our moist vows denied,
Sleep'st by the fable of Bellerus [12] old,   160

---

[4] Arethuse, Mincius (rivers alluded to by Virgil in his pastorals).
[5] Flute.
[6] Triton.
[7] Hippotades (Æolus, god of the winds).
[8] Daughters of the sea-god Nereus.
[9] Camus (the River Cam at Cambridge), sanguine flower (hyacinth, supposed to bear on itself the Greek word for "alas").
[10] Saint Peter, who bears the keys of heaven and wears the miter as first bishop of Rome.
[11] The church of Rome.
[12] Bellerus was said to have lived at Land's End, Cornwall, near where St. Michael's Mount faces cities in France and Spain.

Where the great Vision of the guarded mount
Looks toward Namancos and Bayona's hold.
Look homeward, Angel, now, and melt with ruth;
And, O ye dolphins, waft the hapless youth.
   Weep no more, woeful shepherds, weep no
     more,   165
For Lycidas, your sorrow, is not dead,
Sunk though he be beneath the watery floor;
So sinks the day-star in the ocean bed,
And yet anon repairs his drooping head,
And tricks his beams, and with new-spangled ore
Flames in the forehead of the morning sky.   171
So Lycidas sunk low, but mounted high,
Through the dear might of Him that walked the
    waves,
Where, other groves and other streams along,
With nectar pure his oozy locks he laves,   175
And hears the unexpressive nuptial song,

In the blest kingdoms meek of joy and love.
There entertain him all the Saints above,
In solemn troops, and sweet societies,
That sing, and singing in their glory move,   180
And wipe the tears forever from his eyes.
Now, Lycidas, the shepherds weep no more;
Henceforth thou art the Genius of the shore,
In thy large recompense, and shalt be good
To all that wander in that perilous flood.   185
   Thus sang the uncouth swain to the oaks and
    rills,
While the still morn went out with sandals gray;
He touched the tender stops of various quills,
With eager thought warbling his Doric lay.
And now the sun had stretched out all the hills,
And now was dropped into the western bay.   191
At last he rose, and twitched his mantle blue;
Tomorrow to fresh woods and pastures new.

L'Allegro

Hence, loathéd Melancholy,
  Of Cerberus and blackest Midnight born
In Stygian cave forlorn
  'Mongst horrid shapes, and shrieks, and sights
    unholy!
Find out some uncouth cell,   5
  Where brooding Darkness spreads his jealous
    wings,
And the night-raven sings;
  There, under ebon shades and low-browed rocks,
As ragged as thy locks,
  In dark Cimmerian desert ever dwell.   10
But come, thou Goddess fair and free,
In heaven yclept Euphrosyne,
And by men heart-easing Mirth,
Whom lovely Venus, at a birth,
With two sister Graces more,   15
To ivy-crownéd Bacchus bore;
Or whether—as some sager sing—
The frolic wind that breathes the spring,
Zephyr, with Aurora playing,
As he met her once a-Maying,   20
There, on beds of violets blue,
And fresh-blown roses washed in dew,

Filled her with thee, a daughter fair,
So buxom, blithe, and debonair.
Haste thee, Nymph, and bring with thee   25
Jest and youthful Jollity,
Quips and cranks and wanton wiles,
Nods and becks and wreathéd smiles,
Such as hang on Hebe's cheek,
And love to live in dimple sleek;   30
Sport that wrinkled Care derides,
And Laughter holding both his sides.
Come, and trip it, as you go,
On the light, fantastic toe;
And in thy right hand lead with thee   35
The mountain-nymph, sweet Liberty;
And, if I give thee honor due,
Mirth, admit me of thy crew,
To live with her, and live with thee,
In unreprovéd pleasures free: 40
To hear the lark begin his flight,
And, singing, startle the dull night,
From his watch-tower in the skies,
Till the dappled dawn doth rise;
Then to come, in spite of sorrow,   45
And at my window bid good-morrow,

Milton, *L'Allegro.* In this poem and in the next Milton contrasts the desirable life as it would appear
to the lighthearted and to the contemplative man. Most of the mythological references have been explained
in the *Myths of Greece and Rome,* p. 12.

Through the sweet-brier or the vine
Or the twisted eglantine;
While the cock, with lively din,
Scatters the rear of darkness thin, 50
And to the stack, or the barn-door,
Stoutly struts his dames before;
Oft listening how the hounds and horn
Cheerly rouse the slumbering morn,
From the side of some hoar hill, 55
Through the high wood echoing shrill;
Sometime walking, not unseen,
By hedgerow elms, on hillocks green,
Right against the eastern gate,
Where the great Sun begins his state, 60
Robed in flames and amber light,
The clouds in thousand liveries dight;
While the plowman, near at hand,
Whistles o'er the furrowed land,
And the milkmaid singeth blithe, 65
And the mower whets his scythe,
And every shepherd tells his tale [1]
Under the hawthorn in the dale.
Straight mine eye hath caught new pleasures,
Whilst the landskip round it measures: 70
Russet lawns, and fallows gray,
Where the nibbling flocks do stray;
Mountains on whose barren breast
The laboring clouds do often rest;
Meadows trim, with daisies pied; 75
Shallow brooks and rivers wide;
Towers and battlements it sees
Bosomed high in tufted trees,
Where perhaps some beauty lies,
The cynosure of neighboring eyes. 80
Hard by, a cottage chimney smokes
From betwixt two aged oaks,
Where Corydon and Thyrsis met
Are at their savory dinner set
Of herbs and other country messes, 85
Which the neat-handed Phyllis dresses;
And then in haste her bower she leaves
With Thestylis to bind the sheaves;
Or, if the earlier season lead,
To the tanned haycock in the mead. 90
Sometimes, with secure delight,
The upland hamlets will invite,
When the merry bells ring round,
And the jocund rebecks sound
To many a youth and many a maid 95
Dancing in the checkered shade;

And young and old come forth to play
On a sunshine holiday,
Till the livelong daylight fail;
Then to the spicy nut-brown ale, 100
With stories told of many a feat,
How Faëry Mab [2] the junkets eat.
She was pinched and pulled, she said;
And he, by Friar's lantern led,
Tells how the drudging goblin sweat 105
To earn his cream-bowl duly set,
When in one night, ere glimpse of morn,
His shadowy flail hath threshed the corn
That ten day-laborers could not end;
Then lies him down, the lubber-fiend, 110
And, stretched out all the chimney's length,
Basks at the fire his hairy strength,
And crop-full out of doors he flings,
Ere the first cock his matin rings.
Thus done the tales, to bed they creep, 115
By whispering winds soon lulled asleep.
Towered cities please us then,
And the busy hum of men,
Where throngs of knights and barons bold,
In weeds of peace, high triumphs hold, 120
With store of ladies, whose bright eyes
Rain influence, and judge the prize
Of wit or arms, while both contend
To win her grace whom all commend.
There let Hymen oft appear 125
In saffron robe, with taper clear,
And pomp, and feast, and revelry,
With masque and antique pageantry;
Such sights as youthful poets dream
On summer eves by haunted stream. 130
Then to the well-trod stage anon,
If Jonson's learned sock be on,
Or sweetest Shakespeare, Fancy's child,
Warble his native wood-notes wild.
And ever, against eating cares, 135
Lap me in soft Lydian airs,
Married to immortal verse,
Such as the meeting soul may pierce,
In notes with many a winding bout
Of linkéd sweetness long drawn out 140
With wanton heed and giddy cunning,
The melting voice through mazes running,
Untwisting all the chains that tie
The hidden soul of harmony;
That Orpheus' self may heave his head 145
From golden slumber on a bed

[1] Counts his flock.
[2] Mab (queen of the fairies), Friar's lantern (will-o'-the-wisp).

Of heaped Elysian flowers, and hear
Such strains as would have won the ear
Of Pluto to have quite set free

His half-regained Eurydice.   150
These delights if thou canst give,
Mirth, with thee I mean to live.

Il Penseroso

Hence, vain, deluding Joys,
  The brood of Folly without father bred!
How little you bestéd,
  Or fill the fixéd mind with all your toys!
Dwell in some idle brain,   5
  And fancies fond with gaudy shapes possess,
As thick and numberless
  As the gay motes that people the sunbeams,
Or likest hovering dreams,
  The fickle pensioners of Morpheus' train.   10
But, hail! thou Goddess, sage and holy!
Hail, divinest Melancholy!
Whose saintly visage is too bright
To hit the sense of human sight,
And therefore to our weaker view,   15
O'erlaid with black, staid Wisdom's hue;
Black, but such as in esteem
Prince Memnon's sister[1] might beseem,
Or that starred Ethiop queen that strove
To set her beauty's praise above   20
The Sea-nymphs, and their powers offended.
Yet thou art higher far descended;
Thee bright-haired Vesta long of yore
To solitary Saturn bore;
His daughter she; in Saturn's reign   25
Such mixture was not held a stain.
Oft in glimmering bowers and glades
He met her, and in secret shades
Of woody Ida's inmost grove,
Whilst yet there was no fear of Jove.   30
Come, pensive Nun, devout and pure,
Sober, steadfast, and demure,
All in a robe of darkest grain,
Flowing with majestic train,
And sable stole of cypress lawn   35
Over thy decent shoulders drawn.
Come; but keep thy wonted state
With even step, and musing gait,
And looks commercing with the skies
Thy rapt soul sitting in thine eyes;   40

There, held in holy passion still,
Forget thyself to marble, till
With a sad, leaden, downward cast
Thou fix them on the earth as fast.
And join with thee calm Peace and Quiet,   45
Spare Fast, that oft with gods doth diet,
And hears the Muses in a ring
Aye round about Jove's altar sing;
And add to these retiréd Leisure,
That in trim gardens takes his pleasure;   50
But, first and chiefest, with thee bring
Him that yon soars on golden wing,
Guiding the fiery-wheeléd throne,
The cherub Contemplation;
And the mute Silence hist along,   55
'Less Philomel will deign a song,
In her sweetest, saddest plight,
Smoothing the rugged brow of Night,
While Cynthia checks her dragon yoke
Gently o'er the accustomed oak.   60
Sweet bird, that shunn'st the noise of folly,
Most musical, most melancholy!
Thee, chauntress, oft the woods among
I woo, to hear thy evensong;
And, missing thee, I walk unseen   65
On the dry, smooth-shaven green,
To behold the wandering moon
Riding near her highest noon,
Like one that had been led astray
Through the heaven's wide, pathless way,   70
And oft, as if her head she bowed,
Stooping through a fleecy cloud.
Oft, on a plat of rising ground,
I hear the far-off curfew sound,
Over some wide-watered shore,   75
Swinging slow with sullen roar;
Or, if the air will not permit,
Some still, removéd place will fit,
Where glowing embers through the room
Teach light to counterfeit a gloom,   80

---

[1] Sister of the handsome Prince Memnon, ally of the Trojan. The Ethiop queen was Cassiopeia who was punished by being made into a constellation.

Far from all resort of mirth,
Save the cricket on the hearth,
Or the bellman's drowsy charm
To bless the doors from nightly harm.
Or let my lamp, at midnight hour,   85
Be seen in some high, lonely tower,
Where I may oft outwatch the Bear,
With thrice-great Hermes,[2] or unsphere
The spirit of Plato, to unfold
What worlds or what vast regions hold   90
The immortal mind that hath forsook
Her mansion in this fleshly nook;
And of those demons that are found
In fire, air, flood, or underground,
Whose power hath a true consent   95
With planet or with element.
Sometime let gorgeous Tragedy
In sceptered pall come sweeping by,
Presenting Thebes, or Pelops' line,
Or the tale of Troy divine.   100
Or what—though rare—of later age
Ennobled hath the buskined stage.
But, O sad Virgin! that thy power
Might raise Musæus from his bower;
Or bid the soul of Orpheus sing   105
Such notes as, warbled to the string,
Drew iron tears down Pluto's cheek,
And made Hell grant what love did seek;
Or call up him that left half told
The story of Cambuscan bold,[3]   110
Of Camball, and of Algarsife,
And who had Canace to wife,
That owned the virtuous ring and glass,
And of the wondrous horse of brass
On which the Tartar king did ride;   115
And if aught else great bards beside
In sage and solemn tunes have sung,
Of tourneys, and of trophies hung,
Of forests, and enchantments drear,
Where more is meant than meets the ear.   120
Thus, Night, oft see me in thy pale career,
Till civil-suited Morn appear,
Not tricked and frounced, as she was wont
With the Attic boy to hunt,
But kerchiefed in a comely cloud,   125
While rocking winds are piping loud,
Or ushered with a shower still,
When the gust hath blown his fill,
Ending on the rustling leaves,
With minute-drops from off the eaves.   130

And, when the sun begins to fling
His flaring beams, me, Goddess, bring
To archéd walks of twilight groves,
And shadows brown, that Silvan loves,
Of pine, or monumental oak,   135
Where the rude ax with heavéd stroke
Was never heard the nymphs to daunt,
Or fright them from their hallowed haunt.
There in close covert, by some brook,
Where no profaner eye may look,   140
Hide me from day's garish eye,
While the bee with honeyed thigh,
That at her flowery work doth sing,
And the waters murmuring,
With such consort as they keep,   145
Entice the dewy-feathered Sleep.
And let some strange, mysterious dream
Wave at his wings, in airy stream
Of lively portraiture displayed,
Softly on my eyelids laid;   150
And, as I wake, sweet music breathe
Above, about, or underneath,
Sent by some Spirit to mortals good,
Or the unseen Genius of the wood.
But let my due feet never fail   155
To walk the studious cloister's pale,
And love the high embowéd roof,
With antique pillars massy-proof,
And storied windows richly dight,
Casting a dim, religious light.   160
There let the pealing organ blow,
To the full-voiced choir below,
In service high and anthems clear,
As may with sweetness, through mine ear,
Dissolve me into ecstasies,   165
And bring all heaven before mine eyes.
And may at last my weary age
Find out the peaceful hermitage
The hairy gown and mossy cell,
Where I may sit and rightly spell   170
Of every star that heaven doth shew,
And every herb that sips the dew,
Till old experience do attain
To something like prophetic strain.
      These pleasures, Melancholy, give,   175
      And I with thee will choose to live.

On His Having Arrived at the Age of Twenty-three

How soon hath Time, the subtle thief of youth,
Stolen on his wing my three and twentieth year!

---

[2] Hermes Trismegistus (thrice great), a mythical Egyptian king and magician.
[3] This refers to the unfinished *Squire's Tale* in Chaucer's *Canterbury Tales.*

My hasting days fly on with full career,
But my late spring no bud or blossom shew'th.
Perhaps my semblance might deceive the truth   5
That I to manhood am arrived so near;
And inward ripeness doth much less appear,
That some more timely-happy spirits endu'th.
Yet be it less or more, or soon or slow,
It shall be still in strictest measure even   10
To that same lot, however mean or high,
Toward which Time leads me, and the will of
    Heaven;
All is, if I have grace to use it so,
As ever in my great Task-Master's eye.

When the Assault Was Intended to the City

Captain, or Colonel, or Knight in arms,
Whose chance on these defenseless doors may
    seize,
If ever deed of honor did thee please,
Guard them, and him within protect from harms.
He can requite thee; for he knows the charms   5
That call fame on such gentle acts as these,
And he can spread thy name o'er lands and seas,
Whatever clime the sun's bright circle warms.
Lift not thy spear against the Muses' bower;
The great Emathian conqueror[1] bid spare   10
The house of Pindarus, when temple and tower
Went to the ground; and the repeated air
Of sad Electra's poet had the power
To save the Athenian walls from ruin bare.

To the Lord General Cromwell, May, 1652

ON THE PROPOSALS OF CERTAIN MINISTERS AT THE
COMMITTEE FOR PROPAGATION OF THE GOSPEL

Cromwell, our chief of men, who through a cloud
Not of war only, but detractions rude,
Guided by faith and matchless fortitude,
To peace and truth thy glorious way hast plowed,
And on the neck of crowned Fortune proud   5
Hast reared God's trophies, and his work pursued,
While Darwen[2] stream, with blood of Scots im-
    brued,
And Dunbar field resounds thy praises loud,

And Worcester's laureate wreath. Yet much re-
    mains
To conquer still; peace hath her victories   10
No less renowned than war; new foes arise,
Threatening to bind our souls with secular chains.
Help us to save free conscience from the paw
Of hireling wolves, whose gospel is their maw.

On the Late Massacre in Piedmont

Avenge, O Lord, thy slaughtered saints, whose
    bones
Lie scattered on the Alpine mountains cold;
Even them who kept thy truth so pure of old,
When all our fathers worshiped stocks and stones,
Forget not; in thy book record their groans   5
Who were thy sheep, and in their ancient fold
Slain by the bloody Piedmontese, that rolled
Mother with infant down the rocks. Their moans
The vales redoubled to the hills, and they
To heaven. Their martyred blood and ashes
    sow   10
O'er all the Italian fields, where still doth sway
The triple tyrant; that from these may grow
A hundredfold, who, having learnt thy way,
Early may fly the Babylonian woe.

On His Blindness

When I consider how my light is spent
Ere half my days, in this dark world and wide,
And that one talent which is death to hide
Lodged with me useless, though my soul more
    bent
To serve therewith my Maker, and present   5
My true account, lest he returning chide;
"Doth God exact day-labor, light denied?"
I fondly ask. But Patience, to prevent
That murmur, soon replies, "God doth not need
Either man's work or his own gifts. Who best 10
Bear his mild yoke, they serve him best. His state
Is kingly; thousands at his bidding speed,
And post o'er land and ocean without rest;
They also serve who only stand and wait."

[1] Alexander the Great. Sad Electra's poet is Sophocles.
[2] This and the following are names of battles in the English Civil War.

Paradise Lost

BOOK I

ARGUMENT

This First Book proposes, first in brief, the whole subject,—Man's disobedience, and the loss thereupon of Paradise, wherein he was placed: then touches the prime cause of his fall,—the serpent, or rather Satan in the serpent; who, revolting from God, and drawing to his side many legions of angels, was, by the command of God, driven out of heaven, with all his crew, into the great deep. Which action passed over, the poem hastens into the midst of things, presenting Satan, with his angels, now fallen into hell, described here, not in the center (for heaven and earth may be supposed as yet not made, certainly not yet accursed), but in a place of utter darkness, fitliest called Chaos: here Satan with his angels, lying on the burning lake, thunderstruck and astonished, after a certain space recovers, as from confusion; calls up him who next in order and dignity lay by him. They confer of their miserable fall; Satan awakens all his legions, who lay till then in the same manner confounded. They rise; their numbers; array of battle; their chief leaders named, according to the idols known afterwards in Canaan and the countries adjoining. To these Satan directs his speech, comforts them with hope yet of regaining heaven, but tells them lastly of a new world and new kind of creature to be created, according to an ancient prophecy, or report, in heaven—for, that the angels were long before this visible creation, was the opinion of many ancient fathers. To find out the truth of this prophecy, and what to determine thereon, he refers to a full council. What his associates thence attempt. Pandemonium, the palace of Satan, rises, suddenly built out of the deep: the infernal peers there sit in council.

Of Man's first disobedience, and the fruit
Of that forbidden tree, whose mortal taste
Brought death into the world, and all our woe,
With loss of Eden, till one greater Man
Restore us, and regain the blissful seat,   5
Sing, heavenly Muse, that on the secret top
Of Oreb, or of Sinai, did'st inspire
That shepherd, who first taught the chosen seed,
In the beginning how the heavens and earth
Rose out of chaos: or, if Sion hill   10
Delight thee more, and Siloa's brook that flowed
Fast by the oracle of God, I thence
Invoke thy aid to my adventurous song,
That with no middle flight intends to soar
Above the Aonian mount, while it pursues   15
Things unattempted yet in prose or rime.
And chiefly thou, O Spirit, that dost prefer
Before all temples the upright heart and pure,
Instruct me, for thou know'st; thou from the first
Wast present, and, with mighty wings outspread,
Dove-like, sat'st brooding on the vast abyss,   21
And mad'st it pregnant: what in me is dark,
Illumine; what is low, raise and support;
That to the height of this great argument
I may assert eternal Providence,   25
And justify the ways of God to men.
    Say first—for heaven hides nothing from thy view,
Nor the deep tract of hell—say first, what cause
Moved our grand Parents, in that happy state,
Favored of Heaven so highly, to fall off   30
From their Creator, and transgress his will
For one restraint, lords of the world besides.
Who first seduced them to that foul revolt?
    The infernal Serpent; he it was, whose guile,
Stirred up with envy and revenge, deceived   35
The mother of mankind; what time his pride
Had cast him out from heaven, with all his host
Of rebel angels; by whose aid, aspiring
To set himself in glory above his peers,
He trusted to have equaled the Most High,   40
If he opposed; and, with ambitious aim
Against the throne and monarchy of God,
Raised impious war in heaven, and battle proud,
With vain attempt. Him the Almighty Power
Hurled headlong flaming from the ethereal sky,
With hideous ruin and combustion, down   46
To bottomless perdition; there to dwell
In adamantine chains and penal fire,
Who durst defy the Omnipotent to arms.
    Nine times the space that measures day and night
To mortal men, he with his horrid crew   50
Lay vanquished, rolling in the fiery gulf,
Confounded, though immortal. But his doom
Reserved him to more wrath; for now the thought
Both of lost happiness and lasting pain   55
Torments him; round he throws his baleful eyes,
That witnessed huge affliction and dismay,
Mixed with obdurate pride, and steadfast hate.
At once, as far as angels' ken, he views

The dismal situation waste and wild. 60
A dungeon horrible, on all sides round,
As one great furnace, flamed; yet from those
   flames
No light; but rather darkness visible
Served only to discover sights of woe,
Regions of sorrow, doleful shades, where peace 65
And rest can never dwell; hope never comes
That comes to all; but torture without end
Still urges, and a fiery deluge, fed
With ever-burning sulphur unconsumed.
Such place eternal justice had prepared 70
For those rebellious; here their prison ordained
In utter darkness, and their portion set
As far removed from God and light of heaven,
As from the center thrice to the utmost pole. 74
O, how unlike the place from whence they fell!
There the companions of his fall, o'erwhelmed
With floods and whirlwinds of tempestuous fire,
He soon discerns; and weltering by his side
One next himself in power, and next in crime,
Long after known in Palestine, and named 80
Beëlzebub. To whom the arch-enemy,
And thence in heaven called Satan, with bold
   words
Breaking the horrid silence, thus began:—
  "If thou beest he—but O, how fall'n! how
   changed
From him who, in the happy realms of light, 85
Clothed with transcendent brightness, didst out-
   shine
Myriads, though bright! If he, whom mutual
   league,
United thoughts and counsels, equal hope
And hazard in the glorious enterprise,
Joined with me once, now misery hath joined 90
In equal ruin; into what pit thou seest
From what height fall'n, so much the stronger
   proved
He with his thunder: and till then who knew
The force of those dire arms? Yet not for those,
Nor what the potent victor in his rage 95
Can else inflict, do I repent or change,
Though changed in outward luster, that fixed
   mind,
And high disdain from sense of injured merit,
That with the Mightiest raised me to contend,
And to the fierce contention brought along 100
Innumerable force of spirits armed,
That durst dislike his reign, and, me preferring
His utmost power with adverse power opposed
In dubious battle on the plains of heaven,

And shook his throne. What though the field be
   lost? 105
All is not lost; the unconquerable will,
And study of revenge, immortal hate,
And courage never to submit or yield,
And what is else not to be overcome;
That glory never shall his wrath or might 110
Extort from me. To bow and sue for grace
With suppliant knee, and deify his power
Who from the terror of this arm so late
Doubted his empire—that were low indeed,
That were an ignominy, and shame beneath 115
This downfall; since, by fate, the strength of gods,
And this empyreal substance, cannot fail:
Since, through experience of this great event,
In arms not worse, in foresight much advanced,
We may with more successful hope resolve 120
To wage by force or guile eternal war,
Irreconcilable to our grand foe,
Who now triumphs, and, in the excess of joy
Sole reigning, holds the tyranny of heaven." 124
  So spake the apostate angel, though in pain,
Vaunting aloud, but racked with deep despair
And him thus answered soon his bold compeer:—
  "O prince, O chief of many-thronèd powers
That led the embattled seraphim to war
Under thy conduct and in dreadful deeds 130
Fearless, endangered heaven's perpetual King,
And put to proof his high supremacy,
Whether upheld by strength, or chance, or fate;
Too well I see, and rue the dire event,
That with sad overthrow, and foul defeat, 135
Hath lost us heaven, and all this mighty host
In horrible destruction laid thus low,
As far as gods and heavenly essences
Can perish: for the mind and spirit remain
Invincible, and vigor soon returns, 140
Though all our glory extinct, and happy state
Here swallowed up in endless misery.
But what if he our Conqueror (whom I now
Of force believe Almighty, since no less
Than such could have o'erpowered such force as
   ours) 145
Have left us this our spirit and strength entire,
Strongly to suffer and support our pains,
That we may so suffice his vengeful ire,
Or do him mightier service as his thralls
By right of war, whate'er his business be, 150
Here in the heart of hell to work in fire,
Or do his errands, in the gloomy deep?
What can it then avail, though yet we feel
Strength undiminished, or eternal being
To undergo eternal punishment?" 155

Whereto with speedy words the arch-fiend re-
    plied:—
"Fallen cherub, to be weak is miserable,
Doing or suffering; but of this be sure,
To do aught good never will be our task,
But ever to do ill our sole delight,   160
As being the contrary to his high will
Whom we resist. If then his providence
Out of our evil seek to bring forth good,
Our labor must be to pervert that end,
And out of good still to find means of evil,   165
Which ofttimes may succeed, so as perhaps
Shall grieve him, if I fail not, and disturb
His inmost counsels from their destined aim.
But see, the angry Victor hath recalled
His ministers of vengeance and pursuit   170
Back to the gates of heaven; the sulphurous hail,
Shot after us in storm, o'erblown, hath laid
The fiery surge, that from the precipice
Of heaven received us falling; and the thunder,
Winged   with   red   lightning   and   impetuous
    rage,   175
Perhaps hath spent his shafts, and ceases now
To bellow through the vast and boundless deep.
Let us not slip the occasion, whether scorn
Or satiate fury yield it from our foe.
Seest thou yon dreary plain, forlorn and wild,   180
The seat of desolation, void of light,
Save what the glimmering of these livid flames
Casts pale and dreadful? Thither let us tend
From off the tossing of these fiery waves;
There rest, if any rest can harbor there;   185
And, re-assembling our afflicted powers,
Consult how we may henceforth most offend
Our enemy; our own loss how repair;
How overcome this dire calamity;
What reinforcement we may gain from hope;   190
If not, what resolution from despair."
   Thus Satan, talking to his nearest mate,
With head uplift above the wave, and eyes
That sparkling blazed; his other parts besides
Prone on the flood, extended long and large,   195
Lay floating many a rood; in bulk as huge
As whom the fables name of monstrous size,
Titanian, or Earth-born, that warred on Jove;
Briareos or Typhon, whom the den
By ancient Tarsus held; or that sea-beast   200
Leviathan, which God of all his works
Created hugest that swim the ocean stream.
Him, haply, slumbering on the Norway foam,
The pilot of some small night-foundered skiff,
Deeming some island, oft, as seamen tell,   205
With fixèd anchor in his scaly rind

Moors by his side under the lee, while night
Invests the sea, and wishèd morn delays:
So stretched out huge in length the arch-fiend lay
Chained on the burning lake: nor ever thence 210
Had risen, or heaved his head; but that the will
And high permission of all-ruling Heaven
Left him at large to his own dark designs;
That with reiterated crimes he might
Heap on himself damnation, while he sought 215
Evil to others; and, enraged, might see
How all his malice served but to bring forth
Infinite goodness, grace, and mercy, shown
On man by him seduced; but on himself   219
Treble confusion, wrath, and vengeance poured.
   Forthwith upright he rears from off the pool
His mighty stature; on each hand the flames,
Driven backward, slope their pointing spires, and
    rolled
In billows, leave i' the midst a horrid vale.
Then with expanded wings he steers his flight 225
Aloft, incumbent on the dusky air,
That felt unusual weight; till on dry land
He lights, if it were land that ever burned
With solid, as the lake with liquid fire;
And such appeared in hue, as when the force 230
Of subterranean wind transports a hill
Torn from Pelorus, or the shattered side
Of thundering Etna, whose combustible
And fueled entrails thence conceiving fire,
Sublimed with mineral fury, aid the winds, 235
And leave a singèd bottom, all involved
With stench and smoke: such resting found the
    sole
Of unblest feet. Him followed his next mate:
Both glorying to have 'scaped the Stygian flood,
As gods, and by their own recovered strength, 240
Not by the sufferance of supernal power.
   "Is this the region, this the soil, the clime,"
Said then the lost archangel, "this the seat
That we must change for heaven; this mournful
    gloom
For that celestial light? Be it so, since he,   245
Who now is Sovereign, can dispose and bid
What shall be right: farthest from him is best,
Whom reason hath equaled, force hath made
    supreme
Above his equals. Farewell, happy fields,
Where joy for ever dwells! Hail, horrors! hail 250
Infernal world! and thou profoundest hell,
Receive thy new possessor—one who brings
A mind not to be changed by place or time:
The mind is its own place, and in itself
Can make a heaven of hell, a hell of heaven. 255

What matter where, if I be still the same,
And what I should be; all but less than he
Whom thunder hath made greater? Here at least
We shall be free: the Almighty hath not built
Here for his envy, will not drive us hence: 260
Here we may reign secure, and, in my choice,
To reign is worth ambition, though in hell;
Better to reign in hell, than serve in heaven.
But wherefore let we then our faithful friends,
The associates and co-partners of our loss,   265
Lie thus astonished on the oblivious pool,
And call them not to share with us their part
In this unhappy mansion; or once more
With rallied arms to try what may be yet
Regained in heaven, or what more lost in hell?"
   So Satan spake, and him Beëlzebub   271
Thus answered: "Leader of those armies bright,
Which, but the Omnipotent, none could have
   foiled,
If once they hear that voice, their liveliest pledge
Of hope in fears and dangers, heard so oft   275
In worst extremes, and on the perilous edge
Of battle when it raged, in all assaults
Their surest signal, they will soon resume
New courage and revive; though now they lie
Groveling and prostrate on yon lake of fire,   280
As we erewhile, astounded and amazed;
No wonder, fall'n such a pernicious height."
  He scarce had ceased, when the superior fiend
Was moving toward the shore: his ponderous
   shield
Ethereal temper, massy, large, and round,   285
Behind him cast; the broad circumference
Hung on his shoulders like the moon, whose orb
Through optic glass the Tuscan artist views
At evening, from the top of Fesolé,
Or in Valdarno, to descry new lands,   290
Rivers, or mountains, in her spotty globe.
His spear—to equal which the tallest pine
Hewn on Norwegian hills, to be the mast
Of some great ammiral, were but a wand—
He walked with, to support uneasy steps   295
Over the burning marl, not like those steps
On heaven's azure, and the torrid clime
Smote on him sore besides, vaulted with fire:
Nathless he so endured, till on the beach
Of that inflamèd sea he stood, and called   300
His legions, angel forms, who lay entranced,
Thick as autumnal leaves, that strew the brooks
In Vallombrosa, where the Etrurian shades,
High over-arched, embower; or scattered sedge
Afloat, when with fierce winds Orion armed   305

Hath vexed the Red Sea coast, whose waves o'er
   threw
Busiris and his Memphian chivalry,
While with perfidious hatred they pursued
The sojourners of Goshen, who beheld
From the safe shore their floating carcasses   310
And broken chariot-wheels; so thick bestrewn,
Abject and lost lay these, covering the flood,
Under amazement of their hideous change.
He called so loud, that all the hollow deep
Of hell resounded. "Princes, potentates,   315
Warriors, the flower of heaven, once yours, now
   lost,
If such astonishment as this can seize
Eternal spirits; or have ye chosen this place
After the toil of battle to repose
Your wearied virtue, for the ease you find   320
To slumber here, as in the vales of heaven?
Or in this abject posture have ye sworn
To adore the Conqueror? who now beholds
Cherub and seraph rolling in the flood
With scattered arms and ensigns, till anon   325
His swift pursuers from heaven-gates discern
The advantage, and descending, tread us down
Thus drooping, or with linkèd thunderbolts
Transfix us to the bottom of this gulf?
Awake, arise, or be for ever fall'n!"   330
   They heard, and were abashed, and up they
   sprung
Upon the wing; as when men, wont to watch
On duty, sleeping found by whom they dread,
Rouse and bestir themselves ere well awake.
Nor did they not perceive the evil plight   335
In which they were, or the fierce pains not feel;
Yet to their general's voice they soon obeyed,
Innumerable. As when the potent rod
Of Amram's son, in Egypt's evil day,
Waved round the coast, up called a pitchy cloud
Of locusts, warping on the eastern wind,   341
That o'er the realm of impious Pharaoh hung
Like night, and darkened all the land of Nile:
So numberless were those bad angels seen
Hovering on wing under the cope of hell,   345
'Twixt upper, nether, and surrounding fires;
Till, at a signal given, the uplifted spear
Of their great sultan waving to direct
Their course, in even balance down they light
On the firm brimstone, and fill all the plain: 350
A multitude like which the populous north
Poured never from her frozen loins, to pass
Rhine or the Danube, when her barbarous sons
Came like a deluge on the south and spread
Beneath Gibraltar to the Libyan sands.   355

Forthwith from every squadron and each band
The heads and leaders thither haste where stood
Their great commander; godlike shapes and forms
Excelling human; princely dignities;   359
And powers that erst in heaven sat on thrones,
Though of their names in heavenly records now
Be no memorial; blotted out and rased
By their rebellion from the books of life.
Nor had they yet among the sons of Eve
Got them new names; till, wandering o'er the
    earth,   365
Through God's high sufferance, for the trial of
    man,
By falsities and lies the greater part
Of mankind they corrupted to forsake
God their Creator, and the invisible
Glory of him that made them, to transform   370
Oft to the image of a brute, adorned
With gay religions, full of pomp and gold,
And devils to adore for deities:
Then were they known to men by various names,
And various idols through the heathen world.   375
    Say, Muse, their names then known, who first,
    who last,
Roused from the slumber on that fiery couch,
At their great emperor's call, as next in worth,
Came singly where he stood on the bare strand,
While the promiscuous crowd stood yet aloof.   380
    The chief were those who from the pit of hell,
Roaming to seek their prey on earth, durst fix
Their seats long after next the seat of God,
Their altars by his altar, gods adored
Among the nations round, and durst abide   385
Jehovah thundering out of Sion, throned
Between the cherubim; yea, often placed
Within his sanctuary itself their shrines,
Abominations; and with cursèd things
His holy rites and solemn feasts profaned,   390
And with their darkness durst affront his light.
First, Moloch, horrid king, besmeared with blood
Of human sacrifice, and parents' tears;
Though, for the noise of drums and timbrels loud,
Their children's cries unheard, that passed through
    fire   395
To his grim idol. Him the Ammonite
Worshiped in Rabba and her watery plain,
In Argob and in Basan, to the stream
Of utmost Arnon. Nor content with such
Audacious neighborhood, the wisest heart   400
Of Solomon he led by fraud to build
His temple right against the temple of God,
On that opprobrious hill; and made his grove
The pleasant valley of Hinnom, Tophet thence

And black Gehenna called, the type of hell.   405
Next, Chemos, the obscene dread of Moab's sons,
From Aroer to Nebo, and the wild
Of southmost Abarim; in Hesebon
And Horonáim, Seon's realm, beyond
The flowery dale of Sibma clad with vines,   410
And Eleäle to the asphaltic pool;
Peor his other name, when he enticed
Israel in Sittim, on their march from Nile,
To do him wanton rites, which cost them woe.
Yet thence his lustful orgies he enlarged   415
Even to that hill of scandal, by the grove
Of Moloch homicide: lust hard by hate;
Till good Josiah drove them thence to hell.
With these came they who, from the bordering
    flood
Of old Euphrates to the brook that parts   420
Egypt from Syrian ground, had general names
Of Baälim and Ashtaroth; those male,
These feminine; for spirits, when they please,
Can either sex assume, or both; so soft
And uncompounded is their essence pure;   425
Not tied or manacled with joint or limb,
Nor founded on the brittle strength of bones,
Like cumbrous flesh; but, in what shape they
    choose,
Dilated or condensed, bright or obscure,
Can execute their aëry purposes,   430
And works of love or enmity fulfill.
For those the race of Israel oft forsook
Their living Strength, and unfrequented left
His righteous altar, bowing lowly down
To bestial gods; for which their heads as low   435
Bowed down in battle, sunk before the spear
Of despicable foes. With these in troop
Came Astoreth, whom the Phenicians called
Astarté, queen of heaven, with crescent horns;
To whose bright image nightly by the moon   440
Sidonian virgins paid their vows and songs;
In Sion also not unsung, where stood
Her temple on the offensive mountain, built
By that uxorious king, whose heart, though large,
Beguiled by fair idolatresses, fell   445
To idols foul. Thammuz came next behind,
Whose annual wound in Lebanon allured
The Syrian damsels to lament his fate
In amorous ditties all a summer's day;
While smooth Adonis from his native rock   450
Ran purple to the sea, supposed with blood
Of Thammuz yearly wounded; the love-tale
Infected Sion's daughters with like heat;
Whose wanton passions in the sacred porch
Ezekiel saw, when, by the vision led,   455

His eye surveyed the dark idolatries
Of alienated Judah. Next came one
Who mourned in earnest, when the captive ark
Maimed his brute image, head and hands lopped
    off
In his own temple, on the grunsel edge,   460
Where he fell flat, and shamed his worshipers;
Dagon his name, sea-monster, upward man
And downward fish; yet had his temple high
Reared in Azotus, dreaded through the coast
Of Palestine, in Gath and Ascalon,   465
And Accaron and Gazar's frontier bounds.
Him followed Rimmon, whose delightful seat
Was fair Damascus, on the fertile banks
Of Abbana and Pharphar, lucid streams.
He also 'gainst the house of God was bold: 470
A leper once he lost, and gained a king;
Ahaz his sottish conqueror, whom he drew
God's altar to disparage and displace
For one of Syrian mode, whereon to burn
His odious offerings, and adore the gods   475
Whom he had vanquished. After these appeared
A crew who, under names of old renown,
Osiris, Isis, Orus, and their train,
With monstrous shapes and sorceries abused
Fanatic Egypt and her priests, to seek   480
Their wandering gods disguised in brutish forms
Rather than human. Nor did Israel 'scape
The infection, when their borrowed gold com-
    posed
The calf in Oreb; and the rebel king
Doubled that sin in Bethel and in Dan,   485
Likening his Maker to the grazèd ox—
Jehovah, who in one night, when he passed
From Egypt marching, equaled with one stroke
Both her first-born and all her bleating gods.
Belial came last, than whom a spirit more lewd
Fell not from heaven, or more gross to love   491
Vice for itself; to him no temple stood,
Or altar smoked; yet who more oft than he
In temples and at altars, when the priest
Turns atheist, as did Eli's sons, who filled   495
With lust and violence the house of God?
In courts and palaces he also reigns,
And in luxurious cities, where the noise
Of riot ascends above their loftiest towers,
And injury and outrage: and when night   500
Darkens the streets, then wander forth the sons
Of Belial, flown with insolence and wine.
Witness the streets of Sodom, and that night
In Gibeah, when the hospitable door
Exposed a matron, to avoid worse rape.   505
   These were the prime in order and in might:

The rest were long to tell, though far renowned,
The Ionian gods—of Javan's issue held
Gods, yet confessed later than heaven and earth,
Their boasted parents: Titan, heaven's first-
    born   510
With his enormous brood, and birthright seized
By younger Saturn; he from mightier Jove,
His own and Rhea's son, like measure found;
So Jove usurping reigned: these first in Crete
And Ida known, thence on the snowy top   515
Of cold Olympus ruled the middle air,
Their highest heaven; or on the Delphian cliff,
Or in Dodona, and through all the bounds
Of Doric land: or who with Saturn old
Fled over Adria to the Hesperian fields,   520
And o'er the Celtic roamed the utmost isles.
   All these and more came flocking, but with
    looks
Downcast and damp; yet such wherein appeared
Obscure some glimpse of joy, to have found their
    chief
Not in despair, to have found themselves not
    lost   525
In loss itself; which on his countenance cast
Like doubtful hue; but he, his wonted pride
Soon recollecting, with high words, that bore
Semblance of worth, not substance, gently raised
Their fainting courage, and dispelled their fears.
Then straight commands that at the warlike
    sound   531
Of trumpets loud and clarions be upreared
His mighty standard; that proud honor claimed
Azazel as his right, a cherub tall;   534
Who forthwith from the glittering staff unfurled
The imperial ensign; which, full high advanced,
Shone like a meteor, streaming to the wind,
With gems and golden luster rich emblazed,
Seraphic arms and trophies, all the while
Sonorous metal blowing martial sounds: 540
At which the universal host up-sent
A shout, that tore hell's concave, and beyond
Frighted the reign of Chaos and old Night.
All in a moment through the gloom were seen
Ten thousand banners rise into the air,   545
With orient colors waving; with them rose
A forest huge of spears; and thronging helms
Appeared, and serried shields in thick array
Of depth immeasurable; anon they move
In perfect phalanx to the Dorian mood   550
Of flutes and soft recorders; such as raised
To height of noblest temper heroes old
Arming to battle, and instead of rage,
Deliberate valor breathed, firm and unmoved

With dread of death to flight or foul retreat;   555
Nor wanting power to mitigate and 'suage
With solemn touches troubled thoughts, and chase
Anguish, and doubt, and fear, and sorrow, and
    pain
From mortal or immortal minds. Thus they,
Breathing united force, with fixèd thought,   560
Moved on in silence, to soft pipes, that charmed
Their painful steps o'er the burnt soil: and now
Advanced in view they stand; a horrid front
Of dreadful length and dazzling arms, in guise
Of warriors old with ordered spear and shield,
Awaiting what command their mighty chief   566
Had to impose: he through the armèd files
Darts his experienced eye, and soon traverse
The whole battalion views, their order due,
Their visages and stature as of gods;   570
Their number last he sums. And now his heart
Distends with pride, and hardening in his strength
Glories: for never since created man
Met such embodied force as, named with these,
Could merit more than that small infantry   575
Warred on by cranes: though all the giant brood
Of Phlegra with the heroic race were joined
That fought at Thebes and Ilium, on each side
Mixed with auxiliar gods; and what resounds
In fable or romance of Uther's son [1]   580
Begirt with British and Armoric knights;
And all who since, baptized or infidel,
Jousted in Aspramont, or Montalban,
Damascus, or Morocco, or Trebizond,
Or whom Biserta sent from Afric shore,   585
When Charlemagne with all his peerage fell
By Fontarabbia. Thus far these beyond
Compare of mortal prowess, yet observed
Their dread commander; he, above the rest
In shape and gesture proudly eminent,   590
Stood like a tower; his form had yet not lost
All its original brightness; nor appeared
Less than archangel ruined, and the excess
Of glory obscured: as when the sun, new risen,
Looks through the horizontal misty air   595
Shorn of his beams, or from behind the moon,
In dim eclipse, disastrous twilight sheds
On half the nations, and with fear of change
Perplexes monarchs. Darkened so, yet shone
Above them all the archangel; but his face   600
Deep scars of thunder had entrenched; and care
Sat on his faded cheek; but under brows
Of dauntless courage, and considerate pride
Waiting revenge; cruel his eye, but cast
Signs of remorse and passion, to behold   605

The fellows of his crime, the followers rather
(Far other once beheld in bliss), condemned
For ever now to have their lot in pain;
Millions of spirits for his fault amerced
Of heaven, and from eternal splendors flung   610
For his revolt; yet faithful how they stood,
Their glory withered; as when heavens' fire
Hath scathed the forest oaks, or mountain pines,
With singèd top their stately growth, though bare,
Stands on the blasted heath. He now prepared   615
To speak; whereat their doubled ranks they bend
From wing to wing, and half enclose him round
With all his peers: attention held them mute.
Thrice he essayed, and thrice, in spite of scorn,
Tears, such as angels weep, burst forth; at last   620
Words, interwove with sighs, found out their way.
    "O myriads of immortal spirits! O powers
Matchless, but with the Almighty; and that strife
Was not inglorious, though the event was dire,
As this place testifies, and this dire change,   625
Hateful to utter! but what power of mind,
Forseeing or presaging, from the depth
Of knowledge, past or present, could have feared
How such united force of gods, how such
As stood like these, could ever know repulse?   630
For who can yet believe, though after loss,
That all these puissant legions, whose exile
Hath emptied heaven, shall fail to reascend
Self-raised, and repossess their native seat?
For me, be witness all the host of heaven,   635
If counsels different, or dangers shunned
By me, have lost our hopes. But he who reigns
Monarch in heaven, till then as one secure
Sat on this throne upheld by old repute,
Consent or custom; and his regal state   640
Put forth at full, but still his strength concealed,
Which tempted our attempt, and wrought our fall.
Henceforth his might we know, and know our
    own;
So as not either to provoke, or dread
New war, provoked; our better part remains,   645
To work in close design, by fraud or guile,
What force effected not; that he no less
At length from us may find, who overcomes
By force, hath overcome but half his foe.
Space may produce new worlds; whereof so
    rife   650
There went a fame in heaven that he ere long
Intended to create, and therein plant
A generation, whom his choice regard
Should favor equal to the sons of heaven:
Thither, if but to pry, shall be perhaps   655

---

[1] King Arthur. The following references are all to the medieval romantic heroes.

Our first eruption; thither, or elsewhere;
For this infernal pit shall never hold
Celestial spirits in bondage, nor the abyss
Long under darkness cover. But these thoughts
Full counsel must mature; peace is despaired; 660
For who can think submission? War, then, war,
Open or understood, must be resolved."
    He spake; and, to confirm his words, outflew
Millions of flaming swords, drawn from the thighs
Of mighty cherubim; the sudden blaze 665
Far round illumined hell; highly they raged
Against the Highest, and fierce with graspèd arms
Clashed on their sounding shields the din of war,
Hurling defiance toward the vault of heaven.
    There stood a hill not far, whose grisly top 670
Belched fire and rolling smoke; the rest entire
Shone with a glossy scurf, undoubted sign
That in his womb was hid metallic ore,
The work of sulphur. Thither, winged with speed,
A numerous brigade hastened: as when bands
Of pioneers, with spade and pickax armed, 676
Forerun the royal camp, to trench a field,
Or cast a rampart. Mammon led them on:
Mammon, the least erected spirit that fell
From heaven; for even in heaven his looks and
    thoughts 680
Were always downward bent, admiring more
The riches of heaven's pavement, trodden gold,
Than aught, divine or holy, else enjoyed
In vision beatific; by him first
Men also, and by his suggestion taught, 685
Ransacked the center, and with impious hands
Rifled the bowels of their mother earth
For treasures, better hid. Soon had his crew
Opened into the hill a spacious wound,
And digged out ribs of gold. Let none admire 690
That riches grow in hell; that soil may best
Deserve the precious bane. And here let those
Who boast in mortal things, and wondering tell
Of Babel, and the works of Memphian kings,
Learn how their greatest monuments of fame,
And strength and art, are easily outdone 696
By spirits reprobate, and in an hour
What in an age they with incessant toil
And hands innumerable scarce perform.
Nigh on the plain, in many cells prepared, 700
That underneath had veins of liquid fire
Sluiced from the lake, a second multitude
With wondrous art founded the massy ore,
Severing each kind, and scummed the bullion
    dross;
A third as soon had formed within the ground
A various mold, and from the boiling cells, 706

By strange conveyance, filled each hollow nook,
As in an organ, from one blast of wind,
To many a row of pipes the sound-board breathes.
Anon, out of the earth a fabric huge 710
Rose like an exhalation, with the sound
Of dulcet symphonies and voices sweet,
Built like a temple, where pilasters round
Were set, and Doric pillars overlaid
With golden architrave; nor did there want 715
Cornice or frieze, with bossy sculptures graven:
The roof was fretted gold. Not Babylon,
Nor great Alcairo, such magnificence
Equaled in all their glories, to enshrine
Belus or Serapis their gods, or seat 720
Their kings, when Egypt with Assyria strove
In wealth and luxury. The ascending pile
Stood fixed her stately height: and straight the
    doors,
Opening their brazen folds, discover, wide
Within, her ample spaces, o'er the smooth 725
And level pavement; from the archèd roof,
Pendent by subtle magic, many a row
Of starry lamps and blazing cressets, fed
With naphtha and asphaltus, yielded light
As from a sky. The hasty multitude 730
Admiring entered; and the work some praise,
And some the architect: his hand was known
In heaven by many a towered structure high
Where sceptered angels held their residence,
And sat as princes; whom the supreme King 735
Exalted to such power, and gave to rule,
Each in his hierarchy, the orders bright.
Nor was his name unheard or unadored
In ancient Greece; and in Ausonian land
Men called him Mulciber; and how he fell 740
From heaven they fabled, thrown by angry Jove
Sheer o'er the crystal battlements: from morn
To noon he fell, from noon to dewy eve,
A summer's day; and with the setting sun
Dropped from the zenith like a falling star, 745
On Lemnos, th' Ægean isle: thus they relate,
Erring; for he with this rebellious rout
Fell long before; nor aught availed him now
To have built in heaven high towers; nor did he
    'scape
By all his engines, but was headlong sent 750
With his industrious crew to build in hell.
    Meanwhile, the wingèd heralds, by command
Of sovereign power, with awful ceremony
And trumpet's sound, throughout the host pro-
    claim
A solemn council, forthwith to be held 755
At Pandemonium, the high capital

Of Satan and his peers: their summons called
From every band and squarèd regiment
By place or choice the worthiest; they anon,
With hundreds and with thousands, trooping
    came,   760
Attended; all access was thronged; the gates
And porches wide, but chief the spacious hall
(Though like a covered field, where champions
    bold
Wont ride in armed, and at the soldan's chair
Defied the best of paynim chivalry   765
To mortal combat, or career with lance),
Thick swarmed, both on the ground and in the
    air,
Brushed with the hiss of rustling wings. As bees
In spring-time, when the sun with Taurus rides,
Pour forth their populous youth about the hive   770
In clusters; they among fresh dews and flowers
Fly to and fro, or on the smoothèd plank,
The suburb of their straw-built citadel,
New rubbed with balm, expatiate, and confer
Their state affairs; so thick the aëry crowd   775
Swarmed and were straitened; till, the signal
    given,

Behold a wonder! They, but now who seemed
In bigness to surpass earth's giant sons,
Now less than smallest dwarfs, in narrow room
Throng numberless, like that Pygmëan race   780
Beyond the Indian mount, or faëry elves,
Whose midnight revels, by a forest side
Or fountain, some belated peasant sees,
Or dreams he sees, while over head the moon
Sits arbitress, and nearer to the earth   785
Wheels her pale course; they, on their mirth and
    dance
Intent, with jocund music charm his ear;
At once with joy and fear his heart rebounds.
Thus incorporeal spirits to smallest forms
Reduced their shapes immense, and were at
    large,   790
Though without number still, amidst the hall
Of that infernal court. But far within,
And in their own dimensions, like themselves,
The great seraphic lords and cherubim
In close recess and secret conclave sat;   795
A thousand demi-gods on golden seats
Frequent and full. After short silence then,
And summons read, the great consult began.

PROSE FROM BACON TO PEPYS

For the development of English prose the seventeenth century is of supreme importance. When we read the prose writings of the great Elizabethans, we feel the need of some kind of discipline. The style may be rich and ornate, but it is seldom clear. If, however, we take up the prose of a man like Addison at the beginning of the eighteenth century, we see that in the intervening century English authors had learned to write a prose that is not only pleasing but also clear and distinct. The paragraph as we know it had been invented and developed. The prose writer had learned to plan his work as carefully as does the poet.

No student of English prose can neglect the essays of Francis Bacon. With them he brought into England a literary form that was to occupy some of the most gifted English authors and was to produce some of the finest English literature. Bacon himself did not use the essay form for any great variety of purposes. In his hands essays are used merely for the expression of ideas on all kinds of subjects. As we read them we feel that they are merely abstracts of what he would write if he had a great deal of time. He says as much in a page as the usual writer does in ten, and this means that he has left out all illustrative material and all kinds of elaboration. What we have is a bare, straightforward statement of his ideas about friendship, or marriage, or scholarship. It must be said that there is a great skill used in this unadorned writing. Frequently he has crystallized a whole essay in a single sentence. Even where the sentences are not so memorable, the experienced reader feels that he is reading English that is very heavily charged with ideas. Bacon is not for the lazy reader, but to the thoughtful man or woman the reading of his essays can be a very stimulating experience.

For the half century after Bacon English prose did not take the direction which he had indicated. It was a generation of great sermon writers, such as Jeremy Taylor, and eloquent essayists, such as Sir Thomas Browne. Some of the finest sentences ever written in English appeared in Browne's essay on *Urn Burial* and in his *Religio Medici*.

Possibly because of his importance as a poet, but more likely because of the practical influence of his essay, John Milton's *Areopagitica* is the best known of any prose work of the middle of the seventeenth century. This is perhaps the most persuasive plea ever made for the complete freedom of the press. At times Milton rises to a level of great eloquence in his fervent address to the Lords and Commons of England.

No history of the prose of this century would be complete without mention of Bunyan's *Pilgrim's Progress*. The fervent religious idealism which is expressed by this simple man in plain but extraordinarily imaginative language exercised a profound influence over the readers of English prose for more than two centuries. And it has likewise made a very great impression on our writers, for its expressions and characters have become a part of their traditional background. Its importance in this respect can only be compared with the King James version of the Bible.

The charmingly discursive sketches of fishing life in Izaak Walton's *The Compleat Angler* and the formal scholarly prose of Dryden's critical essays each contributed its part to that development of English prose which we have mentioned.

The casual reader, however, will turn with most eagerness to the pages of a man who apparently had no ambition to be considered a writer of literature. When Samuel Pepys composed his *Diary,* he wrote it in shorthand, presumably for his own amusement. After one hundred fifty years it was transcribed, and for the past century his interest in his own times has been shared by a host of readers.

On the opening day of the year 1660 he begins his *Diary* with the realization that important events are likely to happen very soon. Within the year we see the restoration of Charles II, and in the course of the ten years covered by this record we are taken through the experiences of the Great Fire, the Great Plague, and the war with Holland. We also become acquainted with all of Pepys's friends and learn, as we can in no other way, what life was like in the 1660's.

FRANCIS BACON

Of Truth

"What is truth?" said jesting Pilate; and would not stay for an answer. Certainly there be that delight in giddiness, and count it a bondage to fix a belief, affecting free-will in thinking, as well as in acting. And though the sects of philosophers of that kind be gone, yet there remain certain discoursing wits which are of the same veins, though there be not so much blood in them as was in those of the ancients. But it is not only the difficulty and labor which men take in finding out truth; nor again, that when it is found, it imposeth upon men's thoughts, that doth bring lies in favor: but a natural though corrupt love of the lie itself. One of the later school of the Grecians examineth the matter, and is at a stand to think what should be in it, that men should love lies, where neither they make for pleasure, as with poets, nor for advantage as with the merchant, but for the lie's sake. But I cannot tell: this same truth is a naked and open day-light that doth not shew the masques and mummeries and triumphs of the world half so stately and daintily as candle-lights. Truth may, perhaps, come to the price of a pearl, that sheweth best by day; but it will not rise to the price of a diamond or carbuncle, that sheweth best in varied lights. A mixture of a lie doth ever add pleasure. Doth any man doubt that if there were taken out of men's minds vain opinions, flattering hopes, false valuations, imaginations as one would, and the like, but it would leave the minds of a number of men poor shrunken things, full of melancholy and indisposition, and unpleasing to themselves? One of the fathers, in great severity, called poesy *vinum dæmonum,* because it filleth the imagina-

Bacon, *Of Truth.* Francis Bacon (1561-1626), a son of Sir Nicholas Bacon, was created Baron Varulam and Viscount St. Albans. He had an active life in public office but his fame rests on his contributions to science and philosophy, and on his essays.

tion, and yet it is but with the shadow of a lie. But it is not the lie that passeth through the mind, but the lie that sinketh in and settleth in it, that doth the hurt, such as we spake of before. But howsoever these things are thus in men's depraved judgments and affections, yet truth, which only doth judge itself, teacheth that the inquiry of truth, which is the lovemaking or wooing of it; the knowledge of truth, which is the presence of it; and the belief of truth, which is the enjoying of it, is the sovereign good of human nature. The first creature of God, in the works of the days, was the light of the sense; the last was the light of reason; and his sabbath work, ever since, is the illumination of his spirit. First he breathed light upon the face of the matter or chaos; then he breathed light into the face of man; and still he breatheth and inspireth light into the face of his chosen. The poet [1] that beautified the sect that was otherwise inferior to the rest, saith yet excellently well: *It is a pleasure to stand upon the shore, and to see ships tossed upon the sea; a pleasure to stand in the window of a castle, and to see a battle and the adventures thereof below: but no pleasure is comparable to the standing upon the vantage ground of Truth* (a hill not too commanded, and where the air is always clear and serene), *and to see the errors, and wanderings, and mists, and tempests, in the vale below;* so always that this prospect be with pity, and not with swelling or pride. Certainly, it is heaven upon earth to have a man's mind move in charity, rest in providence, and turn upon the poles of truth.

To pass from theological and philosophical truth to the truth of civil business, it will be acknowledged, even by those that practice it not, that clear and round dealing is the honor of man's nature, and that mixture of falsehood is like alloy in coin of gold and silver, which may make the metal work the better, but it embaseth it; for these winding and crooked courses are the goings of the serpent, which goeth basely upon the belly, and not upon the feet. There is no vice that doth so cover a man with shame as to be found false and perfidious; and therefore Montaigne saith prettily, when he inquired the reason why the word of the lie should be such a disgrace and such an odious charge, "If it be well weighed, to say that a man lieth, is as much to say as that he is brave towards God and a coward towards men." For a lie faces God, and shrinks from man. Surely the wickedness of falsehood and breach of faith cannot possibly be so highly expressed as in that it shall be the last peal to call the judgments of God upon the generations of men; it being foretold, that when Christ cometh, "he shall not find faith upon the earth."

Of Marriage and Single Life

He that hath wife and children hath given hostages to fortune; for they are impediments to great enterprises, either of virtue or of mischief. Certainly the best works and of greatest merit for the public have proceeded from the unmarried or childless men; which, both in affection and means, have married and endowed the public. Yet it were great reason that those that have children should have greatest care of future times unto which they know they must transmit their dearest pledges. Some there are, who, though they lead a single life, yet their thoughts do end with themselves, and account future times impertinences; nay, there are some other that account wife and children but as bills of charges. Nay, more, there are some foolish rich covetous men that take a pride in having no children, because they may be thought so much the richer. For, perhaps, they have heard some talk, "Such a one is a great rich man," and another except to it, "Yea, but he hath a great charge of children," as if it were an abatement to his riches. But the most ordinary cause of a single life is liberty, especially in certain self-pleasing and humorous minds, which are so sensible of every restraint, as they will go near to think their girdles and garters to be bonds and shackles. Unmarried men are best friends, best masters, best servants, but not always best subjects, for they are light to run away, and almost all fugitives are of that condition. A single life doth well with churchmen, for charity will hardly water the ground where it must first fill a pool. It is indifferent for judges and magistrates, for if they be facile and corrupt, you shall have a servant five times worse than a wife. For soldiers, I find the generals commonly, in their hortatives, put men in mind of their wives and children. And I think the despising of marriage amongst the Turks maketh the vulgar soldier more base. Certainly, wife and children are a kind of discipline of humanity; and single men, though they be many times more charitable, because their means are less exhaust, yet, on the other side, they are more cruel and hard-hearted, good to make severe inquisitors, because their tenderness is not so oft called upon. Grave natures, led by custom, and therefore constant, are commonly loving husbands; as was said of Ulysses, *"Vetulam suam prætulit immortalitati."* [2] Chaste women are often

---

[1] Lucretius.   [2] He preferred his little old wife to immortality.

proud and froward, as presuming upon the merit of their chastity. It is one of the best bonds, both of chastity and obedience, in the wife, if she think her husband wise; which she will never do if she find him jealous. Wives are young men's mistresses, companions for middle age, and old men's nurses. So as a man may have a quarrel to marry when he will. But yet he was reputed one of the wise men that made answer to the question when a man should marry, "A young man not yet, an elder man not at all." It is often seen that bad husbands have very good wives; whether it be that it raiseth the price of their husbands' kindness when it comes, or that the wives take a pride in their patience; but this never fails if the bad husbands were of their own choosing, against their friends' consent; for then they will be sure to make good their own folly.

Of Studies

Studies serve for delight, for ornament, and for ability. Their chief use for delight is in privateness and retiring; for ornament, is in discourse; and for ability, is in the judgment and disposition of business. For expert men can execute, and perhaps judge of particulars, one by one; but the general counsels, and the plots and marshaling of affairs, come best from those that are learned. To spend too much time in studies is sloth; to use them too much for ornament is affectation; to make judgment wholly by their rules is the humor of a scholar. They perfect nature, and are perfected by experience; for natural abilities are like natural plants, that need pruning by study; and studies themselves do give forth directions too much at large, except they be bounded in by experience. Crafty men contemn studies, simple men admire them, and wise men use them, for they teach not their own use; but that is a wisdom without them and above them, won by observation. Read not to contradict and confute, nor to believe and take for granted, nor to find talk and discourse, but to weigh and consider. Some books are to be tasted, others to be swallowed, and some few to be chewed and digested; that is, some books are to be read only in parts; others to be read, but not curiously; and some few to be read wholly, and with diligence and attention. Some books also may be read by deputy and extracts made of them by others; but that would be only in the less important arguments, and the meaner sort of books; else distilled books are like common distilled waters, flashy things. Reading maketh a full man, conference a ready man, and writing an exact man. And therefore, if a man write little, he had need have a great memory; if he confer little, he had need have a present wit; and if he read little, he had need have much cunning, to seem to know that he doth not. Histories make men wise, poets witty, the mathematics subtle, natural philosophy deep, moral grave, logic and rhetoric able to contend. *Abeunt studia in mores*.[1] Nay, there is no stand or impediment in the wit but may be wrought out by fit studies, like as diseases of the body may have appropriate exercises. Bowling is good for the stone and reins, shooting for the lungs and breast; gentle walking for the stomach, riding for the head, and the like. So if a man's wit be wandering, let him study the mathematics; for in demonstrations, if his wit be called away never so little, he must begin again. If his wit be not apt to distinguish or find differences, let him study the schoolmen, for they are *cymini sectores*.[2] If he be not apt to beat over matters and to call up one thing to prove and illustrate another, let him study the lawyers' cases. So every defect of the mind may have a special receipt.

JOHN MILTON

Areopagitica

[Milton is here pleading against any restriction on the printing of books.]

. . . I deny not but that it is of greatest concernment in the Church and Commonwealth, to have a vigilant eye how books demean themselves as well as men; and thereafter to confine, imprison, and do sharpest justice on them as malefactors. For books are not absolutely dead things, but do contain a potency of life in them to be as active as

---

[1] Studies develop into habits.   [2] Hair-splitters.

that soul was whose progeny they are; nay, they do preserve as in a vial the purest efficacy and extraction of that living intellect that bred them. I know they are as lively, and as vigorously productive, as those fabulous dragon's teeth; and being sown up and down, may chance to spring up armed men. And yet, on the other hand, unless wariness be used, as good almost kill a man as kill a good book: who kills a man kills a reasonable creature, God's image; but he who destroys a good book, kills reason itself, kills the image of God, as it were, in the eye. Many a man lives a burden to the earth; but a good book is the precious lifeblood of a master spirit, embalmed and treasured up on purpose to a life beyond life. 'Tis true, no age can restore a life, whereof perhaps there is no great loss; and revolutions of ages do not oft recover the loss of a rejected truth, for the want of which whole nations fare the worse. We should be wary, therefore, what persecution we raise against the living labors of public men, how we spill that seasoned life of man, preserved and stored up in books; since we see a kind of homicide may be thus committed, sometimes a martyrdom; and if it extend to the whole impression, a kind of massacre, whereof the execution ends not in the slaying of an elemental life, but strikes at that ethereal and fifth essence, the breath of reason itself, slays an immortality rather than a life. . . .

I conceive, therefore, that when God did enlarge the universal diet of man's body, saving ever the rules of temperance, he then also, as before, left arbitrary the dieting and repasting of our minds; as wherein every mature man might have to exercise his own leading capacity. How great a virtue is temperance, how much of moment through the whole life of man! Yet God commits the managing so great a trust, without particular law or prescription, wholly to the demeanor of every grown man. And, therefore, when he himself tabled the Jews from heaven, that omer, which was every man's daily portion of manna, is computed to have been more than might have well sufficed the heartiest feeder thrice as many meals. For those actions which enter into a man, rather than issue out of him, and therefore defile not, God uses not to captivate under a perpetual childhood of prescription, but trusts him with the gift of reason to be his own chooser; there were but little work left for preaching, if law and compulsion should grow so fast upon those things which heretofore were governed only by exhortation. Solomon informs us,

that much reading is a weariness to the flesh; but neither he nor other inspired author tells us that such or such reading is unlawful; yet certainly had God thought good to limit us herein, it had been much more expedient to have told us what was unlawful, than what was wearisome. . . .

Good and evil we know in the field of this world grow up together almost inseparably; and the knowledge of good is so involved and interwoven with the knowledge of evil, and in so many cunning resemblances hardly to be discerned, that those confused seeds which were imposed upon Psyche as an incessant labor to cull out, and sort asunder, were not more intermixed. It was from out the rind of one apple tasted, that the knowledge of good and evil, as two twins cleaving together, leaped forth into the world. And perhaps this is that doom which Adam fell into of knowing good and evil, that is to say, of knowing good by evil.

As, therefore, the state of man now is; what wisdom can there be to choose, what continence to forbear without the knowledge of evil? He that can apprehend and consider vice with all her baits and seeming pleasures, and yet abstain, and yet distinguish, and yet prefer that which is truly better, he is the true wayfaring Christian. I cannot praise a fugitive and cloistered virtue, unexercised and unbreathed, that never sallies out and sees her adversary, but slinks out of the race, where that immortal garland is to be run for, not without dust and heat. Assuredly we bring not innocence into the world; we bring impurity much rather; that which purifies us is trial, and trial is by what is contrary. That virtue, therefore, which is but a youngling in the contemplation of evil, and knows not the utmost that vice promises to her followers, and rejects it, is but a blank virtue, not a pure.

Since, therefore, the knowledge and survey of vice is in this world so necessary to the constituting of human virtue, and the scanning of error to the confirmation of truth, how can we more safely, and with less danger, scout into the regions of sin and falsity, than by reading all manner of tractates and hearing all manner of reason? And this is the benefit which may be had of books promiscuously read. . . .

For if they fell upon one kind of strictness, unless their care were equal to regulate all other things of like aptness to corrupt the mind, that single endeavor they knew would be but a fond labor; to shut and fortify one gate against corruption, and be necessitated to leave others round about wide open. If we think to regulate printing, thereby to rectify manners, we must regulate all recreations and pastimes, all that is delightful to man. No music must be heard, no song be set or sung, but what is grave and Doric. There must be licensing dancers, that no gesture, motion, or deportment be taught our youth, but what by their allowance shall be thought honest; for such Plato was provided of. It will ask more than the work of twenty licensers to examine all the lutes, the violins, and the guitars in every house; they must not be suffered to prattle as they do, but must be licensed what they may say. And who shall silence all the airs and madrigals that whisper softness in chambers? The windows also, and the balconies must be thought on; these are shrewd books, with dangerous frontispieces, set to sale; who shall prohibit them, shall twenty licensers? The villages also must have their visitors to inquire what lectures the bagpipe and the rebeck reads even to the ballatry, and the gamut of every municipal fiddler, for these are the countryman's Arcadias, and his Monte Mayors.

Next, what more national corruption, for which England hears ill abroad, than household gluttony? Who shall be the rectors of our daily rioting? And what shall be done to inhibit the multitudes that frequent those houses where drunkenness is sold and harbored? Our garments also should be referred to the licensing of some more sober workmasters, to see them cut into a less wanton garb. Who shall regulate all the mixed conversation of our youth, male and female together, as is the fashion of this country? Who shall still appoint what shall be discoursed, what presumed, and no further? Lastly, who shall forbid and separate all idle resort, all evil company? These things will be, and must be; but how they shall be least hurtful, how least enticing, herein consists the grave and governing wisdom of a state.

To sequester out of the world into Atlantic and Utopian polities, which never can be drawn into use, will not mend our condition; but to ordain wisely as in this world of evil, in the midst whereof God hath placed us unavoidably. Nor is it Plato's licensing of books will do this, which necessarily pulls along with it so many other kinds of licensing, as will make us all both ridiculous and weary, and yet frustrate; but those unwritten, or at least unconstraining, laws of virtuous education, reli-

gious and civil nurture, which Plato there mentions as the bonds and ligaments of the commonwealth, the pillars and the sustainers of every written statute; these they be which will bear chief sway in such matters as these, when all licensing will be easily eluded. Impunity and remissness, for certain, are the bane of a commonwealth; but here the great art lies, to discern in what the law is to bid restraint and punishment, and in what things persuasion only is to work. If every action which is good or evil in man at ripe years, were to be under pittance and prescription and compulsion, what were virtue but a name, what praise could be then due to well-doing, what gramercy to be sober, just, or continent?

Many there be that complain of divine Providence for suffering Adam to transgress. Foolish tongues! when God gave him reason, he gave him freedom to choose, for reason is but choosing; he had been else a mere artificial Adam, such an Adam as he is in the motions. We ourselves esteem not of that obedience, or love, or gift, which is of force; God, therefore, left him free, set before him a provoking object, ever almost in his eyes; herein consisted his merit, herein the right of his reward, the praise of his abstinence. Wherefore did he create passions within us, pleasures round about us, but that these rightly tempered are the very ingredients of virtue? They are not skillful considerers of human things, who imagine to remove sin by removing the matter of sin; for, besides that it is a huge heap increasing under the very act of diminishing, though some part of it may for a time be withdrawn from some persons, it cannot from all, in such a universal thing as books are; and when this is done, yet the sin remains entire. Though ye take from a covetous man all his treasure, he has yet one jewel left, ye cannot bereave him of his covetousness. Banish all objects of lust, shut up all youth into the severest discipline that can be exercised in any hermitage, ye cannot make them chaste, that came not thither so: such great care and wisdom is required to the right managing of this point.

Suppose we could expel sin by this means; look how much we thus expel of sin, so much we expel of virtue: for the matter of them both is the same; remove that, and ye remove them both alike. This justifies the high providence of God, who, though he commands us temperance, justice, continence, yet pours out before us, even to a profuseness, all desirable things, and gives us minds that can wander beyond all limit and satiety. Why should we then affect a rigor contrary to the manner of God and of nature, by abridging or scanting those means, which books freely permitted are both to the trial of virtue, and the exercise of truth?

It would be better done, to learn that the law must needs be frivolous, which goes to restrain things, uncertainly and yet equally working to good and to evil. And were I the chooser, a dram of well doing should be preferred before many times as much the forcible hindrance of evil doing. For God sure esteems the growth and completing of one virtuous person, more than the restraint of ten vicious. . . .

Truth indeed came once into the world with her divine Master, and was a perfect shape most glorious to look on; but when he ascended, and his apostles after him were laid asleep, then straight arose a wicked race of deceivers, who, as that story goes of the Egyptian Typhon with his conspirators, how they dealt with the good Osiris, took the virgin Truth, hewed her lovely form into a thousand pieces, and scattered them to the four winds. From that time ever since, the sad friends of Truth, such as durst appear, imitating the careful search that Isis made for the mangled body of Osiris, went up and down gathering up limb by limb still as they could find them. We have not yet found them all, Lords and Commons, nor ever shall do, till her Master's second coming; he shall bring together every joint and member, and shall mold them into an immortal feature of loveliness and perfection. Suffer not these licensing prohibitions to stand at every place of opportunity, forbidding and disturbing them that continue seeking, that continue to do our obsequies to the torn body of our martyred saint. . . .

Methinks I see in my mind a noble and puissant nation rousing herself like a strong man after sleep, and shaking her invincible locks; methinks I see her as an eagle mewing her mighty youth, and kindling her undazzled eyes at the full midday beam; purging and unscaling her long-abused sight at the fountain itself of heavenly radiance; while the whole noise of timorous and flocking birds, with those also that love the twilight, flutter about, amazed at what she means, and in their envious gabble would prognosticate a year of sects and schisms.

What should ye do then, should ye suppress all this flowery crop of knowledge and new light sprung up and yet springing daily in this city; should ye set an oligarchy of twenty engrossers over it, to bring a famine upon our minds again, when we shall know nothing but what is measured to us by their bushel? Believe it, Lords and Commons, they who counsel ye to such a suppressing, do as good as bid ye suppress yourselves; and I will soon show how.

If it be desired to know the immediate cause of all this free writing and free speaking, there cannot be assigned a truer than your own mild and free and humane government; it is the liberty, Lords and Commons, which your own valorous and happy counsels have purchased us, liberty which is the nurse of all great wits; this is that which hath rarefied and enlightened our spirits like the influence of heaven; this is that which hath enfranchised, enlarged, and lifted up our apprehensions degrees above themselves. Ye cannot make us now less capable, less knowing, less eagerly pursuing of the truth, unless ye first make yourselves, that made us so, less the lovers, less the founders of our true liberty. We can grow ignorant again, brutish, formal, and slavish, as ye found us; but you then must first become that which ye cannot be, oppressive, arbitrary, and tyrannous; as they were from whom ye have freed us. That our hearts are now more capacious, our thoughts more erected to the search and expectation of greatest and exactest things, is the issue of your own virtue propagated in us; ye cannot suppress that unless ye reinforce an abrogated and merciless law, that fathers may despatch at will their own children. And who shall then stick closest to ye, and excite others? not he who takes up arms for coat and conduct, and his four nobles of Danegelt. Although I dispraise not the defense of just immunities, yet love my peace better, if that were all. Give me the liberty to know, to utter, and to argue freely according to conscience, above all liberties.

SAMUEL PEPYS

Diary

Bringing in the King [1]

May 21, 1660. [2] By letters that came hither in my absence, I understand that the Parliament had ordered all persons to be secured, in order to a trial, that did sit as judges in the late King's death, and all the officers too attending the Court. News brought that the two Dukes are coming on board, which, by and by, they did, in a Dutch boat, the Duke of York in yellow trimmings, the Duke of Gloucester in gray and red. My Lord went in a boat to meet them, the captain, myself, and others, standing at the entering port. So soon as they were entered we shot the guns off round the fleet. After that they went to view the ship all over, and were most exceedingly pleased with it. They seem to be both very fine gentlemen. News is sent us that the King is on shore; so my Lord fired all his guns round twice, and all the fleet after him, which in the end fell into disorder, which seemed very handsome. The gun over against my cabin I fired myself to the King, which was the first time that he had been saluted by his own ships since this change; but holding my head too much over the gun, I had almost spoiled my right eye. Nothing in the world but going of guns almost all this day.

May 23, 1660. The Doctor and I waked very merry. In the morning came infinity of people on board from the King to go along with him. My Lord, Mr. Crew, and others, go on shore to meet the King as he comes off from shore, where Sir R. Stayner bringing His Majesty into the boat, I hear that His Majesty did with a great deal of affection kiss my Lord upon his first meeting. The King, with the two Dukes and Queen of Bohemia, Princess Royal, and Prince of Orange, came on board, where I in their coming in kissed the King's, Queen's, and Princess's hands, having done the other before. Infinite shooting off of the guns, and that in a disorder on purpose, which was better than if it had been otherwise. All day nothing but Lords and persons of honor on board, that we were exceeding full. Dined in a great deal of state, the Royal company by themselves in the coach, which was a blessed sight to see. After dinner the King and Duke altered the name of some of the ships, viz., the *Nazeby* into *Charles;* the *Richard, James;* the *Speaker, Mary;* the *Dunbar* (which was not in company with us), the *Henry; Winsly, Happy Return; Wakefield, Richmond; Lambert,* the *Henrietta; Cheriton,* the *Speedwell; Bradford,* the *Success.* That done, the Queen, Princess Royal, and Prince of Orange, took leave of the King, and the Duke of York went on board the *London,* and the Duke of Gloucester, the *Swiftsure.* Which done, we weighed anchor, and with a fresh gale and most happy weather we set sail for England. All the afternoon the King walked here and there, up and down (quite contrary to what I thought him to have been), very active and stirring. Upon the quarter-deck he fell into discourse of his escape from Worcester, where it made me ready to weep to hear the stories that he told of his difficulties that he had passed through, as his traveling four days and three nights on foot, every step up to his knees in dirt, with nothing but a green coat and a pair of country breeches on, and a pair of country shoes that made him so sore all over his feet, that he could scarce stir. Yet he was forced to run away from a miller and other company, that took them for rogues. His sitting at table at one place, where the master of the house, that had not seen him in eight years, did know him, but kept it private; when at the same table there was one that had been of his own regiment at Worcester, could not know him, but made him drink the King's health, and said that the King was at least four fingers higher than he. At another place he was by some servants of the house made to drink, that they might know him not to be a Roundhead, which they swore he was. In another place at his inn, the master of the house, as the King was standing, with his hands upon the back of a chair by the fireside, kneeled down and

Pepys, *Diary.* Samuel Pepys (1633-1703) was educated at Cambridge and entered public service shortly before the Restoration. He was influential in placing the English navy on an efficient basis.
[1] Charles II, who is being restored to his throne after eleven years of exile.
[2] At the opening of this selection Pepys is aboard ship off the coast of Holland, waiting for the king and his court.

kissed his hand, privately, saying, that he would not ask who he was, but bid God bless him whither he was going. Then the difficulty of getting a boat to get into France, where he was fain to plot with the master thereof to keep his design from the four men and a boy (which was all his ship's company), and so go to Fécamp in France. At Rouen he looked so poorly, that the people went into the rooms before he went away to see whether he had not stolen something or other. The King supped alone in the coach; after that I got a dish, and we four supped in my cabin, as at noon. So to my cabin again, where the company still was, and were talking more of the King's difficulties; as how he was fain to eat a piece of bread and cheese out of a poor boy's pocket; how, at a Catholic house he was fain to lie in the priest's hole a good while in the house for his privacy. Under sail all night, and most glorious weather.

May 24, 1660. Up, and make myself as fine as I could, with the linning stockings on and wide canons that I bought the other day at Hague. Extraordinary press of noble company, and great mirth all the day. Walking upon the decks, where persons of honor all the afternoon, among others, Thomas Killigrew (a merry droll, but a gentleman of great esteem with the King), who told us many merry stories. After this discourse I was called to write a pass for my Lord Mandeville to take up horses to London, which I wrote in the King's name, and carried it to him to sign, which was the first and only one that ever he signed in the ship *Charles.* To bed, coming in sight of land a little before night.

May 25, 1660. By the morning we were come close to the land, and every body made ready to get on shore. The King and the two Dukes did eat their breakfast before they went, and there being set some ship's diet before them, only to show them the manner of the ship's diet, they eat of nothing else but peas and pork, and boiled beef. I spoke with the Duke of York about business, who called me Pepys by name, and upon my desire did promise me his future favor. Great expectation of the King's making some knights, but there was none. About noon (though the brigantine that Beale made was there ready to carry him) yet he would go in my Lord's barge with the two Dukes. Our Captain steered, and my Lord went along bare with him. I went, and Mr. Mansell, and one of the King's footmen, with a dog that the King loved, (which [dirtied] the boat, which made us laugh, and methink that a King and all that belong

to him are but just as others are), in a boat by ourselves, and so got on shore when the King did, who was received by General Monk with all imaginable love and respect at his entrance upon the land of Dover. Infinite the crowd of people and the horsemen, citizens, and noblemen of all sorts. The Mayor of the town came and gave him his white staff, the badge of his place, which the King did give him again. The Mayor also presented him from the town a very rich Bible, which he took and said it was the thing that he loved above all things in the world. A canopy was provided for him to stand under, which he did, and talked awhile with General Monk and others, and so into a stately coach there set for him, and so away through the town towards Canterbury, without making any stay at Dover. The shouting and joy expressed by all is past imagination. My Lord returned late, and at his coming did give me order to cause the marke to be gilded, and a Crown and C. R. to be made at the head of the coach table, where the King today with his own hand did mark his height, which accordingly I caused the painter to do, and is not done as is to be seen.

Coronation of Charles II

April 23, 1661. About 4 I rose and got to the Abbey, where I followed Sir J. Denham, the Surveyor, with some company that he was leading in. And with much ado, by the favor of Mr. Cooper, his man, did get up into a great scaffold across the North end of the Abbey, where with a great deal of patience I sat from past 4 till 11 before the King came in. And a great pleasure it was to see the Abbey raised in the middle, all covered with red, and a throne (that is a chair) and footstool on the top of it; and all the officers of all kinds, so much as the very fiddlers, in red vests. At last comes in the Dean and Prebends of Westminster, with the Bishops (many of them in cloth of gold copes), and after them the Nobility, all in their Parliament robes, which was a most magnificent sight. Then the Duke, and the King with a scepter (carried by my Lord Sandwich) and sword and mond before him, and the crown too. The King in his robes, bareheaded, which was very fine. And after all had placed themselves, there was a sermon and the service; and then in the Quire at the high altar, the King passed through all the ceremonies of the Coronation, which to my great grief I and most in the Abbey could not see. The crown being put upon his head, a great shout begun, and he came

forth to the throne, and there passed more ceremonies: as taking the oath, and having things read
to him by the Bishop; and his lords (who put on
their caps as soon as the King put on his crown)
and bishops come, and kneeled before him. And
three times the King at Arms went to the three
open places on the scaffold, and proclaimed, that
if anyone could show any reason why Charles
Stuart should not be King of England, that now
he should come and speak. And a General Pardon
also was read by the Lord Chancellor, and medals
flung up and down by my Lord Cornwallis, of
silver, but I could not come by any. And the King
came in with his crown on, and his scepter in his
hand, under a canopy borne up by six silver staves,
carried by Barons of the Cinque Ports, and little
bells at every end. After a long time, he got up to
the farther end, and all set themselves down at
their several tables; and that was also a brave sight:
and the King's first course carried up by the
Knights of the Bath. And many fine ceremonies
there was of the Heralds leading up people before
him, and bowing; and my Lord of Albermarle's
going to the kitchen and eat a bit of the first dish
that was to go to the King's table. But, above all,
was these three Lords, Northumberland, and Suf-
folk, and the Duke of Ormond, coming before the
courses on horseback, and staying so all dinner-
time, and at last to bring up [Dymock] the King's
Champion, all in armor on horseback, with his
spear and target carried before him. And a Herald
proclaims "That if any dare deny Charles Stuart
to be lawful King of England, here was a Champion that would fight with him;" and with these
words, the Champion flings down his gauntlet,
and all this he do three times in his going up
towards the King's table. At last when he is come,
the King drinks to him, and then sends him the
cup which is of gold, and he drinks it off, and
then rides back again with the cup in his hand.
I went from table to table to see the Bishops and
all others at their dinner, and was infinitely pleased
with it. At Mr. Bowyer's; a great deal of company,
some I knew, others I did not. Here we stayed
upon the leads and below till it was late, expecting
to see the fire-works, but they were not performed
tonight: only the City had a light like a glory
round about it with bonfires. And after a little stay
more I took my wife and Mrs. Frankleyn (who I
proffered the civility of lying with my wife at
Mrs. Hunt's tonight) to Axe-yard, in which at the
further end there were three great bonfires, and a
great many great gallants, men and women; and

they laid hold of us, and would have us drink the
King's health upon our knees, kneeling upon a
faggot, which we all did, they drinking to us one
after another. Which we thought a strange frolic;
but these gallants continued thus a great while,
and I wondered to see how the ladies did tipple.
Thus did the day end with joy everywhere. Now,
after all this, I can say that, besides the pleasure
of the sight of these glorious things, I may now
shut my eyes against any other objects, nor for
the future trouble myself to see things of state and
show, as being sure never to see the like again in
this world.

The Great Fire of London

September 2 (Lord's day), 1666. Some of our maids
sitting up late last night to get things ready against
our feast today, Jane called us up about three in
the morning, to tell us of a great fire they saw in
the City. So I rose and slipped on my nightgown,
and went to her window, and thought it to be on
the back-side of Marke-lane at the farthest; but,
being unused to such fires as followed, I thought
it far enough off; and so went to bed again and to
sleep. About seven rose again to dress myself, and
there looked out at the window, and saw the fire
not so much as it was and further off. By and by
Jane comes and tells me that she hears that above
300 houses have been burned down tonight by the
fire we saw, and that it is now burning down all
Fish-street, by London Bridge. So I made myself
ready presently, and walked to the Tower, and
there got up upon one of the high places, Sir J.
Robinson's little son going up with me; and there
I did see the houses at that end of the bridge all on
fire, and an infinite great fire on this and the other
side the end of the bridge; which, among other
people, did trouble me for poor little Michell and
our Sarah on the bridge. So down, with my heart
full of trouble, to the Lieutenant of the Tower,
who tells me that it begun this morning in the
King's baker's house in Pudding-lane, and that it
hath burned St. Magnus's Church and most part
of Fish-street already. So I down to the water-side,
and there got a boat and through bridge, and
there saw a lamentable fire. Poor Michell's house,
as far as the Old Swan, already burned that way,
and the fire running further, that in a very little
time it got as far as the Steele-yard, while I was
there. Everybody endeavoring to remove their
goods, and flinging into the river or bringing them
into lighters that lay off; poor people staying in

their houses as long as till the very fire touched them, and then running into boats, or clambering from one pair of stairs by the water-side to another. And among other things, the poor pigeons, I perceive, were loth to leave their houses, but hovered about the windows and balconys till they were, some of them burned, their wings, and fell down. Having stayed, and in an hour's time seen the fire rage every way, and nobody, to my sight, endeavoring to quench it, but to remove their goods, and leave all to the fire, and having seen it get as far as the Steele-yard, and the wind mighty high and driving it into the City; and every thing, after so long a drought, proving combustible, even the very stones of churches, and among other things the poor steeple by which pretty Mrs. —— lives, and whereof my old schoolfellow Elborough is parson, taken fire in the very top, and there burned till it fell down: I to White Hall (with a gentleman with me who desired to go off from the Tower, to see the fire, in my boat); to White Hall, and there up to the King's closet in the Chapel, where people come about me, and I did give them an account dismayed them all, and word was carried in to the King. So I was called for, and did tell the King and Duke of York what I saw, and that unless his Majesty did command houses to be pulled down nothing could stop the fire. They seemed much troubled, and the King commanded me to go to my Lord Mayor from him, and command him to spare no houses, but to pull down before the fire every way. At last met my Lord Mayor in Canning-street, like a man spent, with a handkerchief about his neck. To the King's message he cried, like a fainting woman, "Lord, what can I do? I am spent: people will not obey me. I have been pulling down houses; but the fire overtakes us faster than we can do it." People all almost distracted, and no manner of means used to quench the fire. The houses, too, so very thick thereabouts, and full of matter of burning, as pitch and tar, in Thames-street; and warehouses of oil, and wines, and brandy, and other things. And to see the churches all filling with goods by people who themselves should have been quietly there at this time. Met with the King and Duke of York in their barge, and with them to Queenhithe, and there called Sir Richard Browne to them. Their order was only to pull down houses apace, and so below bridge at the water-side; but little was or could be done, the fire coming upon them so fast. River full of lighters and boats taking in goods, and good goods swimming in the water, and only

I observed that hardly one lighter or boat in three that had the goods of a house in, but there was a pair of Virginals in it. So near the fire as we could for smoke; and all over the Thames, with one's face in the wind, you were almost burned with a shower of fire-drops. This is very true; so as houses were burned by these drops and flakes of fire, three or four, nay, five or six houses, one from another. When we could endure no more upon the water, we to a little ale-house on the Bankside, over against the Three Cranes, and there stayed till it was dark almost, and saw the fire grow; and, as it grew darker, appeared more and more, and in corners and upon steeples, and between churches and houses, as far as we could see up the hill of the City, in a most horrid malicious bloody flame, not like the fine flame of an ordinary fire. Barbary and her husband away before us. We stayed till, it being darkish, we saw the fire as only one entire arch of fire from this to the other side the bridge, and in a bow up the hill for an arch of above a mile long: it made me weep to see it. The churches, houses, and all on fire and flaming at once; and a horrid noise the flames made, and the cracking of houses at their ruin. So home with a sad heart, and there find every body discoursing and lamenting the fire; and poor Tom Hater come with some few of his goods saved out of his house, which is burned upon Fish-street Hill. I invited him to lie at my house, and did receive his goods, but was deceived in his lying there, the news coming every moment of the growth of the fire; so as we were forced to begin to pack up our own goods, and prepare for their removal; and did by moonshine (it being brave dry, and moonshine, and warm weather) carry much of my goods into the garden, and Mr. Hater and I did remove my money and iron chests into my cellar, as thinking that the safest place. And got my bags of gold into my office, ready to carry away, and my chief papers of accounts also there, and my tallies into a box by themselves.

September 3, 1666. About four o'clock in the morning, my Lady Batten sent me a cart to carry away all my money, and plate, and best things, to Sir W. Rider's at Bednall-greene. Which I did, riding myself in my nightgown in the cart; and, Lord! to see how the streets and the highways are crowded with people running and riding, and getting of carts at any rate to fetch away things. The Duke of York come this day by the office, and spoke to us, and did ride with his guard up and down the City to keep all quiet (he being now

General, and having the care of all). At night lay down a little upon a quilt of W. Hewer's in the office, all my own things being packed up or gone; and after me my poor wife did the like, we having fed upon the remains of yesterday's dinner, having no fire nor dishes, nor any opportunity of dressing any thing.

September 4, 1666. Up by break of day to get away the remainder of my things. Sir W. Batten not knowing how to remove his wine, did dig a pit in the garden, and laid it in there; and I took the opportunity of laying all the papers of my office that I could not otherwise dispose of. And in the evening Sir W. Pen and I did dig another, and put our wine in it; and I my Parmazan cheese, as well as my wine and some other things. Only now and then walking into the garden, and saw how horridly the sky looks, all on a fire in the night, was enough to put us out of our wits; and, indeed, it was extremely dreadful, for it looks just as if it was at us, and the whole heaven on fire. I after supper walked in the dark down to Tower-street, and there saw it all on fire, at the Trinity House on that side, and the Dolphin Tavern on this side, which was very near us; and the fire with extraordinary vehemence. Now begins the practice of blowing up of houses in Tower-street, those next the Tower, which at first did frighten people more than any thing; but it stopped the fire where it was done, it bringing down the houses to the ground in the same places they stood, and then it was easy to quench what little fire was in it, though it kindled nothing almost. Paul's is burned, and all Cheap-side. I wrote to my father this night, but the post-house being burned, the letter could not go.

September 5, 1666. About two in the morning my wife calls me up and tells me of new cries of fire, it being come to Barking Church, which is the bottom of our lane. I up, and finding it so, resolved presently to take her away, and did, and took my gold, which was about £2350, W. Hewer, and Jane, down by Proundy's boat to Woolwich; but, Lord! what a sad sight it was by moonlight to see the whole City almost on fire, that you might see it plain at Woolwich, as if you were by it. There, when I come, I find the gates shut, but no guard kept at all, which troubled me, because of discourse now begun, that there is plot in it, and that the French had done it. I got the gates open, and to Mr. Shelden's, where I locked up my gold, and charged my wife and W. Hewer never to leave the room without one of them in it,

night or day. So back again, by the way seeing my goods well in the lighters at Deptford, and watched well by people. Home, and whereas I expected to have seen our house on fire, it being now about seven o'clock, it was not. I up to the top of Barking steeple, and there saw the saddest sight of desolation that I ever saw; everywhere great fires, oil-cellars, and brimstone, and other things burning. I became afraid to stay there long, and therefore down again as fast as I could, the fire being spread as far as I could see it; and to Sir W. Pen's, and there eat a piece of cold meat, having eaten nothing since Sunday, but the remains of Sunday's dinner.

September 6, 1666. It was pretty to see how hard the women did work in the cannells, sweeping of water; but then they would scold for drink, and be as drunk as devils. I saw good butts of sugar broke open in the street, and people go and take handfuls out, and put into beer, and drink it. And now all being pretty well, I took boat, and over to Southwarke, and took boat on the other side the bridge, and so to Westminster, thinking to shift myself, being all in dirt from top to bottom; but could not there find any place to buy a shirt or pair of gloves. A sad sight to see how the River looks; no houses nor church near it, to the Temple, where it stopped.

September 7, 1666. Up by five o'clock; and, blessed be God! find all well; and by water to Paul's Wharf. Walked thence, and saw all the town burned, and a miserable sight of Paul's church, with all the roofs fallen, and the body of the quire fallen into St. Fayth's; Paul's school also, Ludgate, and Fleet-street, my father's house, and the church, and a good part of the Temple the like. This day our Merchants first met at Gresham College, which, by proclamation, is to be their Exchange. Strange to hear what is bid for houses all up and down here; a friend of Sir W. Rider's having £150 for what he used to let for £40 per annum. Much dispute where the Custom-house shall be; thereby the growth of the City again to be foreseen. I home late to Sir W. Pen's, who did give me a bed; but without curtains or hanging, all being down. So here I went the first time into a naked bed, only my drawers on; and did sleep pretty well: but still both sleep and waking had a fear of fire in my heart, that I took little rest. People do all the world over cry out of the simplicity of my Lord Mayor in general, and more particularly in this business of the fire, laying it all upon him.

PROSE OF THE
NEW CLASSICISM

Although Matthew Arnold has been frequently attacked for calling the eighteenth century the age of prose and reason, it can, nevertheless, be maintained that some of the greatest prose produced in the English language was written during that century.

Beginning in the very early years of the eighteenth century there appeared a long series of periodical essays. These essays came out at stated intervals, usually several times a week. In some newspapers they were all written by a single editor and in others, such as the *Spectator*, they were written by two or more persons in collaboration. These journalistic writings occupied some of the most talented Englishmen of the century, particularly Joseph Addison and Sir Richard Steele at the beginning of the movement and Samuel Johnson and Oliver Goldsmith at a later stage. The habit of receiving and perusing these periodicals produced a generation of intelligent essay readers, and this appreciative public in turn has been a great help in the later development of English prose.

The eighteenth century was a time when satire flourished. Beginning as early as Dryden in the last quarter of the seventeenth century, both poets and prose writers had given themselves over very freely to a fierce criticism of their political and social opponents. With Dryden and Pope this was largely done in verse, but with Jonathan Swift and Daniel Defoe it took the form of prose.

Swift wrote a number of essays savagely attacking political and social conditions, but his masterpiece of satire is *Gulliver's Travels*. In this work he sends his hero into various strange countries, and either by observing the people in these countries or having the people observe him, he brings out comparisons and contrasts that can be applied directly to conditions in England.

Though Defoe is important as a satirist, he is best known as the author of some very realistic fiction. Not to speak of *Robinson Crusoe*, which is familiar to every boy and girl, he wrote a *Journal of the Plague Year*, in which the Great Plague of London is described as if he had been there. Defoe's method of making his stories realistic will be seen in *The Apparition of Mrs. Veal*.

The great prose form developed in the eighteenth century was the novel in the sense that we now know it. It is unfortunate that an anthology cannot include some of these important English novels, but they must be read completely if they are to be appreciated.

After *Robinson Crusoe* the next step in the development of fiction was taken by

Samuel Richardson, who wrote long novels in the form of letters exchanged between the principal characters. These epistolary novels continued throughout the eighteenth century and they may be even found today, but it was not more than ten years after the appearance of Richardson's *Pamela* that Henry Fielding was writing novels without the use of letters. The great English novel tradition which was to be followed by Jane Austen, Scott, Dickens, Thackeray, and George Eliot was well developed and established before 1760.

The literary dictator of the middle years of the century was Samuel Johnson, the author of the *English Dictionary*. Johnson not only wrote periodical essays, plays, poems, and literary criticism, but was one of the greatest of conversationalists. James Boswell, his inseparable companion, recorded many of his most interesting conversations and published them in his great biography. Johnson's influence on English literature is perhaps greater because of his personality than because of his writings themselves.

Even a cursory account of eighteenth century English prose must make some mention of the orations of Edmund Burke. In them we see the clearness and force of eighteenth century prose most effectively employed.

Another important achievement of English prose writing is in the field of history. Edward Gibbon's *Decline and Fall of the Roman Empire* is not only the first history written according to the research technique of the modern historian, but is written with such an excellent command of English that it is one of the enduring monuments of our prose.

DANIEL DEFOE

The Apparition of Mrs. Veal

This thing is so rare in all its circumstances, and on so good authority, that my reading and conversation have not given me anything like it. It is fit to gratify the most ingenious and serious inquirer. Mrs. Bargrave is the person to whom Mrs. Veal appeared after her death; she is my intimate friend, and I can avouch for her reputation for these last fifteen or sixteen years, on my own knowledge; and I can confirm the good character she had from her youth to the time of my acquaintance; though since this relation she is calumniated by some people that are friends to the brother of Mrs. Veal who appeared, who think the relation of this appearance to be a reflection, and endeavor what they can to blast Mrs. Bargrave's reputation, and to laugh the story out of countenance. But by the circumstances thereof, and the cheerful disposition of Mrs. Bargrave, notwith-

standing the ill-usage of a very wicked husband, there is not the least sign of dejection in her face; nor did I ever hear her let fall a desponding or murmuring expression; nay, not when actually under her husband's barbarity, which I have been witness to, and several other persons of undoubted reputation.

Now you must know Mrs. Veal was a maiden gentlewoman of about thirty years of age, and for 10 some years last past had been troubled with fits, which were perceived coming on her by her going off from her discourses very abruptly to some impertinence. She was maintained by an only brother, and kept his house in Dover. She was a very pious woman, and her brother a very sober man, to all appearance; but now he does all he can to null or quash the story. Mrs. Veal was intimately acquainted with Mrs. Bargrave from her

Defoe, *The Apparition of Mrs. Veal*. Daniel Defoe (c. 1661-1731), after a varied career in business and public office, became a voluminous writer of pamphlets, novels, histories, and miscellaneous works.

childhood. Mrs. Veal's circumstances were then mean; her father did not take care of his children as he ought, so that they were exposed to hardships; and Mrs. Bargrave in those days had as unkind a father, though she wanted neither for food nor clothing, whilst Mrs. Veal wanted for both, insomuch that she would often say, "Mrs. Bargrave, you are not only the best, but the only friend I have in the world; and no circumstance in life shall ever dissolve my friendship." They would often condole each other's adverse fortunes, and read together *Drelincourt upon Death,* and other good books; and so, like two Christian friends, they comforted each other under their sorrow.

Some time after Mr. Veal's friends got him a place in the custom-house at Dover, which occasioned Mrs. Veal, by little and little, to fall off from her intimacy with Mrs. Bargrave, though there never was any such thing as a quarrel; but an indifferency came on by degrees, till at last Mrs. Bargrave had not seen her in two years and a half; though about a twelve-month of the time Mrs. Bargrave had been absent from Dover, and this last half-year had been in Canterbury about two months of the time, dwelling in a house of her own.

In this house, on the 8th of September 1705, she was sitting alone, in the forenoon, thinking over her unfortunate life, and arguing herself into a due resignation to Providence, though her condition seemed hard. "And," said she, "I have been provided for hitherto, and doubt not but I shall be still; and am well satisfied that my afflictions shall end when it is most fit for me;" and then took up her sewing-work, which she had no sooner done but she hears a knocking at the door. She went to see who was there, and this proved to be Mrs. Veal, her old friend, who was in a riding-habit; at that moment of time the clock struck twelve at noon.

"Madam," says Mrs. Bargrave, "I am surprised to see you, you have been so long a stranger;" but told her she was glad to see her, and offered to salute her, which Mrs. Veal complied with, till their lips almost touched; and then Mrs. Veal drew her hand across her own eyes and said, "I am not very well," and so waived it. She told Mrs. Bargrave she was going a journey, and had a great mind to see her first. "But," says Mrs. Bargrave, "how came you to take a journey alone? I am amazed at it, because I know you have a good brother." "Oh," says Mrs. Veal, "I gave my brother the slip, and came away, because I had so great a

desire to see you before I took my journey." So Mrs. Bargrave went in with her into another room within the first, and Mrs. Veal set her down in an elbow-chair, in which Mrs. Bargrave was sitting when she heard Mrs. Veal knock. Then says Mrs. Veal, "My dear friend, I am come to renew our old friendship again, and beg your pardon for my breach of it; and if you can forgive me, you are the best of women." "Oh," says Mrs. Bargrave, "do not mention such a thing. I have not had an uneasy thought about it; I can easily forgive it." "What did you think of me?" said Mrs. Veal. Says Mrs. Bargrave, "I thought you were like the rest of the world, and that prosperity had made you forget yourself and me." Then Mrs. Veal reminded Mrs. Bargrave of the many friendly offices she did in her former days, and much of the conversation they had with each other in the times of their adversity; what books they read, and what comfort in particular they received from Drelincourt's *Book of Death,* which was the best, she said, on that subject ever written. She also mentioned Dr. Sherlock, the two Dutch books which were translated, written upon Death, and several others; but Drelincourt, she said, had the clearest notions of death and of the future state of any who had handled that subject. Then she asked Mrs. Bargrave whether she had Drelincourt. She said, "Yes." Says Mrs. Veal, "Fetch it." And so Mrs. Bargrave goes upstairs and brings it down. Says Mrs. Veal, "Dear Mrs. Bargrave, if the eyes of our faith were as open as the eyes of our body, we should see numbers of angels about us for our guard. The notions we have of heaven now are nothing like to what it is, as Drelincourt says. Therefore be comforted under your afflictions, and believe that the Almighty has a particular regard to you, and that your afflictions are marks of God's favor; and when they have done the business they are sent for, they shall be removed from you. And believe me, my dear friend, believe what I say to you, one minute of future happiness will infinitely reward you for all your sufferings; for I can never believe" (and claps her hands upon her knees with great earnestness, which indeed ran through most of her discourse) "that ever God will suffer you to spend all your days in this afflicted state; but be assured that your afflictions shall leave you, or you them, in a short time." She spake in that pathetical and heavenly manner that Mrs. Bargrave wept several times, she was so deeply affected with it.

Then Mrs. Veal mentioned Dr. Horneck's *Ascetick,* at the end of which he gives an account of the lives of the primitive Christians. Their pat tern sne recommended to our imitation, and said, "Their conversation was not like this of our age; for now," says she, "there is nothing but frothy, vain discourse, which is far different from theirs. Theirs was to edification, and to build one another up in faith; so that they were not as we are, nor are we as they were; but," said she, "we ought to do as they did. There was a hearty friendship among them; but where is it now to be found?" Says Mrs. Bargrave, "It is hard indeed to find a true friend in these days." Says Mrs. Veal, "Mr. Norris has a fine copy of verses, called *Friendship in Perfection,* which I wonderfully admire. Have you seen the book?" says Mrs. Veal. "No," says Mrs. Bargrave, "but I have the verses of my own writing out." "Have you?" says Mrs. Veal; "then fetch them." Which she did from above-stairs, and offered them to Mrs. Veal to read, who refused, and waived the thing, saying holding down her head would make it ache; and then desired Mrs. Bargrave to read them to her, which she did. As they were admiring *Friendship* Mrs. Veal said, "Dear Mrs. Bargrave, I shall love you for ever." In these verses there is twice used the word Elysian. "Ah!" says Mrs. Veal, "these poets have such names for heaven!" She would often draw her hand across her own eyes and say, "Mrs. Bargrave, do not you think I am mightily impaired by my fits?" "No," says Mrs. Bargrave, "I think you look as well as ever I knew you."

After all this discourse, which the apparition put in much finer words than Mrs. Bargrave said she could pretend to, and as much more than she can remember, for it cannot be thought that an hour and three-quarters' conversation could be retained, though the main of it she thinks she does, she said to Mrs. Bargrave she would have her write a letter to her brother, and tell him she would have him give rings to such and such, and that there was a purse of gold in her cabinet, and that she would have two broad pieces given to her cousin Watson.

Talking at this rate, Mrs. Bargrave thought that a fit was coming upon her, and so placed herself in a chair just before her knees, to keep her from falling to the ground, if her fits should occasion it (for the elbow-chair, she thought, would keep her from falling on either side); and to divert Mrs. Veal, as she thought, took hold of her gown-sleeve several times and commended it. Mrs. Veal told her it was a scoured silk, and newly made up. But for all this, Mrs. Veal persisted in her request, and told Mrs. Bargrave that she must not deny her, and she would have her tell her brother all their conversation when she had an opportunity. "Dear Mrs. Veal," said Mrs. Bargrave, "this seems so impertinent that I cannot tell how to comply with it; and what a mortifying story will our conversation be to a young gentleman!" "Well," says Mrs. Veal, "I must not be denied." "Why," says Mrs. Bargrave, "it is much better, methinks, to do it yourself." "No," says Mrs. Veal, "though it seems impertinent to you now, you will see more reason for it hereafter." Mrs. Bargrave then, to satisfy her importunity, was going to fetch a pen and ink, but Mrs. Veal said, "Let it alone now, but do it when I am gone; but you must be sure to do it;" which was one of the last things she enjoined her at parting. So she promised her.

Then Mrs. Veal asked for Mrs. Bargrave's daughter. She said she was not at home, "But if you have a mind to see her," says Mrs. Bargrave, "I'll send for her." "Do," says Mrs. Veal. On which she left her, and went to a neighbor's to see for her; and by the time Mrs. Bargrave was returning, Mrs. Veal was got without the door into the street, in the face of the beast-market, on a Saturday (which is market-day), and stood ready to part. As soon as Mrs. Bargrave came to her, she asked her why she was in such haste. She said she must be going, though perhaps she might not go her journey until Monday; and told Mrs. Bargrave she hoped she should see her again at her cousin Watson's before she went whither she was going. Then she said she would take her leave of her, and walked from Mrs. Bargrave in her view, till a turning interrupted the sight of her, which was three-quarters after one in the afternoon.

Mrs. Veal died the 7th of September, at twelve o'clock at noon, of her fits, and had not above four hours' sense before death, in which time she received the sacrament. The next day after Mrs. Veal's appearing, being Sunday, Mrs. Bargrave was so mightily indisposed with a cold and a sore throat, that she could not go out that day; but on Monday morning she sent a person to Captain Watson's to know if Mrs. Veal was there. They wondered at Mrs. Bargrave's inquiry, and sent her word that she was not there, nor was expected. At this answer, Mrs. Bargrave told the maid she had certainly mistook the name or made some blunder. And though she was ill, she put on her hood, and went herself to Captain Watson's, though she knew none of the family, to see if Mrs. Veal was there or not. They said they wondered at her asking, for that she had not been in town; they were sure, if she had, she would have been there. Says Mrs. Bargrave, "I am sure she was with me on Saturday almost two hours." They said it was impossible; for they must have seen her, if she had. In comes Captain Watson while they are in dispute, and said that Mrs. Veal was certainly dead, and her escutcheons were making. This strangely surprised Mrs. Bargrave, when she sent to the person immediately who had the care of them, and found it true. Then she related the whole story to Captain Watson's family, and what gown she had on, and how striped, and that Mrs. Veal told her it was scoured. Then Mrs. Watson cried out, "You have seen her indeed, for none knew but Mrs. Veal and myself that the gown was scoured." And Mrs. Watson owned that she described the gown exactly; "for," said she, "I helped her to make it up." This Mrs. Watson blazed all about the town, and avouched the demonstration of the truth of Mrs. Bargrave's seeing Mrs. Veal's apparition; and Captain Watson carried two gentlemen immediately to Mrs. Bargrave's house to hear the relation from her own mouth. And when it spread so fast that gentlemen and persons of quality, the judicious and skeptical part of the world, flocked in upon her, it at last became such a task that she was forced to go out of the way; for they were in general extremely well satisfied of the truth of the thing, and plainly saw that Mrs. Bargrave was no hypochondriac, for she always appears with such a cheerful air and pleasing mien, that she has gained the favor and esteem of all the gentry, and it is thought a great favor if they can but get the relation from her own mouth. I should have told you before that Mrs. Veal told Mrs. Bargrave that her sister and brother-in-law were just come down from London to see her. Says Mrs. Bargrave, "How came you to order matters so strangely?" "It could not be helped," said Mrs. Veal. And her brother and sister did come to see her, and entered the town of Dover just as Mrs. Veal was expiring. Mrs. Bargrave asked her whether she would drink some tea. Says Mrs. Veal, "I do not care if I do; but I'll warrant you this mad fellow" (meaning Mrs. Bargrave's husband) "has broken all your trinkets." "But," says Mrs. Bargrave, "I'll get something to drink in for all that." But Mrs. Veal waived it, and said, "It is no matter; let it alone;" and so it passed.

All the time I sat with Mrs. Bargrave, which was some hours, she recollected fresh sayings of Mrs. Veal. And one material thing more she told Mrs. Bargrave—that old Mr. Breton allowed Mrs. Veal ten pounds a year, which was a secret, and unknown to Mrs. Bargrave till Mrs. Veal told it her. Mrs. Bargrave never varies in her story, which puzzles those who doubt of the truth or are unwilling to believe it. A servant in the neighbor's yard adjoining to Mrs. Bargrave's house heard her talking to somebody an hour of the time Mrs. Veal was with her. Mrs. Bargrave went out to her next neighbor's the very moment she parted with Mrs. Veal, and told her what ravishing conversation she had with an old friend, and told the whole of it. Drelincourt's *Book of Death* is, since this happened, bought up strangely. And it is to be observed that, notwithstanding all the trouble and fatigue Mrs. Bargrave has undergone upon this account, she never took the value of a farthing, nor suffered her daughter to take anything of anybody, and therefore can have no interest in telling the story.

But Mr. Veal does what he can to stifle the matter, and said he would see Mrs. Bargrave; but yet it is certain matter of fact that he has been at Captain Watson's since the death of his sister, and yet never went near Mrs. Bargrave; and some of his friends report her to be a liar, and that she knew of Mr. Breton's ten pounds a year. But the person who pretends to say so has the reputation of a notorious liar among persons whom I know to be of undoubted credit. Now, Mr. Veal is more of a gentleman than to say she lies, but says a bad husband has crazed her. But she needs only present herself and it will effectually confute that pretense. Mr. Veal says he asked his sister on her death-bed whether she had a mind to dispose of anything, and she said no. Now, the things which Mrs. Veal's apparition would have disposed of were so trifling, and nothing of justice aimed at in their disposal, that the design of it appears to me to be only in order to make Mrs. Bargrave so to demonstrate the truth of her appearance, as to satisfy the world of the reality thereof as to what she had seen and heard, and to secure her reputation among the reasonable and understanding part of mankind. And then again Mr. Veal owns that there was a purse of gold; but it was not found in her cabinet, but in a comb-box. This looks improbable; for that Mrs. Watson owned that Mrs. Veal was so very careful of the key of the cabinet that she would trust nobody with it; and if so, no doubt she would not trust her gold out of it. And Mrs. Veal's often drawing her hand over her eyes, and asking Mrs. Bargrave whether her fits had not impaired her, looks to me as if she did it on purpose to remind Mrs. Bargrave of her fits, to prepare her not to think it strange that she should put her upon writing to her brother to dispose of rings and gold, which looks so much like a dying person's request; and it took accordingly with Mrs. Bargrave, as the effects of her fits coming upon her; and was one of the many instances of her wonderful love to her and care of her that she should not be affrighted, which indeed appears in her whole management, particularly in her coming to her in the daytime, waiving the salutation, and when she was alone, and then the manner of her parting to prevent a second attempt to salute her.

Now, why Mr. Veal should think this relation a reflection, as it is plain he does by his endeavoring to stifle it, I cannot imagine, because the generality believe her to be a good spirit, her discourse was so heavenly. Her two great errands were to comfort Mrs. Bargrave in her affliction, and to ask her forgiveness for the breach of friendship, and with a pious discourse to encourage her. So that after all to suppose that Mrs. Bargrave could hatch such an invention as this from Friday noon to Saturday noon, supposing that she knew of Mrs. Veal's death the very first moment, without jumbling circumstances, and without any interest too, she must be more witty, fortunate, and wicked too than any indifferent person, I dare say, will allow. I asked Mrs. Bargrave several times if she was sure she felt the gown. She answered modestly, "If my senses are to be relied on, I am sure of it." I asked her if she heard a sound when she clapped her hands upon her knees. She said she did not remember she did, but said she appeared to be as much a substance as I did, who talked with her. "And I may," said she, "be as soon persuaded that your apparition is talking to me now as that I did not really see her; for I was under no manner of fear, and received her as a friend, and parted with her as such. I would not," says she, "give one farthing to make anyone believe it; I have no interest in it. Nothing but trouble is entailed upon me for a long time, for aught I know; and had it not come to light by accident, it would never have been made public." But now she says she will make her own private use of it, and keep herself out of the way as much as she can; and so she has done since. She says she had a gentleman who came thirty miles to her to hear the relation, and that she had told it to a room full of people at a time. Several particular gentlemen have had the story from Mrs. Bargrave's own mouth.

This thing has very much affected me, and I am as well satisfied as I am of the best grounded matter of fact. And why we should dispute matter of fact because we cannot solve things of which we have no certain or demonstrative notions, seems strange to me. Mrs. Bargrave's authority and sincerity alone would have been undoubted in any other case.

JONATHAN SWIFT

Gulliver's Travels

PART I

A VOYAGE TO LILLIPUT

CHAPTER I

The Author gives some account of himself and family, his first inducements to travel. He is shipwrecked, and swims for his life, gets safe on shore in the country of *Lilliput,* is made a prisoner, and is carried up country.

My father had a small estate in Nottinghamshire; I was the third of five sons. He sent me to Emanuel College in Cambridge, at fourteen years old, where I resided three years, and applied myself close to my studies; but the charge of maintaining me (although I had a very scanty allowance) being too great for a narrow fortune, I was bound apprentice to Mr. James Bates, an eminent surgeon in London, with whom I continued four years; and my father now and then sending me small sums of money, I laid them out in learning navigation, and other parts of the mathematics, useful to those who intend to travel, as I always believed it would be some time or other my for-

Swift, *Gulliver's Travels.* Jonathan Swift was born in Dublin in 1667 and died there in 1745. He became secretary to Sir William Temple and was eventually made Dean of St. Patrick's in Dublin.

tune to do. When I left Mr. Bates, I went down to my father; where, by the assistance of him and my uncle John, and some other relations, I got forty pounds, and a promise of thirty pounds a year to maintain me at Leyden: there I studied physic two years and seven months, knowing it would be useful in long voyages.

Soon after my return from Leyden, I was recommended by my good master, Mr. Bates, to be surgeon to the *Swallow,* Captain Abraham Pannell, commander; with whom I continued three years and a half, making a voyage or two into the Levant, and some other parts. When I came back I resolved to settle in London, to which Mr. Bates, my master, encouraged me, and by him I was recommended to several patients. I took part of a small house in the Old Jury; and being advised to alter my condition, I married Mrs. Mary Burton, second daughter to Mr. Edmund Burton, hosier, in Newgate-street, with whom I received four hundred pounds for a portion.

But, my good master Bates dying in two years after, and I having few friends, my business began to fail; for my conscience would not suffer me to imitate the bad practice of too many among my brethren. Having therefore consulted with my wife, and some of my acquaintance, I determined to go again to sea. I was surgeon successively in two ships, and made several voyages, for six years, to the East and West-Indies, by which I got some addition to my fortune. My hours of leisure I spent in reading the best authors, ancient and modern, being always provided with a good number of books; and when I was ashore, in observing the manners and dispositions of the people, as well as learning their language, wherein I had a great facility by the strength of my memory.

The last of these voyages not proving very fortunate, I grew weary of the sea, and intended to stay at home with my wife and family. I removed from the Old Jury to Fetter-Lane, and from thence to Wapping, hoping to get business among the sailors; but it would not turn to account. After three years expectation that things would mend, I accepted an advantageous offer from Captain William Prichard, master of the *Antelope,* who was making a voyage to the South-Sea. We set sail from Bristol, May 4, 1699, and our voyage at first was very prosperous.

It would not be proper, for some reasons, to trouble the reader with the particulars of our adventures in those seas: let it suffice to inform him,

that in our passage from thence to the East-Indies, we were driven by a violent storm to the northwest of Van Diemen's Land.[1] By an observation, we found ourselves in the latitude of 30 degrees 2 minutes south. Twelve of our crew were dead by immoderate labor, and ill food, the rest were in a very weak condition. On the fifth of November, which was the beginning of summer in those parts, the weather being very hazy, the seamen spied a rock, within half a cable's length of the ship; but the wind was so strong, that we were driven directly upon it, and immediately split. Six of the crew, of whom I was one, having let down the boat into the sea, made a shift to get clear of the ship, and the rock. We rowed, by my computation, about three leagues, till we were able to work no longer, being already spent with labor while we were in the ship. We therefore trusted ourselves to the mercy of the waves, and in about half an hour the boat was overset by a sudden flurry from the north. What became of my companions in the boat, as well as of those who escaped on the rock, or were left in the vessel, I cannot tell; but conclude they were all lost. For my own part, I swam as fortune directed me, and was pushed forward by wind and tide. I often let my legs drop, and could feel no bottom: but when I was almost gone, and able to struggle no longer, I found myself within my depth; and by this time the storm was much abated. The declivity was so small, that I walked near a mile before I got to the shore, which I conjectured was about eight o'clock in the evening. I then advanced forward near half a mile, but could not discover any sign of houses or inhabitants; at least I was in so weak a condition, that I did not observe them. I was extremely tired, and with that, and the heat of the weather, and about half a pint of brandy that I drank as I left the ship, I found myself much inclined to sleep. I lay down on the grass, which was very short and soft, where I slept sounder than ever I remember to have done in my life, and, as I reckoned, about nine hours; for when I awaked, it was just daylight. I attempted to rise, but was not able to stir: for as I happened to lie on my back, I found my arms and legs were strongly fastened on each side to the ground; and my hair, which was long and thick, tied down in the same manner. I likewise felt several slender ligatures across my body, from my arm-pits to my thighs. I could only look upwards, the sun began to grow hot, and the light offended my eyes. I heard a confused noise about

---

[1] The old name for Tasmania; perhaps Australia is meant.

me, but in the posture I lay, could see nothing except the sky. In a little time I felt something alive moving on my left leg, which advancing gently forward over my breast, came almost up to my chin; when bending my eyes downwards as much as I could, I perceived it to be a human creature not six inches high, with a bow and arrow in his hands, and a quiver at his back. In the mean time, I felt at least forty more of the same kind (as I conjectured) following the first. I was in the utmost astonishment, and roared so loud, that they all ran back in a fright; and some of them, as I was afterwards told, were hurt with the falls they got by leaping from my sides upon the ground. However, they soon returned, and one of them, who ventured so far as to get a full sight of my face, lifting up his hands and eyes by way of admiration, cried out in a shrill, but distinct voice, *Hekinah degul:* the others repeated the same words several times, but then I knew not what they meant. I lay all this while, as the reader may believe, in great uneasiness: at length, struggling to get loose, I had the fortune to break the strings, and wrench out the pegs that fastened my left arm to the ground; for, by lifting it up to my face, I discovered the methods they had taken to bind me, and at the same time with a violent pull, which gave me excessive pain, I a little loosened the strings that tied down my hair on the left side, so that I was just able to turn my head about two inches. But the creatures ran off a second time, before I could seize them; whereupon there was a great shout in a very shrill accent, and after it ceased, I heard one of them cry aloud *Tolgo phonac;* when in an instant I felt above an hundred arrows discharged on my left hand, which pricked me like so many needles; and besides, they shot another flight into the air, as we do bombs in Europe, whereof many, I suppose, fell on my body, (though I felt them not) and some on my face, which I immediately covered with my left hand. When this shower of arrows was over, I fell a groaning with grief and pain, and then striving again to get loose, they discharged another volley larger than the first, and some of them attempted with spears to stick me in the sides; but, by good luck, I had on a buff jerkin, which they could not pierce. I thought it the most prudent method to lie still, and my design was to continue so till night, when, my left hand being already loose, I could easily free myself: and as for the inhabitants, I had reason to believe I might be a match for the greatest armies they could bring

against me, if they were all of the same size with him that I saw. But fortune disposed otherwise of me. When the people observed I was quiet, they discharged no more arrows; but, by the noise I heard, I knew their numbers increased; and about four yards from me, over-against my right ear, I heard a knocking for above an hour, like that of people at work; when turning my head that way, as well as the pegs and strings would permit me, I saw a stage erected, about a foot and a half from the ground, capable of holding four of the inhabitants, with two or three ladders to mount it: from whence one of them, who seemed to be a person of quality, made me a long speech, whereof I understood not one syllable. But I should have mentioned, that before the principal person began his oration, he cried out three times, *Langro dehul san:* (these words and the former were afterwards repeated and explained to me). Whereupon immediately about fifty of the inhabitants came and cut the strings that fastened the left side of my head, which gave me the liberty of turning it to the right, and of observing the person and gesture of him that was to speak. He appeared to be of a middle age, and taller than any of the other three who attended him, whereof one was a page that held up his train, and seemed to be somewhat longer than my middle finger; the other two stood one on each side to support him. He acted every part of an orator, and I could observe many periods of threatenings, and others of promises, pity, and kindness. I answered in a few words, but in the most submissive manner, lifting up my left hand, and both my eyes to the sun, as calling him for a witness; and being almost famished with hunger, having not eaten a morsel for some hours before I left the ship, I found the demands of nature so strong upon me, that I could not forbear showing my impatience (perhaps against the strict rules of decency) by putting my finger frequently on my mouth, to signify that I wanted food. The *Hurgo* (for so they call a great lord, as I afterwards learnt) understood me very well. He descended from the stage, and commanded that several ladders should be applied to my sides, on which above an hundred of the inhabitants mounted and walked towards my mouth, laden with baskets full of meat, which had been provided and sent thither by the King's orders, upon the first intelligence he received of me. I observed there was the flesh of several animals, but could not distinguish them by the taste. There were shoulders, legs, and loins, shaped like those of mutton, and very well dressed, but smaller than the wings of a lark. I eat them by two or three at a mouthful, and took three loaves at a time, about the bigness of musket bullets. They supplied me as fast as they could, showing a thousand marks of wonder and astonishment at my bulk and appetite. I then made another sign that I wanted drink. They found by my eating, that a small quantity would not suffice me; and being a most ingenious people, they slung up with great dexterity one of their largest hogsheads, then rolled it towards my hand, and beat out the top; I drank it off at a draught, which I might well do, for it did not hold half a pint, and tasted like a small wine of Burgundy, but much more delicious. They brought me a second hogshead, which I drank in the same manner, and made signs for more, but they had none to give me. When I had performed these wonders, they shouted for joy, and danced upon my breast, repeating several times as they did at first, *Hekinah degul.* They made me a sign that I should throw down the two hogsheads, but first warning the people below to stand out of the way, crying aloud, *Borach mivola,* and when they saw the vessels in the air, there was an universal shout of *Hekinah degul.* I confess I was often tempted while they were passing backwards and forwards on my body, to seize forty or fifty of the first that came in my reach, and dash them against the ground. But the remembrance of what I had felt, which probably might not be the worst they could do, and the promise of honor I made them, for so I interpreted my submissive behavior, soon drove out these imaginations. Besides, I now considered myself as bound by the laws of hospitality to a people who had treated me with so much expense and magnificence. However, in my thoughts, I could not sufficiently wonder at the intrepidity of these diminutive mortals, who durst venture to mount and walk upon my body, while one of my hands was at liberty, without trembling at the very sight of so prodigious a creature as I must appear to them. After some time, when they observed that I made no more demands for meat, there appeared before me a person of high rank from his Imperial Majesty. His Excellency, having mounted on the small of my right leg, advanced forwards up to my face, with about a dozen of his retinue. And producing his credentials under the Signet Royal, which he applied close to my eyes, spoke about ten minutes, without any signs of anger, but with a kind of determinate resolution; often pointing forwards, which, as I afterwards found, was towards the capital city, about half a mile distant, whither it was agreed by his Majesty in council that I must be conveyed. I answered in few words, but to no purpose, and made a sign with my hand that was loose, putting it to the other (but over his Excellency's head for fear of hurting him or his train) and then to my own head and body, to signify that I desired my liberty. It appeared that he understood me well enough, for he shook his head by way of disapprobation, and held his hand in a posture to show that I must be carried as a prisoner. However, he made other signs to let me understand that I should have meat and drink enough, and very good treatment. Whereupon I once more thought of attempting to break my bonds; but again, when I felt the smart of their arrows, upon my face and hands, which were all in blisters, and many of the darts still sticking in them, and observing likewise that the number of my enemies increased, I gave tokens to let them know that they might do with me what they pleased. Upon this, the *Hurgo* and his train withdrew, with much civility and cheerful countenances. Soon after I heard a general shout, with frequent repetitions of the words, *Peplom selan,* and I felt great numbers of people on my left side relaxing the cords to such a degree, that I was able to turn upon my right, and to ease myself with making water; which I very plentifully did, to the great astonishment of the people, who conjecturing by my motions what I was going to do, immediately opened to the right and left on that side to avoid the torrent which fell with such noise and violence from me. But before this, they had daubed my face and both my hands with a sort of ointment very pleasant to the smell, which in a few minutes removed all the smart of their arrows. These circumstances, added to the refreshment I had received by their victuals and drink, which were very nourishing, disposed me to sleep. I slept about eight hours, as I was afterwards assured; and it was no wonder, for the physicians, by the Emperor's order, had mingled a sleepy potion in the hogshead of wine.

It seems that upon the first moment I was discovered sleeping on the ground after my landing, the Emperor had early notice of it by an express; and determined in council that I should be tied in the manner I have related, (which was done in the night while I slept) that plenty of meat and drink should be sent to me, and a machine prepared to carry me to the capital city.

This resolution perhaps may appear very bold

and dangerous, and I am confident would not be imitated by any prince in Europe on the like occasion; however, in my opinion, it was extremely prudent, as well as generous: for supposing these people had endeavored to kill me with their spears and arrows while I was asleep, I should certainly have awaked with the first sense of smart, which might so far have roused my rage and strength, as to have enabled me to break the strings wherewith I was tied; after which, as they were not able to make resistance, so they could expect no mercy.

These people are most excellent mathematicians, and arrived to a great perfection in mechanics, by the countenance and encouragement of the Emperor, who is a renowned patron of learning. This prince hath several machines fixed on wheels, for the carriage of trees and other great weights. He often builds his largest men of war, whereof some are nine foot long, in the woods where the timber grows, and has them carried on these engines three or four hundred yards to the sea. Five hundred carpenters and engineers were immediately set at work to prepare the greatest engine they had. It was a frame of wood raised three inches from the ground, about seven foot long and four wide, moving upon twenty-two wheels. The shout I heard was upon the arrival of this engine, which it seems set out in four hours after my landing. It was brought parallel to me as I lay. But the principal difficulty was to raise and place me in this vehicle. Eighty poles, each of one foot high, were erected for this purpose, and very strong cords of the bigness of packthread were fastened by hooks to many bandages, which the workmen had girt round my neck, my hands, my body, and my legs. Nine hundred of the strongest men were employed to draw up these cords by many pulleys fastened on the poles, and thus, in less than three hours, I was raised and slung into the engine, and there tied fast. All this I was told, for, while the whole operation was performing, I lay in a profound sleep, by the force of that soporiferous medicine infused into my liquor. Fifteen hundred of the Emperor's largest horses, each about four inches and a half high, were employed to draw me towards the metropolis, which, as I said, was half a mile distant.

About four hours after we began our journey, I awaked by a very ridiculous accident; for the carriage being stopped a while to adjust something that was out of order, two or three of the young natives had the curiosity to see how I looked when I was asleep; they climbed up into the engine, and advancing very sortly to my face, one of them, an officer in the guards, put the sharp end of his half-pike a good way up into my left nostril, which tickled my nose like a straw, and made me sneeze violently: whereupon they stole off unperceived, and it was three weeks before I knew the cause of my awaking so suddenly. We made a long march the remaining part of that day, and rested at night with five hundred guards on each side of me, half with torches, and half with bows and arrows, ready to shoot me if I should offer to stir. The next morning at sun-rise we continued our march, and arrived within two hundred yards of the city gates about noon. The Emperor, and all his court, came out to meet us; but his great officers would by no means suffer his Majesty to endanger his person by mounting on my body.

At the place where the carriage stopped, there stood an ancient temple, esteemed to be the largest in the whole kingdom; which having been polluted some years before by an unnatural murder, was, according to the zeal of those people, looked upon as profane, and therefore had been applied to common uses, and all the ornaments and furniture carried away. In this edifice it was determined I should lodge. The great gate fronting to the north was about four foot high, and almost two foot wide, through which I could easily creep. On each side of the gate was a small window not above six inches from the ground: into that on the left side, the King's smiths conveyed fourscore and eleven chains, like those that hang to a lady's watch in Europe, and almost as large, which were locked to my left leg with six and thirty padlocks. Over-against this temple, on t'other side of the great highway, at twenty foot distance, there was a turret at least five foot high. Here the Emperor ascended, with many principal lords of his court, to have an opportunity of viewing me, as I was told, for I could not see them. It was reckoned that above an hundred thousand inhabitants came out of the town upon the same errand; and, in spite of my guards, I believe there could not be fewer than ten thousand at several times, who mounted my body by the help of ladders. But a proclamation was soon issued to forbid it upon pain of death. When the workmen found it was impossible for me to break loose, they cut all the strings that bound me; whereupon I rose up, with as melancholy a disposition as ever I had in my life. But the noise and astonishment of the people at seeing me rise and walk, are not to be expressed. The chains that held my left leg were about two yards long, and gave me not only the liberty of walking backwards and forwards in a semicircle; but, being fixed within four inches of the gate, allowed me to creep in, and lie at my full length in the temple.

CHAPTER II

The Emperor of *Lilliput,* attended by several of the nobility, comes to see the Author in his confinement. The Emperor's person and habit described. Learned men appointed to teach the Author their language. He gains favor by his mild disposition. His pockets are searched, and his sword and pistols taken from him.

When I found myself on my feet, I looked about me and must confess I never beheld a more entertaining prospect. The country round appeared like a continued garden, and the inclosed fields, which were generally forty foot square, resembled so many beds of flowers. These fields were intermingled with woods of half a stang, and the tallest trees, as I could judge, appeared to be seven foot high. I viewed the town on my left hand, which looked like the painted scene of a city in a theater. The Emperor was already descended from the tower, and advancing on horseback towards me, which had like to have cost him dear; for the beast, though very well trained, yet wholly unused to such a sight, which appeared as if a mountain moved before him, reared up on his hinder feet: but that prince, who is an excellent horseman, kept his seat, till his attendants ran in, and held the bridle, while his Majesty had time to dismount. When he alighted, he surveyed me round with great admiration, but kept beyond the length of my chain. He ordered his cooks and butlers, who were already prepared, to give me victuals and drink, which they pushed forward in a sort of vehicles upon wheels, till I could reach them. I took these vehicles, and soon emptied them all; twenty of them were filled with meat, and ten with liquor; each of the former afforded me two or three good mouthfuls, and I emptied the liquor of ten vessels, which was contained in earthen vials, into one vehicle, drinking it off at a draught; and so I did with the rest. The Empress, and young Princes of the blood of both sexes, attended by many ladies, sat at some distance in their chairs; but upon the accident that happened to the Emperor's horse, they alighted, and came near his person, which I am now going to describe. He is taller by almost the breadth of my nail, than any

of his court; which alone is enough to strike an awe into the beholders. His features are strong and masculine, with an Austrian lip and arched nose, his complexion olive, his countenance erect, his body and limbs well proportioned, all his motions graceful, and his deportment majestic. He was then past his prime, being twenty-eight years and three quarters old, of which he had reigned about seven, in great felicity, and generally victorious. For the better convenience of beholding him, I lay on my side, so that my face was parallel to his, and he stood but three yards off: however, I have had him since many times in my hand, and therefore cannot be deceived in the description. His dress was very plain and simple, and the fashion of it between the Asiatic and the European: but he had on his head a light helmet of gold, adorned with jewels, and a plume on the crest. He held his sword drawn in his hand, to defend himself, if I should happen to break loose; it was almost three inches long, the hilt and scabbard were gold enriched with diamonds. His voice was shrill, but very clear and articulate, and I could distinctly hear it when I stood up. The ladies and courtiers were all most magnificently clad, so that the spot they stood upon seemed to resemble a petticoat spread on the ground, embroidered with figures of gold and silver. His Imperial Majesty spoke often to me, and I returned answers, but neither of us could understand a syllable. There were several of his priests and lawyers present (as I conjectured by their habits) who were commanded to address themselves to me, and I spoke to them in as many languages as I had the least smattering of, which were High and Low Dutch, Latin, French, Spanish, Italian, and Lingua Franca; but all to no purpose. After about two hours the court retired, and I was left with a strong guard, to prevent the impertinence, and probably the malice of the rabble, who were very impatient to crowd about me as near as they durst, and some of them had the impudence to shoot their arrows at me as I sat on the ground by the door of my house, whereof one very narrowly missed my left eye. But the colonel ordered six of the ringleaders to be seized, and thought no punishment so proper as to deliver them bound into my hands, which some of his soldiers accordingly did, pushing them forwards with the butt-ends of their pikes into my reach; I took them all in my right hand, put five of them into my coat-pocket, and as to the sixth, I made a countenance as if I would eat him alive. The poor man squalled terribly, and the colonel and his officers were in much pain, especially when they saw me take out my pen-knife: but I soon put them out of fear: for, looking mildly, and immediately cutting the strings he was bound with, I set him gently on the ground, and away he ran. I treated the rest in the same manner, taking them one by one out of my pocket, and I observed both the soldiers and people were highly obliged at this mark of my clemency, which was represented very much to my advantage at court.

Towards night I got with some difficulty into my house, where I lay on the ground, and continued to do so about a fortnight; during which time the Emperor gave orders to have a bed prepared for me. Six hundred beds of the common measure were brought in carriages, and worked up in my house; an hundred and fifty of their beds sewn together made up the breadth and length, and these were four double, which however kept me but very indifferently from the hardness of the floor, that was of smooth stone. By the same computation they provided me with sheets, blankets, and coverlets, tolerable enough for one who had been so long inured to hardships as I.

As the news of my arrival spread through the kingdom, it brought prodigious numbers of rich, idle, and curious people to see me; so that the villages were almost emptied, and great neglect of tillage and household affairs must have ensued, if his Imperial Majesty had not provided, by several proclamations and orders of state, against this inconveniency. He directed that those who had already beheld me should return home, and not presume to come within fifty yards of my house without license from court; whereby the secretaries of state got considerable fees.

In the meantime, the Emperor held frequent councils to debate what course should be taken with me; and I was afterwards assured by a particular friend, a person of great quality, who was looked upon to be as much in the secret as any, that the court was under many difficulties concerning me. They apprehended my breaking loose, that my diet would be very expensive, and might cause a famine. Sometimes they determined to starve me, or at least to shoot me in the face and hands with poisoned arrows, which would soon dispatch me; but again they considered, that the stench of so large a carcass might produce a plague in the metropolis, and probably spread through the whole kingdom. In the midst of these consultations, several officers of the army went to the door of the great council-chamber; and two of them being admitted, gave an account of my behavior to the six criminals above-mentioned, which made so favorable an impression in the breast of his Majesty and the whole board, in my behalf, that an Imperial Commission was issued out, obliging all the villages nine hundred yards round the city, to deliver in every morning six beeves, forty sheep, and other victuals for my sustenance; together with a proportionable quantity of bread, and wine, and other liquors; for the due payment of which his Majesty gave assignments upon his treasury. For this prince lives chiefly upon his own demesnes, seldom, except upon great occasions, raising any subsidies upon his subjects, who are bound to attend him in his wars at their own expense. An establishment was also made of six hundred persons to be my domestics, who had board-wages allowed for their maintenance, and tents built for them very conveniently on each side of my door. It was likewise ordered, that three hundred tailors should make me a suit of clothes after the fashion of the country: that six of his Majesty's greatest scholars should be employed to instruct me in their language: and, lastly, that the Emperor's horses, and those of the nobility, and troops of guards, should be frequently exercised in my sight, to accustom themselves to me. All these orders were duly put in execution, and in about three weeks I made a great progress in learning their language; during which time, the Emperor frequently honored me with his visits, and was pleased to assist my masters in teaching me. We began already to converse together in some sort; and the first words I learnt were to express my desire that he would please give me my liberty, which I every day repeated on my knees. His answer, as I could comprehend it, was, that this must be a work of time, not to be thought on without the advice of his council, and that first I must *Lumos kelmin pesso desmar lon Emposo;* that is, swear a peace with him and his kingdom. However, that I should be used with all kindness; and he advised me to acquire, by my patience and discreet behavior, the good opinion of himself and his subjects. He desired I would not take it ill, if he gave orders to certain proper officers to search me; for probably I might carry about me several weapons, which must needs be dangerous things, if they answered the bulk of so prodigious a person. I said, his Majesty should be satisfied, for I was ready to strip myself, and turn up my pockets before him. This I delivered part in words, and part in signs. He replied, that by the laws of the kingdom I must be searched by two of his officers; that he knew this could not be done without my consent and assistance; that he had so good an opinion of my generosity and justice, as to trust their persons in my hands: that whatever they took from me should be returned when I left the country, or paid for at the rate which I would set upon them. I took up the two officers in my hands, put them first into my coat-pockets, and then into every other pocket about me, except my two fobs, and another secret pocket which I had no mind should be searched, wherein I had some little necessaries that were of no consequence to any but myself. In one of my fobs there was a silver watch, and in the other a small quantity of gold in a purse. These gentlemen, having pen, ink, and paper about them, made an exact inventory of every thing they saw; and when they had done, desired I would set them down, that they might deliver it to the Emperor. This inventory I afterwards translated into English, and is word for word as follows.

Imprimis, In the right coat-pocket of the Great Man-Mountain (for so I interpret the words *Quinbus Flestrin*) after the strictest search, we found only one great piece of coarse cloth, large enough to be a foot-cloth for your Majesty's chief room of state. In the left pocket we saw a huge silver chest, with a cover of the same metal, which we, the searchers, were not able to lift. We desired it should be opened, and one of us stepping into it, found himself up to the mid leg in a sort of dust, some part whereof flying up to our faces, set us both a sneezing for several times together. In his right waistcoat-pocket we found a prodigious bundle of white thin substances, folded one over another, about the bigness of three men, tied with a strong cable, and marked with black figures; which we humbly conceive to be writings, every letter almost half as large as the palm of our hands. In the left there was a sort of engine, from the back of which were extended twenty long poles, resembling the pallisados before your Majesty's court; wherewith we conjecture the Man-Mountain combs his head; for we did not always trouble him with questions, because we found it a great difficulty to make him understand us. In the large pocket on the right side of his middle cover (so I translate the word *ranfu-lo,* by which they meant my breeches) we saw a hollow pillar of iron, about the length of a man, fastened to a strong piece of timber, larger than

the pillar; and upon one side of the pillar were huge pieces of iron sticking out, cut into strange figures, which we know not what to make of. In the left pocket, another engine of the same kind. In the smaller pocket on the right side, were several round flat pieces of white and red metal, of different bulk; some of the white, which seemed to be silver, were so large and heavy, that my comrade and I could hardly lift them. In the left pocket were two black pillars irregularly shaped: we could not, without difficulty, reach the top of them as we stood at the bottom of his pocket. One of them was covered, and seemed all of a piece: but at the upper end of the other, there appeared a white round substance, about twice the bigness of our heads. Within each of these was enclosed a prodigious plate of steel; which, by our orders, we obliged him to show us, because we apprehended they might be dangerous engines. He took them out of their cases, and told us, that in his own country his practice was to shave his beard with one of these, and cut his meat with the other. There were two pockets which we could not enter: these he called his fobs; they were two large slits cut into the top of his middle cover, but squeezed close by the pressure of his belly. Out of the right fob hung a great silver chain, with a wonderful kind of engine at the bottom. We directed him to draw out whatever was fastened to that chain; which appeared to be a globe, half silver, and half of some transparent metal; for, on the transparent side, we saw certain strange figures circularly drawn, and thought we could touch them, till we found our fingers stopped by that lucid substance. He put this engine to our ears, which made an incessant noise like that of a water-mill. And we conjecture it is either some unknown animal, or the god that he worships; but we are more inclined to the latter opinion, because he assured us, (if we understood him right, for he expressed himself very imperfectly) that he seldom did any thing without consulting it. He called it his oracle, and said it pointed out the time for every action of his life. From the left fob he took out a net almost large enough for a fisherman, but contrived to open and shut like a purse, and served him for the same use: we found therein several massy pieces of yellow metal, which, if they be real gold, must be of immense value.

Having thus, in obedience to your Majesty's commands, diligently searched all his pockets, we observed a girdle about his waist made of the hide of some prodigious animal; from which, on the left side, hung a sword of the length of five men; and on the right, a bag or pouch divided into two cells, each cell capable of holding three of your Majesty's subjects. In one of these cells were several globes or balls of a most ponderous metal, about the bigness of our heads, and requiring a strong hand to lift them: the other cell contained a heap of certain black grains, but of no great bulk or weight, for we could hold above fifty of them in the palms of our hands.

This is an exact inventory of what we found about the body of the Man-Mountain, who used us with great civility, and due respect to your Majesty's Commission. Signed and sealed on the fourth day of the eighty-ninth moon of your Majesty's auspicious reign.

CLEFRIN FRELOCK, MARSI FRELOCK.

When this inventory was read over to the Emperor, he directed me, although in very gentle terms, to deliver up the several particulars. He first called for my scimitar, which I took out, scabbard and all. In the mean time he ordered three thousand of his choicest troops (who then attended him) to surround me at a distance, with their bows and arrows just ready to discharge: but I did not observe it, for my eyes were wholly fixed upon his Majesty. He then desired me to draw my scimitar, which, although it had got some rust by the sea-water, was in most parts exceeding bright. I did so, and immediately all the troops gave a shout between terror and surprise; for the sun shone clear, and the reflection dazzled their eyes, as I waved the scimitar to and fro in my hand. His Majesty, who is a most magnanimous prince, was less daunted than I could expect; he ordered me to return it into the scabbard, and cast it on the ground as gently as I could, about six foot from the end of my chain. The next thing he demanded, was one of the hollow iron pillars, by which he meant my pocket-pistols. I drew it out, and at his desire, as well as I could, expressed to him the use of it; and charging it only with powder, which, by the closeness of my pouch, happened to escape wetting in the sea (an inconvenience against which all prudent mariners take special care to provide,) I first cautioned the Emperor not to be afraid, and then I let it off in the air. The astonishment here was much greater than at the sight of my scimitar. Hundreds fell down as if they had been struck dead; and even the Emperor, although he stood his ground, could not recover himself in some time. I delivered up both my pistols in the same manner as I had done my scimitar, and then my pouch of powder and bullets; begging him that the former might be kept from fire, for it would kindle with the smallest spark, and blow up his imperial palace into the air. I likewise delivered up my watch, which the Emperor was very curious to see, and commanded two of his tallest yeomen of the guards to bear it on a pole upon their shoulders, as draymen in England do a barrel of ale. He was amazed at the continual noise it made, and the motion of the minute-hand, which he could easily discern; for their sight is much more acute than ours: and asked the opinions of his learned men about him, which were various and remote, as the reader may well imagine without my repeating; although indeed I could not very perfectly understand them. I then gave up my silver and copper money, my purse, with nine large pieces of gold, and some smaller ones; my knife and razor, my comb and silver snuff-box, my handkerchief and journal-book. My scimitar, pistols, and pouch, were conveyed in carriages to his Majesty's stores; but the rest of my goods were returned to me.

I had, as I before observed, one private pocket which escaped their search, wherein there was a pair of spectacles, (which I sometimes use for the weakness of my eyes) a pocket perspective, and several other little conveniences; which being of no consequence to the Emperor, I did not think myself bound in honor to discover, and I apprehended they might be lost or spoiled if I ventured them out of my possession.

CHAPTER III

The Author diverts the Emperor, and his nobility of both sexes, in a very uncommon manner. The diversions of the court of *Lilliput* described. The Author has his liberty granted him upon certain conditions.

My gentleness and good behavior had gained so far on the Emperor and his court, and indeed upon the army and people in general, that I began to conceive hopes of getting my liberty in a short time. I took all possible methods to cultivate this favorable disposition. The natives came by degrees to be less apprehensive of any danger from me. I would sometimes lie down, and let five or six of them dance on my hand. And at last the boys and girls would venture to come and play at hide and seek in my hair. I had now made a good progress in understanding and speaking their language.

The Emperor had a mind one day to entertain me with several of the country shows, wherein they exceed all nations I have known, both for dexterity and magnificence. I was diverted with none so much as that of the rope-dancers, performed upon a slender white thread, extended about two foot, and twelve inches from the ground. Upon which I shall desire liberty, with the reader's patience, to enlarge a little.

This diversion is only practiced by those persons who are candidates for great employments, and high favor, at court. They are trained in this art from their youth, and are not always of noble birth, or liberal education. When a great office is vacant, either by death or disgrace, (which often happens) five or six of those candidates petition the Emperor to entertain his Majesty and the court with a dance on the rope, and whoever jumps the highest without falling, succeeds in the office. Very often the chief ministers themselves are commanded to show their skill, and to convince the Emperor that they have not lost their faculty. Flimnap, the Treasurer, is allowed to cut a caper on the straight rope, at least an inch higher than any other lord in the whole empire. I have seen him do the summerset several times together upon a trencher fixed on the rope, which is no thicker than a common packthread in England. My friend Reldresal, principal Secretary for private Affairs, is, in my opinion, if I am not partial, the second after the Treasurer; the rest of the great officers are much upon a par.

These diversions are often attended with fatal accidents, whereof great numbers are on record. I myself have seen two or three candidates break a limb. But the danger is much greater when the ministers themselves are commanded to show their dexterity; for, by contending to excel themselves and their fellows, they strain so far, that there is hardly one of them who hath not received a fall, and some of them two or three. I was assured that a year or two before my arrival, Flimnap would have infallibly broke his neck, if one of the King's cushions, that accidentally lay on the ground, had not weakened the force of his fall.

There is likewise another diversion, which is only shown before the Emperor and Empress, and first minister, upon particular occasions. The Emperor lays on the table three fine silken threads of six inches long. One is blue, the other red, and the third green. These threads are proposed as prizes for those persons whom the Emperor hath a mind to distinguish by a peculiar mark of his favor. The ceremony is performed in his Majesty's great chamber of state, where the candidates are to undergo a trial of dexterity very different from the former, and such as I have not observed the least resemblance of in any other country of the old or the new world. The Emperor holds a stick in his hands, both ends parallel to the horizon, while the candidates advancing one by one, sometimes leap over the stick, sometimes creep under it backwards and forwards several times, according as the stick is advanced or depressed. Sometimes the Emperor holds one end of the stick, and his first minister the other; sometimes the minister has it entirely to himself. Whoever performs his part with most agility, and holds out the longest in leaping and creeping, is rewarded with the blue-colored silk; the red is given to the next, and the green to the third, which they all wear girt twice round about the middle; and you see few great persons about this court, who are not adorned with one of these girdles.

The horses of the army, and those of the royal stables, having been daily led before me, were no longer shy, but would come up to my very feet without starting. The riders would leap them over my hand as I held it on the ground, and one of the Emperor's huntsmen, upon a large courser, took my foot, shoe and all; which was indeed a prodigious leap. I had the good fortune to divert the Emperor one day after a very extraordinary manner. I desired he would order several sticks of two foot high, and the thickness of an ordinary cane, to be brought me; whereupon his Majesty commanded the master of his woods to give directions accordingly; and the next morning six woodmen arrived with as many carriages, drawn by eight horses to each. I took nine of these sticks, fixing them firmly in the ground in a quadrangular figure, two foot and a half square. I took four other sticks, and tied them parallel at each corner, about two foot from the ground; then I fastened my handkerchief to the nine sticks that stood erect, and extended it on all sides, till it was tight as the top of a drum; and the four parallel sticks rising about five inches higher than the handkerchief, served as ledges on each side. When I had finished my work, I desired the Emperor to let a troop of his best horse, twenty-four in number, come and exercise upon this plain. His Majesty approved of the proposal, and I took them up, one by one, in my hands, ready mounted and armed, with the proper officers to exercise them. As soon as they got into order, they divided into two parties, performed mock skirmishes, discharged blunt arrows, drew their swords, fled and pursued, attacked and retired, and in short discovered the best military discipline I ever beheld. The parallel sticks secured them and their horses from falling over the stage; and the Emperor was so much delighted that he ordered this entertainment to be repeated several days, and once was pleased to be lifted up and give the word of command; and, with great difficulty, persuaded even the Empress herself to let me hold her in her close chair within two yards of the stage, from whence she was able to take a full view of the whole performance. It was my good fortune that no ill accident happened in these entertainments, only once a fiery horse, that belonged to one of the captains, pawing with his hoof, struck a hole in my handkerchief, and his foot slipping, he overthrew his rider and himself; but I immediately relieved them both, and covering the hole with one hand, I set down the troop with the other, in the same manner as I took them up. The horse that fell was strained in the left shoulder, but the rider got no hurt, and I repaired my handkerchief as well as I could: however, I would not trust to the strength of it any more in such dangerous enterprises.

About two or three days before I was set at liberty, as I was entertaining the court with these kind of feats, there arrived an express to inform his Majesty, that some of his subjects riding near the place where I was first taken up, had seen a great black substance lying on the ground, very oddly shaped, extending its edges round as wide as his Majesty's bedchamber, and rising up in the middle as high as a man; that it was no living creature, as they at first apprehended, for it lay on the grass without motion, and some of them had walked round it several times: that by mounting upon each other's shoulders, they had got to the top, which was flat and even, and stamping upon it they found it was hollow within; that they humbly conceived it might be something belonging to the Man-Mountain; and if his Majesty pleased, they would undertake to bring it with only five horses. I presently knew what they meant, and was glad at heart to receive this intelligence. It seems upon my first reaching the shore after our shipwreck, I was in such confusion, that before I came to the place where I went to sleep, my hat, which I had fastened with a string to my head while I was rowing, and had stuck

on all the time I was swimming, fell off after I came to land; the string, as I conjecture, breaking by some accident which I never observed, but thought my hat had been lost at sea. I intreated his Imperial Majesty to give orders it might be brought to me as soon as possible, describing to him the use and the nature of it: and the next day the waggoners arrived with it, but not in a very good condition; they had bored two holes in the brim, within an inch and half of the edge, and fastened two hooks in the holes; these hooks were tied by a long cord to the harness, and thus my hat was dragged along for above half an English mile; but the ground in that country being extremely smooth and level, it received less damage than I expected.

Two days after this adventure, the Emperor having ordered that part of his army which quarters in and about his metropolis to be in readiness, took a fancy of diverting himself in a very singular manner. He desired I would stand like a Colossus, with my legs as far asunder as I conveniently could. He then commanded his General (who was an old experienced leader, and a great patron of mine) to draw up the troops in close order, and march them under me; the foot by twenty-four in a breast, and the horse by sixteen, with drums beating, colors flying, and pikes advanced. This body consisted of three thousand foot, and a thousand horse. His Majesty gave orders, upon pain of death, that every soldier in his march should observe the strictest decency with regard to my person; which, however, could not prevent some of the younger officers from turning up their eyes as they passed under me. And, to confess the truth, my breeches were at that time in so ill a condition, that they afforded some opportunities for laughter and admiration.

I had sent so many memorials and petitions for my liberty, that his Majesty at length mentioned the matter, first in the cabinet, and then in a full council; where it was opposed by none, except Skyresh Bolgolam,[2] who was pleased, without any provocation, to be my mortal enemy. But it was carried against him by the whole board, and confirmed by the Emperor. That minister was *Galbet,* or Admiral of the Realm, very much in his master's confidence, and a person well versed in affairs, but of a morose and sour complexion. However, he was at length persuaded to comply; but prevailed that the articles and conditions upon

---

[2] Perhaps the Duke of Argyle, whom Swift had angered by strictures against the Scotch in his political pamphlet, *The Public Spirit of the Whigs.*

which I should be set free, and to which I must swear, should be drawn up by himself. These articles were brought to me by Skyresh Bolgolam in person, attended by two under-secretaries, and several persons of distinction. After they were read, I was demanded to swear to the performance of them; first in the manner of my own country, and afterwards in the method prescribed by their laws; which was to hold my right foot in my left hand, to place the middle finger of my right hand on the crown of my head, and my thumb on the tip of my right ear. But because the reader may be curious to have some idea of the style and manner of expression peculiar to that people, as well as to know the articles upon which I recovered my liberty, I have made a translation of the whole instrument word for word, as near as I was able, which I here offer to the public.

Golbasto Momarem Evlame Gurdilo Shefin Mully Ully Gue, most mighty Emperor of Lilliput, delight and terror of the universe, whose dominions extend five thousand *blustrugs* (about twelve miles in circumference) to the extremities of the globe; monarch of all monarchs, taller than the sons of men; whose feet press down to the center, and whose head strikes against the sun; at whose nod the princes of the earth shake their knees; pleasant as the spring, comfortable as the summer, fruitful as autumn, dreadful as winter. His most sublime Majesty proposeth to the Man-Mountain, lately arrived to our celestial dominions, the following articles, which by a solemn oath he shall be obliged to perform.

First, The Man-Mountain shall not depart from our dominions, without our license under our great seal.

2d, He shall not presume to come into our metropolis, without our express order; at which time, the inhabitants shall have two hours' warning to keep within their doors.

3d, The said Man-Mountain shall confine his walks to our principal high roads, and not offer to walk or lie down in a meadow or field of corn.

4th, As he walks the said roads, he shall take the utmost care not to trample upon the bodies of any of our loving subjects, their horses, or carriages, nor take any of our subjects into his hands, without their own consent.

5th, If an express requires extraordinary dispatch, the Man-Mountain shall be obliged to carry in his pocket the messenger and horse a six days' journey once in every moon, and return the said messenger back (if so required) safe to our Imperial Presence.

6th, He shall be our ally against our enemies in the Island of Blefuscu, and do his utmost to destroy their fleet, which is now preparing to invade us.

7th, That the said Man-Mountain shall, at his times of leisure, be aiding and assisting our workmen, in helping to raise certain great stones, towards covering the wall of the principal park, and other our royal buildings.

8th, That the said Man-Mountain shall, in two moons' time, deliver in an exact survey of the circumference of our dominions by a computation of his own paces round the coast.

Lastly, That upon his solemn oath to observe all the above articles, the said Man-Mountain shall have a daily allowance of meat and drink sufficient for the support of 1728 of our subjects, with free access to our Royal Person, and other marks of our favor. Given at our Palace at Belfaborac the twelfth day of the ninety-first moon of our reign.

I swore and subscribed to these articles with great cheerfulness and content, although some of them were not so honorable as I could have wished; which proceeded wholly from the malice of Skyresh Bolgolam, the High-Admiral: whereupon my chains were immediately unlocked, and I was at full liberty; the Emperor himself in person did me the honor to be by at the whole ceremony. I made my acknowledgments by prostrating myself at his Majesty's feet: but he commanded me to rise; and after many gracious expressions, which, to avoid the censure of vanity, I shall not repeat, he added, that he hoped I should prove a useful servant, and well deserve all the favors he had already conferred upon me, or might do for the future.

The reader may please to observe, that in the last article for the recovery of my liberty, the Emperor stipulates to allow me a quantity of meat and drink sufficient for the support of 1728 Lilliputians. Some time after, asking a friend at court how they came to fix on that determinate number; he told me that his Majesty's mathematicians, having taken the height of my body by the help of a quadrant, and finding it to exceed theirs in the proportion of twelve to one, they concluded from the similarity of their bodies, that mine must contain at least 1728 of theirs, and consequently would require as much food as was necessary to support that number of Lilliputians. By which, the reader may conceive an idea of the ingenuity of that people, as well as the prudent and exact economy of so great a prince.

CHAPTER IV

Mildendo, the metropolis of *Lilliput,* described, together with the Emperor's palace. A conversation between the Author and a principal Secretary, concerning the affairs of that empire. The Author's offer to serve the Emperor in his wars.

The first request I made after I had obtained my liberty, was, that I might have license to see Mildendo, the metropolis; which the Emperor easily granted me, but with a special charge to do no hurt either to the inhabitants or their houses. The people had notice by proclamation of my design to visit the town. The wall which encompassed it, is two foot and an half high, and at least eleven inches broad, so that a coach and horses may be driven very safely round it; and it is flanked with strong towers at ten foot distance. I stepped over the great Western Gate, and passed very gently, and sideling through the two principal streets, only in my short waistcoat, for fear of damaging the roofs and eaves of the houses with the skirts of my coat. I walked with the utmost circumspection, to avoid treading on any stragglers, that might remain in the streets, although the orders were very strict, that all people should keep in their houses, at their own peril. The garret windows and tops of houses were so crowded with spectators, that I thought in all my travels I had not seen a more populous place. The city is an exact square, each side of the wall being five hundred foot long. The two great streets, which run cross and divide it into four quarters, are five foot wide. The lanes and alleys, which I could not enter, but only viewed them as I passed, are from twelve to eighteen inches. The town is capable of holding five hundred thousand souls. The houses are from three to five stories. The shops and markets well provided.

The Emperor's palace is in the center of the city, where the two great streets meet. It is inclosed by a wall of two foot high, and twenty foot distant from the buildings. I had his Majesty's permission to step over his wall; and the space being so wide between that and the palace, I could easily view it on every side. The outward court is a square of forty foot, and includes two other courts:

in the inmost are the royal apartments, which I was very desirous to see, but found it extremely difficult; for the great gates, from one square into another, were but eighteen inches high, and seven inches wide. Now the buildings of the outer court were at least five foot high, and it was impossible for me to stride over them without infinite damage to the pile, though the walls were strongly built of hewn stone, and four inches thick. At the same time the Emperor had a great desire that I should see the magnificence of his palace; but this I was not able to do till three days after, which I spent in cutting down with my knife some of the largest trees in the royal park, about an hundred yards distant from the city. Of these trees I made two stools, each about three foot high, and strong enough to bear my weight. The people having received notice a second time, I went again through the city to the palace, with my two stools in my hands. When I came to the side of the outer court, I stood upon one stool, and took the other in my hand: this I lifted over the roof, and gently set it down on the space between the first and second court, which was eight foot wide. I then stept over the buildings very conveniently from one stool to the other, and drew up the first after me with a hooked stick. By this contrivance I got into the inmost court; and lying down upon my side, I applied my face to the windows of the middle stories, which were left open on purpose, and discovered the most splendid apartments that can be imagined. There I saw the Empress and the young Princes, in their several lodgings, with their chief attendants about them. Her Imperial Majesty [3] was pleased to smile very graciously upon me, and gave me out of the window her hand to kiss.

But I shall not anticipate the reader with farther descriptions of this kind, because I reserve them for a greater work, which is now almost ready for the press, containing a general description of this empire, from its first erection, through a long series of princes, with a particular account of their wars and politics, laws, learning, and religion: their plants and animals, their peculiar manners and customs, with other matters very curious and useful; my chief design at present being only to relate such events and transactions as happened to the public, or to myself, during a residence of about nine months in that empire.

One morning, about a fortnight after I had obtained my liberty, Reldresal, principal Secretary (as they style him) of private Affairs, came to my

---

[3] Queen Anne.

house attended only by one servant. He ordered his coach to wait at a distance, and desired I would give him an hour's audience; which I readily consented to, on account of his quality and personal merits, as well as the many good offices he had done me during my solicitations at court. I offered to lie down, that he might the more conveniently reach my ear; but he chose rather to let me hold him in my hand during our conversation. He began with compliments on my liberty; said he might pretend to some merit in it: but, however, added, that if it had not been for the present situation of things at court, perhaps I might not have obtained it so soon. For, said he, as flourishing a condition as we may appear to be in to foreigners, we labor under two mighty evils; a violent faction at home, and the danger of an invasion by a most potent enemy from abroad. As to the first, you are to understand, that for about seventy moons past there have been two struggling parties in this empire, under the names of *Tramecksan* and *Slamecksan,* from the high and low heels on their shoes, by which they distinguish themselves. It is alleged indeed, that the high heels are most agreeable to our ancient constitution: but however this be, his Majesty hath determined to make use of only low heels in the administration of the government, and all offices in the gift of the Crown, as you cannot but observe; and particularly, that his Majesty's Imperial heels are lower at least by a *drurr* than any of his court; (*drurr* is a measure about the fourteenth part of an inch). The animosities between these two parties run so high, that they will neither eat nor drink, nor talk with each other. We compute the *Tramecksan,* or High-Heels, to exceed us in number; but the power is wholly on our side. We apprehend his Imperial Highness, the Heir to the Crown, to have some tendency towards the High-Heels; at least we can plainly discover one of his heels higher than the other, which gives him a hobble in his gait. Now, in the midst of these intestine disquiets, we are threatened with an invasion from the Island of Blefuscu, which is the other great empire of the universe, almost as large and powerful as this of his Majesty. For as to what we have heard you affirm, that there are other kingdoms and states in the world inhabited by human creatures as large as yourself, our philosophers are in much doubt, and would rather conjecture that you dropped from the moon, or one of the stars; because it is certain, that an hundred mortals of your bulk would, in a short time, destroy all the fruits and cattle of his Majesty's dominions. Besides, our histories of six thousand moons make no mention of any other regions, than the two great empires of Lilliput and Blefuscu. Which two mighty powers have, as I was going to tell you, been engaged in a most obstinate war for six and thirty moons past. It began upon the following occasion. It is allowed on all hands, that the primitive way of breaking eggs before we eat them, was upon the larger end: but his present Majesty's grandfather, while he was a boy, going to eat an egg, and breaking it according to the ancient practice, happened to cut one of his fingers. Whereupon the Emperor his father published an edict, commanding all his subjects, upon great penalties, to break the smaller end of their eggs. The people so highly resented this law, that our histories tell us there have been six rebellions raised on that account; wherein one Emperor lost his life, and another his crown. These civil commotions were constantly fomented by the monarchs of Blefuscu; and when they were quelled, the exiles always fled for refuge to that empire. It is computed, that eleven thousand persons have, at several times, suffered death, rather than submit to break their eggs at the smaller end. Many hundred large volumes have been published upon this controversy: but the books of the Big-Endians have been long forbidden, and the whole party rendered incapable by law of holding employments. During the course of these troubles, the Emperors of Blefuscu did frequently expostulate by their ambassadors, accusing us of making a schism in religion, by offending against a fundamental doctrine of our great prophet Lustrog, in the fifty-fourth chapter of the Blundecral (which is their Alcoran). This, however, is thought to be a mere strain upon the text: for the words are these; *That all true believers break their eggs at the convenient end:* and which is the convenient end, seems, in my humble opinion, to be left to every man's conscience, or at least in the power of the chief magistrate to determine. Now the Big-Endian exiles have found so much credit in the Emperor of Blefuscu's court, and so much private assistance and encouragement from their party here at home, that a bloody war has been carried on between the two empires for six and thirty moons with various success; during which time we have lost forty capital ships, and a much greater number of smaller vessels, together with thirty thousand of our best seamen and soldiers; and the damage received by the enemy is reckoned to be somewhat greater than ours. However, they have now equipped a numerous fleet, and are just preparing to make a descent upon us; and his Imperial Majesty, placing great confidence in your valor and strength, has commanded me to lay this account of his affairs before you.

I desired the Secretary to present my humble duty to the Emperor, and to let him know, that I thought it would not become me, who was a foreigner, to interfere with parties; but I was ready, with the hazard of my life, to defend his person 10 and state against all invaders.

[An outline of the remaining chapters of the voyage to *Lilliput* follows:

The Author, by an extraordinary stratagem, prevents an invasion. A high title of honor is conferred upon him. Ambassadors arrive from the Emperor of *Blefuscu,* and sue for peace. The Emperor's apartment on fire by an accident; the Author instrumental in saving the rest of the palace.—Of the inhabitants of *Lilliput;* their learning, laws, and customs, the manner of educating their children. The Author's way of living in that country. His vindication of a great lady.—The Author, being informed of a design to accuse him of high-treason, makes his escape to *Blefuscu.* His reception there. —The Author, by a lucky accident, finds means to leave *Blefuscu;* and, after some difficulties, returns safe to his native country.]

JOSEPH ADDISON

The Character of Mr. Spectator

*Non fumum ex fulgore, sed ex fumo dare lucem
Cogitat, ut speciosa dehinc miracula promat.*[1]—Hor.

I have observed that a reader seldom peruses a book with pleasure, until he knows whether the writer of it be a black or a fair man, of a mild or choleric disposition, married or a bachelor, with other particulars of the like nature, that conduce very much to the right understanding of an author. To gratify this curiosity, which is so natural to a reader, I design this paper, and my next as prefatory discourses to my following writings, and shall give some account in them of the several persons that are engaged in this work. As the chief trouble of compiling, digesting, and correcting, will fall to my share, I must do myself the justice to open the work with my own history.

I was born to a small hereditary estate, which, 20 according to the tradition of the village where it lies, was bounded by the same hedges and ditches in William the Conqueror's time that it is at present, and has been delivered down from father to son, whole and entire, without the loss or acquisi-

tion of a single field or meadow, during the space of six hundred years; there runs a story in the family, that when my mother was gone with child of me about three months, she dreamed that she was brought to bed of a judge: whether this might proceed from a law-suit which was then depending in the family, or my father's being a justice of the peace, I cannot determine; for I am not so vain as to think it presaged any dignity that I should 10 arrive at in my future life, though that was the interpretation which the neighborhood put upon it. The gravity of my behavior at my very first appearance in the world, and all the time that I sucked, seemed to favor my mother's dream; for, as she has often told me, I threw away my rattle before I was two months old, and would not make use of my coral until they had taken away the bells from it.

As for the rest of my infancy, there being nothing in it remarkable, I shall pass over it in silence. I find that during my nonage, I had the reputation of a very sullen youth, but was always a favorite of my schoolmaster, who used to say *that my parts were solid and would wear well.* I had not been long at the university, before I distinguished my-

Addison, *The Character of Mr. Spectator.* Joseph Addison was born in Wiltshire in 1672 and died in London in 1719. He was educated at Oxford, traveled, held political offices, and wrote periodical essays.

[1] One with a flash begins and ends in smoke;
    Another out of smoke brings glorious light,
    And without raising expectation high
    Surprises us with dazzling miracles.
    —Horace. translated by Roscommon.

self by a most profound silence; for during the space of eight years, excepting in the public exercise of the college, I scarce uttered the quantity of a hundred words; and indeed do not remember that I ever spoke three sentences together in my whole life. Whilst I was in this learned body, I applied myself with so much diligence to my studies, that there are few very celebrated books, either in the learned or the modern tongues, which I am not acquainted with.

Upon the death of my father, I was resolved to travel into foreign countries, and therefore left the university, with the character of an odd unaccountable fellow that had a great deal of learning, if I would but show it. An insatiable thirst after knowledge carried me into all the countries of Europe in which there was anything new or strange to be seen; nay, to such a degree was my curiosity raised, that having read the controversies of some great men concerning the antiquities of Egypt, I made a voyage to Grand Cairo, on purpose to take the measure of a pyramid; and, as soon as I had set myself right in that particular, returned to my native country with great satisfaction.

I have passed my latter years in this city, where I am frequently seen in most public places, though there are not above half-a-dozen of my select friends that know me; of whom my next paper shall give a more particular account. There is no place of general resort wherein I do not often make my appearance. Sometimes I am seen thrusting my head into a round of politicians at Will's, and listening with great attention to the narratives that are made in those little circular audiences. Sometimes I smoke a pipe at Child's, and while I seem attentive to nothing but the *postman,* overhear the conversation of every table in the room. I appear on Sunday nights at St. James's coffeehouse, and sometimes join the little committee of politics in the inner room, as one who comes there to hear and improve. My face is likewise very well known at the Grecian, the Cocoa-tree, and in the theaters both of Drurylane and the Haymarket. I have been taken for a merchant upon the exchange for above these ten years, and sometimes pass for a Jew in the assembly of stock-jobbers at Jonathan's: in short, wherever I see a cluster of people, I always mix with them, though I never open my lips but in my own club.

Thus I live in the world rather as a *Spectator* of mankind, than as one of the species, by which means I have made myself a speculative statesman,

soldier, merchant, and artisan, without ever meddling with any practical part in life. I am very well versed in the theory of a husband or a father, and can discern the errors in the economy, business, and diversions of others, better than those who are engaged in them; as standers-by discover blots, which are apt to escape those who are in the game. I never espoused any party with violence, and am resolved to observe an exact neutrality between the Whigs and Tories, unless I shall be forced to declare myself by the hostilities of either side. In short, I have acted in all the parts of my life as a looker-on, which is the character I intend to preserve in this paper.

I have given the reader just so much of my history and character, as to let him see I am not altogether unqualified for the business I have undertaken. As for other particulars in my life and adventures, I shall insert them in the following papers as I shall see occasion. In the mean time, when I consider how much I have seen, read, and heard, I begin to blame my own taciturnity; and since I have neither time nor inclination to communicate the fullness of my heart in speech, I am resolved to do it in writing, and to print myself out, if possible, before I die. I have been often told by my friends, that it is pity so many useful discoveries which I have made should be in the possession of a silent man. For this reason, therefore, I shall publish a sheetful of thoughts every morning, for the benefit of my contemporaries; and if I can any way contribute to the diversion or improvement of the country in which I live, I shall leave it, when I am summoned out of it, with the secret satisfaction of thinking that I have not lived in vain.

There are three very material points which I have not spoken to in this paper; and which, for several important reasons, I must keep to myself at least for some time: I mean, an account of my name, my age, and my lodgings. I must confess, I would gratify my reader in anything that is reasonable; but as for these three particulars, though I am sensible they might tend very much to the embellishment of my paper, I cannot yet come to a resolution of communicating them to the public. They would indeed draw me out of that obscurity which I have enjoyed for many years, and expose me in public places to several salutes and civilities, which have been always very disagreeable to me; for the greatest pain I can suffer is the being talked to, and being stared at. It is for this reason likewise, that I keep my complexion and dress as very great secrets; though it is not impossible but I may make discoveries of both in the progress of the work I have undertaken.

After having been thus particular upon myself, I shall, in tomorrow's paper, give an account of those gentlemen who are concerned with me in this work; for, as I have before intimated, a plan of it is laid and concerted, as all other matters of importance are, in a club. However, as my friends have engaged me to stand in the front, those who have a mind to correspond with me, may direct their letters to the *Spectator,* at Mr. Buckley's in Little Britain. For I must further acquaint the reader, that though our club meets only on Tuesdays and Thursdays, we have appointed a committee to sit every night for the inspection of all such papers as may contribute to the advancement of the public weal.

Meditations in Westminster Abbey

When I am in a serious humor, I very often walk by myself in Westminster Abbey: where the gloominess of the place, and the use to which it is applied, with the solemnity of the building, and the condition of the people who lie in it, are apt to fill the mind with a kind of melancholy, or rather thoughtfulness, that is not disagreeable. I yesterday passed a whole afternoon in the churchyard, the cloisters and the church, amusing myself with the tombstones, and inscriptions that I met with in those several regions of the dead. Most of them recorded nothing else of the buried person, but that he was born upon one day, and died upon another; the whole history of his life being comprehended in those two circumstances that are common to all mankind. I could not but look upon these registers of existence, whether of brass or marble, as a kind of satire upon the departed persons; who had left no other memorial of them, but that they were born, and that they died. They put me in mind of several persons mentioned in the battles of heroic poems, who have sounding names given them for no other reason but that they may be killed, and are celebrated for nothing but being knocked on the head.

Glaucumque, Medontaque, Thersilochumque.— Virg.

The life of these men is finely described in holy writ by "the path of an arrow," which is immediately closed up and lost.

Upon my going into the church, I entertained myself with the digging of a grave; and saw, in every shovel-full of it that was thrown up, the fragment of a bone or skull intermixed with a kind of fresh moldering earth, that some time or other had a place in the composition of a human body. Upon this I began to consider with myself what innumerable multitudes of people lay confused together under the pavement of that ancient cathedral; how men and women, friends and enemies, priests and soldiers, monks and prebendaries, were crumbled amongst one another, and blended together in the same common mass; how beauty, strength, and youth, with old age, weakness, and deformity, lay undistinguished in the same promiscuous heap of matter.

After having thus surveyed this great magazine of mortality, as it were in the lump, I examined it more particularly by the accounts which I found on several of the monuments which are raised in every quarter of that ancient fabric. Some of them were covered with such extravagant epitaphs, that if it were possible for the dead person to be acquainted with them, he would blush at the praises which his friends have bestowed upon him. There are others so excessively modest that they deliver the character of the person departed in Greek or Hebrew, and by that means are not understood once in a twelvemonth. In the poetical corner, I found there were poets who had no monuments, and monuments which had no poets. I observed, indeed, that the present war has filled the church with many of these uninhabited monuments, which had been erected to the memory of persons whose bodies were perhaps buried in the plains of Blenheim, or in the bosom of the ocean.

I could not but be very much delighted with several modern epitaphs, which are written with great elegance of expression and justness of thought, and therefore do honor to the living as well as to the dead. As a foreigner is very apt to conceive an idea of the ignorance or politeness of a nation from the turn of their public monuments and inscriptions, they should be submitted to the perusal of men of learning and genius before they are put in execution. Sir Cloudesly Shovel's monument has very often given me great offense; instead of the brave, rough English admiral, which was the distinguishing character of that plain, gallant man, he is represented on his tomb by the figure of a beau, dressed in a long periwig, and reposing himself upon velvet cushions, under a canopy of state. The inscription is answerable to the monument; for instead of celebrating the many remarkable actions he had performed in the service of his country, it acquaints us only with the manner of his death, in which it was impossible for him to reap any honor. The Dutch, whom we are apt to despise for want of genius, show an infinitely greater taste of antiquity and politeness in their buildings and works of this nature than what we meet with in those of our own country. The monuments of their admirals, which have been erected at the public expense, represent them like themselves, and are adorned with rostral crowns and naval ornaments, with beautiful festoons of sea-weed, shells, and coral.

But to return to our subject; I have left the repository of our English kings for the contemplation of another day, when I shall find my mind disposed for so serious an amusement. I know that entertainments of this nature are apt to raise dark and dismal thoughts in timorous minds and gloomy imaginations; but for my own part, though I am always serious, I do not know what it is to be melancholy; and can therefore take a view of nature in her deep and solemn scenes with the same pleasure as in her most gay and delightful ones. By this means I can improve myself with those objects which others consider with terror. When I look upon the tombs of the great, every emotion of envy dies within me; when I read the epitaphs of the beautiful, every inordinate desire goes out; when I meet with the grief of parents upon a tombstone, my heart melts with compassion; when I see the tomb of the parents themselves, I consider the vanity of grieving for those whom we must quickly follow; when I see kings lying by those who deposed them, when I consider rival wits placed side by side, or the holy men that divided the world with their contests and disputes, I reflect with sorrow and astonishment on the little competitions, factions, and debates of mankind. When I read the several dates of the tombs, of some that died yesterday, and some six hundred years ago, I consider that great day when we shall all of us be contemporaries, and make our appearance together.

RICHARD STEELE

A Happy Marriage

There are several persons who have many pleasures and entertainments in their possession which they do not enjoy. It is therefore a kind and good office to acquaint them with their own happiness, and turn their attention to such instances of their good fortune which they are apt to overlook. Persons in the married state often want such a monitor, and pine away their days, by looking upon the same condition in anguish and murmur which carries with it in the opinion of others a complication of all the pleasures of life, and a retreat from its inquietudes.

I am led into this thought by a visit I made an old friend who was formerly my school-fellow. He came to town last week with his family for the winter, and yesterday morning sent me word his wife expected me to dinner. I am as it were at home at that house, and every member of it knows me for their well-wisher. I cannot indeed express the pleasure it is to be met by the children with so much joy as I am when I go thither: the boys and girls strive who shall come first when they think it is I that am knocking at the door; and that child which loses the race to me runs back again to tell the father it is Mr. Bickerstaff. This day I was led in by a pretty girl, that we all thought must have forgot me; for the family has been out of town these two years. Her knowing me again was a mighty subject with us, and took up our discourse at the first entrance. After which, they began to rally me upon a thousand little stories they heard in the country about my marriage to one of my neighbor's daughters: upon which the gentleman, my friend, said, "Nay, if Mr. Bickerstaff marries a child of any of his old companions, I hope mine shall have the preference; there's Mrs. Mary is now sixteen, and would make him as fine a widow as the best of them: but I know him too well; he is so enamored with the very memory of those who flourished in our youth,

Steele, *A Happy Marriage*. Sir Richard Steele, born in Dublin in 1672, died in 1729. He was a companion of Addison at Oxford and collaborated with him as essayist. He also wrote plays.

that he will not so much as look upon the modern beauties. I remember, old gentleman, how often you went home in a day to refresh your countenance and dress when Teraminta reigned in your heart. As we came up in the coach, I repeated to my wife some of your verses on her." With such reflections on little passages which happened long ago, we passed our time during a cheerful and elegant meal. After dinner, his lady left the room, as did also the children. As soon as we were alone, he took me by the hand; "Well, my good friend," says he, "I am heartily glad to see thee; I was afraid you would never have seen all the company that dined with you today again. Do not you think the good woman of the house a little altered since you followed her from the play-house, to find out who she was, for me?" I perceived a tear fall down his cheek as he spoke, which moved me not a little. But to turn the discourse, said I, "She is not indeed quite that creature she was when she returned me the letter I carried from you; and told me, she hoped, as I was a gentleman, I would be employed no more to trouble her who had never offended me, but would be so much the gentleman's friend as to dissuade him from a pursuit which he could never succeed in. You may remember, I thought her in earnest, and you were forced to employ your cousin Will, who made his sister get acquainted with her for you. You cannot expect her to be forever fifteen. "Fifteen?" replied my good friend: "ah! you little understand, you that have lived a bachelor, how great, how exquisite a pleasure there is in being really beloved! It is impossible that the most beauteous face in nature should raise in me such pleasing ideas as when I look upon that excellent woman. That fading in her countenance is chiefly caused by her watching with me in my fever. This was followed by a fit of sickness, which had like to have carried her off last winter. I tell you sincerely, I have so many obligations to her, that I cannot with any sort of moderation think of her present state of health. But as to what you say of fifteen, she gives me every day pleasures beyond what I ever knew in the possession of her beauty when I was in the vigor of youth. Every moment of her life brings me fresh instances of her complacency to my inclinations, and her prudence in regard to my fortune. Her face is to me much more beautiful than when I first saw it; there is no decay in any feature which I cannot trace from the very instant it was occasioned by some anxious concern for my welfare and interests. Thus at the same time, methinks, the love I conceived towards her for what she was, is heightened by my gratitude for what she is. The love of a wife is as much above the idle passion commonly called by that name, as the loud laughter of buffoons is inferior to the elegant mirth of gentlemen. Oh! she is an inestimable jewel. In her examination of her household affairs, she shows a certain fearfulness to find a fault, which makes her servants obey her like children; and the meanest we have has an ingenuous shame for an offense, not always to be seen in children in other families. I speak freely to you, my old friend; ever since her sickness, things that gave me the quickest joy before, turn now to a certain anxiety. As the children play in the next room, I know the poor things by their steps, and am considering what they must do, should they lose their mother in their tender years. The pleasure I used to take in telling my boy stories of the battles, and asking my girl questions about the disposal of her baby, and the gossiping of it, is turned into inward reflection and melancholy."

He would have gone on in this tender way, when the good lady entered, and with an inexpressible sweetness in her countenance told us, she had been searching her closet for something very good to treat such an old friend as I was. Her husband's eyes sparkled with pleasure at the cheerfulness of her countenance; and I saw all his fears vanish in an instant. The lady observing something in our looks which showed we had been more serious than ordinary, and seeing her husband receive her with great concern under a forced cheerfulness, immediately guessed at what we had been talking of; and applying herself to me, said, with a smile, "Mr. Bickerstaff, don't believe a word of what he tells you. I shall still live to have you for my second, as I have often promised you, unless he takes more care of himself than he has done since his coming to town. You must know, he tells me that he finds London is a much more healthy place than the country; for he sees several of his old acquaintance and school-fellows are here, young fellows with fair full-bottomed periwigs. I could scarce keep him this morning from going out open-breasted." My friend, who is always extremely delighted with her agreeable humor, made her sit down with us. She did it with that easiness which is peculiar to women of sense; and to keep up the good humor she had brought in with her, turned her raillery upon me. "Mr. Bickerstaff, you remember you followed me one night from the play-house; suppose you should carry me thither tomorrow night, and lead me into the front box." This put us into a long field of discourse about the beauties, who were mothers to the present, and shone in the boxes twenty years ago. I told her, I was glad she had transferred so many of her charms, and I did not question but her eldest daughter was within half-a-year of being a toast.

We were pleasing ourselves with this fantastical preferment of the young lady, when on a sudden we were alarmed with the noise of a drum, and immediately entered my little godson to give me a point of war. His mother, between laughing and chiding, would have put him out of the room; but I would not part with him so. I found, upon conversation with him, though he was a little noisy in his mirth, that the child had excellent parts, and was a great master of all the learning on the other side eight years old. I perceived him a very great historian in Æsop's Fables; but he frankly declared to me his mind, that he did not delight in that learning, because he did not believe they were true; for which reason, I found he had very much turned his studies, for about a twelve-month past, into the lives and adventures of Don Bellianis of Greece, Guy of Warwick, the Seven Champions, and other historians of that age. I could not but observe the satisfaction the father took in the forwardness of his son; and that these diversions might turn to some profit, I found the boy had made remarks which might be of service to him during the course of his whole life. He would tell you the mismanagements of John Hickathrift, find fault with the passionate temper in Bevis of Southampton, and loved St. George for being the champion of England; and by this means had his thoughts insensibly molded into the notions of discretion, virtue, and honor. I was extolling his accomplishments, when the mother told me, that the little girl who led me in this morning was in her way a better scholar than he. "Betty," says she, "deals chiefly in fairies and sprites; and sometimes in a winter night will terrify the maids with her accounts, until they are afraid to go up to bed."

I sat with them until it was very late, sometimes in merry, sometimes in serious discourse, with this particular pleasure, which gives the only true relish to all conversation, a sense that every one of us liked each other. I went home, considering the different conditions of a married life and that of a bachelor; and I must confess, it struck me with a secret concern to reflect that whenever I go off I shall leave no traces behind me. In this pensive mood I returned to my family; that is to say, to my maid, my dog, and my cat, who only can be the better or worse for what happens to me.

SAMUEL JOHNSON

Epigrams

Dr. Johnson used to say, that where secrecy or mystery began, vice or roguery was not far off; and that he leads in general an ill life, who stands in fear of no man's observation.

When a friend of his who had not been very lucky in his first wife, married a second, he said— Alas! another instance of the triumph of hope over experience.

Of Sheridan's writings on Elocution, he said, they were a continual renovation of hope, and an unvaried succession of disappointments.

He used to say, that no man read long together with a folio on his table:—Books, said he, that you may carry to the fire, and hold readily in your hand, are the most useful after all. He would say, such books form the man of general and easy reading.

When accused of mentioning ridiculous anecdotes in the lives of the poets, he said, he should not have been an exact biographer if he had omitted them. The business of such a one, said he, is to give a complete account of the person whose life he is writing, and to discriminate him from all other persons by any peculiarities of character or sentiment he may happen to have.

Dr. Sumner, of Harrow, used to tell this story

Johnson, *Epigrams,* selected. Samuel Johnson (1709-1784) came to London in 1737 and earned his living by his pen. His writing of *The English Dictionary* established him as the literary dictator of his age. The epigrams are taken from Boswell's *Life of Johnson.*

of Johnson: they were dining one day, with many other persons, at Mrs. Macaulay's; she had talked a long time at dinner about the natural equality of mankind; Johnson, when she had finished her harangue, rose up from the table, and with great solemnity of countenance, and a bow to the ground, said to the servant, who was waiting behind his chair, Mr. John, pray be seated in my place, and permit me to wait upon you in my turn: your mistress says, you hear, that we are all equal.

When someone was lamenting Foote's unlucky fate in being kicked in Dublin, Johnson said he was glad of it; he is rising in the world, said he: when he was in England, no one thought it worth while to kick him.

Of the state of learning among the Scots, he said:—"It is with their learning as with provisions in a besieged town, everyone has a mouthful, and no one a bellyful."

When he first felt the stroke of palsy, he prayed to God that he would spare his mind, whatever he thought fit to do with his body.

To some lady who was praising Shenstone's poems very much, and who had an Italian greyhound lying by the fire, he said, "Shenstone holds amongst poets the same rank your dog holds amongst dogs; he has not the sagacity of the hound, the docility of the spaniel, nor the courage of the bulldog, yet he is still a pretty fellow."

When someone asked him, whether they should introduce Hugh Kelly, the author, to him;—"No, Sir," says he, "I never desire to converse with a man who has written more than he has read." Yet when his play was acted for the benefit of his widow, Johnson furnished a prologue.

He held all authors very cheap, that were not satisfied with the opinion of the public about them. He used to say, that every man who writes, thinks he can amuse or inform mankind, and they must be the best judges of his pretensions.

When someone asked him for what he should marry, he replied, first, for virtue; secondly, for wit; thirdly, for beauty; and fourthly, for money.

He thought worse of the vices of retirement than of those of society.

One day, on seeing an old terrier lie asleep by the fire-side at Streatham, he said, Presto, you are, if possible, a more lazy dog than I am.

Being asked by Dr. Lawrence what he thought the best system of education, he replied,—School in school-hours, and home-instruction in the intervals.

I would never, said he, desire a young man to neglect his business for the purpose of pursuing his studies, because it is unreasonable; I would only desire him to read at those hours when he would otherwise be unemployed. I will not promise that he will be a Bentley; but if he be a lad of any parts, he will certainly make a sensible man. He thought the happiest life was that of a man of business, with some literary pursuits for his amusement; and that in general no one could be virtuous or happy, that was not completely employed.

Of a certain lady's entertainments, he said,—What signifies going thither? there is neither meat, drink, nor talk.

Johnson said of the Chattertonian controversy,—It is a sword that cuts both ways. It is as wonderful to suppose that a boy of sixteen years old had stored his mind with such a train of images and ideas as he had acquired, as to suppose the poems, with their ease of versification and elegance of language, to have been written by Rowlie in the time of Edward the Fourth.

Talking with some persons about allegorical painting, he said, "I had rather see the portrait of a dog that I know, than all the allegorical paintings they can show me in the world."

A Scotsman upon his introduction to Johnson said:—"I am afraid, Sir, you will not like me, I have the misfortune to come from Scotland." "Sir," answered he, "that is a misfortune; but such a one as you and the rest of your countrymen cannot help."

Speaking one day of tea, he said,—What a delightful beverage must that be, that pleases all palates, at a time when they can take nothing else at breakfast!

Of a member of parliament, who, after having harangued for some hours in the house of commons, came into a company where Johnson was, and endeavored to talk him down, he said, This man has a pulse in his tongue.

One who had long known Johnson, said of him, In general you may tell what the man to whom you are speaking will say next: this you can never do of Johnson: his images, his allusions, his great powers of ridicule throw the appearance of novelty upon the most common conversation.

Whoever thinks of going to bed before twelve o'clock, said Johnson, is a scoundrel:—having nothing in particular to do himself, and having none of his time appropriated, he was a troublesome guest to persons who had much to do.

Definitions

[FROM THE "DICTIONARY"]

excise: a hateful tax levied upon commodities, and adjudged, not by the common judges of property, but wretches hired by those to whom excise is paid.

Grub Street: the name of a street in London, much inhabited by writers of small histories, *dictionaries,* and temporary poems; whence any mean production is called Grub Street.

lexicographer: a writer of dictionaries, a harmless drudge that busies himself in tracing the original and detailing the significance of words.

network: anything reticulated or decussated at equal distances with interstices between the intersections.

oats: a grain which in England is generally given to horses, but in Scotland supports the people.

patriotism: the last refuge of a scoundrel.

patron: one who countenances, supports, or protects. Commonly a wretch who supports with insolence, and is paid with flattery.

pension: an allowance made to anyone without an equivalent. In England it is generally understood to mean pay given to a state hireling for treason to his country.

pensioner: a slave of state, hired by a stipend to obey his master.

politician: a man of artifice; one deep of contrivance.

thunder: a most bright flame rising on a sudden, moving with great violence, and with a very rapid velocity, through the air, according to any determination, and commonly ending with a loud noise or rattling.

Tory: one who adheres to the ancient constitution of the state, and the apostolical hierarchy of the Church of England, opposed to a Whig.

transpire: to escape from secrecy to notice, a sense lately innovated from France without necessity.

Whig: the name of a faction.

Letter to Lord Chesterfield

["Lord Chesterfield, to whom Johnson had paid the high compliment of addressing to his Lordship the Plan of his Dictionary, had behaved to him in such a manner as to excite his contempt and indignation. The world has been for many years amused with a story confidently told, and as confidently repeated with additional circumstances, that a sudden disgust was taken by Johnson upon occasion of his having been one day kept long in waiting in his Lordship's ante-chamber, for which the reason assigned was, that he had company with him; and that at last, when the door was opened, out walked Colley Cibber; and that Johnson was so violently provoked when he found for whom he had been so long excluded, that he went away in a passion, and never would return. I remember having mentioned this story to George Lord Lyttelton, who told me, he was very intimate with Lord Chesterfield; and holding it as a well-known truth, defended Lord Chesterfield, by saying, that 'Cibber, who had been introduced familiarly by the backstairs, had probably not been there above ten minutes.' It may seem strange even to entertain a doubt concerning a story so long and so widely current, and thus implicitly adopted, if not sanctified, by the authority which I have mentioned; but Johnson himself assured me, that there was not the least foundation for it. He told me, that there never was any particular incident which produced a quarrel between Lord Chesterfield and him; but that his Lordship's continued neglect was the reason why he resolved to have no connection with him. When the Dictionary was upon the eve of publication, Lord Chesterfield, who, it is said, had flattered himself with expectations that Johnson would dedicate the work to him, attempted, in a courtly manner, to soothe, and insinuate himself with the sage, conscious, as it should seem, of the cold indifference with which he had treated its learned author; and further attempted to conciliate him, by writing two papers in *The World,* in recommendation of the work; and it must be confessed, that they contain some studied compliments, so finely turned, that if there had been no previous offense, it is probable that Johnson would have been highly delighted. Praise, in general, was pleasing to him; but by praise from a man of rank and elegant accomplishments, he was peculiarly gratified. . . .

"This courtly device failed of its effect. Johnson, who thought that 'all was false and hollow,' despised the honeyed words, and was even indignant that Lord Chesterfield should, for a moment, imagine, that he should be the dupe of such an artifice. His expression to me concerning Lord Chesterfield, upon this occasion, was, 'Sir, after making great professions, he had, for many years, taken no notice of me; but when my Dictionary was coming out, he fell a scribbling in *The World* about it. Upon which, I wrote him a letter, expressed in civil terms, but such as might show him that I did not mind what he said or wrote, and that I had done with him.' "—BOSWELL, *Life of Johnson.*]

To the Right Honorable the Earl of CHESTERFIELD

February, 1755.

My Lord,

I have been lately informed, by the proprietor of *The World,* that two papers, in which my Dictionary is recommended to the public, were written by your Lordship. To be so distinguished, is an honor, which, being very little accustomed to favors from the great, I know not well how to receive, or in what terms to acknowledge.

When, upon some slight encouragement, I first visited your Lordship, I was overpowered, like the rest of mankind, by the enchantment of your address; and could not forbear to wish that I might boast myself *Le vainqueur du vainqueur de la terre;*—that I might obtain that regard for which I saw the world contending; but I found my attendance so little encouraged, that neither pride nor modesty would suffer me to continue it. When I had once addressed your Lordship in public, I had exhausted all the art of pleasing which a retired and uncourtly scholar can possess. I had done all that I could; and no man is well pleased to have his all neglected, be it ever so little.

Seven years, my Lord, have now past, since I waited in your outward rooms, or was repulsed from your door, during which time I have been pushing on my work through difficulties, of which it is useless to complain, and have brought it, at last, to the verge of publication, without one act of assistance, one word of encouragement, or one smile of favor. Such treatment I did not expect, for I never had a Patron before.

The shepherd in Virgil grew at last acquainted with Love, and found him a native of the rocks.

Is not a Patron, my Lord, one who looks with unconcern on a man struggling for life in the water, and, when he has reached ground, encumbers him with help? The notice which you have been pleased to take of my labors, had it been early, had been kind, but it has been delayed till I am indifferent, and cannot enjoy it; till I am solitary, and cannot impart it; till I am known, and do not want it. I hope it is no very cynical asperity not to confess obligations where no benefit has been received, or to be unwilling that the public should consider me as owing to a Patron, what Providence has enabled me to do for myself.

Having carried on my work thus far with so little obligation to any favorer of learning, I shall not be disappointed though I should conclude it, if less be possible, with less; for I have been long wakened from that dream of hope, in which I once boasted myself with so much exultation,

My Lord,
Your Lordship's most humble
Most obedient servant
Sam. Johnson

POETRY OF THE

NEW CLASSICISM

When Charles II came back to the throne of England in 1660, he brought many changes into English life. For a dozen years he and his companions had been living under the influence of French culture, so that after his return English social life, English drama, and even English poetry became more French than English. Though Milton's great epics appeared after the Restoration, they produced no effect on the immediate history of English poetry. With Dryden, poetry became in a large measure a medium for the expression of social and political satire. If he wrote a narrative poem, it was not "to justify the ways of God to man" but to illustrate the wickedness or absurdity of some political enemy. Occasionally he would compose a beautiful lyric, such as *Alexander's Feast,* but even about such a poem there is a degree of artificiality that makes us admire the workmanship without undergoing any emotional experience.

In addition to the development of poetry for satirical purposes, Dryden perfected the heroic couplet, the five-foot iambic verse that was to be an accepted medium of poetry for two generations. In both these respects Dryden's successor was Alexander Pope.

In spite of a certain revival of interest in Pope, it is hard for us, after the lapse of two centuries, to see why this man should have seemed so important to his own generation. He was a master of the heroic couplet; he knew how to say cruel things in his verse; he was acquainted with the elegances of English society; he knew the conventional ideas of literary criticism and the current books of morality. His ideal of poetry was: "What oft was thought, but ne'er so well expressed." We see all the commonplace moral ideas and critical principles turned into clever heroic couplets. Without having an original thought of his own, he thus became something of a teacher for his generation and he acquired the reputation for wisdom and profound knowledge.

In the light of two centuries all this seems rather thin, and most of us prefer to read our Pope in his playful mood, where he has given us something that no one else could supply. In *The Rape of the Lock* he has had an opportunity to make use of all his gifts in the celebration of trivial things. In such a piece we expect and receive the greatest artificiality of treatment. With this subject such a handling is the only one possible. Perhaps no other poet could ever have done it so well as Pope.

Beginning about 1730 a new spirit seems to be entering English poetry. With

James Thomson's *The Seasons,* which began to appear in 1726, we have not only the first occurrence of blank verse since the time of Milton but also evidences of direct observation of nature. After Pope had been maintaining that the poet should treat "Nature to advantage dressed," it was refreshing to have a description of the seasons as they actually appeared to an honest observer.

In addition to getting away from the restricted heroic couplet, the poets of the new generation revised the ideal of what subjects were proper for poetic treatment. From poetry which deliberately repressed emotional states they went to the opposite extreme and wrote verses the only purpose of which was to express the poet's real or imagined emotions. Melancholy particularly interested the new poets, whose favorite subjects were lonely walks at night or burying grounds at twilight. A part of this movement produced Gray's *Elegy Written in a Country Churchyard* and Collins's *Ode to Evening.*

Meantime, the influence of Pope and Dryden lived on. Much poetry was written throughout the eighteenth century that showed no effect whatever of the new romantic feeling. There was also much that displayed qualities of both schools, the older formalism being somewhat sentimentalized by the new emotional interests. Such a poet was Goldsmith. In *The Deserted Village* we see this peculiar blend so characteristic of the late eighteenth century.

JOHN DRYDEN

Alexander's Feast, or, The Power of Music

A SONG

IN HONOR OF ST. CECILIA'S DAY, 1697

'Twas at the royal feast for Persia won
   By Philip's warlike son—
   Aloft in awful state
   The godlike hero sate
   On his imperial throne;   5
His valiant peers were placed around,
Their brows with roses and with myrtles bound
(So should desert in arms be crowned);
   The lovely Thais by his side
   Sate like a blooming Eastern bride,   10
In flower of youth and beauty's pride—
   Happy, happy, happy pair!
     None but the brave,
     None but the brave,
None but the brave deserves the fair!   15

CHORUS

Happy, happy, happy pair!
   None but the brave,
   None but the brave,
None but the brave deserves the fair.

Timotheus, placed on high   20
   Amid the tuneful quire,
With flying fingers touched the lyre;
   The trembling notes ascend the sky,
   And heavenly joys inspire.
The song began from Jove   25
Who left his blissful seats above—
Such is the power of mighty love!
A dragon's fiery form belied the god;
Sublime on radiant spires he rode
When he to fair Olympia pressed,   30
And while he sought her snowy breast;

Dryden, *Alexander's Feast.* John Dryden (1631-1700) was Poet Laureate and literary dictator of the Restoration period. He wrote dramas, satires, and lyrics, and did much translating.

Then round her slender waist he curled,
And stamped an image of himself, a sovereign of
    the world.
The listening crowd admire the lofty sound;
A present deity! they shout around;   35
A present deity! the vaulted roofs rebound.
        With ravished ears
        The monarch hears,
        Assumes the god,
        Affects to nod,   40
    And seems to shake the spheres.

CHORUS

        With ravished ears
        The monarch hears,
        Assumes the god,
        Affects to nod,   45
    And seems to shake the spheres.

The praise of Bacchus then the sweet musician
    sung,
    Of Bacchus ever fair and ever young.
        The jolly god in triumph comes;
        Sound the trumpets, beat the drums!   50
        Flushed with a purple grace
        He shows his honest face.
Now give the hautboys breath; he comes, he
    comes.
    Bacchus, ever fair and young,
        Drinking joys did first ordain;   55
    Bacchus' blessings are a treasure,
    Drinking is the soldier's pleasure;
        Rich the treasure,
        Sweet the pleasure,
    Sweet is pleasure after pain.   60

CHORUS

    Bacchus' blessings are a treasure,
    Drinking is the soldier's pleasure;
        Rich the treasure,
        Sweet the pleasure,
    Sweet is pleasure after pain.   65

Soothed with the sound, the king grew vain;
    Fought all his battles o'er again;
And thrice he routed all his foes, and thrice he
    slew the slain!
    The master saw the madness rise,
    His glowing cheeks, his ardent eyes;   70
    And while he heaven and earth defied,
    Changed his hand and checked his pride.
        He chose a mournful Muse
        Soft pity to infuse.

He sung Darius great and good,   75
    By too severe a fate
Fallen, fallen, fallen, fallen,
    Fallen from his high estate,
    And weltering in his blood;
Deserted at his utmost need   80
By those his former bounty fed;
On the bare earth exposed he lies
With not a friend to close his eyes.
With downcast looks the joyless victor sate,
    Revolving in his altered soul   85
        The various turns of chance below;
    And now and then a sigh he stole,
        And tears began to flow.

CHORUS

    Revolving in his altered soul
        The various turns of chance below;   90
    And, now and then, a sigh he stole,
        And tears began to flow.

The mighty master smiled to see
That love was in the next degree;
'Twas but a kindred sound to move,   95
For pity melts the mind to love.
    Softly sweet, in Lydian measures,
    Soon he soothed his soul to pleasures.
War (he sung) is toil and trouble,
Honor but an empty bubble;   100
    Never ending, still beginning,
Fighting still, and still destroying;
    If the world be worth thy winning,
    Think, O think, it worth enjoying.
        Lovely Thais sits beside thee,   105
        Take the good the gods provide thee!
The many rend the skies with loud applause;
So love was crowned, but music won the cause.
    The prince, unable to conceal his pain,
        Gazed on the fair   110
        Who caused his care,
    And sighed and looked, sighed and looked,
    Sighed and looked, and sighed again.
At length, with love and wine at once oppressed
The vanquished victor sunk upon her breast.   115

CHORUS

    The prince, unable to conceal his pain,
        Gazed on the fair
        Who caused his care,
    And sighed and looked, sighed and looked,
    Sighed and looked, and sighed again.   120
At length, with love and wine at once oppressed,
The vanquished victor sunk upon her breast.

Now strike the golden lyre again,
A louder yet, and yet a louder strain!
Break his bands of sleep asunder   125
And rouse him like a rattling peal of thunder.
    Hark, hark! the horrid sound
        Has raised up his head;
        As awaked from the dead
    And amazed he stares around.   130
"Revenge, revenge!" Timotheus cries,
    "See the Furies arise!
    See the snakes that they rear,
    How they hiss in their hair,
And the sparkles that flash from their eyes!
    Behold a ghastly band,   136
    Each a torch in his hand!
Those are Grecian ghosts that in battle were slain
        And unburied remain
        Inglorious on the plain.   140
        Give the vengeance due
        To the valiant crew!
Behold how they toss their torches on high,
    How they point to the Persian abodes
And glittering temples of their hostile gods!"   145
The princes applaud with a furious joy;
And the King seized a flambeau with zeal to destroy;
        Thais led the way
        To light him to his prey,
And, like another Helen, fired another Troy!   150

CHORUS

And the King seized a flambeau with zeal to destroy;

        Thais led the way,
        To light him to his prey,
And, like another Helen, fired another Troy.

        Thus, long ago,   155
    Ere heaving bellows learned to blow,
        While organs yet were mute,
        Timotheus, to his breathing flute
        And sounding lyre,
Could swell the soul to rage, or kindle soft desire.
    At last divine Cecilia came,   161
        Inventress of the vocal frame;
The sweet enthusiast from her sacred store
    Enlarged the former narrow bounds,
    And added length to solemn sounds,   165
With nature's mother-wit, and arts unknown before.
        Let old Timotheus yield the prize
        Or both divide the crown;
        He raised a mortal to the skies;
        She drew an angel down!   170

GRAND CHORUS

At last divine Cecilia came,
Inventress of the vocal frame;
The sweet enthusiast from her sacred store
Enlarged the former narrow bounds,
And added length to solemn sounds,   175
With nature's mother-wit, and arts unknown before.
Let old Timotheus yield the prize
Or both divide the crown;
He raised a mortal to the skies;
She drew an angel down!   180

ALEXANDER POPE

The Rape of the Lock

AN HEROI-COMICAL POEM

TO MRS. ARABELLA FERMOR

Madam,

It will be in vain to deny that I have some regard for this piece, since I dedicate it to You. Yet you may bear me witness, it was intended only to divert a few young Ladies, who have good sense and good humor enough to laugh not only at their sex's little unguarded follies, but at their own. But as it was communicated with the air of a Secret, it soon found its way into the world. An imperfect copy having been offered to a Bookseller, you had the good nature for my sake to consent to the publication of one more

Pope, *The Rape of the Lock*. Alexander Pope (1688-1744) because he was a Roman Catholic had no university education, but nevertheless became the chief poet of his age. He spent his life in or near London.

correct: This I was forced to, before I had executed half my design, for the Machinery was entirely wanting to complete it.

The Machinery, Madam, is a term invented by the Critics, to signify that part which the Deities, Angels, or Demons are made to act in a Poem: For the ancient Poets are in one respect like many modern Ladies: let an action be never so trivial in itself, they always make it appear of the utmost importance. These Machines I determined to raise on a very new and odd foundation, the Rosicrucian doctrine of Spirits.

I know how disagreeable it is to make use of hard words before a Lady; but 'tis so much the concern of a Poet to have his works understood, and particularly by your Sex, that you must give me leave to explain two or three difficult terms.

The Rosicrucians are a people I must bring you acquainted with. The best account I know of them is in a French book called *Le Comte de Gabalis,* which both in its title and size is so like a Novel, that many of the Fair Sex have read it for one by mistake. According to these Gentlemen, the four Elements are inhabited by Spirits, which they call Sylphs, Gnomes, Nymphs, and Salamanders. The Gnomes or Demons of Earth delight in mischief; but the Sylphs, whose habitation is in the Air, are the best-conditioned creatures imaginable. For, they say, any mortals may enjoy the most intimate familiarities with these gentle Spirits, upon a condition very easy to all true Adepts, an inviolate preservation of Chastity.

As to the following Cantos, all the passages of them are as fabulous as the Vision at the beginning, or the Transformation at the end (except the loss of your Hair, which I always mention with reverence). The Human persons are as fictitious as the airy ones; and the character of Belinda, as it is now managed, resembles you in nothing but in Beauty.

If this Poem had as many Graces as there are in your Person, or in your Mind, yet I could never hope it should pass through the world half so Uncensured as You have done. But let its fortune be what it will, mine is happy enough, to have given me this occasion of assuring you that I am, with the truest esteem, MADAM,

Your most obedient, Humble Servant,

A. Pope.

CANTO I

What dire offense from am'rous causes springs,
What mighty contests rise from trivial things,
I sing—This verse to Caryl, Muse! is due:
This, e'en Belinda may vouchsafe to view:
Slight is the subject, but not so the praise,   5
If She inspire, and He approve my lays.
    Say what strange motive, Goddess! could compel
A well-bred Lord t' assault a gentle Belle?
O say what stranger cause, yet unexplored,
Could make a gentle Belle reject a Lord?   10
In tasks so bold, can little men engage,
And in soft bosoms dwells such mighty Rage?
    Sol through white curtains shot a tim'rous ray,
And oped those eyes that must eclipse the day:
Now lap-dogs give themselves the rousing shake,
And sleepless lovers, just at twelve, awake: 16
Thrice rung the bell, the slipper knocked the
        ground,
And the pressed watch returned a silver sound.
Belinda still her downy pillow pressed,
Her guardian Sylph prolonged the balmy rest: 20
'Twas He had summoned to her silent bed
The morning-dream that hovered o'er her head;
A Youth more glitt'ring than a Birth-night Beau
(That e'en in slumber caused her cheek to glow),
Seemed to her ear his winning lips to lay,   25
And thus in whispers said, or seemed to say:
    "Fairest of mortals, thou distinguished care
Of thousand bright Inhabitants of Air!
If e'er one vision touched thy infant thought,
Of all the Nurse and all the Priest have taught;
Of airy Elves by moonlight shadows seen,   31
The silver token, and the circled green,
Or virgins visited by Angel-pow'rs,
With golden crowns and wreaths of heav'nly
        flow'rs;
Hear and believe! thy own importance know,   35
Nor bound thy narrow views to things below.
Some secret truths, from learnéd pride concealed,
To Maids alone and Children are revealed:
What though no credit doubting Wits may give?
The Fair and Innocent shall still believe.   40
Know, then, unnumbered Spirits round thee fly,
The light Militia of the lower sky:
These, though unseen, are ever on the wing,
Hang o'er the Box, and hover round the Ring.
Think what an equipage thou hast in Air,   45
And view with scorn two Pages and a Chair.
As now your own, our beings were of old,
And once enclosed in Woman's beauteous mold;
Thence, by a soft transition, we repair
From earthly Vehicles to these of air.   50
Think not, when Woman's transient breath is fled,
That all her vanities at once are dead;
Succeeding vanities she still regards,
And though she plays no more, o'erlooks the cards.
Her joy in gilded Chariots, when alive,   55
And love of Ombre, after death survive.
For when the Fair in all their pride expire,
To their first Elements their Souls retire:

The Sprites of fiery Termagants in Flame
Mount up, and take a Salamander's name.   60
Soft yielding minds to Water glide away,
And sip, with Nymphs, their elemental Tea.
The graver Prude sinks downward to a Gnome,
In search of mischief still on Earth to roam.
The light Coquettes in Sylphs aloft repair,   65
And sport and flutter in the fields of Air.
    "Know further yet; whoever fair and chaste
Rejects mankind, is by some Sylph embraced:
For Spirits, freed from mortal laws, with ease
Assume what sexes and what shapes they please.
What guards the purity of melting Maids,   71
In courtly balls, and midnight masquerades,
Safe from the treach'rous friend, the daring spark,
The glance by day, the whisper in the dark,
When kind occasion prompts their warm desires,
When music softens, and when dancing fires?   76
'Tis but their Sylph, the wise Celestials know,
Though Honor is the word with Men below.
    "Some nymphs there are, too conscious of their
        face,
For life predestined to the Gnomes' embrace.   80
These swell their prospects and exalt their pride,
When offers are disdained, and love denied:
Then gay Ideas crowd the vacant brain,
While Peers, and Dukes, and all their sweeping
        train,
And Garters, Stars, and Coronets appear,   85
And in soft sounds, Your Grace salutes their ear.
'Tis these that early taint the female soul,
Instruct the eyes of young Coquettes to roll,
Teach Infant-cheeks a bidden blush to know,
And little hearts to flutter at a Beau.   90
    "Oft, when the world imagine women stray,
The Sylphs through mystic mazes guide their way,
Through all the giddy circle they pursue,
And old impertinence expel by new.
What tender maid but must a victim fall   95
To one man's treat, but for another's ball?
When Florio speaks what virgin could withstand,
If gentle Damon did not squeeze her hand?
With varying vanities, from ev'ry part,
They shift the moving Toyshop of their heart;   100
Where wigs with wigs, with sword-knots sword-
        knots strive,
Beaux banish beaux, and coaches coaches drive.
This erring mortals Levity may call;
Oh blind to truth! the Sylphs contrive it all.
    "Of these am I, who thy protection claim,   105
A watchful sprite, and Ariel is my name.
Late, as I ranged the crystal wilds of air,
In the clear Mirror of thy ruling Star

I saw, alas! some dread event impend,
Ere to the main this morning sun descend,   110
But heav'n reveals not what, or how, or where:
Warned by the Sylph, oh pious maid, beware!
This to disclose is all thy guardian can:
Beware of all, but most beware of Man!"
    He said; when Shock, who thought she slept too
        long,   115
Leaped up, and waked his mistress with his
        tongue.
'Twas then, Belinda, if report say true;
Thy eyes first opened on a Billet-doux;
Wounds, Charms, and Ardors were no sooner
        read,
But all the Vision vanished from thy head.   120
    And now, unveiled, the Toilet stands displayed,
Each silver Vase in mystic order laid.
First, robed in white, the Nymph intent adores,
With head uncovered, the Cosmetic pow'rs.
A heav'nly image in the glass appears,   125
To that she bends, to that her eyes she rears;
Th' inferior Priestess, at her altar's side,
Trembling begins the sacred rites of Pride.
Unnumbered treasures ope at once, and here
The various off'rings of the world appear;   130
From each she nicely culls with curious toil,
And decks the Goddess with the glitt'ring spoil.
This casket India's glowing gems unlocks,
And all Arabia breathes from yonder box.
The Tortoise here and Elephant unite,   135
Transformed to combs, the speckled, and the
        white.
Here files of pins extend their shining rows,
Puffs, Powders, Patches, Bibles, Billet-doux.
Now awful Beauty puts on all its arms;
The fair each moment rises in her charms,   140
Repairs her smiles, awakens ev'ry grace,
And calls forth all the wonders of her face;
Sees by degrees a purer blush arise,
And keener lightnings quicken in her eyes.
The busy Sylphs surround their darling care,   145
These set the head, and those divide the hair,
Some fold the sleeve, whilst others plait the gown;
And Betty's praised for labors not her own.

CANTO II

Not with more glories, in th' etherial plain,
The Sun first rises o'er the purpled main,   150
Than, issuing forth, the rival of his beams
Launched on the bosom of the silver Thames.
Fair Nymphs, and well-dressed Youths around her
        shone,

But ev'ry eye was fixed on her alone.
On her white breast a sparkling Cross she wore,
Which Jews might kiss, and Infidels adore.　156
Her lively looks a sprightly mind disclose,
Quick as her eyes, and as unfixed as those:
Favors to none, to all she smiles extends;
Oft she rejects, but never once offends.　160
Bright as the sun, her eyes the gazers strike,
And, like the sun, they shine on all alike.
Yet graceful ease, and sweetness void of pride,
Might hide her faults, if Belles had faults to hide:
If to her share some female errors fall,　165
Look on her face, and you'll forget 'em all.

This Nymph, to the destruction of mankind,
Nourished two Locks which graceful hung behind
In equal curls, and well conspired to deck
With shining ringlets the smooth iv'ry neck.　170
Love in these labyrinths his slaves detains,
And mighty hearts are held in slender chains.
With hairy springes we the birds betray,
Slight lines of hair surprise the finny prey,
Fair tresses man's imperial race ensnare,　175
And beauty draws us with a single hair.

Th' advent'rous Baron the bright locks admired;
He saw, he wished, and to the prize aspired.
Resolved to win, he meditates the way,
By force to ravish, or by fraud betray;　180
For when success a Lover's toil attends,
Few ask, if fraud or force attained his ends.

For this, ere Phœbus rose, he had implored
Propitious heav'n, and every pow'r adored,
But chiefly Love—to Love an Altar built,　185
Of twelve vast French Romances, neatly gilt.
There lay three garters, half a pair of gloves;
And all the trophies of his former loves;
With tender Billet-doux he lights the pyre,
And breathes three am'rous sighs to raise the
　fire.　190
Then prostrate falls, and begs with ardent eyes
Soon to obtain, and long possess the prize:
The pow'rs gave ear, and granted half his pray'r,
The rest, the winds dispersed in empty air.

But now secure the painted vessel glides,　195
The sun-beams trembling on the floating tides:
While melting music steals upon the sky,
And softened sounds along the waters die;
Smooth flow the waves, the Zephyrs gently play,
Belinda smiled, and all the world was gay.　200
All but the Sylph—with careful thoughts op-
　pressed,
Th' impending woe sat heavy on his breast.
He summons straight his Denizens of air;
The lucid squadrons round the sails repair:

Soft o'er the shrouds aërial whispers breathe,　205
That seemed but Zephyrs to the train beneath.
Some to the sun their insect-wings unfold,
Waft on the breeze, or sink in clouds of gold;
Transparent forms, too fine for mortal sight,
Their fluid bodies half dissolved in light,　210
Loose to the wind their airy garments flew,
Thin glitt'ring textures of the filmy dew,
Dipped in the richest tincture of the skies,
Where light disports in ever-mingling dyes,
While ev'ry beam new transient colors flings,　215
Colors that change whene'er they wave their
　wings.
Amid the circle, on the gilded mast,
Superior by the head, was Ariel placed;
His purple pinions op'ning to the sun,
He raised his azure wand, and thus begun:　220
"Ye Sylphs and Sylphids, to your chief give ear!
Fays, Fairies, Genii, Elves, and Demons, hear!
Ye know the spheres and various tasks assigned
By laws eternal to th' aërial kind.
Some in the fields of purest ether play,　225
And bask and whiten in the blaze of day.
Some guide the course of wand'ring orbs on high,
Or roll the planets through the boundless sky.
Some less refined, beneath the moon's pale light
Pursue the stars that shoot athwart the night,　230
Or suck the mists in grosser air below,
Or dip their pinions in the painted bow,
Or brew fierce tempests on the wintry main,
Or o'er the globe distill the kindly rain.
Others on earth o'er human race preside,　235
Watch all their ways, and all their actions guide:
Of these the chief the care of Nations own,
And guard with Arms divine the British Throne.
"Our humbler province is to tend the Fair,
Not a less pleasing, though less glorious care;　240
To save the powder from too rude a gale,
Nor let th' imprisoned essences exhale;
To draw fresh colors from the vernal flow'rs;
To steal from rainbows ere they drop in show'rs
A brighter wash; to curl their waving hairs,　245
Assist their blushes, and inspire their airs;
Nay oft, in dreams, invention we bestow,
To change a Flounce, or add a Furbelow.
"This day, black Omens threat the brightest
　Fair,
That e'er deserved a watchful spirit's care;　250
Some dire disaster, or by force, or slight;
But what, or where, the fates have wrapped in
　night.
Whether the nymph shall break Diana's law,
Or some frail China jar receive a flaw;

Or stain her honor or her new brocade;   255
Forget her pray'rs, or miss a masquerade;
Or lose her heart, or necklace, at a ball;
Or whether Heav'n has doomed that Shock must
　　fall.
Haste, then, ye spirits! to your charge repair:
The flutt'ring fan be Zephyretta's care;   260
The drops to thee, Brillante, we consign;
And, Momentilla, let the watch be thine;
Do thou, Crispissa, tend her fav'rite Lock;
Ariel himself shall be the guard of Shock.
　　"To fifty chosen Sylphs, of special note,   265
We trust th' important charge, the Petticoat:
Oft have we known that seven-fold fence to fail,
Though stiff with hoops, and armed with ribs of
　　whale;
Form a strong line about the silver bound,
And guard the wide circumference around.   270
　　"Whatever spirit, careless of his charge,
His post neglects, or leaves the fair at large,
Shall feel sharp vengeance soon o'ertake his sins,
Be stopped in vials, or transfixed with pins;
Or plunged in lakes of bitter washes lie,   275
Or wedged whole ages in a bodkin's eye:
Gums and Pomatums shall his flight restrain,
While clogged he beats his silken wings in vain;
Or Alum styptics with contracting pow'r
Shrink his thin essence like a riveled flow'r: 280
Or, as Ixion fixed, the wretch shall feel
The giddy motion of the whirling Mill,
In fumes of burning Chocolate shall glow,
And tremble at the sea that froths below!"

　　He spoke; the spirits from the sails descend;
Some, orb in orb, around the nymph extend;   286
Some thread the mazy ringlets of her hair;
Some hang upon the pendants of her ear:
With beating hearts the dire event they wait,
Anxious, and trembling for the birth of Fate.   290

Canto III

Close by those meads, for ever crowned with
　　flow'rs,
Where Thames with pride surveys his rising
　　tow'rs,
There stands a structure of majestic frame,
Which from the neighb'ring Hampton takes its
　　name.[1]
Here Britain's statesmen oft the fall foredoom   295
Of foreign Tyrants and of Nymphs at home;
Here thou, great Anna! whom three realms obey,
Dost sometimes counsel take—and sometimes Tea.

Hither the heroes and the nymphs resort,
To taste awhile the pleasures of a Court;   300
In various talk th' instructive hours they passed,
Who gave the ball, or paid the visit last;
One speaks the glory of the British Queen,
And one describes a charming Indian screen;
A third interprets motions, looks, and eyes;   305
At ev'ry word a reputation dies.
Snuff, or the fan, supply each pause of chat,
With singing, laughing, ogling, and all that.
　　Meanwhile, declining from the noon of day,
The sun obliquely shoots his burning ray;   310
The hungry Judges soon the sentence sign,
And wretches hang that jurymen may dine;
The merchant from th' Exchange returns in peace,
And the long labors of the Toilet cease.
Belinda now, whom thirst of fame invites,   315
Burns to encounter two advent'rous Knights,
At Ombre singly to decide their doom;
And swells her breast with conquests yet to come.
Straight the three bands prepare in arms to join,
Each band the number of the sacred nine.   320
Soon as she spreads her hand, th' aërial guard
Descend, and sit on each important card:
First Ariel perched upon a Matadore,
Then each, according to the rank they bore;
For Sylphs, yet mindful of their ancient race,   325
Are, as when women, wondrous fond of place.
　　Behold, four Kings in majesty revered,
With hoary whiskers and a forky beard;
And four fair Queens whose hands sustain a
　　flow'r,
Th' expressive emblem of their softer pow'r;   330
Four Knaves in garbs succinct, a trusty band,
Caps on their heads, and halberts in their hand;
And particolored troops, a shining train,
Draw forth to combat on the velvet plain.
　　The skillful Nymph reviews her force with
　　care: 335
"Let Spades be trumps!" she said, and trumps they
　　were.
　　Now move to war her sable Matadores,
In show like leaders of the swarthy Moors.
Spadillio first, unconquerable Lord!
Led off two captive trumps, and swept the
　　board.   340
As many more Manillio forced to yield,
And marched a victor from the verdant field.
Him Basto followed, but his fate more hard
Gained but one trump and one plebeian card.
With his broad saber next, a chief in years,   345
The hoary Majesty of Spades appears,

---

[1] Hampton Court, a palace a few miles sout' west of London.

Puts forth one manly leg, to sight revealed,
The rest, his many-colored robe concealed.
The rebel Knave, who dares his prince engage,
Proves the just victim of his royal rage.   350
E'en mighty Pam, that Kings and Queens o'er-
     threw
And mowed down armies in the fights of Lu,
Sad chance of war! now destitute of aid,
Falls undistinguished by the victor spade!
   Thus far both armies to Belinda yield;   355
Now to the Baron fate inclines the field.
His warlike Amazon her host invades,
Th' imperial consort of the crown of Spades.
The Club's black Tyrant first her victim died,
Spite of his haughty mien, and barb'rous pride:
What boots the regal circle on his head,   361
His giant limbs, in state unwieldy spread;
That long behind he trails his pompous robe,
And, of all monarchs, only grasps the globe?
   The Baron now his Diamonds pours apace;   365
Th' embroidered King who shows but half his
     face,
And his refulgent Queen, with pow'rs combined
Of broken troops an easy conquest find.
Clubs, Diamonds, Hearts, in wild disorder seen,
With throngs promiscuous strew the level green.
Thus when dispersed a routed army runs,   371
Of Asia's troops, and Afric's sable sons,
With like confusion different nations fly,
Of various habit, and of various dye,
The pierced battalions dis-united fall,   375
In heaps on heaps; one fate o'erwhelms them all.
   The Knave of Diamonds tries his wily arts,
And wins (oh shameful chance!) the Queen of
     Hearts.
At this, the blood the virgin's cheek forsook,
A livid paleness spreads o'er all her look;   380
She sees, and trembles at th' approaching ill,
Just in the jaws of ruin, and Codille.
And now (as oft in some distempered State)
On one nice Trick depends the gen'ral fate.
An Ace of Hearts steps forth: The King un-
     seen   385
Lurked in her hand, and mourned his captive
     Queen:
He springs to Vengeance with an eager pace,
And falls like thunder on the prostrate Ace.
The nymph exulting fills with shouts the sky;
The walls, the woods, and long canals reply.   390
   O thoughtless mortals! ever blind to fate,
Too soon dejected, and too soon elate.
Sudden, these honors shall be snatched away,
And cursed for ever this victorious day.

For lo! the board with cups and spoons is
     crowned,   395
The berries crackle, and the mill turns round;
On shining Altars of Japan they raise
The silver lamp; the fiery spirits blaze:
From silver spouts the grateful liquors glide,
While China's earth receives the smoking tide:
At once they gratify their scent and taste,   401
And frequent cups prolong the rich repast.
Straight hover round the Fair her airy band;
Some, as she sipped, the fuming liquor fanned,
Some o'er her lap their careful plumes displayed,
Trembling, and conscious of the rich brocade.   406
Coffee (which makes the politician wise,
And see through all things with his half-shut
     eyes),
Sent up in vapors to the Baron's brain
New Stratagems, the radiant Lock to gain.   410
Ah cease, rash youth! desist ere 'tis too late,
Fear the just Gods, and think of Scylla's Fate!
Changed to a bird, and sent to flit in air,
She dearly pays for Nisus' injured hair!
   But when to mischief mortals bend their will,
How soon they find fit instruments of ill!   416
Just then, Clarissa drew with tempting grace
A two-edged weapon from her shining case:
So Ladies in Romance assist their Knight,
Present the spear, and arm him for the fight.   420
He takes the gift with rev'rence, and extends
The little engine on his fingers' ends;
This just behind Belinda's neck he spread,
As o'er the fragrant steams she bends her head.
Swift to the Lock a thousand Sprites repair,   425
A thousand wings, by turns, blow back the hair;
And thrice they twitched the diamond in her ear;
Thrice she looked back, and thrice the foe drew
     near.
Just in that instant, anxious Ariel sought
The close recesses of the Virgin's thought;   430
As on the nosegay in her breast reclined,
He watched th' Ideas rising in her mind,
Sudden he viewed, in spite of all her art,
An earthly Lover lurking at her heart.
Amazed, confused, he found his pow'r expired,
Resigned to fate, and with a sigh retired.   436
   The Peer now spreads the glitt'ring Forfex wide,
T' enclose the Lock; now joins it, to divide.
E'en then, before the fatal engine closed,
A wretched Sylph too fondly interposed;   440
Fate urged the shears, and cut the Sylph in twain
(But airy substance soon unites again),
The meeting points the sacred hair dissever
From the fair head, for ever, and for ever!

Then flashed the living lightning from her
    eyes,   445
And screams of horror rend th' affrighted skies.
Not louder shrieks to pitying heav'n are cast,
When husbands, or when lap-dogs breathe their
    last;
Or when rich China vessels fall'n from high,
In glitt'ring dust and painted fragments lie! 450
    Let wreaths of triumph now my temples twine
(The victor cried) the glorious Prize is mine!
While fish in streams, or birds delight in air,
Or in a coach and six the British Fair,
As long as Atalantis shall be read,   455
Or the small pillow grace a Lady's bed,
While visits shall be paid in solemn days,
When num'rous wax-lights in bright order blaze,
While nymphs take treats, or assignations give,
So long my honor, name, and praise shall live!
What Time would spare, from Steel receives its
    date,   461
And monuments, like men, submit to fate!
Steel could the labor of the Gods destroy,
And strike to dust th' imperial towers of Troy;
Steel could the works of mortal pride confound,
And hew triumphal arches to the ground. 466
What wonder then, fair nymph! thy hairs should
    feel,
The conqu'ring force of unresisted steel?

Canto IV

But anxious cares the pensive nymph oppressed,
And secret passions labored in her breast. 470
Not youthful kings in battle seized alive,
Not scornful virgins who their charms survive,
Not ardent lovers robbed of all their bliss,
Not ancient ladies when refused a kiss,
Not tyrants fierce that unrepenting die, 475
Not Cynthia when her manteau's pinned awry,
E'er felt such rage, resentment, and despair,
As thou, sad Virgin! for thy ravished Hair.
    For, that sad moment, when the Sylphs with-
    drew
And Ariel weeping from Belinda flew, 480
Umbriel, a dusky, melancholy sprite,
As ever sullied the fair face of light,
Down to the central earth, his proper scene,
Repaired to search the gloomy Cave of Spleen.
    Swift on his sooty pinions flits the Gnome, 485
And in a vapor reached the dismal dome.
No cheerful breeze this sullen region knows,
The dreaded East is all the wind that blows.
Here in a grotto, sheltered close from air,

And screened in shades from day's detested glare,
She sighs for ever on her pensive bed, 491
Pain at her side, and Megrim at her head.
    Two handmaids wait the throne: alike in place,
But diff'ring far in figure and in face.
Here stood Ill-nature like an ancient maid, 495
Her wrinkled form in black and white arrayed;
With store of pray'rs, for mornings, nights, and
    noons,
Her hand is filled; her bosom with lampoons.
    There Affectation, with a sickly mien,
Shows in her cheek the roses of eighteen, 500
Practiced to lisp, and hang the head aside,
Faints into airs, and languishes with pride,
On the rich quilt sinks with becoming woe,
Wrapped in a gown, for sickness, and for show.
The fair ones feel such maladies as these, 505
When each new night-dress gives a new disease.
    A constant Vapor o'er the palace flies;
Strange phantoms rising as the mists arise;
Dreadful, as hermit's dreams in haunted shades,
Or bright, as visions of expiring maids. 510
Now glaring fiends, and snakes on rolling spires,
Pale specters, gaping tombs, and purple fires:
Now lakes of liquid gold, Elysian scenes,
And crystal domes, and angels in machines. 514
    Unnumbered throngs on every side are seen,
Of bodies changed to various forms by Spleen.
Here living Tea-pots stand, one arm held out,
One bent; the handle this, and that the spout:
A Pipkin there, like Homer's Tripod walks;
Here sighs a Jar, and there a Goose-pie talks; 520
Men prove with child, as powerful fancy works,
And maids turned bottles, call aloud for corks.
    Safe passed the Gnome through this fantastic
    band,
A branch of healing Spleenwort in his hand.
Then thus addressed the pow'r: "Hail, wayward
    Queen! 525
Who rule the sex to fifty from fifteen:
Parent of vapors and of female wit,
Who give th' hysteric, or poetic fit,
On various tempers act by various ways,
Make some take physic, others scribble plays; 530
Who cause the proud their visits to delay,
And send the godly in a pet to pray.
A nymph there is, that all thy pow'r disdains,
And thousands more in equal mirth maintains.
But oh! if e'er thy Gnome could spoil a grace,
Or raise a pimple on a beauteous face, 536
Like Citron-waters matrons' cheeks inflame,
Or change complexions at a losing game;
If e'er with airy horns I planted heads,

Or rumpled petticoats, or tumbled beds, 540
Or caused suspicion when no soul was rude,
Or discomposed the head-dress of a Prude,
Or e'er to costive lap-dog gave disease,
Which not the tears of brightest eyes could ease:
Hear me, and touch Belinda with chagrin, 545
That single act gives half the world the spleen."
   The Goddess with a discontented air
Seems to reject him, though she grants his pray'r.
A wondrous Bag with both her hands she binds,
Like that where once Ulysses held the winds; 550
There she collects the force of female lungs,
Sighs, sobs, and passions, and the war of tongues.
A Vial next she fills with fainting fears,
Soft sorrows, melting griefs, and flowing tears.
The Gnome rejoicing bears her gifts away, 555
Spreads his black wings, and slowly mounts to
   day.
   Sunk in Thalestris' arms the nymph he found,
Her eyes dejected and her hair unbound.
Full o'er their heads the swelling bag he rent,
And all the Furies issued at the vent. 560
Belinda burns with more than mortal ire,
And fierce Thalestris fans the rising fire.
"O wretched maid!" she spread her hands, and
   cried
(While Hampton's echoes, "Wretched maid!" re-
   plied),
"Was it for this you took such constant care 565
The bodkin, comb, and essence to prepare?
For this your locks in paper durance bound,
For this with tort'ring irons wreathed around?
For this with fillets strained your tender head,
And bravely bore the double loads of lead? 570
Gods! shall the ravisher display your hair,
While the Fops envy, and the Ladies stare!
Honor forbid! at whose unrivaled shrine
Ease, pleasure, virtue, all our sex resign.
Methinks already I your tears survey, 575
Already hear the horrid things they say,
Already see you a degraded toast,
And all your honor in a whisper lost!
How shall I, then, your helpless fame defend?
'Twill then be infamy to seem your friend! 580
And shall this prize, th' inestimable prize,
Exposed through crystal to the gazing eyes,
And heightened by the diamond's circling rays,
On that rapacious hand for ever blaze?
Sooner shall grass in Hyde-park Circus grow, 585
And wits take lodgings in the sound of Bow;
Sooner let earth, air, sea, to Chaos fall,
Men, monkeys, lap-dogs, parrots, perish all!"
   She said; then raging to Sir Plume repairs,

And bids her Beau demand the precious hairs:
(Sir Plume of amber snuff-box justly vain, 591
And the nice conduct of a clouded cane)
With earnest eyes, and round unthinking face,
He first the snuff-box opened, then the case,
And thus broke out—"My lord, why, what the
   devil? 595
Z—ds! damn the lock! 'fore Gad, you must be
   civil!
Plague on 't! 'tis past a jest—nay prithee, pox!
Give her the hair"—he spoke, and rapped his box.
   "It grieves me much" (replied the Peer again)
"Who speaks so well should ever speak in vain.
But by this Lock, this sacred Lock I swear 601
(Which never more shall join its parted hair;
Which never more its honors shall renew,
Clipped from the lovely head where late it grew),
That while my nostrils draw the vital air, 605
This hand, which won it, shall for ever wear."
He spoke, and speaking, in proud triumph spread
The long-contended honors of her head.
   But Umbriel, hateful Gnome! forbears not so;
He breaks the Vial whence the sorrows flow. 610
Then see! the nymph in beauteous grief appears,
Her eyes half-languishing, half-drowned in tears;
On her heaved bosom hung her drooping head,
Which, with a sigh, she raised; and thus she said:
   "For ever cursed be this detested day, 615
Which snatched my best, my fav'rite curl away!
Happy! ah, ten times happy had I been,
If Hampton Court these eyes had never seen!
Yet am not I the first mistaken maid,
By love of Courts to num'rous ills betrayed. 620
O had I rather un-admired remained
In some lone isle, or distant Northern land;
Where the gilt Chariot never marks the way,
Where none learn Ombre, none e'er taste Bohea!
There kept my charms concealed from mortal eye,
Like roses, that in deserts bloom and die. 626
What moved my mind with youthful Lords to
   roam?
O had I stayed, and said my pray'rs at home!
'Twas this, the morning omens seemed to tell,
Thrice from my trembling hand the patch-box
   fell; 630
The tott'ring China shook without a wind,
Nay, Poll sat mute, and Shock was most unkind!
A Sylph too warned me of the threats of fate,
In mystic visions, now believed too late!
See the poor remnants of these slighted hairs! 635
My hands shall rend what e'en thy rapine spares:
These in two sable ringlets taught to break,
Once gave new beauties to the snowy neck;

The sister-lock now sits uncouth, alone,
And in its fellow's fate foresees its own;   640
Uncurled it hangs, the fatal shears demands,
And tempts once more thy sacrilegious hands.
O hadst thou, cruel! been content to seize
Hairs less in sight, or any hairs but these!"

Canto V

She said: the pitying audience melt in tears.   645
But Fate and Jove had stopped the Baron's ears.
In vain Thalestris with reproach assails,
For who can move when fair Belinda fails?
Not half so fixed the Trojan could remain,
While Anna begged and Dido raged in vain.   650
Then grave Clarissa graceful waved her fan;
Silence ensued, and thus the nymph began:
    "Say why are Beauties praised and honored
        most,
The wise man's passion, and the vain man's toast?
Why decked with all that land and sea afford,   655
Why Angels called, and Angel-like adored?
Why round our coaches crowd the white-gloved
        Beaux,
Why bows the side-box from its inmost rows;
How vain are all these glories, all our pains,
Unless good sense preserve what beauty gains;   660
That men may say, when we the front-box grace:
'Behold the first in virtue as in face!'
Oh! if to dance all night, and dress all day,
Charmed the small-pox, or chased old age away;
Who would not scorn what housewife's cares
        produce,   665
Or who would learn one earthly thing of use?
To patch, nay ogle, might become a Saint,
Nor could it sure be such a sin to paint.
But since, alas! frail beauty must decay,   669
Curled or uncurled, since Locks will turn to gray;
Since painted, or not painted, all shall fade,
And she who scorns a man, must die a maid;
What then remains but well our pow'r to use,
And keep good-humor still whate'er we lose?
And trust me, dear! good-humor can prevail,   675
When airs, and flights, and screams, and scolding
        fail.
Beauties in vain their pretty eyes may roll;
Charms strike the sight, but merit wins the soul."
    So spoke the Dame, but no applause ensued;
Belinda frowned, Thalestris called her Prude.   680
"To arms, to arms!" the fierce Virago cries,
And swift as lightning to the combat flies.
All side in parties, and begin th' attack;

Fans clap, silks rustle, and tough whalebones
        crack;
Heroes' and Heroines' shouts confus'dly rise,   685
And bass, and treble voices strike the skies.
No common weapons in their hands are found,
Like Gods they fight, nor dread a mortal wound.
    So when bold Homer makes the Gods engage,
And heav'nly breasts with human passions rage;
'Gainst Pallas, Mars; Latona, Hermes arms;   691
And all Olympus rings with loud alarms:
Jove's thunder roars, heav'n trembles all around,
Blue Neptune storms, the bellowing deeps re-
        sound:
Earth shakes her nodding tow'rs, the ground gives
        way,   695
And the pale ghosts start at the flash of day!
    Triumphant Umbriel on a sconce's height
Clapped his glad wings, and sat to view the fight:
Propped on the bodkin spears, the Sprites survey
The growing combat, or assist the fray.   700
    While through the press enraged Thalestris
        flies,
And scatters death around from both her eyes,
A Beau and Witling perished in the throng,
One died in metaphor, and one in song.
"O cruel nymph! a living death I bear,"   705
Cried Dapperwit, and sunk beside his chair.
A mournful glance Sir Fopling upwards cast,
"Those eyes are made so killing"—was his last.
Thus on Mæander's flowery margin lies
Th' expiring Swan, and as he sings he dies.   710
    When bold Sir Plume had drawn Clarissa down,
Chloe stepped in, and killed him with a frown;
She smiled to see the doughty hero slain,
But, at her smile, the Beau revived again.
    Now Jove suspends his golden scales in air,   715
Weighs the Men's wits against the Lady's hair;
The doubtful beam long nods from side to side;
At length the wits mount up, the hairs subside.
    See, fierce Belinda on the Baron flies,
With more than usual lightning in her eyes: 720
Nor feared the Chief th' unequal fight to try,
Who sought no more than on his foe to die.
But this bold Lord with manly strength endued,
She with one finger and a thumb subdued:
Just where the breath of life his nostrils drew,   725
A charge of Snuff the wily virgin threw;
The Gnomes direct, to ev'ry atom just,
The pungent grains of titillating dust.
Sudden, with starting tears each eye o'erflows,
And the high dome re-echoes to his nose.   730
"Now meet thy fate," incensed Belinda cried,

And drew a deadly bodkin from her side.
(The same, his ancient personage to deck,
Her great great grandsire wore about his neck,
In three seal-rings; which after, melted down, 735
Formed a vast buckle for his widow's gown:
Her infant grandame's whistle next it grew,
The bells she jingled, and the whistle blew;
Then in a bodkin graced her mother's hairs, 739
Which long she wore, and now Belinda wears.)
"Boast not my fall" (he cried) "insulting foe!
Thou by some other shalt be laid as low,
Nor think, to die dejects my lofty mind:
All that I dread is leaving you behind!
Rather than so, ah, let me still survive, 745
And burn in Cupid's flames—but burn alive."
"Restore the Lock!" she cries; and all around
"Restore the Lock!" the vaulted roofs rebound.
Not fierce Othello in so loud a strain
Roared for the handkerchief that caused his pain.
But see how oft ambitious aims are crossed, 751
And chiefs contend till all the prize is lost!
The Lock, obtained with guilt, and kept with
pain,
In every place is sought, but sought in vain:
With such a prize no mortal must be bless'd, 755
So heav'n decrees! with heav'n who can contest?
Some thought it mounted to the Lunar sphere,
Since all things lost on earth are treasured there.
There Heroes' wits are kept in pond'rous vases,
And beaux' in snuff-boxes and tweezer-cases. 760
There broken vows and death-bed alms are found,
And lovers' hearts with ends of riband bound,
The courtier's promises, and sick man's pray'rs,

The smiles of harlots, and the tears of heirs,
Cages for gnats, and chains to yoke a flea, 765
Dried butterflies, and tomes of casuistry.
But trust the Muse—she saw it upward rise,
Though marked by none but quick, poetic eyes
(So Rome's great founder to the heav'ns with-
drew,
To Proculus alone confessed in view); 770
A sudden Star, it shot through liquid air,
And drew behind a radiant trail of hair.
Not Berenice's Locks first rose so bright,
The heav'ns bespangling with disheveled light.
The Sylph's behold it kindling as it flies, 775
And pleased pursue its progress through the skies.
This the Beau monde shall from the Mall survey,
And hail with music its propitious ray.
This the bless'd Lover shall for Venus take,
And send up vows from Rosamonda's lake. 780
This Partridge soon shall view in cloudless skies,
When next he looks through Galileo's eyes;
And hence th' egregious wizard shall foredoom
The fate of Louis, and the fall of Rome.
Then cease, bright Nymph! to mourn thy
ravished hair, 785
Which adds new glory to the shining sphere!
Not all the tresses that fair head can boast,
Shall draw such envy as the Lock you lost.
For, after all the murders of your eye,
When, after millions slain, yourself shall die: 790
When those fair suns shall set, as set they must,
And all those tresses shall be laid in dust,
This Lock, the Muse shall consecrate to fame,
And 'midst the stars inscribe Belinda's name.

An Essay on Criticism

PART I

'Tis hard to say if greater want of skill
Appear in writing or in judging ill;
But of the two less dangerous is th' offense
To tire our patience than mislead our sense:
Some few in that, but numbers err in this; 5
Ten censure wrong for one who writes amiss;
A fool might once himself alone expose;
Now one in verse makes many more in prose.
'Tis with our judgments as our watches, none
Go just alike, yet each believes his own. 10
In Poets as true Genius is but rare,

True Taste as seldom is the Critic's share;
Both must alike from Heav'n derive their light,
These born to judge, as well as those to write.
Let such teach others who themselves excel, 15
And censure freely who have written well;
Authors are partial to their wit, 'tis true,
But are not Critics to their judgment too?
Yet if we look more closely, we shall find
Most have the seeds of judgment in their mind:
Nature affords at least a glimm'ring light; 21
The lines, tho' touch'd but faintly, are drawn
right:
But as the slightest sketch, if justly traced,

Is by ill col'ring but the more disgraced,
So by false learning is good sense defaced: 25
Some are bewilder'd in the maze of schools,
And some made coxcombs Nature meant but
    fools:
In search of wit these lose their common sense,
And then turn Critics in their own defense:
Each burns alike, who can or cannot write,   30
Or with a rival's or an eunuch's spite.
All fools have still an itching to deride,
And fain would be upon the laughing side.
If Mævius scribble in Apollo's spite,   34
There are who judge still worse than he can write.
    Some have at first for Wits, then Poets pass'd;
Turn'd Critics next, and prov'd plain Fools at last.
Some neither can for Wits nor Critics pass,
As heavy mules are neither horse nor ass.
Those half-learn'd witlings, numerous in our isle,
As half-form'd insects on the banks of Nile;   41
Unfinish'd things, one knows not what to call,
Their generation's so equivocal;
To tell them would a hundred tongues require,
Or one vain Wit's, that might a hundred tire.   45
    But you who seek to give and merit fame,
And justly bear a Critic's noble name,
Be sure yourself and your own reach to know,
How far your Genius, Taste, and Learning go,
Launch not beyond your depth, but be dis-
    creet,   50
And mark that point where Sense and Dullness
    meet.
    Nature to all things fix'd the limits fit,
And wisely curb'd proud man's pretending wit.
As on the land while here the ocean gains,
In other parts it leaves wide sandy plains;   55
Thus in the soul while Memory prevails,
The solid power of Understanding fails;
Where beams of warm Imagination play,
The Memory's soft figures melt away.
One Science only will one genius fit;   60
So vast is Art, so narrow human wit:
Not only bounded to peculiar arts,
But oft in those confin'd to single parts.
Like Kings we lose the conquests gain'd before,
By vain ambition still to make them more: 65
Each might his sev'ral province well command,
Would all but stoop to what they understand.
    First follow Nature, and your judgment frame
By her just standard, which is still the same;
Unerring Nature, still divinely bright,   70
One clear, unchanged, and universal light,
Life, force, and beauty must to all impart,
At once the source, and end, and test of Art.

Art from that fund each just supply provides,
Works without show, and without pomp presides.
In some fair body thus th' informing soul   76
With spirits feeds, with vigor fills the whole;
Each motion guides, and every nerve sustains,
Itself unseen, but in th' effects remains.
Some, to whom Heav'n in wit has been profuse,
Want as much more to turn it to its use;   81
For Wit and Judgment often are at strife,
Tho' meant each other's aid, like man and wife.
'Tis more to guide than spur the Muse's steed,
Restrain his fury than provoke his speed: 85
The winged courser, like a gen'rous horse,
Shows most true mettle when you check his course.
    Those rules of old, discover'd, not devised,
Are Nature still, but Nature methodized;
Nature, like Liberty, is but restrain'd   90
By the same laws which first herself ordain'd.
    Hear how learn'd Greece her useful rules indites
When to repress and when indulge our flights:
High on Parnassus' top her sons she show'd,
And pointed out those arduous paths they trod;
Held from afar, aloft, th' immortal prize,   96
And urged the rest by equal steps to rise.
Just precepts thus from great examples giv'n,
She drew from them what they derived from
    Heav'n.
The gen'rous Critic fann'd the poet's fire,   100
And taught the world with reason to admire.
Then Criticism the Muse's handmaid prov'd,
To dress her charms, and make her more belov'd:
But following Wits from that intention stray'd:
Who could not win the mistress woo'd the maid;
Against the Poets their own arms they turn'd,   106
Sure to hate most the men from whom they
    learn'd.
So modern 'pothecaries, taught the art
By doctors' bills to play the doctor's part,
Bold in the practice of mistaken rules,   110
Prescribe, apply, and call their masters fools.
Some on the leaves of ancient authors prey;
Nor time nor moths e'er spoil'd so much as they:
Some drily plain, without invention's aid,
Write dull receipts how poems may be made;   115
These leave the sense their learning to display,
And those explain the meaning quite away.
    You then whose judgment the right course
    would steer,
Know well each ancient's proper character;
His fable, subject, scope in every page;   120
Religion, country, genius of his age:
Without all these at once before your eyes,
Cavil you may, but never criticize.

Be Homer's works your study and delight,
Read them by day, and meditate by night;   125
Thence form your judgment, thence your maxims
     bring,
And trace the Muses upward to their spring.
Still with itself compared, his text peruse;
And let your comment be the Mantuan Muse.

   When first young Maro in his boundless mind
A work t' outlast immortal Rome design'd,   131
Perhaps he seem'd above the critic's law,
And but from Nature's fountains scorn'd to draw;
But when t' examine ev'ry part he came,
Nature and Homer were, he found, the same.   135
Convinced, amazed, he checks the bold design,
And rules as strict his labor'd work confine
As if the Stagyrite o'erlook'd each line.
Learn hence for ancient rules a just esteem;
To copy Nature is to copy them.   140

   Some beauties yet no precepts can declare,
For there's a happiness as well as care.
Music resembles poetry; in each
Are nameless graces which no methods teach,
And which a master-hand alone can reach.   145
If, where the rules not far enough extend,
(Since rules were made but to promote their end)
Some lucky license answer to the full
Th' intent proposed, that license is a rule.
Thus Pegasus, a nearer way to take,   150
May boldly deviate from the common track.
Great Wits sometimes may gloriously offend,
And rise to faults true Critics dare not mend;
From vulgar bounds with brave disorder part,
And snatch a grace beyond the reach of Art,   155
Which, without passing thro' the judgment, gains
The heart, and all its end at once attains.
In prospects thus some objects please our eyes,
Which out of Nature's common order rise,
The shapeless rock, or hanging precipice.   160
But tho' the ancients thus their rules invade,
(As Kings dispense with laws themselves have
     made)
Moderns, beware! or if you must offend
Against the precept, ne'er transgress its end;
Let it be seldom, and compell'd by need;   165
And have at least their precedent to plead;
The Critic else proceeds without remorse,
Seizes your fame, and puts his laws in force.
   I know there are to whose presumptuous
     thoughts
Those freer beauties, ev'n in them, seem faults.
Some figures monstrous and misshaped ap-
     pear,   171
Consider'd singly, or beheld too near,

Which, but proportion'd to their light or place,
Due distance reconciles to form and grace.
A prudent chief not always must display   175
His powers in equal ranks and fair array,
But with th' occasion and the place comply,
Conceal his force, nay, seem sometimes to fly.
Those oft are stratagems which errors seem,
Nor is it Homer nods, but we that dream.   180
   Still green with bays each ancient altar stands
Above the reach of sacrilegious hands,
Secure from flames, from Envy's fiercer rage,
Destructive war, and all-involving Age.
See from each clime the learn'd their incense
     bring!   185
Hear in all tongues consenting pæans ring!
In praise so just let ev'ry voice be join'd,
And fill the gen'ral chorus of mankind.
Hail, Bards triumphant! born in happier days,
Immortal heirs of universal praise!   190
Whose honors with increase of ages grow,
As streams roll down, enlarging as they flow;
Nations unborn your mighty names shall sound,
And worlds applaud that must not yet be found!
O may some spark of your celestial fire   195
The last, the meanest of your sons inspire,
(That on weak wings, from far, pursues your
     flights,
Glows while he reads, but trembles as he writes)
To teach vain Wits a science little known,   199
T' admire superior sense, and doubt their own.

PART II

Of all the causes which conspire to blind
Man's erring judgment, and misguide the mind,
What the weak head with strongest bias rules,
Is Pride, the never failing vice of fools.
Whatever Nature has in worth denied   205
She gives in large recruits of needful Pride:
For as in bodies, thus in souls, we find
What wants in blood and spirits swell'd with
     wind:
Pride, where Wit fails, steps in to our defense,
And fills up all the mighty void of Sense: 210
If once right Reason drives that cloud away,
Truth breaks upon us with resistless day.
Trust not yourself; but your defects to know,
Make use of ev'ry friend—and ev'ry foe.
   A little learning is a dangerous thing;   215
Drink deep, or taste not the Pierian spring:
There shallow draughts intoxicate the brain,
And drinking largely sobers us again.
Fired at first sight with what the Muse imparts,

In fearless youth we tempt the heights of arts,   220
While from the bounded level of our mind
Short views we take, nor see the lengths behind:
But more advanc'd, behold with strange surprise
New distant scenes of endless science rise!
So pleas'd at first the tow'ring Alps we try,   225
Mount o'er the vales, and seem to tread the sky;
Th' eternal snows appear already past,
And the first clouds and mountains seem the last:
But those attain'd, we tremble to survey
The growing labors of the lengthen'd way;   230
Th' increasing prospect tires our wand'ring eyes,
Hills peep o'er hills, and Alps on Alps arise!
  A perfect judge will read each work of wit
With the same spirit that its author writ;
Survey the whole, nor seek slight faults to
  find   235
Where Nature moves, and Rapture warms the
  mind:
Nor lose, for that malignant dull delight,
The gen'rous pleasure to be charm'd with wit.
But in such lays as neither ebb nor flow,
Correctly cold, and regularly low,   240
That shunning faults one quiet tenor keep,
We cannot blame indeed—but we may sleep.
In Wit, as Nature, what affects our hearts
Is not th' exactness of peculiar parts;
'Tis not a lip or eye we beauty call,   245
But the joint force and full result of all.
Thus when we view some well proportion'd dome,
(The world's just wonder, and ev'n thine, O
  Rome!)
No single parts unequally surprise,
All comes united to th' admiring eyes;   250
No monstrous height, or breadth, or length, ap-
  pear;
The whole at once is bold and regular.
  Whoever thinks a faultless piece to see,
Thinks what ne'er was, nor is, nor e'er shall be.
In every work regard the writer's end,   255
Since none can compass more than they intend;
And if the means be just, the conduct true,
Applause, in spite of trivial faults, is due.
As men of breeding, sometimes men of wit,
T' avoid great errors must the less commit;   260
Neglect the rules each verbal critic lays,
For not to know some trifles is a praise.
Most critics, fond of some subservient art,
Still make the whole depend upon a part:
They talk of Principles, but Notions prize,   265
And all to one lov'd folly sacrifice.
  Once on a time La Mancha's Knight, they say,
A certain bard encount'ring on the way,

Discours'd in terms as just, with looks as sage,
As e'er could Dennis, of the Grecian Stage;   270
Concluding all were desperate sots and fools
Who durst depart from Aristotle's rules.
Our author, happy in a judge so nice,
Produced his play, and begg'd the knight's advice;
Made him observe the Subject and the Plot,   275
The Manners, Passions, Unities; what not?
All which exact to rule were brought about,
Were but a combat in the lists left out.
"What! leave the combat out?" exclaims the
  knight.
"Yes, or we must renounce the Stagyrite."   280
"Not so, by Heaven!" (he answers in a rage)
"Knights, squires, and steeds must enter on the
  stage."
"So vast a throng the stage can ne'er contain."
"Then build a new, or act it in a plain."
  Thus critics of less judgment than caprice,   285
Curious, not knowing, not exact, but nice,
Form short ideas, and offend in Arts
(As most in Manners), by a love to parts.
Some to Conceit alone their taste confine,   289
And glitt'ring thoughts struck out at every line;
Pleas'd with a work where nothing's just or fit,
One glaring chaos and wild heap of wit.
Poets, like painters, thus unskill'd to trace
The naked nature and the living grace,
With gold and jewels cover every part,   295
And hide with ornaments their want of Art.
True Wit is Nature to advantage dress'd,
What oft was thought, but ne'er so well express'd;
Something whose truth convinced at sight we find,
That gives us back the image of our mind.   300
As shades more sweetly recommend the light,
So modest plainness sets off sprightly wit:
For works may have more wit than does them
  good,
As bodies perish thro' excess of blood.
  Others for language all their care express,   305
And value books, as women men, for dress:
Their praise is still—the Style is excellent;
The Sense they humbly take upon content.
Words are like leaves; and where they most
  abound,
Much fruit of sense beneath is rarely found.   310
False eloquence, like the prismatic glass,
Its gaudy colors spreads on every place;
The face of Nature we no more survey,
All glares alike, without distinction gay;
But true expression, like th' unchanging sun,   315
Clears and improves whate'er it shines upon;
It gilds all objects, but it alters none.

Expression is the dress of thought, and still
Appears more decent as more suitable.
A vile Conceit in pompous words express'd   320
Is like a clown in regal purple dress'd:
For diff'rent styles with diff'rent subjects sort,
As sev'ral garbs with country, town, and court.
Some by old words to fame have made pretense,
Ancients in phrase, mere moderns in their sense;
Such labor'd nothings, in so strange a style,   326
Amaze th' unlearn'd, and make the learned smile;
Unlucky as Fungoso in the play,
These sparks with awkward vanity display
What the fine gentleman wore yesterday;   330
And but so mimic ancient wits at best,
As apes our grandsires in their doublets drest.
In words as fashions the same rule will hold,
Alike fantastic if too new or old:
Be not the first by whom the new are tried,   335
Nor yet the last to lay the old aside.
   But most by Numbers judge a poet's song,
And smooth or rough with them is right or wrong.
In the bright Muse tho' thousand charms conspire,
Her voice is all these tuneful fools admire;   340
Who haunt Parnassus but to please their ear,
Not mend their minds; as some to church repair,
Not for the doctrine, but the music there.
These equal syllables alone require,
Tho' oft the ear the open vowels tire,   345
While expletives their feeble aid do join,
And ten low words oft creep in one dull line:
While they ring round the same unvaried chimes,
With sure returns of still expected rhymes;
Where'er you find "the cooling western breeze,"
In the next line, it "whispers thro' the trees";   351
If crystal streams "with pleasing murmurs creep,"
The reader's threaten'd (not in vain) with "sleep";
Then, at the last and only couplet, fraught
With some unmeaning thing they call a thought,
A needless Alexandrine ends the song,   356
That, like a wounded snake, drags its slow length
   along.
Leave such to tune their own dull rhymes, and
   know
What's roundly smooth, or languishingly slow;
And praise the easy vigor of a line   360
Where Denham's strength and Waller's sweetness
   join.
True ease in writing comes from Art, not Chance,
As those move easiest who have learn'd to dance.
'Tis not enough no harshness gives offense;
The sound must seem an echo to the sense.   365
Soft is the strain when Zephyr gently blows,

And the smooth stream in smoother numbers
   flows;
But when loud surges lash the sounding shore,
The hoarse rough verse should like the torrent
   roar.
When Ajax strives some rock's vast weight to
   throw,   370
The line, too, labors, and the words move slow:
Not so when swift Camilla scours the plain,
Flies o'er th' unbending corn, and skims along the
   main.
Hear how Timotheus' varied lays surprise,
And bid alternate passions fall and rise!   375
While at each change the son of Libyan Jove
Now burns with glory, and then melts with love;
Now his fierce eyes with sparkling fury glow,
Now sighs steal out, and tears begin to flow: 379
Persians and Greeks like turns of nature found,
And the world's Victor stood subdued by sound!
The power of music all our hearts allow,
And what Timotheus was is Dryden now.
   Avoid extremes, and shun the fault of such
Who still are pleas'd too little or too much.   385
At ev'ry trifle scorn to take offense;
That always shows great pride or little sense:
Those heads, as stomachs, are not sure the best
Which nauseate all, and nothing can digest.
Yet let not each gay turn thy rapture move;   390
For fools admire, but men of sense approve:
As things seem large which we thro' mist descry,
Dullness is ever apt to magnify.
   Some foreign writers, some our own despise;
The ancients only, or the moderns prize.   395
Thus Wit, like Faith, by each man is applied
To one small sect, and all are damn'd beside.
Meanly they seek the blessing to confine,
And force that sun but on a part to shine,
Which not alone the southern wit sublimes,   400
But ripens spirits in cold northern climes;
Which from the first has shone on ages past,
Enlights the present, and shall warm the last;
Tho' each may feel increases and decays,
And see now clearer and now darker days.   405
Regard not then if wit be old or new,
But blame the False and value still the True.
   Some ne'er advance a judgment of their own,
But catch the spreading notion of the town;
They reason and conclude by precedent,   410
And own stale nonsense which they ne'er invent.
Some judge of authors' names, not works, and
   then
Nor praise nor blame the writings, but the men.
Of all this servile herd, the worst is he

That in proud dullness joins with quality;   415
A constant critic at the great man's board,
To fetch and carry nonsense for my lord.
What woeful stuff this madrigal would be
In some starv'd hackney sonneteer or me!
But let a lord once own the happy lines,   420
How the Wit brightens! how the Style refines!
Before his sacred name flies every fault,
And each exalted stanza teems with thought!
    The vulgar thus thro' imitation err,
As oft the learn'd by being singular;   425
So much they scorn the crowd, that if the throng
By chance go right, they purposely go wrong.
So schismatics the plain believers quit,
And are but damn'd for having too much wit.
Some praise at morning what they blame at night,
But always think the last opinion right.   431
A Muse by these is like a mistress used,
This hour she's idolized, the next abused;
While their weak heads, like towns unfortified,
'Twixt sense and nonsense daily change their side.
Ask them the cause; they're wiser still they say;
And still tomorrow's wiser than today.   437
We think our fathers fools, so wise we grow;
Our wiser sons no doubt will think us so.
Once school-divines this zealous isle o'er-spread;
Who knew most sentences was deepest read.   441
Faith, Gospel, all seem'd made to be disputed,
And none had sense enough to be confuted.
Scotists and Thomists now in peace remain
Amidst their kindred cobwebs in Duck-lane.   445
If Faith itself has diff'rent dresses worn,
What wonder modes in Wit should take their
        turn?
Oft, leaving what is natural and fit,
The current Folly proves the ready Wit;
And authors think their reputation safe,   450
Which lives as long as fools are pleas'd to laugh.
    Some, valuing those of their own side or mind,
Still make themselves the measure of mankind:
Fondly we think we honor merit then,
When we but praise ourselves in other men.   455
Parties in wit attend on those of state,
And public faction doubles private hate.
Pride, Malice, Folly, against Dryden rose,
In various shapes of parsons, critics, beaux:
But sense survived when merry jests were past;
For rising merit will buoy up at last.   461
Might he return and bless once more our eyes,
New Blackmores and new Milbournes must arise.
Nay, should great Homer lift his awful head,
Zoilus again would start up from the dead.   465
Envy will Merit as its shade pursue,

But like a shadow proves the substance true;
For envied Wit, like Sol eclips'd, makes known
Th' opposing body's grossness, not its own.
When first that sun too powerful beams displays,
It draws up vapors which obscure its rays;   471
But ev'n those clouds at last adorn its way,
Reflect new glories, and augment the day.
    Be thou the first true merit to befriend;
His praise is lost who stays till all commend.   475
Short is the date, alas! of modern rhymes,
And 'tis but just to let them live betimes.
No longer now that Golden Age appears,
When patriarch wits survived a thousand years:
Now length of fame (our second life) is lost,   480
And bare threescore is all ev'n that can boast:
Our sons their fathers' failing language see,
And such as Chaucer is shall Dryden be.
So when the faithful pencil has design'd
Some bright idea of the master's mind,   485
Where a new world leaps out at his command,
And ready Nature waits upon his hand;
When the ripe colors soften and unite,
And sweetly melt into just shade and light;
When mellowing years their full perfection give,
And each bold figure just begins to live,   491
The treach'rous colors the fair art betray,
And all the bright creation fades away!
    Unhappy Wit, like most mistaken things,
Atones not for that envy which it brings: 495
In youth alone its empty praise we boast,
But soon the short-lived vanity is lost;
Like some fair flower the early Spring supplies,
That gaily blooms, but ev'n in blooming dies.
What is this Wit, which must our cares employ?
The owner's wife that other men enjoy;   501
Then most our trouble still when most admired,
And still the more we give, the more required;
Whose fame with pains we guard, but lose with
        ease,
Sure some to vex, but never all to please,   505
'Tis what the vicious fear, the virtuous shun;
By fools 'tis hated, and by knaves undone!
    If Wit so much from Ignorance undergo,
Ah, let not Learning too commence its foe!
Of old those met rewards who could excel,   510
And such were prais'd who but endeavor'd well;
Tho' triumphs were to gen'rals only due,
Crowns were reserv'd to grace the soldiers too.
Now they who reach Parnassus' lofty crown   514
Employ their pains to spurn some others down;
And while self-love each jealous writer rules,
Contending wits become the sport of fools;

But still the worst with most regret commend,
For each ill author is as bad a friend.
To what base ends, and by what abject ways,   520
Are mortals urged thro' sacred lust of praise!
Ah, ne'er so dire a thirst of glory boast,
Nor in the critic let the man be lost!
Good nature and good sense must ever join;
To err is human, to forgive divine.   525
   But if in noble minds some dregs remain,
Not yet purged off, of spleen and sour disdain,
Discharge that rage on more provoking crimes,
Nor fear a dearth in these flagitious times.
No pardon vile obscenity should find,   530
Tho' Wit and Art conspire to move your mind;
But dullness with obscenity must prove
As shameful sure as impotence in love.
In the fat age of pleasure, wealth, and ease
Sprung the rank weed, and thrived with large in-
     crease: 535
When love was all an easy monarch's care,
Seldom at council, never in a war;
Jilts ruled the state, and statesmen farces writ;

Nay wits had pensions, and young lords had wit;
The Fair sat panting at a courtier's play,   540
And not a mask went unimprov'd away;
The modest fan was lifted up no more,
And virgins smil'd at what they blush'd before.
The following license of a foreign reign
Did all the dregs of bold Socinus drain;   545
Then unbelieving priests reform'd the nation,
And taught more pleasant methods of salvation;
Where Heav'n's free subjects might their rights
     dispute,
Lest God himself should seem too absolute;
Pulpits their sacred satire learn'd to spare,   550
And vice admired to find a flatt'rer there!
Encouraged thus, Wit's Titans braved the skies,
And the press groan'd with licens'd blasphemies.
These monsters, Critics! with your darts engage,
Here point your thunder, and exhaust your rage!
Yet shun their fault, who, scandalously nice,   556
Will needs mistake an author into vice:
All seems infected that th' infected spy,
As all looks yellow to the jaundic'd eye.

WILLIAM COLLINS

Ode to Evening

If aught of oaten stop, or pastoral song,
May hope, chaste Eve, to soothe thy modest ear,
   Like thy own solemn springs,
   Thy springs and dying gales;

O nymph reserved—while now the bright-haired
     sun   5
Sits in yon western tent, whose cloudy skirts,
   With brede ethereal wove,
   O'erhang his wavy bed;

Now air is hushed, save where the weak-eyed bat
With short shrill shriek flits by on leathern wing,
   Or where the beetle winds   11
   His small but sullen horn,

As oft he rises, 'midst the twilight path
Against the pilgrim borne in heedless hum—
   Now teach me, maid composed,   15
   To breathe some softened strain,

Whose numbers, stealing through thy darkening
     vale,
May not unseemly with its stillness suit,
   As, musing slow, I hail
   Thy genial loved return!   20

For when thy folding-star arising shows
His paly circlet, at his warning lamp
   The fragrant Hours, and elves
   Who slept in buds the day,

And many a nymph who wreathes her brows with
     sedge,   25
And sheds the freshening dew, and, lovelier still,
   The pensive Pleasures sweet,
   Prepare thy shadowy car.

Then lead, calm votaress, where some sheety lake
Cheers the lone heath, or some time-hallowed pile,
   Or upland fallows gray   3[
   Reflect its last cool gleam.

Collins, *Ode to Evening*. William Collins (1721-1759) studied at Oxford and went to London where he wrote for a living. His later years were obscured by insanity.

But when chill blustering winds, or driving rain,
Prevent my willing feet, be mine the hut
  That from the mountain's side   35
  Views wilds and swelling floods,

And hamlets brown, and dim-discovered spires,
And hears their simple bell, and marks o'er all
  Thy dewy fingers draw
  The gradual dusky veil.   40

While Spring shall pour his show'rs, as oft he
    wont,
And bathe thy breathing tresses, meekest Eve!
  While Summer loves to sport
  Beneath thy lingering light;

While sallow Autumn fills thy lap with leaves,
Or Winter, yelling through the troublous air,   46
  Affrights thy shrinking train,
  And rudely rends thy robes;

So long, regardful of thy quiet rule,
Shall Fancy, Friendship, Science, rose-lipped
    Health,   50
  Thy gentlest influence own,
  And hymn thy favorite name!

Ode

WRITTEN IN THE BEGINNING OF THE YEAR 1746

  How sleep the brave who sink to rest
  By all their country's wishes blest!
  When Spring, with dewy fingers cold,
  Returns to deck their hallowed mold,
  She there shall dress a sweeter sod   5
  Than Fancy's feet have ever trod.

  By fairy hands their knell is rung;
  By forms unseen their dirge is sung.
  There Honor comes, a pilgrim gray,
  To bless the turf that wraps their clay;   10
  And Freedom shall awhile repair,
  To dwell a weeping hermit there!

THOMAS GRAY

Elegy Written in a Country Churchyard

The curfew tolls the knell of parting day,
  The lowing herd wind slowly o'er the lea,
The plowman homeward plods his weary way,
  And leaves the world to darkness and to me.

Now fades the glimmering landscape on the sight,
  And all the air a solemn stillness holds,   6
Save where the beetle wheels his droning flight,
  And drowsy tinklings lull the distant folds;

Save that from yonder ivy-mantled tower
  The moping owl does to the moon complain   10
Of such, as wandering near her secret bower,
  Molest her ancient solitary reign.

Beneath those rugged elms, that yew-tree's shade,
  Where heaves the turf in many a moldering
    heap,
Each in his narrow cell for ever laid,   15
  The rude forefathers of the hamlet sleep.

The breezy call of incense-breathing morn,
  The swallow twittering from the straw-built
    shed,
The cock's shill clarion, or the echoing horn,
  No more shall rouse them from their lowly bed.

For them no more the blazing hearth shall burn,
  Or busy housewife ply her evening care: 22
No children run to lisp their sire's return,
  Or climb his knees the envied kiss to share.

Oft did the harvest to their sickle yield,   25
  Their furrow oft the stubborn glebe has broke;
How jocund did they drive their team afield!
  How bowed the woods beneath their sturdy
    stroke!

Let not Ambition mock their useful toil,
  Their homely joys, and destiny obscure;   30
Nor Grandeur hear with a disdainful smile,
  The short and simple annals of the poor.

Gray, *Elegy Written in a Country Churchyard*. Thomas Gray (1716-1771) spent most of his life quietly as professor of history at Cambridge.

The boast of heraldry, the pomp of power,
  And all that beauty, all that wealth e'er gave,
Awaits alike the inevitable hour.   35
  The paths of glory lead but to the grave.

Nor you, ye proud, impute to these the fault,
  If Memory o'er their tomb no trophies raise,
Where through the long-drawn aisle and fretted
    vault
  The pealing anthem swells the note of praise.

Can storied urn or animated bust   41
  Back to its mansion call the fleeting breath?
Can Honor's voice provoke the silent dust,
  Or Flattery soothe the dull cold ear of Death?

Perhaps in this neglected spot is laid   45
  Some heart once pregnant with celestial fire;
Hands, that the rod of empire might have swayed,
  Or waked to ecstasy the living lyre.

But Knowledge to their eyes her ample page
  Rich with the spoils of time did ne'er unroll; 50
Chill Penury repressed their noble rage,
  And froze the genial current of the soul.

Full many a gem of purest ray serene,
  The dark unfathomed caves of ocean bear:
Full many a flower is born to blush unseen,   55
  And waste its sweetness on the desert air.

Some village Hampden, that with dauntless breast
  The little tyrant of his fields withstood;
Some mute inglorious Milton here may rest,   59
  Some Cromwell guiltless of his country's blood.

The applause of listening senates to command,
  The threats of pain and ruin to despise,
To scatter plenty o'er a smiling land,
  And read their history in a nation's eyes,

Their lot forbade: nor circumscribed alone   65
  Their growing virtues, but their crimes confined;
Forbade to wade through slaughter to a throne,
  And shut the gates of mercy on mankind,

The struggling pangs of conscious truth to hide,
  To quench the blushes of ingenuous shame,   70
Or heap the shrine of Luxury and Pride
  With incense kindled at the Muse's flame.

Far from the madding crowd's ignoble strife,
  Their sober wishes never learned to stray;

Along the cool sequestered vale of life   75
  They kept the noiseless tenor of their way.

Yet even these bones from insult to protect,
  Some frail memorial still erected nigh,
With uncouth rhymes and shapeless sculpture
    decked,
  Implores the passing tribute of a sigh.   80

Their name, their years, spelt by the unlettered
    muse,
  The place of fame and elegy supply;
And many a holy text around she strews,
  That teach the rustic moralist to die.

For who to dumb Forgetfulness a prey,   85
  This pleasing anxious being e'er resigned,
Left the warm precincts of the cheerful day,
  Nor cast one longing lingering look behind?

On some fond breast the parting soul relies,
  Some pious drops the closing eye requires;   90
Ev'n from the tomb the voice of Nature cries,
  Ev'n in our ashes live their wonted fires.

For thee, who mindful of the unhonored dead
  Dost in these lines their artless tale relate;
If chance, by lonely contemplation led,   95
  Some kindred spirit shall inquire thy fate,

Haply some hoary-headed swain may say,
  "Oft have we seen him at the peep of dawn
Brushing with hasty steps the dews away
  To meet the sun upon the upland lawn.   100

"There at the foot of yonder nodding beech
  That wreathes its old fantastic roots so high,
His listless length at noontide would he stretch,
  And pore upon the brook that babbles by.

"Hard by yon wood, now smiling as in scorn,   105
  Muttering his wayward fancies he would rove,
Now drooping, woeful wan, like one forlorn,
  Or crazed with care, or crossed in hopeless love.

"One morn I missed him on the customed hill,
  Along the heath and near his favorite tree;   110
Another came; nor yet beside the rill,
  Nor up the lawn, nor at the wood was he;

"The next with dirges due in sad array
  Slow through the church-way path we saw him
    borne.   114

Approach and read (for thou can'st read) the lay,
Graved on the stone beneath yon aged thorn."

THE EPITAPH

Here rests his head upon the lap of earth
   A youth to fortune and to fame unknown.
Fair Science frowned not on his humble birth,
   And Melancholy marked him for her own. 120

Large was his bounty, and his soul sincere,
   Heaven did a recompense as largely send:
He gave to Misery all he had, a tear,
   He gained from Heaven ('twas all he wished)
     a friend.

No farther seek his merits to disclose, 125
   Or draw his frailties from their dread abode,
(There they alike in trembling hope repose)
   The bosom of his Father and his God.

Ode on a Distant Prospect of Eton College

Ye distant spires, ye antique towers,
   That crown the watery glade,
Where grateful Science still adores
   Her Henry's holy Shade; [1]
And ye that from the stately brow   5
Of Windsor's heights [2] th' expanse below
   Of grove, of lawn, of mead survey,
Whose turf, whose shade, whose flowers among
Wanders the hoary Thames along
   His silver-winding way: 10

Ah happy hills, ah pleasing shade,
   Ah fields beloved in vain,
Where once my careless childhood strayed,
   A stranger yet to pain!
I feel the gales, that from ye blow,   15
A momentary bliss bestow,
   As, waving fresh their gladsome wing,
My weary soul they seem to sooth,
And, redolent of joy and youth,
   To breathe a second spring.   20

Say, Father Thames, for thou hast seen
   Full many a sprightly race
Disporting on thy margent green
   The paths of pleasure trace,
Who foremost now delight to cleave   25
With pliant arm thy glassy wave?
   The captive linnet which enthrall?

What idle progeny succeed
To chase the rolling circle's speed,
   Or urge the flying ball?   30

While some, on earnest business bent
   Their murmuring labors ply
'Gainst graver hours, that bring constraint
   To sweeten liberty;
Some bold adventurers disdain   35
The limits of their little reign,
   And unknown regions dare descry;
Still as they run they look behind,
They hear a voice in every wind,
   And snatch a fearful joy.   40

Gay Hope is theirs by Fancy fed,
   Less pleasing when possessed;
The tear forgot as soon as shed,
   The sunshine of the breast;
Theirs buxom health of rosy hue,   45
Wild wit, invention ever new,
   And lively cheer of vigor born;
The thoughtless day, the easy night,
The spirits pure, the slumbers light,
   That fly th' approach of morn.   50

Alas, regardless of their doom,
   The little victims play!
No sense have they of ills to come,
   Nor care beyond today:
Yet see how all around 'em wait   55
The Ministers of human fate,
   And black Misfortune's baleful train!
Ah, show them where in ambush stand
To seize their prey the murd'rous band!
   Ah, tell them, they are men!   60

These shall the fury Passions tear,
   The vultures of the mind,
Disdainful Anger, pallid Fear,
   And Shame that skulks behind;
Or pining Love shall waste their youth,   65
Or Jealousy with rankling tooth,
   That inly gnaws the secret heart,
And Envy wan, and faded Care,
Grim-visaged comfortless Despair,
   And Sorrow's piercing dart.   70

Ambition this shall tempt to rise,
   Then whirl the wretch from high,
To bitter Scorn a sacrifice,
   And grinning Infamy.

[1] Henry VI, who founded the college in 1440.
[2] Windsor Castle.

The stings of Falsehood those shall try,   75
And hard Unkindness' alter'd eye,
  That mocks the tear it forced to flow;
And keen Remorse with blood defiled,
And moody Madness laughing wild
  Amid severest woe.   80

Lo, in the vale of years beneath
  A grisly troop are seen,
The painful family of Death,
  More hideous than their Queen:
This racks the joints, this fires the veins,   85
That every laboring sinew strains,
  Those in the deeper vitals rage:

Lo, Poverty, to fill the band,
That numbs the soul with icy hand,
  And slow-consuming Age.   90

To each his sufferings: all are men,
  Condemned alike to groan;
The tender for another's pain,
  Th' unfeeling for his own.
Yet ah! why should they know their fate?   95
Since sorrow never comes too late,
  And happiness too swiftly flies.
Thought would destroy their paradise.
No more; where ignorance is bliss,
  'Tis folly to be wise.   100

OLIVER GOLDSMITH

The Deserted Village

Sweet Auburn! loveliest village of the plain,
Where health and plenty cheer'd the laboring
  swain,
Where smiling spring its earliest visit paid,
And parting summer's lingering blooms delay'd:
Dear lovely bowers of innocence and ease,   5
Seats of my youth, when every sport could please:
How often have I loiter'd o'er thy green
Where humble happiness endear'd each scene!
How often have I paused on every charm,
The shelter'd cot, the cultivated farm,   10
The never failing brook, the busy mill,
The decent church that topp'd the neighboring
  hill,
The hawthorn bush, with seats beneath the shade,
For talking age and whispering lovers made!
How often have I bless'd the coming day,   15
When toil remitting lent its turn to play,
And all the village train, from labor free,
Led up their sports beneath the spreading tree:
While many a pastime circled in the shade,
The young contending as the old survey'd;   20
And many a gambol frolick'd o'er the ground,
And sleights of art and feats of strength went
  round.
And still, as each repeated pleasure tired,

Succeeding sports the mirthful band inspired;
The dancing pair that simply sought renown,   25
By holding out to tire each other down;
The swain mistrustless of his smutted face,
While secret laughter titter'd round the place;
The bashful virgin's sidelong looks of love,
The matron's glance that would those looks re-
  prove.   30
These were thy charms, sweet village! sports like
  these,
With sweet succession taught e'en toil to please;
These round thy bowers their cheerful influence
  shed,
These were thy charms—but all these charms are
  fled.
  Sweet smiling village, loveliest of the lawn,   35
Thy sports are fled, and all thy charms withdrawn;
Amidst thy bowers the tyrant's hand is seen,
And desolation saddens all thy green:
One only master grasps the whole domain,
And half a tillage stints thy smiling plain;   40
No more thy glassy brook reflects the day,
But choked with sedges works its weedy way;
Along thy glades, a solitary guest,
The hollow-sounding bittern guards its nest;
Amidst thy desert walks the lapwing flies,   45

Goldsmith, *The Deserted Village*. Oliver Goldsmith was born in Ireland in 1728. After traveling as
a vagabond over Europe, he settled in London as a literary hack. Here he became a friend of Johnson
and his circle. He died in 1774.

And tires their echoes with unvaried cries.
Sunk are thy bowers in shapeless ruin all,
And the long grass o'ertops the moldering wall;
And, trembling, shrinking from the spoiler's hand,
Far, far away thy children leave the land.   50

Ill fares the land, to hastening ills a prey,
Where wealth accumulates, and men decay;
Princes and lords may flourish, or may fade;
A breath can make them, as a breath has made:
But a bold peasantry, their country's pride,   55
When once destroy'd, can never be supplied.

A time there was, ere England's griefs began,
When every rood of ground maintain'd its man;
For him light labor spread her wholesome store,
Just gave what life required, but gave no more:
His best companions, innocence and health,   61
And his best riches, ignorance of wealth.

But times are alter'd; trade's unfeeling train
Usurp the land, and dispossess the swain;
Along the lawn, where scatter'd hamlets rose,   65
Unwieldy wealth, and cumbrous pomp repose;
And every want to luxury allied,
And every pang that folly pays to pride.
Those gentle hours that plenty bade to bloom,
Those calm desires that ask'd but little room,   70
Those healthful sports that graced the peaceful
    scene,
Lived in each look, and brighten'd all the green;
These, far departing, seek a kinder shore,
And rural mirth and manners are no more.

Sweet Auburn! parent of the blissful hour,   75
Thy glades forlorn confess the tyrant's power.
Here, as I take my solitary rounds,
Amidst thy tangling walks and ruin'd grounds,
And, many a year elapsed, return to view
Where once the cottage stood, the hawthorn grew,
Remembrance wakes with all her busy train,   81
Swells at my breast, and turns the past to pain.

In all my wanderings round this world of care,
In all my griefs—and God has given my share—
I still had hopes, my latest hours to crown,   85
Amidst these humble bowers to lay me down;
To husband out life's taper at the close,
And keep the flame from wasting by repose:
I still had hopes, for pride attends us still,
Amidst the swains to show my book-learn'd skill,
Around my fire an evening group to draw,   91
And tell of all I felt, and all I saw;
And as a hare, whom hounds and horns pursue,
Pants to the place from whence at first she flew,
I still had hopes, my long vexations pass'd,   95
Here to return—and die at home at last.

O bless'd retirement, friend to life's decline,
Retreats from care, that never must be mine,
How bless'd is he who crowns, in shades like these,
A youth of labor with an age of ease;   100
Who quits a world where strong temptations try,
And, since 'tis hard to combat, learns to fly!
For him no wretches, born to work and weep,
Explore the mine, or tempt the dangerous deep;
No surly porter stands, in guilty state,   105
To spurn imploring famine from the gate;
But on he moves to meet his latter end,
Angels around befriending virtue's friend;
Sinks to the grave with unperceived decay,
While resignation gently slopes the way;   110
And, all his prospects brightening to the last,
His heaven commences ere the world be pass'd.

Sweet was the sound, when oft at evening's close
Up yonder hill the village murmur rose;   114
There, as I pass'd with careless steps and slow,
The mingling notes came soften'd from below;
The swain responsive as the milkmaid sung,
The sober herd that low'd to meet their young;
The noisy geese that gabbled o'er the pool,
The playful children just let loose from school,
The watch-dog's voice that bayed the whispering
    wind,   121
And the loud laugh that spoke the vacant mind;
These all in sweet confusion sought the shade,
And fill'd each pause the nightingale had made.
But now the sounds of population fail,   125
No cheerful murmurs fluctuate in the gale,
No busy steps the grass-grown footway tread,
But all the bloomy flush of life is fled;
All but yon widow'd, solitary thing,
That feebly bends beside the plashy spring;   130
She, wretched matron, forced, in age, for bread,
To strip the brook with mantling cresses spread,
To pick her wintry faggot from the thorn,
To seek her nightly shed, and weep till morn;
She only left of all the harmless train,   135
The sad historian of the pensive plain.

Near yonder copse, where once the garden
    smiled,
And still where many a garden flower grows wild,
There, where a few torn shrubs the place disclose,
The village preacher's modest mansion rose.   140
A man he was to all the country dear,
And passing rich with forty pounds a year;
Remote from towns he ran his godly race,
Nor e'er had changed, nor wish'd to change his
    place;
Unskillful he to fawn, or seek for power,   145
By doctrines fashion'd to the varying hour;
Far other aims his heart had learn'd to prize,

More bent to raise the wretched than to rise.
His house was known to all the vagrant train,
He chid their wanderings, but relieved their pain;
The long remember'd beggar was his guest,   151
Whose beard descending swept his aged breast;
The ruin'd spendthrift, now no longer proud,
Claim'd kindred there, and had his claims allow'd;
The broken soldier, kindly bade to stay,   155
Sat by his fire, and talk'd the night away;
Wept o'er his wounds, or, tales of sorrow done,
Shoulder'd his crutch, and show'd how fields were
    won.
Pleased with his guests, the good man learn'd to
    glow,
And quite forgot their vices in their woe;   160
Careless their merits or their faults to scan,
His pity gave ere charity began.

  Thus to relieve the wretched was his pride,
And e'en his failings lean'd to virtue's side;
But in his duty prompt, at every call,   165
He watch'd and wept, he pray'd and felt for all:
And, as a bird each fond endearment tries
To tempt its new-fledged offspring to the skies,
He tried each art, reproved each dull delay,
Allured to brighter worlds, and led the way.   170

  Beside the bed where parting life was laid,
And sorrow, guilt, and pain by turns dismay'd,
The reverend champion stood. At his control
Despair and anguish fled the struggling soul;   174
Comfort came down the trembling wretch to raise,
And his last faltering accents whisper'd praise.

  At church, with meek and unaffected grace,
His looks adorn'd the venerable place;
Truth from his lips prevail'd with double sway,
And fools, who came to scoff, remain'd to pray.
The service pass'd, around the pious man,   181
With steady zeal, each honest rustic ran:
E'en children follow'd, with endearing wile,
And pluck'd his gown, to share the good man's
    smile.
His ready smile a parent's warmth express'd,   185
Their welfare pleased him, and their cares dis-
    tress'd:
To them his heart, his love, his griefs were given,
But all his serious thoughts had rest in heaven.
As some tall cliff, that lifts its awful form,
Swells from the vale, and midway leaves the storm,
Though round its breast the rolling clouds are
    spread,   191
Eternal sunshine settles on its head.

  Beside yon straggling fence that skirts the way
With blossom'd furze, unprofitably gay,
There, in his noisy mansion, skill'd to rule,   195

The village master taught his little school:
A man severe he was, and stern to view,
I knew him well, and every truant knew;
Well had the boding tremblers learn'd to trace
The day's disasters in his morning face;   200
Full well they laugh'd with counterfeited glee
At all his jokes, for many a joke had he;
Full well the busy whisper, circling round,
Convey'd the dismal tidings when he frown'd;
Yet he was kind, or if severe in aught,   205
The love he bore to learning was in fault;
The village all declared how much he knew,
'Twas certain he could write and cipher too;
Lands he could measure, terms and tides presage,
And e'en the story ran that he could gauge: 210
In arguing, too, the parson own'd his skill,
For e'en though vanquish'd, he could argue still;
While words of learned length and thundering
    sound
Amazed the gazing rustics ranged around;   214
And still they gazed, and still the wonder grew
That one small head could carry all he knew.

  But pass'd is all his fame. The very spot,
Where many a time he triumph'd, is forgot.
Near yonder thorn, that lifts its head on high,
Where once the signpost caught the passing eye,
Low lies that house where nutbrown draughts in-
    spired,   221
Where graybeard mirth and smiling toil retired,
Where village statesmen talk'd with looks pro-
    found,
And news much older than their ale went round.
Imagination fondly stoops to trace   225
The parlor splendors of that festive place;
The whitewash'd wall, the nicely sanded floor,
The varnish'd clock that click'd behind the door:
The chest contrived a double debt to pay,
A bed by night, a chest of drawers by day;   230
The pictures placed for ornament and use,
The twelve good rules, the royal game of goose;
The hearth, except when winter chill'd the day,
With aspen boughs, and flowers, and fennel gay;
While broken teacups, wisely kept for show,   235
Ranged o'er the chimney, glisten'd in a row.

  Vain transitory splendors! could not all
Reprieve the tottering mansion from its fall?
Obscure it sinks, nor shall it more impart
An hour's importance to the poor man's heart;
Thither no more the peasant shall repair   241
To sweet oblivion of his daily care;
No more the farmer's news, the barber's tale,
No more the woodman's ballad shall prevail;   244
No more the smith his dusky brow shall clear,

Relax his ponderous strength, and lean to hear;
The host himself no longer shall be found
Careful to see the mantling bliss go round;
Nor the coy maid, half willing to be press'd,
Shall kiss the cup to pass it to the rest.   250
   Yes! let the rich deride, the proud disdain,
These simple blessings of the lowly train;
To me more dear, congenial to my heart,
One native charm, than all the gloss of art;
Spontaneous joys, where Nature has its play,   255
The soul adopts, and owns their firstborn sway;
Lightly they frolic o'er the vacant mind,
Unenvied, unmolested, unconfined.
But the long pomp, the midnight masquerade,
With all the freaks of wanton wealth array'd,   260
In these, ere triflers half their wish obtain,
The toiling pleasure sickens into pain;
And, e'en while fashion's brightest arts decoy,
The heart distrusting asks, if this be joy?
   Ye friends to truth, ye statesmen, who survey
The rich man's joys increase, the poor's decay,   266
'Tis yours to judge how wide the limits stand
Between a splendid and a happy land.
Proud swells the tide with loads of freighted ore,
And shouting Folly hails them from her shore;   270
Hoards e'en beyond the miser's wish abound,
And rich men flock from all the world around.
Yet count our gains. This wealth is but a name
That leaves our useful products still the same.
Not so the loss. The man of wealth and pride   275
Takes up a space that many poor supplied;
Space for his lake, his park's extended bounds,
Space for his horses, equipage, and hounds;
The robe that wraps his limbs in silken sloth
Has robb'd the neighboring fields of half their
   growth;   280
His seat, where solitary sports are seen,
Indignant spurns the cottage from the green;
Around the world each needful product flies,
For all the luxuries the world supplies;
While thus the land, adorn'd for pleasure all,   285
In barren splendor feebly waits the fall.
   As some fair female, unadorn'd and plain,
Secure to please while youth confirms her reign,
Slights every borrow'd charm that dress supplies,
Nor shares with art the triumph of her eyes;   290
But when those charms are pass'd, for charms are
   frail,
When time advances, and when lovers fail,
She then shines forth, solicitous to bless,
In all the glaring impotence of dress:
Thus fares the land, by luxury betray'd,   295
In nature's simplest charms at first array'd:

But verging to decline, its splendors rise,
Its vistas strike, its palaces surprise;
While, scourged by famine, from the smiling land
The mournful peasant leads his humble band;   300
And while he sinks, without one arm to save,
The country blooms—a garden and a grave.
   Where then, ah! where shall poverty reside,
To 'scape the pressure of contiguous pride?
If to some common's fenceless limits stray'd,   305
He drives his flock to pick the scanty blade,
Those fenceless fields the sons of wealth divide,
And e'en the bare-worn common is denied.
   If to the city sped—What waits him there?
To see profusion that he must not share;   310
To see ten thousand baneful arts combined
To pamper luxury, and thin mankind:
To see each joy the sons of pleasure know,
Extorted from his fellow-creatures' woe.
Here, while the courtier glitters in brocade,   315
There the pale artist plies the sickly trade;
Here, while the proud their long-drawn pomp dis-
   play,
There the black gibbet glooms beside the way;
The dome where pleasure holds her midnight
   reign,
Here, richly deck'd, admits the gorgeous train;   320
Tumultuous grandeur crowds the blazing square,
The rattling chariots clash, the torches glare.
Sure scenes like these no troubles e'er annoy!
Sure these denote one universal joy!
Are these thy serious thoughts?—Ah, turn thine
   eyes   325
Where the poor houseless shivering female lies:
She once, perhaps, in village plenty bless'd,
Has wept at tales of innocence distress'd;
Her modest looks the cottage might adorn,   329
Sweet as the primrose peeps beneath the thorn;
Now lost to all; her friends, her virtue fled,
Near her betrayer's door she lays her head,
And, pinch'd with cold, and shrinking from the
   shower,
With heavy heart, deplores that luckless hour,
When idly first, ambitious of the town,   335
She left her wheel and robes of country brown.
   Do thine, sweet Auburn, thine, the loveliest train,
Do thy fair tribes participate her pain?
E'en now, perhaps, by cold and hunger led,
At proud men's doors they ask a little bread!   340
   Ah, no. To distant climes, a dreary scene,
Where half the convex world intrudes between,
Through torrid tracts with fainting steps they go,
Where wild Altama murmurs to their woe.
Far different there from all that charm'd before,

The various terrors of that horrid shore;   346
Those blazing suns that dart a downward ray,
And fiercely shed intolerable day;
Those matted woods where birds forget to sing,
But silent bats in drowsy clusters cling;   350
Those poisonous fields with rank luxuriance
    crown'd,
Where the dark scorpion gathers death around:
Where at each step the stranger fears to wake
The rattling terrors of the vengeful snake;   354
Where crouching tigers wait their hapless prey,
And savage men more murderous still than they:
While oft in whirls the mad tornado flies,
Mingling the ravaged landscape with the skies.
Far different these from every former scene,
The cooling brook, the grassy vested green,   360
The breezy covert of the warbling grove,
That only shelter'd thefts of harmless love.
   Good Heaven! what sorrows gloom'd that part-
      ing day,
That call'd them from their native walks away;
When the poor exiles, every pleasure pass'd,   365
Hung round the bowers, and fondly look'd their
      last,
And took a long farewell, and wish'd in vain
For seats like these beyond the western main;
And, shuddering still to face the distant deep,
Return'd and wept, and still return'd to weep.   370
The good old sire the first prepared to go,
To new-found worlds, and wept for others' woe;
But for himself, in conscious virtue brave,
He only wish'd for worlds beyond the grave.
His lovely daughter, lovelier in her tears,   375
The fond companion of his helpless years,
Silent went next, neglectful of her charms,
And left a lover's for her father's arms.
With louder plaints the mother spoke her woes,
And bless'd the cot where every pleasure rose;   380
And kiss'd her thoughtless babes with many a tear,
And clasp'd them close, in sorrow doubly dear;
Whilst her fond husband strove to lend relief
In all the silent manliness of grief.
   O luxury! thou cursed by heaven's decree,   385
How ill exchanged are things like these for thee!

How do thy potions, with insidious joy,
Diffuse their pleasures only to destroy!
Kingdoms by thee, to sickly greatness grown,
Boast of a florid vigor not their own: 390
At every draught more large and large they grow,
A bloated mass of rank unwieldy woe;
Till sapp'd their strength, and every part unsound,
Down, down they sink, and spread a ruin round.
   E'en now the devastation is begun,   395
And half the business of destruction done;
E'en now, methinks, as pondering here I stand,
I see the rural virtues leave the land.
Down where yon anchoring vessel spreads the sail,
That idly waiting flaps with every gale,   400
Downward they move, a melancholy band,
Pass from the shore, and darken all the strand.
Contented toil, and hospitable care,
And kind connubial tenderness are there:
And piety with wishes placed above,   405
And steady loyalty, and faithful love.
And thou, sweet Poetry, thou loveliest maid,
Still first to fly where sensual joys invade,
Unfit in these degenerate times of shame,
To catch the heart, or strike for honest fame; 410
Dear charming nymph, neglected and decried,
My shame in crowds, my solitary pride;
Thou source of all my bliss, and all my woe,
That found'st me poor at first, and keep'st me so;
Thou guide, by which the nobler arts excel,   415
Thou nurse of every virtue, fare thee well;
Farewell! and O! where'er thy voice be tried,
On Torno's cliffs, or Pambamarca's side,
Whether where equinoctial fervors glow,
Or winter wraps the polar world in snow,   420
Still let thy voice, prevailing over time,
Redress the rigors of th' inclement clime;
Aid slighted Truth with thy persuasive train;
Teach erring man to spurn the rage of gain;
Teach him, that states of native strength possess'd,
Though very poor, may still be very bless'd;   426
That trade's proud empire hastes to swift decay,
As ocean sweeps the labor'd mole away;
While self-dependent power can time defy,
As rocks resist the billows and the sky.   430

THE ROMANTIC POETS

We have already observed how the regular classical poetry of the age of Pope continued well on to the end of the eighteenth century. But we have also seen, beginning as early as 1730, a new spirit manifesting itself. Since this new way of looking at life and of expressing it in art and letters came by the end of the eighteenth century to dominate English literature, it is important to look a little more closely at the nature of this Romantic Movement.

Some mention has already been made of the increased interest in the description of nature which began with Thomson's *Seasons* (1726). The romantic melancholy of the writers of "graveyard" poetry has been illustrated by the poems of Gray and Collins. These, however, were only two of the forces that were beginning to show themselves in the 1730's.

A whole series of related currents in the intellectual and spiritual life of England may be expressed by the term "sentimentalism." After a generation of repressed emotions, many people went to the opposite extreme of emotional excess. The new novels which began around 1740 were filled with highly sentimental scenes, and over these scenes even cultivated ladies and gentlemen wept unashamed. This opening up of the flood-gates of feeling for the reading public came at the same time as the great wave of religious enthusiasm caused by the preaching of the Wesleys and George Whitefield. Sentimentalism invaded the domain of scholarship as well. The literary student was no longer content with the well-assured excellence of the old Greek and Latin classics. He began to be fascinated by literatures which up to that time had not been thought worth the attention of scholars. The strangeness and mystery of Oriental tales, the rich imagery of the older Celtic poems and romances, the vigor and masculinity of the Norse hero stories came to him as something new and wonderful and opened up unexplored worlds for the imagination. The peoples who produced these literatures became immensely interesting and were endowed by those who were now first discovering them with a sentimental glamor. At the same time occurred a change in men's ideas towards the Middle Ages. Instead of being thought of as ages of darkness the medieval era now came to be fondly regarded as romantic. Poets interested themselves in gothic castles and cathedrals and stories of chivalry. The intervening centuries were a haze through which the romantic poet saw only pageantry and quaintness and bravery. Novelists delighted in evoking thrills of horror by tales of these olden times so filled with suggestions of the strange and marvelous.

The widened interest in mankind extended itself to primitive peoples. The American Indian, viewed from the safe distance of three thousand miles, became the noble savage and was imagined to possess all human virtues, unsullied by the blight of civilization. "Nature's simple way" came to be prescribed as the remedy for all ills of man or society.

Largely through the influence of Rousseau, this idyllic view of primitive man was extended into a theory of the social contract, in which it was supposed that governments arose in this perfect primitive world through voluntary agreement. The only uncorrupted social state, therefore, was the democracy, where each man had a voice in government. For this aspect of the Romantic Movement the American *Declaration of Independence* is the political and Burns's *A Man's a Man for A' That* the passionate personal expression.

As the age of common sense spent its force, it gave way in some of the ablest writers to a manifestation of mysticism. These men sought to perceive reality, not through their ordinary senses, but by immediate revelation. Many of the poems of William Blake and some of those of Wordsworth attempt to bring these experiences to the reader. Even if the ordinary man finds himself unable to move with under-standing in the rarefied atmosphere which these poets sometimes evoke, he will nevertheless often find that these mystical visions are filled with beauty and emotional intensity.

Many of the forces which we have mentioned had their practical issue in two great political and social upheavals towards the end of the eighteenth century. First, the American Revolution and later the French Revolution served to break up political and social patterns and seemed to prepare the way for a new world compacted of all the romantic dreams of the age. The young Wordsworth threw himself heart and soul into the French Revolution, though later its excesses drove him away in disgust. Some of his contemporaries, however, held firm by the democratic faith through the years of reaction that came at the beginning of the new century. They carried on the ideal and handed it down to the poets of the new Victorian age.

When we speak of the Romantic Revival we are usually thinking of the years 1798-1830. There is no doubt that much of the work of Robert Burns is in a very real sense "romantic." But the first declaration of new literary principles came in the *Lyrical Ballads,* first issued by Wordsworth and Coleridge in 1798. In this small volume we have some of the most characteristic poems of Wordsworth. The actors are of lowly station in life and the language is that of common man. The old artificialities of poetic diction are discarded. Wordsworth shows his romantic point of view when he finds the simplest peasant worthy of dramatic treatment and the highest wisdom issuing from the mouths of babes. It is from his recollections of early childhood that he receives his Intimations of Immortality. And it is from the meadows and the woods that he comes to feel the presence of God.

The young Coleridge is also romantic. But his romanticism goes in the direction of the mysterious and the supernatural. The curse laid on the Ancient Mariner for his killing of the albatross and all the train of strange events that followed gave the poet an outlet for his exhaustive knowledge of rare books of travel and adventure, real and fancied. This quality of the wonder of far-off places and impossible realms is what makes that tantalizing fragment, *Kubla Khan,* a masterpiece of romantic imagination.

Well after the turn of the century a group of three writers came into prominence, Byron, Shelley, and Keats. Lord Byron, the eldest of the group, exercised a profound influence on European literature. Throughout his works several ideas are predominant. His poetry is mostly concerned, in one way or another, with himself. He was the romantic hero, at odds with the world and calling on all sympathetic readers to view what Matthew Arnold calls "the pageant of his bleeding heart." He had a very sincere love of human liberty, so that it is entirely fitting that he met his death helping the Greeks in their struggle for independence. In one way Byron was not a romanticist, for on occasion he could be a bitter satirist. Sometimes he even satirizes himself, for in such poems as *Don Juan* he could write a highly romantic song and then laugh at his own romanticism.

Such a feat would have been impossible for Shelley. He, too, calls on us to share his sufferings, but he is more of an idealist than Byron and is always perfectly sincere. He felt called on to reform the world, but his ideas, though strongly felt, were never thought through to any practical conclusions. He remained to the end the poet of the clouds and skies, and he wrote his greatest poetry when he could wander in spirit with the skylark or the wild west wind.

The third of our trio, the young John Keats, perhaps wrote greater poetry than either of his contemporaries. But he concerned himself little with problems or persons of his own day. In his short six years of poetic activity this youth, born over a livery stable and trained as a surgeon's apprentice, sought one thing only. That was beauty. "A thing of beauty," he says, "is a joy forever." Wherever he might find it, there he sought it. Without a word of Greek he has handed on to us as no other English poet has done the Greek sense of beauty in his *Endymion* and his *Ode on a Grecian Urn*. In like manner we find in his poems expressions of beauty from many other sources, the gorgeousness of old castles, the song of nightingales, and the many colors of autumn.

The most prominent literary form during the Romantic Movement was poetry, but it must not be forgotten that during this period two important novelists were at work. Jane Austen produced her remarkable series of studies of the upper middle classes in such novels as *Pride and Prejudice* and *Emma*. In her hands the novel became a faithful record of a society which she well knew. The other great novelist of her period began as a poet, writing romantic tales of Scotland. But soon Sir Walter Scott discovered that his greatest contributions were not to be more *Lady of the Lake's* but stirring romances which would re-create the glamor of ancient days. During the last twenty years before his death in 1832 he wrote a long series of novels which have maintained their interest through four generations.

ROBERT BURNS

Tam O'Shanter

When chapman billies[1] leave the street,
And drouthy neebors neebors meet;
As market-days are wearing late,
An' folk begin to tak the gate;
While we sit bousing at the nappy,

An' getting fou and unco happy,
We think na on the lang Scots miles,
The mosses, waters, slaps, and styles,
That lie between us and our hame,
Whare sits our sulky, sullen dame,
Gathering her brows like gathering storm,
Nursing her wrath to keep it warm.

This truth fand honest Tam O'Shanter,
As he frae Ayr ae night did canter
(Auld Ayr, wham ne'er a town surpasses,   15
For honest men and bonie lasses).

O Tam! hadst thou but been sae wise,
As taen thy ain wife Kate's advice!
She tauld thee weel thou was a skellum,
A blethering, blustering, drunken blellum;[2]   20
That frae November till October,
Ae market-day thou was nae sober;
That ilka melder wi' the miller,[3]
Thou sat as lang as thou had siller;
That ev'ry naig was ca'd a shoe on,[4]   25
The smith an' thee gat roaring fou on;
That at the Lord's house, ev'n on Sunday,
Thou drank wi' Kirkton Jean till Monday.
She prophesied that, late or soon,
Thou would be found deep drowned in Doon,
Or catched wi' warlocks in the mirk,[5]   31
By Alloway's auld haunted kirk.

Ah, gentle dames! it gars me greet,[6]
To think how mony counsels sweet,
How mony lengthened, sage advices,   35
The husband frae the wife despises!

But to our tale: Ae market night,
Tam had got planted unco right,
Fast by an ingle, bleezing finely,
Wi' reaming swats[7] that drank divinely;   40
And at his elbow, Souter[8] Johnny,
His ancient, trusty, drouthy crony—
Tam lo'ed him like a very brither;
They had been fou for weeks thegither.
The night drave on wi' sangs and clatter,   45
And aye the ale was growing better;
The landlady and Tam grew gracious,
Wi' favors secret, sweet, and precious;
The souter tauld his queerest stories;
The landlord's laugh was ready chorus.   50
The storm without might rair and rustle,
Tam did na mind the storm a whistle.

Care, mad to see a man sae happy,
E'en drowned himsel amang the nappy.

As bees flee hame wi' lades o' treasure,   55
The minutes winged their way wi' pleasure;
Kings may be blest, but Tam was glorious,
O'er a' the ills o' life victorious!

But pleasures are like poppies spread—
You seize the flow'r, its bloom is shed;   60
Or like the snow falls in the river,
A moment white—then melts forever;
Or like the borealis race,
That flit ere you can point their place;
Or like the rainbow's lovely form,   65
Evanishing amid the storm.—
Nae man can tether time nor tide;
The hour approaches Tam maun ride;
That hour, o' night's black arch the keystane,
That dreary hour he mounts his beast in;   70
And sic a night he taks the road in,
As ne'er poor sinner was abroad in.

The wind blew as 'twad blawn its last;
The rattling show'rs rose on the blast;
The speedy gleams the darkness swallowed;   75
Loud, deep, and lang the thunder bellowed;
That night, a child might understand,
The Deil had business on his hand.

Weel mounted on his gray mare Meg—
A better never lifted leg—   80
Tam skelpit on thro' dub and mire,
Despising wind, and rain, and fire;
Whyles holding fast his guid blue bonnet,
Whyles crooning o'er some auld Scots sonnet,
Whyles glow'ring round wi' prudent cares,   85
Lest bogles catch him unawares—
Kirk-Alloway was drawing nigh,
Whare ghaists and houlets[9] nightly cry.

By this time he was cross the ford,
Whare in the snaw the chapman smoored;[10]   90
And past the birks and meikle stane,
Whare drunken Charlie brak's neckbane;
And through the whins, and by the cairn,
Whare hunters fand the murdered bairn;
And near the thorn, aboon the well,   95
Whare Mungo's mither hanged hersel.

[2] Blabber.
[3] Each trip to the miller.
[4] Every time the horse was shod.
[5] Mirk (dark), kirk (church).
[6] It makes me weep.
[7] Creamy ale.
[8] Cobbler.
[9] Ghosts and owls.
[10] Smoored (smothered), birks (birches), meikle (great), stane (stone), whins (furze), cairn (pile of stone), bairn (child), aboon (above).

Before him Doon pours all his floods;
The doubling storm roars through the woods;
The lightnings flash from pole to pole;
Near and more near the thunders roll; 100
When, glimmering through the groaning trees,
Kirk-Alloway seemed in a bleeze;
Through ilka bore [11] the beams were glancing,
And loud resounded mirth and dancing.

Inspiring bold John Barleycorn! 105
What dangers thou canst make us scorn!
Wi' tippenny, we fear nae evil;
Wi' usquabae, we'll face the Devil!
The swats sae reamed in Tammie's noddle,
Fair play, he cared na deils a boddle. 110
But Maggie stood, right sair astonished,
Till, by the heel and hand admonished,
She ventured forward on the light;
And, wow! Tam saw an unco sight!

Warlocks and witches in a dance! 115
Nae cotillion, brent new frae France,
But hornpipes, jigs, strathspeys,[12] and reels
Put life and mettle in their heels.
A winnock-bunker in the east,
There sat auld Nick, in shape o' beast, 120
A towzie tyke, black, grim, and large;
To gie them music was his charge.
He screwed the pipes and gart them skirl,
Till roof and rafters a' did dirl.
Coffins stood round, like open presses, 125
That shawed the dead in their last dresses;
And by some devilish cantraip sleight,
Each in its cauld hand held a light,
By which heroic Tam was able
To note upon the haly table, 130
A murderer's banes in gibbet airns;
Twa span-lang, wee, unchristened bairns;
A thief, new-cutted frae the rape,
Wi' his last gasp his gab did gape;
Five tomahawks, wi' bluid red-rusted; 135
Five scymitars, wi' murder crusted;
A garter which a babe had strangled;
A knife, a father's throat had mangled,

Whom his ain son o' life bereft—
The gray hairs yet stack to the heft; 140
Wi' mair of horrible and awfu',
Which ev'n to name wad be unlawfu'.

As Tammie glowered, amazed and curious,
The mirth and fun grew fast and furious.
The piper loud and louder blew; 145
The dancers quick and quicker flew;
They reeled, they set, they crossed, they cleekit,
Till ilka carlin swat and reekit,[13]
And coost her duddies to the wark,
And linket at it in her sark! 150

Now Tam, O Tam! had thae been queans,
A' plump and strapping in their teens,
Their sarks, instead o' creeshie flannen,
Been snaw-white seventeen hunder linen!
Thir breeks [14] o' mine, my only pair, 155
That ance were plush, o' guid blue hair,
I wad hae gi'en them off my hurdies,
For ae blink o' the bonie burdies!
But withered beldams, auld and droll,
Rigwoodie hags wad spean a foal, 160
Louping an' flinging on a crummock,
I wonder did na turn thy stomach.

But Tam kend what was what fu' brawlie;
There was ae winsome wench and wawlie,
That night enlisted in the core, 165
Lang after kend on Carrick shore
(For mony a beast to dead she shot,
And perished mony a bonie boat,
And shook baith meikle corn and bear,
And kept the country-side in fear). 170
Her cutty sark, o' Paisley harn,
That while a lassie she had worn,
In longitude though sorely scanty,
It was her best, and she was vauntie.
Ah! little kend thy reverend grannie, 175
That sark she coft [15] for her wee Nannie,
Wi' twa pund Scots ('twas a' her riches),
Wad ever graced a dance of witches!

[11] Bore (opening), tippenny (twopenny), usquabae (whiskey), swats sae reamed (ale so foamed), unco (awful).

[12] Strathspeys (a Scotch dance), winnock-bunker (window seat), towzie tyke (shaggy cur), pipes (bagpipes), gart them skirl (make them scream), dirl (vibrate), cantraip sleight (magical contrivance), rape (rope).

[13] Ilka carlin swat and reekit (every old woman sweated and steamed), coost her duddies (cast off her clothes), sark (shirt).

[14] Breeks (breeches), hurdies (hips), burdies (girls), rigwoodie (withered), louping (leaping), crummock (a cane), wawlie (large).

[15] Coft (bought), twa pund Scots (two Scotch pounds, about one dollar), first ae caper, syne anither (first one caper, then another).

But here my Muse her wing maun cour;
Sic flights are far beyond her power;   180
To sing how Nannie lap and flang
(A souple jade she was and strang),
And how Tam stood, like ane bewitched,
And thought his very een enriched;
Even Satan glowered, and fidged fu' fain,   185
And hotched and blew wi' might and main
Till first ae caper, syne anither,
Tam tint his reason a' thegither,
And roars out, "Weel done, Cutty sark!"
And in an instant all was dark;   190
And scarcely had he Maggie rallied,
When out the hellish legion sallied.

As bees bizz out wi' angry fyke,
When plundering herds assail their byke;
As open pussie's mortal foes,   195
When, pop! she starts before their nose;
As eager runs the market-crowd,
When "Catch the thief!" resounds aloud,
So Maggie runs, the witches follow,
Wi' mony an eldritch skriech and hollow.   200

Ah, Tam! ah, Tam! thou'll get thy fairin'!
In hell they'll roast thee like a herrin'!
In vain thy Kate awaits thy comin'!
Kate soon will be a woefu' woman!
Now, do thy speedy utmost, Meg,   205
And win the key-stane of the brig; [16]
There, at them thou thy tail may toss—
A running stream they dare na cross;
But ere the key-stane she could make,
The fient a tail she had to shake!   210
For Nannie, far before the rest,
Hard upon noble Maggie pressed,
And flew at Tam wi' furious ettle;
But little wist she Maggie's mettle!
Ae spring brought off her master hale,   215
But left behind her ain gray tail.
The carlin claught her by the rump,
And left poor Maggie scarce a stump.

Now, wha this tale o' truth shall read,
Ilk man and mother's son take heed: 220
Whene'er to drink you are inclined,
Or cutty sarks run in your mind,
Think, ye may buy the joys o'er dear;
Remember Tam O'Shanter's mare.

Mary Morison

O Mary, at thy window be,
  It is the wished, the trysted hour!
Those smiles and glances let me see,
  That make the miser's treasure poor.
How blithely wad I bide the stoure,   5
  A weary slave frae sun to sun,
Could I the rich reward secure,
  The lovely Mary Morison.

Yestreen, when to the trembling string
  The dance gaed through the lighted ha',   10
To thee my fancy took its wing,
  I sat, but neither heard nor saw.
Tho' this was fair, and that was braw,
  And yon the toast of a' the town,
I sighed, and said amang them a':   15
  "Ye are na Mary Morison."

O Mary, canst thou wreck his peace,
  Wha for thy sake wad gladly die?
Or canst thou break that heart of his,
  Whase only faut is loving thee?   20
If love for love thou wilt na gie,
  At least be pity to me shown;
A thought ungentle canna be
  The thought o' Mary Morison.

To a Mouse

ON TURNING HER UP IN HER NEST WITH THE PLOW,
NOVEMBER, 1785

Wee, sleekit,[1] cow'rin', tim'rous beastie,
Oh, what a panic's in thy breastie!
Thou needna start awa' sae hasty,
    Wi' bickerin' brattle!
I wad be laith to rin and chase thee   5
    Wi' murd'ring pattle!

I'm truly sorry man's dominion
Has broken Nature's social union,
An' justifies that ill opinion,
    Which makes thee startle   10
At me, thy poor earthborn companion,
    An' fellow-mortal!

I doubtna, whiles,[2] but thou may thieve;
What then? poor beastie, thou maun live!

[16] Key-stane of the brig (key-stone of the bridge).
[1] Sleekit (sleek), bickerin' brattle (hurrying clatter), laith (loath), pattle (plow-spade).
[2] Whiles (sometimes), maun (must), daimen icker in a thrave (occasional ear in twenty-four sheaves),
   (rest).

A daimen icker in a thrave   15
    'S a sma' request:
I'll get a blessin' wi' the lave,
    And never miss't!

Thy wee bit housie, too, in ruin!
Its silly wa's the win's are strewin'!   20
And naething now to big[1] a new ane
    O' foggage green!
An' bleak December's winds ensuin',
    Baith snell an' keen!

Thou saw the fields laid bare an' waste,   25
An' weary winter comin' fast,
An' cozie here, beneath the blast,
    Thou thought to dwell,
Till, crash! the cruel coulter passed
    Out through thy cell.   30

That wee-bit heap o' leaves an' stibble
Hast cost thee monie a weary nibble!
Now thou's turned out for a' thy trouble,
    But[2] house or hald,
To thole the winter's sleety dribble,   35
    And cranreuch cauld!

But, Mousie, thou art no thy lane,
In proving foresight may be vain:
The best laid schemes o' mice an' men
    Gang aft a-gley,   40
An' lea'e us nought but grief and pain,
    For promised joy.

Still thou art blest, compared wi' me!
The present only toucheth thee:
But, och! I backward cast my e'e   45
    On prospects drear!
An' forward, though I canna see,
    I guess an' fear.

A Red, Red Rose

O my Luve's like a red, red rose
    That's newly sprung in June;
O my Luve's like the melodie
    That's sweetly played in tune!

So fair art thou, my bonnie lass,   5
    So deep in luve am I;

And I will luve thee still, my dear,
    Till a' the seas gang dry—

Till a' the seas gang dry, my dear,
    And the rocks melt wi' the sun;   10
I will luve thee still, my dear,
    While the sands o' life shall run.

And fare thee weel, my only Luve,
    And fare thee weel a while!
And I will come again, my Luve,   15
    Though it were ten thousand mile.

My Jean

Of a' the airts[3] the wind can blaw,
    I dearly like the west,
For there the bonnie lassie lives,
    The lassie I lo'e best.
There wild woods grow, and rivers row,   5
    And monie a hill between;
But day and night my fancy's flight
    Is ever wi' my Jean.

I see her in the dewy flowers,
    I see her sweet and fair.   10
I hear her in the tunefu' birds,
    I hear her charm the air.
There's not a bonnie flower that springs
    By fountain, shaw, or green;
There's not a bonnie bird that sings,   15
    But minds me o' my Jean.

Auld Lang Syne

Should auld acquaintance be forgot,
    And never brought to min'?
Should auld acquaintance be forgot,
    And auld lang syne?[4]

Chorus.—For auld lang syne, my dear,   5
        For auld lang syne,
            We'll tak a cup o' kindness yet
        For auld lang syne.

We twa hae run about the braes,
    And pu'd the gowans[5] fine;   10
But we've wandered monie a weary fit
    Sin' auld lang syne.

        For auld, etc.

[1] Big (build), foggage (grass), snell (sharp).
[2] But (without), thole (endure), cranreuch (cold frost), a-gley (away).
[3] Airts (directions).
[4] Old long ago.
[5] Gowans (daisies).

We twa hae paidl't i' the burn,[1]
  Frae mornin' sun til dine;   15
But seas between us braid hae roared
  Sin' auld lang syne.

      For auld, etc.

And there's a hand, my trusty fiere,[2]
  And gie's a hand o' thine;   20
And we'll tak a right guid-willie waught
  For auld lang syne!

      For auld, etc.

And surely ye'll be your pint-stowp,
  And surely I'll be mine;   25
And we'll tak a cup o' kindness yet
  For auld lang syne.

      For auld, etc.

John Anderson, My Jo, John

John Anderson, my jo, John,
  When we were first acquent,
Your locks were like the raven,
  Your bonnie brow was brent;
But now your brow is beld, John,   5
  Your locks are like the snow;
But blessings on your frosty pow,
  John Anderson, my jo!

John Anderson, my jo, John,
  We clamb the hill thegither;   10
And monie a canty day, John,
  We've had wi' ane anither.
Now we maun totter down, John,
  And hand in hand we'll go,
And sleep thegither at the foot,   15
  John Anderson, my jo.

To Mary in Heaven

Thou ling'ring star, with less'ning ray,
  That lov'st to greet the early morn,
Again thou usher'st in the day
  My Mary from my soul was torn.
O Mary! dear departed shade!   5
  Where is thy place of blissful rest?
See'st thou thy lover lowly laid?
  Hear'st thou the groans that rend his breast?

That sacred hour can I forget,
  Can I forget the hallowed grove,   10

Where by the winding Ayr we met
  To live one day of parting love?
Eternity will not efface
  Those records dear of transports past,
Thy image at our last embrace—   15
  Ah! little thought we 'twas our last!

Ayr, gurgling, kissed his pebbled shore,
  O'erhung with wild woods, thick'ning green;
The fragrant birch and hawthorn hoar
  Twined amorous round the raptured scene.   20
The flow'rs sprang wanton to be prest,
  The birds sang love on every spray,
Till too, too soon the glowing west
  Proclaimed the speed of wingéd day.

Still o'er these scenes my mem'ry wakes,   25
  And fondly broods with miser care!
Time but th' impression stronger makes,
  As streams their channels deeper wear.
My Mary, dear departed shade!
  Where is thy place of blissful rest?   30
See'st thou thy lover lowly laid?
  Hear'st thou the groans that rend his breast?

Ae Fond Kiss

Ae fond kiss, and then we sever;
  Ae fareweel, alas, forever!
Deep in heart-wrung tears I'll pledge thee;
  Warring sighs and groans I'll wage thee!

Who shall say that Fortune grieves him   5
  While the star of hope she leaves him?
Me, nae cheerfu' twinkle lights me;
  Dark despair around benights me.

I'll ne'er blame my partial fancy;
  Naething could resist my Nancy;   10
But to see her was to love her,
  Love but her, and love forever.

Had we never loved sae kindly,
  Had we never loved sae blindly,
Never met—or never parted,   15
  We had ne'er been broken-hearted.

Fare thee weel, thou first and fairest!
  Fare thee weel, thou best and dearest!
Thine be ilka joy and treasure,
  Peace, enjoyment, love, and pleasure!   20

[1] Burn (brook), dine (dinner time), braid (broad).
[2] Fiere (companion), guid-willie waught (friendly big drink).

Ae fond kiss, and then we sever!
Ae fareweel, alas, forever!
Deep in heart-wrung tears I'll pledge thee;
Warring sighs and groans I'll wage thee!

The Banks o' Doon

Ye banks and braes o' bonnie Doon,
  How can ye bloom sae fresh and fair?
How can ye chant, ye little birds,
  And I sae weary fu' o' care?
Thou'lt break my heart, thou warbling bird,   5
  That wantons through the flowering thorn;
Thou minds me o' departed joys,
  Departed never to return.

Aft hae I roved by bonnie Doon,
  To see the rose and woodbine twine;   10
And ilka bird sang o' its love,
  And fondly sae did I o' mine.
Wi' lightsome heart I pu'd a rose,
  Fu' sweet upon its thorny tree;
And my fause lover staw my rose,   15
  But ah! he left the thorn wi' me.

Highland Mary

Ye banks and braes and streams around
  The castle o' Montgomery,
Green be your woods, and fair your flowers,
  Your waters never drumlie!
There simmer first unfauld her robes,   5
  And there the langest tarry;
For there I took the last fareweel
  O' my sweet Highland Mary.

How sweetly bloomed the gay green birk,
  How rich the hawthorn's blossom,   10
As underneath their fragrant shade
  I clasped her to my bosom!
The golden hours on angel wings
  Flew o'er me and my dearie;
For dear to me as light and life   15
  Was my sweet Highland Mary.

Wi' monie a vow and locked embrace
  Our parting was fu' tender;
And, pledging aft to meet again,
  We tore ourselves asunder;   20
But oh! fell Death's untimely frost,
  That nipped my flower sae early!
Now green's the sod, and cauld's the clay,
  That wraps my Highland Mary!

O pale, pale now, those rosy lips   25
  I aft hae kissed sae fondly!
And closed for aye the sparkling glance
  That dwelt on me sae kindly!
And mold'ring now in silent dust,
  That heart that lo'ed me dearly!   30
But still within my bosom's core
  Shall live my Highland Mary.

Scots, Wha Hae

Scots, wha hae wi' Wallace bled,
Scots, wham Bruce has aften led,
Welcome to your gory bed,
  Or to victory!
Now's the day, and now's the hour;   5
See the front o' battle lour;
See approach proud Edward's power—
  Chains and slavery!

Wha will be a traitor knave?
Wha can fill a coward's grave?   10
Wha sae base as be a slave?
  Let him turn and flee!
Wha for Scotland's king and law
Freedom's sword will strongly draw,
Freeman stand, or Freeman fa',   15
  Let him follow me!

By oppression's woes and pains
By your sons in servile chains!
We will drain our dearest veins,
  But they shall be free!   20
Lay the proud usurpers low!
Tyrants fall in every foe!
Liberty's in every blow!—
  Let us do or die!

A Man's a Man for A' That

Is there, for honest poverty,
  That hings his head, an' a' that?
The coward slave, we pass him by,
  We dare be poor for a' that!
    For a' that, an' a' that,   5
    Our toils obscure, an' a' that;
  The rank is but the guinea's stamp;
    The man's the gowd [1] for a' that.

What though on hamely fare we dine,
  Wear hodden-gray, an' a' that;   10
Gie fools their silks, and knaves their wine,

---

[1] Gowd (gold).

A man's a man for a' that.
  For a' that, an' a' that,
    Their tinsel show, an' a' that;
  The honest man, though e'er sae poor,   15
    Is king o' men for a' that.

Ye see yon birkie, ca'd a lord,
  Wha struts, an' stares, an' a' that;
Though hundreds worship at his word,
  He's but a coof for a' that.   20
  For a' that, an' a' that,
    His riband, star, an' a' that,
  The man o' independent mind,
    He looks and laughs at a' that.

A prince can mak a belted knight,   25
  A marquis, duke, an' a' that;
But an honest man's aboon his might,
  Guid faith he mauna fa' that! [2]
  For a' that, an' a' that,
    Their dignities, an' a' that,   30
  The pith o' sense, an' pride o' worth,
    Are higher rank than a' that.

Then let us pray that come it may,
  As come it will for a' that,
That sense and worth, o'er a' the earth,   35

May bear the gree,[3] an' a' that.
  For a' that, an' a' that,
    It's coming yet, for a' that,
  That man to man, the warld o'er,
    Shall brothers be for a' that.   40

O Wert Thou in the Cauld Blast

O wert thou in the cauld blast,
  On yonder lea, on yonder lea,
My plaidie to the angry airt,
  I'd shelter thee, I'd shelter thee;
Or did misfortune's bitter storms   5
  Around thee blaw, around thee blaw,
Thy bield should be my bosom,
  To share it a', to share it a'.

Or were I in the wildest waste,
  Sae black and bare, sae black and bare,   10
The desert were a paradise
  If thou wert there, if thou wert there;
Or were I monarch o' the globe,
  Wi' thee to reign, wi' thee to reign,
The brightest jewel in my crown   15
  Wad be my queen, wad be my queen.

WILLIAM BLAKE

To the Muses

Whether on Ida's shady brow
  Or in the chambers of the East,
The chambers of the sun, that now
  From ancient melody have ceased;

Whether in heaven ye wander fair,   5
  Or the green corners of the earth,
Or the blue regions of the air
  Where the melodious winds have birth;

Whether on crystal rocks ye rove,
  Beneath the bosom of the sea,   10
Wandering in many a coral grove,
  Fair Nine, forsaking Poetry—

How have you left the ancient love
  That bards of old enjoyed in you!

The languid strings do scarcely move;   15
  The sound is forced, the notes are few.

Introduction to Songs of Innocence

Piping down the valleys wild,
  Piping songs of pleasant glee,
On a cloud I saw a child,
  And he laughing said to me:

"Pipe a song about a Lamb!"   5
  So I piped with merry cheer.
"Piper, pipe that song again";
  So I piped. He wept to hear.

"Drop thy pipe, thy happy pipe;
  Sing thy songs of happy cheer!"   10
So I sung the same again,
  While he wept with joy to hear.

[2] He must not claim that.
[3] Prize.
    Blake, *To the Muses.* William Blake (1757-1827) was of almost equal importance as poet, engraver, and painter. He engraved many of his own poems. He lived in London.

"Piper, sit thee down and write
  In a book that all may read."
So he vanished from my sight;   15
  And I plucked a hollow reed,

And I made a rural pen,
  And I stained the water clear,
And I wrote my happy songs
  Every child may joy to hear.   20

The Lamb

  Little Lamb, who made thee?
  Dost thou know who made thee?
Gave thee life and bid thee feed
By the stream and o'er the mead;
Gave thee clothing of delight,   5
Softest clothing, woolly, bright;
Gave thee such a tender voice,
Making all the vales rejoice?
  Little Lamb, who made thee?
  Dost thou know who made thee?   10

  Little Lamb, I'll tell thee;
  Little Lamb, I'll tell thee:
He is calléd by thy name,
For he calls himself a Lamb.
He is meek, and he is mild;   15
He became a little child.
I a child, and thou a lamb,
We are calléd by his name.
  Little Lamb, God bless thee!
  Little Lamb, God bless thee!   20

The Tiger

Tiger! tiger! burning bright
In the forests of the night,
What immortal hand or eye
Could frame thy fearful symmetry?

In what distant deeps or skies   5
Burned the fire of thine eyes?
On what wings dare he aspire?
What the hand dare seize the fire?

And what shoulder, and what art,
Could twist the sinews of thy heart?   10
And when thy heart began to beat,
What dread hand? and what dread feet?

What the hammer? what the chain?
In what furnace was thy brain?
What the anvil? what dread grasp   15
Dare its deadly terrors clasp?

When the stars threw down their spears
And watered heaven with their tears,
Did he smile his work to see?
Did he who made the Lamb make thee?   20

Tiger! tiger! burning bright
In the forests of the night,
What immortal hand or eye
Dare frame thy fearful symmetry?

Ah, Sunflower

Ah, Sunflower! weary of time,
Who countest the steps of the sun,
Seeking after that sweet golden clime
Where the traveler's journey is done—

Where the youth pined away with desire,
And the pale virgin, shrouded in snow,
Arise from their graves, and aspire
Where my sunflower wishes to go!

WILLIAM WORDSWORTH

Lines

COMPOSED A FEW MILES ABOVE TINTERN ABBEY, ON
REVISITING THE BANKS OF THE WYE DURING
A TOUR JULY 13, 1798

Five years have passed; five summers, with the
    length
Of five long winters! and again I hear
These waters, rolling from their mountain springs
With a soft inland murmur.—Once again
Do I behold these steep and lofty cliffs,   5
That on a wild, secluded scene impress
Thoughts of more deep seclusion; and connect
The landscape with the quiet of the sky.

Wordsworth, *Tintern Abbey*. William Wordsworth (1770-1850) passed much of his life in the Lake
District of Northern England, where he was born. He was educated at Cambridge and lived for a time
in Somersetshire near Coleridge, with whom he published *Lyrical Ballads* in 1798.

The day is come when I again repose
Here, under this dark sycamore, and view   10
These plots of cottage-ground, these orchard-tufts,
Which at this season, with their unripe fruits,
Are clad in one green hue, and lose themselves
'Mid groves and copses. Once again I see
These hedgerows, hardly hedgerows, little lines   15
Of sportive wood run wild; these pastoral farms,
Green to the very door; and wreaths of smoke
Sent up, in silence, from among the trees!
With some uncertain notice, as might seem
Of vagrant dwellers in the houseless woods,   20
Or of some hermit's cave, where by his fire
The hermit sits alone.
                    These beauteous forms,
Through a long absence, have not been to me
As is a landscape to a blind man's eye;
But oft, in lonely rooms, and 'mid the din   25
Of towns and cities, I have owed to them
In hours of weariness, sensations sweet,
Felt in the blood, and felt along the heart;
And passing even into my purer mind,
With tranquil restoration—feelings, too,   30
Of unremembered pleasure; such, perhaps,
As have no slight or trivial influence
On that best portion of a good man's life,
His little, nameless, unremembered acts
Of kindness and of love. Nor less, I trust,   35
To them I may have owed another gift,
Of aspect more sublime; that blessed mood,
In which the burthen of the mystery,
In which the heavy and the weary weight
Of all this unintelligible world,   40
Is lightened—that serene and blessed mood
In which the affections gently lead us on—
Until, the breath of this corporeal frame
And even the motion of our human blood
Almost suspended, we are laid asleep   45
In body, and become a living soul;
While with an eye made quiet by the power
Of harmony, and the deep power of joy,
We see into the life of things.
                                  If this
Be but a vain belief, yet, oh! how oft—   50
In darkness and amid the many shapes
Of joyless daylight; when the fretful stir
Unprofitable, and the fever of the world,
Have hung upon the beatings of my heart—
How oft, in spirit, have I turned to thee,   55
O silvan Wye! thou wanderer through the woods,
How often has my spirit turned to thee!
    And now, with gleams of half-extinguished
      thought

With many recognitions dim and faint,
And somewhat of a sad perplexity,   60
The picture of the mind revives again;
While here I stand, not only with the sense
Of present pleasure, but with pleasing thoughts
That in this moment there is life and food
For future years. And so I dare to hope,   65
Though changed, no doubt, from what I was
      when first
I came among these hills; when like a roe
I bounded o'er the mountains, by the sides
Of the deep rivers, and the lonely streams,
Wherever Nature led; more like a man   70
Flying from something that he dreads, than one
Who sought the thing he loved. For nature then
(The coarser pleasures of my boyish days,
And their glad animal movements all gone by)
To me was all in all.—I cannot paint   75
What then I was. The sounding cataract
Haunted me like a passion; the tall rock,
The mountain, and the deep and gloomy wood,
Their colors and their forms, were then to me
An appetite; a feeling and a love,   80
That had no need of a remoter charm,
By thought supplied, nor any interest
Unborrowed from the eye.—That time is past,
And all its aching joys are now no more,
And all its dizzy raptures. Not for this   85
Faint I, nor mourn, nor murmur; other gifts
Have followed; for such loss, I would believe,
Abundant recompense. For I have learned
To look on Nature, not as in the hour
Of thoughtless youth; but hearing oftentimes   90
The still, sad music of humanity,
Nor harsh nor grating, though of ample power
To chasten and subdue. And I have felt
A presence that disturbs me with the joy
Of elevated thoughts; a sense sublime   95
Of something far more deeply interfused,
Whose dwelling is the light of setting suns,
And the round ocean and the living air,
And the blue sky, and in the mind of man;
A motion and a spirit, that impels   100
All thinking things, all objects of all thought,
And rolls through all things. Therefore am I still
A lover of the meadows and the woods,
And mountains; and of all that we behold
From this green earth; of all the mighty world   105
Of eye, and ear—both what they half create,
And what perceive; well pleased to recognize
In Nature and the language of the sense,
The anchor of my purest thoughts, the nurse,

The guide, the guardian of my heart, and soul 110
Of all my moral being.
           Nor perchance,
If I were not thus taught, should I the more
Suffer my genial spirits to decay;
For thou art with me here upon the banks
Of this fair river; thou my dearest friend, 115
My dear, dear friend; and in thy voice I catch
The language of my former heart, and read
My former pleasures in the shooting lights
Of thy wild eyes. Oh! yet a little while
May I behold in thee what I was once, 120
My dear, dear sister! and this prayer I make,
Knowing that Nature never did betray
The heart that loved her; 'tis her privilege,
Through all the years of this our life, to lead
From joy to joy; for she can so inform 125
The mind that is within us, so impress
With quietness and beauty, and so feed
With lofty thoughts, that neither evil tongues,
Rash judgments, nor the sneers of selfish men,
Nor greetings where no kindness is, nor all 130
The dreary intercourse of daily life,
Shall e'er prevail against us, or disturb
Our cheerful faith that all which we behold
Is full of blessings. Therefore let the moon
Shine on thee in thy solitary walk; 135
And let the misty mountain-winds be free
To blow against thee; and in after years,
When these wild ecstasies shall be matured
Into a sober pleasure; when thy mind
Shall be a mansion for all lovely forms, 140
Thy memory be as a dwelling-place
For all sweet sounds and harmonies; oh! then,
If solitude, or fear, or pain, or grief,
Should be thy portion, with what healing thoughts
Of tender joy wilt thou remember me, 145
And these my exhortations! Nor, perchance—
If I should be where I no more can hear
Thy voice, nor catch from thy wild eyes these
    gleams
Of past existence—wilt thou then forget
That on the banks of this delightful stream 150
We stood together; and that I, so long
A worshiper of Nature, hither came
Unwearied in that service; rather say
With warmer love—oh! with far deeper zeal
Of holier love. Nor wilt thou then forget 155
That after many wanderings, many years
Of absence, these steep woods and lofty cliffs,
And this green pastoral landscape, were to me
More dear, both for themselves and for thy sake!

She Dwelt Among the Untrodden Ways

She dwelt among the untrodden ways
  Beside the springs of Dove,
A maid whom there were none to praise
  And very few to love;

A violet by a mossy stone 5
  Half hidden from the eye!
Fair as a star, when only one
  Is shining in the sky.

She lived unknown, and few could know
  When Lucy ceased to be; 10
But she is in her grave, and, oh!
  The difference to me!

I Traveled Among Unknown Men

I traveled among unknown men,
  In lands beyond the sea;
Nor, England! did I know till then
  What love I bore to thee.

'Tis past, that melancholy dream! 5
  Nor will I quit thy shore
A second time; for still I seem
  To love thee more and more.

Among thy mountains did I feel
  The joy of my desire; 10
And she I cherished turned her wheel
  Beside an English fire.

Thy mornings showed, thy nights concealed,
  The bowers where Lucy played;
And thine, too, is the last green field 15
  That Lucy's eyes surveyed.

Three Years She Grew in Sun and Shower

Three years she grew in sun and shower.
Then Nature said, "A lovelier flower
On earth was never sown;
This child I to myself will take;
She shall be mine, and I will make 5
A lady of my own.

"Myself will to my darling be
Both law and impulse; and with me
The girl, in rock and plain,
In earth and heaven, in glade and bower, 10
Shall feel an overseeing power
To kindle or restrain.

"She shall be sportive as the fawn
That wild with glee across the lawn
Or up the mountain springs;   15
And hers shall be the breathing balm,
And hers the silence and the calm
Of mute, insensate things.

"The floating clouds their state shall lend
To her; for her the willow bend;   20
Nor shall she fail to see,
Even in the motions of the storm,
Grace that shall mold the maiden's form
By silent sympathy.

"The stars of midnight shall be dear   25
To her; and she shall lean her ear
In many a secret place
Where rivulets dance their wayward round,
And beauty born of murmuring sound
Shall pass into her face.   30

"And vital feelings of delight
Shall rear her form to stately height,
Her virgin bosom swell;
Such thoughts to Lucy I will give
While she and I together live   35
Here in this happy dell."

Thus Nature spake.—The work was done.—
How soon my Lucy's race was run!
She died, and left to me
This heath, this calm and quiet scene;   40
The memory of what has been,
And never more will be.

A Slumber Did My Spirit Seal

A slumber did my spirit seal;
    I had no human fears—
She seemed a thing that could not feel
    The touch of earthly years.

No motion has she now, no force;
    She neither hears nor sees;
Rolled round in earth's diurnal course,
    With rocks, and stones, and trees.

My Heart Leaps Up When I Behold

    My heart leaps up when I behold
        A rainbow in the sky.
    So was it when my life began;
    So is it now I am a man:

So be it when I shall grow old,
    Or let me die!
The Child is father of the Man;
    And I could wish my days to be
Bound each to each by natural piety.

Composed upon Westminster Bridge, Sept. 3, 1802

Earth has not anything to show more fair;
Dull would he be of soul who could pass by
A sight so touching in its majesty:
This city now doth like a garment wear
The beauty of the morning; silent, bare,   5
Ships, towers, domes, theaters, and temples lie
Open unto the fields, and to the sky;
All bright and glittering in the smokeless air.
Never did sun more beautifully steep
In his first splendor valley, rock, or hill;   10
Ne'er saw I, never felt, a calm so deep!
The river glideth at his own sweet will.
Dear God! the very houses seem asleep;
And all that mighty heart is lying still!

Composed by the Seaside near Calais, August, 1802

Fair Star of evening, Splendor of the west,
Star of my country!—on the horizon's brink
Thou hangest, stooping, as might seem, to sink
On England's bosom; yet well pleased to rest,
Meanwhile, and be to her a glorious crest   5
Conspicuous to the nations. Thou, I think,
Should'st be my Country's emblem; and should'st
        wink,
Bright Star! with laughter on her banners, drest
In thy fresh beauty. There! that dusky spot
Beneath thee that is England; there she lies.   10
Blessings be on you both! one hope, one lot,
One life, one glory! I with many a fear
For my dear Country, many heartfelt sighs,
Among men who do not love her, linger here.

It Is a Beauteous Evening, Calm and Free

It is a beauteous evening, calm and free.
The holy time is quiet as a nun,
Breathless with adoration; the broad sun
Is sinking down in its tranquillity;
The gentleness of heaven broods o'er the sea;   5
Listen! the mighty Being is awake,
And doth with his eternal motion make
A sound like thunder—everlastingly.

Dear Child! dear Girl! that walkest with me here,
If thou appear untouched by solemn thought,　10
Thy nature is not therefore less divine;
Thou liest in Abraham's bosom all the year,
And worship'st at the Temple's inner shrine,
God being with thee when we know it not.

London, 1802

Milton! thou shouldst be living at this hour:
England hath need of thee: she is a fen
Of stagnant waters; altar, sword, and pen,
Fireside, the heroic wealth of hall and bower,
Have forfeited their ancient English dower　5
Of inward happiness. We are selfish men;
Oh! raise us up, return to us again;
And give us manners, virtue, freedom, power.
Thy Soul was like a Star, and dwelt apart;
Thou hadst a voice whose sound was like the sea;
Pure as the naked heavens, majestic, free,　11
So didst thou travel on life's common way,
In cheerful godliness; and yet thy heart
The lowliest duties on herself did lay.

The World Is Too Much with Us

The world is too much with us: late and soon,
Getting and spending, we lay waste our powers.
Little we see in nature that is ours;
We have given our hearts away, a sordid boon!
This sea that bares her bosom to the moon,　5
The winds that will be howling at all hours,
And are up-gathered now like sleeping flowers;
For this, for everything, we are out of tune;
It moves us not.—Great God! I'd rather be
A pagan suckled in a creed outworn;　10
So might I, standing on this pleasant lea,
Have glimpses that would make me less forlorn;
Have sight of Proteus rising from the sea;
Or hear old Triton blow his wreathèd horn.

On the Extinction of the Venetian Republic

Once did She hold the gorgeous east in fee;
And was the safeguard of the west: the worth
Of Venice did not fall below her birth,
Venice, the eldest Child of Liberty.
She was a maiden City, bright and free;　5
No guile seduced, no force could violate;
And when she took unto herself a Mate,
She must espouse the everlasting Sea.
And what if she had seen those glories fade,

Those titles vanish, and that strength decay;　10
Yet shall some tribute of regret be paid
When her long life hath reached its final day:
Men are we, and must grieve when even the Shade
Of that which once was great, is passed away.

The Solitary Reaper

Behold her, single in the field,
Yon solitary Highland lass!
Reaping and singing by herself;
Stop here, or gently pass!
Alone she cuts and binds the grain,　5
And sings a melancholy strain;
O listen! for the Vale profound
Is overflowing with the sound.

No nightingale did ever chaunt
More welcome notes to weary bands　10
Of travelers in some shady haunt,
Among Arabian sands.
A voice so thrilling ne'er was heard
In springtime from the cuckoo-bird,
Breaking the silence of the seas　15
Among the farthest Hebrides.

Will no one tell me what she sings?—
Perhaps the plaintive numbers flow
For old, unhappy, far-off things,
And battles long ago.　20
Or is it some more humble lay,
Familiar matter of today?
Some natural sorrow, loss, or pain,
That has been, and may be again?

Whate'er the theme, the maiden sang　25
As if her song could have no ending;
I saw her singing at her work,
And o'er the sickle bending—
I listened, motionless and still;
And, as I mounted up the hill,　30
The music in my heart I bore,
Long after it was heard no more.

Ode

INTIMATIONS OF IMMORTALITY FROM RECOLLECTIONS
OF EARLY CHILDHOOD

"The Child is Father of the Man;
And I could wish my days to be
Bound each to each by natural piety."

There was a time when meadow, grove, and
stream,

The earth, and every common sight,
    To me did seem
    Apparelled in celestial light,
The glory and the freshness of a dream. 5
It is not now as it hath been of yore—
    Turn wheresoe'er I may,
    By night or day,
The things which I have seen I now can see no
    more.

    The rainbow comes and goes, 10
    And lovely is the rose;
    The moon doth with delight
  Look round her when the heavens are bare;
    Waters on a starry night
    Are beautiful and fair; 15
    The sunshine is a glorious birth;
    But yet I know, where'er I go,
That there hath passed away a glory from the
    earth.

Now, while the birds thus sing a joyous song,
    And while the young lambs bound, 20
    As to the tabor's sound,
To me alone there came a thought of grief;
A timely utterance gave that thought relief,
    And I again am strong.
The cataracts blow their trumpets from the steep;
No more shall grief of mine the season wrong; 26
I hear the echoes through the mountains throng,
The winds come to me from the fields of sleep,
    And all the earth is gay;
    Land and sea 30
    Give themselves up to jollity,
    And with the heart of May
  Doth every beast keep holiday—
    Thou child of joy,
Shout round me, let me hear thy shouts, thou
    happy shepherd-boy! 35

Ye blessèd creatures, I have heard the call
  Ye to each other make; I see
The heavens laugh with you in your jubilee.
    My heart is at your festival,
    My head hath its coronal, 40
The fullness of your bliss, I feel—I feel it all.
    O evil day! if I were sullen
    While Earth herself is adorning,
    This sweet May-morning,
    And the children are culling 45
    On every side,
  In a thousand valleys far and wide,
  Fresh flowers; while the sun shines warm,

And the babe leaps up on his mother's arm—
  I hear, I hear, with joy I hear! 50
  —But there's a tree, of many, one,
A single field which I have looked upon;
Both of them speak of something that is gone.
    The pansy at my feet
    Doth the same tale repeat: 55
Whither is fled the visionary gleam?
Where is it now, the glory and the dream?

Our birth is but a sleep and a forgetting:
The soul that rises with us, our life's star,
    Hath had elsewhere its setting, 60
    And cometh from afar;
    Not in entire forgetfulness,
    And not in utter nakedness,
But trailing clouds of glory do we come
    From God, who is our home. 65
Heaven lies about us in our infancy!
Shades of the prison-house begin to close
    Upon the growing boy,
But he beholds the light, and whence it flows,
    He sees it in his joy; 70
The youth, who daily farther from the east
    Must travel, still is Nature's priest,
    And by the vision splendid
    Is on his way attended;
At length the man perceives it die away, 75
And fade into the light of common day.

Earth fills her lap with pleasures of her own;
Yearnings she hath in her own natural kind,
And, even with something of a mother's mind,
    And no unworthy aim, 80
    The homely nurse doth all she can
To make her foster-child, her inmate man,
    Forget the glories he hath known,
And that imperial palace whence he came.

Behold the child among his new-born blisses, 85
A six years' darling of a pygmy size!
See, where 'mid work of his own hand he lies,
Fretted by sallies of his mother's kisses,
With light upon him from his father's eyes!
See, at his feet, some little plan or chart, 90
Some fragment from his dream of human life,
Shaped by himself with newly-learnèd art;
    A wedding or a festival,
    A mourning or a funeral;
    And this hath now his heart, 95
    And unto this he frames his song;
    Then will he fit his tongue
To dialogues of business, love, or strife.

But it will not be long
Ere this be thrown aside,   100
And with new joy and pride
The little actor cons another part;
Filling from time to time his "humorous stage"
With all the persons, down to palsied Age,
That Life brings with her in her equipage;   105
   As if his whole vocation
   Were endless imitation.

Thou whose exterior semblance doth belie
   Thy soul's immensity;
Thou best philosopher, who yet dost keep   110
Thy heritage, thou eye among the blind,
That, deaf and silent, read'st the eternal deep,
Haunted forever by the eternal mind—
   Mighty prophet! Seer blest!
   On whom those truths do rest,   115
Which we are toiling all our lives to find,
In darkness lost, the darkness of the grave;
Thou, over whom thy immortality
Broods like the day, a master o'er a slave,
A presence which is not to be put by;   120
Thou little child, yet glorious in the might
Of heaven-born freedom on thy being's height,
Why with such earnest pains dost thou provoke
The years to bring the inevitable yoke,
Thus blindly with thy blessedness at strife?   125
Full soon thy soul shall have her earthly freight,
And custom lie upon thee with a weight,
Heavy as frost, and deep almost as life!

      O joy! that in our embers
      Is something that doth live,   130
      That Nature yet remembers
      What was so fugitive!
The thought of our past years in me doth breed
Perpetual benediction; not indeed
For that which is most worthy to be blest—   135
Delight and liberty, the simple creed
Of childhood, whether busy or at rest,
With new-fledged hope still fluttering in his
      breast—
      Not for these I raise
      The song of thanks and praise;   140
   But for those obstinate questionings
   Of sense and outward things,
   Fallings from us, vanishings;
   Blank misgivings of a creature
Moving about in worlds not realized,   145
High instincts before which our mortal nature
Did tremble like a guilty thing surprised.

      But for those first affections,
      Those shadowy recollections,
   Which, be they what they may,   150
Are yet the fountain light of all our day,
Are yet a master light of all our seeing;
Uphold us, cherish, and have power to make
Our noisy years seem moments in the being
Of the eternal Silence: truths that wake,   155
      To perish never;
Which neither listlessness, nor mad endeavor,
      Nor man nor boy,
Nor all that is at enmity with joy,
Can utterly abolish or destroy!   160
   Hence in a season of calm weather
      Though inland far we be,
Our souls have sight of that immortal sea
      Which brought us hither,
      Can in a moment travel thither,   165
And see the children sport upon the shore,
And hear the mighty waters rolling evermore.

Then sing, ye birds, sing, sing a joyous song!
      And let the young lambs bound
      As to the tabor's sound!   170
We in thought will join your throng,
      Ye that pipe and ye that play,
      Ye that through your hearts today
      Feel the gladness of the May!
What though the radiance which was once so
      bright   175
Be now forever taken from my sight,
      Though nothing can bring back the hour
Of splendor in the grass, of glory in the flower;
      We will grieve not, rather find
      Strength in what remains behind;   180
      In the primal sympathy
      Which having been must ever be;
      In the soothing thoughts that spring
      Out of human suffering;
      In the faith that looks through death,   185
In years that bring the philosophic mind.

And O ye fountains, meadows, hills, and groves,
Forebode not any severing of our loves!
Yet in my heart of hearts I feel your might;
I only have relinquished one delight   190
To live beneath your more habitual sway.
I love the brooks which down their channels fret,
Even more than when I tripped lightly as they;
The innocent brightness of a new-born day
      Is lovely yet;   195
The clouds that gather round the setting sun
Do take a sober coloring from an eye

That hath kept watch o'er man's mortality;
Another race hath been, and other palms are won.
Thanks to the human heart by which we live, 200
Thanks to its tenderness, its joys, and fears,
To me the meanest flower that blows can give
Thoughts that do often lie too deep for tears.

To the Cuckoo

O blithe New-comer! I have heard,
I hear thee and rejoice.
O Cuckoo! shall I call thee Bird,
Or but a wandering Voice?

While I am lying on the grass 5
Thy twofold shout I hear,
From hill to hill it seems to pass,
At once far off, and near.

Though babbling only to the Vale,
Of sunshine and of flowers, 10
Thou bringest unto me a tale
Of visionary hours.

Thrice welcome, darling of the Spring!
Even yet thou art to me
No bird, but an invisible thing, 15
A voice, a mystery;

The same whom in my school-boy days
I listened to; that Cry
Which made me look a thousand ways
In bush, and tree, and sky. 20

To seek thee did I often rove
Through woods and on the green;
And thou wert still a hope, a love;
Still longed for, never seen.

And I can listen to thee yet; 25
Can lie upon the plain
And listen, till I do beget
That golden time again.

O blesséd Bird! the earth we pace
Again appears to be 30
An unsubstantial, faery place;
That is fit home for Thee!

She Was a Phantom of Delight

She was a phantom of delight
When first she gleamed upon my sight;

A lovely apparition, sent
To be a moment's ornament;
Her eyes as stars of twilight fair; 5
Like twilight's, too, her dusky hair;
But all things else about her drawn
From Maytime and the cheerful dawn;
A dancing shape, an image gay,
To haunt, to startle, and waylay. 10

I saw her upon nearer view,
A spirit, yet a woman, too!
Her household motions light and free,
And steps of virgin liberty;
A countenance in which did meet 15
Sweet records, promises as sweet;
A creature not too bright or good
For human nature's daily food;
For transient sorrows, simple wiles,
Praise, blame, love, kisses, tears, and smiles. 20

And now I see with eyes serene
The very pulse of the machine:
A being breathing thoughtful breath,
A traveler between life and death;
The reason firm, the temperate will, 25
Endurance, foresight, strength, and skill;
A perfect woman, nobly planned,
To warn, to comfort, and command;
And yet a spirit still, and bright
With something of angelic light. 30

I Wandered Lonely as a Cloud

I wandered lonely as a cloud
That floats on high o'er vales and hills,
When all at once I saw a crowd,
A host of golden daffodils,
Beside the lake, beneath the trees, 5
Fluttering and dancing in the breeze.

Continuous as the stars that shine
And twinkle on the milky way,
They stretched in never-ending line
Along the margin of a bay; 10
Ten thousand saw I at a glance,
Tossing their heads in sprightly dance.

The waves beside them danced, but they
Outdid the sparkling waves in glee—
A poet could not but be gay 15
In such a jocund company.
I gazed—and gazed—but little thought
What wealth the show to me had brought

For oft when on my couch I lie
In vacant or in pensive mood,   20
They flash upon that inward eye

Which is the bliss of solitude,
And then my heart with pleasure fills,
And dances with the daffodils.

SAMUEL TAYLOR COLERIDGE

Kubla Khan

"In the summer of the year 1797 the author, then in ill health, had retired to a lonely farmhouse between Porlock and Linton, on the Exmoor confines of Somerset and Devonshire. In consequence of a slight indisposition an anodyne had been prescribed, from the effects of which he fell asleep in his chair at the moment that he was reading the following sentence, or words of the same substance, in Purchas's *Pilgrimage:* 'Here the Khan Kubla commanded a palace to be built, and a stately garden thereunto. And thus ten miles of fertile ground were inclosed with a wall.' The Author continued for about three hours in a profound sleep, at least of the external senses, during which time he has the most vivid confidence that he could not have composed less than from two to three hundred lines; if that indeed can be called composition in which all the images rose up before him as *things,* with a parallel production of the correspondent expressions, without any sensation or consciousness of effort. On awaking he appeared to himself to have a distinct recollection of the whole, and taking his pen, ink, and paper, instantly and eagerly wrote down the lines that are here preserved. At this moment he was unfortunately called out by a person on business from Porlock, and detained by him above an hour, and on his return to his room found, to his no small surprise and mortification, that though he still retained some vague and dim recollection of the general purport of the vision, yet, with the exception of some eight or ten scattered lines and images, all the rest had passed away, like the images on the surface of a stream into which a stone has been cast; but, alas! without the after restoration of the latter.

'Then all the charm
Is broken—all that phantom-world so fair
Vanishes, and a thousand circlets spread,
And each misshapes the other. Stay awhile,
Poor youth! who scarcely dar'st lift up thine eyes—
The stream will soon renew its smoothness, soon
The visions will return! And lo, he stays,
And soon the fragments dim of lovely forms
Come trembling back, unite, and now once more
The pool becomes a mirror.'

Yet from the still surviving recollections in his mind, the author has frequently purposed to finish for himself what had been originally, as it were, given to him. Αὔριον ἀδιον ἀσω, but the tomorrow is yet to come."

In Xanadu did Kubla Khan
   A stately pleasure-dome decree;
Where Alph, the sacred river, ran
   Through caverns measureless to man
Down to a sunless sea.   5
So twice five miles of fertile ground
   With walls and towers were girdled round;
And there were gardens bright with sinuous rills
Where blossomed many an incense-bearing tree;
And here were forests ancient as the hills,   10
Enfolding sunny spots of greenery.

But O, that deep romantic chasm which slanted
Down the green hill athwart a cedarn cover!
A savage place! as holy and enchanted
As e'er beneath a waning moon was haunted   15
By woman wailing for her demon-lover!
And from this chasm, with ceaseless turmoil
      seething,
As if this earth in fast thick pants were breathing,
A mighty fountain momently was forced;
Amid whose swift, half-intermitted burst   20
Huge fragments vaulted like rebounding hail,
Or chaffy grain beneath the thresher's flail.
And 'mid these dancing rocks at once and ever
It flung up momently the sacred river.
Five miles meandering with a mazy motion   25
Through wood and dale the sacred river ran,
Then reached the caverns measureless to man,
And sank in tumult to a lifeless ocean;
And 'mid this tumult Kubla heard from far
Ancestral voices prophesying war!   30

The shadow of the dome of pleasure
   Floated midway on the waves;
Where was heard the mingled measure
   From the fountain and the caves.
It was a miracle of rare device,   35
A sunny pleasure-dome with caves of ice!

Coleridge, *Kubla Khan*. Samuel Taylor Coleridge (1772-1834) was born in Devonshire and educated at Cambridge. In his varied life he wrote poems, and literary essays. His last years were rendered ineffective by his use of opium.

A damsel with a dulcimer
  In a vision once I saw.
It was an Abyssinian maid,
  And on her dulcimer she played,   40
Singing of Mount Abora.
Could I revive within me
  Her symphony and song,
To such a deep delight 'twould win me
That with music loud and long,   45
I would build that dome in air,
That sunny dome! those caves of ice!
And all who heard should see them there,
And all should cry, Beware! Beware!
His flashing eyes, his floating hair!   50
Weave a circle round him thrice,
  And close your eyes with holy dread,
  For he on honey-dew hath fed,
And drunk the milk of Paradise.

The Rime of the Ancient Mariner

IN SEVEN PARTS

ARGUMENT

How a Ship having passed the Line was driven by
storms to the cold Country toward the South Pole;
and how from thence she made her course to the
tropical Latitude of the Great Pacific Ocean; and of
the strange things that befell; and in what manner
the Ancient Mariner came back to his own Country.

PART I

*An ancient Mariner meeteth three Gallants bidden to a
wedding-feast, and detaineth one.*

It is an ancient Mariner,
And he stoppeth one of three.
"By thy long gray beard and glittering eye,
Now wherefore stopp'st thou me?

The Bridegroom's doors are opened wide,   5
And I am next of kin;
The guests are met, the feast is set—
May'st hear the merry din."

He holds him with his skinny hand,
"There was a ship," quoth he.   10
"Hold off! unhand me, graybeard loon!"
Eftsoons his hand dropped he.

*The Wedding-Guest is spellbound by the eye of the old
seafaring man, and constrained to hear his tale.*

He holds him with his glittering eye;
The Wedding-Guest stood still,

And listens like a three years' child—   15
The Mariner hath his will.

The Wedding-Guest sat on a stone—
He cannot choose but hear;
And thus spake on that ancient man,
The bright-eyed Mariner: 20

"The ship was cheered, the harbor cleared;
Merrily did we drop
Below the kirk, below the hill,
Below the lighthouse top.

*The Mariner tells how the ship sailed southward with a
good wind and fair weather till it reached the Line.*

The sun came up upon the left;   25
Out of the sea came he!
And he shone bright, and on the right
Went down into the sea.

Higher and higher every day,
Till over the mast at noon—"   30
The Wedding-Guest here beat his breast,
For he heard the loud bassoon.

*The Wedding-Guest heareth the bridal music; but the
Mariner continueth his tale.*

The bride hath paced into the hall,
Red as a rose is she;
Nodding their heads before her goes   35
The merry minstrelsy.

The Wedding-Guest he beat his breast,
Yet he cannot choose but hear;
And thus spake on that ancient man,
The bright-eyed Mariner.   40

The ship drawn by a storm toward the South Pole.

"And now the Storm-blast came, and he
Was tyrannous and strong;
He struck with his o'ertaking wings,
And chased us south along.

With sloping masts and dipping prow,   45
As who pursued with yell and blow
Still treads the shadow of his foe,
And forward bends his head,
The ship drove fast, loud roared the blast,
And southward aye we fled.   50

And now there came both mist and snow,
And it grew wondrous cold;
And ice, mast-high, came floating by
As green as emerald.

*The land of ice, and of fearful sounds, where no living
thing was to be seen;*

And through the drifts the snowy clifts 55
Did send a dismal sheen;
Nor shapes of men nor beasts we ken—
The ice was all between.

The ice was here, the ice was there,
The ice was all around; 60
It cracked and growled, and roared and howled,
Like noises in a swound!

*Till a great sea-bird called the Albatross, came through
the snow-fog, and was received with great joy and
hospitality.*

At length did cross an Albatross;
Thorough the fog it came;
As if it had been a Christian soul, 65
We hailed it in God's name.

It ate the food it ne'er had eat,
And round and round it flew.
The ice did split with a thunder-fit;
The helmsman steered us through! 70

*And lo! the Albatross proveth a bird of good omen, and
followeth the ship as it returned northward through fog
and floating ice.*

And a good south wind sprung up behind;
The Albatross did follow,
And every day, for food or play,
Came to the mariners' hollo!

In mist or cloud, on mast or shroud, 75
It perched for vespers nine;
Whiles all the night, through fog-smoke white
Glimmered the white moonshine."

*The ancient Mariner inhospitably killeth the pious bird
of good omen.*

"God save thee, ancient Mariner,
From the fiends that plague thee thus!— 80
Why look'st thou so?"—"With my crossbow
I shot the Albatross.

PART II

"The sun now rose upon the right;
Out of the sea came he,
Still hid in mist, and on the left 85
Went down into the sea.

And the good south wind still blew behind,
But no sweet bird did follow,
Nor any day, for food or play,
Came to the mariners' hollo! 90

*His shipmates cry out against the ancient Mariner, for
killing the bird of good luck.*

And I had done an hellish thing,
And it would work 'em woe;
For all averred I had killed the bird
That made the breeze to blow.
'Ah, wretch!' said they, 'the bird to slay, 95
That made the breeze to blow!'

*But when the fog cleared off, they justify the same, and
thus make themselves accomplices in the crime.*

Nor dim nor red, like God's own head,
The glorious sun uprist;
Then all averred, I had killed the bird
That brought the fog and mist. 100
' 'Twas right,' said they, 'such birds to slay,
That bring the fog and mist.'

*The fair breeze continues; the ship enters the Pacific
Ocean and sails northward, even till it reaches the Line.*

The fair breeze blew, the white foam flew,
The furrow followed free;
We were the first that ever burst 105
Into that silent sea.

The ship hath been suddenly becalmed.

Down dropped the breeze, the sails dropped down,
'Twas sad as sad could be;
And we did speak only to break
The silence of the sea! 110

All in a hot and copper sky,
The bloody sun, at noon,
Right up above the mast did stand,
No bigger than the moon.

Day after day, day after day, 115
We stuck, nor breath nor motion;
As idle as a painted ship
Upon a painted ocean.

And the Albatross begins to be avenged.

Water, water, everywhere,
And all the boards did shrink; 120
Water, water, everywhere,
Nor any drop to drink.

The very deep did rot—O Christ!
That ever this should be!
Yea, slimy things did crawl with legs 125
Upon the slimy sea.

About, about, in reel and rout
The death-fires danced at night;

The water, like a witch's oils,
Burned green, and blue, and white. 130

A Spirit had followed them; one of the invisible inhabit-
ants of this planet, neither departed souls nor angels;
concerning whom the learned Jew Josephus and the
Platonic Constantinopolitan, Michael Psellus, may be
consulted. They are very numerous, and there is no
climate or element without one or more.

And some in dreams assuréd were
Of the Spirit that plagued us so;
Nine fathom deep he had followed us
From the land of mist and snow.

The shipmates in their sore distress would fain throw
the whole guilt on the ancient Mariner; in sign whereof
they hang the dead sea-bird round his neck.

And every tongue, through utter drought, 135
Was withered at the root;
We could not speak, no more than if
We had been choked with soot.

Ah! well-a-day!—what evil looks
Had I from old and young! 140
Instead of the cross, the Albatross
About my neck was hung.

PART III

The ancient Mariner beholdeth a sign in the element
afar off.

"There passed a weary time. Each throat
Was parched, and glazed each eye.
A weary time! a weary time! 145
How glazed each weary eye!
When looking westward, I beheld
A something in the sky.

At first it seemed a little speck,
And then it seemed a mist;
It moved, and moved, and took at last 150
A certain shape, I wist.

A speck, a mist, a shape, I wist!
And still it neared and neared;
As if it dodged a water-sprite, 155
It plunged and tacked and veered.

At its nearer approach, it seemeth him to be a ship; and
at a dear ransom he freeth his speech from the bonds
of thirst.

With throats unslaked, with black lips baked,
We could nor laugh nor wail;
Through utter drought all dumb we stood!
I bit my arm, I sucked the blood, 160
And cried, 'A sail! a sail!'

A flash of joy;

With throats unslaked, with black lips baked,
Agape they heard me call;
Gramercy! they for joy did grin,
And all at once their breath drew in, 165
As they were drinking all.

And horror follows. For can it be a ship that comes on-
ward without wind or tide?

'See! see!' (I cried) 'She tacks no more!
Hither to work us weal;
Without a breeze, without a tide,
She steadies with upright keel!' 170

The western wave was all aflame
The day was well-nigh done!
Almost upon the western wave
Rested the broad bright sun;
When that strange shape drove suddenly 175
Betwixt us and the sun.

It seemeth him but the skeleton of a ship.

And straight the sun was flecked with bars
(Heaven's Mother send us grace!)
As if through a dungeon-grate he peered
With broad and burning face. 180

Alas! (thought I, and my heart beat loud)
How fast she nears and nears!
Are those her sails that glance in the sun,
Like restless gossameres?

And its ribs are seen as bars on the face of the setting
sun. The Specter-Woman and her Death-mate, and no
other on board the skeleton-ship.

Are those her ribs through which the sun 185
Did peer, as through a grate?
And is that Woman all her crew?
Is that a Death? and are there two?
Is Death that Woman's mate?

Like vessel, like crew!

Her lips were red, her looks were free, 190
Her locks were yellow as gold;
Her skin was as white as leprosy;
The Nightmare Life-in-Death was she,
Who thicks man's blood with cold.

Death and Life-in-Death have diced for the ship's crew,
and she (the latter) winneth the ancient Mariner.

The naked hulk alongside came, 195
And the twain were casting dice;
'The game is done! I've won! I've won!'
Quoth she, and whistles thrice.

No twilight within the courts of the sun.

The sun's rim dips; the stars rush out;
At one stride comes the dark; 200
With far-heard whisper, o'er the sea,
Off shot the specter-bark.

At the rising of the moon

We listened and looked sideways up!
Fear at my heart, as at a cup,
My lifeblood seemed to sip! 205
The stars were dim, and thick the night;
The steersman's face by his lamp gleamed white;
From the sails the dew did drip—
Till clomb above the eastern bar
The hornéd moon, with one bright star 210
Within the nether tip.

One after another

One after one, by the star-dogged moon,
Too quick for groan or sigh,
Each turned his face with a ghastly pang,
And cursed me with his eye. 215

His shipmates drop down dead,

Four times fifty living men
(And I heard nor sigh nor groan),
With heavy thump, a lifeless lump,
They dropped down one by one.

But Life-in-Death begins her work on the ancient Mariner.

The souls did from their bodies fly— 220
They fled to bliss or woe!
And every soul, it passed me by,
Like the whizz of my crossbow!"

PART IV

The Wedding-Guest feareth that a spirit is talking to him;

"I fear thee, ancient Mariner!
I fear thy skinny hand! 225
And thou art long, and lank, and brown,
As is the ribbed sea-sand.

But the ancient Mariner assureth him of his bodily life, and proceedeth to relate his horrible penance.

I fear thee and thy glittering eye,
And thy skinny hand, so brown"—
"Fear not, fear not, thou Wedding-Guest! 230
This body dropped not down.

Alone, alone, all, all alone,
Alone on a wide, wide sea!

And never a saint took pity on
My soul in agony. 235

He despiseth the creatures of the calm,

The many men, so beautiful!
And they all dead did lie;
And a thousand thousand slimy things
Lived on; and so did I.

And envieth that they should live, and so many lie dead.

I looked upon the rotting sea, 240
And drew my eyes away;
I looked upon the rotting deck,
And there the dead men lay.

I looked to Heaven, and tried to pray;
But or ever a prayer had gusht, 245
A wicked whisper came, and made
My heart as dry as dust.

I closed my lids, and kept them close,
And the balls like pulses beat;
For the sky and the sea, and the sea and the sky
Lay like a load on my weary eye, 251
And the dead were at my feet.

But the curse liveth for him in the eye of the dead men.

The cold sweat melted from their limbs,
Nor rot nor reek did they;
The look with which they looked on me 255
Had never passed away.

An orphan's curse would drag to hell
A spirit from on high,
But oh! more horrible than that
Is a curse in a dead man's eye! 260
Seven days, seven nights, I saw that curse
And yet I could not die.

In his loneliness and fixedness he yearneth toward the journeying moon, and the stars that still sojourn, yet still move onward; and everywhere the blue sky belongs to them, and is their appointed rest and their native country and their own natural homes, which they enter unannounced, as lords that are certainly expected and yet there is a silent joy at their arrival.

The moving moon went up the sky,
And nowhere did abide;
Softly she was going up 265
And a star or two beside—

Her beams bemocked the sultry main,
Like April hoarfrost spread;
But where the ship's huge shadow lay,
The charméd water burned alway 270
A still and awful red.

By the light of the moon he beholdeth God's creatures of the great calm,

Beyond the shadow of the ship,
I watched the water-snakes;
They moved in tracks of shining white,
And when they reared, the elfish light   275
Fell off in hoary flakes.

Within the shadow of the ship
I watched their rich attire;
Blue, glossy green, and velvet black
They coiled and swam; and every track   280
Was a flash of golden fire.

Their beauty and their happiness.

O happy living things! no tongue
Their beauty might declare;
A spring of love gushed from my heart,

He blesseth them in his heart.

And I blessed them unaware!   285
Sure my kind saint took pity on me,
And I blessed them unaware.

The spell begins to break.

The selfsame moment I could pray;
And from my neck so free
The Albatross fell off, and sank   290
Like lead into the sea.

PART V

"Oh sleep! it is a gentle thing,
Beloved from pole to pole!
To Mary Queen the praise be given!
She sent the gentle sleep from heaven,   295
That slid into my soul.

By grace of the holy Mother, the ancient Mariner is refreshed with rain.

The silly buckets on the deck,
That had so long remained,
I dreamt that they were filled with dew;
And when I awoke, it rained.   300

My lips were wet, my throat was cold,
My garments all were dank;
Sure I had drunken in my dreams,
And still my body drank.

I moved, and could not feel my limbs,   305
I was so light—almost
I thought that I had died in sleep,
And was a blessed ghost.

He heareth sounds, and seeth strange sights and commotions in the sky and the element.

And soon I heard a roaring wind;
It did not come anear;   310
But with its sound it shook the sails
That were so thin and sear.

The upper air burst into life!
And a hundred fire-flags sheen;
To and fro they were hurried about;   315
And to and fro, and in and out,
The wan stars danced between.

And the coming wind did roar more loud,
And the sails did sigh like sedge;
And the rain poured down from one black cloud;
The moon was at its edge.   321

The thick, black cloud was cleft, and still
The moon was at its side;
Like waters shot from some high crag,
The lightning fell with never a jag,   325
A river steep and wide.

The bodies of the ship's crew are inspired, and the ship moves on;

The loud wind never reached the ship,
Yet now the ship moved on!
Beneath the lightning and the moon
The dead men gave a groan.   330

They groaned, they stirred, they all uprose,
Nor spake, nor moved their eyes;
It had been strange, even in a dream,
To have seen those dead men rise.

The helmsman steered, the ship moved on;   335
Yet never a breeze up-blew.
The mariners all 'gan work the ropes,
Where they were wont to do;
They raised their limbs like lifeless tools—
We were a ghastly crew.   340

But not by the souls of the men, nor by demons of earth or middle air, but by a blessed troop of angelic spirits, sent down by the invocation of the guardian saint.

The body of my brother's son
Stood by me, knee to knee;
The body and I pulled at one rope,
But he said naught to me."

"I fear thee, ancient Mariner!"   345
"Be calm, thou Wedding-Guest!
'Twas not those souls that fled in pain,

Which to their corses came again,
But a troop of spirits blest;

For when it dawned—they dropped their arms
And clustered round the mast;   351
Sweet sounds rose slowly through their mouths,
And from their bodies passed.

Around, around, flew each sweet sound,
Then darted to the sun;   355
Slowly the sounds came back again,
Now mixed, now one by one.

Sometimes a-dropping from the sky
I heard the skylark sing;
Sometimes all little birds that are,   360
How they seemed to fill the sea and air
With their sweet jargoning!

And now 'twas like all instruments,
Now like a lonely flute;
And now it is an angel's song,   365
That makes the heavens be mute.

It ceased; yet still the sails made on
A pleasant noise till noon,
A noise like of a hidden brook
In the leafy month of June,   370
That to the sleeping woods all night
Singeth a quiet tune.

Till noon we quietly sailed on,
Yet never a breeze did breathe;
Slowly and smoothly went the ship,   375
Moved onward from beneath.

*The lonesome Spirit from the South Pole carries on the
ship as far as the Line, in obedience to the angelic
troop, but still requireth vengeance.*

Under the keel nine fathom deep,
From the land of mist and snow,
The Spirit slid; and it was he
That made the ship to go.   380
The sails at noon left off their tune,
And the ship stood still also.

The sun, right up above the mast,
Had fixed her to the ocean;
But in a minute she 'gan stir,   385
With a short, uneasy motion—
Backwards and forwards half her length
With a short, uneasy motion.

Then like a pawing horse let go,
She made a sudden bound;   390

It flung the blood into my head,
And I fell down in a swound.

How long in that same fit I lay,
I have not to declare;
But ere my living life returned,   395
I heard and in my soul discerned
Two voices in the air.

*The Polar Spirit's fellow demons, the invisible inhab-
itants of the element, take part in his wrong; and two
of them relate, one to the other, that penance long and
heavy for the ancient Mariner hath been accorded to the
Polar Spirit, who returneth southward.*

'Is it he?' quoth one, 'Is this the man?
By Him who died on cross,
With his cruel bow he laid full low   400
The harmless Albatross.

The Spirit who bideth by himself
In the land of mist and snow,
He loved the bird that loved the man
Who shot him with his bow.'   405

The other was a softer voice,
As soft as honey-dew;
Quoth he, 'The man hath penance done,
And penance more will do.'

PART VI

FIRST VOICE

" 'But tell me, tell me! speak again,   410
Thy soft response renewing—
What makes that ship drive on so fast?
What is the ocean doing?'

SECOND VOICE

'Still as a slave before his lord,
The ocean hath no blast;   415
His great bright eye most silently
Up to the moon is cast—

*The Mariner hath been cast into a trance; for the an-
gelic power causeth the vessel to drive northward faster
than human life could endure.*

If he may know which way to go;
For she guides him smooth or grim.
See, brother, see! how graciously   420
She looketh down on him.'

FIRST VOICE

'But why drives on that ship so fast,
Without or wave or wind?'

SECOND VOICE

'The air is cut away before,
And closes from behind.   425

Fly, brother, fly! more high, more high!
Or we shall be belated;
For slow and slow that ship will go,
When the Mariner's trance is abated.'

*The supernatural motion is retarded; the Mariner
awakes, and his penance begins anew.*

I woke, and we were sailing on   430
As in a gentle weather.
'Twas night, calm night, the moon was high;
The dead men stood together.

All stood together on the deck,
For a charnel-dungeon fitter;   435
All fixed on me their stony eyes,
That in the moon did glitter.

The pang, the curse, with which they died,
Had never passed away;
I could not draw my eyes from theirs, 440
Nor turn them up to pray.

The curse is finally expiated.

And now this spell was snapped; once more
I viewed the ocean green,
And looked far forth, yet little saw
Of what had else been seen—   445

Like one that on a lonesome road
Doth walk in fear and dread,
And having once turned round, walks on,
And turns no more his head,
Because he knows a frightful fiend   450
Doth close behind him tread.

But soon there breathed a wind on me,
Nor sound nor motion made;
Its path was not upon the sea,
In ripple or in shade.   455

It raised my hair, it fanned my cheek
Like a meadow-gale of spring—
It mingled strangely with my fears,
Yet it felt like a welcoming.

Swiftly, swiftly flew the ship,   460
Yet she sailed softly, too;
Sweetly, sweetly blew the breeze—
On me alone it blew.

And the ancient Mariner beholdeth his native country.

Oh! dream of joy! is this indeed
The lighthouse top I see?   465
Is this the hill? Is this the kirk?
Is this mine own countree?

We drifted o'er the harbor-bar,
And I with sobs did pray—
'O let me be awake, my God!   470
Or let me sleep alway.'

The harbor-bay was clear as glass,
So smoothly it was strewn!
And on the bay the moonlight lay,
And the shadow of the moon.   475

The rock shone bright, the kirk no less,
That stands above the rock;
The moonlight steeped in silentness
The steady weathercock.

The angelic spirits leave the dead bodies,

And the bay was white with silent light, 480
Till rising from the same,
Full many shapes, that shadows were,
In crimson colors came.

And appear in their own forms of light.

A little distance from the prow
Those crimson shadows were;   485
I turned my eyes upon the deck—
O Christ! what saw I there!

Each corse lay flat, lifeless and flat,
And by the holy rood!
A man all light, a seraph-man,   490
On every corse there stood.

This seraph-band, each waved his hand—
It was a heavenly sight!
They stood as signals to the land,
Each one a lovely light;   495

This seraph-band, each waved his hand;
No voice did they impart—
No voice; but oh! the silence sank
Like music on my heart.

But soon I heard the dash of oars,   500
I heard the Pilot's cheer;
My head was turned perforce away,
And I saw a boat appear.

The Pilot, and tne Pilot's boy,
I heard them coming fast;   505
Dear Lord in heaven! it was a joy
The dead men could not blast.

I saw a third—I heard his voice;
It is the Hermit good!
He singeth loud his godly hymns   510
That he makes in the wood.
He'll shrieve my soul, he'll wash away
The Albatross's blood.

PART VII

The Hermit of the wood

"This Hermit good lives in that wood
Which slopes down to the sea;   515
How loudly his sweet voice he rears!
He loves to talk with marineres
That come from a far countree.

He kneels at morn, and noon, and eve—
He hath a cushion plump;   520
It is the moss that wholly hides
The rotted old oak-stump.

The skiff-boat neared; I heard them talk,
'Why this is strange, I trow!
Where are those lights so many and fair   525
That signal made but now?'

Approacheth the ship with wonder.

'Strange, by my faith!' the Hermit said—
'And they answered not our cheer!
The planks look warped! and see those sails
How thin they are and sear!   530
I never saw aught like to them,
Unless perchance it were

Brown skeletons of leaves that lag
My forest-brook along;
When the ivy-tod is heavy with snow,   535
And the owlet whoops to the wolf below
That eats the she-wolf's young.'

'Dear Lord! it hath a fiendish look'—
(The Pilot made reply)
'I am a-feared'—'Push on, push on!'   540
Said the Hermit cheerily.

The boat came closer to the ship,
But I nor spake nor stirred;

The boat came close beneath the ship,
And straight a sound was heard.   545

The ship suddenly sinketh.

Under the water it rumbled on,
Still louder and more dread;
It reached the ship, it split the bay;
The ship went down like lead.

The ancient Mariner is saved in the Pilot's boat.

Stunned by that loud and dreadful sound,   550
Which sky and ocean smote,
Like one that hath been seven days drowned
My body lay afloat;
But swift as dreams, myself I found
Within the Pilot's boat.   555

Upon the whirl, where sank the ship,
The boat spun round and round;
And all was still, save that the hill
Was telling of the sound.

I moved my lips—the Pilot shrieked   560
And fell down in a fit;
The holy Hermit raised his eyes
And prayed where he did sit.

I took the oars; the Pilot's boy,
Who now doth crazy go,   565
Laughed loud and long, and all the while
His eyes went to and fro.
'Ha! ha!' quoth he, 'full plain I see,
The Devil knows how to row.'

And now, all in my own countree,   570
I stood on the firm land!
The Hermit stepped forth from the boat,
And scarcely he could stand.

*The ancient Mariner earnestly entreateth the Hermit to
shrieve him; and the penance of life falls on him,*

'O shrieve me, shrieve me, holy man!'
The Hermit crossed his brow.   575
'Say quick,' quoth he, 'I bid thee say—
What manner of man art thou?'

Forthwith this frame of mine was wrenched
With a woeful agony,
Which forced me to begin my tale;   580
And then it left me free.

*And ever and anon throughout his future life **an agony**
constraineth him to travel from land to land,*

Since then, at an uncertain hour,
That agony returns;

And till my ghastly tale is told,
This heart within me burns.   585

I pass, like night, from land to land;
I have strange power of speech;
That moment that his face I see,
I know the man that must hear me—
To him my tale I teach.   590

What loud uproar bursts from that door!
The wedding-guests are there;
But in the garden-bower the bride
And bride-maids singing are;
And hark the little vesper bell,   595
Which biddeth me to prayer!

O Wedding-Guest! this soul hath been
Alone on a wide, wide sea:
So lonely 'twas that God himself
Scarce seeméd there to be.   600

O sweeter than the marriage feast,
'Tis sweeter far to me,
To walk together to the kirk
With a goodly company!—

And to teach, by his own example, love and reverence
to all things that God made and loveth.

To walk together to the kirk,   605
And all together pray,
While each to his great Father bends,
Old men, and babes, and loving friends,
And youths and maidens gay!

Farewell, farewell! but this I tell   610
To thee, thou Wedding-Guest!
He prayeth well, who loveth well,
Both man and bird and beast.

He prayeth best, who loveth best
All things both great and small;   615
For the dear God who loveth us,
He made and loveth all."

The Mariner, whose eye is bright,
Whose beard with age is hoar,
Is gone; and now the Wedding-Guest   620
Turned from the bridegroom's door.

He went like one that hath been stunned,
And is of sense forlorn;
A sadder and a wiser man
He rose the morrow morn.   625

GEORGE GORDON, LORD BYRON

Maid of Athens, Ere We Part

Ζώη μοῦ, σᾶς ἀγαπῶ.

Maid of Athens, ere we part,
Give, oh, give me back my heart!
Or, since that has left my breast,
Keep it now, and take the rest!
Hear my vow before I go,   5
Ζώη μοῦ, σᾶς ἀγαπῶ.

By those tresses unconfined,
Woo'd by each Ægean wind;
By those lids whose jetty fringe
Kiss thy soft cheeks' blooming tinge;   10
By those wild eyes like the roe,
Ζώη μοῦ, σᾶς ἀγαπῶ.

By that lip I long to taste;
By that zone-encircled waist;
By all the token-flowers that tell   15
What words can never speak so well;
By love's alternate joy and woe,
Ζώη μοῦ, σᾶς ἀγαπῶ.

Maid of Athens! I am gone:
Think of me, sweet! when alone.   20
Though I fly to Istambol,
Athens holds my heart and soul;
Can I cease to love thee? No!
Ζώη μοῦ, σᾶς ἀγαπῶ.

She Walks in Beauty

She walks in beauty, like the night
Of cloudless climes and starry skies;

Byron, *Maid of Athens*. George Noel Gordon, Lord Byron, was born in London in 1788 and died in Greece in 1824. He led a romantic career and through it and his poetry exercised an extraordinary influence on European literature.

And all that's best of dark and bright
  Meet in her aspect and her eyes;
Thus mellowed to that tender light   5
  Which heaven to gaudy day denies.

One shade the more, one ray the less,
  Had half impaired the nameless grace
Which waves in every raven tress,
  Or softly lightens o'er her face;   10
Where thoughts serenely sweet express
  How pure how dear, their dwelling-place.

And on that cheek, and o'er that brow,
  So soft, so calm, yet eloquent,
The smiles that win, the tints that glow,   15
  But tell of days in goodness spent,
A mind at peace with all below,
  A heart whose love is innocent!

The Destruction of Sennacherib

The Assyrian came down like the wolf on the fold,
And his cohorts were gleaming in purple and gold;
And the sheen of their spears was like stars on the
    sea,
When the blue wave rolls nightly on deep Galilee.

Like the leaves of the forest when Summer is green,
That host with their banners at sunset were seen:
Like the leaves of the forest when Autumn hath
    blown,   7
That host on the morrow lay wither'd and strown.

For the Angel of Death spread his wings on the
    blast,   9
And breathed in the face of the foe as he pass'd;
And the eyes of the sleepers wax'd deadly and chill,
And their hearts but once heaved, and for ever
    grew still!

And there lay the steed with his nostril all wide,
But through it there roll'd not the breath of his
    pride;
And the foam of his gasping lay white on the turf,
And cold as the spray of the rock-beating surf. 16

And there lay the rider distorted and pale,
With the dew on his brow, and the rust on his
    mail:
And the tents were all silent, the banners alone,
The lances unlifted, the trumpet unblown. 20

And the widows of Ashur are loud in their
    wail,
And the idols are broke in the temple of Baal;
And the might of the Gentile, unsmote by the
    sword,
Hath melted like snow in the glance of the Lord!

Stanzas for Music

I

There's not a joy the world can give like that it
    takes away,
When the glow of early thought declines in feel-
    ing's dull decay;
'Tis not on youth's smooth cheek the blush alone,
    which fades so fast,
But the tender bloom of heart is gone ere youth
    itself be past.

Then the few whose spirits float above the wreck
    of happiness   5
Are driven o'er the shoals of guilt or ocean of
    excess:
The magnet of their course is gone, or only points
    in vain
The shore to which their shivered sail shall never
    stretch again.

Then the mortal coldness of the soul like death
    itself comes down;
It cannot feel for others' woes, it dare not dream
    its own;   10
That heavy chill has frozen o'er the fountain of
    our tears,
And though the eye may sparkle still, 'tis where
    the ice appears.

Though wit may flash from fluent lips, and mirth
    distract the breast,
Through midnight hours that yield no more their
    former hope of rest;
'Tis but as ivy-leaves around the ruined turret
    wreath,   15
All green and wildly fresh without, but worn and
    gray beneath.

Oh, could I feel as I have felt,—or be what I have
    been,
Or weep as I could once have wept, o'er many a
    vanished scene;

As springs in deserts found seem sweet, all brack-
    ish though they be,
So, midst the wither'd waste of life, those tears
    would flow to me.   20

II

There be none of Beauty's daughters
  With a magic like thee;
And like music on the waters
  Is thy sweet voice to me:
When, as if its sound were causing   5

The charmed ocean's pausing,
The waves lie still and gleaming,
And the lull'd winds seem dreaming;

And the midnight moon is weaving
  Her bright chain o'er the deep;   10
Whose breast is gently heaving,
  As an infant's asleep:
So the spirit bows before thee,
To listen and adore thee;
With a full but soft emotion,   15
Like the swell of Summer's ocean.

PERCY BYSSHE SHELLEY

Hymn to Intellectual Beauty

The awful shadow of some unseen Power
  Floats though unseen amongst us—visiting
This various world with as inconstant wing
As summer winds that creep from flower to
    flower—
Like moonbeams that behind some piny mountain
    shower,   5
  It visits with inconstant glance
  Each human heart and countenance;
Like hues and harmonies of evening—
  Like clouds in starlight widely spread—
  Like memory of music fled—   10
  Like aught that for its grace may be
Dear, and yet dearer for its mystery.

Spirit of Beauty, that dost consecrate
  With thine own hues all thou dost shine upon
  Of human thought or form—where art thou
    gone?   15
Why dost thou pass away and leave our state,
This dim vast vale of tears, vacant and desolate?
  Ask why the sunlight not forever
  Weaves rainbows o'er yon mountain river,
Why aught should fail and fade that once is
    shown,   20
  Why fear and dream and death and birth
  Cast on the daylight of this earth
  Such gloom—why man has such a scope
For love and hate, despondency and hope?

No voice from some sublimer world hath ever 25
  To sage or poet these responses given—
  Therefore the names of Dæmon, Ghost, and
    Heaven,
Remain the records of their vain endeavor,
Frail spells—whose uttered charm might not avail
    to sever,
  From all we hear and all we see,   30
  Doubt, chance, and mutability.
Thy light alone—like mist o'er mountains driven,
  Or music by the night wind sent,
  Through strings of some still instrument,
  Or moonlight on a midnight stream,   35
Gives grace and truth to life's unquiet dream.

Love, Hope, and Self-Esteem, like clouds depart
  And come, for some uncertain moments lent,
  Man were immortal, and omnipotent,
Didst thou, unknown and awful as thou art,   40
Keep with thy glorious train firm state within his
    heart.
  Thou messenger of sympathies,
  That wax and wane in lovers' eyes—
Thou—that to human thought art nourishment,
  Like darkness to a dying flame!   45
  Depart not as thy shadow came,
  Depart not—lest the grave should be,
Like life and fear, a dark reality.

While yet a boy I sought for ghosts, and sped
  Through many a listening chamber, cave and
    ruin,   50

Shelley, *Hymn to Intellectual Beauty.* Percy Bysshe Shelley (1792-1822) came of an upper-class
family. He was educated at Oxford, from which he was expelled for his radical religious views. His
poems reflect these views and his unsettled emotional life. He was drowned off the coast of Italy.

And starlight wood, with fearful steps pursuing
Hopes of high talk with the departed dead.
I called on poisonous names with which our youth
    is fed;
    I was not heard—I saw them not—
    When musing deeply on the lot   55
Of life, at the sweet time when winds are wooing
    All vital things that wake to bring
    News of birds and blossoming—
    Sudden, thy shadow fell on me;
I shrieked, and clasped my hands in ecstasy!   60

I vowed that I would dedicate my powers
    To thee and thine—have I not kept the vow?
    With beating heart and streaming eyes, even
        now
I call the phantoms of a thousand hours
Each from his voiceless grave; they have in
    visioned bowers   65
    Of studious zeal or love's delight
    Outwatched with me the envious night—
They know that never joy illumed my brow
    Unlinked with hope that thou wouldst free
    This world from its dark slavery,   70
    That thou—O awful Loveliness,
Wouldst give whate'er these words cannot express.

The day becomes more solemn and serene
    When noon is past—there is a harmony
    In autumn, and a luster in its sky,   75
Which through the summer is not heard or seen,
As if it could not be, as if it had not been!
    Thus let thy power, which like the truth
    Of nature on my passive youth
Descended, to my onward life supply   80
    Its calm—to one who worships thee,
    And every form containing thee,
    Whom, Spirit fair, thy spells did bind
To fear himself, and love all human kind.

Ozymandias

I met a traveler from an antique land
Who said: Two vast and trunkless legs of stone
Stand in the desert. Near them, on the sand,
Half sunk, a shattered visage lies, whose frown,
And wrinkled lip, and sneer of cold command, 5
Tell that its sculptor well those passions read
Which yet survive, stamped on these lifeless things,
The hand that mocked them and the heart that
    fed.
And on the pedestal these words appear:
"My name is Ozymandias, king of kings;   10
Look on my works, ye Mighty, and despair!"

Nothing beside remains. Round the decay
Of that colossal wreck, boundless and bare
The lone and level sands stretch far away.

Ode to the West Wind

I

O wild West Wind, thou breath of Autumn's
    being,
Thou, from whose unseen presence the leaves
    dead
Are driven, like ghosts from an enchanter fleeing,

Yellow, and black, and pale, and hectic red,
Pestilence-stricken multitudes; O thou,   5
Who chariotest to their dark wintry bed

The wingéd seeds, where they lie cold and low,
Each like a corpse within its grave, until
Thine azure sister of the spring shall blow

Her clarion o'er the dreaming earth, and fill   10
(Driving sweet buds like flocks to feed in air)
With living hues and odors plain and hill—

Wild Spirit, which art moving everywhere;
Destroyer and preserver—hear, oh, hear!

II

Thou on whose stream, 'mid the steep sky's com-
    motion,   15
Loose clouds like earth's decaying leaves are shed,
Shook from the tangled boughs of heaven and
    ocean,

Angels of rain and lightning—there are spread
On the blue surface of thine airy surge,
Like the bright hair uplifted from the head   20

Of some fierce Mænad, even from the dim verge
Of the horizon to the zenith's height
The locks of the approaching storm. Thou dirge

Of the dying year, to which this closing night
Will be the dome of a vast sepulcher,   25
Vaulted with all thy congregated might

Of vapors, from whose solid atmosphere
Black rain, and fire, and hail will burst—oh, hear!

III

Thou who didst waken from his summer dreams
The blue Mediterranean, where he lay,   30
Lulled by the coil of his crystalline streams,

Beside a pumice isle in Baiæ's bay,
And saw in sleep old palaces and towers
Quivering within the wave's intenser day,

All overgrown with azure moss and flowers   35
So sweet the sense faints picturing them! Thou
For whose path the Atlantic's level powers

Cleave themselves into chasms, while far below
The sea-blooms and the oozy woods which wear
The sapless foliage of the ocean, know   40

Thy voice, and suddenly grow gray with fear,
And tremble and despoil themselves—oh, hear!

IV

If I were a dead leaf thou mightest bear;
If I were a swift cloud to fly with thee;
A wave to pant beneath thy power, and share   45

The impulse of thy strength, only less free
Than thou, O uncontrollable! If even
I were as in my boyhood, and could be

The comrade of thy wanderings over heaven,
As then, when to outstrip thy skyey speed   50
Scarce seemed a vision; I would ne'er have striven

As thus with thee in prayer in my sore need.
Oh! lift me as a wave, a leaf, a cloud!
I fall upon the thorns of life! I bleed!

A heavy weight of hours has chained and
    bowed   55
One too like thee: tameless, and swift, and proud.

V

Make me thy lyre, even as the forest is;
What if my leaves are falling like its own!
The tumult of thy mighty harmonies

Will take from both a deep, autumnal tone,   60
Sweet though in sadness. Be thou, spirit fierce,
My spirit! Be thou me, impetuous one!

Drive my dead thoughts over the universe
Like withered leaves to quicken a new birth!
And, by the incantation of this verse,   65

Scatter, as from an unextinguished hearth
Ashes and sparks, my words among mankind!
Be through my lips to unawakened earth

The trumpet of a prophecy! O wind,
If Winter comes, can Spring be far behind?   0

The Indian Serenade

I arise from dreams of thee
In the first sweet sleep of night,
When the winds are breathing low,
And the stars are shining bright;
I arise from dreams of thee,   5
And a spirit in my feet
Hath led me—who knows how!
To thy chamber window, Sweet!

The wandering airs they faint
On the dark, the silent stream—   10
And the Champak odors fail
Like sweet thoughts in a dream;
The nightingale's complaint,
It dies upon her heart—
As I must on thine,   15
O! beloved as thou art!

Oh, lift me from the grass!
I die! I faint! I fail!
Let thy love in kisses rain
On my lips and eyelids pale.   20
My cheek is cold and white, alas!
My heart beats loud and fast—
Oh, press it to thine own again,
Where it will break at last!

The Cloud

I bring fresh showers for the thirsting flowers,
    From the seas and the streams;
I bear light shade for the leaves when laid
    In their noonday dreams.
From my wings are shaken the dews that
    waken   5
    The sweet buds every one,
When rocked to rest on their mother's breast,
    As she dances about the sun.
I wield the flail of the lashing hail,
    And whiten the green plains under,   10
And then again I dissolve it in rain,
    And laugh as I pass in thunder.

I sift the snow on the mountains below,
    And their great pines groan aghast;
And all the night 'tis my pillow white,   15
    While I sleep in the arms of the blast.
Sublime on the towers of my skyey bowers,

Lightning my pilot sits;
In a cavern under is fettered the thunder;
  It struggles and howls at fits.   20
Over earth and ocean, with gentle motion,
  This pilot is guiding me,
Lured by the love of the genii that move
  In the depths of the purple sea;
Over the rills, and the crags, and the hills,   25
  Over the lakes and the plains,
Wherever he dream, under mountain or stream,
  The Spirit he loves remains;
And I all the while bask in heaven's blue smile,
  Whilst he is dissolving in rains.   30

The sanguine sunrise, with his meteor eyes,
  And his burning plumes outspread,
Leaps on the back of my sailing rack,
  When the morning star shines dead,
As on the jag of a mountain crag,   35
  Which an earthquake rocks and swings,
An eagle alit one moment may sit
  In the light of its golden wings.
And when sunset may breathe, from the lit sea
    beneath,
  Its ardors of rest and of love,   40
And the crimson pall of eve may fall
  From the depth of heaven above,
With wings folded I rest, on mine airy nest,
  As still as a brooding dove.

That orbéd maiden, with white fire laden,   45
  Whom mortals call the moon,
Glides glimmering o'er my fleece-like floor,
  By the midnight breezes strewn;
And wherever the beat of her unseen feet,
  Which only the angels hear,   50
May have broken the woof of my tent's thin roof,
  The stars peep behind her and peer;
And I laugh to see them whirl and flee,
  Like a swarm of golden bees,
When I widen the rent in my wind-built tent,   55
  Till the calm rivers, lakes, and seas,
Like strips of the sky fallen through me on high,
  Are each paved with the moon and these.

I bind the sun's throne with a burning zone,
  And the moon's with a girdle of pearl;   60
The volcanoes are dim, and the stars reel and
    swim,
  When the whirlwinds my banner unfurl.
From cape to cape, with a bridge-like shape,
  Over a torrent sea,
Sunbeam-proof, I hang like a roof,   65
  The mountains its columns be.

The triumphal arch through which I march
  With hurricane, fire, and snow,
When the powers of the air are chained to my
    chair,
  Is the million-colored bow;   70
The sphere-fire above its soft colors wove,
  While the moist earth was laughing below.

I am the daughter of earth and water,
  And the nursling of the sky;
I pass through the pores of the ocean and shores;
  I change, but I cannot die.   76
For after the rain when, with never a stain,
  The pavilion of heaven is bare,
And the winds and sunbeams with their convex
    gleams
  Build up the blue dome of air,   80
I silently laugh at my own cenotaph,
  And out of the caverns of rain,
Like a child from the womb, like a ghost from
    the tomb,
  I arise and unbuild it again.

To a Skylark

Hail to thee, blithe spirit!
  Bird thou never wert,
That from heaven, or near it,
  Pourest thy full heart
In profuse strains of unpremeditated art.   5

Higher still and higher
  From the earth thou springest
Like a cloud of fire;
  The blue deep thou wingest,
And singing still dost soar, and soaring ever
    singest.   10

In the golden lightning
  Of the sunken sun,
O'er which clouds are bright'ning,
  Thou dost float and run;
Like an unbodied joy whose race is just begun.   15

The pale purple even
  Melts around thy flight;
Like a star of heaven
  In the broad daylight
Thou art unseen, but yet I hear thy shrill de-
    light,   20

Keen as are the arrows
  Of that silver sphere,
Whose intense lamp narrows

In the white dawn clear,
Until we hardly see, we feel that it is there.   25

All the earth and air
  With thy voice is loud,
As, when night is bare,
  From one lonely cloud
The moon rains out her beams, and heaven is
    overflowed.   30

What thou art we know not;
  What is most like thee?
From rainbow clouds there flow not
  Drops so bright to see
As from thy presence showers a rain of melody.   35

Like a poet hidden
  In the light of thought,
Singing hymns unbidden,
  Till the world is wrought
To sympathy with hopes and fears it heeded
    not;   40

Like a high-born maiden
  In a palace tower,
Soothing her love-laden
  Soul in secret hour
With music sweet as love, which overflows her
    bower;   45

Like a glowworm golden
  In a dell of dew,
Scattering unbeholden
  Its aërial hue
Among the flowers and grass which screen it from
    the view;   50

Like a rose embowered
  In its own green leaves,
By warm winds deflowered,
  Till the scent it gives
Makes faint with too much sweet those heavy-
    wingéd thieves.   55

Sound of vernal showers
  On the twinkling grass,
Rain-awakened flowers,
  All that ever was
Joyous, and clear, and fresh, thy music doth sur-
    pass.   60

Teach us, sprite or bird,
  What sweet thoughts are thine;
I have never heard
  Praise of love or wine
That panted forth a flood of rapture so divine: 65

Chorus Hymeneal,
  Or triumphal chaunt,
Matched with thine, would be all
  But an empty vaunt,
A thing wherein we feel there is some hidden
    want.   70

What objects are the fountains
  Of thy happy strain?
What fields, or waves, or mountains?
  What shapes of sky or plain?
What love of thine own kind? what ignorance
    of pain?   75

With thy clear keen joyance
  Languor cannot be—
Shadow of annoyance
  Never came near thee:
Thou lovest—but ne'er knew love's sad satiety.   80

Waking or asleep,
  Thou of death must deem
Things more true and deep
  Than we mortals dream,
Or how could thy notes flow in such a crystal
    stream?   85

We look before and after
  And pine for what is not;
Our sincerest laughter
  With some pain is fraught;
Our sweetest songs are those that tell of saddest
    thought.   90

Yet if we could scorn
  Hate, and pride, and fear;
If we were things born
  Not to shed a tear,
I know not how thy joy we ever should come
    near.   95

Better than all measures
  Of delightful sound—
Better than all treasures
  That in books are found—
Thy skill to poet were, thou scorner of the
    ground!   100

Teach me half the gladness
  That thy brain must know,
Such harmonious madness
  From my lips would flow,
The world should listen then—as I am listening
    now.   105

JOHN KEATS

On the Grasshopper and Cricket

The poetry of earth is never dead:
When all the birds are faint with the hot sun,
And hide in cooling trees, a voice will run
From hedge to hedge about the new-mown mead;
That is the Grasshopper's—he takes the lead   5
In summer luxury,—he has never done
With his delights; for when tired out with fun
He rests at ease beneath some pleasant weed.
The poetry of earth is ceasing never;
On a lone winter evening, when the frost   10
Has wrought a silence, from the stove there shrills
The Cricket's song, in warmth increasing ever,
And seems to one in drowsiness half lost,
The Grasshopper's among some grassy hills.

When I Have Fears That I May Cease to Be

When I have fears that I may cease to be
Before my pen has glean'd my teeming brain,
Before high piléd books, in charact'ry,
Hold like rich garners the full-ripen'd grain;
When I behold, upon the night's starr'd face,   5
Huge cloudy symbols of a high romance,
And think that I may never live to trace
Their shadows, with the magic hand of chance;
And when I feel, fair creature of an hour!
That I shall never look upon thee more,   10
Never have relish in the faery power
Of unreflecting love!—then on the shore
Of the wide world I stand alone, and think
Till Love and Fame to nothingness do sink.

Bright Star! Would I Were Steadfast as Thou Art

Bright star! would I were steadfast as thou art—
Not in lone splendor hung aloft the night,
And watching, with eternal lids apart,
Like Nature's patient sleepless Eremite,
The moving waters at their priestlike task   5
Of pure ablution round earth's human shores,
Or gazing on the new soft-fallen mask
Of snow upon the mountains and the moors—

No—yet still steadfast, still unchangeable,
Pillowed upon my fair love's ripening breast,   10
To feel forever its soft fall and swell,
Awake forever in a sweet unrest,
Still, still to hear her tender-taken breath,
And so live ever—or else swoon to death.

From Endymion

BOOK I

PROEM

A thing of beauty is a joy for ever:
Its loveliness increases; it will never
Pass into nothingness; but still will keep
A bower quiet for us, and a sleep
Full of sweet dreams, and health, and quiet
     breathing.   5
Therefore, on every morrow, are we wreathing
A flowery band to bind us to the earth.
Spite of despondence, of the inhuman dearth
Of noble natures, of the gloomy days,
Of all the unhealthy and o'er-darkened ways   10
Made for our searching: yes, in spite of all,
Some shape of beauty moves away the pall
From our dark spirits. Such the sun, the moon,
Trees old and young, sprouting a shady boon
For simple sheep; and such are daffodils   15
With the green world they live in; and clear rills
That for themselves a cooling covert make
'Gainst the hot season; the mid-forest brake,
Rich with a sprinkling of fair musk-rose blooms:
And such too is the grandeur of the dooms   20
We have imagined for the mighty dead;
All lovely tales that we have heard or read:
An endless fountain of immortal drink,
Pouring unto us from the heaven's brink.

Nor do we merely feel these essences   25
For one short hour; no, even as the trees
That whisper round a temple become soon
Dear as the temple's self, so does the moon,
The passion poesy, glories infinite,
Haunt us till they become a cheering light   30
Unto our souls, and bound to us so fast,

Keats, *On the Grasshopper and Cricket.* John Keats (1795-1821) was born in London and trained as
a surgeon. He wrote most of his poems between 1815 and 1821. He died in Rome, where he had gone
in hopes of recovering his health.

That, whether there be shine, or gloom o'ercast,
They always must be with us, or we die.

Therefore, 'tis with full happiness that I
Will trace the story of Endymion.   35
The very music of the name has gone
Into my being, and each pleasant scene
Is growing fresh before me as the green
Of our own valleys: so I will begin
Now while I cannot hear the city's din;   40
Now while the early budders are just new,
And run in mazes of the youngest hue
About old forests; while the willow trails
Its delicate amber; and the dairy pails
Bring home increase of milk. And, as the year   45
Grows lush in juicy stalks, I'll smoothly steer
My little boat, for many quiet hours,
With streams that deepen freshly into bowers.
Many and many a verse I hope to write,
Before the daisies, vermeil rimm'd and white,   50
Hide in deep herbage; and ere yet the bees
Hum about gloves of clover and sweet peas,
I must be near the middle of my story.
O may no wintry season, bare and hoary,
See it half finished: but let Autumn bold,   55
With universal tinge of sober gold,
Be all about me when I make an end.
And now at once, adventuresome, I send
My herald thought into a wilderness:
There let its trumpet blow, and quickly dress   60
My uncertain path with green, that I may speed
Easily onward, thorough flowers and weed.

Ode on a Grecian Urn

Thou still unravished bride of quietness,
  Thou foster-child of silence and slow time,
Silvan historian, who canst thus express
  A flowery tale more sweetly than our rhyme:
What leaf-fringed legend haunts about thy shape
  Of deities or mortals, or of both,   6
    In Tempe or the dales of Arcady?
  What men or gods are these? What maidens
    loath?
What mad pursuit? What struggle to escape?
    What pipes and timbrels? What wild
      ecstasy?   10

Heard melodies are sweet, but those unheard
  Are sweeter; therefore, ye soft pipes, play on;
Not to the sensual ear, but, more endeared,
  Pipe to the spirit ditties of no tone;

Fair youth, beneath the trees, thou canst not
      leave   15
  Thy song, nor ever can those trees be bare;
  Bold lover, never, never canst thou kiss
Though winning near the goal—yet, do not grieve;
  She cannot fade, though thou hast not thy bliss,
    Forever wilt thou love, and she be fair!   20

Ah, happy, happy boughs! that cannot shed
  Your leaves, nor ever bid the Spring adieu;
And, happy melodist, unwearied,
  Forever piping songs forever new;
More happy love! more happy, happy love!   25
  Forever warm and still to be enjoyed,
    Forever panting, and forever young,
All breathing human passion far above,
  That leaves a heart high-sorrowful and cloyed,
    A burning forehead, and a parching tongue. 30

Who are these coming to the sacrifice?
  To what green altar, O mysterious priest,
Lead'st thou that heifer lowing at the skies,
  And all her silken flanks with garlands dressed?
What little town by river or sea shore,   35
  Or mountain-built with peaceful citadel,
    Is emptied of this folk, this pious morn?
And, little town, thy streets for evermore
  Will silent be; and not a soul to tell
    Why thou art desolate, can e'er return.   40

O Attic shape! Fair attitude! with brede
  Of marble men and maidens overwrought,
With forest branches and the trodden weed;
  Thou, silent form, dost tease us out of thought
As doth eternity. Cold Pastoral!   45
  When old age shall this generation waste,
    Thou shalt remain, in midst of other woe
Than ours, a friend to man, to whom thou say'st,
  "Beauty is truth, truth beauty"—that is all   49
    Ye know on earth, and all ye need to know.

Ode to a Nightingale

My heart aches, and a drowsy numbness pains
  My sense, as though of hemlock I had drunk,
Or emptied some dull opiate to the drains
  One minute past, and Lethe-wards had sunk.
'Tis not through envy of thy happy lot,   5
  But being too happy in thine happiness—
    That thou, light wingéd Dryad of the trees,
      In some melodious plot
  Of beechen green, and shadows numberless,
    Singest of summer in full-throated ease.   10

Oh, for a draught of vintage that hath been
  Cooled a long age in the deep-delved earth,
Tasting of Flora and the country green,
    Dance, and Provençal song, and sun-burnt
      mirth!
Oh, for a beaker full of the warm South,   15
  Full of the true, the blushful Hippocrene,
    With beaded bubbles winking at the brim,
      And purple-stainéd mouth;
  That I might drink, and leave the world unseen,
    And with thee fade away into the forest
      dim—   20

Fade far away, dissolve, and quite forget
  What thou among the leaves hast never known,
The weariness, the fever, and the fret
  Here, where men sit and hear each other groan;
Where palsy shakes a few, sad, last gray hairs,   25
  Where youth grows pale, and specter-thin, and
    dies;
    Where but to think is to be full of sorrow
      And leaden-eyed despairs,
  Where Beauty cannot keep her lustrous eyes,
    Or new Love pine at them beyond tomor-
      row.   30

Away! away! for I will fly to thee,
  Not charioted by Bacchus and his pards,
But on the viewless wings of Poesy,
  Though the dull brain perplexes and retards:
Already with thee! tender is the night,   35
  And haply the Queen-Moon is on her throne,
    Clustered around by all her starry Fays;
      But here there is no light,
  Save what from heaven is with the breezes
    blown
    Through verdurous glooms and winding,
    mossy ways.   40

I cannot see what flowers are at my feet,
  Nor what soft incense hangs upon the boughs,
But, in embalméd darkness, guess each sweet
  Wherewith the seasonable month endows
The grass, the thicket, and the fruit-tree wild;   45
  White hawthorn, and the pastoral eglantine;
    Fast fading violets covered up in leaves;
      And mid-May's eldest child,
  The coming musk-rose, full of dewy wine,
    The murmurous haunt of flies on summer
    eves.   50

Darkling I listen; and, for many a time
  I have been half in love with easeful Death,
Called him soft names in many a muséd rime,

To take into the air my quiet breath;
Now more than ever seems it rich to die,   55
  To cease upon the midnight with no pain,
    While thou art pouring forth thy soul abroad
      In such an ecstasy!
  Still wouldst thou sing, and I have ears in vain—
    To thy high requiem become a sod.   60

Thou wast not born for death, immortal Bird!
  No hungry generations tread thee down;
The voice I hear this passing night was heard
  In ancient days by emperor and clown:
Perhaps the self-same song that found a path   65
  Through the sad heart of Ruth, when, sick for
    home,
    She stood in tears amid the alien corn;
      The same that ofttimes hath
  Charmed magic casements, opening on the foam
    Of perilous seas, in faery lands forlorn.   70

Forlorn! the very word is like a bell
  To toll me back from thee to my sole self!
Adieu! the fancy cannot cheat so well
  As she is famed to do, deceiving elf.
Adieu! adieu! thy plaintive anthem fades   75
  Past the near meadows, over the still stream,
    Up the hillside; and now 'tis buried deep
      In the next valley-glades:
  Was it a vision, or a waking dream?
    Fled is that music—do I wake or sleep?   80

To Autumn

Season of mist and mellow fruitfulness,
  Close bosom-friend of the maturing sun;
Conspiring with him how to load and bless
  With fruit the vines that round the thatch-eves
  run;
To bend with apples the mossed cottage-trees,   5
  And fill all fruit with ripeness to the core;
    To swell the gourd, and plump the hazel
    shells
With a sweet kernel; to set budding more,
  And still more, later flowers for the bees,
  Until they think warm days will never cease,   10
    For summer has o'er-brimmed their clammy
    cells.

Who hath not seen thee oft amid thy store?
  Sometimes whoever seeks abroad may find
Thee sitting careless on a granary floor,
  Thy hair soft-lifted by the winnowing wind;   15
Or on a half-reaped furrow sound asleep,

Drowsed with the fume of poppies, while thy
    hook
    Spares the next swath and all its twinéd
      flowers
And sometimes like a gleaner thou dost keep
    Steady thy laden head across a brook;   20
    Or by a cider-press, with patient look,
      Thou watchest the last oozings hours by hours.

Where are the songs of spring? Aye, where are
    they?

    Think not of them, thou hast thy music too—
While barréd clouds bloom the soft-dying day,   25
    And touch the stubble-plains with rosy hue;
Then in a wailful choir the small gnats mourn
    Among the river sallows, borne aloft
      Or sinking as the light wind lives or dies;
And full-grown lambs loud bleat from hilly
    bourn;   30
    Hedge-crickets sing; and now with treble soft
The redbreast whistles from a garden-croft;
    And gathering swallows twitter in the skies.

FROM LAMB TO
STEVENSON

Just as the rise of the periodical essay at the beginning of the eighteenth century inaugurated a long and important series of prose writings, so the new literary magazines and critical journals which began to appear shortly after 1800 offered an avenue of publication which stimulated the efforts of an able new generation of essayists.

To most readers the pleasantest writer of essays of the early nineteenth century is Charles Lamb. He was distinctly a city man who enjoyed the companionship of many other London writers. Compelled to make a living as a clerk at the India House and resigned to bachelorhood in order to care for his brilliant, but occasionally insane, sister, he found time for extensive reading and for the writing of some of the most charmingly personal essays in the language. He had become so familiar with the prose writers of the seventeenth century that he thought of them as old friends and almost unconsciously fell into their terms of expression, so that at times his essays have a quaint, archaic flavor. Through them we become acquainted with his sister Mary (whom he speaks of as his cousin Bridget) and, above all, with himself. For Lamb is one of those writers whose personality is quite as important to the reader as anything he wrote.

Two important writers of Lamb's generation were William Hazlitt and Thomas De Quincey. Hazlitt's most important contributions were his critical studies, in which he displayed rare powers of literary judgment. Nevertheless, he is perhaps remembered best by most readers for one or two familiar essays, where we seem to become acquainted with the man himself. He has one excellent account of a prize fight and another of his first acquaintance with Wordsworth and Coleridge. A good illustration of these familiar essays is his *On Going a Journey*. As a master of English prose, Hazlitt has been justly admired. A half century after his death Robert Louis Stevenson was to say, "We are all mighty fine fellows, but none of us can write like Hazlitt."

De Quincey also wrote some critical prose, particularly a very able discussion of the literature of knowledge and the literature of power. His lasting reputation, however, rests on his *Confessions of an English Opium Eater* in which he gives a vivid account of his experiences with the drug. His style everywhere is highly rhetorical, never more so than in the eloquent periods of *Levana and Our Ladies of Sorrow*.

Beginning with about 1830 a new generation of authors arose in England, whom we know as Victorians. Among these were several outstanding writers of the essay. Thomas Carlyle, the first to claim our attention, began his literary work in Scotland, but after his first literary accomplishments he settled in London and wrote busily for half a century. Much of this time was spent with large works taking years of preparation, such as his *History of the French Revolution* and his *Life of Frederick the Great.* His essay, *Labor,* is, however, a good example of his miscellaneous social and ethical writings. Carlyle was one of the most picturesque figures of his generation, and this fact, along with his extraordinary intellectual powers and his vigorous and unconventional manner of writing, impressed his contemporaries to such an extent that he came to be looked upon as a sage or prophet.

A real history of the Victorian essay would certainly discuss the critical and controversial papers of John Henry Newman (later Cardinal Newman), the ethical and æsthetic writings of John Ruskin, and the choice prose of Walter Pater. We are representing the later Victorian period by the writings of Arnold and Stevenson. Matthew Arnold is perhaps the most penetrating literary critic who has written in English. His essays, *Hebraism and Hellenism* and *On Celtic Literature,* have already appeared at appropriate places in this book (pp. 4 and 521, above). In his religious essays he did much toward reconciling new scientific ideas with a truly religious attitude; in his social studies he was a positive force in opposition to the vulgarity of the newly enriched middle classes in England. During his forty years of writing and lecturing he never ceased to use all his efforts in the direction of what he called "sweetness and light," that is, goodwill and intelligence.

Robert Louis Stevenson is perhaps best known for his novels and short stories. His *Treasure Island* is beloved of every schoolboy, and such stories as "Will of the Mill" and "The Sire de Maletroit's Door" appear in many anthologies and maintain undiminished popularity. To many of his readers, however, he is first thought of as an essayist. He tells us how he trained himself as a writer of prose by imitating now one great master, now another. But at the end of all this training there remained something which was his own—a style quite as recognizable as that of any of the masters at whose feet he had sat. There is really a great variety to his productions, as anyone will see who reads his descriptive sketches in his *Travels with a Donkey,* his reminiscences of boyhood in Edinburgh, his literary criticism in *A Gossip on Romance,* his whimsical and homely wisdom in *On Falling in Love,* or his romanticism in *Eldorado.* Many of his readers feel that his greatest achievement is that seemingly pessimistic, but really optimistic, discourse on the basic nobility of man, which he calls *Pulvis et Umbra.* Writers of our own generation are likely to be scornful of Stevenson's elaborate rhetoric, but though it is hard to know how a future generation may judge, it seems safe to say that Stevenson's position as an English essayist is permanently established.

CHARLES LAMB

Dream-Children: A Reverie

Children love to listen to stories about their elders, when *they* were children; to stretch their imagination to the conception of a traditionary great-uncle or grandame, whom they never saw. It was in this spirit that my little ones crept about me the other evening to hear about their great-grandmother Field, who lived in a great house in Norfolk (a hundred times bigger than that in which they and papa lived) which had been the scene—so at least it was generally believed in that part of the country—of the tragic incidents which they had lately become familiar with from the ballad of the Children in the Wood. Certain it is that the whole story of the children and their cruel uncle was to be seen fairly carved out in wood upon the chimneypiece of the great hall, the whole story down to the Robin Redbreasts, till a foolish rich person pulled it down to set up a marble one of modern invention in its stead, with no story upon it. Here Alice put out one of her dear mother's looks, too tender to be called upbraiding. Then I went on to say how religious and how good their great-grandmother Field was, how beloved and respected by everybody, though she was not indeed the mistress of this great house, but had only the charge of it (and yet in some respects she might be said to be the mistress of it, too) committed to her by the owner, who preferred living in a newer and more fashionble mansion which he had purchased somewhere in the adjoining county; but still she lived in it in a manner as if it had been her own, and kept up the dignity of the great house in a sort while she lived, which afterwards came to decay, and was nearly pulled down, and all its old ornaments stripped and carried away to the owner's other house, where they were set up, and looked as awkward as if someone were to carry away the old tombs they had seen lately at the Abbey, and stick them up in Lady C.'s tawdry gilt drawing-room. Here John smiled, as much as to say, "That would be foolish indeed." And then I told how, when she came to die, her funeral was attended by a concourse of all the poor, and some of the gentry, too, of the neighborhood for many miles round, to show their respect for her memory, because she had been such a good and religious woman; so good indeed that she knew all the Psaltery by heart, aye, and a great part of the Testament besides. Here little Alice spread her hands. Then I told what a tall, upright, graceful person their great-grandmother Field once was; and how in her youth she was esteemed the best dancer—here Alice's little right foot played an involuntary movement, till upon my looking grave, it desisted—the best dancer, I was saying, in the county, till a cruel disease, called a cancer, came, and bowed her down with pain; but it could never bend her good spirits, or make them stoop, but they were still upright, because she was so good and religious. Then I told how she was used to sleep by herself in a lone chamber of the great lone house; and how she believed that an apparition of two infants was to be seen at midnight gliding up and down the great staircase near where she slept, but she said "those innocents would do her no harm"; and how frightened I used to be, though in those days I had my maid to sleep with me, because I was never half so good or religious as she—and yet I never saw the infants. Here John expanded all his eyebrows and tried to look courageous. Then I told how good she was to all her grand-children, having us to the great house in the holidays, where I in particular used to spend many hours by myself, in gazing upon the old busts of the Twelve Cæsars, that had been Emperors of Rome, till the old marble heads would seem to live again, or I to be turned into marble with them; how I never could be tired with roaming about that huge mansion, with its vast empty rooms, with their worn-out hangings, fluttering tapestry, and carved oaken panels, with the gilding almost rubbed out—sometimes in the spacious old-fashioned gardens, which I had almost to myself, unless when now and then a solitary gardening man would cross me—and how the nectarines and peaches hung upon the walls, without

Lamb, *Dream Children*. Charles Lamb (1775-1834) was for most of his life a clerk in the India House. His sister Mary kept house for him and made the home a center for the leading literary men of the day.

my ever offering to pluck them because they were forbidden fruit, unless now and then—and because I had more pleasure in strolling about among the old melancholy-looking yew trees, or the firs, and picking up the red berries, and the fir apples, which were good for nothing but to look at—or in lying about upon the fresh grass, with all the fine garden smells around me—or basking in the orangery, till I could almost fancy myself ripening, too, along with the oranges and the limes in that grateful warmth—or in watching the dace that darted to and fro in the fishpond, at the bottom of the garden, with here and there a great sulky pike hanging midway down the water in silent state, as if it mocked at their impertinent friskings—I had more pleasure in these busy-idle diversions than in all the sweet flavors of peaches, nectarines, oranges, and such like common baits of children. Here John slyly deposited back upon the plate a bunch of grapes, which, not unobserved by Alice, he had meditated dividing with her, and both seemed willing to relinquish them for the present as irrelevant. Then in somewhat a more heightened tone I told how, though their great-grandmother Field loved all her grand-children, yet in an especial manner she might be said to love their uncle, John L——, because he was so handsome and spirited a youth, and a king to the rest of us; and, instead of moping about in solitary corners, like some of us, he would mount the most mettlesome horse he could get when but an imp no bigger than themselves, and make it carry him half over the county in a morning, and join the hunters when there were any out—and yet he loved the old great house and gardens, too, but had too much spirit to be always pent up within their boundaries—and how their uncle grew up to man's estate as brave as he was handsome, to the admiration of everybody, but of their great-grandmother Field most especially; and how he used to carry me upon his back when I was a lame-footed boy—for he was a good bit older than me—many a mile when I could not walk for pain—and how in after life he became lame-footed, too, and I did not always (I fear) make allowances enough for him when he was impatient, and in pain, nor remember sufficiently how considerate he had been to me

when I was lame-footed; and how when he died, though he had not been dead an hour, it seemed as if he had died a great while ago, such a distance there is betwixt life and death; and how I bore his death as I thought pretty well at first, but afterwards it haunted and haunted me; and though I did not cry or take it to heart as some do, and as I think he would have done if I had died, yet I missed him all day long, and knew not till then how much I had loved him. I missed his kindness, and I missed his crossness, and wished him to be alive again, to be quarreling with him (for we quarreled sometimes), rather than not have him again, and was as uneasy without him as he their poor uncle must have been when the doctor took off his limb. Here the children fell a-crying, and asked if their little mourning which they had on was not for uncle John, and they looked up, and prayed me not to go on about their uncle, but to tell them some stories about their pretty dead mother. Then I told how for seven long years, in hope sometimes, sometimes in despair, yet persisting ever, I courted the fair Alice W—n; and, as much as children could understand, I explained to them what coyness, and difficulty, and denial meant in maidens—when suddenly, turning to Alice, the soul of the first Alice looked out at her eyes with such a reality of re-presentment, that I became in doubt which of them stood there before me, or whose that bright hair was; and while I stood gazing, both the children gradually grew fainter to my view, receding, and still receding till nothing at last but two mournful features were seen in the uttermost distance, which, without speech, strangely impressed upon me the effects of speech: "We are not of Alice, nor of thee, nor are we children at all. The children of Alice called Bartrum father. We are nothing; less than nothing, and dreams. We are only what might have been, and must wait upon the tedious shores of Lethe millions of ages before we have existence, and a name"—and immediately awaking, I found myself quietly seated in my bachelor armchair, where I had fallen asleep, with the faithful Bridget unchanged by my side—but John L. (or James Elia) was gone forever.

Old China

I have an almost feminine partiality for old china. When I go to see any great house, I inquire for the china-closet, and next for the picture-gallery. I cannot defend the order of preference but by saying that we have all some taste or other, of too ancient a date to admit of our remembering distinctly that it was an acquired one. I can call to mind the first play, and the first exhibition, that I was taken to; but I am not conscious of a time when china jars and saucers were introduced into my imagination.

I had no repugnance then—why should I now have?—to those little, lawless, azure-tinctured grotesques that, under the notion of men and women, float about, uncircumscribed by any element, in that world before perspective—a china teacup.

I like to see my old friends—whom distance cannot diminish—figuring up in the air (so they appear to our optics), yet on *terra firma* still—for so we must in courtesy interpret that speck of deeper blue, which the decorous artist, to prevent absurdity, had made to spring up beneath their sandals.

I love the men with women's faces, and the women, if possible, with still more womanish expressions.

Here is a young and courtly Mandarin, handing tea to a lady from a salver—two miles off. See how distance seems to set off respect! And here the same lady, or another—for likeness is identity on teacups—is stepping into a little fairy boat, moored on the hither side of this calm garden river, with a dainty mincing foot, which in a right angle of incidence (as angles go in our world) must infallibly land her in the midst of a flowery mead—a furlong off on the other side of the same strange stream!

Farther on—if far or near can be predicated of their world—see horses, trees, pagodas, dancing the hays.

Here—a cow and rabbit couchant, and coextensive—so objects show, seen through the lucid atmosphere of fine Cathay.

I was pointing out to my cousin last evening, over our Hyson (which we are old-fashioned enough to drink unmixed still of an afternoon), some of these *speciosa miracula* upon a set of extraordinary old blue china (a recent purchase) which we were now for the first time using; and could not help remarking how favorable circumstances had been to us of late years, that we could afford to please the eye sometimes with trifles of this sort—when a passing sentiment seemed to overshade the brows of my companion. I am quick at detecting these summer clouds in Bridget.

"I wish the good old times would come again," she said, "when we were not quite so rich. I do not mean that I want to be poor; but there was a middle state"—so she was pleased to ramble on—"in which I am sure we were a great deal happier. A purchase is but a purchase, now that you have money enough and to spare. Formerly it used to be a triumph. When we coveted a cheap luxury (and O! how much ado I had to get you to consent in those times!)—we were used to have a debate two or three days before, and to weigh the *for* and *against,* and think what we might spare it out of, and what saving we could hit upon, that should be an equivalent. A thing was worth buying then, when we felt the money that we paid for it.

"Do you remember the brown suit which you made to hang upon you till all your friends cried shame upon you, it grew so threadbare—and all because of that folio Beaumont and Fletcher, which you dragged home late at night from Barker's in Covent Garden? Do you remember how we eyed it for weeks before we could make up our minds to the purchase, and had not come to a determination till it was near ten o'clock of the Saturday night, when you set off from Islington, fearing you should be too late—and when the old bookseller with some grumbling opened his shop, and by the twinkling taper (for he was setting bedward) lighted out the relic from his dusty treasures—and when you lugged it home, wishing it twice as cumbersome—and when you presented it to me—and when we were exploring the perfectness of it (*collating,* you called it)—and while I was repairing some of the loose leaves with paste, which your impatience would not suffer to be left till daybreak—was there no pleasure in being a poor man? Or can those neat black clothes which you wear now, and are so careful to keep brushed, since we have become rich and finical—give you half the honest vanity with which you flaunted it about in that overworn suit—your old corbeau—for four or five weeks longer than you should have done, to pacify your conscience for the mighty sum of fifteen—or sixteen shillings was it?—a great affair we thought it then—which you had lavished on the old folio. Now you can afford to buy any book that pleases you, but I do not see that you ever bring me home any nice old purchases now.

"When you came home with twenty apologies for laying out a less number of shillings upon that print after Lionardo, which we christened the 'Lady Blanch'; when you looked at the purchase, and thought of the money—and thought of the money, and looked again at the picture—was there no pleasure in being a poor man? Now you have nothing to do but to walk into Colnaghi's, and buy a wilderness of Lionardos. Yet do you?

"Then, do you remember our pleasant walks to Enfield, and Potter's Bar, and Waltham, when we had a holiday—holidays and all other fun are gone now we are rich—and the little hand-basket in which I used to deposit our day's fare of savory cold lamb and salad—and how you would pry about at noontide for some decent house, where we might go in and produce our store—only paying for the ale that you must call for—and speculate upon the looks of the landlady, and whether she was likely to allow us a tablecloth—and wish for such another honest hostess as Izaak Walton has described many a one on the pleasant banks of the Lea, when he went a-fishing—and sometimes they would prove obliging enough, and sometimes they would look grudgingly upon us— but we had cheerful looks still for one another, and would eat our plain food savorily, scarcely grudging Piscator [1] his Trout Hall? Now—when we go out a day's pleasuring, which is seldom, moreover, we *ride* part of the way, and go into a fine inn, and order the best of dinners, never debating the expense—which, after all, never has half the relish of those chance country snaps, when we were at the mercy of uncertain usage, and a precarious welcome.

"You are too proud to see a play anywhere now but in the pit. Do you remember where it was we used to sit, when we saw the *Battle of Hexham,* and the *Surrender of Calais,* and Bannister and Mrs. Bland in the *Children in the Wood*—when we squeezed out our shillings apiece to sit three or four times in a season in the one-shilling gallery— where you felt all the time that you ought not to have brought me—and more strongly I felt obligation to you for having brought me—and the pleasure was the better for a little shame—and when the

curtain drew up, what cared we for our place in the house, or what mattered it where we were sitting, when our thoughts were with Rosalind in Arden,[2] or with Viola at the Court of Illyria? You used to say that the gallery was the best place of all for enjoying a play socially—that the relish of such exhibitions must be in proportion to the infrequency of going—that the company we met there, not being in general readers of plays, were obliged to attend the more, and did attend, to what was going on, on the stage—because a word lost would have been a chasm, which it was impossible for them to fill up. With such reflections we consoled our pride then—and I appeal to you whether, as a woman, I met generally with less attention and accommodation than I have done since in more expensive situations in the house? The getting in, indeed, and the crowding up those inconvenient staircases, was bad enough—but there was still a law of civility to woman recognized to quite as great an extent as we ever found in the other passages—and how a little difficulty overcome heightened the snug seat and the play, afterwards! Now we can only pay our money and walk in. You cannot see, you say, in the galleries now. I am sure we saw, and heard, too, well enough then— but sight, and all, I think, is gone with our poverty.

"There was pleasure in eating strawberries, before they became quite common—in the first dish of peas, while they were yet dear—to have them for a nice supper, a treat. What treat can we have now? If we were to treat ourselves now—that is, to have dainties a little above our means, it would be selfish and wicked. It is the very little more that we allow ourselves beyond what the actual poor can get at that makes what I call a treat—when two people, living together as we have done, now and then indulge themselves in a cheap luxury, which both like; while each apologizes, and is willing to take both halves of the blame to his single share. I see no harm in people making much of themselves, in that sense of the word. It may give them a hint how to make much of others. But now—what I mean by the word— we never *do* make much of ourselves. None but the poor can do it. I do not mean the veriest poor of all, but persons as we were, just above poverty.

"I know what you were going to say, that it is mighty pleasant at the end of the year to make all

---

[1] Piscator, the fisherman in Izaak Walton's *Compleat Angler,* and his favorite inn, Trout Hall.
[2] References to Shakespeare's *As You Like It* and *Twelfth Night.*

meet—and much ado we used to have every thirty-first night of December to account for our exceedings—many a long face did you make over your puzzled accounts, and in contriving to make it out how we had spent so much—or that we had not spent so much—or that it was impossible we should spend so much next year—and still we found our slender capital decreasing—but then—betwixt ways, and projects, and compromises of one sort or another, and talk of curtailing this charge, and doing without that for the future—and the hope that youth brings, and laughing spirits (in which you were never poor till now), we pocketed up our loss, and in conclusion, with 'lusty brimmers' (as you used to quote it out of *hearty cheerful Mr. Cotton,* as you called him), we used to welcome in the 'coming guest.' Now we have no reckoning at all at the end of the old year—no flattering promises about the new year doing better for us."

Bridget is so sparing of her speech on most occasions that when she gets into a rhetorical vein, I am careful how I interrupt it. I could not help, however, smiling at the phantom of wealth which her dear imagination had conjured up out of a clear income of poor —— hundred pounds a year. "It is true we were happier when we were poorer, but we were also younger, my cousin. I am afraid we must put up with the excess, for if we were to shake the superflux into the sea, we should not much mend ourselves. That we had much to struggle with, as we grew up together, we have reason to be most thankful. It strengthened and knit our compact closer. We could never have been what we have been to each other if we had always had the sufficiency which you now complain of. The resisting power—those natural dilations of the youthful spirit, which circumstances cannot straiten —with us are long since passed away. Competence to age is supplementary youth, a sorry supplement indeed, but I fear the best that is to be had. We must ride where we formerly walked; live better and lie softer—and shall be wise to do so—than we had means to do in those good old days you speak of. Yet could those days return—could you and I once more walk our thirty miles a day—could Bannister and Mrs. Bland again be young, and you and I be young to see them—could the good old one-shilling gallery days return—they are dreams, my cousin, now—but could you and I at this moment, instead of this quiet argument, by our well-carpeted fireside, sitting on this luxurious sofa— be once more struggling up those inconvenient staircases, pushed about and squeezed, and elbowed by the poorest rabble of poor gallery scramblers—could I once more hear those anxious shrieks of yours—and the delicious *Thank God, we are safe,* which always followed when the topmost stair, conquered, let in the first light of the whole cheerful theater down beneath us—I know not the fathom line that ever touched a descent so deep as I would be willing to bury more wealth in than Crœsus had, or the great Jew R—— is supposed to have, to purchase it. And now do just look at that merry little Chinese waiter holding an umbrella, big enough for a bed-tester, over the head of that pretty insipid half Madonna-ish chit of a lady in that very blue summer-house."

WILLIAM HAZLITT

On Going a Journey

One of the pleasantest things in the world is going a journey; but I like to go by myself. I can enjoy society in a room; but out-of-doors, Nature is company enough for me. I am then never less alone than when alone.

The fields his study, Nature was his book.

I cannot see the wit of walking and talking at the same time. When I am in the country, I wish to vegetate like the country. I am not for criticizing hedgerows and black cattle. I go out of town in order to forget the town and all that is in it. There are those who for this purpose go to watering-places, and carry the metropolis with them. I

Hazlitt, *On Going a Journey.* William Hazlitt (1778-1830) was born in Kent and lived an uneventful life as a literary critic and essay writer.

like more elbow-room, and fewer incumbrances. I like solitude, when I give myself up to it, for the sake of solitude; nor do I ask for

> a friend in my retreat,
> Whom I may whisper, solitude is sweet.

The soul of a journey is liberty, perfect liberty, to think, feel, do just as one pleases. We go a journey chiefly to be free of all impediments and of all inconveniences; to leave ourselves behind, much more to get rid of others. It is because I want a little breathing-space to muse on indifferent matters, where Contemplation

> May plume her feathers and let grow her wings,
> That in the various bustle of resort
> Were all too ruffled, and sometimes impaired,

that I absent myself from the town for a while, without feeling at a loss the moment I am left by myself. Instead of a friend in a post-chaise or in a Tilbury, to exchange good things with and vary the same stale topics over again, for once let me have a truce with impertinence. Give me the clear blue sky over my head, and the green turf beneath my feet, a winding road before me, and a three hours' march to dinner—and then to thinking! It is hard if I cannot start some game on these lone heaths. I laugh, I run, I leap, I sing for joy. From the point of yonder rolling cloud I plunge into my past being, and revel there, as the sunburnt Indian plunges headlong into the wave that wafts him to his native shore. Then long-forgotten things, like "sunken wrack and sumless treasuries," burst upon my eager sight, and I begin to feel, think, and be myself again. Instead of an awkward silence, broken by attempts at wit or dull commonplaces, mine is that undisturbed silence of the heart which alone is perfect eloquence. No one likes puns, alliterations, antitheses, argument, and analysis better than I do; but I sometimes had rather be without them. "Leave, oh, leave me to my repose!" I have just now other business in hand, which would seem idle to you, but is with me "very stuff o' the conscience." Is not this wild rose sweet without a comment? Does not this daisy leap to my heart set in its coat of emerald? Yet if I were to explain to you the circumstance that has so endeared it to me, you would only smile. Had I not better then keep it to myself, and let it serve me to brood over, from here to yonder craggy point, and from thence onward to the far-distant horizon? I should be bad company all that way, and therefore prefer being alone. I have heard it said that you may, when the moody fit comes on, walk or ride on by yourself, and indulge your reveries. But this looks like a breach of manners, a neglect of others, and you are thinking all the time that you ought to rejoin your party. "Out upon such half-faced fellowship," say I. I like to be either entirely to myself, or entirely at the disposal of others; to talk or be silent, to walk or sit still, to be sociable or solitary. I was pleased with an observation of Mr. Cobbett's, that he thought it a bad French custom to drink our wine with our meals, and that an Englishman ought to do only one thing at a time. So I cannot talk and think, or indulge in melancholy musing and lively conversation, by fits and starts. "Let me have a companion of my way," says Sterne, "were it but to remark how the shadows lengthen as the sun declines." It is beautifully said; but in my opinion this continual comparing of notes interferes with the involuntary impression of things upon the mind, and hurts the sentiment. If you only hint what you feel in a kind of dumb show, it is insipid; if you have to explain it, it is making a toil of a pleasure. You cannot read the book of Nature without being perpetually put to the trouble of translating it for the benefit of others. I am for the synthetical method on a journey in preference to the analytical. I am content to lay in a stock of ideas then, and to examine and anatomize them afterwards. I want to see my vague notions float like the down of the thistle before the breeze, and not to have them entangled in the briars and thorns of controversy. For once, I like to have it all my own way; and this is impossible unless you are alone, or in such company as I do not covet. I have no objection to argue a point with anyone for twenty miles of measured road, but not for pleasure. If you remark the scent of a bean-field crossing the road, perhaps your fellow-traveler has no smell. If you point to a distant object, perhaps he is short-sighted, and has to take out his glass to look at it. There is a feeling in the air, a tone in the color of a cloud which hits your fancy, but the effect of which you are unable to account for. There is then no sympathy, but an uneasy craving after it, and a dissatisfaction which pursues you on the way, and in the end probably produces ill-humor. Now I never quarrel with myself, and take all my own conclusions for granted till I find it necessary to defend them against objections. It is not merely that you may not be of accord on the objects and circumstances that present themselves before you—these may recall a number of objects, and lead to associations too delicate and refined to be possibly communicated to others. Yet these I love to cherish, and sometimes still fondly clutch them, when I can escape from the throng to do so. To give way to our feelings before company seems extravagance or affectation; and on the other hand, to have to unravel this mystery of our being at every turn, and to make others take an equal interest in it—otherwise the end is not answered—is a task to which few are competent. We must "give it an understanding, but no tongue." My old friend C——, however, could do both. He could go on in the most delightful explanatory way over hill and dale, a summer's day, and convert a landscape into a didactic poem or a Pindaric ode. "He talked far above singing." If I could so clothe my ideas in sounding and flowing words, I might perhaps wish to have someone with me to admire the swelling theme; or I could be more content, were it possible for me still to hear his echoing voice in the woods of All-Foxden. They had "that fine madness in them which our first poets had"; and if they could have been caught by some rare instrument, would have breathed such strains as the following:

Here be woods as green
As any, air likewise as fresh and sweet
As when smooth Zephyrus plays on the fleet
Face of the curled stream, with flowers as many
As the young spring gives, and as choice as any;
Here be all new delights, cool streams, and wells,
Arbors o'ergrown with woodbine, caves and dells;
Choose where thou wilt, while I sit by and sing,
Or gather rushes to make many a ring
For thy long fingers; tell thee tales of love—
How the pale Phœbe, hunting in a grove,
First saw the boy Endymion, from whose eyes
She took eternal fire that never dies;
How she conveyed him softly in a sleep,
His temples bound with poppy, to the steep
Head of old Latmos, where she stoops each night,
Gilding the mountain with her brother's light,
To kiss her sweetest.

—*Faithful Shepherdess.*

Had I words and images at command like these, I would attempt to wake the thoughts that lie slumbering on golden ridges in the evening clouds; but at the sight of Nature my fancy, poor as it is, droops and closes up its leaves, like flowers at sunset. I can make nothing out on the spot—I must have time to collect myself.

In general, a good thing spoils out-of-door prospects; it should be reserved for table-talk. L—— is for this reason, I take it, the worst company in the world out-of-doors; because he is the best within. I grant there is one subject on which it is pleasant to talk on a journey; and that is, what one shall have for supper when we get to our inn at night. The open air improves this sort of conversation or friendly altercation, by setting a keener edge on appetite. Every mile of the road heightens the flavor of the viands we expect at the end of it. How fine it is to enter some old town, walled and turreted, just at the approach of nightfall, or to come to some straggling village, with the lights streaming through the surrounding gloom; and then, after inquiring for the best entertainment that the place affords, to "take one's ease at one's inn"! These eventful moments in our lives' history are too precious, too full of solid, heartfelt happiness, to be frittered and dribbled away in imperfect sympathy. I would have them all to myself, and drain them to the last drop; they will do to talk of or to write about afterwards. What a delicate speculation it is, after drinking whole goblets of tea—

The cups that cheer, but not inebriate,

and letting the fumes ascend into the brain, to sit considering what we shall have for supper—eggs and a rasher, a rabbit smothered in onions, or an excellent veal cutlet! Sancho in such a situation once fixed upon cow-heel; and his choice, though he could not help it, is not to be disparaged. Then, in the intervals of pictured scenery and Shandean contemplation, to catch the preparation and the stir in the kitchen—*Procul, O procul este profani!*[1] These hours are sacred to silence and to musing, to be treasured up in the memory, and to feed the source of smiling thoughts hereafter. I would not waste them in idle talk; or if I must have the integrity of fancy broken in upon, I would rather it were by a stranger than a friend. A stranger takes his hue and character from the time and place; he is a part of the furniture and costume of an inn. If he is a Quaker or from the West Riding of Yorkshire, so much the better. I do not even try to sympathize with him, and he breaks no squares. I associate nothing with my traveling companion but present objects and passing events. In his ignorance of me and my affairs I in a manner forget myself. But a friend reminds one of other things, rips up old grievances, and destroys the abstraction of the scene. He comes in ungraciously between us and our imaginary char-

_____
[1] Hence, O hence, ye profane.

acter. Something is dropped in the course of conversation that gives a hint of your profession and pursuits; or from having someone with you that knows the less sublime portions of your history, it seems that other people do. You are no longer a citizen of the world; but your "unhoused, free condition is put into circumscription and confine." The *incognito* of an inn is one of its striking privileges—"lord of oneself, uncumbered with a name." Oh! it is great to shake off the trammels of the world and of public opinion—to lose our importunate, tormenting, everlasting personal identity in the elements of Nature, and become the creature of the moment, clear of all ties—to hold to the universe only by a dish of sweetbreads, and to owe nothing but the score of the evening—and no longer seeking for applause and meeting with contempt, to be known by no other title than *the gentleman in the parlor!* One may take one's choice of all characters in this romantic state of uncertainty as to one's real pretensions, and become indefinitely respectable and negatively right-worshipful. We baffle prejudice and disappoint conjecture; and from being so to others, begin to be objects of curiosity and wonder even to ourselves. We are no more those hackneyed commonplaces that we appear in the world; an inn restores us to the level of nature, and quits scores with society! I have certainly spent some enviable hours at inns—sometimes when I have been left entirely to myself, and have tried to solve some metaphysical problem, as once at Witham Common, where I found out the proof that likeness is not a case of the association of ideas—at other times, when there have been pictures in the room, as at St. Neot's—I think it was —where I first met with Gribelin's engravings of the Cartoons, into which I entered at once, and at a little inn on the borders of Wales, where there happened to be hanging some of Westall's drawings, which I compared triumphantly—for a theory that I had, not for the admired artist—with the figure of a girl who had ferried me over the Severn, standing up in a boat between me and the twilight—at other times I might mention luxuriating in books, with a peculiar interest in this way, as I remember sitting up half the night to read *Paul and Virginia,* which I picked up at an inn at Bridgewater, after being drenched in the rain all day; and at the same place I got through two volumes of Madame d'Arblay's *Camilla.* It was on the tenth of April, 1798, that I sat down to a volume of the *New Eloise,* at the inn at Llangollen, over a bottle of sherry and a cold chicken. The letter I chose was that in which St. Preux describes his feelings as he first caught a glimpse from the heights of the Jura of the Pays de Vaud, which I had brought with me as a *bonne bouche* to crown the evening with. It was my birthday, and I had for the first time come from a place in the neighborhood to visit this delightful spot. The road to Llangollen turns off between Chirk and Wrexham; and on passing a certain point you come all at once upon the valley, which opens like an amphitheater, broad, barren hills rising in majestic state on either side, with "green, upland swells that echo to the bleat of flocks" below, and the river Dee babbling over its stony bed in the midst of them. The valley at this time "glittered green with sunny showers," and a budding ash tree dipped its tender branches in the chiding stream. How proud, how glad I was to walk along the highroad that overlooks the delicious prospect, repeating the lines which I have just quoted from Mr. Coleridge's poems! But besides the prospect which opened beneath my feet, another also opened to my inward sight, a heavenly vision, on which were written, in letters large as Hope could make them, these four words, LIBERTY, GENIUS, LOVE, VIRTUE; which have since faded into the light of common day, or mock my idle gaze.

The beautiful is vanished, and returns not.

Still I would return some time or other to this enchanted spot; but I would return to it alone. What other self could I find to share that influx of thoughts, of regret, and delight, the fragments of which I could hardly conjure up to myself, so much have they been broken and defaced! I could stand on some tall rock, and overlook the precipice of years that separates me from what I then was. I was at that time going shortly to visit the poet whom I have above named. Where is he now? Not only I myself have changed; the world, which was then new to me, has become old and incorrigible. Yet will I turn to thee in thought, O silvan Dee, in joy, in youth and gladness as thou wert; and thou shalt always be to me the river of Paradise, where I will drink of the waters of life freely!

There is hardly anything that shows the short-sightedness or capriciousness of the imagination more than traveling does. With change of place we change our ideas; nay, our opinions and feelings. We can by an effort indeed transport ourselves to old and long-forgotten scenes, and then the picture of the mind revives again; but we forget those that we have just left. It seems that we can think but of one place at a time. The canvas of the fancy is but of a certain extent, and if we paint one set of objects upon it, they immediately efface every other. We cannot enlarge our conceptions, we only shift our point of view. The landscape bares its bosom to the enraptured eye, we take our fill of it, and seem as if we could form no other image of beauty or grandeur. We pass on, and think no more of it; the horizon that shuts it from our sight also blots it from our memory like a dream. In traveling through a wild, barren country I can form no idea of a woody and cultivated one. It appears to me that all the world must be barren, like what I see of it. In the country we forget the town, and in town we despise the country. "Beyond Hyde Park," says Sir Fopling Flutter, "all is a desert." All that part of the map that we do not see before us is a blank. The world in our conceit of it is not much bigger than a nutshell. It is not one prospect expanded into another, county joined to county, kingdom to kingdom, lands to seas, making an image voluminous and vast; the mind can form no larger idea of space than the eye can take in at a single glance. The rest is a name written on a map, a calculation of arithmetic. For instance, what is the true signification of that immense mass of territory and population known by the name of China to us? An inch of pasteboard on a wooden globe, of no more account than a China orange! Things near us are seen of the size of life; things at a distance are diminished to the size of the understanding. We measure the universe by ourselves, and even comprehend the texture of our own being only piecemeal. In this way, however, we remember an infinity of things and places. The mind is like a mechanical instrument that plays a great variety of tunes, but it must play them in succession. One idea recalls another, but it at the same time excludes all others. In trying to renew old recollections we cannot, as it were, unfold the whole web of our existence; we must pick out the single threads. So, in coming to a place where we have formerly lived and with which we have intimate associations, everyone must have found that the feeling grows more vivid the nearer we approach the spot, from the mere anticipation of the actual impression: we remember circumstances, feelings, persons, faces, names, that we had not thought of for years; but for the time all the rest of the world is forgotten!

To return to the question I have quitted above. —I have no objection to go to see ruins, aqueducts, pictures, in company with a friend or a party, but rather the contrary, for the former reason reversed. They are intelligible matters, and will bear talking about. The sentiment here is not tacit, but communicable and overt. Salisbury Plain is barren of criticism, but Stonehenge will bear a discussion antiquarian, picturesque, and philosophical. In setting out on a party of pleasure the first consideration always is where we shall go to; in taking a solitary ramble the question is what we shall meet with by the way. "The mind is its own place"; nor are we anxious to arrive at the end of our journey. I can myself do the honors indifferently well to works of art and curiosity. I once took a party to Oxford with no mean *éclat*—showed them that seat of the Muses at a distance,

With glistering spires and pinnacles adorned,

descanted on the learned air that breathes from the grassy quadrangles and stone walls of halls and cottages—was at home in the Bodleian; and at Blenheim quite superseded the powdered cicerone that attended us, and that pointed in vain with his wand to commonplace beauties in matchless pictures. As another exception to the above reasoning, I should not feel confident in venturing on a journey in a foreign country without a companion. I should want at intervals to hear the sound of my own language. There is an involuntary antipathy in the mind of an Englishman to foreign manners and notions that requires the assistance of social sympathy to carry it off. As the distance from home increases, this relief, which was at first a luxury, becomes a passion and an appetite. A person would almost feel stifled to find himself in the deserts of Arabia without friends and countrymen; there must be allowed to be something in the view of Athens or old Rome that claims the utterance of speech; and I own that the Pyramids are too mighty for any single contemplation. In such situations, so opposite to all one's ordinary train of ideas, one seems a species by oneself, a limb torn off from society, unless one can meet with instant fellowship and support. Yet I did not feel this want or craving very pressing once, when I first set my foot on the laughing shores of France. Calais was peopled with novelty and delight. The confused, busy murmur of the place was like oil and wine poured into my ears; nor did the mariners' hymn, which was sung from the top of an old crazy vessel in the harbor, as the sun went down, send an alien sound into my soul. I only breathed the air of general humanity. I walked over "the vine-covered hills and gay regions of France," erect and satisfied; for the image of man was not cast down and chained to the foot of arbitrary thrones. I was at no loss for language, for that of all the great schools of painting was open to me. The whole is vanished like a shade. Pictures, heroes, glory, freedom, all are fled; nothing remains but the Bourbons and the French people! —There is undoubtedly a sensation in traveling into foreign parts that is to be had nowhere else; but it is more pleasing at the time than lasting. It is too remote from our habitual associations to be a common topic of discourse or reference, and, like a dream or another state of existence, does not piece into our daily modes of life. It is an animated but a momentary hallucination. It demands an effort to exchange our actual for our ideal identity; and to feel the pulse of our old transports revive very keenly, we must "jump" all our present comforts and connections. Our romantic and itinerant character is not to be domesticated. Dr. Johnson

remarked how little foreign travel added to the facilities of conversation in those who had been abroad. In fact, the time we have spent there is both delightful, and, in one sense, instructive; but it appears to be cut out of our substantial, downright existence, and never to join kindly on to it. We are not the same, but another, and perhaps more enviable, individual, all the time we are out of our own country. We are lost to ourselves as well as our friends. So the poet somewhat quaintly sings,

Out of my country and myself I go.

Those who wish to forget painful thoughts do well to absent themselves for a while from the ties and objects that recall them; but we can be said only to fulfill our destiny in the place that gave us birth. I should on this account like well enough to spend the whole of my life in traveling abroad, if I could anywhere borrow another life to spend afterwards at home!

THOMAS DE QUINCEY
Levana and Our Ladies of Sorrow

Oftentimes at Oxford I saw Levana in my dreams. I knew her by her Roman symbols. Who is Levana? Reader, that do not pretend to have leisure for very much scholarship, you will not be angry with me for telling you. Levana was the Roman goddess that performed for the newborn infant the earliest office of ennobling kindness—typical, by its mode, of that grandeur which belongs to man everywhere, and of that benignity in powers invisible which even in pagan worlds sometimes descends to sustain it. At the very moment of birth, just as the infant tasted for the first time the atmosphere of our troubled planet, it was laid on the ground. *That* might bear different interpretations. But immediately, lest so grand a creature should grovel there for more than one instant, either the paternal hand, as proxy for the goddess Levana, or some near kinsman, as proxy for the

father, raised it upright, bade it look erect as the king of all this world, and presented its forehead to the stars, saying, perhaps, in his heart, "Behold what is greater than yourselves!" This symbolic act represented the function of Levana. And that mysterious lady, who never revealed her face (except to me in dreams), but always acted by delegation, had her name from the Latin verb (as still it is the Italian verb) *levare,* to raise aloft.

This is the explanation of Levana. And hence it has arisen that some people have understood by Levana the tutelary power that controls the education of the nursery. She, that would not suffer at his birth even a prefigurative of mimic degradation for her awful ward, far less could be supposed to suffer the real degradation attaching to the non-development of his powers. She therefore watches over human education. Now the word *edŭco,* with

De Quincey, *Levana and Our Ladies of Sorrow.* Thomas De Quincey was born at Manchester in 1785 and died in Edinburgh in 1859. He was educated at Oxford, lived for a time in the Lake District, and later settled in London. He made his experience as eater of opium the basis for his *Confessions of an English Opium-Eater.*

the penultimate snort, was derived (by a process often exemplified in the crystallization of languages) from the word *edŭco,* with the penultimate long. Whatsoever *educes,* or develops, *educates.* By the education of Levana, therefore, is meant—not the poor machinery that moves by spelling-books and grammars, but by that mighty system of central forces hidden in the deep bosom of human life, which by passion, by strife, by temptation, by the energies of resistance, works forever upon children—resting not day or night, any more than the mighty wheel of day and night themselves, whose moments, like restless spokes, are glimmering forever as they revolve.

If, then, *these* are the ministries by which Levana works, how profoundly must she reverence the agencies of grief! But you, reader, think that children generally are not liable to grief such as mine. There are two senses in the word *generally*—the sense of Euclid, where it means *universally* (or in the whole extent of the *genus*), and a foolish sense of this world, where it means *usually.* Now, I am far from saying that children universally are capable of grief like mine. But there are more than you ever heard of who die of grief in this island of ours. I will tell you a common case. The rules of Eton require that a boy on the *foundation* should be there twelve years; he is superannuated at eighteen; consequently he must come at six. Children torn away from mothers and sisters at that age not unfrequently die. I speak of what I know. The complaint is not entered by the registrar as grief; but *that* it is. Grief of that sort, and at that age, has killed more than ever have been counted amongst its martyrs.

Therefore it is that Levana often communes with the powers that shake man's heart; therefore it is that she dotes upon grief. "These ladies," said I softly to myself, on seeing the ministers with whom Levana was conversing, "these are the Sorrows; and they are three in number: as the *Graces* are three, who dress man's life with beauty; the *Parcæ* are three, who weave the dark arras of man's life in their mysterious loom always with colors sad in part, sometimes angry with tragic crimson and black; the *Furies* are three, who visit with retributions called from the other side of the grave offenses that walk upon this; and once even the *Muses* were but three, who fit the harp, the trumpet, or the lute, to the great burdens of man's impassioned creations. These are the Sorrows; all three of whom I know." The last words I say *now;* but in Oxford I said, "one of whom I know, and the others too surely I *shall* know." For already, in my fervent youth, I saw (dimly relieved upon the dark background of my dreams) the imperfect lineaments of the awful Sisters.

These Sisters—by what name shall we call them? If I say simply "The Sorrows," there will be a chance of mistaking the term; it might be understood of individual sorrow—separate cases of sorrow—whereas I want a term expressing the mighty abstractions that incarnate themselves in all individual sufferings of man's heart, and I wish to have these abstractions presented as impersonations—that is, as clothed with human attributes of life, and with functions pointing to flesh. Let us call them, therefore, *Our Ladies of Sorrow.*

I know them thoroughly, and have walked in all their kingdoms. Three sisters they are, of one mysterious household; and their paths are wide apart; but of their dominion there is no end. Them I saw often conversing with Levana, and sometimes about myself. Do they talk, then? O no! Mighty phantoms like these disdain the infirmities of language. They may utter voices through the organs of man when they dwell in human hearts, but amongst themselves is no voice nor sound; eternal silence reigns in *their* kingdoms. They spoke not as they talked with Levana; they whispered not; they sang not; though oftentimes methought they *might* have sung; for I upon earth had heard their mysteries oftentimes deciphered by harp and timbrel, by dulcimer and organ. Like God, whose servants they are, they utter their pleasure not by sounds that perish, or by words that go astray, but by signs in heaven, by changes on earth, by pulses in secret rivers, heraldries painted on darkness, and hieroglyphics written on the tablets of the brain. *They* wheeled in mazes; *I* spelled the steps. *They* telegraphed from afar; *I* read the signals. *They* conspired together; and on the mirrors of darkness *my* eye traced the plots. *Theirs* were the symbols; *mine* are the words.

What is it the Sisters are? What is it they do? Let me describe their form and their presence, if form it were that still fluctuated in its outline, or presence it were that forever advanced to the front or forever receded amongst shades.

The eldest of the three is named *Mater Lachrymarum,* Our Lady of Tears. She it is that night and day raves and moans, calling for vanished faces. She stood in Rama, where a voice was heard of lamentation—Rachel weeping for her children, and refusing to be comforted. She it was that stood in Bethlehem on the night when Herod's sword swept its nurseries of Innocents, and the little feet were stiffened forever which, heard at times as they trotted along floors overhead, woke pulses of love in household hearts that were not unmarked in heaven. Her eyes are sweet and subtle, wild and sleepy, by turns; oftentimes rising to the clouds, oftentimes challenging the heavens. She wears a diadem round her head. And I knew by childish memories that she could go abroad upon the winds when she heard the sobbing of litanies, or the thundering of organs, and when she beheld the mustering of summer clouds. This Sister, the elder, it is that carries keys more than papal at her girdle, which open every cottage and every palace. She, to my knowledge, sat all last summer by the bedside of the blind beggar, him that so often and so gladly I talked with, whose pious daughter, eight years old, with the sunny countenance, resisted the temptations of play and village mirth, to travel all day long on dusty roads with her afflicted father. For this did God send her a great reward. In the springtime of the year, and whilst yet her own spring was budding, He recalled her to himself. But her blind father mourns forever over *her;* still he dreams at midnight that the little guiding hand is locked within his own; and still he wakens to a darkness that is *now* within a second and a deeper darkness. This *Mater Lachrymarum* also has been sitting all this winter of 1844-5 within the bedchamber of the Czar, bringing before his eyes a daughter (not less pious) that vanished to God not less suddenly, and left behind her a darkness not less profound. By the power of the keys it is that Our Lady of Tears glides, a ghostly intruder, into the chambers of sleepless men, sleepless women, sleepless children, from Ganges to the Nile, from Nile to Mississippi. And her, because she is the first-born of her house, and has the widest empire, let us honor with the title of "Madonna."

The second Sister is called *Mater Suspiriorum,* Our Lady of Sighs. She never scales the clouds, nor walks abroad upon the winds. She wears no diadem. And her eyes, if they were ever seen, would be neither sweet nor subtle; no man could read their story; they would be found filled with perishing dreams, and with wrecks of forgotten delirium. But she raises not her eyes; her head, on which sits a dilapidated turban, droops forever, forever fastens on the dust. She weeps not. She groans not. But she sighs inaudibly at intervals. Her sister, Madonna, is oftentimes stormy and frantic, raging in the highest against heaven, and demanding back her darlings. But Our Lady of Sighs never clamors, never defies, dreams not of rebellious aspirations. She is humble to abjectness.

Hers is the meekness that belongs to the hopeless. Murmur she may, but it is in her sleep. Whisper she may, but it is to herself in the twilight. Mutter she does at times, but it is in solitary places that are desolate as she is desolate, in ruined cities, and when the sun has gone down to his rest. This Sister is the visitor of the Pariah, of the Jew, of the bondsman to the oar in the Mediterranean galleys; of the English criminal in Norfolk Island, blotted out from the books of remembrance in sweet far-off England; of the baffled penitent reverting his eyes forever upon a solitary grave, which to him seems the altar overthrown of some past and bloody sacrifice, on which altar no oblations can now be availing, whether toward pardon that he might implore, or toward reparation that he might attempt. Every slave that at noonday looks up to the tropical sun with timid reproach, as he points with one hand to the earth, our general mother, but for *him* a stepmother, as he points with the other hand to the Bible, our general teacher, but against *him* sealed and sequestered; every woman sitting in darkness, without love to shelter her head, or hope to illumine her solitude, because the heaven-born instincts kindling in her nature germs of holy affections, which God implanted in her womanly bosom, having been stifled by social necessities, now burn sullenly to waste, like sepulchral lamps amongst the ancients; every nun defrauded of her unreturning Maytime by wicked kinsman, whom God will judge; every captive in every dungeon; all that are betrayed, and all that are rejected; outcasts by traditionary law, and children of *hereditary* disgrace—all these walk with Our Lady of Sighs. She also carries a key; but she needs it little. For her kingdom is chiefly amongst the tents of Shem, and the houseless vagrant of every clime. Yet in the very highest ranks of man she finds chapels of her own; and even in glorious England there are some that, to the world, carry their heads as proudly as the reindeer, who yet secretly have received her mark upon their foreheads.

But the third Sister, who is also the youngest—! Hush! whisper whilst we talk of *her!* Her kingdom is not large, or else no flesh should live; but within that kingdom all power is hers. Her head, turreted like that of Cybele, rises almost beyond the reach of sight. She droops not; and her eyes, rising so high, *might* be hidden by distance. But, being what they are, they cannot be hidden. Through the treble veil of crape which she wears the fierce light of a blazing misery, that rests not for matins or for vespers, for noon of day or noon of night, for ebbing or for flowing tide, may be read from the very ground. She is the defier of God. She also is the mother of lunacies, and the suggestress of suicides. Deep lie the roots of her power; but narrow is the nation that she rules. For she can approach only those in whom a profound nature has been upheaved by central convulsions; in whom the heart trembles and the brain rocks under conspiracies of tempest from without and tempest from within. Madonna moves with uncertain steps, fast or slow, but still with tragic grace. Our Lady of Sighs creeps timidly and stealthily. But this youngest Sister moves with incalculable motions, bounding, and with tiger's leaps. She carries no key; for, though coming rarely amongst men, she storms all doors at which she is permitted to enter at all. And *her* name is *Mater Tenebrarum*—Our Lady of Darkness.

These were the *Semnai Theai* or Sublime Goddesses, these were the *Eumenides* or Gracious Ladies (so called by antiquity in shuddering propitiation), of my Oxford dreams. Madonna spoke. She spoke by her mysterious hand. Touching my head, she beckoned to Our Lady of Sighs; and *what* she spoke, translated out of the signs which (except in dreams) no man reads, was this:

"Lo! here is he whom in childhood I dedicated to my altars. This is he that once I made my darling. Him I led astray, him I beguiled; and from heaven I stole away his young heart to mine. Through me did he become idolatrous; and through me it was, by languishing desires, that he worshiped the worm, and prayed to the wormy grave. Holy was the grave to him; lovely was its darkness; saintly its corruption. Him, this young idolator, I have seasoned for thee, dear gentle Sister of Sighs! Do thou take him now to *thy* heart, and season him for our dreadful sister. And thou" —turning to the *Mater Tenebrarum,* she said— "wicked sister, that temptest and hatest, do thou take him from *her*. See that thy scepter lie heavy on his head. Suffer not woman and her tenderness to sit near him in his darkness. Banish the frailties of hope; wither the relenting of love; scorch the fountains of tears; curse him as only *thou* canst curse. So shall he be accomplished in the furnace; so shall he see the things that ought *not* to be seen, sights that are abominable, and secrets that are unutterable. So shall he read elder truths, sad truths, grand truths, fearful truths. So shall he rise again *before* he dies. And so shall our commission be accomplished which from God we had—to plague his heart until we had unfolded the capacities of his spirit."

THOMAS CARLYLE

Labor

There is a perennial nobleness, and even sacredness, in Work. Were he never so benighted, forgetful of his high calling, there is always hope in a man that actually and earnestly works; in Idleness alone is there perpetual despair. Work, never so Mammonish, mean, *is* in communication with Nature; the real desire to get Work done will itself lead one more and more to truth, to Nature's appointments and regulations, which are truth.

The latest Gospel in this world is, Know thy work and do it. "Know thyself": long enough has that poor "self" of thine tormented thee; thou wilt never get to "know" it, I believe! Think it not thy business, this of knowing thyself; thou art an unknowable individual: know what thou canst work at; and work at it, like a Hercules! That will be thy better plan.

It has been written, "an endless significance lies in Work"; a man perfects himself by working. Foul jungles are cleared away, fair seedfields rise instead, and stately cities; and withal the man himself first ceases to be a jungle and foul unwholesome desert thereby. Consider how, even in the meanest sorts of Labor, the soul of a man is composed into a kind of real harmony the instant he sets himself to work! Doubt, Desire, Sorrow,

Carlyle, *Labor*. Thomas Carlyle (1795-1881) was born in Scotland and educated for the law, but soon turned to writing. In 1834 he moved to London and spent nearly fifty years in active authorship.

Remorse, Indignation, Despair itself, all these, like hell-dogs, lie beleaguering the soul of the poor day-worker, as of every man; but he bends himself with free valor against his task, and all these are stilled, all these shrink murmuring far off into their caves. The man is now a man. The blessed glow of Labor in him, is it not as purifying fire, wherein all poison is burned up, and of sour smoke itself there is made bright blessed flame!

Destiny, on the whole, has no other way of cultivating us. A formless Chaos, once set it *revolving,* grows round and ever rounder; ranges itself, by mere force of gravity, into strata, spherical courses; is no longer a Chaos, but a round compacted world. What would become of the Earth did she cease to revolve? In the poor old Earth, so long as she revolves, all inequalities, irregularities disperse themselves; all irregularities are incessantly becoming regular. Hast thou looked on the Potter's wheel—one of the venerablest objects; old as the Prophet Ezekiel and far older? Rude lumps of clay, how they spin themselves up, by mere quick whirling, into beautiful circular dishes. And fancy the most assiduous Potter, but without his wheel; reduced to make dishes or rather amorphous botches, by mere kneading and baking! Even such a Potter were Destiny, with a human soul that would rest and lie at ease, that would not work and spin! Of an idle unrevolving man the kindest Destiny, like the most assiduous Potter without wheel, can bake and knead nothing other than a botch; let her spend on him what expensive coloring, what gilding and enameling she will, he is but a botch. Not a dish; no, a bulging, kneaded, crooked, shambling, squint-cornered, amorphous botch—a mere enameled vessel of dishonor! Let the idle think of this.

Blessed is he who has found his work; let him ask no other blessedness. He has a work, a life-purpose; he has found it, and will follow it! How, as a free-flowing channel, dug and torn by noble force through the sour mud-swamp of one's existence, like an ever-deepening river there, it runs and flows;—draining off the sour festering water gradually from the root of the remotest grassblade; making, instead of pestilential swamp, a green fruitful meadow with its clear-flowing stream. How blessed for the meadow itself, let the stream and *its* value be great or small! Labor is Life; from the inmost heart of the Worker rises his god-given Force, the sacred celestial Life-essence breathed into him by Almighty God; from his inmost heart awakens him to all nobleness—to all knowledge, "self-knowledge" and much else, so soon as Work fitly begins. Knowledge? The knowledge that will hold good in working, cleave thou to that; for Nature herself accredits that, says Yea to that. Properly thou hast no other knowledge but what thou hast got by working; the rest is yet all a hypothesis of knowledge; a thing to be argued of in schools, a thing floating in the clouds, in endless logic-vortices, till we try it and fix it. "Doubt, of whatever kind, can be ended by action alone."

And again, hast thou valued Patience, Courage, Perseverance, Openness to light; readiness to own thyself mistaken, to do better next time? All these, all virtues, in wrestling with the dim brute Powers of Fact, in ordering of thy fellows in such wrestle, there and elsewhere not at all, thou wilt continually learn. Set down a brave Sir Christopher [1] in the middle of black ruined Stone-heaps, of foolish unarchitectural Bishops, red-tape Officials, idle Nell Gwyn Defenders of the Faith; and see whether he will ever raise a Paul's Cathedral out of all that, yea or no! Rough, rude, contradictory are all things and persons, from the mutinous masons and Irish hodmen, up to the idle Nell Gwyn Defenders, to blustering red-tape Officials, foolish unarchitectural Bishops. All these things and persons are there not for Christopher's sake and his Cathedral's; they are there for their own sake mainly! Christopher will have to conquer and constrain all these—if he is able. All these are against him. Equitable Nature herself, who carries her mathematics and architectonics not on the face of her, but deep in the hidden heart of her—Nature herself is but partially for him; will be wholly against him, if he constrain her not! His very money, where is it to come from? The pious munificence of England lies far-scattered, distant, unable to speak, and say, "I am here,"—must be spoken to before it can speak. Pious munificence, and all help, is so silent, invisible, like the gods; impediment, contradictions manifold are so loud and near! O brave Sir Christopher, trust thou in those notwithstanding, and front all these; understand all these; by valiant patience, noble effort, insight, by man's strength, vanquish and compel all these—and, on the whole, strike down victoriously the last topstone of that Paul's Edifice; thy monument for certain centuries, the stamp

---

[1] Sir Christopher Wren who rebuilt St. Paul's Cathedral. Nell Gwyn, mistress of Charles II, under whom Wren began the work.

"Great Man" impressed very legibly on Portland stone there!

Yes, all manner of help, and pious response from Men or Nature, is always what we call silent; cannot speak or come to light, till it be seen, till it be spoken to. Every noble work is at first "impossible." In very truth, for every noble work the possibilities will lie diffused through Immensity; inarticulate, undiscoverable except to faith. Like Gideon thou shalt spread out thy fleece at the door of thy tent; see whether under the wide arch of Heaven there be any bounteous moisture, or none. Thy heart and life-purpose shall be as a miraculous Gideon's fleece, spread out in silent appeal to Heaven; and from the kind Immensities, what from the poor unkind localities and town and country Parishes there never could, blessed dew-moisture to suffice thee shall have fallen!

Work is of a religious nature—work is of a *brave* nature; which it is the aim of all religion to be. All work of man is as the swimmer's: a waste ocean threatens to devour him; if he front it not bravely, it will keep its word. By incessant wise defiance of it, lusty rebuke and buffet of it, behold how it loyally supports him, bears him as its conqueror along. "It is so," says Goethe, "with all things that man undertakes in this world."

Brave sea-captain, Norse sea-king—Columbus, my hero, royalest sea-king of all! it is no friendly environment this of thine, in the waste deep waters; around thee mutinous discouraged souls, behind thee disgrace and ruin, before thee the unpenetrated veil of Night. Brother, these wild water-mountains, bounding from their deep bases (ten miles deep, I am told), are not entirely there on thy behalf! Meseems *they* have other work than floating thee forward—and the huge winds, that sweep from Ursa Major to the Tropics and Equators, dancing their giant-waltz through the kingdoms of Chaos and Immensity, they care little about filling rightly or filling wrongly the small shoulder-of-mutton sails in this cockle-skiff of thine! Thou art not among articulate-speaking friends, my brother; thou art among immeasurable dumb monsters, tumbling, howling wide as the world here. Secret, far off, invisible to all hearts but thine, there lies a help in them; see how thou wilt get at that. Patiently thou wilt wait till the mad southwester spends itself, saving thyself by dextrous science of defense, the while; valiantly, with swift decision, wilt thou strike in, when the favoring East, the Possible springs up. Mutiny of men thou wilt sternly repress; weakness, despondency, thou wilt cheerfully encourage: thou wilt swallow down complaint, unreason, weariness, weakness of others and thyself—how much wilt thou swallow down! There shall be a depth of Silence in thee, deeper than this Sea, which is but ten miles deep: a Silence unsoundable; known to God only. Thou shalt be a Great Man. Yes, my World-soldier, thou of the World Marine-service— thou wilt have to be *greater* than this tumultuous unmeasured World here round thee is; thou, in thy strong soul, as with wrestler's arms, shalt embrace it, harness it down; and make it bear thee on—to new Americas, or whither God wills!

ROBERT LOUIS STEVENSON

Pulvis et Umbra

We look for some reward of our endeavors and are disappointed; not success, not happiness, not even peace of conscience, crowns our ineffectual efforts to do well. Our frailties are invincible, our virtues barren; the battle goes sore against us to the going down of the sun. The canting moralist tells us of right and wrong; and we look abroad, even on the face of our small earth, and find them change with every climate, and no country where some action is not honored for a virtue and none where it is not branded for a vice; and we look in our experience, and find no vital congruity in the wisest rules, but at the best a municipal fitness. It is not strange if we are tempted to despair of good.

Stevenson, *Pulvis et Umbra*. Robert Louis Stevenson (1850-1894) came of a family of Scotch engineers. He was educated for law but from 1878 on devoted himself entirely to writing novels, essays, and poems. He died in Samoa, where he had gone to regain his health.

We ask too much. Our religions and moralities have been trimmed to flatter us, till they are all emasculate and sentimentalized, and only please and weaken. Truth is of a rougher strain. In the harsh face of life, faith can read a bracing gospel. The human race is a thing more ancient than the Ten Commandments; and the bones and revolutions of the Kosmos, in whose joints we are but moss and fungus, more ancient still.

I

Of the Kosmos in the last resort, science reports many doubtful things and all of them appalling. There seems no substance to this solid globe on which we stamp: nothing but symbols and ratios. Symbols and ratios carry us and bring us forth and beat us down; gravity that swings the incommensurable suns and worlds through space, is but a figment varying inversely as the squares of distances; and the suns and worlds themselves, imponderable figures of abstraction, NH_3 and H_2O. Consideration dares not dwell upon this view; that way madness lies; science carries us into zones of speculation, where there is no habitable city for the mind of man.

But take the Kosmos with a grosser faith, as our senses give it us. We behold space sown with rotatory islands, suns and worlds and the shards and wrecks of systems: some, like the sun, still blazing; some rotting, like the earth; others, like the moon, stable in desolation. All of these we take to be made of something we call matter: a thing which no analysis can help us to conceive; to whose incredible properties no familiarities can reconcile our minds. This stuff, when not purified by the lustration of fire, rots uncleanly into something we call life; seized through all its atoms with a pediculous malady; swelling in tumors that become independent, sometimes even (by an abhorrent prodigy) locomotory; one splitting into millions, millions cohering into one, as the malady proceeds through varying stages. This vital putrescence of the dust, used as we are to it, yet strikes us with occasional disgust, and the profusion of worms in a piece of ancient turf, or the air of a marsh darkened with insects, will sometimes check our breathing so that we aspire for cleaner places. But none is clean: the moving sand is infected with lice; the pure spring, where it bursts out of the mountain, is a mere issue of worms; even in the hard rock the crystal is forming.

In two main shapes this eruption covers the countenance of the earth: the animal and the vegetable: one in some degree the inversion of the other: the second rooted to the spot; the first coming detached out of its natal mud, and scurrying abroad with the myriad feet of insects or towering into the heavens on the wings of birds: a thing so incomprehensible that, if it be well considered, the heart stops. To what passes with the anchored vermin, we have little clue: doubtless they have their joys and sorrows, their delights and killing agonies: it appears not how. But of the locomotory, to which we ourselves belong, we can tell more. These share with us a thousand miracles: the miracles of sight, of hearing, of the projection of sound, things that bridge space; the miracles of memory and reason, by which the present is conceived, and when it is gone, its image kept living in the brains of man and brute; the miracle of reproduction, with its imperious desires and staggering consequences. And to put the last touch upon this mountain mass of the revolting and the inconceivable, all these prey upon each other, lives tearing other lives in pieces, cramming them inside themselves, and by that summary process, growing fat: the vegetarian, the whale, perhaps the tree, not less than the lion of the desert; for the vegetarian is only the eater of the dumb.

Meanwhile our rotatory island loaded with predatory life, and more drenched with blood, both animal and vegetable, than ever mutinied ship, scuds through space with unimaginable speed, and turns alternate checks to the reverberation of a blazing world, ninety million miles away.

II

What a monstrous specter is this man, the disease of the agglutinated dust, lifting alternate feet or lying drugged with slumber; killing, feeding, growing, bringing forth small copies of himself; grown upon with hair like grass, fitted with eyes that move and glitter in his face; a thing to set children screaming;—and yet looked at nearlier, known as his fellows know him, how surprising are his attributes! Poor soul, here for so little, cast among so many hardships, filled with desires so incommensurate and so inconsistent, savagely surrounded, savagely descended, irremediably condemned to prey upon his fellow lives: who should have blamed him had he been of a piece with his destiny and a being merely barbarous? And we look and behold him instead filled with imperfect virtues: infinitely childish, often admirably valiant, often touchingly kind; sitting down, amidst his momentary life, to debate of right and wrong and the attributes of the deity; rising up to do battle for an egg or die for an idea; singling out his friends and his mate with cordial affection; bringing forth in pain, rearing with long-suffering solicitude, his young. To touch the heart of his mystery, we find in him one thought, strange to the point of lunacy: the thought of duty; the thought of something owing to himself, to his neighbor, to his God; an ideal of decency, to which he would rise if it were possible; a limit of shame below which, if it be possible, he will not stoop. The design in most men is one of conformity; here and there, in picked natures, it transcends itself and soars on the other side, arming martyrs with independence; but in all, in their degrees, it is a bosom thought:—Not in man alone, for we trace it in dogs and cats whom we know fairly well, and doubtless some similar point of honor sways the elephant, the oyster, and the louse, of whom we know so little:—But in man, at least, it sways with so complete an empire that merely selfish things come second, even with the selfish: that appetites are starved, fears are conquered, pains supported; that almost the dullest shrinks from the reproof of a glance, although it were a child's; and all but the most cowardly stand amid the risks of war; and the more noble, having strongly conceived an act as due to their ideal, affront and embrace death. Strange enough if, with their singular origin and perverted practice, they think they are to be rewarded in some future life: stranger still, if they are persuaded of the contrary, and think this blow, which they solicit, will strike them senseless for eternity. I shall be reminded what a tragedy of misconception and misconduct man at large presents: of organized injustice, cowardly violence, and treacherous crime; and of the damning imperfections of the best. They cannot be too darkly drawn. Man is indeed marked for failure in his efforts to do right. But where the best consistently miscarry, how tenfold more remarkable that all should continue to strive; and surely we should find it both touching and inspiriting, that in a field from which success is banished, our race should not cease to labor.

If the first view of this creature, stalking in his rotatory isle, be a thing to shake the courage of the stoutest, on this nearer sight, he startles us with an admiring wonder. It matters not where we look, under what climate we observe him, in what stage of society, in what depth of ignorance, burthened with what erroneous morality; by camp-fires in Assiniboia, the snow powdering his shoulders, the wind plucking his blanket, as he sits, passing the ceremonial calumet and uttering his grave opinions like a Roman senator; in ships at sea, a man inured to hardship and vile pleasures, his brightest hope a fiddle in a tavern and a bedizened trull who sells herself to rob him, and he for all that simple, innocent, cheerful, kindly like a child, constant to toil, brave to drown, for others; in the slums of cities, moving among indifferent millions to mechanical employments, without hope of change in the future, with scarce a pleasure in the present, and yet true to his virtues, honest up to his lights, kind to his neighbors, tempted perhaps in vain by the bright gin-palace, perhaps long-suffering with the drunken wife that ruins him; in India (a woman this time) kneeling with broken cries and streaming tears, as she drowns her child in the sacred river; in the brothel, the discard of society, living mainly on strong drink, fed with affronts, a fool, a thief, the comrade of thieves, and even here keeping the point of honor and the touch of pity, often repaying the world's scorn with service, often standing firm upon a scruple, and at a certain cost, rejecting riches:—everywhere some virtue cherished or affected, everywhere some decency of thought and carriage, everywhere the ensign of man's ineffectual goodness:—ah! if I could show you this! If I could show you these men and women, all the world over, in every stage of history, under every abuse of error, under every circumstance of failure, without hope, without help, without thanks, still obscurely fighting the lost fight of virtue, still clinging, in the brothel or on the scaffold, to some rag of honor, the poor jewel of their souls! They may seek to escape, and yet they cannot; it is not alone their privilege and glory, but their doom; they are condemned to some nobility; all their lives long, the desire of good is at their heels, the implacable hunter.

Of all earth's meteors, here at least is the most strange and consoling: that this ennobled lemur, this hair-crowned bubble of the dust, this inheritor of a few years and sorrows, should yet deny himself his rare delights, and add to his frequent pains, and live for an ideal, however misconceived. Nor can we stop with man. A new doctrine, received with screams a little while ago by canting moralists, and still not properly worked into the body of our thoughts, lights us a step farther into the heart of this rough but noble universe. For nowadays the pride of man denies in vain his kinship with the original dust. He stands no longer like a thing apart. Close at his heels we see the dog, prince of another genus: and in him too, we see dumbly testified the same cultus of an unattainable ideal, the same constancy in failure. Does it stop with the dog? We look at our feet where the ground is blackened with the swarming ant: a creature so small, so far from us in the hierarchy of brutes, that we can scarce trace and scarce comprehend his doings; and here also, in his ordered polities and rigorous justice, we see confessed the law of duty and the fact of individual sin. Does it stop, then, with the ant? Rather this desire of well-doing and this doom of frailty run through all the grades of life: rather is this earth, from the frosty top of Everest to the next margin of the internal fire, one stage of ineffectual virtues and one temple of pious tears and perseverance. The whole creation groaneth and travaileth together. It is the common and the god-like law of life. The browsers, the biters, the barkers, the hairy coats of field and forest, the squirrel in the oak, the thousand-footed creeper in the dust, as they share with us the gift of life, share with us the love of an ideal: strive like us—like us are tempted to grow weary of the struggle—to do well; like us receive at times unmerited refreshment, visitings of support, returns of courage; and are condemned like us to be crucified between that double law of the members and the will. Are they like us, I wonder, in the timid hope of some reward, some sugar with the drug? do they, too, stand aghast at unrewarded virtues, at the sufferings of those whom, in our partiality, we take to be just, and the prosperity of such as, in our blindness, we call wicked? It may be, and yet God knows what they should look for. Even while they look, even while they repent, the foot of man treads them by thousands in the dust, the yelping hounds burst upon their trail, the bullet speeds, the knives are heating in the den of the vivisectionist; or the dew falls, and the generation of a day is blotted out. For these are creatures, compared with whom our weakness is strength, our ignorance wisdom, our brief span eternity.

And as we dwell, we living things, in our isle of terror and under the imminent hand of death, God forbid it should be man the erected, the reasoner, the wise in his own eyes—God forbid it should be man that wearies in well-doing, that despairs of unrewarded effort, or utters the language of complaint. Let it be enough for faith, that the whole creation groans in mortal frailty, strives with unconquerable constancy: surely not all in vain.

AMERICAN ESSAYS
AND ADDRESSES

Strictly speaking, American literature is three centuries old, but for practical purposes its history does not begin much before the American Revolution. The rhymed psalms, the doggerel rhymes, and the weighty sermons of the seventeenth and early eighteenth centuries repose undisturbed on library shelves. Even the practical wisdom of *Poor Richard's Almanack* is only a far-off tradition today, and Franklin as an author is known to us only through the pages of his ever-interesting *Autobiography*.

The opening of the American Revolution called forth the best talent from all parts of the colonies. Not only were orators, such as Patrick Henry in Virginia and James Otis in Massachusetts, needed to appeal to their fellow men, but also volunteers for the even more difficult task of framing important political papers. Of the latter class of statesmen, Thomas Jefferson was pre-eminent. It is to him that we owe the *Declaration of Independence* in approximately its final form. He also had much to do with the phraseology of the United States Constitution.

Of nineteenth century oratory in America little can be said here. The great political addresses of Webster are a real part of American literature. But the two outstanding public speeches of the century were not designed as great oratory. One of them was a simple tribute to fallen soldiers and the other was a routine inaugural address as President of the United States.

Such essays as appeared in eighteenth century America were far-off echoes of Addison and Steele. It is not until we come to the *Sketch Book* of Washington Irving that we find that this form has any vitality. In this book, in addition to such favorite stories as "The Legend of Sleepy Hollow" he has a number of delightful sketches, mostly descriptive of his travels.

As the nineteenth century wore on, a large number of writers employed the essay form with success. From all this group we are choosing one representative of the philosophical essay and one of the nature essay. The authors of these works were neighbors in the little town of Concord, Massachusetts, and were almost the same age.

Ralph Waldo Emerson, for fifty years and more, wrote and lectured on a multitude of topics, so that he became an inestimable force in American life—a force which perhaps we do not even yet fully appreciate. He realized as did few men of his generation the vast potentialities of American life and the necessity of boldness

1208

as well as wisdom in our endeavor to develop them. Such an essay as *Self-Reliance* is as important today as it was a century ago when it was written.

Large philosophical concepts of this kind did not interest Emerson's neighbor, Henry David Thoreau. Though he was somewhat of a political rebel when politics affected him personally, his main interest in life was the study of the outdoors. From his camp on Walden Pond near Concord he gave close observation of the life of birds and beasts. A good example of this is his sketch, *Brute Neighbors*.

THOMAS JEFFERSON

Declaration of Independence

IN CONGRESS, JULY 4, 1776
THE UNANIMOUS DECLARATION OF THE THIRTEEN
UNITED STATES OF AMERICA

Preamble

When, in the course of human events, it becomes necessary for one people to dissolve the political bands which have connected them with another, and to assume among the powers of the earth the separate and equal station to which the laws of 10 nature and of nature's God entitle them, a decent respect to the opinions of mankind requires that they should declare the causes which impel them to the separation.

We hold these truths to be self-evident: That all men are created equal; that they are endowed by their Creator with certain inalienable rights; that among these are life, liberty, and the pursuit of happiness; that, to secure these rights, governments are instituted among men, deriving their just 20 powers from the consent of the governed; that whenever any form of government becomes destructive of these ends it is the right of the people to alter or to abolish it and to institute a new government, laying its foundation on such principles, and organizing its powers in such form as to them shall seem most likely to effect their safety and happiness. Prudence indeed will dictate that governments long established should not be changed for light and transient causes; and, accordingly, all 30 experience hath shown that mankind are more disposed to suffer while evils are sufferable, than to right themselves by abolishing the forms to which they are accustomed. But when a long train of abuses and usurpations, pursuing invariably the same object, evinces a design to reduce them under absolute despotism, it is their right, it is their duty, to throw off such government and to provide new guards for their future security. Such has been the patient sufferance of these colonies; and such is now the necessity which constrains them to alter their former systems of government.

Specific Charges against the King

The history of the present king of Great Britain is a history of repeated injuries and usurpations, all having in direct object the establishment of an absolute tyranny over these states. To prove this, let facts be submitted to a candid world:

He has refused his assent to laws, the most wholesome and necessary for the public good.

He has forbidden his governors to pass laws of immediate and pressing importance, unless suspended in their operation till his assent should be obtained; and, when so suspended, he has utterly neglected to attend to them.

He has refused to pass other laws for the accommodation of large districts of people unless those people would relinquish the right of representation in the legislature, a right inestimable to them, and formidable to tyrants only.

He has called together legislative bodies at places unusual, uncomfortable, and distant from the depository of their public records, for the sole purpose of fatiguing them into compliance with his measures.

Jefferson, *Declaration of Independence*. Thomas Jefferson (1743-1826) lived all his life in Virginia. He was active politically from 1769, drafted the *Declaration of Independence,* and had much to do with the writing of the American Constitution. He was President from 1801 to 1809.

He has dissolved representative houses repeatedly for opposing, with manly firmness, his invasions on the rights of the people.

He has refused for a long time after such dissolutions to cause others to be elected; whereby the legislative powers, incapable of annihilation, have returned to the people at large for their exercise; the state remaining, in the meantime, exposed to all the dangers of invasions from without and convulsions within.

He has endeavored to prevent the population of these states; for that purpose obstructing the laws for naturalization of foreigners, refusing to pass others to encourage their migration hither, and raising the conditions of new appropriations of lands.

He has obstructed the administration of justice by refusing his assent to laws for establishing judiciary powers.

He has made judges dependent on his will alone for the tenure of their offices and the amount and payment of their salaries.

He has erected a multitude of new offices, and sent hither swarms of officers to harass our people and eat out their substance.

He has kept among us in times of peace standing armies, without the consent of our legislatures.

He has affected to render the military independent of, and superior to, the civil power.

He has combined with others to subject us to a jurisdiction foreign to our constitution and unacknowledged by our laws, giving his assent to their acts of pretended legislation:

For quartering large bodies of armed troops among us.

For protecting them, by a mock trial, from punishment for any murders which they should commit on the inhabitants of these states.

For cutting off our trade with all parts of the world.

For imposing taxes on us without our consent.

For depriving us, in many cases, of the benefits of trial by jury.

For transporting us beyond seas to be tried for pretended offenses.

For abolishing the free system of English laws in a neighboring province, establishing therein an arbitrary government, and enlarging its boundaries so as to render it at once an example and fit instrument for introducing the same absolute rule into these colonies.

For taking away our charters, abolishing our most valuable laws, and altering fundamentally the forms of our governments.

For suspending our own legislatures and declaring themselves invested with power to legislate for us in all cases whatsoever.

He has abdicated government here by declaring us out of his protection and waging war against us.

He has plundered our seas, ravaged our coasts, burnt our towns, and destroyed the lives of our people.

He is at this time transporting large armies of foreign mercenaries to complete the works of death, desolation, and tyranny, already begun with circumstances of cruelty and perfidy scarcely paralleled in the most barbarous ages, and totally unworthy the head of a civilized nation.

He has constrained our fellow citizens, taken captive on the high seas, to bear arms against their country, to become the executioners of their friends and brethren, or to fall themselves by their hands.

He has excited domestic insurrections amongst us, and has endeavored to bring on the inhabitants of our frontiers the merciless Indian savages, whose known rule of warfare is an undistinguished destruction of all ages, sexes, and conditions.

In every stage of these oppressions we have petitioned for redress in the most humble terms; our repeated petitions have been answered only by repeated injury. A prince whose character is thus marked by every act which may define a tyrant is unfit to be the ruler of a free people.

Nor have we been wanting in attentions to our British brethren. We have warned them from time to time of attempts by their legislature to extend an unwarrantable jurisdiction over us. We have reminded them of the circumstances of our emigration and settlement here. We have appealed to their native justice and magnanimity, and we have conjured them by the ties of our common kindred to disavow these usurpations which would inevitably interrupt our connections and correspondence. They, too, have been deaf to the voice of justice and of consanguinity. We must, therefore, acquiesce in the necessity which denounces our separation, and hold them, as we hold the rest of mankind, enemies in war; in peace, friends.

Conclusion and Declaration

We, therefore, the representatives of the United States of America, in general congress assembled, appealing to the Supreme Judge of the world for the rectitude of our intentions, do, in the name and by the authority of the good people of these colonies, solemnly publish and declare that these united colonies are, and of right ought to be, free and independent states; that they are absolved from all allegiance to the British crown, and that all political connection between them and the state of Great Britain is, and ought to be, totally dissolved; and that as free and independent states they have full power to levy war, conclude peace, contract alliances, establish commerce, and to do all other acts and things which independent states may of right do. And for the support of this declaration, with a firm reliance on the protection of Divine Providence, we mutually pledge to each other our lives, our fortunes, and our sacred honor.

RALPH WALDO EMERSON
Self-Reliance

I read the other day some verses written by an eminent painter which were original and not conventional. The soul always hears an admonition in such lines, let the subject be what it may. The sentiment they instill is of more value than any thought they may contain. To believe your own thought, to believe that what is true for you in your private heart is true for all men,—that is genius. Speak your latent conviction, and it shall be the universal sense; for the inmost in due time becomes the outmost, and our first thought is rendered back to us by the trumpets of the Last Judgment. Familiar as the voice of the mind is to each, the highest merit we ascribe to Moses, Plato and Milton is that they set at naught books and traditions, and spoke not what men, but what *they* thought. A man should learn to detect and watch that gleam of light which flashes across his mind from within, more than the luster of the firmament of bards and sages. Yet he dismisses without notice his thought, because it is his. In every work of genius we recognize our own rejected thoughts; they come back to us with a certain alienated majesty. Great works of art have no more affecting lesson for us than this. They teach us to abide by our spontaneous impression with good-humored inflexibility then most when the whole cry of voices is on the other side. Else tomorrow a stranger will say with masterly good sense precisely what we have thought and felt all the time, and we shall be forced to take with shame our own opinion from another.

There is a time in every man's education when he arrives at the conviction that envy is ignorance; that imitation is suicide; that he must take himself for better for worse as his portion; that though the wide universe is full of good, no kernel of nourishing corn can come to him but through his toil bestowed on that plot of ground which is given to him to till. The power which resides in him is new in nature, and none but he knows what that is which he can do, nor does he know until he has tried. Not for nothing one face, one character, one fact, makes much impression on him, and another none. This sculpture in the memory is not without pre-established harmony. The eye was placed where one ray should fall, that it might testify of that particular ray. We but half express ourselves, and are ashamed of that divine idea which each of us represents. It may be safely trusted as proportionate and of good issues, so it be faithfully imparted, but God will not have his work made manifest by cowards. A man is relieved and gay when he has put his heart into his work and done his best; but what he has said or done otherwise shall give him no peace. It is a deliverance which does not deliver. In the attempt his genius deserts him; no muse befriends; no invention, no hope.

Trust thyself: every heart vibrates to that iron string. Accept the place the divine providence has found for you, the society of your contemporaries, the connection of events. Great men have always done so, and confided themselves childlike to the genius of their age, betraying their perception that

Emerson, *Self-Reliance*. Ralph Waldo Emerson (1803-1882) was born in Boston and educated at Harvard College. After resigning from the Unitarian ministry and traveling for a time, he began a long career of lecturing and essay-writing. He spent his life at Concord and Boston, Massachusetts.

the absolutely trustworthy was seated at their heart, working through their hands, predominating in all their being. And we are now men, and must accept in the highest mind the same transcendent destiny; and not minors and invalids in a protected corner, not cowards fleeing before a revolution, but guides, redeemers and benefactors, obeying the Almighty effort and advancing on Chaos and the Dark.

What pretty oracles nature yields us on this text in the face and behavior of children, babes, and even brutes! That divided and rebel mind, that distrust of a sentiment because our arithmetic has computed the strength and means opposed to our purpose, these have not. Their mind being whole, their eye is as yet unconquered, and when we look in their faces we are disconcerted. Infancy conforms to nobody; all conform to it; so that one babe commonly makes four or five out of the adults who prattle and play to it. So God has armed youth and puberty and manhood no less with its own piquancy and charm, and made it enviable and gracious and its claims not to be put by, if it will stand by itself. Do not think the youth has no force, because he cannot speak to you and me. Hark! in the next room his voice is sufficiently clear and emphatic. It seems he knows how to speak to his contemporaries. Bashful or bold then, he will know how to make us seniors very unnecessary.

The nonchalance of boys who are sure of a dinner, and would disdain as much as a lord to do or say aught to conciliate one, is the healthy attitude of human nature. A boy is in the parlor what the pit is in the playhouse; independent, irresponsible, looking out from his corner on such people and facts as pass by, he tries and sentences them on their merits, in the swift, summary way of boys, as good, bad, interesting, silly, eloquent, troublesome. He cumbers himself never about consequences, about interests; he gives an independent, genuine verdict. You must court him; he does not court you. But the man is as it were clapped into jail by his consciousness. As soon as he has once acted or spoken with *éclat* he is a committed person, watched by the sympathy or the hatred of hundreds, whose affections must now enter into his account. There is no Lethe for this. Ah, that he could pass again into his neutrality! Who can thus avoid all pledges and, having observed, observe again from the same unaffected, unbiased, unbribable, unaffrighted innocence,—must always be formidable. He would utter opinions on all

passing affairs, which being seen to be not private but necessary, would sink like darts into the ear of men and put them in fear.

These are the voices which we hear in solitude, but they grow faint and inaudible as we enter into the world. Society everywhere is in conspiracy against the manhood of every one of its members. Society is a joint-stock company, in which the members agree, for the better securing of his bread to each shareholder, to surrender the liberty and culture of the eater. The virtue in most request is conformity. Self-reliance is its aversion. It loves not realities and creators, but names and customs.

Whoso would be a man, must be a nonconformist. He who would gather immortal palms must not be hindered by the name of goodness, but must explore if it be goodness. Nothing is at last sacred but the integrity of your own mind. Absolve you to yourself, and you shall have the suffrage of the world. I remember an answer which when quite young I was prompted to make to a valued adviser who was wont to importune me with the dear old doctrines of the church. On my saying, "What have I to do with the sacredness of traditions, if I live wholly from within?" my friend suggested,—"But these impulses may be from below, not from above." I replied, "They do not seem to me to be such; but if I am the Devil's child, I will live then from the Devil." No law can be sacred to me but that of my nature. Good and bad are but names very readily transferable to that or this; the only right is what is after my constitution; the only wrong what is against it. A man is to carry himself in the presence of all opposition as if everything were titular and ephemeral but he. I am ashamed to think how easily we capitulate to badges and names, to large societies and dead institutions. Every decent and well-spoken individual affects and sways me more than is right. I ought to go upright and vital, and speak the rude truth in all ways.

.   .   .   .   .

The other terror that scares us from self-trust is our consistency; a reverence for our past act or word because the eyes of others have no other data for computing our orbit than our past acts, and we are loth to disappoint them.

But why should you keep your head over your shoulder? Why drag about this corpse of your memory, lest you contradict somewhat you have stated in this or that public place? Suppose you should contradict yourself; what then? It seems to be a rule of wisdom never to rely on your memory alone, scarcely even in acts of pure memory, but to bring the past for judgment into the thousand-eyed present, and live ever in a new day. In your metaphysics you have denied personality to the Deity, yet when the devout motions of the soul come, yield to them heart and life, though they should clothe God with shape and color. Leave your theory, as Joseph his coat in the hand of the harlot, and flee.

A foolish consistency is the hobgoblin of little minds, adored by little statesmen and philosophers and divines. With consistency a great soul has simply nothing to do. He may as well concern himself with his shadow on the wall. Speak what you think now in hard words and tomorrow speak what tomorrow thinks in hard words again, though it contradict every thing you said today.—"Ah, so you shall be sure to be misunderstood."—Is it so bad then to be misunderstood? Pythagoras was misunderstood, and Socrates, and Jesus, and Luther, and Copernicus, and Galileo, and Newton, and every pure and wise spirit that ever took flesh. To be great is to be misunderstood.

. . . . . .

I hope in these days we have heard the last of conformity and consistency. Let the words be gazetted and ridiculous henceforward. Instead of the gong for dinner, let us hear a whistle from the Spartan fife. Let us never bow and apologize more. A great man is coming to eat at my house. I do not wish to please him; I wish that he should wish to please me. I will stand here for humanity, and though I would make it kind, I would make it true. Let us affront and reprimand the smooth mediocrity and squalid contentment of the times, and hurl in the face of custom and trade and office, the fact which is the upshot of all history, that there is a great responsible Thinker and Actor working wherever a man works; that a true man belongs to no other time or place, but is the center of things. Where he is, there is Nature. He measures you and all men and all events. Ordinarily, everybody in society reminds us of somewhat else, or of some other person. Character, reality, reminds you of nothing else; it takes place of the whole creation. The man must be so much that he must make all circumstances indifferent. Every true man is a cause, a country, and an age; requires infinite spaces and numbers and time fully to accomplish his design;—and posterity seem to follow his steps as a train of clients. A man Cæsar is born, and for ages after we have a Roman Empire. Christ is born, and millions of minds so grow and cleave to his genius that he is confounded with virtue and the possible of man. An institution is the lengthened shadow of one man; as, Monachism, of the Hermit Antony; the Reformation, of Luther; Quakerism, of Fox; Methodism, of Wesley; Abolition, of Clarkson. Scipio, Milton called "the height of Rome"; and all history resolves itself very easily into the biography of a few stout and earnest persons.

Let a man then know his worth, and keep things under his feet. Let him not peep or steal, or skulk up and down with the air of a charity-boy, a bastard, or an interloper in the world which exists for him. But the man in the street, finding no worth in himself which corresponds to the force which built a tower or sculptured a marble god, feels poor when he looks on these. To him a palace, a statue, or a costly book have an alien and forbidding air, much like a gay equipage, and seem to say like that, "Who are you, Sir?" Yet they all are his, suitors for his notice, petitioners to his faculties that they will come out and take possession. The picture waits for my verdict; it is not to command me, but I am to settle its claims to praise. That popular fable of the sot who was picked up dead-drunk in the street, carried to the duke's house, washed and dressed and laid in the duke's bed, and, on his waking, treated with all obsequious ceremony like the duke, and assured that he had been insane, owes its popularity to the fact that it symbolizes so well the state of man, who is in the world a sort of sot, but now and then wakes up, exercises his reason and finds himself a true prince.

. . . . . .

It is easy to see that a greater self-reliance must work a revolution in all the offices and relations of men; in their religion; in their education; in their pursuits; their modes of living; their association; in their property; in their speculative views.

1. In what prayers do men allow themselves! That which they call a holy office is not so much as brave and manly. Prayer looks abroad and asks for some foreign addition to come through some foreign virtue, and loses itself in endless mazes of natural and supernatural, and mediatorial and miraculous. Prayer that craves a particular commodity, anything less than all good, is vicious. Prayer is the contemplation of the facts of life from the highest point of view. It is the soliloquy of a beholding and jubilant soul. It is the spirit of God pronouncing his works good. But prayer as a means to effect a private end is meanness and

theft. It supposes dualism and not unity in nature and consciousness. As soon as the man is at one with God, he will not beg. He will then see prayer in all action. The prayer of the farmer kneeling in his field to weed it, the prayer of the rower kneeling with the stroke of his oar, are true prayers heard throughout nature, though for cheap ends. Caratach, in Fletcher's "Bonduca," when admonished to inquire the mind of the god Audate, replies,—

> His hidden meaning lies in our endeavors;
> Our valors are our best gods.

Another sort of false prayers are our regrets. Discontent is the want of self-reliance: it is infirmity of will. Regret calamities if you can thereby help the sufferer; if not, attend your own work and already the evil begins to be repaired. Our sympathy is just as base. We come to them who weep foolishly and sit down and cry for company, instead of imparting to them truth and health in rough electric shocks, putting them once more in communication with their own reason. The secret of fortune is joy in our hands. Welcome evermore to gods and men is the self-helping man. For him all doors are flung wide; him all tongues greet, all honors crown, all eyes follow with desire. Our love goes out to him and embraces him because he did not need it. We solicitously and apologetically caress and celebrate him because he held on his way and scorned our disapprobation. The gods love him because men hated him. "To the persevering mortal," said Zoroaster, "the blessed Immortals are swift."

As men's prayers are a disease of the will, so are their creeds a disease of the intellect. They say with those foolish Israelites, "Let not God speak to us, lest we die. Speak thou, speak any man with us, and we will obey." Everywhere I am hindered of meeting God in my brother, because he has shut his own temple doors and recites fables merely of his brother's, or his brother's brother's God. Every new mind is a new classification. If it prove a mind of uncommon activity and power, a Locke, a Lavoisier, a Hutton, a Bentham, a Fourier, it imposes its classification on other men, and lo! a new system. In proportion to the depth of the thought, and so to the number of the objects it touches and brings within reach of the pupil, is his complacency. But chiefly is this apparent in creeds and churches, which are also classifications of some powerful mind acting on the elemental thought of duty and man's relation to the Highest. Such is

Calvinism, Quakerism, Swedenborgism. The pupil takes the same delight in subordinating everything to the new terminology as a girl who has just learned botany in seeing a new earth and new seasons thereby. It will happen for a time that the pupil will find his intellectual power has grown by the study of his master's mind. But in all unbalanced minds the classification is idolized, passes for the end and not for a speedily exhaustible means, so that the walls of the system blend to their eye in the remote horizon with the walls of the universe; the luminaries of heaven seem to them hung on the arch their master built. They cannot imagine how you aliens have any right to see,— how you can see; "It must be somehow that you stole the light from us." They do not yet perceive that light, unsystematic, indomitable, will break into any cabin, even into theirs. Let them chirp awhile and call it their own. If they are honest and do well, presently their neat new pinfold will be too strait and low, will crack, will lean, will rot and vanish, and the immortal light, all young and joyful, million-orbed, million-colored, will beam over the universe as on the first morning.

2. It is for want of self-culture that the superstition of Traveling, whose idols are Italy, England, Egypt, retains its fascination for all educated Americans. They who made England, Italy, or Greece venerable in the imagination, did so by sticking fast where they were, like an axis of the earth. In manly hours we feel that duty is our place. The soul is no traveler; the wise man stays at home, and when his necessities, his duties, on any occasion call him from his house, or into foreign lands, he is at home still and shall make men sensible by the expression of his countenance that he goes, the missionary of wisdom and virtue, and visits cities and men like a sovereign and not like an interloper or a valet.

I have no churlish objection to the circumnavigation of the globe for the purposes of art, of study, and benevolence, so that the man is first domesticated, or does not go abroad with the hope of finding somewhat greater than he knows. He who travels to be amused, or to get somewhat which he does not carry, travels away from himself, and grows old even in youth among old things. In Thebes, in Palmyra, his will and mind have become old and dilapidated as they. He carries ruins to ruins.

Traveling is a fool's paradise. Our first journeys discover to us the indifference of places. At home I dream that at Naples, at Rome, I can be intoxicated with beauty and lose my sadness. I pack my trunk, embrace my friends, embark on the sea and at last wake up in Naples, and there beside me is the stern fact, the sad self, unrelenting, identical, that I fled from. I seek the Vatican and the palaces. I affect to be intoxicated with sights and suggestions, but I am not intoxicated. My giant goes with me wherever I go.

3. But the rage of traveling is a symptom of a deeper unsoundness affecting the whole intellectual action. The intellect is vagabond, and our system of education fosters restlessness. Our minds travel when our bodies are forced to stay at home. We imitate; and what is imitation but the traveling of the mind? Our houses are built with foreign taste; our shelves are garnished with foreign ornaments; our opinions, our tastes, our faculties, lean, and follow the Past and the Distant. The soul created the arts wherever they have flourished. It was in his own mind that the artist sought his model. It was an application of his own thought to the thing to be done and the conditions to be observed. And why need we copy the Doric or the Gothic model? Beauty, convenience, grandeur of thought and quaint expression are as near to us as to any, and if the American artist will study with hope and love the precise thing to be done by him, considering the climate, the soil, the length of the day, the wants of the people, the habit and form of the government, he will create a house in which all these will find themselves fitted, and taste and sentiment will be satisfied also.

Insist on yourself; never imitate. Your own gift you can present every moment with the cumulative force of a whole life's cultivation; but of the adopted talent of another you have only an extemporaneous half possession. That which each can do best, none but his Maker can teach him. No man yet knows what it is, nor can, till that person has exhibited it. Where is the master who could have taught Shakespeare? Where is the master who could have instructed Franklin, or Washington, or Bacon, or Newton? Every great man is a unique. The Scipionism of Scipio is precisely that part he could not borrow. Shakespeare will never be made by the study of Shakespeare. Do that which is assigned you, and you cannot hope too much or dare too much. There is at this moment for you an utterance brave and grand as that of the colossal chisel of Phidias, or trowel of the Egyptians, or the pen of Moses or Dante, but different from all these. Not possibly will the soul, all rich, all eloquent, with thousand-cloven tongue,

deign to repeat itself; but if you can hear what these patriarchs say, surely you can reply to them in the same pitch of voice; for the ear and the tongue are two organs of one nature. Abide in the simple and noble regions of thy life, obey thy heart, and thou shalt reproduce the Foreworld again.

4. As our Religion, our Education, our Art look abroad, so does our spirit of society. All men plume themselves on the improvement of society, and no man improves.

Society never advances. It recedes as fast on one side as it gains on the other. It undergoes continual changes; it is barbarous, it is civilized, it is christianized, it is rich, it is scientific; but this change is not amelioration. For every thing that is given something is taken. Society acquires new arts and loses old instincts. What a contrast between the well-clad, reading, writing, thinking American, with a watch, a pencil and a bill of exchange in his pocket, and the naked New Zealander, whose property is a club, a spear, a mat and an undivided twentieth of a shed to sleep under! But compare the health of the two men and you shall see that the white man has lost his aboriginal strength. If the traveler tell us truly, strike the savage with a broad-ax and in a day or two the flesh shall unite and heal as if you struck the blow into soft pitch, and the same blow shall send the white to his grave.

The civilized man has built a coach, but has lost the use of his feet. He is supported on crutches, but lacks so much support of muscle. He has a fine Geneva watch, but he fails of the skill to tell the hour by the sun. A Greenwich nautical almanac he has, and so being sure of the information when he wants it, the man in the street does not know a star in the sky. The solstice he does not observe; the equinox he knows as little; and the whole bright calendar of the year is without a dial in his mind. His note-books impair his memory; his libraries overload his wit; the insurance-office increases the number of accidents; and it may be a question whether machinery does not encumber; whether we have not lost by refinement some energy, by a Christianity, entrenched in establishments and forms, some vigor of wild virtue. For every Stoic was a Stoic; but in Christendom where is the Christian?

There is no more deviation in the moral standard than in the standard of height or bulk. No greater men are now than ever were. A singular equality may be observed between the great men of the first and of the last ages; nor can all the science, art, religion, and philosophy of the nineteenth century avail to educate greater men than Plutarch's heroes, three or four and twenty centuries ago. Not in time is the race progressive. Phocion, Socrates, Anaxagoras, Diogenes, are great men, but they leave no class. He who is really of their class will not be called by their name, but will be his own man, and in his turn the founder of a sect. The arts and inventions of each period are only its costume and do not invigorate men. The harm of the improved machinery may compensate its good. Hudson and Behring accomplished so much in their fishing-boats as to astonish Parry and Franklin, whose equipment exhausted the resources of science and art. Galileo, with an opera-glass, discovered a more splendid series of celestial phenomena than anyone since. Columbus found the New World in an undecked boat. It is curious to see the periodical disuse and perishing of means and machinery which were introduced with loud laudation a few years or centuries before. The great genius returns to essential man. We reckoned the improvements of the art of war among the triumphs of science, and yet Napoleon conquered Europe by the bivouac, which consisted of falling back on naked valor and disencumbering it of all aids. The Emperor held it impossible to make a perfect army, says Las Cases, "without abolishing our arms, magazines, commissaries and carriages, until, in imitation of the Roman custom, the soldier should receive his supply of corn, grind it in his hand-mill and bake his bread himself."

Society is a wave. The wave moves onward, but the water of which it is composed does not. The same particle does not rise from the valley to the ridge. Its unity is only phenomenal. The persons who make up a nation today, next year die, and their experience dies with them.

And so the reliance on Property, including the reliance on governments which protect it, is the want of self-reliance. Men have looked away from themselves and at things so long that they have come to esteem the religious, learned and civil institutions as guards of property, and they deprecate assaults on these, because they feel them to be assaults on property. They measure their esteem of each other by what each has, and not by what each is. But a cultivated man becomes ashamed of his property, out of new respect for his nature. Especially he hates what he has if he see that it is acci-

dental,—came to him by inheritance, or gift, or crime; then he feels that it is not having; it does not belong to him, has no root in him and merely lies there because no revolution or no robber takes it away. But that which a man is, does always by necessity acquire; and what the man acquires, is living property, which does not wait the beck of rulers, or mobs, or revolutions, or fire, or storm, or bankruptcies, but perpetually renews itself wherever the man breathes. "Thy lot or portion of life," said the Caliph Ali, "is seeking after thee; therefore be at rest from seeking after it." Our dependence on these foreign goods leads us to our slavish respect for numbers. The political parties meet in numerous conventions; the greater the concourse and with each new uproar of announcement, The delegation from Essex! The Democrats from New Hampshire! The Whigs of Maine! the young patriot feels himself stronger than before by a new thousand of eyes and arms. In like manner the reformers summon conventions and vote and resolve in multitude. Not so, O friends! will the God deign to enter and inhabit you, but by a method precisely the reverse. It is only as a man puts off all foreign support and stands alone that I see him to be strong and to prevail. He is weaker by every recruit to his banner. Is not a man better than a town? Ask nothing of men, and, in the endless mutation, thou only firm column must presently appear the upholder of all that surrounds thee. He who knows that power is inborn, that he is weak because he has looked for good out of him and elsewhere, and, so perceiving, throws himself unhesitatingly on his thought, instantly rights himself, stands in the erect position, commands his limbs, works miracles; just as a man who stands on his feet is stronger than a man who stands on his head.

So use all that is called Fortune. Most men gamble with her, and gain all, and lose all, as her wheel rolls. But do thou leave as unlawful these winnings, and deal with Cause and Effect, the chancellors of God. In the Will work and acquire, and thou hast chained the wheel of Chance, and shall sit hereafter out of fear from her rotations. A political victory, a rise of rents, the recovery of your sick or the return of your absent friend, or some other favorable event raises your spirits, and you think good days are preparing for you. Do not believe it. Nothing can bring you peace but yourself. Nothing can bring you peace but the triumph of principles.

HENRY DAVID THOREAU

Brute Neighbors

Sometimes I had a companion in my fishing, who came through the village to my house from the other side of the town, and the catching of the dinner was as much a social exercise as the eating of it.

Hermit. I wonder what the world is doing now. I have not heard so much as a locust over the sweet-fern these three hours. The pigeons are all asleep upon their roosts,—no flutter from them. Was that a farmer's noon horn which sounded from beyond the woods just now? The hands are coming in to boiled salt beef and cider and Indian bread. Why will men worry themselves so? He that does not eat need not work. I wonder how much they have reaped. Who would live there where a body can never think for the barking of Bose? And O, the housekeeping! to keep bright the devil's door-knobs, and scour his tubs this bright day! Better not keep a house. Say, some hollow tree; and then for morning calls and dinner-parties! Only a woodpecker tapping. O, they swarm; the sun is too warm there; they are born too far into life for me. I have water from the spring, and a loaf of brown bread on the shelf.— Hark! I hear a rustling of the leaves. Is it some ill-fed village hound yielding to the instinct of the chase? or the lost pig which is said to be in these woods, whose tracks I saw after the rain? It comes on apace; my sumachs and sweet-briers tremble.— Eh, Mr. Poet, is it you? How do you like the world today?

Poet. See those clouds; how they hang! That's the greatest thing I have seen today. There's nothing like it in old paintings, nothing like it in foreign lands,—unless when we were off the coast of Spain. That's a true Mediterranean Sky. I thought, as I have my living to get, and have not eaten today, that I might go a-fishing. That's the true industry for poets. It is the only trade I have learned. Come, let's along.

Hermit. I cannot resist. My brown bread will soon be gone. I will go with you gladly soon, but I am just concluding a serious meditation. I think that I am near the end of it. Leave me alone, then, for a while. But that we may not be delayed, you shall be digging the bait meanwhile. Angle worms are rarely to be met with in these parts, where the soil was never fattened with manure; the race is nearly extinct. The sport of digging the bait is nearly equal to that of catching the fish, when one's appetite is not too keen; and this you may have all to yourself today. I would advise you to set in the spade down yonder among the ground-nuts, where you see the johnswort waving. I think that I may warrant you one worm to every three sods you turn up, if you look well in among the roots of the grass, as if you were weeding. Or, if you choose to go farther, it will not be unwise, for I have found the increase of fair bait to be very nearly as the squares of the distances.

Hermit alone. Let me see; where was I? Methinks I was nearly in this frame of mind; the world lay about at this angle. Shall I go to heaven or a-fishing? If I should soon bring this meditation to an end, would another so sweet occasion be likely to offer? I was as near being resolved into the essence of things as ever I was in my life. I fear my thoughts will not come back to me. If it would do any good, I would whistle for them. When they make us an offer, is it wise to say, We will think of it? My thoughts have left no track, and I cannot find the path again. What was it that I was thinking of? It was a very hazy day. I will just try these three sentences of Con-fut-see; they may fetch that state about again. I know not whether it was the dumps or a budding ecstasy. Mem. There never is but one opportunity of a kind.

Poet. How now, Hermit, is it too soon? I have got just thirteen whole ones, besides several which are imperfect or undersized; but they will do for the smaller fry; they do not cover up the hook so much. Those village worms are quite too large; a shiner may make a meal off one without finding the skewer.

Hermit. Well, then let's be off. Shall we to the

Thoreau, *Brute Neighbors.* Henry David Thoreau (1817-1862) passed his life at Concord, Massachusetts, where he was associated with Emerson and his literary group. He lived alone on the shore of Walden Pond near Concord from 1845 to 1847. This selection is taken from *Walden.*

Concord? There's good sport there if the water be not too high.

Why do precisely these objects which we behold make a world? Why has man just these species of animals for his neighbors; as if nothing but a house could have filled this crevice? I suspect that Pilpay & Co. have put animals to their best use, for they are all beasts of burden, in a sense, made to carry some portion of our thoughts.

The mice which haunted my house were not the common ones, which are said to have been introduced into the country, but a wild native kind not found in the village. I sent one to a distinguished naturalist, and it interested him much. When I was building, one of these had its nest underneath the house, and before I had laid the second floor, and swept out the shavings, would come out regularly at lunch time and pick up the crumbs at my feet. It probably had never seen a man before; and it soon became quite familiar, and would run over my shoes and up my clothes. It could readily ascend the sides of the room by short impulses, like a squirrel, which it resembled in its motions. At length, as I leaned with my elbow on the bench one day, it ran up my clothes, and along my sleeve, and round and round the paper which held my dinner, while I kept the latter close, and dodged and played at bo-peep with it; and when at last I held still a piece of cheese between my thumb and finger, it came and nibbled it, sitting in my hand, and afterward cleaned its face and paws, like a fly, and walked away.

A phœbe soon built in my shed, and a robin for protection in a pine which grew against the house. In June the partridge (*Tetrao umbellus*), which is so shy a bird, led her brood past my windows, from the woods in the rear to the front of my house, clucking and calling to them like a hen, and in all her behavior proving herself the hen of the woods. The young suddenly disperse on your approach, at a signal from the mother, as if a whirlwind had swept them away, and they so exactly resemble the dried leaves and twigs that many a traveler has placed his foot in the midst of a brood, and heard the whir of the old bird as she flew off, and her anxious calls and mewing, or seen her trail her wings to attract his attention, without suspecting their neighborhood. The parent will sometimes roll and spin round before you in such a dishabille, that you cannot, for a few moments, detect what kind of creature it is. The young squat still and flat, often running their heads under a leaf, and mind only their mother's directions given from a distance, nor will your approach make them run again and betray themselves. You may even tread on them, or have your eyes on them for a minute, without discovering them. I have held them in my open hand at such a time, and still their only care, obedient to their mother and their instinct, was to squat there without fear or trembling. So perfect is this instinct, that once, when I had laid them on the leaves again, and one accidentally fell on its side, it was found with the rest in exactly the same position ten minutes afterward. They are not callow like the young of most birds, but more perfectly developed and precocious even than chickens. The remarkably adult yet innocent expression of their open and serene eyes is very memorable. All intelligence seems reflected in them. They suggest not merely the purity of infancy, but a wisdom clarified by experience. Such an eye was not born when the bird was, but is coeval with the sky it reflects. The woods do not yield another such a gem. The traveler does not often look into such a limpid well. The ignorant or reckless sportsman often shoots the parent at such a time, and leaves these innocents to fall a prey to some prowling beast or bird, or gradually mingle with the decaying leaves which they so much resemble. It is said that when hatched by a hen they will directly disperse on some alarm, and so are lost, for they never hear the mother's call which gathers them again. These were my hens and chickens.

It is remarkable how many creatures live wild and free though secret in the woods, and still sustain themselves in the neighborhood of towns, suspected by hunters only. How retired the otter manages to live here! He grows to be four feet long, as big as a small boy, perhaps without any human being getting a glimpse of him. I formerly saw the raccoon in the woods behind where my house is built, and probably still heard their whinnering at night. Commonly I rested an hour or two in the shade at noon, after planting, and ate my lunch, and read a little by a spring which was the source of a swamp and of a brook, oozing from under Brister's Hill, half a mile from my field. The approach to this was through a succession of descending grassy hollows, full of young pitch-pines, into a larger wood about the swamp. There, in a very secluded and shaded spot, under a spreading white-pine, there was yet a clean firm sward to sit on. I had dug out the spring and made a well of clear gray water, where I could dip up a pailful without roiling it, and thither I went for this purpose almost every day in midsummer, when the pond was warmest. Thither too the wood-cock led her brood, to probe the mud for worms, flying but a foot above them down the bank, while they ran in a troop beneath; but at last, spying me, she would leave her young and circle round and round me, nearer and nearer till within four or five feet, pretending broken wings and legs, to attract my attention, and get off her young, who would already have taken up their march, with faint wiry peep, single file through the swamp, as she directed. Or I heard the peep of the young when I could not see the parent bird. There too the turtle-doves sat over the spring, or fluttered from bough to bough of the soft white-pines over my head; or the red squirrel, coursing down the nearest bough, was particularly familiar and inquisitive. You only need sit still long enough in some attractive spot in the woods that all its inhabitants may exhibit themselves to you by turns.

I was witness to events of a less peaceful character. One day when I went out to my wood-pile, or rather my pile of stumps, I observed two large ants, the one red, the other much larger, nearly half an inch long, and black, fiercely contending with one another. Having once got hold they never let go, but struggled and wrestled and rolled on the chips incessantly. Looking farther, I was surprised to find that the chips were covered with such combatants, that it was not a *duellum*, but a *bellum*, a war between two races of ants, the red always pitted against the black, and frequently two red ones to one black. The legions of these Myrmidons covered all the hills and vales in my wood-yard, and the ground was already strewn with the dead and dying, both red and black. It was the only battle-field which I have ever witnessed, the only battle-field I ever trod while the battle was raging; internecine war; the red republicans on the one hand, and the black imperialists on the other. On every side they were engaged in deadly combat, yet without any noise that I could hear, and human soldiers never fought so resolutely. I watched a couple that were fast locked in each other's embraces, in a little sunny valley amid the chips, now at noon-day prepared to fight till the sun went down, or life went out. The smaller red champion had fastened himself like a vice to his adversary's front, and through all the tumblings on that field never for an instant ceased to gnaw at one of his feelers near the root, having already caused the other to go by the board; while the stronger black one dashed him from side to side, and, as I saw on looking nearer, had already divested him of several of his members. They fought with more pertinacity than bull-dogs. Neither manifested the least disposition to retreat. It was evident that their battle-cry was Conquer or die. In the meanwhile there came along a single red ant on the hill-side of this valley, evidently full of excitement, who either had despatched his foe, or had not yet taken part in the battle; probably the latter, for he had lost none of his limbs; whose mother had charged him to return with his shield or upon it. Or perchance he was some Achilles, who had nourished his wrath apart, and had now come to avenge or rescue his Patroclus. He saw this unequal combat from afar,—for the blacks were nearly twice the size of the red,—he drew near with rapid pace till he stood on his guard within half an inch of the combatants; then, watching his opportunity, he sprang upon the black warrior, and commenced his operations near the root of his right fore-leg, leaving the foe to select among his own members; and so there were three united for life, as if a new kind of attraction had been invented which put all other locks and cements to shame. I should not have wondered by this time to find that they had their respective musical bands stationed on some eminent chip, and playing their national airs the while, to excite the slow and cheer the dying combatants. I was myself excited somewhat even as if they had been men. The more you think of it, the less the difference. And certainly there is not the fight recorded in Concord history, at least, if in the history of America, that will bear a moment's comparison with this, whether for the numbers engaged in it, or for the patriotism and heroism displayed. For numbers and for carnage it was an Austerlitz or Dresden. Concord Fight! Two killed on the patriots' side and Luther Blanchard wounded! Why here every ant was a Buttrick,—"Fire! for god's sake fire!"—and thousands shared the fate of Davis and Hosmer. There was not one hireling there. I have no doubt that it was a principle they fought for, as much as our ancestors, and not to avoid a three-penny tax on their tea; and the results of this battle will be as important and memorable to those whom it concerns as those of the battle of Bunker Hill at least.

I took up the chip on which the three I have particularly described were struggling, carried it into my house, and placed it under a tumbler on my window-sill, in order to see the issue. Holding a microscope to the first-mentioned red ant, I saw that, though he was assiduously gnawing at the near fore-leg of his enemy, having severed his remaining feeler, his own breast was all torn away, exposing what vitals he had there to the jaws of the black warrior, whose breastplate was apparently too thick for him to pierce; and the dark carbuncles of the sufferer's eyes shone with ferocity such as war only could excite. They struggled half an hour longer under the tumbler, and when I looked again the black soldier had severed the heads of his foes from their bodies, and the still living heads were hanging on either side of him like ghastly trophies at his saddlebow, still apparently as firmly fastened as ever, and he was endeavoring with feeble struggles, being without feelers and with only the remnant of a leg, and I know not how many other wounds, to divest himself of them; which at length, after half an hour more, he accomplished. I raised the glass, and he went off over the window-sill in that crippled state. Whether he finally survived that combat, and spent the remainder of his days in some Hotel des Invalides, I do not know; but I thought that his industry would not be worth much thereafter. I never learned which party was victorious, nor the cause of the war; but I felt for the rest of that day as if I had my feelings excited and harrowed by witnessing the struggle, the ferocity and carnage, of a human battle before my door.

Kirby and Spence tell us that the battles of ants have long been celebrated, and the date of them recorded, though they say that Huber is the only modern author who appears to have witnessed them. "Æneas Sylvius," say they, "after giving a very circumstantial account of one contested with great obstinacy by a great and small species on the trunk of a pear tree," adds that " 'This action was fought in the pontificate of Eugenius the Fourth, in the presence of Nicholas Pistoriensis, an eminent lawyer, who related the whole history of the battle with the greatest fidelity.' A similar engagement between great and small ants is recorded by Olaus Magnus, in which the small ones, being victorious, are said to have buried the bodies of their own soldiers, but left those of their giant enemies a prey to the birds. This event happened previous to the expulsion of the tyrant Christiern the Second from Sweden." The battle which I witnessed took place in the Presidency of Polk, five years before the passage of Webster's Fugitive-Slave Bill.

Many a village Bose, fit only to course a mud-turtle in a victualing cellar, sported his heavy quarters in the woods, without the knowledge of his master, and ineffectually smelled at old fox burrows and woodchucks' holes; led perchance by some slight cur which nimbly threaded the wood, and might still inspire a natural terror in its denizens;—now far behind his guide, barking like a canine bull toward some small squirrel which had treed itself for scrutiny, then, cantering off, bending the bushes with his weight, imagining that he is on the track of some stray member of the jerbilla family. Once I was surprised to see a cat walking along the stony shore of the pond, for they rarely wander so far from home. The surprise was mutual. Nevertheless the most domestic cat, which has lain on a rug all her days, appears quite at home in the woods, and, by her sly and stealthy behavior, proves herself more native there than the regular inhabitants. Once, when berrying, I met with a cat with young kittens in the woods, quite wild, and they all like their mother, had their backs up and were fiercely spitting at me. A few years before I lived in the woods there was what was called a "winged cat" in one of the farmhouses in Lincoln nearest the pond, Mr. Gilian Baker's. When I called to see her in June, 1842, she was gone a-hunting in the woods, as was her wont (I am not sure whether it was a male or female, and so use the more common pronoun), but her mistress told me that she came into the neighborhood a little more than a year before, in April, and was finally taken into their house, that she was of a dark brownish-gray color, with a white spot on her throat, and white feet, and had a large bushy tail like a fox; that in the winter the fur grew thick and flatted out along her sides, forming strips ten or twelve inches long by two and a half wide, and under her chin like a muff, the upper side loose, the under matted like felt, and in the spring these appendages dropped off. They gave me a pair of her "wings," which I keep still. There is no appearance of a membrane about them. Some thought it was part flying-squirrel or some other wild animal, which is not impossible, for, according to naturalists, prolific hybrids have been produced by the union of the marten and domestic cat. This would have been the right kind of cat for me to keep, if I had kept any; for why should not a poet's cat be winged as well as his horse?

In the fall the loon (*Colymbus glacialis*) came, as usual, to molt and bathe in the pond, making the woods ring with his wild laughter before I had risen. At rumor of his arrival all the Mill-dam sportsmen are on the alert, in gigs and on foot, two by two and three by three, with patent rifles and conical balls and spy-glasses. They come rustling through the woods like autumn leaves, at least ten men to one loon. Some station themselves on this side of the pond, some on that, for the poor bird cannot be omnipresent; if he dive here he must come up there. But now the kind October wind rises, rustling the leaves and rippling the surface of the water, so that no loon can be heard or seen, though his foes sweep the pond with spy-glasses, and make the woods resound with their discharges. The waves generously rise and dash angrily, taking sides with all waterfowl, and our sportsmen must beat a retreat to town and shop and unfinished jobs. But they were too often successful. When I went to get a pail of water early in the morning I frequently saw this stately bird sailing out of my cove within a few rods. If I endeavored to overtake him in a boat, in order to see how he would maneuver, he would dive and be completely lost, so that I did not discover him again, sometimes, till the latter part of the day. But I was more than a match for him on the surface. He commonly went off in a rain.

As I was paddling along the north shore one very calm October afternoon, for such days especially they settle on to the lakes, like the milkweed down, having looked in vain over the pond for a loon, suddenly one, sailing out from the shore toward the middle a few rods in front of me, set up his wild laugh and betrayed himself. I pursued with a paddle and he dived, but when he came up I was nearer than before. He dived again, but I miscalculated the direction he would take, and we were fifty rods apart when he came to the surface this time, for I had helped to widen the interval; and again he laughed loud and long, and with more reason than before. He maneuvered so cunningly that I could not get within half a dozen rods of him. Each time, when he came to the surface, turning his head this way and that, he coolly surveyed the water and the land, and apparently chose his course so that he might come up where there was the widest expanse of water and at the greatest distance from the boat. It was surprising how quickly he made up his mind and put his resolve into execution. He led me at once to the widest part of the pond, and could not be driven from it. While he was thinking one thing in his brain, I was endeavoring to divine his thought in mine. It was a pretty game, played on the smooth surface of the pond, a man against a loon. Suddenly your adversary's checker disappears beneath the board, and the problem is to place yours nearest to where his will appear again. Sometimes he would come up unexpectedly on the opposite side of me having apparently passed directly under the boat. So long-winded was he and so unweariable, that when he had swum farthest he would immediately plunge again, nevertheless; and then no wit could divine where in the deep pond, beneath the smooth surface, he might be speeding his way like a fish, for he had time and ability to visit the bottom of the pond in its deepest part. It is said that loons have been caught in the New York lakes eighty feet beneath the surface, with hooks set for trout,—though Walden is deeper than that. How surprised must the fishes be to see this ungainly visitor from another sphere speeding his way amid their schools! Yet he appeared to know his course as surely underwater as on the surface, and swam much faster there. Once or twice I saw a ripple where he approached the surface, just put his head out to reconnoiter, and instantly dived again. I found that it was as well for me to rest on my oars and wait his reappearing as to endeavor to calculate where he would rise; for again and again, when I was straining my eyes over the surface one way, I would suddenly be startled by his unearthly laugh behind me. But why, after displaying so much cunning, did he invariably betray himself the moment he came up by that loud laugh? Did not his white breast enough betray him? He was indeed a silly loon, I thought. I could commonly hear the plash of the water when he came up, and so also detected him. But after an hour he seemed as fresh as ever, dived as willingly and swam yet farther than at first. It was surprising to see how serenely he sailed off with unruffled breast when he came to the surface, doing all the work with his webbed feet beneath. His usual note was this demoniac laughter, yet somewhat like that of a water-fowl; but occasionally, when he had balked me most successfully and come up a long way off, he uttered a long-drawn unearthly howl, probably more like that of a wolf than any bird; as when a beast puts his muzzle to the ground and deliberately howls. This was his looning,—perhaps the wildest sound that is ever heard here, making the woods ring far and wide. I concluded that he laughed in derision of my efforts, confident of his own resources. Though the sky was by this time overcast, the pond was so smooth that I could see where he broke the surface when I did not hear him. His white breast, the stillness of the air, and the smoothness of the water were all against him. At length, having come up fifty rods off, he uttered one of those prolonged howls, as if calling on the god of loons to aid him, and immediately there came a wind from the east and rippled the surface, and filled the whole air with misty rain, and I was impressed as if it were the prayer of the loon an-swered, and his god was angry with me; and so I left him disappearing far away on the tumultu-ous surface.

For hours, in fall days, I watched the ducks cun-ningly tack and veer and hold the middle of the pond, far from the sportsmen; tricks which they will have less need to practice in Louisiana bayous. When compelled to rise they would sometimes circle round and round and over the pond at a con-siderable height, from which they could easily see to other ponds and the river, like black motes in the sky; and, when I thought they had gone off thither long since, they would settle down by a slanting flight of a quarter of a mile on to a dis-tant part which was left free; but what beside safety they got by sailing in the middle of Walden I do not know, unless they love its water for the same reason that I do.

ABRAHAM LINCOLN

Address at Gettysburg

Fourscore and seven years ago our fathers brought forth on this continent a new nation, conceived in liberty, and dedicated to the proposition that all men are created equal. Now, we are engaged in a great civil war, testing whether that nation, or any nation so conceived and so dedicated, can long endure. We are met on a great battle field of that war. We have come to dedicate a portion of that field as a final resting-place for those who here gave their lives that that nation might live. It is altogether fitting and proper that we should do this. But, in a larger sense, we cannot dedicate, we cannot consecrate, we cannot hallow this ground. The brave men, living and dead, who struggled here, have consecrated it, far above our poor power to add or to detract. The world will little note nor long remember what we say here, but it can never forget what they did here. It is for us, the living, rather, to be dedicated here to the unfinished work which they who fought here have thus far so nobly advanced. It is rather for us to be here dedicated to the great task remaining before us; that from these honored dead we take increased devotion to that cause for which they gave the last full meas-ure of devotion; that we here highly resolve that these dead shall not have died in vain; that this nation, under God, shall have a new birth of free-dom; and that government of the people, by the people, for the people, shall not perish from the earth.

Second Inaugural Address

Fellow-countrymen:—At this second appearing to take the oath of the presidential office, there is less occasion for an extended address than there was at the first. Then a statement, somewhat in detail, of a course to be pursued, seemed fitting and proper. Now, at the expiration of four years, during which public declarations have been con-stantly called forth on every point and phase of the great contest which still absorbs the attention and engrosses the energies of the nation, little that is new can be presented. The progress of our arms, upon which all else chiefly depends, is as well known to the public as to myself; and it is, I trust, reasonably satisfactory and encouraging to all. With high hope for the future, no prediction in regard to it is ventured.

On the occasion corresponding to this four years ago, all thoughts were anxiously directed to an impending civil war. All dreaded it—all sought to avert it. While the inaugural address was being delivered from this place, devoted altogether to saving the Union without war, insurgent agents were in the city seeking to destroy it without war

Lincoln, *Address at Gettysburg*. Abraham Lincoln (1809-1865) was born in Kentucky but moved to Illinois as a young man. He practiced law and held political office. He was President from 1861 to 1865, during the Civil War.

—seeking to dissolve the Union, and divide effects, by negotiation. Both parties deprecated war; but one of them would make war rather than let the nation survive; and the other would accept war rather than let it perish. And the war came.

One-eighth of the whole population were colored slaves, not distributed generally over the Union, but localized in the Southern part of it. These slaves constituted a peculiar and powerful interest. All knew that this interest was, somehow, the cause of the war. To strengthen, perpetuate, and extend this interest was the object for which the insurgents would rend the Union, even by war; while the government claimed no right to do more than to restrict the territorial enlargement of it.

Neither party expected for the war the magnitude or the duration which it has already attained. Neither anticipated that the cause of the conflict might cease with, or even before, the conflict itself should cease. Each looked for an easier triumph, and a result less fundamental and astounding. Both read the same Bible, and pray to the same God; and each invokes his aid against the other. It may seem strange that any men should dare to ask a just God's assistance in wringing their bread from the sweat of other men's faces; but let us judge not, that we be not judged. The prayers of both could not be answered—that of neither has been answered fully.

The Almighty has his own purposes. "Woe unto the world because of offenses! for it must needs be that offenses come: but woe to that man by whom the offense cometh." If we shall suppose that American slavery is one of those offenses which, in the providence of God, must needs come, but which, having continued through his appointed time, he now wills to remove, and that he gives to both North and South this terrible war, as the woe due to those by whom the offense came, shall we discern therein any departure from those divine attributes which the believers in a living God always ascribe to him? Fondly do we hope—fervently do we pray—that this mighty scourge of war may speedily pass away. Yet, if God wills that it shall continue until all the wealth piled by the bondman's two hundred and fifty years of unrequited toil shall be sunk, and until every drop of blood drawn with the lash shall be paid by another drawn with the sword, as was said three thousand years ago, so still it must be said, "The judgments of the Lord are true and righteous altogether."

With malice toward none; with charity for all; with firmness in the right, as God gives us to see the right, let us strive on to finish the work we are in; to bind up the nation's wounds; to care for him who shall have borne the battle, and for his widow, and his orphan—to do all which may achieve and cherish a just and lasting peace among ourselves, and with all nations.

THE VICTORIAN POETS

An intelligent discussion of the English poets of the Victorian age is impossible without some consideration of the age itself and of the forces that made it what it was. By the year 1830 England had adjusted itself to the conditions brought about by the close of the Napoleonic wars. But several new elements were entering into the life of the nation that were to have a profound effect on its thinkers and writers.

With the invention of new machines and new industrial processes at the end of the eighteenth century an entirely new adjustment between laborer and employer became necessary. The establishment of large factories and the concentration of wealth caused acute distress to the lower classes. On the other hand, a new wealthy middle class emerged to challenge leadership of the nation with the older aristocracy.

The greatest advance of the Victorian age was in the field of science. During the 1830's the principles of geology came to be understood, and their implications in connection with accepted theories of the creation of the earth were realized by such thinkers as Tennyson. The most revolutionary scientific pronouncement of the century, however, was the publication of Darwin's *The Origin of Species* in 1859. The consideration of this book made it impossible to avoid a conflict in religious ideas between those who held for a strict interpretation of Christian dogmas as laid down in earlier centuries and those who insisted that religious beliefs must adjust themselves to advancing knowledge. This conflict has, of course, not entirely ended, but after some twenty or thirty years it ceased to have much importance for literature.

Developments of science in other fields, such as chemistry and physics, caused a transformation of the daily life of the people. Railroads and telegraphs and modern household conveniences changed the England of 1830 from an almost medieval type of existence until, by the end of the century, it was in all essentials like that of today. Contacts of all kinds became easier and, though this condition brought about a greater understanding between distant parts of the country and even of outlying parts of the Empire, it also promoted a restlessness among all classes and displayed such contrasts in living as to make for continual dissatisfaction on the part of the underprivileged.

Along with these ill-adjustments there was a serious attempt to meet problems as they arose. Throughout the century, reforms in parliamentary procedure, in the relations of employer and laborer, and in the administration of charity and of unemployment relief came slowly but surely as they were needed.

All these external aspects of Victorian life had their effect on literature. But they were hardly more important in setting the tone of the period than was the character of the royal lady who gave it her name. Queen Victoria stood as a champion for rigidity, not only in morals, but in manners as well. The license of speech, which a generation before permitted all sorts of subjects to be discussed in the drawing-room, now gave way to an extreme reticence, so that many of the works of older authors were frowned on as indecent. The range of what could be discussed in literature was greatly narrowed. This prudery was doubtless a handicap for Victorian literature—a handicap which our present generation has more than overcome.

What with the many changes of the age, all of which seemed at least to be advances, and what with the conscious correctness in social life, the Victorian writer had a great tendency to congratulate himself and his fellows. All appeared to be well in the best of possible worlds. Though a Matthew Arnold here and there may protest, the typical feeling of the mid-nineteenth century Englishman is expressed by Tennyson as follows:

> Her court was pure; her life serene;
>   God gave her peace; her land reposed;
>   A thousand claims to reverence closed
> In her as Mother, Wife, and Queen;
>
> And statesmen at her council met
>   Who knew the seasons when to take
>   Occasion by the hand, and make
> The bounds of freedom wider yet
>
> By shaping some august decree
>   Which kept her throne unshaken still,
>   Broad-based upon her people's will,
> And compass'd by the inviolate sea.

As we look back on it now, Tennyson seems to be the most representative Victorian. From the time when he began to write, around 1830, he had an easy command of poetic expression. At his best he has seldom been surpassed for the musical quality of his verse. It is entirely appropriate that he should have been Poet Laureate, since in his work he shows all the strength and weakness of Victorianism. In such poems as *Ulysses* he achieves a nobility of conception and expression seldom reached in English poetry. But he does not maintain this high level, and he wrote much that will not endure.

His great contemporary, Robert Browning, was felt in his own day to be extremely modern. His wide variety of intellectual interests, his many experiments in meter, frequently grotesque, and his awkward and deliberately obscure passages called attention to himself and made him, especially in his later days, extremely popular. Two generations have now passed and his grotesqueness and obscurity have lost their interest and seem to most critics forced and artificial. Browning also wrote far too much, so that the larger proportion of his output is utterly dead. Nevertheless, he made many permanent contributions to our literature. The most important of these are his dramatic monologues and his lyric poems.

When in 1846 Browning married Elizabeth Barrett, she was already well established as a poet. Though the romantic interest in the marriage of these two poets tends to keep her memory green, it cannot be said that any of her work has maintained vitality except the *Sonnets from the Portuguese* which she wrote as a wedding present for her husband.

In another place we have remarked upon the prose works of Matthew Arnold. In many ways he was the chief literary figure of the Victorian age, for he is almost equally distinguished as essayist and as poet. More than any other poet of his generation he brought into English literature the results of his training in the Greek classics. More and more his poems are coming to be admired for their excellent balance of emotion, observation, imagination, and thought.

The middle of the nineteenth century saw the rise of a group of poets in London who were interested almost as much in art as in literature. They formed the Pre-Raphaelite Brotherhood and banded together to take their artistic inspiration from the simpler painters who had preceded Raphael. Typical of this group was Dante Gabriel Rossetti, who was artist as well as poet. Beauty of color and form is his interest always. Even with religious subjects he is likely to be ornate. His contemporaries called him "fleshly." Though his poems have much beauty, they have suffered in their final reputation because they have little else.

Rossetti's sister, Christina, is by many critics ranked at the head of all women poets of England. She has little, if anything, in common with her brother. She was a person of extraordinary piety, and a large proportion of her poems are devotional and utterly lacking in artistic value. In several poems she expresses with great poignancy her self-abnegation in the face of a hopeless love. She is also the author of a beautiful group of lilting songs for children.

Not all the Pre-Raphaelite poets found their artistic expression in painting. William Morris engaged in almost all other branches of art, particularly fine printing, interior decorating, and the making of beautiful furniture. He was one of the most voluminous of English poets and one of the most skillful writers of the metrical tale. In one of his poems he speaks of himself as "an idle singer of an empty day," but as a matter of fact he took great interest in the life of his time. Though he looked longingly back to the Middle Ages, or let his imagination wander with Jason or Sigurd on their marvelous adventures, he was actively engaged in trying to improve artistic taste and in forwarding the cause of socialism.

Rather more loosely associated with the group was Algernon Charles Swinburne. In his metrical virtuosity and his lusciousness of poetic phrase and imagery he resembles his friend Rossetti. Our present age has been prone to see many weaknesses in his work: the overuse of poetic devices, such as alliteration; the writing of lines that are really nonsense in the desire for a beautiful sound effect; the inability to say much in little, so that his poems repeat themselves and drag tediously on; and finally the fact that he had little to say. While most of this is true, it must not be forgotten that Swinburne expresses real social and philosophical convictions. His is the best poetic statement of the philosophy of Positivism, which to many serious thinkers of his generation seemed the proper solution of the religious conflict we have already mentioned. Swinburne was also interested in the spread of political liberty throughout the world.

As the century wore on toward its close, the forces of Victorianism gradually spent themselves. Before a discussion of two of the later poets, it must be remarked that the age of Victoria produced a number of great novelists. It is a matter of regret that an anthology such as this cannot give examples of the work of such writers of fiction as Dickens, Thackeray, George Eliot, the Brontë sisters, Meredith, and Hardy, not to speak of many important novelists not quite so well known.

We are representing the last decade of the nineteenth century by the poetry of Henley and Housman. Some of Henley's poems were written twenty years earlier than this, but most of them are definitely post-Victorian in spirit. In spite of the fact that he was a cripple, Henley was one of the most robust writers of his time. His poetry ranges from the heroic expression of stoicism in his *Invictus* to the beautiful love lyric, *A Bowl of Roses,* and the calm serenity of *Margaritæ Sorori.*

It was, of course, in this decade that Rudyard Kipling achieved his great popularity, but just as the extravagant acclaim given his red-blooded poems in the nineties has diminished with each year, so a small volume of lyrics which came unnoticed from the press in 1896 has claimed our attention more and more until most critics are finding that Kipling must give way to A. E. Housman as the principal poet of the end of the century. *A Shropshire Lad* contains fewer than fifty poems, and none of them is long. They are expressed in extremely simple language and frequently in such melodious words that the reader may conclude that they are lacking in thought. On further study he will find that they are very closely packed with meaning and especially that the last two lines of many of the poems display the poem's whole philosophy. The vein of pessimism throughout the volume shows a kinship to our own day, and it is entirely possible that that quality contributes to its current popularity. Even the most conservative critic, however, must agree that English poetry was far from dead when it could produce *A Shropshire Lad.*

ALFRED, LORD TENNYSON

Choric Song from the Lotos-Eaters

I

There is sweet music here that softer falls
Than petals from blown roses on the grass,
Or night-dews on still waters between walls
Of shadowy granite, in a gleaming pass;
Music that gentlier on the spirit lies,   5
Than tired eyelids upon tired eyes;
Music that brings sweet sleep down from the blissful skies.
Here are cool mosses deep,
And through the moss the ivies creep,   9
And in the stream the long-leaved flowers weep,
And from the craggy ledge the poppy hangs in sleep.

II

Why are we weighed upon with heaviness,
And utterly consumed with sharp distress,
While all things else have rest from weariness?
All things have rest; why should we toil alone,   15
We only toil, who are the first of things,
And make perpetual moan,
Still from one sorrow to another thrown;
Nor ever fold our wings,
And cease from wanderings,   20
Nor steep our brows in slumber's holy balm;
Nor harken what the inner spirit sings,
"There is no joy but calm!"—
Why should we only toil, the roof and crown of things?

III

Lo! in the middle of the wood,   25
The folded leaf is wooed from out the bud
With winds upon the branch, and there
Grows green and broad, and takes no care,
Sun-steeped at noon, and in the moon
Nightly dew-fed; and turning yellow   30

Tennyson, *Choric Song from the Lotos-Eaters*. Alfred Tennyson (1809-1892) was born in Surrey, the son of an English clergyman. Soon after completing his university work at Cambridge he began writing poetry. Appointed Poet Laureate in 1850, he was raised to the peerage in 1884. See the account of the Lotos-Eaters in *The Odyssey*, p. 71 above.

Falls, and floats adown the air.
Lo! sweetened with the summer light,
The full-juiced apple, waxing over-mellow,
Drops in a silent autumn night.
All its allotted length of days　　　35
The flower ripens in its place,
Ripens and fades, and falls, and hath no toil,
Fast-rooted in the fruitful soil.

IV

Hateful is the dark-blue sky,
Vaulted o'er the dark-blue sea.　　　40
Death is the end of life; ah, why
Should life all labor be?
Let us alone. Time driveth onward fast,
And in a little while our lips are dumb.
Let us alone. What is it that will last?　　　45
All things are taken from us, and become
Portions and parcels of the dreadful past.
Let us alone. What pleasure can we have
To war with evil? Is there any peace
In ever climbing up the climbing wave?　　　50
All things have rest, and ripen toward the grave
In silence—ripen, fall, and cease.
Give us long rest or death, dark death, or dream-
　　ful ease.

V

How sweet it were, hearing the downward stream,
With half-shut eyes ever to seem　　　55
Falling asleep in a half-dream!
To dream and dream, like yonder amber light,
Which will not leave the myrrh-bush on the
　　height;
To hear each other's whispered speech;
Eating the Lotos day by day,　　　60
To watch the crisping ripples on the beach,
And tender curving lines of creamy spray;
To lend our hearts and spirits wholly
To the influence of mild-minded melancholy;
To muse and brood and live again in memory,　　65
With those old faces of our infancy
Heaped over with a mound of grass,
Two handfuls of white dust, shut in an urn of
　　brass!

VI

Dear is the memory of our wedded lives,
And dear the last embraces of our wives　　70
And their warm tears; but all hath suffered
　　change;
For surely now our household hearths are cold,
Our sons inherit us, our looks are strange,

And we should come like ghosts to trouble joy.
Or else the island princes over-bold　　　75
Have eat our substance, and the minstrel sings
Before them of the ten years' war in Troy,
And our great deeds, as half-forgotten things.
Is there confusion in the little isle?
Let what is broken so remain.　　　80
The gods are hard to reconcile;
'Tis hard to settle order once again.
There is confusion worse than death,
Trouble on trouble, pain on pain,
Long labor unto aged breath,　　　85
Sore task to hearts worn out by many wars
And eyes grown dim with gazing on the pilot-
　　stars.

VII

But, propped on beds of amaranth and moly,[1]
How sweet—while warm airs lull us, blowing
　　lowly—
With half-dropped eyelid still,　　　90
Beneath a heaven dark and holy,
To watch the long bright river drawing slowly
His waters from the purple hill—
To hear the dewy echoes calling
From cave to cave through the thick-twined
　　vine—　　　95
To watch the emerald-colored water falling
Through many a woven acanthus-wreath divine!
Only to hear and see the far-off sparkling brine,
Only to hear were sweet, stretched out beneath the
　　pine.

VIII

The Lotos blooms below the barren peak,　　100
The Lotos blows by every winding creek;
All day the wind breathes low with mellower
　　tone;
Through every hollow cave and alley lone
Round and round the spicy downs the yellow
　　Lotos-dust is blown.
We have had enough of action, and of motion
　　we,　　　105
Rolled to starboard, rolled to larboard, when the
　　surge was seething free,
Where the wallowing monster spouted his foam-
　　fountains in the sea.
Let us swear an oath, and keep it with an equal
　　mind,
In the hollow Lotos-land to live and lie reclined
On the hills like gods together, careless of man-
　　kind.　　　110

---

[1] Moly was a magic plant mentioned in *The Odyssey*.

For they lie beside their nectar, and the bolts are
    hurled
Far below them in the valleys, and the clouds are
    lightly curled
Round their golden houses, girdled with the
    gleaming world;
Where they smile in secret, looking over wasted
    lands,
Blight and famine, plague and earthquake, roar-
    ing deeps and fiery sands,   115
Clanging fights, and flaming towns, and sinking
    ships, and praying hands.
But they smile, they find a music centered in a
    doleful song
Steaming up, a lamentation and an ancient tale
    of wrong,
Like a tale of little meaning though the words
    are strong;
Chanted from an ill-used race of men that cleave
    the soil,   120
Sow the seed, and reap the harvest with enduring
    toil,
Storing yearly little dues of wheat, and wine and
    oil;
Till they perish and they suffer—some, 'tis whis-
    pered—down in hell
Suffer endless anguish, others in Elysian valleys
    dwell,
Resting weary limbs at last on beds of asphodel.
Surely, surely, slumber is more sweet than toil, the
    shore   126
Than labor in the deep mid-ocean, wind and wave
    and oar;
Oh, rest ye, brother mariners, we will not wander
    more.

Ulysses

It little profits that an idle king,
By this still hearth, among these barren crags,
Matched with an aged wife, I mete and dole
Unequal laws unto a savage race,
That hoard, and sleep, and feed, and know not
    me.   5
I cannot rest from travel. I will drink
Life to the lees. All times I have enjoyed
Greatly, have suffered greatly, both with those
That loved me, and alone; on shore, and when
Through scudding drifts the rainy Hyades   10
Vexed the dim sea. I am become a name;
For always roaming with a hungry heart
Much have I seen and known; cities of men,
And manners, climates, councils, governments,
Myself not least, but honored of them all;   15
And drunk delight of battle with my peers,
Far on the ringing plains of windy Troy.
I am a part of all that I have met.
Yet all experience is an arch wherethrough
Gleams that untraveled world, whose margin
    fades   20
Forever and forever when I move.
How dull it is to pause, to make an end,
To rust unburnished, not to shine in use!
As though to breathe were life. Life piled on life
Were all too little, and of one to me   25
Little remains. But every hour is saved
From that eternal silence, something more,
A bringer of new things; and vile it were
For some three suns to store and hoard myself,
And this gray spirit yearning in desire   30
To follow knowledge like a sinking star,
Beyond the utmost bound of human thought.
    This is my son, mine own Telemachus,
To whom I leave the scepter and the isle—
Well-loved of me, discerning to fulfill   35
This labor, by slow prudence to make mild
A rugged people, and through soft degrees
Subdue them to the useful and the good.
Most blameless is he, centered in the sphere
Of common duties, decent not to fail   40
In offices of tenderness, and pay
Meet adoration to my household gods,
When I am gone. He works his work, I mine.
    There lies the port; the vessel puffs her sail;
There gloom the dark broad seas. My mariners,
Souls that have toiled, and wrought, and thought
    with me—   46
That ever with a frolic welcome took
The thunder and the sunshine, and opposed
Free hearts, free foreheads—you and I are old;
Old age hath yet his honor and his toil;   50
Death closes all. But something ere the end,
Some work of noble note, may yet be done,
Not unbecoming men that strove with gods.
The lights begin to twinkle from the rocks;
The long day wanes; the slow moon climbs; the
    deep   55
Moans round with many voices. Come, my friends,
'Tis not too late to seek a newer world.
Push off, and sitting well in order smite
The sounding furrows; for my purpose holds
To sail beyond the sunset, and the baths   60
Of all the western stars, until I die.
It may be that the gulfs will wash us down;
It may be we shall touch the Happy Isles,

And see the great Achilles, whom we knew. 64
Though much is taken, much abides; and though
We are not now that strength which in old days
Moved earth and heaven, that which we are, we
    are;
One equal temper of heroic hearts,
Made weak by time and fate, but strong in will
To strive, to seek, to find, and not to yield. 70

Break, Break, Break

Break, break, break,
    On thy cold gray stones, O Sea!
And I would that my tongue could utter
    The thoughts that arise in me.

O, well for the fisherman's boy,   5
    That he shouts with his sister at play!
O, well for the sailor lad,
    That he sings in his boat on the bay!

And the stately ships go on
    To their haven under the hill;   10
But O for the touch of a vanish'd hand,
    And the sound of a voice that is still!

Break, break, break,
    At the foot of thy crags, O Sea!
But the tender grace of a day that is dead   15
    Will never come back to me.

Lyrics from The Princess

Tears, idle tears, I know not what they mean,
Tears from the depth of some divine despair
Rise in the heart, and gather to the eyes,
In looking on the happy autumn-fields,
And thinking of the days that are no more.   5

Fresh as the first beam glittering on a sail,
That brings our friends up from the underworld,
Sad as the last which reddens over one
That sinks with all we love below the verge;
So sad, so fresh, the days that are no more. 10

Ah, sad and strange as in dark summer dawns
The earliest pipe of half-awaken'd birds
To dying ears, when unto dying eyes
The casement slowly grows a glimmering square;
So sad, so strange, the days that are no more. 15

Dear as remember'd kisses after death,
And sweet as those by hopeless fancy feign'd
On lips that are for others; deep as love,
Deep as first love, and wild with all regret;
O Death in Life, the days that are no more!   20

———

Sweet and low, sweet and low,
    Wind of the western sea,
Low, low, breathe and blow,
    Wind of the western sea!
Over the rolling waters go,   5
Come from the dying moon, and blow,
    Blow him again to me:
While my little one, while my pretty one, sleeps.

Sleep and rest, sleep and rest,
    Father will come to thee soon;   10
Rest, rest, on mother's breast,
    Father will come to thee soon;
Father will come to his babe in the nest,
Silver sails all out of the west
    Under the silver moon;   15
Sleep, my little one, sleep, my pretty one, sleep.

———

The splendor falls on castle walls
    And snowy summits old in story;
The long light shakes across the lakes,
    And the wild cataract leaps in glory.
Blow, bugle, blow, set the wild echoes flying, 5
Blow, bugle; answer, echoes, dying, dying, dying.

Oh, hark, oh, hear! how thin and clear,
    And thinner, clearer, farther going!
Oh, sweet and far from cliff and scar
    The horns of Elfland faintly blowing!   10
Blow, let us hear the purple glens replying,
Blow, bugle; answer, echoes, dying, dying, dying.

O love, they die in yon rich sky,
    They faint on hill or field or river;
Our echoes roll from soul to soul,   15
    And grow forever and forever.
Blow, bugle, blow, set the wild echoes flying,
And answer, echoes, answer, dying, dying, dying.

———

Home they brought her warrior dead;
    She nor swoon'd nor utter'd cry.
All her maidens, watching, said,
    "She must weep or she will die."

Then they praised him, soft and low,   5
   Call'd him worthy to be loved,
Truest friend and noblest foe;
   Yet she neither spoke nor moved.

Stole a maiden from her place,
   Lightly to the warrior stepped,   10
Took the face-cloth from the face;
   Yet she neither moved nor wept.

Rose a nurse of ninety years,
   Set his child upon her knee—
Like summer tempest came her tears—   15
   "Sweet my child, I live for thee."

In Memoriam A. H. H.

PROEM

Strong Son of God, immortal Love,
   Whom we, that have not seen thy face,
   By faith, and faith alone, embrace,
Believing where we cannot prove;

Thine are these orbs of light and shade;   5
   Thou madest Life in man and brute;
   Thou madest Death; and lo, thy foot
Is on the skull which thou hast made.

Thou wilt not leave us in the dust:
   Thou madest man, he knows not why,   10
   He thinks he was not made to die;
And thou hast made him; thou art just.

Thou seemest human and divine,
   The highest, holiest manhood, thou.
   Our wills are ours, we know not how;   15
Our wills are ours, to make them thine.

Our little systems have their day;
   They have their day and cease to be;
   They are but broken lights of thee,
And thou, O Lord, art more than they.   20

We have but faith; we cannot know,
   For knowledge is of things we see;
   And yet we trust it comes from thee,
A beam in darkness; let it grow.

Let knowledge grow from more to more,   25
   But more of reverence in us dwell;
   That mind and soul, according well,
May make one music as before.

But vaster. We are fools and slight;
   We mock thee when we do not fear.   30
   But help thy foolish ones to bear;
Help thy vain worlds to bear thy light.

Forgive what seemed my sin in me,
   What seemed my worth since I began;
   For merit lives from man to man,   35
And not from man, O Lord, to thee.

Forgive my grief for one removed,
   Thy creature, whom I found so fair.
   I trust he lives in thee, and there
I find him worthier to be loved.   40

Forgive these wild and wandering cries,
   Confusions of a wasted youth;
   Forgive them where they fail in truth,
And in thy wisdom make me wise.

V

I sometimes hold it half a sin
   To put in words the grief I feel;
   For words, like Nature, half reveal
And half conceal the Soul within.

But, for the unquiet heart and brain,   5
   A use in measured language lies;
   The sad mechanic exercise,
Like dull narcotics, numbing pain.

In words, like weeds, I'll wrap me o'er
   Like coarsest clothes against the cold;   10
   But that large grief which these enfold
Is given in outline and no more.

XXVII

I envy not in any moods
   The captive void of noble rage,
   The linnet born within the cage,
That never knew the summer woods;

I envy not the beast that takes   5
   His license in the field of time,
   Unfetter'd by the sense of crime,
To whom a conscience never wakes;

Nor, what may count itself as blest,
   The heart that never plighted troth   10
   But stagnates in the weeds of sloth;
Nor any want-begotten rest.

I hold it true, whate'er befall;
  I feel it, when I sorrow most;
  'Tis better to have loved and lost   15
Than never to have loved at all.

LIV

O, yet we trust that somehow good
  Will be the final goal of ill,
  To pangs of nature, sins of will,
Defects of doubt, and taints of blood;

That nothing walks with aimless feet;   5
  That not one life shall be destroy'd,
  Or cast as rubbish to the void,
When God hath made the pile complete;

That not a worm is cloven in vain;
  That not a moth with vain desire   10
  Is shrivel'd in a fruitless fire,
Or but subserves another's gain.

Behold, we know not anything;
  I can but trust that good shall fall
  At last—far off—at last, to all,   15
And every winter change to spring.

So runs my dream; but what am I?
  An infant crying in the night;
  An infant crying for the light,
And with no language but a cry.   20

LV

The wish, that of the living whole
  No life may fail beyond the grave,
  Derives it not from what we have
The likest God within the soul?

Are God and Nature then at strife,   5
  That Nature lends such evil dreams?
  So careful of the type she seems,
So careless of the single life,

That I, considering everywhere
  Her secret meaning in her deeds,   10
  And finding that of fifty seeds
She often brings but one to bear,

I falter where I firmly trod,
  And falling with my weight of cares
  Upon the great world's altar-stairs   15
That slope thro' darkness up to God,

I stretch lame hands of faith, and grope,
  And gather dust and chaff, and call
  To what I feel is Lord of all,
And faintly trust the larger hope.   20

LVI

"So careful of the type?" but no.
  From scarped cliff and quarried stone
  She cries, "A thousand types are gone;
I care for nothing, all shall go.

"Thou makest thine appeal to me: 5
  I bring to life, I bring to death;
  The spirit does but mean the breath:
I know no more." And he, shall he,

Man, her last work, who seem'd so fair,
  Such splendid purpose in his eyes,   10
  Who roll'd the psalm to wintry skies,
Who built him fanes of fruitless prayer,

Who trusted God was love indeed
  And love Creation's final law—
  Tho' Nature, red in tooth and claw   15
With ravine, shriek'd against his creed—

Who loved, who suffer'd countless ills
  Who battled for the True, the Just
  Be blown about the desert dust,
Or seal'd within the iron hills?   20

No more? A monster then, a dream,
  A discord. Dragons of the prime,
  That tear each other in their slime,
Were mellow music match'd with him.

O life as futile, then, as frail!   25
  O for thy voice to soothe and bless!
  What hope of answer, or redress?
Behind the veil, behind the veil.

CXXIII

There rolls the deep where grew the tree.
  O earth, what changes hast thou seen!
  There where the long street roars hath been
The stillness of the central sea.

The hills are shadows, and they flow   5
  From form to form, and nothing stands;
  They melt like mist, the solid lands,
Like clouds they shape themselves and go.

But in my spirit will I dwell,
  And dream my dream, and hold it true;   10
  For tho' my lips may breathe adieu,
I cannot think the thing farewell.

Flower in the Crannied Wall

Flower in the crannied wall,
I pluck you out of the crannies,
I hold you here, root and all, in my hand,
Little flower—but *if* I could understand
What you are, root and all, and all in all,
I should know what God and man is.

Crossing the Bar

Sunset and evening star,
  And one clear call for me!

And may there be no moaning of the bar,
  When I put out to sea,

But such a tide as moving seems asleep,
  Too full for sound and foam,
When that which drew from out the boundless
    deep
  Turns again home.

Twilight and evening bell,
  And after that the dark!   10
And may there be no sadness of farewell,
  When I embark;

For tho' from out our bourne of Time and Place
  The flood may bear me far,
I hope to see my Pilot face to face   15
  When I have crossed the bar.

ROBERT BROWNING

Porphyria's Lover

The rain set early in tonight,
  The sullen wind was soon awake,
It tore the elm-tops down for spite,
  And did its worst to vex the lake:
I listened with heart fit to break.   5
When glided in Porphyria; straight
  She shut the cold out and the storm,
And kneeled and made the cheerless grate
  Blaze up, and all the cottage warm;
Which done, she rose, and from her form   10
Withdrew the dripping cloak and shawl,
  And laid her soiled gloves by, untied
Her hat and let the damp hair fall,
  And, last, she sat down by my side
And called me. When no voice replied,   15
She put my arm about her waist,
  And made her smooth white shoulder bare
And all her yellow hair displaced,
  And, stooping, made my cheek lie there,
And spread, o'er all, her yellow hair,   20
Murmuring how she loved me—she
  Too weak, for all her heart's endeavor,

To set its struggling passion free
  From pride, and vainer ties dissever,
And give herself to me forever.   25
But passion sometimes would prevail,
  Nor could tonight's gay feast restrain
A sudden thought of one so pale
  For love of her, and all in vain:
So, she was come through wind and rain.   30
Be sure I looked up at her eyes
  Happy and proud; at last I knew
Porphyria worshiped me; surprise
  Made my heart swell, and still it grew
While I debated what to do.   35
That moment she was mine, mine, fair,
  Perfectly pure and good: I found
A thing to do, and all her hair
  In one long yellow string I wound
Three times her little throat around,   40
  And strangled her. No pain felt she;
  I am quite sure she felt no pain.
As a shut bud that holds a bee,
  I warily oped her lids; again
Laughed the blue eyes without a stain.   45
And I untightened next the tress

Browning, *Porphyria's Lover*. Robert Browning (1812-1889) was the son of a London banker. He
married Elizabeth Barrett in 1846, after which he lived some years in Italy. His poetic career extends
over nearly sixty years.

About her neck; her cheek once more
Blushed bright beneath my burning kiss:
I propped her head up as before,
Only, this time my shoulder bore   50
Her head, which droops upon it still:
    The smiling rosy little head,
So glad it has its utmost will,
    That all it scorned at once is fled,
And I, its love, am gained instead!   55
Porphyria's love: she guessed not how
    Her darling one wish would be heard.
And thus we sit together now,
    And all night long we have not stirred,
And yet God has not said a word!   60

My Last Duchess

That's my last Duchess painted on the wall,
Looking as if she were alive. I call
That piece a wonder, now. Fra Pandolf's hands
Worked busily a day, and there she stands.
Will't please you sit and look at her? I said   5
"Fra Pandolf" by design, for never read
Strangers like you that pictured countenance,
The depth and passion of its earnest glance,
But to myself they turned—since none puts by
The curtain I have drawn for you, but I—   10
And seemed as they would ask me, if they durst,
How such a glance came there; so, not the first
Are you to turn and ask thus. Sir, 'twas not
Her husband's presence only called that spot
Of joy into the Duchess' cheek. Perhaps   15
Fra Pandolf chanced to say, "Her mantle laps
Over my lady's wrist too much," or "Paint
Must never hope to reproduce the faint
Half-flush that dies along her throat"; such stuff
Was courtesy, she thought, and cause enough   20
For calling up that spot of joy. She had
A heart—how shall I say?—too soon made glad,
Too easily impressed; she liked whate'er
She looked on, and her looks went everywhere.
Sir, 'twas all one! My favor at her breast,   25
The dropping of the daylight in the west,
The bough of cherries some officious fool
Broke in the orchard for her, the white mule
She rode with round the terrace—all and each
Would draw from her alike the approving
    speech,   30
Or blush, at least. She thanked men—good! but
    thanked
Somehow—I know not how—as if she ranked
My gift of a nine-hundred-years-old name
With anybody's gift. Who'd stoop to blame

This sort of trifling? Even had you skill   35
In speech—which I have not—to make your will
Quite clear to such an one, and say, "Just this
Or that in you disgusts me; here you miss,
Or there exceed, the mark"—and if she let
Herself be lessoned so, nor plainly set   40
Her wits to yours, forsooth, and made excuse,
—E'en then would be some stooping; and I choose
Never to stoop. Oh, sir, she smiled, no doubt,
Whene'er I passed her; but who passed without
Much the same smile? This grew; I gave com-
    mands;   45
Then all smiles stopped together. There she stands
As if alive. Will't please you rise? We'll meet
The company below then. I repeat,
The Count your master's known munificence
Is ample warrant that no just pretense   50
Of mine for dowry will be disallowed;
Though his fair daughter's self, as I avowed
At starting, is my object. Nay, we'll go
Together down, sir. Notice Neptune, though,
Taming a sea-horse, thought a rarity,   55
Which Claus of Innsbruck cast in bronze for me!

Evelyn Hope

Beautiful Evelyn Hope is dead!
    Sit and watch by her side an hour.
That is her book-shelf, this her bed;
    She plucked that piece of geranium-flower,
Beginning to die too, in the glass;   5
    Little has yet been changed, I think:
The shutters are shut, no light may pass
    Save two long rays through the hinge's chink.

Sixteen years old when she died!
    Perhaps she had scarcely heard my name;   10
It was not her time to love; beside,
    Her life had many a hope and aim,
Duties enough and little cares,
    And now was quiet, now astir,
Till God's hand beckoned unawares,—   15
    And the sweet white brow is all of her.

Is it too late then, Evelyn Hope?
    What, your soul was pure and true,
The good stars met in your horoscope,
    Made you of spirit, fire and dew—   20
And, just because I was thrice as old
    And our paths in the world diverged so wide,
Each was naught to each, must I be told?
    We were fellow mortals, naught beside?

No, indeed! for God above   25
   Is great to grant, as mighty to make,
And creates the love to reward the love:
   I claim you still, for my own love's sake!
Delayed it may be for more lives yet,
   Through worlds I shall traverse, not a few: 30
Much is to learn, much to forget
   Ere the time be come for taking you.

But the time will come—at last it will,
   When, Evelyn Hope, what meant (I shall say)
In the lower earth, in the years long still,   35
   That body and soul so pure and gay?
Why your hair was amber, I shall divine,
   And your mouth of your own geranium's red—
And what you would do with me, in fine,
   In the new life come in the old life's stead.   40

I have lived (I shall say) so much since then,
   Given up myself so many times,
Gained me the gains of various men,
   Ransacked the ages, spoiled the climes;
Yet one thing, one, in my soul's full scope,   45
   Either I missed or itself missed me:
And I want and find you, Evelyn Hope!
   What is the issue? Let us see!

I loved you, Evelyn, all the while!
   My heart seemed full as it could hold;   50
There was place and to spare for the frank young
     smile,
   And the red young mouth, and the hair's young
     gold.
So, hush,—I will give you this leaf to keep:
   See, I shut it inside the sweet cold hand!
There, that is our secret: go to sleep!   55
   You will wake, and remember, and understand.

My Star

All that I know
   Of a certain star
Is, it can throw
   (Like the angled spar)
Now a dart of red,   5
   Now a dart of blue;
Till my friends have said
   They would fain see, too,
My star that dartles the red and the blue!
Then it stops like a bird; like a flower, hangs
     furled: 10
They must solace themselves with the Saturn
     above it.

What matter to me if their star is a world?
   Mine has opened its soul to me; therefore I
   love it.

The Last Ride Together

I said—Then, dearest, since 'tis so,
Since now at length my fate I know,
Since nothing all my love avails,
Since all, my life seemed meant for, fails,
   Since this was written and needs must be—   5
My whole heart rises up to bless
Your name in pride and thankfulness!
Take back the hope you gave,—I claim
Only a memory of the same,
  —And this beside, if you will not blame,   10
   Your leave for one more last ride with me.

My mistress bent that brow of hers;
Those deep dark eyes where pride demurs
When pity would be softening through,
Fixed me a breathing-while or two   15
   With life or death in the balance: right!
The blood replenished me again;
My last thought was at least not vain:
I and my mistress, side by side
Shall be together, breathe and ride,   20
So, one day more am I deified.
   Who knows but the world may end tonight?

Hush! if you saw some western cloud
All billowy-bosomed, over-bowed
By many benedictions—sun's   25
And moon's and evening-star's at once—
   And so, you, looking and loving best,
Conscious grew, your passion drew
Cloud, sunset, moonrise, star-shine too,
Down on you, near and yet more near,   30
Till flesh must fade for heaven was here!—
Thus leant she and lingered—joy and fear!
   Thus lay she a moment on my breast.

Then we began to ride. My soul
Smoothed itself out, a long-cramped scroll   35
Freshening and fluttering in the wind.
Past hopes already lay behind.
   What need to strive with a life awry?
Had I said that, had I done this?
So might I gain, so might I miss.   40
Might she have loved me? just as well
She might have hated, who can tell!
Where had I been now if the worst befell?
   And here we are riding, she and I.

Fail I alone, in words and deeds? 45
Why, all men strive, and who succeeds?
We rode; it seemed, my spirit flew,
Saw other regions, cities new,
   As the world rushed by on either side.
I thought,—All labor, yet no less 50
Bear up beneath their unsuccess,
Look at the end of work, contrast
The petty done, the undone vast,
This present of theirs with the hopeful past!
   I hoped she would love me; here we ride. 55

What hand and brain went ever paired?
What heart alike conceived and dared?
What act proved all its thought had been?
What will but felt the fleshly screen?
   We ride and I see her bosom heave. 60
There's many a crown for us who can reach.
Ten lines, a statesman's life in each!
The flag stuck on a heap of bones,
A soldier's doing! what atones?
They scratch his name on the Abbey-stones. 65
   My riding is better, by their leave.

What does it all mean, poet? Well.
Your brains beat into rhythm, you tell
What we felt only; you expressed
You hold things beautiful the best, 70
   And place them in rhyme so, side by side.
'Tis something, nay 'tis much: but then,
Have you yourself what's best for men?
Are you—poor, sick, old ere your time—
Nearer one whit your own sublime 75
Than we who never have turned a rhyme?
   Sing, riding's a joy. For me, I ride.

And you, great sculptor—so, you gave
A score of years to Art, her slave,
And that's your Venus, whence we turn 80
To yonder girl that fords the burn!
   You acquiesce, and shall I repine?
What, man of music, you grown gray
With notes and nothing else to say,
Is this your sole praise from a friend, 85
"Greatly his opera's strains intend,
But in music we know how fashions end!"
   I gave my youth; but we ride, in fine.

Who knows what's fit for us? Had fate
Proposed bliss here should sublimate 90
My being—had I signed the bond—
Still one must lead some life beyond,
   Have a bliss to die with, dim-descried.

This foot once planted on the goal,
This glory-garland round my soul, 95
Could I descry such? Try and test!
I sink back shuddering from the quest.
Earth being so good, would heaven seem best?
   Now, heaven and she are beyond this ride.

And yet—she has not spoke so long! 100
What if heaven be that, fair and strong
At life's best, with our eyes upturned
Whither life's flower is first discerned,
   We, fixed so, ever should so abide?
What if we still ride on, we two, 105
With life forever old yet new,
Changed not in kind but in degree,
The instant made eternity,—
And heaven just prove that I and she
   Ride, ride together, forever ride? 110

Rabbi Ben Ezra

Grow old along with me!
The best is yet to be,
The last of life, for which the first was made.
Our times are in his hand
Who saith, "A whole I planned; 5
Youth shows but half. Trust God; see all, nor be
   afraid!"

Not that, amassing flowers,
Youth sighed, "Which rose make ours,
Which lily leave and then as best recall?"
Not that, admiring stars, 10
It yearned, "Nor Jove, nor Mars;
Mine be some figured flame which blends, tran-
   scends them all!"

Not for such hopes and fears
Annulling youth's brief years,
Do I remonstrate; folly wide the mark! 15
Rather I prize the doubt
Low kinds exist without,
Finished and finite clods, untroubled by a spark.

Poor vaunt of life indeed,
Were man but formed to feed 20
On joy, to solely seek and find and feast.
Such feasting ended, then
As sure an end to men;
Irks care the crop-full bird? Frets doubt the maw-
   crammed beast?

Rejoice we are allied   25
To that which doth provide
And not partake, effect and not receive!
A spark disturbs our clod;
Nearer we hold of God
Who gives, than of his tribes that take, I must
    believe.   30

Then, welcome each rebuff
That turns earth's smoothness rough,
Each sting that bids nor sit nor stand but go!
Be our joys three-parts pain!
Strive, and hold cheap the strain;   35
Learn, nor account the pang; dare, never grudge
    the throe!

For thence—a paradox
Which comforts while it mocks—
Shall life succeed in that it seems to fail.
What I aspired to be,   40
And was not, comforts me;
A brute I might have been, but would not sink i'
    the scale.

What is he but a brute
Whose flesh has soul to suit,
Whose spirit works lest arms and legs want play?
To man, propose this test—   46
Thy body at its best,
How far can that project thy soul on its lone way?

Yet gifts should prove their use.
I own the Past profuse   50
Of power each side, perfection every turn;
Eyes, ears took in their dole,
Brain treasured up the whole;
Should not the heart beat once "How good to live
    and learn!"

Not once beat "Praise be thine!   55
I see the whole design,
I, who saw power, see now love perfect too.
Perfect I call thy plan;
Thanks that I was a man!
Maker, remake, complete—I trust what thou shalt
    do"?   60

For pleasant is this flesh;
Our soul, in its rose-mesh
Pulled ever to the earth, still yearns for rest.
Would we some prize might hold
To match those manifold   65
Possessions of the brute—gain most, as we did
    best!

Let us not always say,
"Spite of this flesh today
I strove, made head, gained ground upon the
    whole!"
As the bird wings and sings,   70
Let us cry, "All good things
Are ours, nor soul helps flesh more, now, than
    flesh helps soul!"

Therefore I summon age
To grant youth's heritage,
Life's struggle having so far reached its term.   75
Thence shall I pass, approved
A man, for aye removed
From the developed brute; a god, though in the
    germ.

And I shall thereupon
Take rest, ere I be gone   80
Once more on my adventure brave and new;
Fearless and unperplexed,
When I wage battle next,
What weapons to select, what armor to indue.

Youth ended, I shall try   85
My gain or loss thereby;
Leave the fire ashes, what survives is gold.
And I shall weigh the same,
Give life its praise or blame.   89
Young, all lay in dispute; I shall know, being old.

For note, when evening shuts,
A certain moment cuts
The deed off, calls the glory from the gray.
A whisper from the west
Shoots—"Add this to the rest,   95
Take it and try its worth. Here dies another day."

So, still within this life,
Though lifted o'er its strife,
Let me discern, compare, pronounce at last,
"This rage was right i' the main,   100
That acquiescence vain;
The Future I may face now I have proved the
    Past."

For more is not reserved
To man, with soul just nerved
To act tomorrow what he learns today.   105
Here, work enough to watch
The Master work, and catch
Hints of the proper craft, tricks of the tool's true
    play.

As it was better, youth
Should strive, through acts uncouth, 110
Toward making, than repose on aught found
    made:
So, better, age, exempt
From strife, should know, than tempt
Further. Thou waitedst age; wait death nor be
    afraid!

Enough now, if the Right 115
And Good and Infinite
Be named here, as thou callest thy hand thine own,
With knowledge absolute,
Subject to no dispute
From fools that crowded youth, nor let thee feel
    alone. 120

Be there, for once and all,
Severed great minds from small,
Announced to each his station in the Past!
Was I, the world arraigned,
Were they, my soul disdained, 125
Right? Let age speak the truth and give us peace
    at last!

Now, who shall arbitrate?
Ten men love what I hate,
Shun what I follow, slight what I receive;
Ten, who in ears and eyes 130
Match me. We all surmise,
They this thing, and I that; whom shall my soul
    believe?

Not on the vulgar mass
Called "work," must sentence pass,
Things done, that took the eye and had the price;
O'er which, from level stand, 136
The low world laid its hand,
Found straightway to its mind, could value in a
    trice.

But all, the world's coarse thumb
And finger failed to plumb, 140
So passed in making up the main account;
All instincts immature,
All purposes unsure,
That weighed not as his work, yet swelled the
    man's amount:

Thoughts hardly to be packed 145
Into a narrow act,
Fancies that broke through language and escaped;

All I could never be,
All, men ignored in me,
This I was worth to God, whose wheel the pitcher
    shaped. 150

Aye, note that Potter's wheel,
That metaphor! and feel
Why time spins fast, why passive lies our clay—
Thou, to whom fools propound,
When the wine makes its round, 155
"Since life fleets, all is change; the Past gone, seize
    today!"

Fool! All that is, at all,
Lasts ever, past recall;
Earth changes, but thy soul and God stand sure.
What entered into thee, 160
That was, is, and shall be.
Time's wheel runs back or stops; Potter and clay
    endure.

He fixed thee 'mid this dance
Of plastic circumstance;
This Present, thou, forsooth, wouldst fain arrest;
Machinery just meant 166
To give thy soul its bent,
Try thee and turn thee forth, sufficiently im-
    pressed.

What though the earlier grooves,
Which ran the laughing loves 170
Around thy base, no longer pause and press?
What though, about thy rim,
Skull-things in order grim
Grow out, in graver mood, obey the sterner stress?

Look not thou down but up! 175
To uses of a cup,
The festal board, lamp's flash, and trumpet's peal,
The new wine's foaming flow,
The Master's lips aglow!
Thou, heaven's consummate cup, what needst thou
    with earth's wheel? 180

But I need, now as then,
Thee, God, who moldest men;
And since, not even while the whirl was worst,
Did I—to the wheel of life
With shapes and colors rife, 185
Bound dizzily—mistake my end, to slake thy
    thirst.

So, take and use thy work;
  Amend what flaws may lurk,
What strain o' the stuff, what warpings past the
    aim!
My times be in thy hand!   190
  Perfect the cup as planned!
Let age approve of youth, and death complete the
    same!

Prospice [1]

Fear death?—to feel the fog in my throat,
  The mist in my face,
When the snows begin, and the blasts denote
  I am nearing the place,
The power of the night, the press of the storm,
  The post of the foe;   6
Where he stands, the Arch Fear in a visible form,
  Yet the strong man must go;
For the journey is done and the summit attained,
  And the barriers fall,   10
Though a battle's to fight ere the guerdon be
    gained,
  The reward of it all.
I was ever a fighter, so—one fight more,
  The best and the last!
I would hate that death bandaged my eyes, and
    forbore,   15
  And bade me creep past.
No! let me taste the whole of it, fare like my peers,
  The heroes of old,
Bear the brunt, in a minute pay glad life's arrears
  Of pain, darkness, and cold.   20
For sudden the worst turns the best to the brave,
  The black minute's at end,
And the element's rage, the fiend-voices that rave,
  Shall dwindle, shall blend,

Shall change, shall become first a peace out of pain,
  Then a light, then thy breast,   26
O thou soul of my soul! I shall clasp thee again,
  And with God be the rest!

Epilogue to Asolando

At the midnight in the silence of the sleep-time,
  When you set your fancies free,
Will they pass to where—by death, fools think,
    imprisoned—
Low he lies who once so loved you, whom you
    loved so,
      —Pity me?   5

Oh, to love so, be so loved, yet so mistaken!
  What had I on earth to do
With the slothful, with the mawkish, the un-
    manly?
Like the aimless, helpless, hopeless, did I drivel!
      —Being—who?   10

One who never turned his back but marched breast
    forward,
  Never doubted clouds would break,
Never dreamed, though right were worsted, wrong
    would triumph,
Held we fall to rise, are baffled to fight better,
  Sleep to wake.   15

No, at noonday in the bustle of man's work-time
  Greet the unseen with a cheer!
Bid him forward, breast and back as either should
    be,
"Strive and thrive!" cry "Speed—fight on, fare ever
  There as here!"   20

ELIZABETH BARRETT BROWNING

Sonnets from the Portuguese

I

I thought once how Theocritus had sung
Of the sweet years, the dear and wished-for years,

Who each one in a gracious hand appears
To bear a gift for mortals, old or young.
And, as I mused it in his antique tongue,   5
I saw, in gradual vision through my tears,
The sweet, sad years, the melancholy years,

[1] Latin for "look forward."
  Browning, Elizabeth Barrett, *Sonnets from the Portuguese.* Elizabeth Barrett Browning (1806-1861)
was already a noted English poet when she married Robert Browning in 1846. See p. 261 for her translation of Theocritus' *The Cyclops.*

Those of my own life, who by turns had flung
A shadow across me. Straightway I was 'ware,
So weeping, how a mystic Shape did move   10
Behind me, and drew me backward by the hair;
And a voice said in mastery, while I strove—
"Guess now who holds thee?"—"Death," I said.
      But, there,
The silver answer rang—"Not Death, but Love."

VII

The face of all the world is changed, I think,
Since first I heard the footsteps of thy soul
Move still, oh, still, beside me, as they stole
Betwixt me and the dreadful outer brink
Of obvious death, where I, who thought to sink, 5
Was caught up into love, and taught the whole
Of life in a new rhythm. The cup of dole
God gave for baptism, I am fain to drink,
And praise its sweetness, Sweet, with thee anear.
The names of country, heaven, are changed away
For where thou art or shalt be, there or here;   11

And this . . . this lute and song . . . loved yester-
      day,
(The singing angels know) are only dear
Because thy name moves right in what they say.

XLIII

How do I love thee? Let me count the ways.
I love thee to the depth and breadth and height
My soul can reach, when feeling out of sight
For the ends of Being and ideal Grace.
I love thee to the level of every day's   5
Most quiet need, by sun and candlelight.
I love thee freely, as men strive for Right;
I love thee purely, as they turn from Praise.
I love thee with the passion put to use
In my old griefs, and with my childhood's faith.
I love thee with a love I seemed to lose   11
With my lost saints—I love thee with the breath,
Smiles, tears, of all my life!—and, if God choose,
I shall but love thee better after death.

MATTHEW ARNOLD

Shakespeare

Others abide our question. Thou art free.
We ask and ask—thou smilest and art still,
Out-topping knowledge. For the loftiest hill,
Who to the stars uncrowns his majesty,
Planting his steadfast footsteps in the sea,   5
Making the heaven of heavens his dwelling-place,
Spares but the cloudy border of his base
To the foiled searching of mortality;
And thou, who didst the stars and sunbeams know,
Self-schooled, self-scanned, self-honored, self-secure,
Didst tread on earth unguessed at.—Better so!   11
All pains the immortal spirit must endure,
All weakness which impairs, all griefs which bow,
Find their sole speech in that victorious brow.

The Forsaken Merman

  Come, dear children, let us away,
Down and away below.

Now my brothers call from the bay;
Now the great winds shoreward blow;
Now the salt tides seaward flow;   5
Now the wild white horses play,
Champ and chafe and toss in the spray.
Children dear, let us away,
This way, this way!

  Call her once before you go,   11
Call once yet,
In a voice that she will know:
"Margaret! Margaret!"
Children's voices should be dear
(Call once more) to a mother's ear,   15
Children's voices, wild with pain.
Surely she will come again!
Call her once and come away;
This way, this way!
"Mother dear, we cannot stay."   20
The wild white horses foam and fret.
Margaret! Margaret!

Arnold, *Shakespeare*. Matthew Arnold (1822-1888) was the son of Dr. Thomas Arnold, the famous master of Rugby School. He is almost equally important as poet, essayist, and educational reformer. For other works of Matthew Arnold see his essays on *Hebraism and Hellenism*, p. 4, and *On Celtic Literature*, p. 521.
  Arnold, *The Forsaken Merman*. This poem is based on a Scandinavian legend of the mortal woman married to the merman. If she goes to church, the merman loses his power over her.

Come, dear children, come away down;
Call no more.
One last look at the white-walled town, 25
And the little gray church on the windy shore;
Then come down.
She will not come though you call all day.
Come away, come away.

Children dear, was it yesterday 30
We heard the sweet bells over the bay?
In the caverns where we lay,
Through the surf and through the swell,
The far-off sound of a silver bell?
Sand-strewn caverns, cool and deep, 35
Where the winds are all asleep;
Where the spent lights quiver and gleam;
Where the salt weed sways in the stream;
Where the sea-beasts, ranged all round,
Feed in the ooze of their pasture-ground; 40
Where the sea-snakes coil and twine,
Dry their mail, and bask in the brine;
Where great whales come sailing by,
Sail and sail, with unshut eye,
Round the world forever and aye? 45
When did music come this way?
Children dear, was it yesterday?

Children dear, was it yesterday
(Call yet once) that she went away?
Once she sate with you and me, 50
On a red-gold throne in the heart of the sea,
And the youngest sate on her knee.
She combed its bright hair, and she tended it well,
When down swung the sound of a far-off bell.
She sighed, she looked up through the clear green sea, 55
She said, "I must go, for my kinsfolk pray
In the little gray church on the shore today.
'Twill be Easter-time in the world—ah, me!
And I lose my poor soul, Merman, here with thee."
I said, "Go up, dear heart, through the waves; 60
Say thy prayer, and come back to the kind sea-caves."
She smiled, she went up through the surf in the bay.
Children dear, was it yesterday?

Children dear, were we long alone?
"The sea grows stormy, the little ones moan. 65
Long prayers," I said, "in the world they say;
Come," I said, and we rose through the surf in the bay.
We went up the beach, by the sandy down
Where the sea-stocks bloom, to the white-walled town.

Through the narrow paved streets, where all was still, 70
To the little gray church on the windy hill.
From the church came a murmur of folk at their prayers,
But we stood without in the cold-blowing airs.
We climbed on the graves, on the stones worn with rains,
And we gazed up the aisle through the small leaded panes. 75
She sate by the pillar; we saw her clear:
"Margaret, hist! come quick, we are here.
Dear heart," I said, "we are long alone.
The sea grows stormy, the little ones moan."
But, ah! she gave me never a look, 80
For her eyes were sealed to the holy book.
Loud prays the priest; shut stands the door.
Come away, children, call no more.
Come away, come down, call no more.

Down, down, down; 85
Down to the depths of the sea.
She sits at her wheel in the humming town,
Singing most joyfully.
Hark what she sings: "O joy, O joy,
For the humming street, and the child with its toy. 90
For the priest, and the bell, and the holy well.
For the wheel where I spun,
And the blessed light of the sun."
And so she sings her fill,
Singing most joyfully, 95
Till the spindle drops from her hand,
And the whizzing wheel stands still.
She steals to the window, and looks at the sand.
And over the sand at the sea;
And her eyes are set in a stare; 100
And anon there breaks a sigh,
And anon there drops a tear,
From a sorrow-clouded eye,
And a heart sorrow-laden,
A long, long sigh 105
For the cold strange eyes of a little mermaiden,
And the gleam of her golden hair.

Come away, away, children,
Come, children, come down.
The hoarse wind blows colder; 110
Lights shine in the town.
She will start from her slumber
When gusts shake the door;
She will hear the winds howling,
Will hear the waves roar. 115

We shall see, while above us
The waves roar and whirl,
A ceiling of amber,
A pavement of pearl.
Singing, "Here came a mortal,   120
But faithless was she;
And alone dwell forever
The kings of the sea."

But, children, at midnight,
When soft the winds blow,   125
When clear falls the moonlight,
When spring-tides are low,
When sweet airs come seaward
From heaths starred with broom,
And high rocks throw mildly   130
On the blanched sands a gloom—
Up the still, glistening beaches,
Up the creeks we will hie,
Over banks of bright seaweed
The ebb-tide leaves dry.   135
We will gaze, from the sand-hills,
At the white, sleeping town;
At the church on the hillside—
And then come back down,
Singing, "There dwells a loved one,   140
But cruel is she.
She left lonely forever
The kings of the sea."

The Buried Life

Light flows our war of mocking words, and yet,
Behold, with tears mine eyes are wet!
I feel a nameless sadness o'er me roll.
Yes, yes, we know that we can jest,
We know, we know that we can smile!   5
But there's a something in this breast,
To which thy light words bring no rest,
And thy gay smiles no anodyne.
Give me thy hand, and hush awhile,
And turn those limpid eyes on mine,   10
And let me read there, love! thy inmost soul.

Alas! is even love too weak
To unlock the heart, and let it speak?
Are even lovers powerless to reveal
To one another what indeed they feel?   15
I knew the mass of men concealed
Their thoughts, for fear that if revealed
They would by other men be met
With blank indifference, or with blame reproved;

I knew they lived and moved   20
Tricked in disguises, alien to the rest
Of men, and alien to themselves—and yet
The same heart beats in every human breast!
But we, my love!—doth a like spell benumb
Our hearts, our voices?—must we, too, be dumb?

Ah! well for us, if even we,   26
Even for a moment, can get free
Our heart, and have our lips unchained;
For that which seals them hath been deep-ordained!

Fate, which foresaw   30
How frivolous a baby man would be—
By what distractions he would be possessed,
How he would pour himself in every strife,
And well nigh change his own identity—
That it might keep from his capricious play   35
His genuine self, and force him to obey
Even in his own despite his being's law,
Bade through the deep recesses of our breast
The unregarded river of our life
Pursue with indiscernible flow its way;   40
And that we should not see
The buried stream, and seem to be
Eddying at large in blind uncertainty,
Though driving on with it eternally.

But often, in the world's most crowded streets, 45
But often, in the din of strife,
There rises an unspeakable desire
After the knowledge of our buried life;
A thirst to spend our fire and restless force
In tracking out our true, original course;   50
A longing to inquire
Into the mystery of this heart which beats
So wild, so deep in us—to know
Whence our lives come and where they go.
And many a man in his own breast then delves,
But deep enough, alas! none ever mines.   56
And we have been on many thousand lines,
And we have shown, on each, spirit and power;
But hardly have we, for one little hour,
Been on our own line, have we been ourselves—   60
Hardly had skill to utter one of all
The nameless feelings that course through our
        breast,
But they course on forever unexpressed,
And long we try in vain to speak and act
Our hidden self, and what we say and do   65
Is eloquent, is well—but 'tis not true!
And then we will no more be racked
With inward striving, and demand

Of all the thousand nothings of the hour
Their stupefying power;   70
Ah, yes, and they benumb us at our call!
Yet still, from time to time, vague and forlorn,
From the soul's subterranean depth upborne
As from an infinitely distant land,
Come airs, and floating echoes, and convey   75
A melancholy into all our day.

Only—but this is rare—
When a beloved hand is laid in ours,
When, jaded with the rush and glare
Of the interminable hours,   80
Our eyes can in another's eyes read clear,
When our world-deafened ear
Is by the tones of a loved voice caressed—
A bolt is shot back somewhere in our breast,
And a lost pulse of feeling stirs again.   85
The eye sinks inward, and the heart lies plain,
And what we mean, we say, and what we would,
    we know.
A man becomes aware of his life's flow,
And hears its winding murmur; and he sees
The meadows where it glides, the sun, the breeze.

And there arrives a lull in the hot race   91
Wherein he doth forever chase
That flying and elusive shadow, rest.
An air of coolness plays upon his face,
And an unwonted calm pervades his breast.   95
And then he thinks he knows
The hills where his life rose,
And the sea where it goes.

Requiescat

Strew on her roses, roses,
    And never a spray of yew!
In quiet she reposes;
    Ah, would that I did too!

Her mirth the world required;   5
    She bathed it in smiles of glee.
But her heart was tired, tired,
    And now they let her be.

Her life was turning, turning,
    In mazes of heat and sound.   10
But for peace her soul was yearning,
    And now peace laps her round.

Her cabin'd, ample spirit,
    It flutter'd and fail'd for breath.

Tonight it doth inherit   15
    The vasty hall of death.

Dover Beach

The sea is calm tonight,
The tide is full, the moon lies fair
Upon the straits—on the French coast the light
Gleams and is gone; the cliffs of England stand,
Glimmering and vast, out in the tranquil bay.   5
Come to the window; sweet is the night-air!
Only, from the long line of spray
Where the sea meets the moon-blanched land,
Listen! you hear the grating roar
Of pebbles which the waves draw back, and fling,
At their return, up the high strand,   11
Begin, and cease, and then again begin,
With tremulous cadence slow, and bring
The eternal note of sadness in.

Sophocles long ago   15
Heard it on the Ægean, and it brought
Into his mind the turbid ebb and flow
Of human misery; we
Find also in the sound a thought,
Hearing it by this distant northern sea.   20

The Sea of Faith
Was once, too, at the full, and round earth's shore
Lay like the folds of a bright girdle furled,
But now I only hear
Its melancholy, long, withdrawing roar,   25
Retreating, to the breath
Of the night-wind, down the vast edges drear
And naked shingles of the world.

Ah, love, let us be true
To one another! for the world, which seems   30
To lie before us like a land of dreams,
So various, so beautiful, so new,
Hath really neither joy, nor love, nor light,
Nor certitude, nor peace, nor help for pain;
And we are here as on a darkling plain   35
Swept with confused alarms of struggle and flight,
Where ignorant armies clash by night.

Growing Old

What is it to grow old?
Is it to lose the glory of the form,
The luster of the eye?
Is it for beauty to forego her wreath?
—Yes, but not this alone.   5

Is it to feel our strength—
Not our bloom only, but our strength—decay?
Is it to feel each limb
Grow stiffer, every function less exact,
Each nerve more loosely strung?   10

Yes, this, and more; but not
Ah, 'tis not what in youth we dreamed 'twould be!
'Tis not to have our life
Mellowed and softened as with sunset-glow,
A golden day's decline.   15

'Tis not to see the world
As from a height, with rapt prophetic eyes,
And heart profoundly stirred;
And weep, and feel the fullness of the past,
The years that are no more.   20

It is to spend long days
And not once feel that we were ever young;
It is to add, immured
In the hot prison of the present, month
To month with weary pain.   25

It is to suffer this,
And feel but half, and feebly, what we feel.
Deep in our hidden heart
Festers the dull remembrance of a change,
But no emotion—none.   30

It is—last stage of all—
When we are frozen up within, and quite
The phantom of ourselves,
To hear the world applaud the hollow ghost
Which blamed the living man.   35

DANTE GABRIEL ROSSETTI

The Blessed Damozel

The blessed damozel leaned out
   From the gold bar of heaven;
Her eyes were deeper than the depth
   Of waters stilled at even;
She had three lilies in her hand,   5
   And the stars in her hair were seven.

Her robe, ungirt from clasp to hem,
   No wrought flowers did adorn,
But a white rose of Mary's gift,
   For service meetly worn;   10
Her hair that lay along her back
   Was yellow like ripe corn.

Her seemed she scarce had been a day
   One of God's choristers;
The wonder was not yet quite gone   15
   From that still look of hers;
Albeit, to them she left, her day
   Had counted as ten years.

(To one, it is ten years of years.
   . . . Yet now, and in this place,   20

Surely she leaned o'er me—her hair
   Fell all about my face . . .
Nothing; the autumn fall of leaves.
   The whole year sets apace.)

It was the rampart of God's house   25
   That she was standing on;
By God built over the sheer depth
   The which is space begun;
So high, that looking downward thence
   She scarce could see the sun.   30

It lies in heaven, across the flood
   Of ether, as a bridge.
Beneath, the tides of day and night
   With flame and darkness ridge
The void, as low as where this earth   35
   Spins like a fretful midge.

Around her, lovers, newly met
   'Mid deathless love's acclaims,
Spoke evermore among themselves
   Their heart-remembered names;
And the souls mounting up to God
   Went by her like thin flames.

Dante Gabriel Rossetti, *The Blessed Damozel.* Dante Gabriel Rossetti (1828-1882) was both painter and poet. He helped form the Pre-Raphaelite brotherhood, which exerted much influence on Victorian art and literature. He was the son of an Italian poet and the brother of Christina and William Michael Rossetti, who were also poets.

And still she bowed herself and stooped
  Out of the circling charm;
Until her bosom must have made   45
  The bar she leaned on warm,
And the lilies lay as if asleep
  Along her bended arm.

From the fixed place of heaven she saw
  Time like a pulse shake fierce   50
Through all the worlds. Her gaze still strove
  Within the gulf to pierce
Its path; and now she spoke as when
  The stars sang in their spheres.

The sun was gone now; the curled moon   55
  Was like a little feather
Fluttering far down the gulf; and now
  She spoke through the still weather.
Her voice was like the voice the stars
  Had when they sang together.   60

(Ah sweet! Even now, in that bird's song,
  Strove not her accents there,
Fain to be hearkened? When those bells
  Possessed the mid-day air,
Strove not her steps to reach my side   65
  Down all the echoing stair?)

"I wish that he were come to me,
  For he will come," she said.
"Have I not prayed in heaven?—on earth,
  Lord, Lord, has he not prayed?   70
Are not two prayers a perfect strength?
  And shall I feel afraid?

"When round his head the aureole clings,
  And he is clothed in white,
I'll take his hand and go with him   75
  To the deep wells of light;
As unto a stream we will step down,
  And bathe there in God's sight.

"We two will stand beside that shrine,
  Occult, withheld, untrod,   80
Whose lamps are stirred continually
  With prayers sent up to God;
And see our old prayers, granted, melt
  Each like a little cloud.

"We two will lie i' the shadow of   85
  That living, mystic tree
Within whose secret growth the Dove

Is sometimes felt to be,
While every leaf that His plumes touch
  Saith His Name audibly.   90

"And I myself will teach to him,
  I myself, lying so,
The songs I sing here; which his voice
  Shall pause in, hushed and slow,
And find some knowledge at each pause, 95
  Or some new thing to know."

(Alas! We two, we two, thou say'st!
  Yea, one wast thou with me
That once of old. But shall God lift
  To endless unity   100
The soul whose likeness with thy soul
  Was but its love for thee?)

"We two," she said, "will seek the groves
  Where the lady Mary is,
With her five handmaidens, whose names 105
  Are five sweet symphonies,
Cecily, Gertrude, Magdalen,
  Margaret, and Rosalys.

"Circlewise sit they, with bound locks
  And foreheads garlanded;   110
Into the fine cloth, white like flame,
  Weaving the golden thread,
To fashion the birth-robes for them
  Who are just born, being dead.

"He shall fear, haply, and be dumb;   115
  Then will I lay my cheek
To his, and tell about our love,
  Not once abashed or weak;
And the dear Mother will approve
  My pride, and let me speak.   120

"Herself shall bring us, hand in hand,
  To Him round whom all souls
Kneel, the clear-ranged unnumbered heads
  Bowed with their aureoles;
And angels meeting us shall sing,   125
  To their citherns and citoles.

"There will I ask of Christ the Lord
  Thus much for him and me—
Only to live as once on earth
  With Love, only to be,   130
As then awhile, forever now
  Together, I and he."

She gazed and listened and then said,
  Less sad of speech than mild—
"All this is when he comes." She ceased. 135
  The light thrilled toward her, filled
With angels in strong, level flight.
  Her eyes prayed, and she smiled.

(I saw her smile.) But soon their path
  Was vague in distant spheres; 140
And then she cast her arms along
  The golden barriers,
And laid her face between her hands,
  And wept. (I heard her tears.)

CHRISTINA ROSSETTI

Song

When I am dead, my dearest,
  Sing no sad songs for me;
Plant thou no roses at my head,
  Nor shady cypress tree:
Be the green grass above me 5
  With showers and dewdrops wet:
And if thou wilt, remember,
  And if thou wilt, forget.

I shall not see the shadows,
  I shall not feel the rain; 10
I shall not hear the nightingale
  Sing on as if in pain:
And dreaming through the twilight
  That doth not rise nor set,
Haply I may remember, 15
  And haply may forget.

A Birthday

My heart is like a singing bird
  Whose nest is in a watered shoot:
My heart is like an apple-tree
  Whose boughs are bent with thickset fruit;
My heart is like a rainbow shell 5
  That paddles in a halcyon sea;
My heart is gladder than all these
  Because my love is come to me.

Raise me a dais of silk and down;
  Hang it with vair and purple dyes; 10
Carve it in doves and pomegranates,
  And peacocks with a hundred eyes;
Work it in gold and silver grapes,
  In leaves and silver fleur-de-lys;
Because the birthday of my life 15
  Is come, my love is come to me.

Remember

Remember me when I am gone away,
  Gone far away into the silent land;
  When you can no more hold me by the hand,
Nor I half turn to go, yet turning stay.
Remember me when no more day by day, 5
  You tell me of our future that you planned:
  Only remember me; you understand
It will be late to counsel then or pray.
Yet if you should forget me for a while
  And afterwards remember, do not grieve: 10
  For if the darkness and corruption leave
A vestige of the thoughts that once I had,
Better by far you should forget and smile
  Than that you should remember and be sad.

Sing-Song

Who has seen the wind?
  Neither I nor you:
But when the leaves hang trembling
  The wind is passing thro'.

Who has seen the wind?
  Neither you nor I:
But when the trees bow down their heads
  The wind is passing by.

———

The lily has a smooth stalk,
  Will never hurt your hand;

Christina Rossetti, *Song: When I Am Dead, My Dearest*. Christina Georgina Rossetti (1830-1894)
was the sister of Dante Gabriel Rossetti. She lived a retired life of religious devotion.

But the rose upon her briar
  Is lady of the land.

There's sweetness in an apple tree,   5
  And profit in the corn;
But lady of all beauty
  Is a rose upon a thorn.

When with moss and honey
  She tips her bending briar,   10
And half unfolds her glowing heart,
  She sets the world on fire.

De Profundis

Oh why is heaven built so far,
  Oh why is earth set so remote?

I cannot reach the nearest star
  That hangs afloat.

I would not care to reach the moon,   5
  One round monotonous of change;
Yet even she repeats her tune
  Beyond my range.

I never watch the scattered fire
  Of stars, or sun's far-trailing train,   10
But all my heart is one desire,
  And all in vain:

For I am bound with fleshly bands,
  Joy, beauty, lie beyond my scope;
I strain my heart, I stretch my hands,   15
  And catch at hope.

WILLIAM MORRIS

The Haystack in the Floods

Had she come all the way for this,
To part at last without a kiss?
Yea, had she borne the dirt and rain
That her own eyes might see him slain
Beside the haystack in the floods?   5

Along the dripping leafless woods,
The stirrup touching either shoe,
She rode astride as troopers do;
With kirtle kilted to her knee,
To which the mud splash'd wretchedly;   10
And the wet dripp'd from every tree
Upon her head and heavy hair,
And on her eyelids broad and fair;
The tears and rain ran down her face.

By fits and starts they rode apace,   15
And very often was his place
Far off from her; he had to ride
Ahead, to see what might betide
When the roads cross'd; and sometimes, when
There rose a murmuring from his men,   20
Had to turn back with promises.
Ah me! she had but little ease;

And often for pure doubt and dread
She sobb'd, made giddy in the head
By the swift riding; while, for cold,   25
Her slender fingers scarce could hold
The wet reins; yea, and scarcely, too,
She felt the foot within her shoe
Against the stirrup: all for this,
To part at last without a kiss   30
Beside the haystack in the floods.

For when they near'd that old soak'd hay,
They saw across the only way
That Judas, Godmar, and the three
Red running lions dismally   35
Grinn'd from his pennon, under which
In one straight line along the ditch,
They counted thirty heads.
                       So then
While Robert turn'd round to his men,
She saw at once the wretched end,   40
And, stooping down, tried hard to rend
Her coif the wrong way from her head,
And hid her eyes; while Robert said:
"Nay, love, 'tis scarcely two to one;
At Poictiers where we made them run   45

Morris, *The Haystack in the Floods*. William Morris (1834-1896) was artist and decorator as well as poet. He is associated with the Pre-Raphaelite group. He passed his life in London.

So fast—why, sweet my love, good cheer,
The Gascon frontier is so near,
Nought after us."
                But: "O!" she said,
"My God! my God! I have to tread
The long way back without you; then   50
The court at Paris; those six men;
The gratings of the Chatelet;
The swift Seine on some rainy day
Like this, and people standing by,
And laughing, while my weak hands try   55
To recollect how strong men swim.
All this, or else a life with him,
For which I should be damned at last,
Would God that this next hour were past!"

He answer'd not, but cried his cry,   60
"St. George for Marny!" cheerily;
And laid his hand upon her rein.
Alas! no man of all his train
Gave back that cheery cry again;
And, while for rage his thumb beat fast   65
Upon his sword-hilt, someone cast
About his neck a kerchief long,
And bound him.
             Then they went along
To Godmar; who said: "Now, Jehane,
Your lover's life is on the wane   70
So fast, that, if this very hour
You yield not as my paramour,
He will not see the rain leave off:
Nay, keep your tongue from gibe and scoff
Sir Robert, or I slay you now."   75

She laid her hand upon her brow,
Then gazed upon the palm, as though
She thought her forehead bled, and: "No!"
She said, and turn'd her head away,
As there was nothing else to say,   80
And everything was settled: red
Grew Godmar's face from chin to head:
"Jehane, on yonder hill there stands
My castle, guarding well my lands;
What hinders me from taking you,   85
And doing that I list to do
To your fair willful body, while
Your knight lies dead?"
             A wicked smile
Wrinkled her face, her lips grew thin,
A long way out she thrust her chin: 90
"You know that I should strangle you
While you were sleeping; or bite through

Your throat, by God's help: ah!" she said,
"Lord Jesus, pity your poor maid!
For in such wise they hem me in,   95
I cannot choose but sin and sin,
Whatever happens: yet I think
They could not make me eat or drink,
And so should I just reach my rest."
"Nay, if you do not my behest,   100
O Jehane! though I love you well,"
Said Godmar, "would I fail to tell
All that I know?" "Foul lies," she said.
"Eh? lies, my Jehane? by God's head,
At Paris folks would deem them true!   105
Do you know, Jehane, they cry for you:
'Jehane the brown! Jehane the brown!
Give us Jehane to burn or drown!'
Eh!—gag me Robert!—sweet my friend,
This were indeed a piteous end   110
For those long fingers, and long feet,
And long neck, and smooth shoulders sweet;
An end that few men would forget
That saw it. So, an hour yet:
Consider, Jehane, which to take   115
Of life or death!"
             So, scarce awake,
Dismounting, did she leave that place,
And totter some yards: with her face
Turn'd upward to the sky she lay,
Her head on a wet heap of hay,   120
And fell asleep: and while she slept,
And did not dream, the minutes crept
Round to the twelve again; but she,
Being waked at last, sigh'd quietly,
And strangely childlike came, and said: 125
"I will not." Straightway Godmar's head,
As though it hung on strong wires, turn'd
Most sharply round, and his face burn'd.

For Robert, both his eyes were dry,
He could not weep, but gloomily   130
He seem'd to watch the rain; yea, too,
His lips were firm; he tried once more
To touch her lips; she reach'd out, sore
And vain desire so tortured them,
The poor gray lips, and now the hem   135
Of his sleeve brush'd them.
             With a start
Up Godmar rose, thrust them apart;
From Robert's throat he loosed the bands
Of silk and mail; with empty hands
Held out, she stood and gazed, and saw,   140
The long bright blade without a flaw

Glide out from Godmar's sheath, his hand
In Robert's hair; she saw him bend
Back Robert's head; she saw him send
The thin steel down; the blow told well,   145
Right backward the knight Robert fell,
And moaned as dogs do, being half dead,
Unwitting, as I deem: so then
Godmar turn'd grinning to his men,
Who ran, some five or six, and beat   150
His head to pieces at their feet.

Then Godmar turn'd again and said:
"So, Jehane, the first fitte is read!
Take note, my lady, that your way
Lies backward to the Chatelet!"   155
She shook her head and gazed awhile
At her cold hands with a rueful smile,
As though this thing had made her mad.

This was the parting that they had
Beside the haystack in the floods.   160

ALGERNON CHARLES SWINBURNE

Chorus

FROM *Atalanta in Calydon*

When the hounds of spring are on winter's traces,
  The mother of months in meadow or plain
Fills the shadows and windy places
  With lisp of leaves and ripple of rain;
And the brown bright nightingale amorous   5
Is half assuaged for Itylus,
For the Thracian ships and the foreign faces,
  The tongueless vigil, and all the pain.

Come with bows bent and with emptying of
    quivers,
  Maiden most perfect, lady of light,   10
With a noise of winds and many rivers,
  With a clamor of waters, and with might;
Bind on thy sandals, O thou most fleet,
Over the splendor and speed of thy feet;
For the faint east quickens, the wan west shivers,
  Round the feet of the day and the feet of the
    night.   16

Where shall we find her, how shall we sing to her,
  Fold our hands round her knees, and cling?
O that man's heart were as fire and could spring
    to her,
  Fire, or the strength of the streams that spring!
For the stars and the winds are unto her   21
As raiment, as songs of the harp-player;
For the risen stars and the fallen cling to her,
  And the southwest-wind, and the west-wind sing.

For winter's rains and ruins are over,   25
  And all the season of snows and sins;
The days dividing lover and lover,
  The light that loses, the night that wins;
And time remembered is grief forgotten,
And frosts are slain and flowers begotten,   30
And in green underwood and cover
  Blossom by blossom the spring begins.

The full streams feed on flower of rushes,
  Ripe grasses trammel a traveling foot,
The faint fresh flame of the young year flushes   35
  From leaf to flower and flower to fruit;
And fruit and leaf are as gold and fire,
And the oat is heard above the lyre,
And the hoofèd heel of a satyr crushes
  The chestnut-husk at the chestnut-root.   40

And Pan by noon and Bacchus by night,
  Fleeter of foot than the fleet-foot kid,
Follows with dancing and fills with delight
  The Mænad and the Bassarid;
And soft as lips that laugh and hide   45
The laughing leaves of the trees divide,
And screen from seeing and leave in sight
  The god pursuing, the maiden hid.

The ivy falls with the Bacchanal's hair
  Over her eyebrows hiding her eyes;   50
The wild vine slipping down leaves bare
  Her bright breast shortening into sighs;

Swinburne, *Chorus from Atalanta in Calydon*. Algernon Charles Swinburne (1837-1909) came of an upper-class family and was educated in France and at Oxford. For nearly fifty years he produced poems, plays, and works of criticism. He never married, but maintained a home with Theodore Watts-Dunton, the literary critic.

The wild vine slips with the weight of its leaves,
But the berried ivy catches and cleaves
To the limbs that glitter, the feet that scare   55
The wolf that follows, the fawn that flies.

The Garden of Proserpine

Here, where the world is quiet,
  Here, where all trouble seems
Dead winds' and spent waves' riot
  In doubtful dreams of dreams,
I watch the green field growing   5
For reaping folk and sowing,
For harvest-time and mowing,
  A sleepy world of streams.

I am tired of tears and laughter,
  And men that laugh and weep;   10
Of what may come hereafter
  For men that sow to reap.
I am weary of days and hours,
Blown buds of barren flowers,
Desires and dreams and powers   15
  And everything but sleep.

Here life has death for neighbor,
  And far from eye or ear
Wan waves and wet winds labor,
  Weak ships and spirits steer;   20
They drive adrift, and whither
They wot not who make thither;
But no such winds blow hither,
  And no such things grow here.

No growth of moor or coppice,   25
  No heather-flower or vine,
But bloomless buds of poppies,
  Green grapes of Proserpine,
Pale beds of blowing rushes,
Where no leaf blooms or blushes   30
Save this whereout she crushes
  For dead men deadly wine.

Pale, without name or number,
  In fruitless fields of corn,
They bow themselves and slumber   35
  All night till light is born;
And like a soul belated,
In hell and heaven unmated,
By cloud and mist abated
  Comes out of darkness morn.   40

Though one were strong as seven,
  He too with death shall dwell,
Nor wake with wings in heaven,
  Nor weep for pains in hell;
Though one were fair as roses,   45
His beauty clouds and closes;
And well though love reposes,
  In the end it is not well.

Pale, beyond porch and portal,
  Crowned with calm leaves, she stands 50
Who gathers all things mortal
  With cold, immortal hands;
Her languid lips are sweeter
Than love's who fears to greet her,
To men that mix and meet her   55
  From many times and lands.

She waits for each and other,
  She waits for all men born;
Forgets the earth her mother,
  The life of fruits and corn;   60
And spring and seed and swallow
Take wing for her and follow
Where summer song rings hollow
  And flowers are put to scorn.

There go the loves that wither,   65
  The old loves with wearier wings;
And all dead years draw thither,
  And all disastrous things;
Dead dreams of days forsaken,
Blind buds that snows have shaken,   70
Wild leaves that winds have taken,
  Red strays of ruined springs.

We are not sure of sorrow;
  And joy was never sure;
Today will die tomorrow;   75
  Time stoops to no man's lure;
And love, grown faint and fretful,
With lips but half regretful
Sighs, and with eyes forgetful
  Weeps that no loves endure.   80

From too much love of living,
  From hope and fear set free,
We thank with brief thanksgiving
  Whatever gods may be
That no life lives forever;   85
That dead men rise up never;

That even the weariest river
  Winds somewhere safe to sea.

Then star nor sun shall waken,
  Nor any change of light;   90
Nor sound of waters shaken,
  Nor any sound or sight;
Nor wintry leaves nor vernal,
Nor days nor things diurnal—
Only the sleep eternal   95
  In an eternal night.

Étude Réaliste

I

A baby's feet, like sea-shells pink,
  Might tempt, should Heaven see meet,
An angel's lips to kiss, we think,
  A baby's feet.

Like rose-hued sea-flowers toward the heat 5
  They stretch and spread and wink
Their ten soft buds that part and meet.

No flower-bells that expand and shrink
  Gleam half so heavenly sweet
As shine on life's untrodden brink 10
  A baby's feet.

II

A baby's hands, like rosebuds furl'd,
  Whence yet no leaf expands,
Ope if you touch, though close upcurl'd
  A baby's hands.   15

Then, even as warriors grip their brands
  When battle's bolt is hurl'd,
They close, clench'd hard like tightening bands.

No rosebuds yet by dawn impearl'd
  Match, even in loveliest lands, 20
The sweetest flowers in all the world—
  A baby's hands.

III

A baby's eyes, ere speech begin,
  Ere lips learn words or sighs,
Bless all things bright enough to win 25
  A baby's eyes.

Love, while the sweet thing laughs and lies,
  And sleep flows out and in,
Lies perfect in them Paradise.

Their glance might cast out pain and sin, 30
  Their speech make dumb the wise,
By mute glad godhead felt within
  A baby's eyes.

WILLIAM ERNEST HENLEY

Before

Behold me waiting—waiting for the knife.
A little while, and at a leap I storm
The thick, sweet mystery of chloroform,
The drunken dark, the little death-in-life.
The gods are good to me: I have no wife, 5
No innocent child, to think of as I near
The fateful minute; nothing all-too dear
Unmans me for my bout of passive strife.
Yet am I tremulous and a trifle sick,
And, face to face with chance, I shrink a little: 10

My hopes are strong, my will is something weak.
Here comes the basket? Thank you. I am ready.
But, gentlemen my porters, life is brittle:
You carry Cæsar and his fortunes—steady!

Invictus

Out of the night that covers me,
  Black as the pit from pole to pole,
I thank whatever gods may be
  For my unconquerable soul.

Henley, *Before*. He is waiting in the hospital in Edinburgh for the surgeons. William Ernest Henley (1849-1903) was born at Gloucester. In spite of his crippled condition caused by the amputation of a foot, he became one of the most influential editors of his day. His poetry is slight in bulk, since his main energies were devoted to journalism.

In the fell clutch of circumstance   5
    I have not winced nor cried aloud.
Under the bludgeonings of chance
    My head is bloody, but unbowed.

Beyond this place of wrath and tears
    Looms but the horror of the shade,   10
And yet the menace of the years
    Finds and shall find me unafraid.

It matters not how strait the gate,
    How charged with punishments the scroll,
I am the master of my fate: 15
    I am the captain of my soul.

To A. D.

The nightingale has a lyre of gold,
    The lark's is a clarion call,
And the blackbird plays but a boxwood flute,
    But I love him best of all.

For his song is all of the joy of life,
    And we in the mad, spring weather,
We two have listened till he sang
    Our hearts and lips together.

Margaritæ Sorori

A late lark twitters from the quiet skies;
And from the west,
Where the sun, his day's work ended,
Lingers as in content,
There falls on the old, gray city   5
An influence luminous and serene,
A shining peace.

The smoke ascends
In a rosy-and-golden haze. The spires
Shine and are changed. In the valley   10
Shadows rise. The lark sings on. The sun,
Closing his benediction,
Sinks, and the darkening air
Thrills with a sense of the triumphing night—
Night with her train of stars   15
And her great gift of sleep.

So be my passing!
My task accomplished and the long day done,

My wages taken, and in my heart
Some late lark singing,   20
Let me be gathered to the quiet west,
The sundown splendid and serene,
Death.

To W. A.

Or ever the knightly years were gone
    With the old world to the grave,
I was a King in Babylon
    And you were a Christian Slave.

I saw, I took, I cast you by,   5
    I bent and broke your pride.
You loved me well, or I heard them lie,
    But your longing was denied.
Surely I knew that by and by
    You cursed your gods and died.   10

And a myriad suns have set and shone
    Since then upon the grave
Decreed by the King of Babylon
    To her that had been his Slave.

The pride I trampled is now my scathe,   15
    For it tramples me again.
The old resentment lasts like death,
    For you love, yet you refrain.
I break my heart on your hard unfaith,
    And I break my heart in vain.   20

Yet not for an hour do I wish undone
    The deed beyond the grave,
When I was a King in Babylon
    And you were a Virgin Slave.

A Bowl of Roses

It was a bowl of roses:
    There in the light they lay,
Languishing, glorying, glowing
    Their life away.

And the soul of them rose like a presence,
    Into me crept and grew,
And filled me with something—someone—
    O, was it you?

A. E. HOUSMAN

Reveille

Wake: the silver dusk returning
  Up the beach of darkness brims,
And the ship of sunrise burning
  Strands upon the eastern rims.

Wake: the vaulted shadow shatters,   5
  Trampled to the floor it spanned,
And the tent of night in tatters
  Straws the sky-pavilioned land.

Up, lad, up, 'tis late for lying:
  Hear the drums of morning play;   10
Hark, the empty highways crying
  "Who'll beyond the hills away?"

Towns and countries woo together,
  Forelands beacon, belfries call;
Never lad that trod on leather   15
  Lived to feast his heart with all.

Up, lad: thews that lie and cumber
  Sunlit pallets never thrive;
Morns abed and daylight slumber
  Were not meant for man alive.   20

Clay lies still, but blood's a rover;
  Breath's a ware that will not keep.
Up, lad: when the journey's over
  There'll be time enough to sleep.

When I Was One-and-Twenty

When I was one-and-twenty
  I heard a wise man say,
"Give crowns and pounds and guineas
  But not your heart away;
Give pearls away and rubies   5
  But keep your fancy free."
But I was one-and-twenty,
  No use to talk to me.

When I was one-and-twenty
  I heard him say again,   10
"The heart out of the bosom
  Was never given in vain;

'Tis paid with sighs a-plenty
  And sold for endless rue."
And I am two-and-twenty,   15
  And oh, 'tis true, 'tis true.

With Rue My Heart Is Laden

With rue my heart is laden
  For golden friends I had,
For many a rose-lipt maiden
  And many a lightfoot lad.

By brooks too broad for leaping
  The lightfoot boys are laid;
The rose-lipt girls are sleeping
  In fields where roses fade.

Loveliest of Trees

Loveliest of trees, the cherry now
Is hung with bloom along the bough,
And stands about the woodland ride
Wearing white for Eastertide.

Now, of my threescore years and ten,   5
Twenty will not come again,
And take from seventy springs a score,
It only leaves me fifty more.

And since to look at things in bloom
Fifty springs are little room,   10
About the woodlands I will go
To see the cherry hung with snow.

Is My Team Plowing?

"Is my team plowing,
  That I used to drive
And hear the harness jingle
  When I was man alive?"

Aye, the horses trample,   5
  The harness jingles now;
No change though you lie under
  The land you used to plow.

Housman, *Reveille*. A. E. Housman (1859-1936) spent most of his life as a student of the Latin classics. His poetic output consists mainly of two volumes published thirty years apart.

"Is football playing
   Along the river shore,   10
With lads to chase the leather,
   Now I stand up no more?"

Aye, the ball is flying,
   The lads play heart and soul;
The goal stands up, the keeper   15
   Stands up to keep the goal.

"Is my girl happy,
   That I thought hard to leave,
And has she tired of weeping
   As she lies down at eve?"   20

Aye, she lies down lightly,
   She lies not down to weep:
Your girl is well contented.
   Be still, my lad, and sleep.

"Is my friend hearty,   25
   Now I am thin and pine;
And has he found to sleep in
   A better bed than mine?"

Aye, lad, I lie easy,
   I lie as lads would choose;   30
I cheer a dead man's sweetheart.
   Never ask me whose.

When Smoke Stood Up from Ludlow

When smoke stood up from Ludlow,
   And mist blew off from Teme,
And blithe afield to plowing
   Against the morning beam
I strode beside my team,   5

The blackbird in the coppice
   Looked out to see me stride,
And hearkened as I whistled
   The trampling team beside,
And fluted and replied: 10

"Lie down, lie down, young yeoman;
   What use to rise and rise?
Rise man a thousand mornings
   Yet down at last he lies,
And then the man is wise."   15

I heard the tune he sang me,
   And spied his yellow bill;
I picked a stone and aimed it
   And threw it with a will:
And then the bird was still.   20

Then my soul within me
   Took up the blackbird's strain,
And still beside the horses
   Along the dewy lane
It sang the song again: 25

"Lie down, lie down, young yeoman;
   The sun moves always west;
The road one treads to labor
   Will lead one home to rest,
And that will be the best."   30

On Wenlock Edge

On Wenlock Edge the wood's in trouble;
His forest fleece the Wrekin heaves;
The gale, it plies the saplings double,
And thick on Severn snow the leaves.

'Twould blow like this through hold and hangar
When Uricon the city stood: 6
'Tis the old wind in the old anger,
But then it threshed another wood.

Then, 'twas before my time, the Roman
At yonder heaving hill would stare: 10
The blood that warms an English yeoman,
The thoughts that hurt him, they were there.

There, like the wind through woods in riot,
Through him the gale of life blew high;
The tree of man was never quiet: 15
Then 'twas the Roman, now 'tis I.

The gale, it plies the saplings double,
It blows so hard, 'twill soon be gone:
Today the Roman and his trouble
Are ashes under Uricon.   20

On the Idle Hill of Summer

On the idle hill of summer,
   Sleepy with the flow of streams,
Far I hear the steady drummer
   Drumming like a noise in dreams.

Far and near and low and louder   5
   On the roads of earth go by,
Dear to friends and food for powder,
   Soldiers marching, all to die.

East and west on fields forgotten
   Bleach the bones of comrades slain,   10
Lovely lads and dead and rotten;
   None that go return again.

Far the calling bugles hollo,
  High the screaming fife replies,
Gay the files of scarlet follow: 15
  Woman bore me, I will rise.

Epilogue

"Terence, this is stupid stuff;
You eat your victuals fast enough;
There can't be much amiss, 'tis clear,
To see the rate you drink your beer.
But oh, good Lord, the verse you make,   5
It gives a chap the belly-ache.
The cow, the old cow, she is dead;
It sleeps well, the horned head:
We poor lads, 'tis our turn now
To hear such tunes as killed the cow.   10
Pretty friendship 'tis to rhyme
Your friends to death before their time
Moping melancholy mad:
Come, pipe a tune to dance to, lad."

Why, if 'tis dancing you would be,   15
There's brisker pipes than poetry.
Say, for what were hop-yards meant,
Or why was Burton built on Trent?
Oh, many a peer of England brews
Livelier liquor than the Muse,   20
And malt does more than Milton can
To justify God's ways to man.
Ale, man, ale's the stuff to drink
For fellows whom it hurts to think:
Look into the pewter pot   25
To see the world as the world's not.
And faith, 'tis pleasant till 'tis past:
The mischief is that 'twill not last.
Oh, I have been to Ludlow fair
And left my necktie God knows where,   30
And carried half way home, or near,
Pints and quarts of Ludlow beer:
Then the world seemed none so bad,
And I myself a sterling lad;

And down in lovely muck I've lain,   35
Happy till I woke again.
Then I saw the morning sky:
Heigho, the tale was all a lie;
The world, it was the old world yet,
I was I, my things were wet,   40
And nothing now remained to do
But begin the game anew.

Therefore, since the world has still
Much good, but much less good than ill,
And while the sun and moon endure   45
Luck's a chance, but trouble's sure,
I'd face it as a wise man would,
And train for ill and not for good.
'Tis true, the stuff I bring for sale
Is not so brisk a brew as ale: 50
Out of a stem that scored the hand
I wrung it in a weary land.
But take it: if the smack is sour,
The better for the embittered hour;
It should do good to heart and head   55
When your soul is in my soul's stead;
And I will friend you, if I may,
In the dark and cloudy day.

There was a king reigned in the East:
There, when kings will sit to feast,   60
They get their fill before they think
With poisoned meat and poisoned drink.
He gathered all that springs to birth
From the many-venomed earth;
First a little, thence to more,   65
He sampled all her killing store;
And easy, smiling, seasoned sound,
Sate the king when healths went round.
They put arsenic in his meat
And stared aghast to watch him eat;   70
They poured strychnine in his cup
And shook to see him drink it up:
They shook, they stared as white's their shirt:
Them it was their poison hurt.
—I tell the tale that I heard told.   75
Mithridates, he died old.

NINETEENTH CENTURY
AMERICAN POETS

American poetry was even later in development than American prose. The first poet whose work seems destined to live was William Cullen Bryant (1794-1878), who at an unusually early age was producing blank verse of high quality. His *Thanatopsis* is justly regarded as the first important American poem. Throughout his long career he maintained a remarkable uniformity. At his best, in such poems as *To a Waterfowl* and *A Forest Hymn,* he ranks as one of the masters of English verse.

For several decades near the middle of the nineteenth century the focus of poetic production was New England. Although his most important productions were his essays, Ralph Waldo Emerson (1803-1882) wrote a few poems which adequately express his keen mind and sensitive feeling. In a period when most poets were discursive and ornamental, his verse is compact and even overcharged with meaning. These qualities can be seen in such a poem as *Days.*

His contemporary, Henry Wadsworth Longfellow (1807-1882), was much more facile. He wrote a large volume of melodious verse, but much of his poetry shows little depth of thought. A later generation tends to think of him merely as a rhymer of platitudes and an easy-going teller of old tales. The reaction against Longfellow has undoubtedly gone too far. His enormous popularity was not wholly without just cause. Among other things, he was one of the ablest sonnet writers we have had.

A New England poet of great importance in his own day was John Greenleaf Whittier (1807-1892). Much that he wrote has lost interest with the passage of time, but he will continue to be valued for his simple and realistic descriptions of New England farm life. His poetry is not difficult, so that most Americans make their acquaintance with Whittier in childhood and never go further.

In moments of leisure between his work as eminent physician and Professor of Medicine at Harvard and his writing of novels and essays, Oliver Wendell Holmes (1809-1894) composed many poems. Most of them were hurriedly prepared for class reunions and the like and have, of course, been forgotten. But Holmes was a man of great wit and deep feeling and on several occasions displayed these qualities in outstanding poems. The rare combination of humor and pathos in *The Last Leaf,* the rich imagination of *The Chambered Nautilus,* and the ringing passion of *Old Ironsides,* entitle him to a place among the greater American poets.

James Russell Lowell (1819-1891), like Holmes and Longfellow, lived in Cambridge and taught in Harvard College. He wrote much critical prose and took a prominent part in public affairs. Much of his poetry has the same fault as Longfellow's and seems to us now either sentimental or merely rhetorical. It will probably be agreed that his most lasting works are those in which he displays his humor and his homely wisdom, such as his *Biglow Papers* and his *Fable for Critics*.

Outside of New England and New York only one man was producing lasting poetry during the first half of the century. Edgar Allan Poe (1809-1849) achieved considerable distinction as a literary critic, and he wrote short stories which permanently affected that literary form. It is through his poems, however, that he has been of greatest influence on world literature. His mastery of the melodies and harmonies of English verse permitted him to express his emotions and moods so skillfully that he became a model for a whole generation of French poets. These French poets, in turn, are now exerting their influence on American poetry, so that the work of Poe becomes of increasing importance.

The American Civil War marks the beginning of a new era in our poetry. From then on, the whole nation, and not merely the East Coast, was to find poetic expression. The greatest force in this direction was Walt Whitman (1819-1892), whose *Leaves of Grass* had appeared just before the war. Abandoning all conventional metrical forms and also refusing to be limited by the bounds of so-called good taste, Whitman expanded the field of poetic expression until it embraced the whole country, if not the world itself, all men and animals, and all physical qualities or sensations. He preached the gospel of equality and democracy. Whitman had the weaknesses inherent in all pioneer work. His revolt against form caused him to work without plan, so that many of his poems ramble along interminably. In his desire to be all-inclusive he resorts to tedious catalogues in which he feels called on to list all the rivers or all the states, so that we may realize how many there are. But in spite of these failings, Whitman has been the most powerful influence on American poetry of the last half century.

Though we have had an important period of poetic expression recently, it cannot be said to have got under way until the beginning of the twentieth century. During the last decades of the nineteenth century some very musical verse was written by Sidney Lanier (1842-1881), and during those same years a quiet New England lady, Emily Dickinson (1830-1886), was writing some memorable lyrics expressive of her daily life and thought. Lanier's work was enthusiastically greeted in his own time, but most of it seems destined to oblivion. On the other hand, Emily Dickinson's popularity has increased yearly. Though her work was written in the nineteenth century, it seems to belong in spirit to our own generation.

RALPH WALDO EMERSON

The Problem

I like a church; I like a cowl,
I love a prophet of the soul;
And on my heart monastic aisles
Fall like sweet strains, or pensive smiles:
Yet not for all his faith can see   5
Would I that cowlèd churchman be.

Why should the vest on him allure,
Which I could not on me endure?

Not from a vain or shallow thought
His awful Jove young Phidias brought;   10
Never from lips of cunning fell
The thrilling Delphic oracle;
Out from the heart of nature rolled
The burdens of the Bible old;
The litanies of nations came,   15
Like the volcano's tongue of flame,
Up from the burning core below,—
The canticles of love and woe:
The hand that rounded Peter's dome
And groined the aisles of Christian Rome   20
Wrought in a sad sincerity;
Himself from God he could not free;
He builded better than he knew;—
The conscious stone to beauty grew.

Know'st thou what wove yon woodbird's nest
Of leaves, and feathers from her breast?   26
Or how the fish outbuilt her shell,
Painting with morn each annual cell?
Or how the sacred pine-tree adds
To her old leaves new myriads?   30
Such and so grew these holy piles,
Whilst love and terror laid the tiles.
Earth proudly wears the Parthenon,
As the best gem upon her zone,
And Morning opes with haste her lids   35
To gaze upon the Pyramids;
O'er England's abbeys bends the sky,
As on its friends, with kindred eye;
For out of Thought's interior sphere
These wonders rose to upper air;   40
And Nature gladly gave them place,
Adopted them into her race,
And granted them an equal date
With Andes and with Ararat.

These temples grew as grows the grass;   45
Art might obey, but not surpass.
The passive Master lent his hand
To the vast soul that o'er him planned;
And the same power that reared the shrine
Bestrode the tribes that knelt within.   50
Ever the fiery Pentecost
Girds with one flame the countless host,
Trances the heart through chanting choirs,
And through the priest the mind inspires.
The word unto the prophet spoken   55
Was writ on tables yet unbroken;
The word by seers or sibyls told,
In groves of oak, or fanes of gold,
Still floats upon the morning wind,
Still whispers to the willing mind.   60
One accent of the Holy Ghost
The heedless world hath never lost.

I know what say the fathers wise,—
The Book itself before me lies,
Old *Chrysostom,* best Augustine,   65
And he who blent both in his line,
The younger *Golden Lips* or mines,
Taylor, the Shakspeare of divines,
His words are music in my ear,
I see his cowlèd portrait dear;   70
And yet, for all his faith could see,
I would not the good bishop be.

The Snow-storm

Announced by all the trumpets of the sky,
Arrives the snow, and, driving o'er the fields,
Seems nowhere to alight: the whited air
Hides hills and woods, the river, and the heaven,
And veils the farm-house at the garden's end.   5
The sled and traveler stopped, the courier's feet
Delayed, all friends shut out, the housemates sit
Around the radiant fireplace, enclosed
In a tumultuous privacy of storm.

Come see the north wind's masonry.   10
Out of an unseen quarry evermore
Furnished with tile, the fierce artificer
Curves his white bastions with projected roof
Round every windward stake, or tree, or door.

Speeding, the myriad-handed, his wild work   15
So fanciful, so savage, nought cares he
For number or proportion. Mockingly,
On coop or kennel he hangs Parian wreaths;
A swan-like form invests the hidden thorn;
Fills up the farmer's lane from wall to wall,   20
Maugre the farmer's sighs; and at the gate
A tapering turret overtops the work.
And when his hours are numbered, and the world
Is all his own, retiring, as he were not,
Leaves, when the sun appears, astonished Art   25
To mimic in slow structures, stone by stone,
Built in an age, the mad wind's night-work,
The frolic architecture of the snow.

Concord Hymn

SUNG AT THE COMPLETION OF THE BATTLE MONUMENT,
APRIL 19, 1836

By the rude bridge that arched the flood,
    Their flag to April's breeze unfurled,
Here once the embattled farmers stood,
    And fired the shot heard round the world.

The foe long since in silence slept;   5
    Alike the conqueror silent sleeps;
And Time the ruined bridge has swept
    Down the dark stream which seaward creeps.

On this green bank, by this soft stream,
    We set today a votive stone;   10
That memory may their deed redeem,
    When, like our sires, our sons are gone.

Spirit, that made those heroes dare
    To die, and leave their children free,
Bid Time and Nature gently spare   15
    The shaft we raise to them and thee.

Days

Daughters of Time, the hypocritic Days,
Muffled and dumb like barefoot dervishes,
And marching single in an endless file,
Bring diadems and fagots in their hands.
To each they offer gifts after his will,   5
Bread, kingdoms, stars, and sky that holds them all.
I, in my pleached garden, watched the pomp,

Forgot my morning wishes, hastily
Took a few herbs and apples, and the Day
Turned and departed silent. I, too late,   10
Under her solemn fillet saw the scorn.

Terminus

It is time to be old,
To take in sail:—
The god of bounds,
Who sets to seas a shore,
Came to me in his fatal rounds,   5
And said: "No more!
No farther shoot
Thy broad ambitious branches, and thy root.
Fancy departs: no more invent;
Contract thy firmament   10
To compass of a tent.
There's not enough for this and that,
Make thy option which of two;
Economize the failing river,
Not the less revere the Giver,   15
Leave the many and hold the few.
Timely wise accept the terms,
Soften the fall with wary foot;
A little while
Still plan and smile,   20
And,—fault of novel germs,—
Mature the unfallen fruit.
Curse, if thou wilt, thy sires,
Bad husbands of their fires,
Who, when they gave thee breath,   25
Failed to bequeath
The needful sinew stark as once,
The Baresark marrow to thy bones,
But left a legacy of ebbing veins,
Inconstant heat and nerveless reins,—   30
Amid the Muses, left thee deaf and dumb,
Amid the gladiators, halt and numb."

As the bird trims her to the gale,
I trim myself to the storm of time,
I man the rudder, reef the sail,   35
Obey the voice at eve obeyed at prime:
"Lowly faithful, banish fear,
Right onward drive unharmed;
The port, well worth the cruise, is near,
And every wave is charmed."   40

HENRY WADSWORTH LONGFELLOW

Hymn to the Night

I heard the trailing garments of the Night
  Sweep through her marble halls!
I saw her sable skirts all fringed with light
  From the celestial walls!

I felt her presence, by its spell of might,   5
  Stoop o'er me from above;
The calm, majestic presence of the Night,
  As of the one I love.

I heard the sounds of sorrow and delight,
  The manifold, soft chimes,   10
That fill the haunted chambers of the Night,
  Like some old poet's rimes.

From the cool cisterns of the midnight air
  My spirit drank repose;
The fountain of perpetual peace flows there,— 15
  From those deep cisterns flows.

O holy Night! from thee I learn to bear
  What man has borne before!
Thou layest thy finger on the lips of Care,
  And they complain no more.   20

Peace! Peace! Orestes-like I breathe this prayer!
  Descend with broad-winged flight,
The welcome, the trice-prayed for, the most fair,
  The best-belovèd Night!

Serenade

Stars of the summer night!
  Far in yon azure deeps,
Hide, hide your golden light!
  She sleeps!
My lady sleeps!   5
  Sleeps!

Moon of the summer night!
  Far down yon western steeps,
Sink, sink in silver light!
  She sleeps!   10
My lady sleeps!
  Sleeps!

Wind of the summer night!
  Where yonder woodbine creeps,
Fold, fold thy pinions light!   15
  She sleeps!
My lady sleeps!
  Sleeps!

Dreams of the summer night!
  Tell her, her lover keeps   20
Watch! while in slumbers light
  She sleeps!
My lady sleeps!
  Sleeps!

The Day Is Done

The day is done, and the darkness
  Falls from the wings of Night,
As a feather is wafted downward
  From an eagle in his flight.

I see the lights of the village   5
  Gleam through the rain and the mist,
And a feeling of sadness comes o'er me,
  That my soul cannot resist:

A feeling of sadness and longing,
  That is not akin to pain,   10
And resembles sorrow only
  As the mist resembles the rain.

Come, read to me some poem,
  Some simple and heartfelt lay,
That shall soothe this restless feeling,   15
  And banish the thoughts of day.

Not from the grand old masters,
  Not from the bards sublime,
Whose distant footsteps echo
  Through the corridors of Time.   20

For, like strains of martial music,
  Their mighty thoughts suggest
Life's endless toil and endeavor;
  And tonight I long for rest.

Read from some humbler poet,   25
  Whose songs gushed from his heart,

Longfellow, *Hymn to the Night*. Henry Wadsworth Longfellow (1807-1882), Professor of Modern Languages at Harvard University, spent most of his life in travel and in quiet living in Cambridge, Massachusetts.

As showers from the clouds of summer,
  Or tears from the eyelids start;

Who, through long days of labor,
  And nights devoid of ease,   30
Still heard in his soul the music
  Of wonderful melodies.

Such songs have power to quiet
  The restless pulse of care,
And come like the benediction   35
  That follows after prayer.

Then read from the treasured volume
  The poem of thy choice,
And lend to the rhyme of the poet
  The beauty of thy voice.   40

And the night shall be filled with music,
  And the cares that infest the day,
Shall fold their tents, like the Arabs,
  And as silently, steal away.

On Translating the Divina Commedia

Oft have I seen at some cathedral door
  A laborer, pausing in the dust and heat,
  Lay down his burden, and with reverent feet
Enter, and cross himself, and on the floor
Kneel to repeat his paternoster o'er;   5
  Far off the noises of the world retreat;
  The loud vociferations of the street
Become an undistinguishable roar.
So, as I enter here from day to day,
  And leave my burden at this minster-gate,   10
  Kneeling in prayer, and not ashamed to pray,
The tumult of the time disconsolate
  To inarticulate murmurs dies away,
  While the eternal ages watch and wait.

I enter, and I see thee in the gloom   15
  Of the long aisles, O poet saturnine!
  And strive to make my steps keep pace with
    thine.

The air is filled with some unknown perfume;
The congregation of the dead make room
  For thee to pass; the votive tapers shine;   20
  Like rooks that haunt Ravenna's groves of pine
The hovering echoes fly from tomb to tomb.
From the confessionals I hear arise
  Rehearsals of forgotten tragedies
  And lamentations from the crypts below;   25
And then a voice celestial that begins
  With the pathetic words, "Although your sins
  As scarlet be," and ends with "as the snow."

I lift mine eyes, and all the windows blaze
  With forms of Saints and holy men who died,
  Here martyred and hereafter glorified;   31
  And the great Rose upon its leaves displays
Christ's Triumph, and the angelic roundelays,
  With splendor upon splendor multiplied;
  And Beatrice again at Dante's side   35
  No more rebukes, but smiles her words of praise.
And then the organ sounds, and unseen choirs
  Sing the old Latin hymns of peace and love
  And benedictions of the Holy Ghost;
And the melodious bells among the spires   40
  O'er all the house-tops and through heaven above
  Proclaim the elevation of the Host!

How strange the sculptures that adorn these
    towers;
  This crowd of statues, in whose folded sleeves
  Birds build their nests; while canopied with
    leaves   45
  Parvis and portal bloom like trellised bowers,
And the vast minster seems a cross of flowers!
  But fiends and dragons on the gargoyled eaves
  Watch the dead Christ between the living
    thieves,
  And, underneath, the traitor Judas lowers!   50
Ah! from what agonies of heart and brain,
  What exultations trampling on despair,
  What tenderness, what tears, what hate of wrong,
What passionate outcry of a soul in pain,
  Uprose this poem of the earth and air,   55
  This medieval miracle of song!

OLIVER WENDELL HOLMES

Old Ironsides

Aye, tear her tattered ensign down!
　Long has it waved on high,
And many an eye has danced to see
　That banner in the sky;
Beneath it rung the battle shout,　　　　5
　And burst the cannon's roar;—
The meteor of the ocean air
　Shall sweep the clouds no more!

Her deck, once red with heroes' blood,
　Where knelt the vanquished foe,　　　10
When winds were hurrying o'er the flood
　And waves were white below,
No more shall feel the victor's tread,
　Or know the conquered knee;—
The harpies of the shore shall pluck　　15
　The eagle of the sea!

O better that her shattered hulk
　Should sink beneath the wave;
Her thunders shook the mighty deep,
　And there should be her grave;　　　20
Nail to the mast her holy flag,
　Set every threadbare sail,
And give her to the god of storms,—
　The lightning and the gale!

The Last Leaf

I saw him once before,
As he passed by the door,
　And again
The pavement stones resound,
As he totters o'er the ground　　　　5
　With his cane.

They say that in his prime,
Ere the pruning-knife of Time
　Cut him down,
Not a better man was found　　　　10
By the Crier on his round
　Through the town.

But now he walks the streets,
And he looks at all he meets
　Sad and wan,　　　　　　　15

And he shakes his feeble head,
That it seems as if he said,
　"They are gone."

The mossy marbles rest
On the lips that he has prest　　　　20
　In their bloom,
And the names he loved to hear
Have been carved for many a year
　On the tomb.

My grandmamma has said—　　　　25
Poor old lady, she is dead
　Long ago—
That he had a Roman nose,
And his cheek was like a rose
　In the snow;　　　　　　30

But now his nose is thin,
And it rests upon his chin
　Like a staff,
And a crook is in his back,
And a melancholy crack　　　　35
　In his laugh.

I know it is a sin
For me to sit and grin
　At him here;
But the old three-cornered hat,　　40
And the breeches, and all that,
　Are so queer!

And if I should live to be
The last leaf upon the tree
　In the spring,　　　　　45
Let them smile, as I do now,
At the old forsaken bough
　Where I cling.

The Chambered Nautilus

This is the ship of pearl, which poets feign,
　Sails the unshadowed main,—
　The venturous bark that flings
On the sweet summer wind its purpled wings

Holmes, *Old Ironsides*. Oliver Wendell Holmes (1809-1894) was a professor of medicine in Harvard University and one of the most distinguished physicians of his time. In his leisure he wrote both poetry and essays.

In gulfs enchanted, where the Siren sings,   5
  And coral reefs lie bare,
Where the cold sea-maids rise to sun their stream-
    ing hair.

Its webs of living gauze no more unfurl;
  Wrecked is the ship of pearl!
  And every chambered cell,   10
Where its dim dreaming life was wont to dwell,
As the frail tenant shaped his growing shell,
  Before thee lies revealed,—
Its irised ceiling rent, its sunless crypt unsealed!

Year after year beheld the silent toil   15
  That spread his lustrous coil;
  Still, as the spiral grew,
He left the past year's dwelling for the new,
Stole with soft step its shining archway through,
  Built up its idle door,   20

Stretched in his last-found home, and knew the old
  no more.

Thanks for the heavenly message brought by thee,
  Child of the wandering sea,
  Cast from her lap, forlorn!
From thy dead lips a clearer note is born   25
Then ever Triton blew from wreathed horn!
  While on mine ear it rings,
Through the deep caves of thought I hear a voice
  that sings:—

Build thee more stately mansions, O my soul,
  As the swift seasons roll!   30
  Leave thy low-vaulted past!
Let each new temple, nobler than the last,
Shut thee from heaven with a dome more vast,
  Till thou at length art free,
Leaving thine outgrown shell by life's unresting
  sea!   35

EDGAR ALLAN POE

To Helen

Helen, thy beauty is to me
  Like those Nicæan barks of yore,
That gently, o'er a perfumed sea,
  The weary, wayworn wanderer bore
  To his own native shore.   5

On desperate seas long wont to roam,
  Thy hyacinth hair, thy classic face,
Thy Naiad airs, have brought me home
  To the glory that was Greece
And the grandeur that was Rome.   10

Lo! in yon brilliant window-niche
  How statue-like I see thee stand,
  The agate lamp within thy hand!
Ah, Psyche, from the regions which
  Are Holy Land!   15

Ulalume

The skies they were ashen and sober;
  The leaves they were crispèd and sere,

The leaves they were withering and sere;
It was night in the lonesome October
  Of my most immemorial year;   5
It was hard by the dim lake of Auber,
  In the misty mid region of Weir:
It was down by the dank tarn of Auber,
  In the ghoul-haunted woodland of Weir.

Here once, through an alley Titanic   10
  Of cypress, I roamed with my Soul—
  Of cypress, with Psyche, my Soul.
These were days when my heart was volcanic
  As the scoriac rivers that roll,
  As the lavas that restlessly roll   15
Their sulphurous currents down Yaanek
  In the ultimate climes of the pole,
That groan as they roll down Mount Yaanek
  In the realms of the boreal pole.

Our talk had been serious and sober,   20
  But our thoughts they were palsied and sere,
  Our memories were treacherous and sere,
For we knew not the month was October,

Poe, *To Helen*. Edgar Allan Poe (1809-1849), though born of a family of actors, was adopted by a wealthy Virginia gentleman and well educated. In the course of his irregular and distressing life he produced a number of outstanding poems and short stories, besides writing voluminous literary criticism. See his story *The Cask of Amontillado*, p. 1373.

And we marked not the night of the year,
  (Ah, night of all nights in the year!)   25
We noted not the dim lake of Auber
  (Though once we had journeyed down here),
Remembered not the dank tarn of Auber
  Nor the ghoul-haunted woodland of Weir.

And now, as the night was senescent   30
  And star-dials pointed to morn,
  As the star-dials hinted of morn,
At the end of our path a liquescent
  And nebulous luster was born,
Out of which a miraculous crescent   35
  Arose, with a duplicate horn,
Astarte's bediamonded crescent
  Distinct with its duplicate horn.

And I said—"She is warmer than Dian:
  She rolls through an ether of sighs,   40
  She revels in a region of sighs:
She has seen that the tears are not dry on
  These cheeks, where the worm never dies,
And has come past the stars of the Lion
  To point us the path to the skies,   45
  To the Lethean peace of the skies:
Come up, in despite of the Lion,
  To shine on us with her bright eyes:
Come up through the lair of the Lion,
  With love in her luminous eyes."   50

But Psyche, uplifting her finger,
  Said—"Sadly this star I mistrust,
  Her pallor I strangely mistrust:
Oh, hasten!—oh, let us not linger!
  Oh, fly!—let us fly!—for we must."   55
In terror she spoke, letting sink her
  Wings until they trailed in the dust;
In agony sobbed, letting sink her
  Plumes till they trailed in the dust,
  Till they sorrowfully trailed in the dust.   60

I replied—"This is nothing but dreaming:
  Let us on by this tremulous light!
  Let us bathe in this crystalline light!
Its sibyllic splendor is beaming
  With hope and in beauty tonight: 65
  See, it flickers up the sky through the night!
Ah, we safely may trust to its gleaming,
  And be sure it will lead us aright:
We safely may trust to a gleaming
  That cannot but guide us aright,   70
  Since it flickers up to Heaven through the night."

Thus I pacified Psyche and kissed her,
  And tempted her out of her gloom,

And conquered her scruples and gloom;
And we passed to the end of the vista,   75
  But were stopped by the door of a tomb,
  By the door of a legended tomb;
And I said—"What is written, sweet sister,
  On the door of this legended tomb?"
  She replied—"Ulalume—Ulalume—   80
  'Tis the vault of thy lost Ulalume!"

Then my heart it grew ashen and sober
  As the leaves that were crispèd and sere,
  As the leaves that were withering and sere,
And I cried—"It was surely October   85
  On this very night of last year
  That I journeyed—I journeyed down here,
  That I brought a dread burden down here:
  On this night of all nights in the year,
  Ah, what demon has tempted me here?   90
Well I know, now, this dim lake of Auber,
  This misty mid region of Weir:
Well I know, now, this dank tarn of Auber,
  This ghoul-haunted woodland of Weir."

Annabel Lee

It was many and many a year ago,
  In a kingdom by the sea,
That a maiden there lived, whom you may know
  By the name of Annabel Lee;—
And this maiden she lived with no other thought
  Than to love, and be loved by me.   6

She was a child and I was a child,
  In this kingdom by the sea;
But we loved with a love that was more than love,
  I and my Annabel Lee—   10
With a love that the wingèd seraphs of heaven
  Coveted her and me.

And this was the reason that, long ago,
  In this kingdom by the sea,
A wind blew out of a cloud by night   15
  Chilling my Annabel Lee;
So that her highborn kinsmen came
  And bore her away from me,
To shut her up in a sepulcher
  In this kingdom by the sea.

The angels, not half so happy in heaven,
  Went envying her and me;
Yes! that was the reason (as all men know,
  In this kingdom by the sea)

That the wind came out of the cloud chilling, 25
  And killing my Annabel Lee.

But our love it was stronger by far than the love
  Of those who were older than we,
  Of many far wiser than we;
And neither the angels in heaven above, 30
  Nor the demons down under the sea,
Can ever dissever my soul from the soul
  Of the beautiful Annabel Lee:

For the moon never beams, without bringing me
    dreams
  Of the beautiful Annabel Lee, 35
And the stars never rise, but I feel the bright eyes
  Of the beautiful Annabel Lee;
And so, all the night-tide, I lie down by the side
Of my darling—my darling—my life and my bride,
  In her sepulcher there by the sea, 40
  In her tomb by the side of the sea.

JAMES RUSSELL LOWELL

A Fable for Critics

[This poem is filled with a great deal of foolery
which is concerned with persons who have long been
forgotten. But in the part here selected Lowell treats
some of his contemporaries whom we all know.]

There comes Emerson first, whose rich words,
    every one,
Are like gold nails in temples to hang trophies on,
Whose prose is grand verse, while his verse, the
    Lord knows,
Is some of it pr— No, 'tis not even prose;
I'm speaking of meters; some poems have welled
From those rare depths of soul that have ne'er
    been excelled; 6
They're not epics, but that doesn't matter a pin,
In creating, the only hard thing's to begin;
A grass-blade's no easier to make than an oak;
If you've once found the way, you've achieved the
    grand stroke; 10
In the worst of his poems are mines of rich matter,
But thrown in a heap with a crush and a clatter;
Now it is not one thing nor another alone
Makes a poem, but rather the general tone,
The something pervading, uniting the whole, 15
The before unconceived, unconceivable soul,
So that just in removing this trifle or that, you
Take away, as it were, a chief limb of the statue;
Roots, wood, bark, and leaves singly perfect may
    be,
But, clapt hodge-podge together, they don't make
    a tree. 20

But, to come back to Emerson (whom, by the
    way,
I believe we left waiting),—his is, we may say,
A Greek head on right Yankee shoulders, whose
    range
Has Olympus for one pole, for t'other the Ex-
    change;
He seems, to my thinking (although I'm afraid 25
The comparison must, long ere this, have been
    made),
A Plotinus-Montaigne, where the Egyptian's gold
    mist
And the Gascon's shrewd wit cheek-by-jowl co-
    exist,
All admire, and yet scarcely six converts he's got
To I don't (nor they either) exactly know what;
For though he builds glorious temples, 'tis odd 31
He leaves never a doorway to get in a god.
'Tis refreshing to old-fashioned people like me
To meet such a primitive Pagan as he,
In whose mind all creation is duly respected 35
As parts of himself—just a little projected;
And who's willing to worship the stars and the
    sun,
A convert to—nothing but Emerson.
So perfect a balance there is in his head,
That he talks of things sometimes as if they were
    dead; 40
Life, nature, love, God, and affairs of that sort,
He looks at as merely ideas; in short,
As if they were fossils stuck round in a cabinet,
Of such vast extent that our earth's a mere dab
    in it;

Lowell, *A Fable for Critics,* selections. James Russell Lowell (1819-1891) was not only a distinguished poet and essayist but a successful diplomat and literary scholar. He succeeded Longfellow as
Professor of Modern Languages at Harvard.

Composed just as he is inclined to conjecture her,
Namely, one part pure earth, ninety-nine parts
    pure lecturer;   46
You are filled with delight at his clear demonstra-
    tion,
Each figure, word, gesture, just fits the occasion,
With the quiet precision of science he'll sort 'em
But you can't help suspecting the whole a *post
    mortem.*   50

.   .   .   .   .

   There are persons, mole-blind to the soul's make
    and style,
Who insist on a likeness 'twixt him and Carlyle;
To compare him with Plato would be vastly fairer,
Carlyle's the more burly, but E. is the rarer;
He sees fewer objects, but clearlier, truelier,   55
If C.'s as original, E.'s more peculiar;
That he's more of a man you might say of the one,
Of the other he's more of an Emerson;
C.'s the Titan, as shaggy of mind as of limb,—
E. the clear-eyed Olympian, rapid and slim;   60
The one's two thirds Norseman, the other half
    Greek,
Where the one's most abounding, the other's to
    seek;
C.'s generals require to be seen in the mass,—
E.'s specialties gain if enlarged by the glass;
C. gives nature and God his own fits of the blues,
And rims common-sense things with mystical
    hues,—   66
E. sits in a mystery calm and intense,
And looks coolly around him with sharp common-
    sense;
C. shows you how every-day matters unite
With the dim transdiurnal recesses of night,—   70
While E., in a plain, preternatural way,
Makes mysteries matters of mere every day;
C. draws all his characters quite *à la* Fuseli,—
He don't sketch their bundles of muscles and thews
    illy,
But he paints with a brush so untamed and pro-
    fuse,   75
They seem nothing but bundles of muscles and
    thews;
E. is rather like Flaxman, lines strait and severe,
And a colorless outline, but full, round, and clear;—
To the men he thinks worthy he frankly accords
The design of a white marble statue in words.   80
C. labors to get at the center, and then
Take a reckoning from there of his actions and
    men;
E. calmly assumes the said center as granted,

And, given himself, has whatever is wanted.
   He has imitators in scores, who omit   85
No part of the man but his wisdom and wit,—
Who go carefully o'er the sky-blue of his brain,
And when he has skimmed it once, skim it again;
If at all they resemble him, you may be sure it is
Because their shoals mirror his mists and obscuri-
    ties,   90
As a mud-puddle seems deep as heaven for a
    minute,
While a cloud that floats o'er is reflected within it.

.   .   .   .   .

   There is Bryant, as quiet, as cool, and as digni-
    fied,
As a smooth, silent iceberg, that never is ignified,
Save when by reflection 'tis kindled o' nights   95
With a semblance of flame by the chill Northern
    Lights.
He may rank (Griswold says so) first bard of your
    nation
(There's no doubt that he stands in supreme ice-
    olation),
Your topmost Parnassus he may set his heel on,
But no warm applauses come, peal following peal
    on,—   100
He's too smooth and too polished to hang any
    zeal on:
Unqualified merits, I'll grant, if you choose, he
    has 'em,
But he lacks the one merit of kindling enthusiasm;
If he stir you at all, it is just, on my soul,   104
Like being stirred up with the very North Pole.
   He is very nice reading in summer, but *inter
Nos,* we don't want *extra* freezing in winter;
Take him up in the depth of July, my advice is,
When you feel an Egyptian devotion to ices.
But, deduct all you can, there's enough that's right
    good in him,   110
He has a true soul for field, river, and wood in
    him;
And his heart, in the midst of brick walls, or wher-
    e'er it is,
Glows, softens, and thrills with the tenderest chari-
    ties—
To you mortals that delve in this trade-ridden
    planet?
No, to old Berkshire's hills, with their limestone
    and granite.   115
If you're one who *in loco* (add *foco* here) *desipis,*
You will get of his outermost heart (as I guess) a
    piece;

But you'd get deeper down if you came as a preci-
    pice,
And would break the last seal of its inwardest
    fountain,
If you only could palm yourself off for a moun-
    tain.   120
Mr. Quivis, or somebody quite as discerning,
Some scholar who's hourly expecting his learning,
Calls B. The American Wordsworth; but Words-
    worth
Is worth near as much as your whole tuneful
    herd's worth.
No, don't be absurd, he's an excellent Bryant; 125
But, my friends, you'll endanger the life of your
    client,
By attempting to stretch him up into a giant:
If you choose to compare him, I think there are
    two per-
sons fit for a parallel—Thomson and Cowper;[1]
I don't mean exactly,—there's something of each,
There's T.'s love of nature, C.'s penchant to
    preach;   131
Just mix up their minds so that C.'s spice of crazi-
    ness
Shall balance and neutralize T.'s turn for laziness,
And it gives you a brain cool, quite frictionless,
    quiet,
Whose internal police nips the buds of all riot,—
A brain like a permanent strait-jacket put on 136
The heart that strives vainly to burst off a button,—
A brain which, without being slow or mechanic,
Does more than a larger less drilled, more vol-
    canic;
He's a Cowper condensed, with no craziness bit-
    ten,   140
And the advantage that Wordsworth before him
    had written.
    But, my dear little bardlings, don't prick up your
    ears
Nor suppose I would rank you and Bryant as
    peers;
If I call him an iceberg, I don't mean to say
There is nothing in that which is grand in its
    way;   145
He is almost the one of your poets that knows
How much grace, strength, and dignity lie in
    Repose;
If he sometimes fall short, he is too wise to mar
His thought's modest fullness by going too far;

'Twould be well if your authors should all make a
    trial   150
Of what virtue there is in severe self-denial,
And measure their writings by Hesiod's staff,
Which teaches that all has less value than half.

    There is Whittier, whose swelling and vehement
    heart
Strains the strait-breasted drab of the Quaker
    apart,   155
And reveals the live Man, still supreme and erect,
Underneath the bemummying wrappers of sect;
There was ne'er a man born who had more of the
    swing
Of the true lyric bard and all that kind of thing;
And his failures arise (though perhaps he don't
    know it)   160
From the very same cause that has made him a
    poet,—
A fervor of mind which knows no separation
'Twixt simple excitement and pure inspiration,
As my Pythoness erst sometimes erred from not
    knowing
If't were I or mere wind through her tripod was
    blowing;   165
Let his mind once get head in its favorite direction
And the torrent of verse bursts the dams of reflec-
    tion,
While, borne with the rush of the meter along,
The poet may chance to go right or go wrong,
Content with the whirl and delirium of song; 170
Then his grammar's not always correct, not his
    rhymes,
And he's prone to repeat his own lyrics sometimes,
Not his best, though, for those are struck off at
    white-heats
When the heart in his breast like a trip-hammer
    beats,
And can ne'er be repeated again any more 175
Than they could have been carefully plotted be-
    fore:
Like old what's-his-name there at the battle of
    Hastings
(Who, however, gave more than mere rhythmical
    bastings),
Our Quaker leads off metaphorical fights 179
For reform and whatever they call human rights,
Both singing and striking in front of the war,
And hitting his foes with the mallet of Thor;

---

[1] To demonstrate quickly and easily how per-
versely absurd 'tis to sound this name *Cowper*,
As people in general call him named *super*,
I remark that he rhymes it himself with horse-trooper.

Anne hæc, one exclaims, on beholding his knocks,
Vestis filii tui,[2] O leather-clad Fox?
Can that be thy son, in the battle's mid din,   185
Preaching brotherly love and then driving it in
To the brain of the tough old Goliath of sin,
With the smoothest of pebbles from Castaly's
     spring
Impressed on his hard moral sense with a sling?
   All honor and praise to the right-hearted bard
Who was true to The Voice when such service was
     hard,   191
Who himself was so free he dared sing for the
     slave
When to look but a protest in silence was brave;
All honor and praise to the women and men
Who spoke out for the dumb and the down-trod-
     den then!   195
I need not to name them, already for each
I see History preparing the statue and niche;
They were harsh, but shall *you* be so shocked at
     hard words
Who have beaten your pruning-hooks up into
     swords,   199
Whose rewards and hurrahs men are surer to gain
By the reaping of men and of women than grain?
Why should *you* stand aghast at their fierce wordy
     war, if
You scalp one another for Bank or for Tariff?
Your calling them cut-throats and knaves all day
     long
Doesn't prove that the use of hard language is
     wrong;   205
While the World's heart beats quicker to think of
     such men
As signed Tyranny's doom with a bloody steel-pen,
While on Fourth-of-Julys beardless orators fright
     one
With hints at Harmodius and Aristogeiton,
You need not look shy at your sisters and brothers
Who stab with sharp words for the freedom of
     others;—   211
No, a wreath, twine a wreath for the loyal and
     true
Who, for sake of the many, dared stand with the
     few,
Not of blood-spattered laurel for enemies braved,
But of broad, peaceful oak-leaves for citizens
     saved!   215

     .   .   .   .   .

   There is Hawthorne, with genius so shrinking
     and rare

That you hardly at first see the strength that is
     there;
A frame so robust, with a nature so sweet,
So earnest, so graceful, so solid, so fleet,
Is worth a descent from Olympus to meet;   220
'Tis as if a rough oak that for ages had stood,
With his gnarled bony branches like ribs of the
     wood,
Should bloom, after cycles of struggle and scathe,
With a single anemone trembly and rathe;
His strength is so tender, his wildness so meek,
That a suitable parallel sets one to seek,—   226
He's a John Bunyan Fouqué, a Puritan Tieck;
When Nature was shaping him, clay was not
     granted
For making so full-sized a man as she wanted,
So, to fill out her model, a little she spared   230
From some finer-grained stuff for a woman pre-
     pared,
And she could not have hit a more excellent plan
For making him fully and perfectly man.
The success of her scheme gave her so much de-
     light,
That she tried it again, shortly after, in Dwight;
Only, while she was kneading and shaping the
     clay,   236
She sang to her work in her sweet childish way,
And found, when she'd put the last touch to his
     soul,
That the music had somehow got mixed with the
     whole.

   Here's Cooper, who's written six volumes to
     show   240
He's as good as a lord: well, let's grant that he's
     so;
If a person prefer that description of praise,
Why, a coronet's certainly cheaper than bays;
But he need take no pains to convince us he's not
(As his enemies say) the American Scott.   245
Choose any twelve men, and let C. read aloud
That one of his novels of which he's most proud,
And I'd lay any bet that, without ever quitting
Their box, they'd be all, to a man, for acquitting.
He has drawn you one character, though, that is
     new,   250
One wildflower he's plucked that is wet with the
     dew
Of this fresh Western world, and, the thing not to
     mince,
He has done naught but copy it ill ever since;

---

[2] Are these the garments of your son?

His Indians, with proper respect be it said,
Are just Natty Bumpo, daubed over with red, 255
And his very Long Toms are the same useful Nat,
Rigged up in duck pants and a sou'-wester hat
(Though once in a Coffin, a good chance was
    found
To have slipped the old fellow away under-
    ground).
All his other men-figures are clothes upon sticks,
The *dernière chemise* [3] of a man in a fix   261
(As a captain besieged, when his garrison's small,
Sets up caps upon poles to be seen o'er the wall);
And the women he draws from one model don't
    vary,
All sappy as maples and flat as a prairie.   265
When a character's wanted, he goes to the task
As a cooper would do in composing a cask;
He picks out the staves, of their qualities heedful,
Just hoops them together as tight as is needful,
And, if the best fortune should crown the attempt,
    he   270
Has made at the most something wooden and
    empty.
    Don't suppose I would underrate Cooper's abili-
    ties;
If I thought you'd do that, I should feel very ill at
    ease;
The men who have given to *one* character life
And objective existence are not very rife;   275
You may number them all, both prose-writers and
    singers,
Without overrunning the bounds of your fingers,
And Natty won't go to oblivion quicker
Than Adams the parson or Primrose the vicar.
    There is one thing in Cooper I like, too, and
    that is   280
That on manners he lectures his countrymen
    gratis;
Not precisely so either, because, for a rarity,
He is paid for his tickets in unpopularity.
Now he may overcharge his American pictures,
But you'll grant there's a good deal of truth in his
    strictures;   285
And I honor the man who is willing to sink
Half his present repute for the freedom to think,
And, when he has thought, be his cause strong or
    weak,
Will risk t'other half for the freedom to speak,
Caring naught for what vengeance the mob has in
    store,   290
Let that mob be the upper ten thousand or lower.
    There are truths you Americans need to be told,

And it never'll refute them to swagger and scold;
John Bull, looking o'er the Atlantic, in choler
At your aptness for trade, says you worship the
    dollar;   295
But to scorn such eye-dollar-try's what very few
    do,
And John goes to that church as often as you do.
No matter what John says, don't try to outcrow
    him,
'Tis enough to go quietly on and outgrow him;
Like most fathers, Bull hates to see Number One
Displacing himself in the mind of his son,   301
And detests the same faults in himself he'd neg-
    lected
When he sees them again in his child's glass re-
    flected;
To love one another you're too like by half;
If he is a bull, you're a pretty stout calf,   305
And tear your own pasture for naught but to show
What a nice pair of horns you're beginning to
    grow.
    There are one or two things I should just like to
    hint,
For you don't often get the truth told you in print;
The most of you (this is what strikes all behold-
    ers)   310
Have a mental and physical stoop in the shoulders;
Though you ought to be free as the winds and the
    waves,
You've the gait and the manners of runaway
    slaves;
Though you brag of your New World, you don't
    half believe in it;
And as much of the Old as is possible weave in it;
Your goddess of freedom, a tight, buxom girl, 316
With lips like a cherry and teeth like a pearl,
With eyes bold as Herë's, and hair floating free,
And full of the sun as the spray of the sea,
Who can sing at a husking or romp at a shearing,
Who can trip through the forests alone without
    fearing,   321
Who can drive home the cows with a song
    through the grass,
Keeps glancing aside into Europe's cracked glass,
Hides her red hands in gloves, pinches up her
    lithe waist,
And makes herself wretched with transmarine
    taste;   325
She loses her fresh country charm when she takes
Any mirror except her own rivers and lakes.
    You steal Englishmen's books and think Eng-
    lishmen's thought,

<hr/>
[3] Last shirt.

With their salt on her tail your wild eagle is
    caught;
Your literature suits its each whisper and motion
To what will be thought of it over the ocean; 331
The cast clothes of Europe your statesmanship
    tries
And mumbles again the old blarneys and lies;—
Forget Europe wholly, your veins throb with
    blood,
To which the dull current in hers is but mud; 335
Let her sneer, let her say your experiment fails,
In her voice there's a tremble e'en now while she
    rails,
And your shore will soon be in the nature of
    things
Covered thick with gilt drift-wood of runaway
    kings,
Where alone, as it were in a Longfellow's Waif,
Her fugitive pieces will find themselves safe. 341
O my friends, thank your God, if you have one,
    that he
'Twixt the Old World and you set the gulf of a
    sea;
Be strong-backed, brown-handed, upright as your
    pines, 344
By the scale of a hemisphere shape your designs,
Be true to yourselves and this new nineteenth age,
As a statue by Powers, or a picture by Page,
Plow, sail, forge, build, carve, paint, all things
    make new,
To your own New-World instincts contrive to be
    true, 349
Keep your ears open wide to the Future's first call,
Be whatever you will, but yourselves first of all,
Stand fronting the dawn on Toil's heaven-scaling
    peaks,
And become my new race of more practical
    Greeks.—
Hem! your likeness at present, I shudder to tell
    o't,
Is that you have your slaves, and the Greek had his
    helot. 355

.   .   .   .   .

  There comes Poe, with his raven, like Barnaby
    Rudge,
Three fifths of him genius and two fifths sheer
    fudge,
Who talks like a book of iambs and pentameters,
In a way to make people of common sense damn
    meters,
Who has written some things quite the best of
    their kind, 360

But the heart somehow seems all squeezed out by
    the mind,
Who— But hey-day! What's this? Messieurs
    Mathews and Poe,
You mustn't fling mud-balls at Longfellow so,
Does it make a man worse that his character's
    such
As to make his friends love him (as you think)
    too much? 365
Why, there is not a bard at this moment alive
More willing than he that his fellows should
    thrive;
While you are abusing him thus, even now,
He would help either one of you out of a slough;
You may say that he's smooth and all that till
    you're hoarse, 370
But remember that elegance also is force;
After polishing granite as much as you will,
The heart keeps its tough old persistency still;
Deduct all you can, *that* still keeps you at bay;
Why, he'll live till men weary of Collins and
    Gray. 375
I'm not over-fond of Greek meters in English,
To me rhyme's a gain, so it be not too jinglish,
And your modern hexameter verses are no more
Like Greek ones than sleek Mr. Pope is like
    Homer; 379
As the roar of the sea to the coo of a pigeon is,
So, compared to your moderns, sounds old Mele-
    sigenes;
I may be too partial, the reason, perhaps, o't is
That I've heard the old blind man recite his own
    rhapsodies,
And my ear with that music impregnate may be,
Like the poor exiled shell with the soul of the sea,
Or as one can't bear Strauss when his nature is
    cloven 386
To its deeps within deeps by the stroke of Bee-
    thoven;
But, set that aside, and 'tis truth that I speak,
Had Theocritus written in English, not Greek,
I believe that his exquisite sense would scarce
    change a line 390
In that rare, tender, virgin-like pastoral Evangeline.
That's not ancient nor modern, its place is apart
Where time has no sway, in the realm of pure Art,
'Tis a shrine of retreat from Earth's hubbub and
    strife
As quiet and chaste as the author's own life. 395

.   .   .   .   .

  What! Irving? thrice welcome, warm heart and
    fine brain,

You bring back the happiest spirit from Spain,
And the gravest sweet humor, that ever were there
Since Cervantes met death in his gentle despair;
Nay, don't be embarrassed, nor look so beseech-
  ing,—   400
I sha'n't run directly against my own preaching,
And, having just laughed at their Raphaels and
  Dantes,
Go to setting you up beside matchless Cervantes;
But allow me to speak what I honestly feel,—
To a true poet-heart add the fun of Dick Steele,
Throw in all of Addison, *minus* the chill,   406
With the whole of that partnership's stock and
  good-will,
Mix well, and while stirring, hum o'er, as a spell,
The fine *old* English Gentleman, simmer it well,
Sweeten just to your own private liking, then
  strain,   410
That only the finest and clearest remain,
Let it stand out of doors till a soul it receives
From the warm lazy sun loitering down through
  green leaves,
And you'll find a choice nature, not wholly deserv-
  ing
A name either English or Yankee,—just Irving.

         .   .   .   .   .

There's Holmes, who is matchless among you
  for wit;   416
A Leyden-jar always full-charged, from which flit
The electrical tingles of hit after hit;
In long poems 'tis painful sometimes, and invites
A thought of the way the new Telegraph writes,
Which pricks down its little sharp sentences spite-
  fully   421
As if you got more than you'd title to rightfully,
And you find yourself hoping its wild father
  Lightning
Would flame in for a second and give you a fright-
  'ning.

He has perfect sway of what *I* call a sham me-
  ter,
But many admire it, the English pentameter,   426
And Campbell, I think, wrote most commonly
  worse,
With less nerve, swing, and fire in the same kind
  of verse,
Nor e'er achieved aught in't so worthy of praise
As the tribute of Holmes to the grand *Marseillaise*.
You went crazy last year over Bulwer's New
  Timon;—   431
Why, if B., to the day of his dying, should rhyme
  on,
Heaping verses on verses and tomes upon tomes,
He could ne'er reach the best point and vigor of
  Holmes.
His are just the fine hands, too, to weave you a
  lyric   435
Full of fancy, fun, feeling, or spiced with satyric
In a measure so kindly, you doubt if the toes
That are trodden upon are your own or your foes'.

There is Lowell, who's striving Parnassus to
  climb
With a whole bale of *isms* tied together with
  rhyme,   440
He might get on alone, spite of brambles and
  boulders,
But he can't with that buncle he has on his shoul-
  ders,
The top of the hill he will ne'er come nigh reach-
  ing
Till he learns the distinction 'twixt singing and
  preaching;
His lyre has some chords that would ring pretty
  well,   445
But he'd rather by half make a drum of the shell,
And rattle away till he's old as Methusalem,
At the head of a march to the last new Jerusalem.

WALT WHITMAN

Come Up from the Fields, Father

Come up from the fields, father, here's a letter
    from our Pete,
And come to the front door, mother, here's a letter
    from thy dear son.

Lo, 'tis autumn,
Lo, where the trees, deeper green, yellower and
    redder,
Coo! and sweeten Ohio's villages with leaves flut-
    tering in the moderate wind,   5
Where apples ripe in the orchards hang and grapes
    on the trellis'd vines,
(Smell you the smell of the grapes on the vines?
Smell you the buckwheat where the bees were
    lately buzzing?)
Above all, lo, the sky so calm, so transparent after
    the rain, and with wondrous clouds,
Below too, all calm, all vital and beautiful, and the
    farm prospers well.   10

Down in the fields all prospers well,
But now from the fields come, father, come at the
    daughter's call,
And come to the entry, mother, to the front door
    come right away.

Fast as she can she hurries, something ominous,
    her steps trembling,
She does not tarry to smooth her hair nor adjust
    her cap.   15

Open the envelope quickly,
O this is not our son's writing, yet his name is
    sign'd,
O a strange hand writes for our dear son, O
    stricken mother's soul!
All swims before her eyes, flashes with black, she
    catches the main words only,
Sentence broken, *gunshot wound in the breast,
    cavalry skirmish, taken to hospital,*   20
At present low, but will soon be better.

Ah now the single figure to me,
Amid all teeming and wealthy Ohio with all its
    cities and farms,
Sickly white in the face and dull in the head, very
    faint,
By the jamb of a door leans.   25

Grieve not so, dear mother (the just-grown daugh-
    ter speaks through her sobs,
The little sisters huddle around speechless and
    dismay'd),
*See, dearest mother, the letter says Pete will soon
    be better.*

Alas poor boy, he will never be better (nor may-be
    needs to be better, that brave and simple soul),
While they stand at home at the door he is dead
    already,   30
The only son is dead.

But the mother needs to be better,
She with thin form presently drest in black,
By day her meals untouched, then at night fitfully
    sleeping, often waking,
In the midnight waking, weeping, longing with
    one deep longing,   35
O that she might withdraw unnoticed, silent from
    life escape and withdraw,
To follow, to seek, to be with her dear dead son.

O Captain! My Captain!

O Captain! my Captain! our fearful trip is done,
The ship has weather'd every rack, the prize we
    sought is won,
The port is near, the bells I hear, the people all
    exulting,
While follow eyes the steady keel, the vessel grim
    and daring;
    But O heart! heart! heart!   5
        O the bleeding drops of red,
            Where on the deck my Captain lies,
                Fallen cold and dead.

O Captain! my Captain! rise up and hear the bells;
Rise up—for you the flag is flung—for you the
    bugle trills,   10
For you bouquets and ribbon'd wreaths—for you
    the shores a-crowding,

Whitman, *Come Up from the Fields, Father.* Walt Whitman (1819-1892) was born on Long Island
and trained as a journalist. He held various government positions in Washington during and after the
Civil War. Though his *Leaves of Grass* appeared in 1855, he continued to add poems to it throughout
his life.

For you they call, the swaying mass, their eager
faces turning;
Here Captain! dear father!
This arm beneath your head!
It is some dream that on the deck,   15
You've fallen cold and dead.

My Captain does not answer, his lips are pale and
still,
My father does not feel my arm, he has no pulse
nor will,
The ship is anchor'd safe and sound, its voyage
closed and done,
From fearful trip the victor ship comes in with
object won;   20
Exult O shores, and ring O bells!
But I with mournful tread,
Walk the deck my Captain lies,
Fallen cold and dead.

Mannahatta

I was asking for something specific and perfect for
my city,
Whereupon lo! upsprang the aboriginal name.

Now I see what there is in a name, a word, liquid,
sane, unruly, musical, self-sufficient,
I see that the word of my city is that word from of
old,
Because I see that word nested in nests of water-
bays, superb,   5
Rich, hemm'd thick all around with sailships and
steamships, an island sixteen miles long, solid-
founded,
Numberless crowded streets, high growths of iron,
slender, strong, light, splendidly uprising toward clear skies,
Tides swift and ample, well-loved by me, toward
sundown,
The flowing sea-currents, the little islands, larger
adjoining islands, the heights, the villas,
The countless masts, the white shore-steamers, the
lighters, the ferry-boats, the black sea-steamers
well-model'd,   10
The down-town streets, the jobbers' houses of business, the houses of business of the ship-mer-
chants and money-brokers, the river-streets,
Immigrants arriving, fifteen or twenty thousand in
a week,
The carts hauling goods, the manly race of drivers
of horses, the brown-faced sailors,

The summer air, the bright sun shining, and the
sailing clouds aloft,
The winter snows, the sleigh-bells, the broken ice
in the river, passing along up or down with
the flood-tide or ebb-tide,   15
The mechanics of the city, the masters, well-
form'd, beautiful-faced, looking you straight
in the eyes,
Trottoirs throng'd, vehicles, Broadway, the
woman, the shops and shows,
A million people—manners free and superb—open
voices—hospitality—the most courageous and
friendly young men,
City of hurried and sparkling waters! city of spires
and masts!
City nested in bays! my city!   20

When Lilacs Last in the Dooryard Bloomed

1

When lilacs last in the dooryard bloomed,
And the great star early drooped in the western
sky in the night,
I mourned, and yet shall mourn with ever-return-
ing spring.
Ever-returning spring, trinity sure to me you
bring,
Lilac blooming perennial and drooping star in the
west,   5
And thought of him I love.

2

O powerful western fallen star!
O shades of night—O moody, tearful night!
O great star disappeared—O the black murk that
hides the star!
O cruel hands that hold me powerless—O helpless
soul of me!   10
O harsh surrounding cloud that will not free my
soul.

3

In the dooryard fronting an old farmhouse near
the whitewashed palings,
Stands the lilac-bush tall-growing with heart-
shaped leaves of rich green,
With many a pointed blossom rising delicate, with
the perfume strong I love,
With every leaf a miracle—and from this bush in
the dooryard,   15

Whitman, *When Lilacs Last in the Dooryard Bloomed*. Written on the death of Lincoln, as was also
O Captain! My Captain!

With delicate-colored blossoms and heart-shaped
　leaves of rich green,
A sprig with its flower I break.

4

In the swamp in secluded recesses,
A shy and hidden bird is warbling a song.

Solitary the thrush,　　　　　　　　　　20
The hermit withdrawn to himself, avoiding the
　settlements,
Sings by himself a song.

Song of the bleeding throat,
Death's outlet song of life (for well, dear brother,
　I know,
If thou wast not granted to sing thou would'st
　surely die).　　　　　　　　　　　　25

5

Over the breast of the spring, the land, amid cities,
Amid lanes and through old woods, where lately
　the violets peeped from the ground, spotting
　the gray débris,
Amid the grass in the fields each side of the lanes,
　passing the endless grass,
Passing the yellow-speared wheat, every grain
　from its shroud in the dark-brown fields up-
　risen,
Passing the apple-tree blows of white and pink in
　the orchards,　　　　　　　　　　　30
Carrying a corpse to where it shall rest in the
　grave,
Night and day journeys a coffin.

6

Coffin that passes through lanes and streets,
Through day and night with the great cloud dark-
　ening the land,
With the pomp of the inlooped flags with the cities
　draped in black,　　　　　　　　　35
With the show of the States themselves as of
　crape-veiled women standing,
With processions long and winding and the flam-
　beaus of the night,
With the countless torches lit, with the silent sea
　of faces and the unbared heads,
With the waiting depot, the arriving coffin, and
　the somber faces,
With dirges through the night, with the thousand
　voices rising strong and solemn,　　　40
With all the mournful voices of the dirges poured
　around the coffin,

The dim-lit churches and the shuddering organs—
　where amid these you journey,
With the tolling, tolling bells' perpetual clang,
Here, coffin that slowly passes,
I give you my sprig of lilac.　　　　　45

7

(Nor for you, for one alone,
Blossoms and branches green to coffins all I bring,
For fresh as the morning, thus would I chant a
　song for you, O sane and sacred death.

All over bouquets of roses,
O death, I cover you over with roses and early
　lilies,　　　　　　　　　　　　50
But mostly and now the lilac that blooms the first,
Copious I break, I break the sprigs from the
　bushes,
With loaded arms I come, pouring for you,
For you and the coffins all of you, O death.)

8

O western orb sailing the heaven,　　　55
Now I know what you must have meant as a
　month since I walked,
As I walked in silence the transparent shadowy
　night,
As I saw you had something to tell as you bent to
　me night after night,
As you drooped from the sky low down as if to
　my side (while the other stars all looked on),
As we wandered together the solemn night (for
　something I know not what kept me from
　sleep),　　　　　　　　　　　　60
As the night advanced, and I saw on the rim of
　the west how full you were of woe,
As I stood on the rising ground in the breeze in
　the cool, transparent night,
As I watched where you passed, and was lost in
　the netherward black of the night,
As my soul in its trouble dissatisfied sank, as
　where you, sad orb,　　　　　　　64
Concluded, dropped in the night, and was gone.

9

Sing on there in the swamp,
O singer bashful and tender, I hear your notes, I
　hear your call,
I hear, I come presently, I understand you;
But a moment I linger, for the lustrous star has
　detained me,
The star my departing comrade holds and detains
　me.　　　　　　　　　　　　　70

10

O how shall I warble myself for the dead one there
    I loved?
And how shall I deck my song for the large sweet
    soul that has gone?
And what shall my perfume be for the grave of
    him I love?

Sea-winds blown from east and west,   74
Blown from the Eastern sea and blown from the
    Western sea, till there on the prairies meeting,
These and with these and the breath of my chant,
I'll perfume the grave of him I love.

11

O what shall I hang on the chamber walls?
And what shall the pictures be that I hang on the
    walls,
To adorn the burial-house of him I love?   80

Pictures of growing spring and farms and homes,
With the fourth-month eve at sundown, and the
    gray smoke lucid and bright,
With floods of the yellow gold of the gorgeous,
    indolent, sinking sun, burning, expanding the
    air,
With the fresh sweet herbage under foot, and the
    pale green leaves of the trees prolific,
In the distance the flowing glaze, the breast of the
    river, with a wind-dapple here and there,   85
With ranging hills on the banks, with many a line
    against the sky, and shadows,
And the city at hand with dwellings so dense, and
    stacks of chimneys,
And all the scenes of life and the workshops, and
    the workmen homeward returning.

12

Lo, body and soul—this land,
My own Manhattan with spires, and the sparkling
    and hurrying tides, and the ships,   90
The varied and ample land, the South and the
    North in the light, Ohio's shores and flashing
    Missouri,
And ever the far-spreading prairies covered with
    grass and corn.

Lo, the most excellent sun so calm and haughty,
The violet and purple morn with just-felt breezes,
The gentle soft-born measureless light,   95
The miracle spreading bathing all, the fulfilled
    noon.

The coming eve delicious, the welcome night and
    the stars,
Over my cities shining all, enveloping man and
    land.

13

Sing on, sing on, you gray-brown bird,
Sing from the swamps, the recesses, pour your
    chant from the bushes,   100
Limitless out of the dusk, out of the cedars and
    pines.
Sing on, dearest brother, warble your reedy song,
Loud human song, with voice of uttermost woe.

O liquid and free and tender!
O wild and loose to my soul—O wondrous singer!
You only I hear—yet the star holds me (but will
    soon depart),   106
Yet the lilac with mastering odor holds me.

14

Now while I sat in the day and looked forth,
In the close of the day with its light and the fields
    of spring, and the farmers preparing their
    crops,
In the large unconscious scenery of my land with
    its lakes and forests,   110
In the heavenly aërial beauty (after the perturbed
    winds and the storms),
Under the arching heavens of the afternoon swift
    passing, and the voices of children and women,
The many-moving sea-tides, and I saw the ships
    how they sailed,
And the summer approaching with richness, and
    the fields all busy with labor,
And the infinite separate houses, how they all
    went on, each with its meals and minutia of
    daily usages,   115
And the streets how their throbbings throbbed,
    and the cities pent—lo, then and there,
Falling upon them all and among them all, en-
    veloping me with the rest,
Appeared the cloud, appeared the long black trail,
And I knew death, its thought, and the sacred
    knowledge of death.

Then with the knowledge of death as walking one
    side of me,   120
And the thought of death close-walking the other
    side of me,
And I in the middle as with companions, and as
    holding the hands of companions,
I fled forth to the hiding receiving night that talks
    not,

Down to the shores of the water, the path by the
    swamp in the dimness,
To the solemn shadowy cedars and ghostly pines
    so still.   125

And the singer so shy to the rest received me,
The gray-brown bird I know received us comrades
    three,
And he sang the carol of death, and a verse for
    him I love.
From deep secluded recesses,
From the fragrant cedars and the ghostly pines so
    still,   130
Came the carol of the bird.

And the charm of the carol rapt me,
As I held as if by their hands my comrades in the
    night,
And the voice of my spirit tallied the song of the
    bird.

Come, lovely and soothing death,   135
Undulate round the world, serenely arriving, ar-
    riving,
In the day, in the night, to all, to each,
Sooner or later delicate death.

Praised be the fathomless universe,
For life and joy, and for objects and knowledge
    curious,   140
And for love, sweet love—but praise! praise!
    praise!
For the sure-enwinding arms of cool-enfolding
    death.

Dark mother always gliding near with soft feet,
Have none chanted for thee a chant of fullest wel-
    come?
Then I chant it for thee, I glorify thee above all,
I bring thee a song that when thou must indeed
    come, come unfalteringly.   146

Approach, strong deliveress,
When it is so, when thou hast taken them, I joy-
    ously sing the dead,
Lost in the loving floating ocean of thee,
Laved in the flood of thy bliss, O death.   150

From me to thee glad serenades,
Dances for thee I propose saluting thee, adorn-
    ments and feastings for thee,
And the sights of the open landscape and the high-
    spread sky are fitting,

And life and the fields, and the huge and thought-
    ful night.

The night in silence under many a star,   155
The ocean shore and the husky whispering wave
    whose voice I know,
And the soul turning to thee, O vast and well-
    veiled death,
And the body gratefully nestling close to thee.

Over the tree-tops I float thee a song,
Over the rising and sinking waves, over the myr-
    iad fields and the prairies wide,   160
Over the dense-packed cities all and the teeming
    wharves and ways,
I float this carol with joy, with joy to thee, O death.

15

To the tally of my soul,
Loud and strong kept up the gray-brown bird,
With pure deliberate notes spreading, filling the
    night.   165

Loud in the pines and cedars dim,
Clear in the freshness moist and the swamp-
    perfume,
And I with my comrades there in the night.

While my sight that was bound in my eyes un-
    closed,
As to long panoramas of visions.   170

And I saw askant the armies,
I saw as in noiseless dreams hundreds of battle-
    flags,
Borne through the smoke of the battles and pierced
    with missiles I saw them,
And carried hither and yon through the smoke,
    and torn and bloody,
And at last but a few shreds left on the staffs (and
    all in silence),   175
And the staffs all splintered and broken.

I saw battle-corpses, myriads of them,
And the white skeletons of young men, I saw
    them,
I saw the débris and débris of all the slain soldiers
    of the war,
But I saw they were not as was thought;   180
They themselves were fully at rest, they suffered
    not,
The living remained and suffered, the mother
    suffered,

And the wife and the child and the musing comrade suffered,
And the armies that remained suffered.

16

Passing the visions, passing the night,   185
Passing, unloosing the hold of my comrades'
hands,
Passing the song of the hermit bird and the tallying song of my soul,
Victorious song, death's outlet song, yet varying
ever-altering song,
As low and wailing, yet clear the notes, rising and
falling, flooding the night,
Sadly sinking and fainting, as warning and warning, and yet again bursting with joy,   190

Covering the earth and filling the spread of the
heaven,
As that powerful psalm in the night I heard from
recesses,
Passing, I leave thee, lilac with heart-shaped leaves,
I leave thee there in the dooryard, blooming, returning with spring.

I cease from my song for thee,   195
From my gaze on thee in the west, fronting the
west, communing with thee,
O comrade lustrous with silver face in the night.

Yet each to keep and all, retrievements out of the
night,
The song, the wondrous chant of the gray-brown
bird,

And the tallying chant, the echo aroused in my
soul,   200
With the lustrous and drooping star with the
countenance full of woe,
With the holders holding my hand nearing the
call of the bird,
Comrades mine and I in the midst, and their
memory ever to keep, for the dead I loved so
well,
For the sweetest, wisest soul of all my days and
lands—and this for his dear sake,
Lilac and star and bird twined with the chant of
my soul,   205
There in the fragrant pines and the cedars dusk
and dim.

When I Heard the Learn'd Astronomer

When I heard the learn'd astronomer;
When the proofs, the figures were ranged in columns before me;
When I was shown the charts and the diagrams,
to add, divide, and measure them;
When I, sitting, heard the astronomer, where he
lectured with much applause in the lecture-
room,
How, soon, unaccountable, I became tired and
sick;
Till rising and gliding out, I wander'd off by myself,
In the mystical moist night-air, and from time to
time,
Look'd up in perfect silence to the stars.

THE SHORT STORY

The short prose narrative is the most nearly universal of all literary forms. We have observed it in the Egyptian tale of *The Two Brothers,* in the Book of Ruth, and in the story of *Cupid and Psyche.* In the later stage we have seen it in Defoe's *The Apparition of Mrs. Veal.* During the nineteenth century, however, the special form known as "the short story" was perfected. Such tales are highly unified and are told with great concentration. Their purpose is usually to present a character, to depict a setting, or to work out a plot.

In its modern form, the short story was first developed in America. Edgar Allan Poe, in the 1830's and 1840's, wrote a series of stories which fascinated his generation and which served as models for many followers. Some of these, such as *The Gold Bug* and *The Murders in Rue Morgue,* involve the solution of a mystery and were forerunners of the modern detective story. In other tales he bent all his efforts to produce an effect of horror. In all these stories he uses the greatest economy of expression.

At his best Nathaniel Hawthorne (1804-1864) was as great a master of the short story as Poe. Hawthorne's most distinguished work was done in the longer form of the novel. But although *The Scarlet Letter* and *The House of Seven Gables* are among the permanent achievements of American literature, Hawthorne devoted much of his time and thought to the short story. He was especially interested in tales that were based on the history of New England or that give us a picture of some aspect of rural New England life. The combination of the forces of nature and traits of character is handled with great artistic skill, as they lead to the catastrophe in *The Ambitious Guest.*

Among practitioners of the short story form in the second half of the nineteenth century was Herman Melville (1819-1891), the author of *Moby Dick,* one of the greatest American novels. Melville's narrative skill is perhaps best represented by a vivid chapter from this novel, though several of his short stories are well worth reading. Later in the century this form was successfully cultivated by Samuel Langhorne Clemens (Mark Twain), Bret Harte, Henry James, and Hamlin Garland. Beside these a considerable group wrote stories of "local color." Thus New England appeared in the tales of Sarah Orne Jewett, Margaret Deland, Joseph C. Lincoln, and Mary E. Wilkins Freeman; Kentucky, in the works of James Lane Allen; the Tennessee mountains, in the stories of Mary N. Murfree; and the Louisiana French life, in George W. Cable's *Old Creole Days.*

NATHANIEL HAWTHORNE

The Ambitious Guest

One September night a family had gathered round their hearth and piled it high with the driftwood of mountain streams, the dry cones of the pine, and the splintered ruins of great trees, that had come crashing down the precipice. Up the chimney roared the fire, and brightened the room with its broad blaze. The faces of the father and mother had a sober gladness; the children laughed. The eldest daughter was the image of Happiness at seventeen, and the aged grandmother, who sat 10 knitting in the warmest place, was the image of Happiness grown old. They had found the "herb heart's-ease" in the bleakest spot of all New England. This family were situated in the Notch of the White Hills, where the wind was sharp throughout the year and piteously cold in the winter, giving their cottage all its fresh inclemency before it descended on the valley of the Saco. They dwelt in a cold spot and a dangerous one, for a mountain towered above their heads so steep that the stones 20 would often rumble down its sides and startle them at midnight.

The daughter had just uttered some simple jest that filled them all with mirth, when the wind came through the Notch and seemed to pause before their cottage, rattling the door with a sound of wailing and lamentation before it passed into the valley. For a moment it saddened them, though there was nothing unusual in the tones. But the family were glad again when they perceived that 30 the latch was lifted by some traveler whose footsteps had been unheard amid the dreary blast which heralded his approach and wailed as he was entering, and went moaning away from the door.

Though they dwelt in such a solitude, these people held daily converse with the world. The romantic pass of the Notch is a great artery through which the life-blood of internal commerce is continually throbbing between Maine on one side and the Green Mountains and the shores of the St. 40 Lawrence on the other. The stage coach always drew up before the door of the cottage. The wayfarer with no companion but his staff paused here to exchange a word, that the sense of loneliness might not utterly overcome him ere he could pass through the cleft of the mountain or reach the first house in the valley. And here the teamster on his way to Portland market would put up for the night, and, if a bachelor, might sit an hour beyond the usual bedtime and steal a kiss from the mountain maid at parting. It was one of those primitive taverns where the traveler pays only for food and 10 lodging, but meets with a homely kindness beyond all price. When the footsteps were heard, therefore, between the outer door and the inner one, the whole family rose up, grandmother, children, and all as if about to welcome someone who belonged to them, and whose fate was linked with theirs.

The door was opened by a young man. His face at first wore the melancholy expression, almost despondency, of one who travels a wild and bleak road at nightfall and alone, but soon brightened up 20 when he saw the kindly warmth of his reception. He felt his heart spring forward to meet them all, from the old woman who wiped the chair with her apron to the little child that held out its arms to him. One glance and smile placed the stranger on a footing of innocent familiarity with the eldest daughter.

"Ah! this fire is the right thing," cried he, "especially when there is such a pleasant circle round it. I am quite benumbed, for the Notch is just like 30 the pipe of a great pair of bellows; it has blown a terrible blast in my face all the way from Bartlett."

"Then you are going toward Vermont?" said the master of the house as he helped to take a light knapsack off the young man's shoulders.

"Yes, to Burlington, and far enough beyond," replied he. "I meant to have been at Ethan Crawford's tonight, but a pedestrian lingers along such a road as this. It is no matter; for when I saw this 40 good fire and all your cheerful faces, I felt as if you had kindled it on purpose for me and were waiting my arrival. So I shall sit down among you and make myself at home."

Hawthorne, *The Ambitious Guest*. Nathaniel Hawthorne (1804-1864) spent much of his life as a government official at Salem, Massachusetts, and as consul at Liverpool. He was closely associated with the other New England writers.

The frank-hearted stranger had just drawn his chair to the fire when something like a heavy footstep was heard without, rushing down the steep side of the mountain as with long and rapid strides, and taking such a leap in passing the cottage as to strike the opposite precipice. The family held their breath, because they knew the sound, and their guest held his by instinct.

"The old mountain has thrown a stone at us for fear we should forget him," said the landlord, recovering himself. "He sometimes nods his head and threatens to come down, but we are old neighbors, and agree together pretty well upon the whole. Besides, we have a sure place of refuge hard by if he should be coming in good earnest."

Let us now suppose the stranger to have finished his supper of bear's meat, and by his natural felicity of manner to have placed himself on a footing of kindness with the whole family; so that they talked as freely together as if he belonged to their mountain brood. He was of a proud yet gentle spirit, haughty and reserved among the rich and great, but ever ready to stoop his head to the lowly cottage door and be like a brother or a son at the poor man's fireside. In the household of the Notch he found warmth and simplicity of feeling, the pervading intelligence of New England, and a poetry of native growth which they had gathered when they little thought of it from the mountain-peaks and chasms, and at the very threshold of their romantic and dangerous abode. He had traveled far and alone; his whole life, indeed, had been a solitary path, for, with the lofty caution of his nature, he had kept himself apart from those who might otherwise have been his companions. The family, too, though so kind and hospitable, had that consciousness of unity among themselves and separation from the world at large which in every domestic circle should still keep a holy place where no stranger may intrude. But this evening a prophetic sympathy impelled the refined and educated youth to pour out his heart before the simple mountaineers, and constrained them to answer him with the same free confidence. And thus it should have been. Is not the kindred of a common fate a closer tie than that of birth?

The secret of the young man's character was a high and abstracted ambition. He could have borne to live an undistinguished life, but not to be forgotten in the grave. Yearning desire had been transformed to hope, and hope, long cherished, had become like certainty that, obscurely as he journeyed now, a glory was to beam on all his pathway, though not, perhaps, while he was treading it. But when posterity should gaze back into the gloom of what was now the present, they would trace the brightness of his footsteps, brightening as meaner glories faded, and confess that a gifted one had passed from his cradle to his tomb with none to recognize him.

"As yet," cried the stranger, his cheek glowing and his eye flashing with enthusiasm— "as yet I have done nothing. Were I to vanish from the earth tomorrow, none would know so much of me as you—that a nameless youth came up at nightfall from the valley of the Saco, and opened his heart to you in the evening, and passed through the Notch by sunrise, and was seen no more. Not a soul would ask, 'Who was he? Whither did the wanderer go?' But I cannot die till I have achieved my destiny. Then let Death come; I shall have built my monument."

There was a continual flow of natural emotion gushing forth amid abstracted reverie which enabled the family to understand this young man's sentiments, though so foreign from their own. With quick sensibility of the ludicrous, he blushed at the ardor into which he had been betrayed.

"You laugh at me," said he, taking the eldest daughter's hand and laughing himself. "You think my ambition as nonsensical as if I were to freeze myself to death on the top of Mount Washington only that people might spy at me from the country roundabout. And truly that would be a noble pedestal for a man's statue."

"It is better to sit here by this fire," answered the girl, blushing, "and be comfortable and contented, though nobody thinks about us."

"I suppose," said her father, after a fit of musing, "there is something natural in what the young man says; and if my mind had been turned that way, I might have felt just the same. It is strange, wife, how his talk has set my head running on things that are pretty certain never to come to pass."

"Perhaps they may," observed the wife. "Is the man thinking what he will do when he is a widower?"

"No, no!" cried he, repelling the idea with reproachful kindness. "When I think of your death, Esther, I think of mine, too. But I was wishing we had a good farm in Bartlett or Bethlehem or Littleton, or some other township round the White Mountains, but not where they could tumble on our heads. I should want to stand well with my neighbors and be called squire and sent to General

Court for a term or two; for a plain, honest man may do as much good there as a lawyer. And when I should be grown quite an old man, and you an old woman, so as not to be long apart, I might die happy enough in my bed, and leave you all crying around me. A slate gravestone would suit me as well as a marble one, with just my name and age, and a verse of a hymn, and something to let people know that I lived an honest man and died a Christian."

"There, now!" exclaimed the stranger; "it is our nature to desire a monument, be it slate or marble, or a pillar of granite, or a glorious memory in the universal heart of man."

"We're in a strange way tonight," said the wife, with tears in her eyes. "They say it's a sign of something when folks' minds go a-wandering so. Hark to the children!"

They listened accordingly. The younger children had been put to bed in another room, but with an open door between; so that they could be heard talking busily among themselves. One and all seemed to have caught the infection from the fireside circle, and were outvying each other in wild wishes and childish projects of what they would do when they came to be men and women. At length a little boy, instead of addressing his brothers and sisters, called out to his mother:

"I'll tell you what I wish, mother," cried he: "I want you and father and grandma'm, and all of us, and the stranger, too, to start right away and go and take a drink out of the basin of the Flume."

Nobody could help laughing at the child's notion of leaving a warm bed and dragging them from a cheerful fire to visit the basin of the Flume—a brook which tumbles over the precipice deep within the Notch.

The boy had hardly spoken, when a wagon rattled along the road and stopped a moment before the door. It appeared to contain two or three men who were cheering their hearts with the rough chorus of a song which resounded in broken notes between the cliffs, while the singers hesitated whether to continue their journey or put up here for the night.

"Father," said the girl, "they are calling you by name."

But the good man doubted whether they had really called him, and was unwilling to show himself too solicitous of gain by inviting people to patronize his house. He therefore did not hurry to the door, and, the lash being soon applied, the travelers plunged into the Notch, still singing and laughing, though their music and mirth came back drearily from the heart of the mountain.

"There, mother!" cried the boy again; "they'd have given us a ride to the Flume."

Again they laughed at the child's pertinacious fancy for a night ramble. But it happened that a light cloud passed over the daughter's spirit; she looked gravely into the fire and drew a breath that was almost a sigh. It forced its way, in spite of a little struggle to repress it. Then, starting and blushing, she looked quickly around the circle, as if they had caught a glimpse into her bosom. The stranger asked what she had been thinking of.

"Nothing," answered she, with a downcast smile; "only I felt lonesome just then."

"Oh, I have always had a gift of feeling what is in other people's hearts," said he, half seriously. "Shall I tell the secrets of yours? For I know what to think when a young girl shivers by a warm hearth and complains of lonesomeness at her mother's side. Shall I put these feelings into words?"

"They would not be a girl's feelings any longer if they could be put into words," replied the mountain nymph, laughing, but avoiding his eye.

All this was said apart. Perhaps a germ of love was springing in their hearts so pure that it might blossom in Paradise, since it could not be matured on earth; for women worship such gentle dignity as his, and the proud, contemplative, yet kindly, soul is oftenest captivated by simplicity like hers. But while they spoke softly, and he was watching the happy sadness, the lightsome shadows, the shy yearnings of a maiden's nature, the wind through the Notch took a deeper and drearier sound. It seemed, as the fanciful stranger said, like the choral strain of the spirits of the blast who in old Indian times had their dwelling among these mountains, and made their heights and recesses a sacred region. There was a wail along the road as if a funeral were passing. To chase away the gloom, the family threw pine-branches on their fire till the dry leaves crackled and the flame arose, discovering once again a scene of peace and humble happiness. The light hovered about them fondly and caressed them all. There were the little faces of the children peeping from their bed apart, and here the father's frame of strength, the mother's subdued and careful mien, the high-browed youth, the budding girl, and the good old grandam still knitting in the warmest place.

The aged woman looked up from her task, and with fingers ever busy was the next to speak.

"Old folks have their notions," said she, "as well as young ones. You've been wishing and planning and letting your heads run on one thing and another till you've set my mind a-wandering too. Now, what should an old woman wish for when she can go but a step or two before she comes to her grave? Children, it will haunt me night and day till I tell you."

"What is it, mother?" cried the husband and wife, at once.

Then the old woman, with an air of mystery which drew the circle closer round the fire, informed them that she had provided her grave-clothes some years before—a nice linen shroud, a cap with a muslin ruff, and everything of a finer sort than she had worn since her wedding day. But this evening an old superstition had strangely recurred to her. It used to be said in her younger days that if anything were amiss with a corpse, if only the ruff were not smooth or the cap did not set right, the corpse, in the coffin and beneath the clods, would strive to put up its cold hands and arrange it. The bare thought made her nervous.

"Don't talk so, grandmother," said the girl, shuddering.

"Now," continued the old woman with singular earnestness, yet smiling strangely at her own folly, "I want one of you, my children, when your mother is dressed and in the coffin,—I want one of you to hold a looking-glass over my face. Who knows but I may take a glimpse at myself, and see whether all's right."

"Old and young, we dream of graves and monuments," murmured the stranger youth. "I wonder how mariners feel when the ship is sinking and they, unknown and undistinguished, are to be buried together in the ocean, that wide and nameless sepulcher?"

For a moment the old woman's ghastly conception so engrossed the minds of her hearers that a sound abroad in the night, rising like the roar of a blast, had grown broad, deep and terrible before the fated group were conscious of it. The house and all within it trembled; the foundations of the earth seemed to be shaken, as if this awful sound were the peal of the last trump. Young and old exchanged one wild glance and remained an instant pale, affrighted, without utterance or power to move. Then the same shriek burst simultaneously from all their lips:

"The slide! The slide!"

The simplest words must intimate, but not portray, the unutterable horror of the catastrophe. The victims rushed from their cottage, and sought refuge in what they deemed a safer spot, where, in contemplation of such an emergency, a sort of barrier had been reared. Alas! they had quitted their security and fled right into the pathway of destruction. Down came the whole side of the mountain in a cataract of ruin. Just before it reached the house the stream broke into two branches, shivered not a window there, but overwhelmed the whole vicinity, blocked up the road and annihilated everything in its dreadful course. Long ere the thunder of that great slide had ceased to roar among the mountains the mortal agony had been endured and the victims were at peace. Their bodies were never found.

The next morning the light smoke was seen stealing from the cottage chimney, up the mountain-side. Within, the fire was yet smoldering on the hearth, and the chairs in a circle round it, as if the inhabitants had but gone forth to view the devastation of the slide, and would shortly return to thank Heaven for their miraculous escape. All had left separate tokens by which those who had known the family were made to shed a tear for each. Who has not heard their name? The story has been told far and wide, and will forever be a legend of these mountains. Poets have sung their fate.

There were circumstances which led some to suppose that a stranger had been received into the cottage on this awful night, and had shared the catastrophe of all its inmates; others denied that there were sufficient grounds for such a conjecture. Woe for the high-souled youth with his dream of earthly immortality! His name and person utterly unknown, his history, his way of life, his plans, a mystery never to be solved, his death and his existence equally a doubt,—whose was the agony of that death moment?

EDGAR ALLAN POE

The Cask of Amontillado

The thousand injuries of Fortunato I had borne as I best could, but when he ventured upon insult, I vowed revenge. You, who so well know the nature of my soul, will not suppose, however, that I gave utterance to a threat. *At length* I would be avenged; this was a point definitively settled—but the very definitiveness with which it was resolved precluded the idea of risk. I must not only punish, but punish with impunity. A wrong is unredressed when retribution overtakes its redresser. It is equally unredressed when the avenger fails to make himself felt as such to him who has done the wrong.

It must be understood that neither by word nor deed had I given Fortunato cause to doubt my good-will. I continued, as was my wont, to smile in his face, and he did not perceive that my smile *now* was at the thought of his immolation.

He had a weak point—this Fortunato—although in other regards he was a man to be respected and even feared. He prided himself on his connoisseurship in wine. Few Italians have the true virtuoso spirit. For the most part their enthusiasm is adopted to suit the time and opportunity to practice imposture upon the British and Austrian *millionaires*. In painting and gemmary Fortunato, like his countrymen, was a quack, but in the matter of old wines he was sincere. In this respect I did not differ from him materially; I was skillful in the Italian vintages myself, and bought largely whenever I could.

It was about dusk, one evening during the supreme madness of the carnival season, that I encountered my friend. He accosted me with excessive warmth, for he had been drinking much. The man wore motley. He had on a tight-fitting partistriped dress, and his head was surmounted by the conical cap and bells. I was so pleased to see him, that I thought I should never have done wringing his hand.

I said to him—"My dear Fortunato, you are luckily met. How remarkably well you are looking today! But I have received a pipe of what passes for Amontillado, and I have my doubts."

"How?" said he, "Amontillado? A pipe? Impossible? And in the middle of the carnival?"

"I have my doubts," I replied; "and I was silly enough to pay the full Amontillado price without consulting you in the matter. You were not to be found, and I was fearful of losing a bargain."

"Amontillado!"

"I have my doubts."

"Amontillado!"

"And I must satisfy them."

"Amontillado!"

"As you are engaged, I am on my way to Luchesi. If anyone has a critical turn, it is he. He will tell me—"

"Luchesi cannot tell Amontillado from Sherry."

"And yet some fools will have it that his taste is a match for your own."

"Come, let us go."

"Whither?"

"To your vaults."

"My friend, no; I will not impose upon your good nature. I perceive you have an engagement. Luchesi—"

"I have no engagement; come."

"My friend, no. It is not the engagement, but the severe cold with which I perceive you are afflicted. The vaults are insufferably damp. They are encrusted with niter."

"Let us go, nevertheless. The cold is merely nothing. Amontillado! You have been imposed upon; and as for Luchesi, he cannot distinguish Sherry from Amontillado."

Thus speaking, Fortunato possessed himself of my arm. Putting on a mask of black silk, and drawing a *roquelaure* closely about my person, I suffered him to hurry me to my palazzo.

There were no attendants at home; they had absconded to make merry in honor of the time. I had told them that I should not return until the morning, and had given them explicit orders not to stir from the house. These orders were sufficient, I well knew, to insure their immediate disappearance, one and all, as soon as my back was turned.

I took from their sconces two flambeaux, and giving one to Fortunato, bowed him through several suites of rooms to the archway that led into the vaults. I passed down a long and winding staircase, requesting him to be cautious as he followed. We came at length to the foot of the descent, and stood together on the damp ground of the catacombs of the Montresors.

The gait of my friend was unsteady, and the bells upon his cap jingled as he strode.

"The pipe," he said.

"It is farther on," said I; "but observe the white web-work which gleams from these cavern walls."

He turned towards me, and looked into my eyes with two filmy orbs that distilled the rheum of intoxication.

"Niter?" he asked, at length.

"Niter," I replied. "How long have you had that cough!"

"Ugh! ugh! ugh!—ugh! ugh! ugh!—ugh! ugh! ugh!—ugh! ugh! ugh!—ugh! ugh! ugh!"

My poor friend found it impossible to reply for many minutes.

"It is nothing," he said, at last.

"Come," I said, with decision, "we will go back; your health is precious. You are rich, respected, admired, beloved; you are happy, as once I was. You are a man to be missed. For me it is no matter. We will go back; you will be ill, and I cannot be responsible. Besides, there is Luchesi—"

"Enough," he said; "the cough is a mere nothing; it will not kill me. I shall not die of a cough."

"True—true," I replied; "and, indeed, I had no intention of alarming you unnecessarily—but you should use all proper caution. A draught of this Medoc will defend us from the damps."

Here I knocked off the neck of a bottle which I drew from a long row of its fellows that lay upon the mold.

"Drink," I said, presenting him the wine.

He raised it to his lips with a leer. He paused and nodded to me familiarly, while his bells jingled.

"I drink," he said, "to the buried that repose around us."

"And I to your long life."

He again took my arm, and we proceeded.

"These vaults," he said, "are extensive."

"The Montresors," I replied, "were a great and numerous family."

"I forgot your arms."

"A huge human foot d'or,[1] in a field azure; the foot crushes a serpent rampant whose fangs are imbedded in the heel."

"And the motto?"

"Nemo me impune lacessit." [2]

"Good!" he said.

The wine sparkled in his eyes and the bells jingled. My own fancy grew warm with the Medoc. We had passed through walls of piled bones, with casks and puncheons intermingling, into the inmost recesses of the catacombs. I paused again, and this time I made bold to seize Fortunato by an arm above the elbow.

"The niter!" I said; "see, it increases. It hangs like moss upon the vaults. We are below the river's bed. The drops of moisture trickle among the bones. Come, we will go back ere it is too late. Your cough—"

"It is nothing," he said; "let us go on. But first, another draught of the Medoc."

I broke and reached him a flacon of De Grave. He emptied it at a breath. His eyes flashed with a fierce light. He laughed and threw the bottle upwards with a gesticulation I did not understand.

I looked at him in surprise. He repeated the movement—a grotesque one.

"You do not comprehend?" he said.

"Not I," I replied.

"Then you are not of the brotherhood."

"How?"

"You are not of the masons."

"Yes, yes," I said, "yes, yes."

"You? Impossible! A mason?"

"A mason," I replied.

"A sign," he said.

"It is this," I answered, producing a trowel from beneath the folds of my *roquelaure*.

"You jest," he exclaimed, recoiling a few paces. "But let us proceed to the Amontillado."

"Be it so," I said, replacing the tool beneath the cloak, and again offering him my arm. He leaned upon it heavily. We continued our route in search of the Amontillado. We passed through a range of low arches, descended, passed on, and descended again, arrived at a deep crypt, in which the foulness of the air caused our flambeaux rather to glow than flame.

At the most remote end of the crypt there appeared another less spacious. Its walls had been lined with human remains piled to the vault overhead, in the fashion of the great catacombs of Paris. Three sides of this interior crypt were still

[1] This is a description of a coat of arms in technical heraldic terms. A human foot of gold on a field of blue.

[2] No one strikes me with impunity. This is also the motto of Scotland.

ornamented in this manner. From the fourth the bones had been thrown down, and lay promiscuously upon the earth, forming at one point a mound of some size. Within the wall thus exposed by the displacing of the bones, we perceived a still inferior recess, in depth about four feet, in width three, in height six or seven. It seemed to have been constructed for no especial use within itself, but formed merely the interval between two of the colossal supports of the roof of the catacombs, and was backed by one of their circumscribing walls of solid granite.

It was in vain that Fortunato, uplifting his dull torch, endeavored to pry into the depths of the recess. Its termination the feeble light did not enable us to see.

"Proceed," I said; "herein is the Amontillado. As for Luchesi—"

"He is an ignoramus," interrupted my friend, as he stepped unsteadily forward, while I followed immediately at his heels. In an instant he had reached the extremity of the niche, and finding his progress arrested by the rock, stood stupidly bewildered. A moment more and I had fettered him to the granite. In its surface were two iron staples, distant from each other about two feet, horizontally. From one of these depended a short chain, from the other a padlock. Throwing the links about his waist, it was but the work of a few seconds to secure it. He was too much astounded to resist. Withdrawing the key, I stepped back from the recess.

"Pass your hand," I said, "over the wall; you cannot help feeling the niter. Indeed it is *very* damp. Once more let me *implore* you to return. No? Then I must positively leave you. But I must first render you all the little attentions in my power."

"The Amontillado!" ejaculated my friend, not yet recovered from his astonishment.

"True," I replied; "the Amontillado."

As I said these words I busied myself among the pile of bones of which I have before spoken. Throwing them aside, I soon uncovered a quantity of building stone and mortar. With these materials and with the aid of my trowel, I began vigorously to wall up the entrance of the niche.

I had scarcely laid the first tier of the masonry when I discovered that the intoxication of Fortunato had in a great measure worn off. The earliest indication I had of this was a low moaning cry from the depth of the recess. It was *not* the cry of a drunken man. There was then a long and obstinate silence. I laid the second tier, and the third, and the fourth; and then I heard the furious vibrations of the chain. The noise lasted for several minutes, during which, that I might hearken to it with the more satisfaction, I ceased my labors and sat down upon the bones. When at last the clanking subsided, I resumed the trowel, and finished without interruption the fifth, the sixth, and the seventh tier. The wall was now nearly upon a level with my breast. I again paused, and holding the flambeaux over the mason-work, threw a few feeble rays upon the figure within.

A succession of loud and shrill screams, bursting suddenly from the throat of the chained form, seemed to thrust me violently back. For a brief moment I hesitated—I trembled. Unsheathing my rapier, I began to grope with it about the recess; but the thought of an instant reassured me. I placed my hand upon the solid fabric of the catacombs, and felt satisfied. I reapproached the wall. I replied to the yells of him who clamored. I re-echoed—I aided—I surpassed them in volume and in strength. I did this, and the clamorer grew still.

It was now midnight, and my task was drawing to a close. I had completed the eighth, the ninth, and the tenth tier. I had finished a portion of the last and the eleventh; there remained but a single stone to be fitted and plastered in. I struggled with its weight; I placed it partially in its destined position. But now there came from out the niche a low laugh that erected the hairs upon my head. It was succeeded by a sad voice, which I had difficulty in recognizing as that of the noble Fortunato. The voice said—

"Ha! ha! ha!—he! he!—a very good joke indeed—an excellent jest. We will have many a rich laugh about it at the palazzo—he! he! he!—over our wine—he! he! he!"

"The Amontillado!" I said.

"He! he! he!—he! he! he!—yes, the Amontillado. But is it not getting late? Will not they be awaiting us at the palazzo, the Lady Fortunato and the rest? Let us be gone."

"Yes," I said, "let us be gone."

"*For the love of God, Montresor!*"

"Yes," I said, "for the love of God!"

But to these words I hearkened in vain for a reply. I grew impatient. I called aloud—

"Fortunato!"

No answer. I called again—

"Fortunato!"

No answer still. I thrust a torch through the remaining aperture and let it fall within. There came forth in return only a jingling of the bells. My heart grew sick—on account of the dampness of the catacombs. I hastened to make an end of my labor. I forced the last stone into its position; I plastered it up. Against the new masonry I re-erected the old rampart of bones. For the half of a century no mortal has disturbed them. *In pace requiescat!* [8]

HERMAN MELVILLE

Moby Dick

The Chase—Third Day

The morning of the third day dawned fair and fresh, and once more the solitary night-man at the foremast-head was relieved by crowds of the day-light look-outs, who dotted every mast and almost every spar.

"D'ye see him?" cried Ahab; but the whale was not yet in sight.

"In his infallible wake, though; but follow that wake, that's all. Helm there; steady, as thou goest, and hast been going. What a lovely day again! Were it a new-made world, and made for a summer-house to the angels, and this morning the first of its throwing open to them, a fairer day could not dawn upon that world. . . . These warm Trade Winds, at least, that in the clear heavens blow straight on, in strong and steadfast, vigorous mildness; and veer not from their mark, however the baser currents of the sea may turn and tack, and mightiest Mississippis of the land shift and swerve about, uncertain where to go at last. And by the eternal Poles! these same Trades that so directly blow my good ship on; these Trades, or something like them—something so unchangeable, and full as strong, blow my keeled soul along! To it! Aloft there! What d'ye see?"

"Nothing, sir."

"Nothing! and noon at hand! The doubloon goes a-begging! See the sun! Aye, aye, it must be so. I've oversailed him. How, got the start? Aye, he's chasing *me* now; not I, *him*—that's bad; I might have known it, too. Fool! the lines—the harpoons he's towing. Aye, aye, I have run him by last night. About! About! Come down, all of ye, but the regular look-outs! Man the braces!"

Steering as she had done, the wind had been somewhat on the *Pequod's* quarter, so that now being pointed in the reverse direction, the braced ship sailed hard upon the breeze as she rechurned the cream in her own white wake.

"Against the wind he now steers for the open jaw," murmured Starbuck to himself, as he coiled the new-hauled main-brace upon the rail. "God keep us, but already my bones feel damp within me, and from the inside wet my flesh. I misdoubt me that I disobey my God in obeying him!"

"Stand by to sway me up!" cried Ahab, advancing to the hempen basket. "We should meet him soon."

"Aye, aye, sir," and straightway Starbuck did Ahab's bidding, and once more Ahab swung on high.

A whole hour now passed; goldbeaten out to ages. Time itself now held long breaths with keen suspense. But at last, some three points off the weather bow, Ahab descried the spout again, and instantly from the three mast-heads three shrieks went up as if the tongues of fire had voiced it.

"Forehead to forehead I meet thee, this third time, Moby Dick! On deck there!—brace sharper up; crowd her into the wind's eye. He's too far off to lower yet, Mr. Starbuck. The sails shake! Stand over that helmsman with a top-maul! So, so; he travels fast, and I must down. But let me have one more good round look aloft here at the sea; there's time for that. An old, old sight, and yet somehow so young; aye, and not changed a wink since I first saw it, a boy, from the sandhills of Nantucket! The same!—the same!—the same to Noah as to me. There's a soft shower to leeward. Such lovely leewardings! They must lead some-

[8] May he rest in peace.

Melville, *Moby Dick.* Concluding two chapters. Herman Melville (1819-1891) was born and died in New York City. His sea-stories are based upon first-hand adventures.

where—to something else than common land, more palmy than the palms. Leeward! the white whale goes that way; look to windward, then; the better if the bitterer quarter. But good-by, good-by, old mast-head—keep a good eye upon the whale, the while I'm gone. We'll talk tomorrow, nay, tonight, when the white whale lies down there, tied by head and tail."

He gave the word; and still gazing round him, was steadily lowered through the cloven blue air to the deck.

In due time the boats were lowered; but as standing in his shallop's stern, Ahab just hovered upon the point of the descent, he waved to the mate,—who held one of the tackle-ropes on deck—and bade him pause.

"Starbuck!"

"Sir?"

"For the third time my soul's ship starts upon this voyage, Starbuck."

"Aye, sir, thou wilt have it so."

"Some ships sail from their ports, and ever afterwards are missing, Starbuck!"

"Truth, sir: saddest truth."

"Some men die at ebb tide; some at low water; some at the full of the flood;—and I feel now like a billow that's all one crested comb, Starbuck. I am old;—shake hands with me, man."

Their hands met; their eyes fastened; Starbuck's tears the glue.

"Oh, my captain, my captain!—noble heart—go not—go not!—see, it's a brave man that weeps; how great the agony of the persuasion then!"

"Lower away!"—cried Ahab, tossing the mate's arm from him. "Stand by the crew!"

In an instant the boat was pulling round close under the stern.

"The sharks! the sharks!" cried a voice from the low cabin-window there; "O master, my master, come back!"

But Ahab heard nothing; for his own voice was high-lifted then; and the boat leaped on.

Yet the voice spake true; for scarce had he pushed from the ship, when numbers of sharks, seemingly rising from out the dark waters beneath the hull, maliciously snapped at the blades of the oars, every time they dipped in the water; and in this way accompanied the boat with their bites. It is a thing not uncommonly happening to the whale-boats in those swarming seas; the sharks at times apparently following them in the same prescient way that vultures hover over the banners of marching regiments in the east. But these were the first sharks that had been observed by the *Pequod* since the White Whale had been first described; and whether it was that Ahab's crew were all such tiger-yellow barbarians, and therefore their flesh more musky to the senses of the sharks—a matter sometimes well known to affect them—however it was, they seemed to follow that one boat without molesting the others.

"Heart of wrought steel!" murmured Starbuck, gazing over the side, and following with his eyes the receding boat—"canst thou yet ring boldly to that sight?—lowering thy keel among ravening sharks, and followed by them, open-mouthed to the chase; and this the critical third day?—For when three days flow together in one continuous intense pursuit, be sure the first is the morning, the second the noon, and the third the evening and the end of that thing—be that end what it may. Oh! my God! what is this that shoots through me, and leaves me so deadly calm, yet expectant,—fixed at the top of a shudder! Future things swim before me, as in empty outlines and skeletons; all the past is somehow grown dim. Mary, girl! thou fadest in pale glories behind me; boy! I seem to see but thy eyes grown wondrous blue. Strangest problems of life seem clearing; but clouds sweep between— Is my journey's end coming? My legs feel faint; like his who has footed it all day. Feel thy heart,—beats it yet?—Stir thyself, Starbuck!—stave it off—move, move! speak aloud!—Mast-head there! See ye my boy's hand on the hill? Crazed;—aloft there! keep thy keenest eye upon the boats:—mark well the whale!—Ho! again!—drive off that hawk! see! he pecks—he tears the vane"—pointing to the red flag flying at the main-truck—"Ha! he soars away with it!—Where's the old man now? sees't thou that sight, oh, Ahab!—shudder, shudder!"

The boats had not gone very far, when by a signal from the mast-heads—a downward pointed arm, Ahab knew that the whale had sounded; but intending to be near him at the next rising; he held on his way a little sideways from the vessel; the becharmed crew maintaining the profoundest silence, as the head-beat waves hammered and hammered against the opposing bow.

"Drive, drive in your nails, oh ye waves! to their uttermost heads drive them in! ye but strike a thing without a lid; and no coffin and no hearse can be mine:—and hemp only can kill me! Ha! ha!"

Suddenly the waters around them slowly swelled in broad circles; then quickly upheaved, as if sideways sliding from a submerged berg of ice, swiftly rising to the surface. A low rumbling sound was heard; a subterraneous hum; and then all held their breaths; as, bedraggled with trailing ropes, and harpoons, and lances, a vast form shot lengthwise, but obliquely from the sea. Shrouded in a thin dropping veil of mist, it hovered for a moment in the rainbowed air; and then fell swamping back into the deep. Crushed thirty feet upwards, the waters flashed for an instant like heaps of fountains, then brokenly sank in a shower of flakes, leaving the circling surface creamed like new milk round the marble trunk of the whale.

"Give away!" cried Ahab to the oarsmen, and the boats darted forward to the attack; but maddened by yesterday's fresh irons that corroded in him, Moby Dick seemed combinedly possessed by all the angels that fell from heaven. The wide tiers of welded tendons overspreading his broad white forehead, beneath the transparent skin, looked knitted together; as head on he came, churning his tail among the boats; and once more flailed them apart; spilling out the irons and lances from the two mates' boats, and dashing in one side of the upper part of their bows, but leaving Ahab's almost without a scar.

While Daggoo and Queequeg were stopping the strained planks, and as the whale swimming out from them, turned, and showed one entire flank as he shot by them again, at that moment a quick cry went up. Lashed round and round to the fish's back; pinioned in the turns upon turns in which, during the past night, the whale had reeled the involutions of the lines around him, the half torn body of the Parsee was seen; his sable raiment frayed to shreds; his distended eyes turned full upon old Ahab.

The harpoon dropped from his hand.

"Befooled, befooled!"—drawing in a long lean breath—"Aye, Parsee! I see thee again.—Aye, and thou goest before; and this, *this* then is the hearse that thou didst promise. But I hold thee to the last letter of thy word. Where is the second hearse? Away, mates, to the ship! those boats are useless now; repair them if ye can in time, and return to me; if not, Ahab is enough to die— Down, men! the first thing that but offers to jump from this boat I stand in, that thing I harpoon. Ye are not other men, but my arms and my legs; and so obey me.—Where's the whale? gone down again?"

But he looked too nigh the boat; for as if bent upon escaping with the corpse he bore, and as if the particular place of the last encounter had been but a stage in his leeward voyage, Moby Dick was now again steadily swimming forward; and had almost passed the ship,—which thus far had been sailing in the contrary direction to him, though for the present her headway had been stopped. He seemed swimming with his utmost velocity, and now only intent upon pursuing his own straight path in the sea.

"Oh! Ahab," cried Starbuck, "not too late is it, even now, the third day, to desist. See! Moby Dick seeks thee not. It is thou, thou, that madly seekest him!"

Setting sail to the rising wind, the lonely boat was swiftly impelled to leeward, by both oars and canvas. And at last when Ahab was sliding by the vessel, so near as plainly to distinguish Starbuck's face as he leaned over the rail, he hailed him to turn the vessel about, and follow him, not too swiftly, at a judicious interval. Glancing upwards, he saw Tashtego, Queequeg, and Daggoo, eagerly mounting to the three mast-heads; while the oarsmen were rocking in the two staved boats which had but just been hoisted to the side, and were busily at work in repairing them. One after the other, through the port-holes, as he sped, he also caught flying glimpses of Stubb and Flask, busying themselves on deck among bundles of new irons and lances. As he saw all this, as he heard the hammers in the broken boats, far other hammers seemed driving a nail into his heart. But he rallied. And now marking that the vane or flag was gone from the mainmast-head, he shouted to Tashtego, who had just gained that perch, to descend again for another flag, and a hammer and nails, and so nail it to the mast.

Whether fagged by the three days' running chase, and the resistance to his swimming in the knotted hamper he bore; or whether it was some latent deceitfulness and malice in him: whichever was true, the White Whale's way now began to abate, as it seemed, from the boat so rapidly nearing him once more; though indeed the whale's last start had not been so long a one as before. And still as Ahab glided over the waves the unpitying sharks accompanied him; and so pertinaciously stuck to the boat, and so continually bit at the plying oars, that the blades became jagged and crunched, and left small splinters in the sea, at almost every dip.

"Heed them not! those teeth but give new rowlocks to your oars. Pull on! 'tis the better rest, the shark's jaw than the yielding water."

"But at every bite, sir, the thin blades grow smaller and smaller!"

"They will last long enough! pull on!—But who can tell"—he muttered—"whether these sharks swim to feast on the whale or on Ahab?—But pull on! Aye, all alive, now—we near him. The helm! take the helm; let me pass,"—and so saying, two of the oarsmen helped him forward to the bows of the still flying boat.

At length as the craft was cast to one side, and ran ranging along with the white Whale's flank, he seemed strangely oblivious of its advance—as the whale sometimes will—and Ahab was fairly within the smoky mountain mist, which, thrown off from the whale's spout, curled round his great, Monadnock hump; he was even thus close to him; when, with body arched back, and both arms lengthwise highlifted to the poise, he darted his fierce iron, and his far fiercer curse into the hated whale. As both steel and curse sank to the socket, as if sucked into a morass, Moby Dick sideways writhed; spasmodically rolled his nigh flank against the bow, and without staving a hole in it, so suddenly canted the boat over, that had it not been for the elevated part of the gunwale to which he then clung, Ahab would once more have been tossed into the sea. As it was, three of the oarsmen—who foreknew not the precise instant of the dart, and were therefore unprepared for its effects—these were flung out; but so fell, that, in an instant two of them clutched the gunwale again, and rising to its level on a combing wave, hurled themselves bodily inboard again; the third man helplessly dropping astern, but still afloat and swimming.

Almost simultaneously, with a mighty volition of ungraduated, instantaneous swiftness, the White Whale darted through the weltering sea. But when Ahab cried out to the steersman to take new turns with the line, and hold it so; and commanded the crew to turn round on their seats, and tow the boat up to the mark; the moment the treacherous line felt that double strain and tug, it snapped in the empty air!

"What breaks in me? Some sinew cracks!—'tis whole again; oars! oars! Burst in upon him!"

Hearing the tremendous rush of the sea-crashing boat, the whale wheeled round to present his blank forehead at bay; but in that evolution, catching sight of the nearing black hull of the ship; seemingly seeing in it the source of all his persecutions; bethinking it—it may be—a larger and nobler foe; of a sudden, he bore down upon its advancing prow, smiting his jaws amid fiery showers of foam.

Ahab staggered; his hand smote his forehead. "I grow blind; hands! stretch out before me that I may yet grope my way. Is't night?"

"The whale! The ship!" cried the cringing oarsmen.

"Oars! oars! Slope downwards to thy depths, O sea, that ere it be for ever too late, Ahab may slide this last, last time upon his mark! I see: the ship! the ship! Dash on, my men! Will you not save my ship?"

But as the oarsmen violently forced their boat through the sledge-hammering seas, the before whale-smitten bow-ends of two planks burst through, and in an instant almost, the temporarily disabled boat lay nearly level with the waves; its half-wading, splashing crew, trying hard to stop the gap and bale out the pouring water.

Meantime, for that one beholding instant, Tashtego's mast-head hammer remained suspended in his hand; and the red flag, half-wrapping him as with a plaid, then streamed itself straight out from him, as his own forward-flowing heart; while Starbuck and Stubb, standing upon the bowsprit beneath, caught sight of the down-coming monster just as soon as he.

"The whale, the whale! Up helm, up helm! Oh, all ye sweet powers of air, now hug me close. Let not Starbuck die, if die he must, in a woman's fainting fit. Up helm, I say—ye fools, the jaw! the jaw! Is this the end of all my bursting prayers? all my life-long fidelities? Oh, Ahab, Ahab, lo, thy work. Steady! helmsman, steady. Nay, nay! Up helm again! He turns to meet us! Oh, his unappeasable brow drives on towards one, whose duty tells him he cannot depart. My God, stand by me now!"

"Stand not by me, but stand under me, whoever you are that will now help Stubb; for Stubb, too, sticks here. I grin at thee, thou grinning whale! Who ever helped Stubb, or kept Stubb awake, but Stubb's own unwinking eye? And now poor Stubb goes to bed upon a mattress that is all too soft; would it were stuffed with brushwood! I grin at thee, thou grinning whale! Look ye, sun, moon, and stars! I call ye assassins of as good a fellow as ever spouted up his ghost. For all that, I would yet ring glasses with ye, would ye but hand the cup! Oh! oh! oh! oh! thou grinning whale, but there'll be plenty of gulping soon! Why fly ye not, O Ahab! For me, off shoes and jacket to it; let Stubb die in his drawers! A most moldy and over-salted death, though;—cherries! cherries! cherries! Oh, Flask, for one red cherry ere we die!"

"Cherries? I only wish that we were where they

grow. Oh, Stubb, I hope my poor mother's drawn my part-pay ere this; if not, few coppers will now come to her, for the voyage is up."

From the ship's bows, nearly all the seamen now hung inactive; hammers, bits of plank, lances, and harpoons, mechanically retained in their hands, just as they had darted from their various employments; all their enchanted eyes intent upon the whale, which from side to side strangely vibrating his predestinating head, sent a broad band of overspreading semi-circular foam before him as he rushed. Retribution, swift vengeance, eternal malice were in his whole aspect, and spite of all that mortal man could do, the solid white buttress of his forehead smote the ship's starboard bow, till men and timbers reeled. Some fell flat upon their faces. Like dislodged trucks, the heads of the harpooneers aloft shook on their bull-like necks. Through the breach, they heard the waters pour, as mountain torrents down a flume.

"The ship! The hearse!—the second hearse!" cried Ahab from the boat; "its wood could only be American!"

Diving beneath the settling ship, the whale ran quivering along its keel; but turning under water, swiftly shot to the surface again, far off the other bow, but within a few yards of Ahab's boat, where, for a time, he lay quiescent.

"I turn my body from the sun. What ho, Tashtego! let me hear thy hammer. Ah! ye three unsurrendered spires of mine; thou uncracked keel; and only god-bullied hull; thou firm deck, and haughty helm, and Pole-pointed prow,—death-glorious ship! must ye then perish, and without me? Am I cut off from the last fond pride of meanest shipwrecked captains? Oh, lonely death on lonely life! Oh, now I feel my topmost greatness lies in my topmost grief. Ho, ho! from all your furthest bounds, pour ye now in, ye bold billows of my whole foregone life, and top this one piled comber of my death! Towards thee I roll, thou all-destroying but unconquering whale; to the last I grapple with thee; from hell's heart I stab at thee; for hate's sake I spit my last breath at thee. Sink all coffins and all hearses to one common pool! and since neither can be mine, let me then tow to pieces, while still chasing thee, though tied to thee, thou damned whale! *Thus,* I give up the spear!"

The harpoon was darted; the stricken whale flew forward; with igniting velocity the line ran through the groove;—ran foul. Ahab stooped to clear it; he did clear it; but the flying turn caught him round the neck, and voicelessly as Turkish mutes bowstring their victim, he was shot out of the boat ere the crew knew he was gone. Next instant, the heavy eye-splice in the rope's final end flew out of the stark-empty tub, knocked down an oarsman, and smiting the sea, disappeared in its depths.

For an instant, the tranced boat's crew stood still; then turned. "The ship? Great God, where is the ship?" Soon they through dim, bewildering mediums saw her sidelong fading phantom, as in the gaseous Fata Morgana; only the uppermost masts out of water; while fixed by infatuation, or fidelity, or fate, to their once lofty perches, the pagan harpooneers still maintained their sinking lookouts on the sea. And now, concentric circles seized the lone boat itself, and all its crew, and each floating oar, and every lance-pole, and spinning, animate and inanimate, all round and round in one vortex, carried the smallest chip of the *Pequod* out of sight.

But as the last whelmings intermixingly poured themselves over the sunken head of the Indian at the mainmast, leaving a few inches of the erect spar yet visible, together with long streaming yards of the flag, which calmly undulated, with ironical coincidings, over the destroying billows they almost touched;—at that instant, a red arm and a hammer hovered backwardly uplifted in the open air, in the act of nailing the flag faster and yet faster to the subsiding spar. A skyhawk that tauntingly had followed the main-truck downwards from its natural home among the stars, pecking at the flag, and incommoding Tashtego there; this bird now chanced to intercept its broad fluttering wing between the hammer and the wood; and simultaneously feeling that etherial thrill, the submerged savage beneath, in his death-gasp, kept his hammer frozen there; and so the bird of heaven, with archangelic shrieks, and his imperial beak thrust upwards, and his whole captive form folded in the flag of Ahab, went down with his ship, which, like Satan, would not sink to hell till she had dragged a living part of heaven along with her, and helmeted herself with it.

Now small fowls flew screaming over the yet yawning gulf; a sullen white surf beat against its steep sides; then all collapsed, and the great shroud of the sea rolled on as it rolled five thousand years ago.

Epilogue

"And I Only Am Escaped Alone to Tell Thee." Job.

The drama's done. Why then here does anyone step forth?—Because one did survive the wreck.

It so chanced, that after the Parsee's disappearance, I was he whom the Fates ordained to take the place of Ahab's bowsman, when that bowsman assumed the vacant post; the same, who, when on the last day the three men were tossed from out the rocking boat, was dropped astern. So, floating on the margin of the ensuing scene, and in full sight of it, when the half-spent suction of the sunk ship reached me, I was then but slowly drawn towards the closing vortex. When I reached it, it had subsided to a creamy pool. Round and round, then, and ever contracting towards the button-like black bubble at the axis of that slowly wheeling circle, like another Ixion I did revolve. Till, gaining that vital center, the black bubble upward burst; and now, liberated by reason of its cunning spring, and, owing to its great buoyancy, rising with great force, the coffin life-buoy shot lengthwise from the sea, fell over, and floated by my side. Buoyed up by that coffin, for almost one whole day and night, I floated on a soft and dirge-like main. The unharming sharks, they glided by as if with padlocks on their mouths; the savage sea-hawks sailed with sheathed beaks. On the second day, a sail drew near, nearer, and picked me up at last. It was the devious-cruising *Rachel,* that in her retracing search after her missing children, only found another orphan.

HENRY JAMES

Paste

"I've found a lot more things," her cousin said to her the day after the second funeral; "they're up in her room—but they're things I wish *you'd* look at."

The pair of mourners, sufficiently stricken, were in the garden of the vicarage together, before luncheon, waiting to be summoned to that meal, and Arthur Prime had still in his face the intention, she was moved to call it rather than the expression, of feeling something or other. Some such appearance was in itself of course natural within a week of his stepmother's death, within three of his father's; but what was most present to the girl, herself sensitive and shrewd, was that he seemed somehow to brood without sorrow, to suffer without what she in her own case would have called pain. He turned away from her after this last speech—it was a good deal his habit to drop an observation and leave her to pick it up without assistance. If the vicar's widow, now in her turn finally translated, had not really belonged to him it was not for want of her giving herself, so far as he ever would take her; and she had lain for three days all alone at the end of the passage, in the great cold chamber of hospitality, the dampish greenish room where visitors slept and where several of the ladies of the parish had, without effect, offered, in pairs and successions, piously to watch with her. His personal connection with the parish was now slighter than ever, and he had really not waited for this opportunity to show the ladies what he thought of them. She felt that she herself had, during her doleful month's leave from Bleet, where she was governess, rather taken her place in the same snubbed order; but it was presently, none the less, with a better little hope of coming in for some remembrance, some relic, that she went up to look at the things he had spoken of, the identity of which, as a confused cluster of bright objects on a table in the darkened room, shimmered at her as soon as she had opened the door.

They met her eyes for the first time, but in a moment, before touching them, she knew them as things of the theater, as very much too fine to have been with any verisimilitude things of the vicarage. They were too dreadfully good to be true, for her aunt had had no jewels to speak of, and these were coronets and girdles, diamonds, rubies and sapphires. Flagrant tinsel and glass, they looked strangely vulgar, but if after the first queer shock of them she found herself taking them up it was for the very proof, never yet so distinct to her, of a far-off faded story. An honest widowed cleric

James, *Paste.* Henry James (1843-1916) was the son of a cultivated Boston family and brother of William James, the philosopher. He lived abroad most of his life and eventually became a British citizen.

with a small son and a large sense of Shakespeare had, on a brave latitude of habit as well as of taste —since it implied his having in very fact dropped deep into the "pit"—conceived for an obscure actress several years older than himself an admiration of which the prompt offer of his reverend name and hortatory hand was the sufficiently candid sign. The response had perhaps in those dim years, so far as eccentricity was concerned, even bettered the proposal, and Charlotte, turning the tale over, had long since drawn from it a measure of the career renounced by the undistinguished comédienne—doubtless also tragic, or perhaps pantomimic, at a pinch—of her late uncle's dreams. This career couldn't have been eminent and must much more probably have been comfortless.

"You see what it is—old stuff of the time she never liked to mention."

Our young woman gave a start; her companion had after all rejoined her and had apparently watched a moment her slightly scared recognition. "So I said to myself," she replied. Then to show intelligence, yet keep clear of twaddle: "How peculiar they look!"

"They look awful," said Arthur Prime. "Cheap gilt, diamonds as big as potatoes. These are trappings of a ruder age than ours. Actors do themselves better now."

"Oh, now," said Charlotte, not to be less knowing, "actresses have real diamonds."

"Some of them." Arthur spoke dryly.

"I mean the bad ones—the nobodies too."

"Oh, some of the nobodies have the biggest. But mamma wasn't of that sort."

"A nobody?" Charlotte risked.

"Not a nobody to whom somebody—well, not a nobody with diamonds. It isn't all worth, this trash, five pounds."

There was something in the old gewgaws that spoke to her, and she continued to turn them over. "They're relics. I think they have their melancholy and even their dignity."

Arthur observed another pause. "Do you care for them?" he then asked. "I mean," he promptly added, "as a souvenir."

"Of you?" Charlotte threw off.

"Of me? What have I to do with it? Of your poor dead aunt who was so kind to you," he said with virtuous sternness.

"Well, I'd rather have them than nothing."

"Then please take them," he returned in a tone of relief which expressed somehow more of the eager than of the gracious.

"Thank you." Charlotte lifted two or three objects up and set them down again. Though they were lighter than the materials they imitated they were so much more extravagant that they struck her in truth as rather an awkward heritage, to which she might have preferred even a matchbox or a penwiper. They were indeed shameless pinchbeck. "Had you any idea she had kept them?"

"I don't at all believe she *had* kept them or knew they were there, and I'm very sure my father didn't. They had quite equally worked off any tenderness for the connection. These odds and ends, which she thought had been given away or destroyed, had simply got thrust into a dark corner and been forgotten."

Charlotte wondered. "Where then did you find them?"

"In that old tin box"—and the young man pointed to the receptacle from which he had dislodged them and which stood on a neighboring chair. "It's rather a good box still, but I'm afraid I can't give you *that*."

The girl took no heed of the box; she continued only to look at the trinkets. "What corner had she found?"

"She hadn't 'found' it," her companion sharply insisted; "she had simply lost it. The whole thing had passed from her mind. The box was on the top shelf of the old schoolroom closet, which, until one put one's head into it from a step-ladder, looked, from below, quite cleared out. The door's narrow and the part of the closet to the left goes well into the wall. The box had stuck there for years."

Charlotte was conscious of a mind divided and a vision vaguely troubled, and once more she took up two or three of the subjects of this revelation; a big bracelet in the form of a gilt serpent with many twists and beady eyes, a brazen belt studded with emeralds and rubies, a chain, of flamboyant architecture, to which, at the Theater Royal Little Peddlington, Hamlet's mother must have been concerned to attach the portrait of the successor to Hamlet's father. "Are you very sure they're not really worth something? Their mere weight alone—!" she vaguely observed, balancing a moment a royal diadem that might have crowned one of the creations of the famous Mrs. Jarley.

But Arthur Prime, it was clear, had already thought the question over and found the answer easy. "If they had been worth anything to speak of she would long ago have sold them. My father and she had unfortunately never been in a position to keep any considerable value locked up." And while his companion took in the obvious force of this he went on with a flourish just marked enough not to escape her: "If they're worth anything at all—why you're only the more welcome to them."

Charlotte had now in her hand a small bag of faded figured silk—one of those antique conveniences that speak to us, in terms of evaporated camphor and lavender, of the part they have played in some personal history; but though she had for the first time drawn the string she looked much more at the young man than at the questionable treasure it appeared to contain. "I shall like them. They're all I have."

"All you have—?"

"That belonged to her."

He swelled a little, then looked about him as if to appeal—as against her avidity—to the whole poor place. "Well, what else do you want?"

"Nothing. Thank you very much." With which she bent her eyes on the article wrapped, and now only exposed, in her superannuated satchel—a string of large pearls, such a shining circle as might once have graced the neck of a provincial Ophelia and borne company to a flaxen wig. "This perhaps *is* worth something. Feel it." And she passed him the necklace, the weight of which she had gathered for a moment into her hand.

He measured it in the same way with his own, but remained quite detached. "Worth at most thirty shillings."

"Not more?"

"Surely not if it's paste?"

"But *is* it paste?"

He gave a small sniff of impatience. "Pearls nearly as big as filberts?"

"But they're heavy," Charlotte declared.

"No heavier than anything else." And he gave them back with an allowance for her simplicity. "Do you imagine for a moment they're real?"

She studied them a little, feeling them, turning them round. "Mightn't they possibly be?"

"Of that size—stuck away with that trash?"

"I admit it isn't likely," Charlotte presently said. "And pearls are so easily imitated."

"That's just what—to a person who knows—they're not. These have no luster, no play."

"No—they *are* dull. They're opaque."

"Besides," he lucidly enquired, "how could she ever have come by them?"

"Mightn't they have been a present?"

Arthur stared at the question as if it were almost improper. "Because actresses are exposed—?"

He pulled up, however, not saying to what, and before she could supply the deficiency had, with the sharp ejaculation of "No, they mightn't!" turned his back on her and walked away. His manner made her feel she had probably been wanting in tact, and before he returned to the subject, the last thing that evening, she had satisfied herself of the ground of his resentment. They had been talking of her departure the next morning, the hour of her train and the fly that would come for her, and it was precisely these things that gave him his effective chance. "I really can't allow you to leave the house under the impression that my stepmother was at *any* time of her life the sort of person to allow herself to be approached—"

"With pearl necklaces and that sort of thing?" Arthur had made for her somehow the difficulty that she couldn't show him she understood him without seeming pert.

It at any rate only added to his own gravity. "That sort of thing, exactly."

"I didn't think when I spoke this morning—but I see what you mean."

"I mean that she was beyond reproach," said Arthur Prime.

"A hundred times yes."

"Therefore if she couldn't, out of her slender gains, ever have paid for a row of pearls—"

"She couldn't, in that atmosphere, ever properly have had one? Of course she couldn't. I've seen perfectly since our talk," Charlotte went on, "that that string of beads isn't even as an imitation very good. The little clasp itself doesn't seem even gold. With false pearls, I suppose," the girl mused, "it naturally wouldn't be."

"The whole thing's rotten paste," her companion returned as if to have done with it. "If it were *not,* and she had kept it all these years hidden—"

"Yes?" Charlotte sounded as he paused.

"Why, I shouldn't know what to think!"

"Oh, I see." She had met him with a certain blankness, but adequately enough, it seemed, for him to regard the subject as dismissed; and there was no reversion to it between them before, on the morrow, when she had with difficulty made a place for them in her trunk, she carried off these florid survivals.

At Bleet she found small occasion to revert to them and, in an air charged with such quite other references, even felt, after she had laid them away, much enshrouded, beneath various piles of clothing, that they formed a collection not wholly without its note of the ridiculous. Yet she was never, for the joke, tempted to show them to her pupils, though Gwendolen and Blanche in particular always wanted, on her return, to know what she had brought back; so that without an accident by which the case was quite changed they might have appeared to enter on a new phase of interment. The essence of the accident was the sudden illness, at the last moment, of Lady Bobby, whose advent had been so much counted on to spice the five days' feast laid out for the coming of age of the eldest son of the house; and its equally marked effect was the dispatch of a pressing message, in quite another direction, to Mrs. Guy, who, could she by a miracle be secured—she was always engaged ten parties deep—might be trusted to supply, it was believed, an element of exuberance scarcely less potent. Mrs. Guy was already known to several of the visitors already on the scene, but she wasn't yet known to our young lady, who found her, after many wires and counter-wires had at last determined the triumph of her arrival, a strange charming little red-haired black-dressed woman, a person with the face of a baby and the authority of a commodore. She took on the spot the discreet, the exceptional young governess into the confidence of her designs and, still more, of her doubts; intimating that it was a policy she almost always promptly pursued.

"Tomorrow and Thursday are all right," she said frankly to Charlotte on the second day, "but I'm not half-satisfied with Friday."

"What improvement then do you suggest?"

"Well, my strong point, you know, is *tableaux vivants*."

"Charming. And what is your favorite character?"

"Boss!" said Mrs. Guy with decision; and it was very markedly under that ensign that she had, within a few hours, completely planned her campaign and recruited her troop. Every word she uttered was to the point, but none more so than, after a general survey of their equipment, her final enquiry of Charlotte. She had been looking about, but half-appeased, at the muster of decoration and drapery. "We shall be dull. We shall want more color. You've nothing else?"

Charlotte had a thought. "No—I've *some* things."

"Then why don't you bring them?"

The girl weighed it. "Would you come to my room?"

"No," said Mrs. Guy—"bring them tonight to mine."

So Charlotte, at the evening's end, after candle-sticks had flickered through brown old passage. bedward, arrived at her friend's door with the burden of her aunt's relics. But she promptly expressed a fear. "Are they too garish?"

When she had poured them out on the sofa Mrs. Guy was but a minute, before the glass, in clapping on the diadem. "Awfully jolly—we can do Ivanhoe!"

"But they're only glass and tin."

"Larger than life they are, *rather!*—which is exactly what's wanted for tableaux. *Our* jewels, for historic scenes, don't tell—the real thing falls short. Rowena must have rubies as big as eggs. Leave them with me," Mrs. Guy continued—"they'll inspire me. Good-night."

The next morning she was in fact—yet very strangely—inspired. "Yes, *I'll* do Rowena. But I don't, my dear, understand."

"Understand what?"

Mrs. Guy gave a very lighted stare. "How you come to have such things."

Poor Charlotte smiled. "By inheritance."

"Family jewels?"

"They belonged to my aunt, who died some months ago. She was on the stage a few years in early life, and these are a part of her trappings."

"She left them to you?"

"No; my cousin, her stepson, who naturally has no use for them, gave them to me for remembrance of her. She was a dear kind thing, always so nice to me, and I was fond of her."

Mrs. Guy had listened with frank interest. "But it's *he* who must be a dear kind thing!"

Charlotte wondered. "You think so?"

"Is *he*," her friend went on, "also 'always so nice' to you?"

The girl, at this, face to face there with the brilliant visitor in the deserted breakfast-room, took a deeper sounding. "What is it?"

"Don't you know?"

Something came over her. "The pearls—?" But the question fainted on her lips.

"Doesn't *he* know?"

Charlotte found herself flushing. "They're *not* paste?"

"Haven't you looked at them?"

She was conscious of two kinds of embarrassment. "*You* have?"

"Very carefully."

"And they're real?"

Mrs. Guy became slightly mystifying and returned for an answer: "Come again, when you've done with the children, to my room."

Our young woman found she had done with the children that morning so promptly as to reveal to them a new joy, and when she reappeared before Mrs. Guy this lady had already encircled a plump white throat with the only ornament, surely, in all the late Mrs. Prime's—the effaced Miss Bradshaw's—collection, in the least qualified to raise a question. If Charlotte had never yet once, before the glass, tied the string of pearls about her own neck, this was because she had been capable of no such stoop to approved "imitation"; but she had now only to look at Mrs. Guy to see that, so disposed, the ambiguous objects might have passed for frank originals. "What in the world have you done to them?"

"Only handled them, understood them, admired them and put them on. That's what pearls want; they want to be worn—it wakes them up. They're alive, don't you see? How *have* these been treated? They must have been buried, ignored, despised. They were half-dead. Don't you *know* about pearls?" Mrs. Guy threw off as she fondly fingered the necklace.

"How *should* I? Do *you?*"

"Everything. These were simply asleep, and from the moment I really touched them—well," said their wearer lovingly, "it only took one's eye!"

"It took more than mine—though I did just wonder; and than Arthur's," Charlotte brooded. She found herself almost panting. "Then their value—?"

"Oh, their value's excellent."

The girl, for a deep contemplative moment, took another plunge into the wonder, the beauty and the mystery. "Are you *sure?*"

Her companion wheeled round for impatience. "Sure? For what kind of an idiot, my dear, do you take me?"

It was beyond Charlotte Prime to say. "For the same kind as Arthur—and as myself," she could only suggest. "But my cousin didn't know. He thinks they're worthless."

"Because of the rest of the lot? Then your cousin's an ass. But what—if, as I understood you, he gave them to you—has he to do with it?"

"Why, if he gave them to me as worthless and they turn out precious—!"

"You must give them back? I don't see that—if he was such a noodle. He took the risk."

Charlotte fed, in fancy, on the pearls, which decidedly were exquisite, but which at the present moment somehow presented themselves much more as Mrs. Guy's than either as Arthur's or as her own. "Yes—he did take it; even after I had distinctly hinted to him that they looked to me different from the other pieces."

"Well then!" said Mrs. Guy with something more than triumph—with a positive odd relief.

But it had the effect of making our young woman think with more intensity. "Ah, you see he thought they couldn't be different, because—so peculiarly—they shouldn't be."

"Shouldn't? I don't understand."

"Why, how would she have got them?"—so Charlotte candidly put it.

"She? Who?" There was a capacity in Mrs. Guy's tone for a sinking of persons—!

"Why, the person I told you of: his stepmother, my uncle's wife—among whose poor old things, extraordinarily thrust away and out of sight, he happened to find them."

Mrs. Guy came a step nearer to the effaced Miss Bradshaw. "Do you mean she may have stolen them?"

"No. But she had been an actress."

"Oh, well then," cried Mrs. Guy, "wouldn't that be just how?"

"Yes, except that she wasn't at all a brilliant one, nor in receipt of large pay." The girl even threw off a nervous joke. "I'm afraid she couldn't have been our Rowena."

Mrs. Guy took it up. "Was she very ugly?"

"No. She may very well, when young, have looked rather nice."

"Well then!" was Mrs. Guy's sharp comment and fresh triumph.

"You mean it was a present? That's just what he so dislikes the idea of her having received—a present from an admirer capable of going such lengths."

"Because she wouldn't have taken it for nothing? *Speriamo*—that she wasn't a brute. The 'length' her admirer went was the length of a whole row. Let us hope she was just a little kind!"

"Well," Charlotte went on, "that she was 'kind' might seem to be shown by the fact that neither her husband, nor his son, nor I, his niece, knew or dreamed of her possessing anything so precious; by her having kept the gift all the rest of her life beyond discovery—out of sight and protected from suspicion."

"As if, you mean"—Mrs. Guy was quick—"she had been wedded to it and yet was ashamed of it? Fancy," she laughed while she manipulated the rare beads, "being ashamed of *these!*"

"But you see she had married a clergyman."

"Yes, she must have been 'rum.' But at any rate he had married *her*. What did he suppose?"

"Why, that she had never been of the sort by whom such offerings are encouraged."

"Ah, my dear, the sort by whom they're *not—!*" But Mrs. Guy caught herself up. "And her stepson thought the same?"

"Overwhelmingly."

"Was he then, if only her stepson—"

"So fond of her as that comes to? Yes; he had never known, consciously, his real mother, and, without children of her own, she was very patient and nice with him. And *I* liked her so," the girl pursued, "that at the end of ten years, in so strange a manner, to 'give her away'—"

"Is impossible to you? Then don't!" said Mrs. Guy with decision.

"Ah, but if they're real I can't keep them!" Charlotte, with her eyes on them, moaned in her impatience. "It's too difficult."

"Where's the difficulty, if he has such sentiments that he'd rather sacrifice the necklace than admit it, with the presumption it carries with it, to be genuine? You've only to be silent."

"And keep it? How can *I* ever wear it?"

"You'd have to hide it, like your aunt?" Mrs. Guy was amused. "You can easily sell it."

Her companion walked round her for a look at the affair from behind. The clasp was certainly, doubtless intentionally, misleading, but everything else was indeed lovely. "Well, I must think. Why didn't *she* sell them?" Charlotte broke out in her trouble.

Mrs. Guy had an instant answer. "Doesn't that prove what they secretly recalled to her? You've only to be silent!" she ardently repeated.

"I must think—I must think!"

Mrs. Guy stood with her hands attached but motionless. "Then you want them back?"

As if with the dread of touching them Charlotte retreated to the door. "I'll tell you tonight."

"But may I wear them?"

"Meanwhile?"

"This evening—at dinner."

It was the sharp selfish pressure of this that really, on the spot, determined the girl; but for the moment, before closing the door on the question, she only said: "As you like!"

They were busy much of the day with preparation and rehearsal, and at dinner that evening the concourse of guests was such that a place among them for Miss Prime failed to find itself marked. At the time the company rose she was therefore alone in the school-room, where, towards eleven o'clock, she received a visit from Mrs. Guy. This lady's white shoulders heaved, under the pearls, with an emotion that the very red lips which formed, as if for the full effect, the happiest opposition of color, were not slow to translate. "My dear, you should have seen the sensation—they've had a success!"

Charlotte, dumb a moment, took it all in. "It *is* as if they knew it—they're more and more alive. But so much the worse for both of us! I can't," she brought out with an effort, "be silent."

"You mean to return them?"

"If I don't I'm a thief."

Mrs. Guy gave her a long hard look: what was decidedly not of the baby in Mrs. Guy's face was a certain air of established habit in the eyes. Then, with a sharp little jerk of her head and a backward reach of her bare beautiful arms, she undid the clasp and, taking off the necklace, laid it on the table. "If you do you're a goose."

"Well, of the two—!" said our young lady, gathering it up with a sigh. And as if to get it, for the pang it gave, out of sight as soon as possible, she shut it up, clicking the lock, in the drawer of her own little table; after which, when she turned again, her companion looked naked and plain without it. "But what will you say?" it then occurred to her to demand.

"Downstairs—to explain?" Mrs. Guy was after all trying at least to keep her temper. "Oh, I'll put on something else and say the clasp's broken. And you won't of course name *me* to him," she added.

"As having undeceived me? No—I'll say that, looking at the thing more carefully, it's my own private idea."

"And does he know how little you really know?"

"As an expert—surely. And he has always much the conceit of his own opinion."

"Then he won't believe you—as he so hates to. He'll stick to his judgment and maintain his gift, and we shall have the darlings back!" With which reviving assurance Mrs. Guy kissed her young friend for good-night.

She was not, however, to be gratified or justified by any prompt event, for, whether or no paste entered into the composition of the ornament in question, Charlotte shrank from the temerity of dispatching it to town by post. Mrs. Guy was thus disappointed of the hope of seeing the business settled—"by return," she had seemed to expect—before the end of the revels. The revels, moreover, rising to a frantic pitch, pressed for all her attention, and it was at last only in the general confusion of leave-taking that she made, parenthetically, a dash at the person in the whole company with whom her contact had been most interesting.

"Come, what will you take for them?"

"The pearls? Ah, you'll have to treat with my cousin."

Mrs. Guy, with quick intensity, lent herself. "Where then does he live?"

"In chambers in the Temple. You can find him."

"But what's the use, if *you* do neither one thing nor the other?"

"Oh, I *shall* do the 'other,'" Charlotte said: "I'm only waiting till I go up. You want them so awfully?" She curiously, solemnly again, sounded her.

"I'm dying for them. There's a special charm in them—I don't know what it is: they tell so their history."

"But what do you know of that?"

"Just what they themselves say. It's all *in* them—and it comes out. They breathe a tenderness—they have the white glow of it. My dear," hissed Mrs. Guy in supreme confidence and as she buttoned her glove—"they're things of love!"

"Oh!" our young woman vaguely exclaimed.

"They're things of passion!"

"Mercy!" she gasped, turning short off. But these words remained, though indeed their help was scarce needed, Charlotte being in private face to face with a new light, as she by this time felt she must call it, on the dear kind colorless lady whose career had turned so sharp a corner in the middle. The pearls had quite taken their place as a revelation. She might have received them for nothing—admit that; but she couldn't have kept them so long and so unprofitably hidden, couldn't have enjoyed them only in secret, for nothing; and she had mixed them in her reliquary with false things in order to put curiosity and detection off the scent. Over this strange fact poor Charlotte interminably mused: it became more touching, more attaching for her than she could now confide to any ear. How bad or how happy—in the sophisticated sense of Mrs. Guy and the young man at the Temple—the effaced Miss Bradshaw must have been to have had to be so mute! The little governess at Bleet put on the necklace now in secret sessions; she wore it sometimes under her dress; she came to feel verily a haunting passion for it. Yet in her penniless state she would have

parted with it for money; she gave herself also to dreams of what in this direction it would do for her. The sophistry of her so often saying to herself that Arthur had after all definitely pronounced her welcome to any gain from this gift that might accrue—this trick remained innocent, as she perfectly knew it for what it was. Then there was always the possibility of his—as she could only picture it—rising to the occasion.

Mightn't he have a grand magnanimous moment?—mightn't he just say, "Oh, I couldn't of course have afforded to let you have it if I had known; but since you *have* got it, and have made out the truth by your own wit, I really can't screw myself down to the shabbiness of taking it back"?

She had, as it proved, to wait a long time—to wait till, at the end of several months, the great house of Bleet had, with due deliberation, for the season, transferred itself to town; after which, however, she fairly snatched at her first freedom to knock, dressed in her best and armed with her disclosure, at the door of her doubting kinsman. It was still with doubt and not quite with the face she had hoped that he listened to her story. He had turned pale, she thought, as she produced the necklace, and he appeared above all disagreeably affected. Well, perhaps there was reason, she more than ever remembered; but what on earth was one, in close touch with the fact, to do? She had laid the pearls on his table, where, without his having at first put so much as a finger to them, they met his hard cold stare.

"I don't believe in them," he simply said at last.

"That's exactly then," she returned with some spirit, "what I wanted to hear!"

She fancied that at this his color changed; it was indeed vivid to her afterwards—for she was to have a long recall of the scene—that she had made him quite angrily flush. "It's a beastly unpleasant imputation, you know!"—and he walked away from her as he had always walked at the vicarage.

"It's none of *my* making, I'm sure," said Charlotte Prime. "If you're afraid to believe they're real—"

"Well?"—and he turned, across the room, sharp round at her.

"Why, it's not my fault."

He said nothing more, for a moment, on this; he only came back to the table. "They're what I originally said they were. They're rotten paste."

"Then I may keep them?"

"No. I want a better opinion."

"Than your own?"

"Than *your* own." He dropped on the pearls another queer stare; then, after a moment, bringing himself to touch them, did exactly what she had herself done in the presence of Mrs. Guy at Bleet— gathered them together, marched off with them to a drawer, put them in and clicked the key. "You say I'm afraid," he went on as he again met her; "but I shan't be afraid to take them to Bond Street."

"And if the people say they're real—?"

He had a pause and then his strangest manner. "They won't say it! They shan't!"

There was something in the way he brought it out that deprived poor Charlotte, as she was perfectly aware, of any manner at all. "Oh!" she simply sounded, as she had sounded for her last word to Mrs. Guy; and within a minute, without more conversation, she had taken her departure.

A fortnight later she received a communication from him, and toward the end of the season one of the entertainments in Eaton Square was graced by the presence of Mrs. Guy. Charlotte was not at dinner, but came down afterwards, and this guest, on seeing her, abandoned a very beautiful young man on purpose to cross and speak to her. The guest displayed a lovely necklace and had apparently not lost her habit of overflowing with the pride of such ornaments.

"Do you see?" She was in high joy.

They were indeed splendid pearls—so far as poor Charlotte could feel she knew, after what had come and gone, about such mysteries. The poor girl had a sickly smile. "They're almost as fine as Arthur's."

"Almost? Where, my dear, are your eyes? They *are* 'Arthur's'!" After which, to meet the flood of crimson that accompanied her young friend's start: "I tracked them—after your folly, and, by miraculous luck, recognized them in the Bond Street window to which he had disposed of them."

"*Disposed* of them?" Charlotte gasped. "He wrote me that I had insulted his mother and that the people had shown him he was right—had pronounced them utter paste."

Mrs. Guy gave a stare. "Ah, I told you he wouldn't bear it! No. But I had, I assure you," she wound up, "to drive my bargain!"

Charlotte scarce heard or saw; she was full of her private wrong. "He wrote me," she panted, "that he had smashed them."

Mrs. Guy could only wonder and pity. "He's really morbid!" But it wasn't quite clear which of the pair she pitied; though the young person employed in Eaton Square felt really morbid too after they had separated and she found herself full of thought. She even went the length of asking herself what sort of a bargain Mrs. Guy had driven and whether the marvel of the recognition in Bond Street had been a veracious account of the matter. Hadn't she perhaps in truth dealt with Arthur directly? It came back to Charlotte almost luridly that she had had his address.

THE NEW ENGLISH DRAMA

In our earlier discussions of English drama we showed how the great dramatic achievement of Shakespeare and his contemporaries gave way to a rapid decline and how, with the closing of the theaters in 1642, the writing of plays came to a temporary end.

With the restoration of Charles II in 1660 the theaters were reopened. The king and his court returned from their long sojourn in France and brought many innovations to the stage. They opened up elaborate theaters and introduced women actors for the first time. A new generation of playwrights began to write. In catering to a corrupt court they wrote plays that were frequently clever and usually highly immoral. These "Comedies of Manners" held the stage for some forty years until the beginning of the eighteenth century. During this Restoration Period there also appeared a series of heroic tragedies with highly exaggerated situations and characters. From these two types of seventeenth century drama, only two plays seem to have permanent vitality, Dryden's handling of the story of Antony and Cleopatra in his *All for Love* and Congreve's great comedy of manners, *The Way of the World*.

From the appearance of this latter play in the year 1700 until about 1890 British and American drama is an entirely unworthy successor of the great work of Shakespeare and his fellow dramatists. This desert of mediocrity is only broken by an occasional oasis. We still produce and applaud John Gay's *The Beggar's Opera* from the early eighteenth, and Goldsmith's *She Stoops to Conquer* and Sheridan's *The Rivals* and *The School for Scandal* from the later eighteenth century. Some of the great poets of the nineteenth century wrote in dramatic form, but their plays were not meant for the theater. During much of the nineteenth century both English and American theaters were filled with adaptations from the French, Shakespearean revivals, or the cheapest melodrama. The brilliant comic operas of Gilbert and Sullivan, with their clever satire, serve to lighten the melancholy picture of dramatic ineffectiveness.

Such was the condition of the drama in the English-speaking world when, about 1890, the plays of Henrik Ibsen began to exert their influence on the London stage. In our discussion of Ibsen (pp. 810 ff., above) we have seen how he revolutionized the whole of European drama, not only in its technique but also in its subject matter. The stage became a place for conversation, rather than declamation, and serious questions of social and personal ethics were discussed on it.

The first product of the "theater of ideas" in England was Sir Arthur W. Pinero's *The Second Mrs. Tanqueray*. This play has perhaps been overpraised, but there is no doubt that it inaugurated a new era in British and American drama. Aside from a very important series of plays by Pinero himself, the theaters were soon filled with first-rate dramas by George Bernard Shaw, Henry Arthur Jones, and Oscar Wilde. If it were the purpose of this volume to go beyond the nineteenth century, we should have to record the very notable series of plays written for the Irish players, as well as the works of such men as Stephen Phillips, Granville Barker, John Galsworthy, Sir James M. Barrie, and, in America, Eugene O'Neill.

OSCAR WILDE

The Importance of Being Earnest

CHARACTERS

John Worthing, J.P.
Algernon Moncrieff
Rev. Canon Chasuble, D.D.
Merriman (*Butler*)
Lane (*Manservant*)
Lady Bracknell
Hon. Gwendolen Fairfax
Cecily Cardew
Miss Prism (*Governess*)

THE SCENES OF THE PLAY

Act   I. Algernon Moncrieff's Flat in Half-Moon Street, W.
Act II. The Garden at the Manor House, Woolton.
Act III. Drawing-room of the Manor House, Woolton.

Time—The Present.
Place—London.

ACT I

Scene:—*Morning-room in Algernon's flat in Half-Moon Street. The room is luxuriously and artistically furnished. The sound of a piano is heard in the adjoining room.*

Lane *is arranging afternoon tea on the table, and after the music has ceased,* Algernon *enters.*

Alger. Did you hear what I was playing, Lane?

Lane. I didn't think it polite to listen, sir.

Alger. I'm sorry for that, for your sake. I don't play accurately—anyone can play accurately—but I play with wonderful expression. As far as the piano is concerned, sentiment is my forte. I keep science for Life.

Lane. Yes, sir.

Alger. And, speaking of the science of Life, 10 have you got the cucumber sandwiches cut for Lady Bracknell?

Lane. Yes, sir. [*Hands them on a salver.*]

Alger. [*inspects them, takes two, and sits down on the sofa*]. Oh! . . . by the way, Lane, I see from your book that on Thursday night, when Lord Shoreman and Mr. Worthing were dining with me, eight bottles of champagne are entered as having been consumed.

Lane. Yes, sir; eight bottles and a pint.

20 Alger. Why is it that at a bachelor's establishment the servants invariably drink the champagne? I ask merely for information.

Lane. I attribute it to the superior quality of the wine, sir. I have often observed that in married households the champagne is rarely of a first-rate brand.

Alger. Good heavens! Is marriage so demoralizing as that?

Lane. I believe it *is* a very pleasant state, sir. I 30 have had very little experience of it myself up to the present. I have only been married once. That

Wilde, *The Importance of Being Earnest*. Oscar Wilde (1856-1900) was born in Dublin. He was leader of the "Æsthetic" movement of the 1890's.

was in consequence of a misunderstanding between myself and a young person.

ALGER. [*languidly*]. I don't know that I am much interested in your family life, Lane.

LANE. No, sir; it is not a very interesting subject. I never think of it myself.

ALGER. Very natural, I am sure. That will do, Lane, thank you.

LANE. Thank you, sir. [LANE *goes out.*

ALGER. Lane's views on marriage seem somewhat lax. Really, if the lower orders don't set us a good example, what on earth is the use of them? They seem, as a class, to have absolutely no sense of moral responsibility.

Enter LANE.

LANE. Mr. Ernest Worthing.

Enter JACK. LANE *goes out.*

ALGER. How are you, my dear Ernest? What brings you up to town?

JACK. Oh, pleasure, pleasure! What else should bring one anywhere? Eating as usual, I see, Algy!

ALGER. [*stiffly*]. I believe it is customary in good society to take some slight refreshment at five o'clock. Where have you been since last Thursday?

JACK [*sitting down on the sofa*]. In the country.

ALGER. What on earth do you do there?

JACK [*pulling off his gloves*]. When one is in town one amuses oneself. When one is in the country one amuses other people. It is excessively boring.

ALGER. And who are the people you amuse?

JACK [*airily*]. Oh, neighbors, neighbors.

ALGER. Got nice neighbors in your part of Shropshire?

JACK. Perfectly horrid! Never speak to one of them.

ALGER. How immensely you must amuse them! [*Goes over and takes sandwich.*] By the way, Shropshire is your county, is it not?

JACK. Eh? Shropshire? Yes, of course. Hallo! Why all these cups? Why cucumber sandwiches? Why such reckless extravagance in one so young? Who is coming to tea?

ALGER. Oh! merely Aunt Augusta and Gwendolen.

JACK. How perfectly delightful!

ALGER. Yes, that is all very well; but I am afraid Aunt Augusta won't quite approve of your being here.

JACK. May I ask why?

ALGER. My dear fellow, the way you flirt with Gwendolen is perfectly disgraceful. It is almost as bad as the way Gwendolen flirts with you.

JACK. I am in love with Gwendolen. I have come up to town expressly to propose to her.

ALGER. I thought you had come up for pleasure? . . . I call that business.

JACK. How utterly unromantic you are!

ALGER. I really don't see anything romantic in proposing. It is very romantic to be in love. But there is nothing romantic about a definite proposal. Why, one may be accepted. One usually is, I believe. Then the excitement is all over. The very essence of romance is uncertainty. If ever I get married, I'll certainly try to forget the fact.

JACK. I have no doubt about that, dear Algy. The Divorce Court was specially invented for people whose memories are so curiously constituted.

ALGER. Oh! there is no use speculating on that subject. Divorces are made in Heaven— [JACK *puts out his hand to take a sandwich.* ALGERNON *at once interferes.*] Please don't touch the cucumber sandwiches. They are ordered specially for Aunt Augusta. [*Takes one and eats it.*]

JACK. Well, you have been eating them all the time.

ALGER. That is quite a different matter. She is my aunt. [*Takes plate from below.*] Have some bread and butter. The bread and butter is for Gwendolen. Gwendolen is devoted to bread and butter.

JACK [*advancing to table and helping himself*]. And very good bread and butter it is, too.

ALGER. Well, my dear fellow, you need not eat as if you were going to eat it all. You behave as if you were married to her already. You are not married to her already, and I don't think you ever will be.

JACK. Why on earth do you say that?

ALGER. Well, in the first place girls never marry the men they flirt with. Girls don't think it right.

JACK. Oh, that is nonsense!

ALGER. It isn't. It is a great truth. It accounts for the extraordinary number of bachelors that one sees all over the place. In the second place, I don't give my consent.

JACK. Your consent!

ALGER. My dear fellow, Gwendolen is my first cousin. And before I allow you to marry her, you will have to clear up the whole question of Cecily. [*Rings bell.*]

JACK. Cecily! What on earth do you mean? What do you mean, Algy, by Cecily? I don't know anyone of the name of Cecily.

Enter LANE.

ALGER. Bring me that cigarette case Mr. Worthing left in the smoking-room the last time he dined here.

LANE. Yes, sir.   [LANE *goes out.*

JACK. Do you mean to say you have had my cigarette case all this time? I wish to goodness you had let me know. I have been writing frantic letters to Scotland Yard about it. I was very nearly offering a large reward.

ALGER. Well, I wish you would offer one. I happen to be more than usually hard up.

JACK. There is no good offering a large reward now that the thing is found.

Enter LANE *with the cigarette case on a salver.* ALGERNON *takes it at once.* LANE *goes out.*

ALGER. I think that is rather mean of you, Ernest, I must say. [*Opens case and examines it.*] However, it makes no matter, for, now that I look at the inscription, I find that the thing isn't yours after all.

JACK. Of course it's mine. [*Moving to him.*] You have seen me with it a hundred times, and you have no right whatsoever to read what is written inside. It is a very ungentlemanly thing to read a private cigarette case.

ALGER. Oh! it is absurd to have a hard-and-fast rule about what one should read and what one shouldn't. More than half of modern culture depends on what one shouldn't read.

JACK. I am quite aware of the fact, and I don't propose to discuss modern culture. It isn't the sort of thing one should talk of in private. I simply want my cigarette case back.

ALGER. Yes; but this isn't your cigarette case. This cigarette case is a present from someone of the name of Cecily, and you said you didn't know anyone by that name.

JACK. Well, if you want to know, Cecily happens to be my aunt.

ALGER. Your aunt!

JACK. Yes. Charming old lady she is, too. Lives at Tunbridge Wells. Just give it back to me, Algy.

ALGER. [*retreating to back of sofa*]. But why does she call herself little Cecily if she is your aunt and lives at Tunbridge Wells? [*Reading.*] "From little Cecily with her fondest love."

JACK [*moving to sofa and kneeling upon it*]. My dear fellow, what on earth is there in that? Some aunts are tall, some aunts are not tall. That is a matter that surely an aunt may be allowed to decide for herself. You seem to think that every aunt should be exactly like your aunt! That is absurd! For heaven's sake give me back my cigarette case. [*Follows* ALGY *round the room.*]

ALGER. Yes. But why does your aunt call you her uncle? "From little Cecily, with her fondest love to her dear Uncle Jack." There is no objection, I admit, to an aunt being a small aunt, but why an aunt, no matter what her size may be, should call her own nephew her uncle, I can't quite make out. Besides, your name isn't Jack at all; it is Ernest.

JACK. It isn't Ernest; it's Jack.

ALGER. You have always told me it was Ernest. I have introduced you to everyone as Ernest. You answer to the name of Ernest. You look as if your name was Ernest. You are the most earnest-looking person I ever saw in my life. It is perfectly absurd your saying that your name isn't Ernest. It's on your cards. Here is one of them. [*Taking it from case.*] "Mr. Ernest Worthing, B. 4, The Albany." I'll keep this as a proof your name is Ernest if ever you attempt to deny it to me, or to Gwendolen, or to anyone else. [*Puts the card in his pocket.*]

JACK. Well, my name is Ernest in town and Jack in the country, and the cigarette case was given to me in the country.

ALGER. Yes, but that does not account for the fact that your small Aunt Cecily, who lives at Tunbridge Wells, calls you her dear uncle. Come, old boy, you had much better have the thing out at once.

JACK. My dear Algy, you talk exactly as if you were a dentist. It is very vulgar to talk like a dentist when one isn't a dentist. It produces a false impression.

ALGER. Well, that is exactly what dentists always do. Now, go on! Tell me the whole thing. I may mention that I have always suspected you of being a confirmed and secret Bunburyist; and I am quite sure of it now.

JACK. Bunburyist? What on earth do you mean by a Bunburyist?

ALGER. I'll reveal to you the meaning of that incomparable expression as soon as you are kind enough to inform me why you are Ernest in town and Jack in the country.

JACK. Well, produce my cigarette case first.

ALGER. Here it is. [*Hands cigarette case.*] Now produce your explanation, and pray make it improbable. [*Sits on sofa.*]

JACK. My dear fellow, there is nothing improbable about my explanation at all. In fact it's perfectly ordinary. Old Mr. Thomas Cardew, who adopted me when I was a boy, made me in his will guardian to his grand-daughter, Miss Cecily Cardew. Cecily, who addresses me as her uncle from motives of respect that you could not possibly appreciate, lives at my place in the country under the charge of her admirable governess, Miss Prism.

ALGER. Where is that place in the country, by the way?

JACK. That is nothing to you, dear boy. You are not going to be invited. . . . I may tell you candidly that the place is not in Shropshire.

ALGER. I suspected that, my dear fellow! I have Bunburyed all over Shropshire on two separate occasions. Now, go on. Why are you Ernest in town and Jack in the country?

JACK. My dear Algy, I don't know whether you will be able to understand my real motives. You are hardly serious enough. When one is placed in the position of guardian, one has to adopt a very high moral tone on all subjects. It's one's duty to do so. And as a high moral tone can hardly be said to conduce very much to either one's health or one's happiness, in order to get up to town I have always pretended to have a younger brother of the name of Ernest, who lives in the Albany, and gets into the most dreadful scrapes. That, my dear Algy, is the whole truth pure and simple.

ALGER. The truth is rarely pure and never simple. Modern life would be very tedious if it were either, and modern literature a complete impossibility!

JACK. That wouldn't be at all a bad thing.

ALGER. Literary criticism is not your forte, my dear fellow. Don't try it. You should leave that to people who haven't been at a University. They do it so well in the daily papers. What you really are is a Bunburyist. I was quite right in saying you were a Bunburyist. You are one of the most advanced Bunburyists I know.

JACK. What on earth do you mean?

ALGER. You have invented a very useful young brother called Ernest, in order that you may be able to come up to town as often as you like. I have invented an invaluable permanent invalid called Bunbury, in order that I may be able to go down into the country whenever I choose. Bunbury is perfectly invaluable. If it wasn't for Bunbury's extraordinary bad health, for instance, I wouldn't be able to dine with you at Willis's tonight, for I have been really engaged to Aunt Augusta for more than a week.

JACK. I haven't asked you to dine with me anywhere tonight.

ALGER. I know. You are absurdly careless about sending out invitations. It is very foolish of you. Nothing annoys people so much as not receiving invitations.

JACK. You had much better dine with your Aunt Augusta.

ALGER. I haven't the smallest intention of doing anything of the kind. To begin with, I dined there on Monday, and once a week is quite enough to dine with one's own relations. In the second place, whenever I do dine there I am always treated as a member of the family, and sent down with either no woman at all, or two. In the third place, I know perfectly well whom she will place me next to, tonight. She will place me next Mary Farquhar, who always flirts with her own husband across the dinner-table. That is not very pleasant. Indeed, it is not even decent . . . and that sort of thing is enormously on the increase. The amount of women in London who flirt with their own husbands is perfectly scandalous. It looks so bad. It is simply washing one's clean linen in public. Besides, now that I know you to be a confirmed Bunburyist, I naturally want to talk to you about Bunburying. I want to tell you the rules.

JACK. I'm not a Bunburyist at all. If Gwendolen accepts me, I am going to kill my brother, indeed I think I'll kill him in any case. Cecily is a little too much interested in him. It is rather a bore. So I am going to get rid of Ernest. And I strongly advise you to do the same with Mr. . . . with your invalid friend who has the absurd name.

ALGER. Nothing will induce me to part with Bunbury, and if you ever get married, which seems to me extremely problematic, you will be very glad to know Bunbury. A man who marries without knowing Bunbury has a very tedious time of it.

JACK. That is nonsense. If I marry a charming girl like Gwendolen, and she is the only girl I ever saw in my life that I would marry, I certainly won't want to know Bunbury.

ALGER. Then your wife will. You don't seem to realize, that in married life three is company and two is none.

JACK [sententiously]. That, my dear young friend, is the theory that the corrupt French Drama has been propounding for the last fifty years.

ALGER. Yes; and that the happy English home has proved in half the time.

JACK. For heaven's sake, don't try to be cynical. It's perfectly easy to be cynical.

ALGER. My dear fellow, it isn't easy to be anything now-a-days. There's such a lot of beastly competition about. [*The sound of an electric bell is heard.*] Ah! that must be Aunt Augusta. Only relatives, or creditors, ever ring in that Wagnerian manner. Now, if I get her out of the way for ten minutes, so that you can have an opportunity for proposing to Gwendolen, may I dine with you tonight at Willis's?

JACK. I suppose so, if you want to.

ALGER. Yes, but you must be serious about it. I hate people who are not serious about meals. It is so shallow of them.

Enter LANE.

LANE. Lady Bracknell and Miss Fairfax. [ALGERNON *goes forward to meet them. Enter* LADY BRACKNELL *and* GWENDOLEN.]

LADY B. Good afternoon, dear Algernon, I hope you are behaving very well.

ALGER. I'm feeling very well, Aunt Augusta.

LADY B. That's not quite the same thing. In fact the two things rarely go together. [*Sees* JACK *and bows to him with icy coldness.*]

ALGER. [*to* GWENDOLEN]. Dear me, you are smart!

GWEND. I am always smart! Aren't I, Mr. Worthing?

JACK. You're quite perfect, Miss Fairfax.

GWEND. Oh! I hope I am not that. It would leave no room for developments and I intend to develop in *many directions.* [GWENDOLEN *and* JACK *sit down together in the corner.*]

LADY B. I'm sorry if we are a little late, Algernon, but I was obliged to call on dear Lady Harbury. I hadn't been there since her poor husband's death. I never saw a woman so altered; she looks quite twenty years younger. And now I'll have a cup of tea, and one of those nice cucumber sandwiches you promised me.

ALGER. Certainly, Aunt Augusta. [*Goes over to tea-table.*]

LADY B. Won't you come and sit here, Gwendolen?

GWEND. Thanks, mamma, I'm quite comfortable where I am.

ALGER. [*picking up empty plate in horror*]. Good heavens! Lane! Why are there no cucumber sandwiches? I ordered them specially.

LANE [*gravely*]. There were no cucumbers in the market this morning, sir. I went down twice.

ALGER. No cucumbers!

LANE. No, sir. Not even for ready money.

ALGER. That will do, Lane, thank you.

LANE. Thank you, sir. [*Goes out.*]

ALGER. I am greatly distressed, Aunt Augusta, about there being no cucumbers, not even for ready money.

LADY B. It really makes no matter, Algernon. I had some crumpets with Lady Harbury, who seems to me to be living entirely for pleasure now.

ALGER. I hear her hair has turned quite gold from grief.

LADY B. It certainly has changed its color. From what cause I, of course, cannot say. [ALGERNON *crosses and hands tea.*] Thank you. I've quite a treat for you tonight, Algernon. I am going to send you down with Mary Farquhar. She is such a nice woman, and so attentive to her husband. It's delightful to watch them.

ALGER. I am afraid, Aunt Augusta, I shall have to give up the pleasure of dining with you tonight after all.

LADY B. [*frowning*]. I hope not, Algernon. It would put my table completely out. Your uncle would have to dine upstairs. Fortunately he is accustomed to that.

ALGER. It is a great bore, and, I need hardly say, a terrible disappointment to me, but the fact is I have just had a telegram to say that my poor friend Bunbury is very ill again. [*Exchanges glances with* JACK.] They seem to think I should be with him.

LADY B. It is very strange. This Mr. Bunbury seems to suffer from curiously bad health.

ALGER. Yes; poor Bunbury is a dreadful invalid.

LADY B. Well, I must say, Algernon, that I think it is high time that Mr. Bunbury made up his mind whether he was going to live or to die. This shilly-shallying with the question is absurd. Nor do I in any way approve of the modern sympathy with invalids. I consider it morbid. Illness of any kind is hardly a thing to be encouraged in others. Health is the primary duty of life. I am always telling that to your poor uncle, but he never seems to take much notice . . . as far as any improvement in his ailments goes. I should be obliged if you would ask Mr. Bunbury, from me, to be kind enough not to have a relapse on Saturday, for I rely on you to arrange my music for me. It is my last reception, and one wants something that will encourage conversation, particularly at the end of the season when everyone has practically said whatever they had to say, which, in most cases, was probably not much.

ALGER. I'll speak to Bunbury, Aunt Augusta, if he is still conscious, and I think I can promise you he'll be all right by Saturday. Of course, the music is a great difficulty. You see, if one plays good music, people don't listen, and if one plays bad music, people don't talk. But I'll run over the program I've drawn out, if you will kindly come into the next room for a moment.

LADY B. Thank you, Algernon. It is very thoughtful of you. [*Rising, and following* ALGERNON.] I'm sure the program will be delightful, after a few expurgations. French songs I cannot possibly allow. People always seem to think that they are improper, and either look shocked, which is vulgar, or laugh, which is worse. But German sounds a thoroughly respectable language, and indeed, I believe is so. Gwendolen, you will accompany me.

GWEND. Certainly, mamma. [LADY BRACKNELL *and* ALGERNON *go into the music-room,* GWENDOLEN *remains behind.*]

JACK. Charming day it has been, Miss Fairfax.

GWEND. Pray don't talk to me about the weather, Mr. Worthing. Whenever people talk to me about the weather, I always feel quite certain that they mean something else. And that makes me so nervous.

JACK. I do mean something else.

GWEND. I thought so. In fact, I am never wrong.

JACK. And I would like to be allowed to take advantage of Lady Bracknell's temporary absence. . . .

GWEND. I would certainly advise you to do so. Mamma has a way of coming back suddenly into a room that I have often had to speak to her about.

JACK [*nervously*]. Miss Fairfax, ever since I met you I have admired you more than any girl . . . I have ever met since . . . I met you.

GWEND. Yes, I am quite aware of the fact. And I often wish that in public, at any rate, you had been more demonstrative. For me you have always had an irresistible fascination. Even before I met you I was far from indifferent to you. [JACK *looks at her in amazement.*] We live, as I hope you know, Mr. Worthing, in an age of ideals. The fact is constantly mentioned in the more expensive monthly magazines, and has reached the provincial pulpits I am told; and my ideal has always been to love someone of the name of Ernest. There is something in that name that inspires absolute confidence. The moment Algernon first mentioned to me that he had a friend called Ernest, I knew I was destined to love you.

JACK. You really love me, Gwendolen?

GWEND. Passionately!

JACK. Darling! You don't know how happy you've made me.

GWEND. My own Ernest!

JACK. But you don't really mean to say that you couldn't love me if my name wasn't Ernest?

GWEND. But your name is Ernest.

JACK. Yes, I know it is. But supposing it was something else? Do you mean to say you couldn't love me, then?

GWEND. [*glibly*]. Ah! that is clearly a metaphysical speculation, and like most metaphysical speculations has very little reference at all to the actual facts of real life, as we know them.

JACK. Personally, darling, to speak quite candidly, I don't much care about the name of Ernest . . . I don't think the name suits me at all.

GWEND. It suits you perfectly. It is a divine name. It has a music of its own. It produces vibrations.

JACK. Well, really, Gwendolen, I must say that I think there are lots of other much nicer names. I think Jack, for instance, a charming name.

GWEND. Jack? . . . No, there is very little music in the name Jack, if any at all, indeed. It does not thrill. It produces absolutely no vibrations . . . I have known several Jacks, and they all, without exception, were more than usually plain. Besides, Jack is a notorious domesticity for John! And I pity any woman who is married to a man called John. She would probably never be allowed to know the entrancing pleasure of a single moment's solitude. The only really safe name is Ernest.

JACK. Gwendolen, I must get christened at once— I mean we must get married at once. There is no time to be lost.

GWEND. Married, Mr. Worthing?

JACK [*astounded*]. Well . . . surely. You know that I love you, and you led me to believe, Miss Fairfax, that you were not absolutely indifferent to me.

GWEND. I adore you. But you haven't proposed to me yet. Nothing has been said at all about marriage. The subject has not even been touched on.

JACK. Well . . . may I propose to you now?

GWEND. I think it would be an admirable opportunity. And to spare you any possible disappointment, Mr. Worthing, I think it only fair to tell you quite frankly beforehand that I am fully determined to accept you.

JACK. Gwendolen!

GWEND. Yes, Mr. Worthing, what have you got to say to me?

JACK. You know what I have got to say to you.

GWEND. Yes, but you don't say it.

JACK. Gwendolen, will you marry me? [*Goes down on his knees.*]

GWEND. Of course, I will, darling. How long you have been about it! I am afraid you have had very little experience in how to propose.

JACK. My own one, I have never loved anyone in the world but you.

GWEND. Yes, but men often propose for practice. I know my brother Gerald does. All my girl-friends tell me so. What wonderfully blue eyes you have, Ernest! They are quite, quite, blue. I hope you will always look at me just like that, especially when there are other people present.

Enter LADY BRACKNELL.

LADY B. Mr. Worthing! Rise, sir, from this semi-recumbent posture. It is most indecorous.

GWEND. Mamma! [*He tries to rise; she restrains him.*] I must beg you to retire. This is no place for you. Besides, Mr. Worthing has not quite finished yet.

LADY B. Finished what, may I ask?

GWEND. I am engaged to Mr. Worthing, mamma. [*They rise together.*]

LADY B. Pardon me, you are not engaged to anyone. When you do become engaged to someone, I, or your father, should his health permit him, will inform you of the fact. An engagement should come on a young girl as a surprise, pleasant or unpleasant, as the case may be. It is hardly a matter that she could be allowed to arrange for herself. . . . And now I have a few questions to put to you, Mr. Worthing. While I am making these inquiries, you, Gwendolen, will wait for me below in the carriage.

GWEND. [*reproachfully*]. Mamma!

LADY B. In the carriage, Gwendolen! [GWENDOLEN *goes to the door. She and* JACK *blow kisses to each other behind Lady Bracknell's back.* LADY BRACKNELL *looks vaguely about as if she could not understand what the noise was. Finally turns round.*] Gwendolen, the carriage!

GWEND. Yes, mamma. [*Goes out, looking back at* JACK.]

LADY B. [*sitting down*]. You can take a seat, Mr. Worthing. [*Looks in her pocket for note-book and pencil.*]

JACK. Thank you, Lady Bracknell, I prefer standing.

LADY B. [*pencil and note-book in hand*]. I feel bound to tell you that you are not down on my list of eligible young men, although I have the same list as the dear Duchess of Bolton has. We work together, in fact. However, I am quite ready to enter your name, should your answers be what

a really affectionate mother requires. Do you smoke?

JACK. Well, yes, I must admit I smoke.

LADY B. I am glad to hear it. A man should always have an occupation of some kind. There are far too many idle men in London as it is. How old are you?

JACK. Twenty-nine.

LADY B. A very good age to be married at. I have always been of opinion that a man who desires to be married should know either everything or nothing. Which do you know?

JACK [*after some hesitation*]. I know nothing, Lady Bracknell.

LADY B. I am pleased to hear it. I do not approve of anything that tampers with natural ignorance. Ignorance is like a delicate exotic fruit; touch it and the bloom is gone. The whole theory of modern education is radically unsound. Fortunately in England, at any rate, education produces no effect whatsoever. If it did, it would prove a serious danger to the upper classes, and probably lead to acts of violence in Grosvenor Square. What is your income?

JACK. Between seven and eight thousand a year.

LADY B. [*makes a note in her book*]. In land, or in *investments*?

JACK. In investments, chiefly.

LADY B. That is satisfactory. What between the duties expected of one during one's life-time, and the duties exacted from one after one's death, land has ceased to be either a profit or a pleasure. It gives one position, and prevents one from keeping it up. That's all that can be said about land.

JACK. I have a country house with some land, of course, attached to it, about fifteen hundred acres, I believe; but I don't depend on that for my real income. In fact, as far as I can make out, the poachers are the only people who make anything out of it.

LADY B. A country house! How many bedrooms? Well, that point can be cleared up afterwards. You have a town house, I hope? A girl with a simple, unspoiled nature, like Gwendolen, could hardly be expected to reside in the country.

JACK. Well, I own a house in Belgrave Square, but it is let by the year to Lady Bloxham. Of course, I can get it back whenever I like, at six months' notice.

LADY B. Lady Bloxham? I don't know her.

JACK. Oh, she goes about very little. She is a lady considerably advanced in years.

LADY B. Ah, now-a-days that is no guarantee of

respectability of character. What number in Belgrave Square?

JACK. 149.

LADY B. [*shaking her head*]. The unfashionable side. I thought there was something. However, that could easily be altered.

JACK. Do you mean the fashion, or the side?

LADY B. [*sternly*]. Both, if necessary, I presume. What are your politics?

JACK. Well, I am afraid I really have none. I am a Liberal Unionist.

LADY B. Oh, they count as Tories. They dine with us. Or come in the evening, at any rate. Now to minor matters. Are your parents living?

JACK. I have lost both my parents.

LADY B. Both? . . . That seems like carelessness. Who was your father? He was evidently a man of some wealth. Was he born in what the Radical papers call the purple of commerce, or did he rise from the ranks of the aristocracy?

JACK. I am afraid I really don't know. The fact is, Lady Bracknell, I said I had lost my parents. It would be nearer the truth to say that my parents seem to have lost me. . . . I don't actually know who I am by birth. I was . . . well, I was found.

LADY B. Found!

JACK. The late Mr. Thomas Cardew, an old gentleman of a very charitable and kindly disposition, found me, and gave me the name of Worthing, because he happened to have a first-class ticket for Worthing in his pocket at the time. Worthing is a place in Sussex. It is a seaside resort.

LADY B. Where did the charitable gentleman who had a first-class ticket for this seaside resort find you?

JACK [*gravely*]. In a hand-bag.

LADY B. A hand-bag?

JACK [*very seriously*]. Yes, Lady Bracknell. I was in a hand-bag—a somewhat large, black leather hand-bag, with handles to it—an ordinary hand-bag, in fact.

LADY B. In what locality did this Mr. James, or Thomas, Cardew come across this ordinary hand-bag?

JACK. In the cloak-room at Victoria Station. It was given to him in mistake for his own.

LADY B. The cloak-room at Victoria Station?

JACK. Yes. The Brighton line.

LADY B. The line is immaterial. Mr. Worthing, I confess I feel somewhat bewildered by what you have just told me. To be born, or at any rate, bred, in a hand-bag, whether it had handles or not, seems to me to display a contempt for the ordinary decencies of family life that remind one of the worst excesses of the French Revolution. And I presume you know what that unfortunate movement led to? As for the particular locality in which the hand-bag was found, a cloak-room at a railway station might serve to conceal a social indiscretion—has probably, indeed, been used for that purpose before now—but it could hardly be regarded as an assured basis for a recognized position in good society.

JACK. May I ask you then what you would advise me to do? I need hardly say I would do anything in the world to ensure Gwendolen's happiness.

LADY B. I would strongly advise you, Mr. Worthing, to try and acquire some relations as soon as possible, and to make a definite effort to produce at any rate one parent, of either sex, before the season is quite over.

JACK. Well, I don't see how I could possibly manage to do that. I can produce the hand-bag at any moment. It is in my dressing-room at home. I really think that should satisfy you, Lady Bracknell.

LADY B. Me, sir! What has it to do with me? You can hardly imagine that I and Lord Bracknell would dream of allowing our only daughter—a girl brought up with the utmost care—to marry into a cloak-room, and form an alliance with a parcel? Good morning, Mr. Worthing! [LADY BRACKNELL *sweeps out in majestic indignation.*]

JACK. Good morning! [ALGERNON, *from the other room, strikes up the Wedding March.* JACK *looks perfectly furious, and goes to the door.*] For heaven's sake don't play that ghastly tune, Algy! How idiotic you are! [*The music stops, and* ALGERNON *enters cheerily.*]

ALGER. Didn't it go off all right, old boy? You don't mean to say Gwendolen refused you? I know it is a way she has. She is always refusing people. I think it is most ill-natured of her.

JACK. Oh, Gwendolen is as right as a trivet. As far as she is concerned, we are engaged. Her mother is perfectly unbearable. Never met such a Gorgon . . . I don't really know what a Gorgon is like, but I am quite sure that Lady Bracknell is one. In any case, she is a monster, without being a myth, which is rather unfair. . . . I beg your pardon, Algy, I suppose I shouldn't talk about your own aunt in that way before you.

ALGER. My dear boy, I love hearing my relations abused. It is the only thing that makes me put up with them at all. Relations are simply a tedious pack of people who haven't got the remotest knowledge of how to live, nor the smallest instinct about when to die.

JACK. Oh, that is nonsense!

ALGER. It isn't!

JACK. Well, I won't argue about the matter. You always want to argue about things.

ALGER. That is exactly what things were originally made for.

JACK. Upon my word, if I thought that, I'd shoot myself. . . . [*A pause.*] You don't think there is any chance of Gwendolen becoming like her mother in about a hundred and fifty years, do you, Algy?

ALGER. All women become like their mothers. That is their tragedy. No man does. That's his.

JACK. Is that clever?

ALGER. It is perfectly phrased! and quite as true as any observation in civilized life should be.

JACK. I am sick to death of cleverness. Everybody is clever now-a-days. You can't go anywhere without meeting clever people. The thing has become an absolute public nuisance. I wish to goodness we had a few fools left.

ALGER. We have.

JACK. I should extremely like to meet them. What do they talk about?

ALGER. The fools? Oh! about the clever people, of course.

JACK. What fools!

ALGER. By the way, did you tell Gwendolen the truth about your being Ernest in town, and Jack in the country?

JACK [*in a very patronizing manner*]. My dear fellow, the truth isn't quite the sort of thing one tells to a nice sweet refined girl. What extraordinary ideas you have about the way to behave to a woman!

ALGER. The only way to behave to a woman is to make love to her, if she is pretty, and to someone else if she is plain.

JACK. Oh, that is nonsense.

ALGER. What about your brother? What about the profligate Ernest?

JACK. Oh, before the end of the week I shall have got rid of him. I'll say he died in Paris of apoplexy. Lots of people die of apoplexy, quite suddenly, don't they?

ALGER. Yes, but it's hereditary, my dear fellow. It's a sort of thing that runs in families. You had much better say a severe chill.

JACK. You are sure a severe chill isn't hereditary, or anything of that kind?

ALGER. Of course it isn't!

JACK. Very well, then. My poor brother Ernest is carried off suddenly in Paris, by a severe chill. That gets rid of him.

ALGER. But I thought you said that . . . Miss Cardew was a little too much interested in your poor brother Ernest? Won't she feel his loss a good deal?

JACK. Oh, that is all right. Cecily is not a silly, romantic girl, I am glad to say. She has a capital appetite, goes for long walks, and pays no attention at all to her lessons.

ALGER. I would rather like to see Cecily.

JACK. I will take very good care you never do. She is excessively pretty, and she is only just eighteen.

ALGER. Have you told Gwendolen yet that you have an excessively pretty ward who is only just eighteen?

JACK. Oh! one doesn't blurt these things out to people. Cecily and Gwendolen are perfectly certain to be extremely great friends. I'll bet you anything you like that half an hour after they have met, they will be calling each other sister.

ALGER. Women only do that when they have called each other a lot of other things first. Now, my dear boy, if we want to get a good table at Willis's, we really must go and dress. Do you know it is nearly seven?

JACK. Oh! it always is nearly seven.

ALGER. Well, I'm hungry.

JACK. I never knew you when you weren't. . . .

ALGER. What shall we do after dinner? Go to a theater?

JACK. Oh, no! I loathe listening.

ALGER. Well, let us go to the Club?

JACK. Oh, no! I hate talking.

ALGER. Well, we might trot round to the Empire at ten?

JACK. Oh, no! I can't bear looking at things. It is so silly.

ALGER. Well, what shall we do?

JACK. Nothing!

ALGER. It is awfully hard work doing nothing. However, I don't mind hard work where there is no definite object of any kind.

Enter LANE.

LANE. Miss Fairfax.

Enter GWENDOLEN. LANE *goes out.*

ALGER. Gwendolen, upon my word!

GWEND. Algy, kindly turn your back. I have

something very particular to say to Mr. Worthing.

ALGER. Really, Gwendolen, I don't think I can allow this at all.

GWEND. Algy, you always adopt a strictly immoral attitude towards life. You are not quite old enough to do that. [ALGERNON *retires to the fireplace.*]

JACK. My own darling.

GWEND. Ernest, we may never be married. From the expression on mamma's face I fear we never shall. Few parents now-a-days pay any regard to what their children say to them. The old-fashioned respect for the young is fast dying out. Whatever influence I ever had over mamma, I lost at the age of three. But although she may prevent us from becoming man and wife, and I may marry someone else, and marry often, nothing that she can possibly do can alter my eternal devotion to you.

JACK. Dear Gwendolen!

GWEND. The story of your romantic origin, as related to me by mamma with unpleasing comments, has naturally stirred the deeper fibers of my nature. Your Christian name has an irresistible fascination. The simplicity of your character makes you exquisitely incomprehensible to me. Your town address at the Albany I have. What is your address in the country?

JACK. The Manor House, Woolton, Hertfordshire. [ALGERNON, *who has been carefully listening, smiles to himself, and writes the address on his shirt-cuff. Then picks up the Railway Guide.*]

GWEND. There is a good postal service, I suppose? It may be necessary to do something desperate. That, of course, will require serious consideration. I will communicate with you daily.

JACK. My own one!

GWEND. How long do you remain in town?

JACK. Till Monday.

GWEND. Good! Algy, you may turn round now.

ALGER. Thanks, I've turned round already.

GWEND. You may also ring the bell.

JACK. You will let me see you to your carriage, my own darling?

GWEND. Certainly.

JACK [*to* LANE, *who now enters*]. I will see Miss Fairfax out.

LANE. Yes, sir. [JACK *and* GWENDOLEN *go off.* LANE *presents several letters on a salver to* ALGERNON. *It is to be surmised that they are bills, as* ALGERNON, *after looking at the envelopes, tears them up.*]

ALGER. A glass of sherry, Lane.

LANE. Yes, sir.

ALGER. Tomorrow, Lane, I'm going Bunburying.

LANE. Yes, sir.

ALGER. I shall probably not be back till Monday. You can put up my dress clothes, my smoking jacket and all the Bunbury suits. . . .

LANE. Yes, sir. [*Handing sherry.*]

ALGER. I hope tomorrow will be a fine day, Lane.

LANE. It never is, sir.

ALGER. Lane, you're a perfect pessimist.

LANE. I do my best to give satisfaction, sir.

Enter JACK. LANE *goes off.*

JACK. There's a sensible, intellectual girl! The only girl I ever cared for in my life. [ALGERNON *is laughing immoderately.*] What on earth are you so amused at?

ALGER. Oh, I'm a little anxious about poor Bunbury, that's all.

JACK. If you don't take care, your friend Bunbury will get you into a serious scrape some day.

ALGER. I love scrapes. They are the only things that are never serious.

JACK. Oh, that's nonsense, Algy. You never talk anything but nonsense.

ALGER. Nobody ever does. [JACK *looks indignantly at him, and leaves the room.* ALGERNON *lights a cigarette, reads his shirt-cuff, and smiles.*]

CURTAIN

ACT II

SCENE:—*Garden at the Manor House. A flight of gray stone steps leads up to the house. The garden, an old-fashioned one, full of roses. Time of year, July. Basket chairs, and a table covered with books, are set under a large yew tree.*

MISS PRISM *discovered seated at the table.* CECILY *is at the back watering flowers.*

PRISM [*calling*]. Cecily, Cecily! Surely such a utilitarian occupation as the watering of flowers is rather Moulton's duty than yours? Especially at a moment when intellectual pleasures await you. Your German grammar is on the table. Pray open it at page fifteen. We will repeat yesterday's lesson.

CECIL. [*coming over very slowly*]. But I don't like German. It isn't at all a becoming language. I know perfectly well that I look quite plain after my German lesson.

PRISM. Child, you know how anxious your guardian is that you should improve yourself in every way. He laid particular stress on your German, as he was leaving for town yesterday. Indeed, he always lays stress on your German when he is leaving for town.

CECIL. Dear Uncle Jack is so very serious! Sometimes he is so serious that I think he cannot be quite well.

PRISM [*drawing herself up*]. Your guardian enjoys the best of health, and his gravity of demeanor is especially to be commended in one so comparatively young as he is. I know no one who has a higher sense of duty and responsibility.

CECIL. I suppose that is why he often looks a little bored when we three are together.

PRISM. Cecily! I am surprised at you. Mr. Worthing has many troubles in his life. Idle merriment and triviality would be out of place in his conversation. You must remember his constant anxiety about that unfortunate young man, his brother.

CECIL. I wish Uncle Jack would allow that unfortunate young man, his brother, to come down here sometimes. We might have a good influence over him, Miss Prism. I am sure you certainly would. You know German, and geology, and things of that kind influence a man very much. [CECILY *begins to write in her diary*.]

PRISM [*shaking her head*]. I do not think that even I could produce any effect on a character that according to his own brother's admission is irretrievably weak and vacillating. Indeed, I am not sure that I would desire to reclaim him. I am not in favor of this modern mania for turning bad people into good people at a moment's notice. As a man sows so let him reap. You must put away your diary, Cecily. I really don't see why you should keep a diary at all.

CECIL. I keep a diary in order to enter the wonderful secrets of my life. If I didn't write them down I should probably forget all about them.

PRISM. Memory, my dear Cecily, is the diary that we all carry about with us.

CECIL. Yes, but it usually chronicles the things that have never happened, and couldn't possibly have happened. I believe that Memory is responsible for nearly all the three-volume novels that Mudie sends us.

PRISM. Do not speak slightingly of the three-volume novel, Cecily. I wrote one myself in earlier days.

CECIL. Did you really, Miss Prism? How wonderfully clever you are! I hope it did not end happily? I don't like novels that end happily. They depress me so much.

PRISM. The good ended happily, and the bad unhappily. That is what Fiction means.

CECIL. I suppose so. But it seems very unfair. And was your novel ever published?

PRISM. Alas! no. The manuscript unfortunately was abandoned. I use the word in the sense of lost or mislaid. To your work, child, these speculations are profitless.

CECIL. [*smiling*]. But I see dear Dr. Chasuble coming up through the garden.

PRISM [*rising and advancing*]. Dr. Chasuble! This is indeed a pleasure.

Enter CANON CHASUBLE.

CHAS. And how are we this morning? Miss Prism, you are, I trust, well?

CECIL. Miss Prism has just been complaining of a slight headache. I think it would do her so much good to have a short stroll with you in the park, Dr. Chasuble.

PRISM. Cecily, I have not mentioned anything about a headache.

CECIL. No, dear Miss Prism, I know that, but I felt instinctively that you had a headache. Indeed I was thinking about that, and not about my German lesson, when the Rector came in.

CHAS. I hope, Cecily, you are not inattentive.

CECIL. Oh, I am afraid I am.

CHAS. That is strange. Were I fortunate enough to be Miss Prism's pupil, I would hang upon her lips. [MISS PRISM *glares*.] I spoke metaphorically.— My metaphor was drawn from bees. Ahem! Mr. Worthing, I suppose, has not returned from town yet?

PRISM. We do not expect him till Monday afternoon.

CHAS. Ah, yes, he usually likes to spend his Sunday in London. He is not one of those whose sole aim is enjoyment, as, by all accounts, that unfortunate young man his brother seems to be. But I must not disturb Egeria and her pupil any longer.

PRISM. Egeria? My name is Lætitia, Doctor.

CHAS. [*bowing*]. A classical allusion merely, drawn from the Pagan authors. I shall see you both no doubt at Evensong?

PRISM. I think, dear Doctor, I will have a stroll with you. I find I have a headache after all, and a walk might do it good.

CHAS. With pleasure, Miss Prism, with pleasure. We might go as far as the schools and back.

PRISM. That would be delightful. Cecily, you will read your Political Economy in my absence.

The chapter on the Fall of the Rupee you may omit. It is somewhat too sensational. Even these metallic problems have their melodramatic side. [*Goes down the garden with* Dr. Chasuble.]

Cecil. [*picks up books and throws them back on table*]. Horrid Political Economy! Horrid Geography! Horrid, horrid German!

Enter Merriman *with a card on a salver.*

Merri. Mr. Ernest Worthing has just driven over from the station. He has brought his luggage with him.

Cecil. [*takes the card and reads it*]. "Mr. Ernest Worthing, B. 4, The Albany, W." Uncle Jack's brother! Did you tell him Mr. Worthing was in town?

Merri. Yes, Miss. He seemed very much disappointed. I mentioned that you and Miss Prism were in the garden. He said he was anxious to speak to you privately for a moment.

Cecil. Ask Mr. Ernest Worthing to come here. I suppose you had better talk to the housekeeper about a room for him.

Merri. Yes, Miss. [Merriman *goes off.*

Cecil. I have never met any really wicked person before. I feel rather frightened. I am so afraid he will look just like everyone else. [*Enter* Algernon, *very gay and debonair.*] He does!

Alger. [*raising his hat*]. You are my little cousin Cecily, I'm sure.

Cecil. You are under some strange mistake. I am not little. In fact, I believe I am more than usually tall for my age. [Algernon *is rather taken aback.*] But I am your cousin Cecily. You, I see from your card, are Uncle Jack's brother, my cousin Ernest, my wicked cousin Ernest.

Alger. Oh! I am not really wicked at all, cousin Cecily. You mustn't think that I am wicked.

Cecil. If you are not, then you have certainly been deceiving us all in a very excusable manner. I hope you have not been leading a double life, pretending to be wicked and being really good all the time. That would be hypocrisy.

Alger. [*looks at her in amazement*]. Oh! of course I have been rather reckless.

Cecil. I am glad to hear it.

Alger. In fact, now you mention the subject, I have been very bad in my own small way.

Cecil. I don't think you should be so proud of that, though I am sure it must have been very pleasant.

Alger. It is much pleasanter being here with you.

Cecil. I can't understand how you are here at all. Uncle Jack won't be back till Monday afternoon.

Alger. That is a great disappointment. I am obliged to go up by the first train on Monday morning. I have a business appointment that I am anxious . . . to miss.

Cecil. Couldn't you miss it anywhere but in London?

Alger. No; the appointment is in London.

Cecil. Well, I know, of course, how important it is not to keep a business engagement, if one wants to retain any sense of the beauty of life, but still I think you had better wait till Uncle Jack arrives. I know he wants to speak to you about your emigrating.

Alger. About my what?

Cecil. Your emigrating. He has gone up to buy your outfit.

Alger. I certainly wouldn't let Jack buy my outfit. He has no taste in neckties at all.

Cecil. I don't think you will require neckties. Uncle Jack is sending you to Australia.

Alger. Australia! I'd sooner die.

Cecil. Well, he said at dinner on Wednesday night, that you would have to choose between this world, the next world, and Australia.

Alger. Oh, well! The accounts I have received of Australia and the next world are not particularly encouraging. This world is good enough for me, cousin Cecily.

Cecil. Yes, but are you good enough for it?

Alger. I'm afraid I'm not that. That is why I want you to reform me. You might make that your mission, if you don't mind, cousin Cecily.

Cecil. I'm afraid I've no time, this afternoon.

Alger. Well, would you mind my reforming myself this afternoon?

Cecil. It is rather Quixotic of you. But I think you should try.

Alger. I will. I feel better already.

Cecil. You are looking a little worse.

Alger. That is because I am hungry.

Cecil. How thoughtless of me. I should have remembered that when one is going to lead an entirely new life, one requires regular and wholesome meals. Won't you come in?

Alger. Thank you. Might I have a button-hole first? I never have any appetite unless I have a button-hole first.

Cecil. A Maréchal Niel? [*Picks up scissors.*]

Alger. No, I'd sooner have a pink rose.

Cecil. Why? [*Cuts a flower.*]

ALGER. Because you are like a pink rose, cousin Cecily.

CECIL. I don't think it can be right for you to talk to me like that. Miss Prism never says such things to me.

ALGER. Then Miss Prism is a short-sighted old lady. [CECILY *puts the rose in his button-hole*.] You are the prettiest girl I ever saw.

CECIL. Miss Prism says that all good looks are a snare.

ALGER. They are a snare that every sensible man would like to be caught in.

CECIL. Oh! I don't think I would care to catch a sensible man. I shouldn't know what to talk to him about.

They pass into the house. MISS PRISM *and* DR. CHASUBLE *return.*

PRISM. You are too much alone, dear Dr. Chasuble. You should get married. A misanthrope I can understand—a womanthrope, never!

CHAS. [*with a scholar's shudder*]. Believe me, I do not deserve so neologistic a phrase. The precept as well as the practice of the Primitive Church was distinctly against matrimony.

PRISM [*sententiously*]. That is obviously the reason why the Primitive Church has not lasted up to the present day. And you do not seem to realize, dear Doctor, that by persistently remaining single, a man converts himself into a permanent public temptation. Men should be more careful; this very celibacy leads weaker vessels astray.

CHAS. But is a man not equally attractive when married?

PRISM. No married man is ever attractive except to his wife.

CHAS. And often, I've been told, not even to her.

PRISM. That depends on the intellectual sympathies of the woman. Maturity can always be depended on. Ripeness can be trusted. Young women are green. [DR. CHASUBLE *starts*.] I spoke horticulturally. My metaphor was drawn from fruits. But where is Cecily?

CHAS. Perhaps she followed us to the schools.

Enter JACK *slowly from the back of the garden. He is dressed in the deepest mourning, with crape hat-band and black gloves.*

PRISM. Mr. Worthing!

CHAS. Mr. Worthing?

PRISM. This is indeed a surprise. We did not look for you till Monday afternoon.

JACK [*shakes Miss Prism's hand in a tragic manner*]. I have returned sooner than I expected. Dr. Chasuble, I hope you are well?

CHAS. Dear Mr. Worthing, I trust this garb of woe does not betoken some terrible calamity?

JACK. My brother.

PRISM. More shameful debts and extravagance?

CHAS. Still leading his life of pleasure?

JACK [*shaking his head*]. Dead!

CHAS. Your brother Ernest dead?

JACK. Quite dead.

PRISM. What a lesson for him! I trust he will profit by it.

CHAS. Mr. Worthing, I offer you my sincere condolence. You have at least the consolation of knowing that you were always the most generous and forgiving of brothers.

JACK. Poor Ernest! He had many faults, but it is a sad, sad blow.

CHAS. Very sad indeed. Were you with him at the end?

JACK. No. He died abroad; in Paris, in fact. I had a telegram last night from the manager of the Grand Hotel.

CHAS. Was the cause of death mentioned?

JACK. A severe chill, it seems.

PRISM. As a man sows, so shall he reap.

CHAS. [*raising his hand*]. Charity, dear Miss Prism, charity! None of us are perfect. I myself am peculiarly susceptible to draughts. Will the interment take place here?

JACK. No. He seems to have expressed a desire to be buried in Paris.

CHAS. In Paris! [*Shakes his head.*] I fear that hardly points to any very serious state of mind at the last. You would no doubt wish me to make some slight allusion to this tragic domestic affliction next Sunday. [JACK *presses his hand convulsively.*] My sermon on the meaning of the manna in the wilderness can be adapted to almost any occasion, joyful, or, as in the present case, distressing. [*All sigh.*] I have preached it at harvest celebrations, christenings, confirmations, on days of humiliation and festal days. The last time I delivered it was in the Cathedral, as a charity sermon on behalf of the Society for the Prevention of Discontent among the Upper Orders. The Bishop, who was present, was much struck by some of the analogies I drew.

JACK. Ah! that reminds me, you mentioned christenings I think, Dr. Chasuble? I suppose you know how to christen all right? [DR. CHASUBLE *looks astounded.*] I mean, of course, you are continually christening, aren't you?

PRISM. It is, I regret to say, one of the Rector's most constant duties in this parish. I have often spoken to the poorer classes on the subject. But they don't seem to know what thrift is.

CHAS. But is there any particular infant in whom you are interested, Mr. Worthing? Your brother was, I believe, unmarried, was he not?

JACK. Oh, yes.

PRISM [bitterly]. People who live entirely for pleasure usually are.

JACK. But it is not for any child, dear Doctor. I am very fond of children. No! the fact is, I would like to be christened myself, this afternoon, if you have nothing better to do.

CHAS. But surely, Mr. Worthing, you have been christened already?

JACK. I don't remember anything about it.

CHAS. But have you any grave doubts on the subject?

JACK. I certainly intend to have. Of course, I don't know if the thing would bother you in any way, or if you think I am a little too old now.

CHAS. Not at all. The sprinkling, and, indeed, the immersion of adults is a perfectly canonical practice.

JACK. Immersion!

CHAS. You need have no apprehensions. Sprinkling is all that is necessary, or indeed I think advisable. Our weather is so changeable. At what hour would you wish the ceremony performed?

JACK. Oh, I might trot around about five if that would suit you.

CHAS. Perfectly, perfectly! In fact I have two similar ceremonies to perform at that time. A case of twins that occurred recently in one of the outlying cottages on your own estate. Poor Jenkins the carter, a most hard-working man.

JACK. Oh! I don't see much fun in being christened along with other babies. It would be childish. Would half-past five do?

CHAS. Admirably! Admirably! [Takes out watch.] And now, dear Mr. Worthing, I will not intrude any longer into a house of sorrow. I would merely beg you not to be too much bowed down by grief. What seem to us bitter trials at the moment are often blessings in disguise.

PRISM. This seems to me a blessing of an extremely obvious kind.

Enter CECILY from the house.

CECIL. Uncle Jack! Oh, I am pleased to see you back. But what horrid clothes you have on! Do go and change them.

PRISM. Cecily!

CHAS. My child! my child! [CECILY goes towards JACK; he kisses her brow in a melancholy manner.]

CECIL. What is the matter, Uncle Jack? Do look happy! You look as if you had a toothache, and I have such a surprise for you. Who do you think is in the dining-room? Your brother!

JACK. Who?

CECIL. Your brother Ernest. He arrived about half hour ago.

JACK. What nonsense! I haven't got a brother.

CECIL. Oh, don't say that. However badly he may have behaved to you in the past he is still your brother. You couldn't be so heartless as to disown him. I'll tell him to come out. And you will shake hands with him, won't you, Uncle Jack? [Runs back into the house.]

CHAS. These are very joyful tidings.

PRISM. After we had all been resigned to his loss, his sudden return seems to me peculiarly distressing.

JACK. My brother is in the dining-room? I don't know what it all means. I think it is perfectly absurd.

Enter ALGERNON and CECILY hand in hand. They come slowly up to JACK.

JACK. Good heavens! [Motions ALGERNON away.]

ALGER. Brother John, I have come down from town to tell you that I am very sorry for all the trouble I have given you, and that I intend to lead a better life in the future. [JACK glares at him and does not take his hand.]

CECIL. Uncle Jack, you are not going to refuse your own brother's hand?

JACK. Nothing will induce me to take his hand. I think his coming down here disgraceful. He knows perfectly well why.

CECIL. Uncle Jack, do be nice. There is some good in everyone. Ernest has just been telling me about his poor invalid friend, Mr. Bunbury, whom he goes to visit so often. And surely there must be much good in one who is kind to an invalid, and leaves the pleasures of London to sit by a bed of pain.

JACK. Oh, he has been talking about Bunbury, has he?

CECIL. Yes, he has told me all about poor Mr. Bunbury, and his terrible state of health.

JACK. Bunbury! Well, I won't have him talk to you about Bunbury or about anything else. It is enough to drive one perfectly frantic.

ALGER. Of course I admit that the faults were

all on my side. But I must say that I think that Brother John's coldness to me is peculiarly painful. I expected a more enthusiastic welcome, especially considering it is the first time I have come here.

CECIL. Uncle Jack, if you don't shake hands with Ernest, I will never forgive you.

JACK. Never forgive me?

CECIL. Never, never, never!

JACK. Well, this is the last time I shall ever do it. [*Shakes hands with* ALGERNON *and glares.*]

CHAS. It's pleasant, is it not, to see so perfect a reconciliation? I think we might leave the two brothers together.

PRISM. Cecily, you will come with us.

CECIL. Certainly, Miss Prism. My little task of reconciliation is over.

CHAS. You have done a beautiful action today, dear child.

PRISM. We must not be premature in our judgments.

CECIL. I feel very happy.   [*They all go off.*

JACK. You young scoundrel, Algy, you must get out of this place as soon as possible. I don't allow any Bunburying here.

Enter MERRIMAN.

MERRI. I have put Mr. Ernest's things in the room next to yours, sir. I suppose that is all right?

JACK. What?

MERRI. Mr. Ernest's luggage, sir. I have unpacked it and put it in the room next to your own.

JACK. His luggage?

MERRI. Yes, sir. Three portmanteaus, a dressing-case, two hat-boxes, and a large luncheon-basket.

ALGER. I am afraid I can't stay more than a week this time.

JACK. Merriman, order the dog-cart at once. Mr. Ernest has been suddenly called back to town.

MERRI. Yes, sir. [*Goes back into the house.*]

ALGER. What a fearful liar you are, Jack. I have not been called back to town at all.

JACK. Yes, you have.

ALGER. I haven't heard anyone call me.

JACK. Your duty as a gentleman calls you back.

ALGER. My duty as a gentleman has never interfered with my pleasures in the smallest degree.

JACK. I can quite understand that.

ALGER. Well, Cecily is a darling.

JACK. You are not to talk of Miss Cardew like that. I don't like it.

ALGER. Well, I don't like your clothes. You look perfectly ridiculous in them. Why on earth don't you go up and change? It is perfectly childish to be in deep mourning for a man who is actually staying for a whole week with you in your house as a guest. I call it grotesque.

JACK. You are certainly not staying with me for a whole week as a guest or anything else. You have got to leave . . . by the four-five train.

ALGER. I certainly won't leave you so long as you are in mourning. It would be most unfriendly. If I were in mourning you would stay with me, I suppose. I should think it very unkind if you didn't.

JACK. Well, will you go if I change my clothes?

ALGER. Yes, if you are not too long. I never saw anybody take so long to dress, and with such little result.

JACK. Well, at any rate, that is better than being always over-dressed as you are.

ALGER. If I am occasionally a little over-dressed, I make up for it by being always immensely over-educated.

JACK. Your vanity is ridiculous, your conduct an outrage, and your presence in my garden utterly absurd. However, you have got to catch the four-five, and I hope you will have a pleasant journey back to town. This Bunburying, as you call it, has not been a great success for you. [*Goes into the house.*]

ALGER. I think it has been a great success. I'm in love with Cecily and that is everything. [*Enter* CECILY *at the back of the garden. She picks up the can and begins to water the flowers.*] But I must see her before I go, and make arrangements for another Bunbury. Ah, there she is.

CECIL. Oh, I merely came back to water the roses. I thought you were with Uncle Jack.

ALGER. He's gone to order the dog-cart for me.

CECIL. Oh, is he going to take you for a nice drive?

ALGER. He's going to send me away.

CECIL. Then have we got to part?

ALGER. I am afraid so. It's very painful parting.

CECIL. It is always painful to part from people whom one has known for a very brief space of time. The absence of old friends one can endure with equanimity. But even a momentary separation from anyone to whom one has just been introduced is almost unbearable.

ALGER. Thank you.

Enter MERRIMAN.

MERRI. The dog-cart is at the door, sir. [ALGERNON *looks appealingly at* CECILY.]

CECIL. It can wait, Merriman . . . for . . . five minutes.

MERRI. Yes, miss.   [*Exit* MERRIMAN.

ALGER. I hope, Cecily, I shall not offend you if I state quite frankly and openly that you seem to me to be in every way the visible personification of absolute perfection.

CECIL. I think your frankness does you great credit, Ernest. If you will allow me I will copy your remarks into my diary. [*Goes over to table and begins writing in diary.*]

ALGER. Do you really keep a diary? I'd give anything to look at it. May I?

CECIL. Oh no. [*Puts her hand over it.*] You see, it is simply a very young girl's record of her own thoughts and impressions, and consequently meant for publication. When it appears in volume form I hope you will order a copy. But pray, Ernest, don't stop. I delight in taking down from dictation. I have reached "absolute perfection." You can go on. I am quite ready for more.

ALGER. [*somewhat taken aback.*] Ahem! Ahem!

CECIL. Oh, don't cough, Ernest. When one is dictating one should speak fluently and not cough. Besides, I don't know how to spell a cough. [*Writes as* ALGERNON *speaks.*]

ALGER. [*speaking very rapidly*]. Cecily, ever since I first looked upon your wonderful and incomparable beauty, I have dared to love you wildly, passionately, devotedly, hopelessly

CECIL. I don't think that you should tell me that you love me wildly, passionately, devotedly, hopelessly. Hopelessly doesn't seem to make much sense, does it?

ALGER. Cecily!

Enter MERRIMAN.

MERRI. The dog-cart is waiting, sir.

ALGER. Tell it to come round next week, at the same hour.

MERRI. [*looks at* CECILY, *who makes no sign*]. Yes, sir.   [MERRIMAN *retires.*

CECIL. Uncle Jack would be very much annoyed if he knew you were staying on till next week, at the same hour.

ALGER. Oh, I don't care about Jack. I don't care for anybody in the whole world but you. I love you, Cecily. You will marry me, won't you?

CECIL. You silly you! Of course. Why, we have been engaged for the last three months.

ALGER. For the last three months?

CECIL. Yes, it will be exactly three months on Thursday.

ALGER. But how did we become engaged?

CECIL. Well, ever since dear Uncle Jack first confessed to us that he had a younger brother who was very wicked and bad, you of course have formed the chief topic of conversation between myself and Miss Prism. And of course a man who is much talked about is always very attractive. One feels there must be something in him after all. I daresay it was foolish of me, but I fell in love with you, Ernest.

ALGER. Darling! And when was the engagement actually settled?

CECIL. On the 14th of February last. Worn out by your entire ignorance of my existence, I determined to end the matter one way or the other, and after a long struggle with myself I accepted you under this dear old tree here. The next day I bought this little ring in your name, and this is the little bangle with the true lovers' knot I promised you always to wear.

ALGER. Did I give you this? It's very pretty, isn't it?

CECIL. Yes, you've wonderfully good taste, Ernest. It's the excuse I've always given for your leading such a bad life. And this is the box in which I keep all your dear letters. [*Kneels at table, opens box, and produces letters tied up with blue ribbon.*]

ALGER. My letters! But my own sweet Cecily, I have never written you any letters.

CECIL. You need hardly remind me of that, Ernest. I remember only too well that I was forced to write your letters for you. I always wrote three times a week, and sometimes oftener.

ALGER. Oh, do let me read them, Cecily.

CECIL. Oh, I couldn't possibly. They would make you far too conceited. [*Replaces box.*] The three you wrote me after I had broken off the engagement are so beautiful, and so badly spelled, that even now I can hardly read them without crying a little.

ALGER. But was our engagement ever broken off?

CECIL. Of course it was. On the 22nd of last March. You can see the entry if you like. [*Shows diary.*] "Today I broke off my engagement with Ernest. I feel it is better to do so. The weather still continues charming."

ALGER. But why on earth did you break it off? What had I done? I had done nothing at all. Cecily, I am very much hurt indeed to hear you broke it off. Particularly when the weather was so charming.

CECIL. It would hardly have been a really serious

engagement if it hadn't been broken off at least once. But I forgave you before the week was out.

ALGER. [*crossing to her, and kneeling*]. What a perfect angel you are, Cecily.

CECIL. You dear romantic boy. [*He kisses her, she puts her fingers through his hair.*] I hope your hair curls naturally, does it?

ALGER. Yes, darling, with a little help from others.

CECIL. I am so glad.

ALGER. You'll never break off our engagement again, Cecily?

CECIL. I don't think I could break it off now that I have actually met you. Besides, of course, there is the question of your name.

ALGER. Yes, of course. [*Nervously.*]

CECIL. You must not laugh at me, darling, but it had always been a girlish dream of mine to love someone whose name was Ernest. [ALGERNON *rises,* CECILY *also.*] There is something in that name that seems to inspire absolute confidence. I pity any poor married woman whose husband is not called Ernest.

ALGER. But, my dear child, do you mean to say you could not love me if I had some other name?

CECIL. But what name?

ALGER. Oh, any name you like—Algernon—for instance. . . .

CECIL. But I don't like the name of Algernon.

ALGER. Well, my own dear, sweet, loving little darling, I really can't see why you should object to the name of Algernon. It is not at all a bad name. In fact, it is rather an aristocratic name. Half of the chaps who get into the Bankruptcy Court are called Algernon. But seriously, Cecily . . . [*Moving to her.*] . . . if my name was Algy, couldn't you love me?

CECIL. [*rising*]. I might respect you, Ernest, I might admire your character, but I fear that I should not be able to give you my undivided attention.

ALGER. Ahem! Cecily! [*Picking up hat.*] Your Rector here is, I suppose, thoroughly experienced in the practice of all the rites and ceremonials of the church?

CECIL. Oh, yes. Dr. Chasuble is a most learned man. He has never written a single book, so you can imagine how much he knows.

ALGER. I must see him at once on a most important christening—I mean on most important business.

CECIL. Oh!

ALGER. I sha'n't be away more than half an hour.

CECIL. Considering that we have been engaged since February the 14th, and that I only met you today for the first time, I think it is rather hard that you should leave me for so long a period as half an hour. Couldn't you make it twenty minutes?

ALGER. I'll be back in no time. [*Kisses her and rushes down the garden.*]

CECIL. What an impetuous boy he is! I like his hair so much. I must enter his proposal in my diary.

Enter MERRIMAN.

MERRI. A Miss Fairfax has just called to see Mr. Worthing. On very important business, Miss Fairfax states.

CECIL. Isn't Mr. Worthing in his library?

MERRI. Mr. Worthing went over in the direction of the Rectory some time ago.

CECIL. Pray ask the lady to come out here; Mr. Worthing is sure to be back soon. And you can bring tea.

MERRI. Yes, miss.   [*Goes out.*

CECIL. Miss Fairfax! I suppose one of the many good elderly women who are associated with Uncle Jack in some of his philanthropic work in London. I don't quite like women who are interested in philanthropic work. I think it is so forward of them.

Enter MERRIMAN.

MERRI. Miss Fairfax.

Enter GWENDOLEN.

[*Exit* MERRIMAN.

CECIL. [*advancing to meet her*]. Pray let me introduce myself to you. My name is Cecily Cardew.

GWEND. Cecily Cardew? [*Moving to her and shaking hands.*] What a very sweet name! Something tells me that we are going to be great friends. I like you already more than I can say. My first impressions of people are never wrong.

CECIL. How nice of you to like me so much after we have known each other such a comparatively short time. Pray sit down.

GWEND. [*still standing up*]. I may call you Cecily, may I not?

CECIL. With pleasure!

GWEND. And you will always call me Gwendolen, won't you?

CECIL. If you wish.

GWEND. Then that is all quite settled, is it not?

CECIL. I hope so. [*A pause. They both sit down together.*]

GWEND. Perhaps this might be a favorable opportunity for my mentioning who I am. My father is

Lord Bracknell. You have never heard of papa, I suppose?

Cecil. I don't think so.

Gwend. Outside the family circle, papa, I am glad to say, is entirely unknown. I think that is quite as it should be. The home seems to me to be the proper sphere for the man. And certainly once a man begins to neglect his domestic duties he becomes painfully effeminate, does he not? And I don't like that. It makes men so very attractive. Cecily, mamma, whose views on education are remarkably strict, has brought me up to be extremely short-sighted; it is part of her system; so do you mind my looking at you through my glasses?

Cecil. Oh! not at all, Gwendolen. I am very fond of being looked at.

Gwend. [after examining Cecily carefully through a lorgnette]. You are here on a short visit, I suppose.

Cecil. Oh no, I live here.

Gwend. [severely]. Really? Your mother, no doubt, or some female relative of advanced years, resides here also?

Cecil. Oh, no. I have no mother, nor in fact, any relations.

Gwend. Indeed?

Cecil. My dear guardian, with the assistance of Miss Prism, has the arduous task of looking after me.

Gwend. Your guardian?

Cecil. Yes, I am Mr. Worthing's ward.

Gwend. Oh! It is strange he never mentioned to me that he had a ward. How secretive of him! He grows more interesting hourly. I am not sure, however, that the news inspires me with feelings of unmixed delight. [Rising and going to her.] I am very fond of you, Cecily; I have liked you ever since I met you! But I am bound to state that now that I know that you are Mr. Worthing's ward, I cannot help expressing a wish you were—well, just a little older than you seem to be—and not quite so very alluring in appearance. In fact, if I may speak candidly—

Cecil. Pray do! I think that whenever one has anything unpleasant to say, one should always be quite candid.

Gwend. Well, to speak with perfect candor, Cecily, I wish that you were fully forty-two, and more than usually plain for your age. Ernest has a strong upright nature. He is the very soul of truth and honor. Disloyalty would be as impossible to him as deception. But even men of the noblest possible moral character are extremely susceptible to the influence of the physical charms of others. Modern, no less than Ancient History, supplies us with many most painful examples of what I refer to. If it were not so, indeed, History would be quite unreadable.

Cecil. I beg your pardon, Gwendolen, did you say Ernest?

Gwend. Yes.

Cecil. Oh, but it is not Mr. Ernest Worthing who is my guardian. It is his brother—his elder brother.

Gwend. [sitting down again]. Ernest never mentioned to me that he had a brother.

Cecil. I am sorry to say they have not been on good terms for a long time.

Gwend. Ah! that accounts for it. And now that I think of it I have never heard any man mention his brother. The subject seems distasteful to most men. Cecily, you have lifted a load from my mind. I was growing almost anxious. It would have been terrible if any cloud had come across a friendship like ours, would it not? Of course you are quite, quite sure that it is not Mr. Ernest Worthing who is your guardian?

Cecil. Quite sure. [A pause.] In fact, I am going to be his.

Gwend. [enquiringly]. I beg your pardon?

Cecil. [rather shy and confidingly]. Dearest Gwendolen, there is no reason why I should make a secret of it to you. Our little county newspaper is sure to chronicle the fact next week. Mr. Ernest Worthing and I are engaged to be married.

Gwend. [quite politely, rising]. My darling Cecily, I think there must be some slight error. Mr. Ernest Worthing is engaged to me. The announcement will appear in the Morning Post on Saturday at the latest.

Cecil. [very politely, rising]. I am afraid you must be under some misconception. Ernest proposed to me exactly ten minutes ago. [Shows diary.]

Gwend. [examines diary through lorgnette carefully]. It is certainly very curious, for he asked me to be his wife yesterday afternoon at 5:30. If you would care to verify the incident, pray do so. [Produces diary of her own.] I never travel without my diary. One should always have something sensational to read in the train. I am so sorry, dear Cecily, if it is any disappointment to you, but I am afraid I have the prior claim.

Cecil. It would distress me more than I can tell you, dear Gwendolen, if it caused you any mental or physical anguish, but I feel bound to point out that since Ernest proposed to you he clearly has changed his mind.

GWEND. [*meditatively*]. If the poor fellow has been entrapped into any foolish promise I shall consider it my duty to rescue him at once, and with a firm hand.

CECIL. [*thoughtfully and sadly*]. Whatever unfortunate entanglement my dear boy may have got into, I will never reproach him with it after we are married.

GWEND. Do you allude to me, Miss Cardew, as an entanglement? You are presumptuous. On an occasion of this kind it becomes more than a moral duty to speak one's mind. It becomes a pleasure.

CECIL. Do you suggest, Miss Fairfax, that I entrapped Ernest into an engagement? How dare you? This is no time for wearing the shallow mask of manners. When I see a spade I call it a spade.

GWEND. [*satirically*]. I am glad to say that I have never seen a spade. It is obvious that our social spheres have been widely different.

Enter MERRIMAN, *followed by the footman. He carries a salver, tablecloth, and plate-stand.* CECILY *is about to retort. The presence of the servants exercises a restraining influence, under which both girls chafe.*

MERRI. Shall I lay tea here as usual, miss?

CECIL. [*sternly, in a calm voice*]. Yes, as usual. MERRIMAN *begins to clear table and lay cloth. A long pause,* CECILY *and* GWENDOLEN *glare at each other.*]

GWEND. Are there many interesting walks in the vicinity, Miss Cardew?

CECIL. Oh, yes, a great many. From the top of one of the hills quite close one can see five counties.

GWEND. Five counties! I don't think I should like that. I hate crowds.

CECIL. [*sweetly*]. I suppose that is why you live in town? [GWENDOLEN *bites her lip, and beats her foot nervously with her parasol.*]

GWEND. [*looking around*]. Quite a well-kept garden this is Miss Cardew.

CECIL. So glad you like it, Miss Fairfax.

GWEND. I had no idea there were any flowers in the country.

CECIL. Oh, flowers are as common here, Miss Fairfax, as people are in London.

GWEND. Personally I cannot understand how anybody manages to exist in the country, if anybody who is anybody does. The country always bores me to death.

CECIL. Ah! This is what the newspapers call

agricultural depression, is it not? I believe the aristocracy are suffering very much from it just at present. It is almost an epidemic amongst them, I have been told. May I offer you some tea, Miss Fairfax?

GWEND. [*with elaborate politeness*]. Thank you. [*Aside.*] Detestable girl! But I require tea!

CECIL. [*sweetly*]. Sugar?

GWEND. [*superciliously*]. No, thank you. Sugar is not fashionable any more. [CECILY *looks angrily at her, takes up the tongs and puts four lumps of sugar into the cup.*]

CECIL. [*severely*]. Cake or bread and butter?

GWEND. [*in a bored manner*]. Bread and butter, please. Cake is rarely seen at the best houses nowadays.

CECIL. [*cuts a very large slice of cake, and puts it on the tray*]. Hand that to Miss Fairfax. [MERRIMAN *does so, and goes out with footman.* GWENDOLEN *drinks the tea and makes a grimace. Puts down cup at once, reaches out her hand to the bread and butter, looks at it, and finds it is cake. Rises in indignation.*]

GWEND. You have filled my tea with lumps of sugar and though I asked most distinctly for bread and butter, you have given me cake. I am known for the gentleness of my disposition, and the extraordinary sweetness of my nature, but I warn you, Miss Cardew, you may go too far.

CECIL. [*rising*]. To save my poor, innocent, trusting boy from the machinations of any other girl there are no lengths to which I would not go.

GWEND. From the moment I saw you I distrusted you. I felt that you were false and deceitful. I am never deceived in such matters. My first impressions of people are invariably right.

CECIL. It seems to me, Miss Fairfax, that I am trespassing on your valuable time. No doubt you have many other calls of a similar character to make in the neighborhood.

Enter JACK.

GWEND. [*catching sight of him*]. Ernest! My own Ernest!

JACK. Gwendolen! Darling! [*Offers to kiss her.*]

GWEND. [*drawing back*]. A moment! May I ask if you are engaged to be married to this young lady? [*Points to* CECILY.]

JACK [*laughing*]. To dear little Cecily! Of course not! What could have put such an idea into your pretty little head?

GWEND. Thank you. You may. [*Offers her cheek.*]

CECIL. [*very sweetly*]. I knew there must be some misunderstanding, Miss Fairfax. The gentleman whose arm is at present around your waist is my dear guardian, Mr. John Worthing.

GWEND. I beg your pardon?

CECIL. This is Uncle Jack.

GWEND. [*receding*]. Jack! Oh!

Enter ALGERNON.

CECIL. Here is Ernest.

ALGER. [*goes straight over to CECILY without noticing anyone else*] My own love! [*Offers to kiss her.*]

CECIL. [*drawing back*]. A moment, Ernest! May I ask you—are you engaged to be married to this young lady?

ALGER. [*looking round*]. To what young lady? Good heavens! Gwendolen!

CECIL. Yes! to good heavens, Gwendolen, I mean to Gwendolen.

ALGER. [*laughing*]. Of course not! What could have put such an idea into your pretty little head?

CECIL. Thank you. [*Presenting her cheek to be kissed.*] You may. [*ALGERNON kisses her.*]

GWEND. I felt there was some slight error, Miss Cardew. The gentleman who is now embracing you is my cousin, Mr. Algernon Moncrieff.

CECIL. [*breaking away from ALGERNON*]. Algernon Moncrieff! Oh! [*The two girls move towards each other and put their arms round each other's waists as if for protection.*]

CECIL. Are you called Algernon?

ALGER. I cannot deny it.

CECIL. Oh!

GWEND. Is your name really John?

JACK [*standing rather proudly*]. I could deny it if I liked. I could deny anything if I liked. But my name certainly is John. It has been John for years.

CECIL. [*to GWENDOLEN*]. A gross deception has been practiced on both of us.

GWEND. My poor wounded Cecily!

CECIL. My sweet wronged Gwendolen!

GWEND. [*slowly and seriously*]. You will call me sister, will you not? [*They embrace. JACK and ALGERNON groan and walk up and down.*]

CECIL. [*rather brightly*]. There is just one question I would like to be allowed to ask my guardian.

GWEND. An admirable idea! Mr. Worthing, there is just one question I would like to be permitted to put to you. Where is your brother Ernest? We are both engaged to be married to your brother Ernest, so it is a matter of some importance to us to know where your brother Ernest is at present.

JACK [*slowly and hesitatingly*]. Gwendolen—Cecily—it is very painful for me to be forced to speak the truth. It is the first time in my life that I have ever been reduced to such a painful position, and I am really quite inexperienced in doing anything of the kind. However I will tell you quite frankly that I have no brother Ernest. I have no brother at all. I never had a brother in my life, and I certainly have not the smallest intention of ever having one in the future.

CECIL. [*surprised*]. No brother at all?

JACK [*cheerily*]. None!

GWEND. [*severely*]. Had you never a brother of any kind?

JACK [*pleasantly*]. Never. Not even of any kind.

GWEND. I am afraid it is quite clear, Cecily, that neither of us is engaged to be married to anyone.

CECIL. It is not a very pleasant position for a young girl suddenly to find herself in. Is it?

GWEND. Let us go into the house. They will hardly venture to come after us there.

CECIL. No, men are so cowardly, aren't they?

[*They retire into the house with scornful looks.*]

JACK. This ghastly state of things is what you call Bunburying, I suppose?

ALGER. Yes, and a perfectly wonderful Bunbury it is. The most wonderful Bunbury I have ever had in my life.

JACK. Well, you've no right whatsoever to Bunbury here.

ALGER. That is absurd. One has a right to Bunbury anywhere one chooses. Every serious Bunburyist knows that.

JACK. Serious Bunburyist! Good heavens!

ALGER. Well, one must be serious about something, if one wants to have any amusement in life. I happen to be serious about Bunburying. What on earth you are serious about I haven't the remotest idea. About everything, I should fancy. You have such an absolutely trivial nature.

JACK. Well, the only small satisfaction I have in the whole of this wretched business is that your friend Bunbury is quite exploded. You won't be able to run down to the country quite so often as you used to do, dear Algy. And a very good thing, too.

ALGER. Your brother is a little off color, isn't he, dear Jack? You won't be able to disappear to London quite so frequently as your wicked custom was. And not a bad thing, either.

JACK. As for your conduct towards Miss Cardew, I must say that your taking in a sweet, simple, innocent girl like that is quite inexcusable. To say nothing of the fact that she is my ward.

ALGER. I can see no possible defense at all for your deceiving a brilliant, clever, thoroughly experienced young lady like Miss Fairfax. To say nothing of the fact that she is my cousin.

JACK. I wanted to be engaged to Gwendolen, that is all. I love her.

ALGER. Well, I simply wanted to be engaged to Cecily. I adore her.

JACK. There is certainly no chance of your marrying Miss Cardew.

ALGER. I don't think there is much likelihood, Jack, of you and Miss Fairfax being united.

JACK. Well, that is no business of yours.

ALGER. If it was my business, I wouldn't talk about it. [*Begins to eat muffins.*] It is very vulgar to talk about one's business. Only people like stockbrokers do that, and then merely at dinner parties.

JACK. How you can sit there, calmly eating muffins, when we are in this horrible trouble, I can't make out. You seem to me to be perfectly heartless.

ALGER. Well, I can't eat muffins in an agitated manner. The butter would probably get on my cuffs. One should always eat muffins quite calmly. It is the only way to eat them.

JACK. I say it's perfectly heartless your eating muffins at all, under the circumstances.

ALGER. When I am in trouble, eating is the only thing that consoles me. Indeed, when I am in really great trouble, as anyone who knows me intimately will tell you, I refuse everything except food and drink. At the present moment I am eating muffins because I am unhappy. Besides, I am particularly fond of muffins. [*Rising.*]

JACK [*rising*]. Well, that is no reason why you should eat them all in that greedy way. [*Takes muffins from* ALGERNON.]

ALGER. [*offering tea-cake*]. I wish you would have tea-cake instead. I don't like tea-cake.

JACK. Good heavens! I suppose a man may eat his own muffins in his own garden.

ALGER. But you have just said it was perfectly heartless to eat muffins.

JACK. I said it was perfectly heartless of you, under the circumstances. That is a very different thing.

ALGER. That may be. But the muffins are the same. [*He seizes the muffin-dish from* JACK.]

JACK. Algy, I wish to goodness you would go.

ALGER. You can't possibly ask me to go without having some dinner. It's absurd. I never go without my dinner. No one ever does, except vegetarians and people like that. Besides I have just made arrangements with Dr. Chasuble to be christened at a quarter to six under the name of Ernest.

JACK. My dear fellow, the sooner you give up that nonsense the better. I made arrangements this morning with Dr. Chasuble to be christened myself at 5:30, and I naturally will take the name of Ernest. Gwendolen would wish it. We can't both be christened Ernest. It's absurd. Besides, I have a perfect right to be christened if I like. There is no evidence at all that I ever have been christened by anybody. I should think it extremely probable I never was, and so does Dr. Chasuble. It is entirely different in your case. You have been christened already.

ALGER. Yes, but I have not been christened for years.

JACK. Yes, but you have been christened. That is the important thing.

ALGER. Quite so. So I know my constitution can stand it. If you are not quite sure about your ever having been christened, I must say I think it rather dangerous your venturing on it now. It might make you very unwell. You can hardly have forgotten that someone very closely connected with you was very nearly carried off this week in Paris by a severe chill.

JACK. Yes, but you said yourself that a severe chill was not hereditary.

ALGER. It usedn't to be, I know—but I daresay it is now. Science is always making wonderful improvements in things.

JACK. [*picking up the muffin-dish*]. Oh, that is nonsense; you are always talking nonsense.

ALGER. Jack, you are at the muffins again! I wish you wouldn't. There are only two left. [*Takes them.*] I told you I was particularly fond of muffins.

JACK. But I hate tea-cake.

ALGER. Why on earth then do you allow tea-cake to be served up for your guests? What ideas you have of hospitality!

JACK. Algernon! I have already told you to go. I don't want you here. Why don't you go?

ALGER. I haven't quite finished my tea yet, and there is still one muffin left. [JACK *groans, and sinks into a chair.* ALGERNON *still continues eating.*]

CURTAIN

ACT III

SCENE:—*Morning-room at the Manor House.*

GWENDOLEN *and* CECILY *are at the window, looking out into the garden.*

GWEND. The fact that they did not follow us at once into the house, as anyone else would have done, seems to me to show that they have some sense of shame left.

CECIL. They have been eating muffins. That looks like repentance.

GWEND. [*after a pause.*] They don't seem to notice us at all. Couldn't you cough?

CECIL. But I haven't got a cough.

GWEND. They're looking at us. What effrontery!

CECIL. They're approaching. That's very forward of them.

GWEND. Let us preserve a dignified silence.

CECIL. Certainly. It's the only thing to do now.

Enter JACK, *followed by* ALGERNON. *They whistle some dreadful popular air from a British opera.*

GWEND. This dignified silence seems to produce an unpleasant effect.

CECIL. A most distasteful one.

GWEND. But we will not be the first to speak.

CECIL. Certainly not.

GWEND. Mr. Worthing, I have something very particular to ask you. Much depends on your reply.

CECIL. Gwendolen, your common sense is invaluable. Mr. Moncrieff, kindly answer me the following question. Why did you pretend to be my guardian's brother?

ALGER. In order that I might have an opportunity of meeting you.

CECIL. [*to* GWENDOLEN]. That certainly seems a satisfactory explanation, does it not?

GWEND. Yes, dear, if you can believe him.

CECIL. I don't. But that does not affect the wonderful beauty of his answer.

GWEND. True. In matters of grave importance, style, not sincerity, is the vital thing. Mr. Worthing, what explanation can you offer to me for pretending to have a brother? Was it in order that you might have an opportunity of coming up to town to see me as often as possible?

JACK. Can you doubt it, Miss Fairfax?

GWEND. I have the gravest doubts upon the subject. But I intend to crush them. This is not the moment for German skepticism. [*Moving to* CECILY.] Their explanations appear to be quite satisfactory, especially Mr. Worthing's. That seems to me to have the stamp of truth upon it.

CECIL. I am more than content with what Mr. Moncrieff said. His voice alone inspires one with absolute credulity.

GWEND. Then you think we should forgive them?

CECIL. Yes. I mean no.

GWEND. True! I had forgotten. There are principles at stake that one cannot surrender. Which of us should tell them? The task is not a pleasant one.

CECIL. Could we not both speak at the same time?

GWEND. An excellent idea! I nearly always speak at the same time as other people. Will you take the time from me?

CECIL. Certainly. [GWENDOLEN *beats time with uplifted finger.*]

GWEND. *and* CECIL. [*speaking together*]. Your Christian names are still an insuperable barrier. That is all!

JACK *and* ALGER. [*speaking together*]. Our Christian names! Is that all? But we are going to be christened this afternoon.

GWEND. [*to* JACK]. For my sake you are prepared to do this terrible thing?

JACK. I am.

CECIL. [*to* ALGERNON]. To please me you are ready to face this fearful ordeal?

ALGER. I am!

GWEND. How absurd to talk of the equality of the sexes! Where questions of self-sacrifice are concerned, men are infinitely beyond us.

JACK. We are. [*Clasps hands with* ALGERNON.]

CECIL. They have moments of physical courage of which we women know absolutely nothing.

GWEND. [*to* JACK]. Darling!

ALGER. [*to* CECILY]. Darling! [*They fall into each other's arms.*]

Enter MERRIMAN. *When he enters he coughs loudly, seeing the situation.*

MERRI. Ahem! Ahem! Lady Bracknell!

JACK. Good heavens!

Enter LADY BRACKNELL. *The couples separate in alarm. Exit* MERRIMAN.

LADY B. Gwendolen! What does this mean?

GWEND. Merely that I am engaged to be married to Mr. Worthing, Mamma.

LADY B. Come here. Sit down. Sit down immediately. Hesitation of any kind is a sign of mental decay in the young, of physical weakness in the old. [*Turns to* JACK.] Apprised, sir, of my daughter's sudden flight by her trusty maid, whose confidence I purchased by means of a small coin, I followed her at once by a luggage train. Her unhappy father is, I am glad to say, under the impression that she is attending a more than usually lengthy lecture by the University Extension Scheme on the Influence of a Permanent Income on Thought. I do not propose to undeceive him. Indeed I have never undeceived him on any question. I would consider it wrong. But of course, you will clearly understand that all communication between yourself and my daughter must cease immediately from this moment. On this point, as indeed on all points, I am firm.

JACK. I am engaged to be married to Gwendolen, Lady Bracknell!

LADY B. You are nothing of the kind, sir. And now, as regards Algernon! . . . Algernon!

ALGER. Yes, Aunt Augusta.

LADY B. May I ask if it is in this house that your invalid friend Mr. Bunbury resides?

ALGER. [*stammering*]. Oh, no! Bunbury doesn't live here. Bunbury is somewhere else at present. In fact, Bunbury is dead.

LADY B. Dead! When did Mr. Bunbury die? His death must have been extremely sudden.

ALGER. [*airily*]. Oh, I killed Bunbury this afternoon. I mean poor Bunbury died this afternoon.

LADY B. What did he die of?

ALGER. Bunbury? Oh, he was quite exploded.

LADY B. Exploded! Was he the victim of a revolutionary outrage? I was not aware that Mr. Bunbury was interested in social legislation. If so, he is well punished for his morbidity.

ALGER. My dear Aunt Augusta, I mean he was found out! The doctors found out that Bunbury could not live, that is what I mean—so Bunbury died.

LADY B. He seems to have had great confidence in the opinion of his physicians. I am glad, however, that he made up his mind at the last to some definite course of action, and acted under proper medical advice. And now that we have finally got rid of this Mr. Bunbury may I ask, Mr. Worthing, who is that young person whose hand my nephew Algernon is now holding in what seems to me a peculiarly unnecessary manner?

JACK. That lady is Miss Cecily Cardew, my ward. [LADY BRACKNELL *bows coldly to* CECILY.]

ALGER. I am engaged to be married to Cecily, Aunt Augusta.

LADY B. I beg your pardon?

CECIL. Mr. Moncrieff and I are engaged to be married, Lady Bracknell.

LADY B. [*with a shiver, crossing to the sofa and sitting down*]. I do not know whether there is anything peculiarly exciting in the air of this particular part of Hertfordshire, but the number of engagements that go on seems to me considerably above the proper average that statistics have laid down for our guidance. I think some preliminary enquiry on my part would not be out of place. Mr. Worthing, is Miss Cardew at all connected with any of the larger railway stations in London? I merely desire information. Until yesterday I had no idea that there were any families or persons whose origin was a Terminus. [JACK *looks perfectly furious, but restrains himself.*]

JACK [*in a clear, cold voice*]. Miss Cardew is the granddaughter of the late Mr. Thomas Cardew of 149, Belgrave Square, S.W.; Gervase Park, Dorking, Surrey; and the Sporran, Fifeshire, N.B.

LADY B. That sounds not unsatisfactory. Three addresses always inspire confidence, even in tradesmen. But what proof have I of their authenticity?

JACK. I have carefully preserved the Court Guide of the period. They are open to your inspection, Lady Bracknell.

LADY B. [*grimly*]. I have known strange errors in that publication.

JACK. Miss Cardew's family solicitors are Messrs. Markby, Markby, and Markby.

LADY B. Markby, Markby, and Markby? A firm of the very highest position in their profession. Indeed I am told that one of the Mr. Markbys is occasionally to be seen at dinner parties. So far I am satisfied.

JACK [*very irritably*]. How extremely kind of you, Lady Bracknell! I have also in my possession, you will be pleased to hear, certificates of Miss Cardew's birth, baptism, whooping cough, registration, vaccination, confirmation, and the measles; both the German and the English variety.

LADY B. Ah! A life crowded with incident, I see; though perhaps somewhat too exciting for a young girl. I am not myself in favor of premature experiences. [*Rises, looks at her watch.*] Gwendolen! the time approaches for our departure. We have not a moment to lose. As a matter of form, Mr. Worthing, I had better ask you if Miss Cardew has any little fortune?

JACK. Oh, about a hundred and thirty thousand pounds in the Funds. That is all. Good-by, Lady Bracknell. So pleased to have seen you.

LADY B. [*sitting down again*]. A moment, Mr. Worthing. A hundred and thirty thousand pounds! And in the Funds! Miss Cardew seems to me a most attractive young lady, now that I look at her. Few girls of the present day have any really solid qualities, any of the qualities that last, and improve with time. We live, I regret to say, in an age of surfaces. [*To* CECILY.] Come over here, dear. [CECILY *goes across*.] Pretty child! your dress is sadly simple, and your hair seems almost as Nature might have left it. But we can soon alter all that. A thoroughly experienced French maid produces a really marvelous result in a very brief space of time. I remember recommending one to young Lady Lancing, and after three months her husband did not know her.

JACK [*aside*]. And after six months nobody knew her.

LADY B. [*glares at* JACK *for a few moments. Then bends, with a practiced smile, to* CECILY.] Kindly turn round, sweet child. [CECILY *turns completely round*.] No, the side view is what I want. [CECILY *presents her profile*.] Yes, quite as I expected. There are distinct social possibilities in your profile. The two weak points in our age are its want of principle and its want of profile. The chin a little higher, dear. Style largely depends on the way the chin is worn. They are worn very high, just at present. Algernon!

ALGER. Yes, Aunt Augusta!

LADY B. There are distinct social possibilities in Miss Cardew's profile.

ALGER. Cecily is the sweetest, dearest, prettiest girl in the whole world. And I don't care twopence about social possibilities.

LADY B. Never speak disrespectfully of Society, Algernon. Only people who can't get into it do that. [*To* CECILY.] Dear child, of course you know that Algernon has nothing but his debts to depend upon. But I do not approve of mercenary marriages. When I married Lord Bracknell I had no fortune of any kind. But I never dreamed for a moment of allowing that to stand in my way. Well, I suppose I must give my consent.

ALGER. Thank you, Aunt Augusta.

LADY B. Cecily, you may kiss me!

CECIL. [*kisses her*]. Thank you, Lady Bracknell.

LADY B. You may also address me as Aunt Augusta for the future.

CECIL. Thank you, Aunt Augusta.

LADY B. The marriage, I think, had better take place quite soon.

ALGER. Thank you, Aunt Augusta.

CECIL. Thank you, Aunt Augusta.

LADY B. To speak frankly, I am not in favor of long engagements. They give people the opportunity of finding out each other's character before marriage, which I think is never advisable.

JACK. I beg your pardon for interrupting you, Lady Bracknell, but this engagement is quite out of the question. I am Miss Cardew's guardian, and she cannot marry without my consent until she comes of age. That consent I absolutely decline to give.

LADY B. Upon what grounds, may I ask? Algernon is an extremely, I may almost say an ostentatiously, eligible young man. He has nothing, but he looks everything. What more can one desire?

JACK. It pains me very much to have to speak frankly to you, Lady Bracknell, about your nephew, but the fact is that I do not approve at all of his moral character. I suspect him of being untruthful. [ALGERNON *and* CECILY *look at him in indignant amazement*.]

LADY B. Untruthful! My nephew Algernon? Impossible! He is an Oxonian.

JACK. I fear there can be no possible doubt about the matter. This afternoon during my temporary absence in London on an important question of romance, he obtained admission to my house by means of the false pretense of being my brother. Under an assumed name he drank, I've just been informed by my butler, an entire pint bottle of my Perrier-Jouet, Brut, '89; a wine I was specially reserving for myself. Continuing his disgraceful deception, he succeeded in the course of the afternoon in alienating the affections of my only ward. He subsequently stayed to tea, and devoured every single muffin. And what makes his conduct all the more heartless is that he was perfectly well aware from the first that I have no brother, that I never had a brother, and that I don't intend to have a brother, not even of any kind. I distinctly told him so myself yesterday afternoon.

LADY B. Ahem! Mr. Worthing, after careful consideration I have decided entirely to overlook my nephew's conduct to you.

JACK. That is very generous of you, Lady Bracknell. My own decision, however, is unalterable. I decline to give my consent.

LADY B. [*to* CECILY]. Come here, sweet child. [CECILY *goes over*.] How old are you, dear?

CECIL. Well, I am really only eighteen, but I always admit to twenty when I go to evening parties.

LADY B. You are perfectly right in making some slight alteration. Indeed no woman should ever be quite accurate about her age. It looks so calculating. . . . [*In meditative manner.*] Eighteen, but admitting to twenty at evening parties. Well, it will not be very long before you are of age and free from the restraints of tutelage. So I don't think your guardian's consent is, after all, a matter of any importance.

JACK. Pray excuse me, Lady Bracknell, for interrupting you again, but it is only fair to tell you that according to the terms of her grandfather's will Miss Cardew does not come legally of age till she is thirty-five.

LADY B. That does not seem to me to be a grave objection. Thirty-five is a very attractive age. London society is full of women of the very highest birth who have, of their own free choice, remained thirty-five for years. Lady Dumbleton is an instance in point. To my own knowledge she has been thirty-five ever since she arrived at the age of forty, which was many years ago now. I see no reason why our dear Cecily should not be even still more attractive at the age you mention than she is at present. There will be a large accumulation of property.

CECIL. Algy, could you wait for me till I was thirty-five?

ALGER. Of course I could, Cecily. You know I could.

CECIL. Yes, I felt it instinctively, but I couldn't wait all that time. I hate waiting even five minutes for anybody. It always makes me rather cross. I am not punctual myself, I know, but I do like punctuality in others, and waiting, even to be married, is quite out of the question.

ALGER. Then what is to be done, Cecily?

CECIL. I don't know, Mr. Moncrieff.

LADY B. My dear Mr. Worthing, as Miss Cardew states positively that she cannot wait till she is thirty-five—a remark which I am bound to say seems to me to show a somewhat impatient nature—I would beg of you to reconsider your decision.

JACK. But, my dear Lady Bracknell, the matter is entirely in your own hands. The moment you consent to my marriage with Gwendolen, I will most gladly allow your nephew to form an alliance with my ward.

LADY B. [*rising and drawing herself up*]. You must be quite aware that what you propose is out of the question.

JACK. Then a passionate celibacy is all that any of us can look forward to.

LADY B. That is not the destiny I propose for Gwendolen. Algernon, of course, can choose for himself. [*Pulls out her watch.*] Come, dear; [GWENDOLEN *rises*] we have already missed five, if not six, trains. To miss any more might expose us to comment on the platform.

Enter DR. CHASUBLE.

CHAS. Everything is quite ready for the christenings.

LADY B. The christenings, sir! Is not that somewhat premature?

CHAS. [*looking rather puzzled, and pointing to* JACK *and* ALGERNON]. Both these gentlemen have expressed a desire for immediate baptism.

LADY B. At their age? The idea is grotesque and irreligious! Algernon, I forbid you to be baptized. I will not hear of such excesses. Lord Bracknell would be highly displeased if he learned that that was the way in which you wasted your time and money.

CHAS. Am I to understand then that there are to be no christenings at all this afternoon?

JACK. I don't think that, as things are now, it would be of much practical value to either of us, Dr. Chasuble.

CHAS. I am grieved to hear such sentiments from you, Mr. Worthing. They savor of the heretical views of the Anabaptists, views that I have completely refuted in four of my unpublished sermons. However, as your present mood seems to be one peculiarly secular, I will return to the church at once. Indeed, I have just been informed by the pew-opener that for the last hour and a half Miss Prism has been waiting for me in the vestry.

LADY B. [*starting*]. Miss Prism! Did I hear you mention a Miss Prism?

CHAS. Yes, Lady Bracknell, I am on my way to join her.

LADY B. Pray allow me to detain you for a moment. This matter may prove to be one of vital importance to Lord Bracknell and myself. Is this Miss Prism a female of repellent aspect, remotely connected with education?

CHAS. [*somewhat indignantly*]. She is the most cultivated of ladies, and the very picture of respectability.

LADY B. It is obviously the same person. May I ask what position she holds in your household?

CHAS. [*severely*]. I am a celibate, madam.

JACK [*interposing*]. Miss Prism, Lady Bracknell, has been for the last three years Miss Cardew's esteemed governess and valued companion.

LADY B. In spite of what I hear of her, I must see her at once. Let her be sent for.

CHAS. [*looking off*]. She approaches; she is nigh.

Enter MISS PRISM *hurriedly.*

PRISM. I was told you expected me in the vestry, dear Canon. I have been waiting for you there for an hour and three-quarters. [*Catches sight of* LADY BRACKNELL, *who has fixed her with a stony glare.* MISS PRISM *grows pale and quails. She looks anxiously round as if desirous to escape.*]

LADY B. [*in a severe, judicial voice*]. Prism! [MISS PRISM *bows her head in shame.*] Come here, Prism! [MISS PRISM *approaches in a humble manner.*] Prism! Where is that baby? [*General consternation. The Canon starts back in horror.* ALGERNON *and* JACK *pretend to be anxious to shield* CECILY *and* GWENDOLEN *from hearing the details of a terrible public scandal.*] Twenty-eight years ago, Prism, you left Lord Bracknell's house, Number 104, Upper Grosvenor Street, in charge of a perambulator that contained a baby, of the male sex. You never returned. A few weeks later, through the elaborate investigations of the Metropolitan police, the perambulator was discovered at midnight, standing by itself in a remote corner of Bayswater. It contained the manuscript of a three-volume novel of more than usually revolting sentimentality. [MISS PRISM *starts in involuntary indignation.*] But the baby was not there! [*Everyone looks at* MISS PRISM.] Prism, where is that baby? [*A pause.*]

PRISM. Lady Bracknell, I admit with shame that I do not know. I only wish I did. The plain facts of the case are these. On the morning of the day you mention, a day that is forever branded on my memory, I prepared as usual to take the baby out in its perambulator. I had also with me a somewhat old, but capacious hand-bag, in which I had intended to place the manuscript of a work of fiction that I had written during my few unoccupied hours. In a moment of mental abstraction, for which I never can forgive myself, I deposited the manuscript in the bassinette, and placed the baby in the hand-bag.

JACK [*who has been listening attentively*]. But where did you deposit the hand-bag?

PRISM. Do not ask me, Mr. Worthing.

JACK. Miss Prism, this is a matter of no small importance to me. I insist on knowing where you deposited the hand-bag that contained that infant.

PRISM. I left it in the cloak-room of one of the larger railway stations in London.

JACK. What railway station?

PRISM [*quite crushed*]. Victoria. The Brighton line. [*Sinks into a chair.*]

JACK. I must retire to my room for a moment. Gwendolen, wait here for me.

GWEND. If you are not too long, I will wait here for you all my life.

[*Exit* JACK *in great excitement.*

CHAS. What do you think this means, Lady Bracknell?

LADY B. I dare not even suspect, Dr. Chasuble. I need hardly tell you that in families of high position strange coincidences are not supposed to occur. They are hardly considered the thing. [*Noises heard overhead as if someone was throwing trunks about. Everybody looks up.*]

CECIL. Uncle Jack seems strangely agitated.

CHAS. Your guardian has a very emotional nature.

LADY B. This noise is extremely unpleasant. It sounds as if he was having an argument. I dislike arguments of any kind. They are always vulgar, and often convincing.

CHAS. [*looking up*]. It has stopped now. [*The noise is redoubled.*]

LADY B. I wish he would arrive at some conclusion.

GWEND. This suspense is terrible. I hope it will last.

Enter JACK *with a hand-bag of black leather in his hand.*

JACK [*rushing over to* MISS PRISM]. Is this the hand-bag, Miss Prism? Examine it carefully before you speak. The happiness of more than one life depends on your answer.

PRISM [*calmly*]. It seems to be mine. Yes, here is the injury it received through the upsetting of a Gower Street omnibus in younger and happier days. Here is the stain on the lining caused by the explosion of a temperance beverage, an incident that occurred at Leamington. And here, on the lock, are my initials. I had forgotten that in an extravagant mood I had had them placed there. The bag is undoubtedly mine. I am delighted to have it so unexpectedly restored to me. It has been a great inconvenience being without it all these years.

JACK [*in a pathetic voice*]. Miss Prism, more is restored to you than this hand-bag. I was the baby you placed in it.

PRISM [*amazed*]. You?

JACK [*embracing her*]. Yes . . . mother!

PRISM [*recoiling in indignant astonishment*]. Mr. Worthing! I am unmarried!

JACK. Unmarried! I do not deny that is a serious blow. But after all, who has the right to cast a stone against one who has suffered? Cannot repentance wipe out an act of folly? Why should there be one law for men and another for women? Mother, I forgive you. [*Tries to embrace her again.*]

PRISM [*still more indignant*]. Mr. Worthing, there is some error. [*Pointing to* LADY BRACKNELL.] There is the lady who can tell you who you really are.

JACK [*after a pause*]. Lady Bracknell, I hate to seem inquisitive, but would you kindly inform me who I am?

LADY B. I am afraid that the news I have to give you will not altogether please you. You are the son of my poor sister, Mrs. Moncrieff, and consequently Algernon's elder brother.

JACK. Algy's elder brother! Then I have a brother after all. I knew I had a brother! I always said I had a brother! Cecily,—how could you have ever doubted that I had a brother? [*Seizes hold of* ALGERNON.] Dr. Chasuble, my unfortunate brother, Miss Prism, my unfortunate brother. Gwendolen, my unfortunate brother. Algy, you young scoundrel, you will have to treat me with more respect in the future. You have never behaved to me like a brother in all your life.

ALGER. Well, not till today, old boy, I admit. I did my best, however, though I was out of practice. [*Shakes hands.*]

GWEND. [*to* JACK]. My own! But what own are you? What is your Christian name, now that you have become someone else?

JACK. Good heavens! . . . I had quite forgotten that point. Your decision on the subject of my name is irrevocable, I suppose?

GWEND. I never change, except in my affections.

CECIL. What a noble nature you have, Gwendolen!

JACK. Then the question had better be cleared up at once. Aunt Augusta, a moment. At the time when Miss Prism left me in the hand-bag, had I been christened already?

LADY B. Every luxury that money could buy, including christening, had been lavished on you by your fond and doting parents.

JACK. Then I was christened! That is settled. Now, what name was I given? Let me know the worst.

LADY B. Being the eldest son you were naturally christened after your father.

JACK [*irritably*]. Yes, but what was my father's Christian name?

LADY B. [*meditatively*]. I cannot at the present moment recall what the General's Christian name was. But I have no doubt he had one. He was eccentric, I admit. But only in later years. And that was the result of the Indian climate, and marriage, and indigestion, and other things of that kind.

JACK. Algy! Can't you recollect what our father's Christian name was?

ALGER. My dear boy, we were never even on speaking terms. He died before I was a year old.

JACK. His name would appear in the Army Lists of the period, I suppose, Aunt Augusta?

LADY B. The General was essentially a man of peace except in his domestic life. But I have no doubt his name would appear in any military directory.

JACK. The Army Lists of the last forty years are here. These delightful records should have been my constant study. [*Rushes to bookcase and tears the books out.*] M. Generals . . . Mallam, Maxbohm, Magley, what ghastly names they have— Markby, Migsby, Mobbs, Moncrieff! Lieutenant 1840, Captain, Lieutenant-Colonel, Colonel, General 1869, Christian names, Ernest John. [*Puts book very quietly down and speaks quite calmly.*] I always told you, Gwendolen, my name was Ernest, didn't I? Well, it is Ernest after all. I mean it naturally is Ernest.

LADY B. Yes, I remember that the General was called Ernest. I knew I had some particular reason for disliking the name.

GWEND. Ernest! My own Ernest! I felt from the first that you could have no other name!

JACK. Gwendolen, it is a terrible thing for a man to find out suddenly that all his life he has been speaking nothing but the truth. Can you forgive me?

GWEND. I can. For I feel that you are sure to change.

JACK. My own one!

CHAS. [*to* MISS PRISM]. Lætitia! [*Embraces her.*]

PRISM [*enthusiastically*]. Frederick! At last!

ALGER. Cecily! [*Embraces her.*] At last!

JACK. Gwendolen! [*Embraces her.*] At last!

LADY B. My nephew, you seem to be displaying signs of triviality.

JACK. On the contrary, Aunt Augusta, I've now realized for the first time in my life the vital Importance of Being Earnest.

TABLEAU

CURTAIN

CHRONOLOGICAL TABLE
OF AUTHORS AND EVENTS

BEFORE CHRIST

Authors	Historical Events
	Age of Abraham (Palestine), c. 2000
Vedic Hymns (India), 14th century	
Tale of the Two Brothers (Egypt), 14th century	Exodus of Hebrews from Egypt, c. 1300
	End of Mycenæan Age in Greece, 1200?
	Trojan War, c. 1200
Homer, 10th or 9th century	David, king of Israel, c. 1000
Hesiod (Gr.), 8th century	First Olympiad, 776
	Rome founded, 753
	Israelites deported, 721
Sappho, 7th century	Colonial expansion of Greece, 750-500
	Jews carried off to Babylon, 586
Thales, 7th and 6th century	Return of Jews to Jerusalem, 537
Anacreon, 563?-478	Persian Empire in power, 6th century
	Buddha, c. 550
	Confucius, c. 550
	Peisistratus died (Athens), 527
	Battle of Marathon, 490
Æschylus, 525-456	Æschylus wins his first prize for tragedy, 484
Pindar, 522-448	Battles of Thermopylæ and Salamis, 480
Sophocles, 496-406	
Herodotus, 484-425	Age of Pericles, 445-431
Euripides, 480-406	
Thucydides, 471?-400?	Peloponnesian War, 431-404
Socrates, 469-399	
Democritus, 460?-362?	
Aristophanes, 448?-380?	
Xenophon, 430?-352	
Plato, 427?-347	
Demosthenes, 384-322	Philip becomes king of Macedonia, 359

Authors	Historical Events
Aristotle, 384-322	Conquests of Alexander the Great, 336-323
Epicurus, 342?-270	
Zeno, 336?-264?	
Theophrastus, d. 287?	Rise of Rome in importance, 338-290
Theocritus, 3d century	
Plautus, 254-184	Wars of Rome and Carthage, 264-146
Terence, 194-159	Carthage destroyed, 146
Cicero, 106-43	Cæsar's conquest of Gaul, 58-50
Panchatantra (India), 1st century?	
Lucretius, 96-55	
Catullus, 87-54	
Virgil, 70-19	Julius Cæsar assassinated, 44
Horace, 65-8	Battle of Actium, 31
Livy, 59 B.C.-17 A.D.	Augustus Cæsar emperor, 27 B.C.-14 A.D.
Ovid, 43 B.C.-17 A.D.	Birth of Jesus, 4 B.C.

ANNO DOMINI

Authors	Historical Events
Seneca, 2-66	Crucifixion of Jesus, 30
Petronius, d. A.D. 66	
Plutarch, 46?-120?	Nero, emperor, 54-68
Tacitus, 55-120	Eruption of Vesuvius, 79
Juvenal, 60?-140?	Conquest of Britain by Rome, 84
Pliny the Younger, 62?-114?	Trajan, emperor, 98
Epictetus, 95-175	Hadrian; Roman Empire at greatest extent, 117
Apuleius, b. 125?	Marcus Aurelius, emperor, 161
Lucian, 125?-200	Marcus Aurelius' death begins a century of disorder in Rome, 180
	Constantine makes Christianity the official religion of Rome, 313

Authors	Historical Events	Authors	Historical Events
St. Augustine, 354-430	Rome sacked by Visigoths, 410	Erasmus, 1466?-1536	Discovery of America by Columbus, 1492
	Invasion of Britain by Anglo-Saxons, 449	Machiavelli, 1469-1527	Vasco da Gama reaches India by sea, 1498
	End of Roman Empire in the West, 476	Rabelais, 1490?-1553	Henry VIII of England, 1509-47
	Justinian closes schools of Athens, 529	Cellini, 1500-71	Reformation in Germany, 1517-55
Beowulf (England), before 8th century	The Hegira: the beginning of Mohammedanism. The first year of the Moslem calendar, 622	Ronsard, 1524-85	Elizabeth of England, 1558-1603
	Mohammedanism extends from Pyrenees to China, 715	Ercilla, 1530?-1600? Montaigne, 1533-92 Tasso (Italy), 1544-95 Cervantes (Spain), 1547-1616	
	Reign of Charlemagne, 768-814	Bruno, 1548-1600 Dyer, 1550-1607 Spenser, 1552-99	
	Charlemagne crowned Emperor of the West, 800	Raleigh, 1552?-1618	Massacre of St. Bartholomew (France), 1572
	Egbert, first king of England, 828	Lyly, 1554?-1606 Greene, 1560?-92	
	Settlement of Iceland, 874	Bacon, 1561-1626	Defeat of the Spanish Armada, 1588
Firdausi (Persia), 940?-1020?		Lope de Vega (Spain), 1562-1635	
Deirdre, 9th to 11th centuries	Norman conquest of England, 1066	Drayton, 1563-1631 Marlowe, 1564-93	
	First Crusade, 1095	Shakespeare, 1564-1616 Donne, 1573-1631	Virginia settled, 1607
Omar Khayyam (Persia), c. 1100		Jonson, 1573-1637 Gracián, 1601-1658	
Marie de France Aucassin and Nicolete, 12th century	Kubla Khan, 1260	Wither, 1588-1667 Herrick, 1591-1674	Thirty Years' War, 1618-1648
Nibelungenlied, c. 1200 St. Francis, 1182-1226	End of Crusades, 1291	Herbert, 1593-1633	Massachusetts settled, 1620
Sa'di, 1184-1291 Dante, 1265-1321		Carew, 1598?-1639 Calderón (Spain), 1600-81	
Petrarch, 1304-1374	Hundred Years' War, 1337-1453	Waller, 1606-87 Milton, 1608-74	
Boccaccio, 1313-1375 Hafiz, 14th century	The Black Death, 1348	Suckling, 1609-42	Louis XIV of France, 1643-1715
Chaucer, 1340?-1400 Thomas À Kempis, 1380-1471		La Rochefoucauld, 1613-80	
Villon, 1431-after 1463	Constantinople captured by Turks, 1453	Lovelace, 1618-58	Execution of Charles I of England, 1649
Malory, fl. 1470	Cape of Good Hope rounded by Diaz, 1488	Marvell, 1621-78	Restoration of Charles II, 1660
		La Fontaine, 1621-95 Vaughan, 1622?-95 Molière, 1622-73	

Authors	Historical Events	Authors	Historical Events
Pascal, 1628-62		Hugo, 1802-85	
Bunyan, 1628-88		Emerson, 1803-82	
Dryden, 1631-1700		Hawthorne, 1804-64	Queen Victoria, 1837-1901
Pepys, 1632-1703	London Fire, 1666		
Boileau, 1636-1711	New York becomes English, 1674	Elizabeth Barrett Browning, 1806-61	
		Mill, 1806-73	
Racine, 1639-99		Longfellow, 1807-82	
Defoe, 1659-1731		Poe, 1809-49	
Swift, 1667-1745	Rise of Russia, 1689-1796	Gogol, 1809-1852	
		Lincoln, 1809-65	American Civil War 1861-65
Le Sage, 1668-1747			
Addison, 1672-1719		Tennyson, 1809-92	
Steele, 1672-1729		Holmes, 1809-94	
Pope, 1688-1744		Robert Browning, 1812-89	
Montesquieu, 1689-1755			
Voltaire, 1694-1778	English power established in India, 1757-1857	Thoreau, 1817-62	Franco-Prussian War, and unification of Germany, 1870-71
Franklin, 1706-90	Peace of Paris: British dominant in America, 1763	Marx, 1818-83	Unification of Italy, 1871
Goldoni (Italy), 1707-93		Turgenev (Russia), 1818-83	
Johnson, 1709-84		Lowell, 1819-91	
Rousseau, 1712-78		Melville, 1819-91	
Gray, 1716-71		Whitman, 1819-92	
Collins, 1721-59	American Revolution, 1775-83	Flaubert, 1821-80	
		Dostoyevsky, 1821-81	
Goldsmith, 1728-74		Arnold, 1822-88	
Lessing, 1729-81	American Constitution, 1787	Dante Gabriel Rossetti, 1828-82	
Jefferson, 1743-1826	French Revolution, 1789-99	Ibsen (Norway), 1828-1906	
		Tolstoi (Russia), 1828-1910	
Goethe, 1749-1832		Christina Rossetti, 1830-94	
Blake, 1757-1827		Morris, 1834-96	
Burns, 1759-96		Swinburne, 1837-1909	
Schiller, 1759-1805		Zola, 1840-1902	
Chateaubriand, 1768-1848		James, 1843-1916	
Wordsworth, 1770-1850		Nietzsche, 1844-1900	
Coleridge, 1772-1834		Henley, 1849-1903	
Lamb, 1775-1834	Battle of Waterloo, 1815	Maupassant, 1850-93	
Hazlitt, 1778-1830	First railway, 1825	Stevenson, 1850-94	
De Quincey, 1785-1859		Wilde, 1856-1900	Japan's victory over China, 1895
Byron, 1788-1824	Greece independent, 1829		
Shelley, 1792-1822	Beginnings of the Industrial Revolution, c. 1830	Housman, 1859-1936	
		Chekhov, 1860-1904	
Lamartine, 1790-1869		Hauptmann, 1862-	Japan's defeat of Russia and her rise to the rank of a World Power, 1904
Keats, 1795-1821			
Carlyle, 1795-1881	Democratic movement in Europe, 1830-48		
Heine, 1797-1856	English Reform Bill and triumph of democracy, 1832		
Balzac, 1799-1850			World War, 1914-18

INDEX OF MYTHOLOGICAL SUBJECTS

GENERAL INDEX

AUTHORS, TITLES, FIRST LINES

INDEX OF LITERARY TYPES

NORWAY
SWEDEN
FINLAND
Oslo
Stockholm
St. Petersburg
(Leningrad)
NORTH SEA
RUSSIA
Moscow
Edinburgh
Dublin
London
Berlin
GERMANY
BRITISH ISLES
Paris
FRANCE
ITALY
R. DANUBE (Ister)
BLACK SEA
ADRIATIC SEA
Rome
SPAIN
Troy
ARMENIA
ASIA MINOR
MEDITERRANEAN SEA
SICILY
Athens
CRETE
MESOPOTAMIA
TIGRIS R.
EUPHRATES R.
PALESTINE
Jerusalem
MOROCCO
LIBYA
Alexandria
Cairo
EGYPT
AFRICA
ARABIA
SAHARA DESERT
RED SEA
NILE RIVER